THE GOOD THE TOUGH & THE DEADLY

ACTION
MOVIES & STARS
1960s–PRESENT

A | ACTION | A GUIDE TO ACTION MOVIES 1960S–PRESENT

| david j. moore

Schiffer Publishing Ltd

4880 Lower Valley Road • Atglen, PA 19310

Other Schiffer books by david j. moore:

World Gone Wild: A Survivor's Guide to Post-Apocalyptic Movies,
　　978-0-7643-4587-6

Other Schiffer Books on movies:

Graphic Horror: Movie Monster Memories by John Edgar Browning,
　　978-0-7643-4082-6
Alternative Movie Posters: Film Art from the Underground, by Matthew Chojnacki,
　　978-0-7643-4566-1
Pumpkin Cinema: The Best Movies for Halloween, by Nathaniel Tolle,
　　978-0-7643-4723-8

Copyright © 2016 by david j. moore

Library of Congress Control Number: 2015959718

Designed by Justin Watkinson
Cover design by Justin Watkinson
Cover image: Keith Batcheller
Type set in Helvetica Neue LT Pro/Zurich BT/Minion Pro

ISBN: 978-0-7643-4995-9
Printed in China

Published by Schiffer Publishing, Ltd.
4880 Lower Valley Road
Atglen, PA 19310
Phone: (610) 593-1777; Fax: (610) 593-2002
E-mail: Info@schifferbooks.com

For our complete selection of fine books on this and related subjects, please visit our website at www.schifferbooks.com. You may also write for a free catalog.

Schiffer Publishing's titles are available at special discounts for bulk purchases for sales promotions or premiums. Special editions, including personalized covers, corporate imprints, and excerpts, can be created in large quantities for special needs. For more information, contact the publisher.

CONTENTS

FOREWORD BY Craig R. Baxley

I've always thought most stories in the world of action that are told by an insider's point of view are an integral, inescapable truth of the real experience. *The Good, the Tough & the Deadly: Action Movies & Stars 1960–Present* by david j. moore could best be called a "spiritual odyssey" into that world more than anything else, I suppose. I think the following interviews and accounts help put the whole thing in perspective, how the action genre evolved in the late '60s through the early '90s, before CGI. For me, writers like david j. moore and Vern bring a fresh, unbiased point of view that our industry so desperately needs.

Who is the best action movie star? The question is impossible to answer. The short list is maybe two dozen.

In the beginning of my career, I was lucky to work with an actor who was on the top of my list: Sean Connery. Some of the actors that followed reminded me how great he really was. It was 1971, a James Bond film.

Bronson was another one. Charles Bronson. To me he was like Eastwood. He had such a strong presence without saying a word, and he conveyed so much with just a look. I first met him as a kid on the set of *The Travels of Jamie McPheeters* in 1964. I discovered years later that my wife had gone to school with his co-star, Kurt Russell, who I did a picture with 1974. Working with Bronson on *Mr. Majestyk* was an education. Like so many great action stars of his time, his commitment to keeping it real was infectious.

He had tremendous respect for the stuntmen he worked so closely with and would rehearse everything over and over until everyone had it right. An action sequence was like a dance, and he always had to lead. But when it came to driving, he always left it to us.

Flash-forward to 1987: I'm standing in the jungles of Mexico, sweating my ass off next to my producer, Joel Silver . . . who in my opinion, along with Larry Gordon, has had more impact and more to do with shaping the action world over that period than any other producers in the industry. I first met Joel on *The Warriors*—he was Larry's assistant. On that film, I wrote and directed all the fights for Walter Hill, who is also an amazing filmmaker himself. How *Predator* came together was truly epic for several reasons. First of all, I don't think many people realize it had two shooting schedules. The original was for fifty-six days, and after forty-eight days I think Joel and Larry realized there might be a bit of a problem . . . only a little over half the film had been shot. The creature had not been put on film yet, and they hadn't shot any of the major action sequences. The original creature, the Predator, was designed by Boss Films. In my opinion, it was really outrageous: It looked like a horrific, standing, eight-foot ant. The man inside the suit would have to work with four-foot leg extensions and three-foot arm extensions. The performer they had hired to be in the suit was an unknown Jean-Claude Van Damme. So, around day fifty, when they decided they'd better show the studio

something, Jean-Claude tried on the $10,000 head. But there was something nobody realized: He was claustrophobic. He immediately yanked off the head and slammed it down, shattering it completely. Joel fired him on the spot, and yelled, "You're done in this industry, you fuckin' idiot! You'll never work in this town again!" That's when Jean-Claude began his Hollywood career.

Joel had to show the studio something—a major action set piece, something big, or they were going to pull the plug. The first unit was originally going to shoot the guerrilla battle sequence, involving all the principals and a core team of stuntmen with a three- to four-week shooting schedule. Jim and John Thomas had written a fantastic sequence, but then Joel called an audible. He wanted me to rewrite it, and along with the entire cast (when first unit could release them) shoot it in six to seven days, which I did. Apparently, the studio loved the footage, but a couple days later, around day fifty-six, they shut down production anyway.

I then went back to *The A-Team* for the final season. A couple months later I got the call to come back onto *Predator* for the second part of the schedule. Joel and Larry had done their magic and had gotten the studio to let them finish the film. Once again, the shoot was amazing—everyone was excited to be back. A couple months after the film was competed, I got a call to come up to Joel's house. I walked in and realized a production meeting was about to start. All the respective department heads were sitting around the table. He threw a script across the table and said, "This is your next film. You're going to direct *Action Jackson* with Carl Weathers." Three weeks later, with a seven million dollar budget we were in production. Thirty-two days later, we were finished. The shoot reinforced something I already knew: Aside from being an incredible athlete, Carl Weathers is one of the smartest actors/filmmakers I've worked with to date. We've remained close friends ever since.

Next for me was *Dark Angel* (a.k.a. *I Come in Peace*), with Dolph Lundgren. My wife actually wrote the last line, "... and you go in pieces, asshole!" David Koepp wrote the original screenplay under a pseudonym. Why a pseudonym, I couldn't tell you because he hadn't written anything else at that point in time. But once again, I was told we had a great budget and schedule. Uh-huh: six million and thirty days. Okay, I was cool, but when I found out how much they were paying Dolph I knew I was in trouble. So, my casting director Karen Rea found this outrageous talent named Brian Benben to play Dolph's sidekick. Once we started filming, I knew it was coming together, but I needed more to push the envelope. I ripped off the Robocop gun, made it fire more (if that was even possible—the armorer, Randy Moore, thought I was insane, but he made it work even though we melted every firing pin in Texas), then I added more action, and more action. Dolph loved everything, and was a complete player, as was Brian.

Through the years I've been fortunate to work with some of the biggest action stars of their day: Bronson, Schwarzenegger, Weathers, Jim Brown, Mr. T, Lundgren, and later some others like Brian Bosworth. A friend of mine, Lance Henriksen, once said, "We're either going to reach for the stars, or lay down in the mud!"

I remember the day I interviewed with Michael Douglas for *Stone Cold*. His company Stone Group had just shut down two movies and fired both directors. The first was *Radio Flyer*; he hired Dick Donner to replace the original director and gave him three months to prep before they continued shooting with a new budget and schedule. The second film, *Stone Cold*, was a different matter altogether. The director had filmed for weeks. Michael wanted everything completely reshot and the ending completely rewritten. I was hired to replace the director, and was given the remainder of the budget and the shooting schedule to reshoot and complete the film. Unfortunately, the original writer was no longer on the project, so I was given the job of rewriting the entire ending from the time the Huey 212 took off with the Boz, until the last frame. But the real surprise was that Michael didn't want to shut down production, he wanted me to fly to Mississippi and continue filming, with a three-day prep. Sounds crazy, I know, but how do you say no to Michael Douglas? He's an amazing filmmaker, and as it turned out, it was an amazing experience. And come to think of it, I never understood why

"Boz" didn't break out as a major action star. How do some of these stars follow the next? How do you follow another legend?

I'm a third-generation filmmaker. My father, Paul Baxley, along with another stuntman by the name of Davey Sharp, were probably two of the best athletes the business has ever known. Some of the actors my father doubled were Alan Ladd, James Dean, Audy Murphy, and Marlon Brando, who were the action stars of that time. Among the films he did with Brando (with whom he became best friends) was *One-Eyed Jack,* which they co-directed. As an accomplished stunt coordinator, second unit director, and director, it was a hard act to follow. Now my son, Craig Baxley Jr., is following in that tradition. He's an outrageous stuntman, stunt coordinator, and second unit director, and a member of Stunts Unlimited. Obviously, I'm very proud.

I make no excuses for my choices. When it's all said and done, I have a profound appreciation for having lived to experience and share the golden years of action in the motion picture business. How ironic is it that CGI has become the main staple of the action world as we know it today? I think it's important that this era—and more importantly, these action stars—not fade away.

Thanks to david j., and all the other passionate filmmakers and fans and out there for caring. I think we'll always be reaching for the stars.

Craig is currently developing the feature film, The Gingerbread Girl *for Stephen King. Some of his film and television credits include:* Rollerball, Mr. Majestyk, Predator, Action Jackson, Stone Cold, Dark Angel *(a.k.a.* I Come in Peace), The Long Riders, The Parallax View, Reds, Charlie Varrick, The Poseidon Adventure, The Warriors, Heaven Can Wait, Logan's Run, What's Up Doc?, Foul Play, Diamonds are Forever, The A-Team, Dukes of Hazzard, *Stephen King's* Storm of the Century, *Bryan Singer and Dean Devlin's* The Triangle*, Stephen King's* Rose Red*, Human Target, Harper's Island, and Stephen King's* Kingdom Hospital. *His complete credits are available on IMDB.com or IMDBPRO.com.*

INTRODUCTION

Long, long ago, men were men. Before gymnasiums, before porn, before Monday Night Football, men toiled and fought and died wielding axes and swords while defending their villages and lands. Somehow, over time, the world made men into suffering slackjaws who were made to put on suits and ties, commute to work in wheeled boxes and rolling trains, and be kept alive with caffeine, nicotine, Red Bulls, and fast food. The invaders of time and change cruelly mutated men into pale-faced, fluorescent-lit, suit-wearing drones who no longer saw the sun on the plains or the moonlit bloodied fields of battle. The age of masculinity had passed, and by the time that Hollywood began to figure out this unstoppable travesty, it was already too late. Hollywood's belated response to the death of "real men" translated into cowboys and Indians action movies, the John Waynes, the Gary Coopers, and the Audie Murphys. As the years progressed, these films transitioned into the form of the modern action film. In the wake of Vietnam and the "peace, love, and understanding" rallies in the homeland, America reeled over its name-your-own movements, and it wasn't until the early 1980s that the modern action film became something immediately recognizable. With the rise of muscular soldiers, kickboxers, and stalwart, gun-wielding renegade karate cops came back the identity of warriors, fighters, and men.

While actors like Clint Eastwood, Steve McQueen, and Burt Reynolds were establishing themselves as movie stars, headlining mainstream films that became box office successes, they really weren't known as "action stars." They, and

Mexican poster for *Missing in Action*. Author's collection.

almost all of their contemporaries throughout the '60s, '70s, and beyond, were known as "actors" or performers whose films weren't necessarily considered "action" films. What an "action" film is really pertains to the events that happen in the picture, and how they are presented. *Dirty Harry* (1971, Eastwood) can be considered an action film. *Bullitt* (1968, McQueen) and *Malone* (1987,

Reynolds) can also be considered action films. Many of the movies Eastwood, McQueen, and Reynolds starred in are action movies. But these guys are not action *stars*. They're actors. What defines an action star is dependent on who they are in life, where they've come from, and their physical abilities.

In the grand study of *The Good, the Tough & the Deadly: Action Movies & Stars 1960–Present*, I found a common denominator in all or most of the stars I covered, and in the years I spent working on it, I realized that on the greater whole, these stars were bringing to the screen the missing link of physical strength, prowess, and abilities lost in time through the age of industry, Wall Street, socioeconomic depressions, the rise of female empowerment, and gender dysphoria. Political correctness, a fairly modern concept, really didn't apply to the golden age of action stars when Chuck Norris and Sylvester Stallone were obliterating legions of villains of (usually) ethnic descent while casually moving on to the next wave of slayings. Action stars—both male and female—embody a standard found through athleticism, martial arts, and sports, with very few exceptions. In the culling of my search for action stars, I found it to be much easier to cover only those men and women who had made the crossover from professional sports, martial arts, and various other avenues such as bodybuilding, professional wrestling, and stunt work in films. That rule eliminated the fringe action stars like Eastwood, Reynolds, McQueen, and many others who might be considered action stars like Bruce Willis, Kurt Russell, or Mel Gibson, for example. While *Die Hard* (1988) and *Lethal*

Charles Bronson as Paul Kersey in *Death Wish*. Author's collection.

John Rambo sets traps and snares in the forest to stay alive as he's hunted by civilians and policemen in *First Blood*. Author's collection.

Agile and cunning, Frank Martin (Jason Statham) is an action hero in *The Transporter*. Author's collection.

John Matrix (Arnold Schwarzenegger) is a one-man *Commando*. Author's collection.

Shinyuki (John Fujioka) is Joe Armstrong's (Michael Dudikoff) ninja master in *American Ninja*. Author's collection.

Gold medal–winning gymnast Kurt Thomas stars in the cult film *Gymkata*. Author's collection.

Weapon (1987) are integral and influential action films, the stars in them are not (by definition) action stars because in their successive films they would be starring in the likes of *The Story of Us* (1999, Willis), *What Women Want* (2000, Gibson), or *Captain Ron* (1992, Russell), just to name three. Exceptions were made for stars such as Charles Bronson, Sylvester Stallone, Michael Dudikoff, and various others like Jason Statham simply because the greater body of their work is very clearly embodied by physicality and action, and the consensus is that they are without a doubt *action stars*; through their careers they consistently maintain the action star persona with very little variation, and off screen they keep in prime shape, regardless of age. In Bronson's case, once he starred in *Death Wish* (1974) at age 53, his career literally became defined by that one film and his successive films and his image became attached to the persona he displayed in it. One film after another, Bronson was the guy from *Death Wish*, despite the fact that he made dozens of other action films before and after it. With Stallone, two films defined his career: *Rocky* (1976, which he wrote), and *First Blood* (1982, based on a book by David Morrell). Forever after, Stallone's image was irrevocably tied to the two iconic characters from those two films—Rocky Balboa and John Rambo. Action film after action film, Stallone's successful career inevitably veered toward making more sequels to those two films. With Statham (who had been a professional swimmer), his action star career took off when he starred in the martial arts action film *The Transporter* (2002). Spawning two sequels and an unshakable familiarity with the role he played in those films, Statham has become one of the last successful action stars to emerge in the new millennium. Despite not being a real martial artist, he has maintained a visage of being a martial arts–driven action star, and he continues making theatrical releases that feature him in full action star mode.

There's a reason this book had to be written. Since I was very young, going to the movies to see action movies with *action stars* has been an integral part of my life. Watching pictures with *action stars* on video has been just as important and vital. Growing up in the 1980s and early 1990s was the right time to fall in love with action heroes like Rambo, John Matrix (played by Arnold Schwarzenegger in *Commando*, 1985), the *American Ninja* (Michael Dudikoff, 1985), and the dude from *Gymkata* (Kurt Thomas, 1985). This was the VHS era, the time

of the Reagan administration, and then Bush, and then America was changing and VHS was out and DVD was coming in. The mom-and-pop video stores were stocked full of movies starring Dolph Lundgren, Don "The Dragon" Wilson, Billy Blanks, Lorenzo Lamas, Cynthia Rothrock, and all of the other "B" action stars like Olivier Gruner, Jeff Speakman, Brian Bosworth, and David Bradley who weren't making movies with any aspirations higher than they could kick. These were blue-collar movies, movies for men who worked all day, came home tired and wanted to pop an action movie in the VCR or the DVD player and just soak in the explosions, the kung fu, and the stunts. Trust me: There's nothing better at the end of the day than watching ninjas chasing other ninjas or seeing Cynthia Rothrock fighting Richard Norton again and again. It's the sort of thing that moms and dads should raise their children on, like cartoons, cereal, and Flintstones vitamins. These movies—and more importantly, these *stars*—are important. It's not just that they have muscles or can do roundhouse kicks or deliver catchy one-liners after a smackdown, no, it's that they transcend acting and present themselves pretty much as they are in life. They're the real thing. Bruce Lee the martial artist is Bruce Lee the actor. Arnold Schwarzenegger the seven-time Mr. Olympia bodybuilder is Arnold Schwarzenegger the actor. Terry "Hulk" Hogan the WWE wrestler is Terry "Hulk" Hogan the actor. These guys arguably don't act. They just *are* themselves, as they are, as they always will be in the eyes of their fans. You can say that some of them deliver solid, Academy Award-worthy performances on occasion—Stallone in *Rocky* or *Cop Land* (1997)—but that's an exception to the rule. When I watch a movie with "Stone Cold" Steve Austin I'm not expecting a special performance from him. I'm expecting an action movie with some scenes of hardcore fighting, with Austin in the center, stiff-necked and primed for hard-hitting action. Movie after movie, time after time, I know that these action stars are putting almost every effort in keeping themselves in shape and delivering what they can to the best of their abilities in these films, many of which simply don't deserve them in it. For every few great action movies starring an action star like Stallone or Schwarzenegger, there're a half a dozen substandard movies starring the likes of Steven Seagal, Wesley Snipes, or Roddy Piper. I love these guys, all of them, but at some point in all their careers, there's a slip in quality, and an inevitable decline in their

abilities as martial artists, or whatever skills they had as athletes, wrestlers, or whatever. In some instances, while they age and lose muscle mass, agility, and flexibility, men like Stallone and Van Damme have kept up the fight and defy whatever odds are against their bodies and keep themselves in shape and put forth every effort to giving their fans (and their egos) the next film, age be damned.

Theatrical poster for *That Man Bolt*. Author's collection.

It's important to acknowledge action stars and their contributions to cinema because they virtually defined an era, and they helped build empires and movie studios, creating and boosting an economy of action and martial arts films for decades. Countries all over the world have hosted action film productions, stimulating economic growth both on the production side of filmmaking and when these films were made available to see in theaters, to rent, purchase, or stream on the Internet. The stars of these films have become household names, brands really, and are known all over the world for what they can deliver. They have become heroes to impressionable fans, young and old alike, men and women, all across the board. Writing this book wasn't a fan experience for me so much as it was a grafting of my love and appreciation of these men and women in these films to an intensive study on the greater bodies of their work as a whole, all collated and collected into one volume.

Watching thirty Don "The Dragon" Wilson movies in a row over a three-week period was an interesting experience, unlike anything I'd ever

Jean-Claude Van Damme as Leon, the Lionheart. Author's collection.

Steven Seagal plays Forrest Taft in *On Deadly Ground*. Author's collection.

Chuck Norris levels the playing field as Col. Scott McCoy in Aaron Norris's *Delta Force 2: The Columbian Connection*. Author's collection.

done before. I won't tell you that I liked all of the films, but I learned some things about Don Wilson that I'd never known before. I studied *him* rather than the movies themselves, and the same goes for every action star my contributors and I covered in this book. We watched *every single* action film and fringe action film that *every single* real-deal action star ever starred or appeared in with a significant role. This was an exhausting and *exhaustive* process, particularly because we did it in a two-year time span. This is a book for devoted fans of action stars all across the shelf. We go back to the 1960s and early 1970s when Bronson, Jim Brown, Fred Williamson, Jim Kelly, Bruce Lee, and

Tom Laughlin were exploring undiscovered territory and trailblazing for others of their ilk and backgrounds to follow. Others then paved and cemented the path, men like Arnold Schwarzenegger, Sylvester Stallone, Jean-Claude Van Damme, Chuck Norris, and Steven Seagal. These were the titans who rose to prominence and spawned generations of emulators and would-bes. These are the stars I wanted to talk about and study, all the way down the line.

Several guidelines were mapped out as to exactly what *types* of films we'd review because many of these stars have appeared in films that were not deemed "action" films per se, films in various genres including sword and sorcery

or fantasy, outright comedies, or films that were set in ancient times that simply did not pertain to our study. Schwarzenegger's *Conan* films (1982, 1984) and *Red Sonja* (1985) were not reviewed for this book for reasons that felt obvious. Jackie Chan's films prior to his first international crossover *The Big Brawl* (a.k.a. *Battle Creek Brawl*, 1980) largely consisted of Chinese kung fu movies set in ancient China, and were therefore not as pertinent to our study as his films following his English language debut. We encountered many challenges involving Asian martial arts stars, and in order to keep a rein on our coverage, we only included specific action and martial arts stars whose impact on the world of action was felt globally. If they were able to break the world barrier by starring or appearing in an English language film at some point in their careers like Yu Wang did in 1975's *The Man From Hong Kong* (a.k.a. *Dragon Files*), we included those films, knowing full well that the stars had made an impact in their respective native countries and were able to land starring or supporting roles in films that Western audiences would see. In Bruce Lee's case, we made sure to cover *all* of his work because he continues to be an influence on burgeoning martial arts and action stars the whole world over. We wanted to keep our stars and their films limited to more or less *contemporary* action films, with few exceptions. In the case of westerns, we included those that were integral to that star's body of work like Olivier Gruner's *Savate* (a.k.a. *The Fighter*, 1995) or *Shanghai Noon* (2000) with Jackie Chan. We tried hard to keep our study to films set mostly in and around modern times, otherwise our examinations would have exploded with classic kung fu and fantasy films, not to mention westerns, comedies, and dramas. In an obvious case, we included Arnold Schwarzenegger's *Twins* (1988) and *Kindergarten Cop* (1990) because there were action undertones in those movies, but none were found in his comedy *Junior* (1994), which

A fight scene between Inspector Fang Sing Leng (Wang Yu) and Jack Wilton (George Lazenby) in *The Man From Hong Kong*. Author's collection.

Wang Yu performing a dangerous stunt in *The Man From Hong Kong*. Author's collection.

dealt with him as the world's first pregnant man. In the case of *Masters of the Universe* (1987), starring Dolph Lundgren, it was decided that because the movie is generally regarded as a "sword and sorcery" picture, we excluded it, despite the fact that the film is set in different time periods, and that Lundgren's image is still tied to playing He-Man.

Hundreds upon hundreds of films were reviewed for this book, upwards of fifteen hundred. This was done to relate *who these stars are/were* and *what they are/were capable of* as action stars. This book is kind to the stars, and kinder still to the people who love them. It would be unfair to slam many of these movies because many of these movies are so easy to slam. What we did instead is focus on the star, and in lieu of a rating system, we decided to present each film with a more than fair amount of text to review each film equally on the same playing field. A rating system would defeat the purpose. After all the work and all the research, what we've found is that these stars deserve an appreciation of this magnitude—more so now than ever before. In the wake of recent superhero movies like *The Dark Knight* and *Man of Steel* where muscles don't really matter (because they're molded on the suits) and superspy films like *The Bourne Identity* (starring Matt Damon) or the Daniel Craig 007 films, where lean, athletic *actors* can convincingly convey an art of fighting enhanced with camera trickery and hyperstylized editing, the age of the action star is fading. *This* is the time, *this* is the opportunity to lift every action star up in the same way, at the same speed. As a bonus, we've done the best we can in catching up to many of the action stars, performers, and filmmakers we discuss in the book, and we've included exclusive interviews with them. One of the greatest pleasures of working on this project was meeting and interviewing some of our heroes, and in one instance, I traveled in 2013 to the Bangkok, Thailand, set of Isaac Florentine's *Ninja II: Shadow of a Tear*, starring Scott Adkins and Kane Kosugi, to get a first-hand experience of watching a martial arts action film being made. We hope that this book finds every fan of every star featured in it happy and content, knowing that the era of *Good, Tough,* and *Deadly* action stars lives on in the hundreds of films they've made and most importantly, in the hearts of their fans.

david j. moore is the author of *World Gone Wild: A Survivor's Guide to Post-Apocalyptic Movies*. He has written for *Black Belt Magazine*, *Kung Fu Tai Chi*, *Tai Kwon Do Times*, *Fangoria*, *Famous Monsters of Filmland*, *Diabolique*, *FilmFax*, *VideoScope*, *L'Ecran Fantastique*, *Ultra Violent*, *Lunchmeat*, *Flickering Myth*, and *Outlaw Vern*. He has visited movie sets around the world and continues to work as a freelance film journalist.

ABOUT THE Reviews

With a project this intensive and all encompassing, I felt the need to share the experience with several other writers, who would not only lend their voices and opinions in their reviews of these films, but would also help validate the entire endeavor. I called upon some friends and associates who knew and understood—*and valued*—what these action stars have accomplished throughout their careers. Some of my contributors contributed hundreds of reviews, while others only contributed dozens or even just a single review. Also, I did not conduct all of the interviews on my own. Initials found with each review and interview indicate the author.

These are the contributors for *The Good, the Tough, and the Deadly: Action Stars and Their Movies*, in alphabetical order:

(PB) Phil Blankenship
(ZC) Zack Carlson
(CD) Corey Danna
(DH) Duvien Ho
(MJ) Mike Joffe
(DL) Dustin Leimgruber
(MMM) Mike McBeardo McPadden
(djm) david j. moore
(JS) Josh Schafer
(JAS) Jason A. Souza
(V) Vern

It was an incredible challenge to find and review all of the titles that we included in this book. It was a top priority to track down every single movie, starring every single action star we included in this project. With the title of each film, we include the year it was released, the distributor of the title, and who reviewed that title. For example:

Predator

1987 (Fox DVD) (djm)

We predominantly reviewed films and television programs that are available on home video, and we indicate the medium that is most easily and readily available to the public. Therefore, we usually reviewed DVDs and VHS tapes. If we reviewed films on Laserdisc, Blu-ray, or any other medium (including seeing films in festivals, theaters, on YouTube), we simply indicated the distribution company that released the film on home video. If we reviewed titles that are not yet officially on home video in any format, we stated that it is not on video (NOV). We tried our best to find even the most elusive titles to review, and if we could find it, then your chances of finding it too are pretty good.

If we learned anything from reviewing hundreds and hundreds of titles, starring men and women who have crossed over from the world of sports, martial arts, or any other avenue where athleticism played a major role in their careers, it's that being an action star looks like a ton of fun. If only the rest of us could make that crossover.

Ablaze

2000 (Fox DVD) (djm)

A series of out of control fires is plaguing Los Angeles, and a band of heroic firemen are on the case. When the lead fireman is gravely wounded in a rescue, Daniels (Michael Dudikoff) assumes command, but his team is grounded when they're needed most. In the foreground of the confusing plot, a serial arsonist continues to start fires, a hospital is overrun with incompetency while more and more injured people come pouring in, and two detectives (one of whom is played by Ice-T) are on the hunt for the arsonist.

It's amazing that stuff like *Ablaze* managed to get sold and distributed by a company such as 20th Century Fox. I'd wager that about forty-five minutes of footage was actually shot for this thing, and the other forty-five minutes is stock footage from other movies. I can tell you for a fact that the opening action scene involving a car chase (which is great, by the way) was taken from the Bruce Willis movie *Striking Distance*. Other entire chunks are lifted from various other films (it's obvious because the cars look like they're from the '70s), and almost everything involving a fire or streets full of chaos was not shot for this movie. Michael Dudikoff is in the movie, but he probably filmed his stuff in a day or two, and there are a few scenes of him acting heroic, rescuing children from burning buildings, but if you have any love for him and his previous, better-known work, stay far away from this garbage. It's from director "Jay Andrews," who is better known as Jim Wynorski.

Above the Law

(a.k.a. **Righting Wrongs**)

1986 (The Weinstein Company DVD) (djm)

After an entire family is murdered at their home on the day they were to testify against a crime syndicate, a young prosecutor (played by Yuen Biao from *Wheels on Meals*) decides to take the law into his own hands. In the meantime, a foreign female officer (Cynthia Rothrock during her years of making films in Hong Kong) begins an investigation on the case, and the trail leads her to the prosecutor, whom she believes has gone bad.

Biao and Rothrock made several films together (*Shanghai Express* was another one), but *Above the Law* is probably the stronger (and

Cynthia Rothrock as Cindy in Corey Yuen's *Above the Law*. Author's collection.

harder to swallow) film. For a while, it has a light, entertaining tone, and then it has scenes of such graphic violence that it takes time to recover from them, only to have a fresh scene of shocking slaughter thrust at you. There are three heroes in the film (the third is Rothrock's partner, played by the film's director, Corey Yuen), and by the end, they have all been killed. Rothrock's death is the hardest to watch, and the camera never flinches. While Biao and Rothrock are given a great vehicle to showcase their talents and abilities, *Above the Law* will put some viewers off with its downbeat ending. A more upbeat alternate ending exists. Also starring Karen Sheperd (*Mission of Justice*). Yuen also directed Rothrock in *No Retreat No Surrender 2*.

Above the Law

1988 (Warner DVD) (MJ)

"If I find out you're lying, I'll come back and kill you in your own kitchen."

Once upon a time, the landscape of action cinema was dominated by names like Chuck Norris, Sylvester Stallone and Arnold Schwarzenegger. But the landscape changed in 1988 with the arrival of Steven Seagal and the release of *Above the Law*. Fans of action cinema were caught completely off guard in April 1988 when they were introduced to a lanky, soft-spoken actor confidently practicing aikido and Japanese kendō, styles of martial arts that had not been frequently seen on the big screen. *Above the Law* tells the story of Nico Toscani, a Chicago police officer with strong family ties to local organized crime and a mysterious background that includes time spent working for the CIA as an advisor in the early 1970s along the Cambodia/Vietnam border. After disrupting a major drug deal, Nico discovers a cache of plastic explosive. After all of his prisoners are released, Nico begins to suspect that he's stumbled onto a conspiracy involving other government agencies, extending to the upper echelons of power.

Above the Law is one of the most confident debuts of an action star ever produced and still feels like the most personal over twenty-five years later. It's also one of the few action film debuts where the actor was not only the star of the film but also a producer, one of the screenwriters, *and* one of the fight choreographers. Unlike many action films, *Above the Law* has a very personal feel to it, starting in an almost documentary style as the protagonist reveals his background to the audience in a conversational-tone voice-over against a montage of images. Seagal used elements of his own backstory in the creation of Nico Toscani and the opening of the film helps

Japanese poster for *Above the Law*. Author's collection.

to humanize the character almost immediately in a way few action films have done since. Compared to other action stars of the day, Seagal offered something new to audiences: a humble, introspective, articulate man not afraid to take action if his life or the safety of his family is threatened, with an unconventional look for a leading man, a physical presence that is not overbearing, and a natural acting style. The authentic Chicago shooting locations are one of the great strengths of the film, as is the combination of Seagal's personality bouncing off many familiar faces drawn from Chicago's pool of great acting talent, along with the casting of veteran character Henry Silva as the villain. In fact, many elements of style in this film were used in director Andrew Davis's previous film, *Code of Silence*, for action star Chuck Norris. As time passes, *Above the Law* continues to age well, showcasing all the elements that have made Seagal a star, but without the baggage that has accumulated with success.

Abraxas:

Guardian of the Universe

1990 (Mill Creek DVD) (djm)

Jesse Ventura (from wrestling and *Predator*) plays an intergalactic cop named Abraxas, who after ten thousand Earth years of chasing bad guys around the galaxy, ends up on Earth for his last job: To catch and kill a criminal named Secundus (Sven-Ole Thorsen), who raped and impregnated an Earth woman to give life to his progeny, a child who will one day rule the cosmos.

Abraxas isn't the sharpest tool in the shed when it comes to Earth practices (he has *really* awkward conversations), but compared to Secudus, who when hungry orders the entire breakfast menu *and* eats the check, Abraxas is meteorically cooler. Secundus is sort of like The Terminator, but he seems to be more self-aware and has ambitions to govern the galaxies after his long-term plan comes into effect. When Abraxas finds him and confronts him, there's quite a bit of collateral damage to the town and townspeople where they collide. Meanwhile, Secundus's mute child (now a youngster) is exhibiting mind powers, and the clueless mother develops feelings for the blockheaded Abraxas, who shows a special interest in her son. The scene where a shirtless, seated Abraxas tries to tell the silent boy a bedtime story is . . . *weird*.

Held in regard as a "worst movie ever made," *Abraxas* sort of had potential, but as an American-made movie from Damien Lee (who would direct Michael Dudikoff, Jeff Wincott, and Don Wilson in other action movies), it's a bizarre Italian exploitation-esque outing with a less-than-convincing action star at its center. Ventura, who was best known for his professional wrestling at the time, doesn't have the look or the range to play an intergalactic cop, and Thorsen, who recites his lines in a rote fashion, isn't the best choice to play the villain. Still, *Abraxas* has an off-kilter (shall we say) charm to it, and some viewers may find it mildly amusing. Ventura was previously in the fight movie *Thunderground*. His next project after *Abraxas* was the TV pilot *Tagteam*, co-starring Roddy Piper. The same year *Abraxas* was released, Ventura became the mayor of Brooklyn Park, Minnesota.

Absolution

2015 (Lionsgate DVD) (CD)

"I believe that everybody out there is out there to fuck me. So I decided I want to do one thing in my life, one good thing in my life before I die, even if I die in the process. I want to find this guy. I want to find him, and I want to kill him."

John Alexander (Steven Seagal) and his partner Chi (Byron Mann) are hired by a government agency to take out some seedy individuals. Ever the consummate professionals, they do as they're told, lying low and waiting for extraction. While they are out having a drink, the beautiful Nadia (Adina Stetcu) comes running in, fearing for her life. When a group of thugs comes in and tries pulling her away, John and Chi step in and save her. What they fail to realize is the fact these men work for The Syndicate and their boss (Vinnie Jones) is known for being a vicious, sadistic beast. John is torn between saving the girl or breaking his own protocol. He has to do what's right and risks it all for Nadia.

At this point, director Keoni Waxman and Steven Seagal are finally on the same page after making more than half a dozen movies together. The story is simple, the formula is predictable, but something about *Absolution* just works. There're no surprises anymore when it comes to a Seagal film (unless you count being surprised at how bad they can be)—you know what you're getting. The inclusion of Byron Mann (*A Dangerous Man*) certainly elevates this one above some of the others. The action is well staged, bloody, and exciting with Seagal mostly taking a backseat to allow Mann to show off his talents. Seagal throws plenty of stuntmen around here, but never gets hit (as usual). What's great about one of the final scenes in the film is that we get a glimpse of a painting on the wall. It might not mean much to most people, but it will make you smile when you realize the painting is of Seagal himself playing a guitar. Vain? Nah, he's the Mojo Priest! Side note: this is a sequel to *A Good Man* but can easily be viewed out of continuity.

(Editor's note: Lo and behold, Absolution *was given a one-week perfunctory theatrical release across the United States without any promotion or fanfare whatsoever. Perplexing and inexplicable as that may be, it was nice to see Seagal breaking some wrists again on the big screen.)*

Acapulco H.E.A.T.

1993–1994, 1996

(Mill Creek DVD) (djm)

A gaudy, bloated riff on *Mission Impossible*, *Acapulco H.E.A.T.* features an enormous cast of heroic secret agent /spy-type characters, each of whom have their own specialties. The group that calls themselves The H.E.A.T. (Hemisphere Emergency Action Team) responds to terrorist threats and governmental uprisings in South America (they're stationed in Acapulco, obviously), and they go up against slave traders, ninjas, and the typical mumbo jumbo associated with saving the world. The cast includes Catherine Oxenberg, Brendan Kelly, Fabio (yes, *that* Fabio), and a young Michael Worth, who provides the show its only value.

Worth is the martial arts expert of the team, and every episode of this TV series allows him to use his skills a little bit, although the first season is so cluttered with other, useless characters that he's overwhelmed by the nonsense. The second season was vastly pared down and excised most of the other characters, leaving Worth as one of the main stars of the show, and therefore if you take it upon yourself to start watching this show, I'd recommend skipping the first season entirely (or just sampling it), and going directly to the tighter second season. Honestly, this was a really difficult program for me to sit through with its frivolity, silliness, and overall wastefulness, but if you're a fan of Worth's (I am), you should take a quick gander at it and see him at work. Before this show, Worth had starred in several PM Entertainment movies like *Final Impact* and *Street Crimes*. Strangely, this show was canceled after the first season, but was revived more than a year later. If you like this stuff, see also Hulk Hogan's similar *Thunder in Paradise*, which also featured tons of pretty girls in bikinis running around for no reason.

The Accidental Spy

2001 (Dimension DVD) (djm)

A bored exercise equipment salesman named Jackie (or Buck depending on which version you see, played by Jackie Chan) interrupts a bank robbery in the mall he works in, and he makes out with the bag of cash and becomes a media sensation when he turns out to be a hero. He is visited by a private eye, who tells him that he might be the long lost son of a millionaire, and when Jackie meets his dying maybe-father, he is bestowed with a mystery: He must travel to Korea and then to Turkey on a spy-type mission to unlock the key to his past, and quite possibly save the world from some kind of killer virus in the meanwhile.

Starting out as a light comedy, *The Accidental Spy* is confusing in that it has an oddly serious tone once Jackie takes on his mission and starts globetrotting. His attitude seems to be on the somber side, and therefore the sense of adventure and "fun" is milked dry after the first act, despite the big-budget appeal of the foreign locations and the explosive stunts. This feels like a riff on his *Police Story* sequels like *Supercop* and especially *First Strike* but, again, it's either too serious to be funny or slightly too goofy to be serious. It's a weird mix. The climactic stunt chase has Jackie at the wheel of an unstoppable oil tanker, and the final moments of the stunt are heart stopping. The Dimension US release trimmed some minutes from the running time of the original version, which may account for the uneven tone. Directed by Teddy Chen.

Aces: Iron Eagle III

1992 (New Line DVD) (djm)

The continuing adventures of Chappy Sinclair (Lou Gossett Jr. reprising his role from the first two *Iron Eagle* movies) involve him and some of his old pilot cronies, who all make their living flying antique planes for air shows. When a friend of Chappy's is killed in a plane crash in South America, he finds out that his friend might have been transporting drugs for the cartels, but the reality goes much deeper than that. The DEA gives Chappy the go-ahead to lead a search and destroy mission to Peru where a cartel is being used by a German terrorist (Paul Freeman from *Raiders of the Lost Ark*) to carry out a big plan he has. Enter into the picture an incredibly fit woman named Anna (two-time Miss Olympia and star of *Pumping Iron II*, Rachel McLish), whose family is being held hostage by the cartel, and she and Chappy join forces to demolish the cartel by air and land. While Chappy and his old friends (who include Sonny Chiba and Horst Buchholz) are attacking from the air in their ancient planes, Anna is like Rambo on the ground, using booby traps, guns, blades, and grenades to kill the cartel's soldiers.

The director of this movie is John Glen, who'd made all of the James Bond films of the 1980s, and for a while, *Aces* has the look and feel of a Bond movie until it subtly becomes more of a Cannon action movie (though it was a Carolco release), with a washed-out film stock and an old-fashioned score by Harry Manfredini. It's fairly corny in every regard (one villain is brained by a church bell in an unbelievable scene), and its cartoonish plot should appeal to kids and bored adults. What it desperately needs is more McLish, whose first scene has her using her strength to escape her bonds, which is a scene the movie simply cannot top. She looks great on screen, and it was a smart idea to put her in the middle of an action movie, but this is Gossett's franchise. Her next (and last) movie was Albert Pyun's *Ravenhawk*.

Action Jackson

1988 (Warner DVD) (djm)

Peter: "Jackson. Jericho Jackson. There's a nickname associated with it, isn't there? Something like excitement. Uh, enthusiasm? Esprit de corps?"
Jackson: "It's Action."
Peter: "Well, of course. That rhymes."

One of the quintessential action products of the 1980s from producer Joel Silver, *Action Jackson* casts Carl Weathers (*Predator, Rocky*) as Jericho Jackson, a pariah on the Detroit police force who is known for going the extra mile when he loses his temper on the job. With a Harvard Law degree and a little more pizazz than anyone else in his precinct, Jackson has a notable archenemy: A tycoon named Peter Dellaplane (Craig T. Nelson), whom Jackson suspects is knocking off his competition in the automobile industry, is planning to monopolize the auto industry in Detroit and then position himself in a political standing in Washington. Also embroiled in this pulpy yarn are two sultry dames: Patrice (Sharon Stone), Dellaplane's beautiful wife, and nightclub singer Sydney Ash (Vanity), who becomes a target when Jackson realizes that she's Dellaplane's mistress. The final confrontation between Jackson and Dellaplane plays out believably and with utmost satisfaction.

Action Jackson is the gift that keeps on giving. Full of quips, one-liners, and double entendres, it's the perfect companion to other great action movies of the same period like *Lethal Weapon, Die Hard,* and *The Last Boyscout.* Many actors who appear in it are also in at least several other films produced by Joel Silver,

Carl Weathers as Sgt. Jericho Jackson in *Action Jackson*. Author's collection.

Carl Weathers and Sonny Landham in a brawl in *Action Jackson*. Author's collection.

and the score by Michael Kamen and Herbie Hancock should remind you of those films as well. The action is fun, the plot is simple (yet murky), and Carl Weathers shines in his best vehicle film. He would go on to do *Dangerous Passions* and *Hurricane Smith.* Director Craig R. Baxley began his classic action trilogy with *Action Jackson.* His next two were *I Come in Peace* (a.k.a. *Dark Angel*) with Dolph Lundgren and *Stone Cold* with Brian Bosworth.

INTERVIEW:

CARL WEATHERS
(DH AND djm)

Before his breakout role in Rocky (1976) *as the flamboyant Apollo Creed, Carl Weathers played professional football for the Oakland Raiders. He retired from football in 1974 and went after his goal of becoming an actor, and it was a gradual journey for him to become a full-fledged action star with his co-starring role in* Predator (1987), *opposite Arnold Schwarzenegger. The following year, producer Joel Silver gave Weathers his shot at the big time with the Warner Brothers movie* Action Jackson (1988), *which gave him some steam to star in several other notable action projects like* Hurricane Smith (1992) *and the short-lived action/martial arts TV show* Street Justice (1991–1993), *opposite Bryan Genesse. Weathers had a nice run as an action star, but he slowed down considerably in the late 1990s, and hasn't made a full-fledged action film since co-starring with Hulk Hogan in two* Shadow Warriors (1997, 1999) *pictures.*

When's the last time you sat down to watch *Predator*?

In all honesty, whenever this movie's on television, when I'm flipping channels—and you've got a multitude of channels—and if *Predator* happens to be on, how can I go back to whatever I'm watching? (Laughing.) I have to stop and watch it! The action in this movie is probably as good as an action in any movie that's ever been made. Craig Baxley did wonderful work as the second unit director and as the stunt coordinator.

I didn't realize that you were a theater major in college. When did the acting bug bite you and what kept you going forward with acting?

It bit me when I was very young, and when I would walk into those great, old movie theaters. I grew up in New Orleans, so when I would go to the theater or the movies on a Saturday and watch double features, with cartoons and newsreels, it was so magical. The movies I loved were the westerns, which had so much great action in them. They were so larger than life. That was sort of the thing that grabbed me. As I got older, I started looking at films more and more, and so I decided I wanted to major in theater.

You were also a football player, so how did you balance football and theater?

Sydney Ash (Vanity) and Jericho Jackson (Carl Weathers) in Craig Baxley's *Action Jackson*. Author's collection.

I don't know that I ever balanced it. I just found myself doing what I wanted to do. Pretty much all my life, it's been that way. If there was something I was really passionate about, then it was something I would do. Why not do that? Unfortunately, in some of those cases, it might have been better if I hadn't done them, but there are some things that you see and are interested in, and I had a fascination with football. It grabbed me early on. There were athletic heroes that I had. Also, when I was in school, the girls weren't interested in guys who were into Shakespeare. They were interested in the guys who were running around out in the field, doing touchdowns, and stuff like that. So . . . hmmmm . . . that's a discovery: Let's try that!

So you then played professional football in LA. How were you able to get into the film business?

Well, a lot of people don't know this, but I was a free agent. There were a few teams that were interested in me. One of the teams was the Rams, who were in Los Angeles at the time. Of course, I had it designed in my head that I would come to Los Angeles, play for the Rams, and become a movie star. It was just that simple. True story: I called the guy who recruited me for the Rams, and it was on a Friday night. The guy was so drunk that he didn't know who I was. He was having a party. I could hear it in the background —there was so much noise, and he asked me some questions, and he said, "Okay, I'll call you back later." I was so insulted by that. I was all of twenty-one years old. I had another chance to play for another coach, who was coaching somewhere else, and I called him literally within the hour, and said, "I'm coming to Oakland!" And he said, "Great!" And that's how I got to Oakland. But I didn't want to leave LA because that's where movies are made. I went to Oakland and did my time there. When that was over, I went back to Los Angeles. It wasn't through the Rams, but it was back to Los Angeles.

You're back in LA—a former professional athlete—and now you're an aspiring actor. Were you ever frustrated during the period before you got Rocky?

Well, I've had a very unconventional career in a lot of ways. When I decided to come to Los Angeles, I had a play that I was going to perform in San Francisco, and something told me that if I didn't take a chance and come to Los Angeles, that it might never happen for me. So I turned

Sydney Ash (Vanity) riding shotgun to Jericho Jackson (Carl Weathers) in *Action Jackson*. Author's collection.

down this really well-produced play in San Francisco, and I came down to Los Angeles. I knew a few people in LA from San Francisco, and I started working. I did some movies for AIP, Sam Arkoff's company. I started doing a lot of television. Within two and a half years, I think I was on sixteen or seventeen episodics. The AIP movies were blaxploitation movies. And then I got the chance to do *Rocky*, so frustration? I didn't really know frustration. I'm more frustrated today with the quality of what's being made today.

When *Rocky* was released on Friday, no one knew who you were, and on Saturday, everyone was yelling at you on the streets. How did you get involved with *Rocky*?

Well, I went in for an audition around five or six o'clock in the evening. They make you wait all day long. Of course, you're chomping at the bit and you wear yourself out with the tension. It was late in the evening, and I went to what was at that time MGM/UA. I went to Bob Chartoff and Irwin Winkler's offices, and there had to be seventeen or eighteen guys, all waiting out there, these big guys. Some of them I recognized. I felt like I was someone who had just walked in from Iowa, you know? I was just so chomping at the bit for that. Nobody knew who I was. I go in and read for this thing, and the circumstances were good.

When did you realize that you were working on something special?

Ignorance is what happened. As with most of us. After we finished this movie, I saw it and there was a sense of something really special. I told more than one person, "This movie is going to be as big as *Jaws*!" I just had a feeling about what we were doing. It felt so right, so unique. It had a great synergy around all the people involved. After we finished *Rocky*, I was still doing episodic television. Back then, you could be a good guy at the start of the season, and they'd bring you back later in the season, but then you'd be a bad guy. Sometimes I'd do two roles per year on some shows. *Streets of San Francisco, Cannon*, all those. I was doing an episode of *Streets* in San Francisco, sitting on the wharf. I was sitting on a high chair, which I hate those high chairs, I prefer sitting in low chairs so that I can fall asleep, but if you fall asleep on a high chair, you could fall over and kill yourself. So I'm sitting there, doing makeup, and down the wharf comes

this young guy, good-looking guy, and he walks up as I'm sitting in this chair, and he says to me, "Oh, man, I saw a screening of your movie, and it was great! I just finished shooting a movie, and I think it's gonna be as big as your movie is!" I'm sitting there, really smug in my chair, thinking, "*Yeah, right. Sure, pal.*" This guy had just finished *Star Wars*. It was Mark Hamill. So, you just never know.

These days if a movie's a smash hit at the box office over the weekend, a sequel is greenlit right away. When did you become aware that *Rocky* would have a sequel?

I don't remember. It was a little hard to think of doing *Rocky II* without Carl Weathers because it was the rematch. (Laughing.) It wasn't your typical sequel. It was Apollo Creed fights Rocky, so who were they gonna go to? Maybe nowadays they can dream up somebody else. I made a dime on the first *Rocky*, and I made a dollar for the second one, so it was pretty nice. I was pretty happy to see that paycheck. I think I found out, maybe, in '79, something like that. It was an exciting time to find out about it. To reprise that character was fun.

For *Predator*, John McTiernan said that you're a damn good actor and a total pro and he wanted you as Dillon in his new movie. How did *Predator* come into your radar?

I got a call from my manager at the time. When I first read it, Dillon didn't have a name. I came up with his name, thank you very much. It's a great, iconic name. Marshall Dillon. It made sense. It sounded like a macho ass name. Honestly, when I first read the screenplay, I didn't see very much in the role. A lot of the stuff these days is regurgitated and comes from watching other movies and if you look at the call sheets for new movies, it's just full of facilitators. There's nothing to the characters in the scripts. There's nothing

in their hearts. There's nothing that allows you to go anywhere with the role, they're not coming from anywhere. When I read this script, there was just nothing that came off the page. But my manager said, "Why don't you go meet with Joel Silver, he really wants to talk with you." I met with him, and we had a conversation, and he was willing to help make the role special. We tried to put some humor in it, some life into it, and make that character come from some place. And watching it now . . . Arnold is much better in it than he gets credit for. I look at it and think, "Damn, man." And of course, shooting it the way McTiernan did . . . it's a great, macho, over-the-top action film. Thank God we had one woman in it to soften us up.

What was it like working on the set of *Predator*?

Ridiculous! I've said this to many people, but they were all so bent on that set. I was the only straight guy on the set! These guys were mad, they were crazy, they were out of their minds crazy. True. True. To be out there in the jungle every day . . . we drank so much tequila out there.

The first time we see you in the film is in the "*Predator* shake" scene. Where did that scene come from?

It was my idea, of course! I don't know . . . first of all, you're talking about guns. I'm not talking about projectiles, I'm talking about *guns*. You've got to figure out how to not let the other guy upstage you. The way that scene was shot . . . If you notice the way this was shot, the shot showed the back of me. Arnold gets the front shot. I'm just saying. I worked hard to keep up with this guy. Mr. Universe and all that sort of stuff.

Muscles and fitness were obviously a big part of your life then. Were your workout routines more intense as a football player than when you became an actor?

A great fight finale between the corrupt Peter Dellaplane (Craig T. Nelson) and Jericho Jackson in *Action Jackson*. Author's collection.

You know, I actually trained harder after I left football. I fell in love with training. On *Predator*, Arnold brought his entire gym. He set it up in the downstairs room, and if it's there, I'm going to use it! And so did everybody else! There were competitions. We'd get calls at six or seven in the morning to take us to the location to wherever we were going in Puerto Vallarta, and so we'd start getting up earlier and earlier, and earlier. Suddenly, it's four o'clock in the morning and you're in the gym working out. Then there were barbells and dumbbells on the set. You're in the jungle, sweating like a pig, and pumping iron!

Craig Baxley, who would go on to be your director on *Action Jackson* directed that jungle assault scene where you all attack the guerrilla camp. Any comment about Craig?

You cannot imagine how much fun that whole sequence was and how much craftsmanship and how much professionalism and how much intelligence and what a great director Craig was in setting all of that up. We had the best times on that. We shot that in six days.

Any memories of working with a young Jean-Claude Van Damme, who had originally been cast as the Predator?

Yeah, I have memories! I remember how ambitious Jean-Claude was. This guy constantly talked about being a movie star. He wanted to be a movie star, no question about it. The challenge was that the suit of the creature was . . . he was a great kickboxer, and that's what he wanted the Predator to be. But . . . that didn't work.

How did *Action Jackson* become your next movie?

I had this great name for a movie called *Action Jackson*. It was Lorimar's first or second movie, and it did okay for them. I came up with the idea, and within a month, Joel Silver had a script. I thought, "Okay, he's serious."

Did you do your own stunts in the film?

I was crazy, I didn't know any better. I thought I could do it all. We had some great stunt people on that film. They did the real dangerous stuff on it. No matter how careful you are, the strangest stuff can happen.

You did a fantastic TV show called *Street Justice* after your movie *Hurricane Smith*. Say something about working on that great show.

Yeah, it was a really unique show in that it was one of the most demanding jobs I've ever had. I had two and a half days off each year. At the end of each year, I was physically exhausted. By the seventh or ninth episode, you're just fried. And of course, you do twenty-two episodes a year. You're not even halfway through the season, and you're already run down. There were a lot of things about that show . . . you've got to pace yourself. There were always challenges, and it's always about the material, the material, the material. You're grinding twenty-two of those a year. Today, it's different. Nobody's making twenty-two episodes of shows a

A break from mayhem and time for romance in *Action Jackson*. Author's collection.

year anymore. They do runs of ten shows, twelve shows, maybe twenty or eighteen.

You had also worked on a show called *Fortune Dane* in the '80s, which had gotten cancelled early in its run.

It had a lot of potential. I had been given a deal, they had found partners, and it was just unfortunate the way it turned out. We didn't have an entire year commitment. By the time we started making that show, we only had a few scripts in the can. You can't do that. It's hard enough doing a show, you get late scripts. If you're that far behind, it's hard for the writers to come up with good stories. We were finished before we ever started.

In retrospect, were you a little relieved that *Street Justice* ended after those two great seasons?

Well, no, but physically . . . you're not relieved, you just learn that there are certain ways . . . there are a lot of elements of television that a lot of people don't know about. If it's not promoted properly, you know . . .

Any comment about working on *Hurricane Smith*, which was your follow-up to *Action Jackson*? You filmed this in Australia, right?

It was a good attempt, I think, to make a movie. On that movie, I think there were problems on that script. They never really got worked out. If you're there shooting stuff, there's not really much you can do about it. The best part of that movie was that trip to Australia. I got to work with an Australian director and actors.

Early on in your career you got to work with some of the greats like Robert Shaw on *Force 10 From Navarone*, Lee Marvin and Charles Bronson on *Death Hunt*. Talk about working with those guys.

Those guys . . . I learned more from those great actors on those movies than I ever did in the years since. They were pros. They knew how to stand up on screen and do what they did, and they were all people I liked being around too. All of them. Each one of those guys. I have nothing but good things to say about each one of them.

You've also done a number of comedic roles in recent work like *Happy Gilmore* and *Arrested Development*. You seem to work well in comedies.

As an actor, if there's good material, and you feel like it's something you want to do, you do it. I love action movies, I love movies. For me, it's about the movie. I've been very fortunate to do a lot of different kinds of movies and television. Something like *Arrested Development* where there are different audiences that you can reach. I don't have to do action there. Not everyone is necessarily drawn to action or comedy or drama. For me it's always been about doing something that I'm interested in.

I actually like the two movies you did with Hulk Hogan and Shannon Tweed—the *Shadow Warriors* movies.

They were okay. (Laughing.) The best thing about those movies was the director, Jon Cassar. He's fantastic. He's worked on *24* and many other great television shows.

I consider you an action star, and I think a lot of people feel the same way. Any final comment about being an action star?

I was blessed with a certain amount of physicality, and I can handle myself with stuntman on sets, jumping out of cars, and all that. I have certain talents, and maybe if you can develop them and bring them to fruition, and if you can maybe be in the right kinds of movies at the right time . . . I love this stuff. I love what I do.

What would you like to say to your fans?

Well, isn't it nice to have fans? (Laughing.) That's probably the best thing I can say. Some people are entertained by what I've done, so that's at least like getting on base!

Active Stealth
1999 (Paramount DVD) (CD)

"Well, you don't need to kiss the pilot's ass . . . just fondle him a little."

Captain Reynolds (Fred Williamson) and Captain Murphy (Daniel Baldwin) are held hostage by a drug cartel while protecting a member of Congress who is traveling through South America. They somehow manage to get word out that they need help, and a team quickly arrives to save them. Sadly, Murphy's friend and team member Rifkin (Hannes Jaenicke) disappears in the commotion. One year later, intelligence reports that Rifkin is alive and being held by top drug lord Salvatore (Joe Lala). Murphy puts together a small team and has to sneak over enemy lines using the latest technology, including a top-of-the-line stealth jet to transport them. Just when they think things are going as planned, he finds himself double-crossed and out-gunned. This is only a minor set-back for the soldiers since there's a whole group of revolutionaries waiting to lend them a hand.

Fred Williamson (*Hell Up in Harlem*) fans will find themselves highly disappointed after watching *Active Stealth*. The actor only appears in a small capacity and only has one action scene to strut his stuff. He gets to handle a gun during his character's rescue and pops off a few rounds at the enemy. He has a few more short scenes scattered throughout the film, and his character is responsible for setting up the mission. It should also be noted that hardcore wrestling legend Terry Funk (from *Over the Top*) has a featured role as the villain's right-hand man. It was a pleasant surprise to see him in the film. Fred Olen Rey (*Mach 2* with Brian Bosworth) stepped into the director's chair for this mildly entertaining action film.

Acts of Betrayal

1997 (Artisan VHS) (djm)

A pair of FBI agents shows up to collect a chatty material witness, who is due to testify in court against her mobster ex-husband. The witness, Eva Ramirez (Maria Conchita Alonso), resents the position she's in, but when a squad of assassins shows up to kill her and one of the two FBI agents is killed in the crossfire, she has to rely on the other agent, a former Marine named Lance Cooper (Matt McColm), to keep her alive on the way to court. Cooper, who becomes her focal point of verbal punishment, extends his goodwill and protection only so long as he can stand it, and eventually she learns to trust and appreciate him as he continues to save her life time after time over the course of a brutal day and night as they run for their lives.

A standardized thriller with action overtones, *Acts of Betrayal* is yet another disappointing outing for kenpo expert and real-life stuntman McColm, who is held back and restrained from showing off his impressive skills as a martial artist here. The few films he did—*Red Scorpion 2*, *Body Armor*, and *Subterfuge*—were all disappointing for different reasons, but *Acts of Betrayal* is the least satisfying of them all. His co-star, Alonso, plays an incredibly annoying character who complains and mouths off to her protector for the entire length of the picture, which doesn't endear her to the audience in any way. The action in the film is fairly generic, with no standout centerpieces to distinguish it from any other action thriller of its time. A shame. Directed by Jack Ersgard.

Acts of Violence

2010 (NOV) (PB)

A mild mannered doctor (writer/director/producer/star Il Lim) tries to maintain the mundane details of his normal life while seeking retribution on the vicious gang that savagely attacked his beautiful wife (*Eyes Wide Shut*'s Leelee Sobieski, one of Lim's real-life taekwondo pupils). He cracks skulls while unloading groceries, tortures creeps on his way to the office and impales a man while stopping at the corner store to pick up toilet paper. But as Detective Mike (Tom Hanks's look-alike brother Jim) slowly circles in on the crime fighter, our rogue avenger finds solace not with his bloodstained fists but through peaceful contemplation with the mysterious Priest Bill (*Hellboy*'s Ron Perlman).

The world didn't know what hit them when this bizarre mix of brutal violence, screwball comedy and marital drama quietly squeezed onto four Southern Californian movie screens in 2010. Was it a rape revenge fantasy, a pitch-black put-on, or a total joke? And does it matter if the filmmakers can't decide either? Yep, *Acts of Violence* is pretty jaw- dropping stuff, a vanity project disasterpiece filled with stilted performances and more than a handful of questionable decisions. But Il Lim's charm shines through and his athletic abilities are pretty impressive. He's a popular instructor in Los Angeles and you can see why; his physical prowess is beyond reproach. While most will find his directorial debut an amateur mess, fans of oddball auteurs should definitely take a look at the martial arts equivalent of *The Room*.

Adios Amigos

1976 (Trinity DVD) (CD)

"I is the robber, and you is the robbie."

In the good old Wild West, Big Ben (Fred Williamson) is just trying to make his way in a tough world. Things just get harder when he meets Sam Spade (Richard Pryor), a con man who seems to get one over on him every time. He continuously starts trouble, leaving Ben to deal with the mess. Sam eventually offers Ben a cut of his con money but for one reason or another he's never able to fulfill his deal. They go from town to town, each on their own, yet somehow their paths always cross. Various men want to fight with them and all the ladies love them, which just further complicates things. When they upset the wrong people, the chances of either of them ending up with a fist full of cash gets a whole lot slimmer.

Adios Amigos is an entertaining film; it's just a huge mess as far as the story goes. There really isn't a plot to speak of, it just sort of jumps from one scene to the next with very little to no connection whatsoever. Pryor (*Bustin Loose*, *Brewster's Millions*) is comfortable in the wise-guy con man role and has a few funny moments. Williamson (*Black Caesar*) does what he does

best. He's the cigar-chewing tough guy except this time he's always trying to find his way out of trouble caused by his counterpart. There're a couple of brawls and a little bit of shooting but it all sort of feels like an old west stunt show. Williamson served as the film's director, writer, producer, and star so maybe he was still just learning the trade. It could have been so much better, but it's still watchable.

Adventures of Johnny Tao

2007 (MTI DVD) (djm)

In a middle of nowhere town, dreamer and aspiring martial artist Johnny Dow (Matthew Twining) finds his life turned upside down when otherworldly demons invade the area and begin possessing townsfolk. His friend Eddie (Matt Mullins from *Bloodfist 2050*) is possessed by the leader of the demons, and what he's after is a magical carved dragonhead that Johnny's father found and melded onto his guitar. The demons (who have insatiable appetites) lay siege to the town, and Johnny is assisted by a female Chinese warrior named Mika (Chris Yen), who teaches him some vital moves before they go into battle to protect the world.

Matt Mullins as the villain Eddie in *The Adventures of Johnny Tao*. Courtesy of Matt Mullins.

Ultra corny and shot on a low budget, but with its heart in the right place, *Adventures of Johnny Tao* is notable for co-starring Matt Mullins, whose potential as a leading action star and martial artist has thus far gone unnoticed and untapped. He was impressive in the junky effort *Bloodfist 2050*, and in this film he's more of a novelty item than a centerpiece fighter. His co-stars are adequate, and the fight scenes are nothing special, but there's still a very slight sense of charm and bemusement to the proceedings. James Hong has a cameo. Kenneth Scott (*Troum*), who played Raphael in *Teenage Mutant Ninja Turtles II: The Secret of the Ooze*, wrote and directed this film.

Aftershock

1989 (Image DVD) (CD)

After World War III leaves the world in shambles, a tyrannical military leader (Richard Lynch) rules what's left with an iron fist. His next in command, Quinn (John Saxon) makes sure the survivors abide by their rules and if they don't, severe punishment is dealt. One lone hero named Willie (Jay Roberts Jr.) is about to make a huge impression on them when he unwittingly teams up with an alien (Elizabeth Kaitan) who will die if she can't make it to her extraction point. The two of them, along with Gerard (Chuck Jeffries), battle their way across the wasteland to get her there.

Aftershock is overflowing with action heroes and B-movie staples. You have bad guy duties being filled by actors like John Saxon, Michael Berryman, and Richard Lynch. To handle the relentless action they bring in the man with the whitest pants of the apocalypse, Jay Roberts Jr. (*White Phantom*). This hero brings plenty of action to the table, and he isn't alone. Along with Roberts Jr. we have Chuck Jeffries (*Superfights*), James Lew (*High Voltage*), Al Leong (*Die Hard*), and Matthias Hues (*No Retreat, No Surrender 2*) showing up to ignite the screen. This film is never dull, with the bizarre plot twists, the pretty alien, killer landscapes, and nonstop action, *Aftershock* is a cut above the other low rent *Mad Max*-imitation films. The cast is fantastic and director Frank Harris (*Low Blow*) should be commended for delivering such a fun, martial arts–filled, post-apocalyptic romp.

Against the Dark

2009 (Sony DVD) (CD)

"I'm the motherfucker that's gonna do you what you've been doing to everybody else."

The world has become a wasteland of the dead. Well, not exactly dead—they're infected with some sort of virus that has awakened a blood lust in them. There are very few survivors left, and the military is ready to wipe out the area, despite the fact that they have a team of hunters inside. A group of survivors have taken refuge inside an abandoned hospital and the vampire/zombie hybrids are closing in. Tao (Steven Seagal) and his group of fighters find the survivors and risk their own lives in order to save them. Meanwhile, time has run out and two military leaders, Cross (Linden Ashby) and Waters (Keith David), are butting heads over whether to bomb the area or wait to see if the hunters will emerge with the survivors.

Against the Dark is a film that could have been destined for cult film greatness, but instead it's a complete mess with some decent effects. Steven Seagal sort of coasts his way through the film in what mostly amounts to an extended cameo. He mumbles a few lines and swings a sword at the infected vampires, zombies, or whatever they are. The one person who does stand out in the film is Tanoai Reed (Priest), the cousin and occasional stunt double for Dwayne Johnson. He has several impressive fight scenes with the infected using fists and feet, and even has a vicious knife fight against them. The story is sort of convoluted, and it's obvious that some talent was wasted. You can't deny how good some of the practical effects looked

but without anything else to grasp on to, Seagal vs. Vampires was a brilliant idea turned into a missed opportunity. Directed by Richard Crudo.

Agent Provocateur

(a.k.a. **Agent Elite**)

2012 (djm)

A girl named Alex is targeted by a covert, off-the-books organization that contracts out to the government, and the group kills her parents and takes her to a facility to be raised as a killing machine. Years later, Alex (played by newcomer Naomi Karpati) has developed into a kickboxing, nearly emotionless agent, and her handler (played by James Richards, who also directed) feels confident enough to send her out on the field. Her first few assignments (including a random one that is meant to test

Newcomer Naomi Karpati as Alex in James Richards's hard-edged *Agent Provocateur*. Courtesy of James Richards.

Naomi Karpati as the kickboxing killer agent in *Agent Provocateur*. Courtesy of James Richards.

her skills) are complete successes, but when something happens to her handler, she's left without a mentor or supervision of any kind. She goes out into the world and tries to start a life, but the agency that engineered her rashly reacts to her absence as an act of defiance. They send out waves of assassins to kill her, and Alex turns on her killing craft and literally slays everyone who goes up against her. Wave after wave (after wave) of killers are dispatched at her hands, so the agency comes up with a new plan: They place a handsome, normal-seeming guy in her everyday routine, and Alex falls for him, not realizing at first that he's meant to kill her. When she discovers his intentions, she kills him without a moment's hesitation and goes after the agency itself.

Very similar in theme and style to the Gina Carano vehicle *Haywire*, *Agent Provocateur* is really brutal and grungy in its delivery, but it's effective because its star Karpati seems like a genuine, raw talent. From Hungary, Karpati is a fierce kickboxer with an interesting look, and I'd like to see if she's able to continue as an action star. Director Richards also did the martial arts action film *Among Dead Men*. Filmed in Australia.

Agent Red

2000 (Key DVD) (djm)

A patchwork, military-esque exploitation movie starring Dolph Lundgren in a low point in his career, *Agent Red* is a desperate attempt to make something tangible from the severely edited and chopped footage of its initial production, which was begun by screenwriter and director Damien Lee. At least forty minutes of Lee's footage was scrapped and reshoots from director Jim Wynorski and screenwriter Steve Latshaw were ordered, thus tying loose ends together by threads. The story has something to do with some terrorists stealing a weapons-grade virus from a military facility and threatening to launch the virus via submarines, which creates a global threat. A Marine named Matt Hendricks (Lundgren, who delivers perfunctory dialogue and smirks a few times) is called in to quell the threat and deliver the virus back to its origin. Stock footage of submarines and explosions are spliced in to make it seem like it had a big budget, but if you can smell a rat, then the whole movie is a red herring.

Alex (Naomi Karpati) walks away after a beatdown in *Agent Provocateur*. Courtesy of James Richards.

Lundgren throws a few punches and shoots two guns at once a couple of times, but it's obvious that this movie should not have been made. Lundgren has panache and grace in everything he does, and he amazingly manages to walk away from this movie with his dignity intact, but anyone else would have crumpled under the strain of the whole façade. Director Lee has worked with many action stars including Don "The Dragon" Wilson, Jeff Wincott, Roddy Piper, and Jesse Ventura. Wynorski did *The Assault* with Stacie Randall. Screenwriter Latshaw wrote quite a few vehicles for action stars, including *Command Performance* for Lundgren.

Airboss

1997 (Echo Bridge DVD) (CD)

"Come on, evade before I slam this rocket right up your ass!"

When it comes to superweapons, nothing beats the MIG 35, a stealth fighter jet hidden in the Soviet Union at an abandoned air base. Colonel Vlad Kotchev (John Christian) and his assistant Nadia (Kelly Gleeson) decide it's the perfect time to steal it for their own vendetta. The American government learns of this development and assigns Bone Conn (real life Navy Seal Kayle Watson) to head up a team. They also assign fighter pilot Frank White (Frank Zagarino) to accompany them into battle. Conn and White butt heads but soon learn to respect one another. When they learn of the MIG's location, they arm themselves with whatever they can carry and raise some hell.

It would be interesting to see just how long these *Airboss* films would be if they cut out all of the stock footage. To guess, I would say they're comprised of about fifty percent new footage and fifty percent stock footage . . . *each*. And if you watch all of them, you will see much of the same stock footage reused throughout. The only reason to delve into this series is if you're a Frank Zagarino (*Strike Zone*) fan. Most of his action scenes are in fake cockpits with stock air battles but during the finale when the team raids the fortress, there's at least some heavy artillery gunplay and a few explosions. Zags has the military look but is far more deserving of a better project. There are four films in the series, and all feature Zagarino (as well as several other returning cast members) and are directed by J. Christian Ingvordson.

Airboss II: Preemptive Strike

1998 (Echo Bridge DVD) (CD)

"Next time I'm done taking my zero-g piss and the bags full, I'm gonna target your quarters."

Frank White (Frank Zagarino) is back, and this time he finds himself flying a space shuttle on a mission into space. The scientists aboard the shuttle are doing a test on the Ebola virus, possibly turning it into an airborne virus, but they're looking for a cure. When the shuttle lands, the scientists disappear and White thinks everything is a bit fishy. He starts going around and asking questions until he finally finds one of the scientists in a quarantine hospital bed, who tells him the virus was taken. Frank's life quickly becomes threatened after he speaks with a CIA head and feels this guy is crooked. Without too many people he can trust, Frank launches an all-out assault on the crooked operatives in order to reclaim the stolen virus and save millions of innocent citizens.

As enjoyable as it may be, *Airboss II* never quite captures the essence of Zagarino's awesomeness. Made on a shoestring budget and once again directed by J. Christian Invordsen (*Strike Zone*), it's always interesting to see how an action scene can be pieced together using a plethora of stock footage intercut with reaction shots from the actors. There's a lack of Zagarate, but there are a couple of gun battles and some high-flying excitement, so there isn't much else for action fans to complain about. Zagarino has some great dialogue, there's a dash of nudity (Queen of the B's Debbie Rochon appears briefly), and all the stock footage you can eat, *Airboss II* is destined to find a rabid audience somewhere.

Airboss III: The Payback

2000 (Echo Bridge DVD) (CD)

"I swear it, Cain:
I'll kill you deader than hell."

A Russian kingpin steals a large shipment of plutonium with the intent to sell it on the black market to the highest bidder. The American government becomes paranoid of what might happen and decides to assemble a joint task force with the military and the FBI. Buckley (J. Christian Ingvordsen) and Conn (Kayle Watson) are the two military men who team up with agents Murphy (Jerry Kokich) and Daniels (Caroline Strong) to go behind enemy lines. While it's difficult for the four of them to function as a team, they eventually learn it's the

only way to complete the mission. When one of the team members is killed, they bring in hot shot Frank White (Frank Zagarino) to take the place of their fallen comrade, and he's the only one who can help unite the team.

Airboss III is a tough film to sit through. It was shot on a shoestring budget by director J. Christian Ingvordsen who has made a career of directing low-budget DTV action films. The film was billed as a vehicle for Frank Zagarino (*Project Shadowchaser*), but his involvement is barely a supporting role. He shows up once or twice during the first hour of the film for a moment or two then doesn't really get into the action until the finale. He never gets a chance to fight. Some substandard military action is all we get. There is a staggering amount of stock footage that never really mixes well with the real stuff. Zagarino is the only saving grace of the picture and even then, only watch this if you're a hardcore fan.

Airboss IV: The X Factor
(a.k.a. Eco Warrior)

2000 (Echo Bridge DVD) (CD)

"Another pound of pressure on this trigger and you would have shot me in cold blood. You're pretty good with a gun for a hippie chick."

When his commanding officer comes calling, Frank White (Frank Zagarino) just can't tell him no, even if he wants to. The CO's sixteen-year-old daughter has signed up with a group known as the Eco Warriors. They're looking to expose a huge company causing massive damage to the environment. These Warriors don't always operate within the law, so the CO asks White to get on board the ship they're sailing on so he can keep an eye on the girl. When members of the crew start turning up dead, no one trusts anyone because one of them has to be the killer.

Frank Zagarino (*Strike Zone, The Protector*) returns as his White character for the fourth and final time. These movies, directed by J. Christian Ingvordsen (he helmed the previous three entries as well) are all low-budget affairs and only mildly entertaining. The only thing holding these pictures together is Zagarino. The first thirty minutes of the film is almost completely unrelated to the rest of it and has his character captured and being tortured. He has to be rescued by his team since he was drugged with a truth potion. I'm sorry, but the Zags doesn't need rescuing; he should be the one kicking the ass. The final hour with the second story is more entertaining, and Zagarino has some fun moments. It's still light on action but just being able to savor the Zags on screen is reward enough.

Alien Agenda

2007 (Allumination DVD) (djm)

*"Enslave them?
I want to exterminate them!"*

A late addition to Mark Dacascos's line of action and martial arts films, *Alien Agenda* casts him as a *Terminator*-like hero from another planet who is trying to stop fellow aliens from another world from invading Earth. Set entirely on Earth, the events play out in a cat and mouse fashion with Dacascos chasing aliens in human form from one location to the next, where shooting, stabbing, and kickfighting ensue. Nearly indestructible, his character takes a lot of punishment from various other disposable characters. His nemesis is played by Billy Zane, and his greatest ally is a pretty waitress whom he saves from being killed at a diner.

Directed by Jesse Johnson, a stunt coordinator and director in his own right, this film is a surprisingly solid action/science fiction genre picture that should please Dacascos fans more than anyone else. He looks great, is given lots of fight scenes, and he's on screen quite a bit, doing his fair share of physically difficult maneuvers and chase scenes. In an early scene, he fights Darren Shahlavi (*Ip Man 2, Bloodmoon*). *Alien Agenda* is nothing we haven't seen before and done better elsewhere, but it passes the grade. Director Johnson also did *The Last Sentinel* with Don Wilson and *The Package* with Steve Austin and Dolph Lundgren.

Alienator

1990 (Shout Factory DVD) (djm)

*"She's one hell of a woman . . .
on any planet!"*

From exploitation filmmaker Fred Olen Ray, *Alienator* is an ultra low-rent take on *The Terminator* and *Predator*, starring female bodybuilder Teagan Clive as the title character. She's a half-robotic (or maybe all robotic, I'm not certain) bounty hunter, sent to Earth to eliminate an escaped felon named Kol (Ross Hagen), who managed a great exodus from a penal colony in space. He crash-lands in a forest on Earth, disrupting a road trip of a bunch of college students, who run him over with their van. The kids take him to the nearest forest ranger (played by John Phillip Law), who tries to help the guy out, but Kol is being hunted by The Alienator, who has a bazooka laser for a hand and a metallic bikini that repels shotgun blasts. It's all pretty standard stuff.

Teagan Clive struts around the forest, pretending to shoot lasers out of her hand, but the movie's pretty much a stinker, so if you're going to see it for curiosity's sake, good on you. In the movie, she looks like a kid's idea of what

a punk rock alien would look like, but drawn in crayon. There weren't sequels. Clive was later in the post-apocalyptic junker *Interzone*.

Alien Opponent

2011 (Shout Factory DVD) (djm)

The potentially great "Rowdy" Roddy Piper—a former wrestler and the star of John Carpenter's *They Live*—co-stars in this misogynistic frat-house-mentality action movie that concerns a crash-landed alien in a robotic suit that runs amok in a backwoods town. Piper plays a foul-mouthed priest who rallies the local militia into hunting a *Predator*-esque alien, who drops spoors of alien leeches all over the place, and characters that were just named and introduced die in spectacularly gross ways, which is supposed to funny. A mysterious out-of-towner (an entirely boring Jeremy London) joins the hunt, along with a stripper, a gold digger, a soldier looking for his estranged daughter, and a mother and daughter who just recently killed the patriarch of their family for being incestuous and abusive. Piper has a few smackdown scenes, but he meets a grisly fate at the end of a chainsaw after he's turned into a zombie by the leeches.

It's amazing that *Alien Opponent* got made. The whole thing (directed by Colin Theys, who also worked on the effects) is a haphazard effort that feels like a train wreck from the first scenes onward, and even the inclusion of Roddy is sad because he looks depressed in it. After his days as a wrestler, he made a handful of worthy movies (*They Live, Back in Action, Tough and Deadly, Dead Tides*), but the evidence speaks for itself: he's appeared in a lot of bad movies that tarnish his name and reputation. *Alien Opponent* should never be seen by his fans. It's a disgrace.

Alien Uprising (a.k.a. U.F.O.)

2012 (Phase 4 DVD) (djm)

Some young people are out clubbing one night in London when aliens invade Earth, and while it takes them a while to figure out what's going on in the middle of their bacchanal, the streets get chaotic pretty quickly with looters, marauders, and hapless civilians rushing out to stock up on groceries. Michael (Sean Brosnan, the son of Pierce) has just hooked up with the girl of his dreams, a mysterious foreigner named Carrie (Bianca Bree, daughter of Jean-Claude Van Damme), and just when things start going haywire all around them, they are thrust in a trust-me-or-die scenario when they and their friends are literally faced with a full-scale alien attack with spaceships zapping people around them, not to mention encountering some dangerous thugs who want their supplies. To their rescue is a survivalist named George (Jean-Claude Van Damme) who seems to have been expecting such a scenario, but even his survival instincts aren't enough to keep him alive when he's snuffed out by a zapper, leaving those who were depending on him to fend for themselves. The film ends on an unsatisfying cliffhanger.

Populated with thoroughly unappealing characters and an amateurish directing sensibility, *Alien Uprising* is viewing fit for very few, and even those few will be disappointed with how it all turns out. Van Damme's participation isn't really suspect because his daughter is given a lead role, and as a way of christening her, he fights her in a key scene. If you're seeing this movie just because he's in it, you will be upset that he only shows up for a few crucial scenes, but if you're a completist, you will need to track it down. A bit-part player named Joey Ansah has an impressive fight scene with Brosnan (who could turn out to be an action star someday), and Ansah is someone to watch out for. He was the youngest person in the United Kingdom to receive a black belt in ninjutsu, and it's very clear that you and everyone else should pay attention to him. He's the real thing. *Alien Uprising* was directed by Dominic Burns.

Ambushed (a.k.a. Hard Rush)

2013 (Anchor Bay DVD) (djm)

Small-time entrepreneurs turned drug mavens Eddie and Frank (Gianni Capaldi and Daniel Bonjour) step over the line when they kill some goons who work for a real-thing mobster named Vincent Camastra (Vinnie Jones). Camastra warns them to stay away from his turf, but the two young dealers allow ambition and carelessness to get them in more trouble than they can handle. On their trail is a recklessly dirty cop named Jack Riley (Randy Couture), who goes way over the edge in search of drugs to feed his habit. Several other detectives are on a case involving Camastra and the two young dealers, and one of them , Beverly (Carly Pope), is deep undercover as Frank's girlfriend. Detective Maxwell (Dolph Lundgren) is concerned that fellow detective Beverly has gone too far, and when Detective Riley bulldozes through their investigation to score a load of drugs, everything goes berserk, and a whole bunch of people end up dead.

With Lundgren and Couture appearing on screen together outside of an *Expendables* movie, you'd think you'd be in for something special. Wrong. *Ambushed* is a low-grade crime drama with zero appeal. It gives its lead stars secondary roles, and it puts the two young drug dealers front and center as the main characters, which is a massive mistake. None of the characters in the film are appealing. Even Lundgren (who is impossible not to like) is relegated to a one-note role, and his foil played by Couture is a despicable character who's on a downward spiral. At the end of the film, they wrestle each other in the rain (which is the best scene), but what a waste of time to get there. Director Giorgio Serafini also directed *Blood of Redemption* with Lundgren, Jones, and Capaldi. That was also pretty terrible.

American Hunter

1989 (NOV) (djm)

A strip of microfilm that contains all of the secrets of the US government goes missing, and a secret agent named Jack Carver (Christopher Mitchum) is called in to go to Indonesia to track down the culprits before they can sell the film to terrorists. Carver runs afoul of a small-time crime ring that has a badass wetworks enforcer named Adam (played by real-life kickboxing legend Bill "Superfoot" Wallace). Carver works his way through the crime ring, finally facing off against Adam in the finale that first places them on a speeding train, and then at a warehouse.

Action-packed mayhem fills the screen in director Arizal's exploitation exercise *American Hunter*. The whole thing was shot in Indonesia, and the level to which the stuntmen were willing to go to make the action and fight scenes look convincing is apparent in the explosions, stunts, and close-quarter fisticuffs. Bill Wallace's scenes in the movie are the highlights, and his stuff at the end with Mitchum is fantastic and pretty convincing. If you can find this movie out there in the world, it's worth watching.

American Kickboxer

(a.k.a. American Kickboxer 1)

1990 (Cannon DVD) (djm)

If this film and just about any other kickboxing movie were to fight in a ring, this movie would lose, and *hard*. The hero, B. J. Quinn (played by real-life champ John Barrett from *Gymkata*) is really unappealing and hard to relate to. He comes off of winning the title, and at a party afterwards, his nemesis, Jacques Denard (Brad Morris) goads him into hitting someone else on accident, and that person dies as a result. Quinn is sent to prison and barred from ever competing professionally again. When he gets out, he is angry and bitter, and his nemesis is on top in the kickboxing world. The only guy who will give him the time of day is another fighter (played by Keith Vitali from *Revenge of the Ninja* and *No Retreat, No Surrender 3*) who was beaten by Denard. They train together, with the hope that Quinn will get his day in the ring with Denard. As Denard faces very little challenge with his opponents in the ring, he decides to call Quinn out for a fight for $100,000. This gives Quinn his chance to beat his nemesis fairly.

The big failing of the film is the script. It's all very by-the-numbers, and unfortunately, Quinn isn't someone we're rooting for. I was hoping Keith Vitali would have a bigger role, and it should have been him fighting Denard for a rematch at the end. An in-name-only sequel was made but *To the Death*, starring Barrett, is the better answer to a sequel. Frans Nel directed this.

American Kickboxer 2

1993 (Lionsgate DVD) (djm)

"You think you're Dirty goddamn Harry, and you're not making my goddamn day!"

Unrelated sequel to *AK2*, this one is about a wiseass, toothpick-biting cop named Mike (Dale "Apollo" Cook) who is asked by his ex-wife (Kathy Shower) to help her find her daughter who's been kidnapped for a huge ransom. When he arrives to help out, he is upset that his ex also called on the guy who she cheated with during their marriage and is the father of her daughter— David (Evan Lurie), a kickboxer. Mike and David hate each other's guts, but they decide to team up and find the kidnappers anyway. The last thirty minutes of the movie is filled with nonstop action and fighting.

The teaming of Cook and Lurie is ingenious. They're both actors with really rough acting abilities, but their chemistry on screen works. Fans of early '90s straight-to-video martial arts action movies should have a good time with this one. About half of the film was shot in Los Angeles, and the later half was shot in the Philippines, where Cook and Lurie face an onslaught of guys who want to kill them. Jeno Hodi directed it.

American Ninja

1985 (MGM DVD) (djm)

"He possess great skills!"

The quintessential '80s ninja flick that has endeared itself in the hearts of millions of men who were boys when they first watched it on TV, Cannon's *American Ninja* has an innocent charm and a playful, pure quality that recalls a day and age when action movies were still fun and cool. The hero is Joe Armstrong (Michael Dudikoff, who was made a star due to this film), an amnesiac grunt on an Army base in the Philippines who saves the life of his superior's daughter (Judie Aronson) when ninjas attack

The American Ninja (Michael Dudikoff) and the Black Star Ninja (Tadashi Yamashita) face off in Cannon's *American Ninja*. Author's collection.

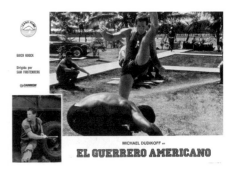

Pvt. Joe Armstrong (Michael Dudikoff) teaches Cpl. Curtis Jackson (Steve James) a lesson in *American Ninja*. Author's collection.

her entourage. It becomes immediately obvious that Joe is skilled in the art of ninjitsu, and his skills are noticed by the Black Star ninja (Tadashi Yamashita). Joe isn't well liked on base, but when Corporal Curtis Jackson (Steve James) begins to like him after losing to him in a fight, Joe gains a friend and sidekick. Joe and Curtis become involved in a 007-type plot centered around a megalomaniac who has built a drug empire near the Army base and whose army of ninja warriors protect his interests. It might as well be a cartoon, but in all seriousness, this is a movie of great import to fans of action and martial arts movies the world over.

It's fairly tricky to tell why *American Ninja* became such a cult hit. Sam Firstenberg, the director, never overplays the comic book aspects of the plot, and the action is more or less "realistic" (no fast cutting, no flashy camera angles, etc.). While this film was playing in theaters, the animated show, *G. I. Joe* was playing on television, and it's no wonder boys fell in love with it. Michael Dudikoff made an engaging and understated introduction to the action movie world with this film. He and Steve James appeared in *Avenging Force* (also by Firstenberg) next. John Fujioka co-stars as Joe's adoptive father.

INTERVIEW:

MICHAEL DUDIKOFF

(djm)

For any young boy who grew up in the 1980s, Michael Dudikoff was a favored staple of the action genre. Star of the cult hit American Ninja *(1985) and other films made for Cannon like* Avenging Force *(1986),* The Human Shield *(1991), and* Chain of Command *(1994), Dudikoff was a busy actor during the 1980s and 1990s. He starred in the Stephen J. Cannell program* Cobra *in 1993 and continued working until the early 2000s before stepping out of the industry to enjoy family life. Few action stars and actors have garnered the mystique Dudikoff generated during his years on screen, and to this very day, he still casts an indelible impression.*

Video promo artwork, featuring Michael Dudikoff in David Worth's *Chain of Command*. Author's collection.

What were you doing before you became an actor?

Before acting, I was trying to make a lot of choices of what I really wanted to do. I really wanted to be a child psychologist. I loved fighting, so I used to train. I was doing jiu jitsu before I even knew what jiu jitsu really was. I went to college and did that whole thing. Finally, one day, I was working as a waiter to pay my way through college, and I was discovered by this guy who had all these beautiful women sitting around the table. I was their waiter. He said, "Hey, you should do modeling." My dad wanted me to go to the military. For me to tell my dad that I was going to go into modeling, there was just no way. My mother was home that day, and I called her and told her about what happened that day, that they wanted me to model, and my mother said, "You do it. Just do it." I said, "Well, what about dad?" "Don't worry about your dad. I'm telling you as your mother to do it." "Okay." I quit my job and took it day by day. I saw what it was all about. It was an adventure. I did it. Max, the guy that discovered me, handed me my first check, and asked me if I wanted to try it out as a career. I said, "Yeah, I'll try it." From that day on, I worked from one modeling job to the next. Elite wanted me really bad. All these modeling agencies, Ford in New York, I wound up going to Italy for *Vogue* and all these different magazines and had a lot of fun.

Did you ever look back and want to return to school at this point?

I wanted to go back to school because I knew that it would be something that I could fall back on. The way it was going, everything was going so fast and I was getting everything I was going up for. There was a commercial agency called Pacific Artists, and they told me that they wanted to meet with me. I didn't know if I wanted to do commercials, I wanted to go to school. So I went over there to meet with them, and I went up for a commercial. I got it. All I had to do was take my shirt off and flash my body, all tan, and it was the right thing at the right time. Then, there was another commercial. Then there was another. Eventually, I totally dropped out of college. I went ahead on this journey that my mother knew that I would be going on, and the whole time I talked to her about it. It was really great for our relationship. She was such a positive person and wanted to see me succeed in some way. I did it, and enjoyed it. I told myself that it shouldn't be about my looks. I had to get out of there.

At what point did you make the transition to acting?

I wanted to learn, and I wanted to grow, I didn't want to just stand in front of the camera and smile. I'm not the *GQ* guy. I just felt that maybe I could act. After the commercials and my success there, an agent saw me. This agent saw me and thought that I should be acting. He heard how well I had been doing, and he liked my attitude. That helped me a lot. I met with him, and he told me about a show. He said, "Have you ever heard of *Happy Days*?" I said, "Oh, yeah." He told me to go in and meet someone at Paramount Studios. There was a part of a boyfriend available. I met the guy at Paramount, and I read for him. I got the part. After I did that show, there was another character named Jason on *Happy Days* available. I played that character. It was a live audience, and I heard all this laughing through the whole thing, and it was the president of Paramount Studios. He put me on a contract because he liked me. I'm going, "Wow! My mom was right. This thing is taking me places." This whole time, my father didn't even know what I was doing. I'd told my mom to just keep it hush-hush. I just kept going.

And you'd had no acting experience before that?

It was on-the-job training. I started going to acting classes and studied seven days a week with three or four different coaches. I was busy learning the craft. I took an improv class and trained a lot. If I was going to do this, I had to be really good at it. I studied and I studied, and it started to pay off. All of a sudden there was a project called *Sawyer and Finn* over at Columbia Studios, and I was up for Huck. I tested for it, and I tested again, and finally I got it. Up to that point I was twenty-four playing sixteen, but when I did Huck, I think I was twenty-nine. We made it work. It was such a kick. I got to work with all of those character actors.

So that led to *Bachelor Party*?

Yeah, with Tom Hanks. Film after film, movies of the week, and traveling. At the same time, I would go home to visit the one I loved the most—my mom, who put me on my journey. She died in my arms. I had to go back and bury her, and then I was back out again on another show. And *another* show. And then my sister passed away. I had to go back out there again. I would come home after a while and my father knew what I was doing after my mom passed away. We became really close. After my sister's death two months after my mom passed away, my father eventually passed away. After my mom passed away, I went to my father's house and he said, "Come on over!" so I went over there and we talked and all of a sudden, he said, "Come on, you want a cold beer?" I said, "Okay, dad. I'll have a cold beer." On the fireplace mantle, where all of his pro bowling trophies were placed, he had a samurai sword and the *American Ninja* poster above the fireplace. He had a mural on the left side of the fireplace that was a collection of all the posters of my films that he'd collected. I didn't even know that he'd known about me. He was my biggest fan. He would ask me, "Did you do that stunt? Did you fall off that roof?" He was so excited. I started doing more stunts in movies because of him. It made an impact on him.

Talk about some of the directors you've worked with over the years. You've worked with guys like Ted Post, Albert Pyun, Sam Firstenberg, just to name a few.

Albert Pyun, what a great guy. He'd come in and always knew what he was shooting. He smiled all the time, a real pro. I only did one movie with him—*Radioactive Dreams*—because he was already on to the next one. He did one movie after another. I look back now, and if I hadn't just taken off the way I did, I would have had more quality time with these guys because I would have loved talking to Albert Pyun, and just talk. We didn't get a lot of that. You're busy doing the movie, but of course you have your coffee in the morning: "How're you doing, Albert?" But you don't get deep. It's pretty shallow when you're just talking about the script and how to make the scene better. You commit yourself to the film and try to do the best job you can. I tried to help out as much as I could. Marlee Matlin and I did a movie together called *In Her Defense*, and the director on that was Sidney Furie. Great guy! An amazing director. I said, "What do you think I should do in this scene?" He said, "Michael! You've got great instincts! Just keep doing what you're doing! I don't wanna tell you anything—just keep doing what you're doing!" That was nice, but I wanted to be directed. A lot of directors never direct their actors. They made their casting choice and they let their actors do their thing. Sam Firstenberg . . . there's a guy in the morning, smiling, singing, not a worry in the world. "Michael! How are you?" He would have the whole day mapped out. He made it seem so easy. Every time I would do a movie with Sam, there were always smiles. If you asked him a

Michael Dudikoff and david j. moore in Hermosa Beach, California. Photo by david j. moore.

question, he wouldn't get upset, he didn't feel that you were challenging him. We would talk about it. That's what I love about him. He was very interested in the collaboration.

You've worked with a lot of stunt guys throughout the years. Bob Bralver, who directed you in *Midnight Ride* had been a well-known stuntman and coordinator before he became a director. Talk about doing stunts yourself versus letting others do stunts for you.

It's funny, but on some movies, I wouldn't do any of the stunts. I'd let the stunt guys do it all.

From everyone I've interviewed who have done pictures with you, the comments I hear about you are all positive. You have a good reputation.

When you're on a set, you make the tone because you're the lead actor. It's just that way. It's a thing that happens. You have to shake the hands and make sure that you don't have an ego. On a movie, you're all having fun, but let's be good. You've got to be careful not to step on the director's vision and have to stand back. I like to work as a team, give it all you've got, and then go home.

Talk about working in the action genre. You were almost always cast as the hero.

What's funny is this: I started out doing comedy. When I did *American Ninja*, which was my first action movie, I did many more. I remember someone was talking to my agent, and he said, "Wait a minute: what do you mean Dudikoff's doing an action movie? He's comedy!" I've done comedy, action, and I played a psychopathic killer in the Sidney Furie movie. I did another TV movie with Susan Lucci where I was a crazy. I always wanted to be a versatile actor. I wanted to do it all. Sometimes you're not given it all with the scripts that you get because the script isn't Shakespeare, so you do what you can with it. You've got to do what the director wants to do. Maybe I did those action movies, but I want to be known as an actor. There were a lot of action guys in the '80s, but they're not actors. I was known as one of the action guys, but I was known to actually act. So that was a plus. I still study acting. Even when you're not doing movies, you should still go to acting classes. You gotta keep going. It can be fun. If you haven't gone in a long time, you go in and realize that that little muscle in there isn't strong enough so you really do have to go in there.

Talk about working for Cannon. What was expected of you as one of their in-house movie stars?

Just showing up. I was at the right place at the right time. They did a worldwide search for *American Ninja*, and I got that part because I was ready. I was able to perform karate, but I was more into aikido and judo, and street fighting. It was very different, but Mike Stone taught me. I got in there and studied and was prepared. I showed up to set early every day. Always. I've never been late. That would give me time to

get to know the director and the stunt guys. Menahem Golan and Yoram Globus wanted to do more movies with me, even after the ten I did. Then [Giancarlo] Parretti became involved, and I remember Menahem pulling me one way, and Parretti pulling me another, and they would each tell me, "I'm gonna make you rich!" It was really hard for me. I just told them, "Listen, guys, I just want to work." I liked them both. I just wanted to work it out with them. The next thing you know, Cannon went under and Parretti went to jail. I was like, "Where do *I* go?" The rug was ripped out from underneath me. I had been successful in so many ways in my acting career, and some people would question that, but I feel that everything I did was a learning experience. Where I went, who I met, who I worked with. I met special people all over the world. They were nobodies who were somebodies. They were real special people. I would not have done anything different. Then, I wanted to step out of the industry a little bit and I wanted to be successful in a marriage and be a successful husband, a successful daddy, and a successful friend. There's so many levels of success, and I got to achieve that. I saw people do things the wrong way.

You're most recognized for your *American Ninja* pictures. Would you address your recognition from this series and talk a little bit about working on them?

First of all, doing those movies . . . I got malaria doing the first one. I had to be in that black outfit and it was 115 degrees. When you have malaria, you sweat profusely. I would have to get undressed, get into another outfit, and I'd fight, and then I'd have to take the wet costume off and put on a dry one. Until finally, after fight after fight and being dizzy, I had a convulsion. They laid me on the hood of a car, and I felt my body jumping like a fish out of water. I found out that I had malaria. I found out when I came home. It was tough, but working over there in the Philippines was great. If I found out that I could work there again tomorrow, I would go. The second one was filmed in Africa. Steve James, what a great guy. All he wanted to was to be the first black action hero. He wanted to make a big impression on the kids. He tried so hard. I remember doing a scene with him where he had his shirt on, and then in the next scene, I would ask him, "Steve, why do you have your shirt off for this scene?" He'd say, "My brotha, let me tell you something: I've worked real hard on this body. My shirt came *off*." I would just laugh and

we'd hug. We were like best friends. We worked out together. We ate together. Just a really great guy. Having him and Sam Firstenberg, it was just so fun to go to work every day. Injury after injury, I'd get hurt and Steve would, too.

You reteamed with James and Firstenberg on *Avenging Force*.

When we did *Avenging Force* in New Orleans, I'd have leeches all over my body from the swamps. I remember there were leeches everywhere. I'd try to burn them off, but I found out that putting salt on them would make them fall off. I was told not to pull them off. I remember one day, I told Sam, "I'm just going to sit here on a chair in the sun" because I was cold. It was a real swamp with huge rats with lice. I didn't realize that while I was sitting there taking a nap, what happened was that all of these lice were attaching themselves to me. I was scratching and it was terrible. It felt like I'd been rolling around in fiberglass.

Sam Firstenberg considers *Avenging Force* his best movie.

I liked it, too.

Do you remember your first encounter with David Bradley, whom you worked with on the fourth *American Ninja*?

You know what, when I first met David Bradley, he wanted to be in the movies so bad. He was working at a car dealership. He was selling Porsches on Wilshire Boulevard. Cannon was right down the street. I was at Cannon doing some ADR work and I took a walk during

The American Ninja (Michael Dudikoff) and the evil Black Star Ninja (Tadashi Yamashita) face to face in *American Ninja*. Author's collection.

Behind the scenes with Steve James, Michael Dudikoff, and director Sam Firstenberg on *American Ninja*. Author's collection.

Shinyuki (John Fujioka) is Joe Armstrong's (Michael Dudikoff) ninja master in *American Ninja*. Author's collection.

Steve James plays the badass Curtis Jackson in *American Ninja.* Author's collection.

lunchtime and met David Bradley just down the street. He said, "Man, I would love to do that martial arts stuff in a movie." I said, "Well, do you do any martial arts?" He said, "Yeah, since I was a kid." I said, "You know what, I'm going to talk about you."

After *American Ninja 2*, your involvement with the series was diminished to the point of simply not being in the series any longer after your co-starring role in Part 4. Any comments on that?

I wanted to do some real big stuff. I wanted to act. I just felt like this ninja stuff wasn't going anywhere. *Ninja Goes to Hawaii* . . . and I don't

For the first and last time, the two American Ninjas (Michael Dudikoff and David Bradley) team up in *American Ninja 4: The Annihilation.* Courtesy of Cedric Sundtrom

Joe Armstrong (Michael Dudikoff) impales a ninja in *American Ninja II: The Confrontation.* Author's collection.

mind doing that stuff, but I wanted some real meat and potatoes. I love to act, and I felt like I wasn't given that opportunity. If anything . . . if I'm frustrated it's only because I didn't get what I was capable of doing.

After your years with Cannon, you worked on the show *Cobra*, which was a Stephen J. Cannell program.

He was amazing. He was a great, successful, and happy man. It was so hard to see him pass on. I went to the funeral. I really enjoyed doing the show with him. He'd heard that my father had passed away, and I was having a hard time dealing with it because I didn't have a lot of friends. I had friends all over the world, but no immediate friends at home. My friend was my dad. When he died, what I really needed was to go to work. Stephen told me that I needed to put all this energy and go to work. So, I said, "Let's try it." So we tried it, and somebody dropped the ball, and it wasn't going as great as we thought it was going. It took off when it started, but the ball was dropped. That happens. You go in one show and you go into another. We shot it in Canada. When Stephen and I first talked, it was going to be called *Viper*, but that was already taken by Paramount. So then we had to change it. Stephen said, "No problem! We'll call it *Cobra*!" We got a Cobra car. We shot a sizzle reel on it, and he sold it in one day and the next day we were working.

When the show was canceled, you went back to movies.

Yeah, that's the whole thing. I never said I would only do film or just TV. I just loved working. I enjoy that whole experience of making movies. Now that I've been successful in my marriage and other aspects of my life, I want to go back and do movies again.

What kind of roles would you be willing to play now?

You know what? I would love to play a very complex character. I love Denzel Washington, and when I see some of the characters he plays . . . the bigger the budget, the more you have the leeway to explore. You can do more than one take. Some of the movies I've done, there's one take so you've got to know what you're doing. One take, boom, next. You ask for another take, and they ask why. When I did the movie with Marlee Matlin, that was done in thirteen days. I had to learn sign language. Every time I would do a line in sign, I'd forget how to do it for the next scene.

My favorite character you ever played was the character in *Soldier Boyz*.

Toliver? Yeah, yeah, yeah. I buzzed my hair for that. I can't tell you my favorite character. Every time I work, I get so into it, and I love everything I do. Can I do better? Yes. You're only as good as the script and the director. Directors can pull a lot out of you. When you do movie after movie after movie, these movies were just going *bam! bam! bam!* There was no time to think about it, I was already on to the next one. My life was

crazy. That movie was a lot of fun. I remember that one. We shot down in the Philippines. I remember they carried the dollies up and down the mountain and through valleys, reservoirs, and crossings. Little Filipino people carrying these things. They were so strong. Great people to work with.

It felt like a different Dudikoff in *Soldier Boyz*.

Some people say that about that movie, but they also say that about another movie I did called *The Silencer*. Some people say that that character was really intense. So many people love that movie. I did two movies with that director, Robert Lee. We shot it in Canada.

You've shot movies all over the world. Say something about working in the Middle East. You shot *The Human Shield* and *Chain of Command* there.

I was there during Saddam Hussein's war. I remember staying in a hotel, and a missile went over our hotel. I was very scared. "Man, I'm going to die." A lot of the people working on the movie were from Tel Aviv, and they carried guns. They'd go, "Michael: You have nothing to worry about." They had it all taken care of. I had to decide not to worry and focus on my work. But they were the warmest, most intelligent and fun people. I would have Sundays off and go to a port and relax and have coffee. You'd be on these cobblestone streets and at noon you'd hear chanting throughout the city, and I'd get the chills. I loved it there. At the time, I could have easily moved there. I really cared about the people and they cared about me. I'd go out to dinners with them and we'd talk all night. I loved that about those people. I miss that. When you go places that are beautiful where the people are beautiful . . . when you get back from a place like Africa where the people have nothing. Poor, poor people, but they are happy, happy people. Beautiful people. I was there during apartheid. Danger? Yes. I saw a necklace being done. A necklace is when they put a tire around a body and they light it on fire.

You saw this?

I saw this. There are a lot of things I've seen. There are a lot of things I've never told of things I've seen because those kinds of things I try to tune out. I don't want that in my brain. You see the things that these people go through and how they live. And they're still happy.

What have you been doing with your time lately, Michael?

I've been working with a lot of different people in a positive way. There are a lot of kids out there with no mommies and daddies, and my wife and I adopted. We let our kids know that they're adopted. At school they have to do a poster board to tell their classes about their life, and we help them and put on the board that they grew up in a little village in the Philippines, where a volcano erupted. We have two little ones. They don't know anything different. They call us mommy and daddy and they can always look at

A WWII tale of adventure, *River of Death* features Michael Dudikoff in a starring role. Author's collection.

the poster board that lets them know where they came from, where their orphanage is. There are so many kids out there with no parents. Every child needs a mommy and a daddy.

You have a legion of fans, Michael. Is there anything you want to say to them?

I do. I'm getting more and more fans. I just want them to be patient, because I do want to do another *American Ninja*. I want to find some really great martial artists and bring the series back. There's so much we can do with *American Ninja*. This is a pop culture phenomenon. Stallone was so smart doing what he did with *The Expendables*. I have fans asking me why I wasn't in that. I didn't have any say so. I didn't get that call. I'm so happy with what he did. He took '80s guys and put them in today's action, and way to go. Hey, I'll get my break. Maybe someday I'll get a blessing. I hope it'll happen. I'd love to work with Stallone. The guy's great. I applaud him. All I've got is time. Just be patient. In the long run, they'll be happy. I get people all the time saying, "I wouldn't have this martial arts studio or this dojo if it wasn't for you and growing up on *American Ninja*. Someday, I'm going to have an academy and a black belt, and I'm gonna have kids, and I'm gonna teach them martial arts. I wouldn't have done it without you." Talk about humbling. That is the biggest compliment I could ever have gotten.

INTERVIEW:
GIDEON AMIR
(djm)

The writing and producing team of Gideon Amir and Avi Kleinberger produced some spectacular results, most notably creating the core characters and outline that would eventually become American Ninja, *produced by The Cannon Group. Amir, who had a relationship with The Cannon Group pre-*American Ninja, *relates his involvement with the creation of the characters that audiences would love for generations down the line.*

How did you become involved with The Cannon Group and American Ninja specifically?

My partner Avi Kleinberger and I had just completed work on *Missing in Action* with Chuck Norris. We were prepping another movie called *King Solomon's Mines* with director J. Lee Thompson. I was his assistant director. Menahem Golan told us to leave that project and go to the Philippines to make a few movies there.

As I understand it, you and Avi came up with the characters in American Ninja. Why don't you talk about that a little bit.

What had happened was that there were a few things working in parallel. They had a script called *American Ninja* that was supposed to be the next Chuck Norris movie. But after *Missing in Action*, Chuck Norris didn't want to do it anymore because he was already a big star. So they had a title but they didn't have a movie. That script they had became another movie that Sam Firstenberg directed called *Avenging Force*. That was *American Ninja*. Also, at the same time, Sho Kosugi didn't want to work with Menahem anymore. After *Flashdance*, Menahem wanted to do an action movie that had a woman element, and that was another movie that Firstenberg directed, and that was *Ninja III: The Domination*. In that movie there was a confrontation between Sho Kosugi and the woman lead, and she beat him in one of the fights, or something, and Sho Kosugi thought that was unacceptable. He didn't want to work with Menahem anymore. Basically, now he had an *American Ninja* title, but he'd lost his ninja. Suddenly, he thought and I thought, "You know something, maybe we can come up with something with an American who is a ninja!" A young, new star. That's how the idea of creating a new persona, which would be the star of this movie, came about. Because we had to shoot in the Philippines, Avi and I thought it would be best if he was a soldier because then we know why he is in the Philippines. This was the origin. He is a lone soldier in the army in the Philippines. Later, we learn that he was in the Philippines before as a kid, so he is kind of drawn to that place. I'm from Israel, so I don't know anything about ninjas, and the introduction that Menahem gave us was that we didn't have to know a lot about ninjas, just that only a ninja can kill a ninja! (Laughing.) When I was in Israel, I went to a naval academy, which was like a boarding school, like a high school. It's a British tradition that you go to these schools and when you finish, you actually go into the army, you're already an officer. In the first

A lesson in humility between Joe Armstrong (Michael Dudikoff) and Curtis Jackson (Steve James) in Sam Firstenberg's *American Ninja*. Author's collection.

year of that school, you suffer a lot because of hazing. There was a young guy in a class next to mine, same age as me, who was rumored to be a young gold medalist of the USSR in wrestling. The big guys in school were actually looking for a confrontation with this guy. There was one who was in his senior year, who was built like a mountain. This was a Dolph Lundgren-type guy. Since it's a naval academy, and we're living on the beach and we don't go home but once a month, a slow confrontation evolved, but it took months for it to happen, but it needed to happen—it was clear. There was a confrontation between this Dolph Lundgren guy and this young wrestler. The guy kicked sand into the wrester's eyes, not once but twice, and the wrestler tells him that he's not interested in fighting him. He says, "Why aren't you interested?" Anyway, the fight starts. In this fight, something amazing happens. The wrestler stepped in front of this huge man and in one split second, the Dolph Lundgren guy finds himself on the ground. It was so quick, we didn't know what happened, and just like in the movies, he gets up and acts as if he'd tripped. Now, he's upset. Now, he's attacking the wrestler, and very quickly, the wrestler has him on the ground and he's holding him there for a moment, and then he leaves him and walks back. Now, the Dolph Lundgren guy is crazy because he's going to kill the wrestler. Now, he really runs into him with the worst look on his face, and the wrestler knocks him down, holds him down, until he can't breathe anymore and he gives up. All these seniors get this guy up and they carry him away, and that was the end of the confrontation. That was the end of them confronting us for the rest of our lives at that school. The wrestler brushed the sand off himself and walked away. (Laughing.) I remember that scene. That scene we built together with our fight coordinator, Mike Stone. With him, we devised the first fight in *American Ninja* where Michael Dudikoff puts the bucket on his head. It has a freakish quality. We wanted to make sure it was understood that this guy was not exactly normal. The real issue is that he doesn't know that. He finds out later.

Why didn't you write the script? Why did the script duties go to Paul De Mielche?

Because we were basically producers. At the time, Avi and I were in the two-four-eight business. They cost two million, they look like they were shot for four, and they make over eight million. We just wanted to move on. We were already prepping the next one. Paul was the scriptwriter. We gave him the title. It was not an issue.

Why didn't you have any involvement with the sequels?

In the Menahem/Cannon world, it all has to do with loyalty, a little Mafia-style. You have to be loyal, and if you're not really loyal, you're not really needed. It doesn't matter if you're talented or not. Besides that, Avi and I went on to do other things. At that time, we didn't really think that we needed to spend our lives with Cannon. It's interesting, but at the same time we were doing these *American Ninja* movies, New Line was doing the Freddy Krueger movies.

Michael Dudikoff in action in *American Ninja*. Author's collection.

Paul DeMielche in Beverly Hills, California. Photo by david j. moore.

Joe Jackson (Michael Dudikoff) shushes Patricia Hickock (Judie Aronson) in *American Ninja*. Author's collection.

It's interesting to see the parallel: They made a movie that was a success, and then they made sure that the second movie was better than the first, and the third is better than the second, etc. With Menahem, it wasn't like that. Since he already saw that *American Ninja* would sell, he would just take a poster to the next Cannes Film Festival, and the idea was to spend less, not more. I couldn't get excited about that.

Are you willing to share the responsibility that you and everyone else involved in the making of these Cannon ninja movies literally help put ninjas on the pop culture radar?

Yeah, we found that out when the *Teenage Mutant Ninja Turtles* started showing up. It was clear that it became mainstream. *American Ninja* brought the martial arts aspect to a wider and a younger audience. In some way, these movies were movies that fathers and sons could enjoy together. That's what made it so appealing. It's not just a martial arts movie, but a tale of a young man.

Is there anything else you'd like to add about the *American Ninja* series and your contribution to it?

Well, first of all, it fell into my lap. I'm happy both Avi and I and Sam Firstenberger did something that created a foundation for it to continue. I'm sorry that we were not part of the rest of it because we could have made it into something more viable. Maybe it will come back because it's a part of culture now. Sometimes these things do come back. Dudikoff was a very nice young man and had good qualities. It had good casting. Sam understood that Dudikoff would do well in this.

INTERVIEW:

PAUL DE MIELCHE

(djm)

Scripter Paul De Mielche was referred to producer Menahem Golan for the task of writing the screenplay for American Ninja *because he'd previously written the film adaptation for Eric Van Lustbader's book* Ninja. *He wrote* American Ninja *in two weeks, and isn't ashamed to admit that he's baffled by the success of the film and that for a time, he was actually embarrassed by the credit. The years have warmed him, though, and he relates his experience of writing the film here.*

How did you become involved with The Cannon Group and ultimately end up writing the screenplay for *American Ninja*?

It's a long story. I had a studio called Cosmopolitan Film Associations in San Francisco. We made short films and educational films. We probably made about 200 various films. None of them were features. I made a half-hour film that was a cartoony drama. I sold it to Paramount. I'd never been down to LA before. I came down and called every studio from a phone booth, looking through the Yellow Pages. This was in 1968. I got an interview with every studio in Hollywood, something that no man will ever be able to do again. Two days later, I sold that film. I got offered to work on stuff, to direct commercials. I made some documentaries for ABC. Zoetrope was happening in San Francisco, and a lot of my old crew was working with Coppola and George Lucas. I went back there and did some shorts for Zoetrope. Chris Pearce was running Zoetrope at the time. Lucas was doing *American Graffiti* and he used a lot of my crew for that. Coppola went off to do *The Godfather*, and I had his office there for a while. Chris wasn't happy, so we decided to become partners. He left Zoetrope and came back to LA. I had ICM for my agents. We raised money to make films with MGM, but we never got anything off the ground. Chris put together something with Marty Fink, a movie called *Stunt Rock* that was directed by Brian-Trenchard Smith. I wrote that script in about a week or so. I went to back to graduate school and began pursuing other things. In the meantime, Chris went to work for Cannon. He slowly became the head of production there, and then he would call me and say, "Can you help me on this project?" Because I'd been in the Marines and studied martial arts, that's how *American Ninja* came about. Chris knew I was into these things. I was approached also to write a ninja movie based on a book by Eric Van Lustbader. It was called *Ninja*. I'd read that book. Because I'd read that book, it was an inspiration to me while I was writing *American Ninja*. Menahem Golan, the producer of *American Ninja* had a good instinct about what was coming next, so he said to Chris that we should do a ninja movie. Chris referred me to him because I knew what I was talking about when it came to ninjas. Avi Kleinberger and Gideon Amir, who created the characters from *American Ninja* had just come over from Israel, and they'd come over because Menahem had told them that if they were ever in LA to come work for him.

Did Avi and Gideon already have a script of *American Ninja* before you came on board?

No, they just had a treatment. It was maybe three to five pages long. It had the basic story. It had a guy who was a ninja! (Laughing.) He had been in some kind of accident, but he didn't know he was a ninja. He had these powers that he was unaware of. I don't remember exactly what the treatment was.

Did Menahem like your first draft?

The movie is the first draft. I wrote it in two weeks. By that time, I'd written like 30 screenplays. I was a journeyman screenwriter. I was sort of embarrassed about *American Ninja* for a lot of years.

How come?

Because it wasn't a great movie. (Laughing.) I'm a better writer than what that movie is. I've written much better scripts that haven't been made, but every writer in Hollywood can tell you that much. The easy thing about Cannon was that they were always in a hurry. First draft, there was nobody there who was smart enough to make any changes. The heads of the studio wanted to pre-sell it, and if they could pre-sell it, the movie would get made.

What are you thoughts on the film?

Every writer is always disappointed when you write a great scene that doesn't end up in the film because they ran out of money. It's not really anybody's fault. The genius of Cannon was that they would pre-sell it, and that's what they would make the movie for, which was usually a low budget. When I saw the film, some of my favorite scenes weren't in the film, so I was disappointed. But I was very impressed by Dudikoff. I thought, "Wow, he pulls it off." It was believable that he could do the things that he was supposed to do.

How about the character that Steve James played? He's a fan favorite. Could you talk a little bit about the relationship his character had with Dudikoff's?

The first thing that was unique was that we brought in a black character. Originally, he wasn't supposed to be black. I grew up in Oakland, so I was trying to get black people into films because I'd been a jazz DJ.... Everyone will probably tell a different story about how Steve James got the role. Unfortunately, he didn't live long enough to have a great career, but he was starting to have a great career.

Did you have any dealings with the casting or the filming?

No. I handed in the script, and that was it.

How come you did not continue with the series?

I was on other projects. A couple of times I got brought in to work on a few scripts for Cannon, and I worked with Dudikoff on lines a few times on other things. Later, some years later, I had a deal to write and direct movies with Cannon. I wrote one for Bronson about an LA private detective. I wrote a script called *Shape Changers* and scouted locations in Israel. Chuck Norris was under contract for Cannon, and I was brought in to write some things for him. There was a movie called *Top Kick*. I wrote three scripts for Chuck. But Cannon was starting to suffer at that time. I think the reason why *American Ninja* had done so well is because MGM released it. Luckily, for Sam Firstenberg, Gideon Amir, and myself, we get residuals from MGM, and they've been very good about that.

This movie is loved all over the world. Would you like to say anything to the fans of this movie?

There's a well-known writer who wrote in an essay that the beauty of ninja movies is you know the difference between the black and the white. They're very moral, in a way. The good guy wins because he's the good guy. There is no gray area. You know why the bad guy is bad and why the good guy is good. *American Ninja* captured that. Now, there's a whole genre of this. It's a pretty standard story. Once in a while, I get a letter from a fan saying how much they love this film. You've probably heard more of these stories than I have. There are stories roaming around *American Ninja*. There's also the bonding element between Michael Dudikoff and Steve James. The person you get into a fight with ends up being your best friend. That happens in the army. *American Ninja* has been good to me. I laugh every few months when I get a check in the mail from MGM. I think to myself, "Wow, this thing has hung on for 25 years!"

American Ninja 2:
The Confrontation
1987 (MGM DVD) (djm)

"American Ninja, I presume? How very nice to meet you!"

The adventures of Joe Armstrong and Curtis Jackson continue with this lightweight sequel that delivers more or less what fans were expecting from a follow-up. Joe and Curtis (Michael Dudikoff and Steve James) are

Michelle Botes as Alicia Sanborn and Michael Dudikoff as Joe Armstrong in *American Ninja II: The Confrontation*. Author's collection.

The cool Joe Armstrong (Michael Dudikoff) in *American Ninja II: The Confrontation*. Author's collection.

dispatched to a tropical island where several United States Marines have disappeared without a trace. Once they get there, they're made fun of for being Army, but when they start producing results, the Marines start taking orders from *them*. More ninjas are thrown into the mix than in the first film: A crazed millionaire (Gary Conway, who also wrote the film) is experimenting on strong, healthy men and turning them into mindless superninjas!

Michael Dudikoff's abilities as a martial artist noticeably improved between this and the first film. Steve James has plenty of moments to shine here, and his character is more than a sidekick, which is nice. Mike Stone plays the evil henchman Ninja, and he also coordinated the fights. Sam Firstenberg directed. The German DVD release is widescreen.

INTERVIEW:
CEDRIC SUNDSTROM

(Questions by david j. moore/conducted by Thorsten Wedekind. Thorsten Wedekind interviewed Mr. Sundstrom on behalf of david j. moore in Johannesburg, February, 2013.)

As the American Ninja *franchise moved on without director Sam Firstenberg, the torch was passed to South African director Cedric Sundstrom for* American Ninja 3: Blood Hunt *and* American Ninja 4: The Annihilation. *These two entries in the series were filmed primarily in South Africa under Sundstrom's direction, and they carried the franchise onward with star David Bradley, who had initially replaced Dudikoff for*

Director Cedric Sundstrom and Michael Dudikoff on the set of *American Ninja 4: The Annihilation*. Courtesy of Cedric Sundtrom

the third entry. When Dudikoff returned for the fourth film, he was paired with Bradley, uniting the two American Ninjas for the first and only time on screen. Sundstrom relates his time directing these two notable films.

Let's talk a little bit about the *American Ninja* films. How did you come to direct *American Ninja 3*?

I had been working with Cannon on about five previous films, during the so-called '80s movie boom period in South Africa, as second unit director—first, the two *Gor* films, then the *Dragonard's*, *Skeleton Coast*, and so forth. The producer on most of them was Harry Alan Towers. In 1988, I had just finished directing a film for him called *Fair Trade*, for The Movie Group—it had a fair amount of action in it and they were impressed. As a result, one day, while I was busy working on an independent film called *The Shadowed Mind*, I got a call from them, proposing that I should direct *American Ninja 3*. Now, I was aware that there had been a part 1 and a 2.

And that 2 had been shot in South Africa . . .

Yes. So I decided to look at a whole lot of martial arts films, from Bruce Lee right across the board, and, in fact, also at *American Ninja* 1 and 2—because, in terms of genre, this was something new to me: my previous directing experience had mainly been on dramas, and that kind of thing. But I realized that if one took it seriously, as a genre, which it was—and I knew the genre was very popular—in terms of doing the comic strip approach, it would work, so I said yes, and we went straight into pre-production on it.

So what had you thought of the two previous entries?

Well, part 1 had been set and shot in the Philippines, and there we had Michael Dudikoff and Steve James doing the kind of "buddy movie," with Steve James also doing the "one-liner" thing. And it was interesting to see how these guys tackled the whole "American Ninja" concept and approached the name—they really seemed to get into that. I must just add here that, in South Africa in the '70s, we had our own two martial arts movies (also involving ninjas), with an actor named James Ryan—he was the equivalent to our Bruce Lee! The first one was called *Kill or Be Killed* and the second one was *Kill and Kill Again*. So I was aware of the genre, and the fact that they'd been made in South Africa.

The question everyone asks is why Michael Dudikoff didn't star in *American Ninja 3*, and how did you come to cast David Bradley?

Well, according to what I heard from Cannon, Michael Dudikoff's contract with them was up, plus I don't think he really wanted to do any more at that point. So Cannon said, "Let's keep Steve James, but find a new American Ninja." So we looked at new people; we held castings in L.A—there was no local casting in South Africa for that part —and one of the people we saw there was David Bradley. A thing that had struck me with Michael Dudikoff was that he was good-looking; he seemed to be able to do the moves, but there's also a vulnerable quality, so I was looking for that. In the casting tapes, they just did a reading —so no physical stuff—but in that reading, Bradley had vulnerability, and had the qualities I was looking for. Then, when I looked at his resumé, I saw that he was, in fact, a black belt, so he'd achieved something, and that reassured me about the physical aspects.

Had he done much acting before this?

No, I don't think so. We then also gave him the billing "and introducing David Bradley as the American Ninja." In the screen test, he wore contacts so that he'd have blue eyes—his eyes are actually brown—and, with blue eyes, there was a quality of Warren Beatty about him. So that's why I decided this is the man I want.

I believe you also had something to do with changing his name.

Yes, his real name is actually Brad Simpson, or something like that, and they didn't really think that was suitable, so I spoke to him, and together we decided to change it to David Bradley. [*TW: Sundstrom had worked with British actor Dai Bradley, and this gave him the idea for the name change; subsequently, Dai Bradley decided to change it to David Bradley, so now there are two actors named David Bradley!*].

Tell us a little about Steve James.

I loved him in part 2—I thought he was very solid, and also a good actor. You know, a lot of people think that these are just action movies, but I think they must have something more than that, other than just the physical skill of doing it. So, I liked what he did, I liked his presence; I liked him as a person, and I really, really enjoyed working with him. Unfortunately, he didn't do *Ninja 4*, which I was a bit upset about.

Was that a possibility—also having him in *Ninja 4*? I suppose maybe having three stars would have been one star too many?

It might have been, but even Michael Dudikoff said, when he came to do part 4, "Where's Steve James? Where's my buddy?" But I really, really thought he was an essential part of it.

Sad that he died so young [*TW: James died 3 years later, in 1993, of cancer, at 41*]—**he was a good actor, and it was a real loss, a career cut short. Did the issue of apartheid ever come up? Because I know he was apparently reluctant to shoot Ninja 2 here, because it was South Africa. Did that issue ever arise with you?**

No, it didn't. In fact, he loved our approach on the set. One day, I wore a T-shirt to set, which had a whole lot of surrounding countries on it, all vehemently against apartheid, and he was astonished that I would dare wear it! I had to convince him that I was allowed to wear what I wanted and that nothing would happen, that I wouldn't be in trouble. So he was certainly aware of it, but otherwise he never brought it up.

Going back to David Bradley—after recognizing the qualities in him that you mentioned earlier, did you feel that they materialized on set and in the film?

Oh yes. Look, it made it easier, in not having to use doubles for the fight scenes, because he knew his moves, and because of the look, and because, underneath it, I think he was also a fairly good actor—or, as we say, a "re-actor." We got on very well; he was very aware of his body, and we, as filmmakers, were very aware of getting the hits, the kicks, absolutely right, and he was, too—if he thought, or we thought, we didn't quite get it, we'd do it again.

He, of course, later went on to also do *Cyborg Cop* and *Cyborg Cop 2*, in South Africa, after *Ninja 4*. In terms of the villain, played by Marjoe Gortner, was that also your casting?

Ah, no, actually not. Other than David, I didn't cast the other imported leads, including Michele Chan, who's ex-South African. She studied at Wits drama school here in Johannesburg, and then went overseas. So, no, I didn't cast Michele, Yehuda Efroni, Steve James, of course, and Marjoe. All the rest of the local actors, support leads and smaller roles, I cast. But I liked Marjoe, because of his background of being an evangelist, and he'd done a couple of movies. An aside here—we were looking for the chief villain, and, because I loved *West Side Story* so much, I asked them to look into the possibility of getting George Chakiris—he would have been quite charismatic in that kind of role. But I also liked Marjoe Gortner.

That was the first film Gortner had done in quite a while, after going through his evangelist phase. Then there were a couple of South Africans in prominent roles, which was nice. Firstly, Evan Klisser.

Yes, Evan J. Klisser. I'll never forget, we were doing a wardrobe call, and, after I'd cast him, I'd told Evan to keep his American accent going, and when he met David Bradley and Steve James, they thought he was from California! He sounded so authentic, they were quite shocked that he wasn't American.

Sean Davidson (David Bradley) as the new American Ninja in Cedric Sundtstrom's *American Ninja 3: Blood Hunt*. Courtesy of Cedric Sundstrom.

Publicity shot for *American Ninja 4*, featuring the two stars, Michael Dudikoff and David Bradley. Courtesy of Cedric Sundstrom

Well, I was pleased that the South Africans, Evan and Adrienne Pearce, got decent billing. On *American Ninja 2*, Michelle Botes was essentially the female lead, but she gets no upfront billing, and is only included in the cast list at the end—which was the fate of so many South African actors during the movie boom years; often, they were much more experienced than the imports, but not accorded the equivalent respect and just taken for granted.

Absolutely! I insisted that not be the case on this one.

Moving on to the writing—did you have any involvement with Gary Conway, the writer of part 3?

Okay, here is a little point of contention. He had, I think, written *American Ninja 2,* and acted in it, and his script for *Ninja 3* was almost a rehash of part 2. So they decided—and I agreed—we should do a rewrite, because we were introducing someone new, and we didn't want him to ape or simply be in the shadow of Dudikoff; we wanted to put new things into it. I was working with a local writer, we were putting ideas together, and then I went down to the set of *River of Death*, which was a bigger movie than *Ninja 3* was, and which Michael Dudikoff was starring in, the last in his contract for Cannon. So I met Dudikoff for the first time there, and then collaborated with its writer, Andy Deutsch, on the rewrites for *Ninja 3*. The funny thing with that was that I'd put two sequences in there, one of which had them accessing the lab with a micro-light—I thought, visually, that would be a nice, creative way to get them there—and then I got a call from LA from Menahem Golan, saying "Cedric, we're just looking at the script—what's a micro-light?" And the other sequence I put in, which he also didn't quite understand, we ended up not shooting. But, to answer your question, no, absolutely no contact with Gary Conway. And then the thing was that the Writers Guild of America came to an agreement on the issue of who had written the script, and, in both versions, I get credited with writing the screenplay.

So there are different credits in different versions?

I think so, but in the main version, that's how it ended up.

Location-wise, you shot in Johannesburg and Durban, right? *Ninja 2* having been shot in Cape Town . . .

That's right. Part 2 was also partly shot in Johannesburg and Pretoria. For part 3, we had to come up with a place (not in South Africa) called "Triana," where the Games took place, and we knew we needed a coastal, tropical feel for that, and then the lab and most of the rest of it was done here, in Johannesburg.

There was a whole extensive sequence in Durban, which was doubling for the Caribbean, shot at the Indian Market, which landed on the cutting room floor. Was there a reason for this?

Yes, we'd put in a whole bit about a Bruce Lee-fundi coming out of the crowd and challenging them, and then there was a whole chase sequence, also involving him. But I think that maybe they thought we were taking away from our leads, by introducing another martial arts expert, so that didn't make the final cut, along with the chase and them ending up in jail. Yes, I think especially when they were coming up with a new *American Ninja*, I don't think they needed that, and it was better.

Tell us a little bit about the budget.

Okay—I have a sneaking suspicion that, since the *American Ninja* films by then already had a built-in fan base, and they were running into some budget problems on *River of Death*, shooting down in Port Edward at the time I was about to start—and definitely a bigger picture than mine —they nipped some of my budget, to pay for the other one. I wasn't privy to the producing level, so I don't know exactly what the budgets were, but I think *Ninja 3* was in the region of 2.5 million, maybe 3 million, possibly more, although you must remember that, with the technicians and other things we could offer, it was still much cheaper to make films here.

Was the budget ever problematic at any stage—making it difficult for you to do what you wanted to do?

No. I was called in once, when they wanted to know why I wanted a thousand extras—I told them it was the opening sequence of the kickboxing tournament, there would be lots of people there, and that you needed to grab them (the audience) straight away, and after I'd explained that to the producers, they signed off on it and let me have my extras.

How did the film do?

In South Africa, it did extremely well. It was the most successful of all the films shot in South Africa during that time. But I also heard reports that it had done well in other territories all over the world and was on television a lot, all over the place. You must remember that, at that time, Cannon still had access to distribution via their cinemas, internationally (in South Africa, it was the Nu Metro cinemas, which had been started by Cannon's Avi Lerner). This seemed to be waning at the time, as well, but, all in all, yes, I think it did pretty well.

Yes, a lot of those Cannon films went straight to video, but the *American Ninja* films all received a theatrical release. I remember being in New York in 1987, and *American Ninja 2* was showing in Times Square, with a huge banner advertising it!

Oh yes—I was always happy about the fact that, while the movie boom was on, at least all of my films saw the inside of a cinema!

Sean Davidson (David Bradley, left) and Curtis Jackson (Steve James, right) blend in the crowd in *American Ninja 3: Blood Hunt*. Author's collection.

You shot *American Ninja 3* towards the end of 1988—when did you start on *American Ninja 4*? Had they already decided they wanted to do another one, and did you start developing it straight away?

American Ninja 4 was 1990—and yes, the writing was already on the wall (with regard to the South African movie boom). Things were starting to wind down, shall we say—in fact, I don't know if they still used the tax incentive at that point—but *American Ninja 3* had done so well, I think they wanted to squeeze one more in, while they could. And, significantly, it turned out that Cannon was still owed one more movie by Michael Dudikoff, whose contract had been renewed in the interim. So they said, "Here comes the challenge—we're bringing Michael back, and they had a script, which they sent me, but unfortunately it had Michael and David Bradley, but no more Steve James, which was a pity.

How did Michael Dudikoff and David Bradley respond to one another?

Initially, I don't think they got on well, to the point that David Bradley resented the fact that Michael had come back, and that, now that he had proved himself as the American Ninja, the other one was coming back. And I think in his mind he didn't adjust to that too well. Michael thought, I am "It" and I'm back, but he was more gracious about it, I think, than Bradley was. There were certain sequences that I shot, using doubles—from behind the double onto David, and then vice versa from a double onto Michael. But there was a scene where they had to be in it together, which was a nice fight scene where Michael seemingly fights with one of the Japanese, who then turns out to be David Bradley—so he was fighting Michael Dudikoff. But, other than that, I kept them apart. There were certain memos going back and forth, that they'd wanted the buddy-buddy thing with Dudikoff and Bradley, but because of David's attitude, they'd lost that in the performance.

If I recall correctly, David Bradley ultimately gets captured, and they send Michael Dudikoff in to rescue him?

Yes, and I don't think David liked that either—he resented the fact that the "other" American Ninja had to come and rescue him!

Did David Bradley and Steve James get on during *American Ninja 3*?

They worked well together. I think Steve understood and also respected the fact that David had a black belt and was very assured; I didn't go through the first two films, to see how many doubles were used, but of course it's much easier when you don't need to use them—when someone can act it and also do the physical stuff.

And the rest of the cast? James Booth?

James Booth—who actually wrote the script under the pseudonym of David Geeves—was an old trouper. I talked to him quite a bit about the script, and at least it wasn't too similar to parts 2 and 3. It was quite different—it had a *Delta Force* feeling with the Arab villain and an ex-colonial running the place—which, as we all know, is quite synonymous with Africa, so that was quite a nice touch.

So James Booth was originally hired to write the script, and was then subsequently included in the cast?

Yes, I think so. And then they also sent me the female lead and Dwayne Alexandre, who filled the sidekick role for David. We had to try a bit of a new approach for them as sidekicks—Dwayne wasn't quite as adept as Steve James had been, so we worked around that and changed things accordingly; but I think James Booth was aware that his script would need to be tweaked in those kinds of ways.

I liked the female lead in part 4, Robin Stille—I think she'd only done one or two horror movies before that, and unfortunately didn't do much after that. And then to round out your lead cast, you had South African veteran, Ken Gampu.

That's right.

And you shot it predominantly in Lesotho?

Right—that was the other proviso. I had the Delta Force coming in from the sea and getting captured and imprisoned, which brings in Bradley and Dwayne, before Dudikoff ultimately comes in and rescues them all. But then they said that Michael Dudikoff was worried about being blacklisted. As you know, around that time South Africa wasn't acceptable as a shooting location

A masked ninja gets the drop on Sean Davidson (David Bradley) in *American Ninja 3: Blood Hunt*. Author's collection.

anymore, until about 1992, so they said we needed to shoot out of the country.

Okay, so he was worried about it at that point, but it hadn't been an issue for *Ninja 2*, obviously.

Yes, I think the pressure had become more intense, and he'd also done quite a few things in South Africa by then, so he didn't want to push his luck. Also, remember that most of those movies were disguised as other places, so that people didn't realize they had actually been shot in South Africa. Anyway, so I had to relocate to Lesotho, which, for those who don't know, adjoins South Africa.

Yes, also, I think the Cannon movie that first drew attention to the shooting-in-South Africa scenario, was *Mercenary Fighters*—probably because it had a slightly more political plot and a more well-known cast, headed by Peter Fonda. That was at the end of 1986, and then the outside world started paying more attention to that situation and what was being filmed here, but *American Ninja 2* had already been shot before that, earlier in 1986.

Remember, also, that these movies fell under the banner of Cannon International, so they could have come from anywhere, and others were brought out by the British Breton Films, Harry Alan Towers's company. But Harry wasn't involved with *Ninja 4*.

Other than this proviso, was there any reluctance from Michael Dudikoff to come back and do *American Ninja 4*?

Not really—when I met him after he arrived in Lesotho, he was very enthusiastic—the only thing he did want to know, was "Where is my buddy? Why isn't Steve James here?" Otherwise, he seemed fine. Another thing about Michael Dudikoff, and how well-known he was—here we were in this rural country in Africa, and we had young kids running up to him, shouting, "Michael Dudikoff! Michael Dudikoff!" They were very aware of him and knew him—and Lesotho only has one cinema! So they definitely knew what *American Ninja* was, and that Michael Dudikoff was coming!

Cannon had already officially declared bankruptcy by the time *American Ninja 3* was released, so did that impact *American Ninja 4*, or was that already lined up?

No, it wasn't already lined up. I think they thought, let's have one last stab, before things collapse completely, and do it with their biggest money-making franchise, while also finishing off Dudikoff's contract at the same time. By that time, they'd just been bought out by the Italians and had already been taken over by them, so that when it came to editing *Ninja 4*, I went to do it in Rome. But, yes, I think it did impact—maybe they couldn't afford Steve James, and just didn't tell us that.

The *American Ninja* movies are all very popular and beloved, all over the world. Why do you think that is?

I think, for the Americans, to acquaint themselves with the mysticism, and certainly with the martial arts, they had Chuck Norris, who was doing that kind of thing, but I think when Avi Kleinberger came up with the concept of *American Ninja*—and remember America's our biggest audience base—they really had something there, and they lived up to it, in that genre—it gave you martial arts, it gave you a little bit of the mysticism, and it certainly gave you the action sequences that they really wanted. So I think that's why it's popular. And then, people said to me, "But how come you got to do it?" and all that kind of thing, and I said, "Listen, if you can't beat the Americans, at least you can play them at their own game!" And that's why I think it was popular.

Are you proud of your contribution, and being involved in the series?

Yes, I am—perhaps a bit more of part 3 than 4, because I am aware that some of the fans felt a bit hard done by 4; they found *Ninja 4* a bit too dark. There was actually a bit more blood and violence, in terms of seeing it, more shooting and explosions, than actual fighting skill.

Which of the two do you, personally, prefer?

Okay—for the innovations—the micro-light, the underwater sequence, and things like that—part 3. In terms of epic scale, part 4 has that arena at the top of the mountain, and we got to do a helicopter shot and things like that. But I think I warm to part 3 more than I warm to part 4. I had Michael walking through lots of scattered bodies at the end of 4, and walking off into the distance, and also the Delta Force being tortured—it had a darker side to it, and I don't know that it's really needed.

Any strange or amusing anecdotes to tell, from either film?

In part 3, we had the art of assuming someone else's identity, by using a mask of that person's face, and Michele Chan, who played Chang Li, was supposed to remove the mask, while in a car, at which point the face of the secretary, played by Adrienne Pearce, would be revealed. Well, Michele came to me, and asked me to please clear the set when she took off the mask. I don't know if it was Chinese culture, but it was quite odd—normally, you only clear a set for nudity! Another thing that comes to mind—also on part 3—during David Bradley's "mind over matter" sequence, where his shirt is off, and his strength is returning to him, without the antidote, because he'd been injected with a virus—when we came to do that sequence, David said he wasn't ready, so I gave him some time, we set up the lights and so forth. As the body pulsed, out of that would come his strength, and then we would see his eyes, and he would be up, and no longer a wimp, because of the mind over matter—well, you cannot, cannot believe—if you look at that sequence—his veins started to pulse! Actually, some people thought we did a special effect, with the lighting, but that wasn't the case—his muscles really seemed to genuinely blow up and give him that strength! He was amazing! He

A

was actually doing that! Remember, I tried to put more mysticism into part 3 than there had been in parts 1 and 2, to take it into another area, so those kinds of things paid off, I think. Also, when he gets his medallion in the title sequence, from the Master—that immediately transported one to Japan—it gave us the essence of Japan. Those were wonderful things, when you get that atmosphere, and it's captured, and it's there.

Any sequences that were particularly challenging or potentially dangerous to shoot?

In part 4, we had a raging river, and the ninjas had to come up from under the water, and surround the Delta Force, before they captured them—we were originally going to do it in the sea, which would have been quite challenging, but here, in this flowing river, they had to go down, the water had to be kind of still, and then they had to come out of that. I'll never forget—we did about three or four takes, with different, varying lenses, and just before we did the last take, of them coming out of the water, this pig's head floated past me in this filthy river! And that seemed to be like an omen—but we got the shot and sequence, and then got out of that water, which could have had any kind of disease in it, very quickly! You are always insured, when you do helicopter shots—because there have been incidents on sets where people have actually died in helicopter accidents—so the cameraman and I, as well as the helicopter, itself, were insured, to get those circular shots at the top of the mountain, in *Ninja 4*. I wouldn't say that's dangerous, but we were certainly insured, for a million rand, for a certain amount of time.

And the stuntmen—were they predominantly South African, or did you bring them in?

We brought in Mike Stone, who was the martial arts expert, and Ed Anders, who was the stunt coordinator, and, between them, they came up with various sequences. It was all very controlled— look, these guys had already done three previous *American Ninja* movies, so they knew what they were doing! A lot of the ninjas in both films were South African stuntmen, however.

Well, I think a lot of the South African stuntmen cut their teeth on these two movies, specifically, as well as on those other Cannon movies—to the extent that they're now considered to be some of the best in the world.

That's right.

Were you offered the opportunity to direct *American Ninja 5*?

No—because, by that time, Cannon was finished. So another producer and David Bradley teamed up to do it. I had absolutely nothing to do with it.

Have you seen it?

I have—but I'm afraid I found it very dull.

Anything you'd like to say to the millions of *American Ninja* fans, all over the world?

I would say to them, cherish and remember those films for the time in which they were made. If we made them now, we would have CGI, we would have all manner of things—remember that those films were actually done in camera, and all the moves were physical. So I don't think they can be re-made. I think we need to hang on to what we loved about them, and that won't change how we feel about them. Today's CGI-heavy action and martial arts movies are completely different. So we must remember them in that time capsule—and I think that's why so many people still love them!

American Ninja 3: Blood Hunt
1989 (MGM DVD) (djm)

"Ninja? Not again!"

With a plot that is strikingly similar to part 2, *Blood Hunt* is less engaging and fun than the previous two entries. Real-life martial arts champion David Bradley replaces Michael Dudikoff as the "American Ninja," although he is a different character. He plays Sean Davidson, who is on tour on the fight circuit in South Africa when he becomes the focus of "The Cobra," a mad scientist with plans to dominate the world by creating a new race of superninjas. Davidson is joined by Curtis Jackson (Steve James), who left the army to follow him on tour. At one point, Davidson is infected with a deadly virus, and he uses ninja magic to cure himself.

Cedric Sundstrom took over directing duties this time, and he would go on to make *American Ninja 4* as well. It's not his fault that *Blood Hunt* is so weak—the script is sillier than usual, and it's hardly credible that Curtis Jackson would be involved in this plot. Gary Conway is credited with the story, most likely because it's the same story as the second film. It's obvious

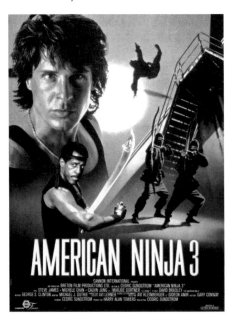

Theatrical Poster for *American Ninja 3: Blood Hunt*. Author's collection.

Ninjas use guns, too—check out this American Ninja (David Bradley) with an AK-47. From *American Ninja 3: Blood Hunt*. Author's collection.

that this film was shot for a lot less money than the previous two. This was David Bradley's first film. He's more than adequate in the starring role. There's a theme song at the end. Mike Stone can be spotted in one scene. The German DVD release is widescreen.

American Ninja 4: The Annihilation
1990 (Cannon DVD) (djm)

The hardest edged entry in the *American Ninja* series is two movies in one. On the one hand it's about Sean Davidson (David Bradley)—now a secret agent—who gets captured in Africa by a ninja cult whose leader, a Muslim extremist, plans to nuke America. That movie is 45 minutes long. The second half is about Joe Armstrong (Michael Dudikoff)—now a teacher in the Peace Corps—who is called back into duty to rescue his friend from captivity in Africa. He sets himself up with weapons, ninja garb, and a straight-shot plan to dive headfirst into the ninja cult, swords and shurikins blazing.

A great entry in the *American Ninja* franchise, *The Annihilation* is definitely more "R"-rated than the previous entries. While still retaining a sense of childlike adventure, it manages to feel more gritty and dangerous than the other films. The prospect of seeing Dudikoff and Bradley fight side by side is dashed, though. They are on screen together for an extremely short amount of time, though they do have a brief fight scene against each other. Steve James is sorely missed in this entry. There's a part for

Sean Davidson (David Bradley) surrounded by evil ninjas in *American Ninja 4: The Annihilation*. Courtesy of Cedric Sundstrom

him in it, and the guy who plays the character James should have played is woefully unsuitable for the role. Cedric Sundstrom directed it, and it appears to be fairly obvious he had a more fun time making it than he did part 3. The end teases another sequel, but the franchise went in a different direction instead. The German DVD release is widescreen.

American Ninja 5

1992 (Cannon DVD) (djm)

Maligned, ignored, and unfairly criticized, the fifth and final entry (rated PG-13) in the *American Ninja* series has the best fights of any of the films in the series, and David Bradley, who stars in it, gives the best performance of his career. At first glance, it appears to be a more-watered down incarnation of the "R"-rated franchise, but it's surprisingly entertaining and engrossing. For reasons unknown, Bradley plays a new character named Joe in this, but it might as well be the Sean Davidson character from parts 3 and 4. He is a martial arts instructor whose friend (Pat Morita) drops off an orphan named Hiro at his doorstep to take care of for a few days. The twelve-year-old orphan is played by Lee Reyes, son of Ernie Reyes Sr. and the brother of Ernie Reyes Jr. and he's an impressive child actor, not to mention quite a little martial artist. When he's put in Joe's care, they end up chasing a woman in peril . . . to South America! Once there, they get into all sorts of trouble, including having to face an onslaught of purple-suited ninjas and a caped superninja, played by James Lew! As silly as some of the events are, Bradley and Reyes have a great chemistry, and the local scenery and fast-paced action adventure heroics really help sell this movie as the most underrated entry in the *American Ninja* franchise.

Bob Bralver, a well-respected stuntman in show business, directed this entry. He also directed *Midnight Ride* with Michael Dudikoff. He managed to get a strong performance out of David Bradley in this film, and Bradley never before or since delivered a more physical and forceful performance. It mystifies me why fans of the *American Ninja* franchise have vilified this movie. Ironically, the ninjas in it are the weakest aspect of the film, and while James Lew is a fine bad guy in it, his costume is ridiculous. Other than that, I enjoyed the film. Tadashi Yamashita from part 1 appears here as "himself."

American Samurai

1992 (Cannon DVD) (djm)

"Why couldn't we have just been brothers?"

An airplane crashes in a remote area in Japan, and a wise Japanese master of swords rescues a white male child from the wreckage. He instructs the child in the ancient art of the samurai, and this upsets the master's own son, who is about

the same age. The master clearly prefers the white child to his own son because his own son is rebellious and full of jealousy and rage. The white son, named Drew, grows up to be played by David Bradley, and the Asian son, named Kenjiro, grows up to be played by Mark Dacascos (in his first film role). Their old father bestows his beloved sword to Drew, who deserves it, and this sends Kenjiro into a fervent rage. Kenjiro joins the Yakuza and years later he steals the sword from Drew and goads and ultimately forces him to fight him in a "Live Blade" tournament where blade masters from all around the world fight to the death for millions of dollars. Kenjiro has the Yakuza kidnap Drew and his girlfriend while they are in Istanbul, and imprisons them both until Drew agrees to fight along with all of the other contestants. From that point on, the film becomes a tournament movie.

David Bradley shines in this film. He looks great and has the chance to showcase his martial arts and swordsmanship. He plays a humble hero, never losing his temper or going too far in his fights. Dacascos is really enthusiastic and crazed in his first film role. He overacts in most of his scenes, but he's most effective when he's quiet and waiting to draw his sword. The rest of the blade masters in the film are all unique, and the fights in the ring are well choreographed and staged. Sam Firstenberg (*Revenge of the Ninja* and *Blood Warriors*, which starred David Bradley) directed this solid film.

American Streetfighter

1992 (EVG DVD) (djm)

Joe Tanner (Gary Daniels) and a buddy botch a robbery and the buddy is killed, while Tanner gets away without notice. He goes to Japan to restart his life as a businessman, and years later, the father of his buddy who was killed resurfaces as a feared Asian drug lord named Ogawa (Gerald Okamura) and he has Tanner's kickboxer brother Randy (Ian Jacklin) targeted for death as revenge. Randy has risen through the ranks as an urban street fighter, but his sure-footed cockiness lands him in a situation he can't get out of. When Joe learns that his brother is in trouble with Ogawa, he travels back to the US to rescue him, but first he has to get himself in fighting shape and in tip-top condition to go up against Ogawa, who is virtually an unkillable samurai.

You've got to hand it to Gary Daniels. He starred in dozens of direct-to-video movies, played the bad guy or second fiddle in half of those, and he still doesn't get the notice he deserves, partly, I feel, because of movies like *American Streetfighter*. He did a lot of cheap movies like this one where some of the sets look like they're someone's garage or basement, where cardboard boxes line the foreground, and where the movie itself looks like it was shot on VHS tape, but despite all that, he remains an interesting action star, a formidable martial artist, and a force to be reckoned with despite how junky the movie may seem. It's easy to dismiss *American Streetfighter*, but it's impossible to dismiss Daniels. His co-star, Jacklin (from *Expert Weapon*) actually looks and sounds like

he could be Daniels's brother. Directed and edited by Steve Austin, who later directed Jacklin in *Expert Weapon* and edited the Daniels vehicle *Full Impact*.

American Tigers

1996 (York VHS) (djm)

A group of international terrorists bomb an American embassy in Asia and the US government comes up with a hackneyed plan: recruit former soldiers who are in state penitentiaries and train them to become a crack commando unit willing to go to Asia to defeat the terrorists. Sounds like a Cannon movie or an Italian exploitation action movie in waiting. Major Sargent Ransom (Sam Jones) is hired to whip a team of death-row inmates in shape before they're sent to war, and he has quite the job on his hands. The group consists of murderers, cast-offs, and never-gonna-amount-to-anything losers, and they have authority issues. Ransom hires Hollywood actress Cynthia Rothrock (playing herself!) to come in and train them, and when her training period is over, the morale of the group actually improves. In a desperate move, the government allocates the mission to a Navy SEAL team, but Ransom makes a deal with his commander: let his men fight the SEALs to see which group is stronger and tougher. Ransom's men win the bet, and they take the mission on. They don't all come home, though.

Don't be misled by the video box. While Rothrock's face is on the cover, the text clearly states that she is featured in a *guest appearance* only. Her small bit in the film is great, and without her the movie wouldn't be nearly as watchable. Don Gibb, from *Bloodsport*, is also featured in a small role. Jones gets first billing, and rightfully so, but his role isn't as physical as it should have been. The men playing the convicts aren't really interesting to watch, and none of them really have any particular skill sets that make them worthy of having the entire movie resting on their shoulders. At nearly two full hours, this film directed by David Worth (*Lady Dragon*, *Chain of Command*) is a marginal effort.

And Now You're Dead

(a.k.a. **Enter the Eagles**)

1998 (Universe Laser & Video DVD) (CD)

Martin (Michael Wong) is a professional thief, the best of the best. An assignment arises where he's asked by a shady businessman known as Karloff (Benny "The Jet" Urquidez) to steal a large diamond in the Czech Republic. It won't be an easy job so he contacts his former partner Mandy (Shannon Lee, daughter of Bruce) to help. They had parted ways years ago when Mandy's sister was killed during an operation gone south. Stealing the diamond will be easy, but when they're double-crossed by Karloff, they'll have to pool their resources in order to get it back. With Martin's brains and Mandy's fists, Karloff will be sorry he double- crossed them to begin with.

Corey Yuen (*The Transporter*) is a brilliant action director; he almost never fails to deliver some amazing feats of excitement from his stars. When it comes to directing an entire film, it usually ends up falling short in every other department. *And Now You're Dead* is no different. The story's weak and confusing, leaving much to be desired. Regardless of its shortcomings, the film needs to be seen for one reason only: Shannon Lee (*High Voltage*). In this film she's very much her father's daughter, showing audiences she has what it takes to be an action star. There are several amazing fight scenes with Shannon, but the one you'll remember most is seeing the daughter of Bruce Lee fight Benny Urquidez (*Wheels on Meals*). It's by far the standout set piece in the film, and both actors deliver some great stuff. The movie as a whole may be a mess, but watching Shannon Lee pick up her father's mantle makes it all worthwhile.

Android Cop

2014 (The Asylum DVD) (djm)

The Los Angeles of 2037 is divided into zones. After "the quake" destroyed much of the outlying areas, Southern California is an urban wasteland. In Zone 12, a group of irradiated survivors are harboring a runaway daughter of the mayor (played by Charles S. Dutton) who wants her found. He goes to the police force, which has only just begun implementing androids into the fold, and the most capable cop is put in charge of the search and rescue. The cop is a badass martial artist named Hammond (Michael Jai White), and when he's partnered with the experimental android named Andi (Randy Wayne), he's outraged. Forced to work together, they have trouble finding a simpatico until Hammond realizes that he's actually an android too! Their mission in the dilapidated ruins of Los Angeles comes to a revelatory boil as Hammond makes his personal discovery, and while it doesn't really impede his job performance, it does put him in a position where he can't really make fun of his partner anymore.

An ultra thrifty production from the notorious exploitation studio The Asylum, *Android Cop* is just about as good as it can be with the script and the budget they were working with. Jai White who was amazing in *Blood and Bone* and *Never Back Down 2* turns in a mouthy, goofy performance, which says to me that he was trying to overcompensate for a lack of direction or a poor script. The physical stuff he does in the movie is okay, but it seems to me that there wasn't much time to get into elaborate fights. The action is generic and the apocalyptic elements are weak, but present. Some of the post-catastrophe landscapes using both practical sets and digital composites are more than adequate. It's a shame the movie isn't special in any way because they could have had something notable here if they'd tried harder. Directed by Mark Atkins.

Angelfist

1993 (New Horizons DVD)

(djm)

A female kickboxing FBI agent is murdered in the Philippines after she takes pictures of some US soldiers getting killed by a group of terrorists, and her sister Kat (played by Catya Sassoon from *Bloodfist IV: Die Trying*) flies to the Philippines to investigate her sister's murder. Kat—also a kickboxing cop—plunges right into the underground kickboxing circuit and makes herself some friends and enemies straight off the bat. She makes a lover out of Alcatraz (Michael Shaner from *The Expert*), who is able to grease some palms for some answers for her, and she makes enemies out of the terrorist organization, which is hoping to assassinate the American ambassador at the kickboxing championships, where Kat has become a frontrunner to become the new champion. In the meanwhile, there are more sex scenes, nude shots, and gratuitous showers than any ten other "R"- rated movies combined.

From producer Roger Corman and director Cirio Santiago, *Angelfist* was designed to be a vehicle for starlet Catya Sassoon, whom Corman was grooming to be a female Don "The Dragon" Wilson, and as the film is enamored with her naked body and pouty face (but not so much with her questionable martial arts abilities), the movie succeeds at least on a lowest common denominator level. Seriously: For an eighty-minute movie (with lengthy opening titles and end titles, that gives you about sixty-five minutes of movie), there are nude scenes and sex scenes every few minutes, leaving precious little else to recommend it. Catya has enough fights in the film, but I'm certain she had a stunt double, and her co-star Melissa Moore (also seen in *The Killing Zone*) has about an equal number of nude scenes and fights on screen as the star. I don't know what else to tell you: Mr. Skin would be happy, but here at the action star headquarters, we're scratching our heads and looking at our watches. Corman recycled this script several other times for other action stars. See also: *Bloodfist, Full Contact, Dragon Fire, Future Kick,* and *Bloodfist 2050*. Catya's next (and last) movie was *Bloodfist VI: Ground Zero*. She would die of a drug overdose some time later.

Angel of Death

2007 (Sony DVD) (djm)

Assassin for hire Eve (Zoë Bell) is stabbed in the skull during a botched job, and in her confusion she accidentally shoots and kills a little girl. Stumbling outside to her ride (with a huge knife sticking out of her head), she's taken to a back-alley doctor who removes the instrument from her person, and hopes for the best. In recovery, Eve begins hallucinating and having scary visions of the girl she killed, and her mistake begins to haunt her. Meanwhile, the little girl's family hires another assassin to hunt Eve down for what she did, and Eve fights for her life while hunting down those who put a contract out on her.

DVD release artwork of *Angel of Death*. Author's collection.

Shot as webisodes for an online outlet, *Angel of Death* is a low-budget martial arts action experiment built around Bell's persona and abilities, which far outshine this movie. She's great looking, she can act (as far as I'm concerned), and she's an incredible physical force to be reckoned with. She displays her martial arts talents and go-for-broke stunt work here, and as a vehicle for her, *Angel of Death* is adequate, but not a showstopper. She fights quite a few people in the film, most notably James Lew from *The Perfect Weapon*. Ron Yuan directed the fights. Written (and based on some comics) by Ed Brubaker. Directed by Paul Etheredge.

Angel of Death (a.k.a. True Justice: Angel of Death)

2012 (Studiocanal DVD R2)

(djm)

Picking up right where *Violence of Action* left off, *Angel of Death* has Elijah Kane (Steven Seagal) helping one of the wounded enforcers under his command to heal after she was shot and nearly killed by a terrorist. His next case has him going after an Egyptian terrorist who might have a nuclear weapon, and he goes undercover as a patron of a brothel the guy frequents. Working with another of his female enforcers (who goes really deep undercover as an abused ex-girlfriend of a man involved with the Mexican cartels), the two of them inch closer to the Egyptian and are able to get them in their grip fairly easily, considering.

Not as satisfying as *Violence of Action*, which had a good bad guy in it, played by Darren Shahlavi, *Angel of Death* feels like the episodic television programming that it actually is, instead of one of Seagal's direct-to-video action movies. From the TV series *True Justice*, it has many of the familiar tropes of the show (terrorists, scenes of Seagal giving orders to his team, flashbacks, Seagal breaking some necks, etc.), but very little replay value, as it is almost immediately forgettable. The next entry in the series is *Dead Drop*. From director Wayne Rose.

Angel of Fury

1992 (Imperial VHS) (djm)

A security expert named Nancy Bolan (Cynthia Rothrock) is tasked to deliver a briefcase with a computer inside it. The computer has top-secret information in it, which a ripped-out, child-killing criminal mastermind named Nick Stewart (Peter O'Brian) is after for various nefarious purposes. Nancy gets into one cliff-hanging climactic action scene after another as she tries protecting the briefcase *and* a young girl from Stewart's henchmen. Sadly, the briefcase remains safe, but the child is killed, which propels Nancy into a fury. Even her boyfriend turns against her, and by the end, she's proven herself to be the expert that her reputation suggests.

With nary a moment of downtime, *Angel of Fury* is chock-full of action and stunt work, and while its story and script (if there was one) are weak, Rothrock remains watchable. The Asian-style action and locales keep the movie popping at all times, with explosions, sprinting, jumping, and grappling every few minutes. This film has a less-than-stellar reputation, but I enjoyed it. Director Ackyl Anwary was the second assistant director on other Rothrock vehicles such as *Lady Dragon* and *Rage and Honor II*. Strangely, this remains the only screenwriting credit for actor Christopher Mitchum, who does not appear in the film.

Angel Town

1990 (Red DVD) (djm)

"That's Mr. Frog to you—Raghead!"

This is Olivier Gruner's first "vehicle" film. Gruner, in real life, was in the French army, having trained in karate, and was later a kickboxing champion. He broke into movies by impressing a producer, and he starred in a string of "B" movies, most of which ended up going straight to video, and none of which really used his talents and abilities the way the first three did (*Angel Town, Nemesis, Savate*). Here, in *Angel Town*, he plays a nice guy named Jacques who comes to Los Angeles to attend a graduate program, and he isn't in LA for one whole day before he is fighting off gang members who are in a turf war in the neighborhood where he's renting a room. He's meek and mild, and prefers not to fight (even though in the film he is a former kickboxing champion), and when the Chicano gang that's harassing his lady landlord's young son gets the picture that Jacques is not to be trifled with, they get *really* aggressive. Gruner tries hard to attend his classes at the nearby campus, but some days he can't make it because he gets into long-lasting bouts with dozens of gang bangers who can't compete with his fancy footwork. The climax of the film has Gruner

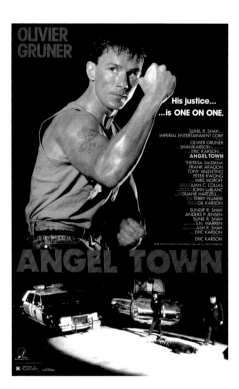

Theatrical poster for *Angel Town*. Author's collection.

(with the help of a vet in a wheelchair, sporting a machine gun, and about a half a dozen students from a nearby dojo, run by his Asian kickboxing friend, played by Peter Kwong) fighting about two dozen gang members. This fight is lengthy and pretty awesome.

Gruner's good-natured and clean-cut demeanor is a genuine, but odd fit for this urban gangland action film. He's different than any other action or martial arts star, but he's almost *too* mild as a screen presence. He has a slight, but muscular build, and his soft voice with its thick accent definitely puts him in the fish-out-water category. He clearly has skills as a martial artist, and his character shows pain and frustration when things go wrong for him and the people he cares about, but he never overacts, which is commendable. The film runs a little too long, but it's a gem of a movie. Gruner was never better. It was directed by Eric Karson, who also made *The Octagon* with Chuck Norris and *Black Eagle* with Sho Kosugi and Van Damme.

INTERVIEW:

OLIVIER GRUNER

(djm)

Born in Paris, France, Olivier Gruner rose to prominence as an action star when Imperial Entertainment discovered him at the Cannes Film Festival during the VHS heyday of the late 1980'. His first film was the slightly biographical action film Angel Town (1990), *and his next two films* Nemesis (1992) *and* Savate (1995) *showcased his impressive abilities as a kickboxer. As the video market began to change, Gruner's run as a bright hope in the field of action stars began fading as he headlined films that made their*

Action star Olivier Gruner at Gold's Gym in Santa Monica, California. Photo by david j. moore.

debuts on video. Gruner's origins are as follows: He was in the French Special Forces, carrying out deadly missions in Somalia and Syria, and shortly thereafter became a world kickboxing champion. After he'd made his crossover as an action star, he became a licensed helicopter pilot, and when his career as an actor slowed down, he returned to kickboxing (and won his fight), and became a bodyguard to one of the richest sheiks in the world. Gruner is the real thing, and his varied accomplishments are an all-around testament to who he is and what he's been able to achieve in life.

From what I understand, you started out in the French Army and later became a professional kickboxer. Is that right?

Yeah, well, I was in the special forces in France. Like the SEALs here. My missions were in Somalia and in Syria. We were based there. We'd spend . . . I can't really talk about it. I'm not sure. My missions were to take over boats, like tankers or fishermen's boats. We were doing that in '78, '79. It's funny because we just found out a couple of years ago that Somalia was taking over tankers, but that happened a long time ago. It's not new. That's what I was doing. From there, I decided to learn a little bit, some martial arts. Obviously, if you are involved in the military you need to know how to defend yourself, hand to hand if you lose your gun. So I went to Shotokan, and I started training in the south of France with a very traditional Shotokan instructor. He was really excellent. I was really picky with who I was training with. So then I went to kickboxing, and from there I went to MMA and judo and jiu jitsu and all that good stuff.

Wow. So you're the real thing. You're actually a for-real badass.

You know the badass? I teach the opposite when you say that. Everybody says, "Oh, you're a badass." I say, "Wait a minute—let's go back a little bit." I got beat up when I was in school. In high school. I was scared. Because I was *not* a badass, that's why I became a badass.

Well, that's how it goes. Isn't that how it goes?

Yeah. Most of the time, that's how it goes. Usually those guys who are really strong in high school, they have that confidence in them, and I was kind of skinny, kind of a nerd. I didn't have that confidence. I had to build that confidence doing something a little bit different.

So, you were discovered at the Cannes film festival?

Yeah. It's very funny. I was living with one American and one British guy—we were living all together. We were traveling France, and we got a job first in the Alps. We had a place, and we'd hang out there. Then we left to another house in the south of France. What we did is we started working with the Cannes film festival. My friend, the American one, said, "Olivier, why don't you put up a poster that you were a champion? Put it on the wall!" I was doing security at the theaters. I'd let people in and out, you know? I said, "Okay!" so I put my poster up. One guy came up and just looked at it, and this was the time when Van Damme was very popular. All the companies were looking for somebody else because Van Damme was very busy. So they needed a backup. I was there at the right time at the right place. Imperial Entertainment asked me to come to LA. I went to an audition, and we started to find projects, and that's the way I started in the movie industry.

That's how _Angel Town_ started?

Yes, exactly. Actually, _Angel Town_ . . . they hired two writers, and they asked me to talk about my past a little bit. There are some scenes in that movie, like the flashback scenes where I was a child, and the gang members gang up on me and beat up on me. That stuff was real. That happened to me. In the entertainment industry, you never know. People ask me how to get into the industry, and you never know. Anybody can be a star. The hard part is to keep yourself on top. It's very hard. Usually, you go up and down and up and down. It's the big rollercoaster.

You just told me that Van Damme was popular and that companies were seeking out the next action star. You came during that period when Van Damme, Steven Seagal, and lots of other guys like Jeff Speakman and Don "The Dragon" Wilson were making one movie right after another. What was it like for you to become an action star, particularly during that period in the late 1980s, early 1990s?

Here's the thing. You have a contract, a two-picture deal, a five-picture deal. It's a business. That's what they used to do. They used to make us sign a ten-picture deal, or a five-picture deal. So when I signed up with Imperial Entertainment, it was a five-picture deal, and it was exclusive. That was hard for me because we were only doing one film every two or three years. Which means that you film one and you have to wait for another year and a half to two years before you film the next one. That's very hard. The '90s were great for people who were good in martial arts, everybody could _become_ a star. You could make these movies. It was the time of the videotape. Kung fu or karate, or whatever you throw in a fight scene, people would buy it and watch it. It was an easier time than what it is now. Now it's more politics, but that time was really good. They tried to lock us up. They wanted us to be part of the company. If you wanted to get out of it, It would have been very difficult, which I did. It was pretty tough. It was not easy.

When Imperial Entertainment was around they were big in the video world, but small in the theatrical realm.

You know what, they were starting to be . . . they wanted to become like New Line Cinema. I think they made a few mistakes, and everybody does, so I can't blame them. . . . They spent twenty million dollars on this film . . . it really crushed them. It's different when you make a four million dollar film, or even a two or three million dollar film, but making a twenty million dollar film is so different. The twenty million dollar film was _Double Dragon_. It crushed them. They had a lot of money, and they were very aggressive in the movie industry, and there's nothing wrong with that, but they jumped from four to eight million dollar films to a twenty million dollar film. At that time, twenty million was a lot of money. It's very interesting. The '90s were very good for us. When I got free from Imperial, I made at minimum two to three films a year. I could have done more than that, but I had to slow down because I didn't want to be overexposed. I turned down a film. (Laughing) . . . I'll tell you the story. I love flying helicopters. I became a commercial pilot. That was really my passion on the side. I passed my helicopter pilot test and then I went to fly commercial, and two days before I passed my exam, Avi Lerner asked me to do a film in South Africa, and I said, "Avi, I'm so sorry," because he wanted me to leave maybe five days later. I told him that I couldn't do it. Everything was good, the money was great, but it took me like two to three months of hard study to get to my commercial license, and then I turned Avi Lerner down. Since I did, I've never worked for him. Avi Lerner produced _The Expendables_. (Laughing). But it was so important for me to become a commercial pilot. It was my dream.

Well, you took a path.

That's it. Sometimes it bites you in the butt.

Let's go back to _Angel Town_. This is probably your best movie because it's so pure. It captures you in your prime, and you were brand new. It feels like an honest movie. It really feels genuine. The fight scenes are interesting and graceful. Can you talk about _Angel Town_ and how you felt about the movie then and now?

You know what, _Angel Town_ . . . just like everything, you have to really fight for what you want. At that time, Van Damme was big and there were a lot of kung fu guys all getting big also. They wanted me to do things that I really didn't want to. I wanted to do Muay Thai, I wanted to use kickboxing, and be different than the other guys. They wanted me to do some jumps because everybody else did jumps. In a street fight, you're never gonna jump. You're going to be spinning and doing a roundhouse kick. If you jump, you're really going to be in trouble. So, I tried to be as pure as possible, and it was not easy to do it. The director was Eric Karson, and he was really good. We worked very close together. I'm glad he really supported me in my vision for the fights in the movie. That really made _Angel Town_ what it is. I'm sure

Steven Seagal had to do the same and fight for what he wanted. Even Van Damme. I think in the movie industry—and in life—you have to fight for what you think is right, and believe for what you think is good and put your vision in your film. That's what makes you special. If everybody does the same thing, then it becomes a uniform. Everybody is different. Jean-Claude is different than me, Steven Seagal is different than us. It's really good to have a variety of martial arts.

What would you say makes you special as a martial artist and an action star?

I think because I've done it for real, like with my military experience, just from my experience doing real things, I think that helps. I really fought, so it's not like I can fake it. Somebody with this kind of experience who can put that on the screen . . . well, I think that's one of my things.

You've worked with some interesting filmmakers: Albert Pyun, Isaac Florentine, Avi Nesher, Philip Roth, and many others. Who do you think has used your unique abilities the best in a movie?

It depends on the screenplay too. I think Avi Nesher, but he did not give me a lot of time to rehearse the fights. Otherwise, I think he gave me the opportunity to really do the things that I wanted to do. At the time of _Angel Town_, I didn't really have a name—I was the new kid on the block. But now it's different. I'm given a lot of freedom when I want to do something. They'll say, "Well, let's try it." That type of thing. I think we have more freedom than when we used to.

When I look at your first three films—I'm talking about _Angel Town_, _Nemesis_, and _Savate_—those three movies captured you in your greatest glory. Those are the three movies that I like the best.

Yeah. I do too. _Angel Town_ was great, don't get me wrong. A lot of people wanted me to do a sequel to _Angel Town_, and _Nemesis_ also, as well. _Savate_ . . . I love westerns. It was cool. The fighting on that was interesting too. There's another movie I like very much too—it's _Mercenary_. They didn't use John Ritter as John Ritter. It was written for somebody else. He was so funny on the set. Sometimes the film is good, or has the potential to be good, but there is something, a decision that was made, and the film is not as good as it could have been.

You did two _Mercenary_ movies.

Yeah. The first one was cool. I liked it. It's funny because nowadays, things are different. The films from the '90s and the films now are different. Then again, it's like a big circle. We're coming back to the '90s with _The Expendables_, the big shootouts. Shooting fifty people with one gun.

I feel like _The Expendables_ are celebrating the old guys rather than creating new ones. I love these movies. How do you feel about them?

Absolutely. Then again, it's pretty cool. They did a really good job. Stallone is excellent. I'm not going to say they're my favorite films to watch, but they're blockbusters. They bring all these guys together. It's pretty cool. Here's the thing: Every time Van Damme goes up, for me it's good too. I have to support what he does as well. If Van Damme goes up, we all go up. That's important.

Talk a little bit about working with Albert Pyun on *Nemesis*. He told me that he had originally written it for a female lead.

Yeah! There was a time when Imperial Entertainment was looking for another show for me. They chose *Nemesis*, and I think it was a really good choice for me to do a film that was a little bit different than a martial arts film. It was more science fiction with a lot of special effects. There was a lot of pyro, and going to different locations was pretty amazing. The good thing about Albert Pyun is that he's a really good director of photography. He knows how to make things beautiful. I remember he was really focused on the set. He really wanted the backgrounds to be perfect. In a good way. He would spend his time making the holes in the walls shinier. He's a pretty hands-on director. Pretty amazing.

It seems like a much bigger movie than it actually is.

Yes! (Laughing.) Yeah. I was bleeding every day. The action scenes were constant in the film. There's a lot of pyro and a lot of stunts every day. So, it was really hard physically, but I got ready for it. With Albert, he gave me a private trainer, a really good guy. We had some really good stunt guys too. I think it's Albert's best film, personally.

How come you didn't come back for part 2?

Well, that was Imperial Entertainment. That was not me. I was attached to the company. I could not do things that I wanted to do. It would have been a great idea, but . . . .

Savate is a fantastic movie. Talk about that one. It was your one and only movie with director Isaac Florentine.

We had such a good time on that film. My parents were there too. I have really good memories on that film. It was a western, so it was a real treat. Isaac is real funny as a director. He's a character. That's what made it so special. You know how Israelis are. We were laughing all the time. But then again, we worked hard as well. I was very impressed with the way he set up the scenes. That was the first time I was with a director who shoots a full scene in one take with a track. He followed the action. There's no cut. Sometimes you say "Action!" and usually directors cover the scene. Isaac was different. He showed me how to use the camera, how to move it, and how to use it in one take and make the scene pretty amazing.

Why didn't you work with him again? He's still working today, making movies.

Yeah, I think he's working with Avi Lerner a lot. I think Avi has some issues with me, I guess. I

think that's what it is. I don't know. You can ask him. I have no clue. When the film is good, it's because the team works. It's never because the actor is great or the director's great. It's because we all get along and we work well together. That's really important. Sometimes to get the good package like that, it's really rare. When a film is successful, you want to keep working with those people.

Your next couple of movies *Automatic* and *Savage* . . . this was the beginning of a reign of straight-to-video movies for you.

Oh, wow. That's where I start to get upset a little bit.

I know this is sensitive, but I just want to be honest with you because I respect you. I just want you to be honest with me as much as you are willing to be. Why don't you talk a little bit about this period of your career as an action star?

Well . . . I asked the director . . . when I read the scripts, they were okay. *Automatic* was not a great script. For me, I didn't see it as a great script. I said, "Are you *sure* this is going to theaters?" "Yeah, yeah, yeah!" I said, "*Are you sure?*" I never worked with this person before. I was beginning. I had a big agent, who said, "You should work with the guy, he's a director who's going up in the business, so you should work with him." I said, "Okay, fine." Sometimes you have to listen to your people as well. I think *Automatic* was pretty good, but the screenplay was not . . . the set-up was not right. It was cheap. It looked cheap. They did spend money on it, but that was the start of the decline. When I had to do it, I said, (sighing) "Okay." When I did it, I had the feeling that I was not making the right movies. I didn't listen to my gut.

So you did these two movies with Avi Nesher, and then it was strictly straight to video for you. Wow.

Yeah. It was a tough era. It was the time, they were paying us a lot of money, and you have the dollar signs and you look at it, and people were saying, "You're not going to be here for a long

time, so you have to take whatever you can." You start to look at it, and you think, "I don't know if that's the right move." It was not an easy decision. You learn from your mistakes.

Even Van Damme and Seagal went straight to video after a decade in theaters.

Yeah, but then again, I never had a chance to work for a big studio. If I'd had the chance, it would have been different. Those guys were smart. They worked with the best people. There's a lot of politics in the movie industry. You know you're making the wrong moves, you know you don't want to make this film, but *you have to*, and I'm sure Jean-Claude and the other guys did the same. Sometimes you have to, for whatever reason.

You did some movies with Philip Roth— *Velocity Trap* and the *Interceptor Force* movies. I looked at *Velocity Trap* and I actually listened to the commentary on the DVD with you and Roth. I was kind of upset with that movie because it didn't give you anything to do. You were just kind of there.

Yeah. Then again, sometimes it's politics. You have a screenplay, you look at it, and you suggest things, but then they sometimes they reject your ideas. There's only so much you can fight for. They can say, "You know what? You're a pain in the ass. Bye-bye." You've got to be careful. There's a fine line.

Later in your career you did *The Circuit* trilogy, which showed that you were still very much in the game. These were hits in video stores.

Here's the thing. The vision I had for *The Circuit* was a little bit different. The script was not good at all. Period. But we tried to cover it with some fight scenes. I talked to Jalal [Merhi, the director] when I was in Toronto doing a TV series, and we agreed to do a martial arts movie in LA. He said, "No, no, no—it's too expensive!" I said, "No, we're going to do a martial arts movie, and it's going to be all underground fighting." And he said, "No, no." We eventually came to LA and shot the first one. The thing is, the casting was not really good. For a movie to be good, it has to fit. Not everything is fitting with that film. But it was one of the most successful films I did because it came out at the right time. The UFC was coming up. Jalal told me that it was out on video, and I went to Blockbuster. This was when we were shooting *The Circuit 2*. I went to the video store in Venice, and I said, "Do you know where *The Circuit* is?" They went, "Over there on the left." I said, "Well, where is it? I can't see it." I was looking for two or three tapes, but we *had a wall* covered with *The Circuit*. I was pretty amazed. It did pretty well. But the film itself . . . you know.

VHS artwork for *Automatic*. Author's collection.

Mike Möller kicking with his entire bodyweight in *Arena of the Street Fighter.*

You directed a movie called *One Night*. I don't know much about it since it's never been released.

That was the hardest thing I've ever done. I worked my ass off, eighteen hours a day acting in front of the camera, directing it, and producing it, all that stuff. It was so hard physically and mentally, and I didn't have any support at all. People actually stabbed me in the back over stupid things. I did everything from the casting to the editing, to the sound, everything. I was there from the beginning to the end. That was the best experience. Most of the time, as the star, you just show up and you leave. But this time, I was there from the beginning to the end. I saw how they make the sound, how we made the first cuts, and we did all the special effects ourselves. That was the best experience, but the worst experience because of the people I was involved with. It could have been great. The film is made, but I don't know what's going on with it. I wish I could make a film about the making of the film. Everything that could go wrong, went wrong. I wish I had a copy. I don't even have leverage of getting a copy of it.

(Editor's note: One Night was released on DVD under the title Re-Generator.)

There was a time in your career as an action star when you would fight guys in movies who kind of seemed like they knew what they were doing. You would get, I dunno, someone like Marc Singer who seemed pretty confident as a fighter, but then later on, in some of these other later movies, you're fighting nameless, faceless thugs who don't look like they belonged there fighting you. Nonprofessionals.

(Laughing.) When you have money, you can pay for good people. When you don't have money, you afford as many as you can. Some guys are good, don't get me wrong, but some guys have no clue. You can't teach them on set because we're limited on time.

When I look at you, I see someone who's still in training, still in shape, and you have the ability, you have the talent, you have the technique, you have everything that you need to make a good action movie, and then I see you in a cheap sci-fi movie where there's only one lame fight scene. I get upset. I'm like, "*Why*?"

I'm glad you're saying that because it's exactly what's happening now. I don't know if it's politics or if people are talking bad behind my back, I have no clue. I've always been on time, I've always worked as hard as I can, I've never been a flake, I don't take drugs, I'm not a drunk, so I'm always ready for it, and sometimes I don't know what it is, to be honest with you. I can't figure it out. My future is a little bit different. I think it's time for me to come back with a good film. I have one chance to come back. I've got to be ready for it. I'm in extremely good shape. I don't know if you know, but I fought in Kazakhstan and I won the belt in MMA, so there's a lot of stuff I'm doing. I grapple a lot. I'm in Vegas, training a lot. I'm in top shape. I have one more shot. I'm going to come back in a really good action picture with a lot of good fight scenes. Like it used to be.

You're still hungry, Olivier!

Oh, yeah. More than before. Remember, I worked with John Ritter when he was at the bottom of his career. Every actor goes up and down, and when they come back, they come back bigger than ever. I have more experience, I've been up, I've been down, and I know exactly what I want now. It's clear. Before it was kind of fuzzy because everybody tells you so many different things, the way they want you to be. You get very confused. Right now, I know exactly what I have to do. And that's *really* good.

How old are you right now, Olivier?

Fifty-two.

You've got time, man. You can do it!

I'm in better shape now than I used to be. I'm not kidding. I'm shredded!

The Apocalypse

1997 (Simitar DVD (CD)

"I will gladly come down there and gore out your eyes before it comes to that. Do you understand me?"

J. T. (Sandra Bernhardt) is the best of the interplanetary pilots in the business and is requisitioned by her old pal Suarez (Matt McCoy) to help head up a mission to an old spaceship long thought to be lost. If they can make it to the ship and salvage it before anyone else, they can relax for the rest of their lives, living off the sweet payday. The two of them can't handle it alone, so they put together a highly skilled team headed up by J. T.'s former flame Vendler (Frank Zagarino). Once on the ship, Vendler double-crosses everyone for his own selfish greed and unknowingly sets the computer on a crash course with Earth . . . and the ship has enough explosives to tear the planet apart.

One of the worst ideas in cinema history was to cast Sandra Bernhardt in an action heroine capacity and have her kick Frank Zagarino's (from *Striker* and *Operation Delta Force*) ass all over the universe. Bernhardt can be brilliant in comedies (*Hudson Hawk,* anyone?) but she's no action star and having her beat the hulking Zagarino is just flat-out insulting. Director Hubert de la Bouillerie made several rotten decisions that contributed to making the film undesirable in any form. It's blasphemous to neuter Zags in any capacity and to accept the fact that he was defeated by Bernhardt is like spitting in the face of his legacy. If you're going to watch this then be sure to follow it up with something far more uplifting, something like *Striker* or *The Revenger*, because this is just a fiasco.

Arena of the Street Fighter

2012 (WVG DVD R2) (djm)

Mike Moeller plays Mikey, a scrapper and short-fuse fighter whose best friend Mathis (Mathis Landwehr) is killed by a rival gang. Mikey prepares himself to enter a street fighting competition, with the prize being respect and bragging rights, but he gets himself into some serious trouble when he kills the rival gang's leader. Sent to prison, he builds himself up as an ultimate fighter, where he reflects on his life as a going-nowhere-but-up fighter.

Ultra simplistic and easy-as-pie scripting make *Arena of the Street Fighter* rely solely on its fights to recommend it. Wall-to-wall fights and brutal encounters, it was cobbled together after star/director Moeller was left with an incomplete film after his producers gave him troubles. He filled in as many gaps as he could and the result is a showcase for his impressive fight styles and athleticism. He may be small in stature, but he more than makes up for it with his bullheaded attitude and aggressive fighting abilities. His co-star Landwehr is an action star in his own right with several notable credits (including *Kampfansage* and *Death Train*) under his belt. Moeller was also in *Kamfansage*.

INTERVIEW:

MIKE MOELLER

(djm)

Relatively short in stature (at 5'3"), Mike *Moeller (Möller) has defied all odds and forced his way into the world of action and martial arts films. Born in a small village in East Germany, he was not allowed to practice martial arts until the Berlin Wall fell, and at the age of thirteen, he joined a taekwondo club and entrenched himself in the art. His first gig was working as a stuntman on a Donnie Yen project that shot in Germany, and as the years have progressed, he's worked on a number of high-profile Hollywood films as a stunt player. His starring role in the ultra low-budget film* Arena of the Streetfighter (2012) *was shot without a script over a several year time span, but anyone with an eye for talent can see that Moeller has that certain magic that makes an action star special.*

Mike Möller as Mikey the street fighter in *Arena of the Street Fighter*.

Tell me a little bit about your background as a martial artist.

I grew up in East Germany and it was not allowed to do martial arts at that time because East Germany was separated from the West. Since I was a little child, I was a big movie fan. In East Germany it was a problem to watch movies. We didn't have the chance to watch these American movies. It was the border. It all changed in 1989 when the wall fell. I was thirteen at the time. The chance to watch all these American movies happened because all these video stores came to East Germany, so I was able to see these Chinese and American movies. I rented all these movies. I started with Sylvester Stallone. The *Rambo* movies. Then, the Schwarzenegger movies. Then, one day I came to a friend's house, and he said, "Go away! I'm watching *Bloodsport*!" I said, "Okay, what is *Bloodsport*?" I went to the video store and I took the movie *Bloodsport* home, and I said, "Wow! What is this? Martial arts meets this great body!" This guy Jean-Claude Van Damme...wow. Then, I started training at home. The problem was that there was no gym and no martial arts school in my area. There was just a few boxing clubs in the city, and I came from a small village. I trained by myself. I did the splits and some kicking. I lifted weights, and I started training like this. Later, when I was sixteen, I left my village because I had to learn a trade in Nuremberg. Then, I joined a taekwondo club. My entry in the martial arts.

At one point did you think to yourself, "I want to be an action star!"?

(Laughing.) Like I said, I was always a huge movie fan. I watched these movies and they influenced and motivated me so much. On every opportunity, my friends would come to me, and we would shoot all our own stuff. One day, my friend came to me with a Super 8 camera, and he said, "Hey, let's shoot some moves from our martial arts school. It was fun—we did some short films. We did short fights and some films.

In 2000, I read in the newspaper that Donnie Yen was in Berlin doing a TV show. He was responsible for doing the martial arts scenes. It was called *Der Puma*. It was eight episodes. I was a huge fan of his. I wrote a letter, because at that time, I didn't have a computer. None of my friends had a computer. All we had was a little camera to shoot our movies and two VCRs to edit them. Our sound system was from a Super Nintendo. So I wrote this letter to the production company, and I got a call from them. They said that I could come to Berlin because they saw my tape. They said that I could train with the guys. I said, "Wow! Perfect! I can train with Donnie Yen!" So I went to Berlin and met with everyone, and also Donnie Yen. There was a mistake in the casting, and I was sent home. They took my picture, and I went back to my factory where I worked, and a few days later the producer from the show called me again and said that they liked my tape because I had a sense of humor and my skills were great. Even though the casting was already completed, the Chinese guys liked me and wanted me back. So, that was my entry. I had a chance to fight the main actor in the last part of the series, and I had three days shooting. Donnie Yen was great.

I saw your film *Kampfansage* with Mathis Landwehr. Talk about working on that film.

It was the same. From 2000–2003, I worked as a freelancer. I heard about this project, and I sent them my tape. I got a call from Mathis, and the director was Johannes Jaeger, who both invited me to train with them. I was on the main stunt team. I worked three months on this movie. I worked on the fights with Mathis.

Don't mess with this man: Mike Möller in *Arena of the Street Fighter*.

So this movie led to your film *Arena of the Street Fighter*, which you starred in and directed. Talk about how this movie happened.

Since 2000, I worked as a stuntman in American movies, for German movies. I did some short movies too with my friends. After maybe six or seven short movies—I said, that's enough for me. I thought I should try a full-length movie like *Kampfansage*. That was hard to realize. I had some friends, and we worked together, but we worked with the wrong people. We started this movie in 2008. The problem was we worked with the wrong people behind the camera. The producers. After two years, I said, "Okay, that's enough." I took my footage under my wing. It was not my intention to be the director, but I had no choice. We'd shot some footage already, and I watched it, and I created a story around the footage. Up to that point, we'd only shot some fight scenes. We shot the movie without a script. It was a shame. It almost looked like the movie would never be finished.

An airborne kick by Mike Möller in *Arena of the Street Fighter*.

You got the attention of Isaac Florentine and Scott Adkins. If they're endorsing you, then clearly the world needs to be paying attention to you. Say something about those guys.

I was a huge fan of Isaac Florentine. He motivated me. He inspired me a lot with his movies. In 2002, 2003, I had a computer, and I sent him an e-mail. I said, "Ah, I respect you so much!" He wrote me back. Since then, we've been in contact. In 2008, 2009, he invited me to come to Bulgaria for the shooting of *Ninja*. It was a great time. I met Scott Adkins on the set, and it was fantastic. Isaac is so friendly. He's a great martial artist. He's supported me all the time. We talk all the time about working together.

What do you want to say to the people who haven't seen your work or *Arena of the Street Fighter*?

I would say it was hard to realize, this movie. We put our hearts and souls into this movie. It's a great movie because I tried to put everything in the movie. Different martial arts styles, different kinds of people, you see brawls to American wrestling, to Hong Kong style, everything. Also, kung fu guys, karate guys, and taekwondo guys. That might be interesting to people. Also, the editing. Every fight is done a little bit differently.

What's next for you, what's after this?

Last year, I worked with Fred Williamson and Lorenzo Lamas in a movie. It's called *Atomic Eden*. I had a lead role in this movie. It's an action movie. I hope I get the chance to do another movie, a better movie than *Arena of the Street Fighter* because this movie was made under bad circumstances. I really hope that we get the chance to do another one with a bigger budget and bigger actors. And a good script. I really hope I can make it.

Lorenzo Lamas, Mike Moeller, and Nico Sentner on the set of *Atomic Eden*. Courtesy of Nico Sentner.

Armor of God

(a.k.a. **Operation Condor 2: The Armor of the Gods**)

1986 (Dimension DVD) (djm)

A pop star turned fortune hunter named Jackie (or sometimes known as Asian Hawk, played by Jackie Chan) goes on a quest to find the separate pieces that are collectively called The Armor of the Gods. He runs afoul of a Satan-worshiping cult who plan on using the ancient armor to perform some kind of unholy ritual, granting them immeasurable power on Earth. Chan, meanwhile, romances a young woman (played by Lola Forner from *Wheels on Meals* with Chan) who has ties to the artifacts.

For unknown reasons, Dimension Films released the sequel to *Armor of God—Operation Condor*—first in the US, and then later released this first film and retitled it *Operation Condor 2: The Armor of the Gods*. It's confusing. If you can put that aside, this first film sets Chan up as an Indiana Jones-styled adventurer, and it places him in crazy situations where he must outstunt himself each time to survive. In real life, Chan hurt himself so bad (he fell and hit his head on a rock, puncturing his skull) in one scene that the production had to halt and the script had to be rewritten to underplay the planned stunts ahead. As a result, the film suffers from a lackluster middle portion, but then the finale featuring Chan fighting the Satan cult (with high-heel-wearing henchwomen) renews interest in the proceedings. The sequel was better. Jackie Chan directed both entries.

Armstrong

1998 (Image DVD) (CD)

Rod Armstrong (Frank Zagarino) is a former Navy SEAL who is now living in Russia and working as a trainer for the FSB (what is essentially the new KGB). He's paid a visit by his old friend Bob Zorkin (Charles Napier), who informs Rod he has a cassette with important info on it, but then they're attacked and Bob is murdered before he can tell him what is on it. Rod tracks the tape to Susan (Kimberly Kates), Zorkin's wife. They find it, and discover footage of the Russian military selling nuclear warheads to the mob. The lead gangster is known only as "Ponytail" (Joe Lara) and he is hot on their trail every step of the way. He wants them and the tape destroyed before it gets into the hands of the proper authorities. Armstrong has a few tricks up his sleeves, and he won't go down without a fight.

The films of Frank Zagarino (The *Project: Shadowchaser* trilogy) tend to be a bit of an acquired taste. The more of them you watch, the more you will appreciate them for what they were meant to be. *Armstrong* starts off with a bang and continues to entertain throughout. There's plenty of gunfire, explosions, nudity, and most importantly: Zagarate! Former Cannon Group mogul Menahem Golem was the director of this Nu Image production. *Armstrong* gives Zagarino another chance to play a character he is comfortable with while also proving he somehow ends up with the greatest character names. Co-star Joe Lara also had a semi-action star career, starring in a number of Nu Image productions.

Around the World in 80 Days

2004 (Disney DVD) (CD)

In 1872, a Chinese man (Jackie Chan) steals a jade statue from the Bank of England to return it back to his village where it belongs. With the police hot on his trail, he finds himself hiding out with ridiculed inventor Phileas Fogg (Steve Coogan). Adopting the name Passportout, the two men find themselves in an adventure that will take them around the world. Along the way they meet significant figures from history as well as pick up a stray in the form of the lovely Monique La Roche (Cecile De France). They have stops in Paris, Turkey, India, China, and the US, all while trying to avoid attacks orchestrated by Phileas's nemesis from the Royal Academy of Science, Lord Kelvin (Jim Broadbent).

Around the World in 80 Days is a surprisingly entertaining family adventure that boasts some terrific action scenes assembled by Jackie Chan (*Police Story*) and his stunt team. The heart of the Jules Vern classic remains intact, but this version is filled with some fantastic martial arts. There's one particular sequence with Chan battling a group of thugs in an art gallery, culminating with a chase through the streets, which is fantastic. It's Chan's classic shenanigans that remind us why he is a living legend. The film mostly belongs to Steve Coogan (*Tropic Thunder*), but Chan as Passportout steals the show. The film also boasts a rather large cameo cast as well. There are hilarious spots by Luke and Owen Wilson (*Bottle Rocket*), Rob Schneider (*Judge Dredd*), Arnold Schwarzenegger (*Commando*), and Sammo Hung (*Martial Law*). It does run a tad bit long but director Frank Coraci (*Here Comes the Boom*) knew when to take a step back and allow Chan to do what he does best.

Art of Submission

(a.k.a. **The Red Canvas**)

2009 (Sun Film DVD) (CD)

Johnny Sanchez (Ernie Reyes Jr.) is a young man with a chip on his shoulder. He trains to be a fighter while his girlfriend is supposed to stay home with their newborn child. Johnny works with his dad, Diego (Ernie Reyes Sr.), but can't handle working in the auto business and quits. He becomes a collector for a drug dealer and ends up in prison. One of the prison guards believes in his potential as a fighter and gets him released after doing five years on the condition he trains to fight in the Red Canvas, one of the most celebrated MMA tournaments in the world. When he gets out, he must confront his family, and come to terms with all the hard trials he's put them through. His family is in financial trouble and his father is in danger of losing the family business, so Johnny will have to grow up real quick and do the right thing. He will fight for them and fight for the respect of his parents.

Art of Submission was a hard film to track down. It's listed under several names including *The Red Canvas* and *Bloodsport: The Red Canvas*. It's a family drama first and tournament action film second. Ernie Reyes Jr. (*The Last Dragon, Surf Ninjas*) is a likable lead and he excels bringing this character to life. The fight scenes are realistically choreographed but the way they were shot sort of masks the fact. There's an overuse of slow motion, high speed, and rapid cuts, while much of it is filmed from outside the cage. It's really bothersome, especially since the action was there—it's just difficult to follow. There's a great fight with Ernie and his father taking on a group of guys in a garage. This scene was shot well, and Ernie Sr. does a fantastic job with the choreography. The elements for a great action film are all here but directors Adam Boster and Kenneth Chamitoff fall a pinch short while still successfully capturing the family drama aspect.

The Art of War

2000 (Warner Brothers DVD) (JAS)

"Appearances are everything . . . politics and deception are built on it."

Wesley Snipes stars as United States government spy Neil Shaw. He is covert to the point of nonexistence; only his immediate supervisor Eleanor Hooks (Anne Archer) and equally stealth spy colleague Robert Bly (genre great Michael Biehn) know his real identity. He is sent on what is proposed as an easy mission by Hooks to eavesdrop on Chinese Ambassador Wu (James Hong) who is to announce the acceptance of an open trade agreement between the United Nations and China. Snipes is broadsided when the leader is assassinated. Naturally, he is suspected as the killer and must fight through the streets of New York with reporter Julia Fang (Marie Matiko) to uncover the mystery and clear his name.

While this film is fun, and Wesley Snipes's mixed martial arts fighting is impressive, it suffers from inconsistency of tone and lacks believability. The film jumps schizophrenically from cerebral political thriller to unrealistic action fest. Motivations are murky, especially as Michael Biehn's Bly character (a professional spy who's acting on orders) starts maniacally explicating the virtues of Sun Tzu's *The Art of War* book as he chases Shaw through the final duel. Couple that with the main villain explaining the "master plan" in the most shoehorned manner possible, and you have an unfortunate disappointment. The actors were great with what they had to work with, and action aficionados will enjoy this despite its flaws. Donald Sutherland co-stars.

The Art of War II: Betrayal

2008 (Sony DVD) (JAS)

Wesley Snipes reprises his role as Neil Shaw, the stealth spy who was bamboozled by his superiors in the original *The Art of War*. This time he's retired and acting as a consultant to a film director (Lochlan Munro) who shoots Hollywood action films and wants to enter politics. Shaw's childhood mentor and sensei named Mother (who is a cross-dresser for no reason related to the plot) is murdered in what is stated as a random act of violence. After Shaw investigates the murder and befriends a beautiful girl named Heather (Athena Karkanis), he realizes that he's being played by those closest to him . . . again.

In a sequel to a film that was already a bit flimsy, *The Art of War II: Betrayal* trudges along at a dull pace. It has the same believability problems as the original, which is ironic since Snipes's character is seen advising the (fictional) film director on how to achieve verisimilitude in an action film. The climax is even more ridiculous than in the original: After a long stream of somewhat reasonable espionage tropes, a cool and collected puppetmaster-type baddie starts randomly shooting a mini rocket launcher in the office building where he does legitimate business. It wasn't even staged as an act of desperation on the villain's part—just a way to gloat and destroy the hero. Would a mastermind do something so dumbfounding and absurd? This is a poorly constructed straight-to-DVD release that even Wesley Snipes, who deserves much better, couldn't save. Director Josef Rusnak also did another Snipes vehicle called *The Contractor*.

Assassination

1987 (MGM DVD) (djm)

A precursor to bigger and better movies like *In the Line of Fire* (with Clint Eastwood) and *Olympus Has Fallen* (with Gerard Butler), *Assassination*, starring Charles Bronson as a seasoned secret service agent assigned to a bitchy first lady (or "One Mamma"), is a half-hearted action movie from The Cannon Group. The newly inaugurated president's wife (played by Bronson's wife, Jill Ireland) is impossibly difficult to deal with, and so the secret service asks Jay Killian (Bronson) to step in and take on protective duties. She shirks all safety protocols and just about gets herself killed several times, and when Killian insists that there is a plot to assassinate her, it takes her forever to realize that he's right. In an extraordinary case, he is forced to take her on the lam and embark on an incognito road trip because there's no one they can trust—including the president, who might be the very man who is trying to kill her.

Light on action, but certainly a palpable thriller, *Assassination* isn't anything special and any fan of Bronson can easily be forgiven for overlooking it. The production values are on par with TV shows that were being produced during its era—stuff like *The A-Team* and *Airwolf*. It's fluff. Bronson looks bored in it. Director Peter Hunt also made *Death Hunt* with Bronson.

Assassination Games

2011 (Sony DVD) (CD)

Vincent Brazil (Jean-Claude Van Damme) is a hitman. He follows his own set of rules, taking most any job as long as the pay is good. Roland Flint (Scot Adkins) has given up the life after his wife was brutally attacked by drug lord Polo (Ivan Kaye). She is in a coma, and Flint spends his time taking care of her. Both men want to see Polo dead. Brazil wants the money, and Flint wants revenge. The two men unknowingly go after him at the same time and kill his brother. Polo flips his lid and puts all of his resources into finding and killing them. They will reluctantly form an alliance to survive, and Brazil will question his loyalty to Flint when money becomes involved.

There's no denying the fact that Van Damme and Adkins have a terrific chemistry, and *Assassination Games* is an intense action thriller. Van Damme has some cool shootout scenes but does very little fighting. His character, though, goes through a major transformation arc, and he is fantastic. Adkins, on the other hand, has some great moments fighting various thugs. They have a short fight against each other that ends before it ever really gets going. The action is solid, the script is well thought out, and their performances are top notch. Director Ernie Barbarash (*Six Bullets*) knows his action and pushes his actors to deliver the audience some high-octane entertainment. Originally shot under the title *Weapon*. Van Damme and Adkins previously appeared together in *The Shepherd*, and later starred in *Universal Soldier: Day of Reckoning* together.

Assassins

1995 (Warner DVD) (djm)

Richard Donner, the high-profile director of all four *Lethal Weapon* movies, made this 133-minute dramatic action movie with Sylvester Stallone as Robert Rath, a lonely and depressive hitman who's known as the best in the business. A young buck named Miguel Bain (a hyperactive Antonio Banderas) enters the picture, taking Rath's hits and becoming a thorn in his side. They both rush to take a high paying mark—a computer hacker who calls herself Electra (Julianne Moore)—and as they convene at the same location at the same time, Electra should pretty well consider herself dead—except Rath is in a midlife crisis and decides to protect her from Bain instead of doing his job and taking the pay. Rath and Electra go on the run and plan an elaborate strategy to trade a sought-after computer disc for millions, but Bain comes after them and seeks Rath's head.

I saw this twice in theaters, somehow blinded by how overwrought and bloated it is, and the few times I've seen it since, I just can't help but realize what a preposterous and overlong movie it is. Stallone is good, but the part is wrong for him, and while I enjoy watching Banderas chew up the scenery and steal the movie right out from under Stallone's feet,

Assassins is easily one of Stallone's worst-written movies (from the Wachowski Brothers, no less!) ever. Donner's usual light touch as a director is entirely absent here and, seriously, this movie is thirty minutes too long. For better results, see Stallone's similar but more entertaining movie *The Specialist*. Stallone and Banderas would team up years later for *The Expendables III*.

Assassin's Code

2011 (Screen Media DVD)

(djm)

Retired assassin Paul Thorn (taekwondo expert Julian Lee from *My Samurai*) is brought back into the fold when a former associate gives him a top-secret disc that the government is hot to get their hands on. Thorn, tired and burnt out from his years as a killer, is pursued by a couple of other assassins, but no one seems to realize that Thorn was the best of the best, and when they go after his old friends and associates, his heart is turned ever colder so he can reach into that deep, dark place to rekindle that killer within him.

Overly talky and convoluted, *Assassin's Code* feels designed to be a vehicle for several performers, but only Julian Lee—who has quietly worked his way through a half a dozen martial arts action films over the years—deserves any mention. It's too bad this film lets him down: he doesn't get to showcase his martial arts skills, and adding insult to injury, his voice was dubbed by someone who speaks English better than he does. I've always liked and admired Lee for working hard and putting his best efforts into his projects, and one of the things I like about him is the way he speaks. The fact that he was dubbed puts a strange damper on the whole movie, which was already tainted by its lack of action. If you go in seeing this movie before seeing any other movie with Lee, you'll probably never want to see anything else he's done. I wouldn't blame you, in that case. Also with Martin Kove and John Savage. Director/writer Lawrence Riggins also wrote *Ironheart*, which was a vehicle for Julian Lee's brother, Britton.

The Assault

1997 (Image DVD) (djm)

After a woman witnesses her husband being murdered by a drug lord, detective Stacy Palermo (Stacie Randall from *Excessive Force II: Force on Force*) steps in and escorts her to a woman's shelter off the beaten path and offers her solace and protection. Hot on their trail is the drug lord and his unruly hordes who have put a death mark on the witness. Palermo and the other women in the shelter, along with a former Marine (played by Matt McCoy) hold the fort and fight off the assault with a few weapons and improvised hand-held objects. It's going to be a long night.

From exploitation director Jim Wynorski,

The Assault is surprisingly enjoyable for an eighty-three-minute movie with no nudity, which is a rarity coming from him. Randall, who was so promising in *Excessive Force II* manages to be nearly as appealing (or even more so) in this film, which doesn't feature as much martial arts action as the other film, but her first scene as an undercover stripper brings down the house with some fancy footwork. This is basically a very low-budget variation on John Carpenter's *Assault on Precinct 13* (which itself was a reworking of *Rio Bravo*), but it sort of works. When the girls blow away dozens of thugs with endless rounds of ammunition without ever reloading, you just have to go with it. It's a shame Randall didn't have a better career as an action star. She could have made it.

The A-Team

1983–1987 (Universal DVD)

(djm)

"In 1972, a crack commando unit was sent to prison by a military court for a crime they didn't commit. These men promptly escaped from a maximum security stockade to the Los Angeles underground. Today, still wanted by the government, they survive as soldiers of fortune. If you have a problem, if no one else can help, and if you can find them, maybe you can hire . . . the A-Team."

A syndicated smash hit in the mid-1980s, *The A-Team* made a star out of Mr. T, who played the muscular, flamboyant B. A. Baracus opposite his teammates Hannibal (George Peppard), Face (Tim Dunigan in the pilot and Dirk Benedict for the rest of the series), and the crazy Murdock (Dwight Schultz). The A-Team are a misfit crew—former Green Berets in Vietnam who are now perpetually on the run from military police for a crime they are obviously innocent of. Over the course of ninety-eight episodes (five seasons), the team helps people in need, and they usually resort to PG-rated violence, resulting in grand fireworks, explosions, and stunt work involving vehicles, helicopters, and airplanes. The chemistry and camaraderie with the perfectly cast foursome is a whole lot of fun to watch, and if you grew up in the era when it played during nonstop reruns, then watching it today will bring back some innocent memories.

As goofy and broad-humored as the show seems today, the novelty of Mr. T's "Bad Attitude" Baracus storming around with his gold chains never really wears off. After his turn in *Rocky III*, Mr. T was a verifiable action star, and he'll always (for better or worse) be associated with this show, which was virtually everywhere with toys, stickers, Velcro shoes, and lunchboxes in the 1980s. Fun guest stars who were on the show include Hulk Hogan, Boy George, and Isaac Hayes. Easy to watch and impossible to forget as a whole, *The A-Team* is a perennial classic. From creators Frank Lupo and Stephen J. Cannell.

The A-Team

2010 (Fox DVD) (JAS)

"Hang on, everybody—I want to try something I saw in a cartoon once!"

The A-Team, based on the 1980s television series, is a wonderfully silly throwback to the days when action stars were charismatic tough guys with a goofy sense of humor. The film feels just as much an homage to 1980s action movies and action stars as it does a salute to the original TV series. The plot focuses on corruption in the ranks of the military, especially as it concerns private contractors during wartime. John "Hannibal" Smith (Liam Neeson), Templeton "Faceman" Peck (Bradley Cooper), Sergeant Bosco "B. A." Barracus (Quinton Jackson), and Howling Mad Murdock (Sharlto Copley) are tricked into taking back stolen US Mint plates from Afghanistan. They are framed and thrown in prison, while a corrupt member of the CIA and some private contractors for the war make money off selling the plates. Of course, the A-Team breaks out of prison to set things right.

The action set pieces in this film are breathtaking, although some scenes could stand a *little* downtime to create contrast between all the mayhem. Still, Liam Neeson's Hannibal Smith flying a tank by shooting the gun turret for navigation is a sight to behold, and UFC star Quinton "Rampage" Jackson takes an admirable turn as B. A. Baraccus. It could in no way be easy to replicate the iconic Mr. T, but Quinton does a great job. He catches the spirit of the character without trying to be exactly like him—not an easy feat for someone who isn't a classically trained actor, but Jackson pulls it off. Bradley Cooper is entertaining as always, doing his charismatic best to claim the heir to his role. Sharlto Copley is absolutely hilarious as the kooked-out Murdock, and is the scene-stealer of this show. *The A-Team* works because the casting is impeccable. Each actor chews the dialogue with comedic irony and with respect to the dramatic tension of the plot. It's a damn fun time at the movies. Now, where's the sequel? From director Joe Carnahan.

Attack Force

2006 (Sony DVD) (CD)

"There's just two things you should know about Marshall Lawson. One, he's a bad motherfucker. And two, he's a bad motherfucker."

Marshall Lawson (Steven Seagal) loses his strike force in a vicious attack. He isn't one to wait around and decides to investigate the attack himself. He stumbles across a secret military program involving the creation of a drug called CTX that can turn an average Joe into a seemingly unstoppable killing machine. When

Lawson gets too close to uncovering the truth, he finds himself a target as both the military and drug runners want him dead.

There should be no arguments that Steven Seagal's *Attack Force* is a complete and total disaster. There really isn't a single redeeming quality to the film. Aside from a decent (and unknown) supporting cast, Seagal turns in one of the most tired and bored performances of his career. The film opens with an interesting premise but things quickly disintegrate when it becomes apparent that Seagal has been placed in a movie he has no right being in. There are only a couple of fight scenes, and they're crammed toward the finale. To call them fight scenes might even be an overstatement since all Seagal does is wave his hands in the air like he just doesn't care. And you can't talk about *Attack Force* without bringing up the fact that most of his dialogue was dubbed by a voice-over actor who sounds nothing like him. One moment we hear Seagal's voice, and the next it's some other guy. It isn't like it's just a line here or there, we're talking full speeches and it's incredibly distracting. It's been stated that some of the story elements were changed after filming was completed and that's why his voice was dubbed later on. Regardless, some of Seagal's other pictures like *Mercenary for Justice* feature bad ADR (Automatic Dialogue Replacement), and basically that suggests that Seagal refuses to do his own voice-over work. An embarrassingly lazy effort that should be avoided by action fans at all costs. Michael Keusch (*Shadow Man* and *Flight of Fury* with Seagal) directed.

Automatic

1994 (Republic VHS) (djm)

This is a not-bad, but nothing-special effort starring Olivier Gruner, who plays a number of roles, all of them "Automatics," which are android men meant to protect humans from danger. In a nondescript, generic-looking future, the next big thing on the market is a controversial android protector manufactured by a company whose every move is spotlighted by the media. When an Automatic (all of them are played by Gruner) is patrolling the company's highrise one evening, he saves a pretty office worker (Daphne Ashbrook) from being raped by her lecherous boss. When the Automatic accidentally kills the guy, everything goes south. The head of the company (John Glover, always smarmy) tries to cover up the situation by hiring some goons to come into the building, murder the woman and destroy the Automatic, and make it all look accidental. Bad idea. The Automatic knows martial arts, and he can take a bullet and keep on going.

What we've got here is a sort of *Die Hard*-hybrid with an android hero. Most of the film takes place in the building and elevator shafts, and there's lots of shooting. Gruner plays the Automatics (he plays at least two characters) so innocently, and at every step he is checking

to make sure the woman he's protecting is all right. When he's kicking someone's ass, he's only doing it after checking to make sure a fight is what they want. The lead goon is played by Jeff Kober. This isn't one of Gruner's worst efforts, but this was the beginning of his junky straight-to-video movies. It was written by "Patrick Highsmith," who is actually Avi Nesher, a frequent collaborator with Gruner. John Murlowski directed it.

Atomic Eden

2015 (NOV) (CD)

"You tell Stoker, if it's war that he wants, it's war he's gonna get!"

Stoker (Fred Williamson) is a mercenary with a mission. In order to complete his current assignment, he will have to assemble a team of not only the best in the business but also people he can trust. He calls in a few favors and assembles the toughest, most badass group of mercenaries loyalty can buy. With David (Mike Möller), Reiko (Hazuki Kato), Heinrich (Wolfgang Riehm), Darwin (Everett Ray Aponte), John (Nico Sentner), Brenner (Dominik Stark), and Laurie (Josephine Hies) by his side, the mission should be a breeze. But it quickly turns into an unwinnable battle with eight people battling against eight hundred, all vying for control of a Nazi doomsday device lost during World War II. With the odds stacked against them, they're ready to risk life and limb to save millions of lives.

The Hammer is back, folks! At seventy-seven years old, Fred Williamson (*Black Caesar, The Messenger*) can still kick ass and take names. Pairing him with rising German action star Mike Möller (from *Arena of the Streetfighter*) was a fantastic (and unexpected) idea. *Atomic Eden* is fast paced, action packed, and above all else, a damn good time. Over the last few years, Williamson has been stuck doing cameos or appearing in bit parts, but here he's front and center, never shying away from the action. With his trademark cigar dangling from his lips, he pummels and blows away the gas-masked villains of the film. He isn't the only one putting a dent in the army of mad men: Möller once again proves himself to be one of the best fight choreographers in the business. He has several major fight scenes showcasing his speed and agility. They're an unlikely duo but they have an undeniable screen chemistry. When the film comes to a close, you want nothing more than to see their further adventures. It was also a pleasant surprise to see *Renegade* star Lorenzo Lamas in a minor role. It's not action-oriented, though it does remind us just how good of an actor he is. Director Nico Sentner set out to make an exciting throwback to the DTV films of the '90s. He easily hit his mark, and for the action alone, this film will be worth revisiting.

Avenging Angelo

2002 (Sony DVD) (djm)

In a period of crisis in his career, Sylvester Stallone hadn't had a hit in several years and after *Eye See You* was shelved, his films *Get Carter* and *Driven* flopped in theaters. The same year *Eye See You* was eventually released in a few theaters and ultimately relegated to video, *Avenging Angelo* bypassed a theatrical release altogether and found a quiet life on DVD and VHS. Stallone plays a romantic bodyguard named Frankie who watches Jennifer (an overly emotional Madeleine Stowe), who is the only daughter of an aging mob kingpin named Angelo (Anthony Quinn in his last movie). Jennifer has no idea that she's Angelo's daughter —or that she's been watched her entire life—but when Angelo is assassinated, Frankie delivers some confession tapes Angelo made for Jennifer, and when she realizes the truth, her world is flipped upside down. Going through a breakup with her philandering husband, Jennifer learns to trust and care for Frankie, whose timely appearance in her life is met with violence as other hitmen vulture around her. Frankie, who's loved Jennifer for decades, protects her from the goons who want to do her harm.

A romantic comedy with some thriller vibes, *Avenging Angelo* was a strange, but understandable choice for Stallone to make at this juncture in his career. It's ultra light (paper thin) and has a goofball tone, but Stallone always plays it straight while his co-star Stowe is all over the place, playing it for laughs. It's an awkward mix. There's barely any action in it, which is almost unforgivable if not for the sincerity of Stallone's performance in an understated role. Bill Conti's score tries to sell the movie as a romantic thriller, but the movie's too weak to sustain any momentum. Stallone's next two movies were the card-playing drama *Shade* (which was given a brief theatrical release) and *Spy Kids 3D*, where he played the villain. Directed by Martyn Burke.

INTERVIEW:

MARTYN BURKE

(djm)

The late 1990s and the early 2000s were rough years for Sylvester Stallone, who had not had a verifiable blockbuster since 1993. The early 2000' were especially trying times, as Stallone had three back-to-back flops with Get Carter *(2000),* Driven *(2001), and the barely released* Eye See You *(a.k.a. D-Tox, 2002), which sat on the shelf for several years. Adding to the hardship, Stallone's follow-up to those pictures was the mob dramedy* Avenging Angelo *(2002), which cast him opposite Madeleine Stowe and Anthony Quinn. From the now-defunct Franchise Pictures,* Avenging Angelo *was surrounded by behind-the-scenes scandals and turmoil, and it never received a theatrical release, making it the first film Stallone starred in that was officially released directly to video. Director Martyn Burke (who'd directed the*

Martyn Burke in Santa Monica, California. Photo by david j. moore.

cable movie hit Pirates of Silicone Valley, 1999) *shares some of his experiences while working with Stallone on that film.*

I remember hearing about *Avenging Angelo* for years before it was eventually released directly to video. I was waiting for it.

So was I. While it was being made, I was being cheered on by Stallone's agents, my agents, the people that made the film, and by the people who produced it because it looked so great. The first screening went great. Then there was this unbelievable silence as to when it was going to come out. What had happened, I am told, is that they'd made so much money in presales. The company that made it—Franchise Pictures—which you must know of . . . Elie Samaha and Andrew Stevens . . . was in such trouble, and they'd made so much money on presales. To have to pay for prints and ads would have risked all the money that they'd made on presales around the world. They decided, "Why should we risk all this money? If the film's a flop, we're gonna lose all this money. We've got it all now." They made a huge profit, and it was safer never to release it in theaters.

Wow. That makes total sense.

I started this film with a budget of thirty million. At the time we started shooting it, the budget had dropped to fifteen million. Half of it disappeared. I don't know all the details here. What I do know is that while I was shooting it, my line producer was being interviewed by the FBI for what had happened with funds. A grand jury was called to investigate. Ultimately, no criminal charges were pressed on this or other films that were related to Franchise. But a lawsuit—and this is a matter of public record—was filed by German investors, and it's the first lawsuit that what they called "pierced the corporate veil," where one person in there—Elie Samaha—was found personally responsible, not his company, for tens of hundreds of millions of dollars. I was in the middle of this. I made the film I wanted to make, but it was the most insane thing. We were supposed to film in Sicily, but the week before, we didn't know if we were going to go to Sicily, and if we didn't go to Sicily we didn't have a film. The money somehow vanished. A producer named Tarak Ben Ammar comes in, and we'd never heard of him. He came in and somehow . . . we never knew what happened. It was all kinds of chaos. Every director will

always have a story that goes, "Oh, my God, it was insane!" Of course, that's the nature of this business, but this one was *way* over the top. I understand that the Italian film crew didn't get paid, or somebody didn't get paid. The producer didn't get paid, and there were huge lawsuits for a long time afterwards. What is important is that I was offered this film. I really believe—and still believe to this day—that Stallone has an incredible role here, and has actually acted a couple of times. As a guy who's more than *The Expendables*, more than the action guy. That was why I was attracted to this.

What was your experience like, working with Stallone?

He's a guy who was enamored with Anthony Quinn. That was my reason for doing it: A different side to Stallone. He and I had all the normal fights that a.) a director gets into with an actor, and b.) you get into with Stallone. That's part of the territory. My challenge doing that was to listen carefully and figure out which ones I thought were good ideas. He wouldn't have gotten to where he is if he wasn't very smart. He would have ideas that no one else would have thought of, which were terrific. The key with him was, which ones work? There's a scene in the film where he's drawing on a kitchen counter. He came to me first thing in the morning the way he always did—it was nose to nose and it was like you were about to weigh in for a prize fight—and I thought it was the dumbest idea I'd ever heard of. Then, when I thought about it, I thought, *Let's try it and see what happens.* I said, "Okay, let's try it." It was *way* better than I thought it was going to be. You know? Working with Sly and Anthony Quinn was . . . and this was Anthony's last film . . . we bonded.

The artwork on the DVD shows Stallone pointing a gun, but I don't think he ever holds a gun in the movie. He might hold a gun, but he never uses one in the film.

I know, and it bugged me. It's not a shoot 'em up movie. It's a comedy love story. They wanted to sell it that way, as an action movie. To my knowledge, it made more money than any other that they made.

Do you think this movie was a good move for Stallone? Personally, I don't think it was.

In retrospect, it wasn't. At the time, it was one of those things where he wanted to change his image because he was in a slump. I think it's probably good that he did it and found out that audiences don't want to see him like that. When I look back on it, it's like when Steve McQueen always wanted to do a film that showed what a capital "A" actor he was. So he chose Ibsen's *Enemy of the People*, the big beard, long hair, and nobody in America wanted to see that film. That's the case with Sly. He's one of these guys who's got a really avid public. Looking back, he made a mistake, and looking back I made a mistake in believing that he could be *so* good— and he's good in this, he did a great job—but nobody wanted to see that. Having said that, to this day I wonder what kind of reception it

would have gotten had it really come out the way it was supposed to. Actually, Warner Brothers was in this film, it was a Warner Brothers film and it was thirty million dollars. When Warner Brothers found out that half of the budget was somehow missing, they pulled out three weeks before we started shooting. (Laughing.) It was an adventure.

So you were dealing with a guy who was still a major movie star at the time—and he's still a major movie star—and you told me that he would get up in your face every morning with his ideas. Were you ever intimidated by him?

The first thing with Sly is that if you show fear or weakness, he will walk all over you. He'll kill you. My attitude is that I thought I knew what I was doing, I thought I knew what I was after, and I could articulate it. I knew when something was off-kilter or heading in that direction. I had no problem with telling him that. He didn't like hearing that. He would respect it, but God help you if you tried to finesse it or you told him that you knew what you were doing and it turned out you didn't. During the course of the film, he and I bonded in a way that helped me tremendously. All the problems we had on this film, had he not been right there, coming in there in the morning . . . he had been pouring over the script all night, doing what he does, he goes over the next day's stuff, and he's got fifteen ideas and they're going well. Sometimes, like so many talented people, he can be his own worst enemy, and he's also smart enough, though, to know if there's a good idea. He will see it. I think I shared with him that attitude. I didn't care if his ideas were better than mine. In the end, I think he would grudgingly admit that he didn't care whose ideas were better than his, as long as they worked. He had the acting courage to go along with that. I found it very exciting to work with him. Part of that excitement was watching him work with Anthony Quinn. They only had a few scenes together. When we were shooting this film, it looked so fabulous. I'm not just talking about the rushes or the dailies, I'm talking about the stuff that's being cut together. We were having the agents, the actors, and everyone else look at this footage, and everyone was so excited. Stallone was doing something that nobody had seen him doing before. People, at the time, loved Sly's character. It's easy now to look back and say, "It didn't work." Now, we can all agree on that. But at the time, and had I been a gambler, I would have thought that this would have had a major impact on his career.

How were you chosen to be the director of this film?

I had just come off a huge cable movie hit called *Pirates of Silicon Valley*. It would been hard to get a bigger hit than that. At the time, it got the highest ratings, and even more than that, it got such a buzz, which to this day, I still get people coming to me about. At the time, I was offered all kinds of *Silicon Valley*-type films, you know? That's the way it works. I wanted to do something completely different. Not that *Avenging Angelo* is a mob movie, but it's a romantic comedy. I had done undercover documentaries on organized crime, I ran stings. This movie that came out recently *American Hustle*, I had done exactly what was in that movie, and I'm not kidding, so close to what's in that movie. We trapped major mafia families on camera. We used them for training films. I kind of knew the mafia. It also seemed like a good idea at the time.

Has *Avenging Angelo* been a profit to you at all?

Not like it should have been. All I can tell you is what I get from the Director's Guild. The residuals . . . it's played all over the place.

Anything else you want to say about the film?

Sly and I had a rather diplomatic falling out in the editing room. He wants to come in and take over. I did not want that. Now, Sly has a tremendous influence, obviously. Let's just say that we had "disagreements." The film that came out is pretty much what I wanted. Sly and I had a real . . . session . . . in the editing room. That's all I'm going to say about it. You've gotta hand it to Sly.

Avenging Force

2986 (MGM DVD R2) (djm)

The dynamic duo from *American Ninja*—Michael Dudikoff and Steve James—reunite for their *Ninja* director Sam Firstenberg under the Cannon banner. Dudikoff plays a retired government agent named Matt Hunter, living in New Orleans, who is buddies with US Senate candidate Larry Richards (James). Richards is targeted by a racist Aryan brotherhood known as Pentangle, whose sole purpose is to strengthen America by murdering and hunting down minorities or those who oppose their mission statement. When Richards is attacked during a Mardi Gras parade, one of his two sons is killed, and Hunter helps foil Pentangle's attempt to assassinate Richards. Hunter assists Richards in finding out who is behind Pentangle, and in the process Richards is murdered, along with his entire family. Hunter's kid sister is kidnapped by Pentangle and is about to be sold into sexual slavery when he jumps into action, saves her, and is forced to play The Most Dangerous Game, where he is hunted through the bayou by masked killers.

Matt Hunter (Michael Dudikoff), wielding a deadly crossbow in Sam Firstenberg's *Avenging Force*. Author's collection.

As far as "B" action movies go, *Avenging Force* is precisely entertaining and perfect genre fodder from a bygone era. Dudikoff and James made a special team, and this entry has the feel and texture of their two comic book-style *American Ninja* movies. This one is every bit the men's adventure pulp yarn it sets out to be. It's shockingly violent at times, and Dudikoff makes a great action hero. The main villain of the piece is John P. Ryan (from *Delta Force 2*), and he chews up the scenery. *Hard Target* with Jean-Claude Van Damme is very similar, and even has the same setting.

INTERVIEW:

SAM FIRSTENBERG

(djm)

Partly responsible for ushering in the era of the ninja craze in the 1980s, Israeli director Sam Firstenberg built a long and lasting career that had its foundation with The Cannon Group, which produced his films Revenge of the Ninja (1983), Ninja III: The Domination (1984), American Ninja (1985), Avenging Force (1986), American Ninja II: The Domination (1987), *and* American Samurai (1992). *He worked with actions stars Sho Kosugi, Michael Dudikoff, David Bradley, and others, and he created a legacy of action films worthy to be proud of.*

How did you get involved with Cannon?

I knew the Cannon people, Menahem Golan and Yoram Globus, before I directed. I was an assistant director with them. I was an assistant director on a movie they produced called *Diamonds*, and some other Israeli movies . . . and *Lepke* with Tony Curtis. Then, at the time, I'd just finished my undergraduate studies. I had been assistant directing for five years, but I didn't want to be doing that anymore. I went back to graduate school in Westchester. When I was in school, I directed a movie called *One More Chance*. When I finished, Golan and Globus acquired Cannon Films. This was in 1979 or 1980. It was a distribution company from New York, and they brought it over here to Los Angeles. Since I'd known them, I showed them my movie, and they distributed it. It was a low-key movie. By then, they'd already done a movie called *Enter the Ninja* with Franco Nero and Sho Kosugi. Menahem, who had directed that film, did not want to direct the second one. They offered it to me, and I said, "By all means!" Am I going to say no? I accepted the challenge. That's how I did *Revenge of the Ninja*.

It seems like Cannon is single-handedly responsible for the ninja craze that took over pop culture in the 1980s, and you directed the most well-known and well-loved ninja movies during that period. *Revenge of the Ninja* and *Ninja III: The Domination* are outrageous and crazy ninja action movies. What did Menahem and Yoram want from you and from these movies—what was their pitch to you?

I'll tell you: First of all, the birth of the Western

ninja movie occurred because Mike Stone came to the office of Cannon. Mike Stone was an instructor and martial artist, a champion. He was a martial arts trainer. He came to Menahem and said, "Let's make a ninja movie!" A western type of ninja movie. Menahem, who had a good imagination, bought the idea. They went to the Philippines and shot *Enter the Ninja*, which already had a script. Mike Stone was the guide. He brought in Sho Kosugi, who played the bad guy. The movie was well received. Because it made money, they wanted to make a sequel. When they came to me, you have to know that I do not come from martial arts. Beside the Kurosawa movies, I'd never seen a martial arts movie. I knew those, but those are high-class martial arts movies. I took it upon myself to make a martial arts movie with an action and western style. They introduced me to Sho Kosugi, who introduced me to the Hong Kong-style martial arts movie. Those movies run very long and have fantastic battles and had thin storylines, and they appeal only to the Eastern audience. But in the West, we like *Bullitt* with Steve McQueen. I thought, let me take this idea of the martial arts and melt it into a regular, Western action movie. With the limitation of the budget, this was what I was trying to do. It's what they expected me to do, and it's what I *wanted* to do.

What was Sho Kosugi like to work with?

He's a marital artist. A black belt, a sensei with his own students and studio. He was already living in Hollywood to make a career here. He's a little different for Japanese society because he's very tall. He's extremely tall for a Japanese. He was kind of involved in the martial arts community in Los Angeles, and that's how he knew Mike Stone. Sho understood the commerciality of making such a movie as we were making. He went along with me, and I learned a lot from him. He went along with the idea that we would use gymnasts and break through the glass into a car. He staged the fights. We had stunt people, but he choreographed the fights. Most of the people he's fighting were his students. He was a major force on the movie.

Director Sam Firstenberg (left) with Sho Kosugi (right) on the set of *Revenge of the Ninja*. Author's collection.

I love that he brought his two sons, Kane and

Behind the scenes shot from *Revenge of the Ninja*, featuring Kane Kosugi (left), Sho Kosugi (center), and Sam Firstenberg (right). Author's collection.

Shane, along with him from movie to movie. What was it like working with Kane?

Kane has gone on to become a big star in Japan. He was a little kid, seven or eight years old, on *Revenge of the Ninja*. Sho had trained him already in martial arts. Working with Kane was very easy. He was very disciplined. He took direction very quickly. The way I remember it, he was very easy to work with.

Talk a little bit about Keith Vitali, who had a supporting role in *Revenge of the Ninja*. He's awesome. He was a real-life champion in his own right, and went on to do a few other martial arts films.

He was known in the martial arts community. He came to the movie, but he was not cast by me, he was already in the mix of putting it together. The whole idea was to have the movie be a "buddy/buddy" movie, which worked really well later in *American Ninja*. The "buddy/buddy" story. This was Sho's idea. Keith had his own fights and his own demonstration in the movie.

Was *Revenge of the Ninja* a modest hit or was it a big hit?

We finished the movie, and Cannon was a pretty new company, and then they showed this movie around and MGM liked the movie. They came to Cannon and said, "We'd like to purchase this

Sam Firstenberg giving directions on the set of *Revenge of the Ninja*, featuring Kane Kosugi and Sho Kosugi (on the right). Author's collection.

movie for distribution." Cannon, which was a tiny company at the time, made big news because MGM wanted to distribute it, and not only that, but they wanted to distribute all of their movies. *Revenge of the Ninja* was the first one. It was a big deal. MGM distributed it, and it was not a *huge* hit, but they did 600 or 700 prints, and they did a "flip/flop" distribution, which is when they took all the prints from the west of the Mississippi and sent them to the east of the Mississippi. They would not distribute one movie across the nation at one time. They would do two movies at the same time, and then flip them. In New York, *Revenge of the Ninja* was number one at the box office. Suddenly, this whole Western ninja movie took off. It's a movie for kids. In the beginning, it was for the adults, but later on—with *American Ninja*—it became for the kids. So, right away, they said, "Let's make another one!"

I never understood the connection between the three Cannon *Ninja* movies. What was the reasoning behind the titles?

The titles were a distribution business, it was never a production business. Sometimes you make a movie under one title, and the distribution changes it to something else. I called them the second ninja movie and the third ninja movie. But, Menahem was a very creative person. He always came up with a twist or an angle. We finished *Revenge of the Ninja,* and then he said, "Next time, let's have a female ninja!" Then we commissioned a writer and we had a script, and at the time *Poltergeist* was out, and so *Ninja III* had a little of *Poltergeist* in it. Within the culture of the ninja, there is a cult of ninja women. There was such a thing, but we didn't go in that direction, so the way to give the female a strong power was to have her be possessed.

I like *Ninja III* despite the fact that it's so weird.

Many people like it. Obviously, it did not have the wide success of *Revenge of the Ninja*.

The star of *Ninja III*, Lucinda Dickey, was in three movies in 1984: *Breakin'*, *Breakin' 2: Electric Boogaloo*, and *Ninja III: The Domination*, and you directed her in two of those (*Breakin' 2* and *Ninja III*). How did she fit all three movies into that one year?

Ninja III was her first movie. We had casting—different girls and actresses came. Many dancers came too. She was good, she had the physique. She's a dancer and an athlete, so we knew she would pick up all the moves we taught her. Heather Locklear was our first choice. Unbeknownst to us, she had another contract with a TV show. Lucinda was number two. So we did the movie. Then, Cannon was preparing *Breakin'*. Shooting was eight weeks on *Ninja III*, and they took her right away when it was done, and she did *Breakin'* while I was editing *Ninja III*. She'd already finished *Breakin'* while I was still editing. MGM picked up *Breakin'* and *Ninja III*, but *Breakin' 2* was distributed by Tri-Star.

Lucinda Dickey in ninja garb in *Ninja III: The Domination*. Author's collection.

The beginning of *Ninja III* is classic. The ninja won't die! He *will* not die! He kills countless cops in that scene where they're shooting him to death, but he simply won't die. What were you guys thinking when you shot that scene? How come that ninja would not die?

I love the police very much. The idea there was that the ninja was super. They have superpowers. Superhuman. This was the idea. They shoot him, and he comes up again. He's indestructible. Another thing was that his inner force is so strong that even though they kill him, they did not kill his spirit and his spirit moves to another person. When you see the Hong Kong movies, they are *way* over the top.

By this point in your career were you starting to see yourself as an action filmmaker?

No, not at all. My first movie, *One More Chance*, is a social drama. I must admit that some of my favorite movies are John Ford and Kurosawa movies, which are action movies. Basically, there are action elements in those movies. Battles, chases, and fighting. But I didn't see myself as a pigeonholed director, but later on I realized that I could not approach any other producer as a director for any other type of movie.

Did that bother you?

Twenty or thirty years ago, maybe. There is something about making action movies that's really pure cinema. Action is creating something on purely visual terms. The action doesn't really happen. No one stabs anybody. Through the visual and cinematic elements, you create the illusion. This is pure cinema. Not every director likes this kind of work, but I enjoy it immensely.

It must have helped a great deal to work with guys who came from the martial arts world—guys like David Bradley, Sho Kosugi, and Tadashi Yamashita (the Black Star Ninja from *American Ninja*)—to assist you on the fight scenes. Talk about working with these guys and building the movies you made around their abilities.

Those guys are champions in their world. Within the world of martial arts, they are famous. When they come to the set, there is a lot of ego and competitiveness, but there is camaraderie at the same time. Sometimes there will be some conflict or some argument. "This is the way to do it!" "No, this is the way to do it!" The right way, the wrong way. Everyone wants to show off more than the others. I also worked with Richard Norton. Later, he had his own career. He was the double of Michael Dudikoff in *American Ninja*.

No way!

Because Michael is not a real martial artist. Norton has two or three scenes. The role of the director is to keep everyone together.

Talk about working on *Breakin' 2*.

The first *Breakin'* was already out. Big success. I was approached because they couldn't get the first director, or whatever. I figured out, when I saw the script, that this was an action movie. There is no difference. What is an action movie? Forty-five minutes of story, forty-five minutes of action. What is a dance movie? The same thing. The structure is the same. A basic story, which is only an excuse to show the action, or in this case, the dancing. From a technical standpoint, I was covered. On the other hand, I was immersed in this hip-hop culture. Most of those kids were Hispanics and African-Americans, and they were really into this culture. I was not part of that culture in the same way that I was not part of the martial arts culture. Adolofo Quinones—Shabba-Doo—was the Sho Kosugi of the hop-hop culture. He tried to keep the dancing pure. On one hand I had the advantage of looking at the movie from the outside, but on the other had, I enjoyed working with the kids and hearing the music on the set all day from morning to evening. They called me "Sam the Sham."

Was it a small production?

No, no, no. It was a *big* production. We shot principle for nine weeks. We had three units on the set. Nine weeks, and we had a little additional photography. Five million dollars, and at that time that was a lot of money for us. The engine that made it big was Tri-Star. Sometime during the second week, they picked it up for distribution. Tri-Star was Columbia. The head of the company wanted to show MGM that they could do an even better job in promoting it. They spent a lot of money on it. Incidentally, it was the summertime. Tri-Star had a movie called *Supergirl*, and they booked 1200 theaters for it. *Supergirl* was coming this weekend, and *Breakin' 2* was maybe two weekends later. They started to sense that *Supergirl* wasn't going to make it,

An undying, unrelenting ninja puts up the fight of his life at the beginning of Sam Firstenberg's bonkers *Ninja III: The Domination.* Author's collection.

so they put pressure on us to finish editing the picture. We edited *Breakin' 2* in four weeks. We edited it around the clock, nonstop. It had been slated for 400 or 600 theaters, but when *Supergirl* bombed, they printed another thousand prints of *Breakin' 2* and put them in the theaters where *Supergirl* was supposed to be playing. Suddenly, we had 1,400 theaters, and it was a big success.

Why was there not a third *Breakin'* movie?

I don't know. There was another breakdance movie called *Beat Street* that Andrew Davis directed. You don't see his name on it, but he directed it. It's a good question. I don't know why they didn't do another one. Imagine if there were a part 3, 4, or 5 like *American Ninja*. It would deteriorate. It was not my decision to not make another *Breakin'*.

Talk about the music in the film. You had Ice-T in there.

The music was produced by a company called Polygram. The music was big already. I guess they were friends with Ice-T. Nobody knew who he was at the time, but he was in the circle of hip-hop. He was the original rapper. Somehow, they brought him to me and I thought he was a good guy. We wrote scenes for him. I used him in another movie. I gave him his first break. In the movie, he wrote one piece for the end, and he regrets it. He said, "It's not real rap."

Right around the time the *Breakin'* movies were made and released, the way people watched movies was changing. There was video and VHS, which was a relatively new thing. I sort of feel like the Cannon-type movies *are* the VHS era.

You are absolutely right. Remember, at the time, there was Cannon and Carolco. There was Crown International too. But Cannon *is* VHS. Cannon invented home video and home video invented Cannon. It happened both ways. Every time new technology comes out, the establishment looks down at the new technology. The networks didn't want to talk about cable, but then cable took off. They thought, "Why would anyone pay for TV?" The beginning of home video, the same thing happened with the studios. Look what happened. The money is in theaters, they said. Why would we spend time copying and making the movies on video? Those Cannon, Carolco,

etc., . . . they entered into the vacuum. "Okay, it's not *big* money, but it's money." Back then, it was all rental business—you couldn't sell the movies on video. Those little video chains were everywhere. Cannon saw money here. They realized that we had to make money for the small screen. We spent money on these films—but not *too* much money. We made the movies exciting enough so that the kids, or whoever, would go to the rental places and rent the movies. Eventually, the studios saw their mistake. Not only that, but it became a gold mine.

After *Breakin' 2* you did *American Ninja*. As I understand it, this was supposed to be a vehicle for Chuck Norris.

Cannon had a deal with Chuck Norris. Menahem said, "Let's make another movie, another ninja movie, but with a twist." The twist was that the ninja would be an American. Chuck Norris was a big star. He didn't want to do it. He didn't want to be covered up in black. So we said, "Let's cast!" We had a script by Paul De Mielche, and it was a buddy/buddy story. We knew already that it would be set in the Philippines because of money. I wondered how we could make it an American story because it was set in the Philippines. We would set it at an American base. This was an open casting call, nationwide. I think we saw 400 young guys. For the Jackson part and for the Armstrong part. When Michael Dudikoff walked in . . . I remember the moment . . . it was like "Whoa! *This* is the American Ninja!" The way he talked, the way he behaved, his body language, everything. He is not a martial artist in the sense that Sho Kosugi or David Bradley is, no formal training but he was very athletic. We had Mike Stone with us, and he choreographed the fights. He said, "No problem, Michael will pick up the moves." Michael Dudikoff had done a few movies already. *Radioactive Dreams* was one of them. Menahem Golan saw what I saw in him. Steve James walked in and he was a martial artist, but a style that I didn't know. When we paired him with Michael Dudikoff, they had good chemistry, and he was hired. Same thing with Judie Aronson, who played the pretty love interest.

***American Ninja* is a quintessential 80s action movie. Did you guys realize you were making something special?**

I get so many letters from fans of *American Ninja*. For Michael and myself, it's like we only made *American Ninja*. People around the world know us for this film. I was in Israel recently where they wanted to do a retrospective of my movies, and the poster of the festival was for *American Ninja*! When we started it, we didn't know that it would become a craze. But there was a good, strong energy to it when we were making it. Michael Dudikoff had trained with Mike Stone before we went to film in the Philippines. It was pretty cheap to film there. We had the resources to do whatever we wanted. We had the cooperation of the military. You saw on the screen that Michael Dudikoff was a movie star. He had this charisma, this energy.

You mentioned that Richard Norton doubled for Dudikoff. Talk about that a little bit.

We were not 100 percent sure if Michael would be able to do everything because he's not a martial artist. We always had doubles anyway, it's too dangerous.

It's interesting that you didn't just cast Richard Norton as the American Ninja. He's Australian, but still . . .

I don't remember why. I don't think he came to the casting. He's a good friend of Mike Stone. From the back, Norton looks exactly like Dudikoff. At the time, I don't know about today. He was the perfect double.

It's interesting. Despite the fact that Michael Dudikoff wasn't a martial artist, his career took off, and he's known for being an action star. *American Ninja* was a huge success, spawning a franchise. It played nonstop on television . . .

Until today! I still get residuals. I still make money from *American Ninja*!

Cannon did the old Hollywood thing by signing a few actors to eight- or ten-picture deals, guys like Charles Bronson, Chuck Norris, and then Michael Dudikoff.

With Michael, it was not a movie contract—it was a salary. He was part of the company, monthly. It was immediately after *American Ninja*; they saw his potential. In my opinion, they could have promoted him much more. When they opened the second *American Ninja*, he was already a name and they didn't realize how big he was with the kids. When the second movie came out, it should have been *DUDIKOFF: American Ninja*. But they didn't. They could have built him up, sent him to parties . . . in Hollywood, you have to build a star. MGM distributed them, and they didn't realize what they had.

Your next film was *Avenging Force* with Dudikoff and Steve James again.

Avenging Force was supposed to be a Chuck Norris movie. Cannon had been working with Chuck Norris to make this movie, but suddenly he didn't want to do it. They couldn't argue with him. The story was a little bit different when he was going to do it—it was going to be about a man and his daughter. We changed it for Dudikoff where it would be a man and his sister because he was too young. Great story. We came back from the Philippines and were still in editing, and Cannon turns to us and they had a good feeling about Michael (because *American Ninja* wasn't out in the street yet), and they took the *Avenging Force* script and asked me if I could make it with Dudikoff. I brought Steve James in. This was a really big movie in terms of budget.

How big?

It was like eight million dollars. What they called twelve million back then. This was almost at the level of Carolco's movies. They always

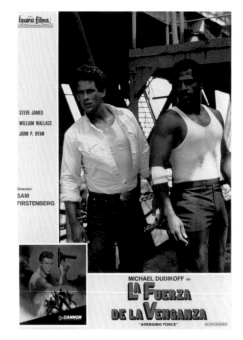

Michael Dudikoff and Steve James as Matt Hunter and Larry Richards in Cannon's *Avenging Force*. Author's collection.

made bigger movies. We went to New Orleans, which was very expensive, unions. Principle photography was eight weeks, and then some more photography. The action sequences are tremendous. We recreated the Mardi Gras. We had to move them twice. We filmed in the French Quarter. They never let anyone film in the French Quarter. That was expensive. We had a sequence in a burning house. We spent days in the marshes. While we were doing it, *American Ninja* came out. We learned how successful it was.

You did a few films with Steve James. You later did *Riverbend* with him. What was he like to work with?

Steve was a good friend of mine. He was a sweetheart of a person, a gentle giant. There are no words to describe how pleasant he was. I'm from Israel, and he married an Israeli woman. When he made *Delta Force* in Israel, he met a woman there and fell in love and married her. They had a daughter. He was a great guy. He had a great love of movies. He had a great collection of movies. He had a great chemistry with Michael Dudikoff on screen.

Matt Hunter (Michael Dudikoff) stands over the body of one of his hunters in *Avenging Force*. Author's collection.

You returned to direct the second *American Ninja* movie. The second one feels bigger. There's a ninja cult on a tropical island, and there's more going on in this film than in the first one. Talk about making *American Ninja II*.

The company switched the writer, which was not so much to my liking. I thought the writer of the original *American Ninja* had this "thing," but they switched the writer for *American Ninja II*. It switched a little to the science fiction side with the creating of ninjas, etc., and the love interest disappeared. This version didn't rise to the popularity of the first *American Ninja*. There are good fight sequences in it. The scene in the arena is really wonderful—again, we had Mike Stone choreographing the fights. We shot it in Africa. The story does not take place there, but we shot it in South Africa. It was a nice experience. Then, the series deteriorated. I was not involved anymore.

Why didn't you continue making the sequels?

I'll tell you, it was not because of me. We made it together with a South African company. It was a Cannon movie, but again, this is the story of killing the chicken that lays golden eggs. They decided that this makes money, so they wanted to see how cheap they could make an *American Ninja* movie for and still make money. They actually commissioned *American Ninja 3* to the South African company, so it was not *really* a Cannon movie. They told the South African company, "You make this movie, and we'll distribute it." This company didn't have any money, so they made it cheap. This company is now Millennium. At the time, it was not Millennium, but they became Millennium. They used a South African director, they didn't call me.

There was a turnaround with the star of the franchise. Dudikoff was out, David Bradley was in.

Michael saw that it was such a low budget. David was already around. He was a good martial artist. He was like another Van Damme.

I like that Bradley came your way eventually even though you never made an *American Ninja* with him.

(Laughing.) Yeah, later. That's how life works. When we worked together, this was the demise of Cannon, the end of Cannon. Then, there was a fraction of Cannon that still existed. Golan created a new company called 21st Century. Globus was involved with MGM. Giancarlo Parretti bought MGM, and he was the guy who bought Cannon. He was an Italian mafia guy, who today is probably still in prison. He got Cannon entangled in finances. He brought about the bankruptcy of Cannon. He was so rich, or he represented so much money, that he bought MGM at some point. He and Golan had a continuation company of Cannon. They wanted to do this martial arts movie, but first they did *Delta Force 3*, which I directed. They wanted to do a martial arts movie to capitalize on the ninja theme. They already knew David Bradley because he'd done an *American Ninja* movie by himself and later did one with Michael Dudikoff. I was called, and they told me they wanted to do another movie with David. I met David, and we said, "Let's make this movie." It was called *Ninja*, but we later changed it to *American Samurai*. David and I went to lunch here in Los Angeles. We worked on the script.

American Samurai introduced Mark Dacascos to the world. Talk about working with Dacascos. How come you guys didn't make another movie together?

I don't know why. Mark was brought in, and he played the bad guy. The conditions were such that we had to make the movie in Israel. The story takes place in Turkey. I saw a couple of guys, but Mark was the most impressive. He had star quality. There were two scripts with the same story, and we chose one over the other. David and Mark are both martial artists. David had a big ego.

I've heard that about him. You must have liked him, though. You guys did several movies together.

Yeah, listen, David Bradley is not so much an "actor" like Michael Dudikoff, but he was a martial artist. He really wanted a singing career like Bruce Springsteen—that's what he really wanted. He played the guitar and the keyboard. He had a little recording studio here in town. He was really trying to make it as a singer, as a musician.

That's interesting. He looks great on screen. He has a forceful presence when he's fighting.

Yes, very strong. I actually had arguments with him because sometimes I would like a double to do some things. It's dangerous for him. You don't want your lead to be out of commission tomorrow. There are many things that I insisted where he used a double, and for David, it was a like a big insult to him. I asked him to step out while the double stepped in, and he would get upset. "No, no! I want to do this!" I said, "But, David, this is dangerous." He would say, "No, I'm going to do this, I can show you!" He would get injured. Michael Dudikoff would get injured too. We all stayed in the same hotels when we worked, it was like we lived together. Afterwards, we would go and eat together. We had a common interest in spicy food. We would try to outdo each other with spicy food. (Laughing.)

You've shot movies all over the world. Talk about shooting on location.

I like to make movies here in town. There is nothing in the world like shooting in Hollywood. The best of the best. The best people, the best crew, the best technical people, the most resources. This is where movies are made. I made a movie called *Quicksand* in India. Bollywood. But it's not Hollywood. You always see a movie where the hero is in Bulgaria or Hungary, but nobody cares. The only exception is when it's in a James Bond movie. But with all the other movies, it has to be an American story. That's

the language of the world of cinema. If Michael Dudikoff was in another country, it was an American story. Same thing with David Bradley. I did *Cyborg Cop* with David in Johannesburg. With *American Samurai*, you don't know where you are. But it's an American story. Shooting in other countries, they are not as advanced. Israel is very advanced because they've shot movies there like *Rambo III*. When we shot *American Ninja* in the Philippines, we used some of the equipment and crew from *Apocalypse Now*. The crew was excellent.

After *American Samurai*, you continued working with Bradley on films such as *Blood Warriors* and two *Cyborg Cop* pictures.

By the time Cannon was in its demise, Nu Image (Millennium) was coming around. I knew the people of Nu Image from *American Ninja II*, and they turned to me. They said, "We want to do something that will be like *American Ninja* and something like *Cyborg*." The word "cyborg" was in because of the movie Van Damme did. They said, "Let's make a movie called *Cyborg Ninja*!" What can we do with a title like that? The story was developed and it became *Cyborg Cop*. *RoboCop* was out, and so that's how the title happened. This idea of a partial human, part machine was out there. We wrote the script accordingly.

I find it interesting that you started out making movies that started trends, and at this point, you're talking about emulating and exploiting other trends.

Right. Again, I can enjoy science fiction, but it's not my favorite. *Cyborg Cop* is really just an action movie with a science fiction slant.

I actually see *Cyborg Cop* as an adventure movie with a science fiction slant.

From the beginning, we didn't want it to have an African feel. We wanted it to have a Caribbean feeling. You might be right.

You've got David Bradley and Frank Zagarino in *Blood Warriors*. Zagarino was also trying to get an action career gong around this time.
I
 was friendly with Zagarino already. I knew him from the circle of guys that included Bryan Genesse. *Blood Warriors* came to me from an Indonesian company because they knew I could

make a foreign movie with American actors. They did a movie with Cynthia Rothrock. David Worth did that movie. They wanted to do an American movie that had no signature of being a movie in another country. The company asked me to get David. They already had Frank. Those were the days when those guys were hot. This was their time. I brought David, they brought Zagarino. It's *The Third Man*.

This was the second wave of the VHS era. You could make anything with a guy who had some martial arts abilities, and it would sell. Talk about the work you guys were doing during this lucrative period, and talk about what you can't do now in terms of getting a movie like *Blood Warriors* financed today.

There was no competition in the field when Cannon and the other Cannons were making movies. There were the studios and there was Carolco, and they did what they wanted to do because studios weren't paying attention to the home video market. But by the time we did *Blood Warriors*, studios already took notice. Van Damme and Seagal became stars, so now you could smell the end. Studios were taking over the home video market. The smaller companies could smell the end. They were getting good money. An actor like Bradley would get $400,000 or $300,000 per movie, which was good. It was a business. But they could never go up to the $800,000 level where Van Damme was at during that time. Van Damme made it into the millions. There was already a feeling that the studios would take over, and they eventually did. When movies like *Batman* were released onto home video, that was almost the end.

And what did that mean to filmmakers like you?

The end of the career. I was at the pigeonholed level of the four million, five million, two and half million movies. The market has become polarized. Either you make over eighty million or 120 million, or you make a movie for a half a million. At the end of this home video era, if you spent five million, you could not recoup the money. Shifts in the market suggested that you must have an event movie to bring the audience in—first to the theater, then on home video. Suddenly, all the television stations in the world could not recoup the money even with all of the commercials that sponsored it. Six million became seven million because of inflation. If you could make a movie under a million, you could recoup the money. But how good is an action movie if you make it for under a million dollars? That's the problem. You'd have an action movie with maybe two fights in it because you don't have the money for action scenes. For guys like me, it was a choice: Either you make it into the "A" movies or you don't. Michael Dudikoff didn't make it, Albert Pyun didn't make it, I didn't make it, David Worth didn't make it. You can go and shoot a movie for four weeks, but what kind of action movie can you do for a million dollars in four weeks? So-called action movies, but they're not really action. We used to produce at least forty-five to fifty minutes of action every movie. If you don't have that, you have ninety minutes of talking. End of the era.

Behind the scenes with David Bradley (left) and Sam Firstenberg (center, with gun) on the set of *Cyborg Cop*. Courtesy of Sam Firstenberg.

Sam Firstenberg (with checkered shirt) and David Bradley (standing, right) on the set of *Cyborg Cop*. Courtesy of Sam Firstenberg.

There's guys like Isaac Florentine who've managed to stay alive in this era. He's made some great low-budget action films over the last few years.

Only because of Nu Image. The only reason why Isaac can make the movies is because of Nu Image's formula. It's not a studio, it's not a major. They make the Stallone movies—*Rambo* and *The Expendables*—but the philosophy of the company is selling, not making. They make movies so that the distribution will have product. They make one big movie and three small ones. Less and less now. They say to the distributor, "Oh, you want *The Expendables*? Well, you must take these three small movies." They make good money if they can sell them as a package.

Because of the way the market is today, there are fewer opportunities for new action stars to rise.

It's not only the market. The kids today have changed. After you see *The Dark Knight*, the visuals in *The Lord of the Rings*, you cannot show them *American Ninja* now. Are you kidding me? This kind of action with someone going through a glass, we cannot rise to the level anymore. The CGI is mind-boggling.

Are you saying that people don't want the type of movies you made anymore?

Well, the *American Ninja* movies are for kids twelve to sixteen years old.

What about me?

Well, yeah, but because you grew up watching them. When I go to see action movies today, the *Bourne Identity* series, I see the fights, and they're blocked—it's all editing. Nobody's doing anything. The whole fight sequence, you don't see anything. You don't feel the pain. When you see *Revenge of the Ninja* or *American Ninja*, when somebody falls on the asphalt, you feel the pain. You know why? Because somebody really fell on the asphalt. Now they shoot with green screen and they add the asphalt later. The kids watching movies now don't know that there can be another kind of action movie.

When you made *Quicksand* with Michael Dudikoff in the early 2000s, did you kind of know that would be it for you guys?

In a way, yes. That was made with Indian money. The producer wanted to do a Western, American feel. That movie is more of a thriller. But, yes. There was a feel that those movies were diminishing. I was approached by others to do the same type of movie in five weeks, but I told them no. I cannot make such a movie in five weeks. We need to explode cars, we need helicopters. That costs money. Michael has come to me, saying, "Can we do something? I want to do something." I don't know why they didn't take Michael in *The Expendables*. He likes to work, he wants to work.

You did another film—*Delta Force 3*—which starred the sons and siblings of famous actors and directors.

I knew Mike Norris from over the years. I was not the original director on this movie. I came in on the first day of shooting, I was not prepared. Somebody else was fired, and I was recruited. I came in on the night before the first day of shooting.

It's a strong film, a very well-made film, and if it had been made today, it would be very relevant.

Yes, it was ahead of its time. Boaz Davidson came up with the story. Everything was there, but I jumped into the water. The only one I knew in the cast was Mike Norris. My first day of shooting was with Mike—I was lucky!

I felt like Mike Norris was the only guy who deserved to be there. Everyone else in the cast was hardly an action star—they were all riding on the coattails of their siblings or parents . . . except him.

It's true. I don't know all the details, but it was the same people who made *American Samurai*.

Did you guys shoot in the same cave where *Rambo III* shot?

It was shot in Israel, so yes, I think so. The first day of shooting was in the cave.

Was *Delta Force 3* a theatrical film or a direct-to-video movie?

I'm not sure. The producers had a deal with Warner Brothers. I guess it's a video movie, but it was big. The action sequences were big. We had everything we needed and we had the cooperation of the Israeli army. We had everything we wanted. There was a lot of pyrotechnics. It was not a cheap movie. Eight weeks of shooting, two units. Good special effects.

Were there ever any projects that you could not do that came to your attention during the period of time when you were making these action films?

My biggest miss—because I rejected it—was *Bloodsport*. (Laughing.) They came to me in between films and they showed me the script called *Bloodsport*, and I read it and it's all in one location. I told myself, and I told them, "I don't want to make a movie in one location. This movie has no chance!" After they made the movie, it was one year on the shelf. It was finished, and they saw the movie and they did not believe in it. It was a year and a half later and they released it, and they still didn't believe in it. So, I passed on that. The other movie I passed on for different reasons was a Chuck Norris movie made in the Philippines. It was one of the *Missing in Action* movies. My wife was pregnant at the time, so I decided to stay in America.

How would you describe your directing style to someone who's never seen one of your movies?

The movies I've directed, they have a tongue-in-cheek type of feeling. You sit there and you say, "Yeah . . . but, no." Sometimes you go to a war or action movie, and it's so real. You feel the horror of war. In a Sam Firstenberg movie, when somebody gets hurt, when a hand is being chopped, it's cartoonish. With a wink. It's action fun. With a grain of salt. This is the feeling of the movies I make. It's in the realm of fairy tales and comic books. I try to use as much cinematic language as possible.

If you were going to recommend only one of your movies to someone, which movie would it be?

American Ninja is the most famous. I like this movie. It's not an action movie. It's a love story. The success is not because the action is spectacular, it's because it's two love stories. One: Between Michael and Judy. It's innocent, they never go to bed. The second love story is between Michael and Steve: buddy/buddy. Two good friends who would do anything for each other. This is the secret of the success of *American Ninja*. A love story, good friendships. But it's not the best movie. From an action point of view, *Avenging Force* is the best movie. It's tremendous. It could have been an "A" movie. It's almost an "A" movie. The visuals are great. If Michael Dudikoff was Tom Cruise, it would be an "A" movie. It was one step away from being an "A" movie. If had not been Cannon, it would be an "A" movie.

Avenging Quartet

(a.k.a. **Avenging Angels**)

1992 (Tai Seng DVD) (CD)

"Hsiong, I must ruin you myself."

Chin (Cynthia Khan) and Lui Chai Feng (Moon Lee) randomly meet and become quick friends. Both of them are mourning over being left by the men they love. Little do they know, these men are one and the same: Hsiong (Waise Lee). He also happens to be in possession of an incredibly expensive painting and Chin is a cop so there's a conflict of interest. Everyone wants to get their hands on the painting, including two Japanese gangsters, Seihaji (female bodybuilder Nishikawa Michiko) and Oshima (Yukari Oshima). To make things even worse, Seihaji was beaten and scarred by her deceased husband because of her affection for Hsiong. Everyone will come together and face off in a bloody battle to the death.

Bringing together four of the hottest (figuratively and literally) women working in Hong Kong action cinema was a brilliant idea. What was upsetting was how they were all pretty much wasted in an incoherent tale too preoccupied with betrayal and lost love to focus on what the audience wanted most: action. For the first hour of the film, all we get is a couple of short burst fights from Khan and Lee. An hour in, there's a weight room fight between Nishikawa Michiko (also featured in *My Lucky Stars*) and Yukari Oshima (*Lethal Combat*) that proves why these action stars are so highly regarded. The finale brings together all four women, and they battle in and around a burning building, which is exciting, but just not enough. From director Stanley Wing Siu.

Theatrical poster of *Babylon AD*. Author's collection.

Babylon A.D.

2008 (Fox DVD) (MJ)

Released in the summer of 2008, *Babylon A.D.* had all the elements of a successful film: A hybrid action/adventure film with science fiction elements, an international cast led by a reliable box-office star, and another well known action star in a supporting role. And yet the film died a quick death at the box office. Based on the novel *Babylon Babies* by Maurice Georges Dantec, a French science fiction writer, *Babylon A.D.* takes place in the year 2058, in a post-apocalyptic world suffering the effects of global warming, political upheaval, and the aftermath of terrorism. The film follows the journey of Hugo Toorop (Vin Diesel), a mercenary and former smuggler hiding out in Serbia as he reluctantly takes a job from a former employer to collect a young woman named Aurora from a small temple in Kyrgyzstan and smuggle her into New York City. For Toorop, this is an opportunity to return home after being branded a terrorist and deported many years back. Toorop quickly discovers that there is more than meets the eye with this young woman named Aurora and her guardian, Sister Rebekah (Michelle Yeoh), as he finds himself in the middle of two factions trying to claim Aurora and her secrets.

Directed by French actor and filmmaker Matheiu Kassovitz (*La Haine*, *The Crimson Rivers*), *Babylon A.D.* had a lengthy development process of five years. The project was initially conceived with actor Vincent Cassel in the lead role. Financing for the film came from 20th Century Fox and Studio Canal. When the film finally went into production in 2006, though, it had a new leading man in the form of actor Vin Diesel, who had dropped out of *Hitman* to take the lead. What happened with this film? According to the director, Fox frequently interfered throughout production and this came to a head during postproduction, where Kassovitz and the studio could not find common ground on the final cut. This ultimately hurt the film upon release as it hardly received any promotion from the studio and was never screened for critics. On the surface, one would think that Vin Diesel was horribly miscast for the lead role in a hybrid science fiction/action film and perhaps this is one of the reasons people stayed away from the film when it was quietly released in theaters in August 2008. And yet Diesel's casting in the film is one of its great strengths as it gave the actor another opportunity to show that he had much more to offer given the right opportunity. While he found early success making action films such as *The Fast and the Furious* and *xXx*, he also showed that he was more than capable of acting, having just worked with director Sidney Lumet on another film (*Find Me Guilty*) most people never saw. It is easy to compare Diesel's career to Telly Savalas, another actor who did not have the looks of a traditional leading man but became an international star and frequently worked in films all over the world. One of the great joys of *Babylon A.D.* is seeing the different international production elements come together to make a truly unique multicultural genre film that really does feel like it's being told on a global scale. The film was shot in locations around the world, including the Czech Republic, Sweden, Norway and France, with an American box-office star in the lead role, a French auteur directing, a largely Eastern European crew, and a stunt unit that includes the work of David Belle (*District B13*) and his parkour stunt team. Run—don't walk—to find the Raw and Uncut version of the film.

Back in Action

1994 (Universal VHS) (djm)

An undercover drug deal goes south when an ex-special forces vet turned vigilante named Billy (Billy Blanks) accidentally interrupts the transaction, which ends up with the murder of a good cop. The dead cop's partner, detective Frank Rossi (Roddy Piper), grows a chip on his shoulder for Billy, who is trying to protect his wayward sister from her drug dealer boyfriend, no matter the cost to his own well being. Frank's investigation into the drug dealers who killed his partner leads him to Billy's sister, who has

Video release poster for the Shapiro/Glickenhaus actioner *Back in Action*. Author's collection.

been targeted by the killers for being a witness. When Frank and Billy continue to cross paths with the same agenda, they reluctantly team up and power through the drug cartel.

What a great idea it was to pair up Roddy Piper with Billy Blanks for an action movie. They look great together and they fight each other several times with spectacular results. They also starred in *Tough and Deadly* together, and both films were sent directly to video despite being nearly "A"-list movies. These were big video releases in their day, and the marketing made them feel like "event" action movies, which they almost were. Look for the infamous McNamara twins (Michael and Martin from *Dragon Hunt*), who get in a fight with Blanks in one scene. Paul Ziller (*Moving Target* and *Bloodfist IV* with Don Wilson) and Steve DiMarco directed. From Shapiro Glickenhaus Entertainment.

INTERVIEW:

BILLY BLANKS

(djm)

The name Billy Blanks has become synonymous with the incredibly successful exercise system he developed known as Tae Bo. But before Blanks become a famous exercise guru whose Tae Bo videos took the fitness world by storm, he was a national karate champion and a very popular martial arts action star with films like Bloodfist (1989), The King of the Kickboxers (1990), Talons of the Eagle (1992) and TC 2000 (1993) under his black belt. His fans might also note that he starred in two films alongside the late wrestling legend Rowdy Roddy Piper: the direct-to-video hits Back in Action (1993) and Tough and Deadly (1995). Blanks eventually left his career as an action star behind to fully pursue developing Tae Bo, and he's currently planning his comeback to action films.

Billy Blanks at the Fit Expo. Photo by Norman Craver.

I think one of the first times I saw you in a movie was when I saw *Driving Force* where you played a bad guy. I thought to myself, Who's this guy? He's so cool!

Oh, thank you.

When did you become interested in the martial arts?

It was when I saw the TV show *The Green Hornet*. It was something that really grabbed my attention as a child. I wanted to be able to do martial arts. At the time, my family couldn't afford it. I went to a youth center in my neighborhood—it was called The Martin Luther King Youth Center. I joined a martial arts youth program at the youth center. I got my black belt when I was sixteen years old. Then I got a chance to compete as a competitor in my own region. I became a champion in my region. I took that chance to step out and join the United States karate team and won the national title. It gave me a chance to travel around the United States with the karate Team. I traveled with that team for five and a half years all over the world. I became a three-time world champion and then won several gold medals.

You became one of the busiest and most successful martial arts action stars of the late '80s and early '90s, which was the pinnacle period of that genre. How did you get started in movies?

It had always been a dream of mine. I went over to the Philippines as a bodyguard for Catherine Bach, who played Daisy Duke in *The Dukes of Hazard*. I was her trainer and bodyguard. While I was there they ended up firing an actor who was in this movie she was starring in called *Driving Force*. They asked me if I wanted to play a part

in the movie, and I said, "Oh, yeah, thank you, I'd like that." I was in the right place at the right time. They needed someone who knew martial arts and they needed someone who looked tough, and I got the part. Eventually, I did a movie with Don Wilson called *Bloodfist* because they needed someone who knew martial arts. So I ended up doing those two movies while I was in the Philippines. That set it off for me.

Shortly after that you did *King of the Kickboxers* with Loren Avedon, and that was such a great fight between you two. That was in the Philippines, too, wasn't it?

That was a great opportunity, too. I came back to the Philippines. They asked me to come in. They just wanted me to play a bad guy. They didn't even give me a script. They just wanted to see what I could do. I came in, showed them what I could do, and as I'm getting in my car to leave, they called my agent and said, "Hey, he got the part, when can we sign him up?" They signed me up for that part, and that really opened up the door for me to play other parts in movies even though it was a bad guy. It gave me an opportunity to be in a movie with Sylvester Stallone—*Tango and Cash*. I was a prisoner in that movie, but Stallone saw that I worked really well, and that started getting me smaller parts to other movies. Then my career really took off.

Being a busy actor is one thing, but being a successful action star is another thing entirely. What was that like for you to be an action star during this period?

It was a dream that came true, to do what Bruce Lee did—to get to be on a movie screen. I tried really hard to stay in really good shape and to hone my martial arts skills. I took acting lessons. I didn't try to be the best actor in the world, but I wanted to be able to enhance my skills and make a lifestyle of it. Then all of a sudden, Tae Bo comes up. It comes out and kind of took me away from the movie industry. I was helping people to try to be in better shape. Now I got another opportunity to do another movie. I've been waiting for that. Since I've been on camera a lot for Tae Bo, I haven't been in the industry for a long time. I'm looking forward to getting back into action films. You know, do a little bit of that now!

When I interviewed Roddy Piper a few years ago—God bless him—he mentioned to me that while you guys were on the set of either *Tough and Deadly* or *Back in Action* you were already developing Tae Bo, and he was kind of observing you while you were working on that. That was the beginning of Tae Bo.

He really encouraged me. He was like, "Billy, you know what? When you got something like that, you work it, you work it, you work it! You give it all you got!" He was so encouraging, God bless him. He gave me a push. I got a chance to do two movies with Roddy. We were always talking on the set. He showed me the things he had to do to become a championship wrestler in that world. He gave me some good pointers.

Those two movies you did with him were the "A"s of the "B"s. Those movies were really good.

Well, thank you. Being around Roddy and watching him work, he was a hard worker and a super athlete. I got a chance to work out with him, and I trained with him. We sat and talked. He empowered me and challenged me to do the same thing that he did with wrestling. He kept saying, "Keep up the good work and work hard. When you have a dream don't quit, don't give up." That inspired me. I used to watch Rowdy Roddy Piper on TV all the time. It was hard for me to believe that I got to do two movies with him at the time. He told me, "Believe it." I said, "Okay." He said, "Believe it. I'm just like you. It takes hard work to be able to do the things that we do. Keep doing hard work and watch what happens."

Very cool.

Yeah, it was.

When he passed away a few weeks ago, Facebook just blew up with the news. Everybody was posting pictures of the two of you together from those movies. He'll be sorely missed.

Roddy really appreciated the love that people had for him. I wrote a big thing about him on Facebook, talking about the love and care he put into me. He didn't really know me that well, but hearing what I'd done with Tae Bo . . . he opened things up for me back in the day. He'd say, "If I can help you in any way, let me know." One time, he wanted me to come back in as his partner. He was going to go back into wrestling. He wanted me to be his partner as his secret weapon, as a tag team. I was going to do it, but something happened and I couldn't do it. That would have been another dream for me, to be able to do something for the WWE. To come out and do it. That would have been really fun.

You had some great on-screen fights with all kinds of fighters and martial artists. You even did *TC 2000* with Bolo Yeung.

On *TC 2000* with Bolo Yeung . . . I actually got to be in a movie with a guy who did movies with Bruce Lee and Jean-Claude Van Damme, and all these other guys. He was my instructor on the movie. He enhanced my abilities. I came in good shape and I wanted to develop my martial arts skills well. Being able to do that with him and Jalal Merhi, who I'd actually done competitions with at the same time, and he said to me, "Hey, Billy, I'm doing this martial arts movie, would you be interested in starring in it?" I said, "I would love to come in." He gave me a shot at a three-picture deal. I also did *Talons of the Eagle* with him. He was the one who really kicked all that stuff off for me, was Jalal. He gave me an opportunity. He helped me out a lot.

What do you consider to be your best on-screen fight?

I think my best on-screen fight was the one with Loren Avedon. That was fun. It had some good choreographers from Hong Kong, and they really used my attributes and they took advantage of my abilities as an athlete. We did some really good things.

Who would you like to do a movie with that you've never been able to work with?

At the time, I really wanted to do a movie with Tony Scott, and I got to do *The Last Boyscout* with him. I played that football player who kills himself. My goal was for Tony Scott to direct me in a movie. I'm looking forward to having Antoine Fuqua direct me. That's my dream. I used to train him before his movie days. I'm hoping that one day I'll get to do an action film with him.

Tell me a little bit about how you developed Tae Bo as a new exercise system.

When I retired from fighting I was trying to find a better way to stay in good shape. In 1975, I won the national title to compete for the United States team. Then I took the theme song to *Rocky* and I put it on. In the projects, I was listening to that theme song. Within two to three minutes I got cardiovascular-itis. At that time I was the national champion. If I couldn't go two rounds or two minutes, I'm not going to be able to do well in the world championship. So what I did was I developed my workouts to music. I started to put together my own stuff to get my cardiovascular on. I did weight training, Karate, boxing, all into one form that would give me the best workout to prepare me for a fight. I did it. I put a Walkman on my ears and I did all this stuff with the Walkman on. Most of the martial artist guys told me, "Hey, Billy, that ain't gonna work." They used to tell me that all the time, but I knew deep inside of me I was developing something. My ex-wife told me, "Billy, you should take that and teach women how to do that. That's a great way for a woman to learn karate and self-defense at the same time." So I went to a hair salon and I told all the women there and said, "Hey, I've got this new exercise called Tae Bo." At the time it was called "Karobics." I put it out there and started doing it. I started getting women in the door. Eventually I changed the name to Tae Bo. When I changed the name to Tae Bo, that's when it really opened the door. The word came from Korean. "Tae" comes from the word leg. The word "Bo" comes from boxing. The whole term became an acronym. "T" is for "Total. "A" stands for "Awareness." "E" stands for "Excellent." "B" stands for "Body." "O" stands for "Obedience." It became this big hit. I didn't expect it to go the way it went. When people really saw that I was trying to help them get into shape and that I was coming from my heart, it really opened up the door for me. It wasn't really about the money, it was about the people. People saw that. My studio back then was nothing special. I had tape to keep the carpet down. It was a run-down place. People came in there and they felt love. Before I knew it, everybody started coming in the place.

Tae Bo really redefined workouts and physical fitness.

Well, I think when Tae Bo came out . . . every generation . . . everybody loves martial arts. I took karate, I took boxing, I took calisthenics, and put them all together into a form of exercise when people were gravitating towards the martial arts. Everybody wants to be a warrior. Deep down inside, everyone wants to be a warrior. They want to feel like they can protect themselves. I thought that if I could put a program together that had those elements in it, it would bring moms, dads, daughters, boys, grandparents, and everyone involved in a workout. It actually revolutionized the whole fitness world.

When Tae Bo took off, you kind of left the movie business behind. You never left entertainment behind, but this was the next chapter for you.

I didn't' want to walk away, but what happened was that Tae Bo took up a lot of my time. I just said, "You know what? I'll just put movies on the back burner," hoping that later on in my career I could get back to doing movies. Now that Tae Bo has settled down, I can get back to doing movies. I'm still developing Tae Bo and making it better every year, but I feel like now with all the experience I've had in front of the camera . . . back when I was doing movies my experience in front of the camera was okay, but now I have a lot more authority about not being so nervous in front of the camera. If I had the opportunity to do another movie I feel that I would be a lot better.

You earlier said that you do have a movie in the works. Would you care to share what that is?

It's set. I'm doing a movie with Jalal Merhi. They haven't given me a working title yet, but it's called *The Tunnel*. It's about the drug cartels. I play a patrol officer on the border, and in the movie I end up shooting the son of the head of a drug cartel, and they come after me. I'm looking forward to it. It's going to be a really good action film. The script is great. I'm looking forward to who they're going to cast in it.

Have you continued to develop Tae Bo or has it become stagnant?

After I came back from Japan—I went to Japan for five years to live—I trained a lot in the martial arts to make my martial arts skills better, focused on meditation and things like that, but when I came back I got involved with The Fit Expo. It will give me a chance to get Tae Bo back out there. To show people that Tae Bo is not dead—it's still alive. It's an opportunity to show that Tae Bo has grown, and you'll see what people have taken from it every day. You're seeing all these different workouts that are based on Tae Bo moves. I'm looking forward to showing people how Tae Bo has grown. I was forty years old when Tae Bo first came out on video. In about two weeks I'll be sixty. I'm still in good shape, still performing well. I teach eight classes a day. I want to show people Tae Bo is still alive for this generation as well as the Baby Boomers. Because there's martial arts in it, it's for every generation.

What would you like to say to your fans, Billy?

Thank you for giving me an opportunity to come to into your households. I've really appreciated it. I'm looking forward to getting back into their households, to give me another opportunity to come back.

Back in Business

1997 (Kinowelt DVD R2) (djm)

An ex-cop named Joe Elkhart (Brian Bosworth) is living quietly as an auto mechanic, routinely calling a psychiatrist on the radio for advice on how to keep down his rage. His buddy Tony (Joe Torry) is still on the force, but is going deep undercover to expose dirty cops in the department, and together, they get involved in a sting operation that gets them both into big trouble with drug runners *and* the dirty cops who know exactly who they're after.

At ninety minutes, *Back in Business* is a long slog through buddy/buddy dialoguing, protracted action scenes, and painfully boring exposition. Bosworth is a pleasure to watch with his good-natured swagger and innocent lunkheaded personality, but the movie just doesn't do him justice. His sidekick is annoying and the action scenes are limp, but it's the story that kills it. Brion James co-stars in a thankless role as Ryker, the clichéd captain on the force, who is ultimately relegated to the villain role. Philippe Mora directed. The German DVD release is widescreen, but in that part of the world, the film is known as *Stone Cold 2: Heart of Stone*, which is mystifying.

Bad Ass

2012 (Fox DVD) (djm)

Aw, man, I *love* this movie. I went to see this opening day in a nice theater in Chino, California, and it was a beautiful day to sit in a dark room first thing in the morning. The theater was completely empty, and I was there to see Danny Trejo on a big screen! I was blown away by it. He plays a good-hearted Vietnam vet named Frank whose hotdog vending business isn't doing so well anymore. He's on the bus one day when some punks make him mad by treating patrons like garbage. They make a move on him, but he lays them all flat with a few *badass* moves. Someone on the bus recorded him on their phone, and next thing he knows, he's all over the Internet (something he doesn't know how to use) and then he's on a morning talk show (he knows what's up with that), and his mom is proud of him. He's a national hero. Months later, his mom passes away and he moves into her house in her ghetto neighborhood. The streets are crawling with scumbags. His best friend (also a vet) is shot dead on the street when he's walking home from the liquor store. Frank gets angry. The cops like him but when he goes out every day and night seeking answers, he causes a stir because most of the guys he questions don't like to give answers.

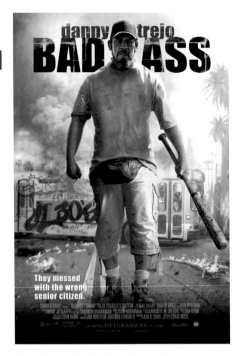

Theatrical poster for *Bad Ass*. Author's collection.

The cops start to see a trend in Frank's methods: Things end up messy, with bad guys on the floor, with witnesses. Instead of just waiting around for the incompetent cops to do their job, Frank gets to the bottom of it, and what he finds out is pretty huge: A crooked politician (played by Ron Perlman) and a midlevel gangster (played by Charles S. Dutton) are in cahoots over some of this and that (and are responsible for the death of his friend), and no one's going to stop them . . . except Frank. He's badass.

Better than the *Machete* movies by millions of footsteps, *Bad Ass* is kinda like what a *Rambo* movie would feel like if Stallone ever loosened up a little bit and moved in next door. Trejo is our Charles Bronson right now, and if only filmmakers like Craig Moss, who wrote and directed this, would catch on to that, maybe Trejo would be a much bigger star. At any given time, Trejo has more than a dozen movies coming out (not all action), but I guarantee that if he would get more offers like this one, his trajectory would be much more interesting. Not that this movie necessarily needed a sequel, but Trejo and Moss teamed up for *Bad Asses*, co-starring Danny Glover. *Bad Ass* might not be entirely credible, but it's a gem.

Bad Ass 2: Bad Asses

2014 (Fox DVD) (djm)

". . . but they're not your typical old guys. Trust me. They're more like badasses!"

Media darling Frank Vega (Danny Trejo) has settled into a nice life as a trainer at a neighborhood gym (which I think he owns), and he's still inspiring people in his actions.

When a young man he's mentoring at the gym is killed by a small-time drug cartel, Frank turns up the heat to get payback. He makes a friend out of Bernie (Danny Glover), a disgruntled liquor store owner who is sick and tired of seeing his neighborhood overrun with thugs and miscreants. When they go head to head with the cartel—run by an Argentinian diplomat (played by Andrew Divoff, who is wasted)—the bad guys are totally unprepared for the elderly badasses who come calling.

As good a sequel as it could have been, I suppose, *Bad Asses* is more or less what you'd expect from it, but I loved the first movie so much that anything less than stellar would have been disappointing. Therefore, I watched this in a slightly sad and depressed state because it nowhere nearly exceeded my expectations. *However* . . . it delivers plenty of (mostly) sincere action and humor, though what's lacking is the pathos of Danny Trejo's character who, while mostly intact this time around, is slightly less endearing and relatable. He looks amazing for being in his late 60s, and when he beats guys up you believe it. I also believe it when he looks gravely hurt and wounded when *he* gets beat up and tossed around. The movie didn't especially need a sidekick for him, but Danny Glover's always nice to have around, so why not? If you were as unhappy with *Machete Kills* as I was, then believe me when I tell you that *Bad Asses* is the better sequel. Craig Moss, who did the first *Bad Ass*, also wrote and directed this one.

Bad Asses on the Bayou

(a.k.a. **Bad Ass 3: Bad Asses on the Bayou**)

2015 (Fox DVD)

Vietnam vet Frank Vega (Danny Trejo) and his liquor store owner buddy Bernie (Danny Glover) go to Louisiana together to attend the wedding of their friend Carmen (Loni Love), who comes from old money. Her father Earl (John Amos from *Die Hard 2*) is a very wealthy owner of a parish, and he treats Frank and Bernie like royalty. On the eve of the wedding, Carmen is kidnapped and held for ransom, and instead of just sitting around waiting for more bad stuff to happen, Frank and Bernie go on the warpath, hijacking a cargo plane, a truck, and at least one car before they fumble and get kidnapped themselves. They beat up a ton of armed thugs (and get beat up themselves a little bit), and eventually they find the compound where Carmen is being held (by a familiar individual). Eventually, old Earl gets in on the action too, and the finale has all the badasses shooting rows of scumbags with never-ending ammunition.

Shot simultaneously with the second film, *Bad Asses on the Bayou* is a very slight improvement on that entry only because it's not as tongue and cheek. It's fairly boneheaded, though, and I miss the character development from the first film, and since the Vega character is surrounded by other grumpy old badasses, the sequels lose focus. Glover as Bernie is perpetually

complaining and riffing on his ailments (which becomes grating almost immediately), but Trejo as Vega (the original badass) never complains, and remains a stalwart hero. The end credits proclaim that these guys will return for *Bad Asses in Bangkok*, but I'd be happy if that didn't happen. Written and directed by Craig Moss.

Bad Blood

1994 (Live VHS) (djm)

One of Lorenzo Lamas's least compelling vehicles during his prime years as an action star, *Bad Blood* casts him as Travis Blackstone, whose wayward brother is marked for death for an insurmountable gambling debt that can only be collected in blood. Travis, who'd once taken the blame of a crime that his brother committed and served a year's prison sentence for him, decides to help him one final time. This entails watching his girlfriend get murdered in front of him, and lots and lots of beatings and fight scenes leading to plenty of deaths.

Unfortunately, *Bad Blood* suffers from familiarity and a mundane script and characterizations. Granted, it was a quickie production and didn't really try to do anything different or special, but even Lorenzo Lamas made some decent films like *Night of the Warrior* around this period that were really interesting and entertaining. In lieu of plot and satisfying action scenes, *Bad Blood* has two gratuitous and nearly soft-core sex scenes. The lead villain is played by martial artist Joe Son, who is currently serving a life sentence for rape, torture, and murder. Tibor Takacs (*Red Line* with Mark Dacascos) directed.

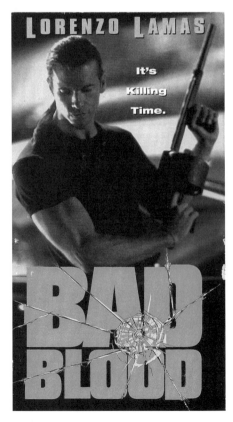

VHS artwork for *Bad Blood*. Author's collection.

Badges of Fury

2013 (Well Go USA DVD) (DL)

"I'm not a grizzled old cop. I'm a nicely aged veteran."

After an unusual string of murders rock Hong Kong, a rookie detective played by *The Sorcerer and The White Snake* star Wen Zhang concludes that they are the work of a serial killer. Together with partner Jet Li, he must track down the culprit before becoming the next target. Things get complicated when Zhang becomes involved with the victims' ex-girlfriend (Liu Shishi) who just might be a suspect herself. The American DVD cover for *Badges of Fury* would have us believe we're in for a dark, edgy cop thriller. Li stands front and center looking pensive, an intense Zhang clutches a pistol, and a massive explosion rolls down the street. The tagline underscores the apparent weight of the proceedings: "Two Cops. One Killer. No Limits." So when the film opens with Zhang wearing a woman's kilt and doing a slap-sticky Scottish jig, the audience can be forgiven for double-checking which disc is in their machine. Heavier on comedy than action, *Badges of Fury* is loaded with shoddy CGI-gags, wacky cartoon sound effects, self-referential in-jokes, and goofy set pieces. Yet despite the zany nature of the action, connecting scenes are often deadly serious in tone. creating a manic-depressive viewing experience. The fights, as choreographed by the usually capable Corey Yuen, are heavy on obvious wirework and fuzzy CGI.

When the film was announced, first-time director Wong Tsz-ming declared that this time Jet Li would be responsible for the comedy while Wen Zhang did the fighting. Despite poster art to the contrary, *Badges of Fury* is indeed Zhang's show from start to finish. Li is nowhere to be found for nearly three quarters of this movie. When he does drop in, it's usually to stand in the background while the younger stars engage in strained rom-com banter. Li does participate at the tail end of most action scenes, repeatedly arriving just in time to save the bumbling Zhang from himself. In their third film together, it seems that Li's job is to help sell Zhang as an action star. He tries his best to service this directive but can't help upstaging the poor kid at every turn. Li's fans won't find much to love in this frenetic, broadly played spoof of cop thrillers. *Badges of Fury* is also known as *The One Detective*, a title that recalls Li's superior *The One* and reeks of more sly misdirection by the marketing team.

The Bad Pack

1997 (Platinum DVD) (djm)

A small Texas town is overrun with white supremacists who are murdering Mexican families in broad daylight, and there's nothing the Mexican townspeople can do about it . . . except pool their funds together to hire some mercenaries to come help them fight off the gang of over 100 killers. They go to James McCue (Robert Davi), who impresses them after they witness him dealing with some hoodlums, and they offer him a job for little up-front money but also the promise of millions that lies within the headquarters of the supremacists. McCue recruits some old pals (played by Roddy Piper, Ralf Moeller, and Brent Huff, amongst others) and they lay siege to the bad guys and get the job done.

What could have turned out to be a dynamite action adventure starring some interesting action guys instead ends up being a pretty big disappointment, despite having some major pluses to it. Co-star Brent Huff (from *9 Deaths of the Ninja*) also directed, and it's a shame he was working with a tiny budget, because the movie could have used a lot more action to keep it engaging. Davi, who heads up the *Expendables*-like cast, is great in a physical role, while Piper and Moeller don't do much to add to the action even though they're the real reason the movie should have been great. It's basically a remake of *The Magnificent Seven*, but it just lags. Too bad.

Balance of Power

(a.k.a. **Hidden Tiger**)

1996 (Cineplex Odeon VHS) (djm)

Good hearted Niko (Billy Blanks) teaches karate to inner city kids when an Asian gangster named Takamura (James Lew) steps into his dojo, demanding protection money. Unafraid of the shakedown, Niko refuses. Next thing he knows, Niko's students are put at risk when Takamura guns down one of Niko's favorite kids. Instead of acting on his rage, he seeks guidance from a much wiser and more steady-minded man than he, an old sensei named Matsumoto (Mako), who teaches him discipline and a way to hone his martial arts abilities. Matsumoto enters Niko in a death match tournament where Takamura is the reigning champion, and Niko is able to get his revenge by working his way up to the brutish and evil Takamura.

What might have been another substandard direct-to-video kickboxer movie starring Billy Blanks, *Balance of Power* surprises by being the best film he ever did. His role has layers, and it's a fun process of seeing him grow as a character. His training montages are actually great to watch and we see Blanks working hard at both the physical extremes and also with his acting. His nemesis played by Lew (from *Red Sun Rising*) is a great bad guy, and when they go against each other, we're really expecting the screen to explode by that point. I enjoyed this one all the way through. Directed by Rick Bennet.

Ballbuster

1989 (Arena VHS) (djm)

Bad guy: "You're crazy!"
Ballbuster: "No, I just don't play by the rules!"

A private eye named Roosevelt "Ballbuster" Prophet (Ivan Rogers) is approached by a distraught woman who swears that she witnessed a murder in her apartment building, but no one believes her story—not even the police. No body ever turned up, and as she is an alcoholic eccentric artist, her story is ruled out. But Ballbuster wants to believe her because it's a case, and when he begins investigating, some goons get in his way, which signifies that something's up. The person who's supposed to be dead is, in fact, still alive, but her husband (the alleged murderer) has a heavy delinquent gambling debt. The few clues Ballbuster is able to gather are rendered inconsequential when his client is kidnapped, and he's forced to abandon all logic and reason to go on a rampage to find her, because by that point he's fallen for her.

This is exactly the sort of thing Fred "The Hammer" Williamson would have excelled at (and would *still* excel at), but former kickboxing athlete Ivan Rogers doesn't command your attention or ignite the screen the way someone like The Hammer would. Rogers (who also produced) shoots a ton of bullets (but only a handful of bad guys) in this movie, and he has a few close quarter brawls, but overall, *Ballbuster* is a disappointment. It needs more karate . . . and ballbusting. Written and directed by Eddie Beverly Jr.

Ballistic

1995 (Imperial VHS) (djm)

"You know what you are, sweetie? You're *ballistic*!"

Renegade cop Jesse Gavin (martial artist Marjean Holden) has the police department divided into those who are for her or against her. She believes that her incarcerated father—a cop who was busted for drugs—was framed by other cops. Her boss (played by Charles Napier) likes her despite her reckless methods, while the other cops on her team hate her guts. She's assigned a case to protect a material witness, but when he's killed on her watch, she's in the hot seat, and on top of that her partner is killed, and all the evidence points toward her. Fired from the force, and with a mountain of odds against her, she starts investigating the other cops in the department (watch for James Lew, who plays the dirtiest cop of them all), and she realizes that she's been set up to give a drug lord named Braden (Sam Jones) free reign in the city. She and her boyfriend (also a cop) go after Braden and his goons (played by Michael Jai White, Cory

VHS artwork for *Ballistic*. Author's collection.

guns . . . a.k.a. *gun fu*), making him one of the absolute best. A deadly micro-pulse bomb has been developed and fallen into the hands of Dragomir (Andrew Divoff), a fellow *ballistica* practitioner and Damian's arch rival. The only person who can defuse the bomb is the lovely Dr. Alexa Zanner (CB Spencer). Assassins are out to kill her but Sloan isn't about to let anyone lay a finger on her. He will protect her for as long as it takes to find the bomb for her to defuse. In the international terrorism game, no one can be trusted, and Damian will come to realize the only person he can count on is himself.

When the low-rent production house The Asylum is involved in a film, it's a safe bet to say you know what you're getting into. Paul Logan (also in *Code Red*) possesses all the required criteria for an action icon—the looks, the moves, the machismo—but he lacks a proper vehicle to showcase these talents. Director Gary Jones is better known for his work in the horror genre so maybe he wasn't the proper choice for this film. The movie dwells too long on drama and romance before getting to the action. If you remember the post-apocalyptic film *Equilibrium*, then you should be no stranger to *gun fu*. Except in this case, it's just not badass at all. It's a killer idea and it's sorta cool but mostly just laughable. Logan's the real thing in desperate need of a vehicle to showcase him.

(Editor's note: I prefer the term gun-kata to gun fu. Just saying . . .)

Bangkok Revenge

2012 (Well Go USA DVD) (djm)

John Foo from *Tekken* stars in this awkward French/Thai film. A little boy named Manit is shot in the head by some corrupt cops who murder his parents in bed because his father is an honest cop who was going to turn all of them in. Manit survives the ordeal, but a kind nurse takes him away and hides him with an old martial arts master because when the corrupt cops find out he survived, they want to murder him in the hospital. Manit recovers from the gunshot wound, but a side effect is that he literally has no feelings (emotional or physical), so he doesn't register when he should feel sorry or sad for seeing something horrible (a puppy getting run over) or when he should be sensitive (after having emotionless sex with a woman). He grows up to be played by John Foo, and he exhibits strong martial arts prowess, thanks to his old and wise master. When Manit learns why his family was murdered, he vows revenge on the corrupt cops, who *are still looking for him* after twenty years! The preposterousness of the plot gets more insane as the movie goes on. On his trail to revenge, Manit encounters a gang of Amazons who love torturing and killing men, and he joins forces with a disgraced French cage fighter (Michael Cohen). Together, they kick and punch a bunch of Thai cops and gangsters.

Jean-Marc Mineo directed this unbelievably silly movie. The fighting is almost nonstop, but none of it is very distinctive. The best fight scene occurs in a moving subway train. Foo isn't a very persuasive actor or hero. He's too fresh-faced and

generic, and it doesn't help that the character he plays here is entirely emotionless and one-note. Still, there is a slight sense of guilty pleasure to movies like this. It will find its audience. It was filmed in English, French, and Thai.

The Bank Job

2008 (Lionsgate DVD) (CD)

"I know you, Terry. And I know your mates. You've always been looking for the big score. The one that makes sense of everything. I have it for you."

Former model Martine (Saffron Burrows) pays a visit to her former flame, Terry (Jason Statham), who is now a used car salesman. Terry's struggling to make ends meet while trying to support a wife and kids. Martine brings him the perfect job: It's a foolproof plan to rob a bank in London. After mulling it over, he assembles his old team, and they do what they do best. Their target is a vault full of safety- deposit boxes, and they hit the mother lode. They don't know Martine has an ulterior motive: One of the boxes contains photos of royalty in compromising positions. So what seemed like the perfect job quickly turns into a flusterfuck when they end up wanted by the police, MI-5, and a group of gangsters ready to kill them to get back what's theirs. Based on a true story.

The Bank Job isn't exactly an action film— it's a heist picture, a brilliantly executed thriller with a fantastic performance by action star Jason Statham (*Homefront*). He's first and foremost an action guy, quite possibly the most prolific currently working in the business. The movie does focus on the heist and the drama surrounding it, so once the finale begins to play out, you can rest assured that our boy blows the dust off his fists and pummels a mobster and his goons. It's not exactly an action fan's dream but it's a very good picture from director Roger Donaldson (*Seeking Justice*).

Bare Knuckles

2010 (Image DVD) (djm)

Down-on-his luck Sonny Cool (Martin Kove) is at a roadhouse one night when he sees a pretty female bouncer beat the heck out of a rowdy patron. Sonny gives the bouncer his card and tells her that he manages female fighters for underground bare-knuckle boxing matches, and that he'd like to be her manager. Samantha (Jeanette Roxborough who is a third degree black belt in Shotokan) is intrigued by his proposal, and with a deaf daughter who needs special (expensive) care, she's willing to take a beating for some extra cash. Sonny shows her around town at the underground tournaments, and Samantha gets in the ring and proves that she can hold her own, but when she goes up against the reigning champ, she gets beaten up and humiliated . . . but she isn't knocked down or

Everson, and Vincent Klyn) and the climax in a warehouse full of cardboard boxes piled to the ceiling is what these martial arts action movies are all about.

What makes *Ballistic* halfway interesting and continually watchable is the great cast. Michael Jai White is there in a thankless silent role as a henchman, but he's incredible to watch. Former bodybuilder Cory Everson (from *Double Impact*) has a couple of great scenes, and she fights Holden in the finale. Vincent Klyn from *Cyborg* gets a couple of fight scenes, and there are other scenes with Nils Allen Stewart, James Lew, Sam Jones, and Richard Roundtree (as the main character's father) to keep things spinning. As for Marjean Holden, she's up to snuff as far as action stars go, but the film itself has a distinctly misogynistic vein running through it. The very first scene of the film features Holden taking a long, soapy shower, and this happens before we even know who she is! This was her only starring vehicle. Directed by Kim Bass.

Ballistica

2009 (The Asylum DVD) (CD)

"The girl I spent the past two weeks with never would have let thousands of innocents die."

Damian Sloane (Paul Logan from *Blazing Force*) is a highly trained CIA operative. He's one of the few who have mastered the art of *ballistica* (a form of hand-to-hand combat using out, which gives Sonny enough encouragement to enter her into "The Show," the high-stakes championship that will make or break the both of them.

Surprisingly endearing and good-hearted for an underground fight movie, *Bare Knuckles* hinges on star Roxborough's performance and physicality, and since the movie is based on her real life, the movie has an air of authenticity despite the film's low budget. She's interesting to look at and she gives it her all, but something strange about the fights in the movie is that they're all so short and lack blood and gristle. Most of the fights are over with one or two punches (which becomes a recurring joke towards the end), but even with that against it, the film is worthy of discovery because Roxborough is cool and she has something special to offer. Fans of nitty-gritty action and UFC-type fight films may want to seek elsewhere for their entertainment, though. Directed by Eric Etebari.

The Base

1999 (Lionsgate DVD) (CD)

"Look, I am a sergeant in the United States Army and during my time in service I've learned two things: Heroes and cowards are both buried under the same goddamn dirt. Do you know what the other one is? Fear, respect, and fear—same word. Now, I will be buried in Arlington one day but until that time, let me be feared as the Godfather of LA!"

Major Murphy (Mark Dacascos) is given a unique new assignment. He is asked to go undercover to investigate Sgt. Gammon (Tim Abell) who is suspected of gunrunning and narcotics distribution from the base. Assuming the fake identity of a Corporal Dalton, Murphy has to be able to play the part and get Sgt. Gammon to trust him before he is brought into the loop. Murphy only has one contact outside the base, Lt. Kelly Andrews (Paula Trickey), a woman who is logging the information until they have enough evidence to bring Gammon down. What Murphy doesn't anticipate is the lengths that Gammon will go to in order to become the Godfather of Los Angeles. Murphy isn't one to give up and isn't afraid to go to similar lengths to bring him to justice.

Mark L. Lester (*Commando, Showdown in Little Tokyo*) is responsible for several classic action films using his expertise and personal seasoning to elevate *The Base* above your typical direct-to-video standards. Even though the story is predictable and mostly generic, the decision to set it within the ranks of the military gives it an interesting hook. Another smart move was casting Mark Dacascos in the lead. He really delivers on both fronts—acting and action—in

this film. The box art and title can be a bit deceiving. It was marketed as a straight-up military type action flick, when it's far from it. Dacascos has several solid fight scenes that are both stylish and believable. Veteran stuntman James Lew (*Action Jackson*) does a terrific job as fight coordinator, giving Dacascos a chance to flash his skills on screen. Being perfectly sinister and likable makes a memorable villain, and Tim Abell embodies that idea with ease and you can't help but feel for the guy. Some of the other performances weren't quite as solid, but are good enough to not be a distraction. Lester knows how to move things along at a pace that isn't too jarring or distracting. Much attention is given to creating tension as well as excitement. For Dacascos fans, *The Base* isn't the best example of his fighting skills but it's still a solid action film.

Batman & Robin

1997 (Warner DVD) (CD)

"There is no defeat in death, Master Bruce. Victory comes in defending what we know is right while we still live."

After a short time of peace and quiet in Gotham City (following events depicted in earlier big-screen adventures featuring the Caped Crusader battling supervillains), a new villain emerges with big plans. While trying to steal millions in diamonds, Mr. Freeze (Arnold Schwarzenegger) is foiled by Batman (George Clooney in a one-shot) and his young sidekick Robin (Chris O'Donnell reprising his role from *Batman Forever*). Freeze escapes only to plan something much more sinister. In South America, botanist Dr. Pamela Isley (Uma Thurman) finds herself in a heated argument with her boss who overturns a shelf containing various toxins. She is drenched in the toxins, transforming her into the superseductress known as Poison Ivy. When she makes her way back to Gotham, she devises a plan to use Mr. Freeze against Batman and to destroy Gotham for reasons that are never made clear. This is one of the biggest challenges Batman has ever faced (it has to be because this is the fourth film in the series and the franchise depended on it), and he can't do it alone. With Robin in tow, they recruit Alfred the Butler's niece Barbara (Alicia Silverstone suiting up as Batgirl) to aid in saving both Gotham City and possibly her uncle, who is dying from a disease known as MacGregor's Syndrome. Only time will tell if they can foil Freeze and Ivy who plan to turn Gotham into the North Pole.

There isn't anything to be said about *Batman & Robin* that hasn't been said before. The film was bad when it was first released and time hasn't been kind to it. It's hard to sit through, but as a historical document it is important because Arnold Schwarzenegger had open-heart surgery the same year this was

released. Schwarzenegger, who was still a box-office titan when this was unleashed, manages to emerge as the only performer in the film who shouldn't have to hang his head in public because of appearing in it. His true identity of Dr. Victor Fries has the most interesting backstory of any character in the film. As Freeze, his costume design is incredibly bulky and gets in the way of his performance a little bit, but he does have a few moments of superhero-like action and his freeze ray is pretty radical considering that of all the guns Arnold has carried and fired in all of his other movies, the one he uses here is the only one that looks like a toy. This is by far the worst *Batman* film ever made and quite possibly one of the worst films in Arnold's arsenal. On the plus side, everyone involved in the picture moved on to bigger and much better things. Director Joel Schumacher made some questionable decisions when making this film, but thankfully this incarnation of the *Batman* universe stopped here, thus leaving the door open for a guy like Christopher Nolan to come in and revamp and reimagine the whole thing.

Battle Creek Brawl

(a.k.a. **The Big Brawl**)

1980 (Fortune Star DVD) (CD)

Jerry Kwan (Jackie Chan) is a simple guy who just enjoys being with his lady Nancy (Kristine DeBell). His father runs a restaurant and his brother is a doctor. Jerry spends the rest of his time training in the martial arts with his Uncle Herbert (Mako). His father doesn't understand the need for martial arts and doesn't support it, but Jerry continues training against his father's wishes. His father ends up being harassed by the mob, which tries extorting money from him, and Jerry keeps foiling their attempts at collecting. When his brother's bride arrives from overseas, the mob kidnaps her and forces Jerry into fighting a tournament in order to get her back safely.

It's no secret Jackie Chan isn't particularly fond of this US-made film. He felt the film would have been a success had he been given the opportunity to direct his own fight scenes. Instead, the fights are slow and repetitive, never a solid representation of what the man is capable of. Director Robert Clouse may have struck gold with *Enter the Dragon*, but *Battle Creek Brawl* just ends up being a missed opportunity for everyone involved. The only thing working for the film is the humor. There are several funny moments for Chan who really hams it up during the fights. There's plenty of action, it's just never on par with what Chan was just beginning to do with his Hong Kong films. It's a fun movie, though, and better than most martial arts films from the US during the timeframe, but it's just not very good as a vehicle for Chan. The music by Lalo Schifrin (*Enter the Dragon*) is so incredibly catchy you will find yourself whistling the tune for days after.

Battle of the Damned

2013 (Sunfilm DVD) (CD)

"Zombies. Killer robots.
Nice town we got here."

A deadly outbreak has turned an Eastern Asian city into a wasteland. The infected are left to run around in search of human flesh. The city has been quarantined, and no one is being let in. The daughter of a prominent businessman is alive, stuck in the middle of the city. They bring in a group of mercenaries to rescue her but they run into some troubles with the infected, leaving one man, Max Gatling (Dolph Lundgren), to finish the mission. Once he finds the girl, he has to convince her to go with him but she won't leave without the small group of survivors she is living with. He follows her to their compound with the intention of using them to help get her out, then leaving them behind. Things don't go as planned and Gatling is left to fend for himself while handcuffed to a lightpost. Once secrets are revealed, the group realizes they need him if they're to survive.

Dreams do come true! Dolph Lundgren (*Red Scorpion*) battling zombies is a brilliant idea. Then when you add a group of killer robots to the mix, you have the recipe for one killer (and fun!) flick. Lundgren delivers some great quips while never letting up on the head stomping. He never fights any live humans but the amount of the infected he takes out is pretty staggering. He not only uses various weapons, he uses some of his martial arts skills as well. And when you begin to think things couldn't get any cooler, a group of obscenely heavily armed robots show up to help him in his quest. Director Christopher Hatton has ported over the robots from his previous film *Robotropolis* and uses them to maximum effect in *Battle*. This movie is great fun and shouldn't be missed.

Beatdown

2010 (Lionsgate DVD) (CD)

Brandon (Rudy Youngblood) is a fighter in an underground fight club. He and his brother Frankie (Jimmy Gonzales) have a good thing going until Frankie is murdered. To add insult to injury, Frankie owed small-time mobster Gino Ganz (Luis Olmeda) $60,000 he expects Brandon to pay. Brandon flees the big city and heads back to the small country town he grew up in to stay with his wheelchair- bound father, Marcus (Danny Trejo). He finds a job working construction and befriends Todd (Jeff Gibbs), who introduces him to the underground fight scene there. He quickly falls for the beautiful Erin (Susie Abromeit) but her brother Victor (Eric Balfour) is overly protective and will do anything to keep them apart—and also happens to be the current champion of the local circuit. Brandon gets some help from veteran fighter Drake (Michael Bisping). Together, they jump

into bare-knuckle brawls and Brandon is willing to risk it all for one large payday.

Beatdown is another Tapout-sponsored film and this one is pretty good. Again, the story is incredibly simple and familiar but the execution is exciting. Rudy Youngblood (*Apocalypto*) has leading man quality and delivers a well-balanced performance. Of course, the film features several real-life fighters like Bobby Lashley (*No Surrender*), Heath Herring (*Circle of Pain*), Mike Swick, and in a featured role, Michael Bisping. Bisping has a cool demeanor about him and his role is mostly acting. He does have one in-ring fight that shows off his skills. There's plenty of action and bare-knuckle fights throughout the film. Youngblood appears to go toe to toe with real fighters. The beatings are brutal and the fights are meant to look realistic. Director Mike Gunther (*Setup*) is also a stunt coordinator and his experience shows in how the fights are handled. It all may be something we have seen before but the acting and presentation are quite slick. Other Tapout-sponsored films include *Circle of Pain, Unrivaled,* and *Death Warrior.*

Behind Enemy Lines

1997 (Orion VHS) (djm)

Two commandos are on a top-secret mission in present-day Vietnam, and their task is to steal several nuclear triggers, but they fail spectacularly. One of them is captured and the other one makes it out, thinking that his partner was killed. A year later, Mike Weston (Thomas Ian Griffith) is a washed-up drunk, reliving that fateful mission a year ago. He is approached by the CIA to go back to Vietnam with a platoon of young, inexperienced soldiers to retrieve the triggers and rescue his partner, who is still alive and in captivity. Sobering up with a fresh resolve, Weston has no time to train his soldiers, so they get right to the mission, and he's got his hands full with the team that was chosen for him: They don't follow orders very well, they make constant mistakes, and they don't respect him until he proves to them that if they don't begin falling into line they will all die behind enemy lines where a formidable army awaits them. Weston ends up getting captured by the Vietnamese and tortured alongside his buddy (played by Chris Mulkey), but his platoon comes and helps them escape, leading to a blast-filled finale.

One of Griffith's better vehicles, *Behind Enemy Lines* gives the star of *Excessive Force* lots of room to showcase his martial arts in the midst of a war-type action film, and he's got some great moments. The best scene has him on trial for murder in a Vietnamese court. He manages to break his bonds, kill everyone in the room, and shred the judge's perch with a machine gun! Movies like this where the hero must depend on a crew of lesser helpers are always a tad bit disappointing because you really just want the hero to do almost all of the damage. Griffith shares the spotlight with a bunch of other guys who don't deserve the time of day. Still, I enjoyed it. It was directed by Mark Griffiths.

Behind Enemy Lines: Colombia

2009 (Fox DVD) (CD)

"There's a special breed of warrior, ready to answer our nation's call. A common man with an uncommon desire to succeed, forged by adversity, he stands alongside America's finest Special Operations Forces to serve his country, the American people, and protect their way of life. I am that man."

With war looming in Colombia, the US government sends in a five-man Navy SEAL team to help facilitate peace talks between the Colombian government and guerrilla fighters. It turns out to be a huge set-up and the leaders of both groups are murdered and the SEAL team is framed for the mess. With two members killed and one captured, Macklin (Joe Manganiello) and Holt (WWE wrestler Ken "Mr. Kennedy" Anderson) are stuck behind enemy lines without any help. Their commander Boytano (Keith David) wants them to make it to the extraction point but SEALs don't leave men behind. If they can prove their innocence, a war could be diverted and they can escape with their lives.

This third entry in the *Behind Enemy Lines* series (which began with Owen Wilson and Gene Hackman) is produced by WWE films and features one of their stars, Ken "Mr. Kennedy" Anderson, in one of the lead roles. If the film had been advertised differently, it could have been much more successful since the real star of the film is Joe Manganiello, who has attained fame for his role on HBO's top-rated vampire series *True Blood.* Manganiello may be the star, but Anderson has all the best action moments. He's the sniper of the group and racks up a nice body count. The film is a little light on the physical altercations so if military action is your thing, then the movie will most likely appeal to you. Anderson has potential as an action star, but sadly, this project falls short. Directed by actor Tim Matheson.

Bells of Innocence

2003 (GoodTimes DVD) (djm)

Jux (Mike Norris), Oren (Casey Scott), and Conrad (David A. R. White) are on a private plane together, with a plan to distribute Bibles on a mission trip, but their plane crashes in the middle of nowhere. They venture out and wander into a strange town that has seemingly drawn them there. The town is under some kind of despotic rule by a demonic figurehead/ cult leader named Joshua (Marshall Teague), and a young girl there reminds Jux of his own daughter, who died in a car accident recently. The three men are treated like the outsiders they are, and when they try to make contact with the outside world, they are met with suspicion and a calculated understanding that they bring unrest to the town. A mysterious figure named Matthew (Chuck Norris) arrives and escorts them to his nearby ranch, where he proceeds to tell them that he's basically an angel, sent to keep this particular town from succumbing to Joshua's evil, which could very well be a harbinger of the end of all things. Jux, Oren, and Conrad are forced to fight for their lives and embrace their faith in Jesus Christ or fall under the might of Satan's minions.

An exceedingly strange faith-based film from Chuck Norris and his son Mike, *Bells of Innocence* is a borderline *Children of the Corn*-type horror film. Chuck plays a secondary character, and his son Mike is more of the lead here, and while Mike gets involved in some action scenes (he kicks and punches some ghoulish characters), the film is sorely lacking in the action that it needs to have to be a solid sell to fans of these two personalities. I'm not really sure Christians (or anyone else) will find this movie entertaining. Other action stars like Gary Daniels and Brian Bosworth have appeared in faith-based films like *The Mark* and *Revelation Road*. *Bells of Innocence* was directed by Alin Bijan.

Belly of the Beast

2003 (Sony DVD) (djm)

All quips referring to Steven Seagal's burgeoning midsection aside, Ching Siu Tung's *Belly of the Beast* is a fairly radical entry for its star, who by this time had done at least three direct-to-video movies, none of which had the style or affection for martial arts this one does. Seagal plays a removed special ops guy named Jake Hopper, whose daughter is coincidentally kidnapped by a terrorist group in East Asia, and when videos start popping up of the masked terrorists holding guns to her head, making demands to the American government, Hopper doesn't just sit around hoping for the best. He gears up, goes to Thailand/Burma and visits an old associate who has since given up a life of violence for a life of peace as a Buddhist monk. His friend (Byron Mann) owes Hopper a favor, so he says goodbye to peace and helps his old pal out, knowing that he'll need backup even when Hopper advises against it. It turns out that the terrorists have darkness on their side as an evil death-worshiping wizard (seriously) has begun making advances in the spirit world against Hopper, but the monks back at the monastery are praying on behalf of Hopper and his friend to overcome any darkness they face. The final battle involving Seagal, a transvestite, and spirit warriors is a doozy.

Pretty wacky and quite simply bizarre for a movie of this type, *Belly of the Beast* makes the most of Seagal and his screen time. He allows himself to undergo a transformation as a martial artist, doing a sidestep advance on his signature aikido and going for a graceful, more unusual (for him) martial art that seems more suited to a Jet Li movie. It's interesting. There's some subtle wirework going on here, but even with doubles, Seagal looks like he's challenged by what he does both physically and in the acting department as he really goes out of his way to appear humble and concerned throughout. Some ridiculous

shootouts and everything-and-the-kitchen-sink fight scenes aside, this is somewhat of an anomaly for him, but it's worth checking out, especially if you're tired of watching his junkier efforts like *Submerged, Flight of Fury,* or *Attack Force.* The director also made a Jet Li movie called *Dr. Wai in the Scriptures With No Words.*

Bending the Rules

2012 (Lionsgate DVD) (CD)

"Even though your face is covered, I can tell you need a hug, huh? Come on, come to papa. No love? Really?"

Nick Blades (Adam "Edge" Copeland) is a corrupt New Orleans cop who takes money on the side and Theo Gold (Jamie Kennedy) is the assistant DA who is out to stop him. The thing is, Blades marches to the beat of his own drummer. He's a good cop that just sort of levitates toward a gray area. Gold is having the worst day of his life. He doesn't get his promotion, his wife leaves him, and to top it off, someone has stolen his father's beloved classic car. Blades finds himself in an unlikely position when the case he is working (unofficially) leads him to Gold and the possibility that he is on a list to be murdered. The two enemies must now work as a team if they are to get the car back and stop a recent string of murders in the area. The only way for them to succeed is to put aside their differences, which is easier said than done.

WWE films make huge mistakes with many of their recent releases: These films are being marketed to the action crowd and contain very little action. *Bending the Rules* is no exception. It was marketed as a buddy action film but there is no action until the final moments. To make matters worse, the heroes were not even involved in it. Pro wrestler Adam "Edge" Copeland (*Highlander:Endgame*) is a likable lead, and this was a good character for him. Not too far of a stretch from his ring persona, Copeland's Nick Blades is a cocky cop who always has something say. Copeland does have natural comedic timing, which serves him well in the film. We barely get to see him lift a finger, though, which is a shame. Jamie Kennedy (*Three Kings*) is the DA who's trying to put Blades away for being corrupt. The two are a mildly entertaining pair. Kennedy is much funnier than this role allowed him to be. Since WWE is playing it safe and marketing these films to a younger audience, that mentality is highly evident in the final product. Director Artie Mandelberg was able to lure some terrific (but, alas, mostly wasted) talent in supporting roles like Philip Baker Hall (*Rush Hour*), Jennifer Esposito (*Taxi*), and Alicia Witt (*Dune*). The movie isn't bad by any means, it's just sorely lacking in the action department. Hopefully, if WWE continues to produce films to showcase their headlining stars, they'll address some of their strategy and realize that they are making mistakes and fix them.

Beretta's Island

(a.k.a. **One Man Force**)

1994 (Live VHS) (djm)

The only movie to star two-time Mr. Olympia Franco Columbu, *Beretta's Island* has him playing a variation of himself, but with some fabrication thrown in there to make it palatable as an action picture. Franco Beretta, an ex-Interpol agent, is asked to go back to his hometown in Sardinia, Italy, because some drug pushers have taken over the area and young people are dying from overdoses. He goes with two American female agents, one of whom is quickly dispatched to set up a plot development so Franco can make some moves on the other (prettier) agent as their case gets halfway interesting. Once in his hometown, Franco shows his partner the sights and introduces her to his family and friends (he's famous in Sardinia, so everyone knows him by name), and once the drug pushers realize that Franco isn't messing around (he chases guys around with his pistol), they turn up the heat and threaten his friends. Barrel-chested and perfectly willing to walk himself into a trap, Franco cleans up his town just in time to enjoy a neighborhood festival.

Columbu, who is famous for several notable reasons, is a close friend and workout partner of Arnold Schwarzenegger, and Arnold was kind enough to donate a day of his time to film a fun cameo for this movie, which appears almost at the very beginning of the film. He works out with Franco and encourages him as he's lifting weights, and the "real" vibe of Franco being in this movie is what makes it charming. It's also one of the reasons why the movie is so goofy . . . but forget about that for a second. Franco, who was in his fifties when he made this, looks like a man half his age, and it's obvious he wasn't meant to be a movie star, but I'm really glad he made this. He co-wrote the script and clearly had it in his heart to show the world the little, cozy corner of the universe where he came from, and the fact that he's running around shooting guns and throwing dynamite at bad guys in his hometown just brought a smile to my face. Yes, it's pretty unintentionally funny with Franco's European overcompensations, but I enjoyed him and his movie for what they wanted to be and how earnest and hard they try to be "for real." PM Entertainment might have made something like this (remember *The Glass Jungle* with Lee Canalito?) once upon a time, but *Beretta's Island* was produced by Columbu himself. It was directed by Michael Preece, who did seventy episodes of *Walker, Texas Ranger* and many other action-star oriented projects like Hulk Hogan's *Thunder in Paradise.*

The whole gang in Robert Radler's *Best of the Best*. Author's collection.

Best of the Best

1989 (Sony DVD) (djm)

"You've learned a lot. We've all learned a lot. As Catherine might say, *The teacher also learns from the students*. Today, you have the chance to be the best martial artists in the world. It's up to you. If you give everything you've got—*everything*—with all your heart, you will be winners. That I promise you. You can be the best of the best."

A Korean American named Tommy Lee (Phillip Rhee), a martial arts instructor for children, is invited to try out for the national karate team to represent the US against Korea. Widower father and factory worker Alex Grady (Eric Roberts) is also given the invitation. They make the cut along with three other men, one of them surly brawler Brickley (Chris Penn). Their coach is hard-as-nails Frank Couzo (James Earl Jones), who drills them and prepares them over a three-month period to face and defeat the seasoned Korean team, the leader of whom killed Lee's brother in the ring when Lee was a child. Along with Couzo, the guys have a spiritual guru in the form of Catherine Wade (Sally Kirkland), who teaches them meditation and balance of the mind and spirit. Faced with out-of-the-ring drama, Grady deals with his son who was hit by a car, and Lee must come to terms with his inner strength before he faces Dae Han, who killed his brother. The final scenes in the film are not what popular competition movies would dish out—instead, we get perhaps the most heartfelt and sincere portrayal of forgiveness and honor ever dealt with in a fight movie this side of *Red Belt*. It's awesome.

Phillip Rhee, who wrote the story and produced this, offers a refreshing take on the kickboxing competition genre. His role is central to the story, but he shares screen time and focus with everyone else in the film. His real-life brother Simon plays Dae Han, and their emotional scene at the end might make any grown man cry. If Roberts had stuck with this type of action film, his career might have taken an interesting (but possibly not as diverse as it ended up being) path. James Lew plays one of the Korean fighters. A pop rock soundtrack (with a theme song!) is generously proportioned throughout. Robert Radler directed this, and he also did the sequel.

INTERVIEW:

PHILLIP RHEE

(djm)

The name Phillip Rhee is synonymous with the Best of the Best *franchise that began in 1989 and carried through unto 1998 with the fourth entry* Best of the Best 4: Without Warning. *Rhee, whose own life story inspired the first film, has been conspicuously absent from the action and martial arts world since 1998, but he's back in several capacities as writer, director, producer, and star in the family-friendly martial arts movie* Underdog Kids. *Rhee has always been one of the most underrated martial arts action stars in the business, and with his return to movies, he took some time out for this interview to discuss his career and his latest endeavors.*

Phillip, I've been a fan of yours for a long, long time. I've seen everything you've done going back as far as the first film you did with your brother Simon—a little movie called *Furious*.

(Laughing.) That's pretty intense! (Laughing.) Thank you, David!

I'm so glad that you're finally back with a new movie. We've waited at least fifteen years for your return. *Best of the Best 4* was your last movie, and that was in 1998! What have you been up to all this time?

Yeah, what happened is that I got into the technology sector. I got involved with the former president of Warner Brothers. We became partners and we created a 3D conversion company. We were converting a lot of movies into 3D. My passion has always been the martial arts, and I always wanted to get back to my roots.

You started directing with *Best of the Best 3*, and you directed the fourth film as well, and now you're back in full capacity with your new film *Underdog Kids*: You star in it, you directed it, you wrote and produced it. You've always been a screenwriter, though. Talk a little bit about all your roles on these films.

When I did *Best of the Best 3* for the Weinstein Brothers, it did really well for them. They wanted me to do part 4, but I didn't have a script or anything for it. Basically they said, "You write it, you direct it, you star in it, and we'll write you a check." The lesson learned is that whatever you do, it's got to come from the heart and don't just choose the money. When I did *Best* number 1, number 2, and number 3, they came from the heart. With 4, I chose the money. Creatively, it was not the best. It was not the best work I could have done. Interestingly enough, someone just sent me a list of the fifteen most inspirational sports movies of all time, and they listed *Best of the Best* on there.

I would put the first *Best of the Best* right after *Rocky*. It's that good.

That film came from the heart. It's based on my story from when I competed in 1980 against the Korean team.

Talk a little bit about what got you excited to write and make *Underdog Kids*.

Underdog Kids is something I wanted to do because it's about families getting together. It's set during the recession when everyone was going through a very difficult time. Parents were getting laid off, getting their cars repossessed. I wanted to make this movie and say that life can be difficult, but don't give up. I grew up with movies like *Rocky* and movies that really inspired people. We don't see that anymore. We see a lot of digital effects, a lot of explosions, and there are no more family movies. It's just animation; no live-action family movies. That's why I started to write it. It's going to be very reminiscent of *Best of the Best*. It's that with kids.

Why didn't you just call it *Best of the Best 5*?

Because we're going to reboot *Best of the Best*. You're the first one to know. We're going to reboot the whole franchise with a new cast. I'm going to bring in elements that nobody has ever seen before. I will produce the picture.

You've never done a family-oriented movie before. Kids these days are used to seeing massive big-budget effects films like *Transformers* and *The Avengers*. Do you think something like *Underdog Kids* will be accepted with kids and families these days?

Yeah, absolutely. When there's a good movie, the movie will find its audience. When *Best of the Best* came out, it became a phenomenon because of word of mouth. Guys like UFC champ Chuck Liddell has said that it's one of his favorite movies of all time. I think this one will do the same. It's a movie with heart. It makes you laugh. I showed it to an audience full of kids, and they laughed like crazy. It will make people cry—not out of sadness, but out of happiness. The greatest gift a filmmaker can give to an audience is to move them emotionally so much that they will cry. If you make them cry out of sadness, that's cheap. If you do it out of happiness, that's the greatest gift you can give to the audience. *Underdog Kids* has that. That's why *Best of the Best*—out of all the martial arts movies out there—is still hung onto by the fans. Remember— it's because of the last scene. Tough guys cry. Not out of sadness, but out of complete happiness. That's really difficult to do.

Did you ever see *Red Belt*?

I did. David Mamet. I enjoyed it.

I wanted to ask you about working with your brother Simon and with James Lew, who are two guys you've continued to work with since *Furious* and *L.A. Streetfighters* (a.k.a. *Ninja Turf*). Talk about working with Simon and James.

James did all the fight choreography and second unit directing on *Underdog Kids*. My brother Simon was a consultant on this movie. Simon just finished working on the new Terminator movie. They are very important. Keeping good relationships is really important. There're a lot of fake people out there. Guys like James and my brother . . . we go back so many years. We always watched out for each other. Over the years, we've each given some people their first big break, and those people go on to become big stars or fight coordinators. It always comes back to you.

I've always wanted to ask you or Simon something. When I saw *Furious* years ago, Simon had the lead role in the film, and you had the secondary role as the villain. It's interesting that you ended up becoming the front and center action star, but Simon works more behind the scenes on films and became a fight coordinator. How did that happen? Did you two have an understanding a long time ago that Simon was supposed to be the big star and you would be the secondary star, or what? It worked out differently for both of you.

My brother is really talented. He comes up with great stunts and fight scenes. For me, I always wanted to be on the creative side of writing and coming up with concepts, developing, and getting things financed. But I think my brother has it much better than I do. He's so busy now. He's doing a Marvel movie . . . he's doing really well. I'm so happy for him. For me, developing projects takes a really long time. You've got to write it, and then you have to rewrite it. I have to put all the elements together and put the financing together. It takes many years sometimes.

Did you get offers in between the *Best of the Best* pictures? Between each entry is a matter of years, sometimes two to four years.

I had a three-picture deal with Warner Brothers. There was a project that I created called *Kato*, and Oliver Stone took me to Warner Brothers. We made that deal. Working in the studio system is just brutal. The development takes many years. I got lost in the shuffle there. I also had a deal with Village Roadshow with the executive producer of *Rocky*. Also with Babaloo Mandel, who wrote *City Slickers*. We made a three-picture deal worth nine million dollars. Then, the CEO changed at Village Roadshow, so we were back down to zero. That's the business. I did get other offers, but they always wanted me to play the bad guy. Bad guys are okay, but the things that I was getting offered didn't excite me.

Is there anything else you'd like to say about *Underdog Kids*?

It's an inspirational picture that both adults and kids can relate to. It's about conquering your fears. Like I said, it's about never giving up. It's a lesson that all of us can relate to.

Phillip, what would you like to say to your fans?

Expect more films to come from me!

The whole gang in Robert Radler's *Best of the Best*. Author's collection.

Best of the Best II

1992 (Fox DVD) (djm)

Phillip Rhee and Eric Roberts return for this strikingly violent sequel. Their characters, Tommy Lee and Alex Grady, have opened up a martial arts studio together, and their buddy Brickley (Chris Penn) is still the wayward, trouble-making friend from the first film. When Brickley enrolls himself in an illegal fight with no rules at "The Coliseum," an underground arena in Las Vegas run by Wayne Newton, he is killed by the champion—a hulking brick wall named Brakus (Ralph Moeller). Witness to the murder is Grady's eleven-year-old son, who tells his dad what happened. Enraged, Alex and Tommy want revenge. They bust into the casino and confront Brakus, wounding his pride in the process. Newton puts a mark of death on Grady's kid, and so Tommy and Alex hightail it to the desert where they train to face Brakus at some point in the future. Brakus, meanwhile, has demanded that Tommy Lee face him in the ring, and when Newton's goons kidnap him, they also end up killing one of his family members (played by Sonny Landham). Forced to fight, Tommy defeats a number of gladiator-type fighters before he is allowed to face Brakus, whom he is essentially forced to kill.

The first film had integrity and heart. Unfortunately, this one goes the wrong way when Chris Penn's character is murdered in front of bloodthirsty spectators. It takes on a fantasy/revenge aspect that dilutes the purity of the first film. That said *Best of the Best II* is still an entertaining film, but more along the lines of lesser movies like *Cage II* or *Kickboxer 3*. Roberts (who receives above-the-title billing) and Rhee (who produced) still make a great team, and the addition of Sonny Landham in

Alex Grady (Eric Roberts, right) fights for the USA in *Best of the Best*. Author's collection.

Eric Roberts plays the underdog Alex Grady in *Best of the Best*. Author's collection.

a great supporting character role enhances the film immensely. Simon Rhee reprises his role as Dae Han, but this time he's an ally of Lee and Grady's. A good action score by David Michael Frank is an asset. Robert Radler returned to directing duties.

Best of the Best 3:
No Turning Back

1995 (Dimension DVD) (djm)

Tommy Lee (Phillip Rhee) visits his sister in the town of Liberty, Middle America, and while there he is shocked to learn that the town is overrun with white supremacists. Their leader (R. Lee Ermey) is trying to buy up more land to facilitate a growing movement, and his subordinate (Mark Rolston) becomes overzealous and takes matters into his own hands. First, he has a local black preacher kidnapped and killed, and then he begins to terrorize local minorities, including newcomer Lee, who won't kowtow to the racist hoodlums. When his sister and his nephew are put in danger, Lee ups the action quotient and goes into action hero gear.

This third entry in the *Best of the Best* series ventures off the *BOTB* reservation a bit, and while Rhee reprises his role from the previous two films, there is a noticeable shift in focus, as Tommy Lee is front and center this time around. His friends from the other films (played by Eric Roberts and Chris Penn) are sorely missed. That said, *No Turning Back* is a solid genre film with good action, nice cinematography, and competent direction from Rhee. Some may find it odd that he's given a sister to rescue, as we'd never known about her from the other films, but wait until you get to the fourth film where he's given a *daughter*! Gina Gershon plays a schoolteacher and Christopher McDonald plays a cop.

Best of the Best:
Without Warning

1998 (Dimension DVD) (djm)

Russian terrorists cause a ruckus in Los Angeles in their quest to claim a computer disc that enables them to print an endless supply of money. A female member of their outfit steals the disc and tries to make good, but she ends up getting herself into a whole lot more trouble than she could have expected. Tommy Lee (Phillip Rhee) is in public with his daughter (?!) when the woman on the run stumbles into him, needing his help. Lee, who has been supporting himself by teaching martial arts defense courses at the local police department, has friends on the force, but it turns out that his most trusted buddy there (Chris Lemmon) is dirty, and Lee ends up killing him in self-defense. The dead cop's partner (played by Ernie Hudson) has it out for Lee, and a cat-and-mouse chase begins. Lee is captured by the Russians because they think he has the disc, and Lee has to use his incredible skills as a fighter to escape, clear his name, and bring the computer disc to the right people.

Even further off the *Best of the Best* reservation than the last entry, *Without Warning* is a suspicious concoction. With Rhee in the Tommy Lee role, it's hard to not call it a *BOTB* movie, but honestly, this one feels like it originated as a stand-alone movie then was retrofitted to bear the *BOTB* moniker. There are several discrepancies this time around that should not be ignored. First, Lee has a daughter this time—as well as a deceased wife—so something's fishy about that. If the events of this film take place ten years after part 3, that's understandable, but it's not made clear. Second, he's teaching martial arts again, which he'd said he'd never do again in part 3. Again, if a considerable amount of time had passed, that is also understandable. What made the original *Best of the Best* film so special was its message and heart. The second film lost that integrity, and the third one found some footing again, but this time around, it's all about action. Phillip Rhee is an underused talent, and I like him in anything he does. He directed this as well as the last entry, and I think it's fair to say he's a pretty good director too. If he ever makes another movie, I hope it's not a *Best of the Best* picture. He's better than that.

Bet Your Life

2008 (Warner DVD) (djm)

A chronic gambler named Sonny (Sean Carrigan) is deeply in debt to every bookie in Vegas when he sees a man get shot to death in an alley by a man in a helicopter. He runs into the nearest casino for shelter, where he's immediately treated like a king, with thousands of dollars of credit, a penthouse suite, and a girl on each arm for good luck. When he goes to his room, the penny drops, and a shadowy millionaire named Joseph (a hammy-as-usual Billy Zane) offers him more than two million in cash to play a game. The game is The Most Dangerous Game (like in *Hard Target* and *Avenging Force*), and all Sonny has to do is survive twenty-four hours and make it back to the casino in one piece to claim his prize. Sonny accepts, and with a fifteen-minute head start, the game is on! With Joseph and his team on his tail every step of the way, his only real help comes from another adversary: a tough female bounty hunter (played by Corinne Van

Ryck De Groot) who realizes that Sonny is worth more dead than alive.

Bet Your Life is the made-for-TV movie that was spawned from the one-season-only reality TV series *Next Action Star* that Joel Silver produced. The reality show featured a bunch of action star hopefuls who ran through various obstacle courses, fell from great heights, and acted like action stars, but ultimately there were only two winners who were given a shot at starring in their own action movie, and *Bet Your Life* is that movie. Sean Carrigan was a boxer for a short time, and his female counterpart Van Ryck De Groot was also a professional boxer. Both of them are given just enough to do in the movie to warrant action star status, but it might have been nice to see them both get their own *separate* movies to see what they could do on their own. Van Ryck De Groot might have done some interesting stuff if she'd been given the chance (she looks incredibly fit and strong and might've achieved Kathy Long-level status). *Bet Your Life* is fun and frothy, and it has some clever moments. I liked it. Directed by Louis Morneau.

Beverly Hills Ninja

1997 (Columbia DVD) (CD)

"I may not be a great ninja, I may not be one with the universe, but I will say this: *No one messes with my brother*!"

He lurks in the shadows, a master of his craft. Gobei (Robin Shou from *Mortal Kombat*) has spent his life training to be the best possible ninja he can be. He's devoted to his clan, never gives up, and he's about to take on one of the most difficult and impossible missions in his short span as a lethal assassin: He must travel to Beverly Hills from Japan in order to protect his brother Haru (comedian Chris Farley). Haru has found himself in the middle of a counterfeiting ring and has let his heart get in the way of his intelligence. Every misstep he makes and any trouble he may find himself in, Gobei is there to save him, taking no credit for himself. At the request of their master, he keeps himself hidden in order to teach Haru how to believe in himself.

Beverly Hills Ninja is a hilarious comedy from the late Chris Farley (*Tommy Boy*)—especially if you're into his brand of humor. It may be tough to take any of the action seriously but martial artist Robin Shou is given at least one humor-free fight during the climax. What's also surprising is just how limber Farley was for his size. He's no Sammo Hung by any means so when he does get into some serious fighting it's quite an accomplishment. Shou is also quite good at being funny; it's a side of him we don't usually get to see. Since just about everything in the film is played for laughs, it's mostly a waste of his talent. He's far more deserving of better roles and Shou always gives 100 percent. With a couple of decent action scenes and plenty of laughs, *Beverly Hills Ninja* is a worthy action comedy hybrid. Director Dennis Dugan is best known for his many collaborations with Adam Sandler.

Theatrical poster for *Beyond Fear*. Author's collection.

Beyond Fear

1993 (Image DVD) (djm)

A competitive martial artist named Tipper Taylor (Mimi Lesseos from *Pushed to the Limit*) retires after a match that left her opponent severely wounded and disabled. On the rebound, she starts up a little business as a wilderness guide for city slickers. Her latest group is a good-hearted bunch, and on the night when they all meet up and stay at a hotel before setting out on the trail, one of the campers uses his video camera to film a couple of thugs murdering a hooker in an adjacent hotel room. When the two killers realize that they were filmed, they try to get the tape from the camper, which leads them on a do-or-die quest to get the evidence over the course of the next few days and nights as Tipper is leading her group through the mountainous wilderness. Since she's the only one in the group who has the skills to fight the two killers off, she has her hands full keeping everyone—including herself—alive.

Very simple and basic, *Beyond Fear* is good if you appreciate Lesseos, who has an honest-to-goodness appeal. She has an incredibly intense and lengthy fight scene with the two villains in the film, and the whole movie is worth watching just for that one scene. Discriminating and demanding viewers will shrug off the low-budget, simplistic quality of this movie (and others starring Lesseos, for that matter), but I think she's great, and though her movies aren't really special, they're interesting simply because she's in them. This one was directed by actor Robert Lyons.

Beyond Forgiveness

(a.k.a. Blood of the Innocent)

1995 (Republic VHS) (djm)

Chicago detective Frank Wusharsky (Thomas Ian Griffith) is at a celebration with his brother when, by happenstance, some Russian thugs are outside conducting business. When his brother is shot and killed by the Russians, Frank takes pursuit of the killers, and loses the guy who seems to have perpetrated the killing. With what little clues he has, he gathers that the Russian mob was behind the (random) killing, and he takes time off to pursue the leads he has to Poland where his brother's killer has fled. Once in Poland, Frank is a fish out of water, but he makes a friend in a portly Polish cop (John Rhys-Davies), who sympathizes with his plight, and it just so happens that they both want to see this particular Russian killer at the end of their gun barrels. Meanwhile, Frank begins to realize that there is a black-market organ transplant ring going on in the midst of his revenge plot, and as he begins to shift his focus to that, he ends up falling in love with a beautiful Polish surgeon who might be involved in the illegal organ transplant ring. As he gets closer to his revenge, he almost becomes an organ donor against his will, as a suave doctor (Rutger Hauer) manages to get the better of him. Good thing Frank has some people watching his back.

A Nu Image production, *Beyond Forgiveness* gives only face-value entertainment. It's got some explosions, some martial arts action, a little sex and nudity, but if you're looking for a standout vehicle from Griffith, you may want to watch *Excessive Force* again. It goes through the motions, and Griffith is okay in it, but any one of his contemporaries like David Bradley, Jeff Speakman, or Michael Dudikoff could have just as easily filled the role and done just as good a job. It's too bad because I really like Griffith, but finding a purely fantastic movie with him as the star isn't easy. His good looks, obvious martial arts talent, and ability to act were criminally underused throughout the VHS boom, and after several nondescript films like this one, he took on supporting roles as villains in movies like *Vampires*, *Kull the Conqueror*, and *Timecop 2*. This one was directed by Bob Misiorowski.

Beyond the Ring

2008 (MTI DVD) (CD)

"Right now you pray for the best, you prepare for the worst, and you expect the unexpected. As long as you're with me, you have nothing to fear."

Andre Lima (Andre Lima, playing himself) is trying to rebuild his life after the death of his wife. He's given up competing and is teaching martial arts full time. He has two children and everything he does is to better their lives. Then the unthinkable begins to happen, and his world comes crashing down. His daughter develops a tumor and the operation is going to cost far more than he can afford. The insurance won't cover the hospital bill so he decides to take the suggestion of his manager Tony De Luca (Gary Busey) and train for an underground fight that could bring him $300,000. The odds are all against the aging fighter, but he will do whatever it takes to save his daughter's life.

This film comes from out of left field and is nothing like you might expect it to be. It's claimed to be based on a true story. Even though much of the acting is wooden, there's something genuine about Andre Lima's (also in *Sunland Heat*) performance. This is an incredibly rare instance where the acting is almost inconsequential since the story is so captivating. There's only one real fight in the film, and it's the finale. It features Lima taking on Justice Smith (*Blood and Bone*) and it doesn't disappoint. Both athletes show off various forms of fighting, especially jiu jitsu. Martin Kove, Gary Busey, and many real life fighters complete the cast in a film directed by Gerson Sanginitto (*Maximum Cage Fighting*).

The Big Boss

(a.k.a. Fists of Fury)

1971 (Shout Factory DVD) (djm)

Cheng (Bruce Lee) moves to Bangkok to live with his cousins for a while, and his first job is working in an ice factory, which is soon revealed to be a front for drug running. Drugs are smuggled out of the factory implanted in the huge blocks of ice, and when Cheng finds out about it, he realizes that he's working for the bad guys. When some workers from the plant go missing, Cheng leads a small movement against the drug cartel, and when the cartel's boss sees that Cheng isn't going to back down, it's war!

Small in scale with little ambition other than to be a simple kung fu movie with a superstar in the making at its center, *The Big Boss* might be best viewed out of context, with its fight scenes obviously being the highlights. The final fight between Lee and "the big boss" is fantastic. The movie itself, not so much, and it's a little long to boot (100 minutes). Directed by Lo Wei, who also did *Fist of Fury* with Lee.

The Big Score

1983 (First Run DVD) (CD)

"I don't think they got a needle big enough to kill the shit you got, baby."

Detective Frank Hooks (Fred Williamson) is out to nail notorious drug dealer Goldy (Michael Dante). When he finally arrests him, a technicality arises and Goldy ends up out on bail. Hooks, along with his pals Davis (John Saxon) and Gordon (Richard Roundtree), get a tip that Goldy will be involved in a huge drug deal. They stake it out, and when the time comes, they pounce on the criminals. Goldy takes off with the money and Hooks is in hot pursuit. Goldy ends up dead and the money disappears with the evidence pointing at Hooks. His superiors suspend him and Goldy's boss, Mayfield (Joe Spinell), wants Hooks dead. With his good name being tarnished, Hooks sets out on his own to find the money, clear his name, and most importantly, take out the trash.

The Big Score is everything that you would expect from a Fred Williamson (*Hell Up in Harlem*) film and more. It was a small-budgeted affair but if you're a Williamson fan, you'll enjoy every minute of it. Williamson rarely plays against type and this film is no exception. He's a tough-as-nails detective out to bring down a group of drug dealers. The film kicks into gear right from the get-go with Williamson springing into action. There are plenty of shootouts along with some fisticuffs. Williamson does show off a bit of his martial arts training in some of the various fight sequences, which is always a treat. The film is also somewhat brutal: There's some extreme violence including several instances of bodies being blown to pieces. If you're a jazz fan, the music in the film will be sure to entertain since artists like Ramsey Lewis and Nancy Wilson perform in the film. There are several genre legends who appear, like Richard Roundtree (*Shaft*), John Saxon (*Enter the Dragon*), and the late Joe Spinell (*Rocky*). It may not be Williamson's best film but it's easy to get lost in the mayhem and have plenty of fun.

Big Trouble in Little China

1986 (Fox DVD) (CD)

"Sit tight, hold the fort, keep the home fires burning. And if we're not back by dawn . . . call the president."

When their leader dies, the Chang Sing gang gives him a traditional funeral, walking his coffin through the streets of San Francisco's Chinatown. They take his body down a back alley only to be interrupted by a semi driven by a blowhard trucker named Jack Burton (Kurt Russell). He ends up being the least of their worries when their archrivals—the Wing Kong—show up. This back alley in Chinatown erupts into a bloody battle between good and evil until things take a turn for the worse when the legendary Three Storms (Thunder, Rain, and Lightning) show up and decimate the Chang Sing. The mastermind of all this carnage is the leader of the Wing Kong, the demon Lo Pan (James Hong). His attempt at securing eternal youth drives him to kidnap a Chinese girl with green eyes, leaving Jack and his pal Wang (Dennis Dun) to save her.

If you've never heard of or seen this film, then close this book and watch it *now*! This film boasts one of the largest collections of martial arts stars assembled in one film up to that time period. These guys are all featured in the numerous fight scenes scattered throughout the picture. Watching them battle one another brings out a childlike giddiness in anyone who has followed them throughout their careers. With Carter Wong (*Hardcase and Fist*), Al Leong (*Rapid Fire*), Jeff Imada (*Double Dragon*), James Lew (*American Ninja 5*), Gerald Okamura (*Ninja Academy*), Eric Lee (*Ninja Busters*), and Dan Inosanto (*Game of Death*), it is clear director John Carpenter (*Escape from New York*) meant business in his goal to deliver action like it had never really been seen before in a film produced in the United States. A bona-fide cult classic, *Big Trouble in Little China* is one of the greatest action/fantasy films ever made. It's a shame we can't call Kurt Russell an action star because he's undeniably awesome.

Billa 2

2012 (TSK DVD) (CD)

"There's a difference between the one who gets the job done and one who wagers his life. Remember that!"

Every crime saga has a beginning, and this film shows how David Billa (Ajith Kumar) rose from his troubled stay in a refugee camp to become the top criminal don in India. Billa takes odd jobs from the criminal underground— everything from moving diamonds to smuggling heroin— with a single goal in mind: to gain power. Each job he takes is skillfully used to propel his standing with other crime bosses. He gradually becomes a feared figure with only one soft spot, his niece. He finds himself some serious competition in Demitri (Vidyut Jamwal from *Commando: A One Man Army*), a no-nonsense arms dealer who quickly catches on to Billa's power trip, making their deal far more personal than he could have ever imagined.

Billa 2 is the prequel to the 2007 film, also starring Ajith Kumar. What stands out most in this picture is the sheer brutality of the fight scenes. Blood is spilled, limbs are hacked, and people are blown up. The most memorable moment comes just before the intermission (films from India still have them) when Vidyut Jamwal's character is introduced and he totally annihilates a large group of men who try to cross him with some incredibly fast and acrobatic fighting skills. Vidyut has such a unique style it's easy to see why he could easily become one of the next great action stars. The final battle in an airplane between him and Kumar is also pretty spectacular. Holding true to Tollywood (Tamil language film from India), there are several upbeat musical numbers to engage you. One of these scenes comes almost immediately after an overly brutal battle; suddenly everyone is singing and dancing all sexy like. This is some crazy stuff for sure, and the action is mouthwatering. Directed by Chakri Toleti.

Billy Jack

1971 (Image DVD) (djm)

"I'm gonna take this right foot and I'm gonna whop you on that side of your face. And you wanna know somethin'? There's not a damn thing you're gonna be able to do about it."

Before Chuck Norris and Steven Seagal made their mark in mass-market action films, Tom Laughlin played a half-breed Indian badass named Billy Jack in four movies. The first one was *Born Losers*, and this second film, *Billy Jack*, was a huge success. In this one, he protects a hippie school for youngsters from a bunch of hypocritical and corrupt police and businessmen who bully the school and ban the kids from coming into town. One of the businessmen's sons is a lecherous, racist scumbag who humiliates the minority students who come to town for ice cream. Billy Jack, who is known for protecting the Indian land in the area, has to rein his temper in when idiots get on his nerves, but when he loses it, he filters his rage through his skills in hapkido. In one scene, a mob of men gang up on him, and he fights most of them off before finally getting clobbered. The subtext of the film (anti-Vietnam and pacifism) is thick, and the action scenes are few and far between, but it's an interesting piece of cinema.

Laughlin wrote, directed, and starred in the film with his wife Delores Taylor, who plays his girlfriend. Her rape scene is rough, and when Billy Jack finds out about it, he chops her rapist in the throat, killing him instantly. You can trace the history of the modern action film back to this single film. Loughlin's persona as Billy Jack became his mantra, and other action stars (especially Steven Seagal) followed his example.

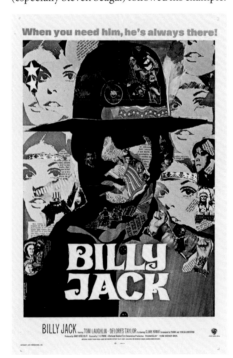

Theatrical poster for *Billy Jack*. Author's collection.

Even his one-liners are great quotables. Followed by *The Trial of Billy Jack*. Some modern viewers will find most of this film boring or outdated, but as far as the action goes, it's hard to beat it.

Billy Jack Goes to Washington

1977 (Ventura Distribution DVD) (JAS)

This film has the late great Tom Laughlin reprising his role for the fourth and final time. This is essentially a '70s remake of the Jimmy Stewart classic *Mr. Smith Goes to Washington*. The story begins with Billy Jack—who is now a hero to the young and radical—being appointed temporary senator as a public relations stunt by a group of political cronies. They expect him to quietly serve as figurehead while appealing to young and minority voters, but his sense of justice disallows this. As he investigates a scandal involving a fellow senator (who is also a family friend, played by E. G. Marshall) involved in the illegal funding of a nuclear power plant where he wants to start a youth camp, the powers that be pull out all the stops to silence him. With the help of his girlfriend Jean (Delores Taylor) and secretary Saunders (Lucy Arnaz), Billy Jack comes to realize it will take more than just martial arts to defend himself and others.

How strange it is that an action series morphed into something that can even be mildly compared to a Frank Capra classic drama (there's only one physical fight in the entire film). That is the audaciousness and awesomeness of this action series. While this film is in no way comparable to *Mr. Smith Goes to Washington* on a technical level, this is the work of an artist being true to his vision and character arc. The film series never lauded violence as an answer, even in the martial-arts-heavy first film (second, if you count *Born Losers*). The spiritual journey Billy Jack makes in each film would be out of sync if he continued to solve everything though violence. This story illustrates a logical outcome for the character. *Billy Jack Goes to Washington* has garnered a lot of negative reviews, which is strange because it's well acted, earnest, and entertaining. It is especially relevant these days as money scandals in Washington have ascended to levels of lunacy. The film deserves a reappraisal, not necessarily as a classic, but as a fitting closure to a solid series that espouses a message of integrity.

Black Belt

1992 (New Concorde DVD) (djm)

Sweet (Mattias Hues), a serial killer with a mother fixation, is stalking and killing women who resemble or remind him of his dearly departed mom. He sets his sights on a pop singer named Shanna (Deirdre Imershein) because her new hit single is a rendition of a song his mother used to sing to him. Shanna is also targeted for death by her spiteful manager, who resents the fact that she won't renew her contract with him. Entering the picture is former cop Jack Dillon (Don Wilson), who sort of stumbles into a job as a bodyguard for Shanna. With two factions dead set against killing her, Dillon has his hands full keeping the hitmen and serial killer just out of reach. He goes on the offensive, and hunts the killer while exposing the plot against her life. In the meantime, he falls for his ward.

Wilson, the star of the *Bloodfist* films, feels right at home in this slightly sleazy, somewhat entertaining grindhouse-style action/serial killer movie. His main opponent, played by Hues (*No Retreat, No Surrender II, Dark Angel*), is big, imposing, and ultra skeezy, which works well for the film. Their final fight is a foregone conclusion, but it works in the context of the picture. Fans of Wilson should be happy. All others may be a little bored, but I enjoyed it. It was written and directed by Charles Philip Moore (writer of *Live by the Fist*), and co-directed by Rick Jacobson (*Dragon Fire*).

Black Belt II: Fatal Force

(a.k.a. **Spyder**)

1988 (New Concord DVD) (djm)

"Listen, Spyder: You're a good cop. You're a little weird, but you get results, and I like that, but you've got to understand when you get into this society shit, you've got to change your methods—that's the way it is!"

The father of a POW soldier stuck in Vietnam for more than a decade is desperate to finance some kind of rescue mission to save his son, but the crew he's hired is corrupt and using him as a source of money. Through convoluted ties, a kickboxing cop named Spyder ("W.K.F. World Kickboxing Champion" Blake Bahner) gets involved because his partner happens to have a recently rescued POW brother who *might* know where the other missing soldier is. Spyder's partner goes to Hawaii to track down his drug-addled soldier brother, who has become a hunted man by the corrupt mercenary crew who want to kill him for reasons that don't make sense. Spyder, an overly protective officer of the law, wants to keep an eye on his partner, and so he follows him to Hawaii and eventually has to avenge him because he gets killed at the hands of the mercenaries.

I don't know what to say about *Black Belt II: Fatal Force*. It's . . . a movie. It's got that going for it, at the very least. From Roger Corman's studio and from producer Cirio Santiago, it's the melding of two different New Concord movies (which were probably semi-coherent), one of which was a martial arts cop movie called

Spyder, starring Bahner, and the other of which seems culled from various Corman/Santiago productions involving a Vietnam POW-driven storyline, possibly *Behind Enemy Lines* or *Eye of the Eagle*. As is, this seventy-seven minute movie is an impossible mess, and it quite spectacularly ruins any chance Bahner might have had at an action movie career. Whether or not he's a world kickboxing champion (I wasn't able to find any evidence to prove it either way), his martial arts abilities consist of throwing a few kicks here and there, but he seems best at punching. So there you go. Bahner was also in *Lethal Pursuit* and *The Contra Conspiracy*. "Directed" by Jim Avellana and Kevin Tent.

Black Belt Jones

1974 (Warner DVD) (djm)

The mafia moves in on an inner-city neighborhood, hoping to strong-arm a midlevel operation into doing its dirty work, with the ultimate goal of acquiring some real estate. They set their sights on a building run and operated by a karate studio, and the owner is stubborn old Poppa Byrd (Scatman Crothers), who refuses all offers and threats from the midlevel thugs. The thugs get aggressive and kill Byrd, which gets Black Belt Jones's attention. Black Belt (Jim Kelly) is a pseudo secret agent and neighborhood do-gooder, and he gets serious about finding the scum who killed his friend. His partner is Byrd's karate-chopping daughter (Gloria Hendry from *Live and Let Die*), and with the help of some trampoline-proficient chicks from the beach, Black Belt Jones invades the mob's headquarters (using trampolines and circus tricks), putting an end to their reign of mayhem. The finale takes place at a carwash, where all of the characters are inundated with soapsuds.

As goofy and funky as they come, *Black Belt Jones* is undeniably dated and hokey, but if you're in the mood for mild theatrics and just-for-fun action, then you can certainly do worse. It reunited star Kelly with his director from *Enter the Dragon*, Robert Clouse, and it's all done under the same Warner Brothers banner. It doesn't really feel like a studio film, though. Kelly made several pictures for producers Fred Weintraub and Paul Heller, and then his star sort of fell out of favor. Making too many movies like *Black Belt Jones* would have done that to anybody.

Black Caesar

1973 (MGM DVD) (CD)

"It's a jungle, and it takes a jungle bunny to run it."

Tommy Gibbs (Fred Williamson) grew up in the ghetto. As a young man, he had a run-in with a crooked cop who accused him of stealing money

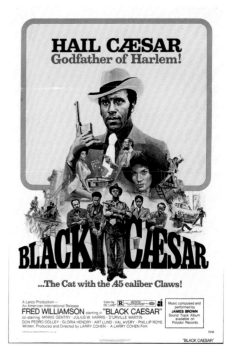

Theatrical release poster of *Black Caesar*. Author's collection.

and then proceeded to break his leg. Tommy didn't like the feeling of being powerless, so years later he's back as a mob hitman. His plans are much more ambitious than that. He quickly begins to rise through the ranks and carves out a nice business for himself. He doesn't waste time taking out the competition any chance he gets. All the power begins to go to his head and the people who really care for him turn their backs. He eventually becomes violent with his girl Helen (Gloria Hendry), which is the beginning of the end for him. Tommy finds himself alone with the mob ready to take him out. The only thing he has going for him are the books with incriminating evidence that he is holding over everyone's head.

Black Caesar may be a small low-budgeted exploitation film but it's played out with strong, well-developed characters and a terrific performance by Fred Williamson. There really isn't any actual fighting in the movie but there's plenty of violent mob-style action. The film is in the same vein as *Scarface* or *Goodfellas*. Writer/director Larry Cohen (*Original Gangstas*) puts a lot of time into developing character and does a fantastic job of building up Gibbs's feelings of alienation as his fall from power begins. The film has minor flaws but still manages to be an engaging portrait of a mob boss. It also boasts a spectacular soundtrack with songs performed by legendary singer James Brown.

The Black Cobra

(a.k.a. **Cobra Nero**)

1987 (djm)

Cop: "You know, Malone,
nobody likes you."
Malone: "Yeah. I know. Sometimes, I
don't like myself either. That's a matter
of opinion. Frankly, I couldn't give a
damn about yours. All I care about is
my work. To finish what I started. And I
usually do."

A woman named Elys (Eva Grimaldi) takes a photo of some criminals in the middle of a crime, and the gang leader (played by Bruno Bilotta, a.k.a. Karl Landgren) marks her for death. Her case is assigned to a detective named Robert Malone (Fred Williamson, ultra cool), who casually participates in protecting her and fending off the attacks of the killer gang. A shootout finale caps this otherwise standard Italian-made riff on Stallone's *Cobra*, which was released the previous year.

Not so much a hybrid movie (like so many Italian films made during the era) as an homage or straight Xerox of *Cobra*, this Stelvio Massi actioner earns its right to be a legitimate original with its nifty camera set-ups, solid action, and a nice, physical performance by Williamson. Sequels followed, but the best one was the first one. Multiple video release companies have distributed this film, but the best way to see it is to watch the uncut Laserdisc (widescreen) from Asia.

Black Cobra

2012 (Lionsgate DVD) (djm)

"Where you get your black belt from? Goodwill?"

T. J. Storm from *The Ultimate Game* stars in this earnest vehicle that casts him as a proficient martial artist named Sizwe whose father has been arrested as a dissident in South Africa. Forced to flee the country, Sizwe smuggles a small cache of diamonds to California, where he hopes to sell them so that he can go back to South Africa to pay corrupt officials for the release of his father. When he gets to California, he meets up with an old college buddy, but he ends up talking to the wrong people about his diamonds, which gets him in big trouble with a crime overlord, played by Cary-Hiroyuki Tagawa.

Some solid fight scenes and an appealing role for T. J. make *Black Cobra* a pretty good late-era direct-to-video offering, but what it lacks in panache and distinction it makes up for with its effort to get as much in there as it can. Some of the fight scenes are really good, but there are deep dips and lags throughout the film where

we meet too many characters for such a small story, resulting in dialogue-heavy plotting and exposition. That said, I still enjoyed it. Directed by Scott Donovan.

The Black Cobra 2

1988 (Legacy DVD) (CD)

Tough-as-nails Chicago cop Robert Malone (Fred Williamson) isn't one to play by the rules. He chases down a perpetrator who quickly takes a hostage to try to save his own tail. Malone doesn't hesitate to take the shot and drops him dead, saving the hostage. His captain is pretty upset about the way the hostage was put in danger, and as a reprimand, Malone is given a break from the job and sent to the Philippines to learn their techniques. He's partnered with Inspector McCall (Nicholas Hammond), and the two men just don't see eye to eye. Malone's wallet is stolen and once they recover it, the circumstances surrounding the death of the thief lead them to a terrorist who is ready to launch an attack on the world.

Say what you will about the *Black Cobra* trilogy, but Fred Williamson (*Boss Nigger*) knows exactly how to deliver the goods to his audience, and he doesn't disappoint with *The Black Cobra 2*. Its success lies in his charisma, charm, and his ability to just keep the audience entertained. Some viewers may consider it to be a low-grade exercise, but when the audience is having so much fun watching it, who the hell cares? There's plenty of action with shootouts, hand-to-hand fights, and tons of brutality. Nicholas Hammond (*Stealth*) was an excellent addition to the cast and some of the best moments in the film are the scenes of interplay between these two characters. Don't miss out on the fun— just watch as much Williamson as possible, particularly in this series.

The Black Cobra 3

1990 (Synergy DVD) (CD)

When a special agent tries to find a stolen cache of weapons, he finds himself in a much more dangerous situation than he expected. After a daring escape, his wounds are far too severe, and he ends up dead. Interpol agent Greg Duncan (Forry Smith) is assigned the case and needs to figure out why the agent was killed. Fellow agent Tracy Rogers (Debra Ward) is assigned to him as a partner, and his other assigned partner has to be outside of Interpol, someone of his choosing, and someone he can trust. That man is Chicago detective Robert Malone (Fred Williamson). He makes the trip to Manila and the three of them begin their investigation. No matter what move they make, the bad guys keep getting the jump on them. Which of them is working for the other side?

The Black Cobra 3 delivers everything you would expect from a Fred Williamson vehicle. Sure, it's way over the top but movies like this are the perfect antidote for those who feel that today's action films are lacking. Williamson is having a blast in his Malone character. There's plenty of ridiculous and violent action with Williamson's signature brand of unorthodox martial arts and gunplay. It's good to see him interacting with a small team and his quips come frequently, while always giving way to action. The man almost never puts down his stogie and delivers one of the best final moments of a film ever. The film was directed by Edoardo Margheriti (*The Black Cobra 2*) under the pseudonym of Dan Edwards.

Black Dawn

2005 (Sony DVD) (DL)

"Devil don't want me, Billy. Just don't want me at all."

Steven Seagal was already several years into his direct-to-video career phase when *Black Dawn* hit rental-store shelves. Seagal reprises the role of Jonathan Cold in this sequel to 2003's *The Foreigner*. Ticking most boxes for a vintage Seagal character, Cold is described as an "ex-CIA, current freelance operative specializing in covert operations and nuclear weapons intelligence." There's an emphasis on the "ex-CIA" part this time as Cold now contracts out his skills to lowlifes with deep pockets. When a deal to sell nuclear materials to trigger-happy Chechen terrorists goes south, our man teams up with his former student (Tamara Davies) to set things right. A derivative, though competently executed, series of car chases, low-grade explosions, and shootouts ensue, culminating in an airborne climax that's a little too ambitious for *Black Dawn*'s modest FX budget. We're told that "Dead or alive, Jonathan Cold is dangerous," but Cold's reputation seems somewhat exaggerated. As demonstrated, his skills include using a white lab coat to infiltrate a prison medical ward and bribing a hacker to look up a baddies' phone records. Most of the time he seems to be coasting on his threatening squint and hoping no one calls the bluff.

Black Dawn is, to date, the sole directing credit for Alexander Gruszynski, whose recent day job has been as director of photography on Tyler Perry films. He moves things along at a brisk pace, keeps the body count high, and shows some flair for staging gunplay. Don't expect any significant martial arts action from Seagal this time as the rare close-quarter fights are executed by an obvious stunt double in a dodgy wig. From his affected *Mojo Priest*-era 'Nawlins accent to his distracted performance, this film typifies the icon's work in the mid-2000s. He just doesn't seem to have his heart in it this time. It's far from the worst of Seagal's DTV films, but *Black Dawn* lacks the production value, high-octane action, and outright fun of his classic '90s output.

The Black Dragon

1974 (Deimos DVD) (djm)

Innocent farmhand Tai-Lin (Jason Pai Piao) leaves his village to make his way in the big city, and he lands a job as a dockworker, loading boxes. When he sees a fellow worker being abused by a taskmaster, he steps in and intervenes, which is a big no-no. The taskmasters gang up on him, and he takes some punishment, but then he snaps, showing that he's a master at martial arts, and he clears the deck of his attackers. This impresses his superior, and he's taken to the big boss, who offers him a job as a taskmaster. He signs a paper with his mark even though he can't read, and he's bound by the contract. After a few days of working for the boss, he's treated to whores, good food, and acceptance, but he starts to realize that he might be working for the bad guys. When some rebels in town make their presence known, they approach Tai-Lin and prove to him that he's working for the wrong side. He saves a girl from prostitution and demands to be let out of his contract, but no dice. With the help of his new friends (who include Rob Van Clief, who became a grindhouse martial arts star because of this movie), he's able to destroy his contract and clean the city up.

Fans of kung fu movies and grindhouse movies in general will enjoy *The Black Dragon* more than others. Van Clief, who is touted as the star of the film, is only in small sections of the movie, but whenever he's on screen, the movie gets better real quick. He would go on to star in *The Death of Bruce Lee* (a.k.a. *The Black Dragon's Revenge*) and *Way of the Black Dragon*. Directed by "Tommy Loo Chung" (Chin-Ku Lu).

Black Dynamite

2008 (Sony DVD) (djm)

"Who the hell is interrupting my kung fu?!"

A verifiable spoof and sendup of blaxsploitation martial arts movies from the 1970s, *Black Dynamite* was produced and written by Michael Jai White who stars as the crass hero who goes on the warpath when his kid brother is murdered by a drug syndicate. Dynamite, a Vietnam vet and a martial arts dynamo (and a lady killer), also has a past with the CIA, and he's asked to infiltrate a crime ring that has an overblown, master plan to spike a new brand of malt liquor with a chemical agent that renders black men impotent and sterile, thus curbing the growth of the African- American race. Only the dynamic Black Dynamite can stop the nefarious plans of the evildoers and have First Lady Pat Nixon swooning at his feet in the White House.

When I saw this theatrically upon its initial release, I didn't care for it at all. I found it too jokey, ironic, and a waste of Jai White's talents. Watching it on video in a second viewing, I was able to invest a little more patience and

forgiveness into it, but I still don't really like it. I don't know why Jai White and his team (such as director Scott Sanders) felt that making a mockery of the genre was more viable than making the real thing, which would have been much more rewarding. Jai White's previous film *Blood and Bone* is one of the best examples reviewed in this book of an action star–fueled vehicle, and *Black Dynamite* is one of the worst. Despite my misgivings with it, the film has garnered a cult reputation and has its fans.

Black Dynamite

2011–2012 (Warner DVD) (djm)

The ultra ironic spoof of blaxsploitation kung fu movies of the 1970s from Michael Jai White was resurrected as a painfully obvious one-note-joke animated series that played on cable television. Over the course of ten episodes, Black Dynamite (voiced by Michael Jai White) and his misfit friends go up against an evil Michael Jackson, solve the serial murders of black porn stars, and get into various perilous situations that require quick, nonsensical thinking from BD and the use of his kung fu skills.

I wasn't a fan of the feature film and so sitting through entire episodes of this animated series was a chore and a half, and its chaotic, ramshackle scripts and misguided sense of humor degrade any chance it might have had at paying homage to the films and the genre it tries to emulate. By endorsing this nonstop mockery, Michael Jai White has lowered his standards, and it's a shame. Fans of his deserve better. From creators Byron Minns and Scott Sanders.

Black Eagle

1988 (Eve Digital DVD) (djm)

Contrary to how this film is marketed now, this was not a starring role for Jean-Claude Van Damme—Van Damme is indeed in it, but he plays the villain. Sho Kosugi (*Revenge of the Ninja*), fresh from his days working for Cannon, stars as a James Bond-type secret agent named Ken Tani who is called into service to retrieve a laser-tracking device from a crashed F-11

Ken Tani (Sho Kosugi) defends the world against evil Russians in *Black Eagle*. Author's collection.

Jean-Claude Van Damme does the splits as Andrei, the villainous Russian muscle in *Black Eagle*. Author's collection.

that lies at the bottom of the Mediterranean. On a tight timetable, Ken has to get to the device before the Russians do, and his biggest competition comes in the form of muscular and agile Adrei (Van Damme), who seems to dog him at every turn. Ken spends a lot of his time running and being chased through the exotic Malta locations, and he tries to spend some time with his two sons (played by Kane and Shane), who become exasperated every time he leaves them in the care of the CIA to go chase bad guys. Kosugi and Van Damme have two fight scenes together, neither of which is conclusive as to who wins, which actually feels appropriate in this case.

Definitely a riff on the 007 movies, *Black Eagle* has almost everything it takes to be a compelling action adventure . . . except a heartbeat. Kosugi's character is boring, and his relationship with his kids in the movie is strenuous at best, and we never see him showing real emotion. Van Damme plays an aloof villain, and we never really get a sense of what he's about. The pacing of the film is a little lackluster, and unfortunately most of the action is accomplished in a rote, by-the-numbers fashion. The beautiful locations help. Eric Karson (*The Octagon*, *Angel Town*) directed it and appears in a small role at the beginning.

Andrei (Jean-Claude Van Damme), the evil Russian, in *Black Eagle*. Author's collection.

Black Eye

1973 (Warner DVD) (djm)

Private eye Shep Stone (Fred Williamson) accepts a case involving a missing teenager, and as he begins his investigation, he encounters some dead bodies, all of which are somehow connected to an antique walking cane with a dog's head at its tip. His path is colored with some interesting individuals including a porno director, a shady Christian pastor, and an elderly antiques collector. Stone (whom everyone knows by name from his days as a cop) is attacked, smacked around, and shot at, but he's a tough dick. He figures it out fairly quickly that it's not the cane that everyone's interested in, but what was *inside* of it: heroin.

Fred Williamson (*Foxtrap*, *Black Cobra*) is incredibly appealing in a cool-breeze role that has him down on his luck and yet perfectly on his game as a tough guy and a romantic leading man. The story isn't especially interesting, but it doesn't matter because Williamson carries it as far as it needs to go. Director Jack Arnold also worked with Williamson on the western *Boss Nigger*.

Black Friday

2001 (Platinum DVD) (djm)

A former mercenary named Dean Campbell (Gary Daniels) leaves his life of killing behind him and becomes a respected attorney. He comes home one day to find that his home has been invaded by terrorists who are threatening to use chemical bombs on the outlying area. It almost seems as though the incident is random, but snarky government agents take Campbell to a nearby compound and prepare to murder him, which is when he snaps himself back into his lethal mode, killing the soldiers who have targeted him for death. Has his past caught up to him, or does all of this have nothing to do with that? It becomes obvious when a former disgruntled associate makes his presence known to him, and then the shit gets real.

Surprisingly stylish and introspective for a direct-to-video actioner, *Black Friday* is a solid vehicle for Daniels, who has just as many moments to act as he does to showcase his fighting abilities. It's worth seeing once. From director Darren Doane, who also did *Ultimate Target* (a.k.a. *Ides of March*) with Daniels.

Black Gunn

1972 (Sony DVD) (djm)

Jim Brown stars as Gunn, a nightclub owner whose Vietnam vet brother Scotty gets into trouble when his ultra militant group steals a book of names and information from the mob. The mob appoints an up-and-comer named Capelli (Martin Landau) to head up a task force to find Scotty and reclaim the incriminating book before it gets out, and Capelli's men

harass Gunn in order to get Scotty's attention. When Scotty is killed, Gunn goes over the edge and forsakes civility and the law by joining the militants and going after the mob. The finale features a bloodbath of epic proportions as Gunn and his armed-to-the-teeth comrades lay siege to the mob's manufacturing drug warehouse.

Pretty entertaining and easy to follow, *Black Gunn* has plenty of roughhousing and gunplay to keep things moving at a good pace. Brown's commanding presence and easy-going panache is on full display here. Some supporting roles—namely Bruce Glover as a thug—really help cement this movie's entertainment value. Fans of blaxploitation action movies and Jim Brown in particular will want to see this. Directed by Robert Hartford-Davis.

Black Horizon (a.k.a. Stranded)

2002 (Lionsgate DVD) (CD)

The Russians and Americans are working together on a space station to create a top-secret device. When the equipment on board begins to malfunction, they find themselves trapped with no way home. NASA enlists the aid of one their best men, Ed Carpenter (Michael Dudikoff), to lead a team into space to attempt a rescue. A meteor shower is threatening the lives of both crews, including causing severe damage to Carpenter's shuttle, ensuring that a return trip in the same shuttle will be next to impossible. On Earth, NSA Agent Jeffries (Ice-T) discovers some crooked officials who have sabotaged the entire mission in order to save their own hides. These officials have changed the launch codes on the escape pods, and he has to twist their arms in order to get them. Meanwhile, in space, Carpenter has to keep his crew from panicking in order to conserve their oxygen and try to conceive an alternate plan in case they can't get the codes.

Who needs *Gravity* when you can watch Michael Dudikoff (*Avenging Force*) in space? This may not be a megabudgeted action flick with state-of-the-art special effects, but it was Dudikoff's swan song in the motion picture industry (so far), which makes it notable. It's too bad because he's really good in it. There's plenty of suspense as the crew tries to survive in space and Dudikoff plays it tough, yet vulnerable. He wears his heart on his shoulder but there's no question he would kick some ass if he needed to. He keeps it calm and is always in control through the duration of the film. Ice-T (*New Jack City*) gets to kick some ass so all of the action bases are covered. The film is surprisingly tame for director Fred Olen Rey (*Active Stealth*) but it's relatively entertaining. One thing's for sure: Michael Dudikoff must make a triumphant return to movies. America needs him!

Blackjack

1998 (Dimension DVD) (CD)

Jack Devlin (Dolph Lundgren) is a former US Marshal who now spends his time working

as a bodyguard for the rich. His old friend Bobby (Peter Kelegan) asks him to watch over his daughter Casey (Padraigin Murphy) since he's being hassled by some mob types. Jack gladly accepts only to be attacked by a group of assassins. He fights them off and protects Casey, but due to the trauma he develops a phobia and has panic attacks when he is confronted with the color white. After some time passes, Bobby and his wife pass away in an unfortunate accident and Jack gains custody of Casey. He begins to rethink his line of work and decides to try something less dangerous. When his pal Tim (Fred Williamson) is injured while on the job, Jack decides to step in and protect supermodel Cinder (Kam Heskin) from the obsessed maniac who almost killed his friend. He will do whatever it takes to protect her, but he will have to battle with his own problem, which is getting in his way of finding the killer.

Blackjack was originally designed to be a pilot episode of a series, but it then wasn't picked up by the USA Network. Instead we have this one-off film directed by action maestro John Woo (*Hard Target*), and it's a mixed bag. There really wasn't enough action to sustain the two-hour runtime but the two major action scenes the film does offer are top notch and everything you would expect from a John Woo film. Lundgren runs around two fisted, stylishly taking out the enemy and using things like trampolines and motorcycles to spice things up. These scenes were great and his character and his ailment were interesting, but the film ultimately has a lackluster pace. Still a solid action flick, *Blackjack* is far more entertaining than most made-for-TV movies.

Black Mask

1996 (Artisan DVD) (CD)

"My destiny, who knows? But if it's hell, then you're coming along."

Tsui Chik (Jet Li) is a survivor of a government experiment to create the perfect supersoldier. Once the project is canceled, he must escape along with some other soldiers. After some time has passed, Tsui resurfaces as an unassuming librarian who is constantly being saved by his cop friend Inspector Rock (Lau Ching-Wan). A string of attacks begins, and Tsui suspects they are led by other supersoldiers he once looked to as brothers. When Yeuk Laan (Françoise Yip) shows her face, he knows it's them. He knows he must jump back into action and bring to life an alter ego for himself, a masked hero known as the Black Mask. He's a one-man fighting machine who tries to keep his friends out of harm's way while trying to keep his identity concealed. The diabolical Commander Hung (Patrick Lung) wants Tsui dead and will do anything to make it happen, even if it means going after the people Tsui cares about.

Black Mask is Jet Li's attempt at a superhero film. It has a few fun moments but the tone of the picture is all over the place, which makes the

US theatrical poster for *Black Mask*. Author's collection.

viewing experience uneven. It's plenty violent with some fantastically staged fight scenes courtesy of Yuen Wo Ping (*The Matrix*). Jet Li is terrific as usual, dispatching the baddies left and right. Director Daniel Lee (*14 Blades*) was a relative newcomer when he did this film and made some noticeable mistakes, but overall, *Black Mask* is an exciting film that may also be one of Li's most violent films with copious amounts of blood, carnage, and severed limbs. Beware the US release: It's horrendously dubbed and the original soundtrack is replaced with rap tracks that never seem to fit into the film. This was released theatrically in the US on the tails of *Lethal Weapon 4* to capitalize on Li's crossover wave.

Black Mask 2: City of Masks

2001 (Sony DVD) (djm)

Kid: "Are you Black Mask?"
Black Mask: "Who's he?"

If you loved the first *Black Mask*, you'll love that they made another one, but you may not like what they made. Black Mask (this time played by Andy On) has his hands full when a new drug is concocted by a scientist hoping to take over the city with his team of bulky wrestlers who have become infected with his drug. Each wrestler has a moniker like "Chameleon," "Wolf," "Claw," or "Iguana," and when infected, they literally become the monster that their name implies. With the city under siege by the hulked-out monsters, Black Mask must don his mask and fight evil.

An interesting cast of martial artists and real-life wrestlers populate this messy and confoundingly stupid movie from director

Tsui Hark, who made some of Jean-Claude Van Damme's worst movies. Scott Adkins from *Undisputed II* plays a bald doctor who has the big climax fight with Black Mask at the end, and wrestler Rob Van Dam plays one of the monsters. Other monsters are played by Tyler Mane, Andrew Bryniarski, and Traci Lords. Adkins doubled for Black Mask in the more intense moments. Movies like *Black Mask 2* give the martial arts genre a bad reputation for a good reason. It sucks.

Black Out

(a.k.a. **Midnight Heat**)

1996 (Platinum DVD) (djm)

A bank executive named John Grey is hit by a car, and he loses his memory. When he wakes up, his wife greets him, and tries to remind him of their life together. Grey (played by Brian Bosworth) begins having violent flashbacks of a life that seems impossible: bank robbing, murder, and a gang life, and he starts remembering fragments of people and phone numbers, which he begins to randomly dial, hoping to find clues to his identity. As his past starts to catch up with him, his former gang members come after him to even an old score, and he soon finds his wife slain in their home. He goes on the lam, making friends with a woman who wants to turn him over to the authorities, and so he must convince her to help him, and stay alive as his ugly past rears its ugly head.

Brian Bosworth (from the classic *Stone Cold*) languished in the made-for-cable and straight-to-video world after his big-screen debut, and most of his following vehicles had him playing characters that were against type. In *Black Out*, he plays a befuddled nice guy, and we only see echoes of his capably mean self, and when he actually engages in fights, he's reluctant and courteous even as he hits people and flips them over. This one bears the mark of a low-budget outing, but it's watchable enough simply because Bosworth is interesting in how he approaches action. The director, Allan A. Goldstein, directed Bosworth in *Virus* as well.

Black Point

2002 (DEJ DVD) (CD)

"I must be missing something here. A woman whacks you over the head, frames you for murder, and now you want to run out and save her? Please tell me you've been drinking again."

Former military man John Hawkins (David Caruso) has finally decided to kick his drinking habit and try to get his life in order after the tragic disappearance of his young daughter. Standing Bear (Gordon Tootoosis) gives him a second chance on the job, and things are looking up. While out on a delivery, he meets

Natalie (Susan Haskell) and they have an instant spark. This could be love at first sight but there's a wrench in the mix: her husband Gus (action star Thomas Ian Griffith). He works for a major crime boss who he is double-crossing for his own personal gain. Hawkins pulls out of his depression now that he has something to fight for, and he tries to help Natalie escape Gus, who is abusing her. No one is exactly who they seem and Hawkins finds himself framed and fighting for his life, struggling to find someone he can trust so he can save the girl of his dreams.

Thomas Ian Griffith (from the dynamic *Excessive Force*) co-wrote the script as well as slithered into the villain role of this film, ravaging through every scene like a madman. What's heartbreaking is the fact that he's the bad guy, so every bad guy must fall by the hands of the hero, and in this case, the hero happens to be David Caruso (*First Blood*). He isn't the ideal opponent, but what can you do? Griffith has very little fight in him, trading the fists for cold-blooded murder. The film is actually rather engaging with a couple of interesting little twists. The cast is (mostly) likable and Griffith is fantastic as a sleazy thug trying to move up the crime ladder. Directed by David Mackay.

Black Samurai

1977 (BCI DVD) (CD)

"Surprise Monkeys!"

Tokie Konuma (Essie Lin Chia) is the daughter of Hong Kong's ambassador who finds herself kidnapped and being held for ransom by an evil warlock and his followers. The ransom may be for money but there's a secret new weapon known as

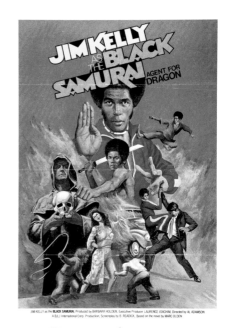

Theatrical poster for *Black Samurai*. Author's collection.

the "freeze bomb" that is part of the kidnappers' hidden agenda. Robert Sand (Jim Kelly from *Black Belt Jones*) is enjoying his vacation when he is called back into duty by a secret government agency known as D.R.A.G.O.N. As soon as Sand jumps to her rescue, people start trying to kill him at every turn. Sand suspects his partner may have double-crossed him, and he has to worry about a voodoo priestess with plans for a ritual sacrifice. The odds are against him but Sand is prepared for anything.

Director Al Adamson (*Dynamite Brothers*) may not have been the greatest filmmaker but he does know how to make a fun movie. This is a WTF-type of film that combines a warlock villain, a ritual sacrifice, high-tech weapons, and Jim Kelly fighting a vulture (seriously!). The movie is just nuts, but Kelly is such a charismatic performer that the action scenes feel genuine. He fights at the top of his game and shows off his incredible skills in various battles. It's a very funny film worthy of laughing at, but it's a bit better than it should be. As long as you don't forget that movies like this are meant to be fun, then you should have no trouble enjoying *Black Samurai*.

Black Thunder

1998 (New Concorde DVD) (djm)

Toward the end of his feature film career, Michael Dudikoff starred in a string of low-budget military-esque thrillers for Roger Corman's company. There was *Strategic Command, Crash Dive, Freedom Strike, Counter Measures,* and the last, *Black Thunder,* which concerns the theft of a highly secret stealth plane with the capability of invisibility. Test pilot Vince Connors (Dudikoff) is called in to go into Libya with a fellow pilot (Gary Hudson from *Marital Outlaw*) where the plane is believed to be, and when they get there, they realize that their colleague (played by Richard Norton) was the thief of the plane, and now that he's working with the enemy, the United States—*and the entire planet*—is at risk because the secret plane is in the wrong hands. It's a mission only Connors can accomplish.

Passable in the action department with lots of air battles fudged with stock footage and clever editing, *Black Thunder* remains watchable and nominally entertaining by having Dudikoff engaging in fisticuffs and gunplay when he's grounded. Most of the scenes of gunfire are obviously shot in sections, revealing (at least to me) that no one is actually shooting at each other in the movie. If you can get past the patch quilt direction (which Corman's factory is notorious for), this is a movie that anyone with a high tolerance for earnest exploitation action movies can enjoy. Co-star Norton once served as Dudikoff's stunt double on the first *American Ninja*. Oh, and there's sex and nudity in the movie, too, for those interested. Rick Jacobson (*Dragon Fire, Full Contact*) directed.

Blade

1998 (New Line DVD) (djm)

"You better wake up. The world you live in is just a sugarcoated topping. There is another world beneath it, the real world. And if you want to survive it, you'd better learn to pull the trigger."

From the Marvel Comics canon, *Blade* stars Wesley Snipes as a half-human, half-vampire badass named Blade, a powerful warrior of the night. He hunts vampires with his arsenal of customized weapons (silver stakes and bullets, garlic bombs, and ultraviolet flash grenades), and the vampire underworld fears him like a plague. He comes up against an ambitious vampire named Deacon Frost (Stephen Dorff), who aspires to unleash a Blood Demon on the world, but in order to do so, he must have the blood of the Daywalker (Blade's other name) to complete the ritual. Between you and me, the Daywalker kicks Deacon's ass.

Snipes was born to play Blade. The only other person who could have played this character correctly was Steve James, but Snipes *owns* it. He's in top form, and his martial arts fight scenes—while incredible stylized—are impressive. Director Stephen Norrington (*Death Machine, The League of Extraordinary Gentleman*) gives the film an extra dose of coolness and pizazz, while ensuring that the star of the film is always the focus. As an action/horror/superhero movie, *Blade* is a complete success. It was a surprise hit and spawned several sequels with Snipes reprising his role, and then later spawned a television series starring Kirk "Sticky Fingaz" Jones. Kris Kristofferson co-stars in the film as Blade's trusty sidekick Whistler.

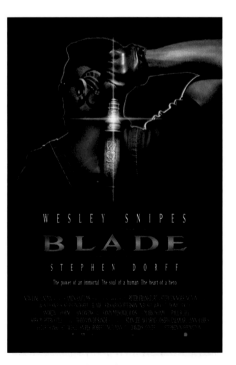

Teaser poster for *Blade*. Author's collection.

Blade Boxer

1997 (Dead Alive VHS) (djm)

Made and released on video at the tail end of VHS, *Blade Boxer* is an obscure to-the-death fight movie that has a tinge of brutality that sets it slightly apart from movies like *Bloodsport* and *Kickboxer*. It stars Kevin King as a cop named Rick, and he's investigating the nasty deaths of fighters whose corpses are being found dumped all over the city. His partner Joe (Cass Magda from *Hawk's Vengeance*) is a martial arts expert who teaches Rick how to defend himself, and when they get too close to the source of the killings, Joe is killed by a "blade boxer" (a fighter who wears a Freddy Kruger glove in the fighting arena), and Rick has to man up and become the fighter Joe taught him to be so that he can get his revenge in the ring.

Really bloody and surprisingly gory for a martial arts movie (like the first *Shootfighter* movie), *Blade Boxer* has an air of strangeness that's hard to describe. It's obviously a very low-budget film, but that shouldn't stop you from watching it if you like these types of movies. I liked aspects of it, despite its goofiness in parts, and the scenes with Magda (who also choreographed the fights) are impressive. The late Dana Plato from *Diff'rent Strokes* is in the film as a love interest, and she has some nude scenes that don't really help the movie. Some few viewers will find something to like about *Blade Boxer*. Everyone else won't be impressed. Directed by Bruce Reisman.

Blade II

2002 (New Line DVD) (djm)

Wesley Snipes, returning as the vampire hunter known as Blade, scored his biggest hit with this sequel. This time, the vampire underworld comes to him for help: A hybrid vampire they call The Reaper (Luke Goss) is running amok, killing humans and vampires alike, and what's worse is that he's turning his victims into more Reapers, who are all immune to the usual things that kill vampires . . . except sunlight. Hard to kill and with a personal vendetta against the oldest vampire around, The Reaper needs to be taken down, which is where Blade comes in. He reluctantly joins forces with the Bloodpack, a crew of badass vampires (who include Ron Perlman and Donnie Yen), and with his sidekick Whistler (Kris Kristofferson) and new groupie Scud (Norman Reedus), the team goes to war with The Reaper and his hordes.

As in the *Alien* franchise, the *Blade* series got a bump up by having a talented director come in to make the first sequel. Guillermo Del Toro, who stepped in to helm this one, manages to give the film an even more distinct comic book flare to it than the first film, and many people prefer this one to the original. Snipes, who is still in perfect form here, looks to be relishing every moment he's on screen, *but* the focus of the franchise began shifting away from him in this entry. With more characters and villains than before, *Blade II* is busy with all kinds of action, character development, and texture. Still, it makes for a really entertaining film. Goss, who is covered in makeup as The Reaper here, went on to become a direct-to-video action star (of sorts) with films like *Interview with a Hitman*, and the *Death Race* sequels to his credit.

Blade: Trinity
2004 (New Line DVD) (djm)

The vampire underworld's greatest foe—Blade (Wesley Snipes)—undergoes his greatest challenge when the media begins picking up on his antics as the vampires he's hunting devise a plan to set him up on live TV. He accidentally slays a human (caught on video!), and all of a sudden, he's public enemy number one. His trusty sidekick Whistler (Kris Kristofferson) is killed (for good this time), and he's captured by the authorities. Sedated, grilled, and incarcerated, Blade seems out for the count until he's rescued by a group of young vampire hunters who call themselves The Nightstalkers. These hunters—Abigail (Jessica Biel) and Hannibal (Ryan Reynolds)—are just as equipped as Blade in terms of savvy weapons and defense mechanisms against bloodsuckers *and* they're more into it than he is, which makes them a valuable asset and ally in his daily fight against the underworld. Their newest and deadliest foe on the street is a freshly resurrected Dracula himself (played by Dominic Purcell), who towers over his minions (played by Parker Posey and wrestler Triple H).

The least satisfying of the *Blade* films starring Snipes, *Trinity* wallows in exposition, dialogue, and build up, and when the action comes in fits and spurts, the film sputters to life only to halt again when the uninteresting story kicks back into gear. Snipes, who produced, looks bored this time around, and his younger co-stars steal his thunder. Purcell, who plays Dracula, is a huge disappointment, and when he manifests himself as a giant monster, it's impossible not to be underwhelmed. The first two *Blade* movies gave Snipes some of the best films of his career, but *Trinity* manages to be one of his worst theatrical efforts thanks to lackluster scripting and direction by David S. Goyer. This was one of Snipes' last theatrical releases before starring in a string of direct-to-video pictures. His next big theatrical release was the drama *Brooklyn's Finest* in 2009.

Blade Warrior
2000 (Pathfinder DVD) (djm)

A cop named Jack quits his job after he realizes there's really nothing he can do on the law's side that will protect the streets from vile criminals who are filtered through a corrupt or lenient justice system. Jack (played by Jino Kang, who also wrote, produced, and directed) goes back to his roots as a hapkido martial arts instructor, and he waits and prepares for the day when the last man he sent to prison is released on early parole. That man is Blades, a martial artist in his

own right who, when released a few years later, goes and calls on some of his allies to hunt Jack and his ex-partner down. When they kidnap and torture Jack's ex-partner and boyhood friend, Jack is finally vindicated to unleash all hell on the guys the system allowed to go free.

Blade Warrior and its unassuming star Jino Kang personify exactly what this book is all about. He follows in the footsteps of the greats—guys like Bruce Lee, Chuck Norris, Jeff Speakman, and Don "The Dragon" Wilson. While their movies basically exist to serve as "vehicles" for the martial artist star within them, the star emerges as the sole reason to see the film. Their unique abilities and talents shine through, and it almost seems that the star isn't really acting. What you're seeing is who they really are. Kang doesn't have a studio behind him in any way. He went out and made this movie all by himself, and it's rough around the edges, but it's a genuine document as it chronicles his abilities at the point in time when he made it, and it's actually pretty amazing. Fans of polished action movies might shrink back if they try watching *Blade Warrior*, but anyone with any sense of daring should earnestly seek it out because Jino Kang is very interesting to watch. His hapkido skills look intimidating, and as a centerpiece star he's competent in ways that other off-the-grid martial arts star-hopefuls like Britton Lee (*Ironheart*), Il Lim (*Acts of Violence*), and Gary Wasniewski (*Thunderkick*) simply aren't. It took Kang another decade to make his next movie *Fist 2 Fist*.

INTERVIEW:
JINO KANG
(djm)

Jino Kang is a rare type of action star. He's only made three movies so far, and each one is a homegrown, carefully constructed film, infused with his own personal philosophies, which showcase his impressive hapkido martial arts abilities. Born in South Korea, he immigrated to San Francisco with his parents in the 1970s, and he currently runs a hapkido school, while making movies on the side. His first film, Blade Warrior (2001), *was begun while he was still in college, and his two successive films,* Fist 2 Fist (2011) *and* Weapon of Choice (2014), *bear his distinctive, personal style.*

Jino Kang at his dojo in San Francisco, California. Photo by david j. moore.

Can you give me a little history of your background in martial arts?

I'm currently a seventh degree black belt in hapkido, of the International Hapkido Federation. I also hold a belt in Kyokushin-kai karate. I received that in the '80s. And also taekwondo. That was in the '90s. And then, just recently, I received a black belt in Gracie jiu jitsu. I was born in South Korea. My father was a master in hapkido. When I was about four, he started bringing me into his studio. That's where all the black belts came in and started training together. Of course, I was just a four year old, running around the mat. I would wake up on the mat with my gi already on. Then, I would just jump into the class, and needless to say, that was history. I started training then. We immigrated to the states in 1971. My father didn't own a martial arts school at that time, but he started teaching from home. Once I became of age in 1981, he said, "I think it's time to open up a hapkido school." We opened up a hapkido institute in California, and that was the beginning of our journey from then to now.

What led you from that point to making your first movie, *Blade Warrior*?

When you're young, you're always watching movies and when you're at that very impressionable age when Bruce Lee hit the screen, I was just enamored with the guy's demeanor and his moves and his charisma. I was interested in it. In 1986, maybe, there was a big tournament from Leo Fong and Ron Marchini, and they said that they had a part in a movie that was available, and I won the part. Once I became a part of the production, I played the part of an FBI agent named Joshua. I had never done any acting before, but I was supposed to showcase what I knew with hapkido. Then, I watched the production and saw how things worked. I thought, *I know I can do this,* but I also thought that I'd better go to school and learn it. I went to college for three years, and they had a great film department. I learned how to make a movie and write a script. I then shot the first ten minutes of *Blade Warrior,* the scene in the grocery store. I shot that while I was attending college. A year after that, I finished the film. We shot every weekend, just about. It took us another year to edit. It was all shot on 16mm film. It was the mid-'90s. By the time we were finished, we switched to digital because that's the way things were going. It took four years altogether. I call it my experimental learning film. We had a lot of fun with it. Ever since then, I was hooked. A distributor picked it up right way.

What was the name of the movie you did with Marchini and Leo Fong?

Ah! It was called *Weapon of Choice*, which is what I ended up calling my newest film.

What happened to that movie?

I don't think they ever finished it, or if they did, it never got distributed. According to Leo Fong. I never got a copy of it.

Jino Kang stars as assassin Jack Lee in *Fist 2 Fist 2: Weapon of Choice*. Courtesy of Jino Kang.

I became familiar with you after *Fist 2 Fist* got picked up by Blockbuster Video and Hollywood Video. It was everywhere. When I got a copy of the movie, I decided to find your first movie *Blade Warrior* and watch that. When I saw it, I was blown away by it. Then, I watched *Fist 2 Fist*. I really, really like *Blade Warrior*. It's a raw little movie, but it's a great showcase for you—whoever you were, I had no idea who you were. I thought, *Whoa, this guy's cool.* That movie is what my whole book is about. You guys are not actors. You're martial artists, you're the real thing. This is who you are.

Thank you so much.

You're welcome. It's a really cool little movie. I want people to see this movie. Talk about making it. Talk about your philosophy a little bit, and how you were able to incorporate your martial arts into it.

My goal was to incorporate martial arts and the book *The Art of War* into it—as best as I could. If a martial artist were faced with a dilemma, how would he handle the situation? Hapkido is a blend of martial arts; it's very eclectic. We had kicks, strikes, weapons, swords, and so on, and it was easier to be more diverse.

Both *Blade Warrior* and *Fist 2 Fist* are very introspective. They're inward movies. This has to be coming from you. They feel personal.

Yeah, they're my own way of telling the stories. They're about how a person can change. When you're in a situation and someone's coming at you directly, you need to bend and redirect in that conflict. That's what I wanted to show in the films. I also watched a lot of martial arts movies, and I don't know why, but a lot of these movies don't think about the plot—they only think about the action. There are only a few really good ones out there that do that. I think anybody can do action, but being able to tell a good story and being able to tell the story that you want . . . and these are all fiction, just so you know . . . the second one, *Fist 2 Fist*, was a personal experience I went through about ten years ago. I incorporated some of my personal life into that film.

What happened in the interim between *Blade Warrior* and *Fist 2 Fist*? There was a long gap between films, and even between *Fist 2 Fist* and your latest one *Weapon of Choice*.

Katherine Celio and Jino Kang star in Kang's *Fist 2 Fist 2: Weapon of Choice*. Courtesy of Jino Kang.

(Laughing.) It's a money issue. It takes forever to finance a movie. Also, in the meantime, I also run a school. It's my bread and butter. I have a very successful martial arts school, so my focus is divided into many things: Martial arts, family, film, and so on. I would like to focus on one thing, but I like them all.

It's an uphill battle making and releasing martial arts action movies these days. That's why I like your movies so much—you're doing them because you love doing them, not so much to make money from them or trying to become a movie star.

Right, right. You're absolutely right. I'm not here to make a quick buck. I'm not working for someone else, making the movie that they want. I want to make the movie the way I want to, and I want to be good at it. It's very tough to put a movie together. I'm in front of the camera and also behind it. Some of the storylines, I have to collaborate with other writers, and I don't mind doing that. Making it personal is the way to go.

Blazing Force

1996 (Wildcat VHS) (djm)

A supernatural entity has taken on human form and walks through Los Angeles, preying on the derelict, stealing their life force. Two buddy cops—Richard Blaze (Tyrone Wade) and Gary Nicholson (James Gordon)—are on a routine call to a hotel where a woman is soliciting herself to customers when they run afoul of Greko, the otherworldly killer. Greko (played by Paul Logan, a Hollywood stuntman and a black belt in Goju-Ryu karate) has a one-track mind—survival—and when the two cops catch him in the act of slaying the hooker for her life force,

he flees, leading to a foot chase throughout LA. When the cops catch up to him, he manages to kill Gary and escape, leaving Blaze behind in a rage. Blaze has been going though some trauma recently: We see an extended flashback (it's kinda random and bizarre) that harkens back to when he had a wife. They're in a forest and they're harassed by some rednecks who threaten to kill them with their bows and arrows. Martial artist Blaze manages to protect her for a while as they're hunted through the landscape, but when his wife is slain, he goes ballistic and loses a bit of his sanity. Flash-forward to him hunting Greko on the streets of LA, and he's a deadly foe to the killer. Lots of martial arts confrontations and strong-looking guys doing katas in the sunset fill the running time.

Filmed on the fly without much of a budget (and probably without permits too), *Blazing Force* is an amateur hour actioner, but it should be commended for trying to incorporate as much genuine fighting in the film as it could contain, and for using Paul Logan (who would go on to star in low-budget action films like *Ballistica*) at an early stage of his career in a film. Most viewers will write this off as garbage, but it's worth watching for two reasons: To see Paul Logan, and to see what kind of fight film you can do without any money. I don't think a single shot is fired in the film, which is funny considering that all the cops had to do was shoot the bad guy instead of spending ten minutes running after him. Directed by Mark J. Gordon.

Blind Fury

1989 (Sony DVD) (djm)

Casino Boss: "If you can't handle it, get me somebody that can! Get me Bruce Lee!"
Henchman: "Bruce Lee is dead."
Casino Boss: "Then get his brother!"

If Rutger Hauer were an action star, then *Blind Fury* would be one of his very best vehicle films, but since he's not, *Blind Fury* would be an anomaly for this book if Sho Kosugi did not have an important cameo appearance in it. Kosugi, the foremost actor/action star from the 1980s who starred in a slew of ninja-themed movies, shows up at the very end of the movie in a ninja-type role. Hauer plays a Vietnam veteran named Nick Parker, who, after being severely wounded and blinded in Vietnam, is nursed back to health by a peaceful village and a nameless patron who trains him to use his senses to protect himself and to use a samurai sword. Twenty years after his injury, Nick is a good-hearted vagabond who walks on foot across the US to visit an old war buddy but ends up becoming the guardian of a pre-teen boy whose mother was killed. Nick accompanies the boy (on foot, by car, and by bus) to Reno, where his father is being held captive by a casino boss using him to manufacture drugs. Along the way, Nick and the boy encounter bad guys who are trying to kidnap the boy to use him as leverage against his enslaved father, but everyone around Nick is shocked to find that he's a formidable sword fighter. The final stage of their quest has Nick faced with an assassin (Kosugi who comes in with complete force).

An Americanized retelling of the Japanese film series *Zatoichi: The Blind Swordsman*, *Blind Fury* is a great little action picture from director Phillip Noyce (*Patriot Games, Dead Calm*). If you're seeing it just because Kosugi is in it, you're seeing it for the wrong reasons and you'll be disappointed because he's only in it for a few minutes. Watch this because it's an underrated gem, and anyone who's had a passing interest in Hauer will be really smitten by him in the film. It's pretty fantastic. Kosugi completists should see it in that case.

Blind Rage

1978 (VideoAsia DVD) (djm)

"Blind?! Now I know you're nuts! How can blind guys rob a bank? Now I've heard everything!"

The United States is sending fifteen million dollars to a bank in the Philippines for relief purposes, and the president of the bank is approached by a mysterious man who offers him a once-in-a-lifetime opportunity. The offer is this: Turn the other cheek when five men heist the fifteen million. But there's a catch: All five men are blind! The president of the bank thinks the plan is crazy, but he agrees anyway. The five blind men are recruited from different corners of the world, and each one of them has particular skills that are essential to pulling off a bank heist. One of them (played by Leo Fong, who also wrote the film) is a martial arts expert, and all five of them are put through a rigorous training regimen to prepare for the heist. When the day is finally upon them, they perform the job (with several glitches; they kill a few innocents) and then flee to Los Angeles where they are supposed to meet up to divide the score. Interpol contacts private eye Jesse Crowder (Fred Williamson, reprising his role from several other films, including *Death Journey*) to help them apprehend the robbers and recover the money. Crowder steps up and stops the suspects from escaping.

Reportedly, this was written in less than a week, and you can believe it. The story is just completely bonkers. Leo Fong (later in *Low Blow*) has some great little moments in the film, but putting Fred Williamson in it at the last ten minutes is just so bizarre that it makes you think they weren't able to sell the movie without tacking on a few extra minutes at the end where Williamson has a fight scene. It's just crazy. And it's even stranger that he is reprising a role he played several times before. He played Jesse Crowder in *No Way Back* (1976), *Death Journey* (1976), and then later again in *The Last Fight* (1983). His footage in *Blind Rage* is not stock footage, so if you're a Williamson completist, just be warned that he doesn't show up until the last ten minutes of this movie, but it's almost worth the wait. Directed by Efren.

Blitz

2011 (Millennium DVD) (CD)

"A word of advice, girls. If you're picking the wrong fight . . . at least pick the right weapon."

"The Blitz" is a serial killer stalking the streets of London, trying to kill off the police force one by one. Detective Tom Brant (Jason Statham) is given the difficult task of trying to find him. Every time Brant starts to make progress, the killer slips through his fingers. He partners up with his newly appointed superior Nash (Paddy Considine) who serves as his voice of reason, able to reel him in if he gets too reckless. "The Blitz" has no remorse and as their friends and coworkers are losing (or close to losing) their lives, the line between what is wrong or right quickly becomes blurred.

Aside from having a rock solid cast, *Blitz* is incredibly disappointing. It's a good-enough police thriller with a fun soundtrack, but it was marketed more as an action film, which was a huge mistake. As a thriller, the story has a few interesting twists, but it offers very few surprises. It does, have some really great characters, but the story they were born into is pretty dull. Statham (*Parker*) plays the tough cop who rarely plays by the rules. It's nice to see him in a straight-up acting role since audiences may sometimes forget that he is really good at it. Paddy Considine is excellent as his superior officer Nash who happens to be a gay man. It's rare to see the theme of homosexuality played against type and it wasn't used as a gimmick, which is refreshing. Also in the mix are Aiden Gillen (*Shanghai Knights*) and the always-outstanding David Morrissey (best known to audiences as The Governor on *The Walking Dead*). There is very little action in the film. We get to see a couple of brutal murders and a foot chase that is relatively exciting. The film opens with Statham dispatching a few hooligans, which is the only real fighting from him. *Blitz* is a decent thriller but Statham has many other films that are more satisfying than this.

The Blonde Fury

(a.k.a. **Female Reporter**)

1989 (DeltaMac DVD) (djm)

As Cynthia Rothrock's last film shot in Hong Kong (and second-to-last film under contract with Golden Harvest), *The Blonde Fury* gives her a great vehicle, and she's the main character, which was a first for her. She plays a character named Cindy (as usual), an international agent who poses as a newspaper reporter in Hong Kong to get closer to a currency counterfeiting ring. She gets herself into all sorts of great fights, and she doesn't get much help from the Hong Kong police, who shrug her off as a Caucasian Westerner female who isn't a threat. They're all wrong. A fight highlight involves her going head

to head with a fighter who greatly underestimates her, and he ends up getting a puncture in the leg from her high heels! Great fight.

As per custom with all of the films Rothrock did in Hong Kong, *The Blonde Fury* has a wafer-thin plot that relies on its impressive fight scenes to stay afloat. It's easy to forget what the stories are about, and most of the films blend together, but Rothrock herself is an alluring presence and every time she's on screen the movie becomes interesting again. *The Blonde Fury* isn't a classic, but if you're into Rothrock, you'll greatly enjoy her screen time in it. Directed by Hoi Mang.

Blood Alley (a.k.a. **True Justice: Blood Alley**)

2012 (Studiocanal DVD R2) (djm)

"Now, I'm six feet, five inches, you must be at least seven feet, huh? Yeah. I really don't wanna make you look bad in front of your boys, I don't, so what I'm gonna do is—rather than knocking you out with one punch, I'm gonna knock you out in three—that way, I'll make you look good."

Now that Elijah Kane (Steven Seagal) is no longer a task-force officer with the police department but is working with the government and with a mostly new team, he's free to more or less perform justice as he sees fit, which allows him to unleash his rage a little more freely and with more style. His latest case involves human trafficking, and once he digs deep into the matter, he finds that it's not just trafficking, but black market organ transplanting. But seriously: Once he gets to the top guys in the ring, he lets loose and kills some dudes without thinking twice about it.

This is the eighth movie compilation from Seagal's *True Justice* TV series, and it's one of the good ones because it's not bogged down by an episodic structure. It more or less feels like one of his (better) direct-to-DVD movies, and it could easily be watched out of sequence from the rest of the series. Still, it's not incredibly memorable, aside from a few brutal hand-to-hand confrontations he has with some thugs. Directed by Wayne Rose, who did other entries in the series. Followed by *Violence of Action*.

Blood and Bone

2009 (Sony DVD) (djm)

"I need you to deliver a message: I want you to tell every motherfucker behind these walls, that if they get the notion to fuck with me—don't."

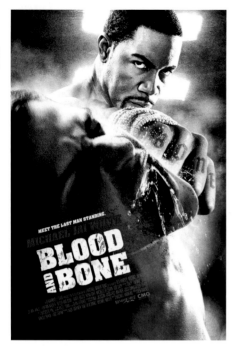

Video release artwork for *Blood and Bone*.
Courtesy of Matt Mullins.

Perhaps the most incredible direct-to-video movie ever made, *Blood and Bone* stars Michael Jai White as a mysterious Ronin-like character known as Bone. Fresh out of prison, he sets up camp in an inner city in a house run by a motherly woman who takes care of orphans. He ventures out into the night, immediately setting his sights on the fight circuit, where he astonishes crowds with his unbelievable martial arts capabilities and aptitude at winning fights with sometimes a single kick or punch. He catches the eye of a rising criminal overlord named James (Eamonn Walker), who rules over a small empire of crime and degradation. As Bone rises to the top of the underground fight circuit, his "manager," Pinball (Dante Basco), sets up a fight with James's top fighter, whom Bone takes down with little to no effort. Furious with the loss, James offers Bone a chance to fight in a much bigger league for a lot more money. As a way of sweetening the deal, James "gives" him a woman, a strung-out beauty who seems to be the object of Bone's attention. This gives Bone leverage in his plan to get some kind of secret revenge on James, who, as it turns out, had Bone's best friend murdered in prison so that he could get to the man's wife, now in Bone's care. Sweet revenge is Bone's plan, and hot damn, he gets it good.

Michael Jai White is, quite simply, the *best* in this movie. He's basically playing a samurai, a quiet, formidable, and unstoppable hero, and he has layers upon layers of coolness and calm that he reveals every time he's on screen. His fighting abilities are varied and astoundingly impressive, and each time he engages in a confrontation, the camera and choreography convincingly capture the minutia of the fights. Director Ben Ramsey (*Love and a Bullet*) and screenwriter Michael Andrews transform the urban streetfighting movie into an almost mythical adventure with spiritual and martial arts undertones. Discover it, and you'll be a Michael Jai White fan forever. Also with Matt Mullins (*Bloodfist 2050*), Kevin "Kimbo Slice" Ferguson, and Gina Carano (*Haywire*).

Director Ben Ramsey in Los Angeles, California.
Photo by david j. moore.

INTERVIEW:

BEN RAMSEY

(djm)

When Blood and Bone *premiered on DVD in 2009, it received little push or promotion from its distributor, Sony Pictures. Starring Michael Jai White* (Undisputed II, Universal Soldier: The Return) *in an amazingly physical performance that showcases his extraordinary martial arts prowess, and featuring cameos by Matt Mullins* (Bloodfist 2050, Kamen Rider: Dragon Knight) *and Gina Carano* (Haywire, Furious 6), Blood and Bone *has garnered an impressive reputation as a real-deal martial arts film that continues to amass a body of fans hungering for a sequel. The film's co-writer and director, Ben Ramsey, has spent years working as a freelance script doctor and screenwriter for such films as* The Big Hit *and* Dragonball, *and his first film as a director,* Love and a Bullet, *set him on the path that would eventually lead him to helming* Blood and Bone.

As far as I'm concerned, *Blood and Bone* is a near-perfect movie. I don't know what could have made it better.

More money, more time.

I think if you'd shot it on film, it might have *looked* a little better, but other than that, it's great. What has been the reaction of this movie over time from the martial arts community and from the world of film and direct-to-video movies?

It's been a very positive reaction. Out of everything I've put out as a writer, *Blood and Bone* has been my biggest hit. Financially, my biggest hit was *The Big Hit*. *Blood and Bone* is hands-down the one I get noticed for. In social settings on Facebook, not a day goes by—almost every single day—somebody from somewhere has something to say about it. "When is *Blood and Bone 2* coming out?" They are demanding *Blood and Bone 2*, and I'm like, "Hey, don't tell me—go tell Sony Pictures." Flood them with e-mails. I have an old script that I tried to get Michael Jai White attached to a long time ago that would be perfect and tailor-made for *Blood and Bone 2*. If they want to go that route, we've already got a script ready. It's been a fantastic response, and just listening to what you've said . . . some people have put it in their top ten martial arts films of all time.

I look at this movie like Michael Jai White's character. It came out of nowhere. When I first saw it years ago, I was blown away by how inauspicious it seemed to be. Where did this movie come from? Who is Ben Ramsey, and why hadn't I heard of you before? I want to know how you were able to make such an incredible movie. You're the secret ingredient of this movie.

Well, it was a combination of everybody. No feature film is a one-man show. It's always a collaborative effort. This movie came to be with me and Mike. I've been friends with Mike for a long time. We always talked about doing something together. He had this script called *Blood and Bone* written by Michael Andrews. Somehow or another, we got somebody that wanted to put the money up. The idea was that we wanted to do a martial arts movie for Mike that was old school, a throwback to what we liked in martial arts movies. No fast cutting. Something that really displayed the talents of the characters. I wanted to do a showpiece for Mike's skills. Until that point, people knew Mike more as an actor than a martial artist. They didn't really know how deep his martial arts background is. How good he is.

It's rare when a director captures the talents and abilities of their action stars in the perfect way. You were able to do that with Michael Jai White in this film.

I'd known Mike for a long time. I knew his sensibilities, and he knew mine. In creating this character, I wanted to do something that played to his sensibilities. From that point on, everything else and every aspect of the film fell into place and formed. We also made the conscious decision—and it was a controversial decision—to say, "You know what? Bone is just going to kick everybody's ass!" We're going to go back to Bruce Lee's style. Maybe somebody might be able to get a lick or a punch in, but Bruce Lee would always kick everybody's ass. From start to finish.

But Michael Jai White made me believe that he could do that. Everything about him suggested that he was untouchable.

Exactly. We wanted to portray that character in that way. I know some people said, "Well, it's boring if the guy just beats everybody up." Sometimes it is, but if you think back to when you were a kid, a child watching your heroes on screen and reading comic books, and you think about what a young boy's fantasy is. A young boy's fantasy is about being strong and about being invincible. No kid thinks about being vulnerable. A young boy wants to grow up and be invincible. There's something about an invincible character that I think touches that inner Hulk.

I'd seen Jai White in *Spawn* and *Universal Soldier: The Return*, but I hadn't really been paying attention to him until *Blood and Bone*. I often wonder why some guys become superstars and why others don't. Why isn't Michael Jai White a huge star?

I don't know. I've worked on A-list movies like *Dragonball*, and for most of my time I've been a writer—I've been working professionally since 1996. Most of that time I've been a script doctor. You can go to every studio in town and find a few of my scripts collecting dust that will never see the light of day. When you get into an A-list meeting, they're not looking at direct-to-video stars—what you would call a "B" star. It doesn't matter if you put him in front of them and say, "Look at this guy! You mean to tell me that people wouldn't want to go to a movie theater and see this guy whuppin' ass?" They have a formula. They have an actor's name, and they have dollars and figures. They have lists in every category, they have foreign numbers. They have a DTV category. It's hard to get a DTV star into the feature world. It's all very systematic.

I remember when *Blood and Bone* was released to video, Jai White had a notable theatrical release with *Black Dynamite*.

Mike was prepping *Black Dynamite* while we were shooting *Blood and Bone*. As soon as we wrapped, he went right on to the next one.

Why didn't *Blood and Bone* get a theatrical release?

Somebody down at Sony said the same thing to me. He was like, "We messed up. We should have released *Blood and Bone* theatrically." That was the plan. Somewhere along the line with their formulaic way of thinking, someone said, "This is one of *those* types of movies in this category." I just said, "Just take the movie out and *test* it! Test it!" They didn't want to spend the money. Both Mike and I were like, "Take this thing up to the Magic Johnson theater and have a screening; it will bring the house down!" We felt real confident when we were making the movie because we put in all the elements that we knew we liked, and I think that's what makes a movie successful—when a director makes the kind of movie that they like. If a director unfamiliar with romantic comedies says, "I think I'll give that a try!" That's what I call creative speculation. When you're making a movie that you like and you know that everybody you know will like, because basically I'm a fanboy and I want to make movies that I want to see . . . if I like what I'm seeing on screen, then I *know* a bunch of other people are going to like it too. The same with Mike. We *know* what the audience is going to like. If we'd had a screening, there would have been people jumping out of their seats, whooping and hollering.

It's interesting that you mentioned directors who make movies outside of their comfort zones. I'm thinking of Steven Soderbergh and his action movie *Haywire* with Gina Carano. Gina had a nice little part in *Blood and Bone*. What was it like working with her?

She was great. I gave her her first film job. She's such a sweetheart. She's such a girly girl. She's really shy.

How did you pitch it to her?

I didn't meet her until the day we shot. We just basically said, "Let's try to get as many cameos as we can." Mike knows all of them. He trains with all the fighters. There was a scene for female fighters. We said, "Let's get Gina," because at the time she was just starting to blow up. They approached her, and they were like, "Hey, we got her!" I had more lines for her, but she was like "No, no, no!"

What movies inspired you while you were making this movie?

The '70s era of martial arts movies. As much as I love Jackie Chan, it was the badasses I liked. Bruce and Sonny Chiba. *Enter the Dragon.* The blaxploitation movies.

Do you consider *Blood and Bone* to be a blaxploitation movie?

Yeah, I consider it a neo-blaxploitation movie. In the sense where *Black Dynamite* was a parody of blaxploitation movies, *Blood and Bone* is a neo-blaxploitation movie. Although it's not about black culture. It has a black male lead in it. There is that one scene in it where Eamonn Walker and Julian Sands talk about race. That, to me, was there because there was a lull between fights, and I thought we should have a verbal sparring match.

Has Michael approached you to work with him again?

Yeah, there are a couple of scripts we're talking about. There's this one called *Rider*, which could possibly be another *Blood and Bone 2* or it could be a dual lead thing with him and Wesley Snipes.

I like that Michael started directing his own movies like *Never Back Down 2*. He'll go do a Tyler Perry movie or *The Dark Knight*, and then he'll go out to shoot *Favela* with Ernie Barbarash. I really like that he'll do one for the prestige, and he'll do one because that's the sort of movie he really wants to be doing.

The people who watch Tyler Perry movies don't realize that Mike started out as a martial artist and a bodyguard and a fighter. He started his life out as a badass. When he got into acting, he kind of put that aside and people only saw him as an actor until they saw him in *Tyson* and saw that he handled himself really well in that. They didn't realize that he was a highly trained martial artist. He's been very smart in how he's handled his career. His love of acting and martial arts is equal, but I think deep down, he really loves martial arts.

There was a time not that long ago when Jeff Speakman and Steven Seagal were making movies that actually were released in theaters. Guys like Dolph Lundgren and Van Damme were huge. That era has passed, and the direct-to-video market has sort of swallowed those guys up. Do you think the era of the action star has passed? Is *Blood and Bone* a last gasp of a dying era?

No, I don't think so. I think it's just in a lull, or about to transition into something else. Right now we're in the special effects stage. Big movies are all about special effects and gimmicks. It's going to get old. I can play my videogames on my big TV and get the exact same experience. Big, digital things going on. Somewhere along the line, people are going to want to connect with something on screen in a more realistic and visceral way. I haven't seen *Fast and Furious 6* yet, but I've been hearing about the fights scenes between Gina Carano and Michelle Rodriguez. I know they've got multimillion-dollar stunts and car crashes and all that, but I keep hearing about the ultimate catfight between two badass chicks, which tells me that people want to see something more real and closer to home. You can blow the hell out of things and have space battles, but at the end of the day, at the end of a great big action movie, it all comes down to a man-to-man fight between the good guy and the bad guy. That's about as personal as you can get. Eventually, it'll make its way back. I talk all the time with my stunt friends and stunt coordinators about the fight scenes in big budget movies and how they suck to high hell. They're lame. The shaky cam thing. They're using actors, and you can't do long takes because the cracks in their skill or form show. In the DTV world, you've got Scott Adkins and Mike, and Gary Daniels. And Matt Mullins.

Yeah, talk a little bit about Matt. He's one of the few action guys I'm really paying attention to these days.

The thing about Matt on *Blood and Bone* is that he came in to just work with Mike. We were originally going to go with Marko Zaror, the Latin Dragon, but he was doing something else. Matt was just training with Mike, and so we were like, "So, who are we going to get for [the character] Price? Well, let's use Matt!" On the page, Price is a vicious beast of a man. Matt is kinda good looking, so I did a quick rewrite and we called him Pretty Boy Price. We changed that, and we changed his style. I said, "You're arrogant, you're flamboyant." I told him to watch Prince Naseem, to get that going. It worked out fantastic. He was a better choice than Zaror. It was a blessing in disguise. He was right in front of us. Just think if you could put all these guys in a big-budget $200 million action movie. Aw, man!

Well, what do you think about *The Expendables* movies?

I like *The Expendables*. They should put Mike in one, but I think they're scared to put him in it. He'd blow everybody away. They'd have to water him down a bit. They had Scott Adkins in one, but he played second fiddle to Van Damme—who did a great job! I loved Van Damme in that. He's mellowing with age. He's aging like a fine wine.

What are you working on now?

I'm working on a project with Rick Yune.

Oh, really? I liked his movie *The Fifth Commandment*.

That was a project I had originally written.

What? Seriously?

(Laughing.) Yeah, there were creative difficulties. I let them have it and do what they wanted with it. I was supposed to direct that. That was when I met Rick. I also have two independent projects that I'm trying to get going on my own. Like I did with *Love and Bullet*, which was written, produced, and directed by me. I funded that out of my own pocket. I'm looking to do the same thing with a project called *Night Angel*. I just shot a teaser trailer and we're going to put it up on Kickstarter. It's a black/Latina version of *The Crow*. My other pet project, which I've been working on for a long time, is called *The Ministry*. It's hard to describe. I can't give it a couple sentence logline.

Is there anything else you'd like to say about *Blood and Bone*?

Just that I'm really blown away by the fan response to the movie. I always equate filmmaking with being a chef. You pour your heart into cooking something up that you think is delicious. Mm, this is good. You put it out there and serve it up to the people, and it's like getting constant compliments to the chef. It's a good feeling. I like that people are enjoying it.

Blood Chase

1989 (NOV) (djm)

An armored car is robbed by a gang of thieves, and years later policewoman Cheryl (Karen Sheperd from *The Shinobi Ninja*) begins to investigate that particular case because her father was one of the thieves and is presumed dead. Cheryl's cop boyfriend John (Andrew Stevens) helps her out in her investigation, but just when they're ready to lay the whole thing to rest, her father's old gang comes after her because they think that her father might have given her the millions they stole before he was killed. Cheryl and John are forced to fight off one wave of thugs after another over the course of a few days, and to survive, they have to turn the tables and hunt whoever's giving the orders instead of just waiting around to be hunted.

Fans of Karen Sheperd (who later appeared in *Eliminator Woman*) should take special notice, as this movie gives her one fight scene after another. *Blood Chase* was shot very cheaply and swiftly in the Philippines from Teddy Page, the same director as *Blood Ring* and *Fist of Steel* with Dale "Apollo" Cook, so if you've seen those or similar types of films made during the era, then you know exactly what you're going to be getting when you sit down to watch it. It's full of crazy action scenes, gunfire galore, kicking, punching, explosions, and a plot that honestly doesn't matter. It's all about seeing Karen Sheperd (who once upon a time beat Cynthia Rothrock in their competition days) in action, and if you care about Andrew Stevens in action too, then you're all set to go.

Bloodfight

1989 (Imperial VHS) (djm)

A former martial arts champion named Kai (Yasuaki Kurata) lives with some regret, and his wife divorces him because she can no longer relate to him. He goes out every day, scouring the streets to find an apprentice. He first attempts to train a hoodlum, who turns out to be a dishonorable jackass, and so then returns his attentions to a young man (played by Simon Yam) who literally refuses any sort of formal training . . . until he's severely beat up and mugged. When he goes to Kai to be trained, Kai grooms him to enter in a deadly "bloodfight" against some of the world's most ruthless fighters—mainly Chang Lee, "The Vietnamese Cobra" (played by Bolo Yeung, virtually reprising his role from *Bloodsport*). When Kai's apprentice is brutally murdered in the ring (it's a pretty shocking scene) Kai spends the next year training himself in earnest to go up against Lee to regain honor and to avenge the death of his pupil.

Filmed entirely in English, but with a predominantly Asian cast who struggle with the language, *Bloodfight* is an undeniable copy of *Bloodsport*, but its few deviations from that film are what make it cool and kinda radical. Bolo's portrayal of the villain is as one-dimensional as most of the characters he played throughout his career, but there's a certain beauty to that. You always know exactly what you're going to get with Bolo. Directed by Shuji Goto.

Bloodfist

1989 (New Concorde DVD) (djm)

Don "The Dragon" Wilson's first starring vehicle, *Bloodfist*, propelled him into direct-to-video stardom. He stars as Jake Ray, a kickboxing champion whose brother is killed in the Philippines. Jake goes to claim his ashes and get revenge. While there, he is approached by his brother's trainer, and Jake trains to go undercover in the same underground arena where his brother fought for cash. In the meanwhile, he falls for a stripper and befriends her brother, also a fighter. By the end, Jake realizes that he's been deceived all along: His brother was murdered by his trainer over a money dispute.

Turkish lobby card for *Bloodfist,* featuring Don "The Dragon" Wilson kicking near a stripper. Author's collection.

Simple, yet effective, this Roger Corman-produced vehicle gives Wilson the opportunity to show his stuff, while keeping it all grounded in a realistic-type setting. It's good that Corman didn't stick him in a futuristic setting his first time out. We see Wilson's moves in fully-lit scenes and the editing allows you to see just about everything you need to see. Some fight scenes were sped up in post-production (not sure why), which is annoying, but Wilson gives a confidant performance regardless. Billy Blanks plays one of the other fighters, but he didn't have any lines. There were nine *Bloodfist* films; Wilson was in the first eight, though only parts 1 and 2 are related. This was remade several times by Corman's company. If this isn't enough for you, see *Full Contact* with Jerry Trimble, or *Dragon Fire* with Dominick LaBanca. Terence Winkless directed *Bloodfist*. He later did *Rage and Honor* with Cynthia Rothrock and Richard Norton.

Bloodfist II

1990 (New Concorde DVD) (djm)

Jake Ray (Don Wilson) kills a guy in the ring and vows to never fight again. He goes off the grid, living a life of pleasure, when he gets a call from an old friend. His friend needs his help in Manila, so Ray goes but finds that his friend has betrayed him. Ray is captured, taken to a secret island, and forced to train to fight in illegal to-the-death matches. He's not the only famous fighter who's in the same situation: He's surrounded by guys from around the world who were duped and captured for their fighting talents. Ray tries escaping, but he's captured again and, finally, when the time comes, he's put to work as a fighter and begins winning fights. Like gladiators, the fighters do-or-die in the ring, and Ray has to take advantage of the little freedom he has to devise an escape.

This not-bad sequel is more of the same, but with even more action and fighting than in the first film. Wilson's role isn't complicated, and his acting style is about as natural as you could ask for. There's less of a love interest this time around, and the focus is on the fighting. Wilson did *Ring of Fire* next. Directed by Andy Blumenthal.

Bloodfist III: Forced to Fight

1992 (New Concorde DVD) (djm)

Jimmy Boland (Don Wilson) is in prison for a crime that he didn't commit. Being half-Asian, he's immediately singled out by the blacks and the whites because he doesn't fit in. He kills a black prisoner for raping his friend (also black), and this puts Jimmy in a tough spot. The blacks want to kill him, and the whites want to include him in their cliques, but he doesn't want to side with either group. His cellmate is a peacemaking, book-reading guru of sorts named Samuel Stark (Richard Roundtree), and once they get to know each other, Stark takes a liking to him. This enrages the blacks even more, and a war begins within the prison walls. Fortunately, the media is visiting the prison on the very day a massive riot starts, and Jimmy manages to prove his innocence, while also proving the guilt of others for several crimes that have occurred in the prison.

Live by the Fist, with Jerry Trimble, tells the exact same story. It doesn't matter which film you see first, or if you only decide to see one, because both of them are pretty good action films. Wilson gives a solid performance here and he looks stronger and in better shape that in his previous films. Oley Sassoon (*Fast Getaway 2*) was the director.

Bloodfist IV: Die Trying

1992 (New Concorde DVD)

(djm)

Repo man Danny Holt (Don Wilson) repos the wrong car one day, and his life is turned upside down from that point on. The car contains a package inside (hidden in a box of chocolates) that some international criminals desperately want. They send in their best man, Scarface (Gary Daniels with long, blond hair), to retrieve the package from Holt's employer, a repo agency. Scarface and a few other baddies kill everyone on the work site, and when Danny comes back to work, he's shocked to find everyone he knows dead *and* his daughter's been kidnapped. The CIA and the FBI enter the picture (the missing package contains a trigger device for nuclear weapons), and Danny quickly learns to trust no one and find his daughter on his own.

If this had been given a slightly bigger budget, it might have been a fun theatrical venture for Wilson as a stand-alone entity (not associated with the *Bloodfist* series). It's entertaining all the way through, and Wilson has a good villain (played by Daniels) to work against. They have several fight scenes, which shouldn't disappoint their fans. "Judo" Gene LeBell has one scene at the beginning as a disgruntled man who has his car repossessed. Cat Sassoon (*Angel Fist, Bloodfist VI*) plays a villain. Amanda Wyss co-stars, and James Tolkan from *Top Gun* has a cameo. Directed by Paul Ziller, who made *Moving Target* with Wilson and *Back in Action* with Roddy Piper and Billy Blanks.

Bloodfist V: Human Target

1994 (New Concorde DVD)

(djm)

Don Wilson stars as an amnesiac federal agent, who is led to believe that he's an international arms dealer. There are men after him, and he goes on the run with a hooker, who is drawn into his unbelievable story (as he learns it as he goes). When he finds out that he's actually working for the FBI, things get even harder for him when his fellow agents (led by Steve James) turn against him. Even the hooker (played by Denice Duff) isn't who he thought she was (she's an agent too!), and he's got to figure things out before he gets himself killed.

Not quite as good as the entries that came before it in the *Bloodfist* series, *Human Target* is still a lot more entertaining and action-packed than a casual Don Wilson fan might expect. Some of the plot developments are preposterous and needlessly complicated for such a low-budget picture, but you just have to roll with it. It definitely feels like a cheap Roger Corman movie. Having Steve James as the villain helps. Future convicted murderer/martial artist Joe Son (*Shootfighter 2*) appears as a villain. Directed by Jeff Yonis.

Bloodfist VI: Ground Zero

1994 (New Concorde DVD)

(djm)

Military courier Nick Corrigan (Don Wilson) delivers a package to a nuclear silo, stumbling upon a terrorist takeover of the silo. An Islamic extremist and his men are bent on launching missiles on American cities, but they need the code keys, which is where Corrigan comes in. He begins killing them off one by one in hallways, and then he's captured, tortured, and tested, but when he breaks his bonds, he saves the day.

Entertaining if you allow it to be, *Ground Zero* really has no business being called *Bloodfist*, but that aside, it's about as fun as the filmmakers intended. Wilson's kickboxing action is on full display, and there's plenty of gunfire and yelling to wake up even the most bored viewer. Cat Sassoon (from *Bloodfist IV*) makes an appearance as a villain. She has a nude scene in the first moments of the film. Rick Jacobson (*Full Contact, Dragon Fire*) directs.

Bloodfist VII: Manhunt

1995 (New Concorde DVD)

(djm)

While on the run from the law, Jim Trudell (Don Wilson) picks up a woman named Stephanie (Jillian McWhirter from *Stranglehold*) who is also on the run. They spend the night together, and when he wakes up in the morning, she's gone and has left a storm of problems on his lap. He is chased by men who think he knows where Stephanie is, but the truth is that he doesn't know anything. He has to keep running and killing in self-defense until he can get to the bottom of who Stephanie is and why people want her dead. When Stephanie comes back into the picture at the end, Jim forgives her for causing him all of the trouble he had to go through. It ends with them laughing together.

The weakest entry in the *Bloodfist* franchise, *Manhunt* feels the most rushed, the cheapest, and the least involving of the bunch. Wilson

is adequate in a boring role, and the action is rushed. The director, Jonathan Winfrey, later made *Excessive Force II: Force on Force* with Stacie Randall.

Bloodfist VIII: Hard Way Out

(a.k.a. **Trained to Kill**)

1995 (New Concorde DVD)

(djm)

School teacher Rick Cowan (Don Wilson) goes home with his teenage son one day after work and finds a bunch of assassins waiting to kill him. In short order, Cowan kills all of them, and he admits to his son that his past as a CIA agent has caught up with him. He flees with his son to Ireland where more mayhem and action greets him with open arms. He has a hard time getting locals to warm up to him ("I hate Yanks!"), and he simply has to fight alongside his clueless son to keep them both alive. The climax is on a ferryboat.

For whatever reason, this last entry in the *Bloodfist* series takes place and was shot entirely on location in Ireland, which sounds nice, but not much is made of the scenery or the culture. It's nice to see Wilson in Ireland, but the plot isn't really interesting. He reteamed with director Rick Jacobson, whom he'd worked with on *Blackbelt, Ring of Fire,* and *Bloodfist VI*. It co-stars Jillian McWhirter, who was also in *Bloodfist VII*. Wilson returned to Ireland to film the superior film *Moving Target*.

Bloodfist 2050

2005 (New Concorde DVD)

(CD)

In the future, Los Angeles has become a filthy and brutal place. Alex Danko (Matt Mullins) heads there to see his brother Johnny (James Gregory Paolleli). Johnny's friend Randy (Glenn Meadows) and girlfriend Nadia (Beverly Lynn) inform him that he had been murdered. The only way for him to uncover the truth is to immerse himself into the fight circuit known as "the Pit." With the help of Detective Marino (Joe Sabatino) and Nadia, he will fight with every ounce of his being to destroy whoever his opponent may be. Whether he is attacked by groups of thugs on the streets or one on one in the ring, they will know that Alex Danko is a force that can't be stopped.

Cirio H. Santiago strikes again with *Bloodfist 2050*, a film we have seen before (actually the fourth time since it was a remake of *Dragon Fire* (1993) and *Full Contact* (1993), which were remakes of the original *Bloodfist* (1989). Matt Mullins was a five-time martial arts champion before starring in the film. He is without question the highlight of the film and the action scenes were surprisingly well done. Each fight shows off just how skillful Mullins is and there is plenty of action. He carries his weight with the best of them. The film runs seventy-eight minutes long and the fight scenes comprise half of the runtime. The other half of the film has a few dialogue scenes and the rest are striptease scenes. Even when there's dialogue being spoken there are cutaways to the topless extras. Jim Wynorski directed the scenes with nudity. The film is perfect for someone with a short attention span. The rest of the cast was passable but the other fighters, most notably Chris Brewster and Monsour del Rosario, had their moments as well. The music is forgettable and the post-apocalyptic sets are barely passable.

Blood For Blood
(a.k.a. **Midnight Man**)
1994 (Avid VHS) (djm)

Officer John Kang (Lorenzo Lamas) has a low-stress job at a youth center, but he's asked to join a murder investigation because he is bilingual in Khmer, the Cambodia language. A Cambodian blood feud is going on in the streets, and certain policemen are targeted for death. The hitman (James Lew) assigned to carry out the killings is a lethal weapon, and when he encounters Kang, it's like hitting a brick wall. It turns out that Kang is a sleeper warrior, the last in a line of secret warriors meant to uphold balance in the world and keep evil from taking over in the world. When Kang "awakens," he is able to fully realize his potential as a fighter and protector.

Not-bad as far as this type of movie goes, Lamas plays it extra-nice throughout, and his scenes with his wife and daughter are ultra genteel and cuddly. James Lew (*American Ninja 5, Red Sun Rising*) is a standout performer in the film, and this is only one of a few action films where he was given a full-fledged role to play

![VHS artwork for Blood for Blood showing Lorenzo Lamas, James Lew, Mako]

VHS artwork for *Blood for Blood*. Author's collection.

rather than being a day player who gets kicked around by the hero. Mako has a co-starring role as a mystic. John Weidner directed.

Blood Hands
1990 (NOV) (djm)

"Oh, God. You finally did it, didn't you? You've stained your hands with blood."

Aspiring kickboxer Steve (Sean Donahue, a stuntman-turned action star) comes home on his birthday to find that his house has been broken into and that his mom is dead and his father (also a kickboxer) has been beaten into a coma. Enraged, Steve embarks on a quest to bloody his hands in a war against the thugs who ruined his life. He trains himself into a trance and becomes a killing machine without an "off" switch, and even his trainer marvels at the transformation. Steve's girlfriend at first resists his Terminator-like metamorphosis, but then she starts to cheer him on and she too begins to feel his urge to get revenge. With some help from some other students in the local kickboxing studio, Steve is able to go all the way and find some closure in murder.

Shot in the Philippines with a very small budget, *Blood Hands* marks an early action vehicle for star Donahue, who does his own stunts and kicks plenty of dudes in the face. Not as polished or as gimmicky as some of his future films like *Parole Violators* and *Roughcut*, it does, however, have enough of what you desire from it to satisfy, and it's entertaining on the same level as any of Dale "Apollo" Cook's action/martial arts movies. In fact, this was directed by Teddy Page, who also made *Blood Ring, Fist of Steel,* and *Blood Ring 2* with Cook. Also, if you're paying attention, you'll hear cuts from the scores to *Come See the Paradise* and *Criminal Law* play on the soundtrack.

Sean Donahue stars in the kickboxing movie *Blood Hands*. Author's collection.

Blood Heat (a.k.a. **Muscle Heat**)
2002 (Tokyo Shock DVD) (djm)

Five minutes into the future (2009!) a new illegal drug is sweeping the streets. It's called "Blood Heat," and it's like an extreme steroid that zips the user into a murderous rage. An underground fighting tournament in Japan has become a venue for desperate fighters willing to die to make a buck, and most of the fighters use Blood Heat to get their rage on. A PTSD-addled US Navy SEAL named Joe (Kane Kosugi from *Revenge of the Ninja*) has drifted into a dark place in his life, and he finds himself aligned with the Yakuza, who sense that he has potential as a fighter in "The Muscle Dome," which is what they call the fight circuit. Joe goes along with it (because why not?), but when he befriends a detective who's trying to bring the Yakuza down, he realizes that he's still human and has feelings, so when the detective is murdered by the guys he's hanging with, he flips his lid and shakes the Earth with his rage.

Blood Heat goes for supercool and ultra stylish with Dutched angles and techno music, but it ends up being almost entirely hollow and vapid, despite star Kosugi's best efforts. This was sort of a coming-of-age vehicle film for young Kosugi, who had been a child action star alongside his father Sho in a bunch of ninja movies in the 1980s, so it's nice to see him as a young adult, showcasing some very impressive skills as a martial artist. That said, the movie is ugly and difficult to find engaging, with virtually emotionless characters and fight scenes that spring from a boring plot. Still, Kosugi's the whole reason to watch it, so if you're a fan, then you should see it. Directed by Ten Shimoyama.

Bloodmatch
(a.k.a. **Bloodchamp**)
1991 (VV DVD R2) (djm)

A deranged amateur kickboxer named Brick Bardo (Thom Mathews) tricks several world champions and fighters of various skills into meeting at a Las Vegas arena, where they are all promptly tied up at gunpoint and strapped to chairs. Bardo's kickboxing brother was killed during a fixed fight, but he doesn't have enough information on who might have been involved in the killing of his brother, so he has all of the fighters he suspects in front of him, and he demands that they fight him to the death. He's already kidnapped and killed the children of his kidnapped victims, so now they have an incentive to fight him back. He fights Benny "the Jet" Urquidez (best scene of the movie), and several others, including a female fighter played by former Playboy Playmate Hope Marie Carlton, who kicks his ass and kills him.

As bizarre as this movie is, it manages to be of interest for several reasons. Albert Pyun directed most of it in a single day on the same arena set where he shot *Kickboxer 2*. It's interesting to see what a guy like Pyun could do under pressure, and it manages to tell a (confusing) story while packing in as many fights as its eighty-plus minutes would allow. Mathews isn't a real-life fighter or martial artist, but Urquidez (who choreographed the fights) is amazing in his single fight scene. What's also interesting is that the main character, who normally would have been the hero, is actually a psychotic villain. It's definitely not for everyone's tastes, but fans of Pyun might find something here to talk about. Vincent Klyn (from *Cyborg*) and Michel Qissi (from *Kickboxer 2*) appear in small roles.

Blood Money (a.k.a. The Stranger and the Gunfighter)

1974 (VideoAsia DVD) (djm)

Wang Ho: "What mean, 'bottom?'"
Dakota: "Ass!"

Two men from opposite ends of the earth are out for the same thing, and so it is inevitable that their roads should intersect. Dakota (Lee Van Cleef) is a gun-for-hire who ended up in jail on his quest to find a lost treasure, and just before he is to be hung, along comes Wang Ho (Kung Fu superstar Lo Lieh), who is searching for the treasure as well. Since Dakota has some knowledge about the treasure, he helps spring Dakota out of captivity, and the two of them team up. Wang Ho reveals to Dakota that the map leading to the treasure has been tattooed on the derrières of several prostitutes in several towns throughout the West, and so the trick is to find the ladies of the night and convince them to share their posteriors long enough to read what's written on them, thus piecing together the complete map. It's a complicated process, namely because one of the prostitutes has a fanatical pimp who catches on to what they're up to, and he takes the initiative to find the treasure on his own.

An awkward mix of spaghetti western clichés and Kung Fu smash-'em-ups, *Blood Money* tries to be funny with its gimmicky premise, but instead ends up being overly silly and spoofish. Lo Lieh (an in-house star for the Shaw Brothers) plays the fish out of water as best he can with little direction, and Cleef turns in a good performance without even trying. But both men look bored with what they're doing, and so will you if you watch this. Directed by Antonio Margheriti.

Blood Money

2012 (XLrator DVD) (djm)

A quiet home video release snuck out into the world, and it pronounced a new "next Bruce Lee" star named Zheng Liu, who is purported to have trained martial arts at a Shaolin academy.

Liu, who plays a depressed (but fierce) character named Zhou in the film, doesn't play a hero in the movie, but he's the central character, which automatically makes the film halfway interesting. Zhou belongs to a Shaolin-trained triad family whose patriarchs are slain in a drug war, and Zhou's sister is kidnapped by an international cartel, which is using her as leverage with the triad. Zhou's brother—the new patriarch and head of the triad—assigns Zhou an assassination gig that takes him to Australia where the Columbian mafia is holding their sister captive. Zhou uses an uncompromising method of killing and assassination to topple the entire cartel while rescuing his sister.

Shot for what looks like millions with impressive looking hardware and locations all around the world, *Blood Money* is the sort of movie that might have gotten made once upon a time after a deal was drawn up on a hotel bar napkin at the Cannes Film festival when movies like this were made by the dozen. It's got an uneven international cast (including Hispanic rapper Pitbull), lots of action, strip bar scenes, a snappy techno score, and a brand new action star in the center who has potential to be a Jet Li-level star, but at this late stage in the action star game, I don't foresee him making too many more movies on quite the same level as *Blood Money*. Is the movie any good? Yeah, kinda. It's too long at 108 minutes, but it's well directed and it's got plenty of action and noise to keep most viewers entertained. Liu's antihero definitely has a mean streak. Some people might find that refreshing. Directed by Gregory McQualter.

Bloodmoon

1996 (Genius Products DVD) (djm)

Gary Daniels stars as a "mindhunter" named Ken O'Hara. There's a masked serial killer out there who's killing martial arts experts to prove that he's the best. The killer (Darren Shahlavi from *Ip Man 2*) happens to be in a bar one night and sees a girl (Brandi Rocci) get assaulted by some lecherous guys. As it is revealed, she's a martial arts expert and lays the guys out. She also happens to be a friend of Ken, so when the killer follows her home and decides to murder her, Ken and a tough cop (Chuck Jeffreys from *Superfights*) are there to fight the killer off. From then on, the film becomes a sort of cat and mouse chase, and there are some impressive close-contact fight scenes involving Daniels, Shahlavi, and Jeffreys.

From Tony Leung, the director of *Superfights*, this is an above-average effort. Keith Vitali, who produced the film, has a quick walk-on role as a thug on a beach who gets beat up by Daniels. Vitali was also in *Superfights*, and also starred in *No Retreat, No Surrender 3*. For a similar-themed film, see the first *Tiger Claws*. That one is also about a serial killer who kills accomplished martial artists.

Blood of Redemption

2013 (E One DVD) (djm)

A powerful mob family's patriarch (played by Robert Miano) is set on retiring, and he encourages his son to leave behind a life of crime. His older son Quinn (Billy Zane) disregards his father's wishes and gets himself arrested and sent to prison for two years, while his other son Kurt (Gianni Capaldi) goes to work for the FBI. Their loyal henchman Axel (Dolph Lundgren) is sort of left out of the loop and out of work for a while until a former associate of the mob family comes back in the picture and sets his sights on the empire. Campbell (Vinnie Jones) has ties to the family, and over the two years while Quinn was in prison, he has laid the groundwork for a silent takeover of the kingdom. When Quinn gets out, he calls on Axel to help him take down Campbell and start a war with him and his camp, but Axel's no dummy: He figures out that Quinn has a secret agenda and that he intends on using him only as a pawn until he's no longer needed. Axel goes to work.

For a Dolph Lundgren movie, *Blood of Redemption* is odd considering that he's not cast in a role that makes him shine. The mafia-esque storyline is nothing special, and with an Aryan action star moving around in it is strange to behold. Lundgren is fine in his quiet role, but he has maybe a dozen or so lines to recite on screen, while narrating the film as it goes along. I didn't care for it. Lundgren and Vinnie Jones also starred in *Hard Rush* (a.k.a. *Ambushed*) the same year. Both that film and this one were directed by Giorgio Serafini and Shawn Sourgose.

Blood Ring

1991 (AIP VHS) (djm)

When her husband runs afoul of the evil promoters of an underground kickfighting circuit, Susan (Andrea Lamatsch) goes to her ex-boyfriend Max (Dale "Apollo" Cook) to help her find her missing spouse. Max is a washed-up alcoholic kickboxer living in Asia, and when he agrees to help her, he finds that helping a girl out isn't as easy as "1, 2, 3." He gets beat up and smacked around, and poor Susan is kidnapped, and so Max has to get back into the fight circuit to find out who's responsible for the anguish. It's a good thing Max is a kickfighting dynamo because some of the guys he goes up against are beasts. Susan's husband is long dead, but it almost doesn't matter because she's already fallen for Max again, and he's more than willing to fill the other guy's shoes. The final fight takes place in a ring that has barbed wire and spikes wrapped around the ropes, so it gets bloody.

As one of the in-house AIP (Action International Pictures) action stars, Dale Cook—a real-life kickboxing champion—manages to deliver one of his best vehicle films with *Blood Ring*. It's ultra simplistic and low budget, but it actually has some unique tidbits that help make it an above-average (for Cook) martial arts film. Fans of gritty to-the-death fight movies should give it a gander and discover

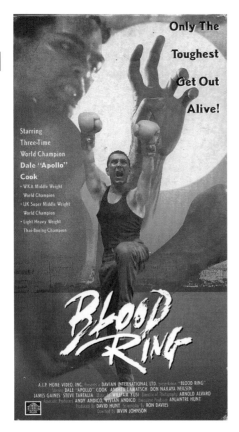

VHS artwork for *Blood Ring*. Author's collection.

Cook for being the diamond-in-the-rough action star that he was. A sequel followed a few years later. Directed by Irvin Johnson (a.k.a. Teddy Page), who also did *Fist of Steel* with Cook.

Blood Ring 2

1995 (NOV) (djm)

Picking up exactly where the first film left off, *Blood Ring 2* starts with Max winning his match in the infamous "blood ring" that concluded Part 1. After killing his opponent, he's taken into custody and shuffled through the corrupt justice system in East Asia and sent to a prison where the warden forces him to fight death matches with other inmates. Fed up with fighting, Max does his best to avoid confrontations, but it's inevitable that he will eventually have no choice but to fight for his life at some point. After a bit of luck, he's able to escape the prison and make a run for it.

Kickboxing champion Dale Cook made a string of "B" exploitation action movies, and his *Blood Ring* pictures were amongst his best. It's a shame that video distribution in North America for this sequel was so spotty because it's pretty good as far as these types of movies go. By this point, Cook had become a better actor and was maturing into an interesting martial arts action star. Sadly, this was one of his last films. Directed by Teddy Page (a.k.a. Irvin Johnson).

Bloodsport

1987 (Warner DVD) (djm)

The movie that put Jean-Claude Van Damme on the map and continues to amass a legion of fans, *Bloodsport* systematically outlines how simple and easy it is to make a movie revolving around a kickboxing storyline. Frank Dux (Van Damme, playing a real-life character) goes AWOL from the military to honor his adoptive father (played by Roy Chiao from *Dragons Forever*), who has passed on a family-developed martial art to him so that he can participate in a secret fighting match known as *The Kumite*. Dux travels to Hong Kong and enters himself in as a representative of his father, and he makes friends with a Vietnam vet named Jackson (Donald Gibb) and an intrepid female reporter, whom he becomes lovers with. His main nemesis in the ring is the hulking Chong Li (Bolo Yeung from *Enter the Dragon*), who is notorious for killing and/or maiming his opponents. Can Dux be the victor of the infamous "bloodsport," or will he fall under the guile of his nasty opponent?

Scripted by Sheldon Lettich (among others), *Bloodsport* pulls off a small miracle by managing to engage the audience with such an elementary and formulaic story. Dux isn't given much dimension (not that he really needs any), and the dialogue is quite simple, but somehow it all works . . . mainly because Van Damme is magnetic on screen and his beautiful butterfly kicks and signature yelling and action poses really sell him as a unique type of martial arts action guy. The score by Paul Herzog (using original songs written for the soundtrack) is essential. The directing is credited to notable second unit director Newt Arnold, but sources have pointed to producer Mark DiSalle and/or director of photography David Worth as being the true director. Co-star Donald Gibb reprised his role in the next entry in the series, starring Daniel Bernhardt. Van Damme would rehash this story in *Kickboxer* and *The Quest*, which was another collaboration with Frank Dux. Bolo Yeung starred in *The Shootfighter* series, which in many ways emulates *Bloodsport*. To this day, countless imitators try to capitalize on the success of this one movie. It worked. There's no denying it.

Bloodsport II

1996 (Lionsgate DVD) (djm)

"It's not about fighting—it's about finding one's self."

Filmed back-to-back with Part 3, this belated sequel to the Van Damme vehicle stars Swiss martial artist Daniel Bernhardt, who astonishingly looks a little bit like Van Damme, but he's taller and leaner. He plays a character named Alex, a debonair thief and martial artist. He steals a priceless sword from an art collector (Pat Morita), who sends men to catch him, and when he's caught, he is sent to a prison someplace in Southeast Asia. As soon as he gets there, he's assaulted and picked on, but he can mostly take care of himself. An elderly inmate (James Hong) takes a shine to him and decides to train him in a powerful form of martial arts. Once he's mastered the art, he is paroled with the sole purpose of competing in the Kumite, an elite fight championship sponsored by the art collector. As a contender, Alex befriends a few fellow competitors (Ron Hall from *Triple Impact* and Don Gibb from the first *Bloodsport*), and he has a small support team behind him when the matches get tougher. The whole story is told by an even older version of James Hong, who relates the story to a bunch of white kids at a karate school.

Bloodsport II is every bit as engaging as Part 1 was. Bernhardt, though really young and inexperienced as an actor at this point in his career, has the magnetism required to make it as an action star, and his star power is on display in this film. He'd go on to do two more *Bloodsport* movies after this one, though in Part 4 he played a different character. Alan Mehrez directed this one.

INTERVIEW:

DANIEL BERNHARDT

(djm)

Tall, dark, and handsome, Daniel Bernhardt worked his way into martial arts action films right at the tail end of the VHS era with the starring role in Bloodsport II (1996), *taking over the franchise a decade after Jean-Claude Van Damme vacated the role. Swiss-born Bernhardt has continued*

Daniel Bernhardt in Santa Monica, California. Photo by david j. moore.

to work since then, starring in direct-to-video fare like True Vengeance (1997), Perfect Target (1997), G2 (1999), *and the TV series* Mortal Kombat: Conquest (1998–1999). *As a supporting player, he's made memorable appearances in bigger films such as* The Matrix Reloaded (2003) *and* Parker (2013), *co-starring with Jason Statham. In his younger years, Bernhardt bore a striking resemblance to Van Damme, but as he's matured, he's become more seasoned and it's interesting to have watched him grow as both an actor and as a martial artist in his varied career.*

Daniel, you've been in the business of making action movies for a while. You got started kind of late in the game, when these types of movies were sort of at the end of their heyday.

I kind of came in at the tail end of the video craze. Remember the time when they just put a face with a guy throwing a kick on the billboard or the DVD box? The Chuck Norris days, the late '80s, the early to mid '90s. I came in . . . I did my first movie in 1995, which was *Bloodsport II*. I came in a little bit late in the game, but it was a pretty cool first movie.

I actually remember when *Bloodsport II* came out in some theaters for a week or two.

Right, right. They only had it for a week to push the video release, which was cool.

I remember the ads in the *LA Times*. They were like half-page ads that week.

Oh, they were? I don't remember.

How did you land the lead role in that movie?

The way I got *Bloodsport II* is kind of a long story. I've always been a martial artist. I started martial arts when I was fifteen years old. I was always very passionate about it. I love training, I love the art, I love everything about it. In my early twenties, I started to be a fashion model. I lived in Paris, London, Milan, and New York, and I was modeling, but I was always very passionate about martial arts. I would always train and do sparring, all around the world. Because of my job as a model, I had the chance to work with some of the biggest masters around the world. I would train with someone in Japan, someone in New York, Paris, so that was all really good. When I was about twenty-seven, I lived in New York as a fashion model, and I had my first brush with the movie business. It was very interesting. I've always believed if you just follow your instinct, it will lead you the right way. I was hired to do a commercial with Gianni Versace, directed by Bruce Weber, who was a very famous photographer. It was a commercial called "Looking for Kicks." No other man than Jean-Claude Van Damme was starring in it. They were looking for fashion models who kind of knew martial arts, who had a certain look, who knew how to move. I auditioned for Bruce, I showed him a couple kicks, and he liked me. He hired me on the spot. A week later, I went to the set, met Jean-Claude Van Damme, which was very exciting because I was a big fan of *Kickboxer* and *Bloodsport*. I was hired to work with him.

He was really cool, he was really nice to us, he said, "Hey, let me see what you guys can do." I was in my late twenties, and I was at the height of my martial arts ability. I just started throwing kicks in the air, and he just looked at me, and he said, "I'll take you last." I did my first fight scene with Jean-Claude Van Damme, but not in a movie—in this commercial directed by Bruce Weber. It was for jeans. I completely fell in love with doing martial arts in front of the camera. At the time, I was living in between New York and Miami because those were the two hotspots for modeling. I flew back to Miami and got all my friends together and said, "Hey, listen guys: I have this crazy idea. I'm going to make a little reel, just how I train, how I box, how I do my martial arts, and just see what happens." One of my friends had a camera, and two other friends kind of knew how to box, and I took them as sparring partners. We went to a famous boxing gym called 5th Street Boxing Gym in South Beach, and I just started hitting the bag, did the splits, did some choreography, and I had no clue what I was doing. It was just hodgepodge. I took the footage back to New York, went to an editing room, put it together and made a four-minute reel, and I sent it out there. Mark DiSalle, who made the first *Bloodsport* movie and the first *Kickboxer*, saw my reel. He picked me out of ten thousand people based on the tape that I'd made.

So they were already making *Bloodsport II* at that time?

They were already making *Bloodsport II*. As I know it, I heard that Jean-Claude couldn't do it or didn't want to do it. He was not available, and they were looking for a new guy to do it. DiSalle approached me. At the time, I was in Paris, and I got a call from a friend of mine, "Hey, uh . . . Mark DiSalle wants you to do *Bloodsport II*." I thought it was a joke. I hung up the phone. He called me back and said, "No, really. They want you." On my way to do some modeling jobs in LA and Mexico, I stopped by the producer's house and met him for a meeting. He basically said, "We want you to do *Bloodsport II*." This was back in 1992, 1993.

The movie came out in 1995.

Yeah. *Then* the big hassle started. Even though I had a deal, now we shot a proper promo reel. It's an interesting reel. We were supposed to shoot the film in '93 or '94. Maybe you remember the whole video crisis started to happen—it started to crash. It was supposed to have a five or six million-dollar budget, then it went down to four million, and then the movie never happened. Basically, I waited for two years for the movie to happen. I moved to LA. I stopped modeling because in those days you couldn't do both. If people knew you were a model, they wouldn't look at you. I felt strongly that I would make it in martial arts movies. I trained for two years and it finally happened in 1995.

Well, it's great that they still went with you and honored their deal with you.

I was very lucky. There was a lot of confusion going on. The original producer, Mark DiSalle,

lost the rights, and it went to someone else, and it went to a new company, and they approached me. It always goes how it goes.

Are we talking about Alan Mehrez now?

Exactly. It was called FM Entertainment. I wish it had been Mark DiSalle who had done it because he did a great job on the first one.

I can't imagine any other actor other than Van Damme in a *Bloodsport* sequel than you. You were the perfect guy for that.

I appreciate that, thank you. That's what he thought. (Laughing.)

A lot of people consider you to be very similar to Van Damme in your style and your look, especially in your early days. Seeing your face on the cover of the video and watching you in certain scenes, it's like, "Oh, wow, this is weird."

You know what, I think it's an honor to be compared to him. When I was younger, I was a big fan of his. I was always inspired by him. I thought he was really, really good in his early movies. He had such a talent, he was so charismatic. I think maybe that's what Mark DiSalle saw when he met me. We're both European, we both have a little bit of an accent. I think we both have a little bit different styles. He comes from a dance background, I believe. I come from more of a taekwondo background. I *love* his kicks. He's a very good kicker. We have a similarity. It's actually funny. He looks *a lot* like my younger brother. If you see us next to each other, we look nothing alike. But I understand when people say that we are similar. Ironically, my younger brother looks much more like him. I'm much taller than Van Damme. Taller and leaner. I like him a lot. I've met him over the years. He's always been really cool with me.

So now you're on the scene with *Bloodsport II* and *Bloodsport III*. You're traveling the world making movies now instead of modeling. What was going on in your mind? Were you thinking that you were going to become an action star at this point?

Never thought about that. My mother told me that when I was younger I told her that I wanted to be an actor. I don't remember that. Something I've known in my life is that I've always followed my instinct. When I smell something, when I feel like there's something that interests me, I just go for it 100 percent I never thought, *I'm going to be the next big action star.* I was just grateful and happy to work. Our business is *so* tough. It's so tough to get a job. When I get a job, I feel like the luckiest guy on Earth.

It's great that you're still here working in films, and not only that, but you're appearing in some of the biggest films you've ever appeared in. You're in *Parker*, and you're even in *The Hunger Games: Catching Fire.*

I got very lucky with *The Hunger Games*.

What's the secret? There has to be more to it than luck.

I think you have to work really hard. You have to be ready. You have to be prepared. Then, you also have to be lucky. Also destiny, maybe. Why was I picked for *Bloodsport II*? If I hadn't trained for my whole life as a martial arts, if I wouldn't have lived in New York at that time, if I wasn't a model at that time, if I hadn't spoken English at that time, I would've never have gotten that shot. You follow your dream, and you make choices. You can go this way or you can go that way. Each way you go, other doors open. My parents told me to get a normal job, but I just felt that there was something out there for me, and I went for it.

I've watched you mature, not just physically, but the roles you're getting now are better and your acting has matured. Even in *Parker* where you don't really have any lines, I can see a much more mature and seasoned version of you that I've never seen before.

Thank you. Actually, I did have lines in *Parker*, but they got cut. (Laughing.) I had a great scene, but it was cut!

You're great in that movie. Even without the lines, you're imposing and you make an indelible impression. I actually like that you're playing bad guys now.

I love it!

Why?

Acting is tough. It doesn't come easy to me. I have an accent. I have to work on it. I studied for a long time. When I did *Bloodsport II*, it was just kind of how I was. I tried to be myself. The one thing I do when I go for something, I find the best people I can to support me. I found the best acting coaches, I find the best martial arts coaches. I put a lot of time into doing what I do. I used to do an hour a day doing my dialogue, two hours a day working on my acting, four hours a day working on my fighting. It's what you have to do. You want to be a great builder; you have to build. You want to be a great martial artist, you have to train. You want to be a great actor, you have to study.

So, in your *Perfect Target* days . . .

A movie I actually like very much.

In those days were you taking acting classes?

Oh, yes! I started right away. Mark DiSalle put me in acting classes right away. It was kind of hard because I had no clue what I was doing. It was just instinct. I felt that my natural instinct wasn't used in the best way by the coaches. I was told to be tough, but that's not me. I'm funny, I'm laughing, I'm light. I've learned over the years . . . like you saw in *Parker*. My character is very light in the beginning. He's smiling. That's what Taylor Hackford, the director, told me. He said, I don't want you tough, I want you charming like James Bond. I want you to walk in the room and smile at the guy before you fight him. That's what I've learned over the years.

Some of the projects you've done seem ill-fitted for you, like *G2* or *Bloodsport IV*.

To be honest, I didn't want to do *Bloodsport IV*. I tried everything to get out of it. At the time, I just didn't like who they brought in as a director, I didn't like the script, but I had a deal with the company. They went in a different way.

That one went in a weird direction.

It was a very strange direction. Even my very close friends were like, "You know, *Bloodsport II* was actually a cool movie. *Bloodsport III*, eh, it was okay. *Bloodsport IV* was just *bizarre*." I had no choice. I tried to get out. I was under contract. The good thing about *Bloodsport IV* was that I met my wife. She was in it.

Was she the one in the sex scene with the revolving bed?

No, the other one! The beautiful one, the tall one with the long, brown hair.

Nice!

That was the best thing about doing that movie. We now have a daughter. We've been together fourteen years. That's destiny. I had to do the movie because I was forced to do it, and something good came out of it.

How about *G2*?

I was approached by the producers, and they were going off the hype of *Mortal Kombat: Conquest*, which was a TV show I'd done in 1998. It was when the whole video market started to die. I met Larry Kasanoff, who is still a very close friend of mine. We totally hit it off. He invited me to parties at his house. He is a total martial arts geek. He just wanted me to be in *Mortal Kombat*. The other producers all liked me, I got the role, and it was one of my favorite jobs to this day. It was one of the best times I ever had. I loved doing a TV show. I was on set every day. I worked every day—fight scenes, acting scenes. I learned so much. While I was doing that show, I was approached by another company to do this movie *G2*, which I got offered. That's very rare, when you get offers. I didn't have to read for it. It was a fun movie to do. What I remember is that it was kind of cool. I liked the character I played. I experimented with my acting. It was like *Highlander* with reincarnation.

You mentioned loving being on a TV series. You shot a pilot for a thing called *Dragon Fire*. What's the story with that?

Yes! Oh my god! I loved that! Awesome! I swear to God! We shot that about four years ago. I was the lead in it. I had to audition for it. I was approached while I was producing a movie. The producer and I had a mutual friend, who told him about me. He told him I was a martial artist and might be able to help out with the fight scenes for this project. The producer and I hit it off over the phone. I told him whatever he needed, I was there for him. I had a lot of experience, and by that point I had done *The*

Matrix Reloaded. The producer wanted to meet me, and I sent him my reel and we met. He liked what he saw, but I was a little bit older than what he imagined. I read for him and I got hired. It was just for a sizzle reel. He did an amazing job. It's outstanding.

That's all it is? A sizzle reel?

That's all it is. They're still trying. It was a very cool concept.

Okay, let's go back a bit. True Vengeance.

True Vengeance. One of my favorite movies I've done. I'm very close with a company called 87eleven. It's an action team, and the two owners are Chad Stahelski and David Leech. At the time, it wasn't 87eleven, but I'd worked with Chad on *Bloodsport II* and *Perfect Target*. Chad came up to me and said, "I have a script. I think it's *awesome*."

VHS artwork for *True Vengeance*. Author's collection.

It was called *Truth or Consequences*. It was written by Kurt Johnstad, who wrote *300*. He's major now. I read the script and loved it. We brought on David Worth to direct it. David and I just hit it off. The producers let me bring in my action guys, so I brought Chad in to do all the second unit and fights. The fight scenes in it are nuts. We did it in a very short time. We were very much inspired by John Woo's *The Killer*. That's what we wanted to make: A hardcore Hong Kong action movie.

I like your fight scene with Miles O'Keeffe with the swords.

It was cool. Miles was cool. I love Miles. A wonderful guy. There was some good acting in there. I really worked hard on that movie.

Director Sheldon Lettich (left), star Daniel Bernhardt (center), and Brian Thompson (right, with sunglasses) on the set of *Perfect Target*. Courtesy of Sheldon Lettich.

Perfect Target. Sheldon Lettich.

That's probably one of my better movies. Very well shot and directed. I brought in my stunt guys. I give a lot of credit to my second unit stunt guys. They coordinated the fights and shot the fights. It was a good script. Sheldon did a really good job directing it. It was shot in Mexico.

It looks like an "A" movie.

Very close. At the time, it was produced by Christian Solomon and Lee Solomon. Look who I'm working with: Robert England.

And Brian Thompson!

Thompson's awesome. It was a great experience.

Did these movies do anything for you? Did they propel you in any direction, because you were stagnant for a long time after these?

Not really. You said something interesting earlier. I came in at the very tail end of that world—you know what I mean? The last years. The last breath. When all those guys like [Olivier] Gruner and Mark Dacascos and David Bradley and [Michael] Dudikoff were just . . .

There were all petering out and dying at that point.

Right. So I kind of came in, and they were like, "Oh, he's the new young guy. . ." I was wasn't *that* young . . . (Laughing.) It was great for me, but then it got tough there for a while.

It's interesting because Steven Seagal and Van Damme made their last theatrical films around the time you were doing movies like *True Vengeance*.

Really? I don't remember. It was very tough for me to get a gig. I had to reinvent myself. When I got the acting bug, I really wanted to become a good actor. My strength now is a little bit of everything. I'm still very good at the martial arts. Now I'm getting smaller roles where they need a guy to do a fight in a big movie. I'll do some lines, so it's a little niche now.

That's what you did in *The Matrix Reloaded*, which must have been huge for you.

Matrix was huge. In my career . . . like I keep saying, it's very tough in this business. Just to be able to work, I'm the luckiest guy. But there's three things I've been very proud of: *Bloodsport II, Mortal Kombat: Conquest,* and *The Matrix.* Even though, after that it was tough and I thought, "Am I in the right game? Should I stop and do something else?" I was never like "It's over, I can't work anymore." Even though if I never worked again, look what I did. Those three. Probably the three coolest franchises in this game, right?

Yeah, you're right. *Bloodsport* pretty much defined that genre.

Bloodsport changed martial arts movies in the mid '80s. And *Mortal Kombat* changed martial arts movies in the mid '90s. Then, *The Matrix* absolutely changed everything. When Chad and I did three or four movies together, and after we finished *True Vengeance*, he got hired to work on *The Crow* after Brandon died, and after that his career went up. He then got hired to double Keanu Reeves on the first *Matrix*. He came back and told me about *The Matrix*, and I thought it sounded so cool. Then when it came out, I went to see it. I was sitting in the movie theater, and I had to sit there and watch it again. I was so blown away. I remember in 2000 or around that time, Chad called me up and told me that they were preparing for *Matrix Reloaded* and were looking for agents. He told me to get ready for an audition. I went to the audition. *Hundreds* of people. *Hundreds!* They looked at every guy who was over 6 feet 1 and had a little bit of a martial arts background. They looked at actors, athletes, and stuntmen. I auditioned for the casting director and got a call back. I auditioned for the Wachowski Brothers—one scene, and everything was top secret. I had to sign a nondisclosure agreement. I was so nervous. Then I got the call I had to audition for Woo Ping. He had approval as well over the agents. Then, I got the job. I got hired, and I was working on *The Matrix Reloaded* for six months over a year and a half. That was so cool.

It was a whole different league.

Again, it was like, "Oh my god. I can't believe I got this gig." We worked really, really hard.

Did that help propel you at all?

Probably not because it was a small role, a supporting role. It was hard to get publicity out of it because all the actors were the stars. All these actors were so much bigger. It helped me a little internationally.

This brings up a good point. The reason why I'm talking to guys like you is because you're the real thing. You do action movies. You know martial arts. I'm not talking to *actors* who learn martial arts for the few movies where they have to learn them to make it look real. Do you know what I'm saying?

Yeah, I do. I worked with Keanu Reeves for six months. The time and passion and energy he put into martial arts was unbelievable. He trained with us every single day, eight hours a day. *Every. Single. Day.* He became so good at it after all this time. Now look what he's doing now. He just did *47 Ronin* and he just directed *Man of Tai Chi*. He really got the bug for martial arts.

You did *The Cutter* with Chuck Norris. A good bad guy role for you.

Loved it! It was really fun because I was very excited to work with Chuck. He's awesome.

That was his last hurrah, basically.

It was supposed to be his comeback movie.

So what happened?

It did really well on DVD. I actually really liked the movie. I had some pretty cool fight scenes with him. He was an absolute gentleman and amazing to work with. What I learned from Chuck was how professional he is. He shows up on set, ready to go. He knows his lines, he works really hard on the fights, he's very safe. We both had stuntmen. First, our stunt guys would do the fight scenes, and we'd step in and we'd do our fight scene. Chuck did almost everything. Very hard worker and dedicated.

He had a cameo in *Expendables 2*. What do you think of those movies?

They're fun. I liked the first one a lot. A fun ride. I love Stallone. He's awesome. I love that guy.

Would you like to be in an *Expendables* movie?

I would *love* to be in an *Expendables* movie. It would be a nice addition to the kind of movies I do. Who knows?

Say something about working on *Parker* with Jason Statham.

I love *Parker*. David Leech from 87eleven called me up and asked me to come train with him, and we were hanging out and training, and I learned so much from these guys. David told me he was doing *Parker* with Jason Statham, and he told me that they were looking for someone to play a Russian hitman, a guy who was 6 feet 5, 250 pounds. That's big. I'm 6 feet 3 and around 200. He asked me if I wouldn't mind auditioning for it, and I said, "Absolutely!" I called my agent and he got me an audition. The casting agent liked me and called me back, and then I met the director Taylor Hackford, a major superstar director.

He's married to Helen Mirren.

Exactly. Actually, it's really funny, but my friends at 87eleven told me that they were looking for a really tough guy so they told me to grow out my facials, and to look really mean, as tough as I can be. So I go in, looking haggard, and I'm just ready to take somebody's head off. The director looks at me and goes, "What are you doing?" "I thought they wanted me to be really tough," I said. He says, "No, I want you exactly the way you were when you walked in—'Hey, how are you, sir?' I want you charming, I want you light, I want you like James Bond." I was like, "Oh." (Laughing.) So I did the audition like that, very light, very charming. I got the job. Taylor Hackford calls me up, "Daniel. I like what you did. I heard you're awesome with the fight stuff, and I want you to do all your own fight stuff." I said, "Of course! I always do my own stunts." Then he said, "I want you to fall off a building, 300 feet." (Pause.) "*Absolutely! No problem!*" That was the deal. I worked with Jason Statham. He was awesome. Nice guy, very hard worker. I think he's actually really good at what he does. Has a great look. We went really hard in the fight scene. I didn't hold back, I threw that guy around, he threw me around. Everything was choreographed, everything was safe, but we went really hard. He never complained. He just said, "Don't hit me." I said, "Absolutely not, I'm a professional." I threw Jason around and he never complained. He was a real good sport.

What's in the future for you?

I got the directing bug. I'm working on a project called *Fetch*. I'm also working on bringing back the *Bloodsport* franchise. I would be the producer on it.

Do you see yourself being an action star for much longer?

It's hard, but it's what I love to do. I'm training almost every day. I'm learning judo, I'm learning grappling, sword fighting, samurai fighting. If I got a job, I would take it. My ideal job is where I can do action.

Is there anything you would like to say to your fans?

How many fans do I have?

Here I am!

Oh, awesome. I love my fans. Because of you guys, I'm here. I can work. When I did *Bloodsport II*, I was invited to fly somewhere in Texas to the premier. It was a huge screening. People lined up around the block. It was my first experience with publicity. They got me a limo, and I got to sign autographs, and there were literally hundreds of people waiting to get my autograph around the block. It was crazy. I remember the publicist was behind me and he said, "We've got ten minutes, and then we have to go!" I was like, "I'm not leaving until everybody has their autograph. They waited in line for an hour." I sat there and shook everybody's hand. I would not leave. It's really important to me to give back.

I feel like you're giving back with these movies you're doing.

I appreciate that. Who are the guys you like right now?

I like Scott Adkins a lot.

He's awesome.

I like Michael Jai White.

Mark DiSalle wanted Michael Jai White opposite me in *Bloodsport II*.

The Ron Hall character?

Yes. He's great. Really nice guy too. He's had a great career. Out of all of us, I have to say, he's had the best career. He does huge movies and comes back and does these smaller movies. He's got a great niche right now.

The guys I really like right now are in that age group. Gary Daniels . . .

Right, right, right.

Do you consider yourself an action star or an actor?

I never considered myself a star at all. I'm an actor who does action movies. I'm very fortunate to work. I love what I do.

Bloodsport III
1996 (Lionsgate DVD) (djm)

"I can insist on having the best. You, sir, are the very best."

Alex (Daniel Bernhardt), the suave art thief and winner of the kumite (a match between elite martial arts fighters) from Part 2, tells the story of this film to his son, who is having troubles at school. Alex tells him that he was offered to enter as the favorite of the new kumite championship, but he turned it down for various reasons at first. When the sponsor of the championship (John Rhys Davis) hears of this, he is angry and has Alex's mentor (James Hong) murdered. This shifts Alex's position and he goes into hardcore training mode. By the time he enters into the competition, it appears to be fairly obvious that Alex will be the best fighter.

This one is more mechanical and predictable than Part 2. It definitely feels like a sequel to the previous entry, but the actual kumite fights are somehow less compelling. For one, Alex is missing his friends and teammates (Donald Gibb as Ray Jackson from parts 1 and 2, Ron Hall as Cliff from part 2), and for another, Alex is more cocky and less willing to *make* friends in this entry. If you really liked Part 2, there's no reason why you won't care for this. It's extremely similar. Alan Mehrez, who directed the second one, did this as well.

Bloodsport 4: The Dark Kumite
1999 (Lionsgate DVD) (djm)

An attempt to redirect the *Bloodsport* franchise in a different direction, *The Dark Kumite* once again stars Daniel Bernhardt from Parts 2 and 3, but he plays a different character here. He's a detective who goes undercover at a prison (by committing a bogus crime so that he can be sentenced by a judge) where prisoners are disappearing. It turns out that some of the toughest convicts are taken to a guy who considers himself a king of sorts (he's surrounded by a harem of women and he sits on a throne), and he has set up his palace to host an underground kumite championship amongst convicts. Through some unbelievable circumstances, Bernhardt ends up competing against the cop-killing psychopath he's been after for months, and guess who wins?

As nutty as they come, *The Dark Kumite* feels like almost anything but an action film. It has surreal moments, nightmare sequences, a sex scene that features a revolving bed, and an overall feeling of *oddness* that is impossible to ignore. Bernhardt, while imposing and finally featuring grown-into good looks, plays an entirely honorable character, and his speeches about the honor of the kumite fall flat. Stafanos Miltsakakis, who fought Jean-Claude Van Damme in the Russian baths in *Maximum Risk*, plays Bernhardt's nemesis here. Their fight is the highlight of the film. None of the other fights in the film make much of an impression. Bernhardt later married his co-star, Lisa Stothard. Directed by Elvis Restano.

Blood Street
1988 (KB Releasing VHS) (djm)

Private dick Joe Wong (Leo Fong reprising his role from *Low Blow*) takes on a gig to find a seductress's missing husband. The case leads him down a violent path involving two separate drug lords who take Wong's meddling and questioning as a threat, but they greatly underestimate him because he's a tough martial artist and a badass. Drug kingpin Boyd (Richard Norton whose face is splashed on the VHS box, but not Fong's) sits back and waits for Wong to come calling, and in the meantime Wong's entire investigation is a sham: The seductress (played by Playboy Playmate Kym Paige) has set him up for reasons that didn't really make much sense in the context of the events that had unfolded up to that point.

There's charm to movies like *Blood Street* (and anything with the participation of Leo Fong), but this time the charm wears off pretty quickly. I was expecting a Richard Norton movie, but with Fong as the hero and Norton as a clueless bad guy who beats up his underlings and fondles half-naked women to fill up the running time, I was disappointed. The whole movie has an improvised, off-the-cuff reality to it, and in some regard that's cool, but it's just not worth your time—especially if you're looking to see Norton kick some ass. Chuck Jeffreys (from *Superfights*) and George Chung (from *Fight to Win*) appear in small roles. Norton, Jeffreys, and Chung all worked together in *Fight to Win*, made the previous year. That one was better. Fong and Chung directed *Blood Street*.

Blood Warriors

1993 (Imperial VHS) (djm)

Weak entry starring David Bradley as a disgraced ex-Marine, who was charged with killing his own brother on the battlefield. He goes to prison for a while and he is mysteriously bailed out and offered a job as a mercenary in Asia. Once he gets there, the sister of one of his Marine pals picks him up at the airport and takes him to her brother's funeral. Confused and wanting to know why he was bailed out, he asks, but the sister (the blonde and indistinct actress Jennifer Campbell) doesn't answer his questions, and instead comes on to him at night in her panties. In the meantime, a gangster has dug up the fresh grave of the woman's brother, and finds it is empty, which angers him. The gangster and his goons kidnap the sister and make a mess of her house, and Bradley is too late to stop them. The gangster tortures her, wanting to know where her brother is, and she insists she thought he was dead. Just then, her brother (Frank Zagarino) shows up with some hired help and rescues her. Back home, a smug Zagarino tells Bradley that he was the one who bailed him out and that now he owes him a favor. Bradley refuses (Zagarino is a creep), and so Bradley gets on his bad side. From then on . . . they are Blood Warriors!

I don't know who to blame for this bad movie. David Bradley wrote it and starred in it, and so maybe I should blame him, but Sam Firstenberg (*American Ninja, American Samurai*) directed it, so maybe he's the culprit. The story is bad. The script is way too talky and there's not enough action. Bradley is kinda corny in his cowboy-ish role (he wears a cowboy hat and plays the guitar), and he only has one or two halfway decent fight scenes. Every time anyone shoots at anything, they find their mark the first time, but every time Bradley is shot at, they always miss. Tons of Asian stunt guys do a lot of falling from heights after getting shot in this movie. One memorable bit has Bradley climbing a scaffold in a city square, and it reminded me a little bit of the scene in *Remo Williams* where Fred Ward was climbing around the Statue of Liberty. Bradley's final fight with Zagarino is okay, but not sensational. *Cyborg Cop* was another Bradley/Firstenberg movie that was released in 1993.

Body and Soul

1981 (MGM DVD) (djm)

"Suggested" by the 1947 movie starring John Garfield, this take on *Body and Soul* was written, produced, and stars Leon Isaac Kennedy who had found success earlier with the boxing action film *Penitentiary*. He plays "Leon the Lover," a svelte fighter who rises to become the most celebrated boxer in the country. His drive for winning comes from his kid sister who has sickle cell anemia, and the only way for her to continue receiving the best medical treatments is if he continues fighting to win. Along the way to the top, he falls in love with a reporter (played by his real wife at the time, Jayne Kennedy) and

he breaks her heart by sleeping around with plenty of ready and willing beauties. It has a happy ending.

From The Cannon Group, *Body and Soul* has an artificiality to it that's hard to shake, and surprisingly the main character isn't likable. Some of the best scenes involve boxing champ Muhammad Ali as Leon's trainer, but the movie is an overall disappointment. Leon is great in the right role, and doing a rehash of this story was the right idea, but the direction it took felt wrong. The boxing scenes are pretty good. Directed by George Bowers.

Body Armor

1996 (Simitar DVD) (djm)

Special security expert Ken Conway (Matt McColm) abruptly quits the gig he's on—working for a rich sleaze who kills a man in front of him—and his manager (played by Clint Howard) is desperate to get him working again. An old flame of Ken's (Carol Alt) comes back into his life and offers him a job: To go undercover at a chemistry lab where a scientist (Ron Perlman) is concocting a deadly virus and an antidote at the same time, which has made the government nervous. The scientist intends to use the virus to infect a percentage of the population and hold the antidote for ransom, which is where Ken figures in. He first poses as a fellow scientist, but then he turns up the action hero within when the scientist kicks his plan into gear.

McColm's career as an action star was short-lived, but his few outings as the lead star (see *Red Scorpion 2* and *Subterfuge* for more) really underwhelmed, despite the fact that he had plenty of potential. He displays some of his kenpo karate skills here, but as in his other films he never gets to unleash his skills or tap into his full potential. The film is especially cheap, and even having Perlman as the villain doesn't elevate it to another level. McColm's leading ladies in the film are attractive (Annabel Schofield is also

DVD artwork for *Body Armor*. Author's collection.

in it), but the script lacks the tenacity to make McColm's character a debonair, sophisticated hero in the James Bond vein. His character is boring. The director, Jack Gill, is a well-known stuntman and stunt coordinator, but he never directed another film.

Body Slam

1986 (MGM DVD) (djm)

Likable loser Harry Smilac (Dirk Benedict from *The A-Team*) has exhausted his appeal as a music promoter and the bill collectors are hounding him day and night. His clients have all dropped him and his Ferrari has just been repossessed. What he needs is a miracle. He happens to run into professional wrestler Quick Rick Roberts (Roddy Piper several years before *Hell Comes to Frogtown* and *They Live*), who is in need of a slick promoter, and so they form an alliance. Lo and behold, Smilac manages to pump up revenue for Quick Rick and his buddy Tonga Tom (professional wrestler Sam Fatu), and just like that Smilac is a success story and the envy of other wrestling promoters. But being who he is, Smilac's gas runs out before he knows it, and his luck is turned upside down all over again when he shows his cards by not knowing how to handle the world of professional wrestling.

Shot on a lark with a script that was probably written on napkins, *Body Slam* is pretty silly stuff and for very unassuming viewers or fans of '80s wrestling. Roddy Piper is fun in a nice little role that is virtually a riff on who he was at the time, and if you like stupid PG-rated comedies like *Police Academy 5* or *Moving Violations*, then this might be up your alley. Stunt guru Hal Needham directed. Figures. Also see *Tagteam* with Piper or *Bad Guys*, another lame comedy that features '80s professional wrestlers (which was also, coincidentally, released in 1986).

The Bodyguard

(a.k.a. **Karate Kiba**)

1976 (Diamond DVD) (CD)

"We all know there's a lot of drugs flooding Japan, corrupting our young, hurting us all. That's why I swear to you now—on my honor—that I will find the rest of the men responsible for this, the drugs too. I will smash them one at a time and put them all out of business."

After Sonny Chiba takes out mob terrorists on a flight to Tokyo, he holds a press conference, letting everyone know he's on a mission. He vows to clear the streets of drugs by taking out the biggest dealer in the country. He offers himself up as a bodyguard to anyone willing to hire him before karate-chopping a bottle in half with his bare hands. He soon meets Reiko (Judy Lee) who would like to hire him. He needs to know she's on the level so he sends his sister (Sue Shiomi) to get evidence from Reiko's car. She's attacked by hitmen who leave her unconscious, naked, and apparently crucified on the shadow of a cross. Chiba needs answers and Reiko is the key. As he begins to protect her, each step they make brings him closer to the men he wants to extinguish, and he's one man who keeps his word.

The film opens with a passage known as Ezekiel 25:17, one many may remember from *Pulp Fiction*, with one major difference: the reference to *the Lord* is replaced with *Chiba the Bodyguard*, immediately thrusting Sonny Chiba to god-like status in an exploitation film filled with bizarre moments. No joke, while a woman is in bed, two men are hiding inside her couch before cutting their way out. There's severed limbs, male chauvinism, and it wouldn't be a Sonny Chiba film if someone didn't get their eye gouged out. There's too much downtime between the action but Chiba fans won't want to miss the fight scene on an airplane where he never loses the cigarette in his mouth. Directed by Ryuichi Takamori (*Kamikaze Cop*).

Boiling Point

1993 (Warner DVD) (JAS)

Boiling Point is about a police officer (Wesley Snipes) who wants to quit the force because he's lost too much . . . his family, his partner, and maybe even his soul. His antagonist is a burnt-out, small-time gangster named Red Diamond (Dennis Hopper, sporting dyed red hair) who owes some upper-tier gangsters $50,000. He is in a mad dash to get the money and manipulates a younger small-timer (Viggo Mortensen) to kill and steal from a hit-man with whom Red has set up a fake exchange deal for the same amount. In the end there are gunfights, Mortensen's character is killed, Red is arrested, and what happens in the police officer's future is only mentioned in a quick scroll before the credits roll. The film is set in Los Angeles.

Boiling Point is anything but what the title suggests. It cruises along with no sense of urgency or palpable excitement. It is a shame that Wesley Snipes committed to so many dull roles because he has the charisma to carry an actioner like nobody's business. Unfortunately, this film is *not* the business. Co-starring Lolita Davidovich and Valerie Perrine.

Boogie Boy

1998 (Lionsgate DVD) (JAS)

Boogie Boy stars martial arts master Mark Dacascos as Jesse Page, a man who's recently out of prison and trying to stay clean. Unfortunately, honor and loyalty to his heroin-addicted ex-cellmate and lover Larry (Jaimz Woolvett) threaten to unravel his goals of starting over. After a violence-marred drug deal, the two escape to the desert to hide with kooky motel owner Edsel (Frederic Forrest) and his ditzy but charming "sort-of-wife" Hester (Emily Lloyd).

Boogie Boy is a strange little cornucopia of a movie. It starts as a claustrophobic urban heroin drama with a strong homosexual subtext, and then switches over to a quirky character study in the desert before finishing with a pretty impressive (but brief) martial arts conflict resolution. Props must be given to Mark Dacascos (from *The Crow: Stairway to Heaven*) as the likable ex-con. He plays the title role with sincerity and conviction. Frederic Forrest is forever likable, and his presence brings a (comparatively) lighthearted, stony Californian charm to the proceedings. This movie is set in a burnt-out Los Angeles, and it *feels* like burnt-out LA. The settings are sufficiently grimy without pretension. Even rocker Joan Jett has a sizable role in the first half, as does ex-porn star Traci Lords. *Boogie Boy* is the genre equivalent of slumming with loony old friends you've outgrown, but still enjoy now and again. Deserves to find a wider cult audience, but not necessarily an audience that watches action and martial arts films.

Book of Swords

2007 (Passworld DVD) (CD)

"That karate shit will get you killed. Go with God, tell him Apollo sent you."

Detective Lang (Ho-Sung Pak) and his partner Lucky (Taimak) are about to make a major bust, one that will make their careers. The heat they end up facing is far more than they can handle. When their backup arrives a massacre occurs killing both Lucky and Lang's little brother. Stricken with grief, Lang leaves the force and disappears for three years. Then guilt begins to set in, and the only way it can be released is to return to Chicago and find out who killed his brother and partner. While in pursuit of the killers, he learns of an ancient manuscript known as the *Book of Swords* and all of the power it holds. He finds himself defending the book while trying to redeem himself for the mistakes he has made in life.

The story, wooden acting, and all-around dullness of anything having to do with dialogue might deter you from watching this, but fans of *The Last Dragon* should rejoice at seeing the long-absent Taimak in action once again. His role is small but the dude still has it. His character is the perfect companion for Ho-Sung Pak (*Fist of the Warrior*) and the two men have a great action scene trying to uphold justice. The film includes appearances by Dan Pesina, Katalin Zamir, and Richard Divizio who all appeared in the *Mortal Kombat* video games.

Borderline

1980 (Columbia VHS) (ZC)

A thematic follow-up to *Mr. Majestyk* and a particularly effective exploration of the US/Mexican border struggle of the time, this Charles Bronson drama puts characters before action and is ultimately better for it. Hold on; I know them's fightin' words in this book, but bear with me. In the year this film was shot, over two million (!!!) Mexican citizens illegally crossed into the United States, a third of whom were immediately caught and sent packing. To attack this subject, most action filmmakers would shape it into pure exploitation, creating a teeth-gritting border war between forces of good and evil. *Borderline* bucks that easy route and instead offers an intelligent, emotionally driven melodrama. . . in which Bronson beats a human trafficker half-dead and shoves his head in a toilet bowl.

Like any typical action picture, you have your heroes (gold-hearted border guards; illegal aliens desperate to make good) and villains (murderous mercenaries; white collar overlords), but the film humanizes all of them in a way seldom seen in two-fisted cinema. This is especially true of Bronson's surprisingly nuanced portrayal of Jeb Maynard, head of the local border patrol and the most compassionate "migra" to ever raid a cargo truck. In his quest to track down the homicidal traffickers, he crosses into Tijuana disguised as an illegal and makes the treacherous trek into his own homeland. It's the sixth time Bronson played a Mexican on screen, and it's a harrowing segment that blurs the film's moral lines perfectly. He's supported by an impressive cast, including Wilford Brimley, a young Bruno Kirby, and Oscar-nominee Michael Lerner, all operating in top form. Beyond that, one of the opening credits reads "Introducing Ed Harris," who provides one of *Borderline's* most memorable moments in two blazing blasts from a sawed-off shotgun. I only wish all important sociological issues were tackled that same way.

Born American

1986 (Image Entertainment DVD)(JAS)

Born American is the first feature film from action director Renny Harlin (*Die Hard 2, Cliffhanger*). It focuses on three American tourists, the leader played by Mike Norris (son of Chuck). On vacation in Finland, the three characters find it a good idea to get drunk and sneak into Russia. While there, they stumble onto a murder mystery, a prison camp, a gladiator-type competition to the death, evil political leaders (from both the United Stated and Russia), freedom- fighting women, and an African-American author (blaxploitation character actor Thalmus Rasulala). It sounds like a blast, but unfortunately the tone does not match the ludicrousness of the plot.

This could have been a humdinger of a popcorn movie but instead takes itself way too seriously considering the absolute nonsense of the proceedings. It's full of half-baked ideas and unlikable characters, which is too bad because there are enough interesting ideas here for three films. One wonders if Eli Roth took this concept to the extreme years later with the *Hostel* series, which are actually more fun to watch (and believe me, that's saying something). To Renny

Harlin's defense, it was his first film, and without it he wouldn't have gone on to make his later, greater films. Any director who has *Die Hard 2* and *Cliffhanger* under his belt can be forgiven for previous sins (but not necessarily for later ones).

The Born Losers

1967 (Image Entertainment DVD) (JAS)

"Whatever they've done to your women . . . you deserve."

The Born Losers introduced Billy Jack (Tom Laughlin) to the world, but this film is not as focused on the Billy Jack character as the subsequent releases in the series. It's really more of a biker film, and uses the then-popular story template to illustrate several societal issues. The story is based on a real-life case of the Hell's Angels motorcycle gang who raped five teenage girls in Monterey, California, in 1964. Billy Jack attempts to stand for and protect one of the girls (Elizabeth James, who also wrote the script), faces the wrath of the gang as a result, receives no community support, and is arrested and eventually shot by the police for his troubles. Racial issues are addressed as Billy Jack is often taunted for his Native American lineage. Eventually, Billy Jack is forced to kill the leader of The Born Losers and is shot by a police officer during the confrontation. There is no happy resolution to the film as the victims are clearly scarred by their experiences.

Using much less of his hapkido martial arts skills than in later releases (except for *Billy Jack Goes to Washington*, which is more of a political drama), this film has a stronger sense of menace and verisimilitude than other entries in the series. There is a surprising amount of focus on the psychological effects of violence (especially rape), and this lends a disturbing air to the proceedings. The Billy Jack character is more fallible in this entry, and even the gang members are somewhat humanized in a few scenes. This is a well-executed, thought-provoking film, though not necessarily a must-see for readers of this book. For those who appreciate dark drama more than action, this is the recommended entry in the series.

Born to Defense

1986 (Miramax DVD) (CD)

"Fuck your atomic bombs! What about my fists?"

At the end of the Second World War, it's time for the Chinese to go back to their lives at home, some hoping to be seen as war heroes. Jet (Jet Li) is off to visit a friend only to find the American soldiers who still reside in China are anti-Chinese prejudices. At a local bar, he finds himself in the ring with one of them, which sparks a feud between him and the other Americans. Each time they confront each other, the actions against him become more and more vicious. He's saved and nursed back to health by a young prostitute named Na (Jia Song) who happens to be the shunned daughter of his friend/mentor Zhang (Erkang Zhao). Even though their friendship becomes strained, Jet can't let the Americans get away with the violence and bigotry, defending the honor of his friends and his fellow Chinese people.

This film has a weak premise and paper-thin story that serves only as an excuse to string together a series of entertaining fight scenes. Jet Li (*Fearless*), fresh from the *Shaolin Temple* series, decided he was ready to direct his first (and to date, only) feature film. Many of the standout fights pits Li against Kurt Roland Petersson (*Bruce Lee's Dragons Fight Back*). They face off several times with each confrontation building upon the next. Most of the battles are one on one and seem to last for long periods of time. You can see the potential in Jet but the star we know and love wasn't quite ready to blossom yet. If you ignore the silly story, there's plenty of action and never a dull moment. It was fun to revisit this entry-level film to see where he began and consider how he has grown into a legend over the years.

Born to Raise Hell

2011 (Paramount DVD) (djm)

Interpol badass Samuel Axel (Steven Seagal) is on the trail of some drug traffickers in Romania when he gets wind of a serial rapist and murderer named Costel (Darren Shahlavi), who is tied to the drug cartel. When his partner is killed, Axel becomes more invested in the case, and he tracks Costel like a bulldozer. When they finally meet, the result is obviously fatal . . . for Costel.

A nondescript entry in Seagal's filmography, *Born to Raise Hell* gives him a role that definitely feels in tune to his reality TV character from *Lawman*. He feels every bit the lawman in this movie, and his dialogue kinda feels realistic, despite the annoying way the movie was put together. Director Lauro Chartrand (a veteran stunt coordinator who later directed episodes of Seagal's television show *True Justice*) never lets things pan out quietly or naturally: quick cuts, pauses, rude lighting interruptions, and other distractions really make the movie ultra modern and cheap. Seagal is okay as far as his later direct-to-video performances go, and his few close quarter fights are good, but choppily edited. His final encounter with Shahlavi (from *G.O.D.* and *The Package*) is surprisingly brutal and amazingly pat. Once again, Seagal's voice is heavily ADR'd by someone else. For more awkward Seagal ADR work, check out *Attack Force, Mercenary for Justice,* and others.

Boss Nigger

1975 (VCI DVD) (CD)

"Thank you for the welcome, ma'am. When you get back to Boston, you be sure and tell my people that you just met two niggers that don't know how to sing or dance."

Bounty hunters Boss (Fred Williamson) and Amos (D'Urville Martin) are on the trail of criminal Jed Clayton (William Smith) when they find themselves in a small town. With no sheriff in sight, Boss takes it upon himself to fill that void, much to the shock of the town's citizens as well as its crooked mayor. The mostly white town has to deal with their black sheriff and abide by all their new rules.

Fred Williamson (*Black Cobra*) starred in a string of westerns during the '70s. One of the standout films from that phase in his career is *Boss Nigger*. It might not be a really great western but it's a solid exploitation film. Williamson and frequent co-star D'Urville Martin (*Hammer*) bust out the charisma and sail on it. They have a terrific chemistry and are hilarious together. The action and violence are rather tame in comparison to other Williamson films. There's very little cursing in the film, which helped to secure its PG rating. So, it was shocking to see partial nudity and to hear the n-word used well over a hundred times. Williamson may be tough, but he isn't afraid to toy around. There are a couple of decent shootouts but no actual fights in the film. It's also great to see his *Hammer* co-star William Smith show up as the main villain. Smith is terrific (as always) and comes off as pretty sinister. The title song needs to be mentioned as well since it's incredibly memorable. The lack of action may be a tad off-putting for action fans, but *Boss Nigger* is great exploitation. This was Williamson's first film as a writer and producer. It was directed by film veteran Jack Arnold (*The Creature from the Black Lagoon*).

Bounty Hunters

1996 (Dimension DVD) (djm)

"There's two things you can do: You can reload . . . or you can reconsider."

This lightweight vehicle for Michael Dudikoff starts off really well, but soon becomes a made-for-TV-quality action film. He plays a former Navy SEAL who's become a down-on-his-luck bounty hunter behind on his mortgage who hangs out with a little kid neighbor. His employer doesn't like him or the fact that he smokes cigars, and his rival is an ex-girlfriend (Lisa Howard). They team up on a case involving the mob, and they spend most of the movie dodging bullets and kicking bad guys in the nuts. Dudikoff shows a light side to his action persona, and he busts out some cool martial arts moves in some close-quarters fight scenes.

George Erschbamer, the guy who made the *Snake Eater* movies with Lorenzo Lamas, directed this. In one scene Dudikoff goes into a video store and there are *Snake Eater* posters in sight. This bears an "R" rating for one scene of nudity, but the violence and profanity are pretty tame. A sequel followed.

Bounty Hunters 2: Hardball

(a.k.a. **Hardball**)

1997 (Dimension DVD)(djm)

A lightweight "R"-rated actioner with star Michael Dudikoff, *Bounty Hunters 2* follows goofball bounty hunter Jersey Bellini (Dudikoff) and his lover/partner B.B. (Lisa Howard) who get the mob's attention when they thwart a jewel heist that was meant to fund further mob endeavors. The boss (played by a slumming Tony Curtis) orders them both killed, but Jersey is some kind of hero, as he always seems to outwit the bad guys and escape just before death comes calling. He survives several bomb blasts (including the obliteration of his house), gunfights, and fistfights, and jumps from tall buildings and makes narrow escapes from racing cars. He and his frustrated partner get the best of the mob and live another day.

It seems like a no-brainer that the *Bounty Hunter* movies (from the Canadian company Cinepix, which brought us the *Snake Eater* movies with Lorenzo Lamas) would have made great lead-ins to a TV series, if not for some mild cursing, some rough violence, and some nudity. After Dudikoff's series *Cobra* was canceled, he should have rolled into another show, and this would have been just right for him. But, alas, he continued making films of lesser and lesser quality, which is a shame. From director George Erschbamer, who did all three *Snake Eater* pictures.

Bounty Hunters

2011 (MPI DVD) (CD)

Former pro-wrestling superstar Trish Stratus makes her feature film debut in the Canadian-lensed action film *Bounty Hunters*. Trish is Jules, a bounty hunter who also works as a bartender in a strip club. As a bounty hunter, she works in a team with with Chase (Boomer Phillips) and Ridley (Frank J. Zupancic). They capture a small-time criminal who makes them a very enticing offer: If they let him go, he will lead them to a mob informant worth $100,000. They take the small timer up on his offer and capture the informant. What they don't expect is that the hitmen on their trail are ready to take them out in order to get the informant back. It's going to take one hell of a plan to get them out of this mess alive.

Bounty Hunters knows exactly what it's supposed to be and it hits the mark. It never takes itself too seriously and zips along at a

lean eighty minutes. The entire cast works well together, and the rapport is undeniable. The humor is hit-and-miss but the action is never disappointing. Trish shows just as much grace and athleticism on screen as she did in the ring. She has several action set pieces but the standout moments are her two fights with co-star Andrea James Lui. To date, this is Trish's only foray into action cinema but hopefully it won't be her last. Directed by Patrick McBrearty.

Bounty Tracker

1992 (Republic VHS) (djm)

Like an "R"-rated extended episode of *Renegade*, this film starring Lorenzo Lamas is similar in theme and tone to his hit show, which ran for five seasons. Here he plays a "bounty tracker" named Johnny Damone, who goes on the hunt for his brother's killer. The killer is an assassin named Eric Gauss (Matthias Hues from *No Retreat No Surrender 2*), who travels with a few accomplices, one of whom is a dominatrix-type hitwoman (Cyndi Pass). Damone makes friends with some neighborhood punks, who help him corner Gauss at a junkyard, where the film's climax takes place.

Generic and simple, *Bounty Tracker* is stock straight-to-video fodder from the early 1990s. It isn't bad, but there's nothing exceptional about it. Lamas's character is likable in the same way his character is in his show *Renegade*, which means he's lacking an edge. In this film, he has a few good fight scenes (the best one is in a dojo), but his fight scene with Hues at the end is a letdown. Director Kurt Anderson (*Martial Law 2: Undercover*, *Martial Outlaw*) seems bored by the material, and most viewers will be bored by this film.

Braddock: Missing in Action III

1988 (MGM DVD) (djm)

"I don't step on toes, Littlejohn. I step on necks."

James Braddock (Chuck Norris) doesn't leave Vietnam right away after fighting his way out of captivity (see *Missing in Action 2: The Beginning*), and he falls in love with a local woman and marries her. During an emergency evacuation out of Saigon, Braddock is separated from her, and he mistakenly believes that she was killed in a fire, so he returns to the States, where he resumes his life. More than a decade later, he is told that his wife is still alive in Vietnam and that he has a son too, which is enough news for him to return to Vietnam to find them. He is told that his family is living behind enemy lines and the only way for him to get to them is to venture into enemy territory. He gears up and prepares for war, and when he finds them, they are all captured and his wife is straightaway murdered in front of him and his son. He's tortured by another evil general—this one named Quok

(Aki Aleong)—and his son (played by Roland Harrah III) is made to witness the horrors. Later, after Braddock escapes, he also takes with him a bunch of imprisoned children (sired by Americans, but abandoned and therefore punished by the Viet Cong), whom he leads through a perilous quest through the jungles to the border of Thailand.

Somehow, this final entry in Cannon's *Missing in Action* trilogy has the smallest impact of the bunch despite being the most sentimental and overly endearing. It gives Braddock something to care about other than captured comrades, but simultaneously the film takes his wife away just when they're reunited, which I feel is cheating. It almost felt like a *Death Wish* movie in that regard. It's manipulative. Norris is okay in the role, but amazingly the picture is underwhelming as an action film *and* as a war movie. It's too bad. It was written by Norris and James Bruner, who collaborated on a number of other projects including the original *Missing in Action* release. Directed by Aaron Norris. The actor who played Norris's son—Harrah III—committed suicide in his early twenties.

Brazilian Brawl

2003 (York DVD) (CD)

"Señor Carlos, something terrible has happened. Someone blew up the farmhouse, your uncle die."

Ruben Rocha (Dan Inosanto) has been struggling to keep his farm afloat but people are afraid to work for him as the corrupt officials want to foreclose on the property for their own personal greed. The villainous sheriff has the farm blown to bits, leaving most of it destroyed. Ruben has family in Brazil who are masters of jiu jitsu, and they head to the US to find out what has been going on. The Rocha brothers (played by real-life siblings: Rigan, Roger, Carlos, John, and Jean Jacques Machado) band together to expose the corruption and pay the back taxes on the farm so they can keep it afloat and in the family.

Brazilian Brawl is an oddity of sorts. It's directed by *Low Blow* star Leo Fong with a story by Geoffrey Lewis (*Double Impact*) and stars the Machado brothers who are cousins to the Gracie family. The movie itself is horrible in every conceivable way with moments of unintentional brilliance that have to be seen to be believed. From the farting debt collector to the ridiculous theme song ("Bad boys, bad boys, bad boys from Brazil") it's hard to tell what was supposed to be taken seriously, but these guys are the real deal. I'm not sure Fong was able to capture the essence of their fighting style but you do get a taste of what they can do, and it's impressive. There're plenty of takedowns, arm bars and grappling displayed, but it's what you would expect from jiu jitsu practitioners. I think we should just call this an interesting idea, but a failed experiment.

Breach of Faith:
A Family of Cops II

1997 (Echo Bridge DVD) (CD)

Paul Fein (Charles Bronson) and his family of cops are back investigating another murder. This time, a priest is murdered and his congregation finds him dead in a confessional. Paul, Ben (played by Joe Penny who replaced Daniel Baldwin), and Eddie (Sebastian Spence) begin to investigate only to learn that the murder is somehow connected to the Russian mob. This puts an obvious strain on their lives since the mob doesn't play around, and their investigation quickly grows dangerous. Daughter Kate (Barbara Williams) has her own dilemma as she helps get a young delinquent boy released, only for him to go back to his criminal ways while daughter Jackie (Angela Featherstone) has decided her path in life is to follow her father's footsteps and she's joined the police academy. Even as the mob is threatening to tear them apart, the family itself couldn't be any stronger.

In his second to last film, Charles Bronson gives another great performance in a work several levels above its predecessor. For a man in his mid-seventies, he showed no signs of slowing down and wasn't afraid to put himself in action. The film dealt with the Russian mob, so there's no choice for our heroes than to get into the action. Bronson looks surprisingly good smacking around Russian mobsters. He even uses a couple of martial arts-styled takedowns. Bronson's character has so much more personality this time around, and it perfectly suits his sensibilities. Other than the *Death Wish* films, *Family of Cops* was his only other franchise. This second film was directed by David Greene of *Fatal Vision* fame. Followed by the third and final film *Family of Cops III: Under Suspicion*.

Breaker! Breaker!

1977 (MGM DVD) (djm)

"The guy's a bad dude—he's punched out half the town!"

Trucker J. D. (Chuck Norris) sends his younger brother on a delivery run through California, abut his brother is waylaid in an enclave town called Texas City, where an insane judge has set up his own law, order, and brand of corrupt justice. After a day of not hearing from him, J. D. travels the same path and ends up in the same town where his brother disappeared. Right away, J. D. meets with resistance and brutality, but what the crazy judge and his corrupt law enforcement aren't counting on is that J. D. is one hell of a fighter! With the help of a single mother living on the outskirts of the town, J. D. is assisted by outlying truckers who respond to a "Breaker! Breaker!" call on a CB radio. The climax has about a dozen big rig trucks bulldozing the town to cinders.

This was Chuck's first solo outing as an action star. Before this he appeared opposite Bruce Lee in *Game of Death* and *The Way of the Dragon*, and in *Slaughter in San Francisco* as Chuck Slaughter. After *Breaker! Breaker!* he starred in *Good Guys Wear Black*. Fans of his may want to check this smallish actioner out, but it's not essential. The director, Don Hulette, also composed the dated music.

Breakheart Pass

1975 (MGM DVD) (djm)

An Agatha Christie-esque thriller/mystery set in the frontier era of America, *Breakheart Pass* takes place almost entirely on a moving locomotive. Charles Bronson plays an undercover secret service agent posing as an outlaw in order to get himself aboard a train speeding through the Rockies. His mission slowly becomes apparent as the lawmen and various civilians aboard the train turn up dead or missing, and he begins to reveal his true intentions. The train's passengers include a Governor (Richard Crenna), a cavalry major (Ed Lauter), and a US marshal (Ben Johnson), and everyone's a suspect when dead bodies of soldiers turn up and an entire train car(!) is unhooked from the rest of the train and meets a terrible end.

Based on a novel by Alistar MacLean, *Breakheart Pass* is light on action, but a mid-point fight scene between Bronson and real-life world champion light-heavyweight prizefighter Archie Moore atop the chugging train is a highlight. Bronson is good in this, and his performance is "light" as far as Bronson performances go. A score by Jerry Goldsmith helps. Directed by Tom Gries, who also made *Breakout* with Bronson and *100 Rifles* with Jim Brown.

Breakout

1975 (Sony DVD) (djm)

Jay Wagner (Robert Duvall) is framed for a murder that took place in South America, and while he and his wife Ann (Jill Ireland) are vacationing, the authorities apprehend Jay and he's swiftly sentenced to more than twenty years in prison. Despondent and desperate, Ann turns to a mercenary to help her break her husband out of prison, but it takes time to set up. Nick Colton (Charles Bronson) isn't cheap, but he can be had, and when he agrees to lead a small team to bust out Jay, he first has to get around the fact that he's attracted to Ann. Once he gets his head around that, he fully commits to the rescue, and the finale of the film delivers great thrills and tension.

One of Bronson's sleeper hits, *Breakout* feels like an influence on movies like *Romancing the Stone* and *Six Days, Seven Nights*. It clearly wants to be an action adventure, but a somewhat grim tone gives it an uneven texture, although the climax is pretty great. Director Tom Gries also did *Breakheart Pass* with Bronson.

Spanish poster for *Breakout*. Author's collection.

Breathing Fire

1991 (AFA Entertainment DVD) (djm)

Bolo Yeung is on the covers of the various video releases of this film, but the real stars are Jonathan Ke Quan (from *The Goonies* and *Indiana Jones and the Temple of Doom*) and Eddie Saavedra (who never did another movie). They play brothers, whose father (Jerry Trimble from *Live by the Fist*) is a bank-robbing killer. They work out and train all the time and have a good relationship despite the fact that Quan is adopted. Their father has provided for them and has given them everything they could ever ask for . . . except the truth. The truth is that he was a cold-blooded killer in Vietnam and slaughtered his adopted son's mother during the war. His brother (played by Ed Neil from *Death Match*), who witnessed the murder, insisted that he take responsibility for the woman's death and take care of her baby boy as a penance. After Trimble pulls off a big robbery, his crew (Bolo Yeung is the silent muscle) turns against one of their own, and the plot thickens. When his sons finally realize what kind of man their father is, their lives are put in danger. Their uncle's strict training in the martial arts helps them a little bit in defending themselves from their father's crew, but when they face their father, things get ugly.

There's a good movie here somewhere. The plot is really cool and Quan and Saavedra are strong kids with some moves. They play older teenagers so it's believable that they could (as a team) go up against someone like Bolo and beat him. Jerry Trimble, who at this point in his career was doing movies like *The Master* with Jet Li, makes a good villain. The script is a little clunky and gives Ed Neil some terrible lines, and the overall picture has the feel of a Hong Kong action movie—there are ultra good guys and ultra bad ones, and plenty of melodrama. Lou Kennedy and Brandon De Wilde directed it.

Brick Mansions

2014 (Relativity DVD) (djm)

A straight-up rehash of France's *District B13* and *D13: Ultimatum*, *Brick Mansions* is the English language iteration from creator/screenwriter Luc Besson. Detective Damien (Paul Walker in his final completed film) takes on a dangerous gig by going into the apocalyptic hell zone known as Brick Mansions of Detroit to retrieve a stolen bomb before it detonates, and he joins forces with the wily Lino (David Belle who reprises his role from the French films), who has reasons of his own to interfere with the drug lords who possess the bomb. They go up against the drug boss Tremaine (RZA), not realizing that the mayor of Detroit and the US government have nefarious plans to nuke Brick Mansions by setting up Damien to unknowingly commit suicide by "saving" the bomb from going off. Leave it to the cop and the parkour-proficient Lino to save the 'hood and turn the tables on the government.

Showcasing Belle's unique martial art-esque running, jumping, flipping, and kicking from buildings and nearby stationary objects, *Brick Mansions* is a parkour-infused action movie if there ever was one. The original French films were leagues more stylish and smooth, and Cyril Raffaelli (who played the part Walker did here) is sorely missed. It's a novel concept to remake those movies into English, but the results are (at times) buffoonish and clumsy (to say the least). Watching a vibrant Paul Walker being athletic and cool casts a strange pallor over the entire film. Still, *Brick Mansions* is fun and entertaining if you can switch your brain off for a while. David Belle deserves more vehicles to feature him displaying his talents as the creator of parkour. Directed by Camille Delamarre, who was the editor of *Transporter 3*.

Bridge of Dragons

1999 (HBO DVD) (CD)

"There's only one problem with that, though: You can't kill Ruechang . . . but I can."

Warchild (Dolph Lundgren) is the perfect soldier working for the insane General Ruechang (Cary-Hirouki Tagawa). He knows just how dangerous Ruechang is but remains loyal since the general was responsible for Warchild's upbringing and training. Princess Halo (Rachel Shane) isn't in love with Ruechang and doesn't want to marry him, especially after learning that her father (the King) was murdered by her betrothed. On the day of her wedding she flees, with Ruechang quickly putting Warchild on the case. He quickly finds her and wants to bring her in. After he witnesses firsthand the evil of his general, Warchild has a change of heart and instead of delivering her to be married, he protects her from her intended at any cost. Warchild teams up with rebels to take down the despot and put an end to his evil reign.

Dolph Lundgren (*The Joshua Tree*) once again delivers an action-packed performance in Isaac Florentine's *Bridge of Dragons*. When the film opens, it just jumps right into the action, filling every frame with fantastic stunt work, messy squibs, constant explosions, and hail after hail of gunfire. And if all this isn't enough for action junkies, Dolph busts out his karate training and beats the crap out of numerous soldiers. There's an exciting final fight between him and Cary-Hirouki Tagawa (*Mortal Kombat*), which is a must-see. As always, Florentine keeps everything moving at a wicked fast pace, barely giving the audience a chance to breathe. As an added attraction, the ferociously gorgeous Rachel Shane (*Meltdown*) gets in on the action with a couple of entertaining fight scenes as well. This is a criminally underappreciated action film from Nu Image, and one that fans of Lundgren and Florentine should make a point to see. Incidentally, this was Nu Image's first movie to be filmed in Bulgaria.

Broken Arrow

1996 (Fox DVD) (CD)

"Would you mind not shooting at the thermonuclear weapons?"

Captain Riley Hale (Christian Slater) is ready and set to go on a routine training exercise with his old pal Major Vic Deakins (John Travolta) when the most unlikely of things happens: Deakins tries to kill him, crashing the plane (a stealth bomber) and the cargo. The cargo just so happens to be some incredibly powerful thermonuclear weapons, and Deakins plans to hold them for ransom from the US government. He doesn't count on Major Hale being such a thorn in his side, especially since he had left him for dead. With the help of local park ranger Terry Carmichael (Samantha Mathis), Hale follows Deakins around, watching his every move and realizing how dangerous he and his pal Kelly (Howie Long, a former NFL player) can be. When it comes to saving the lives of thousands of people, they make sure Deakins's plan falls to shit.

If you're a diabolical genius hellbent on making millions of dollars or destroying part of the country, then you can't do it alone. You need a trusting henchman who either believes in what you're doing or can be bought for the right price to help you achieve your goal. In this big-budget film, Travolta's character has Kelly, a no-nonsense soldier played by Howie Long (next seen in *Firestorm*). After he conquered the NFL (before he became an analyst for Fox Sports), Long set his sights on Hollywood, and John Woo (*Hard Target*) was there to help prepare him. Woo was out to prove to everyone he could deliver a Hollywood-style action film, and it was a huge success. Long's performance is quite memorable, and he really appears to have fun being a bad guy. The introduction of his character (as well as his character's fate) is quite memorable. After being excited by his performance in *Broken Arrow*, several

Fox executives gave him his first leading role in *Firestorm*, which tanked at the box office. Therefore, no more movies starring Howie Long.

Broken Bars

1995 (York VHS) (CD)

Nick Slater (*Enter the Blood Ring*'s Benjamin Maccabee) is one of the best cops around, and when a dirty job needs to be done, he's their man. His boss, Jack Dillon (Joe Estevez), asks him to go undercover in Trabuco Federal Prison to snoop around and try to learn who is behind the heroin trade in Los Angeles. He uses the cover of being an armed robber and finds himself behind bars and bumping heads with Warden Pitt (Wings Hauser). He's one vicious dude who puts together bareknuckle fights at the prison for his own amusement and he tries to lure Slater into his twisted little games. Slater quickly learns the truth behind who is in charge of the heroin trade, and he will have to fight to stay alive in a place where everyone wants him dead.

Broken Bars might actually be Benjamin Maccabee's (also in *Ultimate Prey*) best film. It seemed to have a larger budget and a tad more polish than the pictures he directed himself. You really can't go wrong with a prison action flick chock-full of corny dialogue, silicone breasts, bare chested men beating each other to a pulp, and Wings Hauser. Maccabee sports an unnaturally long ponytail while still creating some of his more impressive fight scenes. When he bursts into action, he far outshines any of his co-stars. We also get to see guys like Paulo Tocha in action appearing alongside his *Bloodsport* co-star Donald Gibb. This is the only feature film that Tom Neuwirth has directed (he also helmed an episode of Lorenzo Lamas' *Renegade*).

Brotherhood of Death

1976 (Anchor Bay DVD) (djm)

Three lifelong friends/brothers—Raymond (Roy Jefferson), Junior (Haskell V. Anderson), and Ned (Le Tari)—are sick of what's becoming of their town in Kincaid County, so they go off to Vietnam and get the hang of smoking and dealing dope to other soldiers while learning guerrilla warfare. Years later, they are discharged and when they go back home, they're disgusted by what's transpired in their very own town: Ku Klux Klan have infested the area and blatantly run over the law. When a black woman is raped by a mob of Klansmen and no one is punished for it, Raymond, Junior, Ned, and the male members of the black community strategize a retribution of the like Kincaid County has never seen. The brothers use their skills as soldiers, planning elaborate traps and dirty warfare tactics to run the Klan from the town.

Starring a slew of professional football players, *Brotherhood of Death* is ultra simplistic, but entirely charming in using a bunch of rough-cut-diamond nonactors and turning them into pseudo-action heroes. The action element is pretty light, but once it gets going toward the end, it really delivers. Jefferson played wide receiver with the Chargers and the Colts. Other players include Mike Thomas (running back with the Redskins) and Mike Bass (defensive back with the Redskins). More athletes are featured in the film in supporting roles. Directed by John Lewis.

Brotherhood of the Wolf
2001 (TVA Films DVD) (djm)

An ultra stylized genre mash-up, Christophe Gans's *Brotherhood of the Wolf* manages to put contemporary martial arts in a period setting (1766, France), but that's just the tip of the iceberg. Under the guise of a creature feature, this epic-length (152 minutes!) French film also gives Mark Dacascos (from *Only the Strong* and *Kickboxer 5*) a great supporting role in a time when Hollywood had nearly forsaken him. Dacascos is the film's greatest asset. He plays an Iroquois warrior named Mani tagging along with a taxidermist knight called Gregorie de Fronsac (Samuel Le Bihan). They become embroiled in a plot thicker than the three-disc DVD set I bought of this film. A "wolf" creature is stalking and terrorizing a large enough French province that the King has heard the horrible tales this beast is engendering. The knight and the Native American are entertained by the court, which sees them as novelties, but the members can hardly believe that they can stop the creature, though they assure everyone they can. They make friends and enemies: A friend in the form of a voluptuous courtesan spy, played by the amazingly endowed Monica Bellucci, and an enemy in the guise of a one-armed hunter, played by Vincent Cassel. It's pretty obvious early on that the hunter is hiding deep secrets (and another arm!) that are revealed in the martial arts–filled finale involving spin kicks, spiny swords, and a goliath of a creature running amok. Clearly, there are more reasons than just Mark Dacascos to see this film, but he's the best one.

Dacascos should always make movies with Christophe Gans. They first worked together on the criminally underseen *Crying Freeman* (one of Dacascos's best), and in this film, Gans gives him the best moments in the film, outshining and outclassing everyone around him in every scene he's in. Dacascos shows in a big-budget movie with great music, editing, and lighting that he's an amazing martial artist and an underrated action star. It's strange seeing Dacascos as an Indian doing flips and kicks in the middle of a crowd of pompous French guys with powder on the faces, but that's one of the many cool things about this movie. It's bizarre to the extreme, and it rightfully garnered a cult following after its limited theatrical release in the US, which is when I first saw it. If you can get past the epic length and the subtitles, this should be top priority viewing, and it's a perfect place to begin watching Mark Dacascos if you're unfamiliar with him.

Brutal Glory
1989 (Quest Entertainment VHS) (djm)

In 1918, Kid McCoy (played by Timothy Brantley), a pickpocket scrapper on the streets of New York, is handpicked by a boxing trainer named Max (Robert Vaughn) to box in his club and train with his best fighters. Kid has an irascible drive to fight and make money, and amazingly his skills as a fighter are unparalleled, despite the fact that he's never been formerly trained. Within months, he's got the attention of the current heavyweight champion (played by South African martial artist James Ryan), who accepts Kid's challenge to fight for the title. In a brutal, bloody match, Kid defeats him and becomes the champion of the world. He and Max come up with a plan to go to Africa and fight under a different name, then slowly build up the new name for himself while making a bunch of cash, but as soon as he arrives he's recognized, and his dishonest plan is dashed. It doesn't matter, though, because boxing promoters are eager to match him with different fighters and the current champ of Africa. As he works his way up the African title-holders, Kid proves that he's the real thing.

This based-on-fact melodrama stars future PhD nutritionist Brantley, who is hard to read as an actor, but the main reason this film is covered in this book is because James Ryan from *Kill or Be Killed* and *Kill and Kill Again* has a nice part in it as a boxer, who is defeated by Kid McCoy and then later cheers him on as a spectator in another fight. Other than that, *Brutal Glory* is a footnote as a boxing film and just a blip on Ryan's career. It was filmed in Africa. Directed by Koos Roets.

Bucktown
1975 (MGM DVD) (djm)

"I don't wanna shoot you, Roy.
I just wanna beat the hell out of you!"

Dean Johnson (Fred "The Hammer" Williamson) comes to Bucktown to bury his brother, who owned a hip, money-making bar. With plans to attend the funeral and leave town, he sees some opportunity in his brother's bar and decides to stay awhile and get it up and running again. But there's a big problem: The corrupt white sheriff in town and his racist deputies might be the guys who killed his brother, and they try to strong-arm him into paying "protection taxes," but Dean isn't about to give in. He calls on some old buddies who quickly heed his call for help, and they go on a murder spree and kill the whole lot of deputies, causing the sheriff to resign his post and relinquish his badge, which Dean's buddies promptly pick up for themselves. With Dean's power-hungry friends in charge of Bucktown, Dean begins to realize that his crew is just as bad as the racist white deputies they

killed, and when they try to rape his girlfriend (played by Pam Grier) and kill his other friends, Dean takes the offensive and has to fight off the guys who helped him in the first place.

Fans of Fred Williamson will love this movie. There's lots of great action in it, and the final fight scene between The Hammer and Thalmus Rasulala is a knockout of a donnybrook. Also, watch for Carl Weathers as one of the goons Williamson has to fight towards the end. *Bucktown* is one of The Hammer's better movies. Directed by Arthur Marks.

Bullet
1996 (New Line DVD) (CD)

"Man, I don't stick nothing up my nose unless it's two legs wrapped around my neck."

Butch Stein (Mickey Rourke) is finally about to find himself back on the streets after doing a stint in prison. It's not an easy transition, and he quickly begins to revert back to his old ways. "Bullet" (as he is known on the streets) has caught the attention of his old archrival Tank (Tupac Shakur) who has an old score to settle, and he wants blood. Butch may not care much about what happens to himself, but he will do anything for his equally messed up brothers Ruby (Adrien Brody) and Louis (Ted Levine). Blood will be shed, but the question is, who will be left standing?

Of course, attention for this film was mostly drawn to rapper Tupac Shakur (*Gang Related*) since it was released just one month after his murder. Mickey Rourke (*Double Team, Iron Man 2*) is the star of the film and he bursts out of the prison gates ready to cause trouble. Not even ten minutes into it, he stabs a fool in the eye. The film is violent without being action packed; it's more like a crime thriller. *Bullet* has a solid one-on-one, bare-knuckled fight where Rourke tangles with one of Tank's men, allowing the star to prove that he still has those amateur boxing skills. The movie itself isn't anything to really get excited over, but many of the performances are standouts—especially Rourke's and Ted Levine's (a criminally underrated character actor). Rourke not only acted in the movie, but served as the music supervisor and contributed to the script (under a pseudonym). Directed by Julien Temple.

Bullet
2013 (Giant Ape DVD) (djm)

"You know, when people wake up in the morning, they see sunshine. When I wake up, I see pieces of shit on the street. And it's my job to clean it up."

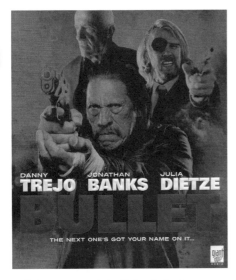

DVD/Blu-ray artwork for *Bullet*. Author's collection.

Danny Trejo stars as a renegade cop and sometime bare-knuckle fighter named Frank, who is a former narcotics addict. His daughter is also an addict, and they attend Narcotics Anonymous together. Frank (who is sometimes known as Bullet to his friends) is out with his grandson one morning when he becomes distracted for a moment, which is just enough time for his grandson to be kidnapped. Immediately, Frank receives a phone call demanding that he perform a task in order to get his grandson back: He must sign a retraction statement that landed a man on death row. The man he sent to prison is due to be executed in a few days, and his father—an evil gangster named Carlito (Jonathan Banks)—has orchestrated several events that will theoretically get his son reprieved and off of death row before his execution. Another big kidnapping he arranged was the daughter of the governor (played by John Savage), who he hopes will call off the execution. Carlito's plan goes wrong because his big mistake was messing with Frank, who goes rogue, gathering up an arsenal and tossing away his badge as he beelines it for Carlito's compound. The last thing anyone from Carlito's side expects is the way Frank carries out his revenge.

Some slick camera work and a more than capable star turn by Trejo are completely and utterly undone by some terrible supporting characters and amateur editing. One of Carlito's henchman is played by a tall German guy who tries to be like Alexander Godunov from *Die Hard*, but the actor (Torsten Voges) ends up coming across more as a caricature than the real thing. Trejo, while a commanding presence, has some lame one-liners in the movie and in one scene mocks his *Machete* movies by shooting down a thug who comes at him with a machete. Unfortunately, this promising package of an action vehicle for Trejo is a big disappointment. It was produced by Robert Rodriguez and directed by Nick Lyon.

Bullet Raja
2013 (T-Series DVD) (CD)

"I, Raja Mishra, son of Ramsharan Mishra, caste Shandilya, district Azamgarh, swear to avenge your death before sunset tomorrow. Otherwise, I'll burn myself alive."

Raja Mishra (Saif Ali Khan) cons his way into a wedding party only to end up saving everyone when he learns of a plot by gangsters to take everyone out so they can cash in on their poppy seed fields. He teams up with the bride's cousin Rudra (Jimmy Shergill), and the two of them clean house. This sets off a chain reaction where the two will then have to avenge the death of Rudra's uncle. These gangsters aren't the type to be shown up so they attack back, killing Rudra. Raja swears revenge no matter the cost, even if all these guys are connected to the government. The politicians need Raja killed so they bring in the toughest cop they can find: Arun Singh Munna (Vidyut Jamwal from the amazing *Commando: A One Man Army*). He and Raja will face off, but they are only pawns in a much grander scheme.

The Bollywood film *Bullet Raja* runs far too long and the obligatory musical numbers aren't particular catchy either. The story's pretty engaging; lead actor Saif Ali Khan is charismatic, and the cinematography is quite grand. None of this matters, though, when Vidyut Jamwal (also in the Bollywood film *Force*) makes his presence known in the film. He has two fantastic action scenes, and he delivers everything you would expect from him. His athleticism is downright jaw dropping, especially when he flips over moving vehicles with ease. Chances are you'll forget just about everything in the film except for him and his unique brand of martial arts action. Directed by Tigmanshu Dhulia.

Bullet to the Head
2013 (Warner DVD) (djm)

Career criminal Jimmy Bobo (an imposing Sylvester Stallone in his mid-sixties) does a job with his partner, and afterwards they are double-crossed by their employer. His partner is killed by a ruthless mercenary named Keegan (Jason Momoa), and Jimmy gets a burn in his gut to get revenge. He forms an uneasy buddy/buddy relationship with an Asian cop named Taylor Kwon (Sung Kang), who has no idea who he's riding around town with. He thinks Jimmy is just a dumb two-bit hood, but Jimmy is a force of nature who not only saves his life on more than one occasion, but gives Kwon a lesson or two in life. Their target is corrupt real estate developer Morel (Adewale Akinnuoye-Agbaje) and his patsy, a cavalier playboy named Marcus Babtiste (Christian Slater), who is in over his head. When Jimmy Bobo and detective Kwon come into their circle of influence, the bodies start piling up. A final incredible axe fight between Jimmy and Keegan sets the screen on fire.

Theatrical release poster for *Bullet to the Head*. Author's collection.

A very back-to-basics exercise in action and banter, *Bullet to the Head* gives Stallone a sweet-tooth role full of juicy moments. His counterpart, played by Sung Kang, is less impressive, but only because he is dwarfed on screen in presence and panache by Stallone. His part was originally offered to Thomas Jane, who lost the part after producer Joel Silver reconsidered the buddy/buddy dynamic. Director Walter Will (*Red Heat, Undisputed, Last Man Standing*) did a solid job on this entertaining "B" movie, made for fans of '70s and '80s action. Unfortunately, it was a gigantic flop when it was released to theaters. It was based on a graphic novel.

Sylvester Stallone as Jimmy Bonomo, a hitman, in Walter Hill's *Bullet to the Head*. Author's collection.

The Bunker
2013 (Inception DVD) (djm)

"I sent him to do ops
—not to cut off fingers!"

A reprehensible motion picture by any standard, *The Bunker*—starring ex-wrestlers Ken Shamrock and Mike Brown—is set in Southern Vietnam in

1965, detailing the madness and degeneration of the human condition during wartime. Technically, it's an "action" movie—with MMA-style beatdowns and neck breaking—but is there a story? If there is one, let it be known here that it wouldn't matter if it did because it would be for naught. Shamrock and Brown play soldiers in Vietnam on a murky, miscommunicated mission that goes south, and two separate platoons collide. One of the platoons has been waylaid in a dingy bunker for far too long, and their cancerous commander has managed to brainwash his men into following him into a death-managed mission where they capture, torture, and murder both Vietnamese villagers *and* fellow American soldiers for infringing on their little death pact. Some of the soldiers in the other platoon are able to fight back, but the hulked out and crazed Shamrock has a ferocious brutality that's hard to best.

I have no idea what this movie was intended to be. It's unrelentingly ugly, unpleasant, and repugnant. Action fans will be appalled at the lack of finesse that's given to the story—or at least an outline of a story—and when the action scenes come on, they're underscored by an ambient music track that doesn't allow the film to have any suspense, character, or arcs. It's all just one big and nasty assault that keeps on going for an hour and a half. If Shamrock or Brown have any fans out there who seek this movie out based on their names and faces on the video box art, they will never forgive them. It does Vietnam veterans a grave injustice, and action and fight movie fans should feel affronted. Written, produced, and directed by Joe Black. Shame.

Busted Up

1986 (MCA VHS) (djm)

Bird (Paul Coufos) is a low-rent boxer with a checkered past, struggling to stay afloat and keep custody of his daughter, whose singer mother (Irene Cara) is fighting to reclaim the girl. Bird's not a great fighter, but he's got heart. He fights with everything he's got, and when the neighborhood youth center is in jeopardy from a corrupt businessman, Bird fights for as much cash as he's able to muster up to placate the businessman, but there's more at stake than Bird realizes. His trainer (played by Stan Shaw) helps him train as hard as he's able, but somehow Bird's luck trickles out. In a twist, he rekindles his relationship with his ex and they actually get married and take vows to stay committed and faithful to each other.

Not as compelling as its follow-up *Thunderground*, *Busted Up* gives Coufos a decent vehicle, but it just doesn't hit the bulls-eye like its sequel does. Both films have a very human element that's endearing and interesting, but the action/boxing themes take a sideline to the drama. Directed by Conrad E. Palmisano.

Cabo Blanco

1980 (Laserlight DVD) (MMM)

"I'm glad you think that cemetery is colorful, because if anything happens to that girl . . . rest in peace."

The notion of Charles Bronson as a romantic leading man is a tough sell (see 1970's *Lola* for proof of that). The notion of Charles Bronson—during his brief career lull between '70s smashes like *Death Wish* and *Telefon* and his '80s reinvention as Cannon Films' go-to splatter-action star—as the romantic lead in an uncredited remake of *Casablanca* is simply . . . impossible. And, yet, here we are in *Cabo Blanco*. Stop us if you've heard a plot like this before: Bronson stars as Giff, an American expatriate who operates a nightclub on the Peruvian island of title. Into his gin joint waltzes French beauty Marie Claine (Dominique Sanda). She's followed shortly thereafter by escaped Nazi Gunther Beckdorff (Jason Robards), who's pursuing sunken gold, thereby setting off a quandary for the dedicatedly neutral Giff—should he simply let Hitler's henchman do his dirty work, or should he risk everything to stop evil, even if it means losing his Parisian love in the process?

Cabo Blanco really is *Casablanca* in daft 1980 drag. If it's not great (which it's not), it is a fascinating curiosity, particularly as one of nine movies Bronson made with director J. Lee Thompson. Alas, even with a few choice violent outbursts that include Beckdorff's sidekick taking a sword to the eyeball, it's hard to imagine that this talky drama came from the same team that gave us the likes of *St. Ives*, *The White Buffalo*, *10 to Midnight*, *The Evil That Men Do*, and *Kinjite: Forbidden Subjects*. As noted earlier, though, here we are in *Cabo Blanco*.

Cage

1989 (Trinity DVD) (djm)

"This is walk away or get carried away!"

In Vietnam, Billy (Lou Ferrigno) saves Scott's (Reb Brown) life, but Billy gets a bullet in the head as a result. Scott watches over Billy in the hospital until he recuperates, but Billy is never the same. Flash-forward to 1989, and Scott and Billy live in a house together and run a dive bar in Los Angeles. Billy is childlike and innocent, and Scott takes care of him. When some thugs cause trouble in their bar, Billy quells the conflict with a few pushes and shoves, and this impresses a couple of businessmen who are in trouble with the Asian mob. The businessmen are deep in debt after betting on losing fighters in an underground cage-fighting ring in Chinatown. They decide to convince Billy to fight for them, but Scott stops them from getting anywhere. When they fool Billy into thinking it's Scott who he would be fighting for, Billy goes along with

Video release poster for *Cage*. Author's collection.

them and begins his fights in the Cage. Once Billy gets in the Cage and starts winning fights, the Asian mob gets upset and decides to take Billy from his handlers. Meantime, Scott is trying to find his buddy, and he joins an undercover Chinese cop (Al Leong) in a quest to put an end to the illegal fighting.

This film has a soft heart. It would be easy to make fun of or laugh at the goofiness of Ferrigno's performance, but he's actually pretty good in this role. Reb Brown is good, too, and when he gets in the cage to fight some fights of his own, he does a pretty solid job of mixing it up. He's not particularly stronger or more agile than anyone else, but his fights look good. The strongest aspect of this picture is the

Billy (Lou Ferrigno) is unleashed in the *Cage*. Author's collection.

relationship Scott and Billy share. I liked the late-'80s, early '90s feel to the movie, and there are some recognizable faces in the cast. Watch for James Shigeta (from *Die Hard*), Branscombe Richmond (from *Renegade* with Lorenzo Lamas), and Danny Trejo in small roles. This was directed by Lang Elliot, who also made the unfortunate sequel.

INTERVIEW:
REB BROWN
(djm)

Throughout the 1970s, '80s, and '90s, Reb Brown appeared in dozens of motion pictures and episodes from many of Universal's episodic television staples. He is perhaps best known for playing Captain America in two made-for-television movies and for starring in a slew of war-themed action films including Strike Commando *(1987),* Robowar *(1988),* Mercenary Fighters *(1988), and* Last Flight to Hell *(1990). With a full, muscular frame, and skills in the martial arts, Brown earned his action star status long ago, but sadly, he's mostly left his career in films behind to pursue other ventures.*

Reb, how did you get involved in the movie business? How did you land your first role on Universal's *Sssssss* in 1973?

Actually, I was working at a bar as a bouncer back then. I was throwing two guys out [laughing], one in each hand. A Hollywood agent was sitting up at the top. He was actually visiting someone over at The Ice House in Pasadena. I was working at The Handlebar Saloon. He looks at me and says, "Hey, kid. You wanna be an actor?" I said, "Just a moment!" as I'm banging these guys' heads together and throwing them out the door. I said, "I don't know," and he said, "That'll

work." Soon thereafter, I ended up working over at Universal. He got me an audition, and they needed someone to play a big football player in that movie, which Dirk Benedict was starring in. So I got it in one day, and that got me my SAG card. In about a two-month period, I talked with this agent about it, and I ended up getting in SAG.

You had a great supporting cast in the *Miami Vice* episode, "Viking Bikers From Hell." Sonny Landham, John Matuszak, and Kim Coats were guests on that episode, too.

I remember a funny story about them. We were going into a hotel, and John was 6 foot 8 and 300 pounds. It was myself, Sonny, and John, and we were going into a hotel, and John said to me, "Look, everyone's looking at us. It's because of these tattoos they put on us." I said, "I don't think that's it, John." Sonny was a great guy too. He was a character and a half. Remember, he was in *Predator*. He was at dinner with the two writers of *Predator*, the Thomas Brothers. He stood up in the middle of the restaurant and started cutting himself with the knife. He was like, "This is what I'm going to do when he comes after me." They were like, "Hey, cool it!" He's a character and a half. Matuszak was funny because he evidently had a terrible temper, okay? He said that he'd start cooling it. We finished doing the show, and he was back in LA, and he said he'd cool it and get real nice. He got into some altercation and [laughing] he got into the street into the traffic, and they said he was running away from the scene. Both Sonny and I called him up and left him a message and said, "Glad to see you cooled down!" It was fun. They were good guys, they really were.

You said that you're comfortable with fighting scenes. Have you had any formal training as a fighter?

I had fourteen amateur heavyweight fights with a 12/2 record, and now I have a black belt in Shindokan karate, and I have a purple belt in Gracie jiu jitsu.

Your training definitely shows in films you did like *Cage*.

I wish I'd trained in jiu jitsu sooner because it would have saved my hands. I bounced in bars for a number of years, and it's a tough way to go. You go to work with a mouth guard and make sure your hands are wrapped. Yeah.

The two *Captain America* movies you did in the late 1970s have made a comeback with the resurgence of interest in superhero movies and Marvel characters. Talk a little bit about working on these movies.

I was at Universal at the time, and I met with Allan Balter, who was the producer of *The Six Million-Dollar Man*, and we had a lunch together, and we just hit it off. He felt that I was right for the role of Captain America, and I ended up doing it, and I had a blast doing it. It's a wonderful character. Captain America is good, he's a consummate hero. It was fun being a superhero. When it was recently released on DVD, it played again on the SyFy Channel, and they played it back to back, back to back again, okay? All of a sudden, I've got a whole new audience. The kids in the neighborhood were asking me if I could really jump that high when I threw the motorcycle up there and stuff like that. It's fun. That was a great experience for me. We had an opportunity to do the series, but Universal lost the rights to it. *The Incredible Hulk* was getting $2,500 an episode for the licensing fee. Whoever was the attorney for our show let it sit on the back burner, and then when it came time when CBS wanted to come buy it for $1,300, he didn't have the information in front of him, or something and he let it go, and then there was a renegotiation where they ended up wanting fifty grand an episode. Yeah. It just destroyed it.

It's interesting that you actually play Captain America's son in the show.

Yeah, they wanted to update it for television a little bit. It came out well in that way. I was exposed to that amazing drug, which was basically a supersteroid, and I had to have it because they almost killed me. I didn't want it, but by doing that, that's what made me a superhero. When I was doing *Captain America*, I was down at Venice Beach. We were filming the second movie, and I came out of my motorhome wearing my Captain America outfit

Reb Brown lets out his signature war cry in *Cage*. Author's collection.

Scott (Reb Brown) is ambushed in *Cage*. Author's collection.

Scott (Reb Brown) is the victor in a cage fight, while Tiger Joe (Al Leong, right) cheers on in *Cage*. Author's collection.

C

and my shield was up, and I was in character, okay? There's this drunk sitting on the wall, and he falls off the wall when he sees me, and when he gets up, he says, "Man, I gotta stop drinkin'!" About a minute later, he realizes that I'm real, and I'm laughing, and he finally says, "Hey, maybe not—he's real!"

Did you keep any parts of your costume?

I don't have the shield—they never let me have that. I did have a couple of the outfits earlier on, but people were interested in them, so . . . I did a PR thing in Venezuela and the motorcycle is still there. Actually, I got a call recently and someone did the motorcycle again and now it's in a museum. They duplicated it. They took some pictures of me with the motorcycle, and I answered some questions. It's pretty cool.

You later did a string of Italian exploitation action films. Any comment about that?

Yeah, I started doing that stuff. I couldn't seem to get into the stuff that I was trying to get. I tested for *Flight of the Intruder*. The character that Willem Dafoe played was written as 6 foot 2 and weighed 220 pounds and was blond-haired and blue-eyed. But . . . they took Dafoe. That's politics. Same thing for *Red Dawn*. Powers Boothe took the role that I tested for. That's a part of what show business is like.

Do you regret doing the films you did in Italy, like *Strike Commando*?

No! They were fun! *Strike Commando* . . . that little film I did for those guys built them a little studio, and everything. They were a wonderful crew. They were very tight-knit. I had a good time with Bruno Mattei, the director. He's known as Vincent Dawn. I did *RoboWar* with him too.

Talk about those two films. *Strike Commando* is basically a rip-off of *Rambo: First Blood Part II*, and *RoboWar* is a rip-off of *Predator*.

Yeah, exactly. I knew what I was going to be doing. Bruno's room was right next to mine, and I could hear him watching *Rambo* one night, and all the different films we were copying. I'd end up doing the same thing the next day. I figured, we were making different movies than those, it was a different ballgame we were playing.

How come you didn't do *Strike Commando 2*? I think Brent Huff took over your role.

Because I was busy at the time. I was doing *Distant Thunder* up in Vancouver. I was supposed to do *Strike Commando 2*, but I couldn't. They were very upset with me, but I was supposed to work only four weeks on *Distant Thunder*, but I ended up working eight. They had to get the other guy. I remember that.

Around that time, you also did *Mercenary Fighters* with Peter Fonda for Cannon. That was a fun movie, and to me all of these action movies you were doing during this time are all sort of related.

Exactly. It was a good market back then. You could do those military movies, and you could have fun

and go to different places. Avi Lerner was actually the producer on that one. He runs Nu Image now. We had a good time there in Africa. We were down there at work one time and there were these baboons there. There's a fruit that baboons eat and it makes them drunk, it's like a kumquat. Up on this hill, they're watching us film while they're eating this stuff. They're laughing and *laughing*! About noontime, they moved down the hill. It was quite funny.

You've shot off so many rounds from so many different guns all over the world doing these movies.

My wife said I should write a book called *Body Count*.

I love how you have a signature yell when you shoot guns. Nobody yells and shoots like you.

That's just something I started to develop on *Uncommon Valor*, if I remember right. I also did it in an alley with a pistol on *Street Hunter*. I've got a picture now that I got from the Internet—I think it's from *Strike Commando* where I've got a bandana around my head, and it says, "His scream can kill rapists in other countries!"

You did two *Cage* movies with Lou Ferrigno and director Lang Elliot. Talk a little about working on these movies.

Lou and I got along really well, and Lang Elliot has been a friend of mine for a long, long time now. The second one wasn't as good as the first one. It was more rushed and we didn't have as much money. I remember doing one fight scene on the first one. We didn't have the technology back in 1988 that they did later on, but I fought from seven o'clock in the morning until seven o'clock at night. By the time we did the second one, I had become more accomplished as a martial artist, which we incorporated into the second film. I remember we had [Jean-Claude] Van Damme's stunt double, and when you do some of those things, you're gonna get hit. It just so happened that in the film I win the fights, which meant I did the most damage towards the end, which worked well for me.

Al Leong was in the first one, and he had a nice part in it. What do you remember about him?

Great guy. Remember him in *Die Hard* where he ate the candy bar? That was great. He played a good guy in *Cage*.

I'm not sure what happened between parts one and two of *Cage*, but Lou Ferrigno's character seems greatly altered. His character was much more genuine in the first one. He was very sensitive and interesting in the first one, but not so much in the sequel.

In the first one he weighed about 260-some pounds. In the second one he was about 315. He was getting ready for contests and stuff, so as far as the chemistry in his body goes, it was different.

Ah, I see. Well, you guys worked really well together in the first one. Your friendship really shone through. In the second one, you guys hardly had any screen time together.

Scott (Reb Brown) and Billy (Lou Ferrigno) restrain Tin Lum Yin (James Shigata) in *Cage*. Author's collection.

I remember we'd play around like friends in the first one, and we'd punch each other a little bit, and one time I punched him, and he looked at me and said, "You're *strong*, Reb." I worked out with him a couple of times at the gym, and boy, he's a strong man. My wife laughed because he was the only man she's ever seen who could put a plate of food on his chest and eat off his chest. He's a big dude.

How come you guys didn't do a part 3? The end of part 2 suggested that there would be another sequel.

Well, I don't think they ever got the funding for it. It just didn't work out. It would've been fun to do.

Your co-star in the war movie *Last Flight to Hell* was Chuck Connors. What do you remember about that film or working with Connors?

I remember when I first met him, I got teary-eyed because he was *The Rifleman*, which I'd seen as a kid. We got along beautifully. I'm sorry to see his passing in recent years. He said something to me when we were on the set. There was an eighteen-year-old girl in the film, and he goes, "Hey, Reb. You got any of that?" I said, "No, Chuck, I'm married." He said, "Good. There's a chance for me!" That's about it. He was a really good dude, though.

Steve James was the star of *Street Hunter*, which you played the villain in.

Ah! Steve. I really miss him. I think about him every day. He was a wonderful human being. He used to tell his pop that I was the white Steve James. [Laughing] We were filming the movie, and we were working late. In two weeks' time, we did four weeks of work. We were doing the fight scene, and Steve and I were watching the guys change the set, and I looked at him and started singing the seven dwarfs work song. Pretty soon, the whole crew was singing it, too. We just laughed. Everything about Steve was great.

You took a long break between movies. The horror film *Night Claws* is your first movie in over a decade.

Yeah, I kinda dropped out. If you see me physically, I don't fit into the normal roles of the father or grandfather, okay? I'm big and physical, and most of the people that play those roles don't look like me. A lot of times, I'm bigger and in better shape than the guys who are playing the lead. That's just something that I'm not going to change about myself.

Cage II: The Arena of Death

1994 (Summa VHS) (djm)

Billy (Lou Ferrigno) and Scott (Reb Brown) return for this pointless sequel, which was also directed by Lang Elliot. The Asian mob fool Billy into thinking Scott is dead, so they use his sadness and anger to get him to fight and kill people in illegal cage fights in Chinatown. Billy seems more intelligent this time, and Ferrigno seems to have forgotten how to play him. He's also put on even more muscle this time around, and the mob gives him daily steroid injections that ultimately harm him. Scott runs around town looking for the place where the fights are conducted, and he joins an old martial arts master who teaches him how to fight more effectively. When Scott enters the Cage to surprise Billy that's he's still alive, Billy doesn't recognize him at first and hits him a few times. When he finally recognizes him, they hug for a long time, confusing their bloodthirsty audience. It's silly.

In this entry, the fights get started almost immediately, and there are hardly any breaks in between. There's enough time for Billy to fall in love with an Asian hooker (played by Shannon Lee, Bruce's daughter) who massages his muscles after each fight, but not enough time between Scott and Billy. James Shigeta returns as the Asian mob leader, and Gerald Okamura (from *Ninja Academy*) and James Lew (from *Lethal Weapon 4*) are in it, too. The ending suggests that there would have been a part 3 if this one had been a success. Thank goodness it wasn't.

The Cannonball Run

1981 (HBO DVD) (V)

"This infrared is the cat's ass!"

Hal Needham's second Burt Reynolds-led franchise (after *Smokey and the Bandit*) is a broad, all-star ensemble comedy written by *Car & Driver* editor Brock Yates, telling the story of an illegal cross-country race like the one that he actually started and competed in. It's a great cast (of particular interest to action fans are a young Adrienne Barbeau in a black Lamborghini Countach and Roger Moore as a guy who thinks he really is James Bond), and Needham's fellow stuntmen get plenty of work in the form of police chases, off-roading, fiery explosions, a motorcycle skydive, and cars crashing into a swimming pool, through walls, off a bridge, etc. In one scene Reynolds and sidekick Dom DeLuise land a small plane in the middle of a town just to pick up a six-pack at a corner market. The large crowd seen down the block in the background seems to indicate that the whole town came out to watch the stunt.

There's plenty to enjoy here, but if I'm in the mood for an ode to old school stuntwork I'd rather watch Needham's own *Hooper* or Brian Trenchard-Smith's *Deathcheaters*. A lot of the comedy here is uncomfortably dated, especially everything about Reynolds and DeLuise

Jackie Chan might be a little out of his comfort zone in the screwball comedy *Cannonball Run*. Author's collection.

kidnapping Farrah Fawcett by pretending to be paramedics and drugging her. It's supposed to be cute even though Burt has to calm her fears by saying "A gang bang? We're racers, not rapists." This makes it into the book by being one of Jackie Chan's first English language roles. I know a lot of people dislike *The Big Brawl* but this makes you appreciate it because as an introduction of Chan to America this is about as low as you can go. He plays "Japan's #1 Race Car Driver Jacky Chan." As far as I can tell the change in nationality is just to feed into Japan's reputation at the time as a creator of electronic gadgets. Chan and Michael Hui race in a "fully computerized" Subaru hatchback, wearing infrared goggles for night vision and eventually using a rocket engine that launches it into the air. Jackie does get to fight briefly in a brawl at the end, bowing to and knocking over Peter Fonda two different times. Other than a few decent kicks in that scene the only good that came out of the movie for Chan was that it inspired his longstanding tradition of showing outtakes during the credits of his movies.

Cannonball Run II

1984 (Warner DVD) (V)

"Whatta you want, ching chong man?"

Director Hal Needham and some of the cast returned three years later to rehash the same jokes about wacky cross-country street racing. This time Burt Reynolds and Dom DeLuise impersonate military officers and bordello belly dancers instead of medical professionals. Instead of kidnapping Farrah Fawcett they pick up Marilu Henner and Shirley MacLaine, who are pretending to be nuns. Frank Sinatra (as himself) joins returning cast members Sammy Davis Jr. and Dean Martin for the last on-screen appearance of the Rat Pack. Susan Anton and Catherine Bach replace Adrienne Barbeau and Tara Buckman, playing the same Lamborghini driving seductresses. *Code of Silence/Above the Law* villain Henry Silva has a small part as a mobster, and NFL player turned TV's *Hunter* Fred Dryer shows up as a California Highway Patrolman. There seem to be fewer elaborate stunts but more lowbrow jokes and some corny allusions to *Lawrence of Arabia*, *The Godfather*, and *Jaws*. Most importantly Jackie Chan returns, this time racing in a Mitsubishi and partnered with Richard

Kiel from *The Spy Who Loved Me*. Their car blasts fire out of the back and can go underwater, eject trash, and emit an oil slick. It even has a periscope and torpedoes. If he ever has downtime he can play the Atari 2600 version of Pac-Man on his computer screen using a calculator ruler as the controller. He gets an arguably slightly better fighting showcase this time when he beats up a bunch of bikers at a farmers' market. At least he's the main character in the fight and he gets to use a chain as a weapon, if not other objects. Also he chops a watermelon in half with his hand. In another climactic fracas he fights side-by-side with Reynolds for a bit and then shakes hands with him.

Though it received an impressive eight nominations, *Cannonball Run II* was robbed of any Golden Raspberry Awards, losing out to Cannon Films' *Bolero* for Worst Picture and other major categories.

Capital Punishment

1991 (eve DVD) (djm)

An early starring vehicle for martial artist Gary Daniels, *Capital Punishment* casts him as a street fighter named James who takes a gig for the Drug Enforcement Agency. They want him to be under the tutelage of a deadly sensei named Nakata (played by *American Ninja*'s Tadashi Yamashita), who also moonlights as a drug lord. As James learns under Nakata, he also enters himself into a tournament fight against another pupil of Nakata's (played by Ian Jacklin from *Expert Weapon*) who he thinks he accidentally kills in the ring. As it turns out, Nakata has set James up and his supposedly dead pupil is alive and ready to take James down in another fight.

The best scenes in the movie feature star Daniels acting alongside Yamashita, whose very presence in the film adds a flavor of authenticity. On the whole, *Capital Punishment* is average, but fans of Daniels may want to see it no matter what. Directed by David Huey (*Full Impact* with Daniels).

The Capitol Conspiracy

(a.k.a. **The Prophet**)

1998 (New Concorde DVD) (djm)

A CIA agent named Maddox (Don Wilson) is assigned a hot female partner named Taylor (Alexander Keith), and they begin an investigation involving human test subjects from the 1960s under a secret government umbrella. They find out which children were experimented on and, strangely, those who were part of the experiment are being found murdered in the present day. Maddox, meanwhile, realizes that *he* was one of the test subjects, and he comes to understand that the children chosen were gifted with clairvoyance. He suspects that his partner is working against him, and when he's proven right, a plot unfolds, revealing that the government is covering its tracks and tying up loose ends.

Fairly downbeat for a direct-to-video action movie, especially one starring Don "The Dragon" Wilson, *The Capitol Conspiracy* relies on sex and nudity to sell it, and fans of Wilson will be a little mystified by its murky plot and serious tone. There's plenty of hand-to-hand combat (there's even a bar fight), but it doesn't really feel like an action movie. Director Fred Olen Ray, an expert at sleazy exploitation, casts horror queen Barbara Steele as the head of the CIA, but otherwise, this is strictly for hardcore fans of Wilson's.

Captain America

1979 (Shout Factory DVD)

(CD)

"I'm grateful for that. But I'm not grateful for the fact that for the rest of my life I'll never really know how long I'll have."

After responding to a phone call from his deceased father's old friend, former Marine and aspiring artist Steve Rogers's (Reb Brown) life is about to change forever. The old friend, Jeff Hayden (Dan Barton), is murdered before Steve can get there and Steve learns the assailants were looking for something. He quickly finds himself in the middle of this mess due to his father's research in the 1940s—he had developed a serum known as FLAG (Full Latent Ability Gain), though it had never been successfully tested. Now the serum is about to get a second chance. Whoever killed Hayden wants Steve dead, too; he's run off the road in the middle of the night and left to die. He's rescued by Dr. Mills (Len Birman), but there's nothing he can do. Steve is fading fast and in order to save his life, he has to go to extreme measures and try the serum. He's saved from the brink of death and has gained new, superhuman abilities. As reluctant as he may be, Steve will use his super strength to go after the killers as well as give birth to a new hero: Captain America.

Chris Evans and Matt Salinger weren't the first to pick up the Cap's shield. Before them was Reb Brown (*Cage, Strike Commando*). His version of Steve Rogers differs significantly from the others. The film is set in the present day, and his character isn't very excited about being given the serum. His Steve Rogers is more of a California kid and an aspiring artist. Comic book fans didn't exactly embrace the changes but it was successful enough to spawn a sequel released later the same year. Reb Brown gives a decent enough performance but his character feels more like Evel Kneivel than a superhero. *Captain America '79* was a made-for-TV movie airing January 19, 1979, on CBS and directed by Rob Holcomb.

Captain America II: Death Too Soon

1979 (Shout Factory DVD)

(CD)

"I'd like you to remember something when you get out of jail, pal. The old people around here are my friends. And if I ever hear they have problems again, I'm coming after ya, you got that?"

The diabolical mastermind known as Miguel (Christopher Lee) has set up shop at a prison in Oregon. He's kidnapped Professor Ian Ilson (Christopher Cary) who has developed a formula to accelerate the aging process. Miguel plans on using the formula to get a billion-dollar ransom from the United States government. Who better to start snooping around than Steve Rogers—a.k.a. Captain America—(Reb Brown)? He follows a lead to a small town where everyone seems to be hiding something from him. Once he discovers the truth it will lead him directly to Miguel for their final showdown.

Originally airing on CBS over the course of two nights in November of 1979, this sequel to *Captain America* wastes no time getting started and as a result is a hundred times more entertaining than its predecessor. Reb Brown (*Street Hunter*) is much more relaxed in the role and gets to spend more time in the red, white, and blue tights. He races (and flies) around on his special motorcycle while tossing his signature shield around. There are some pretty impressive stunts and by adding the legendary Christopher Lee to the cast it automatically becomes worthwhile. Since they don't have to go through the whole origin in this film, we jump right into the exciting stuff and director Ivan Nagy is able to craft a much tighter film. Skip the first one and jump right into this family-friendly adventure.

Carjack

1996 (NOV) (CD)

"Is that all you got? Showtime!"

Conan Lee from *Gymkata* stars as a man who works in an auto shop trying to make ends meet while caring for his sick mother in the hospital. He has a group of friends led by Rico (Fabian Carrillo), who all steal a car and end up with a large amount of cocaine. The drug dealers aren't too pleased with what has transpired and set out to kill them all unless they get their junk back. Conan becomes involved to help his friends but bad guy Nick (Loren Avedon) puts him right in the middle of everything and holds his girlfriend hostage until he's satisfied. Conan proceeds with caution, ready to unleash a deadly assault on the men who have wronged him and his friends.

Carjack is almost impossible to find since it was never officially released. The film feels incomplete, the editing is choppy, the music feels out of place, and the coloring varies from scene to scene. Conan Lee (also in *Prince of the Sun*) wrote, directed, and starred in this, but it's the final battle between him and Loren Avedon (from *No Retreat, No Surrender 2*) that makes the whole picture feel worthwhile. There are a few solid fights scattered throughout, and there are appearances by fellow action stars Fabian Carrillo (from *Latin Dragon*) and Leo Fong (from *Ninja Assassins*). In all honesty, the film is a mess and the only thing that holds it together are a couple of decent kicks and the end fight, which is cool except it ends abruptly. The funny part is that Conan Lee is billed as himself and all the characters in the movie compare him to Jackie Chan.

Catch the Heat

1987 (MGM DVD) (djm)

This Trans World Entertainment release stars martial artist/dancer Tiana Alexandra as an undercover cop named Checkers who has a chip on her shoulder that stems back to the brutal death of her sister who was raped, degraded, and killed by thugs. Checkers has a personal grudge against men who treat women badly, and her latest case involves women who are found murdered and mutilated on the streets of San Francisco. She traces the source to Argentina, where women are groomed as entertainers and then given breast augmentations, but instead of silicone, they are filled with drugs and shipped off to the US where they are murdered and harvested for the drugs. Going undercover as a dancer and endearing herself to the kingpin behind it all (played by Rod Steiger), Checkers goes on a vendetta against the drug ring responsible for the deaths and mutilations of many women.

Marginal by most standards, *Catch the Heat* is a notable experience for having the spunky Alexandra in the center of it all, and while she's not really in the league of the Cynthia Rothrocks of the action world, she's kind of an interesting personality if you can work with her ditsy antics and unusual martial arts abilities. Physically, she's very slight, but her background in dance and martial arts shines through. On par with many Cannon releases of the era, *Catch the Heat* is a product of its time. Director Joel Silberg did Cannon's *Rappin'* and *Breakin'*.

Cellular

2004 (New Line DVD) (CD)

Jessica Martin (Kim Basinger) starts her day off like any other day until her home is invaded by five attackers led by Ethan (Jason Statham), who promptly takes her hostage. They lock her up in an attic and all she has is a broken phone. She's somehow able to twist and tap some wires in order to get it working enough for it to randomly call the cell phone of a guy named Ryan (Chris Evans). She convinces him she needs help so he takes the cell phone to the police station and talks with Sgt. Bob Mooney (William H. Macy). With trouble breaking out in the police station, Ryan has to make a decision and ends up helping her on his own. He has to break laws and risk his life to try and find her. The real question they both have is why was she taken, and the only person who can answer the question is Jessica's husband. It's a life or death chase across the city and Ryan is risking it all for a complete stranger.

Jason Statham (*Revolver*) can be just as convincing as a villain as he is a hero. He really sinks his teeth into the role of a crooked cop trying to cover his ass. The film boasts an all-star cast including Kim Basinger, William H. Macy, Jessica Biel, and Chris Evans. As short of an exchange as it may be, you still get to see *The Transporter* beat the crap out of *Captain America*. The hardcore action elite will also be excited to see action star Matt McColm (from *Red Scorpion 2*) in a featured role. *Cellular* is thrilling and expertly brought together by late director David R. Ellis.

Chain of Command

1993 (Cannon DVD) (djm)

Michael Dudikoff goes to the Middle East again, this time as an antiterrorist operative named Merrill Ross. He's recruited by a sexy agent to oppose a Death Squad that is trying to topple an international oil conglomerate located in Qumir. Ross is a pretty likable character, even managing to deflect the hot agent's come-ons, and he makes running around and shooting an AK-47 look fun. There are scenes back in a control center where R. Lee Ermey barks orders to people sitting at computers.

This was one of Cannon's later releases. It's not as good as *The Human Shield*, but it's similar. David Worth (*Lady Dragon*, *True Vengeance*) directed it.

Chain of Command

(a.k.a. **Echo Effect**)

2015 (Lionsgate DVD) (djm)

After serving out his duty to his country, soldier James Webster (Michael Jai White) comes home to a warm welcome, and after a reunion with his brother and members of his old squad, he's thrust into a funk when his brother is found dead the next day. Suspecting that his bro was into bad business with shady people, James begins retracing his brother's steps, and when one of his own squad members is found (on the same day) with his throat slit, James gets the idea that something serious is going on. After an encounter with a thug (whom James kills without mercy), an expensive hitman/cleaner named Peters ("Stone Cold" Steve Austin) is called in to do something about James and find out where millions of dollars are hidden. As James investigates, more thugs come after him (whom he's able to dispatch without nary a hiccup), but the truth begins to crystallize: His old friend Lt. Ross (Max Ryan) is in cahoots with some government

spooks who have embezzled more money than anyone could possibly hide in the obvious spots, but James's brother had a plan to make everything clear in due time, if he hadn't been killed.

Okay, let's see here: Michael Jai White from *Blood and Bone* is your star and Steve Austin is going to be your villain. Knowing that these guys were already in a movie once (the underwhelming *Tactical Force*) should soften you up a little because you should at least have a sense of what you're going to be getting (good stuff), but what unfolds in *Chain of Command* is a perfect example of what should never happen when guys like these make a movie together: Their talents are cruelly wasted—more so with Austin than with Jai White, who at least gets to do some martial arts in the movie. Austin is seen walking across the screen, sitting at a desk, or standing stock-still in his few scenes in the picture, and he has one good (pretty great, actually) speech, which he delivers to a frightened secondary character, who is then shot point-blank in the head, so essentially the speech was for nothing. Jai White and Austin never fight each other in the movie, which is cheating, and fans of Stone Cold are going to be spitting mad at how he wasn't used the way they expected him to be. The quality of the film is so bad that every bullet squib is computer generated (including the ones that are supposed to be making contact on the characters), and there's one moment where Jai White jumps through a window, but even the glass is CGI (it's obvious), so that should tell you how cheap this thing is. They couldn't afford to break a window. These two major action stars deserve better, but they took the project on, so where does that leave their fans? Upset, as I was after I watched it. Written and directed by Kevin Carraway.

Champions

1996 (Ardustry DVD) (djm)

After killing an opponent in an MMA tournament, William Rockman (Louis Mandylor from the TV series *Martial Law* with Sammo Hung) goes off the grid. When he finds out that his brother was killed in a similar fashion in an extreme fighting sport, Rockman joins the sport hoping for some kind of revenge, knowing full well that his life is on the line. The promoter of the sport is a slimy scuzzbag named Max (Danny Trejo), who encourages fighters to kill each other in the ring to drum up controversy and press, and since this film is set ten minutes in the future the media eats up the craze of the extreme sport featured in the film. Other fighters are played by Ken Shamrock (a real-life wrestler), Paco Christian Prieto (*Only the Strong*), Fabian Carrillo (*Latin Dragon*), and Lee Reherman (from TV's *American Gladiators*).

Excessive sex and nudity cheapen this otherwise standard fight movie where big, beefy guys throw each other around and break each other's necks. There are some nice touches of humor and originality here and there, but for the most part this isn't presented in any new or fresh way. Louis Mandylor is adequate in the lead (he has some Muay Thai fighting skills in real life, but doesn't make the cut as an action star), but the film's best assets lie with his supporting cast of players. Directed by Peter Gathings Bunche.

Chaos

2005 (Lionsgate DVD) (CD)

Conners (Jason Statham) is a suspended detective who's asked to help with a hostage situation within a bank. Lorenz (Wesley Snipes) has the place locked down and is always one step ahead of the authorities. Conners finds himself paired with rookie Shane Dekker (Ryan Phillippe) when everything goes wrong in the back, and Lorenz escapes with his crew. This baffles them when they realize that Lorenze broke into a bank but stole absolutely nothing. The question they need answered is: What were Lorenz and his crew doing in there? The detectives soon realize that the criminals were planting a virus in their systems, which would allow them to steal millions without raising any suspicion. The principles of the Chaos Theory are applied to their flawless plan. As the bodies pile up, Dekker questions everything he knows and digs as deep as he can in order to find the truth.

Chaos isn't the type of film you would expect to see Jason Statham (*The Mechanic*) and Wesley Snipes (*Drop Zone*) to be in together. It's still an action film but it's more about the thrill of the chase than any actual confrontation. In actuality, neither actor really carries the film; that task belongs to Ryan Phillippe (*The Way of the Gun*). The story tries a little too hard to be clever but it's never really hard to figure out. There is, however, plenty of action. With Snipes and Statham involved you might hope to see some stellar martial arts action or a final showdown between the two of them. Alas, it isn't to be. In fact, the two of them barely have any actual screen time together. There are many shootouts and a couple of short scuffles but no real fight scenes. While Statham and Phillippe turn in solid acting performances, Snipes is a bit flat. We already know that he can be a very animated villain, but he just never really delivered in this film. Statham was a little laid back but still brings his A-game to the show. It is nice to see how the film unfolds over the course of one day, and there is a solid chase scene at the halfway point. It's not an edge-of-your-seat type of flick but it's passable. It's also notable for being Statham's first direct-to-video movie. Directed by Tony Giglio.

The Chaperone

2011 (Samuel Goldwyn DVD) (CD)

"You know, Larue, at this point I think the best thing for you to remember is the three essentials. Confront it, be truthful, and sleep with your back against the wall!"

Ray Bradstone (Paul Levesque) is being released from prison. He did seven years for a bank robbery and is ready to turn over a new leaf. He wants nothing more than to connect with his daughter Sally (Ariel Winter) even though his former love, Lynne (Annabeth Gish), wants to forbid it, not trusting him or his intentions. Following the advice of radio personality Dr. Marjore (Lucy Webb), he keeps at it. With the rejection and his lack of employment, he begins to second-guess himself, turning to his old partner in crime, Larue (Kevin Corrigan), who has the perfect bank job to bring him in on as the driver. In the middle of the robbery (which is happening right in front of his daughter's school) he realizes that the whole enterprise is wrong, and he bails mid-robbery. He quickly goes to the school bus and volunteers to be a chaperone for a field trip to New Orleans. With no place to go, the robbers disperse and the bag of money ends up on the bus while Larue and his crony Goldy (Kevin Rankin) not only want the money, but want to get their revenge on Ray. They follow the bus and will do anything to get back that cash.

Pro wrestler Paul Levesque (*Inside Out*) has a lot to prove if he wants to be an action star. He has all the requirements he needs; the one thing he has been sorely lacking is the proper vehicle in which to display his talents. *Inside Out* has a few nice moments but it's more of a crime thriller than an action vehicle and *The Chaperone*, while moderately entertaining, only gives us a tiny glimpse at what he could be. He plays a part that he was well suited for, though the execution and direction suggests that the entire movie is geared more towards a younger audience. As a family film, the story is a bit silly, but it really does work to show a father's longing to reconnect with his estranged daughter. Levesque is a decent enough actor, better than many wrestlers-turned-actors, with charisma and a complete dedication to the role. This, along with how the father-daughter relationship is handled, makes the film worthwhile. Ariel Winter (*Kiss Kiss Bang Bang*) plays his daughter, Sally. Since you immediately connect with Levesque's character, Sally tends to be a pinch unlikable at first. As the story progresses, you see things from her point

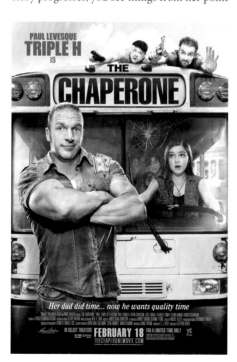

of view and her behavior becomes justifiable. She ends up being a major force in the film's charm, and the overall effect of the proceedings is a tad heartwarming. Directed by Stephen Herek (*Bill and Ted's Excellent Adventure*).

Chato's Land

1972 (MGM DVD) (djm)

Half-breed Chato (Charles Bronson) is minding his own business at a saloon when a racist sheriff threatens him, and Chato doesn't hesitate to shoot the sheriff dead in self-defense. A hanging party goes out to catch him, but he leads them on an odyssey of death, as he takes them through Apache country where he knows the lay of the land. The posse's leader (played by Jack Palance) eventually gets the picture that their trek is useless, and when his team begins turning against itself with infighting, murder, and bad decisions, Chato ultimately wins.

Kind of one-note and unimaginative, *Chato's Land* might as well be a slasher set in the Old West, with a justified (but vindictive, and rightfully so) killer eliminating his hunters one by one. The conclusion is pat and abrupt, and more or less unsatisfying. Bronson barely says a word in the movie, and he is unfortunately not on screen very often. Directed by Michael Winner, who made *The Mechanic* and the first three *Death Wish* movies with Bronson.

Chavez: Cage of Glory

2013 (Crystal Sky DVD) (djm)

Hector Echavarria (*Extreme Force*) plays an unemployed palooka named Hector in the fight circuit on the ground level. His gets his ass kicked every night for handfuls of five-dollar bills, and when his young son requires a crucial heart operation, he gets desperate and is blessed when a top-tier MMA world championship organization comes calling on him. They like his fighting spirit and they offer him a once in a lifetime opportunity: Fight the reigning champion "The Cage" (real-life fighter Heath Herring) for the world title for a hundred thousand bucks. Hector's wife doesn't like the idea, but what choice do they really have? He trains in earnest with his priest brother (Steven Bauer), and he's harassed by a local gang, led by Mando (Danny Trejo), who wants him to wear gang colors during his fight. Hector's one chance at glory is marred when Mando murders his brother in cold blood, but it only makes him that much more determined to win.

The warning signs that *Chavez: Cage of Glory* is going to be a tough sit-through are written on the poster. Echavarria, the star, also wrote the film and directed it, and it's about as convincing as a commercial for fast food: You know what it tastes like before it's even advertised, and it tastes pretty stale. The script is as basic and clichéd as fight movies go (they kill his brother *and* his son needs an operation?!), but it stands its ground, and Echavarria (now in his forties) is unashamed of making movies like

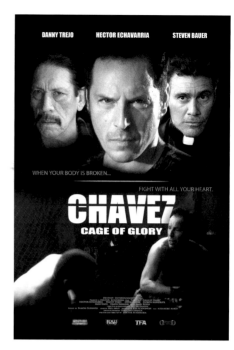

this where he's the center and where he wins. The supporting cast goes through the motions, and even the fight scenes aren't very convincing. This was released in theaters, surprisingly.

Checkmate (a.k.a. Deep Cover)

1997 (Ti DVD R2) (djm)

An ATF operation goes south at a cultish military compound, and when Special Agent Kate Mason (Cynthia Rothrock) is blamed for the deaths of the two daughters of the compound leader, her life is endangered. She takes time off to spend a spell with her father, a small-town sheriff, but as her luck would have it, her father is beholden to members of the same fanatical cult leader, who gives orders from behind bars. When her identity is revealed, several hits are attempted on her life, and when her father is slain, she takes her authority to the next level.

An obscure Cynthia Rothrock vehicle that never received proper distribution in the US, *Checkmate* is a justly ignored film for several reasons. It was shot on crummy video stock using a steadycam, which gives it an off-the-cuff sensibility that might feel okay for direct-to-video movies made in 2014, but at the tail end of the '90s, it wasn't used properly and was a novelty. Rothrock herself almost feels like a secondary character, and much of the film features despicable, scuzzy characters that treat women terribly, and indeed in the climax the bad guys get the better of Rothrock and crucify her (!) before she manages to turn the tables and get her revenge. Also, the soundtrack is not so subtly inspired by *Pulp Fiction* and Tarantino's ultra cool films of the era, so the movie has a painfully dated vibe. Despite some earnest action and kung fu scenes that feature the star showcasing her abilities, *Checkmate* should only be sought out by her most devoted fans. Directed by Nicholas Celozzi.

The Chemist

2015 (NOV) (djm)

A hitman takes on an upstart apprentice who is destined to receive the contract to snub out his mentor. We've seen it before in films like both versions of *The Mechanic*, and yet somehow we always see it again in new films because it's a fallback idea for action movies. It's just one of those things that works. In Art Camacho's *The Chemist* (not as good a title as *The Mechanic*, but whatever), French kickboxing champion and former special forces soldier (for real) Olivier Gruner from *Savate, Angel Town, Savage,* and most recently *Sector 4*, plays a depressed assassin named Ronus Steele who takes on an apprentice because he seems to understand that he's on his way out of the profession and deep down he wants to settle and have a family, and so he frequents a bar where he has his eye on a cute young woman attending a nearby college.

By day Ronus trains Blaine (Steven Dell), a total tool of a man who thinks that killing people for money is cool, and whose hot-for-killing girlfriend Trinidad (Nina Bergman, sexy as hell) wants to go along with Blaine and Ronus to observe them killing their marks. By night, Ronus drinks alone until he works up the nerve to talk to Gabriela (Stephanie Gerard who almost sinks the movie with her inexperience as an actor), but then both Ronus and Blaine get a contract to kill Gabriela, who is somehow tied to an earlier contract that Ronus completed. Since he's become slightly attached to the girl, he tries to work his way around killing her, but with Blaine and Trinidad eager to close the contract, Ronus has to juggle more than just his feelings this time around. His boss Claxton (Patrick Kilpatrick) doesn't have the patience to let Ronus make up his mind to do his job or not, and so he gives Blaine the contract to kill Ronus. Will the mentor outwit and outmuscle the apprentice and by some miracle save the woman he's developed feelings for? Things don't always turn out happily-ever-after, especially for a hitman with a guilty conscience.

Olivier Gruner has always been one of the underrated martial arts action stars. His first three films (*Angel Heart, Nemesis,* and *Savate*) were his best, and he quickly fell into an undesirable groove of starring in mostly crummy (I've seen them all, believe me) direct-to-video films that didn't deserve his talents. His acting and thick accent haven't really "improved," over the years, but you could say that about any of his peers who've crossed over from the world of martial arts and sports from other countries. Their rough acting and accents are just part of who they are. What you see and hear is what you get with these guys. Their talents lie in being themselves, by being interesting athletes and performers of their designated martial arts. Gruner is part of a dying breed of real-thing action stars, and he's actually become more interesting as he's gotten older because you can see how hard he's trying to stay strong and relevant in his respective genre. He has no other genre to turn to like Stallone or Schwarzenegger have. If you want to compare him to anybody, compare him to Jean-Claude Van Damme, but while Van Damme achieved "A" status for nearly

a decade, Gruner was never quite able to get to that level. It's admirable to see him still going for it, and he's the best thing about *The Chemist,* which, on the whole, is needlessly confusing and badly directed. Apologies to Mr. Camacho, who has done some solid work over the years (*The Power Within* and *Recoil* are his best movies), but *The Chemist* has the markings of a director who has never made a movie before. There are incredibly irritating visual flairs all throughout (some people call this technique "avid farting"), and there were whole stretches of the film where I didn't know what was going on or why. Another detriment is co-star Stephanie Gerard, who is not only miscast, but given too much to do. Someone this inexperienced and awkward on camera should never be given more than a few lines of dialogue at a time, but she was cast in the leading lady role, which was a huge mistake. On the other hand, Nina Bergman as the vixen/villain absolutely shines in her underwritten role. This is someone who will have a long and interesting career if she's careful about whom she works with from here on out. For anyone unfamiliar with her, check out the *Wonder Woman* short film she starred in for director Jesse V. Johnson. Rounding out the cast are dependable action guys like Kilpatrick and Martin Kove, who both do what they can do with throwaway roles. Also, mysteriously in the cast are a gaunt-looking Richard Grieco and Sasha Mitchell (the star of *Kickboxer 2–4*), who both must have done Camacho a favor by showing up for wordless, thankless roles as two sinister looking guys sitting around a poker table. We see flashes of them playing a game, but are never quite able to understand why it matters that we see them, as they serve little purpose to the plot.

If there're a few reasons to see something like *The Chemist,* then that should be enough. You've got Gruner, Bergman, and some action (most of which is obscured by dark shaky cam photography), and you've got a CGI-exploding helicopter at the end. I remember talking to a well-known director of some beloved action films from the 1980s, and he told me that when it came to the point in his career where the budgets had shrunk so much that he couldn't afford to blow up real cars anymore, that's when he knew his career was over. And yet, Art Camacho and others in his peer class have pressed on, budgets be damned, and have found ways to blow up a helicopter using cheap computer-generated effects. That's where we're at with these types of films, and you know what? It's almost always worth it.

Chinango

2005 (Allumination DVD) (djm)

Starring Chilean martial artist Marko "The Latin Dragon" Zaror, *Chinango* casts him as Braulio, the progeny of monk-ish protectors throughout the ages who search for a mysterious medallion that grants its possessor unlimited power. He finds the item buried beside the grave of an Asian monk, and when he reveals his find, bad guys come after him, hoping to obtain it. Good-hearted and quick to trust, Braulio becomes romantically involved with the daughter of a Shaolin mystic, who may or may not be working

for the villains who are after him. Occasionally, there's a martial arts duel between Zaror and one or more bad guys at a time.

If you've seen some of Zaror's later films like *Kiltro, Mirage Man,* or *Mandrill*, then watching *Chinango* afterwards might be a step back for you. It's very rough around the edges, features awkward Spanish dubbing in place of Zaror's voice, and the ultra low-budget aesthetics and leery camera work might put off even the most dedicated fans of the star's talent and abilities. There's certainly a great reason to see the film—Zaror himself—but if you're looking for something that will expand your action and martial arts filmography, *Chinango* is fairly disappointing. Peter Van Lengen co-wrote and directed it.

China O'Brien

1990 (Fortune Star Media DVD R2) (djm)

"You see that? She's one of them chop suey fighters!"

Cynthia Rothrock at the peak of her condition and career plays her most recognized role, *China O'Brien*, where, as a disgraced city cop, she returns to her small hometown, now overrun with corrupt politicians and evil men who disregard the law in favor of power and money. Her father, an old timer sheriff, is murdered right in front of her, and her next step is to run for sheriff and turn the town upside down with her kickboxing skills and no-nonsense methods of law and order. She deputizes an old flame (Richard Norton) and a one-handed biker named Dakota (Keith Cooke), and the three of them make it their business to clean up the town.

A thinly disguised remake of *Walking Tall* (which was also remade in the Jerry Trimble vehicle *One Man Army*), this entertaining actioner gives Rothrock and her two male co-stars a solid vehicle to showcase their incredible abilities. Director Robert Clouse (*Enter the Dragon, Gymkata*) directed this Golden Harvest production, which was the last film Rothrock made for them. A sequel was made immediately thereafter. The French Region 2 DVD release is widescreen.

INTERVIEW:

CYNTHIA ROTHROCK

(djm)

The quintessential female action star, Cynthia Rothrock was a dominant force in the action and martial arts genres throughout the late 1980s and all through the 1990s, headlining in the hits No Retreat, No Surrender 2 *(1987),* China O'Brien *(1990),* Martial Law *(1990),* Tiger Claws *(1991),* Lady Dragon *(1992), and* Rage and Honor *(1992), but ironically her beginnings in motion*

Cynthia Rothrock in Los Angeles, California. Photo by david j. moore.

pictures started in Hong Kong following her five-year run as a real martial arts champion. Her contract with Golden Harvest extended from the mid-1980s through 1990, and during that period she worked with Hong Kong superstars Sammo Hung, Yuen Biao, Michelle Yeoh, and Jackie Chan, who produced a film she co-starred in called The Inspector Wears Skirts (1988). *Her most prolific partnership has been with frequent co-star Richard Norton, who quickly became as well known and respected as Rothrock during the heyday of straight-to-video action and martial arts films. Rothrock's contribution to both the Hong Kong action genre and Hollywood's golden age of VHS glory is unparalleled, and her status as one of the greatest action heroines (known for her signature scorpion kick) is forever cemented.*

After your contract with Golden Harvest had run its course, you did *Martial Law.* **This was after your last two Golden Harvest films,** *China O'Brien 1* **and** *2,* **correct?**

Yes.

By the way, did you film those two movies back to back?

Yeah, we shot them at the same time . . . which was difficult. (Laughing.) We never knew if we were in Part 1 or Part 2. They would say, "Oh, here, we got this office for Part 2!" But wait a minute: we don't even have the second script! They would say, "Okay, but it doesn't matter. Let's just shoot it!"

How did *Martial Law* **come to you, and what did you think of embarking on this next phase of your career?**

I think I was in Hong Kong at the time and Pierre David and his company that did *Martial Law* was in Germany, and all my movies were skyrocketing there. He said, "Who's this girl? I've got to meet her, I've got to do a film with her." So he contacted me while I was in Hong Kong, and he found me and told me that as soon as I got back to the States that we would do *Martial Law.* It was exciting for me because I knew that I was finishing my contract with Golden Harvest, but I was coming into a whole different career now in the United States.

Was *Martial Law* **the first movie you did in Los Angeles, then?**

It was.

What was it like to be partnered up with an American lead actor? In this case, it was Chad McQueen. You were in the "girlfriend" role.

It took a while, until I did *Fast Getaway,* for people to think [at that time] of women in action selling. It was kind of like, "Oh, well, yeah, they add to it," but we still had to be the girlfriend and the boyfriend has to come in and save us. I don't know what the first one was that I did where it came to the point where they said, "Well, let's just try it with her as the lead."

Would you consider *Rage and Honor* **your first lead here in the US?**

I don't know. I was kind of the co-lead with Richard Norton. I guess *Lady Dragon.*

Yeah, let's talk about *Lady Dragon.* **That was a David Worth picture. He was an established cinematographer on some of Clint Eastwood's movies. You ended up working with him three times. This one and** *China O'Brien* **really changed your path and put you in the spotlight.**

China O'Brien was actually number two in England under *Rain Man.* That was a huge success. But, you know, I loved working with David Worth on *Lady Dragon.* He was very creative. He was not only the director, but he was the DP at the same time. You're in a country that none of us really had shot in before. We were dealing with different cultures, different languages, the stunt team from Indonesia . . . we all bonded together because we were all in this crazy world where they didn't even have dressing rooms or bathrooms. A movie actress knocking on those people's doors, asking to use their bathrooms. I'd put a little stool in the corner and that's the makeup chair. It was really kind of crazy, the primitive conditions. I think that's why all of us became such good friends because all you do is laugh about it. It was funny. You just make the best of it. Considering the circumstance, I think he pulled off a really good film.

Talk about working with Richard Norton. He's been in so many of your movies, including *Lady Dragon.*

The first time I met him was on *The Millionaire's Express,* which was the second movie I did in Hong Kong. We were the only two foreigners, really, who spoke English. We became friends quite quickly. Then, by the time *China O'Brien* came around, we were really good friends. I think at that point, people began seeing us as a good team and a good seller. If Cynthia and Rich are going to be in it, it's gonna make a lot of money. To this day, he's one of my best friends. I knew that if I was going to do a film with Richard—whether we were on the same side or not—it was going to be a good film. If we had a fight together, it would be really tough and strong. He's like a comedian; he likes to pull pranks. It's never boring with Richard around. When I did *Lady Dragon,* they said, "Who would you like to be in this?" I said, "Richard."

I remember seeing this movie you two did called *Magic Crystal.* **It's a really oddball movie.**

Magic Crystal is funny because you don't have a script, so you don't really know what the movie is about, and you don't know what scene you're doing until you get there. Sometimes, they don't even know what they're doing and they're writing the scenes at that moment, so there's a lot of downtime. It's very cheap to shoot in Asia; it's not like an American movie where you're on a schedule. It was funny because I remember this one scene we were in a cave and the director said, "Look up at the ceiling." We said, "Why?" He said, "Look up." When we saw the movie, we realized that it was being invaded by aliens, so I'm looking at the alien. It makes a big difference when you're on the set and you're looking at holes in the ceiling. I remember on that film we were working so hard—we were working over twenty-four hours. We were so dead tired. The director wanted to finish the scene we were shooting, and we shot in Taiwan, we shot in Greece. When we were in those areas, we were on a schedule. I hurt my knee on that film, so I had to switch all my kicking to my left thigh. We were doing a fight scene where we were so tired that Richard came up and instead of ducking and crossing his sword, I split his arm open. There were a lot of little mishaps. When we saw the movie, we saw the alien, which we didn't see on the set, and Richard and I saw it at a midnight showing. When we saw it, I remember we were cracking up. We thought they were going to put in special effects, but they put in an alien that didn't really talk! The thing is that we had some good fight scenes in the cave. I did traditional kung fu, I did Eagle Claw, Snake, so I like the fight scenes in that. I remember when we were doing the spear scene that's when I hurt my knee. I stabbed a guy in the groin with a spear!

What's the deal with actors in Hong Kong action movies having their own names as their character names? You're always Cyndi.

When I grew up, I was Cyndi. When I started competing professionally, I went as Cynthia, because I thought Cynthia was a little bit more professional. When I went to Hong Kong, it was easy because I went as Cyndi again. That was my name, so that's what I was called.

You were supposed to do an *Armor of God* **movie with Jackie Chan, but he was badly injured on that film, so he ended up producing** *The Inspector Wears Skirts,* **which is something you appeared in.**

What happened was that I was supposed to do *Armor of God* with him, and that's when he got hurt and had that brain surgery. So, Golden Harvest put me with Yuen Biao in *Righting Wrongs* instead. I was supposed to be the bad person in *Armor of God.*

That's interesting. You're always the hero. Did it ever come up again for you to play a villain again?

I was a villain in *Shanghai Express.*

VHS artwork for *Fast Getaway 2*. Author's collection.

A fight in a public place in *Martial Law 2*, featuring Cynthia Rothrock. Author's collection.

Yeah, you were a bandit!

And I was a villain—kind of—in *Fast Getaway*.

Okay, yeah, all right.

I just did a movie with Don Wilson called *White Tiger*, and I'm pretty bad in that. That's probably my nastiest role.

Oh, cool. I'm looking forward to that. You've pretty much stuck to playing the hero, which is great.

You know, it works. Like in *Rage and Honor*, Richard Norton and I thought we should have a love scene, but the director was like, "No, no, no. That doesn't go in action pictures." (Laughing.) At that time, there was this formula, and they wanted to stick to what just worked.

I wanted to mention the VHS boom and the glory days of action stars. Talk about working during this time when you and many of your contemporaries were finding much success in this action and martial arts genre.

It was intense. I remember getting to a point of going from one film to another. I was like, "If I'm going to do another film, I'm going to go *insane*!" I needed to take a break. I was so popular back then. Actually, up until I had my daughter, I was working pretty much nonstop.

And when was that?

1999. That's why I stopped. When she was three, I did *Outside the Law*, but I didn't really do too

much in between there. I did a couple things here and there, but then when she went to school, I stopped and said, "Okay, it's time to be mom." Now she's a teenager and has her own life and her own friends, and now it's time for me to go back to work. So I started doing some things.

I'm sure you've noticed it, but the market for "B" action films has all but died since you've been away. The last ten years have seen a drastic change. What do you think happened?

I think what happened is that they were so popular that everybody wanted to do them, then they started doing them really cheaply, and the scripts started getting really bad, the action was bad. They were getting bad. The quality wasn't as good. Then independent studios started folding, and then the big studios started doing action pictures. Then it was hard for little independent pictures to compete. The independent world kind of died, but I think it's coming back again. I think it's because it's not as expensive. People are using the Cannon cameras to shoot. People are shooting movies for fifty to a hundred thousand now. You're seeing that.

During that lucrative period in your career when you were doing all these movies, were you paying attention to your competition at all? I'm not just saying the Kathy Long variety of competition, but everybody else working in your field.

I don't think I had time. I really didn't. I don't even think I've seen a lot of films that action stars have done, even to this day.

Any action stars you've admired over the years that are still around?

When I first started training in kung fu, I was into Jackie Chan. I grew up with him as my idol. I trained in New York City in Eagle Claw. I would go there every Sunday. I would commute from Pennsylvania. I would go to Chinatown and see movies, and a lot of the time, they would have Jackie Chan movies. *Snake in the Eagle's Shadow* was one of them. I would see him and go home and try to remember all the moves. He was my inspiration. I never thought then that I would do films.

Now that you *have* done an incredible amount of films, do you look back and think, "I actually did this." Has it sunk in?

(Laughing.) Sunk in! For a while it didn't, but it has now. When I did my first picture *Yes, Madam!* with Michelle Yeoh, I thought I would just do the one picture. I thought that was it. I'd be on the poster, and someday I'd show my kids, "Look, I was in a movie!" I never really thought I would have a big action career. That movie became a big hit, and then I got offered another one, and then when I did *Millionaire's Express*, I thought, "Oh, maybe this will be my career." My goal was to be five years in a row undefeated in women's form, and I finished my fifth year when I shot *Yes, Madam!*, so it was time. That was my goal, to quit undefeated #1. All of a sudden, *Millionaire's Express* came around, and I was like, "Okay: This is what I'm going to do now."

The playing field was so open—even to this day—for female action stars. It's almost always been virtually uninhabited. Every once in a while a Kathy Long or a Gina Carano will come out and do a movie, but you were the dominant female force in martial arts action movies.

(Laughing.) I don't know. A lot of people ask that, and the only thing I can think of is that I think I come across as likable on the screen. When people like you, they want to see more of you. There are certain people that you like on film, and then there's others where you don't. I am blessed in that I have the likability factor. I would get people coming up to me, going, "Oh, could you be a lawyer next time in your next film because I'm a lawyer, and I want you to be my daughter's hero." People related to me. I was just this all-American girl that knew how to fight, and if I could do it, they could do it. It wasn't like I was big and strong and manly. So I think it was a relatable factor and my fighting style was good. I like the Jackie Chan style. To try to do things that are a little bit different, a little more complicated, a little more fancy.

Well, your movies are generally pretty fun. They stayed fun. Would you agree?

I would have to say that when I look back on my career, sometimes you can't tell if a movie is going to be good or not. You read the script, you don't know if the direction will be good, what the budget will be, how the other actors are going to be, until the whole thing comes together. I would say probably 98 percent of the films I've done, I had a great time. I loved working with the people, and I had a really, really good experience.

You've shot all over the world. Do you prefer shooting films abroad, or . . .

Um, well, I think there was a period where I loved traveling and going foreign, but then there was a time when it was nice to shoot at home. I don't think I have a preference. When I had my daughter, I liked being here.

The first movie I ever saw you in was *No Retreat, No Surrender 2*. I saw it in theaters when it came out. I was a kid. I was completely devastated when you got killed in the movie. It still hurts!

(Laughing.)

Foreign poster for *No Retreat, No Surrender 2*. Author's collection.

Promo artwork for *Sworn to Justice*. Author's collection.

You've been killed a few times in your movies. Your death in *Above the Law* is incredibly brutal. Any comment about dying on screen?

Well, actually . . . I don't know if you know the story or not about *Above the Law*, but there're two versions—one where I die and one where I don't. The first one is the one where I die. They showed it in Thailand and the Philippines, and the people got up and walked away. They were outraged. "You can't kill her! You can't kill her!" They felt like I'd really died. I was shooting *China O'Brien* at the time, and Yuen Corey called me back and said, "We've got to shoot this scene over. We're not gonna kill you." So there's the scene where I get the spear in the throat, and then there's the one where I'm in a sling in a boat and seeing Yuen in the water, because he died in the other version as well. People were just depressed because both of the heroes died. They'd never seen that before and they didn't like it.

Talk about *No Retreat, No Surrender*. I really like that movie.

Yeah, that was a very early on experience for me. It was the third film I did. It was in English, which I wasn't used to. We were in Thailand, and we had three different crews. We had a Thai crew, a Chinese crew, and an American crew. It took a long time. I think we were there five and a half, six months. It had its problems, it had its issues. There were fights amongst the different groups. It was kind of funny because when I did that movie, I thought that Kurt McKinney [from *No Retreat, No Surrender 1*] was going to be in it, but Loren Avedon ended up being in it because Kurt dropped out at the last second, and they never told us. When I got to Thailand, Yuen Corey introduced me to Loren as the character name, and I thought he was Kurt McKinney, and I thought, *Wow! He sure looks different in person!* They never told me that the cast was changed. They actually didn't tell Yuen Corey that Van Damme was changed to Matthias Hues. Van Damme didn't want to do it because he got *Bloodsport*, and he talked Kurt McKinney out of doing it as well. That's the story I heard.

I wanted to bring up one of your latest ones, *Sworn to Justice*. You're image was starting to change a little bit, and you're given a sexier, sultrier role to play in it. You had a producing credit on this movie.

Yeah. You know what? Paul Maslak was the director of *Sworn to Justice*, and he and the producers basically said, "We want to do something different. We want to make you look more sexy rather than tomboyish." They took a lot of care as to my wardrobe and what I looked like, the acting. They put me with an acting coach. That was a good challenge for me. It was different than anything else I'd done. I had to study my dialogue. I was a therapist in the movie, so I had to study these technical terms, and to me, I loved it. It was something that I really wanted to work at. I worked with actors like Brad Dourif on that movie. I was in awe of him. In my mind, that's one of my better performances. I also brought in some Hong Kong guys to do some of the choreography. I wanted to get a little Hong Kong action in it.

Another film you did, *Irresistible Force*, is one of your very best movies. It really mystifies me why this wasn't turned into a TV series.

It was supposed to. At that time, CBS went through all these changes. I went in and met with them, and I remember a producer told me that they were going to set me up with an acting coach. They didn't want to do a movie with a lot of violence, because at that time it was not a good time for action pictures on TV. I went in and I did a good job, and there was so much pressure because I knew they wanted to say, "She's not good." So I go in and there's all these suits watching me read a scene. You know? But they were like, "You're okay, we like her." Kevin Hooks, the director, kept getting directions like, "She can't kick to the head, there can't be any blood . . ." He was like, "Are you kidding me? I have this girl, and you don't want her to kick?" Kevin was really creative. I think at that point, CBS was like, "Let's just get it done." They were looking at the footage, and they were concerned it was too

violent for children. Kevin came up short with it. He thought they would give him some more time to shoot some more footage. When he came back to LA, they didn't do that. It came up short, it wasn't long enough for a pilot for TV, and technically they decided they would rather bury it. It was bad timing. It was before its time.

Outside the Law was one of your later vehicles. You had some creative control with this one.

That was the first one I did after I had my daughter. I wasn't sure how I was going to do that. How am I going to take my baby and go to Puerto Rico and shoot there for a couple months? It was a test for me. I brought my mom, we had a condo on the beach, and I found out that I could do it. For me, it was a test to see if I could still do movies and be mom at the same time. That was an amazing crew. We had such a great time. When certain movies end, you feel really sad, almost upset and crying because everyone's leaving. That was kind of how that one was. Everyone really got along.

You got James Lew to play the bad guy in it.

I love working with James. First of all, he's a brilliant choreographer and such a good martial artist. He's very professional and such a good actor. I was so glad when he came. I think he came a little bit later.

You had a little bit part in the Sally Field movie *Eye for an Eye*.

Yeah, just a bit.

That was a big Paramount movie directed by John Schlesinger. How did that happen?

Somehow, I met the casting director, and she called me in for that. I had to do some stuff in front of the director. They said they would hire me as a technical assistant for Sally Field. And I would have a part. It was a strange experience for me because I was on a big set. When I got there I saw that the stunt coordinator didn't really like me there. I would go to tell Sally Field how to do stuff, and she wasn't a martial artist in the film, so I was teaching her how to kick, but she was kicking the guy in the head. Her technique wasn't good. Her foot was coming off the ground, her hands were coming out . . . it wasn't believable. As I was teaching her, the stunt coordinator came in and contradicted some things I was saying, and from there she had something against me. I would just sit there and the director would tell me to tell her how to do some things, and I would go in there and she just didn't want me to tell her how to do it. It was kind of different. I went from being the star to . . . you know, helping the star making them feel good about themselves. I didn't know how to handle that because she wasn't receptive to me. I was trying to be nice . . . yeah.

In *American Tigers*, another David Worth movie, you play yourself. You train a bunch of miscreants to go on a *Mission Impossible*-type task. It's a cameo role, but you definitely made an impression.

They called me and said, "Do you want to come in and play yourself?" I said "Okay!" I just went in and shot for a day. It was fun.

There are a few titles that you are credited as starring in, but I haven't been able to find any proof that you were in them. I'm going to throw you some titles: *Jungle Heat.*

Jungle Heat. I think that was a Leo Fong movie. He was a funny guy from the Philippines. What happened was that I was going to shoot *China O'Brien* and I had three days to shoot a movie prior to it. I went in and for two and a half days they didn't do anything. And then on the third day, they said, "Okay, we're going to shoot you." Then they said, "Okay, we need more time." I didn't have any more time, I had to leave. So what they ended up doing was they had someone in a ninja suit play me for the rest of the film.

Oh! Is that *24 Hours to Midnight?*

Is that *24 Hours to Midnight?* What is *Jungle Heat,* then? Hold on, I'm thinking. I don't think it exists. On *24 Hours to Midnight,* they had about five minutes of footage of me, and called me the lead. They had some girl take her top off. That wasn't me. Aw, man. I hated that. I think with *Jungle Heat,* they used some footage from another movie and used that. Back in the day, there was a lot of crookedness that went on. I had Godfrey Ho shoot something, and then it would end up in another movie in Hong Kong. I wouldn't get paid, and I wouldn't even know he did it.

You did a couple of movies with Godfrey Ho. *Honor and Glory, Undefeatable,* **and** *Manhattan Chase.* **Any comment about those movies or Godfrey Ho, other than what you just said?**

(Laughing.) You know, I got paid a lot of money to do those movies. The problem with doing those movies is that they didn't pay anybody else. They would have people from the local schools come in and the girl who played my sister in *Honor and Glory* had to go to work and couldn't do a scene with me, and I was like, "Are you kidding me?" I had this big scene where my sister dies, and people couldn't remember their lines. It got to the point where actors were putting their lines on other people's foreheads. It was crazy, you know what I mean? That movie *Undefeatable* has gotten something like thirteen million hits because it's so bad. People have started thinking of it as a cult film.

I like it.

A lot of people like it. See, I die when I see it. It became like this weird cult classic.

All right. Here's another obscure title: *Rapid Fire.*

I don't know what that is. I think that's one of those where they took footage from something else, because it's not one I've ever done.

No Witnesses.

I don't think I've heard of that one. Someone did something sneaky there.

You played a mother in the Fred Williamson movie *Night Vision,* **and I think that was the first time you did that. You've played a protector of children in movies like** *Prince of the Sun and Angel of Fury,* **but I wanted to know what you think of playing a mother.**

I would be up to it a lot more now because of my experience and what I know. I know kids. I have the feeling of what it's like to love a child. Back then, I didn't. I would love to do a role like that now. Back then, it was the same thing where they liked seeing me play a cop. I did so many movies where it starts off in some underground scene and I come in as a hooker. It was a formula. It worked.

What sorts of roles or movies are you hoping to do now? What sorts of roles have you not played that you would like to play?

I'd like to play in a science fiction film. An apocalyptic movie, something where I get to wear a costume. Something like *Lord of the Rings.* I would love to play in a horror film. I would love to be in something with vampires or zombies.

Have you ever been invited to go back to Hong Kong to do another movie?

No, I haven't. When I stopped in '99, Yuen Corey was shooting films here, Sammo Hung was doing a TV series here, everybody I'd worked with started working here. I would love to work with Corey again. We had a great working relationship.

What do you have in the works?

I did this one film called *Santa's Summer House.* It's a very small film with me and a bunch of action people. Daniel Bernhardt, Gary Daniels, Kathy Long, and me. I'm a big Christmas nut. They asked me to do it, but they asked me to do the Kathy Long part. I read the script, and I said to my daughter, "Oh my God, I would love to play Mrs. Claus!" When my schedule cleared up, I went back and told them I could do it, but that part had already been cast. They then asked me if I wanted to play Mrs. Claus. I went, "Thank you God!" It was one of the most fun times I've ever had. I like that opportunity to play characters. We shot the whole thing in three days. We had to act like we were doing a play. One take. I was pleasantly surprised. I did another movie with that director, David DeCoteau, called *Badass Showdown.* I was happy that he liked my acting so much that he asked me to come back and do another one. It was a good acting role.

I saw your newest film, *Mercenaries.* **It was nice to see you on screen with Zoe Bell and some other tough action girls like Kristanna Lokken. Would you like to say something about that one?**

It was interesting. It was on my way to the Arnold Schwarzenegger fitness class, and I was getting an award there, and I got a call the night before saying, "Oh, we want you to play this part in this movie." They wanted me to be there on Saturday, but getting this award was really important for me because it was from Arnold. It's the most prestigious award I've ever gotten. They said, "Okay, we can push it to Sunday, but you need to be here on Sunday." I got

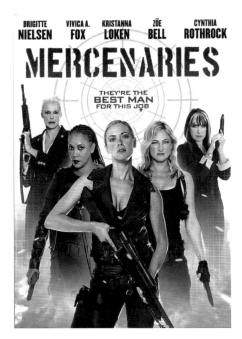

Promotional card for The Asylum's *Mercenaries.* Author's collection.

my award and went straight to the airport. I read the script on the way. My first day of shooting, I had like seven or eight pages of dialogue. Oh, my goodness. I loved the script. I play the head of the CIA. It's good because it's a women's action picture. I would have loved to have done more fighting in it. If they do a Part 2, I would love to be in it. It was a fun part for me.

What do you want to say to your fans? You have fans all over the world.

They've stuck with me all this time. I feel like I have more fans now than I did back then. I have six Facebook pages and they're all full. I'm glad that they've stuck with me. I have something that's coming up that's an "A"-list movie, and I'm hoping it goes. If it does, it will accomplish my dream of being in an "A"-listed movie, and my career will take off again. It's a good possibility.

You're still training.

I am. I still teach and do seminars. I travel around the world, teaching. Teaching is my first love. I love knowing that people walk away having learned something. I haven't stopped doing that. I've been doing that for the past few years now.

How come you never directed a movie?

I don't think I could. I honestly don't. I became a photographer, though. It's a whole other world. I'd like to choreograph. I actually worked with the girls on the new *Charlie's Angels,* the TV series. I trained them when they were in LA. That was fun too. I also do a lot of adventure trips. I do a lot of hiking, backpacking, rappelling, extreme adventures.

Any last comments about being an action star?

It's tough. It's not easy. First of all, you're always open for injury. You get hurt, so you need to be able to go along with all the bruises and injuries that come with it. Every martial artist wants to be an action star, but there are only so many action movies that are made. It's actually a small number. It's a hard industry to get into. It's hard to break out into that field. Even harder for women.

China O'Brien 2

1990 (Fortune Star Media DVD R2) (djm)

"I bet you like beating up on men, don't cha?!"

A man in witness protection living in Sheriff China O'Brien's town is targeted for death, and he has nowhere to turn but to her for protection. A scumbag killer has broken out of prison to exact vengeance on the man who testified against him, and he has a team of followers who do his bidding. They make their way to O'Brien's hamlet, and they cause some chaos. O'Brien (Cynthia Rothrock) and her two deputies (Richard Norton and Keith Cooke) fend of an onslaught of bad guys in a series of action confrontations. The best fight of the film is between Cooke and Billy Blanks, who plays a goon.

The charm and genuineness of the first film wore off by the time the same team reunited to make the sequel. Robert Clouse returned to directing duties, but this entry lacks a compelling arc and the fights feel lackluster in comparison with the first film. The look, tone, and identity of the film and the characters feels the same, but it suffers from being *too* familiar and unoriginal. Rothrock and her co-stars look like they're having fun, though.

China Strike Force

2000 (Miramax DVD) (CD)

Darren (Aaron Kwok) and his partner Alex (Leehom Wang) are sent to investigate a crime when they run afoul of two up-and-coming crime lords. Coolio (Coolio) and Tony (Mark Dacascos) are going against the wishes of crime boss Ma (Siu-Ming Lau), who is old fashioned and wants nothing to do with them. They smuggle drugs into the country anyway, with plans to take over Ma's territory. Darren and Alex team up with the beautiful Norika (Norika Fujwara) to stop them before the drugs hit the streets.

China Strike Force has an awful lot going for it yet manages to be painfully uneven and sort of ridiculous. The director, Stanley Tong (*Supercop*), is a brilliant action filmmaker. He knows how to up the stakes and give the audience some real thrills. There are several moments in the film that will excite the audience, but the story is weak with a real lack of character work. Mark Dacascos (*Crying Freeman*) plays a villain in the film and he's nowhere to be found during the thrilling finale, which features a fight scene involving Aaron Kwok (*The Storm Riders*) and Coolio (*Gangland*). Though it is a Hong Kong production, it was produced to be more appealing to an international audience.

Dacascos does have a few exciting fight scenes and the film exhibits some incredible stunt work. There's just far too much dialogue when there should have been a lot more action. There's a great car chase and several extended fight scenes that make the film worthwhile. Tong really outdoes himself with one of his most breathtaking fight sequences set upon a glass platform suspended from a high-rise building. You might have to wade through a bit of muck, but the action is really exciting.

Chinese Zodiac (a.k.a. **CZ 12**)

2012 (Universal DVD) (djm)

Jackie Chan plays JC or Asian Hawk once again after playing him years before in *Armor of God* and *Operation Condor*. He's a globetrotting adventurer who hires out to high-paying clients who desire certain ancient artifacts to be found or stolen from their current owners. He and his team are after twelve Chinese bronze heads, modeled after the Chinese Zodiac, and each of the heads is in a different part of the world having been pillaged centuries previously from China. Chan's quest leads him to a perilous jungle full of pirates and rival adventurers, who challenge his claim on several of the heads, which are hidden in a wrecked ship wedged in a cavern between two cliffs. Later, when Chan has managed to collect all of the missing heads, he is betrayed by his employer (played by a slumming Oliver Platt), whose son has kidnapped several siblings of Jackie's crewmembers. The climax has Chan skydiving without a parachute to save a plummeting bronze head headed straight towards an erupting volcano.

Childish, tedious, and entirely bewildering considering Chan's stellar reputation, *Chinese Zodiac* clearly shows that he's lost touch with his fans, despite the fact that he salutes them in the end credits featuring a montage of all of his greatest feats over the years. His work as a director *and* a performer in this film mark his worst ever, with an entirely confusing story, confounding dialogue, and stupid characters that belong in a cartoon. His energy level is extremely low (it's easy to tell), and even children will be bored or insulted by the low intelligence quotient of this film. There's a late-in-the-game fight scene that sparks a mild level of interest, but fans of Chan will be appalled by this movie on the whole. A sinking feeling in the gut tells me that his next best move is simply to not play the game any longer.

Chino

1973 (Amazon DVD-on-Demand) (V)

"Mr. Valdez, you are crude, insensitive, and vulgar. You're not a man at all. You're a horse!"

In his last collaboration with *Magnificent Seven/The Great Escape* director John Sturges, Charles Bronson plays Chino Valdez, a loner horse breeder living on what he thinks is open range but finds out is the property of a rich jerk named Maral (Marcel Bozzuffi from *The French Connection*). One day a naive blond runaway named Jamie (Vincent Van Patten from *Rock 'n Roll High School*) wanders by, and though he's terrified of Chino—who has such a bad history in town that a bartender gives him a free bottle and begs him to leave—he ends up hanging out with Chino and entertaining him enough to be hired as his only employee. Meanwhile Chino tries to teach Maral's proper sister Catherine (Jill Ireland) how to ride a horse and falls in love with her, which gets him into some serious trouble.

This is mostly a sweet movie with a great, folky theme song and mariachi-tinged guitar score by Guido and Maurizio De Angelis. But I have to note that I was thrown off by the crazy sex scene right in the middle. Catherine sits and watches two horses having sex. Chino comes over and they exchange nervous glances. Suddenly she tries to run away and he grabs her, they hit at each other, and he violently pins her down. Then, of course, she changes her mind and they begin to gently kiss. Hey Chino, I'm glad it worked out, but Paul Kersey would've blown your head off for that one. Not cool. But if you can get past a rapey horse orgy scene then I bet you will enjoy this story of a man who cannot be tamed. Catherine calls him a horse (both before and after seeing his schlong) and the comparison is apt. Like he says proudly of his mustang Buck, he's only as gentle as he wants to be. So when he (spoiler) abandons his American dream of a wife, stove, and laundry wringer in favor of setting his house on fire and riding off, it's kind of a happy ending in a *Fight Club* sort of way.

Chocolate

2008 (Magnolia DVD) (DL)

Director Prachya Pinkaew (*Ong-Bak: Muay Thai Warrior*) achieves new heights of bizarro awesomeness in this gonzo cocktail that blends dizzying martial arts action with neurodevelopmental disorders and Hallmark movie sentimentalism. *Chocolate* (a.k.a. *Zen, Warrior Within*) tells the story of Zen (Yanin "Jeeja" Vismistananda), the autistic daughter of a cancer-stricken ex-gangster moll/debt collector named Zin. As Zin's medical bills mount, Zen and her adopted brother Moon uncover their mother's old ledger and set out to collect from a series of shady bosses. But first they must fight their way through a seemingly endless army of martial arts–trained stock boys and factory workers. Luckily, the symptoms of Zen's autism include razor sharp reflexes and the ability to assimilate instantly any fighting style thrown her way. Way cooler skills than Rain Man's toothpick counting. Zen's ass-kicking rampage draws out Zin's jealous ex-lover, a Thai gangster named Number 8, who schemes to take down Zen, Zin, and Zin's exiled Yakuza boyfriend.

Third degree dan black belt in taekwondo Jeeja Vismistamanda (best known as Jeeja Yanin) is a revelation in her debut film. She brings tremendous life and pathos to a virtually wordless role and dazzles as a refreshingly feminine, but no less lethal, action star. Pongpat Wachirabunjong (*Ong Bak 2* and Steven Seagal's *Belly of the Beast*) is sufficiently intimidating as Number 8, whose Lady Boy hit squad could command a movie of their own. As directed by Pinkaew, *Chocolate* is a glossy, well-paced affair that moves along quickly once it gets past some clunky, front-loaded backstory. The action is brilliantly choreographed and beautifully shot, unfolding in long takes and wide angles to allow full appreciation for the artistry part of the martial art. Countless kicks and punches connect for real and several falls look genuinely painful. A wince-inducing montage of real on-set accidents plays under the end credits, demonstrating the lengths to which the stars and stunt people went for realism. As we know, pain is temporary and film is forever. In the case of *Chocolate*, the ends justify the pain.

Christmas Bounty

2013 (Warner DVD) (djm)

A private school in upper Manhattan has a pretty female teacher named Tory (Francia Raisa), who is about to get married to another teacher, a wealthy WASP who has no idea who Tory used to be before becoming a teacher. Her family business (in New Jersey) is a bounty-hunting operation involving her mother, father, and her brother, and her ex-boyfriend (played by Mike "The Miz" Mizanin playing a bounty hunter) is still pining after her, despite the fact that she dumped him and moved away to start a new life. Her past catches up to her when her family needs her help on a bounty snatch-and-grab, and out of obligation she suits up and gets her action side on, putting her fiancé in harm's way, and it isn't long before her ex is stepping in to help her out and confuse her feelings. A weak finale that involves crashing (literally) a mob wedding reveals that Tory is still in love with her ex, and she embraces her past and leaves her swanky life in Manhattan behind.

A slapdash effort from ABC Family, *Christmas Bounty* (at 73 minutes) is little more than a cash-in during the holiday season. Its Christmas themes are entirely inconsequential to the plot and to call this an "action" movie isn't a lie, but it's a stretch. Mike "The Miz" (from WWE's *The Marine 3: Homefront*), while not the main character, has a prominent role, and he is featured in several PG-restrained fights here, so this is relevant to the genre of action films featuring real-thing action stars, but there's no genuine reason to see it. It's in a rush to tell a boring story, and the lack of a clear villain and a central conflict (other than a watery romance) weighs this feature down irredeemably. "The Miz" needs to choose better projects if he's going to stay afloat in the movie business. WWE Studios produced this. Directed by Gil Junger.

Chronicles of Riddick

2004 (Universal DVD) (MJ)

"In normal times, evil would be fought by good. But in times like these, well, it should be fought by another kind of evil."

Prior to his enormous and early box-office successes, Vin Diesel was working his way up the ladder in Hollywood with notable supporting roles in films such as *Saving Private Ryan* and *Knockabout Guys* and a significant turn providing the voice for the robot in *Iron Giant*. And then he really captured the attention of audiences around the world in *Pitch Black* with one of the roles that would help ensure his status as an international star, anti-hero Richard B. Riddick. On the surface, *Pitch Black* was just another disposable genre film stocked with a cast of cannon fodder but in the hands of writer/director David Twohy the project became something else entirely, challenging the expectations of the audience and surprising them by making Riddick the unexpected hero of the piece and becoming a surprise hit for Universal pictures at the box office in 2000. Coupled with the even greater box office returns of *The Fast and the Furious* and *xXx*, Diesel was now in a better position to choose his next project and he chose to return again to play the role that helped make it all possible. *Chronicles of Riddick* begins five years after the events of the first film and begins on an isolated planet on the edge of the universe where Riddick has been hiding out to keep his friends safe from the usual attention he tends to attract. When Riddick discovers that his position has been revealed and a new contract has been put on his head, he overwhelms the mercenaries sent to capture him and steals their ship, taking it to Helion Prime, the home planet of Imam (Keith David), one of the few survivors of the first film and the only person to know where Riddick had been hiding. Riddick arrives on New Mecca, and Imam introduces him to Aereon (Judi Dench), a member of the Elemental race, who is responsible for the new contract on Riddick. Aereon is aware that Riddick is the last surviving member of the Furian race and hopes that Riddick will be able to stop the advance of the Necromongers, a sect of warrior priests with mysterious origins that has been slowly cleansing and conquering all of the planets in the galaxy while expanding the borders of its empire. Before Aereon can get into much detail, the Necromonger fleet arrives on New Mecca and begins its invasion. Reluctant to get involved in the affairs of others, Riddick finds himself having to make a difficult choice when the Necromongers arrive at Imam's door.

Expectations for *Chronicles* were very high. Diesel's profile had increased significantly and *Pitch Black* and Riddick had developed quite a following in a short amount of time. In an unprecedented move, Diesel had participated with the development of an animated film and a video game to help bridge the gap between the two films. Fans expecting a sequel with a similar structure to the first film were surprised to discover a different film altogether as writer/director David Twohy and Diesel went in a much different direction, choosing

to expand Riddick's Furian origins and opening up the story on a galactic scale instead of just taking place in just one location. For many people, this became a challenge, and as a result the film did not perform as expected at the box office but, like *Pitch Black*, performed extraordinarily well on home video. With shades of Frank Herbert and Clive Barker, *Chronicles* is actually one of the better genre sequels of all time, expanding the world of its protagonist and his place in the universe, increasing the personal stakes and offering a greater challenge than what has come before, especially to an audience expecting a different kind of film. To really enjoy the film, though, seek out the unrated Director's Cut, which is a longer version of the film and helps to further explain some of the details of Riddick's backstory. This is one of the rare genre sequels that actually rewards the viewer on multiple viewings, thanks to the combination of its unique production design, clever writing and Vin Diesel's star power holding it all together.

Chuck Norris: Karate Kommandos

1986 (Warner DVD) (djm)

Hanna Barbera produced a limited run of thirty-minute cartoon episodes centered around Chuck Norris's persona, name, and action hero image in the mid-1980s, and the result was the short-lived series, *Karate Kommandos*. Norris himself introduces each episode (always seen in a gym), and his cartoon doppelgänger is a cross between Doc Savage and Rambo. He is the commander of a group of martial arts-styled heroes, one of whom is a kid sidekick named Too Much. Their main nemesis is a half-man, half-cyborg named Claw, who is like Cobra Commander in that he is the leader of a nefarious organization known as VULTURE. All five episodes are chock full of action, karate kicking, and animated stunts and explosions. The last episode features voodoo and the walking dead.

I remember this show spawned a toy line that seemed to long outlive the show. I used to think that the series lasted much longer, but only five were produced, which is a shame. It's a little strange to think that Norris lent his image for a kid's cartoon while at the same time he was starring in R-rated movies like *Invasion U.S.A.* and *Code of Silence*. Ah, the 80s. The episodes were directed by Charles Nichols and John Kimball. For more Hanna Barbera action star shenanigans, see *Mr. T.*

C.I.A. Codename: Alexa

1992 (Echo Bridge DVD) (CD)

A group of supposed terrorists infiltrate a funeral and steal the body. The body contains a deadly microchip that crime boss Victor Mahler (Alex Cord) wants to get his hands on. Things go south and a bloody shootout ensues. No nonsense detective Nick Murphy (O.J. Simpson) captures one sole member of the terrorists, a woman named Alexa (Kathleen Kinmont). He discovers this woman is far more deadly than anyone could have expected. What he isn't prepared for is the interference by CIA operative Mark Graver (Lorenzo Lamas) who takes her to a secret facility where he forces her to turn on Mahler and work for him. Mahler wants the power to strike fear in the nation and Graver can't stop him without Alexa. The two of them, along with help from Murphy, pull out all the stops to try to bring him down.

C.I.A. Codename Alexa is all about Kathleen Kinmont (*Renegade*). This film was fashioned to be a showcase for her talents and yes, she's talented. She does a fine job carrying the film and handles the action with ease. She looks comfortable holding a weapon and would most likely stomp down any man who might get in her way. Lorenzo Lamas (*Bounty Tracker*) takes a bit of a step back to let his then-wife Kinmont enjoy the spotlight. It doesn't mean he doesn't have his moments. The film opens with a decent shootout featuring Lamas as well as two decent one-on-one fights during the finale. The chemistry between those two is undeniable and is a major reason why the film works. The film was directed by Joseph Merhi (*To Be the Best*) for PM Entertainment.

C.I.A. 2: Target Alexa

1993 (Platinum DVD) (CD)

Agent Mark Graver (Lorenzo Lamas) shows up to do a job at a secret facility where he is supposed to help transport a top-of-the-line nuclear guidance system when it's stolen right from under his nose. Alexa (Kathleen Kinmont), the ex-terrorist from the first *C.I.A.* film, now lives a quiet life with her daughter. They have a small ranch where they have horses, and life is good. Then, while shopping for groceries, she finds herself involved in a robbery. She kills one of the assailants and ends up in jail. The authorities make it clear she will be going away and they will be taking her daughter from her. Graver interferes and gets her immunity if she comes out of retirement and helps him retrieve the guidance system as well as a microchip that controls the device. The thing is, the man who has the chip, Franz Kluge (John Savage), also happens to be the father of her child.

C.I.A. 2: Target Alexa follows a very similar premise to the first film but ups the ante a bit as far as the action is concerned. Once again, Kathleen Kinmont (*Gangland*) is front and center with several solid fight scenes. She spends most her time using her fists and feet instead of weapons. Lorenzo Lamas (*The Swordsman*), on the other hand, spends most his time using his sidearm and various other guns. He has a couple of short scuffles during the finale but not much else. Instead, Lamas spent much of his energy as the director of the film. It was his first work in this capacity, and he delivers a solidly entertaining film that is once again a PM Entertainment production.

Circle of Pain

2010 (Lionsgate DVD) (CD)

Former MMA champion Dalton Hunt (Tony Schiena) has given up the ring to live a simpler life; after accidentally causing a horrible accident, he's vowed never to fight again. But five years pass and current champion Colin Wahle (Heath Herring) is on the verge of breaking Hunt's record. RFC owner Victoria Rualan (Bai Ling) sees an opportunity to dig up some dirt on Hunt and force him back into the ring, but he refuses. Hunt just wants to be a father to his daughter and win back the love of his life. Victoria does everything in her power to threaten Hunt, even going after his family. Hunt decides he has to fight Wahle and end it once and for all. His wheelchair-bound best friend, Wyatt (Dean Cain), introduces him to Willy (Louis Herthum), the only man who can help train Hunt and have him ready for the fight of his life.

Circle of Pain is another notch on the belt for a series of Tapout-produced films that were obvious attempts to milk the Tapout brand. Sadly, this film does nothing to further the brand nor does it do much to excite the audience. The story is nothing more than a *Rocky* rehash set in the MMA world. There are numerous fights throughout the film featuring real-life fighters such as Kimbo Slice, Frank Mir, Roger Huerta, and Heath Herring. Tony Schiena (who is a real-life martial arts champion) plays the lead and has a fine quality about him, but he's never really pushed to his limits. The fights are underwhelming and never raise the level of excitement to the point where the audience might become breathlessly invested. Music video director Daniel Zirilli (*Locked Down*) called the shots on this film, which heavily relies on nudity and incessant fighting to keep up its momentum and lacks heart.

The Circuit

2002 (Velocity DVD) (djm)

Dirk Longstreet (Olivier Gruner) is the only man who was able to leave The Circuit alive. The Circuit is one of those impossibly secret underground clubs where fighters fight to the death for thousands of dollars. Longstreet was a champion when he left, and he's been in hiding for a number of years in suburbia. When the gangsters who run The Circuit find out where he's been hiding, they take his brother and force him to re-enter The Circuit. The new undisputed champion is Kwan, a flamboyant killer who wants nothing more than to kill Longstreet in the arena. Kwan (played by James and Simon Kim) is actually a name shared by two men, twins who cheat by fooling the other fighters by sort of tagging themselves out and relieving themselves in between matches. When Longstreet gets to the point of almost killing one of the brothers in the arena, the other one comes out to save his brother and reveals their secret. Longstreet beats them both.

Simplistic and hearkening back to the glory days of straight-to-video kickboxing movies of the 1990s, *The Circuit* is very much as advertised. Gruner was still in great shape at this point, and the fight scenes are adequate, if repetitive. The supporting cast is fairly impressive for a movie this cheap. Billy Drago, Bryan Genesse, and Loren Avedon (who doesn't fight) all make more-than-cameo appearances. Jalal Merhi directed this and the two sequels that followed. He shows up in two scenes as a cop who sits at a desk.

The Circuit 2

2003 (First Look DVD) (djm)

Dirk Longstreet (Olivier Gruner), a retired fight circuit champion, is living a quiet life with his beautiful wife, a reporter, and he's loving it. The case she's currently on involves a to-the-death fight tournament within a prison, and when the warden realizes that a reporter is investigating his main source of income, he has her assaulted and raped to the point of being comatose. Dirk is informed of his wife's condition, and he immediately seeks out justice, but when the police offer him little hope, he joins forces with his friends (played by Jalal Merhi and Lorenzo Lamas) to help him get incarcerated at that prison under an alias so that he can find out whom to blame for his wife's precarious condition. Once within the prison walls, he speedily works his way up the fight circuit, and as the new champion, he becomes feared and looked upon as a valuable commodity. It's fairly clear to him (and the audience) whom he needs to go after, and once his purpose has been fulfilled, his next plan is to escape.

Livelier than the first *Circuit* movie, this sequel is incredibly preposterous, but I enjoyed it for giving Gruner a good role to play, with copious amounts of fights and some nice bantering between him and his co-stars Lamas and Merhi. Lamas has a nice sidekick role, getting to show off his kicks a few times, but Merhi (from *Tiger Claws* and *Operation Golden Phoenix*) doesn't get physical. Michael Blanks (from *Dragon Fire*, and Billy Blanks's brother) has a supporting role as an inmate. Merhi directed.

The Circuit III: Street Monk

(a.k.a. The Circuit 3: Final Flight)

2006 (Universal DVD R4) (djm)

Dirk Longstreet (Olivier Gruner), a former MMA champ who's been put through the ringer over the course of his adventures chronicled in *The Circuit* movies, faces another challenge when he rescues a teenage girl from being kidnapped on the beach by a bunch of thugs. After saving her life, she clings to him and won't let him alone because she's really got no other place to go. It turns out that a strip club owner has been keeping her as a slave and has plans to use her in his club, but the crazy, convenient catch is that his club also serves as a venue for middle-stakes MMA/kickboxing tournaments, and when he finds out that Longstreet is a semi-famous fighter, he puts extra effort into capturing the girl and using her as leverage to make Longstreet fight in the ring. Longstreet, being a heart-of-gold guy with nothing in life left to lose, goes up against the best fighter in the club, a fancy fighter named "Spider" Webb, played by James Lew!

With this third entry in Jalal Merhi's *The Circuit* trilogy, Dirk Longstreet's varied life and times as a fighter sort of come to an inconclusive and unsatisfying finale. *Street Monk* (a much better subtitle than this movie deserves) is a standard entry in the genre and doesn't really expand on the hidden "circuit" world like the second film did, and understandably the budget they were working with didn't allow them to be ambitious or very original, which is too bad. Gruner is good here, but his character has gotten less appealing, and his fights aren't really notable. His final fight with James Lew (from *Blood for Blood* and *Red Sun Rising*) is rushed and ultimately a cop-out. I think the time has passed for a fourth *Circuit* movie, but if they ever do another one, I want to see Dirk Longstreet in Bulgaria, living off the grid and getting into trouble somehow with the guys from the *Undisputed* movies. A cross-pollination! Jalal Merhi and Loren Avedon appear in small roles in *Street Monk*.

City Cops

1989 (VV DVD R2) (djm)

FBI agent Cindy (Cynthia Rothrock) finds herself smack in the middle of a case involving a strip of microfilm that a female gangster (Japanese bodybuilder Michiko Nishiwaki from *My Lucky Stars*) wants, but the gangster and her goons have to go through Rothrock and two goofball cops to get to the witness who has the microfilm. Rothrock endures an unending stream of sexist remarks and inappropriate behavior from her peers, and by the end she has incredibly developed feelings for one of the two cops. In one scene she gives him an oil rubdown that dares you not to call it awkward. The final scene of the film has some of Rothrock's best fights ever, as she faces an onslaught of white-coated goons (she's wearing yellow), and her climactic fight with Nishiwaki is a highlight.

Instantly forgettable (aside from the fights) and indistinguishable from other films of its type from its period, *City Cops* is incredibly similar to *Yes, Madam!* which was another Rothrock vehicle set in Hong Kong featuring a plot revolving around a strip of microfilm. Rothrock is the only real reason to see this one, and she looks great and proves that she's an incredible force of nature. If you're easily offended by political incorrectness, steer clear of this film. For some reason, there is title confusion. Some video releases list it as being *Fight to Win*, but that is inaccurate. *Fight to Win* is a completely different film starring Rothrock. That film was released in 1987. *City Cops* was directed by Chia Yung Liu.

City Hunter

1992 (Shout Factory DVD) (djm)

If Jackie Chan made *Last Action Hero*, *City Hunter* is more or less what that movie would be. Chan plays a cocky private eye (inspired from a famous anime character) named Ryo Saeba—best known as City Hunter—who has a cute, but an untouchable assistant, and a legion of adoring female followers who swoon whenever he's around. He takes a case where he's got to find the runaway daughter of a publishing maven, and his adventure gets him into scuffles with several villains, who are played by Richard Norton and Gary Daniels. One memorable fight reenacts different combat scenarios inspired by the arcade game *Street Fighter*.

Incredibly overbearing in its ultra comedic delivery, *City Hunter* is a misfire of gargantuan proportions. Not a single minute in the movie is played straight. Chan and other actors mug for the camera, and the chintzy comic book stylizations like garish lighting and pratfall, circus-like underscoring ruin what might have been an interesting vehicle for the star. The highlights of the movie come from Daniels and Norton, who try to fit in this otherwise unredeemable movie. Chan fights them both in memorable scenes, and Daniels in particular makes an indelible impression as a Speedo-wearing henchman. Director Wing Jing's vision for the film clashed with what Chan had in mind, and they've yet to work together again as a result. Jing later directed the Jet Li movie *Meltdown*. Norton would go on to play the bad guy in another movie with Jackie called *Mr. Nice Guy*.

City of Fear

2000 (City Heat DVD) (djm)

A martial arts proficient journalist named Steve Roberts (Gary Daniels) travels to Bulgaria to visit his old pal Charlie, who—to Steve's shock—has died literally just a day or two before Roberts arrives. It seems that Charlie was into some serious business about a cure for AIDS or some kind of viral preventative, and when Steve starts asking questions, he's approached by the Bulgarian government to cease and desist. He persists despite the unknown dangers that are bound to follow him, and he makes friendly with Charlie's stripper girlfriend, who knows just exactly what kind of man Charlie was. As Steve pieces together that Charlie was involved with the Russian mafia, he gets himself in a heap of trouble as bad guys think he might have some information on the cure Charlie was keeping to himself.

So-so action and plotting make *City of Fear* a standard outing for star Daniels, who (as always) gives the movie everything that's required of him. I never feel like Daniels half-asses it; he's always in great shape, the characters he plays aren't too complicated, but he never delivers a lackluster performance despite how lackluster the movie might be. He's a true professional, and his work in this picture shows that. It's from Nu Image. Directed by Mark Roper, who made *Queen's Messenger* with Daniels, and *High Adventure* with Thomas Ian Griffith.

Class of 1999 II: The Substitute

1994 (Vidmark VHS) (CD)

Jenna McKensie (Caitlin Dulany) is one of the last of the good teachers in the world trying to do the right thing when she witnesses one student kill another in cold blood. She wants to testify against him in court even though she is advised against it by her boyfriend Emmet (Nick Cassavetes). Sanders (Gregory West) and his group of thugs have different plans for her. Enter John Bolen (Sasha Mitchell), a substitute teacher who travels from school to school to take out the trash. He is the last surviving android from a test batch produced by the government (see *Class of 1999* for more on this) and has a mission that he must complete. He also has an ex-agent (Rick Hill) on his trail to make sure that his mission is a success.

As a sequel, *Class of 1999 II: The Substitute* fails on almost every level. There are only a few very thin threads that tie it to the first film, which is a great cult classic though not technically an "action" film. This movie even goes so far as to use several minutes of footage from Part 1 to pad out the running time while helping to tie them together. There isn't much time spent within the school and the only real special effects we see are from those reused scenes. Spiro Razatos (*Fast Getaway*) is best known for his work as a stunt coordinator, and this was his second (and last) time as a feature director. The script by Mark Sevi (*Sci-Fighters*) takes several clever twists but takes a while to find its footing. Sasha Mitchell (star of *Kickboxer 2-4*) plays John Bolen ,and he takes his role seriously; he jumps right into playing this cyborg role and shows little to no emotion. His character is supposed to be the last of the cyborg teachers, and his dry, monotone delivery is a constant reminder of what he's attempting to play. He has a few decent fight scenes with many of the troubled students. Actually, the students are just practice dummies for him, as we rarely see anyone actually fight back. There are a couple of decent shootouts and the final confrontation with Bolen and the heroine played by Caitlin Dulany is fitting. She turns in a solid performance even though her character plays the victim right up until the end when the tables get turned. It's not nearly as exciting (or even needed) as its predecessor, but *Class of 1999 II: The Substitute* is simple escapist entertainment. It settles somewhere in the middle of not-real-good but not-too-bad either. Both of the *Class of 1999* films are in-name-only sequels to *Class of 1984*, with the first two directed by Mark L. Lester.

Clementine

2004 (Tai Seng DVD) (CD)

"I didn't come here to fight. I come only to get my daughter!"

Kim (Jun Lee) is a former cop who also happens to be a taekwondo champion. The only thing important to him in life is his eight-year-old daughter, Sa Reng (Seo-woo Eun). He's an alcoholic mess and has a hefty gambling debt. He finds himself mixed up with a group of gangsters who coax him into underground fighting. Soon he begins to refuse fights, especially when they're with the current champion, Jack Miller (Steven Seagal). It's not something he really wants to do but when his daughter is kidnapped, he's forced back into the ring in order to save her. If he wants her back, though, he'll have to throw the fight.

For the first thirty minutes of this picture we get to see some nicely staged (and bloody as all hell) action featuring the picture's star Jun Lee (*Enemies and Foes*). He's a talented and convincing performer and delivers a decent performance. The most unique thing about this film is the glorified cameo by action superstar Steven Seagal, who had only recently begun starring in direct-to-video movies. He spits out a couple of short lines at the end and fights the film's star. This is a huge departure for Seagal since this is just a cameo and he plays the villain. But this is Seagal we're talking about so he ends up being an honorable one. There's some cool action in the first part of the film, and the final duel was nicely done, but this movie is filled with so much crying in the middle portion that it becomes unbearable. Never released stateside. Directed by Du-yeong Kim.

Cliffhanger
1993 (Sony DVD) (djm)

After a string of flops including *Oscar* and *Stop! Or My Mom Will Shoot*, Sylvester Stallone revitalized his action career with the amazing *Cliffhanger*, directed by Finnish director Renny Harlin, who had just done *Die Hard 2: Die Harder*. Stallone plays a mountain climber/mountain ranger named Gabe Walker, who experienced a harrowing accident involving the death of a climber that ended his relationship with his girlfriend Jessie (Janine Turner) and his friendship with fellow ranger Tucker (Michael Rooker). Tucker's girlfriend died as a result of the split-second decision that Gabe made on that fateful day. Gabe returns to the mountains nearly a year later, with the hope of reconnecting with Jessie, but something big is happening out there in the ranges that supersedes any relational conflict: Terrorists have hijacked a plane containing 100 million dollars and due to some unforeseen issues, the money—in three separate suitcases—is lost midflight amidst the ranges just before the plane crashes in the middle of a national park. Sadistic terrorist Qualen (a superb John Lithgow) and his team of mercenaries make a distress call, instigating a rescue team led by Tucker and Gabe, who are taken captive and forced to lead them all around the freezing snow-capped peaks to find the three suitcases. Gabe manages to

Foreign release poster for *Cliffhanger*, featuring artwork by Renato Casaro. Author's collection.

Gabe Walker (Sylvester Stallone) dangles on a cliff in Renny Harlin's *Cliffhanger*. Author's collection.

Cliffhanger will have you on the edge of your seat. Gab (Sylvester Stallone) jumps for his life. Author's collection.

Sylvester Stallone traverses a chasm via rope in *Cliffhanger*. Author's collection.

escape (coatless and without a weapon) and cause the terrorists untold amounts of grief as he foils their plans of escape.

    Cliffhanger is a grade "A" action movie propelled by an "A" grade action star, and the sheer audacity and scope of this movie (it was shot on 70mm film) is astonishing and jaw dropping. Stallone's star never shone brighter than it does here, and he goes for broke on the physical front: he's shown climbing impossible

Gabe Walker (Sylvester Stallone) wields millions of dollars in a case, and uses it to block an avalanche in *Cliffhanger* Author's collection.

Jessie (Janine Turner) and Gabe (Sylvester Stallone) share a calm moment in *Cliffhanger*. Author's collection.

peaks and crags, he runs, he jumps, he dives, he fights for his life, and he saves the day. The action (very "R"-rated!) is unrelenting, and the death-defying stunts are absolutely amazing. Filled with convincing, seamless special effects and pyrotechnics, *Cliffhanger* is the sort of action star–driven entertainment that we simply don't get anymore. Cherish it. The same summer *Cliffhanger* was released, Arnold Schwarzenegger's *Last Action Hero* was being hyped and flaunted, but Stallone emerged the clear winner of 1993. From Carolco.

Close Range
2015 (XLrator Media DVD) (DH)

While the era of big-screen high kicking and martial arts ended in the '90s with Jean-Claude Van Damme and Steven Seagal going straight to video, director Isaac Florentine and athletic star Scott Adkins have almost single-handedly been keeping the genre alive. After well-received efforts like the *Undisputed* sequels and the *Ninja* series (both from Nu Image/Millennium), Florentine and Adkins are back with *Close Range*, a low-budget action fest bound to please hardcore fans. A modern-day spaghetti western, the Chad Law and Shane Dax Taylor scripted flick finds the mean mugging Adkins as Colton MacReady, an AWOL soldier who rescues his kidnapped niece from a powerful Mexican cartel. MacReady accidentally comes into possession of a flash drive containing sensitive material and becomes the target of a well-armed hit squad.

    After an office set opening sequence that sees Adkins dispatching multiple goons via kicks, knees, joint locks and several stab wounds, the

Close Range press release poster. Author's collection.

action shifts to a secluded farmhouse. The setting highlights the low budget while showcasing bounds of fists, feet, blades, and bullet-infused mayhem. There are plenty of impressive stunts like jumping on and over a moving car and running up a wall while a truck crashes into it. The fights have evolved from *Undisputed*'s overlong kickboxing style matches into mixed martial arts–infused scraps with chokes, throws, and acrobatic grace. It's all impressively choreographed but looks incredibly staged, harkening back to Florentine's overly frenetic work on the *Mighty Morphin Power Rangers* franchise. Adkins has surpassed the cinematic physical chops if not the charisma of his idol Jean-Claude Van Damme but does well enough looking mean and grunting dialogue in between fight scenes. In true '90s throwback fashion there's a nonsensical shirtless scene to show off Adkins's time in the gym. Familiar faces Nick Chinlund (Con Air) and Jake La Botz (Rambo) lend credibility to the barely there story as we wait to be pummeled by the next action overload.

Cobra

1986 (Warner DVD) (djm)

Cop: "Cobretti, do you know
you have an attitude problem?"
Cobretti: "Yeah, but it's just a little one."

Renegade cop Marion Cobretti (Sylvester Stallone) is unleashing a spray of lead in *Cobra*. Author's collection.

"You're the disease. I'm the cure," says Cobretti (Sylvester Stallone) in *Cobra*. Author's collection.

Target practice at the range. Cobretti (Sylvester Stallone) takes aim in *Cobra*. Author's collection.

Justice from the bed of a truck in *Cobra*, featuring Sylvester Stallone at the height of his career. Author's collection.

The look of law enforcement: shades, a tan, and a bad attitude. Sylvester Stallone is action personified in *Cobra*. Author's collection.

Gigantic billboards throughout Los Angeles announced the arrival of Sylvester Stallone as *Cobra*, a macho cop whose methods would land him in prison in real life, but in the movies, he's just a cop with "an attitude problem." He's on the trail of The Night Slasher, a dreaded killer who slays men, women, and children randomly and without rhyme or reason. He suspects that the killer is actually more than one person—several people, in fact—and though his superiors think he's crazy, he finds a witness—a fashion model named Ingrid (Brigitte Nielsen)—who may be the next victim on The Night Slasher's list. The Night Slasher is indeed a collective: A crazed (and pumped-up) man (Brian Thompson) is leading a cult of axe-wielding psychos who believe in his plan of creating a new society by killing the weak, and his main source of intel comes directly from the police department. His girlfriend is a cop, and because of her, they're always one step ahead of Cobretti.

Cobra is an outmoded, outdated movie that would be laughed at and scorned if it were to be released as-is today. Stallone (in his prime) struts around as his incredible action star self here, and while I still dig all that, it does seem pretty ridiculous now. He says with dead seriousness, "You're the disease, and I'm the cure." It's really hard to take that seriously now. George P. Cosmatos (*Rambo: First Blood Part II*) is credited as the director, although Stallone ghost directed it. The soundtrack is full of pop songs of the day. It was based on a book by Paula Gosling, which was later made into another movie called *Fair Game*, starring Cindy Crawford.

Cobra

1993 (Mill Creek DVD) (djm)

Ex-Navy SEAL Scandal Jackson (Michael Dudikoff) goes AWOL after he refuses to follow orders that would have gotten a bunch of innocent people killed, but he's found and shot in the face and left for dead. He wakes up in a hospital with a slightly altered face and a new identity (kinda like Remo Williams) and is recruited by a secret anti-crime unit that goes by the name "Cobra." Scandal is attracted to the idea and to the woman who recruits him (played by Allison Hossack), so he goes with it and joins the team. Over the course of twenty-two episodes, Scandal and his partners (the boss is played by gruff James Tolkan) help people in need, mostly poor people who can't afford to hire detectives.

Cobra starts off pretty great, with a movie-like set-up and scenario, but after a half a dozen episodes, the plots become ultra simplistic and silly, and anyone with less than half a brain can follow the scenarios, which basically connect the dots. It's a shame that a TV show with a guy like Michael Dudikoff (who had just ended his tenure at The Cannon Group, which collapsed in the early 1990s) couldn't sustain much interest because the producers had everything they needed to keep a show like this going for years. Dudikoff, who is usually very physical in every episode, isn't given much direction, and he lets his comedic side shine more than his action hero persona. Some interesting guest stars pop up now and again, and almost-action star Sam Jones plays a bad guy in one of the earlier shows. From Stephen J. Cannell, who helped make Mr. T a star with *The A-Team*.

Cocaine and Blue Eyes

1983 (Sony DVD) (CD)

"You got a hot buttered rum, you get a kiss on the cheek, and a Merry Christmas. Can't have everything."

Michael Brennan (O. J. Simpson) is a private detective in San Francisco who is about to stumble upon the case to make his career. After a chance meeting with a stranger in a diner, he gives the man a ride on Christmas. When the new year rolls around, the police find a man murdered . . . the same man Brennan gave a ride to. The cops find his business card on the body and now they think he's somehow involved. He then finds a letter in the mail from this same man asking him to find his missing girlfriend for him. Money talks and there's a down payment included so off he goes to find this woman. He soon finds himself in all sorts of trouble and the mystery of this missing girl will eat away at him until he learns the truth.

It's too bad nothing ever came of this proposed pilot episode executive-produced by star O. J. Simpson (*Firepower*). This could have been a perfect ongoing vehicle for the former football player. It's all about the mystery, but there's a pinch of action in this thing. Simpson dukes it out with a group of thugs in an alley. He beats the crap out of them until one busts out the weapons and our hero has no choice but to kick it in gear and just runs the bastard down. Director E. W. Swackhamer was able to make a career out of working on television films and series. He's good at what he does and if there had been a pinch more action, it could have been more memorable, and possibly led to a series.

Code Name Phoenix

2000 (Paramount VHS) (CD)

In the future, the world has become a peaceful utopia. Sadly, nothing lasts forever and a new virus rears its head, threatening everything the population has achieved. The virus has been genetically engineered to keep humans from aging. Everyone on the planet wants it and will go to extreme lengths to get it. The only hope is to send in Special Agent Lucy Chang (Jeanne Chinn) to keep the virus from being sold to a makeup company. She's caught, and the company has her pegged as a wanted fugitive. US Marshal Jake Hawkins (*Raven*'s Jeffrey Meek) is on the case and hunts her down. He quickly learns the truth about her innocence and the two of them team up to keep the peace in the new world.

It's always a shame to see something like *Code Name Phoenix*, a solidly entertaining pilot to a television show that sadly never made it past this stage. It works as a standalone film but there was room to explore and to expand the futuristic universe. Martial artist Jeffrey Meek is such a likable presence he could have carried this thing on his own but pairing him with the lovely Jeanne Chinn (from *Lethal Weapon 4*)

was a fantastic idea. Meek's character is more of a weapons expert (though he does see his fair share of fisticuffs) while Chinn handles the majority of the hand-to-hand action. It's fast-paced, funny, and could have easily sustained itself over several seasons. Jeff Freilich (*Naked City: Justice with a Bullet*) directed this TV movie/pilot for the UPN, which originally aired in March of 2000.

Codename: Vengeance

1987 (Video Treasures VHS) (djm)

A Middle Eastern shah's wife and hemophiliac son are kidnapped by a Moroccan terrorist named Tabrak (played by South African action star James Ryan), who plans on executing them both to set an example. A washed-up mercenary named Monroe (Robert Ginty, who simply cannot pass the action star quota) is dug up in some hellhole by the American embassy, and he's asked to get a crew together to rescue the woman and child before their execution. Monroe gets cleaned up and goes into overdrive on his quest to rescue them in the deserts of Northern Africa. His final confrontation with Tabrak in a cave is fairly disappointing because I know that James Ryan is a badass, and in his final scene he considerably restrains himself.

Codename: Vengeance is a so-so actioner from director David Winters, who would later re-team with Ryan on the slightly better action movie *Rage to Kill*. I don't have a problem with Ryan (from *Kill or Be Killed* and *Kill and Kill Again*) playing a bad guy, but it's rough sitting through a movie knowing that a guy like that can kick ass, but plays a character in it who never really does. The action is okay, with tons of gunfire and grenade explosions, and the whole thing is reminiscent of the stuff that Cannon made in the 80s with Chuck Norris and Michael Dudikoff. Nothing against Robert Ginty, but he had nothing on those guys. At least he gets a sex scene with Shannon Tweed here.

Code of Silence

1985 (MGM DVD) (djm)

"When I want your opinion, I'll beat it out of you."

A drug bust is botched, and detective Eddie Cusack (Chuck Norris) is put to the test for being in charge of the operation. One of his subordinates (played by Ralph Foody, the black-and-white movie gangster from *Home Alone*) accidentally killed an innocent man during the drug bust, and he covered it up by planting false evidence, which puts the heat on Cusack's unit. Cusack takes the high and moral road, while his entire unit turns against him, and when the drug lord they're up against— Camacho (Henry Silva)—gets serious about

"When I want your opinion, I'll beat it out of you." says Eddie Cusack (Chuck Norris) in *Code of Silence*. Author's collection.

Renegade cop Eddie Cusack (Chuck Norris) gives a beating in *Code of Silence*. Author's collection.

Chuck Norris as Eddie Cusack in *Code of Silence*, an Andrew Davis picture. Author's collection.

Villain Comacho (Henry Silva) and hero Eddie (Chuck Norris) in *Code of Silence*. Author's collection.

getting revenge, Cusack finds that he has no one to back him up (not that he especially needs it). He commandeers a prototype robot cop to assist him when he decides to go up against Camacho and his men in a warehouse.

One of Norris's best films, *Code of Silence* gives him plenty of room to be Chuck Norris while also giving everyone around him an opportunity to shine too. It was scripted by Michael Butler and Dennis Shryack, who also wrote the superior buddy action movie *Fifty/Fifty* with Peter Weller and Robert Hayes. They clearly know dialogue and the flavor of Chicago, as everyone speaks and acts like any real human would in that part of the US. The director, Andrew Davis, should be credited for making every nook and cranny as authentic as possible, and it's no surprise that he would later become a big director in Hollywood. His next films were *Above the Law*, *The Package*, *Under Siege*, and *The Fugitive*. The best scene in the film (and there are several great ones) has Chuck faced against about twenty guys in bar. It's a doozy. David Michael Frank did the score.

Code Red

2013 (E-One DVD) (CD)

"But you're fine with shooting and burning other people's children, right? Here's your privilege: die human."

It was thought that during World War II Stalin had a nerve gas created, one so deadly it would turn the most gentle of humans rabid. No one knew of this gas until the present day when a war diary is found. After a report comes in from NATO, doctor Anna Bennett (Manal El-Feitury) confirms a recent infection, and the government sends in special forces operative John McGahey (Paul Logan from *Blazing Force*) to locate the gas. An explosion rocks the city, unleashing the deadly gas on the population, turning them into rabid beasts. Anna becomes separated from her daughter while John finds and protects her. They're stuck in the middle of an outbreak, and they'll need a miracle if they're to make it out alive.

Director Valeri Milev (*Re-Kill*) has an interesting outlook and gives the picture plenty of style (some really impressive POV shots) without forgetting about the story. There's nothing real original about the picture, but the execution makes it stand out. What Milev does do well is pull out a strong performance from action star Paul Logan (also in *Ballistica*) who is well suited for the role. Even though there's an emotional depth, Logan still gets to show us he's a highly capable action star. He's involved in a fight with a couple of soldiers and also decimates the infected with whatever he can get his hands on. *Code Red* is an action-oriented horror flick: one you go into with low expectations but walk out feeling entertained.

Cold Harvest

1999 (Image DVD) (CD)

In a not-too-distant future, much of the Earth's population is dying off due to a plague. There are only six humans left on the planet who are capable of producing the antibodies in order to cure it. Villain Little Ray (Bryan Genesse) attacks the convoy they are being transported in and attempts to kill everyone in it. Oliver (Gary Daniels) and his wife Christine (Barbra Crampton) are the only ones who escape, and they are hunted down by Little Ray and his men. Christine takes off to safety while Oliver is murdered in cold blood. After finding out what the convoy was carrying, it comes to light that the only person left harboring the antibody to save the human race is the unborn child that Christine has no clue she is carrying. She soon meets up with Oliver's twin brother Roland (Gary Daniels) who is a bounty hunter going after Little Ray. With much more at stake than he could have imagined, he sets out to put an end to Little Ray.

Cold Harvest is a post-apocalyptic western with heavy doses of hard-hitting martial arts action, making it a must-see slice of cinema. Isaac Florentine strikes again with a film that's filled with deliciously cheesy dialogue and overflowing with the type of action you'd expect from him. Gary Daniels (*Fist of the North Star*) brings his usual charisma to the table. He has several neat shootouts and plenty of hand-to-hand brawls that show off his prowess. It's also a solid showcase for his acting talents, portraying dual roles. The real stand-out in the film is Bryan Genesse (*Death Train*) as the villain Little Ray. He really took the time to spruce up this character with some rather interesting quirks and mannerisms. He creates a memorable bad guy for Daniels to get revenge on. It's also a real treat to see Barbra Crampton (*Re-Animator*) appear as the female lead. The fight scenes are fast-paced, well edited, and expertly choreographed. Florentine spends plenty of time playing up the western aspects of the film, which work amazingly well with the post-apocalyptic wasteland of the future. He ties it in with the martial arts segments to create a truly unique experience. A shout-out should also be given to the stuntmen who worked on the film. They don't just take falls when they get hit; they're launched through walls and hit everything they can on the way down. This film is without question a high point in the careers of everyone involved.

Cold Sweat

1970 (Synergy DVD) (CD)

"Killing him wouldn't be murder. It would be like cleaning a cesspool."

Joe Martin (Charles Bronson) appears to be your average, run-of-the-mill, hard-working American living in France renting boats. He lives with his lovely wife Fabienne (Liv Ullman) and her young daughter. Their life is picture-perfect

until one day Joe's past catches up with him. Joe's last name really isn't Martin, it's Moran and he was a former sergeant in the army who was imprisoned during the Korean war. He made friends with a group of black-market sellers in the pen, and they planned a daring escape. Things go perfectly until one of them, Katanga (Jean Topart), murders a German officer. Joe doesn't want any part of it and escapes on his own, leaving the rest of them to be recaptured. Now they're back and are going to force him to help transport drugs. He refuses but they have some serious leverage (his wife and step-daughter), so refusing is out of the question.

Charles Bronson (*Chino, Hard Times*) looks pretty ripped in this film. He gives a fantastic, laid-back performance, one you won't forget. The great thing about Bronson is his smile, the one that says, "You're an idiot for fucking with me. You just don't know it yet." He smacks these guys around left and right but it's the final car chase through the twisting and turning mountains everyone will remember. Staged by the legendary Remy Julienne (*Armor of God 2: Operation Condor*), it's a marvelous example of why he's so good at what he does. With Bronson in top form, Remy delivering the goods, and Terence Young (*Thunderball*), a director responsible for some of James Bond's greatest adventures, this movie found the recipe for success.

Cold Vengeance

(a.k.a. **Sometimes a Hero**)

2002 (Velocity DVD) (djm)

Small-time hood and enforcer Jimmy Hood (Josh Barker) has had enough of his life in crime, but his "family" won't let him go. He goes home to his mother, who chastises him for being a lowlife and loser, and his only solace is the hope of finding love. When his boss orders him to blow up an ice skating ring, he refuses because he's fallen in love with the sister of an ice skater, who has been targeted for death. Jimmy has to deal with the consequences of such a refusal, and he now has to protect the woman he loves and her sister from the team sent to do his job. His rival is Russ Fortus (Darren Shahlavi), who gives him a hard time when the clock starts ticking. With help from his partner (Bryan Genesse), Jimmy is able to save the day . . . and the woman he loves.

Directed by Jalal Merhi (*Operation Golden Phoenix*), *Cold Vengeance* is an incredible bore. It saves the action and martial arts fight scenes for the last ten minutes of the film, and with guys like Genesse and Shahlavi in the cast, that's a *huge* mistake. It's boring as hell, and the last-ditch effort to make it interesting at the end comes too late to save it. Josh Barker isn't a very good lead either. Real-life kickboxing star Luraina Undershute has a supporting role (and a fight scene) as well. She married Shahlavi after the film wrapped.

Collateral Damage

2002 (Warner DVD) (djm)

"You want collateral damage, huh? I'll give you fucking collateral damage!"

Firefighter Gordy Brewer (Arnold Schwarzenegger) witnesses his family get blown to bits when a terrorist known as "The Wolf" (Cliff Curtis) executes a terrorist attack in Los Angeles. Wounded and grieving, Gordy is enraged that the government works at a snail's pace in making headway in capturing The Wolf, so he takes it upon himself to plan an elaborate strategy of revenge by traveling to Colombia where the terrorist is already planning his next attack on American soil. Out of his element and without a paddle, Gordy is captured by The Wolf's soldiers and goes through the usual interrogation/torture routine before he escapes and tracks him back to the US. The government becomes annoyed with Gordy's heroics, but when he brings them The Wolf's girlfriend (Francesca Neri) as an asset, they pay attention to what he has planned. Just before The Wolf makes his move against Washington in a grand attack, Gordy realizes that their asset is actually working *against* them, and he's able to foil their plot single-handedly, while also emerging a hero.

The controversy surrounding this by-the-numbers actioner is that it was set to be released late 2001, but when the September 11 attacks occurred, it was hastily postponed due to its sensitive nature of terrorism against the United States. Even if September 11 hadn't happened, *Collateral Damage* would have been an exceptionally weak outing for Arnold, whose character deliberately never picks up or uses a gun in the film. His final blow to the villain at the end involves impaling him with an axe to the chest. Fitting, I suppose, in that he's a firefighter, but there are several instances where he could have used a gun and he didn't. Director Andrew Davis has worked well with action stars like Chuck Norris (in *Code of Silence*) and Steven Seagal (in *Above the Law* and *Under Siege*), but his work here with Arnold is tepid and forgettable. *Collateral Damage* was the last of a string of flops for Arnold after *End of Days* and *The 6th Day* before he became The Terminator again in *Terminator 3: Rise of the Machines*, which was his last starring film before becoming the governor of California.

Commando

1985 (Fox DVD) (djm)

Bad Guy: "Your daughter's safe, Colonel. Whether she stays that way is up to you. My people got some business with you. If you want your kid back, then you gotta cooperate. *Right*?"
Matrix: "Wrong!"

Commando is a defining moment for Arnold Schwarzenegger. After his sword and sorcery movies (the *Conan* films and *Red Sonja*), he had

Arnold Schwarzenegger is John Matrix (with bazooka) in *Commando*. Author's collection.

to prove that he wasn't just The Terminator. A shot of him gripping a grenade and the hilt of a knife while strapped up and camouflaged was featured on posters and became one of the most recognized and iconic images of the 1980s, and rightfully so. Arnold stars in the film as a retired soldier named John Matrix, who is forced back in the game when a South American dictator wannabe has his daughter (Alyssa Milano) taken captive from their home and flown to a private island. Matrix is supposed to go to a South American country to perform an assassination in exchange for his daughter, but Matrix doesn't play by the rules. He manages to make for himself an eleven-hour window to sort out how to get the drop on his daughter's kidnappers and create an alliance with a stewardess (a cute Rae Dawn Chong), who helps bail him out of trouble more than once and helps him fly to the island where he obliterates the bad guys and saves his daughter.

One of the all-time great action movie vehicles, *Commando* is a connect-the-dots actioner if you think about it, but it stands shoulders higher than its emulators for a number of reasons. Arnold (in pristine shape and ultra confident) is a standout in a fairly simple role, and the script (by Joseph Loeb III, Matthew Weisman, and Steven E. de Souza), with direction by Mark Lester, is clever,

witty, and unexpected. People love *Commando* because of the great lines and the outrageous action, and it's mostly due to the way it's all handled. James Horner's gritty urban action score gets the tone embedded in the first moments of the movie. A cool rock song by The Power Station plays over the end credits. It's one of the best end credit songs ever. A sequel would have been great, but it's probably a blessing that we only got the one because it's almost perfect as is. Lester later did *Showdown in Little Tokyo* with Brandon Lee and Dolph Lundgren. You can tell the same guy did both movies.

Commando: A One Man Army

2013 (Reliance DVD) (CD)

"Let's complete that joke of yours—you'll die with a smile. What did Mike say in Pat's ear when he died? Bang!"

During a routine helicopter training exercise, Karan (Vidyut Jamwal) and his fellow commandos crash in Chinese waters. The wreckage, as well as all the human remains, washes away, leaving a lone survivor. Karan is thought to be a spy by the Chinese and he's imprisoned for a year. The Indian government (his native country) wants to avoid an international incident by brushing it all under the rug, forgetting Karan even existed. While being transferred, he bravely escapes to a small town where he finds himself defending a young woman named Simrit (Pooja Chopra) from AK 74 (Jaideep Ahlawat), the local crime lord who runs everything. All of the locals fear him but when Karan stands up to him, he will do whatever it takes to get Simrit for himself and make an example out of the soldier who showed up in his town.

While the story is pretty generic, *Commando* ends up being quite impressive in the action department. Yes, it's a Bollywood film and twenty to thirty minutes of the two hour runtime is devoted to flashy singing and dancing. What it does have

Spanish poster for *Commando*. Author's collection.

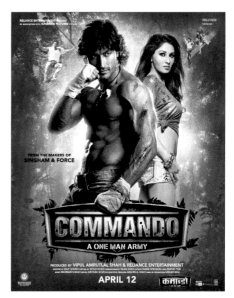

Theatrical release poster for *Commando: A One Man Army*. Author's collection.

is Vidyut Jamwal, a martial artist from India who isn't afraid to do his own stunts. Some of the action is just amazing, and Jamwal is just as limber as he is skilled in kalaripayattu (an Indian martial art system). He leaps over cars, bounces off surfaces, and jumps through windows, and it's all amazing stuff. The excessive singing and dancing takes some getting used to but it's well worth your time to see this guy in action. It'll be interesting to see where he goes from here. Directed by Dilip Ghosh.

Commando Squad

1987 (TWE VHS) (djm)

A badass commando federal agent named Clint (Brian Thompson) gets himself captured in South America in his one-man drug war against a former federal agent turned bad (William Smith). Clint's former partner Cat (Kathy Shower with a funky black wig) is meanwhile tearing up the streets of Los Angeles with her *Ms. .45* tactics on the boulevard, and when she finds out that Clint has been captured and needs her help, she goes to South America to rescue him. Once they've been reunited, it's up to them to put an end to the drug trafficking and save themselves from explosions, gunfire, and close-quarter combat.

As far as cheap exploitation action movies go, *Commando Squad* plays it safe all the way, but it does, at the very least, give Brian Thompson (so good as the bad guy in *Cobra*) his first starring vehicle as an action star. That said, the movie is *still* disappointing because it doesn't have enough of him or enough action in general. Former *Playboy* playmate Kathy Shower, who downplays her natural assets by keeping her clothes on at all times and by hiding her naturally blonde hair, is cast as a kickass action heroine, and the movie really belongs to her. William Smith as the villain and Sid Haig as his muscle would usually go over well in a movie like this, but even so, the movie is lacking a certain oomph and pizazz. From director Fred Olen Ray, who filmed one scene at the historic Hollywood Book and Poster Company on Hollywood Boulevard. Brian Thompson deserved better.

Command Performance

2009 (First Look DVD) (djm)

"Dying's easy. Rock and roll is hard."

The Soviet president "commands" a multiband concert to be put on for the birthday of his daughter, and several hot bands in Moscow convene at a giant arena for this big bash. Terrorists take the opportunity to crash the party, kill a bunch of civilians, and hold the president and his daughters hostage, but there's one guy they didn't count on pissing on their parade: Joe (Dolph Lundgren), the drummer for one of the rock bands. Joe isn't just a drummer (though he's a good one at that); he's got fighting skills that suggest he has a past in the military

or in the special forces, and he's the only hope the president and his daughters have of living to see tomorrow.

From Nu Image, *Command Performance* is a fun action film in the vein of *Sudden Death* and the *Die Hard* movies. Lundgren is such a badass in it that there should be a little franchise built around his character. Lundgren co-wrote (with Steve Latshaw, who wrote *Mach 2* with Brian Bosworth) and directed this, and it's as good as any other movie he did around the same period like *The Russian Specialist* and *Direct Action*. It's a nice vehicle for him, and he uses his strengths in the film to the best of his abilities. The next year, Lundgren co-starred in Nu Image/Millennium's *The Expendables*.

INTERVIEW:

STEVE LATSHAW

(djm)

The late 1990s saw the emergence of low-budget action thrillers, financed by exploitation film groups like Royal Oaks and Andrew Stevens's Franchise Pictures, and action stars like Brian Bosworth, Jeff Speakman, Michael Dudikoff, and Dolph Lundgren starred in various films of this type during the lucrative period when these films were being produced by the dozens. Steve Latshaw wrote the scripts for many of these films, and he was the "go-to" writer for these companies when they were able to get guys like Dudikoff, Bosworth, and Speakman to star in them.

You wrote a handful of military thrillers, starring the likes of Michael Dudikoff and Brian Bosworth for Royal Oaks in the latter half of the 1990s. Talk about that a little bit.

Here's the short version. I'd been in LA for a year, and Fred [Olen Ray] said, "Would you like to try your hand at writing?" I wrote a movie called *Invisible Dad* for Fred and Andrew Stevens. Everybody liked it. Andrew came to me and said, "I've got this political thriller that has action, adventure, and it takes place on a space shuttle. It's called *Scorpio One*. I need a rewrite on it." I read it, and I told him, "I can't rewrite this. It's just not filmable." He said, "Well, what would you do?" I said, "Well, there's an old Alistair MacLean novel from the '60s called *Ice Station Zebra*. If I were going to do a space shuttle movie, I would remake that. He said, "Fine, do it." He loved it; everybody loved it. They made the movie with Jeff Speakman. Suddenly, I became the go-to guy at Royal Oaks who wrote military films. They were hybrids with military action and intrigue. So I did a countless stream of those. It was a nonstop working relationship for about ten years.

You wrote *Mach 2*, one of Brian Bosworth's films.

I wrote that in 1999. That was one of the busiest years I've ever had. It was a movie that Fred directed. It combined a disaster plot with a terrorist takeover with terrorists who were going to crash a Concorde into Paris. We put in the vice

president of the United States as a character in there. These movies all had a certain . . . we call them "stock footage" movies, okay? *Mach 2* is a classic example. Franchise Pictures spent about a million and half dollars on this thing. We'd come up with a concept, usually based around available stock footage. In the case of this, it was like, "Hey, we've got access to a lot of Concorde footage from *Airport '79*. So let's write a movie about it!" Okay? I did a movie with Fred called *Submerged* that's about a 747 at the bottom of an ocean. That's because they'd made a deal to get all the stock footage from *Airport* from the '70s.

Wow!

Or we'd just come up with a general idea for an action film and we'd troll the libraries to see what was available. Paramount or Columbia or whoever would have all these movies you could buy footage from. We'd just sit there with a stack of videotapes and we'd go, "Hey! There's an action sequence from this movie! Let's throw it in!" Then, the casting, they'd usually get somebody like a Michael Dudikoff or Treat Williams or Brian Bosworth, and they'd usually pay them a quarter of a million or two hundred thousand to work for ten days. Okay? Then they'd bring in a name—someone who was very famous like a Dennis Hopper or Cliff Robertson or a Roy Scheider—and they'd pay him to work for one day as the vice president. Then you'd have a bunch of recognizable actors who would work cheap. You put a good cast and crew together and make a movie. Most of the money went to the cast. We did a bunch of those like that. We did one called *Extreme Limits* with Treat Williams, and we used stock footage from *The Long Kiss Goodnight*, and we used the entire climax from that. All of the helicopter and plane crash footage was from *Cliffhanger*. At the time, Franchise Pictures was actually *making* a Renny Harlin movie called *Driven* with Sylvester Stallone. I always wondered if Renny Harlin knew that on the other side of the lot, we're making this other movie with footage that he shot. Plus, we had this huge helicopter chase on a train that was from a Gene Hackman movie called *Narrow Margin*. We had all this stuff for this movie. Treat Williams walked up to me on the set and said, "I really like the scene where the helicopter is chasing the Jeep down the mountain." I said, "Thank you." And he said, "And I like the movie it came from too." In *Mach 2*'s case, they wanted another action sequence that would kill off Michael Dorn's character, and we're all sitting around trying to figure out what to do. Someone said, "What about *Ronin*? There's some good car chases in that." Someone else said, "Oh, no, that's a Frankenheimer movie. He won't let anyone buy stock footage from his films." I said, "Well, there's an old United Artists movie with Charles Bronson called *The Mechanic*, and there was a good car chase in France in that one." I didn't think anyone would go for it. They went for it, and said, "Not a bad idea." So they found a 35-year-old Fiat to match the Fiat in *The Mechanic*. We used a 1973 chase to kill off Michael Dorn! That's how we made all those things.

Why didn't Fred Olen Ray use his name on some of these movies? He uses a pseudonym.

Andrew Stevens, who produced many of these things, was extremely loyal. He liked using the same people over and over again because we were all reliable. The foreign buyers would start asking questions like "Why are the same people making all these movies? Can't you hire some different directors and some different writers?" It happened to me on a movie called *Gale Force*, which was another Treat Williams and Michael Dudikoff movie. Andrew said, "You're a woman for this movie." I said, "What do you mean?" "Well, the German buyers want a woman writer. Try to write like you're a woman writer for this one." I just wrote in my standard style and I gave them my ex-wife's maiden name for the credit. I did that on another movie called *Black Horizon*, another Michael Dudikoff movie. It was a half-assed remake of *Scorpio One*.

You recently wrote *Command Performance* with Dolph Lundgren. This felt like a big movie.

It's the biggest film I've been involved in, certainly the biggest paycheck. It's gotten the best reviews of my career. It was a wonderful collaborative experience with Dolph. He very much is a writer. He's like Clint Eastwood in that he's gradually moving into writing and directing.

What was it like working with Dolph Lundgren?

Dolph is a very smart, intelligent man. He's an MIT graduate. He knows his stuff. He's very charming. Like most Europeans, he's unfailingly polite. We'd sit down in a room to write, and he would go, "Can I get you something to drink? You need a refill? Is that chair good for you?" It was an Old World courtesy. Andrew Stevens put me in touch with Dolph because they were doing *Missionary Man*. Dolph was writing and directing *Missionary Man*, but he wanted another writer on it, and Andrew suggested me. I read the script, I sent my notes in, and I told him that I thought the script was already pretty good. I said, "If you think you need me, I think it would be a waste of your money." Apparently, that impressed whomever I was talking to because Dolph said, "I would like to work with you in the future." So, like anything else you hear in Hollywood, you just take that and say, "Fine. Sure. My ass." Sure enough, three months later, I get a call from Dolph, "Hey, I'm staying at the W in West Hollywood, and I'd like to talk to you about a project." So I go over there, and we talk about stuff. We ended up talking about westerns the first time we met, which was when we met about *Missionary Man*. He would quote lines from *Unforgiven*. He told me about working with Roger Moore on *A View to a Kill*, and that he ended up on that movie by accident. It's funny. So, anyway, at the W, which was the second time we met, we talked about these three movies he had made a deal to make in Russia. He told me to take a look at these three treatments he had and told me to pick the one I wanted to help him with. I looked at all three of them, and *Command Performance*, the one about the ex-biker turned rock and roll drummer saving the concert hall, looked like the one that could be the most fun. It had humor. I said, "Let's do it." We agreed to do it and split the fee 50/50. I told him my plans for it, the budget range, etcetera. It was on spec, but I couldn't say no. The story was good. A lot of actors will say, "I want to collaborate with you," but

they'll sit there and you're supposed to take notes and they babble for twenty minutes and they want you to do the heavy lifting. *Command Performance* was a detailed, twenty-page treatment he had. It was what you see in the movie. It was there. He did the treatment himself. It was a great starting point. We started working on the script, and we worked on it for about a year. I would send him the first draft, and then two or three months later, he would send me a return draft. He busted his ass on it. He took my long, first draft, which was about 130 pages, and he cut 30 pages out, but he didn't cut out any of my good stuff, which was great. I wrote the line, "Dying is easy, rock and roll is hard." It was a back and forth thing. He would periodically keep me updated on the production, and then it looked like it wasn't going to happen. It was still a fun experience. I thought that at least he'd be able to sell it one of these days. Then I got a call from him saying, "We gotta meet. We're set up. Nu Image is going to do it." The deal happened very quickly. It was a matter of days. Contracts were signed, I got a check for exactly the amount he said I was going to get. No questions asked. The only thing I asked was, "You don't have to pay me, but I'm so in love with this script, let me stay on and make changes during the filming." Periodically, he'd send me the script, and he'd say, "Look at this, help me make this scene real." He got the film made. I was invited to a screening with him and some buyers, and it was a great experience.

Dolph is a better action star now than he ever was.

Here's the thing: A lot of these guys are in pretty bad shape. I worked with Van Damme. That was an odd experience. He seemed to be a very nice guy, he was certainly very nice to me. But I could see how he could be very difficult. It was for a project that eventually became *In Hell*. I'd been approached by a company to do a massive rewrite with the director. We were going to do *Bloodsport* meets *The Shawshank Redemption*. It was going to be his theatrical comeback. The script we wrote was a wonderful life-affirming thing that also had lots of action in it. Van Damme really liked it, but for some reason right towards the end of development, Warner Brothers suddenly didn't guarantee a theatrical release, so the film didn't happen at Warner Brothers, and it ended up at Millennium where it was no longer going to be a forty million dollar movie, but ended up being made for five or six. I worked with Jeff Speakman, Dudikoff—who I did a lot of movies with and is a very sweet guy—but Dolph still has the potential to be a major theatrical star, and he may end up doing that. Audiences love him the way they don't love some of these other guys. He's in great shape, and he's a very talented actor.

The Condemned

2007 (Lionsgate DVD) (djm)

"Sounds like you had a hard life . . . good thing it's over."

"Stone Cold" Steve Austin as condemned prisoner Conrad, Tory Mussett as Julie in WWE's *The Condemned*. Author's collection.

Ten condemned prisoners from around the world are culled to "participate" in a streamed to-the-death competition. The players are dropped on a tropical island, are given some weapons to use, and cameras set up throughout the environment capture the action up close, brutal, and personal. One player—Jack Conrad ("Stone Cold" Steve Austin in his first vehicle film)—is a wrongfully convicted Delta Force commando—and he literally doesn't flinch when he's forced to play the game and when the monsters he's up against challenge him to fights. Another one of the players—played by Vinnie Jones—is an absolute animal, a heartless, ruthless killer who turns out to be Conrad's biggest competition. In addition to the action, there is a side story about the callous man who runs the illegal event, and the people working under him who develop a conscience. Hearkening back to the glory days of The Cannon Group and the 1980s style of pure action and adrenaline-charged filmmaking, WWE Films' *The Condemned* is pretty fantastic on most counts. The big sin it commits is a consistent usage of the "shaky cam" effect, which spoils some of the close encounter fights on screen, but repeated viewings and some forgiveness should smooth out the issue. Steve Austin makes for

German lobby card of *The Condemned*, featuring Steve Austin as Conrad. Author's collection.

a great muscle-bound action hero, and while this movie was a gigantic flop at the box office, it was a great segue for him from the world of professional wrestling to film. As a result of its box office failure, Austin then became a direct-to-video action star. Most of his movies failed to match the grandeur of *The Condemned*, which is a shame because he has so much potential to be one of the biggest and best action stars working in today's video/movie market. Nathan Jones (from *The Protector* and *Muay Thai Fighter*) plays one of the imposing contestants in the film. He has a fight with Austin. Director Scott Wiper would later helm the WWE direct-to-video effort *The Marine 3: Homefront*. I'd love to see him direct a movie with John Cena.

The Condemned 2: Desert Prey

2015 (Lionsgate DVD) (djm)

""Tanner, you're a one-man wrecking crew. You did what half my force couldn't do."

A bounty hunter named Will Tanner (Randy Orton from WWE's stable of wrestlers-turned-action stars) and his crew bust an illegal gambling den run by a maniac named Cyrus Merrick (Wes Studi), who takes homeless men and hooks them up to chairs where they're slowly drained of life but somehow makes a gambling game of it. Tanner kills Merrick even though he wasn't supposed to, and the mistake lands him in court, where the judge orders him to cool it, and in his humility he decides to quit the life of a violence-prone bounty hunter and visit his father in the desert. His dad (played by Eric Roberts) lives a simple life fixing cars, and Tanner comes to him with his head hung low, and for a day or so, they're able to enjoy each other's company Tanner (who has gotten a gig towing cars on the highway) responds to a call of someone whose car dies in the middle of nowhere. As it turns out, Tanner knows the driver from his days as a bounty hunter, but something's not right: His friend pulls a gun on him, and his friend ends up dead after the confrontation. Instead of just waiting around, Tanner goes on the run. That's when the plot reveals itself: Cyrus Merrick's understudy—Raul Baccaro (Steven Michael Quezada)—has taken on the mantle of maniac by orchestrating a grand revenge on Tanner and all his buddies, whom he blames for his boss's death, and holed up in a massive warehouse with dozens of high-end gamblers willing to bet tens of millions on the fates of "the condemned," Baccaro has made it so that Tanner will be forced to fight to the death every single one of his former team members in the desert. The entire "game" is caught on camera via intrusive drones that fly around the action, and when Tanner is pushed, he pushes back with everything he's got, and even though he doesn't ask for help, his dad comes along for the ride to protect his son.

I was really looking forward to seeing this one. I was lucky to get to see it in a theater, and watching it on a big screen brought me back to the early '90s when The Boz had his shot with Stone Cold and when Dolph was in *Army of One* (a.k.a. *Joshua Tree*). That said, *The Condemned 2* is a paltry effort when compared with the first entry with Steve Austin. One of the major problems with this movie is that Randy Orton (who's fine) is pitted against much less distinct opponents, none of whom look like they would ever have a prayer against him in a fight. When he finally fights Quezada, it's a joke because nothing we've seen from Quezada promises a good fight. One of the charms of the first film was that each and every "contestant" in the game the characters were forced to play looked beastly and deadly, and so you knew going right in that you're going to get some tasty action. The action in *The Condemned 2* is adequate (when it's at its best), but the story is weak and the villain is miscast. Still, there were a few brawls, thanks to Orton, and Orton himself looked more relaxed here than he did in his previous movie, *12 Rounds 2: Reloaded*, which was directed by this film's director, Roel Reine. I'm really hoping that someday soon that WWE's films will get around to putting two of their stars in the same movie at the same time to give their films a much needed boost in the action department. But I'll be there no matter what if they keep doing them the same way.

Confessions of a Pit Fighter

2005 (Lionsgate DVD) (CD)

Eddie Castillo (Hector Echavarria) has just spent the last seven years of his life in prison for killing a man in a street fight. He's ready to start a new life and live by the law. The only family he has is his little brother David (Rick Medina), who has fallen into the world of underground pit fighting. A circuit has formed with some high rollers calling the shots, especially Argento (Armand Assante) and Lucky (Flavor Flav). In a big-money fight with Argento's top muscle, Matador (Quinton 'Rampage' Jackson), David is killed. Eddie is devastated, as is David's pregnant girlfriend Angel (Yvonne Arias). Eddie wants revenge so he reluctantly steps into the world he abandoned while in prison and begins to earn money to help with his unborn nephew. While trying to win big in the fights, his probation officer McGee (John Savage) offers to look the other way for a cut of the winnings. Eddie has no choice but to play along and continue on with his plan for vengeance.

Confessions of a Pit Fighter is pretty generic and predictable as far as the story goes. The action is good with some solid bare-knuckle fighting in the streets. Hector Echavarria (*Unrivaled*) is an action star, no matter how you look at it. While most of his films are of the pedestrian and predictable sort, he has a star quality about him and he belongs on the screen. The action scenes are all done without wires, with choreography by Art Camacho who also served as the film's director. The picture stands out for its Latin influence and with the East LA setting. We're also treated to a bloody brawl between Echavarria and Quinton Jackson, who worked with him on *Death Warrior*. *Pit Fighter* is worth checking out.

Contour (a.k.a. **The Agent**)

2006 (Indican DVD) (djm)

Obviously inspired by the kind of Hong Kong action comedies that Jackie Chan is best known for, *Contour* is a step in the right direction for its director, choreographer, and star, Eric Jacobus. With a budget of only a few thousand dollars, this film is mostly kindling for the fire until the incredible climax that goes on for something like twenty minutes. Jacobus plays a down-on-his luck guy who gets embroiled in a far-fetched plot involving the prince of a tropical island who is willing to pay a large reward for a task. Slapstick humor and goofy acting make the film pretty unbelievable and hard to swallow, but luckily Jacobus and his crew of stuntmen-friends invested lots of time and energy on crafting meticulous and dangerous fight scenes.

Jacobus would later refine and rethink his filmmaking technique into the much-better film *Death Grip*. *Contour* is of interest, though, if watching Jacobus and his pals get crazy with their skills is something you want to check out after watching *Death Grip*.

Contract Killer (a.k.a. **Hitman**)

1998 (Sony DVD) (CD)

"I should tell you something about a killer. A killer may not be required to kill one person. Someone might want to dismember his target. A left hand is worth $8,000 and a leg is worth $10,000. If he wants both, we should give him a twenty percent discount. That's $16,000."

A Yakuza crime boss who is about to be assassinated sets up a revenge fund to be awarded to the first person who can turn in the body of "The King of Killers," an assassin with no known affiliation and a secret identity. Fu (Jet Li) is a low-rent assassin who has trouble killing anyone since he is such a nice and humble guy. He takes on the task of trying to find this unknown assassin. He meets Lo (Eric Tsang), a con artist who acts as Fu's manger. Lo may be able to talk his way out of almost any situation but knows nothing about being a hitman. The police want to put an end to all of this and Detective Chan (Simon Yam) is at the front of the movement. The power hungry son of the slain crime boss has taken over the business and his plans are much more dangerous than anyone could have imagined.

Aside from feeling like the premise was stretched a little too far, *Contract Killer* is an off-beat comedy with a few excellent action scenes courtesy of Jet Li (just prior to his Hollywood breakthrough, *Lethal Weapon 4*). The focus is on the humor (much of which may be lost in translation), so action is secondary. Watching Li take out bad guys with his fists and feet never gets old. There's a unique match with Li fighting Paul Rapovski (*Extreme Challenge*) who uses little lights as weapons. You won't be blown out of the water with this one but it's fun enough to watch at least once, and it has Simon Yam in it, which is a big plus. Directed by Wei Tung (*Magic Cop*).

The Contractor
2007 (Sony DVD) (djm)

An assassin named James Dial (Wesley Snipes who barely says a word in the movie) is called in to snipe an international terrorist who is being arraigned in London, and he performs the job, but his escape gets messy when his contact/driver is killed by the London police. Wounded after a car crash, Dial retreats to a safe house, which is inhabited by an old woman and a twelve-year-old girl who takes a liking to him even though she should be afraid of him. He's bleeding, wielding a weapon, and sirens are blaring outside when they meet, but never mind. She likes him. She helps him with getting supplies and even though he continues to shrug her off, she keeps helping him. Meanwhile, Dial's boss is working with the police to find and kill or capture him because Dial has become a liability for the American government. The British detective on his trail is played by the lovely Lena Heady (from *Dredd*).

Muted and uninvolving until the last act, *The Contractor* isn't special in any way, but by the end I realized that I kinda liked it. Snipes is okay in the movie, though this movie could have starred anyone, and except for a last-second fight scene, there is almost no action at all, aside from a car chase and some periodic shooting. But I liked the London locations, I liked the awkward relationship between the girl and Snipes, and ultimately, the movie made sense in a way that many direct-to-video action movies of this caliber simply don't. It delivers what you want from it, at a level that I was willing to accept. Directed by Josef Rusnak (*The Art of War II* with Snipes).

Convict 762
1997 (York DVD) (CD)

"I've seen men blind themselves so they didn't have to see him, slit their own throats to deny him the pleasure, men who thought they forgot about fear long before they reached this hellish rock."

In the darkness of space, the all-female crew of a spaceship are about to return to Earth when Reno (Tawny Fere) makes a navigational mistake and leads them all into a meteor storm. They won't be able to make it home, having burned through too much fuel, so they make an emergency landing on a penal colony. It seems to be abandoned—everyone has either fled or been killed by an escaped convict known only by his number: 762. There are only two men alive on the planet: Vigo (Frank Zagarino) and Mannix (Billy Drago), both of whom accuse the other of being the notorious villain. Once the women in the crew begin dying, they will have to

decide who is telling the truth or the ladies may end up dead . . . just like the rest of the colony.

The film has a clever story and it's refreshing to see this sort of picture carried by a group of talented and strong women. It's mostly a (generic) character play so the inclusion of action star Frank Zagarino (*The Protector, Cy Warrior*) is a bit of a waste. He's given very little screen time and we only see him in action during the final moments. He faces off with resident baddie Billy Drago who growls, scowls, and grins his way through an otherwise thankless role. Zagarino makes the best of his limited appearance and at least gets to show off in front of a group of gorgeous ladies. Directed by Luca Bercovici.

Cop Land
1997 (Lionsgate DVD) (djm)

After a string of high-profile box-office flops, Sylvester Stallone returned to his dramatic roots and starred in the intense drama *Cop Land*, which casts him in an unattractive and shockingly dumpy light. He plays Freddy Heflin, the half deaf and seemingly slow-witted sheriff of a quiet town in New Jersey, where a flock of New York cops and detectives live. Heflin, who lost his hearing in one ear as a teenager when he saved the life of a drowning local woman (Annabella Sciorra), has let life pass him by until an internal affairs officer (played by Robert De Niro) comes to him with a case involving a young cop named Murray Babitch (Michael Rapaport), who shot and killed several unarmed black teens on a bridge, and then later supposedly jumped off the bridge in remorse. The fact is that Babitch is alive and well, being harbored by fellow detectives Ray Donlan (Harvey Keitel), Jack Rucker (Robert Patrick), and Figgis (Ray Liotta), who each have a truckload of sins they're hiding. When Heflin is mocked, derided, and shredded by his fellow officers for being a simpleton and for not being a real man, he decides to make a deadly serious choice to bring Babitch to the authorities and to shed his old skin and become a warrior. The violent finale has a wounded and (completely) deaf Heflin walking down the street with a shotgun and pistol like a cowboy.

Stallone's haters will repent when they see *Cop Land*. He has absolutely no ego in his role, and his down-to-earth performance is probably his best ever. To see the biggest action star in the world cower his head in shame here is to see a real-thing actor in pristine form. He's surrounded by the best actors in the business, and while the movie isn't really Academy Award-worthy, it does bring out the best in everyone involved. James Mangold wrote and directed it. After this, Stallone took a hiatus for a few years and returned with *Eye See You*, which was shelved for years. His next release was *Get Carter*.

Counterforce
1987 (IVE VHS) (djm)

A team of American mercenaries is hired to protect an exiled revolutionary in the Middle East from a dictator (played by Robert Forster) whose encroaching forces are putting the lives of the revolutionary and his family at risk. The team's leader (George Kennedy) assigns his squad (played by the great George Rivero, Isaac Hayes, Andrew Stevens, and Kevin Bernhardt) to stick to the revolutionary (played by Louis Jourdan) through his campaign to appeal to his followers, but when an attempt is made on his life, the mercenaries turn the tables and go on the offensive.

Very similar to Stallone's future *Expendables* franchise, *Counterforce* is a really fun vehicle for highlighted Mexican action star Rivero, who gets to show off just how game he is in a movie that he's perfectly suited for. The supporting "B" cast only makes the movie better. If this is your first encounter with Rivero in a movie, make your next one *Fist Fighter*. Directed by J. Anthony Loma.

Counter Measures
1998 (Platinum DVD) (CD)

"I've read Fuller's file. I'm sure he's trying to get a message to us. If the Odessa's been taken, God help the hijackers."

Jake Fuller (Michael Dudikoff) is a Navy medic who recently lost his brother in a confrontation with Russian spies. A short while later, Fuller finds himself as a consultant on the Russian sub known as *Odessa*. The problem is that terrorists who are ready to blow up the world if their demands aren't met are controlling the sub. There are plenty of nuclear weapons aboard ready to launch at the flip of a switch. Fuller is the type of guy who wants to avoid violence at all costs but when lives become threatened, he will give it everything he's got to save the day and survive. With few resources and even less time, he and Lt. Swain (Alexander Keith) make their way through the sub to find the villainous Captain Petrov (James Horan) who is ready to make the world his personal playground.

Michael Dudikoff (*Chain of Command, Avenging Force*) knows his audience and almost always delivers a film that's worth watching. His persona always ends up being highly likable with an unparalleled charm. His performance in *Counter Measures* is no different; his character wants to be a pacifist but circumstances prevent him from being able to follow that ideal. His character is quite resourceful and for a portion of the film his only weapon is a corkscrew (for which he finds several uses). It wouldn't be a Fred Olen Ray (*Black Horizon,* also with Dudikoff) film without at least one scene of gratuitous nudity (which is delivered very early on). Dudikoff eventually begins to fight his way through the terrorists, taking them on one by one. He is unrivaled when it comes to likability even if the film only ranks as passable.

Cover-Up

1991 (Artisan DVD) (CD)

"Gentleman, we are going to start a fucking war."

Mike Anderson (Dolph Lundgren) is an American reporter who is sent to cover an attack on a US naval base that was supposedly committed by a group known as Black October. While trying to uncover the truth, he must also confront some old friends whom he parted ways with years before including Colonel Cooper (John Finn) and his ex-lover Susan Clifford (Lisa Berkley), who are now a couple. Cooper knows something is up, but he's murdered before revealing what he knows, leaving Mike alone to butt heads with his former CIA boss, Lou Jackson (Louis Gossett Jr.). He soon learns of a plan that will leave thousands dead, and he has to race against the clock to save them.

Cover-Up was an early vehicle for Dolph Lundgren (*Rocky IV*), and while it's a slow film, it gave him the opportunity to focus more on his acting ability rather than how many different ways he can rip someone apart. It has an intriguing storyline, one that requires the viewer to be patient and to work *with* the film rather than just watching it. The question is: Would Dolph's fans really want to work that hard to enjoy it? The film is really light on action and some people may be turned off by the political intrigue and covert cover-ups. Dolph is excellent in the film, playing a really likable and vulnerable character. At the time the film was released, people weren't expecting something like this from him. He spends much of the movie being chased, with constant attempts being made on his life. One of those assassination attempts turns into a solid brawl in a hotel room. That is the only real fight to speak of. Everything else is tension building to brief moments of excitement. Supporting him in the film was Lisa Berkely (who never made another film), John Finn (*Turbulence*), and Academy Award–winner Louis Gossett Jr. (*Iron Eagle*). *Cover-Up* isn't a high point in Dolph's filmography but he did prove to the world that he can act just as well as he can kick some ass. Directed by Manny Coto.

Crackerjack

1994 (Republic VHS) (djm)

Thomas Ian Griffith stars as Jack Wild, a cop suffering from PTSD after he watched his wife get killed. His performance on the job is uneven, and he's forced to take a leave of absence. On a vacation trip to the Rocky Mountains with his sister and her husband and child, he's thrust into *Die Hard* mode when a group of terrorists take over the remote hotel he's staying at. Their objective is a cache of diamonds, and they plan on blowing up one of the mountains, causing an avalanche to cover their tracks. Wild must tap into his inner reckless force to face the terrorists, and once he gets going, he's nearly impossible to stop.

VHS artwork for *Crackerjack*. Author's collection.

Griffith was great in *Excessive Force*, which he also wrote, and in *Crackerjack* he's sort of doing the same thing, but with less focus. The problem with *Crackerjack* is that the script is boring and the director, Michael Mazo (*Time Runner* with Mark Hamill), doesn't give the movie the pizazz it needs to be exciting. It's got a sort of *Cliffhanger* vibe to it, but exploitation producer Lloyd Simandl cuts too many noticeable corners for *Crackerjack* to be a contender. One sore point I have is the chintzy music score. It's terrible. A cheap, unimaginative score is an obvious clue as to how the movie is going to play to an audience. This was the beginning of Griffith's downward spiral into direct-to-video territory. After *Excessive Force* he should have followed up with something fantastic. *Crackerjack* isn't fantastic. Christopher Plummer and Nastassja Kinski co-star.

Crackerjack 3

1999 (Lionsgate DVD) (djm)

"Why waste bullets when you've got a neutron bomb?"

Good ol' boy Jack Thorn (Bo Svenson) hangs up his hat and retires from the CIA, but not before he meets his successor, Marcus Clay (Olivier Gruner), a cocky agent who gloats to Jack that things will be a *lot* different now that he's retiring. Jack goes to his cabin in the woods and begins his retirement by fishing, and in no time, the world's safety is at risk when Marcus betrays the US government by hijacking a bomb, which he and his team threaten to detonate on American soil. Jack is alerted to all

this when Marcus sends some men to kill him so that he won't retaliate on some kind of mission against them, but being the ex-Navy SEAL that he is, Jack manages to turn the situation around by capturing one of Marcus's assassins and torturing him into revealing information. Jack's idea is to recruit former military cronies (most of whom are senior citizens now) and launch an attack-and-destroy mission against Marcus and his team.

Several things: First, this is not a sequel to either of the two previous *Crackerjack* films. There is no relation whatsoever to the Thomas Ian Griffith vehicle or the second film with Judge Reinhold. Second, this is one of Olivier Gruner's worst films, despite the fact that he has a rare opportunity here to play a villain. Finally, this is barely an action film. Gruner, who had a great beginning as an action star in films like *Angel Town* and *Savate*, is demeaned and diminished in this film; in his final scene he engages in a losing fist and kick fight to Bo Svenson, who looks like he can barely go out for a jog, let alone take on a real-life kickboxing champion and a for-real French special forces soldier (Gruner was both). *Crackerjack 3* is a painful movie to sit through. Gruner's most devoted fans should avoid it. Everyone else should be advised to know that Gruner's career was unfortunately wasted on garbage like this. Anyone else who's curious, just understand that movies like this one are what drag some action stars to a bottomless level. Directed by Lloyd A. Simandl, who made a small fortune making movies in Eastern Europe featuring naked women in captivity.

Crack House

1989 (MGM DVD) (djm)

Beautiful Melissa (Playboy Playmate Cheryl Kay) chose the wrong guy to give her heart to: Rick (Anthony Geary), a Latino gangbanger in her neighborhood. When Rick gets popped for retaliating on the black gang that killed his brother, Melissa is pretty much easy game for other gang members (both blacks and Latinos), who take advantage of her. While Rick is rotting in prison, Melissa becomes a drug slave for a low-level black gang member, whose overlord Steadman (a buff and imposing Jim Brown) kills him and steals Melissa as his own personal sex slave, pumped up with drugs. As Melissa is degraded and tortured in her own personal dungeon by Steadman, Rick hears about what's become of his girlfriend and he makes a deal with a detective (Richard Roundtree) to be released if he can help bring Steadman to justice. With Rick on the streets again, he's going to head straight into Steadman's horns and do his best to bring down the crack house.

From The Cannon Group, *Crack House* is ultra exploitative and sleazy, and it's hard to root for Jim Brown's character, despite how badass he is. We watch him leer over nude Kay, and it's implied that he rapes and tortures her, not to mention the other female slave under his fist in the film. Still, it's a solid villain turn for him, and his tussle with a much weaker Geary in the climax plays out believably (Geary is thrown around like a ragdoll). From director Michael Fischa.

Cradle 2 the Grave

2003 (Warner DVD) (djm)

After Jet Li's one-two punch of *Lethal Weapon 4* and *Romeo Must Die* with Joel Silver, they teamed up again with *Cradle 2 the Grave*, which is in the same Hollywood vein. Li plays a mysterious Chinese cop named Su who is after some precious black stones that are worth millions, but have been stolen by a jewel thief named Fait (played by a deadpan DMX) and his crew (featuring Anthony Anderson and Gabrielle Union). Fait's score is heisted by another crew working for a deadly assassin-type named Ling (Mark Dacascos). Ling has organized an auction for the black stones, and it's Su's job to get to them before they reach anyone's hands because when ignited by lasers, they become more powerful than plutonium. Su and Fait team up (with help by comedy relief, courtesy of Tom Arnold) and save the world.

Slick and full of intrusive rap songs, *Cradle 2 the Grave* was made to turn a quick profit, but movies like it that were made around the same time (*Romeo Must Die, Exit Wounds*, etc.) weren't really made to last. They capitalized on the post-*Matrix* interest in martial arts, but they cheat angles, use terrible editing, and ultimately fail the stars featured in them. I like elements of *Exit Wounds, Romeo*, and *Cradle* (which were all directed by Andrzej Batkowiak and produced by Silver), but they'd be better films and easier to watch a decade later if there were no rap songs or wires in the fight scenes, and if they gave a little more room to the main stars instead of stifling them with dumb supporting players. The best scene in *Cradle* features Li in a fighting cage, and his first opponent is played by Randy Couture (a real MMA fighter), but as he easily defeats him, about a dozen more MMA fighters rush in to fight Li. The final fight scene between Li and Dacascos is good, but it's intercut with several other lame fight scenes, so it's a waste. After this, Li made *Unleashed*, which didn't make any of the mistakes that ruined his Silver films.

Crank

2006 (Lionsgate DVD) (CD)

"Listen, I've been fatally poisoned, there's probably a psychopath heading over there to torture and kill you as we speak, but don't bother getting out of bed, I'll be there in a flash . . . . Maybe you could fry me up a waffle or something, okay?"

Chet Chelios (Jason Statham) is a dead man. He wakes up to find out that he was poisoned with a rare Chinese concoction that will kill him when his body slows down. The only thing that will slow the poison down is to keep his adrenalin up. Trying to stay alive, he heads out on the streets to find Verona (Jose Pablo Cantillo), the man responsible. He seeks advice from quack Doc Miles (Dwight Yoakam), and with his girlfriend

Eve (Amy Smart) in tow, he does whatever he can to keep his adrenaline up while trying to find his killer.

The term *adrenaline-fueled* is often used to describe action films, but if you are referring to the movie *Crank*, never has it been more appropriate. The movie takes maybe the first five minutes of screen time to explain what's going on, then we're off and running. Statham (*Chaos*) gives one of his finest performances, and while it really isn't a traditional action film there is plenty of fighting, chases, and shootouts to keep us entertained. The directing team of Mark Neveldine and Brian Taylor (*Gamer*) turn everything up by several notches and go for broke, turning this into a stylishly assembled motion picture. When the central character and his impossible predicament shifts into overdrive, so does the camera. It whips in, out, and around the action at a blistering pace. The story is thin yet still pretty solid, with Statham holding everything together at the seams. He puts all of his energy into hoarding the screen and he manages to command your attention every moment. *Crank* is filled with equal amounts of humor and action, and it takes the viewer on one incredibly fast-paced ride that leaves you feeling exhausted once the credits roll.

Crank 2: High Voltage

2009 (Lionsgate DVD) (CD)

"Chev, I'm a certified heart surgeon, well at least I was. I lost my license after I fucked up my ex-wife's vaginal rejuvenation procedure in our basement, but that's irrelevant right now."

Picking up directly after the events of the first film, Chev Chelios (Jason Statham) finds himself kidnapped by gangsters with his indestructible heart replaced by an artificial one. When the battery pack is destroyed, Chev must use various means to send small bursts of electricity into the heart for it to keep ticking. All the while he's on the search to find the party who stole his heart . . . because he wants it back.

The original *Crank* film was a moderate hit for Lionsgate when it was released in 2006. The sequel *Crank 2: High Voltage* didn't do nearly as well. While the first film was a crazy, adrenaline-fueled beast, this second film is more or less complete lunacy, tied very loosely together by virtually the same thread that made the first one so original. The events that take place in the film are so incredibly bizarre and psychotic, the only way to really swallow everything is to just imagine you're watching a cracked-out superhero film. We see a man get a shotgun shoved in his ass, a stripper who has her breasts deflate when the implants seep out after being shot, and a fight scene with our unkillable hero best described as a *kaiju* throwdown. The action is pretty much nonstop with bloody shootouts and a couple of fight scenes for good measure. The directing team

of Nevaldine/Taylor (*Gamer*) return with their unique visionary style that might be too much for some, but the hyperkinetic ADD-addled style is their trademark, and it's undeniably pretty unique. Many actors return from the first film like Dwight Yoakam, Efren Ramirez (who returns as the twin brother of his character from the first film who was killed), and the incredibly sexy and adorable Amy Smart (*The Reunion*). Joining the cast this time are Corey Haim (*Fast Getaway*), David Carradine (*Project Eliminator*), and the hilarious Bai Ling (*The Crow*). The film may go too far over the top for some, but no one can say it's dull.

Crash Dive

1997 (Platinum DVD) (CD)

The U.S.S. *Ulysses* is a nuclear submarine designed by former Navy SEAL James Carter (Michael Dudikoff). While the sub is out at sea, the crew answers a distress call and saves the lives of what they believe to be a few sailors in need of rescuing. Once safely aboard, the sailors turn out to be terrorists with the intention of capturing the nukes on board. The only way the government can save the lives of the men on board is if they can get someone on the ship. The only person who knows every nook and cranny of the ship is Carter. With the terrorists threatening to unleash the nukes, he has to get on board to reprogram the missiles. The terrorists are a crafty bunch and make things incredibly difficult for Carter. But with a son at home, Carter isn't willing to go down easy.

At some point in their careers, most action stars will have done at least one *Die Hard*-type movie on a bus, ship, phone booth, etc. *Crash Dive* is, unfortunately, one of those movies where the formula doesn't work. The film is highly predictable; it's easy to see where everything is headed and its ending is no surprise. It does, however, have one thing going for it that may keep you interested and that's Dudikoff himself. His character and persona are just so darn likable that you can't hate the film. He plays an ex-soldier retired from duty in order to care for his young son, so he has something to lose, which raises the stakes. Where the film falters is in the rather tired action scenes. There are a few short scuffles and a shootout or two but none of it is memorable. It just felt like everyone was going through the motions without really ramping up the excitement. Dudikoff gives a solid performance, but his co-star Catherine Bell (*Men of War*) is sadly underused. Some of the special effects are surprisingly well-rendered. *Crash Dive* is mainly just a time-killer. It was directed by Andrew Stevens.

Creed

2015 (Warner DVD) (djm)

The long lost son of Apollo Creed (played by Carl Weathers in the first four *Rocky* movies), Adonis Johnson (Michael B. Jordon) got a rough start on life as he was living as an orphan in juvenile halls, group homes, and under the state. Apollo's wife Mary Anne (Phylicia Rashad) eventually took him in as her own son, but no one could take the fighter out of him as he grew up with a fighter's spirit. Even living in the lap of luxury in Creed's home couldn't dissuade him from pursuing low-level fights in Tijuana, and cutting all ties to the world that didn't revolve around boxing, Adonis relocates to Philadelphia to pursue training with his father's greatest opponent and ally, Rocky Balboa (Sylvester Stallone). Showing up unannounced at Rocky's humble Italian eatery, Adonis surprises him with some knowledge only Apollo would have known, and sensing that he's not being glammed by just some palooka off the street, Rocky takes a good look at the kid and actually considers training him, as he's obviously ambitious (but also humble, but not without some issues). Adonis moves into an apartment building and begins dating a young woman named Bianca (Tessa Thompson) who's going deaf, and he spends every spare minute training and thinking what it would be like to fight the champion of the world, "Pretty" Ricky Conlan (real boxing champ Tony Bellow), who is scheduled to fight one final fight in his boxing career before going to prison. An unexpected opening in Conlan's slate leaves a slot open for a contender, and after Rocky gives Adonis a fight with a local champ, Adonis wins the match, proving that he's not just a pushover. When the media catches on that Adonis is Adonis Creed, the son of the famed Apollo, there's a small frenzy as he's considered to fight Conlan. Just as Adonis is picking up some heat with Rocky in training sessions, Rocky collapses and is rushed to the hospital, where he is told he has cancer. Exhausted with life and lonely without his beloved Adrian and his best friend Paulie, Rocky decides not to take chemo treatments, which would ultimately spell his doom, but Adonis convinces him to fight for his life. Given the slot to go up against Conlan, Adonis has virtually the same shot that Rocky had once upon a time with Apollo, and so the parallel is uncanny.

Stallone gave over the reins to his franchise to young director Ryan Coogler, who was still in his twenties when he made this. Coogler's sensibilities are a little edgier than anything we've seen from a story featuring Rocky Balboa, and though Rocky isn't the main character this time, the story is in his world and in his backyard, which still feels more or less like it belongs to him, despite the fact that the world is clearly moving on without him. Adonis is a worthy pupil for Rocky, and he deserves Rocky's tutelage, but even with all the pluses, *Creed* falters somewhere in the telling, and especially in the ending that tries to mirror the original Rocky. Adonis is a good character and should have been given his own unique fist-pumping climax (and his own music theme, for that matter), but it was admirable watching Stallone allow himself to look cancer-ridden and beaten down by chemo treatments. As a result, he was nominated for Best Supporting Actor by the Academy, his first nomination since he was nominated for Best Actor (for the same role) in 1977.

Crime Story

1993 (Shout Factory DVD) (djm)

Grittier than most of the movies Jackie Chan had done up to the point of its release, *Crime Story* forsakes comedy and goes straight for the jugular. Jackie plays a straight-laced, high-strung detective named Eddie who's on a kidnapping case that could be a lot easier to solve if his partner wasn't dirty and part of the kidnapping scheme. His partner—Detective Hung (Kent Cheng)—is working against him every step of the way, and when Eddie figures out that he's dirty, his investigation gets even more complicated when thugs come out in droves to kill him, on Detective Hung's orders.

"R"-rated in tone, texture, and delivery, *Crime Story* is a refreshing vehicle for Jackie who hadn't done something this ballsy since starring in James Glickenhaus's *The Protector*. His close calls with explosions, escapes, and falls from great distances almost take a back seat to the edgy thriller vibe of the film. The movie is much more concerned with showing Jackie dealing with realistic situations than putting him through flaming hoops and trapeze-artist stunts, which is great. Fans of his more well-known films like *Police Story* and *Rumble in the Bronx* should check this one out. Director Kirk Wong would later direct the American action movie *The Big Hit*. Jackie did some uncredited directing work on *Crime Story*.

Crisis

1997 (Platinum DVD) (djm)

This is the last film David Bradley (*American Ninja 3, 4, 5* and *American Samurai*) made, and it's awful. He stars as a hitman who calls it quits to spend time with his brother. As soon as he reunites with him, they both get forced to do a job for the mob. The mob doesn't realize that Bradley is supposed to be a badass, but they tie him down and restrain him anyway. For the next hour, the film takes place in a single location (a medium-sized house in suburbia), where characters move around, chatting and getting angry at each other. In the last few minutes, Bradley is freed by a sympathetic female character, and he beats up the main villain in a brawl. The credits roll.

Jalal Merhi, who is usually in front of the camera as an action star himself, directed this junky movie. It hardly qualifies as an "action" picture. Bradley looks incredibly bored and tired of making movies in this thing. He never made another one. Merhi and Bradley previously worked together in *Expect to Die*. If you're a Bradley fan, steer clear of both films.

The Crocodile Hunter: Collision Course

2002 (MGM DVD) (djm)

"Well, that's one poacher that just learned a valuable Steve-o lesson: *Don't muck with it!*"

Animal Planet's go-get-'em adventurer and one-of-a-kind crocodile hunter Steve Irwin got his shot at the movies with this one-off actioner that recalls some of the fun movies Jackie Chan made during the '90s in Australia. Irwin plays himself, alongside his real-life wife Terri, and the film follows their exploits through the outback of Australia as they encounter deadly snakes, killer spiders, lost "joeys" (kangaroos), and a menacing crocodile. Their extremely busy day saving rarified species that could easily kill a human being with one sting or bite is interrupted by some government agents who are trying to find a piece of a fallen satellite that a crocodile swallowed. In the midst of his jaw-dropping antics with the lethal creatures, Irwin dodges the agents like Indiana Jones and saves the day, saves the world (or Australia), and protects the wildlife he so loves.

In my mind and by my estimation, Irwin was a stuntman. Nobody in their right mind would jump out of exploding helicopters, off of rooftops, or deliberately flip their car in the air, only to (also deliberately) *stay* in the car while it blows up, crashes multiple times, or is set on fire while the movie world around them is exploding and coming apart . . . and yet that's exactly what stuntmen do. Irwin did the same sort of thing, but with death-dealing creatures, and he allowed everything he did to be caught on camera. In this movie, he wrestles with crocodiles, holds venomous snakes by their tails, and antagonizes horrifyingly poisonous spiders to get a rise out of his audience, and it all works. If he'd lived longer, he might have made more movies and become a sort of *Crocodile Dundee* meets Jackie Chan action star, but sadly he was killed by a manta ray in 2006 when he swam too close to it and was stung hundreds of times, piercing his heart. *The Crocodile Hunter: Collision Course* isn't a fantastic movie by any means, but it's a novelty of an action film, and it can be considered very unique for having a star in the center of it who was fearless and dedicated (and more than a little bit crazy) to deliver death-defying thrills to his fans. Directed by John Stainton, who had worked with Irwin on several of his documentaries.

Crooked

2006 (Lionsgate DVD) (CD)

Danny Tyler (Don "The Dragon" Wilson) and Phil Yordan (Olivier Gruner) are two police detectives who are given the task of finding call girl Angel (Diana Kaufman) after she witnesses the murder of a protected witness who had information that would have put mobster Nugentti (Michael

Cavalieri) behind bars. She sees Nugentti pull the trigger so now there is a price on her head. Tyler and Yordan do everything they can to keep her safe, but no matter where they go, Nugentti's crew always seems to find them. Captain Rouse (Gary Busey) is doing what he can to find the mole in the department who's tipping the mob off, but to no avail. The only thing they can do is stay ahead of the game and do what they can to keep Angel alive.

Action fans should enjoy the hell out of *Crooked*. There are plenty of shootouts, hand-to-hand fighting, cheesy one-liners, and even a little nudity for good measure. The only thing missing from the film was a major car chase which is completely forgivable. It stars two icons of the genre: Don "The Dragon" Wilson (the *Bloodfist* series) and Olivier Gruner (*Savate*), as reluctant partners who must protect a witness to a murder. The film is a throwback to the buddy-cop films that dominated cinemas during the glory days of action and martial arts movies. Wilson is the by-the-book cop while Gruner is the wild card. Seeing the two of them together is a treat, and under the direction of Art Camacho they seem to be having a great time. The action is mostly nonstop with both men getting equal amounts of time to showcase their martial art skills. They spend a little amount of time trading quips and have no problem using their guns either. Also turning in cool performances are Gary Busey (*Lethal Weapon*), Martin Kove (*Steele Justice*), and the one and only Fred "The Hammer" Williamson (*Original Gangstas*). Each of these guys has at least one moment to remind viewers exactly who they are, and fans should dig their moments. Negative reviews aside, I had a great time with it.

Crossfire

(a.k.a. **Not Another Mistake**)

1988 (Nelson VHS) (djm)

Richard Straker, a broken and bitter Vietnam vet, has lived off the grid since the war ended. His days consist of drowning himself in alcohol and living day to day without any purpose. A bit of destiny comes calling when he's offered the chance to return to Vietnam with the prospect of rescuing some MIAs, and it doesn't take long for him to get back into the zone again. Sobered up with a mission, a mandate, and a crew, Straker

Richard Norton is enveloped by an explosion in *Crossfire*. Courtesy of Richard Norton.

Anthony Maharaj's *Crossfire* stars Richard Norton as Richard Straker, a soldier on a mission in Vietnam. Courtesy of Richard Norton.

Richard Straker (Richard Norton) plans an attack in *Crossfire*. Courtesy of Richard Norton.

(played by Richard Norton) leads a team back into the jungles, searching for captives. When they find two, they're faced with a vindictive Vietnamese general with an endless force, and the film concludes with one of the bleakest endings this type of movie has ever seen.

Surprisingly grim and serious for a clear riff on *Rambo: First Blood Part II* (complete with a bureaucratic betrayal at a crucial moment), *Crossfire* is a really good vehicle for Australian action star Norton, who actually plays an Australian 'Nam vet in this film. The action is plentiful, with some fine martial arts footwork thrown in for good measure, but the dénouement is shockingly abrupt and pretty realistic. Fans of *Rambo* and *Missing in Action* should like this one. Norton worked with the director Anthony Maharaj several other times: *Kickfighter, Return of the Kickfighter,* and *Death Fight*.

The Crow

1994 (Dimension DVD) (djm)

"So you're him, huh? The avenger. The killer of killers. Nice outfit. Not sure about the face, though."

Grunge rocker Eric Draven (Brandon Lee) is murdered along with his girlfriend, Shelly, on Devil's Night, the night before Halloween. A year later, Draven is brought back from the grave, and he systematically hunts down each and every reprobate who had something to do with his death. The gang he hunts answers to Top Dollar (Michael Wincott), a callous and bored overlord of the dark, rainy city. As The Crow (as he might as well be called) works his way to Top Dollar, he rekindles several small relationships he had when they were brutally interrupted a year before. The most important friend he has is a young preteen girl who's practically an orphan, and this relationship helps even out an otherwise bleak and melancholy story.

No matter how many times you watch *The Crow*, it always seems to have a strange effect. On the one hand, it's Brandon Lee's best film and best performance, but on the other hand, it's immediately tragic and profoundly unsettling to think that he died on the set of this film while shooting it. It's an eerie film to begin with, and adding the shocking reality to it just compounds the proceedings. That said, Lee uses some martial arts (but not much) in the film, and relies heavily on brute force and crazed intention, which makes him incredibly compelling to watch in the picture. It's based on a cult comic book series, and all of the sequels and spinoffs that followed pale in comparison to it. Mark Dacascos played Draven in the television series *The Crow: Stairway to Heaven*, which is the best of the sequels/spin-offs. Alex Proyas directed *The Crow*.

The Crow: Stairway to Heaven

1998–1999 (TV Guide DVD) (CD)

"I'm Eric Draven. I was murdered, I came back. I don't understand how or why any better than you do. When I need to, I turn into what you saw. I believe I'm supposed to set things right in this world or at least try. Any more questions?"

Eric Draven (Mark Dacascos) is a struggling musician, but he has everything he needs in his lady Shelly Webster (Sabine Karsenti). Sadly, the two of them are brutally murdered, and the killers are left to roam the streets. On the one-year anniversary of their death, Eric comes back, powered by a mystical crow, to set the wrong things right in order for him to be reunited with his love. Back from the dead, he has gained the ability to heal from fatal wounds, can develop psychic connections, and has grown more powerful. He uses these newfound abilities to get his revenge on the ones who wronged him. His journey doesn't end there: Until the time comes for him to be reunited with Shelly, Draven must seek out those who need help, people who can't help themselves, and do what he can to solve their problems. Then when his work is done and he helps enough people, he will be allowed to cross over and finally rest in peace.

After the enormous success of the feature film of *The Crow* with Brandon Lee, producer Edward Pressman tried his best to mimic the success through sequels and a television series. This series starts out as a remake of the original film. The first two episodes retell Draven's story but the series tries to set itself apart by changing up the mythology a bit. It takes them a few episodes before they start to develop an ongoing storyline, and unfortunately it isn't a very good one. In fact, most of these stories are ridiculous and destroy the emotional connection viewers may have begun to have towards it and the characters. The undead Eric Draven is put on trial for the murder of his girlfriend—so silly. There are stories involving a female Crow—Shelly's spirit crossing over and possessing the body of a woman—and bad guys trying to become a Crow, time traveling through portals, and so forth. The one thing the series does do right are the action scenes and having Mark Dacascos (*Only the Strong, Sanctuary*) in the lead role. There's martial arts action in almost every episode and Dacascos is somehow able to sell the ludicrous stories with a very strong performance. Fans of the film will hate everything this show stands for but if you're devoted to the greatness of Dacascos, you may be able to suffer through the twenty-two episodes produced just to see the man in action. The show was canceled, and it was left with an unresolved cliffhanger, leaving fans with loads of unanswered questions. Tibor Takacs, who directed several of the episodes, has worked with Dacascos on other projects like *Sabotage, Sanctuary,* and *Red Line.*

Crying Freeman

1995 (JY DVD) (djm)

Christophe Gans's faithful feature adaptation of the anime series of the same name is richly produced and well cast. Mark Dacascos plays Yo, a potter who is taken captive by a secret cult who hypnotizes him and turns him into a

Mark Dacascos stars in director Christophe Gans's *Crying Freeman.* Author's collection.

An acrobatic flip from *Crying Freeman,* featuring Mark Dacascos. Author's collection.

Theatrical release poster for *Crying Freeman.* Author's collection.

killing machine and renames him Freeman. He performs assassinations against his will (which is why he cries), and he falls in love with a woman he should have killed. The police are after him, and when he is on an extended mission to infiltrate the Yakuza, things get complicated.

For various unknown reasons, this film was never shown or made available in the US. It was a hit in Europe and around the world. Mark Dascascos is very good in a sensitive role, and the last act of the movie has him showcasing his extraordinary physical abilities. Incidentally, he later married his co-star, Julie Condra Douglas. He reteamed with director Gans on *Brotherhood of the Wolf.*

Cutaway

2000 (Artisan DVD) (djm)

In the tradition of *Point Break* and *Drop Zone,* the made-for-cable film *Cutaway* features heavy doses of breathtaking skydiving stunt work and law enforcement officers who go to extremes to catch bad guys. A US Customs agent named Cooper (Stephen Baldwin) takes an undercover

gig at a skydiving school to ferret out a drug-smuggling ring run by the enigmatic "Redline" (Tom Berenger) and his partner "Turbo" (Dennis Rodman). As Cooper ingrains himself in the skydiving "cutaway" culture, he loses all sense of his former life and just about crosses over, leaving his duties as an officer of the law behind. His sense of identity blurs as he lives his life on the edge, becoming Redline's right hand man when Turbo is killed during a skydive accident.

Cutaway is a rare movie that showcases an extreme sport and doesn't cheat the audience with cheap effects or editing techniques. It's a full-throttle stunt show, with real skydiving on display every few minutes, while still retaining a story that manages to stay involving. Co-star Dennis Rodman (a former NBA player who had fared much worse in action movies like *Double Team* and *Simon Sez*) is given just enough screen time to warrant that his face be put on the video box, but his part in the film is perfect for him, and he doesn't botch it up with bad acting or lame dialogue, which is great. Director Guy Manos holds world records for skydiving and has performed aerial stunts on films such as the Wesley Snipes vehicle *Drop Zone.*

The Cutter

2005 (Sony DVD) (djm)

Moore: "Did you have to throw him out of the window, Shep?"
Shepherd: "I needed some air."
Moore: "Could have made a call before you pulled a *Die Hard*."

An inauspicious "R"-rated return to movies for Chuck Norris, *The Cutter* concerns an elderly jeweler named Teller who is kidnapped and forced to cut some incredibly rare diamonds in the rough that date back to the Old Testament. A mysterious millionaire has fulfilled his lifelong mission by locating the diamonds and an ancient breastplate in Egypt, and his henchman (a well cast Daniel Bernhardt) is a ruthless expert at killing, torture, and manipulation who has now gotten the attention of John Shepherd (Norris). Shepherd, a bachelor private eye, is a last-resort tracker when the police can't find certain missing persons. Teller's niece Elizabeth (Joanna Pacula) hires Shepherd to help her find her uncle, and in his process, they run afoul of deadly hitmen, disgruntled policemen, and dead bodies that suddenly start piling up.

To date, *The Cutter* is Norris's last starring vehicle. He looks good in it, and he doesn't shy away from the physical stuff, showcasing some hard-hitting action. He has two good fights with the imposing Bernhardt, who some might remember from the *Bloodsport* sequels. At this point, Norris had mellowed out considerably from seven long seasons of *Walker, Texas Ranger* and a handful of TV movies, but *The Cutter* hearkens back to his days at Cannon. Watch quickly for Deron McBee (from *The Killing Zone*) in a small role. It was directed by Bill Tannen, who directed Norris in Cannon's *Hero and the Terror*, and it definitely feels like it was done in the same vein. It was released directly to video and was produced by Nu Image.

Cyberjack

1995 (Echo Bridge DVD) (djm)

In 1995's vision of the future, everyone is into cyberspace and computer hacking. Remember, this was the time when awkward cyber-hacking and virtual reality movies like *Virtuosity, Lawnmower Man 2,* and *Johnny Mnemonic* were being made and released. *Cyberjack* is the same nonsense, with crazy-looking Brion James as a cyber terrorist breaking into a high-rise building to steal a fancy computer super virus from the mainframe. He and his team act like they're in a *Die Hard* movie, while the janitor (Michael Dudikoff) kills them off, one-by-one. The janitor is actually a former tough cop who disgracefully left the force after his partner was murdered by guess who? Yup: Brion James. So this is a good time for payback.

Shot for peanuts, this ugly looking straight-to-video garbage doesn't give Dudikoff much to work with, and there are moments where he seems slightly retarded because of the lines he's made to say. He seems really out of place in this techno-babble movie. James, however, seems right at home. Robert Lee directed this, and later reteamed with Dudikoff on *The Silencer*.

Cyber Tracker

1993 (Red DVD) (djm)

In a dank and cinematically familiar future world where robotic android police are programmed to kill criminals on sight, a secret service agent named Eric Phillips (Don Wilson) is protecting the creator of the Cyber Tracker units because his life is being threatened by an anti-robotic movement in society. When his boss's number-one bodyguard Ross (Richard Norton) sees Eric as a threat, Eric is targeted by a Cyber Tracker to hunt him down and kill him. Eric goes into hiding and joins the underground pro-human faction, which lives like outlaws on the outskirts of society. He falls for the resistance leader (a TV reporter with a secret identity), and he helps them uncover a plot, which reveals that the man Eric was protecting is actually a cyborg himself. The highlight of the film features Wilson and Norton in an intense fight that had me riveted.

A product of its time, *Cyber Tracker* is not really original as far as these low-budget science fiction action movies go, but it tries hard to deliver exactly what you think you're going to get by looking at the box art and reading the synopsis. It doesn't shortchange you on fighting, robots, and murky futuristic-looking sets and smoky alleyways. It's got everything a Don Wilson movie should have circa 1993, and having Norton around as the heavy is always a good idea. This was an Imperial release directed by Richard Pepin (*Firepower, Cyber Tracker 2*).

Cyber Tracker 2

1995 (Trinity DVD) (djm)

Eric Phillips (Don Wilson, returning from part 1) is now married to the reporter who was secretly the leader of the underground resistance against the implementation of Cyber Trackers (robots programmed to kill criminals on sight) in society. A criminal mastermind named Paris Morgan (Anthony De Longis) has a grand scheme to cast facial molds of Phillips and his reporter wife on some Cyber Trackers, who go throughout the city, killing people. Phillips, his wife, and their crew of resistance fighters have to stop the killing machines while trying to prove their innocence and stop Morgan from fulfilling his plan.

Nonstop action with a seemingly bigger budget than the first film, *Cyber Tracker 2* really follows *Terminator 2* as its inspiration, with similar scenes, chases, and situations. It sort of forgets that it's set in the future sometimes, and the scenery isn't nearly as murky or smoky as in the first one. Several cast members returned, and new additions are played by Nils Allen Stewart (*Mars, Timecop*) and Peter Kent (Arnold Schwarzenegger's body double for many years). De Longis is best known for playing Blade in *Masters of the Universe*, but he also played villains in movies like *Final Round* (with Lorenzo Lamas). He fights Wilson in the climax, but it's a disappointing encounter. In real life, De Longis is an accomplished martial artist, sword master, and whip trainer. Richard Pepin returned as director.

Cyborg

1989 (MGM DVD) (CD)

In a plague-ravaged wasteland, a cyborg named Pearl (Dayle Haddon) is carrying information that scientists in Atlanta need to cure humanity. A vicious "pirate" leader Fender (Vincent Klyn) wants the information for his own selfish agenda. Before Pearl is kidnapped by Fender, she meets a "slinger" named Gibson (Jean-Claude Van Damme), and asks him to escort her. But Gibson is knocked out, and Fender takes off with Pearl. Gibson befriends a young lady named Nady (Deborah Richter) who hates the pirates as much as he does. Together they trek across the wasteland doing whatever it takes to save Pearl

Gibson Rickenbacker (Jean-Claude Van Damme) is a wasteland warrior in Albert Pyun's *Cyborg*. Author's collection.

and to get the cure into the proper hands. Fender doesn't make things easy for Gibson and we learn what it is that fuels Gibson's hatred for him. It's a fast-paced and brutal chase through a world that's in desperate need of a hero.

With *Cyborg*, director Albert Pyun was able to craft a highly entertaining post-apocalyptic martial arts film that doesn't feel like a knock-off of better known films like *The Road Warrior*. Films like *Mad Max* and *The Terminator* were influential on low-budget genre films during this time period but *Cyborg* managed to be its own beast. The movie speeds along at a rapid pace with some great fight scenes and iconic imagery that cemented the movie's place as an action classic. Make no mistake: this is no perfect film. The acting is poor, and there are several plot holes and a few continuity errors. The special effects in the film are great fun, though there aren't an abundance—just enough to make for a few interesting (and somewhat bizarre) sequences. You have to remember that Van Damme was still the new action guy in town, and the action he delivered was new to audiences at that time. His performance is subtle and there is an innocence behind his eyes that grew dim during his studio years in Hollywood. There are plenty of well-choreographed fights and action scenes that have stood the test of time and they remain exciting to watch. Every hero needs a formidable foe and Fender Tremolo is quite possibly one of the most memorable screen villains of the last quarter century. Former pro-surfer Vincent Klyn will forever be remembered for his near-white eyes and menacing growl. With his chiseled face and physique, he almost comes off as being indestructible. It's hard to contain the excitement when he and Van Damme finally do clash in the finale. Watch out for future action stars Ralf Moeller, Matt McColm, and Stefanos Miltsakakis in small roles. *Cyborg* was a financial success and spawned two sequels, the first of which starred a young Angelina Jolie and Karen Sheperd. Both sequels were pretty far removed from the original, shying away from martial arts. Pyun's "Director's Cut" is a reenvisioned version, and contains the original score by Tony Riparetti, which was replaced by a score by Kevin Bassinson in Cannon's theatrical cut.

Cyborg 2

1993 (Trimark DVD) (CD)

"If you want to dine with the devil, you'll need a long spoon!"

In 2074, cyborgs have replaced humans in almost every aspect of life. The Pinwheel Corporation has developed a liquid explosive called Glass Shadow and filled a prototype model known as Cash Reese (Angelina Jolie) with it. The corporation plans to use her and the explosive to destroy the leaders of rival company Kobayashi. Cash was designed to be as close to human as possible, so she begins to develop feelings for her combat trainer Colt (Elias Koteas). Together, they escape the evil clutches of Pinwheel, helped

C

by Mercy (Jack Palance), someone they can only communicate with by television. The two love birds try to escape death while being hunted by hired killer Danny Bench (Billy Drago) and rival assassin Chen (action star Karen Shepard from *The Shinobi Ninja*). Love isn't all they need in this world . . . they'll need a miracle if they're going to survive.

Angelina Jolie nabbed her first starring role in 1993 at the ripe old age of eighteen. For most people, the attraction of seeing the future superstar in an early performance would be enough but add Karen Shepard (also seen in *Operation: Golden Phoenix*) to the mix and you have something pretty special. Shepard's role is small but pivotal; she has a terrifically aggressive fight scene against Jolie and Koteas's characters, and it's easily the film's highlight. The story is rubbish, the effects are corny, and the acting feels inexperienced, so director Michael Schroeder made a brilliant decision by tossing in screen legend Jack Palance (*Tango and Cash*) to liven things up a little. It's all a really bizarre mix and it's an "in name only" sequel to the Van Damme classic with no connecting factors at all (sorry, a dream sequence just doesn't count). Director Schroeder also made *Cyborg 3: The Recycler*, which had a small role for action star Evan Lurie (*Guns and Lipstick*).

Cyborg Cop

1993 (Vidmark VHS) (djm)

With a title like *Cyborg Cop*, you'd think you'd be getting something like *RoboCop*, but this is nothing like that film. I suspect that anything with the word "cop" in the title would sell in 1993. What we have here is a strange genre mash-up. David Bradley plays a guy named Jack Ryan whose brother is a DEA agent who goes to a third world country to bust a drug dealer. While there, his brother's team is wiped out by a cyborg created by a local mad scientist, played by a very hammy John Rhys-Davies, who wants to take over the world with his unstoppable cyborgs. A cyborg cuts off Bradley's brother's arm and soon he becomes a likely candidate to become a cyborg himself. Back at home, Bradley gets a microcassette in the mail with a message from his brother just before he was captured. Bradley decides to go to the third world country (it looks like Haiti or Jamaica, or possibly Africa) to search for his brother, and as soon as he gets there he is chased by the authorities for being a suspected drug dealer. A hot blonde reporter (Alonna Shaw) happens to be there at the same time covering a story about the mad scientist, and she hitches a ride with him even though he doesn't want anything to do with her. At this point, the movie turns into a sort-of clone of *Romancing the Stone* (lots of bantering while being chased, lots of stunts and searching for clues, some sexual tension), which is strange considering we know where the movie will end up: With Bradley fighting some cyborgs (including his brother) and confronting the mad scientist in his secret laboratory.

Bradley is best when he's fighting guys. He looks good while holding a machine gun (he spread fires it, which is interesting), and while his acting is sometimes a little uneven, I don't blame him because the movies he was in (like this one) are pretty preposterous, almost in the style of the Italian rip-offs. Still, *Cyborg Cop* has some fun moments, and squeezes in a soft sex scene (naked reporter on top, of course), and Sam Firstenberg, the director, does what he can with a goofy storyline. This was produced by the Nu Image guys (Avi Lerner, Trevor Short, Danny Lerner). It was also released the same year as *Blood Warriors*, another David Bradley/Sam Firstenberg movie.

Cyborg Cop 2
(a.k.a. **Cyborg Soldier**)

1994 (Image DVD) (djm)

"The time of the cyborgs has arrived!"

David Bradley plays Jack Ryan again from *Cyborg Cop*, but this picture feels like an in-name-only sequel. It's very similar to part one, but this time instead of taking place in a third world country, it has a more urban feel. Bradley goes head-to-head with a psychopath named Starkraven (Morgan Hunter), who is put behind bars, but is then used for a secret government experiment that turns him into a lethal cyborg soldier. Just as in *Universal Soldier* and *RoboCop* before it, saying a person's memories are erased just before turning him into a robotic minion doesn't make it so. Starkraven isn't a mindless cyborg for long. He turns against his programmers and amasses an army of like-minded cyborg soldiers who plan on taking over the world. Bradley, with the not-needed assistance of a female government agent, has to clean up the government's mess.

As usual, Bradley is best when he's fighting, and in this film, he seems to be having fun acting smart-alecky and crass. He's clearly not taking the film very seriously, and it almost offsets the violent nature of the picture. There are lots of explosions and shootouts, as per the usual requirement. Sam Firstenberg, who directed several films with Bradley (including part one), also made this. It was from Nu Image. *Cyborg Cop 3* was made without Bradley or Firstenberg, and it is better known as *Terminal Impact*.

Cyclone

1987 (Shout Factory DVD) (djm)

"It looks more like a battleship than a motorcycle!"

An engineer named Rick (Jeffrey Combs) working for the government on a top-secret weaponized motorcycle called a Cyclone is killed by some assassins, and his hot girlfriend Teri (Heather Thomas from TV's *The Fall Guy*) is left with the bike and a truckload of problems when the assassins come after her. One of the assassins—Rolf (the late great Dar Robinson)—captures her and tortures her, but when she escapes she mounts the Cyclone and uses its laser cannons to unleash holy hell.

From exploitation director Fred Olen Ray, *Cyclone* is of note for being stuntman Robinson's last completed feature, and he's great in it. After his menacing villain role in *Stick*, his turn in this film is welcome (and similar). Much of this movie is focused on Thomas and her skin-tight jeans (not an issue), so the male target audience will enjoy the movie for that alone. Aside from that, it's pretty silly.

Cy Warrior:
Special Combat Unit

1989 (NOV) (djm)

A government-made cyborg (Frank Zagarino) is awakened during an experiment, and it goes on the lam, not really knowing what for or why. Without any orders or logic other than to survive, it ends up in the care of an orphaned boy and his older sister, who live in the outskirts of the city. The government comes up with a plan to retrieve their expensive tech. They hire a crazed bounty hunter named Hammer (a manic Henry Silva) and his team of mercenaries to hunt down the Cy Warrior before it ends up in enemy hands. The several encounters Hammer has with the cyborg result in staccato gunfire and explosions.

From celebrated makeup effects artist Gianetto De Rossi, *Cy Warrior: Special Combat Unit* is strictly for fans of Italian-made exploitation movies or for fans of action star Zagarino, who is no stranger to playing robots. His part in the *Project Shadowchaser* movies is similar to the one he plays here, only this time he actually seems to develop feelings, as the kid he sidekicks with and his sister begin to care for him. It's hard not to laugh at something like this, so if you decide to track it down, good luck trying not to. The last scene is pretty awesome.

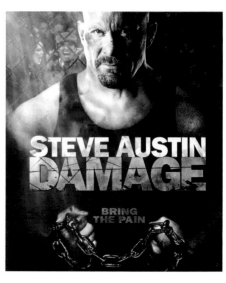

DVD artwork for *Damage*. Author's collection.)

Damage

2009 (Fox DVD) (CD)

Travis Brickner (Steve Austin) gets an early parole from prison. He's ready to turn over a new leaf and get to work. He finds a construction job, though his foreman has a thing against ex-cons, making it tough for him. He accidentally lands himself a parttime gig as a bouncer in a local bar. There he befriends the beautiful Frankie (Laura Vandervoort) who has a boyfriend who may have work for him. Reno (Walton Goggins) has an eye for talent when it comes to fighting and thinks Brickner may be able to make some cash. Reno has made many enemies in the underground fighting circuit and owes tons of money. Brickner turns him down until he learns that the daughter of the man he once killed is in need of a heart transplant that costs $250,000. He embarks into the violent world of underground fighting to save the girl, his friends, and ultimately find redemption.

Damage isn't just about the damage that Steve Austin (*The Condemned, The Expendables*) causes during the brutal underground fights depicted in the film, it also refers to just how damaged each character is emotionally. There is an investment in the characters and the roads they have travelled that sets this picture apart from the rest of the pack. Much like *The Condemned*, this film feels tailor-made for Austin, and he is excellent in the role of Brickner. There is a bit of depth to his character and the charisma he is known for in his wrestling career shines through in this film. He is not known for being a stylish fighter—he's more of a brawler. The fight scenes in the film reflect that, and they don't disappoint. There is plenty of brutal bloodshed that plays out more realistically than expected. Austin seems somewhat stiff at times in his movement (quite possibly do to the damage his body took during his years in the ring) but that isn't really important. There are some hilarious moments when Austin conveys what he is thinking with a certain look. Austin is surrounded with some terrific talent, too. Walton Goggins (*Django Unchained*) and Laura Vandervoort (*Into the Blue 2*) play an unlikely couple just as damaged as Brickner, and the trio forms this dysfunctional family with Brickner as the father-figure. Another important component of action films like this is music and the final piece in the score by Peter Allen is the perfect denouement to the beatdown. Director Jeff King (*Driven to Kill* and *Kill Switch* with Steven Seagal) put together a solid action picture with a bit of a heartbeat and a hero you can cheer for.

A Dangerous Man

2009 (Paramount DVD) (CD)

"So let me go, just let me go on by, or I'll fuck you up ugly."

Shane Daniels (Steven Seagal) has been recently released from prison after serving six years for a crime he didn't commit. He was cleared of all charges and the government apologized for the mistake. Even though he's a free man, he will never get back the time he lost. Once released, he isn't out to waste any time, but he finds himself in a predicament: A young girl named Tia (Marlaina Mah) is being held captive, and Shane comes to her rescue. He saves her, helps the son of a Russian mobster, and comes into possession of a duffel bag full of drug money. While trying to keep Tia safe, Shane must fight off Chinese mobsters and corrupt police officers. He has to dig deep into his special forces training to earn back some of what he has lost.

Seagal (*Above the Law*) can still manage to surprise an audience and deliver a solid action film, despite the bad press and even worse movies he's had in his later career. In this film, we can still see the spark he once nurtured to a flame in the early part of his career. He appears to be almost inspired here, and he easily delivers the goods. When someone is stabbed, the blood spurts, and his blows are lethal. Seagal may actually be the last of the invincible action stars. He takes on thug after thug, throwing them around effortlessly, and no matter how good his opponent is, he never gets hit. Director Keoni Waxman has done a number of other projects with Seagal, most notably the TV series *True Justice*, which was broken up into a series of direct-to-video releases starting with *Deadly Crossing*.

Dangerous Passion

1990 (Artisan DVD) (CD)

"I never admire a weapon in someone else's hand."

Kyle Western (Carl Weathers) is a security expert who has taken a job working for Lou (Billy Dee Williams), a man who has ties to organized crime. Lou slowly begins to offer Kyle more and more money in hopes he will clean up Lou's messes. Kyle is stuck covering up two murders, but that doesn't stop him from falling for the boss's wife, Meg (Lonette McKee). Kyle and Meg plot to run away together but Lou appears to have a hold on both them and their money. Kyle forms a plan to get them both out from under Lou's grasp, regardless of the damage it causes.

This was Carl Weathers's follow-up to the brilliant *Action Jackson* and pales in comparison. It's a relatively entertaining picture, and who doesn't want to see Billy Dee Williams (*The Empire Strikes Back*) and Weathers trading tough-guy dialogue? This was some sort of made-for-television movie (there's no cursing, but there's nudity), and it's really light on the action. We don't get to see Carl toss anyone around until the last twenty minutes or so, and he looks great doing it. There just wasn't enough of that going on, and I know director Michael Miller is no fool when it comes to action—he directed the Chuck Norris classic *Silent Rage*. Another issue with the film is that it's hard to believe the Kyle character would risk so much for a woman who was bat-shit crazy and a pain in the ass. I guess she was just that good, maybe better than this film.

VHS artwork for *A Dangerous Place*. Author's collection.

A Dangerous Place

1994 (PM VHS) (djm)

An "R"-rated movie that is really a PG-13 movie at heart, *A Dangerous Place* is PM's answer to *The Karate Kid*, but with more heightened violence and heavier thematic content. Teenager Ethan Keyes (T. J. Roberts from PM's *Magic Kid* and *Tiger Heart*) experiences a huge blow when his older brother is found hung by the neck in the school gymnasium. Both he and his brother were heavily into martial arts, but when his brother recently left the Lions dojo (peacefully run by Mako) to join the Scorpions (overseen by a vindictive sensei, played by Marshall Teague), his brother's lifestyle and habits drastically changed. As it turns out, his brother was murdered by a gang of Scorpions, whose ringleader is played by a cold-hearted Corey Feldman. Ethan decides to get to the bottom of his brother's supposed suicide by joining the Scorpions and going head-to-head with every member of the gang—including Feldman and Teague, the sensei, who both can't believe how tough he is given his stature and age. As the tagline of the movie proclaims, "High school can be a dangerous place . . . and a deadly experience," and Ethan finds that out for himself.

Ted Jan Roberts was one of only a few martial arts teen stars from the '90s (Ernie Reyes Jr. was another that comes to mind) who deserved to make the crossover from kid movies to adult-oriented movies, and *A Dangerous Place* with its "R" rating deserves some attention for being fairly genuine and intense. I don't know how kids were able to rent this back in the day, but if they had been able to, I'm sure they would have enjoyed it. It's one of T. J.'s best movies. He was also in *The Power Within*. Directed by Jerry P. Jacobs.

Dark Angel

(a.k.a. **I Come in Peace**)

1990 (Shout Factory DVD)
(CD)

". . . and you go in pieces, asshole!"

Jack Caine (Dolph Lundgren) is sick and tired of the drug trade, especially having to deal with Victor Manning (Sherman Howard). While on a stakeout, he leaves his post to stop a robbery, which is a huge mistake. Everyone involved in the drug deal—including his undercover partner—ends up dead. When it comes time to investigate the massacre, Jack finds himself partnered with straight-laced FBI agent Larry Smith (Brian Benben). They find a mysterious flying disc that they believe to be the murder weapon. It's like nothing they've ever seen before, so when they pair it with a string of mysterious murders, things begin to get weird. There's an evil alien known as Talec (Matthias Hues) who is using alien technology to create a superdrug for use on his planet. It involves pumping humans full of heroin then extracting the resulting fluids from the brain. Jack and Larry throw the rule book out the window and follow Talec's trail. It won't be an easy task but they will do whatever it takes to stop him.

 Dark Angel has become a cult classic, and it's easy to see why. The film is fast paced, fun, and offers loads of excitement. This was the second in a trio of classic action films directed by Craig R. Baxley (the others were *Action Jackson* and *Stone Cold*). Lundgren gets to do everything we expect from him. There are some insane shootouts and several hand-to-hand fights where he shows off his martial arts skills. Matthias Hues (*TC 2000*) never really fights in the film but he is all over the place slaying humans and blasting off some badass alien weapons. It may feel a little dated at times (mostly because of the music) but *Dark Angel* is a must-see action classic. The film was released as *I Come in Peace* in the United States (to avoid confusion with two other films with similar titles).

INTERVIEW:

MATTHIAS HUES

(CD)

In order to have a great action film, the hero needs to confront a worthy villain. Many actors have jumped into the shoes of a villain at one time or another, but it takes a certain type of person to build a career on it. One of the most recognizable screen villains in martial arts and action pictures throughout the 1980s and 1990s is German-born Matthias Hues. At a towering and muscular 6 feet 5 inches, he received his first break in film as a replacement for Jean-Claude Van Damme in No Retreat, No Surrender 2 (1987), *then further cemented his path as a screen villain when he was*

Matthias Hues plays Yuri, the Russian in *No Retreat, No Surrender 2*. Author's collection.

cast in the Dolph Lundgren action/sci-fi hybrid Dark Angel *(a.k.a.* I Come in Peace*) (1990). Before making it to the big screen, Matthias was a pentathlon champion in his native Germany, went into hotel management, and became a gymnasium owner. He has starred in films with action greats like Bolo Yeung, Lorenzo Lamas, Billy Blanks, Cynthia Rothrock, and many more.*

Were you athletic as a child?

No, not really. I was tall and awkward, which made me decide to join the track and field team in my city. Being teased about my small chest all the time inspired me when I was fifteen to start lifting weights in the weight room of the athletic department. To this day, I never miss one workout, unless I am sick or traveling. When other kids went to the pool in the summer, I joined them, but had to leave early to make it to the gym. Same in winter; I walked against the will of my mother through ice and snow for over an hour to reach the athletic department. It became my life and job as I started to compete for Germany in the pentathlon.

At what age did you begin studying the martial arts?

Martial arts came to me about the same time. I first trained in judo then taekwondo. I wasn't too interested in it at first, since it took time away from my track and field, but loved doing judo competitions on the weekends. I was such a strong young child at sixteen with my training that it was bizarre how easy it was to win my rounds on the mat. Taekwondo was a different thing. People are tall in Germany and extremely good with their legs. It's not too easy to score against a quicker and lighter guy with your height. The best fighters were around the 180 to 200 pound mark and about 6 foot 4, powerful, and fast. It's all about the whip effect—loose, speed, and the right angle will make a kick a good one. Too much muscle will slow you down in the end.

When did you realize that hotel management wasn't your passion?

Pretty early on while I was living in Paris. I worked so many hours and my gym time suffered tremendously. I realized it's a world of excess food, wine, and other influences that would not fit into my lifestyle. I worked out in a gym that was all about actors, fashion models, dancers, and so on. It quickly became my world and invited me to think what I might really be about. This gym changed my life without me

knowing it yet. I was treated a little like a star, not knowing why. French movie stars, dancers, and models took me in, had me around, and wanted to be close to me. I felt some pull in that direction . . . but I wasn't so sure since I felt so unpolished and had nothing to offer really, so I thought, "Why would they want to hang with me?" It made me think and I used that little pull I had and opened my own gym. I had many people from Paris and the USA follow me to Germany to kick-start my place. It was an instant success, given the colorful people I imported. We were all so different, and you were exotic if you had come from a country like Germany. But soon this wasn't enough for me. I realized you could actually achieve anything in this world if you don't hesitate. I went one afternoon to see *Rocky 4* with Dolph Lundgren and instantly knew I had to leave town to be an actor in Hollywood. By then, I owned my second gym. I left a week after I had seen the movie. I didn't even sell the gym, I was convinced I didn't need money since I knew I would be in the movies and this would be my new life. I never even gave it a second thought. I gave the key to my gym to a friend who needed a job since he just had two baby girls and said, "Good luck, see you later. I'm off to Hollywood."

Your first film appearance was in *No Retreat, No Surrender 2* in a role that was originally meant for Jean-Claude Van Damme. What was the audition process like and were you nervous being on a set for the first time?

I had just moved to LA and joined Gold's Gym as part of my plan to be with the movers and shakers in town like Arnold, Stallone, Hulk Hogan, and many others. Everyone in the action field seemed to work out there. I joined the family so to speak and was treated with open arms from day one. I was at home. Soon, a call came in from Thailand. The producer, Roy Horan, desperately needed to replace Van Damme, who had walked off the film. The idea was to call Gold's and find someone from Europe like Van Damme. The manager, Derek Barton, had picked up the phone with the producer on the other end, and immediately thought about me as I had just sat in his office telling him I wanted to be an actor.

 He sent me up to meet Roy and the writer, Maria Cellino, for a screen test. I wasn't even close to what Van Damme represented; I was quite the opposite with long blond hair, more like He-Man, who wasn't at all this polished martial artist who was famous for his splits. Maria Cellino told the producer that he must hire me or she would not allow the movie to be made. She told him, no matter what, I was their guy. So Roy Horan hired me against his will and was rather upset about it all. The pressure was on from day one in Thailand. No one really wanted me to be on the set, knowing I wasn't this "show and tell" martial arts fighter like Van Damme. It came to the point that the director, Corey Yuen, stormed off the set on my first actual take, cussing in Chinese. But throughout the filming, I somehow created my own style. I used my size and speed until I eventually ended up doing all my own stunts. Eventually, all the stunt people and fighters embraced me as one of their own, since they only respect people who do not mind getting hurt and take risks without complaining. As a matter of fact, in the Chinese film world, it's an honor to take punishment, so getting hurt is what I was after. I needed to feel the pain. I wanted to be one of the tough guys, to learn to take it, and stay with it until it was over. I have to say, it was a tough lesson of survival and discovering your own strengths and weakness. I just worked through it with a single goal in mind. It was to set me up for the rest of my career; I knew I would always have to go the extra mile if I wanted to be successful and respected.

How was your experience working with Loren Avedon and Cynthia Rothrock?

Both of them know their stuff like no one else. It's safe and a joyride to work with both of them. They're total pros and the best in the world. My respect goes out to both of them. I was in awe a lot as I watched, and I thought, "I wish I could do that."

Big Top Pee Wee **has gone on to become a family classic. What was it like being a part of this film?**

Amazing, is all I can say. It was one of the best times in my life. They had a real circus set up. There were people so colorful and nice from all around the world, the exotic animals, and our amazing star Pee Wee Herman. It seriously made me proud to be an actor even if I only had a small role. I was there every day throughout filming and we all became a tight family.

Dark Angel **(a.k.a.** ***I Come in Peace***) **has also become an action classic. How did you find yourself as a part of this film?**

This one is special all the way. The call went out in Hollywood to find athletes who wouldn't mind doing their own stunts. They needed two: one to play the Dark Angel and the other to be the Alien Cop. They wanted both to be taller than Dolph and able to jump cars, or other higher obstacles. It's not something someone can master easily. When I walked in the room, it was filled with sport giants, basketball, track and field stars, and pretty much anyone who was over six foot five and fast on their legs. I was called in eventually and there was chemistry at first sight with the director Craig R. Baxley. His face instantly lit up. More or less, all I had to do was sit down. He shook my hand and said, "Today is your lucky day. I will hand you a career and stardom, because you will take the role of a lifetime today. But you need to be willing to kill yourself for it—no limits, if asked to jump just say *how high?*" He went on telling me that this role was actually designed for Dolph to play but he decided to take the role of the police man instead, which the director thought was a huge mistake for Dolph but it was my chance, at entry level, to be a new action star. He was in my corner from the moment we met, and I decided right then and there he would own me. I'd kill myself on the set if needed. It ended up being something I later regretted a little as Baxley took it literally nearly every day. I was overhearing on a daily basis someone telling him that it was nuts and that I might not make that stunt, and over time it made me a little hesitant. I did become quicker as he kept telling me to run faster or jump higher so the fire or explosion wouldn't catch me. All this

was done with those white contact lenses that nearly made me blind. There was no hole in the pupils of the contacts so everything was white fog. Running over exploding cars and jumping through windows on fire was all done mostly by instinct. I just hoped it would work out as I had rehearsed it first without the contacts.

What was your impression of Dolph Lundgren and Craig R. Baxley?

I loved both! I was in awe of Baxley. He's the real deal, old school, someone to look up to, someone you want to please when you're shooting. Dolph was a legend already. We're both from Europe so we're laid back and felt like we knew each other. It seemed like we spoke one language. He's my age or close. He's an athlete and a pro. I loved his comeback in *The Expendables,* by the way. He's come a long way and seems to get sharper with age and isn't afraid to takes chances in his acting, which I love.

The film is pretty widely known by two titles, which do you prefer?

Dark Angel!

You worked with Albert Pyun on ***Kickboxer 2***. **Do you have any interesting stories from that production?**

Yes, Tong Po hits real hard! Wow! Jimmy Nickerson, the fight and stunt coordinator from *Rocky*, knows his shit! Benny Urquidez from the Jet Center is a legend and I'm a huge fan. He kicked my ass in the training camp every day. So was Gene LeBell. He was nearly breaking my jaw everyday back then with his locks. He bet me $10,000 if I could escape his locks. I didn't think he could hold me down. I was so strong at that time, not many people could keep me on the mat. He was over seventy and I still have problems now with my jaw since I wouldn't give up. But there's no chance in hell anyone on this planet could escape that old legend's clutches while being on the mat in one of his chokeholds. I love this man, he taught me how to be humble.

Neil Vargas (Matthias Hues) throws a kick at David Sloan (Sasha Mitchell) in *Kickboxer 2.* Author's collection.

You did ***Blackbelt*** **for Roger Corman's New Concorde Pictures. What's it like being on a Corman set? Did you enjoy working with Don "The Dragon" Wilson?**

Don is an ace, one of my favorites in the business, the real deal, a gentleman, and a pro. He's so nice, you wonder if you actually could kick his ass. He's so unassuming. Big mistake, do not try it. He'll kill you in an instant. I never tried. See, when you fight on film it's like making love without the happy ending. You just never really get to it. It leaves you with the thought of how it might be for real. Him? I would skip. Billy Blanks, I would skip him as well. Dolph? I would be curious to fight for real. It would be a close match-up in terms of height, size, and speed. He would be scary to fight, but it would be worth it.

Talons of the Eagle **marked the first time you worked with Billy Blanks and Jalal Merhi. Was there an instant chemistry once the cameras started to roll?**

Yes, it was instant and amazing, all of it. I love Billy, super safe, fast, and a pro. I trust him with my life. Jalal is a real amazing kung fu fighter. It's not my world in terms of fighting style, since kung fu is something I never trained in, but I admire it. He's an amazing guy, producer, actor, and businessman all in one. I learned a lot from him.

You followed that with ***Mission of Justice***, **which is a pretty fantastic film. Any fun memories from that shoot?**

Jeff Wincott is amazing and I'm totally in awe of him. He has it all, and I miss seeing him. He should be making a comeback and most likely he will. Brigitte Nielsen and I were like fire and ice. We kept the set alive with our drama every single day. We started dating and had this steaming, heated, and destructive kind of an affair. We held up production a lot since we lived it up 24/7. The producer was a mess every day, not knowing how to handle us. We were crazy in those days but we got the job done, we never let anyone down. We just kept the set busy with our antics and had too much fun, pulling everyone deep into it with our pranks. But the film was a blast in the end for all of us with insanely long hours that turned us into giggling kids. The entire set was sleep depraved. Fighting Jeff was total fun but I enjoyed watching him the most with his stick work in the underground gauntlet scene. That was as impressive live as it was in the finished film.

Age of Treason **was a completely different type of role for you. Do you feel like that experience helped you to grow as an actor?**

Yes, thanks for asking, I loved that show. We had high hopes for it. It was, at that time, the most expensive pilot shoot in the history of the network. For me, as an actor, it would have been a huge chance to grow if it had been picked up. You could look at years of filming and sharpening your tools that way, but it wasn't so. I remember being offered a deal to star on *Hercules* a few years earlier. It was between Kevin Sorbo, Lou Ferrigno, and myself, but in the end Kevin won the battle for the role. I just remembered being the first one called in for it and getting an offer. But this is the film business. You never know till you're on the set if you're the lucky one and then you don't know if it will succeed. If it does, you're so blessed and you need to run with it and make it your own while you can.

How did you enjoy facing off with Lorenzo Lamas in *Bounty Tracker*?

Lorenzo is one of the nicest and most humble guys I've met in the business. Period. What a class act. He's also an amazing fighter and fighting with him was a breeze. Safe, fun, and amazing team work. He had some great ideas without ever pressing them on you. He also had long hair and a great build which made for a terrific match-up. We had good chemistry from day one.

The *Talons* gang reunited for *TC 2000*. This time Bolo Yeung was added to the mix. Did his addition push the rest of you to up your game?

Bolo is a legend and we all felt it. We were in awe of him. It was like we were waiting for him to show up and do miracle type things. And he did just that. He's quiet, polite, mysterious, and not easy to get to on any level. He's just too withdrawn and calm. You would think he's just like he is in the movies, but of course he's a real gentleman with no aggression or temper. He's just a cool guy who knows he can hurt you but won't unless you challenge him. Fighting him was a treat for me. He was calm, knows how to handle pressure. With other strong muscles coming at him he never lost his cool or ultra mysterious aura. It was like fighting the guy from *Enter the Dragon* or *Double Impact*. You somehow didn't think this was a movie; it felt

VHS artwork for *Death Match*. Author's collection.

like watching a movie and there's Bolo now and he's after you. I was kind of waiting for Bruce Lee or Van Damme to appear. It felt that surreal, and it was an honor to be killed by him.

You did back-to-back tournament fighting films with *Death Match* and *Fists of Iron*. Though the stories were similar, they each had their own flavor and the action scenes had a different feel to them. What's your take on these films?

Yes, both films felt completely different. The fighting was unique as well. One was more cage fighting, out to kill, the other was more light touch entertainment or how you might see it in a millionaire's house in Malibu. These fights do go on in real life. Some of my friends were flown to some island to do blood sport type events for crime and mob bosses. Their guests brought plenty of money for betting purposes. So what you see in the movie is the real deal. Maybe that's why these films have found a fan group since they are based on reality.

***Alone in the Woods* showed that you could do comedy just as well as action. Would you like to do more comedies?**

Well, yes, in a way. It's always fun to do something new or different. I'm truly a fan of these types of films. Comedic timing is something completely different, and it's somewhat easy if you just relax into it. A lot of times you actually play it straight if everything around you is set up to be funny or corny. It takes practice like everything else. If you do things long enough you eventually get the feel for it.

***Droid Gunner* and *Hostile Environment* were rare hero roles for you. Did you enjoy being the hero or do you prefer being the bad guy?**

No, it's fun, except the movies weren't really films. I mean they were what they represent: a genre, low budget, and limited. I admire the directors and how they get this type of film made and they all do a great job. You're just frustrated or you feel a sense of potential but you're limited with the budget, so everything goes down a notch. Being the hero in a bigger budgeted film is much more rewarding. But like I said, you really must do your homework working on a lower budgeted film when being the lead as there will be no distractions through expensive action, explosions, or elaborate sets. So you have to be convincing somehow.

***Legion of the Dead* was also a bit of a departure for you but it's a really fun to watch. Could you talk a bit about this film and working with Darren Shahlavi and Olaf Ittenbach?**

Darren is one of the most talented upcoming martial arts fighters out there. Olaf is also multitalented and has carved out a nice market for himself in the horror splatter world. I hope he uses his talents to do more action films.

You have several upcoming projects like *Angel of Death*, *1066*, and *The Rogue*. Can you tell us anything about these?

Well, I can't say too much. I'm not sure if any of these films will actually happen. It's been a while since I was approached by the producers, and it remains to be seen if these will be shot anytime soon. I hope so, as they all sounded like a win/win in my mind. Great stories, ideas, and scripts, so I hope they happen.

Were you ever a witness to any major accidents on a set? You would think that with all the fighting and explosions people would get hurt more often, even with all the safety measures taken?

I've never seen anything go wrong, but I've heard some horror stories on the sets of other films where someone had their head chopped off. Some stories are so tragic that I needed to forget them fast so I wouldn't get spooked doing similar action. Like in Florida, when I was waiting for a boat to race towards us, it had to hit a ramp then get catapulted in the air like a rocket flying directly towards us. The actors in the shot were in the line of fire so to speak. Just before that stunt, I found out that right there in Florida where we were shooting, a stuntwoman lost her head while her husband did the same stunt and the boat's propellers caught her. In our case, the boat raced up way too fast, went up in the air, and was an unstoppable projectile—we barely could escape. So yes, it's never really safe.

You always seem to work with many of the same people. Was this a coincidence or did you guys sort of stick together over the years?

No, it's pure coincidence, but we all like each other and are always happy to be working once more as a team. This is really a tight community and action guys do harvest a lot of respect for each other due to their skills.

Have you thought about doing more work behind the camera?

I am actually. Check it out, offgridpictures.com. You'll see all the films I am set to produce in the next few years. All are tailor made, with my girlfriend and I producing with our writing partner Leslie Carleton, to bring you more high-end action films with bigger budgets and interesting concepts. What worked before is what we concentrate on. Films like *Taken* or *The Transporter* are films that hit the right nerve for viewers, and we created a slate of films in that genre area.

Do you feel that we still have action stars? The genre has changed so much over the years and I guess you can say that they don't make them like they used to. Who do you consider to be a modern action star?

Well I see Jason Stratham as one, The Rock, even Stallone still has it in my eyes. People will always want to see action stars, but they don't come so easy these days as you so observantly noticed yourself. It's more subdued and normal. Now Ryan Gosling has a six pack and is taking over. But I must say, these new types are very convincing as well. I love Liam Neeson. He isn't a super hero but I do believe him being real when he kicks ass. So I feel there's a market for them all. If you are a good, powerful actor, and your action is believable, you will find your fans. Best example, Russell Crowe in *Gladiator*. For me, as an actor still out there, I train harder now than I ever have in my life and I'm ready to keep the shape and edge for many years like Stallone. It's never too late to be big, ripped, and dangerous so you can kick some ass and make it look real.

You have many fans all over the world, is there anything that you would like to say to them?

I love you, I really do. Thanks for it all, I truly could not have done it without you, and I will do everything in my power to stay true and real, making you believe in something good because I believe in it myself. Moving mountains isn't just a saying as I found out over the years, even though they're steep at times. I want to thank you from the bottom of my heart and I feel stronger just having you ask me these questions as I need a lot of support on this journey as film making isn't the easiest job in the world. You need to be very lucky at first, then strong, in top shape both mentally and physically.

Dark Assassin

2006 (Cinema Vault DVD) (djm)

Derek Wu (Jason Yee) gets out of prison and is looking forward to starting a new life. The crime syndicate he once worked for is under fire by an unknown entity: Members of the gang are being hunted down dead one by one, and whoever's doing the killing is making it look like Derek is responsible. With his former gang after him and a police force that wants him back in prison, Wu has to figure out what's going on and make sure whoever set him up will pay.

Ultra low budget and made with the best of intentions, *Dark Assassin* is Jason Yee's first feature film foray into martial arts action. He bears a striking resemblance to Bruce Lee (and he knows it because he pays him homage several times), and in an extended fight scene that appears to have been shot in one take, he takes down at least a dozen guys. The climax has Yee facing the film's villain, played by real-life MMA fighter Cung Le (who would later become an action star in his own right with *Dragon Eyes*). The final fight is easily the best scene in the film, but Yee ends the film on an abrupt note, which is unsatisfying. His next film, *The Girl From the Naked Eye,* was more ambitious, but just as homegrown and independent. He wrote and directed both films.

Dark of the Sun

1968 (Warner DVD) (djm)

Two mercenaries—Curry (Rod Taylor) and Ruffo (Jim Brown)—are hired to lead a rescue mission in the Congo where some civilians are being held captive by vicious rebels. Also on the agenda is for the mercenaries to recover a

cache of huge, uncut diamonds, but first they have to assemble a team to assist them in the do-or-die attempt. Once they've got their team together (one guy is an alky, another is a Nazi, etc.), their trip is planned, and they board a train and ride straight into the combat zone through the Congo. One imperiled stage after another, Curry and Ruffo (who's always got Curry's back) scrape their way through to accomplishing the mission, and the biggest challenge they face is not so much the rebels, but the evil, racist Nazi scum they have on their team.

Based on a book by Wilbur Smith (a great novelist who writes adventure stories set in Africa), *Dark of the Sun* is good, manly stuff and a fine vehicle for Jim Brown, whose role is integral to the story. There's plenty of fist-smashing action and shootouts, and fans of movies like *The Dirty Dozen* and *The Expendables* should make this a priority at some point. It may not have an entirely satisfying ending, but it's fairly realistic. Jack Cardiff (who was the DOP on *Rambo: First Blood Part II*) directed.

Dark Vengeance (a.k.a. **True Justice: Dark Vengeance**)

2010 (Optimum DVD R2) (djm)

Elijah Kane (Steven Seagal) and his team of undercover cops land a case involving a serial killer who slays pretty strippers (from a particular gentleman's club) and hangs them publicly in a ritualistic fashion. Kane allows his two female cops to go undercover within the club to pose as strippers/biker chicks to see if they can sniff out the killer. Kane himself scopes out the club and gets a lap dance, but not before he profiles all of the shady characters throwing money at the dancers. One of the suspects is the son of a famous writer who writes vampire novels, and he becomes the prime suspect. Kane beats the snot of him when he proves himself to be the killer.

This is the second compilation film from Seagal's TV series *True Justice*. It almost feels like a legitimate movie on a smaller scale as Seagal's *The Glimmer Man*, but it ends on a weird, cliffhanging note implying that perhaps they got the wrong guy when another dead woman is found. The most interesting aspect of this entry is that Seagal's character Kane is challenged by several of his inferior detectives, to the point where he comes to blows with one of them (Kane wins, obviously). The next time we see that other detective, he's on the straight and narrow with Kane again. It's a weird, jarring thing to know that Kane's guys aren't just "yes" men, following his every word and command. The next entry in the series is *Street Wars*. Directed by Keoni Waxman.

Daylight

1996 (Universal DVD) (djm)

A commuter tunnel underneath the Hudson River collapses, trapping over a dozen survivors in a subterranean wreckage, and a disgraced

medical emergency chief named Kit Latura (Sylvester Stallone) is the only human alive who can save them. He does the impossible by finding a way into the wasted lair that used to be the tunnel, and when he gets there to help the survivors find a way out, he's immediately hated when he is recognized for the disgraced figure of society that he has become. The group of survivors include a bunch of convicts (one of whom is played by Stallone's real son Sage), a family of three, an elderly couple, a police officer, and an attractive young playwright, who fills the love interest role for Latura. The film features deadly escapes from breakaway props, perilous explosions, waterfalls, and various other deathly manifestations caused by the impending obliteration of what remains of the tunnel.

For a Stallone vehicle, the film is careful to restrain him within the confines of what constitutes a "disaster film" with all of the formulaic genre trappings these types of films contain. Disaster films were the flavor of Hollywood in the mid 1990s (like they were in the late 1970s), and *Daylight* certainly delivers on the technical aspect with state-of-the-art special effects and thrills. Most of the characters in the film are right out of the book of clichés (there's even a dog in peril), but Stallone, who is incredibly watchable in his physical role, manages to elevate the film with his charisma and pathos. Released in the height of the Christmas season of 1996, *Daylight* bombed, contributing to Stallone's falling out of favor during the period. His previous several films, *Judge Dredd* and *Assassins* were also expensive flops. He made a career comeback with his next one, *Cop Land*. *Daylight* was directed by Rob (*The Fast and the Furious*) Cohen.

Day of the Panther

1987 (Celebrity Video VHS) (djm)

Jason Blade, the newest member of an elite martial arts school called Panther, is inducted into an international spy ring that does top secret jobs that only James Bond and the like could ever hope to be called upon to perform. Blade (played by Edward John Stazak) and his partner are on their first assignment when thugs working within a drug empire in Australia kill his female partner. Blade's boss tries to redirect Blade's anger by introducing him to the boss's pretty daughter Gemma, a dancer played by Paris Jefferson. Blade and Gemma have some chemistry and in the middle of the mayhem building up around them, Jason Blade has just enough time to kindle a romance with his new girlfriend.

From Australian director Brian Trenchard-Smith (*The Man From Hong Kong*), *Day of the Panther* is a quickie flick with a lot of fight scenes involving star Stazak, whose style of martial arts is limited to basically the same three moves. Stazak's on-screen presence isn't exclamatory in any way—he's handsome to a fault, he smiles and smirks a lot, and when he fights he doesn't always look convincing. The best scenes of the movie aren't always where you'd expect them to be (i.e. the fight scenes), but some of the scenes involving co-star Paris Jefferson are cute and fun. *Day of the Panther* was shot back-to-back with *Fists of Blood* (a.k.a. *Strike of the Panther*).

D.C. Cab

1983 (Universal DVD) (djm)

Joel Schumacher's directing debut came in the form of this ensemble comedy/action movie, showcasing Mr. T (who was a hit on TV's *The A Team*) and David and Peter Paul, of the Barbarian Brothers. The story revolves around a struggling taxicab company in Washington, DC, and all of the misfit drivers who work there. An orphaned teenager named Albert Hockenberry (Adam Baldwin) goes to visit his surrogate uncle Howard (Max Gail), a Vietnam vet who has a hard time keeping his cab business afloat. His drivers get robbed on a daily basis, and some of them are more trouble than they're worth. Mr. T, Gary Busey, The Barbarian Brothers, Bill Maher, Charlie Barnett, and Paul Rodriguez all play the drivers, among others. The plot is pretty thin, but when Albert gets kidnapped by a team of thugs who steal a child for ransom (he's at the wrong place at the wrong time), the cab company comes to his rescue, with one-on-one fights, ruses, and dim-witted heroics. Mr. T figures in the action predominantly.

For a lightweight action comedy, this one's pretty "R" rated, with crude humor, profanity, and nudity, but it's surprisingly bereft of action. The Barbarian Brothers have smallish roles, but the brand of humor they became known for isn't on display. Mr. T is no-nonsense as usual, and the rest of the motley cast does what they can with their roles. Mr. T was in *Rocky III* and *Penitentiary II* the previous year. Schumacher also wrote the script.

Theatrical release poster for *D.C. Cab*. Author's collection.

Dead Drop

(a.k.a. **True Justice: Dead Drop**)

2012 (Studiocanal DVD R2)

(djm)

Following *Angel of Death*, this entry in Steven Seagal's *True Justice* series picks up immediately after that one and carries on with Elijah Kane (Seagal) on a mission to stop some Russian terrorists who have a nuclear weapon and plan on using it. Turns out, one of Kane's own associates from his old team—Marcus (played by Adrian Holmes)—is a double agent (shocker!), working against Kane. Up until this point, Kane had always been at odds with Marcus (see the previous films/episodes for more on that), so when Kane finally gets wise to him, their confrontation is fairly satisfying.

Not as dramatically linear or cohesive as some of the other *True Justice* movie compilations, *Dead Drop* at least brings some closure to some story threads left dangling from previous entries. Compared to some of Seagal's feature films like, say, *The Patriot*, *Dead Drop* has loads more action and wrist snapping, but it still doesn't quite feel like a genuine movie. Don't just see this and ignore the rest of the *True Justice* movies, or you'll be completely bewildered by the whole affair. Directed by Keoni Waxman, a frequent Seagal collaborator. The final *True Justice* title is *Deadly Assassin*.

Dead in Tombstone

2012 (Universal DVD) (djm)

Murderer: "What the hell?!"
Guerrero: "Now you're talking!"

Guerrero Hernandez (Danny Trejo) and his half-brother Red (Anthony Michael Hall) have a plan to rob a bank holding millions in gold, and so they take their gang to the small town where they easily heist the score. Instead of riding off into the sunset as planned, Red double-crosses his brother and convinces their gang to turn against him, murdering him in cold blood. Guerrero finds himself in hell, at the mercy of the devil (a bloated and sick looking Mickey Rourke), who torments him. Guerrero pleads with him and makes a deal to return to Earth for one day to kill his brother Red and the entire gang that murdered him, gladly allowing the devil to reap their souls. The devil accepts, and one year to the day of his death, Guerrero returns as a black-coated revenger, taking one step at a time to kill the gang one by one, finally making his way to Red. But there's a big problem: the devil is having fun playing around with the rules of the game.

From prolific director Roel Reine, who made *Pistol Whipped*, *The Marine 2*, and *12 Rounds 2*, *Dead in Tombstone* is theatrical-quality entertainment, giving its audience plenty of bang for its buck, and an engaging sense of style to boot. Trejo is dry as usual, but it's great seeing him as an antihero sans the irony found in his *Machete* movies, and there's some good looking special effects and stunt work to keep things exciting. This was shot in Romania on the same sets as *Ghost Rider: Spirit of Vengeance*, which this film strangely resembles.

Deadly Assassin (a.k.a. **True Justice: Deadly Assassin**)

2012 (Studiocanal DVD R2)

(djm)

After killing one of his own men for being a turncoat spy, Elijah Kane (Steven Seagal) takes his covert task force on the run when he and his whole battalion are hunted by various government organizations, including the FBI, for killing his own man. Kane, while reacting to his hunters with nary an eyebrow twitch when confronted by them, warns each of them that he's one of the good guys, but no one listens, and he has to break some arms and wrists to prove that he's not to be messed with. As a result of the miscommunication, the remainder of Kane's team encounters some very close calls with police and task forces as they run out of places to hide.

The final movie compilation of Seagal's TV series *True Justice*, *Deadly Assassin* tries to wrap everything up in a cool and tidy fashion, and the final frame of the series is abrupt, but appropriate, with Kane's team captured or in trouble and Kane vowing that he'll make all things right. All things considered, the entirety of *True Justice* blends together and it's difficult to tell each episode/film compilation apart from one another, but it gave Seagal a chance to be a part of an ensemble, which is nice. This entry was directed by Wayne Rose.

Deadly Bet

1992 (Madacy DVD) (djm)

Filmed on the heels of other PM Entertainment movies like *Final Impact* and *Street Crimes*, *Deadly Bet* stars Jeff Wincott from *Martial Outlaw* and *Martial Law II*. He plays a compulsive gambler named Angelo Scala, who ends up in huge trouble with an underground fighting circuit when he wagers that he can beat Rico Darby (Steven Vincent Leigh from *Ring of Fire* and *Sword of Honor*) in a kickboxing fight, but he loses big time. As part of his wager, he put his girlfriend (Charlene Tilton) up as collateral, and so he not only loses the fight, but his girl too. Months in the hole for upwards of tens of thousands of dollars, Angelo goes on an alcoholic binge and takes wetworks jobs for bookies and gangsters. One day in a drunken stupor, he realizes that he's squandered everything away that's ever meant anything to him, so he dumps his booze and begins working out in earnest and living a clean lifestyle. Impressed with his change, Rico allows him to enter a fight tournament again for big money and with the hopes that Angelo can win his girl back. With everything that he's got, Angelo fights like he means it this time and wins.

For at least an hour, Jeff Wincott's character is an unlikable son of a bitch, so it's hard to root for him until he *finally* makes a turnaround. At that stage (at about an hour and ten minutes in), my patience had almost been exhausted, so *Deadly Bet* is an iffy gamble. I like Jeff Wincott, and he's one of the most criminally overlooked action stars of the 1990s, so if you feel the same about him, you might want to give this a try despite its faults. Gary Daniels appears in a fight early on in the movie. Directed by Richard W. Munchkin, who made *Out for Blood* with Don Wilson and *Guardian Angel* with Cynthia Rothrock.

Deadly Crossing (a.k.a. **True Justice: Deadly Crossing**)

2010 (Optimum DVD R2) (djm)

Steven Seagal plays Elijah Kane, the leader of an elite undercover squad of cops in Seattle. When an immigrant family is shot dead at a convenience store, the only witness is a young girl, who swears that the killer is someone Kane is familiar with: a fellow officer of the law. As Kane and his crew build a case against the cop (a racist woman), another case is brewing: a Russian mobster (played by Gil Bellows) is in town, and he's looking to recruit several attractive women for his heroin operation, and two of Kane's crew happen to be extremely gorgeous women who are used to going dangerously undercover. When the mobster suspects the two women of being police, the sting goes haywire, and Kane and his crew have got to bulldoze through some formalities to get their man.

Deadly Crossing is made up of the first two episodes of the television series *True Justice*, a weekly fictional program starring Seagal. Strangely enough, the series has never gotten syndicated airtime in the US, but overseas the show was broken up into individual movies that went directly to video. The pace of this compilation is a bit uneven and doesn't really lend itself to a single film, as it has two more or less complete stories mashed up into one. The production qualities aren't bad, and Seagal seems to be into it, but it's an inauspicious entryway into fictional television for him. Concurrently, he also starred in the "reality" TV show *Lawman*, which covered his exploits as a sheriff in Louisiana. The next compilation movie in the *True Justice* series is *Dark Vengeance*. Directed by Keoni Waxman.

Deadly Currency

1998 (Aurora VHS) (CD)

"I should get paid by the punch."

There's never a shortage of money in Las Vegas, especially during Super Bowl week. Millions are going to be stashed away and it belongs to mob boss Mario Verelli (William Smith). Fed up with his father's villainous ways, Verelli's son Jason (James Zahnd) devises a plan to walk away with the small fortune. He can't do it alone, so he assembles a small team, including Rico (Deron McBee, a former American Gladiator), a former FBI agent looking for a quick payday. Just as the

heist is about to go down, he learns his former partner already has a sting operation in place to take down Verelli and his crime syndicate. Their lives are all a huge mess and everyone is willing to fight to keep the cash.

If you have any doubt as to the type of film this is, just pop the tape into the VCR and hit play so all the nude female bodies can sear themselves into your impressionable mind. Aside from all the nudity, cult favorite William Smith (*Red Dawn*) steals the show as a twisted mob boss with a taste for classical music. Bodybuilder Deron McBee (*Ring of Steel, Enter the Blood Ring*) is finally given his chance to snag the spotlight and he gives a solid performance. The unfortunate thing about the film is that it's too talky and there's very little action. Aside from a few small scuffles, McBee is never able to show off his fighting abilities, which is a shame. Even with a nonexistent budget, the script is engaging enough to keep you interested, and Smith fans won't want to miss his powerhouse of a performance. Directed by Marque Case Chantal.

Deadly Engagement

2003 (Next Video DVD) (CD)

"What harm could an eleven-year-old and a file clerk possibly do to us?"

Paul Gerard (Olivier Gruner) is a hard working paper clerk who has to go away on business leaving his wife and son home alone. Mia (Daniela Krhut), his wife, is a famed physicist who knows how to program the codes for a top-secret bomb that has been stolen by Vukov (John Comer) to sell on the black market. Vukov sends his goons to kidnap her, leaving her son Danny (Max Norlin) alone. He's an eleven-year-old computer genius who quickly locates and identifies her assailants and feeds the information to his dad. Paul isn't just any old clerk, he has military training and he's going to get his wife back.

In lieu of delivering the hardcore action, exploitation director Lloyd A. Simandl puts the good stuff on the back burner in favor of some softcore action. The film almost plays out like a Women In Prison (W.I.P.) picture, with more skin and breasts on display than kicks and fists. Action star Olivier Gruner (*Angel Town, Savate*) does his absolute best, delivering several entertaining, short burst–like fight scenes. The movie entertains on a nominal level, but it pays no attention to logic with moments so ridiculous you won't believe they happened. It takes Gruner two nights hiking through the woods to get to his wife, and then his son shows up on his bicycle. There could have been an interesting subplot with the son and how adept he is with computers, but that was ignored in favor of all the girl-on-girl action. If you prefer heavy petting to heaving hitting then grab yourself some fruit snacks and take a peek.

Deadly Impact

1984 (Revok DVD) (djm)

A young couple has figured out a way to beat the odds in Las Vegas (using computers), and a local crime ring begins to notice they are reaping heavy harvests. When the couple runs into trouble, a 'Nam vet cop named George (Bo Svenson) and his helicopter pilot buddy (also a Vietnam vet) Lou (Fred Willaimson) get into the mix by butting heads with the thugs in question.

A disappointment for fans of co-star Williamson, who spends most of his scenes acting scared and reluctant to fight (seriously?!), *Deadly Impact* indeed has some grindhouse action and violence, but it really belongs to Svenson, who takes charge and keeps encouraging his pal to shoot bad guys and chase after them. Still it's kind of goofy hearing Williamson squeal, "Let me outta the damn car!" when he's stuck in the passenger seat during a high-speed chase. Directed by Fabrizio De Angelis.

Deadly Intent

1988 (MGM DVD) (djm)

A ruddy archaeologist named Raymond (Lance Henriksen) returns home from a bloody expedition in the Amazon, and his benefactors hold a home-coming party for him at a swanky art gallery, where he expresses regret at returning empty handed, but the truth is deep and dark: He recovered a precious gemstone at a great price—he killed and backstabbed his fellow archaeologists who were on the expedition with him, and he's keeping the stone for himself! When he leaves the party that night, he's followed by a mysterious stalker, who runs him off the road, resulting in his death by a fiery car explosion. Raymond's wife Laura (Lisa Eilbacher) mourns his death, but she knows deep down that her husband was a liar and a cheat, and indeed his secrets are going to haunt her over the next few days as various ne'er-do-wells begin stalking and hounding her for the gemstone. One pair of stalkers comes in the form of a married couple—Curt and Francesca Slate (Fred Williamson and Persis Khambatta)—who literally tie and gag her to a chair and torture her to give up the stone she doesn't know anything about, but she's saved by an old friend of her husband's named Jeff (Steve Railsback), who is as mysterious as everyone else. There's some action and intrigue, but this is mainly a thriller.

If you're going to track this movie down because action star Fred Williamson is in it, you're going to be disappointed. He's in the film in a strictly supporting capacity, and if you adhere to Williamson's own imposed rules that he will only appear in a movie if he doesn't die in it and if he gets the girl at the end of it, then you're *really* going to be let down because he dies rather easily and he doesn't get the girl. That said, there's some entertainment value to a movie that has a murky *Raiders of the Lost Rip-Offs* vibe to it. Directed by Nigel Dick.

VHS artwork for *Deadly Outbreak*. Author's collection.

Deadly Outbreak

1995 (Live VHS) (djm)

After *The Perfect Weapon* and *Street Knight*, Jeff Speakman starred in this Nu Image production set in Israel. He plays a US Embassy first sergeant named Dutton Hatfield, who meets a group of scientists at the airport and escorts them to a chemical plant, where they proceed to lock the facility down and kill all the workers within. They make the demand that they will use the deadly chemicals in the plant to launch a terrorist attack if the government doesn't pay them a half a billion dollars. Hatfield is the only man to stop them, and he kills them off one by one, until the last few take to the road, leading to a bus/helicopter chase.

Those who saw *Street Knight* and were disappointed by the lack of action will be glad to know that *Deadly Outbreak* features Speakman in full action mode again. There's plenty of kenpo-style fights, and there's an equal measure of hand-to-hand fighting and gunplay. Loud, simple, and predictable every step of the way (with a surprising emphasis on misogyny), this one gives him a good-enough vehicle to showcase his persona. He also has quite a few quips and one-liners. Ron Silver plays the lead heavy, but he's not given much to do. Speakman also plays a dad to a ten-year-old kid. This wasn't released theatrically. Director Rick Avery has a long history as a stuntman and stunt coordinator. He also directed Speakman in *The Expert*.

Deadly Ransom

1998 (York DVD) (djm)

The ingredients are here to make a good action film, but unfortunately it's a big disappointment for star Loren Avedon (*King of the Kickboxers*), especially considering that he helped write and produce it. He plays a Navy SEAL whose wife is kidnapped while they are on vacation in Brazil. She is held for a fifty million dollar ransom by his scumbag uncle, played by Brion James. Avedon gathers a few badass soldiers around him, and they plan a rescue.

For a ninety-minute movie, I was shocked at how little action there is in it. Avedon only displays his martial arts prowess twice in the film, and the fight scenes aren't really impressive or interesting. The film looks good, appears to have been shot on nice locations, and has a decent score by Terry Plumeri but, alas, it's a time-waster. Directed by Robert J. Hyatt.

Deadly Reckoning (a.k.a. **The Company Man**)

1998 (Cheezy Flicks DVD) (CD)

Ernest Gray (Frank Zagarino) is a seemingly harmless man who runs a used bookstore with his eleven-year-old daughter Jennifer (Rebecca Ayre Doughty). One afternoon they're viciously attacked by a group of well-armed men (and one woman) led by Van Guilder (Matthias Hues) who are hell-bent on killing Gray. Turns out Gray has a hidden cache of weapons and is highly skilled. He and his daughter escape, and he confesses to her that he's a former CIA agent who has retired to take care of her. The men after him were hired by Control 5 (Robert Vaughn) who wants them to retrieve a disc Gray might have that contains information that could be used to make millions. With help from two former colleagues, Lewis (Bryan Genesse) and Marianna (Elizabeth Giordano), Ernest (who was known as Napoleon when he was an agent) has to defend his daughter and protect the information he has acquired before he's able to go back to his quiet life.

Director Art Camacho (*Half Past Dead 2*) is known for delivering solid action on a limited budget and *Deadly Reckoning* is no exception. Sure, the script is predictable and chock-full of horrible dialogue, so thankfully we have Frank Zagarino (*Never Say Die, Terminal Impact*), Matthias Hues (*Dark Angel*), and in an extended cameo Bryan Genesse (Zagarino's co-star in *Terminal Impact*) to bring the thunder. Zagarino delivers the two-fisted gunplay and not to be outdone by Genesse (who has a great fight scene with a random villain), he trades blows with the Swedish beast Hues. The film falters when it comes to the story, but it's the action and the action-centric cast that makes this one worthwhile. The picture wouldn't be complete without a gorgeous woman for the hero to hook up with and Elizabeth Giordano (Mrs. Zagarino) is breathtaking.

Deadly Shooter

(a.k.a. **The Shooter**)

1997 (Vivendi DVD) (djm)

Michael Dudikoff stars as the strong, silent type of drifter cowboy in this direct-to-video western directed by Fred Olen Ray. Michael Atherton (Dudikoff) is a former soldier of the Civil War who is known for being a formidable gunman, and when he stumbles upon a scene involving several men lashing a naked woman tied to a tree, he kills all the men but one and rescues the helpless woman. The woman, named Wendy (Valerie Wildman), is a whore at the local saloon, and she'd been taken by the Krants gang and condemned to death for slighting one of them. When the head of the Krants gang (William Smith) finds out that his son was among those killed by Atherton, he vows vengeance and spares no expense to capture and kill him. Atherton, who doesn't want anything to do with anybody, is thrust into a story he knows nothing about, and when he's captured by the gang, he's whipped, tortured, and crucified. Wendy, the whore he saved, manages to save him from dying of exposure, and she nurses him back to health, and when he's recovered, he modifies his gun and gets to revenging.

Fans of westerns may enjoy this rather generic movie, but Dudikoff fans will most likely be disappointed by it. He's not really at the center of attention, and his role doesn't flatter him. For a Fred Olen Ray picture, it's not as sleazy or cheap looking as some others of his, but it *does* have a totally gratuitous sex scene between minor characters who don't contribute much to the plot. Randy Travis plays a villain, Nils Allen Stewart appears as a member of the Krants gang, and Andrew Stevens plays the chronicler of Atherton's tale.

Deadly Target

1994 (Mill Creek DVD) (djm)

As Gary Daniels was working his way up the direct-to-video food chain, he made *Deadly Target*, which is on par or slightly better than many of the films he'd made up to this point in his career. He plays a Hong Kong detective named Charles Prince who travels to Los Angeles to extradite a Chinese criminal for a big trial. While in LA, he's assigned a local cop as a partner to keep him in line, but they encounter wave after wave of Asian gangsters who make Prince's job an obstacle course. Chinatown's deadliest killers are out to make him their next target.

Most notable for having a great supporting Asian cast that includes the likes of James Lew (in a bit part), Al Leong (also a bit), Ron Yuan (from *The Girl From the Naked Eye*), and Philip Tan (from *Lethal Weapon 4*), *Deadly Target* is fine for fans of Daniels, but others may find it too simplistic or indistinguishable. I thought it was okay, but anyone looking for a stellar vehicle starring Daniels may want to fast forward a few years and go directly to *Recoil*. From PM Entertainment. Directed by Charla Driver.

Death Before Dishonor
1986 (Anchor Bay DVD) (djm)

Bureaucrat: "I'm sorry, sergeant, but you realize this doesn't change anything."
Burns: "It does for me."

A Vietnam vet, Master Sergeant Joseph "Gunny" Burns (Fred Dryer, a former Rams player in the NFL) is a take-no-shit kind of guy, and when he's given the task to lead a security detail in the Middle East after a dignitary and his entire family are slain, he culls a squad of young commandos to join him. As soon as he gets there with his team, a jihad is declared and his men and other American sympathizers are in harm's way as they become hunted by suicide-ready killers. When Burns witnesses firsthand the degree to which the terrorists are willing to go, he jumps into action, killing a bunch of them, and thus putting himself in hot water with the American bureaucrats who are only thinking about diplomacy. Fed up with diplomacy when his commander (played by Brian Keith) and one of his young Marines are captured, Burns bulldozes through red tape with every gun blazing, with his remaining Marines backing him up.

While Fred Dryer was in the middle of making the hit TV show *Hunter*, he went out and shot this adequate actioner that was perfectly suited for his sensibilities. Sadly, he isn't given much to do other than shooting guys up real good, but it would have been nice to see him get into some tussles because it's obvious he would be good at it. After *Death Before Dishonor* he returned to *Hunter* and sort of stayed there for the rest of his career. We were robbed of a potentially awesome action movie career. Sasha Mitchell, who would later star in *Kickboxer 2-4*, has a memorable role as one of Dryer's Marines. Prolific stuntman Terry Leonard directed this. It remains his only directing effort to date.

Death Cage
1988 (Image DVD) (djm)

Joe Lewis from *Jaguar Lives!* co-stars as the main villain in this Hong Kong martial arts movie starring Robin Shou, who would later go on to star in the *Mortal Kombat* movies. Lan Si Han (Shou) is a fantastic kickboxing fighter who upsets a mob boss named Mr. Kent (Lewis) by winning against his best fighters. Mr. Kent rigs a few fights so that Lan's home gym loses business, thus making Mr. Kent's gym the place where most fighters want to train. When Lan works himself back up the fight circuit, Mr. Kent is enraged and forces Lan to fight him in a "death cage" tournament where the losing fighter pays for his loss with his very life. The final fight gets bloody.

Lewis's voice was dubbed into Chinese, but anyone can see that he was acting in the frantic, theatrical Chinese style (red-faced yelling, finger pointing, etc.). He looked like he'd gained some weight since *Jaguar Lives!*, but when he fights

Robin Shou, he looks like a beast. This is a minor effort, only of interest to fans of its stars. Directed by Robert Tai.

Deathcheaters
1976 (Madman Films DVD R4) (djm)

Two Vietnam veteran buddies have gone into stunt work in the motion picture business, and there's almost nothing that they won't try. Steve (John Hargreaves) is a ladies man and balances out his reckless life with romance with his steady girl, and Rodney (real-life stuntman Grant Page) is a bit more solitary and therefore has free rein to get as crazy as he wants to. The two of them are quite a pair, and they're so outrageous in their willingness to try anything, that they accept an offer from the government to undertake a dangerous mission to the Philippines to retrieve some secret documents from a Filipino criminal, which entails some gonzo stunts and daredevil bravado.

The sheer audacity of this film from director Brian Trenchard-Smith is appealing, and the only few other movies I can compare it to are Trenchard-Smith's own pseudo documentary *Stunt Rock* (also starring Page) and Quentin Tarantino's *Death Proof*. Casting stuntman Page in this thing was a stroke of genius, and anyone can see that he defied death at every opportunity. *Deathcheaters* isn't a classic by any means, but it's a fun time, and co-star Page made a great action star. He was also in *The Man From Hong Kong*, also directed by Trenchard-Smith.

Death Dimension
1978 (Mondo Crash DVD) (CD)

Brilliant scientist Dr. Mason (T. E. Foreman) has created a freeze bomb for the twisted crime lord known as The Pig (Harold Sakata). When he realizes what he has been doing was wrong, he sacrifices himself in order to allow his female assistant to get away with all his files. The Pig is furious and sends all of his best men out to find her. Captain Gallagher (George Lazenby) puts his best man on the case: Detective Ash (Jim Kelly). His methods may be a bit unorthodox but there is no denying that he produces compelling results. He quickly finds himself in the thick of it all, and people he cares about are caught in the crossfire. He and his partner Li (Myron Bruce Li) have their fists and feet primed and ready to destroy everyone in their path to retrieve the information and save the young assistant.

Director Al Adamson (*Dynamite Brothers*) isn't exactly known for his finesse as a filmmaker but he's still able to deliver some schlocky fun for us to enjoy. *Death Dimension* is pretty much a mess, but it's how Jim Kelly (*Three the Hard Way, Enter the Dragon*) was able to shine regardless of the material he was given. His charisma and martial arts skills are on full display here and he shows them off in several action scenes sprinkled

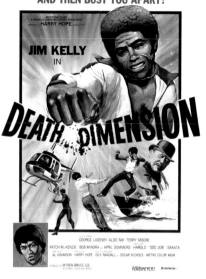

THAT MAN FROM "ENTER THE DRAGON" IS BACK TO BUST YOU... AND THEN BUST YOU APART!

JIM KELLY IN DEATH DIMENSION

Theatrical release poster for *Death Dimension*. Author's collection.

throughout the movie. The fights themselves may not be very memorable, but some of his signature moves are. When he throws a series of punches near the end of the film, you really get a sense of how fast he really was. While it's far from being the best representation of his screen work, *Death Dimension* offers up some great late-night entertainment and features performances from former James Bond actor George Lazenby (*On Her Majesty's Secret Service*) as well as *Goldfinger*'s Odd Job himself, Harold Sakata.

Death Fight (a.k.a. Rage)
1994 (Platinum DVD) (djm)

Stepbrothers Jack and Chiang grow up hating each other, and while Chiang becomes a rich businessman who stages to-the-death fights in his secret arena in Thailand, Jack is on the opposite spectrum, living a modest life in Bangkok with his wife, an attorney. When Jack (Richard Norton) is framed for murdering his mistress (played by Tetchie Agbayani from *Gymkata*), his wife (played by Karen Moncrieff) must draw all the facts from him before she can defend him in court. As his feud with his half-brother Chiang (played by Franco Guerrero) is hashed out, Jack realizes that his brother is trying to put him away to lay claim to their father's fortune, while also spiting him. Out on bail, Jack goes to everyone he knows to search out clues as to what's really going on, and he's drawn in closer and closer to his half-brother's death ring where a fight with his champions await.

Fairly standard and predictable as far as this type of movie goes, *Death Fight* is most notable for featuring some intense fights between Norton and two fighters: First with Ron Vreeken from *Rage and Honor II*, and second with Chuck Jeffreys from *Fight to Win* and *Superfights*. The Norton/Jeffreys fight is really impressive. Other than that, this is strictly for Norton's fans or those interested in movies with to-the-death fight themes. Director Anthony Maharaj collaborated with Norton on other films like *Kick-Fighter* and *Return of the Kickfighter*.

Death From Above

2012 (Naedomi DVD) (djm)

A couple of roughhousing buddies are out on a hunting trip when one of them accidentally unearths an ancient Druidical stash in the woods, leading to a discovery of an evil amulet that changes one of them into Thule, a vengeful god of the underworld. Thule (former wrestler and Olympic gold medal winner Kurt Angle) goes on a murder spree as he seeks out several other evil amulets that will grant him unlimited power and dominion over mankind. On his trail is a chosen warrior named Herzog (former wrestler Psycho Sid Vicious), who is tracking him down to stop his quest from coming to fruition. They have a brief confrontation at the conclusion, while several hillbilly onlookers gape in wide-eyed wonder.

Kurt Angle, whose vehicle film this is, had done a few ultra low-budget action films before this one with the same director Bruce Koehler, and whatever fans he has will probably be willing to forgive the fact that his movies don't really reward in the way of action or spectacle. Angle's strongpoints come in the way of his one-note physical feats of brawling, and when he's not smacking opponents down in this film, he's delivering lines of dialogue like The Terminator. Action fans will be disappointed by *Death From Above*, and the crowd that pays to see Angle in movies *might* get their money's worth. I watched it, wondering who his fans might be, and I got my answer when I realized that all or most of the characters in the film drove monster trucks, drank beer, sported tattoos, and listened to heavy metal music. Angle also starred in *End Game* and *River of Darkness*.

Death Grip

2012 (The Stunt People DVD) (djm)

For anyone who hasn't watched a movie with Eric Jacobus, *Death Grip* is the best place to start. Jacobus wrote, directed, edited, and starred in this back-to-basics action film. He plays a guy named Kenny, whose brother, Mark, has been institutionalized for many years due to his autism. When he picks him up from the institution to come live with him, they try bonding a little bit, which proves to be a bit of a challenge. Kenny gets a call to fill in for a friend, who is supposed to be catering at a museum where the last silver coin that Judas was paid to betray Jesus is on display. Kenny takes the gig and brings along his brother, and while doing the job, a Satan-worshiping cult breaks in and tries to steal the coin. Enter the Jacobus! Kenny, who has skills in martial arts, manages to thwart the

Poster artwork for *Death Grip*. Courtesy of Death Grip, 2013 ©Eric Jacobus.

cult's plans for sacrifice and dastardly intentions, but one of the beautiful things about this film is that it never goes overboard and Jacobus never glorifies his abilities. We see him as he imagines the fights will go, and then we see the fights as they play out, which are never as elaborate as he wishes they were.

Carefully nuanced and calculated, *Death Grip* has a surprisingly fresh and honest sense of humor, and some of the bravura fight scenes are elaborate and intensive. Where the film's weaknesses lie are in the lighting, some of the camerawork, and in a stretch of time where not much is going on. Still, this is a solid vehicle film for one of action film's most underrated and unknown action guys. Jacobus is a talent to watch out for.

INTERVIEW:

ERIC JACOBUS

(djm)

The world has yet to learn the name Eric Jacobus. Ladies and gentlemen, hear the name and speak it because he's here, and he's about to break through. Working way off the grid and completely off the

Kenny (Eric Jacobus) looks over his shoulder, ready to fight, in *Death Grip*. Courtesy of Death Grip, 2013 ©Eric Jacobus.

radar, Jacobus, a practitioner of hapkido, has been building himself up through impressive short films and totally independent feature films, namely with the two pictures Contour *(2006) and* Death Grip *(2012), both of which he wrote, directed, and starred in. He's already appeared in the second season of* Mortal Kombat: Legacy *(2014) as Stryker, and he's on a clear and calculated path of action stardom.*

It's obvious you're really into Hong Kong movies; your movies hearken back to the glory days of Golden Harvest.

I discovered Jackie Chan when I was around seventeen or so. That's about the time when his movies were being released in my hometown in theaters.

We're talking *Rumble in the Bronx* and *Supercop*?

Yeah. I saw *Rumble in the Bronx* and *Operation Condor* in a theater. I guess that was around early high school. I really loved it. Nothing really was happening during that time period, and come 2000 or so, I called up my friend who was also a Hong Kong movie fan, and he was the only one I knew in my hometown—Redding—that I could say, "Hey, do you want to try this out—to make a Jackie Chan movie?" It sounds absurd. We had a video camera, we had a computer, and I thought we knew how to edit video. "Let's just try it out!" I thought I knew how to put a fight scene together. I'd watched enough of them—I'd watched like 500 Hong Kong films by that point. I got really obsessed with it. I lived like four hours from Chinatown. I would go down there and spend almost my whole paycheck. Whatever I could get my hands on. I loved it. I wanted to do it. That was it. We started a group—The Stunt People. The name just kind of came to us. The idea was that we were everyday guys. Our movies have always had that everyday guy feel. That's what we go for. We don't try to do . . . we're not trying to be Bruce Lees. We're trying to be action stars that can identify with the common man. Like Jackie Chan or the early vaudeville guys.

Exactly. I don't see you guys running from explosions. I see you guys fighting in close quarters, on streets, in warehouses. I definitely saw the Jackie Chan influence in your movie *Contour*. Your movie *Death Grip* reminded me a little bit of *Heart of Dragon*.

Yep.

Where have you gotten your training? You can't do that stuff unless you train hardcore.

I started taking martial arts when I was twenty. Before that I did a little gymnastics. And weight lifting. When I started training, I did taekwondo for two years. Then I took up hapkido, and I've been doing that ever since. It's known as a throw-heavy style. The kind you see at the end of *Game of Death*. What I do focuses on a lot of punching, a lot of kicking, a lot of throwing, a lot of grappling.

D

Kenny (Eric Jacobus) in action in *Death Grip*. Courtesy of Death Grip, 2013 ©Eric Jacobus.

Eric Jacobus wrote, directed, and starred in *Death Grip*. Here, he's featured in combat. Courtesy of Death Grip, 2013 ©Eric Jacobus.

You mentioned earlier that there was nothing going on in the world of action movies when you became swept away by Jackie Chan. This was when guys like Seagal and Van Damme were just beginning to do straight-to-video movies and Schwarzenegger was doing stuff like *Batman and Robin* and *End of Days*. Not a good time to be an action star. Why do you think that was happening?

I think I have a good answer. For Hong Kong action stars, it had something to do with the handover, and I think that's why people from Hong Kong were starting to do stuff in the US. I know some Hong Kong people who moved to the US because of that. This was around 1997. In America, I think it had to do with the borders suddenly dropping in terms of trade, so the entertainment industry just seemed to go over. When the Berlin Wall fell, it was hard to come up with a new enemy. Before that, it was easy. You had South American dictators, you had drug cartels, you had the Russians. It was easy to make an action movie. Find the bad guy and kill him. But who was the bad guy in 1995? Well . . . I don't know. We wanted to do business with Russia, so we couldn't make them the bad guys anymore. Globalization . . .

That happened with the Bond movies too.

Absolutely. It was blatant. In some countries, it still is blatant. They're doing it with Japanese and British. Because they have a very nationalistic film market. Action films require a villain. There was like a five-year period where we didn't know who to beat up.

I like that. Growing up were there any specific movies or entertainment figures that you aspired to?

There were two main sources of inspiration to me. The first one was vaudeville. Laurel and Hardy, The Marx Brothers, Charlie Chaplin, and Buster Keaton. I loved all of those because they were very physical. I'm not very good at audio comprehension. I'm better at visual comprehension. I understood physical comedy more than normal comedy. Early on, I idolized Arnold Schwarzenegger. That's why I got into weight lifting. My dad had bought me a weight set. I used to spend the summers in the garage. *Commando, Total Recall, Terminator 2*. Those were the big ones. John Connor was totally me in *Terminator 2*. I wanted to be that kid. Now I want to be Arnold. (Laughing.)

Let's talk about your movie *Contour*. It's a very simple movie, very inexpensive, but the fight scenes are really intense. The climax has an incredible fight scene that goes on for something like twenty minutes. How did you get this movie going?

In the early 2000s nothing was coming out, but *Ong Bak* came out and that was a big deal. That was great. The newcomers weren't really delivering. Donnie Yen hadn't picked up at that point yet. The martial arts was aching and craving for fight scenes. I really wanted to do a *Dragons Forever*. I threw together a script that was like forty pages long. It was ridiculous. I just wanted to do an action movie. The last paragraph in the script said something like, "a seventeen minute fight in a warehouse." (Laughing.) I thought all I needed then was a warehouse. I knew a guy who had one and we filmed there for like sixty days.

Oh my gosh. Sixty days?

Sixty days. But we're talking like two- or three-hour days. We would shoot only when all of our schedules were aligning. Had we been able to do ten- or twelve-hour days, we wouldn't have taken as long.

Did anyone get paid?

. . . uh, none of us. (Laughing.) I had done a movie about a year beforehand with a producer who had been trying to put together a production company, and they wanted to acquire films. I told them, "Oh, I've got a film I want to make. I just need some money to do it." He said, "Is three thousand bucks enough?" I said, "Make it five!" They gave me five thousand bucks to do this movie, and in exchange, they owned it. Five thousand bucks to me was great. I was out of college and broke. That money all went to food, a couple locations, and paying guys for gas.

You guys are really dedicated, man. I had to wait until the end credits to appreciate *Contour*.

(Laughing!)

It took me about halfway through to realize what you guys were trying to do, and then when it was over I realized that you were all the real thing. You guys were hurting, you guys were in pain. That's why Jackie Chan always did the outtakes at the end. I appreciated the movie then. You guys are cool.

Thanks.

So, did Indican distribute your movie at that point?

That was actually a different company. I think they ended up paying six thousand dollars to the production, and then after I was editing it while we were shooting it. It took a year to shoot it. I had a finished cut and I had a "making of" and all this stuff. I just wanted to release the DVD, so what do I do next? They said, "Well, now we need you to wait." So I sat there for a few months. I was itching to release this. I said, "Let's just show this in a theater." I showed it in a place called The Four Star Theater. Packed the house with 200 people. They loved it. I said, "Guys, we really need to release this thing. What can I do?" They said, "We'll sell it to you for a little bit more than what we paid you." So I bought it back. It was mine. I immediately released it, direct-to-consumer DVD. I made all the money back. I made a thousand DVDs at the local DVD company. We did the artwork for the DVD, we did the authoring for the DVD. It took me a month to author the DVD. I packed it full of special features. I took the disc to a disc making plant. We sold those, and they sold really quick. We sold them at Comic Con, at screenings, online. Orders just came in.

When did Indican become involved?

We went to an action festival. The fact that it was shown at a festival meant that it existed. Suddenly it was on all these lists. "It's an action movie!" It was categorized. There are distribution companies that will look at that list to fill their catalogues. Indican saw our film on that list and they wanted a screener. They were the first ones we talked to, and they took it in 2007. I've been very happy with them.

There was a long gap between *Contour* and *Death Grip*. I don't know if it was a long gap to you, but it felt like a long gap to me. What happened in the meantime between the two projects?

It was an eternity. Let me say that the reason that *Contour* was made the way that it was made—in the sense that we shot it over the course of a year. We shot sixty days in the warehouse and another forty outside, elsewhere. That's the most relaxed shoot that you can ask for. There were days when we'd go to the warehouse and couldn't think of anything to shoot. "Oh, well . . . I've got to go to work at two anyway. . . ." Suddenly when you turn twenty-five, twenty-six, you meet a girl, you get married, you have a kid, you have a full-time job, and then you can't shoot like that anymore. We realized that putting together a production like *Contour* again was going to be impossible. Especially since I had to pay the bills now. I wanted to make my own living. So, it was five years of developing a great script. The thing that people say about *Contour* is, "Good action, crappy everything else." So I had to improve everything else. That meant that I had to learn how to write a good script. That took a *long* time. Even after *Death Grip*, I don't know what I'm doing half the time. I commend anyone who can write a good script. I wanted to work on my acting, too. I took acting classes. I got some acting jobs. Jobs where I didn't have to do any fighting. I just had to *act*. I got hired to do acting and fighting. I was able to improve during that time. I didn't want to make another *Contour*. If I made *Contour* and then *Contour 2*, I might not really make a dent. Plus, after *Contour,* things started speeding up in the martial arts world. The thing that I kept doing is writing. I wrote a script for a year and I realized how bad it was. I threw it away and started all over. That script ended up being *Death Grip*. The stars aligned at that time. We decided to make it a legitimate production that we'd shoot in forty-five days. Let's get some money to do it, let's get insurance. Let's have lighting. We needed a good camera. That was another thing—no one knew what the hell kind of camera to use during that time period.

How much did *Death Grip* cost, what kind of camera did you use, and where did you film it?

It cost about a hundred thousand. We used the Sony FS100. It was nice and small and cheap. We used the hell out of it. The cost breakdown: Thirty thousand goes to the cast and crew, of which I didn't take any. Then ten thousand for the equipment. Ten thousand for insurance. That's half the budget. About seven thousand for catering. It goes quick. We got the money from private equity.

You were saying earlier that a good action movie needs a good villain. I like that the villains in *Death Grip* are Satan worshippers. They're a cult of Satanists! That's kinda cool!

The key elements to make a good action movie, you've got to know who your villains are going to be. They have to be worth killing. I was raised

Kenny (Eric Jacobus) is surrounded by a Satanic cult in *Death Grip*. Courtesy of Death Grip, 2013 ©Eric Jacobus.

A wounded Kenny (Eric Jacobus) is fighting for his life in *Death Grip*. Courtesy of Death Grip, 2013 ©Eric Jacobus.

Catholic. I could resonate with that. I remember reading about the thirty silver coins of Judas. The silver that he was paid to betray Jesus. I thought it'd be cool to have one of those coins floating around somewhere. The Satanic cult floats around, recovering these coins. That was my inspiration for that.

What's your idea of who the hero should be? I like the hero you play in this movie. I like your character's relationship to the guy who played your brother. That guy was really good. He didn't overact in any way. Even your acting is understated in the film. Everything is calculated very specifically in the movie, even the humor. Talk about that.

Well, I cast myself as the hero, because it was the easiest thing to do. I feel like often an action movie isn't going to get made unless you do it yourself. If you want to find the perfect director, if you want to be an action star, that's going to make you look like a douchebag. That's an issue. The easiest thing is if you're both the actor and the director. I appreciate your comments about the acting and all that. Nathan, who played by brother, he was the actor of the group. I told him to play autistic, without really knowing what that meant. I had my idea of what that would be, but then he came back and showed me what his idea of what that would be, and it was like, *Whoa. That's WAY better than I expected.* I really didn't need to direct him much. He brought up my game. That's great. I struggled with how I was going to fit in this market of action movies. I had to make something that would be accepted by an audience. It wouldn't work if I was playing a six foot tall supermodel or something. I had to put my strengths on camera. I've got some physical ability. I think I'm able to show some humanity as well. I can get the audience on my side.

I love that you allowed your character to get beat up in the movie. You're not Steven Seagal.

If I were 6 foot 2 like Steven Seagal, I could probably get away with not getting beat up. People might buy it. It's tough when you're 5 foot 6, 5 foot 7 on a good day. I'm 5 foot 9 in heels. I'm gonna get beat up. I also wanted to play with it. In *Contour* there were these really intricate fight scenes, and I decided that I would put the audience in Kenny's head in *Death Grip*. I wanted to show them what Kenny's thinking.

That happens a lot in the movie.

It happens a lot, maybe more times than people want, but it was an experiment. I wanted to try it out. Everyone has a vision in their head of how they're going to fight. You rarely lose a fight when it's in your own head. But then when you show the reality of it, it's much more brutal. You get beat up. It's much more Korean feeling, you know? That was a good way of showing his ego in the film. His ego is crushed all the time. The only way he can really win at the end in that end fight is that he realizes that he can't beat this guy in his own head. That's what allows him to realize that he *can* beat this guy. That's his character arc.

Nice. Were the *Sherlock Holmes* movies with Robert Downey Jr. in your head at all?

Yeah, yeah. Sherlock Holmes is a genius. Kenny's not a genius. He's very vulnerable, very unstable. We took it in that direction. Yeah, that was our first influence.

Tell me some challenges of making a movie like *Death Grip* in forty-five days.

Oh, where do I start? There's always a challenge to flex your muscles and innovate. A lot of the challenges come early on. Production is easy. Shooting is easy. The beginning part, getting the right idea, an original idea, that's tough. I found that writing a screenplay was hard. When I thought I had a screenplay, I would pitch the entire screenplay. I would sit down and pitch the whole thing, "My movie's about this! And this!" But in my own head, I don't even know what the story is. I don't even have an idea. I just want to do an action movie. I don't have the skill set yet to pitch an idea to somebody. That was always tough. Coming up with that script—that was the challenge.

The market is tough right now for action movies. Studios are only doing big action movies and that's it. There aren't many more movies around like *Death Grip* being made.

Yeah, exactly. The alternatives to big action movies are low-budget action movies in other countries. Bulgaria, Indonesia. In America, nobody really does these. Nobody knows how to do it cheap. If you use SAG or whatever, suddenly, you're doing a two million dollar movie. If you do a hundred thousand dollar action movie, you might as well do it for nothing. The perception of action movies in the market is that it's gotta look big. Martial arts movies can get away with a lot more. The chop sockie theater-type look. Grindhouse-looking things. That's a recent thing. The martial arts movie is much more refined than it used to be. The audience is getting used to that.

It's like they don't even want to be called "martial arts movies" anymore.

No. It puts them in a different bucket. An exploitation bucket. The major change that's happened is that MMA has gone from 5 percent popularity to 100 percent popularity. Around the world and in the US. Every part of the population knows what MMA is. In my hometown when I was doing *Contour*, they didn't know what a roundhouse kick was. Now everybody knows. They watch MMA at the bar or at the casino, they watch it at work, or they watch it at home. We're all wearing MMA shirts of MMA schools. In my hometown!

What do you think MMA has done to promote martial arts?

First of all, MMA has primed America for the martial arts movie. Martial arts movies used to be foreign to America. They're not quite foreign anymore. They're seeing their own type of people doing martial arts on TV. They can imagine themselves throwing roundhouse kicks. The average viewer has a closer connection to martial arts than before. What they're also used to now is that MMA fights are not shot like a Van Damme movie—they're shot like a Hong Kong movie. It's a long take for five minutes from a wide angle. It's not about the feeling of the fight, it's about seeing the technique. And the character drama. The fact that people want to see moves now in a martial arts fight and they like it—that's perfect. They would eat a martial arts movie alive. All you'd need to do is to show them the character drama and give them fights you can see. That's why I did *Death Grip* the way I did.

Why don't you think more guys are shooting films the way you've just described to me how MMA fights are shot?

Interesting question. I shoot a fight scene like it's science. In the course of twelve years of doing this, we figured out what angles are good for roundhouse kicks. Which angles look best for punches. We've developed a vocabulary. The only way you can act on that is if the choreographer and the cameraman are literally talking to each other, figuring out where to put the camera, where to put the fighters. That's something you don't usually get with Hollywood shoots. There's that communication missing in those productions. Typically, in Hollywood they just shoot the full fight scene. Coverage style.

What films have you seen lately that have gotten your attention. Everyone loves *The Raid*.

Flashpoint was really interesting in terms of MMA. People are mimicking it. Donnie Yen has a special thing about him. That was a big one. I liked *Ip Man 2*. The end fight with Darren Shahlavi was great.

What do you think of Scott Adkins?

Scott Adkins. He's the world's hope. He has a vocabulary that is unparalleled. For someone of his size and his acting ability, it's incredible. I can't wait to see what he's got coming next. I really liked *Expendables 2*. It felt like the action company did a great job on it. I liked the fight with Jason Statham in the church. That was one of the best fight scenes that have been in an American movie in a long time. It was creative.

Would you be opposed to being the third guy or the fourth or fifth guy in an action movie that you're not putting together?

When I'm doing my projects, I'm obviously going to put myself in the lead. I want to push myself that way. But I would love to work on anything.

It seems like *Death Grip* should be getting you some gigs. It's a great showpiece for you.

It's getting me somewhere. It's still new. It hasn't been distributed yet. That's what we're going for. If I send people the knife fight from *Death Grip*, it's enough for them to look at me. After they see that, they want to see the movie. After they see the movie, they say, "Okay, you can make an action movie." So let's do something. I'm able now to talk to Scott Adkins, I'm able to talk to

Gary Daniels. Making the deal is another thing. But I've got my foot in the door. I'm not going about it in a conventional way. I'm not living in LA so I'm not auditioning for anything. I'm just trying to push my projects and trying to get big names attached to them. There aren't many people who can tell me what to do.

You're thirty now, right?

Yeah.

How many more years can you be someone who keeps doing this?

Fifteen.

I hope you can get to a place where you can be doing at least one movie a year.

I would love to. We've got four we're working on right now, at once. We're trying to throw them all at the wall and see which one sticks. Different budgets, different casting options. Different distribution ideas. The whole video market is in chaos. Nobody knows what the hell is going on. Should we do a two hundred thousand dollar movie? Should we do a five million dollar movie?

Is there anything else you'd like to say?

I want to say that the reason why I make these movies is for fans, for people who want to see them. I don't want to do them for myself. It is a labor of love. I love watching these movies. That's why I made *Death Grip*, and I've heard the criticism. I listen. For *Contour*, I took the criticism and made *Death Grip*. Now I'm getting new feedback, and overall the criticism has been much better. I don't get defensive about that. I need to build up my skills and make the best movie that I can. I make them for the fans, and I want to thank them.

Death Hunt

1981 (Anchor Bay DVD) (MJ)

Released in the United States in May 1981, right before the summer would begin, *Death Hunt* offered fans of action cinema the possibility of great entertainment by bringing two of the toughest men in cinema together again—Lee Marvin and Charles Bronson, two veterans of one of the greatest action films of all time, *The Dirty Dozen*. Surprisingly, the two men had not worked together since 1967 and had been busy finding success with their own careers. *Death Hunt* is a period piece, taking place in Canada, 1931, and is based on a true story, telling the fictionalized account of solitary trapper Albert Johnson (Bronson) and the greatest manhunt in Canadian history, led by Sergeant Millen (Marvin) of the Royal Canadian Mounted Police. The general public was immediately drawn to the story as it was the first time in history that airplanes were used by authorities to track down a wanted fugitive. In the film, Johnson is a trapper in the Yukon Territory, living a quiet life in the wilderness inside a log cabin he made with his own hands. Coming into town one day for a

supply run, Johnson comes across an organized dogfight. One of the dogs is badly injured and Johnson forcefully takes it away, paying the owner, Hazel (Ed Lauter), a local trapper, for his trouble. Claiming the dog was stolen from him, Hazel gathers some of his friends and follows Johnson back to his cabin, where they attack him. Defending himself, Johnson kills one of the men after they kill the dog he has been trying to nurse back to health. Hazel returns to town and reports the crime, which attracts the attention of Edgar Millen and the RCMP. Millen leads a posse to Johnson's cabin and after meeting him, begins to suspect that there is more to Hazel's story. Torn between his duty and his growing respect for Johnson, Millen must decide how to proceed with Johnson.

For younger fans of action cinema, it's difficult to imagine that action films were once made featuring leading men who did not use their hands and feet to resolve their problems. Well, occasionally, they used their hands to make fists but mostly they used guns and high explosives. These films frequently starred rugged men who actually looked like they had done some living and not men who looked like little boys who had perhaps only recently discovered the benefits of shaving. *Death Hunt* is a special film, released in the twilight years of stars Charles Bronson and Lee Marvin. These were men who were not just stars of the box office but also capable of acting and they could do their work sometimes by just standing still and letting the camera capture them. Directed by Peter Hunt, a legendary director and editor of motion pictures, *Death Hunt* was shot on location in Canmore and Drumheller in Alberta, Canada, and not on studio soundstages. This is an important detail that sets the film apart from many of its peers as the location is almost another character in the film, enhancing the performances of all the actors as the manhunt for Albert Johnson extends deeper and deeper into the Yukon Territory. While the tone of the film is a little shaky, this is a solid action film that delivers on its promise, showing two titans of the cinema together one last time before the faces of action cinema would change in the 1980s to become familiar ones like Norris, Stallone, and Schwarzenegger. Also, watch for future action star Carl Weathers in an important role in the film.

Death Journey

1976 (CD)

"I'm not gonna kill you, baby, you're too good in the sack for that. I'm just gonna bruise you up a little."

After two witnesses who were about to testify against a big-shot gang leader end up dead, two attorneys feel they need the help of one man to protect their star witness Finley (Bernard Kirby). The man for the job is one tough son of a bitch and his name is Jesse Crowder (Fred Williamson). They need him transported from

Los Angeles to New York where he can appear in court. Crowder agrees but has no idea just how difficult the job will be when there are hitmen waiting around every corner to take Finley out. Crowder is up for the challenge and nothing gets by him, not even a pretty lady. But whatever move Crowder makes, it seems someone is waiting for him. Crowder begins to suspect that someone is ratting him out, and he plans to make them pay.

Death Journey brings back the character of Jesse Crowder, which Fred Williamson (*Hammer*) first portrayed in *No Way Back* (released earlier the same year). There's no shortage of action in the film with Williamson having plenty of opportunities to show off his martial arts skills in various fights with multiple opponents. Aside from the action, he finds the time to take on multiple women as well, while leaving his shirt unbuttoned throughout the entire film. It's not a very notable film for its star but it delivers everything you would expect from him. It feels more like a low-budget rush job but with Williamson also on board as the director he's able to at least keep it together long enough to entertain with the action and some snappy dialogue.

Death List

2006 (Dragon DVD) (CD)

"You bastard! You left me for dead and you killed my master. Today, I'm gonna kill you!"

Night (Ara Paiaya) lives his life as a hitman. While on a job, he finds himself double-crossed. Left for dead and having lost his memory, he's nursed back to health and finds himself in the hands of a martial arts master. He begins to train vigorously so he can obtain the skills necessary to defeat the man responsible for trying to end his life. Night will have to do battle with disappearing ninjas and dozens of highly skilled men ready to take him out the first chance they get.

Death List has almost no production budget and it shows. What it does have is passion for the genre. Ara Paiaya (who now goes by the name Bradley Paiaya) is a major fan of martial arts cinema. It's almost impossible to decipher what is going on in the movie, but once the action starts, there's no mistaking the talent of Paiaya (also the director) who pays homage to different films, though it's clearly Jackie Chan who is his main inspiration for this stuff. There are fight scenes around a car that are pretty impressive and reminiscent of things Jackie did in films like *Police Story 2* and *Twin Dragons*. It appears as if the film has no budget but it never takes itself too seriously and is injected with a healthy dose of humor. Having handled all the major tasks on the film himself, it might be interesting to see what Paiaya could do with more experience and a bit of cash. Much later, he directed the Gary Daniels movie *Skin Traffik*.

Death Machines

1976 (Rhino DVD) (djm)

A minor theatrical grindhouse release from the mid-1970s, Paul Kyriazi's *Death Machines* is really only notable for one reason: Ron Marchini from Kyriazi's later (and better) film *Omega Cop* has a showcase role in it. Marchini—along with several other brainwashed martial artists, each with his own ethnicity—are culled from a pool of contestants to become "Death Machines" that will do the bidding of an evil mastermind. One of their first missions is to annihilate everyone at a martial arts studio, and the sole survivor of that attack is Frank (John Lowe), who has an arm chopped off in the encounter with the Death Machines. He spends time in recovery and vows vengeance against the secret club of villains, but ultimately he isn't up to par with the might of the brainwashed assassins.

Watchable only for diehard Marchini enthusiasts, I'd recommend *Death Machines* to only a sparse handful of viewers who revel in '70s kitsch and nostalgia. No disrespect to Marchini or Kyriazi, but this was a difficult movie for me to see to its conclusion. Marchini has a couple of fight scenes in the film, but I'm not sure they're worth watching in the context of the rest of the film. Stick to *Omega Cop*.

Death Match

1994 (Monarch VHS) (CD)

"And Tommy O'Brian looks right in the guy's face, and he tells him—laughing, right in his face—Stealing from me ain't nothing to lose your head over, and proceeds to decapitate the guy right there in the basement. The guy was screaming for his mother, there was blood every place. That was my grandfather. God, he was brutal, but very effective."

John Larson (Ian Jacklin) and Nick Wallace (Nick Hill) are a couple of dockworkers trying to earn a living. After a run-in with arms dealers, Larson decides to look for work elsewhere while Wallace decides to earn a quick buck working for Landis (Martin Kove) and Vanik (Matthias Hues) as a fighter in an underground circuit. Wallace doesn't realize he's expected to kill his opponent and walks out on a fight. Landis and Vanik don't take kindly to this, beating him to a pulp before they make him disappear. Larson finds out his friend is missing and heads back to the city to find him. With the help of reporter Danielle Richardson (Renee Allman), they work their way into the underground fighting circuit to find out Wallace's whereabouts—if he's even alive.

Ian Jacklin (*American Streetfighter*) isn't the strongest actor but he doesn't have a problem delivering the goods when it comes to action. *Death Match* is an underground fight film so there's plenty of action. The fight choreography is above average and exciting. Matthias Hues (*Fists of Iron*) has a couple of great fights as well, always towering over his competition. Martin Kove (*The Karate Kid*) turns in a great performance as the lead villain and has some of the best dialogue. Also in the cast are martial arts greats like Eric Lee (*Big Trouble in Little China*), Benny "The Jet" Urquidez (*Dragons Forever*) and Michelle "Mouse" Krasnoo (*Kickboxer 4*). The film was directed by Joe Coppoletta (*Walker, Texas Ranger*) who manages to keep things tight and exciting. Also of note, this was the first film composed by future two-time Academy Award nominee Marco Beltrami (*The Hurt Locker*).

The Death of Bruce Lee (a.k.a. Black Dragon's Revenge)

1975 (BCI DVD) (V)

"I'll definitely let you know who did it."

Shortly after the unexpected passing of the greatest icon in martial arts cinema, a San Francisco millionaire claiming to be a Lee family friend hires Ron "The Black Dragon" Van Clief (playing himself) to investigate what happened. He flies to Hong Kong and recruits his old 'Nam buddy (Charles "The Latin Panther" Bonet) to help out. They interview people who knew Bruce Lee and investigate different theories. For example: They beat up a guy to disprove his claim that he killed Lee with the Iron Fist. They clash with other groups of fighters who are also investigating or trying to cover up the truth, and fight a lady who uses poisonous snakes as throwing weapons. My favorite move is when a guy throws a big rock at Van Clief but he catches it and twists it in half.

It's interesting to see where blaxploitation intersects with Bruceploitation, but this is like a poor man's Jim Kelly movie. I like the outrageous '70s fashion and swagger, especially when the Black Dragon challenges the Latin Panther by pulling off his bow tie and tossing it away without looking at it. But it's an amateurishly made movie with bland locations and mostly unimaginative fights. You also have to wonder about the taste of a guy who actually knew Bruce Lee playing himself in a fictional exploitation of the legend's death. Or maybe it helped him to deal with the tragedy to find no answers and have a master teach him "you find out that the universe is true by letting things alone." This was an early film for director Lu Chin-Ku, who went on to helm Shaw Brothers favorites like *Holy Flame of the Martial World* and *Bastard Swordsman*.

Death Proof

2007 (Dimension DVD) (djm)

Stuntman Mike (Kurt Russell) is a serial killer. He scopes out groups of pretty young women and plans an elaborate vehicular homicide by way of his "death proof" stunt car that he has

136

rigged to withstand any crash. We see him vulture around a group of gorgeous (and cool) gals, and we watch as he charms (albeit with a dose of swag and creepiness) the girls, and then we witness him brutally slaying all of them in one incredible moment of smashed car-on-car carnage. Fourteen months later, we see him scoping out his next group of girls, but this time, he has no idea who he's up against. The new group includes two stuntwomen (like him, only crazier), one of who is Zoë Bell, playing "Herself." Bell, who is out on a joyride with her gal pals on a Dodge Challenger (on the hood, in fact), finds that she's on the ride of her life when Mike comes careening on the road to kill them all in one fell swoop. Bell and her friends (who include Rosario Dawson and Tracie Thoms) manage to out-muscle and out-drive Stuntman Mike and turn the tables on him, giving *him* the ride of *his* life.

Quentin Tarantino's *Death Proof* is a masterstroke of action, dialogue, and kinky horror. The first half of the film is a masterpiece all on its own, but the second half—which introduces Zoë Bell as the focal point as she's riding virtually without protection on the hood of the speeding Challenger—actually drags a bit until the spectacular car stunts get going. Bell, who had worked for Tarantino as Uma Thurman's stunt double in *Kill Bill*, is a delightful rough-cut diamond in this film. As "Herself," she's cute, fearless, and when she throws some punches and a fatal kick in the last shots of the film, we can clearly see that she was an action star in the making. Thanks to Tarantino, Bell was given her first big-screen action role (though it's small), and I'm still waiting for Hollywood to fully use her as a commodity. She would go on to star in low-budget films like *Angel of Death* and *Raze* (which also stars Tracie Thoms), but she's still sitting on the bench as far as I'm concerned. She should be starring in major action films. *Death Proof* is a great introduction to her.

INTERVIEW:
ZOË BELL
(djm)

There's a whole world of adventure bubbling up from the person that Zoë Bell is. Her life has been a travelogue of great gigs—from doubling Lucy Lawless for the stunt and martial arts scenes

Zoë Bell in San Diego, California. Photo by david j. moore.

on the long-running hit show Xena: Warrior Princess, *to doubling Uma Thurman in Quentin Tarantino's* Kill Bill—*and when Tarantino decided that she would play a lead role in* Death Proof *(essentially appearing as herself), her career trajectory took on a new direction. In just a few years, the New Zealander has found herself in a niche as a female action star, headlining the hard-hitting action and martial arts films* Angel of Death *and 2014's* Raze, *which casts her as an ex-soldier named Sabrina who is captured and forced to fight other women to the death. Her work in* Raze *will elevate audience's perception of her as an actress, but more importantly she has cemented her status as a real-deal action star, with acting chops to boot.*

What was it about *Raze* that appealed to you? Was it your character?

It was twofold, really. What appealed to me about Sabrina was that she seemed like a phenomenal character. She was fierce, an atypical woman especially for this day and age, but in an action film, she was going through a massive emotional journey as well. Her character arc was almost the most interesting thing for me. The movie's concept also appealed to me. It was something I hadn't really come across before. Also, it happened after I was on the project, so I'm finding this hard to answer. I came on the project and I was going to play a cameo role in the short film, but they were bringing me on as a producer because it had female action in it and they wanted to use my expertise, if I may talk about myself in such a manner. Once I came on board and once we were all in place and shooting the short, that's when the story started to unfold and that's when the feature started to unfold and come about. It essentially came about through my . . . through this character Sabrina, who I had created for the short. It all happened in kind of a reverse order. I can't really say that the character of Sabrina "drew" me to the project because she kind of developed once we had already started, if you know what I mean. I'm sorry, that's probably really complicatedly worded.

Teaser poster for *Raze*. Author's collection.

Forced to fight, Sabrina (Zoë Bell) is a force to be reckoned with in *Raze*. Author's collection.

No, I understand exactly what you're saying. I sat there and watched *Raze* and was surprised to see that it combined the 1990s kickboxing tournament movie with the dungeon-set *Hostel/Saw* type of movie. It wasn't at all what I was thinking it would be. You're obviously from the world of action, but you had to step into this deep, dark place. Talk about that transition for you.

Like I said before, I'd done quite a bit of work on Sabrina as she wasn't fully fleshed out when we started, so I had to explain to myself just how dark her past had been, which was not daunting so much as it was liberating. I had created this whole world of her past. It really was useful to me. In the short film, there was really only one fight, but I knew exactly why she was there, I knew exactly how she felt about it, I knew exactly why she wanted to get out, I knew exactly why she was trying to fight. When it was turned into a feature, I was really equipped. Once I read the feature script, I went, "*Holy shit!* This is going to be massive for me." Challenging for me as an actor, but personally for me to go into the places . . . that's the thing that makes our movie largely different. It's that so much of the story and so much of the movie is about the emotional truth and the emotional journey these women are going through. Which makes it that much more horrific. The absolute *anguish*, the absolute *horror* that these women are going through. Knowing that, it was definitely like *I'm going to have to find a lot of dark places and I'm going to have to spend a lot of time there*. As the lead, I think I had two days off from the whole film. I was the producer anyway, but as an actor there were only two days where I wasn't on the call sheet. I was definitely prepped for it to be intense and exhausting. It's absolutely those things, but it was also incredibly satisfying even though I was getting home at midnight and having to get up again at four in the morning. I was waking up in the morning fired up. I was so enjoying myself. There was a sense of purpose. It was an exhausting process, but ultimately it was so fulfilling both as a producer and as an actress.

I've seen the other films where you were the star or the lead, and I'm absolutely bewildered why you haven't been given the opportunity to star in more films . . .

(Laughing.) Bewildered. That's a good word.

No, really. It's amazing that you haven't been given the opportunity to star in more movies. I'm thinking, of course, of *Death Proof* and *Angel of Death*, which I thought was a really cool little movie.

Yeah, thanks.

Raze is only the third time where you're front and center. I kind of want to know what this means for you as an actress, and how you've been able to grow not just as an action star but as an actress as well.

Thank you. I love you. You're asking me very real, serious questions that make me feel like I'm being taken very seriously. I appreciate it. I recently looked at my showreel and I was like, "Oh my God, I've done a lot of work!" and that was quite satisfying, but also watching the progression—and it's clear to me just watching it—that these steps that happen and these experiences you have as an actor that teach you—like fundamentally change you—like something *clicks*, and *Raze* was absolutely a moment like that. So was *Angel of Death*. It's funny. You're right. These three movies are where the most fundamental changes have happened. I think it's because when you're carrying a movie, there's a massive—there's much more responsibility. At least that's how it's translated in my head. When you're carrying the film, that's a big deal beyond just having or doing a good performance. This is cool. You're right. I hadn't thought of this before. *Death Proof* was obviously the first one. *Angel of Death* was the second time I was the lead of a film, but it was the first time I was really carrying the whole thing. In *Death Proof* I was one of . . . you know . . . the key cast. *Angel of Death*, I just remember realizing how much preparation was going to be of service to me, and just preparing *the shit* out of it. I made the same decision with *Raze*. I want to be better in this movie than I was in the last movie. Everybody's always wanted to be in a movie and act, and I get this opportunity and so I wanted to work my hardest and I wanted to *at least* improve or *at least* find some other depths that I couldn't access before. And I don't just mean like *In this one I need to cry more!* (Laughing.) I needed to find a level of truth to that character. I, honestly . . . the difference I feel the most is that I have conquered the ability to do my job, so I'm not scared as much as I am anxious in anticipation for knowing or trusting that I can commit 100 percent to this process. *Am I capable of this process* is now *Show me what you got, boy!* It's a different kind of enjoyment, I guess.

I'd like to talk a little bit about the action star concept itself. There was a time when people like Cynthia Rothrock, Karen Sheperd, and Mimi Lesseos built careers making action movies . . . there's just so few of you guys out there. What do you think happened? There're so few female action stars to begin with, but now it seems like there's even fewer. When you get a chance to do one, it's like one every couple of years rather than two or three a year. What's up with that?

You know, you could theorize all day long about it. The natural progression of the nature of this business. The female action thing is sort of a weird one. I think I have a slightly skewed vision of it too because for the first four years of my career I was doubling Lucy [Lawless] on *Xena* every day. I was doing female action every day. Every week there was always at least one other female character that was kicking ass, so it was the opposite of what was going on in the industry. It didn't occur to me because there was work for *me*. I don't know. There was a period of time when it seemed sort of cool when there was that phase—that girl power phase—when *Charlie's Angels* got reinvented . . . that kind of stuff . . . it was like it was being treated as a fad. It was like bellbottoms instead of denim. I feel like there's a possibility now—*right now*—that there could be a movement that has some real staying power when we put some people in there—like myself—or Gina Carano or Ronda Rousey—actually casting these women who are known by audiences to be capable of fighting. The concept of why these women are worthy of putting in a movie is because *they can fight*. To me, that feels like there's a little more weight in it and a little less about chicks looking hot while they're kicking ass. Not that these women aren't hot, but it's about the coolness of knowing that these women can kick your ass. It's really like what the male action stars from way back when—the man could feel it that *he could do it* because he's doing it. Like the *Die Hard*s and the *Lethal Weapon*s—these weren't comic book heroes, these are your everyday guys who could kick ass. That's something I like about *Raze* is that these are everyday women in a situation that forces them to find death within themselves instead of *I've been training in martial arts my whole life* . . . you know. That's one of the things we wanted to do differently.

Who do you think Raze is for? It's a difficult movie to watch. It's not an expected film in any way. Even the ending is polarizing. What do you think?

Ummm . . . it is a movie between expectations. It's an interesting place to fit. That's what we were going for. So, yeah. It can come as a disadvantage if someone is trying to put the movie somewhere. We've had people on both sides. *Oh my God, I just couldn't find a way to connect* and then there are the ones who say *Oh my God, I've never seen a movie where I was so engaged.* Some people love the end, and some people hate the end. It just polarizes. I've never heard someone say that if it was on a plane that they'd watch it again. The ending . . . the boys were all in cahoots about the ending. My memory was that there was a lot of back and forth about it. My concern was that it needed to be paid off, but you also don't want it to be clichéd. You don't want to disappoint your audience either way. It's one thing to shock them and making them feel bad, but disappointing them . . . That's not really where you want to go. The boys all wanted it to end the way it did. Clearly, I agreed with them.

Do you regret the decision now?

DVD release artwork of *Angel of Death*. Author's collection.

I got to a place with the movie with the limitations of money and time . . . I'm so proud of the movie we have. I don't have a regret.

I wanted to talk about Angel of Death a little bit. It's the sort of movie that really doesn't get made anymore.

I had an absolute blast shooting that movie. I worked with really lovely people. Ed Brubaker just loves to write this kind of story, and he does it so well. It was so fun and collaborative. John Norris, the producer, was the most generous producer on the planet. Just a great team. It was just kind of *cool*. It wasn't trying to be anything other than it was. It was an ambitious shoot. Ron Yuan, the stunt and fight coordinator, knows exactly what he's doing so it was superefficient. I had a real blast. It was the first time I dived into a character that wasn't myself. In *Death Proof* I was clearly playing a Quentin-ized version of myself, which is . . . not me. I don't chase men down and beat them to death. But Eve [in *Angel of Death*] was a character that was not silly. She didn't grow up with my life, and so I really enjoyed that. I remember writing her backstory, and I wrote it in the first person, "My name is Eve . . . " and she started talking about it. It was an experience where I felt like I *got it*. That's so fun, that part of acting, the make-believe.

What sorts of martial arts do you practice, or do you know?

I am the perfect example of being the offspring of stunt fighting. I started with taekwondo—that was my first introduction into the martial arts. That's my foundation. I did it for about two and half or three years before starting on *Xena*, so that's where I learned kicks and where I learned punches. As a stunt person, a) you have to mimic different styles, and b) you have to mimic certain actors and their personal styles and the way that they swing. So I basically, I've gotten to the point—the most concise I can say—I am a martial arts mimic. I've done loads of martial arts. I've done Krav Maga . . . I've done just about all of them, and anytime I work with someone who has one that I've not played with before, I'll play around with it. But I've never studied. I just don't have the space because my job takes up . . . you know what I mean? My job is to be able to mimic them as best I can. I fake it for a living, basically. (Laughing.)

You could have fooled me, man. I thought you were some kind of martial arts master.

That's my job. Listen, when I'm training in these things, I'm training for real. I'm training with people, I'm in a ring, but I would feel dishonest if I said that I've studied taekwondo for years and that I have a blah blah belt in aikido. Because I haven't. I've practiced all of them, and I love them all.

You worked with Gary Daniels on *Game of Death*. Do you have any memories of working with Daniels, who is very much a martial artist?

Oh, yeah! He's such a sweetheart. We enjoyed having each other to chat with in trailer times. He's the quintessential action star hero guy. I really enjoyed listening to him talk about his career, his life in Asia. We never got to fight, which was always sort of a bummer. I would love to do a movie opposite him. It's so fun to watch an actor approach action in the same way that I do. He is a fighter, he does do that, and that's where he's from. He can hit the ground in the middle of a fight and keep going without it freaking him out. That's just what he does.

Your role in that movie was relegated to a bit part. I really wanted to see you fight Wesley Snipes, or something, you know what I mean?

Yeah, me too! There were scheduling problems on that movie. Most of that movie ended up being shot in a very short amount of time. There was meant to be a fight in there, and I wasn't meant to die so quickly. I was like, "We can shoot a fight in like a half an hour!"

***Death Proof* is the movie you're really known for. It put you on the map as far as putting you in front of the camera front and center. Any comments about working with Tarantino, working on this movie, and how it propelled you on a different career path?**

Well, yes, of course. I worked on the *Kill Bill* movies, and this was his little brainchild that I knew very little about until the script was finalized. It came as a shock to me. He talked about me working on the movie, but I really had no concept as to the capacity. I had never talked to him about wanting to be an actor, so it wasn't even on my radar that it was something he was considering. When a) my friend Quentin asks something like that of me, there's no way I'm going to say no, and b) when Tarantino wants you to play a character in his movie, there's no world where you'd *want* to say no. Having said that, I was terrified going into it. I was very conscious of how green I was as an actor. I'd never done it before. I was also very conscious that if Quentin had made that decision, then it was something he wanted and that he knew better than I did. Working with Quentin . . . I had already greased my working

relationship with him, and we were on the same page, had the same on-set language. We'd worked with each other long enough that that was already in place, which was a very comforting thought. He's such an actor's director. So much of my experience—knowing what I know now—at the time I knew nothing. He said to me, "Don't take acting classes—Just learn the script inside out, 'cause I know what I want to get from you and I know you have it." So I was like putty in his hands on that movie. I did everything he told me to do because I didn't know what I was doing. So much fun. He's such a conscientious director. In terms of casting, he was conscious of what would be best for the movie, which means what would be best to support *me* and what kind of people he would surround me with as well as what characters. He considered all of it, which was good because I wasn't considering. *Death Proof* definitely put me in a different direction because it didn't just put me on the map as an actor, but in my head it put in the possibility of me being an actor. It put it in the forefront for me to the point of considering it. Deciding that I should get representation, not really understanding what that means. I'm pretty sure I would never have started a career in acting if it weren't for *Death Proof*. Pretty sure I wouldn't have. It's taken me a while to wrap my head around it. I think I'm getting there now. Having someone like Quentin get behind you and say, "I think you should consider *this* . . . ." Holy mackerel! I should definitely consider that! Yeah. I certainly wouldn't be where I am if it hadn't been for Quentin.

Just say something about . . . I don't know what you can say because I don't even know how to ask . . . but that stuff where you're on the hood of the car . . . that's so crazy. It's like watching *Star Wars*. It's like, *How did they do that*?

(Laughing.) Um . . . yeah. Quentin and I have discussed how much I'm allowed to say. When it first happened, people were posting stuff online where they were doing Ship's Mast . . . I was like, "Oh my God, people are going to die." My compromise in saying how we did it is by saying that there was a safety. There was a safety for performance reasons, but what enabled us to make it so terrifying was that I was safe to throw myself around the car because I had a safety in place. The camera could get in close, the camera guy could come in while we were doing all the craziness. We could all push limits because we had the safety in place. If the safety hadn't been in place, that sequence would be so much more boring. I wouldn't be able to move without the fear of actually coming off at any given minute. And it enabled us to go at speeds that it feels like we're going. We're not faking it. It was *awesome!*

I'm happy with that. That's a satisfactory answer. Do you want to say anything else about *Raze* and how you're hoping it will perform when it comes out?

Of course, as a producer, I want everybody to see it and I want everyone to love it, I want to make heaps of money, and as an actor I want it to be supersuccessful so that everyone puts me in heaps more action movies . . . that's my ultimate hope. But, it's definitely a very specific movie. I

know there's an audience out there for it. We've already found some of them. I just want to give it to those who will appreciate it the most because those who appreciate it really get a kick out of it. I hope it makes people think a little bit. There are fights in it that you've not seen before. I just hope it has an effect on people. The word "hope" feels so sort of hopeless. When I say "hope" it sounds sort of weak. I look *forward* to it having an effect on people. As you make the point—at your "bewilderment"—that this movie could reach the right people and give them the faith that I can carry a movie . . . I would love that.

I consider you an action star. I don't know if you consider yourself an action star or an actor or what, but you can answer that within this question . . . but I know that you have fans out there and I'm one of them. Is there anything you want to say to those who look up to you or consider you a role model? To your fans: Is there anything you want to say to them?

Yeah, truthful: Thank you. A lot of the fans I've had have been around since before *Death Proof*. The *Xena* days. There's a documentary called *Double Dare* that a lot of people watched and were affected by. I think the thing that makes . . . it's so weird to for me to even say the term "my fans" . . . my *support group* (laughing) . . . they seem to be fans of what I represent more than me being famous in any way, which is what means the most to me. People say the sort of things like, "You make me want to be a better woman," or "I'm glad my daughter has a role model like you." Those have really hit home. It makes me want to continue doing what I can because to be that to people . . . I try and I hope that me staying as true to being myself as possible can be a part of that so that my need to be something for other people doesn't start feeding into some form of dishonesty. I've tried putting this in words before, and I always seem to stumble around it. It sounds kind of cheesy to say thank you to your fans, but I really mean thank you for being the *kind of* fans you are and for being fans of what you are fans of as opposed to being fans of me because I've worked with Quentin or because I'm on a screen somewhere. You make me proud to be the person I am, you know? Yeah.

Death Race
2008 (Universal DVD) (CD)

Jensen Ames (Jason Statham) is framed for murdering his wife and ends up in a maximum-security prison. Warden Hennessy (Joan Allen) has masterminded a televised car race within the prison walls that includes spruced-up vehicles equipped with weapons that inmate contestants can unleash on each other, with a full pardon as the ultimate prize. When Ames tires of Hennessey's game, he plots with his fellow inmates to escape and bring her down.

The only thing that really saves *Death Race* from being a complete mess is the stellar casting. With a film like this, you don't need a complex plot to take away from the action, which is predominantly in the form of loud, weapon-equipped vehicles trying to rip each other to shreds. There are some decent race sequences and the inventive design of the cars makes for some solid eye-candy. It's surprising to see how seriously the cast takes the dumb script. Make no mistake, this is a forty-five million–dollar "B" movie with respectable talent hamming it up on screen. In the lead role, Statham scales back his *Transporter*-style persona, and the two actual fight scenes in the film are pretty weak, considering his capabilities. The highlight of the film is Joan (*Face/Off*) Allen as the evil warden who is the mastermind behind the race. Her demeanor is perfectly sinister while she still tries to be the consummate professional. When she finally snaps, we are treated to some of the best dialogue in the film. Ian McShane (*Pirates of the Caribbean: On Stranger Tides*), Tyrese Gibson (*Fast Five*), Robin Shou (*Mortal Kombat*), and Natalie Martinez (*The Baytown Outlaws*) all elevate the material they're given. *Death Race* is all flash and no substance. Paul W. S. Anderson (*Mortal Kombat*) writes and directs to the best of his ability but the film never feels like anything more than random scenes from a video game. This was a very loose remake of the Roger Corman- produced and Paul Bartel-directed *Death Race 2000* from 1975.

Death Riders (a.k.a. True Justice: Brotherhood)

2011 (Studiocanal DVD R2) (djm)

Seattle's best task force is on the Yakuza's ass when a downtown nightclub hosts some syndicate meetings, and Elijah Kane (Steven Seagal) and his team come in and bust things up. The Yakuza (with members played by Hiro Kanagawa and Byron Lawson) underestimate Kane, and they cast their net far and wide to see who Kane is and where he came from. He's unlike anything they've ever encountered before, and when forced to fight, Kane invariably lays his foes down in furious bouts that result in neck breaking and ass whuppings. One scene has a Yakuza guy wielding a samurai sword, and Kane uses just his hands and aikido skills to get the better of the guy. Meanwhile, Kane gets sidetracked when everyone inside a bank is held hostage by a desperate gunman, whose house was just foreclosed on. Kane walks in the bank and is yelled at by the gunman, who points an automatic weapon at him. Kane simply has a calm, rational conversation with the man, who eventually lowers his gun and relents to Kane's good sense. It's a pretty great scene.

Death Riders (terrible title that has nothing to do with the movie) is the fifth compilation of episodes of Seagal's TV series *True Justice*. It bears the mark (as the other collections do) of being spliced together, which makes it confusing at times, but this one had some of the better moments of the entire series. It's worth checking out even out of context from the series. Seagal wrote it, and Wayne Rose (who did thirteen episodes of the series) directed. *Urban Warfare* is next.

Death Ring

1993 (New Line VHS) (djm)

When ex-special forces commando Matt Collins (Mike Norris) wins a grueling televised survival competition, an eccentric billionaire named Danton Vachs (Billy Drago) takes notice and has him and his fiancée kidnapped and brought to his remote compound in the wilderness. Vachs stages a "Most Dangerous Game" hunt once in a while, where high-paying clients gather to hunt down and kill a man. They all assume that Collins will be a pushover, but when the hunt begins, Collins turns the table on them all by hunting and killing *them* one by one. Towards the end of the game, Collins teams up with a former survivor of the game (played by Don Swayze), and together they topple Vachs's little empire. A big rescue by Collins's war buddy (played by Chad McQueen) is undermined by Collins's ability to bring down the house in his own way.

A somewhat clever concept to make a movie starring relatives of better-known stars, *Death Ring* might have been a promising vehicle for Norris (whose previous films *Born American* and *Survival Game* underwhelmed), but unfortunately, the movie relies too much on build-up and dialogue to be the action-packed adventure it ought to be. Drago is appropriately slimy as usual, but Swayze and McQueen don't really add much. Branscombe Richmond and George Cheung also appear. Norris contributed to the story. Other action star movies in the same vein are *No Contest* with Jeff Wincott, *Final Round* with Lorenzo Lamas, and *Hard Target* with Jean-Claude Van Damme. Directed by R. J. Kitzer, who co-directed *Hell Comes to Frogtown*.

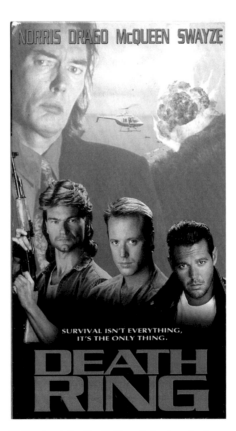

VHS artwork for *Death Ring*. Author's collection.

Death Train

2003 (Velocity DVD) (CD)

"So, we have a hero on the train. Who is it? Can anybody tell me anything about who he is? Is he . . . is he a porter, is he a bartender, is he a happy passenger on his way to fucking Seaworld?"

Ryan (Bryan Genesse) and his security team are hired to protect millions in diamonds being transported on a train. A group of criminals makes their way on board and await their opportunity to strike—and their plan goes off without a hitch. Weaver (Bentley Mitchum from *Delta Force One: The Lost Patrol*) and his team of criminals to escape with the riches. The train is derailed and the only survivor is Ryan, who only has one thing on his mind . . . revenge. He quickly sets out to find Weaver and captures him with the help of a friend on the Mexican police force. The only problem is that he'll have to be transported back to the United States by train. Weaver is a resourceful bastard and manages to escape. He and his crew take the passengers on the train hostage, giving Ryan an opportunity to put these criminals down for good.

Production house Nu Image has put out some fantastic action films, and even though Bryan Genesse (*Cold Harvest*), one of their in-house stars, is great, even he can't seem to save this train wreck. Actually, the story and action are pretty solid for a film of this budget, but the film's weaknesses are far more noticeable than they should be. Genesse has some decent one-liners, goes through plenty of ammo, and gets to fight a bit. He does everything right, so maybe director Yossi Wein (*Merchant of Death*) didn't have all the resources he needed to make a completely satisfying film. They did the best they could with what they had and delivered a mediocre action picture. Not a career highlight for Genesse.

Death Train

2006 (Image DVD) (CD)

"I'm sorry to inform you but you are all my prisoners."

Sandra (Bettina Lamprecht) is a single mother trying her best to get an operation for her son Joey (Joey Stetz) who has a rare blood disease. Their insurance won't cover the costs, and she needs to come up with 100,000 euros to save his life. A church offers the two of them a chance to travel by train with other pilgrims to Lourdes, where the Pope will be making an appearance. But a group of terrorists, led by Lennart (Arnold Vosloo), break into a facility and steal a virus that can wipe out thousands. They're disguised as monks and get on the same train, which also has real monks on it too. A couple of those monks are traveling with a young protégé Lasko (Mathis Landwehr), a former soldier who is still haunted by those days of fighting. The senior monks know what they must do since they belong to a secret sect of the church that isn't afraid to fight in the name of the Lord. When one of the monks gets killed, the others recruit Lasko to join their ranks. If he is to save the day, he will have to fight. With all the lives of everyone on the train at stake, he has to decide fast or risk losing them all.

Death Train (aka *Im Auftrag des Vatikans*) was a made-for-German-television pilot starring action star potential Landwehr (*Kampfansage*). The film is big for what it is, with some very impressive set pieces. It was an obvious set-up for a television series that ran for two seasons in Germany. Mathis plays Lasko with a bit of reserve. For most of the film he holds back and there is very little fighting until the end of the second act, which isn't to say that this is a boring movie. We learn about Lasko's past and why he has become a monk and sworn off violence. When the time comes, he doesn't hold back, becoming "The Fist of God." Mathis is without question a star on the rise. He has all the qualifications you could ask for and he is just waiting to be discovered by the world. He gets to show off his fighting abilities as well as his acting chops. It's also a treat to have Vosloo (*Hard Target*) as the lead villain. The story may be silly and familiar, but it's a fun concept that's highly enjoyable. Director Diethard Kuster knows how to work an action crowd, keeping the audience at bay for a while before unleashing the goods. This is a really solid vehicle for Landwehr and a high mark for German television.

Death Warrant
1990 (MGM DVD) (djm)

An undercover French Canadian cop named Louis Burke (Jean-Claude Van Damme, slightly miscast) goes after the psycho killer known as The Sandman (Patrick Kilpatrick from *Under Siege 2: Dark Territory*) because he killed his partner. When he's done what he set out to do, Burke is asked to go undercover at a hellhole penitentiary where inmates are "disappearing." Set up with a bogus backstory and a new identity, Burke becomes an inmate at the prison, where of course he's immediately attacked, tortured, and picked on for wanting to make friends with a black inmate (played by Robert Guillaume). Being a proficient martial artist and a silent-type badass, Burke makes plenty of enemies, but in the meantime his investigation leads him to a discovery that the warden and his guards are running an illegal organ donor transplant scheme, using the inmates as the "donors." Burke, who has a very rare blood type, is the next "donor" on the list if he doesn't solve his predicament in time. A wrench is thrown in his plans when The Sandman—who is basically an unmasked Michael Myers or Jason Voorhees because he simply won't die—is brought into the prison as a prisoner and immediately sets his sights on brutalizing and humiliating Burke.

Van Damme's second studio film in the same year (the other one was *Lionheart* for Universal), *Death Warrant* feels completely familiar, but obvious studio tampering and trimming truncate what might have been a slightly more interesting film. Van Damme, who looks great in the movie, has a hard time delivering his dialogue, and his understated performance is so subtle that you wonder how he was directed. Director Deran Sarafian (*Gunmen, Terminal Velocity*) doesn't really go for much other than in-your-face outrageousness and ultra slick gloss. Not one of my favorite Van Damme movies, *Death Warrant* still has its fans and followers. Watch for veteran stuntman Al Leong in one scene. Written by David S. Goyer, who also wrote *Kickboxer 2* and the *Blade* movies. Mark DiSalle (*Kickboxer, The Perfect Weapon*) produced it.

Death Warrior
2009 (Lionsgate DVD) (CD)

"If I didn't love you so much, I wouldn't have a reason to keep on fighting."

MMA champion Reinero (Hector Echavarria) is on the verge of ending his career—just a couple more fights and it's over. He has one last battle in store with his old pal Wolf (Quinton "Rampage" Jackson), which will make them both loads of cash. Someone has a different idea and each of these men is suddenly forced to fight in an underground fighting circuit. Only one of them will get out alive: All of the top fighters are being forced to fight, pitting friend against friend. The villain gives fighters an incentive to stay in the circuit, and in Reinero's case, they have his wife. She is injected with a poisonous serum and given only days to live. The bad guys have an antidote but Reinero will have to survive the brutal matches if he wants to save her life. It's easy to satisfy a market if you know what your audience craves. If it's sex and violence, then the output from Tapout Films is the perfect remedy for a boring evening. These films have a pattern: fight, dialogue, nudity, then more fights. *Death Warrior* is competently shot with some decent performances from the supporting actors. The star of these films is the fighting itself, and there's plenty of it. Hector has the goods to be a solid action star, but he just needs to move one step above these films. During the action scenes, he looks fantastic and really shows his talent. Other fighters featured in this film are Keith Jardine (*Recoil*), Quinton "Rampage" Jackson (*The A-Team*), George "Rush" St. Pierre, and Rashad Evans (*Locked Down*). The film was directed by Bill Corcoran (*Street Justice*) from a screenplay by Echavarria and Eamon Glennon. This is a decent flick but will probably go down best with beers and bros.

Death Wish
1974 (Paramount DVD) (djm)

"I mean, if we're not pioneers, what have we become? What do you call people who, when they're faced with a condition of fear, do nothing about it—they just run and hide?"

Charles Bronson was in his early fifties when he starred in Michael Winner's *Death Wish*, from the novel by Brian Garfield. It made Bronson a bona fide movie star—better late than never. He plays Paul Kersey, a New York architect who is at work when his wife and daughter are brutally assaulted at home. His wife is killed and his daughter is left for dead after being raped. When Kersey talks to the police, they tell him there's nothing they can do—they have no leads and no description of the attackers. His daughter has been rendered catatonic, and her son-in-law (a businessman) has no clue how to deal with their situation. Kersey, a vet from the Korean War, but a conscientious objector, re-evaluates his stance on violence and gets himself a handgun. He goes out at night, finds trouble, and shoots muggers dead on the spot. He does this several nights running, and the New York police department begins spinning a story to the press that the streets have a dangerous vigilante on the loose. Crime goes down. The cops don't want to apprehend him because he's doing their job for them. The brass on top wants the vigilante to relocate, but only because they don't want the heat if they kill him. So Kersey pretty much has a free rein until he gets caught. At the end, he is in another city, seriously considering continuing his brand of justice.

Before Golan/Globus began pressing sequel sausages from their Cannon factory, there was this sincere and thought-provoking feature. It raises questions, it challenges the viewer to consider Kersey's plight, and it kicks ass. Bronson is great in it. When he loses everything, he tries to move on, and gets angry when someone checks him on it. As far as Bronson movies go, it is one of the best, and in a way, it pigeonholed him into making more movies that were just like it. This was the movie where Bronson became typecast from here on out. Most of the movies he did after this (even up

A thug thinks he can get the better of Paul Kersey (Charles Bronson) in *Death Wish*. Author's collection.

to his later years) were similarly themed, and it created a subgenre of vigilante action films. The *Death Wish* sequels have entertainment value, but don't hold a candle to the first one. Part 2 was released eight years later. Vincent Gardenia plays the detective on his trail. The Kevin Bacon film *Death Sentence* was based on the same book.

D

Death Wish II

1982 (MGM DVD) (djm)

"You know what we've got here, don't you? A goddamn vigilante!"

Architect Paul Kersey (Charles Bronson) has relocated to Los Angeles, and he has his traumatized daughter (who was raped in the first film) in a psychiatric hospital, where she is making slow progress back to a semblance of normalcy. While out on a field trip to the park with her and his new lady friend (played by Jill Ireland, Bronson's wife), he attracts undue attention from a pack of multiracial hoodlums. They steal his wallet and they go to his house before he arrives, where they rape and murder his housekeeper, club him unconscious, and kidnap his daughter. When he comes to, he calls the police, who assure him that they'll do everything they can to locate his daughter, but he knows that the only way he's going to get results is to go after the thugs himself. When his daughter is found raped and killed, he locks himself into a sociopathic mindset where he basically lives and breathes the streets of skid row until he lasers in on the skuzz who have brought out the dormant killer within him.

Calling this a retread won't help even if it is one. *Death Wish II* is the first crank in the machine that Bronson allowed himself to become when The Cannon Group (Menahem Golan and Yoram Globus) signed him to a multipicture deal. Bronson became as much an action star in the 1980s as Stallone, Chuck Norris, or Schwarzenegger. Every movie he did throughout the 1980s featured him holding guns on the poster, and while *Death Wish II* and its successive sequels were basically remakes of each other, they really made an icon out of Bronson/Kersey in that he literally didn't have to say anything while on screen to get the point across that if you wronged him or society in any way, he would blow your brains out. They each have merit and plenty of moments to savor, but with this first sequel, it becomes immediately obvious that this is a film for capital, with little regard as to what was becoming of Bronson's character. His career, however, was in full swing. Vincent Gardenia (from the first film) and Laurence Fishburne co-star. Director Michael Winner would return for Part 3.

Charles Bronson as Paul Kersey in *Death Wish 3*. Author's collection.

Death Wish 3

1985 (MGM DVD) (djm)

Bennett: "What are you doing?"
Kersey: "Thinning the herd."

Paul Kersey (Charles Bronson), best known as "The Vigilante" throughout several densely populated cities across the United States, makes his way to New York to visit a friend in need. The very afternoon he arrives in his friend's dilapidated neighborhood, hoodlums who have overrun the block and daily terrorize, pillage, and vandalize the apartment complex where his buddy lives kill his friend and make off with whatever meager valuables he owned. Kersey is accosted by the police and brought downtown and questioned over the killing of his friend, and as soon as the cops realize that he's the infamous

Ed Lauter as Richard Shriker and Charles Bronson as Paul Kersey in *Death Wish 3*. Author's collection.

Paul Kersey (Charles Bronson, left) is the neighborhood vigilante in Michael Winner's *Death Wish 3*. Author's collection.

In the shadows and in the alleyways lies vigilante Paul Kersey (Charles Bronson) in *Death Wish 3*. Author's collection.

"Vigilante," the top cop—Striker (Ed Lauter)—vows to keep an eye on him and throw the book at him if he's caught doing what he's famous for. He tells him, "Mr. Vigilante! Last damn thing I need is a vigilante! Dude, you're in big trouble!" Instead of going back home, Kersey hunkers down in the apartment complex, befriending Bennett (Martin Balsam) and other benevolent tenants in the building who need his help, and he wages war with the gangs who have brought the neighborhood down to apocalyptic standards.

A wild and crazy attitude settles in early on in *Death Wish 3* that gives it an outrageous afterglow, and it's difficult to take any of it seriously, but it's the perfect sequel to *Death Wish 2*. Gavin O'Herlihy (from *Willow* and *Never Say Never Again*) plays the creepy leader of the multiracial gang who becomes the focus of Kersey's rage. Some of the best parts in this movie are the most ridiculous ones. The finale is about as insane as anything Cannon produced during the era—in the same league as some of the stuff that goes on in *Invasion U.S.A.* Bronson purists may not like the *Death Wish* sequels, but fans of action movies won't be disappointed. Directed by Michael Winner (*Death Wish 1-2*, *The Stone Killer*).

Death Wish 4: The Crackdown

1987 (MGM DVD) (djm)

Thug: "Who the fuck are you?"
Kersey: "Death."

Career vigilante and borderline sociopath Paul Kersey (Charles Bronson) has relocated to Los Angeles with an architectural firm, and he's been dating again. His girlfriend of two years (played by Kay Lenz) is a ballsy journalist with a pretty teen daughter. Dodging commitment, Kersey is, however, still willing to keep an eye on his girlfriend's daughter who is dating a punk who smokes weed and has a general lack of respect for the niceties of dating a pretty girl he obviously doesn't deserve. One night, the girl goes out and takes some cocaine she's offered and she overdoses and dies. Kersey, sensing that her jackass boyfriend had something to do with it, goes out and hunts him, not realizing that the kid actually cared for the girl and that his loose ties to a street gang played a much bigger part in the girl's death. Kersey shoots down the thug who was directly responsible for the girl's overdose, and the next day he receives a weird note in the mail implying blackmail. When a prominent gentleman in society named Nathan White (John P. Ryan from *Avenging Force*) comes forward to Kersey with a threat to kill the scum of society or else, Kersey is sort of attracted to the idea despite the fact that he's being blackmailed to do it. Provided with all the resources and information he would need to carry on a midnight rampage night after night, Kersey uncovers a conspiracy: Dirty cops—including the bogus "Nathan White"—are setting him up to kill all the rival gangs in the area so that they can secretly run drugs and make a few million on the side. Unwilling to be their pawn or their scapegoat, Kersey goes after the cops and kills them all, turning himself into a "most wanted" criminal.

Much slicker than the previous two entries, *The Crackdown* is almost machine-like in its efficiency, but as much as it achieves its objective, it is a soulless, heartless monstrosity of such proportions that there's really very little humanity left of its central character. Bronson, who looks great and still pounces and sprints when he's required to in the film, displays a lack of interest and his character, who had grace and panache in the first film, is devoid of any traits that resemble a dimensional creation. The first scene involves him having a nightmare where he declares himself "Death," which is interesting in retrospect, but the episode of his life chronicled in this film is pretty depressing considering every living soul he's ever cared about has been stripped away from him in the cruelest fashion. As an action entertainment, it certainly has its merits, and if you're a fan of Bronson's Cannon years and of mechanical vigilantism on film, then there's no reason why you won't enjoy it on at least a base level. Watch for character actor/action star Danny Trejo in one scene. J. Lee Thompson (*10 to Midnight*, *Messenger of Death* with Bronson) directed.

Death Wish V: The Face of Death

1993 (Final Cut Entertainment DVD) (djm)

Cop: "You're not thinking of going back to your old ways, are ya?"
Kersey: "Is that such a bad thing?"

After murdering dozens of street thugs and hoodlums over his lifetime, Paul Kersey (Charles Bronson looking pretty tired) has tried a final time to live a normal life and settle with a woman, this time a socialite named Olivia (Lesley-Anne Down), who had once been the mistress of a mobster named Tommy O'Shea (Michael Parks from *The Hitman*), and they've had a daughter together who, now as a preteen, lives with her. O'Shea becomes determined to take the girl away from Olivia, and he hires goons to menace her. After her face is maimed, Kersey goes after the guys responsible, but that only infuriates O'Shea further, and so he has Olivia murdered. Kersey, with a hardened heart and a broken soul, hits the street, but his focus is only on the mafia this time, and he goes after the killers one by one, working his way to O'Shea, whom he eventually dunks in a vat of acid.

Trite subject matter aside, *Death Wish V* is the nadir of Bronson's career. Blatantly extreme and outrageous for the sake of being so, it drags Kersey through the mud *again*, and I don't know why any audience would want to put themselves through that kind of punishment. Fans of Bronson should shrink back from seeing him go through the motions yet again, and it's sad to think that his career path led him down this dark, cold alley so close to his retirement. Bronson's heart clearly wasn't in it, and the story is just terrible. Too bad. From Menahem Golan's 21st Century Film Corporation, which was an offshoot of Cannon. Directed by Allan A. Goldstein.

The Defender (a.k.a. The Bodyguard from Beijing)

1994 (Dimension DVD) (CD)

"The most important duty is being an effective bodyguard for the Nan Hai government headquarters. Our duty is to protect the lives of our clients. I may die, but I mustn't make any mistakes."

Allan (Jet Li) is part of an elite group of bodyguards trained by the Chinese government to do whatever they must in order to keep their assignment alive. A businessman hires him to protect his girlfriend Michelle (Christy Chung) who was a witness to a murder and is about to testify. She isn't too thrilled with having him watch everything she does and isn't afraid to let him know it. Allan just goes about his business and does his job, never making any mistakes. Once the attacks on her life start rolling in, they begin to bond in a way they had never expected. During an attack at the mall, Allan kills a hired gun who was impersonating a guard. The man's brother, Wong (Collin Chou), who is a highly decorated elite soldier, is none too happy and sets out to get his revenge on Allan, going straight after Michelle.

As far as Jet Li films go, *The Defender* is just mediocre. It plays out almost as if it were an Asian version of the Kevin Costner and Whitney Houston film *The Bodyguard*. It's light on action,

and for a good portion of the film Christy Chung's character is just terribly unlikable. Jet Li does his best in the film with very little martial arts action until his showdown with Collin Chou (*Badges of Fury*, also with Li). There are several gun battles, which may have been exciting in 1994 but haven't held up well up over time. Director Corey Yuen (*The Transporter*) knows how to use Jet Li's talents and abilities better than anyone and most of their collaborations are memorable, but *The Defender* is probably their weakest outing. The final battle with Chou is by far the shining moment of the film and skipping the rest of it to watch those final moments won't hurt anyone.

The Defender

2004 (Visual Entertainment DVD) (CD)

"You messed with the wrong country and you fucked the wrong president!"

The president of the United States (reality personality Jerry Springer) is doing all he can to protect the country. The biggest threat around is renowned terrorist Mohamed Jamar (Geoffrey Burton) who has been missing for months and plotting an attack, putting the president in a position where he must decide how to proceed against him without turning him into a martyr. He has the head of the National Security Agency, Roberta Jones (Caroline Lee Johnson), working to keep him invisible. A secret meeting is arranged in an empty hotel in Bucharest, and her team is up to the challenge. Heading them up is Lance Rockford (Dolph Lundgren) who has been working as her personal bodyguard. The meeting appears to be going off without a hitch—no one even knows they're there. Without warning, they're ambushed by unknown assailants, cornering them within the hotel. They will have to call upon all of their training to keep everyone safe, find a way out of the building, and keep the United States safe from an impending attack.

This is yet another score for Dolph Lundgren (*Silent Trigger*, *Hidden Assassin*). This is the first film where he decided to take the plunge and do double duty as both actor and director. The man knows the genre better than anyone, and he emerges as a more than capable filmmaker. He never tries to cram the movie with an abundance of subplots or convolute it with too much backstory. What he delivers is a lean action film full of thrills and excitement. Lundgren is as confident behind the scenes as he is on the screen. As his team battles its way through the hotel, he mixes things up with high-octane shootouts and then breaks it up just a bit when he has to kick some ass the old-fashioned way. After the first twenty minutes or so, the action rarely lets up. Lundgren directed *The Russian Specialist* next.

The Delta Force

1986 (MGM DVD) (CD)

"Sleep tight, sucker!"

A group of Lebanese terrorists hijack a Boeing 707 traveling through several European countries before landing in New York City. The terrorist leader Abdul (Robert Forster) forces the pilot to land in Beirut to refill. The hostages are segregated in the plane, focusing on the Jews, while demands are made to the US government. The government wastes no time dispatching its most elite unit, The Delta Force, headed up by Colonel Alexander (Lee Marvin) and Captain McCoy (Chuck Norris). Once they arrive at the airfield, a mistake is made and a massacre is imminent if they don't get on the ball immediately. The climax has McCoy riding around a missile-outfitted motorcycle and eliminating the threat almost single-handedly.

Theatrical poster for *The Delta Force*. Author's collection.

After a moment of silence, Chuck Norris launches a missile into a truck, it explodes, and so does Alan Silvestri's fantastic calypso electronic score that will bring any action fan to their feet. *The Delta Force* is part of the reason why many of us look to Chuck Norris as an American hero. He may not have fought in any real wars but he was (and still is) the cinematic embodiment of patriotism and hope. For the first half of the film, Chuck sort of takes a back seat to the terrorists and the hostages, played by an all-star cast. There's some strong emotional moments from actors like Shelley Winters, Lainie Kazan, George Kennedy, Martin Balsam, and several others. Once the team launches their attacks, it's nonstop action time. Chuck uses very little martial arts in the film but when he does he makes every blow count. The great Steve James (*American Ninja*) has a small role in the film but it's always a pleasure to see the late actor appear. Sadly, this was the final film to star the legendary Lee Marvin who passed away shortly thereafter. Menahem Golan (*Over the Top*) directed the picture for Cannon Films. *The Delta Force* is one of the best action entries from the era and one that fills the audience with adrenaline and patriotism. Cue the calypso!

Delta Force Commando

1987 (djm)

"My mission was easy. I came here to tell you to kiss my black ass!"

A soldier named Tony (Brett Baxter Clark) is on R&R with his pregnant wife on an Army base in Puerto Rico when some Latin revolutionaries break into the base and steal a nuclear bomb. During the commotion, Tony's wife is shot and killed, propelling Tony into a rage. He jumps in a car being driven by Captain Samuel Beck (Fred Williamson), and Tony basically carjacks him. They take pursuit, leading to some carnage, but the bulk of the bad guys get away, leaving Tony fuming. Later the next day, he hijacks a jet just as Captain Beck lands it during a routine drill, and the Air Force and Army go ballistic when they think Captain Beck and Tony have gone rogue, but the reality is pretty simple: Tony wants revenge for the death of his wife, and Captain Beck is just frustrated that this crazy soldier keeps holding him at gunpoint. Their jet is shot down in South America by the same revolutionaries (led by Mark Gregory from *1990: Bronx Warriors*), and they get separated after they jettison from the exploding plane. Beck is captured and tortured, and Tony rescues him, leading to an extended chase that involves gunfire, explosions, and runaway, flaming vehicles.

Not bad for a cheap Italian exploitation movie, *Delta Force Commando* gives its two leads plenty of opportunities to exert themselves physically, and even though their two characters hate each other at first, by the end they've basically formed a bromance. Director Pierluigi Ciriaci also did the sequel.

Delta Force Commando 2

1990 (Live VHS) (CD)

"Why me and not somebody else? I'm on the verge of getting away from it all and you reach out and drag me back. Why?"

The theft of six nuclear missiles from a convoy and the murder of a man in a European hotel sets off a chain of events, showing the American government just how real the terrorist threat is. Captain Sam Beck (Fred Williamson) has been accused of being negligent but something more is happening at the military facility: a mole may just be the culprit. Meanwhile, former Delta Force leader Brett Haskell (Richard Hatch) is coaxed out of retirement to go after known terrorist Juna (Giannina Facio), but the problem is that he has a romantic history with her. As much as he wants to turn down the assignment, he takes it on anyway, knowing there is far more at stake than having to confront an old flame.

It happens to the best of them—a time when an actor needs to eat so they take on a role for one reason only: money. You will get the feeling right away that Fred Williamson (*The Black Cobra*) worked on *Delta Force Commando 2* to buy some groceries. There's nothing wrong with that, and the hardcore fans won't care as long as they get to see their hero in action. Fred's role is tiny and barely worth your time, but the Fred-aholics will need to include this in their collections. There's mild action, a couple of surprising (and bloody) deaths, plus Fred (and his mile-long stogie) who only really has one moment of air combat to show for the action. This movie is a cash grab from director Pierluigi Ciriaci (who did the first *Delta Force Commando*).

Delta Force One: The Lost Patrol (a.k.a. D.F. One: The Lost Patrol)

1999 (Warner DVD) (djm)

How can a movie starring Gary Daniels and Mike Norris under Joseph Zito's direction suck? How can that be possible? Yoram Globus—half the producing team of Cannon's Golan/Globus partnership—produced this meandering, lackluster action movie with a moniker that sounds like it belongs to a series. After Sam Firstenberg's pretty decent *Delta Force 3* (also with Mike Norris), you'd think that anything with a "*Delta Force*" in the title would at least halfheartedly make an attempt to make it matter, but not so with *The Lost Patrol*. Filmed in Israel with only the minimum effort taken to give its audience more bang for its buck, it has a thin story about a team of commandos (who include Daniels, Norris, and Bentley Mitchum) on the run in the Middle East after their other team members are slaughtered in an ambush (an awkward, clumsy scene of failed pyrotechnics). Their mission to stop a nuclear missile from launching is bombarded with captures, sidetracking, and stories and jokes by campfire. A last-minute action scene following their escape from incarceration involves only the smallest modicum of martial arts, and a final freeze frame almost suggests that they all die from an explosion.

I do my best not to trash on movies starring the likes of action guys like Daniels and Norris, but when a movie like *Delta Force One: The Lost Patrol* comes along, I feel like I have a duty to tell the world how I really feel. All of the right elements were in place to make a solid military actioner, but it utterly collapses before your very eyes. I don't know if this is Zito's fault or if Globus is to blame, but even if the script was bad there should have been some pizzazz thrown in, or at the very least they should have allowed Daniels and Norris some leeway to showcase their abilities. Skip this one. Fans of its stars won't miss a thing.

Col. Scott McCoy (Chuck Norris) twists a Marine's leg in *Delta Force 2: The Columbian Connection*. Author's collection.

Delta Force 2:
The Columbian Connection
1990 (MGM DVD) (djm)

"Shit! Always the hard way!"

A superior sequel to the Menahem Golan-directed original, *Delta Force 2* is a step up in every way. Chuck Norris returns as Scott McCoy (now a colonel), who is ordered to go to South American to rescue some DEA agents who've been taken prisoner by an untouchable drug lord named Ramon Cota (Billy Drago). This time, McCoy doesn't really have a team to back him up, and he has a flare of vengeance in his heart to fuel his mission. His buddy and partner is killed early on by Cota, and hell hath no fury like Chuck Norris on a mission. Cota has a penchant for killing people himself rather than

Col. Scott McCoy (Chuck Norris) dangles from a helicopter in the finale of *Delta Force 2: The Columbian Connection*. Author's collection.

Billy Drago, Richard Jaeckel, and Chuck Norris in *Delta Force 2: The Columbian Connection*. Author's collection.

letting others do his dirty work—and he *enjoys* it, which makes his evil that much more skeezy. The finale has McCoy and Cota tied to ropes from a helicopter, and the entire sequence is thrilling.

The Delta Force wasn't necessarily a movie that needed sequels, but *The Columbian Connection* is far better than it could have been. Director Aaron Norris (Chuck's brother) gives Chuck all the attention, which is a wise decision this time around. We can feel his anger and frustration in some scenes like the infamous training montage where he puts the hurt on about a dozen trainees. Drago is good as usual being the creepy villain. He made several movies with Norris. He was also in *Invasion U.S.A.* and *Hero and the Terror*. The score by Frederic Talgorn mixes synthesizer music with a full-bodied orchestral sound. On a sad note, five crewmembers were killed in a helicopter accident during filming. Written by Lee Reynolds (*Jackie Chan's Who Am I?*). More *Delta Force* movies followed. The region 1 DVD is full frame, but the region 2 DVD is widescreen. The MGM region 1 Blu-ray is preferred.

Delta Force 3: The Killing Game
(Cannon DVD) (djm)

Cannon cobbled together the sons of famous actors and directors to star in this fairly competent companion piece to the first two *Delta Force* films, starring Chuck Norris. Nick Cassavetes (son of John Cassavetes) heads a team of commandos trying to stop a fanatical jihadist from inciting terror in America. The team goes to the Middle East to join forces with a couple of Russians and a local woman, who is their greatest asset. The Russians are led by a stalwart soldier, played by John Ryan, who replaced Gregory Peck's son, Tony, in the role. Other members of the team are played by Mike Norris (Chuck's son), Matthew Penn (son of director Arthur Penn), and Eric Douglas (son of Kirk Douglas, and brother of Michael Douglas). The only one of them that can fight is Mike Norris, and the film gives him a few scenes to showcase his abilities. Douglas plays an explosives expert, and his character has the most personality. The locations and level of action scenes are perfectly in line with the films Cannon was making at the time. Certain scenes were shot on some of the same locations as *Rambo III*.

Surprisingly relevant for today's turbulent times, *DF3* is a solid enough actioner with a nice grainy texture. Sam Firstenberg (*American Ninja, American Samurai*) directed this from a script written by Boaz Davidson and Gregg Latter. A tagline for the film reads, "Younger and tougher . . . because they have to be!" These guys aren't tougher than Chuck Norris or Lee Marvin, but it's a novel idea to throw some sons of famous people up there and call them "tough." At least Chad McQueen isn't in it.

Hero John Spartan (Sylvester Stallone) is in the same predicament as villain Simon Phoenix (Wesley Snipes) in *Demolition Man*. Author's collection.

Demolition Man
1993 (Warner Bros. DVD) (CD)

"He's finally matched his meet. You really licked his ass."

John Spartan (Sylvester Stallone) is a tough as nails cop who will stop at nothing to capture the diabolical Simon Phoenix (Wesley Snipes). It's 1996, and Spartan is trying to rescue a group of hostages that Phoenix has hidden in an industrial building. After the building explodes, the bodies of the hostages are found in the ashes, and Spartan is blamed for their death. Both men are sentenced to the CryoPrison where they will serve out their sentences in a cryogenic freeze-state. In the post-natural apocalypse year of 2032, Phoenix is mysteriously resuscitated and escapes into the new nonviolent world and goes on an unheard-of crime spree. The San Angeles Police are at a loss and come up with the idea to revive the man who captured him in the first place: John Spartan. With the help of Officer Lenina Huxley (Sandra Bullock), Spartan has to readjust his twentieth-century attitude and capture Phoenix no matter how much damage he causes.

A large part of why *Demolition Man* is such a terrific film is the ridiculous outlook of the future that it provides us with. It should also be considered one of Stallone's finer moments. It was a genius idea to take the type of character he was comfortable with playing and transplant him into a far-flung and bizarre alternate future where Arnold Schwarzenegger is the president, Taco Bell is the last restaurant standing after the

After being woken from cryo-sleep, Simon Phoenix (Wesley Snipes) goes nuts in *Demolition Man*. Author's collection.

other franchises collapsed (in some markets it was changed to Pizza Hut), profanity is outlawed, and going to the bathroom involves using three sea shells. It was a refreshing change to see him own the film in this weird futuristic setting. Equally as memorable is the over-the-top energy of Wesley Snipes (on a roll after *Passenger 57*) as Simon Phoenix, the villain of the film. Snipes, sporting a bleached blond crew cut, has some great moments, showing off his skills as a martial artist and his action star potential. The cast includes Denis Leary, Benjamin Bratt, and Nigel Hawthorne. This is equal parts satire and action, with director Marco Brambilla expertly balancing the two. Of course, action is the main attraction and there is no shortage in that department. The two main characters play cat and mouse for much of the running time but the final confrontation is as good as we could hope. The film has near flawless production design, a bombastic music score (by Elliot Goldenthal), and top-tier special effects. The action scenes are well staged and the pop cultural references in the script are well placed and relevant (especially circa 1993). It's a shame that Marco Brambilla has only one other feature film (*Excess Baggage* with Alicia Silverstone) on his resume since he proved with *Demolition Man* that he was a force to be reckoned with.

Derailed
2002 (DEJ DVD) (CD)

Jacques Kristoff (Jean-Claude Van Damme) has to hide his true profession from his family in order to protect them. His line of work is very dangerous, but they believe him to be in banking. Jacques is actually a special agent assigned to watch over and transport Galina Konstantin (Laura Harring) who is in possession of a biological weapon (much like smallpox). Jacques's wife Madeline (Susan Gibney) and two children (Jessica Bowman and Van Damme's real life son Kristopher Van Varenberg) decide to surprise him for his birthday. Things go really wrong when a group of terrorists board the train they're traveling on to get Galina and the vials. Jacques is the only hope to save the people on the train. He has very little time to become a hero after one of the vials breaks open and spreads the virus throughout the train.

Though the film suffers a bit from budget constraints, it still manages to entertain. It follows in the footsteps of *Under Siege 2*, but is actually a better film. Van Damme was just starting to settle into the direct-to-video arena and is very good in the movie. He uses his fists and feet far more often than any weapon. We get some cool action sequences as he makes his way through the terrorists one by one. The only real sore spot is a sequence on the train involving a motorcycle. Director Bob Misiorowski (*Air Panic*) experiments with style; some of his attempts work, while others fail. Some of the effects and miniatures just don't mesh well with the action and diminish the payoff. Overall, it's entertaining and Van Damme has plenty of time to chase the bad guys and kick some ass. Stefanos Miltsakakis (from *Cyborg* and *Maximum Risk*) has a role as a heavy. Boaz Davidson wrote the story.

Desert Heat (a.k.a. Inferno)
1999 (Sony DVD) (CD)

"Gadzooks! Bloody well bled all over back here. He bloody well bled all over. However, not to worry. Some Spic and Span, a little elbow grease, several yards of Saran wrap, and everything will be as good as new."

Eddie Lomax (Jean-Claude Van Damme) has reached his end. He has a snazzy looking motorcycle he's riding to give to his friend Johnny Six Toes (Danny Trejo), and then he intends to take his own life. Instead, the motorcycle breaks down in the desert, leaving him with his gun and his thoughts. While firing his gun into the nothingness of the desert, he upsets a group of local thugs who assault him and leave him for dead, stealing his motorcycle. Thankfully, his old friend Johnny finds him and nurses him back to health. In town, the locals live in fear of the two rival gangs that have turned their home into a ghost town. Eddie wins over the locals, including waitress Rhonda (Gabrielle Fitzpatrick), old Eli (Bill Erwin), and Jubal Early (Pat Morita). They band together to rid the town of all the scum that has been festering all these years.

This was a film Van Damme wasn't quite suited for. It was directed by John G. Avildsen (*Rocky*) under the pseudonym Danny Muldoon. It has a *Twin Peaks*/*Yojimbo* vibe with a bizarre sense of humor. There are a few moments or lines that work, but it's never enough. The supporting cast featuring Pat Morita, Jamie Pressley, Larry Drake, Danny Trejo, and others try their best but something just never clicks in the film. Van Damme was slightly miscast, never fully encompassing what the director was after. There're a few fight scenes and shootouts that fail to really capture any excitement. *Desert Heat* looks fantastic with some really beautiful photography and unique camera movements, but it's a sore misstep.

Desert Kickboxer
(a.k.a. Desert Hawk)
1992 (HBO VHS) (djm)

Released directly to home video under the 21st Century Film Corporation (the company Menahem Golan formed after Cannon folded), this stars John Haymes Newton (TV's *Superboy*) as Joe Highhawk, a disgraced kickboxer who now lives in a trailer in the desert and works as a border deputy. When a secretary for a gangster embezzles millions of dollars from her boss, she goes on the run with her mentally slow brother. The secretary, Claudia (Judie Aronson from *American Ninja*), is pursued by a bunch of thugs and her boss (Paul Smith), none of whom expected anyone to save her. Highhawk comes to her rescue.

Fans of the *Undisputed* sequels and *Ninja*, all with Scott Adkins, may be interested to see where the director of those films got his start.

Isaac Florentine, who is the foremost director working in today's "B" action genre, directed *Desert Kickboxer*, and it bears the mark of a filmmaker who loves the genre and respects it. John Newton is no Scott Adkins, and he never really returned to the martial arts/action genre, but he's competent in the role, and he looks the part. It's not a bad film. Check it out.

Desert Warrior
1988 (Digiview DVD) (CD)

"We can't give up. We're all dying of nuclear contamination. If we don't get fresh food, fresh water, and a clean woman soon, we're gonna die."

After the third world war, life has become incredibly difficult to sustain. Survivors have broken off into tribes, but almost all of the women are contaminated with radiation and cannot bear healthy children. Zerak (*The Incredible Hulk*'s Lou Ferrigno) is the ever-loyal servant to the leader of his tribe; he patrols the wasteland looking for uncontaminated women to offer to his superior. Racela (Shari Shattuck) and her father live with a secret society in an area safe from the radiation. They're captured by a vicious tribe only to be saved by Zerak. Since he's a servant, he takes her to the leader of his tribe who wants to force himself upon her. Zerak begins to realize he has been wrong all along and decides to become a turncoat and fight for good.

Desert Warrior has the happiest of happy endings in the history of happy endings. Sure, this is a spoiler but everyone hugs and makes up before walking off into the sunset. Lou Ferrigno (also in *Cage*) is best used as the strong and silent type. He partakes in various battles and always comes out on top. He makes marks with his sword, tosses some fools around with his big meaty paws, and just for good measure, he has his little laser blaster for a last resort. It would be incredibly easy to slam this movie, but instead of going that route, we've decided to embrace and celebrate it. Director Jim Goldman never made another film after this one (who knows why), but at least he gave us *Desert Warrior*.

Destroyer
1988 (Virgin VHS) (CD)

"You don't want to hurt me, Malone. This is what we've been waiting for. It's just you and me now."

The notorious serial killer Ivan Mozer (former NFL lineman Lyle Alzado) is on death row awaiting his execution. Having been convicted of the rape and murder of over twenty victims, his final day has arrived, and he's spending his last moments strapped to an electric chair. When the switch is flicked on, everyone thinks he's toast but there's a prison riot in full swing and the power goes out. Everyone assumes he's dead and goes on with their lives. Months later, the prison is abandoned and a film crew has taken residence to shoot an exploitation movie there. Everything seems to be going smoothly until bodies begin showing up and a young couple Susan (Deborah Foreman) and David (Clayton Rohner) come to learn Ivan never died. He's living in the walls and in the darkest spaces of the prison, ready to pounce on anyone who will try to disrupt his solitude.

Alzado (from *Neon City*) is the lead villain in this supernatural horror film directed by first timer Robert Kirk. It feels as if Alzado's character was being groomed to be the next Jason Voorhees or Freddy Krueger. He doesn't necessarily fight anyone; it's more along the lines of attacking them, using various weapons including a jackhammer. Plenty of blood is shed, and it includes a brilliant shower scene with plenty of skin. Alzado appears to be having a blast and he's the only reason the film should be viewed. Many of us will remember the fantastic VHS box cover with him shirtless on the cover brandishing the giant power tool. Sadly, the most memorable thing about the film was the box. Otherwise this is just a by-the-numbers slasher with a brilliant villain and ho-hum execution. *See No Evil*, starring WWE wrestler Kane, is similar.

Detective Malone

(a.k.a. **Black Cobra 4**)

1991 (Editoria Elettronica DVD R2) (CD)

Caleb Sakur (Karl Landgren) has a very important agenda as the leader of a terrorist organization. He needs to be the strongest, most powerful person on the planet and the only way to do so is be on the cutting edge of technology. He has an idea but the only way to see it to fruition is to locate and kidnap scientific engineer Barry Wilson (Ronald Russo), who is forced to create a device to give the terrorists an advantage when it's time for them to attack. While stopping them may be a job for the military, it's Chicago cop Robert Malone (Fred Williamson) who is tough enough to destroy everything they've built.

Detective Malone can barely be called a movie, let alone boast how it stars Fred "The Hammer" Williamson (*Bucktown*). Fred is in the film all right, but his scenes were all stolen from the previous films. Malone is seen swinging his arms a bit, firing his gun, hanging out, or even smiling at the camera. Director Bob Collins (a pseudonym for Umberto Lenzi) seems to think his audience is stupid and uses actors from the original *Black Cobra* who have aged, trying to convincingly splice the old footage with the new, but it doesn't work. Fred gets to kick a bit of ass but it's ass he's already kicked before. The real Fred Williamson wasn't too happy about this shady endeavor, but I believe he was able to collect a paycheck for it anyway.

Detention

2003 (Lionsgate DVD) (CD)

"Tick tock, we're in the school.
Tick tock, get the van.
Tick tock, blow the fucker up."

After serving his time in the Gulf War, Sam Decker (Dolph Lundgren) returns to pursue a career at an inner-city school where the students are as tough as they come. He wants to make a difference, but no one else seems to care. Fed up with the school district, he resigns, ready to move on with his life. His final duty at the school is to watch over the troublemakers in detention. It sounds like an easy enough job—until a group of armed men (and a woman) use the school to hide a huge shipment of cocaine. The criminal leader, Chester Lamb (Alex Karzis), thinks it will be an easy front to hide the drugs but it quickly turns into a battle of wits when he and his well-armed gang must face off with Decker and a group of unarmed students. Chester is going to find out real quick just how resourceful Decker can be.

Detention is everything it should be and more—a ridiculously fun action flick with Dolph Lundgren (*The Punisher*) kicking asses inside a high school. Really, who wouldn't want to have Dolph as their teacher? He's a guy we could all learn something from. This has one of the best chase scenes ever: A disabled teenager in a motorized wheelchair is being chased by a villain on a motorcycle through the hallways of a high school, opening fire on one another. Somehow, director Sidney J. Furie (*Direct Action,* also with Lundgren) is able to wrangle in all these oddball elements, creating one of Lundgren's more memorable films. Dolph isn't one to disappoint so he's quick to fight when he needs to *and* there are several shootouts. There's action right out of the gate and the excitement never lets up. Production house Nu Image scored another for the team with *Detention*.

The Detonator

2005 (Sony DVD) (djm)

Wesley Snipes plays Sonni Griffith, a formidable CIA agent stationed in Eastern Europe, who's after an international arms dealer. He gets sidetracked in a separate mission involving Nadia, the beautiful wife of a terrorist (played by Silvia Colloca), who has ties to the arms dealer Sonni has been chasing. There is a stash of thirty million dollars that the arms dealer is looking to steal from Nadia, and just when Sonni begins to trust her, she reveals herself to be more than she seems, her betrayal severing the trust he's extended towards her. As it turns out, the terrorists have kidnapped Nadia's young son, which explains her sketchy behavior. Sonni—using his impressive martial arts skills and his well-trained abilities as a field agent—saves Nadia, exposes a rat in the agency, and kills the terrorists. It's all in a day's work.

Snipes delivers a solid, forceful, and physical performance in *The Detonator*, which is a passable enough actioner, but it's not very distinct in the way that, say, Jean-Claude Van Damme's similar-themed direct-to-video movies are. It goes through the motions with drab Eastern European backdrops on display, and it does almost everything right except be original or amazing. It also has a strangely unsatisfying ending. Some of the ADR voice-over work that was supposed to be performed by Snipes was done by someone else. It made me think of several of Steven Seagal's direct-to-video films where he did the same thing. Po Chih Leong (*Out of Reach* with Seagal) directed.

Detour to Terror

1980 (Sony DVD) (CD)

It's time to hop on a bus and take a leisurely ride to Sin City, a place to gamble and have a good time. Everyone aboard is relaxed and excited while Lee Hayes (O. J. Simpson) is at the wheel and taking everyone to play. It's a perfect trip—until they're run off the road by three men in dune buggies. These men believe there's a woman aboard who is worth quite a bit of coin. The bus has flat tires and is stuck in the middle of the desert. The kidnappers toss her into their vehicle and then proceed to take anything of value and disappear. Lee has to keep this eccentric group of people focused, otherwise they may succumb to the heat and dehydration. He has a plan and maybe if he's lucky he can get them out alive. They better roll soon since the kidnappers (including a very young looking Lorenzo Lamas) discover one of the passengers has a postage stamp worth ninety grand and they're coming to get it.

This made-for-television film was produced during a time when television films were all the rage. It's a run-of-the-mill thriller, offering some fun moments and an exciting conclusion. Who better to rally a misfit group of people on a bus than O. J.? While most of his time is spent commanding and organizing, he does take charge of the bus and partakes in a chase through the desert where he tries to take out the kidnappers in their dune buggies. It was also fun to see Lorenzo Lamas (*Snake Eater, Renegade*) in an early role, though he never really gets to show off the talents that would define his action career a few short years later. He and O. J. would appear together again in *C.I.A.: Codename Alexa*. Directed by Michael O'Herlihy.

Diamond Dogs

2007 (Sony DVD) (CD)

"Alright, you got fifteen minutes to undo a very bad first impression."

Xander Ronson (Dolph Lundgren) is down on his luck and in debt to the tune of $20,000. An eccentric collector named Chambers (William

Shriver) comes to town and offers him an exceptional amount of money to be his guide. It's a tough offer to turn down but Chambers is asking an awful lot. He's in search of a Buddhist artifact known as the Tangka worth millions of dollars. It's rumored to be cursed but no one really believes in all the ancient mumbo jumbo surrounding its legend. Unfortunately for them, things are about to get deadly when competing cutthroat treasure hunters close in on their trail. Ronson is a former special forces soldier so he's always one step ahead of the game, even if he's dealing with something far more powerful than any of them thought possible.

Diamond Dogs was a troubled production from the get-go, which resulted in director Shimon Dotan (*Coyote Run*) stepping away from the job, leaving Dolph Lundgren (*The Punisher*) to pick up the pieces. Overall the film is pretty good, though it does feel as if it's lacking something. Lundgren turns in a solid performance and has a few decent action scenes. The film could have been Dolph's attempt at bringing an Indiana Jones-type of adventure flick to the screen but it doesn't quite make the grade in that regard. The mythology aspect of the story is quite interesting and the exceptional cast elevates the picture into an entertaining ninety minutes. This may be the only film in which you will see Dolph being spooned by a woman, his *Expendables 2* co-star Nan Yu.

Die Another Day
2002 (MGM DVD) (CD)

"The same person who set me up then has just set me up again, so I'm going after him."

MI-6 agent 007 James Bond (Pierce Brosnan) is on an undercover mission in North Korea trying to do an arms deal with Colonel Moon (Will Yun Lee) when Moon's assistant Zao (Rick Yune) discovers Bond's true identity. While Moon is killed and Zao is captured, 007 is taken by Moon's father. In North Korean custody and tortured for a year, Bond is then traded back to his country in exchange for Zao. There's someone within the agency who has betrayed him and he wants to know who it is and why. MI-6 will not support him, so he goes rogue and starts his search with the one person who survived the whole ordeal in the first place: Zao.

More than any other Bond film starring Pierce Brosnan, *Die Another Day* feels more like a Roger Moore-era Bond film with all the crazy gadgets and completely over-the-top action. This was Brosnan's last time portraying the iconic character in this fortieth anniversary film. Director Lee Tamahori (*Next*) made a wise decision when hiring martial artist Rick Yune (*Ninja Assassin, The Fifth Commandment*) to portray one of the big bads. Rick brings an energy to the film with his unique look (he has diamonds embedded in his face) and steals the show with an amazing car duel in an ice castle. Sadly, they never really give him an opportunity

to showcase his martial art skills. It's a real shame, and there were plenty of opportunities to do so. This wasn't Bond's finest hour but it has some exciting set pieces and Madonna's theme song is pretty rad (Yep, I said it!).

Die Fighting
(a.k.a. **The Price of Success**)
2014 (NOV) (CD)

"You might be wondering: Am I insane? The answer is, I don't know. I like to say no but does a crazy person know if he's crazy?"

The Z Team is a group of four stuntmen who are waiting for their big break in Hollywood to come along when a mysterious stranger casts them in their own action movie. The catch is that it's all reality based. This so-called filmmaker has kidnapped their wives, and they will have to follow his script if they want to have a happy ending. His script leads the team deep into the underbelly of Los Angeles where they will have to steal money, fight hordes of thugs, and ultimately have to kill. They have no choice but to follow his instructions, even if it means turning against one another.

Fabien Garcia wrote, starred, edited, directed, and choreographed *Die Fighting*, his first feature film. His team consists of Jess Allen, as well as brothers Laurent and Didier Buson (Didier appeared in *Merantau* with Iko Uwais). These guys together have crafted an action heavy thriller so full of spit and vinegar you won't be able to get enough. The story plays second fiddle to the breathtaking set pieces and each cast member has a moment to show off his skills. The thing is, Fabien is truly the star and he has the best moments. He has to fight a school full of marital artists (much like Bruce Lee in *The Chinese Connection*) and even has to down some whiskey in order to use his drunken style (like Jackie Chan in *Drunken Master*). These scenes easily demonstrate just how amazing this guy is and combining him with the Z Team is a match made in martial arts heaven. This is just a beginning for these guys, and I can't wait to see what they do next.

Direct Action
2004 (First Look DVD) (djm)

Frank Gannon (Dolph Lundgren) has been a member of the Direct Action police force for as long as it's been around, and his unit is comprised of the baddest asses on the force. They're like The Untouchables—they're allowed to use excessive force if need be, and Gannon is respected and understood as the best of them. Over time, he begins to be ostracized by his team because everyone else begins siphoning drugs from various busts, and even his captain—Stone (Conrad Dunn)—is dirty and willing to kill Frank, especially on the fated day Frank is due to

appear in court to give his testimony against his entire team. On said day, Frank is assigned a new partner—a young woman named Billie (Polly Shannon)—and since she's entirely clueless as to what's going on, when Frank is all of a sudden being hunted down, she quickly takes his side against the other cops.

Dolph is great in this. His laid-back attitude and go-easy wardrobe and hairstyle really help him to come across as a realistic guy, and he's not so much an "action hero" as he is a guy just doing his job and kicking ass and taking names. *Direct Action* renewed my faith in him as a direct-to-video star in a time when he was making bad movies like *Hidden Agenda* and *Retrograde*. The production values of this film are pretty good for such a small urban action film, and there wasn't a single time while watching it when I wasn't in the moment. From Nu Image, this was directed by Sidney J. Furie, who also made *Detention* with Lundgren the previous year.

Direct Contact
2009 (First Look DVD) (CD)

Mike Riggins (Dolph Lundgren) is a former American soldier doing time in a Russian prison for arms smuggling. Clive Connelly (Michael Pare), who is an attaché for the American consulate, shows up and offers Mike the chance to start over with a clean slate. An American girl named Ana (Gina May) has been kidnapped by Russian mobsters and he wants Mike to rescue her. He takes the assignment and rescues her only to find out she was never kidnapped. Connelly is playing Mike, and there has to be a reason everyone is after this girl. Not knowing who to believe or trust, he has to follow his instincts and do what's right instead of just collecting the small fortune he is being offered for turning over the girl.

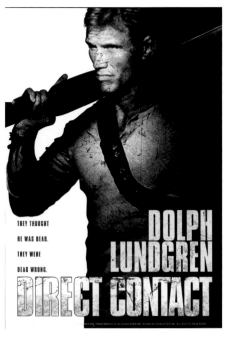

Video release poster for *Direct Contact*. Author's collection.

Direct Contact has you screaming out loud with excitement during certain moments in the film. This is one of those Dolph Lundgren (in a career upswing following *The Russian Specialist*) flicks you just have to love. There are some amazing moments of ass-kickery and no one but Lundgren could pull off some of the things he does in this movie. While being chased by two SUVs and a tank, he's able to escape with nothing but a motorcycle. He beats to a pulp everyone who gets in his way, *and* saves the girl, who is putty in his fingers. All of this is neatly wrapped up in a highly bloody package, ready to knock your socks off. There's just enough story to keep things moving and the action is literally nonstop with very little breathing room. This should come as no surprise since the film was brought to us by Nu Image/Millennium's producer/director Danny Lerner (*Traitor's Heart*).

The Dirty Dozen
1967 (Warner DVD) (djm)

One of the great ensemble WWII-set action movies of all time, *The Dirty Dozen* stars Lee Marvin as Major Reisman, who has landed a mission nobody wants to lead simply because it's close to impossible. The Army wants him to train twelve convicted prisoners who all have extended and/or death sentences, and lead them to Nazi Germany where they will do the unthinkable: Kill a mansion full of German officers in one fell swoop. The trick is not to survive the mission, but to instill a sense of hope, discipline, and camaraderie in the men who are fighting for the promise of a pardon. Amongst the misfits are Wladislaw (Charles Bronson), who speaks German, and Jefferson (Jim Brown), who is one of the brawniest men in the bunch. Other guys in the group are played by Donald Sutherland, John Cassavetes, Telly Savales, and Clint Walker.

At two-and-a-half-hours long, *The Dirty Dozen* is mostly the build-up to the mad-dash, suspense-filled finale that kills off most of the central characters during their mission, but Bronson and Brown (who I focused on) both shine in standout roles that feature them in great physical shape with plenty of dimensional arcs to make their characters interesting. It's easy to see where Stallone got his inspiration for *The Expendables*. I would love to see a remake of *The Dirty Dozen* someday with guys like Thomas Jane, Tom Hardy, and Ryan Gosling . . . and someone like Stallone or Mel Gibson in the Major role. It doesn't hurt to dream. Three made-for-TV sequels followed decades later.

Displaced
2006 (MTI DVD) (CD)

"I had a close encounter with an alien today. I mean, I was this close to an alien today."

When soldier John Marrettie (Malcolm Hankey) meets Stel (martial artist Mark Strange), he has no clue the man is actually an alien. Not the creepy looking type, no: His race all looks human. Stel and his sister are sent to Earth to locate a file containing information on the whereabouts of their father. They're intercepted by a money-obsessed military leader who plans on selling the file to the highest bidder since there's also information in it about alien technology. His sister is murdered, leaving Stel alone—until he meets John. They quickly team up—with one being the brains and the other, the brawn—and they try to keep the information from being sold into the wrong hands.

It's amazing to see what people can do with little money, plenty of ambition, and group of dedicated individuals who are willing to hang in for the long haul. Action star Mark Strange (from *The Medallion*) and director Martin Holland spent six years trying to get this film completed. While the end result is a mixed bag, there's plenty to be excited about. Strange also did the fight choreography, and there's some pretty exciting action to behold, and lots of it. I didn't always agree with the rapid cut editing style; it was difficult to make out what was happening during some of the action. The washed out, drab look of the film was ugly to look at, but with a smart concept and continuous action it still remains a winner.

District B13
2004 (Magnolia DVD) (djm)

In the near future, the French government has fenced off a portion of Paris to keep an unruly demographic isolated from society. This zone is called District B13. One man in the district is trying to keep the drug pushers and warlords clear of his building, but it constantly results in him making enemies. Parkour expert Leito (David Belle) makes one enemy too many when he upsets a drug lord by disposing of a million bucks worth of drugs, and as retaliation, the drug lord has Leito's sister kidnapped. Leito takes it upon himself (as usual) to go after the drug lord himself, and when he delivers him up to the authorities outside of the district, he himself is reprimanded and jailed while the drug lord is set free with Leito's sister in hand to boot, which shows just what kind of dystopian society Leito is living in. Six months later, a missile ends up hijacked by the same drug lord in B13, and he's holding it for ransom while the timer is ticking down to zero. With just a few hours to defuse it before the entire area is leveled, the government puts their best cop—a martial arts dynamo named Damien (Cyril Raffaelli)—on the case, but they team him up with Leito, who gets a free pass out of jail if he leads Damien to the drug lord. As reluctant

partners, Leito and Damien make an unstoppable team against the warlords and marauders of the nearly apocalyptic landscape of B13.

Co-writer and creator Luc Besson (*Leon the Professional*, *The Fifth Element*) has a knack for dreaming up some cool action scenarios and vehicles for actors and performers with talents that go beyond just acting. He created *The Transporter* series for Jason Statham and wrote the script for *Kiss of the Dragon* for Jet Li, which should give you an idea of where he's at in terms of action. *District B13*, which casts David Belle (the creator of parkour) and Cyril Raffaelli (a Shotokan and wushu expert) as unlikely allies, is an exemplary execution of style and action, mixing parkour stunts and martial arts in equal measure. Belle and Raffaelli work great together, and their on-screen footwork and action is really something special. The sequel reunited them five years later, but this one is the better entry. This was remade with Belle in English as *Brick Mansions*. Directed by Pierre Morel, who later directed *Taken* and *From Paris With Love*.

District 13: Ultimatum
2010 (Magnet DVD) (djm)

The adventures of Leito (David Belle) and Damien (Cyril Raffaelli) continue with this fun sequel to *District B13*. This time, factions within the French government want to obliterate the undesirable District 13, which is seemingly posing a threat to society by just *existing*, and so an elaborate ruse is devised to make it appear that a gang in the district has mercilessly killed two policemen on patrol. This creates a media sensation, and public opinion is swayed against

Cyril Raffaelli in *District 13: Ultimatum*, a Magnet release. Photos courtesy of Magnet Releasing.

David Belle and Cyril Raffaelli in *District 13: Ultimatum*, a Magnet release. Photos courtesy of Magnet Releasing.

David Belle and Cyril Raffaelli in *District 13: Ultimatum*, a Magnet release. Photos courtesy of Magnet Releasing.

the district. A plan is put together to nuke the entire area, but Leito and Damien team up when they are given damning evidence proving that the government was behind the killings of the policemen and the deception behind the entire case, which has been falsified. They race against time, while uniting all the gangs in the district to help them stop the president from pressing the button that will obliterate their home.

A little looser in structure than the first film, *Ultimatum* is still a fun sequel, which follows the beats and rhythms of the world Luc Besson created with this franchise. Belle and Raffaelli could easily go on to become major action stars if the right doors keep opening for them. They're more interesting to watch than most of the action guys coming out of the factory these days. Directed by Patrick Alessandrin.

The Divine Enforcer

1992 (Prism VHS) (djm)

"Repent or pay the price!"

A mentally deranged serial killer (played by Don Stroud) is stalking the streets and kidnapping pretty women and strapping them to a chair in his dungeon basement, where he hooks them up to IVs and turns them into drug addicts so that he can hear them whimper and beg for more drugs as he systematically rapes, degrades, and murders them. The only hope the city has is a cadre of vigilante priests who operate under the Monsignor (Erik Estrada), who encourages them to go out and seek justice in the name of the Father, the Son, and the Holy Spirit. Their newest addition is Father Daniel (martial arts guy Michael Foley), who has a personally handcrafted collection of knives and guns, all fashioned and adorned with crucifixes. Along with Father Thomas (Jan Michael Vincent, who reads his lines from a cue card, a fact that is barely concealed), the team of priests makes it their personal mission to bring down the serial killer, one karate chop at a time.

Ultra sleazy and unappealing, *The Divine Enforcer* is pretty much torture porn before there was such a thing, but a huge problem it has is that the Father Daniel character, played by newcomer action star Foley (who had small roles in *Lionheart* and *Desert Kickboxer*), is just about

as deranged as the serial killer. When he gets a crazy look in his eye before attacking scumbags, you've gotta start wondering who the good guy is. Foley gets to show off his martial arts skills a few times (but not nearly as often as he should), and the rest of the cast (including Robert Z'Dar and Jim Brown in bit roles) is pretty much wasted. I had a difficult time with this purely misogynistic trash, but some guys might like it. Directed by Robert Rundle.

DNA

1997 (Platinum DVD) (CD)

"They say that God is dead, that he choked to death with pity for mankind. What do you think, Ash?"

There's a small village in the jungles of Borneo where Dr. Ash Mattley (Mark Dacascos) has devoted his time to helping as many people as he can. He's paid an unexpected visit by Dr. Carl Wessinger (Jurgen Prochnow) who has completed research Mattley gave up long ago. The research, if used properly, could cure the world's most vicious diseases. The thought of all the good he could do leads him to assist Wessinger only to learn that Wessinger's intentions are dark: He has found the remains of what is believed to be a mythical creature and discovered it's an alien life form out for blood. Fast forward and the only hope the village has of survival is Dr. Mattley—and he has a few tricks to pull out of his hat in order to save it.

DNA is a poor man's *Predator*. It's sleekly produced, was shot in the Philippines, and it's much better than expected. Director William Mesa (*Galaxis*) uses his confident skills to pit Mark Dacascos (*Only the Strong, Operation Rogue*) against an ancient alien beast. The effects work by KNB is impressive until it's in the sunlight. The alien looks like the bastard child of Pumpkinhead and H. R. Giger's Alien design. Dacascos has these short burst fights but nothing to get real excited about. As decent as the film may be, there are too many missed opportunities for action but Dacascos pulls another one out of the gutter using only his charm. It's a likable enough movie even if it's predictable and quite honestly a rip-off.

DOA: Dead or Alive

2006 (Dimension DVD) (djm)

Based on a popular videogame, *DOA* was marketed to horny teen boys, but dumped to theaters before its perfunctory video release shortly thereafter. It stars several incredibly attractive and fit actresses (including Jaime Pressly, Holly Valance, Sarah Carter, Natassia Malthe, and Devon Aoki) as invited contestants in a fight tournament on a secret island, hosted by an enigmatic millionaire/scientist/martial artist named Donvan (played by Eric Roberts). One of the women is a ninja princess, and her

royal escort is played by Kane Kosugi from *Revenge of the Ninja* and *Pray For Death*. There are fights, sexy outfits, and computer generated and wire-enhanced stunts.

I've seen this movie twice, and it's obvious that the real reason to see it is to watch the pretty girls do their thing in sometimes little more than a bikini or bra and panties, but if that isn't your thing, then watch it for the fight choreography by director Corey Yuen (*No Retreat, No Surrender, The Transporter*). Co-star Kosugi doesn't have much of a part, but he's certainly involved (and has a few fight scenes), but the whole affair is of little consequence. Teenagers will like it. Horny ones will be teased to no end. Robin Shou from *Death Cage* and *Mortal Kombat* has a small part as a pirate.

Doberman Cop

1977 (VideoAsia DVD) (CD)

"If a bunch of you fucking cops come at me, I still won't give her up!"

Sonny Chiba plays Joji Kano, a cop who appears to be a bit of a country bumpkin. He comes from the island of Okinawa to assist the big city cops in trying to solve a series of murders involving young women. One of these girls (they are all believed to be prostitutes) comes from the same island and Joji is intent on finding out what actually happened to her because he doesn't believe she's dead. The mainland cops all think Joji is crazy (which he is) but he knows what he's doing and he's one of the best cops Japan has to offer. With a trail leading him to a wannabe pop star and some evil gangsters, Joji will find the truth— no matter what.

When Clint Eastwood uttered his famous line about how a .44 Magnum could blow a man's head clean off, he forgot to demonstrate. Sonny Chiba (*Karate for Life*) wanted to prove he was dirtier than Harry and blows some sucker's head clean off. The kung fu fighting takes a back seat to oddball shenanigans (Chiba being molested by a stripper on a stage) and explosive shootouts. Rest assured: he never abandons his roots and there are several extended fight sequences for good measure. The film really does feel as if it's a Japanese *Dirty Harry* clone, but it was based on the manga *Doberman Deka*. The film was directed by legendary filmmaker Kinji Fukasaku (*Battle Royale*) who helped shape the film into not just a vehicle for Chiba but a key entry in '70s badass cinema.

Dogs of Chinatown

2010 (All Aces Media DVD) (djm)

Just as he's about to commit suicide, Jack (Eric Jacobus) looks outside his window and sees a Chinese woman being accosted by some thugs.

He goes outside, uses his gun to shoot and kill the men harassing the woman, and he saves her life. She takes him to her "family," which is the biggest Triad in town. The boss gives Jack an enforcement job, and in no time, Jack has moved to assassinations, and then he becomes one of the Triad's most trusted guys, working hard to make the boss happy. He's trained in martial arts, given a nice paycheck, and he begins developing a relationship with the woman he saved, who also happens to be the boss's mistress. When she's taken captive by the Italian mob, Jack goes after her, but he pays the ultimate price.

If you're not familiar with Eric Jacobus, I highly recommend seeking him out as an action star. His later film *Death Grip* was pretty fantastic, and while *Dogs of Chinatown* is an earlier effort, it's still entertaining and surprisingly effective despite how low-budget it is. It's got off-the-wall humor that works, and the fight scenes—while not completely off the handle—are decent. Jacobus is a rising post-millennial hope in the action world, and *Dogs of Chinatown* isn't a bad place to get acquainted with him. Written and directed by Micah Moore.

Dollar For the Dead

1998 (Warner DVD) (djm)

A nameless "cowboy" (played by Emilio Estevez) is being hunted by a guy named Reager (*Firestorm's* Howie Long), along with Reager's posse of regulators. Cowboy picks up a chatty sidekick named Dooley (a fun William Forsythe), who tells his new pal about some lost gold and the four separate gun holsters that make up a map that leads to the treasure. Dooley already has one of the holsters and knows where to get at least one more, and so Cowboy gives Dooley the benefit of the doubt because he really doesn't have anything better to do. Reager, meanwhile, is closing in on his quarry, and the story behind his pursuit has something to do with the fact that Cowboy killed his son the same day Reager murdered Cowboy's family. There's bad blood there, and so we know there's going to be retribution . . . but not before Cowboy gets his hands on all four holsters and ends up in a peaceful village overrun with bandits who harass the local priest. Is Cowboy really a guardian angel . . . or just a nameless gunslinger out to fill his saddlebags with gold?

Gene Quintano's *Dollar For the Dead* is a ton of fun. It was made for cable (TNT), which pretty much heralded the close of the theatrical careers of both Emilio Estevez and ex-NFL star Howie Long, who had just suffered a flop with *Firestorm*. Estevez is great in the movie, and Long gets to show once again that he was a perfect candidate to be an action star. Though he's the villain, he displays incredible brute strength in the movie, and it's kinda sad to know that this was pretty much his last hurrah (*3000 Miles to Graceland* doesn't really count). If you've seen some of Quintano's other movies like *National Lampoon's Loaded Weapon 1* or *The Musketeer* (which he scripted), then you should have a fairly good idea what sort of cinematic universe *Dollar For the Dead* is in. Incidentally, this movie was originally going to be a theatrical

vehicle for Bruce Willis to star in. Side note: There are two slightly different versions of this movie. Warner Brothers released a DVD on demand of the same version that aired on US television, and Prism Leisure released a slightly altered cut with some sex and nudity. Either version works.

The Donor

1995 (WarnerVision/Imperial VHS) (CD)

"My life? What life, Mike?
I wasn't meant to be a victim.
I'm not gonna be a victim."

Living on the edge is the only way stuntman Billy Castle (Jeff Wincott from *Martial Outlaw*) knows how to live. He drinks too much, partakes in extreme sports, and he loves the ladies. While on vacation with two of his buddies, he meets a gorgeous girl in a bar. They hit it off right away and they quickly take off to her motel room for a night of smoldering hot sex. When he wakes up in the morning he finds himself bleeding and he's missing a kidney. He's naturally freaked out by the incident and goes to the hospital. He begins having nightmares about the ordeal, and he can't let it go. The only way for him to put it in his past is to begin a search for the person who did this to him. It's happening to other men as well, and Billy Castle will put an end to it all.

The Donor is a horror/thriller from director Damien Lee (who would pair again with Wincott on *When the Bullet Hits the Bone*) who takes a chance by casting Wincott as the lead, a departure from his action star status at the time. It's a decent mystery, and Wincott has a likable enough persona to keep you interested. That said, the lack of action slows it down, and it would have been far more interesting if a little more combat had been thrown in. The urban legend aspect of the film is fun and an abundance of skin will most certainly entice a male demographic, but anyone coming in thinking it will be the type of martial arts action film Wincott was known for will be disappointed.

Doom

2005 (Universal DVD) (djm)

"*Big* fucking gun."

Some space Marines are sent to Mars on the Olduvai Research Station, where an archaeological site was uncovered, revealing that an ancient humanoid race lived there long before human history began. A distress signal from the station is sent, and the Marines (who include Dwayne "The Rock" Johnson and Karl Urban) are warped to the station, where they systematically begin evacuating people off the station and get to the real issue:

Vile creatures are running amok in the hallways and in the air vents, eating people and causing a zombie-like virus to spread. In typical stalk-and-slash fashion, the Marines are killed off one by one, until The Rock gets more than a little homicidal and takes his mission mandate too far, and Urban has to be the one to stand up against him.

About as well produced as a movie based on a videogame can be, I suppose, *Doom* makes you wonder if The Rock was really right for this film. He's too big for it (literally), and it's distracting to see him bark orders incessantly and use hard profanity (it's his first "R" rated movie) because all the time you're thinking that he was miscast. He doesn't even get first billing, which is strange. His final fight with Urban is okay (wrestling figures in), but fans of his will probably be disappointed to see that he's ultimately the villain. If you've played the videogame (I played *Doom 3*), you'll notice some appropriate choices made to the production design and the creature effects, but the movie is staggeringly unimaginative and boring. The Rock only makes it worse. It was directed by Andrzej Bartkowiak (*Cradle 2 the Grave* and *Romeo Must Die* with Jet Li).

Double Blast

1993 (Vidmark VHS) (djm)

Emulating in equal measures *3 Ninjas*, *Home Alone*, and *Indiana Jones*, this family movie features badass Dale "Apollo" Cook in the softest movie of his career. After hard "R" movies like *Fist of Steel*, he looks and seems a little out of place in "PG" territory. He plays a kickboxer

VHS artwork for *Double Blast*. Author's collection.

whose martial arts-proficient kids (teenage girl and a ten-year-old boy) are kidnapped by some softy bad guys (Joe Estevez, Robert Z'Dar, and some others) because the kids saw the bad guys kidnap an archaeologist (Linda Blair). The bad guys are after some treasure in a mountain, and they use Blair as their guide. The kids escape, but Cook is already on the trail of the bad guys anyway, so by the time he meets up with them the movie is already almost over, but with just enough time for him to fight Ron Hall (*Raw Target, Triple Impact,* both with Cook) in an impressive fight scene.

Not really for fans of martial arts and action movies, per se, but perfectly suitable for kids who might get a kick out of it, although I think kids today are a little more sophisticated than what *3 Ninjas* can give them. *Double Blast* is fairly low-rent, but for its time it might have been worth the rental. Cook enthusiasts may want to see it. John Barrett (*American Kickboxer 1, Gymkata*) appears in one scene as a trainer.

Double Dragon

1994 (Universal VHS) (CD)

Millionaire Koga Shuko (Robert Patrick) has one half of an ancient Chinese talisman that, once merged with the other half, will give ultimate power of the Double Dragon to the owner. That other half is in the possession of Jimmy (Marc Dacascos) and Billy (Scott Wolf) Lee, two teenage brothers who don't have a clue what it is capable of. Once their guardian Satori (Julia Nickson) is killed, the two brothers, along with freedom fighter Marian (Alyssa Milano), do whatever they can to protect their half. At some point they will have to stop running and use their skills to stop Shuko for good.

Imperial Entertainment sunk twenty million dollars into this film, and it was the ultimate cause for their demise. *Double Dragon* may not be a good film by most standards, but as long as you have fun watching it, then it shouldn't matter. It's a goofy action movie based on a classic video game. This film might be most appealing to young kids, especially those into shows like *Mighty Morphin Power Rangers*. Even though many of the performances are way over the top, it still seems like everyone is having a good time. There's some interesting post-apocalyptic/punk-like production design, and the world they created looks pretty great. Director James Yukich is best known for his work as a music video director, and it's apparent in his style. The story is really simple and ties together the action in a way that keeps the movie moving without feeling slow. The main attraction here is Marc Dacascos (*Crying Freeman*). This was one of his early vehicle roles and you can tell that he would go on to star in finer films. Scott Wolf does a fine job as Billy, the mouthier of the two brothers. Robert Patrick (*Zero Tolerance*) has no trouble chewing up his scenes as Koga and sporting the most outrageous hairdo of his career. Alyssa Milano as Marian could have been given a bit more to do but she's adequate with what she was given to do. Michael Berryman, Jeff Imada, Al Leong, Andy Dick, Vincent Klyn, and many others appear in co-starring roles. This film has been a punching bag for

Scott Wolf and Mark Dacascos (in the air) are brothers in *Double Dragon*. Author's collection.

critics and the general public over the years. That said, *Double Dragon* never takes itself too seriously and after twenty years, maybe it's time to lighten up a bit and enjoy the film for what it offers: a fun time.

Double Duty

2009 (NOV) (djm)

MJ: "The Corps has been very good to me, sir, but it's time I led a civilian life."
The General: "What's in it for you? You're a Marine."
MJ: "Yes, sir! But somewhere deep down inside, sir, I'm a woman. A woman with needs."

Seasoned Marine MJ (Mimi Lesseos from *Streets of Rage*) yearns to leave soldiering behind to start a fresh life, hoping to find true love. She visits her best friend Sophia (Susan Duerden), who is a socialite, and while on her visit MJ is hypnotized at a party. When she awakens she is a prim and proper lady, but if someone snaps their fingers, she's back to being a blowhard Marine, without a trace of grace or class. Sophia and her maybe-gay friend Craig (Tom Sizemore) play tricks on her to confuse her and from one second to the next she's My Fair Lady, but then she's back to being the exact opposite. When Sophia hosts the auction of a priceless Fabergé egg at her home, a group of thieves (led by great character actor/martial artist Anthony De Longis) crash the party, and the only hope the party has of ridding it of the bad guys is MJ, who is in a confused state when she's an on-again, off-again martial arts-proficient Marine.

Long unreleased, *Double Duty* is a screwball comedy at heart, with action undertones. Mimi Lesseos (also in *Personal Vendetta*) wrote and produced (and performed the end title theme

song, too!), so she's always front and center, giving herself the spotlight. There's an undeniable oddness to how politically incorrect the movie is at times, but fans of Mimi won't care because she gets in on the action at every opportunity and she even gets undressed a few times. As it is, *Double Duty* is an odd duck. It's not for everyone. Directed by Stephen Eckleberry.

INTERVIEW:

MIMI LESSEOS

(djm)

In a genre dominated by men, it's a rare and welcome thing to find a strong female announce herself as a verifiable action hero, and no woman has said it as loudly with her films as Mimi Lesseos. With a muscular, imposing frame and a background in wrestling, kickboxing, and martial arts to boot, Lesseos made her mark in action cinema with a string of low-budget films (which she also wrote) where she was the star front and center. It's a shame that she wasn't able to prolong her short reign as a direct-to-video action star because when she was displaying her hard kicks and lethal punches, no man could withstand her force.

How did you get your career started as an action star? Was it an easy transition from wrestling and fighting, or was it a long, drawn-out struggle to get your foot in the door?

Really, how it first began, I always wanted to be an actress. My whole, entire life. I was born and raised in Hollywood, second generation. My mom was born and raised in Hollywood. I always wanted to be an actress, but it doesn't always work out that way. There're many detours. You can go the other way, where the detour will lead you to your dream if you continue. I never expected to be a pro fighter—*ever*. But my uncle is Gene LeBell, so he sort of helped me go into the arenas and see all

Promo artwork for *Personal Vendetta*. Author's collection.

the fighters, the tough boxers, and the wrestlers. It sort of gave me an inspiration. He'd put me in a headlock and say, "Come here, you ugly kid! Come here!" My goal, my dream, though, was to be an actress. To follow that dream, I got to be the martial artist that I am. I started with judo, then I started kenpo karate, and full contact, and I went all around the world fighting. Then I got a name for myself. It was "Magnificent Mimi." I was in AWA . . . Japan was probably the biggest highlight in my fighting years because the fighters in Japan went all out. I mean, *they're nuts!* Absolutely crazy for training. They would train four to five hours before they had a match! Americans are exhausted by that point. When I would travel to Japan, it sort of gave me that high inspiration to be a *really* good fighter. I never threw my dream of acting away. It just brought me into another realm where I could be really good at what I was doing at the moment. Like the song, "Love the one you're with." Do it! If you're thrown into a different career than what you're expecting, *do it well.* Damn well. That way you can back up who you are.

When you started doing movies, you wrote them and produced them, as well as starred in them. That's unusual.

When I retired from the circle of fighting, it was around 1990. I really focused on producing and starring in movies. My very first one was *Pushed to the Limit.* I wrote the script because it was a self-told story, but movie-ized. With that, I ran out of money, and I couldn't get the audio and the soundtrack done. I only had enough for principle photography. So I took on a competition in Japan, and producing a film drives you to want to kick anybody's ass. It's a very hard process when you're producing a film. It was my first film, and I pulled in all my favors. I financed it myself. I financed my house to produce it. I ran out of money, took the competition in Japan, and by that point I was so wound up that I won the competition, won the money, and back then if you were a fighter in Japan, you were like a rock star. You're on the front page of *everything.* What I did was, I utilized that and cut myself a trailer from the footage that I had, and I brought it to the largest distributor in Japan, which was Gaga. Because I had gotten all that publicity in Japan and had that footage, I was able to make a sale of my film. I came back home with a very large sale from Japan and because of that, I was able to find a distributor here. Then I was able to finish my movie. I then was able to do a movie a year. I would put the money I earned into another movie.

You only made a handful of films. Was this a lucrative period for you as an action star? Why didn't you make more movies?

Well, in the '80s you could make a film and sell it to the world. It was a roller coaster. You were able to sell movies like Kool-Aid. But then, the video market . . . it was good, but then it started deteriorating after a while. Video was not the happening thing anymore. I was able to sell two hundred or two hundred and fifty thousand units in just one sale. Not anymore. It depends on the quality of the movie. You can't just put anything out there anymore.

Well, it was great seeing you in your movies while it lasted. When you kick a guy, he flies across the screen. Some of the fights in your movies look fantastic.

I coordinated most of the fights, but I also brought in some coordinators. What I do is I don't just bring in stunt guys. I bring in martial artists who don't just want air kicks. They want contact. It gives a better reaction. Hell yeah, it hurt.

I really liked *Beyond Fear* where you're in the forest as a tour guide.

That was a very interesting movie because there were a lot of tricky weather moments. We went up to the forest for that one, and it was written for sunny, exterior scenes, but then this big, huge flash flood comes along—real weather. It rained on us hard. It stormed and flooded our RVs, and our cameras got washed away. It was a major thing. You have to be very creative as a filmmaker when that stuff happens. Exterior scenes become interior tent scenes.

One of your movies, I think it was *Streets of Rage*, was directed by Danny Elfman's brother Richard, who had done *Forbidden Zone*. How did he of all people become the director of this film?

Rick is an interesting filmmaker. I actually dated him for a while there.

Ah, well there you go . . .

He was a wild man. You think I'm a wild woman . . . he was a wild man. He was a lot of fun and I really respect him. As a matter of fact, there were a couple of times where I chased him down the street because he was yelling at the crew so much. (Laughing.) Just don't yell at my crew. Please don't yell. (Laughing.) If you ever got a quote from Rick, he'd probably say, "Mimi's handshake

Promo artwork for *Streets of Rage*. Author's collection.

is better than any studio network—ever. That her handshake and her word are gold." With all the fighting and all the fuss and the stomping, he made a good friend.

Any comment about your latest film *Double Duty*, which is still unreleased?

Tom Sizemore was an amazing actor. He did a role for it that he's never done before. He played a feminine, almost gay kind of character. We had a great cast. I wanted to put a movie together where I was a tough, military broad, but who turns into a feminine, nontough, nonviolent person who doesn't even know she can fight. She gets hypnotized with the snap of a finger. The whole movie, they're messing with me because I'm hypnotized. I just wanted to show the two characters that I have. In real life, I'm very soft, very feminine, but in the movie she's a badass and she kicks ass. I wanted to bring both of those out. All my fans think that I'm just a badass, and I *am* a badass, but I'm a woman. I don't let my soft side out too often in my movies. I wanted to do that with *Double Duty*, but not disappoint my fans.

Say something about your stunt career. You've worked on some "A" films like *Million Dollar Baby* and *Man on the Moon*.

Yeah. I stopped doing the pro fighting and did stunts. They hire me as Mimi Lesseos, but not as a double. I get hired to play characters. I was also in *Green Hornet* and *Gangs of New York*. It's really fun to do stunts. I don't have to produce those films, I'm not the actual "star" of those films, which is nice. Everybody's eyes aren't on me. I'm not on camera every second. To me, doing stunts is a lot of fun because you go in and get attention and you still get to kick ass. I don't have all that responsibility as a producer. When I was doing stunts for *Malcolm in the Middle*, I doubled Jane Kaczmarek every season. I'm usually the sexpot, hot babe kicking ass. Doubling someone as goofy as Jane Kaczmarek, who's like Carol Burnett, and I had to imitate that. I was this goofball, and that was kind of cool.

Is there anything that you would like to say to your fans?

Oh, my goodness. What I would like to say is keep on keeping on. Keep dreaming your dream and dive in. Never forget about Mimi or Magnificent Mimi . . . oh, my God, I'm going to cry! (Laughing.) What makes me want to make more movies—oh, my God, stop! (Crying.) Talking about the fans makes me very emotional. My fans are my inspiration to make more movies. Because they look up to me and like my work. It's an extremely powerful and emotional feeling I get when I talk about my fans.

Double Impact

1991 (MGM DVD) (djm)

"There's two of them!"

Twin brothers Chad and Alex are separated as babies immediately after their dignitary parents are murdered by the Hong Kong mafia in Hong Kong following a major development deal gone bad. Years later, Chad (Jean-Claude Van Damme), who's been raised by his guardian, Frank (Geoffrey Lewis), in France and Los Angeles, has become a bit of a dandy, working at a gym, studying martial arts, and spending all his money on fine clothes. Frank does some research and finds out where Alex (also Van Damme) was raised and now lives: Hong Kong. Not knowing that he has a twin brother, Chad accompanies Frank to Hong Kong, thinking they're going on vacation, and they barely have time to step off the plane when small-time hoods and crooks think Chad is Alex. When he finally meets his small-time criminal brother, they clash, but when Frank lays it all out that their parents were killed by the mafia on the order of a British businessman, the two brothers plan out a revenge to regain their honor. They have a notable adventure together, and it's fun seeing Van Damme playing two clearly defined separate characters.

Released on the coattails of *Lionheart*, *Double Impact* was a solid stepping stone for its rising star. The film looks really good, and the script is surprisingly coherent and moderately intelligent enough that when action occurs, it's never in excessive amounts or gratuitous. Van Damme's acting is pretty good, considering English isn't his strong suit, and he clearly has a grasp on who he's playing at all times. Director Sheldon Lettich (also the director of *Lionheart*) gives the film a nice, wide-open scope, featuring great views of Hong Kong and other areas where the film is set. Arthur Kempel delivers a good action score, and there are times when I thought that it is a real shame that action movies today aren't afforded the same time and budgets that even a "B" movie like *Double Impact* was given once upon a time. Van Damme, in this film, shows that he's a movie star. The few movies he did after it only helped him retain his stardom. He co-wrote the script with Lettich. Bolo Yeung and Evan Lurie are in it as villains. Later, Van Damme would play twins again in *Maximum Risk*, and again in *Replicant* where he fights an evil clone of himself.

Double Tap

2011 (NOV) (CD)

"So the real question my friend is, do you want to be fucked or do you want to be superfucked?"

Bobby Giovanni (martial artist Fabian Carrillo) is a tough LA detective who doesn't play by the rules. While he's off dealing with some black market dealers, his wife is brutally murdered. The shocking event sends him into a downward spiral, eventually leading to a pain-killer addiction. He's so lost in his own pain, he can't pull himself together and he's unable to care for his own children. The need for revenge is eating away at his very soul and only after he brings retribution to those responsible can he have any peace. It's a long road, and he plans to walk alone but there are people around him who want to see him succeed in getting some sort of closure, like Captain Spears (Richard Tyson). Bobby has time to reflect, and if he can pull himself together long enough he will find the road to redemption has always been there all along, right in front of him; all he needs to do is follow it.

Even though *Double Tap* is a low-budget affair, there's something else at work here pushing the film into the realm of absolute entertainment. Sure, it could use some fiddling with from an editing standpoint but this role really does allow Fabian Carrillo (*Latin Dragon*) to lose himself and just go. It's more about the personal journey, allowing the action to take a backseat. The film is bookended by two solid fight scenes with Fabian showing the world just how dangerous he can be. Director Ryan Combs (*Caged Animal*) is a miracle worker when it comes to getting the maximum bang for the buck. The main issue with the movie is all of the needless flashbacks. These moments are meant to elicit a dramatic response while the character is reflecting, but these moments only take the audience out of the moment and interrupt the flow of a scene, especially during the final action confrontation. *Double Tap* is a solid outing that sat on the shelf for over four years but is finally completed for all to see. It's available on iTunes.

Double Team

1997 (Sony DVD) (djm)

Emulating the globetrotting superspy-antics of the James Bond pictures, *Double Team* is the inevitable movie that Jean-Claude Van Damme would make with Hong Kong director Tsui Hark. He plays a retired secret agent named Jack Quinn, who is pulled back into "the game" when his arch nemesis Stavros (Mickey Rourke) resurfaces. Stavros is so cunning and so lethal that he's one of those terrorists who thinks twelve steps ahead of everyone else. He says

Jack Quinn (Jean-Claude Van Damme) and his wife Kathryn (Natacha Lindinger) in *Double Team*. Author's collection.

Agent Jack Quinn (Jean-Claude Van Damme) encounters other agents who want to kill him in Tsui Hark's *Double Team*. Author's collection.

things like, "Kill her in sixty seconds," which is a minute faster than everyone else around him is thinking. When Quinn botches an assassination attempt on him, Quinn is wounded and when he recovers he finds himself on The Colony, a place where spies are exiled if they screw up. The Colony is like The Village—that place where Agent Number Six is sent in *The Prisoner*—and there's no escape from it. Quinn and all of the other exiled agents are still forced to work counterterrorism while in The Colony, and he spends the next several months planning his elaborate escape so that he can be back home in time for his son to be born. When he escapes (the best scenes of the movie involve him planning his exodus), he enlists the help of Yaz, a freakish variation of the "Q" character from the James Bond movies. Yaz, played by Dennis Rodman, is basically there to bounce one-liners off of Quinn, who makes jokes at his expense: "Who does your hair? Siegfried or Roy?" Together, they become the "Double Team" of the title, and the climax has them running around a coliseum in Rome, with a shirtless Stavros and a Bengal tiger dogging them at every turn.

A product of its time, *Double Team* has its merits, but the core idea of the film—retelling *The Prisoner* with Jean-Claude Van Damme at the center—is incredibly appealing and should have remained the focus. The original script was called *The Colony*, but as these things go, the movie became bloated by adding in unnecessary elements . . . like Dennis Rodman. Having Rodman (who was a big basketball star at the time) in the film only makes it kitschy and a novelty (even then), so the movie suffers for it. The highlight of the film is Mickey Rourke who was in the process of reinventing himself with a buffed-out body and a sort-of new face. He plays the thankless role of the villain with some pathos, and he manages to make him interesting and sympathetic. Director Tsui Hark helped ruin Van Damme's theatrical career with this film and their next one, *Knock Off*. Rodman starred in his own action movie *Simon Sez*, which was amazingly a theatrical release.

D

Double Trouble

1991 (Columbia/Tristar VHS) (djm)

"Oh, now who said body builders were big and dumb?"

David and Peter Paul play estranged twin brothers on opposite sides of the law. David is a maverick LA cop whose partner is killed and framed for drug use, and Peter is a rich jewel thief living high off of his spoils. David busts Peter red-handed and the department wants Peter to be David's new partner for a while as he might have some information that could lead them to an international criminal (Roddy McDowall) who has a penchant for killing his henchmen when they screw up. The two huge brothers fumble their way to their goal, but not without getting punched around, shot, and mistaken for each other on more than one occasion.

The Pauls have taken heavy doses of criticism over the years for their handful of marginal movies, and perhaps rightly so, but movies like *Double Trouble* and *Think Big* have their charms. The two guys managed to stay in the game a lot longer than some other action guys, and their movies have an odd playful innocence about them. There's not a lot of cursing, no sex or nudity, and the bloodletting and violence is kept to a minimum, despite the "R" rating on some of their movies. Kids will like this stuff more than adults will. The director, John Paragon, played Jambi the Geenie in the original *Pee Wee's Playhouse*. He later directed *Twin Sitters* with the Paul's. Kurt Wimmer (*One Man's Justice*) cocreated the story and co-wrote the screenplay for *Double Trouble*.

Down 'n Dirty

2001 (City Heat DVD) (CD)

"You know what kind of gun I carry? A Desert Eagle, the most powerful handgun made in Israel. I know what you're wondering, you're wondering if I'm really holding a loaded gun at your head. Now that wouldn't be very nice of me, would it?"

After a four-year hiatus, Fred Williamson brought back Dakota Smith (previously seen in *Night Vision*) for another round of stomping out the bad guys. This time, Dak witnesses his partner being murdered. The killer escapes unseen, leaving Dak with tons of questions and revenge on his mind. He finds there are some rotten apples in his department who want to see him go down. Dak knows there's corruption in the inner circle on the force and it all leads right to district attorney Mickey Casey (Gary Busey), who isn't taking too kindly to Dak's prodding so he has people out trying to put an end to him.

Luckily Dak still has a friend on the force in Detective Jerry Cale (*Police Academy*'s Bubba Smith) who is willing to risk his own career in order to help out his pal.

If you love The Hammer, then you know exactly what you're getting when popping this baby in the playa. Not only is Fred at his best, but he treats us all by inviting a few friends to take the journey with him. We get appearances from Gary Busey, David Carradine, Sam Jones, Charles Napier, Tony Lo Bianco, Andrew Divoff, and the amazing Bubba Smith. Watching him and Fred together is reason enough to experience the film but we all know that Williamson is the real attraction. If we go over the Williamson checklist, we know he smokes stogies, loves music, defies authority, and the ladies love him. As usual, he directs himself in an '80s style action/thriller, giving the fans exactly what they hope for.

Dragon (a.k.a. Wu Xia)

2011 (Anchor Bay DVD) (CD)

"The human body is very magical—it can fool people. You see, you must die."

There have been two deaths in a small village that Detective Xu Bai-Jiu (Takeshi Kaneshiro) just can't seem to let go of. A simple villager named Liu Jin-Xi (Donnie Yen) who works in a paper mill managed to take out both of these criminals by accident and becomes a hero in the village. But something doesn't sit right with Bai-Jiu, and he analyzes every clue he can find in order to unveil the truth. In doing so, a man's life is turned upside down, hurting the family he loves, and exposing his village to an evil clan bent on finding out if Jin-Xi is actually a missing gangster named Tang Long. member of the clan known as Master of the 72 Demons. Though he longs for a quiet life with his wife and children, his past will threaten all which he holds dear.

This is such a unique film for Donnie Yen (*Tiger Cage*). It plays out very much like an episode of *CSI* or something when the detective character is trying to obtain clues. Yen is much more subdued, and his performance is rather strong as a man being pulled in two different directions. This is very much a tragic character story, which eventually pits Yen against cinematic legend Jimmy Wang Yu (*The Man From Hong Kong*). The film has a beauty and style all its own and the score combines the traditional with a heavier rock sound. It may take a while for the rumbles to begin but Yen has a few tricks up his sleeve, delivering several fights that combine moments we expect from him with a far different take on the fight front. Director Peter Chan (*The Warlords*) takes a traditional martial arts film and gives it a modern spin. The story is very similar to the David Cronenberg film *A History of Violence* and Renny Harlin's *The Long Kiss Goodnight*.

Dragon and the Hawk

2000 (Inferno Films DVD) (djm)

Dragon Pak (Julian Lee from *My Samurai* and *Little Bear and the Master*) comes to Los Angeles from Hong Kong to look for his MIA sister, who stopped sending letters months ago. He begins showing her picture around, is taken advantage of for being a foreigner, and gets himself into trouble with the law pretty quickly because when people slight him, he uses his taekwondo on them. Finally, after being duped and dumped on by everyone else, a renegade policewoman named Hawkins (people call her "Hawk," played by Barbara Gehring) decides to help him because there have been other young women who have disappeared on her beat, and when they team up they're able to get somewhere on the case. A foreigner named Therion (a terrible actor named Trygve Lode) has been kidnapping women that society has cast off and uses them for a devious scientific experiment, and Dragon's sister is clearly under Therion's umbrella of evil. When the two modern avengers get onto his megalomaniacal scheme, they level the playing field and get to hand out some justice.

I would love to recommend *Dragon and the Hawk* and every other earnest martial arts action movie that seeps out of the woodwork, but there are massive problems with this movie. It feels like it was made at least a decade earlier than when it was shot, which isn't a bad thing, per se, but it's not a good selling point to a crowd that craves cutting edge action, clean cinematography, marketable stars, and some sophistication. Every movie I've seen with Julian Lee can be accused of being a waste of time, but I actually really like the guy. He's so good-hearted and on the side of righteousness in his films that it's easy to dismiss him as being out of date or boring, but when he's on screen I enjoy watching him. He's like an ambassador of good will sent from a distant, faraway and forgotten village, and when he's crossed by bad guys, he goes to work with his martial arts, but he's the type of guy to help the bad guys get up after knocking them down first. So if you can watch something as amateur as *Dragon and the Hawk* and see through it and straight to its heart where Julian Lee wears it on his sleeve, then maybe—just *maybe*—you will be able to enjoy it on a very elementary level. The cast and crew are hopeless and cannot be redeemed as he can, though. Directed by Mark Steven Grove.

Dragon Eyes

2012 (Warner Bros. DVD) (CD)

A mild-mannered stranger named Hong (Cung Le) shows up in the town of St. Jude Square for seemingly unknown reasons. While looking for an apartment, he is attacked by a group of thugs. He dispatches the thugs with ease, setting into motion a series of events that he is masterminding. Mr. V (Peter Weller) is a corrupt police detective who's running the town's criminal activity and thinks Hong would be a welcome addition to head up his crime syndicate. Hong must draw upon all the skills and knowledge introduced to him by Tiano (Jean-Claude Van Damme) while they were in prison. Not only does he want to clean up the streets of St. Jude, but he must forgive himself for the mistakes he made in the past in order to become a better man.

Dragon Eyes belongs to real-life fighter Cung Le (*The Man with the Iron Fists*) while Van Damme is merely a supporting character, which is a refreshing change for the veteran action star. For the majority of his career, he has carried the weight of dozens of films on his shoulders and it's about time he gets to take a step back and play a multi-layered character who, while minor, sets the lead character off on a life-changing journey. Le, if used to proper effect, is someone to keep an eye on. He carries this picture with relative ease and has plenty of opportunities to show off his fighting skills. There's loads of action with him taking on numerous large groups of thugs with spectacular results. Van Damme doesn't really fight much, though we get to see his character Tiano handing down his knowledge to Le's Hong. Director John Hyams (*Universal Soldier: Regeneration*) knows how to use the talent with best results in a film. *Dragon Eyes* has a solid story (ripped straight from the classic *Yojimbo* and *A Fistful of Dollars*) with interesting characters and plenty of martial arts action. If that wasn't enough, Peter Weller (*Robocop*) turns in a terrific performance as the twisted Mr. V. Some of the best scenes in the film (aside from the action) feature Weller chewing up some great dialogue and spitting it out in his distinctive style. *Dragon Eyes* is an exciting film and the perfect vehicle for placing Cung Le in the spotlight.

INTERVIEW:

CUNG LE

(djm)

Former Sanshou kickboxer and current middleweight competitor in the Ultimate Fighting Championship, Cung Le, a Vietnamese immigrant, worked his way to the top as a Strikeforce Middleweight Champion before segueing into acting in several notable action films. He had a memorable fight with Channing Tatum in Fighting *(2009), and then appeared as a fighter in the post-apocalyptic video game adaptation of* Tekken *(2009). In 2012, he was the lead in John Hyams's* Dragon Eyes, *co-starring Jean-Claude Van Damme. Le, proficient in Sanda, Viet vo dao, taekwondo, and wrestling styles, continues to fight professionally and if all goes well for him, he will be a predominant force in the world of action and martial arts films for years to come.*

Your movie *Dragon Eyes* hearkened back to the golden age of action movies. The VHS era.

Yeah. I'm glad you felt that way. It was what the producers, Courtney Solomon and Moshe Diamant, wanted. To try to make it as realistic as possible. With the budget and the time we had, I think we came pretty close.

Theatrical poster for *Dragon Eyes*, signed by John Hyams and Cung Le. Author's collection.

I would agree. How was the project pitched to you?

First of all, my agent wanted a vehicle for me to sink my teeth in to star in, to show that I could carry a movie on my own. With an eye for action. I met Moshe three years before we ever did the project, and then finally he came forward and wanted to pair me up with Van Damme to make it easier to sell, and at the same time build me. He gave me the chance to carry my own movie, and at the same time let me choreograph all the action. That was my shot. Thanks to my agent.

If I'm not mistaken, Joel Silver had something to do with the film as well.

Yes, I believe Joel was also the executive producer, and he had the power to say "Yay" or "Nay" to the project. He gave me a chance, too. As far as the film being in the '80s style, it was my manager who told me that he wanted me to study these movies and to come up with my own action. He told me that the '80s were done, so to just give it a "Cung Le" feel. I evolved the action to next generation action. It's hard to evolve any action with this budget, but I actually cast most of the stunt guys and brought in my own buddies who were big names and everything started coming together. I brought my friends together. My hands were tied with some things I wanted to do, but I'm just proud I was able to get it done.

It's interesting that you said the action has a "Cung Le" feel because I became interested in you after I saw *Dragon Eyes* for that very reason. I did feel that the movie bore a signature style of fighting, and I wasn't really familiar with you before I saw it, so now I think I get where you're coming from in terms of action and being an action star. What would you say is "the Cung Le style"?

Someone who would come off the screen and not only make things believable . . . like when people say, "That was a cool ass move!" It can only be done in the movies, right? I want people to say, "Wow! That was a cool ass move, and you know that dude can really do it because he does it in his fights." That's the Cung Le feel.

I read a quote about you that said that your style of fighting is technically simplistic yet explosive and brutally practical. I thought that was perfect because whoever said that kind of knew your style from your real fights, and I'm wondering—I'm asking you—how do you translate that into a movie?

Well, you know, with all the years of martial arts and experience that I've had from so many different bouts, being able to work with legendary Hong Kong producers . . . I think Hong Kong movies—like the Shaw Brothers era, the Bruce Lee era—they gave martial arts more of an identity in film, especially Bruce Lee. He's the godfather of them all. I just feel like when you take an actor and that actor dedicates himself for three to six months and works on it, sure he's an actor and he can deliver the action, but if it comes down to the guy who's editing it and the music and the sound to make it come to life . . . now if you have someone with the knowledge, with the experience that I've come across through the years and put something together for a sequence, and I'm doing it, I can feel like I can deliver it. If you've never been hit in real life on a regular basis . . . I've seen it a million times. I see it when I spar. I see guys get hit all the time. I know how it feels. I know how to react to it. I react to it all the time. I think just with my experience, I was able to connect easily to Yuen Woo-Ping, Donnie Yen—especially Donnie Yen. He was a lot more open-minded to opinion. Woo-Ping was more like, "I know how it's done. I'm Woo-Ping, and this is how you do this, and this is how it's going to get done." Which is great because he's a master at his art. For me, I like to have an open mind like Donnie Yen and evolve, evolve with the times. Now with MMA being so big and the general audience is more educated about fighting and mixed martial arts and martial arts because it's everywhere on TV, you've got to really sell the action now for the audience.

Do you think today's audience wants the '80s style of action movies or do you think audiences are more into the new style of the quick cuts and the frantic editing?

I think audiences are content with what they're getting right now. It's just because they haven't had a chance to see anything different. That's why MMA is so big. Wow, it's as real as it gets. When I go watch a movie, I want to escape reality for a little bit. To stay in the zone for ninety minutes. To enjoy a movie. Whether it's good action or bad action, I really don't want to think about it. But I'm in the business, so I go, "Holy crap! That could have been so much better!" When Bruce Lee came out, he had that power, that presence, and he was so dynamic and so fearless on screen. There was a big void, and then Chuck Norris did his thing, and yet no one could bring to the screen what Bruce Lee brought to the screen. Then Van Damme came to the big screen. His kicks were so graceful, visually cool. Then Seagal came with the arm breaking and the aikido-type deal. Then, the Shaw Brother era came back, and we got Jackie Chan and Jet Li, who exploded onto the scene. Right now, we have Tony Jaa from *Ong Bak*, and there's Tony Jaa 2.0 with *The Raid*. Again, these are fast action, hard hitting. It's the same moves done with a different choreograph, and shot to compliment that style. What I tried to do with *Dragon Eyes*, the best I could . . . if I'd had the right budget, and if I'd had the right team, people would have been like, "Holy shit! What the hell was that?!" I haven't seen anyone use judo. It hasn't been utilized right in movies. Wrestling hasn't been utilized right in movies. If we'd had the right time, the right team, the right budget, I feel like we could have taken it to the next level and evolve movie fighting to another level.

You've stayed away from making cage fighting tournament movies so far, which I think is a wise decision. Was this a conscious decision or has it just worked out that way so far?

I sat down with my team, and we talked about it. I'm already an MMA fighter. Why am I gonna have to go and betray an MMA fighter and do this low-budget movie where I actually fight better inside a cage with someone else whether I win or lose? I'm always both guns blazing, and I leave it all inside the cage, and I get more of a reaction than putting together a fight that might compete against someone watching UFC. Until you're inside the arena, and the crowd is cheering, and you're walking out, whether you're on the outside or on the inside of the cage, it's a different feel. You can't get that same emotion from a person watching it close or an athlete fighting. Why compete against that? I feel like you've got to give yourself a chance to win. If you're gonna be the next action guy, you have to pick and choose your battles. You've got to pick and choose your script and your character to take it to the next level.

When you worked with Van Damme on the few scenes you had together, what was he like? Did he give you pointers?

Actually, Van Damme was a really cool guy to me. I picked his brain, but he really picked my brain on nutrition. He asked me a lot of questions about fighting. Most of the time I spent with him was answering *his* questions. He wanted to know what kinds of vitamins I was taking, and I took him to a vitamin store, and he walked out with about a thousand dollars worth of vitamins. He does need to work a little bit on his control because he did break someone's nose and chipped someone's tooth on the set, and I definitely had to keep my hands up and when we did our little simulation for the movie, his kicks were coming at a high velocity. You'd say, "Oh, he's a real fighter—he can take it!" I think that's why our scenes came out really good. It was definitely a great experience to work with him. I'm a big fan.

What movies inspired you when you were training when you were younger?

I think the biggest movie that inspired me was *Bloodsport* and there was another one called *Lionheart*. And *Enter the Dragon*.

At what point in your life did you decide to become a martial artist?

When I was ten years old, my mom put me in martial arts because I was being picked on a lot. I went to a martial arts school where there were all these young kids who had black belts. That's when I realized that I really had to get into this.

While you were growing up, were you renting VHS tapes of action movies, or did you go to the movies much?

I grew up in the era of VHS! I rented a lot of action movies like the Shaw Brothers' *36 Chambers Shaolin*, which is a classic. *5 Deadly Venoms. The One-Armed Swordsman.* Things like that.

So you had a lot to talk about with RZA when you made *The Man With the Iron Fists*.

Definitely. RZA and I really hit it off good. He called me little brother. I felt like when I came into the office to meet him, he said, "I want you to play Bronze Lion." I read the script, and I was like, "I can play two characters in here." He was like, "Bronze Lion is your character." I was like, "Okay. Bronze Lion it is." We worked out the little details, and I would have done that project for free. I got a chance to work and meet a lot of great people like Eli Roth and Dave Bautista, and all the producers. Russell Crowe and Lucy Liu. I became really good friends with all of them. I usually make friends on every movie I work on. Like Channing Tatum on *Fighting*. We became pretty tight. He was very athletic. I think he's one of those guys who could take a path of doing action movies, but why do all those action movies when you can kiss all these beautiful girls? (Laughing.)

***Fighting* was a great little movie. What are your thoughts on that one?**

I put together a little fight scene, and I didn't get credit for it, and that's when I realized that I had a knack for putting together fight scenes. I think that's where it started. I feel like *Fighting* could have been so much better. We had so many guys throwing punches and kicks, and Channing's character should have had a different style. It should have been wrestling with fighting. It would have been a lot more dynamic. It would have had a different feel. I'm not trying to put it down, I'm just saying that I think the actors they surrounded Channing with were not real fighters, so the actors can't really compete against guys who can really fight. I'm not sure what you feel, but when my character came on throwing the kicks and stuff like that, for Channing to slam me and to put the wrestling stuff on me, that was my input, and the movie got away from that with the other fight scenes.

Your scene in that movie is the best scene in the movie. It definitely made an impression on me. I wanted to ask you how you feel about putting guns in the hands of martial arts action stars in their movies? Steven Seagal, Van Damme, Chuck Norris used guns. Are you going to be a gun guy?

Guns bring a cool element to the action hero. You've got to have a variety. You've got to have the right flavor to have the guns. You've got to have the right style to handle guns. Nowadays, even actors who are not real martial artists are starting to get into it. It adds another element for them. They educate themselves with gun specialists on how to walk, how to move, how to draw their gun, and I think that's very important and visually important for the viewer.

Is there any action star you're really paying attention to right now?

Donnie Yen. His style is very visually exciting to watch. I heard he just made a *Flashpoint Part 2*, and I'm curious to see how that comes out. I haven't really seen anyone else come to the table except Tony Jaa. He does some pretty amazing stuff. His stunt guys are so good that he's able to kick and punch at them. The first *Ong Bak* is his masterpiece. There was one shot in *The Protector* that was pretty amazing, the one that was done in one shot where he's coming up the stairs.

What's in the future for you? Are you going to continue fighting?

I'm getting ready to fight in Macau. After that, I've got to put a little more focus on my movie career because I feel like I have a lot more to offer. I have an element of martial arts and action that people haven't seen, and hopefully I'll get a chance to develop it and produce it, and people will say, "Holy shit! That's the evolution!"

Dragon Fight

1989 (Tai Seng DVD) (CD)

Jimmy (Jet Li) is part of a traveling martial arts team that has just finished putting on a show in San Francisco. When it's time to go back home to Hong Kong, his friend Tiger (Dick Wei) isn't as keen to head back. He plans on defecting but Jimmy attempts to stop him. In the process, Jimmy misses his plane while Tiger finds himself mixed up with a group of mobsters. He kills a cop and Jimmy is wrongly accused of the murder. In a foreign country with no one to turn to, Jimmy escapes police custody and finds help in one of his admirers, a Chinese immigrant named Andy (Stephen Chow). While all of this is happening, Tiger is quickly moving up the ranks in the crime family doing all kinds of dirty work. This isn't settling well with Jimmy and when he meets up with his former friend again, it's an all-out war.

Jet Li (from *The Master*) was just a youngster in *Dragon Fight*, but you could easily see that he had something special. If you throw the flimsy plot out the window and focus on the physical altercations, then this movie is a great start to making your way through Jet's oeuvre. It's enjoyable to watch how the action sort of builds up throughout the film until it finally culminates in a one-on-one showdown between Li and Wei. The final thirty minutes of *Dragon Fight* is almost nonstop fighting. There's a standout scene with Jet fighting a large group of guys in a small party store. The place gets leveled but the interior is two floors and the stuntmen make sure both floors are used. *Dragon Fight* is just a straight-up, basic fight film that stays away from wirework and delivers the real deal. Directed by Billy Tang.

Dragonfight

1990 (Warner VHS) (djm)

"Whatever's happening here's so far beyond us. It's so far beyond two idiots out there, chopping each other up with swords. There are people up there, lady. Playing games with human lives to rule the world. That's why this has to stop. I can't stop the next one and the next one, but I damn well can stop this one. The only way to win the game is not to play."

Five minutes into the future, and corporate takeovers are fought between gladiators in a game called "Dragonfight," which is usually fought in an honorable fashion between two warriors in full armor. Two competing corporations stake every dollar on their two chosen fighters: the insane Lochaber (Robert Z'Dar) and the rational Falchion (Paul Coufos from *Busted Up*). Falchion, a seasoned gladiator, has decided to walk the straight and narrow, despite the fact that the corporation behind him is paying him millions to win their battle. This enrages Lochaber, who begins killing innocent civilians on the battleground to draw Flachion back into the fight. In a weird twist, Falchion ends up killing Lochaber several times throughout the film, but Lochaber's corporation also has a witch on their side who keeps resurrecting him.

An oddball movie to be sure, *Dragonfight* might resonate with viewers who enjoyed *Robojox*, which has a similar storyline, but as a vehicle for Coufos, it's strange because the movie was marketed around the face and name of Michael Pare, who appears in some office scenes as one of the corporate executives. Robert Z'Dar plays a deranged warrior, which feels right, but Coufos, who fared so well in *Busted Up* and *Thunderground*, is slightly miscast in this oddly confused movie. Still, it has some good fights in it. Warren Stevens directed it.

Dragon Fire

1993 (New Concorde VHS) (CD)

"They say that a rat has an outside chance. The fox is an underdog but the snake is a frontrunner, the favorite."

In the future, Los Angeles has become an apocalyptic hellhole. Laker Powers (Dominick LaBanca) heads there to see his brother Johnny (Dennis Keiffer) who has just won a fighting tournament and was killed. When Johnny's friend Eddie (Harold Hazeldine) and his sister Marta (Pamela Pond) meet Laker, they inform him that his brother was just recently murdered. The only way for him to uncover the truth is to immerse himself into the fight circuit known as "The Alley Fights." With the help of a mysterious man named Slick (Kisu), he will fight with every ounce of his will to find and destroy whoever killed his kin. Whether he is attacked by groups of thugs on the streets or one-on-one in the ring, they will know Laker Powers is a force that can't be stopped.

Dragon Fire is the fourth time Roger Corman and company used what is essentially the same script that inspired *Bloodfist* with Don "The Dragon" Wilson. With each remake, there's an attempt at launching a film career for a real-life martial artist. This time out it's Dominick LaBanca (*Street Survival*) in his first starring role. Dominick really doesn't look like a martial artist but when the time comes for an ass kicking, he delivers. The film plays out much like the 2005 remake *Bloodfist 2050* (with Matt Mullins): It's light on the dialogue and heavy on the fights. We can't forget to mention an appearance by cult director Jim Wynorski (*Hard to Die*) and an abundance of bare breasts displayed during the strip-club scenes (which Wynorski probably directed). It's short, fast-paced, and solidly entertaining . . . just don't expect to be surprised by anything. You know the story, and Kisu did a fine job with the choreography. Directed by Corman regular Rick Jacobson (*Bloodfist VIII: Trained to Kill*). If you like this, try tracking down the same movie, but done slightly differently, called *Full Contact* with Jerry Trimble.

Dragon Fury

1995 (Monarch VHS) (CD)

"You want a fight? You got one."

A vicious plague is wiping out the population of the Earth in the year 2099. The plague isn't the only thing the humans have to worry about: Vestor (Richard Lynch) is an evil warlord hellbent on ruling the land with an iron fist—marauding, slaying, and scheming. One man has had enough, one man is strong enough to fight back against him, and this man is Mason (Robert

Chapin with a mullet). After having his family murdered by the hands of Vestor's men, he meets a loony inventor named Milton (Chuck Loch) who has a time machine ready to send someone back before the events that led to the spread of the plague. If he can change these events then maybe he can save the future. With his sidekick Regina (Chona M. Jason) in tow, they have thirty-six hours to change history but they will have to fight off Fullock (T.J. Storm), Vestor's right-hand man whose skills match Mason's, if he is to return to his time with the vaccine.

Robert Chapin (*Ring of Steel*) has become a very successful visual effects artist and stuntman in Hollywood but he got his start as an action star. *Dragon Fury* is a discovery with this underappreciated action star. With his golden mullet and perpetual lack of a shirt, he barrels through enemies with swords and fists. Written and directed by David Heavener (*Twisted Justice*), the plot is mostly an excuse to string together action scene after action scene and to throw an occasional bare breast at the audience. Chapin has a great presence and he's a fantastic fighter, even if Heavener doesn't always effectively capture the action. It was followed by *Dragon Fury II* the following year.

Dragon Fury 2

1996 (Silver Lake VHS) (CD)

"Now, normally it's against my creed to kill a woman. Why don't we go hand to hand? And when I'm finished with ya, how bout you give me a little taste?"

After being cryogenically frozen for fifteen years, our hero Mason (Robert Chapin) is given a second chance at life. The scientist who did so needs his help with a gang known as the Dragons. Their evil leader Molech (Mike Norris) is in search of a computer with technology to rule the world. Mason is confused after his long slumber, and joins Molech in his quest. The future's only hope is Crystal (Cathleen Ann Gardner) who is as tough as any man. She is the only one who can help Mason to remember his past and to realize he's fighting for the wrong side. When the two of them finally join forces, they will become unstoppable.

Swordsman Robert Chapin (*Ring of Steel*) returns to his most popular role as Mason, and boy is this one odd film. It references the original but sort of takes a weird left turn and ignores what happened at that film's conclusion. The fighting is essentially non-stop and there is barely a dull moment. It isn't exactly well choreographed and all the fights seem to take place in the exact same outdoor set. Chapin and his flowing locks are worthy heroes and Cathleen Ann Gardener is surprisingly quite the tough gal. She also isn't afraid to shed her clothes in a love scene that never seems to end. Action star Mike Norris (*Born American*, *The Rage Within*) puts on his best scowl in the film for this no-budgeted quickie from director Bryan Michael Stoller.

Dragon Heat

(a.k.a. **Dragon Squad**)

2005 (The Weinstein Company DVD)(JAS)

Dragon Heat is a stylized action film about a group of young Interpol agents. The hunt for elusive enemies Panther Duen (Doi-yung Ng), Petros Angelo (Michael Biehn), Ko Tung-Yuen (Jun-ho Heo), and a host of other baddies begins when a group of terrorists violently free local crime lord Tiger Duen (Ken Tong) who is en route to court in which he will be convicted on the strength of several testimonies. It is later revealed that Angelo is involved so he can exact revenge on Tiger Duen for killing his brother. The agents who lost the crime lord vow to find those responsible, and eventually receive the help of elder police officer Kong Long (Sammo Hung). Through a series of action set pieces infused with martial arts and stylish gunplay, the Interpol team is able to find and kill the enemies.

The action in this is fun to watch, and it is refreshing to see the villain humanized in much the same way Sammo Hung's villain was in the great *Kill Zone*. Biehn's bad guy character is not nearly as mean as Hung's villain was in the other film, and he has the relatable motivation of revenge over a dead brother. Biehn's character, along with protagonist Kong Long (again Sammo Hung), are the emotional anchors of the film. Unfortunately, these two are drowned out amongst too many characters and a convoluted plot. Add to this an overly stylized camera style, and you have a somewhat messy affair. Still, it's worth watching for the fight scenes and the scene-stealing Sammo Hung and Michael Biehn. Daniel Lee (*Black Mask* with Jet Li) directed. Incidentally, Steven Seagal was the executive producer.

Dragon Hunt

1990 (NOV) (djm)

"Hunters—take notice! Although the twins are vastly outnumbered, they are masters of kung fu and kickboxing. Complete professionals. They're also skilled woodsmen. The twins can survive in the bush in the harshest of conditions. Don't underestimate them!"

Real-life twins Martin and Michael McNamara from *Twin Dragon Encounter* star in *Dragon Hunt*, an overly earnest vehicle for two of the most sincere non-actors to make martial arts action movies. They run afoul of an insane megalomaniac who has a private army of ninjas and rednecks, and their goal is world domination, but first they have to get rid of "the twins," who stand in their way. The big plan to get rid of these two guys (who sport mustaches and perpetual grimaces) is to capture them and force them to play The Most Dangerous Game in a forest. This gives the twins plenty of time

to rig traps, sharpen sticks into spears, and plan for attack as the hordes of ninjas and ruffians go chasing after them. One of the overlord's underlings tells his boss, "The ninjas aren't supposed to fight at night!" The overlord growls back, "Well, give them flashlights!"

So, yeah. Movies like this exist and people make fun of them. Movies like this, in almost every essence, were made to be made fun of, but just . . . *enjoy* it. Laugh all you want. I did. But there's a certain indefinable glory to movies like this. These two guys—the McNamaras—they really believed that they were going to be major martial arts action stars. They *might* have been in another universe. Who knows? They look like they were in their forties when they made this, but they were in incredible shape, and they tried *real* hard to be badass. The synthesizer soundtrack really goes into gear when these guys are making their traps, and the songs are kinda cool in a radical VHS sort of way. Nothing in this movie makes sense, nor should it. It's bound to be an inspiration to guys like Astron 6 who lampoon this stuff endlessly. For me, there is no lampooning it. It is perfect. It is exactly the right movie that these two guys could have made with what they had to offer. Anything else or anything more would have been a disappointment. The twins appeared in the Billy Blanks/Roddy Piper movie *Back in Action* next. Directed by Charlie Weiner.

Dragon Princess

1976 (Diamond DVD) (CD)

Kazuma Higaki (Sonny Chiba) is attacked by fellow martial arts master Hironobu Nikaido (Bin Amatsu) simply because he wants to take Higaki's place as the top fighter. Nikaido doesn't play by the rules and brings in four other masters to cripple Higaki and stab him in the eye. Shamed, Higaki and his daughter Yumi (Sue Shihomi) flee to New York where he rigorously trains her to be the best fighter she can possibly be so that when the time is right she will go back to Japan and seek revenge. After her father passes away many years later, the adult Yumi makes her way back to join a tournament, funded by the vicious Nikaido. When he realizes just how good she is, Nikaido recruits four of the best fighters to wipe out the competition. Yumi is no amateur and calls upon all of her training to get the revenge her family deserves.

Sonny Chiba (*The Bodyguard*) fans may be disappointed when they sit down to watch *Dragon Princess*. His presence may be felt throughout the film but he only appears in the first fifteen minutes. It opens with a great fight scene with him doing the things we love to see him do, but then the film quickly shifts its focus to Sue Shiomi's (*Sister Street Fighter*) character as she fights her way through a series of fighters with dedication and conviction. Chop-socky fans will eat this film up with the hilarious dubbing, ridiculous story, and endless succession of neatly choreographed fight scenes. Brilliant grindhouse madness brought to us by director Yutaka Kohira (*New Female Prisoner Scorpion: Special Cellblock X*).

Video release promo for *Dragon Hunt*. Author's collection.

Dragons Forever

1988 (Showbox DVD R2) (djm)

A playboy lawyer named Jackie Lung (played by Jackie Chan) has a client who is a drug lord, and when the drug lord tells him to get a concerned citizen off his back, Chan looks into it and sort of falls for the innocent woman whose main concern is that Chan's client is polluting her neighborhood with toxic chemicals. When Chan takes her side, he teams up with two buddies (who don't know each other and clash at first), played by Sammo Hung and Yuen Biao, to help him make the right choices. The two of them assist Chan as he goes up against the drug lord, who has a seriously badass henchman, played by Benny "The Jet" Urquidez. The final fight in the drug lord's chemical factory is insane, but the end to the film is abrupt.

Some romantic subplots bog down this otherwise amusing and intense martial arts film. Chan, Hung, and Biao had previously appeared in *Project A, My Lucky Stars,* and *Wheels on Meals*. Both Hung and Chan fight Urquidez here, and Chan also fought him in *Wheels on Meals*. Urquidez, who was a champion kickboxer in real life, later made some appearances in a few action movies like *Bloodmatch* and *Kickfighter*. *Dragons Forever* is essential mainly because he's in it. Without him, it wouldn't be nearly as special. Hung directed. Corey Yuen choreographed the fights.

Dragon Tiger Gate

2006 (Tai Seng DVD) (CD)

"We train in martial arts to protect people, not to hurt them. No matter what happens, we must never use our skills to do bad things."

The Dragon Tiger Gate is a martial arts academy that was created to train children in various techniques. These children are to use these skills in order to uphold justice. Tiger Wong (Nicholas Tse) is a disciple of the school who is eating in a restaurant where local mobster Ma Kun (Kuan Tai Chen) is meeting a rival family. They are there to discuss a plaque known as the Luocha Plaque, which will give the owner power over others in the Luocha Cult. Tiger interrupts the meeting and a fight ensues. During the fight, one of his friends takes the plaque leaving Tiger to battle the only person tougher than he is: Dragon (Donnie Yen). Tiger is beaten, but his life is spared. Later that night, Tiger is once again with his friends when Dragon returns to take back the plaque. During a large fight, Dragon and Tiger meet Turbo (Shawn Yue), who is another great fighter. When the plaque is returned to Ma Kun, he gives it to the cult leader Shibumi (Ya Kuan) to signify his retirement. Shibumi isn't satisfied with it and finally goes off the deep end. His reign of terror is just about to begin and the only way he can be stopped is if Tiger, Dragon, and Turbo unite.

Donnie Yen (*Shanghai Knights*) spent years as a celebrated screen fighter but it wasn't until his union with director Wilson Yip (*Ip Man*) that he became an international sensation. *Dragon Tiger Gate* was the sophomore pairing of these two and was every bit as exciting as *Kill Zone* (their first outing) and had a completely different tone. It was based on a comic series known as *Dragon and Tiger Heroes*, created by Wong Yuk-Long. Yen will always be at his best when he isn't using wirework, but since this is essentially the Chinese equivalent to a superhero film, it features wire stunts and non-enhanced stunts equally. Yen is such a powerhouse and has a commanding presence; he sets himself apart from his contemporaries. Within the first thirty minutes, there are two major fight scenes, staged with brilliance by Yen himself. Early in the picture, the fights are more like one versus two dozen, while in the second half the fights are much more intimate. Action packed with an intriguing story, *Dragon Tiger Gate* is cinematic adrenaline.

Drive

1997 (Med USA Pictures DVD) (djm)

"I'm not a bad guy, okay? Just relax and drive!"

If you're only going to see one movie starring Mark Dacascos, then see *Drive*. It follows the buddy/buddy formula, and gives Dacascos lots of room to show us what he's capable of as a martial artist and performer. He plays a human experiment named Toby Wong, who has been genetically engineered to move and think faster and be the ultimate weapon. He goes AWOL, and the corporation that "made" him has put a bounty on his head. Some goofy (a little *too* goofy) mercenaries, played by John Pyper-Ferguson and Tracey Walter, are on his trail until he hooks up with a barfly named Malik (Kadeem Hardison), whose car becomes their stagecoach to adventure and nonstop action. Eventually, the corporation (run by James Shigeta from *Die Hard* and the *Cage* movies) sends a more-high-tech supersoldier after them, and that leads to the last of many incredible fight scenes.

Steve Wang (*The Guyver*) directed this, and it's a shame he didn't go on to direct more action films. It's done in the Hong Kong style, with lots of close-call stunts and meticulous choreography. My one complaint is that it runs a little long. I watched the 112-minute director's cut, rather than the 100-minute producer's cut (which is available on Allumination DVD). Brittany Murphy is in the film too, and she's cute in it, but she disappears at one point and never returns, which I found strange. Kadeem Hardison also appears in *Instinct to Kill*, with Dacascos.

INTERVIEW:
STEVE WANG
(CD)

Most people tend to think of Steve Wang as an effects artist, a monster maker, and sculptor whose work has appeared in films like Alien: Resurrection *(1997) and* Blade: Trinity *(2004), as well as being one of the men responsible for creating the Predator creature in John McTiernan's* Predator *(1987). On top of his accomplishments as a creature designer, he is also a distinguished director with a style that combines the best elements of American and Hong Kong action styles, melding them together in way very few are able to do. He also directed the underappreciated action classic* Drive, *starring Mark Dacascos, and he brought the Japanese hit show* Kamen Rider: Dragon Knight—*starring American martial artist Matt Mullins—to American television.*

Steve Wang in Los Angeles, California. Photo by david j. moore.

Talk a little bit about your background in special effects and how you got started.

I started doing sculpting and mask-making when I was fourteen years old. I used to collect masks as a kid, when I was ten, then at fourteen I started making masks. This was 1980 so there were no schools or the Internet so I learned from monster magazines. I found out that in order to do sculptures you had to do molds, so I went to the store and bought some cheap clay and started sculpting. Then about five years later I moved to LA to get into the film industry so in order to get a job I scrambled to studios and landed *Invaders From Mars*, directed by Tobe Hooper. From then on I just kept working, doing stuff like *Predator*, which received some Academy Award nominations, and I just worked on dozens of movies after that, making creatures.

When did you decide to get into directing?

When I was eighteen, I had a friend who was going to school and majoring in film. He was always coming to my house telling me stories about films he wanted to make and he really didn't do any of these films but it all sparked my interest. I wanted to know what the big deal was about making a movie so I helped a friend out once, learned a few things, then decided to get some friends together, wrote a quick little script, and we shot this thing. Then I realized that people will talk about it; you watch it with your friends, and it's a cool experience but making it is a pain in the ass. You have to organize so many things and half of them always flake on you. Then you have to deal with the technical aspects like shooting the film, and everything else. Then six months later you have a thirty-minute film. I thought, *Wow, this is really cool!* So I started making all these short little films, and then eventually when I was twenty-three or twenty-four, I decided to direct my first feature film that I financed myself called *Kung Fu Rascals* and it has kung fu monsters, martial arts, and stunts I really shouldn't have for this small of a movie. It took ten months to shoot it on the weekends. I financed it myself and it cost about $40,000. I would spend five days a week planning shots then shoot them on the weekends with my friends. We shot for ten months then it took another six to edit and do post on it. That eventually led to other opportunities like codirecting *The Guyver* with my good friend Screaming Mad George, and then *The Guyver 2*, and *Drive*.

In *Kung Fu Rascals*, you played around with camera tricks like forced perspective and other illusions. Did you carry those over to any of your other projects when you had a bit of a budget to work with?

Yeah, I used those in every one of my films. I love special effects, forced perspective, and trick photography—especially when creating an imaginary world and when you don't have the money for high-end special effects. CGI has become the go-to effects technique and we didn't have that at the time, so when we approached it we approached it the old-fashioned way, using forced perspective and miniatures; we even used miniatures in *The Guyver 2* and *Drive*. I like using anything that helps to sell it. Like in *Drive*, when our heroes blew up the camper—that was a combination of things using a forced perspective shot through the window of a car, and it looks great. It's just a combination of different things. People believe it when the hotel explodes. Half of that stuff is miniatures.

Was *Drive* a project you developed or was it brought to you?

It was actually brought to me. What happened was, after *Guyver 2*, I got a call from one of the executive producers of *The Guyver*, a guy name Aki Komine, whom I'd become friends with over the years. He called me up and he had been making a lot of the *American Yakuza*-type movies. Viggo Mortenson was in one of them and Russell Crowe was also in one them before they were stars, so he got in touch with me and I sent him a copy of *Guyver 2,* and he was really impressed. He told me we needed to make another movie together so he introduced me to these guys who just did another adaptation of a Japanese anime called *Fist of the North Star,* which they'd made with Gary Daniels, and they wanted to do another one, like a reboot and wanted to know if I was interested. I was, so I got together with Nathan Long, who'd written *Guyver 2* with me, and we wrote another *Fist of the North Star* script called *Legend of the North Star.* It was pretty epic and crazy and we got the project approved and then we went to Romania to scout locations for a week and when we came back we realized the timing wasn't going to work out. Where we wanted to shoot, it was going to be covered in snow for the next five months and we needed it to be post-apocalyptic and dry so we had to postpone the film. Overseas Film Group who was financing the project came to me with another project that was ready to go if I wanted to do it in the interim, which was called *Road to Ruin,* which eventually became *Drive.* It was written by Scott Philips, and I already had that script for about six months, but I hadn't had a chance to read it. I went home and read it and I thought the writing style and dialogue were really well done, but what I had a problem with was that there was all this driving and machine gun action. I didn't think there was any way we could make this film for two million dollars. I went back and suggested we turn this into a martial arts film—still with some driving, so I re-wrote the script and but kept the road movie aspect and turned it in to them. They loved it and Scott came on board and polished it and that was the film we made.

When did Mark Dacascos come on board?

Mark came on board pretty early on. I knew about Mark for a while. The producer and I met with him. I was always sold on him, and after our conversation, everyone was sold. It was pretty easy getting him in but we did run into a scheduling conflict and Mark became unavailable but there were delays and we were shifting things around and everything worked out fine. It just ended up we only had two weeks of preproduction and then we started shooting the film. It was kind of crazy! We literally ended up making the film on the fly. There was literally

no time to prep; it was really that crazy. Nobody really met until they were on set. We were watching demo tapes on set and just saying, "They're good, let's bring them in." That's how we did it; Tracey Walter, I never met him until he showed up on set. I knew Tracey's work so I knew he was great. But other actors, I never knew or met until they showed up to work on set.

Did Mark and Kadeem Harrison know each other beforehand or did their friendship originate on this film?

They had never met before. We were looking for an African-American actor and a lot of different names came up and I saw a picture of Kadeem and thought he looked good, he looked the part but I wasn't familiar with his work at the time. I was shown some clips of his and I thought he was a solid actor so he came in and I met with him and we got along great. He knew I was into Hong Kong action movies, and we had all the same loves. He really wanted to do an action movie and break away from the sitcom mold he had. I never looked at him with some preconceived notion, I looked at him as a good actor and he fit the part and when we cast him, this was supposed to be a buddy movie, so I took Mark and Kadeem and said, "Let's take a few weeks and go hang out." We hung out, put stuff together, and just really got along and a friendship developed between all of us. By the time we got on set that friendship translated to the screen. You really get the sense that these two guys will become good friends and that's what happened. We're still good friends to this day. We all work on different projects but Mark will come visit me on set or Kadeem will visit. Mark became a huge part of the second half of *Kamen Rider* and Kadeem made a surprise visit. It was nice that it translated so well in the film and we have maintained that friendship over the years.

How closely did you work with choreographer Koichi Sakamoto and Mark to bring the fight scenes to life?

It's funny you should ask. The only scene that was prechoreographed and rehearsed was the handcuff scene in the quarry. We had a day to work out everything then we brought Mark and Kadeem in to rehearse it which was really important since Kadeem had never done anything like it before and Mark was an actual competition fighter so when it came to doing stunts and fighting, he was generally really careful, almost to a fault. So I would have to tell him to be a bit more calloused and not so afraid to hurt somebody. We had to get him comfortable working with Kadeem so he wouldn't be afraid of hurting him by accident. So he started doing the stuff, he was looking great, and we had such a good time. When we got on set that day and shot it, everything looked so natural but because we had no time in preproduction, we literally would just drag Koichi and his stunt team to a location and shoot for like three or four hours so we could see what we could do and use every conceivable angle. I wouldn't write anything extra into the script; we would go into the hotel room and I'd say, "Okay, here's the space, we have the batons and

if he gets hit one time the fight is over. There's the challenge, go choreograph something." Then the team would choreograph something while I took notes, did storyboards, and then I would come back and check on them. They would show me some stuff and I would say, "That was great, I like this." So we would sort of make things up as we went, and we would rework some of the stuff. A lot of the stuff, like the garage fight, was literally choreographed the day before and some of it was done on the spot. Koichi had come up with some stuff but I wouldn't have seen it until the next morning while we were shooting it. It continued throughout the film, he would do this, this, and that. If this part didn't work for me I would make a suggestion, then we would start shooting. Near the end of that fight, I told him things were looking a bit repetitive, so we dropped all of it and had him jumping over here and over here, and then off this thing, so he took some notes. We went to lunch then came back and started shooting. It was a very hectic pace but his team was so good and in tune and we spoke the same language so it was very easy to improvise and figure things out and there were no surprises. I know how to shoot stuff, he knows how to shoot stuff, so when we would choreograph the fights, we knew exactly how to shoot it. For five and a half weeks of the shooting schedule I was shooting twenty-two hours a day. I was literally getting no sleep. There was just so much to do and so little time to make this movie and I actually camera-operated all the fights myself so I was doing this half-asleep and would doze off between set-ups. I would shoot the thing then fall asleep right behind the camera. We would move the camera over here, put the lens on, then rehearse it. I would fall asleep for five minutes then they would wake me up and I would shoot it. That's how the entire film was made. It was pretty crazy.

The film opens with this amazing fight scene and then each consecutive fight tops the previous one. How were you able to keep up that intensity?

When I was writing the script and coming up with the ideas for the fights, I would think about how we could make each one interesting and I would come up with a situation and think about how we could allow it to be creative or how we could create an environment to allow some original ideas. When you go into a shoot, everyone knows to shoot the end action scene first, because you always run out of time. When we did *Drive,* we couldn't do that—it just didn't work out that way. The set we were shooting at was such an enormous set. And unfortunately when we started shooting, it was just being built so we literally had only the last week to shoot on that set. Generally, if the film doesn't come together, you at least have a big ending. I think the more you do, the better you will have an understanding of the logistics. The more you do, hopefully you're learning, you become a better storyteller. You'll just know where to put important scenarios to elevate the film and the excitement.

Drive is one of the best martial arts films ever produced in America. Why do you think it was treated so poorly here?

Thank you, but that's one I'm still trying to figure out. This might sound kind of silly but I think there were higher powers at work here. It really was a dream team, the producer was 100 percent behind us, the actors were fantastic, we had a great stunt team and a great production team. We all worked so hard on the set . . . it was a happy set, you know? The cut that was released in the UK was actually my original cut, so when we finished the film, we tested it, and tested it, and tested that cut so when the scores came back it was incredible. People just loved this movie. And even women loved this movie with all the comedy and they loved Mark. So essentially, we had a hit on our hands as far as we knew. The investor took it to the film market in Italy and a week later I took a call from him. He said, "Are you ready for some bad news?" I said, "What bad news?" He said, "It's about the movie, nobody wants to buy it." I thought it was impossible. I made the film for the foreign audience and I know what they like. They like action, comedy, and special effects—they respond to that. There's one hour of action in an hour and fifty minute movie. How could they possibly not enjoy this? About two years later they took it away from me and they butchered it, changed the music then just released it to HBO. It just died and disappeared. I later found out, this guy named Brian White who was working for what I think was Medusa Distribution and this label called Hong Kong Legends, he was a huge fan of Drive. He contacted me and said they had my film but wanted to release the director's cut of it. He said, "We want to do all of the interviews and everything. I've never been wrong about anything before when it comes to Hong Kong action movies. My friend Rick Baker from England and I were at the film market and saw your film. We were there selling Jet Li movies and John Woo movies and people were saying Drive was the prize of the market." So when they saw it, they thought it was going to be a huge hit because it was the perfect Hong Kong/American crossover. Miramax had made a theatrical offer to the distributor but because there were no big names in the film, the offer wasn't huge, it was more like they believed in the film and they'll spend money on promoting it but you won't get much money up front. You can expect to get your money after it's successful. The investor said "No, I want the money up front." He thought if he kept the film, cut it shorter and changed the music, it would be a bigger hit. I don't know how he came to that conclusion but that's what he decided. He never sold the film, refused all the offers, and came back to spend another year butchering it up. People were asking me why I changed the film and why I didn't sell it the first time and there was nothing I could do about it. He literally just killed the film. After it came out directly to HBO, it just died. So they had to lie to me about everything because if they had told me the truth, I never would have cooperated. I wouldn't have cooperated with them anyways because they butchered it. I didn't own the movie but they really did butcher and kill it. So anyways, Brian from Hong Kong Legends put

out my version of the film and it was huge—it even beat out some James Bond collection that was released the same time. It was high up on their top ten list. The European market is a tenth of the US market so if you sell 100,000 copies, it's like selling a million here. The investor didn't even think we would sell a thousand copies so when he heard we sold 100,000 and they were still selling, he couldn't believe it. He really fucked up. I still have all the papers saying how well the film did when that DVD was released and this guy just destroyed it. So that's what happened in a nutshell, and it still can't get a proper release here in the US. So now you have this new Drive film out with Ryan Gosling which was a success, putting the last nail in my coffin.

I saw and own the U.K. release and that version is far superior and really builds the relationship between the two lead characters. It's baffling why anyone would cut so much out.

You don't need to have any common sense or any talent to have money and distribute films or to invest in movies. So many of these people come in thinking they know more than the filmmakers, but they don't. They make stupid decisions and they kill your movie. You go into these projects, give it your heart and soul like a baby, working your ass off to do the best job you can, make the best film that you can, only to have someone step in and kill it, not giving a shit. It's heartbreaking, and I'm amazed so many people can still make movies in these conditions. I think I've reached my limit. It's on my terms or no film at all. It's not worth it. It's completely not worth it.

I guess I don't need to ask my next question about why you haven't made a feature since.

(Laughing.) Well, I did produce a TV series with my brother called Kamen Rider: Dragon Knight, which has a lot of the same connections from Drive. Aki Komine came to me with the idea because he knew I was a huge fan of Kamen Rider as a kid. I even met the creator of it when I was twenty-one so I was really excited about doing it and it would give me the opportunity to executive produce a project of this scale, and I spent two years doing it. It was a hell of a learning experience but there are good things and bad things about working in television. The bad thing is you literally have no time; the turn-around time on these shows is so quick, you have a block of scripts which all have to make sense within the grand story arc, each script has to go out to the director of the episode and they literally have one week to get it into production. There's a lot of running around, helping to write the stories, the editing, sound mixing, and all of this stuff, plus producing the show. I was also directing episodes and doing the action unit some of the time. I would be shooting action for someone else's episode and be prepping my next fifteen days of shooting and be right back to shooting again. So you really have to shoot in your head most of the time and try to keep everything in perspective while making it up as you go. That was challenging and I had learned so much with Kung Fu Rascals so I knew it was going to happen that way. I trained myself early making

my little movies so when I would walk on set I would figure out what we were doing then do it very quickly. That's the downside of doing a TV show, but the upside is having forty episodes to tell your massive story, and it was amazing. I loved that, and at the end of the two-year run you can go back and watch this giant, massive, epic story with all these characters which is something you don't get to do when making a feature film. So it's a trade-off, but I could do TV forever. It's crazy and you don't get any rest, but it's satisfying. After that, my brother and I created a couple of more kids shows which we shopped to all the major networks and one time we thought one was going to get picked up, but it didn't. After two years of that I just decided it was time to stop doing this. I had been doing it for fifteen years before this so I didn't want to waste any more time in my life. I then got back into my effects stuff. Effects are still one of my first loves and it has always treated me well. I'm always busy—all year long. So I just had to go where I was being called. I'm still very successful, still really busy and making a comfortable living. It's been nice. As far as why I haven't directed any more movies, it's not like I haven't tried. I have a lot of filmmaker friends who are always working and always busy, and I'm not talking big movies—these are small films, guys like Isaac Florentine. I have no idea what his secret is but he's always working. I don't have that success making other people's films so I don't get calls very often to do them. I can't tell you why other than maybe it wasn't meant to be. But that's fine. I'm not bent out of shape about it. I don't have to make movies or I'll die. I'm doing something else that I love which is why I came to LA to begin with and I'm still doing it. If I ever make another film I won't have anything to do with it, you know what I mean? I'll just get a call out of the blue asking me to make this movie. I think that's how it will happen, and that's how it always happens. I've come so close to getting my own films off the ground. There was one called Men of Action that a couple of friends wrote which I did an overhaul on and it's really good. Mark Dacascos was on board to star in it and we were so close to getting it made. We were literally gonna start production in a week then, and then . . . nothing. There was a Steven Seagal film I was going to direct; we were two weeks from preproduction and then the whole thing fell apart. So, I don't know what to say about that other than other people have had better luck than I have had.

For a show that was aimed at a much younger audience, Kamen Rider: Dragon Knight had a very in-depth and intricate story. How were you able to keep it all in check and still appeal to the target audience?

We had to do it all in a sneaky way. As a kid, the show really engaged me with all the characters and as silly as some of these shows were, I remember there being so much depth to the characters that at the end of a series, I would be brought to tears. These shows were always about the characters, to like the characters and what they do. You would root for them or be afraid something bad would happen to them, and these shows and characters were really important

162

in my life. When I decided I wanted to be a storyteller, I had gone to a Robotech convention, and there was this panel with the actors there, and it was packed. It was standing room only and I looked around the audience and there were these little kids in there and sixty-five-year-old men. I noticed the broad age of the audience for this cartoon, which made a statement. It was really incredible how it attracted kids of all ages so when I did *Kamen Rider* I took that to heart. I wanted to make a show that kids could love but be smart enough so the adults could watch it. I wanted the parents to sit down with them and enjoy it, too. I didn't want to insult the children—I hate shows that do that. So I wanted to make a show that would work that way. In the beginning, we had to deceive the network a little bit by making the show light with a little bit of seriousness to it, and then after the first five or six episodes the tone starts to change. Then it starts to become a totally different show and that was our way of slowly turning up the heat without being noticed. It combined all the things I loved as a kid in a superhero show and it was hard to do since we had half the budget for an episode as a *Power Rangers* episode. It was shot here in the United States (which was more expensive), so we had to get really resourceful with how we could do the show when we only had three days to shoot each episode. It was tough but there were compromises throughout and some stuff we just couldn't do. So we just tried to be cocky with one episode so we could put more action in another and still made sure to keep the story moving so it would all balance out.

Matt Mullins—the star of the show—is one of those guys who is just waiting for a breakout role. What do you have to say about him?

I love Matt Mullins! He is an awesome human being! He's genuinely a good guy. He works with children, and the guy has a heart of gold. He has no ego whatsoever and is supertalented. He had a tough upbringing as a kid and was taken in by a martial artist who mentored him and shaped him up. He grew up to be a really responsible, good human being. He gave all that back and still does by devoting his time to training young kids, teaching them discipline, teaching them respect, and all the things that are important in life. I can't say enough good things about Matt Mullins. He's just an incredibly easy human being to get along with, incredibly talented, and when we would start working we had so much fun. He's just like Mark Dacascos; he's another one of these guys who deserves to break out. These guys have such an impact on people, and they will continue to do that. I wish them both the best, and I'm sure Matt is going to do well over time. He doesn't just live to do movies or TV, he's out there in the martial arts world working to get kids exposed to all this awesomeness. He gets excited about stuff, he has a little troupe called Sideswipe and they do all kinds of shows and it's a great show, you should see it. I have no doubt that he will do well.

All of the works you have directed have gone on to be cult favorites. What are your thoughts on that?

Yeah, it's funny. I think it's my curse! (Laughing) It's true; everything I've done has gone on to be a cult film. I wonder if cult is a nice way of saying that these are unsuccessful films people like? (Laughs.) I had a filmmaker friend who has passed away now, Donald G. Jackson, and his claim to fame was a series of rollerblade movies, but that is what he would set out to do. His goal in life was to make cult movies and he would go out and try to make these cult movies but was never successful. I'm not sure why, maybe he was trying too hard to do it, making things crazy for the sake of being crazy. When I make my kind of crazy, it's crazy because it's something I like. My whole thing was that I want to make big, successful, commercial action films, but then the irony is that my films became cult movies. I can't explain it, but it must just be my taste.

What in your career has been most rewarding to you?

I'm proud of a lot of the things I've done, like *The Guyver 2*. I'm really proud of that film, though it's far from a perfect film. I don't even think it qualifies as a really good film but I'm proud of it because of all the things I had to go through to get it made. *Drive* is the other one I'm really proud of. I really killed myself making that film but it's so much fun and the fact that so many people like it, holding it in high regard, makes me so proud of what we did. Then *Predator* is another one. It was a really superfast shooting schedule, and we had so little time to build that thing and now it's this superhuge movie monster, an icon and I can't escape it. Everywhere I go there are *Predator* fanboys. I'm very grateful to have been a part of it and it's certainly helped my career, being one of the guys who built the *Predator* is really cool, and I'm proud of that.

Do you have anything you would like to say to the fans who have supported you over the years?

I'm surprised I still have fans as far as films are concerned. From the bottom of my heart I really appreciate their support, and I'm honored that they still watch my films. I hope someday I'll be able to keep making them or at least make some of the films I really want to get off my chest. And it will probably end up being another cult movie.

Driven

2001 (Warner DVD) (djm)

The movie that reunited star Sylvester Stallone and director Renny Harlin (who did *Cliffhanger*), *Driven* is an impossibly misguided movie that gets my vote as the worst movie of Stallone's career. Joe Tanto (Stallone, who also scripted) is a veteran race car driver, who is pulled back to the big leagues by a former associate (played by a wheelchair-bound Burt Reynolds). Tanto is misinformed by thinking he's wanted back to race for the championship, but the reality is that he's needed as a backup teammate to help a rookie boy wonder driver (played by Kip Pardue who has no business being in movies whatsoever) beat a determined competitor

(played by Til Schweiger). Tanto teaches the rookie some life lessons and proves that he's the guy who should be winning the races instead.

What a calamitous venture *Driven* is! The movie market hadn't seen a racing movie like this since *Days of Thunder*, and the prospect of seeing Stallone (whose career was lagging at this stage with flops like *Eye See You* and *Get Carter* just behind him) in such a film—directed by Renny Harlin, no less!—sounded appealing, to say the least. Instead of a full-blooded, hot-headed action movie, we got an inconsequential throwaway potboiler filled with lame romantic subplots, choppy, unconvincing racing scenes, and actors (aside from Stallone) who were terribly miscast. The entire thing is a fiasco. This could have been fantastic stuff, and the teaser trailer made it look a lot more entertaining than it ended up being. Stallone's next few films, *Avenging Angelo* (which went directly to video), *Shade* (a drama that was barely released in theaters), and *Spy Kids 3D*, didn't do him any favors either. And to make matters worse, *Driven* is stuffed with junky pop songs instead of a legitimate music score, which dates the film to a time when pop music was in the doldrums. This movie is simply impossible to like.

Driven to Kill

2009 (Fox DVD) (CD)

"Don't worry, my baby. You're going to be well and those who did this to you will cry tears of blood. This I promise you."

Ruslan (Steven Seagal) is a former Russian mobster who lives a quiet life as a crime novelist. His daughter Lanie (Laura Mennell) is getting married and he goes to attend her wedding. His ex-wife Catherine (Inna Korobkina) is married to Terry Goldstein (Robert Wiseden), an attorney who usually defends some pretty shady characters. Moments before the wedding their home is attacked. Catherine is killed and Lanie is just barely alive. Ruslan shows up to find his daughter just barely clinging to life and because of his past, he fakes her death in order to keep her safe. The question is, who exactly ordered the hit on his family? His first suspect is the husband-to-be Stephan Abramov (Dmitry Chepovetsky), the son of a mobster named Mikhail Abramov (Igor Jijikine). He has to quickly find out who's innocent and who's guilty since his brand of justice involves doling out pain from his fists and automatic weapons.

If every film Steven Seagal made was as good as *Driven to Kill*, the man could quite possibly find his way to the top once again. The story is a simple revenge plot, but it's done in a manner that never pulls back and is highly brutal. He never really strays from his usual formula, but the execution is spot-on. Director Jeff King (*Kill Switch*) is able to bring out the best in him. The action scenes are directed with surety and are just bloody good fun. Halfway through the film, Seagal faces off with a thug in a strip club. Knives are pulled, and the ensuing knife fight is incredible. This is a perfect example of how a generic script can become a fantastic film. Seagal brings his "A" game and delivers punishing action, bloody shootouts, and an end battle that knocks your socks off.

Driving Force

1989 (Academy VHS) (CD)

Steve (Sam Jones) is an out-of-work engineer seeking employment. His daughter Becky (Stephanie Mason) is all he has in the world, and he'll do anything to take care of her . . . even if it means taking a crappy job as a tow truck driver. Set in a post-apocalyptic future, towing companies are in a constant struggle to make a buck by stealing jobs from each other, and some of the drivers resort to making sure there is plenty of work by causing motorists and their vehicles to befall various calamities. Steve quickly runs afoul of roughneck driver Nelson (Don Swayze) and his two cronies (Billy Blanks and Robert Marius) who leave him battered in the road. Luckily, Harry (Catherine Bach) comes by and checks on him. There is chemistry between them, and romance blossoms. Violence escalates when Steve starts his own company and outsmarts Nelson's tow team at every turn. This sends Nelson over the edge and the lengths he will go to wreak havoc have no bounds.

Driving Force is such a weird movie. It comes off and was marketed as a straight-up action film. The action bits mostly bookend the proceedings, but the middle portion unfolds in a soap opera-like (but engrossing) fashion. Sam Jones (*Fists of Iron, American Tigers*) is incredibly likable as Steve and his chemistry with both Bach and Stephanie Mason are spot on. You can't help but root for him every step of the way. His demeanor is cool, and he does what he has to (resorting to violence) when necessary. Don Swayze and his crew (including martial arts legend Billy Blanks from *TC 2000*) are seriously despicable villains. Swayze is the perfect embodiment of a character with nothing to lose and who would do anything to prove himself superior. *Driving Force* is able to break the mold of what is expected for most post-apocalyptic action films and turn it into something like *Days of Our Lives*—with action! It was shot in the Philippines, which is evident in the backdrop. Some pretty fun car chases take up most of the action. This one is a real surprise, and Jones proves in this film that he's a solid action star.

Drop Zone

1994 (Paramount DVD) (CD)

"Well, what other kind of jump is there? There's only one kind of jump and I did a sweet one, if I must say!"

US Marshal Pete Nessip (Wesley Snipes) is transporting a prisoner by air with fellow marshal (and brother) Terry (Malcolm Jamal Warner) when a hijacking takes place. The terrorists responsible are led by former DEA agent Ty Moncrief (Gary Busey) and are all highly skilled skydivers. It's actually a daring prison break, and they spring Nessip's prisoner Earl Leedy (Michael Jeter). In the mayhem, Terry is murdered, and the terrorists escape with their target. Nessip ends up being the fall guy, and the blame lands on his shoulders. He can't let it go, and needs to find his brother's killer. He enlists the help of Jessie Crossman (Yancy Butler), who happens to be one of the best skydivers in the business. Together they have a common interest and set out to expose the truth of what really happened on that plane.

Drop Zone is nothing but a studio-driven, by-the-numbers action/thriller that is slightly elevated by a likable cast and adequate direction by John Badham (*Blue Thunder*). The plot is highly predictable, and it only takes moments to figure out where it's headed and what will happen. Star Snipes (*Demolition Man*) does what he can to breathe life into a rather uninteresting character with mixed results. He's enjoyable but the character is pretty one-dimensional. As far as action movies go, it was sort of disappointing. There's one good fight where he takes on several guys in a bathroom but other than that, everything is kind of scattershot. To have the film set in the midst of the world of skydiving was a good idea, and it affords viewers the opportunity to see some pretty stunning aerial photography, which shows off some skilled divers. There are some chintzy-looking effects shots thrown in to spice things up, but ultimately with poor results. We tend to forget just how talented of an actor Gary Busey (*Lethal Weapon*) is, with the way he currently portrays himself in the media. He knocks it out of the park as the villain and tends to be a bit of a scene-stealer every time he's on screen. With only one all-out fight scene and some scattered mayhem, *Drop Zone* is a letdown. It's already proven that it won't last the test of time.

Dr. Wai in the Scriptures with No Words

1996 (World Video DVD) (CD)

"I love to be a pile of shit. If only a flower is willing to be placed on it."

Serial novelist Si-Kit (Jet Li) is on the outs with his wife Cammy (Rosamund Kwan), which is causing him great stress. With all these distractions, he's finding it incredibly difficult to write and has developed a case of writer's block. His friend Shing (Takeshi Kaneshiro) and their assistant Yvonne (Charlie Yeung) decide to ghost write the next story in the "King of Adventurers" saga. The story within the story puts Dr. Wai (Jet Li) in search of a box with supernatural powers in which the Scripture With No Words must be contained in order to have the future foretold. He sets off on an epic adventure with his friends to unite them while trying to keep their findings out of the evil clutches of Hung Sing (Collin Chou).

This 1996 feature film won a Golden Horse Award for "Best Visual Effects" which was very welcomed since the production went overbudget when a fire destroyed sets worth millions of dollars. Jet Li (just two years away from *Lethal Weapon 4*) plays both Si-Kit and Dr. Wai, otherwise known as the "King of Adventurers." As Si-Kit, he's nothing but a writer and never gets into a scuffle. In fact, he won't even slap his own wife. In the Dr. Wai story, he is much more agile and ready to throw some punches. Wires may aide him, but under the direction of Ching Sui-Tung (*Belly of the Beast* with Steven Seagal) they have some fun with the action. There's a fair amount of slapstick thrown into the early fights, and we are treated to a final battle with large flaming bullwhips. No matter who it is, whenever an action star dresses in drag, they always make the ugliest women.

Dual

2008 (Cinema Epoch DVD) (CD)

"When I was a boy I used to wonder; if I listened real hard, could I hear the sound of hate? Not the screaming and shouting, not the crack of a gunshot, but does it actually have a sound?"

It's the late 1800s and Luke Twain (Michael Worth) is traveling the countryside alone. He stumbles into a town where the entire population has been murdered. He's devastated by the discovery and buries all of the bodies. He hangs around the town for a while trying to gather his wits in order to go off and seek revenge on those who did it. He soon discovers he's not alone: Ember (Karen Kim) has been there hiding all along and they quickly fall for one another. A mysterious stranger (Tim Thomerson) shows up in town, participating with Luke in a psychological duel to uncover the truth of what really happened in the town.

This film was a passion project for action star Michael Worth (*U.S. Seals II*) and a far departure from what we expect to see from him. Worth stars (he also wrote the script) and spends the majority of the screen time alone. He steps out of his comfort zone and stretches himself as an actor. *Dual* is a little slow moving, but the story is engaging enough to keep you interested. The only action in the film occurs near the end with a good old wild west shootout. Director Steven R. Monroe (The *I Spit on Your Grave* remake) has a style all his own and there are some wonderful shots in the film. It's a different sort of film, and it won't satisfy every action fan out there. Fans of Michael Worth should check it out.

Dubbed and Dangerous Trilogy

2001-2004 (Paiaya DVD) (CD)

"Okay, now listen up. Everything's been organized for the escape of Big Al from the maximum security prison tomorrow. We've got some chill time from being evil, so let's play some football."

Ara Paiaya made his writing, directing, and acting debut with this trilogy of short films about special agent Ara, the best in the business. After terrorists blow up a train, he's assigned to find the men (and women) responsible. Over the course of these three films, Agent Ara has to fight his way through gangsters and terrorists in order for him to save the world. *Dubbed and Dangerous* is a loving ode to not only martial art films but also pictures like *The Matrix*, *Austin Powers*, and many others.

These micro-budgeted action films pride them-selves on delivering in the action department, despite of not having much money to play with. Set pieces are expertly staged and Ara Paiaya (later in features like *Death List*) isn't afraid to let his audience know just how much he loves Jackie Chan. He really knows what he's doing when it comes to action, but the fighting balances the fine line between homage and plagiarism. The story is almost nonexistent, but what makes it particularly fun is all of the English-speaking actors are dubbed in English. Most of the voices were done by Ara himself and the results tend to be pretty funny. You can see the growth from picture to picture and the final one has cameos from martial arts film historian and sometime actor Bey Logan, as well as Freddy Krueger himself, Robert Englund. Don't be fooled: these guys make very brief appearances and they're just there to lend their names to the project. These are crudely patched together little flicks (shot on video), but they're charming, and the dedication Ara and his crew show is quite admirable.

He doesn't need a deadly weapon: He is one! Action star James Lew. Photo by david j. moore.

Eastern Condors

1986 (Fox DVD) (djm)

After the Vietnam War, the Pentagon convenes a meeting comprised of a bunch of Chinese prisoners who are told to take on a do-or-die mission: Go to Vietnam and destroy a munitions base that the US left behind after the war. The Chinese team (played by Sammo Hung, Yuen Wo Ping, Corey Yuen, and Haing Ngor, amongst others) can earn their freedom, and so they all go along with the mission, armed and prepared for battle. When their plane crashes behind enemy lines, they're captured by the Viet Cong and tortured, but they manage to escape and join with the local Vietnamese (Yuen Biao plays a local commando) and three female rebel commandos, who help them complete their mission.

I have no idea why more people don't know about *Eastern Condors*. It's Hong Kong's answer to *The Dirty Dozen* and it mirrors Stallone's 2008 film *Rambo* in ways that should be seen to be believed. Incredibly violent, tense, and with balls-to-the-wall action, it packs an incredible wallop. Hung, who also directed, looks slimmer and more agile here than he usually does, and some of the gunplay and explosive stunt work will make you sit up in your seat. Fans of *The Expendables* and *Rambo* should definitely check this one out.

Easy Money

1987 (Universe Laser & Video Company DVD) (CD)

Michelle Yeung (Michelle Yeoh) has all the money and riches she could ever want or need. She is smart, sophisticated, and knows how to manage her wealth. These qualities are what makes her a successful businesswoman . . . *but* . . . she likes to steal. And not just petty theft, mind you. She enjoys plotting and planning out elaborate heists. After a close call robbing the Hong Kong Jockey Club, she draws the attention of police detective Ken (Kent Cheng). With him close on her tail, she meets Lam (George Lam), a guy who spends his time investigating insurance fraud. They quickly form a bond with one another, and Lam can't help but fall for the lovely lady, even though she may be a bit of trouble.

After making this film, Michelle Yeoh (an international superstar from *Tomorrow Never Dies* and *The Touch*) took five years off from the business to raise a family with her then-husband, producer Dickson Poon. *Easy Money* is mostly a half-baked attempt at remaking *The Thomas Crown Affair*. There are some neat ideas when the characters pull off the heists but overall the film lacks a sense of fun and action. Yeoh is as beautiful and lithe as always but her gracefulness and fierce spirit are missing from this film. As a completist, you won't want to miss seeing the film but be warned of the overly long interludes and ho-hum pacing. We love Michelle, and every chance we get to see her on a screen is worth the effort, but this one is far less memorable

than something like her vehicle *Royal Warriors* or *Magnificent Warriors*. This was a transitional period for her and when she returned to the screen in *Supercop*, she became the action star we all know and love. Directed by Stephen Shin.

18 Fingers of Death!

2004 (Screen Media DVD) (djm)

A passion project for character stuntman, martial artist, and actor James Lew (*Red Sun Rising*, *American Ninja 5*), *18 Fingers of Death!* pays slight homage to his idol Bruce Lee and pokes fun of half of the action stars he worked with throughout his career. Shot in the faux-documentary style of *This is Spinal Tap*, the camera follows him on his quest to find financing for his next action film, *18 Fingers of Death!* He plays an aging action star (of more than 800 films) named Buford Lee, and we see him living humbly in an apartment full of mementos from his career and we see him trying to recruit other action stars like Don Wilson and Lorenzo Lamas (who basically play themselves) to co-star in his film. Bokeem Woodbine plays Billy Buff (a take on Billy Blanks whom Lew worked with on *Balance of Power*) and Pat Morita shows up as an old man who says some words of wisdom to Buford.

Calling this a spoof of action films wouldn't be accurate. It's spoofy and crude to be sure, but Lew seems to be making light of being an action star in general, while commenting on the hardships of his business. It's a telling sign that this is the only feature film he's ever directed, and you'd think a well-respected and highly regarded stunt and fight coordinator and actor such as he would have gone on to direct more films of his own, but as of this writing, *18 Fingers of Death!* remains his only directing credit. It's silly, childish, offensive, and mostly unfunny, but if you're a fan of Lew and of "B" action films, it might be of interest. Lew is to be commended for making this film of his own volition and with his own money, but it could have been so much funnier and telling.

INTERVIEW: JAMES LEW

(djm)

Anyone who's watched about a dozen martial arts or action movies from the 1980s or 1990s has most likely seen character actor and stuntman James Lew get pummeled by the star of the film, and after seeing dozens of these pictures, there should be a point where Lew begins to emerge as a mainstay in the genre. "It's that guy again! It's James Lew!" With over 100 credits as either an actor or stuntman (or stunt coordinator), Lew is a true perennial in the action industry, and he deserves a one-of-a-kind award for having taken so many hits on screen.

Stunt man and action star James Lew in Los Angeles, California. Photo by david j. moore.

You've been in so many movies, and you're *still* making movies. I think most people who watch the movies that you're in don't even realize that you're in all of them. Does that ever bother you somewhere in the back of your mind?

I just enjoy this business so much. Just getting to play is always an honor and a blessing. So, I'm happy. Whenever I'm on the set, I am at home. It feels so comfortable. I like being the stunt guy who gets the crap beat out of him, or coordinating and getting to create. The best way I can describe getting to direct is like being God. How good is that? Acting, of course, I just have fun getting to pretend I'm somebody I'm not. It's such a pleasure.

You got into stunt coordinating fairly early in your career. It was John Carpenter who let you do some stuff behind the scenes on *Big Trouble in Little China*, right?

That was my first studio movie. It was an amazing experience. I got involved in the preproduction. At that time, I was like a curious kid, walking around each department . . . the props department, and then my favorite department was the guy sitting at his desk doing these drawings. He was the storyboard artist. I was so curious, so mesmerized. "What are you doing?" He showed me. I got a quick lesson. From then on, I put it into practice. I would go to the set, then I would *draw* the set, map it out, then I did my attempt at drawing, which is really horrible drawings (stick figures), but I knew instinctively how to frame where the fights should be with the different angles. Carpenter would say, "Okay, what do you have?" I would have all these sheets of paper, and I would give him different fight sequences. I would say, "Here, let's shoot this one," and he would say, "Yeah, go ahead, take it!" He would pretty much let me run with it. Sometimes I would try to push for a little more violence, and he'd go, "No! We can't shoot this one!" So I'd say, "Okay: Next!"

How have other directors over the years helped influence your style of coordinating fights, and the way that you now direct?

You know what, as far as action and fight choreography, I actually watched a lot of dancing, like musicals. The way they shoot it. You see the moves. They never try to hide it. No shaky cams, no up-your-nostrils close-ups. It goes back to the Hong Kong style. You think of the action like you would think of the ballet. You want to see the motion, but at the same time you want to capture the violence of it. That was helpful. I like Jackie Chan's stuff. When I got to be on the set with Jackie, I got to see him break it all down. Mini-masters. American filmmaking seems to always want to shoot a big, wide master shot for the entire fight, which doesn't work. Something's going to go off in the middle or at the end, so you'll have to start it all over again anyway. The camera has a very specific sweet spot, so if you're a little bit off . . . it's like getting good dialogue. You want to get the very best performance. Another thing, when I've done second unit . . . I discovered this when I was working with Mark Dacascos on a TV series: We would go off and do some second unit fight action. We would shoot it and when we would see it edited and finally put together, "Oh, they used that! We didn't want that!" So I told myself that I would shoot exactly to a point that within ourselves, we'd be cutting. When we'd shoot the second unit stuff, we'd shoot only exactly what we'd want for the cut. In a sense, forcing the editor to use certain cuts. Trying to outsmart them.

You mentioned Jackie Chan and Mark Dacascos. Would you mind talking about them in regard to the films you worked on with them?

Jackie Chan is absolutely the living legend. Here's the consummate filmmaker, not only just an actor, but a stuntman, a director, producer. He has his hands on every single part of production. His passion behind it is what's so impressive. He loves filmmaking. When he's not on set, he's constantly categorizing and cataloging ideas. He'll look at a location and say, "Oh, that'll be a great place for a stunt." He'll jot down, make a drawing, make a picture, and put it in a file. He is a great influence on me in that he takes the whole picture. He knows all the parts that make the entire movie come together. You know exactly what the director is asking for, what the DP is looking for. I think that's really important to take your performance *and* your career to another level. Mark Dacascos is probably my favorite person to work with. When we were doing *The Crow: Stairway to Heaven*, he'd say, "What'd you come up with now to make me do?" But, he's fantastic because I know I can push his limits. He'll come through and do some crazy move. He executes it better than I could ever imagine. Perfect. It's a pleasure because often I end up working with action stars who are limited to a dozen moves, and they're afraid to try something else. It's understandable because they don't want to look bad on film. It's forever. With Mark, I can unleash my creativity and just have fun. And he has so much fun on set, so that actually is contagious.

You've worked with everybody. A lot of these guys have previous reputations. How do you adapt your styles in coordinating fights to those who aren't that comfortable, as you said, with stretching their limitations?

Just like you, as a writer, you do your homework. You do your research on what your subject has done. So I do my homework before I go to a film set on what these actors have done. I get a sense of how their rhythm is. What side is stronger for them. I look at stuff, and I go, "That looks *okay*." It's best to use the very best of your actors. Just getting inside their head. I would like to have an introductory meeting with them, just to get a feel for them. It's still a character they're playing, and it should fit their idea of what their character should have. By doing that, it all goes back to making the actor feel comfortable. I want what's in their best interests. If they don't look good on screen, I don't look good. Once you get that confidence and trust, it makes a difference. Even as a director: If your actors trust you, they'll follow you. I've been pretty fortunate with that. I worked with Jean-Claude Van Damme on *Timecop*. They had me put together some of the fight stuff on that, so I put together moves, showed Jean-Claude, and he said, "Oh, no, I won't do that." I said, "Jean-Claude, just try it. We'll look on the monitor, we can watch it, and if you think it looks really bad for you, we can change it." Luckily, he said, "Okay," and we tried it, and he came back and he kind of smiled and said, "Oh, that looks pretty good." Again, it goes back to the idea that they have this persona to protect. It's them up there. Their fans will look at it, and they can say, "You suck, Jean-Claude." But that's something they need to protect. It's their business.

You've worked with all these action guys. They want to look good, and if they don't look good, they feel insecure. Talk about your experience with working with all of these guys.

I try to relate to them as my understanding as an actor. They know where I'm coming from because I know where they're coming from. If you base it on the drama or the comedy or the emotion of the scene . . . I'm for every technique and every move in a fight. It's exactly like dialogue. The better you write the dialogue that fits the character, it just makes more sense to actors. I try to create what they call beats within the scene. When you say a line, what are you trying to get from this person? When you throw this kick, what are you trying to get? Just stun him? Kill him? What's your emotion here? I think that by getting that into them, it gets their juices flowing. They feel more confident. It's the martial spirit. It comes out in their eyes. You're not just saying lines. The audience will feel it. There's not better emotional content than in Bruce Lee. When you get him pissed off, you know *you're gonna get your ass kicked!*

All roads lead right back to Bruce Lee.

He's, to me, the king of all. Love him!

I just had a question, but I don't think I want to go there . . .

You can go there.

It's a silly question. I was going to say something about stroking these guys' egos . . .

It's your attitude on how you look at it. I don't see it as stroking their ego. I think it's stroking their confidence. All these guys have insecurities. It's absolutely amazing. The bigger the star, the better looking they are, they are just filled with insecurities. Maybe because people expect so much from them. They're told they're perfect, so if they do anything less than perfect . . . Somebody who's not so big can get away with doing something not so good. Most of the time, the guys that play the villains, the bad guys, they're the mellowest dudes ever. They have less to lose.

You are usually cast as the villain. I can't think of more than one or two movies where you were the hero.

Not too many. I'm usually shot, stabbed, thrown off buildings . . .

Talk about that: being cast—typecast, literally!

I think early in my career I started questioning that. *Why don't I get to be this guy? Why don't I get to play this character?* It's the realization that . . . welcome to America. This is not Asia. The white guy needs to be the hero. Everybody else is the villain, so it's something you just can't take personal. It's business. Most of the time, if it's not written that an Asian guy is the good guy, what can you do about it? The best way to look at it is to go there and do the best you can, and hopefully from that you shine. There might be a chance somewhere else that you can do something else.

I'm curious why you haven't gone to Asia to be an action star?

That's a great question. Way back, I got to know Jackie [Chan]. My best friend is very close with Jackie. His manager at that time asked me that same question. He said, "Hey, why don't you come over here to Hong Kong and do movies?" And I said, "Two things. I don't speak Chinese. It would be a horrible challenge for me to go there and try to do something like that. And second, home is here. I guess I just can't think of going away from home. I would be such an outsider." I actually got to do this movie in Taiwan. This producer brought me over there. It was originally called *Young Dragon*, but they changed it and redubbed it and added some reshoots. I knew the executive producer. We went to Taiwan, there was the script, and there I was, a Chinese American surrounded by all these Chinese actors. They did their dialogue in Chinese, and I would respond, "Yeah, what's happenin'?" (Laughing.) I had no idea what they were saying, and they had no idea what I was saying. Then they redubbed my voice into Chinese. That was one of the best experiences for me. The fight coordinator would lay out huge fight scenes—forty, fifty moves—and I really learned how specific and exact they want your moves. I had the toughest time doing that type of fight. Every single move flows into the next one. Finally, I got it and coming back to America, the fight scenes were so easy. This was right before *Big Trouble in Little China*. I showed some of that footage to John Carpenter in my first meeting with him, and that's really what sold me to him. I was able to do Chinese style, but being an American added a bonus. I was the ideal guy.

You worked with Carpenter a few times. You were part of Hershey's gang in *Escape From L.A.*

Yeah, yeah. That was a great time, but unfortunately, the movie is . . . totally different than *Escape From New York*. You do a sequel, you should do it in the same tone. It was campy.

I'm going to throw some names of action stars, and it would be great if you could say some words about each of them. First one: Thomas Ian Griffith in *Ulterior Motives*.

Tom is great. He's such a solid actor. What people don't realize is that he comes from a real background in martial arts. He's a very solid person. He cares about the other people he works with. It makes people work harder.

Jeff Speakman. *The Perfect Weapon*.

Yeah. Jeff Speakman. That was his first movie. I don't think he was quite trained or used to doing movie fights. So I got tagged constantly. He's good. He's the real deal. He hits hard. He did a couple of moves right here to my solar plexus, and he hit me so hard right between there that my chest got real concave. I couldn't straighten up. I told the coordinator, "Man, give me a moment." I couldn't straighten up. Jeff is really good. Really fast. I finally figured out his system 'cause I don't like to get hurt. His moves are so fast like a machine gun. You have to train your body to be like a split-second ahead in anticipation. You just have to go with each hit. Boom, baboom, boom. So you're not letting it smack you that hard.

James Lew (left) and Jeff Speakman (right) in the middle of a fight scene in *The Perfect Weapon*. Author's collection.

You weren't like, "Dude. *Stop* hitting me."

There's no . . . that's all he knows. I remember it was my turn to do this one move where they wanted to do a pick-up shot where they wanted me to do a side kick. I'd been beat up all day, the stunt coordinator goes off to the side, and I smiled like this at him. He just shook his head. I went, "Aw, man." I just wanted to tag him a little bit. But I didn't. Unfortunately, your job as a "stuntman" is to eat it sometimes. That's part of your paycheck.

Steven Seagal. You've done a couple of things with him.

I've done a *bunch* of movies with Steven Seagal. I've taken every smack, every form of punishment from him. I coordinated a couple of commercials with him. One was with Nils Allen Stewart. I got

him on it because he's big. After Seagal knocks me down, he's got Nils by the hand, and I'm trying to watch from the ground. I see Seagal has his arm around him. So, he just cranks his arm and I hear this pop! I went, "Oh, man . . . " He popped Nils's bicep. I went, "Oh, man . . . " Seagal likes to play hard. My guys don't like working with him because there's so much punishment.

Let me ask you something. In the '80s and '90s, we had the rise of the action star. Even straight-to-video guys had their time in the sun. We had guys like Van Damme and Seagal, and in the late '90s, we saw the decline of the action star. Even guys like Stallone. Even he did some straight-to-video movies. You've been through the VHS era, you've been through the DVD era, and you're still here, and you're still working in the download era. What are your thoughts on the rise and fall of the action star and how it might relate to the medium they're represented on?

You know, I don't think it's the medium that has changed. I think what's happened is movies like *The Matrix*. Now you have an actor who is trained to do this stuff. Great camera stuff and wires, and you make this guy look *pretty damn good*. He looked great.

He didn't need the muscles.

Yeah, yeah. The camera tricks, the choreography. That was pretty much the nail in the coffin. An action guy who's not really that great of an actor became obsolete . . . now the studios want the name actors because the budgets are bigger.

They can turn Matt Damon into an action star.

Yeah, and Matt Damon, I thought he was fantastic in *The Bourne Identity*. The first one. I loved the first one. Absolutely flawless choreography, the way it was edited, the story. I loved it. These actors train daily before production starts. You see the difference. Now, because the stakes are higher, the studios don't want to take the chance on martial artists.

How has that affected your career?

Well, it's definitely great as far as being on the coordinating side. Part of my job is that I want to come on as the trainer too so that I can assist on other things than choreography. It's better than sending the actors off to a martial arts studio. That's actually been good for me.

I want to talk about a few movies where you actually played characters rather than just being the guy that gets thrown around.

I still die. (Laughing.)

That's okay. I can deal with that. Let's talk about a few movies that come to my mind. *American Ninja 5*.

Okay. The director called me and said, "I've got a great part for you." It was the lead villain. It was a little on the comic book side because they were gearing this particular *American Ninja* for a younger audience. You don't want to have a bad guy that is too real, and by adding the red cape and the tights, and all that goofy stuff, it lessened the realism of it. I had a great time. We shot it in Venezuela. The people there were great. My character's name was The Viper. The people there couldn't pronounce that, so they called me The Veeper. I got to work with David Bradley. I had a lot of fun with him and we became friends. Also Lee Reyes, I just treasured. He was the little kid. He was just fantastic at martial arts. I thought he was great as an actor. He had charisma.

The director was a stunt guy.

Bob Bralver.

Talk about working under the "American Ninja" banner.

I guess the pressure was off because they weren't trying to make—in the true sense—a sequel. This was going to be a little bit of a departure. We were just there to have fun. It was probably because it had nothing to do with the other *American Ninja* movies that we had free license to do whatever we wanted.

Was that the first time you worked with Pat Morita?

I think we worked on some little thing. He was great. During off time, he was playing the piano in the hotel, entertaining, drinking, singing. Years later, I wrote my little movie *18 Fingers of Death*, and he was the only guy I could imagine playing a certain part.

David Bradley. Any final comments about working with him? He was the real thing as far as action stars go. He seemed charismatic.

It's a good and bad trait for people to be passionate. In fact, it's always good. To be passionate about whatever you do. But, sometimes, if you don't keep it in check, it gets in your own way, and in this business you have to be someone that people like to work with and spend a minimum of twelve hours a day with. Constantly you're butting heads with that person. Because David is a perfectionist, and he knows what he wants, but when he sees that it doesn't come out the way he likes it, it probably really bothered him. That's a frustration that maybe turned him off to the entire business. I think he just got fed up with it. Like I said, I understand. It's his face up there. When people make fun of the movie, how can you not take it personally. "Oh, you're in that shit movie!" *Aw, great.* But like I said, I got along great with David. We were friends.

Red Sun Rising with Don "The Dragon" Wilson. Another good part for you.

Yeah, that was one of the highlights of my career. Don was absolutely instrumental in having me play that part. A lot of times, when working with a star, I hear, "Oh, I think I should be the only one doing this move or this high kick." Because they're just trying to protect themselves. They don't want you to shine more than they do. Don was completely supportive that I do my

best stuff. He was beyond encouraging. It made sense. The greater the villain, the greater the hero. Eventually, if he kicks my butt, and if I'm pretty damn good, that means he's better.

Talk about Don Wilson. He made an incredible number of movies in a row. He was an incredibly busy actor while also maintaining a real fighting career. What do you think the secret is for the longevity of some of these action guys? Why do you think some guys are able to keep going where guys like Speakman sort of tapered off?

Hmm. I thought Jeff Speakman would roll along and have a long career. He had a great shot. Right place, right time. Sometimes, it's really hard to tell. A Don Wilson movie is *Don Wilson*. You know what to expect. I think once he got his core audience, they were never disappointed. They're going to get this: Don Wilson.

I wanted to mention _Martial Law 1_ and _2_. You had bit roles in both of them, but I wanted to mention that Chad McQueen was the lead guy in the first one. You had a fight with him. In the second one, you fought Cynthia Rothrock and Jeff Wincott.

That's right. I was there on the first one for maybe a day. The second one, maybe two days.

I really like Wincott. He's fantastic. Talk about working with these people. You did a couple of movies with Rothrock and Wincott.

I knew Cynthia from back in the tournament days. Competition stuff. She was always the sweetheart darling of the martial arts world. Look at her career. Just awesome. I don't know

Jeff Wincott (with sticks) is putting the beat down on James Lew in *Martial Law 2*. Author's collection.

how many she's done. A lot. She worked hard and got her bumps and bruises.

Did you ever have a problem hitting her?

You don't hit. You don't touch. At the point when you're hired as the bad guy, you just go in and get your ass kicked. She always kicks my ass. I got to coordinate this little movie with her called *Outside the Law* in Puerto Rico. She called me and wanted me to work on this movie. It was an absolute pleasure working with her. She wanted to add some cool acrobatic stuff, and I told her straight out that I didn't know too many females that were at that level. Most of the female martial artists and action girls were good with certain things, but were lacking with that explosive energy. So I brought a buddy of mine to double Cynthia. She just said, "Whatever it takes to make me look good."

Brandon Lee. You worked with him on _Showdown in Little Tokyo_.

Yes. Fantastic human being. I remember we were just hanging out and talking on the set. He was very appreciative. He said, "Look, I'm barely half Chinese, and I'm cast as this Asian guy, and how lucky am I to be playing the lead?" I found that was pretty humbling. I think before that, he had a period of denial where he didn't want to be known as Bruce Lee's son. A lot of people—rich kids—are like "I want to make it on my own!" But that was the same kind of conflict. But once he embraced it, he really embraced it. He was really good. He really worked at it and trained. He was really serious about his acting. In *Showdown in Little Tokyo* he does that famous foot sweep while I'm doing a round kick, so one leg is up and he actually contacts my base foot, and it's on the wet sauna floor so I'm *going*. There's nothing I can do. The way they wanted me to fall, partly in the water, people always say to me, "I thought you broke your back on that." Like I said, I don't like getting hurt, so I know how to cheat it.

You worked on some Andy Sidaris movies.

Yeah! I loved Andy! He was always very positive. They were all superlow budget.

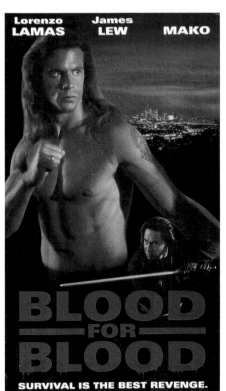

LORENZO **LAMAS**   JAMES **LEW**   **MAKO**

BLOOD FOR BLOOD

SURVIVAL IS THE BEST REVENGE.

VHS artwork for *Blood for Blood*. Author's collection.

Lots of naked ladies, though.

And he made no excuse for that. He would say, "It's time to shoot the titty scenes. It's time! It's in the script!" I totally respected him. He would put his house up to finance each movie. When the movie would make its money back, he would pay off his house again. He did great, though. That was his thing. He just rotated these movies. He wasn't a dirty old man, he loved his wife.

Was it fun to work with all those *Playboy* and *Penthouse* models?

Oh, it's a job! (Laughing.)

You've worked with guys like Tom Cruise and Johnny Depp, too.

Tom Cruise. My first experience working with him was on *The Last Samurai*. Probably one of the easiest stunt jobs that I've ever had to do. There's a scene where he's going through the village on a rickshaw. Because there were a lot of people and it was in and out and there was a very valuable passenger—Tom Cruise—they wanted a stunt guy pulling the rickshaw. They wanted a certain timing with the camera, and it was pretty technical. I got to do that. I got to rehearse for two or three days with a stunt double on the rickshaw with the DP, tracking, doing the exact take. On the shooting day, Tom Cruise was there and there were hundreds of people in the village, so I got to be there maybe like a week.

In Japan?

No, it was here. Warner Brothers. Awesome set! I walked in when they'd fully dressed everything, and I was like, "Wow! I'm in Japan!" I got to listen to Tom Cruise all day, he called his mom, "Hey, mom!" Then he said, "Oh, I'm so excited, my kids are going to come!" I said, "You want me to give them a ride?" He got so excited. "Could you? Would you give them a ride?" He was like a little kid. The nicest guy. Then I got to work with him on *Collateral*. It was supposed to be three nights in the nightclub. When I got there, they fired the DP. It turned out to be almost three weeks of shooting. Nights. Tom Cruise was always happy. Every night. Every day. He's a superstar.

You told me that you've known Michael Jai White since he was young.

Since he started. When he was first getting started.

You worked on *Black Dynamite*, which was his baby.

Yeah, Michael is a tough, tough son of a bitch. He's a real fighter. He played opposite Seagal in *Exit Wounds*. Mike was telling me that they had all these badass dudes on that movie and they'd all try to intimidate Seagal.

Do you watch action movies at all? Do you keep tabs on some of the guys you've worked with?

I love action movies. That's why I'm in this business. It's homework, but it's not homework. I love the new Korean action movies. Great, great stuff. *The Man From Nowhere*. Really intense. Pushing the envelope as far as stories. Creative.

Anybody you're thinking could be the next big thing in action and martial arts?

When I first saw Tony Jaa, I was so excited. Finally, we have Jackie Chan, Bruce Lee, and Jet Li all in one. The real kick-ass fighting, the acrobatics, the stunts. The full package. But unfortunately, he's been tied into the production company there, so they've had a grip on him. This new kid from *The Raid* has real charisma. If given the right vehicle, he might have a shot. Guys who have a French accent like Jean-Claude are cool. English accents like Statham are cool. German, Spanish, you name it. But an Asian accent trying to speak English does not translate into being a hero. Jackie works his comedy. Other than that, unfortunately you can't be ladykiller. Bruce Lee was on another level. Even with his accent . . . he had a mix of everything.

You did a pretty good Bruce Lee accent on *18 Fingers of Death*.

Well, cool. It was a tribute to Bruce.

How about Phillip Rhee?

He had theatrical release for *Best of the Best*, but I think that's what we were talking about and how it all changed, being an action star. It wasn't enough. You had to be a movie star. He just couldn't get financing for another project. It faded as time went on. *Best of the Best* was too long ago. He's tried to do some other business ventures. He's trying to do another *Best of the Best*.

Billy Blanks.

I was on his last movie. *Balance of Power*. I play the lead villain. Mako was in it. We shot it in Toronto. It's one of those fight-to-the-death movies. Billy had like .5 percent body fat. He was ripped. I've never seen anybody jump as high as Billy. Very accurate. After that he got way busy with Tai Bo.

Chuck Norris. You did an episode of *Walker* with him.

Chuck is a legend. I went in through casting, and it was for the lead villain. I booked it, and the coordinator told me that I would have a fight with Chuck. I was like, "Oh, cool, okay." The next day, I get to the set, and I was told that Chuck didn't want to do a fight. I was like, "You're kidding! I'm the bad guy, we've got to do a fight!" I had to fight another guy, a guest star. I was so close. He was getting to the point where he had the perfect stunt double. I never got to fight Chuck Norris.

Are there any guys you would have loved to work with?

Bruce Lee. I've worked with everybody else except Bruce Lee. Never even got to meet him.

Do you think it's harder to become an action guy in today's market?

Absolutely. Now, they have "A" list actors doing action. Now we have Liam Neeson. Here you have an "A" list actor doing action now, and it's really good. I try to pitch things, and the first thing you always hear from a financier or a producer is "Who's in it?" It's not "What's it about?" It's "Who's in it?"

You got to direct a movie that you also starred in, the spoof *18 Fingers of Death*. What made you want to make this movie?

It pretty much sums up how everybody should look at their business career or life. How to create your own destiny. Because there weren't some opportunities for me or for other minorities, so I kept thinking about what I could do. Instead of complaining, I did my own thing. I knew I wasn't going to get a lot of money for it, so I decided to write it and thought how I could make it in the mockumentary style. It was cheaper to do it that way. One of my favorite movies is *This is Spinal Tap*. I thought that shooting style was perfect for this. I went out to meetings. I went to great meetings. I went to Universal. They loved my script, but it was too small. I was asked, "Who do you have in it?" That's when I realized I wasn't going to get outside financing. I decided to make it no matter what. I got in contact with an investor, and I pitched him, and I told him that I would bring in my own money. My nickel and dime savings, the credit cards, so we did it. I called in a lot of favors. I called Lorenzo Lamas, Don Wilson, a bunch of people.

How do you feel the movie turned out?

I've gotten great responses. So far, just good reactions. I'm happy with the performances everybody gave me. It would have been nice to have had a little more time to shoot it. Without deep pockets, the budget stopped right there. We had some technical setbacks. It was the toughest thing I've ever done in my life, but I wouldn't trade it. I'm fairly happy with it. There are a couple things I would like to redo. At a certain point, I just had to let it go. I had to move on.

Any final words on being an action star?

Create your own projects. Now with technology and all the things available, there's no reason why you can't get something going. It's a long shot, but at least it's a shot. If you're passionate, and you love it, you should do it.

El Condor

1970 (Warner DVD) (djm)

Jim Brown and Lee Van Cleef star in this adequate western adventure that pushes hard for an "R" rating. Brown plays a convict named Luke, who escapes his hard labor camp and chases a story he heard about a place called "El Condor" where tons of gold is supposed to be. He bamboozles a rapscallion misfit named Jaroo (a great Lee Van Cleef, who easily steals the movie from Brown), who joins Luke on his quest to find the gold. Jaroo recruits an army of Apache Indians to raid El Condor (a heavily guarded outpost that guards Mexico's national reserve of gold), but first Luke has to whip an Apache brave in a fistfight if the Apaches are going to follow him into battle (best scene in the movie). When their raid on the fortress is botched, both Luke and Jaroo are captured and tortured, but they manage an easy escape and convince the only woman in the compound (played by Mariana Hill who has an eyebrow-raising nude scene) to join them in their attack against the soldiers, which tips the scales in their favor.

A fun, rousing first half is undone by a lackluster second, but what makes *El Condor* watchable is its two appealing stars. Brown's physicality, brute strength, and manly appeal should go over well with his fans and newcomers to him, and Van Cleef (not an action star, but welcome in any movie) is just great in his scoundrel role. Brown and Van Cleef would reunite for another western called *Take a Hard Ride* a few years later. Some of the violence and stunt work in the movie is shocking, and there's a surprising amount of nudity in the film. Maurice Jarre did the score. Directed by John Guillermin.

El Gringo

2012 (Warner DVD) (djm)

Part of After Dark's Action series (produced by Joel Silver), *El Gringo* is a lark of an action flick, starring *Undisputed II* and *III*'s Scott Adkins as a nameless gringo caught in a corrupt Mexican town with a bag full of cash. No matter how hard he tries, he can't for the life of him get a glass of water or a ticket out of town, and when the local gang and the corrupt sheriff realize that he's lugging two million in cash, he becomes a running target as every bad guy in town tries to gun him down on the street. In the chaotic mix is an American DEA agent (played by a slumming Christian Slater) who is more enemy than ally to The Gringo, who—while not without flaws—is a good guy at heart. He manages to get a local buxom barmaid (Yvette Yates) on his side, and she tends to him as he comes back to her wounded and battered. As scraped up and smashed around as he gets, The Gringo has a skill set of surviving unparalleled to none, and he emerges as some kind of action hero the likes of which we rarely get in these types of movies anymore. Basically, it's a throwback to the early '90s when Van Damme and Steven Seagal were on top.

Given a brief theatrical release and an oh-so-slight marketing push, *El Gringo* could have done better business had the public been given a chance to discover it theatrically. Once upon a time, movies like this were in multiplexes all over the country, and stars like Scott Adkins were big deals. I like *El Gringo* despite its distracting directorial flourishes (with quick cutting and annoying, flashy editing techniques), and with its spry, go-get-'em pace and upbeat tone, this movie will likely be enjoyed by newcomers to the genre and by anyone who's never seen a movie with Adkins. It's flawed and over the top, but so what? It's a good time at the movies. Directed

by Eduardo Rodriguez, who also did the Dolph Lundgren movie *Stash House*, which was another After Dark Action movie.

Eliminators

1986 (Shout Factory DVD) (CD)

"Adios, you walking junkyard."

Abbott Reeves (Roy Dotrice) is a mad genius with dreams of ruling the world. He plans on achieving this by going back into time to set things in motion. He uses a "mandroid" (Patrick Reynolds) to test the time travel process. Once his work is done, Reeves orders his sidekick Takada (Tad Horino) to dismantle the droid. He feels too much compassion for the machine that has regained some of its human emotions and sacrifices itself to save him. The mandroid was previously a pilot named John who was severely injured in a plane crash years ago. He stands up to rebel against his evil creators with the help of scientist Dr. Nora Hunter (Denise Crosby), the sleazy but faithful Harry (Andrew Prine), and a renegade ninja named Kuji (*Gymkata*'s Conan Lee). They will band together to learn the truth of Reeves's motives and save the world from his vicious rule.

If you were a child of the '80s who grew up on the "B" movies playing in a constant rotation on HBO or the Z Channel, then the chances that you've seen (and love) *Eliminators* increases exponentially. Produced by Charles Band and distributed by Empire Pictures, the project paired him with director Peter Manoogian whom he would collaborate with many times over the following years. For most of us, this film was our introduction to Conan Lee (also in *Carjack*). He doesn't appear until the final reel but his presence is felt immediately. He helps our heroes go after the bad guys after he learns of his father's death. He fights with a sword, exploding shurikens, and feet while defeating humans and tiny robots. How can you turn away from a film about a funny man, a pretty lady, a ninja, and cyborg centaur? You don't.

Eliminator Woman (a.k.a.

Terminator Woman)

1992 (Vidmark VHS) (djm)

Designed as a vehicle for Karen Sheperd (*Cyborg 2, Mission of Justice*), first and foremost, *Eliminator Woman* takes place in Africa and casts her alongside Jerry Trimble from *Full Contact* and *Live by the Fist*. They play LA cops who go to Africa to talk to a witness who might be able to testify against a big-time gangster who is living there. The gangster is played by Michel Qissi from the first two *Kickboxer* movies. Shepherd and Trimble are forcefully separated and each has to fight his and her way back to each other, and they have a final confrontation with Qissi and a bunch of his men.

The setting helps this movie. Watching Trimble and Sheperd kickfight with a lot of able African stuntmen is pretty cool. There's lots of gunplay and an adventuresome atmosphere to the entire movie, and the only thing I wanted more of was Qissi himself, especially considering that he also directed it. Sheperd and Trimble get about equal screen time. The video box prominently displays Sheperd and Qissi, but nothing of Trimble. The title doesn't really mean anything.

INTERVIEW:

KAREN SHEPERD

(CD & djm)

The heyday of action pictures during the 1980s and 1990s was a world dominated by men, with very few exceptions. Female martial artists like Cynthia Rothrock, Kathy Long, Mimi Lessos, and Karen Sheperd are the rare exceptions, carving a place for themselves in the action and martial arts world and making names and reputations for themselves as action heroes on film. Shepard made it a conscious decision to try to open doors for women, not only in film, but in the arena of competitive martial arts as well. For two consecutive years, she was rated #1 Women's Black Belt Forms Champion, which didn't exist for women until she came along. Once she conquered that world, she set her sights on film. With over twenty credits on her resume, appearing in martial arts action films like Mission of Justice *(1994),* Eliminator Woman *(1993),* Operation Golden Phoenix *(1994), and* Above the Law *(1986), she's proved that she is truly a master of her craft.*

At what age did you begin your journey into the world of the martial arts?

I was about seventeen. I took my first classes in tai chi chuan and Shotokan karate. Talk about opposite ends of the spectrum! I fell in love with martial arts movement. The movements felt natural to me and I knew, from the beginning,

Action star Karen Sheperd in a claw pose. Author's collection.

that I had found my niche. Later, I migrated to kajukenbo, then on to Wun Hop Kuen Do where I presently hold a seventh degree black belt.

Was there a particular moment, incident, or person that influenced you in your career path?

I was sitting in a car at the drive-in movies watching Bruce Lee in *Fists of Fury*. I was mesmerized! I wanted to do what he was doing more than anything. I thought, "Why can't a woman do that?" I went back and watched it a few more times, taking my tape recorder with me to record his unique fight vocals. I'd go home and play make-believe, choreographing fights and pretending I was in a film. I'd go see Chinese martial arts films and was inspired to see women like Cheng Pei-pei, and Angela Mao up there on the big screen kicking ass. I wanted nothing more than to be part of this exotic club of martial arts actors.

What sort of opportunities opened up for you (and other women) when you became the first #1 Women's Black Belt Forms Champion?

I felt not only that it could mean my entrance into the exotic club I had dreamed of, but that it would help draw more women to compete. That is why I fought to establish the first official ratings for Women Black Belt Forms Competitors. Men and women were rated separately for sparring but not for forms. I seized the opportunity to "right the wrong" and contacted Renardo Barden, the editor of *Karate Illustrated* magazine. At the time, they were the only ones with a ratings system in place. The result of my meetings with him and of me working with tournament promoters and organizing a petition of female competitors was the establishment of separate ratings for Women Forms competitors in 1979. Seeing my picture and my name in the #1 "Top Women Kata" spot on page 34 of *Karate Illustrated* magazine [May 1980, Volume 11, No. 5] was a real victory. *Inside Karate* soon followed suit with the "Star System" and soon more women came out of the woodwork to compete since there was a title to be had. That was my goal. I knew more women wanted to compete but were too intimidated to compete with men, as many expressed to me on the tournament circuit. I won the title for 1979 and again in 1980. I received nice exposure, including magazine covers and television coverage, which attracted the attention of film producers, which led to offers. I was the first woman to win Grand Champion at the U.S. Open in St. Petersburg, Florida in November, 1980, and it made the national evening television news. I was the first American female martial arts champion to star in an action film, following the likes of Chuck Norris and Joe Lewis. In summation, magazine covers, television interviews and film opportunities opened up for me. As for other women, competition with a title to be won opened up to them as well as more exposure and film opportunities for them, too.

When did you find yourself being bitten by the acting bug?

I'll never forget that moment. As I was lying in six feet of snow in the mountains of Japan with an arrow stuck in my arm—movie magic—and freezing my buns off, waiting for the camera to reset (on *Shinobi Ninja*, my first film)…the bug bit. I realized that I was happier than I had ever been in my life. I loved being in front of the camera. I loved the pressure. I loved everything about it. It all felt natural to me and even to this day, I am happiest being on set.

The Shinobi Ninja was your first appearance in a film. How was that opportunity presented to you?

I was fresh off of two years holding the #1 Women's Forms title (1979 and 1980), when Tadashi Yamashita phoned me and said he wanted me to co-star in his next film. Soon after, I was on a plane to Tokyo with Eric Lee.

You had a pretty stellar fight scene with Cynthia Rothrock in Above the Law. What was it like doing that sequence with her? Were the two of you acquainted beforehand?

It was an incredible learning experience, and I am thankful it came early in my career. That sequence, which took two weeks to film, taught me to be a very tough film fighter. They would show us thirty to forty choreographed moves, then say: "Okay, now do it." That was a lot of moves at one time to memorize, and there was huge pressure to get it quickly. We had very little rehearsal time. It was very different from American film and television where you were given ten to fifteen moves at once, at most. American productions had more cuts and inserts whereas Hong Kong productions had lengthier wider shots. Also, they were into more contact and speed, constantly shouting, "Harder! Faster!"
When I auditioned for that film, I didn't know Cynthia was going to be in it. I actually turned it down four times. The pay offer was jokingly bad, and I had offers pending in the USA. Their fifth offer, which I accepted, came with more money and the promise of a three-picture deal. Cynthia and I had met on the national tournament circuit, and we were the top two women's forms competitors at the time. The last time I had seen her, before I arrived in Hong Kong, was at one of my last tournaments before retiring: the Diamond Nationals in Minneapolis, Minnesota, on May 2, 1981. Not only did I beat her, but so did Belinda Davis. Cynthia was pretty miffed that she only got third place. She seems to have "forgotten" that defeat, as she claims to be "undefeated," which is clearly a lie. I tried to contact her about her claim, but she ignored me, choosing to sweep my victory under the rug. The truth is there in black and white in *Sport Karate* magazine [Volume 4, No. 5, May 1981 page 28]: "The nation's top-rated woman, Karen Sheperd, continued her dominance by defeating Belinda Davis of San Jose, Cynthia Rothrock and Lori Clapper of Florida." The results are posted on page 39 and then there's that awesome centerfold shot of me on pages 26-27. So, yes, we were well acquainted beforehand.

Corey Yuen, the director of Above the Law, has gone on to be a staple of the Hong Kong film industry as a choreographer. What was your experience like working with him?

He is very knowledgeable and knew what he wanted and how to get it. Corey did not speak much English, so we really weren't able to converse much but he was able to communicate direction, gave some to me in Mandarin (which I have a basic understanding of), and I picked up some key directional words in Cantonese, so it all worked. He turned out a "stellar" scene, as you said, and many seem to think it still holds up as one of the best film fights between two women.

Mission of Justice was another really fun film you appeared in. Do you have any good stories from that production? It starred guys like Jeff Wincott, Matthias Hues, and James Lew. How was it being the only woman who could go toe-to-toe with any of them?

We filmed in Los Angeles, and I was able to take my dad on set with me for the first time. We walk on set, and there's Brigitte Neilsen … this blonde Amazon goddess with boobs spilling everywhere holding one of the guys on her lap. My dad got a kick out of that. She was funny and kind. I liked her. It was the first time I filmed at home and a few of the stuntman were surprised at my strength. They didn't expect to be hit with such force by a woman. There was only one person there who knew what I was capable of, and that was Jeff Pruitt, the stunt coordinator, and he was very respectful and supportive. One stuntman in particular wanted more pay after we rehearsed a fight because he realized it wasn't going to be a piece of cake fighting me. It was fun filming at home for a change.

Eliminator Woman was sort of your film and your moment in the spotlight. How did you enjoy being the lead?

I enjoyed working on that film. I never have thoughts of being the lead, but rather of just being in a film, on location, working with a team … just working! I am so thankful for having had the opportunity to spend a few months in Africa. After wrap, I flew to Kenya and camped on the Serengeti. I've never slept better in my life, with the sounds of the wild animals all around. Africa is truly magical.

That was Michel Qissi's first film as a director. How do you think he fared? I heard a story that the original director of that film was fired. Any memories of that director?

I thought Michel did a pretty good job. I felt really bad for Robert Davies, the original director. It was very uncomfortable to witness the film being wrestled away from him. He'd show up on set every day, thinking he was still the director but he'd hang out in the background while Michel took over. It was awkward for a while. Robert was nice to me, and I had nothing against him.

Jerry Trimble was your co-star who also happens to be highly underrated. How was your relationship working with him?

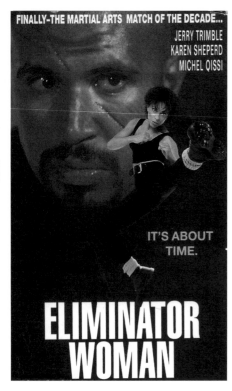

FINALLY-THE MARTIAL ARTS MATCH OF THE DECADE...

JERRY TRIMBLE
KAREN SHEPERD
MICHEL QISSI

IT'S ABOUT TIME.

ELIMINATOR WOMAN

VHS artwork for *Eliminator Woman*. Author's collection.

I thought we worked well together. Jerry was very professional and is a talented martial artist and actor.

Why do you think you weren't given the chance to have more starring roles in more of these action movies?

I was given the chance. I just didn't take them. I was being offered projects but the scripts were bad and the pay ridiculous. I didn't want to get stuck taking every low-budget film offered to me. I decided early on to gamble on holding out for better roles. It was my conscious decision to stay in the US to study acting and to pursue mainstream projects. My mindset was, "If I'm going to do this thing, then do it right . . . study hard and hold out for better opportunities." It was never about the money for me. I was willing to struggle, financially, rather than do projects I didn't care for. You have to be brave to say, "No."

In addition to appearing in *America 3000*, you were also responsible for some of the fight choreography on that film. How did you approach those scenes and how did you enjoy it? You've got to tell at least one story from this movie. I love this movie!

Oh, I have so many stories! A good story is about how I got that role. I saw a full-page ad in the *Hollywood Reporter* about this upcoming film in preproduction. I wrote a letter to the director, David Englebach, and basically told him I thought I was perfect for his film. He called me into a meeting at Cannon Films and gave me the role of "Keva." I was also the fight-trainer for the girls. We were sent to Israel two weeks ahead of filming to train with the horses and for me to give some basic fight training to the girls. Once we started filming, it was realized

that our stunt coordinator was not capable of choreographing the final melee fight, which was essential to the story. They asked me if I could do it. At the time, I didn't have much experience choreographing, so I suggested to Menahem Golan (the producer) that he bring Ernie Reyes Sr. over to choreograph, but I would be happy to assistant-choreograph. That way, Ernie could focus on all those fights, and I was able to focus on my character and enjoy Israel.

When did you first meet Jalal Merhi, who directed you and starred alongside you in *Operation Golden Phoenix*?

I first met him when he picked me up at the airport in Beirut, Lebanon, to begin filming *Operation Golden Phoenix*.

How was your experience working on that film?

I feel fortunate to have experienced Lebanon, but I wouldn't want to go back. That is a dangerous location. There's something about being guarded with guys with machine guns that shakes you or being told not to point your camera towards the Syrian army (ever-present in the hills above Beirut) or they'd shoot you, and always being escorted in the heart of Hezbolah territory for fear of being kidnapped. Despite that, it was fun hanging out with James Hong. Talk about a career! He's probably worked with every actor in the business. He's a real hoot! Originally, my part was supposed to be bigger, but I was badly injured and had to cease filming and fly home. If you watch my fight scene in the ruins, you'll see me jumping off a rock doing a kick. I blew out my knee on that one, popped the ACL off the bone. Jalal took me to have the knee X-Rayed in Baalbek and the machine was so old, the doctor had to kick it to get it to work. All I could think of was . . . *get me back home!*

Could you tell us a bit about your experience on *Cyborg 2*? Is it true that the role was originally intended to be male?

The part of "Chen" was written for a man. My manager convinced the producers to give me a shot. I auditioned three times and won the role . . . much to James Lew's disappointment, as he had also read for the role. I have such good memories of working on *Cyborg 2*. The legendary Jack Palance recited Russian poetry to me in his trailer on our first day of filming. I helped train Angelina Jolie for the action. We had a couple of weeks before filming to prep some fight moves. I taught her how to make a fist. She was wonderful to work with, had an open mind and natural ability. She was also wonderful to work with as an actor, very present and giving. Elias Koteas was pretty cool, not thrilled about me licking his face but he was a good sport. Greg Nicotero made my body prosthetic for my electrocution scene. It was awesome to see his effects shop and, wow, has he come a long way as a producer and director.

Though it's not exactly an all-out action film, *Boogie Boy* was something you did with Mark Dacascos. How is he to work with?

If you can stop laughing between takes, he's great to work with. It's a riot for me to work with Mark. I used to give him rides on the back of my motorcycle when he was about eight years old. We also worked together for years in a stage show so we go way back with a life full of laughter, antics, and experiences. The stories I have about Mark would take up your whole book! Aside, he is an extremely talented martial artist and actor, a real cut-up on set but takes his work seriously.

Do you feel that the roles for women in action films have changed for the better over the years?

Oh, absolutely the roles for women in action films are for the better. Now, it's acceptable for women to do anything that men can do in film. When I began, producers were hesitant to put women in lead action roles because they didn't think it was good for box-office sales. I have always felt that audiences wanted to see women in action but the producers were slow to recognize that. From day one, I had a large fan-base that wanted more. I was definitely ahead of my time, but it had to start somewhere.

What was the toughest experience you ever had on a set and why?

Above the Law (a.k.a. *Righting Wrongs*) in Hong Kong was the toughest experience I've had on set in many ways. Physically, it was tough as Corey wanted us to make a lot of hard contact. We were taken to a doctor in the evenings after wrap to have our bruises massaged out with his special formulation of Dit Da Jow. That process was extremely painful, but it worked. The production people were not exactly above-board with me. They lied about the three-picture deal just to get me there. They did not pay me as promised, and I had to halt filming for about an hour until they deposited a very late payment with my agent in LA From day one, they were not very courteous towards me. Imagine being alone with no one on your side, everyone around you speaking a language you don't, no one is translating for you, and your contract is not being honored. I was quite young, and it seemed they felt they could take advantage of me. It's the only time I ever held up production. I've never encountered such unprofessionalism anywhere. The scene was completed. and I said my thank-yous and goodbyes and gave small gifts to various crew members, including a leather passport cover to Cynthia, and I headed home. The only good thing about that experience was the knowledge I gained about film fighting and my meeting with Jackie Chan. He was very courteous and gracious to me.

You were the stunt double for Nia Peeples on *Walker, Texas Ranger*. What was it like working on the show with that cast and crew? What was your impression of Chuck Norris?

I loved working in Texas. The crew was wonderful and took good care of me. Chuck was always so nice to me. He was my head judge when I won First Place Chinese Style over men and women at the N.K.C. Finals in Oklahoma, November 1980, so we go way back.

I got to feel his ability when I doubled Joan Jett for one episode and was very impressed with his power and control. I enjoyed working on *Walker*. I love barbeque and Texas is the place! The work on *Walker* was fun and easy, doing different things each week, meeting new actors and stunt performers and seeing many old martial arts friends passing through.

You also doubled Eliza Dushku on both *Buffy* and *Angel*. How was your experience with that and do you have any stories you could share from either show?

Eliza was great to work with. She was bold and not afraid of the action. I enjoyed watching her work. She had an intense energy and really went for it. Sara Michelle Gellar was a little more fragile than Eliza and I had to be careful not to hurt her but she was professional and respectful with me, as was David Boreanaz. David really appreciated heavy action and was always quick to dole out compliments when we'd have a good fight together or when watching me crash through stuff like walls, crates, glass, and things like that.

You've been a guest star on numerous shows like *Hercules*, *V.I.P*, and *Criminal Minds*. Is there any performance or role that you were particularly proud of?

I am partial to my role as The Enforcer on *Hercules, The Legendary Journeys*. From day one, it was a dream job. I thought I was going to an audition for the role at Universal Studios. When I walked in, the entire production team was sitting in a circle and welcomed me as the guest Sstar! The producer, Rob Tapert, was a fan of martial arts films and having seen my previous work, had written the role tailored to me. He was the most open-minded producer I ever worked for. I made a number of suggestions regarding my character, and he was most accommodating. My husband and I even rewrote my final scene in my second episode. I presented it in a production meeting in New Zealand with the cast and Rob Tapert and our director, TJ Scott. Everyone loved it, and it was added to the script. A company is only as good as its top people. Rob Tapert and Kevin Sorbo's open-mindedness and positive attitude influenced the entire crew and made it a pleasure to work with them every day. Even the costume designer, Nigla Dickson, asked for my input regarding my costume. I'm proud to say that my costume was designed by an Academy Award-winner. TJ and I worked together to develop my character. As soon as I put Nigla's fabulous costume on, it was like magic . . . the character "appeared" and TJ and I took it from there.

Criminal Minds was special too because Joe Mantegna and Paget Brewster were so welcoming. Right before we shot the scene, Paget told me that my audition blew away the competition. The director and producers didn't even want to see any more auditions after mine. That was so sweet of her, and it boosted my confidence. I gave Joe some tomatoes from my garden, and we had a lovely chat about Italy, cheese, wine, and tomatoes. He is very warm and personable. It's always fun to work on a network show and everyone there embraced me and made me feel welcome.

You've worked all over the world and in some pretty exotic locales. Where was your favorite place to work?

I'd have to say New Zealand was my favorite place to work. I had my own apartment, and I'd go horseback riding on the beach on my days off. My dad came with me on my second episode, and we toured the southern island and flew by helicopter on to a glacier. It was beautiful.

There weren't too many female action stars during the height of the VHS period. I can think of only a few: Rothrock, Kathy Long, Mimi Lessos, and you. Were you paying attention to your contemporaries and what sort of work they were producing?

Regarding action films, I've always said, "I just make 'em. I don't watch 'em." I prefer watching character-driven, human-interest films, comedy, drama, suspense. I did watch the work of Jackie Chan but come on . . . who didn't?

Could you tell us a bit about your theater work?

Theater is thrilling because it is totally in the moment and there are no retakes. I find new things about my characters in every performance so it is ongoing research during the run of the show. My first experience in theater was playing Bilbo Baggins in *The Hobbit*—hairy toes and all. I've played leads in various shows such as David Rabe's *In the Boom Boom Room* and Tennessee Williams's *Summer and Smoke*. Finding the right role in the right theatre is a challenge but I'm always on the lookout because theater is the best workout an actor can have.

Aside from acting or the martial arts, do you have any other passions that you are currently pursuing?

I am passionate about painting, animals, and tomatoes. I grow exotic, heirloom, organic tomatoes. I'm a "tomatomaniac" and for about three months every year I go AWOL and get lost in my garden. I grow way more than I can consume and my biggest joy is presenting beautiful baskets full of every shape, size and color of tomatoes to friends. I also love animals and my furry kids keep me busy, but I occasionally volunteer my time helping animal rescue groups. I'm currently building a website for one now. My other passion is painting. My work is very avant-garde, an artistic and physical expression of my martial arts. I've recently begun a new series called, *Karen Sheperd's Martial Art*, my "art" with a martial flair. They're quite unique, and I've already been approached to sell them at a showing.

You have a large fan base that has supported you and your career. Would you like to take the time to say anything to them?

Be kind to all animals. They are a privilege and a blessing. Also, I'd love to say that I consider the loyalty and admiration of my fans a huge compliment and am honored by it. Thank you so very much! I make an effort to answer everyone and the best place to contact me is via my website at KarenSheperd.com or my Facebook Fan Page

Empire State
2013 (Lionsgate DVD) (djm)

Set in the early 1980s, *Empire State* stars Liam Hemsworth as Chris Potamitis, a down-on-his-luck security guard at an armored truck company who gets desperate to make money when he begins to accrue a heavy stack of bills related to his father's illness. He manages to pilfer some cash from the storeroom, and when he tells his buddy Eddie (Michael Angarano) about it, Eddie brags to a local mobster that Chris can get more money anytime. The mob forces Chris to help them plan a robbery, and before he knows it, Chris is in the middle of several bad situations involving various parties and their plans to rob the armored car company. The NYPD steps in, and detective James Ransone (Dwayne "The Rock" Johnson) suspects Chris of being involved. When Chris inadvertently saves Ransone's life during a botched robbery, Chris is cast in a different light. Eventually, Chris's circumstances and Eddie's unbelievably foolish actions lead them both to a place where Ransone is easily able to link the robberies to them, and they're sent to prison.

Based on a true story, *Empire State* doesn't really qualify as an "action movie," but Johnson's participation and role lend themselves to giving the film an action star/movie persuasion. Johnson's role is minor, but he has several scenes in the film where he's wielding weapons and firing them, and the DVD box art clearly wants consumers to consider the film a movie "starring The Rock," but it's really not about his character at all. Fans of his will be disappointed. The film itself is nothing special; it's a docudrama with a foregone conclusion. Dito Montiel, who directed the fantastic *Fighting* with Channing Tatum and Cung Le, directed it.

End Game
2009 (First Look DVD) (djm)

A muscular killer is brutally slaying young women in and around a Pittsburgh neighborhood, and detectives on his trail stumble across his identity, but aren't quite prepared to face him as an adversary. The killer (played by WWE star Kurt Angle) has a sex and death fetish, and he gets to know his victims before he kills them. The bull-headed detective after him is a devoted family man, and he's not surprised when he finds that his family has not only been threatened by the killer, but that they've been assaulted and kidnapped as well. The conclusion isn't a big deal, but what surprised me was how effective Angle was in his death scene.

Shot for what looked like nothing, *End Game* is a by-the-numbers serial killer movie with very slight undertones of action, as it features the bulky Angle in a very physical role. This is an early feature for him, and he's actually pretty impressive, and it's interesting that his successive films *River of Darkness* and *Death From Above* are all fringe action films, with horror themes. Angle obviously has potential as an action star, but he hasn't really tapped into it yet. All three of his films were directed by Bruce Koehler.

End of Days

1999 (Universal DVD) (djm)

"So the Prince of Darkness wants to conquer the earth, but he has to wait until an hour before midnight on New Year's Eve. Is this Eastern time?"

A celestial sign appears in the sky in the late 1970s, and the Vatican is clued in to a certainty: a fated female child is being born that night, and her destiny is to become Lucifer's bride and ultimately the mother of the anti-Christ. Agents of the Vatican are sent out far and wide to search for her, but Satan's minions have already located her in New York, and they surround her as she grows up, ensuring her safety until the day when The Devil comes calling for her. Several days before New Year's in 1999, The Man (Gabriel Byrne) shows up to begin his search for his young, unsuspecting bride, Christine (Robin Tunney), and at the same time the city streets are crawling with wackos and crazies who seem to be on to the grand scheme of Christine's destiny. Suicidal cop Jericho (Arnold Schwarzenegger) stumbles on several strange cases that all seem to be connected . . . to Christine who, as innocent and unsuspecting as she is, starts experiencing startlingly demonic visions of The Man coming to her. Jericho, a faithless man after his wife and daughter were murdered years ago in a home invasion, slowly becomes aware that the cases he's on and Christine's predicament all point to the supernatural and indeed the Devil himself, which throws him a curveball he's hardly able to catch. When it comes time for him to have a showdown with Satan (who eventually reveals his true visage as a computer generated gargoyle), Jericho suits up and straps on an armful of guns and grenades that he thinks will hold back The Man.

This was the first movie Arnold did after open-heart surgery and starring in back-to-back flops (*Jingle All the Way* and *Batman and Robin*). It's also the first time (spoiler!) we see him die on screen as a human. Posters promoting the film showed him hanging his head (also a first for him), and it was an unsettling experience for me seeing this for the first time in a theater on opening day. He looks more seasoned and worn out than ever before, and his first scene in the film has him pointing a gun to his own head. Later in the film, he's crucified, and finally at the end he dies by impaling. The film should be appealing to horror and gore fans, but action aficionados and Arnold enthusiasts might be out of their element. It was geared as his comeback, but it just doesn't connect on the

same level as say *Eraser* does. Earlier in 1999 I saw Stallone's intended comeback movie *Eye See You* at a test screening, and that too showed its star in a suicidal, morose manner, also in a horror-centric surrounding. It was not a great year to be an action star. Peter Hyams directed and photographed *End of Days*, which remains his biggest production to date. He also directed Jean-Claude Van Damme in *Timecop*, *Sudden Death*, and *Enemies Closer*.

Enemies Closer

2014 (Lionsgate DVD) (djm)

A plane full of heroin crashes in a lake in the middle of a national park, and a band of cutthroats, led by a drug lord named Xander (Jean-Claude Van Damme), trolls the park and kills most of the rangers stationed there. With the coordinates in hand, the killers need a guide and a diver to help them retrieve the stash, and they set their sites on the last ranger in the park—Henry (Tom Everett Scott), a former disgraced soldier. When the killers come calling on him, he's already got his hands full—a mysterious man named Clay (Orlando Jones) has him at gunpoint, and is about to kill him over an old grudge stemming back to Henry's soldiering days. When the killers show up, bullets fly and if Henry and Clay are going to survive the night, they'll have to team up to defeat their common enemy.

From director Peter Hyams, who'd previously worked with Van Damme on *Timecop* and *Sudden Death*, this low-budget lightweight effort casts Van Damme as an outlandish villain the likes of which we've never seen him play before. As refreshing as that might be, the rest of the movie is a lame exercise of stalk, shoot, run, and duck, with the occasional fight thrown in. At less than ninety minutes, the movie barely has the time to be boring, but a terrible script and wrong casting sink it. The hero should have been played by the likes of Scott Adkins or Michael Jai White, and seeing the lanky Everett Scott (obviously not an action star) try to fight Van Damme is laughable. Van Damme's hamming about the ills of the burning of fossil fuels and the consumption of meat are pretty hilarious for a while, but the rest of the movie could have used as much energy and pizazz as he was showing. Strangely, this picture was given a one-week theatrical engagement across the United States. It's perplexing considering that some of Van Damme's later better efforts were relegated to video. Ah, well.

The Enforcer (a.k.a. **My Father is a Hero**)

1995 (Dimension DVD) (CD)

Kung Wei (Jet Li) is a family man at heart and has a dying wife and a son he's very proud of. But his life of crime is keeping him from his family—in order to help his wife he's out earning money to pay for her medicine. His adolescent son Siu Ku

(Mo Tse) is sort of filling in at home but refuses to believe his father is a criminal. While Kung is pulling off a heist, things go south, and he takes a hostage to make it out, a woman (who happens to be an inspector from Hong Kong) named Fong (the late Anita Mui) who right away realizes there is something different about him. He escapes and leaves her unharmed, though deep down she knows he is a cop who has gone far too deep undercover. Kung is close to crazed madman Po Kwong (Rongguang Yu), and no matter what happens he can't give up his cover. But when his son finds himself smack-dab in the middle of his father's situation, Kung, Siu, and Fong will have to team up in order to take down Po.

The Enforcer is one of Jet Li's better films and intertwines all the best elements from Hong Kong movies of that period. There's plenty of wirework, weapon use, and gunplay to showcase the talents of the star. Jet's fights are fast and fantastic. He uses a combination of weapons and hand-to-hand fighting. What really stands out is a scene where he is aided by Mo Tse. He ties a rope around his son's waist and swings him around like a lasso to fight off enemies. It's a great scene and so much fun to watch. Director Cory Yuen (*Above the Law, No Retreat, No Surrender*) uses Jet as his muse while choreographing fights, and the two are naturally at the top of their game when they're together. The film is brutal and the way the child is treated at times can be a bit much, but the action is exciting and very memorable. It's as much a family drama as it is an action film.

Enter the Blood Ring

1995 (NOV) (djm)

A virtually unknown video effort from virtual unknowns, *Enter the Blood Ring* stars Israeli martial artist Ben Maccabee (a.k.a. Benjamin Kobby) as a struggling father named Luke who is in a custody battle over his daughter. To make as much money as he can to support her and fund "an operation" she needs (to be performed in Australia for whatever reason), he fights in a deadly kickboxing ring every night against opponents who are bigger and more imposing than he is. Various real-life martial artists play some of the fighters, and action guys like Deron McBee (performing under his alter ego "Malibu" from his American Gladiator days) show up for some fight scenes.

Top-billed "star" Robert Z'Dar appears in some disjointed interludes where he sits around the fighting arena, making leering faces at the fights, but the real star of the movie is Maccabee, who tries hard to be convincing and persuasive as an action star. It's a shame that the movie he's in here (and every other movie he starred in) has a terrible script and poor direction. Still, it has heart, but anyone who makes the effort to track this down needs to have incredibly low expectations in order to appreciate it. Tom Oliver directed.

Enter the Dragon

1973 (Warner DVD) (djm)

"Man, you come right out of a comic book!"

This is the movie that virtually sums up what the "action movie vehicle" is all about, and it remains a classic example of an action and martial arts film more than forty years after it was made. Bruce Lee starred in this film when he was thirty-three and he was dead by the time it was released in theaters. He plays a cocky agent hired by the British Secret Service to enter a martial arts championship hosted by a criminal mastermind named Han on his island paradise in Asia. Lee goes, but his ulterior motive is to avenge the death of his sister, who was killed because of Han's evil. Also on the island are Roper—a gambler (John Saxon)—and Williams—an Afro-American badass (Jim Kelly in his first role). Han (Shih Kien) and his henchmen Bolo (Bolo Yeung) and Oharra (Bob Wall) provide the film with some of the most memorable moments. Once the martial arts competition begins, Lee and the gang kick into full gear, and the film unfolds like a great James Bond film.

The perfect blend of East meets West, *Enter the Dragon* is a miracle of a film in that it captures Lee in the state of his just-barely-tapped glory. Every martial arts hopeful wanted and still wants to be him, and executives and producers are still on the lookout for "the next Bruce Lee." The fights in this film are only special because of the way he performed in them, and while his co-stars also shine, this one will always belong to him. The director, Robert Clouse, worked with Jackie Chan on his first crossover vehicle, *The Big Brawl*. Clouse remade *Enter the Dragon* in the '80s as *Gymkata*.

Enter the Ninja

1981 (MGM DVD) (djm)

"Mr. Parker! I want my black ninja, and I want him now!"

Menahem Golan, director and producer at The Cannon Group, saw potential in bringing Japanese ninja movies to Western audiences, and *Enter the Ninja* (which he directed) is the first big Westernized ninja movie that made a dent in Western consciousness. After this came *Revenge of the Ninja* and *American Ninja*. In this film, Franco Nero plays Cole, a newly inducted master of *ninjutsu*, and his rival, an embittered Hasegawa (played by Sho Kosugi, in his first notable ninja movie), holds a grudge against him for not being Japanese. Cole leaves the ninja clan to visit an old war buddy, Frank (Alex Courtney), who's living in Manila on a plantation. Frank and his wife Mary Ann (Susan George) are being harassed by a wealthy businessman because the plantation is sitting in the middle of an oil field. Cole helps them out by fighting off the thugs who come calling

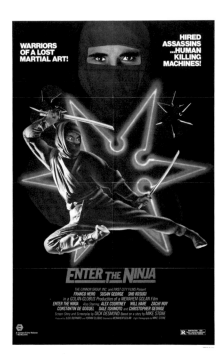

Theatrical release poster for *Enter the Ninja*. Author's collection.

during the night, but when the problem escalates to the point when Cole's rival Hasegawa is called in from Japan to eliminate them, shit gets real.

Watching *Enter the Ninja* is amusing. I'm not sure if it was amusing the first time I saw it when I was much younger, but this stuff is pretty ridiculous now. I love ninjas, I love Kosugi who's always so serious, but Franco Nero as a white garbed ninja? I'm not sure I love that. And his buddy Frank is the biggest wet blanket *ever*. His hot wife sleeps with Cole during the night, and the next morning Frank is talking about how he feels like a man again. It's painful. The villain (played by Christopher George) is an idiot. He screams and hollers for help while ninja stars are being flung all around him, and it's just cartoony. In 1981, *Enter the Ninja* was probably badass. Sho Kosugi's first appearance in a big movie is still pretty great. In 2015, *Enter the Ninja* is goofy like *really* goofy. But that's okay, right?

Entre Llamas

(a.k.a. Into the Flames)

2002 (Fries DVD) (CD)

Max (Marko Zaror) is fresh out of the police academy, graduating at the top of his class. His uncle helps him get a job on the police force and everything seems to be on the right track. He has a beautiful wife and a nice home, but when he's exposed to the corruption on the force, things take a terribly wrong turn. While spying on his superiors who are partaking in a shady deal, he accidentally blows his cover, and he's taken hostage and tortured. He's left for dead but he still has a little bit of life left in him. After four months in a coma, he disappears with his wife only to launch a full-on assault to expose the corruption on the force and try to bring back honor to the badge.

Chilean action star Marko Zaror (from *Kiltro*) has yet to make a seminal picture, one his fans will remember for the rest of their life. Every legend has a beginning and *Entre Llamas* was his first film as a lead actor. *Entre Llamas* feels more like a true crime drama than an unadulterated action picture. His talents as a screen fighter and stuntman are only used for a few short moments to craft an entertaining (yet far too short) fight sequence. Zaror went on from here to do some pretty fantastic work with pictures like *Mirage Man* and *Mandrill*. This film was more like an acting exercise for him, a chance to show that he has charisma and a presence. To date, this is the only film to be directed by Carlos Victorica Reyes.

Epoch of Lotus

2000 (NOV) (CD)

"They say that in your deepest darkest moments, when confronted by what you fear, something within you begins to change."

In a future where life as we know it no longer exists, one woman is on a quest to enlighten those in captivity with help from a book known as the *Lotus Sutra*. The government sends the assassin Mortis (Ho-Sung Pak) to eliminate this woman but when he has the opportunity, he cannot bring himself to complete the task. She somehow unlocks memories of his past, revealing the truth of who he is and how their lives have always intersected. With a newfound purpose, he will protect her and fight off anyone who attempts to cause her harm.

With limited funds and resources, director Vincent Lee should be commended for capturing action star Ho-Sung Pak's (*Book of Swords*) best performance in this short film. The characters only speak in their mind—telepathically, if you will, but it's an engaging little story with solid performances, and there's an exciting final duel between Pak and T. J. Storm (from *Black Cobra*). The action and stunts are top-notch for such a short film, very much influenced by films like *Crouching Tiger, Hidden Dragon. Epoch of Lotus* has only recently been made available online by producer Audrea Topps-Harjo.

Equalizer 2000

1987 (MGM/UA VHS) (CD)

In a post-apocalyptic world, Slade (Richard Norton) is out to avenge the death of his father. Both men have sided with The Ownership (the new ruling government), and when Slade's father is killed in a routine firefight, Slade wants to help but is forbidden by Colonel Lawton (William Steis). Against orders he does what is right and in turn is shunned by The Ownership, becoming their enemy. Slade is hit by a thug and taken hostage. He soon earns the rebels' trust and becomes one of them, and he even falls for the foxy rebel Karen (Corinne Wahl). Finally, with the help of one superweapon, he vows to take them all down.

Equalizer 2000 was the first collaboration between director Cirio Santiago (*Bloodfist 2050, Future Hunters*) and action star Richard Norton (*China O'Brian 1* and *2, Under the Gun*). Of the three films they have done together, this is arguably the best. From the opening frames of the film, the action is nonstop. With Norton's martial arts background, it's surprising to see that the focus of the action involves firearms and fast weapon-laced cars over martial arts. In that respect, there is some slight disappointment, but overall we are treated to a blast of a film. Norton can take out any and all enemies that come his way. He doesn't speak much, but he is all business here and not only can he use his hands and feet but he totes around the centerpiece weapon (the Equalizer!), which he uses with ease against an endless horde of villains. Along for the ride is William Steis (*Raiders of the Sun*) as bad guy Lawton and a very young Robert Patrick (*Terminator 2, Hong Kong '97*) in one of his first roles. As for the love interest, Corinne Wahl is a bona fide stunner and a real pleasure to watch. There are some memorable musical cues from composer Edward Achacoso that send off the heroic vibe. *Equalizer 2000* is an action-packed post-apocalyptic masterpiece that delivers on all fronts. The version I viewed was the "R"-rated US cut. There is another version of the film that has an additional ten minutes added in to the film that was released in the UK through New Dimension.

Eraser

1996 (Warner DVD) (djm)

"Smile: You've just been erased!"

US Marshal John Kruger (Arnold Schwarzenegger) is a legend in his field. With slick precision and apparent ease, he's a one-man operation in facilitating the "erasing" of material witnesses and relocating them before they meet grisly fates. When

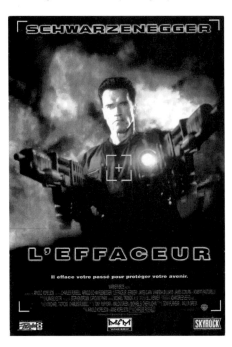

French poster for *Eraser*. Author's collection.

a fellow US Marshal (played by James Caan) turns against him to get to his latest witness (played by Vanessa Williams), Kruger first has to understand the sudden about-face before he can engage his enemy. It turns out that Lee Cullen (Williams) has uncovered a major arms deal where an enhanced, handheld supergun (a "rail gun") has been illegally mass-produced and sold to a foreign faction, which intends on using it for terrorism. Lee has been targeted for death, and only Kruger can protect her, while also protecting the integrity of his country.

Released in the heat of the summer of 1996 (against *The Cable Guy*, of all things), *Eraser* is arguably the last big-budget action movie Arnold Schwarzenegger starred in that really capitalized on his youth and physicality to the best of his abilities. It's a movie that's just big enough to fit his persona, and he has some solid, signature lines like "You're luggage!" after he shoots an alligator point blank. While it's a significant dip from the superior *True Lies* (released in 1994), *Eraser* has plenty of playback value and popcorn thrills. Directed by Chuck Russell.

Escape from Alaska

(a.k.a. **Avalanche**)

1999 (Millennium DVD) (CD)

While out tagging wildlife for the Environmental Protection Agency, Dr. Lia Freeman (Caroleen Feeney) and her boyfriend Jack (C. Thomas Howell) are caught in the middle of an avalanche and buried beneath the snow. Their best friend Neal (Kenpo expert Thomas Ian Griffith) is a helicopter pilot and heads out to look for them with a search party. They find Jack dead but Lia is nowhere to be found. The search team leaves to aid the people in town who are affected by the avalanche while Neal searches through hell and high water to rescue Lia. He finds her, and she survives, but the trauma causes her to become reclusive. Two years later, the two of them reunite when a large corporation wants to extend an oil pipeline above a city, which could turn out to be dangerous. The crooked executives will do whatever it takes to proceed as planned and the only way to do so is to get Neal and Lia out of their way.

Thomas Ian Griffith (*The Karate Kid Part III, Excessive Force*) takes on a belligerent restaurant patron, a polar bear, and an avalanche in this movie. When there's no one else to fight, the filmmakers put him up against a natural disaster and we see how that transpires. Director Steve Kroschel is obviously trying to get an environmental message across, and that agenda becomes the focal point of the film. Griffith has a very brief fight scene where he's arguing with a lady friend while fighting the town bully. He uses a technique where he fights by pretending to not know how to fight. Films like this with huge ambitions on a tiny budget rarely work but there's something endearing about this one; the use of miniatures during the disaster scenes hearkens back to old school filmmaking. *Escape From Alaska* is an interesting little action picture. I enjoyed it.

Escape From Atlantis

1997 (Universal VHS) (djm)

Lighthearted family fare released directly to television, *Escape From Atlantis* stars *The Perfect Weapon's* Jeff Speakman as single father Matt Spencer, whose three teenaged kids are spiraling out of his control. As a knee-jerk reaction, he takes them on a family vacation to Bermuda, but a storm offsets their ship (helmed by character actor Tim Thomerson) and they end up in ancient Atlantis. The Spencers get split up and Claudia Spencer (teen actress Mercedes McNab) ends up in a kingdom that opposes the Atlantians, and they worship her as a goddess. Craving that kind of attention, she unwittingly becomes a pawn for their campaign of war, and Matt and his two sons—along with the entire population of Atlantis—engage in a war that they can only win by learning new tactics . . . which Matt can teach them from his experience as a soldier (he knows kenpo karate!).

Harmless and inauspicious, *Escape From Atlantis* is like *Captain Ron* meets *Hercules: The Legendary Journeys* meets *The Perfect Weapon*. It's extremely light on action, which is lamentable, but it's cool seeing Speakman in a family-oriented movie. The fantasy elements are slight, but present, and the teen drama is overstated and overly prominent. Take that as you will. Directed by Strathford Hamilton.

Escape Plan

2013 (Lionsgate DVD) (djm)

Ray Breslin (Sylvester Stallone) is a one-of-a-kind escape expert. He's hired for exorbitant sums of money to be incarcerated in maximum-security prisons to find the weak spots in the systems, and he *always* finds a way to escape. His latest gig (for double his usual pay) lands him in a supersecret prison for the most dangerous criminals in the world. He has no idea where the prison (dubbed "The Tomb") is, and his team of helpers (who include Amy Ryan and Curtis "50 Cent" Jackson) are out of the loop, which puts Breslin in a really dangerous spot because there's no one to help him on the outside. The warden of The Tomb is the ice-cool Hobbes (Jim Caviezel), who designed the prison based on Breslin's textbook of escapes and methods, and so Breslin's next move must

Two peas in a pod: Rottmayer (Arnold Schwarzenegger) and Ray Breslin (Sylvester Stallone) are prisoners in The Tomb, a top-secret prison in *Escape Plan*. Author's collection.

be to first make an ally on the inside. He makes a buddy in the form of Rottmayer (Arnold Schwarzenegger), a German terrorist who is as desperate to get out of hell as Breslin is. Together, they slowly form a plan of escape, and literally crack The Tomb wide open with their sheer brawn and will to overcome.

If *Escape Plan* had been made over a decade earlier it might have been an event. The sad truth is that Sly and Arnold's core fans have either abandoned them or simply no longer desire to support their big screen ventures any longer, which is a tragedy. Seeing these two guys spar with each other (physically and mentally) is a treat, and while they'd briefly appeared alongside each other in *The Expendables* pictures, they spend more time together on screen in this film, and I doubt we'll see anything like this from them again. Arnold steals the show, no doubt about it, and he shows more vitality and panache here than he did in *The Last Stand*, which came out the same year. Where *Escape Plan* succeeds in part as a buddy/buddy action-ish movie, it also fails to live up to any expectations you might have. It lacks scope, and the direction by Mikael Hafstrom is quite nearly half-hearted. It needed a director like Renny Harlin or a producer like Joel Silver to push it over into the event category. Still, it's absolutely impossible not to enjoy *Escape Plan* if you have any love for its stars, but there's still a touch of melancholy that taints it.

The Evil That Men Do

1983 (Sony DVD) (djm)

A sadist doctor known as "The Doctor" is a high commodity in third world countries, and his latest gig is in a Central American country where soldiers and government officials flock to watch him perform electrocutions and torture rituals on local dissidents. The local revolutionaries are desperate to be rid of the vile doctor (played by Joseph Maher), and they send an emissary to visit a retired hitman named Holland (Charles Bronson) who lives on a private island, hoping to convince him to take on one more job and kill the doctor. Holland, a serene man now with no need for money, accepts the mission once he has a complete grasp of who the doctor is, and he undertakes his task with the utmost determination. Once he's connected to the revolutionaries, he begins his campaign—killing the doctor's bodyguards and soldiers one by one—until his final mark presents itself.

Shockingly downbeat and grim, *The Evil That Men Do* is an *anti*-action movie, with brutal realism and ugliness tainting the waters of entertainment here, but fans of this era of Bronson's output may be interested to see the only theatrical feature he did in the 1980s that wasn't produced by Cannon. It was made in between *Death Wish 3* and *10 to Midnight* and was directed by J. Lee Thompson, who directed a total of nine outings with Bronson.

VHS artwork for *Excessive Force*. Author's collection.

Excessive Force

1993 (New Line DVD) (djm)

"Die with a little dignity."

The film that put Thomas Ian Griffith (a kenpo expert) on the map, *Excessive Force* is a rare first outing by an action star potential that perfectly captures the star's abilities and charisma. Griffith (who scripted and produced) casts himself as a Chicago cop named Terry McCain, a cop so tough and brutal that he's suspended for using excessive force on bad guys. On a recent bust, he thrashed a bunch of drug dealers who worked for a local mobster (Burt Young), and a suitcase full of three million dollars was confiscated. The mobster puts a hit on McCain and his partners (Tom Hodges and Tony Todd), and when the partners are both murdered, McCain goes after the mob single-handed. His captain (Lance Henriksen) can't stop him, and his best friend (James Earl Jones) and his ex-wife (Charlotte Lewis) can only stand by and watch as he becomes the prime suspect of a murder he didn't commit. When McCain realizes that his captain is his enemy, he brings out the excessive force in spades.

In the same way that *Above the Law* gave Steven Seagal the perfect vehicle to begin his career in action films, *Excessive Force* was a great way for Griffith to make his mark and put his own stamp on the genre. Unfortunately, Griffith didn't have the same trajectory as some of his peers, but like Jeff Speakman (also a kenpo specialist), he starred in a few solid action films before taking supporting roles in films where someone else was the star. He played the villain in big films like *Kull the Conqueror* and *Vampires*. His script for *Excessive Force* has some great character moments in it, and it's so much better than the scripts for other action films of its time. He also wrote *Night of the Warrior*, which ended up starring Lorenzo Lamas. Jon Hess (*Mars* with Olivier Gruner) directed *Excessive Force*. An in-name-only sequel with a female lead followed.

VHS artwork for *Excessive Force II: Force on Force*. Author's collection.

Excessive Force II: Force on Force

1995 (New Line DVD) (djm)

"Where you going, Lethal Weapon?"

A hard-hitting special agent named Harly (Stacie Randall) is betrayed by her partner and lover Frank Lydell (Dan Gauthier), and after making love, he shoots her in the head, leaving her for dead. Years later, Harly is a cop with a bullet lodged in her brain, and she experiences intense headaches and dizzy spells that will eventually result in her death if she doesn't have a major operation. As is, Harly is an untouchable, yet extremely attractive woman with a bad attitude, and her superiors on the force don't really know how to handle her excessive force tactics in the line of duty. Her ex-lover Lydell has meanwhile planned an extensive terrorist attack on the city of Los Angeles by laying siege to the police force, and when Harly gets wind of the plot and who is behind it, she focuses her rage on the man who made her the killing machine she has become.

Surprisingly adequate for an in-name-only sequel to the Thomas Ian Griffith vehicle, *Force on Force* brings Stacie Randall to the forefront of the action heroine limelight. She was a contender to take on the mantle held for so long by Cynthia Rothrock, but it just wasn't in the cards for her. She displays some impressive martial arts skills here, but the movie just didn't make much of an impression on the home video market to help propel her career forward. She also starred in *The Assault*, which was released the following year. Fans of female martial arts action stars should give *Excessive Force II* a try. It was directed by Jonathan Winfrey (*Bloodfist VII*).

The Executioner

1974 (Adness DVD) (djm)

Ryuichi Koga is from a long line of Koga ninjas, the elite class of assassins in Japan. Ryuichi is raised by a strict ninja master who instructs him how to dislocate his arms, legs, and take the sort of punishment that no mortal man should ever be able to withstand, and when he becomes a man (to be played by Sonny Chiba) he becomes fed up with living a cloistered life in a monastery and he leaves the clan to try to live a little while he's still young enough to enjoy it. But there's a big problem with his plan: It doesn't work because his role and purpose is more important than his desires, and he's immediately drafted by the government (which oversees and sponsors his ninja clan) to undertake a mission. His first gig is to work with two other assassins to topple a drug empire that is smuggling narcotics into Japan. The other two assassins aren't as tough as Ryuichi, but as a team they're pretty unstoppable.

Some outrageous violence (eye popping, bone breaking, screaming while attacking) makes the grindhouse classic *The Executioner* a fun viewing experience, and fans of Chiba will get enough of him to be satiated. He goes through his usual extreme motions as an overly dramatic martial artist here, but it's fun to watch. Some of this stuff is just plain bonkers, but anyone who's seen this sort of thing before will feel right at home. Directed by Teruo Ishi.

The Executioner 2
(a.k.a. **Karate Inferno**)
1974 (Adness DVD) (djm)

A jewel and its owner—a rich heiress named Sabine—are taken by kidnappers and thieves. A group of mercenary thieves are hired to steal the jewel and the girl back. The leader of the mercenaries is Ryuichi Koga (Sonny Chiba, reprising a role he already played), and his team of immature misfits are on the case, but not before they screw around and take forever to formulate a plan. They manage to reclaim the girl, but not the jewel, and so they devise an impossible plan—involving aerial feats—to get the jewel back, but their plan gets them caught and sent to prison.

It's hard to argue over a stupid plot that only takes eighty-five minutes to tell, but what *The Executioner 2* desperately needed was more action. The climax is definitely action packed, but it takes more than an hour of oddball comedy and slow buildup to get there. You could do worse, I suppose, but it's not an essential Chiba film. Directed by Teruo Ishii.

Executioners
1993 (Tai Seng DVD) (CD)

"You and I are inseparable. Your money and intelligence with my military power makes us the best rulers. The world will belong to us soon."

Things have changed greatly since we last saw *The Heroic Trio*. Wonder Woman (Anita Mui) has given up her crime fighting ways to take care of her young daughter. Invisible Girl (Michelle Yeoh) has devoted her life to atoning for her past evils and doing the best she can to uphold justice. Thief Catcher (Maggie Cheung) is still out trying to make money so she really hasn't changed much. The world, however, has become a post-apocalyptic wasteland and uncontaminated water is in short supply. A disturbingly deformed madman is in control of what's left of the safe water, and his intentions are not in the best interest of the survivors. The three lady heroes set out to uncover the truths and bring everything full circle to save humanity.

Executioners is an entirely different animal than its predecessor. There was a dark humor running rampant in *The Heroic Trio,* and it's discarded this time in favor of something far more serious and bleak. Instead of keeping our trio united, they spend the majority of the film separated. Director Johnny To returns with action direction by Ching Sui Tung, and neither disappoint in their respected areas, bringing a unique vision to the screen. Michelle Yeoh (*The Touch*) never lets her audience down and, as always, brings her beauty and grace to the proceedings. There seems to be less action in this one but they make sure every bit counts. Each of the women has their own moments to shine, as they all should. This is a worthy sequel to an action classic, which was released only seven months after the first one.

Executive Decision
1996 (WB DVD) (CD)

"I think we're looking up the ass-end of a dead dog, but it's worth a try."

Just a few moments after a commercial airline flight takes off, it's hijacked by terrorists led by the elusive Nagi Hassan (David Suchet). The United States government is holding one of his comrades, and Hassan demands the man's release. Intelligence expert David Grant (Kurt Russell) has enough intel to believe Hassan's plans are much more horrifying than originally assessed. He believes there's a missing nerve agent that could act as a poor man's nuclear bomb and Washington DC may very well be the target. Lieutenant Colonel Austin Travis (Steven Seagal) has devised a plan to get his team on the plane but he needs Grant there to guide them. Planting them on the plane is highly dangerous and Travis is killed (!), leaving Grant and several of the soldiers on the plane with less than four hours to find the bomb and nerve agent. Meanwhile, flight attendant Jean (Halle Berry) has several run-ins with the terrorists before discovering Grant, and she silently does what she can to help. With time running out and the US government ready to blow the plane out of the sky, every moment will count.

This is a rare film where Steven Seagal (*Ticker*) isn't the star and is merely a bit part player. It was a decision he should make more often since it always ends up being a great choice. He played similar small (but pivotal) roles in films like *Machete* and the Korean action/drama *Clementine* with great success. Before his untimely on-screen demise, he does very little fighting. The film opens with his team storming a terrorist hideout and he manages to knife several of them in one quick moment, which is basically the end of any real fighting from him. Still, his death comes as a much needed jolt. The film is a solid thriller, and Kurt Russell (not an action star by this book's definition), is always welcome in any movie, in any capacity. Directed by Stuart Baird (*U.S. Marshals*) whose claim to fame is editing such high-profile films as *Skyfall* and Richard Donner's *Superman,* amongst many others.

Exit
1996 (Republic VHS) (djm)

An exotic dancer named Diane (Shannon Whirry from *Mach 2* with Brian Bosworth) has just been proposed to, but her evening is about to get rough. A two-bit masked crew hoping to make out with the strip club's takings for the night has just made a ruckus on the floor, killing a patron and threatening to kill more if they don't cull enough money to make their effort worthwhile. When one of the robbers is shot and killed by the bartender, the second-in-command (played by David Bradley of *American Samurai* and *American Ninja* fame) steps up to finish the job. Everyone's chances of surviving the night just got worse because he's willing to die for just a few thousand extra bucks. Diane (who's dressed in stripper attire through most of the film) and an ex-cop patron manage to get the drop on the two remaining robbers and give themselves the exit they desperately need to make it through the night.

Slightly more sultry than sleazy, *Exit* was certainly a departure for the versatile Bradley, who shucked his heroic image for an unattractive thug in this low-budget thriller with action undertones. He gets into a few brawls (and even kicks a guy a few times), but this is as far away from *American Ninja* as he could probably get at the time, which is most likely exactly what he wanted. It's too bad, because Bradley should have been a bigger star, and *Exit* didn't do him any favors. If you want to see a really radical role for Bradley, check out the horror film *Lower Level*, where he played a psychotic security guard. Ric Roman Waugh who, much later, made the film *Snitch*, starring The Rock, directed this.

Exit Wounds
2001 (Warner DVD) (djm)

Detective Orin Boyd (Steven Seagal), a not-very-liked detective on the force, manages to save the Vice President's life almost by accident when a bunch of assassins make an attempt on his life. Boyd, at the right place at the right time, throws the VP over a bridge into a river, but he's later scorned because the VP couldn't swim—luckily the VP survived. Busted for his actions, Boyd is transferred to another department—a bad neighborhood with an unstable squad of cops to protect it—and he's hazed and shunned.

He begins to suspect that half the cops in his department are manufacturing and dealing drugs, and there's only one other cop whom he can trust (played by Isaiah Washington) aside from his chief (Jill Hennessy) who doesn't warm up to him very easily. At first Orin makes an enemy out of a slick streetwise operator named Latrell Walker (DMX), but they eventually realize that they're on the same side, and when they start playing offense together, they yield undeniable results.

Producer Joel Silver gave Seagal the big screen comeback he needed after his star began to wane and was beginning to headline direct-to-video movies like *The Patriot* and *Ticker*. The box office take of *Exit Wounds* proved that audiences were still into Seagal. Slimmer and more in tune with his role than he'd been for years, Seagal looks great in the film and his sense of humor really works in it. One fight scene in particular in the film involves a WTF wire trick, but other than that, his fights look genuine. The climactic fight scene involves Seagal and villain Michael Jai White swinging swords at each other, and the director Andrzej Bartkowiak (*Romeo Must Die, Cradle 2 the Grave*) makes the same mistake he did in *Cradle 2 the Grave*: He intercuts two separate fight scenes together—one between Seagal and Jai White, and the other between DMX and another character—and it ruins both fights. It's an ideal proposition to have Seagal fighting Jai White, but the on-screen results are poor. Still, there are more things to like about this entry than dislike, and it was a fine form return for Seagal. He squandered his comeback with his next film *Half Past Dead*.

Expect No Mercy

1995 (Legacy Entertainment DVD) (djm)

"I guess heroes aren't what they used to be."

Billy Blanks and Jalal Merhi reunite for the third and last time (after *Talons of the Eagle* and *TC 2000*), this time as cops trying to track down a "computer warlord" (Wolf Larson), who has an army of followers. Larson runs a "virtual arts academy" that's really a school of assassination, and Blanks and Merhi have to get used to using virtual reality games to work themselves into the fanatical army. They gain the trust of the army's technician (Laurie Holden, way before *The Walking Dead*), and she helps them take down her crazy boss. The finale has Blanks fighting Larson in an arena-type area, and Merhi fighting Anthony Delongis (from *Final Round*) on a rooftop.

The virtual reality angle really cripples this movie. The entire premise hangs on the VR gimmick, and the whole thing is rather awkward. Zale Dalen, the director, doesn't really make things interesting or original. Merhi directed and starred in another virtual reality action movie called *Expect to Die* with David Bradley. That one was worse.

Expect to Die

1997 (Platinum DVD) (djm)

Made during the virtual reality craze of the mid-1990s, *Expect to Die* is painfully outdated and inconsequential. Jalal Merhi (*Tiger Claws, Operation Golden Phoenix*) plays Justin Blake (yeah, sure), an undercover detective who's trying to find a killer who is using a virtual reality game as his means of murder. The killer is Dr. MacIntyre (David Bradley, playing against type), who created the game, and is killing people to promote and perfect the sequel. Merhi and his partner (Evan Lurie, who played the villain in Merhi's *Tiger Claws III*) go up against MacIntyre's syndicate, and they face plenty of opposition.

Merhi is a love-him-or-hate-him action guy. He never really had the charisma or the chops to give himself an edge over many of his co-stars, and given the fact that he almost always cast himself as the hero against bigger and more established stars like David Bradley, Cynthia Rothrock, Loren Avedon, and others, it's difficult not to consider him egotistical and vain. In *Expect to Die*, he doesn't give himself the best fight scenes, per se, but he does make sure Evan Lurie's character is killed and he doesn't allow Bradley to use his martial arts. Their final fight is more of a brawl, which is interesting, but telling of Merhi's thinking. Bradley signed up for another Merhi film, *Crisis*.

The Expendables

2010 (Lionsgate DVD) (djm)

After Sylvester Stallone made an unlikely one-two punch comeback with *Rocky Balboa* and *Rambo*, he used the momentum he had to get the all-star, dream team, smash-up *The Expendables* rolling. It's basically *The Dirty Dozen* teaming action heroes from the '80s and '90s with the current breed of action guys. Jason Statham stands next to Randy Couture, Jet Li fights Gary Daniels, "Stone Cold" Steve Austin fights Stallone, Terry Crews shoots a cannon of a gun, and Dolph Lundgren gets to fight Li a few times, too. There's a cameo scene with Arnold Schwarzenegger and Bruce Willis where they crack wise with Stallone, and it's a too-brief,

The Expendables: Barney Ross (Sylvester Stallone), Yin Yang (Jet Li), Toll Road (Randy Couture), Hale Caesar (Terry Crews), and Lee Christmas (Jason Statham). Author's collection.

"Stone Cold" Steve Austin (center, with pistol) is Paine in *The Expendables*. Author's collection.

Posing for the camera: Jet Li, Jason Statham, Sylvester Stallone, Randy Couture and Terry Crews in a publicity shot for *The Expendables*. Author's collection.

Jet Li, Sylvester Stallone, and Dolph Lundgren on a day off from shooting bad guys in *The Expendables*. Author's collection.

but fun scene. The plot is textbook *Rambo* stuff involving a dictator in a small South American island who is being shadowed by a dirty CIA agent (Eric Roberts) who wants to harvest cocaine in the fields of the island. The action scenes are bombastic and filmed a little too close to the action for comfort, but it's all in good fun. If this is the movie to reintroduce these guys to a new generation, I see no problem with that.

Stallone directed this, and it's clearly his show. The plot revolves around his character, as it does in part 2, but he gives the other characters a bigger sandbox to play in with that film. The director's cut of this first one has a few more moments for the characters to be funny or interesting, and I'd recommend seeing that

Jason Statham as Lee Christmas in *The Expendables*. Author's collection.

version. Mickey Rourke is also in the film, but he doesn't get involved in the action. The best parts of the film are just seeing these guys still in ridiculous shape and watching them do what they do best. It's not a classic, but it's everything it should and needs to be.

The Expendables 2 (a.k.a. The Expendables 2: Back For War)
2012 (Lionsgate DVD) (djm)

"Never count out a classic!"

Action movie dream teams simply do not get better or more fantastic than the one lined up in Simon West's *EX2*. Barney Ross (Sylvester Stallone) and his expendable team of mercenaries (Jet Li, Dolph Lundgren, Terry Crews, Randy Couture, Jason Statham, and newcomer Liam Hemsworth who is their new sniper) take on another mission to pay off their debt to the solemn Church (Bruce Willis, who seems to *want* to have fun, but his character is a stick in the mud). After an explosive first twenty minutes, the film cools down for about five minutes before shifting the action to Bulgaria, where a new villain named Jean Villain (a welcome return to the big leagues by Jean-Claude Van Damme) has laid claim to tons of weapons-grade plutonium. When one member of their team is killed, Ross and his badass compatriots "track 'em, find 'em, and kill 'em." The final showdown throws in a few extra Expendables in the mix to keep things lively:

Theatrical poster for *Expendables 2*. Author's collection.

Arnold Schwarzenegger, Willis, and Chuck Norris show up and blow stuff up real good. There are two final fights: Jason Statham fights Scott Adkins (*Undisputed 3*) and Stallone goes head-to-head with Van Damme. Both fights are good, but they're over far too soon, which is disappointing.

It is a nice, comfortable feeling I'm getting now that I've finally seen Van Damme, Chuck Norris, Arnie, Sly, and the gang all duke it out in the same movie. Amazing that Dolph Lundgren walked away with all of the best moments. Van Damme showed us and the world that he's worth more than everyone's been giving him over the last decade, and it was fun to hear Chuck crack a Norris joke. The only little qualm I had with it was that Scott Adkins got the Gary Daniels end of the stick, meaning that he was sort of shuffled to the side and his big fight scene with Statham felt rushed and was poorly lit. Arnold and Willis get more screen time, which is nice, and there are a few too many references to each star's movies, but how is any fan of the films that helped spawn *The Expendables* franchise not going to be happy to soak in the pure fun of this entry?

Producer/director Boaz Davidson in Hollywood, California. Photo by david j. moore.

INTERVIEW:
BOAZ DAVIDSON
(djm)

Israeli born director/producer/writer Boaz Davidson is one of the most important filmmakers in the movie market as far as action stars as concerned. He has either written, produced, or directed movies starring the likes of Chuck Norris, Sylvester Stallone, Arnold Schwarzenegger, Mark Dacascos, David Bradley, Scott Adkins, Gary Daniels, Jason Statham, Michael Worth, Jean-Claude Van Damme, Steven Seagal, and dozens of other action stars and guys on the fringe. Davidson is one of the executive producers of the production company Nu Image/Millennium, and has been in the business long enough to see action stars rise, fall, make comebacks, and disappear into the ether. His latest crop of action star–fueled films include Rambo *(2008) and all three* Expendables *pictures.*

You did a few movies with Cannon and have worked with many of the world's greatest action stars. Say something about directing and producing movies during the height of the VHS boom.

We made a lot of movies, and in those days video was very big. We had our action guys. We had Joe Lara, Michael Dudikoff, all those guys. And Van Damme. Chuck Norris, too.

You directed a movie called *Blood Run*, which was retitled *Outside the Law*, and this was one of David Bradley's only nonmartial arts/action movies. What was it like working with Bradley?

I had so many problems with this movie. Unbelievable problems. David Bradley was one of the main problems. I couldn't control him. He had problems with the leading lady. I had to make peace with him all the time.

Theatrical banner poster for *Expendables 2*. Author's collection.

He was known for doing action; I mean he was the *American Ninja* at that point. What sorts of problems did you have with him? In fact, what other problems have you had with other action guys in other movies, if any?

He didn't want to do that anymore. He didn't even want to do the love scene with the girl we cast, so we had to put in a double. It was okay for him to make love, but not with her. Crazy, funny things happened on *Expendables* too. In the second *Expendables*, Mickey Rourke was supposed to be in it. But he was supposed to be killed by Van Damme. He said, "Um, no problem, I'm ready to die, but this motherfucker is not killing me. If somebody else wants to kill me, fine, but not that guy." When Van Damme was offered the part, he said, "I want to have a fight in the movie with Statham." Statham said, "No problem, but if I fight with him, I kill him." Stallone heard this. "No fucking way. *I'm* killing him!"

What is it about the action genre that appeals to you? Your company Millennium seems to work exclusively in the action genre.

The truth is we don't do only that, but we do a lot of action movies. They are much easier to sell because in those days . . . first of all with buyers around the world, they didn't have too much time or patience to read the script, so if they see a poster with explosions on it, they like it. Today, it's much more difficult to sell a drama. If you go back to the Cannon days, we did a lot of art movies.

The smaller action movies are almost nonexistent today.

The low-budget action movie doesn't exist. *Ninja 2* will be one of our last low-budget action movies. We don't do this kind of movie anymore because there is no room for this kind of movie anymore. A big company cannot survive making movies like this. Today, people are looking for movies with movie stars or something special.

It's interesting that you say "movie stars." What is a movie star? What is your definition of that?

A star is like the stock market. A movie star is somebody who is up here today, and tomorrow is down. But he's a movie star. You can sell a movie with him.

***The Expendables* was a great idea, and those two movies were big hits for you guys. But then, Stallone's movie *Bullet to the Head* bombs. Schwarzenegger's movie *The Last Stand* bombs.**

Everybody's movie bombed. And Statham [in *Parker*].

Jason Statham's movie *Parker* bombed, too, yeah.

Together, they work. Separately, they don't work. Thing is, movie stars—especially action movie stars—at that age, making movies . . . let's face it: the movie star ages and so does his audience. Age is a big factor.

Statham's not that old.

No, no. He's younger.

So what's going on?

Well, his movies were never big hits when you look at them. He always had a ceiling.

Like thirty or forty million.

Yeah, around there.

Who's your hope for the future of action films?

I love Scott Adkins. His biggest exposure was in *Expendables 2*. He's great. He's very physical. He's one of those rare actors who can act and do martial arts. This question is coming up again and again. "Who is the next guy?" I don't know.

Talk about working with some of the directors whom you've worked with. Guys like Isaac Florentine.

Look, Isaac is very close to me. He comes from martial arts, and he's a good student of action movies and the martial arts. We started out together on *American Cyborg*. He did second unit. Even in one of the scenes, he was in it. I've worked with him on many, many movies. I think we have a very good relationship. Isaac found Scott Adkins. This is a good match. Unfortunately he hasn't broken into the big movies. I think he's ready to break in.

What is it like working with Stallone on these last few movies you've done together?

Stallone is a pure delight to work with. Sly is a filmmaker. He's very good to work with. He has a plan. It's really great to work with him. I go to so many film sets where the director says, "I think we should put the camera here," and then the actor comes and says, "I think we should put the camera there." This doesn't happen when Stallone is on set. He knows how to use the elements of the story to make the thing work.

What's the plan for *Expendables 3*? Bigger, better, more guys . . .

Bigger, better, more guys. We're still looking. Also, younger. A younger generation.

The Expendables 3
2014 (Lionsgate DVD) (djm)

Christmas: "When I joined,
I joined for the whole ride."
Barney: "I know you did.
The ride's over."

Barney (Sylvester Stallone) and his posse of "expendable" mercenaries—Christmas (Jason Statham), Toll Road (Randy Couture), Hail Caesar (Terry Crews), and Gunnar (Dolph Lundgren)—stage a great escape for one of Barney's original expendables, Doc (Wesley Snipes), and with that out of the way the movie then moves right into their next mission: Eliminate an arms dealer in Somalia. When Barney realizes that their target is an ex-expendable named Stonebanks (Mel Gibson), he goes ballistic and botches the mission, putting his men in mortal danger. Hail Caesar is seriously wounded, they lose their target, and they're reassigned a new boss: Drummer (a very game Harrison Ford), who announces that his predecessor Church (Bruce Willis who is absent) will no longer be their handler. Barney is told to capture Stonebanks, who has committed crimes against humanity, and with a guilty conscience, Barney retires his team and takes time out to assemble a new one. With the help of an old comrade, Bonaparte (Kelsey Grammer), Barney brings a younger and even more expendable crew (played by real boxer Victor Ortiz, real MMA fighter Ronda Rousey, Glen Powell, and Kellan Lutz) together. These kids have no idea what's in store for them as their bull-headed leader leads them straight into yet another botched mission that gets all of them captured except Barney, who stubbornly refuses to call his old team to help him rescue the new guys. Thankfully, Barney's competition in the game, Trench (Arnold Schwarzenegger, who gets more screen time than ever), has decided to be a team player and makes the call to help out. When the *whole* gang—including Yin Yang (Jet Li) and even a new guy named Galgo (Antonio Banderas, Stallone's co-star in *Assassins*)—shows up to help Barney, the action heats up as Stonebanks throws most of Eastern Europe's armies at them.

With a bigger-than-ever roll call of action guys and actors (some of whom haven't done this sort of thing in a while), *Expendables 3* pulls off a minor miracle and manages to be the best of the series. The action takes a secondary position to what goes on between the characters, which is what makes this one so crisp. There are *so* many characters this time around that it's a wonder that several of the guys agreed to return (Jet, Dolph, and Randy aren't given much to do this time), and even a few of the new guys like Powell and Ortiz aren't given well-defined traits or skills aside from shooting stuff real good or climbing stuff and jumping off. The big additions this time are from Mel Gibson, who snarls and gives Stallone a run for his muscle in their key scenes together, from Harrison Ford who looks like he's having more fun in this than in the last six or seven movies he's been in, and from Antonio Banderas who sorta feels like he's in the wrong movie altogether, but since his part was written for Jackie Chan, you can see that he's having a fantastic time riffing with Sly because he's just so happy to be there. Wesley Snipes is there too, but for some reason he seems reserved and held back, and Ronda Rousey gets to show some of her abilities as a fighter, but her climactic fight is intercut with several other key fights (including Statham's, which is a common cardinal sin of these three films). I don't really have much to say about Kellan Lutz, as Millennium/Nu Image is desperately trying to create an action star out of him (not going to happen, guys), so the less said about him the better. As busy as *Expendables 3* is, it amazingly never loses its focus, which is on the team, and even while the team continues to expand, the joy of watching them get into action together is what these movies are all about. If this is the last one, I'm really glad they saved the best one for last. Directed by Patrick Hughes.

The Expert

1995 (Boulevard Entertainment DVD) (djm)

A sociopath named Kagan (Michael Shaner) breaks into the home of a woman and kills her. As he's leaving the house, the woman's brother, John Lomax (Jeff Speakman), is driving up and he sees the killer leaving. Lomax, a former special ops expert, identifies Kagan in a line-up, and Kagan is put on trial for murder. Instead of receiving the death penalty, a psychologist argues that he deserves special treatment, and he is interred in a prison where he has the leeway to prove the psychologist wrong—he is every bit as dangerous as she argues he isn't. Dissatisfied with the justice system, Lomax breaks into the prison where Kagan is being held, and he makes sure justice is served.

Pretty strange for an action film, *The Expert* isn't the best vehicle for Speakman, whose kenpo abilities aren't really the focal point. He gets into a few fights, but the film is script and plot heavy, with maybe too many characters than it needed. Shaner (from *Bloodfist*) isn't a good match for the overpowering Speakman, who doesn't face any real competition in this film. The score by Ashley Irwin is grandiose and awesome, especially for a film of this stature. James Brolin plays the warden of the prison. It was directed by Rick Avery, who also worked with Speakman on *Deadly Outbreak*.

Expert Weapon (a.k.a. American Dragon)

1993 (Simitar DVD) (djm)

After murdering a police officer during a crime spree, Adam Collins (Ian Jacklin from *Death Match* and *Ring of Fire II: Blood and Steel*) is apprehended, incarcerated, and sentenced to death. During his imprisonment, he's "recruited" by a secret, off-the-books government agency and trained to be an assassin. With his ingrained fighting sense and streetwise attitude, Adam is more or less a decent candidate to perform these government jobs, but he clashes with his recruiter Janson (Sam Jones who played *Flash Gordon*), who keeps calling him a maggot. When the agency kills Adam's girlfriend, he goes ballistic and turns the tables against the guys who trained him.

From the low-budget production company Cine Excel (which did some projects with Gary Daniels), *Expert Weapon* is pretty much the only time Jacklin got a chance to star in something, and while that's a noble notion, the film is pretty dismal and it doesn't really offer its promising

star a chance to shine. The movie is ugly, chintzy, and cheap to the point that the movie barely has a music score to heighten the action scenes or help play on emotions. It relies on a sex scene, ho-hum action choreography, and a star-hopeful to carry the film to its predictable conclusion, resulting in a junky effort. From director Steven Austin, who did *American Streetfighter* (another poor effort) with Gary Daniels.

The Extendables

2014 (ITunes) (CD)

"I show you, I did not retire: I got extension."

Vardell Duseldorfer (*Cobra*'s Brian Thompson) was once the nation's hottest action star. Having succumbed to fame, drugs, and women, he's looking for a project to propel him back to the top. He quickly finds himself as the director and star of a film called *Hard Times on Mars* shooting abroad. Once on the set, VD (his nickname) starts reverting back to his old ways: doing drugs, attempting to fornicate with young starlets, and changing things up just because he feels like it, making it difficult for his crew. *The Extendables* chronicles the difficulties of making a film with a star who hasn't come to terms with his checkered past and must conquer his inner demons if he's to find himself on top again.

Brian Thompson (also in *The Order*) gives an intro to the film saying it is all based on his true experiences working with several different action stars over the course of his career. He essentially combines JCVD, Arnie, and Sly to create his VD character and does a pretty solid job of doing so. The problem is that the film is supposed to be funny and falls seriously short. It's like watching one long, boring dick joke. There are a few cool cameos but these guys just sort of show up for a minute then they disappear. Guys like Martin Kove, Kevin Sorbo, and Mark Dacascos appear throughout and deliver a couple of mildly entertaining lines then they disappear. Thompson wrote, directed, starred, and edited his little passion project, but with little to no action and jokes consistently falling flat, maybe he's better suited for kicking ass.

Extraction

2013 (Sony DVD) (CD)

"All right, we got four bullets left, we got thirty minutes 'til extraction, and the entire infernal prison is out to kill us. You ready?"

It won't be an easy task but the US military has assembled a black ops team to extract Rudolf Martin (Falk Hentschel), a man with information that will help them capture a major terrorist threat. The tricky part will be busting him out of

a maximum security prison in Chechnya. There appears to be a mole in the military since the team is ambushed immediately upon entrance. The only survivor is Mercy (Jon Foo from *Bangkok Revenge*), and he's determined to get Martin himself. The prison warden Ivan Rudovsky (Vinnie Jones) has another idea. He releases the entire prison population on him, but Mercy is one of the elite and he won't go down without a fight.

This is the first film produced by streaming service Crackle, and it's a damn good one. It feels quite a bit like *The Raid* but manages to be highly entertaining throughout. Jon Foo (also in *Tekken*) is an action star on the rise and has proven time and again that he's a serious force in the business. Once the film moves into the final act, Foo has some great fight scenes with fantastic choreography. He's surrounded by a great supporting cast with Vinnie Jones, Sean Astin, Joanne Kelly, and the always-brilliant Danny Glover watching his back. Writer/director Tony Giglio (*Chaos*) spins an engaging tale leaving the film wide open for a sequel. Jon Foo deserves a character he can develop over a series of films, and hopefully this will be the one.

Extraction

2015 (Lionsgate DVD) (djm)

A badass CIA agent named Leonard Turner (Bruce Willis) is duped by some bad guys and his wife ends up dead, and his son Harry survives by pure luck. Years later, Harry (Kellan Lutz) has worked hard to follow in his father's footsteps as a CIA operative, but circumstances have sidelined him and he's never been able to work in the field, despite his excellent test scores and his aptitude. When his dad (who's retired) is kidnapped by some terrorists over a military-grade device known as "Condor," the CIA drags their heels in saving him, so Harry takes it upon himself to save him all on his own. His ex-lover (also a CIA agent) Victoria (Gina Carano from *Haywire* and *In the Blood*) joins him in his mission, and while keeping an eye on him and making sure he gets out of his scrapes and brawls with thugs and bad guys, she also gets in on the action. They get to Leonard (who spends most of the movie strapped to a chair) and save the world.

Almost instantly forgettable, the barely theatrically released *Extraction* heavily implies that Bruce Willis is the star, but being in his declining era of his career, he's barely there, and when he's required to be on screen he mutters his lines with his signature scowl. Co-star Gina Carano, who was so great in her previous films, is given a few fights to show off her feats of physicality, but her character is beholden to star Lutz, who actually emerges more appealing here than he was in *Expendables 3*. Carano's character is more a damsel in distress than the hero, but when she unleashes in a few scenes it's clear that she's the star who deserved more screen time. She also appeared in a small role in a film called *Heist* (co-starring Dave Bautista) the same year, but that movie didn't really feature any action in it, so it is not covered here. Carano is a talent that should never be wasted. Directed by Steven C. Miller.

Extreme Challenge

2001 (Ingram DVD) (CD)

"Hey, woman, stop fooling around. Go home, make love not war. If you come up here I'll crush you."

In the near future, a sports company has created a martial arts competition like no other. With the help of modern technology, they bring the unique fights to the Internet for the first time ever. It's an elimination challenge where the fighters compete in an obstacle course–like environment with the intention of eliminating as many other players as they can. Everyone has something to prove, including two students of the same master—Fang Jin (Jun Ngai Yeung) and Kin Kuang (Ken Chang). They're both fighting for their own reasons but first they have to realize what is actually most important to them. Money is thrown around and pockets are greased. There is more to life than taking a bribe to throw a fight—things like honor and respect. Once they learn this, one of them could take the whole thing.

Extreme Challenge offers up some fantastic fight sequences and little else. The story is paper-thin and the English-dubbed dialogue is just ludicrous. The film does take pride in showcasing different styles of martial arts as well as various weapons. *Extreme Challenge* is of note mostly for the fact it features an early performance by Scott Adkins (*Ninja*). He only appears briefly in the film but has an exciting fight with Jun Ngai Yeung. It's a fight that focuses on weapons work and Adkins shows off his skills using nunchuks while Yeung uses a staff. The scene is a highlight of the film. There are many excellently staged sequences but the story never really draws you in. Director Stephen Tung Wei (Jet Li's *Contract Killer*) delivers the excitement from an action standpoint but fails to engage the audience with realistic characters or a story.

Extreme Counterstrike

2012 (MW Films DVD) (djm)

Gary Wasniewski from *Thunderkick* and *Kill Factor* returns as renegade agent Sean Kane (the same character from those previous films), but this time Kane is a psychologically damaged man, filled with bloody flashbacks involving the death of a child. When a terrorist bombs London, Kane is sent to Los Angeles where the terrorist and his cronies are thought to be, and while there he drinks himself into a stupor, beats up and murders petty criminals to numb the pain, and eventually finds the terrorist—and stops him from blowing up Los Angeles.

From co-directors Wasniewski and Leo Fong, *Extreme Counterstrike* is a much more sobering film than their previous two efforts, and with the use of great-looking stock footage and better cameras, at least their film looks halfway presentable, despite terrible sound editing. The action isn't doled out as frequently as it was on *Kill Factor*, and Wasniewski does his damnedest to act according to script, but the biggest problem with the film is the script itself. Most fans of action and martial arts films will find this film appallingly bad, but if you're going to do an intensive study on action stars all across the board, then you would be remiss if you neglected Gary Wasniewski.

Extreme Force

2001 (Razor Digital DVD) (djm)

Thieves for life Marcos (Hector Echavarria) and Cole (Youssef Qissi) are on a roll with their heists, but when Marcos wants out of the life, Cole gets crazy and forces him to do one more job—and then he betrays him and leaves him for dead right in the middle of the heist. When Marcos regains consciousness, he finds that the man whom they were stealing from—Kong Li (Michel Qissi, who also directed)—has helped nurse him back to health with only one purpose for the kindness: To find Cole and reclaim the treasure that he stole. Marcos is kind of a smartass about the whole thing, but he grows to like Kong Li despite his deadpan demeanor and utter seriousness about life. They grow to trust each other in the midst of their grand plan to get revenge on Cole, who has gone off the rails.

Okay, let me explain something about Hector Echavarria. It's no secret that he's what most would call "a bad actor." It's not a big deal to me. Most action stars are bad actors. So I look past the acting and I see their strengths as martial artists or athletes, and when I look at Echavarria in his movies, I see the same exact guy in all of his films. He's a good martial artist. He kicks high and gracefully. He works hard, I can see that. *But* . . . he tends to play egotistical characters who are really difficult to find appealing. He plays that kind of guy in *Extreme Force*, and his co-star Michel Qissi (who virtually played the same character in the first two *Kickboxer* movies, but this time he's a good guy) is almost silent throughout the whole movie, quashing any ego he might have with a forceful, wordless presence. Every time Echavarria opens his mouth, I want to tell him, "Hey, take a note from Michel. Tough guys are tougher when they're quiet." Most fans of action and martial arts movies will be challenged to be won over by Echavarria's swagger and bravado in any of the films he's been involved in, and *Extreme Force* is no exception. I liked aspects of it. Echavarria is a guy who could be making some interesting movies. *Extreme Force* isn't very interesting.

Extreme Honor

2001 (MTI DVD) (CD)

"I sincerely sympathize with your dilemma, I do. But you see, I am not a hypocrite. I truly believe whether it's an adult or a child, everyone must die when your time comes. You see, Mr. Brascoe, dying is the bottom line to life."

Sometimes things happen and you have no control over the outcome. Former Navy SEAL John Kennedy Brascoe (Dan Anderson) is about to find this out not once, but twice. First, in an operation gone bad, he takes the fall for his partner Cody (Olivier Gruner) who accidentally kills a child. Second, his son is dying of leukemia and his condition is only growing worse. Working for a private security firm, Brascoe learns of an experimental treatment that could prolong his son's life. The price tag on the treatment is five million dollars, money he just doesn't have. He enlists the help of a few friends, including former SEAL Sparks (Michael Madsen), to devise a plan and swipe money from corrupt businessman Baker (Michael Ironside). It's a daring plan but he and his team are just crazy (and well trained) enough to pull it off.

Extreme Honor does a few things right but makes one huge mistake: They forgot to put in the action. The cast is actually rock solid with brilliant talent like Michael Madsen (*Kill Bill*), Martin Kove (*Steele Justice*), Antonio Fargas (*Superfly*), Michael Ironside (*Total Recall*), Sarah Shahi (*Bullet to the Head*), and action star Olivier Gruner (*Angel Town*). Gruner's appearance basically serves as bookends to the film. He does have a single fight scene with Dan Anderson so his talents weren't completely wasted. The story has its heart in the right place and director Steven Rush succeeds in making a decent picture, but it is just sorely lacking in the action department, making it unnecessary viewing.

An Eye For an Eye

1981 (Optimum DVD R2) (djm)

San Francisco cop Sean Kane (Chuck Norris without facial hair) leaves the force in disgrace and anger after a sting goes bad, leaving his partner dead. He does some investigating on his own, and when his dead partner's reporter girlfriend is murdered later, he seeks help by joining forces with her father, played by Mako (*The Perfect Weapon*), who is a master at martial arts. Together they get involved in investigating what Mako's daughter was working on and they discover that a major drug cartel is operating within the city, and that her boss (Christopher Lee) is the head of the cartel.

Fairly simple and no-nonsense, *An Eye For an Eye* gives Norris plenty of room to flex his abilities as an action star, and he's never less than convincing. The climax features a fight between him and Professor Toru Tanaka, who plays the murdering muscle who killed the reporter. Richard Roundtree (*Shaft*) is wasted in a small role as Norris's disgruntled captain. There are some nice shots of the Golden Gate Bridge. The director, Steve Carver, would later direct Norris in *Lone Wolf McQuade*. The MGM DVD release is full screen, while the Region 2 Optimum DVD is widescreen.

Eye See You (a.k.a. **Detox**)

2002 (Millennium DVD) (djm)

A serial killer who has targeted policemen and their families is on a rampage, and he has set his sights on tormenting FBI agent Jake Malloy (Sylvester Stallone), who is an ex-cop. When the killer brutally slays Malloy's beautiful girlfriend (Dina Meyer) and gets away with it, Malloy plunges into a deep, alcoholic-infused depression and attempts suicide. On a fragile rebound, he commits himself to an intensive rehab facility in rural Wyoming in the dead of winter. Along with ten other law enforcement officers on the rebound (including the likes of Robert Patrick, Robert Prosky, Courtney B. Vance, Jeffrey Wright, and Sean Patrick Flannery) and staff members (including Kris Kristofferson, Polly Walker, Tom Berenger, and Stephen Lang), Malloy quickly realizes that the serial killer has preceded him and is amongst the patients, killing them off one by one, saving him for last.

Sylvester Stallone stars as Jake Malloy, who is being hunted by a serial killer in *Eye See You*. Author's collection.

Jake Malloy (Sylvester Stallone) is faced with a serial killer, who is hunting him in *Eye See You*. Author's collection.

The serial killer dramatic action movie *Eye See You* features Sylvester Stallone as a law enforcement officer who's life is turned upside down when he's been targeted by a psycho killer. Author's collection.

In 1999, I saw a test screening of this movie under the title *The Outpost*. When the film started, the audience cheered when Stallone came on the screen, and by the time it was over, I watched people bolt for the exits, cursing the film and tearing it apart in the lobby. I went home in a deep funk, mulling over my own feelings for the film, and the more I thought about it, the more angry I became that Stallone had chosen this as his comeback movie after a two-year hiatus following *Cop Land*. I waited several years for the film to actually see a legitimate release, and it wouldn't see the light of day until 2002, when it snuck out into a few theaters and was eventually released to video under the lame title *Eye See You*. It's not a good vehicle for Stallone, who gets to act depressed and enraged, but ultimately this stalk-and-slash action hybrid is a slog to get through, especially seeing as how the great supporting cast is ultimately wasted (literally and figuratively). In the meantime, Arnold Schwarzenegger had made an against-type action movie called *End of Days* where his character is suicidal and morose. Imagine my disillusionment during the early years of the new millennium. Stallone's next film was the flop *Get Carter*, but it was released years before *Eye See You*, as was *Driven*. After *Eye See You* (which was originally produced by Brian Grazer and Imagine Entertainment) was finally released, Stallone's next release was *Avenging Angelo*, which debuted on video. This was his worst era. Jim Gillespie, who had done the weak post-*Scream* slasher *I Know What You Did Last Summer* directed *Eye See You*.

Michael Jai White stars in the Ernie Barbarash action film *Falcon Rising*. Author's collection.

Falcon Rising (a.k.a. **Favela**)

2014 (djm)

Suicidal ex-soldier John Chapman (Michael Jai White) drinks a bullet every week if the bullet he puts in his gun to play Russian roulette with doesn't fire. That's where he's at . . . until his social worker sister goes to Brazil and is beaten and maimed nearly to death by unknown assailants. An old Army pal named Manny (Neal McDonough) is working in Brazil for the US State Department, and he helps point John in the right direction. A loose canon, John has itchy trigger fingers and an even shorter fuse, and when he bulldozes into a plot concerning human trafficking, which his sister also stumbled onto, he gets the undivided attention of several corrupt cops (played by Lateef Crowder from *Undisputed 3* and Jimmy Navarro) and the Yakuza. The Yakuza has a stronghold in Rio, and they are behind John's sister's predicament (she spends most of the movie in a coma), and when John gets it in his gut to go after those responsible, he doesn't leave anyone standing.

Filmed in Puerto Rico, *Falcon Rising* gives you what you came to see. Whenever Jai White does one of these types of movies, he's pretty much the best there is, and he does exactly what you're hoping he will in this one. It's got the right amount of action, some intense dramatic moments, and a simple plot that never gets lost in the telling. Director Ernie Barbarash (*6 Bullets, Assassination Games*) knows his audience well enough not to shortchange them, and the climactic fight between Jai White and Crowder, Navarro, and Masashi Odate, the actor plays the Yakuza boss, is an excellent capper to an otherwise enjoyable action movie. Sequels are promised. This one got a brief theatrical release.

Fallout

1999 (Genius DVD) (CD)

"Do you think I want to go through with this? *Do you*? My family, my brothers and sisters have known nothing but war for a decade, now occupation. I can change this. You have child, wouldn't you do the same?"

With a trip to a space station on the horizon, veteran astronaut J. J. Hendricks (Daniel Baldwin) is having a problem—he can't seem to land the new prototype shuttle in the simulation. His boss decides it's in Hendricks's interest to stay on the ground, letting Amanda McCord (Teri Ann Lin) take his place. She's dispatched to fix the computer systems, but quickly finds out they were never broken but were just sabotaged under the orders of Russian astronaut Captain Previ Federov (action star Frank Zagarino) who takes the space station hostage and threatens to blow up satellites over major cities until his comrades are released. The only person who can get up there quick enough to stop him is Hendricks, but he'll have to overcome his fears if he is to save the world.

Fallout is incredibly light on action, and putting Baldwin in the lead role was a mistake. The movie is dull even if there are several worthy mentions in the picture. Aside from the exceptional editing and mediocre script, our man Frank Zagarino (*Airboss, Warhead*) stretches his acting chops and delivers one of the most bizarre Russian accents I've ever heard. It isn't bad, but I guess you could call it inconsistent. Accent aside, he's still a great villain and he is without question the most interesting character and a real scene-stealer. Directed by Rodney McDonald (*Sonic Impact*).

Family of Cops

1995 (Echo Bridge DVD) (CD)

Paul Fein (Charles Bronson) is a police detective in Milwaukee, Wisconsin. One son, Ben (Daniel Baldwin), is also a dectective, while his other son Eddie (Sebastian Spence) is a uniformed street cop. He also has two daughters: Kate (Barbara Williams), who is an attorney, and Jackie who finds herself in a position no one would ever want to be in. Jackie (Angela Featherstone) wakes up in the bed of a very rich married man only to find he has been shot to death. She has no recollection of what happened, and didn't hear any gunshots. Naturally, she calls her father and brother who will do whatever it takes to clear her name. Things become complicated for everyone when Ben is shot and the killer disappears. Paul won't let go, and he will tear the town apart until he finds his man.

Bronson (*Death Wish*) was in his early seventies when he starred in the first of what would eventually become a trilogy of made-for-

TV films. Even at his advanced age, the essence of what made him so great in his heyday (a disputable period for fans) was still very much evident. *Family of Cops* is more of a thriller than an action picture, but Bronson is given a couple of great tough-guy moments, including giving a mobster one of the best bitch-slaps ever. Also, he isn't afraid to take a pool stick and show an opponent how easy it is to snap it over his head. If you can get over the fact that it's a predictable film, it's still decent entertainment and the legendary Bronson only made two more films after this before he passed away in 2003. This one was directed by veteran director Ted Kotcheff (*First Blood, Hidden Assassin*).

Family of Cops III:
Under Suspicion

1999 (Echo Bridge DVD) (CD)

The Fein family has been through the ringer. They've been accused of murders and targeted by the Russian mafia. With all of this turmoil, it's a surprise they're able to keep their personal lives in check. Paul Fein (Charles Bronson) is still the patriarch, and everyone looks to him for advice. His daughter Kate (Barbara Williams) finds herself on her own and pregnant, his son Eddie (Sebastian Spence) blames himself for the near death of his partner during a raid, his other daughter Jackie (Nicole de Boer) has graduated to rookie police officer, and his other son Ben (Joe Penny) is working alongside his father. They're investigating the murder of a prominent banker who has connections within the local government. Going after these men could have some serious repercussions, especially for Paul, who gets thrown off the case after the current chief ends up murdered and it looks as if Paul is somehow involved. With assistance and support from his family, he sets out to find the truth and do what must be done to clear his name.

While it may not be a great film, *Family of Cops III* is the cinematic farewell of a Hollywood legend. Charles Bronson (*Assassination, Breakout*) was seventy-six when he filmed this, and you can tell he was struggling a little bit. His supporting cast steps up to help the actor through to the finish, and the result is that this is the best film in the series. This trilogy is only a blip on a career spanning five decades but somehow serves as a fitting swan song. Bronson never gets too physical in this one, choosing to take a step back while still finding himself in the middle of several shootouts. There's a bit of cheesiness to these flicks, but it's interesting to see how these characters grow and how their lives have changed since the previous entry. There's a great moment for the star when he goes to a private club with his lady friend. Every person his character is investigating is in there, and he just goes in, sits down, and orders a bottle of champagne. He calmly just hangs out and smiles as all these criminals get flustered that he's there. It's great. Directed by Sheldon Larry.

Fast and Furious

2009 (Universal DVD) (CD)

"It starts with the eyes. She's gotta have those kind of eyes that can look right through the bullshit, to the good in someone. Twenty perfect angel, eighty percent devil. Down to earth. Ain't afraid to get a little engine grease under her fingernails."

Brian O'Connor (Paul Walker) has moved on from the events that took place in *2 Fast 2 Furious* and is now working with the FBI. He's working on a huge case to try and bring down heroin smuggler Arturo Braga (John Ortiz). In Panama City, Dominic Toretto (Vin Diesel), who is still on the run from the law, hears news that his girlfriend, Letty (Michelle Rodriguez), was killed on a job. Toretto quickly makes his way to LA to investigate the circumstances of her death. The road leads to Braga, which brings him face to face with his former friend O'Connor. The two men reluctantly team up to achieve a common goal and infiltrate Braga's operation. While on the hunt for Letty's killer, they have to deal with their personal issues with each other, allowing time for Brian to make amends with Toretto's sister Mia (Jordana Brewster). When it comes to Letty, both men are willing to risk everything in order to avenge her death.

It took eight years after the release of the first film to reunite the cast for this entry that rebooted the series and send it on its current trajectory. Though Paul Walker (*Running Scared*) took the reigns for the 2003 sequel *2 Fast 2 Furious*, this was the first in the series that featured Vin Diesel (*Riddick*) returning in a star capacity (he had a cameo in *The Fast and the Furious: Tokyo Drift*). It was a welcome return and under the helm of director Justin Lin (*Tokyo Drift*) they were able to breathe new life into the series. The movie never forgets where it came from: there are plenty of fast cars and racing, but with the added action elements and character detail, this was the start of when the series began heading toward the fifth (and best) installment. The action scenes are top-notch and the final chase through the underground tunnels is just badass, leading directly into the perfect set-up for *Fast Five*.

Fast & Furious 6
(a.k.a. **Furious 6**)
2013 (Universal DVD) (djm)

Following the events of *Fast Five*, *Fast & Furious 6* reassembles all of the characters from that entry and injects them into another impossible adventure. This time, international cop Hobbs (Dwayne "The Rock" Johnson) needs world-class criminal Dominic Toretto (Vin Diesel) and his misfit crew to help him track and bag another globetrotting criminal named Shaw (Luke Evans), who has ties to Toretto's former

Hobbs (Dwayne Johnson) and his partner Riley (Gina Carano) are bulked up and ready for action in *Fast and Furious 6*. Author's collection.

The chase is on! Riley (Gina Carano) trails Hobbs (Dwayne Johnson) in *Fast and Furious 6*. Author's collection.

Riley (Gina Carano) fights Letty (Michelle Rodriguez) in the finale of *Fast and Furious 6*. Author's collection.

flame, Letty (Michelle Rodriguez), who was presumed dead in earlier entries in the series. Toretto gets his gang together, and they all agree to stage an incredible plan to bring Shaw down with the proviso that they will all be given full pardons for their crimes, enabling them to go back home to the US. Along for the ride in this entry are a few newcomers, including MMA fighter Gina Carano (from *Haywire*). She has plenty of maneuverability to show off her moves in two fight scenes with Rodriguez.

Fans of the series that keeps on giving will have a blast with *Furious 6*. The post-end credit sequence (spoiler alert) features a set-up involving Jason Statham as the villain of the next film. Diesel and Johnson make a good team, and if you're not engrossed with the cars and the

Dominic Toretto (Vin Diesel) in *Fast and Furious 6*. Author's collection.

chases, then you have the fisticuffs and high-flying stunts to get you involved. As far as top-of-the-line studio movies go, this one has it all. Returning cast members include Paul Walker, Jordana Brewster, Tyrese Gibson, Ludacris, and Sung Kang from *Bullet to the Head*. Justin Lin is the director.

Fast and Furious 7

(a.k.a. **Furious 7**)

2015 (Universal DVD) (djm)

The blue-collar über-franchise from Universal Pictures speeds along with this 7th(!?) iteration of more of the same, but even bigger and more explosive than before. Former outlaw and alpha male to a band of former outlaw misfits Dominic Toretto (Vin Diesel) is on the warpath to avenge the death of his comrade Han (Sung Kang), who is killed in Tokyo (see: *The Fast and the Furious: Tokyo Drift*) by a vengeful ex-special forces maniac named Deckard Shaw (Jason Statham), who has a grudge against Toretto and his gang. Shaw has made it his mission in life to kill everyone in Toretto's circle (and even blows up his house for the hell of it), and that goes for his allies too—including buffed out Agent Hobbs (Dwayne Johnson), who is knocked down and out by Shaw's ruthless cunning. Toretto is offered a chance by a government spook named Mr. Nobody (Kurt Russell!) to find Shaw by using a device called "The God's Eye," which can locate any human being on the planet in a matter of moments, but first Toretto must rescue the computer hacker who created the device, and then take his whole crew to the Middle East to salvage the device from a billionaire's headquarters. With his pals (excuse me, his family) Brian O'Connor (Paul Walker), Roman (Tyrese Gibson), Tej (Ludacris), and Letty (Michelle Rodriguez), Toretto performs several mission impossibles to get what he needs to find Shaw and have a street brawl with him. If I haven't mentioned it yet, Tony Jaa (from *Ong Bak* and *The Protector*) and Ronda Rousey (the MMA champion from *Expendables 3*) have small, supporting roles where they get to showcase the stuff they're famous for.

Before this was completed, star Paul Walker was killed in a fiery car crash, and as a result, this entry has an elevated sense of poignancy to it, especially in the denouement where his

character is tactfully and gracefully retired from the franchise. That said, the movie is noticeably compromised (most people don't seem to notice, but it's impossible for me to deny it), and the focus of the film shifts to Vin Diesel's character, giving Walker's character a smaller, supporting role. It's not the movie's fault that the film had to shift focus and scramble a reworked story together to get it done, but even amidst some great action star moments (particularly the scenes with Statham as the villain and Johnson, who is also just a supporting character this time), it was difficult for me to get into the gigantic mess of vehicular carnage the movie throws at you. It was nice seeing Tony Jaa in his first English-language crossover (his memorable line: "Too slow!"), but if you're looking for a great vehicle for Rousey, you'll be disappointed to see that she's only got one scene where she fights Rodriguez (and loses, dammit!). Vin Diesel fans will be overjoyed that this is essentially his biggest action star film so far. Directed by James Wan.

The Fast and the Furious

2001 (Universal DVD) (CD)

"I live my life a quarter mile at a time. Nothing else matters for those ten seconds or less: I'm free."

Brian O'Connor (Paul Walker) is a rookie Los Angeles detective who has gone undercover to find out who is responsible for a string of high-speed robberies of trucks filled with electronics. He's led to Dominic Toretto (Vin Diesel), who is like the king of the street racers. He infiltrates Dominic's crew with hopes of gaining the evidence to land a conviction. Brian doesn't expect to find himself feeling like he is a true part of this world, but also has fallen for Dominic's sister Mia (Jordana Brewster). With the threat of a rival gang, Brian has to choose a side and decide if he's going to play by the rules or take a chance with the criminal element.

No one suspected that this movie would end up spawning a juggernaut of a franchise, with more than two billion in worldwide grosses. Looking back at this first film, it's easy to see why it was successful, but it really isn't anything spectacular. Most of the action in the film is derived from racing cars at crazy speeds through the mean streets of LA. If you're a car aficionado then this is the franchise for you. The first few films in the series are all about the souped-up cars and racing them for money. Though the characterization of the recurring characters is sort of light, there's an undeniable likability to each of them. It's best to describe the film as pop-culture junk food. Vin Diesel owns his character and through successive entries in the franchise has given his character Toretto a mythical quality. In this first film, Toretto's heart is in the right place even though he chooses to operate outside the law. This first entry is fun but with each progressive film the stakes grow higher and the stories more complex and interesting. *2 Fast 2 Furious* was next, but Diesel's next appearance was in a cameo in *The Fast and the Furious: Tokyo Drift*. His next star turn in this franchise was in *Fast and Furious*. Directed by Rob Cohen, who shepherded Diesel's next big film *xXx*.

Faster
2010 (Sony DVD) (djm)

Lily: "He's really that good?"
Killer: "Good's not even the right word. I mean, the dude's completely artless. I mean, there's no sophistication to him *whatsoever*. But he's *pure*, you know? No fear, no hesitation. There's *nothing*."
Lily: "He as fast as you?"
Killer: "No. He's *faster*."

Dwayne "The Rock" Johnson stars as a nameless character that the movie refers to as "Driver." We see him get his parole from a ten-year stretch for bank robbing, and the first thing he does is begin a killing spree of the men who killed his brother, also a bank robber. Unafraid of having his actions caught on tape, Driver immediately gets the media's attention and a manhunt is on to catch him before he makes it to his next victim. A "Killer" (another nameless character) is hired to take him out in the meantime, and even he can't stop the bulldozer that Driver is on. Two detectives (played by Billy Bob Thornton and Carla Gugino—not sure if they were given names) are on the case, and they figure it out pretty quickly who Driver is after, so the trick is to get to his next target before *he* does. There's a plot here, and it makes some sense, but with all the character exposition and drama, why aren't these guys named?

I've seen *Faster* twice. Once on opening day, and once to review it here. The first time, I left angry and disappointed because it was resoundingly clear that The Rock was never going to live up to the action star he should be. *Faster* should be his *Commando* or his *Raw Deal*, but it's more concerned with style and drama than action, and while he's a beast of a man who has more potential than any of his peers to be the biggest and best action star working in the business these days, he doesn't have the edge or take the risks that Arnold or Stallone did when they were in their prime. The second time I saw it, I was able to forgive its dulled dramatic formulas and just let it play out, but when the movie should soar in a carefully set up action scene like the key moment between The Rock and a bad guy in a bathroom in a strip club, the movie just stops, drops, and rolls over. And the "Killer" character is all wrong. He's too young, for one. He's also a whiner. Finally, his relationship with Lily (Maggie Grace), his girlfriend, is more evidence that the movie wants you to care about characters we should care less about. The movie's about Driver, so we should be with him every step of the way, but there is so much unnecessary detail about all these characters and more (we even get to know Billy Bob's son's character, but what for?), and all I wanted from the film was for The Rock to dominate the picture, but he's virtually a supporting player. Just add *Faster* to the list of disappointments from The Rock. Directed by George Tillman Jr.

Fast Five
2011 (Universal DVD) (CD)

"All right, listen up! The men we're after are professional runners. They like speed and are guaranteed to go down the hardest possible way so make sure you have your funderwear on. We find them, we take them as a team, and bring them back. And above all else, we don't ever—*ever*—let them get into cars."

While being transported to prison, Dominic Toretto (Vin Diesel) is busted out by his sister Mia (Jordana Brewster) and friend, former FBI agent Brian O'Connor (Paul Walker). They quickly flee the states and find themselves working a job in Rio lifting cars, transported by DEA agents, from a train. They're quickly double-crossed by the other guys working on the job with them, and the deaths of the agents are blamed on the Torettos and O'Connor. This puts them at the top of the most wanted list and directly in the sights of DSS agent Luke Hobbs (a hulking Dwayne "The Rock" Johnson). Toretto and his crew go after Hernan Reyes (Joaquim De Almeida), the corrupt businessman who put them in their current position, and they attempt a heist for the record books. The whole gang shows up to support and assist.

Fast Five is the entry in the *Fast and the Furious* franchise that left behind the car racing stuff and transitioned the property into a whole different level with a much broader mass appeal. New character Luke Hobbs played by Dwayne Johnson (on a career roll after doing too many family-friendly movies like *The Tooth Fairy*) steals the show and helps propel the movie into a verifiable action hero movie. If there ever was a character deserving of his own film, it's the one he plays. The action is amazing, and it defies all laws of gravity. They throw everything into the movie: car chases, fist brawls, gunfights, exotic locations, stunts galore, and a healthy dose of humor. The highlight of the film is a brutal brawl between Johnson and Diesel, who surprisingly holds his own against the former wrestling superstar. These guys throw each other through tables, windows, doors, and even walls, ripping each other apart. The film culminates with one of the most exciting (and ridiculous) car chases ever filmed with two speeding cars slinging a giant safe in between them, decimating the entire Rio de Janeiro police force in the process. Director Justin Lin (*Fast and Furious, Furious 6*) outdoes himself with the film and helped to streamline and popularize one of the most successful movie franchises of all time.

Fast Getaway
1991 (Paramount VHS) (CD)

Sam (Leo Rossi) is the leader of a group of bank robbers. Though he is the leader, his teenage son Nelson (Corey Haim) helps to plan the heists as well as some intricate escape routes, preparing for all occasions. The other two members of the team, Lilly (Cynthia Rothrock) and Tony (Ken Lerner), have grown tired of Nelson and split from the group. Nelson and Sam are better off on their own. Sam wants to go straight and get Nelson into a normal life routine but they find themselves working a job that could make them rich. What they fail to realize is that Lilly has other plans that ends up putting Sam in jail and Nelson on his own. Thankfully, Sam has an old friend in town named Lorraine (Marcia Strassman) who takes Nelson into her custody until they can bust out Sam. But then Lily and Tony kidnap Nelson, leaving Lorraine and Sam to devise a plan to rescue Nelson.

As silly as *Fast Getaway* is, a running theme throughout the film keeps things together: family. The relationship between father and son is rather sweet and enjoyable, even though the dialogue tends to be hokey. Corey Haim (*Demolition High*) and Leo Rossi (*Relentless 1-4*) have some endearing moments, and that's what makes the film work. It doesn't hurt that the villain of the story, Lilly, is none other than martial arts sensation Cynthia Rothrock (*China O'Brian, Lady Dragon*). She seems to be having fun in the type of role she rarely plays. It's a shame though that her only real fights are with nonfighter Leo Rossi, as well as with some living room furniture. There are also solid turns by Ken Lerner (*Undisputed II: Last Man Standing*) and Marcia Strassman (*Welcome Back, Kotter*). The film never seems to take itself too seriously and tries to be fun. While much of the dialogue is groan-worthy, it's still an entertaining piece of genre cinema. While it's short on fist-to-fist type action, there are a couple of really terrific chase scenes that show off some talented stunt driving. Unfortunately, the story is filled with plot holes, some questions are never answered, and incidental characters are introduced in a big way then never seen again. If you suspend logic for a bit, you can have a good time with *Fast Getaway*. It was followed by a sequel in 1994.

Fast Getaway II
1994 (Live VHS) (CD)

Nelson Potter (Corey Haim) has given up his life of crime and moved on to the security business. He and his partner, Patrice (Sarah Buxton), hire themselves out to test a bank security system. Shortly after the test, the bank is robbed, and it looks as if Nelson is the culprit, but in fact he is being framed by his father's former partner, Lilly (Cynthia Rothrock), who holds a grudge against him. To make matters worse, psychotic FBI agent Rankin (Peter Liapis) has it in for Nelson because of his past endeavors with his father, Sam (Leo Rossi), who has been locked up in prison and wants nothing more than to find a way out so he can help his son. Nelson and Patrice are quickly on the run and looking for some answers so they can clear his name.

Fast Getaway II offers up more of the same hijinks that were on display in the original film except it's just not as fun. It lacks the heart of the first film though Corey Haim and Leo Rossi both try to reignite the father/son relationship that made the first film so endearing. Rossi's involvement this time is a bit more limited, and the two share very little screen time together. It really isn't until the final act that we get to see that father and son dynamic again. It also seems that the characters changed a bit too much from the first film. Ken Lerner and Cynthia Rothrock reprise their roles, but Lerner has a much smaller role while Rothrock gets to show off a bit more in this one before she basically disappears from the film. The crazed FBI agent Rankin played by Peter Liapis (*Wanted*) takes over the lead villain role late in the story. Though it may have had a few clever ideas for the heist, the rest of the film never really finds its focus. If you are looking for some sort of continuation or answered questions from the first film, be prepared to be disappointed. We're never really clear as to why Sam is in jail or what happened to Lorraine (Nelson's mother), who is barely mentioned. Rothrock has a few good moments and a couple of decent chase scenes but nothing on par with the chases in the previous entry. *Fast Getaway II* may have a few fun moments but overstays its welcome rather quickly. It was filmed on location in Tucson, Arizona.

Fatal Blade (a.k.a. Gedo)
2000 (Universal DVD) (djm)

A Yakuza underboss in Los Angeles is lax in his position, and when some merchandise is stolen under his regime, the Yakuza send their best assassin to LA to murder the men responsible for the slight. Domoto (Kiyoshi Nakajo), the silent and deadly assassin, does his job, but he's caught by a couple of LAPD detectives who are on a stakeout that night. One of them—Richard Fox (Gary Daniels)—is proficient in martial arts, but Domoto gets the best of him in their first encounter. Fox's partner saves him, and once back at the station, their boss decides to let the Japanese man go on a technicality. Circumstances, though, send Fox's partner out after Domoto, leading to a high-speed chase, and in a turn of events, the cop is killed by another Japanese Yakuza. Fox is enraged and vows a personal vendetta against Domoto, even though he wasn't the one who killed his partner. When Fox gets the facts straight, he ends up trusting Domoto enough to tentatively team up with him to go after the guys who were responsible, while also cleaning up the irresponsible Yakuza underboss's empire.

One of Gary Daniels's better vehicles, *Fatal Blade* has the look and feel of a theatrical production along the lines of movies like Jeff Speakman's *The Perfect Weapon* or *Street Knight*, at the very least. The story, while kind of familiar, is played out believably and convincingly, much to the credit of the writers Bill Zide and N. Sakai. The action is good, with lots of good fights throughout, and the uneasy alliance of the cop and the assassin is cool. The actors were all well cast, and even James Lew from *Night of the Warrior* and *The Perfect Weapon* has a small role. I liked this one a lot more than many of Daniels's other films during this period in his career. Directed by Talun Hsu.

Fatal Deviation
1998 (Rising Sun DVD) (CD)

Jimmy Bennett (Jimmy Bennett) has spent ten long years away from home in a reform school. He learns of his father's death and finds his way back to learn the truth behind what happened. He quickly runs afoul of the local gang, showing no mercy as he beats up several guys who are harassing a lovely young lady named Nicola (Nicola O'Sullivan). This gets the attention of Nicola's ex—Mikey (Mikey Graham)—who wants Jimmy to disappear forever. A mysterious monk has been watching Jimmy for a specific reason: to send him an invitation to an underground fight tournament known as the Bealtine. Mikey's father Loughlan (Michael Regan) is the head of the gang and wants to recruit Jimmy into their ranks. He refuses, and the gang kidnaps Nicola whom he has been dating since he rescued her. With so much at stake, Jimmy will have to harness his strength to defeat the evil that is destroying his hometown.

Fatal Deviation is Ireland's first martial arts film. It was put together on a shoestring budget and was shot on SVHS. It stars real-life martial artist Jimmy Bennett (later in *Max Havoc: Curse of the Dragon*) who also wrote, produced, photographed, and directed second unit. This is an amateurish effort but hey, at least they tried. There's plenty of fighting and action throughout the film with the best stuff saved for the tournament near the end. Bennett is clearly a Jean-Claude Van Damme fan and numerous scenes are obvious homages to his work. Even Bennett's build is very similar to JC's. Cracked.com named this the worst film ever made, but don't take their word for it—watch and judge for yourself.

Fatal Revenge
1990 (NOV) (CD)

Palmer (Michael Land) and his partner Tae (Britton Lee from *Ironheart*) are cops about to make the bust of their lives when things go bad and Tae is killed. His brother Jung (Julian Lee, later in *My Samurai*) has a vision of the death and quickly hops on a plane to find out what happened. He and Palmer team up to try and find the drug dealers responsible for the murder. While working undercover, Palmer's girlfriend Linda (Sandra Greenberg) finds herself mixed up with the men they're looking for and ends up being kidnapped. Their quest for revenge quickly turns into a rescue mission, and there's nothing in the world to stop them.

I can almost guarantee in a few years someone will discover this movie and it will become a cult classic. There's so much to love about it I don't even know where to start. How about with the crazy rap songs used like "Doom Rap" and "Let's Get Nasty?" These need to be heard and should be released for the world to hear. All the characters in the film are quick to sling insults and curse. Everyone is yelling at everyone, calling each other names, or cursing up a storm throughout the entire film. This flick has more memorable one-liners than most films

could only dream of. Then you have Julian Lee (also in *Assassin's Code*). He may struggle with the English language while speaking, but as far as the international language of ass kicking, this guy is fluent. Did I mention this movie is funny as hell? Some of the humor may be unintentional but when it's funny, it's *laugh out loud* funny. This undiscovered gem was directed by Philip Roth (*Total Reality* with Olivier Gruner).

Fearless
2006 (Universal DVD) (djm)

As a boy, Huo Yuanjia wants to be the best at wushu, but forsaking his father's example of showing mercy, Huo (played as an adult by Jet Li) grows up to be a fierce pugilist and the champion of his village. He takes on all challengers, no questions asked. When he kills a worthy challenger, that challenger's martial arts school takes revenge by slaughtering Huo's wife and child, sending Huo careening into a deep, dark depression. He travels far and wide as a vagrant, nursing his soul back into working order, and when he returns to his hometown years later, he fights a few more bouts to regain his honor and bring the art of wushu into the forefront of the various styles being practiced in a burgeoning Chinese economy where Western styles are influencing the people. When he enters into a championship as an older, wiser fighter, Huo reveals himself to be a changed-for-the-better man.

An epic length (141 minutes) martial arts extravaganza, *Fearless* gives star Jet Li a good role to play, while also giving him plenty of opportunities to show his fans that he still had the goods. He fights a massive Nathan Jones (a professional wrestler later featured in Tony Jaa's *The Protector*) and sword master Anthony De Longis in separate featured fights. The excessive length (I reviewed the director's cut of the film) might cause some viewers to scuttle in their seats, and if that doesn't do it, then maybe the subtitles will. Still, *Fearless* has undeniable appeal as a study of martial arts. From director Ronny Yu.

Fearless Tiger
(a.k.a. Black Pearls)
1991 (Imperial VHS) (djm)

Every action guy starts someplace. This was Jalal Merhi's first starring vehicle. He plays a collegiate named Lyle whose brother overdoses on a new street drug known as Nirvana. Lyle leaves his supermodel girlfriend (Monika Schnarre) to go study martial arts in China, and his mentor is a mysterious brute played by Bolo Yeung. Lyle, now fully equipped to take on the role of an avenging brother, joins a tournament to work his way to the guys who are responsible for his brother's death.

If this is the first movie you see with Merhi, you'll probably never want to see another one. He's a terrible actor in it, and his martial arts prowess isn't impressive. He produced and co-wrote the film and it's incredibly obvious how he wanted to be seen and considered as an action star. His future films like the *Tiger Claws* trilogy and the three he did with Billy Blanks (*Talons of the Eagle, TC 2000,* and *Expect No Mercy*) almost all feature him as a heroic cop who faces foes whose martial arts abilities outshine his own. Still, I give him a lot of credit for going out there and financing, directing, and starring in his own movies. He worked with a lot of the same people from movie to movie. The villain in this one is played by Lazar Rockwood, who went on to appear in three more of Mehri's films. There are two different scores for this film. Nash the Slash and Gary Koftinoff composed the score for the Cineplex Odion release (1991), and Varouje (a frequent Mehri collaborator) did the music for the Imperial release (1994).

15 Minutes

2001 (New Line DVD) (CD)

"She stripped me, man. A bag lady. Stripped all my clothes off. Grabbing me all in my nuts, it was disgusting."

America the beautiful, home of the brave, and land of the free. A country where you can come on down and be anything you want to be. Oleg Razgul (real-life Sambo champion Oleg Taktarov) has dreams of becoming a famous director. He leaves Russia with his friend from the Ukraine, Emil Slovak (Karel Roden), and they find themselves trying to make it big in New York City. Oleg finds a camera (actually, he steals it) and the two set off on a crime spree. He's a serious filmmaker and stays behind the camera while Emil murders anyone who pisses him off. Their moment in the spotlight is about to be cut short by a hard-boiled New York detective and an unorthodox arson investigator (Robert DeNiro and Edward Burns). Their only hope is to embrace the media and use it to gain fame and notoriety.

This was the film to give Russia-born MMA fighter Oleg Taktarov (later in *Predators*) his first real standout role. He's constantly shooting, but just not the type of shooting we would want to see—he has a camera in his hand and never really uses his fists. The man does make quite an impression and his character and Karel Roden's are the most interesting in the film. Director John Herzfeld (*2 Days in the Valley*) should be commended for taking a chance with him because it certainly paid off. The film is light on action, but heavy on suspense, and having the presence of Taktarov makes it pretty legit.

The Fifth Commandment

2008 (Sony DVD) (djm)

When he was a child, Chance Templeton witnessed his family being slaughtered by a ruthless assassin, and he is adopted by another hitman named The Jazzman (Keith David), who raises him along with his other son, Miles. As he grows up, Chance (played by Rick Yune from *Die Another Day* and *The Man With the Iron Fists*) is trained to become an assassin near to perfection. But Miles (Bokeem Woodbine) has become a bodyguard to high-paying clients, and when Chance receives a hit order to kill a Jennifer Lopez-type pop star, he has reservations because his brother is her bodyguard. He joins his brother against his replacement killers, and the consequences of his actions have manifold repercussions.

Written and produced by its dynamic leading star, *The Fifth Commandment* gives Yune the solo vehicle he deserves. He plays a conflicted hero of few words, and his real-life taekwondo and boxing skills are evident in several fight scenes. The direction by Jesse Johnson (*Alien Agent, The Package*) elevates this direct-to-video release to a more mainstream and respectable level. It's very much in the vein of *Taken*, but some might find this film more honest and compelling. It was shot in Thailand.

Fighting

2009 (Universal DVD) (CD)

"In the words of the late, great, Marvin Gaye: Let's . . . get . . . it . . . on!"

Shawn MacArthur (Channing Tatum) is a country boy from Alabama selling bootlegs on the streets of New York to make ends meet. He has a chance meeting with Harvey Boarden (Terrence Howard), who catches him in a fight and sees his potential. The two men enter into a business agreement where Harvey will set up the fights and all Shawn has to do is show up and kick some ass. He isn't quite prepared for the caliber of fighters he's pitted against, guys like Dragon Le (UFC fighter Cung Le) who are out for blood, and Shawn quickly learns that he's fighting for his life. When his nemesis from high school appears (now a famous MMA fighter), Shawn sees it as a chance to finish off a demon from his past.

Cung Le (*The Man with the Iron Fists*) has a small, nonspeaking role in *Fighting* and he delivers the most memorable fight. Like him or not, Channing Tatum (*21 Jump Street*) is a decent lead in this ho-hum action flick. The story is pretty straightforward; it's not bad, but it's very familiar. Getting to see Le in the picture was by far the highlight, and the fight doesn't disappoint. I'm lying: you know who wins the fight and it's just plain wrong. Cung Le should have been Channing all over his Tatum but instead we have to watch our hero fall. Director Dito Montiel (*Empire State* with The Rock) delivers an entertaining action film as long as you head in with low expectations.

Fighting Fish

2004 (Universal Benelux DVD R2) (CD)

"Fights are bad for business . . . and bad for health insurance."

When he gets news of his brother's death, A-ken (Kim Ho Kim) travels from Hong Kong to Rotterdam to investigate the circumstances surrounding it. His brother was murdered because of gang affiliations, a life A-ken has long left behind, but the truth is hard to find since the gang leader wants to just leave well enough alone. The leader's son, Koh (Chung-Huen Lam), wants to help and gives A-ken some information that could help him find his brother's killer. What he doesn't expect is to fall in love with a woman named Jennifer (Chantal Janzen). From two totally different worlds, they find it difficult to be together. The Asian gang members feel A-ken is betraying his people by dating a white girl,and her brother Marc (Ron Smoorenburg) just wants him to walk away so she isn't dragged into the gang life. A-ken has to decide which path to take, and in the meanwhile get to the issue of solving his brother's death.

The Netherlands is probably the last place you'd expect to find a martial arts action film, but this is where *Fighting Fish* hails from. This is the first (and only) feature from director Jamel Aattache, who also co-wrote the script with the star Ho Kim (whose only feature this is as well). With no wirework whatsoever, and fight choreography from star Kim, the action scenes are done well yet still feel a little on the unpolished side. Kim has a unique fighting style, showing off his Wing Chun and wushu training. The action mostly takes place during the first and final portions of the film, while the romantic subplot occupies much of the middle portion. The most impressive of the action scenes occurs between Kim and Smoorenburg (*Jackie Chan's Who Am I?*) when they face off against one another. It's an interesting first effort, maybe not a must-see for everyone, but there's some talent at work here.

The Fighting Fist of Shanghai Joe (a.k.a. My Name is Joe, a.k.a. The Dragon Fights Back)

1973 (Transworld Entertainment VHS) (djm)

"It's gotta be him. Ain't no one else who fits the description from Frisco to Kansas City."

A violent spaghetti western/martial arts hybrid, starring an unknown martial artist named Chen Lee (real name: Mioshini Akira Hayakawa), who plays a Chinese immigrant who finds himself in frontier America, looking for work. He's met with disgust, racism, and trepidation, and when he defends himself with impressive martial arts skills in several confrontations, he's despised and spat on. When he finds some honest work, he's faced with the reality that Americans aren't going to warm up to him. He then befriends a pretty blonde woman, but he's discriminated against and has a mark of death put on his head. A band of bounty hunters come after him, and Scalper Jack (a cold-blooded Klaus Kinski) is amongst the cutthroats who make him their business. The blood-soaked finale has Joe killing off the bounty hunters one at a time. He gouges out the eyes of one of the guys.

The Fighting fist of Shanghai Joe will make some purveyors of spaghetti westerns and martial arts films happy, but general viewers will be bored, confused, and fed up with it. It has a murky story and a lame script, and Chen Lee, while engaging in some of the fights (a few which are cheated by camera angles), doesn't really shine in the lead role. If all you've got to hang on to in a movie like this is the shocking violence, then you're in trouble. Directed by Mario Caiano.

Fighting Mad
(a.k.a. **Death Force**)
1978 (Synergy DVD) (CD)

"Let your mind and blade be as one. As one, shall you live, eat, and sleep. A mistress shall it be to you."

Vietnam vets Doug (James Iglehart), McGee (Leon Isaac Kennedy), and Morelli (Carmen Argenziano) are finally finished with the war and are on their way home. They make a pit stop in the Philippines to deliver a coffin full of gold when they decide splitting the money two ways is more beneficial than splitting it three. McGee and Morelli slit Doug's throat, tossing him overboard. He isn't dead, though; he washes ashore on an island, only to be nursed back to health by two stranded Japanese soldiers who've been there since World War II. One of them is a samurai and takes the time to pass his knowledge on to him. Back in LA, McGee and Morelli have moved up the ladder and have become the new top dogs in the criminal underworld. Morelli has even tried to move in on Doug's wife Maria (Jayne Kennedy), who isn't very receptive. When he finally makes his way back to LA, Doug will be ready to make them all pay.

James Iglehart (*Savage!*) is a beast of a man and totally nails it in the role of a man out for revenge. He has such a dominating presence it couldn't have been easy to find the perfect actor to face off with him in the film, but director Cirio H. Santiago (*Bloodfist 2050*) was smart enough to nab fresh, young star Leon Isaac Kennedy (future action star of the *Penitentiary* trilogy) to be the main nemesis, and he rules! He's such a sleazy character, well deserving of the vengeance about

to be unleashed on his sorry ass. There're plenty of well-staged action scenes, many of which include some brutal beheadings, deserving of your fist pumps. This flick is severely underrated and easily one of Santiago's masterpieces. Both actors elevate this thing to cult status and beyond. A true action classic.

Fight the Fight
2011 (Lionsgate DVD) (djm)

Sammo Hung and his real-life son Sammy Hung play father and son in this sensationalized account of a real martial art known as choy li fut, a secret art closely guarded by a martial arts school. It's set in modern times, and Sammy goes to England to university, and right away he makes a friend, played by Sho Kosugi's son Kane from *Revenge of the Ninja*. The two friends join a martial arts academy. A competing school threatens to take over the academy, and the matter is to be settled by a martial arts tournament. Sammy and Kane train and prepare for the fight of their lives to protect the secret art of the school.

Fairly pedestrian and overly sentimental and romantic to the point of distraction, *Fight the Fight* has some so-so fight scenes to keep the movie watchable. It's cool to see Sammo the elder share some moments on screen with his son, but anyone looking for a gem will have to look elsewhere. Directed by Tommy Lor.

Fight to Win
1987 (KB Releasing VHS) (djm)

A young martial arts student named Ryan Kim (George Chung) and his elderly teacher each own a rare statue; the two statues go together and have one other mate. Armstrong (Richard Norton) owns the third statue. He comes into their dojo, and when he realizes that Kim and his master own the two statues, he begins causing trouble for them. As a way of placating Armstrong, Ryan and his teacher set up a fighting competition with one of their statues up as a prize for the winner. Ryan fights Armstrong's champion (played by Bill Wallace from *L.A. Streetfighters*), and Ryan is disgraced when he loses. Not satisfied with just two statues, Armstrong has his men steal the third statue from Ryan's teacher. At a loss, Ryan gathers his friends and tries to come up with a plan to steal the statues back, but his teacher has an even better idea: He hires a special trainer to get Ryan into the proper shape to face Armstrong. The trainer? A perky martial artist played by Cynthia Rothrock. Ryan has trouble believing that she's any threat, but when she begins to humble him by beating him repeatedly in training sessions, he rethinks his options and viewpoint and begins to get with the program. Together with his new teacher and several of his friends (who include Chuck Jeffries from *Superfights*), they go after Armstrong and get the statues back.

Extremely simplistic and about as basic a movie as can be, *Fight to Win* grew on me. Chung, who also directed, starts off in the movie as an unlikable smartass, but by the end he's a self-deprecating ham whose abilities as an actor and martial artist noticeably improved as the movie went on. Rothrock and Norton greatly enhance the technicality of the fight scenes in the film, and without them the movie would just be a cheap effort with way-below-the-line names to keep it afloat. Jeffries and Wallace have smallish roles. A minor effort, but worth tracking down if you're a fan of either Rothrock or Norton. Not to be confused with Rothrock's *City Cops*, which bears the name *Fight to Win* on some video releases.

Final Impact
1992 (Trinity DVD) (djm)

Nick Taylor (Lorenzo Lamas) is a retired former kickboxing champion who runs a gym. He's always on the lookout for new talent, and when cocky Danny Davis (Michael Worth) steps into his gym, looking to impress him, he opens his eyes and sees nothing but untapped potential. He takes him on as an apprentice, and his real motive is to get back at the reigning kickboxing champ, Jake Gerard (Jeff Langton), who disgraced him in his final fight. When Danny begins winning fights and working his way up the chain, Nick senses that his opportunity for revenge is nigh. Nick's longsuffering gal pal Maggie (played by a sensitive and affecting Kathleen Kinmont, Lamas's ex-wife) sees what this revenge plot is doing to him, and she begins distancing herself from him. In a moment of rash impulse, Nick challenges Jake Gerard to a back alley (no rules) fight, and Nick loses terrifically and tragically. His ward, Danny, takes him to the hospital where Maggie comes to see him . . . just before he dies! Danny steps into the ring for the championship fight with Jake, and he wins.

A definite change of pace for Lamas, who at this point was at the peak of his action star days, *Final Impact* gives him more of a dramatic action role than a straight-up heroic role, which in this case was played by Worth (*Fists of Iron, To Be the Best*). Not only is it shocking to see Lamas die in this film, but he dies well and believably. Worth is good in his role, but in an early scene he fights Gary Daniels (who doesn't have lines), and it's obvious to see that Daniels should have been given a bigger part. Joseph Merhi (*Rage and Riot* with Daniels) and Stephen Smoke directed.

Final Reprisal
1988 (HDMV DVD R2) (djm)

A platoon in Vietnam goes on a mission, which ends with an innocent little girl's death. The girl's father is a Viet Cong commander, and he spends the next few years stewing in rage and contemplating how he's going to exact revenge on the American soldiers who were responsible for his daughter's senseless murder. Former solider David Callahan (Gary Daniels in his very first film role) has lived with the guilt of leading the team that killed that little girl, but he's moved on with his life and has started a family of his own, living in peace in Eastern Asia. When his wife and child are kidnapped, and then subsequently murdered by militant soldiers working under orders of that commander in Vietnam, he fuels his anger by forsaking all advice from friends and the police and goes back to Vietnam to get his revenge. Once there, he's captured and tortured (electrified, hung upside down, and humiliated), and when he's forced to fight one of his former soldiers to the death (the one who killed the girl, in fact), he's pushed to his absolute limit, but he dupes his captors and goes off the rails killing the commander and his soldiers.

Gary Daniels, who would become an action and martial arts perennial in low-budget films from around the world, got his start with this very low-budget actioner filmed in the Philippines. He does his best in it (he's very young in it), and despite the film's incredible shortcomings, he showcases his martial art abilities and emerges more or less unscathed to pursue a busy career in the genre. His next film *The Secret of King Mahis Island* was filmed directly after this, also in the Philippines. Directed by Teddy Page (Hemingway), who also did *Blood Ring* with Dale "Apollo" Cook.

Final Round

1993 (World Vision VHS) (djm)

"I'm a big fan of Chuck Norris. Let's move!"

A precursor to bigger and better films like *Hard Target* and *The Condemned*, *Final Round* carried on the tradition of stories inspired by *The Most Dangerous Game*. Lorenzo Lamas stars as a motorcycle mechanic and boxer-on-the-side badass named Tyler, who impresses some scouts at a bar when he protects the honor of a woman he just met, played by Kathleen Kinmont. The scouts work for a millionaire sicko named Delgado (Anthony DeLongis) who broadcasts via satellite a snuff program where gladiators (who are equipped with cameras on their heads) hunt weaponless civilians to the death. Delgado makes a fortune on the underground gambling circuit with his network of wealthy clients, and when he has Tyler and his new girlfriend kidnapped and forces them to play the game, the bets are on! When the tides begin turning in Tyler's favor (a first for a player), Delgado senses that his assets are in danger and so he ups the ante and enters the game himself to ensure that Tyler loses.

A familiar story and an undercooked script hurt this otherwise basic and by-the-numbers action flick. Lamas plays a character that feels very similar to his *Renegade* persona (which he took on in other films like *Bounty Tracker*), and Kinmont (who was his real-life wife at the time and who co-starred with him in several other films and projects) delivers as well as a co-star and love interest can, but the film needed *more* co-stars and contestants involved with the

dangerous game to liven up the events. It was an arbitrary process to show Lamas killing off most of the hunters, and it got a little redundant and predictable after the first few kills (which tended to be on the gory side). Whip-wielding DeLongis (from *Masters of the Universe*) isn't given enough to do to make his villainous character interesting, and his final fight with the star is disappointing. Lamas and the director George Erschbamer also collaborated on the *Snake Eater* trilogy.

Fire Down Below

1997 (Warner DVD) (djm)

"Now, how you wanna do this? You wanna play this all the way? I'll have 300 agents come up here into this little hick town and crawl up every orifice you got. When it's over, you can go to your favorite proctologist and get a soothing ointment and rub it on the hole that hurts the most. How do you want it? *How do you want it?*"

A soft-talking agent working for the Environmental Protection Agency named Taggert (Steven Seagal) rides into a small Appalachian community, pretending to be a missionary. He asks people if they need their porches fixed, then promptly repairs them with a smile on his face. The tight-knit community doesn't take kindly to him at first, but when he reveals himself to be an agent working for the government, they take a different stance. He is intent on bringing a billionaire tycoon in the town (played by Kris Kristofferson) to justice for illegally disposing thousands of gallons of toxic waste into the ecosystem, and he's risen to the top of the tycoon's hit list. What nobody is expecting is that Taggert is a grade "A" badass with a penchant for snapping wrists, smashing heads, and breaking bones.

A flop at the box office, *Fire Down Below* is one of Seagal's better theatrical efforts. He plays a likable character who shows a softer side while playing guitar alongside country music star Marty Stuart, and he shows that he has a way with kids and pretty women. The movie has enough action to please Seagal's fans, and I was impressed with a truck chase that had me on the edge of my seat. Marg Helgenberger plays the love interest, and other country stars including Randy Travis and Travis Tritt appear as well. Director Felix Enriquez Alcala is known for directing episodes of television shows. After this film, Steven Seagal starred in *The Patriot*, which debuted on video and cable.

Firehawk

1993 (Live VHS) (djm)

A sketchy mission in Vietnam turns even sketchier when the platoon's chopper is downed behind enemy lines. Chopper pilot Stewart (Martin Kove from *Steele Justice*) and his men

realize that they've been sabotaged by one of their own, but who? With the Viet Cong pressing in and one of them a betrayer, things just got FUBAR. As it turns out, Stewart has some intel that a plane with a nuke on board crashed in the jungle, and their whole mission has something to do with the nuke, so when his men realize that he has an agenda, the whole mission is compromised. Once they get taken captive by the Cong, it's a do-or-die deal when they're faced with torture.

A so-so Vietnam action film from producer Roger Corman and director Cirio Santiago, *Firehawk* will remind you of when Martin Kove got slugged by Stallone in *Rambo: First Blood Part II*. In fact, this could very well be a prequel to *Rambo* (not really, but why not?). Kove acts alongside Matt Salinger (from Albert Pyun's *Captain America*) and T. C. Carson here. If you like seeing Kove be a slimy bastard, then look no further than *Firehawk*. His final scene is pretty great.

Firepower

1979 (Avid VHS) (CD)

"This is a Walther P38 with a silencer on it . . . no one will hear you die."

On the day of her husband's birthday, Adele (Sophia Loren) is witness to his death in a major explosion. Knowing the authorities will do little to catch who did it, she enlists the aid of an old flame, someone she hasn't seen in twelve years, Jerry Fanon (James Coburn). Money talks, and he quickly jumps on the case but not without hiring some backup first: his pal Catlett (NFL star O. J. Simpson). She knows her husband's killer is Karl Stegner (George Touliatos), a man her husband was going to testify against. He lives in a heavily guarded fortress in the Caribbean so Fanon and Catlett will have to plan their attack carefully so they can kidnap Karl and bring him to justice.

Aside from having an amazing cast, *Firepower* grows dull way too quickly. It's light on the action and feels more like a 007 rip-off than anything else. O. J. Simpson (also in *Detour to Terror*) is never really given much to do other than follow Coburn around. The film does have one great moment with Coburn and Simpson interrogating a suspect on a boat. They have him tied up, and they throw him over the ledge, partially dangling him in the ocean. The best part is they're pouring fish guts and blood all over him as a school of sharks close in. It's so badass you wish there would have been more moments like this in the film. Instead, we only get a few more static and uninteresting shootouts, which is disappointing, especially since the film was directed by Michael Winner who made *Death Wish* a few years earlier.

F

Firepower

1993 (Trinity DVD) (djm)

A team-up with Gary Daniels and Chad McQueen might have seemed like a great idea at the time they made this, but looking at these two guys together in a movie now is like watching that terrible Harrison Ford movie with Josh Hartnett, *Hollywood Homicide*. It's hard to watch someone with talent and abilities being forced to perform next to someone who has none of either. In Chad's case, he brings zilch to the table except his dad's good name, and it's too bad because Gary Daniels has all the talent and far outclasses him even when Daniels is beheaded three-fourths into the movie, leaving McQueen to carry the rest of the movie— which is a huge mistake. The film is a fringe apocalyptic movie, taking place slightly into the future, when a place called "The Hellzone" is left to the criminals and the scuz of the Earth to live in as they wish. Cops are afraid to go there to track down criminals, but when an evil mastermind named The Swordsman (a ridiculously steroidal James Hellwig, who was The Ultimate Warrior in professional wrestling) takes refuge in the Hellzone, two cops, Baniff and Sledge (McQueen and Daniels), follow him in. They pose as fighters who want a shot in a to-the-death kickboxing ring where The Swordsman reigns supreme. While there, they win some fights (Daniels is flashy and cool, whereas McQueen seems to win by pure luck), and they eventually get their shot at fighting The Swordsman, who unbelievably kills Sledge (chop, chop) with a sword, putting Baniff into a rage. The final fight between The Swordsman and Baniff is pretty sloppy, and not in a million years would McQueen be able to kill The Swordsman, who not in a million years would have been able to kill Gary Daniels.

Pretty junky by most standards, *Firepower* is super low-budget and ugly. The sets are cheap, and the script is terrible. The fight scenes are obviously staged, and there's not enough of Daniels. Admittedly, he wasn't as badass in this as in some of his later work, but he's the only good thing going in this movie. Gerald Okamura has an uncredited role as a fighter named Professor Tenabe. Directed by Richard Pepin.

Firestorm

1998 (Fox DVD) (djm)

Smokejumper Jesse Graves (former NFL Raider Howie Long) is a specialist firefighter who jumps out of planes into raging infernos and rescues people in peril. He's called into action when a forest fire gets out of control, but meanwhile there's a plot unfolding: A master criminal named Randall Shaye (William Forsythe) and a bunch of convicts have staged a clever escape in the midst of the (planned) forest fire as they are being transferred via bus, and in their trek on foot to the Canadian border, they kidnap an innocent bird watcher (played by Suzy Amis), who also happens to be the daughter of a tough marine. so she's no pushover. As Jesse moves in on trying to rescue them, they turn on him,

Jennifer (Suzy Amis) is safe with fireman Jesse (Howie Long) in Dean Semler's *Firestorm*. Author's collection.

Ex-NFL player Howie Long plays the heroic fireman Jesse in *Firestorm*. Author's collection.

propelling him into action mode as he escapes them and rescues their captive, who turns into a formidable ally as they struggle to survive the spreading inferno.

Released theatrically with very little promotion or push from 20th Century Fox, *Firestorm* was a decent vehicle for Howie Long, who had just begun his career in movies with a supporting role in *Broken Arrow* opposite John Travolta and Christian Slater. In *Firestorm* he

Firefighter Jesse (Howie Long) gets into a heap of trouble when escaped prisoners run rampant through a burning forest in *Firestorm*. Author's collection.

relies heavily on his physicality, but the film never really ignites with the explosiveness it needed to warrant more films with him as the star. He became a supporting actor in movies from here on out, which is a shame. I think it might have been cool to see him star, like Brian Bosworth, in some direct-to-video movies, but it just wasn't to be. Director Dean Semler is best known as a director of photography on films like *The Road Warrior* and *Razorback*, but his next film as a director was *The Patriot* (starring Steven Seagal), which was released on video the same year as *Firestorm*. Long next appeared in the action western *Dollar for the Dead*.

Firewalker

1986 (MGM DVD) (djm)

Chuck Norris went in a PG direction with *Firewalker*, which is his answer to *Romancing the Stone* and *Raiders of the Lost Ark*. He and Lou Gossett play Max and Leo, two bumbling adventurers who get caught up in a treasure hunt somewhere in South America. Their benefactor is a cute blonde (Melody Anderson from *Flash Gordon*) who has a map leading to native gold in a cave. They get captured by an evil Indian (Sonny Landham), get into cantina fights, traverse rivers full of crocodiles, and have a blast being the guys they are. Norris shows off his signature kick several times in slow motion.

Anyone familiar with Cannon's *Indiana Jones* rip-offs like *Treasure of the Four Crowns* and *King Solomon's Mines* will feel right at home seeing Chuck Norris in this lightweight adventure. He cracks jokes, laughs, and romances a pretty blonde while being Lou Gossett's best buddy. It's as fun and innocent as action films get. J. Lee Thompson (who did a bunch of films with Charles Bronson like *Death Wish 4* and *St. Ives*) directed this. John Rhys-Davies (from *Raiders of the Lost Ark*) shows up in a cameo. Gary Chang did the electronic score.

The Firing Line

1988 (Mill Creek DVD) (CD)

"Puta! It gives me great pleasure to get rid of you meddlesome fools."

Mark Hardin (Reb Brown from *Cage*) is a military advisor for the armed forces in Central America who helps to capture a rebel leader, believing he's doing the right thing. But the leader is brutalized and murdered, leaving Hardin to question the Army's motives. He kills the general responsible for the death, and he's quickly captured and tortured. In a daring escape, Hardin is joined by the gorgeous Sandra Spencer (Shannon Tweed), and the two of them join forces with the rebels and help them capture a radio tower in order to expose the evil within the government.

The Firing Line's script has some of the most hilarious dialogue you'll ever hear. It's also loaded with stock footage, but at least we have

The Reb in military mode. He kills men with his bare hands, trains a (mostly female) rebel army, manages to be bulletproof, and gets his mitts on softcore goddess Tweed. It's all in a day's work for our (super?) hero who is also sporting a killer stash, which is a good look for him. Director Jun Gallardo (*Commando Invasion*) is a veteran of over fifty films, and this was his last. For whatever reason, it manages to be entertaining and charming for a crisp ninety minutes.

First Blood

1982 (Lionsgate DVD) (MJ)

> "You don't seem to want to accept the fact you're dealing with an expert in guerrilla warfare, with a man who's the best . . . with guns, with knives, with his bare hands. A man who's been trained to ignore pain, ignore weather, to live off the land, to eat things that would make a billy goat puke."

After the enormous critical and box-office success that followed *Rocky* in 1976, Sylvester Stallone found himself in a difficult situation. After playing an iconic character like Rocky Balboa so early in his career, even after struggling just a few years prior to get small parts in television and film, Stallone had become an international star but his fans had a difficult time accepting him in any other role. Attempts to improve his craft as an actor in films such as *F.I.S.T.* and *Paradise Alley* met with a lukewarm response at the box office. Returning to play Rocky Balboa in more sequels seemed to be the only way to ensure continued success at the box office, and so Stallone struggled to find other projects to develop and other roles to play that might strike the right balance with his fans.

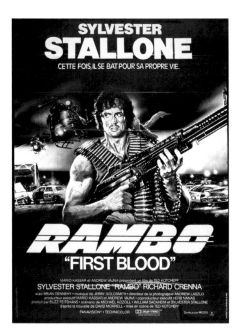

Foreign release theatrical poster for *First Blood*, with artwork by Renato Casaro. Author's collection.

John Rambo sets traps and snares in the forest to stay alive as he's hunted by civilians and policemen in *First Blood*. Author's collection.

Harassed, tortured, and belittled for being a Vietnam veteran, John Rambo (Sylvester Stallone) is booked for being a vagrant in *First Blood*. Author's collection.

He finally struck gold in the form of another seemingly underdog hero cut from the same cloth as Rocky but with a much harder edge. Based on the 1972 novel by David Morrell, *First Blood* tells the story of Vietnam veteran John Rambo, hiking through Washington state and pausing near the town of Hope to visit one of his comrades from the war only to find out that his friend died years back. Passing through town and hoping to stop for a bite to eat, Rambo is insulted by the local sheriff, Will Teasle (Brian Dennehy), and abruptly escorted out of town. Ignoring the sheriff's advice, Rambo starts walking back to town and is swiftly arrested by Teasle for vagrancy. Unknown to Teasle and his deputies, Rambo is still haunted by the events of the war. As Teasle's sadistic deputies mistreat him as they process him for incarceration, Rambo begins to have flashbacks of his time spent in a prison camp during Vietnam, which trigger his survival instincts and combat training. Rambo escapes from jail and makes a run for it, sparking an intense manhunt that will have unintended consequences for both men . . . and the entire town.

First Blood offered Stallone the first unique opportunity to get out from under the shadow of Rocky Balboa. It's easy to forget that Stallone not only starred *Rocky* but also wrote the screenplay for it and then directed three films, including two of the *Rocky* sequels, before coming to the role of Rambo. On the surface, the roles were not too different. Both men were underdogs, and there was an expectation that audiences would continue to root for Stallone in a similar role. But

Rambo had more of an edge. He was a trained soldier who had killed for his country. Rambo also offered him an opportunity to address the plight of Vietnam veterans in the United States at the time, still a tender subject with audiences less than a decade after our withdrawal from Vietnam and failure to win that war. *First Blood* also offered Stallone the opportunity to play against seasoned actors like Brian Dennehy and Richard Crenna, which helped to illustrate his great strengths as both actor and star. Directed by Ted Kotcheff (who would later direct *Hidden Assassin* with Dolph Lundgren), *First Blood* was shot on location in British Columbia, with still-impressive outdoor stunt work, including Stallone himself performing the majority of his own stunts in addition to giving one of his strongest performances. With a running time of less than ninety-five minutes, the film still holds up as one of the greatest action movies of all time and one of the defining action films of the 1980s.

First Encounter

1997 (Leo Films VHS) (djm)

A space crew encounters an alien ship, adrift in the cosmos. They are ordered to attempt communication with it, and when that fails, the captain (Trevor Goddard from *Men of War*) orders his men to board the vessel and see if there are any aliens aboard. Security officer Lieutenant Edward Ganz (Roddy Piper) balks at his orders, declaring that he intends to annihilate the aliens (if there are any), and half of the crew sides with his argument, while the other half sides with the captain, including the captain's main squeeze (played by Stacie Randall). When they actually encounter the alien species (they look like giant rubber ants), some mild action ensues.

Let me be straight with you: No one on planet Earth ever needs to see this movie. It's a colossal waste of time, and it's most likely a complete embarrassment for the actors, most notably Roddy Piper, who probably wished this movie never existed. It was shot for what looks like a few thousand bucks, with awful special computer effects, terrible scripting more suited for the pornographic industry, and the whole movie feels incomplete and cobbled together like some of Roger Corman's worst productions, just without the nudity or the action. Piper completists will be appalled, and fans of Randall (from *Excessive Force II: Force on Force*) will be equally disappointed. Trevor Goddard and Piper were in *Dead Tides* the same year. Goddard died of a drug overdose shortly thereafter. This was written, produced, and directed by Redge Mahaffey.

Fist Fighter

1988 (IVE VHS) (djm)

A drifter named C. J. Thunderbird (George Rivero from Lucio Fulci's *Conquest*) is on a quest to find the man who murdered his friend in a bare-knuckle boxing fight. He hears that the killer, Rhino (Matthias Hues), is in a small town in South America somewhere, beating opponents right and left in underground tournaments, so he quietly goes on the road, making a few bucks here and there in arm-wrestling matches along the way. When he makes his way to where Rhino is engaged in a partnership with the local crime lord, C. J. declares his interest in fighting the champ. He's pitted against a lesser challenger to test his worth, and when C. J. proves he's got the sand and grit to take on Rhino, he's given a date and time and five-to-one odds. He takes a rapscallion trainer on (played by Edward Albert), and they hit the bricks and train . . . *hard*. C. J. is determined to win his fight, and when the fight is on, it looks as though he's going to demolish Rhino, but the corrupt local police disrupt the bout and steal the collected wagers and the fight ends inconclusively. In a twist of events, both C. J. and his trainer are thrown in a dungeon hell of a prison and the only way C. J. is going to see the light of day again is for him to fight in the prison circuit to win his and his trainer's freedom. When he faces the grotesque champion known only as "Beast," he wins and gains his freedom. At last C. J. can face Rhino and gain respect, vengeance, and redemption.

After seeing dozens upon dozens of direct-to-video kickboxing movies and other movies of that ilk, watching something called *Fist Fighter* did not excite me in the least. But here's the deal, readers: *Fist Fighter* is that golden brick in the Great Wall of fight movies. It shines. The lead guy George (Jorge) Rivero is unbelievably awesome in the film. He was fifty when he made this and not only does he look phenomenal in it, but he has that Charles Bronson quiet cool about him that completely elevates this underrated film. Even Matthias Hues turns in a solid performance as the villain. This is as masculine a film as you're ever going to get, and every hardcore fan of these types of pictures should make it a top priority to track it down. Watch for professional wrestler Billy Graham in a crucial, cameo role at the beginning of the film. Rivero and Hues also made *Death Match* together. Directed by Frank Zuniga.

Fist of Fury

(a.k.a. **The Chinese Connection**)

1972 (Fox DVD) (DH)

"This time you're eating paper, next time it's gonna be glass!"

After TV's *The Green Hornet* was canceled, talented but frustrated martial artist-turned-actor Bruce Lee headed to Hong Kong to become the master of his own destiny. Lee would alternate between star, writer, producer, and choreographer on several low-budget kung-fu flicks for legendary producer Raymond Chow before securing Hollywood financing for his final feature film *Enter the Dragon*. But before *Enter the Dragon* cemented his mythic status in the world of martial arts and cinema, Lee starred in the inspired-by-true-events, racially charged *Fist of Fury*, a.k.a. *The Chinese Connection*. The

film opens at the funeral of Huo, the greatest Chinese boxer 1930s Shanghai has ever known. Huo's former student Chen Zhen (Lee) arrives in a white suit, coiled like a spring, ready to weep or lash out at any moment, despondent and suspicious of the mysterious circumstances surrounding his master's death. There's no time to grieve, however, as the local Japanese martial artists show up at Huo's school, parading a framed sign claiming the Chinese are "Weak men of Asia." Constantly belittled and literally slapped in the face, Huo's disciples choose not to fight back in respect for their dead master's desire to keep the peace. Determined to find the truth, Zhen takes the sign back to the Japanese dojo where he challenges the karate gi-clad bullies, taking them on one, two, and thirty at a time like a furious kicking, punching, and screaming tornado. The nunchuks come out, and it's hardcore Asian on Asian crime with Zhen stomping the entire dojo and making two of the fighters eat pieces of the insulting paper sign. On his way home, Zhen is confronted with more disrespect as a park posts a "No dogs or Chinese allowed" sign. This sign is quickly broken along with the faces of several Japanese supporters.

Lee's penultimate feature-length performance is another showcase of the star's on-screen charisma, sense of humor, physique and fighting prowess, despite the film's overly long running time. Following the first terrific fight scene, there's a ponderous middle act wherein Zhen goes into hiding, finds out that the Japanese poisoned Huo, then starts killing those involved and stringing them up in the streets. The Japanese eventually bring in a formidable, metal- bending, hard-drinking, mustachioed mountain of a man from Russia, but he too is no match for Chen Zhen's speed, skill, and determination. Disappointingly, Lee only has two fight scenes in the film, albeit two big, complicated, multi-opponent, rough-and-tumble, back-and-forth affairs that highlight the gone-too-soon star's well-rounded philosophy of combat. There are punches, kicks, throws, arm bars, and chokes galore in Lee's signature fast, brutal, and technical style. If only the scenes not featuring Lee were as exciting...

(Editor's note: See also Fist of Legend *with Jet Li and* Legend of the Fist: The Return of Chen Zhen *with Donnie Yen for variations of the same story.)*

Fist of Glory

1991 (Vidmark VHS) (djm)

"Hey, the rules are different here —they fight to the death, understand?"

Real-life kickboxing champion Dale "Apollo" Cook made his film debut with this tournament-to-the-death fight movie. Cook stars as a soldier named Reynolds in the Vietnam War who is wounded in battle and then spends months recuperating. When he's released, he wanders around Saigon for a while, looking for members of his platoon. His best buddy Lee (Maurice

Smith) has been taken in by a small crime syndicate who have pumped him full of heroin and have him hooked. Lee's mind is half gone from the drugs, and he's forced to fight in Muay Thai to-the-death fight matches for more drugs, and when Reynolds finds him, his buddy doesn't recognize him. In order to get close to him, Reynolds must enter the fight circuit and work his way up to Lee, and by the time he gets to that point, Lee's mind and body are ravaged almost beyond repair. The two friends are finally able to make a connection, and they make a grand escape from the circuit together, only to turn right back around and get revenge on the drug peddling scum who imprisoned Lee and caused them the trouble.

For at least twenty minutes, I had no idea what this movie was about. The first segment shows the platoon in action, but their mission was vague, and I couldn't tell what was going on. Later, when Cook's character went looking for his friend, I realized that this was another kickboxing movie using the Vietnam War as a backdrop, which was fine, but the contemporary vibe of the whole movie threw me for a loop. For one, there's synthesizer pop music that plays in the strip club scenes, and modern-looking appliances and hardware abounds. That aside, *Fist of Glory* is a not-bad first outing from athlete-turned-action star Cook, who looks like he's trying to do his best. In his later movies, he loosened up a great deal and looked like he didn't care how he acted on screen. The director—Jo Mari Avellana—also did *Black Belt II*.

INTERVIEW:

DALE "APOLLO" COOK (djm)

Oklahoma-based former action star Dale "Apollo" Cook had an incredible run in the world of competitive fighting before his ten-movie stint as an action guy. With multiple world titles in the realm of kickboxing and shoot boxing, and with a seventh degree black belt in taekwondo, Cook was offered the lead role in a Vietnam action movie called Fist of Glory *(1991), which was a picture Don "The Dragon" Wilson was set to star in but had to back out of at the last minute. After that film, Cook starred in a string of "B" martial arts action films with titles like* Blood Ring *(1991),* Fist of Steel *(1992),* and *American Kickboxer 2 (1993), which all featured him as the lead. Not known for being a great actor but certainly for his intense, brutal fighting abilities, Cook retired from the movie business when the industry edged out quite a few action guys when smaller, independent movie companies like AIP went out of business. These days, he produces MMA, cage fighting, and kickboxing events in Oklahoma.*

You've told me that you've starred in ten of the worst movies ever made. I don't agree with you, but I understand why you would say such a thing. Why do you consider these movies to be so horrible?

They were pretty low-budget movies, mostly made in the Philippines. We were working with $300,000 budgets. You can only do so much. Another thing is, it's always the same kind of storyline. The kickboxing genre was hot at the time for a few years. We were just churning them out.

Does that make them the worst movies ever? I think they're fine for what they are.

(Laughing.) I don't know. I think some of my movies are fun, yes, but the acting was pretty bad. Who starred in ten movies worse than mine?

You came from the world of competitive kickboxing and were a world champion. How did you get involved with AIP and action movies?

I was fighting in Japan on a pretty regular basis. I had a buddy, Maurice Smith, who went on to become the UFC heavyweight champion, and at the time he was the defending world heavyweight kickboxing champion. We fought around the same time in Japan, and this one time he gets a phone call after a fight, and he tells me he's going to the Philippines to make a movie with Don Wilson. Don Wilson had just signed with Roger Corman so he couldn't play the lead in this movie. Did he know anyone else that could take that spot? Someone who had kickboxing skills, and he said, "Yeah, he's sitting right here!" He handed me the phone, and a week later I'm starring in a movie shooting in the Philippines. That movie was called *Fist of Glory*. We spent a couple weeks on location in the jungle with no one to talk to but each other. The Chinese producer just liked my jokes, so I starred in his next nine pictures. His name was David Hung. He goes by David Hunt. He sold movies to AIP and Vidmark Entertainment. He was the producer.

So you were thrust into the world of "B" action movies. You'd never had any formal training as an actor, but your skills as a fighter were finely tuned, which certainly shows in your movies. Did the directors you worked with ever give you any advice or direction in terms of your acting?

At the time, I was fighting at the highest level of kickboxing all over the world, and that's what I was doing for a living. For me to step onto a movie set, where you can do more than one take and where no one is really going to hit you, I was so relaxed and confident. I just had fun with it. There was a little direction in the first movie, but after that, to be honest, David was letting me write my own lines—which were corny as hell. They kinda let me have some fun and let me do what I wanted to do. It was a blast. If you make ten pictures, and you win every fight and never miss a shot, and always get the girl, that's gotta be fun. That's kinda how it was.

At what point did you realize that you could actually make a career out of making "B" action movies, and at what point did you realize that that career was over?

I've never realized I had a career in this! I never pursued this. This pursued me. As long as they were willing to pay me money and ask me to come to the Philippines for a month, I was good to go. But I *never* considered this a career, and I had no idea there were going to be ten pictures. I expected it to end after every single one of them. They made money, so that was good for David and our relationship. We became great friends.

Clearly, they made money because you did so many of them. But it's funny how you responded to me initially that these were the worst movies ever made. People obviously really liked these movies.

(Laughing.) I'm probably talking as much about my acting as I am about the budgets. You know, I guess when you look back on it, those Bruce Lee movies weren't made for a whole lot more than that. If it served the purpose of showing entertaining fight scenes and a little bit of comedy, then I feel proud about some of the stuff we did. The movie I felt the most involved in was *Double Blast*. It co-starred Linda Blair, and it was the only PG-rated film that I did. I'm most proud of that because the whole script was my idea. We took *Home Alone* and *The Karate Kid* and married them together. Vidmark bought it and it made a lot of money

I was going to bring that up later. It was like *Home Alone* meets *3 Ninjas*, with the kids.

Yeah, yeah. Exactly.

I liked *Raw Target*, which was one of the last movies you did. That's one of your better movies.

I was certainly in the best shape of my life when I did that one. I took my shirt off at every opportunity in that movie. It was fun. It had some interesting characters to work with in there. The film itself? The lighting was pretty horrible. It was pretty dark. It was a little bit of a storyline. I like the *American Kickboxer 2* movie I did with Evan Lurie. Working with some of those people was great. As much as I hated the director, I ended up respecting him. He brought a lot of direction to the film, which a lot of those films was lacking. I usually got to do whatever the hell I wanted. There needed to be a director and a leader there who'd say yes to some ideas and no to bad ones.

How did John Barrett end up with a cameo as your trainer in *American Kickboxer 2*? He'd been the star of the first film.

For that movie, we actually shot a week in LA. John has a karate school in that area. I think someone just suggested that and thought it was a great gesture to get him involved in it.

Do you have any memories of making Blood Ring?

Yeah, Blood Ring 1 and 2. I never think of myself as any kind of an actor, I'm just confident in front of a camera—I just go. I had a character to play other than a prizefighter or a futuristic character. In that movie, I have a drinking problem. In that regard, I felt like I had an opportunity to at least give a half-assed attempt at a performance.

How about *Triple Impact*? That one was basically a comedy.

VHS artwork for *Fist of Glory*. Author's collection.

VHS artwork of *Triple Impact*. Author's collection.

VHS artwork for *Fist of Steel*. Author's collection.

It was fun working with Ron Hall. I think that was the first movie we did together. I had a friend of mine, Bridgett Riley, come on as well. She played the female lead. I thought she did a good job.

Talk about working with Ron Hall, who co-starred with you on several of your movies. He's clearly underrated as an action guy.

He was great for the camera. I'm telling you what, he knew how to sell a shot. He knows how to make a hit look great when he's delivering it. He's so flexible and so athletic. He can always add some spice to a fight scene because he can do things that the average Joe can't do. I may be able to knock everybody on that movie set out in the ring, but I can't do some of the athletic moves that Ron Hall can do.

Talk about your post-apocalyptic movie *Fist of Steel*. Many people know you just from this one movie.

It was like *Mad Max*! It was. What I hate about the memory of doing that one was the thought of being three weeks in the damn sun. When you're trying to sell that it's a futuristic movie, or an apocalyptic movie, everything's got to be sand dunes. You're out in a sand dune area all day. Everyone was sunburned. What was fun about that movie was that I got to get some of my personal black belt students involved as characters in the movie. And friends from the kickboxing world like Don Nakaya Nielson. There were great character roles in that movie.

Talk about being the hero in this film. I mean, you get crucified in this movie!

(Laughing.) Yeah, it was a dark kind of movie. A lot of that came from the Chinese influence. My co-star in that was Cynthia Khan, who was a huge female action star in China. They really catered to her. Sometimes Chinese movies don't have a happy ending.

Where did you film this movie? Was it in the Philippines?

Yeah, it was way up in the north. Some beach area. We found a shitload of sand.

Do you think you'd survive in a post-apocalyptic environment should the apocalypse occur in your lifetime?

Oh, so long as I have my foam rubber nunchucks, I'm down!

Talk about the VHS-era of action stars and action movies where guys like you were able to make your movies.

For me in particular, it was an exciting time where I was making movies and fighting all over the world, defending my world championships. My fights were on ESPN or on national and international television. For me at home in Tulsa, Oklahoma, we didn't even have a professional big-league sports team. I would come home after making a movie or a fight overseas, and my fights were huge here. I was like the major-league sports team for about a decade. My friend Don Wilson was instrumental in getting me started. When Maurice suggested me, he called Don and asked him, "Can Dale do this?" And Don said, "Oh, hell yeah!" You've seen that he had a great career, and he's still got a great career. He lasted long after the kickboxing movie phase passed. It was a golden age for a lot of us. I never took acting classes, I never went to LA, I never moved anywhere. I stayed right here at home. I didn't pursue it at all. For a guy who's not pursuing it to make it, you know it was a golden time.

Do you have any plans to return to movies?

No, no!

Over and out?

Over and out.

You've got fans out there, Dale. Anything you want to say to them?

If they've enjoyed my movies, I'm honored. I had a hell of a lot of fun.

Fist of Legend
1994 (Vivendi DVD) (djm)

Teacher: "What style was that?"
Chen: "Don't worry—I'll show you!"

One of Jet Li's most celebrated films, *Fist of Legend* is set in 1937 in Shanghai during the Japanese occupation. Li plays a student named Chen Zhen who comes home from Kyoto when he learns that a Japanese fighter had killed his master during a duel. Once Chen is home, he investigates and discovers that his master was poisoned before his fight, and that bombshell puts him in danger, as the Japanese now consider him a threat. His martial arts school is divided: Some are with Chen, and others are with the rightful master to the school but Chen gracefully declines leadership to pursue a romance with a Japanese girl. But all distractions are put aside and Chen is in for the fight of his life when he accepts a duel with the Japanese militant who is directly responsible for the death of his master.

A handful of knockout one-on-one martial arts scenes have given *Fist of Legend* a notable reputation as one of the great modern kung fu movies, and as one of Li's best. It covers the same ground as Bruce Lee's *The Chinese Connection*, and was later chronicled in Donnie Yen's *Legend of the Fist: The Return of Chen Zhen*. The story is no big deal, but the fight scenes are worth watching out of context. Directed by Gordon Chan, who did *Thunderbolt* and *The Medallion* with Jackie Chan.

Fist of Steel (a.k.a. Eternal Fist)
1992 (AIP VHS) (CD)

The love of Amp's (Dale "Apollo" Cook) life is murdered by the treacherous post-apocalyptic overlord Mainframe (Don Nakaya Neilsen), and he is left for dead, staked to the ground. He manages to escape only to meet up with the lovely Wild (Cynthia Khan), a woman whose village was destroyed by the same horde that turned Amp's world upside down. He agrees to teach her to fight so together they can make their way through the fighting league in order to carve a path to Mainframe. It won't be easy, as there is trouble around every sand dune, but as long as they keep fighting, maybe that revenge they're looking for will be fulfilled.

It's a wonderful thing to live in a world where films like *Fist of Steel* exist. Is it a bad movie? Yes, in every sense of the word. Everything you shouldn't do when making a film was probably done when making it. Even though it's a bad movie, it really is great and memorable. It's entertaining from beginning to end in many different ways. The script could have been written by a twelve-year-old, but it isn't the story that really matters here. The number of fight scenes in it is ridiculous—one every five minutes or so. Seriously, more than two-thirds of the film is continuous fighting. Dale "The Apollo" Cook (*Blood Ring*, *Triple Impact*) is a fighter, not an actor. He more than compensates for his lack of acting skills when his fists and feet are flying. The real treat (in my opinion) is Hong Kong action star Cynthia Khan in her only English language role. Her movements are always elegant, graceful, and deadly. Their chemistry as actors never really works but as a team fighting for revenge, you couldn't ask for anything better. There are so many things wrong (yet they feel so right) with the film that it isn't even worth worrying about. There are continuity errors, awful dialogue, and no real production design. The only thing that even remotely looked as if any money had been spent on it was the costumes. It was also a bizarre choice (though maybe necessary) to dub over Khans's voice. This movie is silly fun from beginning to end and should be further recognized for being a nonstop action fest.

Fist of the North Star

1995 (First Look DVD) (CD)

The Earth has become a nuclear wasteland and Lord Shin (Costas Mandylor) has become the evil dictator, ruling with an iron fist. A lone wanderer, Kenshiro (Gary Daniels), travels the wasteland, helping those in need. The town of Paradise Valley needs his help. After restoring the sight of a blind girl, he becomes his destiny to be the successor of the Fist of the North Star, a mystical moniker bestowed on only one. Ken and Shin have a violent past together, and it becomes Ken's quest to put a stop to all the torture that Shin's army, the Crossmen, have inflicted on the lands, and to bring Shin to his knees.

Fans of the classic anime *Fist of the North Star* were outraged when the live-action film was released. Many hated the liberties it took with the origin story and the not-so-subtle changes. Revisiting the film now, it can be incredibly entertaining. In 1995, CGI effects were not widely used and for this film, some terrific practical effects and makeup techniques were put into use to bring the gore featured in the anime to life. While not nearly as graphically violent as the anime, there's still plenty of blood and other extras to be as over the top as the story is meant to be. Gary Daniels (*Recoil*) plays Kenshiro, and he somehow manages to be the perfect choice for the role. The fight scenes are brutal with limbs being smashed and or bended in ways they were never meant to be. With arterial spray spritzing from gaping wounds at every blow, what more could you ask for? Maybe a little less convincing of a casting choice (but still solid) was Costas Mandylor (*Gangland*) as Lord Shin. He's at his best in this film and is so badass that when he bleeds, his blood turns to fire. The film also features Clint Howard (*Barb Wire*), Melvin Van Peebles (*Sweet Sweetback's Badass Song*), Malcolm McDowell (*Class of 1999*), and Chris Penn (*Rush Hour*). Just throw out your preconceptions of the anime, sit back, and enjoy an insanely fun film, which accomplishes everything it set out to do. Director Tony Randel is best known for directing the horror films *Hellbound: Hellraiser II* and *Ticks*. The magnificent score by Christopher Stone elevates the film immeasurably. This was never released theatrically in the US.

INTERVIEW:

GARY DANIELS

(djm)

An action star perennial who deserves to be celebrated, Gary Daniels has stood the test of time, and with an expansive body of work that stretches almost three decades, he has proved that he's the genuine article time and again. With a background in professional kickboxing (he was the Lightweight Kickboxing Champion of the World) and in taekwondo and ninjitsu, Daniels worked his way up from the VHS days of starring for movies made by the production companies Cinepix and PM Entertainment, while also working with Roger Corman's New Concord and then with Nu Image/Millennium. He's played both heroes and villains equally, and his most recognized roles are as Kenshiro in Fist of the North Star (1995), *and in the action star dream project,* The Expendables (2010).*

I recently watched one of your later films called *Forced to Fight*. It struck me while watching it that you're literally one of the last action heroes from the golden age of VHS who has stood the test of time. You're still starring in or appearing in action-oriented feature films, despite the fact that the home video market has crashed and low-budget action films are being made less and less these days. And to top that off, you're in still in incredible shape. My first question: Do you consider yourself an action star? If so, what does that entail for you as an actor and a martial artist? If not, is there anyone out there who you might consider "an action star?"

Me, '"an action star?" No, definitely not! It's fans that can make you or call you a star, but for me, all that I can do is strive to be a working actor, which means that I need to consistently train, work hard on my craft, and strive to work on better movies with accomplished actors, writers, and directors. My goal is to make films that entertain the people that pay to see my films and to be able to help the directors I work with to achieve their vision. There are other action actors in the martial arts genre that I respect for their work such as Donnie Yen, Tony Jaa, Jackie Chan, and Sammo Hung to name a few that are still around but to use the word "star" just seems so superficial.

I wanted to ask you a question about some of the filmmakers you've worked with, guys like Albert Pyun, Joseph Merhi, and Isaac Florentine. These are some of the unheralded directors who've made notable movies in the genre you're known for. Would you say some words about working with these guys and others you'd care to mention?

I've been fortunate enough to work with a real mixed bag of directors in my career. They all have their own style and way of doing things. Some focus more on the fighting, some more on the narrative or story, and some more on developing characters, and others focus more on the technical aspects of directing like the blocking of scenes, the placement of cameras and so forth. They all have the best of intentions and most are usually inhibited by the budgets that we work with. Of course I have my own vision of how I think the scripts should be adapted and applied so I don't always agree with them all, but I always give 100 percent regardless. You mentioned a few names so I will try to answer my best. Joseph Merhi—he was one of the owners of PM Entertainment. A great guy, one of the nicest guys I have met in my twenty-five-plus years in the business. A very intelligent man who came to the US with nothing—he couldn't even speak English, and he built an independent studio that produced over 200 films. I always enjoyed working with Joseph. He knew what his buyers and his audience wanted: action, action, and more action—and he delivered! He's still a dear friend of mine to this day. Albert Pyun—a nice guy, very easy-going with a distinct vision. Isaac Florentine—a fifth degree karate black belt. He was one of the two best directors for martial arts action in the US back in the '90s . . . the other being Steve Wang. Isaac has a flair for the fantastical with his fight scenes. Not my cup of tea, but he's been very successful in the genre. I would like to give a shoutout to some lesser-known directors that I have enjoyed working with although they may not have the recognition: Jeff Burr, Keoni Waxman, Richard Martin, Mark Roper, Dwight Little, Jonas Quastel, and more recently there are two directors that I have worked with that I believe are more than just good directors, but also good film makers: Wych Kaosayananda, a man who went through a rough learning curve (like many of us), but he's a brilliant writer, a great director, a DP, and a producer. I have learned so much from this man about making films. And a great guy to boot. I believe this man will be at the top of his game sooner rather than later. Also, there's Roger Ellis Frazier,who's another great writer/director/producer who brings more to his films than just punches and kicks. These last two really understand about not shooting action for the sake of action, but really deliver action scenes that are born out of the narrative and only when it works for the story and the characters.

You've either fought (on screen) or acted alongside some of the greatest names in the action and martial arts genre—men like Jackie Chan, Tadashi Yamashita, Richard Norton, Don Wilson, Sugar Ray Leonard, and any number of the cast of *The Expendables*—and I wanted to know if there were any of these people (or others that I didn't list here) who made a notable, affirming impact on your life.

All the actors you mentioned have been a pleasure to work with, but other than Jackie Chan I can't honestly say any of them had an affirming impact on my life except maybe Sylvester Stallone as he was one of those action actors I watched and admired growing up. Bruce Lee had a huge impact on my life. Also, my kung fu teacher Sifu Winston Omega had a huge impact on my life. Of course you learn from every experience you have in your life and from everyone you meet . . . sometimes positive and sometimes negative but you absorb and learn from them all.

F

I recently did an interview with Zoe Bell, and I asked her what it was like to work with you, and she told me how much she enjoyed working with you and hearing your stories about working in Asia. You've filmed all over the world. What places on Earth do you most enjoy doing a movie, and why?

Well, yes I have been very fortunate that this business has taken me all over the world, and traveling to other countries and visiting different cultures is the best education in the world. I do enjoy working in Asia. The people are always so respectful—whether it be China, Thailand, the Philippines, Hong Kong, or Japan. It's all been very humbling. But I've always had good experiences with the local people whether it's been in Asia, Europe, or Africa. Traveling is definitely one of the fringe benefits of this job. It's always interesting to see how different countries approach the art of filmmaking. As I said: it's been a great education in life and work. I think at one time the different countries each had their own focus and beliefs on what made a good film. Some focused more on action and fighting and some focused more on the scope of the film and others more on drama, but as Hollywood goes more global and US films are shooting all over the world now, I think the differences are becoming less and less. By the way, Zoe was great to work with. She was very professional and a lovely lady.

In preparing for this interview, I've been watching just about all of your movies over a year's time span, and I saw an early one you did called *The Secret of King Mahi's Island*, which must have been quite an adventure for you. You seemed so young in it, but it was clear that you had potential (even then) to become a leading man in action films. Do you remember anything about your time making that particular movie, and what was going through your head in those days? Did you ever think or dream to believe that you'd become one of the busiest and most respected action stars in the world?

(Laughing.) I can't believe you saw *The Secret of King Mahi's Island*! It was the second film (and the last one I completed) on a six-picture deal I had with a company in the Philippines. After that one they asked me to do soft porn! Anyway, it was quite an experience. I was so young, and other than a year of acting classes I really had no experience, and it shows in that film! I was pretty awful in it. It was an *Indiana Jones* kind of film if I dare compare it with those movies, and I had a blast making it in remote jungles and caves in the Philippines, but there were so many troubles on that film. The director quit after the first week due to personal problems and a very inexperienced guy took over. We got it finished eventually but . . . it wasn't my finest hour. I almost died on that film when I was escaping from some bad guys shooting at me and I had to jump into a deep river. I was wearing a burlap rucksack that immediately filled with water and dragged me to the bottom. I was so disoriented but managed to get it off and back to the surface which seemed a mile away as I was running out of air. Welcome to filmmaking! I was a kid with

a dream in those days—always very determined. I never even thought that I would achieve my goals someday . . . the thought never entered my head. I have had the same goal since I was eight years old when I saw *Enter the Dragon* and Bruce Lee for the first time. In fact, even though I have had some limited success over the years, I am still chasing my ultimate goal and won't—*can't*—quit until I get there.

There are a few of your movies I'd like to single out for questions. I'll list the titles, and if there's anything you'd like to say about working on these films, please jump in and say some words about any memories you might have from that movie. First movie: *Recoil*.

Recoil—that was a PM movie that followed their tried and true formula of action, action, and more action. I really enjoyed making that film and working with Spiro Razatos. It was my third film with him as the stunt co-coordinator. He is one of the best in the business. That film has some incredible action sequences comparable to some much bigger budgeted films of that time. We often had three units running, so I would be jumping from one unit where I was doing dialogue to a second unit where I would do a fight scene and then jump to a third unit where I would shoot a bunch of guys, and back to one again. It was crazy fun.

Knights.

That was like my second film, which came very early in my career. It was memorable for a couple of reasons. Getting to work and hang out with Kathy Long who was the women's world kickboxing champion at the time was great; she is one of the nicest ladies you will ever meet. Working with Lance Henrikson and getting so many acting tips from him and then getting to sit around campfires at night having barbecues while Kris Kristofferson sang and played guitar was all pretty cool. My part was supposed to be bigger but on my way out to Colorado where we filmed I got a call from my manager saying that Golden Harvest had called and wanted me in their next Jackie Chan film, *City Hunter*. The dates I had to fly to Japan coincided with my time in Colorado so I had to ask Albert Pyun's permission to go because I was contracted to do *Knights*. After waiting a couple of weeks Albert rearranged my schedule on *Knights* so that I could go to Japan. I will be forever grateful to Albert for allowing me to go.

Fist of the North Star.

I was under contract with Overseas Film Group to do a couple of films based on a character I had created called Union Jack—which never got made—when the owner, Robbie Little, was approached by Tohei of Japan to co-produce *Fist of the North Star,* and I was asked to play the lead. I jumped at the opportunity, as I had been a fan of the Manga. So I immediately started training super hard to put on muscle to try and look like the Kenshiro as portrayed in the comics. I originally wanted Koichi Sakamoto and Alpha stunts to do the action directing but at that time Robbie didn't want them so I was

Gary Daniels is . . .The Fist of the North Star. Author's collection.

fortunate to hire my sifu Winston Omega to do the choreography, but unfortunately I didn't get to shoot the fights how I wanted to. The director had his own ideas. That film was shot long before all the CGI technology we have today, and although I think it looked pretty good I can only imagine what it could be like if it was remade today.

Riot.

That one was another PM film directed by Joseph Merhi with some terrific action coordinated by Spiro Razatos. It was a simple story that was inspired by the LA riots. There was no worldwide web back in those days—or if there was it was very new—and I always wonder what would have happened to these films and my career had we gotten the Internet exposure that independent films get in this day and age. In *Riot* I got to work with boxing legend Sugar Ray Leonard who was such a nice, humble man. And again I got to work with my sifu as the fight choreographer.

Bloodmoon.

In the '80s and '90s the best martial arts action films were being made in Hong Kong and there was one company called Seasonal Films whose owner Ng See Yuen (who had produced the three films that made Jackie Chan a superstar) was making Hong Kong–style action films but with Western leads. I had wanted to work with him so badly, and when I met the writer of these films—a great guy named Keith Strandberg—I had my opportunity. I think Keith recommended me to Ng and I was offered *Bloodmoon*. We shot in North Carolina in the summer of 1996, I think. It was super hot and humid. There was an unusual atmosphere in Wilmington where we stayed as Brandon Lee had just lost his life on the set of the *The Crow* there and everyone was talking about it. Let me tell you that whenever I work with a director from Hong Kong and his crew they are the most physically demanding films I have ever worked on. I'm not complaining, but you certainly earn your pay. We had a great cast with Darren Shalahvi and Chuck Jeffreys, and one of the producers was ex-karate champ actor Keith Vitali, so we really had a great time making that film, and it had some of the best fights I have ever filmed.

Cold Harvest.

That was my only film with director Isaac Florentine. It was a futuristic western. Isaac wanted to homage John Woo and Sergio Leone so we shot a martial arts western in South Africa. I liked working with Isaac, and it was an interesting experience. Not many times does an Englishman get to play a cowboy! And I got to play twins to boot! The action director was Akihiro (Yugi) Noguchi, one of the Alpha stunts team members that I had wanted to use on *Fist of the North Star*. The Alpha stunt team was the nearest thing to Hong Kong action directors that we had in LA back in the '90s, so with Isaac and Yugi on board I knew we would get some decent fighting. I had wanted to work with Isaac again but he obviously never felt the same as he has gone on to have much success . . . but we have never worked together since.

I've got to mention *The Expendables*. This was a monumental event for fans of action stars. I'm going to be honest, okay? With all of those guys in that movie, the one I was most excited to see on a big screen was you. It actually meant everything to me that Stallone understood that you belonged in that movie, even if it was just for a small part. Talk about working with Stallone and that incredible cast.

I've done a lot of interviews about working on *The Expendables*. It is a film that attracted a lot of attention with its great cast. I was offered the role as Mr. Stallone was looking for an actor that could deliver lines but did not have to be doubled when it came to the action. The stunt coordinator/second unit director Chad Stahelski—who I have known for years and worked with previously—recommended me and after having a meeting with Mr. Stallone, I was offered the part. The first five weeks we shot in Brazil and I remember the first night I was on set being directed by Mr. Stallone . . . he was walking around the set chewing on a big cigar. I was just thinking how surreal is this?! I'm working with Rocky! I'm working with Rambo! He's a guy I have watched and admired since my youth. It was a pretty cool moment. Originally my part was a small stunt role but Mr. Stallone kept adding scenes for me and by the end of the fifth week in Brazil Mr. Stallone put his arm round my shoulder and said, "You're doing a great job. I wanna make your part bigger, but I gotta do it without adding days to the schedule." I was so honored. By time we got to New Orleans they had done some rewrites on the script and I had a new character name and more scenes. Not everything I shot ended up in the final cut of the film but I wasn't complaining. It was a great experience and an opportunity to work with and learn from one of the best action stars of our generation.

THE EXPENDABLES

Gunnar Jensen (Dolph Lundgren) threatens The Brit (Gary Daniels) in *The Expendables*. Author's collection.

You've worked with Steve Austin and Dolph Lundgren a few times now. When I met Steve Austin, I mentioned that fight you two guys had in *Hunt to Kill*. His response was, "Yeah, Gary Daniels. He's *badass*." Talk about working with these two guys and how you're able to work both of your different styles into a movie fight.

Well, to be completely honest when I worked with Dolph on *Retrograde* it was a very positive experience as originally I had been cast as the main villain, but Dolph changed that and when I was asked to choreograph a fight with the new main villain, all my work was cut and I was told to just hit the guy with a two by four. This is something you have to accept and respect. Every lead man has a vision for his films and you have to respect that the film is being financed on his name so if your styles contradict then you have to be prepared to step down. I have read stories that say Dolph and I never got along, but that's not true. I understood the situation and respect him for the career he has had. And we got along fine on *The Expendables*.

I first met Steve on *The Expendables*. I'm not a fan of wrestling so I really didn't know who he was but pretty much all of our scenes were together—with Eric Roberts—and although he is a very intimidating-looking bloke, he is actually one of the funniest, nicest guys I have ever worked with. I had a blast working with him. The following year I was in Detroit working on *Game of Death* with Wesley Snipes when Steve called me and asked if I would go up to Vancouver to work on *Hunt to Kill* and I didn't hesitate. So this time we were adversaries and I was asked to choreograph a fight between Steve and me. Obviously we are from completely different backgrounds so it was a challenge to choreograph a fight where I could use my strengths and he could use his. We both had to look good, and Steve needed to be the victor. We shot it in the Golden Needles National Park in the Vancouver winter. It had been raining and snowing the whole shoot and it was freezing the day of the shoot and we shot in a forest with the most uneven ground with tree roots sticking out of the ground: not ideal conditions, but Steve is a true professional. He never complains about anything. It's always a pleasure to work with guys like him.

You've got quite a few films already in the pipeline or in the works. Are there any titles you'd like to mention?

Right now I have two films to be released where I play the lead. One is *Skin Traffik,* which also features Mickey Rourke, Michael Madsen, Eric Roberts, Jeff Fahey, Darryl Hannah, and Alan Ford. We shot it in Vancouver, LA, England, Scotland, and Amsterdam. I haven't seen that one myself yet. And the other one is called *Misfire*, which was shot in Mexico. In two weeks I go back to Mexico to shoot an action-packed feature tentatively titled *Bull Pen*. And I have two other films lined up after that!

Have you ever thought about directing a film?

Yes, I really want to direct a film. I'm in the process of writing a script at the moment, which is taking me longer than I thought but if I ever get it completed and can raise the funds, I will direct that one.

Is there anything you'd like to say to your fans?

Well, if I have any fans left out there I would like to say thank you for sticking by me. My career has had its ups and downs, and I'm now entering a new phase. I will always give 100 percent, and I hope the best is yet to come.

Fist of the Warrior

2007 (Lionsgate DVD) (CD)

"So I guess now you say,
Holy cocaine, Batman!"

Lee Choe (Ho-Sung Pak) is a hit man who's ready to leave that life behind now that he's found love with Sarah (Robin Paul). She doesn't know his dark secret but at the same time, he wants to be honest with her. The mobster he works for, John Lowe (Peter Greene from *Under Siege 2*), is not too happy about this decision, and he vows that Lee will pay a heavy price for leaving. After Lee and Sarah disappear, they are found by Lowe's hired guns and Sarah is murdered, sending Lee into a inconsolable rage. In the meantime, Detective Barnes (Roger Guenveur Smith) is doing favors for the crime family, and Lee will use him in order to get closer to Lowe and his men. What they did to him was unforgivable, and he has every intention in making all of them pay with their lives.

Fist of the Warrior isn't exactly the showcase Ho-Sung Pak deserves. He has the looks, the moves, and the talent to be an above-the-line action star, but this movie fails to really give him an outlet. The story is all over the place and tends to focus more on the cop and the mobster. The acting by all is pretty solid but the audience deserves more action from Ho-Sung Pak. The fights he does have are impressive and stylish but they aren't shot very well, which is an issue many cheap direct-to-video martial arts movies have. A major issue is the fact that he has doesn't have any opponents in the film who are martial artists. He fights his way through guy after guy without a satisfying final showdown. This one's filled with promise and Ho-Sung Pak deserves a showcase worthy of his talents. It was directed by Wayne Kennedy.

Fists of Blood
(a.k.a. **Strike of the Panther**)
1988 (Celebrity Video VHS)
(djm)

Filmed back to back with *Day of the Panther*, *Fists of Blood* follows superspy Jason Blade (Edward John Stazak) on his extended adventure involving the rescue of an enslaved rich girl who's been forced to prostitute herself to high- paying clients. When that mission is over, his next one connects to the first film (covered in *Day of the Panther*), only this time it's more personal, as the drug ring he's after kidnaps his dancer girlfriend (played by Paris Jefferson), who spends the whole movie in a leotard, even while tied up. Featuring ninjas who wear hockey masks, a hero who wields nunchucks, and a goofy dance sequence, *Fists of Blood* is only marginally better than its predecessor.

From director Brian Trenchard-Smith (*The Man From Hong Kong*), this nondescript entry in the martial arts action genre is pretty dispensable. Trenchard-Smith is a more than competent filmmaker, whose great catalog of films include *Escape 2000*, *Dead-End Drive-In*, and *Night of the Demons 2*, but his work on the Jason Blade series isn't the best reflection on his abilities. They lack a genuine front-and-center action star . . . Stazak is very wet behind the ears and his abilities as a martial artist are adequate, but he just seems miscast in these films. Lacking an outrageous element that makes most of Trenchard-Smith's work so enjoyable, the Jason Blade movies can easily be skipped.

Fists of Iron
1995 (Live VHS) (CD)

Dale Hartwell (Michael Worth) makes his living as a mechanic. He's a lot smarter than he lets on, but he enjoys his job and he's content. He has a daughter that he thinks the world of, and he's fairly adept at swinging his fists around in practice. His friend Matt (Nicholas Hill) takes him to a mansion where there's some underground fighting going on. Matt decides he can get in the ring against Victor "The Destroyer" Bragg (Matthias Hues), but sadly things don't go his way. Due to his sustained internal injuries, Matt passes away. Dale is broken and disturbed about the situation and mulls over revenge, but he is in no way ready to take on Bragg. He meets Daniel (Eric Lee) and Tyler (Sam Jones) at a local bar. They're both former fighters who previously had run-ins with Gallagher (Marshall Teague), the man behind the fights. Together they will have to instill all their knowledge into the young fighter since they all want to taste that sweet revenge.

Fists of Iron is a perfectly safe bet of an action movie. It's essentially just another tournament fighting film but the pieces all fit together nicely. Michael Worth (*To Be the Best*) is a likable lead with plenty of charisma that carries the picture. He's a skilled fighter, and the action scenes are exciting. Matthias Hues (*TC 2000*) is a great villain here (as usual) and a formidable foe. Art Camacho (*Crooked*) was the fight choreographer on the film, which was directed by Richard Munchkin (*Deadly Bet*). *Fists of Iron* follows a very familiar premise but manages to be a step higher than the rest; it's entirely satisfying.

Fist 2 Fist
2011 (Screen Media DVD) (djm)

Hapkido instructor and counselor at a neighbor-hood youth center, Ken Min (Jino Kang from *Blade Warrior*) has a dark past that is about to catch up to him. His former associate in crime Tokyo Joe (wrestler and NFL player Bill Duff) is about to be released from prison, and the only thing he has in mind is revenge. When Tokyo Joe is released, he recruits a new crew to assist him on his grand scheme to kill Ken, kidnap his girlfriend, and take over the neighborhood. Ken, who understands what's coming for him, is prepared to face the man he betrayed, but Ken's a different man than he used to be. He's also incredibly proficient in martial arts, and nobody—not even Tokyo Joe—realizes that he's such a force to be reckoned with. With the help and support of a few of his young students, Ken is able to defend his studio from these thugs, but after Ken's wife is abducted, he is forced to compete in an underground fight tournament, where Tokyo Joe hopes to humiliate and emasculate him in front of a bloodthirsty audience.

Writer/director/star Jino Kang is really interesting to watch. This is only the second film he did (*Blade Warrior* was the first), and you can see where he's coming from as a writer and an action guy. He's not exactly what most would consider a leading man type, but he's got a cool, controlled demeanor, and his abilities as a fighter are undeniable. His movies have a slow-burn effect, and I think a mature, seasoned fan of these types of movies will appreciate him in the same way that I do. It's a shame he hasn't made more movies. *Weapon of Choice* was his next film.

Fist 2 Fist 2: Weapon of Choice
2014 (djm)

An in-name-only sequel to *Fist 2 Fist*, *Weapon of Choice* stars Jino Kang (from *Blade Warrior*) as a retired hitman named Jack whose past comes back to haunt him. Some thugs break into his house and kidnap his adopted daughter, and he's too late to stop them, but not too late to kill a few of the invaders and leave a body count for the police to mull over. We learn that Jack's daughter's maternal father is a lower-level crime boss living in San Francisco, and now that he's figured out where she is, he's come to seek her out and reclaim her, despite the fact that she

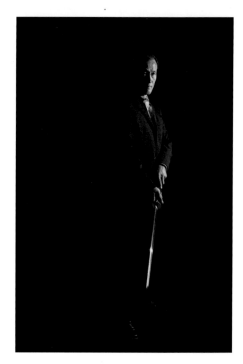

Jino Kang as Jack Lee in *Fist 2 Fist 2: Weapon of Choice*. Courtesy of Jino Kang.

has no memories of him. She's only known Jack as her father, and as we see her in captivity and degraded by her predicament, we can plainly see that she's been taught martial arts and survival tactics by Jack, who she knows will come save her. Jack becomes involved with an FBI agent (Katherine Celio), who helps him recover from a bad wound sustained from a fight with some bad guys, and using her resources as a field agent, she's able to bring him several steps closer to recovering his daughter.

Star/writer/producer/director Jino Kang only makes one movie every once in a while, and when he does, the product he comes up with is always worth watching. More seasoned than ever, Kang knows his limitations and his strong suits, so *Weapon of Choice* is his most accomplished (and best-looking) movie yet, but the dense storyline and plotting takes a big second place to characterizations and the fight scenes, which are sprinkled sparsely throughout the movie, but come in heavy doses towards the last act. Kang's introspective scripts usually feature him in laconic, no-nonsense roles (which is great), and while his films tend to be plot-heavy and rely on drama to tell his stories, all three of them are excellent vehicles for him to display his talents and abilities as a hapkido martial artist. The last fifteen minutes of the movie are jam-packed with one realistic and brutal fight scene after another. Out of his three films, *Weapon of Choice* might be his most viable and commercial, even with a running time of an hour and forty minutes.

Flash Point
2007 (Well Go USA DVD) (djm)

Inspector Jun Ma (Donnie Yen) has been warned by his superiors that he's using too much excessive force while on duty. Everyone knows that Ma has a higher arrest rate and has solved more cases than any of his peers, so it's difficult for anyone to tell him to slow down. His latest case involves three Vietnamese brothers who are in business together as a mini drug cartel, and their big plan is to cash out just before the mainland takeover of Hong Kong. Ma captures one of the brothers, which spurs a retaliation from the other two, and very quickly the situation escalates to the point where the oldest brother Tony (Collin Chou from *The Matrix* sequels) stages a death hit on Ma and his entire squad at a party. Ma survives and kicks his investigation/revenge trip into high gear, leading to an incredible sixteen-minute fight scene that finishes the film.

I saw this theatrically in a brief US run, and I remember being taken aback by the style of fighting used in the film. Star Yen and his director Wilson Yip infuse mixed martial arts into the movie, which at that point in time hadn't really been done to the best of its abilities on film before. Watching it again on video only made me realize that they were ahead of the wave (or just in time), and it makes the movie that much more interesting. Action packed for an eighty-eight-minute feature, *Flash Point* upped the bar for fight scenes and gave Yen one of his best vehicles to date. Yen and Yip also worked on *Kill Zone*, and then later on the two outstanding *Ip Man* movies.

Flight of Fury

2007 (Sony DVD) (CD)

"There used to be something called self-defense, but seems like when you defend yourself, if you do it too good, you get into trouble."

John Sands (Steven Seagal) is an Air Force pilot who was wrongly imprisoned and his memory set to be erased because of all the military secrets he's privy to. Once out, he finds himself at the mercy of the military once again. John's protégé, Ratcher (Steve Toussaint), steals a top-secret military jet known as the X-77. It's a stealth bomber that has the ability to disguise itself from any and all surveillance. The military wants John to go to the Middle East and get the jet back. He's given twenty-four hours, and if he succeeds, they'll wipe his slate clean. He's partnered up with Rick Jannick (Mark Bazeley) to go in and get the plane. A SEAL team is sent in beforehand, only to be killed by a terrorist group co-led by a woman named Eliana (Katie Jones). Once John and Jannick land in Afghanistan, they're separated, and Jannick is captured by Eliana, leaving John alone with time running out and a mission to accomplish.

When Steven Seagal (*The Patriot*) makes a good film, it's really good. The same philosophy can be applied to when he makes a bad film. With the exception of a few above average action scenes during the first and third acts, *Flight of Fury* is simply uninteresting and bland. The story is predictable and the supporting cast is

forgettable. Seagal just sort of shows up and does his thing without putting in much effort. There's a decent fight during the first twenty minutes with Seagal foiling a robbery at a convenience store. During the last twenty minutes there's a similar battle with terrorists in the airplane hangar. Everything else is instantly forgettable. This isn't one of Seagal's shinier moments, and by avoiding it you may be better off. Michael Keusch, the director, also directed Seagal in *Shadow Man* and *Attack Force*.

The Forbidden Kingdom

2008 (Lionsgate DVD) (CD)

Jason Tripitikas (Michael Angarano) is an awkward teenager obsessed with martial arts films. He frequently buys bootleg movies from a shop run by Old Hop (Jackie Chan). Jason is confronted by a group of punks and forced to help them rob Old Hop's shop so they can make away with some loot. In the robbery, Old Hop is shot and his dying wish is for Jason to deliver an ancient staff to the rightful owner. He runs off with the staff only to fall off the roof of the building. When he awakens, he finds himself in ancient China where he must help fulfill a prophecy. He learns of the prophecy when he meets Lu Yan (Jackie Chan), who tells Jason the story of the Monkey King (Jet Li) and how the staff can free him. They set off on their journey where they meet the Silent Monk (Jet Li). Lu Yan and the Monk realize Jason is the chosen one from the prophecy and must teach him martial arts so he can battle the evil Jade Warlord (Collin Chu) and resurrect the Monkey King.

This really wasn't the type of film fans were hoping for when pairing action legends Jet Li (*Fist of Legend*) and Jackie Chan (*City Hunter*) for the first time. It was an American-

US poster for *The Forbidden Kingdom*. Author's collection.

produced fantasy/martial arts film from Rob Minkoff who also directed Disney's *The Lion King*. Chan pretty much plays against type here and much of, if not all, his fighting was wire enhanced. Jet Li plays the type of role he is rather comfortable in. There is a pretty epic fight scene with the two legends battling each other. It's solid entertainment but longtime fans will have trouble not thinking about how that fight would have looked if both men were still in their prime. There's plenty of action and some rather stunning cinematography to whet the palate. It's a good film though, playing out much like *The Neverending Story* or *Warriors of Virtue*. It's a safe film for most of the family and on that level, it delivers.

Force

2011 (MoserBear DVD) (CD)

"It's late at night, you're out with a girl, you're roaming without papers, you remove a police barricade knowing that it's kept there for a purpose. What kind of a friend does that make you?"

Yash (John Abraham) and his undercover police unit have single-handedly wiped out all the major drug families in the city. By doing so, they have left the playing field open for Vishnu (Vidyut Jamwal), one of the most vicious criminals India has ever seen. Yash and his team have killed Vishnu's brother, sending the criminal into a bloodthirsty rage. With nothing left to lose, he begins to take out the special unit and their families one by one. Yash can't stand by and watch this happen, especially since he recently married Maya (Genelia D'Souza) and will do anything to protect her. Vishnu is well connected and it's almost impossible for them to hide anywhere, so Yash will have to gather up all his strength and knowledge in order to stay alive.

At nearly two and a half hours, *Force* tends to drag but only for a few minutes. The final hour of the film is action-packed and filled with suspense. John Abraham (*Dhoom*) is a great lead; he brings a much-needed intensity to his role as the toughest cop on the force. In fact, he's so resilient he tosses motorcycles at criminals as if they were weightless. It will take one hardened S.O.B. to go against a cop like this, and Vidyut Jamwal (*Commando: A One Man Army*) is pure T.N.T. When this guy is in action, you can't for one second peel your eyes away from the screen. His time in the film may be limited but he leaves his mark in every scene, building up to a battle of the titans when he finally has the showdown with Abraham. Just remember: this is a Bollywood picture so you will have to sit through several musical montages, including a duet, soapy romance, and a pinch of comedy, so be patient and hang in there. I promise: you will be rewarded. Nishikant Kamat directed.

Forced to Fight

2011 (Image DVD) (djm)

Watching *Forced to Fight* should bring back memories of other fight-for-revenge-and-money movies like any number of the *Bloodsport* and *Kickboxer* sequels from the 1990s. Gary Daniels stars as Shane Slavin, a former kickboxing champion whose brother gets in deep with a mini-mogul and crime boss (Peter Weller), and Slavin is . . . forced to fight for his brother's freedom from debt. Slavin, who has settled down as a loving father, husband, and auto mechanic, has to relearn and retrain how to fight, but even in top condition (Daniels was forty-nine when he made this) he has to rethink his fighting techniques because his opponents don't fight fair or clean. Weller's villain streams the illegal fights on the Internet from servers in the Ukraine, and he doesn't hesitate to murder anyone who disagrees with him or interrupts his business. There comes a point when Daniels is told to take a few dives, and by the end of the film he has been beat up so bad and brought to such a dilapidated state that it's a wonder that he is able to walk away of his own volition and strength.

Shot in Canada and in Romania, *Forced to Fight* is absolutely familiar to fans of the kickboxing genre, while updating the fighting styles to the MMA set. Daniels, while sporting frosted highlights in his hair, proves for the umpteenth time that he's a physical force to be reckoned with. The dramatics in the film are melodramatic at best, with some clunky dialogue and delivery by some of the actors, and all the fight scenes take place in the same basic black-draped dungeon set with the same crowd of bloodthirsty extras, but if you're watching this picture you're probably willing to forgive its shortcomings. Weller, who is fully capable of playing evil characters such as he plays here, gives the role more gusto than it probably deserves. He played a similar role in *Dragon Eyes*, starring Cung Le. Jonas Quastel directed this film.

Forced Vengeance

1982 (Warner DVD) (djm)

Security enforcer and bagman Josh Randall (Chuck Norris) is working and living in Hong Kong when his life is turned upside down when his employer and friend is murdered by a crime syndicate. Randall is framed for the crime, and he finds himself on the run. He takes his girlfriend, Claire (Mary Louise Weller), and another woman (who the syndicate is after) with him, and they have a price on their heads, so the chase gets interesting. When he is forced to go off on his own, his girlfriend is raped and killed and the other woman is taken captive, which sets the final act of the film in motion: Randall embarks on . . . *Forced Vengeance*.

Chuck Norris fans should appreciate the amount of action and solid one-liners he delivers, but casual martial arts and action movie fans may find the film a little lackluster. Personally, I found it to be perfectly satisfactory, albeit a little shocking when the girlfriend character is brutally raped and slain, but it gives

Chuck Norris sandwiched between two beauties in a publicity still for *Forced Vengeance*. Author's collection.

the film an edge and an aura of unpredictability that I found refreshing. The Hong Kong locations add to the exotic and dangerous nature of the film, and Norris (who is constantly called a cowboy because of his attire) works well while being surrounded by the Asian locales. His final fight with his girlfriend's rapist and killer is the highlight of the film. James Fargo, the director, did several films with Clint Eastwood including *The Enforcer* and *Every Which Way But Lose*.

Force: Five

1981 (Scorpion DVD) (djm)

Force: Five is one of those movies I waited years to see, and when I finally watched it, I was really disappointed. I had high expectations: It's from director Robert Clouse, who made *Enter the Dragon* and *Gymkata*, two of my favorites, and it stars some great martial artists like Richard Norton, Joe Lewis, and Benny "The Jet" Urquidez. How could this movie let me down? The story is simple, and that's fine. An evil reverend (Master Bong Soo Han from *Kill the Golden Goose*) has brainwashed

Spanish poster for *Force: Five*. Author's collection.

The team of heroes (featuring Richard Norton, left, and Benny "The Jet" Urquidez, back) in the Robert Clouse actioner *Force: Five*. Author's collection.

an army of average citizens into forking over their bank accounts and savings to fund his cause. One young woman (played by Amanda Wyss from *Better Off Dead*) has a concerned father who hires a team of mercenaries to rescue her from the reverend's cult. The team's members consist of Norton, Lewis, and Urquidez, amongst some others. The best parts of the movie involve the introductions of each of the mercenaries. Norton beats up a bunch of guys in a pool hall; Urquidez does some crazy stuff to some thugs in an outdoor shopping area. I thought, "Oh, man, this is gonna be good!" But then the movie gets redundant and ugly, focusing on the evil reverend's torture methods, and there were no surprises. The fights get to be lackluster, and attempts at humor fall flat.

This was an early effort from Norton and Urquidez (who would both appear together again in *Kick Fighter*), so I can't blame them, but Joe Lewis had already starred in *Jaguar Lives!* so what was *his* excuse? Clouse turned in what feels like a halfhearted attempt at an action movie with generic set-ups and forgettable action scenes. I'd really hoped that this would be something special. Still, Urquidez is great in it. Norton is fun, too. Also with Bob Schott from *Gymkata*.

Force of Execution

2013 (Anchor Bay DVD) (djm)

A Mafioso named Mr. Alexander (Steven Seagal) who lives on a hacienda compound has a trusted right-hand man named Roman (Bren Foster), who botches an important job, but he was set up, so Mr. Alexander doesn't hold it against him. However, to save face and to make amends, Roman is turned over to the people who set up the job, who now brutally maim and torture him, crushing both of his hands and arms beyond recognition. Roman, an honorable man and an incredible martial artist, receives the punishment like a man. Six months later, he's living like a bum in back alleys and he comes to the aide (despite not having the proper use of his hands) of his friend, a Hispanic fry cook (played by Danny Trejo) who is being attacked by hoodlums. Roman comes to realize that Mr. Alexander has never lost track of him and has his friends and trusted associates (Trejo's character is one of those) all over the place. So when Mr.

Alexander announces his retirement as "The Iceman" (Ving Rhames) muscles into town, Roman steps up to help his old boss settle some scores in a final showdown.

Surprisingly multilayered and story-driven, *Force of Execution* is a fantastic stepping stone for martial artist and budding action star Bren Foster, who had a small, supporting role in *Maximum Conviction*, a previous movie starring Seagal. He's got a great, show-stopping role here, and kudos to Seagal for passing the reigns to him. As for Seagal, his antihero role here is understated and subtle, and while he breaks some bones, he's sort of in the backseat this time, which is great. I'm definitely looking forward to seeing more of this guy Bren Foster. Directed by Seagal regular Keoni Waxman.

A Force of One

1979 (Anchor Bay DVD R2) (djm)

Some cops are getting picked off by a martial artist when they get wind of a drug ring in the city, and after an investigation turns up no leads, the police enlist a karate champion named Matt Logan (Chuck Norris) to help them with the case. He teaches them some moves and how to protect themselves, but when two more of them get killed, things get interesting. Logan becomes convinced that someone in the martial arts community is the killer, and when it is revealed that the killer is the man he has been training to fight against in the ring, all hell breaks loose!

A solid actioner with a good role for Norris, *A Force of One* is exactly what you'd expect it to be. The action and fight scenes are straight-up and honest, and the cop procedural elements are a little hokey, but fitting. Norris has an on-screen son who is killed towards the end, which adds an element of revenge to the plot that feels right for this type of film. Bill Wallace, a former middleweight karate champion, co-stars as the main heavy. Dick Halligan directed. The Region 2 DVD release is widescreen.

The Foreigner

2002 (Sony DVD) (djm)

After making a notable and promising comeback to theatrical feature films with *Exit Wounds* and *Half Past Dead*, Steven Seagal began shooting sub-par movies in Eastern Europe and started his reign as one of the kings of direct-to-video action flicks. *The Foreigner* was the first of many such pictures, and since Tri-Star released it, it seems apparent that it was first intended to play in theaters before going to video. The story is a complete mess. Seagal plays a "foreigner" named Jonathan Cold who travels the world as a so-secret agent, doing ultra intense missions where his superiors won't even tell him what he's supposed to be doing in plain English because actually telling him what his missions are about would entail better writing from the authors of

the screenplay. Cold's latest assignment involves him trying to recover a black box with top-secret intel from a plane crash, and as soon as he embarks on his quest, there are other elements playing against him. There are assassins upon assassins and double-crosses, triple-crosses, and shootouts galore set to techno music on the soundtrack. This is one of those movies where the star probably agreed to do the film based on a paragraph premise.

Seagal is all wrong for this movie. He was already past his best days as an action star, but that shouldn't be an excuse to headline in something as confounding as *The Foreigner*. It's an inconsequential, disposable little movie that has no idea what to do with its star. While he engages in a couple of fights, it's simply not enough to keep viewers engaged. I remember buying *The Foreigner* on DVD when it first came out and being overwhelmingly disappointed by it. There are a number of movies that Seagal has starred in that his fans should never see. This is one of them. A sequel, *Black Dawn*, was made a few years later. Directed by Michael Oblowitz.

Forest Warrior

1996 (Gaiam DVD) (djm)

A gruff wilderness man named John McKenna (a grizzled Chuck Norris) is on the warpath when his Native American wife is slain by nasty villains. He tracks them down in the forest, and he nearly gets his revenge, but he's overcome by the odds, and he dies, fading into legend. Generations later, a group of kids are congregated in the very forest where McKenna was killed, and around the campfire, they tell stories about him, contemplating the possibility that he might still be alive. Meanwhile, a corporate entity is threatening to tear down the trees of Tanglewood Mountain, where McKenna's protective spirit dwells, and when the kids try to protect the land from the thuggish land developers, their very lives hang in the balance as the goons don't discriminate adults from children. Just as the scales are tipped in the villains' favor, the shape-changing specter of John McKenna (with his eighteenth-century garb and awkward sense of humor) returns to aid the kids and put an end to the tyranny of modern expansion.

What could have easily been a straightforward action fest with slight supernatural elements takes a fairly radical sharp turn towards farce, comedy, and tomfoolery. Chuck Norris participates in some signature action scenes that incorporate his martial arts, but as soon as the kids start fighting back, the movie turns into *3 Ninjas*, with pratfalls, silly sound effects, and a superstar who basically winks at his audience to let them know that it's all in good fun. But there's a problem with that. After Norris became a TV star, his persona became associated with "clean" entertainment that delivered positive messages, and while I'm all for that, *Forest Warrior* is a diluted movie with a star who but only five years previously was starring in Cannon's hard "R"-rated movies *The Hitman* and *Delta Force 2*. *Forest Warrior* (directed by Chuck's brother Aaron) is okay for the family, but not necessarily okay for fans of his "R"-rated days.

Fortune Dane

1986 (Starmaker VHS) (djm)

After a career in football, Fortune Dane (Carl Weathers) embarks on a career in law enforcement, which makes him a minor celebrity in his precinct even with bad guys, who use his fame as a punchline. When Dane's acquaintance (played by David Rappaport) is killed along with several others in a casino, Dane mourns him by investigating the incident. As it turns out, the massacre had a motive, and the hitman who committed the act may have been working for Dane's own father, the owner of a bank. As Dane closes in on the hitman (played by Sonny Landham, who would later co-star with Weathers in *Predator*), the action intensifies.

The Starmaker VHS tape is comprised of a two-part pilot of a television series that lasted only six episodes. Weathers would later star in a very similar television series called *Street Justice*, co-starring Bryan Genesse, which lasted two full seasons. As this pilot movie stands alone to represent the canceled show, it's fine for network programming and an acceptable vehicle for its star, who gives it his all. The best part about the whole thing is the title sequence, which features Weathers working out, undressing, taking a soapy shower, and then dressing himself again. Directed by Nicholas Sgarro and Charles Correll.

4Got10

2015 (Cinedigm DVD) (djm)

After a bloody shootout at a drug deal gone bad in the desert, a guy named Brian Barnes (Johnny Messner) wakes up wounded and with a memory loss of who he is or how he came to be in the middle of this unfortunate situation. A sheriff (Michael Pare) and his rookie deputy show up to gauge the aftermath, and when the sheriff decides to steal the leftover drugs and cash (both totaling over six million), the sheriff murders his deputy, but then gets shot by the guy with amnesia, not realizing that guy was still alive. Barnes jumps in a van with all the goods, drives off, and tries to remember the whole set-up. Meanwhile, the sheriff survives and is taken to the hospital to have surgery, and a DEA agent named Rooker (Dolph Lundgren) is called in to investigate the strange circumstance in which the sheriff survived a shooting that left his deputy dead by the sheriff's own gun. Add to the mix a ruthless drug lord (Danny Trejo), whose son was actually the deputy who was killed, and you've got an explosive mix of dangerous characters who are all basically after the same thing: the truth and the cash.

A nifty enough premise that might have looked okay on paper, but as a film, *4Got10* (terrible title) is a piece of low-rent garbage from filmmakers who still think flashing nom de plumes like "The Kid" and "The Broad" across the screen every time a new character is introduced is cool. The entire movie adds up to a sack of hot air, and action star Lundgren is relegated to supporting status, and this might be the first time I've ever seen him look like he's in physical pain when he walks to wherever his marks were on set. He doesn't get into the action much, and with Trejo in the role of "The Drug Lord" his role is interchangeable with any other twenty films he's done in the last decade. But, seriously: *4Got10* is a turkey, and certainly amongst Lundgren's worst.

Foxtrap

1986 (Orion VHS) (djm)

Private eye Thomas Fox (Fred "The Hammer" Williamson) lands a case that pays more money than he's ever earned on any job. A young heiress has fled the country, and her last known whereabouts is in France, and his job is to find her with only that clue. He takes the first flight to Cannes (where the 1985 Cannes Film Festival is underway), and once he starts asking questions about the girl, he begins to realize that some bad guys are on his trail, ahead of him, behind him, and all around, making sure that he doesn't find her. Once he finds her, it becomes apparent that she is a high-class call girl, and he's been lied to from the very beginning, but he brings her back anyway to collect the rest of his money. When he delivers her, his employer (played by Christopher Connelly) has her killed for reasons that don't really concern Fox, but what *is* of concern to him is that if he doesn't kill his employer first, he'll be the next one to die.

What struck me about *Foxtrap* is that Williamson (who also directed) allows himself to get beat up a lot, which I found surprising. Guys get the drop on him all the time in the movie (even a gay guy, who manages to prove a point to him after making a slur), and he complains at one point that he keeps getting knocked out and hit in the head. That said, Williamson is sure to give himself at least one gratuitous sex scene with a French starlet (of which there are several throughout the film), and by the end of the picture, he is in good Hammer form, stomping on long cigars, shooting up villains, and living to carry on his legacy to a proposed sequel called *The Fox and the Cobra*, which sadly never materialized. Released smack in the center of a prolific career in action films, Williamson's *Foxtrap* is certainly what it advertises, and its only shortcomings are made up for in its earnest delivery. I liked it.

Freedom Strike

1998 (Allumination DVD) (CD)

Tom Dickson (Michael Dudikoff) is the head of a special ops team known as Freedom Strike. He leads the team on a mission to shut down the nuclear capability in Syria. Once a ceasefire has been reached, the American president (played by James Karen) meets with various leaders to sign an agreement that will bring peace. An American journalist unknowingly brings in two terrorists as his camera crew, who attempt to assassinate the president, but instead the Syrian president is shot in the mayhem. The terrorists use the incident against the US, threatening a nuclear war. The president thinks the only way out is to strike first with the nukes regardless of any collateral damage.

Dickson knows how precise his team is and talks the president into allowing them to go in first and stop the terrorists before they can strike at the US.

Freedom Strike isn't much better than most of Dudikoff's other late-career military thrillers. It was a step above *Crash Dive* but overall we pretty much know the story and have seen it all before. There's a bit more hand-to-hand fighting in this one, which is fine, but it's still a bit sporadic and not consistently entertaining. Dudikoff is likable as always and seeing Tone Loc (*The Adventures of Ford Fairlane*) in the film was a treat. While not one of Dudikoff's best, it's still passably watchable. Directed by Jerry P. Jacobs (*A Dangerous Place*).

From Noon Till Three

1976 (MGM DVD) (djm)

Graham Dorsey (Charles Bronson) and his gang of bank robbers prepare to pull off a heist that will make them all rich. He has a dream the night before that spooks him, and he gets the feeling that he should let the guys go off and do the robbery without him. They ride up to a beautiful home on a hill, hoping to score one more horse (because Dorsey's horse had to be put down), and the woman of the house—Amanda (Jill Ireland)—lies to them, telling them that she doesn't have a horse to spare. Dorsey backs up her story, which puts him in a position to sit the robbery out. His gang rides off to town, and Dorsey spends the afternoon with Amanda—from noon till three. In those three hours, Dorsey manages to melt her icy heart (she's a bitter widow) and fall head over heels in love with her. They make love, go swimming in a nearby creek, have lunch, and dance the hours away. By three o'clock, news arrives that Dorsey's gang was captured and will be hung in expediency, but Dorsey has to leave because the authorities were alerted that he was staying with Amanda, and in a strange turn of events, he switches places with a traveling dentist, who is killed and thought to be Dorsey, while Dorsey himself is apprehended for being a salesman who swindles money from simple folk, and he's put in prison for a year. Meanwhile, Amanda thinks he's dead, and within a year's time, Amanda's story has become a bestselling novel and play, and her tale of love has inspired hearts all over the world. She goes back to being an icy-hearted widow of sorts, and when Dorsey eventually gets out of prison and visits her, things get strange and almost surreal for him as she doesn't believe he's who he says he is, as his legend and her memory of him have been blown out of proportion in her mind. The end of this film is shockingly depressing, and it left me in a stupor.

A radical film from Charles Bronson, *From Noon Till Three* is like no other movie ever made. Is it an action movie? No, not really. It's not really a comedy or a drama either, so what is it? It's a movie unique unto itself, and because Bronson plays a gunslinger/bank robber in the film, I've decided to review it here, but I'm not certain it would appeal to many of his fans, or anyone else reading this book. If you're a Bronson completist, you absolutely must see it. If you

want to see something that will shatter your mind and explode your heart, see it. Bronson is fantastic in it. It's one of his best performances, but it just astounds me that he and his wife Jill Ireland readily agreed to appear in it together. It's devastating. Written and directed by Frank D. Gilroy, who also wrote the novel it is based on.

Fugitive Mind

1999 (Avalanche DVD) (djm)

American Ninja's Michael Dudikoff stars in this conspiracy thriller about an everyman named Robert Dean who begins having horrific waking nightmares and visions that suggest he is either having a mental breakdown or that his mind has been tampered with. As he begins to lose his cool and cause scenes with those people who care about him the most, a plot thickens: He was part of a covert government experiment when he was in the military, and his whole purpose in life is to assassinate a senator. Just like in *The Manchurian Candidate*, Robert is turned on by a code phrase, and just like that he becomes a machine, but luck is on his side when he accidentally runs into a former girlfriend (played by Heather Langenkamp), who tries to get him to remember who he is and the day he was taken from her years ago.

Having Dudikoff engage in some brawls and chases helps this low-budget effort from director Fred Olen Ray, and I stayed interested until the very end. Dudikoff is almost always very watchable, and while *Fugitive Mind* is a bit of a potboiler, it does have two good leads and some action, which keeps things moving. It isn't for everybody, but if you're a Dudikoff completist like me, then maybe someday you'll want to see it.

Full Contact

1992 (Columbia Tristar VHS) (djm)

Luke Powers (Jerry Trimble, former kickboxing champion) comes to the slums of Los Angeles to visit his brother, but finds out that his brother was just killed after an illegal kickboxing match. Angry and vengeful, Powers begins his own investigation into his brother's murder and decides to enter in the underground fight circuit to get to the bottom of things. He takes on a trainer and makes a few friends (one of whom is a stripper). After fighting his way through all of the toughest fighters, Powers discovers that his trainer is his brother's murderer.

Shot in and around a crumbling, urban area of Los Angeles, this tight little fight movie is actually pretty good. It's got some great character moments and takes its time allowing you to get to know the characters a bit before shoving you into the fight scenes. Trimble is good in one of his better roles. The director, Rick Jacobson, remade this as *Dragon Fire* (1993), a post-apocalyptic fight movie starring Dominic La Banca, who plays "Laker Powers." *Full Contact* is much better. Robert King and Beverly Gray wrote both films. If you pay attention, you'll notice that Michael Jai White has a small role in this film.

Full Impact (a.k.a. American Streetfighter 2)
1993 (eve DVD) (djm)

Gary Daniels (working here for Silver Screen International and Cine Excel Entertainment) stars as an ex-cop turned bounty hunter named Jared Taskin who is obsessed with finding a serial killer of women who goes by the name "Death Touch" in the media. Taskin's life was cruelly disrupted by Death Touch years previously, and he's vowed to catch and/or kill him come hell or high water, but his former chief on the force puts up blockers every time Taskin wants to get in on an investigation. With his incredible skill at martial arts, Taskin fights his way through cops and scumbags to his primary target, who happens to be his best friend and his former partner.

Daniels literally fights every male character he meets in this movie. If he isn't butterfly-kicking two bad guys at once, he's punching, dodging, or being flipped around by thugs, and *Full Impact* would be a skeleton of a movie if you took the fights out of it. At almost ninety minutes, it probably has seventy minutes of fighting in it. It's nuts. Daniels was in his longhaired bleached blond phase here, and his fans will find plenty of what they like best about him here. All others may become exhausted after fifteen minutes of it. It's cheap, but it delivers. Directed by David Huey (*Capital Punishment* with Daniels) and Marc Messenger.

Furious
1984 (Leomark DVD) (djm)

An introspective fighter named Simon (Simon Rhee) lives in the wilderness with a band of children, whom he trains (silently) in kung fu. His mate is killed by a mountain man who is after a piece of an amulet which, when connected with two other pieces, forms a magic talisman. Simon leaves the comfort of his haven and embarks on a spiritual journey, which leads him to the city, where the cunning Spiritual Master (Phillip Rhee) lives and is surrounded by followers. Spiritual Master (his character's name) gives Simon plenty of advice and wisdom, but it's all to fool him into relinquishing his piece of the amulet. When Spiritual Master reveals himself to be evil, Simon follows him to the end of the world where they have a fantastical battle over the magic talisman.

Shot in seven days and featuring early film roles for the brothers Rhee, *Furious* is a lost curiosity that has been all but forgotten. It has the feel of a student film, with abstract, odd touches like having one mystical character shooting chickens from his fingertips, and other characters behaving strangely (like, why does Simon live with a bunch of children in the wilderness?). Religious and mystical elements

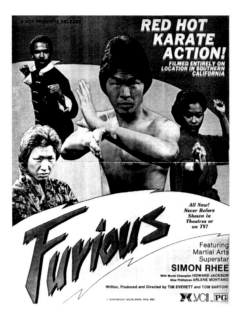

Promotional poster for *Furious*. Author's collection.

abound. It's interesting to see the Rhees in the early stages of their careers. It appeared to be that Simon was being groomed to be the action star, and Phillip was relegated to be a second-tier supporter, but as things turned out Phillip became the star with his *Best of the Best* series and Simon became *his* support. Look fast for future action star Loren Avedon (*King of the Kickboxers*) as a martial arts fighter. This was released theatrically in the US for a week. A VHS release happened, and then it faded into obscurity. Two versions of this film exist: One with a classical music underscoring, and the other with more upbeat music from porno movies. I saw the version with the classical music. Directed by Tim Everitt.

Future Fear
1997 (New Concorde DVD) (CD)

In the future, a virus has virtually wiped out the human race. This attack was orchestrated by General Wallace (Stacey Keach) who is trying to create a superior race. Dr. John Denniel (Jeff Wincott) is a scientist who has developed a cure that involves harvesting fetuses to extract the blood from them. His ex-wife Anna (Maria Ford) disagrees with his decision to allow them to grow to term but it may be the only way to save humanity. General Wallace has the upper hand as he plays one side against the other, and it's really a race against time to see which side will be victorious.

Future Fear is what happens when good performers chose the wrong project. There isn't anything that can be recommended about this Roger Corman production. It's plagued with major problems, the most important being the lack of any real cohesive story. It confusingly jumps around in the timeline and never really settles on one story to tell. Flashbacks happen so frequently that you are consistently losing your place in the film. This is the one and only

film directed by Lewis Baumander and his inability to successfully weave a story may be the reason. Bona fide action star Jeff Wincott (*Martial Outlaw, Martial Law II*) can be a solid and exciting lead in the right project. He's a decent actor and without question can handle his action scenes. None of this is evident in *Future Fear*; he mostly just quotes *Alice in Wonderland* and eats sandwiches and apes Bruce Willis in *Die Hard*. This is without question the least likable film on his resume. His character has several altercations with his ex-wife and more than anything else these confrontations are played for laughs. Maria Ford (*Ring of Fire 1* and *2*) is the ex-wife who is out to get him. There is little to no action, some ridiculous dialogue, and a serious lack of production value. All the talent involved has much more entertaining product for us to sample than this. Sadly, *Future Fear* is just a forgettable mess.

Future Hunters
1986 (Avid Home Entertainment VHS) (JS)

The more attentive and voracious action fans will recognize Australian-born Richard Norton as the prolific martial arts instructor and action movie all-star who once served as a bodyguard for Mick Jagger but is probably most well-remembered for his first on-screen role as Kyo, the deadly masked ninja in the final fight of the Chuck Norris classic *The Octagon*. Between his early '80s roles in flicks like *The Octagon* and *Gymkata* and the explosively prolific latter half of his career where he continues to act, produce, and be a highly sought-after fight choreographer, Norton played a part in this obscure yet satisfying VHS-only 1986 Cirio H. Santiago action flick. Norton's role, however short-lived, is that of Matthew: a *Mad Max*-styled character in a post-holocaust world who's desperately trying to attain the spear that pierced Christ during his crucifixion. It's told that this godless artifact possesses the power to transport the holder back in time before the holocaust, and should it be placed back in its sheath, its evil reign shall cease and stop the holocaust from ever happening. I guess you could say the power of Christ compels him?! I just couldn't help myself. Matthew dishes out a heaping helping of automatic gunfire and ass-kicking action (with entertaining retaliatory attacks) before he gets his hands on the spear, which then transports him to the past, giving him the chance to save the world. This is where the movie mutates into what feels like a completely different flick. Matthew happens upon an anthropologist and her boyfriend named Slade (played by Robert Patrick a.k.a. T-1000 in one of his first roles!) and after saving the girl from a gang of rapist bikers is mortally wounded; his world-saving quest is passed to the two hapless twenty-somethings. Exit Norton. The plot from then on consists of the anthropologist girlfriend dead-set on cracking this mystery ("This could be my BIG find!") and dragging Slade along as they set out to find a missing professor who is a scholar on the subject of the spear. This sends them through a mildly thrilling adventure across the globe filled with bumbling hit men, decent low-budget action, and perfunctory chase scenes. However, aside from Norton's opening performance, there are some serious highlights: a slow-mo kung fu fight scene featuring Bruce Le and Jang Lee Hwang, plenty of fire power mixed with spears and swords via ancient tribes on the attack, and what might be an unintentionally funny Nazi undertone.

This one warrants a view not only for the curious layout of the flick, but also for the wide array of low-budget action entertainment. One question remains: can they stick the spear back in the sheath and save the world? You'll have to feed this one to your VCR to find out, my friends. One more interesting note: Norton and Patrick met again on screen just one year later in *Equalizer 2000* (another Santiago flick), but this time, Norton's character was named Slade. Gotta admit: it's one meaty moniker!

Future Kick

1991 (New Concorde DVD) (CD)

"There are only two things I'm gonna take: your body and your soul!"

Walker (Don "The Dragon" Wilson) is a Cyberon, a member of a race of androids created to protect the world from crime. Eventually his race realizes that the corporate world is full of criminals and they turn on their creators. A corporate police force is put into place and the humans destroy all the Cyberons, except for one: Walker. When the creator of a virtual reality simulator is murdered by a man who harvests organs to sell to the corporate companies, his wife Nancy (Meg Foster) sets out to find the truth. With the world being so dangerous and corrupt, she can't do it alone. She meets Walker and offers him $500,000 to track down who was responsible for her husband's death. He takes the job and will see it to the end . . . even if he ends up extinct.

Future Kick is a Roger Corman-produced action film that was written and directed by Damian Klaus. For one reason or another, this was his one and only film. Don "The Dragon" Wilson (*Bloodfist*) is the sole draw to see the film, but even he isn't able to save it. It's a mess from the start with a paper-thin plot and overly slow pacing. Wilson isn't given much to do and rarely takes off his bulky sunglasses. During the finale, he has a showdown with the late Chris Penn (*Best of the Best*), but unfortunately little else happens. In fact, for an action film, there are more bared breasts per minute than fights, so if that's up your alley, then *Future Kick* will be perfect for you. Wilson's fans might want to stick to his *Bloodfist* movies instead.

Futuresport

1998 (Sony DVD) (CD)

"Yes, man, get it, man! All right, that's enough. Oh, excuse me, I really hate to break up this beautiful moment but don't you have a game to play?"

In the year 2025, Obike Fixx (Wesley Snipes) has created a new pastime known as Futuresport that's used to keep gangs from fighting and to settle their differences. Tre Ramsey (Dean Cain) was the first breakout star of the game. As time has passed, the fame and fortune have turned his life into a popularity contest. The Hawaiian Liberation Organization is bent on causing a global war. When Tre loses the championship, he begins to question his worth, but with the help of reporter and former flame Alex Torres (Vanessa Williams) he is able to see the man he wants to be. He comes up with a plan to stage a game that will keep the two factions from going to war but only if the HLO can play by the rules.

Futuresport was a made-for-television film that debuted on ABC. It was a big deal at the time since Wesley Snipes (*Passenger 57*) was at the height of his career. The film itself is sort of hit and miss. There are some strong ideas and the actual sport of the title was fully realized in concept, but we just don't get to see much of it until the final moments of the film. The main issue is that the script is weak. Thankfully, the cast is able to make it watchable, even if it doesn't offer up much else. Dean Cain (*Max Havoc: Ring of Fire*) does a great job as Tre Ramzey, who takes a highly unlikable character and transforms him into a hero. Every lost hero needs a woman to help him find who he is and Vanessa Williams is a perfect fit for her character Alex Torres. Snipes (who also produced) sports some crazy dreads and a thick Jamaican accent. There is little to no action except in very short doses at the end of the film. It was directed by Ernest Dickerson (*Surviving the Game*).

Future War

1994 (Eve Digital DVD) (djm)

Before Daniel Bernhardt starred in the *Bloodsport* sequels, he starred in this awful exploitation movie that he probably wished he'd never done. He plays a nameless character from another world who thinks that Earth is heaven. He battles dinosaurs (obviously puppets) with martial arts, and he befriends a nun and some other assorted characters who live in buildings furnished with lots of cardboard boxes. Bernhardt spends most of his screen time hitting and kicking dinosaurs and a cyborg-styled assassin (Robert Z'Dar).

This movie would be a blemish on anyone's record, and it's an embarrassment any way you look at it. Bernhardt is hardly to blame—he looks very young and skinny in it and his English is appropriately rusty (remember, he's playing an alien). The story makes no sense whatsoever, and the cheapness of it recalls the collected works of Donald G. Jackson (*Hell Comes To Frogtown*). This was directed by Anthony Doublin.

Gale Force

2001 (Artisan DVD) (djm)

The first ten minutes of this movie are unbelievable. If you thought no one had the balls to rip off *Last Action Hero* (which rips off an entire genre), then think again. Treat Williams plays a tough cop named Sam, who is introduced in an extended action scene in the exact same way Schwarzenegger was introduced in his first scene in *LAH*. It turns out that the whole action/chase scene was literally lifted from *LAH* and inserts were shot to make it look like Treat Williams was doing all the driving and shooting. I'm dead serious. It's an incredible first ten minutes. After the title sequence, the film goes on a completely different track. Williams, who has been suspended for his insane behavior in the first ten minutes of the movie (see it and believe it), is offered the chance to be a part of a reality television show similar to *Survivor* where real people are on a tropical island searching for buried treasure in teams. The catch is that a team of pirates (real soldiers who would only be playing the part of pirates) make it that much more difficult for them to find the treasure. To make matters worse, a "gale force" storm is about to sweep through and kill all of them.

Jim Wynorski directed this film under the pseudonym Jay Andrews, and he explained on the commentary how he was able to incorporate the footage from *Last Action Hero* into the footage he shot. Michael Dudikoff plays the leader of the soldiers who pose as pirates, and it's one of the few times he's played a villain. The soldiers, as it turns out, end up forming a *Cliffhanger*-type plot to steal the money for themselves and kill everyone on the island. Tim Thomerson is in it too as one of the contestants on the show. He has the best fight scene in the film. As far as "action" movies go, this isn't a very good one, but it exceeded my expectations as an exploitation film, and it's surprisingly entertaining.

Gallowwalkers

2013 (Lionsgate DVD) (djm)

In a fantastical, forlorn, and distant alternate Old West, a cursed gunslinger known as Aman (Wesley Snipes) walks the desert wastes carrying his curse: every soul he guns down will return to haunt him until he kills them again with a blade. By now, a small legion of his victims has banded together to hunt him down, and their leader, the skinless Kansa (Kevin Howarth), is hellbent on relieving Aman of his soul. Aman takes on an apprentice named Fabulos (Riley Smith) to help him on his quest, and a final showdown between them and the undead horde brings them to the brink of an uncertain destiny.

It sounds cool, right? Everything about *Gallowwalkers* suggests that it would turn out to be the movie that brought Wesley Snipes from the direct-to-video doldrums and back onto the glorious big screen, but it just wasn't meant to be. Filmed in Namibia, Africa, in 2010, this was the last movie he shot before being sent to prison for tax evasion. Originally slated to star Chow Yun-

Fat, this confusing and profoundly muddled movie lacks any coherence or relevance, despite being intriguing from the first frames. Snipes is okay in the film, but the film itself just doesn't work. Writer/director Andrew Goth fills the film with interesting looking undead creatures, which would be more suited to a *Hellraiser* movie than an action film, so horror and sci-fi fans may be interested. Action fans and Snipes devotees will be disappointed.

Game of Death

1978 (Shout Factory DVD) (djm)

Billy Lo (Bruce Lee) is a burgeoning kung fu action star making movies and romancing his singer girlfriend (played by Colleen Camp) when a crime syndicate demands that he sign a contract with them, with the intention of extorting him. He refuses, and they make an attempt on his life, so he makes the decision to fake his death to fool the syndicate. Gathering his strength, he plans an elaborate revenge on them, taking on the champions of the syndicate one by one.

This is the infamous movie that was patched together and released five years after Bruce Lee's tragic and untimely death. Lee had shot and directed footage for a film he had intended to make before *Enter the Dragon*, but he left the production to star in that film instead. He died before *Enter the Dragon* was released, leaving behind an unfinished film with several key fight scenes (mostly) completed. In the interim, the director of *Enter the Dragon*, Robert Clouse, was brought in to re-edit and film new scenes to connect what Lee had intended. The results are painfully conspicuous and obvious, as the few minutes Lee appears in are basically just the fight scenes at the very end of the film. Two doubles were used to pose as Lee throughout the film—one of whom was Yuen Biao—but neither one is remotely adequate as a stand-in. Scenes of the doubles wearing huge sunglasses or fake beards—or cowering in shadows—are what constitute Lee's appearance, and it's embarrassing. Lee's climactic fight scenes with Bob Wall, Dan Inosanto, and Kareem Abdul-Jabbar are just a taste of frosting on what might have been a delicious cake. Sadly, this patchwork film is only good for viewing Lee's fights out of context. There is controversy over "lost footage" that Lee had shot for what was intended for a film called *The Game of Death*, and documentaries have covered the topic. Chuck Norris is billed in the finished product, but his appearance in it is linked only by stock footage from *The Way of the Dragon* with Lee, so don't be fooled. Sammo Hung also appears in a fight scene with Bob Wall. The best thing about the movie (aside from Lee's fights) is the cool James Bond-esque score by John Barry.

Game of Death

2010 (Sony DVD) (djm)

Diabetic CIA agent Marcus Jones (Wesley Snipes) takes a job bodyguarding a wealthy broker named Frank Smith (Robert Davi), who has a heart attack on the way to an important appointment. A band of cutthroat ex-CIA agents gone rogue have been planning to take Smith hostage and steal all of his money (around 100 million), but his heart attack diverts their plan as Marcus rushes him to the hospital. The rogue agents (who include Gary Daniels and Zoë Bell) raid the hospital, killing anybody who gets in their way of kidnapping Smith, but Marcus throws a huge wrench in their gears as he defends his client.

Surprisingly (almost shockingly) entertaining and fulfilling as a vehicle for Snipes, *Game of Death* is probably his best film to be released directly to video. He puts in extra effort to perform in some great action and fight scenes, and his co-stars Daniels and Bell are both welcome in the film as the villains. The final fight between Snipes and Daniels is pretty good, but the best fight in the film has Snipes taking on several guys on in a packed psych ward. If Snipes had made more movies like this one, he might have made his way back to the big screen if he hadn't served prison time. The script by Megan Brown is solid, with lots of little character quirks (such as his diabetes), and the direction by Giorgio Serafini (*Hard Rush* and *The Blood of Redemption* with Dolph Lundgren) is more than satisfactory. Simon Rhee also appears.

Game Over

2005 (Maverick DVD) (CD)

"Seems like fighting is the only thing I'll be good at."

Victor Know (Andre McCoy) has just recently been released from prison. He has a son he has never met and his wife has left him. He has grown frustrated with trying to find a job when no one wants to hire a felon. Things reach an all-time low when Vic saves Violet (Latrice Harper) from being attacked. She hires him as her personal driver but it's just not enough to get by. Victor finds himself joining an underground fighting league, one run as if it were a video game. The catch is, he never knows who or when he will fight. He can be attacked at any time, which is beginning to make his life hell. No money in the world is worth missing the chance to spend time with his son but "The Ref" (Daz Crawford) isn't going to back down and Victor will have to fight for his life until the game is over.

Game Over is one of those high-ambition projects with an incredibly low budget. The way the fight club in the film is proposed—the idea of being watched at all times, never knowing when or who—is a cool idea. There are many fights in the film with adequate choreography, but only one or two stand out. McCoy fights a flamboyant

stylist who keeps pricking him with needles, and that was interesting and odd. There's also a fight involving playing cards that stood out from the rest of the fights. The moment everyone will be waiting for is the showdown between McCoy and Crawford, but it's a letdown. The film looks cheap and the acting doesn't get much more wooden than what's on display here. If you like this, also see *T.K.O.* with both McCoy and Crawford. Directed by Peter Sullivan.

The Game Plan

2007 (Disney DVD) (CD)

"Hi, we've never met before. You were married to my mom, Sara. Sara Kelly. My name is Peyton. I'm your daughter."

Joe Kingman (Dwayne Johnson) is one of the top players in the NFL. He's selfish, obnoxious, and has a tough time relating to others. All he seems to care about is money, fame, and himself. Then one afternoon, he hears a knock at the door and it's Peyton (Madison Pettis), the eight-year-old daughter he never knew he had. Joe isn't very receptive to her being there but his ex-wife is in Africa for a month and according to Peyton, he needs to watch her. Things immediately change for Joe, in ways he never expected. He has always been alone, and having Peyton there forces him to change his ways. With a championship game coming up, he has to decide what is more important to him in life: football or his daughter. It won't be easy for someone who is so self-centered to learn to love someone other than himself.

When Dwayne Johnson (*Snitch*) gets it right, he can be the perfect lead for a family film. *The Game Plan* is a sweet film that Johnson helps to carry with the help of the adorable Madison Pettis (*Mostly Ghostly*). Johnson can balance humor and drama far better than many would expect. The only action present in the film is during the football scenes. There's no fighting at all, just some rough-looking tackles. The film is still endearing and has tons of heart, which tends to be rare in films today. Director Andy Fickman (*Race to Witch Mountain*, also with Johnson) is able to lead the cast on a truly uplifting and funny film. Since this was a hit, Johnson went on to star in several other family-centric action-type films, which is where he seems to be most comfortable.

Gangland

2001 (Razor DVD) (CD)

In 2010, a nuclear holocaust has wiped out much of the population and in the fallout, a plague is now eating away the flesh of many of the survivors. A brilliant scientist (played by Tim Thomerson) has discovered a cure. He and his family must flee Atlanta and deliver it to those who can help, but things take a quick change when they are kidnapped by Lucifer (Vincent Klyn), the leader of the gang who wants it for himself to divvy out as he pleases. The brother of a guy named Jared (Sasha Mitchell) is murdered, and Jared is captured by Lucifer's gang and thrown into a cell. In the neighboring cell is Derek (Costas Mandylor). Jared wants to avenge his brother's death, and Derek has a plan to help him. After a daring escape, they team up with Alexis (Kathleen Kinmont) to plot out an intricate plan to infiltrate the stronghold, save the scientist, mankind, and put an end to Lucifer's evil reign.

A riff on Albert Pyun's *Cyborg*, Art Camacho's *Gangland* has no new twists or surprises to make it feel fresh, but what it does offer up is a cast composed of genre favorites doing the things that they do best. The DVD cover art is misleading, and while Ice-T and Coolio do appear in the film, their scene is incredibly short and unrelated to the core plot. The real stars of the film are Sasha Mitchell (*Kickboxer 2, Class of 1999 II*), Costas Mandylor (*Fist of the North Star*), and Kathleen Kinmont (*Renegade, CIA: Codename Alexia*). Each of the actors does a fine job in their respective roles, especially delivering where it counts: the action scenes. While the fights are not overly stylized or brutal, they manage to entertain on a basic level. What are three heroes without a villain? In the role of gang leader Lucifer, we have none other than Mr. Vincent Klyn (from *Cyborg*) himself. While his role here isn't nearly as iconic as his part in *Cyborg*, he is still be a formidable foe. The always-reliable Tim Thomerson plays it straight and can just bring a smirk to your face by being present. Kristanna Loken from *Terminator 3* has some flashback scenes. The production design and music are rather underwhelming but since the cast is so likable it's easy to forgive. Director Camacho wore several different hats in the production including fight choreographer, co-producer, and stuntman. This type of commitment is commendable even if the end result was not his best work. If anything, it's a rather interesting film on the resumes of some great talent.

Get Carter

2000 (Warner DVD) (djm)

Jack Carter (Sylvester Stallone) is a bruiser working in Las Vegas for a local gangster when he hears about his brother's accidental death. He leaves his job to attend the funeral in Seattle, and right away he gets in everybody's business, asking around, poking and prodding for answers on why his brother was drinking and driving that night, particularly since his brother wasn't known for drinking. His brother's family barely knows Carter, and when he ingratiates himself into their lives, he sort of rubs everyone the wrong way. As he delves deeper into his brother's affairs, he uncovers a sordid and checkered path, which gets uglier and more shocking as he goes along. Amongst his brother's associates are a porn maven (played by Mickey Rourke), a shady billionaire (Alan Cumming), a drug-addled escort (Rhona Mitra), and the owner of a nightclub where his brother worked. The nightclub owner (played by the original Jack

Jack Carter (Sylvester Stallone) in the remake of *Get Carter*. Author's collection.

Cyrus Paice (Mickey Rourke) and Jack Carter (Sylvester Stallone) in *Get Carter*. Author's collection.

A bruiser out for revenge, Jack Carter (Sylvester Stallone) can take a hit in *Get Carter*. Author's collection.

In *Get Carter*, this elevator is too small for the three of these guys, including Sylvester Stallone (center). Author's collection.

Carter, Michael Caine) is the key to the mystery, and when Carter comes to understand that his niece (Rachel Leigh Cook) was filmed while being raped, he works himself into a rage, willing to hunt anyone and everyone down to reclaim her honor and avenge his brother's death.

Meant as a follow-up to Stallone's *Eye See You*, which was supposed to be his comeback after a long hiatus from movies since *Cop Land*, *Get Carter* ended up being his re-entry since *Eye See You* was shelved after disastrous test screenings (under the name *The Outpost*). This was a really bad time for Stallone. Warner Brothers took out full color spreads in the Los Angeles Times to promote it, and when it was released, it grossed less than seven million over the weekend, tapping out at under 15 in its entire release, which was a disaster. It was a departure for Stallone (after his dramatic turn in *Cop Land*), which in retrospect might have been a mistake at the time. As it is, I like the film for giving Stallone a strong role to play, though it's fairly one-note, but ultimately his star power shines through. The directing style (from Stephen Kay) is a little too modernized and frenetic in the editing for no good reason, but the earnest performances by the interesting cast makes up for the film's shortcomings. Stallone's next theatrical release was *Driven*, which also didn't do him any favors.

Get Smart

2008 (Warner DVD) (CD)

"I don't know. Were you thinking, *Holy shit, holy shit, a swordfish almost went through my head*?"

Maxwell Smart (Steve Carell) is an analyst for a covert government agency that supplies the best spies available. Smart dreams of becoming an agent one day, much like his co-worker Agent 23 (Dwayne Johnson). The agency is attacked and The Chief (Alan Arkin) has no choice but to promote Smart to operational status, and he's partnered with Agent 99 (Anne Hathaway). Though she's displeased with the decision, she's a trouper—even when Smart's ineptitude continually causes them to have their covers blown, amongst other blunders.

The villainous group KAOS seems to be behind it all, and the two agents will have to infiltrate their inner sanctum, which becomes a nearly impossible task because of Smart's bumbling, bombastic klutziness. With time running out and the president's (James Caan) life in danger, Smart will have to wise up if he's to save the day.

Steve Carell (*Evan Almighty*) is no Don Adams (the original Maxwell Smart on the cult hit TV series from the '60s) and this film version fails to capture what many loved about the original program. It tries far too hard to be funny and by jamming one joke after another down our throats, it just irks. Dwayne Johnson's ability to be genuinely amusing is impressive but he's only a minor character in the film. He has a couple of short action scenes, one of which involves some intense (and impressive) stunt work. It was an interesting turn for him (and his first film where he dropped "The Rock" from his credit), but this role could have been played by anyone—he's much better than this. Despite that, the film was a huge success and it helped propel him forward in a time when his career was becoming stagnant. Also featuring appearances by the underused Terry Crews (*The Expendables*) and WWE wrester Dalip Singh (*The Longest Yard*), who manages to be a scene-stealer. It's directed by Peter Segal who was also responsible for *The Longest Yard* remake.

Ghost Rock

2003 (Lionsgate DVD) (djm)

A western with some martial arts action, *Ghost Rock* is a low-budget vehicle for star and screenwriter Michael Worth from *To Be the Best* and *Final Impact*. He stars as a drifter cowboy named John Slaughter who wanders back to his hometown Ghost Rock, which has been overtaken by a nasty lawman named Jack Pickett (Gary Busey). Years previously, when John was a boy, he saw his whole family and half the town get murdered by Pickett and his men, and so John's mission is to seek revenge and put order back to it any way he knows how, which is mainly to use his martial arts skills, which he picked up over the years from an Asian mentor, played by James Hong. On John's side is a vengeful ghost named Savannah Starr (played by Jenya Lano from the underrated post-apocalyptic movie *Deathlands: Homeward Bound*), who goes around slaying bad guys right and left before John has a chance to do it all himself.

Michael Worth is an underrated action star, with only a handful of martial action films under his belt. *Ghost Rock* is something that he drummed up out of his own volition and it's an interesting little movie. It's not as crazy a western hybrid as say Gene Quintano's *Dollar for the Dead* or Sam Raimi's *The Quick and the Dead* (which this movie emulates in more ways than one), but when Worth starts busting out his martial arts moves, I definitely raised my eyebrows in surprise. Some people will enjoy it more than others. I had a good time with it. Directed by Dustin Rikert.

G.I. Joe: Retaliation

2013 (Paramount DVD) (djm)

The belated sequel to the big-budget hit from 2009 (*G.I. Joe: The Rise of Cobra*), *Retaliation* stars Dwayne "The Rock" Johnson as Roadblock, one of the secondary characters from the cartoon series. He and Duke (Channing Tatum, the star of the first film) and the rest of the Joes are on a mission, when they are attacked and wiped out by Cobra forces on the order of the president of the United States (Jonathan Pryce), who is actually a genetically modified Cobra agent known as Zartan. With Duke and all of the other Joes dead, Roadblock and only two other G.I. Joes (who include Adrianne Palicki as Lady Jaye) survive and have to *keep* surviving in order to save ninja-like Snake Eyes (Ray Park) from captivity so that he can help them bring Cobra to its knees. In the process of saving Snake Eyes, they make allegiances with Storm Shadow (Byung-hun Lee) and Jinx, both formidable martial artists who help them lay siege to Cobra's infrastructure. Later on, Roadblock calls on the original G.I. Joe, played by Bruce Willis, and together, as a team, they go up against Cobra Commander and his forces.

A major disappointment as a sequel and as an action film, *Retaliation* bears the brand of a desperate studio in search of a franchise. I wasn't a big fan of the first film, but it had elements that I appreciated. The first misstep of this movie is that it literally kills off its roster of potential stars and characters in the first quarter of the film. Roadblock was never a central character in the cartoon, and Dwayne Johnson is too big of a personality to carry a movie that should have relied on an ensemble but instead revolves around his character. By the time Bruce Willis's character was introduced, the movie had completely exhausted my goodwill towards it, and it was sad to realize that Paramount was hinging the *G.I. Joe* franchise on such an ill-guided and purposeless script. Some nice moments of clever stunt and martial arts action (the scene with the bungee cables astride a mountain involving a score of ninjas, for instance) help cut a compelling trailer, but overall, *Retaliation* is one of the more impressionable big-screen travesties I've seen in a long time. Korean actor Byung-hun Lee (from *I Saw the Devil* and *Red 2*) commands your attention every time he's on screen, and Ray Stevenson (from *Punisher: War Zone*) appears as the villain Firefly. He has a fight with Johnson. Directed by John Chu.

G.I. Joe: The Rise of Cobra

2009 (Paramount DVD) (CD)

It's never easy for a young boy to brave the streets alone. Cold and hungry, he wanders around trying to find someplace he can score something to eat. Looking into the windows of strangers, he finds one open and sees a feast spread out on the table. He tries to sneak in only to be confronted by another child, one with fighting abilities much like his. The boy's master (Gerald

Okamura from *Ninja Academy*) stops the fight between the two boys and invites the little thief in for dinner, giving him the name "Snake Eyes." The other boy is known as "Storm Shadow," and the two quickly become rivals. They grow up and go their separate ways, but not before Shadow kills their master and disappears. Snake Eyes (Ray Park, who played Darth Maul in *Star Wars: Episode 1*) takes a vow of silence and eventually becomes part of an ultra secret team (which requires him to conceal his identity), swearing to protect the world from terrorists. Four warheads with the potential to wipe out billions have gone missing and Storm Shadow (Byun-Hun Lee) and his team are behind it. The two childhood rivals will once again do battle, but this time, it will be to the death.

Ray Park (a gold medalist in wushu) is one of the most underused talents working in action and martial arts films today. Though we never see his face, Park delivers an electric performance as Snake Eyes, giving the audience everything they could want from a live-action version of the character, which is based on a toy line and a cartoon series. Park brushed up on his wushu skills for the film and it shows in the various fight scenes he is featured in, most notably the final battle with Byun-Hun Lee (from *I Saw the Devil* and *Red*). The film never quite captures what the whole G.I. Joe phenomenon was, but Park is once again a standout. Also featuring Dennis Quaid, Channing Tatum, and Marlon Wayons, amongst others. Directed by Stephen Sommers (*The Mummy*).

The Girl From the Naked Eye

2011 (Naedomi DVD) (djm)

Jason Yee from *Dark Assassin* starred, produced, and co-wrote this earnest vehicle film that prominently showcases his abilities as a martial artist and as an actor. *The Girl From the Naked Eye* takes its cues from pulpy mystery novels and comic books (namely *Sin City*), and it gives its down-on-his-luck hero Jake (Yee) some fighting skills, but he's the not the type of character who can always fight his way out of trouble. He gets beat up a lot and is forced to comply with a high criminal element, and he doesn't have a lot of luck. Jake loses his boss's Mercedes in a poker game, and he spends the next several years of his life working to pay off his debt working as a "driver" to call girls, including a sixteen-year-old runaway named Sandy (Samantha Streets), whom he has feelings for. When she's murdered in her apartment, Jake first goes after the owner of the Naked Eye—the nightclub where she worked—but when that lead goes nowhere, he goes after the next guy up on the food chain. Jake, whose luck ran out long ago, has nothing to lose by going for revenge, but he's got to keep himself alive if he's going to go all the way.

So much goes right with *The Girl From the Naked Eye* that it pains me to say that several things derailed it for me. First of all, Jason Yee is excellent. He looks great, he can act, and he's a more than capable martial artist and can handle action. Second, the movie looks great. It's well lit, edited, and scored. The supporting cast is good, too: Ron Yuan, a veteran stunt guy and fight choreographer, co-stars as the nightclub owner, and other supporting parts are played by Dominique Swain and Sasha Grey. But here's the problem: It seems to understand the material it was inspired by, but by throwing an incredible amount of sex, nudity, and profanity in its short running time (eighty-four minutes), it proves to be disingenuous. I would have loved to see the same movie—still "R"-rated but with a scaled-back portion of the elements that made the movie feel like it was made by misogynistic teenagers. I'm looking forward to seeing what Yee will do next. Hopefully it's a more mature project than *The Girl From the Naked Eye*. He's got potential.

G.I. Samurai (a.k.a. Time Slip)

1979 (Mill Creek DVD) (djm)

A modern Japanese squadron of soldiers literally slips through time several hundred years to the past to the warring era of shoguns and clans. The squad—fully equipped with jeeps, a truck, a tank, a helicopter, and tons of ammo and rocket launchers—quickly realize that they have been misplaced by cruel fate, and they are thrust into the middle of a war between two warring factions, intent on supremacy. The leader of the squadron—Lieutenant Iba (Sonny Chiba)—allows his men to interfere in the initial battle, and the realization hits him that he can give one warring side a massive upper hand, thus setting the course to change history. He befriends the Shogun of one of the sides—Kagetora (played by Isao Natsuyagi)—and the two of them (along with Iba's heavy and far superior artillery) are an unstoppable force. When Iba gets it in his head to conquer the land by his own design, he alienates Kagetora and infighting begins to set in with his own camp of time travelers. With a major battle to fight for supremacy, Iba and his men engage in a bloody (and incredible) war with the opposing Shogun and his army.

An interesting and introspective epic-scale action film with star Chiba at the center, *G.I. Samurai* is a fairly impressive pulp story with a jaw-dropping battle scene about ninety minutes in. Iba and his men take on thousands of samurai in one long battle, and watching them use machine guns, grenades, the helicopter, the tank, and their jeeps against the hordes is impressive. When Iba faces the opposing Shogun sword to sword (and using other weapons) the battle climaxes with a beheading. At times, the film dips into depraved melodrama (the soldiers take advantage of the women of the period and turn against themselves, murdering out of boredom), but at its heart, the film is a treatise on ambition and backstabbing. Directed by Kosei Saito.

Gladiator Cop: The Swordsman II

1994 (Monarch VHS) (djm)

A woeful motion picture by any standard, *Gladiator Cop* is something that by all intents and purposes shouldn't exist. A shirtless and tanned Lorenzo Lamas holding a sword graces the video box, but Lamas didn't shoot a single day on this film, and when he found out it was made and released to video without his permission, he sued and got the same amount of money he was paid for the original *Swordsman*. All of his short scenes in *Gladiator Cop* are outtakes and snippets from the first film, so scenes of him in this sequel show him driving, inspecting dead bodies in silence, and having seizures from the striking visions he sees (not to mention a truncated sex scene). Much more time is devoted to new footage that focuses on another character: a sleazy elderly millionaire who is seeking Alexander the Great's sword and who goes to several underground sword fight competitions where the fighters (who look like gladiators) fight to the death. In an incredibly obvious and conspicuous move, the filmmakers throw Lamas's character in a few of the fight scenes, but the actor who doubled him wears a full face mask every time, making it painfully clear that Lamas had nothing to do with the film.

An interesting fact about this film (other than the legal ramifications) is that it was "written" and directed by Nick Rotundo, who edited the first film. He later made a movie called *G2* with Daniel Bernhardt that has the same exact plot of this film, and not only that, but character actor James Hong (*Operation Golden Phoenix*, *Big Trouble in Little China*) plays the same exact character (named Parminion) with the same motivations in both films, which is strikingly odd. Knowing that, I highly advise avoiding both films.

The Glass Jungle

1989 (City Lights VHS) (djm)

If you wondered what happened to Lee Canalito, Sylvester Stallone's co-star in the underrated wrestling movie *Paradise Alley*, it took him nearly a decade to star in another film, which ended up being this unfortunate effort from Joseph Merhi and Richard Pepin, who would go on to form PM Entertainment, a factory of action films throughout the 1990s. Canalito (who was a real boxer) plays a palooka cabdriver, who might have had a chance at a boxing career once upon a time. He picks up a fare one afternoon who ends up getting him in the middle of a situation that sort of alters his destiny. He's asked to deliver a bag containing a bunch of cash, and when he is reluctant to do the "job," the FBI steps in and asks him to do it despite the danger involved. When he pisses the bad guys off, they kidnap his cute French girlfriend, which stirs him to go after the villains on his own, against the FBI's warnings. He uses his brutish strength (but not much smarts) and some archery equipment to accomplish his goals.

Poor Canalito. The years following *Paradise Alley* weren't real kind to him. He seems slower and more sluggish than he was in that film, and his awkward, Frankenstein-ish gait gives him a strange, uncomfortable presence on film. When he's engaged in some brawls, it's obvious that the choreography is wrong for him because his movements don't flow and his belated responses in the fights give away his inexperience as an on-screen fighter. There's a sleazy vibe running through the whole movie, which might be of some appeal to certain viewers, but I was put off by the whole thing. It's a shame to see Canalito in this. He waited too long to try movies again. Written and directed by Joseph Merhi and photographed by Richard Pepin.

The Glimmer Man

1996 (Warner DVD) (djm)

LA detective Campbell (Keenen Ivory Wayans) is following a trail of victims, all murdered by the same killer. Families are crucified together in their homes, and Campbell needs help because his case is going nowhere. Detective Cole (Steven Seagal) is transferred from New York to assist, and Cole has a penchant for Eastern philosophies and soft-spoken rules of wisdom that throw Campbell for a loop, particularly when Cole's methods actually begin yielding results. Cole suspects that the Russian mafia is somehow involved, and a conspiracy is brewing that neither of them quite understand until all of the clues are pieced together. When Cole's ex-wife is crucified by the serial killer, Cole takes it personally and drives his hits home harder than ever.

A murky and needlessly confusing plot for a simple premise bogs *The Glimmer Man* down a bit, but with Seagal in the center (at a prime stage of his career), the film still manages to be entertaining. He had just done *Under Siege 2: Dark Territory* (his most expensive film to date), and *The Glimmer Man* was a noticeable step down for him, despite having decent production values. Wayans doesn't add anything interesting to his role, and anyone else could have played his part with the same amount of effort. My favorite scene of the film has Seagal taking a lie detector test. Fans of Seagal will be surprised to see that he gets a bloody nose during the climactic fight. Directed by John Gray.

Global Effect

2002 (First Look DVD) (CD)

"No doctor, taking a shit without toilet paper is a mistake. This is a goddamn disaster!"

In a small South African village, a deadly virus surfaces and wipes out the town's entire population. The government levels the village in hopes of containing it to the one incident. A small boy escapes the blast but is found nearby, dead from the virus. Dr. Sera Levitt (Madchen Amick) researches the body and is able to create a vaccine. This discovery sparks interest from known terrorist Nile Spencer (Joel West), who kidnaps the doctor as well as nabbing the virus and vaccine for a deadly plan he's ready to implement, which includes spreading the virus across the continent. Luckily for the human race, the government has recruited Marcus

Poynt (Daniel Bernhardt) to lead a small team behind enemy lines to rescue Dr. Levitt. Once he realizes the severity of the situation, he will have to make a choice: follow his orders or save the lives of millions.

Global Effect has an intriguing premise and is surprisingly well acted for a minuscule-budgeted action thriller. Far too much of the film's runtime is wasted on scenes of politicians delegating in the Pentagon when it should have focused more on the men in the field, who are obviously much more interesting than anyone in a suit. Daniel Bernhardt (*Bloodsport 2, Parker*) is a fantastic hero but is only able to deliver on the goods later in the flick and not nearly as much as we would like to see. Eventually the time comes for him to save the day (but only after an entire city is leveled), and he is able to partake in a few decent physical exchanges, though nothing to write home about. It succeeds at being a decent thriller but leaves much to be desired when it comes to action, which is frustrating since we know Bernhardt is capable of much better. Also with South African action star James Ryan from *Kill or be Killed*. Directed by Terry Cunningham (*The Con Express*).

Golden Needles
1974 (MGM DVD) (djm)

A little golden statue with acupuncture needles sticking out of it has been a prized and coveted artifact through the ages, and those who've possessed it usually end up dead because someone else comes along and kills for it. Legend has it that the needles (when applied to skin in key areas) provide sexual bliss. The statue ends up in Hong Kong, where a minor adventure takes place involving a mercenary named Dan (Joe Don Baker) who is commissioned to find it and carry it to its next buyer, but when various factions chase him around and fight him for it, he calls on his best friend Jeff (Jim Kelly) to help him out.

Silly and instantly forgettable, *Golden Needles* is a throwaway movie that sadly doesn't use Jim Kelly nearly enough. The director, Robert Clouse, worked with Kelly on the films *Enter the Dragon* and *Black Belt Jones*, but their work here is merely a footnote. Baker hardly qualifies as a martial artist or action star, despite the fisticuffs he gets into here. If you're looking for better Clouse/Kelly films, you know where to go.

Golgo 13
1977 (BCI DVD) (djm)

Based on a manga comic strip, *Golgo 13* stars Sonny Chiba (*The Street Fighter*) as the mysterious assassin Golgo 13 whose latest assignment has him hunting a crime lord, which may be one of his toughest assignments. An intrepid cop is on Golgo's trail, and they have several close encounters, but the final one, where they resolve not to kill each other and walk away worthy adversaries, takes the cake.

Chiba's presence in this slapdash movie helps, but only a little. He was probably hired for just a handful of days, and most of the time we see him he's aiming rifles at distant targets, so whenever he gets up and uses his martial arts on some thugs, the movie perks up, but only nominally so. For his hardcore fans only. Directed by Yukio Noda, who also made *Soul of Bruce Lee* with Chiba.

Good Cop, Bad Cop
(a.k.a. **Black Dawn**)
1997 (Avalanche DVD) (djm)

Ex-cop Jake Kilkanin (Lorenzo Lamas) is visited by his old boss, who asks him to take a job searching for an elderly banker who was kidnapped by a Mexican cartel and taken south of the border. The banker's wife, who witnessed the kidnapping, joins Kilkanin on the search, but only because she can help out with some clues—Kilkanin is a bit of a blow hard, who prefers working alone, so having a partner puts a damper on his style. Constance (Catherine Lazo), Kilkanin's new partner, ends up saving his life a few times after they cross the border and encounter cartel hit men, and as they inch closer to the cartel leader (played by Marco Rodriguez), they realize that the cartel is actually a Satanic cult, drawing Kilkanin and Constance closer so that they can perform a ritual to bring forth a new era of blood and destruction on the world.

The wacky *Good Cop, Bad Cop* looks pretty good on the surface, with lots of well-staged shootouts and a good performance from Lamas (who doesn't use martial arts in the movie), but when the doomsday cult story kicks in, the movie goes haywire and is never able to repair itself. The director John DeBello is the creator and director of all four *Killer Tomatoes* movies (and the producer of the ensuring TV series), so I wouldn't put too much stock in his basket. As a vehicle for Lamas, it's about on par with a handful of other movies he made during the mid '90s.

Good Guys Wear Black
1977 (HBO DVD) (djm)

A commando unit who engaged in numerous missions in Vietnam together is being systematically hunted down in the present day. The leader of the unit, John T. Booker (Chuck Norris), now teaches classes at a university, and he's approached by an attractive Senate reporter named Margaret (Anne Archer), whom he quickly falls for despite the fact that he's never able to fully trust her. They begin tracking down the remaining members of his team, who are killed sometimes in front of Booker's eyes, and so he begins suspecting that Margaret is playing against him and leading him towards his doom. When she is killed in a plane crash (also in front of him), he realizes that he has no idea who his enemy is, and his life depends on finding answers before he is assassinated as well.

Following *Breaker! Breaker!*, this dated vehicle showcased Norris in a type of role that he would become comfortable in. He plays a Vietnam vet in full action mode, doing the sort of thing he is best known for, but unfortunately *Good Guys Wear Black* feels much grounded in its day and age, with a poor music score and hazy photography. The story is complicated, too, and when the big reveal comes at the end, it's disappointing. Soon-Tek Oh, one of the actors in the film, went on to co-star in several other Norris vehicles including *Missing in Action 2: The Beginning* and *The President's Man*, and he always played a bad guy. Also, this film's title has no relation to the plot whatsoever. Ted Post (*The Human Shield*) directed.

A Good Man
2013 (Lionsgate DVD) (djm)

A special ops point man named Alexander (Steven Seagal) calls it quits when an innocent girl dies in his arms after a military strike in the Middle East goes south. He retreats into seclusion in Eastern Europe and becomes a handyman at an apartment complex, where the most challenging thing he does is help people open their doors when they get locked out. A young woman and her kid sister living in his building are having some issues with an American man (played by Victor Webster) who works with the Russian mafia, and when the guy is targeted for death by an Asian mobster, Alexander steps in to protect the two females and keep them from harm. When the younger girl is kidnapped, Alexander sort of recruits the American to help him retrieve the girl, and when Alexander faces the Asian (played by Tzi Ma), he realizes that he's an old enemy from his past.

One of Steven Seagal's best direct-to-video efforts, *A Good Man* doesn't mess around with flash cuts, abrasive music, or a confusing plot. It's incredibly straightforward and sincere, delivering old-school action for fans of Seagal and action films of the 1990s. Seagal's character walks around with a samurai sword in his coat (even while he's in the Middle East on his mission), and when he unsheathes it, he uses it every time to devastating effect. Kudos to longtime collaborating director Keoni Waxman, whose previous projects with Seagal collectively underwhelmed (aside from *Force of Execution*). This is easily their best film together, and it should be ranked fairly high on any list that rates the star's films. Co-star Webster is a taekwondo champion in real life.

The Goonies
1985 (Warner DVD) (djm)

You might have heard this one before: Some misfit kids get their hands on a treasure map and think they can find a pirate's booty somewhere in the caves of Oregon. Teens Mikey (Sean Astin), Mouth (Corey Feldman), Data (Ke Huy Quan), Brand (Josh Brolin), Chunk (Jeff Cohen), Stef (Martha Plimpton), and Andy

(Kerri Green) join for the adventure of their lifetime as they are pursued by a small-time crime family—the Fratellis (played by Anne Ramsey, Joe Pantoliano, and Robert Davi) and their dirty secret, the disfigured Sloth (a hulking John Matuszak, a former NFL player). By the time the adventure comes to a crescendo and the pirate treasure is revealed, Chunk and Sloth have become an inseparable tag team, and they save the day.

A crucial growing-up movie from the 1980s, *The Goonies* has worked its way into the hearts of millions of 30-something adults who watched it over and over in the heyday of VHS, but it's also worth noting that John Matuszack gave the deformed Sloth life in a way that not too many of his contemporaries might have been able to do. Heavily made-up with a mechanical headpiece, he's able to give the lovable character a personality and a physicality that is instantly relatable and yet entirely inimitable. After this, Matuszack made some TV appearances, but it would be a few more years before he would get his own action movie to star in called *One Man Force*. Incidentally, that was released the same year he passed away from heart failure. *The Goonies* had a great team behind it: Steven Spielberg wrote the story and produced it, Chris Columbus wrote the screenplay, and Richard Donner directed it. It's a classic.

Gorgeous

1999 (Sony DVD) (CD)

Bu (Shu Qi) is a gorgeous young Taiwanese girl who is holding out hope for a fairy tale romance. Her neighbor proposes to her, but this isn't what she wants. One day she sees a bottle floating in the water with a romantic message in it. This could be the answer to her dreams, and she follows it all the way to Hong Kong. She soon finds the bottle's owner: Albert (Tony Leung), and he's a hunk who happens to be gay. The two strike up a friendship and Bu decides to stay there a little longer, and then meets millionaire playboy C. N. Chan (Jackie Chan). The fairy tale romance she always wanted is now happening, and everything seems magical. During their romance, Chan is battling with his longtime business rival who has hired a fighter to fly in and teach him a lesson. When truths are revealed, will hearts be broken or will true love prevail?

For years, superstar Jackie Chan talked about stepping away from action pictures to focus more on dramatic roles. So once his deal was up with Golden Harvest he found a script to nurse to fruition, and that movie became *Gorgeous*. It's first and foremost a romantic comedy but it does have some action elements, including a near-ten-minute competitive fight with stuntman/martial artist Bradley James Allan (*Who Am I?*, which was another movie with Jackie). With an overly long two-hour running time, there are only a couple of minor scuffles (one on a boat and the other in an alley) worth mentioning, though it's the two fights with Allan most viewers will remember. Jackie served as a producer, editor, and writer, but it was directed by Vincent Kok.

The Green Hornet

1966 (ABC Television) (CD)

"You know, if we ever meet up with that masked kung fu man again, I want him."

After the death of his father, Britt Reid (Van Williams) inherits the family business, the *Daily Sentinel*, a newspaper. Britt harbors a secret identity; he dons a mask and calls himself "The Green Hornet" and fights crime. Along with his high-kicking sidekick Kato (Bruce Lee), he keeps an eye out for evil doers and protects the innocent. The police consider him a criminal but Hornet and Kato operate on a whole different level to uphold the law. There are only two people who know their true identities: district attorney Frank Scanlon (Walter Brooke) and Britt's receptionist Casey (Wende Wagner). They travel around in an battle-reinforced Imperial Crown sedan they call the "Black Beauty." Together, they are a duo like no other—Hornet with his detecting abilities, and Kato with his martial art skills—and criminals better beware because the Green Hornet is ready to strike!

Without *The Green Hornet*, Bruce Lee might not have had the opportunity to venture into vehicle films. This television program was the launching point for his career. It may not have been a large success stateside, but in Hong Kong the series was widely known as *The Kato Show* and from there, history was made. The show is a campy mixture of mystery and action playing out over twenty-six half-hour episodes on ABC. When you think about the program, the first thing that comes to mind will always be Bruce Lee, and it's easy to see why. At the time, nothing like what Bruce could do had been seen on television, and in each episode, he has a few moments to show off his stuff. International superstardom was just a second away. Bruce has very little dialogue in the series—usually nothing more than a few lines per episode—but it doesn't matter. This was the birth of a man who became a legend. The series lacked a recurring villain and each episode is self-contained (with the exception of a few two-parters), making it easy to just jump in and watch it at whatever point you please. It sort of feels a bit like the Adam West *Batman* series (there were even a few Green Hornet and Kato crossovers), with the added excitement of watching Bruce Lee at the beginning of his (far too short) career. The duo faced everything from art thieves to the brainwashed, and even a *Green Hornet* imposter, all in the name of good fun. Lee's first film appearance after this was in the James Garner movie *Marlow*.

Green Street 3: Never Back Down

2013 (Lionsgate DVD R2) (djm)

Danny (Scott Adkins) owns a gym and keeps himself fit and ready for trouble if and when it comes calling. He learns that his younger brother was brutally killed in a gang fight, and so he drops everything to return home to bury him. While visiting his distraught mother, he goes to his old stomping grounds and rekindles old alliances with his former gang on Green Street. Danny begins asking around and investigating his brother's death, and he quickly learns that things have changed since he left the gang: There's a fight circuit that all of the gangs now compete in for supremacy, and his brother died during one of the bouts. Re-initiating himself into his gang, Danny whips his mates into shape and they work their way to the top spot in the circuit as the toughest gang around. All the while, he hones in on the brute who killed his brother.

Unrelated (for the most part) to the previous two *Green Street* pictures, this third entry is packed with donnybrooks and roughhousing of the most brutal variety. Casting Adkins in the film was an inspired idea, and his part in the film is basically the main reason to watch it. It very quickly becomes apparent that the character he plays is not untouchable or invulnerable to getting hurt. Every guy in the movie is beat down, smacked up, and pummeled to some degree, but it's great seeing Adkins (as always) use brawling skills as well as his martial arts. This is simple stuff, but it's well done. I considered myself lucky to see it in a theater. Directed by James Nunn.

Gridiron Gang

2006 (Sony DVD) (CD)

"They didn't beat you—they beat a team that never played before. But on this day, it's gonna be different. On this day, you're gonna have Mustang Pride, you're gonna go out there, you're gonna put your helmets on, buckle your chin straps, and hand out thirty-eight ass whuppins! Do you understand?"

It's no surprise when young men who spend their time in detention centers fall back into the same corruptive crowd when they are released. They end up back in detention centers, in prison, or in the grave. Sean Porter (Dwayne Johnson) is sick and tired of investing his time in these kids only to lose them once they exit the gates of Kilpatrick Detention Center. He's a former football player and decides the sport may be the best outlet for them to be a part of a team, learn self-esteem, show off their pride, and even walk away with some discipline. It won't be an easy task; these kids are tough (some are even killers) but when they find someone like Porter believing in them with every ounce of his being, they begin to forget they were losers and begin to act like the winners they have the potential of being.

Dwayne Johnson (*The Rundown*) knows how to kick some ass. We've seen him tossing guys around the ring (in wrestling), riding a giant bumblebee (in *Journey 2 the Mysterious Island*), and even seen him fight pygmies (in *The Rundown*). In *Gridiron Gang*, he kicks just as much ass, but just not in the traditional sense. He takes all these kids and psychologically kicks their asses until he whips them into shape. He smacks the snot out of them with words, beating them with intelligence and knocking them out with pride. This is an entirely different type of action film, but it most certainly is one. The addition of the brutal football scenes only adds to its action credibility. Johnson gives a great, heartfelt performance, all of which is based on the true story of a man who never gave up on a group of troubled kids who eventually learned to be a winning team, on and off the field. The film is inspiring and if we had more people in the world like Sean Porter, it surely would be a less violent place. Directed by Phil Joanou (*State of Grace*).

Grosse Pointe Blank

1996 (Hollywood Pictures DVD) (djm)

A freelance hitman named Martin Blank (John Cusack) is already facing a midlife crisis at age twenty-eight: He's bored and exhausted with killing people and the prospect of attending his ten-year high school reunion in Detroit beckons him, if only to rekindle an old flame with Debi Newberry (Minni Driver), the girl he stood up for prom to join the Army. His latest hit mission happens to be Debi's dad, but that doesn't stop him from trying to enjoy the festivities of his reunion and meeting up with old friends. With government agents shadowing him wherever he goes, a rival named Grocer (Dan Aykroyd) pressuring him to join a union of assassins, and a mark on his head, Martin is going to have a hell of a time trying to survive the week if he's going to win Debi's heart.

World-renown kickboxing legend Benny "The Jet" Urquidez from *Force Five, Kick Fighter,* and *Bloodmatch* has a plum role as a hitman sent to kill Martin Blank, and in his three choice scenes he more than makes an impression: He shines. His big fight scene with John Cusack at the high-school reunion is fierce and deadly, and it probably went on his showreel to prove that he was one of the best in the business. As for the film, it's a personal favorite of mine, if only for the fact that it literally kept me from dropping out of school so that one day I could attend my high-school reunion. The sad fact is that my high-school reunion was a drag, and who knows what might have been if I'd dropped out to pursue other ventures? With a snappy, sentimental script by Tom Jankiewicz, Cusack, and Steve Pink, *Grosse Point Blank* was one of the best films of the 1990s. Directed by George Armitage.

Ground Rules

1997 (Digiview DVD) (djm)

"New ground rules: There *are* no rules!"

A new sport known as Battle Ball is sweeping the stage of underworld sports. The game is fairly simple: It's like polo, but the players are on dirt bikes and the riders have metal scoops to sweep

Video artwork for *Ground Rules*. Author's collection.

up a steel ball while they ride, hoping to throw the ball in a hole in the back of a racing dune buggy. Just about anything goes in the game, so other riders can knock you off your bike, run over you, or whatever it takes to win the game. The biggest and brightest star of the game is thrown off his bike and becomes paralyzed, and so the game has lost its champion. A lowly mechanic (played by Sean Donahue from *Blood Hands*) thinks he can get into the game and win, but first he needs a sponsor, and as luck would have it his ex-girlfriend's father is the creator of the game, and so he has a way in . . . but there's a problem: A germaphobe gangster (played by Richard Lynch) is muscling into the Battle Ball business and is forcing the sport to be more edgy and violent, which puts all the players at even greater risk.

A late '90s entry in the direct-to-video pantheon of action flicks, *Ground Rules* has plenty of motorcycle and car stunts in the vein of *The Dukes of Hazard*. It lacks hand-to-hand combat, which is one of the main appeals of watching a movie with Sean Donahue, but knowing that Sean did all or most of his own stunts (he's a stuntman too) gives the movie-viewer some satisfaction. The plot is thin and some of the dramatics are weak, but it's all in good fun. Frank Stallone has a supporting role in the film as a biker in the game. Directed by Sean's father, Patrick.

Grudge Match

2013 (Warner DVD) (djm)

An endearing concept and the on-screen pairing of Sylvester Stallone and Robert De Niro, who both starred in renown boxing movies (*Rocky/Raging Bull*), might tickle some fancies. Stallone plays "Razor" Sharp, and De Niro plays "The Kid" McDonnen, two former boxing champs who have held a bitter feud for decades. In their primes, they each beat each other for the title, but they never fought a tiebreaker, and when Razor abruptly

retired, Kid never got his chance at a comeback. Razor lost his fortune (and his two true loves: boxing and his girlfriend) and became a blue-collar worker, while Kid became an entrepreneur and lived the good life. When a scrappy promoter named Slate (Kevin Hart) comes calling on Razor to lend his voice to a videogame for an easy paycheck, Razor isn't properly warned that his nemesis Kid will be at the recording studio on the same day at the same time. This inopportune meeting results in a ruckus and a donnybrook, which in turn becomes an Internet sensation. With their names in the limelight again, Slate pushes for them to have a rematch fight with a sweet payday that Razor desperately needs after losing his job and with mounting bills that need to be paid. Against his better judgment—and the warnings of his trainer "Lightning" (Alan Arkin)—Razor trains harder than ever because "it's the best we got." As their fight looms closer, Kid develops a relationship with his estranged son (played by Jon Bernthal), and Razor reconnects with his ex-girlfriend (Kim Basinger), who cheated on him with Kid decades ago. Once the fight is on, it becomes apparent that it doesn't really matter who wins, because they both fight with honor and respect.

Stallone's determination to put every ounce of physical effort into keeping himself in as tip-top shape as his age will allow is really a wonder to behold, and this might be the first time I've seen him, on screen, groan and sink to a seat with exhaustion. His counterpart, played by De Niro, isn't in shape in the movie and he plays that up, but it's interesting to see them together again (after *Cop Land*) and essentially doing riffs on their famous boxing characters. I don't know how many more movies Stallone is going to do where he insists on taking his shirt off and performing feats that men half his age wouldn't dare try (like towing a semi with a rope and his brute strength), but I'm willing to go as far as he's willing to, forever and always. It's just a shame that all three of his 2013 releases (the others: *Bullet to the Head* and *Escape Plan*) were flops. Directed by Peter Segal (*Get Smart* with The Rock).

G2

1999 (Avalanche DVD) (djm)

"I can't close my eyes without seeing the sword!"

An embarrassingly awful rehash of *Highlander*, this movie stars Daniel Bernhardt (*Bloodsport 2-4*, *Parker*) who is at the mercy of a terrible script and an amateur director. He plays a reincarnated warrior/protector of an ancient sword, and his lifelong enemy through the ages is Parmenion (James Hong), who killed him once over the sword and wants to see him dead again. Bernhardt finds himself drawn to compete in an underground sword-fighting and martial arts completion (to the death!), where Parmenion sees him and realizes that their destinies are about to collide once more. In the mix is a female detective (just like in *Highlander*), who is on a case concerning the ancient, magical sword.

Bernhardt looks more mature here than he did in the first few *Bloodsport* sequels he was in, but unfortunately this film was a wasted opportunity for him. He displays some fine martial arts skills, but when the sword-fighting elements kick in, the movie really lets him down. James Hong spends all his screen time giggling and wailing awful dialogue ("Today you die, Macedonian!"), and Bernhardt's fighting partners aren't up to par. Written and directed by Nick Rotundo, who curiously was the editor of the similarly themed Lorenzo Lamas vehicle *The Swordsman* and the director of that film's sequel. The similarity of those films with *G2* is uncanny.

Guaranteed on Delivery
(a.k.a. **G.O.D.**)
2001 (Velocity DVD) (djm)

Filmed in eleven days, *Guaranteed on Delivery* starts off well and goes downhill. The set-up is simple: a security guard named Ray (Jalal Merhi) is on his post at a bank when some high-tech terrorists come in and rob the place. His wife happens to be visiting him, and she is shot and killed in the commotion. The robbers get away. To make matters worse, he is relieved of his job and asked to turn in his gun. His buddy Norman (David Carradine) tries to cheer him up by encouraging him to go into business for himself. So Ray sells everything he has and buys a van and becomes a courier for high-paying clients who only hire drivers who are willing to transport valuable goods and are willing to take a risk. One day he realizes he's transporting human cargo—kidnapped women—meant for the slave trade, and he decides to do something about it. His clients also happen to be the men who robbed the bank on that fateful day when his wife was killed. He calls his friend Norman and they go to work, revenging and carrying out justice.

Like I said, it starts off okay. The film looks better than it should, the actors are fine (Carradine adds a nice touch to a small part), but the martial arts action stuff is terrible. The main villain is played by Olivier Gruner (from *Nemesis* and *Savate*), but he never shows off his abilities as a fighter. The star, Merhi, is okay in the lead, but when he goes up against other serious martial arts fighters like Darren Shahlavi (from *Bloodmoon* and *Ip Man 2*), he embarrasses himself by winning fights on screen that he obviously wouldn't have won in real life. The choreography is sloppy, and it shows. There might have been a good opportunity to feature a fight between Merhi and Gruner towards the end of this picture, but sadly, it wasn't meant to be. Merhi later directed Gruner in *The Circuit* trilogy. *G.O.D.* was directed by Dean Rusu.

The Guardian
2000 (NOV) (CD)

Paul Randall (Frank Zagarino) is a security expert who is hired by the wealthy Steve Layton (Bryan Genesse) to protect his dad, Ted, who he believes to be in danger. Paul's mother was recently murdered, and the cops seem to think he is somehow connected. Paul has his old friend Win (Robert Saunders) do some investigating to help clear his name while Paul does his job protecting Ted (Dale Wilson). The assassination attempts begin and Paul does what he does best to keep Ted alive. Soon, information comes to light connecting the death of Paul's mom to these attempts and Paul wants answers . . . even if it means risking everything he has.

There's no denying the fact that Frank Zagarino (*Alien Chaser, The Protector*) and Bryan Genesse (*Live Wire: Human Timebomb, Street Justice*) are absolutely dynamic when they appear together on screen. In this one, Zags is the hero, and he's constantly butting heads with Gens. *The Guardian* is less action and more thriller, but we are treated to a killer fight between these two action heroes in a weight room. While the fight is on the short side, you will feel the instant gratification when they butt heads. It's a shame this film is difficult to find as it's really good. It's chock full of twists and turns, and we get to see just how good both of these men can be from an acting standpoint as well. Director Gerry Lively (who was also responsible for the Zagarino masterpiece *Shattered Lies*) delivers a highly entertaining film on a very limited budget.

Guardian Angel
1994 (Universal DVD) (djm)

A more than adequate vehicle for Cynthia Rothrock, *Guardian Angel* casts her as a cop, Christine McKay, who loses two partners in a row in the line of duty, the second of whom was her fiancée. She leaves the force in disgrace and becomes a bodyguard for a cocky playboy who is a sweetheart deep down. Turns out that her employer has been marked for death by his ex-girlfriend, who also happens to be the woman who killed McKay's fiancé in cold blood. McKay gets her revenge.

Made in the day and age when low-budget action movies were able to use plenty of explosions, car crashes, and helicopters, *Guardian Angel* is exactly what it should be. In this movie, Rothrock plays a character who is sort of the flipside to the Mel Gibson character, Martin Riggs, in the *Lethal Weapon* films: she lives in a trailer, talks to her dog, and has a mean edge. Still, it's fairly lightweight and modestly entertaining. Directed by Richard W. Munchkin, who made several films with Don Wilson and Jeff Wincott.

Guardians of the Galaxy
2014 (Disney DVD) (djm)

"I am Groot!"

Peter Quill, a child going through terrible tragedy in 1988, is abducted by aliens, and twenty years later he's a rapscallion space adventurer who calls himself "Star Lord," but really he's just an insecure kid who values his cassette Walkman more than all the treasures of space. Quill (played by Chris Pratt) recovers a handheld metal orb from a deserted planet, and in that instant he becomes an infamous outlaw, and when bounty hunters from all corners of the galaxy come after him, he develops a reputation for quick thinking, being a slippery prisoner, and making friends and enemies equally. At first, he makes enemies of the Amazonian warrior Gamora (Zoe Saldana), the revenge-minded convict Drax (Dave Bautista), the raccoon bounty hunter Rocket (voiced by Bradley Cooper), and Rocket's incredible tree-like bodyguard Groot (voiced by Vin Diesel), but in time they all become his most trusted friends and allies in protecting the galaxy from the megalomaniacal Ronan (Lee Pace), a galactic warlord on an errand for the most feared tyrant of space, known as Thanos, to retrieve the metal orb that contains an "infinity stone," which could potentially bring about the end of all things if in the wrong hands.

Easily the best and most entertaining science fiction fantasy adventure since the glory days of the '80s, *Guardians of the Galaxy* is incredibly well cast and gives each character equal attention and screen time to shine. Mention should be made of former wrestler Dave Bautista, who spends the entire film bare-chested and covered in alien-styled makeup, and Vin Diesel, who repeats the same line "I am Groot" over and over, with varied intonations and inflections, which should remind genre fans of Chewbacca in the *Star Wars* franchise. This isn't just a movie for fans of Bautista or Diesel, obviously, but for people who love movies, comic books, and science fiction . . . but fans of Bautista and Diesel will walk away very pleased. Guaranteed. Director James Gunn has a blast in this sandbox, and here's hoping we get many more adventures of the *Guardians*.

Guns and Lipstick
1995 (Anchor Bay DVD) (djm)

Seasoned private eye Danielle Roberts (Sally Kirkland) was a cop before she became a gumshoe, and she doesn't have many friends on the local police department: they resent her and would love to see her behind bars over anything they can pin on her. Her latest client is a stripper who hires her to protect her from a stalker, but when her client turns up dead, Roberts is immediately in the hot seat with the cops. With no evidence against her, she goes to her client's brother Andy (played by Evan Lurie from *American Kickboxer 2*), who is devastated by the news of his sister's death. Roberts decides to solve the death of her client on her own without a retainer just for honor's sake, and Andy—a martial arts expert who performs katas to get his days started—tags along with her to make sure she's got her back covered because everywhere she goes she gets in trouble. With hitmen on her trail (one of them is played by Sonny Landham, and another one is played by Jorge [George] Rivero) and dirty cops at her throat, she's going to need a gung ho karate bodyguard to help her survive the week.

From Jeno Hodi, the director of *American Kickboxer 2*, *Guns and Lipstick* is a great vehicle for Kirkland, but it should have been a better vehicle for "B" action star Evan Lurie, who only gets minimal screen time with Kirkland. It would have been great to see Lurie go up against Landham (from *Predator*) or Rivero (from the underrated *Fist Fighter*), but Kirkland (who obviously isn't an action star) gets most of the good moments. If anyone is curious about Evan Lurie, you may want to see *American Kickboxer 2* or *Hologram Man* before seeing this film.

Guns for San Sebastian

1968 (NOV) (JAS)

"I'll make it quick. I am not a priest. If you ever need money, there's a price on my head."

Guns For San Sebastian is a thoroughly enjoyable tale set in Mexico about an atheist outlaw named Leon Alastray (Anthony Quinn) whose life is saved by a priest. Feeling obligated, Alastray accompanies the priest to a small town terrorized by an Indian tribe. The priest dies en route, and the town mistakes the sun-dazed Alastray for the priest. The leader of the marauding tribe, Tecio (Charles Bronson), believes the members of the village are traitors for adopting the culture and religion of the Spanish. Alastray eventually teaches the villagers to fight for themselves and helps them not only to survive, but to regain their dignity.

With a simple story, *Guns For San Sebastian* stands above other pedestrian westerns of the time due in no small part to the menacing coldness of Bronson's Tecio, the likable Quinn's reluctant hero Alastray, the realistic Mexican locations, and the sweeping awesomeness of Ennio Morricone's spaghetti-tinged score. The action never seems superfluous, and the stunts are quite astounding, considering the film's low budget. There is an authenticity here that effectively transports the viewer to a grittier time. This is a solid little film that is positively worth searching out.

Gutshot Straight

2014 (Lionsgate DVD) (CD)

Jack (George Eads) is a professional gambler in Vegas. He's down on his luck and owes mob boss Paulie Trunks (Steven Seagal) a large chunk of change. Paulie's enforcer Carl (Vinnie Jones) is ready to make him pay up the hard way but Paulie has a soft spot for the guy. When things seem their darkest, a mysterious stranger named Duffy (Stephen Lang) shows up at the casino and offers Jack a job. He invites Jack back to his house and wants to pay him to have sex with May (AnnaLynne

McCord) while he watches. The two men duke it out until Duffy accidentally dies. Jack doesn't know what to do so May offers her help in hiding the body, thus beginning a whirlwind night unlike anything he has ever had to endure.

The thing about *Gutshot Straight* is how all of these veteran actors are cast against type. Action superstar Steven Seagal (*The Glimmer Man*) as a Marlon Brando-esque mob boss is a delicious entry in the actor's canon of characters. Sadly, the opening credit sequence may actually have more screen time than he does. This isn't really an action film (more of a thriller) but the performances by everyone in the cast really make this a worthwhile effort. George Eads is a highly likable lead and carries the film with ease. Seagal has a short action moment before the end credits role, and he once again proves how even in a small character role, he adds a bit of pizazz to anything he does. Directed by Justin Steele.

Gymkata

1985 (Warner DVD) (djm)

Whoever grew up watching action and martial arts movies in the VHS era should remember watching *Gymkata*. Starring real-life gold medalist gymnast Kurt Thomas, this film is one of the very few that defined my childhood. Thomas plays Jonathan Cabot, an Olympian who is approached by the Secret Service to follow in his father's footsteps as a secret agent and go to a remote country called Parmistan, which is on the border of Russia, and enter a life-or-death game. The winner of the game is granted one request, and the Secret Service wants Cabot to ask for the right to set up a satellite system in that country that would be the first warning system in the event of a nuclear strike against the United States from Russia. Cabot agrees, and as soon as he does, he is trained to become a lethal fighter. His unique

abilities in gymnastics are sort of integrated into a new form of martial arts . . . *Gymkata*! He is joined on his journey to Parmistan by the princess of that country, and they are besieged by ruthless killers who want to make sure that he never enters the game. Once they're in the king's court (it's very feudal and medieval), Cabot has a chance to size up his competition. Richard Norton plays the king's most trusted assistant, and this is the guy Cabot will have the most trouble with. Once the game begins, the movie accelerates into iconographic territory. The final stage of the game leads into a town full of the criminally insane and everyone there is a crazed lunatic running around with pitchforks, knives, and other assorted sharp objects. Cabot is surrounded, besieged, and grossly outnumbered. He finds the nearest stationary gymnastics horse in the town square and does *a lot* of damage to the crazies who are out to kill him. The film ends with Cabot triumphant.

First of all, there's no other action movie like this one. Yes, it is a loose remake of *Enter the Dragon*, which was directed by Robert Clouse, this film's director, *but* it's radically different in tone, style, and execution from any other vehicle action film in the history of movies. Second, the fact that Kurt Thomas never made another action movie before or after this one works to the film's benefit because he's really different and his style of fighting (while completely bogus) is actually very cool to look at and—in the context of this film—works beautifully. The sound effects, the mood, and the bizarre tone of the entire film make *Gymkata* an unforgettable viewing experience. The weird locations and local extras help make an indelible impression, and the heroic score by Alfi Kabiljo elevates the film to a whole other level. I love everything about this film, and fans of unique, interesting martial arts movies must check it out. It also stars John Barret as the ill-fated Gomez, Conan Lee, and Tadashi (*American Ninja*) Yamashita.

Production release insert for *Gymkata*. This artwork was never used again for the film. Author's collection.

Theatrical poster for *Half Past Dead*. Author's Collection.

Half Past Dead

2002 (Sony DVD) (djm)

Undercover FBI Agent Sasha Petrosevitch (Steven Seagal) and his thug partner Nick (Ja Rule) are sent to New Alcatraz prison as convicts on the eve of a high-profile prisoner's execution. The convict to be executed knows the whereabouts of a stash of hundreds of millions of dollars worth of gold bars, but he won't tell anyone where it is before he dies. Sasha's mission is to gain the man's trust quickly, but just when the execution is scheduled, a band of highly equipped and trained terrorists break into the prison, kill the guards, and lay siege to the place, taking the condemned man hostage, hoping that he will tell them where he hid the gold. It's up to Sasha and his buddy Nick to stop them before anyone else is killed, and in the complicated process of doing so, they are hoping that the condemned man will confide in Sasha, who ultimately reveals that he's with the FBI.

A jumbled mess with lame action and terrible music, *Half Past Dead* was Steven Seagal's final starring picture that played in theaters in the US. Following his superior film *Exit Wounds*, *Half Past Dead* pretty well squanders the goodwill audiences had gained back for him, and it's a shame that he didn't pick something more interesting to follow up with. The production design and camerawork work in tandem to give the film a completely artificial texture, and it hasn't aged well over the years. Some of the action is clearly inspired by *The Matrix*, but it falls short of delivering anything remotely so compelling. Seagal turns in an intentionally humorous performance, but even so, this movie doesn't deserve him at that stage of his career. It feels like one of his later direct-to-video movies. Written and directed by Don Michael Paul, who is also known for acting in some films. Followed by a direct-to-video (but Seagal-less) sequel.

Half Past Dead 2

2007 (Sony DVD) (CD)

"Let me get this straight. You got transferred here, so you could break out and find some gold?"

After the events at New Alcatraz in *Half Past Dead*, prisoner Twitch (Kurupt) has kept a low profile, keeping his nose clean. He hasn't been able to get paroled but has a plan to get himself transferred that will bring him just a little bit closer to his goal. There's $160 million in gold hidden, and he is one of only two people who know where to find it. The only other person that knows is Hubert (Jeff Krebs), who is also incarcerated at New Alcatraz. Once Twitch is transferred to the new prison, he tries to keep to himself, but it's not easy. A gang war is about to erupt, and Twitch is stuck in the middle. The only person he can turn to is Burke (Bill Goldberg), a fellow inmate who is trying to just do his time

and get out. When a prison riot erupts, both men find themselves framed for murders they didn't commit by the riot's mastermind Cortez (Robert Madrid), who is also holding Twitch's fiancé and Burke's daughter hostage. Together they must prove their innocence and save the ones they love before they can even think about that incredible payday.

Oddly enough, with only two characters returning from the first film (neither of which were main characters), *Half Past Dead 2* manages to be a much better film than the original. There's no mistaking the type of film that this is, and it never pretends to be anything other than a schlocky (but fun) "B" movie with a cast willing to go the extra mile to deliver a highly entertaining sequel. It very loosely follows the same set-up as the first film, but quickly heads off into its own territory. There's no Steven Seagal this time; in his stead, we get former WWE/WCW wrestler Bill Goldberg (*Universal Soldier: The Return*) who is just a complete beast. He may be limited to the types of roles he can play, but director Art Camacho (*Gangland*) gives him a role that suits him well. He gets plenty of opportunities to show off a very similar fighting style to what we are used to seeing from him in the ring. He's partnered up with returning cast member Kurupt, who is still an annoying little weasel but redeems himself in the end. Camacho (who worked second unit on the original) keeps things energetic throughout the film with plenty of action and a decent story that keeps you interested. If you enjoy watching inmates beat the pulp out of each other, then you can't go wrong with *Half Past Dead 2*.

Hammer

1972 (MGM DVD) (CD)

"Some of this soul is gonna rub off on you, yet. Now come over here and give me a big sloppy kiss."

B. J. Hammer (Fred Williamson) is a dockworker who dreams of being a fighter. He finds himself a manager who pushes him and can get results. The problem with his manager, Big Sid (Charles Lampkin), is that he's corrupt and also a drug dealer. Hammer has money in his pocket, and girls are throwing themselves at him. As he begins to fall for Lois (Vonetta McGee), it becomes painfully clear that as he rises through the ranks, the mob has their hand in fixing the fights. Hammer isn't about to let his reputation become tarnished, especially after being asked to take the fall in a fight. The mob might think they own him, but Hammer isn't about to be owned by anyone.

It's sort of a shame that *Hammer* isn't held in as high regard as similar films from that era like *Shaft* or *Super Fly,* especially since it's just as great as they are. Williamson (*Black Caesar*) is at his best here in one of his first starring roles. Released in 1972, it's an obvious product of the times, but it's always entertaining and has some hilarious dialogue that you will find yourself

quoting to your friends. Since Williamson plays a boxer, there are plenty of solid brawls for the audience to enjoy, including in-ring battles and some street brawling. The boxing scenes are good, though they never reach the excitement of something like *Rocky*. The brawls outside the ring (especially the first time we see him fight) look pretty realistic. He looked to be in the best shape of his career and didn't really bother wearing a shirt for the first half of the film. He played the quintessential hero, with the male characters fearing him, the women loving him, and the kids worshiping him. He's accompanied by a solid cast with appearances by Vonetta McGee (*Shaft in Africa*), D'Urville Martin (*The Big Score*), and the always enjoyable William Smith (*Hell Comes to Frogtown*). *Hammer* is an action classic that should be revisited. Directed by Bruce D. Clark.

Hangfire

1991 (MGM DVD) (djm)

Cutthroat convict Kuttner (Lee de Broux) and his gang (which includes Lou Ferrigno and Lyle Alzado) manage to bust out of their bonds during a prisoner transfer and they invade a small town, causing untold ruckus and damage. Sheriff Ike Slayton (the late Brad Davis) and his buddy Billy (Ken Foree)—both Vietnam veterans—are the town's best hope against the cold-blooded killers loose in the area, despite the fact that the National Guard has been called in. Slayton's wife Maria (Kim Delaney) has been taken hostage by the killers, and Slayton takes it as personally as can be, and his reaction is to rely on his experience as a soldier to reclaim his wife and set the town straight.

A great premise is squandered as the running time clicks on. There's action in the movie, but so little of it comes from co-stars Ferrigno (*The Incredible Hulk*) and NFL player Alzado (*Neon City*), who are both virtually relegated to being muscular buffoons by allowing themselves to be overtaken several times by Brad Davis and Ken Foree! Still, some fans of action movies (but not necessarily fans of action stars or fans of Ferrigno or Alzado) might enjoy this picture. It was directed by Peter Maris.

Hardcase and Fist

1989 (Image DVD) (V)

"Don't leave me like this! Finish me! McAll, you sonofabitch!"

Ted Prior (from *Deadly Prey*) and Carter Wong (from *Big Trouble in Little China*) star as embattled cellmates who unfortunately are named McAll and Lee, not Hardcase and Fist. McAll is a cop framed by his crooked partner, and Lee is a kung fu master busted for murdering a guy his stripper girlfriend cheated with. They get threatened by the gangs and the warden and eventually much too late in the movie they bust

216

out and have some car chases, shootouts, and martial arts fights. Lee tries to make up with his girlfriend but instead watches her do a g-string fire-eating dance and then gets into a giant strip club brawl. Meanwhile, McAll makes no attempt to prove his innocence. His enemy kidnaps his girlfriend and threatens to bite her, so he shoots the guy's car, sets him on fire, and ignores his cries to put him out of his misery.

This is an extremely amateurish movie with stiff acting and dialogue, numerous scenes and shots that go on agonizingly longer than they should, and laughable use of scratchy stock footage to represent memories of the Vietnam War. But for such an unprofessional movie it does manage to get some production value from prison scenes with real inmates and some decent stunts. The fire gag at the end is especially impressive (though an earlier one apparently went so bad that they felt they had to awkwardly composite smoke over it). In fact, the ending—from a car flipping and burning to Lee smiling and holding a fist up in victory—almost justifies the whole movie. The other highlight is director/producer/co-writer/music editor Tony Zarandast's performance as Tony Marino, a mob hitman hired to "ice" McAll and torn about it because the "god damn altar boy" saved his life in 'Nam. Zarandast's sincere attempt to play an Italian American badass despite his thick Iranian accent is made even more charming by an obvious fake mustache.

The Hard Corps

2006 (Sony DVD) (djm)

Sauvage: "You and I need to talk about my severance package."
Barclay (flipping him the bird): "Why don't you sever this?"
Sauvage: "You don't seem to understand. I want you to name a place and make sure to bring some ice packs and some painkillers. Because it's going to hurt."

Writer/director Sheldon Lettich and star Jean-Claude Van Damme reunited for this great vehicle featuring Van Damme as a PTSD-rattled soldier who becomes a bodyguard for a former heavyweight champion turned business mogul. Philippe Sauvage (Van Damme)'s best friend—a Vietnam vet—is a bodyguard for a millionaire mogul named Barclay. Barclay (Raz Adoti) has an enemy in the form of a famous gangster rapper named Singletery (Viv Leacock), a fresh parolee with a plan to assassinate Barclay. The first assassination attempt fails, though Sauvage's friend is killed. Barclay's sister Tamara (Vivica A. Fox) then hires Sauvage to protect her brother at all costs. The police are no help, and Sauvage has a hard time getting his employer to trust him, but when he starts showing results and making sense in how he handles his boss's safety, Sauvage becomes an essential asset to him. All clashes with his boss aside, once they start working together they become a great team—the hardest of the Hard Corps.

It mystifies me that this one wasn't released in theaters. It's a great action film, and it might have put Van Damme back on the map if it had gotten more of a push. He works really well with Lettich—their films *Bloodsport, Lionheart,* and *Double Impact* are fan favorites, and their direct-to-video efforts *Legionnaire* and *The Order* are solid entries as well. *The Hard Corps* will reinstate faith in Van Damme as an action star if any of his fans have fallen by the wayside.

Hard Hunted

1992 (Malibu Bay Films DVD) (djm)

"I have a contact in Arizona. He's reliable. He's Asian."

Bikini-clad super agents Donna Hamilton (Playboy Playmate Dona Speir) and Nicole Justin (Playboy Playmate Roberta Vasquez) get their hands on a jade artifact that has a nuclear trigger stashed within it, and all manner of trouble comes their way. A fellow sexy agent dies to bring them the artifact, and when arms dealer Kane (R.J. Moore) sets his sights on the trigger, he sends his "contact in Arizona" Raven (legendary stuntman/martial artist Al Leong) to retrieve it. With Raven on their tails (nice tails, by the way) in a sophisticated helicopter, Donna and Nicole are going to have to take arms, strap on their bikinis extra tight, and stand their ground to survive . . . because they're *hard hunted*!

As disposable as any number of Andy Sidaris's repertoire of titles, *Hard Hunted* is best watched in a vaguely horny state, but if you're watching it simply because Al Leong is in it, you may be on the wrong frequency. The girls look pretty amazing with or without bikinis. Leong actually has a decent sized role, but he's been better in other things. The movie desperately needed the kickboxing talents of Harold Diamond to pep things up. This was the seventh entry in Sidaris's Bullets, Bombs, and Babes series. It followed *Do or Die* and preceded *Fit to Kill*.

Hard Justice

1995 (Image DVD) (djm)

One-track-minded ATF agent Nick Adams (David Bradley) gets himself in a situation that will scar him forever: Asian gangster Jimmy Wong (Yuji Okumoto from *Red Sun Rising*) takes an innocent woman hostage after an explosive confrontation with Adams, and when Adams miscalculates a risk, the woman ends up dead. While recovering psychologically, Adams is told that his partner was killed in a prison while on an undercover assignment as a prisoner. Adams demands that he be sent to the same prison so that he can find his partner's killer, and once he gets there, he sets boundaries with the other

prisoners, who immediately jump on his case to hurt him, tame him, and make him their bitch. What no one in the prison—including the warden (played by Charles Napier from *Rambo: First Blood Part II*)—is prepared for is that Adams is a formidable fighter and a cop to boot. His secret gets out when Jimmy Wong is sent to the same penitentiary, and Adams lacks any allies on the inside to back him up when all of the inmates are out to get him. He's got to escape fast before he's killed, and his escape plan entails a lot of action.

Hard Justice feels similar to the Jean-Claude Van Damme vehicle *Death Warrant*, but with David Bradley (of the *American Ninja* sequels and *Outside the Law*) at the center, it has its own feel and texture. It was around this time that Bradley strayed away from using martial arts in his movies, but he uses it to the best of his abilities in this film, and sadly it was his last martial arts-fueled performance. Much of the action in the film is obviously inspired by John Woo's signature style, and fans of Woo's films will be entertained. Director Greg Yaitanes worked well in the action genre, but his career followed a trajectory that featured lots of television work. From Nu Image.

Hard Luck

2006 (Sony DVD) (CD)

After being released from prison, Lucky (Wesley Snipes) wants to leave behind his former life peddling drugs on the street. But no matter how hard he tries, things just never seem to go his way. Once he's back in New York, some of his old friends from his criminal past try to lure him back into the life. He shows up at a strip club for his friend's birthday only to find out the whole party was a ruse for another shady deal. It quickly turns sour and people are getting blown away, but Lucky sees a chance. There are two cases containing a total of $500,000, and he swipes them both. He grabs an unwilling hostage, a stripper named Angela (Jacquelyn Quinones), and escapes. They won't be able to relax for long since the mob, crooked cops, and two serial killers aren't far behind, guaranteeing this will be one of the craziest experiences of their lives.

Hard Luck reunites Wesley Snipes with his *New Jack City* director and co-star Mario Van Peebles. This is an odd film (especially for Snipes), but it's highly entertaining from start to finish, and it's got some action too. There're a couple of shootouts and a car chase, and Snipes finally busts out his fists during the finale. Quinones and Snipes share some great banter as he holds her hostage, showing a side of Snipes we don't always get to see. The cast also includes Cybil Shepard and Luis Guzman in fun roles. *Hard Luck* might not be essential Snipes, but it's worth seeking out. His fans might be surprised by it.

Hard Target

1993 (Universal DVD) (djm)

"Let me review the tactical situation for you gentlemen. Boudreaux is wounded. He's been pursued and harried across miles of open country. Now he's cornered and outnumbered twenty to one. He's an annoying little fucking insect, and I want him stepped on—*hard*!"

Chance Boudreaux (Jean-Clade Van Damme with interesting looking hair extensions) is a drifter, looking for work after his military career ended badly. He's been hanging around New Orleans, getting to know the lesser element very well, and when a despondent young woman named Natasha (Yancy Butler) comes looking for her father, who may have been homeless, he shows her around and escorts her (for a price) as protection while they look for him. When her father turns up dead, Chance catches on pretty quickly that he was murdered and that there is a series of deaths of vagabond Vietnam vets going around. A band of mercenary-type hunters led by the suave and dignified Emil Fouchon (a sublime Lance Henriksen) gives homeless vets the chance to run for their lives with a payday dangling at the end of the race, but the hunters always find their quarry at the end of a gun, arrow, or other weapon. When Chance gets himself in the sights of the hunters, the most dangerous game is on!

Director John Woo's first big-screen crossover in America, *Hard Target* is *still* the best movie that he made stateside, even when he had much bigger budgets for movies like *Broken Arrow, Face/Off,* and *Windtalkers.* His style is all over this fun movie, and it remains one of Van Damme's best films. The setting is cool, Van Damme plays it easy does it, and the action is pretty fantastic without being heavy handed, which is something so many of Woo's Hong Kong pictures have trouble with. Graeme Revell's score is almost iconic to me. Woo directed *Black Jack* with Dolph Lundgren around the same time.

Hard Ticket to Hawaii

1987 (Malibu Bay Films DVD) (djm)

The second entry in Andy Sidaris's "Bullets, Bombs, and Babes" series (which spanned twelve films!), *Hard Ticket to Hawaii* stars Playboy Playmates Dona Speir and Hope Marie Carlton as Donna and Taryn, two sexy superspies who love James Bond movies and globetrotting while on the job. Their latest mission takes them to Hawaii, where they get into some dangerous situations while trying to recover a stash of diamonds from a villain (played by Rodrigo Obregon) who has no idea that a lethal, venomous snake is slithering around near his property. But seriously: the snake is pretty close

to the size of the one from *Conan the Barbarian,* and if it comes in contact with anyone, it will eat up its victim and spit out the bones. Donna and Taryn are in only slightly over their heads with this mission, so they call on allies Rowdy (Ronn Moss) and Jade (real-life kickboxer Harold Diamond from *Rambo III*), who help them blow shit up and kick bad guys in the face.

How can guys not enjoy stuff like *Hard Ticket to Hawaii*? It's basically a porno without the hardcore stuff, and it's got explosions, nice locations, Harold Diamond, and tons of T & A. Diamond's role is small, but he has his moment to show off his kickboxing skills, and he also reprised his role in the sequel *Picasso Trigger.* There's a cool theme song, too!

Hard Time on Planet Earth

1989 (NOV) (djm)

"Negative outcome. *Not good*."

Martin Kove from *Steele Justice* stars as an alien soldier who is unjustly exiled to Earth for crimes against his planet's council, and once on Earth, he takes the name "Jesse" and becomes a fish out of water. His sidekick is a funny floating robot sentry known as "Control" who can manipulate computers to give him currency or help him out with information as he plods along a directionless course. Jesse is a good-hearted hero, so over the course of thirteen episodes, he helps people out with their troubles, and even goes to Disneyland in one episode.

When *Hard Time on Planet Earth* was on TV, it was my favorite show, and ever since then it's languished in Disney's vaults (it aired on ABC). Bootleggers still carry it, so if you ever stumble upon it, make sure to pick it up and see one of Martin Kove's best works as an action star. It's done very much in the episodic "PG" vein of '80s television, but if you like movies like *Starman* and *The Terminator,* then you should enjoy this, as it melds the two and makes a fun hybrid. Kove was never better, and it's a shame that this project may have contributed to the decline of his career. Jim and John Thomas (the screenwriters of *Predator*) created this show.

Hard Times

1975 (Columbia DVD) (djm)

Lucy: "What does it feel like, to knock somebody down?"
Chaney: "It makes me feel a helluva lot better than it does him."

Chaney (Charles Bronson), a proletarian vagabond drifting through shantytowns during the Great Depression, sees a way to make some cash: bare-knuckle boxing. His ticket into the circuit is to find a manager, and he finds Speed (James Coburn),

a scrappy promoter looking for his next fighter. In Chaney, Speed finds more than he could have ever dreamed . . . Chaney is a dynamo even at a seasoned age, and as a man of few words, Chaney is a good fellow, generous, and gracious almost to a fault. In between fights, Chaney tries romancing a chilly moll named Lucy (Jill Ireland), but when that goes nowhere, he befriends a cat. The story is simple, but the payoff is a hundred fold.

An early outing from director Walter Hill, who would find enormous success with the films *The Warriors, 48 Hours,* and *Red Heat, Hard Times* is a great, great dramatic action piece for Bronson, who had shot into stardom (at age fifty-three) the previous year with the release of *Death Wish.* Bronson's quintessence of manly cool and silent but deadly aura was never more perfectly personified than in *Hard Times,* where he displays a convincing fighter's physique and a vocabulary of few, but well-chosen words. His co-stars Coburn and Strother Martin as a shady, but likable doctor along for their road trips are in the "A" class, just like this movie. A+

Hard to Kill

1990 (Warner DVD) (djm)

"We're outgunned and undermanned, but we're gonna win. And I'll tell you why: Superior attitude, superior state of mind. We'll get 'em, buddy. Believe me. Every fuckin' one of 'em."

Steven Seagal's second movie out of the gate, *Hard to Kill* features Seagal in a sympathetic action role where he's gunned down beside his wife after obtaining evidence against a politico, who conspired to kill a senator to further his own gain. In a coma for seven years, cop Mason Storm (Seagal) wakes up, weak and virtually helpless, but when it's revealed that he's awake—and not dead as originally believed—goons come out in droves to kill him. With the help of a hot nurse (played by Kelly Le Brock, who would marry and then later divorce her co-star), Storm gets himself back into workable shape again and begins hunting the now-senator (played by William Sadler who would later play the lead villain in *Die Hard 2: Die Harder*) and a cadre of dirty cops on his payroll.

Mason Storm (Steven Seagal) is . . . Hard to Kill. Author's collection.

You'll always be Hard to Kill if you're always out for justice. Featuring Steven Seagal. Author's collection.

They couldn't kill him. They only made him angry. Steven Seagal stars as Mason Storm, and Kelly LeBrock co-stars as Nurse Andy in *Hard to Kill*. Author's collection.

We sympathize with Seagal's character every step of the way in this film. We watch him as he witnesses his family getting attacked, and then he's taken down and we see him gradually build himself up, which is all presented believably. Seagal uses his background in Asian philosophy and martial arts to great effect in the film, and the amount of action in the movie is plentiful and satisfying. It's simple, but it's exactly what it should be. At one point in the movie Seagal busts in on a bunch of bad guys and says, "How's the action, boys? Mind if I play?" Seagal had arrived in Hollywood and was there to stay. Bruce Malmuth (*Pentathlon*) directed.

Hawk's Vengeance

1996 (Dimension DVD) (djm)

The brother of a British special forces soldier named Eric Hawke (Gary Daniels) is killed while on duty as a cop, and when Hawke hears about it, he takes leave from duty to comb the criminal underbelly of his brother's beat to find who killed him and why. With the help of his brother's sexy partner (played by Jayne Heitmeyer), Hawke begins honing in on a gang of white supremacists led by a martial arts master named Garr (Cass Magda, an expert in Indonesian silat), who gives Hawke a run for his money when they face off in a death fight atop a high-rise building.

The Gary Daniels factor in *Hawk's Vengeance* is at work here: He's in prime shape, he plays a hero, there are plenty of fight scenes (and a sex

Video release poster for *Hawk's Vengeance*. Author's collection.

scene), and it's all done effectively. Filmed in Canada, this Cinepix feature isn't necessarily distinguishable from other movies Daniels made with PM Entertainment or other similar studios, but it has a decent villain in Cass Magda, who gives the film an interesting flare when the fights are on. Magda didn't really do much else, although he was in the film *Blade Boxer* the following year. *Hawk's Vengeance* is from director Marc F. Voizard, who made *Marked Man* with Roddy Piper.

Haywire

2011 (Lionsgate DVD) (djm)

Black Ops agent Mallory Kane (Gina Carano) finds herself at a crossroads when her handlers and the agency she works for turn against her and want her dead. She can run and hide (which she does), or she can take the offensive and go after the figures who are hunting her down (which she *also* does). She embarks on a globetrotting adventure through Europe to seek some answers, and she ends up on an estate owned by her father (Bill Paxton), where her

MMA star Gina Carano stars as the deadly agent Mallory Kane in Steven Soderbergh's *Haywire*. Author's collection.

handlers (who include Ewan McGregor and Channing Tatum) are waiting to kill her, but everyone always underestimates her incredible martial arts skills and her intuition. She makes it tough on anyone who isn't on her side.

The script by Lem Dobbs and the direction by Steven Soderbergh suggest that audiences really needn't concern themselves with the blank slate story but simply focus on Mallory and *what* Mallory is: a badass. The plot exists purely to give her movement, and we follow her in flashback and in real time, and every moment of her adventure is filled with fluidity and action. Carano, a real-life mixed martial arts fighter, fills the role of Mallory in a way only an unseasoned actor can. She's perfect for the role. Her acting is delightfully simple, and her physicality is everything. She's the real Jason Bourne. We see her (no doubles that I can detect) beat guys up in brutal fights, and she does everything in master shots, which works well for the film. Soderbergh, who is known for taking different genres and making them his own (sometimes experimentally), manages to make an action star out of Carano, but he does it in a nonchalant, unflinching and nonsensational way, which is jarring at times, because in this day and age when action stars are a dying breed to see something like *Haywire* in the guise of an indie thriller is actually kind of crazy. Carano is a talent and a force to be reckoned with. Her name should be shouted from rooftops and put in blaring lights. She's a real-deal action star. Fans of action and martial arts films might find *Haywire* a little too obtuse and artsy to fully enjoy (that would be me), but fans of *action stars* should definitely check it out. Carano's amazing. Her next appearance in an action film was several years later in *Fast and Furious 6*.

Heart of Dragon

1985 (Fox DVD) (djm)

A rising star in the SWAT team, Ted (Jackie Chan) has one thing holding back his dreams and ambitions: His mildly retarded brother Danny (Sammo Hung), who at thirty years of age, still acts like a child and has the mental capabilities of a kindergartner. Every time Ted gets the chance to advance in his career, he has to consider the ramifications of what that would mean for Danny. With a struggling romance with a nice girl, and an extremely trying relationship with Danny, Ted just can't get a break. When Danny finds a stash of loot hidden by some gangsters, Ted has to protect his brother from the consequences of being in possession of the loot, and after some grave misunderstandings, Danny is kidnapped and used as collateral for the loot, which Ted now has. With the help from his SWAT brethren (working outside the limits of the law), Ted takes on the mob . . . and pays a price for doing so.

A surprisingly sincere dramatic turn for both Chan and Hung, who both turn in solid "A" performances, *Heart of Dragon* is not just a drama, but a hardboiled action thriller that goes the distance, particularly in the action-packed finale. It's astonishing that Hung also directed the film because when you see him on screen, he's so convincing as the character he plays. If you like this, see also *Death Grip*, starring Eric Jacobus.

Heatseeker

1995 (Vidmark VHS) (djm)

A Japanese corporation builds technically advanced cyborgs capable of martial arts abilities, and they plan to enter their prized creation Xao (Gary Daniels) into a televised fight competition as a "sure thing" winner against other corporations who intend on having their best cyborg fighters in the running. The one element that's lacking in the match is an all-human fighter, and the current champ is Chance O'Brien (Keith Cooke from *China O'Brien*), who refuses to fight . . . until the corporation kidnaps his girlfriend and forces him to accept the terms. When he finally engages and fights his way to Xao (who has psychologically messed with him by making his girlfriend fall in love with him), the corporation—and the media—is shocked to find that Chance is clearly the superior fighter.

From action maestro and "B"-movie master Albert Pyun, *Heatseeker* is pretty good entertainment—especially if you're a fan of these types of movies and of its two stars. Cooke shines in the heroic role, and he has a light touch in the acting department and his physique and martial arts abilities equally match those of co-star Daniels, whose stoic, villainous turn must have been a cinch. It would have been great to see these two guys team up on something again, but for whatever reason, Cooke dropped out of the movie business. A shame.

Hellbinders

2009 (Maverick DVD) (djm)

A bored soldier-for-hire named Max (Ray Park from *G.I. Joe: The Rise of Cobra*) takes a job that leads him to Satan, chained in a basement. Literally. Along the way, Max becomes an ally of two guys—one guy is the last of The Knights Templar, and the other dude is a ninja named Ryu (Johnny Yong Bosch from *Death Grip*). The three of them are ultimately the last and only hope humanity has of ridding the world of evil and protecting the souls of mankind from being taken by a cult that intends on unleashing Satan from his prison. I don't know, guys. I had no idea what was going on. Sorry.

Framed around comic book-style panels and techno music, *Hellbinders* makes a lot of noise but says hardly anything at all and, believe me, I tried listening. Ray Park, who at that point had co-starred in some huge blockbusters, gets to play a character without a mask or makeup, which is cool, but Yong Bosch does most of the martial arts fighting in this movie, which is great, but we needed to see more action from Park. The story is nonsense, and I stopped trying to follow it less than halfway through the movie. It's so serious and blisteringly sincere that some of the dialogue made me (despite trying not to) laugh out loud. Woefully bereft of a sense of humor,

the movie failed to either impress or interest me. Directed by three (!) guys: Mitch Gould, Hiro Koda, and David Wald.

Hellbound

1993 (Cannon DVD) (djm)

A fairly radical opening act set during the Crusades where King Richard the Lionhearted and his knights imprison Satan's chief warrior in a cavern is followed by Chuck Norris kicking some thug's ass in Chicago. Norris is Frank Shatter (cool name), who sort of stumbles onto a murder case involving a rabbi who had his heart ripped out of his chest. Frank and his partner Calvin (Calvin Levels) are sent to Israel to escort the rabbi's corpse to the authorities, but when they get there they realize that the rabbi's killer is already there, committing more murders. The killer is the ancient demon warrior (played by Christopher Neame), who has been resurrected and is committing murders to piece together a talisman that could bring about the end of the world. When he faces Frank Shatter, he's up against a whole new type of Lionheart.

This was the last theatrical film Norris made before becoming a TV star. If you're familiar with *Walker, Texas Ranger*, you'll be dumbfounded when you see his female co-star in the show is also his lead co-star in this film. Sheree J. Wilson, who is virtually playing the same character here as in the show, has a damsel-in-distress moment where Norris saves her life. Also, Norris's partner, played by Calvin Levels, is surprisingly similar to the character Clarence Gilyard Jr. played on the show, and not just because he's black. When you see Norris, Levels, and Wilson on screen together, it's really hard not to do a double-take. This was filmed in Israel. Aaron Norris directed it.

Hell Comes to Frogtown

1988 (Anchor Bay DVD) (CD)

"Eat my lead, froggies!"

After a nuclear war wipes out most of the population, a new government is run by women. The human race is on the verge of extinction (due to infertility) and Sam Hell (Roddy Piper) is recruited by the government to rescue a group of fertile women being held by a group of mutant frogs. He signs a contract that lands him in a male chastity belt, and he's led off into battle with his handlers Spangle (Sandahl Bergman) and Centinella (Cec Verrell). It's never as easy as it sounds. They find themselves having run-ins with Captain Devlin (William Smith), and they're ultimately held captive by the mutants. Sam Hell plays by his own set of rules and if things go his way, then just maybe they'll make it out alive.

Theatrical poster for *Hell Comes to Frogtown*. Author's collection. .

"Rowdy" Roddy Piper is always at his best when he's playing an antihero type of character and *Hell Comes to Frogtown* is a unique and truly bizarre one-of-a-kind film. It's sort of light on the action but when you have a film that takes place in a post-apocalyptic future where the world is overrun by large human-like mutant frogs that are holding the last of Earth's fertile woman captive and he's the last sterile man brought in by the government to impregnate them, how could you go wrong? The film may have been produced on a small budget but the makeup effects look pretty terrific and cool. It should be noted that the effects wizard Steve Wang (who directed the superb Mark Dacascos film *Drive*) was the man responsible for the design and application of the creature effects. The film never for a second takes itself seriously and tries to accomplish one thing: force the audience to have fun. That's all it really needed to do and being awarded cult film status is the grand prize. Piper plays it over the top, and in this film it works. His performance works best when he's alongside Sandahl Bergman (*Conan the Barbarian*), who plays the government agent leading his character to the fertile women. They have a love/hate type of relationship that toys with building a sexual tension between them. The great William Smith (*Eye of the Tiger*) also makes an impression as Sam's nemesis who wants nothing more than to see him dead. Donald G. Jackson (*The Roller Blade Seven*) was a "B"-movie prince and *Hell Comes to Frogtown* was his masterpiece. Before he passed away in 2003, he managed to make three sequels, the first of which was *Return to Frogtown* with Lou Ferrigno and Robert Z'Dar as Sam Hell.

Hell's Heroes (a.k.a. Inglorious Bastards 2: Hell's Heroes)
1987 (Video Asia DVD) (djm)

"This goddamn war's a fucking waste. I'll be glad to go home."

The Vietnam war is raging and a US Senator (played by Chuck Connors) visits to get some good PR, but when he and his entourage are decimated by the Viet Cong, only one solider survives: Darkin (Miles O'Keeffe), a cynical, fed-up warrior, who just wants to go home. After surviving the attack, he wanders around the jungle, stunned and piecing together his memory, and when he's picked up by the allies, he's taken to his superiors and put on trial for deserting his post. Tried for crimes he didn't commit, he's court marshaled and stuck in a camp of reject soldiers until the government can figure out what to do with them. Biding his time, he clashes with Feather (Fred Williamson), another fallen soldier, but realizing that there may be an opportunity to redeem himself and the names of his fellow disgraced soldiers, Darkin takes it upon himself to lead them all on an unsanctioned mission to blow up a bridge and slaughter an enemy battalion before they reach the US Army bases and cause untold damage.

Much more a vehicle for Miles O'Keeffe (who I wish we could call an action star) than for co-star Williamson, but Williamson has a few moments that are enough for us to include it on his wide roster of action films. In typical Italian-made fashion, *Hell's Heroes* is over the top and absurd with ridiculous moments (especially the ending, which has a title card that reads: "They will go to heaven for sure now because they have been living in hell"), but fans of Vietnam-exploitation movies might get what they're looking for. Directed by Stelvio Massi.

Hell Up in Harlem
1973 (MGM DVD) (CD)

Picking up at the exact moment *Black Caesar* ended, the story begins with Tommy Gibbs (Fred Williamson) on the verge of death. Thankfully, his father Papa Gibbs (Julius Harris) gets to him in time. While Tommy is getting his strength back, Papa is out on the streets helping him settle the score so they can rise to power together. Mr. DiAngelo (Gerald Gordon) is out to put a stop to their reign and taps one of Tommy's own men to initiate the double-cross. There's no turning back and Tommy finds himself once again in a position where it's him or everyone else and he's not going to stay put. There may be a hit out on his head but he won't go down without a fight.

Where *Black Caesar* was more of a crime thriller, *Hell Up in Harlem* is a straight-up action film. Fred Williamson (*Black Cobra*) is back in the shoes of Tommy Gibbs and he couldn't be much better. In the first film, he never raised a fist to anyone, but that's all changed now.

Here, he has no problem hitting or kicking the enemy in any number of action sequences scattered throughout the film. Along with all the fighting, there are shootouts galore with plenty of cartoonish-looking blood. Much of the cast from the original film returns to reprise their roles including Gloria Hendry, D'Urville Martin, and of course, Gerald Gordon, who shines during the first half of the picture. Larry Cohen returns as the writer/director, and this time he goes for excitement instead of the slow burn. It was a bold and smart move to make both films so different while still maintaining what made the character so intriguing in the first place.

Hercules in New York
(a.k.a. Hercules Goes Bananas)
1970 (ZC)

Say what you will, Arnold Schwarzenegger's first movie is one humdinger of a zinger. Thrown out of Mount Olympus by a magic bolt from Zeus, young Hercules (guess who) is sent to Earth. There, he battles sailors until he's rescued by Pretzy the pretzel vendor (Arnold Stang). While learning about the strange and exotic customs of mankind, Herc calamitously interferes with college sports, forklifts, young romance, and film exhibition. He's eventually visited by other gods (Mercury, Atlas, Samson), but most of the movie focuses on his bizarrely inflated torso committing widespread buffoonery on the streets of Manhattan. Just to provide a barometer, the most riveting scene takes place when Hercules boxes an escaped grizzly bear in Central Park, only, the bear is just a skinny guy in a gorilla suit and bear mask.

The film's producers decided to credit their bulging lead as "Arnold Strong" after they deemed his last name as completely unpronounceable. They also provided him the additional indignity of redubbing his voice with a velvet-throated radio personality (for posterity, Schwarzenegger's unintelligible vocal recording was restored for the DVD release). But let's be honest: the hero of the film is Pretzy, played by supreme nerd Arnold Stang. The chinless, bespectacled, turtle-headed character actor is on fire, dishing out googly-eyed double-takes and zany gapes that counterbalance the aimless dead-eyed performances from everyone else on screen. Without him, all hope would be lost.

Hero and the Terror
1987 (MGM DVD) (djm)

"You came up against a monster, and he beat 'ya. That's heavy shit."

Plagued by nightmares of a homicidal killer of women he arrested in the past, Danny O'Brien (a weary and stressed-out-looking Chuck Norris) is plunged back into a real nightmare when the killer, known as "The Terror" (Jack O'Halloran

from the first two *Superman* films) escapes his confinement and begins killing women again. Danny's wife is very pregnant, and his life is full enough as it is, but when the mayor of Los Angeles (Ron O'Neal from *A Force of One*) comes to him and asks him to head the task force to stop The Terror, Danny enlists his friend and fellow cop (played by Steve James) to help him. The Terror takes up residence in the rafters of The Wiltern Theater, a concert hall, and the film takes on *Phantom of the Opera* proportions when the police comb the rafters and attics of the concert hall looking for the crazed killer.

Similar to Norris's previous film, *Silent Rage*, Cannon's *Hero and the Terror* features a silent, unstoppable killer twice Norris's size and strength, culminating in a smackdown only Norris can walk away from. The best aspect of the film is showing Norris in a tired, dilapidated state, and yet we see him working out and trying to be on his game despite the stress his character is experiencing. The scene where Steve James faces The Terror is a big disappointment, and it only goes to show that James was rarely given the opportunity to shine past the sidekick roles he usually played. Billy Drago plays a small role as a psychiatrist. Director William Tannen later worked with Chuck Norris again on his last solo vehicle to date, *The Cutter*.

The Heroic Trio
1993 (Dimension DVD) (CD)

"Don't give me that shit! I almost got killed because of your so-called justice."

There's an epidemic of missing babies in Hong Kong, and the culprit is an invisible phantom. The police are baffled and don't know how to handle the situation. Local superhero Wonder Woman (Anita Mui) is trying her best to help find who it may be. Thief Catcher (Maggie Cheung) is willing to help, but only if the price is right. Which leaves Number 3 (a.k.a. Invisible Woman, played by Michelle Yeoh): she's the one stealing the children but she's under the control of the Evil Master (Yen Shi-Kwan), who is trying to breed the next Emperor while turning the others into mindless (and murderous) minions. There's no way he can be stopped unless they band together. If this is going to happen, then Thief Catcher and Wonder Woman will have to do anything they can to break the hold Evil Master has over Invisible Woman.

To this day, *The Heroic Trio* remains a perfect example of why there was nothing like Hong Kong cinema in the early '90s. It's an awesomely bizarre masterpiece that showcases the talents of three of the most amazing women to work in the Hong Kong industry: Maggie Cheung (*Police Story,*) Michelle Yeoh (*Supercop*), and the late Anita Mui (*Rumble in the Bronx*). The story is unique and confusing simultaneously, but the action is incredible, unlike anything we've seen before. The wirework in the film is superb and each of the women has her moment to shine. Michelle Yeoh is in top form, playing the troubled character with serious moral decisions to make—this is a layered performance, topped off with her amazing physical agility. Directed by Johnnie To and followed by a post-apocalyptic sequel, *Executioners*, which was released later the same year.

Hidden Agenda

2001 (Lionsgate DVD) (djm)

A private agent for hire named Jason Price (Dolph Lundgren) takes on a job protecting the leader of a crime syndicate, who says that "a cleaner" has been hired to kill him. Price uses his resources and his small agency's manpower to find out what's going on, but something personal distracts him: a childhood friend of his is killed, and he tries to piece together some open-ended clues to find out who killed his buddy. As the two cases he's on converge, he discovers that his friend faked his own death and that "the cleaner" supposedly hunting down his client doesn't exist. Also, the woman working with Price (played by Maxim Roy) might be about to betray or kill him and, realizing this, he must put all the pieces together or risk getting himself killed.

Lundgren's career as an action star reads like an adventurer's road map. He's played He-Man, The Punisher, hitmen, soldiers, mercenaries, and cops. Many of his films are great action-tastic genre films, but when he stars in movies like *Hidden Agenda*, it's immediately apparent that he did them for the money and to fill a void instead of trying to do something that remotely had a chance to be special. The script, story, and direction of *Hidden Agenda* are all completely watered down and forgettable. His character isn't interesting, and the action in it is boring. It's too bad. Lundgren is a talent that should never be wasted. Director Mac S. Grenier never made another action film. Lundgren also starred in a movie called *Hidden Assassin*. That one was better.

Hidden Assassin

1995 (Dimension DVD) (CD)

When in New York, the ambassador to Cuba is assassinated. This murder could set off a chain of negative events when the US/Cuba summit takes place in Prague. The CIA brings in federal marshal Michael Dane (Dolph Lundgren) to capture who they believe to be the killer. Her name is Simone (Maruschka Detmers), a seemingly harmless woman with a past who now owns a club with her friend Marta (Assumpta Serna). Dane and his partner Alex (John Ashton) plot to take her in, but she's much more resourceful than they imagined. Once she's in custody, Dane begins to think she's innocent and the murder of the ambassador is part of a much more sinister plan conceived to set her up for the fall. He finds himself in a position where he doesn't know who he can trust; he just knows he will do anything to bring down the real assassin and clear Simone's name.

Hidden Assassin was originally titled *The Shooter* before it was acquired by Miramax. They're notorious for acquiring films for US distribution and chopping them up before releasing them, and this one is no exception. The international cut of the film runs nearly fifteen minutes longer than the version released in the US. Dolph Lundgren (*Men of War*) is the star of the film, so viewing either version is mandatory . . . even if it breaks you. The movie takes some time to get moving and it's painful to watch his character being made a fool of by this woman who is able to evade him for more than half of the picture. Despite some frustration, there are some fun action scenes (mostly intense shootouts), as well as an intriguing story. It was directed by Ted Kotcheff (*First Blood*).

High Adventure

2001 (e-m-s DVD R2) (djm)

"We all do a little thieving now and then . . . "

Chris Quartermain (Thomas Ian Griffith), the grandson of the infamous treasure hunter Allan Quartermain (of *King Solomon's Mines*), is carrying on the tradition of adventure in his bloodline, and his latest globetrotting adventure entails searching for Alexander the Great's gold helmet. Along for the ride is his benefactor (played by German actress Anja Kling), who doesn't quite realize the trouble they will find themselves in until a secret band of warriors guarding Alexander's booby-trapped temple enters the picture. Quartermain, proficient in sword fighting and fisticuffs, and with a general sense of the do-or-die mentality that made his grandfather a legend, manages to out-adventure everyone around him and save the day, win the girl, and obtain some treasure.

Kenpo martial artist Griffith from *The Karate Kid Part III* and *Ulterior Motives* turns in a breezy but physical performance in this lightweight action adventure that mimics *Indiana Jones and the Last Crusade*. It's a shame that by this point in Griffith's career he was starring in smaller, less demanding films, but I always enjoy watching him in anything he does, even this "PG"-rated picture. He later teamed up with the same director, Mark Roper, for a similar treasure-hunting action adventure called *The Sea Wolf*, which might as well be a sequel to this. Griffith's fans might be put off by the family-friendly tone of these two films and the lack of martial arts action in them. They're of interest, however.

Highlander: Endgame

2000 (Miramax DVD) (CD)

Connor MacLeod (Christopher Lambert, reprising the role that pretty much defined his career) has grown tired of his immortal life and never has it been more apparent than after he

witnesses the death of his friend Rachel. He learns of a place known as the Sanctuary, a haven where immortals can go to leave it all behind, a place to just rest on holy ground, where the game of killing other immortals never comes into play. Jacob Kell (Bruce Payne) is as ruthless as they come and he returns to the Sanctuary with his group of immortal mercenaries (one of whom is played by Donnie Yen) to kill all who reside there, including, as it first appears, Connor. Duncan MacLeod—Connor's cousin, also an immortal (played by Adrian Paul)—doesn't believe for a second that Connor is dead and does some investigating into the matter. With the help of a few friends, Duncan and Connor reunite but it's all about business. Villain Kell is far more powerful than either of them, and to end to his vicious reign, one of them will have to make the ultimate sacrifice to save the other.

Through five films and a long-running television series, the world of *Highlander* has had a mixed past. This is the film that attempted to bring the world of the TV program into the world of the film franchise, but with disappointing results. It was great to see the stars of both mediums—Christopher Lambert (*Mean Guns*) and Adrian Paul (*The Breed*)—but their on-screen union isn't what makes the film worth mentioning. It's the fact that martial arts sensation Donnie Yen (*Ip Man*) appears in the film as a mercenary working for the Jacob Kell character. Everything in the film pales in comparison to the two exciting fight scenes he participates in. He single-handedly takes on a group of masked men, and then a bit later he has a sword fight with Adrian Paul, which develops into a hand-to-hand fight. Yen has these few short moments to show why he's an amazing talent. There's also a brief appearance by WWE star Adam Copeland (*Breaking the Rules*). Doug Aarniokoski (*The Day*) directed this film in Bulgaria.

High Voltage

1997 (A-Pix VHS) (CD)

"There's an old saying: *If you cut the dragon, you better slay him*. So far, you've only cut him."

A group of young thieves, led by Johnny (Antonio Sabato Jr.), decide to hit a bank in Little Saigon thinking it will be their last job. What they don't know is the bank is a front for Vietnamese mobster Victor Phan's (George Kee Cheung) money-laundering business. They barely escape with their lives and have nothing to show for it. Phan doesn't like being targeted so he goes after Johnny, Sam (Mike Mains), Molly (Amy Smart), and Larry (Lochlyn Munro). Johnny becomes close with the bank's manager, Jane (Shannon Lee), who is being abused by Phan. He wants to help her out, and they hatch a plan that will cost Phan his money and his life. They just have to keep their heads in the game if they want to succeed.

Direct-to-video action helmer Isaac Florentine knows exactly what he wants and how to shoot it. *High Voltage* may have some corny dialogue and incidents in the story that leave you scratching your head, but the action is top notch and never lets up. If you're a fan of early '90s Hong Kong action films, then you can't go wrong with it. *High Voltage* has numerous extended shootouts that are reminiscent of the heroic bloodshed era that John Woo helped popularize. Almost everyone runs around two-fisted, sliding over tables, and propelling themselves through the air using various surfaces. Then out of nowhere, there is an incredible bar brawl where everyone knows martial arts and some of the tumbles look just plain brutal. The action scenes were choreographed with an expert's eye by Koichi Sakamoto (*The Guyver: Dark Hero*). The fights are furious while the shootouts attempt to be more balletic. The acting in the film is decent with a truly eclectic cast. Antonio Sabato Jr. (*The Base 2*) proved that he can headline an action film with this. Along for the ride are Shannon Lee (*Cage 2*), Amy Smart (*Crank*), Lochlyn Munro (*Art of War II*), James Lew (*Rush Hour 2*), and William Zabka (*Shootfighter*). This film really is all about the action. Who really cares about the limp story when everything else falls perfectly in place? Florentine knows how to entertain where it counts, and *High Voltage* never lets you take a breath and delivers the excitement every step of the way.

Hijacked

2012 (Anchor Bay DVD) (djm)

When the first *The Expendables* was released, I was expecting former UFC champ Randy Couture to break off and do films of his own straightaway, but it took a while before that happened. He appeared in the abysmal *Scorpion King 2* and had a cameo in David Mamet's *Red Belt*, but he was out of the picture until he did *Hijacked*, a cheap straight-to-DVD movie that disappoints on almost every level. He plays a government agent who gets on a plane to oversee the transfer of a billionaire from one location to another, but everything goes wrong. The billionaire (Craig Fairbrass, who is miscast) locks himself in his cabin on the plane when terrorists take over and start killing people. There's only a handful of passengers aboard in the first place, so there's not much suspense, and there aren't too many hiding places, which makes it that much more obvious that this won't be another "*Die Hard* on a plane" film (which might have worked better than this, actually). Couture is mostly mute and motionless for much of the film, and when he's free to move around, he kills one or two guys, none of which are any match for him. The blood in the film is weak sauce CGI nonsense, and when it was over, I got angry.

The pedigree of this film is bottom of the barrel. The director is Brandon Nutt, who made a junky slasher before this, and the writer is Declan O'Brien, who wrote and directed the direct-to-video *Wrong Turn* sequels. Nothing hurts worse than when a champ like Couture sinks to the low level of appearing in cannon fodder like this. He looks great in the film, and you can tell he's being held *way* back. Dominic Purcell and Vinnie Jones co-star.

Hired to Kill

1990 (Hollywood DVD) (CD)

"Either you go on a little Mediterranean cruise with us, dance a little, kill a little, have a barrel of fun or every camel jockey from here to Mecca is gonna be blowing smoke up your pretty ass."

Frank Ryan (Brian Thompson from *Commando Squad*) is the best mercenary money can buy. He's called in by an old associate named Thomas (George Kennedy), who's ready to give him a new assignment. At first it sounds pretty simple when he's asked to travel to Cypra and rescue a man known as Rallis (Miguel Ferrer), a rebel leader being held captive. The catch is that he has to pose as a gay fashion designer who is about to reveal a new line of fashion. He isn't alone either—he has to put together a team of super sexy women who can kick ass and pose as models for his fashion show. Once they have assembled as a team, they'll have to take out the evil president of the country, Michael Bartos (Oliver Reed), who is holding their target.

After watching this film you'll realize someone in Hollywood is an idiot for not giving Brian Thompson (also in *Cobra*) more lead roles in the same vein as this. He's perfectly capable of carrying a film and spewing one-liners, and he sure as hell can handle the action. *Hired to Kill* is a politically incorrect romp with some seriously odd-ball moments. It drags for a spell in the middle, but it delivers everything you could possibly want from it. It might be a tad difficult for Thompson to keep up with his seven gorgeous co-stars, but he pulls it off. There's tons of gunfire, a pinch of kung fu fighting, a dash of girl-on-girl, and a sprinkle of man-on-man (a bizarre and funny moment) action brought to the screen by director Nico Mastorakis (*Ninja Academy*).

The Hitman

1991 (Cannon DVD) (djm)

Chuck Norris stars as Cliff Garrett, a cop who was shot and left for dead by his corrupt partner (Michael Parks). Three years later, Garrett is working deep undercover as a hitman for the Italian mafia, and his boss (Al Waxman) is at war with an Iranian syndicate that is moving in on his territory. When Garrett's boss makes an alliance with Garrett's former partner, Garrett's identity is compromised, and those he cares about—a girlfriend and a bullied black kid who lives next door—are put in jeopardy.

Really violent and downbeat, *The Hitman* is one of Norris's grittiest movies. The violence is fairly graphic and bloody, and the few tender character moments involving Norris and the neighbor boy help offset the nasty scenes of torture, dismemberment, and foul play. Still, this is one of Norris's most serious and down-to-earth movies since *Code of Silence*. It was directed by his brother Aaron.

Hollow Point

1996 (Allumination DVD) (djm)

From Nu Image, *Hollow Point* stars Tia Carrere (from *Kull the Conqueror*) as FBI agent Diane Knox, who is on an endgame mission to find and capture a criminal mastermind named Thomas Livingston (John Lithgow, playing a friendlier version of his character in *Cliffhanger*). A rogue-ish DEA agent (or so he says) named Max Perish (Thomas Ian Griffith, also from *Kull the Conqueror* and *Excessive Force*) gets in Knox's way by going after Livingston in a reckless, slapdash manner, and despite their best efforts to work apart, they end up working together. They pick up an unlikely ally in a hitman named Garrett (a really wacky Donald Sutherland), who has a grudge against Livingston and is willing to pair up with the two agents because they're really after the same thing.

Just a few years after Thomas Ian Griffith starred in some really interesting and smart martial arts action movies like *Excessive Force*, he was relegated to direct-to-video movies that downplayed his martial arts abilities and allowed him to squander his talents on projects that had no idea what to do with him. *Hollow Point* is such a movie. Even if it weren't zany, spoofy, and awkward in almost every way, it still wouldn't have enough action in it. There are a few times when he uses his kenpo abilities, but the movie's virtually a comedy, and so it's a waste. It's not quite on the level of *Hudson Hawk*, but it's close. Sidney J. Furie—the director of *Direct Action* with Dolph Lundgren and *The Rage* with Lorenzo Lamas—made this.

Hollywood Vice Squad

1986 (Image DVD) (djm)

A bunch of misfit cops played by Leon Isaac Kennedy (from the *Penitentiary* trilogy), Carrie Fisher, Ronny Cox, Cec Verrell, and Evan C. Kim hit the Hollywood streets as a vice squad, intent on arresting prostitutes, pimps, and sex traffickers. Several story threads intersect and collide, as the team is after a missing teen girl (played by Robin Wright in her first film role) who is being used as a drug-addicted hooker by a notable kingpin (played by Frank Gorshin). There's some unexpected action (pretty violent), silly comedy, and depressing drama. Strangely, it kinda works.

An odd mixture of farce, comedy, drama, and action gives Penelope Spheeris's *Hollywood Vice Squad* an interesting flavor, but it doesn't use co-star Leon Isaac Kennedy enough. He's got some nice little moments, but just when the movie needed him to spring into action, he's sidelined. Still, if you love movies like *Angel*, *Vice Squad*, *Hardcore*, and *Fear City*, then you'll probably have a good time with this.

Hologram Man

1995 (Trinity DVD) (CD)

"I understood that one, you little computer maggot. How 'bout I put a bullet in this ear and out the other, then we'll see how much brains you really got."

Slash Gallagher (Evan Lurie) is a terrorist of sorts who murders a prominent political figure only to be taken down by rookie cop Decoda (Joe Lara). He's taken and sentenced to holographic stasis where he's essentially turned into a hologram and kept in a little jar. Five years later when Gallagher is up for parole, one of his cronies creates a problem in the mainframe and Gallagher's released, more powerful than before. He escapes with his gang and the president sends Decoda to stop him. Since he's a hologram, it's almost impossible to kill him, even if he's wearing a rubberized skin to contain the energy of the hologram. Decoda will have to fight fire with fire if he's to stop the madman's rampage.

This moderately budgeted action film from PM Entertainment and director Richard Pepin (*T-Force*) defies summarization. Who do we have to thank for this? Well . . . Evan Lurie (*T-Force, American Kickboxer 2*) of course! He co-wrote the script based on his idea, and it's a really wild one. There isn't a dull moment in the picture. It opens with a brilliant gunfight, pausing only to cut to some hot and heavy banging (complete with soft-core nudity), then cutting to another explosion-filled action scene. This all happens within eighteen minutes. No expense was spared on the action; there's an abundance of high-tech weapons and explosions that would make Michael Bay jealous. Lurie is the highlight—his over-the-top performance as the villain is quite memorable even if he only gets to fight in a couple of short sequences. It's a weird combination of *Demolition Man* and *Wes Craven's Shocker*, and it isn't an easy feat to pull off, but somehow it's ridiculous and relevant all at the same time.

(Editor's note: Co-star Lara also had a career in action films, starring in movies like American Cyborg: Steel Warrior *and* Steel Frontier, *but he wasn't particularly buff and he didn't come from martial arts or sports, so we decided not to cover his career in this book.)*

Homefront

2013 (Universal DVD) (djm)

After a drug bust goes wrong, DEA agent Phil Broker (Jason Statham) quits and relocates to a Southern town and tries to make a life with his daughter (Izabela Vidovic), who is still in grade school. While in school one day, she is picked on by a bully, whom she plainly warns to leave her alone, and when he persists she gives him a beating he won't soon forget. This event changes hers and her father's lives forever. The bully's

HOW FAR WOULD YOU GO TO PROTECT YOUR HOME?

JASONSTATHAM   JAMESFRANCO   WINONARYDER   KATEBOSWORTH

HOMEFRONT

Theatrical release poster for Millennium's *Homefront*. Author's collection.

mother (Kate Bosworth) is an unforgiving, spiteful tweaker whose brother Gator (James Franco) is the local drug lord whom everyone knows not to mess with. She seeks his help on getting some revenge on Broker and his daughter, and what starts out as being a tit-for-tat disagreement turns into something much bigger. Gator finds out that Broker is ex-DEA, and he makes a deal with a much bigger drug cartel to give them Broker (who killed their leader's son in the botched drug bust) in exchange for wider drug distribution rights. A wave of killers invade the town hunting Broker and his daughter, but this isn't just anybody they're up against.

Similar to the Thomas Jane iteration of *The Punisher*, this solid Statham vehicle was based on a book by Chuck Logan and adapted by Sylvester Stallone for the screen. Stallone had wanted to star in the film himself years earlier, but other projects came up in the interim, and so he passed it over to Statham, who certainly fits the bill. That said, *Homefront* still isn't able to give Statham the "A"-list project he needs to put his career on another level. Produced by the Nu Image/Millennium folks, who also backed Statham in *The Mechanic* and in *The Expendables* pictures, this one is certainly on par with those. Also starring Frank Grillo and Winona Ryder. Directed by Gary Fleder.

Honor

2006 (Monteray DVD) (CD)

"Out on the street, in the joint, or in the ring, you've got to fight to stay alive. You've got to earn your respect!"

Ray (Russell Wong) has become a feared man. Growing up on the streets, he's become a hardened criminal. People are afraid to leave

their homes because of him, and local businesses are being hit up for cash on a daily basis. LT Tyrell (Roddy Piper from *Jungleground*) is a retired police officer who is about to open a new bar. Ray was responsible for Tyrell son's death, so the blood is obviously bad between them. Tyrell's adopted son Gabriel (Jason Barry) has come back to town after serving time in the military. He and Ray were once best friends, but now they're mortal enemies. Ray is ready to claim the town as his own, and Gabe is planning to bring the war home and destroy Ray's entire criminal operation, including his underground fight club.

Honor is a superlow-budget action film with little to surprise an audience, but somehow does it right and manages to be moderately entertaining. The main attraction is the number of martial art celebrities in minor roles, including Don Frye, Rorian Gracie, and Rener Gracie. It's always a pleasure to see Roddy Piper (also in *Back in Action* and *Tough and Deadly*) appear on screen, and he gives a genuinely heartfelt performance. There's an awful lot of action in the picture, and Piper luckily gets a couple of great scenes, with the best one taking place during an extortion attempt at his bar. The final action scene lacks focus since there are four one-on-one fights happening simultaneously, but seeing all the different styles at play is interesting. Since the film is directed by David Worth (*Kickboxer, Lady Dragon*), we are at least given an action-packed presentation.

Honor Among Thieves

(a.k.a. **Farewell, Friend**)

1968 (Lionsgate DVD) (djm)

Two men serving in the French Foreign Legion end their tour of duty and go their separate ways. A mercenary by trade, Franz (Charles Bronson) looks for his next gig, and he sets his sights on cracking a safe that might hold a fortune. Dino (played by Alain Delon) goes back to his work as a respectable doctor. The safe that Franz wants to crack is located next door (in the same building!) to Dino's office, and when they find themselves in a serendipitous situation where they both have the same idea—to raid the safe—their worlds collide once again. When their heist doesn't work out according to plan (the safe is empty and a man has been murdered in the building), they have to hide out in the building over the weekend to avoid getting caught, but that means that both of them are going to get on each other's nerves and get into fisticuffs a few times. When the weekend passes, they attempt to escape . . . but get caught. With a cool-headed Franz being interrogated by the cops, and Dino trying to formulate another plan, will these guys find themselves behind bars, or will one of them take the fall for the other? Is there, indeed, honor among thieves?

Sharp and classy, *Honor Among Thieves* was amongst a batch of films that Charles Bronson made in Europe in the late '60s and early '70s. It's leagues better and more entertaining than his dramatic thriller *Someone Behind the Door* (which we did not review for this book for lack of action), and it gives him some pretty fantastic character moments to shine. He does a neat trick with a stack of quarters and a full cup of liquid several times throughout the film, but the last time he does it is better than any of the fistfights he engages in here. Speaking of fistfights, Alain Delon holds his own against him in a long fight scene in a hallway. Light on "action," but heavy on character arcs, *Honor Among Thieves* is a solid effort from director Jean Herman.

Honor and Glory

1993 (Imperial DVD R2) (djm)

"You chase honor, I'll chase glory."

Reporter Joyce Pride (Donna Jason) is visited by her FBI agent sister Tracy (Cynthia Rothrock), who helps Joyce on a story dealing with a ruthless banker named Jason Slade (John Miller), who is clearly raging on steroids. When Slade isn't killing minions with his martial arts prowess, he's chasing after a key that can launch a nuclear arsenal, and he's already got a billion-dollar deal in place with a Middle Eastern buyer. One of Slade's men—Jake Armstrong (Chuck Jeffries)—no longer wants any part of Slade's evil plans, so he joins the Pride sisters in taking Slade down.

Director Godfrey Ho reunited several of the key actors from this film for his next one, *Undefeatable*. *Honor and Glory* isn't a great showcase for Rothrock, but it does offer some nice moments for Chuck Jeffries (from *Superfights* and *Fight to Win*, also with Rothrock). Miller's performance in this film is off the handle. He makes the movie worth watching. Otherwise, the movie is silly and junky. *Undefeatable* is better.

John Miller plays the psycho villain in Godfrey Ho's *Honor and Glory*. Courtesy of John Miller.

Hostile Environment

(a.k.a. **Watership Warrior**)

2000 (Laser Paradise DVD) (CD)

In the near future, toxic waste has obliterated the world's water supply. There are only a select few who know how to clean the water, and they are the ones who are in power. One such person is the evil Minna (Brigitte Nielsen), who has set up her base on a giant battleship. She holds hundreds of people as slaves on her ship doing all the dirty work. Jennifer (Rochelle Swanson) is part of a rebel group in desperate need of a leader, and she turns to Mike Erikson (Matthias Hues), a man who isn't about to take any guff. While the two of them plot to overtake the ship, Jennifer's brother Rocky (Darren Shahlavi) makes his way to them to help.

When you have guys like Matthias Hues (*Dark Angel*) and Darren Shahlavi (*Bloodmoon*) in lead hero roles, it actually kind of makes the world a more pleasant place to live in. Both these guys are fantastic, and it makes you wonder why they haven't been offered more. It was great to see the majority of the action falling into the martial arts arena, and the finale brings these two action stars together, fighting groups of men, side by side. Hues is such a large man but he moves with the speed of someone half his size. Darren's style is reminiscent of a young Van Damme, flexible and full of kick. David Prior (*Raw Justice*) has been a stable of DTV releases for many years and this is most certainly one of his best efforts.

Hot Potato

1975 (Warner DVD) (djm)

A US senator's daughter is kidnapped by an Asian crime lord in Rangoon, where she is held captive for a king's ransom. A team of secret agents led by Jones (Jim Kelly) is sent in to save her and eliminate the crime lord. He teams up with an Asian agent (Irene Tsu), who surprises him with her go-get-'em prowess and strength. They traverse rivers, fight off ninjas, and shoot rockets and fireworks at a stampede of the crime lord's henchmen. The ending finds them saving the senator's daughter.

Unfortunately, at this point in Jim Kelly's career, the films he was making were already becoming sub-par and made the deadly mistake of turning martial arts into comedy. When he jump-kicks or flips, the sound effects suggest silliness and tomfoolery, which is a big no-no. Much of *Hot Potato* mocks itself and the genre, all while Kelly is doing his best to make a straight action film. It was filmed in Thailand. Oscar Williams, who wrote *Truck Turner*, wrote and directed it. It was remade (at least in part) as *Force: Five*.

House of the Rising Sun

2011 (Lionsgate DVD) (djm)

Former detective and recent parolee from a penitentiary Ray Shane (pro wrestler Dave Bautista) has sold his brawn to the mafia, who have stationed him at a strip club called House of the Rising Sun, and his job is basically to stand around the door, doing security work. When some armed thugs get the drop on him at the entrance, they hold him at gunpoint and proceed to rob the club, which has several hundred thousand dollars of mob money stashed in the back room. In the commotion, the club owner's son is shot and killed. Left picking up the pieces, Ray is blamed for the whole fiasco, and because Ray is a former detective, his boss demands that Ray use what little skills he has to find out who robbed him and killed his son. As Ray ventures out and calls on some shaky alliances with some of his former cop friends, he finds that a mob middleman (played by Dominic Purcell) is hunting him down and trying to frame him for several murders, including the boss's son. With cops, mobsters, and an encroaching sense of doom on his tail, Ray must turn up his brute force to get results, and the climax unfolds in a credible fashion.

On the one hand, fans of Dave Bautista will be pleased to see that he's been given a lead role in a movie that requires him to act (first and foremost) while doing some physical stuff like sprinting, bashing up bad guys, and using a pistol to kill some on-screen vermin. But on the other hand, *House of the Rising Sun* is a film that many of his fans will be disappointed with. Shot on digital video and on a very low budget, it showcases Bautista as a vulnerable physical brute, but it doesn't really make him shine or prove that he's any kind of hope for the world of action stars. The tone is grim, the characters around him are pretty vile, and while a few supporting turns by Amy Smart and Danny Trejo add some bright moments throughout the picture, an overall sense of indistinguishability mars what might have made an engrossing and gritty little action movie. As a stepping stone for its star, *House of the Rising Sun* is close to what it should be, but not nearly the launching pad it might have been. It was directed by Brian A. Miller.

The Human Shield

1992 (Cannon VHS) (djm)

Captain Doug Matthews (Michael Dudikoff), a CIA Marine instructor, makes an enemy for life while in Iraq in the mid 1980s: General Ali Dallal (Steve Inwood), who slaughters innocent villagers on a whim in front of him. They get into a fight, and Matthews scars Dallal's face with a knife, inciting a hatred that will burn for years to come. Matthews flees Iraq, restarting his life in the States. Five years later, on the precipice of the Gulf War, Matthews's brother Ben and his family are trying to leave Iraq after a business trip, but General Dallal has Ben kidnapped in order to entice his brother Doug to return to Iraq so that he can get his revenge on him. When Doug learns of his diabetic brother's kidnapping, he secretly smuggles himself into the country and sneaks his way around, trying to find the best way to save his brother before he's murdered or goes into a diabetic coma.

I saw this theatrically when it was briefly released in theaters in 1992, and watching it now it's amazing how simple it is. Dudikoff remains a stalwart hero, and his films with Cannon gave him the roles his persona was best suited for. *The Human Shield* isn't action packed or full of special effects; it's a dramatic action film with startling violence, casting the hero into a tragic adventure. Director Ted Post never glorifies the action or heroics, but instead makes everything more or less realistic. The Middle Eastern locations and local talent on screen lend themselves to a dangerous foreign excursion on film. It's still pretty good.

Hunter

1984–1991 (Mill Creek DVD)

(djm)

One of the most consistently present television shows throughout the 1980s and 1990s (via re-runs), *Hunter* cast former New York Giants and LA Rams NFL star Fred Dryer as Sgt. Rick Hunter, a chili dog–loving renegade cop wielding a .44 Magnum (and in later seasons a Heckler and Koch P9S 9mm). His partner is the very cute Sgt. Dee Dee McCall (Stepfanie Kramer), who backs him up, but there's never any romance between the two. They go after cop killers, drug dealers, good guys gone bad, and everything in between. Hunter usually settles his quarrels with his gun, but there are plenty of times where he's required to use fisticuffs and brute strength to knock down bad guys.

Over the course of 153 episodes, Rick Hunter switched his gun and his car several times, and when Dee Dee moved on (after the sixth season), he was assigned new partners (also females). The show was so popular that it spawned several TV movies: *The Return of Hunter* (1995), *Hunter: Return to Justice* (2002, with Kramer finally reprising her role), and *Hunter: Back in Force* (2003). There was a short revival of a new *Hunter* series with Dryer and Kramer in 2003, but it was cancelled shortly thereafter. Dryer was never able to shake off his *Hunter* image (which was essentially a riff on Dirty Harry), and the only feature film project he took on during his reign as that character was *Death Before Dishonor*. Frank Lupo created the show.

The Hunt for Eagle One

2006 (Sony DVD) (CD)

While making a routine fly-by, a US Marine helicopter is shot down by Philippine rebels. The pilot, Captain Amy Jennings (Theresa Randle), is captured by the al Qaeda–backed rebels, and she's tortured. General Lewis (Rutger Hauer) takes on responsibility for the situation, and a

rescue team is quickly dispatched. Leading the team into the danger zone is Lt. Matt Daniels (Mark Dacascos), a highly trained and respected Marine who has a tough and qualified team that's ready to go. When it's revealed that the rebels not only have Jennings but are also preparing a biological attack, he won't quit until the mission has been accomplished.

The Hunt for Eagle One makes one serious mistake: it lacks of any real character development. Because of that, it's sort of tough to become invested in the story. It isn't any fault of the actors who do whatever they can to get into character. Mark Dacascos (*Crying Freeman*) is a far better actor than he is given credit for, and he does his best with his no-nonsense character. Since the dialogue in the film is mostly limited to military jargon, he uses facial expressions in order to convey emotion and does so very well. Most of the film's emotional baggage is left to be carried by Theresa Randle (*Bad Boys*) who plays the role of the captured Marine captain. In a male-dominated picture, her character is put through the ringer and still comes out on top (by far the strongest and most developed). Rutger Hauer is given even less to do as the general. He's there to hand out orders and to give a bit of motivation. There are no fist fights or martial arts action to speak of in the film. Everything plays out in a strategic and war-like manner. Even though there's no shortage of gunfire and explosions, the action remains relatively bloodless. The story is really straightforward and offers no surprises. Director Brian Clyde does a solid job behind the camera, keeping it all together when it could have easily fallen apart. The script is weak but the directing and acting are solid enough to at least warrant a single viewing. It was produced by Roger Corman and Cirio Santiago. The sequel, *The Hunt for Eagle One: Crash Point,* was filmed back-to-back with this film and was released shortly after it.

The Hunt for Eagle One: Crash Point

2006 (Sony DVD) (CD)

Terrorists have stolen an encoder device that allows them to lock out a pilot's controls mid-flight and to take over a plane completely by remote control. They've hijacked three passenger planes and have begun crashing them into designated targets. Colonel Halloran (Jeff Fahey) calls in his special strike force that's headed by Captain Matt Daniels (Mark Dacascos) to try to locate the device. They find out that the terrorists plan to crash one of the planes into a US military intelligence airbase and that time is running out. With the help of Captain Amy Jennings (Theresa Randle), they cross enemy lines to do what they do best.

The Hunt for Eagle One: Crash Point is a huge step up from its predecessor. It suffers from much of what crippled the first film but this time so much is done right that it's a solidly entertaining film. Dacascos (*Sanctuary*) is back as Daniels, but this time he has been promoted to a Captain's rank and yet he's still a man of few words. Thankfully, he is actually given the

opportunity to show off some fighting skills in this entry. The first film lacked any hand-to-hand combat, but this time he has a couple of short (but decent) fights. The explosions and gunfire dominate the screen as he leads his team into violent action. Theresa Randle also returns as Captain Jennings. Much like in the first film, her character is the most developed and she proves herself once again. Daniels is less of a machine this time around, and we get to glimpse his humanity. The story also raises the bar and has a solid hook, with threatening villains who seem to have a grudge not only with Americans but with Daniels as well, making the plot more personal (which is a plus). Any good sequel should feel like it has evolved and *The Hunt for Eagle One: Crash Point* does just that. Rutger Hauer is missing from this one, replaced with the great Jeff Fahey (*Machete*) who gives his character the perfect amount of authority while still being compassionate. *Crash Point* made the effort to be a better film, and it succeeds, with much of the credit going to director Henry Crum (*Barbarian*) doing his best to make it happen.

Hunt to Kill

2010 (Anchor Bay DVD) (CD)

After the death of his partner, US Border Patrol officer Jim Rhodes (Steve Austin) takes a transfer from Texas to the mountains of Montana, living a simple life while trying to raise his rebellious daughter Kim (Marie Avgeropoulos). Meanwhile, a group of thieves pull off a heist making away with millions of dollars in bonds. Their leader, Lawson (Michael Hogan), double-crosses his team and takes off with the loot. The second-in-command Banks (Gil Bellows) takes the initiative with the rest of the team to track Lawson down. That leads them to Rhodes. When the double-crossed team arrives in Montana, they take Kim hostage and force Rhodes to lead them through the mountains. What they don't know is that Rhodes will stop at nothing to outsmart them and do whatever it takes to save his daughter.

With *Hunt to Kill,* Steve Austin (*Damage, The Package*) finds himself in a role that works best for him. This is his *Commando*. The plot is pretty cut and dry, but Austin is able to bring his in-ring charm to the screen and pulls out a solid performance to create a truly entertaining film. Austin is surprisingly believable in the lead as a father and survivalist. He has several other solid actors along for the ride including his *The Expendables* co-stars Gary Daniels (*Fist of the North Star*) and Eric Roberts (*Best of the Best*) in a cameo. Though done on a fairly small budget, the film was competently shot in Vancouver, using the scenery to maximum effect. The film is predictable but has a certain energy. Most of the fighting is kept to quick altercations that are exciting enough, but the real question is: Does Austin fight Daniels? Yes, he does and it's the highlight of the film. It is a solidly choreographed scene and thankfully, it's shown without much rapid editing and with plenty of wide shots to take it all in. These guys go all out, and it pays off. Gil Bellows (*The Shawshank Redemption*) is the lead heavy, and he makes sure that the audience loves to hate him. There are plenty of clichés and the one-liners come at a rapid pace (the final one is the real treat), which only adds to how great of a time you can have while watching this film. Keoni Waxman (*A Dangerous Man* and other movies with Steven Seagal) pulls together a solid direct-to-video actioner while bringing out the best in his performers.

Hurricane Smith
1992 (Warner DVD) (djm)

Construction worker Billy Smith (Carl Weathers) learns that his mother passed away, and he needs to get in touch with his sister to settle their mother's estate. He travels to the last place he heard she was—Australia's Gold Coast—and immediately realizes that she's missing and possibly dead. He trolls the underbelly of the area, picking up information that reveals that his sister was an in-demand prostitute, and that her sadistic pimp (Jurgen Prochnow) may have killed her when she tried to escape her situation. Targeted by the lesser element for asking too many questions, Billy must turn on the hurricane within him not only to stay alive and protect a hooker he's fallen for but also to get some damn fine revenge.

After Carl Weathers headlined in the Joel Silver-produced action-tastic *Action Jackson*, he didn't jump aboard another action movie—instead he starred in *Dangerous Passion*, a TV thriller co-starring Billy Dee Williams, and the TV show *Street Justice* with Bryan Genesse. *Hurricane Smith* was a too late and not-good-enough return for him in an action role, and it wasn't released theatrically in the US. It's light on action, but in the last act there are some stunts and explosions. Still, Weathers doesn't look like his heart is in it this time. Directed by Colin Budds.

Hyper Space
1989 (Simitar DVD) (djm)

A space crew wakes up from suspended hibernation so they can perform their task: dumping nuclear waste from Earth into space. It isn't long before they realize that they're screwed: Out of fuel and twenty-two years away from home, they begin to panic because their only way home is a shuttle fit for one. Their leader (Richard Norton) tries to keep a level head, but other members of the crew (Ron O'Neal, Don Stroud, Lynn-Holly Johnson, and others) begin fighting amongst each other—*and dying!* Someone on the crew is killing the others, and when the big reveal proves that at least one of them is an android, things get intense.

Light on action and suspense and long in tedium and chitchat, *Hyper Space* isn't Norton's finest hour, but he's usually at the center of attention and he's given a few fight scenes. He has several flashbacks to his life as an enforcer (or cop, or something), and he fights pro wrestler Big John Studd. Professor Toru Tanaka is also featured in his flashbacks. Don Stroud (*License to Kill*) gets the honor of fighting Norton in the last scene. Only die-hard Norton fans need bother with this one. Directed by David Huey (*Full Impact* with Gary Daniels).

I Am Omega
2007 (Echo Bridge DVD) (CD)

"Word about her is already out there. And if she does make it to Antioch, or they get her anywhere they can make a cure, then we go back to the way it used to be: taking care of the sick, and the idiots and the slackers, and make this world the piss hole that it was."

Loosely based on Richard Matheson's popular novel *I Am Legend*, *I Am Omega* takes place in a post-apocalyptic future where human life is near-extinct and the planet is overrun by virus-infected, mutant humans. Renchard (Mark Dacascos) lives alone, fighting to survive in the dying world. Much to his surprise, he's contacted on a webcam by a survivor named Brianna (Jennifer Lee Wiggins) who is trying to find a group of other survivors who call themselves Antioch. She's asks for his help, but he turns her down. Soon, two men show up claiming to be from Antioch and ask Renchard to escort them in saving the girl who's of special interest to them. It seems she's immune to the virus and her blood could save the human race. He decides to go along, but time is running out. He's rigged the entire city to blow up, intending to wipe out the plague and save humanity.

The Omega Man and *I Am Legend* were both based on the same source material, and to cash in on *Legend*'s release, the exploitation studio The Asylum title-smashed the two flicks and delivered *I Am Omega*. The first half of the film sort of mirrors those titles, but the second half is the most fun. Mark Dacascos (*Cradle 2 the Grave, Crying Freeman*) is the picture's driving force and manages to turn copper into silver. If you've ever wanted to see him crush zombies, there's plenty of it here, and the final

DVD artwork for The Asylum's *I Am Omega*. Courtesy of The Asylum.

fight between him and Geoff Meed (who also scripted) was better than expected. Director Griff Furst (*Universal Soldiers,* another Asylum title) didn't deliver a classic by any means, but it wasn't nearly as bad as expected. Dacascos makes it work, which, in turn, makes it watchable.

Ice Station Zebra
1968 (Warner DVD) (CD)

"I once killed a man called Jones, though not for that reason, of course."

James Ferraday (Rock Hudson) is the commander of the US military submarine known as the USS *Tigerfish*. He's called on a mission to investigate a disturbance on Ice Station Zebra (a scientific weather station) but there may be ulterior motives at play. British agent Mr. Jones (Patrick McGoohan), Marine commander Captain Anders (former NFL star Jim Brown), and a Russian defector known as Vaslov (Ernest Borgnine) will all accompany him on his mission. The sub must travel underneath the ice and then break through it to reach the station. Once there, it quickly becomes obvious that there's more to the mission than meets the eye and someone is a traitor. A capsule from a satellite has crashed there, and people will kill to acquire what's in it.

Ice Station Zebra was a huge success upon its release and but the reason for that is baffling. The film is excruciatingly long, and everyone just keeps talking and talking. There's no excitement at all until the final moments. Keep in mind that you have to sit through over two hours of dialogue before you get a glimpse of any action. Jim Brown (later in *Slaughter* and *much* later in *Mars Attacks*) has a small but pivotal role in the film, and you only get to see him in action for a few short moments when he's swinging a crowbar at Ernest Borgnine. The film is better known for its innovative camera work and the fact that it was nominated for two Academy Awards. It was based on the novel by Alistar MacLean and directed by John Sturgess (*Chino* with Charles Bronson).

I Escaped from Devil's Island
1973 (Shout Factory DVD) (CD)

"I'll come up with something sweet for him. I'll make him lick the blade that cuts his throat."

Devil's Island was a penal colony for French Guiana in the late 1800s through the early 1900s. It was controversial because of the brutal treatment of prisoners. There were a few notable real-life escapes but this film is a fictional account of how convict Le Bras (Jim Brown) devises a plan to escape the island with a few friends in tow. He's sick and tired of the harsh treatment he receives on the island prison, so he skillfully takes the time to put together the pieces of the puzzle before making his escape. Getting off the island is proves to be relatively easy, but surviving afterwards is far more difficult. With a huge ocean separating him from freedom, he will have to stay strong in order to survive.

When Roger Corman heard the feature film *Papillon* (based on the best-selling novel) was in the making, he and his brother Gene wasted no time nabbing director William Witney (who worked on many classic television shows) and rushing into production and releasing this film before the other made it to the screen. This is a Corman picture, so you get what you expect, and giving the lead role to Jim Brown (*100 Rifles, Slaughter*) was the best choice he could have made. He was in fantastic shape and is amazing on the screen. His character will lay waste to anyone who will interfere with his chance to escape. Brown has a great brawl with a man and practically snaps him in two. Once he escapes, he and his group encounter lepers, natives, and man-eating sharks. This is highly entertaining drive-in fare, and Brown just destroys it with his no-nonsense portrayal.

The Immortal

2000–2001 (Image DVD) (CD)

During the seventeenth century, Raphael "Rafe" Caine (Lorenzo Lamas) suffered through the worst tragedy of his life when his wife was murdered by demons who also took his daughter. Rafe is stricken with rage and grief until he meets Goodwin (Steve Braun), the world's biggest coward, and they set out to get revenge. Rafe learns he's the chosen one, a man destined to fight the forces of darkness. He's trained to fight by Yashiro (Robert Ito), and along with Goodwin, they are granted eternal life. Four hundred years later they're still on the job when they meet a scientist named Dr. Sara Beckman (April Telek), who unknowingly creates a device with the ability to identify demons. Sara eventually joins their team, and the three of them set out to rid the world of evil while tracking the worst of the worst—Mallos (Dominic Keeting)—the demon responsible for his wife's death and the only one who knows where his daughter is.

Right from the get-go, the show bares a striking resemblance to *Highlander*. It's not a clone but does borrow from it in tone and structure. While the majority of each episode takes place in a modern time period, they do offer flashbacks, giving a look into the lead character's motivations and origins. The show only ran for twenty-two episodes (one season) and a major issue for this low-budget show was having too much ambition and not enough scratch to make it all work. The effects are horrible and draw you out of the story. The pilot for the series sets up a perfect mission for the characters and the episodes that deal with the ongoing arc are always the best. Several of the stand-alone episodes have many things going for them but sometimes the stories feel a bit dumbed down. The chemistry between the three

leads was the glue holding the show together, and Lorenzo Lamas (*Renegade*) knows what his fans enjoy and he delivers many great action scenes throughout the entire season. It runs the gamut, too, with sword fights, double-fisted shootouts, and all sorts of hand-to-hand throw downs for good measure. It was also cool to see former wrestling superstar Bret "The Hitman" Hart show up as a recurring character and a thorn in the side of Rafe. Even though it was canceled, the final episodes wrap up the series quite nicely. Overall, *The Immortal* is a show many will forget about, but for Lamas fans, it was a worthy follow-up to *Renegade*. For more *Highlander*-inspired material starring Lamas, see also *The Swordsman*.

Immortal

2006 (The Stunt People DVD) (djm)

A knight from the Crusades harnesses an ancient power that grants him immortality, and through the ages he looks for pupils to whom he can pass his knowledge and power. In the 1980s he finds three young men talented enough in the martial arts that he sees potential in them. Over two decades, he teaches them his powers, and they are granted immortality. But in those years, one of them (played by Eric Jacobus, who would break out a few years later with his film *Death Grip*) turns against the others and has ambitions of ruling the world with his power and immortality.

An overly ambitious independent movie shot on a camcorder, *Immortal* has a story reminiscent of *Highlander*, but its young cast and crew bit off more than they could chew with this ninety-eight-minute feature. It's filled with nonstop martial arts sequences and brawls, which is the obvious selling point, but most viewers will be put off by the whole endeavor because of how silly and amateur it is. Jacobus and his team of stunt people made a great showreel that they could use to get other gigs and show what they could do physically, but otherwise, *Immortal* is pretty much a home movie with some great fighting. Jacobus and Chelsea Steffensen directed.

Immortal Combat

1993 (Simitar DVD) (djm)

Roddy Piper and Sonny Chiba! Just those two guys appearing in the same scene together is enough for me to recommend the otherwise forgotten *Immortal Combat*. They play partners on the force, and they're on a case involving a serial killer who carves a ritualistic mark on women's bodies before killing them. Their boss orders them to cool down after getting into trouble too often, and John (Piper) takes a "vacation" by hunting down the killer to a tropical island, where a scientific facility uses a local flower to concoct a serum that has healing abilities. The head of the corporation is a psychotic woman (played by Meg Foster) who holds open auditions for soldiers/bodyguards, which is where John sees

his opportunity. He goes to one of the auditions along with a guy he just met and befriended (played by Tommy "Tiny" Lister), and he gets a glimpse of the serial killer (played by the hulking Deron McBee from *The Killing Zone*), who is the head henchman on the island. John meets a pretty female journalist whom he saves three (!) times from being killed, and when John finds himself overwhelmed by sheer numbers of bad guys, he's saved by his surprise arrival partner JJ (Chiba), who is actually a badass ninja.

I don't know what I was expecting when I sat down to watch *Immortal Combat*, but I ended up being pretty surprised by the whole thing. It's exactly of its time and era of direct-to-video martial arts movies, but it has twice the star power and at least three times the amount of action in it that I was hoping to get. Chiba, while a little challenged in the language department, looks like he's having a great time in the movie, and Piper is like a big kid in a playpen that's a little too small for him. He's all over the place, but he's fun to watch. I liked the movie, but it's a little too long. Fans of the two stars should be reasonably happy with it. Directed by Daniel Neira. The *Cyborg Cop* movies with David Bradley are extremely similar.

The Incredible Hulk

1978–1982 (Universal DVD) (CD)

"Mr. McGee, don't make me angry. You wouldn't like me when I'm angry."

David Banner (Bill Bixby) is a doctor working within the Culver Institute when he and his wife Laura are in a car accident. He desperately tries to save her life but doesn't have the power to do so. Traumatized by the event, he devotes his life to learning how to tap in to a human's inner strength. After months of research, he learns there's a connection between high levels of gamma radiation and the phenomena of inner strength. He decides to expose himself to gamma activity to see if his findings are right. He overdoses on gamma, and he eventually finds himself transforming into a giant green monster with superhuman abilities. Confused by what he is becoming, David seeks help from his old friend Dr. Elaina Marks (Susan Sullivan) to conduct some tests. They're soon confronted by glory hound tabloid reporter Jack McGee (Jack Colvin) who thinks something is fishy and wants answers. A fire breaks out in the laboratory, and Elaina loses her life despite the attempt of David's new alter ego, The Hulk (bodybuilder Lou Ferrigno), to save her. Thought to be dead, David sets out to find a way to control his transformations, or better yet, find a cure. He travels from place to place, putting the needs of others before his own and helping those who can't fight back. He has to stay one step ahead of the law since the monster is being blamed for Elaina's death, and he has to cover his tracks because McGee will stop at nothing to expose the truth.

The *Incredible Hulk* ran for a whopping five seasons on CBS before being canceled. The show itself was a huge success and to this day, people love it even if it distanced itself from the comics from which it was birthed. Many of us watched this show as kids and something we may have missed (besides the fact that it's at times painfully cheesy) was how mature many of the stories were and how the characters dealt with the situations—especially during the second season with episodes dealing with child abuse, mental problems, and even racism. That season was by far the most polished, but began a slow decline once entering season three. Lou Ferrigno's (later in *Desert Warrior*) name will forever be synonymous with this series. The Hulk is like a bundle of rage and Lou portrays it brilliantly, but it's the more subtle moments that really drive home just how multifaceted the character was. You feel for him, you even ache for him, and Lou should be commended for his serious work in the show and not just his physical ability. Pairing him with Bill Bixby really brings out the overlooked layer of the show. Also of note is the season four episode, titled "King of the Beach," where Lou stars in the episode as a second character. This was the only time during the series that he appeared sans makeup. Ultimately, *The Incredible Hulk* is a human drama disguised as a comic book action show (there's plenty of action). When the series ended after having only seven episodes in the fifth season, NBC bought the rights from CBS and resurrected it after a six-year hiatus as a trio of TV movies, *The Incredible Hulk Returns*, *The Trial of the Incredible Hulk,* and *The Death of the Incredible Hulk*. The movies never quite captured the magic of the first couple of seasons but were interesting because they featured other Marvel characters on screen for the first time like Daredevil and Thor. The music by Joe Harnell, especially the piano bit played at the end of each episode, invokes a feeling of loneliness and is darkly beautiful. Not everything about this show was great, but there are many great things and it was intelligently handled to appeal to both adults and children.

Inglorious Bastards

1978 (Severin DVD)(JAS)

"A gang of deserters, cutthroats, deserters, and thieves . . . you don't even deserve to be called soldiers!"

Enzo G. Castellari's late '70s "B"-movie war epic *Inglorious Bastards* is a cartoonishly violent and quickly paced actioner, which is a bit surprising considering it sprang from the cynical '70s. The movie stars Bo Svenson, the go-to genre hunk of the time, and ex-Oakland Raiders/Kansas City Chiefs football star and blaxploitation pioneer Fred Williamson. The film centers on a group of American soldiers in Europe during World War II who are arrested for separate crimes ranging from thievery to murder. While being taken to jail, a German air raid happens to kill most of the American captors and sets the surviving

prisoners free. They plan to slither their way to neutral Switzerland, but after a series of near-death escapes, they are commissioned (out of necessity) by an American colonel to steal a bomb from the Nazis. The Bastards agree to the job and of course find a code of honor and latent morality as the mission progresses.

The movie chugs along at an exciting and humorous gait with the help of some quirky characters and the charm of Mr. Williamson. This is astonishingly effective action, especially considering its mild budget. The antihero sentiment found its way into director Quentin Tarantino's heart. He loosely reworked the film in 2009 (with a title change to *Inglorious Basterds*) with a much darker (but no less entertaining) tone.

In Hell

2003 (Sony DVD) (ZC)

After annihilating the man who killed his wife, Kyle LeBlanc (Jean-Claude Van Damme) is thrown into a particularly roguish Russian prison. Here, the turnkeys organize vicious bare-knuckle boxing bouts to entertain the warden and his high-society friends. After showing his prowess while defending a fellow inmate, LeBlanc is inducted into the prison's battle hierarchy and forced to conquer increasingly powerful opponents until he's lost any semblance of humanity.

Director Ringo Lam deserves much credit for his contributions to action cinema, including the legendary *City on Fire* (best known as the movie that Quentin Tarantino brazenly lifted from to write *Reservoir Dogs*). Additionally, his *Prison on Fire* films are defining works that changed the genre forever. That being said, this movie reeks. It's a ludicrously unfocused, mustache-twirling melodrama that revels in every stereotype prison films have to offer: rape, machismo, sewage, corruption, escape, bad food . . . the works. It confuses relentless hopelessness with artistic impact, but shoving your lead character in increasingly unsavory scenarios only evokes a response when you actually care about his survival. The fights have palpable impact and a couple of the actors do their damnedest, but the tone is constantly waylaid by heavy-handed dialogue and even CGI fairies (really). Don't be discouraged . . . if you need to see Van Damme smash some face behind bars, there's always *Death Warrant*.

Inside Out

2011 (Lionsgate DVD) (CD)

After thirteen long years in prison, A. J. (Paul "Triple H" Levesque) finally finds himself on the outside ready to walk the straight and narrow. He is hoping to start a business making pickles. His best friend Jack (Michael Rapaport) has other plans. He wants things to go back to the way they were when they worked for his father

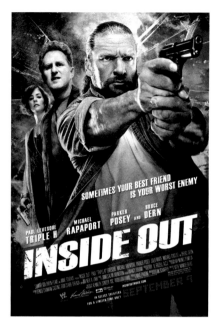

The theatrical release poster for *Inside Out*. Author's collection.

Vic (Bruce Dern), an unlikely mob boss. Jack accidentally kills a man when collecting money and A. J. finds himself in a position he doesn't want to be in: instead of turning his back, he chooses to help Jack, who only makes matters worse by keeping the $250,000 he was collecting for his father. A. J. tries his best to clean up the mess but Vic is through with his son and wants him dead. With the police closing in, A. J. doesn't have much time to set things right. To top things off, Jack is married to Claire (Parker Posey), the woman A. J. was with before he entered prison, the woman he loves. With a mafia hitman hot on his tail, A. J. will have to rely on his wits to save the people he cares about.

Of the recent batch of films released by WWE Films, *Inside Out* may be the best one to date. That isn't to say that it's great or of any special note. It's good but it's still far too short on the action. Paul "Triple H" Levesque would make a great action hero. He has all the qualities you could ask for, but he's never been given a vehicle or had a director who knows how to cater to his strong points. He still seems a bit stiff at times, but that could be adjusted. He is an strong force and the one action scene in the film is exactly what one would hope for. His character does have a likable charm and some interesting quirks. To balance out Levesque's inexperience, we get veteran actor Bruce Dern (*Last Man Standing*), as well as independent film royalty Michael Rapaport (*True Romance*) and Levesque's *Blade: Trinity* co-star Parker Posey. The story is intriguing and moves along at a steady pace. The only complaint (aside from the lack of action) was that the ending sort of feels forced. Much like Artie Mandelberg's follow-up film *Bending the Rules*, all the elements were in place: it was just missing that one important ingredient: action. Hopefully, Levesque will eventually find himself in a film where he can be showcased in the proper manner. That said, *Inside Out* is still worth a look.

The Inspector Wears Skirts

1988 (Universe Laser and Video DVD) (djm)

A top female cop named Hu (Sibelle Hu) is asked to form an elite squad of female cops, and she is given a short amount of time to do it. The squad is put together and they train unbelievably hard for that duration. Their final test is when they are visited by a guest teacher, Madam Lo (Cynthia Rothrock), who takes them outside of the training compound and puts their abilities to the test on a ship. They fail miserably, but they are given another chance to prove their worth. They are asked to supervise and guard an auction house where precious jewels are being sold. A group of thieves have a plan to rob the jewels, but what they don't count on is coming face to face with the female squad, who are formidable enough (with the help of Madams Hu and Lo) to stop them. The final fight involving Hu, Rothrock, and the other girls is the highlight of the film.

Not as compelling as most of the other pictures Rothrock co-starred in during her years in Hong Kong, *The Inspector Wears Skirts* is a footnote in her career, and if not for her involvement, the film would be lost in obscurity. It spends an inordinate amount of time on sorority-style hijinks, pratfalls, and jokes, but none of it means anything without the action. Jackie Chan produced it. Wellson Chin, who also made *Prince of the Sun* with Rothrock, directed it.

Instinct to Kill

2001 (First Look DVD) (djm)

This is a psycho-killer thriller with Mark Dacascos playing a personal defense instructor to a woman (Melissa Crider) whose cop husband (Tim Abell) is a serial killer of women. When Crider turns her husband in, he plots his escape from prison, and when he escapes, his only thought is to make his wife suffer. Crider turns to Dacascos (who plays a former cop) for help, but she has a lot of issues with holding a gun, etc.

A lot of time is devoted to the creepy husband, effectively played by Abell. He is truly an evil character, and he's almost like The Terminator. He has a one-track mind, kills without emotion, and continues coming even after being wounded. Dacascos underplays his character, but he's still very physical here. He's not invincible, and Abell seems to match him by sheer force and will. An unpleasant vibe and misogynistic tone mars the film. Kadeem Hardison, who co-starred with Dacascos in *Drive,* has a smaller role here as a detective. Directed by Gustavo Graef-Marino.

Interceptor Force

1999 (York DVD) (djm)

"Okay, so big deal—you're a badass."

Olivier Gruner (*Nemesis, Angel Town*) plays the leader of a team of secret mercenaries who are assigned to track down and kill or capture a *Predator*-esque alien who's crash-landed in a dusty Mexican town. The alien is computer generated when it's on screen, and we only see it a few times because it spends the rest of the time in an invisible state. Gruner is given plenty of fight scenes here (even one in a stripper bar!), and the alien opponent is adaptable, it seems, because its fight skills aren't too shabby.

The cast of *Interceptor Force* is slightly average. It co-stars Ernie Hudson and Brad Dourif (who probably shot their scenes in a day), Glenn Plummer, and William Zabka from *The Karate Kid.* The sad truth about this movie and movies like it is that falling or fallen action guys appear in them to fill a void. These types of movies rarely utilize the star's potential, and sadly, most of them aren't worth the price of a one-dollar rental. Filmmakers like Phillip Roth (who directed this) make movies like these for a dime a dozen, and I suspect stars like Gruner will be exploited by filmmakers like him for as long as they feel they need to be working. Roth also made *Velocity Trap* with Gruner. Astonishingly, *Interceptor Force* had a sequel, also by Roth and starring Gruner.

Interceptor Force 2

2002 (Image DVD) (djm)

Olivier Gruner returns as Sean Lambert, an interstellar cop/soldier who is called into duty to stop an otherworldly being from causing a nuclear apocalypse on Earth. The alien can shape-shift and take on the guise of anyone it comes in contact with, which makes Sean's task a little daunting at first, but he has a team to back him up. Using his martial arts prowess and dauntless attitude, Sean helps save the world from the alien menace.

Made to appease a low common denominator, which doesn't mind watching low-budget SyFy Originals, *Interceptor Force 2* has lots of action in it, and some computer-generated alien stuff that most likely fulfilled SyFy's requirements of having a creature appear before every commercial break. Some people won't mind watching this, and certain fans of Gruner's will appreciate that he's at the center of attention almost all the time, but this just isn't something that you're going to remember a few days later. Phillip Roth directed. He worked with Gruner several times on other films like the first *Interceptor Force* and *Velocity Trap.*

Interzone

1987 (TWE VHS) (CD)

"I'm gonna hit you so hard your dog's gonna die."

Swan (Bruce Abbott) is one of those guys who always finds himself getting into trouble. After winning the future's version of Russian roulette, he finds himself in the company of Panasonic (Kiro Wehara), a monk helping to protect his temple from an evil gang led by Mantis (female bodybuilder Teagan Clive) and Balzakan (John Armstead). The gang wants to control this temple (this area is known as the "Interzone") since it's one of the last places to avoid nuclear contamination after World War III. There also happens to be talk of a treasure hidden within it, and they want it all. With the lovely Tera (Beatrice Ring) by their sides, Swan and Panasonic will fight with all their knowledge to keep these villainous thugs from overtaking the Interzone.

This is one goofy movie but it has a sense of humor, which goes a long way. Bruce Abbott (from *The Re-Animator*) is a great bumbling hero and if this film had been more successful, maybe we would have seen him cast in similar roles. The real attraction, though, is the mesmerizing Teagan Clive (also seen in *Alienator*). She doesn't really get her hands dirty until the final moments, but she's a marvel to behold. This woman can maintain her bodybuilder physique and still manage to exude femininity. Director Deran Sarafian (*Death Warrant* with Jean-Claude Van Damme) may have slapped this thing together, and as bad as it is, it still can entertain a simple mind for ninety minutes. Fred Olen Ray reportedly worked on it post-production.

In the Blood

2014 (Anchor Bay DVD) (djm)

*"Survivors have scars.
Losers have funerals."*

After their wedding, Ava (MMA star Gina Carano) and Derek (Cam Gigandet) go to the Caribbean for their honeymoon. Everything is fine until they go to a nightclub together. A tough Hispanic drug lord (played by Danny Trejo) gets a little too grabby with Ava, and she unleashes her inner beast, which she's suppressed and kept hidden from her husband. She beats up a bunch of guys in the club, and her husband realizes that she's been keeping a secret from him. She was raised by "an outlaw" (played by Stephen Lang in flashbacks), and she learned at a young age to defend herself to survive, and to kill if necessary. After the nightclub incident, a circumstance leads to a grave injury for Derek, and Ava loses track of his ambulance, leading to a frantic search all over the Caribbean island for him. With no leads, few clues, and only resistance from the corrupt local authorities, Ava has to

Theatrical poster for *In the Blood*. Author's collection.

switch on her inner revenger and track down those responsible for the disappearance—and possible murder—of her husband. It gets bloody.

As a second solo vehicle for the impressive Gina Carano (after her starring role in *Haywire* and a supporting role in *Fast 6*), *In the Blood* is a good follow-up, but for whatever reason 20th Century Fox, which co-distributed the film, decided to dump it to the home video market instead of giving it a deserved wide theatrical release. It was given a perfunctory, dismissive one-week theatrical engagement, but it seems like a slap in the face to Carano who really put forth her best effort into delivering a forceful, dedicated performance that has her delivering solid MMA-style action and dramatics that are more than within her capabilities. I saw this in its theatrical exhibition, and it had me yelling out loud during some of the action scenes. It's pretty good stuff. There's no reason why this can't find a big audience. John Stockwell directed.

In the Name of the King 2: Two Worlds

2011 (Fox DVD) (CD)

"I have a feeling in the Black Forest, size does matter."

Teaching self-defense classes to a bunch of kids is exactly how Granger (a grizzled been-there, done-that Dolph Lundgren) would like to continue living his life, but that's just not in the cards for him. At home after a day of work, he's attacked by hooded men who appear from out of nowhere. Luckily, he's assisted by a woman who opens a portal that whisks them away to medieval times. She's killed, but he's saved

and taken to the king (Lochlyn Monroe) who tells him of an ancient prophecy in which he is supposed to play an integral part. Granger embarks on a journey with a small band of fighters and a medic (Natassia Malthe) to battle the "Dark Ones" and soon learns everything he was told is a lie and the truth is far more unbelievable than he could have ever imagined. A stranger in a strange land, Granger uses his wits and special forces training to survive.

It's pointless to say whether or not *In the Name of the King 2* is a good movie. The name of the notorious director will help you to decide. Uwe Boll (of *Bloodrayne* and the first *In the Name of the King* with Jason Statham) has been called just about everything under the sun, but the fact that he had the wherewithal to cast Dolph Lundgren (*Masters of the Universe*) in the film and pit him against a fire-breathing dragon deserves some sort of honorable mention. There's plenty of action and over-the-top medieval dialogue to melt the mind with. Lundgren plays the sort of character he's comfortable with, which gives the movie a certain credibility. Lundgren injured himself on the first day of filming, which resulted in the use of a stunt double during most of the scenes where he's seen running. On the final day of shooting there was another accident (an explosion on set) that injured six people. Not a highlight in his career, but he does battle a dragon. For more Lundgren versus dragons action see *Legendary: Tomb of the Dragon*.

Into the Sun

2005 (Sony DVD) (CD)

"This one is so sharp. I'll use it tonight. This kills very well."

When the governor of Tokyo is murdered, the CIA office stationed there calls in their former operative Travis Hunter (Steven Seagal) to investigate. They believe the Yakuza was involved, but not the run-of-the-mill variety of the Yakuza. This is a new breed: a vicious Yakuza family has teamed up with the Chinese Triads to take over the criminal underworld. Hunter discovers the leaders of the two gangs: Kuroda (Takao Ohsawa) and Chen (Ken Lo), who are both planning on taking over the drug trade and killing off anyone who may get in their way. Hunter is well respected in the Asian community, and he's able to talk his way into getting the information he needs to stop them. Kuroda is a loose cannon and when word gets out there's an American looking for him, things get real messy when Hunter faces off against this mortal enemy.

Into the Sun is a better-than-average Seagal film with beautiful locations, a strong supporting cast, and several exciting action scenes. Seagal delivers exactly what you would expect from him. You can always get a sense if he is really into the film or not and he seems to be trying here. A good portion of the dialogue is in Japanese and the majority of it was filmed in Japan with a largely Japanese cast (blink and you'll miss Chiaki Kuriyama of *Kill Bill* fame). Seagal has a

solid battle with Jackie Chan's friend and former bodyguard Ken Lo (*Drunken Master II*), which is unexpected (but welcome) and there's some brutal swordplay towards the end of the film. It has several cheesy moments (one of the final shots, for example) but this one's a little gem. The director was one-timer mink (yes, he has just one name and it is in lowercase), but some scenes were shot by director Don E. FountLeRoy, who would go on to direct *Today You Die* and *Urban Justice* with Seagal.

Invasion U.S.A.

1985 (MGM DVD) (djm)

"If you come back in here, I'm gonna hit you with so many rights, you're gonna beg for a left."

The ultimate Chuck Norris movie, *Invasion U.S.A.* boggles my mind. A group of Russian terrorists, led by the insane Rostov (Richard Lynch, who's great), invades America via Cuba. When they land in the Everglades, they immediately begin a systematic slaughter of innocent American civilians at Christmastime. They bomb suburban neighborhoods, pose as policemen while they gun down innocents in the streets, and terrorize shopping malls. The National Guard steps in and martial law is declared, but the problem only escalates as civilians turn against authorities. Who's to stop Rostov and his horde of men? Matt Hunter! Hunter (Norris) is a former military hero, now turned alligator wrangler in the bayou, and he's the only man who's ever been able to put the fear of God into Rostov. Armed with Uzis, grenades, a rocket launcher, and his black truck, Hunter is like a force of nature in Rostov's path. He shows up every single time he's needed (including a

Chuck Norris stars as Matt Hunter in the Cannon picture *Invasion U.S.A.* Author's collection.

Matt Hunter (Chuck Norris) emerging from wreckage in *Invasion U.S.A.* Author's collection.

time when terrorists plant a bomb on a school bus!), and he sets an elaborate trap for Rostov and his men, putting all of them in the same place at the same time. It's a blast!

The only way for this movie to get made was for it to be directed by Joseph Zito (*Missing in Action*, *The Prowler*), and for it to be financed and released by Cannon in 1985. Any other director, and any other studio and year, and this movie would not exist. It's one of the most insane action movies ever made, with incredibly ballsy moves. What other "popular" mainstream movie would show American families getting blown up in their homes while decorating Christmas trees? I'm willing to forgive the fact that Norris appears like Superman every single time someone needs saving (like, hey, how did he know which mall to go to?), and so should you. *Invasion U.S.A.* is the best movie Norris made during his hot streak of good movies, which included *Lone Wolf McQuade*, *Missing in Action*, *The Delta Force*, and *Code of Silence*. It has great action set pieces and some iconic moments. Billy Drago, who's in it for only a few moments, gets his balls shot off. The whole movie's awesome.

Ip Man

2008 (Well Go USA DVD) (CD)

"I'm just a Chinese man."

This is a semi-autobiographical account of the life of Grandmaster Ip Man (Donnie Yen). Living in Foshun, he has established a martial arts school where he's famous for teaching wing chun. He lives a good life with his wife and son and is well respected in the community. When Japan invades China in 1937, he loses everything and has to struggle on the streets to find food and shelter for his family. He eventually finds a job in a coal mine where many of his former students now work. Japanese General Miura (Hiroyuki Ikeuchi) is plucking these fighters from the mines and bribing them to fight for food. When one of Ip's friends is murdered, he quickly jumps to defend the honor of his people. This sets off a chain of events that will culminate with a final battle between Miura and Man.

Director Wilson Yip (*Kill Zone*) knows exactly how to bring out the inner beast inside Donnie Yen (also in *Shanghai Knights*) who just completely explodes and blows everyone away with his performance. There's a strong and compelling story here that will easily captivate you. When it comes to the action, no one can top Yen in this film. His battle against ten Japanese fighters will be remembered as one of the most breathtaking fights ever captured on celluloid. The speed at which he punches is just unbelievable! This is the sort of movie you show to someone who might not be a martial arts fan, and I can guarantee that they will forever after change their tune. Donnie Yen and Wilson Yip followed it up with a sequel in 2010.

Ip Man 2

2010 (Well Go USA DVD) (CD)

"Is winning more important than having dinner with your family?"

This sequel picks up with Ip Man (Donnie Yen) leaving mainland China to try and make a life in Hong Kong. He opens a school where he can focus on teaching Wing Chun. Man's good nature keeps him from enforcing payment from his students, so he continues to struggle financially. The local martial arts teachers have banded together and don't think he should be allowed to teach in their town. They issue him a challenge, and he must defeat them if he is to continue. These teachers are led by Master Hung (Sammo Hung) who matches skills with Man. These two masters learn respect for one another with Hung allowing Man to continue as he was. That is until the Western boxer Mr. Miller (*Bloodmoon*'s Darren Shahlavi) comes to town, degrading the Chinese, and laughing at their martial arts. He challenges everyone, and the ailing Master Hung steps up to put him in his place, but Mr. Miller may prove to be a much more formidable foe than anyone could have imagined and Grandmaster Ip Man will have to face his toughest challenge yet.

Once again, Donnie Yen (*Iron Monkey*) and Wilson Yip (*Dragon Tiger Gate*) team up to bring us another action masterpiece telling (fictional) tales in the life of Ip Man. This time out we learn about Man and his move to Hong Kong. As interesting as the guy may be, the action scenes are every bit as exciting in this one as they were the first time out. We're treated to seeing Yen take on dozens of cleaver-wielding fisherman, an epic confrontation with Sammo Hung (*Heart of Dragon*) on top of a table, and the final battle with Darren Shahlavi (also in *The Package*) playing a boxer. This fight is interesting because a stipulation is set during the bout and Ip Man is unable to use his feet. There's never a dull or disappointing moment in the film even if it does tend to mirror *Rocky IV*.

Darren Shahlavi in Hollywood, California. Photo by david j. moore.

INTERVIEW:

DARREN SHAHLAVI

(djm)

Of Persian and English descent, Darren Shahlavi has a distinctive look and style all his own. He's appeared in dozens of motion pictures and television programs, but most people might recognize him as the villainous boxer Twister in the Donnie Yen-starring film Ip Man 2 *(2010), which was a breakout role for Shahlavi. Since then, he's had more front-and-center roles than evere, and his star is rising. He's co-starred in action and martial arts films alongside Jean-Claude Van Damme (in the upcoming* Pound of Flesh, *2015), Steven Seagal (*Born to Raise Hell, *2010), Gary Daniels (*Bloodmoon, *1997), Steve Austin (*Tactical Force, *2011), and many others including Michael Jai White and Scott Adkins. In 2012, he was the star of the made-for-TV movie* Aladdin and the Death Lamp *(which is not reviewed here), and it's obvious that he has star quality. He's one of the most promising up-and-coming action stars of this downloadable age, and every time you see him in a feature or TV show, you should definitely pay attention.*

The first time I saw you in a movie was in *Bloodmoon* with Gary Daniels, where you played the bad guy. That's kind of a recurring thing with you—you play bad guys. Why do you think that is?

Because I don't think I look like a traditional leading actor. I mean, all the stuff I audition for . . . I guess I got known for playing bad guys. On my reel, I'm playing all bad guys. Pretty much the only movie where I've played the good guy was in *Aladdin*. That's recent.

You were good in that.

They ran out of money for visual effects. There were a lot more shots that needed visual effects. It wasn't in the budget, and it kind of screwed up the story. It got pretty shitty by the end of it. I guess the traditional Michael Dudikoff, Gary Daniels, blond hair blue eyes, the traditional kind of white guy, good guy . . . those guys look like good guys. I don't look like a traditional good guy. Times are changing. Vin Diesel became a big star, The Rock, and other people like that. They kind of look like a different ethnicity. At the end of the day, the kinds of people who watch these kinds of movies are of ethnic minority. The people who know me and watch these kinds of movies, they come from all kinds of diverse backgrounds. So, we'll see how that goes. But once you play a couple of bad guy roles, that's where people want to put you, isn't it? Those types of roles. I'm pushing to play a different type of role. We'll see what happens.

I'd love to see you as the main bad guy in more movies. You're usually like "Hitman #3." But every time I see you, I'm like, "There's that guy again! It's Darren Shahlavi!" I always want to see you do more in these movies. Have you gotten that from any fans?

Yeah, all the time. People are always saying that. I had this big discussion with my agent. This is kind of getting ridiculous right now. I read film reviews, and they always say, "Darren Shahlavi is so underused." And I am! But at the end of the day, I need to make money. I'm not a waiter, I don't have any other kind of job. Years ago I was working at the door, but I still have to work. When I get people who know me that ask me to do work, you see if it's an okay part, then you hope you're going to get a chance to do fight scenes. With these low-budget movies, you think you're going to get a good amount of time to do fight scenes, but you really don't. I've had to do fight scenes within two hours. You can't really get a chance to show what you can do in those sorts of movies. Yeah, I do need to be used more. I was living in Vancouver. Everything I auditioned for I was too dark for those roles, I wasn't dark enough for the ethnic roles. I'm half Persian, half English. I have a British accent, so there are no parts that require a guy with any actor who's half Middle Eastern, or maybe Spanish or Italian. I've played a couple of Spanish guys and things like that, but there's no roles that are written for me, and when they cast roles, it's for 6 foot 1 with blue eyes or a black guy or an Asian guy. There are no roles for a guy that looks or sounds like me.

You became a stunt guy at some point in your career. How did that start?

What I did is I stopped acting for awhile and just did stunts. I went through a divorce and then in 2005, my friends were doing *The Chronicles of Riddick*. I was doing nothing, and nothing was happening with my acting career. I was doing silly little parts here and there. I did three Uwe Boll movies, and I was underused. I was in *Bloodrayne*. I had a scene that didn't really pan out. Then I did *Alone in the Dark* and my fight scene with Christian Slater got cut. Then I was going to be in *In the Name of the King*, and Uwe told that I wasn't big enough, that he needed names. So he put ten names in it and it made 2.3 million opening weekend. So there you go. Now he's gone back to doing smaller movies and sequels. He's making money. I needed to make some money. I was going through a divorce, and you go through this stuff and you realize that you kind of have to bankroll your career. My friends contacted me about *Chronicles of Riddick*, and they wanted me to double Vin. Bobby Brown, the stunt coordinator, said, "Look, I can't have an actor doubling an actor." So they brought me in to double the Lord Marshall, the bad guy. I was

one of four doubles, who Vin's fighting when he's teleporting. In that week I made over ten grand. In that week, I was like, *You're not making that kind of money acting. Silly little parts for movies that nobody sees.* So, then I worked on *Blade 3*. A friend was looking for stunt actors/bad guys for *The Hard Corps*, the Van Damme movie, which Sheldon Lettich directed. I was asked to come in and help out. I knew some boxing and stuff, so I went in to help them audition people. So I went in and helped them choreograph some fights with them. Sheldon walked in and said, "Hey, he moves just like Jean-Claude!" I'm a fan of Van Damme, and I like doing impersonations of people, so I was kind of impersonating Van Damme a little bit, so Sheldon said I should double Jean-Claude. I was like, "Yeah, that's why I'm here." So they hired me to double Van Damme on *The Hard Corps*. I was helping with the fight choreography, and then I got a call from a friend who was doing *300*. He said that he wanted to hire me to work on *300*. Three months working on a Warner Brothers movie. I was like, "Aw, shit!" I was stuck doubling Van Damme on this movie now, so he said, "All right . . .." I told him I'd ask them if they could find someone else to double Van Damme. He said, "If you find someone else, I'll keep a spot open for you." So I spoke with the coordinator, and I said, "You don't really need me on this. I just got a call to work on *300*. Can I leave if I can find another double?" Then, he was like "No problem." They found someone to double Van Damme, and I called and asked if the spot was still open on *300*, so I went and worked on that. I'd been working at that time for like fifteen years as an actor, and on *300* I made more money on that movie in three months that I'd made in fifteen years. Then I got a call to work on *A Night at the Museum*, the first one and the second one. I made enough money doing stunts on those big movies that I could go, *Okay, now I don't need to do a small part in this movie or that movie. I could be picky and choosey because I had a lot of money in the bank, and I'm only going to do movies that help me advance my career.* I'd kind of given up my dream on acting in action movies. It was tough. I was doing stunts on *The Day the Earth Stood Still* and the stunt coordinator on that always calls me and brings me in, and I was supposed to do a scene where I'm coming down and grab Jennifer Connelly and take her up in the air. He said, "Yeah, we're going to do it on a crane, and we're going to do it on a wire and take you up in the air." I thought, *Okay, um . . .* For the whole week before we were shooting that, I kept looking up and it was like 200 meters or something, and I just thought, *I can't do this. I'm scared of heights.* I thought *I don't want to do this.* The week goes by and I'm concerned about it. They were going to pull me up really high on a crane. So I decided that I wanted to act again. I started training really fucking hard. I thought really hard about what I really wanted to do with my life. I had a vision of what I wanted to be and what I wanted to do.

Is this the point when *Ip Man 2* came your way?

My friends would call me on the weekend, and I would say, "Oh, I'm training, I can't go out." They'd say, "Oh, what are you working on?" I

said, "I've got a movie coming up in Asia." "What movie?" "I, uh . . . I only know the Chinese title." I didn't have the movie, nothing. I just had this vision in my head that something was going to happen. I started watching Donnie Yen's movies again. I used to go down to the gym down in Vancouver, and I would take my portable DVD player with me. I watched *Flashpoint*, and one day I got *Ip Man*, and I'm getting ready to watch it at the gym, and I get a phone call from Hong Kong. They're casting for the bad guy role in *Ip Man 2*, and they liked me in a movie called *Tai Chi 2*, this movie I did before *Bloodmoon*. And of course I did a movie called *I Spy* with Eddie Murphy. So I watched *Ip Man* and called them back, and I said, "Man, this movie's fucking amazing!" They called me back two days later and told me that they thought I looked a little too modern. They wanted me to take photographs where I looked like a boxer like from the 1950s. So I slicked my hair to one side, took some pictures and made them sepia and some in black and white, and I sent them off. They called me back and said, "Okay, we want you." I'd been training. It just fucking *happened*. At that time, I was writing a script that I potentially wanted to shoot with me as a lead. A lot of it was born out of my confusion, just frustration. The character was a little biographical. It was about an actor who goes back to Asia and all this action stuff happens. It was kind of parallel to me getting *Ip Man 2*. It was a bizarre situation. Since I did *Ip Man 2*, things have just happened. I've been working since then.

Let's backtrack to *Bloodmoon*. Working with Gary Daniels. What was that like?

Working with Gary was fantastic. I met him maybe twenty years ago. I was like seventeen. We were going to go to this event called "Clash of the Titans" in England. I was really familiar with him, and Gary was the new big star in martial arts movies. You look at him, and you can see his skills and abilities. I really liked his movies, so when I got to meet him, I was really excited. I get there and work with him, and he was just the nicest guy. So professional. Fantastic with the choreography with the fights, and all that stuff. We both had the same upbringing and the same kind of dreams. He'd been to Hong Kong for work, and so had I, so we got along really well, and it was great working with him. I got a check for $2,500 as a signing bonus for the role.

Let's flash forward a few years to the Jalal Merhi era. How did you end up working with Jalal?

I'd done this movie called *Hostile Environment* with Matthias Hues, and the producer on that also produced all of Jalal's movies. That producer wanted to sign me to a three-picture deal. At that time, I had a few things, but I should have done it. I didn't sign it. It was the end of that time of the straight-to-video market. They wanted me to be in *G.O.D.*, but I couldn't do a bigger role because I was still shooting a movie in Germany. So he said, "How about you come in and just do one fight scene with Jalal? Just work one day?" It paid a lot of money to fly into Canada to shoot just one day. I'd never been to Canada before. Jalal let me choreograph that fight.

That scene made me mad. How could Jalal beat you in a fight?

Well, it would have been a much better fight if I'd had a bigger role. We didn't really have any time. Jalal is a great producer. He should get back in the business. I sent him a message and said, "We should remake one of your movies."

That's a great idea!

Let's relaunch *Tiger Claws*! Reboot one of his old movies. Now that the distribution for movies is changing, it's viable to start making those kinds of movies again. With on-demand. This is why nothing happened with my career and I never took off is because it was at the end of straight-to-video, and DVD was coming out, and nobody knew about distribution and the internet and stuff and how that was going to happen. It was the end of all those PM Entertainment companies. All those movies just stopped.

They're coming back now, but they're being done so cheaply now. I like stuff like *The Package* and things like this, but they're . . . different. They're not shot on film, they're all digital, you know what I mean?

Yeah.

You were in *Alien Agent* with Mark Dacascos. Talk about working with him.

Mark is amazing.

That was a good fight between you guys.

Yeah, that was a quick one. Mark choreographed that. We only had two hours to do it. Jesse Johnson, the director, shot it really fast. I've been a big fan of Mark's for a long time. I kept quoting lines from *Drive*. I nearly worked with him a couple of times. I met with a producer about twelve years ago, and we were talking about doing *Brothers of the North Star*, and he wanted me and Mark. Mark was going to do a movie called *Rohan,* which was based on a French comic book. It's kind of like Tarzan, but he's got blond hair. Christophe Gans was going to do it. I'd been in talks with the casting director to play his brother in that. Unfortunately, it never happened. They had artwork for it and everything.

Talk about working with Jesse Johnson on *Alien Agent* and *The Package*.

Jesse's the best. I love that he comes from a stunt background. He's a film historian. He really knows movies. As a director, he's very acutely aware of the characters, the performances, the nuances, how to tell a story, how to put it together, how to shoot the action . . . how to get the most bang for your buck. He's so prepared. He's going to be a really big director.

You've worked with Steve Austin a couple of times.

Yeah!

Your work in *Tactical Force* was one of the better things about that movie. Your fight with Michael Jai White was pretty good. But the way it was cut together . . .

Yeah. You know what I hate? When directors shoot the fight scene, but then every time you get to a pivotal point in the fight, you cut away to something else. It's like watching a porno movie and watching two people fuck and just when they spin around and get to something else, you cut to a different scene. Same thing with a fight scene. You want to see the progression of the fight. We're telling a story when we're choreographing a fight. There are two characters, and we're playing together. Bruce Lee and Chuck Norris in *The Way of the Dragon*. Imagine if when you just get to a certain point where Bruce is knocking Chuck to the ground, they'd cut away to Bob Wall doing something else? It ruins the momentum of the fight. That's what happened on *Tactical Force*, that's what's happened on a bunch of movies that I've done. They just cut away to something else. Let us show the fight and tell the story.

Was your experience on *The Package* better?

The Package was awesome. We had more time, and what Jesse does is he'll shoot the whole fight wide and then he'll go in for a medium shot and then a tight shot. That one was a lot better.

There were some great guys in that one. Jerry Trimble was in there, Dolph Lundgren, you and Steve.

Working on a movie like that is cool because I really like Steve. Number one, he's got no ego. He's always asking questions. He's like, "I'm just learning this stuff." We went in his trailer, and he asked me about acting. He knows who he is in his world, and he knows that movies are something that he's got to learn. He's really interesting. He asks really smart questions. He picks things up very quickly. He wants to do the best performance. He doesn't just turn up, knowing that he's the name, just do his thing and go back to his hotel. He works really hard at it. He took Jesse's direction, and Jesse really knows how to work with these guys. Same with the fight scenes. Steve was really open to stuff. He was a real joy to work with.

How about Steven Seagal? You worked with him on *Born to Raise Hell*.

I really enjoyed working with Steven. I'm sure you'll hear all kinds of stories about him. The thing with Seagal, when I got called to work on it, I was in Shanghai working with Donnie Yen and Sammo Hung. So I flew in from Shanghai. I literally wrapped like three o'clock in the morning, and by seven in the morning I was on my way to the airport to catch a flight to Romania. Steven knew that I'd just finished working with Donnie and Sammo. He's known those guys for a long time, so I got his respect right away, so he was awesome with me. We didn't really have any scenes in *Born to Raise Hell* until our fight at the end. He was pissed, and rightly so, that they'd scheduled the fight for the

end of the day, when really with a big end fight scene, it's better to schedule it for the beginning of the day to make sure we get everything. It was very, very rushed. He had to leave, too. That was a fight scene that was kind of done in like three hours.

Did he hurt you?

No, he didn't. For the first time ever I had a stunt double on that one. He threw my stunt double for the crashes. He liked working with me because I could move around. When he turns me around, he didn't have to use any force. As soon as he's got my arm, twisting it around and moving me, I'm propelling myself. It's kind of a good dance. He was really great.

You worked with him on *True Justice*, his TV show, right?

Yeah, what happened to that? I was going to do a movie called *Maximum Conviction* with Steve Austin and Steven Seagal, and somebody didn't want me in the movie because I was in *Tactical Force*, and that movie didn't turn out very well at all, and I found out that they didn't want anybody who was in *Tactical Force* to be in Steve Austin's other movies. So Steven Seagal told the producer, "Hey, if we're not going to use Darren in this, we'll get him on *True Justice*." A few months later, Jesse called me about working on *The Package*, and I thought, well, they didn't want me on *Maximum Conviction* because of *Tactical Force*, but they hired me anyway on *The Package*, and later that same week I was hired on *True Justice*.

Are you picking anything up from these guys who were "A"-list blockbuster stars at some point in their careers?

I don't think Steven Seagal likes doing the movies that he's doing. Everybody's got to pay the bills. To me, he still comes across as being very natural when he acts. His fight scenes have never been the kind of fights where he gets hit, or anything like that. He just beats people up and he enjoys doing that, and I think that he has fun with that. Do I get anything out of that? I know how I want to work, and I enjoy working my ass off, and I enjoy going to the hotel every night and getting in a hot bath and relaxing my muscles.

You're forty, right?

Yeah.

There's got to be an expiration date, right?

Well, Steven was thirty-seven when he did *Above the Law*, and I was thirty-seven when I did *Ip Man 2*. So, I was always thinking that when I'd hit my mid-thirties, *I'd better make it pretty soon*. Steven was one of those guys that I looked at and realized that he didn't make it until he was thirty-seven. So, I still had a good amount of time. I train harder now than when I was in my twenties. Another thing is, I feel like I'm an actor now. I wasn't an actor when I was doing *Bloodmoon* and stuff like that. I didn't know how to act. *Bloodmoon* was the first movie I ever did with live sound. I was concerned with how my voice was going to sound. If I had made it ten years ago, I wouldn't have a career now. I'd have been doing those kinds of action movies, relying on the physicality, not performance. I'd be washed up now. I think it's better that I'm doing these movies *now*, that I'm having success *now*, so that I can appreciate it.

Do you think your *Aladdin* movie hurt you?

No, because obviously nobody's seen it. (Laughing.) It can't hurt me. The only thing I would have done differently is we should have put some fight scenes in it.

Right! Exactly!

I was kind of happy that I was hired to do a movie just because I was an actor.

And you were the lead, which was awesome.

They were talking of it as being a TV series. SyFy wants contemporary. They don't want to spend that kind of money on locations and sets and costumes. I really wanted *Aladdin* to be like the *Hercules* TV show. Every episode somebody else has got the lamp. We could time travel. There's no reason why Aladdin couldn't time travel to New York. It would have been really cool. I was happy that I was hired to be the lead in a movie where I don't even have to throw one kick. They paid me a really good amount of money to do it, too.

What sorts of projects would you like to be doing in the future?

Well, what I want to be doing is these martial arts action movies, but also playing the right hand to the bad guy in a studio film. The guy that comes in and does the action, that type of stuff. Also, acting in smaller parts in more interesting films that tell stories. As an actor you just want to act.

What is it about action and martial arts that appeals to you?

Well, when I was a kid . . . when we're kids we all want to be more heroic. Bigger and more muscular, more of a man. You go back and dream what you might have done in a fight that happened earlier, and stuff. You get to act out those scenarios in movies. All the guys I watched when I was growing up like Van Damme, Seagal, Jackie Chan, you watch their movies and you want to be able to play those kinds of characters. Young boys grow up wanting to do that stuff. Everybody else grows up and finds a normal kind of a job in life, and I guess there's just some of us where there's something wrong with us to want to continue wanting to play and create. I don't know why I want to do this. I just feel like I'm getting better at it.

(Editor's note: In January 2015, Shahlavi tragically passed away in his sleep due to a heart condition. His final completed film role is in the forthcoming Kickboxer Vengeance. *He will be missed.)*

Ironheart
1992 (Imperial VHS) (djm)

A Korean cop named John Keem (newcomer Britton Lee who never made another movie) goes after a pinstriped villain named Milverstead (Richard Norton), who uses a nightclub as a way to lure attractive, single women to inebriate themselves enough so that they can be tricked and taken captive to be sold throughout the world as sex slaves. Keem is on Milverstead's doorstep with revenge on his mind because Keem's partner was earlier killed by Ice (Bolo Yeung), Milverstead's hulking goon. When a young woman is taken prisoner at the nightclub, Keem reluctantly uses a pretty civilian decoy to help him entrap his target, but when that goes south, Keem has to go the extra mile to get his man . . . which proves more difficult than it should be because it turns out that his own boss is working against him and working *with* Milverstead for a fat paycheck.

Despite the fact that Bolo's face and name are brazenly splayed on the VHS box cover for *Ironheart*, Bolo in fact only plays a supporting role, and this guy Britton Lee is the actual star of the show. Lee produced the film as well as starred in it, and his fight scenes are mostly quick, one-sided matches that leave him generally unscathed. His one deadly encounter with Norton ends with Norton screaming just before Lee chops his head off, and then his finale fight with Bolo is astonishingly over and done with after a few terse blows and kicks. Needless to say, Lee's mark in action and martial arts cinema remains only a blip. Director Robert Clouse helmed a handful of great action movies like *Enter the Dragon, Gymkata*, and *China O'Brien*. This was his last movie.

Iron Man 2
2010 (Paramount DVD) (CD)

"If you try to escape or play any sort of games with me, I will tase you and watch *Supernanny* while you drool into the carpet."

Ivan Vanko (a revitalized Mickey Rourke after *The Wrestler*) is the son of a dying physicist and is equally as talented as his father. His father, Anton (Eugene Lazarev), was the former partner of Howard Stark, the brilliant scientist and businessman. He had Anton banished to Russia for attempting to commit treason, and Ivan wants his revenge. He designs and builds amazing electrified whips and attacks Howard's son Tony (Robert Downey Jr.), who has recently revealed to the world that he is the hero Iron Man. He can't do it all on his own—he needs help, equipment, and funds—so he teams up with weapons contractor Justin Hammer (Sam Rockwell), who has his own score to settle with Stark. After they've combined their skills, Tony Stark may be in way over his head.

Pairing Mickey Rourke (also in *The Expendables*) with Sam Rockwell (*Charlie's Angels*) was a stroke of genius. Rourke's best moment occurs when he activates his whips for the first time while RDJ's Tony Stark is racing a car. The set piece was shot brilliantly, with cars flipping, flying, and exploding in the background. And walking down the middle of the racetrack is Ivan Danko looking like a complete boss. Aside from his prison escape scene and the finale, we don't get to see much more action from him. The best fight scene in the film belongs to Scarlett Johansson (*The Avengers*) who has a wicked hand-to-hand brawl with a group of armed guards in a hallway. Rourke was hot off the success of his Academy Award–nominated performance in *The Wrestler* so this was a welcome turn for one of Hollywood's bad boys in a film directed by John Favreau (*Iron Man*).

Iron Thunder (a.k.a. Contemporary Gladiator)
1989 (Vivendi VHS) (CD)

"The reason for me living is to get some pussy. There's nothing more rewarding or fulfilling to me than to lay between some soft brown legs. Now if in the process, we can promote and sell some tickets, that's fine!"

Anthony "Amp" Elmore has spent his life trying to be the best martial artist he can be. This is the true story of the man and his rise to the top. He dreams of being the karate kickboxing champion, but it's a sport many were unfamiliar with at the time. We learn Elmore's story from the man himself, from his college beginning, his run as a carpet salesman, and finally to the devoted martial artist who would defy the odds and popularize the championship. It was never an easy road and we get to see all the struggles he would have to endure in order to make his dreams a reality.

Anthony Elmore is a one-man show on this film based upon his life experience. He wrote, directed, starred, and even sang some of the songs in it. It's hard to tell how much of it is to be taken seriously and how much was meant to be funny. The afro on this guy is pretty outrageous at the beginning of the film but it shrinks as time passes. There's very little action in the movie, though it does culminate with a large tournament fight with Elmore competing for the title he'd always dreamed of having. There's plenty of hilarious dialogue, most of which comes courtesy of his best friend Kingfish (George M. Young), with his over-confidence and his obsession with women. "The Amp" is a tough talker and self-promoter and this was his only film role. He has since, however, opened a very successful carpet business in Memphis, Tennessee.

Irresistible Force

1993 (Fox VHS) (djm)

"Great: Seven thousand cops on the force, and I gotta pick the only broad with a death wish!"

Sergeant Harris Stone (Stacy Keach) is fed up with having partners on the job who are quick to draw their gun on suspects, so he entreats his boss (Paul Winfield) to assign him a female partner. He's given Charlotte "Charlie" Heller (Cynthia Rothrock), a borderline dropout for failing her field test . . . for being overly aggressive. On their first day out together, they stop a robbery in progress, and cause more damage to the place being robbed than the robbers did. They're both suspended, and later that evening they stop off at a public ceremony where a new shopping mall is being opened (complete with high-tech security systems), and Harris notices something fishy going on. Charlie goes into the mall just when terrorists take over the place and hold everyone inside hostage. Harris, outside, becomes her only ally when the authorities come to lay a full-fledged assault on the mall. Charlie, smart and fully proficient (being an ex-Navy SEAL) in martial arts and combat, takes on the terrorists one by one until she's virtually cleared the place of vermin in a *Die Hard* fashion.

VHS artwork for *Irresistible Force*. Author's collection.

Made for network television, but still cinematic and highly entertaining, *Irresistible Force* is a great vehicle for Rothrock. It would have been a great TV series for her. Directed by Kevin Hooks after he did *Passenger 57* with Wesley Snipes, this action film runs at a fleet pace (at seventy-seven minutes in length), and it holds up even in today's jaded market.

The Italian Job

2003 (Paramount DVD) (CD)

"I trust everyone. It's the devil inside them I don't trust."

In this 2003 remake of the 1969 comedy/thriller *The Italian Job* (with Michael Caine), Mark Wahlberg plays Charlie Crocker, a thief extraordinaire who masterminds the perfect heist of $37 million in gold. Just when Charlie's crew is about to celebrate, their partner Steve (Edward Norton) leaves Charlie and his team for dead and takes off with the gold. A year later, Charlie brings together his team of Lyle (Seth Green), Left Ear (Mos Def), and Handsome Rob (Jason Statham) with the intention of getting their revenge on Steve for killing their partner John (Donald Sutherland) and taking off with the gold. Charlie needs a secret weapon so he enlists the aid of John's beautiful daughter Stella (Charlize Theron), who happens to be a master at cracking safes. This heist isn't just about the money—it's about payback—and Steve will have to pull out every trick he knows if he plans on making a getaway.

This take on *The Italian Job* is a near-perfect popcorn flick with tons of excitement and laughs. With a film like this with such a big cast, it's tough to be a standout—everyone is an important piece to the mosaic. To this day, women are still talking about Handsome Rob. Jason Statham, hot on the heels of the first *Transporter* film, is one charming son of a bitch. The character is a perfect match for him, and the cast meshes incredibly well. Statham spends much of his time behind the wheel of a car. and the car chases are badass (no CGI). Director F. Gary Gray (*Law Abiding Citizen*) may have made a few missteps in his career but *The Italian Job* isn't one of them.

Jackie Chan Adventures

2000–2005 (NOV) (CD)

"I am the keeper of the talismans. I am the apocalypse of which legend speak. And I am . . . for once and for all: Your executioner!"

In the year 2000, the WB Network debuted *Jackie Chan Adventures*, an animated series following the, uh, adventures of Jackie Chan. In the series, Jackie is an archaeologist who helps his uncle with an artifacts shop. His young niece Jade comes to live with them in the United States and ends up being a handful for them. Much of the series focuses on Chan's quest to find and protect twelve talismans. Each of the talismans contains a special ability, and once combined, can unleash a vicious demon known as Shendu. The Dark Hand is a criminal organization (led by a mastermind named Valmont) trying to find the talismans before Jackie and his crew do. Recruited by Section 13 (a top-secret law enforcement team), Jackie travels the globe battling various evils unleashed as the talismans (and various other objects) exchange hands.

The show was a big success for the WB and ran for ninety-five episodes (five seasons), spawning a line of books, a comic book series, various action figures, and even a video game. The show captures the humor and action many associate with his films (even better than most of the films he shot in the US.). Long-time Jackie Chan fans will catch tiny references to his film work and many of the episode titles are variations of film titles. At the end of each episode, the real Jackie Chan appears to answer questions asked by kids. They're all interesting little segments and you get to learn a bit about the man (though us hardcore fans will already know the answer to most of them). For an animated series, the show had a pretty fun storyline (Chan borrowed a bit from the story for *Chinese Zodiac*) with an interesting group of characters. The thing is, after five seasons it grows repetitive with them collecting talismans, *and then* there are Oni masks to collect, as well as Chi powered relics, so it grows old sort of quick. It's definitely fun for a while but the kids will dig it and everything is wrapped up nicely in the final episodes. Chan doesn't voice his animated likeness but the voice cast is pretty impressive with actors like Julian Sands, Adam Baldwin, Clancy Brown, David Carradine, and Lucy Lui appearing throughout the series.

Jackie Chan's First Strike

(a.k.a. **Police Story 4: First Strike**)

1997 (New Line DVD) (djm)

Supercop Jackie (Jackie Chan) is asked to accompany an important witness to the Ukraine, and he agrees on the provision that he *only* observe her until she gets off the plane. As soon as they get off the plane, things get wonky. A rogue nuclear

J

scientist is somehow involved, and all of a sudden everyone is running around shooting at each other, and Jackie is smack in the middle of it all. Jackie joins forces with the Russians to travel to Australia where the nuclear scientist has family, and his mission is to wait around until the scientist returns. But Jackie, being honest and tired of all the espionage, implores the scientist's family to be up front with him and alert him when their sibling comes calling. This action gets him into some trouble, and the Russians turn against him, which in turn allows the plot to go on autopilot as Jackie gets into more action.

Released theatrically in the US, *First Strike* is 007-lite, with incredible death-defying stunts and Mickey Mouse–style plotting and intrigue. Some memorable stunts featuring Jackie in extreme peril are the highlights, as usual. It's pure fun, and anyone who turns a nose up at it has lost the ability to just have a good time at the movies. At eighty-five minutes, the film's fleet pace won't let any one become bored. Nathan Jones (who later appeared in *Muay Thai Giant, Fearless,* and *The Protector*) had his first role here as a hitman. Directed by Stanley Tong (*Supercop, Rumble in the Bronx*).

Jaguar Lives!
1979 (Arrow DVD R2) (djm)

Secret agent, karate expert, and all-around adventurer Jonathan Cross (real-life karate champion Joe Lewis) is called upon to globe trot on his next mission. His code name is The Jaguar, and his enemies know him as such the worldwide over. He travels to Asia and the Middle East, with a short interlude in Paris, and his enemy includes a mustachioed Christopher Lee who, as a way of psyching him out, shows him the tombstone that bears his name, with an empty grave waiting for him. Cross has just as many allies as enemies, and his closest friends include actors such as Barbara Bach, Donald Pleasence, and Joseph Wiseman, all of whom co-starred in various James Bond films (Lee too). Jumping from one pitfall and fight scene to another, Cross proves that he is a secret agent worthy of a sequel, which unfortunately never got made.

The best scenes of this movie feature Lewis when he's fighting. The best scene features him fighting a cocky villain, played by Anthony Delongis, who would go on to become a famous whipmaster and fencer in real life, training the likes of Michelle Pfeiffer in *Batman Returns* and Harrison Ford in one of the Indiana Jones movies. Joe Lewis, who was a household name in the martial arts circuit, didn't have much of

a career in action movies after this. He's sort of in the Chuck Norris class of acting and action, and the producers obviously wanted him to be the next big thing, otherwise why would they go to the expense of surrounding him with 007 alumni in a 007-wannabe movie? It looks like they spent money on it, if not in casting, then in exotic locations. It's no classic, but it's the kind of thing that helps to define what a "vehicle" movie is and how an athlete or martial artist fits into such a film. Lewis was in *Force Five* next. The director was Ernest Pintoff, who made a career out of directing episodes of television programs.

JCVD
2008 (Peace Arch DVD) (djm)

For years (nearly a decade), I lamented the fall from grace that defined the latter era of Jean-Claude Van Damme's career. I'd seen every single one of his films theatrically from *Timecop* to *Universal Soldier: The Return*, and when he started doing direct-to-video movies like *Desert Heat* and *Derailed*—inferior action movies that were beneath him—I yearned for him to find his way to a deserved comeback, but I knew it would be a long time coming, but when that day came, it would be glorious. *JCVD* isn't an action spectacular or even a mass-market appeal movie, but anyone who's ever been a true fan of Van Damme will feel vindicated for the long wait between theatrical releases for the star, and for believing that he's always been capable of delivering a performance that outclasses 99 percent of his peers in any of their best movies where they delivered their most stellar performances. He basically plays a version of himself in this movie—a haggard, exhausted "B" action star on the verge of a nervous breakdown. He's lost custody of his only daughter who's embarrassed by him, and he's just relinquished a part in a direct-to-video movie to Steven Seagal. His week only gets worse when he walks into a bank/post office in Belgium, and he finds that the place is in the middle of being robbed by a bunch of second

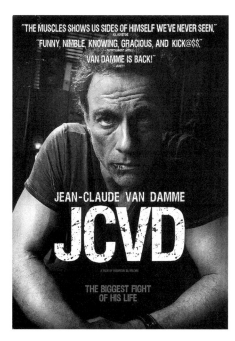

rate thieves. He's instantly recognized (after all, he's the biggest movie star to come from that country), but his celebrity status gets him into trouble when the police mistakenly assume that he's the instigator of the robbery in progress. All of a sudden, he becomes infamous, but as he's held against his will at gunpoint by the robbers, he laments his status in life and contemplates what he believes he's worth—not only to the world, but to himself.

Van Damme delivers a once-in-a-lifetime performance in a once-in-a-lifetime movie, and while it's not a "great" movie per se, it does, however, contain his greatest moments ever captured on film. He's absolutely clear and precise in his acting (most of his lines are in French), and it's immediately obvious that this is much more than "the muscles from Brussels" here . . . this is a full-fledged actor, completely in command (for once in his life) of his art, process, and purpose, and it's pretty amazing to think that he of all action guys was able to pull this off at that stage in his career. It certainly helped move him in the direction of a comeback (which, in turn, led to his crucial role in *Expendables 2*), but honestly, this is where it's at. Director Mabrouk El Mechri (who would later do the Bruce Willis film *The Cold Light of Day*) also co-wrote the script. Van Damme produced.

Jian Bing Man
2015 (NOV) (djm)

Let's just get this out of the way: Despite being heavily featured in the trailers, marketing, and posters, Jean-Claude Van Damme is neither the star nor the co-star of the new Chinese megabomb known as *Jian Bing Man* (English translation: *Pancake Man*). His name is spoken once early on in the film as a teaser that he might show up at some point, and you're sitting there waiting for your favorite action star to show his face in some capacity, and in the last five minutes he at last appears to add the only star quality this hopelessly immature and lost in translation motion picture has going for it. He does the splits (why wouldn't he since that's what he was paid for?), throws a butterfly kick, gets thrown on his face by the star who's wearing a yellow cape, and in the last seconds of the film before the credits roll Van Damme gets the last line: "Iron Man didn't kick my ass!" as if that's supposed to validate The Pancake Man's awesomeness. I'm telling you, guys, I really hope Van Damme got a million bucks for this garbage because if he didn't then there's no justice.

A quick backstory of my appreciation and devotion to Van Damme's work: The first time I saw one of his films in a theater was *Timecop* in 1994. I've been a fan ever since, seeing all of his theatrical releases any time he's been given one. I was there for everything from *Maximum Risk* (twice) to *Knock Off* and *Universal Soldier: The Return*, and I've sought out every screening of his latest film at every nook and cranny festival if it was playing in a theater within a hundred mile radius. I saw *JCVD* in a theater, I went out of my way to go see *Welcome to the Jungle, Swelter, Universal Soldier: Day of Reckoning, Dragon Eyes, Enemies Closer, Pound of Flesh,* and I even went to see *Kung Fu Panda 2* because he did the voice of an alligator in it. If the powers that be decide that Van Damme

J

gets a theatrical release, I make sure I'm there no matter what. So when I found out that *Jian Bing Man* was getting a theatrical release —playing at the Puente Hills Mall AMC Theater—I made sure I was there for the preview night before the opening night. I figured I'd be the only guy in the theater (same as I was when I saw *Universal Soldier: Day of Reckoning*, *Dragon Eyes*, and *Enemies Closer*), but I was absolutely floored when I entered the auditorium—it was packed! Almost every single seat had been taken by a crowd of young Asians (Chinese, I'm guessing educationally), and I had to find a seat in the last row in the back, next to a happy guy who looked excited to watch the film. After four or five trailers for exclusively Asian films, Jian Bing Man started.

The crowd went wild for this garbage, including the guy sitting next to me who kept looking over to me, wondering why I wasn't as thrilled as he was. From the first frames, the audience laughed uncontrollably, clapped, cheered, and had a great time. The guy next to me kept ribbing me, trying to get a response out of me, but it just wasn't happening. I almost wanted to run to the foot of the auditorium to take a photo of everyone in the theater having a such a good time because I was not only the only gweilo in the place, but also the only person not laughing. As in Chinese opera and theater, almost everything in these modern films from that region takes great pains to oversimplify drama, mystery, and comedy to the point of nullifying any sense of personal gratification for going on a cinematic journey along with characters you're supposed to care about. Silly characters are ridiculously broad, with massively broad strokes coloring their temperature when they're in comedic situations. Gay characters (forget subtlety) are parodies of gay characters, and romantic, leading characters are hopeless romantics with melodramatic subplots who are sometimes allowed long, drawn-out (and in slow motion, no less) flashbacks to childhood for no good reason. To top off all of this cinematic ineptitude, the main character (played by the film's director Da Peng, who is just cute enough to play the lead, but just nerdy enough to have everyone in the film consider him a loser) dreams of becoming a superhero known as Pancake Man, whose sole superpower is to throw raw eggs at bad guys. We get slow-mo shots of eggs crashing on grimacing faces, and Pancake Man (who sort of looks like Cyclone from *He-Man* and the *Masters of the Universe*) flips around and zooms off into the ether from whence he came. For me, this was not a superhero movie, a comedy, or a spoof of any sort. It is a sad and confounding state of affairs to realize that this is what millions of Chinese people are eating up, and to know that this has made over a hundred million dollars and broke every record in its native country just bewilders me.

As for Jean-Claude Van Damme, he plays himself playing a nameless villain Pancake Man fights at the very end of the film. The fight lasts maybe two or three minutes at most. If you saw and were disappointed by Van Damme's appearances in *Welcome to the Jungle* and *Swelter,* you'll be glad (I guess) to hear that he kicks more and does more of what you're hoping he'll do in this thing. It's just over so quickly. It's not worth the price of admission, frankly, unless you're a diehard fan (like I've always been). A funny thing about the film is that a Chinese pop band (four dudes with ultra stylish hair and make-up) shows up immediately after Van Damme gets knocked out by Pancake Man, and their purpose in the film was simply to upstage him for the bigger-and-better cameo (at least to the Chinese audience, who cheered when these guys came into the picture), and one of their songs plays on the soundtrack to highlight their gorgeousness. When Pancake Man greets them (they have no purpose in the film other than simply to appear and disappear), they smile and chat with him for a second, and that's when I noticed their teeth. The true mark of communism is bad teeth, and that's when the film got my first and only laugh. I dunno, guys. This movie's the pits, but if you feel you need to go there, then go there. I did. And I'll never forget the experience.

Jill the Ripper

2000 (Sony DVD) (CD)

"You can't go from flowers and a kiss to a punch in the stomach."

Matt Sorenson (Dolph Lundgren) is an ex-cop who makes his way back home to Boston after his brother is murdered. His body was found bound and mutilated, and Matt deals with it in his own way . . . by hitting the bottle. His brother was a powerful politician who had a secret life no one ever knew about. Matt's former colleagues seem to think it was the work of a prostitute, and he becomes driven to find the truth as the bodies begin to pile up around him. His brother's widow Irene (Danielle Brett) seems to know more than she's letting on, and the truth about their obsession with bondage and S & M emerges. Learning this, Matt must submerge himself into a world he knows nothing about, dealing with shady characters and pushing himself to the edge to find the woman responsible for the murders.

Jill the Ripper is quite possibly the most daring film in Dolph Lundgren's (*Sweepers*) library and it's also has him playing one of the more interesting and complex characters he has ever portrayed. Matt has a real mean streak, he's a bully, and he isn't afraid to beat a woman. It's a nice twist to see his character go through so much and to see this sadistic side emerge as this perverse world overtakes his life. Thankfully, it doesn't get in the way of some ass-kicking . . . not even dogs are safe from his wrath. The film, directed by Anthony Hickox (*Storm Catcher,* also with Lundgren), is based upon the novel by Frederic Lindsay. We see Dolph in a down low state here, but it's worth it; this crime thriller delivers the action, thrills, titillation, and graphic carnage we would hope to see from the pairing of this actor and director.

Jingle All the Way

1996 (Fox DVD) (CD)

"I'm not a pervert! I just was looking for a Turbo Man doll!"

Howard Langston (Arnold Schwarzenegger) devotes the majority of his time to work, leaving his family to wish he was around more for them, especially his son Jamie (Jake Lloyd). Howard keeps making promises to his family and not keeping them, which upsets not only Jamie but also his wife Liz (Rita Wilson) as well. Jamie wants a toy for Christmas called Turbo Man and it's the most sought after toy of the season. Howard sets out on a quest on Christmas Eve to find the action figure for his son. It turns out to be a nightmare when he goes toe-to-toe with rival father Myron (Sinbad) to obtain what turns out to be the last figure left. While he is off trying to find and claim the toy, Liz and Jamie are left at home with neighbor Ted (Phil Hartman), who is on the prowl to win Liz's affection.

As ridiculous as the movie is, *Jingle All the Way* manages to capture the spirit of the holiday and is a fun film for the whole family. This may not be the type of film Arnold's fans want to see him in, but he does seem to be enjoying himself and it's infectious. As far as action goes, there's a hilarious fight where he takes on dozens of Santa Clauses, including WWE wrestler Paul "Big Show" Wight and his *Red Heat* co-star Jim Belushi. Arnold also has the chance to knock out a crazed reindeer—see *Conan the Barbarian* for more Arnold-punching-animal action. Director Brian Levant (*The Spy Next Door*) was somehow able to transform an action hero into a buffoon but kids will enjoy it. Arnold did *Batman and Robin* next.

Jinn

2014 (Freestyle Releasing DVD) (djm)

A supernatural action/fantasy adventure hybrid, *Jinn* concerns an ancient prophecy stating that a savior will be born to protect the world from the evil "Jinn" race, which has set its sights on destroying humanity since time began. One Jinn in particular has reserved its right to hunt down the bloodline of a particular hunter through the ages, and in the present day, the Jinn has come to kill off Shawn (Dominic Rains), who has no idea that he is a descendant of a long line of hunters. His wife (Serinda Swan) disappears during an assault by the evil Jinn, and two men who have been protecting him his whole life without his knowledge save Shawn and clue him in on the grand, epic tale he is a part of. One of the men is a good Jinn named Gabriel (played by gymnast Ray Park), and the other guy is a priest who assigns Shawn with holy weapons to do battle with the supernatural entities who are after him. While Gabriel uses superpowers and martial arts to protect Shawn, Shawn himself must muster up his own courage and strength to defeat the evil force that has laid siege to his life.

Of interest for a variety of valid reasons, *Jinn* is a fun, adventuresome horror-ish action adventure with a good-sized part for Ray Park, who is best known for playing Darth Maul in *Star Wars Episode 1*. Park's role is pivotal, and he engages in several martial arts battles, displaying his wushu skills in at least two scenes. I enjoyed *Jinn* not just because Park was in the film (although that didn't hurt), but because it's exactly the sort of movie that is rarely done on quite this scale—or with this amount of skill—anymore. It does mostly everything right, and if there's a sequel (as the end credits promises there will be), I will be ready and willing to pay to see it. Ajmal Zaheer Ahmad wrote and directed it.

Johnny Mnemonic
1995 (Sony DVD) (CD)

Johnny (Keanu Reeves a few years prior to *The Matrix*) is a "mnemonic" courier of important information; he has an implant installed in his head that allows him to transport vital information. He's hired by a group of businessmen who uploads data into his head, and though the amount of information exceeds his capacity, he takes it on anyway thinking it will all be transferred out once it is delivered. The group is then slaughtered by Yakuza who want the information Johnny's transporting, but they aren't the only ones who now are after Johnny: also in pursuit is Takahashi (Takeshi Kitano), the boss of the Pharma-Kon Corporation who knows there's a cure to NAS (nerve attenuation syndrome), the plague that has destroyed mankind. He hires an eccentric mercenary named Street Preacher (Dolph Lundgren) to find Johnny before the Yakuza. With the help of Jane (Dina Meyer), Johnny is taken deep into the underground where they meet a motley bunch of characters who will help them save Johnny before the information in his head gets him killed.

No other action star on Earth could have pulled off the role of a Bible-quoting assassin that Dolph Lundgren takes on in this film. Lundgren had recently played He-Man and The Punisher, and here he brilliantly delivers his lines as if he were proselytizing to a congregation of untold legions. Where else can you see Lundgren being attacked by a psychic dolphin? While Reeves may be the star on the video box, it's the eclectic group of supporting characters that give the film some backbone. The cast includes Udo Kier (*Blade*), Ice-T (*Surviving the Game*), and Takeshi Kitano (*Zatoichi*). This film was based on the cyberpunk story by William Gibson, who also wrote the screenplay. This was director Robert Longo's first and only feature film credit. Lundgren is by far the best reason to watch it. A Japanese version also exists.

John Wick
2014 (Lionsgate DVD) (djm)

After John Wick's wife dies, he receives a final gift from her: a cute puppy named Daisy. John (played by Keanu Reeves) just starts to care for the puppy when some home invaders get the drop on him (they want his car), beat him, and leave him for dead . . . and kill Daisy. When he comes to, he busts out a sledgehammer and breaks some concrete in his basement, unearthing his past. Armed with weapons and geared with gold Krugerrands for currency, John begins his quest of revenge, but it's complicated: The man who stole his car is Iosef Tarasov (Alfie Allen), the impetuous son of Viggo Tarasov (played by Michael Nyqvist), the most powerful Russian mobster in the city. The complications are manifold when it's revealed

that John Wick is not just a regular Joe: He's *John Wick*, the man who's known for killing boogeymen, an unstoppable powerhouse of a hitman whom everyone either knows or has heard of and steers way clear of. When Viggo understands that his son committed an unforgivable sin against John, he hires every assassin available to take out John, and the body count starts to pile up as John makes his way forward.

Here's the deal: Keaunu Reeves isn't an action star. With starring roles in *Point Break, Speed, The Matrix, 47 Ronin*, and *Man of Tai Chi*, he clearly appeals to an audience craving action, but for me he's a guy like Liam Neeson or Matt Damon who learn their moves in rehearsals and are consummate professionals and make everything look good. That's fine, good for them. The reason why *John Wick* works for me is because martial artist/action star Daniel Bernhardt from *Bloodsport 2, 3, 4,* and *Parker* plays a featured heavy, and his several scenes where he goes up against Reeves are moments to cherish. Bernhardt is one of the reasons why this book needed to be written. You see him on screen, and your jaw drops. When he moves, you watch. It doesn't matter that he's a supporting player because he makes the whole movie worth watching. Reeves is great, and the movie is fun entertainment, but the real joy of the film (and other films where Bernhardt and others of his ilk are sidelined by big name actors) is watching the real professionals at work. Stuntman and stunt choreographers Chad Stahelski and David Leitch directed this film. It's a great first effort.

Joshua
1976 (Catcom DVD) (CD)

"You ever kill a man before? Do you know what it feels like to kill? I killed in the war. People I didn't even know."

Joshua (Fred Williamson) is a soldier who fought for the Union during the Civil War. Now the war is over, he is ready to return home to build a new and better life for himself and his mother. When he gets in town to see her, he finds out he's too late. His mom has been murdered by a gang of white thugs. Joshua is filled with rage and finds out he is only a few hours behind them. He sets out to find them, carrying his mother's only possession—a rifle that had belonged to his father. Hot on the trail, he takes his time and will never give up until each one of them is dead.

Joshua is a solid (though flawed) effort written by and starring Fred Williamson (*Active Stealth*) and directed by Larry G. Spangler (*The Soul of Nigger Charley*). The film has very little dialogue, which isn't an issue since the story is as simple as they come. Things get rolling as soon as the movie begins and never really stop moving. There are several overly long moments of people riding their horses with some rather generic western music playing over and over again. Those moments slow things down a bit, but Williamson is fantastic. He is the silent hero, a man who won't quit until he gets his revenge. For the first half of the film, his character is hawk-like, watching the gang from a

distance. Then he swoops in to pluck them off one by one. He has a solid fight scene with one of the thugs and comes up with a couple of inventive kills for the bad guys. This is a decent flick but let's face it, we are only watching it to see "The Hammer" in action, and he delivers.

Joshua Tree
(a.k.a. **Army of One**)
1993 (Shout Factory DVD)
(djm)

Following the success of *Universal Soldier*, Dolph Lundgren was cast as the hero in *Joshua Tree*, the first feature directed by stuntman and stunt coordinator Vic Armstrong, who doubled Indiana Jones, James Bond, Superman, and other big-screen heroes for major motion pictures. Lundgren plays a wrongly convicted racecar driver named Wellman Santee, who went into bad business with a corrupt cop (George Seagal). On his way to prison in a transport vehicle, Lundgren manages to escape and go on the lam with a gorgeous hostage (Kristian Alfonso), who also happens to be a cop. They drive through the desert and end up in Joshua Tree, California, where Santee grew up. He tries to set things right, and in the process, he gains an ally (and hot sex partner) in his hostage, who realizes that the cop on their tail is a corrupt, lying murderer. Some intense and well-choreographed John Woo-style shootouts and car chase scenes elevate this "B" action movie to another level.

The very fact that Vic Armstrong directed and shot this movie with his brother Andy should clue you in to the realization that this movie will be special. It's not anything more than advertised, but it's a great-looking, exciting road movie with lots of good action. The only thing that bothers me about it is that from one moment to the next, we are expected to believe that Lundgren's character is a marksman and a badass killer. If you can get past that, then there's no reason why this film won't work for you. Joel Goldsmith's jazzy action score helps the film quite a bit as well. Unfortunately, this film wasn't released theatrically in the US, but received a direct-to-video debut, which might be why many people have yet to discover it.

Journey 2:
The Mysterious Island
2012 (Warner DVD) (CD)

"Big man's not afraid of anything. I love lizards . . . when they're boots and belts."

Sean Anderson (Josh Hutcherson) gets himself in trouble by breaking into a satellite facility. His stepdad Hank (Dwayne Johnson) helps him by keeping the police from pressing charges, but he wants to have a breakthrough with the kid. The moment comes when he finds out Sean is trying to decode a message containing information leading him to the mysterious island Jules Vern wrote about. Hank wants to bond with him a bit so the two embark on a trip to the island of Palau with the help of locals Gabato (Luis Guzman) and his daughter Kailani (Vanessa Hudgens). Together, they search for the mysterious island but must cut their trip short when they realize the island is about to be completely flooded. After they find Sean's grandfather, Alexander (Michael Cain), who has been living on the island, they will have to race against time and find their way home if they want to survive.

Journey 2 is a perfect example of an incredibly fun family experience. Dwayne "The Rock" Johnson (*Snitch*) is an absolute blast in the film. This isn't exactly filled with action, and it's more like an adventure, where the characters must travel across an island filled with unexpectedly large creatures and bizarre obstacles inspired by the stories of Jules Vern. Johnson never really fights, though he does have the chance to land a *thunder cookie* across the jaw of a giant lizard. He also sings and has a hilarious moment showing off the "peck pop of love." The script by Mark and Brian Gunn (brothers to writer/director James Gunn) hits all the right beats while director Brad Peyton (*Cats & Dogs 2*) helps to create a visually beautiful film with eye-popping effects that you can really appreciate when watching the film in 3D. Brendan Fraser had been approached to star in this sequel to 2008's *Journey to the Center of the Earth*, but when a deal couldn't be made, Johnson was offered the lead role instead. It paid off, evidentially, because the film was a huge hit.

Judge Dredd

1995 (Hollywood Pictures DVD) (CD)

"Emotions: there ought to be a law against them."

In the future, a new law system is put into place where the power of judge and jury is given to the police, making them judge, jury, and executioner on the spot. When the top lawman of Mega City One, Judge Dredd (Sylvester Stallone), is framed for a murder he didn't commit, he is sent to a prison colony. With the help of Fergee (Rob

Judge Joseph Dredd (Sylvester Stallone), sans helmet, in *Judge Dredd*. Author's collection.

Schneider) and fellow Judge Hershey (Diane Lane), they set out to find who is responsible for the murder, only to have someone from Dredd's past re-emerge to destroy him.

Judge Dredd is not a very successful film. It takes a much-loved comic book and unique concept and turns it into a brainless action film. Stallone (*Over the Top*) does his best, but this role was not very well suited for him. There's no question that he delivers all of the action beats but as far as what was required to play the iconic Dredd, he was either miscast or the material wasn't adapted properly. Deviating too much from the comic (character and tone wise) was a huge mistake. One of the character's signatures is the fact that he never removes his helmet. In this film, his helmet is removed about ten minutes in and then only seen sporadically thereafter. When the studio paid for a name like Stallone, then you better believe the audience will see him. Also, the comic relief sidekick seemed forced and unnecessary. Director Danny Cannon (*The Young Americans*) tries too hard with this film, never giving it a real edge. In 2012, director Pete Travis brought *Dredd 3D* to the big screen with Karl Urban as the titular character. It was a reboot and not a remake; that *Dredd* film is fantastic and what the fans had been waiting for.

Jungleground

1995 (Image DVD) (djm)

An apocalyptic hell zone known as Jungleground has been cordoned off from the rest of the city, and once you go in, it's fairly likely that you'll never come out again. Gangs rule the streets, and they live by a special brand of rules. Vice detective Cornel (Roddy Piper) is asked to go into Jungleground to investigate the death of an undercover cop, and as soon as he goes in, he's captured by a major gang (The Rockers), and he's forced to play The Most Dangerous Game. He's given a few seconds head start to run for his life, and then the gang chases him, hoping to kill him before he leaves Jungleground. Since this is a movie, we know that he'll survive the night, kill the gang members one by one, and escape with his life. There's nothing new here.

It's really hard to get onboard with this movie. The actors look too unblemished and clean to be gang members, and there's nary a trace of authenticity or menace about any of them, and the Jungleground itself looks like a Hollywood set. There's no fear, no sense of danger in this movie, which is a huge mistake. Roddy Piper is pretty good in a physical role, but it's a foregone conclusion that he's going to get the better of his situation because none of the guys hunting him look like they can take him on. I like that his name is Cornel, which I'm fairly certain is an homage to Cornel Wilde and his movie *The Naked Prey*, which is a *Most Dangerous Game* variation. Other than that, this movie's got nothing going for it. Directed by Don Allan, who hasn't done another movie to date.

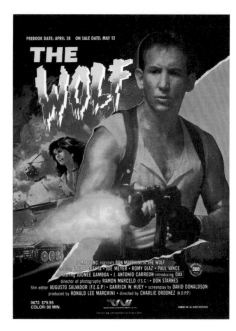

Video Promo poster for *Jungle Wolf*. Author's collection.

Jungle Wolf (a.k.a. Forgotten Warrior, a.k.a. The Wolf)

1986 (Trans World Entertainment VHS) (djm)

A US ambassador is kidnapped by a southeast Asian terrorist organization and held captive in a jungle camp, and the United States government asks former P.O.W. Vietnam vet Steve Parrish (Ron Marchini) to go out to the Philippines on a secret mission to save the ambassador. He leaves his son behind and embarks on a Rambo-esque campaign through the jungles, hunting down the terrorists one by one, and he has help in the form of a female revolutionary, who later dies in a memorable scene that recalls the scene in *Rambo: First Blood Part II* where Rambo's girlfriend is shot down in front of him. Much of *Jungle Wolf* emulates the formula of *Rambo*, with Marchini as a one-man commando, setting traps, gunning down dozens, and speaking only monosyllabic lines of heroic standoffishness.

Marchini, a real-life karate champion, made a small career for himself as a direct-to-video action star, headlining fare like *Death Machines, Omega Cop,* and *Karate Cop,* and this first *Jungle Wolf* entry spawned a three-picture franchise. The next one was *Return Fire*. Directed by Charlie Ordoñez.

Kamen Rider: Dragon Knight

2009 (NOV) (djm)

A teenager named Kit Taylor (Stephen Lunsford) stumbles across an advent deck that gives him the ability to transform into a "Kamen Rider," a kung fu warrior with supernatural powers. He attracts the attention of General Xaviax (William O'Leary), who is from another dimension and is building an army of Kamen Riders to fight his interdimensional war for him. Xaviax wants Kit to join his cause, but when another Kamen Rider named Len (Matt Mullins) shows up to convince Kit otherwise, Xaviax has his hands full trying to eliminate Len while still trying to turn Kit over to his side. It's an ongoing saga of good and evil, with martial arts battles galore and a fantastical element to keep things colorful.

This forty-episode television series lasted only a single season, but it comes from a long line of *Kamen Rider* brand-name shows produced in Japan. This particular series was developed by Steve Wang (who directed *Drive* with Mark Dacascos) and aired on the WB network in the US. Real-life martial artist Matt Mullins, who plays the second-lead character, is featured throughout the show, and the show allows him to showcase incredible feats of martial arts. Those unfamiliar with Mullins should try to seek out certain episodes to see what he can do. This is the best body of work Mullins has to his name so far, and his feature film credits like *Bloodfist 2050*, *Blood and Bone*, and *The Adventures of Johnny Tao* pale in comparison to his work on this program. Other than Mullins, the show isn't really my cup of tea. It's more for fans of stuff like *Ultra Man* and *Power Rangers*. Mark Dacascos appears in several of the episodes.

INTERVIEW:

MATT MULLINS

(djm)

Matt Mullins exemplifies what it means to be an action star. A true martial artist with everything it takes to make it as a star—five martial arts titles, good looks, great skills, a hunger to succeed—but today's market for action stars has weeded out most of the up-and-comers and would-be action guys striving to make their mark. Despite the odds, Mullins has accrued a solid resume of action and martial arts projects like Bloodfist 2050 *(2005),* Kamen Rider:

Dragon Knight *(2008–2010), and* Wrath of Vajra *(2013), and he has a starring film called* White Tiger *(co-starring Don "The Dragon" Wilson and Cynthia Rothrock) in the can. It wouldn't take much to push Mullins over the edge and into action movie stardom, so only time will tell . . .*

You're one of the last martial arts guys to have been hand-picked by Roger Corman to star in one of his productions, *Bloodfist 2050*. Talk about how that happened.

The way that got started with Roger Corman was that I had done a show called *XMA*. It was Extreme Martial Arts, and it was on the Discovery Channel. In that program, it featured me doing all types of martial arts; it was kind of a Hollywood-esque version of what martial arts is. It looked at everything from how we generate power to how a technique is done. It was a huge international success. Basically, what *Sports Science* is now, *XMA* was the pilot for that show. There was a good storyline behind it as well. Not that my life is a great story, but it was a story of my coming up in the world of martial arts, and they did a really good job with it. Roger Corman saw it, and I received an email from him the next day. He asked me if I wanted to come in for a meeting about a film. I went in, and he was really cool. I'd been really familiar with him mostly from the Don Wilson movies—the *Bloodfist* series—and talking to Roger was nice. I got to go the Philippines, and for me at that time it was really exciting. It was a huge opportunity. I went out there and I ended up working on the film for about two months. It was shot on film. I got to work with Cirio Santiago, may he rest in peace. It was a really cool and interesting time to be there because it was right at the end of that era of making movies in a certain way to make a certain amount of return. It was a really great experience. I learned more working on that set than years and years of acting class.

Just a technical question about *Bloodfist 2050*: Did you film all of the wasteland scenes with the car racing and stuff, or was that footage from other Santiago/Corman productions?

That was stock footage. We were trying to follow the formula of having a certain amount of action, a certain amount of sex, car chases, and things that people would like. A certain amount of stock footage was spliced in as we went. I didn't do any of the driving or additional sequences that you see in the film.

How was this movie pitched to you? Did Corman say, "Let's do *Bloodfist* in the future!"

When Roger told me about the film, he told me that it would be the ninth in the series. He said that he wanted to relaunch the brand. He wanted to usher in a new generation of action. He let me read the script, I enjoyed it, and I read some lines for him, and then it was a done deal. It was easy-going. It was cool.

You started off as the star in your own film, which is sort of the way it used to be back in the VHS era. What happened after *Bloodfist 2050*? Did you think you'd keep going on in that direction?

Matt Millins (seated) on the Philippines set of *Bloodfist 2050*. Courtesy of Matt Mullins.

I'd been working on acting and being in TV and film ever since I was sixteen. Simultaneously, I'd been doing martial arts, and I never actually thought I'd be able to do both of the things I love at the same time. I was fortunate enough with *Bloodfist* to do that. Six months later, I did another film called *The Adventures of Johnny Tao*, which was a really fun film. The concept and the ideas behind that were really cool. The choreographers, who included Marcus Young and J. J. Perry, had done so many different films that I was a fan of. J. J. had just gotten back from doing *Undisputed II* with Scott Adkins. He showed me some of the action that he'd developed for that film. It was really fun working on two specific characters. I got to play the lead villain on the film. Everyone had such determination to make a great film. They worked their butts off. That film was one of the most fun times I've ever had on a movie set. No one wanted this movie to get lost on the racks in video stores. Why it never blew up to the level that it should have, I'll never be sure. Everyone put in the work to make the best project possible.

What movies inspired you while you were growing up? Which movies made you want to be a martial artist?

My first "martial art" movie was *The Karate Kid*. I was hooked ever since then. I was thirteen years old when I started martial arts. *Ninja Turtles*, Van Damme, I liked some of Steven Seagal's movies. Van Damme had that great personality on film. Today's action stars have sort of lost that. The Rock has that. He has a little bit more fun with his characters—he's not just so hardcore all the time. You've got to have a great personality. *Bloodsport* is my favorite martial arts movie. My favorite *movie* is *The Crow* with Brandon Lee. I would watch it over and over. The first Jackie Chan movie I saw was *Cannonball Run*. I don't remember him in between the time when *Rumble in the Bronx* came out. Then, I was immediately a fan of his. He was so

K

unique. I never got a chance to meet Jackie, but I've met Sammo Hung a few times, and I trained with him once or twice. It was really fun to see how that version of cinema and action was brought to life.

Were scripts coming your way after you made *Bloodfist* and *Johnny Tao*? What were you looking for as an actor?

After *Bloodfist*—even though it was a starring role—and even though *XMA* had done really well, scripts don't just roll your way. There was this idea that "Why should we hire this guy when we can hire him to be the double?" I had to fight to get these roles. Even with *Johnny Tao*, I went through six rounds of auditioning to get the role. It's easier to get those meetings on a lower budgeted film than anything beyond that. It was hard to break through. I continued to do the best work possible. I kept getting comments that I was so young. I was only twenty-three or twenty-four at the time.

You just made a movie called *White Tiger* with Cynthia Rothrock and Don Wilson. Talk about that.

Yeah, and Joe Lewis actually. He passed away recently. That was his last project ever. It was pretty incredible to work with someone who was the cornerstone of American martial arts. He basically created American-style kickboxing. It eventually became as huge as it is. It was very cool to work with him and to hear his rants and raves about martial arts. Working with Don Wilson was really fun. He just has such a great personality. There's a really cool air about him. He's seen it, been around it all. Being able to hear it all was great. Cynthia has been around and has worked in American cinema, Hong Kong cinema—it was a dream to work with her. I hope the movie comes out at some point. There were production issues, unfortunately. A couple months after that, I got a chance to work on a movie in China called *The Wrath of Vajra*. I got to work with a mainland China production. That was really interesting. It was a huge-budgeted movie. It was something like

forty million Chinese dollars. That meant like a 200-million-dollar movie here in the States. It's a period piece.

You're definitely going in the right direction with your career. You're working with the best of the best in the action world. I've seen you in *Blood and Bone*, *Mortal Kombat: Legacy*, and *Metal Hurlant Chronicles*. You're part of a core group of guys who are doing great things in the action world right now. Guys like Michael Jai White, Darren Shahlavi, and Scott Adkins. Talk about working with these guys.

It's cool to be a part of a group of guys who are still making the action that's not CGI action. It's us doing it. Us doing the action that you see. All of us want to put out an amazing product. Whatever it takes to do that, we go out and do it. Everybody's got their own personality. Working with Michael Jai White is amazing. It's amazing how fast he is considering how big he is. He's an incredibly gifted athletic individual. And an amazing actor. Darren Shahlavi, same thing. A really good actor, and also someone who's worked in Hong Kong cinema, Thailand, and everything in between. With Scott, we're very much on a similar trajectory as far as the films and projects we've been involved in. It's really cool to see what he's done and learn from the type of action that he puts on screen, the way that he presents himself.

Talk about working with some of your stunt and fight choreographers like Larnell Stovall and J. J. Perry.

There's been a lot of fight choreographers who've been a lot of fun to work with. Larnell has a great martial arts mindset. He's great from an action standpoint, but he's also a great viewer. He'll

Matt Mullins and Michael Jai White on the set of Ben Ramsey's *Blood and Bone*. Courtesy of Matt Mullins.

think, "What will the audience think or see from this viewpoint?" He'll know what movie fans and martial arts fans would want to see. There are times when people will look at a fight scene and when they see it, they'll be like, "Oh, that would never work! It's not real!" There's a fine line you have to dance between it being real and it being visual. If you want it to be real, you need to watch some MMA, and sometimes the knockouts are impressive, and sometimes not. It has to be somewhere in between. J. J. Perry pumps you up. When he tells you to do something, you want to just *kill* it. It's very motivating. I got to work with a coordinator in Thailand—his name is Kazu Nada. He's a really outstanding martial artist. He knows how to capture action in a certain way. He helps enhance the story with his great camera movements. I worked with another guy, named Peng, on *The Wrath of Vajra*, and he did the fights in *Kick Ass* and *Scott Pilgrim vs the World*. It's a cross between the traditional Hong Kong style with the MMA style.

How do you adapt your style and persona to what coordinators or directors want from you with each project?

With a lot of the scripts I've gotten, I try to make a collaboration. I'll try to research different people who are like my character. It's acting. For *Blood and Bone*, I remember for [my character] Price, the director wanted me to be super ridiculously confident. Cocky. I watch videos of the boxer Prince Naseem. He was this real-life cocky boxer. When you watch him, you're like, "Oh, that guy: He's a dick!" But you love to hate him. Even when I was fighting, there were guys who would have these mannerisms when they fight. I worked on them and would see what worked on them and what didn't. I try to do that with all my characters.

Talk about working on *Blood and Bone*. That movie blew me away.

Blood and Bone was the first of the MMA movies to come out. It had everything in it. J. J. Perry coordinated all that. It had really good visuals, a great interpretation of MMA. It did a really good job of taking that unpredictable action and putting it in a movie. Michael Jai White was huge. Gina Carano was in it. It had really great cameos in it. What the director, Ben Ramsey, did was put all the old and current artists in the same movie.

Your role was pivotal in the movie.

I actually beat Michael Jai White in the movie. He kicks my ass, but I won the fight! It's all fake, but when you're up against someone like him . . . he *so* strong. To make it seem like you hit him, it's hard! It's really hard. He doesn't move. You've really got to work hard at selling it. He's an amazing martial artist. Even doing that first headlock . . . it was hard getting my arms around him. He's *that* big. He's amazingly fluid and fast. When he goes for stuff, he goes for it. He's one of the best on-screen fighters there is. Period.

What happened with the fights on the episode you did on *Metal Hurlant Chronicles*? It's not that I didn't like the episode, but the fights were lackluster.

DON "The Dragon" WILSON JOE LEWIS MATT MULLINS CYNTHIA ROTHROCK

WHITE TIGER

GORILLAPICTURES.NET

Promo artwork for *White Tiger*. Author's collection.

Fast. So fast. Not enough time. We had less than two hours to do the whole thing. We cut things out, we only had one or two angles. It was extremely rushed. Very limited production time. With *Blood and Bone*, we shot the last fight over two whole days. Some of the fights we did on *The Wrath of Vajra* took seventeen to twenty days. One action sequence. On *Metal Hurlant*, we had great cameras, great costumes, but just not enough time. One day for three fights.

You were the center of attention for your Johnny Cage segment on *Mortal Kombat: Legacy*, which was an impressive web series. Why aren't you in the second season of that series?

They didn't bring me back. Plain and simple. It was a production decision. It wasn't the director's decision. The higher-ups felt like they needed a bigger name.

Man, that sounds exactly like the episode.

That was the whole point. It really was. It's art imitating life. The irony of it is so crazy. My episode was one of the most successful. It had the most hits outside of the first and last episodes. Not enough of a fan base. They went with Casper Van Dien. It's really too bad. They made me re-audition. They made me reread the lines. I actually talked to the stunt coordinator. I was like, "What can I do?" I would have died to play that part again. I even went down to Atlanta to work with a choreographer to put together a video to show them that they had to keep me for this character, but at the end of the day it came down to numbers. It was really unfortunate. It hit me for a big loop. We were all on this path together: Myself, the director Kevin, Larnell, Michael Jai White. I was pushed aside. I understand because it's business, but on another level . . . the fans will never understand why this happened.

***Kamen Rider: Dragon Knight* is probably the best place for someone to see you in action. It's your biggest body of work, and as far as I'm concerned, you're the best reason for anyone to watch the show. Talk about working on this show. You worked with Steve Wang, who did—**

Drive! Yeah, *Kamen Rider* was the little ship that could. Steve had this project, and he was a very big fan of *Kamen Rider*. He wanted to bring it to America. He wanted to make it happen. He shot an eight-minute preview, and I came in for an interview. I actually crashed the audition. The Japanese producers decided to make the pilot into a series, and they recast everyone who was in the pilot except for me. We ended up making the show. Working with Steve was awesome. If anyone knows how to create badass, it's Steve. If you're drinking coffee, he can make it look like an epic, martial arts movie. He can create things quickly. It's incredible. He has a unique skill set. I wish he would do more. He hasn't done anything since *Kamen Rider*. I got to work with Alpha Stunts on that. It was cool, because I watched *Power Rangers* growing up. The show was fun. What they did on a shoestring budget was unheard of. They produced forty episodes for nothing. Unfortunately, it got lost on the CW channel; they kept changing the times. I went everywhere they would take an interview, and

I promoted it as much as I could. I went to Florida, to Ohio, to Palm Springs, anywhere they would do an interview because I really wanted the show to be a success. It didn't stay on the show for more than two seasons, which was a disappointment.

What's next for you? What are you hoping to do in the future?

It's hard to say. You never know what the next thing is. I'm going to keep pushing for those jobs. The industry—it doesn't matter what level you're at—when your job is over, you've got to find another job. For me, it's about putting out work that will spark interest.

Do you think you'll be able to survive as an action star in today's world?

One of the great things about doing martial arts in general is that you don't have to just work in film. I've done twenty-five videogames, too. I take on different jobs that expand me in different directions. You have to wear different hats in this business. That's how you survive. What is "making it?" Is "making it" making a 200 million dollar film? Maybe. "Making it" to me is being able to work consistently, and having fun while doing it. I feel like I have something really unique that audiences haven't seen yet, and I've only scratched the surface. I just need a little bit of a shot, just a little bit more of a push, and then all of a sudden I'll explode. Martial arts have helped my life in more ways than I could ever have imagined. Find what you love, and go do that shit.

Kampfansage
(a.k.a. **The Challenge**)
2005 (Image DVD) (CD)

"What do you want to do now? Kill me? Or fuck me?"

In the year 2045, wars have given way to a new age where much of modern technology has fallen by the wayside. Jonas (Mathis Landwehr) is a martial arts master who was left for dead by Bosco (Christian Monz), who was also responsible for the death of Jonas's master. Jonas is also in possession of a book that contains all the martial arts secrets of various long-dead masters. Jonas sets out to find Bosco and destroy him. It isn't something he can do on his own since Bosco has a large army of disciples ready to do his bidding. Jonas meets and becomes friends with Vincent (Volkram Zschiesche) and Linda (Esther Schweins). They want Bosco's reign of terror to end and are willing to risk their lives for Jonas's mission. They will have to put together an army by showing the scared citizens that if they stick together, they can and will make a better future for everyone.

Long winded and full of flaws, *Kampfansage* has some things going for it. It can't be denied that the filmmakers behind this picture are all incredibly talented individuals who show an

incredible amount of promise. A large amount of CGI is mixed with some old-fashioned matte work, creating a bit of a bizarre and unique looking post-apocalyptic world. There is also a lot of experimenting with camera angles that helped to create some interesting set pieces. On the negative side, the filmmakers relied too heavily on their camera trickery and stylizations, resulting in migraines for the viewer. The two leads, Mathis Landwehr (*Death Train*) and Volkram Zschiesche, are rather charismatic, as well as talented fighters. The core of the story surrounds Landwehr's character Jonas, so he is in the spotlight most of the time. He has a unique style that tended to rely on stick fighting and acrobatics while Zschiesche's style is a bit more traditional with tiny doses of humor. The villain was played with just enough menace by Christian Monz, who appears to be a very talented fighter. Mathis was the chief choreographer and was able to bring out the best in his inexperienced (at least on screen) fighters. *Kampfansage* was released as *The Challenge* in the US. It also claimed to be the first martial arts film from Germany.

INTERVIEW:
MATHIS LANDWEHR (CD)

When it comes to martial arts and action cinema, Germany is the last place you might think of. That all changed in 2005 when Kampfansage *(a.k.a.* The Challenge)*, was released to audiences worldwide. That film also put its star Mathis Landwehr into the spotlight.* Kampfansage *quickly led him to other work in films like* V for Vendetta, Perfect Hideout, *and* Death Train. *He has also worked extensively on German television, even having his own series that featured his* Death Train *character and was called* Lasko: The Fist of God. *Though it only ran for two seasons, it was still an excellent stepping stone for a young action star on the rise. He and other German performers like Mike Moeller (*Arena of the Streetfighter*) are paving the way for these types of films in their native country.*

When did you first become interested in the martial arts?

It's kind of classic: when I saw my first Bruce Lee movie.

Do you also have a gymnastics background?

Yes, I started when I was six years old and did it intensively till I was fourteen.

I had heard that you worked a bit in theater. Could you tell me about that?

My mother is a theater director and scenographer. My father is a doctor of philosophy and writes pieces. They gave me the chance to be on stage when I was still a kid, but I soon realized that I wanted to do films.

When did you decide that you wanted to be in film?

The first impulse for me that I wanted to make movies was in fact watching Charlie Chaplin's *The Circus* when I was about five or six. We shot our first "action clips" when I was eight or nine years old on HI8 .We edited them on the video recorder. It was really elaborate! The "martial arts flavor" came with Bruce Lee and Jackie Chan.

What films or stars influenced you growing up?

All of the Chaplin movies (my father loved them), Takeshi Kitano, Jean-Paul Belmondo, Clint Eastwood, Jackie Chan, and of course Bruce Lee

When did you meet guys like Volkram Zschiesche and start making short films?

We went to the same school. I think we finally became friends when I was sixteen. Two years after that we started filming together.

How did the feature film *Kampfansage* finally become a reality?

It was a really, really long process. We did two shorts before we got the chance to do a whole feature. To boil it down, it's really hard to do these kinds of movies in Germany, even today, but we kept on training hard and pushing the producer by rewriting the script over and over again.

You were also the primary fight choreographer on the film, correct?

Yes.

I'd read that this was considered the first German martial arts film. Did it spark interest in other German filmmakers to make these types of films?

It actually did, but almost all of them didn't make it to the point of actually shooting a movie or a series, because as I said, Germany is not an easy place for that and if you really mean it, you have to have a lot of patience.

There were many other talented martial artists in the film, most notably Mike Moeller. Where did you find them?

We met at the auditions for the film! Mike is so talented!

How do you feel it was received when it was released?

That's a difficult question. There were those who hated it, but there were also those who liked it. I felt great. I'm glad that there are still many people who really love that movie, even if I have to admit that I will never watch it again. We were kids back then.

How did you end up as a stunt performer on *V for Vendetta* and how was the overall experience?

David Leitch and Chad Stahelski, two of the most influential choreographers and action directors today, gave me the job after an audition. It was a great experience. I saw for the first time how American movies are shot. More money, more time, more precision. But after all, everybody puts his pants on one leg at a time.

Where you approached for *Lasko-Im Auftrag des Vatikans* (*Lasko: The Fist of God*) or did you audition?

I did an audition but the director saw *Kampfansage* and wanted me.

Arnold Vosloo, who plays the villain in that series (which was released as *Death Train* in the US) is such an underappreciated actor. What was it like working with him?

He was great. He is such a polite man. And he really did a good job, especially when we were fighting on a moving train!

The film was obviously a success, so how did it end up spawning the series several years later? Or was it always meant to be a series?

It was meant to be a series, but it took two more years to get the green light. It's almost a joke, but even today I have to really struggle for shooting any kind of action project in Germany.

How did working on the film differ from doing the series?

Shooting a movie is not so hard. Shooting a martial arts series is one of the hardest experiences I ever had in my life. Most of the people don't know how you feel after a day of shooting action. It's not like a workout. You can't warm up so your muscles get sore quicker. Simultaneously, I had to prepare all the other action sequences plus the drama scenes. I couldn't rest after shooting for the day.

Did you choreograph the fights on the series as well?

Yes, together with Ulrik Bruchholz and stunt coordinator Ramazan Bulut.

Lasko—Die Faust Gottes ran for two seasons. Is television something you would like to continue to do?

Yes, I love TV shows. But I want to produce them myself. There are so many things I would have done differently.

Can you talk a bit about your involvement in *Urban Fighter* (aka *Arena of the Street Fighter*) with Mike Moller?

Actually I had only a few shooting days for a feature called *Straight Blast*. There were some problems finishing the movie due to discrepancies between the producers, so the material was used for *Urban Fighter*.

You played a mentor to him in the film. Is that how he actually sees you, as sort of a mentor?

No, it's the other way around. Mike is probably the most experienced "martial arts veteran" in the German action film industry.

Kingz is an incredible short film you were in. What are your thoughts on it?

I love it! It was an exhausting shoot, though.

It has such a bizarre concept that by mashing up the two genres that if it were made into a feature film, it could quickly become an international cult classic. Are there any plans to do so?

The *Kingz* concept doesn't belong to my company, so I can't tell you. Unfortunately, the two heads of this project have separated. But I know that they had planned to do a feature.

Land of Giants is another short/teaser that has a unique concept. How has the reception been so far?

It was actually really good. We went to the film market in Cannes twice and found great partners.

You used a crowd-funding campaign to complete it. Is that ever something you would consider trying for a feature film version or have other options become available to you?

No. I think it's a good way to initialize a project and to see if there's any interest in what we are doing. We shot the teaser to raise money for the whole series.

Do you consciously choose or create projects that mix martial arts with other genres?

Yes, it's what I've always wanted to do.

Do you have anything that you are currently working on that you would like to talk about?

Since I founded Roundhousefilm.com in 2011, there are three projects I am working on intensively. These are: *Trespasser*, *Land of Giants*, and *Karateman*. It's kind of a brew of over five years producing and finding the right projects and people to make this become a reality.

Is there anything that you would like to say to your growing fan base who might read this?

I would like to thank them from the bottom of my heart for their support, and I hope I can inspire them a little.

DVD artwork for *Kampfansage*. Author's collection.

Karate Bear Fighter

1977 (ADness DVD) (CD)

"You were scared of your own reflection in me."

Sonny Chiba returns as his real-life karate master Mas Oyama in the second chapter of his (fictionalized) life story. This time out, Mas has been shunned by the karate community for his hard drinking and his bastardly ways when he's approached by an old friend to work as a bodyguard for the Yakuza. While working for these troublemakers, he befriends a young boy and takes care of him while the father is in the hospital. To add more weight on his shoulders, two of Mas's friends are murdered, and he sets out on a bloody rampage to avenge them.

Sonny Chiba (*The Executioner*) wastes no time getting started, once we're through the opening credits. He kicks ass for like fifteen minutes straight. The movie then starts to slow down and a few weird things happen (like when he confronts an old man walking down a dirt road and he does a flip over him) before we get back to the brutality. If beating the crap out of a bull wasn't enough, this time he fights a bear. It really is a sight to behold and bloody as hell. The final battle is terrific, and Chiba's signature eye gouge isn't forgotten. Why are Japanese men so emotional in these movies? When they cry the tears pour, when they're mad, the veins bulge on their neck, and when they're horny, they're steam trains. Director Kazuhiko Yamaguchi returns from the first film and the duo round out the trilogy with *Karate for Life*.

Karate Bullfighter (a.k.a. Champion of Death)

1975 (Adness DVD) (CD)

"Weapons? These hands? Then aren't your guns weapons? Aren't they?"

Sonny Chiba (from *The Executioner* and *Dragon Princess*) was given a rare opportunity to take the lead role in a film based on the history of his real-life instructor and founder of Kyokushin karate, Masutatsu Oyama. *Karate Bullfighter* is the first in a trilogy of films that gives a fictionalized account of the man's life. After spending time alone training, Oyama (played by Chiba) comes back to the city to participate in a martial arts tournament. He has no problem defeating anyone and quickly wins the title. With the win, he discovers just how weak modern karate is and grows disgusted. After trying to go back to his old ways in solitude, he will have to face off with those who oppose him, including a gangster willing to end Oyama's life.

The film was meant to glamorize the life of a man who is a legend in the martial arts world. The film isn't nearly as well-known to American action fans as it should be, but Sonny Chiba is just a frightening beast in the movie. His character

is downright scary; he kills a man, he rapes a woman (who then falls in love with him), and there's the moment like nothing you will ever see in a martial arts film: Sonny Chiba fighting a bull. This really happened—the real Oyama battled a real bull on numerous occasions. Chiba gives a brilliant performance and the level of action and choreography far exceeds most films in the same genre released during this time period. Director Kazuhiko Yamaguchi (*Karate for Life*) directs one of the best films of his career while allowing Chiba the opportunity to give the proper respect to the man responsible for his life and career. The sequels were *Karate Bearfighter* and *Karate For Life*.

Karate Commando: Jungle Wolf 3

1993 (NOV) (djm)

This obscure actioner stars Ron Marchini as a character named Jake Turner, an American expatriate living in East Asia, living off kickboxing matches in the streets and helping out when old friends come calling. His old commander (played by Joe Estevez) needs his help in rescuing a captured female DEA officer, who is being held by sadistic goons, the leader of whom looks like a one-eyed pirate. With the help of his buddy (played by Ivan Rogers from *Ballbuster*), Marchini goes into the jungle and the pair take on a two-man rescue mission, the likes of which seem familiar if you've seen anything else with Marchini in the lead.

Those looking for a third installment of Marchini's *Jungle Wolf* series will be as confused as I was when it was revealed that he is playing a different character in *Karate Commando*. To add more confusion, his character has a crucial flashback from the first *Jungle Wolf*, which really threw me off. I took this film as a completely new story, and that flashback was added, I thought, to pad out the running time, never intending to link the other *Jungle Wolf* movies, but then this film bears the *Jungle Wolf* brand, so who knows? Obscure as it is, *Karate Commando* is really for Marchini's most dedicated fans. Marchini is credited as the co-director with Charlie Ordonez, who made the first *Jungle Wolf* with him.

Karate Cop

1991 (Digiview DVD) (CD)

This is the follow-up to the 1990 action film *Omega Cop*. Ron Marchini reprises his role as John Travis, one of the last cops from the Special Police who is alive and still trying to maintain some sort of order in a post-apocalyptic future. When Rachel (Carrie Chambers) runs afoul of a local gang, she must run to safety while her friend Mica (Vibbe Haugaard) tries (unsuccessfully) to fend them off. Rachel escapes only to be surrounded by the gang. Then, from a foggy doorway, out steps Travis, who saves the day. Rachel offers Travis a hot meal in return for a ride back to her base camp. He agrees, only to learn that she is in charge of a group of children known as The Freebies and needs to ask a favor of him: Their camp is home to a teleporter that can

be repaired with a crystal. Only a few exist, so John is given the mission to find the crystal that would enable the teleporting system to become functional. Lincoln (D. W. Landingham) is the evil leader who has plans of his own to horde the teleporter for his own wicked needs.

Marchini serves as a writer, producer, and the star of the film. He was also well past his prime at this point in his career. While he was able to pull off some rather impressive fight scenes, they were shot with far too many close-ups to be exciting. Marchini, as an actor, has little to no charisma whatsoever. Since the plot was fairly minimal, his dialogue results in nothing more than corny one-liners and silly quips. When done properly they can be fun, but in this case they just don't work. The rest of the acting in the film isn't much better. Thankfully, the villains play it *way* over the top which helps make the viewing experience much more entertaining than it should have been. There is a cameo by David Carradine, but the entire sequence had no real reason for being there other than to show him off for a few quick moments. The film looks cheap and rushed, the score is terrible, and an emotionless statue of a star carries the film. It was directed by Alan Roberts.

Karate Cops (a.k.a. Hawkeye)

1988 (KB VHS) (djm)

Long forgotten and/or ignored, *Karate Cops* stars George Chung (who also wrote, edited, and directed) as a wry Asian cop named Hawkamoto (Hawk or Hawkeye as a handle). We see him test for his black belt, and he passes with flying colors, but his police chief is fed up with him for skipping

VHS artwork for *Karate Cops*. Author's collection.

work to focus on his extracurricular activities. He's assigned a new partner named Charles (played by Chuck Jeffreys who bears an incredibly striking resemblance to Eddie Murphy) who also knows martial arts, but isn't really interested in working with a partner. Hawk is racist, arrogant, and egotistical, but after being taught a lesson by his partner, they become friends and a good team. They go up against a small-time mafia ring working in and around Las Vegas and get their hands dirty while taking out the trash.

Chung did a handful of low-budget movies throughout the mid to late 1980s and early 1990s, and his best one was *Fight to Win*, but he has some nice moments in this one, which is equally Jeffreys's picture. Both of them worked together on *Fight to Win*, and they had an interesting dynamic while on screen. This movie was somewhat ahead of its time. Years later Jackie Chan and Chris Tucker did the enormously popular *Rush Hour*, which you have to admit is very similar to this. *Karate Cops* isn't great (or even very good, really), but it's got something going for it. You'll know what I mean if you see it. Side note: Richard Norton's name and face appear on the video box cover, and I kept expecting him to show up in the movie. That's the kind of operation Chung and Leo Fong (who produced) had going back in those days.

Karate for Life

1977 (ADness DVD) (CD)

"With that spirit, you can do anything."

Karate for Life completes Sonny Chiba's trilogy about his real-life master, Masutatsu Oyama. After the events of the last film (*Karate Bear Fighter*), Oyama has taken to challenging various masters to fight him so he can prove how strong his karate is. After laying waste to over one hundred fighters, he travels to Okinawa to compete in a ring against foreign fighters. What he won't do is throw the match like he's expected to do. He ends up pissing off the mob, which quickly sends their muscle out to try to kill him. Oyama will have to prove once and for all that karate is his life and send these scumbags straight to hell.

Of the Oyama trilogy, this one is by far the most fun, entertaining, and badass. Within the first ten minutes of the film, Sonny Chiba (*Karate Warriors*) single-handedly takes on one hundred and one opponents. It's a phenomenal scene and part of the title sequence. There is minimal dialogue, just enough to move the story along, before Chiba is presented with more asses to whoop. If you're a young problem child, watch out because he will slap you straight. In the final battle, he pays tribute to the great Bruce Lee and delivers a sequence that borrows heavily from the finale of *Enter the Dragon*. He completes the trilogy along with director Kazuhiko Yamaguchi. and they definitely saved the best for last.

The Karate Kid

1984 (Sony DVD) (djm)

Teen Daniel Larusso (Ralph Macchio) and his mother relocate from New Jersey to Los Angeles, and he has trouble adjusting to his new life at the local high school. Tough bullies who learn karate from the Cobra Kai martial arts school run by hard-edged, show-no-mercy Vietnam vet John Kreese (Martin Kove) pick on Daniel and beat him up almost daily. Daniel has no one to turn to for solace, which is where his apartment's resident handyman Mr. Miyagi (Pat Morita) comes in. Miyagi is a soft-spoken WWII vet who teaches Daniel in unconventional ways how to defend himself and prepare for a martial arts tournament against the Cobra Kai school. Miyagi's "wax on, wax off" methodology is like Zen wisdom to Daniel, who is obstinate, but respectful and hungry to be taught. Meanwhile, Daniel kindles a romance with a cute rich girl named Ali (Elisabeth Shue).

A massive hit when released in theaters, *The Karate Kid* is still every bit the classic underdog story of a kid from the wrong side of the tracks making good. Inspirational, funny, touching, and exciting, it's one of the great '80s teen movies that spawned sequels, spin-offs, a remake, and rip-offs. Even a cartoon series followed. Director John G. Avildsen (*Rocky*) knew exactly what to do with this material and make it work like gangbusters. Macchio is great as the lanky teenager who learns how to be a winner. Shue as the love interest is perfect. Kove as the villainous Vietnam vet sensei is exactly right. All ages will enjoy it for all time.

The Karate Kid

2010 (Sony DVD) (CD)

"Kung fu lives in everything we do, Xiao Dre! It lives in how we put on the jacket, how we take off the jacket. It lives in how we treat people! *Everything* . . . is kung fu."

Sherry (Taraji P. Henson) must make a life-altering decision to uproot her son Dre (Jaden Smith, son of Will) from Detroit and move to China for a better position at work. Dre isn't too excited but goes along with his mother only to find himself alienated in a country he knows nothing about. He quickly meets a young girl named Meiying (Wenwen Han) and does his best to impress her. Her friend Cheng (Zhenwei Wang) doesn't like this foreigner and promptly begins to bully him. He and his friends beat Dre every opportunity they get, which becomes too much for Dre to handle. One day during an attack, he's saved by the handyman at his apartment complex, Mr. Han (Jackie Chan). Han agrees to take Dre to speak with the teacher of the boys only to find out Master Li (Rongguang Yu) is the reason the boys act the way they do. Han gets Li to call his boys off but only if Dre will compete against them in an upcoming martial arts tournament. Li agrees and Dre begins his training with Han and his unconventional

methods. Han and Dre form a bond during their training, but if he is to defeat the bullies at the tournament he will have to learn a few things about himself as well as help Han to come to terms with his own personal demons.

Jackie Chan (*Dragons Forever, Rush Hour*) proves once and for all he's more than just a stuntman but a damn fine actor as well. His performance here is top notch and moving, more so than in any of his other English-language films. He's the anchor of the picture, and without him it would never have succeeded. The story of the remake doesn't deviate much from the 1984 except for a few minor details, but the film's title is utter nonsense as Han is teaching Dre kung fu and not karate. Chan does have an interesting fight scene with a bunch of preteen boys. It's fun to view since he never once hits them and just uses all of their attacks against them. Be sure to check out the alternate ending on the disc since it's a fight between Jackie and Rongguang Yu (*The Myth*); it's worth watching. *The Karate Kid* is a surprisingly strong remake that some may prefer to the original. Directed by Harald Zwart (*Agent Cody Banks*).

The Karate Kid Part III

1989 (Sony DVD) (djm)

The saga of underdog karate kid winner Daniel LaRusso (Ralph Macchio) and his humble Japanese mentor Mr. Miyagi (Pat Morita) concludes with this third entry, which is most notable for introducing kenpo expert Thomas Ian Griffith to motion pictures. Daniel and Mr. Miyagi have just returned from Japan (see *Part II* for more on that), and Daniel has been invited to compete in another karate championship match, but this time he only has to fight in one bout with whoever climbs to the top to go against him, the champion. Disgraced Vietnam vet and former sensei of the Cobra Kai school of martial arts John Kreese (Martin Kove) is despondent over his devastating loss to Miyagi and Daniel (see *Part I*) when he's visited by an old Vietnam buddy named Terry Silver (Griffith), who has made a name for himself in business. Silver and Kreese come up with a plan to deceive Daniel and humiliate him in front of everyone at the tournament. Daniel ends up turning his back on Miyagi to train with the sadistic Silver, unbeknownst to him that Silver is, in fact, his enemy. But don't worry: Mr. Miyagi saves Daniel, and their training together gets him back on track to be a winner.

I love the original *The Karate Kid*. It might be one of my favorite growing-up movies of all time. I wanted to be Daniel LaRusso. But I don't care for the sequels. Like the middle *Rocky* sequels, they forget what made the first film so special and they're sensationalized and feel assembled by a committee who think that pop songs and overly heated conflict and violence will be acceptable as content for the fans who loved the original. What makes *The Karate Kid Part III* slightly interesting to watch is that newcomer Ian Griffith is in it and that the producers thought (rightfully) that he was interesting on film; his part in it—though way too evil and nasty to be a villain in a *Karate Kid* movie—is meaty and gave him his first shot at being a martial arts figure on film. The villains in this movie are way too broadly drawn to be convincing, and the only actor who *isn't* unconvincing is Mr. Miyagi who, as played by Pat Morita, manages to give the movie more grace than it deserves. Most of the characters are simplistically written (by Robert Mark Kamen), and almost all of the actors overdo it—including Macchio. Shortly after this film was released, Griffith would take on an action hero persona and would star in several good martial arts action films including *Excessive Force*, which he also wrote. John G. Avildsen (*Rocky*) directed. *The Next Karate Kid,* starring Morita and Hilary Swank, was released in 1994.

Karate Warriors

1976 (Xenon VHS) (CD)

"You're nothing but a fool! I'm going to make you suffer the way Goro did when they cut off his arm. I'll cut off your arm!"

Sonny Chiba is a lone stranger who comes to town only to find himself smack-dab in the middle of a gang war. He learns the two gangs are after a large amount of heroin that has gone missing so he does what he does best and plays both factions against one another to cancel each other out. While he's doing this, he befriends a young boy who has a samurai as a father. This samurai works for one of the feuding gangs and the two titans will have to face off against each other, and even if they respect each other, only one can walk away alive.

Director Kazuhiko Yamaguchi (*Sister Streetfighter*) reteams with Sonny Chiba (*Dragon Princess, The Street Fighter*) to deliver what is easily described as a remake of the classic Akira Kurosawa film *Yojimbo*. It follows the same basic formula in a modern setting with loads of karate action. There's far too much shaky camera work, but when they show off Chiba's skill by running some slow motion, then speeding it up again, all is forgiven. Every time Chiba fights, it's frightening because he's such an unpredictable force he could rip someone's head off their shoulders at any second. He lays waste to dozens of men and all they ever really manage to do is to tear his sleeves off. *Karate Warriors* is one of his best pictures. Just beware that the little boy has the most annoyingly dubbed voice ever recorded.

Kazaam

1996 (Mill Creek DVD) (CD)

"Grab my belly and make a wish."

Max (Francis Capra) is a bit of a loner who's being bullied by some local kids from school. He tries to get them off his back by giving them a key that he says will lead them to some goods.

When they realize the key is junk, they want some sort of retribution. They chase Max into an old building where he falls through a floor and discovers a boom box. This isn't just any boom box; it houses a genie named Kazaam (NBA superstar Shaquille O'Neal) who is ready to grant him three wishes. As the two of them begin to develop a friendship, Kazaam doesn't want to go back into his box and begins to pursue a career in rap music. Meanwhile, Max is trying to reconnect with his estranged father who has found himself entangled with some mob men. As the threat of people getting hurt becomes a reality, the two unite to put a stop to it while learning more about themselves and each other.

Kazaam is every bit the train wreck you may have heard it to be. There are plenty of laughs in the film, none of which were intentional. Most of the humor comes in the form of watching a seven-foot-tall black man chasing a young white boy, stalking him, sneaking into his bed while he sleeps, showering in his bathroom, and even planting several unwanted kisses on him. There is however a rather cool fight scene at the end with Shaq taking on the thugs. Shaq-Fu is in full effect as he takes them down one by one (including a blink-and-you'll-miss-him James Lew). Shaq was in *Steel* next. Directed by Paul Michael Glaser (*The Running Man*).

The Keeper

2009 (Fox DVD) (djm)

Detective Rolland Sallinger (Steven Seagal) is betrayed and nearly killed by his corrupt partner over a stash of drug money, and while in the hospital, Sallinger is nearly killed by him again. Sallinger kills his partner in self-defense (while lying in his bed hooked up to tubes!), and when he's fully recovered, his department forces him to take an early retirement. Luckily, he finds a job bodyguarding the debutante daughter of a wealthy businessman who has many enemies. The young woman learns to trust Sallinger and take his good advice, but someone in her inner circle is trying to kill her and take what belongs to her father: a lucrative uranium mine.

The Keeper doesn't raise any eyebrows in the plotting or action department. Seagal goes through the motions (sometimes with a smirk on his face), and the whole affair is a little lackluster and disappointing. It's nice to see him on native soil rather than in Eastern Europe as in so many of his recent films, but it's just not enough to recommend this film. This marks Seagal's first collaboration with director Keoni Waxman, who would go on to be Seagal's #1 director in his direct-to-video era. Their next picture was *A Dangerous Man*.

Kenner

1968 (Warner DVD) (djm)

A smuggler named Roy Kenner (Jim Brown) lands on the shores of Bombay with revenge on his mind. He's searching for a man who murdered

his partner, and during his search he encounters some trouble. Cornered in an alley, he's saved by a little boy named Saji (Ricky Cordell), who gives him a quick place to hide. When the trouble's over, Saji (who's half Indian and half white) asks Kenner tons of questions because he's looking for his long-lost American father. Saji is completely innocent and ignorant about how the world works, and Kenner doesn't really want to be bothered by the kid, and so he gives him a couple of bucks to go away. Saji, a heartsick child in search of his "father" (whose picture he keeps as a shrine, but in reality the picture is just a page torn out of an American magazine) goes home to his mother Anasuya (Madlyn Rhue), who has tried to protect his innocence as best she can, but Saji is at a crossroads in his life. When he runs into Kenner again, it's a completely different situation: Kenner has been wounded by some cutthroats, and Saji takes him to his mother who nurses him to health. Over a few weeks, Kenner has developed feelings for Anasuya and Saji, and he tries to work out his issues with revenge while being a father figure and husband substitute to the poor mother and child.

Billed as a "family picture," *Kenner* is a "G"-rated film, but it features violence, shocking death, and themes of prostitution, which wouldn't be suitable for family audiences today. Jim Brown, in one of his best roles, gets to roughhouse with thugs and killers in the film, while also showing his sensitive side, and the mix is very interesting. The relationships that are cultivated in the film are believably conveyed, and the movie shows some authentic Indian life. Fans of Jim Brown definitely need to check this one out, but it's not really for kids. Directed by Steve Sekely.

The Kick

2011 (Lionsgate DVD) (djm)

A family of taekwondo practitioners is aiming to compete in the Olympics when the eldest son, Tae Yang (played by Tae-joo Na), is in the wrong place at the right time when a band of thieves tries to steal an ancient Thai artifact from a museum. Tae Yang and his sister thwart the thieves and become national heroes, but the thieves retaliate and target their whole family for death. The patriarch of the family sends them all to live in the country with some relatives, and while in hiding they continue to train and hone their skills in the martial arts. Tae Yang falls for a local girl (who he might actually be related to) named Wawa (played by Jeeja Yanin from *Raging Phoenix*), who also happens to be a kickboxing champion and Muay Thai dynamo. When the thieves find out where Tae Yang and his sister are living, they lay siege and the fight is on!

From Prachya Pinkaew, who directed *Chocolate* with Yanin and *Ong-bak* with Tony Jaa, *The Kick* is easy enough to digest, without a hint of irony or pretense. His skills as a director of complicated martial arts sequences are on full display here. Scores of intensive and dangerous-looking fighters go full-bore and enliven an otherwise substandard story that is pretty much inconsequential. Yanin only has a supporting role here, but it's easy to see that she's a star.

Kickboxer

1989 (Lionsgate DVD) (JS)

When it comes to action films, Jean-Claude Van Damme is an undeniable household name. JCVD's early action films like the modern martial arts essential *Bloodsport* and the Albert Pyun cult classic *Cyborg* were the spark that ignited the opportunity for Van Damme to help create the late '80s essential *Kickboxer*. JCVD not only choreographed the fight scenes for this flick, he also gained his first writing credit, and though the plotline isn't groundbreaking, it's entirely engaging and allows room for everything you want and need from an exemplary martial arts–driven action flick. *Kickboxer* spins the tale of US champion kickboxer Eric Sloane (played by real-life kickboxing heavyweight-title winner Dennis Alexio) and his brother Kurt (Van Damme) as they travel to Thailand for Eric to battle the much feared and menacing champion Tong Po. Things go terribly awry after Po pulls some illegal maneuvers on Eric, who is left wheelchair-bound for the rest of his life. Kurt vows to exact revenge and earns his chance to train with the best master in Thailand: the much revered Xian Chow.

The training sequences take up a bulk of the running time in *Kickboxer,* but the merciless, barbarous, and ultimately transforming methods of Master Chow make for great-paced entertainment and allow Van Damme to show off his top-tier physical prowess. However, *Kickboxer's* cinematic finesse and re-watchability don't just come from Van Damme's adept action performance. *Kickboxer's* cohesive combination of action, drama, thriller, and comedy elements make it one of the most well-rounded and accessible action flicks of the era. Though the part where Kurt defeats a tree blow by bloody blow is utterly brutal and the final fight against Tong Po is slow-motion martial arts glory, perhaps the most amazing scene in *Kickboxer* is the mid-point bar fight. Master Chow gets Kurt all sauced up on endless rounds of something called "Kiss of Death," asks Kurt to dance to some "American Disco," and surreptitiously starts some shit with the other fighters in the bar. What unfolds is quite possibly the most entertaining drunk dancing/expert ass-kicking scene in all of cinema. Don't miss it. *Nok su kow!*

Kickboxer 2: The Road Back

1991 (Lionsgate DVD) (djm)

Following the off-screen murders of his brothers Kurt (played by Jean-Claude Van Damme in the first film) and Eric, the youngest brother David (Sasha Mitchell from *Death Before Dishonor*) is struggling to keep his kickboxing gym afloat. His bills are way past due, and when he gets an offer to fight professionally again, he stubbornly refuses. After reconsidering, he takes on a fight simply to pay his bills. His fight with his opponent (played by Matthias Hues) goes incredibly well, and he not only wins enough money to pay off his bills, but he garners a lot of fans . . . and enemies. Tong Po, the vicious fighter who murdered his two brothers (in a striking flashback scene) is called in from East Asia to regain the honor of Thailand

by staging a fight with Sloan's best friend to get Sloan's attention. When his friend is brutally killed by Po (played by Michel Qissi from the first film) in the ring, Sloan's blood runs high and hot. After another unfortunate incident where his gym is burned to the ground and he's wounded in the leg, Sloan seeks training from his brother Kurt's trainer, Xian Chow (Dennis Chan), and together they build up his character and his fortitude to face a mortal enemy.

The fights in this film are incredibly tense and believably staged and play out in a convincing manner. Mitchell's acting is a little rough around the edges, but he made a fine full-fledged entry into the world of martial arts and action films with this picture. Director Albert Pyun made sure to give the film plenty of time to set up the characters before thrusting them straight into fight scenes, and the film is well shot. The screenplay by David Goyer (who went on to write *Blade* and *Batman Begins*) is solid, and if only the future sequels took the kickboxing genre as seriously as this film did, then there might be more respect paid to the genre. That said, this film is populated with good character actors such as Peter Boyle, Cary-Hiroyuki Tagawa, John Diehl, and "B" action star Vince Murdocco (from *L.A. Wars*) and they all help the film stay credible.

INTERVIEW:

SASHA MITCHELL

(djm)

When he took over the Kickboxer *franchise after Jean-Claude Van Damme stepped away from it, Sasha Mitchell became an action star, though in retrospect he has never seen himself in that way. He has a black belt in taekwondo and a muscular figure that goes with the territory of being an action star, and while his career in that realm was short-lived with only a handful of action films on his resume, Mitchell (who does not have representation) seems genuinely humbled by the "action star" label, and he's even willing to consider making a comeback.*

You had done *Death Before Dishonor* **with Fred Dryer before you did the boxing film** *Spike of Bensonhurst,* **and then your next big feature after that was** *Kickboxer 2.* **Let's talk a little bit about** *Death Before Dishonor.*

Sasha Mitchell in Burbank, California. Photo by david j. moore.

Yeah, we filmed it in the Middle East. It was a lot of fun. That was my first feature. It was directed by Terry Leonard, which was amazing, a big honor to work with him. He holds all the records for everything. He was what the stunt business was built on. He was amazing. This was his directing debut. I had gotten out of military school, so I already knew all the drills and stuff. I got lucky and they let me do it.

What did you pick up from that experience? Were you thinking of staying in the business of working in movies?

On that movie, I was just trying to keep up. I was just trying to keep everything together. I think that's what happens on any movie. You just try to do the best you can. I don't think I ever stopped and looked around. I was only eighteen. I turned nineteen walking around Israel one day.

Spike of Bensonhurst **was a great movie for you even though it's not really an action thing. You gave the best performance of your career in that film.**

That was Paul Morrissey. That was amazing. David Weisman produced it.

Talk about the boxing stuff in that picture. Say something about the physical aspect of working on that movie.

Physically, I ran everywhere. Running and cycling. I was always a big cyclist. Even growing up in LA and New York, my friends and I would always cycle at night. 5Ks at night. Every night. To the beach and back. Training in that movie, the boxing, I trained with Rob Compono. He was a pro boxer. He was the Italian boxer in the movie that was like, "I'm gonna kill you!" Everybody in New York and in the military school and those I worked out with knew boxing. Boxing was just . . . always. Back in LA, I was training with Benny Urquidez. He put me with another guy who trained with pro fighters. Benny worked with me on *Kickboxer 2,* but he was working on *Diggstown* when we did *Kickboxer 3.* The window that we had, he couldn't go, so he put me with Shuki Ron.

Since you brought up Benny Urquidez, in *Kickboxer 2,* **you're wearing his shirt in the movie.**

Yeah, always. I asked if I could, and we put it in. We love Benny. He's like family. Twenty years ago, I moved him in the house that he's in now. We went and got a truck and got a bunch of friends and I was like, "We're moving you today." (Laughing.)

How did you go from *Spike* **to** *Kickboxer 2?* **You became an action star just like that.**

It was Albert [Pyun], 100 percent Albert came over to my house, and we just stood outside talking about it for hours, working on my trees. I was working on bonsai trees the day he came over. And we talked forever. . . I've done bonsai trees my whole life. Albert and I just talked and talked, and he put me with Benny. I worked with all those guys in the movie, every day for like twelve weeks. Matthias Hues is a bodybuilder in

Buddies Xian Chow (Dennis Chan) and David Sloan (Shasha Mitchell) in *Kickboxer 2*. Author's collection.

great shape, but with little or no flexibility, and I had to do spinning wheel kicks to his face. He had to look like he got hit and not flinch. We worked together every day, and they made him look good. And he felt good doing what he did. We got that kick. They put the camera between us on the ground, facing both of us, one at a time. He was unbelievable to work with. Really nice guy.

***Kickboxer 2* launched you into a different career path. This was the era when these kickboxing karate movies were all over the market—in theaters and in video stores everywhere. Talk about how this movie sort of changed your course.**

Well, I don't know. I think because I started with *Death Before Dishonor* . . . then Albert brought me in. I love that guy. I was doing TV at the time and comedy. Comedy and action are the same. You talk, talk, talk, and then you fight, or you talk, talk, talk, and there's a punchline. I was doing both. We brought a bunch of kickboxing episodes into *Step by Step*, the show I was doing. I got to bring all those fighters from the Jet Center into the TV show. We used Dale Jacoby. He did a bunch of action movies. I think my pattern for movies stayed the same. For action movies, when they don't have money to blow

Sanga (Cary-Hiroyuki Tagawa) and David Sloan (Sasha Mitchell) in Albert Pyun's *Kickboxer 2*. Author's collection.

The final battle: David Sloan (Sasha Mitchell) and Tong Po (Michel Qissi) fight to settle a score in *Kickboxer 2*. Author's collection.

up buildings or to blow up cars, but the formula needs twenty-two minutes of fighting, so we do three minutes here, eight minutes there, and five minutes there. When they don't have money to blow things up, they call fighters. Sometimes they don't even have permits.

***Kickboxer 2* is the best of your action movies. It had a really cinematic quality to it. It was a pure movie—there was just something special about it. The fourth one was kind of cool too where you get out of prison and go to Mexico. Talk about the second one a little bit, and mention some of the guys you worked with like Michel Qissi and Cary-Hiroyuki Tagawa.**

Yeah, Michel. He was a French guy. They did a really good job with his makeup. They made him look like an Asian guy. His friend played his character in *Kickboxer 4*. It was really fun working with Cary Tagawa. Benny and I brought so much spirit to everything we did. It was a blast working with those guys. I had so much fun. The fourth one that you liked was because of Albert. We did it in only ten days.

What?! You're kidding me.

The producer—God bless him—was having a lot of trouble with money. He fell in love with some girl, and that's why we did *Kickboxer 3* in Brazil. Albert was busy, so we shot it somewhere else, which is probably why you didn't like it. Albert came back to do *Kickboxer 4*, and he waived his salary and gave the producer all the rights to *Kickboxer 3* just so he could make a little money

Tong Po (Michel Qissi) takes a kick to the gut from David Sloan (Sasha Mitchell) in *Kickboxer 2*. Author's collection.

again, which is why when they did *Kickboxer 5*, they didn't have Albert or myself in it. It's one of those things. I didn't know what was going on. The reason that *Kickboxer 2* looks good is because Albert was really going for that warm Fuji film look. You could really feel the love and the spirit with the kids. He had time to shoot it.

Talk about doing *Kickboxer 3*, which you shot in Brazil. This one felt like a sequel to a sequel, but your character had altered really noticeably. With each movie, your character was considerably different. You almost felt like a different guy in each movie, but your buddy in the movies, played by Dennis Chan, seemed like the same guy.

I love Dennis! He's a big director in China. He went right back to that. *Kickboxer 3* . . . yeah, I dunno. The director that they hired, Rick King, had never done an action or a fight movie before. So it was kind of rough. I liked how the fighting looked. We did it with Shuki, and we had a lot of good fighters. I dunno. I liked the story, I liked Brazil, I liked the fighting, but it was hard with Rick's style of directing. You've got to know how to film fights. You really do. They're not easy. It was a lot of filming to get it.

The thing about the third film is that you start killing people in it. You shoot a lot of people. Talk about that. You went from kicking to shooting.

Oh, yeah. They wanted it more lethal. More deadly. That had nothing to do with me. In the first *Kickboxer* that we did with Albert, I was a reluctant guy who was not into it, I was really only a teacher in the movie. Then by the end of that movie, he's been dragged into the whole thing. Then, when I get to Brazil my heart took over and I had to rescue these kids, so my character evolved, but he had some of his same qualities where he loved kids and didn't want to see them get hurt.

With *Kickboxer 4*, your character had been beaten down by the world and you're now an ex-con. You had accepted your fate, and your whole purpose was revenge in the film.

I remember the fighters in that film. We shot it in ten days, so I can't really remember the plot real well. I remember we shot in a jail, and we got to use a lot of Brazilian fighters, and I remember working with them. There was no stunt coordinator on the movie, but there were all these fighters, and these fighters were really proud. Their students are in the movie because they're in the movie too, and I had to get in there and address everyone as "Sir." We had to honor all the fighters and their different styles when we would shoot our fight scenes together. I just don't really remember the plot that well. I remember there was naked stuff in there. I couldn't do that stuff because I was married, and they filmed this whole thing with this guy and some girl, and they pretended it was me. They painted my tattoos on him. It was ridiculous. I don't know. With Albert I would do anything.

After the *Kickboxer* movies, you did *Class of 1999 II: The Substitute*.

Oh yeah, that was a lot of fun. That was great. We finally got to blow something up! It was like, *Wow! We blew up a car!* (Laughing.) There were a lot of good stunts in that and some good action. I didn't really understand the whole robot thing, but there was another movie before, so they set up the robot teacher thing.

Did you ever watch these movies that you did after the fact?

Yeah, I watched them, but like once. I couldn't really watch myself. I can't stand listening to my voice. It sounds like I'm asleep. I don't understand my voice at all. I used to watch the TV show I did. That was funny. I'd come home, and we'd have filmed on Friday night when it was on. My kids watched it.

At this point in your career it seemed like you could've gone on to do a lot more action movies, but after *Class of 1999 II*, you dropped out of the business. What happened there? Why did the action career abruptly end?

I did one called *Gangland*, which was filmed on the *Jurassic Park: The Lost World* set. That was post-apocalyptic. But I don't know. I liked acting. Every time anyone ever offered me a movie, I would do it. When people call me up . . . like, that's how I did that movie *Slammed!* They called me up, and I went in for a meeting. They were like, "Oh my God! You want to do this?" I was like, "Sure." They put me in a movie. I did one recently with Albert, a vampire movie with sword fighting. He was like, "I need some good kicking and fighting, and I need some jokes. It's too serious." That was fun. I don't know. I was married for a long time. I could afford a housekeeper to take care of the kids when I wasn't there, and then after I got divorced, it was just the kids and I. There were four of them. The youngest one was just six months old, and I was raising them alone, so I didn't have time to go looking for acting jobs. I had to work. I had to feed them. I was cooking in restaurants, and at farmer's markets. I was cooking on the weekends, and I was welding and building e-mail servers and networks during the week. Anything I could do for my kids. I never really stopped to look around for an agent. I don't even have one now. Even when I was working really hard in movies, I would just go home afterwards and take care of my kids. I never did the Hollywood scene. Twenty years went by so fast. My youngest is a senior in high school now.

So what are you doing now, Sasha?

Same thing! I've worked for a lot of different companies. A lot of them are in the clothing business. I built their e-mail servers, I built their networks. When you called me I had a laptop taken apart all over me. I'm also a welder. I do structural welding. High beams and walls, architectural stuff like gates. You know, whatever. I do anything I can do to get by.

Do you ever look back on your career as an action star and think to yourself, *You know what? I was an action star.*

No! (Laughing.) No, not at all. I don't think of it that way. When I think of action stars, I think of a whole other arena than what I was in. I was

the guy they would call when they didn't have the budget for somebody like Bruce Willis. He's an action star. With all those cop movies he did. He was a great action star. I tried to make people laugh and tried to have a good time, but I don't think I was ever like a big action star.

Well, as far as I'm concerned, you are.

(Laughing.) Well, thanks. That's really cool. I had a really good time. It gave my children a really good life when I was doing it. It just got hard when I didn't have time to go look for jobs and get acting stuff going. That was it. After the divorce, my wife emptied our bank accounts, took my tools, took everything. She even took the toys. *Everything.* I just started from scratch. I didn't have time to play around and look for acting jobs. It might have been smart to have spent time doing that, though. When you need diapers, you need to work.

When we met, I was shocked at how you look physically now. You are in incredible shape. Your physique is massive now. You don't look like you did when you were in your twenties. How do you keep in shape?

I never stopped working out. Ever. That was one thing that helped me keep my sanity through all these years. When you don't want to let anyone know how you're feeling or let the kids know what you're feeling, you just go to the gym. All my life, I've always trained. Even when I was a kid. The first thing I ever bought in my life was a weight bench. I saved up and bought myself a weight bench, and my dad bought me the weights. I didn't even realize they didn't come together.

Is there anything you would like to say to your fans? I know you've got some because you're talking to one right now.

Ah, man. I love you guys. I wish things could have been different. I wish I could've kept looking for acting jobs and doing them, but it's who you know now. I don't know anybody. Acting was a lot of fun. Now, I'm only suited to be a dad. I'm forty-five. I'd be a dad in a TV show. It was a lot of fun, and I appreciate everyone who watched me. I had a lot of fun doing it.

Kickboxer 3: The Art of War

1992 (Lionsgate DVD) (djm)

A departure in tone and structure from *The Road Back*, this entry has David Sloan (Sasha Mitchell) and his sidekick and mentor, Xian Chow (Dennis Chan) flying to Rio de Janeiro for a championship fight against a new challenger. Considering that Sloan had little to no interest in fighting for money ever again at the end of Part 2, this is a noticeable and conspicuous change to his character. But moving on, while he and Xian are exploring the city, they are accosted and robbed by a pair of street ruffians, a boy named Marcos (Noah Verduzco) and his older sister Isabella (Alethea Miranda). When Sloan sets them straight, he takes a shine to them, and he and Xian become their unofficial wards and

protectors. Meanwhile, a scuzzy entrepreneur named Lane (Richard Comar) offers Sloan a half a million dollars to take a fall in his fight, and in his spare time, he has his men kidnap attractive young girls from the streets so he can prostitute them, which adds to his business capital. In order to entice Sloan to take the fall in his fight, he takes Isabella hostage and threatens to sell her virginity to the highest bidder if Sloan doesn't comply. Enraged, Sloan and Xian (with the boy Marcos in tow) scour the favelas for leads on where the girl may be held captive, and they procure an arsenal to make their intentions well known. By the end of the film, both Sloan and Xian (and the boy too) have become cold-blooded murderers, and it gets to the unbelievable point where they begin bragging about how many men they've killed.

A stretch as far as the *Kickboxer* films go, this sequel-to-a-sequel is fun if you're willing to simply go with the flow, but if you're thinking about the characters and how much they've changed and how far they're willing to go to get what they want, then it will be a rough viewing. Mitchell, while engaging to a certain point as the character he's best known for playing, looks uncomfortable holding firearms and he seems much more at home when he's using martial arts to put people down than when he's shooting them. The Brazilian locations are nice. Directed by Rick King, who directed *Terminal Justice* with Lorenzo Lamas.

Kickboxer 4: The Aggressor

1993 (Lionsgate DVD) (djm)

Ignoring the events of Part 3, *The Aggressor* finds a framed David Sloan (Sasha Mitchell) in prison, receiving taunting letters from his arch nemesis Tong Po (Kamel Frifia, who replaced Michel Qissi), explaining to him that his wife has been taken captive and is being raped and tortured on a daily basis. While in prison, Sloan faces onslaughts of challengers, and he has become a hardened con. The DEA comes to him with a deal: He will be released on the condition that he travel to Mexico to enter in a championship fight sponsored by Tong Po—and held at Po's fortified drug compound—so that he can bring Po down. Sloan takes the deal with revenge in mind, and he hitchhikes his way across the border. Along the way, he encounters plenty of lowlifes who make his journey interesting, and he sort of picks up a spunky, badass, sidekick teenage girl called Mouse (Michelle Krasnoo) who thinks she has the chops to enter the competition. Once he enters into the arena, Sloan is eventually recognized by Po, and his wife's life hangs in the balance.

The grimmest and most downbeat entry in the *Kickboxer* series features a relentlessly pessimistic tone while virtually changing Sloan's worldview and demeanor. His sidekick and mentor from the previous films, played by Dennis Chan, is absent and sorely missed, and the recasting of Tong Po is a little jarring, but after awhile Kamel Frifia (one of Jean-Claude Van Damme's protégés) makes the role his own, and you learn to accept him. Albert Pyun's direction for this entry feels somehow more personal than his previous *Kickboxer* effort, but I also found the film to have a misogynistic flavor that was a bit upsetting. Mitchell's performance in the film is his strongest by far, and Tony Riparetti's electronic score is interesting. The end of the film suggests that a different sort of sequel would be made than the one that was produced and followed a few years later with Mark Dacascos in the lead.

Kickboxer 5: Redemption

1995 (Lionsgate DVD) (djm)

Hardcore fans of the *Kickboxer* series will probably be pissed that the franchise moved on without Sasha Mitchell, and even worse, the filmmakers made the decision to kill off his character off screen. This entry (the last of the series) stars Mark Dacascos as Matt Reeves, a martial arts instructor who was friends with David Sloan, the role that Mitchell played in the previous three films. Reeves discovers that Sloan was murdered by a disgraced former kickboxer named Negaal in South Africa. Negaal (played by James Ryan from *Kill or Be Killed* and *Kill and Kill Again*) has set up a kickboxing federation that caters to his goal of eliminating kickboxing champions and stripping them of their titles unless they bow down to his rules. Reeves has another friend who is killed by Negaal, and that's when Reeves decides to go to South Africa and face Negaal himself. He joins with another fighter (Geoff Meed, who later reteamed with Dacascos on *I Am Omega*), and they face the challenge of Negaal and his legion of men.

Not so much a "kickboxing" movie as a straight-up action movie with plenty of martial arts, *Kickboxer 5* is better than it should be, and Dacascos is appealing as usual. By this point in his career, he had done *Only the Strong* and *Double Dragon*, and taking the lead in the fifth entry of this series might not have been the best move. It was directed by Kristine Peterson.

Kick Fighter

(a.k.a. **The Fighter**)

1989 (AIP VHS) (djm)

Left stranded in an East Asian cesspool after the Vietnam war, Ryan Travers (Richard Norton) and his sister Katie (Erica Van Wagener) now live on the streets, with only Ryan's scavenger skills and ability to pick pockets and gamble to keep them afloat. When Ryan is caught stealing, he is sent to prison for years, where he learns some fighting skills, and when he's released, he finds his sister living with a kind elderly gentleman who considers himself her guardian. Over the years, Katie has developed a severe heart condition requiring extensive surgery, and so Ryan takes to the streets again, with the hopes of working his way to the top of the street-fighting circuit for money and eventually to the big leagues where "The Jet" (played by Benny "The Jet" Urquidez) reigns undefeated.

A publicity shot from *Kick Fighter,* featuring Richard Norton and Benny "The Jet" Urquidez. Courtesy of Richard Norton.

Ryan Travers (Richard Norton) gets ready to fight in *Kick Fighter.* Courtesy of Richard Norton.

Exactly what you should expect from an AIP release from this period, *Kick Fighter* gives Norton a part that's perfectly suited for him, and it's fun to see him scrapping on the streets of Vietnam or Thailand, or wherever this little movie was filmed. He loses a few of his fights, but when he gets good at fighting (or "kick fighting"), he's a powerhouse, taking on Benny "The Jet" in a slam-bang finale. Without any pretensions (because it can't afford them), *Kick Fighter* is a solid effort from director Anthony Maharaj, who worked with Norton on *Death Fight* and *Crossfire*.

Kill and Kill Again

1981 (Scorpion DVD) (djm)

James Ryan stars as Steve Chase, a mercenary/adventurer who takes on a mission when the daughter of a kidnapped scientist comes calling. She tells him that a crazed dictator has taken her father to force him to derive a serum to brainwash fighters and martial artists to create an unstoppable army of soldiers, who will ultimately lead him to creating a master race. Chase assembles his "old team" of mercenaries, and we watch him visit his old friends and convince them all that he's on a worthy cause. Once they're a team again, they go

after the megalomaniacal dictator (who sports a weird paste-on beard), and Chase must confront his seasoned champion, The Optimus.

Much better and certainly more focused than the haphazard *Kill or Be Killed*, this follow-up/sequel has a fun spirit and an easy structure that was clearly right for its era of grindhouse releases. James Ryan, who at the time was emerging as a "B" action star, showcases his assured skills as a martial artist, and he's obviously emulating Bruce Lee and perhaps some other Hong Kong stars of the era, while still bringing his own self-assuredness to the role. This is light "PG"-rated fare, but still a good time at the movies. Ivan Hall directed.

Kill 'Em All

2012 (Well Go USA) (djm)

"Let the freak show begin! Hahahahaha!"

A handful of assassins are kidnapped, drugged, and thrown into a locked warehouse, where they groggily wake up and told via a disembodied voice on a megaphone that they will all fight to the death. The fights are randomly selected, and after each match, the winner is allowed to choose a weapon from the locked "weapons chamber," which considerably cuts down the odds. Gabriel (Johnny Messner) is a suicidal hitman with nothing left to lose. The Kid (Tim Man) is a lethal martial artist with everything to gain, Som (Ammara Siripong) is an assassin with an agenda, Carpenter (Joe Lewis) is a washed-up hitman who probably knows this will be his last gig, and other characters populate the warehouse. Once Gabriel, Som, and The Kid realize that their best bet is to work together instead of against one another, the tides turn against their captor (played by a hammy Gordon Liu) and his legion of ninjas.

Kill 'Em All isn't meant to tell a cool story or make movie stars out of its mostly up-and-coming cast of young martial artists. Instead, its purpose is to showcase the talents of its very game cast, with an emphasis on Tim Man, who also coordinated the fights. Man would later fight Scott Adkins in *Ninja II: Shadow of a Tear*, but watch this movie to see more of what he can do. Also in the cast is kickboxing legend Joe Lewis (the star of *Jaguar Lives!*) and stuntman Brahim Achabbakhe, who would later be featured in the Keanu Reeves movie *Man of Tai Chi*. Directed by Raimund Huber.

Killer Elite

2012 (Universal DVD) (djm)

A team of off-the-grid killers (with guys played by Jason Statham, Robert De Niro, and Dominic Purcell) is under investigation by a covert government organization for their slew of killings throughout the world, and one agent—played by Clive Owen—makes it his mission in

Danny (Jason Statham) is amongst the *Killer Elite*. Author's collection.

German lobby card for *Killer Elite*, starring Jason Statham. Author's collection.

life to hunt the killers down and put an end to their business. When Hunter (De Niro, playing Statham's seasoned mentor) is kidnapped by a dying sheik, Danny's (Statham) only option is to take on one final killing mission at the behest of the sheik in order to have Hunter released. It is during that mission that the intrepid agent Spike (Owen) gets too close for comfort.

An old-fashioned and involving globetrotting action adventure, *The Killer Elite* is a competent film, and it reaches beyond Statham's fan base and should appeal to those viewers who might be turned off by stuff like *The Transporter* and *Crank*. Much like Statham's more mature films *The Bank Job* and *Redemption*, it doesn't just feature action for action's sake; it has what Statham's fans crave, but it exceeds expectations and delivers a solid thriller with plenty left over to please several demographics. Despite how good it is, it was not a success at the box office (like most of Statham's movies). Directed by Gary McKendry, and based on a true story.

The Kill Factor

2009 (Sky Dragon DVD) (djm)

A hooded killer is stalking the streets of Los Angeles and putting chokeholds on innocent women, slaying them within seconds. When the media catches on that there's a serial killer on the loose, detective Sean Kane (Gary Wasniewski from *Thunderkick*) is put on the case. Kane is a self-proclaimed strong arm of God's law, and he skirts the rules and kicks, punches, and wisecracks his way through a cadre of thugs, punks, and lawbreakers, working his way to a martial arts instructor who specializes in teaching chokeholds to students looking to learn self-defense. The instructor is obviously the culprit behind the killings (no surprise, guys), and when Kane faces off against him in a dojo, the killer's chokehold is no match for Kane's thunderkick!

From writer/director Leo Fong, who did his absolute best to make a real movie here, *The Kill Factor* is similar to Fong's once-upon-a-time starring vehicle *Low Blow*, but much cheaper and goofier, despite Wasniewski's best efforts. Just like Fong's character in *Low Blow*, Wasniewski's character thwarts purse-snatchers, saves innocent women, and basically ignores his boss. The look of *The Kill Factor* is reminiscent of reality television. This is an obscure little movie, but if you're intrigued I encourage you to seek it out. Compared to Wasniewski's previous movie *Thunderkick*, it's pretty great.

Killing American Style

1989 (Cinema Epoch DVD) (djm)

"I'll kill them—American style!"

A team of robbers, led by Tony Stone (played by an enthusiastic Robert Z'Dar) get themselves caught and incarcerated, and when they're being transferred to their correctional facility, they are rescued by an associate, who leads them to what they believe to be an abandoned house in a desert community to lay low for awhile. It turns out that the home is occupied by a family, whose patriarch is a kickboxing teacher named John Morgan (played by real-life kickboxing champ Harold Diamond). When John comes home to find that these thugs have raped his wife, he goes into a frenzy, killing them off (there are three total) one by one in violent encounters. Meanwhile there's a detective (played by Jim Brown) on the case, and he gets to the aftermath of Morgan's brand of justice just a hair's breadth too late.

From Amir Shervan, the director of the infamous *Samurai Cop*, *Killing American Style* isn't as overtly outrageous as that film, but it's still pretty bonkers. Gawkers of bad action movies should have a good enough time watching it, while others looking for kernels of genuine awesomeness will have to dig deep. Star Harold Diamond is the real thing as far as being a kickboxing champ. His biggest claim to movie fame was stick fighting with Sylvester Stallone at the beginning of *Rambo III*. Co-star Jim Brown

is given a thankless, action-less role. Two years later Shervan directed Diamond in the obscure action film *Gypsy*.

Killing Down

2006 (Maverick DVD) (djm)

Army intel officer Steven Down (Matthew Tompkins) is in South America in the late '80s with some American college students who are farming and helping revolutionaries with their cause when some guerrillas invade their village, slaughter the students, and take Down captive. Tortured in captivity for months, he never gives up any information, and years later he suffers from PTSD and nurses a deep-seated hatred and need for revenge that remains unfulfilled. He spends most of his time researching the Contra initiative and the murky politics of the Reagan era, and when he finally thinks he's found the man who tortured him, he closes in on him, with the help of a mysterious undercover agent (played by Sheree J. Wilson from *Walker, Texas Ranger*), who may or may not be on his side. At last, Down might have found his quarry, but his uneven mental state may be his worst enemy.

A very earnest attempt to make an action star out of martial artist/stuntman Matthew Tompkins, *Killing Down* tries its best to cover its ultra low budget with a convicting performance by its star. Tompkins, who sorta looks like a bulked up Casper Van Dien, is clearly a good martial artist, but he rarely gets the chance to show off what he can do. Most of the time, he's asked to be enraged, to run and duck, or to simply act (which is all fine), but this is a movie that absolutely needed to showcase more action to warrant more films with him as the star. If you're going to try to make a new star, you need to let him shine. A dark and depressing vibe permeates *Killing Down*, but it's not without its merits. Tompkins has worked in Hollywood as a stuntman and as an actor for several decades, but so far this was his only starring vehicle. Directed by Blake Calhoun.

The Killing Grounds

(a.k.a. **Children of Wax**)

2007 (Dimension DVD) (CD)

In a Turkish community in Berlin, children are being found murdered and with mannequin-like makeup. The local Turkish gang, led by Murat (Daniel Bernhardt), believes it's the skinheads in town doing it. Even though the skinheads deny the accusations, a war is about to erupt over the murders between the two gangs. Kemal (Armand Assante) is a detective who is working the case. He grew up in the streets and was friends with Murat at one point. While trying to find the killer, he tries to convince Murat that a war isn't the answer. When evidence comes to light that the skinheads are innocent, the rest of the Turkish gang doesn't care and still wants their war. Sadly, nothing Murat can say will stop them. Things get personal for Kemal and he will do whatever it takes to find the truth.

This is sort of a strange film. It was directed by Ivan Nitchev (*Journey to Jerusalem*) but was written and produced by Menahem Golan, co-founder of the now defunct Cannon Films, for Nu Image. The story works on most levels, though certain aspects never really seem to belong, most notably the love affair between one of the Turks and a skinhead woman. There are several solid performances throughout, namely Armand Assante (*Judge Dredd*) and Daniel Bernhardt (*Bloodsport 2*), who are both really damn good. From an action standpoint, Bernhardt has one fight scene during the first several minutes that is impressive and for the rest of the film he is able to show off his acting chops. Otherwise, *The Killing Grounds* is a pretty standard thriller with a few inspired moments. It's worth a view.

Killing Machine
1975 (Adness DVD) (djm)

A Japanese spy named Doshin (Sonny Chiba) returns to his village after World War II, and finds that his hometown is overrun with raiders, warlords, and rapists who have taken advantage of the humble people who live there. Doshin, a martial arts master, doesn't just sit idly by while children go hungry and women are raped and used (against their will) for prostitution. He takes action and hurts the oppressors by castrating them, breaking their bones, and humiliating them one at a time. The people of his village flock to him for martial arts lessons so that they can defend themselves, and he ultimately creates a lasting legacy.

Based on a true story, *Killing Machine* is okay entertainment if you're a real fan of Chiba's, but while trying to cover its bases as a true story it gets bogged down in heavy-handed drama and theatrics. Some of the supporting characters have emotional arcs and sad stories, and so Chiba's character is usually there to console, lift up, and bury his friends when the story requires him to. Other than that, there's enough going on here to keep you interested. Directed by Noribumi Suzuki.

The Killing Machine
2010 (Anchor Bay DVD) (CD)

"That's the funny thing about fate . . . if you don't follow, it will drag you where it wants to go."

Edward Genn (Dolph Lundgren, who also directs) works for an investment company. He's divorced and has a daughter whom he loves very much. But he's also a Soviet-trained assassin forced to work for the mob and while in Hong Kong, his cover is blown and he quickly finds that the tables have turned. He becomes a target, along with his family, and they go on the run and look for a safe place to stay. In order to save his loved ones, he must confront the demons of his past.

Lundgren seems to know exactly what his audience expects from him, and he delivers in spades with *The Killing Machine* (previously titled *Icarus*). It's an obvious homage to the action films of the '80s or 90s but still feels relevant and is highly entertaining. There's no shortage of action, and things get rolling right away. This isn't light action either; Lundgren goes all out with the blood as he shoots, fights, and maims anyone who gets in his way or keeps him from protecting his family. He also is completely believable in the role. It was really important to bring some emotional weight to the story in order to bring it above being just another "B" movie. There's also a great villainous turn for Bo Svenson (*Inglorious Bastards*). In the short moments when the action slows down, there are some genuinely strong scenes as Edward tries to be a father to his daughter. Lundgren has proven yet again that his directing skills are superb, and he knows how to craft an action film without the resources afforded for a Hollywood film. He keeps things practical, and it suits the picture perfectly. This sort of picture may have been done before, but it accomplishes everything it sets out to do while delivering great entertainment.

The Killing Man
(a.k.a. The Killing Machine)
1994 (A-Pix DVD) (djm)

A sedated and handcuffed man with a considerable amount of martial arts abilities and lethal skills wakes up in a room where the only furniture is his hospital bed. A nameless man gives him food and refuses to answer his questions. A television screen with violent images plays on a loop near his head, and later, a beautiful woman comes in and strips naked in front of him, giving herself without question to him, and he realizes that he is part of some kind of experiment. The man, named Harlin Garret (Jeff Wincott of *Martial Law II* and *Mission of Justice*), has been detained and brainwashed by a shady covert government man (played by Michael Ironside), who tells him that he is a test subject, meant to go out into the streets and perform assassinations and killings without hesitation and without remorse. Harlin's first test is when an armed thug from the streets is brought into his quarters, and Harlin must prove that he can kill on order, which he does without much issue. Wherever Harlin is from and whatever his training, it is obvious that he is an expert at what he does, but something about the whole set-up irks him, and when he's unleashed on the streets to become a "killing man," he backtracks and ends up going after the secret government organization that created him.

Edgy and lean for a fairly high-concept action movie, *The Killing Man* bears with it a stigma of being incredibly low budget and oddly underpopulated, which gives it an unusual flavor. Jeff Wincott, who always manages to elevate the projects he stars in, took on some

interesting vehicles in his career as an action star, and this one has a sort of film noir aura to it, but with martial arts and some sex scenes. It would have been great if this movie had been bigger and shown the web of conspiracy revolving around his character, but what we're shown is hardly enough, and therefore it's difficult for me to say that this movie is a complete success. It gives Wincott a risky-ish movie to star in, and like some of his other films such as *No Exit*, it goes off the action and martial arts reservation a bit and may alienate fans of the genre. Michael Ironside, a dependable character actor from movies like *Red Sun Rising*, adds exactly what he tends to add to films like this, which is something but just not enough to make it justifiable to see it based on his name alone. The director was David Mitchell, who did *Mask of Death* with Lorenzo Lamas and *Last to Surrender* with Roddy Piper.

Killing Streets
1991 (Vestron VHS) (CD)

"There's no deal. I'm taking the hostages home. It's over."

Craig Brandt (Michael Pare) is a Marine working in Lebanon. He's about to take some down time with his lady friend when they're interrupted by terrorists who are quick to kill her and nab him. In the US, Craig's twin brother Chris (also played by Pare) wants some answers. It's being reported that Craig is dead, but his twin intuition is telling him otherwise. He leaves behind his coaching gig for a high-school basketball team in Ohio and jumps on the next flight to Lebanon. Once there he basically runs into a brick wall when it comes to getting information about what happened. He begins to do his own investigating and learns he was right, but he will need some serious firepower if he's to rescue Craig. He'll need some help, and the only person he can turn to is US Government employee Charlie Wolff (Lorenzo Lamas), who reluctantly agrees to help him blast through the terrorist compound.

On paper, this film sounds like it could be brilliant, pairing two direct-to-video titans like Michael Pare (*Streets of Fire*) and action star Lorenzo Lamas (from *Renegade* and *The Rage*) in an action picture like *Killing Streets*. Though the film has a few inspired moments, it's way too long and (quite honestly), it's boring. Pushing the hour and fifty minute mark, this thing will put you to sleep while you wait for the good stuff. To trim the fat and deliver a ninety-minute masterpiece would have been a better strategy. Lamas only appears briefly in the film, but it's the finale where we get to see the action, the heavy artillery, and plenty of explosions. The film was produced by Cannon's Menahem Golen and directed by Stephen Cornwell (*Marshall Law* with Jeff Wincott).

The Killing Zone
1991 (Madacy DVD) (djm)

"Don't talk to me about laws or rules! There aren't any!"

A drug lord's brother is killed by another prisoner while incarcerated, and when the drug czar—Carmen Vasquez (James Dalesandro)—finds out about it, he goes after everyone who helped put him in prison in the first place . . . namely Sam and Garret Bodine, the DEA agent and his nephew who originally made the bust. Garret (played by Deron McBee from *Cage II* and *Immortal Combat*) has big problems of his own: He was wrongly convicted of a crime and is serving hard time, but he's released under the proviso that he help capture Vasquez who is creating a "killing zone" in Los Angeles in his quest for vengeance. The cops need the Bodines together again to bring peace back to the streets.

Pretty fun and slightly above the margin for these types of movies, *The Killing Zone* (from PM Entertainment) gives former *American Gladiator* McBee a decent vehicle to flex his impressive muscles. As the lead guy, he never oversteps his capabilities and he's surrounded by competent co-stars who do more than their share of supporting him. There's plenty of action and nudity, and most guys looking for a better than expected direct-to-video action experience should enjoy this. Written and directed by Addison Randall, who also wrote the similar movie *L.A. Wars*, starring Vince Murdocco.

Kill or Be Killed
(a.k.a. **Karate Killer**)
1976 (Media VHS) (djm)

A crazed German named Von Rudloff—a Nazi holdover—has built a mini-empire in the Namibian Desert, and his whole goal in life is to have a conquering army of karate fighters. He has champions from all over the world kidnapped and brought to his fortress, and one fighter, Steve Hunt (James Ryan), is always on the verge of leading some kind of revolt against his captor and guards. As Von Rudloff leads his "team" to fight in a tournament against a Japanese army, Hunt and his fellow captives finally sense their opportunity of escape, and they overtake Von Rudloff's men (who include a crusty dwarf who makes it clear that he has the hots for Hunt).

Sort of old-fashioned in the sense that its filmmakers had no idea what they were doing but knew that they at least had a real martial artist star and a karate tournament concept to build from, *Kill or Be Killed* launched South African James Ryan into the public consciousness, at least in the grindhouse circuit. Filled with crazy nonsense and confusing mayhem, this movie is really only good for watching its star in his early stages. He's interesting to watch. The director was Ivan Hall. Ryan and Hall returned with *Kill and Kill Again*, which really wanted to be a sequel to this.

Killpoint
1984 (Mill Creek DVD) (djm)

"I'd like to oblige you of your rights."

A psychotic gunrunner and his cadre of goons get the attention of the Riverside police department when their crimes leave messy collateral damage and dead civilians in their wake. Lieutenant James Long (Leo Fong) is assigned to the case, and Long's world was recently shattered when his wife was raped and murdered by a crazed biker gang. Already on edge, Long goes on the hunt for the gunrunner (played by Cameron Mitchell), and it doesn't take much police work for him to figure out that the biker gang responsible for his anguish is working for his quarry and his cold-blooded killing henchman Nighthawk (Stack Pierce, who does most of the slaying in the film). Long poses as a buyer of the illegal arms and he's put through the ringer to gain the trust of the gang, but when he finally unleashes his fury, there's nothing the bad guys can do to stop his wrath.

A moderate exploitation outing from Crown International, *Killpoint* is a decent vehicle for Fong, who is not a typical looking (or sounding) action hero. His big, floppy hair and his monotone accent are a little disarming until he starts kicking dudes in the face. He looks mean, and despite his goofy appearance, he's kinda cool. He has a couple of great fight scenes with character action/stuntman James Lew (who went on to be in tons of martial arts movies), and the ending is good, although it's not as awesome as the ending of Fong's next movie, *Low Blow*. Fong, Mitchell, and director Frank Harris made *Low Blow* next.

Kill Switch
2008 (First Look DVD) (djm)

Two serial killers are on the loose in Detective Jacob King's corner of the universe. King (Steven Seagal, speaking softer than ever) is on to both killers, and since the cases are unrelated, it's amazing that he's able to keep both guys straight. One of the killers targets young women, and when their corpses turn up, they have astrological symbols carved on some part of their bodies. The other killer is just a maniac, haphazardly going after anyone who annoys him, and when he's on his rampage, he goes after King and his girlfriend, who also happens to be a detective. King certainly has his hands full, and when he's not chopping dudes in the throat or slamming their mouths on tabletops, knocking out their teeth, he's remembering a childhood trauma when a predator killed his twin brother.

Despite terrible editing in the action scenes and a completely out-of-nowhere ending, I really liked *Kill Switch*. Seagal seems to be enjoying the world he inhabits in this film, and the action scenes (though terribly put together with obvious stunt doubles) are brutal as hell. The film doesn't add up correctly, though, and

the ending throws the whole film into a bizarre perspective—he goes to Russia and meets up with a secret wife and children we never knew he had. Even with all that against it, I think it's still one of Seagal's better direct-to-video movies. He also wrote it, but goodness knows who edited it. Directed by Jeff King (*Driven to Kill* with Seagal and *Damage* with Steve Austin).

Kill the Golden Goose
1979 (CustomFlix DVD) (CD)

"Ever since Captain Karate took over this division, every broad in here's become a lethal weapon."

Mauna Loa (Ed Parker) is a killer for hire, and he's one of the best. He's hired by a corrupt official to take out three specific targets: all witnesses about to testify before a Senate committee. Loa isn't given much time to prep but takes the job anyway since the money is good. Once in town, he begins to seek out his targets, but his former friend Captain Han (Master Bong Soo Han) is hot on his trail. Han isn't about to let Loa complete his contracts and dives head first into a search that will take him deep into the Los Angeles underground. As the bodies begin to pile up, Han and Loa will face off against one another in the battle of the century.

Kill the Golden Goose may not be a great action film but it's a highly important one. It's the only film that featured Senior Grand Master of American Kenpo Ed Parker (Jeff Speakman's teacher) in a lead role. Joining him in the picture is a man who was known as "the Father of American Hapkido," Master Bong Soo Han (*The Trial of Billy Jack*). Director Elliot Hong (*They Call Me Bruce?*) brings these two titans together in a film that tends to be light on the action and overly talky for two men with no formal training as actors. Master Bong may have the best fight in the film (about thirty minutes in), but the finale between him and Parker is what everyone will want to see. It's a moment in action history worth viewing even though the film is mostly of interest to hardcore martial arts fans who know and respect what these men accomplished in their lives.

Kill Zone
2005 (The Weinstein Company DVD) (JAS)

Kill Zone is a dark action-drama that stars martial arts film stalwarts Simon Yam and Donnie Yen as Hong Kong police officers, and the iconic Sammo Hung (Kam-Bo) as the cruel but complex villain Wong Po. The story concerns cancer-plagued officer Chan Kwok-chung (Yam) and his attempts to dethrone criminal warlord Wong Po at all costs. Against the better judgment of his soon-to-be successor Ma Kwun (Donnie Yen), Kwok-chun alters a videotape in an effort to link

Po with a murder he didn't technically commit. This of course backfires on Kwok-chung, and along with other police-related mistakes, results in the deaths of the entire police squad. While technically victorious, Wong Po realizes the cost of his lifestyle in a twist that is best not revealed here, as it would spoil the impact.

This is a wonderfully mean and meaningful film in that it cruelly illustrates the danger of compromising personal values to combat injustice. The philosophy of the story is that the ends don't always justify the means, and each character pays dearly to learn this. There is a moral ambiguity in its character portrayals, showing the "good guys" as sometimes despicable, and the villain as sometimes empathetic and loving. *Kill Zone* has a strong moral message that forces the audience to consider whether good people can fight evil with more evil. It doesn't hurt that the film has a lot of kick-ass action along the way, especially the very intense knife-fight alley scene between Kwun and fluid knife assassin Jack (Wu Jing), whose movements are so quick they seem almost ballet-like . . . a butcher ballet, that is. Donnie Yen is the perfect opponent for Jing's level of skill, and he engages in the fight with his own style of close-contact weapon combat, blocking and attacking with a dagger that is like an extension of his arm. This scene is an interesting contrast to a final fight in which the large (yet amazingly agile) Hung goes toe-to-toe with Chan; the fight is unpredictable, absurd, perfectly executed, and a bit disturbing in its climax. It's a perfect crescendo to a perfectly paced film. Highly recommended.

Kiltro

2006 (Magnet DVD) (CD)

A beautiful young girl named Kim (Caterina Jadresic) is about to be raped by thugs when she's rescued by Zamir (Marko Zaror). After he helps, Zamir finds himself in love with her and as a way of showing his affection, he beats up any man who tries to date her. Sadly, his approach doesn't work but he isn't willing to give up. When a man named Max Kalba (Miguel Angel De Luca) arrives in town to seek vengeance on the "Sect" of martial artists that had wronged him many years ago, Kim's father is the focus of his wrath. Zamir and Kim go on the run and are taken in by a dwarf who is a "Zeta" master. Zamir must learn to be a master as well if he is to have any chance at all to defeat Kalba. In his quest to reach this elevated state, he tries his best to win over Kim, the only person he truly loves.

This was the directorial debut of Ernesto Diaz Espinoza, who would later collaborate with star Marko Zaror again on *Mandrill*. The film itself is a bit flawed but the reason to watch *Kiltro* is that it's the cinematic birth of one of the next great action stars: Zaror is an amazing talent. His skills are jaw-dropping and his fight choreography in the film is hypnotic. When he fights during the first half of the film, it's a more stylized street martial art than we're used

to seeing. There's a great scene in a Korean martial arts school where he must take on twenty students at once, which might remind viewers of *The Chinese Connection*. When lives are at stake and he reaches a new level of enlightenment, the fighting is much more brutal and Zaror is able to take on more than twenty opponents at a time. With each subsequent film, he has grown in every aspect, as has his director with whom he has collaborated on two more occasions (*Mandrill* and *Mirage Man*). Both actor and director are on the rise and at the beginning of what will most likely be exciting careers.

Kindergarten Cop

1990 (Universal DVD) (djm)

"You kids are soft. You lack discipline. Well, I've got news for you: You are *mine* now! You belong to *me*! You're not going to have your mommies around behind you to wipe your little tushies! Oh, no. It's time now to turn this mush into muscles. No more complaining. No more 'Mr. Kimble, I have to go the bathroom.' NOTHING. There *is* no bathroom!"

Pure genius! Let's get The Terminator and put him in a kindergarten class. Let's have him scream at them, work them out, and have them fall in love with him. Holy moly, it works! Detective John Kimble (Arnold Schwarzenegger at his peak) is on the trail of a killer named Cullen Crisp (an indelible Richard Tyson) who, along with his evil mother (Carroll Baker), is trying to find his six year-old son. Crisp gets a lead that his ex-wife (who fled with their son years ago) is living in Astoria, Oregon, and he and his mother make their way there, but Kimble has already beaten him to the punch. Along with his partner Phoebe (Pamela Reed), Kimble is already in Astoria, posing as a kindergarten teacher for a few weeks to ferret out Crisp's son and his mother, who might be one of the other teachers, played by Penelope Ann Miller. Amidst the chaos of the classroom, Kimble is able to get the other teacher to fall in love with him, and the kids end up thinking he's the greatest. He deals with all the headaches of kindergarten mayhem, while saving the lives of the children and Crisp's son and ex-wife.

Pretty radical for a "family" movie, *Kindergarten Cop* is violent and hard-edged, while still very cute and funny. I saw this several times in theaters in 1990, and I loved it as a ten-year-old, and I still love it. The first fifteen to twenty minutes are like an "R"-rated cop movie with Arnold, and then it switches gears to *Twins* territory, and then it veers back to the "R"-rated vibe towards the end. Director Ivan Reitman, who did *Twins* and then *Junior* with Arnold, did a fantastic job making an action movie for adults that most kids would enjoy.

Kindergarten Ninja

1994 (Legacy DVD) (djm)

Philanderer, drunkard, and all-around jackass of a man Blade Steel (former NFL player Dwight Clark) gets pulled over while swigging on a beer, and he's promptly arrested for DUI. The judge slams him with a sentence that seems woefully inappropriate: Ninety days of community service . . . working with children! In heaven, God takes notice and gives Bruce Lee a one-time-only offer: go back to Earth, turn Blade's life around by some miracle, and earn his wings in heaven. Bruce (played by this movie's director, Anthony Chan) takes the gig and visits Blade, gives him some martial arts coaching lessons (because he's gonna need 'em), and puts him in the care of a blind karate master (played by this film's writer, George Chung), who picks up where Bruce left off in his training. Once Blade begins subbing in a kindergarten class, he realizes that the neighborhood is overrun with a drug cartel, led by a guy named Machete who uses kids from his kindergarten class (!?) to sell drugs on the streets. Blade and his blind master get their ninja groove on and pound the pavement with their Bruce-inspired kickers.

Since this might be the only review of this movie to ever appear in a published book, let me be clear that it's not something most people will ever need to see. I wanted to see it because George Chung from *Fight to Win* and *Karate Cops* wrote and co-starred in it, and I'm glad I took ninety minutes to watch it. It's basically an amateur knockoff of *Kindergarten Cop*, populated by non-professional actors who fly into walls of cardboard boxes every time they're hit or kicked, but that's got its own small appeal. Movies like this never get a chance in a mass-market mentality, and while maybe that's deserved, it should be said that George Chung, working outside the mainstream, deserves a modicum of respect for some of his efforts. *Kindergarten Ninja* is an easy target. I'll go on the record by saying this: I watched it, and it made me chuckle a few times. It ain't so bad.

The King of Fighters

2009 (Well Go USA DVD) (djm)

"Who am I?
I'm the new King of Fighters!"

Similar in notion to movies like *Mortal Kombat* and *DOA: Dead or Alive*, *The King of Fighters* concerns a secret martial art tournament to be held in "another dimension" with an ultimate prize. The tournament is invitation-only and when a carefully selected group of fighters are chosen one at a time to fight a potential adversary, they are each shocked to find a villain named Rugal (*Star Wars Episode 1: The Phantom Menace*'s Ray Park) has overtaken the council behind the tournament and is killing off the competitors as they rise to meet the challenge. His goal is to reign over all the dimensions and ultimately take over Earth once he's become the

"King of Fighters." One of the competitors—Mai (Maggie Q)—and her boyfriend Iori (Will Yun Lee) are in possession of an ancient sword with unusually strong power, but the sword rightfully belongs to Kyo (Sean Faris), who reluctantly joins Mai and Iori on their quest to rid the alternate dimension of the evil Rugal, who wants to get his meaty claws on the sword.

I dunno, guys. Kids might like *The King of Fighters*, but anybody else better be warned. It's a slog. The Dutched camera angles and techno-type music was old back in 1997 when *Mortal Kombat: Annihilation* came out in theaters, and more than a decade later, they're still doing the same thing. It's great seeing wushu champion Ray Park without a mask on for a change, but this movie isn't worth seeing just to watch him. This is from the director of *The Medallion* with Jackie Chan and *Fist of Legend* with Jet Li. Also with Francoise Yip from *Rumble in the Bronx*.

King of the Kickboxers

1990 (Imperial VHS) (djm)

Jake Donahue watches his kickboxing brother win a big match in Thailand, and on their way home to celebrate, they are stopped by a gang of ruthless thugs led by a crazed killer named Khan (Billy Blanks in a breakout performance). Jake witnesses his brother get murdered by Khan, and the story flashes forward ten years. Jake is now a smart aleck New York cop who uses unconventional methods (martial arts) to bag criminals. Jake (Loren Avedon, following his success from the *No Retreat, No Surrender* sequels) is offered the chance to go to Thailand to follow a case leading to a gang of snuff filmmakers who murder martial artist champs on camera. Once in Thailand, Jake has a time of it working his way to the point where the snuff filmmakers approach him for a "star-making role" and once he's gotten to that point he knows that he will be facing Khan one way or another. Jake trains with the only man who survived a fight with

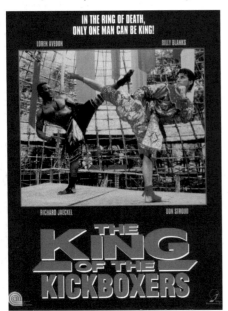

Video release poster for *King of the Kickboxers*. Courtesy of Loren Avedon.

Khan, a washed-up drunk in the jungle, played by Keith Cooke (*Heatseeker*). The final fight between Avedon and Blanks is staged in a Thunderdome-type set-up, and it's a doozy.

Lucas Lowe (*No Retreat, No Surrender 3*) directed this really entertaining "B" action movie. One scene has a television playing *No Retreat, No Surrender 3*. Avedon is given a lot to do in the film, and he impresses as a fighter. His character is a little too cocky for my taste, but it fits the film. There is sequel confusion about this movie. Lowe directed *American Shaolin*, which is known as *King of the Kickboxers II: American Shaolin*, and Avedon made a film called *Fighting Spirit*, which is known as *King of the Kickboxers 2*. Neither film is a legitimate sequel to *King of the Kickboxers*. Stick with the original.

King of the Kickboxers 2

(a.k.a. **Fighting Spirit**)

1992 (Seville DVD) (djm)

Billy's sister is assaulted and nearly raped and blinded by a gang of hooligans, and Billy (played by Sean Donahue from *Ground Rules*) goes into a rage and seeks revenge. His buddy David (Loren Avedon from *No Retreat, No Surrender 2 & 3*) is a happy-go-lucky guy with just enough fighting abilities to back his friend up in fights, but it's Billy who's the kickboxing dynamo. As Billy gets deeply entrenched in his revenge scheme, he becomes overwhelmed and is eventually killed (spoiler!), which sets the film on its next course. David breaks the terrible news to Billy's emotionally damaged and physically marred sister, and he resolves to train in martial arts and become a better fighter than his fallen friend to finish revenging where he left off.

I made this movie sound slightly better than I should have. The truth is that it's woefully amateurish and just barely watchable enough to not disgrace stars Donahue and Avedon. The *King of the Kickboxers* title is obviously wrong and has nothing to do with the first film, and as an in-name-only cash grab it fails miserably. Avedon is so skilled as a martial artist (you can see it) that he should have been making the type of movies Jeff Speakman or Don "The Dragon" Wilson was making during the era. Co-star Donahue dominates the first half of the film, and even he deserved better movies than this. Filmed in Eastern Asia and filled with old, stock music scoring that sounds like it's from the '70s. Directed by John Lloyd.

Kingz

2007 (Vimeo) (CD)

"My homie is a full-blown psychopath..."

Two young thugs, Olli (Olli Banjo) and Mathis (Mathis Landwehr), have a large pack of a white powder, presumed to be cocaine, which they must deliver to a nightclub where notorious

drug lord Luca (Bela B. Felsenheimer) takes up residence. Everything seems to go according to plan until Olli spots his sister Nadine (Claire Oelkers), who shouldn't be there. Things quickly go awry, and the events that transpire are nothing that anyone expected.

The short film *Kingz* takes elements of science fiction, horror, and martial arts films, throwing them all into the pot with everything mixing and working in an unexpected way. There are plenty of great effects with a unique monster and the story is compelling and original. There's an excellent fight scene that features Mathis Landwehr (*Death Train*, also the fight choreographer). It's a fast-paced and brutally fun smackdown that truly shows off the talents of Landwehr. The unknown German cast couldn't be more perfect. As an interesting side note, Mike Moeller (*Arena of the Street Fighter*) worked as a stuntman. The film is the brainchild of Benni Diaz and Marinko Spahic who both have worked extensively in the effects field (most notably on Lars Von Trier's *Melancholia*). Just judging by this short film, these guys deserve to have some money thrown their way so that they can make a full-length feature. The story moves and transitions flawlessly and when it's over you wish for more. This is a real hidden gem and you can watch it online for free on Vimeo. It's in German and subtitled in English.

Kinjite: Forbidden Subjects

1989 (MGM DVD) (djm)

"Who appointed you avenger of my department? *Who gave you a flaming sword?*"

The last of Charles Bronson's features from Cannon, *Kinjite* is a shockingly kinky thriller that features the star as a racist detective named Crowe. When a horny Japanese businessman molests his daughter on a packed transit bus, Crowe doesn't refrain from biting his tongue before spouting off to his partner (Perry Lopez) and his boss that he'll have nothing to do with helping Asians in need of police assistance. When the very man who molested his daughter experiences a personal crisis when his own daughter is abducted by a low-level exploiter of minors, Crowe's chief assigns him the case. Not realizing that the Japanese man (James Pax who played Lightning in *Big Trouble in Little China*) is the pervert responsible for his daughter's molestation, Crowe takes the case because it also connects to several other cases he's on. In one scene, Bronson makes a pimp swallow his own Rolex!

Ultra sleazy and pulpy, but surprisingly multilayered, *Kinjite* follows two storylines that intersect, and when Bronson's character is revealed to be a racist, overprotective father/cop, the movie becomes more interesting. There's enough fisticuffs and gunplay to satisfy Bronson fans, but making a movie just like this today would not be possible. Aside from *52 Pick-Up*, this was Cannon's sleaziest movie. Directed by J. Lee Thompson, who also made *Firewalker* with Chuck Norris and *10 to Midnight* with Bronson, amongst others.

Kiss of the Dragon

2001 (Fox DVD) (djm)

A chilling secret agent from Hong Kong named Liu Jian (Jet Li) is called in for a quick job in Paris, but the job severely goes south when a deranged police inspector (Tcheky Karyo) reveals himself to be setting Liu up for a gruesome murder. Liu goes on the lam, while the inspector sends out his forces to kill him, and Liu's only hope of redeeming himself from being framed for the murder is to prove that he didn't do it and that the inspector is behind everything. Liu's hope lies (at least in part) with a battered American prostitute named Jessica (Bridget Fonda), who knows the inspector well enough to provide evidence against him, but first she must survive the night and reclaim her daughter from an orphanage with Liu's help.

Easily Jet Li's best English-language movie, *Kiss of the Dragon* provides him with a fantastic vehicle to flex around in. The Paris locales and the top-notch direction by Chris Nahon give him plenty of support and every single action scene he's in is a knockout. The action is directed by Cory Yuen (*No Retreat, No Surrender, Above the Law*), and some of the action stuff designed for the film is unbelievably cool. A standout scene (and there are several) has Li fighting about two dozen guys in a dojo with sticks. While Fonda's role is fairly thankless, it is interesting that she's co-starring in a movie written by Luc Besson, who wrote and directed the film *La Femme Nikita*. Fonda starred in John Badham's remake of *Nikita: Point of No Return* in the early 1990s. Cyril Raffaelli (*District B13* and *District 13: Ultimatum*) has a notable fight scene with Li here. Newcomers to Li may want to start here for their education if they're not adventurous enough to start with *Fist of Legend*.

A fight between Liu Jian (Jet Li) and a thug in *Kiss of the Dragon*. Author's collection.

Hooker with a heart of gold Jessica (Bridget Fonda) is passed out in Liu Jian's (Jet Li) arms in *Kiss of the Dragon*. Author's collection.

Knights

1993 (Paramount VHS) (CD)

When she's a child, Nea's (real life kickboxing champ Kathy Long) family is slaughtered (except for her little brother) by the evil cyborg Job (Lance Henricksen). The cyborgs need blood to survive, and they plan on getting as much as they can to sustain eternal life. Years later, Nea must face Job again when his men try taking out her village. This time, a renegade cyborg with different programming, named Gabriel (Kris Kristoferson), shows up to kill all the other cyborgs. Gabriel trains Nea to help him and when he's blown apart and taken by Job's henchman, David (Gary Daniels), she must call upon all her training in order to stop them and save her friend.

It really is a shame that this wasn't a more successful film. Director Albert Pyun envisioned it as a trilogy and it completely feels like it's just the first part of a much bigger story. So we will never know how it truly ends, which is fine since the first movie is such a blast. Just looking at Kathy Long, there should be no question that she could and would rip you apart if she had to. This was her first starring vehicle, and she was perfectly cast as Nea. Her acting skills are somewhat wooden though Pyun smartly cast actors like Kristoferson and Henricksen to even out Long's rough edges. She shines when she's in her element. There's always plenty of action in Pyun's core action films, and *Knights* is no exception. Vincent Klyn from Pyun's *Cyborg* has a small role, and Gary Daniels appears in a small but pivotal part. Pyun makes excellent use of his locations and really captures the beauty of the deserts. The story was somewhat typical of Pyun's sci-fi works from that time period (cyborgs trying to take over the world) and his longtime musical collaborator Tony Riparetti creates an amazing score. It has a much larger and heroic sound than much of the synthesizer music that films of this type are usually saddled with. *Knights* is a highlight of Pyun's career.

Knights of the City

1985 (New World VHS) (djm)

"You guys don't wanna dance —you wanna rock!"

A breakdancing street gang known as the Royals shares a dream to make it big as an R&B group that mixes dancing in their act, but they have a huge hurdle to overcome: They're basically thugs and no record company will ever consider listening to their demo tape. When their leader—Troy (Leon Isaac Kennedy from the *Penitentiary* movies)—lands his whole crew in the slammer over a night, they impress a record executive who is spending the night in the drunk tank. They sing their asses off while in jail, and he gives them his card and says to look him up when they

get out. Over the next week or so, they polish their act and make an impromptu visit to the exec's office, getting stonewalled by his daughter (played by a very foxy Janine Turner in her first film role), who feels a sexual attraction to Troy. When the exec finally sees them, a record deal is considered, but first the Royals must enter in a dance/band competition and prove they can do their stuff. Their biggest challenge is facing off against The Mechanics, a rival gang that is willing to commit murder to win the competition . . . or to get revenge if they lose.

A time capsule action/breakdance movie with tons of topical music, *Knights of the City* was Leon Isaac Kennedy's baby: He had a hand in the script, he produced, and as the star he gives himself the best moments in the film, leading up to a satisfying ten-minute gang fight between himself and the leader of the other gang. They start off tied together by a rope, and when they get separated, their gangs riot and all hell breaks loose. A much longer cut was originally assembled after initial production (Sammy Davis Jr. was a character, but then got cut out), but it sat on the shelf for too long and the breakdance movie phase went out of style, so the film was cut to shreds. As it stands, the film is pretty entertaining, and it's a good vehicle for Kennedy, who turns in a very physical performance. It's silly stuff, but it's a good time. Music video filmmaker Dominic Orlando directed.

Knock Off

1998 (Sony DVD) (djm)

Jean-Claude Van Damme's second and fatal collaboration with director Tsui Hark resulted in the hyperstylized and confusing mess that is *Knock Off*. Van Damme plays a happy-go-lucky businessman named Marcus Ray who peddles knock-off clothes in Hong Kong. His partner Tommy (Rob Schneider) reveals himself to be working for the CIA on a major case, which involves the Russian Mafia and an attack against the United States. When Ray realizes that the Mafia is using the buttons on his knock-off jeans as micro-bombs, Ray and Tommy are thrust in the middle of an incredibly confusing plot that has them engaged in action.

Along with Van Damme's and Tsui Hark's *Double Team*, I firmly believe *Knock Off* helped topple Van Damme as a theatrical marquee name. From the start, *Knock Off* has him delivering stupid dialogue, which casts him in a buffoonish light. The plot is incoherent and idiotic, which is strange considering that the script was by Steven E. De Souza, who wrote the script for *Die Hard*. De Souza also wrote and directed the Van Damme turkey *Street Fighter*, but *Knock Off* is a whole different brand of bad. The Hong Kong-style aesthetics are lost in translation here, and even with some clever stunts and interesting-looking fight scenes, the movie doesn't have a leg to stand on. Needless to say, Van Damme began making movies that were released directly to video after this.

K

Knockout

2010 (Phase 4 DVD) (djm)

Displaced teen Matthew (Daniel Magder), who has just moved to a new neighborhood with his mom and stepdad, is picked on for being nerdy at his new school. He has an interest in boxing because his grandfather was a former contender, but he just can't seem to get a grip on how boxing works. When he goes out for the boxing team at school he's picked on harder and beat up more severely than ever, until the school janitor, a muscular former fighter named Dan ("Stone Cold" Steve Austin), takes an interest in him and begins encouraging and training him in how to defend himself. The only way for Matthew to make the team and stand up for himself without getting his lights knocked out is to work hard and become a real-thing fighter.

With a nod to *The Karate Kid*, the lightweight *Knockout* knows exactly what it is and doesn't have any pretensions. It's refreshing to see Austin in a "PG"-rated movie, and his role is understated, yet integral. There's nothing offensive about the film, and families can enjoy it together. WWE Entertainment produced a similar film called *Legendary*, starring John Cena, around the same time. This was directed by Anne Wheeler.

Knucklehead

2010 (Vivendi DVD) (CD)

"You're right, Todd. If only my voice was three octaves higher . . . I looked as good as you in a dress, maybe —just maybe—I'll get adopted."

Eddie Sullivan (Mark Feuerstein) is a former fighter who gave up the sport after throwing a match. Now he finds himself in some deep trouble with local crime boss Memphis Earl (Dennis Farina). After racking his brain for ideas, he accidentally meets a lovable oaf named Walter (Paul "The Big Show" Wight). He's a grown man still living at an orphanage and has accidentally caused severe damage to the place, which is now being closed down by the state. Walter feels responsible and wants to do something to fix the whole situation. Eddie has the idea of trying to turn Walter, who is a massive seven-foot tall, 450-pound teddy bear, into a fighting machine. He convinces head nun Sister Francesca (Wendie Malick) to let Walter come with him as they travel from state to state creating an Internet buzz. As a precaution to make sure Eddie doesn't screw the orphanage out of any money, Francesca sends along her assistant Mary (Melora Hardin) to keep him in line.

Knucklehead isn't going to do much to change whatever opinion you may have of WWE Sudios, but it's an endearing little picture and pro wrestler Paul "The Big Show" Wight (*Jingle All the Way*) gives a surprisingly sweet and funny performance. The film is obviously geared to be more family-friendly, which helps to make it just a bit more enjoyable than one would expect. The humor is harmless, and if you find the idea of a very large man pooping in a (far too) small bathroom on a bus funny then you've got a winner. Wight is perfectly cast in the film and has great comedic timing. Most of the action throughout the film is played out for humor's sake but the fights in the final moments feature Wight more focused and showing why he is such a popular talent in professional wrestling. Directed by Michael Watkins.

Kung Fu: The Movie

1986 (Warner DVD) (djm)

"I know a thousand ways to take a life. I know not one to give it."

More than a decade after the TV series *Kung Fu* ended, David Carradine returned to his most famous role in this made-for-TV movie. As Shaolin monk Kwai Chang Caine, he finds himself at the center of a conspiracy to frame him for murder, and as he's on trial, he realizes (very wise is he) that a man from his history has targeted him for a past wrong. A Manchurian warlord known as The Manchu (played by Mako) has staged the entire conspiracy to do Caine in because when Caine was very young, he killed The Manchu's son (we see this in flashbacks to the old series). As a way to plunge the knife deeper, The Manchu has found Caine's long-lost son he never knew he had (played by a young Brandon Lee), and has hypnotized him to kill Caine should his plan fall apart. When Caine escapes his bonds after being declared guilty of a crime he didn't commit, he must face his hypnotized son before taking on The Manchu.

A court procedural structure bogs down this otherwise interesting movie that has Carradine's wise kung fu master realizing for the first time that he is not on a journey alone but with a son he never knew he had. Brandon Lee's role is relegated to a small, supporting status, and the movie could have easily used more of him, but I'm just glad that we got as much of him in it as we did. Lee also made *Legacy of Rage* the same year. In 1993, a follow-up series called *Kung Fu: The Legendary Journeys* was made with Carradine, but not with Lee. Directed by Richard Lang, who worked on the original series.

Kung Fu Killer

2014 (Well Go USA DVD) (djm)

After killing a man in a martial arts duel, martial arts instructor Hahou Mo (Donnie Yen) is sentenced to five years in prison. Three years later, a well-known pupil of Mo's is killed in another duel, and Mo insists that he knows who the killer is. When the police question him in prison, he lists a handful of other people who will most likely be the killer's next target, and when one of those men is killed in another duel by a mysterious killer just like Mo said would happen, the police get him out of jail to assist their investigation before another name on the list is crossed off. As it turns out, there's a "Kung Fu Killer" on the loose, serial killing masters of their craft in the martial arts, and somehow Mo is connected to the killer. The only way Mo is going to catch the killer is if he escapes custody and works on his own, and when he encounters the deformed killer (played by Baoqiang Wang), the two are nearly evenly matched and have a major showdown on a busy freeway with trucks and cars whizzing by.

A step down from some other of Yen's starring vehicles like *Kill Zone* and *Flashpoint*, but about on par with *Special ID*, *Kung Fu Killer* is worth watching for the final fight alone, but to get there you have to slog through overly simplistic plotting, boring characters, and silly melodramatic tragedies that pinpoint character motivations. As per usual for modern Chinese action cinema (I can't speak for Chinese cinema outside of this genre), the entire endeavor seems geared for the underclass masses, so there's zero sophistication and constant reminders of what is going on in case you forgot what happened ten minutes ago. Fans of Yen will want to see this, but casual purveyors of kung fu action movies should skip it. Yen coordinated the stunts, while John Salvitti helped out with the MMA-oriented fights. Directed by Teddy Chan.

Theatrical poster for *Kung Fu Killer*. Author's collection.

Lady Dragon

1992 (Sterling DVD)
(djm)

Kathy Galagher (Cynthia Rothrock at her peak) has become a wandering vagabond in search of vengeance against the man who murdered her husband on their wedding day. She participates in bloodsport fights for quick cash while she's living in Asia. She's visited by an old friend (Robert Ginty, *The Exterminator*), who sort of tips her off to where her nemesis, Ludwig Hauptman (Richard Norton), is living. She insinuates herself into Ludwig's circle, but she's found out before she can get revenge, and Ludwig punishes her for it: he rapes her and beats her to a pulp and leaves her for dead. She's rescued by a cute Asian boy and his mute grandfather, who nurse her back to health, and she slowly begins to train herself back into shape. When she's ready to try going after Ludwig again, she takes a different approach, but she's discovered *again*, and Ludwig's bright idea is to settle the score by fighting to the death. This being a Rothrock vehicle, we get to see her take Norton down.

David Worth, director of films such as *True Vengeance* and *Kickboxer*, gives the film a little *too* much visual flare by showing us the best contact scenes in repetition sometimes three or four times in a row. It should also be noted that many of the fight scenes have been sped up in the editing room, which is annoying. Rothrock and Norton move fast enough for my eyes and for the camera, so it's a disappointment to see their best moments have been so obviously cheated. The film itself is typical of the shot-in-Asia, straight-to-video action films from the period, and it doesn't really offer anything truly spectacular or worth noting. Rothrock, as usual, is competent in the type of role she was accustomed to playing, and Norton is perfectly adequate in a smarmy villain role. Worth also directed the in-name-only sequel.

Lady Dragon 2

1993 (Imperial VHS) (djm)

Unrelated to Part 1, but once again starring Cynthia Rothrock, *Lady Dragon 2* casts her as "The Golden Angel," a red-headed kickboxing champion named Susan whose husband is a soccer hero in his native Asian country. While traveling back home by plane, some jewel thieves stash hot diamonds in their luggage, and the thieves follow them home. The three thieves are a dangerous bunch. Their leader is played by Billy Drago, who gives an incredibly entertaining and unsettling performance. They show up at their house, maim Susan's husband

The Director Of KICKBOXER Brings You The New Dragon

She Fights Fire With Fire

CYNTHIA ROTHROCK
LADY DRAGON

Home video release poster for *Lady Dragon*. Author's collection.

and rape her, demanding the diamonds. Susan doesn't have a clue what they're talking about, but she later learns that her husband found them and wanted to keep them. When Drago begins taunting her by calling her and insinuating that he'd love to rape her again, she begins to take the offensive. She tracks the thieves down one by one (one of them is played by Sam Jones from *Driving Force*) and brutally kills them. When it's just down to her and Drago, the film feels extra familiar if you've seen any of the *Death Wish*-type movies that this movie feels inspired by.

The tone and execution of this movie is grim and downbeat. Rothrock plays a victim, then an avenger, but her reward for her revenge is strangely unsatisfying. The best performance is clearly by Drago, who has never been creepier or more sinister than he was in this film, and he makes a great foil for the heroine. David Worth (*True Vengeance, Chain of Command*) directed and photographed this.

Land of the Free

1998 (Madacy DVD) (CD)

Frank Jennings (Jeff Speakman) is working as a campaign manager for a politician who is running for a seat in the Senate. He's approached by some agents who believe that his employer Aidan Carvell (William Shatner) has plans to build his own army to try to overthrow the government. They want Jennings's help in obtaining evidence to help convict Carvell. Reluctant at first, Jennings goes along with it and quickly finds out that it's all true and agrees to testify in court. Carvell will go to any lengths to make him pay for his betrayal, even if it means going through his family and hitting him where it hurts.

Land of the Free suffers from numerous setbacks, none of which are Jeff Speakman (*The Perfect Weapon, Street Knight*). The film had a noticeably small budget, a horribly misused score, and some questionable acting from supporting cast members, but if you set those aside, it's actually a pretty damn fun movie. It lacks a satisfying final battle but many of us will derive some sort of pleasure from watching Speakman beat the smug face of William Shatner. Speakman actually has quite a few action scenes, and the bus chase in the film boasts several spectacular jumps, crashes, and explosions. Hell, he even straps on a John McClane fire hose and takes a dive off a building, all in the name of entertainment. Speakman looks good, is full of energy, and most importantly, seems to be having fun in this, and it's infectious enough for the audience to feel it, too. Directed by Jerry Jameson.

Laser Mission

(a.k.a. **Soldier of Fortune**)

1989 (Blue Laser DVD) (djm)

Brandon Lee (*Rapid Fire*) stars as a devil-may-care mercenary named Michael Gold, who goes on a mission to Africa to escort an elderly professor who is the world's foremost expert on lasers. When they meet, both he and the laser expert (a hammy Ernest Borgnine) are captured by bad guys. Gold escapes from confinement, and spends the rest of the movie trying to save the professor from his captors, who are trying to use a giant laser and the world's largest diamond for nefarious purposes. With the help of a ditzy blonde secret agent (with perky boobs), Gold gets into one adventure after another on his way to saving the professor.

Filmed on location in South Africa and featuring lots of explosions, car chases, and fisticuffs, *Laser Mission* is an inauspicious vehicle for star Lee, who never uses martial arts in the movie. His later films, *Showdown in Little Tokyo* and *Rapid Fire,* showcased his talents much better than this film, but he looks like he's having fun in it. The director, BJ Davis, is a much-respected stuntman and stunt coordinator. Almost all of the video versions of this film are released by companies who distribute movies that are in the public domain, and therefore it is difficult to find a decent transfer of it. I watched the 16 × 9 letterboxed version from Blue Laser, which is a DVD-on-demand company through Amazon.

Last Action Hero

1993 (Sony DVD) (MJ)

"Something is rotten in the state of Denmark, and Hamlet is taking out the trash."

In 1993, Arnold Schwarzenegger was on top of the world following a string of box-office hits that included *Total Recall, Kindergarten Cop,* and *Terminator 2: Judgment Day.* Expectations were incredibly high for *Last Action Hero,* which had at its core a reunion of Schwarzenegger and director John McTiernan (*Die Hard, Hunt For Red October*) following their successful collaboration in 1987 with *Predator. Last Action Hero* tells the story of young Danny Madigan, the world's biggest fan of Jack Slater, the world's greatest action hero, played in the film by Schwarzenegger. With the gift of a magic ticket, Danny finds himself able to enter the film world of his favorite hero and interact with its inhabitants. Fatally precocious, Danny allows the magic ticket to fall into the hands of one of Slater's greatest enemies, who uses the ticket to return to the real world and start wrecking havoc. At the top of his list of Things To Do is to kill Arnold Schwarzenegger, thus ending the threat of Jack Slater in his own world and more sequels in our world. The only way to end this threat is to convince Slater that Danny isn't crazy and get him to return to our world to stop this shared threat.

L

At the time of the film's release, *Last Action Hero* became Arnold's first significant box-office failure after years of great success. Heightened expectations for the film were raised even higher by ad campaigns that did not accurately hint at the contents of the film but seemed to promise what fans had come to expect from Schwarzenegger and McTiernan: quite simply, a great action film and a great popcorn film. What the film ultimately delivered was an opportunity for the star and the director to wink at the audience and have some fun with the conventions of not just the genre of action films but Hollywood in general, especially the Hollywood of the day, which was known for ever-inflating budgets and the ever-escalating demands of its box-office stars. Nevertheless, the film never loses sight that we all love to go to the movies. With the passing of time, the film has aged well, both as a showcase for Arnold and his star power and the steady hand of director McTiernan. The film's supporting cast is stacked to the rafters with great talent, including Charles Dance as the villain, Robert Prosky as the surrogate father/projectionist we all wish we had, and even Sir Ian McKellen taking a turn as the Grim Reaper, stepping right off the screen from the print of a Bergman film to wreak havoc in the real world. To this day, the film still polarizes fans but is required viewing for fans of the star, who was at the height of his popularity when he made this film. Incidentally, exploitation filmmaker Jim Wynorski licensed the opening car chase from the film and used it in the Michael Dudikoff/Treat Williams action picture *Gale Force*.

The Last Dragon

1985 (Sony DVD) (djm)

Leroy Green (Taimak) is a humble, innocent martial arts student who quests for "The Glow," a mystical power attained through enlightenment. Living in the big city is hard for him, though: His family thinks he's weird, he's bullied by a thug who calls himself Sho'nuff—the Shogun of Harlem—(played by Julius Carry III), and his Asian master leaves him to his own devices to seek his destiny. Leroy idolizes Bruce Lee but struggles to become a man, and when he inadvertently becomes the bodyguard of a local celebrity named Laura Charles (Vanity), he learns pretty quickly to step up his game and become the man she needs him to be. While saving her from a scuzzy record producer who tries to muscle her into compromising her integrity, Leroy attains The Glow and defeats Sho'nuff.

A bona fide cult film with a legion of fans, *The Last Dragon* is one of the most important martial arts films of the 1980s because it reignited an interest in martial arts in the black community, while having a crossover appeal. Taimak is really good in a seemingly simple role, and he manages to avoid being campy when it would have been incredibly easy to go that way. Outlandish costumes, over-stylized dialogue, and pop songs abound, but this is one of the most unique action/martial arts films of its era. It can be compared to movies like *The Golden Child* and *No Retreat, No Surrender*, but it's really

its own thing. Ernie Reyes Jr. (*The Rundown, Teenage Mutant Ninja Turtles II: The Secret of the Ooze*) has a small, but memorable role as a kid who kicks ass. Also watch out for Glen Eaton, whose next film *Trained to Kill* made an action star out of him. Taimak showed promise as a martial artist/action star, but he didn't continue in that direction. Michael Shultz directed.

INTERVIEW:

TAIMAK

(djm)

Every generation has its own touchstone, inspirational film, and The Last Dragon *(1985) is such a film for thousands of fans the world over. Filled with exciting action, bizarre, mystical elements, an ultra hip Motown soundtrack full of pop songs, and a lead star who popped from the screen, the film has garnered an incredible cult following and is more popular now than ever before. Taimak (last name: Guarriello) was chosen to play the lead character Leroy Green, who seeks the mystical power of "The Glow," and the film becomes an adventure as his quest leads him on a path of honor and discovery through various trials and tribulations. Taimak's background in martial arts includes studying goju karate, Goju-Ryu (his teacher was Ron Van Clief, the African American star of* The Black Dragon), *jiu jitsu, and taekwondo, and he was a lauded kickboxing competitor in his younger years. Even though he was virtually a "one-hit wonder" action star, Taimak has maintained his strength, vitality, and positive outlook. Maybe he found* The Glow.

Theatrical release poster for *The Last Dragon*. Author's collection.

The Last Dragon has garnered an incredible cult following. This is a favorite movie for many, many people. Why do you think this movie has endured so strongly?

Well, I guess it's similar to *Rocky*. It's one of those characters that's endearing. He succeeded after such a struggle. I think that appeals to everybody out there. That was the fundamental, basic concept of the film. Obviously, all the comedy and all the great actors, and all the people who were in charge of it—Michael Schultz and Barry Gordy—they were behind it, and with the music and with the originality, and all of us together as an ensemble is what made it last.

It's a really unique movie. Finding "the glow" . . . it has a mystical element, and that mystic action adventure was kind of in during the mid-80s. I remember The Golden Child with Eddie Murphy and Big Trouble in Little China with Kurt Russell had similar themes. When you read the script for The Last Dragon, what were your thoughts?

I was a kid. I wasn't mature enough to go too deep. I'd won a kickboxing title, and I was contemplating what I wanted to do with my life because there was no money in kickboxing, and I was contemplating whether or not I should go back and continue my education in physical therapy. I wanted to start a business so that I could eventually get a school. Then, when this film came up everybody told me that I was perfect for it. That's what happened. When I read the script . . . I saw that I would fight everybody. I was more serious about the fight scenes. (Laughing.) But I thought it was very funny and a great story.

What was your audition like? Did you have to show them that you could do martial arts?

They already knew about me as a martial artist. They were just interested in my acting. They'd known that I'd only done a few school plays. Basically, they wanted to make sure that all of those scenes were going to be strong. At first, it was very challenging because I didn't have a structure [of acting], but they worked with me.

After this movie, I would have assumed that you would have gone on to do more movies of this type and become a big action star. What happened? How come you didn't continue?

There are many reasons. Some of them I am accountable for. Some of them the industry is accountable for. If you think about—especially back in the 80s—having a leading man of color to be a hero and a positive character wasn't . . . you'd rarely find something like that. Hollywood didn't put so much attention into that. That was partly the reason, and that's still an issue in Hollywood. Also, I was very young. There was a dynamic in Hollywood that I wasn't prepared for. I'm prepared now because of maturity.

Talk about your martial arts background a little bit. Did your interest in martial arts intensify after the film? It seems like you have a lifelong passion for martial arts.

Yeah, sure. Honestly, when I was very, very young, like five years old, I was reading a lot of comic books and I got fascinated with being big and all the muscles and stuff. I told my aunt, "I want to have big muscles like this guy." What happened was, when I turned six, my father let me study karate with his friend in New York. That was my first taste of martial arts. I didn't get started until after we moved to Europe—my parents moved to Europe—and I started again when I was about twelve. I saw a Bruce Lee commercial, actually, and that was what put the passion in me. It got me really curious about martial arts. At first I was doing aikido, but I wanted to kick like Bruce Lee, so I started taekwondo. And I competed in taekwondo tournaments, and I really got interested. When I was about fifteen, I saw a movie that Ron Van Clief was in called *The Black Dragon*, and I'd never seen a man of color star in a martial arts film before. I'd only seen an Asian guy. I said, "Wow, I'd like to meet that guy one day." Then my father said, "Oh, I know Ronnie!" So before you know it, I ended up training with Ron Van Clief. I got my black belt with him, and I ended up training with him for many years. During that time I was kickboxing at one of the only kickboxing academies in New York. It was a really interesting time. After the film, I pulled away from a lot of that and I wanted to learn some more stuff about film,

Taimak stars as *The Last Dragon*. Author's collection.

and I started focusing on a lot of different things. I ran marathons, I biked all the way up to Bear Mountain in New York, and I just fell more into the fitness side of training. I started studying Shaolin because I'd always been interested in Shaolin kung fu. I did some of that. I then met a Japanese master and studied jiu jitsu, and that focused on your chi manipulation. For the past couple of years I've been interested in Brazilian jiu jitsu, and I find it really fulfilling physically and mentally.

Talk a little bit about your character in *The Last Dragon*, Leroy Green. You just mentioned to me that you developed an interest in martial arts because of Bruce Lee, which parallels your character in the film.

Yeah, he was a dragon. And so am I. The year of the dragon. He was the first one to really captivate on screen. Before him there were a lot of Asian martial arts stars, but they were kind of caricatures, and the only one who ever came close to Bruce Lee was Sonny Chiba in his Street Fighter series. These were charismatic guys who showed martial arts skills. They showed high advanced martial arts skill. It was just a natural thing. He showed a spiritual side. He blended a lot of his training with his philosophical ideas. I'd been studying a lot of that, too. Trying to make the connection between your life, your training, and how philosophy connects the whole thing. Even though I grew up in New York around all these tough guys, I did still retain a lot of naiveté. I guess that in a way was how I was similar to the character in the movie. I wasn't as streetwise and knowledgeable. It's hard to explain. I don't know. That's the only way I saw myself similar.

Would you like to say anything in particular about *The Last Dragon*?

I want to send my blessings to Julius Carry and Leo O'Brien, who played my little brother. It was very sad when they both died. Julius's mother called me an hour after he died. It was a shock. The real shock was Leo O'Brien. He was only forty-one. He was great. You never know when you're going to be taken off this planet. It just reminds me to make the best of what you have while you're alive, to get over all the minutiae. They touched my heart and contributed so much to that film. Everybody involved in the movie was fantastic.

Little kids come up to me wanting autographs at conventions. Their parents have showed it to them. It's transcended time. It's like the movie came out yesterday.

Is there anything you would like to say to the fans of this movie and to people who have always wanted to know what became of you?

Yeah, sure. The fans are human beings, they are people. They see me doing something that touched their heart, and I made them chuckle . . . for me as a person and as a martial artist and as an actor, that is my goal, is to make somebody's day a little better. I want them to know that I've always been training since *The Last Dragon*, and I've also been improving myself as an actor. I've got a short film right now with Rob Howard's company, Imagine, and that is where I'm at right now. You can like my fan page on Facebook. I think what I'd like to give my fans is that for me, life has been a lot of ups and downs. I was so young when I got in this business, and I went through that struggle, but I've come to a place now where I have embraced everything—every part of it. That's been the biggest growth for me, to really transcend whatever obstacles I've had, and to find harmony within it. That's what's been my biggest prize is to give myself that freedom. Thank you for the support. It's not over. There will be a lot more coming.

The Last Fight

1983 (Thorn-Emi VHS) (CD)

"Is fat meat greasy? That's my business to know what's going on in the fight game. I smell a dive."

Andy "Kid Clave" Perez (Ruben Blades) is a singer and boxer. Things are looking up for him until his gambling debt to Joaquin Vargas (Willie Colon) becomes too much to handle. The two make a deal where Vargas will take fifty percent of Perez's fight money. When Perez's manager is killed, he needs to find out who was responsible, and the only man for the job is Jesse Crowder (Fred Williamson). With Jesse in hot pursuit of the killers, Perez learns he has a life-threatening blood clot in his head possibly ending his chances of the title shot he's been dreaming of. Crowder can work miracles when it comes to catching the bad guys, but what happens with Perez is out of his control.

Fred Williamson brought back one of his most beloved characters to the screen, Jesse Crowder, five years after the 1976 film *No Way Back*. Crowder has been one of the best representations of Williamson's screen work, and with *The Last Fight*, he writes, directs, and stars alongside a fantastic cast including Ruben Blades

(*Predator 2*), Willie Colon (*Vigilante*), Joe Spinell (*Rocky*), and legendary boxing promoter Don King. The acting is top-notch and Williamson's script is possibly the best he's ever written. It's an action thriller set in the boxing world and features real life personalities as well. One of the best scenes in the film has Williamson and a lady friend walking across the street only to have him get nailed, crashing through the windshield, and then literally just getting up. He brushes himself off and puts his arm around the girl, and that's exactly why we love Fred Williamson.

Last Flight to Hell

1990 (AIP VHS) (djm)

This substandard AIP junk stars Reb Brown in the type of role he mastered. In less than three years, he had appeared in nearly a dozen movies about Vietnam or other modern wars that featured him wielding heavy machine guns while he traipsed in the jungle or other war-torn parts of the world. In *Last Flight to Hell* (a decent title, but not fitting for this film), he escorts a young woman through a southeastern Asian country to help her find her father who has been kidnapped for a large ransom. It turns out that her father has vital information that would implicate Reb Brown's friend (a grizzled Chuck Connors) in a series of drug deals. Connors and Brown shoot at each other while running and ducking in the jungle.

Made with Italian money and by an Italian director (Ignazio Dolce, credited to Paul Robinson), this has a cheapness and artificiality that is impossible to shake off. The dubbing is spotty, and Brown's character and performance are one-note and blasé. If you liked Reb Brown's *Strike Commando* or *Mercenary Fighters*, you may be more inclined to enjoy this.

Last Man Standing

1995 (Trinity DVD) (djm)

Detective Kurt Bellmore (Jeff Wincott from *Martial Outlaw*) and his partner Frank Kane (Jonathan Banks from *Bullet*) score a pretty big bust, but when the hundreds of thousands in drug money disappear before it's accounted for, Kurt won't let the matter slide—especially when he knows that a fellow detective is most likely responsible for the discrepancy. His partner Frank warns him to just let it go, but Kurt is persistent, and on their next bust Frank is shot dead, and Kurt suddenly finds himself the target of some fellow cops and the drug running scum who are in cahoots. Kurt and his pretty wife (Jillian McWhirter from *Stranglehold*) take it on the lam together and prepare for all-out war.

Last Man Standing is the perfect action movie for audiences who shy away from martial arts in their action movies. It has *just enough* martial arts action to satisfy fans of that type of movie, but what it's really got going on are big-scale stunts and huge explosions that will satiate any appetite hungry for action. One of Jeff Wincott's biggest and best vehicle films (almost on par with *Mission of Justice*), PM Entertainment's *Last Man Standing* takes "B" action to a nearly "A" level with jaw-dropping stunts (a few of which had me wincing and yelling at my screen), and it spreads the action across a surprisingly big canvas for a relatively small story. It has a high tempo *Speed*-ish score and a sex scene early on to get any full-blooded male in the right frame of mind. Joseph Merhi (*Riot, Magic Kid*) directed.

The Last Witch Hunter

2015 (Lionsgate DVD) (djm)

A Viking witch-hunting warrior named Kaulder (Vin Diesel) is cursed to live eternally by a powerful witch queen (Julie Engelbrecht), and so through the ages, he slays witches and amasses a fortune as the decades turn to centuries. A sect of monks (or are they priests? doesn't matter) known as the Dolans aide him through the ages, and in current times, Kaulder's Dolan is #36 (played by Michael Caine), but when #36 dies under suspicious circumstances, Kaulder seeks the aide of a witch named Chloe (Rose Leslie), who can help him to remember a suppressed memory that would help put his curse in perspective. When he's assigned Dolan #37 (Elijah Wood), Kaulder realizes that #36 was not killed, but cursed for the knowledge of what became of the witch queen's heart all those centuries ago. A powerful witch named Belial (Olafur Darri Olafsson) is aiming to perform a ritual with the (still pumping) witch queen's heart, and by doing so will resurrect her and every witch Kaulder defeated over the centuries. With an impending major mess looming ahead of him, Kaulder must rely on his tried and true witch hunting skills to save the world one more time.

Intended to kick-start a franchise with star Diesel at the forefront, *The Last Witch Hunter* is basically a revamped riff of *Highlander*, complete with swords and all that jazz. It's exactly as advertised with little variation away from what you would expect from it, and Diesel is good in a role that doesn't require much of him. The special effects are good, and the movie entertains. What more do you need from something called *The Last Witch Hunter*? Unfortunately, it was a big flop, so we won't be seeing sequels. From director Breck Eisner.

L.A. Streetfighters
(a.k.a. **Ninja Turf**)
1985 (RCA VHS) (djm)

Young (Jun Chong) is a college student by day and a leader of a multiracial gang by night. He has a feud with another local gang, whose leader Chan (James Lew) is bitter about losing in a fight against Young witnessed by tons of spectators. Young is approached by scouts who work for a drug kingpin, and they offer him a job: bodyguarding the kingpin. This opens up a slew of possibilities for Young's gang, and he brings his crew onboard with him as extra protection to the kingpin. One night his crew gets the idea to steal a suitcase full of cash that belongs to the drug kingpin. Young supports the idea, and once they've double-crossed their employer, the gates of hell open and they are hunted down by not only Chan's gang but also two seasoned enforcers (one of whom is played by Bill Wallace) employed by the kingpin. The finale is quite brutal and bloody as Young and his right-hand-man Tony (Phillip Rhee) take on all comers.

Moments of truth and honesty of Korean life, and life in general, in the youth-centric set of the mid-1980s gives *L.A. Streetfighters* an interesting texture, and while fantastical at times, it has a gritty, unexpected power to it. The film is just as much a showcase for Rhee as it is for Chong, and while Rhee might be better known for going on to star and produce the *Best of the Best* series, Chong deserves a look in this film. The director, Richard Park (Woo-sang Park), received a posthumous career boost when his next film *Miami Connection* was rediscovered.

The Last Sentinel

2007 (Echo Bridge DVD) (CD)

"You've come to the best place in the world for dying. Consider yourselves dead already."

In the not-too-distant future, the world has been turned into an apocalyptic battlefield. Tallis (Don Wilson) is the last of a special unit of electronically enhanced soldiers. When a group of resistance fighters fail in their mission, they leave behind one of their own, a young woman. The girl (Katee Sackhoff) is reluctant to trust Tallis but with the fate of the human race at stake, she doesn't have much choice. The drone police have wiped out much of the population. Tallis has a history with the drone police since his unit was originally sent to stop them. He helps to train the young rebel to prepare her for the final battle. What he doesn't expect is the elite force of drones that they will have to fight to destroy the drones' central command.

The Last Sentinel was a much more entertaining experience than expected. The main issue with the film is the lack of focus on the story. The flashbacks were kind of distracting and overly drawn out, pulling you from the main story. Thankfully, the action is nonstop, which is really a blast. The amount of gunfire in the film is dizzying. Early on there is so much gunfire that it drowns out much of the dialogue. A late entry in the Don "The Dragon" Wilson (the *Bloodfist* series) oeuvre, this picture gives him an opportunity to show himself as a formidable aging action star—certainly a contender. He does what he does best and goes through all the necessary motions. The film is of interest to action fans for his involvement and because his co-star is fanboy dream girl Katee Sackhoff of *Battlestar Galactica* fame. Her character suffers the most from the lack of focus and never really feels like a part of the story, more like a bit part player. And the way she just reappears in the film's climax is just silly. The film also features Keith David (*They Live*), Bokeem Woodbine (*The Fifth Commandment*), and Steven Bauer (*Scarface*). Their scenes really amount to little more than extended cameos. For a small-budget science fiction film, some of the effects look really good and the costume designs for the drones are really interesting. There is a lack of any real main villain, which causes the film to suffer a bit, but overall it's a fairly fun and exciting ride. Fans of Wilson (who also co-produced) should enjoy it.

The Last Stand

2013 (Lionsgate DVD) (djm)

Infamous drug cartel leader Eduardo Noriega (Gabriel Cortez) stages an elaborate escape from federal custody, and he flees using an ultra expensive sports car that can outrun a helicopter. Agent John Bannister (Forest Whitaker) is immensely frustrated that Noriega escaped on his watch, and he quickly has to form a plan to capture Noriega before he makes his way to Mexico. He makes a call to a border town where the tired sheriff answers the phone and barely acknowledges the agent's warning that trouble might be headed his way. The sheriff, Ray Owens (Arnold Schwarzenegger), is dealing with problems of his own. There has been suspicious activity in his town since a group of truckers arrived and made camp in the outskirts, and suddenly there's a murder to solve and a hailstorm of trouble is about to crack the town wide open. When Owens realizes that all the trouble is related to the escape of Noriega, he and his few deputies (who include Luis Guzman, Jamie Alexander, and a too-goofy Johnny Knoxville) fortify the town and arm themselves to the teeth with a Gatling gun and all sorts of weaponry. When the war reaches their small town, they're ready to fight!

Thai poster for *The Last Stand*. Author's collection.

Intended as a big-screen comeback for former Governor (of California) Schwarzenegger, *The Last Stand* made headlines by losing millions. It's too bad, really, because it's a fun ride without any pretensions, and it simply aims to please. At turns, it's shockingly violent, and then becomes silly and pedestrian, but ultimately it accomplishes what it sets out to do. For Arnold fans, it's a little sad to see him so haggard and over-the-hill, but at the same time, it's great to have him back killing bad guys. I enjoyed the film a great deal, and I saw it theatrically in a theater in Bangkok, Thailand. It made me proud to be an American. It was directed by Korean Jee-woon Kim, who made the intense action/serial killer film *I Saw the Devil*.

Last to Surrender

1999 (Lionsgate DVD) (djm)

Narcotics cop Nick Ford (a foul-mouthed Roddy Piper) watches his partner get killed by a Chinese gangster, and he's then teamed up with a Chinese cop named Wu Yin (Han Soo Ong) to chase the killer to Asia. They travel to the Burmese jungles to track the gangster down where he's joining up with an army, and Nick and Wu have to figure out each other's strengths and weaknesses before they can properly get along to face their enemy. Wu is captured and tortured and Nick comes in and saves him, leading to a prolonged action chase in the jungle. It's a little like *No Retreat, No Surrender 2*.

A rough and shoddy first-third is smoothed out with an unexpectedly exciting and fun final two-thirds as a usually spunky Piper in a strange environment with a foreign partner livens up the film. Their banter is belabored and awkward at times, but the movie picks up the pace and manages to redeem itself despite the incessant cursing and basic storytelling. Han Soo Ong had bit part roles as fighters in various martial arts action films like *Tiger Claws II*, *The Quest*, and *Bloodsport II*. He never made another movie after *Last to Surrender*. It was directed by David Mitchell, who also made *The Killing Man* with Jeff Wincott and *Mask of Death* with Lorenzo Lamas.

The Last Warrior

2000 (Artisan DVD) (CD)

"It was a time of milk and honey, hardbodies and hotrods, chaos and cappuccino."

Green Beret Nick Preston (Dolph Lundgren) finds himself as an unlikely leader of a group of misfits after an earthquake has caused a rip in the San Andreas Fault that leaves California broken off as a desert island. With few resources, they attempt to live as normal a life as possible. The earthquake left Preston with memory loss, and inner turmoil threatens to break the group apart, but when one of them ends up captured by a rogue group of prisoners, Preston steps up to the plate in to save her and learns of a terrifying plot that threatens the life remaining on earth.

As far as Dolph Lundgren films go, *The Last Warrior* (also released under the title *The Last Patrol*) is amongst his lesser works. It's saddled with an overly slow-moving storyline that may turn off many viewers. Voice-over narration in a film isn't always a bad thing but it just seems that far too much was revealed in the film using that device, which is draining. The only way to describe the film would be to call it a post-apocalyptic action film even though the action (what little there is) doesn't make an appearance until the final thirty minutes or so. There are a couple of interesting ideas, like the mutant goat milk, but they're never fully realized. The fights were well choreographed and director Sheldon Lettich (*The Hard Corps*) knows action. He's a solid director who works to give the film a unique look with lots of sunlight and very little darkness. This is the weakest film on his directing resume, but it's still passable. It's admirable that much of the film's focus was on developing an atmosphere and adding attention to the building of character. Dolph's character Preston has an interesting backstory that's delivered with conviction by the actor. The rest of the cast are relative unknowns who don't go the extra mile to be convincing, but aren't completely bad either. *The Last Warrior* is for Lundgren completists (or fans of the production company Nu-Image) only.

Latin Dragon

2004 (Screen Media DVD) (CD)

"Come on, come on, just do it. Come on, it's like the commercial, right? Be all you can be. Reach out and shoot someone. It's late, I'm starving!"

Danny Silva (Fabian Carrillo) has just made it back to his hometown after being away for many years. Things aren't the same, and it seems like the street gangs are slowly taking over. The gang violence has escalated, and people are afraid. After a run-in with a few of these thugs at the local convenience store, Danny meets up with his brother Rafael (Luis Antonio Ramos), who happens to be a cop. One gang leader, Paco (Robert LaSardo), is the hired gun to corrupt millionaire businessman Bishop Thorn (Gary Busey). Things get serious when his lady friend Claudia (Joyce Giraud) is taken by Thorn's right-hand man, Frank (Lorenzo Lamas), after a notebook with important information ends up missing. Danny can't stand by any longer and decides to take matters into his own hands.

Fabian Carrillo comes out of nowhere and delivers a highly entertaining action film. *Latin Dragon* feels a bit like a stepping stone and hopefully leads to bigger and better things for him. He has the skills and presence to be a mainstay in the genre. He may look like Ray Romano, but the guy has some solid fight scenes. There are several group battles as well as some one-on-one fights, including a decent showdown with Lorenzo Lamas. Lamas takes the backseat

and has fun in a rare villain role. Director Scott Thomas (*Silent Assassins*) infuses the film with Latin flair, helping to set it apart from the rest of the pack.

L.A. Wars

1994 (Monarch VHS) (djm)

"I *love* this kung fu shit!"

Renegade cop Jake Quinn (kickboxer Vince Murdocco from *Ring of Fire* and *To Be the Best*) is a loose canon and is let go from the force. He becomes a bouncer at a bar and one day he saves the life of a pretty woman who is about to be killed by some hitmen. The woman happens to be the only daughter of the biggest crime lord on the West Coast. She takes him to meet her father, who asks him to name his price as a gift for saving his girl. What does he ask for? A job . . . as her bodyguard. He gets the gig, but he pisses her former bodyguard off, and the rivalry is so thick you can smell it. Meanwhile, Jake goes back to the police chief and makes a deal to get his badge back and work undercover to help topple the drug czar's empire, and he spends most of his time protecting his ward, who has fallen hard for him. Even when hitmen are out to kill/kidnap her, she still swoons at his kickboxing heroism. It turns out that her former bodyguard has plans to betray his boss by making a dirty deal with a competing drug lord, and only Jake can bring an end to the "L.A. Wars."

Similar to *The Killing Zone*, starring Deron McBee, *L.A. Wars* was Vince Murdocco's "one

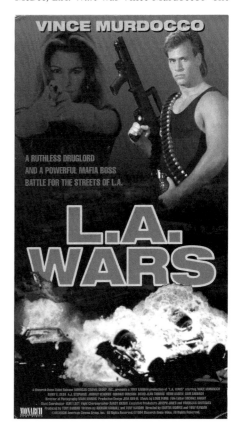

VHS artwork for *L.A. Wars*. Author's collection.

L

hit wonder" effort as a centerpiece star in a martial arts action movie. He co-starred in a number of action films of the era, and while some might wonder why he didn't star in more films, I think it's safe to say that *L.A. Wars* pretty much encapsulates what he was able to offer as a direct-to-video action guy. He's got a killer mullet, an asshole-ish attitude, some kickboxing moves, and a way with the ladies. He's almost like the dude in *Samurai Cop.* He's unbeatable. Addison Randall (*The Killing Zone*) wrote it and Martin Morris and Tony Kandah directed it.

The Lazarus Papers

2010 (Green Apple DVD) (DL)

The Lazarus Papers opens with the gushing credit "Lunaflex Productions Proudly Presents," but no amount of hard selling can elevate this sleazy fever dream of a movie. It opens in a fictional southeast Asian country with seasoned DTV action star Gary Daniels (*City Hunter, The Expendables*) and his army of child soldiers massacring the residents of a poor village and kidnapping women for the sex trade. His prized abductee (Krystal Vee of *Scorpion King 3*) numbs herself with drugs and contracts HIV before being chosen to participate in a convoluted mail-order-bride scam. She turns the tables, steals a suitcase of money from the scammed groom, and escapes captivity with another groom-to-be who suffers from a terminal heart condition (the twitchy John Edward Lee). The psychotic Daniels pursues them across the country as the ill-fated duo falls implausibly in love. Still following all this? Forrest Whitaker's brother Damon plays an ineffectual cop bringing up the distant rear. And Danny Trejo appears as a mystical healer bouncing back and forth between life and death in what seem to be outtakes from a completely different movie.

The ensemble cast is a wildly diverse mix that director Jeremiah Hundley proves incapable of corralling. Daniels is a formidable presence but his one-note character is so vile that his scenes are excruciating. The mixed martial arts skills that made him famous are downplayed in favor of bullets. Trejo discards his strong but silent persona to stretch himself as an actor, and the results are not pretty. Wrestler Tommy "Tiny" Lister serves up a grotesque performance as a drooling, Tex Avery-pitched rapist. *The Lazarus Papers* is the directorial debut of bit part actor Hundley who you may know from his role as Guard #5 in the short film *No Horizon* or his more prominently billed portrayal of Reporter #1 in the never-aired 2011 *Wonder Woman* pilot. He also wrote the incoherent script that defies sensible synopsis. Hundley is clearly trying to say something profound with the uneasy fusion of brutal hyper-violence and new age mysticism, but his message—like the majority of his film—is totally indecipherable.

Legacy of Rage

1986 (Fox DVD) (djm)

Brandon Ma (Brandon Lee pre-*Showdown in Little Tokyo*) is an honest, hard worker with a burgeoning relationship with a woman he intends to marry. His best friend is Michael (Michael Wong), who has ties to a crime family, and on a fateful day when Brandon is framed for the murder of a police officer, everything changes for both of them. Brandon is sent to prison for eight years, and Michael steps up in the crime family and eventually becomes a boss. While Brandon is stuck in prison, his pregnant girlfriend takes on a sugar daddy and they go to Brazil when her safety is threatened by Michael, who tries to rape her. While in prison, Brandon makes buddies with a guy who was an arms dealer, and after their sentences are up, they're both released. When he finds out that Michael framed him, he calls on his arms dealer buddy and they go after the entire crime family who set him up. When Brandon realizes that his old pal Michael has kidnapped his girlfriend and the son he never knew he had, he shows Michael no mercy.

Along the same lines as the Arnold Schwarzenegger films *Raw Deal* and *Commando*, *Legacy of Rage* is a great vehicle for the up-and-coming action star Brandon Lee. In an early scene he has a back alley fight with Bolo Yeung, who, in a sense, passed the torch to the son of Bruce, whom he appeared with in *Enter the Dragon*. The action is brutally intense in *Legacy of Rage* and Brandon is nicely able to balance both action and drama, as the film forces his character to go through some heavy-duty emotions. Brandon's next film was *Laser Mission*. Ronny Yu, who would go on to do some horror films like *Bride of Chucky* and *Freddy vs Jason* directed this.

Legendary

2010 (WWE DVD) (MMM)

"Not all legends are about victory. Some are about struggle, finding out who you are, and your reason for being."

Professional wrestling superstar John Cena stars in *Legendary*, a production by professional wrestling offshoot WWE Studios that's about, of all things, amateur wrestling. From the start, with its small-town Oklahoma setting, intimate family dynamics, and acclaimed actors on the order of Patricia Clarkson and Danny Glover in the cast, *Legendary* is a decided departure for Cena from his two previous big-screen WWE showcases, the globetrotting action-blast *The Marine* (2006) and the near-horror kidnapping thriller *12 Rounds* (2009).

Cena plays Mike Chetley, a booze-broken, down-on-his-luck former local wrestling legend and older brother of picked-on teenage bookworm Cal (Devon Graye). When young Cal announces he wants to follow both Mike and their deceased father into the family tradition of competitive grappling, mom Sharon (Clarkson) flips out. Eventually, of course, she lightens up, just a bit, after Mike's old coach Red Newman (Glover) assures her he'll keep an eye on him. Mike agrees to quit drinking and fly right in order to secretly train his kid bro, and their montages provide the bulk of *Legendary*'s energy and impact, building up to the inevitable championship. Will the mat make a man out of Cal as he attempts to take the title? No spoilers here, but we do witness Mama Sharon finally come around during the big bout when she shouts, "Squeeze it, Cal! Squeeze it!"

Legendary: Tomb of the Dragon

2013 (Lionsgate DVD) (djm)

A cryptozoologist named Travis Preston (Scott Adkins) and his team are asked to track down a creature known as a Cryptid, long thought to be extinct, in China, and when they get there, Travis is met by his former colleague-turned-nemesis, Harker (Dolph Lundgren), who is famous for killing the rare animals he's tasked with locating. Travis and his team (mostly inexperienced youngsters) compete with Harker and *his* team (a bunch of cutthroat mercenaries), leading to a heavy body count by the special effects–filled finale.

Geared for kids and adults who don't mind a bloodless adventure with the likes of Lundgren and Adkins in lead roles, *Legendary* is a safe movie every step of the way, but it's *boring*. The dragon creature in the movie is unimpressive looking, and other computer-generated creatures/animals like a huge, hulking bear in the prologue are slightly more impressive. Adkins is a great action star, and he's asked to carry this picture, but the movie needs more Lundgren, who plays the villain. The budget looks sizable enough to allow the production to film on location in China, and it was released in 3D in certain territories, but I can't imagine why. Directed by Eric Styles.

The Legend of Drunken Master

1994 (Dimension DVD) (djm)

A Jackie Chan classic, *The Legend of Drunken Master* tells a simple story about the son of an apothecary who has an amazing skill of "drunken boxing," which gets him undue attention in his village when he accidentally ends up with a jade artifact that the British government wants to procure. When Wong Fei-hung (Chang) bumbles upon the artifact, his family encounters trouble as he nearly destroys his father's good reputation by getting drunk and displaying his incredible drunken boxing skills against a group of Chinese conspirators who are working with the British to recover the jade artifact. When Fei-hung makes a spectacle of himself, he is disgraced in front of the whole town, and he must work himself back into shape and regain his honor by fighting for his family, for his village, and for his country.

Full of Jackie's signature comedy, death-defying stunts, and jaw-dropping martial artistry, *The Legend of Drunken Master* is easily one of his best films, and he manages to (seemingly) effortlessly balance comedy, action, and even drama as the film goes through its course. Technically, it's a sequel to Jackie's *Drunken Master* (1978), but it works very well as a standalone. Lung Ti, who plays Jackie's father in *The Legend* is actually only a few years older than Jackie, which makes for odd trivia. Also with Anita Mui (*Rumble in the Bronx*) as Jackie's stepmother, and Ho-Sung Pak and Andy Lau also have supporting roles. Released theatrically in the US in 2000. Directed by Jackie Chan and Lau Ka Leung.

The Legend of Nigger Charley
1972 (Blax Film DVD) (CD)

"I ain't taking no shit from no white man again. Toby, I'm a free man and that's the way I'm gonna die."

Charley (Fred Williamson) is a blacksmith working on a plantation with his mom and lady friend. Things are good there, and Mr. Carter (Allan Gifford) treats his slaves decently and takes care of them. When Mr. Carter falls ill, his dying wish is to set Charley free. Houston (John P. Ryan), who manages Carter's estate, won't have it. He already has buyers set up to get rid of all the slaves when Carter finally passes away. Houston beats Charley to a pulp, which sends him into a rage before he is to be sold. Charley gets his revenge by beating Houston to death and he goes on the run with fellow slaves Toby (D'Urville Martin) and Joshua (Don Pedro Colley). They find themselves in a small town hiding from bounty hunters. They end up having to protect the people from a crazed priest and a half-breed Native American woman Charley falls for. He's had it being a slave, and nobody's going to stop him from doing what he wants.

Once again, Fred Williamson (*Active Stealth, Three Days to a Kill*) delivers a highly entertaining western that offers viewers exactly what they should expect from him. There are fistfights, gunfights, knife fights, horse-riding shootouts, and if that wasn't enough there's plenty of word sparring. Williamson is his normal, everyday badass self, but he also slows it down a bit to give a pretty solid performance, very down to Earth and human. While it may be a low-budget effort, there's no denying it should be remembered as a minor classic, especially since it was originally released by Paramount. The title suggests it would be nothing more than an exploitation piece but it's a PG-rated romp with plenty of action and fun. Directed by Martin Goldman.

Legend of the Dragon
2005 (Cinema Epoch DVD) (CD)

"You've got it all wrong. This fight is not about money; I want to prove my father's ideal, to prove my courage, but more important, I believe that tai chi can defeat karate."

Dragon Ki (Sammo Hung) has had to make a difficult decision, one that will forever change his life. He has a loving wife and a young son, but he chooses to leave them both behind to pursue his lifelong passion for the martial arts and live in a village where he can master tai chi. Years later, his adult son Ki Fung (Xiaoming Huang) decides he too would like to learn self-defense, so he grabs his best pal Robert (Timmy Hung), and they head off in search of Dragon Ki. When father and son meet they quickly bond and Fung learns the truth about why his father left. The reunion will be short lived because the two of them will have to show off their skills against two other karate masters.

The description I've given makes the move sound more far more exciting than it is. Sammo was in the middle of a hot streak with films like *Kill Zone*, *Dragon Heat*, and *Twins Mission* but then there was *Legend of the Dragon* that is painfully dull. There are a couple of training montages and two fights in the whole thing. Neither are very exciting and Sammo is only in one. The scene was shot with too many close-ups of the action, and they never really capture anything of interest. The comedy isn't funny, the action is mediocre at best, and the romance is just headache inducing. If you must see everything Sammo does, then fine, but avoid it if you can. The film also co-stars his real son, Timmy Hung. Directed by Gwing-Gai Lee.

Legend of the Fist:
The Return of Chen Zhen
2010 (Well Go USA DVD) (CD)

Seven years have passed since the death of a man who had become a legend with the Chinese people: Chen Zhen (Donnie Yen). He died defending the honor of his people after the Japanese invaded during the First World War. Then one day, a stranger shows up in Shanghai and partners with Liu Yu-Tian (Anthony Wong) in a nightclub. The stranger is the masked hero Chen Zhen, who is keeping his true identity a secret so he can infiltrate and destroy the Japanese who have created an assassination list of prominent Chinese men and women. He begins to fall for the lovely Fang (Shu Qi), a hostess at the nightclub. He isn't aware that she is actually a spy feeding information to Colonel Chikaraishi (Ryu Kohata) of the Japanese army. In order to put a stop to all the madness, Chen dons a mask and goes after those who are harming his people.

Even though the film has a few pacing issues, *Legend of the Fist* offers up plenty of brutal action from Donnie Yen (*Flashpoint*). Yen previously played the character of Chen Zhen in a TV series based on *Fist of Fury*. Bruce Lee (*Enter the Dragon*) originated the character and Yen goes to great lengths to honor Lee's legacy as well as put his own personal stamp on the character. The action scenes are spread throughout the film, and Yen takes on hundreds of attackers and obliterates them all. In most of the fights Yen is in his masked hero costume, which looks very much like the one Lee wore in *The Green Hornet*. There's some light wirework but nothing too over the top. The final battle is incredible with Yen finding himself in a one-versus-a-legion sort of situation where he really channels his inner Bruce Lee and just explodes. This film has some seriously memorable sequences and is directed by the great Andrew Lau (*The Storm Riders*).

Legionnaire
1998 (Sterling DVD) (djm)

Richly produced with a healthy budget, *Legionnaire* was the first movie Jean-Claude Van Damme starred in that ended up going directly to video in the US. It takes place in the 1920s, and he plays Alain, a champion boxer in France who refuses to take a dive on a fixed fight. After he defies the gangsters who fixed the fight, he flees for his life and joins the French Foreign Legion. Whisked off to Morocco, he is thrust into a vigorous and brutal training program along with sixty other soldiers,

Jean-Claude Van Damme stars as a boxer forced to become a Legionnaire. Author's collection.

Legionnaire is one of Jean-Claude Van Damme's most underrated pictures. He plays a boxer named Alain Lefevre in the 1920s. Author's collection.

and he makes friends with a few of the men who have equally compelling stories about how they landed in the Legion. His battalion is sent (on foot!) to a remote outpost in the desert to revenge a squad of soldiers who were tortured and killed by a native Arabian clan who resent the presence of the French occupation. Faced with an impending attack by the natives, the Legionnaires must learn to get along with each other, face their fears, and become the soldiers they signed up to be. When Alain is ultimately the last soldier standing after the bloody siege, he is saluted by the Arabs for being brave. The film ends on an unresolved note.

Legionnaire is really good, which is surprising considering that it was dumped to video. I understand why it wasn't distributed in theaters in the US, but it's a shame that more of Van Damme's fans haven't seen it or dismiss it. He's quite good in a dramatic role that doesn't require him to use martial arts at all. It's a physical role, but there's no high-flying heroics here. This is done on a grand, epic scale, in the old-fashioned style, with a sumptuous score by John Altman and great cinematography by Doug Milsome. Director Peter MacDonald also directed *Rambo III*, and the screenplay by Sheldon Lettich (*Double Impact*) and Rebecca Morrison is compelling and informative. This is one of Van Damme's most underrated films. Van Damme also played a Legionnaire in *Lionheart*.

Lessons for an Assassin

2001 (Smooth Pictures DVD) (djm)

Shannon Lee, the daughter of Bruce Lee, graces the video box art for *Lessons for an Assassin*, and you'd think you'd be getting a full-blown vehicle for her with it, but you'd be mostly mistaken. She plays a henchwoman to a covert government goon (played by Michael Dorn from *Mach 2* with Brian Bosworth), who recruits and trains criminals to be secret agents and assassins. Their latest project is a piece of work named Gavin Matthews (Robert Vitelli with dyed blond hair and goatee). Matthews learns martial arts and survival skills from Fiona (Lee), who takes a shine to him when he turns out to have more potential than any of the other recruits, and gradually, they grow attracted to each other, despite the rules. Matthews (who is purported to have an exceptionally high IQ) learns that the agency that has recruited him is actually an evil organization, and when he tries to convince Fiona, she at first doesn't believe him, but when her boss tries to kill her, she joins Matthews in bringing the curtain down. Finally, we get to see Shannon Lee get in on the action.

Shot on a shoestring budget, *Lessons for an Assassin* has potential, but the focus should be on Lee's character rather than the other guy. The story would have been more fascinating if we'd seen the story through her eyes, and watched her build up to a big realization and then explode with fury. Seeing Bruce Lee's daughter in action has some novelty to it, but her previous vehicle *And Now You're Dead* (shot in Hong Kong) was better. Directed by Ines Glenn and James Dudelson.

Lethal

2005 (Image DVD) (CD)

Samantha Stewart (Heather Marie Marsden) is an FBI dropout who now does odd jobs for Kordell (John Colton), a friend of her late father's. These jobs are of the dangerous type, involving shady individuals and lots of firearms. After her father's passing, she is left to care for her teenage sister Heather (Jennifer MacIsaac), who doesn't seem to care about anything but boys. Samantha accompanies Kordell on a side job in which she learns the location of a top-secret package everyone wants to get their hands on. Kordell is taken by Russian mobster Federov (Lorenzo Lamas of *Renegade* fame), and the only way she can get him back is by teaming up with FBI agent Ethan Marshall (Frank Zagarino from *Striker*). Marshall isn't keen on the idea but goes along with it. Samantha isn't prepared for what she's in for when her sister is kidnapped by Federov and she finds herself doing his bidding in order to get her sister back.

With "B" action guys Lamas and Zagarino in notable roles, there is a certain level of expectation going in that just isn't delivered. Heather Marie Marsden (*House Under Siege*) is cast in the lead as the heroine, which is fine, but let's be honest and say that all we really want to see is Lamas and Zagarino fight each other at some point, but it never happens. On the action front, however, there's plenty to go around. Both Lamas and Zagarino have entertaining fight scenes with Marsden and the gunfire is almost endless. Lamas, as the villain, steals the show; he's obviously having a blast (even if his Russian accent is a little off). Some of the fight scenes were obviously sped up but the choreography is tight and the shootouts are as stylish as they can be on a limited budget. The script gets bogged down with backstory and hokum, but the movie knows what it is and manages to be an entertaining slice of action meringue.

Lethal Justice (a.k.a. True Justice: Lethal Justice)

2010 (Studio Canal DVD R2) (djm)

The fourth DVD release from Steven Seagal's *True Justice* TV series, *Lethal Justice* follows Elijah Kane (Seagal) and his crew of undercover cops in Seattle as they deal with several subplots. An Aryan brotherhood has targeted an African American politico and makes an attempt on his life (and just about succeeds with a car bomb), making way for one of their own members to run for office. Kane puts one of his guys undercover with the brotherhood to ferret out if they are responsible for the attempted assassination, while a female member of his team targets a serial sex offender in the neighborhood. Once those plotlines are more or less evened out, a third one presents itself when men are being shot dead by a sniper, and as Kane suspects one of his former

soldiers from his days as a special ops leader in the Middle East, there is a race to find the killer before more men are shot down in the streets.

Lethal Justice manages to be a fairly cohesive compilation from the *True Justice* show, whereas many of the other film collections from the program are choppy and confusing. Seagal is good in it (and consistent, which is important), and his team treats him like a surrogate father at times. Followed by *Death Riders*. Directed by Wayne Rose (*Blood Alley*, another *True Justice* collection).

Lethal Weapon 4

1998 (Warner DVD) (djm)

"Why do you always gotta make shit complicated?

The last entry in Richard Donner's beloved *Lethal Weapon* series is most notable for introducing Asian superstar Jet Li to the Western world. Longtime buddy cops Riggs (Mel Gibson) and Murtaugh (Danny Glover) are coasting through their jobs as semi-celebrities in their department when they break a case involving human trafficking. Murtaugh takes an entire Chinese family home with him even though it's entirely illegal (they're all undocumented aliens), and it jeopardizes his own family and household when a Chinese enforcer named Wah Sing Ku (Jet Li in a star-making performance) makes a house call, threatening the lives of his wife, kids (one of whom is pregnant), and Riggs's girlfriend (also pregnant) Lorna (a returning Rene Russo). This is the breaking point for Riggs, who makes it a personal vendetta to bring down the Chinese Triad gang before they're able to complete a major transaction that could put Los Angeles in a sorry state if even more gangs began operating in earnest.

With at least two too many faces on the movie poster than it should have, *Lethal 4* is easily the most bloated film in the series, with padding to accommodate unnecessary characters like Leo Getz (Joe Pesci, who was great in the second film, but overstayed his welcome by the third one) and Detective Butters (Chris Rock, in a garish supporting role as Murtaugh's son-in-law). Even more burdensome is having Riggs and Murtaugh worry about old age together while preparing to welcome new additions to their families. *Lethal 4* is carrying so much weight that it barely has time to consider the heart and soul that made the first (classic) film so vibrant, but it sparks to life when Jet Li comes on the screen to beat the two heroes to a pulp. And that's another thing: When Riggs confronts Li and other martial artists in the film, he completely forgets that he knows martial arts, too. Remember that fight scene he had with Gary Busey in the rain in the first film? Why doesn't he pull some of that mojo out to fight Li in this film? He's a straight-up brawler (which is not enough to overcome his opponents here) this time around, which is just bizarre. All said, *Lethal 4* is entertaining on a very superficial level, and if you have any real love for the first film (or for Part 2, which is pretty fantastic), then this one should feel more than a little inadequate. Jet Li's career as an international crossover action star skyrocketed after this. Thankfully, there weren't any more *Lethal Weapons*, otherwise, there'd be three or four more faces on the posters each time. If you pay attention you'll notice some Asian action guys in *Lethal 4*. Watch for: James Lew, Simon Rhee, Conan Lee, and Philip Tan, amongst others.

Liberator
2012 (Amazon VOD) (CD)

"I mattered once. Eagle across your chest, you know. That stands for something."

Ed Migliocetti (Lou Ferrigno) is just an ordinary guy trying to make a living and hoping to grow a connection to his adult daughter. He's having trouble adjusting to an average life since he spent his professional career as The Liberator, a superhero on a team of superheroes who worked for the government. An incident happened (we're never told exactly what) and Ed was the fall guy while the others continued their work. He writes a tell-all book exposing the truth behind his disgrace and proving his innocence. The government is ready to put an end to him, but he isn't going down without a fight.

There's some great stuff in this eighteen-minute short film, but the fact that there's only eighteen minutes is also its downfall. It's a gritty, adult-oriented, superhero story that tackles the aging superhero idea. Lou Ferrigno (*The Incredible Hulk*) may have found the role of his career. This is a pilot for a proposed web series and whether or not it continues remains to be seen. Director Aaron Pope sets up a great story and delivers one killer action scene with Ferrigno skillfully and stylishly dropping a dozen or so soldiers. It's an exciting moment, but knowing it's a short that delivers only a tiny portion of a much larger story may keep some viewers away. Also appearing in a tiny (non-action) role is Don "The Dragon" Wilson. Ferrigno, well into his sixties, is still very much a significant performer, and he proves here that he's a star no one should ever forget.

Liberty and Bash
1989 (Fries Hone Video VHS) (djm)

Three buddies from their soldiering days have all adapted to different walks of life. Liberty (Miles O'Keeffe) is a straight-arrow cop. Bash (Lou Ferrigno) is a fitness guru and the leader of a group of street vigilantes, and Jesse, well, he gets himself killed by drug dealers. Liberty and Bash team up for the first time in ages to find out who killed Jesse and why. The bodies pile up!

Fairly straightforward for a direct-to-video effort with just the minimum amount of action to keep viewers watching, *Liberty and Bash* needs

a lot more Ferrigno, I'll tell you that. Ferrigno gets just enough screen time to put his face alongside O'Keeffe's on the video box, but he's only given a few scenes to show off his brawn. He spends some time yelling at guys to work harder at the gym, but when he gets involved in a street brawl, I got real interested real quick. This is O'Keeffe's movie all the way, and it's a shame I'm not covering all of his movies because I like him. In someone else's book about action stars, I implore you to cover everything he did. This was directed by Myrl A. Schreibman.

Lionheart (a.k.a. **A.W.O.L.**)
1990 (Universal DVD) (djm)

"Wrong bet!"

Legionnaire Leon Gaultier (Jean-Claude Van Damme) deserts his post in Africa to try to make it to Los Angeles before his brother dies from wounds inflicted in a drug deal gone bad. Leon hops on the first ship he sees and as a stowaway he's forced to work hard labor. He eventually jumps ship, lands in New York, and without a penny to his name or a green card, he stumbles into the underground fight circuit, where he immediately causes a sensation with his martial arts abilities. He picks up a scoundrel of a manager—a been-there-done-that guy named Joshua (Harrison Page)—who introduces him to the big leagues of the fight circuit. There he meets a vixen named Cynthia, who stages high-stakes fights, but before he can get to work for her, he goes to Los Angeles with the little money he's earned, and he tries being a good Samaritan to his sister-in-law and his niece. When Cynthia comes down to LA, she begins putting Leon to work, fighting bigger and badder opponents, until he faces the undefeated champion of the circuit: Attila (Abdel Qissi from *The Quest*).

Legionnaire Leon (Jean-Claude Van Damme) goes AWOL to find his brother's killer in New York City in *Lionheart*. Author's collection.

A water fight in *Lionheart*, featuring Jean-Claude Van Damme and Paco Christian Prieto. Author's collection.

Life or death: a fight in *Lionheart*. Author's collection.

This was the movie that got me into Van Damme. It's bigger and slicker than *Bloodsport* and *Kickboxer*, and it gives Van Damme more room for dramatics. Director Sheldon Lettich manages to evoke a sense of scope and fills the screen with a solid supporting cast and fighters who are well matched against his star. Harrison Page is great as a genuine sidekick, and there're plenty of moments where he's stealing the scenes away from Van Damme. John Scott's big, orchestral score gives the film a wonderful texture, and without it the movie might just be a run-of-the-mill tournament film. One of Van Damme's very best films, *Lionheart* was co-financed by Imperial Entertainment, and one of the producers was Eric Carson (also in the film as a doctor), who helped make Oliver Gruner a star with *Angel Town*. Also starring Michel Qissi, Brian Thompson, Billy Blanks, Paco Christian Prieto (from *Only the Strong*), and Deborah Rennard. If you look closely, you can spot future action star Jeff Speakman (*The Perfect Weapon*)

L

The big mojo Attila (Abdel Qissi) and Leon (Jean-Claude Van Damme) in the climactic fight in *Lionheart*. Author's collection.

at the very end of the film. The Universal DVD release is full screen, but the Italian DVD release is widescreen.

INTERVIEW:
SHELDON LETTICH
(djm)

A filmmaker who has worked with some of the greatest action stars of all time, Sheldon Lettich is (partly) responsible for Bloodsport *(1988),* Rambo III *(1988),* Lionheart *(1990), and* Only the Strong *(1993), all featuring larger-than-life action heroes. Lettich has had a very successful career in action and martial arts cinema, and though he's no longer making "A" Hollywood blockbusters, he's found a niche in the direct-to-video niche market, where stars like Jean-Claude Van Damme and Dolph Lundgren continue to thrive.*

Sheldon, you've done some great action movies, and you've worked with the best of them: Jean-Claude Van Damme, Dolph Lundgren, Daniel Bernhardt, Sylvester Stallone, and Mark Dacascos. What compels you to keep returning to the action and martial arts genre?

Well, it's actually a very simple explanation. It's a field that I just happened to fall into many years ago. These are the kinds of things that people get pigeonholed in. It's not that this is specifically what I wanted to do, but I wrote a few action films that became very popular, so I pretty much got pigeonholed as an action movie guy. That's why I've been doing those.

Sheldon Lettich in Los Angeles, California. Photo by david j. moore.

You got started with *Bloodsport*, which made a big splash, and to this day it's a hit. Sam Firstenberg told me that he turned it down because he was confident that it wouldn't be a success and how much he's regretted that decision.

Menahem Golan thought the same thing. He thought that it would be a complete flop. He wanted to go straight to video with it. I had a big argument with Menahem about that because I had actually gone to see him about another film, another script that I had written. You know who Leon Isaac Kennedy is?

Of course! I interviewed him.

Oh, well, Leon and I were working on some things back then. He had done *Penitentiary 3* with Menahem, and Menahem wanted to do another movie with him, another action movie. Leon and I had written a script called *Striker's Force*, which Leon wanted to be a sequel to *Lone Wolf McQuade*. It was turning out really good, so we decided to just make it a stand-alone. Leon was wondering who he could co-star with in it. *Lone Wolf* was Leon with Chuck Norris and David Carradine. I had just met Jean-Claude right around the same period of time. I introduced Jean-Claude to Leon, and Leon really liked him and thought he had a lot of potential. He also knew that Jean-Claude had a three-picture deal with Cannon. Leon and I go into meet with Menahem, and there was a short film I had made called *Firefight*, which got me my first directing deals, and it was going to be with Cannon Films. Menahem wanted me to direct a film for Cannon, and Leon had proposed making *Striker's Force* that film. He submitted the script, and they liked it, and we go in to meet with Menahem and we said, "How about getting Jean-Claude to be the co-lead in the movie?" This was before *Bloodsport* had opened. Menahem said, "Um . . . I like the script, and I like the rest of the package, but I don't like Van Damme. I saw *Bloodsport*, it's a terrible movie. He's a joke. He's never going to make it. He's just going to lose me money. I think you should put a real movie star in this movie. And that real movie star is Michael Dudikoff." So anyway, we argued with him for about two hours. I told him that *Bloodsport* was going to do better than *Missing in Action 3*, and that was their big "tentpole" for that summer. Menahem's reply to me was, "You're dreaming, my friend!" (Laughing.) Cut to the chase, *Bloodsport* did make more than *Missing in Action 3*! And Menahem changed his tune after that. Meanwhile, we couldn't get the movie made with Jean-Claude, and then the script was submitted to Michael Dudikoff, but Michael didn't like it! It had a number of elements . . . we had some white supremacy things, we had some things go on between Leon and whoever his white co-star was going to be. Michael thought it was too controversial. We almost got it made a few other times, with other people, but that's one of those that never got off the ground.

So what happened after *Bloodsport* and the big success it created for you, Cannon, and Van Damme? *Lionheart* and *Rambo III* happened shortly thereafter.

Rambo III I wrote before *Bloodsport* came out. I was hired to write it a couple of years before *Bloodsport* was released. I was already writing action projects beforehand. We finally got *Bloodsport* released, and it just surprised the hell out of everybody. Jean-Claude was having trouble getting arrested, although he did get cast in *Black Eagle*. He was basically playing the villain to Sho Kosugi. What's interesting is that when he got the offer to do that, he went to Menahem—and I actually went with him—and he told Menahem, "Look, I'm being offered this other movie called *Black Eagle*, but I have a three-picture deal with you. So I want to ask you permission before I take it." Menahem told him, "Go ahead and do it! Don't call us, we'll call you!" He was really not interested in Jean-Claude at all. He thought he was just terrible in *Bloodsport*. We had become pretty good friends during the production of *Bloodsport*. Jean-Claude and Frank Dux called me from Hong Kong, and they were having some problems with the producer, who was making a lot of changes with the script. He was ripping pages out, so they called me to commiserate. We ended up talking quite a bit, and so when Jean-Claude came back to LA, one of the first things he did was come by my apartment, and we just hit it off right off the bat. We planned to do some other things. Here's a little piece of hidden Hollywood history: I was very good friends with Sam Raimi and Rob Tapert and Bruce Campbell, those Detroit guys for many, many years. I introduced Jean-Claude to Sam Raimi, and Sam really liked him. Sam thought he had a lot of potential. When they had the first screening of *Bloodsport* on Hollywood Boulevard, we all went to the Warner Hollywood Theater, and Jean-Claude was signing *Bloodsport* posters. Sam was there and Frank Dux. Then we all went over to my apartment and had a party there. Jean-Claude had written a rough outline for a project about a science-fiction story called *Atlas*. It was like Spartacus in the future. Sam really liked the idea. Sam was working with Dino De Laurentis at the time. Dino had a company that made *Evil Dead 2*. It was called DEG. They liked this project that we brought them. They liked my film, so they accepted me as the director, and they liked Jean-Claude, and they liked Sam's endorsement of Jean-Claude. I brought another player into the mix called Chuck Pfarrer, and Chuck ended up writing *Darkman* and *Hard Target*. Chuck and I had the same agent, and I had met him via my agent. Chuck had been a Navy SEAL and I had been in the Marine Corps, so we hit it off. I introduced him to Sam and Jean-Claude and the guys. Anyway, we all liked the idea of *Atlas*, and Chuck and I were hired to write the screenplay, which we did. Jean-Claude was going to star. Sam and Robert were going to produce. We were already starting to talk about special effects and art direction and things like that, and then DEG ran into a financial crisis. Suddenly, they didn't have the money to make a slate of movies. It all petered out. Sam has tried to revive the project a few times, but it just never ended up happening. Interesting little digression: I was in this shop getting a poster of *Rambo III* framed. This guy comes in there, and he sees the poster, and he goes, "Oh, did you work on that?" When he realized that I co-wrote it, he said, "Hey,

Leon (Jean-Claude Van Damme) becomes a street fighter in *Lionheart*. Author's collection.

One of many fights that Leon (Jean Claude Van Damme) wins in *Lionheart*. Author's collection.

A fight to the finish in *Only the Strong*, featuring Paco Christian Prieto (left) and Mark Dacascos (right). Author's collection.

I'm having a party tonight. You want to come to it?" So I invited a bunch of friends—Sam Raimi, Boaz Yakin, and some others, and I met Quentin Tarantino there. Quentin was working at Imperial Entertainment, which produced *Lionheart*. He was working there doing sales to video stores all across the country. Quentin would call the mom-and-pop stores and try to sell movies from Imperial Entertainment. When I first met him, the first thing he said was, "Hey, uh, you co-wrote one of my favorite movies! *Thou Shalt Not Kill . . . Except!*" That was one that I made with these Detroit guys. That's how I ended up introducing Quentin to Scott Spiegel. Scotty had just made a low-budget horror movie called *Intruder*.

Let's move towards your film *Only the Strong*. I love Mark Dacascos. He's awesome. Talk about working with Mark versus working with Jean-Claude.

Well, I've got some interesting stories about Mark. Mark had been introduced to me by his manager. I liked him, but I didn't know what to do with him. I'd looked at something he did called *American Samurai*. An opportunity was presented to me to make a martial arts movie about Capoeira. We had this story called *Only the Strong*, but it did not involve Capoeira, and it took place in New York City. The producer specifically wanted to make a Capoeira movie. The writer and I reworked it to take place in Miami and it would have Capoeira in it. Then we needed a star. I thought that Mark would be the perfect guy for this. The producers were very

hesitant because he'd never starred in anything. They had other people they were trying to put in it like Sasha Mitchell. I stuck to my guns and said, "Mark's the guy." We shot a screen test in 35mm with Mark, and we finally got him into the movie. I guess one difference between Mark and Jean-Claude is that I fought for Mark to be in *Only the Strong*, and with Jean-Claude, it was the opposite because Jean-Claude fought for me to direct *Lionheart*. He had made a deal when he made *Black Eagle*, and the producers had liked him, and wanted to do another movie with him. He had pitched them this idea called *Wrong Bet*, which is what *Lionheart* ended up being called. Jean-Claude had seen my short film, and saw how I was introducing him to all these people like Sam Raimi and how I was trying to help him be a star. I really believed in Jean-Claude. After I met Mark, I just had faith that this guy could make it as an action star. Jean-Claude brought me to the producers of *Lionheart*. He got me my first directing job.

That actually leads me to my question. Since you've worked with all these actions guys—even Dolph Lundgren—what makes an action star special? I can see it when I see it, but you see these guys before they're in their hit movies.

A larger-than-life quality. A heroic quality. There's something about them that makes them shine. They cast a glow when they enter the room, and they cast an even bigger glow when you see them on film. When you see Jean-Claude in a scene with other people, your eye goes to Jean-Claude. Unless he's in a scene with someone who's equally stellar, your eye automatically goes to him. It's something that Sam Raimi noticed. When we'd go out to dinner, people would be looking at him. He'd be in a group, all eyes—especially women—would be looking at Jean-Claude. There was something about him that radiated stardom. It's kind of hard to quantitatively put my finger to, but it's something that Jean-Claude had in spades. I saw that in Mark. When I met Dolph, he was already a star. A few years ago, I met Scott Adkins, and I'd seen him in an Isaac Florentine movie. Isaac really discovered this guy. The most impressive thing about the movie I saw—*Special Forces*—was this British guy, Scott Adkins. Then I met him in Belgium. I told him, "I'm in Brussels, do you want to come and visit for a day?" He took the Euro Star over and we hung out for a day. I could see that he had some of those star qualities. In every case, people will disagree with me. I was pushing Scott Adkins a few years ago, and we almost had a few projects set up. I had some projects I wanted Scott to be in. Scott read the scripts, wanted to work with me, but then the producers wouldn't be able to put the projects together because nobody knows who Scott was. He eventually did get his breaks, and I think he's on his way now. It was tough with Scott, just like it was tough with Jean-Claude and Mark Dacascos.

What about Daniel Bernhardt?

Daniel I met through a producer who was trying to get a movie going. I liked Daniel a lot. We really hit it off. They specifically wanted to do a movie with me and Daniel. This producer had a script that was so far off the mark from what that movie turned into, but it was something that was very inexpensive to acquire. We ended up with something that we thought was sellable to shoot in Mexico. Daniel and I got along great while we were making the movie. We tried to do a number of things afterwards. He got me involved in a possible *Bloodsport* sequel. They didn't want it to be a continuation of the *Bloodsport* sequels that Daniel had made, they wanted to reinvent it. They were going to call it *Bloodsport: A New*

While AWOL from the Foreign Legion, Leon (Jean-Claude Van Damme) works in the belly of a ship, shoveling coal in *Lionheart*. Author's collection.

Director Sheldon Lettich on the set of *Only the Strong*. Author's collection.

Beginning. Daniel was going to star in it, and he was going to direct it also, which I was fine with. We ended up writing a script, but the financier decided that he didn't want to make it unless it would open theatrically. I told them, "Quite honestly, you're not going to open this theatrically. You're going to have a hard time with that unless you've got Van Damme in it." This was a few years back when Van Damme was still in his forties. Even so, the way we wrote the script, it would have been very suitable for him. So he said, "Well, let's get Van Damme!" I said, "I don't think Van Damme really wants to do a *Bloodsport* sequel because all these sequels had been made already. Then by a crazy coincidence, I'm in Santa Monica meeting with the financier, and Jean-Claude calls me on his cell phone and *he's* in Santa Monica. So I told him, "Hey, I've been working on this *Bloodsport* sequel. The producer would love to have you in it, but I told him that you wouldn't be interested because there's already been three of them made." He said, "I would *love* to be in a *Bloodsport* sequel! Can I meet you guys?" So I arranged the meeting, and it took off and it looked like it was going to happen. They actually had a contract and everything. The only issue became that Jean-Claude did not want Daniel directing the movie if he was going to be in it. So he suggested that I direct it. This led to some conflict with Daniel because Daniel thought that I'd sold him out. Anyway, at the end of the day, it spun out of control and it didn't happen. That financier is still trying to get a sequel to *Bloodsport* made. He hooked up with Ed Pressman, who produced *Legionnaire,* and they hired Robert Mark Kamen to write the script. Apparently, they've got a pretty well-known director attached. The story is going to take place in Brazil and is going to feature mixed martial arts.

You brought up *Legionnaire,* which I loved. This came out during the decline of these "A"-list action stars like Van Damme and Seagal when they started to do movies that went directly to video. That's always interested me. It scared me when it started happening. What do you think happened during that period of time when even Stallone's movies weren't going to theaters?

The studios started taking a different tack during that time. When *Speed* came out, I had directed *Only the Strong* for Fox. They were pretty happy with the way the film turned out, but they were the studio that had put *Speed* together. They were looking for a director. They sent me the script, I read it, I really liked it, and I had a discussion with them about it. I asked them who would be playing the lead. They told me Keanu Reeves. Well, I was taken aback because he was the guy who co-starred in *Bill and Ted's Excellent Adventure.* I just didn't see him as this LA cop. What they were doing was different than what they'd done earlier, which is to take a guy like Van Damme and Seagal, who are established martial artists, or guys like Schwarzenegger, who's a world-famous body builder, guys who had the physical chops already, and teaching them to do some acting to do these movies. But they decided instead to get some actors—people who are established and proven as actors—and

let's teach them how to do a little bit of this action stuff—and we'll get stunt doubles to fill in for them for the stuff that they can't do, and let's see if that formula is going to work. You can't deny that the formula was working because *Speed* did really well. Guys like Ben Affleck and Matt Damon, and Keanu Reeves and Mark Wahlberg would do these action movies and stunt doubles would do the hard stuff. In the middle, there would be car chases and stuff like that. Whereas Van Damme and Seagal and Schwarzenegger would "wow" us with their physicality, and so would Stallone. It was just a different tactic the studios were trying. There does seem to be a certain nostalgia now for guys like Dolph and Chuck Norris. They started getting away from people like that and going towards actors.

You've worked in both stratums—you've done "A" list theatrical features, and you've done dome direct-to-video "B" movies. I know these guys you've worked with have egos, but have you noticed that they're wounded at all when you find that you're working with them on direct-to-video movies?

Absolutely. All of them felt wounded by that. I think that's one of the reasons why Seagal got so grossly out of shape. It's probably one of the reasons why Wesley Snipes started having substance-abuse problems. Because they were "A" list stars in studio films, and suddenly they're being relegated to the straight-to-DVD world. Even Stallone. Who would have ever thought that Stallone would be doing straight-to-DVD movies like *Avenging Angelo*? Stallone has pulled himself back from the brink, of course. But, for a while there, he was in straight-to-DVD world. Same with Van Damme, Seagal, and Snipes. Dolph. Dolph was making films theatrically once.

When you're preparing a movie with say, Van Damme, doing something like *The Hard Corps*—which is another great movie . . .

Thank you! I really like that movie.

It's great. It came at the right time for him. There was a period there when his first few direct-to-video movies after *Legionnaire* like *Desert Heat* were terrible. I was getting really despondent, but then all of a sudden he was making good movies again like *Second in Command* and *The Hard Corps.* He's been making the best movies of his career. He not only looks great, but he's trying hard. He's going for it.

Right, right.

So when you're preparing these movies like *The Hard Corps* or *The Order,* what kind of discussions do you guys have? Is there full disclosure that these movies will be going directly to video all over the world, or what?

No, no. Generally, whether or not the producers are lying to themselves or not, the intention generally is to try to go theatrical. I think some of the stuff that Jean-Claude has been doing in the last few years . . . well, the producers always tell him, "Oh, it's going theatrical," even if they

Behind the scenes shot with Jean-Claude Van Damme (center) and Sheldon Lettich (right) on the set of *The Order.* Courtesy of Sheldon Lettich.

know it's going to be tough to do. *JCVD* ended up opening theatrically. But then when a movie like that opens and doesn't do well, it proves the bean counters correct because the bean counters are saying, "Van Damme is not going to be able to open a movie theatrically. When that comes true, it's harder for Jean-Claude to go theatrical unless he puts some extraordinary effort to make sure it goes theatrical. It's hard to do.

I understand. I thought something like *The Hard Corps,* which had a cross-cultural urban sensibility, would do something at the box office if money was spent on advertising it.

Here's what happened with that: The intention was to go theatrical with it, but it's all about cast. The producer told us that we were going to get Cuba Gooding Jr. to play the boxer. Now, with Van Damme, Cuba Gooding, and Vivica Fox, I think that was a pretty good package there that could have gone theatrical. Then, we also interviewed DMX, who wanted to play the villain. That would have made a *really* strong package. Then we had problems with that. The producer had also worked with Wesley Snipes, and I was saying to them, why don't we get Wesley in this with Van Damme. He would have been perfect to play the boxer. The answer I got was that Van Damme was going to cost three million. Wesley's going to cost at least three million. There's six million dollars right there. We were playing to the same audience. People who come see Van Damme movies will also come see Wesley Snipes movies. I was told that you don't get more people just because you have two big stars in it. I think he was dead wrong about that. Look what happened with *The Expendables.* With Stallone, Schwarzenegger, and Bruce Willis, you could say that the same crowd is going to see their movies, but you're not going to get any extra people. Well, wrong about that. That movie did great. If we would've had Wesley or Cuba . . . but the producer said that we wouldn't be able to get Cuba because he'd want too much money, too. The numbers were off. We ended up getting a really good actor, who's British, actually, but nobody in the world knew who the hell he was. They didn't even put his face on the poster because he didn't bring anything box-office wise. That hurt that film. With DMX, he wanted to be in the movie—he actually flew into LA to meet with me, and everything was ready to be drawn up into a contract, and the next day I get a call from his attorney, who says, "Oh, by the way: We forgot to mention something. DMX has to start a prison sentence like two weeks after you're to start shooting, but it's no problem! You can just start shooting his scenes in those two weeks and he goes and does his prison sentence." We were all saying, *What the fuck?!* Well, what if we don't start exactly on that start date? What if we're a week behind? Or what if we go over, or what if we need to shoot more scenes? He's in prison for sixty days! What if he starts a fight or gets in a fight in prison and his sentence gets extended? We're totally screwed! The bond company said forget about it: You're not getting DMX. We had a good cast. You know a movie does well when you get residuals, and I'm still getting residuals from that movie. That movie has not stopped playing since they had a TV debut of it. It's always playing somewhere, and I'm getting money from it, more so than some of these other movies I've done. If we would have had one more good element in the cast, then I think we wouldn't have had a problem taking a chance with it with a Screen Gems release. It did amazingly well on DVD. I got a photo at my local Blockbuster where they had a whole wall of nothing but that movie. It was an interesting combination of Jean-Claude and Vivica Fox. People wanted to see that. If we'd had Wesley Snipes or Cuba Gooding, it would have been a huge hit.

I know that *Legionnaire* was intended to go to theaters too, right?

Yeah. It was a twenty million dollar movie. Basically, Peter MacDonald, the director, screwed up something very, very crucial to the film working as a movie. He totally messed up the ending of that film. It was supposed to have an action ending where Jean-Claude and the British guy survive the attack on the fortress, and they go back to rescue the girl and the girl gets rescued in a blazing shootout. It was going to be an action finale, which is what you're supposed to have with a movie like that. Peter MacDonald disagreed, and he wanted it to . . . I don't know what he wanted. He's also a guy who didn't necessarily want to make action movies. Politically, he's very far left, very ultra liberal, and here he is directing *Rambo III*, which he basically directed by getting the original director thrown off the project. He undermined the director, who was Russell Mulcahy, who's done a bunch of great stuff.

To escape the law, Alain Lefevre (Jean-Claude Van Damme) joins the French Foreign Legion in *Legionnaire*. Author's collection.

I heard that Stallone kicked Mulcahy off.

That's because Peter undermined him. Peter was on the movie as the second unit director. Anyway, it was all engineered by Peter MacDonald. That's why Mulcahy got kicked off. Peter didn't want to make these war-like revenge films. So here was his chance to upend what should have been an action ending on *Legionnaire*, which was an action movie. He wanted to make a statement and have a nonviolent ending. His nonviolent ending—which was ridiculous—is that Van Damme goes back to the bar, which is owned by the gangster, walks in, holds out his hand to the girl, and the girl's hand is in front of the gangster, he walks out with her. That was just fucking ludicrous! He had his way. That's the ending they shot. When people saw that ending, they said, *What the fuck is this?* It made no sense at all. They ended up having to recut the ending, and you've seen the ending—it's hard to figure out what it's all about. That really hurt the movie. The studios that were seeing the film, who were interested in releasing it theatrically, were all baffled by the ending. They even said, "Shoot another ending that makes more sense for this movie, and we'll consider it." The budget—twenty million dollars—had already been spent and allocated. There was no more money to spend. Without shooting a new ending—and they certainly couldn't use the ending that Peter had shot—because that was even more infuriating than the ending that was on there—so the only alternative they had was to go straight to DVD.

Wow. I noticed that you were the only one who did a commentary for the DVD, not MacDonald.

Yeah, he wasn't interested because he didn't give a fuck about the movie. For him, it was really . . . he's a second unit director and a cinematographer. He's very good at what he does. But he didn't have any passion for the project. I didn't know what his trip was. All I knew is that he didn't want to participate with the commentary. I was willing. I came up with the idea and wrote the initial screenplay and everything. I was happy to do a commentary. I knew a lot about the French Foreign Legion. I spent a lot of time researching it. I worked on the script over a period of a year. I went to France, went to Morocco, went to the headquarters of the French Foreign Legion. It's a very accurate film. I was involved in picking the costumes, picking the weapons, designing the fort, all of this stuff. There's a great deal of authenticity to it. It's a good movie overall.

Why didn't you direct it?

Peter did the same thing to me that he did to Russell Mulcahy. I was supposed to direct it. Peter kept undermining my decisions so that he would ultimately direct the movie. There you go.

Little Bear and the Master

2008 (Seminal Films DVD)

(djm)

The Ute Reservation in Colorado is an idyllic place for the last Ute American Indians to try to rebuild their culture and nurture their customs. But there's a problem: Poachers are slaughtering the few remaining black bears that are left on the reservation for their gall bladders, which are fetching exorbitant prices on the black market. One young lad named John "Little Bear" (Cameron Keluchie) takes it upon himself to scour the wilderness and seek out the poachers who are damaging the ecosystem. When he comes upon a team of poachers, he's overwhelmed by the possibility of being shot and killed, but a mysterious Asian man, who comes out of nowhere and fights off the poachers with his taekwondo skills, saves him the trouble of putting his neck on the line. The Asian man—a Korean named Lee (played by Julian Lee from *My Samurai*)—is living illegally on the reservation as a vagrant, and Little Bear is intrigued by him and befriends him. As it turns out, Lee recently killed a man in self-defense and wanders the Earth in penance, and now that he's stumbled on a purpose to help Little Bear protect his land, he stays on as a helper and a friend. When the small-crime organization gets wind of Lee and Little Bear cutting off their supply of bear gall bladders, they call in a specialist to handle the problem. When the heavy hitter (played by Frank Zagarino from *Striker*) comes to town to take care of Lee, he's just as surprised as everyone else is when Lee proves that he's got what it takes to fight off a bully of any size.

Little Bear and the Master is a sweet and genteel family film that won't be to most people's tastes. It's got a "G" or "PG" rating feel to it, and even though it has a few kickass fight scenes featuring Julian Lee, and then later with Zagarino, it still might put some viewers off by how it manages to avoid violence, profanity, and a rough tone. It's a nice film, and I really enjoyed it, but not necessarily because it aimed for a certain family demographic, per se, but because it gave Julian Lee a really solid vehicle. I like this guy. I liked him in the film *My Samurai*, too. He's one of those off-the-grid action guys (like Jino Kang, for example) who only makes a movie every handful of years, but when they make one it's got quality. I'd happily recommend *Little Bear and the Master* to anyone who is patient enough to invest ninety minutes into something that was made with care, concern, and a purpose to entertain the whole family. And if that's not enough, just wait until Frank Zagarino shows up in the finale. His scenes are worth waiting the whole film for. Written and directed by Fred Dresch.

Live by the Fist

1992 (New Concord DVD) (djm)

> "The name of the game . . . is survival."

Former real-life kickboxing champ Jerry Trimble made a handful of movies for Roger Corman and Cirio Santiago in the 1990s, and *Live by the Fist*, at less than eighty minutes, is great fun. He plays a former Navy SEAL named John Merril looking for work in Asia, and in the first five minutes of the movie he gets into a fight with a group of thugs who are trying to rape an innocent woman. The thugs kill the woman and at the end of the fight, he's been knocked out and framed for the woman's murder. He's quickly put on trial and found guilty in the corrupt court, and his sentence is life imprisonment on an island somewhere in southeast Asia. Once there, he immediately gets into fights with guys who want to rape him, and the only person he gets along with is his cellmate, Uncle, played by George Takei, who is working on a plan to have their cases appealed by a human rights organization. Turns out that the prison is a hellhole run by a sadistic warden and guards who are known for torture and murder. Merril has his hands full trying to keep himself alive and fit enough to take on everyone who wants to kill him.

This movie doesn't waste a minute. Trimble looks like a real fighter, and his fighting style is photogenic. He takes plenty of hits, but he emerges heroic and able. The other films he did with Corman and Santiago are *Stranglehold* and *One Man Army*. He also did a few Chinese martial arts movies. He made *The Master* with Jet Li. *Bloodfist III: Force to Fight* with Don "The Dragon" Wilson tells the same story as *Live by the Fist*.

INTERVIEW:
JERRY TRIMBLE
(djm)

The heyday of the direct-to-video action era produced a slew of unique martial artists and champions who crossed over and made careers as action stars, and Jerry Trimble (nicknamed "Golden Boy" in the kickboxing world where he became the kickboxing champ of the world with a record of

Jerry "The Golden Boy" Trimble in Santa Monica, California. Photo by david j. moore.

thirty-six wins and only two losses) had a solid stint as a lead star in films produced by Roger Corman, amongst others. With films like The Master *(opposite Jet Li, 1989),* Full Contact *(1993),* Live by the Fist *(1993), and* One Man Army *(1994) on his resume, Trimble transitioned into stunt work and supporting roles in much bigger, blockbustery features, and continues to work in various capacities in motion pictures and television.*

How did you make a transition from your kickboxing career into action movies?

My first film was in 1990. It was right before I won the US title. I was signed with Jim Abernathy. He put the bug into my ear about sending me to Hollywood. He signed five world champions. His goal was to take us champions to Hollywood and get us into movies and into action movies. It was all about Chuck Norris at the time. Drugs got ahold of Jim. He was the Dana White of kickboxing. When that fell through, I decided to sell everything I owned and follow up on that. I moved to California in 1990, and within four months I found a manager, I started teaching at one of Chuck Norris's studios, and I was sent to my first few auditions, and I landed two lead roles. The first one was *The Master* with Jet Li, and the second one was *Breathing Fire* with Bolo Yeung. It took off from there. Martial arts—that was my hook. When I did *The Master* and *Breathing Fire*, I booked both roles in one week. They both started at the same time, so the two production companies were working together to schedule it so that I could do both movies. I'd do twelve hours on one, I'd go to the other one and do twelve hours. I did that three or four times and it got to the point where I told my manager that I didn't mind working on both films, but I wanted to know if there was anything we could do. He went to them after the third time I did that because it was taking a toll on me. They worked it out so that I didn't have to do that anymore.

What do you remember about Bolo?

Bolo was great because most of the time he was silent. And then he'd make a joke. When he'd make a joke—because he was so silent and menacing—it would make it that much funnier. It was so funny. He's still around, still kicking.

No one in the US really knew who Jet Li was when you made *The Master* with him. You play the role of the villain, and you're pretty imposing in it. You tower over him in the film. Also, your fighting style is different in that movie than in anything else you were in. Talk about making that film.

It was shot in LA. It was interesting. Tsui Hark was the director. As far as my style in the movie goes, I was working with the Hong Kong crew. These guys are balls out on everything they do. Tsui said, "Jerry, I want you to make your own method of kung fu, kind of your own tweak on a style, but keep your kicks the way that they are." It was more or less my own style. I come from a taekwondo background, and boxing. I sparred with different guys from all styles, so I kind of took a little from those guys, and I tweaked it for my own style when I did those fight scenes. The twirling of the hand motion? I didn't know what

the hell I was doing! (Laughing.) Working with Jet was interesting. We didn't really get to know each other. He couldn't speak a lick of English. Maybe a couple words here and there. It's funny because on the set, we had the crew placing bets on who would win in a real fight. They'd come up to me and go, "Hey, uh, Jerry, a fight between you and Jet . . . who do you think?" This went on the whole time. It was interesting because there were times where we would be doing the fight scenes, he'd tag me, and I'd be like, "Okay." He'd tag me again, and I'd be like, "Okay." So I'd hit a little bit harder on the body, and then we'd slip a couple times, and it was a little silent thing going on between us. But there was really no communication. From what I knew he was cool, everything was great. I got along great with the stunt crew. They were incredible.

How about some of the stuff on the high-rise building where you're hanging?

Those were my own stunts, I did all those. We were hanging from maybe twenty stories, I think. We were on wires. We were doing the fight scenes on wires. We were doing them hanging vertical, and then we would lie on a platform when we did the end scene where he swished and hit me and I fell down. We were doing that on a platform that was horizontal.

After or during the period when you did *The Master* and *Breathing Fire*, was it your intention to become an "action star?"

Yeah, that's what I wanted. When I got into the business, I realized I was lucky because I was a world champion. If I hadn't been a world champion, it would have been a hell of a lot harder. The fact that I was a world champion and that I could kick the way that I could kick . . . when I went on auditions and they would say, "Okay, let's see you do your stuff," and once I'd do my shadow boxing and kicking, that was it. After I did my first few films as the lead, then it got to the point where I wanted to get out of that. In the beginning I wanted to be an action star. A big action star. But the roles I was getting, the scripts . . . oh, wow. They were horrendous. I've come a million miles since then. I started getting into acting classes, then I started thinking that I could still do these action roles—the roles I'd been doing there with so much fighting—I wanted to do some action roles that had some depth to them, but they weren't coming. So then, I started putting the energy out there, and I believe whatever you put out there, you're gonna get back. *Heat* was the first step out of that genre. It was a rush to be on the set with Al Pacino, Robert DeNiro, and Val Kilmer. We did that action scene in downtown LA walking a block back and forth with Val Kilmer each time, just talking to him. I thought, "This is where I want to be. I could care less if I do another kick!" It was weird. But then when I did other films without fighting, then I kinda missed it. It would have been great to do both, but with a little bit of fighting. Things started changing. I didn't want to be an action star anymore, I wanted to be an actor. *Heat* wasn't a juicy role, but it was a role where I was able to step out of the genre. I just did an action movie last year called *The Package* with Steve Austin, and that was my first fight scene, first action movie in a long time. It felt *good*! It felt really good. It was cool. Everyone keeps saying, "You need to get in *Expendables 3*!" I'm like, "Yeah . . . " I wouldn't turn it down, I would be honored to be in it, but, you know?

It's interesting that *Heat* came to you when it did, because the vehicle martial arts movie was already dying at that point.

Exactly, yeah. It was perfect timing.

I'd like to know how you then became the leading star of films for Cirio Santiago. I mean, nobody knew what *The Master* was or that it even existed until Jet Li became a star many years later.

I was the bad guy for my first three films. *Breathing Fire* and *King of the Kickboxers* were the other ones. Then I got introduced to Cirio. Interesting guy, right there. When I got introduced to him, I had put a flier up for kickboxing classes. The picture was a vertical sidekick pose. Rick Jacobson called, and I went in for Roger Corman. I got the lead role in *Full Contact*. It was for New Horizons. Rick Jacobson did it. After that, that's when I got introduced to Cirio. I don't know how many movies I did with him. Four, five?

Several.

Yeah, and Cirio and I hit it off great. Great relationship.

Did you have some kind of a deal with Corman to make multiple pictures?

No, no. I think Don Wilson signed a contract with him, but no, I never signed a contract with him. He just called me every six months or so and would tell me, "Cirio wants to make another movie with you," and boom. It was great money at the time, and I loved working with Cirio and I loved working with the crew. It was a lot of work. Fifteen- or twenty-hour days. Three weeks.

When you were doing these pictures, when did you have time to train and work out?

The training is on your off-days, which was rare. When there was a day off, we would go to a dojo, or if it was in the Philippines, we would go to a karate school there. The first thing I'd ask Cirio was, "Find me a gym." First and foremost. But on these films we were doing push-ups, we were doing kicking pads, all kinds of targets, so we were working out on set when we weren't doing anything. Those action scenes we would do over and over and over. There's like ten guys in a fight scene. That in itself was training.

How old/young were you when you were doing these pictures?

I retired from the ring when I was twenty-eight, that was my last fight. So I started doing movies right after that.

Wow. You played a father of two teenagers in *Breathing Fire*.

I know! That was funny. Everyone on set kept calling me Michael Douglas. Every time. When I moved to Canada—I work in Vancouver now—they call me Sean Penn in Canada. It's so funny. I asked my mom, "Are you sure you didn't fool around with the Douglases?"

Let's go back to *Full Contact* for a second. This movie has the exact same story and characters as several other Roger Corman productions, including Rick Jacobson's own *Dragon Fire*. Were you aware of this?

Dragon Fire, yeah. Yeah, I dunno. Roger Corman found a way to copy the same movie. *Live by the Fist*, the movie I did . . . Don Wilson did it as *Bloodfist*. Instead of George Takei in the prison, it was Richard Roundtree. I'd sit there and watch it because somebody had told me, "You need to check this out, man! You and Don Wilson are doing the same damn movie!" I'd look at it and be amazed. It was the same dialogue! There were little bits and pieces that were changed, but he did it!

Did that bother you?

Uh . . . no. I was like, "Eh, no big deal." I knew these films weren't going to be a career maker for me. It was just a step in the right direction.

You did an interesting action movie called *Terminator Woman* or *Eliminator Woman* depending on which release you're looking at. Talk a little bit about that one.

We filmed that one in South Africa. The director on it got fired and Michel Qissi took over as director. Michel was the greatest guy to work with. He was an incredible director. The original title was *Backlash*. I don't know what these marketing people think.

Are you proud of these low-budget action films you starred in?

Yeah, yeah, um . . .

Are you embarrassed by them?

No, not embarrassed. I look back at it, and I wished I'd gotten into acting classes a lot sooner. But once everything started taking off, it was like boom, boom, boom! I was averaging two or three movies a year until 9/11 happened. Then nothing happened. That's when I got into stunts. Jesse Johnson, the nephew of Vic Armstrong told me, "Hey, listen, my uncle's casting for *Charlie's Angels*." I gave them my reel, they looked at it and said, "Yes!" I worked six weeks on *Charlie's Angels*. It paid really good money, and I had a fight scene with Drew Barrymore. Those earlier movies, I look at them as a learning experience. I don't know, it's weird. People tell me, "I loved you in this movie!" I'm like, "Really?" There's a following for these. There's a big fan base. I'm flattered and I'm grateful, and I'm blessed to have been a part of all these films. But am I proud of my acting? No! Am I proud of my action?

Yes! A fan of mine posted a video tribute of my movies on Facebook, and it moved me. I was like, "Wow!" It was a compilation reel, and it had a lot of my kicking, and I was looking at myself, and I called my wife over, "Honey, honey, come look!" She started laughing. She's like, "Look at your hair, look at your mullet!" I'm like, "Don't look at that, look at the kicking! That's what it's about!" I was impressed.

You've gone on to do some stunt work on some very high-profile movies like *Mission Impossible III* and *The Green Hornet*.

The Green Hornet was the last big film I did. The fight scene that Michel Gondry did in *The Green Hornet* with Jay Chou . . . I thought it was going to be a big fight scene, but he condensed a lot of the stuff. The good thing about that shoot was that we had Vic and Andy Armstrong doing the stunts. The fight with Jay inside the SUV, we were flying down the highway, it was like drop down, BANG, BANG, BANG, it was like maybe four or five shots, and then they threw me out, and when I saw it I was like, "WHAT?! That's all we got?"

That was like a hundred million dollar movie.

Yeah! And then they cut the hell out of it.

Talk about *The Package*, your latest. You had a nice fight with Steve Austin in it.

The director, Jesse Johnson, is an incredible guy. Jesse's put me in his last five, six films. I played a hit man. It was a cool role. I had a fun fight scene. Jesse was like, "Are you up for a fight scene with Steve Austin?" I went, "Dude, I can do it!" My training has been consisting more of boxing and weights, but not so much kicking. I'm still stretching, though. I went home and started stretching like a banshee. I stretched on a wall. I found out how tall Steve was and I marked it on my door, and as I was stretching on the wall, I was like, "Yeah, okay: I can kick him." Good thing I didn't have to kick Dolph Lundgren because that guy's like 6 foot 5. It was fun to get back into the action because I hadn't done it in a while. I'm getting that spark to get into action films again.

What do you think of guys like Stallone and Schwarzenegger coming back and doing these *Expendables* movies?

More power to them. I think it's great. It's inspiring. The fact that they can go that long and look that good doing what they do, it's inspiring to me. I'll bet you that they don't walk the way that they walk when they're doing those movies. They probably walk a *little* bit slower.

Do you have a favorite movie of yours? I like *Live by the Fist*.

You like *Live by the Fist*? I like *Live by the Fist*, too. (He picks up my VHS copy of *Full Contact*.) Look at this. I mean, were they stoned when they did the marketing for this? When I saw this cover picture for the first time, I was sure someone in Roger Corman's office didn't like me. What were they thinking? I don't get it. *Full Contact* I like.

Eliminator Woman I liked. That was one of my favorite movies that I've done. *One Man Army*, I dunno. John Travolta says that with every movie he does he has a different walk for each character he pays. With me, it was like a different hairdo. I had a ponytail in one, a mullet in another one . . . but I can fight like nobody's business on film.

Live Wire: Human Timebomb

1995 (New Line DVD) (CD)

"Never deal with a bald Cuban."

Parker (Bryan Genesse) is a wisecracking FBI agent who is staking out a large international drug deal. After the deal takes place, he shows himself, and all hell breaks loose. It becomes apparent that the deal actually involved a very valuable microchip. It's used as an implant in humans to turn them into perfect killing machines. Cuban General Arnaz (Anthony Fridjohn) is the mastermind behind it, and when a trade for the microchip goes bad, Parker finds himself captured with the chip implanted in him. With his memories suppressed, Parker becomes a puppet for Arnaz, doing all his dirty bidding. With a meeting of delegates on the horizon, a plan is hatched to turn Parker into a human time bomb, one that will take them all out in one fell swoop. Will Parker come to his senses and defeat the chip in his body, or will Arnaz succeed in his plan?

Bryan Genesse (*Cold Harvest*) is the only thing saving *Live Wire: Human Timebomb*. The film opens with a large, extended (but uneven) shootout. After the first forty minutes or so, the story picks up, and Genesse really gets to show off his skills. There are numerous shootouts as well as some really nice action scenes. One in particular has Genesse squaring off with an assailant in a rather intense knife battle. Director Mark Roper (*Queen's Messenger*) is able to pull off some nice work on the production side with a modest budget. Not exactly a classic but Genesse is pretty solid in this film, making it worthwhile.

Lockdown

1990 (Vidmark VHS) (djm)

A homicidal maniac named Garrett (Richard Lynch from *Invasion U.S.A.*) frames a good cop named Taylor (Chris De Rose) for a murder, and Taylor is sent to prison for years. Taylor's partner on the force McBride (Chuck Jeffreys from *Karate Cops*) uses his time wisely on the outside by trying to figure out who framed his partner, and it doesn't take long for him to figure out that Garrett is the guy, but the trick is to prove it while keeping his imprisoned partner's morale high. Taylor, meanwhile, manages to escape from prison (in a halfway believable scene), and when he's out he makes a quick visit to his family, and then he's off to rendezvous with his partner and they go after Garrett, who is an entirely unpredictable loose cannon.

For a straight-to-video action movie with zero pretenses, *Lockdown* is kinda cool if only to see Eddie Murphy-lookalike action star Jeffreys get angry and throw his lightning-fast spin kicks at scumbags and then do Eddie Murphy impressions. Jeffreys is easily one of the most underrated action stars featured in this book, so the few times he had a chance to star in a film are real treats to watch. Richard Lynch is always a great bad guy, and while the material holds him back a little bit in this one, he's still a pretty frightening villain. Co-star Chris De Rose was a police officer in real life before becoming an actor. Directed by Frank (*Killpoint, Low Blow*) Harris.

Locked Down

2012 (Lionsgate DVD) (CD)

"You will eat, sleep, shit, and piss when I tell you to. Understood, fuck monkeys?"

Hard-working cop Danny (Tony Schiena) has taken down many criminals while working undercover. He lives his job, and the job defines him. After finishing a huge bust, life seems to be good for him. Things take a turn for the worse, though, when police bust into his apartment and accuse him of being crooked. He finds himself in prison, but not just any prison—a prison where many of the inmates have a vendetta against him. The prison isn't run by the warden—oh no, that would be too easy. It's run by gangster Anton Vargas (Vinnie Jones). Though he's incarcerated, his reach still stretches across the country and he's making a killing by running underground fights-to-the-death in the basement of the prison. Internal affairs agent Gwen (Sarah Ann Schultz) is doing everything in her power to clear Danny's name while he's forced into fighting. With the help of his cellmate Irving (Dave Fennoy), he prepares for the fight of his life.

The Tapout brand brings us another entry in their series of sponsored action films with *Locked Down*. This one is brought to us from Daniel Zirilli, the director of their previous film *Circle of Pain*. This one is a tad bit more entertaining but still suffers from feeling like a music video. The excessive use of slow motion is distracting and detracts from the action. Tony Schiena (*Circle of Pain*) brings the beatings and was responsible for choreographing his own scenes. None of the fights are fast-paced enough, a side effect of the incessant slow motion. The film features a stable of UFC fighters like Rashad Evans (*Unrivaled*), Kimbo Slice (*Circle of Pain*), Forrest Griffin (*13*), and Lance "The Snake" Cartwright. This is a mildly entertaining romp, and Tony Schiena will grow on you after a while.

Lock Up

1989 (Lionsgate DVD) (djm)

Good-hearted mechanic Frank Leone (Sylvester Stallone) is on his last six-month stretch of a prison sentence for aggravated assault, and his

fellow inmates (and the guards) at the minimum-security prison all really like him. From one day to the next, though, he is yanked out of his cell and transferred to a maximum-security hell hole where he is made to endure harsh punishments inflicted by the spiteful Warden Drumgoole (Donald Sutherland), who has long held a grudge against Leone for a past event. The story behind that isn't as important as Leone's current situation: he is cruelly harassed by other inmates on the order of Drumgoole, and he's pushed to his absolute limit, with the hope on Drumgoole's part, that Leone will commit some sort of offense that will knock his sentence up indefinitely. Leone, who has only to outlast the punishment during his present sentence, makes a few friends on the inside, but his goodwill towards a fellow inmate (a newbie) gets him in trouble and lands him in the hole for six weeks. When he emerges after the extreme torture, fellow inmate Chink (Sonny Landham, always welcome) pushes him to further extremities, and finally Leone is forced to make an escape attempt when his girlfriend on the outside is threatened. The escape attempt is merely a ruse for Leone to move in on the evil Drumgoole, who is behind all of the wrongdoing towards him, and it's up to Leone to prove to all of the guards (many of whom are corrupt and scuzzy) that Drumgoole is an evil son of a bitch and that Leone is maxed out on goodwill.

No matter how many times I watch *Lock Up*, it's always shocking to me at how hopeless it feels. Stallone was on top of the world when this was made (it came out after *Rambo III* and before *Tango and Cash*), so it's amazing that he starred in a movie where he's brutally beaten and punished for the entire length of the picture. His character is so inherently likable that it's no wonder someone out there hates him so badly, but Sutherland's character is the polar opposite of his, which makes for an old-fashioned black-and-white character study. It's not really an action movie, per se, but Stallone engages in some close quarter physical attacks (namely with Landham), so it definitely emerges as an action-oriented drama. It's a brutal watch, though. Stallone, interestingly, has played incarcerated characters more times than any of his contemporary action stars. He was in the concentration camp Nazi soccer movie *Victory*, played a POW in *First Blood* and its sequels, and in the same year as *Lock Up*, he played a character who is imprisoned in *Tango and Cash*. Years later, he played an escape expert in the prison movie *Escape Plan* with Arnold Schwarzenegger. *Lock Up* was directed by John (*Out For Justice*) Flynn.

Logan's War: Bound by Honor

1998 (Madacy DVD) (djm)

As a child, Logan witnessed the murder of his parents. But what's more is he had a psychic intuition that danger was coming before the event happened, so he's blessed (or cursed) with that ability. Years later, Logan (played as an adult by Eddie Cibrian) is under the care of his uncle Jake (Chuck Norris), who has taught him martial arts and how to be a soldier, and when he comes of age, Logan abandons his uncle to seek revenge for the death of his parents. He knows who the killer is (played by Jeff Kober, always a good villain), and he ingratiates himself to the clique of thugs to get close to his parents' killer. But even with his psychic ability, Logan gets in over his head, which is when his uncle Jake comes to rescue him.

A made-for-TV movie with certain cinematic sensibilities, *Logan's War* is a solid little action movie with just enough screen time from Chuck Norris to warrant a viewing. It was shot during his days playing *Walker, Texas Ranger*, and he looks good and gives a nice, physical performance. Director Michael Preece worked with Norris on another TV movie called *The President's Man*. Preece also did the Franco Columbu vehicle *Beretta's Island*.

Lone Tiger

1996 (Platinum DVD) (CD)

"Explain to me how you let a little rice-eating, slant-eyed, Buddha head stab you in your ass!"

Chuji Kurenai (Bruce Locke) has left Japan to spend some time in Las Vegas. He isn't there to catch a show or gamble but to learn the truth about his father's death. Fifteen years prior, his father was murdered in cold blood. Chuji grew up in an orphanage and was raised by a martial artist who taught him all he knew. Now, Chuji will have to fight if he's to find the killer. He goes by the name Tiger and wears a tiger mask in honor of his father. He's soon discovered by underground fight promoter Bruce Rossner (Richard Lynch from *Invasion U.S.A.*) who recruits him with promises of large sums of cash. Tiger doesn't care about the money, he just wants his chance to fight Dark Tiger (Matthias Hues from *Death Fight*), the same man his father was to fight fifteen years ago and a possible lead to understanding what really happened to his dad.

I'm not sure words can describe just exactly what *Lone Tiger* actually is. It's an action film to be remembered for several reasons, including the facts that the hero wears a giant tiger mask during his battles and that it's got a good-guy turn for Matthias Hues (*I Come in Peace*). Richard Lynch (*Dragon Fury*) also gives a memorable, standout performance. The fight scenes are poorly shot and the choreography is very slow, however. Watching this film may make you realize that Hues would have been a titan had he decided to take on the world of professional wrestling in real life. It might have been a missed opportunity for him. He has a few cool action scenes in a wrestling ring, and Lynch appears to be have a blast, but other than that, the film is pretty empty. Directed by Warren Stevens (*Dragonfight* with Paul Coufos).

Texas Ranger J. J. McQuade (Chuck Norris) is about to give drug kingpin Rawley Wilkes (David Carradine) a severe beating in *Lone Wolf McQuade*. Author's collection.

Lone Wolf McQuade

1983 (MGM DVD) (djm)

Texas Ranger J. J. McQuade (Chuck Norris) works alone, and when he's chastised by his boss for being *too* good at what he does, he is assigned a partner, a young Hispanic whose life he'd previously saved. McQuade locks horns with an arms-dealing maven named Rawley Wilkes (David Carradine), who lives on a hacienda and likes to show off his martial arts prowess in front of crowds. Not willing to do things by the book, McQuade messes with Wilkes's business and inadvertently gets Wilkes's main squeeze (Barbara Carrera) interested in him for all the right reasons, which obviously puts a stick in Wilkes's craw. Wilkes has McQuade's daughter kidnapped and his dog/wolf murdered, and that's all McQaude needs to develop a one-track mind in toppling Wilkes' mid-level empire and showing him who's the best. With the help of his partner and a rogue FBI agent (played by Leon Isaac Kennedy), McQuade doesn't have to Lone Wolf it anymore.

A precursor to *Walker, Texas Ranger*, this spaghetti western–themed martial arts movie is one of Chuck's very best movies. Working under the direction of Steve Carver, whom he'd worked with on *An Eye for an Eye*, Chuck personified the strong, silent type he became known for and really set the standard for himself with this film. Strangely, the film needs more Carradine and Leon Isaac Kennedy (from the *Penitentiary* trilogy), who are both relegated to popping up only when the plot needs them to appear. The final fight between Norris and Carradine doesn't disappoint. A strong Italian score by Francesco De Masi adds immense flavor to the film.

The Longest Yard

2005 (Paramount DVD) (CD)

"And that's the truth! With some cheese on it. There ain't no meatloaf between these buns."

Former NFL quarterback Paul Crewe (Adam Sandler) spends most of his days getting drunk after being banned from playing pro ball. He was accused of throwing a game, though it was never proven. After getting wasted, stealing his girlfriend's car, and leading the police on a high-speed chase, Crewe finds himself thrown into a maximum-security prison. The warden forces him into putting together a prison team to face his all-star team of guards. With the help of "Caretaker" (Chris Rock) and a tough old former player Nate Scarborough (Burt Reynolds), they assemble a team like no other in history. These guys are the toughest of the tough, but none of it will be important if they can't come together as a team. When the warden and his guards see they are becoming an actual threat, they'll do anything to break the team's spirits but Crewe won't give up so easily and stays strong to inspire his team.

The Longest Yard is a comedy first and foremost but is important to action fans because of its enormous cast. By enormous, I mean both the quantity and the individuals' girth. These guys are all minor characters but most, if not all, have a moment or two to shine. From the world of professional wrestling, the film features Steve Austin (*Hunt to Kill*), Kevin Nash (*The Punisher*), Bill Goldberg (*Half Past Dead 2*), and the 7 foot 2, 400 pound Dalip "The Great Khali" Singh (*MacGruber*). Each actor has a moment or two to have their laughs and to get dirty on the field. Nash may have had the largest speaking role but Goldberg and Singh have the most screen time. Austin is a bit underused in the film. From the world of pro football we have Terry Crews (*The Expendables*), Michael Irvin, Bill Romanowski, Bob Sapp (*Conan the Barbarian*), and the great Brian Bosworth (*Stone Cold*). Director Peter Segal (*Grudge Match*) manages to pull out some pretty strong performances from the athletes while the veteran actors like Sandler, Reynolds, and Rock just sort of coast through. The football scenes are pretty brutal but aside from that, the film is about laughs and not action. It's well worth viewing to see all the sports personalities on screen, as they don't disappoint.

Looney Tunes: Back in Action

2003 (Warner DVD) (CD)

"This is unacceptable. We cannot have nine-year-olds working in sweatshops making ACME goods, when three-year-olds work for so much less."

Bugs Bunny and Daffy Duck have never changed over the years. Their love/hate relationship is the same as always but the executives over at Warner Brothers feel Bugs is the more marketable star. Daffy doesn't take too kindly to this and decides to quit once and for all. Escorted out by Vice President of Comedy Kate (Jenna Elfman), he has a run-in with wanna-be stuntman (current security guard) DJ Drake (Brendan Fraser), who later takes him into his home. DJ soon finds out his father Damien (Timothy Dalton) is actually a spy (and not just an actor who plays one); his father is kidnapped by the chairman of the evil ACME company, Mr. Chairman (Steve Martin). DJ and Daffy quickly team up with Kate and

Bugs to rescue DJ's father. The chairman may throw every obstacle he can at them, including his hired muscle Mr. Smith (professional wrestler Bill Goldberg), but Bugs and Co. may have a few tricks of their own.

The most entertaining part of *Looney Tunes: Back in Action* is trying to catch all the cameo appearances packed into the ninety-minute runtime. The amount is staggering, and some of them are quite surprising. There's plenty of cartoon shenanigans to make kids happy, but the movie never quite captures the true spirit of why we loved these characters in the first place. Bill Goldberg (*Half Past Dead 2, Santa's Slay*) is mostly just wasted in this role. He isn't given much to do or say and never has a great moment to impress; he's mostly subdued. He takes his orders from Steve Martin's character so I guess that's something you won't ever see again. It was directed by Joe Dante (*Small Soldiers*), who pays homage to his roots, making this worth a view, but purveyors of action cinema and fans of Goldberg will be disappointed.

Los Bravos
2001 (Spartan DVD) (CD)

Hector Riviera (Hector Echavarria, *Chavez: Cage of Glory*) is a family man who works hard at his job. He has a wife and son whom he loves more than anything. The thing about Hector is, he has a past. The friends he used to run with are all being murdered, execution-style. His long-lost friend Tomas (Louis Lacoviello), shows up to tell him about the murders. Hector is skeptical until Tomas ends up dead and all the evidence points to Hector. He quickly finds himself on the run and looking for answers. A mysterious assassin named Reaper (Ryan Watson) is responsible for the deaths but he isn't working alone. He was hired by DeFuego (Michel Qissi from *Kickboxer*), who is a vicious killer with a link to Hector's past. Things go horribly wrong when DeFuego has his men kidnap Hector's wife and son, sending Hector on a rampage until his family is safe.

As a whole, *Los Bravos* is on the bottom of the barrel. It's obviously a low-rent affair with little to no production value. The acting from much of the cast is poor and unconvincing. The story is familiar and predictable with some truly horrible dialogue. So with all that against it, why invest your time? Acting may not be Echavarria's strong point but thankfully there's plenty of action and this man delivers. There are several solid match ups, including Echavarria versus Watson as well as the finale with Echavarria against Qissi. Director Paulo Schultz does an adequate job but his inexperience is apparent. In the right hands with a stronger director and choreographer, Echavarria could become a solid force in action cinema. The fight scenes are good but they just don't quite reach their full potential. There wasn't enough variation in the moves, and key attacks are repeated too often. Having said that, there are brief moments of brilliance in some of Echavarria's moves, so it's easy to see his potential. It was also nice to see an appearance by martial arts legend Bill "Superfoot" Wallace (*The Protector*).

The Lost Medallion: The Adventures of Billy Stone
2013 (Bridgestone DVD) (djm)

Billy Stone, the son of an archaeologist working on a site in eastern Asia, and his orphaned friend Allie accidentally unearth an ancient gold medallion that has mysterious powers. Billy (Billy Unger) and Allie (Sammi Hanratty) are chased by goons who want to steal the medallion, and the two kids are magically transported back in time hundreds of years to the point in history when the medallion was first lost. They find themselves on a tropical island where a peaceful tribe is under threat of an evil warrior named Cobra (Mark Decascos). When Cobra finds out that the medallion is in the hands of these kids, he sends his men to take what he believes should be his. Whoever is in possession of the medallion is the rightful king of the land, and so the fact that Billy wears it around his neck is cause for strife in the region. Young prince Huko (Jansen Panettiere), who's the same age as Billy and Allie, becomes jealous of Billy, but the story takes them all on a lesson-learning experience of humility, love, and sacrifice. Along for the ride is the wizened hermit Faleaka (James Hong, who looks like he's having fun), a caring sidekick to the kids while they get themselves involved in the adventure of their lifetimes.

Told in a storybook fashion, *The Lost Medallion* is an inspirational adventure that surprises with its good-natured, everyone-is-loved-by-God message, and kids and adults who enjoy stories revolving around archaeology and treasure hunting should have a good time watching this. A similar film called *The Seventh Coin* was made in 1993. *The Lost Medallion: The Adventures of Billy Stone* was shot in 2010, and sat on the shelf until its release in 2013. Fans of Mark Dacascos might be interested in seeing him here, but he only has a few quick scenes where he displays his martial arts abilities. This was directed by Bill Muir.

Love and Bullets
1978 (itv DVD) (djm)

An Arizona detective named Charlie Congers (Charles Bronson) is given a mission no one wants: travel to Switzerland to locate and guard a mobster's moll named Jackie (Jill Ireland), who has a hit out on her life. He's meant to keep her safe so that she can go back to the States to testify against the mob, but the irony is that she's completely innocent and doesn't know a thing about the mafia or the kingpin she slept with. Charlie develops feelings for her despite how clueless she is, and when the hitmen start turning up and making attempts on her life, he thinks fast and improvises, making handy weapons out of household objects. In one instance, he makes a blowgun from furniture and appliances.

A melancholy and stilted vehicle for Bronson, *Love and Bullets* isn't very rewarding for fans of its star or of action movies in general. With a few choice moments for its two stars (who were married in real life), it goes down a certain path and tries to give us what some would expect from Bronson (a theme of vigilantism with police procedural drama), but it's lacking a compelling center and a sense of escapism. In some ways, the movie has a pallid objective, which is accomplished on some levels, but it just isn't any fun at all. Henry Silva plays a hitman, and Rod Steiger co-stars as the kingpin. Directed by Stuart Rosenberg.

Low Blow
1986 (Mill Creek DVD) (djm)

An Asian private eye named Joe Wong (Leo Fong) stops eating his lunch or whatever he's doing every day to stop robberies, chase down and beat up purse snatchers, and crack wise because that's what he does. His latest gig involves the daughter of a concerned father, who tells him that she's joined a cult in the middle of nowhere, and she needs rescuing. Wong and his jalopy car make the trip to the commune, and he tries to make it seem like he's a journalist, but it isn't long before leader Yarakunda (Cameron Mitchell acting spaced out) and his right-hand woman Karma (Akosua Busia) are onto him, and he's being chased around. He recruits a motley crew of misfits (a Vietnam vet, an ex-cop, and a fist fighter) to help him save the girl for the fee the woman's father is willing to pay, and the bunch of them get in on the action. The final scene of the film is priceless.

A Crown International release, *Low Blow* is a gem. If there's anyone out there who hasn't heard of Leo Fong, it's time to acquaint yourself with him. He has starred in, produced, and directed (very) low-budget martial arts action movies for decades. *Low Blow* is easily his best movie. It's a laugh riot, but only in the best way. It's nothing to make fun of, but to celebrate. Fong deserves more attention. Future action star and creator of the Tai Bo exercise system Billy Blanks appears in an early role. He says to Fong, "I'm gonna kill you, Chinaman!" Director Frank Harris previously worked on another Fong picture called *Killpoint*. The sequel to *Low Blow* is *Blood Street*, co-starring Richard Norton. The Mill Creek release is 16 × 9 widescreen and comes in a collection with other action movies from Crown.

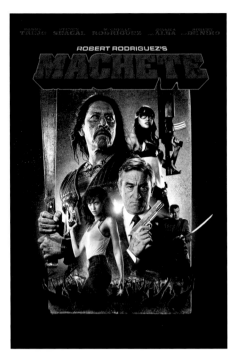

Theatrical artwork for *Machete*. Author's collection.

Machete

2010 (Fox DVD) (djm)

"You just fucked with the wrong Mexican."

A one-track-minded Federale named Cortez (Danny Trejo) earns his nickname "Machete" for obvious reasons, and he garners a reputation that precedes him. He goes after a drug lord named Torrez (Steven Seagal), but he's duped and beaten within an inch of his life, and Torrez beheads Cortez's wife in front of him as punishment. Years later, Cortez is living as a vagabond, taking day labor jobs as they come, and he's offered a job by a mysterious man with ties to a senator named McLaughlin (Robert DeNiro), who has declared war on illegal aliens in the state of California. Cortez is set up to make it look like he's trying to assassinate the senator, which gives McLaughlin a favored edge in the coming election, but Cortez doesn't take these matters lightly. He gears up and joins forces with an INS agent named Sartana (Jessica Alba) and a revolutionary named Luz (Michelle Rodriguez), and they unleash the floodgates of Machete's wrath. Torrez, who has links to the despicable senator, faces off against the only man who can take him in a fair fight (fought with a machete and a samurai sword), and the finale is . . . satisfying.

Inspired by the faux trailer featured in the Quentin Tarantino/Robert Rodriguez flop *Grindhouse*, this nearly spoofy action movie finally gives long-time supporting tough guy Danny Trejo the starring vehicle he's always deserved. The result isn't entirely to my liking, but I appreciate Trejo's performance because he's playing it absolutely straight. The tone of the film is wildly uneven. At times, it's a straight-up action movie (the first fifteen minutes), but then it swerves into farce and then back to a real action film from one scene to the next. Machete is a cool character. He deserves a film to be built around him, but this effort isn't one to last the test of time. Director Robert Rodriguez (and co-director Ethan Maniquis) has a hard time finding a balance for the movie, which probably plays best as a comedy. Casting Steven Seagal as the villain is a small stroke of genius, though. His death in the film is classic. Trejo was in his late sixties when he made this. After this film, he seemed to star in dozens of movies, most of which were throwaway direct-to-video films, but he starred in one called *Bad Ass* that blows *Machete* away. Check that one out.

Machete Kills

2013 (Relativity DVD) (djm)

"Oh, Machete. I've heard of you. People sing songs about you."

Cortez Machete (Danny Trejo) and his muse Sartana (Jessica Alba) are on a secret mission when Sartana is slain by a masked terrorist. Machete wallows in despair until the president (Charlie Sheen) forces him to go on a death-defying mission involving a terrorist who plans to blow up the planet with a mega nuclear missile that cannot be disarmed because the trigger is wired to his heartbeat. Machete then goes to the man who armed the missile, a madman named Voz (Mel Gibson), who is a sort of cult leader with plans to repopulate the human race in outer space. Voz likes Machete and offers him a job: to have himself cloned and be his personal bodyguard in space. When Machete refuses, Voz throws his army of clones (all played by Marko Zaror from *Kiltro*) at him, but Machete doesn't flinch at shedding blood, beheading, or dismembering enemies, so Voz's task is much harder than he anticipated. The film ends with a promise of *Machete Kills Again . . . In Space!*

Far less punchy or inspired than the first entry (which isn't a classic by any means), *Machete Kills* is less a film this time than a concept of situations stacked on top of each other. It's less funny this time, and the novelty wore off somewhere in the interim when Machete was on hiatus. Director Robert Rodriguez's low-budget sensibilities aren't that endearing this time around, and the novelty of seeing Mel Gibson square off with Danny Trejo is just strange and a little bit sad. The best part of the movie is Marko Zaror, who has had an impressive career as "The Latin Dragon," starring in films like *Kiltro*, *Mirage Man*, and *Mandrill*. His role in *Machete Kills* is self-perpetuating, so he never goes away, which is fine by me. We honestly don't need to see Machete killing in space. We're good here.

Mach 2

2001 (Paramount DVD) (djm)

In a period of decline as an action star, Brian Bosworth (from *Stone Cold* and *Black Out*) starred in Fred Olen Ray's inferior "action" movie *Mach 2*. The Boz plays an Air Force captain named Jack Tyree, who is accompanying a senator on a Concorde flight. Mid-flight, the plane is hijacked by a team led by actor Michael Dorn from *Star Trek: The Next Generation*. The only guy who can prevent the senator's death and the imminent threat to the White House is Jack, but there's a big problem: He doesn't know how to fly a plane!

Aside from a few fits and starts of action scenes that feature Bosworth throwing some guys down and dodging some bullets, *Mach 2* is more or less a boring movie set in one location. Decent writing by Steve Latshaw (Dolph Lundgren's *Command Performance*) and a passable music score prevent the movie from being a total disaster, but movies like this need a bigger budget and more action to keep me or anyone else engaged. Bosworth deserved much better vehicles than this. A good supporting cast helps nominally. Also with Shannon Whirry, Lance Guest, and Cliff Robertson. Director Ray is credited under the pseudonym Edward R. Raymond.

Maggie

2015 (Lionsgate DVD) (djm)

The world is in the midst of an apocalypse the media has dubbed "The Turn," in which much of humanity has succumbed to a "necro-ambulant" condition . . . a scientific way of saying that people everywhere are turning into flesh-rotting zombies. Martial law is declared, countries are on lockdown, and if you're bitten by one of the walking dead you're closely watched by family members over the course of about two weeks, after which time you are either terminated by a loved one or interred into a mass holding pen, a filthy quarantine zone where zombies are free to munch on each other until they completely phase out. It's been a little while since the initial outbreak, so the sight of slowly turning neighbors or family members (or even strangers at the hospital) doesn't elicit the shock and awe it might have at the outset but, rather, seeing ordinary people in their transition from human to zombie conjures deep emotional sadness and distrust, because science hasn't been able to pinpoint exactly how long it takes for people to turn yet.

Humble, hard-working farmer Wade Vogel (Arnold Schwarzenegger) has been searching for his missing sixteen-year-old daughter Maggie (Abigail Breslin) for two weeks throughout a devastated urban apocalyptic landscape (this was filmed in Louisiana) and finds her in a depressed, half-empty hospital for the infected. She's only just been bitten, so there's still time to make whatever amends they need to before she's completely turned. Back at their dilapidated homestead, Wade and his wife Caroline (Joely Richardson) do their best to make Maggie comfortable as her symptoms worsen. She loses her appetite altogether before gaining it back with a vengeance and loses an index finger in a simple accident. Meanwhile, her flesh is rotting and her lungs completely give out. As if watching his daughter deteriorate isn't bad enough, Wade seeks every option available on what to do when the hour arrives when she will become dangerous. Knowing there will be no easy way out of it, Maggie gives him the strength to do her final favor.

Simplistic, unpretentious, and emotionally draining, *Maggie* is an up-close and personal voyage of humanity during a zombie apocalypse. It's depressing, and yet it prides itself on its deliberate effort to humanize the monsters Hollywood and pop culture have exploited through mass-appeal blockbusters, video games, and comic books. This movie strips away the myth of the zombie and puts souls in them, and we watch characters slowly go through a bereavement period as they stand by, waiting for their loved ones to take their final breath. What makes the movie really stand out is that Arnold Schwarzenegger is the star of it. He's played fathers before, but never so touchingly or with as much depth. If you've paid attention to his career, you will have seen him play some deeply emotional characters twice before—once as a suicidal detective in *End of Days* (1999), and more recently as a jaded task enforcer out for the revenge of the murder of his family in *Sabotage* (2014)—and *Maggie* gives him even more to work with and allows him to plunge into dark emotional territory that he bravely treads, emerging topside with all the pathos, wisdom, and strength he's accrued as an actor and a father over the past several decades. He's the best aspect of the film, and if it wasn't for him (because the role could have been played by dozens of working name actors, honestly), the movie would merely be a curiosity in the pantheon of zombie apocalypse films. It's different for that type of picture, but it's not a game changer, but for Arnold it's serious business and a stern reminder that he deserves to be treated with utmost respect as an actor and not just as an action star. He's still got it, and any of his fans who ignored his last several films (shame on you if you did!) should make the effort to support this one in any way you can.

The script by John Scott III makes every attempt to demystify the horror genre by presenting us with characters we care about, particularly that of Maggie herself, and as played by Breslin—who is shown in various stages of decay—never appears or acts as anything less or more than an average teenager. With the dread of knowing her fate, her character tries to accept what is coming, and even when in the end we expect her to rage in hunger, her actions are surprisingly human. The direction by first-timer Henry Hobson is understated (perhaps frustratingly so) and grounded in a terrible, devastated future, but it's the apocalypse of the heart that he's most concerned with.

Magic Crystal

1986 (Mei Ah Entertainment DVD) (djm)

A child named Pin-Pin (who's practically still in Pampers) obtains a glowing green crystal rock that has magic powers. It talks to him and sprouts tiny little legs and walks around, and Pin-Pin falls in love with it as if it were a pet. His father is a secret agent (played by Andy Lao), who is being chased by a rogue force of the KGB led by evil Karov (Richard Norton), who wants the magic crystal. Lao (whose character is named Andy Lo) is helped by a female Western agent named Cindy Morgan (Cynthia Rothrock), who goes through great lengths to assist him in fending off the KGB agents on their trail. Meanwhile, Pin-Pin's safety is threatened when bad guys come to his house to search for the crystal, and that's when the crystal's powers are revealed: it can cloud men's minds like The Shadow and make itself invisible and forcefully suggest individuals to do things they don't want to. To make matters even more ridiculous, the film's climax takes place in a Temple of Doom–style chamber where the Crystal's origins are revealed: it is from another world, and in fact is the pet of an alien that has been stranded on Earth for thousands of years. If you think about it, this portion of the movie is strikingly similar to *Indiana Jones and the Kingdom of the Crystal Skull*.

Made for children, *Magic Crystal* features some good fights, the best being between Norton and Rothrock, and while it might appeal to fans of its stars, the film has an odd sense of appeal for anyone who enjoys weird movies. The *Indiana Jones* angle comes late in the game, but it's a might-as-well element that makes it even more bizarre and fun. Kien Shih (a.k.a. Shih Kien) from *Enter the Dragon* has a supporting role. Directed by Jing Wong.

Magic Kid

1992 (Universal DVD) (djm)

Brother and sister kids Kevin and Megan go to California to visit their uncle Bob (Stephen Furst), a washed-up Hollywood agent and all-around schlub. Kevin (Ted Jan Roberts) is an aspiring martial artist and dreams of starring in a movie with Don "The Dragon" Wilson, which uncle Bob keeps assuring him is a distinct possibility. While cajoling his niece and nephew, he ducks and dodges his intent bookies, who are after him for over ten grand. Kevin, sensing an opportunity to flex his martial arts prowess in public, kicks and smashes the thugs who come after his uncle, which gets old rather quickly when the realization that his uncle is a loser hits him in the face. Ultimately, uncle Bob wins over his kin when he miraculously redeems himself by doing everything he can to arrange for Kevin to meet his hero, Don Wilson. The end of the film has Kevin starring in a movie with "The Dragon" as his sidekick.

Family-friendly and endearing to a fault, *Magic Kid* reminds me that the world was a better place when movie kid characters aspired to meet an action star such as Don Wilson. It's incredibly wonderful to think that once upon a time, kids actually watched movies starring the likes of Wilson, Dudikoff, and others of their ilk. *Magic Kid* is simple entertainment, and it's perfect, I suppose, for dads who have sons who care what their dads like. Otherwise, I'm not sure it has a place in the world anymore. Kid star Ted Jan Roberts made a few martial arts-themed films, including *Magic Kid 2*. The co-founder of PM Entertainment (a studio that made dozens of martial arts and action movies throughout the 1990s), Joseph Merhi, directed it. He also directed *Riot* and *Rage* with Gary Daniels.

Magic Kid 2

1994 (Trinity DVD) (CD)

Kevin (Ted Jan Roberts) has now become a movie star. Being fourteen and famous isn't easy for him. His Uncle Bob (Stephen Furst) is managing his career and the boy's life is run by the studio. Bob knows it's not what is best for Kevin but goes along with it because he's blinded by the money Kevin is bringing in. Kevin's in the middle of filming a movie called *Ninja Boy*, and once the movie is finished he can start high school. The producer is a shady character and wants to milk Kevin for everything he's worth. He wants to force Kevin to do the sequel so he would miss going to high school. Kevin takes off and visits his tutor where he's able to be a kid, which is all he really wants. Hugo wants his movie finished and sends thugs out to find Kevin, and Uncle Bob begins to see where he went wrong.

For a family film, there's plenty of martial arts action with *Magic Kid 2*. Ted Jan Roberts (*The Power Within*) was just a young teenager at this time and his skills were on par with many action stars of the era. With fight scenes choreographed by Art Camacho (*Recoil*), the action is kept light-hearted and playful. Most of the fighting is for the faux movie within the movie, and Roberts is put through the motions. Most of the fighting is one on one, but he also gets to use his nunchucks on several occasions. The movie is harmless and there's a genuine sweetness to the film and how Roberts plays Kevin. This one's entertaining for the whole family.

Magnificent Warriors (a.k.a. Dynamite Fighters)

1987 (Fox DVD) (djm)

Hong Kong superstar Michelle Yeoh (who would later star in *Supercop* and *Tomorrow Never Dies*) plays a scrappy adventurer named Fok Ming-Ming, who is on a mission to rescue a Chinese spy from the Japanese army in 1938. She's a full-time mercenary and a part-time aviatrix, and her skills in martial arts are unparalleled. In the first great scene of the movie, she's delivering a shipment of guns to a small, enclosed village somewhere near Mongolia, and when the entire village turns against her, she uses a whip and a Gatling gun to push the waves of assailants away, while still managing a grand escape. This movie's full of great, cinematic fights and explosive thrills.

Old-fashioned and exciting, *Magnificent Warriors* is a blast. Anyone can see that star Yeoh (real name Yang Zi Chong) is someone to watch out for. Her athleticism is astonishing, and her skills as a fighter are amazing. She looks great in action, and this is one of her standout movies. Fans of contemporary Hong Kong martial arts action movies should seek it out. If you're not already a fan of Yeoh, this movie might make you one. Directed by David Chung.

A Man Apart

2003 (New Line DVD) (djm)

Former gang bangers Sean and Demetrius (Vin Diesel and Larenz Tate) cleaned up and became hardboiled DEA agents, partners. After seven years on a case trying to capture a major drug lord operating through Mexico and Los Angeles, they score the head honcho through sheer determination. After some celebratory nights, the new drug lord on the streets—a guy calling himself El Diablo—has a hit put out on Sean and his wife. When hitmen kill his wife and wound him, Sean loses consciousness and wakes up much later, days after his wife's funeral. Enraged and inconsolable, Sean goes off the rails in his quest to bring El Diablo down. Due to his carelessness and uncontrollable temper, Sean gets three fellow officers killed in a botched sting, and his partner Demetrius becomes afraid for him and where his recklessness has him heading. Sean is suspended, which lowers his inhibitions even further, and

Sean Vetter (Vin Diesel) is A Man Apart. Author's collection.

Vin Diesel stars as Sean Vetter in F. Gary Gray's *A Man Apart*. Author's collection.

as he nearly single-handedly goes after the drug empire, he becomes an unstoppable bulldozer, consequences be damned.

One of Vin Diesel's best vehicles to date, *A Man Apart* is well written and surprisingly well acted, and it's got enough action and thrills to satisfy even those who aren't really into Diesel. He delivers his best performance here, and I can't imagine any other action star in the role he plays. Director F. Gary Gray (*The Italian Job*) infuses an urban action mentality with an awful lot of heart for what might otherwise have been a direct-to-video movie if it had been handled differently. For whatever reason, this flopped at the box office. Go figure.

Mandrill

2009 (Magnet DVD) (djm)

Raised by a Lothario uncle who weaned him on secret agent action movies, Antonio grows up to be a suave bounty hunter known as "Mandrill," a martial-arts proficient professional (played by Chilean Marko Zaror from *Mirage Man*) who lasers in on his targets with nary a hitch. Always at the forefront of his mind is the horrific incident he witnessed as a child: the murder of his parents at the hands of nefarious scum. Every time he's on a job, Antonio is scoping out clues as to who might have left him an orphan, and one day he spies the beautiful daughter of his next target, and he's shocked to find that she carries his mother's locket music box. This leads him to believe that her father killed his parents, which immeasurably complicates their budding romantic entanglement. Target aside, Mandill must choose the course of his destiny by deciding how to handle his conscience if he kills his lover's father.

Super stylish, but shot on a very limited budget (just like Zaror's previous films including *Kiltro*), *Mandrill* is almost two movies in one because while it seems sincere in the first half, it becomes almost farcical and spoofish in the second half. Zaror is a superb martial artist and has tons of potential as an action star, and in each of the films I've seen him in, he shines in his roles, which he seems to have fashioned just for himself. Writer/director/editor Ernesto Diaz Espinoza worked with Zaror on *Kiltro* and *Mirage Man*, and they're a good working team. Their next film is called *The Redeemer*. Some viewers will enjoy *Mandrill* more than others.

The Man From Hong Kong

(a.k.a. **Dragon Files**)

1975 (Madman Films DVD R4)

(djm)

Brian Trenchard-Smith's "Ozploitation" cult hit, *The Man From Hong Kong* is a balls-to-the-wall action extravaganza starring Wang Yu from the Hong Kong martial arts films *The One-Armed Boxer* and *The One-Armed Swordsman*. Here he

Inspector Fang Sing Leng (Wang Yu) schools Jack Wilton (George Lazenby) in *The Man From Hong Kong*. Author's collection.

A high-flying stunt in *The Man From Hong Kong*, featuring Wang Yu. Author's collection.

plays a James Bond–styled inspector named Fang Sing Leng who goes after an international drug maven named Jack Wilton (played by George Lazenby, who *was* 007 in *On Her Majesty's Secret Service*). Inspector Leng has time to romance a philandering journalist (Rebecca Gilling) while globetrotting and getting into one spectacular stunt and chase after another. The best scene has him fighting real-life stuntman Grant Page (from Trenchard-Smith's *Death Cheaters*) in a kitchen. The scene goes on for what feels like ten minutes, and it's a doozy.

Blatantly modeled after the big-budget 007 movies, *The Man From Hong Kong* doesn't quite make an international star out of Wang Yu, but at least it made the attempt to do so. Sammo Hung appears in some scenes at the beginning. This film is notable for its gonzo stunts and spectacularly insane action scenes. Lazenby is set on fire in one scene, and it's obvious that they didn't use a double. Movies like this simply do not get made anymore. It's too bad, because it's pretty great. Yu's next English-language action/martial arts film was *International Assassin*, also with Lazenby, released in 1976.

Manhattan Chase

2000 (Force Entertainment DVD R4) (djm)

Hitman Jason Reed (Loren Avedon) is busted by tough cop Nancy (Cynthia Rothrock), and sent to prison. Years later, he is released and he tries to go straight and desperately attempts to reconnect with his family and son, who whines that he feels abandoned by him. Jason is approached by his old cronies, who tempt him with getting back into the mob, but he makes an honest attempt at a new life. By accident, he saves a woman from being killed by a drug boss (who happens to be someone from Jason's past), and this sets the plot in motion. Through unlikely circumstances, Nancy, the cop who busted Jason years previously, becomes involved in Jason's actions and decisions, and they become unlikely allies against the mob.

Seemingly shot over a period of just a few days and with virtually no money, rehearsals, or script, *Manhattan Chase* is an embarrassment for its two leads. Godfrey Ho, who directed Rothrock previously in films such as *Undefeatable* and *Honor and Glory*, put this film together in a slapdash fashion, and it shows. The saving grace of the film are the several fight scenes involving the leads, but even out of context the fights don't add much to a dismal effort that should not have been attempted in the first place. Awkward direction, dialogue, acting, and a woefully inappropriate sex scene make this a film to avoid. Avedon does a fairly good job in the film despite how terrible his dialogue is, and his fights and acting in it are better than what we saw in his previous vehicle films *Deadly Ransom* and *Silent Force*, so if you're an Avedon completist, you may have an interest in *Manhattan Chase*. Rothrock's role is small.

Man of Tai Chi

2013 (Anchor Bay DVD) (djm)

A mysterious businessman named Donaka Mark (Keanu Reeves) stages to-the-death fights for a host of high-paying consumers. His latest fighter has second thoughts about fighting for Mark (who doesn't hesitate to kill fighters when they don't cooperate), and he goes to the police as an informant against Mark, but then Mark kills him before any evidence can be brought up. Mark has his eye on his next potential fighter: a tai chi champion named Chen Lin-Hu (Tiger Hu Chen), a good-hearted student of the art of tai chi who struggles at his courier job and devotes most of his time and money to his master, an old man intent on living in a crumbling temple that has been condemned by the government. Mark offers Chen a "security position" that turns out to be a fighting position that pays incredibly well, and Chen takes the offer if only to help his master rebuild his temple to code and to give his poor parents some money to live on. As Chen fights increasingly brutal opponents, his skill level is upped immeasurably, but his fighting style becomes clouded by anger and

rage, which causes his master to shun him. Now a "dark chi" fighter, Chen becomes immersed in the fight circuit until the day Mark forces him to kill his opponent. When Chen refuses to kill, Mark turns against him, and they have to deal with their issues—one on one.

It's surprising that Reeves chose this old-fashioned kickboxing tournament movie as his directorial debut. Reeves even casts himself as the creepy villain, which is even more surprising considering his "A" listing in Hollywood. *Man of Tai Chi* doesn't have any pretensions. It's low budget, shot way off Hollywood's radar, and is packed with one-on-one fights. It's pretty fun considering that these types of movies rarely get released to theaters anymore, especially with someone of Reeves's caliber on the poster. Tiger Hu Chen doesn't look like much on screen, but Reeves knew what he was doing when he cast him as the lead: he's perfect for the role, and he certainly appears to know his stuff when fighting. I'm not a fan of wire usage in martial arts movies, and this film commits the wire sin, but other than that, there's no reason why purveyors of '80s and '90s tournament movies won't enjoy *Man of Tai Chi*. Iko Uwais (from *The Raid*) and Brahim Achabbakhe (from *Kill 'Em All*) appear in small roles as fighters.

The Man With the Iron Fists

2012 (Universal DVD) (JAS)

The Man With the Iron Fists is a wonderfully entertaining mess. It is busy, convoluted, and a hell of a lot of fun. After a lengthy opening of colorful characters bouncing around and performing all manner of martial arts, the plot coalesces into a nifty story about a man named Blacksmith (Wu Tang Clan producer and director RZA) who is forced to make weapons for a kaleidoscope of treacherous villains, and a warrior named Zen-Yi (actor, Olympiad, and taekwondo expert Rick Yune) who is bent on revenge against the thieves who killed his father. Blacksmith is eventually forced to create his own weapons—literal iron fists—after he loses his arms to villain Brass Body (Wrestler and UFC fighter-turned-actor Dave Bautista). With the help of Blacksmith and undercover emissary Jack Knife (Russell Crowe), Zen-Yi searches for his father's killer.

It is gratifying to see several famous martial artists displaying their formidable talents. Many of the stunts are real, and the authenticity comes across on screen even for a fantastical film such as this. Rick Yune (from *The Fifth Commandment*) has a natural hero persona with his genuine smile and good-guy aura, and martial arts expert Cung Lee's menacing betrayer Bronze Lion is played to great effect. Dave Bautista brings a different kind of darkness, exuding genuine danger with his menacing scowl and herculean physique. This guy will continue to have a long career portraying all manner of villainously evil characters. These characters contribute to the dramatic impact of a film that could have easily been ineffective and silly. Overall, *The Man With the Iron Fists* is a rousing success . . . just don't expect much nuance. A direct-to-video sequel is forthcoming, also from RZA.

The Marine

2006 (Fox DVD) (djm)

Soldier: "How do we get around them?"
The Marine: "We don't. We go through them!"

WWE superstar John Cena got his chance at being an action star with the WWE-produced film *The Marine*. He plays an uber-pumped Marine named John Triton, who after disobeying direct orders in the field in Iraq, is discharged from service. He goes home to his cute wife (Kelly Carlson), who encourages him to hit the bricks and get an honest job. His first day as a security guard ends with him being fired for being too aggressive, and he goes home with his head down. He takes his wife on a short road trip, where they end up at the wrong place at the wrong time. While filling up on gas at a station, they encounter a band of jewel thieves who don't hesitate to kill cops when they feel threatened. Their leader (played by Robert Patrick) orders his men to pile into Triton's SUV, and they drive off, taking Triton's wife hostage. Triton, who was blasted back by a gas explosion, picks himself up and takes pursuit of his wife's captors. Thus begins his perilous adventure to save her life and redeem himself as a soldier.

To capitalize on Cena's popularity with youngsters, the decision was made to ground *The Marine* in a PG-13 world with little blood, sparse profanity, and a general sense of "clean" action, which stunts the movie's potential to be a real-thing event. Cena's first outing as a centerpiece star is certainly promising, and he was definitely given a few signature moments to show his heavy-lifting wrestling abilities. His physique is amazing, and given the right vehicle, he could blow his contemporaries away. Unfortunately, all of his films thus far have been PG-13 efforts and he's not yet found the right project to make a true believer out of me. The home video release of *The Marine* touts an "Unrated" moniker on its cover, but I saw the film theatrically as well as on video, and I see no difference in the cuts. It was directed by first-timer John Bonito. Several unrelated sequels were released directly to video. Cena's next film was *12 Rounds*.

The Marine 2

2009 (Fox DVD) (djm)

Ted DiBiase Jr. steps in the eponymous role of The Marine previously incarnated by John Cena. This time, his name is Joe Linwood, and he takes a vacation to Thailand with his pretty wife (Lara Cox), who is on a working vacation. Her boss is a prick who is hosting a swanky party at an exclusive and secluded resort on the coast, and when terrorists crash the party and hold the billionaire boss for ransom, Joe is in a position where he can save his wife and perform some heroics to save the day. Receiving no help from the corrupt police or from incompetent mercenaries, Joe relies on his military training and on the encouragement of a crusty boat captain (played by Michael Rooker) to do the job no one else can. It's basically *Die Hard*.

Well produced for a direct-to-video release, *The Marine 2* looks and feels like a theatrical production, certainly on the same level as the first film. The lavish locales and rich native scenery of Thailand lend value to the way the movie ends up looking. DiBiase Jr. is adequate in a physical role, although he doesn't have much charisma on screen (that I can detect), but I'm sure his wrestling fans won't notice. Surprisingly, the fight scenes in the film where he displays his signature wrestling moves aren't very well choreographed and look boxy and clunky, but the shootouts and subsequent bloodletting more than make up for the inadequacies of the awkward wrestling stuff. This one definitely feels more like an "R" rated movie than the first one. The villain is played by New Zealander Temuera Morrison, who was Jango Fett in the *Star Wars* prequel movies. Roel Rene (*12 Rounds 2*) directed.

The Marine 3: Homefront

2013 (Fox DVD) (djm)

Mike "The Miz" Mizanin plays Sergeant Jake Carter of the United States Marines, who comes home for a few weeks to visit his family. His hometown in middle America hasn't changed much, but his family seems to have moved on without him while he's been on duty. His older sister is dating his best friend (a cop), and his younger sister (played by Ashley Bell) is going out with a guy he doesn't approve of. While on a date with her boyfriend, his younger sister witnesses a murder in an open field, and she and her friend are kidnapped. The men who committed the murder are planning a terrorist

Video promo for *The Marine 3*. Author's collection.

attack on a corporate building in town, and now that they have Jake Carter's sister as a hostage, they've just risen to the top of his things to do. With no help from the FBI, Carter sets his sights on the terrorists and plans a bloody revenge for the wrongs they've done to his family.

From Scott Wiper and WWE Entertainment—the team that brought us *The Condemned*—this hard "R"-rated exercise in direct-to-video action is a disappointment on several levels. "The Miz" is a more convincing Marine than either John Cena or Ted DiBiase Jr., but he's not given enough action to showcase his wrestling techniques. The best fight of the movie has him squaring off against Darren Shahlavi (from *Ip Man 2*), which is a great little fight, but aside from that, the action in the film is all very basic and formulaic. The terrorists in the film (led by actor Neil McDonough who fought Dwayne Johnson in *Walking Tall*) are on a lame "Listen to us!" mission, so the movie has a limp, moody quality to it because we know exactly how and when they're all going to die at the hands of the Marine. There are some nice directorial flourishes (some cool hand-held shots and first-person shooter moments), but there's nothing really new or exciting here. I say bring John Cena back for another entry and let Scott Wiper direct him. That might be interesting.

The Marine 4

2015 (Fox DVD) (djm)

Ex-Marine Jake Carter (Mike 'The Miz' Mizanin) is floundering after his service in the military, and he takes a gig in the private sector on a security detail for a young whistle-blower named Olivia Tanis (Melissa Roxburgh), who absolutely doesn't understand how much her life is in danger. On a routine pick-up in a remote location, Carter's entire team is ambushed by a band of ruthless mercenaries who have been hired to murder Tanis and anyone who gets in their way, but Carter manages to escape with Tanis in tow. This sets off a cat-and-mouse chase through a forest wilderness, which gives Carter just a hair's edge of an advantage as he's able to set traps and get the drop on the mercenaries who are out to kill his ward.

On par with the third *Marine* picture, which also starred The Miz as the same character (this is the first sequel to have character continuity), *The Marine 4* has lots of action from start to finish, and The Miz gets to throw in some of his signature wrestling moves for good measure. The major deficit of the film is the character played by Roxburgh, who consistently screws herself and her protector over with terrible choices, bad behavior, and a serious lack of good sense. Also appearing in the cast (as a mostly silent mercenary) is Summer Rae (a.k.a. Danielle Moinet), who is also a wrestling star. From WWE Studios. Directed by William Kaufman, who you should keep an eye out for. His next picture is a direct-to-video sequel to *Jarhead*, starring Scott Adkins.

The Mark

2012 (Pure Flix DVD) (MMM)

The mark of *The Mark* is nothing short of the Mark of the Beast, as referred in a Biblical prophecy regarding the donning of a specific code-bearing device that will be required of anyone who seeks to buy or sell anything during the Christian end-times. In the case of Iraq-vet-turned-soldier-for-hire Chad Turner (Craig Sheffer), the mark comes in the form of a biometric computer chip implanted into him by the Avanti Corporation, which plans to equip the world's entire human population with just such a get-up. Complicating matters is Antichrist figure Phillip Turk (Ivan Kamaris), who dispatches Joseph Pike (action star Gary Daniels), a machine-gunning martial arts expert, to hunt down and extract the implant.

The Mark hits high gear when Pike boards an airliner that's transporting Turner and the precious chip contained inside him. Shootings, stabbings, hand-to-hand combat and general mayhem rock the flight, turning *The Mark* into the *Die Hard 2/Passenger 57* of faith-based direct-to-DVD apocalypse movies. Sheffer is rock-solid in the lead, but *The Mark* is Gary Daniel's show all the way. The real-life former world kickboxing champion and super-prolific "B"-flick dependable really unloads in this over-the-top role, turning a movie that might have been as dull as a church sermon into an unexpected hell of a good time.

The Mark 2: Redemption

2013 (Pure Flix DVD) (MMM)

Craig Sheffer as Mark-of-the-Beast-implanted soldier Chad Turner and Gary Daniels as merciless mercenary Joseph Pike return from the Christian apocalypse thriller *The Mark* to continue their ass-whomping battle for the biotech-controlled soul of humanity while the world literally starts collapsing around them. *The Mark 2* never attains the highs of the first film, but it brings a gorgeous and two-fistedly capable leading lady on board in the form of Sonia Couling as Dao, a flight attendant who's sympathetic to Turner's situation.

With much discussion of the New World Order and a more specific endorsement of prayer as a weapon and shield, *The Mark 2* ups its own faith-based factor, which would be fine if it didn't also dial down the action. Alas, that is what happens. Stick with the original *Mark*, but if you get stuck watching the sequel, don't worry: it's not the end of the world.

M

Marked For Death

1990 (Fox DVD) (djm)

Hatcher: "One thought he was invincible, the other thought he could fly."
Max: "So?"
Hatcher: "They were both wrong."

DEA agent John Hatcher (Steven Seagal) is ordered some R&R by his boss, and while on vacation, he visits his old war buddy Max (Keith David), who coaches ball in a neighborhood where a Jamaican drug lord named Screwface (Basil Wallace) has planted some bad seeds. Hatcher tries ignoring the bad mojo, but Max can't ignore the problem any more. When they're hanging out at a nightclub, a drug deal goes bad and a bunch of people are killed in the crossfire, which places Hatcher in a position to snap some wrists and keep the massacre from getting worse. In that one action, Hatcher gets the attention of Screwface, who puts a mark of death on him. When attempts are made on Hatcher's life and the lives of his loved ones, he decides he's had it with ignoring the issue, and he and Max go to war with the Jamaican drug cartel, going so far as to follow the root of the problem to Jamaica.

From director Dwight H. Little, who had done several horror films before doing this, *Marked For Death* has a rough edge and graphic gore (cut to shreds on the editing room floor), which gives the film an interesting texture, particularly for a Steven Seagal vehicle, his third out of the gate. The first scene of the film has him sprinting after a hoodlum (played by Danny Trejo, incidentally), and the pace of the picture never lets up. There are some fantastic moments throughout the movie, and Seagal's fans will undoubtedly be happy with it. It was his first film outside of his string of movies for Warner Brothers. Little did *Rapid Fire* with Brandon Lee next.

Marked Man

1996 (Live VHS) (djm)

Roddy Piper stars as Frank Stanton, a hard-working auto mechanic whose wife is run down by a drunk driver right in front of him. In anger, he kills the driver, and as a result he's sent to a minimum-security prison for manslaughter. While on the inside, the prison guards encourage him to get into fights with other prisoners for the sport of it, and he becomes the best fighter in prison. Corrupt, and with an evil agenda, the guards kill an inmate on the inside, and if Stanton doesn't break out of prison ASAP, he'll be framed for the murder and will be stuck inside forever. He sees his chance and he breaks free, and in order to clear his name, he's got to keep himself alive, which means that he causes some collateral damage along the way. He even kills a cop, which doesn't help how the media sees him. On the run, with cops and reporters on his trail, he's not just a marked man . . . he's desperate to make things right.

Released a few years after *The Fugitive*, starring Harrison Ford, *Marked Man* is similar, but obviously smaller and with less going on. It's not complicated, and Piper delivers an incredibly physical performance with lots of sprinting and running, punching, body slamming, and as much exertion as he's willing to display. One of the villains of the film is played by Miles O'Keeffe (from *True Vengeance*), and he fights Roddy in the climax. This film is a minor entry in the annals of direct-to-video cinema, but if you like Roddy, you should dig it. It was directed by Marc Voizard, who did *Hawk's Vengeance* with Gary Daniels.

The Marksman

2005 (Sony DVD) (djm)

A terrorist lays siege to a nuclear power plant in eastern Europe and takes hostages, threatening an attack. The US sends a crack commando unit to quell the situation (priority being the nuclear reactor), and when the team is duped as soon as they land, the only hope they have is a mysterious "marksman" named Painter (Wesley Snipes), who travelled with them, but managed to get away when they were captured. The film becomes a series of stalk/escape scenes as Painter eludes the terrorists and turns the tables on them by hunting them.

As a vehicle for Snipes, *The Marksman* is a complete failure, but as a typical genre outing with action as its selling point, it manages to please on a nominal level. Snipes is wasted in a role anyone could have played; he's sort of sidelined by the film, which places him in the foreground rather than in the center, and he has maybe a dozen or so lines to recite, none of which are compelling or quotable. It's a shame to see him cast in such a forgettable film. The locations (shot in Romania) are indistinct and drab. Marcus Adams directed.

Marlowe

1969 (Warner DVD) (djm)

Philip Marlowe (James Garner), private detective extraordinaire, is on a case for a young female client looking for her missing brother. As Marlowe closes in on his quarry, bad stuff starts happening and people turn up dead, usually with an icepick in their back. He's visited by Winslow Wong (Bruce Lee in a standout role), a mysterious emissary of a rich man, who wishes to pay Marlowe to look the other way and quit the case, but being the sly, intrepid detective that he is, he shrugs Wong and his $500 bribe off, resulting in a pretty hilarious scene where Wong takes it personally and trashes his office with some serious kung fu. When Wong is ordered to offer Marlowe a final bribe, Marlowe insults him, resulting in an unexpected turn of events. Whoever is trying to kill Marlowe has ties to the entertainment industry, but when his search results in learning that his client's brother has been murdered, Marlowe's next move is to solve the murder and bring the mystery to a satisfactory conclusion.

Raymond Chandler's famous character Philip Marlowe has been played on film by some great actors like Humphrey Bogart, James Caan, and Powers Boothe, to name just a few, and James Garner did a fine job of bringing him up to date in the late 1960s. The grit, gristle, and noir nostalgia of the character is still very much intact, and having Bruce Lee come in to do two show-stopping scenes was a stroke of genius. This was before he became a martial arts icon with his films *Way of the Dragon* and *Enter the Dragon*. From director Paul Bogart.

Mars

1997 (Avalanche DVD) (djm)

Olivier Gruner, star of solid movies like *Angel Town* and *Savate* and real-life kickboxing legend, lowered his standards as an action star by appearing in garbage like *Mars* and *Velocity Trap* in the late 1990s. One wonders if it was out of necessity or by choice, but either way, this film didn't really require him to do much more than wear dark sunglasses and look intimidating. In *Mars*, he goes to the red planet to avenge his brother's death, and he has a few poorly choreographed fight scenes with nameless goons, who get in the way of finding his brother's killer. Most of the movie shows him running down long corridors or moving from place to place, with nary an action or fight scene in sight.

For Gruner completists only, this film was directed by John Hess, who directed the far superior Thomas Ian Griffith vehicle *Excessive Force*. Nils Allen Stewart, a recognizable stuntman and familiar screen villain from *The Quest, Timecop,* and *Raw Target*, appears in a small role.

Mars Attacks!

1996 (Warner DVD) (CD)

Former heavyweight boxing champion Byron Williams (Jim Brown) had lost it all. Seeing him unable to get out of his downward spiral, his wife, Louise (Pam Grier), divorced him. Byron left Washington to get his life straight while Louise toughed it out, raising their two sons, Cedric (Ray J) and Neville (Brandon Hammond), on her own. After some time, though, Byron has a spiritual awakening and puts his demons aside. He finds himself working as a celebrity greeter in a Las Vegas casino, saving money to make his way back to Washington so he can prove to his family he has changed, and hopefully get a second shot with them. Then something bizarre happens, something no one could have ever predicted: Martians attack the Earth! With Vegas falling around him, he leads a small band of survivors to an airfield so they can escape. But at the airfield, an army of vicious aliens will await him. Armed with only his fists, he will have to reach deep inside and perform a selfless act—putting the lives of endangered strangers before his own.

While watching *Mars Attacks*, you will anxiously await the moment when Jim Brown (*Original Gangstas*) decides to open a very large can of whupass on the aliens with the oversized brains. Be patient—it happens, and it will fill you with utter excitement. The only thing missing is the chance to see Brown crushing intergalactic skulls side by side with one of the baddest and most beautiful women to ever grace the silver screen, Pam Grier (who co-starred with him in *Original Gangstas*). Brown still has the opportunity to throw down with the small army and a glorious moment occurs, creating one of the most memorable sequences in the film. A cast full of major stars like Jack Nicholson, Pierce Brosnan, Danny DeVito, and Michael J. Fox populates this Tim Burton extravaganza.

The Martial Arts Kid
2015 (NOV) (djm)

Remember when Don "The Dragon" Wilson and Cynthia Rothrock were the king and queen of direct-to-video movies in the 1990s? It got to the point where they would literally have a new release every few months, and at one point Don Wilson had upwards of five brand-new titles in less than a year. Those were the glory days of martial arts action films, and the action movie market has quaked in their absence and in the drought since they were the reigning champs of the genre.

If you've followed these two stars, you'll have seen that they've never completely gone away. They've remained busy, but not necessarily prolific, since coming into their seasoned years, and in fact Don Wilson has delivered the best performances of his film career in his latest pictures *The Last Sentinel* (2007), *White Tiger* (2015), and this family-friendly film, *The Martial Arts Kid*. Wilson, who has long relied on his "World Kickboxing Champion" status to go above his name, no longer needs the moniker to herald his skills, because he's finally come into his own as an actor, and it's more believable than ever when he throws his kicks and punches. He looks like he's taken enough punishment as well, and so when he gets into a scrape on screen now that he's in his 60s it looks edgy and you can see that he's still got it where it counts. He's finally playing characters who are human, who have interesting arcs, and are relatable. With Rothrock, she's always played more or less the same character, and no one has ever really allowed her to play mothers or anything beyond a woman out for justice or a cop, detective, or avenger of some kind, and so it's wholly refreshing to see that in *The Martial Arts Kid* both she and Wilson (who have appeared in three films together) play husband and wife, and they're both given material that goes beyond the thankless kicking and punching stuff and gives them something tangible to work with.

The Martial Arts Kid—which in some small ways resembles the two Magic Kid movies with Don Wilson and Ted Jan Roberts—stars appealing young actor Jansen Panettiere as a troubled high-school kid named Robbie, who as an orphan must go to live with his aunt Cindy (Rothrock) and uncle Glen (Wilson), a couple of interesting people that never had a chance to get to know Robbie until now. As it turns out, both Glen and Cindy run a martial arts studio

and a restaurant on the beach, and they've clearly had some fieldwork as government employees, teaching astronauts about enduring pain. Whenever there's trouble on the beach with bullies or hooligans, it's Aunt Cindy who quells the issue with her signature scorpion kick, throat jabs or over-the-shoulder toss. Glen is a little more laid-back, but he too gets into fisticuffs with the bad element if he happens upon a thug trying to ruffle the feathers of a shop keep, but Glen's motto is "right makes might" and puts honor above muscle every time.

Attracted to their way of living, Robbie begins training with Glen and Cindy, and when he finds himself falling for a cute girl in class (played by Kathryn Newton), his advances are met with the utmost bullheadedness by her bully boyfriend, who is a disciple of the ruthless Coach Kaine (TJ Storm from The Ultimate Game), a practitioner of "extreme fighting" at a local dojo. With a bully making fists at Robbie, Glen and Cindy have to teach their nephew how to defend himself honorably before he's crushed by the bully and his knuckle-dragging friends. The climax is a free-for-all fight with almost the entire cast, but it culminates in a nicely edited and balanced confrontation between Glen and Coach Kaine at a batting cage with baseballs being chucked at them at fifty-five miles per hour.

Nuanced, funny, and suitable for families who haven't forsaken the prospect of watching something together that has some good, solid action in it, *The Martial Arts Kid* was a nice surprise, especially considering that its target demographic is the "PG" set. While the movie made me cringe a couple of times with awkward scripting, I found the film to be perfectly palatable and digestible, and it superseded every expectation I had of it. Director and co-writer Michael Baumgarten pulled off a really entertaining family movie starring the best in the "B" business and gave everyone in the movie something they should be very proud of.

Martial Law
1990 (Media VHS) (djm)

Cynthia Rothrock plays second fiddle to Chad McQueen, who stars as a cocky cop named Sean Thompson who is after a crime lord named Dalton Rhodes (David Carradine). Rhodes isn't just the type to send others to do his dirty work: he challenges his competitors to one-on-one fights, and in one scene he kills Professor Toru Tanaka with a *Kill Bill*-style hand trick to the chest. Rothrock plays McQueen's lover and partner, Billie, and she backs him up when he needs it. The best scene of the movie has Rothrock fighting Benny Urquidez (*Wheels on Meals*) in an alley. James Lew (*American Ninja 5*) shows up in that scene, but he fights McQueen. The good supporting cast also includes John Fujioka (*American Ninja*) and Philip Tan (*Lethal Weapon 4*), who has an extensive fight scene with Rothrock at the end.

Similar to several other films made during the VHS action boom period of the late 1980s and early 1990s (most notably *Tiger Claws*, also starring Rothrock), *Martial Law* doesn't really

deliver a slam-bang entry in the action genre, but it's certainly on an average level. Steve Cohen (S. E. Cohen) directed this. He later made another buddy action film, *Tough and Deadly*, starring Roddy Piper and Billy Blanks. *Martial Law 2* was made without McQueen.

Martial Law
1998-2000 (NOV) (djm)

"The guy we're looking for is a martial arts expert. *That guy* looks like a cook!"

Syndicated television's answer to *Rush Hour* with Jackie Chan and Chris Tucker, *Martial Law* casts Sammo Hung (a longtime associate of Chan's) as Hong Kong cop Sammo Law, who is sent to Los Angeles to apprehend a notorious Chinese criminal. When that job is done, he is allowed to join the LAPD, which is something he has trepidations about, but he quickly adapts and gets his groove on. His partners on the show come and go (there were issues with casting that were never properly ironed out), including Louis Mandylor (only in the first season), Tammy Lauren (first five episodes only), Kelly Hu (through the whole show), and Arsenio Hall, who came in almost halfway through the first season and made it through to the conclusion. Hall takes the comedy relief role, and he's always trying to teach Sammo about popular culture and English grammar.

Mostly enjoyable if you're a fan of Sammo's, *Martial Law* needed much more focus to sustain a proper following, but if you drop in and out of the show for various, random episodes, it's easy viewing. During its second and final season, *Martial Law* crossed over into the eighth and final season of *Walker, Texas Ranger*, as well as another show called *Early Edition*. A fun aspect of *Martial Law* is that most of the episodes have stunt outtakes during the end credits. A total of forty-four episodes were produced. From creator Carlton Cuse.

Martial Law 2: Undercover
1991 (Universal VHS) (djm)

An improvement over Part 1, *Martial Law 2* features Cynthia Rothrock, returning as kickboxing cop Billie Black, and Jeff Wincott (*Mission of Justice*) as Sean Thompson, a tough martial arts expert recently promoted to detective. Thompson blows his cover at a nightclub where a small-time kingpin is scheming to raise the stakes and put himself amongst the major crime lords of the district. Thompson turns to his former partner and friend Billie to go undercover at the club as a bartender to investigate a lead. Billie and Thompson end up exposing a cadre of dirty cops going straight to the top of their precinct: their boss (played by Billy Drago) is in deep with the kingpin. Nearly nonstop action and close-quarter fights keep things lively.

M

Promo stills for *Martial Law 2*, featuring Jeff Wincott and Cynthia Rothrock. Author's collection.

Detective Sean Thompson (Jeff Wincott) is in a fight with a man twice his size in *Martial Law 2*. Author's collection.

The story is more involving this time around, and Wincott and Rothrock make a good team. Rothrock is given more to do here than she was given the first time, and Wincott impresses not only with his abilities as an actor but also as a full-fledged martial artist and fighter. He has two intense fight scenes with Evan Lurie (*American Kickboxer 2*), and another fight scene with some guys where he uses some kenpo sticks. Career movie stuntman and supporting actor James Lew (*American Ninja 5*) has a nice fight scene with Rothrock in the film. He also appeared in the first film (as a different character, I assume). Director Kurt Anderson later worked with Wincott on *Martial Outlaw* and with Lorenzo Lamas on *Bounty Tracker*.

Martial Outlaw

1993 (Republic VHS) (djm)

Two brothers—Kevin and Jack—work for different law enforcement agencies, and while DEA agent Kevin (Jeff Wincott) upholds the law, LAPD cop Jack (Gary Hudson) uses the law to commit crimes and profit from drug deals. Jack has gotten himself into the uneasy graces

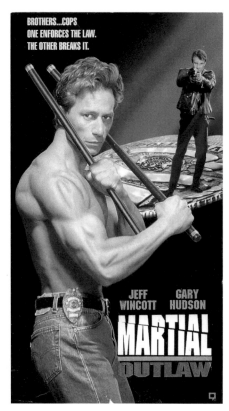

BROTHERS...COPS
ONE ENFORCES THE LAW.
THE OTHER BREAKS IT.

JEFF WINCOTT   GARY HUDSON

MARTIAL OUTLAW

VHS artwork for *Martial Outlaw*. Author's collection.

of the Russian mob, which is about to bring a boatload of drugs into Los Angeles, and he puts his brother Kevin at the top of the mob's hit list. When Kevin is captured, the Russians pit him against a bunch of their best fighters, and when he lays them all down with his surprisingly effective martial arts abilities, he's only got to get through the badass Russian henchman (played by Stefanos Miltsakakis from *Cyborg* and *Maximum Risk*) before he can actually face off against his treacherous brother.

By-the-numbers and without a spark of inspiration, *Martial Outlaw* is another disappointment from director Kurt Anderson and Jeff Wincott, who made the equally discouraging *Open Fire* together. Wincott looks good on film, and his acting is certainly efficient enough, but the downbeat plotting and generic scripting do nothing to elevate him or embrace him. His counterpart (played by Hudson) is entirely one-dimensional, which makes him a boring villain bound for a certain fate. For better Wincott films, try *Martial Law II: Undercover* (also directed by Anderson) or *Mission of Justice*.

Masked Rider

1995–1996 (CD)

"For a top banana, you should be more appealing!"

Dex (Ted Jan Roberts from *Tiger Heart*) is a young boy from a planet called Edenoi. With only moments left before it's about to

be destroyed by an evil ruler known as Count Dregon (Ken Merckx), his grandfather passes down to him the power of the Masked Rider (a suit of armor that gives him superhero-like abilities). With Edenoi gone, Dregon wants to use the Earth as a breeding ground for his overgrown, walking maggots. Dex is dispatched to the Earth only to be found by a family with two adopted children. The Stewarts waste no time in taking the boy into their home and treating him like one of their own. Dregon only has one real goal: to have the Masked Rider body armor for himself . . . and nothing will ever get in his way of trying. And while Dex may have full control of the costume, learning to act human is a pinch more difficult, especially when he learns English by watching countless hours of television. He doesn't waste any time telling his adopted family the truth about his mission, and as crazy as that sounds to them, they still accept him unconditionally. Dex is also surprised that his furry little pal from Edenoi—Ferbus—has tagged along for the ride. Now, these two aliens are protectors of human life and the Earth.

Masked Rider was really nothing more than a possible cash grab for Saban Entertainment (who also gave us the mega-hit *Mighty Morphin Power Rangers* franchise). It followed a similar model where they used footage from the Japanese *Kamen Rider Black RX* series and partnered it with new footage shot in the US with an American cast. The majority of the action is then courtesy of this Japanese series and showcases some pretty extravagant fight sequences with various twisted looking creatures. Teen action star T. J. Roberts (who found "B" movie success with pictures like *Magic Kid*) eventually gets to show off his technique outside of the costume. He never failed to impress with his action skills but this show is mostly a bust for adults. Each episode is formulaic and predictable; the same thing happens in every installment. Count Dregon sends some sort of creature to try and stop Dex while Ferbus gets into all sorts of trouble; i.e. the day is saved, then everyone learns an important lesson, and they laugh: The End. The Ferbus character was created and designed to capitalize on the Ferbie craze of the time period, and it's painfully obvious. The show does teach important lessons to children, the action is pretty spectacular, and T. J. Roberts doesn't disappoint on the action front. *Masked Rider* is fun for a few episodes, but watching all forty is more than any mortal human being should have to endure. For completists only.

Mask of Death

1995 (Lionsgate DVD) (djm)

Detective Daniel McKenna (Lorenzo Lamas) is shot in the face by a mobster named Lyle Mason (also Lamas), who is on the run from the FBI. McKenna's wife is murdered, and Mason is killed in a fiery car crash. McKenna wakes up in the hospital and is approached by Agent Jeffries (Billy Dee Wiliams) who offers him an opportunity: Since he looks a lot like Mason already, why not get a little plastic surgery to make the transformation complete and fool the mob into thinking that Mason is still alive? A whole plan is hatched for McKenna to infiltrate the mob under the guise of Mason, and McKenna has to learn how to become a cold-blooded killer. He fools even his ex-partner (played by Rae Dawn Chong), but he soon makes an ally of her when he reveals his true identity.

With elements of better films like *Remo Williams: The Adventure Begins* and the big-budget action film *Face/Off*, *Mask of Death* has a fair beginning, but it becomes a grating and tedious picture to watch due to a lame script and lackluster direction. Lamas tries, but the film is populated by unappealing characters who resort to streams of profanity rather than actual discourse. David Mitchell directed. He also did *Last to Surrender* with Roddy Piper and *The Killing Man* with Jeff Wincott.

The Master

(a.k.a. **The Master Ninja**)

1984 (Trans World Entertainment VHS) (djm)

This television program that lasted twelve one-hour episodes helped launch Japanese martial artist Sho Kosugi into the limelight in the United States. He plays a ninja villain named Okasa who is chasing his American master John Peter McAllister (Lee Van Cleef), a Korean war veteran and a ninjutsu expert, across the US as he is searching for his long-lost daughter. McAllister has picked up a new protégé named Max (played by Timothy Van Patten), who is helping him track down his daughter. From one episode to the next McAllister and Max help pretty women out of bad situations by using their ninja skills. Occasionally, Okasa shows up and interferes with their plans, but McAllister invariably manages to get the best of Okasa.

I love shows like *MacGuyver, The A-Team,* and *The Master*. I grew up on this stuff. As corny and simplistic as they are now, I can sit back and relax and not have to worry about anything but pretty girls getting saved by ninjas. That's what this show is all about. Watching Lee Van Cleef don a goofy looking ninja suit is about as ridiculous as things get, and when his stunt double starts doing cartwheels and dodging bullets, I just revel in the absurdity. Co-star Kosugi also served as a technical advisor and weapons craftsman, but it's a shame he wasn't on screen for more than a few episodes. The Trans World VHS releases were around in video stores for years, and all six of the tapes brazenly used his name and face to sell rentals, despite the fact that he was barely in the show. His son Kane (from *Revenge of the Ninja* and *Ninja II: Shadow of a Tear*) appears in one of the last episodes. Other notable guest stars include Demi Moore and Kathleen Kinmont. Many of the episodes were directed by Gordon Hessler who would go on to direct *Pray for Death, Rage of Honor,* and *Journey of Honor,* all with Sho Kosugi. The theme music for *The Master* was composed by Bill Conti, and anyone who's heard his score for *For Your Eyes Only* will notice the resemblance.

The Master

1989 (Dimension DVD) (djm)

Jet Li (as a character named "Jet") comes to Los Angeles to visit his marital arts instructor, but runs into trouble with local gangs and a kickboxing champ (Jerry Trimble) who is also a former student of his instructor. Jet impresses the local gangs, but the kickboxing champ wants to see him humiliated . . . or dead. The climax features Jet and Jerry on a rooftop of a sky rise, and it doesn't disappoint.

This might actually appeal more to Trimble's fans than Li's. While Li is the hero, it feels more like a showcase for Trimble, who was brand new to movies. Li looks very young while Trimble looks appropriately sinister and villainous. It's mostly lightweight, with some comedy, but some of the violence is pretty bloody. It's better than Li's later Americanized *Romeo Must Die* and *Cradle 2 the Grave*. Billy Blanks appears as a thug in one scene. Tsui Hark directed it.

The Master Demon

1991 (Digital Video Dreams DVD R2) (djm)

"A man is not responsible for this! It is a demon!"

In an ancient place, in another time, two celestial warriors are duking it out with swords. One is a demon, the other a heavenly warrior. The demon (played by Gerald Okamura with half a face) is trying to cross over to Earth to wreak unholy havoc, and the angel/man (played by Eric Lee) is simply trying to stop him. When the demon's hand is cut off during the fight, the demon retreats for thousands of years, and the warrior encloses the severed appendage in a sacred box where it is kept until it ends up in a museum in modern times. During a tourist walkthrough, the box is disrupted and the demon is unleashed again, prompting a new battle for the fate of mankind. The warrior must face off against the demon and his minions (one of whom is played by a gigantic, buff woman in a thong), and they go to war one more time.

The Master Demon feels like it was made on the fly as a riff on *Big Trouble in Little China,* and I swear that if you pay attention to some of the plot developments and pay *very* close attention to some of the characters that you will see the similarities. That said, it's pretty much a shambles, but who cares? If you're reading this book and reading this review in particular and have any love for guys like Eric Lee and Gerald Okamura, then you'll want to go out there and find a copy of this movie to watch some day. You should. It's bonkers. Lee and Okamura also crossed swords and fists in *Weapons of Death.* Check that one out, too! Filmed in 1988 (watch for a marquee playing Luc Besson's *The Big Blue*). Directed by Art Camcho and Samuel Oldham.

The Master Gunfighter

1975 (Ventura DVD) (djm)

Tom Laughlin (from the *Billy Jack* movies) plays Finley, the Master Gunfighter in this odd western directed by Laughlin's son Frank. Finley (whom everyone calls Master Gunfighter) lives with a tribe of Indians on the coast of Northern California, and when several wealthy dons hatch a plan to steal a shipment of gold (which is meant to serve as taxes to the government), the plan turns into a mass murder plot involving the systematic slaughter of the tribe of Indians who stand in the way of the greedy dons. As Finley becomes aware of the plot, he makes a stand against the Dons, despite the fact that Don Paulo Santiago (Ron O'Neal from *Eye For an Eye*) is his brother-in-law. Finley, while known as a "master gunfighter," is also a master swordsman, a skill he picked up in the Far East in the years when he exiled himself from California when Paulo first betrayed his trust. Now a proficient samurai *and* gunfighter, Finley is a one-man executioner against the killers and scum who intend on murdering his tribe.

An unusual hybrid of a western and samurai film, *The Master Gunfighter* is a likely and conspicuous outing from star Laughlin, who will always be remembered for playing the iconic Billy Jack. His character here is cool, commanding, and mysteriously awesome, but the pace of the film is aggravatingly lackluster, and even when the fight scenes and violence comes in jolting spurts, the film still never finds its footing on solid ground. Laughlin is a unique action star, and his body of work deserves to be studied, but many will find his vehicles difficult to get into. I like *The Master Gunfighter,* but it's a misfire. Barbara Carrera (*Lone Wolf McQuade*) co-stars.

Masterblaster

1985 (Prism VHS) (djm)

For $50,000, anyone can join the game of Masterblaster: an elaborate paintball gauntlet where paying players hunt other players in a booby-trapped forest in an idyllic wilderness. This year's contestants include a policewoman, a novelist, several backwoods hillbillies, an actor, and an ex-soldier named Jeremy Hawk (played by martial artist Jeff Moldovan) who did a two-year stint in the Mekong Delta in Vietnam. Before Hawk arrives at the game site, we've seen that he can more than handle himself: at a quick stop at a backwoods bar, he's singled out for being a biker by some inbreds, and he makes short order of the pack of guys by breaking some pool cues over their necks and throwing them all out the window. Once the Masterblaster game begins, it looks like Hawk will easily pick the others off in the friendly game, but when an unseen killer stalks and slays the players one by one using the booby traps and other deadly weapons at his (or her) disposal, the game stops being fun and an agenda reveals itself.

Mostly fun and mindless action entertainment, the low-budget *Masterblaster* starts off in the same vein as *Tag: The Assassination Game* or *Gotcha!* and

M

ends up feeling a little like *The Zero Boys*, but with more focus on star Moldovan, who contributed to the script. Up to this point in his career (and after this project), Moldovan made a career out of being a stuntman and fight coordinator on feature films and TV shows. His portrayal of an emotionally withdrawn 'Nam vet feels sincere and his prowess as a physical force is impressive on screen. The movie itself dips a little too deep in unconvincing slasher tropes, but when it's on action mode, it's at its best. Moldovan would co-star in a few negligible Italian-made action films after this, but he would mostly be relegated to the sidelines. Directed by prolific stuntman Glenn R. Wilder.

Max Havoc: Curse of the Dragon

2004 (Westlake DVD) (CD)

Sports photographer Max Havoc (Mickey Hardt) is looking for a change of scenery. After speaking with his boss, he's given an assignment in Guam to take pictures for an ad campaign. Once there, he meets up with his old friend Tahsi (Richard Roundtree) who was once his kickboxing coach. Many years before Max was a kickboxer but left it all behind when he accidentally killed a man in the ring. Tahsi is now an antique dealer and has acquired a very rare jade dragon, which he sells to Jane Goody (Joanna Crupa). There are some vicious people who want the jade dragon for themselves and will do anything to obtain it. When lives are taken, Max will have to spring back into action to save Jane while being confronted at the same time by a few demons from his past.

Max Havoc: Curse of the Dragon is a simple yet poorly conceived film with very little to offer besides a couple of surprisingly well-choreographed fight scenes. Mickey Hardt (*Vampire Effect*) is a bit dry as an actor but has a charming demeanor, so he's likable. The only reason the film is worth watching is to see him in the numerous action scenes in which he takes on various opponents. Also in the cast are David Carradine (*Lone Wolf McQuade*) and rising Vietnamese action star Johnny Nguyen (*Cradle 2 the Grave*). The film spends far too much time on pointless dialogue and has an excessive amount of stock footage. Though Albert Pyun (*Cyborg*) is the credited director, he had some help from Isaac Florentine (*Ninja*) who directed some of the final scenes to fill out an otherwise weak story. The film is better known for the controversy it created in Guam (it was funded by the government and producers failed to pay the money back) than anything else. It was followed by the sequel *Max Havoc: Ring of Fire* in 2006.

Max Havoc: Ring of Fire

2006 (Westlake DVD) (CD)

"Aw Max, I gotta tell ya, I'm a little disappointed. I thought you'd be a little tougher but maybe you've lost that killer instinct."

Retired kickboxer-turned-photographer Max Havoc (Mickey Hardt) has booked himself a job for a magazine taking pictures of a beautiful young tennis player named Suzy Blaine (Christina Cox). The shoot is set to take place at a lush resort where everything is being arranged by the owner, Roger Tarso (Dean Cain). Before Max can begin, a young boy steals his camera case. He follows up a lead and finds the boy living in a mission with Sister Caroline (Rae Dawn Chong). She explains to Max all the troubles they have been having with a local gang before he witnesses firsthand the severity of the problem. No one knows the identity of the gang's leader (who calls himself "Tiger") except the young boy who witnessed his brother being killed by him. Max and Suzy see a chance to make a difference and will sacrifice themselves in order to protect the child.

The Max Havoc character has so much potential and Mickey Hardt (*Max Havoc: Curse of the Dragon*) has all the skills necessary to be an action star. It's a shame neither film in the franchise was able to capture what could have been a really solid and entertaining series of "B" action films. *Ring of Fire* has a great cast and a better script than the first entry, but this one suffers from something very unexpected: The lighting is so atrocious it's almost impossible to see what's happening. When you can make out what's going on, Hardt is able to show off his kickboxing skills in several nicely choreographed scenes. The film is a little slow moving at times but has spirit and excitement. Director Terry Ingram (TV's *Relic Hunter*) delivers a better film than the predecessor, with the exception of the bad lighting.

Maximum Conviction

2012 (Anchor Bay DVD) (djm)

"Remember, man. It ain't over 'til we're dead."

A maximum-security prison is being decommissioned and a team of private contractors is tasked with clearing the cellblocks out while maintaining complete order and efficiency. Partners Steele (Steve Seagal) and Manning (Steve Austin) and their team are going about their business without incident until some things start going haywire. Someone on their team is working against them and *for* a group of mercenaries who come into the prison to extract two female prisoners, one of whom has valuable information, so secret that it's never quite made clear what she knows. The leader of the mercenaries is played by Michael Pare (from *Streets of Fire*), and he's a ruthless badass in his own

Video release promo for *Maximum Conviction*. Author's collection.

right, so when his plans are stonewalled by Steele and Manning, he's puzzled because this sort of thing never happens to him. Since this is a movie where Seagal and Austin are teammates instead of playing against each other, it should be fairly obvious that any opposing force against them will be met with the utmost brutality. It's a bloodbath.

From the cover of the video box, it's not really clear if the two Steves are friends or enemies. Since it turns out that they're on the same side, it's too bad that they didn't cast more awesome bad guys to fight them, but Michael Pare (almost, but not quite, an action star) is more than welcome in any movie, but when he faces Seagal in a fight, it's almost hilarious at how overpowered he is. My biggest issue with the film is that Seagal and Austin only have one scene where they're in the same shot (it's near the beginning). The last scene of the film has some clearly fudged doubling going on, and Austin and Seagal have a conversation with each other, but they are never framed in the shot at the same time. I hated that. Another crucial scene with Seagal and the main actress in the film is also fudged with doubling. Stuff like this irks me because it would be so easy for Seagal to show up to the set to shoot these crucial scenes with his co-stars. Other than that, *Maximum Conviction* is almost what it should have been. It's adequate. Director Keoni Waxman has worked with both Seagal and Austin before. He did *Hunt to Kill* with Austin, and *The Keeper, A Dangerous Man, Force of Execution,* and several episodes of *True Justice,* all with Seagal.

Maximum Impact

2008 (Brightspark DVD) (CD)

"There is a difference—I don't kill innocent people or sell our country's secrets to the scum of the Earth. And I'm only going to kill you and your boyfriends here."

Agent X (Ara Paiaya) is assigned to help save Katie Tang (Raquel Paiaya), a woman responsible for designing one of the toughest firewalls to hack. She has fallen into the hands of Pirani

M

(Adam Davidson), a former agent who has an encoded flash drive with info he desperately wants to sell for the big bucks. The only person who can decode it is Katie. Agent X tries to stay one step ahead of the game, but somehow Pirani is able to foil his rescue attempts. With a mole in the Department of Justice and assassins on his tail, he quickly learns he has no one to count on except himself.

Ara "Bradley" Paiaya is best suited for humorous action roles as opposed to something as serious (in tone) as *Maximum Impact*. It takes itself really seriously, but there's still something intriguing about this fellow. Some of the action scenes are really well done and they're surprisingly exciting, but then just when you think you're about to get a payoff, you see something that calls the bluff and you just sit there shaking your head. This movie also has an unnecessarily long end credits—eighty percent of the credits are just Ara Paiaya's name rolling over and over again. An injection of humor can go a long way and could have possibly saved this supposedly five million dollar feature (at least according to Imdb.com, though I call bullshit). There are a couple of neat stunts and some interesting touches in the choreography, but not enough to warrant a search to track this down.

Maximum Risk

1996 (Sony DVD) (djm)

One of Jean-Claude Van Damme's last and best studio theatrical releases, *Maximum Risk* casts him in two roles, as he plays twins (again). In the prologue, Russian gangster Mikhail (Van Damme) is killed by some corrupt FBI guys, and then we meet his twin brother, a French cop named Alain Moreau (also Van Damme), who had no idea that he had a twin. Alain tries to solve his brother's murder by going back to the source: his mother, who tells him that yes, he had a twin. He then begins searching for clues as to who his brother was and how he became a gangster, and ultimately who killed him and why. When he figures out that his brother was trying to find him and give him some dirty secrets of the Russian mob and their ties to the FBI, both the mob and the bad Feds come after *him* because they think he might catch on to the secrets his brother knew. He travels to New York where he meets Mikhail's girlfriend Alex (a super

Detective Alain Moreau (Jean-Claude Van Damme) is hunting his twin brother's killer in *Maximum Risk*. Author's collection.

Lots of vehicular mayhem to enjoy in *Maximum Risk*. Author's collection.

sexy Natasha Henstridge), who doesn't realize at first that Alain is not his brother, but when he comes clean (before he has sex with her), she helps him solve the big mystery. Lots of stunts and martial arts action keeps things interesting.

From Hong Kong director Ringo Lam, *Maximum Risk* has a great James Bondian vibe running through it, with nice foreign locales, a strong hero, a supermodel-looking leading lady, stunts galore, and bad guys who have lots of henchman. The best henchman is played by Stefanos Miltsakakis, who fights Van Damme several times in the movie, but their best scene together is their last one in an elevator. Miltsakakis also appeared alongside Van Damme in *Cyborg* and in *Derailed*. I really like *Maximum Risk*, and I enjoy Van Damme's understated performance in it. It's one of his movies that I return to now and again and fondly remember seeing in a theater (twice). Director Lam would later reunite with his star for the films *Replicant* and *In Hell*.

McCinsey's Island

1997 (Monarch VHS) (djm)

Officially retired from protecting the world, former secret agent Joe McGrai (Hulk Hogan) lives on a tropical island, enjoying life with his jet skis and his sidekick talking bird. His old partner Walter (Robert Vaughn) shows up and warns him that their former nemesis Alanso Richter (Grace Jones) is on the island with a crew of henchman, and they're going to torment them until they lead them to a stash of buried pirate treasure somewhere on the island. Joe, who recently captured a giant turtle with an etched map on its shell, gets worked up and decides that they'd better find the treasure before anyone else does, and as he finds a priceless diamond (about the size of a grapefruit!), the game is afoot when Alanso captures one of his friends.

I can't believe this movie was directed by Sam Firstenberg! The man who made *Revenge of the Ninja*, *American Ninja*, and *Avenging Force* made this . . . movie. Not for one second can we possibly believe that Hulk Hogan is a former secret agent in this PG-rated picture. When he sees the map carving on the turtle's shell he says something like "I think it's safe to assume that this was etched by a human." As an action movie, this is fabulous stuff for little kids with great attention spans. Hogan gets into some clumsy wrestling matches, but it's all very

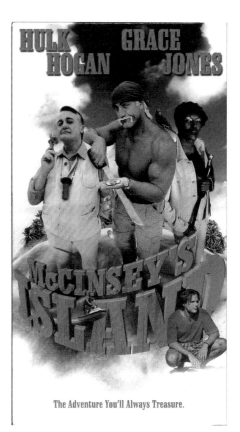

VHS artwork for Sam Firstenberg's *McCinsey's Island*. Author's collection.

comedic and silly. Grace Jones as the villain is basically doing a parody of her character in *A View to a Kill*. Everyone involved seems to have accepted filming this movie for its value as a tropical island vacation getaway.

Mean Johnny Barrows

1976 (Movie Ventures DVD) (CD)

"How do you measure a man's worth, Nancy? Is it by what he owns, his dreams, or what he wants from life?"

Johnny Barrows (Fred Williamson) is a GI who is dishonorably discharged from the military after striking his superior officer. Back in civilian life, he's mugged and arrested by racist cops. He eventually gets released and finds himself starving on the streets. In an Italian restaurant, he is offered a job by mob boss Mario Racconi (Stuart Whitman). He doesn't want to involve himself in that kind of work and turns down the offer. He lands a job as a gas station attendant but the owner treats him like a slave. One day he has enough and flips out on his boss. Mr. Racconi and his girl Nancy (Jenny Sherman) continue to visit him, always treating him with respect. When Barrows lands in jail for a second time, Nancy is quick to bail him out. The Racconis find themselves in a mob war with the Da Vinci family who want to peddle drugs to the kids. The Racconis want nothing to do with the stuff so all

M

hell breaks loose. When Nancy is kidnapped by the Da Vincis, it's time for Barrows to get mean.

Mean Johnny Barrows sort of moves at a slow pace but is well worth sitting through to enjoy the payoff. Much of the film builds on how rough Barrows's life has become. Fred Williamson (*Black Cobra*) plays the character sympathetically and you sort of feel bad for the guy. So when the time comes that he is thrust into action, the violence more than makes up for the slowness of the first half. Williamson gets to do a bit of everything in this one—not only on screen, but behind the scenes as well. As the director, he skillfully balances the drama and action. There are several bloody shootouts and Williamson uses his fists just as frequently. While the choreography was nothing extravagant, there's that Williamson charm that just makes you smile. Another solid effort from a legendary performer.

Mean Machine

2001 (Paramount DVD) (CD)

"Oh right lads, you wanna be nothing—prisoners . . . numbers . . . that's fine. But you win out there today, and you'll have something to remember forever, talk about it over and over, because up and down the country there are cons that are pig-sick of not being here in your shoes . . . just to have one crack at those bastards next door!"

Danny Meehan (Vinnie Jones) was a soccer superstar until he blew it by throwing a game. He begins to drown his troubles in the bottle and finds himself doing a year in a maximum-security prison. Once inside, he finds out quick that they don't like celebrities and he finds it tough to adjust. The warden wants him to coach his soccer team made up of guards, though head guard and current coach Burton (Ralph Brown) warns him (with force) not to. Instead, Meehan pitches the idea of assembling a team of inmates to go against the guards. This idea is embraced by everyone, especially the inmates since this will be their one and only chance to get at the guards. The ragtag group of misfits that includes the psychotic Monk (Jason Statham), Billy the Limpet (Danny Dyer), and Hayter (Nick Moss) can't win without the cooperation of the resident mob boss and his cronies. It's going to take more than a bunch of tough guys to win; they'll have to unite as a team if they are to beat the guards.

Mean Machine is a remake of the 1974 Burt Reynolds film *The Longest Yard* (which was also remade in 2005 with Adam Sandler). With executive producer Guy Ritchie (*Snatch*) and producer Matthew Vaughn (*Kick-Ass*), the film has an overtly cool persona, much like the works of these fantastic directors. Vinnie Jones (*Locked Down*) is the perfect actor for this role since he spent many years himself as a pro football (soccer) player in the UK. He's fantastic in the role and adds an element of authenticity to it. There's plenty of action and a nice drinking game, which involves punching the opponent in

the face and then doing a shot to see who can last the longest. Also in a very memorable role is Jason Statham (*Blitz*), who steals every scene he's in. He plays a crazed killer who plays the game extremely roughly and has daydreams of beating the guards. Though the 2005 remake is fun, this is the superior film. Directed by Barry Skolnick.

The Mechanic

1972 (MGM DVD) (ZC)

There's no shortage of articles that cover the crucial impact Charles Bronson had on film and culture as a whole. But what they all oddly fail to mention is that *he was the greatest human being who ever lived.* I've done my research and determined this to be an indisputable fact. And *The Mechanic* is his absolute apex. Bronson plays Arthur Bishop, an ice-cold hitman/"mechanic" for a powerful but nebulous global crime ring. He inherited the job from his late father, a legendary fixer who taught him the tools of the trade. As Bishop reaches middle age, he similarly takes on eager protégé Steve McKenna (Jan Michael Vincent), who may be even more heartless than Bishop himself. It's a fairly simple premise for a crime masterpiece, and that's what makes *The Mechanic* perfectly effective. There's no dialogue for the first fifteen minutes of the film, a trick that few Hollywood productions have dared pull since. Your protagonists murder lifelong friends, and stand by unaffected as a teenager slits her wrists. Through all the bombings, bullets, and dazzling motorcycle collisions, it's this emotional detachment that guides the movie into places other thrillers won't tread.

Though Bronson allegedly disliked working with "pretty" co-star Vincent, the dual non-emoters have a transfixing reptilian chemistry. Their characters almost seem competitive in their quest to detach themselves from our species. In fact, Bishop's lone moment of humanity takes place in an interaction with his quasi-ladyfriend (played by Bronson's actual wife, Jill Ireland). Without revealing too much, it's a subtle, unexpected scene that reveals volumes about the character, and not necessarily what you'd expect from a collaboration between Bronson and pugilistic director Michael Winner. The pair ended up completing six movies together before the rampaging, irresponsible hostility of *Death Wish 3* ended their relationship entirely. (PS: That movie is *raaaaaaging.*)

The Mechanic

2011 (Sony DVD) (CD)

Arthur Bishop (Jason Statham) is a gun for hire, the best in the business. When he's hired to punch someone's ticket, he can make it look like no one else had ever been there. When he receives orders for his next job, the target is Harry McKenna (Donald Sutherland), his friend and mentor. Bishop finds himself torn between his job and personal feelings. The decision will be the toughest one he will ever make. In comes Steve (Ben Foster), Harry's troubled son, who wants revenge for Harry's murder. Bishop takes him in

Arthur Bishop (Jason Statham) is on the run after a hit in Millennium's *The Mechanic*. Author's collection.

Teacher and pupil: Arthur Bishop (Jason Statham) and Steve McKenna (Ben Foster) in *The Mechanic*. Author's collection.

Being a hitman is a lonely profession. Just look at Arthur Bishop (Jason Statham) in *The Mechanic*. Author's collection.

Jason Statham plays Arthur Bishop, and Ben Foster plays Steve McKenna in the remake of *The Mechanic*. Author's collection.

as an apprentice, keeping his secret to himself. The film develops into a character study between these two, building to a final double- and triple-cross, exposing these guys for who they really are.

The Mechanic is a loose remake of the 1972 film of the same name starring Charles Bronson and Jan Michael Vincent, which was based on a book by Lewis John Carlino. In this incarnation, Jason Statham has taken over the Bishop role in the type of film he is most comfortable in. Whether or not you're willing to nominate Statham as the current heir to the action hero throne, he possesses a charisma both sexes can identify with. Even though he plays a cold-blooded killer (with brutal and defining martial arts skills), he is still likable and really delivers the action. His co-star, Ben Foster, luckily has a strong character to work with and he does a fine job playing with the big boys and could possibly hold an action film on his own. The film's best scene features a great one-on-one brawl between him and an opponent who towers over him. The story, while familiar, works well, despite its flaws. When you pay to see a movie starring Statham you generally know what to expect and *The Mechanic* delivers where it matters. Director Simon West (*The Expendables 2, Con Air*) is no stranger to action and is able to hold it all together. Though not a big hit in theaters, a sequel (with Statham) is in the works.

The Medallion (a.k.a. Highbinders)

2003 (Sony DVD) (djm)

A magical medallion makes it through the ages of time without getting into the wrong hands . . . until the evil Snakehead (Julian Sands) sets his sights on it in the present day. Snakehead sends his goons to kidnap a mysterious, ethereal child who possesses the medallion, but Hong Kong cop Eddie Yang (Jackie Chan) saves the child in a heroic, selfless act and dies in the process. As a thank-you gift, the child blesses Yang, and as a result Yang is brought back from the dead with supernatural powers to protect the medallion from any villainous comers. Snakehead must do battle with the now-powerful Yang to obtain that which he covets most.

A telling theatrical poster featuring beautiful co-star Claire Forlani and Jackie Chan striking kung fu poses kept me away from this movie for years until I watched it to write this review. After Chan's disastrous team-up with Jennifer Love Hewitt for the abysmal *The Tuxedo*, I wasn't in a hurry to watch another movie where Chan was paired up with another lovely looking Caucasian actress with zero martial arts abilities. *The Medallion* is (sadly) just as bad—or worse—than *The Tuxedo* for a myriad of reasons. The martial arts action (choreographed by Sammo Hung) is completely aided and abetted by wires and CGI enhancement, which discounts everything that happens in the movie, and the buffoonish story clunks and clatters from the first frames to the last. It's almost entirely irredeemable. But you knew that when you saw the poster, didn't you? Directed by Gordon Chan (*Thunderbolt* with Chan). For similar-type films check out *Prince of the Sun* with Cynthia Rothrock or *The Lost Medallion* with Mark Dacascos.

Meltdown

1995 (Sony DVD) (djm)

A mad bomber named The Doctor and his terrorist minions bomb a school bus full of children and some teachers, and they get away with it. A cop, whose wife was on the bus, is haunted by the incident and he quits the force and becomes the bodyguard for a movie star. Kit (Jet Li), the bodyguard, performs all of his employer's stunts in his movies, and he's sort of bored by the whole thing. His employer, Frankie Lane (Jacky Cheung), is a good-for-nothing playboy who goofs around all day and fools everyone into thinking that he's a martial arts master when Kit is the one who's really dangerous. Meanwhile, as Frankie and Kit check into a swanky hotel during a break from making a new movie, The Doctor and his terrorists sweep into the place and kill a bunch of people in the lobby and lock the hotel down and hold everyone in it hostage as if this were a *Die Hard* movie. Sensing both an opportunity to save his employer and also to get revenge, Kit springs into action and helps save the day.

Irresponsible direction by Wong Jing (*City Hunter*) really upsets this way-too-goofy and way-too-violent film. After the jarring first few minutes where a busload of children is blown apart, the next scene has the Frankie Lane character (modeled after Jackie Chan) acting silly, signaling that we're in for a comedy, but then the film veers excessively to the side to showcase mind-numbing violence with bloodletting, mayhem, and explosions galore, particularly in the last act. Jet Li's role is relegated to almost a humorless sidekick, while the annoying Jacky Cheung grates in his riff on Jackie Chan. Incidentally, this was *supposed* to be the first on-screen pairing of Chan and Li, but after Chan had a bad experience working with director Jing on *City Hunter*, he opted out. His image is lampooned pretty heartlessly in this, and Li reportedly personally apologized to him later.

Memorial Day

1998 (Artisan VHS) (djm)

"I understand this is war, sir. I'm anxious to get started."

From Royal Oaks Entertainment, this Jeff Speakman vehicle spends an inordinate amount of time on characters in closed sets, looking at television screens or talking on the phone, and when that stuff gets boring, there's lots of stock footage of submarines and satellites in space, shooting lasers. Speakman stars as a brainwashed operative named Edward Downey, who is tortured for the first half-hour of the movie and then unleashed by his corrupt boss who wants a presidential candidate assassinated, but when Downey starts to get visions and some of his memory back, he realizes that he's working for the wrong side. He goes rogue and he helps foil a gigantic plot to cause untold damage to the United States of America. He uses his kenpo skills too, thank goodness.

Unfortunately for Speakman's most devoted fans (that would be me: hello!), *Memorial Day* is a sad movie because it's easy to see that he's being held back considerably and that the movie is way beneath him. There's nothing wrong with the way he acts in the movie, and his fighting skills are up to par, but the movie just fails as it tries to accommodate him. The script by Steve Latshaw (who also wrote *Command Performance* for Dolph Lundgren and *Mach 2* for Brian Bosworth) really goes to great lengths to piece together a convoluted plot framed around some stock footage of military hardware and explosions from other movies. I tried to make sense of the story, but I stopped paying attention to the details and just focused on Speakman, who by this point in his career should have been making solid movies that showcased his amazing abilities as a martial artist. *Memorial Day* isn't a complete waste, but if you're a fan of his and have never seen it, you'll be disappointed by it. The director, Worth Keeter, also did *Scorpio One* with Speakman.

Men of War

1994 (Dimension DVD) (djm)

A washed up mercenary named Nick Gunar (Dolph Lundgren) is approached by some businessmen to undertake a mission in far east Asia. Reluctant at first to take the job, he eventually decides to do it with the proviso that he can recruit his own team. Assembling a motley crew of expendable soldiers cobbled from his past, they travel to this exotic island far removed from modern civilization. Gunar and his men are meant to persuade the islanders into signing over their island for money, but the islanders have been through it all before—they have no interest in money, and they're willing to die fighting to keep anyone from taking their island away from them. It turns out that the island has a valuable natural resource (something about bird excrement), and it comes to the point when Gunar's men turn against each other when they realize that they won't get paid if they don't just kill the islanders already. Gunar ends up taking up a cause by siding with the natives, and his team divides in half—those who will fight with the natives, and those who'll fight to kill them. The final battle is bloody.

Amazingly underrated and mostly ignored, *Men of War* is undoubtedly one of Dolph's best films as well as an incredibly bloody action/war film from screenwriter John Sayles. It has a rich, epic scope, and it's criminal that it wasn't given a theatrical release in the US. Fans of Lundgren's will note that he plays a mercenary named Gunar here. He also plays a similar (but somewhat more degraded) character named Gunnar in *The Expendables*. His cohorts and compadres in *Men of War* include Tiny Lister, B. D. Wong (who steals the movie), and Trevor Goddard, amongst others. It was directed by Perry Lang.

M

Merantau

2009 (Magnet DVD) (djm)

Yuda (Iko Uwais who would later star in *The Raid: Redemption*) is at the time in his life when he must embark on a "Merantau" quest to find his own way in life and become a man of honor. He leaves his family behind in their quiet village in Indonesia and travels to Jakarta where he immediately encounters trouble. Equipped with his skills in silat (a traditional martial art native to Indonesia), Yuda defends himself and the honor of a local young woman who is being harassed by thugs. He gets the attention of the leader of the gang, and while that's a bad thing, Yuda shrugs off the experience as just his first day in the city. Without a home or lodging, Yuda sleeps in a construction yard, and his next day is comprised of more of the same: He encounters more thugs who are harassing the same woman, and as it turns out, the woman has been targeted by a human slave trafficking ring, and only Yuda in his innocence and unmatched skills in fighting can attempt to save her. The head of the ring is lead by a cantankerous Caucasian named Ratger (Mads Koudal, a practitioner in Muay Thai fighting), whose rage is only matched by his cruelty. When Yuda throws himself utterly and completely against the trafficking ring, he may have committed himself to more than he's equipped to handle.

Down and dirty (and pretty exhausting) for a martial arts fight movie, *Merantau* is notable for introducing star Iko Uwais to the world, while writer/director/editor Gareth Evans (G. H. Evans) also introduced himself as the new kid on the block. As a first effort, *Merantau* is extremely well shot and directed—though too long—and its statement on what fate has in store for innocent virginal Muslim heroes is startlingly depressing for a mostly jaw-dropping action entertainment. Director Evans and Uwais teamed up several years later for the game-changing film *The Raid: Redemption* and that film's sequel.

Mercenaries

2014 (The Asylum DVD) (djm)

"We go PMS from hell on this place!"

A riff on *The Expendables*, starring or featuring several well-known female action stars, The Asylum's *Mercenaries* wastes absolutely no time in revving its engines and going full speed ahead. The president's daughter is kidnapped by some terrorists in the Middle East, and the head of the CIA (Cynthia Rothrock) quickly forms a plan to recruit some mercenaries to spearhead a mission to rescue the first daughter. Her mercenaries are cast-offs of society, all serving extended sentences in various penitentiaries, and here's the roster: Clay (Zoe Bell), Kat (Kristanna Lokken), Raven (Vivica A. Fox), and Mei-Lin (Nicole Bilderback). The ladies are informed of the mission, given a once-in-a-lifetime opportunity to redeem

Promotional card for The Asylum's *Mercenaries*. Author's collection.

themselves, obtain a presidential pardon, and stretch their legs on the battlefield. When they're off and running, they butt heads with the terrorists, whose leader Ulrikia (played by a surprisingly well-cast Brigitte Nielsen) is well up to the challenge of facing fellow female warriors.

As low-rent and cheap as the film is, *Mercenaries* is a delightfully fun romp, with lots of digital effects and enhancements that almost make it seem like you're watching something with a budget. Casting Zoe Bell alongside Lokken and Rothrock is a great move for The Asylum, and it's a shame that they weren't all cast in one of Millennium's *Expendables* flicks. Rothrock's role is relegated to bossing the recruits around, but it's obvious that she could still handle herself well in an action scene even well into her fifties. Director Chris Olen Ray (son of Fred) makes the whole thing work somehow, and despite the strangely familiar Californian landscapes filling in for Middle Eastern locales, *Mercenaries* ain't chopped liver.

Mercenary

1996 (Lionsgate DVD) (djm)

Multi-millionaire Jonas Ambler (John Ritter) holds a party on his yacht, celebrating a controversial Iraqi author who is the guest of honor. A group of terrorists crash the party, slaughtering dozens, including the author and Ambler's wife. While in recovery, Ambler begins planning his revenge. He tries hiring a mercenary named Hawk (Olivier Gruner), but Hawk backs off when Ambler insists on going along on the mission to kill the terrorists, led by Phoenix (Martin Kove). Later, when one of Hawk's men is framed for drug smuggling, Hawk turns to Ambler to bail his friend out in exchange for spearheading the mission to the Middle East to kill the terrorists. Much to Hawk's chagrin, Ambler slows his team down, complains, and

gets them into some trouble when his feelings get in the way, but by the end of the mission, Ambler has become a pseudo commando.

Mercenary is as complete a package as a low-budget action film can be. It's got a cool martial arts action star (Gruner) at the center, with plenty of explosions, stunts, excitement, and martial arts action all the way through. Gruner, who plays a one-note character, is a compelling action star, who after a real-life career as a French Commando became a champion kickboxer *and then* chose acting as a follow-up. The way he plays a mercenary in this film feels oddly real. His co-stars include Robert Culp, Ed Lauter, and Nils Allen Stewart, who appeared in *Mars* with Gruner. Director Avi Nesher also did *Savage* with Gruner. A sequel, starring Gruner, followed a few years later.

Mercenary II: Thick and Thin

1999 (Touchstone VHS) (djm)

When a businessman named Charlie Love (Robert Townsend) goes missing in South America, his partner Patricia van Lier (Claudia Christian) hires renowned mercenary Hawk (Olivier Gruner) to go find him. He goes to get him, immediately realizing that he has been set up and that Love didn't want to be found, and as a result of the "rescue" mission, they are hunted down by a team of killers in the jungle. Hawk sets traps while Love makes wisecracks, and they eventually find themselves in deeper waters as they encounter natives in the jungle, creating more conflict and comedy relief as Hawk has to get them out of one awkward situation after another.

What made the first *Mercenary* work was that it had more than one gimmick up its sleeve to keep it interesting. There was all kinds of action, stunt work, and locations to keep it involving, but *Mercenary II* is a one-trick pony, with just the jungle location and only two guys at the center of the film. It's a shame that only Gruner is worth watching. Townsend outstays his welcome as soon as he starts talking in the first scene of the film: his character is annoying, idiotic, and obscene next to Gruner, who keeps his cool and always remains fascinating. Unfortunately, the action this time is unimaginative and boring, and the music score acts like the whole movie is a cartoon. If you liked the first one, don't see this one. Directed by Philippe Mora (*Back in Business* with Brian Bosworth).

Mercenary Fighters

1988 (MGM DVD) (djm)

T. J. Christian (Reb Brown from *Cage*) is a mercenary living the good life until his buddy (Ron O'Neal) offers him a job in Africa. When they get there, their boss (Peter Fonda) puts them to work straightaway, killing African rebels who oppose a dictator president. When T. J. realizes he's fighting for the wrong side, he changes course by joining the rebels. He gets a chance to go Rambo on his own team.

M

This is Reb Brown's picture, despite Peter Fonda getting top billing. This is slightly better than similar-themed films being made at the time from exploitation markets. Cannon released this towards the end of their run in Hollywood. Another Cannon film released a few years later, *Fifty/Fifty*, starring Peter Weller and Robert Hayes, is very similar. Riki Shelach Nissimoff directed this.

Mercenary for Justice

2006 (Fox DVD) (CD)

"I don't touch a gun. And guns don't touch me. That's why I'm still alive."

Mercenary John Seeger (Steven Seagal) and his team are battling French soldiers during a coup while holding the French ambassador and his family hostage. While Seeger is fighting for his life, certain members of his team take it upon themselves to wipe the family out. In the process, his best friend Radio Jones (Zaa Nkweta) is killed. Seeger vows to take care of Jones's family for him and heads to see them once he's back in the States. But shortly after his visit, they are kidnapped by crooked CIA guys John Dresham (Luke Goss) and Anthony Chapel (Roger Guenveur Smith) with the intention of forcing Seeger to complete a job: the son of a prominent gunrunner is being held in a South African prison and Seeger has to head the team that will bust him out. With the help of Maxine (Jacqueline Lord), Seeger devises a plan to get his friends back and take out the bad seeds in the CIA.

Love him or hate him, Steven Seagal has had a long and prolific career as an action star. With *Mercenary for Justice*, he brings us a film that—for better or worse—is just a mediocre DTV action film with better-than-average production values. Seagal sticks to his usual formula and plays the role as only he can. There's much more gunfire than aikido, but there are a couple of nice fight scenes in which a single hand is never laid on the star while the bad guys are tossed around and beaten to a pulp right before he snaps their necks. This time out, he's surrounded by an above-average supporting cast, which surprisingly helps to carry the film to its limp finish. You can't go wrong when casting Luke Goss (*Death Race 2* and *3*); his presence can elevate almost any film he's in, though he really isn't given much action in this picture. Roger Guenveur Smith (*King of New York*) plays a decent villain with a smarmy, can't-be-bothered attitude, and he's one of the more memorable villains in a Seagal film. The story was a bit too convoluted and needlessly confusing during the first half of the film. Director Don E. FauntLeRoy (*Urban Justice*, *Today You Die*—both with Seagal) spent much of his career as a cinematographer and he brings those skills to directing. The film looks and feels much larger than it is, and you could say that it is even theatrical quality.

Merchants of War

1989 (Platinum DVD) (djm)

The government offers two expert commandos a cakewalk gig: go to Africa to take pictures of a terrorist group and return the photos safe and sound. Well, the job doesn't go smoothly at all. Nick Drennon (Asher Brauner) and Frank Kane (Jesse Vint), the two commandos, land right in the middle of a full-scale combat zone and are captured almost immediately. Tortured by their terrorist captors, they are put through humiliating trials, but Drennon escapes and makes it back to America where his friends and fellow commandos were already planning to stage a search and rescue mission for him and Frank. Mobilizing a handful of the best of the best (who include martial arts action star John Barrett from *American Kickboxer* and *To the Death*), they go back to Africa and rescue Frank from the sadistic terrorist holding him captive.

A very minor entry in this book, *Merchants of War* is fairly negligible, but it's valid simply because co-star Barrett gets to do some stuff toward the end of the film, including using some martial arts in a few quick scenes. If there are any Barrett completists out there, you may need to see this. It's not a bad movie, but he's hardly in it. When the movie finally gets to him, you begin to wonder why he wasn't cast as the lead, instead of Brauner. Barrett also coordinated the stunts in the film. Peter M. Mackenzie directed.

The Messenger

1986 (MGM VHS) (CD)

"I would've stayed in jail for twenty years if I thought it would have kept her alive."

The time has come for Jake Sebastian Turner (Fred Williamson) to get out of prison. A former Green Beret and professional thief, he's ready to live a straight life with his lady, Sabrina (Sandy Cummings). She seems to have racked up a bunch of enemies while Jake was in prison: she has developed a drug problem and owes some shady characters money. While out at a party, Sabrina is gunned down in front of Jake. He feels like nothing can be done and the cops are useless, so he sets off on his own to take out every last scumbag who killed her, and—if he's lucky—bring the entire crime organization down in the process.

With as many films as Fred Williamson (*Original Gangstas*) has been a part of, you're bound to come across some that are disappointing. *The Messenger* is one of those films. There's still a lot to enjoy but something was missing from the final product. It feels rushed and clipped when it should have relished the premise and the star at the center of it. The production values are pretty low and the acting of the supporting cast is fairly rough around the edges. The story is generic, but it really doesn't matter much since we get to see plenty of Williamson chewing on a cigar and kicking

some ass. There are shootouts, pistol whippings, and, if that isn't enough, he throws ninja stars to boot. *The Messenger* isn't one of his better flicks, but it definitely has its moments.

Messenger of Death

1988 (MGM DVD) (djm)

Somewhat of a potboiler for a Cannon picture starring Charles Bronson, *Messenger of Death* begins with an incredible amount of daring dread, as it shows a faceless man shotgunning three defenseless women and a half a dozen children in the privacy of their own home. Startling and upsetting, this prologue might have had theater patrons running for the exits. It then introduces a newspaper reporter named Garret Smith (Bronson), who becomes drawn to the case. It involves a Mormon sect based in Colorado, and the slain victims were related to a man who had split from the sect and may have started a feud with the minister. As Smith does his investigating, his life is put in danger and he is forced to defend himself several times. A scene in a bathroom where he fights a knife-wielding thug reminded me of a scene in *Faster* with Dwayne "The Rock" Johnson, but the one in *Messenger of Death* is better. Bronson uses a trashcan to attack his assailant, and then he throws the guy out the window!

Bronson's years at Cannon yielded some interesting action/thriller films like *10 to Midnight* and even the *Death Wish* sequels had some merit, but *Messenger of Death* feels like an extended pilot episode of a TV series, with excessive blood and violence. It works on a very basic level, but it's far from one of Bronson's better efforts. J. Lee Thompson (*Murphy's Law* with Bronson) directed.

Metal Hurlant Chronicles: Second Chance

2014 (Shout Factory DVD) (CD)

"Alright, Joe, the moment of truth. Get in, get rich, get out, that's all you're gonna do. Then you can shove that last container up your boss's ass."

Smuggler Joe (Scott Adkins) decides it's time to throw caution to the wind and try his luck at a casino in space. Things haven't been exactly going his way lately: having lost his cargo, he needs a big win. He jumps into a game with criminal Xero Trobes (Kamel Laadaili) who likes to raise the stakes a bit. Joe sweetens the deal by agreeing to bet his eyeballs, a bet he will end up regretting. He quickly loses the game but Trobes is kind enough to give him time to come up with some cash to buy his eyes back. Joe comes up with a plan, but it may all backfire in his face.

Since each episode of *Metal Hurlant Chronicles* is self-contained, you get an interesting mix of talent and stories. The episode *Second Chance* stars Scott Adkins (from *Undisputed III* and *Ninja*) in a role that allows him to flex his acting chops more than his fighting skills. It's an interesting tale but lacks any real excitement. Scott Adkins in any project is always a good thing, but this particular episode will leave action fans wanting something more. Directed by Guillaume Lubrano.

Metal Hurlant Chronicles:
The Endomorphe
2014 (Shout Factory DVD)
(CD)

The Meccamorphs are a workforce of cyborg miners created by humans to harvest fuel to run the planet. One day they rebelled against the humans and began to destroy everything. A small group of humans held up in a bunker are protecting a young boy and his pet bunny. He's the last hope for the human race and they have to escort him to the Meccadrome (a huge beam of light), where he will turn into a Golem and save them all. The Meccamorphs are hot on their trail so they will have to move quick if they are to deliver the child to his destiny.

This is one of the best episodes of the *Metal Hurlant* TV series. It's action-packed, has cool creature designs, and three amazing action stars (Michael Jai White, *Android Cop*, Darren Shahlavi, *The Package*, and Michelle Lee, *Blood and Bone*), who sell the story. They have a killer fight scene (there's only one, but the episodes are only twenty minutes long) against the Meccamorphs; it's well choreographed and somewhat bloody. There's a nice twist ending and the whole episode has a stellar visual style to it. The episode was directed by Guillaume Lubrano.

Metal Hurlant Chronicles:
King's Crown
2012 (Shout Factory DVD)
(djm)

An incredible line-up of contemporary action guys were cast for this half-hour episode in the science fiction anthology series based on the adult comic book known as *Metal Hurlant* (or *Heavy Metal*). This episode features four warriors (played by Scott Adkins, Michael Jai White, Darren Shahlavi, and Matt Mullins) who are competing in a fight-to-the-death tournament with the prize being the crown to a kingdom of a wasted world. The former king has just died, and his last will stated that the next king must be the victor of this particular barbaric tournament. Shahlavi has a fight with Adkins, Mullins has a fight with Jai White, and the final fight is between Adkins and Jai White.

With fights coordinated by Larnell Stovall

Scott Adkins and Matt Mullins on the set of *Metal Hurlant Chronicles: King's Crown*. Courtesy of Matt Mullins.

(*Undisputed II* and *III*), and a line-up of the best action guys working in the business, *King's Crown* is more than just a little disappointing. The fights are restrained and clipped where they should be full-throttle and brutal, and the choreography is obviously lackluster. It's great seeing the guys all together, but this is not the place to start watching any of their work. As a concept, it's great. As a result, it's totally underwhelming. Guillaume Lubrano directed.

Miami Connection
1987 (Drafthouse Films DVD)
(djm)

As fate would have it, this gem was a lost film for twenty-five years until the Alamo Drafthouse discovered it and gave it a theatrical and video release in 2012. It was self-financed by a Korean martial arts instructor and motivational speaker named Y. K. Kim during the boom of the VHS, and it gave him a chance to showcase his taekwondo skills as one of the film's central stars.

Theatrical poster for *Miami Connection*. Author's collection.

In the film, Kim is a member of a rock band called Dragon Sound, which becomes the focal point of a ninja cult and a mafia running drugs in Miami. Through a crazy chain of encounters, Dragon Sound thwarts the mafia's plans to properly distribute cocaine on the streets and, thus, there's an all-out war on the streets when a motorcycle gang of ninjas and thugs put a mark of death on the members of the rock band.

It's truly unbelievable that this film sat on a shelf for so long. It has great energy, insane comedy (some of which is unintentional), and some bravura action and fight scenes that must be seen to be believed. It's not on the level of, say, some of the better Jackie Chan vehicle films, but it's certainly better than Jackie's *The Protector* or dozens of other ninja flicks that were released during the period. It's more fun than almost all of Sho Kosugi's ninja efforts. The soundtrack is killer!

Midnight Ride
1990 (Cannon VHS) (djm)

This one is a change of pace for star Michael Dudikoff. He plays a cop named Lawson with a cast on his leg, and he can't seem to keep his Russian wife (Savina Gersak) from leaving him. He tries following her anyway, which leads to him commandeering all sorts of vehicles to find her as she takes a road trip to stay with one of her family members. She picks up a psychotic hitchhiker named Justin (Mark Hamill) who seems nice at first but quickly shows his true nature. Lawson, who was basically a stalker husband for a while shifts into the hero mode as he realizes that his wife is being held hostage by a psycho. Most of the movie involves car chases and vehicular stunts—one scene has Dudikoff strapped on the hood of a car while Hamill cackles and makes weird jokes.

While not necessarily an "action" movie, this thriller works because of the way the two leads play their characters. One might wonder what the movie would be like if they had switched roles and let Dudikoff play the psycho. That would have been a completely different movie—maybe a more interesting one. This was a quiet Cannon release. It was directed by Bob Bralver, a stunt coordinator and the director of *American Ninja 5*.

The Minion
1998 (Touchstone DVD) (CD)

"I've always been a warrior, but not always for God."

It's the dawn of a new millennium when a subway crew discovers a tomb that houses a mysterious key. Archaeologist Karen Goodleaf (Francoise Robertson) is called in to investigate. When a mysterious man shows up in the tomb trying to kill her, she realizes that there is something more to it. In comes Lukas (Dolph Lundgren), a Templar Knight who was trained to protect and hide the key from the minions of the Antichrist. Hundreds of years ago, the Antichrist was locked away and the key was hidden since there's no way to kill him. The two come up with a plan to hide the key in toxic waste. Since the minions must use a human host, it's impossible for a human to survive in order to find the key in the waste. The heroes' quest is far more difficult than they can imagine, but if they give up it could mean the end of the human race.

How is it even possible that there is a film where Dolph Lundgren gets to play a Templar Knight trying to hunt down the Antichrist? The concept is just ludicrous and the fact that it actually exists should be a dream come true. Sadly, the film fails to live up to the concept, achieving only a mediocre payoff. It's unfortunate when a film falls short due to budgetary constraints, and this may very well be the case with *The Minion*. Lundgren is excellent as usual, playing a mysterious priest who was trained to protect the world from evil forces. The story works well and the movie keeps moving at a decent pace but something important is missing. We never really get to see the minions jump from body to body, we never see the true form of the evil, nor do we get to see the Antichrist. There is, however, plenty of action. Lundgren has to fight off all the different incarnations of the minion as it body-jumps, and he has a really cool metal spiked glove that he uses to punch his victims in the back of the head. There are various brawls, shootouts, and even a sword fight. So it's well worth viewing, but it's just missing that extra special element that could have elevated it to cult status. Directed by Jean-Marc Piche.

Miracles (a.k.a. Black Dragon, a.k.a. Mr. Canton and Lady Rose)

1989 (Media Asia DVD) (CD)

"A mistake, I have too much sympathy but no ability trying to help Madam Rose create miracles. You're right, I can't measure up!"

Kou Chen-Wah (Jackie Chan) has just moved from the mainland to 1930s Hong Kong. He's down on his luck and swindled out of the last of his money. After buying a lucky rose from Madame Kao (Kuei Ya-lei) he accidentally ends up taking the place of a slain gangster, inheriting his fortune. As he begins to fall for feisty lounge singer Luming Yang (Anita Mui), they feel the need to repay Madame Kao. Her daughter is marrying into a very rich and powerful family, so Kou and Luming devise an elaborate plan to make her appear to be rich and powerful, a far cry from the lowly street vendor she really is. As brilliant and generous as their plan may be, they lie, kidnap, and deceive anyone who threatens to expose their good deed. While trying to stick to

the plan, Kou still has to deal with being the head of a crime family and fend off fellow mobster Tiger (Chun Hsiung Ko) and his goons. One thing is certain: Kou always repays a debt and will fight to get a happy ending.

Jackie Chan has always showed his admiration for icons like Buster Keaton and Charlie Chaplin in his films; there have been numerous times throughout his career when he has paid homage to them. With *Miracles*, Chan directs a full-fledged film inspired by Hollywood's classic era. It's a big, flashy, and beautiful extravaganza filled with drama, comedy, musical numbers, and most importantly Chan's trademark action and stunt work. Even though they take a backseat to the shenanigans, the fights are expertly staged and the final fight in a rope production warehouse ranks as some of Chan's best work. *Miracles* is one of Chan's more interesting films and finely captures the glitz and glamor of Hollywood's yesteryears.

Mirageman

2007 (Magnet DVD) (djm)

This Chilean effort stars Marko Zaror (from *Kiltro* and *Mandrill*) as an emotionally damaged man named Maco, who was assaulted as a child. In addition to the assault, he witnessed his parents getting killed and watched his younger brother get raped by a street gang. As a grown man, Maco is a withdrawn bouncer at a nightclub, who spends every spare moment training in martial arts and imagining himself as some kind of superhero. One night he comes across a family being robbed, and he goes into the house and stops the attackers from raping a woman by using his skills as a martial artist. Wearing a blue ski mask, Maco's identity is kept a secret, and when he sees on the news the next day that a famous reporter was saved in her home by a masked avenger, suddenly Maco becomes a media sensation. He gets it into his head to continue his campaign as a masked hero—calling himself "Mirageman"—and he sets up a website and offers his services to those who need his help. Naive and innocent, Maco is suckered into some bad situations where thugs have set him up, and on several occasions, he's surrounded and beaten down, but invariably, he gets the better of his assailants by his sheer skill as a fighter. The climax involves a serious betrayal by the reporter he saved, and his last campaign to topple a pedophilia ring in the city ends in tragedy.

Grungy and disarming, *Mirageman* has zero pretensions and achieves a lot with limited means. Zaror (who barely speaks in the movie) is a talent to watch out for. I've been impressed with him in the few films I've seen him in, and his martial arts prowess is really impressive. In this film, he almost always fights with a mask on, but his style is unmistakable. An uneven tone (it's really goofy while being ultra serious) might upset some viewers, and a downbeat ending could turn even more viewers off. I enjoyed it for being exactly what I was hoping it would be. Zaror rocks. Written, directed, and edited by Ernesto Diaz Espinoza, who also made *Kiltro* and *Mandrill* with Zaror.

INTERVIEW: MARKO ZAROR (djm)

A Chilean native, Marko Zaror is an anomaly. He pushed himself to become a martial artist in a country where martial arts isn't widely practiced, and when he relocated to Los Angeles to pursue modeling, he was noticed by a stunt coordinator at a gym, and the next thing he knew he was being considered to double Dwayne "The Rock" Johnson in his first action film The Rundown (2003). *With the money he made from that fortunate gig, he was able to complete a martial arts film he'd been shooting in Mexico called* Chinango (2005), *and after that film quickly found distribution, he was able to leverage himself into his next project,* Kiltro (2006), *which he shot in Chile (the first Chilean martial arts film) with his childhood friend Ernesto Diaz, a burgeoning director. With several vehicle films under his belt, Zaror landed a plum role as a Mel Gibson's henchman in the Robert Rodriguez film* Machete Kills (2013). *Zaror's trajectory seems headed upward, and here's hoping that he'll make many more films in the years ahead.*

I just watched a little movie you were in called *Hard as Nails*.

Hard as Nails!

Yeah, I watched it last night. You had a couple of scenes in it. You have a fight scene, and there's a scene where your car blows up.

(Laughing.) That was actually my first American experience. When I just arrived to LA they invited me to be a part of this gym where all the stunt people in the stunt community trained. I heard about this job. They were like, "Yeah, just come over and hang out! Come to the set. Do you want to be a part of this?" I was like, "Yeah, for sure!" They called me to be the stunt double for the lead guy. Right? They liked me a lot, the look, and they saw me doing some moves on stage and then they were like, "Yeah, why don't we put him as the bodyguard of the bad guy?" Where you see the bad guy, you see Marko standing there. Don't say anything, just stand there and maybe we can use him for a fight or something. That was really cool for me because they gave me an opportunity to be in front of the camera. I threw some kicks and started little by little, creating my demo around those images.—the car, where I'm driving, and when I'm doing the backflip off the wall, and when I'm doing a butterfly twist... and when I'm shooting with the gun. It was so funny.

You come from a part of the world where martial arts isn't really prevalent as far as I can tell. Talk about getting into martial arts while growing up in Chile.

Yeah, and I would even say from Latin America. Martial arts films... yeah, man... what can I say... it's like... I'm so thankful that I was so inspired since I was a little kid by a man named Bruce Lee. I'm thirty-five, so back in the day there was no YouTube, no access to any media,

M

and I remember I saw his film *Enter the Dragon* on TV. Before that, my mother was a black belt in karate. She was like the first woman to be in karate in Chile. Or the first black belt, or something. I remember my game as a kid was fighting. When I first saw Bruce Lee, it was so clear that my life or my path would have something to do with that. It never stopped, man. I started training. The only access I had to his work or his philosophy was through his movies. There were no documentaries about him. I started looking obsessively for a martial arts instructor to start learning. It became very intense. I was dedicated. I went to high school, and I remember that I didn't care about the classes. I was doing stretches in the back of the room. My mother was like, "Oh, what am I going to do with this kid? He's going to be trouble." In Chile, there really weren't movies fifteen years ago. When I was fifteen, it was twenty years ago. There were no films or any movie industry or anything. Not even now! To dream to be an action or movie star or being involved in the backstage for a movie was something beyond any dream. Nothing. It was the bottom of the world. It's the end. I didn't know that. It was not in my dreams to make a movie. I just knew that my life would be related to martial arts. I knew it from the moment that I saw that movie. I started training on the national team of taekwondo. I did traditional kung fu and karate, and I tried to train myself in these different doctrines, you see? Without even knowing the philosophy of Bruce Lee—because he didn't believe in the style; he wanted to find himself within the martial arts—without even knowing all that, I was following the same direction, you see? Through his movies, that's the way he impacted my life. It was so like the truth. Without him telling me or without reading any book, I was trying to find myself in different styles. Then, I started getting access to more material about him. YouTube started happening, and I started realizing that I felt like we were connected. It's weird, man. It's crazy, you see? That's why when you see all my movies, there's always a Bruce Lee energy hiding somewhere in my movies. If you're a fan, you can recognize that, you see? In *Kiltro*, when I grab the nunchucks, I tried to do the same shot of one of his posters. Just to acknowledge him. If a kid is watching this movie and doesn't even know who Bruce Lee is, they'll know that this is the continuation of him. This is my way of saying, "Thanks, man. Thanks for inspiring my life." It's very strong, man. That's the only way I can explain why a Chilean man is able to do everything I've done. Life gave me all the signals.

You made a couple of action movies in Mexico. How did those movies happen?

I did some low-budget movies in Mexico, yeah. That's when I realized that everything was real.

You made *Chinango* while in Mexico?

(Laughing.) Yes! I arrived in Mexico and lived one year there. I received a scholarship to star in soap operas. I met Jose Luis Mosca, a martial arts guy who is from Chile, but he was living in Mexico. He did really low-budget video movies and soap operas. He was the one who showed

me that this was real. He turned my impossible dream to being possible. He'd done some really bad low-budget movies, but he was doing action and he was on the poster with his leg like this. This was real. It wasn't another world. I had to learn to act, and I went to LA to make *Hard as Nails*, and then I got the call to come back to Mexico to do *Chinango*. It was kind of at the same time. The date they put on the Imdb[.com] is not true. I was nineteen or twenty when I did that movie. What happened is that I had met this director who said, "Let's do this movie. I got some money and we're going to do the first martial arts movie!" My friend Jose would do action movies, but he would be like a gangster and throw one kick in the movie. This director had never directed a movie before. We played around and did some choreography. I did not know how to do choreography or anything. That's how we came up with *Chinango*. Then I came back to LA to work as a stunt double for The Rock on *The Rundown*. With the money I made on that, I put it into *Chinango* so we could finish it. We added a couple more fight scenes. We needed more action.

You just glazed over your gig on *The Rundown*. That was a huge steppingstone for you to double The Rock. How did you get that job?

Yeah, because I was still trying to understand the *Hard as Nails* and *Chinango* thing. When I received the *Hard as Nails* job, everything started happening. I had a little demo. I started running into some friends who were really in the industry, people who were really known stunt doubles like Arnold Chon who was a big inspiration to me. He introduced me to Andy Cheng, who used to work on the Jackie Chan team. He was the action director of *The Rundown*. He saw me training at the gym and asked me, "Marko, do you want to work as a stunt double?" I was like, "Yeah!" I didn't even know for sure what that was. It was for doubling The Rock. That was a big deal for me. It was the big break. What happened on that job was that I was working at a fitness center teaching martial arts classes, and when Andy offered me that job, I quit. I was living the dream, trying to pay the rent and going through all the struggles day by day. I remember I started as a dishwasher at a restaurant and then I moved up as a waiter. The story. It was very nice. I used to wake up every morning and see the Hollywood sign. In Chile, you've got to understand: You see the map and you go, "Where is Chile?" And then you understand that for me, walking one hour to the bus to drive one hour to go to work as a dishwasher and then coming back to wake up with this Hollywood sign on your window. It was strong. I was excited. Then I used to clean the gym so that I don't have to pay for the gym. Right? That was Ken's Karate Studio. I'm never going to forget Master Ken. He gave me the opportunity to train at his gym. So, I quit my job, but then SAG and the community said, "No, no, no! Marko cannot do this job. He's from Chile. He has a working visa that said *modeling visa*, or something totally different. Why would we give a job to this guy if we have tons of stuntmen that can do this job?" Andy Cheng was like, "No, no, no. This is *Marko*! He's 6 foot 2, he weighs

200 pounds and he can do the acrobatics and the martial arts." They obligated him to do a big casting session to cast someone else to take the job. That took three months. To prove that I was the one for the job. I was like, "Oh, man, it's so hard to get to this point." Then I had to deal with all this. I was getting ready to go back to Chile. It happened that no one else was able to match those conditions or had the right skin color. That's how I got my working visa. With that money I was able to finish *Chinango*.

What happened after *Chinango*? How did *Kiltro* get started?

We sold *Chinango* to a distributor in the US. It was a very good deal. We did the movie for something like $20,000. We were able to sell it very good. There were some investors who said, "Let's make another movie!" Then we tried to make it, but we realized that with the same amount of money, we couldn't make the same kind of movie in the US. In that moment, we said, "Why don't we go to Chile and make it?" My friend Ernesto Diaz, who is a director from Chile, was staying with me in the US. He was trying to get into the industry. We were like, "With this money, we can do a much better movie in Chile." That's how we did *Kiltro*. More investors from Chile added to the budget.

Kiltro **is such a radical movie. It's not like any other movie of that type. It's so different. That was the first movie I saw you in. I'd never heard of you before. "The Latin Dragon." I was like, "Where did *this* guy come from?"**

(Laughing.)

Talk about your relationship with Ernesto. You've done three or four movies with him now.

We were friends from high school. I was the crazy karate boy. In the break, everybody was playing soccer and I was doing sit-ups and

DVD artwork for *Kiltro*. Author's collection.

M

practicing my kick. Ernesto was playing with his camera. Because we were these weird kids, we became friends. In English classes, they said, "Work for next week is you have to do a video or a book in English. A real book or a real video in English." Ernesto and I were like, "Let's make a martial arts movie in English!" That's how we became friends. We did a movie with fights. When I was living in the US I got my first leading acting role through a casting agency for a little independent Mexican film called *Into the Flames*. They were needing an assistant director, so I called Ernesto and told him, "Man, this is a great opportunity—they're not going to pay you because it's really low budget—but if you come over here and do this it will be a really good experience for you." You see? He came to the US and he worked on this movie, and he decided to stay. We started developing projects together. He wrote a script for me and we got the money, and that's what we decided to make in Chile. That was *Kiltro*. That was script was so cool.

From then on it seems that you and Ernesto worked hand in hand to develop projects for you to star in.

Yeah, I became more of a developer. As a martial artist . . . I gotta be honest. I don't like going to the auditions. As a martial artist, I'd rather develop my projects. To be more involved in what I want to communicate. The only way to do that is to do low-budget, independent movies. After my name was out there, they called me for *Undisputed III*. That was a big break as a martial artist. After *Kiltro*, I didn't go back to LA to keep doing stunts. I developed instead *Mirage Man*. You see? After that, *Mandrill*. Then that gave me the chance to be known. They called me for *Undisputed III*. They wanted me to fight Scott [Adkins].

If you're working with Isaac Florentine, you're working with the best. You're in the club.

(Laughing.) That was a great experience, man. I'm never gonna forget that. Scott is the best. He's such a cool guy. I remember talking with Scott at the trailer and telling each other how we were watching YouTube videos of each other without even knowing each other. "Oh, wow, he can do this move! Okay!" There was tension when I

Isaac Florentine directing Marko Zaror and Scott Adkins (back facing) on *Undisputed III*. Courtesy of Maroody Merav.

Marko Zaror (left) and Isaac Florentine (right) rehearsing a fight scene in *Undisputed III*. Courtesy of Maroody Merav.

arrived at that set, kind of like the challenge before a fight. Then to work together for the movie, we became such good friends. I really like Scott, man. We had a really cool time. One of the best experiences of my life. Isaac is the best. So passionate. He's such a perfectionist.

What was it like for you to work for Isaac after working with Ernesto several times?

In Chile, we're always fighting with the budget, with how we can solve this problem with the shooting. No time to do any action. We're *trying* to make a movie. I'm wearing a lot of hats on those movies. I'm acting and I'm coordinating the action. I'm trying to teach everyone how to fight. There were no stuntman. On *Kiltro* I trained a group of ten guys for four months to learn how to fight in front of a camera. That was hard. Then, you've got teach them how to do the basic things in front of a camera. From there, going to Isaac in Bulgaria . . . I just had to worry about my character. Everybody was so professional. I had to bring my abilities, but they made me look even better. It's a different feel. It was a release. I tried to observe and learn as much I could. I knew that at some point I would do another movie.

Talk about *Mirage Man*. It's a unique action movie. It's melancholy. You play a damaged character.

Ernesto and I wanted to go back and tell a nice story with a handheld camera with some fighting. I didn't use any wires, but *Kiltro* was kind of like a Japanese animation. All that took away from the martial arts. It was a waste of money. We could have done much more with that money. Let's go do a little movie, and we did this movie. I told Ernesto, "What happens if someone in real life goes to the street, puts on a mask, and becomes a superhero? No powers. It's just real. What would be the real scenario?" That was the mentality for that movie. Everything we did for that movie was based on that concept. How would he change his outfit on the street? Ernesto was like, "Yeah, but why would he do that?" So he came up with the story. It was psychological. He was trying to create this hero to help his brother. We just did it. That story

DVD artwork for *Mandrill*. Author's collection.

surprises. That movie won so many festivals and audience awards. All over the world. Every place that we show that movie. It was so surprising. It looked really raw and low budget, but it was very strong, man. Business-wise, it did the best business of all the other movies we did, and it looked so cheap! That's how the industry is. You never know. Then we decided to do *Mandrill*. But the money was not good in Chile at that time. The returns were not that good. Ernesto and I decided not to produce any more movies because I cannot guarantee investors will make their money back. But I decided to keep training because as a martial artist, that's a part of my life. Maybe no more movies. If they call me, maybe okay. Then they called me for *Undisputed* right after *Mandrill*.

How did you get a nice supporting role in *Machete Kills*? You got to play Mel Gibson's henchman. You were the best part of the movie!

A long time passed after *Undisputed*, and I got a call from Robert Rodriguez. He saw *Mandrill*. Life sometimes acts in ways you can't understand. Sometimes later you understand. Man, anything that has happened is just gratitude. Man, it's beyond . . . what can I say? When I was with Ernesto making *Mirage Man*, we watched *El Mariachi*. Our mentor on movie-making on a low budget was Robert Rodriguez. Ernesto said, "Imagine one day making a movie with Robert Rodriguez!" When you say that . . . it's something that you know is impossible, but it became real. The moment that I arrived on the set of *Machete Kills* to the moment I left, I was kind of in a trip. It was unreal. I was so happy, man. With Mel Gibson . . . I remember watching *Braveheart*, saying, "It's so strong!" There are no words in my vocabulary to tell you how that movie made me feel. When I was shooting that movie with him, it was too strong, man. I didn't care what happened next. I've been so blessed with all the opportunities I've had. How I've been treated. Grateful.

Isaac Florentine and Marko Zaror behind the scenes shot from *Undisputed III*. Courtesy of Maroody Merav.

M

What's next for you, Marko?

I'm about to start shooting a movie. The movie is called *The Redeemer*. It's another movie with Ernesto. After all these years, we're ready. One of the reasons why my movies didn't do good business is—I believe—that we were not in good hands with the people who made the sales and the strategy. Now we are with one of the most known and recognized sales agencies. They brought *The Raid* and *The Raid 2*. Our movie is low budget, but it's better than *Mirage Man* and *Mandrill*. It's one step forward. We are prepared. We are in the right hands. We have the best people now. We have to give it one more try. I've been working hard on the fight choreography for four months already. I'm bringing Jose Mosca, the guy who gave me the opportunity in Mexico. He's my main bad guy. It's very magical, man. We're trying to apply everything I've learned from Isaac and Andy Cheng to do one step further. To try to evolve. To try to do the best fights possible. I'm very involved with this one. I'm very excited. We'll see what happens.

Everybody's got their own unique on-screen fighting persona and style. What's the Marko Zaror style? Why do you think people keep coming back for more of your films?

Hmm. That's a hard question, man. For one, style. What's my style? I don't believe that there is any one style that is my style. I don't know, man. As a human being, you're unique, and as a martial artist, you're also unique. So, I don't see myself doing any style. It's a very hard question. I don't know, man. Maybe people come to see my honesty in my movies. I'm just doing what I love to do in front of a camera. I try to share my learning process, my different movies, and my passion. Maybe it's that. I always see myself as a martial artist and not as an actor. I don't want to do a part with no martial arts because then I would have to worry about my career as an actor. I don't want to have to do one comedy or a drama so that I can do a martial arts movie. I don't care about my career. See? I have a beautiful life in Chile. I don't have the need to be making movies and movies and movies. Maybe *Machete* was my last movie and I didn't even know it. I would be so thankful of what life gave me up to that point. I don't care if I never do another movie. If life keeps bringing me the opportunity to express myself in a project that I love, I'll do it! I don't care if they pay me or don't pay me. Yeah, if it happens that they can pay me, that's better, but it's not about that. It's about if I really believe in what I'm doing.

What do you want to say to your fans, Marko?

I want to say thanks for the support. I promise that I will do all that is in my power in this existence or in this life that I will stay honest and I will never stop enjoying what I'm doing. I cannot promise you that I'm going to do a lot of movies because I cannot promise you that, but I can promise you that when you see me in a movie, you will see someone that is passionate and someone who is enjoying what he loves to do. That I can promise. Thanks for the interview, man. It means a lot.

Misfire

2014 (Image DVD) (djm)

The ex-wife journalist of a DEA agent named Cole (Gary Daniels) is taken by a Mexican cartel and her current husband is charged with her disappearance. Cole meets with the guy while he's incarcerated, gets some info on what happened, and decides to investigate on his own. A photographer friend of his ex-wife (played by Vanessa Vasquez) insists on helping Cole find her friend, and the two of them go to Tijuana to pick up the pieces. To get back at the cartel, Cole kidnaps the leader's son and has some leverage to get his ex-wife back.

Gary Daniels, as usual, is fit to kill and manages to supply his character with some dimension, but *Misfire*—which was entirely shot on handheld digital video—only has a handful of characters, and therefore it lacks suspense during the action scenes because when characters are shooting at each other or running away, there's usually a suspicious lack of extras, and when there are some people in the background, they barely notice that the characters in the movie are in life-or-death situations involving gunfire. It's weird. The events that happen in *Misfire* happen almost entirely without notice from anybody but the people playing the lead roles in the movie. The nameless, faceless passersby weirdly don't react to gunfire or martial arts happening in the streets. If you can get past that quibble, the movie is nominally effective, but when it's finished I did a double-take because it didn't have a satisfying conclusion. Cole's ex-wife is rescued, but she never spoke a word in the movie, so there's very little payoff with that. The whole movie had a strangely suspicious vibe to it. Directed by R. Ellis Frazier, who has another project called *Rumble* with Daniels already in the can.

Missing in Action

1984 (MGM DVD) (djm)

Vietnam veteran James Braddock (Chuck Norris), who suffers from PTSD, agrees to go back to the People's Republic of Vietnam on a bogus diplomatic mission, where he's promptly brought up on war crime charges. He sneaks out of the hotel where he's staying in Saigon and does some recon work. He finds out that American MIAs are still being held captive deep in the jungle, and he plans a mission to rescue as many as he can on the sly. He recruits an old expat (M. Emmet Walsh) buddy to help him with transportation through the rivers, and he starts a war with the Vietnamese government, who adamantly swear that no American soldiers are being held prisoner.

Less a martial arts action movie than an out-and-out war film with heavy political implications, *Missing in Action* is a no-nonsense drama heavy on heroics with Chuck Norris as a one-man revenger on the side of right. His scenes as a civilian portray him as an embittered, suffering vet, and when he takes on his mission, he's a force of nature to be reckoned with. The war scenes (both in real-time and in flashbacks)

are fairly vivid, though stylized through the Cannon filter. The Cannon Group had just begun their partnership with Chuck, who would go on to make nearly a dozen films as their biggest contracted star. *Missing in Action 2* and *Missing in Action* were filmed back to back (in that order), but *Missing in Action* was deemed the better film and therefore released first. The story by Lance Hool and John Crowther was adapted in script form by James Bruner. Joseph Zito directed. He worked with Chuck again on *Invasion USA*.

INTERVIEW:

JAMES BRUNER

(djm)

No one wrote more movies for Chuck Norris than James Bruner. Not only that, but he wrote some of his very best films including An Eye For an Eye *(1981),* Missing in Action *(1984),* Invasion USA *(1985),* The Delta Force *(1986), and* Braddock: Missing in Action III *(1988). Bruner's days as a screenwriter at The Cannon Group yielded some great material, and in addition to his work there, he worked on some other interesting action-oriented projects including* American Ninja *(1985),* Sword of Heaven *(1985), and* POW: The Escape *(a.k.a.* Behind Enemy Lines, *1986). All these years later and Bruner's work on these films continues to amass interest as pop culture embraces his lines of dialogue on T-shirts and bumper stickers.*

How did you get involved with Chuck Norris and your script of *An Eye for an Eye*?

I'm from Wisconsin. I came out here to Los Angeles, but not to work in movies, although I made Super 8 movies when I was in high school. I loved movies, but I never thought in a million years that I'd be involved in making them. I ended up in LA to do a job that had nothing to do with movies. That job didn't work out, and I was literally sitting at the beach—I had an apartment in Hermosa Beach—it was March and I didn't want to go back to Wisconsin because it was still freezing there. I had met this girl, and I said that I'd written articles for some gaming magazines, and she said, "Oh, you've written some stuff. I need to write a screenplay." She had something going on at Warner Brothers. This was a thousand years before the Internet

James Bruner in Pasadena, California. Photo by david j. moore.

and there wasn't a book out there on how to write a screenplay, and I didn't know anybody in the business. I'd never even seen a screenplay. I found a book at a university written in the 1940s on how to write a screenplay. I picked it up and it hadn't been off the shelf in literally forty years. The format of the screenplay was basically the same. So I started writing a screenplay. I wrote a western, and by the time I finished it—it took me a long time—I'd lost track of that girl. I drove to Beverly Hills and I had a pocketful of dimes and I went through the Yellow Pages and I looked up agencies. I was clueless. I started dialing at the "A's" and by the time I got to the "B's," someone said, "I'll read your screenplay." Oh great! I got nice rejection letters. It was a western, and no one was doing westerns. I had a background in martial arts in taekwondo and kung fu, and I had an idea for an action movie. I went back to Wisconsin for Christmas, and I wrote this first draft. In the meantime I'd met some guys who'd broken into the business. One guy knew a character actor who had been in a movie and had done dialogue in that movie. I told the actor, "Hey, you've been in a movie, and I wrote this screenplay. Can you read it?" He read it and he said, "You know what? I just did a movie with Chuck Norris called *A Force of One*, and Chuck's looking for something. I'll give him your script." By March, I got a call and they told me that they liked it, but that it was too short. It was only seventy pages. They wanted me to write another twenty-five pages. So I sent the revised script in, and by June I had eight dollars to my name. I get a call from this character actor guy [Mel Novak], and he said, "We're going in tomorrow to Avco/Embassy Pictures and we're taking your script *An Eye for an Eye*." I was like, "Wow! This is great!" He took it to Chuck, and the original script was more what John Woo did in the 90s: There was a combination of martial arts with the guns, but at that time Chuck Norris didn't want to do the gun stuff, so they took out the gunplay. One of the best parts of this whole experience was that at the cast and crew screening, I was introduced to this girl, and we hit it off and we've been married ever since. The movie was a hit. Chuck jumped up a little, but the phone didn't ring for me. My girlfriend knew Chuck through karate school, and she would see Chuck and he asked her, "Hey, are you still going out with that guy James Bruner, who wrote *An Eye for an Eye*?" She said, "Yeah!" Chuck said, "I want to write another movie." That movie ended up being *Missing in Action*.

The way I understand this is that *Missing in Action 1* was filmed after *Missing in Action 2*. You didn't write Part 2, right?

Correct. What really happened . . . Chuck had a brother killed in Vietnam, so he had always wanted to do something about vets. He read a book about MIA soldiers. He wanted to do a movie about a soldier who goes back to Vietnam. I wrote the film on spec, and I was introduced to an ex-special forces guy. He knew a lot about all that. He was heavily involved in that in real life. I got a lot of stuff from him. Chuck tried to set it up, but we didn't get anywhere. He called me up one day, and he said, "I've got a producer interested in *Missing in Action*. He

read the script, and he liked it. Can you have lunch with him?" I said, "Yeah, okay." It was a producer named Lance Hool. Lance loved the script. Chuck called later and said, "We're going to Cannon Films. They want to do the movie." I thought, *Oh, this is great!* I didn't hear back from them until five in the afternoon. That was weird. Chuck called me from his car on his way home and said, "I don't know how to tell you this, but I went in and they handed me a script called *Missing in Action*, but it wasn't the script that you wrote. It was written by these other guys. I told them I would do the movie, but that they would have to buy *your* script." What happened is Lance found out that Cannon had read and liked this other script called *Missing in Action*. They were interested in doing it, but they needed a star. Cannon had not optioned the script, so Lance optioned it immediately, so when he went to Cannon, he said, "I own the script." While they were filming that movie, I got a call and they told me, "You need to fly down here right away—they want to do a sequel. They want you to write it." They were going to film a trailer for the next movie. I went down there, and wrote a trailer, which was based on my original screenplay, and we showed part of the ending and it made a great trailer. They still wanted to do the sequel, so I took the original script I'd written and revamped it a bit so it worked more on their budget. Joe Zito shot the movie in the Philippines. They finished *Missing in Action 2*, which was my script, and Warner Brothers had made a deal with Cannon to distribute the first film. They looked at the first movie and they decided not to distribute it. So Cannon pulled out of the deal and looked at the film I wrote, and decided to put it out under Cannon Films and they already had a release date, which was the end of 1984. That was a number one hit. It did quite well. They put the first one out as a prequel the following year.

Talk about the subject matter of the *Missing in Action* movies. They touch on a controversial subject matter. The first two films in that series were pre-*Rambo: First Blood Part II*.

My friend, as I said, was involved in that in real life. He had looked for soldiers who were MIA in southeast Asia. I knew a lot about it from him. Plus I had a number of friends who had been in Vietnam. I never joined up or got called up. They were treated so poorly after the war. No one had

Col. James Braddock (Chuck Norris) and his pal Jack Tucker (M. Emmet Walsh) go back to 'Nam to rescue P.O.W.'s in *Missing in Action*. Author's collection.

James Braddock (Chuck Norris) has returned to Vietnam to rescue prisoners of war in *Missing in Action*. Author's collection.

ever done anything really positive for them at that point. It was a big issue. People were trying to raise awareness that there could be guys still being held over there. It was a big deal. People wanted to see that, but for it to have a happier ending. When I saw it in theaters, people actually stood up and cheered.

Where do you draw the line between entertainment and exploitation? The first *Missing in Action* movie you wrote is a lot more entertaining than Part 2, which felt exploitive and nasty. I watched *Missing in Action 3* the other night, and Braddock goes through so much pain and awful stuff—even seeing his wife get killed right in front of him—it feels like a *Death Wish* sequel. What else can we put this guy through for the sake of entertainment?

I can't really speak for the second film, and I would agree with you on that. My *Missing in Action* was gritty, but it was also . . . I don't think we ever really set out to do exploitive things. Some things did feel like they were pushing the envelope for the sake of doing something. I think we were just trying to think of something that worked for the story, something that would affect the audience. One of the differences, I think, between those movies and movies that are being made now, is that you would always root for the hero. The hero may have been flawed, but they were good guys. Nowadays there are these dark heroes that you don't really like. That's just me being a little old-fashioned. No one ever asked me to come up with something controversial, but maybe it ended up that way.

What sort of feedback from veterans and the media did you get after the release of the two *Missing in Action* movies you wrote?

Very positive feedback for the first one. It showed veterans in an honorable light. We got positive reaction for the third one even though that one has an interesting backstory. Some critics liked them, but we were also accused of warmongering. We were doing *Invasion U.S.A.* by the time *Missing in Action* was completed and was going to come out. We were in Chicago to see Chuck because he was doing *Code of Silence* with Andy Davis, and Cannon had arranged a screening of *Missing in Action* for Chuck, Joe Zito, Andy Davis, and a few other people. It was the first time we saw the completed movie. After the end of it, we were all feeling so pumped up. It turned out so good. Chuck's manager at the time turned to me when it finished and said in my ear, "I don't think it'll hurt his career." I didn't say anything. Did we see the same movie? It still plays on regular television and pay television. When people find out that I wrote *Missing in Action*, they always go, "Oh, I love those movies!" They're still playing all these years later.

You wrote Chuck Norris's most iconic movies. You wrote the trinity: *Missing in Action*, Invasion U.S.A., and The Delta Force.

You mentioned to me that you'd written an article about *American Ninja*. Here's the real story about *American Ninja*: Menaham had done *Enter the Ninja* and he wanted to do *American Ninja*, starring Chuck Norris. I have an ad from the trade papers announcing Chuck Norris as the *American Ninja*. I was hired to write it. Chuck said, "I do *not* want to do a ninja movie!" He'd just done *Missing in Action* and it hadn't come out yet. He was moving away from martial arts movies and was trying to do regular action movies. I said, "Okay, I have an idea." I laid out the storyline for *Invasion U.S.A.* The kicker part was that Chuck's character was ex-CIA and his code name was American Ninja. The first draft of the screenplay was called *American Ninja*. During the movie, someone would say, "His code name used to be American Ninja!" I turned the script in and everyone was really happy with it, and Menahem read it and looks over at us and says, "Of course we cannot call this movie *American Ninja*!" We were like, "Of course not—we never wanted to call it that!" I came up with the *Invasion U.S.A.* title, and we used that. I actually did a major rewrite on *American Ninja*.

Is that true?

(Nodding.)

Wow, that's the first I'm hearing about that.

No one knows. It was a thing where the script was in trouble. I did that a lot for Cannon. I didn't ask for credit.

How did you write a script with Chuck Norris in mind? You gave him one-liners that are now a part of pop culture. All of those "I don't step on toes, I step on necks" lines. Those are on T-shirts now.

With Chuck, he's great at action and good at one-liners, but acting isn't really a strong suit. The way you'd have to tell the story, basically, is with sidekicks and other characters. Chuck gets the good lines. That's the general process of doing a movie with him.

Terrorists don't stand a chance against Matt Hunter (Chuck Norris) in *Invasion U.S.A.* Author's collection.

Chuck is such a badass in *Invasion U.S.A.* that the villain of that movie has nightmares about him. That's the only movie I can think of where the villain has nightmares about the hero. It scares him to death—almost literally. Tell me more stories about the making of this movie.

Yeah. There was a longer version. Chuck and Aaron [Norris] both had input for the script. Before we shot it, Chuck called me from New York and said, "Someone had left me a ticket to this off-Broadway play. There was a note saying, 'This play stars a woman who had been an extra in *A Force of One*. She has a one-woman play, and she'd love it if you'd come to see it.' Well, I went to see it, and it was fantastic! She would be great to play the reporter in *Invasion U.S.A.*" I said, "What's the woman's name?" He said, "Whoopi Goldberg." I'd never heard of her, and no one else had either. Chuck thought it would be great to cast her. The studio said "No." The woman they hired was nice, but her acting skills were weak. That character really told the story. She tied everything together. A lot of the emotional connections came from her. When we saw the rough cut of the movie, we cut a lot of her scenes out. The final version was a little choppy.

This movie has terrorists bombing shopping malls and blowing up neighborhoods at Christmastime. This is an insane movie.

If someone really did this, obviously there would be bigger repercussions, but I tried to think of what could plausibly happen. Having a million-man army would cause chaos. There were some serendipitous things that happened during the location scouting. We shot in Georgia and Florida. One of the things is that they found World War II landing craft so that cool scene when the landing craft comes up on the beach and all these guys come out, you know, it was possible because we found that stuff. They were originally going to be coming in on regular boats. It would have been boring. In Atlanta, we found a shopping mall that was going to be renovated. The company said, "Oh, yeah, you can come in and break stuff and run over stuff." I was able to write stuff because of that. Everything in these movies is real. Real stunts. The other thing that happened is that the Atlanta airport was extending runways, so they bought out this whole subdivision and they were going to bulldoze those homes. So, I had a scene like that already in the script, but it was going to cost too much. But we had the perfect locations

Savior of the free world, Matt Hunter (Chuck Norris) is cuffed and wrongly accused in *Invasion U.S.A.* Author's collection.

for that stuff. It was totally fun to do it. One guy had to stop all these bad guys. There was a lot of room to do some fun stuff.

Is there ever a point where you can go too far on a movie like this?

Probably. I don't know if we hit it or not because it worked for the audience. I just watched it recently. I'd forgotten some of the things we did.

You rolled right into *The Delta Force*, which was another of Chuck Norris's franchises. Talk about doing that one.

It started out as a completely different movie. The special forces guy I knew told me about the Delta Force, and he had originally trained the Delta Force who went into Desert One. He told me that no one knew about them, so I thought, *Wow—what a great movie!* I pitched that to Menaham at Cannon right after *Missing in Action*, and he was like, "Nah, nah, nah." I thought, "Eh, whatever." A year later, Menaham calls me from New York and says, "I just read this little article in *Newsweek* about the Delta Force! I want you to write the movie! This is the movie: Chuck Norris and Charles Bronson! *The Delta Force*!" I was like, "Chuck Norris and Charles Bronson? Holy crap! It's the best idea ever for an action movie in history!" I wrote it for Chuck and Bronson. It was about a bus full of tourists that was hijacked in Egypt, amidst the ancient ruins. The Delta Force comes in—Chuck and Bronson, basically—two of them against a thousand terrorists. Zito was going to direct it. We thought it was going to be really good. I don't know what happened; Chuck didn't agree, Bronson didn't agree—somebody didn't agree. Then the TWA hijacking happened in Beirut, and all of a sudden everything changed. Menaham decided, because he had directed some films, that he would direct it. I rewrote the script. I was following the news and writing things basically as they happened. They needed another star, so they got Lee Marvin. He was old. It was his last movie. I was there when Lee and Chuck met for the first time in Menahem's office. Lee was there first. He was a really good comedian. Chuck walks in. Lee Marvin's 6 foot 2, Chuck is not that tall. Lee being a super professional, takes a look at Chuck, shakes his hand and says, "You know, Chuck, I'm kind of what they call a *slouch actor*." He puts a hand on Menahem's desk, so that he and Chuck are at the same eye level. "I kind of like to do this kind of thing," he says. Anyway . . . Having Lee play that part was great.

Were you happy with the final cut of the film?

The original version of the movie was about five hours long. They should have saved it because it would have been a great miniseries. They filmed a ton of stuff. It was over five hours. At that point, the hostage situation still wasn't over. He looks at me and says, "Well, we don't have a third act." He then said to me, "I want you to go to Beirut and go to the airport and find out what's going on!" I said, "I don't think that's such a good idea." Luckily, he rethought it.

Were you asked to work on *Delta Force 2*?

I was. Michael Winner was going to direct *Delta Force 2*. He did some of Bronson's better movies. I had written a treatment for it, and they wanted me to go down to London to meet with Michael, but he insisted that I stay in London to write the whole script. It was a thing where I would be writing ten pages a day, and Michael sat there and rewrote the pages. It was one of those things. The script turned out *awful*. It was so bad that when I got back to the story department at Cannon, and they said, "What happened to you?" I said, "No, this is Michael Winner's script!" They said, "Oh my God, we thought something had happened to you!" For whatever reason, that's what happened, and someone else ended up doing it.

Anything else you want to say about *Braddock: Missing in Action III*?

I actually think that my original script for *Braddock* is the best script I've ever written. It went through some financing problems, and it went from being a bigger picture—Zito was going to direct it again—to having three or four different directors. The script got watered down. I don't like the movie. The bad guys are so hokey. None of that was in the original script. I got into a fight with Menahem because my writing deal was somehow tied into Aaron Norris's directing deal. The payments. I never figured out why. After I wrote three drafts, Menahem wanted me to take fifty percent. The good thing about Cannon is that they made a lot of movies. The bad thing was that they didn't pay all that well. It was great getting things made. I said, "No, I'm not going to get paid half when I already did all the work." He didn't offer me anything else like directing my own movie or something else, and it had something to do with paying Aaron. He said, "If you don't take half the money, you'll never work here again." That's it.

In the midst of your work at Cannon you wrote a little action/martial arts movie with Tadashi Yamashita called *Sword of Heaven*. Talk a little bit about that one.

It was a spec script I wrote. Mel Novak, who introduced me to Chuck, also introduced me to Tadashi. We became friends. He was an amazing martial arts guy. I came up with this story idea for him. I wrote the script. We had foreign sales already. Tadashi had brought in one of his students to help produce it, and that guy went off the rails. Someone else rewrote the script. The movie ended up being awful. There're a few

good action moments. I have a writing credit on it, but it's a terrible movie. It would have been great. I don't even think it came out theatrically.

You also wrote a movie called *P.O.W.: The Escape*, which starred David Carradine.

Someone else wrote the original script, and they had me do a rewrite and then when they were done with principle photography, I got called in to help them write some additional scenes for additional footage they would have to shoot. They needed the movie to make sense. The director was a great guy, Gideon Amir. They had a limited budget. It worked okay.

Anything else you want to say about working on all of these films in the golden era of action stars?

It was a great experience for me. Just coming up with an idea, pitching the ideas, and having the studios going, "We're going to start shooting in three months!" It was a lot of fun. Good people. The thing that makes me feel good—even today—is that they're still playing and people are still enjoying them.

Missing in Action 2:
The Beginning
1985 (MGM DVD) (djm)

Colonel James Braddock (Chuck Norris) and a platoon of soldiers are captured in Vietnam during a mission, and declared "Missing in Action." They spend years in captivity under the rule of a vindictive and evil Vietnamese colonel named Yin (Soon-Teck Oh), who has a personal grudge against Braddock because he won't sign a

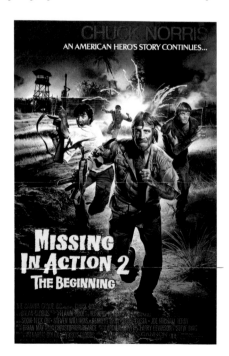

Theatrical release poster for Missing in Action 2. Author's collection.

bogus confession declaring that he's a criminal. Yin holds Braddock's team responsible for Braddock's obstinacy, and tortures them day-in and day-out for years on end. After years of grueling and inhumane treatment, Braddock finally snaps when Yin tricks him into signing the confession in exchange for medicine for one of his men who has malaria, but Yin kills the defenseless guy anyway. Braddock plans his escape, and when he's free from the prison, he builds up his strength and an arsenal to annihilate his captors and level the prison camp, while setting his fellow inmates free.

Filmed before *Missing in Action*, but released after it, *The Beginning* is tough to watch at times, and I'd hesitate to call it "entertaining." It almost feels like exploitation at times (actually it *is* exploitative in some ways), but if you're looking at it from an action movie perspective, it has some redeeming qualities. Norris is good in a pretty thankless role, and his co-stars (including Oh, who plays a horrible villain) are all game for what amounts to a prison camp movie with some payoff. It's easy to understand why Cannon (which produced all of the *Missing in Action* movies) decided to release this one second even though it was intended to be the first. Lance Hool directed. *Braddock: Missing in Action III* was next.

Missionary Man
2007 (Sony DVD) (CD)

M

"I will break your nose with this knee. And there is nothing you can do about it."

A mysterious stranger known as Ryder (Dolph Lundgren) rides into town on his motorcycle. He's there to pay his respects to his friend J. J., who has passed away. The Indian reservation on which J. J. lived has grown corrupt and, according to his family, J. J. was murdered by John Reno (Matthew Tompkins), the local crime lord. Ryder takes it upon himself to help clean up the streets of the town while spreading the word of God (literally) to those who will listen. The greedy Reno has plans for a casino to be built and J. J. got in the way, leading to his death. Ryder doesn't take kindly to his friends being hurt so he keeps one step ahead of the enemy at all times.

Missionary Man should have been the first entry of a trilogy. The way the story plays out and how it ends lends itself to being the perfect set-up for a continuing story. All we have is the one film, and it's really damn fun. It's a modern-day western heavily influenced by the likes of Clint Eastwood and *Pale Rider*. Star Lundgren (*Battle of the Damned*) fights his way through the bad guys while still finding time to sit with the local kids to teach them about the Bible, which is interesting. Lundgren put a lot of energy into this picture as he contributed to the script, and was also the director and the star. He even made it a point to perform all his own stunts. Dolph should never quit; he's a one of a kind and *Missionary Man* delivers the goods.

Mission of Justice

1992 (RAAM DVD R4) (djm)

A shady California mission—purporting to do good in the neighborhood with "peacekeepers" patrolling the streets, looking for trouble to quell—has a solid reputation in the media, as its leader Rachel Larkin (Brigitte Nielsen) is a candidate for a local election. What's really going on is that Larkin is building up an army of willing soldiers to do her bidding if and when she requires a dirty job to be done. She has the owner of a gym murdered because he won't bend to her will, and the best friend of the murdered man happens to be a disgruntled former cop named Kurt Harris (Jeff Wincott), who quit the force because his superiors got one of his witnesses killed over a bad judgment call. Harris decides to join the "peacekeepers" at their Mission of Justice, and he must first go through an intense initiation phase where he must survive a gauntlet of peacekeepers who wield sticks. Not only does he survive the initiation process, but he passes it with flying colors, which impresses Larkin, who hires him as a personal bodyguard. When Harris becomes aware of the evil going on in Larkin's camp, he uncovers the truth about her and proves that she had his friend murdered.

This is quite easily the best movie Jeff Wincott starred in. He shines in a spectacularly physical role, which requires him to exhibit his impressive skills as a martial artist while still grounding him in a real-world environment faced with a challenging task. His initiation scene would turn anyone watching it into a fan of his, and nothing else in the film measures up to that moment when he begins fighting those dozens of guys with sticks. Another highlight in the film is the casting of Karen Sheperd (from Eliminator Woman) as Wincott's former partner. She's given some great fight scenes, and I

actually think this is a better vehicle for her than Eliminator Woman was. Brigitte Nielsen comes off pretty well in the film, too. Her character's brother is played by Matthias Hues, who has a nice fight scene with Wincott towards the end. If you want to begin your Jeff Wincott journey, start with Mission of Justice. It was directed by Steve Barnett.

Mister T

1983–1986 (Warner DVD) (djm)

Hanna-Barbera's animated Mister T features episodic adventures of a group of gymnasts whose coach, Mr. T, helps them get out of trouble. They go around the world competing in championships, and with each episode, they help foil jewel heists, spar against megalomaniacal masterminds, and find treasures in exotic locations like South America. In each episode, Mr. T in his gold-chained, Mohawk-sporting cartoon persona helps the kids learn valuable life lessons.

In the solve-a-mystery-every-week tradition of Scooby Doo, Mister T lasted two seasons (thirty episodes) over a three-year time span. Mr. T himself introduces and concludes each episode—just like Chuck Norris later did in his own animated show, Chuck Norris Karate Kommandos, which was also produced by Hanna-Barbera. I remember buying Mister T breakfast cereal when I was a kid. It was basically Captain Crunch with Mr. T as the mascot.

Money Train

1995 (Columbia VHS) (CD)

"You're right on the edge. You're a wreck looking for someplace to happen. I'll be there and I'll fuck you dead."

Transit cops John (Wesley Snipes) and Charlie (Woody Harrelson) spend all their time on patrol, keeping the subways safe. They're constantly bumping heads with Captain Patterson (Robert Blake) who is more concerned with his money train (a single rail car used for collecting and delivering money) arriving on time than anything else. Charlie tends to get into trouble (he has a $15,000 gambling debt to the mob), and John has spent his life bailing him out of trouble, but this time Charlie's on his own. They're both vying for the affection of their new partner Grace Santiago (Jennifer Lopez), but it's John she has a connection with. When Charlie catches them together, the resentment he feels towards his foster brother and partner sends Charlie over the edge. He devises a plan to rob the money train on his own, and he has no idea the ruckus he will cause. This will leave John in a tough position: to let Charlie go down on his own or risk his career trying to save him.

Money Train was the much anticipated follow-up pairing of stars Snipes (Art of War) and Harrelson (Natural Born Killers) after the highly successful dramedy White Men

Can't Jump. This film tones the comedy way back and focuses more on the action. It's entertaining enough, though it suffers in the story department. The two stars make a solid duo and it doesn't hurt to have Jennifer Lopez (Out of Sight) in the mix as their new partner and love interest for Snipes. There are big-scale action set pieces scattered through the film; the highlight has Snipes fighting some mob thugs in a strip club dressing room. Directed by Joseph Ruben (The Stepfather).

Mortal Challenge

1997 (New Concorde DVD) (CD)

"There's no help in Death Row! It's kill or be killed!"

In the near future, Los Angeles has been devastated by an earthquake and has cracked right down the middle. Social classes have divided as well, with the filthy rich on one side and the poor on the other. Private dick Jack (Timothy Bottoms) has been hired to find the daughter of a rich businessman but then Jack and some local punks are taken captive. Jack and the punks are tossed into a game of death—a fight to the finish—and they try to find a way out. On the run in the maze-like complex, they try to elude the vicious attacks of a half-human, half-cyborg known as Grepp (American Kickboxer 2's Evan Lurie) when they find the missing girl. They may be in this together . . . but getting out will be an entirely different challenge.

The entertainment value of this film skyrockets if you imagine George W. Bush playing the lead character Jack. This isn't as difficult as you might think since the resemblance between the former president and Timothy Bottoms (who portrayed him twice) is pretty uncanny. Evan Lurie (Expect to Die) appears in a nonspeaking role stocked with some serious artillery. He pops up from time to time to give our heroes something to do when they're hiding out; he stomps through the picture wearing some crazy cool glasses as a character somewhere in between Robocop and The Terminator. The film is action packed and features several other martial artists like Vince Murdocco (L.A. Wars), Nicholas Hill, and Darren E. Scott. This was Lurie's final screen appearance and the only film to be directed by Randy Cheveldave.

Mortal Enemies

(a.k.a. Pirate Brothers)

2011 (Lionsgate DVD) (CD)

After a gang member murders his brother, a young boy, Sunny, is brought to an orphanage. There he meets a kindred spirit, and they quickly bond like brothers. Eventually, they are separated

Theatrical poster for Mission of Justice. Author's collection.

M

when they're adopted. The kindred spirit is Verdy (Verdy Bhawanta) who grows up and takes over his father's company where he has developed a top-secret microchip about to be unleashed upon the world. Meanwhile, the Sunny (Robin Shou from *Death Cage* and the *Mortal Kombat* features) is running with a gang of pirates who are plotting to kidnap Verdy until they can get their hands on the microchips. Things aren't as they appear to be, and Sunny is actually working for Interpol and is deep undercover within the gang. Verdy's fiancée is kidnapped in his place and the two estranged friends will have to put aside their differences if they are to save her life.

Robin Shou finally has the chance to shine in *Mortal Enemies*. It takes its time getting to the action but those who stick around will not be disappointed. Shou is now in his fifties and doesn't look a day over thirty. With fight after fight he just grows more and more impressive. Playing his partner in the film is newcomer Verdy Bhawanta who explodes in his feature film debut. Watching the two of them fight side by side is exciting and interesting since their styles are so distinctly different. While Shou is more wushu-based, Bhawanta has studied several different arts, but it's capoeira he showcases in this film. Both stars are brilliant. Director Asun Mawardi was smart enough to craft this film to showcase the newcomer and almost reinvent a veteran who was long overdue for resurgence.

Mortal Kombat

1995 (New Line DVD) (djm)

Raiden: "So you're going to win the tournament?"
Liu Kang: "Yes, I am!"
Raiden: "Show me how!"

Based on an immensely popular videogame, *Mortal Kombat* concerns an interdimensional fight tournament that decides the fate of humanity. A batch of human fighters are invited to participate in the competition, but all of the humans are staggeringly underprepared when they realize that their matches are against magical creatures, gods, and shape-shifting monsters. The lightning god Raiden (Christopher Lambert, who easily steals the show) is sympathetic to the humans, and he singles one of them out: a monkish warrior named Liu Kang (Robin Shou from *Death Cage*), who it seems has a destiny to fulfill. Liu Kang's human companions, Johnny Cage (a Hollywood action star) and Sonya Blade (a no-nonsense soldier), can only watch and behold as Liu Kang uses his inner spirit and martial arts prowess against the evil host of the "Mortal Kombat" Shang Tsung (Cary-Hiroyuki Tagawa), who has declared war against humanity.

Nonsensical, but fun to a degree, *Mortal Kombat* did several things right: it cast Hong Kong action star Robin Shou in the lead role, and he emerges fairly well in a Hollywood production that is just right for him. The direction by Paul W. S. Anderson (who would

later helm *Resident Evil, Soldier,* and *Death Race*) is necessarily flashy and stylish, and the fights are well shot and choreographed. Other notable martial artists, bodybuilders, and fighters in the cast include Keith Cook (*Heatseeker*), Trevor Goddard (*Men of War*), and John Fujioka (*American Ninja*).

Mortal Kombat: Annihilation

1997 (New Line DVD) (djm)

Liu Kang (Robin Shou), the victor of the battle that decided the fate of humanity in the first film, is stuck with his human companions in the dimensional rift where magic creatures and god-like monsters threaten to bring humanity to its knees in a war that an evil overlord named Shao Kahn (Brian Thompson) desperately wants. Raiden—a god of lightning (James Remar, who replaced Christopher Lambert)— forsakes his godhood in order to join Liu Kang and his friends in their fight against the monstrous horde.

Directed by John Leonetti, who was the cinematographer on the first *Mortal Kombat*, this woeful sequel has nonstop nauseating action, with enough flash, techno music, and inconsequential plotting to make casual viewers feel sick. I was always on the verge of not liking the first film, and so it's an easy call for me to say that *Annihilation* is a disgrace. It chucks out most of what made the first film watchable (especially Christopher Lambert) and replaces it with green screen–enhanced digital monstrosities. There's plenty of fighting here, but the movie's such a mess that it's just about irredeemable. Star Shou is relegated to a supporting role. Other martial artists and bodybuilders in the cast include Deron McBee (*Enter the Blood Ring*), Ray Park (*Star Wars: Episode 1*), and Keith Cook (*King of the Kickboxers*). I ditched school to see this theatrically on a depressing, rainy afternoon. I went home in a foul mood.

Mortal Kombat: Conquest

1998–1999 (CD)

"It's the most noble of weapons, a mystical blend of warrior and steel. Man forges the blade, and the blade forges man."

Taking place centuries before the storyline from the feature films, *Conquest* follows monk Kung Lao (Paolo Montalban), the most recent victor of the Mortal Kombat fighting tournament. He defeated the evil Shang Tsung (Bruce Locke), leaving him imprisoned in a dimensional void known as Outworld. Lao is living a peaceful life with his girlfriend Jen, waiting to take her hand in marriage. The forces are always at work and though Shang is banished from the Earth Realm, he's able to use sorcery and sends his minions to torment Lao. Jen is killed, leaving him without purpose until he teams up with her former guard Siro (Daniel Bernhardt), and a common thief

they meet along the way, Taja (Kristanna Loken). With guidance from the thunder god Raiden (Jeffrey Meek), they set up in a small town and battle the evil threatening to take over. Shang Tsung may be their main threat but many others are waiting in the wings for their opportunity to wreak havoc. United, Lao, Siro, and Taja will fight the forces of evil while learning more about each other and perfecting their skills.

Mortal Kombat: Conquest began its run in syndication before being picked up by the cable network TNT. It was a moderate success and many believed it would have been picked up for a second season. The cost to produce the show proved to be too much, though, and after only twenty-two episodes, the show came to an end. The ending of the series is a cliffhanger but it somehow manages to be a satisfying conclusion. While the show flaunted weak storytelling and cheap effects, the fight scenes tended to be done well, especially with star Bernhardt (from the *Bloodsport* sequels). Throughout the series, he fought numerous battles, took on multiple opponents, and had plenty of opportunities to show off his athleticism. The only other martial artist in the cast is Jeffrey Meek (from the martial arts–themed TV series *Raven*), who portrayed the characters of Raiden and Shao Kahn. He isn't featured in the action as much as Bernhardt, but he does have a few moments during various episodes (mostly near the end of the season) to do his thing. It wasn't until the final episodes that the story and action really got interesting. The show was geared towards an adult demographic, but has a teen mentality. Fifteen hours is way too much time to devote to this series, but there's some solid action to watch, and fans of the franchise will get their fill.

Mortal Kombat: Legacy

2011 (Warner DVD) (djm)

Nine short segments (up to ten minutes each) comprise this first season of webisodes showcasing the origins of the best-known characters from the *Mortal Kombat* videogame. Michael Jai White plays Jax, Darren Shahlavi plays Kano, Matt Mullins plays Johnny Cage, and other actors such as Jeri Ryan and Ian Anthony Dale portray other characters. Some of the episodes cross over into each other, but generally the segments are stand-alones. Mullins and Shahlavi shine most of all.

Fans of the games and films received this series with open arms because it takes the characters back to their roots and grounds them in a hyper-realistic universe, giving them equal, careful attention. The tone is "R"-rated, and the action and fights are fairly intense. The director, Kevin Tancharoen, is clearly a devoted fan of the franchise, and if you're going to start anywhere in the *Mortal Kombat* universe, this might be the best place.

M

Mortal Kombat: Legacy II

2013 (Warner DVD) (CD)

It has begun! The tenth Mortal Kombat tournament is about to dawn. Liu Kang (Brian Tee), once a guardian for the Earth Realm, has left the order to be with the woman he loves. This causes some friction between himself and Kung Lao (Mark Dacascos), a man he considers to be a brother. When his woman is killed, Liu Kang chooses a remarkably dark path, one Kung Lao will try to save him from. In period Japan, two clans have spent decades feuding with one another. Bi-Han (Eric Steinberg) and Hanzo Hasashi (Ian Anthony Dale) were childhood friends who were banned from playing together by their feuding families. As adults and after the death of Bi-Han's brother Kuai Liang (Harry Shum Jr.), the two come together to form a truce to end the fighting. When a supernatural force wipes out Hasashi's family, it's believed Bi-Han and his clan were responsible. In their rage, they create their alter egos: Bi-Han adopts Sub-Zero and Hasashi becomes Scorpion. Raiden (David Lee McInnis) and Shang Tsung (Cary-Hiroyuki Tagawa) summon their fighters to Outworld, where the fighters are set loose to find themselves in elimination matches to the death. With all of their personal issues on the table, the fighters are all ready to do whatever it takes to survive.

Mortal Kombat: Legacy II is a much different season than the first. The first season mostly dealt with standalone origin stories for fan favorite characters, while this time there is more of a cohesive storyline. With the success of the first installment, more money was spent on the production and it shows. There are more effects, elaborate camera set-ups, and the fights look spectacular. The much-needed addition of Mark Dacascos elevates the production, but sadly it ends before he gets a chance to fight. He's fantastic as Kung Lao and the rivalry between him and Liu Kang is nicely represented. There's no denying the chemistry between Brian Tee and Dacascos, with their storyline being the highlight. As Kurtis Stryker, Eric Jacobus (from *Death Grip*) is completely wasted. Jacobus is a seriously talented fighter and actor with skills that have been relatively untapped. His character is underused and only gets into the action for a few moments. This is where *MK: Legacy II* fails: there's far too much filler. The Liu Kang and Kung Lao rivalry and the Sub-Zero/Scorpion rivalry will excite and draw viewers in. The rest of the characters like Stryker, Johnny Cage, Mileena, Katana, etc. just have throwaway moments leading up to the main rivalries. What's even more frustrating is the abrupt ending that will leave fans salivating for a third entry. Director Kevin Tencharoen has an amazing vision for rejuvenating this franchise, but it just needs a little fine-tuning.

Moscow Heat

2004 (Lightning Entertainment DVD) (djm)

"With all due respect, sir, I'm not a runner—I'm a bodybuilder."

A good cop (played by Adrian Paul of *Highlander: The TV Series*) is killed by a Russian arms dealer named Klimov (Richard Tyson) on American soil, and the cop's father Rod Chembers (Michael York) wants nothing but revenge for the death of his son. Rod hops on a plane headed to Moscow, buys a gun from a gangster, pays for some information, and heads straight for the nightclub where Klimov is known to hang out. When Klimov figures out that he's being hunted, all hell breaks loose and some people are shot and Rod is arrested and questioned by an elite cop named Vlad (Russian bodybuilding champ Alexander Nevsky), who finds him amusing because of how stubborn he is. Rod insists that he "found" the gun he was carrying when he was arrested, but Vlad doesn't buy that. Despite that, he ends up helping Rod by hunting Klimov because his partner was shot and killed by the known arms dealer, and if they work together maybe they can get him.

An obvious riff on *Red Heat*, *Moscow Heat* is surprisingly slick for a straight-to-video effort, and it uses its Russian locations really well, providing some much-needed production value to an otherwise by-the-numbers actioner. If you pay attention to Nevsky, you'll get some goosebumps when he starts to remind you of Schwarzenegger, but his acting is really rough and he needs to clock in some more hours in front of a camera to push his physicality over the edge. The movie gives him a handful of fight scenes, and he handles himself well enough to pass the grade. He even makes a reference to Schwarzenegger at the end of the film. His next movie was *Treasure Raiders*. The director of this film is Jeff Celentano, who had a supporting role in *American Ninja 2: The Confrontation*.

Moses:
Fallen, In the City of Angels

2005 (Tiberia DVD) (CD)

"Hebrew? What the fuck—is that the fucking Hebrew? Boss, what the fuck is he saying? The Jew took your brother out?"

After serving time in the Israeli military, Moses finds himself on the streets of Los Angeles. He's haunted by the death of a child during a firefight. Now, he's taking jobs as a hitman, eliminating anyone when the price is right. There's something inside he doesn't understand, all the killing just isn't right. Even though he looks at it as cleaning up the streets, deep down he knows it's wrong. The woman he works for, Mrs. Mier (Addi Kaplan) is keeping a secret. She's actually the Archangel Gabriel and wrongfully sends Moses to kill a man named Lucky Palermo (Hank Garrett). Lucky's brother Julius (Tony Digerlando) wants vengeance, for he is actually the Dark Angel, Lucifer himself. He sends his daughter Angel Eyes (Penny Ray) to kill Moses, but instead she falls in love with him. They flee the city with the help of a homeless Vietnam vet but they can only hide for so long before the Devil finds them.

The idea of an Israeli soldier working as a hitman who is actually a fallen angel sentenced to life on Earth is brilliant. Writer/director/star Benjamin Maccabee (*Enter the Blood Ring*) may not have the budget guys like Van Damme or Seagal get, but he tries. He has ambitious ideas and does his best each and every time he makes a movie. *Moses* takes itself too seriously and suffers from being really lengthy at 125 minutes. If this film was put under a knife and then sewn back together (minus about thirty to forty minutes) it could have been a highly unique actioner. Even with the outlandish story, there just isn't enough action to hold your attention. Maccabee is a risk-taker and this gives him an edge, one we just can't ignore.

Moving Target

1996 (A-Pix VHS) (djm)

Sonny McClean (Michael Dudikoff) is a schlubby bounty hunter who can't keep his pregnant woman happy. She complains that his job is too dangerous, but he continues to pay the bills while everyone around him treats him like a second-rate citizen. He gets an offer from an elderly couple to find their son who skipped bail, and this particular job appeals to him because he actually feels like someone believes in him for a change. When he finds the bounty, his life immediately takes a turn for the worse because this particular bounty is being hunted down by a faction who wants him dead, and when Sonny is knocked out after an intense chase, he finds that not only is the bounty dead but he has been framed for the murder. Faced with a murder charge and a death note on his head from the mob (the murdered man was related to the don), Sonny only has a few days to clear his name and find the real culprit of the killing, while still maintaining some kind of normalcy with his pregnant girlfriend (played by Michelle Johnson).

The video box prominently displays Michael Dudikoff running with a pistol in his hand while co-star Billy Dee Williams runs beside him with a shotgun. Williams is in the movie in a small role as a lawyer/detective friend of Dudikoff's character, but he never holds a gun and he never runs. Incorrect marketing aside, *Moving Target* is a vehicle that might have suited Don "The Dragon" Wilson in his heyday, but Michael Dudikoff (*Avenging Force*) looks tired, bored, and miscast in it, which is too bad because I like Dudikoff as an action guy. His character in this film is too naive and too likable to inhabit the gritty world he is a part of. The next year he would go on to play another bounty hunter in a very similar film called *Bounty Hunters*. *Moving Target* was directed by Damien Lee (*Abraxas: Guardian of the Universe*). Incidentally, Don Wilson starred in a film called *Moving Target*, but the story was entirely different and was set in Ireland.

Moving Target

2000 (New Concorde DVD)

(djm)

Ray Brock (Don Wilson) goes to Ireland to meet a woman whom he met online. As an afterthought, he buys a case of beer at a pub to give to his friend, but it turns out that each bottle of beer holds a nuclear detonator. The IRA want their detonators back, and they chase Brock around and are surprised when he turns out to be a formidable kickboxing champion who can fight better than any of their best men. They kidnap his friend and kill all of her co-workers in cold blood, and Brock becomes the number one suspect in the killings. He and a new acquaintance (his friend's pretty roommate) have to redeem his good name and save his friend from a brutal death.

Fun for most of the way, *Moving Target* reunites star Wilson with his director from *Bloodfist IV*, which had virtually the same story and set-up as this film. Paul Ziller, his director, works well with him, and the tone in this one is breezy and light. It helps to have Wilson in a nice setting, and the Irish cast and locations are better used here than in his other film set in Ireland, *Bloodfist VIII*. Fans of Wilson will be happy, and newcomers to his films will be pleasantly surprised.

Mr. Majestyk

1974 (MGM DVD) (ZC)

Lee Marvin once said, "If I appeal to anyone, I hope it's the man who picks up the garbage." This may be the single greatest sentence ever uttered by an actor, but Bronson conveyed the same message in nearly every role he played. Chief among these is Vince Majestyk: devoted rancher, melon farmer, and champion for the rights of migrant workers. When the livelihood of his employees is challenged, Majestyk steps up in the most masculine way, slamming the butt of his rifle in the crotch of a seedy lowlife (Paul Koslo). This lands him on a bus to the county jail alongside career criminal Frank Renda (Al Lettieri). When Renda makes his getaway, Majestyk is dragged into an all-out war. Whether shotgunning hoods or driving his dented Chevy through the desert brush, our hero "just wants to get those melons in on time"!

This wildly intense assault on fruit harvesting was directed by Richard Fleischer and penned by none other than Elmore Leonard, who manages to consistently distract from the film's ludicrous premise. The action is '70s-sweaty and palpable throughout, and

the dialogue is whip-smart (even when one of Bronson's earliest lines is, "You sayin' I busted the toilet?"). While this definitely ranks among one of Bronson's most memorable films, it's the villainous Al Lettieri who steals any scene he's in. His vein-bursting performance is fueled by feral rage, and every line is spat with mush-mouthed venom. Sadly, he died at age forty-seven of a heart attack, but it's clear that he lived and performed with such power that the world just couldn't hold him.

Mr. Mean

1977 (Magnum VHS) (CD)

"Mean is a personality trait, not necessarily my character."

After tying up a few loose ends on a previous assignment, Mr. Mean (Fred Williamson) finds himself ready to embark on a new adventure. He's contacted by an old associate, then asked by an Italian mafia boss to take someone out. Killing isn't usually his business but the price is right. When the mark, Huberto (Lou Castel), learns of the contract on his head, he in turn takes a contract out on the man who was hired for the job: Mr. Mean. What ensues is a cat-and-mouse game of who kills who first but what Huberto fails to realize is that Mr. Mean lives up to his name utterly and completely.

Even the untouchable Fred Williamson (*Black Cobra*) can take a few missteps and sadly *Mr. Mean* is one of them. At the time, the film's main selling point was the fact that the then-popular band The Ohio Players composed the soundtrack. The music is smooth, hip, funky, and really jazzy so the chances are that the music will be more memorable than the film. Williamson never strays from the type of character he's most comfortable with, so he just essentially kicks some ass then charms the gals right out of their pants. He spends a bit more time out of his pants as well, parading around in a black Speedo for several scenes. Even if it's a bit disappointing, it's still The Hammer and his hardcore fans won't want to miss it. This was another one-man show film for Williamson who also produced, wrote, and directed.

Mr. Nanny

1993 (New Line DVD) (CD)

"Ooohhh, the dynamic duo, Wimpy and Gimpy."

Sean Armstrong (Terry "Hulk" Hogan) is a former pro-wrestler who takes a job as a bodyguard when his friend Burt (Sherman Hemsley) presents it to him. The job isn't exactly the type of bodyguard job he was expecting: he's guarding children. The children's father, Alex Mason (Austin Pendleton), is in possession of a microchip that madman Tommy

Thanatos (David Johansen) wants to get his hands on. The catch is that Thanatos is a former nemesis of Armstrong's, which makes the hunt so much more enticing to him. Before he can even worry about dealing with Thanatos, Armstrong will have to deal with the two children who are having the time of their lives pulling as many pranks as they possibly can on him. So, first he has to survive the children before he can even worry about taking care of Thanatos.

For whatever reason, Terry "Hulk" Hogan (*No Holds Barred*) took the family film route when entering into his acting career. For better or worse, he was able to mix his style of action in a family-friendly approach that is far more appealing to young children than adults. He plays a former wrestler in the film, which isn't much of a stretch for him, and he uses his wrestling skills in the few fight scenes there are in the picture. It's hard to take it very seriously when a sweaty Hogan is battling in a purple tutu. Through much of the film he takes beating after beating by the two children he was hired to protect. As an adult, you might find yourself laughing at how ridiculous the film is but children will most definitely enjoy the humor. Michael Gottlieb (*Mannequin*) directed the film from a script he wrote with Edward Rugoff. *Twin Sitters*, starring Peter and David Paul, was released the following year and bears a striking resemblance to this one.

Mr. Nice Guy

1998 (New Line DVD) (djm)

A well-liked celebrity chef named Jackie (Jackie Chan) is at the wrong place at the wrong time when some thugs chase a female journalist down because she has a videotape that can incriminate their boss, a mogul named Giancarlo (Richard Norton). Jackie saves the journalist and incites the thugs to chase *him* down because they think he now has the tape. What follows is an extended chase that carries the action-packed scenario to its conclusion.

Nothing's more fun than watching Jackie Chan do his crazy stuff for real in a movie, and the lightweight *Mr. Nice Guy* is 100 percent Chan doing exactly the kind of stuff he's famous for. Having Richard Norton in the film is nice, although the tone the film sets for the villains is pretty much on par with the tone Saturday morning cartoons set. Nothing is serious, everything is for fun, and if you're looking

Jackie Chan is up to his insane stunts in *Mr. Nice Guy*. Author's collection.

In *Mr. Nice Guy*, the villain is played by Richard Norton. Author's collection.

Mr. Nice Guy features Jackie Chan as a celebrity chef who goes on the run after some circumstances force him to. Author's collection.

A fight scene in *Mr. Nice Guy*, featuring Jackie Chan (center) and Richard Norton, far right. Author's collection.

Stunts galore in *Mr. Nice Guy*, this one featuring Jackie Chan hanging from pipes at a construction site. Author's collection.

for an action film that will resonate, *Mr. Nice Guy* might not be the right movie for you. The director, Sammo Hung (also a famous action star), appears in a few comedic scenes as a disgruntled bicyclist.

Mr. X

1995 (BCI DVD) (djm)

A Hong Kong wedding of a member of a Triad gang turns into a massacre when a Yakuza boss puts a mark of death on him. The Triads retaliate and in days, the streets of Hong Kong are awash in blood. An American "cleaner" is called in to squelch the escalating war, and when Mr. X (kickboxing legend Joe Lewis) begins performing his job, both sides realize that he's somewhat of a pale horse, riding in and bringing death with him. The climax is a virtual scene-for-scene rehash of Mark Goldblatt's *The Punisher*.

From director "Ed Woo" (a.k.a. the very prolific Godfrey Ho), *Mr. X* is a violent actioner with gunfire and explosions galore, and it's surprisingly entertaining as a brainless tit-for-tat action movie. Lewis's role is prominent and front-and-center, and he doesn't shy away from getting into the action. He has an extended fight scene with a gigantic steroid-infused muscleman, who finally collapses after being kicked around for ten minutes by the less-exhausted Lewis. If you're into Joe Lewis, seek *Mr. X* out and enjoy.

Muay Thai Giant

2008 (Magnet DVD) (djm)

The 6 foot 11 Australian wrestler Nathan Jones from *Fearless* and *The Protector* stars in this lightweight "family" movie about a big loser named Barney who wins a vacation to Thailand in a raffle. As soon as he lands, he's duped by a couple of scammers who get him drunk, steal his passport, his clothes, and any chance he might have of getting back home. Dejected and clueless, Barney wanders the streets shirtless and shoeless and bumbles his way into a situation involving two street urchin girls who are being harassed by thugs. The girls thank him for helping them in the fight (his method of fighting is to just swing his massive form around and knock people over) and, feeling sorry for him, they take him home to the monastery where they live. The monk who runs the place agrees to let him stay until he can get a new passport, and they feed him, clothe him, and teach him Muay Thai fighting. Within a week, the two girls have figured out how to make the mild-natured Barney into a raging beast: they feed him a spicy dish called *somtum*, and it's an instant way to get him to pulverize any enemies. Through some random occurrences, Barney and the two girls run afoul of international criminals, who pose a threat to them, but all of their problems are solved when the girls feed him somtum. He goes berzerk and saves the day.

Once upon a time something like *Muay Thai Giant* might have been given a token theatrical release and gone on to build a cult following around a community of fans who enjoy movies like *Crocodile Dundee* and *3 Ninjas*. It's simple-hearted, with the right amount of sentimentality and action to make kids happy, but some of the violence in it is "R"-rated, which sort of kills its chances at a life at daycares. Jones, who is impressive on screen, delivers a fun, game performance, allowing himself to be trampled on and abused, and he never comes across as ironic

or self-aware. He looks happy to be in a movie focused on him, and there's really no vanity to any of it. One of the girls in the movie—Sasisa Jindamanee—is a real-life Muay Thai champion. Directed by Somsak Techaratanaprasert.

The Mummy: Tomb of the Dragon Emperor

2008 (Universal DVD) (CD)

"Today you awake to a world in the grip of chaos and corruption. I will restore order. I will retake what is mine. I will crush any idea of freedom. I will slaughter without mercy. I will conquer without compassion. I will now lead you past the Great Wall. Once you cross, you will be indestructible!"

In ancient China, a man known as Qin Shi Huang (Jet Li) uses his strength and wits to become the emperor after uniting the kingdoms into a single empire. He and his second in command, Ming Guo (Russell Wong), take control and order the construction of the Great Wall of China. He builds so he can bury beneath it the bodies of his fallen enemies. As age begins to creep up on him, the emperor begins to dabble in sorcery until he meets Zi Yuan (Michelle Yeoh), a sorceress who knows the secret to eternal life. He falls in love with her but she wants to share her life with Ming Guo instead. In a fit of rage, the emperor has Ming killed and in return, Zi curses the emperor and his army. They're turned to stone and buried deep within a hidden tomb. Thousands of years later, he awakens and is brought to General Yang (Anthony Wong) with whom he hopes to reign. It won't be easy, as adventurer Rick O'Connell (Brendan Frasier reprising his most successful role) and his family poke their noses where they don't belong.

This big-budget blockbuster-hopeful is jam-packed with adventure and CGI effects, making it the most entertaining film in the series (this is the third entry). It also doesn't hurt having three of Hong Kong cinema's most familiar faces in major roles in the movie. Director Rob Cohen (*The Fast and the Furious, xXx*) knows how to do these huge action scenes with loads of activity and special effects, but as far as seeing two people in an honest fight, there's just far too much frenetic editing for any of those scenes to be completely satisfying. Jet Li, who at this point had enjoyed a successful string of minor English-language hits like *Romeo Must Die, Cradle 2 the Grave,* and *Kiss of the Dragon*, has a couple of very short battles, including one with the always delightful Michelle Yeoh (who had already starred in *Tomorrow Never Dies*). Li seems to be having a blast as the villain, and who better to have by his side than Anthony Wong from John Woo's *Hard-Boiled*. Li spends much of his time in a stony, blocky CGI incarnation, but the visuals and his villainous performance help to elevate this one above the previous two entries in the series.

Murder at 1600

1997 (Warner Brothers DVD) (CD)

"Yeah, and your duties can send an innocent man to jail for the rest of his life. You wanna live with that?"

Harlan Regis (Wesley Snipes) is a homicide detective from Washington, DC. He's called to the White House to investigate the murder of secretary Carla Town (Mary Moore). He finds it tough to do his job when everything he needs is classified. He's paired up with secret service agent Nina Chance (Diane Lane), and together they begin to unravel the biggest cover-up in government history. With the United States on the verge of war with North Korea, the president is having trouble deciding what course of action to take. This isn't the best time for a scandal of that magnitude to erupt in the White House so the pressure is on to clean up the mess quickly. Harlan finds there are people high up in the government involved in the case and an innocent janitor is being framed for the murder. He and Nina can't let it go and set out to find the truth no matter the cost.

Murder at 1600 is a thriller with political overtones and a few moments of action. The story is intriguing enough to draw in the casual viewer and the film is elevated by terrific actors. Snipes is really good as Harlan Regis. He spends much of the film running for his life but has a cool one-on-one battle near the end. The fight showcases some really quick blocking that looks outstanding on film. Aside from those few moments, Snipes actually spends much of the movie getting his ass kicked. The audience has to let it slide since we all know it wasn't a balls-out action film. Director Dwight Little (*Rapid Fire*) knows how to ramp up the suspense and does so with ease. Even though this is very light on the action, the story and acting are enough to hold your interest.

Murder in the Orient

1974 (Falcon Home Video VHS) (djm)

"You hit like my grandma! Come on!"

A stash of gold is buried during World War II in the Philippines, and decades later, a cult of bad guys that go by the name of The Golden Cobras has been quested with finding the gold, but the only map that leads to the score is engraved on the blades of two lost samurai swords. A secret agent played by Ron Marchini (who would later star in movies like *Death Machines* and *Omega Cop*) has been stationed in Manila, and he bides his time between missions by sleeping with other men's wives. He gets wind of the gold,

and when the wrong woman dies as a result of his philandering, he is hunted by The Golden Cobras. He aligns himself with a local martial arts instructor, played by Leo Fong. They join forces and go after the two swords, and in the middle of their adventure, they have to deal with scores of bad guys who rush at them and die in slow motion. One scene has Marchini ripping a guy's trachea out in the finale.

Most viewers will find *Murder in the Orient* a chore to sit through, but anyone who's ever watched a movie with either Marchini or Fong *and enjoyed* the experience will definitely need to watch this film at some point. It's great to see these future "B" martial arts action stars together on screen, fighting side by side. The film is cheap, ugly, and poorly made, but at less than eighty minutes, it's worth a small investment of time. It's fun. Directed by Manuel G. Songo.

Murphy's Law

1986 (MGM DVD) (djm)

"Remember what I told you:
Don't fuck with Jack Murphy!"

After a small-time carjacker steals his car and crashes it, detective Jack Murphy (Charles Bronson) catches up to Arabella, the young thief (Kathleen Wilhoite), and she turns around and kicks him in the balls. She gets away. Murphy's an alcoholic—he drinks on the job, catches his ex-wife's stripper act as often as possible, and follows her around, moping and getting himself in trouble at work for slacking or using excessive force. When he later catches Arabella by accident, he throws the book at her, and it's just his luck when his ex-wife is shot dead with his gun later that night, and *his car* is seen driving away from the incident . . . *with him inside it* to boot! He wakes up, bewildered, and then the cops bust down his door and cart him off to jail for the murder of his ex, and Arabella the thief is there in the same cell hanging out, waiting to be arraigned. Murphy is cuffed to Arabella, and instead of waiting around to be put through the system for a crime he didn't commit, Murphy breaks out of jail with Arabella chained to him. Together, they are forced to become buddies as Murphy figures out his situation: A psychotic woman he helped institutionalize a decade ago is hunting down everyone who contributed to her pain and suffering, and she has planned out an obstacle course for Murphy because he's the one she hates the most. The woman (played by a buff Carrie Snodgress) is hunting Murphy down every step of the way, and when Arabella gets in the way, she doesn't flinch when it comes to collateral damage. The only way Murphy is going to stop her and clear his name, while saving Arabella, is to tap into that renegade cop within him and shoot to kill.

Right up Cannon's alley—and keeping in tune to Bronson's action star persona (especially during the '80s)—*Murphy's Law* is pretty good for an unexpected buddy/buddy movie. Wilhoite, whose first film this was, is super spunky and loudmouthed, but she comes across as endearing

despite her annoying insults to Bronson, who seems like he can barely tolerate her. Snodgress is a great villain, and when Bronson dispatches her, it's pretty satisfying. Sort of overshadowed by the *Death Wish* sequels, *Murphy's Law* has its rewards. Directed by Bronson regular J. Lee Thompson (*10 to Midnight*).

Musketeers Forever

1998 (Prism Leisure DVD) (djm)

Some ex-secret service agent buddies (one of whom is played by Lee Majors) pool their resources together and open up a nightclub in Nevada, but being on a Native American reservation, they come into a situation where a nasty gangster tries to swindle the local tribe into building a gigantic casino using dirty money. The secret service guys (who are in their twilight years) call on their younger crony D'Artagnan (Michael Dudikoff) to join them in helping the Indian tribe rid themselves of the gangster who is bullying them into selling their land.

Surprisingly violent and sexually frank for a movie that could have easily been a made-for-TV movie with some tweaks, *Musketeers Forever* has a seed of an intriguing premise and two of the most likable stars in the genre you could get, but it's a failure. The treatment of updating *The Three Musketeers* is less than halfheartedly handled, and while it has some action in it, the movie is just not palatable. The direction by Georges Chamchoum is abysmal.

My Lucky Stars

1985 (Fox DVD) (djm)

My Lucky Stars is virtually an anime cartoon brought to life. Jackie Chan plays a cop everyone calls Muscles, and he's after a villain who has a ninja cult that backs him up. Yuen Biao plays Ricky, Muscles's partner, and when they run afoul of the ninja cult, Ricky is captured by the ninjas. In the meanwhile, a group of goofball convicts (the leader of whom is played by Sammo Hung, who also directed) is paroled under the condition that they help the police go after the ninjas, but there's a big problem with that scenario: the convicts are pretty much good for nothing except cracking jokes and acting like children (poop jokes, pratfalls, silly games galore). When Muscles teams up with the ex-cons, everyone is surprised that Kidstuff (Hung) actually knows how to fight, and there's a happy ending.

Some solid, exciting fight scenes enliven this otherwise boneheaded comedy. Whenever Chan appears on screen (he's hardly in it), the movie's pulse jumps up and the film comes alive again. Fans of Yuen Biao will lament that his screen time is even shorter than Chan's. The best scene of the film features a girl-on-girl fight between Sibelle Hu and Japan's first women's bodybuilding and power-lifting champion Nishiwaki Michiko, who looks incredible in the film. Chan, Hung, and Biao appeared a number of times on screen together in films like *Wheels on Meals*, *Dragons Forever*, and *Project A*. *My Lucky Stars* had a sequel called *Twinkle, Twinkle Lucky Stars*. The prequel to this film is *Winners and Sinners*.

My Lucky Stars 2:
Twinkle, Twinkle Lucky Stars
1985 (Fortune Star DVD R3) (CD)

"It doesn't hurt at all. My whole damn body is numb."

Kidstuff (Sammo Hung) and his band of fools are back at it when an informant sends evidence in a letter to a young woman named Yi-Ching (Rosamund Kwan). Three assassins are dispatched to intercept the evidence and take Yi-Ching out. The chief inspector (Sibelle Hu) takes Yi-Ching to stay with Kidstuff while they try to stop the assassins. Fellow detectives Muscles (Jackie Chan) and Ricky (Yuen Biao) are protecting a double agent who's involved with the same group. All of them have to band together in order to stop the assassins while bringing down one of the top drug operations in Hong Kong.

There's so much silliness in this film it's tough to remember there are some really amazing action scenes sprinkled throughout. Jackie Chan (*Project A*) and Yuen Biao (*The Iceman Cometh*) are only bit part players here. They show up a few times to kick some asses around but most of the film has the Lucky Stars group chasing girls and trying to see them naked. Also appearing in the film are Richard Norton (*Raiders of the Sun*), Michelle Yeoh (*Supercop*), Andy Lau (*The Legend of Drunken Master*), and Yasuaki Kurata (*Fist of Legend*). The movie belongs to Sammo; his fights with Norton and Kurata are classic. You will never see anyone his size be so limber or able to turn a couple of tennis rackets into lethal weapons the way he can. Sammo also served as the project's director. It's always great seeing Biao, Chan, and Hung together, even if it's only in small increments.

My Samurai
1988 (Imperial VHS) (djm)

A young martial arts student named Peter (John Kallo) witnesses a murder by a corrupt cop, and he goes to his master Young Park (Julian Lee) for help. Evidence is altered to make it look like the kid and his teacher did the killing, and so they go on the run while the media labels them outlaws. A crime lord (played by Mako) is in cahoots with the corrupt cop, and so everywhere Peter and Young turn, they face overwhelming odds. But it's a good thing Young is a force to be reckoned with, because when the bad guys try to fight/kill them, he manages to lay them all out cold. The

A behind-the-scenes shot from *My Samurai*, featuring Julian Lee and Terry O'Quinn. Courtesy of Julian Lee.

A press photo from Imperial's *My Samurai*. Courtesy of Julian Lee.

crux of the story is really about getting Peter to "man" up and become a confident fighter, and by the end of the film he can face his father (played by Terry O'Quinn).

Shot in '88, but not released until the early '90s, *My Samurai* will turn a lot of viewers off by its simplistic and amateur style, but I liked it. Star Julian Lee (a South Korean martial artist who has continued making martial arts action films in the independent circuit) delivers a deadpan, honest performance, and I would liken him to Jino Kang (also South Korean), who made the films *Blade Warrior* and *Fist 2 Fist*. That's a complement, trust me. Lee also produces his own films, and some other titles of his are *Dragon and the Hawk* and *Little Bear and the Master*. Bubba Smith from *The Wild Pair* has a cameo here. Directed by Fred Dresch.

The Myth
2007 (Sony DVD) (djm)

In between some of his Hollywood films, Jackie Chan makes several films in his native China, and *The Myth* is such a film. He plays an archaeologist named Jake, who has vivid dreams and visions of what might be a past life: In ancient China, a general (played by Chan with a serious face) has been assigned the arduous task of escorting a Korean princess to his emperor, but he's faced with a dissenting army and the battle that goes with it. Jake becomes obsessed with his visions, which correlate to his current quest, and unsurprisingly there's a villain on his trail, hoping to catch up to him before he finds his quarry.

Unhampered by a large budget, but crippled by an uninvolving story and blasé characters and an uneven tone, *The Myth* is a pretty massive disappointment. Chan alternates between too-serious and bored-looking, and the few fight scenes usually involve him wielding a sword or floating around, courtesy of wirework. The story and direction by Stanley Tong (*Rumble in the Bronx*, a better vehicle for Chan) are lackluster. It needed to be more fun.

Myths and Legends:
The New Alliance
2010 (CD)

"The truth is, Sofia and I went to another dimension and Sofia got caught."

Martin (Christian Seve) spends his days and nights obsessed with the card game known as Myths and Legends. When he pieces together his cards, he notices some tiny markings that come together and form a symbol. Somehow when the sun shines and the cards are aligned properly, he opens a portal into the world portrayed on the cards. He and his friend Sofia (Paulette Seve) travel into the other dimension, where she is captured by the evil ruler Chronos. Martin is tossed back into the real world and will have to convince his friends to help him in order to rescue her. Each of them choose a card from the deck and enter the portal where they are equipped with the powers and abilities represented on the card they hold. This isn't a mission they can do alone; they will have to enlist the help of warrior Marimoto (Marko Zaror from *Kiltro* and *Mirage Man*) to put an end to Chronos's vicious reign.

Marko Zaror is one of the greatest, underused talents working in action films today. Whether he is the star or just a supporting character (like in *Undisputed III* and *Machete Kills*), the movie is better for having him in it. In *Myths and Legends*, Zaror never utters a single word of dialogue but he doesn't need to. He's perfect as a mythological warrior helping a group of kids battle evil to save their friend. There's one battle scene with Zaror and his followers taking on an onslaught of enemies. It's a cool scene but it's far too short for fans of Zaror, whom I'd imagine would expect and hope for more. Regardless, the movie itself is tons of fun and if you've ever played a card game like Magic: The Gathering or even Myths and Legends, you will find yourself drawn into the colorful world represented here. Directed by Jose Luis Guridi.

Nature Unleashed: Fire

2004 (Echo Bridge DVD) (CD)

"Gotta wonder though, what kind of idiot would come up with that brilliant idea, huh?"

A group of dirtbikers head out into the woods for fun and a little bit of danger, until one of them has a nasty accident and breaks their leg. They're deep into the woods with no help until forest ranger Jake (Bryan Genesse) is helicoptered in to save the day. A freak accident leaves him stranded in the woods with the bikers. The plan is to bike out until they end up trapped within the woods, surrounded by a raging fire decimating everything in its wake. There's something different about this fire; the way it has them trapped suggests it wasn't accidental. Someone has intentionally set the flames to trap them there. Jake, who is haunted by an incident in his past, will have to overcome his own issues if he's to lead these young adults to safety.

For a film with major ambition and little money (from Nu Image), *Nature Unleashed: Fire* is a surprisingly entertaining romp through a forest inferno. There couldn't have been a better lead for the picture than Bryan Genesse (*Cold Harvest, Street Justice*). Sadly, after suffering a serious injury on the set, he had to semi-retire from action pictures. The movie has just about everything you could want from an action film. There are plenty of motorcycle stunts, Bryan gets to show off his fighting technique a bit, manly showboating, and a pinch of romance. It's a fast-paced ride through a manmade disaster with a likable cast directed with care by Allan A. Goldstein (*Death Wish V*). A similar faction film called *Firestorm* stars ex-NFL player Howie Long.

Nautilus

2000 (MTI DVD) (CD)

"I will pay you $10,000 to make sure this happens. If he refuses or in any way jeopardizes this operation, you are to put a bullet in his head. Ready to go back to work, Levine?"

Captain Brin (Christopher Kriesa) and his daughter Ariel (Miranda Wolfe) have watched the world crumble after a giant drilling station known as Prometheus starts a chain of events leading to total devastation. They've built a time-traveling submarine (the *Nautilus*) and go back to stop the apocalypse from happening. But in the past, they meet with opposition from the developers of the giant drill who find the story ridiculous and who are also having problems with a terrorist group. Stuck in the middle of this crazy mess is security expert/mercenary Jack Harris (action perennial Richard Norton) who was hired to keep the developers safe. As the terrorists make their move, he learns the truth from the *Nautilus* crew: an unseen fault line is in range and if the drill is set off, it will launch a series of earthquakes, the beginning of the end. The terrorists want to blow the Prometheus to smithereens, which will result in the same thing. It's all one big flustercluck but Harris isn't your average mercenary . . . he's the *best*.

Nautilus would feel right at home if it were a film made for the SyFy Channel. It's nowhere near as bad as it should have been but not exactly as good either. The effects are poor, and the story isn't really engaging. The film does have a saving grace: his name is Richard Norton (*Gymkata, China O'Brian*). He has a way of spreading his charm through a film that otherwise has very little. The opening sequence is the most fun and exciting part with Norton partaking in a one-man rescue mission. He doesn't really get to fight much again until the finale, thought that particular scene is lackluster. Norton fans won't want to miss this movie, however; it's a decent time and our Australian hero is in tip-top shape. Directed by Rodney McDonald, and written by C. Courtney Joyner (*Class of 1999*).

Nemesis

1992 (Imperial VHS) (CD)

Alex Raine (Olivier Gruner) is a partly human police assassin who is trying to stop the Red Army Hammerheads from smuggling information when their leader Rosaria (Jennifer Gatti) leaves him for dead. He is rebuilt and seeks her out in Baja, where he is reunited with his former lover and handler Jared (Marjorie Monaghan), who is there to bring him back in. He refuses, only to be kidnapped by his former boss Farnsworth (Tim Thomerson), who coaxes him into a new assignment by telling him that a bomb has been implanted in his heart: ff he doesn't agree, he will be killed. He then meets Julian (Deborah Shelton), who is working with Jared. She informs him that Farnsworth isn't who he says he is and that the fate of humanity lies in Alex's hands. She gives him a jamming device to keep the bomb in his heart from exploding. Without much time or not knowing who to trust, he dives headfirst to risk his life to save humanity.

It's surprising that *Nemesis* doesn't have a larger cult following. I remember seeing it for the first time when it was originally released to the home video market, and I flipped over it. It's a standout in the genre for several reasons. It was one of the first American productions that drew inspiration from the Hong Kong and John Woo style, reflected in everything from the wardrobe to characters double-fisting their guns. Director Albert Pyun assembled one of his best casts for the film. Olivier Gruner (*Angel Town, Savate*) does a fantastic job in his second feature film; he is relatable and believable in this action/fantasy type of role. Pyun wisely filled out the rest of the cast with genre veterans and future stars. Tim Thomerson (who is an incredible villain in the film), Brion James, Thom Matthews, Cary-Hiroyuki Tagawa, Vince Klyn, a very young (and nude) Thomas Jane, and Jackie Earle Haley all make memorable appearances. There is more gunplay than martial arts here, but it's all stylized and exciting. In 1992, practical effects were still widely used, and this film has no shortage of some really spectacular stuff. The animation sequences at the end should remind viewers of their love for films of that era. *Nemesis* may rip off *The Terminator* a little bit and the plot is overly convoluted, but I dare a filmmaker to make a film this rich and entertaining in today's market. It's still Gruner's best movie vehicle and it stands as a highlight in Pyun's long and varied career. Incidentally, Gruner's role was originally written for actress Megan Ward. The sequels went in completely different directions and starred bodybuilding champion Sue Price.

Nemesis 2: Nebula

1995 (WarnerVision VHS) (CD)

Seventy-three years have passed since the cyborgs overthrew humans in war. When a special DNA strain is developed, it looks like it could be what the humans have been waiting for. It is injected into a volunteer, and her baby becomes the key to saving mankind, but in order to save the child she travels back in time to 1980 in East Africa. She is killed, but her baby is raised by a native tribe to become the perfect hunter: Alex (Sue Price). She doesn't know much about her past other than a single clue—the necklace she wears around her neck, which was given to her by her mother. The cyborgs send an assassin named Nebula to track and find Alex. His mission: terminate her. Alex will call upon all her knowledge to try to defeat the deadly foe.

Nemesis 2: Nebula is a slow moving and disappointing sequel (more of a restart of the franchise) that pretty much ditches everything that was enjoyable about the original, including the star. This film gives Sue Price, a female bodybuilder, her first starring vehicle, and her physique looks molded out of the finest materials. She is a marvel to look at but her acting isn't particularly award-worthy. It takes far too long to get the movie rolling, and by the time the action hits, most viewers may have shifted their attention elsewhere. Price does a fine job in the physical department, and there are some slick acrobatic shootouts that keep things moving. If you can make it to the final twenty minutes, there are some nicely choreographed gunfights and a couple of spectacular stunts. The Nebula creature of the title is a poor man's Predator. You never really get a good look at the creature until the film's final moments. The sets and locations were pretty minimal: lots of desert, a small village, and an abandoned mining site. There is very little dialogue, and the script is mostly a hodgepodge of elements from *The Terminator* and *Predator*. As always, Tony Riparetti's score elevates the material, adding a very crucial element in making the film stand out. The budget for this film was considerably smaller than that for the first *Nemesis* film, and the special effects that I found so terrific in that movie are non-existent here. *Nubula* is a missed opportunity and the original is a far superior film. Director Albert Pyun usually has a much better eye. More sequels with Price followed.

Nemesis 3: Time Lapse

1996 (Imperial VHS) (CD)

"I don't want your shit,
I want your molecules."

Shortly after the events of *Nemesis 2: Nebula*, Alex (once again played by Sue Price) awakens with amnesia caused by a head wound. As she makes her way through the desert, she tries to put the pieces together and remember everything that had happened. What she fails to realize is that there are more cyborgs sent from the future to try to destroy her, including Farnsworth 2 (the returning Tim Thomerson). Alex eventually finds out that she is part of a family and has many sisters born of the same mother, all with mutated powers that can be used to save humanity in the future.

Unfortunately, the *Nemesis* films grow progressively worse with each entry. There were some technical issues with *Nebula*, but it was able to find some footing in the final reel, which made up for the thin plot and drawn-out and thin first half. With *Time Lapse*, the plot is even thinner and stretched out even longer. It is a far tougher viewing experience trying to keep it all in perspective. Real-life bodybuilder Sue Price is still a marvel to look at and having Tim Thomerson returning as Farnsworth 2 is a nice touch. Some viewers will get a kick out of director Albert Pyun's shenanigans—dune buggies turn into digital blobs when they take off, and twin cyborg assassins characters named Ditko and Ramie (played by Debbie Muggli and Ursula Sarcev) turn to each other and laugh one of the most bizarre laughs ever captured on screen. When Alex first meets Farnsworth 2, he bizarrely keeps morphing back and forth between a human and cyborg without explanation. The CG effects look horrible and cheap. On some of Pyun's earlier films (but not this one), he managed to make a cheap film look like a multi-million-dollar venture. No matter how you look at it, *Nemesis 3* is a lesser effort from the director. The film was an obvious set-up for the fourth entry into the series.

Nemesis 4: Death Angel

(a.k.a. **Cry of Angels**)

1996 (CFP VHS) (CD)

"Say ten Hail Marys and go to cyborg hell."

Long after the cyborg war, the cyborgs and humans now live in peace. Alex (Sue Price) is an assassin, doing whatever jobs she is assigned, and she's the best at what she does. Her boss Bernardo (Andrew Divoff) feels she has reached her limits, and it's time for her to retire before she gets sloppy. She agrees to do one last job. But she is led astray and kills the wrong target, the son

of a vicious mobster who puts a $100,000,000 bounty on her head. When other assassins begin to show up to collect on the hit, Alex isn't about to go down without a fight. With the help of her ex-lover Johnny Impact (Simon Poland), she will find out who double-crossed her and get her revenge.

The *Nemesis* films degraded in quality with each passing installment. Nothing in this film really resembles anything in the previous films. The only constant (at least from the last two films) is former bodybuilder Sue Price. She spends her time killing people with her thighs and running around naked. She's a special effect all on her own, but . . . *wow*. There's an incredibly bizarre cyborg sex scene too (the highlight of the film). The story is much more basic and cohesive than the previous two entries. Price was in amazing shape, and she pulls off what little action there is with ease. Albert Pyun is once again in the director's chair, doing the best he can with limited resources. He's gone on the record to name this his favorite of the *Nemesis* films.

Neon City

1991 (Vidmark VHS) (CD)

It's 2053, and the world has become a radioactive wasteland. It's not easy making a living in this dangerous new world but Stark (Michael Ironside) has no issue working as a bounty hunter. There're plenty of people to bring in, and he lands himself a red-starred convict, a whole different class of criminal and one that brings an exceptionally high bounty. It's a young woman named Reno (Vanity), and she has to be transported to Neon City if he is to collect the money. They board a passenger transport vehicle driven by an old friend of Stark's named Bulk (NFL star Lyle Alzado). As they trek across the wasteland, each of the passengers harbors a secret, all of which come to light during the trip. Their pasts may end up being the least of their worries when they cross through forbidden territory, and they're constantly attacked along the way by nomadic marauders. Stark is a resourceful guy, and he begins to realize money isn't everything and what he's found is worth keeping.

Neon City is a bit of a *Mad Max* clone that takes the high road and develops its own identity. Made on a tight budget, the film is a vivid, exciting, and playful romp through a world on the verge of extinction. In a rare leading role, Michael Ironside owns every scene he's in. The film exceeds expectations with the supporting cast led by the dream-worthy Vanity (*The Last Dragon*) and former NFL tough guy Lyle Alzado (*Hangfire*). Aside from a few shootouts and some fancy driving during the chase scenes, Alzado sort of takes a back seat. Thankfully, it doesn't mean he didn't leave an impression. He gives a solid and sweet performance, one that is very memorable. Sadly, this was his second to last film; he passed away the following year when his last film, *Comrades in Arms*, hit video store shelves. *Neon City* was directed by actor-turned-director Monte Markham (*Baywatch*).

A publicity shot from Michael Jai White's (center) *Never Back Down 2*. Author's collection.

Never Back Down 2: The Beatdown

2011 (Sony DVD) (djm)

Nearly an in-name-only sequel to 2008's *Never Back Down*, *The Beatdown* showcases Michael Jai White (from *Blood and Bone* and *Universal Soldier: The Return*) as a supporting character *and* as the director of the film. He plays a former UFC champ named Case Walker, whose career collapsed when he was sent to prison for a few years over a crime, and who is slowly building himself up—not as a fighter this time, but a *teacher* in the vein of Mr. Miyagi. He coaches four misfit college boys who each have their own reasons for training hard in MMA-style fighting. Mike (Dean Geyer) is a star wrestler, but he's having emotional problems after his father walked out on him and his mother. Zack (Alex Meraz) has a damaged retina and can no longer box, so now he wants to try MMA even at the risk of losing his eyesight. Tim (Todd Duffee, a real MMA fighter) is trying to enter an event called The Beatdown to get money so his mom won't have to work at a strip club. Justin (Scottie Epstein) is a victimized comic book store clerk who desperately wants to learn to defend himself. Case works all four of the boys hard, grooming them to be good fighters, while also trying to instill some wisdom in them. But Justin crosses over to the dark side after he gets a taste for hurting people, and Case shuns him from the group. In revenge, Justin frames Case for a crime he didn't commit and the the other three boys have to help Case defend himself. The film climaxes at the big Beatdown event, where Justin must face his three ex-friends, who can't wait to humble him.

The only element that connects this film to Part 1 is a secondary character named Max Cooperman (played by Evan Peters), an entrepreneurial college student who organizes the Beatdown fight. This sort of film has been made and remade dozens upon dozens of times, but what makes this one stand out is the way Jai White portrays his interesting and sympathetic character and how he relates to the boys. There are some really fantastic moments for Jai White to shine, and when the film settles in for the big Beatdown tournament, that's when the movie becomes ultra conventional and predictable. I had a great time with it, regardless. I'm ready for a third installment with Jai White in the center. *Now*, please.

N

Never Say Die

1994 (Image DVD) (djm)

An ex-special forces soldier named Blake (Frank Zagarino) is trying to live a quiet life as a boat repairman in the bayou. His life of solitude and peace is grossly interrupted when the entire congregation of a religious cult commits mass suicide under the shepherding of the evil Reverend James (Billy Drago), who is a former soldier as well, and a former associate of Blake's. The cult's headquarters is just a few miles from where Blake lives, so when a commando unit comes in to find and kill or capture the Reverend, Blake is hard-pressed to not get himself involved. A politico's daughter was amongst the Reverend's flock, and indeed she's the only survivor of the massacre, so she clearly needs to be rescued from the psychotic Reverend, who plans on killing her in a spectacular fashion. Blake gets in on the action.

Filmed in South Africa under the Nu Image banner, *Never Say Die* features a bulked up Zagarino in a *Commando*-esque role that has him setting traps in the swamps, throwing grenades, shooting automatic weapons, and driving boats at high speeds. It's exactly what the action doctors ordered. It's not particularly memorable, but it feels right when you're watching it. It was filmed shortly after another Zagarino movie called *Terminal Impact*, which had the same director as this film: Yossi Wein.

Never Surrender

2009 (Lionsgate DVD) (djm)

Self-assured champion of cage fights Diego Carter (Hector Echavarria) is seduced into fighting in an illegal circuit. As a "perk," he's given a different woman to sleep with every night, but he doesn't quite seem to understand that he's a prisoner in the circuit. He has new living arrangements in a heavily guarded compound, and the women who sleep with him every night are slaves, answering to an imposing Russian animal named Seifer (Patrick Kilpatrick), who sees potential in Diego as a moneymaker. When Diego ends up falling in love with one of his sex partners, he begins asking questions and then the big picture comes into focus: Seifer is a sadistic warden running both the prison of fighters and the sex slaves who keep his prisoners happy, and when anyone begins asking too many questions or offers resistance, the punishments are severe. Diego is lucky enough to have friends on the outside who care about him and come looking for him when he's been off the radar for months, and before long, Seifer and his MMA-proficient henchman have a task on their hands when Diego and his pals (also MMA guys) declare war.

The DVD box cover proudly shows off some minor supporting players in the film who happen to be major names in the world of mixed martial arts fighting—names like Quinton "Rampage" Jackson (from *The A Team* movie), Heath Herring, Anderson Silva, and George

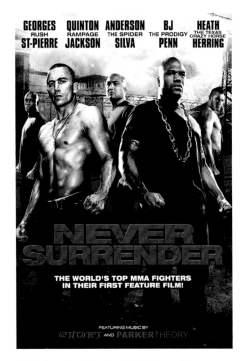

Publicity artwork for the DVD release *Never Surrender*. Author's collection.

"Rush" St.-Pierre, but the star (and the director) of the film, Hector Echavarria, is nowhere to be seen on the cover despite giving himself top billing, which he actually deserves. *Never Surrender* is a vanity project if there ever was one. He wins every single fight in the film *and* he has graphic simulated sex with several nubile young women in different scenes when the fighting gets monotonous. His ego is front and center, and it's hard to root for the guy when we know he also directed the film. Echavarria is amazing. He manages to get these little movies financed and gets real-deal fighters in his films, *and* he casts himself as the hero every single time. I have no idea how he does it, but he's still doing it. Several years later he directed and starred in the theatrical release *Chavez: Cage of Glory* that cast him alongside Danny Trejo and James Russo, who has a small role in *Never Surrender*. Kilpatrick was in that one too.

The New Barbarians (a.k.a. Warriors of the Wasteland)

1983 (Shriek Show DVD) (CD)

"One wants to exterminate all human beings so life will be erased from this planet, right? Well, now you know how I'm different. Me, I wanna live."

In a post-apocalyptic world, a man known only as Scorpion (Giancarlo Prete) wanders the wasteland just trying to survive. He helps out when he can and won't take any crap from the vicious scavengers known as "The Templars." He was a former member who left the crazed group in order to live. He rescues a young woman and takes on a partner when he meets his old acquaintance Nadir (Fred Williamson). A helpless band of survivors find themselves about to be destroyed by The Templars and it's up to Scorpion and Nadir to save them.

The New Barbarians is so bad it's phenomenal! So much of this movie is just ridiculous, but it has a large following for being so much fun. It's even hard to comprehend some of the events that take place in the film. The good thing is that the film is action packed and rather brutal. Unfortunately, you can tell that a few of the effects shots may have been botched, but at least they tried. Fred Williamson may play second fiddle to Prete but he still has all the best moments. He never fights, but he does have a bow and arrow with exploding arrow tips he enjoys using. He also has many of those signature Williamson moments where the ladies can't resist him. He has a few great facial expressions that are priceless. From Enzo G. Castellari, who also directed Williamson in *Inglorious Bastards* and *1990: Bronx Warriors*, which was another post-nuke exploitation actioner.

New Police Story

2004 (Lionsgate DVD) (CD)

Inspector Chan (Jackie Chan) and his team are called to investigate a warehouse hideout inhabited by a group of high-tech thieves led by the sinister and misunderstood Joe Kwan (Daniel Wu). Chan's entire team is murdered before his eyes as Kwan forces him to play a sick game to save their lives. He ends up being the only survivor, and a year later he's fallen into darkness, living by the bottle. His fellow cops and superiors blame him for their deaths and he's the laughing stock of the precinct. When new transfer Frank Cheng (Nicholas Tse) shows up, his goal is to help Chan track down these killers and bring them to justice. Chan's relationship with his girlfriend Sun Ho (Charlie Yeung) is suffering and he's falling apart at the seams. Frank isn't going to give up on him, and the two of them enter into a vicious cat-and-mouse game with Kwan and his gang . . . and all of them are willing to die in order to win.

At a time when Jackie Chan's American work was becoming ridiculous and trite, *New Police Story* came around to remind us why he's legendary. It's a solid film with an engaging story, exciting stunts, and several outstanding fight scenes to show audiences he can still deliver where it counts, even though his age may have caused him to scale the fighting and stunts back a little. Unrelated to the previous *Police Story* films, this reboot gives Chan the opportunity to flex his acting muscles while still delivering (on a smaller scale) some solid action. At times, he may go a little bit overboard in the acting department but somehow it still comes together in an entertaining package. Frequent Chan collaborator Benny Chan (*Shaolin*) crafts a fine thriller and knows his star well. A worthy offering.

N

Nighthawks

1981 (Universal DVD) (MJ)

"There is no security."

After Rocky Balboa and before John Rambo, there existed a period of time where Sylvester Stallone struggled to find success at the box office in a role other than the one that made him famous around the world. Stallone took a chance on the script for *Nighthawks* because something in the material resonated with him. Perhaps it was the opportunity to play a character as far as he could get from Rocky and show audiences that he had more to offer. *Nighthawks* tells the story of international terrorist Wulfgar (Rutger Hauer) as he escapes from Europe after bombing a department store in London and arrives in New York with the intention of carrying on his reign of terror. In pursuit is Peter Hartman (Nigel Davenport), an Interpol officer familiar with Wulfgar and his tactics, who arrives in New York and begins to assemble an anti-terrorist team made up of specialists from Europe and local law enforcement to prepare a response for Wulfgar when he next surfaces. Assigned to the team are Deke DaSilva (Stallone) and Matthew Fox (Billy Dee Williams), two New York detectives from the Decoy Squad, their knowledge of the local criminal element considered to be a valuable asset to Hartman's team. DaSilva immediately objects to Hartman's methods as he tries to teach the men that they have to suppress their natural instincts and training as law enforcement when dealing with men like Wulfgar and should instead shoot to kill when dealing with men who have such little regard for human life. In the course of chasing down their leads, DaSilva and Fox accidentally stumble upon Wulfgar in a nightclub with disastrous results, beginning a cat-and-mouse pursuit that causes Wulfgar to both fixate on DaSilva and accelerate the time table for his terror plans.

One of the niches in action cinema in the early 1980s was the rogue cop movie, made popular in films like *Dirty Harry* and *The French Connection*. In fact, *Nighthawks* was initially conceived as a sequel to *The French Connection* for 20th Century Fox, but Gene Hackman had ino interest in playing Popeye Doyle again and Universal acquired the rights to the story, which was then reworked into this film as a vehicle for Stallone. It was a very troubled production, though. The original director left the project and director Bruce Malmouth (*Hard to Kill* with Steven Seagal) took over. When Malmouth was not able to make it to set on his first day of production, Stallone directed the scene himself and there is some speculation that he may have directed other scenes as well. In postproduction, the film was cut radically for violence by Universal and the MPAA. The initial cut of the film was two and a half hours, and the running time for the theatrical release was under 100 minutes. The theatrical trailer and lobby cards for the film hinted at scenes that were no longer in the film, especially those with actress Lindsay Wagner, cast as DaSilva's girlfriend, and more time spent with Wulfgar and Shakka, played by

actress Persis Khambatta. Yet what remains of the film is still compelling and perhaps ahead of its time in depicting how a terrorist attack would affect a major metropolitan city like New York and showing anti-terrorism tactics for responding to such an attack. Stallone does all his own stunts in the film, including a riveting cable-car sequence. This is a star vehicle, and Stallone's performance and the casting of Rutger Hauer as Wulfgar in his first American film make for good cinema as DaSilva chases Wulfgar around the city and the tension continues to build up to their inevitable confrontations.

Night Hunter

1996 (New Concorde DVD) (djm)

When he was a boy, Jack Cutter's parents (the dad is played by James Lew) are killed by a pack of vampires. Jack (Don "The Dragon" Wilson) grows up to be a vampire hunter with emotional issues who wears a black duster coat in the big city, and he's the plague of the vampire underworld. When he gets the attention of the police, *he's* the one being hunted, but when he gains the trust of a cop and a female journalist, he has allies in his fight against the bloodsuckers. Cutter crosses a vampire name off a list he maintains, and there's only a few names left on his list: Those who killed his parents. His final fight with the last group of vampires (in the world?) takes a huge toll on him, and he manages to save the lives of his new friends in the process.

A slight move in a new direction for Don Wilson, *Night Hunter* is at least outside of the norm for a star who is known for his kickboxing films. While still on the same low-budget scale as most of his New Concorde/Roger Corman-produced action films, *Night Hunter* manages to give its star a different sort of role. The biggest fault of the film is its terrible, shaky camera work every time a fight scene starts up. The camera literally *shakes* when characters begin hitting and kicking each other. Melanie Smith plays the appealing reporter character, and Maria Ford (from the *Ring of Fire* films with Wilson) co-stars as a vampire. Vince Murdocco from *Ring of Fire* and *Kickboxer 2* has a small role. It was directed by frequent Wilson collaborator Rick Jacobson, who made several of the *Bloodfist* films.

Night Man

1997–1999 (NOV) (djm)

Jazz musician Johnny Domino (stuntman-turned-action star Matt McColm) is struck by lightning in a freak accident and he gains a super power: the ability to sense evil on a strange frequency that only he can pick up. He receives help from a scientist (played by Patrick MacNee), who crafts a special suit that allows Johnny to fly around and help people in need. As the caped crusader Night Man, Johnny (who no longer needs to sleep due to his newfound power) is basically a variation on Batman, coming out

only at night to aid the innocent and fight evil. Over two full seasons (44 episodes total), Glen Larson's *Night Man* (which had a brief run as a comic book) is in the same vein as other TV shows like *The Flash* and *Mantis*, but it also gave star Matt McColm (who'd had a run as a martial arts action star with *Red Scorpion 2* and *Body Armor*) a lot of exposure on a level that he'd never had before (or since). The show is geared for kids, with limited violence and comic book style heroics, and while most of the action for McColm involves him in a heavy-looking suit with a cape, the best scenes of the show are when he's out of costume and in plain clothes. Incidentally, McColm also played Batman in a series of OnStar commercials.

Night of the Kickfighters

1988 (AIP VHS) (djm)

A scientist mogul (Adam West) creates a high-tech laser that some terrorists are interested in stealing, and they kidnap his daughter to leverage her for the laser. He hires a covert mercenary group to find her and retrieve her before she's hurt or killed. The mercenaries are led by kickboxer Brett Cady (Andy Bauman), who leads his cartoon-variety friends to undertake the dangerous mission to rescue the damsel in distress.

Fans of low-on-the-rung "B" martial arts action movies should be familiar with guys like Ron Marchini and Dale "Apollo" Cook, but Andy Bauman might not be so familiar. A nondescript (but muscular) everyman, Bauman was plucked

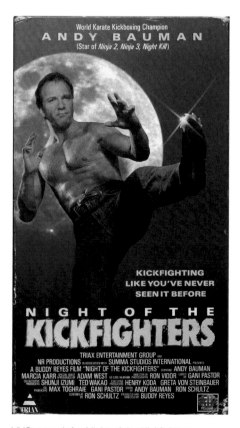

VHS artwork for *Night of the Kickfighters*. Author's collection.

from obscurity to star in (and apparently co-write) this Action International entry, which is probably best left undiscovered. Bauman, a "world karate kickboxing champion," graces the cover of the video box, but he doesn't show up in the film until at least thirty minutes into it. The inane plot and "action" carries on, and when he's required to show up, he ambles into it and throws a few kicks and punches, but it's really quite amazing how little the filmmakers invested themselves into creating a new star. In the era of direct-to-video action stars, Bauman is barely an afterthought, if even that. His co-star characters in the movie resemble the *Defenders of the Earth*, with a black fighter, a magician, and a guy with nunchuck guns. The title of the film means absolutely nothing. Directed by Buddy Reyes.

Night of the Warrior

1991 (Trimark DVD) (djm)

In a smoky, dark portion of Los Angeles, a kickboxer named Miles Keane (Lorenzo Lamas) wins his last illegal fight to finally pay off the bank so he will completely own a trendy nightclub he runs. By day, he is a freelance photographer, combing the back alleys and streets to find interesting subjects to photograph, and by night he is a fighter, a nightclub boss, and a lover. He quits his gig as a fighter, which infuriates the gangsters who bet and win on his fights, and they force him to fight one more time (they kidnap his mom, played by Arlene Dahl, Lamas's real mother). Meanwhile, he's begun romancing a waitress (Kathleen Kinmont, his real-life wife at the time) and becoming embroiled in a murder plot where he's the chief suspect. His final fight is with James Lew (*Blood For Blood*), and the fight is intense and memorable.

Strange, kinky, and compelling, *Night of the Warrior* has my vote for the best film Lamas starred in. I attribute the direction by Rafal Zielinski for the film's ultimate success. It's got a sleek, ultra cool (albeit a tad bit outdated) vibe running through it, and Lamas's character is a little on the creepy side, but the script is above average and the trendy aspects of the film give the film an interesting flavor that none of Lamas's other films had. As usual, he rides a motorcycle in the film, but nothing else feels like a holdover from his other films, despite the kickboxing theme. His relationship with Kinmont in the film is sexy, and their chemistry really burned bright here. Interestingly, Thomas Ian Griffith (*Excessive Force*) wrote and produced this film, and he would later go on to become an action star in his own right.

Night Vision

1997 (Xenon DVD) (djm)

A serial killer who videotapes the daily routine of his (female) victims before he kills them delivers his "The Life and Death of" videos to the police department as a way of taunting them. A beat cop named Dak Smith (Fred Williamson) gets the killer's attention when he tries to pull him over on a routine stop, and after a deadly encounter that could have killed him, Dak emerges as the first eyewitness of the killer. From that point, Dak is assigned a partner named Kristen O'Conner (Cynthia Rothrock), a take-no-nonsense cop with aggression issues. Together, they delve into the serial killer case, while trying to maintain some semblance of a life. Dak is an alcoholic and Kristen is a single mother, and they support each other when things get hard and stressful. Throw in the serial killer (who has friends who do his bidding), and you've got a solid exploitation movie.

What makes this movie work is the script and the lead actors. Robert Forster plays Williamson's and Rothrock's boss, and when the three of them interact, the movie is at its best. Williamson delivers a solid performance in a well-written role, and Rothrock, while stuck in the partner role, manages to embody her character with more than just her action hero persona. She throws some kicks and punches in the film, but she's not invincible or untouchable. It's also worth noting that this is her first time playing a mother in a movie. The serial killer element makes the movie feel a little sleazy and exploitive, but that's exactly what the movie is going for. Directed by Gil Bettman (*Never Too Young to Die*).

9 1/2 Ninjas

1991 (Republic VHS) (djm)

The ninja movie subgenre of action films got several spoofs in the late 1980s and early 1990s. There was the *Police Academy* riff *Ninja Academy* with Gerald Okamura and there was also *9 1/2 Ninjas*, which (wouldn't you know it?) has a cameo by Okamura as a blind ninja master. Since Okamura (who is what we consider an "action star") only has a cameo (the best scene in the film), this movie falls on Tommy "Tiny" Lister to carry it as an action star, but his role is relatively minor, so if you're looking for a solid role from an action star, then *9 1/2 Ninjas* is not a great place to get your fix. It's a ramshackle spoof of ninja films, while also a semi-spoof of the Zalman King movies, namely *9 1/2 Weeks*, but it's a failure any way you look at it. The story? A tycoon named Gruber (Robert Fieldsteel) is after a pretty woman named Lisa (Andee Gray) who has some evidence that could put an end to his business, and so he hires a cadre of inept ninjas to assassinate her. To her rescue is short-tempered Joe Vogue (Michael Phenicie), who was taught as a child by a blind master (Okamura) in the ninja arts. Vogue ends up trying to teach the bubble-headed Lisa some ninja tricks, and as a team, they foil slo-mo attacks from crying, slipping, and ridiculously untrained ninja assassins, and so Gruber hires the menacing Cutter (Lister, who growls and basically plays Zeus from *No Holds Barred* again) to do the job.

I dunno, guys. Maybe I have no sense of humor, but *9 1/2 Ninjas* isn't funny. At all. The funniest scene in the movie is when blind Okamura advises his kid pupil to see the world through his eyes, and the kid closes his eyes and bumps into a tree. Kinda funny for a second, but then the movie kicks in, and it's just dumb. It's not worth it to see either Okamura or Lister pass on through, so skip it. See *Ninja Academy* instead. Directed by Aaron Worth (Barsky).

9 Deaths of the Ninja

1985 (BCI DVD) (djm)

An effeminate terrorist confined to a wheelchair named Alby the Cruel (played by Blackie Dammet) and his henchwoman Honey Hump (Regina Richardson) plan a hostage takeover of a school bus full of children and their teachers traveling in the Philippines. They hold them for ransom, and an anti-terrorist group known as DART is called in to retrieve the hostages while killing or capturing the terrorists. The DART team consists of a ninja named Spike Shinobi (Sho Kosugi), a gung-ho commando named Steve Gordon (Brent Huff), and a pretty explosives expert named Jennifer (Emilia Crow). Lots of wacky action and ninja shenanigans ensue.

After his years at Cannon as their reigning ninja star, Sho Kosugi went off and did some weirder than usual action films, but *9 Deaths*

Brent Huff, Emilia Crow, and Sho Kosugi in a publicity shot of *9 Deaths of the Ninja*. Author's collection.

Spike Shinobi (Sho Kosugi) is clearing the field in *9 Deaths of the Ninja*. Author's collection.

Sho Kosugi in ninja garb in *9 Deaths of the Ninja*. Author's collection.

Guess who? Sho Kosugi! (from *9 Deaths of the Ninja*). Author's collection.

Ninja locked in combat in *9 Deaths of the Ninja*, featuring Sho Kosugi. Author's collection.

of the Ninja is definitely the most bizarre. The villain, Alby the Cruel, is comedic to the extreme, and you can never take him seriously for a second. He speaks with a preposterous German accent and has a giant thug for a lover, and his henchwoman Honey Hump screams and hollers as if she were in some kind of slapstick comedy. Kosugi and his action hero co-stars are moderately convincing in their roles, but this is all very cartoonish and absurd. The movie begins with a James Bond–style credit sequence featuring an original song that plays while Kosugi poses with a sword amidst scantily clad dancers. His real-life sons Kane and Shane appear in the film as well. Director Emmett Alston directed several other ninja pictures with names like *Force of the Ninja*.

1990: The Bronx Warriors

1982 (Shriek Show DVD) (CD)

In the future, the Bronx is a "no man's land" ruled by ruthless gangs out for blood. The police have sworn off the area, and anything goes on the mean streets. The rules change when Anne (Stefania Girolami) takes refuge there. She is set to take over The Manhattan Corporation, the world's largest arms manufacturer. Anne is attacked by gang members, only to be saved by Trash (Mark Gregory), who is a leader of a rival gang. Everyone wants to get their hands on her, because if they control her, they have the weapons. The government sends in crazed police officer Hammer (Vic Morrow) to burn down the place. Trash tries to protect Anne the best he can but with the rival gangs, traitors, and the police closing in there is only one person he can turn to: the Ogre (Fred Williamson). They reluctantly join forces against a common enemy and together they fight to survive.

Directed by Enzo Castellari (*Warriors of the Wasteland*), *1990: The Bronx Warriors* really only amounts to being a cheap *Escape From New York* rip-off but, in all its silliness, manages to be a highly entertaining trip into a violent world. While the acting may be questionable, the violence is over the top with a solid performance by Fred Williamson (*The Messenger*). His appearance is more of an extended cameo, but during the film's final act, he has some great martial arts/weapons fights that won't disappoint his fans. Watching Williamson behead an assailant will bring joy to those who admire him. *1990: The Bronx Warriors* is a film that well deserves its cult status.

Ninja

2009 (First Look DVD) (djm)

Nu Image produced this old-school *American Ninja*-type actioner starring Scott Adkins as an adopted orphan who learns the art of the ninja from Sensei Takeda (Togo Igawa) at a prestigious school in Japan. Casey (Adkins) has a rival, who is resentful and spiteful towards him, and when it comes time for Takeda to choose a successor, the rival, Masazuka (Tsuyoshi Ihara), disgraces himself by losing his cool in a routine exercise with Casey. Banned from the school, Masazuka becomes a ninja assassin for hire, and he takes

From the Nu Image film *Ninja*, featuring Scott Adkins. Courtesy of Nu Image, Inc.

a job offered to him by a cult, which plans to rule the world by controlling a valuable natural resource. When Casey is away performing a task for Takeda, Masazuka returns and kills the sensei and everyone at the school. It is up to Casey and Takeda's daughter to restore honor to the art of the ninja.

Director Isaac Florentine brings the 1980s style of simplicity back to the action film. In *Ninja*, we're treated to a non-pretentious plot and superhero antics that hearken back to the glory days of Cannon. Adkins is in pristine condition here, and while the script by Boaz Davidson doesn't give him anything interesting to say, Adkins shines despite the silliness of the story. Computer generated blood isn't my favorite method of carnage, but there's a lot of it here. Florentine and Adkins worked on several other projects, namely *Special Forces*, *Undisputed 2* and *3*, and *Ninja II: Shadow of a Tear*.

Ninja II: Shadow of a Tear

2013 (Millennium DVD) (V)

Nakabara: "The man who seeks revenge should dig two graves."
Casey: "They're gonna need a lot more than that."

Isaac Florentine and Scott Adkins reteam for a more down-to-earth follow-up to their underrated (even by themselves) white ninja story. I miss the only-a-ninja-would-understand motivation of the first one (they were stubbornly fighting over a box of old weapons, not trying to save the world or anything), but you have to appreciate the directness of an old-fashioned revenge story. When Casey Bowman's peaceful

Tsuyoshi Ihara plays the treacherous Masazuka, and Scott Adkins plays the heroic Casey in Isaac Florentine's *Ninja*. Courtesy of Nu Image, Inc.

Captured and stripped down, Casey (Scott Adkins) is about to unleash his inner ninja in *Ninja II: Shadow of a Tear*. Courtesy of Nu Image, Inc.

Casey (Scott Adkins) is about deliver pain in *Ninja II: Shadow of a Tear*. Courtesy of Nu Image, Inc.

life as a ninjutsu sensei in Japan is shattered by the murder of his wife he kills the guys who he thinks did it and takes a sabbatical in Thailand to train with an old friend named Nakabara (ninja movie royalty Kane Kosugi). But before he knows it, he's in a one-man war with Goro (Shun Sugata), a drug kingpin who schismed off of their clan and might've been the true wife-killer.

I could take or leave the grittier feel of part II, since I appreciated the first one's Cannon-esque goofy touches like the hooded corporate cultist bad guys. But this one definitely looks better, nicely shot on location in Thailand, with none of the artificial looking soundstages and green screens from the first movie. There are multiple high-quality villains (including a torture-happy general played by Vithaya Pansringarm of *Only God Forgives*), though none have a point of view as relatable as the first film's Masazuka. On the other hand, Adkins's screen-presence-while-not-playing-Russian has definitely improved since the first one, making Casey a more compelling anti-hero than before. He spends most of the movie in civilian clothes, but uses stealth, trickery and improvised weapons and eventually dons a ninja costume and tools stolen from a grave! There are numerous excellent fight sequences in all the classic locations: alley, bar, mountaintop fortress. He has knife fights, throws grenades, gets shot at, and fights a bunch of guys while high on meth (long story). And he fights a cobra. I wish I could've seen this with a crowd in one of its handful of film festival screenings, but in my living room it's still very effective and a reminder that if you want to see a new English language movie with lots of clearly filmed action you're going to have to go directly to video.

INTERVIEW:

SCOTT ADKINS on *Ninja 2: Shadow of a Tear*

(djm)

It's weird meeting action stars in person. I've met more than I can count now, and every one of them is different, but I knew Scott Adkins would be cool. We'd previously met face to face when I did an hour-long Skype interview with him in 2012 after I saw him in Expendables 2, *and he was incredibly gracious and generous with his time. In that interview, I was shocked at how well versed he was in "B"-action movies, and we talked about not only his movies and career but also the careers of guys like Jeff Speakman and Michael Dudikoff. He joked to me how upset he was when he saw Jeff Speakman's second or third movie and that Speakman wasn't delivering on the martial arts front like he did on his first movie. "Fuck you, Jeff Speakman!" he joked, which I thought was hilarious.*

It was Scott Adkins himself who opened the door to me when I visited the set of his latest film Ninja: Shadow of a Tear. *He sent me an email a few months before filming and told me that he and Isaac would be making a sequel to their 2009 film* Ninja *and that they would be filming in Bangkok, Thailand. I immediately got in touch with Isaac and the producers at Millennium, and in no time, I was on board with full approval to visit the set. On my first day on the set, Scott warmly greeted me, and he reminded me of that joke he made about Jeff Speakman. "Remember when I said, Fuck you, Jeff Speakman!" he asked me. From that moment on, I knew that I was welcomed, and I spent the next few days getting in his way, trying to find out what it really means to be a real-thing action star. In various stages, I watched him rehearsing his lines, I saw him stretching on exercise mats and practicing a few kicks and flips; he had warned me that he'd injured himself a few days previous during a fight scene. He was wearing a back brace during down times on the set, and he'd remove it when it came time to fight before the camera.*

When he finally summoned me to have lunch with him in his trailer on the last day of my visit, I sat down with him and prepared to conduct my official set visit interview. As I fumbled about with my tape recorder, he put on a video for me that stunt coordinator Tim Man had assembled, which featured the run-through of the climactic fight in the film. We watched the video, and he kept pointing out things that he liked about it, and asked me what I thought. "Dude, this movie is going be amazing," I said. As I asked him the following questions related to Ninja: Shadow of a Tear, *I couldn't help but notice the enormous pile of spaghetti he was eating for lunch. Action stars eat BIG.*

What can people expect from *Ninja 2*?

It's a full-on martial arts film, as was the first one. There was a hell of a lot of martial arts fighting in the first one. I think there's actually more in this one. More from just me—I think I've got about twelve fights in it, ranging from really

Action star Scott Adkins with the scrapes, sweat, and bruises to prove it, on the Bangkok, Thailand, set of *Ninja 2: Shadow of a Tear*. Photo by david j. moore.

long to short and sweet. It's definitely a very physical part. I was disappointed with the first one, at least with my performance. My character Casey was kind of bland. He was a bit of a wet blanket. That was the character in the script. I tried to perform the character as it was on the page, and so when we watched it back, there wasn't much about the character—there wasn't much of an edge. What we've done with this one is we've taken him to a darker place. Everything that he holds dear is taken from him, and when you think of good ninja movies you think of the revenge storyline. We're definitely going down

Enraged, Casey is an unmasked ninja. Courtesy of Nu Image, Inc.

Scott Adkins returns as Casey in *Ninja II: Shadow of a Tear*. Courtesy of Nu Image, Inc.

that track. He's also grown more into himself. He's a bit wiser, he's a bit cooler. He's full of anger and vengeance in this one.

The first film had a larger-than-life comic book style. What are the stylistic choices being made in Part 2 that will give it a unique style of its own?

No CGI, no silly bat wings. No silly ninja cult. This one is a bit more down and dirty. The other one was a bit more clean and pristine. This one is in Thailand, partly in Burma. It's grittier and dirtier. The martial arts in this film will be much flashier than what we did on the first *Ninja*. Another mistake we made with the first *Ninja*—and I don't want to put it down too much because it's got a lot going for it—was that we tried to make the fights more realistic in the first one . . . a lot of it was very basic. We're really going for the flash in this one, the same way we did in *Undisputed 3*. We're trying to make the fight scenes very flashy and very entertaining—we want to give you those big "Wow!" moments.

What's the hardest part—acting or action?

Action is the hardest part, make no mistake about it. You smash yourself up completely. I've already gotten injured. I hurt my back a bit. When you make as many action films as I do, with all probability is that on one of them you're gonna get hurt. I did get hurt on the one fight, and I've been doing my best to recuperate as quickly as possible. If it's a normal drama, you go home and work on your lines for the next day, you come in and you work all day . . . you could be sitting at a table, you're having a domestic with your partner, and she's slapping you in the face, but it doesn't happen just once, it happens again, again, and again. And then the next day you're probably going to have some bruises. But when you're smashing yourself on concrete, when you're throwing spinning kicks, when you're trying to raise the bar to do things that haven't been seen before, you hurt yourself. I'm sacrificing my body for what I love to do, and I'm happy to do that, but it's not easy. That, in turn, makes the acting harder because you're fucking knackered! You're absolutely shattered. And you still have to go home and work on your lines for the next day.

This is your . . . eighth movie with Isaac Florentine?

I think this is the seventh. He helped us a little with *El Gringo*. We'll say this is the seventh. We're very comfortable with each other. When we did the first shot of the first fight sequence, and I thought, "Man, just that bit looks better than any of the action I've done in the last three years since *Undisputed 3*." I feel very comfortable that he's going to be able to deliver. If you're going to do an action or martial arts film, that's what you want. Also, we know each other so well. He knows the way I work, and I know the way he works. I know what he wants me to do in front of the camera. I know how he wants to shoot it. I can also be very blunt with him, and he's the same with me. We don't have to beat around the bush. He's not going to hurt my feelings because I know he's got my best interests at heart.

Nakabara (Kane Kosugi) and Casey (Scott Adkins) square off in *Ninja II: Shadow of a Tear*. Courtesy of Nu Image, Inc.

Talk about working with Kane Kosugi, your co-star.

Yeah, brilliant. Been a fan of his for a long time. What he did in *D.O.A.* and *Muscle Heat*. I watched *Black Eagle* a lot when I was a kid during my Van Damme fascination. And, of course, I'm a big fan of his dad, Sho. We've only just started this fight, and just to see his movement and watch him pull it off—you can see he's really got that form, that samurai look about him, which I struggle at. I'm more of a kickboxer—that's my bread and butter, so I have to adjust to the Japanese ninja style. He's definitely got that. He's a very nice guy—I'd heard he was, and he's doing a great job with the acting. I wanted him in *Ninja 1*, actually.

Tim Man is coordinating the fights, and I've been observing him, and he's incredible. He's also in the film. Talk about Tim.

I knew who he was, I've seen his kicks, and he's brilliant. But I didn't know if he could choreograph or not. We said, "Well, does he have any stuff to show us?" He sent over some stuff he had done. Another thing was that we had to use someone who was in Thailand. So we said, "Okay, let's give Tim Man a shot." What he and his team started to do was send over these previews of the fights we were going to do. I've worked with a lot of the best stuntmen in the world, and he's up there. I knew I was in good hands. He and his partner, Brahim [Achabbankhe] are as good as anyone I've ever worked with.

What can fans of yours and fans of martial arts films or even fans of the first *Ninja* look forward to when they settle down to watch *Ninja 2*?

You're going to get brilliant fights, and you're going to get the best people in the business doing what they love to do. We hope we pulled the story off. You never know until you see it. You never know. I don't care how big the budget is. I've worked on films and thought, "This is gonna be great!" and it turns out to be not so great. I've been on films and thought, "This is gonna be shit!" and it turns out to be pretty good. You never know. You hope you've got a story that pulls the audience in and make them care about what's going on. You follow Casey on his journey, and hopefully it means something.

Does this feel like a sequel to you, or does it feel like a completely different movie?

I

I think the sequel *should* be a completely different movie. You take elements that made the first one work and made it successful. It feels the same, but it's very different. It's not a bad thing that it feels different. A lot of people thought there should have been more ninja stuff in the first one. It's going to be a great martial arts film.

Are ninjas back?

No, I don't think so. Let's be honest: Ninjas are a bit cheesy. There is a good time and place for a ninja movie. You've got to do a ninja movie the right way. A modern-day ninja movie is always going to be slightly cheesy. It's going to be a bit tongue-in-cheek. I think that's why he's not running around in the daylight in a ninja suit for most of the movie. We save the ninja suit for when it's dark and when he needs to slay people silently. There's more to this film than just the ninja stuff. That's why we base it in reality with these martial arts schools.

Anything you want to say about shooting in Thailand?

I love it. The stunt guys are brilliant. They don't mind taking a hit.

INTERVIEW:

ISAAC FLORENTINE on *Ninja 2: Shadow of a Tear* (djm)

On the set of Ninja: Shadow of a Tear, *director Isaac Florentine is completely in his element while making his latest martial arts action film, starring Scott Adkins and Kane Kosugi. I've been invited to observe several days of filming on the set in Bangkok, Thailand, and my first day consists of watching an intense dialogue scene between Adkins's character and his mentor, played by Kosugi. Both of them are dressed in Japanese robes during their scenes together, and the dojo set is decked with traditional Japanese tapestries and artifacts. I interact with the crew as they move lights around, and in between takes I chitchat with Adkins, Kosugi, and Florentine, who all take time out to address my questions, comments, and attempts at humor. Florentine, whom I've interviewed before, is incredibly gracious to me, and he thanks me several times for visiting the set. We both agree on the fact that movies like the ones he makes aren't given the attention or the fair criticism that they deserve, and I've made it my prerogative to give him and his peer filmmakers like Jesse Johnson, Ben Ramsey, and Ernie Barbarash, the attention that they should be getting. I interviewed Florentine for a few minutes about* Ninja: Shadow of a Tear *on set, and while this is not a comprehensive interview on his career, it does shed some light on what his intentions are with making this particular film.*

Director Isaac Florentine, on the Bangkok, Thailand, set of *Ninja 2: Shadow of a Tear*. Photo by david j. moore.

Isaac, what's brought you back to the world of *Ninja* again?

About a year ago, one of the sales people at Nu Image came up with the idea to do a sequel to *Ninja*. He was the first one who said, "Let's do a sequel!" It was just a remote idea. I came up with some ideas, the producer, Boaz Davidson, came up with some ideas, and David White, the writer who had written my *Undisputed* movies, came up with some ideas, and this is how *Ninja 2* was born.

How come Boaz didn't write this film? He was the writer on the first one.

His hands are full right now.

Was it obvious to bring Scott Adkins back for this film, or did you have to convince him that a sequel to *Ninja* was a good idea?

In this industry, nothing is obvious, but it *was* obvious because he was in Part 1, he should be in Part 2.

Does this one feel like a sequel to you, or is this a completely different movie?

Director Isaac Florentine on the set of *Ninja II: Shadow of a Tear*. Courtesy of Nu Image, Inc.

Story-wise, it's a sequel, but style-wise, this movie . . . the first one was more in the comic book style, this is more in the realistic style. No wires, no fantasy . . . the character is in a more realistic world, and Scott's character is becoming darker in this movie. It's a sequel, but not in the same style.

How do you intend to amp up the action and present the martial arts in this film? What are your intentions as far as the action and fighting goes?

We have a very good team, which was a nice surprise. It's not a big-budget movie, as you know. One of the restrictions I had was that I had to use local people, which is not a bad thing because movies like *Ong Bak* were done here. I used all of their people. It was a really nice surprise to have Tim Man and Brahim Achabbankhe come in and coordinate the fighting. Tim is from Sweden and Brahim is from France. Working with them is a joy. They are innovative, creative, responsible, and the most amazing thing is how organized they are. When they came, they sketched the action and showed me what they could do, and I knew I could sleep really, really well.

How did Tim and Brahim become a part of *Ninja 2*?

My assistant is a relative of Prachya Pinkaew, the director of *Ong Bak,* and she saw them working on a movie last year that was shot here in Bangkok, and that movie was called *Kill Them All.* She was impressed by how they worked, and she popped their names in to me. Scott [Adkins] had heard about them, and I'd kind of heard about them. All of the elements were there. It was an opportunity for all of us to work together. It's been a very good experience. I'm very pleased with them.

This is your eighth movie working with Scott. Talk about working with him again on this film.

You're talking to someone who's worked with him so many times. We each know our strong sides and our weak sides. Scott and myself have worked together so many times that we don't have to say a lot or explain a lot.

Kane Kosugi has been in the action movie world since he was a child. Why bring Kane into *Ninja 2*? Talk about working with him.

It's been several years since I wanted to work with Kane. This was the right opportunity to work with him. I knew 100 percent that he would deliver—I had complete confidence in him. He's a rare combination of someone who has feet on two continents. He's American, but he's lived in Japan for so many years that he can be Japanese. He can play both characters. He can play the Japanese character, but he doesn't have the baggage of struggling with the accent. He can up the action, too.

Talk about Mika Hijii's character in this film and how she relates to the story?

In the first film, it was about Scott and Mika before they got married. In this film, he hears that she's pregnant and basically she gets murdered. He blames himself for her murder. So now he has a chip on his shoulder, and it totally changes his personality.

So this is *The Dark Knight* of the *Ninja* franchise.

Kind of. Look, the first *Ninja* was . . . the idea of Batman . . . in a way, Batman is a ninja. The idea was that a ninja can become Batman. That was the first one.

It sounds like you guys are packing in as many fights as you possibly can into this film. Talk about the fights.

There's a lot of fights in this movie. Someone counted fifteen fights. I didn't count them. It's action packed! There will be some nice, coherent action in this film. Action that you can see. We emphasize the beauty and the dynamic of the fighting, but not the violence of it. It's clear, it's coherent, it's technical. I like the action to always be clean and coherent because I like to see the technique. Myself, coming from martial arts and being a martial arts aficionado, I like to see the beauty of it.

INTERVIEW:

ROSS CLARKSON on *Ninja 2: Shadow of a Tear* (djm)

One of the pleasant surprises while visiting the Bangkok, Thailand, set of Isaac Florentine's Ninja: Shadow of a Tear, *was hanging out with the cinematographer, Ross Clarkson. I had lunch with him several times over the course of the few days I was on set, and I found him to be jovial and consistently likable, despite the fact that I could clearly see that he was under pressure with the restraints of a tight budget and schedule for the film. Clarkson, an Australian living in Hong Kong, got his big break working with Ringo Lam and has shot numerous films with some of the greatest action stars in the business, including Dolph Lundgren, Michael Jai White, Jean-Claude Van Damme, and of course Scott Adkins. I would periodically ask him about working with guys like Van Damme, and he would drop a funny line about him, or some of the others, and even told me that Van Damme was his best man at his wedding. Clarkson was a never-ending trove of great stories, but most of them were off the record. After lunch one afternoon, he showed me the rough footage of some of the action scenes for* Ninja 2, *and asked me what I thought. I was in awe. Even the rough footage looked amazing. On my last day on set, I asked him what his next project was, and he told me that he was going to be making his directorial debut on a Gary Daniels action film, and as an afterthought, he hooked me up with Daniels' email, which I thought was incredibly cool of him. It's guys like Ross Clarkson who make action stars look great on film, and his work on* Ninja: Shadow of a Tear *is going to blow you away.*

Scott Adkins in ninja wardrobe in *Ninja II: Shadow of a Tear*. Courtesy of Nu Image, Inc.

You've filmed seven of Isaac Florentine's films. You keep coming back for more. Why?

You'd wonder why, wouldn't you? Isaac has got a lot of talent. He needs the right crew to work with him. There's a total reason why I work with him all the time. I understand what he wants, when he gets a little bit stressed. It doesn't bother me at all because I come from Hong Kong. There's the support there. At the end of the day, hopefully it looks good.

You've worked with a bunch of action stars in your career—Dolph Lundgren, Van Damme, Michael Jai White, and Scott Adkins a few times now. What is it like working on these action and martial arts movies?

It's challenging. It's fun. Because you've got these guys jumping all over the place doing really cool stuff. And just to try to keep the camera on them while they're doing all this, to work with them—it's very exciting. From a camera operating point of view, it's quite a challenge because they're pretty quick.

I'm going to name a few movies you've worked on. Just saw a few words about working on these movies. First one: *Direct Contact*.

That was Dolph Lundgren doing *Die Hard*. Blow up everything. It had a lot of scenes from other movies. I shot all the other movies. (Laughing.) There's a taxi chase from *Derailed*. Bits and pieces.

Russian Specialist.

That was Dolph's second directing one. He let me have a lot of influence on him. He accepted a lot of ideas. We spoke about everything a lot. Worked through it all. The story, camera angles, everything. It showed. It's a good-looking film.

Replicant.

Replicant was a great film. Ringo Lam always brings out the best in Van Damme. Especially the end ambulance chase. For a one-car car chase, it was fantastic. It took at least seven days and four ambulances to destroy to finish it. That was a lot of fun, that one. And Michael Rooker, he agreed to hang on the side of the ambulances as we're gonna hit four cars. And I said, "Dude, I'm coming with ya!" So I strapped myself on the ceiling so I can look over at the side of his face as we hit four cars. It was quite fun!

You've worked with Scott Adkins a few times.

He's got a huge potential. He just needs the right vehicle to blast off. *Undisputed II* should have gone to the cinema. I met one of the guys who was at the meeting. I met one of them at a boardroom table where there were eight to ten people. There was only one who was against it not getting a release. If that had gotten released, it would have changed a lot of people's careers. But it didn't. Not only did it not, but it was held back, too. That was a huge bummer.

Talk about working on *Ninja 2*.

This time it's a little more personal for the character. He's out for blood. There's a different motivation. We're playing Japan, Thailand, and Burma, so it's a bit more dirty and down to earth.

What can fans of Scott Adkins, Isaac Florentine, and action movies in general expect from this movie?

It's got the most number of fights I've done on a film. Out of a thirty-six days schedule, there's ten days of not fighting.

INTERVIEW:
TIM MAN on *Ninja 2: Shadow of a Tear* (djm)

When I met Tim Man, the stunt and fight choreographer on the Bangkok, Thailand, set of Ninja: Shadow of a Tear, *my first thought was, "Wow, this guy's short!" He has a distinct look about him, and he speaks with an unusual accent. He is of Chinese and Swedish descent. Man, trained in judo, jiu jitsu, taekwando, Viet vo dao, boxing, and wushu, has worked on several Thai martial arts productions including* Ong Bak 2 (2008) *and* Kill 'Em All (2012). *He was tasked with not only creating all the fights for* Ninja II, *also handling all the stunts, and he co-stars in the film as well as a villain named Myat. As I tried to get to know him over the course of several days, I found him to be immensely knowledgeable in action movie terms, and we'd quiz each other over action stars we like and their movies. We discussed the merits of guys like Keith Cooke, Tony Jaa, Gary Daniels, Billy Blanks, and all sorts of other guys, and it was obvious that he was a hardcore fan of "B"-action and martial arts movies. He was always in good humor, and in between takes, he'd sit down next to me and carry on our conversation.*

During filming, I was astounded at his professionalism and focus. He would dole out wordless directions to his team of stuntmen, who responded to his gestures and his hand motions. I watched him silently describe the movements of fragments of a fight scene to his team, who simply nodded their understanding, and when director Isaac Florentine would call "Action!" Man's team would reply with their physical feats of motion during the fights before the camera. It

Fight coordinator and action star Tim Man on the Bangkok, Thailand set of *Ninja 2: Shadow of a Tear*. Photo by david j. moore.

was amazing. Scott Adkins and Kane Kosugi, the stars of the film and the focus of the scene, would gravitate towards Man's intensity during the brief moments where he would (again, wordlessly) describe the martial arts movements the scene required, and I stood there watching him in his element. There's a good reason why Florentine ultimately chose him to choreograph the fights for the film.

Tim, tell me about your character, Myat, in *Ninja 2*.

He is on the right hand of another character named Goro. He's his personal bodyguard. Goro is one of the main bad guys in the movie.

Talk about what you're doing with the fights on this movie. I can already tell that you're doing some pretty spectacular things.

Well, there's a lot of fight scenes in this movie. I'm creating all the fights, I'm handling all the stunts, planning the safety of the stunts.

How are you making the fights special and unique? The stuff in the first *Ninja* was impressive. What are you doing to make the fights in this film even more spectacular?

I had a discussion with Isaac. He told me that he didn't want the fights to be so Japanese. He wanted them to feel a little more like his *Undisputed* movies and *The Raid*. In the first previews I did, I went more in that direction, but when Isaac saw them, he went, "Nah—it needs to be more Japanese!" I was like, "Okay . . . ." I was a bit confused. It took a while before I understood what Isaac wanted. Once I understood what he wanted, it was pretty easy to find the style that he was looking for.

What is the style he was looking for?

It's basically a Japanese style, but more realistic and more brutal in the way that his *Undisputed* movies were, but still different from the first *Ninja*. With a mix of *Ninja* and his *Undisputed* movies.

The first *Ninja* was quite bloody, but Isaac was telling me that they're going for a PG-13 rating for this film. How are you able to adapt that rating to the style of the fights and the brutality in this film?

N

I actually didn't know that until a week or two before shooting, so everything I'd planned was to be bloody and stuff, so I had to take down the blood, but we kept what I'd planned.

How'd that make you feel to know that the film would be PG-13?

I'm okay with that, but I'd rather see the movie with NOT a PG-13. It would be more awesome, you know?

You're obviously familiar with Isaac's work, right?

Yeah, big fan. The way he shoots his movies, I think he's amazing. Most of the directors I've seen, they direct a fight scene—I'm talking about the western directors—they basically cover the action. They set up a master shot and they pick some stuff up to cover the action, but Isaac is actually directing the action. He's telling us where the camera is gonna come, and how we're gonna move. It's good to see this. It's not often that you see this.

Talk about working with Scott Adkins.

What can I say? Everybody knows Scott. He's supertalented. He can do everything. I just show him the choreography, and he knows it. He doesn't need to practice much—he's got everything down. He's an easy guy to work with.

Stunt coordinator and actor Tim Man (left) and Scott Adkins on the set of *Ninja II: Shadow of a Tear*. Courtesy of Nu Image, Inc.

Talk about working with Kane Kosugi.

He's a real humble and nice guy. He's very respectful.

I think it's interesting that you're acting in the movie, *and* you're coordinating the stunts. Tell me how you're able to juggle that.

Luckily, it's a small part in the movie, so I'm focusing on the fights. By the end of the movie, I think is when I'll be filming most of my part, so luckily I can focus on the fights now, and then my part later.

Tell me a little bit about your background as a martial artist.

I started when I was six years old. I started with judo and jiu jitsu. At that time, it was just playing around. I didn't understand why I did it. But

then, when I was eight, I started Taekwondo, and I met my teacher. I basically started training really hard. I trained in his family style, which was a Vietnamese style, Viet vo dao. From there, I did boxing, I did wushu, stuff like that.

How did you get your start in the movies?

I was doing a lot of shows. I was called up when I was in Sweden to do some background stuff for a shooting. On that, I met a stunt coordinator. We started talking, and over a few years, we talked and I started being his apprentice. He taught me everything about cameras.

How are filmmakers using your look? You look different than anyone else in the movies. You're very distinct looking. Are you going to be the bad guy forever? Do you want to play a good guy once in a while?

I don't know. I like playing the bad guy. It's much more fun. I don't mind playing the bad guy.

Say something about *Kill 'Em All*.

I'd just made a movie in Italy. It was the first martial arts action comedy ever in Italy. When I was doing that movie, the director contacted me and asked me if I wanted to do the action for this movie *Kill 'Em All* in Thailand. There was this character The Kid that they were having trouble finding an actor for. He asked me if I would do it, and I did it.

What can fans of action movies and martial arts movies expect from *Ninja 2*?

Oh, a lot of action! A lot of good fights. Scott always brings a lot of good energy to the fights.

Ninja III: The Domination
1984 (Scream Factory DVD)
(djm)

Cop: "You're a ninja!"
Ninja: "It doesn't matter!"

In what might be the most insane ninja epic of all time, the first fifteen minutes of this film has a crazed ninja assassinating people on a golf course, and then when the cops start chasing him, he climbs a tree, jumps onto a helicopter, jumps *off* the chopper, buries himself under a few feet of dirt, and gets shot about a hundred times . . . and he still lives long enough to transfer his soul into a Jazzercising dancer who moonlights as a worker for the phone company. The dancer, Christie (Lucinda Dickey from the *Breakin'* movies), begins dating a persistent cop, and she starts having prolonged blackouts. When the cops who shot the ninja dead begin turning up murdered, Christie's new boyfriend is concerned that other ninjas are on the loose. He takes Christie to a Chinese healer (James Hong) to help her get over her blackouts, and while being treated, the healer unwittingly taps

Theatrical poster for *Ninja III: The Domination*. Author's collection.

Yamada (Sho Kosugi, right) is an avenging ninja in Sam Firstenberg's *Ninja III: The Domination*. Author's collection.

Sho Kosugi is about to plunge the blade home in a scene from *Ninja III: The Domination*. Author's collection.

into the "black ninja" inside her. A full-on *Exorcist* interlude ensues. Meantime, a secret ninja cult calls upon its top ninja (Sho Kosugi) to dispense of the "black ninja" who is causing the police force so much grief. The final confrontation between Christie, the exorcised "black ninja," and the good ninja is so cartoonish it belongs on a short list of glorious climaxes.

The ninja/horror mash-up combination is an uneasy one. Still, this is the only movie I can think of that has a ninja being shot countless times, and enough life left to muster a soul transfer. It's incredibly awesome. Sam Firstenberg, who is a wise master of ninja cinema, directed this film from Cannon. Lucinda Dickey, great legs and a pretty face aside, never made another action film. Kosugi made more ninja movies. This was the last of his "Ninja" series with Cannon. 9 Deaths of the Ninja was not related.

Ninja Academy

1989 (Omega DVD) (djm)

In the tradition of *Police Academy*, Nico Mastorakis made a martial arts rip-off of the same type with *Ninja Academy*. A martial arts master (played by Gerald Okamura, who plays his role straight, which is the best thing about the movie) is given the task to keep a ninja school running, and when he puts an ad in *Black Belt Magazine* for open enrollment, a band of misfits come knocking on his door. One rich kid has a Vietnam vet dad who forces him to take the ninja program, hoping that he'll learn some discipline; one bullied street mime takes the class to toughen up; one valley girl hoping to pick up on guys joins the school; a James Bond secret agent–type takes the class to bide his time between missions; and various other cliché types join the program. Once they've faced Okamura and his strict code of conduct, the first thing most of the guys do is go and peep on the nudist colony down the road. There's some action, too: A nutjob militant and his band of soldiers come in and threaten the school, and the misfits (who've amazingly learned some moves by then) help defend it.

Ninja Academy isn't really my cup of tea, despite being made in the '80s with music of that era and being a lightweight sex comedy. I usually like that type of movie, but Mastorakis only made one good movie (*The Zero Boys*), and everything else he did had an apparent desperation to it. In addition to Okamura, James Lew and Art Camacho have small roles.

Ninja Apocalypse

2014 (Naedomi DVD) (djm)

"Surviving?! C'mon—it's time to *flourish!*"

Years after "The Great War" (a nuclear apocalypse) rendered Earth an inhospitable desert wasteland, humanity evolved and the survivors divided into clans. Those clans became strongholds of ninja warriors, and each ninja has developed his or her own mutant power. Some ninjas can conjure fireballs and toss them, other ninjas can control the elements, while others can shapeshift, and so on. Over time, the ninja clans turned against one another and there was unrest in the wastelands. One ultra ninja named Fumitaka (Cary-Hiroyuki Tagawa, a sort of mascot for these types of movies) has the respect of all the ninja clans, and he calls a summit meeting in his vast, subterranean redoubt, where all the clans convene to hear his proposal of a lasting peace treaty. The Lost Ninja Clan (a ragtag group that the other clans despise) shows up to hear Fumitaka out, but when he's assassinated in front of the clans, The Lost Ninja Clan is framed for the killing. Hiroshi (Ernie Reyes Jr. from *Surf Ninjas*), the zealous leader of another clan, spearheads a hunt-and-destroy mission to eliminate The Lost Ninja Clan, and the rest of the film is a sort of riff on movies like *The Warriors* and *Resident Evil* where the heroes (The Lost Ninja Clan) are systematically hunted down by other ninjas . . . and zombies, too.

When something like *Ninja Apocalypse* comes around, you begin to question certain things about life. Is something like this supposed to fill a void in someone's existence? Does endeavoring to create a film like this give someone's life meaning? How is anyone supposed to take this seriously? The tone of the film is without a trace of irony, and you watch it thinking, *How did this happen? Is this for real?* At the very least, it gives unknown actors and young martial artists a chance to cobble a nice demo reel from their scenes, and Ernie Reyes Jr. (no longer looking like a teenager) has a halfway engaging fight at the very end of the picture. I'm not really sure who the audience is for this movie, though. Fans of post-apocalyptic movies will be perplexed by it, and fans of ninja movies and martial arts films will wonder what it all means. It's pretty bonkers. Directed by Lloyd Lee Barnett, who has done some special effects work on much bigger-budgeted films like *Avatar.*

Ninja Assassin

2009 (Warner DVD) (CD)

"This is not my family. You are not my father. And the breath I take after I kill you will be the first breath of my life."

Mika Coretti (Naomie Harris) works in law enforcement doing research. Investigating the various murders of politicians, she starts to believe they are being committed by ninja. When she starts getting too close to the truth, she becomes a target. Thankfully, rogue ninja Raizo (Korean pop star Rain) shows up to save her. The two form a bond, and she learns of how he defected from his clan after being brutally trained as a child. They now want him dead as well, as he is considered a traitor. Clan leader Ozunu (martial arts legend Sho Kosugi) sends out his ninja assassins, led by Takeshi (Rick Yune from *The Fifth Commandment*), tracking them to Los Angeles, leaving a bloody trail in their wake.

Director James McTeigue (*V for Vendetta*) and producers the Wachowski Brothers (*The Matrix*) should be given some serious credit for convincing a major studio to invest $40 million in an ultra violent ninja film with a cast of relative unknowns. Rain (next in *Speed Racer*) is the lead while Rick Yune (*Die Another Day*) takes a backseat to portray one of the villains. One of the best fights in the film is between the two of them during the finale. Also of note is the inclusion of legendary '80s action star Sho Kosugi (*Enter the Ninja*) who plays the clan leader and main antagonist. It's great to see him on screen again; he has been sorely missed. The problem with the movie is how much it relies on CGI for blood, action, and other things. This is no masterpiece, but there are a few cool set pieces and it's a treat to see action guys like Kosugi and Yune given prominent roles in a major motion picture.

Ninja Assassins (a.k.a.

Enforcer From Death Row)

1978 (Star Treasures VHS) (CD)

"How much, and who do I kill?"

T. L. Young (Leo Fong) is a man awaiting his last moment on Earth, sitting on death row. His life is remarkably spared when the World Organization for Peace needs a man of a certain skill-set to protect them from assassination by a vicious terrorist organization. The terrorists have a deadly gas they plan to unleash in the Philippines to wipe out the entire population. After being given a fake execution and a new identity, Young finds himself battling ninjas and trying to save the world. Young is the man for the job, and no one can stop him.

This is a tough film to pin down since it has been released under so many different titles (along with the two listed above there is *Ninja the Enforcer* and *Ninja Nightmare*). Leo Fong (*Low Blow* and *Blood Street*) delivers the chops and kicks with a vicious fury. He plucks out eyes with the same intensity as Sonny Chiba. The movie is the true definition of silly, but broken English and kung fu fighting make this a must-see. The final field brawl is kind of spectacular and goofy all at the same time. It takes a little too long to get to the action stuff, but once it does you will have a good time beholding the Fong.

Ninja Busters

(a.k.a. Shadow Fight)

1984 (Garagehouse Releasing DVD) (djm)

A couple of good-hearted losers (played by Eric Lee and Sid Campbell) keep getting themselves in trouble by running into bullies and lying that they are friends of Bruce Lee's. Finally, they get the idea that to get girls, maybe they should take some martial arts classes, and so they join a club and take lessons from the born-200-years-too-late samurai master sensei (played by Gerald

Okamura), who teaches them that to get girls, first you must have discipline and fortitude. The two bumbling idiots manage to learn and excel in the martial arts (various styles including taekwondo and hapkido), and when the whole martial arts school runs afoul of a group of ninjas working for a local crime syndicate, the two likable morons manage to make their school proud by helping to fend the villains off with honorable and impressive fighting skills. It also doesn't hurt that the two buddies have made allies of the bully biker gang who used to beat them up.

A lost "B" movie gem from director Paul Kyriazi (who also made *Weapons of Death, Death Machines*, and later *Omega Cop*), *Ninja Busters* is strictly PG-rated fun stuff for fans of late grindhouse-era shenanigans, but it's a good little vehicle for Eric Lee (also in *Weapons of Death* and *The Master Demon*) and the no-nonsense Gerald Okamura (also in those two movies). It's strange that a small distributor hasn't picked this up for even a VHS or limited DVD release. It's perfectly suitable for fans of the genre.

Ninja Masters

2009 (Lions Gate DVD) (DL)

Ninja Masters was known internationally as *Coweb* before being renamed for American release and each title raises its own valid question. What the hell is a Coweb? And why is a film totally devoid of ninjas called *Ninja Masters*? Unfortunately, those unsolved mysteries are far more compelling than anything in the actual movie. *Ninja Masters* follows Yi Yi, a former martial arts instructor turned bodyguard (Luxia Jiang), as she searches for the powerful couple whose bodies she failed miserably at guarding. With a skinny guy called Fatty at her side, she is drawn into a series of Internet-streamed fights that climax with a "surprising" twist that will surprise no one except the clueless Yi Yi. Neophyte director Xin Xin Xiong (an actor in *Once Upon a Time in China* and *Black Mask*) opens strong with an imaginatively shot wushu vs. wrestling fight and a girl-on-girl battle in a shallow in-ground pool. But the action becomes repetitive and the story predictable. Unless you think the running "skinny/fatty" gag is a real knee-slapper, there's no humor to found either. An all grown-up Kane Kosugi (*Revenge of the Ninja, Pray for Death*) brings some much-needed energy to the last act as Yi Yi's final opponent, but it's too little too late.

Best known as a finalist on Jackie Chan's competition series *The Disciple*, Luxia Jiang was essentially a reality TV star when she shot, this and it shows. The first-time actress doesn't have the charisma necessary to carry an entire film, and she isn't given much help from her director. Poorly conceived fight scenes include a clumsy battle on bamboo scaffolding and an absurd showdown with hip-hop dancing bad guys. *Ninja Masters*'s greatest flaw is the obvious cautiousness of its stunt team. Pumped-up sound effects do little to cover the yawning chasm of air between countless blows and their intended connections.

Ninja's Creed (a.k.a. Royal Kill)

2009 (Lionsgate DVD) (CD)

A royal soldier, Adam (Alexander Wraith), is sent to the United States to protect the sole heir to a Himalayan kingdom from a ruthless assassin (professional wrestler Gail Kim). The heir, Jan (Lalaine), is unaware of her legacy, having grown up with her adopted father (Eric Roberts) since she was a small child. Once Adam finds her, the two run and hide until the assassin locates them and Adam will have to face the truth about his legacy . . . or something to that effect, I dunno.

Never before have you witnessed a train wreck like *Ninja's Creed*. The story is almost completely incoherent with very little action. Aside from the filmmaker, no one knows for sure exactly what's happening, but you get the feeling they just tried to salvage whatever footage they had, slapped it together, and then added voice-overs to attempt to explain everything. Seventy percent of the dialogue is delivered without seeing the actors' faces. It even goes for a wacky surprise ending to try to show how clever it wants to be. Putting the inconsistencies aside, the film *does* co-star WWE and TNA wrestler Gail Kim. Fans of hers will want to see the movie regardless of how it turned out. She looks stunning and has a couple of decent fight scenes where she's able to drum out some punishment. Sadly, this is the only film on her resume, and if anyone is worthy of another shot at a better movie, it's her. *Ninja's Creed* features two Academy Award–nominated actors (Eric Roberts and Pat Morita in his final role) but fails to feature any damn ninjas! Directed by Babar Ahmed.

(Editor's note: Amazingly, I saw this theatrically in an empty theater, where I sat watching it in awestruck amazement. When it was over, I requested a refund for the pain and misery I had to endure, but I was denied.—djm)

Ninja Warriors

1985 (Avid VHS) (djm)

"Anything to do with ninja is serious!"

I love movies like *Ninja Warriors*. I grew up on this stuff. It has a hero named Steve (Ron Marchini) who rocks sweatpants and a wifebeater shirt. He has shuriken stars on his belt, and he smirks at his own wisdom and the stupidity of others. He's a ninja! A team of scientists is creating a serum or something that makes men into compliant drones, and the government is hearing rumors of ninjas breaking into their facilities to steal important memos. This won't stand, so they call on Steve because everyone *knows* he's a ninja! When they call on him, he arrives in the bureaucrat's office, and the first thing he does is look up at the ceiling knowingly. Everyone looks up, but sees nothing. He takes a ninja star from his belt and throws it at a spot he sees, and he kills a tiny recording device! He smiles while everyone looks at him in amazement.

Ron Marchini, who had found some moderate success with the theatrical feature *Death Machines*, is an acquired taste. I like him in *Omega Cop* and the first two *Jungle Wolf* movies. As Steve the ninja, he's . . . the best he can be in the role, I guess. It doesn't require much of him, but what he offers is pretty funny. He seems to be really into it, and when he's in action and fight mode, he's clearly got what it takes to play Steve the ninja. Anyone who has never seen a move starring Marchini should see the ones I mentioned before trying to watch him here. If you start here, you'll never be able to see past *Ninja Warriors*. Directed by John Lloyd, who made *Fighting Spirit* (a.k.a. *King of the Kickboxers 2*) with Loren Avedon.

No Code of Conduct

1998 (Dimension DVD) (CD)

Jake Peterson (Charlie Sheen) is one dedicated detective. He's so dedicated to his job that he's endangering his own personal life. He and his wife Rebecca (Meredith Salenger) have been separated for a while, even though he wants nothing more than to be with her. In a sting operation gone bad, a fellow officer is killed, and Jake takes it personally. He isn't the only one: his father Bill (Martin Sheen) is part of the same unit and wants justice just as much. The two of them, along with Jake's partner Paul (*Only the Strong*'s Mark Dacascos) set out to find the killer and unknowingly stumble upon a much larger case involving police corruption, public officials, and $50 million in uncut heroin.

This is an action film directed by Bret Michaels (yes, the same Bret Michaels who had every rocker chick in America talking dirty to him) who co-wrote the script with Sheen and a few others. Their choice to include Mark Dacascos (*DNA*) in their film was a masterstroke. Sadly, this is strictly an acting role, and he is totally second fiddle to Sheen. He throws a punch (maybe two) and disarms an assailant attacking with a knife. That's it until the finale, and even then it's Sheen who is in the spotlight. Thankfully for Dacascos, he doesn't always need to fight to be entertaining. His natural charisma shines through, making you wish he had a more substantial role. Either way, the film has moderate entertainment value and director Michaels did a stand-up job, even if he failed to unleash Mark's furious skills as a martial artist.

No Contest

1994 (Sony DVD) (djm)

"She's like a Bruce Lee with boobs!"

A beauty pageant is hijacked by a band of terrorists, demanding 10 million in diamonds for the release of one of the contestants, whose wealthy father is a politico. The beauty contestants are all strapped with wristbands loaded with explosives, so they all have to stick together. Sharon (Shannon Tweed), a former beauty queen, is amongst the hostages, and having some experience as a martial artist movie star (her career after winning beauty pageants) gives her a slight edge over the terrorists, who include the megalomaniacal Oz (Andrew Dice Clay) and Ice (Roddy Piper), who takes a special dislike to some of the girls, whom he enjoys tormenting. Once on the loose in the building, Sharon kills the terrorists one by one, using her sexy charms, her brutal karate skills, and an Uzi.

Not bad for an unabashed riff on *Die Hard*, *No Contest* really tries to make an action star out of sexy Tweed, who would also go on to star in other movies like *Shadow Warriors* where she used martial arts. But the problem with that is that it's fairly obvious when fight doubles are used for her, so it's easy to discount her as an action star, but nice try. Roddy Piper, who was in the midst of his years as a formidably dependable action star, shines in a good villain role, and while he gets kicked around by Tweed's character a lot, he keeps getting back up to pursue her and throw her clear across the room a couple of times. It's fun. Also with Robert Davi as an ex-commando who tries to help Tweed. Directed by Paul Lynch.

No Exit
1995 (RAAM DVD R4) (djm)

A university professor named John Stoneman (Jeff Wincott) teaches nonviolence and nonaggression, despite the fact that he holds multiple black belts in various martial arts. His philosophy is severely put to the test when some hooligans mug him and his wife. When they stab her in the stomach (she's pregnant), he goes berserk and kills the guys. The incident makes the news, catching the attention of a billionaire who lives in the Arctic. The billionaire secretly holds to-the-death fight competitions and broadcasts the matches on an untraceable airwave, and he culls warriors from across the globe and forces them to fight. He has Stoneman kidnapped and brought to him, where he is groomed to go up against his current champion, Darcona (Sven-Ole Thorsen), a hulking mass of death-dealing badness. Stoneman contemplates his predicament and his options, and then he seizes the day by embracing the animal he must become to regain his freedom.

Fairly by-the-numbers despite having intriguing philosophical themes, *No Exit* isn't as fun or action packed as it could be, namely because it stops and actually asks questions in between the fights. The focus is on Stoneman's thought process and how he deals with his turmoil. That sounds good on paper, but when on film, it's just . . . not exciting. Wincott (*Mission of Justice, Martial Law II*) is certainly up to the task, and the movie is good for him, but there's a reason no one's heard of it. Damien Lee (*Terminal Rush* with Roddy Piper and Don Wilson) directed.

No Holds Barred
1989 (WWE DVD) (djm)

Hulk Hogan's big vehicle film, *No Holds Barred*, casts him as a slightly fictitious version of himself as a famed wrestler named Rip. He goes out in public looking like a luchador without a mask, and an insane television executive named Tom Brell (Kurt Fuller, never more scuzzy) demands a meeting with him with the intention of hiring him as his network's star attraction. Rip gets a bad vibe from him and refuses him to his face, which enrages Brell to the point of hatching a plan to find an even stronger fighter than Rip. He holds a "Tough Guy" competition, and a crazed, monstrous fighter known as Zeus (Tommy "Tiny" Lister) steps in the ring, annihilating all potentials. Zeus goads Rip on TV, causing a spike in Brell's ratings and stirring a media sensation, but Rip continues to refuse to fight him . . . until Zeus maims his brother. When Rip takes Zeus on in the ring, there's *No Holds Barred*!

This is a really strange movie. I thought it was great when I saw it in a theater in 1989, but looking at it now, I can't help but wonder what the World Wrestling Federation was thinking when they produced it. It presents the world of wrestling as a virtual freak show, with its front and center wrestling stars cast as completely outlandish and monstrous action figures, with zero personalities. Hogan does what he can with an impossible role, but he doesn't come across as manly, heroic, *or* very likable, which is really too bad because he certainly has a distinct look about him, and he has a legion of fans. Tiny Lister (with an odd unibrow) is cast in another impossible role in the film; he grunts, screams, and pounds his chest like a mutant gorilla through the whole film (which scared the crap out of my nine-year-old self), but I think he plays to the extreme, which is unnecessary. He might be better suited in a hard "R"-rated Stallone or Schwarzenegger film than this movie, which was marketed to families and kids. Sexy Joan Severance (*Bird on a Wire*) plays the love interest in the film, but again, she's cast in an impossible role. What woman in her right mind would fall for Rip, who looks like a carnival strongman and acts like a twelve-year-old child? Directed by Thomas J. Wright. Hogan was in *Suburban Commando* next.

No More Dirty Deals
1993 (Magic Studios VHS) (CD)

"One more fucking word out of you. and I'm going to blow your brains all over this place. If that word is bimbos then your dicks are going with it."

The life of speedboat mechanic Travis McCloud (Von B. von Lindenberg) is about to take a drastic turn when he meets Sean Holloway (Taimak). Holloway seems to be made of cash

and wants some high-tech gadgetry installed in his boat. He's impressed with McCloud's work, and the two become quick friends. Even though McCloud is curious as to how Holloway made his money, he fails to realize the guy is nothing but a thief. Hollway's the head of a group of criminals (they consist of nearly nude women) who do his dirty work for him. Soon, Travis is arrested for a crime he didn't commit. When a friend gets him released, he starts to search for the truth and wants nothing more than to find out who let him take the fall for something he knew nothing about.

One thing there isn't a shortage of in *No More Dirty Deals* is the thong. Every five to ten minutes we're treated to a lovely young lady in a thong. But there's a shortage of just about everything else in the film. This is no joke, the star of the film is a man with flowing blond hair named Von B. von. His character should be more heroic, but instead he's a bit of a weenie. The real fun comes from *The Last Dragon* star Taimak, who allows his performance to explode so far over the top; you're not sure if he's actually lost it or not. What many of us really want is to see is the guy in action, and the film is seriously lacking in this department. He does kick some ass while wearing some bizarre face paint and going nutzoid. There's even a scene with him boxing, just plain old boxing. What's great about this scene is the fact that the ring is inside a strip club. A boxing ring: every good strip club should have one. Directed by David J. Schweitzer.

No Retreat, No Surrender
1985 (Universal DVD R2) (djm)

A knee-jerk reaction to *The Karate Kid*, this low-budget film is best known for giving Jean-Claude Van Damme one of his first roles. He's only in it for two scenes, but he makes an impression. The story is simple: Jason (Kurt McKinney) studies at his father's dojo, but when his father is humiliated

Jean-Claude Van Damme plays Ivan the Russian in Corey Yuen's *No Retreat, No Surrender*. Author's collection.

The splits! Jean-Claude Van Damme shows off one of his signature skills in *No Retreat, No Surrender*. Author's collection.

and wounded by an enforcer (Van Damme) of a crime syndicate, Jason's relationship with his dad is altered. His father quits teaching martial arts and moves his family to Seattle, where teenage Jason has to rebuild his life. He idolizes Bruce Lee so much that he virtually worships him at his gravesite. Lee's ghost visits him and becomes his mentor until Jason is finally able to accomplish the physical feats he aspires to. A local dojo bars him from training there (because of lies a bully tells about him), which makes life even harder for him. He finally gains his dad's respect by saving his dad's life outside a bar. The film's big climax centers around a martial arts tournament in a boxing ring, and lo and behold, Van Damme is the guy annihilating everyone who opposes him, including all of the guys at the local dojo. Jason rushes in to save a guy's life, and manages to beat Van Damme.

Filmed in such a way that mirrors silent movie theatrics and Hong Kong-style filmmaking, *No Retreat, No Surrender* is fun and ridiculous. The theme song, *Hold on to the Vision*, plays about five times on the soundtrack. Several sequels followed, but each one is unrelated to the one that came before it. Corey Yuen directed the first two.

No Retreat, No Surrender 2

1987 (Universal DVD R2) (djm)

Made in 1987, but released to theaters two years later, this in-name-only sequel stars Loren Avedon as a skilled kickboxer named Scott who is looking for his friend in Thailand. His friend Mac (Max Thayer), is one of those expatriates who lives in bars and makes his living by gambling. When Scott's girlfriend is kidnapped for having political connections, Scott and Mac enlist a plucky pilot named Terry (Cynthia Rothrock, who steals the show) to fly them to Cambodia where the girl is being held. Her captor is a Russian militant (Matthias Hues) who controls an army. What ensues is basically

a *Missing in Action*-style rescue, and the climax is a great sequence between Avedon and Hues, which involves alligators.

I saw this film when it was briefly released in theaters, and it made an impression on me. Rothrock, unfortunately, has a smaller role, and the film would have been even better if she'd been in it more. As it is, it's a solid action adventure with tons of fighting and explosions. Corey Yuen, who did the original film, also directed this one. After this he made movies with Jackie Chan and Jet Li in China, and later directed *The Transporter* with Jason Statham.

INTERVIEW:
LOREN AVEDON
(djm)

VHS artwork for *No Retreat, No Surrender 2*. Author's collection.

With movie star good looks and black belts in taekwondo and hapkido, Loren Avedon got a lucky break when he was offered the lead role in Corey Yuen's No Retreat, No Surrender 2 (1987), *co-starring Cynthia Rothrock. He was signed for a three-picture deal with Hong Kong producer Roy Horan, which yielded his best work to date:* No Retreat, No Surrender 2, No Retreat, No Surrender 3: Blood Brothers (1990), *co-starring Keith Vitali, and* The King of the Kickboxers (1990), *alongside newcomer Billy Blanks. After his contract ended, his career took on a sub-par trajectory, with smaller villain roles opposite Don "The Dragon" Wilson and Jalal Merhi in underwhelming movies that didn't measure up to his earlier films. He's slowed down considerably as an action star and has since gone into stunt work.*

Tell me how you got started in the movie business.

I was a black belt and people called the studio for guys who could kick and punch and fall down. The Hollywood stunt guys didn't have any technique. That's how I got bitten by the bug. Then I would do these little movies with this Korean director. My thing was martial arts. I got introduced to acting because it was a challenge like the martial arts—like taekwondo. I didn't think I was very good at it, and I think many people would agree that I'm not. I don't know. The movies I did were for entertainment. I was never going to be doing the kinds of lines that Laurence Olivier would get. Or Robert DeNiro. People and writers like that. So I made the best of it. Doing martial arts at that school was where I got bitten by the bug. I showed up on these little sets and saw all the activity, and I got introduced to acting that way. Soon, the phone started ringing. There was a guy looking to replace Kurt McKinney and Jean-Claude Van Damme in *No Retreat, No Surrender 2*. Jean-Claude had scared Kurt out of going to Thailand

to do it. The Chinese are really tough. They are very demanding. I think that Jean-Claude was worried about it. He got Kurt worried. Kurt was on a soap opera at the time. Because they were going to do the next one in Thailand, they were worried that there would be more unaccounted abuse. That's how they found me. I jumped on a plane, and I starred in my first film. I went from zero to hero.

I remember seeing *No Retreat, No Surrender 2* in a theater.

Yeah! Shapiro Glickinhaus Entertainment got behind it and released it in like 2,500 theaters. At the same time, *Red Scorpion* came out with Dolph Lundgren. We did a better per screen average than *Red Scorpion*. I still have the poster and the ticket stub from the movie. I went to watch myself in it! I was sweating bullets through the whole thing! I came out and I was drenched. I thought something more was going to happen after that.

The evil Russian in *No Retreat, No Surrender 2* is played by Matthias Hues. Loren Avedon (right) plays the hero Scott Wylde. Author's collection.

What do you mean?

I thought because I was coming out in 2,500 theaters, that the phone is going to ring! But, it turns out that the three-picture deal I had was with Seasonal. If I had done something else, they wouldn't have used me on the other two films. I didn't know that, but that's why they never used Van Damme or Kurt again. When they find their talent, they sign them to a three-picture option.

What was the deal with the title? It didn't have anything to do with the first film.

It's about marketing. In Europe and overseas it had a different title. In Germany it was *Karate Tiger*.

Talk about working in Thailand and working with Cynthia Rothrock and Matthias Hues. It looked like you were all having a lot of fun, but I'm sure it was grueling.

It was. Yes, it was. I was so wet behind the ears. I showed up on the set, and everything was built. Corey Yuen, the great action Hong Kong director, and the action team were sitting there twiddling their thumbs while the production was trying to find the leads, which were me and Matthias. It was the middle of the night when I arrived, and Corey met me in the hallway with the producer. He said something to me in the hallway, and they threw a few punches and kicks at me to see my reaction. The next morning they had the camera set up outside, and they had Matthias and I come up and do a screen test right there in Bangkok in front of the hotel. Even though we'd signed the deal, we still didn't have the film until Corey looked at us and said, "Okay, these guys will do." Then we started the film. The first scene that was shot was me and Max—that's why I look so healthy in the scene—looking over how we're going to save my fiancé, and Cynthia helps out and so on and so forth. We're talking to each other, having this moment—my mentor and I. Thank God for Max Thayer. He was such a great guy to have there. We hit it off instantly. But I had to carry this movie. It was very hard, quite demanding. I got very ill quite a few times. They would bring out lunch in a plastic bag—soup or whatever was in it. The food came in a rickety old truck. That was lunch. They would tell me, "Loren! Don't eat too much because you're fighting after lunch!" I can't eat this shit anyway, so don't worry about it! They were worried about me having a full stomach, but I was already hurling anyway. *No Retreat, No Surrender 2* was an amazing experience. Cynthia was so nice. She's a sweet gal and very talented. Hwang Jung Lee, who was in *Drunken Master* and Snake in *Eagle's Shadow*, taught me the fights. He would show me some things and gave me some confidence. I remember distinctly I got ill in the middle of Thailand, and he came along and asked me what he could do for me. He brought me hot water, and he helped me. He did some pressure points on me. He said, "Bring me some fried rice so we'll both be sick!" This was the kind of guy he was. The Hong Kong guys were scared to death of him because he had this power. When we were training, he did this little kick on my hand, and my elbow bent, and I swear that if he'd done it full force, he would have ripped my arm off. This was just a little Korean guy! They threw me in front of the camera, and I didn't know what was going on. There are three or four languages on set, and it's probably good that I didn't understand some of the things being said! It was phenomenal. They brought me to Hong Kong to do some things later. It was a whirlwind experience. It was tough to come back to the real world.

An action-packed finale featuring Loren Avedon (left) and Matthias Hues (right) closes Corey Yeun's *No Retreat, No Surrender 2.* Author's collection.

What happened in between *No Retreat, No Surrender 2* and *No Retreat, No Surrender 3*?

A lot of frustration! I'll tell ya! I went back to teaching taekwondo. I taught the day classes. Ron Reagan Jr. was one of my students. Lorenzo Lamas was one of my students. Rebecca Ferrati. I was hustling and bustling because they didn't pay me very much on that film. Basically, for almost two years, I did this. I didn't know what to do. I was so driven to do that again. It's like being a soldier, being in a firefight, and once someone's shooting at you, and you're shooting back at them, you're like, "What can top that?" I had all this high level of martial arts going on, and all of these incredible people there. Wow. At twenty-two, twenty-three, it was hard for me to readjust. So then I went to do *No Retreat, No Surrender 3*, and Keith Vitali—bless his heart—broke his arm just before we started shooting. I'd been practicing all these techniques, and the Chinese guys wanted to see what we could do. We all went to a studio where there was no padding on the ground. They had glued some padding on the concrete. I was doing all these triple kicks, doing all these fancy things, and then it was Keith's turn. He's like, "Uh, okay . . . ." But the dude who'd been holding the bag for him to kick had stepped away. I went, "Uh, oh. This is not gonna be good." But I didn't say anything because he's a high-level martial artist. If he can do something . . . you know? So he jumped up and tried to do a double side kick and he went straight down and broke his arm in three places. That was two days before we were supposed to start shooting. And bless his heart, Keith took painkillers and was in bed for a week, but we changed the schedule around and they came to me and said, "Loren, do you know anybody who can play your brother?" I was like, "Oh, my gosh. Six months of training, six hours a day . . . . " I didn't want to be disloyal, so I told them, "No, I don't know anybody." My heart dropped. Thank God they rearranged things. Keith put on a half cast, but he was in a lot of pain.

That scene at the end in the hangar—that was an amazing scene. Did he do okay during that scene?

You know what? He was, but he would have to stop and have to wince for a minute. There's a shot in there where he grabs his arm. I've got to hand it to the guy. He's an amazing martial artist.

He's one of those guys who I wished could have been a bigger star in movies.

He did that movie *Wheels on Meals* with Jackie Chan. He did *American Kickboxer*, which we were supposed to do together, but I didn't like the script. I don't know what happened. If I had done that movie, I wouldn't have been able to do *King of the Kickboxers*. They wouldn't have hired me for it. It all worked out.

King of the Kickboxers was on a whole different level. I really like that movie a lot. Talk about working on that movie.

King of the Kingboxers was the end of my three-picture deal. They found Billy Blanks, thank God. He was ready, willing, and able. They actually read Don Wilson for that part.

They read Gerald Okamura. First of all, some of the scenes and some of the acting I'm not pleased with. I was giving the director what he wanted. He wanted me to scream and whatever. Overact. After fighting with him, I just did what he wanted. Working on that movie, coming to Thailand again, was unreal. We had Keith Cooke there. If you've seen videos on him, he's just unbelievable. And then we had Billy Blanks who could pick the buttons off your shirt—he's that fast. I remember Billy said, "Hold your hand in the air—I'm going to jab it twice before you can move it." He did it. Holy shit! How can a man with that mass move that fast? Let me tell you— being kicked by that dude . . . (whistles). That was some pain! There's one shot where he does an axe kick drop kick on the back of my shoulder, and he must have hit a lung point or something because it just dropped me. He was the one who was concerned. "Loren, Loren, are you all right?" I was on the ground, barely breathing, trying to say, "I'm fine, I'm fine." He was so humble. That guy was so generous. He said, "Loren, this is your movie. Whatever you want to do, we're going to do it." We worked very well together.

Prang (Keith Cooke) and Jake Donahue (Loren Avedon) prepare to train in *King of the Kickboxers.* Courtesy of Loren Avedon.

Talk a little bit about your persona in these movies. You tend to play a cocky, smart-aleck character.

That was essentially me . . . period. The thing about it is every actor has a facet of themselves that they show within their character. You're playing a character, but basically when they hire an actor to play a role it's because he *is* that character. I was kind of a cocky bastard. Temper with that the fact that you have to have some *cojones* to go to the middle of wherever and throw yourself into God knows what. You have your passport taken away when you get to the location. You've got to stick it out. As a martial artist, when you square off against somebody, you've got to pull that part of you that is invincible, and that part of you *will* talk back, and *will* strike back, and be the part of you that *does* it. My dad would say, "You're such a smart ass!" I would say, "Well, I wonder where I got that from?" That's part of my character—being cocky. Tempered with age, I hope.

What happened after the three-picture deal?

In 1991, I was pretty much a free ranger. PM Entertainment talked to me about doing some stuff. I think my next movie was *Fighting Spirit*.

Video artwork for *King of the Kickboxers 2*. Author's collection.

Yes! There's sequel confusion about King of the Kickboxers. Some video releases list Fighting Spirit as King of the Kickboxers 2, but there's another King of the Kickboxers 2 called American Shaolin.

(Laughing.) It's a marketing ploy!

Which is the true sequel?

Um . . . you know something, I don't know. I have no idea. *Fighting Spirit* came along because there was this chap in the Philippines who wanted to make a movie, and he wanted me. They paid my rate, and I hopped on a plane. When I got there, I read the script, and I went, *Oh, my God!* We promptly rewrote the script. We made it make more sense. That's pretty much *Fighting Spirit*. I don't know how they got away with calling it *King of the Kickboxers 2*.

You started playing the bad guy around this point in your career. You started working with Jalal Merhi in movies like Operation Golden Phoenix.

Well, you know people were chiding me about the fact that I wasn't the star in these movies anymore. They said, "You're going to ruin your career." I was like, "Wait a minute: Work is work." So I shouldn't do anything because I'm not the star? What's running me? Am I an actor? A martial artist? Am I just going to wait for the phone to ring, hoping that something miraculous is going to happen? I wanted to show some versatility. Jalal I had met at the film market. He had hired Billy Blanks for *TC 2000* and some other movies that he did. I didn't particularly like Jalal when I first met him. I thought, *Who is this guy?* Again, it was part of my cockiness. It hurt me. I would be too honest. I didn't know who this guy was, but we got to talking and his writer loved me. With Jalal, he's Lebanese. It's "I love you, I kill you, I love you, I kill you." You never know what you're going to get. But Jalal is a terrific guy, don't get me wrong. When you're dealing on a professional level—the guy has a huge ego, and we all do—in that business . . . when I went to do

Operation Golden Phoenix, I knew James Hong was going to be there, and I knew I was going to get to go to shoot in Lebanon and shoot in the Middle East. I'm either an adventurer or I've got a death wish, I don't know which. I had a four-month-old baby, and I was married. First of all, there was no American Embassy because it got blown up. I went with the Canadian crew. They stamped my passport, and there I was. Working over there and having that experience was mind blowing. It was awesome. The shame about that—and in Jalal's defense—some film lab in Toronto burned something like ten thousand feet of the footage that we had shot. There was only one film company in Beirut, and they owed the lab over there money. We couldn't process the dailies to see what we really had. We got it back, and then it all got lost in a fire. To have that raw footage gone forever . . . that was that. There were Syrian tanks checking people's identification every half a kilometer. There were no police. You could do whatever you wanted to over there. I asked, "Can I go to Israel?" They told me, "Fifty/fifty chance you'll make it by land." Wow! Then, when Jalal and I did *Tiger Claws 3*, the thing about playing a baddie . . . it was a blast. It was so much fun to do. I went to that level. Bad guys think that everybody else is an idiot because no one else around them is willing to do what he wants them to do.

I saw you playing Lex Luthor in that movie. You had those otherworldly beings at your disposal. That's how I saw you in that movie.

There it is! Success!

At this point in your career—and I'm talking post Silent Force and post Deadly Ransom, which were your last vehicle movies—at the point when you did Tiger Claws 3 you had veered away from doing the high kicks and the extreme physical exertion. Was this because of age?

Well, let me tell you why you didn't see that in *Tiger Claws 3*. Because when Jalal got in the editing room and saw me executing technique, versus him and everybody else, I have to say this: I was throwing things with power and accuracy and speed. I was blasting people with beautiful lines. There was a scene where I fight three people, and that scene is gone. It's not in there. I did a jump split back kick. It's not in there. Same thing with the Don Wilson movie I did, *Virtual Combat*. Andrew Stevens directed that. I did some stuff in that film . . . I love Don, but I did some stuff that made him look like he was standing still. They cut it out! The thing about it—my view was always this: If I'm that good then that means that everybody will be that good and the movie will be *great*! If they choose not to use a shot or cut it out, I have no say.

It makes sense. I noticed that in Virtual Combat. You had a couple of fights with Don Wilson in that. I could see that something was up. Something didn't feel right.

I was at one of my peaks during that time. Physically and as a martial artist. I was throwing my leg so fast. Art Camacho, the stunt coordinator, was like, "What was that you just

did?" Art is a great guy. Don has tremendous power. It looks slow and laborious, but it's not. When you're doing stunts on film, there's a different way in how you execute your technique. I was doing all this flashy stuff, and I was kicking him so fast and in so many ways, but it's just not there. It wasn't there because it wouldn't be believable if I was doing that and Don beat me. A lot of the flashy stuff, and the helicopter kicks and things, I was still doing those, but I wasn't the star, so . . .

Talk about your last two vehicle projects, Deadly Ransom and The Silent Force. I watched both of these. Talk about making these movies and what you think of the final products.

Silent Force was a labor of love. My buddy had this script called *Asian Task Force*. There was this Filipino actor who was slated to star in it. They had "X" amount of dollars to do it. My buddy came to me and said, "Loren, we can rewrite this and you can be Frank Stevens." I said, "Sounds great, let's do it." Sure enough, once I was on board, there were a couple of others who came on board. David May, the director, had been an actor. He rewrote the script, and our plan was to produce this film and then on the sales of that film create our own production company and make one to three action films per year. What ended up happening was that the guy who funded the film was an insurance executive who had more money than he knew what to do with, so he financed a movie. His accountant was put in charge of the books and in charge of the production. What she did was she took our idea and made it her own. She is now banned from the American Film Association. She took our dream, and she tried to make it happen. Basically, *The Silent Force* was stolen from us. It didn't really get released until 2000. We shot that movie in 1995. It had been sold under another name by this nefarious person, and it was not delivered, and because sales were made on future films, which were not delivered, this movie had to be taken back somehow, some way in a legal way. We really wanted to get the financier his money back. Our dreams of creating our own production company and everything we had wanted to do was torn away by this other person. Later on, I got a phone call from this guy who told me, "Loren, we've got a deal to make *Deadly Ransom*," and my deal was that I'd get to handle the action. I didn't get to do ninety-nine percent of what I was promised to do, but it was financed and it was a chance to go to work. At least I'm still there, the lead. It was a SAG film in LA. I jumped on board. That company ended up falling apart a year later.

Do you feel that your fans were let down by these two movies?

You know, that's a good question. I hope they aren't or weren't let down. I got paid because you gotta pay the bills, but you also want to know that people who watch you are entertained. You want to feel like you did a good job. I always try no matter how big or how small to make my . . . when I'm on screen, they're gonna be watching me, you know? I was going to have that charisma. *Silent Force* . . . the DP didn't really know how to shoot action. We had a limited time and a limited budget. We knew that we were going to have some great action and do the best we could do. Maybe I let some people down because the bar was set so high with the Hong Kong movies I did. That's something that you can only control so much. I can't compete with Seasonal Films. I'm the producer dealing with a western crew and ideals and values, unions, the system. There was not the freedom or the skill level with the action. The fighters and the people who did their jobs on both of those films did great. But a film can be made or broken in the editing room, through the lens. This is one of the reasons why I wanted to be involved in the action. I wanted the set to be turned over to me. If you can get the crew up for it, the camera shows it. I did that on *Deadly Ransom*. The director didn't like me in the driver's seat. He and the DP took their sweet ass time getting ready. It's sad when you have people in different departments who you're working with who don't necessarily have your best interests—or the film's best interests—at heart. I'm not blaming anything on anybody. I'm just saying that I was committed to doing the best job that I could do. I wanted to do the action, but I also didn't want to step on anyone's toes. You get what you get at the end of the day. There were things that I had to bargain for. I got J. J. Perry to do stunts, and he's since gone on to be one of the biggest stunt choreographers in Hollywood. I gave him his first two jobs. The director wouldn't let me have J. J. unless I let him have this actress that he wanted. "Okay, fine." There's always compromise. I gotta say that the reason why the Hong Kong movies stand out so much—especially with the action—is because that is what their bread and butter was. Their creativity is still today difficult to parallel.

What have you been up to these days, Loren? I know you're living in Hawaii . . .

You have to know what your shelf life is. You have to know what your potential is and what you want to pursue. The thing about LA . . . I was a single father. Me being there for my daughter was more important to me than my career or anything else. I went back to LA to do stunts. I have an Emmy for an episode because I was part of the team for *Chuck*. I was broke in 2001. I was down to zero. A buddy in the stunt players directory gave me a call to be on a show called *The Agency*. He needed somebody to double this Russian guest star. My buddy was doubling Spike on *Buffy*, and the stunt coordinator on that had always been a fan of mine, and he was just a wonderful guy. My buddy calls me and knows that I was living on credit. He asked me if I wanted to show up and do this double for a stunt. I arrived on the set of *The Agency*, and I got looked up and down. He said, "You'll do." Afterwards, he said, "What are you doing on Tuesday?" I said, "Working for you?" "Yeah, I'll give you a day on Tuesday. too." I got hired. I was back at zero, starting all over again in stunts. I then got hired on the next episode, and then I

got hired on *Buffy* and started hustling. I got in through the side door. I didn't want to compete with the actors. I didn't have an agent, I had been off the radar for a while. I started getting bit by the bug again. I would show up on the set and people would say, "What are you doing here?" I would say, "I need a job." That kind of thing. I had to eat a lot of crow. People started to hire me. The stunt community is amazing. Wonderful people. I got back into the biz by stunting. I did a movie called *Risk Factor* that should be coming out soon. It took years to complete. I had always dreamed of living in Hawaii on the big island. There's something about this area that just makes me feel completely at peace. In LA it's just a rat race. I can't deal with that. In my heart, that is not the place that it used to be. I literally picked up and built a house on a plot of land I bought. There wasn't enough reason to stay in LA. Here I am.

Say something to your fans.

Wow. First of all, I have to think about that. It's an honor that I can be seen on celluloid. That I'm associated with the golden age of Hong Kong filmmaking. I am just thrilled about it. People find me on Facebook and tell me that I'm the reason they started martial arts. What I want to say to my fans is how grateful I am. I've been so lucky to do what I did. I hope they know how much I enjoyed doing it and that I'm glad they enjoyed watching it and that I've inspired them in some way. That is the greatest feeling. I could never ask for more than that.

No Retreat, No Surrender 3: Blood Brothers

1989 (Universal DVD R2) (djm)

Loren Avedon and Keith Vitali star as feuding brothers who have to get along to avenge their father's death. Avedon (who played a different character in part 2) is a martial arts instructor with a bad attitude, and Vitali is a playboy CIA agent, whose father (also a CIA agent) is murdered by a white-haired creep named Franco who has a following of thugs. Franco (played by Rion Hunter from *Cage*) has plans to assassinate President George Bush, and it's up to the two martial arts–proficient brothers to stop him.

Like all of the *No Retreat* movies, this one has a really entertaining vibe to it. More than the others, though, this has heavily orchestrated fight and stunt scenes done in the Hong Kong style. A set piece at an airport hangar is a highlight. Avedon and Vitali are appealing and are both given a lot of screen time to showcase their abilities. The script is weak, but my guess is that if you've made it this far into the series, you won't mind. Lucas Lo directed this. He also did *King of the Kickboxers* with Avedon.

No Rules

2005 (Sherdog DVD) (djm)

A prizefighter named Kain Diamond (Tom Sizemore) tells his young son Kurt to grow up to be an astronaut—anything but a fighter. When Kain is killed in front of his son and daughter in a home invasion, Kurt (played by newcomer David Dunn) wears the memory like a millstone around his neck, and he grows up to be a formidable fighter. As an adult, he's a stick of dynamite, ready to fight anyone who is willing to throw down some cash. He seeks his father's old trainer (played by Philip Tan from *Lethal Weapon 4*) to prepare him for an upcoming championship. A local martial arts studio challenges Kurt for the use of the insignia he wears that belonged to his father, but there's something more to it than that. The studio is run by a sinister brotherhood (whose leader is played by Randy Couture), who years previously killed Kurt's father over some trade secrets of his fighting methods, and now that Kurt is in possession of the secret MMA takedown moves, the brotherhood has targeted him for death. With a championship ahead of him, a death cult brotherhood on top of him, and everything to prove that he's got what it takes to measure up to his dad, Kurt uses everything he's learned to take vengeance and become the man he thinks he should be.

Strangely, this film never received a proper video release, but it's certainly on par with similar direct-to-DVD titles from Tapout like *Beatdown, Never Surrender,* and *Locked Down.* It features real MMA/UFC fighters like Couture and Frank Shamrock, and it has comparable production values and testosterone-driven rock songs and enough on-screen sexuality to satiate most male viewers. The fights are nonstop, and star David Dunn doesn't have much charisma or skill as an actor, but he certainly measures up in the incessant simulated beatings that ensue. "Judo" Gene LeBell and Pamela Anderson appear in cameos. Directed by Gerry Anderson.

No Tomorrow

1999 (Splendid Entertainment DVD R2) (djm)

An office worker named Jason (Gary Daniels) is convinced by his wild coworker Davis (Jeff Fahey) to live on the edge and join him on a dangerous arms deal that turns out to be a disaster. With his buddy Davis dead, Jason manages to live through the ordeal and impress a government agent (played by Gary Busey), who offers Jason a job. Jason takes the gig and gets involved in a case where some major arms deals are going down, and when he immerses himself in the lifestyle, living on the edge is where he feels most alive. He even falls in love with a woman whose alliances are on the shady side, and when the adventure is over, he seeks her out to settle down with her.

Directed by rapper Master P, *No Tomorrow* is a shambles. I'm telling you, this movie has everything it needs to be a great little action movie. You've got Gary Daniels, Gary Busey, Jeff Fahey, and supporting parts played by Frank Zagarino and Pam Grier. You've got some money for explosions, car crashes, and even some spliced footage from *Air America* where a huge plane crashes and explodes. You've got all this, and you still don't have a halfway decent movie? How did *that* happen? Well, let's see . . . you didn't allow Gary Daniels to throw any punches or kicks. That's bad, Master P. Not cool. You didn't let Jeff Fahey or Gary Busey unleash their inner crazy. Why not? They're there, you should let them go hog wild. You hired Frank Zagarino, but didn't give him anything to do but show up a few times and say some lines. Say *what?* Oh, and you've got Pam Grier in a room, talking to FBI guys a few times. *WOW.* Great way to waste your cast. And the story? Meh. From PM Entertainment.

No Way Back

1976 (NOV) (CD)

Jesse Crowder (Fred Williamson) is a man with a price. If the price is right, hell, he'll do just about anything. He's a private dick with a burning lust for all the groovy chicks. But business is business, and when he's offered a job to look for this fella named Pickens (Charles Woolf) who disappeared with his girlfriend Candy (Tracy Reed) and a bag of cash, he's in no position to refuse. He sets off on his search to find the couple but danger seems to be lurking around every corner. It seems low-rent gangster Bernie (Stack Pierce) wants the money for himself so he sends his goons to get rid of Crowder. Even with all the women begging for more, he still manages to keep one step ahead of the enemy.

No Way Back was the first film to introduce Jesse Crowder to audiences. The character garnered enough success that star/director Williamson brought him back three more times. *Death Journey* (1976), *Blind Rage* (1978), and *The Last Fight* (1983) followed. This first appearance is by far the best. He shoots and fights his way through the gangsters with his shirt wide open and neck scarf tied around his neck. There's a great slow-motion shot of Williamson doing some sort of jump kick and blasting the enemy directly on top of his head. It's a moment that has to be replayed a couple of times to fully appreciate it. As usual these films are filled with colorful dialogue and a bevy of gorgeous women to show us mortals how a true Adonis operates. Williamson also scores a hat trick on the picture as star, writer, and director. This is one of his top efforts. The theme song by The Dells is pretty funky.

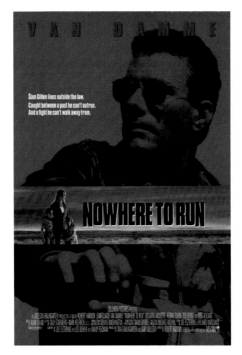

Theatrical poster for *Nowhere to Run*. Author's collection.

Nowhere to Run

1993 (Sony DVD) (djm)

In a rare dramatic turn, Jean-Claude Van Damme plays an escaped convict named Sam, who ends up squatting on the outskirts of a farm owned by a struggling single mother named Clydie (Rosanna Arquette), who is being threatened by a land developer (Joss Ackland) to sell him her land. Sam emerges from the shadows to help her fend off the hired thugs sent to scare her into submitting to the evil businessman. In so doing, he becomes a surrogate father figure for her two little kids (one of whom is played by Kieran Culkin) and a love interest for her, which amazingly feels right and convincing in the context of the story. When Sam's identity is revealed, he must decide whether or not he should flee the authorities or stay and help the family he has come to love and also face the consequences.

From Robert Harmon, the director of *The Hitcher* and the *Jessie Stone* movies with Tom Selleck, *Nowhere to Run* has some subtle stylistic flourishes, but it's surprisingly grounded for a Van Damme vehicle—particularly at this prime stage of his career. He had just done *Universal Soldier* and his next film was *Hard Target*, so it's interesting to see him in this quiet, relatively sensitive film. He uses brawling tactics when he's pushed to fight, but he never kicks anybody. It has the feel of a western or a Harlequin Romance novel. Joe Eszterhaus, Leslie Bohem, and Randy Feldman wrote the screenplay.

Chuck Norris stars as Scott James in *The Octagon*. Author's collection.

The Octagon

1980 (Anchor Bay DVD R2) (djm)

A complicated plot and some voice-over work muddies the waters of this generally entertaining movie starring Chuck Norris. Norris plays Scott, an orphan whose master chose him over his treacherous brother Seikura (Tadashi Yamashita from *American Ninja*). Seikura has grown up to be a member of a terrorist group that trains people to be ninjas who will one day take over the world. Scott infiltrates the terrorist group (Richard Norton plays a thug in a few scenes) and there's a final confrontation between the two sworn enemies/brothers.

Eric Karson directed this film, and it's engaging to a point. Lee Van Cleef shows up in a few scenes to give Norris a few directives, and when Norris isn't romancing the leading ladies, he's fighting ninjas. Norris's real-life son Mike plays a younger version of him in several scenes in this film. Karson also made *Black Eagle* with Sho Kosugi and Jean-Claude Van Damme and *Angel Town* with Olivier Gruner.

Omega Cop

1990 (Southgate VHS) (CD)

John Travis (Ron Marchini) is one of the last of a small group of law enforcement officers who works for the Special Police in a future overrun by criminals. He and his fellow officers stumble upon a public auction of slave women and decide to stop it. His team is wiped out in the process and his captain, Presscot (Adam West), refuses to send him backup. With a small group of women he has sworn to protect, Travis will fight his way back to the bunker so he can get them to safety.

Ruthless warlord Wraith (Chuck Katzakian) has his own agenda to take back his property (the women), kill Travis, and put an end to the Special Police.

With tough guy lines like, "That's the butt of my gun, anyone want the front?" you know that there is great fun to be had. Ron Marchini's lack of on-screen charisma in the sequel *Karate Cop* was surprising since he was much more likable here. The fight scenes are entertaining enough, with wide shots capturing the action so you can see a master showing off his craft. It's a fair guess that Adam West was around for maybe a day or two of shooting since all of his scenes take place in the same room. There are also appearances by character has-beens Troy Donahue and Stuart Whitman who show up for a few moments. Chuck Katzakian has one of the greatest voices of any screen villain, though there is never a question as to who will win the final fight since he appeared to be quite on in his years. The music choices are all over the place: there is standard synthesizer underscoring going on but there are moments when they try to make Travis look like a futuristic cowboy and the music reflects that. There's even some sort of retro 1950s or 1960s type of oldies music that Travis listens to on a cassette tape when in his jeep. The one-liners come rapidly and there is a fairly solid attempt at giving the audience a bit of backstory. Director Paul Kyriazi previously worked with Marchini on *Death Machines*.

Once Upon a Time in the West

1969 (Paramount DVD) (djm)

Westerns have never really been my thing. I like some of them a lot, but it's rare when I see one that I want to watch all over again as soon it's over. *Once Upon a Time in the West* is probably my favorite western. I love this movie. Charles Bronson plays a nameless character known as The Man—or Harmonica—and he has one life goal: To kill a coldblooded, icy-eyed killer named Frank (Henry Fonda). All we know about The Man is that he's in no hurry to kill Frank, and we meet him close to the end of his journey, which is apparently the most interesting part of his quest because we also meet some great side characters who are a part of his plot of vengeance. There is Cheyenne (a wonderful Jason Robards), a rapscallion bandit who gets blamed for a massacre that Frank committed. We also meet Jill (Claudia Cardinale), who has traveled thousands of miles to meet her new husband, only to find him slaughtered along with his children—the unforgivable crime that Cheyenne is being hunted down for. When The Man comes into this story, everything just eases blissfully into a pulpy, violent yarn that makes you yearn for the days of great storytelling and moviemaking.

From Sergio Leone, who made Clint Eastwood an international star with *A Fistful of Dollars* and its two sequels, *Once Upon a Time in the West* is arguably Charles Bronson's best movie, featuring his most iconic character. It's astonishing to think that he was in his late forties when he made this. It would be several years yet down the road for him until he made his star-making hit with *Death Wish*. Even if you don't enjoy westerns as much as others do, this film is everything that a motion picture should be. From Ennio Morricone's classic score, to the wry, succulent script by Leone and Sergio Donati (from a story by Bernardo Bertolucci and Dario Argento), this is a great, essential film.

On Deadly Ground

1994 (Warner DVD) (djm)

"My guy in DC tells me that we are not dealing with a student here. We are dealing with a professor. Anytime the military has an operation and fail, they call this guy to train the troops, okay? He's the kind of guy that would drink a gallon of gasoline so he can piss in your campfire. You can drop this guy off at the Arctic wearing a bikini underwear without his toothbrush and tomorrow afternoon he's going to show up at your poolside with a million-dollar smile and a fistful of pesos. This guy's a professional, you got me? He reaches this rig, we're all going to be nothing but a big goddamn hole in the middle of Alaska! So let's go find him and kill him and get rid of the son of a bitch!"

After the success of *Under Siege*, Steven Seagal had some power in Hollywood, and he used it to leverage *On Deadly Ground* as his first (and so far only) directing effort. He plays a complacent roughneck named Forrest Taft, who works for an evil businessman named Michael Jennings (Michael Caine), who has become a hated man in the media for his ruthless dealings in the oil industry. Taft looks the other way when Jennings lies about vital matters that result in the cover-

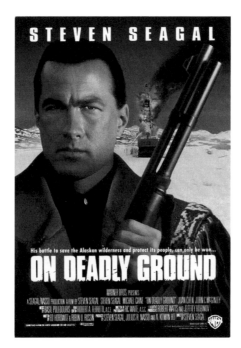

Theatrical poster for *On Deadly Ground*. Author's collection.

Forrest Taft (Steven Seagal) plays around with a dude before breaking his arms in *On Deadly Ground*. Author's collection.

This is the face most stuntmen see when they get hurt by Steven Seagal. From *On Deadly Ground*. Author's collection.

Forrest Taft (Steven Seagal) is on the warpath in *On Deadly Ground*. Author's collection.

ups of deaths on oil rigs and the spilling of oil in the Alaskan environment. When Jennings orders Taft's death for knowing too much, Taft barely escapes with his life, and is saved by a tribe of Eskimos in the wilderness. Nursed back to health and given a spirit vision that entails his destiny as the savior of the environment, Taft spearheads a war against Jennings that brings hellfire and brimstone boiling and bursting all around them.

Well-produced and lavish in production value, *On Deadly Ground* is great for giving us a glimpse into Steven Seagal's mind and how he sees himself. Some of the stuff in this movie is classic Seagal material, and it's pretty much the only movie you'd ever really need to see if you'd want to summarize Seagal's talents, persona, and charisma into one movie. There's a scene near the beginning of the film that really amazes me: He's in a honky-tonk bar, and some big guys are picking on an Eskimo man, and they finally get on Taft's nerves. They pick a fight with him, and he takes them all on, singling out the leader of the bullies (played by Mike Starr), who he then proceeds to teach a lesson on what it means to be a man. It's priceless. Nils Allen Stewart (*Mars*), Sven-Ole Thorsen (*The Running Man*), and Shari Shattuck (*Out For Blood*) also appear in the film. Basil Poledouris did the score.

The One

2001 (Sony DVD) (CD)

"I am Yulaw! I am nobody's bitch! You are mine!"

There isn't just one universe, there are many, a multiverse. In each of them, lives another version of ourselves. Yulaw (Jet Li) a former officer of the MVA (a multi-universe police force that patrols those jumping from universe to universe) kills a version of himself only to discover that each time you kill yourself in a universe, the energy that is released divides itself among the remaining ones. Yulaw wants to be the only version of himself left. His strength is superhero-like and the only alternate-self left standing in his way is Gabriel Law (Jet Li). He is a police officer who has noticed an increase in his own strength over the last couple of years. Yulaw attempts to kill Law but two officers from the MVA—Roadecker (Delroy Lindo) and Funsch (Jason Statham)—foil the attempt. When bodies start piling up, Law becomes a wanted man: he's the innocent being blamed for the wrath of Yulaw, despite the fact that his wife (Carla Gugino) is trying to protect him. When the unthinkable happens, Law will harness all of his abilities and do anything to stop Yulaw once and for all.

Despite the fact that the story has several plot holes, *The One* is an excellent showcase for its star Jet Li (*Kiss of the Dragon*). He sometimes struggles with handling the English language but he convincingly manages to embody different personas, which is essential to the story. There is plenty of hand-to-hand combat, much of which is enhanced with some snazzy CGI effects. Most of the effects were pretty seamless and quite an accomplishment, particularly with the final fight scene in which Jet Li fights another version of himself. It was interesting to see how both characters, played by the same actor, used two distinctly different fighting styles. Yulaw uses xingyiquan, which is a more offensive style of fighting, and Law uses baguazhang which uses more circular movements. There are several scenes that are pretty interesting where you can see them practicing these styles. While Jason Statham is in it, he hadn't quite broken through as an action star yet. He's able to play an interesting and sympathetic character without having to rely on his action skills. The movie has a rocking soundtrack featuring such acts as Disturbed, Linkin Park, and Papa Roach (with an equally bombastic score from Trevor Rabin). Director James Wong co-wrote the script with his long-time partner Glenn Morgan, with Dwayne Johnson originally set to star. If you're willing to suspend your rational thought for ninety minutes, then you can have a great time with *The One*.

One Down, Two to Go

1976 (Anchor Bay DVD) (djm)

"You may be good in kung fu, but I'm an expert in gun fu!"

The mob are using a series of karate tournaments to hedge bets and rig outcomes, and when martial artist Chuck (Jim Kelly) finds out about it, he and his promoter Ralph (Richard Roundtree) go after the lowlifes who are ruining the integrity of the sport. Chuck is shot twice and Ralph is unable to get the results they'd hoped, so they call on their friends Cal and J (Fred Williamson and Jim Brown), who heed their plight and show up, guns and fists at the ready. Once in town, they immediately get into some scuffles (a bar fight, a few shootouts), and by the time it's all over, the mob infrastructure in the town has been quelled and the four friends can laugh about it like it was all a cartoon.

The team-up of these four blaxploitation stars is a great idea coming so soon after *Three the Hard Way* (1973) and *Take a Hard Ride* (1975), which also featured Williamson, Brown, and Kelly. *One Down, Two to Go* is pretty simple stuff, but it gets a lot better when Williamson and Brown show up about thirty-five minutes into it. Frustratingly, Jim Kelly is underued in it, and he spends at least an hour off screen, and when he's on screen, he's incapacitated on a bed. A shame. Williamson directed.

100 Rifles

1969 (Fox DVD) (djm)

Yaqui Joe (Burt Reynolds) is being hunted by Sheriff Lyedecker (Jim Brown), and when he finds him about to be executed in Mexico for crimes against the Mexican military, Lyedecker helps him escape, only to apprehend him later. The Mexican government sends their best man Verdugo (Fernando Lamas, father to Lorenzo) after them, and Verdugo's main motivation is that he thinks Yaqui has thousands of dollars hidden away somewhere from a bank robbery, but the truth is that the money was spent on 100 rifles to arm a revolution against the Mexican military. Lyedecker ends up siding with the revolution—led by Yaqui and his partner Sarita (Raquel Welch)—and as a team they are almost unbeatable.

Sexy and full of roughhousing, *100 Rifles* went down in the history books for featuring an early interracial love scene (between Brown and Welch), but if you're looking for gun-blasting, fist-smashing action from Brown, you won't be disappointed. Jerry Goldsmith provided the cool western score, and Tom Gries (*Breakheart Pass*, *Breakout*—both with Charles Bronson) directed.

One in the Chamber

2012 (Anchor Bay DVD) (djm)

A seasoned hitman named Ray Carver (Cuba Gooding Jr.) is unable to complete his latest murder mission, and the Eastern European mobsters he was supposed to assassinate come after him. Another hitman known as "The Wolf" (Dolph Lundgren) is called in to mop up Carver's mess, and it is inevitable that Carver will run into The Wolf at some point and clash. While Carver is a mostly down-to-earth human being with feelings and scruples, The Wolf is the complete opposite: He's a tad bit flamboyant with some panache in the way he kills, and he doesn't hesitate in killing anyone if there's a payday to be had. In their first encounter, Carver gets the best of The Wolf (hard to believe) and doesn't kill him off, which throws The Wolf for a loop. Rethinking his adversary, The Wolf decides to (sort of) team up with Carver against their employers and score a huge payday.

Shot in Romania and in the Czech Republic, *One in the Chamber* feels like so many other direct-to-video actioners starring the likes of Wesley Snipes, Jean-Claude Van Damme, and Steven Seagal, and while it's passably entertaining it never hits the bull's eye. Gooding Jr.'s role might have been better filled with one of those names, and it's difficult to accept that he'd get the better of Lundgren, who towers over him in every way. Lundgren doesn't show up until almost thirty minutes into the picture. Directed by William Kaufman, who'd worked with Gooding Jr. on *Hit List*.

One Man Army

1993 (New Concord DVD) (djm)

Walking Tall is blatantly ripped off in this Cirio Santiago-directed movie starring Jerry Trimble (*Live by the Fist*). Trimble plays a guy named Jerry (nice) who comes back home to attend his grandfather's funeral, but he gets into all sorts of trouble right away: his hometown has become a cesspool for gambling, prostitution, and lawlessness, and he takes it upon himself to run for sheriff against the corrupt, current sheriff. He wins, and immediately begins his reign as a One Man Army against the thugs and bad guys in his town.

I suppose the absence of a two-by-four in Trimble's hands is replaced by his martial arts abilities and high kicks, which works for me. The film is cheap, as per the producer's—Roger Corman—standards for this type of movie. It's also very short (less than eighty minutes), so it's all over very quickly. Trimble was capable of more, but this film uses him as much as it can despite not being very special.

One Man Force

1989 (Maple DVD) (djm)

Chief: "You didn't have probable cause!"
Jake: "I have all the cause I need!"

LAPD detective Jake (played by former defensive lineman for the Oakland Raiders John Matuszak) is a loose cannon. When his partner (played by Sam Jones) is killed on a bust, Jake goes off the rails and steps all over procedure to get revenge. His chief (played by an exasperated Ronny Cox) doesn't have a prayer in reining Jake back; if anything stands in his way—man, woman, or household appliance—he plows through it or knocks it down to get to where he's going. A sideline case he's on involving the disappearance of a young woman (played by pop star Stacey Q) leads him to the same guys who killed his partner. Those guys are played by Richard Lynch and Charles Napier. Great supporting cast!

John Matuszak, who is probably best known for playing Sloth in *The Goonies*, appeared in a handful of movies in his (unfortunately) short life. *One Man Force* is his solo action vehicle that has just enough room for him to flex his boisterous, larger-than-life personality. He looks massive and imposing, and when he hits a punching bag, the bag looks petrified. While the film is not very memorable or distinctive, fans of '80's cop and action movies will probably find some things to enjoy about it, and those unfamiliar with Matuszak outside of *The Goonies* should give this a gander at some point. It's kind of fun. He was a beast! Written, produced, and directed by Dale Trevillion. From Shapiro/Glickenhaus Entertainment. David Michael Frank (*Showdown in Little Tokyo*) did the score.

One Man's Justice

(a.k.a. **One Tough Bastard**)

1995 (Artisan DVD) (djm)

Drill sergeant and combat instructor John North (Brian Bosworth) is devastated when his wife and daughter are murdered at a convenience store for being at the wrong place at the wrong time. Their killer is a lowlife named Marcus (Jeff Kober) who works for a corrupt FBI agent named Savak (Bruce Payne), whose objective is obtaining some military prototype guns that can shred cars with a single clip. When North sets his sights on Marcus, the trail leads to Savak, and when he gets too close, Savak uses his influence to frame North for peddling hard drugs, which lands North in jail for a time. Desperate to clear his name and avenge his family, North escapes and goes straight for the jugular, no matter the cost to his own life.

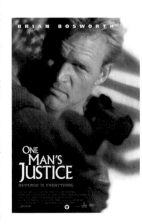

Video poster for *One Man's Justice*. Author's collection.

Tinged with tragedy and a melancholy theme, *One Man's Justice* is a solid vehicle for Bosworth, whose previous film *Stone Cold* put him on the map as an action star. *One Man's Justice* loses a lot of credibility with the corrupt FBI agent character, played by Payne. He looks like a Hollywood villain (nose piercings, long, blond hair, a hint of an accent), and he behaves irrationally, and there's no way such a person could exist in the real world. He reminded me of the character Gary Oldman played in Luc Besson's *Leon* (a.k.a. *The Professional*). Other than that, there's some good action and fight scenes here, and if you liked *Stone Cold* and want to see Bosworth in another decent action film, seek this one out. It's not a classic, though. Kurt Wimmer (*Equilibrium*) directed it.

On Fire

(a.k.a. **Forgive Me Father**)

2001 (Digiview DVD) (CD)

"When they pulled his corpse out of that burning car, I could have sworn I heard him laughing at me."

For twelve long years, Father Virgil Garrett (Ivan Rogers from *Ballbuster*) has lived a quiet life. One day he receives a newspaper with a particular article circled, detailing a murder. The man murdered was Virgil's brother. A rage grows within him, and he walks away from his church, just like he walked away from his old life twelve years ago, the life of an assassin. His brother was a doctor and did nothing but help people so Virgil sets out on a murderous rampage trying to learn the truth. And when he does, those people better pray to the Lord since they're about to meet their maker.

Watching *On Fire* is like going on a trip with your family and your dad takes the scenic route. You get to see a couple of cool things but it takes forever to get there. You could easily trim forty-five minutes from the run time of this film and most likely you would end up with a far more rewarding experience. Ivan Rogers (*Two Wrongs Make a Right*) gives a subtle performance, appearing in the dimly lit shadows as he plucks villains out of this world. There's no real fighting in the movie, but it does deliver some pretty solid squib work and prosthetics. I love how Rogers carries himself in the film, and he gets all the best moments. Then again, why wouldn't he? He also wrote, directed, and starred, so why the hell not, right?

Ong-bak

2005 (Fox DVD) (djm)

"The fucker never gives up!"

A village on the outskirts of Bangkok experiences a crisis: The stone head of their Buddha statue is stolen by an errand boy of a crime lord in Bangkok, who had instructions to buy a small item from the monks of that village, but when they refused to sell the item, the errand boy desecrated their god in retaliation. The monks send their greatest warrior, Ting (Tony Jaa), to Bangkok to retrieve the Buddha's head, and Ting's willing to go to any extreme to bring balance back to his village. Once in Bangkok, Ting experiences a culture shock: crime is rampant, and being an innocent he is susceptible to kindness and virtue, and therefore he's an easy mark. He's quickly thrown into a pit fighting ring run by the crime lord he's after, and he reveals himself to be not only a superior fighter but the main attraction in the freak show that comprises Bangkok's underbelly.

Ong-bak came out of nowhere. The very fact that this received a wide theatrical release (with zero promotion or fanfare) in the US is an astonishment, and it heralded the arrival of a new action star in Tony Jaa. He's got the humorless no-nonsense approach of Jet Li and the balls-to-the-wall, no-holds-barred, no-stuntman mentality of Jackie Chan, but he's got the forceful martial arts talent in Muay Thai fighting that's all his own, and when he puts the beatdown on guys it should remind you of Steven Seagal's finest hours when he put the hurt on countless stuntmen. The movie itself is as simplistic as they come, but it has no pretensions and should make even the most jaded martial arts action fans raise their eyebrows a few times. Luc Besson helped distribute it outside of Thailand. Jaa's next movie was *The Protector*. Two non-related sequels to *Ong-bak* were made, starring Jaa, but they were set in ancient times and therefore are not reviewed for this book. Directed by Prachya Pinkaew.

Only the Strong

1993 (Fox DVD) (djm)

From director Sheldon Lettich (*Lionheart*, *Double Impact*), this lightweight tough-teacher movie features Mark Dacascos as an ex-special forces soldier named Louis who learned capoeira (a martial art that incorporates dancing) while on missions in Brazil. He applies for a job at his old high school back home and is surprised to find out that gangs and drugs have overrun the premises. His favorite teacher, Kerrigan (Geoffrey Lewis, *Double Impact*), watches Louis deal with some drug dealers on campus, and as a result, he gets him a job on campus as a sort of physical education teacher. Louis then has to figure out a way to coach some jaded kids in capoeira, which they all find ridiculous until they realize that it rocks. The funny thing about

0

the film is that the tough drug lord (played by Paco Christian Prieto from *Lionheart*) in the neighborhood also happens to be a capoeira master, so he has something in common with Louis. They have two fight scenes in the movie.

It's hard not to like *Only the Strong*. It's in love with capoeira so much that it almost seems convinced that it was going to be the next big thing in martial arts. A lot of Brazilian songs are on the soundtrack. Dacascos is easy-going in the role. Stacey Travis is his co-star. Dacascos later did a war movie called *Only the Brave*. Don't let that confuse you.

INTERVIEW:
MARK DACASCOS
(djm)

With a prestigious background in martial arts, Mark Dacascos was born to become an action star. A self-proclaimed "chameleon of martial arts," he's built an impressive body of work around his abilities as a martial artist, as well as his abilities as an actor. Starring in stellar action films like Only the Strong *(1993),* Crying Freeman *(1995),* Drive *(1997), and* Brotherhood of the Wolf *(2001), Dacascos is multi-faceted, as he's found great success as The Chairman in* Iron Chef America *on the Food Network.*

I've never heard the story of how you got discovered.

My first movie was called *Dim Sum*, with director Wayne Wang. After living in Hawaii and Colorado and California and Hamburg, Germany, and in Taiwan, I made my way back to San Francisco Chinatown when I was eighteen. I was teaching martial arts and aerobics classes for my mother in her school. On my lunch break, I was walking with my girlfriend on our way to

Mark Dacascos plays Louis, an ex-special forces soldier in *Only the Strong*. Author's collection.

lunch, and these two guys stopped me and they asked me if I was an actor, and I said, "No," and they asked me if I would like to try out acting and be in a movie, and I said, "Absolutely not, thank you very much." They insisted on giving me a card so that if I changed my mind, they would be happy to audition me. It was very pleasant. I told my mom about what happened, and she told me that life is a big adventure and that I should try something new and try something different. I said, "Okay," and I went to the audition and had no idea how to audition. I'd never taken an acting class, I'd never studied Shakespeare, and I'd never done a play in school. I started off in Hawaii and then I went to Colorado to school up until the sixth grade. After that it was Europe. And there I was auditioning for these professionals, and for whatever reason, I got it. The first day on set I see this beautiful Chinese girl by the name of Joan Chen, and Joan spoke perfect English and perfect Chinese and was studying German. I went to school in Germany so I spoke German, I spoke English, and I was studying Chinese. So the director, Wayne, wanted us to improvise in German. The whole idea was that I was her boyfriend and I was supposed to have been gone for a couple of months and this was the first time I'd gotten to see her in a long time, and he wanted us to talk and have this make-out scene in this car on this street out in Chinatown. I remember him telling me what to do, and I asked him, "Well, how do you want me to kiss her?" And he said, "Well, how do you kiss your girlfriend?" I said, "Uh, French kiss." He goes, "Well, do that." I went, "Okay . . . " You know? I was excited, but I was also like, *Wow, I don't even know this girl!* So he calls action, I go up to her, we improvise in German, and then we start making out, and you know, it's a little weird because people are watching, and then I hear somebody yell, "Cut!" and I keep going. "Cut!" I keep going. "Cut! Stop!" Oh! Stop! I didn't know what "cut" is. That was my first experience ever on camera. Making out with Joan Chen. I thought, *This acting thing . . . hmmm . . . me likee!* (Laughing.) That was when I was eighteen years old. I'm forty-eight now. I can say that in terms of acting, I love it more now than ever because I'm starting to understand it a little bit more because of life experience and taking tons of classes. It takes talent, but it also takes discipline and training and constantly trying to improve yourself.

Looking back on all the years you've been involved in the movie business, would you say that you're an actor or an action star?

Well, I never even considered myself an action star. I've only considered myself an actor because the way I fight off-camera is completely different from how I would fight in a tournament or on the street. So, everything that I've done on camera is as a character, not as Mark Dacascos. If you see me in *Only the Strong*, it's me being a capoerista, and I remember people going, "Oh, he's not a real capoerista," and I go, "Yeah, I'm not a real capoerista." I'm not trying to be a real capoerista, I never said I was a real capoerista, I am a student of capoeira like my character is a student of capoeira. The masters are at the beginning of the movie and at the end of the movie. I am a soldier in the movie, a special

forces soldier who's learned some capoeira, he's a fighter, and that's the character I tried to portray. In *Drive*, he's a kung Ffu guy. He's a Hong Kong-style kung fu guy. A bionic guy. That's what he does, and that's the way he fights. If you look at the character I'm playing right now on *Hawaii Five-o*, I play a character named Wo Fat, and he's a killer, so whatever works, he does. In *American Samurai*, he's a samurai.

How much do you prepare for the different styles for some of these movies? For example, how long did it take you to adapt to the capoeira style in *Only the Strong*?

Only the Strong came around in an interesting way. I'd heard about capoeira for years, and a friend of mine had tried to get me with this teacher for a long time, but things got in the way, but what really triggered my entrance to capoeira was heartbreak. My girlfriend and I broke up, and I needed to do something that would inspire me and get me out my depression. I loved martial arts, but I needed something to shake it up, so I called my friend and he sent me down to Amen Santo, who is also the teacher in *Only the Strong*. He's my real teacher. I was in the parking lot at Santa Monica Airport, and even before I made it to the hangar where they were teaching, you could hear the music and the beats. I remember thinking, *This sounds so cool!* I had good vibes. I walk in there and people were doing cartwheels and doing kicks and jumping, and it just made me so happy. So I took classes for two months on my own before I even heard about the audition. Serendipity. My agent told me that he had an audition for me, and it had something to do with

Paco Christian Prieto (left) plays the villain Silverio in the Sheldon Lettich film *Only the Strong*. Mark Dacascos (right) plays Louis Stevens, the hero. Author's collection.

Ex-special forces soldier Louis (Mark Dacascos, left) learns the martial art capoeira in *Only the Strong*. Author's collection.

this martial art called capoeira, and I went, "Hey! I just started classes two months ago!" So I did the audition for Sheldon Lettich, I got the part, and then we were supposed to shoot in July, but a hurricane hit down in Miami, and so we got pushed back to October. So as a result, I had a good eight months of training, and Sheldon also wanted me to be a little more buff, so I had a weight coach and lifted weights every day plus capoeira training. In reality, I was a good high-level beginner. Fortunately, I'd already been a gymnast and I'd been studying martial arts all my life in different styles, so I had a strong basis.

How about for something like *Drive*, which featured high-intensity fights?

This is the thing, as a martial artist and somebody who has a lot of passion for martial arts, and staying healthy, I've never let myself go, and I've never had to go from zero to a hundred. If a hundred is my optimal, and zero is not doing anything, I try to keep myself going at a good eighty-five already, so it's only fifteen percent I've got to work up to. I'm about to start shooting *Mortal Kombat: Legacy* Season 2, and we're going to shoot in about a week and half, so by then I want to drop down about five pounds. Anything that jiggles, I'm getting rid of. I've got five pounds to drop in about ten days. I can do that easily. That's where I like being: eight-five to ninety-five at all times. Not only is that good for me if I have to do movies, but that's just a healthy lifestyle. Period. It's a good example for my children, and less medical expenses.

Talk a little bit about doing movies where the entire film is centered around you. Some of the movies you've done, the movie doesn't revolve around you.

No, right.

And you're not Steven Seagal, where he has one style throughout his whole career. You adapt.

First of all, anytime you're number one on the call sheet, there's a huge amount of pressure. You set the tone and the sensibility of the set. You and the director. I take that very seriously. I work very hard, and I expect everybody else to do the same, to give 100 percent. I have to tell you, working with Steve Wang on *Drive* was one of the best experiences I've ever had. He is so incredibly creative and has so much passion. I love the character I played. We worked our butts off. We worked many more hours than we should have. We all wanted to give it. It started with Steve. He did not go home. He did first unit, second unit back to back. That was his baby. Since he was working that hard, he wanted *us* to work that hard, and we *wanted* to work that hard. It was a great collaboration. It's one of the few movies where I watch the fight scenes and I go, "Ah! They did it right!" I love it. Action-wise, by far it's my favorite.

You get an interesting credit on *American Samurai*. You're billed as "Introducing Mark Dacascos" in that one. Say something about working on that movie. You worked with director Sam Firstenberg and David Bradley on that one.

Officially, that was probably my first movie. Technically, I worked on *Dim Sum*, but my part and Joan's part got cut out. As far as being on camera, *American Samurai* was my first movie. The story of that film takes place in Istanbul, but we shot it in Tel Aviv and Jerusalem. I had a fantastic time. We were in Israel for three months plus, and Guy Norris was our stunt coordinator, and he was great. Sam Firstenberg was very professional, and I enjoyed my experience with him. Easy to work with, gave me direction, and I'd do it. I didn't hang out a whole lot with David Bradley, but when we were on set, we worked. He had some issues with some of the fight stuff, and he worked it out with those guys. We never had any problems. I worked four to six weeks with a kendō master to prepare for the role. Someday, I'd like to go back to kendō.

I noticed in the credits that you doubled at least one other actor in the movie for the stunts.

I doubled the ninja; there's a ninja that flips into the scene. They asked me if I could do it and I said, "No problem!" (Laughing.)

Weren't you in *Angel Town* with Oliver Gruner?

As a stunt guy. Not as an actor.

How was your experience with Sheldon Lettich on *Only the Strong*?

Also a great experience. He liked me and wanted me for the part, but I had to get approved by 20th Century Fox, so he prepared me as much as he could. We went in for the screen test, and it went well and obviously I got it. He was easy to work with. That was my first lead in a big movie.

By the time *Double Dragon* came around, did it occur to you what the future was presenting to you? You were already what I would call "an action star." You were on the track, moving up.

That's a good question. That's a very good question, thank you. This is how I see it as an older guy, looking back: You were saying that Steven Seagal is known for his hands and his aikido. Jean-Claude is known for his big kicks and his flexibility. I didn't want to be known for anything in particular. In my mind, I wanted to be known as the chameleon of martial arts. That could be detrimental, and also a huge advantage. Detrimental because people don't know what to expect. They cannot count on you doing any one particular thing. It was never my intention to be a big action star. I just wanted to be a working actor, and I just wanted to do everything I could possibly do to be the best performer I could, and if that meant that the role required me to do fighting, I already had a lot of experience. If not, I would have to work my butt off to make up for getting my acting up to par. In *Double Dragon*, which was based on a videogame, this guy I'm playing is a teenager. Career wise, an agent or manager might say it was a big mistake because I went from being a muscular dude in *Only the Strong* to dropping almost fifteen pounds on a 5 foot 9 frame. That's a lot of weight. I grew my bangs out and played a skinny teenager. Because why? It's post-apocalyptic, we

don't have a lot of food. He *should* be skinny. What happened is that people saw me in *Only the Strong*, and when they saw me in *Double Dragon* they thought I was sick or thought, *Oh, he doesn't look like an action guy.* What does an action guy look like? We see movies and we get a stereotypical version of what an action guy is supposed to look like, but then you see Jackie Chan, who is pretty svelte, or Jet Li. Some look like stereotypical action stars, but others don't. That was the deal with me. Because I'd travelled all over the world and had seen tough guys who didn't look like tough guys, I wanted to be one who could change his appearance. That was my whole goal. I certainly did not reach for status, nowhere close to Jean-Claude or Steven Seagal. But I'm still happy because I still have a really interesting career. In just one year of my life in my career, I'm playing Wo Fat on *Hawaii Five-o,* I'm playing The Chairman on *Iron Chef America* on the Food Network, and I'm playing Kung Lao on the *Mortal Kombat* series. Three completely different characters in three completely different genres. *And I love that!* That's what I wanted.

Are you comfortable with the action star label if people see you that way?

I take it as a huge complement. I don't see myself that way, but if they want to see me that way, thank you! I love that! I don't see myself as anything other than father, husband, friend, martial artist, actor.

I *want* to call you an action star. You are.

Thank you! I appreciate that. I'll honor that.

What martial arts are you into right now?

For the last six years, I've been studying Muay Thai, and I love it. I love the impact. It's all real. I'm training two to three times a week, and I do yoga on the off-days.

The author with Mark Dacascos in Sherman Oaks, California. Photo by Kady Moore.

Why did you do *Kickboxer 5* at the point you did it in your career? It was the end of a franchise, and you might have been starting other franchises at that stage.

I did not like the title whatsoever. What I did like was the character, I liked the humanity to it. I liked the adventure of being in Africa. I loved Kristine Peterson, the director. She was lovely. I was not keen on the title, but the story and the character I liked. We had a lot of talent there.

Was that a good move for you?

Eh, I don't think it made a difference one way or the other. I don't think it hurt me.

Well, you certainly looked good doing your stuff in it. You always elevate the movies you're in.

Well, thank you. I had a good time on that. I was there for three months, and while I was there I took a safari, and while I was on safari, I got the call to do *Crying Freeman*, and I was *stoked* because I liked the title, I loved the story, the character.

Crying Freeman is definitely one of your best movies. That was a memorable character for you.

I love playing characters with stuff going on. He was an assassin with innate skills that he didn't know about, he doesn't want to kill, but he can't help himself because of the hypnosis. He's an artist, he's in love with someone . . . he's got stuff going on. I love stories that are full. I don't watch a lot of action movies—I love action movies—but I don't watch a lot of them because usually the story is compromised because they want to put in more action. Look at *Enter the Dragon*. The whole set-up with Bruce Lee's sister, and there's stuff going on. He always had some sort of story going on. That's what a lot of action movies are lacking. The movies I've done that I like the most have something going on.

Just a technical aside, but I don't include guys like Liam Neeson or Matt Damon in this book because they're actors and they learn how to fight for the movies they're in for that time. Then they go on and do *We Bought a Zoo*, or whatever. How do you feel about these guys having quick cuts and cheat angles to sell their abilities on screen? I mean, if you're going

Freeman (Mark Dacascos) is an assassin in *Crying Freeman*. Author's collection.

to call it an "action movie," it should have someone like Mark Dacascos in it.

Well, thank you, sir. This is the thing: I guess I look at it in the context of the story in the film. I love *The Bourne Identity* and *Taken*. And I love them in those movies because for the purpose and the context and sensibility of the story, they worked. For example, if Matt Damon took a wushu pose in between his fights in *The Bourne Identity*, it would not have worked. If I want to look for Hong Kong action, I would go to that kind of movie for it. The way I adapt to each character for the story, as an audience member, I do that as well. I get into context.

Crying Freeman should have been your big hit movie. That was the one that should have launched you to another level.

Thank you! I appreciate that. Most Americans have never even heard of it. Career wise, it was one of my biggest joys because I loved that character and the director is brilliant. I met my wife on that picture. It's one of the biggest disappointments because while it was a huge success in Europe, it never—to this day—was released in North America. *Crying Freeman* elevated my career, so to speak, in Europe and Central Asia and in Russia, and in America no one has even heard about it. It's one's of those things that's absolutely a disappointment, but what can you do?

That's what happened with *Drive*, too. Another great movie that nobody saw.

Thank you, yeah. There was a lot of talk about getting a feature release, but for whatever reason it did not happen. We got an HBO release, and it was a huge hit in Russia. It was a bigger hit than *Executive Decision* in Russia. It's like I have two different careers: One foreign and one domestic.

Why do you think Europe, Asia, and Russia embrace these types of movies so much?

David, I don't know. It's a good question.

You worked with Tibor Takacs several times. You did *Red Line, Sabotage, Sanctuary,* and several episodes of *The Crow: Stairway to Heaven* together.

Great guy. The way we met, I auditioned for a movie called *Deadly Past*, and I got it, and Tibor had me put on glasses, and some hair extensions

in there and I played a quirky bartender in it. Fortunately, we worked together again on those other films. We get along really well.

Sabotage was a much better movie than it should have been, you know what I mean?

Thank you. We had Tony Todd, Carrie-Anne Moss, and Graham Greene. It was a great cast.

Let's talk about you doing *The Crow* TV series. That was important because you followed Brandon Lee. Were you nervous about that?

Well, sure. I knew Brandon as a kid. I think he did a fantastic job with the movie. When I had an opportunity to do it on TV, what are the disadvantages? People would compare it to Brandon, and how would I be able to beat that? If he didn't do a great job, they wouldn't be doing a TV show. In a way, we're doing this because of that, out of respect, tribute, homage. He left a great legacy. There's no way a TV show can match the grand scale of the movie. What can I do? I'm not Brandon Lee, I'm Mark Dacascos, so I can give them the best Mark Dacascos possible in portraying this. How can I make this work? I gave my all, my best take on the character. I *loved* this character. It was a great piece of material to work with.

That was a big commitment for you to work on this show for twenty-two episodes, and I'm sure you were committed to more than that.

I love being on a show for a long time. I like going for the truth and honesty. I like getting intense. With *The Crow*, I liked having the opportunity to show this character's arcs, his nuances of playing both Eric Draven and The Crow. There was love, there was action, there was music, there was poetry, there was drama. It was a dream role. I miss part of that.

The Brotherhood of the Wolf was another great role for you in a big movie that should have launched you in a huge way, but it wasn't as big as it could have been. Talk about working on that one.

Well, here's the thing: You saw it. Let's be honest . . . a lot of people aren't into foreign films. It's the second or third highest grossing French movie ever. The fact is: it's in a foreign language. They aren't as big as English-speaking films. That was a choice Christophe, the director, made. He wanted a French story with an all-French cast except me. He knew the cost and the disadvantage of that, and I love that. Over here, those who were open to foreign films saw it and liked it. The mass audiences did not. Bottom line.

You did *Cradle 2 the Grave* with Jet Li, a big Warner Brothers movie produced by Joel Silver. How did that happen?

Lots of happiness for me. I enjoyed the heck out of working with Jet Li. Huge disappointment in the fight scene. I don't know if you know how I was chosen for that film. Jet Li on his website asked his fans worldwide: Who would they want to see him fight next? The fans chose me. So he

Mark Dacascos cradles Julie Condra in *Crying Freeman*. Author's collection.

asked Joel Silver to ask me to be in the film. I was a huge Jet Li fan, so absolutely yes. One of the reasons why I went to Taiwan when I was seventeen to be a Shaolin monk was because I had seen Jet Li in *Shaolin Temple*, his first film. Huge inspiration. Jet Li, Bruce Lee, and Jackie Chan: Huge idols.

I was happy to work with Joel Silver and Jet Li. The problem was that we choreographed this fight scene and Corey Yuen did a great job, and Jet Li's a fantastic fighter, and we spent over a week on this one fight scene, but what did the editors and the company do? They cut it to pieces! And then they intercut two other fight scenes into it! Any energy we have building up between these two guys, mano-a-mano, is dissipated and washed away when you have two other fight scenes going on at the same time. They killed us. When I saw Jet Li at the New York premiere, I said, "Jet, how's our fight?" He goes, "No comment." He hugged me and that was that. Then I saw the fight scene and it *broke my heart.* It broke my heart, David. With *Crying Freeman* not being shown in America, with *Drive* not being on a big screen in America, and a fight scene with Jet Li that was cut to pieces, those are my three heartbreaks in my career.

You were up for *Dragon: The Bruce Lee Story*, right?

I was asked to audition for *Dragon*, but quite honestly, I'm a huge Bruce Lee fan, and I never saw myself being able to play Bruce Lee. So I humbly and gracefully declined the audition. I did not have the tools, the confidence, or the wherewithal to pull that off. I didn't want to waste their time. I told Jason Scott Lee, "Thank God you got it." He was fantastic.

You worked with Cirio Santiago on some of his last movies, *The Hunt For Eagle One* and the sequel. Talk about that a bit.

He was a lovely man. Being in character and being in the Philippine jungles a lot for those two movies, I didn't see him a lot. The interaction I did have with him was very personable, very professional. He got the movies done in a place that wasn't that easy to shoot in. When you're shooting for hours in the jungle, it's logistically hard to get resources, but he made it doable.

Rutger Hauer was in one of those. You've worked with him a few times.

Yes! He's a crazy guy, and it's always an adventure. You never know what's going to come out his mouth, and I love it.

This is kind of a weird thing for me to say, but when you do something like *Only the Brave*, which is a war movie you did, as a fan of yours I think to myself, *Oh, I wish he'd done an action or martial arts movie instead.* You're getting older, and it's getting more difficult, I would imagine, to do martial arts movies, but when you take the time to do something that *isn't* a martial arts movie, I wish you'd make that *one more* action movie instead.

You know what I love that you just said? You're not afraid to speak the truth. We're all getting older. I'm forty-eight now. I know that. A lot of people are shy about that.

This is it, man.

I love that, I love that! Thank you, I appreciate that. When I read that story and took that movie, I asked for the audition. I'd been researching that story—a true story—for years. My grandfather married a Japanese woman in Hawaii, and he was a racist who fell in love with a Japanese girl! So anyway, I love the whole story about Japanese Americans fighting in World War II while their families are in internment camps. When I was told that this movie was being made, I *asked* for the audition. I'm only a quarter Japanese, so a part was written specifically for me. I was doing *Nomad* in Kazakhstan at the time. That story meant so much to me. But I love that there are people out there who want to see me move. Trust me, if there's a good story out there for me, I want to move for you. I *really* do. I'm motivated by the heart, by the story. If I don't get that, it's not going to happen. Sometimes I get the audition, but maybe I didn't do good enough. Or, for whatever reason, I'm just not asked to audition. There are so many variables involved. The thing is, I'm forty-eight . Can I still do a double back? I can say, "No," because I haven't done one in years, but can I still do a standing back or a butterfly twist right now? Yes. If I worked on a double back for two weeks, I can do a double back. I also want to write, I want to direct, I want to do movies like *Taken* and *The Bourne Identity* and do the action with a solid storyline, or I want to direct and find young guys who can do all the things that I used to want to do. You know what I mean? There are other things that I haven't done yet that I want to try.

I Am Omega was a very small exploitation movie, but the fact that you're in it and you're putting way more into it than anybody else would makes it a pretty good little movie. Talk about *I Am Omega*.

Thank you, David. My good friend Jeff Mead wrote it, and while I was in Serbia doing this other movie, he called me and said he had this movie going and he sent me the script, and I loved it. He said, "We're doing this on a mini, mini budget, guerrilla-style. You're in it, and the director's cool." It was a good platform for me to work on my acting, and it gave me the chance to do a part that I don't usually get to play. I did it, and I had a blast. I just jumped in. It was a tiny budget, and there're some issues like sound quality that could be improved, but as far as the experience, I had a blast.

You mentioned that you want to direct. Might that be a possibility in the near future?

There's a movie I did called *Boogie Boy*. Pretty dark film, but I loved the writer/director. He's writing a script for me right now. Tons of action, but deep characters. I gave him certain criteria, and I think he's hitting the marks. I'm also working on a different version of *Rush Hour*. I'm also working on a story based on my own life.

Say something to your fans.

I think I've had an incredible adventure as an actor, and it is all because of the fans. Without the fans, I would not have a career, I would not still be working, so to all of you who've watched me and supported me over the years, my deepest and most heartfelt aloha and thank-you.

On the Edge
2002 (City Heat DVD) (CD)

"Gentleman, I don't give a shit about your cover. If I find out that Slim's involved in my family's murder, he won't just be undercover, he'll be underground!"

When a rising young basketball star, Jo Harris (Derrick Franklin) buys some drugs, he unknowingly sets off a chain of events, changing the lives around him forever. He owes drug dealer Slim (Ice-T) a nice chunk of change and doesn't have the flow to pay him. Slim sends the cavalry out to kill Jo but they go to the wrong house and kill the wife and son of Rex Stevens (Bernie Casey). Rex is stricken with grief, and he wants answers. Jo doesn't know what to do; he desperately tries to keep his problems from his father Frank (Ron O'Neal), and he goes to his dad's old pal, retired detective-turned-private eye Dakota Smith (Fred Williamson, reprising his role from *The Rage Within*). Compared to the freshly comprised team of Dak and Rex, Slim is just small beans but they will have to go through him in order to identify the *real* villain and take down whoever is responsible for all the pain and suffering.

Director/star/co-writer Fred Williamson once again delivers a highly exciting actioner, and he brings along another batch of friends to play with. This was the final screen appearance of *Superfly* star Ron O'Neal, and he brings an awful lot of character to his role. Bernie Casey has always been a powerhouse of an actor, and he has several moments where he reminds us of it. Jim Brown (*Slaughter*) makes a cameo appearance but never gets to have fun with the other guys. Then of course we have Fred back again as Dakota Smith. This is one of his great characters. He runs around two-fisting his guns as if he were Chow Yun-Fat and makes sexy with the ladies. Just be forewarned: Don't look too close during the love scene or you will catch a peek of why they call him The Hammer.

Oosaravelli

2011 (Bhavani DVD) (CD)

"Everyone is born as zero. Life gives them a chance to become a hero. Most fail to use it. I too failed to use it. Life will also give you a chance to become a hero. Don't leave the chance. You'll know the day when it comes."

Tony (N. T. Rama Rao Jr.) is the type of guy who will do anything to get his hands on some money. On his way home he meets a beautiful young girl named Niharika (Tamannaah Bhatia) who is being kidnapped by terrorists. He immediately begins to fall for her but he must put his feelings aside in order to save her. After the ordeal is behind them, Tony continues to try to get her to fall in love with him. When her feelings begin to sway in his favor, the truth of who he really is becomes revealed. With a slew of criminals all trying to kill him, including the vicious Bhai brothers (action star Vidyut Jamwal and Prakash Ral), nothing is what it seems and there are far more shades to this twisted story.

Maybe it's because I'm still new to the Bollywood scene, but this is one overly long and confusing movie. There's much to enjoy: some catchy tunes, excellent action, and some decent offbeat humor, but damn, this thing is just one convoluted mess. Supposedly it was inspired by the Johnnie To film *Vengeance*, but the similarities are very slim to say the least. There are, however, some fantastic fight scenes and shootouts sprinkled throughout the two hour and forty minute runtime. Vidyut Jamwal (great in *Commando: A One Man Army*) is criminally underused and appears only in a supporting capacity. Even in such a small role he's able to bring his unmistakable charisma to every scene he appears in. *Oosaravelli* is not an essential film, but director Surender Reddy at least knows how to stage an exciting action scene.

Open Fire

1994 (Republic VHS) (djm)

Jeff Wincott (from *Martial Law II* and *Martial Outlaw*) plays a former FBI agent named Alec McNeil, who now works for the phone company. His father runs a chemical plant, where some terrorists break in and make demands. Their mandate is that they require a criminal mastermind named Kruger (played by Patrick Kilpatrick) be released from prison, or they will wreak havoc on the ecosystem. The FBI quickly bows to their demands, have Kruger released, and fumble about as Kruger systematically makes the authorities looks stupid. After all, he was the one who planned the takeover of the chemical plant, and his

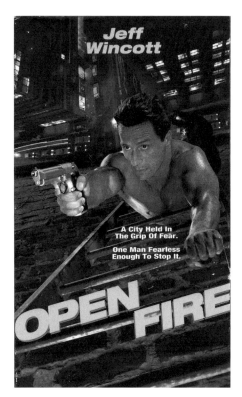

VHS artwork for *Open Fire*. Author's collection.

every move suggests that he'd planned his release long before he was even incarcerated. McNeil is nearby, so he drops in on the FBI's flustercluck and he offers his services, which they refuse. He goes renegade and infiltrates the structure where Kruger now holds sway. As McNeil kills off Kruger's men one by one, Kruger gets nervous and begins his escape plan, which involves several ruses for the FBI to chase after. The climax has McNeil grappling onto the roof of a truck, and a standardized shootout ensues once he plants his feet on the ground.

In the wake of *Die Hard* and its first sequel, some obvious rip-offs were spun from the exploitation and straight-to-video market, as well as from big studios, which were making movies like *Under Siege* and *Speed* as their response to the can't-loose formula. *Open Fire* is 100 percent inspired by *Die Hard*, but it becomes painfully obvious that the filmmakers didn't have a clue as to how to springboard from the initial set-up and premise. All credibility collapses as the villain is ten steps ahead of everyone else (evidenced by the cassette tape ploy that is used several times throughout the film), and while Wincott is impressive as a "B"-movie action star, he is punching and kicking his way through a movie that doesn't deserve his talents and abilities. This is precisely the sort of direct-to-video movie that flooded the market in the mid-1990s, and there is a certain nostalgia to be found in watching them now, but movies like *Open Fire* are why the genre never garnered proper respect from critics and consumers alike. The director was Kurt Anderson, who made *Martial Law II: Undercover* and *Martial Outlaw* with Wincott and *Bounty Tracker* with Lorenzo Lamas.

Operation Cobra (a.k.a. Inferno)

1997 (New Concorde DVD)

(djm)

Interpol agent Kyle Connors (Don "The Dragon" Wilson) is on a mission when his partner Trevor (Rick Hill) is killed in front of him. He vows revenge, and he travels to India to forage for answers as to how things got so botched. It turns out that Trevor is still alive and has nefarious plans of terrorism, and so Connors alters his mission and becomes a one-man force to thwart his ex-partner's plans. Trevor's henchman (Evan Lurie) happens to be a formidable martial artist, and the woman Connors thought was on his side—agent Callista Sinclair (Tane Mclure)—is a backstabbing bitch intent on killing Connor on the order of her lover, Trevor. It's got action and fights, too.

From exploitation specialists Fred Olen Ray and Roger Corman, *Operation Cobra* is incredibly derivative and sultry, with several simulated sex scenes (involving erotic thriller starlet McClure) that *might* raise the bar for fans of soft-core sex movies, but fans of action and martial arts films will be groaning for the wrong reasons. Wilson has a nice fight scene with co-star Lurie, whom he fought in *Ring of Fire 2*, but otherwise, this one's a forgettable potboiler. Rick Hill is better known as the star of the first and fourth *Deathstalker* movies.

Operation Condor

(a.k.a. Armor of God 2)

1991 (Dimension DVD) (djm)

Jackie Chan returns as the Indiana Jones-type adventurer known as Asian Hawk (or Jackie), and this time he goes on a quest for a stash of gold that Hitler stockpiled somewhere in the Sahara desert. Along for the ride are two attractive women (played by Carol Cheng and Eva Cobo), who mostly get in his way when trouble comes calling. The villain is a wheelchair-bound guy with a crew of treacherous henchmen who eventually turn against him, and Jackie teams up with him when they each need an ally. The finale of the film takes place in some kind of high-powered jet hangar with wind turbines spinning, causing Jackie and a host of villains to fight each other in mid-air. It's entertaining.

The sequel confusion of this movie is due to the fact that Dimension released this film in US theaters in 1997 *before* releasing the first film, *Armor of God*. Several years later, Dimension released *Operation Condor 2: The Armor of the Gods*, which is entirely misleading. See *Armor of God* before seeing *Operation Condor* to see these two films in order. Both films are lightweight action entertainment. Fans of Chan will have fun. Kung fu fans might find them too breezy. Chan directed both films.

0

Operation Delta Force

1997 (Hollywood DVD) (CD)

"All right, gentlemen, we are going in seven, neat and tight. And we will be coming out seven, neat and tight."

Those pesky terrorists just can't seem to keep their filthy little paws out of other people's business. A small group of them invade a military facility and steal a vicious strain of the ebola virus with plans to use it as leverage to get what they want. An elite military unit is assembled and dispatched to retrieve it before anything happens. Johan Nash (Joe Lara) won't give up so easy, but the vile containing the virus becomes compromised, and ebola begins to spread like wildfire. Time is running out for the team, and they have to catch Nash as soon as possible since he still has the vile containing the cure. Tipton (Ernie Hudson), Lang (Jeff Fahey), and McKinney (Frank Zagarino) will all have to be on the same page if they are to complete their mission on time and stop the spreading of this superstrain of the virus.

When it comes to action star Frank Zagarino (*Armstrong, The Protector*), it really should be all or nothing. He just doesn't get the opportunity to be all he can be in films where he is essentially just a bit part player. You don't get the whole experience when he has limited screen time. Zagarino has one great moment in this film when the team finds themselves surrounded with no place to go. Just as the enemy is about to lay waste to them, a small, all-terrain vehicle comes flying out of the jungle with The Zagarino behind the automatic weapon obliterating everything in his path. If it had been filled with those types of moments, then this thing could have been a certified classic. It was entertaining enough to spawn four sequels (all written by Danny Lerner), and it didn't hurt having action maestro Sam Firstenberg (*American Ninja*) behind the camera for this Nu Image release.

Operation Delta Force 3: Clear Target

1998 (Image DVD) (CD)

"Stupid fucks, who the fuck they think they're dealing with here? You just got yourselves a war!"

The Delta Force is in full attack mode when they're given a mission to destroy a multi-million-dollar cocaine stash belonging to a malicious kingpin named Salvatore (Danny Keogh). During the strike, one of the team members is killed in an explosion. They have a hard time dealing with the fact that the man responsible is still out there but there's nothing they can do. Salvatore has invested money in a bright young computer analyst who is able to

hack in and help hijack a US military submarine to be used as a weapon to destroy New York. The government reassembles the Delta Force team and sends them in to retrieve the sub and to bring Salvatore in, dead or alive.

These types of movies have only one goal in mind when they're conceived and it's to be action packed. Without question, *Operation Delta Force 3* delivers exactly that. And to keep things fresh, director Mark Roper (*Nature Unleashed: Volcano*) adds the capable direct-to-video martial arts action star Bryan Genesse (*Live Wire: Human Timebomb, Cold Harvest*) to the cast. The sole purpose of the film is to focus on action so any character dimension is thrown out the window in favor of spent rounds and grenades. Genesse isn't really given a chance to show off his action skills until the finale, but when he's unleashed, he beats the enemy senseless in a gritty, painful, and bloody brawl. It's easily the best scene in the film, which helps to build into the intense climax. Production house Nu Image has always delivered the goods with these types of films and *Operation Delta Force 3* carries on their stellar tradition.

Operation Golden Phoenix

1994 (Universal VHS) (djm)

Part James Bond globetrotting adventure, and part Indiana Jones treasure hunt, with enough well-shot and choreographed fight scenes to fill two movies, *Operation Golden Phoenix* should appeal to fans of Hong Kong action adventure films like *Supercop* and *Operation Condor*. Jalal Merhi directed and starred in it, and he plays a former US agent who is set up by his partner (Loren Avedon) to take the fall for stealing a priceless amulet, which is rumored to be one of two connecting pieces that leads to ancient treasure in Lebanon. Instead of just sitting idly in prison, Merhi escapes, travels to Lebanon, and gets the support of a royal bodyguard of a princess to track the amulet down. Turns out that Avedon is working for an international gangster (James Hong, who dies laughing at the end), and they have both of the pieces of the puzzle. The final showdown at some ruins leads to some of the better fights in the film, but it's fairly easy to tell that Avedon is the more fluid martial artist, and that Merhi works that much harder to make himself look better than his opponents. Still, this is probably Merhi's best work as an action star.

Avedon and Merhi made several pictures together. Avedon was the villain to Merhi's hero in *Tiger Claws III*, and Merhi cast him in his *Circuit* series, which starred Olivier Gruner. As a director, Merhi was able to deliver a product that he could sell to his distributors, and fortunately, *Operation Golden Phoenix* is one of his better products. As an actor, it's sometimes difficult to see him as the hero because he doesn't have much charisma, his martial artistry pales in comparison to some of his co-stars and his persona isn't very interesting, but this film gives him a chance to look good, and he manages to shine a little bit. I would be proud of this film if I were he.

Operation Rogue

2014 (Sony DVD) (CD)

A group of terrorists have stolen all the ingredients to build a chemical weapon they plan on unleashing at an upcoming political summit. Marine Captain Max Randall (Mark Dacascos) and his elite team are sent in to stop them and bring the terrorist leaders out alive. Things don't go exactly as planned, and the leader's son is killed. Vowing revenge on the US, the terrorists kidnap Captain Wallace's (Treat Williams) daughter Jenna (Sofia Pernas) and threaten to cut off her head if their demands aren't met. Going against the rules, Wallace sends Randall in to rescue her and stop them before they use their deadly weapon.

Produced by the legendary Roger Corman and directed by Bryan Clyde (*The Hunt for Eagle One,* also with Dacascos), *Operation Rogue* was a real surprise and a step in the right direction for star Dacascos who'd spent the last few years hosting *Iron Chef* and appearing on *Dancing with the Stars*. The film builds character, offers a compelling story, and most importantly features plenty of action. Since it is a military actioner, I was worried there would be a lack of martial arts fighting, but the action gods have answered our prayers and Dacascos delivers. This doesn't have *Drive*-caliber action, but it most certainly gets the adrenaline pumping, and now Dacascos can still bring it home. Clyde has grown as a director and moves the story along quickly without compromising the action and gets plenty of bang for what little bucks Corman was willing to shell out.

The Operative

2000 (Lionsgate DVD) (djm)

A Cold War secret agent for the US named Alec Carville (Brian Bosworth from *Stone Cold*) is stuck in Russia when the Red Curtain falls and communism collapses. The KGB arrests him, and his government abandons him for over a decade, and when he's finally released, he's plopped in front of a former KGB honcho, who forces him to do a job that could very well end his life and start up some kind of retro-Cold War action. Alec accepts the mission (something about a renewable energy source), and some mildly perilous situations ensue.

After Pierce Brosnan helped resuscitate the James Bond franchise, it was fairly clear that the world was in dire need of a good villain to fuel the plot of a halfway decent action movie. In the Val Kilmer-starring film *The Saint* and in the Vin Diesel movie *xXx*, I felt a little exhausted with the same sort of bad guys and the same sort of plot that the old Bond movies gave us, and with this movie *The Operative*, the bad guy sits in a chair most of the time and orders Bosworth to do whatever it is that he doesn't want to do. It's boring. The whole movie is boring, which is really too bad because Bosworth should have been in slam-dunk movies, and it's sad knowing that the only really great one he did was his first one (*Stone Cold*). *The Operative* is a cheap, useless actioner that doesn't deliver any thrills or acceptable action scenes, but worse, it wastes its star by putting him in the middle of a dumb plot without a good villain. Directed by Robert Lee, who did *Cyberjack* and *The Silencer* with Michael Dudikoff.

The Order

2001 (Sony DVD) (CD)

"It beats a messiah complex any day!"

Rudy (Jean-Claude Van Damme) is an adventurer who makes his living by stealing artifacts that people are willing to pay very large sums of money for. His father Oscar (Vernon Dobtcheff) finds and deciphers an ancient text that belongs to a religious sect known as The Order. Within the text is a map to a treasure hidden beneath Jerusalem. Oscar travels there only to disappear. Rudy jumps on the next plane to try to find his father. The last person his fatehr had talked to was his old friend Walt Finley (Charlton Heston), and he is there to meet Rudy at the airport. People are quick to try to stop Rudy, and Finley is murdered. With the local police seemingly in on all the shenanigans, Officer Dalia Barr (Sofia Milos) realizes that something is wrong and risks everything to help Rudy find the truth.

As Jean-Claude Van Damme's (*Cyborg*) box-office power began to fade, he inched his way into a series of direct-to-video films. After a few theatrical flops, he found himself starring in projects that were much better than some of his theatrical pictures, and *The Order* is one of them. The movie has much more in common with *Indiana Jones* than, say, *Bloodsport*, but it's a seriously fun adventure film that hits all the right beats. This was obviously a project that Van Damme was very invested in since he co-wrote the script with Les Weldon (*Replicant*). He plays a thief who goes after artifacts, selling them to the highest bidder (who usually ends up being a shady character of some sort). It really feels like he is having fun with the role. The character is materialistic and goofs around, but when things get serious, he has no problem jumping into action. The fights are excellent; they're infused with a dash of humor and play out a bit more like something Jackie Chan would do. The odd thing about the film is that it features an extended cameo by legendary actor Charlton Heston (*Planet of the Apes*). It was sort of a strange inclusion for a Van Damme film, but his character is integral to the plot. There's also some solid work from Ben Cross (*The Russian Specialist*), Vernon Dobtcheff (*Indiana Jones and the Last Crusade*), and Brian Thompson (*Lionheart, Cobra*). The score by legendary composer Pino Donaggio (*Blow Out*) is a standout. It was directed by frequent Van Damme collaborator, Sheldon Lettich (*Double Impact*).

Original Gangstas

1996 (MGM DVD) (djm)

"Well, there goes the neighborhood."

Before *The Expendables* there was *Original Gangstas*, starring the biggest and best names from the blaxploitation genre of the 1970s. Fred Williamson (*That Man Bolt*), Jim Brown (*Black Gunn*), Pam Grier (*Foxy Brown*), Richard Roundtree (*Shaft*), and Ron O'Neal (*Superfly*) are the headliners, and they even threw in some cool white guys from that era like Robert Forster (*Vigilante*), Charles Napier (*Rambo: First Blood Part II*), and Wings Hauser (*Vice Squad*). The story's pretty straightforward: Jake (played by Brown) returns to Gary, Indiana, after his son is gunned down in a drive-by shooting. John (played by Williamson) also returns to Gary when he hears the news because his father was targeted by the same gang that killed Jake's son. John left Gary years ago to pursue a career in the NFL, and both he and Jake belonged to the same gang when they were teens, so basically they were the *original* gangstas of Gary. They console Laurie (Grier), the grieving mother of Jake's son, and together they formulate a plan to try to make peaceful amends with the coldblooded gang that has overrun the streets of Gary, but when that goes bad, they round up other "original" gangstas Slick (Roundtree) and Bubba (O'Neal), who gladly participate in the *Death Wish*-styled vengeance they have in mind. Kowtowing politicos of Gary (played by Napier and Hauser) and a street detective (played by Forster) can do nothing to stop the bloodbath the OG's unleash.

For the most part, this whole movie is a build-up leading to a pretty satisfying conclusion that gives the central stars their moments to shine. Clearly, this movie belongs to Williamson, Brown, and Grier, which is fine, but fans of everyone else who make appearances in the movie will be disappointed. Shot on a relatively low budget under Larry Cohen's direction (with uncredited work by Williamson), *Original Gangstas* delivers more or less what you hope it will. It's not a huge crowd-pleaser, but it's just about what the doctor ordered.

INTERVIEW:

FRED "THE HAMMER" WILLIAMSON

(CD)

One of the pioneers of blaxploitation action films, Fred "The Hammer" Williamson played professional football for the NFL with the Pittsburgh Steelers (1960) and the AFL with the Oakland Raiders (1961–1964) and the Kansas City Chiefs (1965–1967) before he began making feature films, which launched him as a verifiable action star and sex symbol. For over thirty years, he kept himself in the action game, starring or

Director Nico Sentner and Fred Williamson on the set of *Atomic Eden*. Courtesy of Nico Sentner.

appearing in several films every year until he was in his late sixties, and even until this day he remains busy appearing in low-budget action films. With black belts in kenpo karate, Shotokan karate, and taekwondo, he usually uses his own blend of martial arts in his films, laying "the hammer" down on the bad guys. He appeared in a number of films with his fellow blaxploitation titans Jim Brown and Jim Kelly, and he made a slew of films in Italy during the lucrative Italian movie boom of the 1970s and 1980s. With his signature mustache and cigarillo, Fred Williamson is one of the great "B" action stars.

At what point did you decide to give up a career in architecture to pursue film and television?

I couldn't smoothly make the transition after being a football player for six months out of the year, six months on, six months off. My time was unregulated so once I left football and went to work full time sitting at a desk, doing nine to five and all that shit, it just didn't suit my personality, man. One night I'm watching television and about nine months of that architectural stuff, I had to find something else and I didn't know what to do. I was watching television and I saw Diahann Carroll had a TV show called *Julia*. The guest star for the week was playing her new boyfriend. So I said, "Shit, I'm better looking than any of those guys." I went to Hollywood to be Diahann Carroll's boyfriend on the *Julia* show and that's what I did. It took me about a week to establish a contract for me to be the boyfriend.

What was it like making movies in the 70s during the time when black action films were thriving?

I had a plan when I went to Hollywood, and I was going to be the same kind of man I was when I was playing football. I decided if I was going to go into the business it was going to be on my terms and I was going to be a hero. There were no black heroes in my era growing up, no one to look up to. The only person we had was Sidney Poitier, he was a damn good actor, but not the hero type so if I was going into the business, it was going to be "Hammer style." When I was doing the *Julia* show, we were filming on the 20th Century Fox lot, and one day a guy comes by and says, "Hey, you're the Hammer right?" I said, "Yeah." So he said, "I'm doing a movie with some football shit in it and I don't know shit about football. Would you direct the football stuff and put the football stuff together?" Lucky for me the movie was *M.A.S.H.*, and I played Spearchucker. I was like, "Shit, this is nothing. You guys make money by standing up here and saying lines: this is easy." So I called a press conference and said I was going to make films. I'm not doing any more television, and I'm not doing comedy. I told them I had three rules: If you want me in your movie I won't die in the movie, I win all my fights in a movie, and I get the girl at the end of the movie . . . IF I want her. Give me two out of three of those and you got me in your movie. They thought I was crazy like, "Who the fuck is this guy?" I knew I could pull it off so I went to Paramount, I says, "Hey, Paramount, you never had a black cowboy, ever." They said, "This is true." I told them, "Give me $500,000 and I'll make a western." They said, "You can't make a movie for $500,000." I said, "Give me the money, I'll show ya." They said, "Okay, I'll give you $500,000 to make a movie. What's the name of it?" I said, "It's *The Legend of Nigger Charley*." He about fell out of his goddamn seat and that's the reaction I expected. If I make this movie, that was the reaction I wanted from the public. I knew coming into the business that blacks needed heroes and I wasn't going to be the comic because ninety percent of the blacks in the business at that time were comics. Everybody was funny, coming from Mars and landing in America for the first time think all black people are funny. We're not all funny; some of us can kick some ass. *Nigger Charley* was the beginning of it. After that there was *Black Caesar*, *Three the Hard Way*, and it was the foundation of the strong black character I was going to play. What I sell is an image. I'm a black Clint Eastwood who knows martial arts or a black Charles Bronson with a big gun. Those are the characters I play, and I don't stray from that image. That image is always marketable. I don't sing, I don't dance, and I don't tell funnies. I can, but I won't do them in my movies because that's not what my fans want to see.

The films you did in the '80s were some of my favorites, *The Big Score*, the *Black Cobra* films, the post-apocalyptic films. What's your take on this period in your career?

You see what happened was all the black guys disappeared. You see all these black actors fucked up. They had the chance to extend their careers but in the '70s all they were doing was retribution movies—they wanted to kick whitey's ass. That's all they talked about in the films, "Let's kill the white motherfucker." You see me, I killed black people, white people, yellow people, I killed everybody. So my films didn't quite fit into that genre of black exploitation. The only reason they tried to lump me in there was because I'm black. But my subject matter or my themes had nothing to do with killing whitey. I kill everybody. I'm an equal opportunity ass-kicker.

One of my all-time favorite films came out of this time period, William Lustig's *Vigilante*. You and Robert Forester were amazing. How do you remember the film?

Vigilante for me was the chance to write the monologue in the beginning. Lustig told me he was going to do a vigilante picture so I just told him to start it up and use my image to open the movie the right way. I come out of a dark room

Hazuki Kato, Mike Moeller, Fred Williamson, and Nico Sentner on the set of *Atomic Eden*. Courtesy of Nico Sentner.

Fred "The Hammer" Williamson and Nico Sentner posing for the camera on the set of *Atomic Eden*. Courtesy of Nico Sentner.

and start spouting off at the mouth to a bunch of people, telling them how we had to take our city back. That was me utilizing my image, so it was a perfect vehicle for me.

It seemed like every decade gave birth to a recurring character for you. The '70s was Crowder, the '80s was Malone, then the late '90s was Dakota Smith. Each one seemed to represent the decade they were prominent in. Was this intentional?

Most definitely intentional, I wanted an identity like Dirty Harry. I started with Jesse Crowder but the story about Crowder is weird, man. When I was in high school looking for my identity, and I was watching these two guys who were seniors. One guy was named Jesse Crowder, and the other was Eugene Greenwaldt. They were football players. They would tell everyone in school to say hi to them but I never seen either of them fight or get angry, but everyone was afraid of them. They had a style about them that scared the shit out of people. Maybe they were just dumb or stupid but you would walk down the hall and say, "Hey, Jesse." You would walk away from them and say, "Damn, that was a cool dude but maybe he's dumb." But he had a cool image and people were afraid of him and that was who I wanted to be. I didn't want to be the guy who went to the party, I wanted to be the guy who the party came to. So when I came up with Jesse Crowder, I was inspired by this guy. But guess what Jesse Crowder does: He sues me. I'm using that name and this guy wants to get paid. This guy just ruined my bubble, man. I had to get a lawyer and counter-sue or he would have won. We go to court in Chicago and my lawyer pulls out five phone books and opens them all up to the name Jesse Crowder and there were like

2,000 Jesse Crowders, and asked, "Which one of these are you?" We embarrassed this guy in court and all he had was some rinky-dink lawyer. We won, but I had to give up Jesse Crowder. I gave this guy something to be proud of, and in town he was proud to be Jesse Crowder. He had all my posters with the name on them to show people. I thought he would be proud since I was doing the name justice. Then he sues me.

Talk a little bit about marketing your films in Europe.

When I started making my own films, they started to tell me my films weren't doing good business in Europe. I knew that was bullshit. My films were just as big over there as they were over here. And the reason I found out was because companies like AIP were selling every film with a black star in it for $3,000 across the board no matter what the film was as long as there was a black star. That's because these distributors in the foreign market were outsmarting the folks over here and playing against their prejudices by saying these black films weren't gonna make money over here. I wasn't going to sell my movies for $3,000. The first one I tried to sell at the Cannes Film Festival was *Adios, Amigos* with Richard Pryor. I paid to have a table set up with my posters and flyers, I had a bunch of girls in their t-shirts and the first offer I got was from Greece for $3,000. I said, "No, no, no, no, nooooo, $25,000". They wouldn't shell that money out, so after eight days I still had all my movies and on the very last day I had $275,000 to $300,000 in sales. Then these distributors would come to me and say, "Don't tell anyone what I just paid for this film." So I knew my films were doing well so I decided to stay in Europe for a little while. The first movie I did was *Inglorious Bastards* with Bo Svenson. Enzo Castellari and I were making films like *1990: Bronx Warriors* and they were trying to get me to replace Woody Strode who was very popular over there. So the first films I did over there were those sorts of films. Since Clint had just left, I wanted to take over and fill that void and do the police action stuff so I did the three *Cobra* films and they were equal to what I was doing in the states. .

What can you tell me about your character in *Atomic Eden*?

Stoker is a tough guy, a leader, he kicks ass, takes no stuff, does a little martial arts, slaps a few people around, wins the fight, and I don't get the girl because they're all too young, man. I didn't get a love scene because they had all them young chicks in there. It's a role where I'm a badass, he followed my rules, so I was in the movie.

I was excited to learn you were starring in the film with Mike Moller, who's a very talented action star on the rise. What were your impressions of him?

You're right you know—it's true. He's got presence, and the camera sees it. You can't hide from the camera. You either have it, or you don't. The camera catches it and it likes Mike the way it likes me. If it likes you and what you have is marketable or sellable, you're on your way.

Are you still practicing the martial arts? Can you tell me a bit about your discipline and background?

Yeah, of course. I have four black belts and I just came from New Jersey. I got a trophy and an award for being a sensei. I'm still connected to the martial arts, I studied with Bruce Lee when I was in Hong Kong, Aaron Banks in New York, so I'm very active. It's how I stay in shape. Why do you think I look as good as I do, I don't look the age that I am.

After forty-five plus years in the business, how would you sum up your career?

I'm not even there yet, man. I'm not even close to doing the things I want to do. It's hard to find money and people who will believe in you. It's frustrating, man.

Orion's Key

1996 (Image DVD) (CD)

"We found it, you homo ignoramous! Almost died for it!"

Also known as *Project Shadowchaser IV* or *Alien Chaser*, this is the final film in the "B"-movie franchise to bring Frank Zagarino's albino-like cyborg (except in this one he's an alien) to the screen. This time out he's awoken from a deep slumber by archaeologists who have an agenda of their own. Michael (Todd Jensen) and Corinne (Jennifer MacDonald) are working day and night in the desert of South Africa for a big find to help pay their son's medical bills. They soon discover an artifact worth millions, and people will kill to get it. The recently awoken alien assassin wants it for himself to make an elixir to save his people. The young married couple find themselves in major danger as their boss and his thugs try to kill them to get it, but the vicious alien may get his hands on it first.

Who's more menacing than a pissed off Frank Zagarino? A pissed off Frank Zagarino with alien strength, that's who. This film is more of an oddity than it is an action film. There are a few entertaining moments and a pinch of action, but this one seemed to spend its time preaching to the choir. Zagarino (in spiked blonde hair and dressed head to toe in leather) spends the film running through the desert chasing the young couple and anyone who stands in his way. He fights some folks off, but he's so strong that they can't really be considered fights. One thing is for sure: the final moment in the film is bizarre as all hell and damn creepy (I have my reasons). Directed by genre veteran Mark Roper (*City of Fear* with Gary Daniels) and brought to us by those kooky kids over at Nu Image.

Oscar

1991 (Touchstone DVD) (CD)

"If it's Poole you want, it's Poole you'll get. But, Lisa, you've got to cross the finish line on this one! This is your third fiancé today and it ain't even lunch yet!"

Angelo "Snaps" Provolone (Sylvester Stallone) is one of the most feared gangsters in 1930s Chicago. He rules with an iron fist, and no man would dare to cross him. Things take a bizarre turn when his father falls ill. His father's final wish is for him to give up his life of crime and go straight. Angelo agrees, but it won't be easy. He decides to go into the banking world and tries his best to get everything right except the people around him might drive him back to the darkness. He finds out his accountant has stolen $50,000 from him, his daughter is pregnant with the chauffeur's baby, and he has the most important meeting of his life with the board of bankers. A tough-as-nails detective has his house staked out, waiting for him to make a mistake so they can take him in. In one afternoon he could lose it all if he isn't able to pool all of his resources to save his family and career.

Sylvester Stallone (*Cobra*) isn't the first name to come to mind when thinking about a farce—which *Oscar* most certainly is—but if you give the movie a chance you may find yourself chuckling at the madcap shenanigans coordinated by legendary director John Landis (*An American Werewolf in London*). It's funny: Stallone has made his career out of beating the bad guys into submission, and in this film he's constantly fighting to do the exact opposite. And you know what? He really has a handle on the material, and he's hysterical. Thankfully, this isn't another *Rhinestone* and succeeds as a classic comedy with plenty of twists and turns within a solid story. This isn't a one-man show either; the ensemble includes Marissa Tomei, Chazz Palminteri, Tim Curry, Don Ameche, Vincent Spano, and many more. Together, this group delivers a film worth a second (or first if you haven't seen it yet) look. Stallone's next movie was the comedy action flop *Stop! Or My Mom Will Shoot!*

The Other Guys

2010 (Sony DVD) (CD)

New York City has always been a place where crime has run rampant, a place where people have been afraid to walk the streets at night. Then two men came along with a dream. These two men weren't afraid to put their lives on the line every single moment of every single day to clean up the scum and protect the fine people of the thriving metropolis: detectives Danson (Dwayne Johnson) and Highsmith (Samuel L. Jackson). These two men have risen far above their peers to become living legends, fighting for truth, justice,

and any fine lady who may want to repay them with . . . well, you know. This is the story of their reign as top cops and the shocking tragedy of their fall, and the two schlub detectives (played by Will Ferrell and Mark Wahlberg) who are tasked with replacing them.

The Other Guys quickly opens with Sam Jackson's (*The Long Kiss Goodnight*) guns blazing and Dwayne Johnson (*Snitch*) clinging to the roof of a suspect's car while in high pursuit. This is the film we want to see. Every moment these two men share the screen together, they're a dynamite duo. They're not afraid to shoot up a vehicle, crash through a bus, or even blow up the entrance to Trump Tower and still walk away with the keys to the city. The action is incredibly over the top but always fun and unique. Director Adam McKay (*Step Brothers*) builds a dynamic showcase for its lead actors to run away with and have fun. The first ten minutes of the film belongs to Johnson and Jackson, but the remainder belongs to *The Other Guys*, Ferrell and Wahlberg, whose bumbling characters can't live up to the legacy of their predecessors as they fumble their way through their tasks. It's a novel concept.

Out For a Kill

2003 (Sony DVD) (djm)

Steven Seagal plays an archaeologist named Robert Burns. Burns finds some ancient artifacts in eastern China, and some drug smugglers plant a stash of product inside the artifacts just before they're shipped off to the US, which creates a huge mess when the authorities think he's trying to smuggle drugs out of China. He's waylaid in court and then prison for a spell, but he manages to get out and go after the narcotics ring that put him in this compromising position. When he starts meddling (by smacking thugs around and causing scenes in restaurants when he's threatened), the drug mafia targets him for death, but they end up murdering his wife instead. This, as any fan of Steven Seagal would understand, is absolutely the wrong thing to do to Steven Seagal. He goes ballistic and literally takes on one bad guy on the mafia chain at a time until he makes it to the top guy, whom he throws a samurai sword at from a building above and *beheads* him on the street below! Talk about an ending!

As wacky and goofy as this movie is at times, it's an interesting little outing for Seagal, who seems miscast at certain portions of the movie, but then the movie veers right into his comfort zone again and feels perfect for him. *Out For a Kill* at the very least has a title that feels tailor-made and Frankensteined together for Seagal (i.e. *Out for Justice/Hard to Kill*), and it should please forgiving fans, but it won't stick with you. Filmed in Bulgaria. Directed by Michael Oblowitz, who did Seagal's previous direct-to-video effort *The Foreigner*.

Out for Blood

1992 (Madacy DVD) (djm)

Lawyer John Decker (Don Wilson) is out with his wife and child one evening when they are killed by a group of thugs in front of him. He is beaten to a pulp and left for dead. When he recovers, he vows revenge and trains himself to be a ruthless martial artist who goes out at night after defending the law, looking for the thugs who made his life a living hell. As a vigilante, he stirs fear in the hearts of criminals, and he becomes a media sensation known as "Karate Man." He tries starting his life anew by courting a comely art gallery owner (Shari Shattuck), but he becomes distracted when he finally comes across the men who killed his family.

One of Wilson's stronger films, *Out for Blood* feels more in tune to the vibe and spirit of big-screen efforts by Wilson's competition and contemporaries at the time of its release. If it had starred Steven Seagal, Jean-Claude Van Damme, or Jeff Speakman, this movie would be better remembered. I liked it for giving Wilson more to work with as an actor, and there are moments where he goes through various stages of suffering and anger, which works well for the film. For other stars, *Out for Blood* might have been a minor effort, but for Wilson, it's a high point. His director, Richard Munchkin, also did several of the *Ring of Fire* movies with him.

Out For Justice

1991 (Warner DVD) (djm)

Gino (Steven Seagal in his prime) is an Italian Brooklyn cop who has uneasy alliances with the mob, but when his partner is gunned down in the street in front of his family by a crazed, low-level mobster named Richie (an intense William Forsythe), Gino goes over the edge, breaking limbs, laws, and every rule in the book to get his revenge. But there's a big problem: Richie and his cronies are perpetually high on coke and suicidal, so their methods are wildly dangerous and unpredictable, making their bloody path hard to trace, and it isn't helping that the mob is on their own warpath to kill Richie before Gino does.

This is some serious stuff. When Steven Seagal made *Out for Justice*, his star was almost at its peak, and he was a force to be reckoned with on screen. This is one of his best, most indelible movies. Every second he's on screen, you're looking at him, studying him, and thinking, *This guy's awesome. How did he end up getting fat and doing crummy direct-to-video movies? How is that possible?* He's a superstar in *Out for Justice.* Seagal aside, John Flynn's kinetic direction is incredible. All of the characters feel real. The locations are authentic and interesting. The music by David Michael Frank is great. The fight scenes are brutal and hilariously unexpected. If you're a casual fan of Seagal's and have never seen this, it's time you do. You will cross over. Flynn also did *Lock Up* with Stallone.

Out of Reach

2004 (Sony DVD) (djm)

A former covert government spook named Billy Ray Lansing (Steven Seagal) lives way off the grid in the wilderness like a mountain man, but his one connection to the outside world is with a teenage girl named Irena, who lives in an orphanage in Eastern Europe. Billy Ray sponsors her and sends her letters, and their pen pal relationship is sweet, but when he receives a letter from the orphanage, telling him that Irena was adopted suddenly and would no longer be sending him letters, he suspects something sinister. He flies to Europe, visits the orphanage, and with just a little bit of investigating he comes to understand that the orphanage is a front for human trafficking, and that Irena was sold to a crime organization. This obviously doesn't sit well with him, and he goes after her, working his way to the top of the ring to rescue her.

Everything is in place for a halfway decent Steven Seagal vehicle. It's all there. Seagal was only a few years into his direct-to-video era, and he still has his moves, his looks, and his swagger, but there are whole stretches of the film where he doesn't have his voice. This is one of a handful of films he starred in where he didn't do his ADR (voice-over dubbing) work, so there are entire scenes where he's talking with someone else's voice. It's incredibly tacky. The action scenes are good, however. The final battle between him and the lead villain (played by Matt Schulze from *The Transporter*) involves swords, and the choreography is solid. *Out of Reach* should make most of Seagal's fans reasonably happy, and while it's not entirely distinctive, it gives Seagal a chance to show his softer side as he plays several key scenes with children. Directed by Po-Chih Leong, who also did *The Detonator* with Wesley Snipes.

Outside the Law

(a.k.a. **Blood Run**)

1994 (Image DVD) (djm)

Alcoholic detective Brad Kingsbury (David Bardley) is brought on a case involving a murdered young woman, who may or may not have been slain by her lover, a bisexual vixen named Tanya Borgman (Anna Thomson), who makes it very clear that she has several unplayed cards up her proverbial sleeve. Kingsbury, who is failing as a father and as a policeman, spirals into obsession in the case, and finds himself drawn to Borgman's world, ultimately succumbing to his lust and sleeping with her. As he loses himself in her sultry embrace, he also loses his grip on the case, and a surprise springs itself on him, revealing the killer to be someone he wasn't expecting.

In the wake of *Basic Instinct* and the Sharon Stone-esque erotic thrillers of the early 1990s, *Outside the Law* presents no new twists or spins on the well-worn genre, but it does give David Bradley (of the *American Ninja* sequels) a chance to delve into the cop procedural genre, with room to flex his acting muscles a little bit. Director Boaz Davidson (who's produced dozens of action films under the Nu Image/Millennium banner) had a difficult time with Bradley on the set, and Bradley refused to perform in sex scenes with actress Thomson, who was given a body double in the erotic scenes. At this point in Bradley's short career as an action star, he was already veering away from the martial arts and doing erotic-type thrillers. He was also in *Exit* with Shannon Whirry.

Outside the Law

2001 (Sony DVD) (djm)

Cynthia Rothrock plays a secret agent named Julie Cosgrove who is burned by her superiors while on a job in Colombia, and she's hunted down for knowing too much. Her fiancé is murdered, and she flees to Florida to sort out her options, but before becoming comfortable, she reluctantly gets pulled into helping out a couple of people who need protection from a local drug dealer and advice on how to stop him from getting away with murder. The drug dealer (Jeff Wincott) is basically a woman-beating bully who has no idea what he's up against when Rothrock steps into his world, and even the local law enforcement (represented by a smarmy Dan Lauria, the best actor in the film) is clueless with how to deal with her. The drug cartel calls a topnotch enforcer (played by James Lew) to come in and deal with Rothrock personally, and she makes everyone understand that not only is she a contender, but that she operates . . . *Outside the Law!*

A decent set-up and opening act becomes diluted with stilted situations and a dull script. Rothrock is good in a part that seems tailor-made for her, but the draggy pace only picks up slightly when Lew shows up in the last act. Wincott doesn't get in on any of the action, which is a disappointment, but it's nice to see him in another Rothrock vehicle (they were in *Martial Law II* together as partners). Jorge Montiesi directed.

Overkill

1995 (Vidmark VHS) (djm)

"I prefer a stand-up fight any day to the one we're playing."

Known for his use of excessive force and disregard for rules, narcotics cop Jack Hazard (Aaron Norris in his one-shot action movie vehicle) is given a mandatory vacation leave. He decides to go to South America to drink mojitos on the beach, and maybe he'll get laid, but another American notices his badge and begins to pester him to help him with a problem he has. Hazard shrugs the desperate guy off, but when he literally stumbles upon the poor guy getting beat up by a thug, he steps in and teaches the attacker a lesson. As it turns out, the guy he saves has been targeted by some corrupt policemen who are working for a rich businessman (played by Michael Nouri), who has staged a "most dangerous game" where he and some others are planning to hunt some tourists through the jungle for the hell of it. Once Hazard gets involved, the stakes get higher because it's obvious that he can handle himself, and the hunters quickly become the hunted as Hazard sets elaborate traps (a little *too* elaborate, if you ask me) to thin the herd.

If we lived in another dimension and if things worked out just a little differently, Aaron Norris would have been a big "B"-movie star and his brother Chuck would have been Aaron's go-to director on all his films. While you're watching *Overkill* you're bound to do a double-take or two and marvel at how similar Aaron is/was to his brother—at least in 1995. He has the mullet, the face, the voice, the attitude, and even the martial arts skills that Chuck did at the time, and it's absolutely dumbfounding to me that Aaron didn't do at least a half a dozen more movies. As far as I'm concerned, this is a Chuck Norris movie with a dude who might as well be Chuck Norris. It's uncanny. The movie's got a lot in store for fans of the genre, and Aaron kicks ass. His character isn't really all that likable, but so what? He's on vacation and he didn't want to be bothered, and he's disgruntled through the whole thing, and I would be too if I'd had to set traps in the jungle instead of getting laid by the local talent. Director Dean Ferrandini never directed another movie, but he worked on the stunts for a slew of pictures directed by Aaron.

Over the Top

1987 (Warner DVD) (djm)

"Here we are, ladies and gentleman! We're approaching the most important event of this unique and exciting competition. The final phase in the world of arm wrestling—we call this OVER THE TOP!"

Sylvester Stallone made headlines when he accepted Cannon's exorbitant offer of millions to star in this movie that puts arm wrestling at its center and tries to (more or less) retell the story of *The Champ*. Stallone plays down-on-his luck humble everyman Lincoln Hawk, a loner truck driver who left the lap of luxury behind when he left his rich wife, who had just had their son Michael. Years later, Hawk's ex-wife (Susan Blakely) is dying and her final wish is for Michael (David Mendenhall) to get to know his father, and so Hawk surprises his son at his graduation from a military academy. Embarrassed by his blue-collar, out-of-nowhere dad's appearance, bratty Michael is affronted by his father, who desperately tries to make a connection with his boy. As they're traveling on the road to meet up with Michael's mother at the hospital, Hawk reveals himself to be a bit of a hustler as he takes on challengers in diners and truck stops to arm wrestle for cash prizes. Further offended, Michael leaves his dad and goes to live with his cash-heavy uncle Jason Cutler (a disgruntled Robert Loggia who never seems to *not* growl in every scene he's in), who forbids Hawk from ever seeing his son again. After a violent confrontation with some of Cutler's bodyguards, Hawk is arrested and jailed, but he's released under the stipulation that he will relinquish custody rights to Cutler, who agrees to pay his bail in that case. Hawk relents and goes to Las Vegas to compete in the "Over the Top" arm-wrestling championship where some seriously ogerish dudes compete to win $100,000, plus a brand new big-rig truck. Hawk's biggest competition is the hulking Bull Hurley (Rick Zumwalt), who towers over him . . . and plays dirty. Just when the tables are turning against Hawk, his repentant son finds his way to the tournament and cheers dad on.

I probably watched this movie twenty-five times growing up. There's something about Stallone's humility in the film that appeals to me, especially since the other Stallone film I watched over and over growing up was *Rambo: First Blood Part II*, where he's mowing down Russians with machine guns. Lincoln Hawk is a great character for him, and even watching it in today's cynical, make-fun-of-everything world, I refuse to retrofit my opinion of it because it's the perfect '80s star-driven vehicle where one man's stardom really defines the film and gives it more than any other "actor" could have given it. The original story of the film (by Gary Conway, who wrote *American Ninja 2*) was reportedly much darker and less sensational than Stallone's revision, but I like it this way. It's predictable, but endearing (to a fault, maybe), and Stallone shines in it. The soundtrack is jam-packed with pop rock songs that glorify America, and the whole film and everything about it is the epitome of Reagan-era decadence, and yet . . . it's still a very small film, with a little story, and that's what makes it so great. A number of body builders and wrestlers are featured in the cast, including Magic Shwarz and Terry Funk. Several of these guys also appeared in the Cannon film *Penitentiary III*, starring Leon Isaac Kennedy, which was made soon after this.

Pacific Inferno

1979 (Gemstone DVD) (CD)

"That's all fine, Totoy, but I ain't no hero."

It's the final days of World War II and troops are about to leave the Philippines. Clyde Preston (Jim Brown) is a diver in the US Navy who is coerced into leading a small team of divers into Manila Bay to search for the sixteen million dollars in silver General MacArthur dumped there in order to keep it from falling into the hands of the Japanese. Clyde and his group want to destroy the whole project but can't do it alone. They must team up with the local resistance movement if they are to have any chance against the Red Army. The Japanese begin to catch on to their plan, so Clyde and his team will have to move quickly if they want to get away with their lives and stop the enemy once and for all.

Jim Brown (*Mars Attacks, Black Gunn*) doesn't play the type of characters who do well when forced into doing anything. That said, he plays Clyde Preston as sort of a reserved guy who takes the nice approach, plotting and planning until he finds the right moment to strike. Directed by Rolf Bayer (*The Kill*) and shot in the Philippines, *Pacific Inferno* is a movie strictly for hardcore fans of Brown's. With an intriguing story and strong performances, it's a shame the movie wasn't more exciting. Thankfully, in the last act, things pick up a notch and Brown does what he does best: he takes out a handful of armed Japanese soldiers with his bare fists and charges through even more of them with a bomb tucked under arm, much like his early days in the NFL.

The Pacifier

2005 (Disney DVD) (djm)

Navy SEAL Shane Wolfe (Vin Diesel) is wounded on a superspectacular mission, and as a result, the man he was supposed to protect went missing. On the rebound, Shane is assigned to the missing man's household where he's supposed to protect his family (namely five rambunctious children, one of whom is still a baby) and search for a secret disc that has military secrets. Over several weeks, Shane whips the kids into shape and teaches them respect and discipline (while learning to change diapers and tell bedtime stories) using his ultra strict military code of "It's my way—the highway is not an option!" By the end of his tenure of babysitting, he's learned to love the kids—and they him—and he saves the day and keeps the country safe by thwarting the bad guys who threaten them all.

A surprise hit when released theatrically and subsequently to video, *The Pacifier* was clearly a smart move for the then-burgeoning action star Diesel, who had found success with *Pitch Black, The Fast and the Furious*, and *xXx*. *The Pacifier* is just cute enough and has *just* enough action in it to satisfy Diesel's fans, while creating new ones in the kid and family demographic, who will most likely find

P

this really entertaining. It doesn't pander to its audience, but instead treats its viewers fairly by allowing Diesel to mostly play it straight while softening his tough image a little bit, which is fine. I'm glad he didn't keep making more movies like this the way The Rock did with movies like *The Tooth Fairy*, but if he had, he probably would have had even more blockbusters. From director Adam Shankman.

The Package

2012 (Anchor Bay DVD) (djm)

Tommy Wick (Steve Austin) is a good-hearted bruiser who collects debts for his boss, a small-time bookie and businessman. If a guy needs his nose broken for not paying up, Tommy is the man to call. When Tommy is told to deliver a package to The German (Dolph Lundgren), Tommy doesn't hesitate. But there's a problem: some thugs who work for another crime boss try to take the package from him before he delivers it. What's the package? Whatever it is, it's contained in a diary, wrapped with rubber bands. And Tommy doesn't let *anyone* take it away from him. But the plot thickens: The German is dying of some kind of disease, and Tommy's rare blood type is a perfect match for The German's, so the package is, in fact, Tommy himself. Once he figures this out, the movie gets that much more compelling.

Some great action guys star in this film. Austin gets the hero role, and he plays it at about the best of his abilities as an actor. He utters short sentences, he stands his ground when guys try to beat him up, and he gets the last word. Lundgren can play The German role in his sleep. He looks tired and pale, stabs and shoots guys, and he mixes a smoothie while people painfully die around him. Jerry Trimble from *Live By the Fist* makes an auspicious return to action as a thug who has a nice little fight with Austin in an alley. Darren Shahlavi from *Bloodmoon* and *Ip Man 2* also has work to do in the film as a mercenary sent to kill Austin's character, and he and Austin have a fight scene by a pool that ends too soon. All of that should make this movie better, but for whatever reason, the pacing and energy is slow and lethargic. There's no "*Wow!*" moment when there should have been at least two or three with this cast. All of the fights in it go like this: A guy hits, the guy he's hitting takes the hits and then hits back, and back and forth until a guy is down or dead. It was directed by Jessie V. Johnson, who has made better movies like *The Fifth Commandment* (with Rick Yune) and *The Last Sentinel* with Don Wilson.

INTERVIEW:

JESSE JOHNSON

(djm)

So few directors working in the direct-to-video market are giving it their best when tasked with helming actioners starring the likes of Jean-Claude Van Damme, Steven Seagal, or "Stone Cold" Steve

Director Jesse Johnson in Sherman Oaks, California. Photo by david j. moore.

Austin. One such filmmaker is Jesse Johnson. The nephew of the infamous stuntman Vic Armstrong, Johnson has been in the movie business for several decades, working as a stuntman and stunt coordinator on big films like Charlie's Angels, Mission Impossible III, *and* The Amazing Spiderman. *He began his journey as a director when he directed the low budget direct-to-video film* Pit Fighter, *starring Dominiquie Vandenberg. Other impressive titles on Johnson's resume as a director are* Alien Agent *with Mark Dacascos,* The Last Sentinel *with Don "The Dragon" Wilson,* The Fifth Commandment *with Rick Yune, and 2012's* The Package, *starring Steve Austin and Dolph Lundgren. Clearly, Johnson is building an impressive list of action films, all starring some of the best in the business.* .

How did The Last Sentinel come about as a project for you? It was a really good vehicle for Don, one of his best.

I was called in. They had a director and they had a script, they'd actually been on preproduction on it. Don Wilson, who was the lead actor, had found the money. Basically he'd had a falling out with the director. I drove over there and listened to him and got him talking about himself, which is pretty easy to do with Don . . . he'd talk about the fight game and get very excited

Promo artwork for *The Last Sentinel*. Author's collection.

and animated. I'd written the script for *The Last Sentinel* a few years earlier for a friend of mine, Dominiquie Vandenberg [*Pit Fighter*], but we'd never been able to finance it. It was about a guy who didn't speak a lot, had a lot of shooting, martial arts, action in it. I worked really, really hard with Don. We tried to surround him with as many solid actors as possible.

You've worked on some huge movies as a stunt coordinator. How was it to transition from bigger films to this low-budget action movie?

We don't really approach anything too differently. Obviously, people are being paid a lot more on those bigger ones, but you don't ever try to water it down. You approach it with the same level of professionalism. Rehearsal time. It's really a mental mindset. You commit to something even if it's a slightly smaller scale. You're not gonna have fifty guys, you're gonna have five. You try to make it as good as possible. I'm very lucky in that I can go backwards and forwards between the two types. When I did *The Package*, I was coming off *The Master* and *Lincoln*, which I helped put together the big battle scene at the beginning. I did *Thor* with Kenneth Branagh. I've had the opportunity to work with some of the best directors, not only alive, but in the history of filmmaking. I'm able to watch them and their techniques, and then apply them to my kind of movies. The economy at that level is incredible. When you're talking about Spielberg, you're talking about one take and move on, but there's an awful lot of rehearsal time and preparation. You're talking about someone who's at the very top of their game, but there's no sense of waste or no sense of them throwing money at things to fix them. That's the wonderful thing you come away with. You're also talking about incredible humility that these guys have at that level. Yes, the budgets are different, but you don't change your mindset when you're making a movie.

When do you think you'd finally found your niche or your style as a filmmaker?

I'm still learning.

I liked The Fifth Commandment. Rick Yune did a solid job in that. He wrote it and produced it as well, right?

It was certainly his baby. I worked enormously hard on it. We stepped off the plane in Thailand—myself, the ADm and Rick, and there was a huge Thai crew that was assigned to us. We tried to make as good a film as possible. Rick was the boss, and also the lead actor, which, at the time, I wasn't really equipped mentally to deal with. It's good to know whom you're serving. He asked me to make my kind of movie, and then would change his mind beforehand. What he should really do is direct a film himself. He should get an AD to trust him, and a stunt coordinator to work with him, perhaps a second unit director who can guide him because he has such a clear idea of what he wants. He could probably do that. We had a blast doing it. I felt there were elements in the story that should have been strengthened before we shot, but at the end of the day it was probably a journeyman production for me.

P

Are the films you've directed designed to be released directly to video? I saw _The Package_ in a theater, but it was the only theater showing it.

In my mind, they're all destined for the movie theater. You cannot go out and aim to make a direct-to-DVD movie. You can't do that. If you start honing yourself back and second-guessing . . . there are some people who work that way, but not me. I go out there, and I make the best damn movie I possibly can. The best performances, the best camera angles, the best action. I do everything it takes, and I take it very personally. You are held back by your cost sometimes because it's very expensive to release a movie in theaters. If you have a cast that has made movies theatrically and has failed theatrically, or if you have direct-to-DVD names, no one is going to release it theatrically. You know that going in.

You've worked with a lot of action guys who've made movies in the theatrical release world, but whose stars have fallen and now exclusively make movies for video. Talk about that.

There's a myriad of reasons why they make these movies. They have bills that need to be paid. Divorces, and trials and tribulations they go through. They say yes to a script that's terrible, which they know is terrible, and it's an ever-decreasing circle. There's very few who manage to buck that. Steve [Austin] is doing really well at the moment. He's being very careful about what he says yes to. The next three films he has to act in, he's also producing, which gives him creative control. We're talking about a script at the moment. He has an enormous amount of influence over it. This is exactly how you reinvent yourself, by taking control of these things. We were working on a fifteen-day schedule on _The Package_ . . .

You had a bunch of great action guys in that one: Jerry Trimble, Darren Shahlavi, Lundgren, and Austin. Talk about working with these guys.

What I like about Darren is that he's a guy who's continually honing his craft. He works like a madman five days a week at the gym learning these techniques. That's how you survive, that's how you create yourself. Darren is all of that. He's also working on his acting. To me, his performance in _The Package_ was so head and shoulders above what he did for me in _Alien Agent_, which I thought was good at the time. Jerry Trimble is the same way. I've worked with him as a stuntman in probably eight or nine movies. He's just a phenomenal human being with a broad scope of knowledge of humanity. This is a guy who's lived more lives than more people can hope to live. From "The Golden Boy" to being in Roger Corman pictures, to motivational speaker, and now working as a Hollywood stuntman. Most people would be happy to have one of those. I love him. I think he's fantastic.

Promo artwork for Jesse Johnson's _The Package_. Author's collection.

Talk about the personas of some of the guys you've worked with. They carry with them their reputations from their glory days as action stars.

I come from a stunt background where I've dealt with a lot of champions, fight guys, motorcycle guys, guys who are at the very top of their game. You talk to a champion a little differently than how you talk to a normal human being. They love being treated like normal people right up to the moment where you actually treat them like a normal human being. There's a certain amount of deference, but also a sense of simpatico in that they know what I've done before as well, so I can at least pretend that I can come close to what they've done. They're type "A" personalities. It takes a certain amount of energy to deal with them. If you engage these guys and look them in the eyes and talk to them . . . with Steve [Austin], I'd watched his earlier movies and I honestly couldn't get through most of them, and so when I sat with him on the set [of _The Package_], he'd been really working on the character, and I sat with him quietly, and I asked him, "What was the deal with the other movies? Because what you're doing here is acting, and when I watched your other movies I didn't see the Steve I'm seeing here." He said, "Yes, you've got no idea. They didn't even talk to me. They put me in a position where the tape was on the floor and then kind of walked off and left me to do my thing." The only thing that he could work out was that perhaps they were intimidated or scared by him.

He's untapped potential as far as I'm concerned.

That's _exactly_ what I felt, and it made me happy when I thought about it a little more. He's got incredible charm and an incredible sense of humor. It's very rangy, it's very distinct to south Texas, and he's a little nervous of it when he's around people who are ostensibly more educated or whatever. In actual fact, he's twice as smart as they are, and once you bring that out, it's a very sharp wit and very interesting. Most of the cool lines in _The Package_ weren't in the script. The lines that Steve gave were improv—he came up with those on set. They're wonderful. No one knows Steve like Steve does. If you're brave enough to kind of talk to him and engage him and find a common ground with him and a character and make him aware of that, you get a pretty cool performance. I think we can really do some stuff together. His first professional fight, he got paid forty bucks. I mean, these guys beat the shit out of each other. Pound for pound. They're performing like gladiators. Ground-pounding and smacking. He would also engage the audience. He would play the bad guy. Those guys know how to perform. If you can tap into that and bring it into the forefront, you're gonna have something really good. As you said, he's got so much untapped potential.

Talk about _Alien Agent_ with Mark Dacascos.

I did two for SyFy: _The Last Sentinel_ and _Alien Agent_. There were certain things that were required of them like monsters . . . I dunno . . . I would love to work with Mark again. I worked my balls off on that script. The only thing they let me touch was the action. There's way too much dialogue in it. You don't need action stars talking about their inner self. Especially with someone who's as good an actor as Mark Dacascos is. He can do that page of dialogue with a look over and a look back, and the audience feels it. We had a very overwritten script in terms of dialogue. I rewrote the action, and I think we had some fun action in it. But action without story is nothing; it's the worst thing in the whole world. When you talk to film buffs and talk about the best action sequences, they'll say Shane for the gunfight, and all of those films were an hour and fifteen minutes of character development and then an action scene. You feel the jeopardy that they're in. You feel the excitement when they overcome. That's why that action scene worked so beautifully. The films were not personal for me at this point. They didn't get personal until _The Butcher_, which if there is ever a film I would like to go back and remake, it would be _The Butcher_. We did that film in such a hurry. I sat down with Eric Roberts and we went through the script with a red pencil and took out huge chunks of the movie because we didn't have the time to do it all, which was very sad for me. That was my homage to the '70s action movies like _Point Blank_.

The year 2013 was a really bad year for action stars and their movies. Big action guys like Stallone, Schwarzenegger, and Statham all had flops. Why do you think that is?

It's not just 2013. You're talking about an audience who at one time had nothing else but VHS action movies or DVDs to have a look at, but there are now beautifully designed and wonderfully animated videogames, and you're competing with these things. And the audience has stopped going to movie theaters. Why should someone pay to see someone blow things up when you can be immersed in a first-person shooter at home? Especially if the movie's story is not that good. The big and dumb movies are done. At one point, these guys filled theaters. But now their audience is playing videogames. The only way to get them back in is to raise the level and the quality of the movie. That's my theory why movie theaters are being taken over by the _Twilight_-type movies. Pictures like _The Package_ are a hell of a lot of fun. It's made money for the guys who produced it, so it's found its market.

Is there anything else you want to add about any of your movies?

Well, I hope people enjoyed _The Package_. In terms of it being a complete movie, I really do enjoy it. If anyone wants to know me through my work, I highly recommend watching it. But the next one is going to be even better. At the moment, what I'm desperately trying to do is to take a film that has action in it, and make it personal, and make it important to me, to make it resonate with an audience to a degree where they don't notice the budget. It's taken me six or seven pictures to learn that craft.

Pain & Gain

2013 (Paramount DVD) (CD)

"Jesus Christ himself has blessed me with many gifts, one of them is knocking someone the fuck out."

Bodybuilders Adrian (Anthony Mackie) and Daniel (Mark Wahlberg) hatch a scheme to get wealthy entrepreneur Victor Kershaw (Tony Shaloub) to sign over his fortune to them. In order to make sure all the bases are covered, they enlist the help of ex-convict Paul (Dwayne Johnson), who has become a born-again Christian. Daniel seems to think he has everything figured out, but intelligence isn't his strong point. Each of the men comes to the situation with a unique perspective: Daniel believes in the American way, Adrian must deal with his steroid-induced impotence, and Paul is now a full-blown believer. The one thing holding the three of them together is their devotion to bodybuilding. They go ahead with their crazy plan only to have their stupidity shine through and crack the plan wide open. The kidnapping is just the beginning of their descent into crime as each of the three quickly becomes unhinged.

Though the film feels like it runs a bit too long, *Pain & Gain* is actually director Michael Bay's best film. It's nowhere near great, but it's saved by the strong performances from the three leads. Thankfully for us, Dwayne Johnson (*The Tooth Fairy*) is far more successful at stealing the film than his character is at kidnapping. Johnson proves he can do it all. He's fantastic at action, can pull off being funny without trying, and is genuinely a good actor. He only has one real brawl, which takes place as a flashback to his time in prison. The fight is also of note since it featured an uncredited appearance by one of Johnson's former WWE pals, Kurt Angle (*Death from Above*). Apart from the fight, Johnson's character goes on a downward spiral and steals every moment he's on the screen. The film's based on a true story, and it might be interesting to see just how closely it mirrored the real events.

Paper Dragons

1996 (Trinity DVD) (djm)

Two hoodlums (played by Jeremy Renner and this film's director and writer Adolfo Swaya) double-cross a drug lord and kill some of his enforcers, and as they try to escape the drug lord's wrath, only Paul (played by Swaya) manages to escape. With his partner in crime dead, Paul hides at a monastery, where the monks are practicing kung fu. The head monks (played by James Hong and Victor Wong, both who were in *Big Trouble in Little China* together) are at odds on what to do with the

fugitive. When it's decided that he will stay and learn the ways of Buddhism and practice martial arts while he's hiding out, Paul quickly adapts to the lifestyle of a monk by shaving his head, eating little, and doing chores and meditating regularly. He learns martial arts from a young monk (played by Ernie Reyes Jr.) and he gets good enough at it that when two dirty cops on the drug lord's payroll come looking for him, he's ready to fight for his life and defend the monastery from impending violence.

Somehow, *Paper Dragons* feels like a very personal effort from Adolfo Swaya, who casts himself in the lead. He surrounds himself with competent and dependable Asian actors, and it's always good to see the underrated action star Reyes Jr. in a nice supporting role. It's weird seeing a young Jeremy Renner in a thug role, but he's there so if you're a fan of Renner, then take a gander at him here in a small part. *Paper Dragons* is nothing spectacular or particularly special, and even with Reyes Jr. in it, it's (at best) a very slight and mild entertainment.

Paradise Alley

1978 (Universal DVD) (djm)

"Listen: I just bet a hundred bucks against that monkey, and I ain't got a dime. Now if you don't win, these creeps are gonna try to drag me in the alley and tie knots in my spine. Not that I can't handle it, but who needs the midnight exercise?"

After the enormous success of *Rocky*, Sylvester Stallone had some leeway in Hollywood, and he was able to write, direct, and star in the period piece drama *Paradise Alley*. Set in the 1940's in Hell's Kitchen, Stallone plays a scrapper named Cosmo Carboni, who encourages his younger brother—a hulking ice deliveryman with a heart of gold named Victor (played by real boxer Lee Canalito)—to wrestle at a dive called Paradise Alley for cash. They enlist their older brother Lenny (Armand Assante), a disabled World War II vet, to be Victor's manager, and off they go winning fights one right after another. Victor's showdown with a monster of a wrestler (played by real wrestling champion Terry Funk) goes for twenty-two rounds, ending in a spectacular climax.

Very unusual for a Stallone vehicle, *Paradise Alley* is a forgotten movie filled with snappy dialogue, realistic characters, and some solid acting by the whole cast. Stallone is the star, but Canalito, who plays his mentally slow muscular brother, is the real focus. He's a gentle giant, played with sensitivity, but as a fighter he's a bulldozer. Canalito didn't have much of a career in movies. Aside from his boxing career, he went on to star in the low-budget actioner *The Glass Jungle*. Hardcore fans of Stallone might not even know *Paradise Alley* exists. I remember seeing it when I was very young and not quite getting into it. Watching it now, I can appreciate it and see what a good writer and director he is. He also sings the title song, which is . . . adequate.

Parker

2013 (Sony DVD) (djm)

The best way for Jason Statham to stay in the big-league game of action heroism is by making movies for filmmakers in the "A" market. In the case of *Parker*, he starred under Taylor Hackford's direction. Hackford, who is known for films like *Against All Odds, Proof of Life*, and *Ray*, does a fine job giving Statham a solid vehicle to star in, and also making a fairly mainstream heist movie with crossover appeal. Statham plays an antihero named Parker, who is stiffed and left for dead by a crew of bad guys after a heist. Once recovered, he hatches a plan to stiff *them* after they pull off their next job—stealing fifty million in jewels in Palm Beach. In the mix is a desperate real estate agent (Jennifer Lopez), who figures out that Parker isn't who he says he is, and a mob assassin (Daniel Bernhardt) sent to kill Parker before he gets to his old crew.

The best scene in the film is the amazingly brutal fight scene between Statham and Bernhardt. Casting Bernhardt (*Bloodsport 2–4*) in this small role was an inspiration. Statham is usually really good in his films, but it immensely helps when he goes head-to-head with guys who are equally as skilled and imposing as he is. Parker is a good character, and the Donald Westlake stories that inspired him have been adapted for other films like *Point Plank* with Lee Marvin and *Payback* with Mel Gibson. This stuff is nothing new, but it's entertaining. Hackford is certainly capable of better, but matched with Staham, he seems to be having a pretty fun time.

Parole Violators

1994 (Digiview DVD) (djm)

Thug: "The fuck? Where the fuck did you come from?"
Miles: "Through the window, asshole!"

A former cop named Miles Long (all kinds of connotations there) has become a nighttime avenger, a vigilante who follows ex-cons around with his video camera, hoping that they'll violate their parole by robbing liquor stores or kidnapping someone. Needless to say, he gets on the nerves of every ex-con he comes in contact with. When Miles (played by stuntman-turned-action star Sean Donahue) begins following a just-paroled child-murderer thug named Chino, he eventually catches him trying to kidnap a little girl from a park, and the game is on. Chino retaliates by kidnapping the daughter of Miles's girlfriend (played by Pamela Bosley, who is willing to do just about anything a role requires of her). Miles goes off the rails and starts carrying his police-issued handgun again instead of his video camera. He goes straight for Chino's hideout and tries to rescue the little girl, but instead of getting retribution, Chino gets away and the girl nearly drowns and goes into a coma! With the girl in a coma at the hospital and his girlfriend beat up and bedraggled, Miles (who has also taken quite a beating) gives his plot of revenge one last

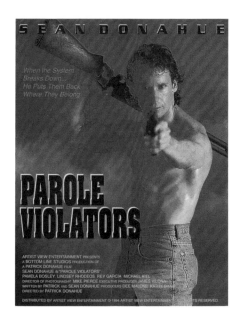

Video release poster for *Parole Violators*.
Author's collection.

engine rev and goes up against an entire gang of Chino's allies all by himself.

Heralded as a so-bad-it's-good masterpiece (like *Samurai Cop*, for example), *Parole Violators* has some undeniably goofy moments, but if you're watching it to study Sean Donahue instead of to make fun of it (which, admittedly, would be very easy to do), the movie has a gung-ho action heroism going on that should appeal to fans of these late '80s, early '90s "B" action movies with sex, nudity, explosions, and martial arts. It's got all that and some unintended humor, so there you go. Donahue gives the movie everything he's got, and he's a worthy action star for those interested. Directed by his father, Patrick.

Passenger 57
1992 (Warner DVD) (djm)

Cutter: "Charlie, you ever play roulette?"
Charles: "On occasion."
Cutter: "Well, let me give you a word of advice—always bet on black."

John Cutter (Wesley Snipes) is a self-assured security specialist who is aboard a plane when master criminal Charles Rane (Bruce Payne) is escorted onto the plane by two FBI agents taking him to Los Angeles in handcuffs. As Rane breaks free of his bonds and stages a hostage takeover of the plane (he has inside help with weapons), only Cutter can match Rane's intensity, and when Cutter defuels the plane mid-air, Rane is forced to land the plane, setting the next stage for their tête-a-tête. Once on the ground, Cutter manages to get Rane off the plane, leading to a chase through an amusement park. Once they're both on board the plane again, the film finds Cutter going head to head with Rane's crew of hired terrorists (who include Elizabeth Hurley), and finally Cutter can face Rane himself, which yields a fun beatdown that Rane clearly deserves.

"Always bet on black": Wesley Snipes (left) plays John Cutter and Bruce Payne (right) plays Charles Rane in *Passenger 57*. Author's collection.

Wesley Snipes headlines the Warner Brothers film *Passenger 57*. Author's collection.

Other than for *Blade*, Wesley Snipes is probably best known for this film. At a fleet pace and short running time (eighty-four minutes), *Passenger 57* emulates the Joel Silver-produced blockbusters of the era like *Die Hard* and the *Lethal Weapon* sequels (complete with a Michael Kamen-esque score by Stanley Clarke). If you pay attention, you'll notice the shortcomings and the lack of overkill so common in films of its type, but it keeps its focus on Snipes, whose first out-and-out action film this was. He uses martial arts quite a bit, which was a departure for him at the time. Before this film, he was known for dramas like *New Jack City* and *White Men Can't Jump*. Bruce Payne, who adds a lot to the film as the psychotic villain, went on to play numerous bad guys in movies like *Sweepers* with Dolph Lundgren and *One Man's Justice* with Brian Bosworth. Directed by Kevin Hooks, who did the TV movie *Irresistible Force* with Cynthia Rothrock the next year.

The Patriot
1998 (Touchstone DVD) (djm)

Dr. Wesley McClaren (played by Steven Seagal) is an immunologist who lives in a quiet Montana community where some militant white supremacists are stirring up a storm of trouble when they get their hands on a deadly virus, which they use to infect the town with hopes of garnering attention and a ransom for a cure that they have and think will work. The townspeople rapidly become infected and start dying, but McClaren and his daughter (played by young Camilla Belle, who would grow up to be a starlet) are immune. The military gets involved and suddenly the town looks like an apocalyptic zone with Hazmat-suited soldiers walking around, quarantining the whole area. McClaren kills some bad guys while trying to find a cure, which he realizes is linked to the flowers he uses in the tea he drinks. The final scene shows helicopters dropping loads of flower pedals down on the town, alerting everyone to use them in their tea.

There's a good reason why *The Patriot* ended up being the first movie Seagal starred in that was not released in theaters. It's very skimpy on action, and it's nearly ninety minutes of dramatic suspense, with nary an action set piece or a "wow" moment for Seagal to engage in. Directed by famed cinematographer Dean Semler, who filmed *Razorback* and *The Road Warrior*, *The Patriot* is a beautiful-looking film, but it's kinda boring. It premiered on cable TV and then shortly thereafter made its way to video. Seagal's days on the big screen were virtually over, but Joel Silver would give him a chance at a comeback with *Exit Wounds* not long after. Incidentally, Jean-Claude Van Damme had his first direct-to-video release with the costly *Legionnaire* around the same time as *The Patriot*. This was clearly a time of transition for action stars. Semler's next directing effort was *Firestorm* for Fox, starring football star Howie Long.

Penitentiary
1979 (Xenon DVD) (djm)

Marten "Too Sweet" Gordone (Leon Isaac Kennedy in the role that made him a bona fide action star) is at the wrong place at the wrong time, and in a blink of an eye he finds himself an inmate at a penitentiary for years of his life. The warden runs an illegal boxing ring among the fittest, most able prisoners, and Too Sweet volunteers to fight because he knows he'll gain favor with the warden, and the prisoners will respect him and leave him be if he can defeat the reigning champ Half Dead Johnson (Badja Djola), who is a monstrous, molesting beast of a convict. Too Sweet's journey to the top is a trek through hell, but he manages to keep his dignity and his humanity intact as he makes it through.

This first entry in Jamaa Fanaka's exploitation trilogy is leagues better than its sequels for dozens of reasons, mainly because its foundation comes from a humble, hungry, and independent spirit. Shot for peanuts by film school students while Fanaka was still learning how to make films, *Penitentiary* is a grungy, yet winning story about a guy whose destiny takes a turn for the worse, but he overcomes despite it all. Star Kennedy went on to become a busy action star with films like Cannon's *Body and Soul* and MGM's *Lone Wolf McQuade* under his belt before leaving the movie business behind to become a Christian minister. Good for him.

P

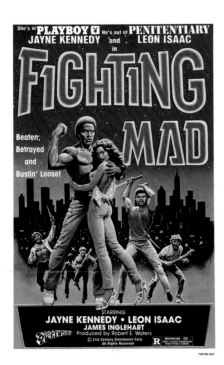

Theatrical poster for *Fighting Mad*. Author's collection.

INTERVIEW:

LEON ISAAC KENNEDY

(djm)

For a time, Leon Isaac Kennedy was one of the leading African American actors in cinema. He had starred in a major hit, the independent prison boxing film Penitentiary, *released in 1979. A resounding success,* Penitentiary *spawned two sequels, the last of which was financed and distributed by The Cannon Group, which had already dealt with Leon on the boxing film* Body and Soul *(1981). He went on to co-star alongside Chuck Norris and David Carradine in* Lone Wolf McQuade *(1983), and would write and produce the film* Knights of the City *(1986), which remains his greatest heartbreak in his career in the motion picture industry. He had humble beginnings, working his way up from a disc jockey, and then through several television programs, finally landing his big break in Cirio Santiago's jungle action film* Death Force *(a.k.a.* Fighting Mad, *1978), and he later married his co-star in that film, Jayne Kennedy. Although Leon has since retired from acting and gone into ministry, his mark in the exploitation and action film market remains undeniably undisputed.*

Tell me a little bit about your background and how you became involved in the movie business.

I'm from Ohio. When I was in the 10th grade, I was on my way to always thinking I was going to be a doctor. That's what I thought and that's what my family thought. I had always gotten good grades, and schoolwork always came easy to me. And so we had a pre-med class for people who were interested in that type of thing. In one week, things changed. They took us to a hospital and the hospital was rather depressing with

the smell and so on, and within the same week some people asked me to be in the school play. I enjoyed being in that play. So I changed course that week and announced to all my friends that I was going to be a movie star, a writer, and a producer. However, at that time there weren't many roles available for dark-skinned blacks, let alone a light-skinned black. The industry would usually use a dark-skinned black over a light-skinned black to let everyone know that, "Hey, we're using a black person." So I had to come up with a plan in order to be a movie star. The plan was to become an on-air personality, then I'd get my own TV show, and from there I would work my way into doing movies. So I was a fifteen-year-old kid with a plan. When you don't have a plan it's like being on an elevator and you want to get to the seventh floor but you don't push that seventh-floor button. Somebody else will get on that elevator and push the button for the basement, ninth floor, or penthouse, so you end up going up and around but you never get to your seventh floor. I followed my plan, which called for a third-class license to be a disc jockey. If you are a DJ back east, you were a sort of movie star at that time. Long story short, nine months later I became the weekend DJ and the youngest DJ in the history of Cleveland. By the time I was eighteen, I had a TV show but it wasn't until I was twenty that I had a syndicated TV show called *Outta Sight*, which was something like *Laugh-In*, a comedy show with sketches with musical entertainment. *Outta Sight* became the first syndicated black show in television history —years before *Soul Train* became syndicated. So I was following my dream, working out my plan, and then finally I came out to Los Angeles and started working towards movies, and by the time I was twenty-four I ended up being in major motion pictures.

What are your memories of making your first movie, *Fighting Mad*?

My head gets cut off in that particular film. They had to do a mold of my face, so they had to put some kind of mixture on my face and make a mold of it. They didn't get it quite right; when they pulled it off my face, it was pulling my eyelashes and my eyebrows off, and I thought maybe they were pulling my eyelids off. It was excruciating. (Laughing.) I didn't want to holler because I was playing a macho part! Jayne came running into the room and said, "You've got to stop doing that! Just cut it off of him!" That was one memory.

You're best known for playing Too Sweet in the *Penitentiary* trilogy. How did the first movie come your way?

As far as *Penitentiary* goes, I did not know [director] Jamaa Fanaka. I think he came to one of my clubs or something or maybe he knew me as a disc jockey. Long story short, he left a script for me, and it was *Penitentiary*. At that time the Too Sweet role was not offered to me. It was offered to Glynn Turman, one of my favorite actors and the star of *J.D.'s Revenge*. The other role of the guy who was deflowered, Eugene, was the role Jamaa had in mind for me. Nevertheless, I prepared myself for the role of

Eugene. However, I wanted to do the part of Too Sweet so I prepared for the possibility of playing that role as well.

How did you approach the role of Too Sweet, not really knowing if you would actually get that role?

I wasn't as spiritual then as I am now, but I still believed in positive prayer, positive action, and positive thoughts to get positive results. Wanting the role of Too Sweet and preparing for the role of Too Sweet are two different things. So I decided to really get into shape. I started going to the gym three or four times a week to build my physique. I also began rehearsing the part of Too Sweet just in case I got that call. When they were not able to pay Glynn the amount he wanted . . . . the first *Penitentiary* film was done with a very small budget, and Glynn said he couldn't take the role for the amount offered, and so he passed on it and said something about going on a honeymoon with Aretha [Franklin]. Glynn told Jamaa he would do something with him in the future. And Wilbur White, who played Sweat Pea said during rehearsals that I would make a great Too Sweet. Jamaa looked at me and asked, "You think you can play this part?" And I said, "I'm already ready for it." Then he said, "You think you can do all the boxing and fighting? Why don't you take your shirt off and let me see your muscles?" So I took my shirt off and the muscles popped out. You see, I wanted to forge my body like Bruce Lee, who is one of my heroes, and I achieved that level of definition and high-toned physique with my workouts. So then Jamaa says, "Well, let me see some of your boxing moves." Little did Jamaa know that my father had been a professional boxer. So naturally I knew a thing or two about boxing and I showed Jamaa a few boxing moves. After Jamaa saw what I could do, he said, "This is gonna be Too Sweet." And so that rehearsal was the beginning of a lifelong friendship. I loved Jamaa, his work, his family. We remained very close.

Describe the idea behind Penitentiary a little bit.

In the original script Too Sweet was supposed to get killed. But I suggested to the [director] Jamaa that we should infuse some hope into this movie. You know, why not have Too Sweet fight his way out of the penitentiary? Give some hope to other people by having a happy ending. Jamaa was open to this idea of mine. In the original script Too Sweet was supposed to fall in love with the prostitute that put him in jail. And I let Jamaa know that this would make Too Sweet look dumb. Jamaa protested saying, "There's got to be a love affair in the movie!" I said, "Let the love affair be between the old man and Too Sweet. Let the two of them bond." Jamaa loved this idea so he reedited the script and we were ready to roll. The whole idea of *Penitentiary* was, for me and Jamaa, to break into the film industry.

This film came out at the tail end of the blaxploitation era of films. Were you guys challenged at all by the fact that the movement had sort of moved on?

At the time, black exploitation films had come and gone, yes. Let me tell you my thoughts on black exploitation. From my point of view, black exploitation films were a wonderful training ground for black artists. You know, from black exploitation films came Richard Pryor, Cecily Tyson, Pam Grier, Rudy Ray Moore, and the list goes on and on. Despite this great wave of talent, the black community frowned upon the black exploitation film. So that's why so many people questioned the purpose of making *Penitentiary*. I told the naysayers that my purpose was to show how I could be a leading man and Jamaa could be a good director of a major motion picture. So we believed in our abilities but we had no money. With no money, I (although being the star) had to pay for the food for everybody. Also, we were kicked out of many shooting locations because we couldn't afford the location fees.

How long was the shoot for that film?

It took an extremely long time to shoot. We had to buy film loops called short ends and this caused huge time delays because you had to reload the camera constantly. Sometimes we worked sixteen- to twenty-hour days; it was exhausting. On my lunch break, I would go off by myself and, despite being extremely fatigued, I would imagine my name on a marquee and that would keep me going, baby! Despite the struggles, Jamaa would exude so much energetic enthusiasm that the actors and even the film crew—who were not very often getting paid— were energized and inspired to push on, work hard, and complete the film. Eventually, this tiring adversity of shooting the film paid off to the tune of eighteen million dollars in box-office sales. Made for less than half a million bucks, we had the last laugh.

You returned some years later for the sequel. Mr. T was your co-star in the film.

I knew Mr. T back when he worked as a bouncer in Chicago nightclubs. I remember the first time I saw him. He came walking in with this mohawk. I said, "Who in the heck is that?!" He was as flamboyant then as he was seen by the public later. Before he did *Penitentiary II*, Mr. T had already done *Rocky III*. Jamaa and I knew that he was going to be a huge star, so we decided to try and acquire Mr. T for *Penitentiary II*. Our thinking was, "Let's work with Mr. T, finish the film, and release it after *Rocky III* had its run in the theaters." We strongly suggested to the heads of United Artists that releasing *Penitentiary II* after *Rocky III* was not only a sound business decision, but a smart one. But unfortunately, when dealing with studio execs in charge of marketing, especially when it comes to promoting a "black film," they didn't know or understand the market or the promotional aspects of such a market. Those who released the first film knew how to nurse that film in coming out with different ad campaigns, in different sections of society. They knew the white market, the black market, the college market, they knew how to saturate the various markets with the appropriate advertising. So, regretfully, United Artists did not listen to our advice, and they released *Penitentiary II* before *Rocky III*.

Your next film was Cannon's *Body and Soul*, which was also a boxing film. That was a remake of a John Garfield movie. You also wrote this film. Talk about making this one.

They saw a niche for me, and they're really not looking for you to stretch that much. I had a meeting with Menahem Golan at Cannon. Basically, he said, "According to our research, if you take your shirt off and if you fight, and if you make love with some women, there's going to be a hit movie. So that's what we want. We want a boxing film, we want lovemaking, we want a strong lead. We're going to give you a million dollars to do it." The way that white executives looked at a so-called black movie, they didn't really look at the whole film. So many times you deliver a film and it's not at all what you wanted it to be. *Body and Soul* had some great emotions and things, but they were unfortunately cut out. But I think it's a good film.

***Penitentiary III* was your next film with Cannon. This one's pretty outrageous. It's the most "Cannonized" of the three films for sure.**

Penitentiary III was a long-awaited film. Every year we had gotten offers to do another one, but it depended on the budget. I'm talking with Menahem one day and pitching him an idea, which was another film with Chuck Norris. Chuck was tied up at the time, so Menahem said, "You know, Leon, why don't you do *Penitentiary III*? That's what we want. We want you to do it. Based on the title and your name, I can pre-sell it. We'll be in the profit before it even comes out." So I called Jamaa and brought him over and introduced him to Menahem, and he made both of us co-producers. I wrote a lot of that script and gave it to Jamaa to work it into the version that he was working on. It got homogenized together, and we ended up with a script that everybody was happy with. It was no longer just boxing. It went to another level.

This movie is so over the top. Only in the world of movies would this movie happen. It's crazy.

Correct!

One of the most important movies you made was Lone Wolf McQuade with Chuck Norris and David Carradine. What can you tell me about working on this movie?

That was one of the easiest going sets I have ever been on. Yoram Ben-Ami was the producer, and the director ran a smooth operation. Every single day was so effortless the way they did this film. Chuck is an A-1 gentleman. Always has been. I remember with that particular film, up for the part was O. J. Simpson, Carl Weathers, Howard E. Rollins Jr., so there were a lot of heavyweights that were up for the movie. My agent called and told me, "Well, they want you. You beat out everybody for the part. They did research and found out that you have a really big following all over the world." I was very happy to be in an action film with Chuck and David. When I got there, to show you what type of gentleman that Chuck is: He and Yoram were out at the airport at 10:30 that night to meet me and make me feel welcome. That's the way that was. Everybody was so nice, so cordial.

What do you remember about working with Chuck Norris on that film?

One of the things I remember is that Chuck and I used to work out in the morning. It was great fun to work out with him. He was a real champion when it came to martial arts. He had worked with Bruce Lee. I had never met Bruce, but he was one of my heroes. When I first saw *Enter the Dragon*, I said to myself, "That is one of the greatest athletes I have ever seen." I was fascinated to hear all of Chuck's Bruce Lee stories. In the interim, I was very good friends with Mohammed Ali. I had traveled all over the world with him, to Manila and to other countries. We were very good friends. Chuck was a big fan of Ali, so I would tell him Ali stories every morning as we were working out together. It was very hot in El Paso, but it was a great shoot to be on.

Any memories of working with David Carradine on that film?f

I had seen David maybe two months before he passed away. I was down at the Beverly Hills Hotel, and I was in the Polo Lounge, and he was sitting at the bar. I said hello to him, and he hugged me, and he looked at me and he said, "Leon, it's been over twenty years dammit! You still haven't changed!" He was always very cordial to me. We did not spend as much time as Chuck and I did. He was not as talkative as Chuck is. We enjoyed each other's company, and we respected each other. Every time we'd seen each other socially, we'd gone out of our way to talk with each other. As a matter of fact, we had also planned to do other films together, but just never found the right vehicle to make it work.

What do you think of this resurgence of Chuck Norris with all the one-liners and his career come-uppance with *Walker, Texas Ranger*?

I think it's great! Chuck never really went away. He had a long-lasting film career and the TV show. That's an interesting story: The TV show *Walker, Texas Ranger* is really *Lone Wolf McQuade* on TV. When we were doing that film, people approached Chuck, and then they asked me, if we would be interested in doing a TV series. At that time, neither one of us was interested in doing TV. Then years later, they did something—a pilot or something—with his son, actually called *Lone Wolf McQuade*, or something near to it, but I don't know what became of that. But, *Walker, Texas Ranger*, if you look at it, it's *Lone Wolf McQuade*.

How do you feel about your part in the movie? It's a relatively small role, and your part doesn't really kick in until at least halfway into it.

Well, that's the way it was written. The character is in and out, really. It was amusing to me because I think that character got shot three times in the same leg or something. I did mention it to Steve, the director. For whatever reason, they had me shot several times in the same area.

Did that movie help your career? Up to that point, you'd played the lead in the *Penitentiary* movies.

Yeah, I think it helped the career. First of all, I was glad to be in someone else's film than just my own. To be part of an ensemble piece with someone like Chuck who'd had a long string of hits, I thought it was a good thing to do.

You wrote and produced *Knights of the City*. Not a lot of people talk about this movie, but it was perfect for you.

Knights of the City was the film that broke my heart. After that, I really was thinking about doing some other things until I had enough money to totally produce a film, inside out. By that I mean this: I did a lot of different things. I starred, I wrote, I produced. If you have a script, you want to protect it, so you become the producer. If you're starring in something you wrote, you certainly want to protect it, so I became the producer. So, *Knights of the City* . . . I used to think that if you wrote it, produced it, and starred in it that you'd pretty much have total control. We delivered a class act film. We delivered a hit. That film should have made over a hundred million dollars, and gotten rave reviews. First of all, you've got to remember the climate. This was just after *Flashdance*. All the breakdancing movies had come out. Michael Jackson had just done "Beat It." I knew we had to get this film done quickly. One thing about Cannon films was that if they had an idea, they ran with it and got the film made quick and released to the marketplace. We had independent money behind *Knights of the City*. We shot it in Florida. We had over a hundred street kids doing street numbers, and I'm talking about some of the best street dancing you've ever seen. I had Sammy Davis Jr. come in. He was so busy back in those days. He was a supporter of *Penitentiary*. He went on Johnny Carson and told everyone that it was one of the best movies he'd ever seen. He told me back then, "If you ever want me, just let me know." When I was putting *Knights of the City* together, I had a character that was a street person, a wino. This character was like when I was growing up—there weren't a lot of homeless people, but every neighborhood had a wino, a bum that was out on the streets. I called him and I said, "Are you ready for an Academy Award performance? I just wrote what's going to get a nomination for you. At the end of the movie, we're going to find out that you're my father." He said, "I'm in! But the problem is that I only have three days in the whole year where I'm free." I told him that I'd work the film around him, that I'd fly him in and work him sixteen hours a day. It would be like he was there for two weeks. He was in. He gave a great performance. It would have brought tears to your eyes. But you never saw it in the movie! It got cut out. How in the hell can you cut Sammy Davis Jr. out of a movie? But that's what these people did. How can you cut some of the greatest breakdancing that you've ever seen? We had a killer soundtrack. Killer tunes by Stevie Wonder, KC and the Sunshine Band, Smokey Robinson, and many other people. We had the Fat Boys in there. Kurtis Blow. This would have broken

some rappers in films. None of this is in the film as it should have been. What happened was that after we shot it, the producer was charged with racketeering and laundering money, and he went to prison. The film got turned over to some associates. I wanted the film to be put out immediately. You gotta ride this wave. So, a whole year went by, and it took so long and it finally ended up being an independent deal. They finally made a deal with New World. At that point, New World had had some failures when it came to breakdance films, so they decided that it wasn't going to be a breakdance film. It's going to be a gang film. They cut out all the dance numbers, they cut out the music scenes. I said to them, "How could you do this? The reason why those other breakdance movies didn't do well is because the scripts were terrible. They weren't good films. I suppose if your last comedy didn't do well, you'd cut out all the damn jokes for your next comedy!" That's what they did with *Knights of the City*. It was certainly not the film that I delivered. Out of any film that I've ever been involved with, that was the very best one, and that was the one that hurt the most. Sammy died being a little peeved with me because he had given me the only three days off he had in the whole year, and he said to me, "Leon, how could you let them cut me out of the film?"

Is there an uncut version of the film that exists?

Unfortunately, no, it's gone.

What have you been up to since you retired from acting?

When people don't see you on the screen, it's like your whole life has stopped, but actually it hasn't. I've just transcended into other things. One of them is ministry. I have spent a great deal of my time in ministry. It started out as my way of giving back. Anything negative or tragic that had happened to me, it's really in reverse. God has been so good to me. I wanted to give back. The best way to do that was through the way of Jesus. So I go around the world speaking and doing what I can to help folks. That takes up a good 70 percent of my time. Then I've done my entrepreneurial things. I've done a lot of buying and selling houses. It really goes back to *Knights of the City*. I just wanted to make enough money so that if I really want to do something I can put up my own money and I can market it and distribute it myself, and no one is ever going to butcher one of my films ever again.

What would you like to say to your fans?

I'm a Hollywood historian. I have followed Hollywood from its very beginning. I always get a kick out of running into people who can give me interesting information. There are many stars that have been manufactured by Hollywood or agents and managers have helped push them to another level. With me, it was really the opposite. I was just the people's star. For some reason the public liked me and my films. So that was always quite touching to me. I was a star that the people made.

"Too Sweet" (Leon Isaac Kennedy) gets a boxing lesson from Mr. T (played by himself) in *Penitentiary II*. Author's collection.

Penitentiary II

1982 (Xenon DVD) (CD)

"I'm gonna be somebody, Ellen. I'm gonna get respect. I'm gonna talk to the kids about the insanity in this world. I'm gonna make a difference in this dirty, rotten world."

Too Sweet Gordone (Leon Isaac Kennedy) is freshly released from incarceration, now trying to get his life in order. He has moved in with his sister, her husband, and son. Things are good for Too Sweet—he even has a girlfriend he's madly in love with. As part of his probation, he has to work in a boxing gym, but he refuses the attempts of the owner to get him to box. He's sworn off boxing and wants to keep on the straight and narrow. His former cellmate and rival Half Dead (Ernie Hudson) is out of prison and has a score to settle with him. He kills Too Sweet's girlfriend, which begins to drive Too Sweet off the deep end. He reels himself in because he realizes he doesn't want to throw his life away: he wants to *be* somebody. With the help of Mr. T (Mr. T), Too Sweet again starts training to box. When he's ready, he finds himself as a visitor in the prison boxing circuit, fighting for respect in a world he had left behind.

Penitentiary II is an improvement over the first entry in the sense that it's not afraid to have some fun. Humor plays a much bigger part (both intentional and unintentional) and the motley cast of characters is much more colorful. Hell, the film features one of the most colorful personalities of the '80s in a major role, Mr. T (filmed after *Rocky III* but released before). He spends most of his time training Leon Isaac Kennedy's (*Hollywood Vice Squad*) Too Sweet to be a better boxer but he also has a great backroom brawl with Ernie Hudson (*The Crow*). Kennedy himself ups his energy and charisma level tenfold and delivers the type of memorable performance that is perfectly well balanced between acting and action. Writer/ director Jamaa Fanaka is back as the director, and he too had improved as an artist and delivers a fantastic action/exploitation hybrid.

Penitentiary III

1987 (Warner Bros. VHS) (CD)

"I'm nobody's pea brain. I'm nobody's property, and I always like to look a man straight in the eye when I tell him to kiss my ass."

Too Sweet (Leon Isaac Kennedy) has had it rough over the years. He was wrongfully sentenced to prison, only to be released and have his girlfriend murdered. Some time has passed and now things are good until his water is laced with a new drug that causes him to lose control during a match until he beats his opponent to death. Back in prison, he becomes a pawn for a gangster who wants him back on the boxing team. Too Sweet wants to hang up his gloves and never fight again. When his friend Roscoe (Steve Antin) is nearly murdered in the ring, Too Sweet needs to step up and set things right. With an unlikely coach, Sweet begins training to take on Hugo (Magic Schwarz). The training just might not be enough because these guys don't play by the rules.

Only Cannon Pictures could have brought a film like this to the screen. This is quite possibly one of the most bizarre action films to be released in the height of the 1980s action craze. Leon Isaac Kennedy (*Lone Wolf McQuade*) once again delivers a solid performance. His fighting style is much different in this film than the previous two. He incorporates a bit of the martial arts into his technique. There are two fights that really stand out in the picture, one of which pits Kennedy against the late Raymond Kessler who was a former wrestler known as the Haiti Kid. Kessler, a dwarf in fantastic shape, plays a monstrous character known as The Midnight Thud. Watching them fight is exciting and strange all at the same time. The final battle with Hugo is strange on a completely different level. Kennedy becomes a man possessed and looks like he's in need of an exorcism more than anything else. Jamaa Fanaka (*Penitentiary*) returns to direct and takes the film to a highly unlikely level of absurdness. This is a good thing since *Penitentiary III* is as crazy as they come and one you won't want to miss. Many actors in this film also appeared in Cannon's *Over the Top*, released around the same time.

Pentathlon

1994 (Anchor Bay DVD R2) (djm)

After winning the gold medal in the pentathlon event at the Olympics in Asia in 1988, East German athlete Eric Brogar (Dolph Lundgren) escapes his guards and coach (David Soul) and defects to the United States, but not before he is shot and his best friend is killed. Once in America, Eric loses his purpose and his drive for life, and when the Berlin Wall falls within a year's time, he realizes what a mistake he made by betraying

his country. His bitter coach goes on the warpath and kills Eric's father and plots to go to America to kill Eric as well. In the meantime (five years later), Eric has hit rock bottom: He's become a smoker and an alcoholic, spending his days working as a fry cook at a dive burger joint run by Roger E. Mosely (T. C. from *Magnum P.I.*). When Mosley figures out who his fry cook used to be, he gets excited and begins to motivate him into training again for the next Olympics. Working up his will to succeed and join the human race again, Eric trains harder than ever and reconnects with a former girlfriend (Renee Coleman), and the future seems bright. Just when he's beginning to turn over a new leaf, his former coach enters the picture in a *Die Hard*-style fashion: he has an organized crew, and they have a plan to frame Eric for the assassination of the German ambassador at a peace rally. Eric has to muster every ounce of courage and strength he has left to stop that from happening, while still protecting himself and his friends from the terrorists.

Not so much an "action" picture as it is a suspense film featuring Lundgren in a more-or-less dramatic role, *Pentathlon* has a strong opening act and a feeble finale that settles for a predictable and violent showdown. Lundgren pulls off a German accent and demeanor, and he deserves credit for taking the extra effort to create a three-dimensional character. We see him swimming, running, shooting, horse riding, and fencing, all convincingly. He also produced it. Bruce Malmuth (*Hard to Kill*) directed it.

Perfect Target

1996 (Platinum DVD) (djm)

A thin line separates this "B" action film from being an "A" action film. Sheldon Lettich, who is best known for *Only the Strong* with Mark Dacascos and *Lionheart* and *Double Impact* with Jean-Claude Van Damme, directed it, and it's fairly solid. Daniel Bernhardt stars as a washed-up expatriate hanging out in Latin America betting on cockfights when some former friends and colleagues ask him to join their team in protecting the reigning president of Santa Brava, a small, nearby country. He accepts, and when the president is assassinated on his watch, he is framed for the crime and is forced to retreat into the jungles where the guerrillas plan to depose the new president: the evil wife of the dead president. Bernhardt joins the revolutionaries and teaches them how to fight.

The villains are really good here. Robert Englund (in a non-horror role) is Bernhardt's backstabbing former boss, and the lead heavy is played by Brian Thompson from *Cobra* and *Lionheart*. Those two guys make a good team, and Bernhardt is well cast against them. This could very easily have been a movie starring Van Damme, but Bernhardt fits the bill quite well. The film looks good, is nicely paced and edited, and the score by David Michael Frank (*Above the Law, Showdown in Little Tokyo*) really elevates the movie and makes it better.

A fight in a dojo between Jeff Speakman (left) and James Lew (right) in *The Perfect Weapon*. Author's collection.

The Perfect Weapon

1991 (Olive DVD) (djm)

"It's break time, guys."

From the opening training montage (set to "I Got the Power" by C + C Music Factory), we can tell that the star, Jeff Speakman, is going to be interesting to watch. Speakman, an expert in kenpo, a full contact form of martial arts, made a handful of vehicle films before petering out, and his signature weapons of choice are sticks that he uses in lightning-fast fashion. The story for this one is supersimple. He plays a guy named Jeff (why complicate things?) who works construction and fondly remembers his adoptive father (Mako), who taught him kenpo to help discipline him. When he returns home to check up on family, he finds that his kenpo master is being bullied by the Korean mafia. When Mako is killed, Jeff does the obvious thing: he begins a quest for vengeance. He takes on a sort of kid sidekick (smart aleck Dante Basco from *Blood and Bone*), who is street-wise and knows the right people. The Korean mafia has a strongman named Tanaka (played by . . . Toru Tanaka), who head-butts people to death. The final fight between him and Jeff is okay, but the film has some great fight scenes between Jeff and lots of other guys, including James Lew (*American Ninja 5*).

Speakman was supposed to be the next great hope for action movies, but something just didn't work out for him. He had incredible skills and looked great doing what he does, but after this Paramount release, he did *Street Knight* for Cannon, which was a collapsing studio at the time. He appeared in *Lionheart* with JCVD, but *Perfect Weapon* is the only film he did that perfectly captured him at the height of his skills and appeal. He played characters who were kinda cocky and self-assured, which may be a little off-putting, but then again, Steven Seagal had a lot of longevity acting the same way. In this film, Speakman uses sticks and knives, and he pole vaults in one scene. The tag line was "Full contact, no protection: No problem." Believe it. With Al Leong, James Hong, and Cary Hiriouki-Tagawa.

P

Jeff Sanders (played by Jeff Speakman) trains to be The Perfect Weapon. Author's collection.

INTERVIEW:
JEFF SPEAKMAN
(djm)

When Paramount's The Perfect Weapon *arrived in theaters in 1991, it heralded the arrival of the next big action star: Jeff Speakman. Unlike Steven Seagal, Chuck Norris, and Jean-Claude Van Damme, Speakman stood out because of his radically unique style in the martial arts. An eighth degree black belt in kenpo karate, Speakman had a once-in-a-lifetime shot at becoming the world's next big action star, but after* The Perfect Weapon, *his next film* Street Knight *(1993, from Cannon) wouldn't arrive for two more years, which is an eternity in Hollywood, and just like that, he began making films that went directly to video. With ten starring action films under his black belt, Speakman soldiered on, creating Kenpo 5.0 and founded American Kenpo Karate Systems. .*

My first question for you about your career is what drew you to Kenpo? It's an interesting martial art when it's translated on screen.

I'd been studying Japanese Goju-Ryu with Lou Angel for five years prior and working my way through college in Joplin, Missouri, which is where I met Mr. Angel. When it came time for me to graduate, and very generously on his part, he said that if I wanted to study martial arts that I should study kenpo from Ed Parker in Los Angeles, he's the best in the world. So I said "Okay," and I did that. I sold my car to pay for the U-Haul to move to LA and I had a letter of recommendation from Lou Angel. He'd known Ed Parker from the late '60s, early '70s. I found Mr. Parker in Long Beach, and I bowed very deeply to him to show respect and I handed him this letter, and he was so pleased that his old friend Lou Angel thought to send him one of his black belts that he gave me his phone number and told me to call him in two weeks. That got me started in kenpo. It was years later when I was thinking about that—the story I just told you—it really made me appreciate Lou Angel. As a master instructor in the martial arts, he was more concerned for my personal development and my personal growth, so he sent me who he thought was the best, as opposed to sending me to do more Goju-Ryu. You come from a traditional system like that, seldom do you have someone with the objectivity to send one of his black belts with whom he's working with every day away from there—across country—nd not only go to

a different style of martial arts, but to a very non-traditional style of martial arts. Very unusual. But it was really Lou Angel's concern for me as a person that led him to do that.

How did you end up doing a bit part in the Jean-Claude Van Damme movie *Lionheart*?

I volunteered my services to do what's called a reader. You're the other actor in the audition room. You're reading the lines to all the actors who come in and audition. You will be there for however many days and work all day free. They'll buy you lunch, but that's it. In exchange, they'll give you a little bit part in a movie. That's exactly what I did. No one knew that I knew karate when I did that movie. I was a complete unknown. I wanted to prove that I could get hired as an actor, that karate would come second. That's how I approached it.

Were you observant on the set of *Lionheart*? ?

Yes, of course, when I was on the set, especially as a beginning actor, you're paying attention to everything and trying to learn by watching working actors. Set etiquette and how movies are made is quite different than how it's taught in school. So, the best thin—one of your best teachers—is just hanging around a movie set. Watching. Get a chair and get the hell out of the way and just sit there hour after hour and watch how everybody does their job and how actors act. How directors relate to actors. If you ever get a chance as an actor, one of your jobs—in my opinion—is to make life easy for the director . . . because you'll get hired again. Actors have an opposite approach. They want to know what their motivation for opening the door is. "My character wouldn't do that." Okay, that's a question under some circumstances, but by and large, just shut up and open the door.

How did that segue into your major debut, *The Perfect Weapon*? How did that happen?

As fate would have it, I was studying regularly at an acting workshop in Burbank called The Creative Actor's Workshop. One of the instructors there was also a writer. We became friends. It turns out that he wrote Van Damme's second movie, *Kickboxer*. Because we became friends and he wrote a martial arts movie, he wanted to come down and watch me teach at the West LA school one night, which he did, and that was his first time to see kenpo. So, as soon as he saw me, he went to the guy who was the director and the producer of Van Damme's three movies, *Bloodsport, Kickboxer,* and *Death Warrant* and said, "You've got to see this guy Speakman and you've got to see this kenpo stuff! I've never seen anything like it!" After pursuing him, Mark DiSalle came to the West LA dojo and watched this and that was it. When he saw kenpo, he realized that this was the next thing for film.

How were you chosen to be the star of the film? Why didn't they go to a Van Damme or to an established star?

Well, it started with this three-picture deal I had with Mark DiSalle. Right after that, a connection he had with the guy who was the president of production at Paramount—Gary Lucchesi—got him in with Paramount because he was able to

make Van Damme a star. So DiSalle went in and met Gary Lucchesi and said, "I've got the next action star and I've signed him to a three picture deal." Then, Paramount bought that deal with Mark DiSalle attached, which he had every legal right because it was in my contract to sell my option, as it were. So Paramount came in and *The Perfect Weapon* was developed and written for me. So we took off. That's just what DiSalle was in the business of, and Paramount wanted to do that, and circumstances were that they were ready to sign off and let DiSalle make it with the next guy. So before we did that, Gary Lucchesi, president of Paramount, and two other executives came to the West LA school and watched me do a demo one night . . . with DiSalle, of course. After they saw the demo, they said, "Okay, we're in." Then they saw that I'd actually been studying acting for five years, I'd worked as an actor, I'd been hired on a TV series for one day called *Hunter*, and so they went, "Okay, wow." Then we did a screen test at Paramount. After the screen test was done —it was actually a scene from the script for The Perfect Weapon—we went ahead and Paramount went ahead and bought all three options from DiSalle.

Well, how come Paramount didn't continue making movies with you then?

You just asked . . . the BIG QUESTION. As fortunate as everything I just laid out for you was —it was really unique—then the exact opposite of that happened. Working with DiSalle was a nightmare, and Paramount actually lost its CEO when I was there, and an interim CEO came in and that's usually bad news for everybody who signed on a multiple picture deal because the studio won't want to make another movie star out of somebody that the preceding group tried to make out of because that other group will always get the praise, if you will. So you're in an uphill battle from day one. Even though *The Perfect Weapon* was a huge success and made a lot of money and launched my career, the people who came in the interim were not action movie folks and they didn't like DiSalle, and to get DiSalle out they had to pay him a lot of money just to walk away. So instead of doing that we actually read a script that Paramount sent to us, and it was a great, great script, and it would have been absolutely perfect for my second movie. We were engaged in it—they hired a writer for a lot of money, and he was doing a lot of rewrites to [fashion it for me], and in the middle of that the interim head of the studio put that script in turnaround, which is when they take scripts and put them out there to other studios and say, "Hey,

Jeff Speakman is . . .The Perfect Weapon! Author's collection.

look, we've put two hundred thousand into this script and we don't want it—if you pay two hundred thousand you can have it." It sort of becomes available. The next day after this guy did that, all of us —my legal guys and my agents—jumped on the phone and called Paramount and said, "What the hell are you doing?! This is Speakman's movie. We picked it! You picked it! You gave it to us and you've already spent $250,000 hiring a writer to make it a Jeff Speakman movie! What the hell are you doing?" The guy who was temporarily running the studio was like, "Oh, shit! Sorry! I fucked up, let me go get it back." Fox bought it and would not sell it back to him. They made that movie, which was supposed to be my second movie at Paramount, and the name of that movie was *Speed*.

No way!

It was the movie that made Keanu Reeves a star. We were rewriting it so that the bus would stop and Speakman would have to get off the bus and fight guys and get back on the bus—we were doing all that. We lost it. And consequently, there went my career.

Let's go back to The Perfect Weapon for a minute. You said that you had problems with Mark DiSalle. What were the issues there?

It wasn't with me. The problem was a business sort of a thing between Paramount and DiSalle, which I wasn't a part of. The only thing when it became an issue with me is when DiSalle wouldn't back off and Paramount wouldn't pay him a million bucks to walk away. I went to DiSalle and said, "Look, it's really none of my business what happened in there, but if you don't knock this shit off, they're not going to do anything." Of course, he's a businessman and so he continued to hold my contract as leverage and Paramount subsequently passed on doing the second Speakman movie, but they would not let me out of the contract because, again, if another studio picked me up and paid off DiSalle and made me a star, then that other studio would get the credit. So, Paramount just let me sit on the shelf and let me just dwindle.

Wow. Yeah, it was like two more years until Street Knight.

And see, DiSalle had the options. So, he wouldn't let go and let Paramount do it, so he had "X" number of months to exercise his option, which he did at the very last moment, and put together the second movie, *Street Knight*, so that's why I went from Paramount to Cannon. It was released through Warner Brothers, but it wasn't the direction we wanted to go, but here's the truth: I was still doing movies. Here we are, ten movies later.

Talk about working with Mako and Tanaka on Perfect Weapon.

Yeah, boy, wasn't that incredible, huh? Toru Tanaka, that was his stage name. The truth is that he was a Hawaiian. His name was actually Charles Kalani and he grew up on the island with Mr. Parker. So when he was called upon by Paramount with this, he was hooking up with his old friend, Ed Parker. When they were together, it was Hawaiian home week. That was great to work with a legend like

Jeff Speakman's breakout action film *The Perfect Weapon* made him an instant action star. Author's collection.

that. And Mako: A beautiful, well-trained actor, who was a gentleman. He was very kind. It was all good. It was different shades of good and great.

Talk about Street Knight. This was the last movie Cannon released in theaters before it completely folded.

Yeah, it had a tremendous amount of potential. It was directed by a phenomenal director, Albert Magnoli, who also did Prince's *Purple Rain*. He had a great eye. He was classically trained, a brilliant director. I got along with him beautifully. We became very good friends. *Street Knight* turned out to be a disaster because in order for DiSalle to exercise his second option with Speakman and not lose me from the contract, he only had so much time, so Cannon was able to come up with a certain percentage of the budget for the movie and then the worst of all possible scenarios happened. You're two weeks into filming, everything is going great, the scenes look phenomenal, it's got a beautiful look to it, and then the suits start showing up on the set and the rest of the money isn't coming, so you have to make these slashes, and then it was just a nightmare. So that's why there are certain—like the opening scene of that movie—we shot the opening scene first, which seldom do you do, but in this case it so happened that the scheduling was that we did the opening scene of the movie. You watch that and it looks like a big movie. Really, really well done. Beautifully lit. And then you see things that are compromised like crazy. The movie went south because of that. The story I just told you is altogether too common. Money gets yanked or money doesn't come through or whatever. Then the suits start showing up and pages get torn out and the movie's compromised.

Is that why there's less fighting in that movie than in The Perfect Weapon?

Exactly right. A lot of money goes into the fight scenes. With *The Perfect Weapon*, in that movie was the taekwondo fight scene. We had one full twelve-hour day and another half day. One and a half day. We had eighteen hours. Three cameras, three crews, every length and light that you can imagine for just that fight scene that turned out to be two minutes of film. And I had final edit and sound check, and I've had the same thing in all my movies since then. Then when you're on a movie like *Street Knight* and the money gets yanked, you have to try for the same thing in six hours instead of eighteen. With one camera, instead of three. With very limited lens package and crew. Everything

pays a terrible price. In the editing room you wind up with less because you had less to work with. That's just the way the world works.

Both The Perfect Weapon and Street Knight were released theatrically, and you were announced as the next big action guy. What was that like, being hailed as an action star in this period when action guys like you and Van Damme and Steven Seagal were viable. Nowadays, these guys aren't making theatrical releases anymore. This type of movie has been relegated to video. What was that like for you?

It was a very surreal experience, to be honest with you. Not just to have the opportunity to do that, but to be picked up by Paramount, of all studios, which was not known for doing martial arts action movies. It was even more bizarre. Of course, it was an obvious opportunity that I was well aware of, and I did my very best to deliver on all levels, and I'm very proud of the work I've done—both there and in every movie I've done. I've approached every movie with the same seriousness, if you will. But it was a tremendous event. I was devastated that before *The Perfect Weapon* was released, Ed Parker died. So, it was a very bittersweet time in my life because he wasn't there to see it. He saw edited fight scenes and loved it beyond compare, but he never saw the whole film. It was very tragic, but at the same time, it was tremendous. Two extremes. It was a very duplicitous time of my life. To go to all the theatrical releases of my movie, to see it develop and to watch it all go down, it was gratifying beyond measure, but it had this element to it where as a martial artist, my feeling was, Now what the hell am I going to do? Once you've been mentored and taught by someone of Ed Parker's stature, one of the first questions that comes to your mind is, What the hell am I going to do now? Where do I go now? Who do I study from? As it turned out, there was really nobody for me to study from. So I wound up, in a sense, continuing studying from Mr. Parker by how he taught me. I became what you might call "self-taught," which ultimately led to what I've been able to develop in these last few years this version of kenpo, which is called Kenpo 5.0, where now we've taken kenpo to the ground where there was zero ground stuff before. It took me years to figure it out. I came to the conclusion that . . . see, after Mr. Parker died, in December of 1990—March of 1990 is when *The Perfect Weapon* came out—he had written an article about me that was to be published in *Black Belt* magazine, and the irony was that in March there was on the one side of the page a Jeff Speakman article written by Ed Parker, and the flipside of that page was his obituary. In that article, he wrote, "I never gave Jeff complete answers to his questions. I always gave him half answers and made him figure out the rest for himself." I thought to myself, That's really incredible because for three and a half years, he'd been doing exactly that and I never saw it. I was so encumbered by trying to learn from him. When you get an opportunity to learn from a master instructor, you want to pay attention. You want to try the best you can. After reading that, in the published magazine, I realized that a true martial arts master isn't someone who teaches, but a master is someone more of a guy who helps you to discover the art yourself. And then you own it. Ultimately, then you can perhaps contribute to advances in that art, which is exactly what we feel we have done here.

P

Well, you certainly made your mark in motion pictures. You put kenpo on the screen like nobody else. When I think of kenpo I think of Jeff Speakman. Do you think you've accomplished putting kenpo on screen?

Yes, very much so. I certainly think I did that with *The Perfect Weapon*, and I continued to do that with my subsequent movies. The one I'm doing soon, which is called *Lido*, which will be all Kenpo 5.0 specifically. So, I will continue to do that. Additionally, I've franchised martial arts schools in fifteen countries. We're the largest kenpo organization in the world. Because of this Kenpo 5.0, many people are coming in because now it's the ultimate mix off the standoff art. Now we know how to do kenpo on our backs, which is something we could never do before.

You worked with director Rick Avery a few times on the films Deadly Outbreak and The Expert. Talk about working with him.

Yes, Rick is a very accomplished martial artist. He received a fifth degree black belt many years ago. He's a phenomenal athlete and so accomplished in the film business. All my movies, Rick has done the stunt coordinating for me. He's done second unit on my movies too. He also directed the one I did in Israel, *Deadly Outbreak*. There was another film I did, *The Expert*, where we unfortunately had to fire the director about three quarters of the way into it, and Rick went from second unit director to the director, and he finished the film, and he did a phenomenal job. Because he did such a great job, I had him come do my next movie, which was *Deadly Outbreak*.

That was a Nu Image/Millennium movie.

Yup. That's exactly right. That was a wonderful experience. I had never been to Israel before. I was there for almost three months. Rick did, once again, a fantastic job. He and I are very close friends. I just can't say enough about him.

This was the period when your movies were going directly to video. What was that like for you?

I just swallowed the jagged pill. It was how things were being one. I focused on *If I keep delivering my martial arts in these lesser movies—if you will—then eventually someone will see that and figure it out that they should give me another shot*. Which is exactly what we believe is happening here with my next movie *Lido*, which we're hoping will be my return to the big screen. I've never ever taken anything—any of the movies or my opportunity to study with Ed Parker or the opportunity to travel around the world or having schools around the world —I've never taken anything for granted. I've lived every day as though I were alive, and I appreciated everything. I've been grateful. I've done my absolute very best to deliver on all fronts. Certainly, with that kind of energy and perseverance, it will pay off. I'll get a chance to get back out there in a big way again because I feel like I should be. I feel like I should be out there contributing in that way. I will be.

Is there anything you would like to say to your fans?

Yes, something very important. As you know, I've gone through cancer. I've come out the other end of it, survived it. I took radiation and chemo treatments. I'm about eleven weeks out from treatment, and so far they say that the cancer is gone and there's no sign of it. To speak directly to my fans: The extraordinary thing that transcends the horribleness of the cancer and what I went through, the fact that I learned that there are so many people out there throughout the world who care and who are my fans and who are my friends . . . my students and other martial artists whom I've never met . . . all came together to help me get through this with their support—whether it was a donation to my medical fund or whether it was well wishes and just letting me know that they're there. It was that extraordinary bit of strength that I was able to glean from that experience that allowed me to walk down the hallway every day to go to my radiation treatment, which was no fun and no day at the beach. It's what I learned from. It was something great and beautiful. I've been able to take from that horrible experience. Metaphorically, that's how I've always approached life. One day, this will end for all of us. The question that's in front of you is "What are you going to do with these heartbeats that you have? Are your contributions to the common good?" I really feel like I've made tremendous contributions because those people would never have come to my aide if they didn't feel something very positive from the movies I've done and the way I've led my life. That's my gratitude to everyone who taught me that lesson. The cancer wasn't the most important thing. The cancer was an opportunity for me to learn about the connectedness that we all have. The work I have done truly has been appreciated around the world. That, I am very grateful for.

Personal Vendetta

1995 (Image DVD) (djm)

"Another bad guy bites the dust at the hands of the karate cop!"

The incredible Mimi Lesseos wrote, produced, and starred in *Personal Vendetta*, which casts her as a battered wife who is beaten so badly one night by her creep husband (played by Timothy Bottoms) that she has leverage enough to have him sent to prison for several years. During that time, she learns to defend herself and she trains to become a police officer. She turns out to be a highly formidable and valuable asset to the force. She falls in love with her partner and ends up uncovering a human trafficking ring in the city. When her husband is let out of prison for good behavior, she's forced to enact her personal vendetta against him when he comes calling on her with nefarious intentions.

Like all of the movies that Lesseos starred in, *Personal Vendetta* is suited to her abilities and her persona, though in this one she allows herself to be shown more vulnerable and against-type situations. When she starts kicking ass, she looks like a beast and no one can go up against her

without getting some ribs cracked. Some more demanding and sophisticated viewers might be turned off by the movies that Lesseos made, but I like her and her movies are incredibly easy to digest, so I don't really have anything to complain about. Directed by Stephen Lieb (*Blind Vengeance*).

Phase IV

2002 (Fox DVD) (CD)

Simon Tate (Dean Cain) is a journalism student and a family man. He harbors dreams of playing football again while still caring for his wife and daughter. He finds it strange that there have been four murders at the university in four unrelated incidents. His friend Dr. Roanic (Stephen Coats) is the prime suspect but Tate believes his friend to be innocent. Before Roanic is killed in a police chase, he leaves a clue for Tate that will lead him to the truth. The clue leads Tate to a cure for AIDS, which would cost pharmaceutical companies billions if it were to get out. The cover-up goes further than Tate could have ever imagined, and he'll be lucky to get the story out without sacrificing his life. Hot on his trail is Detective Birnam (Brian Bosworth), a grunt working with the government to cover the whole thing up. Tate has a few tricks up his sleeve and maybe he can get the truth out there before anyone else is murdered.

Phase IV is better than it should be, and the story is actually pretty frightening. If a cure for AIDS were to be found, just think of all the money lost when no one would need treatment pills anymore. Non-action star Dean Cain (*Futuresport*) is the star of the film, but it's great to see Brian Bosworth (*Stone Cold, One Man's Justice*) taking on the villain role. He spends most of the film chasing characters down and it's not until the end that he gets a chance to fight. He and Cain go toe to toe in a solid life-or-death brawl. Since this is Cain's vehicle, Bosworth loses. A pity. Directed by Bryan Goeres.

Picasso Trigger

1988 (Malibu Bay Films DVD) (djm)

"Didn't I tell you, Jade?
I got a black belt in *shotgun!*"

Playboy models Donna Spier and Hope Marie Carlton return as action-tastic spies Donna and Taryn in Andy Sidaris's *Picasso Trigger*, which is more or less the same movie as *Hard Ticket to Hawaii*, but with some more characters thrown into the mix. This time, Donna and Taryn start off in Paris, hunting for an elusive work of art known as "The Picasso Trigger," but in reality The Picasso Trigger is an assassin named Salazar, and another secret agent named Travis (played by Steve Bond) is on his trail, and when they both end up in Hawaii, the plot then includes Donna, Taryn, and kickboxer Jade (Harold Diamond from *Killing American Style*), who join in the adventure.

With even more explosions, shootouts, and nudity than *Hard Ticket to Hawaii*, *Picasso Trigger* is every bit as fun as its predecessor, but it still doesn't give Harold Diamond a lead role. Most of the time, he walks around, lifts weights, or takes girls' shirts off, but if you're hoping to see more kick-fighting action from him, you'll have to seek elsewhere. That said, he does have a great fight scene in the movie where he kicks a dude in the face so hard, the guy flies out a window and falls fifty stories to his death. The last scene of the film shows all of the heroes laughing like the end of a cartoon episode. Watch quickly for Keith Cooke (as Keith Hirabayashi) in a small role. The next movie in the series is *Savage Beach*, which had roles for James Lew and Al Leong.

Pistol Whipped

2007 (Sony DVD) (djm)

"You know what really is amazing to me? A guy that can walk into an urban territory, a five-star hotel full of bodyguards, take care of business with extreme prejudice, and walk out in one piece like a fucking ghost."

After Steven Seagal's stellar return to form in the direct-to-video *Urban Justice*, his next movie *Pistol Whipped* did an okay job as a follow-up, but the last act is a complete mess and ruined what might have been another stellar effort. Seagal plays Matt, an alcoholic gambling addict, whose life is in a shambles after his wife divorces him, taking his daughter and remarrying, this time to his former partner on the police force. Without a job or a family, and with zero luck (not to mention over a million dollars of outstanding markers), Matt is bailed out by a mysterious "old man" (played by Lance Henriksen in two scenes) who gives him a job he simply can't refuse: to kill nefarious criminals who go unpunished in society. Matt takes the gig and begins a series of hits, but when his final hit turns out to be his former best friend and his ex-wife's husband, he begins to seriously rethink whom he's working for and if his friend is actually worth killing (he is, in fact).

Some murky plotting and some strange, off-kilter acting choices by Seagal upset the tone of this otherwise "B"-rate action movie. I like the story—that's where the movie succeeds, but some of the all-of-a-sudden twists and oh-we're-in-a-big-shootout scenes made me wonder if I'd been paying close enough attention, but it's the same situation in so many of Seagal's direct-to-video movies. I never had to second-guess the plotting of his core theatrical releases (until *Exit Wounds* and *Half Past Dead*), so why are these direct-to-video movies so needlessly convoluted? *Pistol Whipped* has some good stuff going on, but it's still not up to par with his great ones. Roel Reine (*The Marine 2*) directed it.

Pitch Black

2000 (Universal DVD) (djm)

A space vessel carrying a light crew and a handful of passengers in suspended hibernation crash-lands on a desolate planet with three suns. Every few decades the planet undergoes a period of "pitch black" during a rare eclipse, and it just so happens that the stranded survivors of the ship are about to be subjected to a grueling few days and nights of terror as they encounter the planet's chief predator—a legion of flying alien creatures partial to the dark. Their only hope comes from an unlikely source: a prisoner condemned to death named Riddick (Vin Diesel in a star-making role) has an ability to see through the dark. Riddick's strength, cunning, and unpredictability make him a sort of antihero the likes of which hasn't really been seen in movies lately. He's dangerous, but only in the best way, and he emerges a hero, despite his best efforts not to become one.

Diesel, who had previously appeared in *Saving Private Ryan* in a small role, became an action star when he headlined this film. From here on out—with few exceptions—he starred in films that relied on his physicality and strong persona. Riddick is a role he obviously cherished, as he would go on to reprise the role several more times in *The Chronicles of Riddick* in 2004 and *Riddick* in 2013. Writer/director David Twohy wrote and directed all three films. Diesel became a household name with his next film, *The Fast and the Furious*.

Pit Fighter

2005 (Fox DVD) (CD)

"What more triumphant an end can there be than to be raked by the fiery rash of a hundred marksmen's cartridges, blistered where I stand like bleeding, shredded hamburger? If I could only choose . . . "

Jack Severino (Dominiquie Vandenberg) has no memory of his past. After being nursed back to health by Manolo (Steven Bauer), he needs to work and find himself a trade in order to pay back his debt. He discovers that he is an expert fighter and quickly finds himself in a brutal underground fight club, raking in the money for Manolo and himself. The only memory of his past is of Marianne (Stana Katic), which keeps him sane. As bits and pieces of his memory come back, he quickly learns that the person he was isn't the man that he has become. He must embrace the truth in order to set things right.

Pit Fighter is a movie that may have been overlooked upon its release but it deserves a better fate than disappearing on a video store shelf somewhere. What starts out as a typical underground fight film quickly turns into a much deeper story about a man trying to remember who

he is, only to find out that his past is far darker than he could have imagined. Dominiquie Vandenberg (*Green Street Hooligans 2*) is an unlikely lead yet manages to be very engaging. It takes a little bit to warm up to him as a screen presence and once you do, he really ends up delivering an intense performance. He has the look of a villain and the heart of a hero. His character has some unique traits that you don't see often in action films like this. For example, during his fights, he allows his opponents to beat him to a pulp before he knocks them so they don't feel like they have lost face. Steven Bauer plays his only friend and manager, a man who lives in poverty and sees Vandenberg's Jack as a way to the big time. Bauer is able to make you feel for him, even if he is a tad bit skeezy. Rounding out the cast is Stephen Graham (*London Boulevard*), Andre "Chyna" McCoy (*T.K.O.*), Stana Katic (*Quantum of Solace*), and Fernando Carrillo (*Spin*). It's also very interesting to see Scott Adkins (*Undisputed II: Last Man Standing*) in a strictly acting capacity. It's nothing more than a cameo to help move the story along, but it would have been nice to see him in action. The fight scenes are less about style and more about finishing the job. There are some very bloody moments with no shortage of brutality in the underground fights. Director Jesse Johnson (*The Package, The Last Sentinel*) has a knack for taking a predictable premise we've seen before and turning it in to a highly entertaining B-movie extravaganza.

Platoon Leader

1988 (MGM DVD R2) (djm)

"What's it like? You go out on patrol, and you kill a few of them. Then they kill a few of yours. Then you go back to base. Eat. Sleep. Next day, same thing."

Lt. Jeff Knight (Michael Dudikoff) is flown into the jungles of Vietnam where he quickly realizes the horrors of war. His subordinates don't like him because he graduated from West Point and has never seen or dealt with real combat before, but that changes quite suddenly when he's wounded and brought to the brink of death. He's flown out, recuperates, and gets right back in the action. They learn to respect him, and his hard casing becomes accepted.

Some have accused *Platoon Leader* of being an outright rip-off of *Platoon*, but I'm not sure I'd agree with that. It's a straight-up, simplified (and extremely gory) look at combat in Vietnam, and it doesn't bite off more than it can chew. The characters are well defined, and Dudikoff, while fresh from his first two *American Ninja* movies, is capable of portraying his not-too-complicated character. The score by George S. Clinton is heroic and memorable. It was directed by Aaron Norris, who made many movies with his brother Chuck. It's based on a book by James R. McDonough.

Plato's Run

1997 (Echo Bridge DVD) (CD)

"You took away the love of my life, now I'm gonna take you away."

Plato Smith (Gary Busey) is a former Navy SEAL who has retired and is trying to reconnect with his daughter Kathy (Maggie Myatt). Money is tight and his business is failing, so when he's contacted by former fling Marta (Tiana Warden) about a job, he really can't refuse the money. He's asked to rescue two escaped prisoners in Cuba. He and his buddy Sam (Steven Bauer) pull off the job without a hitch . . . or so they think. Plato ends up framed for a murder he didn't commit. He goes on the run and finds that arms smuggler Alex Senarkin (Roy Scheider) is behind it all. Plato won't go down without a fight, but he can't do it alone; he needs to bring in his whole team. Senarkin takes Kathy hostage, and Plato's old pal Dominic (Jeff Speakman from *The Perfect Weapon*) is just the man to help rescue her.

Gary Busey's (*Under Siege*) character makes one major mistake right at the beginning of the film. There's a bar brawl, and it's quite apparent who the real muscle in the team is and of course it's Jeff Speakman (who is a kenpo expert). Instead of keeping Speakman around, he is sent on his way and Steven Bauer (*Scarface*) becomes Busey's character's right-hand man. Long after the shit hits the fan, they finally decide to call in Speakman, who uses a series of stealth techniques to dispatch the enemy one by one and essentially saves the day. If Speakman was the lead, this would have been a much different film. He would have been a one-man army and wouldn't have needed to wait for any reinforcements. As it stands, Busey does a solid job as an action hero (even though he's not an action star) and helps to deliver a fun action flick courtesy of Nu Image and director James Beckett (*Ulterior Motives*).

The Player

2015 (NBC TV) (CD)

"Saving an innocent woman, wife beater gets what he deserves, not a bad day. You said you wanted to do good. Well, power, Mr. Kane, power when used properly, can do good."

Alex Kane (Philip Winchester) is a former secret operative and FBI agent who is now working as a security expert in Las Vegas. His life as a secret operative led him to a very dark place inside his head. His only way out was when he met his wife, Ginny (Daisy Betts), who gave him a new lease on life. They split up but remained on the best of terms, good enough to eventually rekindle their romance and try it a second time. In the middle of the night, a man breaks into their home and kills Ginny. Alex goes after the man only to be hit by a car driven by Cassandra King (Charity

Press poster for *The Player*. Author's Collection.

Wakefield). She takes Alex to meet her employer, Mr. Johnson (Wesley Snipes). He's a pit boss who runs a only-in-the-movies-or-on-TV high stakes game, totally unlike any other. He and Ms. King are part of this game; they have the high-tech capability of being able to predict a crime before it happens. They must inject a player into the equation, and see if he can stop the crime before it happens. The underground game is then bet upon by high rollers, so everything rides on the player's shoulders. They're in need of a new player and the man they want is Alex. He's reluctant to play along but he sees it as an opportunity to do good and help the innocent people who would become victims if he didn't. He also has another agenda: Some evidence comes to light that his wife might still be alive. Alex will do whatever it takes to win each game and save lives while Mr. Johnson and Cassandra use their equipment to help him learn the truth about what really happened to his wife.

NBC's *The Player* has taken a beating. As of this writing, the original thirteen-episode order was cut back to nine, which is a shame since the series has an incredibly likable cast, interesting premise, and some killer action scenes. Philip Winchester (*Solomon Kane*) has all the makings of being an action star. His looks and physical capabilities are front and center in each episode. Wesley Snipes, on the other hand, is most certainly there in every episode, but he takes a bit of a backseat in this series. This isn't a bad thing, as his character is meant to be mysterious and we learn tidbits about him in each episode and his character rests in a gray area, but we're never really sure if he's one of the good guys or if he has an agenda. It's not until the fifth episode of this season where his action skills are displayed. He has a great one-on-one fight with Will Yun Lee (*Die Another Day*). His showcase continues on in the following episode as well. Aside from the action, Snipes has the chance to don disguises and show off his range a bit, thus proving that the show is a terrific showcase for him. Whether or not the show continues after this first season remains unclear, but either way, each episode is a blast and worth taking the time to watch.

INTERVIEW:

WESLEY SNIPES

(djm)

A practitioner of the martial arts since his pre-teens, Wesley Snipes had already established himself as an actor by the time he began showing what he could do as an action star. When he starred in the Warner Brothers action film Passenger 57 *(1992), he'd already earned a fifth degree black belt in Shotokan*

karate and a second degree black belt in hapkido. His career as an action star then took off, with a string of big-budget films with major studios, and when he starred as the half human/half vampire Marvel Comics character Blade in 1998, his popularity soared. It's strange that just a few years after that, he was already relegated to starring in direct-to-video fare like 7 Seconds (2005) and The Marksman (2005). When news broke that he was being sent to prison for income tax evasion, Snipes's career was put on hold, and he served a three-year sentence (2010–2013), which was a terrible blow for the star and for his fans. As soon as he was released, Sylvester Stallone brought him on board to co-star in The Expendables 3 (2014), his first theatrical film since his supporting role in the drama Brooklyn's Finest (2009). In this interview conducted at 2015's San Diego Comic Con, Snipes discusses his next frontier as he makes his transition to the small screen:*

I've got to say, man, that it's great to have you back. We've missed you.

Thank you!

You were great in *Expendables 3*.

Yeah, that was fun. I tried to add a little bit of comedy to it.

You going to be in the next one?

Yeah, from what I hear. My character could be blown up in a car accident—he died in a car bomb!

You're best known for your action films, but you've also done dramas and comedies, and now you're moving into your first television show. Talk a little bit about your transition to TV.

This one affords me the opportunity to explore all of those genres. There will be some high, dramatic action, some emotional scenes, and some opportunities for comedy as well. There will also be some martial arts in this piece as well. Then I get to play different characters, use disguises. I'll see if I can create a real library of interesting characters, even if they're only in one episode. It's fun for the actor in me. It's like repertory theater classes. I wanted to do this, but I never got the chance to pull it off. I like that there are do-overs in television. If you don't get it right in episode two, you can get it right on episode four or six. It's intriguing to me as a theater guy. I like the prep and I like to develop the character. I like getting into characters in a deeper way.

Do you like playing a character like this where you don't really know what's coming for you from episode to episode?

Yeah, because you can explore your full range of your talents as an actor. You have to be just as convincing as the bad guy as the nerd or the tech guy or the non-aggressive type of character. It's a nice challenge for me. You have eight days to do it for each episode.

How would you compare your character in *The Player,* to say . . . Blade?

Oh, he could definitely go toe-to-toe with Blade.

Talk about the action aspects of the show. This is what your fans are expecting.

We are bringing what we do in feature films to the small screen. We're keeping it as emotionally engaging and as visually dynamic as possible. I'll be bringing a couple of my martial arts buddies to the table. We'll be adding both male and female martial artists to the show. This is pure popcorn entertainment.

What martial arts styles and disciplines would you like to bring into this show?

We're going to reference some more regional things, some exotic systems out of Japan, exotic systems out of Indonesia, the Filipino kali and stick work. We're going to bring these to the table. Not a whole lot of wushu. It will be much more combat oriented. The Krav Magas of the world. Some systems that people have never heard of. It will definitely be exciting to look at.

This show is set in and around Las Vegas. Are you much of a gambler?

The biggest gamble I've made is pursuing an acting career. Other than that, I'm not a gambler. I lost my Sunday school shirt money at three-card monte at 125th Street, and I've been traumatized ever since!

Pocket Ninjas

1997 (Simitar Entertainment DVD) (CD)

"I swear I will take revenge . . . scout's honor!"

Cobra Khan (Robert Z'Dar from *Samurai Cop*) is the most feared hooligan in town. He and his group of trusty gang members (known as "Stingers") rule with iron fists. They begin to pollute the environment with a toxic waste that will eventually cause irreparable damage. Enter the White Dragon (Gary Daniels), who uses a mask to fight evil—but he can't do it all alone. He enlists the aid of his three best students: Tonya (Sondi), Steve (Brad Bufanda), and Damien (Joseph Valencia). Each dons a different-colored dragon mask, and they help defend the people of their town. The Stingers can't handle all their plans being foiled so they kidnap the mother of one of our heroes, who band together one last time to rescue her.

Trying to make sense of the plot in *Pocket Ninjas* is a pointless endeavor. What you can do is sit back and relish just how bizarre it is. You'll find yourself mystified, wondering why you're watching it in the first place. But if you're a completest (like us), then this is a must-see. Star Gary Daniels (*Hawk's Vengeance, American Streetfighter*) appears as the White Dragon, as well as the teacher of the three kid heroes. The movie shows Daniels training in various locations, over and over again. In fact, the majority of the film's runtime is filled with training montages. Dave Eddy was brought in to replace original director Donald G. Jackson (*Hell*

Comes to Frogtown) when producers felt his take on the material wasn't working. The film essentially ended up being a patchwork of both directors' footage. It was released in foreign territories in 1994 before finding its way to the US market in 1997.

Point Blank

1998 (Sterling DVD) (djm)

A bunch of hardened criminals (including Danny Trejo, Kevin Gage, and Michael Wright) stage a big escape while they're being transported by bus through Texas, and they end up with an arsenal. Bunkered down in a shopping mall full of helpless hostages, the convicts make demands (helicopters, cash, etc.), and wait for stuff to happen. When they're bored or frustrated, they murder hostages for the hell of it. The police force hasn't a clue how to handle the situation, so the FBI is called in, and while the FBI is getting a plan together, a former Texas Ranger and ex-military commando named Rudy Ray (a bulked-up Mickey Rourke, the year after his stint on *Double Team* with Jean-Claude Van Damme) is called in because his brother Joe Ray (Gage) is one of the convicts in the mall. Rudy Ray doesn't wait for a plan to formulate; he gets himself in the mall by going through the roof and killing some guys (and booby-trapping the corpses), and in no time at all he's getting himself in some *Die Hard* situations.

A straight-to-video riff on *Con Air* and *Die Hard* with a buff head-hanging hero, *Point Blank* is interesting for fans of Rourke, who does some martial arts in the film (or at least his body double does), and he even performs several backflips as a getaway method. Rourke was never more an action star than he was here, and while the film dips deeply into melodrama and stupid plotting, it has just the right amount of stuff in it to make it valid action star material. Rourke and Trejo go toe to toe several times, and that alone is worth the price of a rental or a purchase. Directed by Matt Earl Beesley, who never directed another feature.

Police Academy

1984 (Warner DVD) (MMM)

"I was a florist . . . you know, flowers and shit."

The ensemble nature of the raunchy, "R"-rated slapstick blockbuster *Police Academy* plays well upon the strengths of its individual cast members who play incoming ragtag cadets. Steve Guttenberg is the irreverent class cut-up, Kim Cattrall supplies heartthrob duties, Tim Kazurinsky embodies coiled-up nerdishness as only he can, and David Graf as hothead gun-nut Tackleberry establishes the one archetypal character who would appear in every incarnation of the *Police Academy* franchise (in time that would include seven big-screen adventures, a live-action TV series, an afternoon kids' cartoon,

and a line of toys). In addition, human sound effects machine Michael Winslow made such an impact that, thirty years on, he's still referred to as "the sound effects guy from *Police Academy*." It's a role that literally only he could play, a distinction that also fits florist-turned-lawman Moses Hightower, who's portrayed to six-foot-seven, 265-pound perfection by pro football legend Charles Aaron "Bubba" Smith.

Police Academy, of course, is primarily focused on comedy, but legitimate action arises when the law enforcement candidates must contend with an actual citywide riot. Here, Bubba towers most high (pun intended); previously his sheer hugeness set up most of his scenes and then, during the climax, Hightower gets to kicking bad-guy ass and tickling our funnybones. As amusing as *Police Academy* was at the time, the film's "*Animal House* goes to cop school" nature packs an even greater wallop now. That's due to hilariously un-PC gags such as a porn star Georgina Spelvin making a strategic cameo on her knees and the repeated humiliation of two hyper-macho blowhards in an S&M gay bar called the Blue Oyster. On top of wild humor, *Police Academy* also made sure to satisfy mid-'80s audiences' cravings for some well-done slam-bangs among all the ha-ha-ing. By way of Bubba Smith as Moses Hightower—a role he'd continue to perform in five sequels—*Police Academy* remains a massively arresting success.

Police Story

1985 (Shout Factory DVD) (djm)

One for the record books, *Police Story*, directed by and starring Jackie Chan, tells the story of intrepid cop Chan Ka-Kui, who is assigned a task to arrest a notorious drug lord. When he manages to accomplish the task single-handedly after an incredible foot chase, he's thrust into the public limelight as some kind of shining example of what a Chinese cop should be. When the drug lord is exonerated after a botched trial, Chan takes it upon himself to redeem himself and bring the obviously guilty man to justice.

Filled with almost nonstop stunts and jaw-dropping action—not to mention comedy antics—*Police Story* was a pioneer film in that it was one of the earliest martial arts cop movies made in Hong Kong. Jackie goes above and beyond the call of duty as he puts himself through painful and death-defying odds to give his audiences way more than they paid for. Some scenes have him falling great distances through glass, others have him dangling from a bus while cars rush towards him at deadly distances and speeds, and he's constantly in the middle of intricate and complicated fight scenes where he's outnumbered and outgunned. During the shoot, after a dangerous fall, he stopped breathing and was rushed to the hospital. Chan, the consummate professional and perfectionist, managed to deliver an outstanding entertainment with *Police Force*. A number of sequels and spin-offs followed.

P

Police Story 2

1988 (Shout Factory DVD) (CD)

"That's the way it goes. We said it'd be a tough case. We're dealing with an organized bunch of criminals here. I wished they'd blown me up instead. I don't like putting lives at risk."

Kevin Chan (Jackie Chan) may not always play by the rules but there's no denying he can get things done. Despite this, the damage he caused in *Police Story* has forced his superiors to demote him to a street cop. The crime lord he had put away is now free and continuing to harass Chan and his girlfriend May (Maggie Cheung). Hong Kong is being plagued by a gang of bombers who are blackmailing a group of real estate owners for 10 million bucks. Chan quits the force only to be lured back in when the bombings escalate. It takes one tough cop to handle all of the mayhem occurring in town.

Depending on which version of the film you watch, your reaction may be different. In the case of *Police Story 2*, the shorter version actually plays much better. The longer version (which adds an additional thirty minutes to the runtime) adds more character, humor, and a few odds and ends, but it doesn't make it the better version. Jackie Chan (*Project A*) is a one of a kind and has several fantastic fight and stunt sequences in the film. By far the most memorable is when Chan faces a group of thugs in a playground. It's a fast and vicious assault that has Chan and his stuntmen taking hits and falls with such force it's amazing there were no serious injuries. Chan is known to be a bit of a control freak so he serves as the director, writer, star, and stunt coordinator, and even sings the theme song. *Police Story 2* is a good film with some breathtaking action and is certainly a highlight in Chan's career.

Police Story 2013

2013 (Universe Laser DVD) (CD)

"Who lives? Who dies? It's up to you."

Captain Zhong (Jackie Chan) is trying to find a club where his daughter Miao (Tian Jing) has asked him to meet her. After the death of his wife, they've grown apart and he wants nothing more than to mend things with her. Being a cop, he put his career before his family and his efforts may now be too little too late. Once inside the club, things seem off but the owner Wu Jiang (Ye Liu) tries to set him at ease. A situation arises in the club and—always a cop—Zhong tries to defuse it. Everything goes to hell, and the club turns out to be a fortified building with Wu holding everyone hostage. Zhong appears to be the main target and being the cop that he is, he has plenty of enemies, but the real reason behind this massive plan will shock them all.

If you put Jackie Chan in a film and call it *Police Story*, fans are going to expect a certain type of film, and it should be delivered. This is not a *Police Story* movie in any way, shape, or form. It was a mistake to do so and a bit misleading. The movie itself isn't bad; Chan gives a great performance, but the film drags on too long and lacks punch. Think about it: a group of criminals have a fortified club with the police locked out and the only hope for the hostages is a washed-up cop trapped inside. This should have been Chan's *Die Hard*, but alas, it just wasn't to be. He has one fight scene with Liu Hailong, and it's a brutal one-on-one, last-man-standing affair. At his age we can't expect the lavish stunts and lightning-quick action he was once capable of, so to see him branch out and try other things is refreshing. Director Sheng Ding (*Little Big Soldier*, a historical picture with Chan) may have made a poor choice with the title but the film does showcase the star as an actor and it mostly succeeds as a thriller.

Pound of Flesh

2015 (Odyssey DVD) (djm)

A former kidnap and rescue agent named Deacon (Jean-Claude Van Damme) flies to the Philippines to donate a kidney to his niece, who's dying. Instead of going straight to his hotel for the night, he goes to a nightclub, picks up a hooker, has sex with her, and when he wakes up after being drugged, he realizes that he was operated on and that one of his kidneys has been stolen! He calls his distraught brother George (John Ralston) and a munitions buddy (Aki Aleong), who try to help him piece together what happened so that they can (hopefully) reclaim his kidney before it ends up in someone else's body. Over the next twenty-four hours, Deacon encounters all sorts of thugs working in the organ black market, namely a pimp/henchman named Goran (Darren Shahlavi), who might be Deacon's match in a fight if Deacon weren't so haggard and run down with pain. With the hooker who duped him in tow, Deacon, George, and their munitions pal sidekick get closer to the truth, and every second that passes is precious time as they try to get Deacon's kidney back.

Pound of Flesh is Van Damme's attempt to do a time crunch action movie in the spirit of *Crank* and *Taken*. Director Ernie Barbarash, who worked with Van Damme on *Assassination Games* and *Six Bullets*, gives his star plenty of opportunities to act, and while that's fine, the movie moves at a much slower pace than those two films, and drab shooting locations throughout China and the Philippines gives the film a pasty aura. Shahlavi, who passed away of a heart attack before the movie was released, livens the movie up whenever he's on screen, but the movie needed much more of him. There are nonsensical plot developments (like why does the hooker have to look exactly like George's dead wife?) that goof up the dramatic tension, and some of the acting by the supporting cast is wildly uneven. All said and done, this is the weakest collaboration between director Barbarash and star Van Damme. The fights were coordinated by John Salvitti, and look out for Brahim Achabbakhe early on in the film as a fighter.

The Power Within

1995 (Echo Bridge DVD) (djm)

Ted Jan (T. J.) Roberts from *Magic Kid* and *A Dangerous Place* stars in this kid-friendly martial arts fantasy movie from PM Entertainment. He plays a bullied high-school kid named Stan, who can't for the life of him get a prom date. His buddy (Keith Coogan) is always encouraging him to ask the class babe (Karen Valentine) out on a date, but then her ex-boyfriend (a stupid jock) beats Stan up in front of the whole school. What Stan doesn't realize is that he has a destiny that is about to reveal itself to him: An old Asian mystic has been watching him and is about to bestow a terrible, life-changing gift upon him—a sacred ring that will transform him into a martial arts dynamo. When Stan encounters the mystic (played by Gerald Okamura), the gift is passed to him, and from then on Stan doesn't have trouble with bullies anymore . . . because he can defend himself and prove that he has a power within! In the shadows is another watcher: a villain named Vonn (William Zabka from *The Karate Kid* and *Shootfighter*), who possesses an identical ring to Stan's, but Vonn plans to unite the rings and become a god. Will Stan be man enough to face evil and defeat it?

Similar to *Double Dragon*, but not as noisy or ambitious, *The Power Within* is a mystical action adventure feature that is inherently watchable if you're a kid at heart. It's well made for a low-budget movie, and T. J. Roberts is pretty good (as usual) in a role that is perfectly suited for him. It's really a shame that we didn't get to see him make these kinds of movies as an adult. If PM Entertainment had kept making movies, I suspect he would have stayed with them as one of their in-house stars. Don "The Dragon" Wilson appears as himself in a cameo. Directed by Art Camacho, who also made *Magic Kid* with T. J. and Wilson.

Pray For Death

1985 (MGM DVD) (djm)

"You cannot escape your shadows, my son. You will *always* be a ninja!"

A successful Japanese businessman named Akira Saito (Sho Kosugi) hides the fact that he's a ninja from his wife and children, and when his wife suggests that they move to America to start a business, he agrees. Relocated to Houston, Texas, they try opening a shop downtown, but some dirty cops hid a priceless bejeweled necklace in the shop before Saito bought the storefront, and they come looking for it, harassing Saito and his family. The mafia, meanwhile, is also after the necklace, and they send their hitman, Limehouse (James Booth), to intimidate Saito, who isn't having it. He goes to the police, but gets no help from them, and when he's pushed even further—when his wife and one of his sons are targeted and injured—he has had enough of the bureaucracy and dons his ninja garb and handles things his own way . . . and the streets of Texas will never be the same!

Theatrical poster for *Pray For Death*. Author's collection.

Akira Saito (Sho Kosugi) is a ninja who just wants to settle down in *Pray For Death*. Author's collection.

Sho Kosugi plays family man/ninja Akria Saito in *Pray For Death*. Author's collection.

Pray For Death stars Sho Kosugi as Akria Saito, a ninja pushed to the limit. Author's collection.

Sho Kosugi is undoubtedly *the* ninja of the 1980s, and *Pray For Death*, which followed his days at Cannon, is right in line with his more famous ninja films *Enter the Ninja*, *Revenge of the Ninja*, and *Ninja III: The Domination*. He designed the weapons used in the film, and there's plenty of "R"-rated ninja carnage to fill at least one other movie. In a notable scene, another ninja slips on a sword and dies. It's just that kind of movie. Kosugi's real-life sons Kane and Shane appear as his sons in the film, and Kane gets in on some of the best action. Peggy Abernathy sings the memorable theme song "Back to the Shadows." Gordon Hessler, who directed, would work with Kosugi several more times. Their next one was *Rage of Honor*.

Predator

1987 (Fox DVD) (djm)

"There's something out there waiting for us . . . and it ain't no man."

A team of commandos is called in to do a one-day job in the jungle: To perform a quick rescue and go home. What ends up happening is way beyond any of their expectations. A "Predator" from outer space is on a hunting trip and he's collecting trophies, picking off the commandos one by one. Invisible and armed with advanced weapons none of the soldiers can match, it stalks them in the jungle, sizing them up, and when it's down to the last man—the leader, Dutch (Arnold Schwarzenegger)—he's finally got a worthy opponent. Dutch sets traps and calls the monster out for a final tête-à-tête. Can a man ever hope to kill a behemoth of a hunter?

A verifiable classic, John McTiernan's *Predator* has all the accoutrements—courtesy of producer Joel Silver—to cement its status as one of the all-time great action star vehicles. No one else on Earth could have starred in this movie except Arnold. He's larger than life, and he's surrounded by an awesome group of tough guys—Carl Weathers (who would go on to do *Action Jackson* next), Bill Duke (who was in *Commando*), wrestler Jesse Ventura (*Abraxis*), and the great Sonny Landham from *Fleshburn*. The gigantic Kevin Peter Hall from *Harry and the Hendersons* plays the Predator, which was designed by Stan Winston. The creature has since gone on to be an iconic movie monster. Jean-Claude Van Damme was originally cast as the Predator, but he was fired after creative differences.

Just imagine if he *had* played the Predator . . . Weird, right? Sequels and spin-offs were made without Arnold, which is too bad. The script for *Predator 2* was written for him, but he starred in *Total Recall* instead. McTiernan and Arnold later teamed up again for *Last Action Hero*.

Predators

2010 (Fox DVD) (djm)

"We're gonna need a new plan."

Waking up in freefall, mercenary Royce (Adrien Brody) is disoriented, and when his chute opens, he lands in the middle of a jungle. Another disoriented man named Cuchillo (Danny Trejo) is on the ground, ready to kill whoever brought him to this place, and the two of them realize that there are several others in the same predicament, including Russian Spetsnaz soldier Nikolai (Sambo champion Oleg Taktarov), death row inmate Stans (Walton Goggins), doctor Edwin (Topher Grace), guerrilla soldier Isabelle (Alice Braga), and several others. They form a team out of necessity because none of them can figure out how they got to this jungle or what's going on. When they realize that they're on another planet, that's when things get real interesting for them. Royce understands before anyone else that they've been brought to a game reserve and that they're being hunted by otherworldly "predators," and the only way they're going to survive and find a way off the planet is to work together, despite their differences.

A nice welcome return to what made 20th Century Fox's *Predator* franchise so appealing in the first place, *Predators* gets a motley bunch of badass characters and fills them with more than capable actors—and even two action stars (Trejo and Taktarov). It would have been ideal to have someone like John Cena or "Stone Cold" Steve Austin in the Royce roll, but Brody's acting chops were more or less enough to compensate for the fact that he's not an action star. Both Trejo and Taktarov are great in their small, respective roles, and the action, effects, and music score by John Debney should bring fans of the original *Predator* back into the fold. Robert Rodriguez produced, and Nimrod Antal directed.

The President's Man

2000 (Madacy DVD) (djm)

When the president of the United States is out of options, he has a last-case resort: Vietnam vet Joshua McCord, officially known as "The President's Man." McCord (Chuck Norris) spends his days as a college professor, and when he's called upon to undertake one-man missions of such import as rescuing the first lady from terrorists who've taken her hostage, he is an efficient and well-oiled machine, never a skip in beats or a slip-up. He gets to a point in his career where he feels the pull to retire, but before he can, he must recruit a successor. His secret agent daughter, Que (Jennifer Tung), is his only teammate, and she suggests looking into a disgraced soldier named Deke Slater (Dylan Neal), who is prone to following his instincts over the orders he's given, and we see how his actions led to not only a court marshal and a seven-year prison sentence, but also to killing a fellow inmate in self-defense. McCord has him released on a probationary term, where he must train and prove himself a worthy "President's Man" before McCord allows him to undertake a mission. McCord's first task for him ends with a question mark as to Slater's abilities to follow orders and not his instincts, but his second mission confirms that McCord trusts him to carry the mantle and become the most trusted man to the commander in chief.

A late vehicle for Chuck Norris, who by this time had become a major TV star thanks to *Walker, Texas Ranger*, *The President's Man* is a lark of a film, and thoroughly entertaining considering that it was made for television. With nonstop action and a generous portion of seemingly death-defying stunts, it goes an awful long way to please its audience. Underscored by a big, brassy James Bond-type soundtrack, it constantly keeps things engaging, and it fooled me into thinking that it was *almost* a theatrical-level release. Soon-Tek Oh from *Missing in Action 2: The Beginning* plays a small part as a villain. Chuck's son Eric directed it with Michael Preece.

The President's Man 2:
A Line in the Sand
2002 (Madacy DVD) (djm)

Joshua McCord (Chuck Norris) still hasn't retired, despite the fact that he has found the perfect successor in Deke Slater (Judson Mills, who replaced Dylan Neal). As "The President's Men," they are asked to undertake the most dangerous missions of all. Their latest mission requires them to capture a Muslim extremist who plans to set off a nuclear bomb on US soil, and after a death-defying capture of the terrorist, the son of the extremist is left with a mandate by his father to detonate the bomb in Dallas, where he is being held by the government. This propels McCord and Slater into accomplishing a task with such urgency that we're constantly reminded that a bomb will go off if they don't get to it first and disarm it.

Not as fun as the first entry, *A Line in the Sand* feels like a weak couple of episodes of *24*, and with Chuck Norris taking a back seat to Judson Mills (who has a black belt in taekwondo in real life), the movie loses potency and its Chuck Norris-y awesomeness. Norris looks bored this time, and his spunky sidekick eats up the spotlight, for better or worse. The President is played by the late Robert Urich. Directed by Eric Norris.

Prince of the Sun
1990 (York VHS) (djm)

Buddha, who has inhabited the body of a man for decades, is transferred to another body when the man dies. The monks around the man are desperate to find the next "Living Buddha," and when the next one in line is a little boy there is a race of sorts to get to him before an evil, magical monster finds him and casts him into outer darkness. A protector is assigned to help the boy travel to a holy place where the boy can transcend into a state that will reveal his true self and power. The protector is played by Cynthia Rothrock, and she spends most of her screen time in a monk's garb, and she does some fancy footwork in the film. Along for the adventure is a bickering couple (Sheila Chan and Conan Lee) who cross paths with "the Living Buddha," and they unwittingly help the boy fulfill his destiny.

Extremely hokey and irritating, *Prince of the Sun* feels like a quickie shot for peanuts and without much of a script, despite the purported multimillion-dollar budget. Rothrock remains mostly silent for much of the film, and the only real reason to see the movie at all is to watch her fight. Conan Lee (from *Eliminators* and *Gymkata*) is in it mostly for laughs, and the little boy is crude, nasty, and unlikable. The version I saw was poorly dubbed, and the film stock used for the movie was grainy and washed out. Directed by Wellson Chin (*The Inspector Wears Skirts* with Rothrock) and Yi-Jung Hua.

The Prisoner
(a.k.a. **Island of Fire**)
1990 (Sony DVD) (djm)

Sammo Hung, Jackie Chan, and Andy Lau star in this hardboiled dramatic action movie set in and around a maximum-security prison. They each have their separate stories that explain how and why they ended up in prison, and we see them plan a grand escape. We watch them as the warden and his cruel guards torture them, and our hopes are crushed as the climax builds to a surprisingly grim conclusion.

There are several existing versions of this film. The definitive version is the original, uncut film, which fleshes out the characters and has an epic, expansive length, but I watched the truncated, dubbed US DVD version. While (as I understand it) the story and situations have been considerably altered in this shorter version, I feel more or less confident that I understood the basic elements of the plot. The pessimistic tone and shockingly downbeat aspects of the film will take fans of Chan and Hung aback. While there're some expectedly intense martial arts encounters, the focus is on the dire circumstances of each of the characters and how the system pretty much destroys them. Chan's role is diminished, and anyone looking to see a movie where he's the star should look elsewhere. Also with Wang Yu from *The Man From Hong Kong*. Directed by Chu Yen Ping.

Project A
1983 (Dimension DVD) (djm)

In late nineteenth-century Hong Kong, the coast guard is having a hard time dealing with free-ranging pirates, who cause untold damages to shipping freighters. They recruit young men willing to die to keep the seas safe, and one man's dedication is noticed above the others. Dragon Ma (Jackie Chan, who also directed) is singled out and given a promotion, and through a series of events, he goes undercover and finds out that the coast guard has some dishonest officials, who have been bribed by the pirates. Dragon (along with two buddies, played by Sammo Hung and Yuen Biao) is able to get the best of the pirates and reveal the rotten apples.

Some highly distinguishable fight scenes elevate *Project A* to a near "A" level of action entertainment, but even after watching it several times throughout the years, I still struggle to remember the film. A fight scene in a clock tower is a highlight, as well as the finale involving the three stars matched against the pirate horde. Dick Wei, who played the pirate overlord, appeared in a number of other films starring Jackie Chan. Chan, Hung, and Biao also appeared together in *Wheels on Meals, My Lucky Stars*, and *Dragons Forever*. They made a great team. Side note: Danny Trejo voiced the main villain in the dubbed American release.

Project A 2
1987 (Dimension DVD) (CD)

"We're victims of your heroism!"

After Dragon Ma (Jackie Chan) has defeated the pirates (see the first film for more on that), he finds himself a local hero. He's promoted to be the new police chief in the Sai Wan district. Once in charge, he notices how crime has run rampant and many of the police officers are on the take. He's ready to shape everyone up and rushes straight after the local triads. While the triads turn out to be far more powerful than he originally thought, he still has to fight for his life against a small group of pirates who want revenge on Dragon after he killed their brothers (the villains from the first film). He eventually finds himself in an unlikely position and teamed up with a group of revolutionaries who are trying to put an end to the corruption in the government, and together they just might have the evidence to do the impossible.

Project A 2 is a far more serious film than the original (it does have a fair share of humor, just not as abundant) but Jackie Chan (*Wheels on Meals*) was in his prime for this film and crafts a truly phenomenal experience. Chan took this beast on himself: directing, writing, and starring in a masterpiece of action cinema. The movie moves a little slower than the original, and I would be lying if I said the presence of Sammo Hung (*Eastern Condors*) and Yuen Biao (*The Iceman Cometh*) wasn't missed. Chan's love for Buster Keaton-esque humor is evident here, especially during a scene where a scaffold falls over and he is luckily standing in the right spot. All of the fight scenes are outstanding, but the twenty-minute finale will leave you in awe of Chan and his stunt team. This is the type of film to be included in a curriculum in a class teaching Action 101: it don't get much better than this.

Project Eliminator

1991 (Image DVD) (CD)

"War is one universal shitstorm!"

Dr. Markson (Joshua Bryant) has developed a weapon that could change the rules of war but then he destroys it when he realizes he wants to get out of the arms business. The weapon is so advanced and deadly that he brings in two former special forces soldiers, Ron Morrell (David Carradine) and John Slade (Frank Zagarino), to watch over him and his daughter Jackie (Hilary English). The crooked Agent Willis (Drew Snyder) hires mercenary Elias (Brett Baxter Clark) to kidnap Markson and his daughter but Slade ends up being a bigger pain than he anticipated. They eventually succeed in the kidnapping, but you can't keep a good man down. Slade is a machine that just can't be stopped, and anyone getting in his way will be sorry.

Project Eliminator won't go down in history as being some sort of masterful accomplishment, but if you can't have a good time with it then you're reading the wrong book. Frank Zagarino (*Trained to Kill*) returns as John Slade in this sequel to the 1987 film *Striker*. Zagarino is in top form and hits every beat he should as an action star. There are several fight scenes and buckets full of spent ammunition. It also delivers a solid climactic fight scene between Zagarino and Brett Baxter Clark (*Delta Force Commando*). Joining him in the shenanigans this time around is the late and great David Carradine (*Lone Wolf McQuade*) playing an old military buddy who offers Slade a job opportunity. The story is an obvious excuse to go from set piece to set piece while never taking itself too seriously. The body count is high, the quips come frequently, and the hero goes to hell and back walking away with just a bloody lip. Much of the music is pretty generic but there's a great opening song called "Never Look Back" that really sort of sets the tone for the rest of the picture. Directed with a burst of energy by H. Kaye Dyal (*Trained to Kill*), you can't go wrong with *Project Eliminator*.

Project Purgatory

2010 (Maverick Entertainment DVD) (djm)

A virus besieges the globe, and nukes are set off to eradicate the infected, who mutate into zombie-like stragglers with only a modicum of intelligence and reasoning. The fallout from the radiation only makes things worse, and survivors hole up in redoubts and underground shelters, where they bide their time over the following year. One noninfected survivor named Shinji (martial artist Andre "Chyna" McCoy, who always wears dark sunglasses even though most of the movie takes place in the shadows) goes around the urban wastelands, slaying "Radvics," which is what the zombies are now called. A group of survivors watches him on the warpath and is impressed with his survival skills, and so they invite him into their safe haven where maybe a dozen of them live with a scientist who is working on a cure. Shinji reluctantly joins the group, but he's immediately drugged and thrown in a cell so that his health can be monitored. It's not a good start to a positive, trustful relationship, and so the group has already made an enemy out of their best hope to stay alive in the coming weeks when their unstable community reveals itself to be full of racially partial members—black, white, and Asian—who quite honestly all deserve to die for putting personal prejudices ahead of any other priorities. When Shinji gets loose in the redoubt, he slays the racist German militant in the shelter (who has already caused untold damage to the group), and then it's time to face the invading Radvics, who come pouring in.

Low tech, low brow, and appealing (maybe) to the lowest common denominator, *Project Purgatory* is a slapdash hack job that doesn't even feel finished, as it ends at the seventy-five minute mark on a cliffhanger. Star Chyna McCoy (from *Game Over* and *TKO*) has some appeal as a martial artist/ action star, but most of the fights he engages in are with zombies, so there's little payoff seeing him breaking the necks of slow-moving gut munchers. The movie was shot for peanuts, with bad lighting, terrible sound, and annoying techno music on the soundtrack, so if you've read this far into the review then you might be this movie's core audience. As an apocalyptic movie, it's trash. As an action film, it has some little merit, but not much. Written and directed by Xavier Kantz, who did another awful post-apocalyptic action movie called *Wasteland*.

Project: Shadowchaser

(a.k.a. **Shadowchaser**)

1992 (Prism VHS) (djm)

A hospital the president's daughter is visiting is taken over by terrorists who are using a billion-dollar cyborg as their point man. The cyborg is known as Romulus (played by a buffed out Frank Zagarino), and his creator (Joss Ackland) is called in to help talk him out of the hostage situation. Also in the mix is a just-thawed-out-from-cryogenic-stasis prisoner named Desilva (Martin Kove), who the authorities think is the architect of the hospital, so when Desilva is treated like an important asset to the rescue of Sarah, the president's daughter (played by Meg Foster), he's bewildered, confused, but glad to be amongst the living. He goes along with the rescue team, but the entire commando is killed, leaving him as Sarah's only hope for rescue. Just like in *Die Hard*, he crawls around in the ventilation shafts, using elevators and hidey-holes to get the drop on Romulus's unit of terrorists.

The first part of a trilogy, all of which star Zagarino as the same relentless cyborg with a bleached white flattop, *Project: Shadowchaser* is adequate in the action department, but a vanilla sense of direction keeps it from obtaining any ounce of distinction. Zagarino's take on the cyborg character is okay (he certainly looks perfect for it), but he's not really given the direction to do anything remotely unique with it, which is a shame. Kove plays his part this side of hammy. If he'd done something like what he did in *Steele Justice*, this might have been something special. The next movie in the series was better. They were all directed by John Eyres.

Project Shadowchaser II: Night Siege

1994 (Image DVD) (djm)

An alcoholic janitor named Frank Meade (Bryan Genesse in great shape a few years after *Street Justice*) goes to work at the nuclear power plant, sasses his hot boss (Beth Tousaint), and gets his ass fired. He sticks around anyway, riding out the day, and good thing, too: Terrorists have overrun the place and are using an android (a massive Frank Zagarino, totally pumped out) to comb the halls and shoot anyone who resists. The terrorists are demanding a ransom or else, and so Meade stalks the air vents and elevator shafts and gets the drop on the bad guys one by one, using his pretty impressive martial arts skills. His final fight with Zagarino the robot is pretty cool.

Genesse was a cool and underrated action star, and so was Zagarino, for that matter. Both of them had some luck for a while when they were making movies for Nu Image (which this movie was for), and *Shadowchaser II* was one of two movies they did together. The other one was *Terminal Impact*, and that one was more fun. *Shadowchaser II* is a basic *Die Hard* clone, but it goes through the motions in the right way, making sure that its two central stars get their time in the spotlight. The next entry in the franchise took place way in the future and featured a glorified cameo by Zagarino. John Eyres did all three pictures.

Project : Shadowchaser III

(a.k.a. **Project Shadowchaser 3000**)

1995 (Image DVD) (djm)

A space crew can't avoid a collision with another spaceship, and in the chaos, several members of the crew are killed. When they get their bearings, they board the other ship and find that everyone has been murdered. A rogue android (played by a buffed out and bleached white haired Frank Zagarino) systematically hunts them all down, while helping to spread a contagious disease.

For Zagarino completists only, *Shadowchaser III* is the sort of thing Roger Corman used to produce, but with boobs, and so this production from Nu Image (without boobs) isn't any fun. Zagarino, a star for Nu Image at the time, only appears in a few scenes, but he's compelling when he's there, but when he's not, the movie sags. He went on to do *Orion's Key* later. Directed by John Eyres, who did all the *Project: Shadowchaser* movies, which are technically unrelated despite the fact that Zagarino kinda played the same android in all of them.

P

Billy Wong (Jackie Chan) goes all out when he fights! From James Glickenhaus' *The Protector*. Author's collection.

The Protector

1985 (Shout Factory DVD) (djm)

Jackie Chan's second attempt (not counting *The Cannonball Run* movies) at crossing over to the US as an action star, *The Protector* casts him as a humorless New York detective whose partner is killed in front of him. He is assigned a new partner (Danny Aiello), and they travel to Hong Kong to nab a drug lord who kidnapped an American woman. They get into some bad scrapes, and Aiello is captured and tied to a chair, where he spends most of the finale of the movie. Jackie saves him, and there wasn't a sequel.

From James Glickenhaus, the director of the nasty *The Exterminator*, this vehicle for Chan has a completely different feel than any of his other works. It's downbeat, foul-mouthed, ultra violent, and sexist. Chan is good, but it appears (at least, to me) that he was reigned in and restrained from being the Chan everyone loves. For that reason, *The Protector* is essential viewing. It's an anomaly, and it's worth watching to see a great action star a little

Cop Billy Wong (Jackie Chan) uses what's available to stop the bad guys in *The Protector*. Author's collection.

Watch Jackie Chan cross a river without getting wet in *The Protector*. Author's collection.

out of his comfort zone. It still has some interesting stunt and set pieces (watch Chan cross a river on a motorcycle without getting wet), but the tone is completely different for him. Two versions exist of this film. There was the version released by Warner Brothers, and the Golden Harvest/Jackie Chan cut, which has slightly more martial arts action in it. His next English language crossover film, *Rumble in the Bronx*, was ten years later, and that proved to be the hit he needed in the US.

The Protector

1998 (Raven VHS) (djm)

A man wakes up, frightened and overwhelmed that he can't remember who he is. The Man (Steven Nijjar) is immediately thrust into a violent odyssey where people are trying to kill him, but one guy named Cole (Frank Zagarino) is trying to protect him. As The Man comes to realize, he was working with Cole (a former outlaw), and during a heist Cole accidentally killed an innocent child, the son of a brute named Gunther (Matthias Hues). Gunther is hunting Cole and The Man, and is using The Man's own son as bait, but since The Man doesn't have a memory of his life before a head injury, the threat isn't as imminent.

You gotta love Frank Zagarino. He rarely shows emotion and might as well be The Terminator in most of his movies, but when he shows a little humanity, it's funny because it almost doesn't become him. He gets to have a long, drawn-out duke-it-out session with Hues, who is great at getting beat up by good guys. Steven Nijjar gave himself the lead role (he produced this), but there's a good reason why he never made more movies (his acting is . . . questionable). He also worked on movies like *TC 2000* and *Expect No Mercy*. Only see *The Protector* if you want to complete your Zagarino or Hues collection. Directed by Boon Collins and Fabian Lloyd.

The Protector

(Tom Yum Goong)

2005 (The Weinstein Company DVD) (djm)

A sect of monks is tasked with protecting a family of elephants, and one of the protectors has a son

Kham (Tony Jaa) encounters the hulking T. K. (Nathan Jones) in *The Protector*. Author's collection.

From director Prachya Pinkaew, *The Protector* stars Tony Jaa as the humble Kham. Author's collection.

An intense action scene from *The Protector*. Author's collection.

named Kham (Tony Jaa) who grows up alongside one of the younger elephants. Kham treats this animal like a brother, so when many years later his father is murdered by poachers and his brother elephant is stolen, Kham travels to Australia to bring him back home. It's a good thing Kham is a proficient Muay Thai fighter because the people he's up against are brutal and lethal. Kham uncovers an illegal operation going on in an elite restaurant where wealthy clientele are served endangered animal species from a secret menu, and when Kham believes that his "brother" has been served up as food, he loses all rationale and control, annihilating all comers as he works his way up to the top gangsters who have wronged him.

Heavy handedness aside, this dynamic Tony Jaa vehicle is a good follow-up from his breakout success *Ong Bak*. Jaa plays a perpetually innocent soul here, and despite the carnage he wreaks, he still manages to emerge as child-like and pure. There's a great scene shot in one take as he works his way up the floors of the restaurant/brothel, and this

Jackie Chan does his own stunts (as usual) in *The Protector*. That's him in the sky on a motorcycle. Author's collection.

When Kham's (Tony Jaa) elephant is taken from him, he tracks it down because he's The Protector. Author's collection.

Tony Jaa is airborne in this scene from *The Protector*. Author's collection.

one scene sort of places this movie on a high shelf where movies with the best fight scenes of all time dwell. This movie has lots of great fights in it. Jaa has a fight with Jon Foo (*Bangkok Revenge*), one with Lateef Crowder (later seen in *Falcon Rising*), and then another one (a brutal one) with the gigantic Nathan Jones from *Muay Thai Giant* and *The Condemned*. Some of the stuff we see in the movie looks like it hurts terribly, and everything between Jaa and Jones looks deathly serious. Two versions of this movie exist: The US theatrical cut is eighty-three minutes (I saw that version in theaters), and the international version is 110 minutes, which pads out the time with a longer prologue and some other filler scenes. Either version is worth watching. Prachya Pinkaew, who directed *Ong Bak*, did a pretty impressive job here. The sequel, which arrived a number of years later, is nuts.

The Protector 2
2013 (Magnet DVD) (djm)

Tony Jaa returns as Kham, the elephant-loving man who when pushed past his breaking point becomes a skull-crushing avenger. In this sequel, Kham's elephant (whom he calls his little brother) is stolen from him by some shady businessmen who want to use the animal as a live bomb to be presented as a gift to two dignitaries at a peace meeting. Kham has a limited amount of time to save his elephant before the bomb goes off (the bombs are planted in the tusks, which have been severed and reattached), and his biggest task is to get through a barrage of fighters who've been branded and brainwashed by a villain named Mr. LC (RZA). While Kham goes through dozens of bad guys to get to his elephant, he is being pursued

Tony Jaa in *The Protector 2*, a Magnet release. Courtesy of Magnet Releasing

by an Interpol agent and a pair of twin girls (both played by JeeJa Yanin from *Chocolate* and *Phoenix Point*), who think he's up to no good. There are scenes of Jaa dodging dozens of motorcycle raiders, and another extended scene of him grappling the roof of a car as it's being chased and rammed by all kinds of traffic. The best moments of the film feature Jaa fighting the fight coordinator, Marrese Crump, who makes an indelible impression as one of the main villains.

Filmed over a period of several years, *The Protector 2* is bound to make Jaa's fans happy, and even his most devoted followers will be willing to forgive the wackiness that might very well mar it for non-fans. In one scene, Jaa and Crump have a long fight where their bodies become light sabers (complete with *Star Wars* sound effects), and the last scene has RZA incinerated by the tusk bombs while Jaa and his elephant embrace lovingly after all the trauma they went through. I saw this theatrically in 3D. It's pretty crazy. Directed by Prachya Pinkaew.

Puncture Wounds
(a.k.a. **A Certain Kind of Justice**)
2014 (Lionsgate DVD) (djm)

"I'd find the men who killed his family, and I'd put them away. Then I'd wait for John to turn himself in because that's what he'll do. He won't run from what he's done. He's just not wired that way. He believes in justice, and if you can't deliver it, well then, you can be sure as hell John will."

Iraqi war veteran John (Cung Le from *Dragon Eyes*) comes home after a harrowing tour of duty and takes up residence at a dumpy apartment complex near where his family lives. Not long after, he steps into a confrontation involving a battered prostitute named Tanya (Briana Evigan), who "belongs" to a white supremacist drug lord named Hollis (an imposing and dangerous looking Dolph Lundgren). John kills several men in the confrontation and saves the girl, but he incites the curiosity of the police and—more importantly—the wrath of Hollis, who sends his goons to take revenge on John by having his family raped and degraded before being burned to death in a fiery explosion. John

won't stand by as justice is left to the incompetent system, so he enlists his only friend: an amputee veteran, who has been waiting for some kind of purpose to present itself to him after years on the sidelines. The two of them go after the heart of Hollis's drug manufacturing and get themselves more attention than they can handle when they stir the bull, who comes in horns blazing.

From Giorgio Serafini, the director of the inferior Dolph Lundgren vehicles *Ambushed* and *Blood of Redemption*, *Puncture Wounds* manages to correct the wrongs of those two films by giving Lundgren a great villain role that he seems to relish and by allowing star Cung Le to spread his wings as a burgeoning action guy. This is without a doubt Cung's movie, and he manages to dig his heels and toes into the role, committing to the emotional devastation his character goes through, while still focusing on his martial arts abilities when he plows through bad guys. With a pessimistic, downbeat tone, *Puncture Wounds* may turn some viewers off, but ultimately I enjoyed it despite its grim nature and the bittersweet ending. If Cung can find more vehicles like this to star in, then there's no reason he won't become one of the fiercest action stars working in the business.

The Punisher
1989 (Artisan DVD) (djm)

From the Marvel Comics library, the Dolph Lundgren-starring version of *The Punisher* has been unfairly ignored for decades—strange, considering the recent resurgence of comic book characters, The Punisher character itself, and even Dolph's own comeback following his turn in *The Expendables* movies. After playing *He-Man* in Cannon's *Masters of the Universe*, he was tapped for this modestly budgeted film from New World Pictures, and his take on it was pretty good, despite the fact that the producers and director Mark Goldblatt ultimately decided he shouldn't wear The Punisher's signature skull shirt. As Frank Castle/The Punisher, Lundgren wears face paint and has dyed black hair to make him look sinister, sallow, and dark, and he spends most of the film in a monotone mindset, as befitting a midnight avenger, seeking justice for his family's slaughter at the hands of a mafia. A detective named Berkowitz (Lou Gossett Jr. who would co-star with Lundgren again in *Cover Up*) believes his deceased partner Castle is the vigilante the media has labeled The Punisher, and as he gets closer to the truth, The

Frank Castle (Dolph Lundgren) is *The Punisher*. Author's collection.

Punisher virtually turns himself in after redeeming himself by rescuing a bunch of kidnapped sons and daughters of crime lords who are under siege by the overzealous Japanese Yakuza. Mafioso Franco (Jeroen Krabbe) busts The Punisher out of incarceration only to force him to help him rescue his only son, who is being heavily guarded by ninjas and bodyguards.

Filmed in Australia and nicely directed by well-known editor Goldblatt, who cut movies like *The Terminator, Commando,* and *Rambo: First Blood Part II, The Punisher* was unfortunately never released to US theaters when New World went bankrupt. Released to video and relegated to "B" movie status, it was a catalyst for turning Lundgren into a direct-to-video star. After this, he had a few theatrical releases like *Showdown in Little Tokyo* and *Universal Soldier,* but if *The Punisher* had been released to theaters as intended in the same climate as Tim Burton's *Batman,* things might have turned out differently for him. As it is, this remains a solid vehicle for him, and it's one of several of his films that garnered cult status. Boaz Yakin, who wrote and directed *Safe* with Jason Statham many years later, scripted this. More *Punisher* movies—starring Thomas Jane and Ray Stevenson in the title role— followed, and all three movies are really good for different reasons. Is Lundgren the definitive Frank Castle? You decide.

INTERVIEW:
MARK GOLDBLATT
(djm)

Mark Goldblatt's name on the credits of a movie usually signifies that the picture is going to be BIG. After co-editing films like Piranha (1978) *and* Humanoids From the Deep (1980), *he segued into one of the most prolific and most in-demand editors in Hollywood, cutting Joe Dante's* The Howling (1981), *James Cameron's* The Terminator (1984) *and* Terminator 2: Judgment Day (1991), *not to mention some of the biggest action blockbusters of the 1980s and 1990s like* Rambo: First Blood Part II (1985), Commando (1985), *and Michael Bay's* Armageddon (1998). *In 1988, Goldblatt tried his hand at directing, and his first effort was New World's* Dead Heat (1988), *starring Treat Williams and Joe Piscopo as two cops who are killed and return to duty as zombies. Combining* Lethal Weapon-*styled action and a hybridized horror flavor, the film flopped at the box office, but Goldblatt was offered another New World picture: the first film adaptation of Marvel's* The Punisher (1989), *starring Dolph Lundgren and Lou Gossett Jr. Both back-to-back films he did for New World are now considered cult classics, and here he looks back on his successful career.*

How did you get your start as an editor? As I understand it, you started out doing some things for Roger Corman.

I was a film buff at an early age growing up in New York. I watched lots of movies all the time. I directed movies—started shooting my own 8mm movies and editing them, among other things, so I was kind of self-taught. I loved genre pictures. I was a big fan of the *Flash Gordon* serials. Buster

Crabbe. Science fiction and horror. That was with me forever, and that was my hobby, basically, movies. By the time it came time for me to figure out what to do with my life, I joined a film society in high school, and then I went to college, but I didn't really study film there because the film department was kind of small. I was a philosophy major. I did join a film society there and programmed 35mm screenings. Then I became a film critic for the paper. And I continued to make my films, and I decided that if I was going to work in movies for a living that I would need some training. So I went off to London in the 1970s, and in those days it was pretty inexpensive. I went to a film school there called London Film School where I studied everything. I learned editing, sound, you name it. It was very much a trade school, not an academic. By the time I was done, I knew all kinds of stuff, and I also knew that I liked editing a lot. I found out I was pretty good at it. Then it was time to come back to the United States, which I did. I came to Los Angeles where I only knew a handful of people. I just started beating on doors and found an entry-level job as a production assistant—getting coffee, doughnuts, and bagels and stuff. It was on a movie called *Hollywood Boulevard.* That was 1976. Joe Dante and Allan Arkush were the directors. Roger Corman owned the company that made the picture. Jon Davison was the producer who gave me the break. They hired me at no pay. After a few eighteen-hour days, I told them, "You've got to pay me! This is insane!" So they gave me $60 a week, non-retroactive. But it was a great job. I met a lot of people. I got another job right away that paid more. Finally, I got an editing job somewhere. Joe Dante was going to edit a movie, and he was going to have me as his assistant. I became his associate editor. He got another picture to direct called *Piranha* that I co-edited with him. He gave me a big break on that. That was successful so I started getting more and more offers. I went from that to *Humanoids From the Deep.* There was something in between those called *Spirit of the Wind.*

Yeah, say something about that film.

That's a really good movie. It's a movie about a guy named George Attla, who had polio as a child. It's his life story. He rose above his deformity to become the dog sledding champion of the world. This movie was made independently by a guy named Ralph Liddle, and another guy named John Logue, who shot the picture. They'd shot the whole picture but they needed to have it edited. I'd done *Piranha,* and this job wasn't for much money, but I ended up working with these guys out of their garage. We put this movie together. It was really nice. Chief Dan George was in it. Slim Pickens was in it. It was pretty much a homemade film. It was selected to go to the Cannes Film Festival that year. We had to fly ourselves there. We all got second-hand tuxedos. The picture was financed by a Native American tribe. There were rights issues all across the board. It played in Westwood for a week, and it won the very first Sundance Film Festival, but at that time it was called the US Film Festival. It was shown on the Disney Channel, and then it disappeared. I would get requests to loan out my 16mm print of the film. I know there's a French DVD out now. I think the ownership issues have been ironed out now. It's a good movie.

So you went from that to *Humanoids From the Deep.*

Yes, from the snow to the water.

You did a Golan/Globus film *Enter the Ninja* shortly thereafter.

That was the first picture I did for them. I had done *The Howling,* but it hadn't been out yet. I was brought in to take over this movie. It went very quickly. They were very happy over there at Cannon. That picture went out, and I ended up doing a few more pictures for them down the road. Menahem Golan, the head of the company, was also a director. He directed *Enter the Ninja,* and then I did *Over the Brooklyn Bridge* and then *The Ambassador,* which was one of J. Lee Thompson's last pictures. It had Rock Hudson and Robert Mitchum. Very good cast. It was based on an Elmore Leonard novel. Cannon transposed it to take place in Israel. It was based on the novel *52 Pick-Up.* Cannon made *52 Pick-Up* a few years later, which John Frankenheimer directed. Adam Greenberg was the DP, and he also shot *The Terminator,* which I also edited.

Your work on *The Terminator* began your relationship with James Cameron. Talk a little bit about working with Cameron on the two *Terminator* pictures.

Well, they were different experiences, of course, but both good. The first one was in 1984. It was Jim's first real movie. He had done *Piranha 2,* but I don't even think that had come out when we were working on *The Terminator.* He wrote *The Terminator,* and I read the script. I knew Gale Anne Hurd, the producer. She used to be Roger Corman's assistant for a while, and then she went on to be a producer. She introduced me to Jim. I'd known him before, but she was very instrumental in me doing that movie. Jim and I hit it off, and so we got together and did the picture together. I knew the script was great, but none of us knew what an impression the picture would create. That was pretty amazing.

Was there much footage you had to excise from the first cut?

No, not really. Just a couple of subplot scenes that we had to take out, but that was just because we felt we could live without them. Everything that we took out is in the current DVD. That was pretty much the movie. We shot the script. That was a good one.

How clear was Cameron's vision for that film in the early stages?

His vision was very precise. He had originally made a drawing of the exoskeleton. That was his first vision that came to mind before he wrote the script. He's a painter, so he can draw. The script was very tight. He knew how it was going to go together. I remember the executives were concerned because he wasn't shooting coverage. I said, "He doesn't need coverage. He knows exactly what he's doing! I see exactly how it's going to come together. It's going to be great!" You could see that he knew what he was doing. A lot of people just shoot a lot of stuff, but he didn't need to do that.

It's considerably shorter than the second film.

Oh, yeah, much shorter. The second film was much huger. A much bigger canvas. They were both great to work on. It was a privilege to do those films.

How did *The Terminator* change the course of your career? Were you thinking at this point that you wanted to become a director?

That changed my career. It took me out of the independents, out of the "B" pictures. I went from that to *Rambo: First Blood Part II* to *Commando* with Fox and Joel Silver, to *Jumpin' Jack Flash*, and then I kind of wanted to get into directing. I would do pitch meetings for different projects. I did second unit directing on *RoboCop*. Somebody sent me the script of *Dead Heat*, and I really liked it. So I went for that and got that job.

***Dead Heat* wasn't a hit, so I'm curious why New World Pictures offered you another film to direct, which was *The Punisher*.**

Well, they had already offered me the other one.

Ah, I see.

They liked *Dead Heat* and were very high on the movie before it came out. I had a multi-picture deal with them. They had offered me *The Punisher* a lot earlier. I wasn't sure about it. I wanted more work done on the script, but they were happy with the script they had. So I didn't do it. They had another director, and after some time he fell out so they asked me again.

There's a scene in *The Punisher* where Frank Castle, played by Dolph Lundgren, shoots up a casino and all the slot machines. This scene is almost identical to the scene you edited in *Rambo: First Blood Part II* where Rambo shoots up a control center. Any comment on that?

Yes, it is, isn't it? (Laughing.) Well, I didn't edit the scene in *The Punisher*. The idea was to shoot it up! You shoot up the room, and then you shoot up the particulars in the room! I will cop to that. Although, I don't know if it was intentional. I think I was influenced by the very fast editing that we did in *Rambo II*. There's no question about that.

Where were the old carnival scenes shot?

That was shot at a place called Luna Park. Actually, that scene in the script doesn't take place at an amusement park. In the script, it takes place at a place where you buy tractors. There's a battle on these giant tractors, but I didn't know how we would shoot that. I found this place off the road called Luna Park, which is what you see in the movie. I thought it looked really cool. We checked it out, and basically we put together an action scene at that location. Visually we could get some mileage out of it.

The scene where The Punisher is stretched out and tortured is basically in every action movie ever made, every James Bond movie ever made. How important is this kind of scene for action movies?

The Punisher (Dolph Lundgren) is not to be trifled with. Author's collection.

I don't know. I guess it's an archetype. It's cool because it basically shows that the hero is chained and completely under subjugation. It doesn't look like there's much hope left until he get out of it and turns the tables. You don't have to have it. It's the old torture scene.

It seems to work! There's a unique twist in the film where The Punisher and the bad guy team up towards the end of the movie. Can you talk about that and say something about Jeroen Krabbé a little bit. He plays a good villain.

He's a perfect actor. A Dutch actor. I first saw him in *Soldier of Orange*, and I got to know him a little bit because he and I both worked with Paul Verhoeven. I remember he was in *Jumpin' Jack Flash*, which I also worked on. The idea was that we wanted his character to be a very likable guy who has the capacity to be very ruthless. He's a very likable bad guy.

He's the lesser of two evils in the film.

Compared to Lady Tanaka? Yeah, she's even more ruthless than he is. I remember that Gianni Franco, his character, blackmails The Punisher to help him, although The Punisher does go after the kids to do the right thing. But he says, "Remember: When this is over, you're dead!" The Punisher must carry out his vendetta. Quid pro quo. There's a point at which they teamed up, and in a strange way there is a camaraderie. Franco keeps putting out these little quips, and offers him body armor, but he doesn't react and doesn't want to get too close to him.

It's my favorite scene in the movie, when they team up.

Frank Castle (Dolph Lundgren) and his enemy Gianni Franco (Jeroen Krabbe) reluctantly team up in the climax of Mark Goldblatt's *The Punisher*. Author's collection.

Yeah, it's pretty cool. They had good chemistry together. After Tanaka is killed, Franco realizes that he has to kill The Punisher or The Punisher will kill him. So in that scene where The Punisher is wounded, and Franco attacks him, Franco plays dirty. He tries to gouge his eyes out and step on his wound. He shows his true nature.

Talk a little bit about working with Lou Gossett. His best scene has him hitting the guy after he asks to use the restroom.

Right, right, right. That's a funny moment. Lou was great. He improvised the little pizza thing. The way he reacted, stuff like that. He's a pro. He's a hard worker.

He and Lundgren did two movies together.

What was the other one?

***Cover-Up.* It was right around the same time. It went straight to video, just like *The Punisher*.**

Well, Dolph's pictures—with a couple of exceptions—pretty much did, didn't they? That's the way it is. You have no way of knowing. You make the movie and hope for the best.

Are there any subtexts in this movie with the East versus West? Guns versus swords?

Nothing on a conscious level that I can think of. If anything, I always think that the Eastern philosophy has a kind of a spiritual spine to it. Very often, Eastern religion and the way you live your life are inextricably tied together in a very organic way. Whereas Western religion is based on other things. Forgiveness. Guilt. A lot of guilt. There's more mysticism in the Eastern way. But that's not subtext.

There's the scene in the film where the guy with the mace is fighting The Punisher. The scene takes place in the dojo. You used a red filter.

Oh! Yeah. The red filter was because of the emergency lighting.

Anything interesting about that fight? It's a great fight.

I thought they came up with great fights. The two guys—the two fighters—were actually found by Robert Kamen. Robert Kamen is actually a martial artist, among other things. He also wrote *The Karate Kid*. He is a devout karate person. He went to a dojo in Tokyo and found these guys. I trusted him implicitly because he knows this stuff. I don't. They were real fighters. Dolph, of course, was a kickboxing champion. We worked out these pretty intricate fights. We covered them in different ways, with wider cameras and static shots. We used a steadycam so we could move around with the action. Dolph didn't use very many stunt doubles. He mostly did his own thing.

What is it about vigilantes living in subterranean lairs? The Ninja Turtles did the same thing and that came out around the same time.

P

Well, turtles are one thing, but The Punisher is living below the stratum of life. He's living in this basement in the dark. Damp, dark where the refuse goes. It's also a place to hide. If you think about The Phantom of the Opera, he was living in the sewers of Paris. There's something about that low, smelly refuse-laden, non-naturally lit environment that feels deadly.

Was this intended to be a franchise?

Well, I don't think there was an intention one way or the other, but if the picture was successful, sure! Definitely. We had a character who could go on.

What did you think of the other *Punisher* films that came much later? Did you see them?

I did, actually. I know Jonathan Hensley, who directed the one with Thomas Jane. He wrote *Armageddon*, which I worked on. He's married to Gale Hurd, whom I've known for decades. I think he did a pretty interesting take on *The Punisher*, actually. I'm one of the few people who liked the neighbors in that film. They were eccentric. They reminded me of the comics.

What can you tell me about Stan Lee's involvement in your *Punisher* film? His name is up there.

We met with him before we did the picture. We discussed it. I don't know if he had any input with the script. He wished us well. And then we showed it to him when it was done. I remember the one thing I did get out of him was that he thought that the picture was too violent.

The Punisher is a unique character, but he's even more unique in the comic book world because he's an "R"-rated character. Any comment on that?

It's a fine line. It's not intended for kids. Some kids can take it, and some kids can't. The Punisher is a killer. He's there to kill people. I'd say you have to . . . I wouldn't show it to my twelve year-old. It's an action picture! It's an adventure! It's a comic book!

The *Batman* movies are just as dark, but those don't have the language or the blood.

The thing is that Frank Castle—and certainly in the comic books at the time—he's completely gone. He's living in the sewer. Batman is living in two worlds, isn't he? *The Dark Knight* is very dark. By the way, the reference to Batman in our film—and a lot of people didn't like that we referenced Batman—I liked the way Batman sounded. When we made this picture, *Batman* was made before our film, but it came out after. That line was just a nod to the fact that there *was* a *Batman* picture. I didn't worry that we crossed over from the Marvel universe to the DC universe. Someone asked me about it and I told them, "I'm just referring to a fictional character." I think the line just got misunderstood.

Do you have any recollections of working with Dolph Lundgren?

We all went out one night after a hard day's work and went and did karaoke. I think he might have done an Elvis tune. That was great fun. There's a

Barry Otto as Shake and Dolph Lundgren as Frank Castle in Mark Goldblatt's *The Punisher*. Author's collection.

scene where Dolph is walking down the corridors with Jeroen, and there's a ninja hiding behind a fake wall, and Dolph just senses that he's there and he throws a knife in the wall. There was one take where the guy comes plummeting out, and fell on Dolph, and they went flying. It was an outtake. It was funny.

How come you didn't direct any more movies after this?

Well, there's the issue that *The Punisher* didn't get a theatrical release in the United States. I had done one movie that didn't make very much money. And then I did another one that didn't get a theatrical release. On video it did pretty well. Those were the early days of direct to video. A lot of the stuff I was offered I just didn't want to do. I needed to work and make a living. In fact, over the course of my directing career—because so much time is spent trying to get the picture going—I needed to get editing jobs. I went back to editing. Once you're doing that, it's hard to reposition yourself. I directed one episode of a show called *Eerie, Indiana*, which Joe Dante was doing. He recommended me. I did the episode that was a werewolf story. It was a lot of fun. I think we shot for like five days.

How did you go about casting editors for your two films as a director? Tim Wellburn was the editor on *The Punisher* and Harvey Rosenstock was your editor on *Dead Heat*.

Well, I knew Harvey from cutting *Commando*. Harvey was down the hall cutting *Moonlighting*. Tim was recommended to me. I had seen some movies that he had cut. I had seen a picture he had cut called *The Chain Reaction*, which was a picture that was made after *Mad Max*. George Miller was one of the producers on that. Tim was also one of the editors on *The Road Warrior*. I liked him so much that I recommended him to Stuart Gordon who hired him for *Fortress*.

Why didn't you cut your own movies?

I didn't think it was a good idea. That said, I did come in and cut some scenes. Tim nailed so many scenes perfectly that they were done. I didn't need to cut anything.

What if The Punisher dies? Who would punish the guilty?

Wow. There you go. There's a good question.

Pursuit

1991 (HBO VHS) (djm)

Some terrorists in South Africa steal a box of gold belonging to the government, and a soldier of fortune named Jake Cody (James Ryan from *Kickboxer 5: Redemption*) is called upon to lead a mission to retrieve the gold and kill the terrorists who stole it. When Cody is approached for the job, he is deep in training and meditation, and by the looks of things, he pretty much lives off the land, eating in the shade of trees, and ignoring the world. Coaxed back from retirement, he recruits an old friend and a few others, and once they begin their mission, they reluctantly allow a female journalist to join them. When they retrieve the gold, the prospect of riches corrupts Cody's men, and they turn against him and run off with the treasure. He and the journalist are left high and dry in the bush, and a cannibalistic tribe of natives captures them, and when they manage to free themselves, Cody locks into his killer mercenary self and gives his old friend a final goodbye.

South Africa's action star offering to the world—James Ryan—made a name for himself with the films *Kill or Be Killed* and *Kill and Kill Again*, and while he certainly has a certain appeal to him with his own brand of martial arts and action, he emerges as sort of a wet blanket in the bland *Pursuit*, which has an unusual regional flavor. He displays some of his martial arts abilities here and shoots guns and tells stories by the campfire, but he's so incredibly melodramatic in the film and the movie's big centerpiece moments are underwhelming. The climax is abrupt, too. I literally had to rewind the tape a few minutes because I thought I'd missed something. I didn't. It just ended. Directed by John H. Parr.

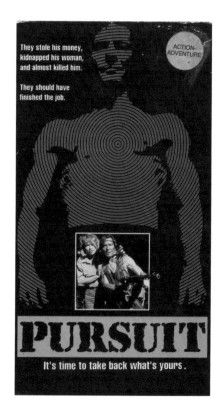

They stole his money, kidnapped his woman, and almost killed him.

They should have finished the job.

ACTION-ADVENTURE

PURSUIT

It's time to take back what's yours.

VHS artwork for *Pursuit*. Author's collection.

P

Pushed to the Limit

1992 (Image DVD) (djm)

"Try me! I'm pushed to the limit!"

The inimitable Mimi Lesseos (a former martial arts champion and pro wrestler) wrote, produced, and starred in this earnest action movie that casts her as a grieving sister of a man who was murdered by a crime syndicate for knowing too much about an underground fight tournament known as "the Kumite," which should sound familiar to anyone who's a fan of movies starring the likes of Jean-Claude Van Damme. Mimi (playing a character named "Mimi") hungers for revenge, and she takes on martial arts classes full time to have a chance to enter the Kumite, fight her way to the top, and in the process achieve some sort of justice. When she eventually starts fighting in the ring, she realizes that the rules have been thrown out the window and contestants tend to die violent, gladiatorial deaths, so her challenge is all the more grave.

Lesseos is pretty amazing to look at. She's a modern-day Amazon, with a tall, muscular frame and an incredible body, and so when she starts to attack with her martial arts abilities, the whole effect is very convincing. The few films she starred in (*Personal Vendetta* and *Streets of Rage* are two others) all bear her genuine talents as a fighter. While all of her films are weakened by sub-par writing and nearly crippling production values, I like them because I like Lesseos. She might have been a contender against other female action stars like Cynthia Rothrock and Karen Sheperd if her films had found better distribution. Her movies have remained largely undiscovered, which is a shame. This one was directed by Michael Mileham.

Queen's Messenger

2001 (Indies Home Entertainment DVD R2) (djm)

In this sequel to *Witness to a Kill*, Gary Daniels reprises his secret agent role of Captain Anthony Strong, who is tasked with delivering a package (handcuffed to his wrist) to an emissary of the British government stationed in Kazakhstan, where turmoil is brewing. Once he gets there, he's not even out of the airport when he's attacked by a terrorist group working for a warlord named Ben Samm (Christoph Waltz before his days with Tarantino). Strong manages a heroic escape on a motorcycle, and then joins up with an American female journalist who is doing a story on Samm, and the rest of the picture involves Strong romancing the journalist while saving her life time and again (007-style) from the terrorists.

Enjoyable for fans of James Bond films and especially for followers of Gary Daniels, *Queen's Messenger* is sort of in the lighthearted spirit of the '80s and '90s Bond films, while making sure Daniels gets to show off what he can do. The plot and the story don't really make much sense, but honestly, who cares? This sequel was better than the first film *Witness to a Kill*, and yet it still (to this day) has not received distribution in North America, which is very strange. Directed by Mark Roper (who did *High Adventure* and *The Pirate's Curse* with Thomas Ian Griffith).

A Queen's Ransom (a.k.a. International Assassin)

1976 (Shout Factory DVD) (djm)

An IRA terrorist (George Lazenby) hires a team of killers (one is played by Jimmy Wang Yu from *The Man From Hong Kong*, another is played by Bolo Yeung from *Enter the Dragon*) to assassinate Queen Elizabeth on her trip to Hong Kong. As the team prepares for their big day, some infighting occurs (i.e. some fights between Wang Yu and Yeung), and they have to deal with a band of refugees (one of whom is played by Angela Mao Ying, also from *Enter the Dragon*) who have stored a treasure in gold in a cabin where the terrorists are organizing their plan. As the big day closes in, the terrorists get tangled up with the refugees, and their plan becomes compromised.

A Golden Harvest production that reunites Wang Yu and Lazenby from *The Man From Hong* (which is leagues more entertaining than this film), *A Queen's Ransom* is only going to be rewarding to the most patient viewers. A muddled story and all-over-the-place plotting keeps the film from being anything special, but if you really enjoyed *The Man From Hong Kong*, you may want to check it out anyway. Directed by Shan-Hsi Ting.

The Quest

1996 (Universal DVD) (djm)

The last of Jean-Claude Van Damme's films distributed by Universal, *The Quest* is an old-fashioned adventure with a storybook feel. He plays a streetwise rapscallion named Christopher Dubois, who protects a bunch of street urchins in 1920s New York. He's forced to flee after a scuffle with the police, and he ends up as a stowaway on a ship bound for Asia. An aging British admiral named Lord Dobbs (Roger Moore) is now a pirate on the high seas, and he seizes control of the ship Dubois is on. Dobbs sees potential in Dubois as a fighter, and he sells him to a Muay Thai teacher in Siam. Six months later, Dubois has virtually become a gladiator unparalleled in skill, and he runs into Dobbs again, who is ready for his next adventure. Dubois proposes a quest: They will all go to Tibet, where an elite fight tournament is going to take place—a championship amongst the greatest fighters in the world, with the prize being a gigantic golden dragon. Dobbs, Dubois, a pretty female American journalist, and some other friends agree to the quest, and they all go to Tibet and by a miracle, Dubois is allowed to enter the tournament. It's *Bloodsport* from there on out.

Van Damme is credited as the director of this film, which is interesting. The film is really entertaining and has an almost epic scale to it, so if he directed it all by himself, then kudos to him. He came up with the story with Frank Dux (who was the inspiration for *Bloodsport*), and he surrounds himself with a cast of solid character actors like James Remar and world-class fighters, all of whom have their own distinct and stylized variations of the martial arts. The bookended prologue and epilogue, which show the Van Damme character as an old man, aren't really necessary, but there you go. I saw this theatrically in 1996 and loved it. It still holds up.

Theatrical poster for *The Quest*. Author's collection.

Quicksand

2002 (New Concorde DVD) (CD)

Randi Stewart (Brooke Theiss) is a sergeant in the Marines and is stationed on the same base as her father, General Stewart (Dan Hedaya),though the two have a troubled relationship. Meanwhile, her brother Gordon (Douglas Weston) has a promising political career and tries to distance himself from her to keep his reputation intact. Randi has issues and has begun talking to the base psychiatrist, Bill Turner (Michael Dudikoff). Turner has taken a liking to Randi but keeps his distance (despite her advances). When Randi's father is murdered, everyone is quick to suspect her as they had a public spat in which she threatened him. She's afraid of what everyone thinks and goes directly to her psychiatrist Turner. He believes everything she says and decides to do a little investigating himself, even though certain parties are out to get his confidential files. He will do whatever it takes to uncover the truth.

Of all the action stars covered in this book, Michael Dudikoff (*American Ninja*) comes off as being the most down-to-Earth on screen. Even in a film like *Quicksand* where there is little action and it feels like he's holding back his inner fury and could annihilate another person in a split second, he's just too good of a guy to do it. This film reunites him with his *American Ninja* (amongst several others) director Sam Firstenberg. It's less of an action film and more a military conspiracy thriller shot on a small budget on location in India. Despite a few minor technical issues and a score that feels wildly out of place, *Quicksand* is an engaging movie and Dudikoff gives an excellent performance. It was one of his last films as a leading star.

Theatrical release poster for *Race to Witch Mountain*. Author's collection.

Race to Witch Mountain

2009 (Disney DVD) (djm)

"Couple of kids, big wad of cash —what could go wrong?"

In his second family-oriented movie, Dwayne Johnson (no longer calling himself "The Rock") plays a Vegas cab driver/ex-getaway driver for the mob named Jack Bruno, whose life is about to take a turn for the worse when two blond children (brother and sister, played by Annasophia Robb and Alexander Ludwig) end up in his taxi, throwing a wad of cash at him and asking him to drive them to a remote location in the Nevada desert. Needing the cash (but not the headache), he takes the kids where they need to go, but the fare turns out to be way more trouble than it's worth. It quickly becomes apparent that the two kids are actually stranded extraterrestrials being hunted by an intergalactic soldier *and* government (human) spooks, hoping to tag, bag, and file them away in a scientific facility. Good-hearted Jack (and a sweet scientist, played by Carla Gugino) chaperone the two imperiled aliens back to their spacecraft so that they can go home.

A frenetic pace, a bombastic score by Trevor Rabin, and mid-level blockbusterish special effects nearly convince me that *Race to Witch Mountain* is a bona fide real-deal entertainment, but every time I see a movie with The Rock, I have to reevaluate my stance before committing to an opinion. This is a competently made motion picture, with explosions, thrills, and a big action star in the center of it, but is this a good vehicle for him? Not really, no. Anybody could have played his part in this movie. Jim Carrey could have played it. Anybody. So, does having The Rock in the movie make it better? Again, no, not really. More often than not, he takes on projects that don't suit him, which is the real problem I have with him. Occasionally, he'll do a role that actually feels like it was fashioned for him (*The Rundown, Fast Five*), but he's never really found his footing as an action star, and it actually feels deliberate, as if he doesn't *want* to be an action star . . . and there's the rub. *Race to Witch Mountain* (which is a remake/reboot of a delightful pair of movies from the later '70s) is good enough to fool an audience who doesn't care that The Rock is a delinquent action icon in waiting, but it's not good enough for me. Fans of this man deserve a full-fledged action vehicle where he's finally and completely come into his own, but honestly, we still haven't gotten that movie. Directed by Andy Fickman, who also did *The Game Plan* with The Rock (which is something no fan of his should ever see).

Rage

1995 (Universal DVD) (djm)

Mild-mannered schoolteacher Alex Gainer (Gary Daniels) is driving home one day when he's carjacked. The man who robs him is on the run from a secret government agency that takes men and women from different walks of life and experiments on them by giving them superhuman fits of strength, though a side effect symptom for most of the "volunteers" is rage. When Alex is mistaken for the fugitive, he's taken to a facility and given the experimental drug, and when he wakes up, he explodes with rage and escapes. A nationwide manhunt begins as Alex is chased by law enforcement officers who try to kill him on site because he's in a violent rage. Endowed with a newfound ability to survive explosive chases and death-defying stunts, Alex also has an incredible new skill in martial arts.

One of the most expensive films in the history of PM Entertainment, *Rage* is really impressive for showing some amazing— AMAZING—stunts that rival some of the things that have been done in the Tom Cruise-starring *Mission Impossible* films. One long scene has star Daniels dangling at the edge of a high-rise without a harness, and a helicopter shoots at him until he's able to swing himself from the edge of the building to the helicopter, which leads to another scene where he falls thousands of feet to his (we would think) death. The whole scene is carried out with the utmost professionalism, and I was breathless by the time it was over. The rest of the film plays out fairly expectedly, and fans of Daniels should be happy. Joseph Merhi (*Last Man Standing* with Jeff Wincott) directed.

The Rage

1997 (Echo Bridge DVD) (CD)

FBI Agent Travis (Lorenzo Lamas) has been trailing a serial killer for quite some time. The killer likes to rape and mutilate women, and the body count is rising. He's assigned a new partner, Kelly McCord (Kristen Cloke), who is fresh from the academy on her first field case. The two don't see eye to eye on anything, and meanwhile the psychotic killer Art Darcy (Gary Busey) finds new victims, even viciously attacking McCord. Travis begins to realize he has developed feelings for his partner and blames himself for not being there, vowing never to let anything happen to her again. They soon realize Darcy isn't a traditional serial killer and travels with a group of Vietnam vets who have a vendetta against just about everyone. Travis and McCord break every rule in the book trying to stop them, much to the dissatisfaction of their superior Agent Taggart (Roy Scheider). Darcy isn't a killer who plays by the rules, so they do what they must to stop him.

The Rage has some really high points, but unfortunately, it has some really low points as well. The film suffers from being overly dramatic. Maybe it wouldn't have been so noticeable if the score didn't play to a soap opera sensibility, but it is and it does. Lorenzo Lamas is very likable in the film from an acting standpoint. The movie has plenty of action but it's mostly of the cat-and-mouse type, with the good guys constantly in some sort of chase with the bad guys. Lorenzo has two short fight scenes, both which were disappointing since his opponents weren't up to him physically. It's a decent thriller with a fantastic death scene for the villain. Directed by Sydney J. Furie (*Direct Action*).

R

Rage and Honor

1992 (Sony DVD) (djm)

Australian cop Preston Michaels (Richard Norton) moonlights as a bodyguard to rock stars in LA when he witnesses a murder on the street involving dirty cops. He teams up with Kris Fairfield (Cynthia Rothrock), a karate instructor with ties to the police *and to* the top guy behind the crime wave in the city. Her brother happens to be Conrad Drago (Brian Thompson), the kingpin with a slightly crazed bent, whose moll was caught on tape while murdering someone. The videotape in question is the object on which the plot centers, and Preston and Kris have to deal with a slew of dirty cops, an Amazon gang (which includes Kathy Long!), and Drago himself.

Norton and Rothrock teamed up for the umpteenth time to deliver a mostly entertaining rock 'em, sock 'em actioner with more humor than was expected. Norton is constantly reminded by other characters that he's Australian, and he's made fun of, belittled, and teased, and when he rolls with it, the movie finds some of its best moments. The supporting cast is good, and Toshihiro Obata from *Showdown in Little Tokyo* and *Red Sun Rising* has a decent fight scene with Norton. Kathy Long (*Knights*) makes her movie debut here, but it's just a bit part. She later made *Under the Gun* with Norton. Terence H. Winkless (*Bloodfist*) directed.

Rage and Honor II:
Hostile Takeover

1992 (Sony DVD) (djm)

Cynthia Rothrock and Richard Norton team up again for this better-than-usual sequel. They play the same characters, and the continuity of seeing them meet up again under coincidental circumstances is actually (surprisingly) believable. Kris Fairfield (Rothrock) has joined the CIA, and she's sent to Jakarta to pose as a banker to get close to a money-laundering operation, and disgraced Australian police officer Preston Michaels (Norton) is slumming as a bartender until he impresses a young guy named Tommy Andrews (Patrick Muldoon) when he takes on a bunch of guys at once in the bar. Tommy begins training with Preston, and they become friends. Preston's father (the corrupt banker Kris is investigating) is holding a party, at which Kris and Preston are in attendance, and when they see each other again, things start happening. Goons are out to kidnap Tommy for ransom, but Preston stops them, and not long after that Tommy's father is murdered, which leads to some not-so-surprising revelations. This is the point when the bad things that have happened suggest that Tommy is a mastermind deceiver and crime lord. Preston and Kris have to fight for their lives before Tommy (and his henchmen) kills them and gets away with billions in cash and diamonds.

Fairly slick and filled with action and explosions, *Rage and Honor II* feels more like a vehicle for Norton than for Rothrock, but however you see it, it's always good seeing these two together. Ron Vreeken (*Among Dead Men*) plays the lead heavy in the film, and anyone who's

a fan of Matthias Hues will be upset to see Vreeken do a part that Hues could have done better. Stunt coordinator Guy Norris directed.

Rage of Honor
(a.k.a. **Top Fighter**)

1986 (MGM DVD) (djm)

Narcotics agent Shiro Tanaka (Sho Kosugi) brings down a major drug-smuggling operation in Argentina, but his partner is killed as a result. When Tanaka goes home, his girlfriend is kidnapped by Havlock, a vicious killer (played by Lewis Van Bergen) who tortured and murdered his partner. Tanaka follows Havlock to Argentina (rogue, against orders), intent on saving his lady and enacting an honorable revenge. When he parachutes out of the plane, he finds himself near Iguazu Falls, one of the seven natural wonders of the world, and his first task is to survive an attack by native pygmies, who crawl out of the jungle to slay him. Being a ninja (of sorts), Tanaka survives the pygmies, and gets straight to business by laying siege on Havlock's operation and compound.

What makes *Rage of Honor* interesting are the locations—the film gets some nice shots of Iguazu Falls. Despite the outrageous segment involving killer pygmies, it's a fairly standard ninja-type affair with Kosugi in command of the action. The film picks up midway and never lets up, with jungle action, ninja fights (with explosive shurikens!), and explosions galore. Director Gordon Hessler worked with Kosugi on the TV show *The Master* and on the films *Pray For Death* and *Journey of Honor*. The German DVD release is widescreen.

Rage to Kill

1988 (Worldvision VHS) (djm)

A Caribbean island is overtaken in a militaristic coup led by a crazed general (Oliver Reed), and a number of hostages are corralled in a holding area where they await an uncertain fate. Amongst the detainees is a courageous race car driver named Blaine Striker (South African action star James Ryan), who along with an elderly CIA agent stages a daring escape and assault on the soldiers who have overrun the island paradise.

MAŠINA ZA UBIJANJE

Mercenary Blaine Striker (James Ryan) is about to shoot a few rounds in *Rage to Kill*. Author's collection.

Blaine Striker (James Ryan, second from the right) is leading a revolution in *Rage to Kill*. Author's collection.

MAŠINA ZA UBIJANJE

Some commandos plan a strike on a dictator in *Rage to Kill*, featuring James Ryan, center). Author's collection.

By the numbers and without distinction, *Rage to Kill* is a time waster featuring martial arts star Ryan (from *Kill or be Killed* and *Kill and Kill Again*) in a full-blown Rambo-esque role that doesn't require him to showcase his skills in martial arts. Big-name star Reed appears to be drunk for several of his scenes that show him cavorting with nude starlets. You know exactly what you're getting by the video box artwork that features a giant fireball engulfing the core actors, who are holding machine guns. Directed by David Winters, who also worked with Ryan on *Codename Vengeance*.

The Rage Within

2001 (Deltamac VCD) (CD)

"If you lay one hand on them, so help me God, I'll kill you twice!"

Police detectives Billy Rains (Mike Norris) and Darren Steel (David Rael) have had a long and successful run as partners. Billy has decided to call it quits and live a quiet and relaxing life. On Billy's final day, they run afoul of a heist gone wrong and give the assailants chase. Just when they think they have the bad guys, Billy is gunned down. Steel swears he will get revenge and finds himself working undercover in the gang responsible, working for the leader, Keller (Richard Norton). His new partner Dakota Smith (Fred Williamson) has his back but his true identity is discovered, and Keller is going to make the both of them pay when he kidnaps Steel's wife and Smith's daughter. These two cops are tough as they come and if he wants to play dirty, then these two are game.

The Rage Within is a hidden gem from director Mike Norris (*The Delta Force 3*) and it's notable for many reasons. It's a difficult film to locate but it features the return of Fred Williamson as Dakota (a character previously seen in *Night Vision*), a villainous turn for Richard Norton (*Mr. Nice Guy*), and more car chases than a man can handle in one film. There's some great stuff here and plenty of action with guys doing cartwheels off platforms before attacking, people being thrown off moving vehicles, and The Hammer blowing shit up with a shotgun. The story isn't important; it's the fact that this thing is so much fun you can't deny its infectiousness. It should also be noted there's an appearance by Ron O'Neal (*Superfly*) and the great Andrew Divoff (*Nemesis 4*).

Raging Phoenix

2009 (Magnet DVD) (djm)

"The penalty for stealing my flower is death!"

Women are being kidnapped all over Bangkok, and when one young woman named Deu (Jeeja Yanin from *Chocolate*) is taken, she's rescued by a group of men whose wives, girlfriends, and sisters were all taken at one point. Wanting to help the misfit guys out, she learns martial arts from them, and they induct her into their clan of sorrow. They go on the hunt for the evil cult that abducts women, and when they finally find their way into their lair, they realize that the women have been harvested for their scents and pheromones to produce an ultra rare perfume. Deu and her new male compatriots fight the fight of their lives to rescue the comatose women under captivity from the bodybuilding queen of the perfume cult.

At two full hours, *Raging Phoenix* is overlong by at least twenty minutes, but you get to see some stuff you've never seen before. The martial arts featured are radically unique and interesting to watch. JeeJa Yanin is one of the more interesting female martial artists working in (more or less) mainstream action films. Every time you see her in a movie she looks different, and she's adapted a new on-screen martial arts ability, so it's not easy to peg her. This movie is all over the place humorwise, so emotionally it's difficult to register, but it's worth a look. From director Rashane Limtrakul.

Raid on Entebbe

1977 (Wham USA DVD) (CD)

"Remember, these terrorists are killers. They will try to kill the hostages so your first shots must be accurate!"

It's 1976, and terrorists for the Popular Front for the Liberation of Palestine hijack a plane, which lands at Entebbe Airport in Entebbe, Uganda. The Israeli government, who won't give in to the terrorists, bring in General Dan Shomron (Charles Bronson) to plan a top-secret mission to attack the terrorists and get the hostages to safety. The raid will take place on the Jewish Sabbath—a very controversial move—and the team will have to be extra careful not to stir up a fuss. Shomron puts his team through vigorous training in hopes of getting the hostages out alive.

Director Irvin Kershner had a long career directing action classics like *The Empire Strikes Back* and *Robocop 2*, but this film is based on true events and lacking in the action department. The film boasts an all-star cast with the likes of Yaphet Kotto, Martin Balsam, John Saxon, Robert Loggia, and a very young James Woods. It's Charles Bronson (later a Cannon-contracted action star with movies like *Death Wish 2* and *Assassination* to his credit) we are all interested in, and he takes a back seat. He gives the orders but doesn't carry them out himself. It's a strong performance, but this won't be a film he will be remembered for. He's more of a supporting character, while the film focuses mostly on the deliberation between officials figuring out how to stop the terrorists. It's fun to see all these great actors looking so young, but the novelty runs out of steam quickly.

The Raid: Redemption

2011 (Sony DVD) (djm)

A SWAT team in Jakarta is thrust into a top-secret mission to snatch a drug lord from a tenement building, but the team has absolutely no idea what's in store for them. Right from the start, the mission is FUBAR when their presence becomes known, and as they try to work their way up the building, the drug lord (Ray Saketapy, with a dead-eyed drawl) makes an announcement on the loud speaker that anyone who helps kill the SWAT team will get free room and board for the rest of their lives. One cop named Rama (Iko Uwais from *Merantau*) is formidable enough to stay alive from one floor to the next, while most of the rest of his team is slaughtered in ambushes and blitzes from the gun- and machete-wielding tenants in the building. Rama's brother Andi (Donny Alamsyah) works for the drug lord, but when he realizes that his brother is part of the SWAT team, he starts working against his boss to help his brother survive. When the life-and-death encounters start happening, the screen sizzles.

The Raid: Redemption took the world by storm. Writer/director/choreographer Gareth Evans (*Merantau*) is a Welshman working in the Indonesian action and martial arts world, and his work is vibrant and essential. While *The Raid: Redemption* doesn't really have much of a story or even characters with dimensions, the direction of the film and the editing take the genre to another stratosphere. Ultra dark and impossibly violent (almost to the point of being videogamey), it presents one rocking action scene after another, and they all look *brutal*. This is an action movie to wake people up. Subtitles aside, it's a kick in the gut to the Hollywood industry that forgot how to make movies like this. The intensity Evans is able to sustain for the entire length of the picture is almost unbearably harrowing. His star Uwais could go places with the right shepherding. He next appeared in a small role in Keanu Reeves's *Man of Tai Chi*.

The Raid 2

(a.k.a. **The Raid 2: Berandal**)

2014 (Sony DVD) (djm)

Survivor of the bloody raid in the first film, Rama (Iko Uwais) barely has a chance to get back to his life when he goes deep undercover to expose dirty cops working with the crime organizations in and around Jakarta. He goes to prison for two years(!), thinking he's only going to be gone for a few months, but in the interim he makes a close alliance with Ucok (Arifin Putra), the son of the boss of one of the major syndicates. When they are released from prison, Ucok's father gives Rama a full-time gig as an enforcer, which firmly plants him in the thick of things. When Ucok becomes too ambitious and makes a deal with a competing syndicate—and ultimately murders his own father to get a leg up—Rama is left to survive on his own terms and bring down the entire syndicate himself (and damn his original mandate!), or die trying.

Director Gareth Evans is in his early James Cameron days with *The Raid 2*. At two-and-a-half hours, it is an epic crime drama with incredible, jaw-dropping martial arts action set pieces, most of which feature star Uwais in peak form. From a chaotic prison riot to a balls-to-the-wall car chase, *The Raid 2* showcases some unrelenting action, and then it pauses for a while and revs up its motors to jump full speed ahead for a show-stopping finale. I saw this theatrically with a blood-crazed audience who screamed, shouted, and got to their feet during the action scenes. All said and done, I found it exhausting, and to be quite honest I felt numb afterwards. Still, this is an impressive work of action cinema.

Raiders of the Sun

1992 (New Concorde DVD) (CD)

After a nuclear war has destroyed life as we know it, a group of people calling themselves the Alpha League attempts to form a democratic society. Gunpowder is a hot and rare commodity, and to maintain peace and fend off the traitor Clay (William Steis), they send a man named Brodie (Richard Norton) to search for a mine that is rumored to exist. In his search he meets up with and saves Sierra (Lani Lobangco), whose village happens to rest on one of those mines. Brodie's comrade Talbot (Blake Boyd) is on a search of his own, for his wife Vera (Brigitta Stenberg) who has been kidnapped by the same traitor. Brodie and the villagers must defend the mine while Talbot will do whatever it takes to get his wife back.

As capable as Richard Norton is as a martial artist and action star, there is nothing to recommend about *Raiders of the Sun*. It was hard to sit through any way you slice it. Unless you have a fetish for constant explosions, then this one can be skipped. There are a few minor fight scenes that show a tiny glimpse of what Norton is capable of, and it's a shame he wasn't surrounded with other fighters who could have gone toe to toe with him, which would've made a much more exciting film. Blake Boyd plays second fiddle to Norton but is able to hold his own. Most of the action is comprised of shootouts and explosions, without much style. There isn't anything that really stands out about the locations, just bland desert wasteland environments (shot in the Philippines). The music tends to drone on with the exception of the end theme rock song. Richard Norton is much more talented than this film allowed him to be so this one stung a bit. This may fall into the so-bad-it's-good category, so if that tickles your fancy then maybe it will sit better with you. Ultimately, this was a rather bizarre *Mad Max* rip-off and the amount of explosions (and little people) was mind numbing. Director Cirio Santiago fared better directing Norton in other post-nuke films like *Equalizer 2000* and *Future Hunters*.

Rambo: First Blood Part II

1985 (Lionsgate DVD) (djm)

Rambo: "Sir: Do we get to win this time?"
Trautman: "This time it's up to you."

Incarcerated and cast off by society, John Rambo (Sylvester Stallone) is given a rare opportunity at redemption: His former superior and friend Colonel Trautman (Richard Crenna) offers him a mission to Vietnam behind enemy lines—to *take pictures* of a Viet Cong camp to see if there are any American POWs being held captive there. Accepting the mission, Rambo meets the bureaucrat who's calling the shots: Marshall Murdock (Charles Napier) and his team of mercenaries (who include Martin Cove), and concluding that there's no one he can trust but Trautman, Rambo goes to Vietnam and begins his mission. His guide through the jungle (not that he needs one) is a pretty soldier named Co (Julia Nickson), who leads him to the camp where he finds about a half a dozen POWs. He rescues one, and when Rambo is betrayed by Murdock and left in the open to be captured by the Cong, Trautman warns Murdock that when Rambo comes for him he won't show him mercy. Russian soldiers who have allied themselves with the Vietnamese forces torture Rambo, and as he's pushed to his limits with pain and degradation, he breaks free and becomes a one-man army against the world.

Sylvester Stallone's biggest box-office hit to date, *Rambo: First Blood Part II* made an icon out of Rambo, who at this point became a full-fledged action hero. Stallone was at the peak of his powers in 1985 with the #2 and #3 biggest box-office hits (*Rocky IV* was the other one), and where *First Blood* laid the groundwork for him as an action star, *Rambo II* elevated him head and shoulders above his peers. Chuck Norris had already starred in two *Missing in Action* films by the time *Rambo II* had been released, but it was *Rambo II* that became one of the most copied films in the exploitation market ever. After this film became a huge hit, a toy line and a cartoon spin-off series were produced (using Jerry Goldsmith's themes), despite this film's "R" rating. In many ways, *Rambo: First Blood Part II* defined a generation of action films, and it arguably set off a boom of action stars, all of who hoped to become "the next Stallone." George Pan Cosmatos directed it. He later reteamed with Stallone on *Cobra*.

Rambo III

1988 (Lionsgate DVD) (djm)

Bureaucrat: "If it can be done, I want you to know up front that if you're captured, or if any of this leaks, we'll deny any participation or even knowledge of your existence."
Rambo: "I'm used to it."

Pardoned for his previous crimes, John Rambo (Sylvester Stallone) is now living in Thailand among a group of monks, and to help finance the building of a new temple, he stick fights for money, using some new Muay Thai skills. His old comrade Colonel Trautman (Richard Crenna) comes to him to ask for help on a mission to Afghanistan, but he turns the offer down. Trautman goes ahead with the mission on his own and gets captured by Russians who are systematically slaughtering the Afghan rebels (Mujahideen—holy warriors) on an ethnic cleansing campaign. When Rambo is called on to help rescue Trautman, he accepts the mission without hesitation and goes to the Middle East to begin the quest to free his friend and former commander. The finale has Rambo in a Soviet tank playing chicken with an Aerospatiale Puma helicopter (which was originally built for John Milius's *Red Dawn*). It's a great scene.

Where *Rambo: First Blood Part II* was a runaway blockbuster smash, *Rambo III* was a massively budgeted box-office disappointment. It went through a regime change in the early stages of filming: Director Russell Mulcahy (*Highlander*) was notoriously fired, and the second unit director Peter MacDonald was promoted to the director's chair. As it is, *Rambo III* is equal parts action *and* adventure with a pristine Stallone as a dashing Rambo riding horses, stick fighting, and using a dash of martial arts in an environment where we're not used to seeing him. Many fans consider this entry the worst of the series, but it's my personal favorite. I love seeing Rambo out of his comfort zone, and while the film is a virtual rehash of part II, I still find this one to be richer, more interesting, and a lot more entertaining than the previous film. Rambo, now an action icon, has become slightly self-aware (which I don't necessarily like), with lots of short quips and one-liners. He doesn't have a big speech at the end of this film like he did in the previous two, which is fine. Stallone wrote the script with Sheldon Lettich, who is best known for his work with Jean-Claude Van Damme. Director MacDonald later helmed the epic desert action film *Legionnaire* with Van Damme. Stallone left this character alone for two decades (a wise decision), and revisited it with *Rambo*.

Rambo

2008 (Lionsgate DVD) (djm)

"Any of you boys want to shoot, now's the time. And there isn't one of us that doesn't want to be someplace else. But this is what we do, who we are. *Live for nothing.* Or *die for something.* Your call."

In the twenty years that John Rambo had been cultivating his manliness and "fuck the world" attitude, the world and the movie business seemingly moved on without him, but what we didn't quite understand is that we *needed* Rambo—desperately—to come and save the day and bring back action heroes with an unbridled vengeance. When Sylvester Stallone stepped back into his best role as Rambo (a year after reprising his role as *Rocky Balboa*), no one could have expected what Stallone would have done, and that is to stick a Rambo-bladed sabre up the ass of action

John Rambo (Sylvester Stallone) is tortured with his own knife in *Rambo: First Blood Part II*. Author's collection.

The great stick fight scene at the beginning of *Rambo III*, which features Sylvester Stallone using some Muay Thai skills. Author's collection.

After nearly two decades, Sylvester Stallone returned to his best role as Rambo. Author's collection.

John Rambo sneaks up on a guy who's about to be gutted in *Rambo*. Author's collection.

One of only a few scenes of serenity in *Rambo*. Author's collection.

John Rambo (Sylvester Stallone, center) takes a band of mercenaries up river in *Rambo*. Author's collection.

Missionary Sarah (Julie Benz) needed Rambo (Sylvester Stallone) to save her in *Rambo*. Author's collection.

and war movies and twist the hilt so hard and with so much force that there's no way Stallone or any other action star of his caliber could ever deliver a worthy follow-up. But that's okay because no one should. *Rambo* stands alone. Stallone's bulkier, angrier, and more isolated hero finds

himself piloting a boat full of white missionaries to Burma (against his stern advice), and the sole woman in the group (played by Julie Benz) makes an impression on him because she speaks to his heart and his humanity, where no one else could. When he leaves them to their devices to tend and minister to the victims in a genocidal area of Burma, they are captured and tortured by a sadistic warlord who believes himself untouchable . . . until John Rambo and a team of mercenaries go in to retrieve the missionaries. At that point, even the seasoned mercenaries fear Rambo, whose speeches he delivers at the point of an arrow, stretched at eye point, ready to impale. Not only has Rambo had enough time to contemplate his purpose in life, but he has embraced the animal within him, the machine that was always there and ready to be turned on for killing.

It doesn't matter how may times I watch *Rambo*, I always love it like it was the first time. I saw it opening night at the Cinerama Dome in Hollywood, and I couldn't stop myself from yelling and stomping my feet throughout the whole thing. The second and third times I saw it in theaters, I still couldn't contain myself. I watch it at home, and I'm like a spectator at a gladiatorial arena. The blood drives me wild. Stallone's greatest achievement as a director, but not necessarily as a writer and actor, *Rambo* is the great, fulfilling film that now occupies the gaping void where action stars used to dwell, but emptied out over time. It is a return, a hearkening back, a reminder. It is exactly what the world and Hollywood requires because this is what we crave from our heroes. Thank you, Sylvester Stallone. You're my hero.

Rapid Exchange

2003 (DEJ DVD) (CD)

"I think that money is just little green pieces of paper that is always looking for a new home anyway."

Some high-end thieves plan their next heist, and the goal is a big fat wad of cash to the tune of 250 million. That's a hell of a prize package, but it sure won't be easy scoring it. Planning a heist is tough, but it's much harder when the place you have to break into is an airborne 747 jet. That means the heist will take place between two jets in mid-air. The stakes don't get much higher than that, but thieves Brooks (Matt O'Toole) and Ketchum (Lorenzo Lamas) are up to the task. Their leader, Newcastle (Lance Henriksen), assigns them to a team with Daltry (Wayne Pere) and Sophie (Aviva Gale). They don't exactly get along with each other and trust is a huge issue. If they want that money, they won't have a choice.

Lorenzo Lamas (*Latin Dragon*) is tailor-made for films like *Rapid Exchange*. While some of the story aspects may be a tad stretched, it comes together in a way that's not only a perfect fit but also highly entertaining from beginning to end. It's less an action film and more of a heist flick: It's a risky job with high stakes, playing out in an interesting and exciting fashion. It's obvious that the script by Tripp Reed and Sam Wells was

given plenty of time to be mapped out with all the twists and turns at just the right moments. It's easy to tell when an actor is enjoying himself or having fun with a role, and Lamas seemed to be having a blast. This is a great role for him, and he does a terrific job. In a much smaller role, Lance Henriksen (*Stone Cold*) delivers his all. He is one of those character actors who never phones in a performance. Much of the cast was unknown but they are all interesting, especially Matt O'Toole (*Safe*) and Aviva Gale (*The Movie Hero*). There are no real shootouts and only one small fight during the finale. None of that matters, though, since the film is a fun time. It may have been done on the cheap, but it looks like every single penny was put on the screen. With a solid cast, stellar script, and a director like Trip Reed (the direct-to-video *Walking Tall* movies with Kevin Sorbo) at the helm, *Rapid Exchange* excites and entertains.

Rapid Fire

1992 (Fox DVD) (djm)

"Jake! Why don't you take those fists of fury of yours outside—you're making the old man nervous!"

College student Jake Lo (Brandon Lee) has a perpetual chip on his shoulder, and yet he has a lackadaisical sense of humor that people find appealing. When he's at the wrong place at the wrong time, he witnesses a murder being committed by a Mafioso (Nick Mancuso) muscling in on his drug distributor. Lo is hunted down by the Mafia, and when put in a safe house under federal

Jake Lo (Brandon Lee) blows off some steam in *Rapid Fire*. Author's collection.

Brandon Lee shows what he was capable of as an action star in *Rapid Fire*. Author's collection.

Nobody puts Jake Lo (Brandon Lee) in a corner in *Rapid Fire*. Author's collection.

Some thugs corner Jake Lo (Brandon Lee) in *Rapid Fire*. Author's collection.

custody, the federal agents turn on him when they're offered enormous amounts of money to kill him. On the run from everyone, Jake must turn to a likable cop named Mace Ryan (Powers Booth) for help. Ryan takes a shine to him, and together they go up against the mob *and* the powerful drug supplier (played by Tzi Ma) and his henchman (played by a silent Al Leong).

Rapid Fire is easily Brandon Lee's best action movie. It really is an amazing little film, totally underrated and criminally overlooked in lieu of his next (and last) film *The Crow*. He shows what a great martial artist he was in this film, and it's a promise of things that sadly never happened. The action is fierce and plentiful, and the fights are interesting and believable. The final fight between Lee and Leong is a highlight. Director Dwight H. Little did *Marked For Death* with Steven Seagal previous to this, and he later did *Murder at 1600* with Wesley Snipes.

INTERVIEW:

AL LEONG
(CD)

One of the most overlooked and dangerous jobs in the movie business is that of the stuntman. The average movie patron tends to forget how important they are to the industry, and more often than not, the stuntmen don't get the recognition they rightfully deserve. Then there are men like Al Leong. An actor, a stuntman, and an author, Leong spent more than two decades appearing (as either a stuntman, actor, or both at the same time) in major motion pictures such as Lethal Weapon *(1987),* Action Jackson *(1988), and as the candy bar-stealing terrorist in the perennial classic* Die Hard *(1988). Many viewers*

may also recognize him as a guest star from various syndicated television shows like Magnum P.I., Simon and Simon, *and* The A-Team. *He's worked alongside many action genre greats such as Brandon Lee, Bruce Willis, Jean-Claude Van Damme, and David Carradine, and he later ventured into stunt coordinating and directing. With his long, black hair, Fu Manchu mustache, and goatee, it is hard to miss him in almost every major action film from the 1980s and 1990s. Health issues have forced him into retirement but he is still as passionate about film as he ever was, and has every right to be proud of his rich legacy. In 2010, he released his autobiography,* The Eight Lives of Al "Ka-Bong" Leong. *Having survived brain cancer as well as two strokes, Leong has proven that the man who fell victim to many of Hollywood's tough guys on screen is far stronger and inspiring in real life than his on-screen persona. Al was generous enough to take the time to answer some questions about his career in front of and behind the camera.*

Can you give a brief history of your martial arts background and how you broke into the film industry?

Fred Phillips and I had a custom car paint shop. A friend of mine got in the movie biz as a grip, and he sort of talked me into trying it. I applied at Warner Bros. and it just so happened to be a busy time, and I was hired within a couple weeks. I worked on the lot for a few months then ended up on Vine Street on the Merv Griffen/Steve Allen lot setting up the two shows. After so many month, I ended up doing feature films and low-budget films. The director came to me and asked if I knew martial arts. He then asked if I could teach four girls a routine as cheerleaders, and I said yes. After a few hours, the girls were asked to do the routine, and the director told me to go up and do it with them. A week later I worked on another film and was asked to run through a set-up with fake rain in swimming fins and with one of these jobs I got my SAG card. What I was going to do with it, I had no idea.

Talk a little bit about your stints on episodic television shows like *Magnum P.I., The A Team,* and *Knight Rider.*

First of all, Bob Minor, Craig Baxley, and Jack Gill are the great stunt guys from *Magnum P.I., The A-Team* and *Knight Rider. Magnum* was shot in Hawaii and just to go there was great. I do believe in one episode, Magnum picks me up on his shoulder and throws me over the bar, which I think he actually did. Also, I am a stunt guy and not an actor. Craig and his stunt guys were always great. Craig would come to me and ask if I could do this, and we would try it. Jack was always on top of the game. Sometimes strange things are in the script, like jumping on the car and trying to beat it up. You really can't beat working on jobs with great coordinators, and I have worked with great ones.

Having worked with John Carpenter numerous times, how would you describe him as a director?

What I really like about the man is that he's a real person.

Big Trouble in Little China was a major film with a predominantly Asian cast. How was it being able to work with so many of your colleagues at once?

Working with all the guys on *Big Trouble* was great. And equally important is the people behind camera: the crew. As you see, I was not on the poster because I got into an argument with the guy that put it together. John was so great, he gave many Asians opportunities, even behind camera. That is how this guy got his job, because John was so nice.

Do you have any stories from the classic back alley fight sequence?

Before the alley fight began, John walked the alley and asked what door I wanted [to go through]. We talked about putting James [Lew] through the glass, so John told the guys behind us to put in breakaway glass and a breakaway door.

Many people remember you from *Die Hard* as the terrorist with a sweet tooth. Did the idea of you stealing the candy bars originate from you, was it scripted, or just thought up on set?

From what I remember, I asked McTiernan if it was okay to take the candy. It definitely was not in the script, but it was a well-written story.

You were in two quintessential big-screen action films from the 1980s that both spawned franchises: *Lethal Weapon* and *Die Hard.* When you were acting in these films, did you get the sense that you were appearing in something particularly special?

The story is very important to me. Whenever I can, I like to get the script and read it first. And if I know the story is no good, I'll try to leave the show. Fifty percent of the time I can do it, and yes, I passed up a lot of money. Some people say you have been in great films but I think it is because I will leave movies when I sense they are not working. And no, there is no way of knowing what will happen after you leave the set of a movie.

What was your overall experience like on *Lethal Weapon* working with Mel Gibson and Gary Busey?

Both Mel and Gary were great. The helicopter in the air was great because there were two choppers flying way too close, with one filming us. The pilot asked me what I was doing, and I said I was getting ready to jump if things go wrong. He said you don't want to jump, you want to ride it out. It was exciting when he was bouncing the chopper on top of the car—that pilot was great. The guy that picked me up after Mel kills me was an LA Hell's Angel member, another great guy to work with.

What was your impression of Bruce Willis on the set? Were you at all concerned with the casting decision? It's fairly well-known that Richard Gere was offered that role first.

On *Die Hard,* Bruce was great. He is one of these guys that walks in and can memorize everybody's name. I mean everybody's name. The electrician, grips, and everybody else. I mean, I have trouble

R

A classic fight scene between Minh (Al Leong) and Jake Lo (Brandon Lee) in *Rapid Fire*. Author's collection.

Al Leong and Brandon Lee have at it in *Rapid Fire*. Author's collection.

trying to remember my own name. I had no idea someone else besides Bruce was supposed to do the part. I was brought on by Joel Silver after he used me on *Lethal Weapon*. I was originally introduced to Joel Silver by Craig Baxley, who directed a Carl Weathers film I was on, *Action Jackson*. As far as the casting, I knew nothing about that.

Is it true that your final fight with Brandon Lee in *Rapid Fire* was shot in a single day? Was it pre-choreographed before you arrived or was it something the two of you worked out on the set?

Yes, the fight was shot in one day. I would say a fight like this would normally take three to five days to do. And no, it was not pre set-up, it was put together on the spot by Jeff Imada, Brandon, and me. I was also working with Craig Baxley in Hawaii [at the same time]; he was shooting a pilot for a TV series called *Raven*. The producers were nice enough to let me go in the middle of shooting. It actually became three days because of flying time. The director for *Rapid Fire* was great and so was the crew. Of course Brandon and Jeff are always great to work with. The producer was an asshole. At the end he made sure I didn't get paid because he made it a point to let the Screen Actors Guild know I was working another job. It was a lot of fun doing the fight because a lot of the time you are under control by someone who knows nothing about fighting and you end up with a mess.

Having worked with Brandon Lee more than once, what was your impression of him and the legacy he left behind?

I really miss him. He was an incredible man.

Scott (Reb Brown) is the victor in a cage fight, while Tiger Joe (Al Leong, right) cheers on in *Cage*. Author's collection.

You've had scenes cut from films like *Ghost of Mars* and *Lethal Weapon 4*. Does it bother you when you have put so much into a scene like that only to have it removed?

Fights get cut all the time. I don't mind what they decide to do. On *Lethal Weapon 4* there were two reasons to cut me. One was because I was killed in part one. The other is Jet Li is in it, and you can't go against the effects they will back him up with.

How was your experience working on the film *Cage* when your performance hinged mostly on your acting skills and not fighting skills?

I'm not sure if I remember *Cage*. I think it was a quick throwaway film.

You tended to work on films with the likes of James Lew, Jeff Imada, and other great stuntmen. Would you guys recommend each other for jobs, or was it just coincidence that you all worked in the same circles, with the same groups of people?

I would always want to work with people I know because I know what they can do, and this is true with anybody out there when they look for people.

Steele Justice is such a great action movie. What do you remember about working on that film and working with Martin Kove?

I don't remember much about *Steele Justice*. I do remember Martin was fun to work with.

Other great action films you worked on around the same period were *Action Jackson* and *The Perfect Weapon*. Any memories of working on those two films?
I
I don't remember anything on *The Perfect Weapon* but *Action Jackson* was a lot of fun with everyone like Craig T. Nelson, Carl Weathers, James Lew, and of course Craig Baxley as director.

Talk a little bit about working with director Andy Sidaris on his T & A action films. That must have been fun.

Andy and his wife are great people. Andy knows what he wants and writes it on the plane as we fly to the locations. It's always great to work with people who love what they are doing.

How did you find yourself moving into the role of stunt/fight choreographer? Was it what you wanted or something that you just sort of fell in to?

The business is weird. I could have stepped up the action from day one but a lot of time it's who you know.

Do you have a method to choreographing a fight sequence?

When I set up a fight, I have a million notes. Some directors couldn't care less, others love it. Whenever I can, I try to find out what the actor likes or wants to do.

When choreographing something like a sword fight with actors who have no experience, what are some of the steps you take to train and prepare them? Was this something you went through when working with Duane Johnson and the cast of *The Scorpion King*?

On *The Scorpion King*, and all the others, I always start with foot movements first. Then hand movements, and finally the weapons. The Rock and Mike [Clarke Duncan] were fantastic to work with. Both of them needed no help. I was so sorry to hear of Mike's passing. The rest of the cast and crew were excellent and Billy Burton, the stunt coordinator, was great. He originally hired me some twenty plus years ago on *Simon & Simon*. Also, The Rock is a pro wrestler so things with him were very easy.

Your stint as choreographer on *Kung Fu: The Legend Continues* was plagued with behind-the-scenes problems. Do you regret the experience, or did you just see it as living and learning?

On *Kung Fu*, David Carradine and the other actors and crew were great. The two main writers were lost. The producer and stunt coordinator on season four were total idiots. I didn't learn anything except that it's truly who you know.

How were you approached to write episodes of *Kung Fu: The Legend Continues*?

When they asked me to come back and do season four, I told them I had written episodes of the show and if they wanted me back they would have to buy one, and they did.

You directed a film called *Daddy, Tell Me a Story*. Not much is known about this film. What is the film about, and why did you choose this as your directorial debut?

Daddy, Tell Me a Story became *Scarecrow's Dream* after an actor did not want to come back for pick-up shots. The whole story had to be changed and a million shots now couldn't be used. I had written about thirty scripts in the past and this was mostly a non-action script and that is why I wanted to do it. At the time of the shoot, video cameras where just coming in. If I would have waited another two years, I could and would have shot it in video for a lot cheaper. The film is about a young P.I. looking for a missing boy that is supposed to have his brain transplanted in a young girl's head. He only has so many days left to find the boy or his company has to pay out three million dollars. He talks to the father of the girl who denies any such transplant ever happened. He even speaks to the doctor who owns the big hospital where this had to have happened. He also talks to a thug who may have been involved and the mother of the missing boy and finds nothing.

What film are you most recognized from?

I think I'm recognized most from *Big Trouble*, *Rapid Fire*, *Lethal Weapon*, and *Die Hard*.

Do you have a film or role that is a favorite or are particularly proud of?

Big Trouble and *Rapid Fire* were the most fun casts. I could actually do some things which allowed the fights to be more real.

You've been in many great films that don't get the same recognition as others. How was your experience working on *Joshua Tree* and *Dark Angel* (a.k.a. *I Come in Peace*) with Dolph Lundgren?

Joshua Tree was a waste of time and I really don't remember it. *I Come in Peace* was fun because Craig Baxley is always a blast to work for.

Who choreographed the fight between you and Mark Dacascos on *Double Dragon,* and what are your thoughts on that film?

The fight with Mark and I was sort of put together between the both of us. Mark is an amazing guy, and I had so much fun shooting the movie.

Koga Shuko (Robert Patrick, center) is the villain in *Double Dragon*. Directly behind him is one of his henchman, played by Al Leong. Author's collection.

Having appeared in major studio films with stars like Willis, Gibson, and Jean-Claude Van Damme as well as in the direct-to-video market with guys like Gary Daniels, Jeff Wincott, and Lundgren, was there ever an instance where you were incredibly impressed or disappointed by some of the action stars you worked with and their fighting styles?

The stuff I did that went straight to video I just don't remember them at all. And no, it does not bother me if someone has a different approach or style.

Did you ever have a favorite person to work with or someone you never had the chance to but wish you had?

The people that I would have liked to work with are Bronson, Stallone, and Eastwood. I'm surprised Eastwood did that film [*Letters From Iwo Jima*] with all those unknown Asians. He did a great job, but I didn't care for those Asians. I wish he would have used more established Asian actors.

Why do you think Chow Yun Fat was never really accepted as an action star in the states when *The Replacement Killers* was such a perfect vehicle for him?

The Replacement Killers and Chow Yun Fat are great! I wrote in my book [*The Eight Lives of Al "Ka-Bong" Leong*] that Asians themselves are a good portion to blame. They don't support themselves. I don't depend on the Asian community to back me up. They're not there. Also, the Asians have no music that the American market is interested in. I feel that's a big thing. They have actors that can do the job but if your own people don't support you and the music's not there, you have nothing.

What is your take on modern action films and action stars? Is there anyone you've got your eye on, in terms of who's the real thing and deserves more recognition?

I think the effects today are looking very good. This allows anybody to do almost anything or at least look like they can. I don't follow actors the way everyone else does. There are a lot of great people and stunt guys out there.

Is there anything you'd like to say to your fans and those who've admired you and enjoyed watching you throughout the years?

I love all the people out there, and I think things will look better, and I wish the best for everyone.

Raven

1992–1993 (NOV) (djm)

From Frank Lupo, the creator of *The A-Team* and *Hunter*, *Raven* was an interesting TV series that starred martial artist Jeffrey Meek, who had once played Remo Williams in a pilot for a failed TV series. In *Raven*, he plays a half-Japanese samurai/ex-special forces assassin named Jonathan Raven, who witnessed his parents getting killed by a secret clan of ninjas known as The Black Dragon. The clan takes him in and forces him to become one of them, and he trains to be a ninja, with hopes to turn against them one day and get revenge. When he's of age, he falls in love with a Japanese woman, who bears him his son, but The Black Dragon kills her right after she sends the boy away to safety. Not knowing where his son is, Raven is despondent and even more enraged at The Black Dragon, and he joins the special forces to filter his rage. As an

assassin for the US government, Raven racks up a body count and quits the gig to focus on finding his son. Stationed in Hawaii with a rapscallion sidekick—private investigator Ski Jablonski (Lee Majors)—Raven closes in on The Black Dragon while helping people in need of protective services. It's basically *Magnum P.I.* and *Burn Notice* meets *American Ninja*.

Over the course of two short seasons (twenty episodes total), *Raven* is a great showcase for star Meek, who shows that he's a very capable martial artist and actor, and he looks good doing both. It's a shame that the show was canceled so soon because it could have gone on to become one of the better (and edgier) shows of the 1990s. The pilot episode is two hours and was directed by Craig R. Baxley, who directed *Action Jackson, Dark Angel* (a.k.a. *I Come in Peace*), and *Stone Cold*. The show features some of the best Asian stuntman and action guys working in the business at the time, including Cary-Hiroyuki Tagawa, Al Leong, and James Lew.

Ravenhawk

1996 (Columbia Tristar VHS) (djm)

The striking and astonishingly built Rachel McLish from *Aces: Iron Eagle III* and *Pumping Iron II: The Women* stars in Albert Pyun's criminally neglected and forgotten *Ravenhawk*. McLish plays Rhyia Shadowfeather, a Native American woman who as a young girl was forced by evil thugs to kill her parents. The thugs were hired by a businessman intent on removing Rhyia's family and tribe off their land to make room for a nefarious plan involving

VHS artwork for *Ravenhawk*. Author's collection.

nuclear waste disposal. Charged with the murder of her family, Rhyia is institutionalized and sent to a women's penitentiary, and decades later she manages to escape and begin her ritualized hunt of the men who sadistically eliminated her family and stole her freedom. The man behind it all is a rich guy named Philip Thorne, played by the always reliable William Atherton from *Die Hard*.

Ravenhawk is easily one of Albert Pyun's best movies. It was beautifully shot on location in Utah, Arizona, and New Mexico, and the action, though sparse, is pretty great. There's a scene where McLish has been captured and is being dragged in the desert behind a motorcycle, and she manages to position herself in a way where she's able to spring up and fly up onto the driver, knocking him off the bike. It's a fantastic scene. McLish was an amazing looking woman and a certifiable action star in every way, but sadly she only made two features after being the focus of the documentary *Pumping Iron II*. I would have loved to see her in a few more movies. Director Pyun worked with some notable female action stars like bodybuilder Sue Price in *Nemesis 2-4* and kickboxing champion Kathy Long in *Knights*. The laserdisc of *Ravenhawk* is widescreen.

Raw Deal
1986 (Fox DVD) (MJ)

"You should not drink and bake."

Made in the wake of enormously successful films like *The Terminator* and *Commando*, this 1986 action film from the De Laurentiis Entertainment Group finds Arnold Schwarzenegger playing a more traditional leading man in this slice of noir helmed by director John Irvin (*The Dogs Of War, Hamburger Hill*). *Raw Deal* tells the story of Mark Kaminsky, a disgraced former FBI agent hiding out as a small-town sheriff, who gets the chance to get his old life back when Harry (Darren McGavin), his old boss, tracks him down and asks for his help. During the course of guarding a key witness in an FBI investigation into a Chicago mobster, Harry's son, also an FBI agent, is killed. Suspecting corruption inside the FBI, Harry vows to get his own revenge and turns to Kaminsky for help, which requires Kaminsky to go undercover in the Chicago mob and identify who was responsible for the death of Harry's son.

Looking back on Schwarzenegger's filmography, *Raw Deal* is an important step forward in his development as an action star and as an actor. *Raw Deal* is the very definition of a star vehicle. If you take Arnold out of the film, it becomes just like any other action film of the day. But his presence invigorates the material and makes it better. In *Raw Deal*, for the first time, Arnold gets to play a role that doesn't hinge on his physicality but requires more of him an as actor, as he plays against veteran actors such as McGavin, Sam Wanamaker, Paul Shenar, Robert Davi, and Ed Lauter. For the first time, Arnold gets to play a role where he is married, and he also has another love interest in the form of actress Kathryn Harrold. While *Raw Deal* retains the elements that made *The Terminator* and *Commando* successful, it also

shows new aspects of Schwarzenegger as an actor, including his burgeoning talent for comedy, which he would continue to develop in future projects.

Raw Target
1995 (Platinum DVD) (djm)

"Yeah, I know who you are, Mr. Kickboxer. And I don't want any of that vigilante crap—that's not the way we do things around here!"

Dale "Apollo" Cook plays Johnny Rider, a disgraced kickboxer whose last fight in the ring left his opponent dead. He hitchhikes around, looking for trouble, and ends up in a town where a small-time hood named Rod (Nick Hill) is running things. Johnny becomes Rod's enforcer only because he knows that Rod murdered his brother and that's the best way he knows to work his way to revenge. Meanwhile, two cops are closing in on Johnny: One of them (Ron Hall) is the brother of the man Johnny killed in the ring, and the other is a beautiful detective who ends up falling in love with him, leading to a *looong* sex scene. Nonstop fight scenes fill the running time of this fairly enjoyable actioner.

Cook isn't known for being a good actor, but his style of acting and his character in this movie almost make him seem up to par with his peers in the action movie world. He's not too cocky or self-assured in this one, and his fights are pretty intense in it. His leading lady (Mychelle Charters) is very pretty and his co-stars, Ron Hall and Nick Hill are quite good. Hall co-starred with Cook several times, most notably in *Triple Impact* and *Double Blast*. It was directed by Tim Spring, who also did *Double Blast*.

Raze
2013 (IFC DVD) (djm)

A dungeon lair in a remote location holds fifty young athletic women, all of whom have been kidnapped and are told via a disembodied voice that they must fight each other in pairs and only one of them can walk away alive. The women are shown creepy footage of their loved ones and told that if they lose the fight and die their loved ones will be systematically murdered. The incentive is to survive but, as it quickly becomes clear, there is no shortage of women willing to fight to the death to ensure the survival of their husbands, children, or siblings. One woman named Sabrina (Zoë Bell from *Angel of Death* and *Death Proof*) is a former POW from a Middle Eastern war, so she's able to withstand the psychological torture longer than most of the women imprisoned around her, and when she's forced to fight, she goes through the trials with a brutal determination because she's fighting for her daughter. Her biggest enemy in the prison (aside from the brutish guards and her captor) is a psychopath named Phoebe (Rebecca Marshall), who *enjoys* killing other people. When

The theatrical release poster for *Raze*. Author's collection.

Sabrina manages to get the better of her captors, she turns the tables and goes after the masterminds behind it all: a crazed couple (Doug Jones and Sherilyn Fenn) who are intent on creating a maenad (frenzied female warriors, from Greek mythology), and when they encounter Sabrina, their wildest hopes are manifested in her rage.

A kickboxing tournament movie in the guise of a torture porn horror film, *Raze* is an interesting experiment. As a vehicle for Bell, it works until the very end of the film, which ventures down an unbelievable path, leading to an unsatisfactory conclusion. When her character is unleashed upon the beasts, the film should have just run wild, but that wasn't what transpired. In the film we see Bell engage in five brutal fights (and then some), and while the fights and choreography aren't glamorized in any way, we do get to see her in an unvarnished glory. There were times when I wanted to look away from the screen. It's *that* brutal in certain scenes. Fans of clean, well-lit action may have a hard time watching *Raze*. It isn't pretty. Also starring Tracie Thoms, who previously appeared in *Death Proof* with Bell. Directed by Josh C. Waller.

Ready to Rumble
2000 (Warner DVD) (CD)

"There's a lot of glare coming off that dome of yours, squirrel nuts!"

Gordy (David Arquette) and Sean (Scott Caan) are wrestling fanatics. They are preparing to go to the WCW Monday Nitro event where they get to see their hero Jimmy King (Oliver Platt) defend the World Heavyweight title against Diamond Dallas Page (played by himself). King has made a few enemies in his career, and one of them is show runner Titus Sinclair (Joe Pantoliano), who has a plan to take away King's title and ban him for life. Gordy and Sean are devastated by this calamitous news, so they set out on a quest to find King, and when they meet him for the first time, they realize what a disappointment he is (he's a drunken louse). The two of them help King get one last shot at the title, but first he has to make amends with the ones he crossed, like his wife, son, and most importantly, fellow wrestler Goldberg (Bill Goldberg), who may be the only person who can help save his ass when the odds are against him.

Ready to Rumble is a goofy comedy filled with infantile humor, scantily clad ladies, and oily men rolling around the ring together. It's all rather harmless fun and does offer up quite a few chuckles. What's so great about the film (at least for wrestling fans) is getting to see so many real-life wrestling personalities featured as full-fledged characters. Guys like Sting, Sid Vicious, DDP, Randy Savage, Perry Saturn, and many others get to do what they do best as well as ham it up for laughs. It's Bill Goldberg (Half Past Dead 2) who stands out heads above the rest, though. He has the best entrance and gets to toss around plenty of bodies during the triple-decker cage match finale. The film holds up pretty well, and there's a pinch of nostalgia for those of us who thrived on one of the most exciting times in wrestling history. Directed by Brian Robbins.

(Editor's note: In 1986, the film Bad Guys, starring Adam Baldwin and Mike Jolly featured a storyline about two misfit cops who get booted off the force, join professional wrestling, and make a splash as "bad guys" in the ring. That film featured cameos by famous wrestlers like Toru Tanaka, Gene LeBell, and Robert Remus (Sgt. Slaughter). It is not reviewed here, however, because the roles by the wrestlers were too small.)

Recoil

1998 (Trinity DVD) (djm)

A band of bank robbers is interrupted by a legion of cops who surround the bank on the street. The thieves won't back down—an intense shootout ensues, leading to a chase where one robber escapes via a motorcycle, but Detective Ray Morgan (Gary Daniels) takes pursuit with his partner. The chase picks up intensity as more policemen join in, but the cyclist is eventually thrown off his bike, and Morgan shoots him dead out of reflex. The action is caught on tape, and the footage is brought to the dead man's father, who is a vindictive mobster. Morgan and his whole family are targeted for death, and after a shocking scene where his family is killed, he spends time brooding and strengthening his resolve to seek revenge. While in that contemplative state, his partner is murdered, which cinches it for him. He goes after what remains of the mobster's family, bringing the patriarch to his knees.

One of Gary Daniels's best and most vibrant movies, Recoil (from PM Entertainment) looks, sounds, and feels like a major Hollywood release. The production values, editing, cinematography, and score are all top-shelf, and if this had been given a theatrical release, it might have elevated the star's status during that period. Director Art Camacho (Half Past Dead 2) uses Daniels to the best of his abilities here, and Daniels himself doesn't use his martial arts until nearly an hour into the movie, which is great because then it actually means something.

INTERVIEW:

ART CAMACHO (CD)

Many big-name action and martial arts stars have found themselves working with Art Camacho in one capacity or another. He's worked as a stuntman, fight choreographer, producer, and director. Having made it through a rough childhood, Camacho was able to better himself through his passion for the martial arts, which eventually led to him working in motion pictures. The legendary PM Entertainment gave him some of his first opportunities as a choreographer and director, which gave birth to a cinematic legacy that has spanned three decades with no signs of slowing down. Having directed modern action entries like Recoil (1998), Redemption (2002), *and* Half Past Dead 2 (2007), *Camacho is one of the few who still abides by a more traditional style of directing, one that doesn't include excessive use of gratuitous computer effects or quick cutting. With so many stories to tell and learn from, Camacho shares a few of his memories here.*

What led you to training in the martial arts?

There were several factors that led to my training in martial arts but the two main ones were getting beat up by rival gang members and of course being introduced to the great Bruce Lee. Bruce Lee died long before I discovered his movies, but I can't forget the first experience I had watching my first Bruce Lee film, which was *The Chinese Connection.* It was one of those experiences that almost seems like it was fated to happen. I was in my teens, and my life began to spiral away. I grew up in a barrio and gangs and drugs were all around. I was barely hanging on by a thread in school. I was failing almost every class, and I cut classes so much that one day I was picked up by the local cops and taken home. Then one night I decided to walk to the local liquor store around midnight. The next thing I remember was someone calling out to me, and I turned around and got smashed over the head with beer bottle. What happened next was surreal. I remember fists and heavy shoes slamming into my body and face and smelling my own blood as it was pouring from my face, head and mouth, and

Art Camacho in Burbank, California. Photo by david j. moore.

thinking how warm the blood felt pouring down my face. When this was happening, I didn't feel any pain whatsoever, just the hard impact of the hits. Shortly after that, as I was recovering with eleven stitches over my right eye and several wounds all over my face and head, I saw one of my first Bruce Lee movies, and that was it. I started training at first to beat the crap out of people. I had so much pent-up hostility—and still do to this day—but as I got more and more involved in the martial arts, my outlook on life began to change. I was never a stellar martial artist. In fact, I was always one of the slowest learners in class. It wasn't until years later that I began to channel my martial arts into movies.

Did you ever compete competitively?

I only competed a few times in sparring. I did not do too well and felt it was very confining for me, and I never pursued it. I did however get into some amateur boxing matches and that was more my style.

How did you manage to get your start in the film industry?

Ever since I could remember, I always had an affinity for film and didn't know how to break in until one day when I decided to give it a shot. I quit a steady job I had and just jumped into doing some extra work in movies to get an idea of what it was about and that led to eventually doing some non-union films as an actor/stunt fighter, and I was hooked. My sifu (master), Eric Lee, was one of the first people to give me an opportunity to work in movies.

You started out as an actor. How did that lead to stunt work and fight choreography?

I began doing small parts and then some leads in independent action films, and I got them because of my acting and martial arts skills. It was very fun and rewarding but those roles in films were few and far between so when I started getting asked to do stunt fights in films, I jumped at the chance. I had already had some experience behind the camera directing and producing Spanish language commercials, and so when I started doing fights on film I understood the camera, which is very important. I did my job so well I kept getting asked to appear in films and then on one film in particular I not only performed my role but I also helped coordinate the other fighters and fights and made things run so smooth by helping the director get the shots he needed. That impressed the co-director/writer so much that he asked me if I was interested in choreographing his next project. I wasn't sure about it at first until I consulted with my sifu, Eric Lee, and he encouraged me to take the job. From then on in, I became in demand in the independent circles as a fight choreographer.

When choreographing a fight, what is your method and how do you piece it together?

The very first thing I do once I get a movie is read the script. I do this to understand the characters and their strengths and weaknesses. I then consult with both the star and the director to get a feel for the tone and what type of fight action they're looking for. Then I review the locations and also

R

how they intend to shoot the fight. It's only after I have an understanding of all these elements that I begin the physical choreography. Every film is different and the physical approach I use varies with the style and the tone of a film. For instance, I just finished an MMA action drama. With this film I was going for a gritty feel and look to it so I staged it in such a way that you really get a visceral response to the fights, whereas in a film I did with Don Wilson some years back called *Sci-Fighter*, that was more of an over-the-top action family film so we made it a little more spectacular and stylized with techniques and editing. I kept the camera in place to capture the impact and see the different martial arts techniques, whereas in the MMA film it is a little bit grittier. I shot the MMA film with master shots and handheld cameras, which gives it a more visceral feel.

Does the choreography of the fights differ when you're actually directing the film?

It does differ because as a director/choreographer it is completely my vision and I can move much faster as opposed to when I am working to fulfill someone else's vision. The end result is the same but just the process is different.

How were you introduced to Don "The Dragon" Wilson?

It was on *Ring of Fire*. Eric Lee was the choreographer and he needed some martial arts stunt fighters for a big fight scene in Chinatown and he called me up and asked if I wanted to get paid for getting my butt kicked on a movie, and I jumped at the chance. I remember meeting Don Wilson at Eric Lee's house for the first time, and I was star struck. I could not believe how down to Earth he was and how generous he is as a person. I ended up working on *Ring of Fire* and many others with Don including *Out for Blood* in which he proceeded to demolish me, but I enjoyed every minute of it.

How has your professional working relationship with him evolved over the years?

I started out as a stunt fighter in his movies and for several years became his fight choreographer. We traveled all over making movies, including India. Don and I got along as martial artists, peers and eventually friends. I ended up directing him in three films in addition to choreographing the fights for over twenty of his films.

The Power Within was your first film as a director. How was that experience and were you ready for what you were getting into?

You know something funny? I never asked any producer to direct movies; I just naturally gravitated towards doing it without the credit, but in about a year, two producers asked me to direct movies for them, and the one I chose was PM Entertainment's *The Power Within*. I was actually slated to direct *Fists of Iron*, starring Michael Worth, but I had too many commitments at that time. I ended up being the choreographer on it. Richard Munchkin did a great job on it. I was ready to direct features, but I didn't know that at the time and I was so stressed out about it. You have to imagine, I am a high-school dropout, ex-gang

banger and all around screw-up and here I am in the director's seat. I was so afraid of being fired on my first day. One thing I did have going for me is experience because I had not only choreographed the fights for over thirty features but also directed over 100 Spanish commercials prior to getting into directing. I was very blessed to have started out very early in life. The stress eventually eased up and I got into the zone of it all and began to flourish with my vision. I am still very proud of that first film. It is an indescribable feeling to direct a movie because I am not a trained director and I only go by instinct. The movie itself plays out in my head and the shots come to me.

You've also spent some time working in television with shows like *L.A. Heat* and more recently *Banshee*. How has the medium evolved and changed over the years from the perspective of a stunt guy?

It really hasn't changed much. It is pretty much the same in the sense that many of the really good shows still rely on good old-fashioned human bodies to do the fight action and in terms of getting the jobs themselves, it's the same except it's become much more of a clique in the stunt community than ever before. When I started out I was giving so many people opportunities to hone their craft and create careers for themselves and unfortunately that is much different now. It is next to impossible to get in unless you're really lucky. Skill matters, but what matters more is being in with the right people.

You directed Michael DePasquale Jr.'s passion project, *The Cutoff*. How did that come about?

I had met Michael a few years before through Don Wilson and we got along great. We became close friends, and when he was putting this film together he asked if I could help him. I was drawn to the story and Michael's passion for the project but the script needed some work so we all set out to make it great. It was awesome working with Danny Lane who I think is great writer as well as great martial artist. To this day this was one of my best experiences. It wasn't like work at all. It felt like we were just a bunch of martial artists and artists just going out there and having fun.

How was your experience working with Gary Daniels on *Recoil*?

Gary is first and foremost an incredible martial artist and a really good actor. We had known each other for years and had worked together on *Firepower* prior to this. *Recoil* was a challenge in that it was one of PM Entertainment's tent pole films. So even though I had a great time working with Gary, it was a very stressful film to work on.

The chase scene at the beginning of *Recoil* was pretty spectacular. What was it like filming that sequence and what sort of time and preparation was put into it?

We had at one time three full units running simultaneously and I had an incredible stunt coordinator and second unit director guiding and working with me. In fact I remember the scene where we filmed a limousine splitting in two. We were sitting and discussing the scene involving the

limousine. The stunt coordinator wanted to have it roll down the river bed in the finale but I thought about it and I realized that was boring. I looked at the length of the limo and asked, "Why not split it in two?" I got a weird look from everyone for a few moments, but then the stunt coordinator said, "Absolutely!" He meticulously planned the stunt and we did it. We sawed it in half and anchored it to the highway and had a cable attached to Gary's double, and right when the eighteen-wheeler hits the car, the cable yanks the stuntman and the thirty gallons of gasoline explodes as the eighteen-wheeler goes through the car. It was spectacular.

Any other stories from your time with PM Entertainment?

I can't say enough good things about that company, especially about Joseph Merhi. He is a throwback to the Louie B. Mayor type of producers who lead with their gut. To Joseph, a handshake is just as good as any contract on paper. I remember my early experiences with them were so great. PM Entertainment not only got me my SAG card but they gave me my first fight choreography job and my first directing job. In the PM Entertainment days you had to know your craft or learn it quick. If Joseph saw potential in you, he would put you into these really precarious situations to give you the opportunity to either "sink or swim". I remember the first time he officially had me direct the fight action. It was on *To Be the Best*. It was the opening fight on the roof of a casino in Las Vegas. I had choreographed the fight featuring Michael Worth and Manuel Sanchez and was ready to step back and let him direct when he came out to the center of the rooftop and told me in a loud voice, "Art, you direct this fight!" He then turned to the first assistant director, Jerry Jacobs (who is now producing with Lionsgate pictures and was a director himself), "Jerry, don't help him. I want him to do it on his own." I felt sick to my stomach but after a few moments Joseph left the set. I turned to the camera guy and said, "Well, you heard him, ummm . . . put the camera . . . there," and I pointed to a random corner and the cameraman told me, "Wouldn't it be better here?" and he pointed to a better location. "Umm . . . okay!" and it was on! After the first couple of stumbles I was cooking. It was shortly after that time that I became PM's go-to guy for fights. And one day on the set of *Magic Kid*, Joseph came up to me and asked me if I wanted to direct movies. I didn't know if he was serious or what, so I nonchalantly said, "Yeah, that'd be cool." Within two weeks I was a feature film director.

Walk us through your day on a film like *Gangland*. You directed, produced, did the fight choreography, and performed stunts on the film. How is that humanly possible?

Now that movie kicked my butt big time! I had worked for Dominion before and I knew that things can get chaotic but we had an impossible delivery date for the movie and went in with a script that was incomplete! So I would sit down every morning with the actors and we would literally be writing the scenes of the day and tweaking the script as we went along. Anything that could go wrong, did go wrong! Our effects shots didn't work as planned and one morning this disgruntled crew member organized a set stoppage for reasons I never did figure out. My line producer and I got in front of the crew and told them to go ahead and quit. I had a back-up crew just in case. Fortunately for them they stayed on to work. Same thing happened on *Point Doom*, but in that case they were threatening to steal our generator and that ticked me off. I had hired two great martial artists as personal assistants on that movie and I told them that if anything went down I wanted them to back me up. My plan was to take out the biggest guy on the set myself if he caused any problems and have them back me up if anyone jumped in. Yeah, pretty crazy, huh? Fortunately, it didn't come to that but I was fired up so much it reminded me of being back in the barrio. So many things went wrong on *Gangland*. If it hadn't been for my great cast—Costas Mandylor, Sasha Mitchell, and Kathleen Kinmont—I don't know If I would have made it through the shoot. I was choreographing fights every day on the spot and the actors would learn them and perform them with no more than a few minutes' practice while I was having to deal with minute details such as lunch for the crew, locations permits, and everything else.

You had a really large cast of genre favorites in *Gangland*, some of whom you just mentioned. Were they all offered roles or was there an audition process?

For the leads, no one auditioned. We knew who we wanted and got them. The opening scenes with Ice T and Coolio were shot long after principal photography was finished. And the two were just offered their roles. The funny thing is that I shot them for so many hours that Ice T actually had barely enough time to go home and pack up to fly out to New York to do his first day on *Law and Order*. For all the smaller roles, we auditioned actors. But many films in this time period were already pre-cast or had actors attached for the lead roles.

What can you tell us about your experience doing *13 Dead Men* with Lorenzo Lamas?

13 Dead Men was a film that I was not going to do. It was an impossible schedule and the initial script made no sense. In fact, York Entertainment had given me a deposit check that I refused to cash for several weeks because I wasn't sure I would do the movie. I had wanted to work with Lorenzo again and Mystikal but the script didn't make sense, so one day I asked the producer to give me a crack at the script and I spent two days mulling it around until it came to me. I started writing, and by around nine o'clock in the evening I had written forty pages! I sent it to producer and he loved it, so it was back on. I worked with another writer finishing it and then polishing it in a matter of two weeks and then we shot the movie on a schedule of eleven days! Lorenzo, as always, was a pro; he not only delivered in his acting performance but in his fight scenes.

Can you talk a bit about working on *Half Past Dead*? Do you have any stories about working with guys like Steven Seagal, Ja Rule, or Mike Moeller? You appear in the film as well.

To be honest, when I got the call to meet for *Half Past Dead*, I really didn't think I was qualified for what the director had in mind. He was looking for someone from the Hong Kong-style of screen fighting. I still took the meeting and was gracious, but every time he'd bring someone's name up like Donny Yen, I would tell the director to just hire whomever he was referring to. I meant it because these guys are my idols. But after a few weeks I got a call and they told me they had hired Xin Xin Xiong and the stunt coordinator from *Resident Evil*. I told them, "Great, now why are you calling me?" The studio still wanted me on board. I didn't see any position for me but they really wanted me to work on this film so they made me an offer I couldn't refuse. It was great working with Steven and I not only worked with Ja Rule but I trained him a bit in screen fighting. He was awesome. I also met and worked with some great talent from Germany, including Mike Moeller. Mike impressed me not only with his skills but with his overall humility. He was an incredible martial artist, but he wasn't used enough in this film in my opinion. I had no intention of appearing in the movie but they needed someone at the last minute so I filled in.

Your film *Redemption* is one of Don Wilson's films, and certainly a high mark in your career as well. Talk about directing this film and working with all of the great action guys in the cast like Richard Norton, Sam Jones, Steven Vincent Leigh, and Ms. Cynthia Rothrock.

Redemption was a film I was not slated to direct. In fact, I almost turned it down. They had offered it to another director and he wanted too much money for the film and they came to me and told me the other guy was too expensive. I wasn't going to take the job just because I was cheaper than the other guy, so we went back and forth and finally agreed to a fee that I thought was fair. I did it because I believed in the film. If I hadn't believed in it, I would've kept turning them down. I'm glad I did direct it because in spite of all the issues we had, it still worked. There were some really crazy incidents on that film that I will share one day that will blow people away. We had a physical fight on the set. An actor who kidnapped a production assistant, a producer who promised to fund pick-ups, but reneged at the last minute, and so on. But I kept my head in the game and forged ahead, working with a bunch of great people including the ones you just mentioned and one of my favorite actors, James Russo. Again, a challenging film but the saving grace was my friend Don Wilson and a really strong premise and script. Half the time on these films I have to troubleshoot in almost every area.

With *Sci-Fighter*, you make it a point to show off different fighting techniques. What were you trying to show the audience?

The general idea behind the *Sci-Fighter* action was to showcase not only different techniques but different iconic martial artists as well and make it action-driven without being too violent. To me, there is a difference between fight action and violence. That film came about because Don Wilson wanted to do a real family film, and it was going to be Bill Gottlieb's first film (Bill

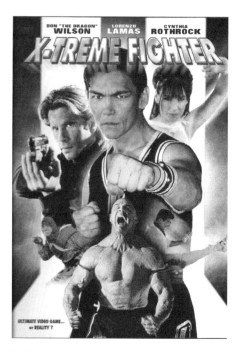

DVD cover art for *X-Treme Fighter*. Author's collection.

Gottlieb is president of Gorilla Pictures). As with other Don Wilson films, we called in a bunch of friends to help out. I did want to feature many types of martial arts and icons in that field, but more importantly I wanted to tell a story of a dysfunctional family. As much as *Sci-Fighter* is about action, it also focuses on a family dynamic. I felt that way because if you don't care for the people and their plight you, as an audience member, will not go on this journey with them.

You worked with Jeff Wincott on several films and he's certainly an underrated performer. What was your impression of him?

Jeff is a great guy and a hard worker. I really am surprised that he didn't do bigger projects. He's got a sort of Paul Newman-esque charm about him on screen, and he's got sort of an everyman persona. He's a great actor and a really good on-screen fighter.

R

Crooked was a film loaded with talent. Can you talk a bit about being with that group of guys on set?

Crooked was an extreme challenge from the onset. We had a script that had many strong points but it needed some work. So we kept on working on it even during shooting. This was a Don Wilson vehicle but as we proceeded to move forward we began attaching other talent including Olivier Gruner, who is also a great screen presence and Fred "The Hammer" Williamson. I ran into Martin Kove as we were filming, and we wrote him into the film. Another actor that we attached was good old Gary Busey. He was definitely a handful to work with, to say the least. One of the most challenging actors I've encountered, actually. Deep down he's a really good guy but you have to dig real deep to find it. So as usual it was up to me to maneuver my way through several cinematic minefields and get at the core of the movie. But you know, what has made it really worth doing was my friendship with Don. He and I have been through thick and thin together from films shot in India to films shot on top of moving trains, and when you work with friends, it makes it all worthwhile. People on the outside would be shocked at what it takes to get films made from inception to completion.

How did you end up as director of *Half Past Dead 2?*

That was one of the quickest films I have been involved with. It was simply a phone call from Andrew Stevens, the producer, and he said, "Hey, how would you like to direct this sequel?" It was that simple. However, as it always is, it came back to script. The story and concept were there but the script needed a lot of work. Also, it was made for Sony Pictures, so the challenges are different when you work for a studio. Many approvals from top to bottom are needed as opposed to indie producers where you just go to them directly on the set and you have your answers. But overall it was great working on this and especially working with Bill Goldberg. He is truly a rare talent. I think he managed to find the right balance in his role.

Why do you think Bill Goldberg hasn't gone on to be a bigger action star?

I ask myself the same thing. He really looks great on camera and comes across very strong and has some depth about him. It's much like Gary Daniels, who's also a pretty good actor and has some presence. It's really something intangible. I remember years ago meeting Cuba Gooding Jr. before he became successful. He was acting and I was doing stunts on a project and he was interested in training with me for a boxing project that he was about to do. He told me that his agent was really hooking him up with jobs and that he was on his way. We never got a chance to train but he did have something about him that was likable and that intangible quality I mentioned. Bruce Lee had that. If you look at Bruce Lee's choreography, it's great but not out of this world but he had that "it" quality about him. With Bruce Lee, you never felt the need to cut away for insert shots. The camera loves him so much that you want him to stay on camera all the time and even the way he executes the simplest of techniques its exciting to watch. Same thing with Steven Seagal.

You're one of the few directors who seems to prefer to keep things real in your grittier action films. How do you feel about the current state of the action film and the excessive use of CGI and fast cutting?

I think part of my preference in keeping things real on screen is that visceral quality to the action. Because to me, and again it's just my preference, I just get so removed from the action when it's CGI unless it is a surrealistic film or a superhero type of movie. It works great in *The Avengers* and *Superman*, but when you're making a contemporary action film, it takes you out of the moment. Don't get me wrong, you enjoy it but you have to suspend reality for the action then go back into the drama,

whereas if you have a gritty visceral fight you stay into the characters and the movie. I am working on a *Batman* type of project right now and we will get a little over the top, but not too much because the person doesn't have superpowers. Also, I feel you have to find the right balance between long shots and quick edits on a fight. Sometimes if the shot is too long it gets boring and slows down the pace but, on the other hand, if you have too many cuts you feel cheated because you can't get into the fight action and it's just an assault on the senses because along with quick cuts comes the loud pounding of bone-crunching sound effects to mask something. But in the batch of superhero-type films it's great because you're watching a live action cartoon and you buy into it the minute you sit in front of the screen. The exception to the rule of long boring shots is Bruce Lee; he's so poetic and exciting to watch. I don't know of anyone else who has as much raw charisma as he did.

You seem to have shifted your focus in recent years to producing. Was that a conscious decision or are you just waiting for something to catch your interest?

The last three films I've directed were so grueling and challenging that I really got burned out. The producers were more interested in getting out a product and I was more interested in making a great movie and sometimes those two goals come into conflict and I didn't feel I was able to do my best anymore under those circumstances, so I took a step back. I love doing stunts and choreography but as a director, I get so emotionally invested in each film and it becomes very personal and if I can't accomplish what I set out to do due to circumstances beyond my control, it eats me up. And I was getting offered very, very bad scripts to work with so I turned down a couple films, and then I decided to wait until I found a project that would really get me going. Recently I have found my passion for directing again and just shot my first short film and now I'm in talks on two other full-length features. I got that burning passion that I had in the beginning of my career again.

You recently produced two Spanish language action films, *Once Upon a Fight* and *Cage Fight*. Could you talk about your involvement with those?

I was working on developing a science fiction *Expendables*-type of movie with some spiritual overtones when one of my friends and student Willy Ramos approached me with the idea of doing a couple Spanish action films. I was really intrigued with the idea. I knew I couldn't put in the time to direct them, but I gladly helped him produce them. They were experimental films to see if there's a niche market for these types of movies, and so far we've had moderate success . . . enough to warrant my directing a couple films for this untapped market. In addition to the business side, I've always wanted to do films for Latinos as well as the general market.

You've also been dabbling in a South African television show. What is you interest in the South African industry?

I've had many people reach out to me from various countries to work with them in helping develop marketable action projects in their prospective markets, and I really want to support them in any way I can because I know that there is such a strong pool of talent out there waiting to be discovered.

What's your favorite acting role you have taken in someone else's film? What was it that connected with you?

The best time I had was on the film *To Be the Best*. It was great. I was acting in it, fighting, and choreographing, and even directing the fight action. It combined all my passions. Even though the role was small it connected with me because it was an underdog type of role. All my life I've been an underdog in everything I set out to achieve. I'm not complaining. I've worked so hard for everything I have and put myself out there so many times to get doors slammed in my face, and I've been ridiculed for believing in the possibilities, and that's why some of these projects resonate with me.

What can you tell us about your upcoming acting role in William Lee's *Architect of Chaos?*

This is strictly an acting role with some action but no directing responsibilities, which is great because that is a huge task. It's a cool script, and I really like William Lee's energy and passion. That's the usual criteria unless it is a "payday" type of project where you do it primarily for the money.

At one point you were attached to a film called *The Unforgiven*, which would have brought together actors like Don Wilson, Cynthia Rothrock, James Lew, and Martin Kove. Is this film something you are still pursuing or is it in development hell?

The Unforgiven has gone through so much. First off, there was an option purchased and when the funding didn't come in on time the option expired and then it went into limbo and now there is another source pursuing it on a larger scale. So it is, in essence, in development hell. I tell everyone, "It ain't real until I'm on the set calling action." But I am hoping to do this film because I feel this can be a really strong movie. It will have some real strong spiritual messages underlying the story, characters, and action.

What does the future hold for you, sir?

I am currently working on creating a slate of pictures to produce, and I will direct some of them but others I will find great new directors with great visions to helm them, and overall I am hoping to keep doing stunt fighting workshops to help others in the martial arts community and to discover new talent.

Here's your chance to address your fans. What would you like to say to them?

I want to first off thank everyone for many of the kind words I have received on my work over the years and for watching my movies or reading my articles. I came up in the barrio and dropped out of school at sixteen and really had the bleakest of futures ahead of me, and the martial arts literally changed my life. I am not where I aspire to be but whenever I feel myself complaining, I look back and thank the Lord for granting me the gift of living a dream. If not for people watching, buying, or renting my movies, I would not be working in this industry, and I owe a deep debt of gratitude to everyone. From the bottom of my heart, I thank you for even considering me important enough to do this interview.

Recoil
2011 (Vivendi DVD) (djm)

Shopkeeper: "Where'd you learn to fight like that?"
Varrett: "From fighting."

Ex-cop Ryan Varrett ("Stone Cold" Steve Austin) has long left the force for the high and lonely road of vigilantism, and he drives across the country looking to punish the guilty who have slipped through the cracks of the justice system. He ends up in a desoalte town called Hope, where he systematically goes after a scuzz named Rex (Noel Gugliemi), whom he kills in an outlandish stunt. Rex's druglord brother Drayke (Danny Trejo) goes on the warpath to avenge his brother's death, and Varrett must stand his ground and face the force of power that Drayke's little drug and gun empire throws at him. With little help from the corrupt law enforcement in the town, Varrett comes to care a little bit for a young widow named Darcy (Serina Swan), and if he's going to survive his stay in Hope, he's got to make sure she survives, too.

I was blown away by *Recoil*. Steve Austin's track record as an action star is spotty due to the fact that he's been in some junky efforts like *Tactical Force* and *The Stranger*, but *Recoil* is one of his best—if not his very best—action film. The script by John Sullivan (who has written some low-budget horror films) is surprisingly smart and believable, and the direction by Terry Miles feels assured and accomplished. The action scenes are tight and convincingly planned out, and Austin's character behaves in a realistic fashion. His final fight with Trejo (who's very good in the film) is great. MMA fighter Keith Jardine (from *Tactical Force*) has a nice fight with Austin at about the halfway point. This one is highly recommended.

Redeemer
2015 (Dark Sky DVD) (djm)

The assassin living a double life makes a mistake: He accidentally kills the child of his mark, and it alters the course of his destiny. The hitman—Pardo (Marko Zaror, the Chilean martial arts action star from *Kiltro*, *Mirage Man*, and *Mandrill*)—has the tables turned on him in that moment of error, and his mark—Alacran (Jose Luis Mosca)—takes that

split-second to enter full rage mode, taking Pardo down. Alacran imprisons the murderer of his son and kidnaps Pardo's wife and forces Pardo to kill her in a sick and twisted torturous fashion. He crucifies Pardo, but allows him to survive in the midst of his own torment, leaving him a gun with a single bullet in the spun chamber so that he can contemplate the chance of suicide. Pardo, who gives fate more than several chances to end his life, somehow manages to survive one day at a time, and with what he believes is God's permission, he goes on a crusade of personal penance as The Redeemer, a one-man vigilante force who goes from town to town throughout Chile, creating a legend in his wake. He ends up in a little backwater beach town where an American drug lord wannabe named Bradock (a miscast Noah Segan, who provides the paltry comedy relief) has planted his roots to start up his burgeoning drug trade. Pardo comes into town like The Man With No Name, but as soon as he runs afoul of Bradock's lackeys, the action heats up as he takes them out one by one (or all at once, depending on the scene) until everyone realizes that he's the legendary Redeemer, which causes them to scatter in fear. To cap off the odds, the sadistic Alacran arrives in town to finish Pardo off, and the climactic fight between them concludes in a satisfyingly teeth-shattering crescendo.

The whole reason movies like *Redeemer* are made is to showcase the physical talents and abilities of stars like Marko Zaror. On the surface, movies like this are a dime a dozen, shot on small budgets, filled with mediocre acting, and filmed in and around dusty, ugly locations, but if you look a little deeper you'll find that movies like this are what make the martial arts and action genre so appealing. The entire spectrum of these genres exists simply to be the vehicle for the star—the real-life champion of the martial arts, of bodybuilding, of professional sports—and without that star the movie would essentially be worthless. Marko Zaror—if you've ever seen him in anything (he also had supporting action roles in *Undisputed III* and

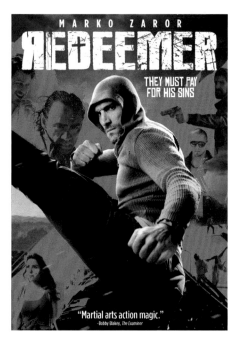

Press poster for *Redeemer*. Author's collection.

Machete Kills)—gleams like a sword blade when he's on screen. Acting-wise, he's not there yet, but that doesn't matter because when he's moving and doing his incredible kicks and flips (if you want to compare him to anybody, compare him to Scott Adkins) he's a wonder to behold. In *Redeemer* he's pretty much playing the silently heroic and downtrodden cowboy who mutters his self-righteous lines to crowds of villains who can amazingly understand what he said to them moments before he kicks their teeth out, so it's a cliché type of role to play, but if you're going to look at it that way, then the whole movie is a cliché and you won't be interested. If martial arts action films are your thing, then Marko Zaror should definitely be on your radar and *Redeemer* is as good a place as any to get started with its rising star. Ernesto Diaz Espinoza, who collaborated with Zaror on *Kiltro*, *Mirage Man*, and *Mandrill*, wrote and directed this one as well.

Redemption
2002 (Dominion DVD) (djm)

Cop John Sato (Don Wilson) makes some judgment calls that get him in trouble, and he clashes with one of the cops in his unit—Tom (Richard Norton)—who presses him to the point where they come to blows. Sato's partner, Erin (Cynthia Rothrock), is killed when she disobeys Sato's order, and Sato is let go. Depressed and emotionally vulnerable, he turns to a local gangster named Leggio (Chris Penn) for work, and he begins hanging around a high-class hooker (Carrie Stevens) to boost his self-esteem. As he begins making some good money, he sees an opportunity to redeem himself by thwarting a major heist by an Asian gang, and he saves the lives of his former partners on the force.

Surprisingly multifaceted for a direct-to-video effort, *Redemption* has a great cast that surrounds star Wilson with their welcome presence. The script is solid, the characters feel real, and the action takes a backseat to an engrossing story. Every character in the film feels like he or she belong there, and the actors (who also include Sam Jones, James Russo, Gerald Okamura, and Steven Vincent Leigh) are perfectly chosen. Director Art Camacho (*Gangland*) does a really good job with this one. It's one of Wilson's best pictures.

Redemption
(a.k.a. **Hummingbird**)
2013 (Lionsgate DVD) (djm)

In an interesting career move, Jason Statham stars as an AWOL soldier named Joey who lives among the homeless in London, getting beat up by thugs on a daily basis. One night, he literally falls through the roof of a building while being chased, and he comes to find that the owner of the swanky apartment he's found himself in won't be back for nearly half a year. He cleans himself up, uses the absent man's bank account to help realign his path, and he begins working for an Asian mobster as a bruiser. Accruing a large nest egg, he decides to

R

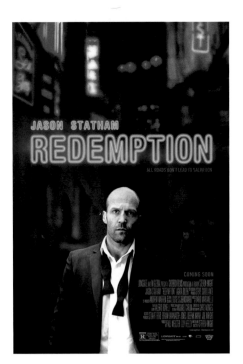

Theatrical release poster for *Redemption*.
Author's collection.

help those individuals who made him feel human when he was homeless, and those include a young woman whom he had feelings for, and a nebbish nun who fed him every night. When the young woman turns up slain, Joey turns to the nun (played by Agata Buzek) to help him find the girl's killer, and in turn, he ends up falling a little in love with the nun. Seeking assistance from the Asian mafia, Joey goes on a revenge trip, despite how it affects his relationship with the nun, who, as it turns out, has some very serious secrets of her own.

If you're used to seeing Statham in his *Transporter* persona, you might find *Redemption* a little too radical to handle. It might remind some viewers of his best movie *Safe*, but it's not as action-focused as that film, and many will find it to be a tad strange for Statham. I really enjoyed it. Director Steven Knight gives Statham a lot to work with, and Statham himself comes across as a full-fledged actor, despite the fact that he ends up relying (as usual) more on his physicality than his acting abilities (which he has). There are slightly surreal touches throughout the film, but everything points to Statham's broken hero's psyche. It's one of his best films, up there with *Safe*.

Red Heat

1988 (Lionsgate DVD) (MJ)

"Very strange city. The crime is organized. The police is not."

The year 1988 was very good for Arnold Schwarzenegger. Following his ever-increasing returns at the box office from hit films such as *Raw Deal, Predator,* and *The Running Man,* 1988 would see the release of two films from the popular star, *Red Heat* and *Twins*. One of the

formulas in action cinema at the time was the buddy picture, which first yielded great success at the box office in 1984 with *48 Hrs*, featuring two characters with opposing viewpoints who reluctantly have to team up to achieve a common goal. Both *48 Hrs* and *Red Heat* are directed by Walter Hill, known for explosive action and great storytelling in films such as *The Warriors, Southern Comfort,* and *The Long Riders. Red Heat* tells the story of Russian policeman Ivan Danko (Schwarzenegger), who comes to Chicago to extradite Viktor Rosta (Ed O'Ross), a crime lord from his country who, unknown to the Chicago police department, is also responsible for killing Danko's partner. Forced to babysit Captain Danko is Art Ridzik (James Belushi), an unorthodox Chicago policeman who is one step away from losing his job. When Rosta escapes from custody, killing Ridzik's partner in the process, the two mismatched policemen must work together to get Rosta back.

The success of *Red Heat* hinges on the casting of Schwarzenegger and Chicago native James Belushi as reluctant partners and the end result is more than satisfying. The actors became lifelong friends and would work together on other projects in the future. Along with many familiar faces from Walter Hill's regular stable of actors, including Brion James, Peter Jason, and Luis Contreras, the film also has a great villain, played by Ed O'Ross, who is more than a match for Schwarzenegger. The film benefits strongly from location shooting in Chicago and, more importantly, Soviet Russia, being one of the first American productions to shoot there during the Cold War. While *Red Heat* was more along the lines of what Schwarzenegger's fans had come to expect in 1988, *Twins* was a gamble that paid off in more significant ways, by showing that the star had more to offer as an actor, capable of playing comedy *and* drama. This served to increase the size of his fan base to include people of all ages and ensure greater success at the box office in the future.

Redline

1997 (Nu Image DVD) (CD)

"Never fuck with a man's dreams!"

In a dark and violent future, small-time smugglers John Wade (Rutger Hauer) and Merrick (Mark Dacascos) have made off with a bunch of fantasy chips (virtual reality) for the cyber-addicts to feast on. It appears to be smooth sailing when Wade is double-crossed by his supposed friend. Merrick shoots him in the head and leaves the body, making off with the goods and the cash. When Wade's body is discovered by the police, they use modern technology to bring him back to life and question him about the crime family his former partner is a part of. He quickly escapes and sets out on a quest to find Merrick and score the revenge he so desperately needs.

How did Mark Dacascos (*Sanctuary*) end up with the short end of the stick? Rutger Hauer has all the fun being a badass and scoring the ladies. Most the women in *Redline* have two things in common: they're gorgeous and naked. They're naked so often Hauer has to fight them: He literally dukes it out with a couple of naked fighters. Tibor Takacs, who previously directed Dacascos in *Sanctuary*, fashions a decent film with a fair amount of action, including a cool scene where Merrick cuts off a man's fingers with a samurai sword then shoves them in the guy's mouth. Dacascos has his fair share of screen time but fans of the underrated action star may be a bit disappointed. There're some great ideas and enough action on display, but it's just not overly memorable.

Red Scorpion

1989 (Synapse DVD) (djm)

Just about every one of the big action stars of the 80s had their go at making their own *Rambo*, and *Red Scorpion* was Dolph Lundgren's shot. He's a tough, take-no-shit Spetsnaz Soviet agent named Nikolai who is ordered to go into Africa to appeal to rebels who are fighting the Russians. His ultimate goal is to assassinate the leader of the rebels, but when his plan goes awry, the leader entrusts him with a mission of heart and soul, rather than of mind and body, and Nikolai is sent away into the blazing African desert where he is rescued by a kindly bushman who emblazes a skin scar of a scorpion on his chest. From then on, Nikolai becomes the Red Scorpion who fights for the rebels. With the aide of a foul-mouthed "ugly American" reporter (M. Emmet Walsh), Nikolai takes on the Russians and blows stuff up real good.

Joseph Zito, who made *Invasion U.S.A.* and *Missing in Action,* directed this troubled film. It was a difficult shoot and millions were

Lt. Nikolai Rachenko (Dolph Lundgren) in *Red Scorpion*. Author's collection.

After being baptized by the sun and the sting of the scorpion, the Spetsnaz soldier Nikolai (Dolph Lundgren) becomes a good guy in *Red Scorpion*. Author's collection.

Dolph Lundgren and some big guns in *Red Scorpion*. Author's collection.

The ritual of pain in *Red Scorpion*, featuring Dolph Lundgren. Author's collection.

poured into it while African politics kept the production and crew on hold for months on end. There are graphic torture scenes and lots of dangerous stunts, which Dolph apparently performed himself. The scope and size of this film is nearly on par with *Rambo III*, which was released the year before. Brion James co-stars, and Jay Chattaway did the music.

Red Scorpion 2

1994 (Universal VHS) (djm)

After the financial debacle that was *Red Scorpion*, producer Jack Abramoff managed to do an in-name-only sequel, this time starring stuntman and kenpo blackbelt martial artist Matt McColm. He plays a secret agent named Nick Stone, who is tasked with assembling a misfit commando team to bring down a potential terrorist named Andrew Kendrick, who proposes a new world order to his legion of followers. Kendrick's mission is akin to Adolph Hitler's, but Kendrick has an artifact—the Spear of Destiny (the spear that pierced Jesus Christ on the cross)—to help lead him to victory. Stone and his unruly band of fighters must learn to work together to function as one cohesive unit to stop Kendrick, and their boss, Colonel West (Michael Ironside), assigns them a trainer and a sort-of mascot named Sam Guiness (Jennifer Rubin) to quick them into shape. Lots of explosions and gunfire commences.

The last thing I want to do is to overtly criticize movies like *Red Scorpion 2*, but it's hard *not* to when I can clearly see where movies like this miss the mark. The big problem with this film is that there are too many characters in it. If you're going to introduce an action star—namely Matt McColm, who looks like a movie star, acts like an action star, and moves like Jeff Speakman—the best thing that could have happened is letting him take the movie over. Unfortunately, the movie is helplessly bogged down with too many sidekicks and partners, and the focus of the action is never solely on McColm where it should have been. He gets to have a few nice fights, and the finale fight between him and

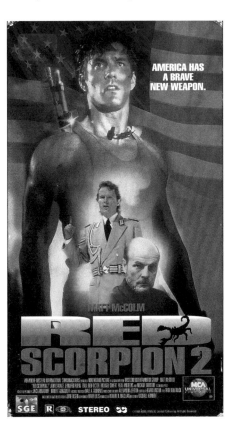

VHS artwork for *Red Scorpion 2*. Author's collection.

Vladimir Kulich (from *The 13th Warrior*) is pretty cool. McColm starred in *Subterfuge* next. Directed by Michael Kennedy (*The Talons of the Eagle* with Billy Blanks and *The Swordsman* with Lorenzo Lamas).

Red Serpent

2003 (Echo Bridge DVD) (CD)

"Why don't you take your money and get the hell out of here before I lose my sense of humor?"

Steve Nichols (Michael Pare) is a businessman who deals in medical supplies. Accompanied by his young daughter, he takes a trip to Russia to finalize a deal. The deal ends up being with Hassan (Roy Scheider), a feared drug lord who wants Nichols to smuggle drugs with the medical supplies. He refuses, and Hassan has Nichols's daughter kidnapped. By chance, Nichols meets Sergei Popov (real-life Sambo champion Oleg Taktarov), a former spy whose family was slaughtered by Hassan. Sergei is itching for revenge, and so the two men team up to hit Hassan where it hurts and get the girl back to safety.

If you read other reviews about this one, people hate it. It's even been called one of the worst films ever made. I challenge the claim—it isn't the greatest, but I'll call it a perfect "B" action film. It has two likable leads in Michael Pare (*The Philadelphia Experiment*) and Oleg Taktarov (also in *15 Minutes* and *Predators*), a decent story, fighting, explosions, and boobs. You can't ask for much more, and you get exactly what you should. Oleg has a few cool moments, but there was a missed opportunity by not including a rough and vicious brawl between him and action star Deron McBee (from *Deadly Currency*), who plays a henchman for Hassan. This is a fun film. Director Gino Tanasescu has never made another film.

Red Sun

1971 (Optimum DVD R2) (djm)

A train carrying some precious cargo is robbed by a band of outlaws, but the biggest score comes in the form of a priceless samurai sword meant as a gift to the president of the United States from the emperor of Japan. A Japanese ambassador and two samurais guard the sword, but that isn't enough to stop Gauche (Alain Delon), the left-handed leader of the bandits, from shooting one of the samurai down without any honor. Gauche betrays his right-hand-man Link (Charles Bronson) and leaves him for dead, and when Link regains consciousness, his first and only agenda is to hunt Gauche down and kill him, but not before reclaiming the booty. The ambassador of Japan gives his remaining samurai Kuroda (Toshiro Mifuni) one week to recover the precious sword, and he is forced to

Link Stuart (Charles Bronson) with a Japanese blade at his throat, held by the samurai Kuroda Jubie (Toshiro Mifune) in *Red Sun*. Author's collection.

Charles Bronson plays the gunslinger Link Stuart in *Red Sun*. Author's collection.

Sexy time: Ursula Andress is the prostitute Cristina in *Red Sun*. Charles Bronson plays the gunslinger Link Stuart. Author's collection.

Cowboy vs. samurai, featuring Charles Bronson and Toshiro Mifuni in *Red Sun*. Author's collection.

join Link on his like-minded quest. The outlaw and the samurai join forces (reluctantly), and while they're virtually enemies at first, they become allies and friends along the way.

This East-meets-West action adventure set in the West (but filmed in Spain) unites two badasses of cinema. Bronson and Mifuni (from Akira Kurosawa's epic samurai films like *Yojimbo* and *The Seven Samurai*) are fantastic in their meaty roles, and the action is wonderfully entertaining. Supporting cast mates Delon, Ursula Andress (who has several brief nude scenes), and Capucine all add great flavor to this unusual western. Directed by Terence Young (*Dr. No, From Russia With Love, Thunderball*), who had worked with Bronson on the thriller *Cold Sweat*. Their next picture together was *The Valachi Papers*.

Red Sun Rising

1994 (Imperial VHS) (djm)

A half-Japanese detective named Thomas Hoshino (Don Wilson) travels to America to seek answers and ultimately revenge for the death of his partner. His partner's killers are now in the US causing trouble in the streets of Los Angeles. He buddies up with a racist female detective named Ryder (Terry Farrell), and they face Hoshino's deadliest foe: Blue-eyed Jaho (James Lew), who has mystical powers and can kill with a single "death touch." Jaho's boss (played by Soon-Tek Oh) taunts the police force to stop them, and Ryder's Captain (Michael Ironside) is powerless. Hoshino seeks counsel with an old teacher of his (Mako), who instructs him how to harness the power of the "death touch" so that he's evenly matched with Jaho.

The best part of seeing this film is watching James Lew in the lead villain role. Lew, a stuntman and character punching bag from nearly eighty films since the 1980s, rarely got the opportunity to show off his abilities as an actor, and it's great to see him in a lead role. He has some great moments in the film (his blue contact lenses are used to good effect), and the lead-up to his fight with Wilson is carefully set up and executed. Wilson's fans will be pleased with the final result. Directed by Francis Megahy.

Re-Generator (a.k.a. One Night)

2010 (Ytinifni Pictures DVD) (CD)

"Now you listen to me, General, and you fucking listen good, motherfucker, 'cuz you owe me! I own you, do you understand?"

The weekend's here and it's time to party when a group of teenagers load their cars with booze and head out on the best camping trip ever. When they aren't getting drunk, they plan to get laid, then maybe drink some more. Their plans suddenly become derailed when The Beast (Olivier Gruner) shows up. He's a genetically enhanced government experiment trained to kill everything in sight (unless they have a special chip implanted), and he has the ability to regenerate. He was on a plane being transported when it crashed near the woods where the kids are camping. One by one he hunts down the innocent kids, butchering them senselessly. The government knows they have really messed up and will have to resort to extreme measures to sweep this one under the rug.

Olivier Gruner (*Automatic, Savage*) returns to the screen in this low-budget thriller he produced and directed. He's also responsible for the story, which is a mash-up of *Friday the 13th* and *Universal Soldier*. It's not a particularly good one but the idea is there, and it has potential. Audiences don't want to see Gruner running through the woods offing teens with an axe. If he's going on a rampage, his hands and feet are much more sufficient weapons than anything else he could use. His screen time is limited, with most of it going to the teens who quickly meet their demise. It also seemed like a waste to have someone like Paul Logan (*Ballistica*) in the picture and never have him face off with Gruner. Patrick Shanavian served as a co-director to Gruner and the two of them do their best, but it seems budget constraints may have prevented them from fully realizing their vision.

Remo Williams: The Prophecy

1988 (NOV) (djm)

Fred Ward and Joel Grey starred in the overlooked cult gem *Remo Williams: The Adventure Begins*, which was based on a series of men's adventure novels called *The Destroyer*. Ward played Remo Williams, a befuddled New York beat cop who is inducted into a top-secret government hit squad where he is trained in the art of sinanju, a lost Korean martial art that gives him very nearly supernatural powers and abilities. His trainer is the ancient Chiun (played in the film by Joel Grey), who resents the fact that he has to teach a white man the sacred art that should rightfully be passed onto another Korean. The film was a flop at the box office, but producer Dick Clark resurrected it for television for this pilot, which was intended to ignite *Remo Williams: The Adventure Continues*. This time, martial artist Jeffrey Meek (more slender and loveably cute than Fred Ward) plays Remo, and Roddy McDowall plays Chiun. The story is told over a forty-five-minute span, and it quickly tries to recap the events of the film, while moving forward with Remo's training (he can dodge bullets and glide in the air), and Chiun is faced with the reality that he's stuck with Remo. When Remo is gravely wounded by an assassin, Chiun helps nurse him back to working order, and they seek revenge.

If you're a fan of the feature film (I am), then there's a certain glee to be found in watching the ongoing adventures of its happy-go-lucky hero and his fish-out-of-water father figure, even though the whole endeavor of seeing them together again on a television-episode budget is not as endearing as it's meant to be. Jeffrey Meek (later in the martial arts show *Raven*) doesn't even try to mimic Fred Ward, and his take on

R

Remo is very "cute" and "safe," but it's nice to see that he gets to use his martial arts (on roller skates!) at least once in the episode. Relegated to obscurity, *Remo Williams: The Prophecy* only aired once on television, and a series did not follow, sadly. Directed by Christian I. Nyby II.

Renegade

1992–1996 (Mill Creek DVD) (djm)

Reno Raines (Lorenzo Lamas) is a renegade cop with long, flowing locks and taekwondo skills who is framed for the murder of his girlfriend by dirty cops after testifying against them in court. With a bounty on his head, Raines goes on the lam on his Harley and makes friends out of two road-tripping bounty hunters who believe his story. The bounty hunters—Bobby Sixkiller (Branscombe Richmond) and his sister Cheyenne (Kathleen Kinmont)—agree to induct Raines into their clique and allow him to hunt down bounties with them. On the road and with a new identity as Vince Black, Raines goes around towns and cities helping out where he can and bringing bad guys to justice while getting himself into one bad scrape after another.

From Stephen J. Cannell, who also brought Michael Dudikoff to the small screen with *Cobra*, *Renegade* was a five-season hit show with a simple, easy-to-follow episodic structure that really put Lorenzo Lamas on the map as a mass-market "B" action star. Over the course of 110 episodes(!) Lamas was able to get in as much action and roundhouse kicks as each forty-five-minute episode could contain, and his pulpy, romance novel-esque appeal was a big success all over the world, where the show ran on syndication for years after it was over. It's astonishing to realize that Lamas kept this show going for five years while also carrying on a full slate of direct-to-video movies in the off seasons. As a whole, *Renegade* is a satisfying body of work for one of the hardest working action stars of his era. Kinmont (who was his real-life wife for a while) dropped off the show during the fourth season, but Richmond was in every episode alongside Lamas. Some notable action stars and stunt people appeared as guest stars in the show's run, including Michael Jai White, Jesse Ventura, Nils Allen Stewart, James Lew, Cary-Hiroyuki Tagawa, Al Leong, Fred Williamson, Brian Thompson, Danny Trejo, Peter Kent, Trevor Goddard, Sugar Ray Leonard, Marjean Holden, and Martin Kove as the long-lost brother of Lamas's character. Creator Cannell also appeared in a bunch of the episodes as the dirty cop hunting Lamas down.

Replicant

2001 (Lionsgate DVD) (djm)

"If this thing turns out to be anything like the original, we're going to regret it."

A vicious serial killer named Garrotte (Jean-Claude Van Damme in a change of pace) targets single mothers and kills them in front of their children, and then burns their corpses. Detective Jake Riley (Michael Rooker from *Cliffhanger* and *The 6th Day*) has been after him for three years, but he's up for retirement and gives up the chase . . . until Garrotte calls him on the phone and begins taunting him. An anti-terrorist government agency approaches Riley with an unprecedented opportunity: They've cloned Garrotte from some of his DNA, and they offer Riley the chance to use the "replicant" as a sort of telepath to find his original self. The replicant version of Garrotte is innocent and childlike (but with all the strength and agility of his doppelgänger), and Riley treats him terribly out of resentment and anger, but eventually he learns to care for him and protect him against Garrotte who, when faced with his clone, goes into a rage.

The first time I saw this movie was when it was originally released directly to video, and I resisted it. Watching it a second time, I realize now that it's actually really good, and it gives Van Damme a strong, challenging role, which is rare for him. It's got some martial arts action and acrobatics, but it's more of a serial killer thriller. The scenes with both Van Dammes on screen fighting each other are cleverly edited, and they convincingly play out. Director Ringo Lam previously worked with Van Damme on *Maximum Risk*. Their final movie together was *In Hell*.

Reptilicant

2006 (NOV) (djm)

A group of treasure hunters/mercenaries are seeking a stash of diamonds somewhere on Alcatraz Island, but they are assaulted by a body-snatching alien that looks like a giant reptile in its genuine form. As their team is systematically slaughtered by the alien, a secret agent/interrogator named Ryan Moore (martial artist Gary Daniels) is left to contend with a pile of bodies that he simply can't explain, even with the full confession from the lone survivor of the team. When the last survivor turns out to actually be the alien, Ryan must kickbox the alien to death . . . or die trying to survive.

There's a good reason why *Reptilicant* has never been released to video in North America: It's *terrible*, and frankly, nearly unwatchable. Gary Daniels manages to keep a straight face and perform his scenes and action stuff with complete conviction, which not only makes him a good sport, but also a consummate professional. If anyone else had starred in this disaster of a movie, I would have had to turn it off early on. Daniels completists need not bother tracking this obscurity down. Directed by Desi Singh.

Rescue Me

(a.k.a. Street Hunter)
1992 (Cannon VHS) (djm)

When this film was released, the *Los Angeles Times* ran full-page ads announcing its opening. It was the last movie Michael Dudikoff starred in (*Ringmaster* doesn't count) that was theatrically released in the US. He plays a Vietnam vet named Mac McDonald who helps a teenager named Fraser (Stephen Dorff) save a cheerleader (Ami Dolenz) he likes from two moronic kidnappers. They go on a road trip on Mac's motorcycle, and they bond like father and son, which is a first for both of them.

The action is minimal—typical run, shoot, duck, tumble stuff—and it has the feel and texture of a late 1980s, early 1990s action-lite picture. Dudikoff is appealing in a role suited for him, and his relationship with Dorff isn't particularly special or interesting, but by the end, I was willing to admit that I enjoyed the film as a whole. It was released at the tail end of Cannon's demise. It was directed by Arthur Allan Seidelman.

Retrograde

2004 (First Look DVD) (CD)

In the future, John Foster (Dolph Lundgren) is about to lead a team of genetically unique humans on a trip back in time to prevent a disaster that will alter the future. Moments before they time-travel, John is double-crossed by members of his crew who have a differing view of life. John jumps back to present day and is injured by his treacherous crewmates who followed him. He is nursed back to health by a biologist named Renee, who's been doing research aboard a large cruise ship—a crucial factor to the viral outbreak that changes the future. After one of the crew members becomes infected, everyone aboard the ship teams up, including deck hand Markus (Gary Daniels), to stop the soldiers from the future and to contain the virus before it spreads.

It's important to keep in mind that *Retrograde* isn't the movie that you might want it to be. With action stars Dolph Lundgren (*Red Scorpion*) and Gary Daniels (*Fist of the North Star*) attached, you'd expect it to be heavy in the martial arts arena. Instead, this is more of a straightforward science fiction film with a pinch of action thrown in. The movie itself isn't really bad, but it's a letdown in the sense that we don't get to see these guys do what they do best. As it stands as a low-budget sci-fi picture, it's mildly entertaining with a good cast and visual effects, which are on par with some of today's top-selling video games. The story was well crafted and aside from a slow first half, the pacing during the second half mostly makes up for it. Lundgren turns in an adequate performance, and Daniels has one very short fight during the finale and the rest of his screen time is just as a secondary player. Lundgren is more involved in the action with a couple of short and sadly uninteresting fights. These two guys barely have any actual screen time together; they don't fight each other, nor do they fight together. There is a bit of gunplay as well, but nothing overly exciting. *Retrograde* is something to watch when you want to pass the time.

Return Fire: Jungle Wolf II

1988 (AIP VHS) (djm)

Vietnam vet Steve Parrish (Ron Marchini) has resettled with his son, and has tried to adjust back into normalcy when his former commander (played by Adam West) has Parrish's son kidnapped when Parrish interferes with "The Agency" and his drug empire. Parrish, an expert at killing and setting bombs and traps, goes after his boss and the drug cartel, killing most of them by explosions.

After some flashbacks from the first film (which ended on a cliffhanger), *Return Fire* improves on the first film by giving Marchini slightly more iconic moments where he uses a rad-looking shotgun, which he uses to blow away Adam West (from the '60s *Batman* TV show) at the end. This is strictly an AIP production all the way, with ugly office building sets and rickety cars getting pummeled in wrecks and grenade blasts, but it's one of Marchini's more entertaining movies. Strangely, though, he doesn't use a lot of martial arts in it, which is usually his specialty. Directed by Neil Callaghan.

VHS artwork for *Return Fire: Jungle Wolf II*. Author's collection.

Return of the Street Fighter

1974 (Diamond DVD) (djm)

Less a sequel to *The Street Fighter* than an extension of that film, *Return* features the ruthless mercenary Terry (Sonny Chiba) on the trail of the Yakuza, which has betrayed him after he does a job they hired him for. With a hit out on him, Terry goes berserk and shows no mercy when he goes up against the hired killers on his trail. One fight scene after another, Terry proves that it's a massive mistake to double-cross him.

An already short running time is padded with extensive flashbacks from the first film, so *Return of the Street Fighter* is really simple and short, but if you're looking for outrageous fight scenes and unbelievably brutal encounters, look no further. In one scene Terry hits a guy so hard in the head that his eyes pop out! More *Street Fighter* movies followed. *Sister Street Fighter* was next. Shehiro Ozawa directed.

Return to Frogtown

1992 (York DVD) (CD)

Ranger John Jones (Lou Ferrigno) is one of the elite, a Texas Rocket Ranger (essentially a Texas Ranger who patrols by flying around with a rocket pack). He is captured by the mutant frog people who reside in the apocalyptic watering hole of Frogtown. His partner Sam Hell (Robert Z'Dar in a role originated by Roddy Piper in *Hell Comes to Frogtown*) teams up with Spangle (Denise Duff) to fly over enemy lines and save Jones. What should be a pretty cut and dry mission turns into something far more sinister when it's revealed that the frogs have also imprisoned Dr. Tanzer (Brion James) and forced him to develop a serum to convert humans into frogs. Sam Hell is still every bit the hero he has always been and risks it all to save the human race.

Robert Z'Dar (*Tango & Cash, Killing American Style*) is no Roddy Piper and this sequel is a shadow of what the original film was. The budget is not even close to that of the previous film, and it shows. The effects are laughable at times, though some of the frog makeup manages to get a passing grade. "B" movie lovers have embraced the lunacy of this film, but Lou Ferrigno (*The Incredible Hulk*) fans will be disappointed in how little he's given to do in it. He would have been a more interesting lead but as it stands, he gets to beat and shoot a handful of mutant frogs while flying around in a rocket suit (blatantly ripped off from *The Rocketeer*). The Sam Hell character is so far removed from the version Roddy Piper played that he should have just been a different character entirely. Director Donald G. Jackson (creator of the insane *Roller Blade* series) continued his frog saga with *Toad Warrior* and *Max Hell: Frog Warrior*, none of which feature action stars.

The Reunion

2011 (WWE Studios DVD) (CD)

Sam (John Cena) is a cop on suspension. Leo (Ethan Embry) is a bail bondsman losing money. And Douglas (Boyd Holbrook) is a thief just out of prison. The three of them are estranged brothers who share the same father. Their sister Nina (Amy Smart from *Crank*) is the only one of the siblings who has forgiven their father for being a drunk. He's since passed away, and his dying wish was to bring the family back together with the reward of a large inheritance. Nina is left in charge and in order to get their hands on the money they must run a business together for one year. They go into the bail bonds business and head to New Mexico to catch a fleeing criminal who has left Leo with a $250,000 debt. What they don't expect to find while on their search is an adventure involving a kidnapping. They could easily take the reward for giving information on the kidnapped businessman, and then go their separate ways. Will they take the money and run, or will their father's final wish be fulfilled?

The Reunion (originally titled *Blood Brothers*) isn't an all-out action movie. There are action elements that are entertaining but the film really is, at its core, a family drama. Some moments work better than others, but there is an interesting dynamic between John Cena (*The Marine*), Ethan Embry (*Eagle Eye*), and Boyd Holbrook (*The Host*). At times they are really believable as siblings; unfortunately, it's not always enjoyable watching them interact. Of course, the majority of the action (what little there is) mostly belongs to Cena. He has

Theatrical release poster for *The Reunion*. Author's collection.

a couple of short fight scenes where he displays many of the skills used in his wrestling career. I will say that his acting improved since his first couple of films. Embry and Holbrook each have a couple of moments for them to shine in a few action spurts with a firearm or other weapon. There are some other really good performances from the likes of Gregg Henry (*Payback*) and Michael Rispoli (*The Sopranos*). The film was written and directed by Mike Pavone, who has also had his hands in other WWE productions. *The Reunion* is mildly entertaining but drags in the middle, making it entirely too easy to lose interest. This was given a brief theatrical release before arriving on DVD.

Revelation Road: The Beginning of the End

2013 (Pure Flix DVD) (MMM)

Normally, films made by faith-based studios about the Christian end-times contain only a handful of action sequences, cannily sprinkled throughout the drama to heighten suspense. Just see any versions of *Left Behind*, or the '70s drive-in chestnut *A Thief in the Night* for examples. *Revelation Road: The Beginning of the End* bolts from the boilerplate, though, beginning with hints of a *Mad Max* feel and with former Seattle Seahawks hotshot turned fitfully prolific "B"-movie star Brian Bosworth as its psycho biker villain, Hawg. We first meet traveling bulletproof-vest salesman Josh McManus (David A. R. White), who foils a gun store stick-up attempted by the Barbarians (Hawg's outlaw motorcycle gang) by busting out martial arts skills and high-powered weapons savvy, both of which indicate a mysterious ass-kicker past. Naturally, McManus will have to answer to Hawg, but a bigger, darker picture looms as freak lightning strikes and sudden earthquakes plague the Earth. The movie isn't called *Revelation Road* for nothing: it's a reference to the Bible's wrap-up chapter that kicks off with the rapture and gets really rocky for those who don't vamoose into Heaven.

All told, *Revelation Road* is a stylish-looking, serviceably entertaining set-up for future installments in the franchise. Bosworth rocks his Harley well, and there are welcome supporting turns by low-budget reliables Ray Wise, Eric Roberts, and Steve "Sting" Borden. Just don't go in expecting the apocalypse. That comes later.

Revelation Road 2: The Sea of Glass and Fire

2013 (Pure Flix DVD) (MMM)

The Rapture is at hand at the beginning of *Revelation Road 2: The Sea of Glass and Fire*, but Earthly vengeance remains foremost on the mind of Brian Bosworth as Hawg, the fur-clad, monster-hammer-swinging president of the Barbarians outlaw motorcycle organization. Never mind that good people are instantly disappearing and the plates of the planet itself are rumbling with cosmic violence: mysterious badass-turned-traveling salesman Josh McManus (David A. R. White) cannot get home until he finally contends with the full brunt of Barbarian rage. It was McManus, after all, who put a fatal hurt on three biker members while thwarting their robbery of a roadside munitions store. Even with the apocalypse starting to rain down, Hawg simply can't let that insult go.

What came to a slow boil in the first *Revelation Road* hits a decent simmer here. McManus is a solid hero with a dark history, and Hawg is a conflicted villain whose bad attitude and worse behavior may actually be his wrong-headed attempt to seek salvation. Such moral gray areas are a bit more than one might expect from a cheap Christian end-times saga, as is the stylish, borderline *Mad Max* milieu of the *Revelation Road* films. They may or may not win over converts, but Brian Bosworth running wild on a Harley hog is always sufficient to satisfy action-flick true believers.

Revenge of the Kickfighter (a.k.a. Return of the Kickfighter)

1987 (AIP VHS) (djm)

An inappropriate and confusing title notwithstanding, *Revenge of the Kickfighter* has a Rambo-eque vibe, but it's unusual for a back-to-Vietnam war movie and deserves to be seen on its own terms. A platoon of American soldiers on a mission in Vietnam during the war slaughters an entire village on their squad leader's orders. They recover a stash of gold bars from the village and horde it for almost two decades before spending it, for fear of unleashing their dark secrets. Then, out of the blue, the whole commando unit becomes systematically hunted down and killed one by one by a mysterious killer, and the old squad leader hires a young Australian-but-American soldier to investigate. Brad Cooper, the soldier who is called in to assist (played by an impressively fit Richard Norton), goes to Hong Kong to find the original squad's Vietnamese translator, and when he convinces him to help find the killer, an old acquaintance and arch enemy of the translator resurfaces. The finale is action packed.

Solid enough for fans of jungle war movies with lots of explosions, gunfire, and some martial arts fighting, *Revenge of the Kickfighter* (which has no relation to Norton's other film called *Kick Fighter*) is a good little actioner. There's lots of overdubbing and overly dramatic flare, but if you're out there watching movies called *Revenge of the Kickfighter* then you're obviously willing to forgive almost as many shortcomings as these movies have. Norton is a consummate professional, and anything he does he does with gusto. He's really good in this movie. He looks great, and he's got more than enough energy to keep you focused on him when some of the stuff around him gets lackluster. Anthony Maharaj, who directed it, also made a similar (but much more depressing) movie with Norton called *Crossfire*.

Revenge of the Ninja

1983 (MGM DVD) (djm)

"This is no job for the police! It's something I'll have to do! Only a ninja can stop a ninja!"

In the early-to-mid 1980s Cannon was on a roll making movies about ninjas. This one, the second in a series that started with *Enter the Ninja*, stars Sho Kosugi as a man whose family was slaughtered in Japan by a bunch of evil ninjas. It turns out that his Caucasian friend (Arthur Roberts) set him up. This not-so-good friend wants Kosugi to come to the US to front a business with him so that the friend can smuggle in heroin and make a lot of money. Kosugi is left with only his infant son, and so

Spanish poster for *Revenge of the Ninja*. Author's collection.

Sho Kosugi (right) in *Revenge of the Ninja*. Author's collection.

he agrees to go the US to start a business with his evil white friend. Nearly ten years pass and his friend has gotten rich, and Kosugi has raised his son (played by his real-life son, Kane) in the art of the ninja. When his son sees how evil and conniving his father's friend is, all hell busts open as the boy is hunted by a masked ninja out to kill him. Turns out the kid has some mad ninja skills! When his father comes to his aid, the masked ninja's true identity is reveled: His evil white friend who had his family slaughtered! Ninjas fight on rooftop! Action!

Sho Kosugi in silhouette as the ninja in *Revenge of the Ninja*. Author's collection.

R

If you grew up in the '80s and watched VHS videos all day long like I did, then movies like *Revenge of the Ninja* hold a special place in your heart. They're pure fantasy, but such glorious fantasy. This movie and its prequel/sequel are probably to blame for thousands of boys dressing up as ninjas at Halloween. *American Ninja* too. I was one of those kids. Thanks, Cannon. And a special thank-you to Sam Firstenberg, who directed this, its sequel *Ninja III: The Domination*, and the first two *American Ninja* movies. He is the king sitting on the throne of ninja movies. It should also be mentioned that Keith Vitali (who would later star in Cannon's *American Kickboxer*) has a nice showcase role as a buddy of Kosugi's. Vitali was in *Wheels on Meals* with Jackie Chan following *Revenge of the Ninja*.

INTERVIEW:

KANE KOSUGI

(djm)

The son of famed Japanese martial artist and action star, Sho Kosugi, Kane grew up on movie sets with his father, who played his dad in several films including Revenge of the Ninja *(1983),* Pray For Death *(1985),* 9 Deaths of the Ninja *(1985),* Black Eagle *(1988),* and *Journey of Honor (1991).* Kane and his brother Shane were taught martial arts almost from birth, and in the films they were in togather, they were always right in on the action beside their father, who is famous for playing ninjas. As Kane grew up, he moved to Japan to work full time as an actor in martial arts and action films, and only recently did he return to the States to appear in *D.O.A (Dead or Alive) (2006) and* War *(2007), starring Jason Statham and Jet Li. He returns in* Ninja: Shadow of a Tear, *starring Scott Adkins, and his role in the film gives him plenty to work with as both an actor and a martial artist. I spent several days on the Bangkok, Thailand set of* Ninja: Shadow of a Tear, *and I found Kane to be one of the nicest, most humble actors I've ever met.*

Tell me a little bit about your role in *Ninja 2.*

I play Nakabara, the senpai, the elder. A one-year senior of the main character, played by Scott Adkins. Our characters both trained in

Martial arts action star Kane Kosugi on the Bangkok, Thailand, set of *Ninja 2: Shadow of a Tear.* Photo by david j. moore.

martial arts. We didn't have the same teacher, but I started a little earlier than him, so he has kind of a respect for me. I'm kind of his friend and his mentor, and I've helped him through his tough time. His wife was killed, so I help him out. Nakabara has a lot of faces. He's really deep. He's wise. He knows a lot of Japanese proverbs. He's been in the martial arts for as long as he's been alive. He's a master. He's a good guy on the outside, but deep down, he's got a lot of layers. He's interesting.

What is your impression of Isaac Florentine, your director?

He's great. I'd met him once more than ten years ago. I've always wanted to work with him. We always talked about it. There've been a few opportunities, but it hasn't happened until now. When I heard about this project, I emailed him right away and I asked him if it was really him who was directing it. It was, and that's all I needed to know, basically. I've always looked forward to working with him. From everything I've heard from a lot of martial artists, from all the movies he's done . . . he's been in the business a long time and he knows what he's doing. A lot of directors who've done action movies don't really know martial arts. They're mostly just directors. When it comes time to do the action parts, they turn it over to the action director. They block everything, and the director takes a break. But hearing from everyone and talking with Isaac, he's a martial arts encyclopedia. He knows everything about martial arts, and he also trains in martial arts. He knows what looks good. It's really rare to have someone like that. I haven't had too many opportunities to work with someone like that.

How hands-on is he in terms of the action and fight scenes so far on this film?

I've only done a little bit so far, but I've seen what he's done on it so far. He's very hands-on. He knows what he wants. He knows where to put the camera, and he knows how to talk to the actors. He's been making everyone feel comfortable. That's really important—even if you have really a good fight scene, if it doesn't match with the actor or their style, the actor may be uncomfortable and it may be hard for them, but he's great about making us feel comfortable.

Tell me a little bit about Tim Man and his team. They're doing the fight choreography and some of the stunts.

I've been practicing with Tim. I'd never worked with him before. I got this part, and I talked with Isaac, and he said, "Tim Man is our action director." He sent me his website, and I watched him in a fight, and it was really good. I came here to Thailand and practiced with Tim, and he's really good. His team is really, really good. They can move. They've been training a long time.

Talk a little bit about working with Scott Adkins.

Scott is cool. I was a little nervous at first. I was really looking forward to working with him. I'd been hearing about him for the longest time.

Friends or foes? Scott Adkins as Casey and Kane Kosugi as Nakabara in *Ninja II: Shadow of a Tear.* Courtesy of Nu Image, Inc.

Isaac always wanted us to work together. I've seen his work. There's no one who can move like him, especially a non-Asian action actor. I've always wanted to work with someone who can actually move who isn't a stuntman. It was exciting. I was thinking, "Shoot, I better start training because I don't want to get my butt kicked by him." (Laughing.) He's really down to earth. Before the movie started, he sent me an email saying, "Let's do a great action scene together." He's really easy to get along with. He's the star of the movie . . . I should be the one going up to him, but he's always coming up to me, making me feel like I'm at home. It's really rare.

Which movies of Scott's have you seen and were impressed by?

Undisputed II. I've seen parts of *Ninja.* I didn't want to see the whole thing because I didn't want to put an image to what this film should be. But then, it's completely different. I've worked with a lot of stunt guys who've worked with him. A few actors as well. I'd heard about him from a lot of people, and I saw a lot of clips of him on YouTube.

What can we expect from *Ninja 2?*

What Isaac is trying to do and seeing how the shooting is going . . . I heard that the first *Ninja* had a lot of computer graphics . . . but Isaac wanted to go back to the old days, with real action. That's what we're doing. No wires. The human body and what we can do. A lot of times, nowadays, movies use wires and computer graphics, so you'll see the difference. Kind of like with *The Expendables* and bringing the '80's back. It's nice to see that. After all the high-tech, computerized stuff, it's nice to go back and see the real thing again. Plus, it's got a story to it. It's got a few twists. It's going to be really action packed. There's more than fifteen fight scenes. Scott's got a lot on his hands!

Are you enjoying filming in Thailand?

I've been here more than ten times, working on a lot of Japanese projects. So, I know the crews are really good. It's really Hollywood standards. I've worked on a lot of tough shoots. Working in Asia . . . we go twenty-six hours straight. I've done twenty-six hours nonstop action. It's crazy. That was on a movie called *Blood Heat.* I've done Chinese movies where we've gone on only four hours of sleep for three days in a row. Those were tough, too.

You mentioned bringing the '80s back to new movies. You've come from the '80s school of filmmaking. You did a bunch of movies with your dad in the Cannon years. You worked with Jean-Claude Van Damme on *Black Eagle*. What does it feel like working on these movies now versus working in action and martial arts movies when you were a kid? Does it feel the same, or have you noticed a difference?

It's harder now. The audience has seen lots of stuff now. They're smart. They know what's fake and what's not. They know what's wire and what's real. They've seen so many action movies that it's hard to surprise them. I think that's important. You don't want to go to the movies and see something you've already seen. You want to see something that touches you and surprises you, something that makes you forget about your worries. You want to be entertained for two hours. It's harder and harder for people to get into movies. When I go to an action movie, I look for something that I haven't seen. The way they shoot the action or the way it's done. It's important to surprise the audience.

Let's go back a bit. What was it like being Sho Kosugi's son, working on movies with your dad, who was basically a ninja?

It was cool. (Laughing.) I'd like to say I got a lot of girls, but I didn't. Friends would always ask me about my dad and what it was like being in movies. It was fun. I enjoyed it a lot, and I'd always wanted to be an actor. It's something I love. I fell in love with it right away. When I first saw my dad in a movie, and when I was actually in a movie. The first movie I did with my dad was *Revenge of the Ninja*, and the first movie I saw my dad in was *Enter the Ninja*. He played a bad guy in that movie, but even playing the bad guy he looked like a hero to me. It was because of that that I wanted to be an actor.

Was martial arts and acting a choice for you and your brother Shane, or were these things chosen for you by your father?

Martial arts was something that I had to do. Our parents wanted us to do martial arts until a certain age. They wanted us to learn stuff. Like martial arts or learning to play the piano. We really didn't have a choice in it. When we were little kids growing up, we just wanted to play. Now that I look back on it, I'm really thankful that they forced us to do the things that we did. Acting was something that we wanted. They gave us the opportunity to do it. If we really didn't want to, we didn't have to.

You told me you were six years old on *Revenge of the Ninja*.

Yes.

As a kid, you were pretty convincing as a martial artist.

Yeah, I started when I was a year and half old. By that time on that film, I was six and I'd competed a lot. I trained a lot. It wasn't difficult at all, actually, to be on that movie.

Does it seem preposterous now when you watch it or think about it? You were beating up full-grown men in that movie.

(Laughing.) It looks funny. I recently pulled out the *Revenge of the Ninja* DVD and I watched it for the first time in over ten years. It was actually surprisingly good. The action wasn't bad. My dad's action was great. Even if it came out right now, it would still be pretty cool. My fight scene was okay. For a six-year-old, it was okay.

That's part of the charm of these movies you were in with your dad. You do some action in these "R"-rated action films, but you don't get killed, You don't get hurt—not really—so kids can watch these movies.

Maybe little kids can look up to these movies and be inspired.

You were part of that pop culture thing that was all about ninjas.

Yeah, after I went to Japan and worked for twenty years, ninjas started coming back with *Ninja Assassin* and Isaac and Scott's *Ninja*. I always wanted to do a ninja movie as an adult, because the first movies I did as a kid were about ninjas. It's cool to come back with it. This is an opportunity. I'm really thankful to Isaac and Scott for bringing me on board.

Do you remember working with Sam Firstenberg, your director on *Revenge of the Ninja*?

Honestly, I don't remember. I remember the main actress.

The blonde?

Yes. I remember the action scenes were tough. I remember when she was hitting me with the stick. The staff. I cried because it really hurt. She

had to do it over and over again. I remember that really, really clearly. (Laughing.) I remember bits and pieces of that film.

Do you remember seeing yourself on a big screen when the movie came out?

Yeah. I went with a friend of the family. He used to babysit us. He took us, and that was the first time I saw it. I remember going to the popcorn stand and the guy at the counter said, "Hey, you look like that kid in the movie." I remember him saying, "Oh, yeah, all Asian kids look alike." (Laughing.) For some reason, I didn't see the movie with my dad. He was shooting movie after movie.

Your next movie was *Pray for Death*, right?

No, it was 9 *Deaths of the Ninja*.

9 *Deaths of the Ninja!* I love that movie!

That was in the Philippines. I don't really remember too much about it. *Revenge of the Ninja* was tough. It was a lot of action scenes. I was in that movie a lot. For 9 *Deaths of the Ninja*, it was more of a vacation for me and my brother. We weren't in it that much. We were just there, kind of hanging out. I remember my dad used a crossbow in it.

Was it a package deal when producers called on your dad to be in a new movie? "Okay, we need you because your dad is starring in a new ninja movie? We need you to play his kids!"

No, I don't know. We would do them if my dad thought we could play his sons. If the story called for it.

That kind of leads into *Black Eagle*, where your dad played the hero to Van Damme's villain. Van Damme was pretty new at the time. What was it like working with Van Damme?

At the time, I didn't know of him. I'd never seen anything with him. He was very charismatic. He was in really, really good shape. He was a nice guy. I was just a kid, eating my crackers, and he asked me, "Hey, I'll arm-wrestle you for those cookies." So I arm-wrestled him. I lost, even with two hands. I didn't think about that film much, but when I look back on it, I think it was a cool experience working with Van Damme. He was nice to me.

What was it like working with your dad several times?

Growing up, it's cool. He was gone a lot, working for long periods of time. So it was nice to hang out with him. It was great doing what I loved to do. It was fun. It was better than going to school.

Have you ever stopped to think that you were a part of a time and era and in specific movies that helped impact the "B"-action movie world?

Not really when I was growing up. Not until I was in junior high. I think the first time I realized that my dad was an icon was when we went into a

Young Kane Kosugi in *Revenge of the Ninja*. Author's collection.

An action scene from *Revenge of the Ninja*, featuring Kane Kosugi. Author's collection.

Foot Locker and we were buying shoes, and they were like, "Hey, you're Sho Kosugi, can you sign our backboard?" Remember the old days when they'd have a basketball rim inside the store? They had him sign it, and I was like, "My dad is famous." Until then, he was just my dad. When I worked on *Journey of Honor*, that was the first time I realized, "Wow, I'm getting paid, and I need to start taking this seriously. I can't play around anymore." It was when I realized I was a professional. We shot that in Malta, and we shot at least three months. I remember we travelled that whole summer through the old Yugoslavia. Yeah, they built big ships, had costumes, and a Japanese staff of over twenty people came over—it was an epic movie.

What happened with your career after *Journey of Honor*?

That was when I was fifteen or sixteen. I graduated high school, and then I went to Japan. I worked on TV in Japan. I did two movies that my dad directed when I went to Japan. We did a movie called *The Fighting King*. I started working there and worked on TV for a long time.

You came back into my radar when *D.O.A.* came out with Eric Roberts and all the pretty girls.

Yeah, I'd been working in Japan for a while, and I was really busy, but I was enjoying it. I was learning things I'd never have learned if I'd stayed in the States. But my heart was always to work in Hollywood. When I turned thirty, I knew it was time that I should start going back. I thought maybe I should start working in the States again. It took me about half a year to find a manager and an agent, and then I met up with the producers of *D.O.A.* I auditioned for it, and I got it. It was a fun shoot. I was really excited. I little later, I did *War*, the Jason Statham, Jet Li movie. The director of *D.O.A.* was Corey Yuen, and he was the action director on *War*. They wanted me to fight with Jet Li, and I got to do a small fight scene with him. There're more and more opportunities for Asian actors now, but the auditions I usually go to are for bad guys. They just want the bad guy look.

Do you have the bad guy look?

Well . . . they want the cliché look. You have to look really bad. It's been an experience going through everything. My heart's still in Hollywood, but I decided to keep working in Asia. There's still so much for me to learn.

How often do you train?

I train fairly often in martial arts. I've been working in different styles since I've been in Japan. Growing up, I did Japanese karate, taekwondo, but when I went to Japan, I started stunt training, wushu, break dancing, just any kind of style that will make my action my own. I work out a lot. I don't bulk up as much as I did when I was in my twenties. I just try to make my body flexible so that I can move so that I don't get injured easily. I do that kind of training. Before I do a movie, I try to train every day if I can.

Is there anything else you want to add about your career or anything else?

My goal is to always do better in the next movie, and then the next. The fight scenes we do in *Ninja 2* will be the best fights I've ever done. I hope everyone will enjoy it.

The Revenger

1990 (AIP VHS) (djm)

A nightclub saxophone player named Michael (Frank Zagarino) takes a ride with the wrong friend one night after doing his set, and the ride turns into a bloodbath as his friend (played by Arnold Vosloo) turns out to have stolen a stash of drugs from a kingpin. The cops kill Michael's buddy, and Michael is sent to prison for being an accessory. Five years later, he's released and he isn't home a full week before the kingpin (played by Oliver Reed) kidnaps his wife and ransoms her for the money that the stolen drugs would have yielded. Michael is helpless in his situation, so he turns up his brute strength and does what a desperate ex-con would do: He goes *revenging!*

From Cedric Sundtrom, the director of *American Ninja 3* and *4*, *The Revenger* was shot in South Africa with local actors, and as a result, the American video release dubbed over almost everyone's accent. It gives the movie a slightly hokey quality that it really didn't need, but aside from that, this is a fair actioner with the muscular Zagarino (who has a workout montage during the opening credits) in the lead role. This isn't going to garner too many new fans for Zagarino, but if you're already a fan then *The Revenger* should be easy viewing.

VHS artwork for *The Revenger*. Author's collection.

Revolver

2005 (Sony DVD) (CD)

"One thing I've learned in the last seven years: in every game and con there's always an opponent, and there's always a victim. The trick is to know when you're the latter, so you can become the former."

After doing seven years in solitary confinement, Jake Green (Jason Statham, fresh from *The Transporter*) is finally back on the streets. The man responsible for his imprisonment, Dorothy Macha (Ray Liotta), is now a bigwig casino boss, worth millions of dollars. Jake challenges him to a game and walks away with a ton of Macha's money, seriously pissing the man off. After Jake blacks out trying to get away, he's saved by Zach (Vincent Pastore) and Avi (Andre Benjamin). They let Jake know he suffers from a rare blood disease and only has three days to live. If he wants to survive he has to do everything they tell him to do, no questions asked, including giving away every last penny he has. Even though he feels this to be some sort of con, he goes along with it hoping he will get his revenge in the end.

After the romantic travesty known as *Swept Away*, director Guy Ritchie returned to the crime genre only to craft a film far smarter and more complex than many would have expected. It may be a tad off-putting with its dreamlike quality and non-linear storytelling, but over multiple viewings, you can really appreciate exactly what Ritchie was going for and the performances by action star Statham (from Ritchie's crime caper *Snatch*) and Liotta (*Goodfellas*) are outstanding. The film isn't about physical altercation; these battles are all fought with smarts and wit. Statham is all business here and the way his character maneuvers his way through these gangsters is just like someone trying to outwit their opponent in chess. This review was written after viewing the UK version (Red Bus DVD R2); the US release differs significantly with scenes rearranged and with an alternate ending. The former is the director's preferred cut.

Riddick

2013 (Universal DVD) (djm)

This long belated sequel to *The Chronicles of Riddick* finds the former renegade criminal Richard P. Riddick (Vin Diesel) complacent and bored as the Lord Marshall of the Necromongers (see *Chronicles*), and when he returns to his home planet Furya he finds that it is an apocalyptic wasteland. He is betrayed and left for dead by his own army, and completely alone and stranded on the desolate planet, he builds up his strength and plans his escape. Months later, he has gained a sidekick in the form of a dog-like creature, and he sends out a distress call, making it very clear that he is the one making the call, which entices several squadrons of bounty hunters to visit the planet to find and capture or kill him. His plan is

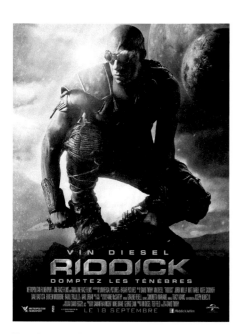

French poster for *Riddick*. Author's collection.

simple: Kill the bounty hunters and steal one of their ships to escape. He makes his plan explicitly clear to the hunters, who underestimate him, and as he narrows the playing field, the plot begins to thicken: The planet is undergoing a severe storm, which will cast a flow of rain and waters upon the surface, thus introducing a host of water-kindred creatures who come out in droves to eat anything that moves. Riddick is systematically captured by the bounty hunters, then he convinces them to free him in exchange for their protection (remember: he can see in the dark), and they strike a deal that grants him his freedom should they survive the night. It becomes very familiar in the last act.

I loved the first half of this film. Riddick, who has become an iconic antihero in the Snake Plisskin mold, is left virtually to his own devices for nearly half the film, as he wordlessly builds a plan of escape over the course of time. When the bounty hunters (who include Katee Sackhoff and Dave Bautista) show up, the movie sags considerably, and the last act with the creatures feels forced and all too expected. Diesel knows this role inside and out, and it was his choice to carry the franchise onward. He looks great in the role, and his physicality is essential to playing it. He has a fight scene with Bautista that should raise a few eyebrows. Written and directed by David Twohy, who made the first two films in the series. Unfortunately, this will probably be the last film in the franchise, as its box-office take was pretty weak.

Rider on the Rain

1970 (905 Entertainment DVD) (JAS)

Rider on the Rain stars Charles Bronson as mysterious Army Colonel Harry Dobbs who is tracking down a serial rapist who escaped a military stockade. Seemingly bent on terrorizing the rapist's latest victim Mellie Mau (Marlene

Jobert), Dobbs employs bizarre methods and mind games to garner information from her. Mellie becomes aware that Dobbs is in search of more than just the escaped convict, and eventually begins to identify with him as he opens her eyes to the falsity of her existing world. Through a sort of cruel mental conditioning, Dobbs sharpens her wits, exposes what a cheating liar her husband is, and generally helps her to see the oppression and lies of those she thought she loved. Mellie fights back and eventually outwits Dobbs, their rivalry becoming a rite of passage to a character who, possibly representing many oppressed women, will never be taken advantage of again.

If one can stand the rather slow pace, there is a lot to be admired about this film. It is uneven and the plot is difficult to follow, but the exchanges between Bronson and Jobert are mesmerizing once they finally take flight. For fans of the era, it has 1970 written all over it, from the loungey jazz score to the funky duds the women characters don; it also has a heavy dose of female empowerment subtext within its rather confusing plotline. Recommended for cinephiles, Bronson fans, or sociology majors. There's not much action in it, though.

Ring of Fire

1991 (Madacy Home Video DVD) (djm)

Johnny Wu, a respectable doctor, has a brother who is intent on participating in underground fights for cash. Johnny (Don "The Dragon" Wilson) tries his best to talk his brother (Steven Vincent Leigh) out of fighting in a deadly Muay Thai match where the fighters put broken glass on their taped fists, but his brother goes ahead and does it anyway. His brother is killed, and the real issue is that the fighter who killed him is the brother of the woman Johnny has fallen in love with.

More a romantic drama than an action/martial arts movie, *Ring of Fire* is certainly good viewing for the right, select audience. It's more concerned with throwing in as much sex and nudity as it possibly can than in showing fights, and I'm sure that's great for some people. When I watch a Don Wilson movie or a kickboxing movie, I'm more interested in the fights. *Ring of Fire* is weak on the action, and it's obviously a very low-budget movie, but if you're a fan of Wilson or of Gary Daniels, who has a role as a fighter, you may be willing to forgive its shortcomings. Also with Vince Murdocco (who later starred in *L.A. Wars*). It was directed by Richard Munchkin (*Guardian Angel, Out For Blood, Deadly Bet*) and Rick Jacobson (*Full Contact, Dragon Fire, Black Thunder*). I can't imagine why this movie required two directors. It was followed by two sequels.

Don "The Dragon" Wilson in Los Angeles, California. Photo by david j. moore.

INTERVIEW:

DON "THE DRAGON" WILSON (djm)

The most popular direct-to-video martial arts action star of the 1990s, Don "The Dragon" Wilson made thirty back-to-back movies at the height of the VHS and early DVD era. A professional boxer and kickboxer with more than seventy wins on his record, Wilson became a superstar in the video market when he signed a contract with Roger Corman, starring in eight successive Bloodfist *(1989–1996) movies, not to mention dozens of others for other studios like PM Entertainment in titles like* Ring of Fire *(1991),* Out For Blood *(1992), and* Magic Kid *(1993). He also appeared as a martial arts-proficient thug in face paint in 1995s biggest blockbuster,* Batman Forever *(1995). Undeniably successful as both a real-life fighter and a "B"-movie action star, Don Wilson's certainly made his mark in the genre.*

Don, you've made a *lot* of movies . . .

Well, I starred in thirty movies . . . if you want to count *White Tiger*. In *White Tiger*, I didn't actually consider myself the star. I considered it a buddy picture, like a Mel Gibson/Danny Glover kind of a thing. Although, I'm a much bigger star than who you would say is the star of the film, which is Matt Mullins. Basically, the buyers didn't know him, so they needed names. Cynthia Rothrock, who's also in the movie, and I are names. She only worked a few days. We have an action sequence together. That is one of the only movies I've done in twenty-five years where I was what you would call "an actor for hire." I did not work on the script, I did not cast it, I did not hire the director. I will go in the editing room to work on my scene with Cynthia, possibly. Maybe. Now I know why other actors do the "actor for hire." Michael Madsen told me, "Do the job, do the best you can, and go to the next gig." For me, when I've always done a movie, I've always been the star, and I feel responsible for the quality. I want to make sure the director is experienced, and the music . . . even down to the posters. From the third film on, I've been in creative control with things like the artwork. I've edited two films myself. The directors went on to other things . . .

R

Which two?

Operation Cobra and *Whatever it Takes.* I was able to go in and re-cut things, mainly fight action. I cannot really recall playing around with the drama of my films. Whatever the directors like, I usually like, pretty much. The fight action, yeah. I've gone in and recut the fight action on many films.

You did one right after another during that stretch of years when you were making them.

I did five in thirteen months.

You were the number one direct-to-video action star in the 1990s.

My pictures were in *Time* magazine for being one of the top direct-to-video action stars. Now, when you get to *Time* magazine that means you're pumping out some movies! I did five movies all in the same genre—martial arts action—released in thirteen months. *Entertainment Weekly* did a little story on me, and to their knowledge no one had ever done that before. No one had starred in five American action films that were released in thirteen months. All in the same genre. One of the reasons is that this was a different time. The video era. They used to call it "feeding the video monster." There were 30,000 video stores. After customers had rented that one video they came for, the Tom Cruise movie or the Brad Pitt movie, they would get something else. They needed new product all the time. Basically, I would have a movie come out that would compete with another one of my movies. It was almost like I was a TV star and not a movie star.

How familiar were you with the movie business when you got started?

As a kickboxer, I didn't really know the movie business. All my friends who were experienced told me that it would kill my career. What saved me is that I would work on the quality of the films as a co-producer.

Can you stop and think back on any of your memories of working nonstop and think back on any one particular film that you did?

You know what? I spent a thousand hours on those sets. It's all the same genre, so if there's a certain amount of story and a ton of fight scenes . . . there are specific moments that stand out, but as far as the four weeks, twelve hour days, eighteen hour days—I worked a twenty-three hour day once on a movie called *Bloodfist IV: Die Trying*—I don't remember the movies very well.

What's with the *Bloodfist* titles? Only the first two are related.

I asked Roger Corman what it meant, and he said, "If Don Wilson's in it, there's martial arts." There was never a connecting reference to any character I played in those.

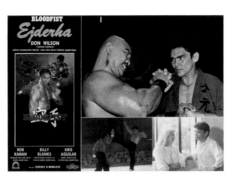

Turkish lobby card for *Bloodfist,* with a montage of scenes featuring Don "The Dragon" Wilson in a bout with a bald nemesis. Author's collection.

Don "The Dragon" Wilson and Billy Blanks in the middle of a fight in *Bloodfist.* Author's collection.

Well, I liked that you played the same character in the *Ring of Fire* movies. There was actually a progression to the guy you were playing.

Those were real sequels. We tried. We even had the same girl in the first two, but she died off by the third one.

The girl in the third one was great.

Yeah, Bobbie Phillips. She was phenomenal. She'd done martial arts action. I met her at a party. We'd already started work on the script for *Ring of Fire 3*, so I thought in a commercial sense that people like to watch the beginning of relationships. They like seeing people fall in love. Maria Ford [from Parts 1 and 2] and I were supposed to be married in the movies, and you don't have a lot of married couple sequels. Maria's a friend, but I killed her off in the series. Then I meet the Bobbie Phillips character.

You've made movies all over the world. I just watched two you made in Ireland—*Bloodfist VIII* and *Moving Target*—what's that been like for you, filming on location?

Those two you mentioned were a lot of fun. I opened Corman's studio up there in Ireland. He's had a studio there for ten years. He had a deal with the Irish government. What the Irish got out of it is that they have a whole crew that are trained—actors, directors. They can make the whole movie there in Ireland. My film was the first one ever done. We brought in people to train the Irish people. Stunt coordinators, choreographers, ADs, editors. We trained the Irish. I left after the movie was done, and I came back years later to do another film, and I got to see what they had learned, and they were great. David Carradine did one, and I came in right behind him.

You also did a movie in India. *Operation Cobra,* I believe.

Well, that came about because Ashok Armritraj was the producer, and that was his hometown. He thought he would shoot a film in his hometown. All the local actors were cast, and he asked me to do it, and we were friends since *Red Sun Rising*. I liked that he came from sports. He's a tennis player. He's been doing studio films for years now. I believe his first film as a silent investor was *Double Impact*, a Van Damme movie. He made money, so in his mind the movie business was a way to make money. He then produced *Red Sun Rising* with my manager, and that made money. Eventually, I did some movies with Andrew Stevens, and he and Ashok formed their own company, and that was Franchise. I did *Virtual Combat* and *Terminal Rush* with them. I helped start many businesses. PM Entertainment was one. I did six films with them. I got them going. Great guys.

This was the golden era for guys like you and companies like PM.

This was the golden era. There is nothing but gratitude for me and Van Damme when it comes to the movie business. He ignited the business with *Bloodsport*, and I did *Bloodfist*, which is basically a rip-off. You could say that Van Damme is almost responsible for my beginnings in movies.

You've gone on the record about your misgivings of Van Damme's claims that he was a martial arts champion.

My problem with Van Damme is that he came to this town saying that he was a world kickboxing champion. I *am* a world kickboxing champion. We didn't make big money, but at least we had something we could say. It's like being an Olympic gold medal winner. It means something. If someone else is going around saying that he's a gold medal swimmer, and you know for a fact that he doesn't even know how to swim, would that bother you when you've worked eighteen to twenty years of your life to win a gold medal? You know for a fact that he's never even had one race. That's what bothered me about Van Damme. A lot of people would say, "Oh, you're just jealous of his career." No! If I wanted to be jealous about his career, why don't I badmouth Tom Cruise? I've never said a bad word about Tom Cruise. Van Damme's thing and mine . . . has nothing to do with the film business. Lying is a commandment. There's something wrong with people lying about your background. He wanted the prestige of being a real fighter. It was printed that he was a world kickboxing champion middleweight fighter. I read an article where Van Damme was asked how he powers his punches. He said, "Well, you've got to have big arms, you have to lift weights, and curl." I said, "That is so far wrong. The power comes from the hip. You don't use muscle when you punch." There's nothing wrong with a guy saying he's a medical doctor until he starts giving out medical advice. Then there's something wrong. The last time Van Damme and I were in the same area was in Cannes, and I was in the lobby. I hadn't even checked into my room. The press was there and Van Damme was in the lobby, and they wanted to get a picture of the "two world champions together." That's the way they put it. A photo op. I said, "No, I refuse." My agent was in the room, and he got mad. That's one of the sell-your-soul-to-the-devil kind of things.

When you were making all these movies, were you ever conscious of what was going on with your contemporaries? Were you keeping tabs on other action stars?

A little bit. A little bit. Just to see what they were doing. I wanted mine to be my own kind. Everybody—I feel—has their own certain thing that they can do better. I remember Jet Li did the aerial thing. The wirework. Not so much Van Damme, not so much Seagal. In the beginning, anyway. Jackie does the comedy. Certain people do certain things. My little niche was that I was a real fighter. Guys knew that I'd knocked out forty-eight professional fighters. I told my choreographers and directors, "Look, when I land a technique, even though it's just a movie and it's fake, I want it to look like if it was real life that it would do some real damage." I wanted mine to be more realistic. I think that's what separated me from the other guys. Early on, I would use techniques that I actually used in the ring. Two to the body, one to the head. I was one of the first guys who was doing body shots. Everybody else was to the face. It looks more dramatic if you hit a guy in the face. I would work the body and go to the head. In *Bloodfist* I was doing leg kicks. Nobody was kicking to the legs in 1988. It turns out that it's not very cinematic, by the way. It just doesn't look exciting on film. If all I did were leg kicks, I'd be out of business.

Did any of your movies go theatrical?

My first film was theatrical. It was one of the top 100 independent films of all time when it was released. It was released by Roger Corman. MGM released the video. They sold like 60,000 cassettes. It was successful, but I got into a catch 22 very early on. *Bloodfist* was theatrical, *Bloodfist II* was theatrical, *Bloodfist III* was limited theatrical, then it went right to video. Those kinds of movies would lose money in theaters and make money on video. Roger Corman went, "Why release it to theaters? Don Wilson is so popular on video, people will go right out to rent the movies without me losing money in theaters." That's how I became one of the top direct-to-video stars of the '90s.

Was acting something you thought would be a good career while you were still fighting early on?

Um, here's the thing. I never thought for one minute that I would act in my life. I had no intention, it never crossed my mind. In 1979, Chuck Norris came to one of my fights, and he's the guy who said to me, "You should think about it." It worked out for him. He did a movie with Bruce Lee, he had a deal with Cannon, he had a great career. He's real famous from an eight year run on TV. He's the only one who's done it in the martial arts business.

Was TV ever an option for you at any point?

Yeah, it was. Aaron Spelling guaranteed me a two-year commitment for a TV series, an action series. I turned it down.

Really?

Yeah. As many right choices I've made in this town, I've made many wrong ones. It was obviously wrong. I went in there with my agent and said, "No." At that time, I was doing film, and at that time, lower-budget guys like myself were getting looked at by studios. I thought doing TV would ruin my image. What TV stars—back then—were doing big films? Bruce Willis did it. I was trying to pattern myself after Chuck Norris. Nobody took a lateral sideways move into TV. Looking back, it was a bad choice.

What was the show about?

We didn't get to that point. I was also offered a show with a writer, John Fusco, and it was green-lit. I got the call from the William Morris Agency. They said, "Break open a bottle of Dom Perignon!" They were going to throw in a car too because the Chrysler Corporation bought all the ads for thirteen episodes. It was going to be like the old days: All the commercials were going to be for one company. John Fusco was the showrunner. He wrote *Young Guns* and *The Forbidden Kingdom*. I think the other actor was going to be Dean Cain. Dean Cain's dad had directed *Young Guns*. It was a story about two half-Asian brothers, whose parents are murdered, and it's set in Japan. One is trained in jiu jitsu, and the other is an LA cop. I come in and I'm like Batman. By day, I'm a college professor, and by night I'm doing this ninja stuff. I'm a high-tech ninja. They wrote the pilot, and it was green-lit. Here's what happened. Two or three months later, 9/11 happened. It was supposed to be shot in New York. Chrysler pulled the plug.

How did you land a role in *Batman Forever*?

Joel Schumacher saw me in a movie. *Bloodfist III*, I believe he mentioned. He thought that all the kids were playing martial arts videogames, and he thought Batman and Robin should know martial arts. So he asked me if I would come in for three months to work as a main bad guy with Tommy Lee Jones, and I said that I couldn't because I had a contract. I was signed six movies in advance. Those schedules were set. I was locked in. That was one of the bad things about a contract. No actor does that. I had the offer to be in what would end up being the highest-grossing film of the year. You couldn't get a better offer than that. So he said, "What can you do?" I said, "I know I'm going to get beat up in the movie. It would be cool to have a disguise." I told him, "I'll just come in and do a fight scene. I can take one week off of anything if it's planned right." He shook my

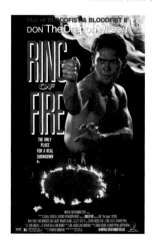

Video promo poster for *Ring of Fire*. Author's collection.

hand and I left. A couple weeks later, I get a call from my agent. He said, "Joel wants to meet with you in his office." I went, "Oh, okay." I drive to Warner Brothers, and I went to his office, and he hands me a sealed folder with my name on top, and says, "Here. Read this." The script was treated like a CIA document. It did not leave the office. I read the scenes I was in, and it was exactly what I had asked for. I was a skull-faced character, the leader of the gang, and I do one fight. That way I could be in the movie, get all the advantage of it, but not have to get sued by these B-movie companies. I cannot say he wrote the scene for me. I just said, "Can you do that?" We shook hands, and that was it. I did the scene. I've run into him once since then. It was after he had done the second one. I saw him at the mall at the Beverly Center. He said, "Don, I could have used you in the second one."

I thought your movie *Night Hunter* was an interesting film for you.

The hair was real. I grew that hair. It took me a while. That came about from *The Crow* and *The Professional*. The guy Leon. He was shy. Stunted. My character was a kid whose parents were killed, and he trained his whole life to get revenge. He's not good with people. The look came from *The Crow*. The heavy metal, the jacket. You'll see in this movie that a lot of the scenes are in the day. This was a vampire movie. Vampires can't come out in the day! Ours can. Ours have suntans. We had to change the myth because of the budget. What happened—and this is hearsay—Ashok was doing another movie with Brian Bosworth. That movie was not looking good, and so he needed to spend more money on their stunt package, which was the car crashes, the shootouts, so he took it out of our movie. Our budget went down, and we could not afford to shoot at night. All the lights and set-ups slow everything down. When you shoot in the day, you use available daylight. We had to change everything. Vampires are horror movies, bloody movies, and that's what we shot. We made it scary, bloody, gory. You'll never see that. We shot it to be horrific, but the horror element was so brutal. Ashok, who is an Indian Hindu, watched it at his home privately, and he couldn't watch it. It freaked him out. He wanted all the blood cut out. Whole scenes were cut. That's what happened. We planned it to be an action horror movie, but all the blood was taken out. It was not the movie we set out to make.

Your movie *The Capital Conspiracy* was also interesting. It's a downbeat movie, particularly for you.

It was based on fact. The CIA hired what they called "remote viewers" to tell them where the Russian missile silos were. They'd take like five guys and told them to draw the geographical locations. These guys would draw five pictures that looked the same. I don't know what remote viewing is. Psychic stuff. The genesis of that movie was that my brother read a book about remote viewers. I think it was called *Psychic Warriors*. One of the hit shows at the time was *X-Files*. We did the same thing. A guy and girl. My partner turns out to be the bad guy.

R

One of my favorites of yours is one of the last ones you did, *The Last Sentinel*.

I was a few weeks from shooting another movie called *Microwave Park*, and suddenly that fell through. I told my agent, "We need a basic action movie." We didn't have a script. I told him to look through his client list. We didn't have time for rewrites and all that stuff. We had this stunt coordinator and writer named Jesse Johnson. He brought an action script with no martial arts in it. I read the script and put some martial arts and a samurai sword in it. I knew it was going to be a success because Jesse had done stunts on movies like *War of the Worlds*. He's worked on the big ones. He knows the pyro guys, the stunt guys who would do the high falls. Everything that needed to be safely on my budget, Jesse could do it, and he did. He shot that movie in eighteen days. We sold it as a three and a half million-dollar movie. It was made for considerably less than that. It was real successful. We cast it right. Katee Sackhoff had a show called *Battlestar Galactica*. It was currently on the SyFy Channel while we were shooting it. We had a draw there. We had the sci-fi fans and the martial arts fans. I helped with the sales overseas, while Katee helped domestically.

Are you happy with the film?

Oh, yeah. Very happy. We considered doing a series at one time.

You've worked with a lot of amazing action stars. All of them, really. Who would you like to work with that you haven't worked with yet?

Chuck Norris! I worked with him on *Walker*, but I want to do a real movie with him. He's always said that he's open to it if the script is right. I would like to do something like *Unforgiven* where we're not playing young guys. Like a *Rambo* thing where I have to go get my old commander. Chuck would play the mentor guy. We would team up. I have my idea about it.

Do you feel like you've left your mark in the world of action films? Are you glad you did all these films?

If Chuck Norris had never been in a movie, if I had never done a line of dialogue, you would know we were martial arts champions. If Van Damme had never done a movie, if Steven Seagal had never been in a movie, if Jeff Speakman had never been in a movie, the odds that anyone would know them and their accomplishments in martial arts would be very slim. I think Van Damme was a member of the Belgian team, Jeff Speakman was a high ranking kempo guy, but name ten kempo guys.

What would you like to say to your fans, Don?

Thank you. I had a great career as a fighter. You know, I had a fight scheduled in Istanbul, but they missed their second payment. Everyone says, "You're still training?" I say, "You know what? I can't totally get out of shape." They paid some of the money, and as soon as they pay me the rest of the money, the fight would be back

Promo artwork for *Red Sun Rising*. Author's collection.

on. That's all it would take. I'm a mercenary. I don't fight for my ego or trophies or for titles. It's just the most ridiculous thing when people tell me that I'm fighting for the wrong reasons. The money you get from a movie, the money you get from a fight, the money you get is for your family. When you're fighting for your ego and for bragging rights and all that, that's twenty-year-old fighters. I don't need that anymore. Just pay the money that's well worth it to me. I still like the lifestyle. I love that my only responsibility is to train. I'm getting ready to do an action scene for a movie called *The Scorpion King 4*. I've never seen these other *Scorpion King* movies, but I'm getting ready to go to Romania to shoot this. The main thing is, thank you for your support.

Ring of Fire 2: Blood and Steel

1993 (Madacy DVD) (djm)

Don Wilson returns as Johnny Wu, a doctor who has incredible kickboxing skills. He's out with his fiancée (Maria Ford from Part 1), when she is wounded in a botched armed robbery. While in the hospital, she is kidnapped by the gang that botched the robbery because Johnny killed the gang leader's brother. Johnny investigates the gang and finds them "underground," living beneath the city in a bizarre labyrinth of strange populations and customs. He is forced to fight in the fight circuit before he can reach the gang leader—Kalen (Ian Jacklin from *Final Round* and *Expert Weapon*)—who presides over a mini-empire of derelicts and ruffians. When Johnny defeats Kalen's champion Predator (Evan Lurie from *American Kickboxer 2*), Kalen flees, with Johnny in hot pursuit. Backing Johnny up are his buddies from the first film, and they provide much of the comedy relief. Some action topside rounds out the climax.

Stranger than the first film to be sure, *Blood and Steel* has an alternate reality feel to it, but it's still enjoyable if you're willing to just let it happen. Wilson is faced with some bigger and stronger opponents, and there's plenty of fight scenes to keep things lively. There's no sex or nudity this time around, which is a wise decision on the filmmakers' part. The first film had *way* too much of that going on. It was directed by Richard Munchkin, who co-directed the first one, and its fights were choreographed by Art Camacho, a director in his own right.

Ring of Fire 3: Lionstrike

1994 (Madacy DVD) (djm)

The third and final entry in the *Ring of Fire* series finds Dr. Johnny Wu (Don Wilson) a widower with a young son to take care of. In the first scenes of the film, he is on his lunch break, practicing his kickboxing on the roof of the hospital where he works. The nephew of a criminal being treated at the hospital stages a daring escape for his uncle, a mobster being watched and guarded by police. A group of hired killers invades the hospital, kills a bunch of doctors and bystanders, and a helicopter swoops down on the roof to whisk the old criminal away. Johnny Wu doesn't let that happen. He kills the bad guys and blows up the helicopter! And that's just the first ten minutes of the movie! After that, the plot kicks in. A group of Russian terrorists have made an alliance with the Italian mob (run by Robert Costanzo from *Die Hard 2* and *Undisputed III*) to steal a computer disc that would give them the capability to control a nuclear arsenal. A couple of two-bit hoods are hired to steal the disc, but Johnny Wu is there (on accident) to put a wrench in their gears. A bag is switched (again, by accident), and Wu ends up with the disc. He goes on a fishing vacation with his son to an idyllic mountain area, and the terrorists track him down. While with his son, he meets a badass female sheriff (Bobbie Phillips) who has her hands full averting the undue attention of bikers and ruffians. When the terrorists come to town, Wu has to save his son, who is kidnapped as ransom, and keep the pretty sheriff alive.

Part *Cliffhanger*, *Die Hard*, and any number of movies starring Don Wilson, *Ring of Fire 3* is one of his best movies. I like that it follows his character on a completely different adventure while still retaining the *Ring of Fire* brand. That was something I never really understood about the *Bloodfist* movies. They should have either kept on going with the character he played in the first two films, or dropped the *Bloodfist* moniker all together. As it is, *Lionstrike* gives Wilson everything he needs to flex his martial arts and his sensitive side, in equal measure. Some of the villains are on the annoying side, but it doesn't matter. If you're only going to see one *Ring of Fire* movie, see this one. It was directed by regular Wilson collaborator Rick Jacobson (*Black Belt*, *Bloodfist VI*, *Bloodfist VIII*). Wilson came up with the story.

Ring of Steel

1994 (Universal VHS) (djm)

Olympic fencer Alex Freyer (Robert Chapin from *Dragon Fury*) accidentally kills an opponent while in competition, and he drops out of the world of competitive fighting. Some time later, he gets a mysterious offer to join a sword-fighting circuit known as the Ring of Steel, run by a nameless millionaire, played by Joe Don Baker. Alex gladly joins the circuit—to prove that he's the best and to quell the pain and remorse he still feels over that awful accident. When he's forced to fight to the death, he refuses, so his girlfriend is taken hostage to make him go over the edge. Alex, using some martial arts techniques and his skills with swords, fights with everything he's got to redeem himself and save his girlfriend . . . and to put an end to the Ring of Steel.

From Shapiro Glickenhaus Entertainment, *Ring of Steel* was more or less Robert Chapin's introduction to the world of direct-to-video action and martial arts movies. He only made a handful, but this one was his best one (close second would be the first *Dragon Fury*), and it had Universal as its distributor, which was a big deal. This movie was also amongst a wave of martial arts sword-fighting movies that included *The Swordsman* (with Lorenzo Lamas), *G2* (with Daniel Bernhardt), and the *Highlander* franchise, which was all over the map. David Frost directed this.

Rio Conchos

1964 (Shout Factory DVD) (djm)

Notable for being the first film Cleveland Browns running back Jim Brown appeared in in a supporting (but significant) role, *Rio Conchos* stars Richard Boone as Lassiter, an ex-Confederate Army soldier who has all but given up on life after Apaches raped and murdered his wife and child. Lassiter is forced to lead a small convoy to Mexico to intercept the sale of rifles to Apaches, and his team consists of Captain Haven (Stuart Whitman) and a buffalo soldier named Ben Franklyn (Brown), who both back him up despite their individual misgivings about Lassiter and the mission itself. A rousing, violent finale incorporating chaotic gunplay and explosions amidst an Apache skirmish closes this otherwise standard western.

Jim Brown trail-blazed for blacks in the world of motion pictures. Though *Rio Conchos* isn't an entirely memorable movie, it was certainly a steppingstone for one of the greatest black action stars in the history of film. The movie isn't bad; it's just unremarkable. A strong score by Jerry Goldsmith is a highlight. Directed by Dordon Douglas.

Riot

1969 (Olive DVD) (djm)

The prisoners in the isolation block at a prison stage a riot and take several guards hostage. The warden is away on vacation, and over a period of several tense days, the tension escalates. The leader the prisoners look to is Red Fraker (Gene Hackman). Fraker's violent temper and impulsive nature is evened out by a cool-headed inmate named Cully Briston (Jim Brown), who is only serving a five-year sentence. Cully and Red are able to work with each other as their fellow inmates get out of hand, and every second of every day they are watched by armed snipers, who are perched on high, just waiting for them to slip up or give away their intentions. As Red formulates a grand escape plan, Cully is just trying to keep his cool and let the press and the authorities know that he had nothing to do with all of this. Eventually, the prisoners get restless, and Red's plan of escape is spectacularly botched, but astonishingly, Cully sees his chance to escape and manages to be the only prisoner to do so.

Definitely more of a drama/thriller than an action film, *Riot* was an early starring role for pro NFL fullback Jim Brown, who was, at the time, breaking boundaries for African Americans all across the board. His performance in this film is calculated, focused, and pretty impressive considering how new he was in the acting world, and while he does showcase his physique and physicality throughout this film, the movie really isn't about being an action star. That's the beauty of Jim Brown: He's an action star when he's just *acting*. Directed by Buzz Kulik and based on a book by Frank Elli.

Riot

1996 (Universal DVD) (djm)

At Christmastime, riots erupt in a major metropolitan area, and gangs take over the streets. Several supermodels are carjacked and are taken hostage by a vicious gang, intent on getting several million dollars for their ransom. Two majors in the military—also buddies for life—are called upon to go into the city to pay the ransom and save the girls. Major Shane Alcott (Gary Daniels) is a martial arts expert, and he has no idea that one of the girls is a former flame of his, and Major Williams (world-famous boxer Sugar Ray Leonard) is an adept fist fighter. When Shane encounters some distress while in the riot zone, his buddy tries to save him, but gets killed. Now alone and enraged, Shane faces not just one gang, but two of them who want the ransom money and won't hesitate to kill him for it.
A fleet pace and lots of explosive action and high-flying kicks help elevate *Riot* from the rest. From PM Entertainment and director Joseph Merhi (co-founder of PM and director of *Rage* and *Magic Kid*), this tightly wound direct-to-video film looks to have a bigger budget than many theatrical releases of the time. Daniels is rock-solid in a role he's well suited for, but Sugar Ray Leonard, who is well cast, isn't used nearly enough. Patrick Kilpatrick (*Open Fire*) co-stars

as the leader of an Irish gang, and Charles Napier has a bit part at the beginning. Similar films in the same vein would be Universal's *Trespass* and *Judgment Night*. *Jungleground* with Roddy Piper is also comparable, but not as good.

Ripper Man

1994 (Turner Home Entertainment VHS) (djm)

Ex-cop turned novelty stage hypnotist (?!) Mike Lazo (Mike Norris, son of Chuck) is pretty much a flop at whatever he does, but he actually *does* know the art of hypnotism (and martial arts too), which is what gets him noticed by a creep named Charles (Timothy Bottoms). Charles pays him thousands of dollars to put him under hypnosis to see if he's been reincarnated, and as it turns out, Charles is the reincarnated form of the infamous killer Jack the Ripper. Fueled by this knowledge, Charles goes on a vicious killing spree, eviscerating women of all walks of life, and the police are appalled by the grisly aftermaths he leaves in his wake. Mike realizes that he knows who the killer is, but his former chief and associates at the police department think he's a big joke, and in a twist, Charles makes it look like Mike is, in fact, the killer. Faced with murder charges and a looming, stalking shadow over his reality, Mike absolutely *must* man up and recall his martial arts training to defeat the monster that could very well destroy or end his life.

A slow cooker, *Ripper Man* makes a fatal mistake by giving us a lead character who's pretty much a wimp, and when he brings out his

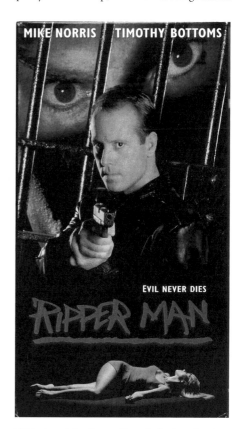

VHS artwork for *Ripper Man*. Author's collection.

fighting skills, I'd get excited for a few moments, only to be disappointed again when characters beat him down with very little difficulties. I like Mike Norris (from *Born American* and *Death Ring*) as an action guy, but he never really had the ultimate, awesome movie that he needed to push his status over the top. *Ripper Man* is weak and really goofy, and I'm fairly certain most purveyors of action and fans of his will end up not really enjoying it. Written and directed by Phil Sears.

Rising Sun

1993 (Fox DVD) (JAS)

"We're the cops! Why are we running?"

Rising Sun stands as an engaging, if dated, thriller filled with the red herrings and wrong turns one has come to expect from movies based on Michael Crichton books. This noir-action film, about a murder committed during a party at a Japanese-American company, concerns three police officers with (surprise!) conflicting personalities. Wesley Snipes, Sean Connery, and Harvey Keitel are immensely entertaining as the bickering cops, which is a testament to Philip Kaufman and Michael Crichton's snappy script writing. Web Smith (Snipes) is a short-tempered police officer who is just young enough to be open-minded to the Japanese culture he must infiltrate, while John Connor (Connery) and Tom Graham (Keitel) are polarized in their approach. Connor has worked on previous police cases with the Japanese and has appropriated their social mores to his tactical advantage, whereas Graham is the odious loudmouth who tramples all over their customs in the name of "police work." Smith and Connor eventually discover that Graham is on the take and abetting the real murderer by trying to pin it on the son of a wealthy Japanese businessman (Cary-Hiroyuki Tagawa). In the midst of this we are treated to a labyrinthine plot bolstered by amusing verbal exchanges between the male leads.

With a strangely bouncy tone for such subject matter, *Rising Sun* is an engaging thriller buoyed by strong performances from all involved. Connery brings a stateliness and class to the aura of scuzz and violence, Keitel is hilariously profane as a prejudiced investigator, and Snipes is the endearing everyman who grows into wisdom with the help of his mentor. His brief displays of martial arts are impressive, and the same goes for real-life martial artist Tagawa, who shows his strong athletic chops in a few scenes. Overall, this is an engrossing film with enough surprises to satiate those who like their thrillers a little on the grown-up side. It's also a lot of fun to see what was considered "cutting-edge" technology at the time this was made.

Risk Factor

2015 (NOV) (CD)

Alex Granger (Jalal Merhi) is a very well respected photographer. He spends his time with a lovely girlfriend and is constantly surrounded by beautiful women. It's a lifestyle he has grown accustomed to until Eve Armitage (Elise Muller) walks in his studio door. Eve knows Alex has a past. He was a former operative in the CIA known for his work in surveillance. She offers him a huge chunk of change to jump back into the game and do what he does best. He's never told that her partner Damon Ramsay (Brett Halsey) is a major arms dealer. After he agrees to do the job his old pal Rick D'Angelo (Loren Avedon) shows up to put in his two cents. His methods are sometimes questionable but he gets things done. The two of them partner up like old times, dancing with death while attempting to shut down a major shipment of illegal weapons.

Risk Factor was shot on a nonexistent budget back in 2011 and is just now seeing the light of day (on Amazon Instant). As uneven as the picture may be, it really doesn't matter much since we're treated to the reunion of two amazing action stars—Jalal Merhi (*Talons of the Eagle*) and Loren Avedon (*King of the Kickboxers*). Their real-life friendship always shines through in their screen work and this film is no exception. The movie tends to drag a bit but when the men spring into action things heat up. Merhi doesn't fight much until the end but Avedon is just as energetic now as he was in the '90s. The thing most endearing about the film is even though it's modern, it looks and feels as if it were a '90s DTV action film. It captures the aesthetic of why we love those films. This is by no means the highlight of their careers, but it's great seeing them together again and it delivers a couple of fun action scenes. Ignore the horrible CGI muzzle flashes and explosions; just enjoy the rest. Directed by Frank A. Caruso.

Riverbend

1989 (Prism VHS) (djm)

Director Sam Firstenberg and star Steve James (both of *American Ninja* and *Avenging Force*) reunited for the final time for *Riverbend*, which casts James as a Vietnam veteran named Quinton who is on his way to a court marshal, just after his tour of duty. He and several of his men (also about to be court marshaled for a war crime they didn't commit) manage to escape before their trial and end up in a town in Georgia that is overrun with racism and corruption. The sheriff is an evil, spiteful man who rapes black women and murders their husbands in cold blood in front of the whole town, but no one has the sand to stand up against him . . . not even his own deputies, who find him deplorable! When Quinton and his men show up, they take the opportunity (because they're pretty much damned already) to declare war on the sheriff by holding every white man, woman, and child in it hostage and demanding that the media and the FBI come into the town and investigate the mistreatment and unsolved deaths of blacks in the town. This creates a very dangerous situation, putting Quinton and his men (and everyone who follows them into guerrilla-style battle) at the center of attention when the military is called in to rescue the white hostages. It's a mess.

Steve James was awesome in everything he did. He was convicting in his acting, and his physicality was always impressive. He rarely got the chance to star in films (check out *Street Hunter*), so when he did get a vehicle, it was always something to savor. *Riverbend* is pretty close to being a terrible movie, which is truly a shame. It has all the ingredients to be excellent, but the script clubs you over the head with racist tropes and an overly despicable character in the form of the sheriff, who is so awful, so disgusting that in the context of a "B" action movie, he overpowers it to the point of distraction. The action in the movie is fine (especially a scene where James takes the sheriff to an alley to beat the shit out of him), but the biggest flaw of the film is that it wants to be taken seriously. The chintzy score ruins any attempt the movie makes to be sincere, and if the sheriff character were written a little more sensitively and with a careful hand, this movie might have been something. For James, it was an attempt to elevate him to "star" status, but Firstenberg's direction wasn't deft enough to gauge the material correctly. Others might appreciate this movie more than I did.

River of Darkness

2010 (Green Apple DVD) (djm)

A river town experiences a bout of terror when corpses of its inhabitants begin turning up in grisly murder scenes. Clues begin pointing to the impossible: The killers might very well be the vengeful ghosts of two brothers who were killed years ago. The town sheriff, a bruiser named Logan (played by pro wrestler Kurt Angle), is on the case, and the superstitious townsfolk are sure that he will botch up the investigation and unleash more mayhem than the town deserves. Sure enough, the two zombified brothers (played by pro wrestlers Kevin Nash and Psycho Sid Vicious) are on a killing spree, and apparently only Sheriff Logan has the sand to stand up to them, fight them, and survive.

More of a stalk-and-slash horror movie with slight action overtones than a straight-up action movie, *River of Darkness* is surprisingly effective as a horror outing, but as an action movie it left me wanting. Star Kurt Angle (from *Death From Above* and *End Game*), doesn't really exert himself too much, which is weird because he's a wrestler and when wrestlers get to star in movies they *exert* themselves. I kept expecting a smackdown between him and the zombie slashers, but their big scene at the end felt truncated and chopped, which was a big disappointment. Director Bruce Koehler and star Angle also worked together on *End Game* and *Death From Above*.

R

Adventurer John Hamilton (Michael Dudikoff) in *River of Death*. Author's collection.

River of Death

1989 (Cannon VHS) (djm)

This minor effort from Cannon tries going for "swashbuckling adventure," but ends up feeling closer to Cannon's *Allan Quartermain and the Lost City of Gold* than the likes of Indiana Jones. It's set in the Amazon jungles, where a former Nazi (Donald Pleasence) hires a ne'er-do-well guide named Hamilton (Michael Dudikoff) to take him through the most treacherous parts of the Amazon to help him find a lost Incan city of gold. The ex-Nazi's worst enemy is another Nazi (Robert Vaughn), who now resides in the lost city, posing as a god of some kind, and he commands a legion of native Indians who thwart all invaders from coming into the city. Dudikoff is just tough enough to survive the adventure. The same can't be said of Pleasence.

This movie played countless times on network television in the early 1990s. For some reason it seemed really old and dated even

Michael Dudikoff stars as John Hamilton in Cannon's *River of Death*. Author's collection.

Not quite Indiana Jones or even the American Ninja, Michael Dudikoff plays John Hamilton, an adventurer-for-hire who travels to the Amazon in *River of Death*. Author's collection.

when it was a recent release. It shamelessly bares the Cannon mark, and Dudikoff as its lead actor seems to have star power despite the film's lackluster energy. It was based on a book by Alistair MacLean. Steve Carver directed it.

Road House 2

2006 (Sony DVD) (djm)

The Black Pelican Road House is in a prime location in a turbulent parish in Louisiana, and a drug lord (played by Richard Norton from *Gymkata*) wants the establishment so that he can run drugs in and out of it. His underling Wild Bill (Jake Busey) is a petulant little snit whose haphazard methods attract undue attention from the law, and in comes DEA agent Shane Tanner (Johnathon Schaech), who steps in to oversee and manage his wounded uncle's Road House in the interim while his uncle (played by an uncharacteristically physical Will Patton) recuperates in the hospital after Wild Bill makes an attempt on his life. Shane's very presence in the parish is an affront to Wild Bill and his scary boss, and all hell breaks loose when good people die at the Black Pelican to scare Shane off. The renegade DEA agent brings it on and goes toe to toe and fist to fist with Wild Bill and his kickboxing boss.

Road House 2 is 100 percent better than it has any right to be, and if you go in with zero expectations like I did you may end up having a really good time with it. Schaech's physical performance is surprisingly good, and his stunt double Sam Hargrave, who is an up-and-coming action star in his own right, has appeared in movies like *Blood and Bone*. Richard Norton, who virtually steals the show with his incredible fight scene with Schaech at the very end of the film, is only featured in a handful of scenes, but if you need an excuse or a reason to watch this, then watch it just to see him—it's worth it. This is a great showcase for fight coordinator J. J. Perry, who has coordinated fights on dozens of films, including several for Isaac Florentine. Director Scott Ziehl is a direct-to-video filmmaker for hire, and he made another really good one called *Exit Speed*, if anyone cares.

The Road Raiders

1989 (NOV) (djm)

"Am I going nuts or is there an echo in this jungle?"

A made-for-television pulpy action adventure in the vein of *Zone Troopers* or any number of fun men's adventure novels, *The Road Raiders* is set on the eve of World War II on a Pacific Island where a handful of misfit American soldiers are stationed. Charlie Rhodes (Bruce Boxleitner from *Tron*) owns a hopping gin joint, but his tenure as the owner is pretty much up when the war starts, and he's branded a traitor by the

Japanese, who threaten to imprison him and his sidekick Harlem (Reed R. McCants). Charlie hastily gets a bunch of other Americans who are also in a pickle, and they hop in a plane, hoping to escape the turmoil. The plane crashes in the jungle, and the bunch of misfits survive and have to escape the encroaching Japanese soldiers, who are out to get them. The misfits include a schizophrenic, a genius (played by Stephen Geoffreys), two meatheads (played by David and Peter Paul, otherwise known as The Barbarian Brothers), and some other guys. When the Americans are pushed into a corner, they do an "A-Team" job on the parts of the plane and create several functional armored cars, equipped with machine guns, and they burst out of the jungle, guns blazing.

This movie has slipped through the cracks over the years, but anyone who's a Barbarian Brothers completist should try to track it down as they add some fun stuff to this old-fashioned action movie. One of the brothers repeats everything the other one says immediately after he says something, so they're a constant echo team, which is funny, but then when they get in the cockpit of several of the Mad Max-inspired makeshift vehicles, they're action heroes, looking like crazed apocalyptic warlords with machine gun staccato coming from their itchy trigger fingers. As their roles are minor, most viewers or interested parties may want to skip it, but it's an entertaining movie nonetheless. Directed by Richard Lang.

Roaring Fire

1982 (Bonzai DVD) (CD)

"What are you, a salesman? A thief? That's it: You're a thief."

Young Joji (Hirouki Sanada) is about to learn things about his past he never saw coming. The man he has always believed to be his father is dying. With his last breath, he informs Joji that his real parents are long dead but he has a sister and twin brother living in Hong Kong. Joji packs his bags and sets out to find them. He quickly finds his sister, Chihiro (Sue Shiomi), who is blind as a bat but can kick anyone's ass. She's staying with their uncle who just so happens to dabble in the crime world. His uncle tries to convince him to cross over to the dark side, but Joji refuses, sending his uncle into a rage, retaliating by trying to have Joji killed. A mysterious magician (*The Street Fighter*'s Sonny Chiba) and his ventriloquist dummy may just end up being the savior Joji needs to stop his drug-dealing uncle for good.

This isn't really a Sonny Chiba (also in *Karate for Life*) film; it belongs completely to Hirouki Sanada (later in *The Wolverine*), and he delivers plenty of great action to feast your lazy eyes on. Chiba (in his flashy white suit sporting a mustache to make most Canadian mounties jealous) shows up to fight alongside Sanada for one brawl but his most memorable stuff is when he works his dummy. The dummy has an odd design and the English-dubbed voice makes it sort of frightening. Also appearing in the picture is former professional wrestling superstar Abdullah the Butcher. He has a larger role than Chiba and actually fights Sanada in one of the more hilarious moments of the film. Directed by Japanese exploitation legend Noribumi Suzuki.

Robin-B-Hood

2006 (Vivendi DVD) (djm)

Two thieves—Fong (Jackie Chan) and Octopus (Louis Koo)—make a living robbing from others, and when they are propositioned to steal a baby from a wealthy family for a considerable sum of money, they take the job, not realizing how it will alter the course of their destinies. They steal the adorable baby and keep him in their apartment for a time before they are supposed to turn him over to their employer, and during that time, they have to deal with the poopy diapers, the screaming, the feeding, and the general *Three Men and a Baby* tropes that the movie requires them to go through before they actually begin to care for the child despite their immaturities and bachelorisms. When they give the baby up to the shady characters who hired them, they immediately feel remorse and try to right their wrong and steal the baby back, but that gets them into a ton of trouble. They have to contend with a horde of goons, who lock them in a freezer—*with* the baby, and then the movie takes a horrible left turn when it becomes inevitable that the baby freezes to death, creating heart-rending drama when the two goofball thieves try to resuscitate the poor child, leading to a terrible epilogue where the two guys find themselves in prison for kidnapping and murder . . . only to have a junky twist ending where the baby is revealed to still be alive and smiling and the two guys are only serving a short prison term for kidnapping.

I kind of hated this movie. It's hard not to like Jackie Chan, but dude, seriously, *Robin-B-Hood* made me want to pull my hair out. First of all, Chan (who wrote and produced) is way too old to be playing a guy like the one he plays here. Second, the baby stuff is grossly mishandled and it was reprehensible what they did to the poor little guy on screen, and then to see him die and have Chan and co-star Koo cry over him and try to do CPR on him is just the pits. There's action in the movie, but this is just not the way to make a "lighthearted" martial arts "comedy" that deals with the kidnapping, manhandling, and mistreatment of a child. Sorry, Jackie: I'm not laughing. Directed by Benny Chan, who did the far superior Jackie Chan movie *Who Am I?*

Robowar

1988 (NOV) (ZC)

With the dawn of spaghetti westerns, Italian exploitationeers established a tradition of Xeroxing popular genres at bargain rates. From countless knock-offs of *The Road Warrior*

to *Escape from New York* (to even *Flight of the Navigator*), the boot-shaped nation has managed to remain the undisputed pioneers in cinematic coattail-riding. And of their countless professional apers, director Bruno Mattei (a.k.a. "Vincent Dawn") takes the cannoli. Like his contemporaries, Mattei seemed to derive genuine pleasure from distilling the thrills of Hollywood's finest into a more blue-collar, less palatable concentrate. But where other filmmakers pilfered specific sections of popular work, Mattei brazenly released films like 1989's *Terminator 2* (which had no legal relation to James Cameron's series). It's this plagiaristic fearlessness that's on blazing display in his masterpiece *Robowar*... which is essentially *Predator* with the alien replaced by Robocop.

Unless you're a joyless, suicidal wreck, that sounds like a very good time. And it is, especially due to a head-spinningly anti-logical script by *Troll 2*'s Rosella Drudi and Claudio Fragasso, the latter of whom even appears on screen as this film's titular "Robo." He's malfunctioned and is now being tracked by an elite military task force named BAM, an acronym for "Big-Ass Motherfuckers." While only some of these motherfuckers are actually big, they're all led by Major Murphy "Killzone" Black (action star Reb Brown from *Cage*), a pillar of emotionless, relentless firepower. His ethnically diverse mercenary squadron has seen/done/killed it all, until they run up against an unstoppable purveyor of mechanized homicide. What follows is a symphony of jungle explosions, Uzi fire, and death shrieks, punctuated by homophobic zings from characters named "Blood" and "Masher." As IQ-decreasing as *Robowar* is, its purity and innocence have made it a legend of euro-exploitation. Every time we see the android on screen, a synthesized voice-over drones robobabble that sounds like "BIDDY BIZZLE ZORP . . . GREAZY." Its costume is basically a studded wetsuit, motorcycle helmet, and codpiece. The credits misspell characters' names and/or switch them at random. The soundtrack is composed of Casio sample beats and tone-deaf bar rock. It's a rare example of a movie that fearlessly revels in its own idiocy, plagiarism, and limitations, yet still comes out on top. Fearlessly macho, completely braindead, and 100 percent greazy.

Rocky

1976 (MGM DVD) (djm)

"I was nobody. But that don't matter either, you know? 'Cause I was thinkin', it really don't matter if I lose this fight. It really don't matter if this guy opens my head, either. 'Cause all I wanna do is go the distance. Nobody's ever gone the distance with Creed, and if I can go that distance, you see, and that bell rings, and I'm still standin', I'm gonna know for the first time in my life, see, that I weren't just another bum from the neighborhood."

Only once in a lifetime does something like *Rocky* happen to a man. For Sylvester Stallone, *Rocky* was the project that created him. He was born to play Rocky Balboa (a character he created in the script he wrote)—a palooka from Philadelphia, a dreamer, a gentleman, a good-hearted boxer who is given a Cinderella's chance to fight the world heavyweight champion for the title: Apollo Creed (Carl Weathers). The circumstances that lead up to Rocky's lottery's chance to fight the champ play out while he's struggling to maintain dignity while fighting in dives for thirty bucks a pop and being a debt collector for a local bookie by day. He's got a crush on a shy woman who works in a pet shop, and Rocky's heart is always worn plainly on his sleeve. When the chance to fight Creed presents itself (believably), Rocky humbly takes on the opportunity, training for his life to "go that distance" with the champ, and the whole neighborhood roots for him as he gives it everything he's got. When the climactic fight is on, it's obvious that Creed didn't take Rocky seriously, and even though Creed wins by technicality, the whole world embraces Rocky as the winner.

As well worn as the story is, *Rocky* is an all-time classic with an instantly recognizable score by Bill Conti, and even Stallone's haters will have a hard time arguing how great he is in it. Every detail and moment in the film is authentic and pitch-perfect, except (ironically) the final fight, which has a staged quality to it. Director John G. Avildsen won best director, and the film won best picture at the 1977 Academy Awards. Stallone would go on to an incredibly successful career as an action star, but he wouldn't grow his action star feet for a few more years. He would never be able to shake the Rocky image, which has never really been a major issue because he would take on another image that would stick with him just as hard when he would later star in *First Blood*. You're either a Rocky fan or a Rambo fan. I like the *Rocky* movies, but I *love* the *Rambo* pictures exponentially more.

Rocky II

1979 (MGM DVD) (djm)

Creed: "What are you afraid of, Tony?"
Tony: "Honest?"
Creed: "Yeah, honest."
Tony: "He's all wrong for us, baby. I saw you beat that man like I never saw a man get beat before, and the man kept coming after you. Now, we don't need that kind of man in our life. I know what you're feeling. Let it go. *Let it go.* You're the champ."

The inevitable sequel to the Academy Award–winning smash hit that made Sylvester Stallone an international star, *Rocky II* is focused on the rematch title between Apollo Creed (Carl Weathers) and the "nobody" who went the distance with him, Rocky Balboa (Sylvester Stallone, a little more svelte than he was three years ago). Balboa marries his sweetheart Adrian (Talia Shire), bonds with his brother-in-law Paulie (Burt Young), and prepares to face Creed for a bout that will change the course of his destiny. Under the tutelage of his trainer Mickey (Burgess Meredith), Balboa trains harder than ever because his opponent knows what he's up against, and a media frenzy sparks as they prepare for their title bout.

The pre-release poster blazed "The Rematch of the Century" across the top, which pretty much sums up the tone of the movie. It builds to a great big climax, which we know will end up in Rocky's favor, but the appeal of the *Rocky* series is that we get to know the characters quite a bit before the big fights. In this entry, we see Rocky hit hard times as he struggles to find a job after his first fight with Creed. He spends the money he made on that fight—and from the few sponsorship commercials he attempts to act in—and he's left with mounting bills and responsibilities that he simply can't contend with if he doesn't get back in the ring soon. The drama builds, and Stallone's script allows the characters to really get into the groove of their situations. *Rocky II* is a worthy sequel because at this point the series hadn't gotten so sensational yet; it's grounded in a more or less real world with still-real-enough characters. The next three sequels were really intensified and lost touch with the humility of the world these characters came from. *Rocky Balboa*, which came years later, was a worthy sequel that felt in tune to the first two films in the series.

Rocky III

1982 (MGM DVD) (djm)

"Look, man. When you beat me, I hurt all over, and I didn't want to know from nothing or nobody, not even my kids. Hell, every fighter knows that hurt. And we get sick inside trying to live with it, so don't back off now. Make it right for yourself, or you'll be sorry you didn't. We held the greatest title in the whole world, babe. You lost that fight, Rock, for all the wrong reasons. You lost your edge. All right, I know your manager dying had you all messed up inside. But the truth is, you didn't look hungry. Now, when we fought, you had that eye of the tiger, man, the *edge*. And now you gotta get it back, and the way to get it back is to go back to the beginning. You know what I mean? Maybe we can win it back together. Eye of the tiger, man!"

Rocky III announced the arrival of Sylvester Stallone the action star. Here it is. This is where he really emerged as a verifiable movie star—a sculpted, gleaming jewel of a movie star, and from here on out, he would headline in larger-than-life action films, each one bigger than the last. As a *Rocky* film, Part III is a slick, adrenaline-charged popcorn flick. It resembles

the previous two movies, but only because it has carryover actors and characters. Rocky Balboa, we learn at the beginning of the film, has fought ten title defense matches, and he's remained the heavyweight champion of the world for several years running. Rocky's physique is no longer that of a bookie's debt collector, but that of a chiseled statue, every muscle protruding, every ounce of fat chipped away. He lives a lavish life with his wife and son, and his trainer Mickey (Burgess Meredith) lives in the home, always there in Rocky's corner. When Rocky announces his retirement to the world, a rising star in the boxing world named Clubber Lang (Mr. T in a dynamic, star-making role) taunts him and goads him to accept one final challenge before making his exit. Rocky takes the challenge, not realizing that Clubber Lang is a dynamo, and when they meet in the ring, Rocky is trounced upon and embarrassingly loses in the second round. To top off the devastating loss, Mickey dies, leaving Rocky without a mentor. In his downward spiral of depression, Rocky's biggest ally comes when his former adversary Apollo Creed (Carl Weathers) visits him and offers to train him for a rematch against Lang. With Rocky and Apollo training together, there's nothing that can stop them in obtaining that "eye of the tiger!"

A blockbuster in every way, *Rocky III* is *The Road Warrior* of the *Rocky* movies. It left the humility and the grounded space of the first two films and creates its own space in a Hollywoodized sequel Valhalla. It has the best fights (easily) of the whole series. Stallone fights Hulk Hogan in one memorable scene in an exhibition fight, and then he fights Mr. T twice. The climactic fight is a whopper of a donnybrook. The editing is much tighter in the fight scenes, which helps quite a bit, and the team-up of Rocky and Apollo is a great, novel idea. It would have been ideal for the series to end here, but the juggernaut that this series became would simply not stop. More power to Stallone. He made a boxer into an action hero the world over. Mr. T appeared in *Penitentiary II* the same year.

Rocky IV

1985 (MGM DVD) (djm)

"No, Stallion, maybe you *think* you're changing, but you can't change what you really are. And you can forget all this money and stuff you got all around you, man, 'cause it don't change a thing. You and me, we don't even have a choice. See, we're born with a killer instinct that you can't just turn off and on like some radio. We have to be right in the middle of the action 'cause we're the warriors. And without some challenge, without some damn war to fight, then the warrior may as well be dead, Stallion."

The year 1985 was huge for Sylvester Stallone. He had two massive hits at the box office: *Rambo: First Blood Part 2* and *Rocky IV*. In both films, he fights evil Russians. In *Rocky IV*, Rocky Balboa is no longer an underdog. He's barely the same character he was in the first two films. Ultra lean and slick, Rocky is an action hero 100 percent. His adversary is Ivan Drago, played by Dolph Lundgren, in his first big role. Drago is virtually a cyborg in the film: He's been manufactured by the Russians to prove to the world that their fighter is stronger and more superior than any living fighter, and they make a proposal to Rocky via the media: An exhibition fight matching the undefeated American champion and the latest technical marvel from Russia will prove to the world who's warrior is the strongest. Rocky isn't too keen to accept the challenge, and so his best friend and trainer Apollo Creed (Carl Weathers) jumps at the chance to step back into the limelight, and the Russians accept. The fight between Creed and Drago is a disaster: Drago kills Creed in the ring, and the aftermath has Rocky reeling with a focused rage. He accepts the next challenge from the Russians, and he goes to Russia to train. The final fight lasts at least twenty minutes and even though Drago pummels Rocky, he goes the distance and is victorious.

It's interesting watching the progression and the degeneration of Stallone's dearest character through the *Rocky* series. The first two are intimate and more or less "realistic" and honest. The third one announced the arrival of a sculpted action star and pitted Rocky against adversaries who were freakish and outlandishly strong. Part 3 felt like it had a big budget and got away from the intimacy of the characters and what made them so interesting in the first two. *Rocky IV* is the shortest entry in the series, and it barely has the legs to stand on, let alone remind you why Rocky as a character matters so much. The movie is filled with unnecessary trappings like pop songs on the soundtrack, incidental and lame distractions like showcasing a state-of-the-art robot that Paulie (Burt Young) receives as a gift, and several training montages that focus on Drago's calculated power. Drago is generally considered one of Rocky's greatest adversaries (and a fan favorite), but as much as I love Dolph Lundgren, I consider him to be Rocky's worst adversary. Even though Rocky delivers a heartfelt speech about "change" at the end, the whole point of the movie is lost amidst a too-conscientious production that forgot who Rocky was and why we should care what happens to him. Stallone, the action star, is endearing and essential in many of his projects, but not so in *Rocky IV*. He also directed.

Rocky V

1990 (MGM DVD) (djm)

The most baffling of Stallone's *Rocky* movies, *Rocky V* starts off immediately after the events of the previous entry, but everyone in the film looks at least five years older and more depressed. Rocky (Sylvester Stallone) is suffering from brain injuries after his impossible victory over Ivan Drago from

Part IV. He visits doctors who tell him that he has to retire. His brother-in-law Paulie (Burt Young) squanders his fortune on a bad business move, and Rocky is forced to liquidate all of his assets in order to keep his family from living on the streets. They move back into the old neighborhood in Philly, and Rocky tries to get Mickey's old gym back in working order. Rocky's son (Sage Stallone) is picked on at school, and the poor kid can't win his dad's attention because Rocky has found an up-and-comer to train and invest his heart in. The young boxer is a hothead named Tommy Gunn (the late Tommy Morrison, a real boxer at the time), and he has issues with anger that Rocky seems to understand, and for a while they are like father and son, spending their days together in training. As Tommy works his way up the circuit, Tommy is seduced by an unsavory promoter, and Tommy betrays Rocky and in so doing becomes the heavyweight champion of the world. The promoter goads Tommy into forcing Rocky to fight him for a championship title, but Rocky rejects him, inciting a street brawl that serves as the film's climax.

So many things are wrong with this movie, it would take pages for me to relate how misguided this story is. Stallone, at this point in his amazing career, had lost touch with who Rocky Balboa is, and it was showing by *Rocky III*, but in this entry the story—while keeping most of the core characters together and giving them stuff to do—is so far gone that it literally doesn't realize that Rocky is a champion of the people. The fact that he takes on a protégé (an everyman, also of the people) who betrays him so cruelly and heartlessly says something about where Stallone was at emotionally when he wrote the screenplay for this movie. It's an angry, sad movie, and its moral compass comes in the form of a weird ghostly flashback involving Mickey (Burgess Meredith who looks at *least* five years older than when we last saw him). Rocky has not only lost his way as a character, but Stallone clearly lost touch with the audience of his character as well. With his heart always worn on his sleeve, Rocky Balboa is a hero for the ages, but in *Rocky V* he was no longer an action hero—or even a champion. He was a suffering man with a broken ego. It's a painful movie to watch. Fans of Stallone will be dumbfounded by it and fans of *Rocky* should be outraged. John G. Avildsen, who directed the first film, returned as the director.

Rocky Balboa

2006 (MGM DVD) (djm)

"You know, I talk and I talk, and sometimes I think what I'm saying is true, and then, you know, I look at myself and I'm not even sure what is true anymore 'cause it's like, I pushed this crazy idea about fighting—I mean, what's it all about? Do I really care about standing toe to toe and all that stuff, or like my kid says, is it just like, ego? Or am I like this old pug who's just trying to replace old pain with new pain? I don't know. I . . . don't know."

After years of flops and then a significant absence from the spotlight, Sylvester Stallone made a great comeback with what might be his most poignant and personal movie yet. *Rocky Balboa* brings his most beloved character back in a profound way. Rocky, now the humble owner of a small Italian eatery in Philly, is lonesome after his sweetheart Adrian passed away, and his son (Milo Ventimiglia, who bears a striking resemblance to Stallone) is mostly estranged and running the rat race in the big city. Rocky tells the same tired stories to his customers, and after a while, he's exhausted of the routine, so much so that when a glimmer of a possibility that he can fight again presents itself, he jumps at the chance with gusto. A computer simulation estimated that the current heavyweight champion of the world, Mason "The Line" Dixon (real boxing champion Antonio Tarver) would lose against Rocky Balboa in his prime. This creates a stir in the media, and Dixon's managers think it would be a novel idea to ask Rocky to fight the current champ in an exhibition fight. Rocky must first jump through the legalities of even entertaining such a notion, but he manages to convince the league that he's fit to fight, and once the game is on, he trains for the fight of his life.

Here's why *Rocky Balboa* is one of Stallone's very best movies—and the best sequel to the original *Rocky*: It's honest. Stallone had never been this humble on screen before. In the first *Rocky*, he was desperately hungry and his heart burned bright. In *Cop Land*, he was trying to erase his action star image, and while that was a great performance, it's got nothing on what he does in *Rocky Balboa*. Stallone is entirely self aware of who he is, how far he's come in life, the ups and downs, and never before or since has he revealed a glimmer of the man who actually has gone through all of his enormous highs and lows. The Rocky he wrote here is the most appealing to me, because he remembers every detail of his life. He remembers falling in love, he remembers having nothing, and he remembers winning, but after all the years, he's beginning to forget what winning felt like. While far removed from the bloated days of *Rocky III* and *IV*, this one pumps vibrancy into an old franchise and gives it new life. Stallone is awesome beyond compare here. It has the most heart, and on top of that, it has a kickass training montage. Bill Conti's score for this film is the best of the whole series. This was a surprise hit for Stallone (who also directed), and it paved the way for his next film, *Rambo*. With those two movies combined, he delivered two of the best movies of his whole career. In a surprising turn of events, a follow-up/spinoff called *Creed* was made in 2015 with Stallone's participation.

Romeo Must Die

2000 (Warner DVD) (djm)

After Jet Li made a spectacular crossover as the ruthless villain in *Lethal Weapon 4*, producer Joel Silver cast him as the hero in *Romeo Must Die*. Li plays a wrongfully convicted police officer named Han, who breaks out of his prison in China when he hears that his brother was killed in America. In the US, he confronts his gangster father (who committed the crime he took the

blame for), demanding to know who killed his brother. There's a racial war going on between two heavy-hitter syndicates in the city, and the leaders (black/Asian) are blaming each other for the death of Han's brother, who was considered royalty in the Asian community. Han doesn't follow anyone's rules and begins hanging out with Trish O'Day (the late pop singer Aaliyah), who is the only daughter of Isaak (Delroy Lindo), the leader of the black syndicate. This causes strife and unrest, and Han's methods only amplify the problem.

A half-hearted redux of *Romeo and Juliet* with a heavy reliance on hip-hop songs on the soundtrack and wires in the action scenes, *Romeo Must Die* is a product of its time. Li tries to jump in there and play with the material as best he can, but after Joel Silver's huge smash with *The Matrix*, it was inevitable that the gravity-defying stunt work from that movie would creep into urban action movies. Watching the pint-sized Li participate in a gladiatorial football match with huge dudes three times his size—and using martial arts and *Crouching Tiger* wires to help him defeat his foes—is just . . . strange. A treat in the film is that Russell Wong from the martial arts TV series *Vanishing Son* plays a villain here. Director Andrzej Bartkowiak would later direct Li again in *Cradle 2 the Grave*, and *Exit Wounds* with Steven Seagal.

Rome 2072:
The New Gladiators
(a.k.a. The New Gladiators)
1984 (Troma DVD) (djm)

"Violence pays, and it's about to pay big."

A dystopian Roman future sanctions violence in the media, and all the TV shows push real violence (happening live) as far as it can go. The biggest show on the air features "Kill Bike" gladiators who ride around an arena with weaponized motorcycles, and the best gladiator of them all is Drake (Jared Martin), whose wife is murdered by a competing station, hungry for higher ratings. They frame him for the murder, and he's cast in a cell with other condemned prisoners, who will all be given a last chance to redeem themselves by fighting for their lives against each other. Fred Williamson, who in the '80s had made a nice niche for himself in the Italian film market, plays one of those guys. They are tested and trained to the brink of death, and one scene shows four of them gripping a pull-up bar for hours, for fear of dropping to the electrified ground. As their big game day approaches, they all realize that the system is corrupt, and they band together and fight their way out.

Lucio Fulci's *The New Gladiators* is a little slow and lacks excitement, but it does have a murky, futuristic atmosphere tinged by the Italian flare that makes movies of this type watchable. Williamson's role is small, but he gets in on the action, so it's a valid entry for him. He

R

appeared in another Italian action movie called *Warrior of the Lost World* around the same time, but it's not included for review here. The Troma DVD looks atrocious, so I reviewed the widescreen Japanese laserdisc instead.

Rope-A-Dope

2013 (The Stunt People DVD)

(djm)

From director/editor/writer/star Eric Jacobus (*Death Grip, Contour*), this short film (about thirteen minutes) packs a wallop. The Dope (Jacobus) wakes up, goes out for a walk to get his breakfast, and he's assaulted by a martial arts gang and gets knocked out. He wakes up, remembering the previous day, but it's *the same* day all over again. He goes outside, gets his breakfast, and is assaulted by the gang again, only he has a little bit more reflex response this time. He gets knocked out again. When he wakes up again, he relives the same day ad infinitum until he gets better at defending himself. Finally, on his last day in his time loop, he not only manages to have mastered his art as a fighter, but he defeats the martial arts gang and is victorious. What a great, hilarious little movie this is. Highly recommended.

Jacobus, who is one of the unsung rising stars of the martial arts world in film, is doing an incredible job working outside the limelight and under no supervision of any kind. He's creating great work for himself, and he's one of the few guys who actually should be paid attention to. His movie *Rope-A-Dope* has won numerous film festival awards and can be seen in its entirety on YouTube.

Roughcut

1994 (NOV) (djm)

Sean Donahue from *Parole Violators* and *Blood Hands* starred and directed this slick action picture that casts him as a disc jockey who is in the wrong place at the wrong time when he witnesses a murder. While on a hunting trip in the California wilderness with his buddy, Garrett (Donahue) stumbles onto a double-cross between a diamond smuggler named Caine (Richard Lynch) and a thief who brought him the diamonds. When Caine kills the other man, Garrett runs for cover, but Caine and his goons realize they've been made, and so they hunt Garrett and his buddy through the forest. After Garrett gets away (and with the stash of diamonds to boot!), his buddy is slain and Caine vows to hunt down the remaining witness come hell or high water. Fleeing to safety, Garrett calls on his best friend—a renegade cop named T. J. (Shawn Flanagan)—to help him hunt down the murderers who are after him. It's a two-man job to take down the toughest scumbags in town.

If you've seen anything with stuntman-turned-action star Donahue then you know that he usually gives it his all in the physical department, with high falls, close-call car

smashes, and plenty of scenes where he dives through plate glass windows while shooting guns and kicking guys in the face. *Roughcut* is a step up from the wacky *Parole Violators*, and it perplexes me why it was never properly distributed. With a good bad guy (Lynch, always a smarmy, dependable villain), straight-up action scenes (and plenty of them), sex, nudity, and explosions galore, this should be on every "B"-action movie lover's list of movies to track down if only there were copies of it to find. It took more digging, emails, and phone calls to get myself a copy to watch than I care to admit, but it was worth the quest. If you've never seen a movie with Donahue, make this one the first one . . . and good luck to you.

Royal Warriors

(a.k.a. **In the Line of Duty**)

1986 (Fox DVD) (CD)

Three unlikely heroes form an alliance while on a hijacked plane. Hong Kong police officers Michelle (Michelle Yeoh), Michael (Michael Wong) from air security, and no-nonsense Tokyo detective Yamamato (Hiroyuki Sanada) have no choice but to team up on the flight in order to foil the hijacking attempt and to save the innocents on the plane. What they aren't ready for is the backlash from the remaining members of the notorious gang that organized the hijacking. When Yamamato's family is brutally murdered, the three of them band together but there's more to it than they had expected, and their lives (as well as those of many other innocent people) mean nothing to these madmen and their revenge.

Royal Warriors cemented Michelle Yeoh's status as an action star, and the film remains a classic in the pantheon of Hong Kong action cinema. Hot off the success of *Yes, Madam!* (co-starring Cynthia Rothrock), Yeoh moves into this role with ease, delivering an electric

and emotional performance. It's action packed with fight scenes, car chases, gun battles, and breathtaking stunts popularized by Jackie Chan during the same time period. There's a nightclub battle, which goes toe to toe with Jackie Chan's *Police Story* in the amount of glass shattered per second. There's also a staggering number of innocents caught in the crossfire who die violent deaths. Yeoh has moved past these sorts of films as she's gotten older, and she's grown into an amazing actress, but these early Hong Kong efforts are unforgettable classics. Director David Chung also did *Magnificent Warriors* with Yeoh.

Rumble in the Bronx

1995 (New Line DVD) (djm)

"No fear. No stuntman. No equal."—tagline

After years of being a box-office star all over the world—*except* the United States—Jackie Chan finally caught a break when New Line Cinema distributed *Rumble in the Bronx* in theaters across the US. Chan plays Keung, who comes to New York to attend his uncle's wedding, and he stays on for a week while his uncle goes on his honeymoon. He hangs around the neighborhood and helps with protecting his uncle's former grocery store, which now has a new owner: Elaine (Anita Mui), who finds it exasperating when hoodlums thrash the place when Keung tries to discourage their unruliness. Keung is targeted by a multiracial gang (who act like *Road Warrior* rejects), and he befriends the gang's moll, an exotic dancer named Nancy (Françoise Yip), whose disabled younger brother has no idea that he has a stash of stolen diamonds in his wheelchair cushion. Some pinstriped goons begin harassing the neighborhood, looking for the diamonds, and Keung makes peace with the gang to stop the goons from killing or hurting anyone they care about.

As silly as the movie may seem with goofy acting, bad dialogue, and wacky dubbing (I reviewed the US theatrical release), *Rumble in the Bronx* is a ton of fun with Chan at the peak of his career. This was a fine transition for him into the US market—much better than his previous US crossover attempts *Battle Creek Brawl* (*The Big Brawl*) and *The Protector*. A slightly altered

The action in *Rumble in the Bronx* is nuts. Jackie Chan is on the right. Author's collection.

Jackie Chan is about to spring into action in *Rumble in the Bronx*. Author's collection.

Jackie Chan throws one of a zillion kicks in *Rumble in the Bronx*. Author's collection.

Holding on for dear life, Jackie Chan grips a handle of a hovercraft in *Rumble in the Bronx*. Author's collection.

unrated international cut exists. Director Stanley Tong also worked on the stunts in the film. Tong and Chan also collaborated on *Supercop, First Strike,* and *The Myth.*

The Rundown (a.k.a. Welcome to the Jungle)

2003 (Universal DVD) (djm)

After starring as The Scorpion King in two back-to-back Universal films, Dwayne "The Rock" Johnson was given his first straight-up action movie to carry on his own, but they still gave him a comedy relief sidekick. In *The Rundown,* he plays a nice-mannered bruiser/bounty hunter named Beck, who desperately wants to retire and go into the restaurant business. His leash is pulled one last time, leading him on a final adventure to catch his employer's wayward son, a likable treasure hunter named Travis (Seann William Scott) living in Brazil. When Beck comes calling, Travis gives him a hard time, stringing him along on a hackneyed scheme about a golden treasure known as "El Gato," which is something that Indiana Jones would clearly go after and get himself into a heap of trouble trying to obtain. Same deal goes for Beck and Travis, as they get the attention of a slave master and gold hunter named Hatcher (Christopher Walken), who has dozens of mercenaries at his side and several thousand indigenous workers/slaves under his whip. Taking the chase to the jungles of the Amazon, Beck and Travis run afoul of a pygmy tribe who give Beck The Rundown of his life as they muster up an ass

The Pygmy Manito (Ernie Reyes Jr.) flies around and kicks Beck (Dwayne "The Rock" Johnson) with full force in *The Rundown*. Author's collection.

Some action in *The Rundown,* featuring Dwayne "The Rock" Johnson. Author's collection.

Seann William Scott as Travis and Dwayne "The Rock" Johnson as Beck in *The Rundown*. Author's collection.

Dwayne "The Rock" Johnson, Rosario Dawson, and Seann William Scott in *The Rundown*. Author's collection.

Spanish poster for *The Rundown*. Author's collection.

wupping that he's never had before. Leave it to camaraderie and a good old-fashioned buddy/buddy formula to keep things light and lively.

The Rundown was almost the right vehicle for The Rock to make following his lame-duck movies *The Mummy Returns* and *The Scorpion King,* but what's lacking is an edge. To this day, he has never made "the right vehicle" as far as I'm concerned, and I'm still waiting for his *Commando,* his *Terminator,* his *Rocky* or *Rambo.* When he got

R

going as an actor, he made a string of safe PG-13 movies, and by the time he did the "R"-rated *Doom* where he played an underdeveloped villain, I sensed that his heart wasn't in the right place to commit himself to the action genre. He then squandered years away making PG-rated family movies and even when he tried "edgier" movies like *Faster*, it was too little and too late to win me over. *The Rundown* is adequate, and he has everything it takes in the movie to be a bust-out action star in it, but it's just not the event movie or the 100 percent satisfying ride it needs to be. There's a lot of back-and-forth silly banter between him and William Scott, which is time consuming and strenuous, and while Walken is a great bad guy, the movie needed a nasty henchman and some *blood*. The best scene of the movie has The Rock fighting a pygmy, played by Ernie Reyes Jr. from *Surf Ninjas*, and what this scene really proves is that Reyes Jr. was robbed of a bigger action movie career. Watch closely at the very beginning of the film for a cameo by Arnold Schwarzenegger who just about literally passes the torch to the star of the film. "Have fun," he says. Directed by Peter Berg. The Rock's next movie was the PG-13 *Walking Tall*.

The Running Man

1987 (Lionsgate DVD) (CD)

"You cold-blooded bastard, I'll tell you what I think of it. I'll live to see you eat that contract, but I hope you leave enough room for my fist because I'm going to ram it into your stomach and break your goddamn spine!"

By 2017 America has become a police state where all cultural activity is censored by the government. The most popular show on television is a reality show called *The Running Man*, a sport program where criminals must run for their lives from gladiators who are waiting to kill them. Ben Richards (Arnold Schwarzenegger) is a helicopter pilot for the police who is framed for a massacre of innocents he actually tried to prevent. He is captured and thrust into the game show by its sadistic host Damon Killian (Richard Dawson). These gladiators are tough but Richards isn't a man who will go down easily, and he fights with all he has, every step of the way.

The Running Man is a classic action film from the '80s, though it doesn't quite hold up as well as many might assume. Schwarzenegger does what he does best and just pulverizes the gladiators in many different (and sometimes pretty gory) ways. As far as one-liners go, they come fast and loose. Several of the gladiators were played by former sports personalities, most notably Toru Tanaka (*The Last Action Hero*) who was a former WWE wrestler, legendary NFL star Jim Brown (*Slaughter*), and Arnie's *Predator* co-star Jesse Ventura. Sadly, Ventura never gets into the action. Tanaka and Brown are both memorable in their roles of Subzero and Fireball, respectively. Of course, both characters fall victim to the mighty Schwarzenegger, but each of them left their marks on the film with their unique looks and costumes.

The film was originally to be directed by Andy Davis (*Under Siege*) who was replaced a week into filming by Paul Michael Glaser (*Kazaam*).

Running Red

1998 (Mill Creek DVD) (djm)

Jeff Speakman plays a Russian commando named Gregori, who turns his back on his ranking officer when he is given an order to kill an innocent child. He quits the military, goes to America, and restarts his life. Now married and with a young daughter, his heroic actions during a robbery are caught on video by a bystander, and suddenly his face is on the news. His former commanding officer seeks him out and disrupts his life, making demands and threats that he do certain heinous deeds in exchange for the safety of his family, who have no idea the level of his skills as a highly trained killer. He's got a limited amount of flexibility to formulate a plan to save his family, while still protecting himself from the Russians who have a scheme to assassinate an American politico.

One of Speakman's last efforts as a real-deal action guy, *Running Red* (from Joseph Merhi's PM Entertainment) isn't as sad as it could have been, but Speakman just petered out at some point when he was given second- and third-rate scripts to work with, resulting in weak movies with short bursts of his amazing kenpo martial arts abilities. In this film, he doesn't even try a Russian accent, even though it would have been interesting to hear him take one on, and his character is pretty bland. His wife is played by Angie Everhart, who seems totally disinterested. It was directed by Jerry P. Jacobs (*Freedom Strike* with Michael Dudikoff).

Rush Hour

1998 (New Line DVD) (CD)

"Damn, Chin, this is some greasy shit. You ain't got no better food, like some chicken wings, some baby back ribs, some fries or something?"

Detective Lee (Jackie Chan) unravels a plot to steal ancient Chinese artifacts on the final night of British rule in Hong Kong. Chinese Consul Han (Tzi Ma) couldn't be more excited. Later, when Han and his daughter Soo Yung have moved to the United States, criminal Juntao shows up to seek revenge. Juntao kidnaps Soo Yung (Julia Hsu), leaving Han in a state of panic. The FBI is quickly on the case but Han wants his friend Lee to assist them. Agents Russ (Mark Rolston) and Whitney (Rex Linn) don't want Lee getting in their way so they enlist the help of the LAPD to send over a babysitter. Detective Carter (Chris Tucker), a loud-mouthed troublemaker last seen blowing up half a city block, is enlisted to hang around Lee. Carter and Lee don't like each other but quickly learn to get past their differences when the FBI's efforts grow inept and Soo Yung's only hope of survival lies in their hands.

For longtime Jackie Chan fans, *Rush Hour* will be a bit of a disappointment. He doesn't completely abandon what we have come to expect from him but there is a really solid attempt at making him more appealing to the masses. Pairing him with Chris Tucker (*Money Talks*) was a brilliant marketing idea. While it may be nowhere near as energetic as some of Chan's past films, it manages to successfully bring back the buddy-cop formula for a modern, nonassuming audience. Tucker can go either way for people. If you find his brand of humor off-putting, then it's best you stay away from the film. He has some very funny dialogue and his bug-eyed delivery can be hilarious in just the right doses. Chan's fights have the same tone and style that we are used to, except they are much slower and less inspired this time. The two leads need little to no direction on screen and genuinely seem to have fun working together. Chan's fish-out-of-water act never really gets old and plays a major part in the hilarity. The two superstars have an amazing supporting cast that includes Tzi Ma (*Rapid Fire*), Mark Rolston (*Best of the Best 3*), Chris Penn (*Best of the Best*), Philip Baker Hall (*Bending the Rules*), Elizabeth Pena (*Blue Steel*), and Tom Wilkinson (*Batman Begins*). Longtime Chan fans may enjoy seeing frequent collaborator and Chan bodyguard Ken Lo (*Drunken Master 2*) show up in a minor role. The music has a sort of Chinese/hip-hop influence and is fused well by veteran composer Lalo Schifrin (*Enter the Dragon*). *Rush Hour* might not be close to being Chan's best work but it is perfect family popcorn fare. The film was a huge success, grossing over $244,000,000 worldwide and spawning two successful sequels. Brett Ratner directed all three films

Rush Hour 2

2001 (New Line DVD) (CD)

"Don't be messing with me, Lee. I will kick your ass. I'll hit you so hard you'll end up in the Ming Dynasty. I mean it, I'll bitch-slap you back to Bangkok!"

While on vacation in Hong Kong, Detective Carter (Chris Tucker) wants some more excitement as well as more ladies. Inspector Lee (Jackie Chan) has his own agenda and is after triad leader Ricky Tan (John Lone) who may be responsible for the deaths of two Americans in a bombing at the embassy. As they push deeper, they uncover a counterfeiting ring that takes them back to Los Angeles. Things get more complicated when Secret Service agent Isabelle (Rosalyn Sanchez) informs them that they are about to blow her undercover status. It doesn't stop them and they will go to great lengths to keep Tan from attaining his goal.

Rush Hour 2 improves on the formula established in the first film in almost every respect. Chan and Tucker return, picking up were the first film left off, finding the two unlikely partners in a brand-new globetrotting adventure that has them going from Hong Kong to Los Angeles, then to Las Vegas. No time is wasted and the action and laughs come fast and frequently. It really felt like Chan was given a bit more room to fashion some

R

really exciting fights. They were filmed in a way that allows viewers to take in all the movement and not jump from shot to shot. Tucker has some classic moments that will have you laughing out loud. You may catch yourself rolling your eyes at his character's stupidity, but the words that come out of his mouth are really funny. It's also a treat to hear Chan saying things that are so out of character for him. When Inspector Lee says to Carter that he "will bitch-slap you back to Africa," you may find yourself asking out loud if he just actually said that: It's side-splittingly funny. The lack of any major fight in the finale keeps this film from being truly special. John Lone (from *The Hunted*) is an excellent villain and his hench-woman played by Zhang Zi-Yi (*Crouching Tiger, Hidden Dragon*) should have been able to fashion an incredible final fight that could have been a showstopper. Instead, they take a different route that feels more like a missed opportunity. Other than that, *Rush Hour 2* is an absolute blast that delivers on the action and hilarity. Make sure you watch the credit sequence since the blooper reel is classic. Once again, Brett Ratner did the directing duties.

Rush Hour 3

2007 (New Line DVD) (CD)

"In case you missed it man, people are trying to kill me! I'm covered in shit and some French cop whooped my ass with some yellow pages, man. So don't tell me it ain't none of my business."

While making a speech in front of the World Court, Ambassador Han (Tzi Ma) is the victim of an assassination attempt. That quickly brings Carter (Chris Tucker) and Lee (Jackie Chan) back into action when they promise Han's daughter Soo Yung (Zhang Jingchu) that they won't quit until they find who was responsible. They quickly find out that it's all triad related, and they find themselves in Paris protecting a young woman who has a secret list of triad leaders' names. To make matters worse, a man from Lee's past named Kenji (Hirouki Sanada) shows up and turns out to be the most vicious criminal they have had to face.

Rush Hour 3 reunites Jackie Chan and Chris Tucker for a third outing, except this time, the results are mixed and the finished product is disappointing. The chemistry is still there, but it just feels like this third outing is more of a rush job than anything else. Many of the jokes are recycled and not quite as funny the third time around. The story attempts to go full circle by bringing back characters from the first film. It sort of works, but the film needed a bit more to really feel like the stakes had been raised. What *Rush Hour 3* does have that its predecessors lacked is a final fight between Chan and a single opponent. It is also a rare turn for Chan since it is a sword fight (atop the Eiffel Tower, no less). There is less of Chan showing off and more of Tucker running his mouth this time, but he's not quite as naturally funny. The biggest laughs come once again during the blooper reel that runs during the end credits. Joining our

heroes this time out are Max Von Sydow (*Never Say Never Again*), Noemie Lenoir (*After the Sunset*), and Hiroyuki Sanada (*The Promise*), who ends up being the strongest villain of the series. The big surprise is the addition of Yvan Attal (*Munich*) as a cab driver with dreams of being an American spy. This is by far the weakest entry in the series but it still manages to offer up few fun moments and a chuckle or two. Aside from the finale, there really is only one other shootout/fight that manages to feel inspired. Brett Ratner returned as the director.

The Russian Specialist

2005 (Sony DVD) (CD)

Nick Cherenko (Dolph Lundgren) is former Spetznaz (Russian special forces), living a simple life as a mechanic with his wife and son. Life is wonderful until Aleksandr Popov (Ivan Petrushinov) arrives in town. Nick's wife and son are killed in the crossfire of a gang war Popov is responsible for. Nick goes after him and leaves Popov for dead. Nick migrates to the US, and years later he is confronted by a woman who knows exactly who and what he is. She wants him to find her daughter. He declines only to change his mind when he finds out that Popov is not only still alive, but also responsible for the daughter's disappearance. He is offered a large sum of money and back to Russia he goes. He puts together a small team of men that includes William Burton (Ben Cross), who has a person on the inside. Rescuing the daughter Julia (Olivia Lee) is the easy part; collecting the rest of the cash and keeping Julie safe ends up being a bloody affair.

The Russian Specialist is a rare sort of film. It's exciting and packs an emotional punch, and it also proves just how great Dolph Lundgren can be in the right role. So who was the director smart enough to tailor this character to his strengths? Well, it was Dolph Lundgren! He hits a homerun here. While the story is simple, he's able to convey more emotion with a single look than many of his action star contemporaries. He has the face of a tortured man, one who has been through hell and back, and that fire fuels him. Nick Cherenko is one of Lundgren's best characters and with this film he proves to the world his place in the action pantheon. *The Russian Specialist* is a near-perfect example of what an action film should be. The film plays much like a modern day *Death Wish* with plenty of graphic violence and mayhem to please even the most jaded fan. We are treated to solid performances from Ben Cross, Olivia Lee, and Ivan Petrushinov as the despicable Popov. The film's success lies totally within the hands of Lundgren. This is one of his best acting performances, and as a director, he slyly gives us strong characters grounded within the real world and action that is believable and bloody. He has an expert eye and knows his own limitations. This is a truly great action film that may have been overlooked and deserves much more attention. The film was released in foreign territories as *The Mechanik*.

Sabotage

1996 (Warner VHS) (djm)

Much better than most movies of its ilk, *Sabotage* is an involving action/intrigue film starring Mark Dacascos as Michael Bishop, a former black ops sniper who was almost killed in the field by a rogue agent named Sherwood (Tony Todd). Several years later Bishop is working as a bodyguard to a wealthy businessman who is killed right in front of him . . . by Sherwood. This leads to the involvement of and investigation by the FBI, and the agent assigned to the case is Agent Castle (Carrie Anne Moss), who doesn't trust Bishop. Through hard work and determination, Bishop and Castle begin working together to find the rogue group who hired Sherwood to assassinate the businessman. Bishop gets into a couple of close-quarter fights with some bad guys, and faces off with Sherwood later on.

I was consistently surprised at how much I enjoyed this film. Tibor Takacs (*The Gate*) did a really good job keeping things interesting, and his big coup came when he hired good actors to fill the roles. Aside from those I already mentioned, Graham Greene plays a pivotal role, and all of the characters are three-dimensional. Dacascos has several scenes that feature his extraordinary physicality and prowess at martial arts, and both Moss and Todd make him look even better. Takacs later worked with Dacascos again on *Red Line* and *The Crow: Stairway to Heaven*. This was one of the better efforts from Imperial Entertainment.

Sabotage

2014 (Sony DVD) (djm)

A tough-as-nails DEA enforcement team led by John "Breacher" Wharton (Arnold Schwarzenegger) steals ten million in drug money during a major bust, but before they can divvy up their spoils, their loot is stolen right out from under them. They spend the next half-year in suspension during an investigation on their tactics, and when that period is over without repercussions, they get back in the game. Two separate story threads unfold: First, Breacher's team is being hunted down one by one by (they think) the drug cartel they stole from, and a separate investigative team is scrambling to assist in finding the truth, but Breacher and the rest of his crew are withholding vital information that could help, which leads to the second plot point: Two years previously, Breacher's wife and son were kidnapped by the cartel and raped, tortured, and murdered on camera, and Breacher has an endgame agenda to carry out his revenge against the cartel. Who is behind the killings of Breacher's team, and will Breacher be able to carry out his plan before anyone can stop him?

From David Ayer, the director of the urban cop/crime dramas *Harsh Times, Street Kings,* and *End of Watch, Sabotage* is a fairly radical vehicle for Arnold, who at this point in his career has massive odds against him if he's ever going to make a proper, triumphant comeback as an action star. *Sabotage* doesn't do him any favors.

S

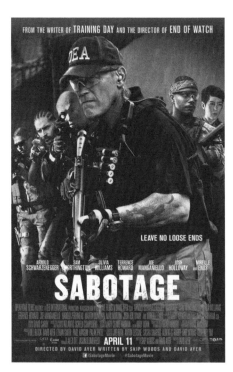

Theatrical release poster for *Sabotage*. Author's collection.

Ayer uses him as a mascot to tell the same sort of story he always tells—corruption in the police force, showing masculinity in its most obvious, clichéd state of overcompensation, etc.—and the film emerges as a sensational take on police procedurals that have more or less been covered better in TV shows like *The Shield*. Watching Arnold shepherd a bunch of roughnecks (played by Terrence Howard, Sam Worthington, Joe Manganiello, Josh Holloway, and an electrified Mireille Enos) isn't as endearing as it wants to be, and witnessing him sit in a dark corner, smoking a cigar while watching the snuff videos of his wife being raped, tortured, and murdered puts a damper on the whole proceedings. *Sabotage* isn't supposed to be pretty, but it wasn't supposed to be dour or depressing either. Fans of Arnold will be divided by it.

Safe

2012 (Lionsgate DVD) (djm)

One of Jason Statham's very best pictures, *Safe* casts him as Luke Wright, a former cop turned cage fighter, who just about kills a guy in the ring, thus setting the course of his destiny. It was a fixed fight, and he was supposed to take a dive, and the Russian mob kills his wife as punishment and forces him to live as a vagabond. Homeless and suicidal, he drifts through New York, and on a fateful day he happens to notice a little Chinese girl being pursued by the same Russians who killed his wife. He saves the girl (and kills the Russians), and just like that, he becomes the focus of attention for several factions who are looking for the girl. The girl—named Mei (Catherine Chan)—was stolen by the Chinese mafia and enslaved and put to work by using her ability to memorize numbers, and she's got

an incredibly long number in her head that everyone in town wants . . . including a squad of corrupt cops led by a deadly captain (played by *Robocop 3*'s Robert John Burke). Luke finally finds his purpose in life—to protect Mei and keep her safe—while almost literally clearing the city of its underbelly.

A sharp, smart script and snappy direction by Boaz Yakin (the writer of Dolph Lundgren's *The Punisher*) propels *Safe* into "A" movie territory. Statham is a busy and formidable action star, but rarely has he gotten the opportunity to star in something as good as this film. He gets to *act* as well as show us what he's capable of as an action guy, and the action in the film is pretty fantastic. Oddly, this was a flop in theaters, which is confounding. A film he did later called *Redemption* (a.k.a. *Hummingbird*) was equally good and also featured him as a homeless badass. That film flopped too. James Hong has a supporting role here as a Chinese crime boss.

Saf3

2013 (NOV) (CD)

"We all know this is dangerous work. We're a different breed. We eat, drink, sleep what we do: It's a part of us."

In Southern California, a multi-agency unit of individuals has formed to help people in some of the most dangerous situations—ones that involve air, fire, and water. This unit has the best people from the Coast Guard, the fire department, and the Los Angeles lifeguards. Their mission is simple: work together as a team and save the lives of those in need. And most importantly, they must have each other's back. After losing their leader, they are given a replacement: John Erikkson (Dolph Lundgren), who comes in and takes over, picking up the torch of his fallen friend. While the group bonds outside the job, Erikkson tries to teach them to trust one another and to be better people as well as to be the top rescue unit in the country. Each week as they learn something about themselves, they are faced with various challenges and natural disasters that they must respond to while they hopefully save lives.

For a first foray into a lead role on series television, *SAF3* (pronounced SAFE) may not be the best fit for veteran action star Dolph Lundgren (*Battle of the Damned*). The focus of the show isn't so much on him as it is on the young and fresh-faced (or more concise: buff and sexy) cast of men and women his team is comprised of. While Lundgren is without question the high point of the series, the rest of it focuses a bit too much on soap opera-like drama. Each episode opens with an inspiring quote and then concludes with a dedication to someone who has risked his or her life for others. Each episode follows a simple formula: Start with team drama and then quickly shift to dangerous rescue attempts. The young cast seems overwhelmingly inexperienced but what

you may find interesting is the inclusion of real-life hero J. R. Martinez. He was a soldier who served in Iraq in 2003 and was severely burned over thirty-four percent of his body (including his face) when his vehicle was bombed. The show pays tribute to men and women like him who risk themselves for others. It excels with the carefully plotted-out rescues, with much attention given to detail. Make no mistake: Each episode is sure to contain some sort of musical montage that includes all sorts of pretty people in skimpy clothes, much like co-creator Gregory J. Bonann's previous series, *Baywatch*. Lundgren only appears in just over half of the first season's episodes with his character being given the most interesting story arc. The only action we ever see in the show is the team springing to help those in need. *Saf3* misses the mark in the character department and the previously mentioned soap opera drama is difficult to digest, but at least the program has its heart in the right place.

Samurai Cop

1989 (Cinema Epoch DVD) (djm)

Long-haired cop Joe Marshall (Matt Hannon) is a wonder to behold. He has the magic touch with women, he gets along with his black partner, Frank Washington (Mark Frazer), despite the fact that he's a racist, arrogant human being, and he knows the deadly art of the samurai because he was raised by great Japanese masters. He and his partner run afoul of a Yakuza kingpin and his deadly serious lackey Yamashita (Robert Z'Dar), and suddenly they are at war against each other, inciting their police chief to yell at them in expletive adjectives. Meanwhile, Marshall finds time to bed several gorgeous women including a sexy helicopter pilot and the Yakuza's main squeeze, who desperately falls in love with him. It's easy being Joe Marshall. It's just not easy to understand why he's the center of attention.

Samurai Cop is a glorious motion picture. It's bad for all the right reasons, and it's great for all the wrong ones. It's star, Matt Hannon, is not a real-deal action star, but he certainly pretends to be, and if this film had been made and released in any other universe other than our own, it might be an action classic. It co-stars Gerald Okamura, who is known for starring or co-starring in dozens of notable action and martial arts films, namely *Ninja Academy* and *Big Trouble in Little China*. He fights Hannon in one scene, but it's impossible to fathom that Hannon would have won the fight. After his fight scene with Okamura, he has another one (with swords!) with Z'Dar, who is playing a Japanese man. If you can prepare yourself to experience one of the greatest bad movies of all time, by all means rush to see *Samurai Cop*. In all sincerity, it's a special movie, and one that fans of action and martial arts movies should attempt to watch at some point. It was incompetently directed by Amir Shervan. Side note: Hannon was long thought to be deceased but emerged in 2014 to announce a sequel to *Samurai Cop*. God bless him.

S

San Andreas

2015 (Warner DVD) (djm)

Ray (Dwayne Johnson), a rescue helicopter pilot stationed in Los Angeles, is on his way to pick up his college-aged daughter Blake (Alexandra Daddario) to spend some time with her before his wife Emma (Carla Gugino) divorces him and moves in with a rich architect when "the big one" (and how!) strikes, splitting land mass apart right along the San Andreas fault line. Not wasting a moment, Ray uses his helicopter to rescue his wife from a collapsing building, and then the two of them try to make their way to San Francisco where Blake is biding time, but in the midst of the sequential earthquakes (the biggest one reaches past a 9 on the Richter scale), San Francisco is absolutely pummeled by wreckage, chaos, and a tsunami. A seismologist/professor named Lawrence (Paul Giamatti) predicted the earthquake, and he warns everyone on the news that the quake will be felt globally and cause even more damage throughout the Unites States. Ray and his wife brave all sorts of incredible perils on their way to a photo finish rescue of their daughter, but they encounter marauders, impossible destruction, and mayhem on a massively cinematic level.

Fun from start to dénouement (which shows that California split in *Escape From New York* style), *San Andreas* is a solid, big-budget apocalyptic rollercoaster that offers nothing new to the genre, but gives you everything you expect from it, no expense spared. It's basically a gigantic CGI extravaganza, but if you can dig it, then dig in. Johnson emerges as a stalwart action hero, and he fared better in this than in many of his more recent outings. I watched this on an IMAX screen in 3D and had a blast. Written by Carlton Cuse and directed by Brad Peyton.

Sanctuary

1997 (Lionsgate DVD) (CD)

Luke Kovak (Mark Dacascos) is a former CIA agent who's living his life under the assumed identity of priest John Connelly. He wants to put his past behind him, but it's easier said than done. When former team member Rachel (Kylie Travis) shows up, things get complicated. His current life is threatened by CIA team leader Dyson (Alan Scarfe) and new protégé Dominic (Jaimz Woolvett). Luke comes into possession of a video tape that implicates Dyson in the death of a female agent, and he reluctantly gets drawn back in to work, but only to do what he must to set things right.

Sanctuary has an interesting premise but it seems to drag on far too long. There's very little action, but Mark Dacascos (*Instinct to Kill*) manages to at least keep your attention through the course of the film. He gives an emotionally subdued performance, but when push comes to shove, he eventually unleashes his fury. Hardcore Dacascos fans may end up disappointed in the lack of hand-to-hand fighting. He has a few quick hits or kicks until a short final fight with Jaimz Woolvett (*Boogie Boy*). The film

is overly stylish and a tad convoluted with many fashbacks. It's unfortunate that the most interesting plot device comes during the final moments. Not a high point of Dacascos's career but not the worst either. It was directed by Tibor Takacs, who previously worked with Dacascos on *Sabotage* and *Redline*.

Santa's Little Helper

2015 (Fox DVD) (djm)

"You're probably bad news, but you're by far the best looking bad news I've seen all week."

Dax "The Ax" (WWE wrestler turned action star Mike "The Miz" Mizanin) is a heartless go-getter who enjoys shutting businesses down, and on the fateful day he visits the orphanage he grew up in to inform the proprietors that he'll be personally closing their doors, he's shocked to find that when he gets back to the office that his boss has fired him. Since he's just bought a new sports car and a swanky new house, the creditors come calling on him (a day after he gets fired, which all feeds into the silliness of the plot), and when Santa Claus himself hand picks him (unbeknownst to him, of course) for a special position at the North Pole (something about the "Ho-Ho-Ho" job), Dax is visited by an attractive looking elf named Billie (Annalynne McCord) who tells him that he's been selected by a famous individual to join the team. Thinking he's got a chance at redemption, Dax goes through the rigmarole of Billie's tests to prove that he can handle pressure without resorting to violence or anger, and after a few off-the-wall tests (like going into a biker bar with a silly elf hat and telling all the bikers he defaced their bikes) and passing them one after another with only minor hiccups (he does a pretty good job of defending himself in the bar, but is about to get pummeled before Billie intervenes using magic), Dax is finally told that he'll be working for Santa Claus. Upon hearing the news, he refuses to accept it until Billie proves that she's an elf, and then she whisks him to the North Pole where he meets Santa, Mrs. Claus, and a jealous elf warrior (played by Mizanin's fellow professional wrestler who goes by Paige) who wants the job he's been chosen for. A final test involving an obstacle course decides who will ultimately become Santa's "little helper," and Dax goes above and beyond showing his good will and cheer when he also helps save the orphanage back home.

Mike "The Miz" Mizanin's second Christmas movie out of four (so far) starring role vehicle projects (he was also in *Christmas Bounty*), *Santa's Little Helper* doesn't aim very high and should appeal to bored or lazy viewers who might happen to catch it on television, but it won't ever need to be watched a second time. The Miz gets into several situations where his physicality comes into play (not including one where he's all but forced to dance half-naked in front of a bunch of old people), but just like in *Christmas Bounty*, this is hardly an action film and his male fans will be scratching their heads, wondering why he's not plowing into opponents like he does in *The Marine 3* and 4.

For an action star crossover who's only done four movies altogether, to have two of those be hokey holiday movies is a telling sign of where his career seems to be headed. Still, he's one of the only contemporary WWE superstars who've done four movies in two years. Most of his peers are at least two movies behind him. Directed by Gil Junger, who also did *Christmas Bounty*.

Santa's Slay

2005 (Lionsgate DVD) (CD)

"We're trapped in a closet on Christmas with Santa trying to murder us. How fucked up is that?"

Santa (pro wrestler Bill Goldberg) isn't exactly the man you think he is. He's actually a demon who lost a bet against an angel, sentenced to become the gift bringer we all know and love. After a thousand years have passed, the bet's over and all hell's about to break loose on Christmas. Santa would much rather kill those who were naughty (or even nice) than anything else. Teenager Nick (Douglas Smith) thinks his grandfather (Robert Culp) is a bit of a nut. He tries to teach Nick the origins of Santa from a book known as "The Book of Klaus." The text explains the bet, the thousand years of delivering presents, and the whole scenario. When bodies start piling up, Nick begins to see the truth, and just like that, Santa ends up on his tail and Nick enters into a dangerous game of cat and mouse with Old Saint Nick.

Who would want to make a movie about a Santa who would burn down a gentleman's club full of strippers? No one wants to see that! Actually, the only thing worth watching in the film is Bill Goldberg (*Half Past Dead 2, Ready to Rumble*) as the slaying Santa. Director David Steiman comes up with a slew of different ways for him to off people, many of which are laugh-out-loud funny, while other slayings just miss the mark. This is Goldberg, after all, so he has a tendency to use his physical abilities to take people out, and it's probably fair to assume that that's what his fans are expecting to see. Goldberg is able to give the film a few nice moments. Other wrestlers/action guys who've made films in the horror genre are Lyle Alzado in *Destroyer* and Kane (a.k.a. Glenn Jacobs) in *See No Evil*.

Santa With Muscles

1996 (Vivendi DVD) (djm)

"Santa, you slay me."

A health guru with a slant of militaristic nuttiness named Blake (Terry "Hulk" Hogan) is playing a paintball game with some associates when he upsets some policemen, leading them on a high-speed chase. Once on foot, he escapes into a shopping mall and ends up falling and hitting his head hard enough that when he wakes up in a Santa suit, he believes he's the real Santa. With the encouragement of a crook dressed as an elf, he sits down on Santa's throne in the middle of the mall while the crook tries to use his ATM card to clean out his account. Since this is just a few days before Christmas, Blake gets to deal with the crowd of children who sit on his lap, listening to their wishes. In those moments, a couple of thugs cause a ruckus in the mall, and he steps up and saves the day, turning himself into an urban hero Santa Claus. A media sensation, he goes off *really* thinking he's the real thing, and he stops by an orphanage, where only a few kids and their social worker remain after all the other kids have been adopted. Soon Blake realizes that the land the orphanage is sitting on is very valuable: In the caverns below the building lies a cache of rare gemstones that can perpetuate energy, which is why a megalomaniacal scientist (played by Ed Begley Jr.) in the neighborhood has begun harassing the occupants of the orphanage, and exactly why Blake embraces his inner Santa to protect the innocent and bring joy to everyone he meets.

Basically, this Hallmark Channel-esque holiday movie tries to be *3 Ninjas, Home Alone,* and *Suburban Commando* all at once, with a kid-friendly Hogan acting kinda goofy and running around in a Santa suit through most it. That said, it's not very festive, with some strong PG violence involving bazookas, shooting, fistfights, and smack-downs, but it's pretty harmless. Hogan was almost good at this sort of thing by this point in his career as an action guy. Look for a young Mila Kunis is a small role as one of the cute kids at the orphanage. Directed by John Murlowski, who did *Automatic* with Olivier Gruner.

Savage

1995 (Republic VHS) (djm)

One of the strangest and most inexplicable sci-fi action films from the straight-to-video era of the 1990s, *Savage* stars a mostly mute Olivier Gruner. It begins with him loving on his family when some thugs break into his home, murder his wife and child, and then burn his house down. Wounded and comatose, he enters a psychiatric hospital, and many years later, he snaps out of his trance and escapes the hospital, wandering around the desert for an indeterminate period of time. He comes upon a mystical cave and an alien visits him and gives him a mission . . . to save the world. He then wanders back into a futuristic civilization and a patrol car runs him over, thinking he's Tarzan (he's wooly and feral). He's taken into custody, where he freaks out and escapes. We then learn the plot: A crazy eccentric businessman has been collecting data on extraterrestrials (who created Atlantis), and he's closing in on discovering the knowledge that would make him a god. He only has a few employees (because this is a low-budget movie), and his best employee is a hot hacker (played by Kristin Minter, who has a sex scene). The businessman seems to know that someone is going to be hunting him soon,

so he makes preparations for the arrival of "the Savage." Gruner spends a lot of time being a fish out of water, as he (I guess) has become a completely different person than the one he was before. Now that he knows a "savage" form of martial arts, he causes a lot of damage to people who get in his way.

Wildly uneven, this borderline junky film is a take-it-or-leave-it effort, and fans of Gruner will want to see it for the sake of watching him try brutality over his usually graceful style of martial arts. The production values are about on par with his previous film, *Automatic,* and after *Savage,* his films got cheaper and less expressive of his talents as an action star. His frequent collaborator Avi Nesher wrote and directed this one.

Savage Beach

1989 (Malibu Bay Films DVD) (djm)

Federal agents Donna (Dona Speir) and Taryn (Hope Marie Carlton) are back for another action adventure that takes them to the South Seas. Their plane crashes on a deserted island, which happens to be the very island where some buried Japanese gold is hidden, and a Japanese soldier from World War II has been guarding the island all by himself for decades. In the meanwhile, a revolutionary named Martinez (Rodrigo Obregon, who played another character in *Hard Ticket to Hawaii*) has set his sights on claiming the gold for himself to fund the revolution in his country. *But that's not all!* Some US naval commandos also get themselves on the island to claim the gold for themselves, *and* some terrorists get to the island to get the gold before anyone else. The island gets busy with action and skinny-dipping.

The fourth film in Andy Sidaris's franchise of "Bullets, Bombs, and Babes," but only the third to feature Playboy Playmates Speir and Carlton, *Savage Beach* is notable for featuring a big role for stuntman/action star Al Leong (in fact, maybe it's one of the biggest he ever got to play). Though he dies a death by impalement, Sidaris used him again in one of the sequels, *Hard Hunted.* In addition to Leong, James Lew appears in *Savage Beach.* That said, if you're watching these Andy Sidaris movies because Al Leong or James Lew are in them, you're clearly watching them for the wrong reasons. Enjoy!

Savate (a.k.a. The Fighter)

1994 (Prism DVD R2) (djm)

"Damn Frenchman's good!"

Former real-life French commando Olivier Gruner followed up *Nemesis* with this unusual western/martial arts film. He plays Charlemont, a foreign legion officer in 1865, who goes AWOL and ends

up in the US. The people of the old west don't take very kindly to him. He gets waylaid by bandits, who kill his horse, but he makes short order of them with his savate (French kickboxing) skills. A kindly brother and sister (Ian Ziering and Ashley Laurence) take him in, and he helps them with a problem they have: A greedy and wealthy landowner (R. Lee Erme) wants their land, and everyone else's land in the area, too. Erme's best man, Mitchum (Michael Palance), is not up to Charlemont's skills as a fighter, but he doesn't have to be because he's a quick draw. This being a straight-to-video movie from the 1990s, there has to be a kickboxing match thrown in somewhere to get the rentals. So, yes, there's a kickboxing match ("the tough man tournament"), and the winner gets $500, which will help the persecuted landowners pay a nasty tax to get the greedy landowner off their back. Gruner enters the contest, and his arch nemesis, a sadistic monocle-wearing German played by a hammy Marc Singer, is his only real competition. Their final fight is memorable.

The director is Isaac Florentine, who later made *Bridge of Dragons* with Dolph Lundgren, *The Shepherd* with JCVD, and films with Scott Adkins, Michael Jae White, and Gary Daniels. Clearly, Florentine has a taste for martial arts and action films, and it shows. His films are usually a cut about the rest, and *Savate* is better than average. It showcases Gruner's unique style, and these were the days before quick cutting, so everything is on the table in full view. Gruner's big setback is his soft voice with a thick accent. He looks great on screen, and in this film he's shirtless most of the time. Typical. The score by Kevin Kiner is very good.

INTERVIEW:

ISAAC FLORENTINE (djm)

One of the best filmmakers in the action and martial arts film market is Isaac Florentine. With over a dozen feature credits directing the likes of Olivier Gruner, Michael Worth, Shannon Lee, Michael Jai White, Jean-Claude Van Damme, Gary Daniels, Bryan Genesse, Marko Zaror, and Scott Adkins, Florentine has built an impressive resume in a dying niche market where he still continues to nurture up-and-coming action stars. His films have very strong foundations in the martial arts, and fans of these types of films are able to recognize Florentine's flare for directing and deeply appreciate his style.

Director Isaac Florentine. Photo by david j. moore.

S

At what point did you realize that you wanted to become a director?

I always loved movies. I grew up in a country where there was no TV station. In small-town Tel Aviv, there were theaters everywhere. Because the movies had subtitles, it didn't matter what language it was in. You go and judge the movie by itself. I stumbled onto spaghetti westerns as a kid. I remember when I saw *The Good, The Bad, and the Ugly*. It was the music that caught me. Then you see the closeups and the wide lenses, and you see the sweat on their faces. It was monumental. It was totally new. Because it was so new visually, I got interested. I wanted to know what made it so different from the typical American movies. It's the style. For a child, the style is something abstract. My brother said, "Look, there's a director behind this." I started to dive a little bit deeper into movies. Later came the exploitation and blaxploitation movies. Charles Bronson was big in Europe. *Violent City* and *Cold Sweat*. Those movies had the biggest impact on me, the Italian films. They captivated me. When I finished high school I went into the army. When I finished the army, I went to a university. I wanted to study cinema. I enlisted with the film and television department. I remember when the first kung fu movie came to Israel—it was *Five Fingers of Death*. I saw it and I did not like it. It was bad movie making, the fights were terrible, it was too violent and too cheesy. I remember thinking, "I don't think I ever want to see another kung fu movie." By then, I was already training in karate. Then, *Fists of Fury* came out. I remember my teacher saying, "This is a good movie." There were articles in *Black Belt* magazine about Bruce Lee. I went and I saw it, and it was then called *The Chinese Connection*. This movie really changed my life. I was blown away, but not by the story. By Bruce Lee. By his charisma, his persona, and of course, the fight scenes. It was like "Wow!" It was a revelation. I walked home, and it was like walking on clouds. At that point, I wanted to try and do a martial arts movie. I used to go and watch other martial arts movies, and I would write on a pad the fighting techniques, and try them later in the dojo. .

How did your first film *Desert Kickboxer* come around as an opportunity?

One of the reasons why I went to film school —this was the early '80s—video was really at its infancy. One way to do a movie was on 16mm. One of my goals in going to film school was to do a short film. I knew that if I was a good student, that the money for the film would be covered by the university. After three years, I came up with a script that was an action script. You have to understand that the environment where I came from—especially then—students were very pretentious, they all felt that they were the next Fellini or Bergman. I was the only one who was there who had short hair, went to karate school, and wanted to do action movies. I didn't come as an intellectual. I came with a certain goal to see if I could do action movies. I was a black sheep, but I was accepted. So I wrote a script, and in order to get the funds—and some of the funds come from the Ministry of Commerce—and

they said, "What is this? It's like a comic book." They were used to dramas and political movies. They didn't think I was serious. I was rejected. My teachers at the university went back to those people and said, "Look, before you reject him, watch his work. Go and see some of his shorts he did while he was a student." So I was called again, and I showed them my short—one, two, three minute movies—and they liked it. They had a certain look and feel. I got the funds to shoot my script called *Farewell, Terminator*, which was a futuristic thing. It was very cheesy. It was influenced by Walter Hill's *Streets of Fire* and *Mad Max*. It was a twenty-seven- or twenty-eight-minute movie. I shot it with a Bolex camera. All the sound was put in later. The movie was done, and I put it in a festival, and I was sure that it wouldn't win anything. I was lucky. It was a grueling day at the festival seeing movie after movie after movie—they were all political and inspired by Fellini. By the end of the day people were tired, and when my movie came on, it was an action movie from beginning to end. It was refreshing. The audience loved it. Two days later, the results were announced, and my movie took all the prizes from the festival. Suddenly, I was in all the national papers and on television. The movie was getting exposure, and one of the people who saw it was Menaham Golan. At that point, I was running my karate school. I was thinking what would be next. I didn't want to be teaching the same thing—how to close a fist, how to stand—to white belts. We live only once. I wanted to do what some people call stupid action movies, and my wife reluctantly said yes. I tore her up from her dream and brought her to America. One of my students knew a producer here and an actor named Paul Smith. I met Paul and his wife—he opened his house to us, and he tried to hook me up with some producers he knew. Putting egos aside, I started as a floor sweeper as a production assistant. I started to make my way into the industry. I became a fight choreographer. I even played a double for Ray Sharkey on a movie. Menahem remembered my movie *Farewell, Terminator*. I wrote a western called *Savate*. To shoot this movie, it would cost about a million and a half. I felt this in my gut. I needed to come up with something that would cost two to three hundred thousand. When I met Menahem—this was after Cannon was closed—he had a company called 21st Century. Menahem came to me and asked me if I had an idea for a movie, I said yes, and that's how *Desert Kickboxer* happened. This was in 1991. I was standing next to an elevator, and I realized, "I am going to make my first American feature." It's a low-budget movie. The guy that was the DP was a guy who was with me when I was in high schoo—he photographed my student film. I remember Menahem's partner came to me on the set before shooting the movie, and he said, "Isaac, you know something: Let's elevate the script from two hundred and fifty thousand to three-eighteen." It's a big bump! I had sixteen days to shoot. I call my friend, and he said, "With this kind of movie, don't even think how much you'll earn, because you earn nothing. Say yes to everything."

This is how Desert Hawk—that was the original title—was done. One of the terms of the movie was that I had to bring Paul Smith

into the movie because he could sell it. I went to Paul, and he told me it's a war to make a movie, so it's better to go to war with your friends. It's really true. We shot it in Vasquez Rocks. I shot it in July when the nights were short. My decision was that no matter what I would finish on time and on budget. I'm always committed to that. It takes ten years to build a reputation and only ten seconds to destroy it. We finished the movie, and HBO bought it on the spot. They were very happy with it, but they changed the title to *Desert Kickboxer*— - what a terrible name!

The title was of its time. Kickboxer movies were in. So that led to your next film, *Savate*, starring Olivier Gruner.

Yes. By then, it was already written. That movie was influenced by a few things. I told you that I liked spaghetti westerns. Second, I am a history buff. I love history. How could I come up with an angle that wasn't just martial arts, but also a western? Savate was a martial art that was developed in the 1820s. Napoleon III had already opened a school to teach his officers self defense, and savate was taught there. Charlemont was an officer in the French army in Mexico in 1865, and he comes to Texas after the Civil War, and it's a great period. You can combine the western with a European hero with French martial arts. It's a great opportunity. I wanted to do it as a spaghetti western. I wanted to homage Charles Bronson from *Once Upon a Time in the West* with the harmonica. This was the story behind *Savate*. How did this movie happen? Every movie I've done until now I say it's a miracle. After *Desert Hawk*, the producers of *The Power Rangers* brought me to work on the series, and they gave me carte blanche. They told me to experiment. If it doesn't work today, shoot it again tomorrow. I was the fight choreographer, second unit director, and later I became the main director. That season with carte blanch experimenting really brought me up. You can think of things to push the envelope. Shooting stuff in reverse, split screen, forced perspective. This was the pre-CGI age. At that time, a producer took an option on my script of *Savate*. I got a phone call that they wanted to do the movie. I had a dilemma in that I had to leave the series. It was a dream. I went and did the movie. It was done for a million and a half. Since everyone wants to be in a western, I was able to bring R. Lee Ermey, who wanted to ride horses. Same thing with James Brolin.

Talk a little about working with Olivier Gruner, who was pretty new at the time. He had already done *Angel Town* and *Nemesis*. *Savate* and these two movies are still his best movies, and he agrees with that as well.

First, Olivier is a great guy. Warm heart, but he's a tough guy. He came after doing *Angel Town*, a movie I really loved. The fact that I come from a martial arts background cuts a way for me talk with actors. Why? Because there's a way of shooting action, and there's also a way of communicating. If you're talking to a director who knows your craft like you know it—I train avidly, every day—when a director goes to do an action scene, they are sometimes hesitant on how to do it. Olivier liked the character.

He loved it. He understood that it would be an opportunity to do something different. The concept of doing action when I came to America was that you shoot a master and then you cover it. For me, coming from a different point of view, I use every frame of footage. I edit before I shoot. Olivier had seen other directors shoot a master. But when it comes to action, you cannot shoot a master of a fight because A, the camera will not be in the right place, and B, people will get tired because the technique looks sloppy. I told Olivier that I wasn't going to shoot masters, and he wanted me to shoot masters because that's the way the other directors had done with him. In the beginning, I shot one master so that he would feel good. Then I said, "Fine. Let's do it my way now." Slowly, slowly, he started to see that it was working. He was new, also. He needed to feel comfortable. Something about Olivier is that he had a military background. There's a fire scene in the movie, and I had Ian Ziering in the movie, and he got excited during the fire scene, and he accidentally hit Olivier straight in the nose, and he broke it. There was such a crack. It was a short shoot, and such a low budget, so Olivier decided to keep shooting even though the whole side of his face was swollen. The next day, we shot him in profile.

***Savate* and all of your other movies haven't gotten theatrical releases. Any comment on that?**

Test screenings are an industry standard. We can do a test screening anywhere in the United States, and you will more or less get the same grade anywhere you do it. It's pretty accurate. When we did *Undisputed 2*, it was test-screened. It scored very high, something like eighty-nine percent in favor. The target audience was eighteen to twenty-five. It's a genre movie. For

Director Isaac Florentine on the set of *Undisputed III*. Courtesy of Maroody Merav.

Mykel Shannon Jenkins, Scott Adkins, and Isaac Florentine on the set of *Undisputed III*. Courtesy of Maroody Merav.

Marko Zaror (left) and Isaac Florentine (center) on the set of *Undisputed III*. Courtesy of Maroody Merav.

sure, it would go to theaters. We had a studio behind this movie. New Line Cinema was behind it. New Line was at the meeting, and they wanted to put it in over a thousand theaters. They gave it over to their specialists to figure it out. We did another screening in New Jersey. Same results. They wanted to show it on 800 to 1,200 screens. My movie was going to theaters. It was approved by New Line, and an hour later, it was disapproved. What happened in that hour . . . people from the film department came and said that they had vetoed it in favor of going to the video department. A movie that they had just released in theaters called *Running Scared* with Paul Walker was a big flop. They didn't want to look bad with another flop. It was a big revelation for everyone. Avi Lerner, the producer, went back to New Line and said that he wanted to take it to theaters. New Line said, "No problem." But if they were going to do that, they wanted this amount of money for us to get the rights back. He said, "Okay." He brought it to Harvey Weinstein, who was surprised that a black guy was not behind the camera, but a Jewish guy. Harvey really liked the movie, but he didn't want to pay anything up front. So Avi went back to New Line, and they released it on video. It was a great release. They did an amazing release.

It must have been a big enough hit for it to warrant another sequel.

Yes. There was a festival—and I didn't know that movies like this could go to festivals—it was in Action Fest. Nu Image pressed for *Undisputed III* to be released at the festival. The movie wasn't supposed to be at the festival because it had distribution. The festival liked the film. The company that released *Ong-Bak* came to me and told me that *Undisputed III* was the best martial arts movie they had ever seen. They wanted to take it to theaters. But it was too late because it was already with the other end of Warner Brothers, which now had New Line. That distributor wanted to get it from Warner Brothers, but they said no. They didn't want this movie—which was supposed to be a video release—to be picked up by another company and released to theaters. They mishandled it. The *LA Times* did a review, and it had a full-color page in the Sunday calendar section.

In the late 1990s, there was a significant shift in the action movie world. Guys like Stallone, Seagal, and Van Damme, who had been big box office draws, were suddenly making direct-to-video movies. I feel like the action movie world suffered. What do you think happened during this period?

Here's what happened: Video was hot, especially DVD. It was very profitable to do something that would go to the DVD market. For instance, it was good economics—this was something I learned with Nu Image—if you're doing a movie that costs "X" amount, let's say three million, you have to spend another eight million if you want to see it in theaters. Now, if you put the same movie in the DVD market, it will make six to seven million. So you have a profit of three to four million. If you're going to spend another eight million for it to be in theaters, you have eleven million you have to recoup. This movie can flop or it can succeed and succeed big. Why take the risk when it's obvious you can make the profit on video and keep going? This is how Nu Image used to operate until the video market died, which is why Nu Image is now doing big movies because it's the only way to survive.

So the little movies are obsolete now.

They're obsolete! All of the companies that used to do little movies are obsolete. In many ways, I am The Last of the Mohicans. Why can I survive? Because I've done so much, and I have a reputation and I have a following. I've seen other filmmakers and even actors . . . when the silent movie died . . .

So movies like *The Shepherd* aren't going to be made anymore, is that what you're telling me?

Who knows? The market is now in limbo. All of those illegal downloads . . . *Undisputed II* was released almost a year after it was released in Europe. *Ong-Bak* was released almost a year after it was released in Europe. By then, everybody and their mothers had seen bootlegs of these movies. I remember when I did *Ninja*, I went to Israel and I saw bootleg DVDs of it at the market.

What are the numbers for the revenues for a movie like *The Shepherd*? I've never been able to find the statistics for movies like that.

I know that *The Shepherd*—at least what I heard from Moshe Diamant—went straight to DVD and was one of the biggest grosses for Sony's straight-to-DVD market.

How much did *The Shepherd*, for example, cost to produce?

I think it was something between nine to twelve million.

Really?!

You have to understand one thing: Jean-Claude is a star, and he gets a chunk.

Nine to twelve million? I can't believe that.

I couldn't believe it either. For me, as a director, I never ask, "How much does it cost?" I ask, "How many shooting days are there?"

Do you shoot on film or on digital?

Now I shoot on digital. The last movie I did on film was *Ninja*. After that, I started shooting on the RED. But back to *The Shepherd*, I asked why there were so few shooting days. What's going on here? I shot it for thirty-two days, and I was supposed to shoot it for thirty-six, something like this.

That sounds okay.

Not when you do action. Especially when you do intricate action. When I shot *Undisputed II*, I was supposed to have thirty-six days. And then, I get a call one day, and I heard that New Line was going to distribute it, and they gave me a few more days. For *Undisputed III*, I shot for thirty-two days with one unit. You feel the crunch.

It seemed like in the 1980s and early 1990s, anyone who had martial arts abilities or muscles could have their shot at making an action movie and build a career from that . . .

I'll tell you why. The video market was so hot that you could do garbage and you could get picked up and keep making movies.

It's getting more rare for that to happen these days. That's why when a guy like Scott Adkins comes around, it's amazing to me that he can make it and keep starring in movies.

You're right. Menahem Golan gave chances to people like Van Damme and many others. Scott is a different story. Around 1998, 1999, I opened a company with a friend to document martial arts—or martial arts aficionados. We used to get a lot of VHS tapes, and we'd see people who were good actors who could not move, good martial artists who could not act, bad martial artists that could not act, or martial artists who were martial artists per se, but there is something that they lack, which is screen fighting, which is a totally different art than martial arts. One day came a VHS, which my partner saw, and he said, "Isaac, you should see this!" I said, "No, no, I'm not interested." He said nothing; he was very polite. By the end of the day, he came to me and said, "I think you need to see this guy." I said, "Okay, quickly." he puts on the VHS, and I'm sitting there and watching it, thinking, "Okay, he looks good, good physique . . . now let's see his martial arts. Hey, the guy's good. Now lets see how he does with screen fighting . . . Whoa! He knows the tricks of the trade. Wow, he's really good. Can he act?" Then come dramatic scenes. "Wow!" So I call him and leave him a message. "I don't know you, or whatever, but I would love to work with you." I took the tape to Boaz Davidson and showed it to him. Then, we said, "Okay, let's give him a role in our next movie!" That movie was *Special Forces*. It's not a bad movie. He comes in and steals the show. This is how Scott started with me. I trusted him so much, that when the

Boyka character was created for *Undisputed II*, I wanted to bring him. Everybody thought I was crazy. He's a small guy, he's British, he's good looking, how could he play a big Russian guy? I believed in him. My editor, whom I had worked with for many years, told me that I was killing my career. Boaz told me, "I trust you, but I think you are doing a mistake." I said, "Boaz, I trust Scott." I told Scott, "Don't shave or cut off your hair. Let's see what you can do." We cut his hair, and we found his character. We raised his shoes a little bit. We put him in a thick jacket that made him look bigger, and we put a thin jacket on Michael [Jai White] to make him look smaller. The scenes where they are together, Michael didn't have shoes on, and Scott had the pair of shoes that made him taller. You cheat.

Scott has got some moves, that guy.

He's got some moves. He's the whole package. He's got a great gymnastics background, he's got martial arts and has done them since childhood. He knows the genre. He was a stuntman in Hong Kong, so he knows the tricks of the trade. I also had to fight for him when I wanted him for *The Shepherd*. Sony didn't want him. They said no. We had to make the role smaller for them to say yes. Jean-Claude was worried about him at the beginning. The fight was supposed to be much longer. He wanted it to be shorter. He came to me afterward and said, "Isaac, I made a mistake. He makes me look great!" By now, they've done four or five movies together.

I liked *Ninja*. Talk about that one.

Ninja was not a good movie. The story doesn't work. The problem is that the hero is too much of a hero. He has no weaknesses. Problem number two is that the baddies were some kind of a cult. Nu Image had done a movie in Bulgaria called *The Code* where the baddies were Russian mobsters. They were supposed to be the villains in *Ninja*, but Nu Image didn't want to do the same thing again with *Ninja*. It was changed to a cult. I knew in my gut that it wasn't right. Also, *Ninja* was done on purpose like comics. Computer generated, and I think I pushed the envelope too far and made mistakes. If you don't make mistakes, you never learn.

I like the film because it brought me back to the Cannon days—the *American Ninja* feel of action movies.

Yes. Sam Firstenberg, the director of those movies, is my best friend.

You also worked with Gary Daniels on *Cold Harvest*. Talk about that one.

The thing with those guys like Gary is that they had a potential. Scott has potential and I hope he becomes a big star. What happened with Gary is that in this city [Los Angeles], most of the people that you meet worry only about their butts. They don't want to take risks with actors, with directors. Why? If you're sitting in a studio with a good salary, and you are about to hire an actor or a star or a director, you're taking a bold risk if you decide to hire a "B" movie actor or a

"B" movie director, and the movie flunks, you're out on the line and you're kicked out. But if you take a risk on the best commercial director or the best MTV director . . . What happens is that people go with names, the for-sure names. Therefore, people like Gary, who has the look and the moves, never had a chance. I get this. They niche you. I met Ed Pressman for the remake of *Bloodsport*. It was supposed to be a five-minute meeting, but we sat for two hours. I hooked him up with Robert Mark Kamen, who wrote the script for it. I was booted out. I was told that the studio would not approve me. I understand that. This is the way of the world. That doesn't mean that it doesn't frustrate me, or whatever. The minute that they niche you . . . this is the way it goes in this town.

Any particular memories about making *Cold Harvest*?

This was my first movie with Nu Image. I shot it in South Africa. We shot it nights on skid row Johannesburg. I didn't know that nights in South Africa can be freezing cold. It was a thirty day shoot. I was promised thirty-six, but unfortunately it got down to thirty days. You do what you can. It was hard on the crew. It was a tough movie. In those fights, I brought in Akihiro Yugi Noguchi as the fight choreographer. I worked with him on *Power Rangers*. His team is as good as the Jackie Chan team. They did a lot of stuff in Japan. Amazing. People don't know how good they are. It was a great experience. It was a pleasure working with Gary. Let's compare him to Olivier. When I worked with Olivier, he didn't so much understand angles. Gary understands the camera. He knew exactly which lens, where to put the camera. He understood how we were going to cut it. He came from Hong Kong movies, so he understood what we were going to do. Scott is the same way.

What do you think of these *Expendables* movies that are giving these guys the exposure that they've so long been denied?

I think it's wonderful. Look—ha!—they deserve it. You said it yourself. They *deserve* it. The mainstream—they don't know. Occasionally a movie like *The Raid* comes into the mainstream. Why is it in the mainstream? Because the producer knows that he can release it the way that he wants it. It gets exposure in film festivals, and then it goes to theaters. They are about to do an American remake of *The Raid*. I met the producers. Why did I meet them? Gareth Evans, the director of the original, said that he was inspired by my *Undisputed* movies when he did *The Raid*. So I met those guys. Of course, they go with a different director, and of course they don't want to make it into a martial arts movie, and of course they want to take stars and get them doubles. So why do you want to make a remake of a movie like this? Why do you call it *The Raid*? What attracted people to that movie is that those guys do everything in the movie. Why do people like my movies? Because those guys are doing everything. Once you understand martial arts and you understand cinema, you can do it and it's safe. Yes, they're busting their butts and they're working hard, but they're willing to do it. It's rewarding for me for all of those years that I invested in martial arts. Everybody is willing to go the extra mile—the whole crew. When we did *Undisputed II*, for instance, the first movie that Scott did in Bulgaria, the crew didn't know him. The first weeks, we only shot dialogue, dialogue, dialogue. For the crew, it was cold, snowing, whatever. We went to the studio to shoot the action by the third week. I remember I'm thinking I wanted to prepare the crew for Scott because I knew it would change the energy. I told Scott, "Show them what you are going to do." Then he does this amazing flip, and everyone quiets down. The people realize that the fights in this movie will be totally different. You could see the energy coming. That was it. Suddenly the motivation of the crew was high.

Talk about working with Michael Jai White on *Undisputed II*.

Michael is for real. There're a few guys, in a sense like me, who are karate geeks. He knows the history of martial arts. He does traditional karate, one of the few, and boxing, and he's doing it amazing. And he's a very good actor. I knew him years before. He once came to a screening I did of a movie called *High Voltage*. Out of the blue. Just to see it. Always a gentleman. I didn't see *Undisputed* in theaters. I love Walter Hill. When Nu Image came to me to do *Undisputed II*, I told them I watched the first one and that the people who did it really love boxing. I went to Nu Image and told them I would do it as a mixed martial arts movie. They didn't know what that was because it was just starting. Boaz trusted me and knew I knew action, so he told me to do what I wanted. Then, I said I wanted to bring Michael Jai White as the lead. I brought him, and they looked at him and they weren't sure. I said, "He's the guy—he's perfect!" When I'm talking to Michael, it's completely different than I how I talk to other actors because we're into the same movies. "In this scene, you are like Lee Van Cleef in *For a Few Dollars More* . . . Do this and this." Here's the thing with Michael. He's an amazing martial artist, but we had to hold his horses because he's a boxer in the movie. He cannot kick. Even at the end when he's using some mixed martial arts, we had to limit him. It wouldn't work if he's suddenly doing those amazing kicks. He got to do it in *Blood and Bone*.

You worked with Van Damme on *The Shepherd*. Say something about working on that film with him.

In 1998 or 1999, one day I'm sitting at home, and there's a phone call. "Isaac, this is Jean-Claude Van Damme. I got your phone number from Sam Firstenberg. I love your films. Let's meet." I said, "Sure, no problem." Here we are an hour later in Chatsworth. The ice was broken. I speak French, he speaks French. I'm coming from karate, he's coming from karate, we know the same people. We became friends. My wife and kids know him. So when *The Shepherd* came, it was an opportunity to work together. We worked with people we trusted on this movie. Jean-Claude is one of the hardest-working people I've ever worked with. Did you see *JCVD*? Amazing movie. He made it after *The Shepherd*. I think

he deserved an Oscar for this movie. I think he shines in this movie because it's in French. It's easier for him. He has no fear.

You also worked with Dolph Lundgren on *Bridge of Dragons*.

I met Dolph in Sweden in 1979 or 1980. It's a long story. He was working as a bodyguard or a bouncer at a nightclub. Years later, nineteen years later, Nu Image wants to do a movie with Dolph—this was my second movie with Nu Image. I fly with the producer to New York. We get to the office, and Dolph is looking at me. He starts to recognize me. The ice breaks. He studied at MIT. He's superintelligent and supernice. The thing is, people coming from the martial arts are usually nice people. Martial arts are about honor and discipline. In order to become a good martial artist, you have to put ego aside. The same with Dolph. It was a pleasure. The biggest compliment he game me was after three weeks of shooting. He had just made a movie with John Woo called *Black Jack*. He said he enjoyed working with me more than he enjoyed working with John Woo. That for me was a big compliment. That was the first movie Nu Image made in Bulgaria. All of this white hair you see on my head is from that movie. It was totally new. In Hebrew you say, "Somebody is learning to shave on your beard." Ouch. That's this movie. If we would do it now, it would be a much better movie.

I'm a little confused about your involvement with *Max Havoc*. Albert Pyun is credited as the director, but you had something to do with it, right?

Here is the story with *Max Havoc*. The movie was done. The producer came to me and said, "Can you help me here? I cannot sell it like this." I told him that I would help him on the condition that my name would not be on it. What I did was shoot a little bit of the beginning, some scenes in the middle, and a little at the end. The majority of the movie was Albert's. Everybody was fighting everybody before I came. I was brought as a gun for hire to connect the movie together. We brought Richard Roundtree and David Carradine. You can never fix something that is broken. You can fix the car, but the bump will always be there. The one good thing about this was that the fight choreographer was J. J. Perry. I knew him years before. I looked at the fights in this movie and they were good fights, but they were not shot right. Albert must have only had time to do the master. I brought J. J. to *Undisputed II*. Now he's one of the top choreographers in Hollywood. Same thing when I brought Larnell Stovall for *Undisputed III*. They never really had the chance before. I believe in giving people the chance. They can flourish.

What do you hope to do in the future?

I love this genre. I'd like to do stuff that has more layers historically. More period pieces related to the genre. In many ways, a lot of the contemporary stuff being done is synthetic and is being recycled. Remember, I'm a gun for hire. When I get the script, I am the carpenter who has someone else's blueprints. I get to build the cabinet. I can try to fix the crooked road before we build it: "Let's fix it."

I think there's a need for the movies you do.

I remember Michael Jai White and I were talking about it. Audiences love a genre movie, what I call a matinee movie. Horror films have their audience, but action audience can captivate everyone in the world. There's a good, there's a bad. The good doesn't have to always be good. He can be someone with his own sense of justice, but it's the right thing to do. I think it gives some kind of satisfaction to people around the world.

Sci-Fighters
1996 (Image DVD) (CD)

In the year 2009, Detective Cameron Grayson (Roddy Piper) is on the trail of master criminal Adrian Dunn (Billy Drago). The thing is, Dunn is supposed to be dead and no one wants to believe Grayson. As Grayson tries to piece together the puzzle, he befriends Dr. Kirbie Younger (Jayne Heitmeyer). She is studying a strange virus that has been found in a recent rape victim. Once the evidence becomes clear, Grayson must find Dunn before the criminal hurts anyone else. Dunn, fresh from escaping a prison planet, is out to pay back Grayson for their turbulent history. If Grayson can defeat his own personal demons, he just might be able to get that revenge he craves and save humanity in the process.

The title *Sci-Fighters* isn't really a good representation of what the film is about. It's a science fiction/action hybrid with some great makeup effects and terrific performances from the three leads in the film. It's not exactly all action, but time was taken to flesh out characters and give careful consideration to the plot and pacing. Roddy Piper (*Back in Action*) as Grayson, a damaged man who tries to forget his past by submerging himself in work, turns in a really solid performance. Aside from gunplay, he has a couple of short (but fun) fight scenes. He plays incredibly well off actress Jayne Heitmeyer (*Hawk's Vengeance*) who injects some brains and beauty into the story. Billy Drago (*Delta Force 2*) gives a truly incredible performance as a despicable man who has become a monster. He's frightening and sort of sad at the same time. His character also goes through a physical transformation. He's a strange-looking man to begin with, and with the added makeup effects, he quickly becomes someone many of us would fear. It may not have nonstop action but *Sci-Fighters* is really good entertainment that has slipped through the cracks. Directed by Peter Svatek.

S

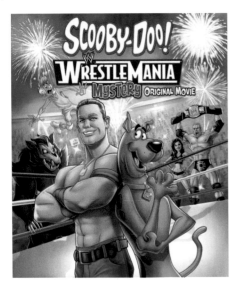

Press poster for *Scooby-Doo! WrestleMania Mystery*. Author's collection.

Scooby-Doo!
WrestleMania Mystery

2014 (Warner DVD) (djm)

Scooby-Doo, Shaggy, and the rest of the gang team up with WWE's biggest contemporary wrestlers for this breezy (and fun!) animated original movie. The gang wins tickets to see WrestleMania live at WWE City, and even though Fred, Daphne, and Velma aren't really "into" wrestling. Scooby's and Shaggy's enthusiasm for the whole enterprise fuels their trip. Something is amiss right away when they roll their mystery van into WWE City: A horrific "ghost bear" is plaguing the city and by all evidence it is trying to make sure that WrestleMania doesn't happen this year. The gang teams up with John Cena, Mike "The Miz" Mizanin, Paul "Triple H" Levesque, and even the scary Kane (a.k.a. Glenn Jacobs) to help them solve the mystery of what (or who) the ghost bear is.

An all-star roster of voice talents bolster this cash tie-in (directed by Brandon Vietti) to WWE wrestling, and seeing bulked-out animated versions of each wrestler makes this Scooby adventure worth watching. Dads and their impressionable sons and daughters can share a bucket of popcorn and watch this without flinching. Even Vince McMahon, the mascot of WWE, makes an appearance. In the mid 1980s Hulk Hogan lent his image to an animated series called *Hulk Hogan Rock 'n' Wrestling*, but he did not provide his voice talents to it, which is why I don't cover it in this book.

Scorpion

1987 (Mill Creek DVD) (djm)

"Do you have stock in this newspaper, or something? It says you're a hero again."

Steve Woods (played by Tonny Tulleners) is a hero of a bygone era. He is a Vietnam vet who once led a rescue mission to reclaim POWs, and now as a federal agent, he's the guy they call when no one else can do the job. He lives on a houseboat, he wears short shorts, he has a porno mustache, wears big black shades, and he knows some serious karate. He's the real thing. When he's called in to quell a terrorist takeover of a grounded airplane, he boards the plane without a weapon, is yelled at by the terrorists, and in a split second, he's handled the situation with such ease and speed that it's some kind of movie miracle that he doesn't even attempt to deliver a one-liner, a quip, just something to make light of what he just did, but he's not that guy. He walks off the plane, and gets on with his life . . . until the next job. The next job has him overseeing a team that is supposed to protect a valued witness, a Middle Eastern terrorist who will be leading the government to a major terrorist organization, and when that goes bad and ends up with Steve's best friend dead, Steve, with his laser determination and his ability to get any job done despite his feelings (which he has), catches up with the culprit responsible for his friend's death. I should also mention that Steve is the kind of guy who wordlessly tosses his gun aside when he has the opportunity to use his bare hands and feet to kick their ass instead of shooting them.

A wonder to behold, *Scorpion* is exactly the sort of movie that guys like Astron 6 and hipster filmmakers like to parody and glorify when commemorating '80s action films. It's got an amazing synth score, some unbeatable moments of macho cool, and the star—Tonny Tulleners—looks like the Marlboro Man. Tulleners, who lamentably never made another movie, is the only man on Earth who beat Chuck Norris three times in martial arts competitions. How's that for a moniker? I love everything about *Scorpion*. Tulleners, with his rough edges and unseasoned acting capabilities, should have made a dozen more movies, but he would have always been in Chuck's shadow, which is an irony I cannot comprehend. This was from Crown International. William Riead wrote and directed it.

Scorpion

2008 (Anchor Bay DVD) (djm)

"That night, I made up my mind to change myself, to turn myself into a nightmare, to become a lean, mean, winning machine. An uncaged animal. To rekindle the noble art I possessed, and all that bullshit. To hit and hit and smash with all the rage inside me, to scorch whoever's in my way, to transform into a beast, to truly become the scorpion."

Angelo (played by French actor Clovis Cornillac) is a highly skilled Muay Thai boxer, but when his trainer chooses a lesser fighter to represent the gym in an underground fight tournament, Angelo alters the course of his destiny by fighting the other fighter in a street fight, resulting in the other man's death. Angelo goes to prison for six years, and when he gets out, he squanders away six months in a drunken stupor. He ends up getting the attention of a strip-club owner who remembers him from years ago, and he offers him the chance to regain his honor by fighting for cash in underground bouts. When Angelo manages to rekindle his mojo by getting into impeccable shape and great fighting condition, he fights hard, winning every fight and works his way up to a champion UFC fighter named Elias (played by real UFC fighter Jerome Le Banner), who senses that Angelo might give him a run for his money in the ring. When the final fight is on, Elias shows Angelo respect even when it looks like he might lose, but at the last second, everything changes . . .

While I was watching *Scorpion* (which is in French, by the way), I could have sworn Clovis Cornillac was the real thing, but he's just an actor. When I realized I'd made a mistake by focusing on him, I quickly rebounded and tried to focus on Le Banner, who has had an illustrious and impressive fighting career. He was interesting, too, but his role was pretty diminished in the film, which was obviously about Cornillac's character. I enjoyed the film either way, and despite some heavy-handed thematic material about a girl Angelo is interested in, the film is dramatically even and has some great fight scenes in it. The final fight climax was great, and I liked the way it panned out. If you're a fan of Le Banner's fight style and personality, you may be disappointed by how little he's in it, but if you stick with the movie to the end, you'll be rewarded. Directed by Julien Seri, who made the French films *Yamakazi* and *The Great Challenge*, both of which deserve viewings.

Scorpio One

1998 (RHI Entertainment DVD) (CD)

"Tell me, Wilford, are your spy boys ever going to figure out what the hell's going on before another American dies on this thing?"

Space station Scorpio One is in turmoil when the entire crew ends up dead and things appear to have been sabotaged. The government needs to know what happened, so they decide to send up a new group of astronauts, including Jared Stone (Jeff Speakman) and his team. The shuttle launches without a hitch but as soon as it docks on Scorpio One, everything quickly begins to fall apart. Power is lost, people are killed, and no one seems to know who the culprit is. Stone quickly finds a disc containing the information people were killed for. An attempt is made on his life, but he narrowly escapes. Commander Wilson (Steve Kanaly) can't believe someone from their team is behind it. Stone has to jump into action if he wants to save everyone before their oxygen runs out.

Director Worth Keeter (*L.A. Bounty*) had spent a lot of time working on various incarnations of *The Power Rangers*, so it's a shame there wasn't more action in *Scorpio One*. It plays out mostly like a political thriller with a few quick action scenes near the end. When Speakman (*The Perfect Weapon*) starts to swing his fists, things begin to pick up. He's rather good in the film and his fights are solid. Only his fans should seek this one out.

Sea Wolf (a.k.a. Pirate's Curse)

2005 (Platinum DVD) (djm)

Towards the end of Thomas Ian Griffith's career as an action star, he starred in two adventure movies: *High Adventure*, in which he played Allan Quartermain's grandson, and *Sea Wolf*, in which he is a likable modern pirate, descended from a long line of pirates. With a sinking love life and a group of bad guys on his trail over a theft of a stash of diamonds, Jeffrey Thorpe (Griffith) takes a job offer from a beautiful woman who needs him to find buried Mexican gold that once belonged to Montezuma. With nothing to lose, he embarks on the quest, and instantly finds himself in trouble again when the woman turns out to have an evil twin sister who tricks him. This gets him caught by the same group of villains who were after him in the first place, and he finds himself stuck in a situation where he's forced to dig up the treasure while also digging a grave for himself. Luckily, the woman who hired him saves his life, and the movie has a happy ending.

Extremely lightweight for an action movie, *Sea Wolf* is almost a made-for-TV movie quality film, but exotic locations and a fun, energetic performance from Griffith help save it. Griffith, who is best known for embarking on a promising martial arts action career following his stellar breakout film *Excessive Force* couldn't seem to maintain that career trajectory and took on supporting roles in bigger movies and starring roles in action-ish movies like this one where he wasn't required to use his martial arts training but only asked to run, jump, and avoid getting shot. I like *Sea Wolf*, but most people who watch it will have no idea whatsoever that Griffith is a much-valued (in my eyes) talent who has been criminally underused in movies. South African director Mark Roper has worked with a number of action stars including Bryan Genesse and Gary Daniels. He also directed *High Adventure* with Griffith.

Second in Command

2005 (Sony DVD) (djm)

In Moldavia, a crisis is brewing. A new president is elected to the Eastern European country, and a militia rises up to depose him and assassinate him. A former Navy SEAL named Sam Keenan (Jean-Claude Van Damme) is called in on a favor to come to the US embassy and lead a rescue mission to the presidential palace, secure the new president, and bring him back to the embassy. Once the president is safe in the embassy, Keenan fortifies the embassy and prepares for an imminent attack from the outlying militia who begin using RPGs and blunt force tactics to lay siege to the stronghold. Waiting for reinforcements from the United States Marines, Keenan and a dozen US Marines hold the fort down as the embassy is pummeled. Facing opposition from within the embassy by bureaucrats and a dwindling supply of ammunition, Keenan and the Marines hunker down and prepare to fight with everything they have to stay strong and keep the President alive.

After *Wake of Death*, Van Damme's direct to video efforts picked up steam, and *Second in Command* is the beginning of a long stream of solid titles he starred in. This and *Wake of Death* are really where his comeback started. It took a while, but once his fans picked up on the fact that he wasn't messing around anymore with junky movies like *Desert Heat* and *Derailed*, Van Damme became the best and hardest-working action star in the direct-to-video market. While relatively small in scale and set in and around one central location, *Second in Command* is what Van Damme needed at a crucial point in his career to gain traction. His next one was even better: *Hard Corps*.

The Secret Agent Club

1996 (Platinum DVD) (CD)

"This toy business, it's cutthroat."

Ray Chase (Hulk Hogan) comes off as nothing more than an overgrown oaf with a good heart. His wife passed away several years ago and all he has left is his son, Jeremy (Matthew McCurley). Jeremy never gets to spend much time with his father since he's always on business trips for his toy-making business. What Jeremy doesn't realize is that his father is moonlighting as a secret agent, working on classified missions and keeping the world safe. One day his dad arrives home with a highly dangerous ray gun that he took from vicious female arms dealer Eve (Lesley-Anne Down). She sends her cronies to apprehend Ray and steal back the ray gun. Jeremy then discovers his father's secret and must round up his friends so they can risk their lives to save his father.

The Secret Agent Club is mostly a derivative effort that will only appeal to youngsters. Hulk Hogan (*Mr. Nanny*) seems to be enjoying himself, though, and has a few watered-down fight scenes, including one with Richard Moll (*Sidekicks*). The special effects don't look particularly special and much of the over-the-top humor tends to be a bit much. The film does have some heart, and Hogan has a solid chemistry with child actor McCurley. This is a blemish on Hogan's film career, but the kids will love it. Director John Murlowski (*Automatic*) manages to create a low-budget *True Lies* clone for the little ones.

The Secret of King Mahi's Island

1988 (NOV) (djm)

Eclipsed by '80s treasure-hunting classics like *Jungle Raiders, The Further Adventures of Tennessee Buck,* and *Hunters of the Golden Cobra*, this completely ignored and forgotten movie starring martial artist and future *Expendables* co-star Gary Daniels isn't nearly as bad as some might assume. Daniels (in his first starring role) plays a mercenary/adventurer named Chuck, who joins a woman on a trek through the jungle to find a lost treasure before some bad guys do. They encounter killer natives and plenty of pitfalls, all while traversing deadly landscapes including a murky Amazonian river, as villains race them to recover the treasure first. Daniels uses his martial arts to dispatch plenty of guys who deserve it.

Shot in the Philippines, *The Secret of King Mahi's Island* is strictly for fans of *Raiders of the Rip-Offs*-type movies. It's just over sixty minutes long, with a lengthy prologue and set-up. There's enough action to keep it moving. If you want to see where Gary Daniels started, feel free to seek this one out. Directed by Jim Gaines.

S

Sector 4: Extraction

2013 (Lionsgate DVD) (djm)

"A mercenary who gives a fuck . . . "

After Nash (played by French martial arts star Olivier Gruner) and his team of mercenaries are called in to pull off a deadly mission in Iraq, the entire team is captured by al Qaeda, except for Nash, who makes it out alive. He goes back home to his family with his head hanging, and his family situation is bad enough that his own wife asks him to knock on the front door next time he comes home. With unresolved issues back in Iraq, he decides to go back and rescue his team all by himself, but first he has to get his head in the game and train (and train *and train*) to get himself in the best shape of his life. Once he's ready and has been given the blessing of his "boss" (played by Eric Roberts), Nash goes to Iraq, buys guns from gunrunners, and risks all kinds of exposure when he enters enemy territory. With the intel he has, he infiltrates the al Qaeda compound, kills some bad guys, and saves the few members of his team that are still alive after the rest of them have been tortured and murdered.

A surprisingly strong entry for star Gruner (who also directed), *Sector 4* gives him a great vehicle to show that he's still in the game. Now in his 50s, Gruner has seen the highs of action stardom with great movies like *Angel Town, Savate,* and *Nemesis*, but then he was relegated to starring in some terrible direct-to-video action/sci-fi films that barely showed what he was capable of. Gruner, a real-life French special forces soldier before becoming a kickboxing champion, has always been the real deal as far as action stars go, and *Sector 4* has a hint of realism to it, and it shows a glimpse of his own personality, which has always been a rare thing to see in his movies. I really enjoyed this one, and if you've been waiting for Gruner to find a solid vehicle to star in, check this one out. It's a definite step in the right direction for him.

See No Evil

2006 (Lionsgate DVD) (djm)

WWE wrestler/personality Kane (real name: Glenn Jacobs) was given his shot at the big screen in the slasher *See No Evil*, which casts him as the relentless, emotionally damaged killer Jacob Goodnight. He dwells in a decrepit hotel, where a bunch of young adults are performing a day of community service. The kids are all in for a night of adrenaline-charged terror as Goodnight hunts them down one by one, plucking their eyes out and keeping them as trophies. Most of the kids are pretty defenseless against the hulking killer, and even their police escort falls prey to their psychopathic host.

Certainly not an "action" movie by any standard, but notable for starring a WWE athlete who has a large following, *See No Evil* is a pretty unpleasant stalk-and-slash movie (produced

by WWE Films), even by standards associated with these types of movies (which I generally appreciate). Kane is featured in all his hulking glory, and he's pretty scary as an unstoppable killer. He was also featured in a small role in the spoofy action movie *MacGruber* a few years later. Director Gregory Dark made a name for himself in the adult film industry and in the world of music videos. Followed by a sequel, also produced by WWE Films.

See No Evil 2

2014 (Lionsgate DVD) (djm)

Set just hours after the events of the first film, Part 2 takes place at the morgue in the middle of the night as mass murderer Jacob Goodnight (WWE's Glenn "Kane" Jacobs) is wheeled in on a stretcher along with his dozens of victims (see Part 1 for that). Only three people are on duty: Amy (Danielle Harris), Seth (Kaj-Erik Eriksen), and a wheelchair-bound attendant (played by Michael Eklund). Amy is about to celebrate her birthday, and Seth is still working up the nerve to ask her out, and when Amy's friends surprise her at the morgue with an impromptu birthday party, the night should be fun . . . until Jacob Goodnight rises from his slab to resume his killing spree, turning out to be a major party pooper.

Not as hyper-stylized as the first film, and not nearly as fast paced or "fun," Jen and Sylvia Soska's *See No Evil 2* is a downbeat, depressing, and generally lackluster riff on the first film, giving Kane his chance to throw young adults around like they're toys. Since Kane hadn't done a starring vehicle film in the eight-year hiatus since the first film, it might be accurate to assume that he's a one-trick pony with these slasher movies (which are basically variations of *The Terminator*). He's a huge beast, and he has presence on screen, but he deserves better

material to star in. If there's a *See No Evil 3D*, I hope Jacob Goodnight's remaining eye comes flying out at the end.

INTERVIEW:

GLENN "KANE" JACOBS (djm)

A WWE superstar, Glen "Kane" Jacobs has amassed a fan base by portraying a villain people love to hate. He made his crossover into films with the slasher picture See No Evil *(2006) from WWE Studios, and his movie career stalled until he made a brief appearance in the spoof* MacGruber *(2010). He reprised his role as the killer Jacob Goodnight in* See No Evil 2 *(2014) from WWE Studios and the directing team Jen and Sylvia Soska, and his future in films is up in the air, as he is considering a career in politics (he's a devout Libertarian supporter of Ron Paul). Whatever is in store for Glenn Jacobs, action and horror fans have more Kane to fear with* See No Evil 2.

What can horror fans expect from *See No Evil 2*? Has anything changed that we should watch out for?

It's beautifully shot, and also I think this time Jacob has . . . the story . . . even though Jacob's mom is the villain, it delves a little more into Jacob's mind. You understand why he does what he does. I think the characters are very well rounded. I think this one has a little more emotional depth than the first movie did. Even though the first movie was good, this one's pretty great.

It's been a while since the first *See No Evil*. Were you ever thinking that a sequel was not going to happen?

I didn't really. I was surprised it took this long because the first movie was a commercial success for WWE Studios. It did pretty well. I was surprised when a year went by and then a couple years, and *Oh, forget about it, they're never going to do another one.* Then I just got a call out of the blue. I was more than surprised; I was shocked.

Would you want to steer towards doing more movies or politics?

(Laughing.) I don't know. Okay, earlier I was asked this question: "Which is scarier—horror movies or reality?" Reality is much scarier, okay? I have a lot of fun acting, I really do. I find it rewarding in a different way than wrestling. At the end of the day, at WWE, what we're trying to do is we're trying to entertain people. We want people to have a good time, and that's very rewarding to me, to have that opportunity. The politics deal . . . you're dealing with scumbags most of the time. Yeah, so . . . I don't know, I really don't know. I'm probably just going to stick with acting. But maybe not, who knows? The door's always open.

Would you be down for playing different kinds of characters, say in an action movie rather than another *See No Evil* type of film?

I would. One of the things that the [Soska] twins and I really lobbied for was for Jacob not to be more the silent type, who never says anything and just walks around and that's it. We wanted him to have some emotional depth, and for him to have some dialogue, and to find out what's going on inside his head. Not only does that make the movie much better, but to me it's much better because he's not just a stunt guy they stick a mask on. No offense to anyone. With Kane, he's a very dark character often. But the most fun I've ever had as Kane is when I did stuff with Daniel Bryan. I went from being the meanest guy, the darkest guy on the show to being the funniest guy on the show. As a performer, or as a wrestler, it's that variety that really keeps you going. When it gets to the point where you could almost do something in your sleep because you've done it so much, that's not as much fun or a challenge intellectually. If they say, "Here's something completely different that you've never done before: Can you pull it off?" That's where things become interesting.

Did anything strange or out of the ordinary happen on the set of *See No Evil 2*

I think the set [an old abandoned mental institution] had a lot of history. Everybody on the crew who'd worked there before . . . *X Files* had filmed stuff there, and they all had a story. The creepiest one, was that one day there was a little girl on the set, and everyone's talking to her and stuff, then someone goes, "Who's girl was that?" She was gone, and it wasn't anybody's little girl. Yeah. You hear these stories.

Can you talk a little bit about the differences between Gregory Dark who directed the first film and the Soska twins, who directed you in this film?

Sure. Gregory directed the first movie, which was shot in Australia. We had a really great crew. I've been blessed to be surrounded by such great people in both movies I've done. Gregory was more of a behind-the-camera, technical guy. The difference with the twins is, you have that aspect of that, but then you have one of them who is out there with you. At first, I thought, *Okay, we're going to have two people direct this movie—how is that going to work?* It's the kind of deal where they almost finish each other's sentences. The one behind the camera is like psychically telling the other one out there on the set to tell everyone what to do because they're so connected. They don't have to say anything out loud! Seriously! You'd be getting notes from the one on the set with you, but they weren't talking to the other one! The one behind the camera would say, "Okay that was perfect, let's move on." *How does that work?!* I think they're great, and they keep telling me not to say this, but they're great and wonderful. They're great students of the game. Their enthusiasm excites me. Frankly, anytime you go on to a project like this . . . I think we shot for fifteen days . . . so everything is (slapping his hands) like this, and

you get behind schedule, but they were the ones who weren't stressed, they were the ones who kept everyone going. They kept the ship afloat. I have nothing but good things to say about them. They're huge WWE fans. When we met, they were freaking out, and I was like, *This is not good.* But then they got that out of the way, and they were great, they were fantastic.

Have you ever entertained the possibility of directing a movie yourself?

I wouldn't know what to do! Way down the road, maybe. It's just a different way of expressing your creativity. Maybe at some point. I don't think I quite qualify to do that. (Laughing.)

7 Seconds

2005 (Sony DVD) (CD)

" . . . places to go, people to kill . . . "

Professional thief Jack Tulliver (Wesley Snipes) has put together the perfect team to pull off a daring heist. Everything seems to be going smoothly when they are unexpectedly foiled by an opposing group that was somehow tipped off to their plan. His crew is killed off, but Tulliver narrowly escapes with his life and with a sealed briefcase with the goods inside. He highjacks Sergeant Kelly Anders's (Tamzin Outhwaite) car and makes a clean getaway. When Anders reports back to her superiors, they suspect she may be in on it. She's angry and heads out to clear her name while Tulliver begins to follow any lead he can in order to learn the truth about why he and his team were set up. They'll both accomplish their goals only if they trust one another and team up . . . which in these types of movies leads to some interesting conflict.

For a direct-to-video thriller, *7 Seconds* is able to hit all the right notes without any trouble. Wesley Snipes (*The Expendables 3*) is comfortable in the role and appears to be having a good time. The film is bookended by two solid car chases through the streets of Bucharest, Romania. Snipes brings wit and cockiness to his character, which is something that his fans are likely going to enjoy. Though the fight scenes are on the short side, they're exciting for what they are. Snipes has a fun banter with co-star Tamzin Outhwaite (*Great Expectations*), and their chemistry is good. Director Simon Fellows (*Second in Command, Until Death*—both with Jean-Claude Van Damme) delivers a straightforward (and fun) action flick that delivers in all the right places.

Shadow Man

2006 (Sony DVD) (djm)

A semi-retired ex-intelligence agent named Jack Foster (Steven Seagal) is teaching martial arts in Asia and enjoying a fairly quiet life with his young daughter until the day he takes

a trip to Eastern Europe with his daughter. She's kidnapped virtually in front of him, and he spends the next few days going after the government spooks and mafia thugs who are trying to leverage his daughter for a little cylinder with a prototype virus he has (and was hired to hand-deliver, which is why he was in Eastern Europe). The female agent hired to kidnap his daughter realizes that she was working on the wrong side, and she turns coat and helps Jack recover the girl before time runs out.

On the surface, *Shadow Man* is just another crummy direct-to-video hack job for Seagal, but if you look just a little past the terrible DVD box art and the generic story, you'll find that it's actually one of his better post-theatrical career films. He's entirely present in the movie, appearing in nearly every scene, and when he gets to engage in fight scenes it looks like him, and it looks good. There are some interesting character development moments throughout the film, and I really like the way the movie allows him to actually seem like a person rather than just throwing another government spook profile at us through other government agent characters' conversations. He's not just a "shadow man" like the title would suggest, but a martial artist instructor who can crack a watermelon open with his chi (it's all established early on, but it works). Also, the movie has some other good actors like Eva Pope as the attractive hit woman/kidnapper agent who seems to grow as a character the longer she's allowed to be on screen. Also in the picture is Imelda Staunton as an ambassador who has a couple of scenes with Seagal (just one where they're actually captured on camera together, though). Ultimately, *Shadow Man* is the movie *Skyfall* should have been. Yes, *Skyfall*, the worst James Bond movie ever made. There's some stuff in here that reminded me of *Skyfall*, but everything in *Shadow Man* was better. In one scene Seagal makes a shotgun out of household appliances to kill a bunch of armed bad guys who think they have the drop on him, and it's a pretty badass scene. In *Skyfall*, James Bond made explosives out of a shotgun and some light bulbs, but it was stupid. Also, in *Skyfall*, Bond cries when his boss, M, dies in his arms. In *Shadow Man*, Seagal doesn't cry, and even if Imelda Staunton's character died in his arms, he wouldn't cry. He'd put her aside and go break some arms. *Shadow Man* is a better movie than *Skyfall* hands-down. Directed by Michael Keusch.

Shadow Warriors (a.k.a. Assault on Devil's Island)

1997 (Platinum DVD) (djm)

A group of Navy SEALs are assigned a mission where they must save a group of US gymnasts who were kidnapped by a South American drug lord named Carlos Gallindo (Billy Drago). The SEALs are comprised of Mike McBride (Hulk Hogan), Roy Brown (Carl Weathers), and the beautiful Hunter Wiley (Shannon Tweed), and their leader McBride is a bit of a blowhard when it comes to socializing and going by the book.

When he gets angry, he's a gung-ho warrior, with two guns blazing. When they capture Gallindo, they take him to his compound where his henchmen (played by Trevor Goddard and Billy Blanks) are keeping the gymnasts in a watery dungeon. Hoping to make an exchange, the SEALs are given the full henchman-revenge treatment as they go to war against them.

Made for cable and outfitted with a relatively low budget, *Shadow Warriors* is sort of a pilot movie for a franchise that only lasted one more film. As a vehicle for Hogan, it's adequate, but it's interesting to note that he's playing the role completely straight without a trace of humor, which is different for him. He looks to be in great shape in the film, and his usual golden locks are dyed brown, which is also unusual for him. His co-stars Weathers and Tweed (who has a nude scene and prances around in a bikini and/or panties and bra often) are good company to have in this otherwise standard entry. Martin Kove also shows up for some scenes as their ally. The highlight of the film is a fight scene between Hogan and Billy Blanks, who is underused here. Name confusion for this film is well deserved: Some video releases have given this film the title *Shadow Warriors 2*, which is very confusing because it's the first film in the franchise.

Shadow Warriors 2 (a.k.a. Assault on Death Mountain)

1999 (Spartan DVD) (djm)

Former SEALs Mike McBride (Hulk Hogan), Roy Brown (Carl Weathers), and Hunter Wiley (Shannon Tweed) have quit the military and formed a mercenary group, and their first job as a team involves the rescue of a young girl kidnapped by a millionaire living in the Alps. After their daring rescue, their next mission is to stop a terrorist (Gerald Plunkett) from bombing several US cities with a new gas toxin. McBride, who is having trouble staying focused due to some PTSD trauma, is captured after he goes rogue, and he is injected with the toxin, putting him in a deeper funk. His pals (who include Martin Kove as a likable weapons supplier) rescue him, and they save the day.

Slightly better than the first *Shadow Warriors*, this one has a strong rescue scenario for the first thirty minutes, and when their next mission kicks in, it becomes a little tedious because we've seen this sort of thing so many times before. Hogan, who is deadly serious to the point of being hilarious, looks strung out and fatigued throughout the whole thing, and his dyed-brown locks give him a heavy-metal rocker look. The biggest surprise of the film is Shannon Tweed, who amazingly outclasses and outfights anyone else in the movie. If it hadn't been for her reputation as a soft-core porn star, she might have made a formidable action heroine. Sequel confusion continues to plague this series. This entry, although the second in the series, is sometimes known as *Shadow Warriors*. DVD releases have confused the continuity of the two films in the series, so let these reviews set the record straight.

Shanghai Express (a. k. a. The Millionaire's Express)

1986 (The Weinstein Company DVD) (djm)

Part screwball comedy and part East-meets-West action film, *Shanghai Express* takes place in the early 1900s and has Sammo Hung (who also directed) playing a likable bandit on the run from the law. He ends up in a western town, a crossroad of fates where a "millionaire's express" train is due to dock. On the train are three Japanese samurai who have stolen a priceless work of art, and on their trail is a horde of bandits, amongst them Richard Norton and Cynthia Rothrock. The town has gotten wind that trouble is coming their way, and the townsfolk elect a sheriff (Yuen Biao from *Above the Law*) to help them maintain order. Once the train arrives, all hell breaks loose, and we get to see some nice fights. Rothrock and Hung have the best one.

Hung is equally talented behind and in front of the camera. His comedic timing and martial arts prowess are impressive. Biao (who is essentially the hero of the film) plays a one-note character, so it's hard to care about him, but he performs some incredible stunts here. The real reason why this film is important is because of Rothrock's and Norton's small contributions to it. They both have very little screen time here, but they are memorable, and without them the movie would suffer. This isn't essential to fans of action and martial arts films, but fans of Rothrock and Norton should pay attention.

Shanghai Knights

2003 (Touchstone DVD) (CD)

Chon Wang (Jackie Chan) has made quite a name for himself as a sheriff in Carson City, Nevada, when a package arrives from his sister Chon Lin (Fann Wong) with news that their father has been murdered. Picking up from the plot of the first movie, *Shanghai Noon*, Chon travels to New York to visit his pal Roy O'Bannon (Owen Wilson) and collect his share of the reward money from his previous adventures. He wants to use the money to get to London, England, where his sister has tracked their father's killer. Of course, it isn't as easy as it sounds, and they soon find themselves in London looking for Lord Nelson Rathbone (Aiden Gillen), who is the man responsible. They learn that he's been working with Wu Chow (Donnie Yen), a man from Wang's past who wants the Imperial Seal—the same seal that Wang's father died protecting—for himself. Without Roy O'Bannon by his side, Chon Wang may let revenge consume him but, together, they have what it takes to set things right.

Shanghai Knights is the sequel to *Shanghai Noon,* and Chan and Wilson energetically reprise their respective roles here. It tops the original in almost every way. The first film was a terrific attempt at bringing Chan to American

cinemas, and this one just cements how well this particular formula can work for him. The only thing that keeps it from being a perfect film are the lackluster final fights. If he had been facing anyone other than Hong Kong action legend Donnie Yen (*Iron Monkey*) at the climax, then it would have been more acceptable. Instead, just as the excitement builds, it's over far too soon (in 2004 the legends faced each other once again in *The Twins Effect II* with a better end result). Chan's other fight scenes in the film are incredibly fun, paying homage to some of his previous films as well as Fred Astaire. At this stage, he was still the king at mixing comedy with action. Many will still prefer his Hong Kong output, but the *Shanghai* films are perfect introductions for new audiences to see what he can do. His foil, Owen Wilson, is just as funny in this one as in the first. He has great comedic timing and knows exactly how to deliver a line with the right amount of cockiness. Joining Chan and Wilson is Fann Wong (*Dance of the Dragon*) as the lovely and deadly Chon Lin, who also has an eye for O'Bannon. She actually has several rather impressive fights in the film, and her character has a strong will and is highly motivated to avenge the death of her father. While somewhat similar to the first film, *Knights* really delivers a fun, entertaining time. There's no reason why it won't leave you with a smile on your face.

Shanghai Noon

2000 (Touchstone DVD) (CD)

> "You've almost killed me like seventeen times already . . . eighteen, nineteen, twenty. You're on fire today!"

Chon Wang (Jackie Chan) is a Chinese imperial guard tasked with locating and rescuing Princess Pei Pei (Lucy Lui), who has been kidnapped and taken to the American west. He feels

Shanghai Noon theatrical release poster. Author's collection.

responsible for the incident and needs to make things right. In Nevada, Wang comes close to finding her when he is sidetracked by likable outlaw Roy O'Bannon (Owen Wilson) and his band of robbers. The two men reluctantly team up only to find out that they are wanted criminals. The crooked Marshall Van Cleef (Xander Berkley) is hot on their tails, and to make matters worse, he has teamed up with Lo Fong (Roger Yuen), Pei Pei's kidnapper. The ransom is ready to be paid in gold, but the problem is, it's the old west, and the rules are not what Wang are used to.

Shanghai Noon is one of Jackie Chan's most entertaining films shot and released for the American film market. It's a perfect family-friendly popcorn film that keeps the laughs and action rolling at a blistering pace. Owen Wilson (*Behind Enemy Lines*) has a certain type of charm that's perfect against the fish-out-of-water Chan. Chan never strays too far from his comfort zone, creating action scenes that are both exciting and funny. It has always been a specialty of Chan's to mix humor with action, paying homage to the likes of Buster Keaton and Charlie Chaplin, and this film is no exception. There are some great set pieces that showcase his talents but it's not until the finale when things really get amped up with his battle against Roger Yuan (*Bulletproof Monk*). Even Lucy Liu (*Kill Bill vol. 1*) gets in on the action, if only for a short bit. As Princess Pei Pei, she is more like a damsel in distress for much of the picture, but she shows her true strengths later on. The old west setting brings out an entirely different vibe from Chan's previous buddy film *Rush Hour*, even though it's virtually the same premise; it just works much better here. It really felt like Chan had more behind-the-scenes control this time out and that inexperienced director Tom Dey (*Showtime*) was in a position to follow his lead. With a fun western-inspired score (by Randy Edelman) and a couple of heavier tracks from the likes of Aerosmith, Kid Rock, and ZZ Top, *Shanghai Noon* is one incredibly fun stroll through the old west with two great compadres.

Shark Alarm (a.k.a. Shark Attack in the Mediterranean)
2004 (Image DVD) (CD)

Ever since the violent death of his wife by a giant shark, Sven Hansen (Ralf Moeller) has been struggling. One day things take a turn for the worse when a body is found that appears to have been mauled by a shark. Sven finds a gigantic tooth near where the body was found, identical to the one found in the body of his wife. He takes the tooth to the proper authorities but no one believes his story about a supposedly extinct thirty-five-foot shark (known as a Megalodon) being the culprit. He quickly finds out that there's more at stake than he realized and someone out there is willing to kill him so no one finds out. With the help of marine biologist Julia Bennet (Julia Stinshoff), it's a race against time to stop the gigantic beast from terrorizing their beaches and to expose the cover-up before anyone else gets hurt.

It may be low-budget, cheesy, and at times just plain ridiculous, but *Shark Alarm* is pure fun. With crazy shark movies at an all-time high, *Shark Alarm,* starring former Mr. Universe Ralf Moeller (*Best of the Best 2, The Bad Pack*), fits in nicely with the trend. The version available in the United States is horribly dubbed, but it doesn't matter because the film offers plenty of excitement with car chases, Moeller tossing around security guards, giant CGI sharks eating people, and a helicopter dueling the beast. Moeller is far better than what he's given to do here, but you can't go terribly wrong with this one.

Shark Lake
2015 (Screen Media DVD) (djm)

Small-time criminal and negligent father Clint Gray (Dolph Lundgren) is arrested after a sloppy car chase where he drives his van into Lake Tahoe. He's promptly sent to prison for selling exotic animals on the black market and for putting his daughter Carly in harm's way. Five years later and with a better outlook on life, Clint is paroled, and he's humbled that the tough female cop—Meredith Hernandez (Sara Malakul Lane)—who arrested him adopted his daughter Carly (played by Lily Brooks O'Brient) and is doing a damn fine job being a mother to her. All Clint wants from Hernandez is an opportunity to meet with his daughter and try to make amends, but knowing the kind of man he used to be, she keeps her distance from him and tries to get a court order against him. But this is just family drama; there's a bigger issue at stake when Lake Tahoe is revealed to be the buffet bar for a trio of bull sharks who have been biding their time for the right moment to start chowing down on human legs, arms, and whatever else is poking through from the surface. As it turns out, when Clint drove his van into the lake, there was a pregnant shark in the cab, and

Shark Lake press release poster. Author's collection.

now that it's five years later, the mamma shark has been keeping her two offspring company and now's as good a time as any to start the feeding frenzy. With Clint on the path to redemption, and Officer Hernandez on the warpath to save the lake from any more fatalities, the future is pretty bright for these characters.

If you're going to make a movie called *Shark Lake* and have it star someone as towering and iconic as Dolph Lundgren, the very least the filmmakers could have done is have him wrestle with one of the creatures in the same (or similar) way that Richard Keil wrestled and bit one in *The Spy Who Loved Me*. What a showstopper that would have been. But, alas, that wasn't to be. *Shark Lake* is a nice enough time-waster with Dolph going through the motions and giving his slightly interesting role some panache, but all the stuff with the computer-generated sharks is merely adequate. He gets to tussle with one and gets bit on the shoulder, but being the true grit that he is, he winces and passes it off as a flesh wound. The whole look and feel of the movie is strictly direct-to-video with a late '90s feel to it, and that's not necessarily a bad thing. First-time director Jerry Dugan has a difficult time with pacing and giving his movie enough energy to carry your interest, but if you're devoted to Dolph you'll sit there and go the distance despite how pedestrian it feels. He has a nice three-way fight scene with a couple of home invaders in one scene, but other than that, there's not much in the action category. Amazingly, this received a one-week theatrical release, which accounted for three theatrical releases for Dolph in 2015. The other two were *Skin Trade* and *War Pigs*. That's impressive.

Shattered Dreams
1998 (Digiview DVD) (djm)

Mel (Sean Donahue), a security guard, is framed for a crime perpetrated by his co-workers, and when his wife is killed in a car chase, he is caught and blamed for the crime. Sent to prison for three years, Mel is eventually paroled and tries to find a decent job so that he can regain custody of his teenaged son. The same men who framed him once realize that it would be incredibly easy to frame him again for a similar crime (robbery), and when he gets wise to their scheme, he has no one to turn to for help but himself. With a detective on his back (played by Erik Estrada) and a parole officer hovering around him, Mel has to prove that he's always been on the right side of the law . . . or he's going to be framed and sent to prison again.

One of Sean Donahue's "bigger" movies, *Shattered Dreams* has a slightly bigger budget than his previous films like *Parole Violators* and *Blood Hands*, but it's not as interesting or as distinct as those. He engages in some fun action scenes (the one in the wine cellar was pretty great), but the movie looks suspiciously underpopulated and could use some more extras in the background. Sadly, this was Donahue's final starring vehicle. He also directed it.

Shattered Lies

2002 (Arts Alliance DVD) (CD)

"Talk? Maybe later, that comes after the cigarette. That Viagra you took while you were still out should be kicking in any time now. Betcha never been raped before, huh Roger?"

Mia Reed (Elizabeth Giordano) is a cop . . . sort of. She spends her time pushing papers but it's not what she wants to do. The only way she can make things happen is by going behind her superior's back and try her hand at an undercover sting. She dresses as a hooker and heads out to the streets where she picks up a man who calls himself John Smith (Frank Zagarino from *Striker*). She quickly learns he isn't who he says he is when they're attacked at a hotel by two men. When John finally comes clean to her, she learns that there's three million dollars out there waiting for the taking. He needs Mia's help to find the money but his motives might not be what they seem.

Shattered Lies may be Frank Zagarino's (also in *Deadly Reckoning*) masterpiece. It has several car chases, shootouts, explosions, fist fights, a Zag-oatee, and some very pretty ladies. It's easy to see the chemistry between Zagarino and Giordano—they seem to be at their most natural and are having fun together . . . it's no wonder that they're a married couple in real life. I'm not sure if it was music supervisor Steve Edwards who did the bizarre rap songs in the film but they must be heard. If those weren't enough, we even get a panty-sniffing, bisexual female villain who gives a man Viagra and rapes him (it's implied, never shown). Zagarino abandons his Zagarate for boxing as his go-to fighting style and he seems almost energized by this. With cameos by Martin Kove, Jack Scalia, and James Russo, director Gerry Lively brings to life a fantastic example of the perfect "B" action film.

The Shepherd: Border Patrol

2008 (Sony DVD) (djm)

Jack Robideaux (Jean-Claude Van Damme), a homicide cop from New Orleans, relocates to New Mexico and becomes a border patrol agent. He's a man of few words, and his superior and others around him aren't sure what to make of him. Right away, he gets into a mess involving a rogue special forces unit that has plans to smuggle in millions worth of heroin from Mexico, and when Jack becomes the wrench in their plans, they set their sights on him. He's captured and tortured, and when he breaks free, he is the only thing stopping them from accomplishing their goals.

From director Isaac Florentine (*Desert Kickboxer, Ninja*), this surprisingly cinematic entry with Van Damme is a thoroughly entertaining direct-to-video effort. Van Damme really puts himself out there with this one: He gets into lots of close-quarter fights, and his

final fight with Scott Adkins, who appears as one of the lead villains, is excellent. This was the first time Van Damme and Adkins appeared on screen together. Later, they co-starred in *Assassination Games, The Expendables 2,* and *Universal Soldier: Day of Reckoning.* Florentine's sure directing hand gives *The Shepherd* an added touch of pizazz, and fans of his will be very happy. It feels like a theatrical production most of the time. Van Damme's next film was the pseudo-documentary drama where he played himself—JCVD.

Shinjuku Incident

2009 (Sony DVD) (CD)

"Who do you live for? Your brothers? Your ex-girlfriend? Or for me?"

Steelhead (Jackie Chan) is an illegal immigrant living in Japan. He spends his time working odd jobs and running from the police. His old pal Jie (Daniel Wu) takes him in, and they live together with other Chinese immigrants. While on a job, Steelhead finds himself in the middle of a raid but then happens to save the life of Inspector Kitano (Naoto Takenaka), who promises to do him a favor one day. Steelhead's life changes when he realizes he must resort to crime in order to get ahead. He moves up the ranks and enters into a deal with the Yakuza, and then everything begins to fall apart.

This was a huge departure for Jackie Chan and not everyone seemed to be on board with his portrayal of an immigrant turned mobster. This is really a strong performance by Chan and he proves once and for all that he's more than just a stuntman. The character may not have been particularly well written, but he's able to give his character an extra dimension. He basically abandons the persona we all know and love, even getting down and dirty in a rare sex scene. Since this is a gangster flick, there's plenty of graphic violence. Without any stylized action, this is meant to be more realistic and in your face (where else will you see Chan hack off an arm with a machete?). Derek Yee (*The Great Magician*) struggles a bit to keep the film compelling through its two-hour runtime, but overall he succeeds at delivering something Chan can be proud of.

The Shinobi Ninja

1981 (Burbank Video VHS) (djm)

"It is quite possible that that man is a ninja!"

An ancient feud between two Japanese ninja clans has stretched into the 1980s, and the US government calls in Ken Suzuki (played by

American Ninja's Tadashi Yamashita), the last of the Koga ninja clan, to put a stop to the Ega ninja clan's reign of terror. The Ega clan has been targeting US spies and slaughtering them in the field for their top-secret information, and only Suzuki can save the world. Suzuki hesitantly works with two other US agents—Lee (Eric Lee from *The Weapons of Death*) and Smith (Karen Sheperd from *Blood Chase*)—and as a team they manage to slay the Ega horde intent on killing them.

For the most part, this is a corny early '80s ninja movie that predated the ninja craze started and perpetuated by Cannon, but it's a great showcase for Tadashi Tamashita, who would later be recognized for his work in *Gymkata* and *American Ninja*. Co-stars Lee and Sheperd are also given plenty of fight scenes, and the best one is in the snow, where they kick-fight a bunch of skiing ninjas. This would be an easy target for *Mystery Science Theater 3000*, but as is, it's pretty outlandish and absurd already. Directed by Luk Chuen and Syuji Gotho.

Shootfighter:
Fight to the Death

1993 (Columbia Tri Star VHS) (djm)

"In shootfighting—as in nature—only the strong survive!"

The VHS world craved a movie like *Shootfighter*. It was meant to be. Young Ruben (William Zabka from *The Karate Kid*) runs a small martial arts studio, where his seifu Shingo (Bolo Yeung) teaches him and other students martial arts. Things are a little rough for Ruben because he borrowed too much money to keep his studio running, and now thugs are harassing him and his girlfriend (played by former Bond girl Maryam D'Abo). Ruben's best friend Nick (Michael Bernardo) comes to town to help him out a little bit, and they get a mysterious invitation to fight in a "shootfighting" match south of the border for several thousand dollars. They go and win their matches, but something's going on that they don't realize: Mr. Lee (Martin Kove), who runs the illegal matches, has a lifelong grudge against Shingo, and he's using Shingo's students to lure him to the ring, where Mr. Lee was once disgraced in front of an audience by Shingo himself. As Ruben and Nick become locked into more fights, the danger quotient is upped considerably as the fights become more vicious and deadly—hearts are ripped out of chests, necks are broken, throats are slashed with blades, and so forth. With the understanding that only one man will become the champion, Ruben and Nick are forced to fight each other to the death . . . but Shingo arrives just in time to challenge Mr. Lee in exchange for a reprieve for his two students.

Pretty gory for a chop sockie '90s kickboxing-type tournament movie, *Shootfighter* surprised me when it started getting extreme and never looked back. There's a good cameo by "B" action star John Barrett (from *American Kickboxer 1* and *To the Death*), and when he's brutally dispatched, I was ready for almost anything. The best part of watching this movie is seeing Bolo Yeung be nice to a bunch of children, and he even plays basketball with a kid. He's the hero here, and that's awesome. Zabka became a real-life black belt in Tang Soo Do since appearing in *The Karate Kid*, and you can kind of tell that his martial arts skills improved by the time he made this movie. Directed by Pat Alan, whose only directing credit this is.

Shootfighter 2

1996 (Columbia Tri Star VHS) (djm)

Check out the VHS cover, guys! It's exactly the same as Part 1, only yellow! *Shootfighter 2* is an unfortunate sequel for so many reasons. The first film (made three years earlier) came out right at the cusp of the kickboxing craze. It was about two friends who get into illegal bloodsport matches, and their seifu, played by Bolo Yeung, comes and saves them. This sequel is pretty much a Xerox copy, but glummer, murkier, and more boring. It arrived three heartbeats after the fervor for kickboxing movies died, so it doesn't have much of a pulse, either. Fighters Ruben (William Zabka) and Nick (Michael Bernardo) are approached by a grieving father, whose son died in a "shootfighting" match (a martial arts duel to the death), and the father wants to organize a "sting" within the fight circuit to redeem his dead son by bringing the killers to justice. Ruben

THE ULTIMATE FIGHT TO THE DEATH!

2

SHOOTFIGHTER

KILL OR BE KILLED!

VHS artwork for *Shootfighter 2*. Author's collection.

and Nick's seifu Shingo (Yeung, not as fun as he was in the first movie) advises against it, but they go ahead and enter in the secret circuit anyway. As the plot reveals a big twist (Shingo's younger brother is the head honcho of the illegal fights), the fights carry on, but none of it is even mildly compelling this time around. Shingo comes to the rescue . . . again.

As I was watching *Shootfighter 2*, I kept noticing the villain, played by Joe Son. I'd seen every movie Son was in, and every time I'd seen him, I paid special attention to him for some reason. He had small villain roles in the Lorenzo Lamas movie *Bad Blood*, a Don "The Dragon" Wilson picture, *Bloodfist V: Human Target*, and even one of Dolph Lundgren's movies called *Joshua Tree* (a.k.a. *Army of One*). I looked him up, and I was shocked to realize that he's serving a life sentence without parole for torture and rape, and in his first month of serving his life sentence, he'd killed his cellmate. Pretty grim. When he was acting in all these movies, fighting Bolo Yeung, Lundgren, Lamas, and Wilson, he'd already committed the crime for which he'd be sentenced years later. That's all I could think about while watching this forgettable little movie. I wonder how often Son thinks about it. Paul Ziller (*Bloodfist IV: Die Trying, Back in Action*) directed it.

Showdown

1993 (Imperial VHS) (djm)

Beat cop Billy (Billy Blanks) and his partner answer a domestic disturbance call, and in a scuffle, Billy kills a guy accidentally. He takes it hard, and years later he's living a low-key lifestyle, working as a high-school janitor. He sees a new kid named Ken (Kenn Scott) getting harassed by a bunch of bullies, and he tries to encourage Ken to defend himself. But there's a big problem: The bullies are students of Lee (Patrick Kilpatrick), a sadistic sensei at a local dojo, and it was Lee's younger brother that Billy killed all those years ago. Lee has transformed himself into a mind-controlling master of the martial arts, and his students are conniving and manipulative punks. When Ken tries to befriend Julie (Christine Taylor) at school, he's beat up by her boyfriend Tom (Ken McLeod). Billy takes the initiative and begins training Ken in the martial arts, and he builds him up to a point where he can not only defend himself against Tom, but also beat him at his own game of fighting. It comes to a crescendo when one of Lee's associates tries to lure Ken into an illegal gambling den where young fighters fight for cash, and Ken takes the bait, ending up in Lee's clutches. Billy comes to rescue him, but as it turns out, Ken's abilities have vastly improved and he does his own fighting for himself.

From director Robert Radler, who made the first two *Best of the Best* films, *Showdown* is *The Karate Kid* for the "R"-rated crowd, with brutal, dirty fights and beatings galore. The language isn't too harsh, but it definitely earns its restricted rating with the violence. Patrick Kilpatrick (who played The Sandman in *Death Warrant*) is an evil, love-to-hate-'em bad guy, and Billy Blanks

(from *TC 2000*) is a stalwart good guy, so it's easy to choose a side and pick a team. Young Kenn Scott displays some impressive abilities as a martial artist, and while he wouldn't go very far as an action star, he would much later direct the film *The Adventures of Johnny Tao*, starring Matt Mullins. Watch out for a fun action scene between Blanks and stuntman James Lew at one point in the film. Also, Brion James appears in the film as the school principal.

Showdown in Little Tokyo

1991 (Warner DVD) (djm)

"That's perfect! I'm partnered with a homicidal maniac on a personal vendetta of family vengeance!"

Sgt. Chris Kenner (Dolph Lundgren), a specialist in Japanese culture, is on a case in Little Tokyo, Los Angeles, when he realizes that he might be in over his head. He upsets the Yakuza, which is running a drug empire in LA, and even worse, the head of the Yakuza is Yoshida (Cary-Hiroyuki Tagawa), the man who killed his parents in Japan when he was a boy. Kenner is assigned a new partner—the cocky Johnny Murata (Brandon Lee), who doesn't know a thing about Japanese culture, despite the fact that he's half Japanese. Together, they troll the underbelly of LA, looking for clues to a young woman's brutal murder while getting in the Yakuza's business, which obviously puts them in harm's way. As Murata wisely exclaims in one scene, "This must sound strange for being a cop, but let's get the fuck out of here!"

At only seventy-six minutes long, *Showdown in Little Tokyo* manages to pack everything inside to make it a really entertaining buddy/buddy movie. There's plenty of action, fighting, comedy, sex, nudity, and explosions to fill at least two movies. Mark L. Lester (*Commando*) directed with a tongue-in-cheek attitude, and Lundgren and Lee make a great team. Tagawa is a despicable villain, and the film caused some controversy when it was released because of the negative way it depicts Asians. Two years later, *Rising Sun* with Wesley Snipes and Sean Connery took some flack for the same reason. Many well-known stunt actors like James Lew, Al Leong, Simon Rhee, and Toshishiro Obata have small roles in the film. Brandon Lee made *Rapid Fire* next. The region 1 DVD is full screen, but the region 2 DVD is widescreen.

Sidekicks

1986–1987 (NOV) (djm)

Disney/ABC aired *Sidekicks*, a half-hour show that spanned twenty-three episodes, which was a fantastic vehicle for martial artist prodigy Ernie Reyes Jr., who had previously co-starred in *Red Sonja* and *The Last Dragon*. He plays Ernie Lee, "The Last Electric Knight," the last of an ancient bloodline of superlative karate fighters from a lost village in China. His ailing grandfather Sabasan (Keye Luke) entrusts him to the care of a savvy detective in Los Angeles named Jake Rizzo (Gil Gerard from *Buck Rogers*). When Sabasan passes on into the spirit world, Ernie is adopted by Jake, and the two become "sidekicks" who get into all sorts of trouble together as they stop kidnappings, foil robberies, and find stashes of cash that the mob has hidden. Ernie never says no to a fight, but he possesses wisdom and compassion and an uncanny fighting ability. The ghost of his grandfather visits him to give him wit and witticisms, and he has no shortage of friends (watch for a very young Giovanni Ribisi in some of the episodes).

I love *Sidekicks*. It's a shame that Disney hasn't put it on DVD. It shows a kid in peril every single episode (which might be a problem these days, I guess), but if you grew up in the '80s, it's a must-see—especially if you're a fan of Reyes Jr. who would go on to star in *Teenage Mutant Ninja Turtles II: The Secret of the Ooze* and *Surf Ninjas*. It's very simple programming for young people, but it works. Ain't nothing to complain about here. If you know where to look, *Sidekicks* is available out there as a bootleg.

Sidekicks

1992 (Alliance DVD) (CD)

Barry (Jonathan Brandis) is an awkward kid. He struggles with asthma and spends much of his time daydreaming. He dreams about fighting alongside his hero, Chuck Norris (Chuck Norris). At school, he's constantly being picked on and the girl he crushes on, Lauren (Danica McKellar), feels sorry for him. He lives with his father, Jerry (Beau Bridges), who works hard to make ends meet. His teacher, Noreen Chan (Julia Nickson-Soul), takes an interest in him and brings him under her wing. Barry wants to learn the martial arts so she introduces him to her uncle, Mr. Lee (Mako). Lee sees the potential in him but Barry's daydreams still seem to get in the way of his concentration. When the local martial arts tournament comes around, he decides to enter to prove to everyone that he is growing up and learning discipline.

Sidekicks is a solid family film with plenty of action and lightheartedness for everyone. Who didn't daydream about fighting alongside one of your heroes as a kid? Chuck Norris (*Missing in Action*) recreates scenes from many of his films with Barry in tow. They're laugh-worthy moments that may strike a cord with longtime fans. This means Chuck is fighting the baddies with his fists, feet, and other various weapons (though tamed down for a PG-rating). He does have a rather entertaining tournament-style fight with Joe Piscopo (*Dead Heat*). The film was directed by his brother Aaron Norris (*The Hitman*), who hit all the right marks with this. *Sidekicks* works for the whole family! *Magic Kid*, starring Don "The Dragon" Wilson is similar.

The Silencer

2000 (Trimark VHS) (djm)

Slow-moving and uninspired, this movie about a young punk FBI agent named Jason (Brennan Elliot) who goes deep undercover to infiltrate a terrorist group gets slightly more interesting when he is mentored by a seasoned hitman named Quinn (Michael Dudikoff). When Quinn puts some pieces together and realizes that Jason is with the FBI, he doesn't threaten or want to kill him—he wants to protect him! Evidently, Quinn sees himself as a father figure to Jason, which didn't really work well for the film. Quinn, meanwhile, is trying to nurture a relationship he has with a schoolteacher, and his intimacy and trust issues continue to keep them apart. A showdown with a bad politician leaves Quinn no option other than to sacrifice himself for Jason, but the ending offers some hope that Quinn is still alive someplace.

Unfortunately, this is a completely forgettable film, and Dudikoff, though a little older and wiser-looking, isn't given much to work with. His co-star, Elliot, is too green and pretty to be interesting as an actor, and the plot requires that they bounce off each other a little bit. The tone of the film is a little depressing, and it's a letdown. Director Robert Lee worked with Dudikoff on the cheap futuristic movie *Cyberjack*, another weak entry.

Silent Assassins

1988 (Music Bank DVD R2) (djm)

An LAPD detective named Sam Kettle (Sam Jones) investigates the murder of a Korean family, whose little daughter survived but was kidnapped by the murderers. The murders are tied to another kidnapping: that of Dr. Terrence London, a biochemist with top-secret information on a germ warfare device. The terrorists are holding the little girl and the doctor hostage (they threaten to kill her if he won't comply with their demands), and Sam Kettle begins his investigation in earnest when some kooky things start happening. The terrorists have employed a Playboy-type model (Rebecca Ferratti) to assassinate anyone who gets in their way, and a relative of the deceased family (Phillip Rhee, who also produced) joins forces with Kettle to save the biochemist and the little girl.

Silly, derivative, and hokey, *Silent Assassins* is a cheapjack effort that fails to give either Sam Jones or Phillip Rhee the vehicle that he deserved. Rhee (who would later star and produce and/or direct the *Best of the Best* entries) is more of a comedic sidekick here, and a later scene features him in an intense and impressive fight in a men's restroom. Linda Blair is completely wasted as Jones's girlfriend. Mako has a cameo. Directed by Lee Doo Yong and Scott Thomas (*Latin Dragon* with Lorenzo Lamas).

Silent Force

2001 (Leisure Entertainment DVD) (djm)

Loren Avedon's final star vehicle to date, *Silent Force* is indistinguished and instantly forgettable. At least it's better than his previous effort, *Deadly Ransom*. Here he plays a member of an elite drug enforcement task force known as The Silent Force, and after his entire team and superior are killed by the Asian gang that they've been after, he goes on a killing rampage to avenge his comrades. He has a few close-quarter fights with some guest fighters, and one scene even features Matthias Hues, who famously fought Avedon in *No Retreat, No Surrender 2*.

The entire film is hampered by an overall sense of cheapness and tedium. The plot is barely there, and the characters are woefully underwritten, and even Avedon (who produced) isn't interesting in his role. Some recognizable Asian character actors such as George Cheung (who gets shot by an exploding arrow in *Rambo: First Blood Part II*) help a little bit, but when it's all said and done, *Silent Force* doesn't make much of an impression. Directed by David May.

Silent Hunter

1995 (Image DVD) (djm)

Jim Parandine (Miles O'Keeffe) is a good cop who is with his wife and daughter when a band of bank robbers carjacks them and shoots them all and leaves them for dead. Jim survives, but his family dies. Months later, Jim has retreated to the snowy mountains, where he lives in a log cabin in a small town. The local sheriff, Mantee (Fred Williamson, who also directed), is a single man who has plenty of girlfriends in town, and he's a pretty likable guy. The same bank robbers that we saw earlier come into the town to lie low, but they rob a local grocer of his stash of grenades and kill him, which doesn't do them any favors. They try to use a helicopter to get away, but their chopper crashes in the middle of nowhere, and they hike to the closest cabin they can find, which is where Jim is trying to live a quiet life. He recognizes them, and just at that point, they recognize him as well, so there's really no suspense when they force him to guide them to the Canadian border. On their trail is Sheriff Mantee, who pursues them relentlessly.

A low-rent variation on *Cliffhanger* and the Thomas Ian Griffith vehicle *Crackerjack*, Williamson's *Silent Hunter* is lacking in suspense, star power, and action. I have nothing against Miles O'Keeffe (who isn't an action star by my definition), but the part he plays here would have been better suited to Ian Griffith or Lorenzo Lamas, who both would have added an extra flare for martial arts action. Williamson, who has a glorified cameo appearance, doesn't really do much, but a pivotal scene has him involved in a crucial action-oriented fight with the bad guys. If you're a diehard Williamson fan, I suppose you may want to see *Silent Hunter*, but it's entirely nondescript and forgettable.

S

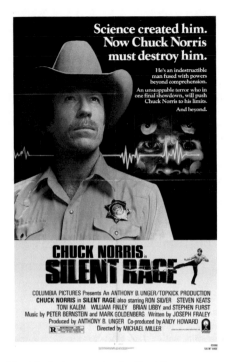

Theatrical release poster for *Silent Rage*. Author's collection.

Silent Rage

1982 (Sony DVD) (djm)

A borderline slasher, *Silent Rage* casts Chuck Norris as Texan Sheriff Stevens, a precursor to *Walker Texas Ranger*. Stevens responds to a 911 call and captures a homicidal maniac (Brian Libby) who had been renting a room in a house. The maniac has been part of an experiment at a nearby research and medical facility, and his doctors (who include Ron Silver and William Finley) have been working on a serum that would help regenerate wounded flesh and organs. When Stevens is forced to put the maniac down, the corpse is taken to the hospital, where it proceeds to heal itself and come back to life. Without letting the sheriff know about it, the doctors continue to pump the killer full of healing formula and when he wakes up he goes right back out to kill again and again. Sheriff Stevens already has enough to worry about in his small town: a gang of bikers terrorize the area and his good-for-nothing partner (Stephen Furst) makes matters worse, so it's all up to Stevens to make the town safe again. The final fight between Norris and Libby (who keeps getting back up after being kicked more times than anyone else in any other movie starring Chuck Norris) ends with Libby getting kicked into a deep well. This being a horror movie by any other name, the killer is still alive when the credits begin rolling.

It's a little odd to see Chuck Norris in a movie of this type. It's a grindhouse flick with a nasty edge, but fans of Norris should get plenty of satisfaction out of seeing him do his kicks and punches ad infinitum throughout the film. He's a slightly more playful and forgiving character here, and he's even willing to tolerate his shlubby partner's antics, which is beyond comprehension. He also has time to play a lothario with a secretary in the movie (played by Toni Kalem), and their love scenes might surprise fans of *Walker Texas Ranger*. An odd hybrid film from the Chuck Norris filmography, *Silent Rage* should be a must-watch at some point. It was directed by Michael Miller, who is best known for directing TV adaptations of Danielle Steel's novels.

Silent Trigger

1996 (Fox DVD) (CD)

"Those who don't remember the past will be condemned to live it again."

A shooter (Dolph Lundgren) is given a job to assassinate a female politician. He and his spotter (Gina Bellman) run into some difficulties and the shooter refuses to pull the trigger. They separate and quickly find themselves on the run and live by their wits to stay alive. Several years later in a high-rise that is still under construction, the two meet again under very similar circumstances. The agency they work for has given them orders, and they're to be carried out exactly as planned. Once again things don't quite work out that way and not only do they have to battle other highly trained marksmen, but they also have two security guards with their own agendas trying to take them out. Even though they are working together, the limits of their loyalty to each other are tested.

Filled with distracting flashbacks, *Silent Trigger* may be a bit uneven and sometimes slow, but it still manages to come off as being a slick and entertaining action film. Director Russell Mulcahy (*Highlander, Resident Evil: Extinction*) injects enough life into it with his keen eye, making it worthy viewing. Lundgren can almost always elevate a film with his presence and that is no different here. His performance is a bit subdued, and he manages to give his character a bit more substance than he may have had otherwise. With his lumbering stature and ultra physical persona, some viewers may be frustrated to see him spending most of his screen time behind the scope of a sniper rifle. There is very little hand-to-hand fighting aside from one brief (but welcome) sequence. Some of the best action moments come during the finale, and there is no skimping on the bloodshed. His co-star (the spotter) is the lovely Gina Bellman (TNT's *Leverage*). Her character is the most fleshed out, as we see her grow from a rookie to a more seasoned pro faced with some very difficult decisions. Also in the cast are Conrad Dunn (*Death Warrant*) and Christopher Heyerdahl (*Highlander: The Final Dimension*), who play the security guards in the building where most of the events play out during the climax. The way the flashbacks are presented detracts from the overall enjoyment of the film, taking viewers out of the main story arc every ten minutes or so. It still manages to be better than expected even if some of the CGI explosions look really bad. The film was originally written and produced as *The Algonquin Goodbye*.

Silverhawk

2005 (Screen Media DVD) (djm)

Rich socialite by day and masked avenger by night, Lulu Wong—a.k.a. Silverhawk—encounters a megalomaniac named Alexander Wolfe (Luke Goss from *Blade II*) whose ambitions to rule the world are cut short when Lulu (played by Hong Kong superstar Michelle Yeoh from *Royal Warriors*) dons her superhero garb and goes to war with him. Using her unlimited resources to help fight crime, she's a virtually unstoppable force, but this time she's got an ally in a popular policeman who also happens to be an old friend. Against them are Wolfe's henchmen—most notably a thug named Morris, played by Michael Jai White. Lots of acrobatic, wire-enhanced, Cirque du Soleil-inspired fights ensue.

Silverhawk was a chore for me to sit through. It's handsomely produced, with lots of money on the screen with anime-style action (i.e. lots of colorful, stylized lighting, garish costumes, expensive-looking hardware, etc.), but it panders to the audience and assumes we're all preteens. Yeoh seems to be too old to be playing a silly socialite, and the comedic, cutesy aspects of the story should have been chucked out for a more intense focus on the conflict. Both Luke Goss and Michael Jai White are drowned out by the theatrics of the whole production, so they're both wasted, which is a crime. Yeoh's fans will be disappointed. Directed by Jingle Ma, who is a well-known cinematographer of many Hong Kong martial arts films including *Rumble in the Bronx*.

Simon Sez

1999 (Sony DVD) (CD)

"What happened to you, clown face, huh? A bird shit on your eye?"

Simon (Dennis Rodman) is an Interpol agent who accidentally meets up with Nick (Dane Cook), an old CIA acquaintance. Nick (basically a moron) needs Simon's help to deliver a briefcase and to retrieve the kidnapped daughter of a very wealthy American executive. The daughter, Claire (Natalia Cigliuti), isn't even aware she has been kidnapped and refuses to go with them. The briefcase contains a disc with military secrets the kidnapping villains will stop at nothing to retrieve.

Is there really anything positive to say about *Simon Sez*, a flop vehicle for former NBA bad boy Dennis Rodman (*Double Team*)? Well, it does feature two incredibly gorgeous women, Emma Wiklund (*Taxi*) and Natalia Cigliuti (*Kill Speed*). And it also features Xin Xin Xiong (*Once Upon a Time in China*) in a minor role, and he also serves as the action director. No matter how anyone looks at it, it's still a huge failure on every level, a virtual embarrassment for everyone involved. Rodman tries his best to be an action star but falls way short. There's plenty of action and some of the fight scenes

S

are entertaining enough to watch, especially with Wiklund and Xiong. Aside from their few shining moments, the rest of the film just hurts to watch. Dane Cook (best known as a comedian) plays one of the most annoyingly unfunny characters ever committed to celluloid. *Simon Sez* isn't worth trudging through. Watch *Double Team* again instead. The director, Kevin Elders, is best known for creating the *Iron Eagle* franchise.

Sin City

2005 (Dimension DVD) (CD)

"I'll stare the bastard in the face as he screams to God, and I'll laugh harder when he whimpers like a baby. And when his eyes go dead, the hell I send him to will seem like heaven after what I've done to him."

Tough guy Marv (Mickey Rourke) finds himself in bed for a night of hot passionate sex with the gal of his dreams, Goldie (Jaime King). He spends the night sleeping next to her but when he awakens, she's dead. He's obviously been framed, and he flees the scene just as the police arrive. He's a wanted man but he visits his parole officer Lucille (Carla Gugino), who tries to talk some sense into him about going after the killer. Marv has a condition, and he tends to imagine things if he doesn't pop his pills. Her warning doesn't stop him—it just fuels his flame, but it's all turned upside-down when he's attacked by a woman who's the spitting image of the slain Goldie.

In 2005, director Robert Rodriguez (*Machete*)—along with comic book icon Frank Miller—brought to life Miller's graphic novel *Sin City*, which boasts a visual style never seen before. The cast included major players in Hollywood like Bruce Willis, Clive Owen, and Jessica Alba, but it was Mickey Rourke (later in *The Expendables*) as Marv, the tough-talking beast of a man, who owns this picture. He's an imposing force in the film, smashing faces through brick walls, driving in a car while dragging a man across the pavement, and obliterating a group of men with a hatchet. Rourke *is* Marv and this is one of the roles for which he will forever be remembered. The film is broken up into vignettes; his is called "The Hard Goodbye" and features some incredible talent like Clive Owen, Rutger Hauer, and Elijah Wood. Rourke also rubs elbows (or maybe not, since much of the film was shot without sets using green screen and with the actors shooting their scenes weeks apart) with some of Hollywood's most beautiful women like Rosario Dawson, Jaime King, and Carla Gugino.

Sin City: A Dame to Kill For

2014 (Dimension DVD) (djm)

Nine years after the first film, Robert Rodriguez and Frank Miller made *A Dame to Kill For*, which, more or less, tries to recapture the magic of the first film. Various vignettes revolve around the central story of hard-luck case Dwight (Josh Brolin), who has had the sheets pulled out from under him by "a dame to kill for" named Ava (Eva Green, usually nude or mostly nude in the movie), who wants nothing more than to dupe all of the men she comes across by seducing them for money, power, and bragging rights that she's superior to them. Her bodyguard Manute (Dennis Haysbert, virtually playing a cyborg) beats Dwight to a pulp, and so he crawls to Marv (Mickey Rourke), a local barfly barbarian who sympathizes with him and joins him on a bloody quest to right Dwight's wrongs, but as usual, Marv is an outdated, outmoded caveman who allows himself to be used if only to feel alive for a while. Marv's own personal hell is watching untouchable stripper Nancy (Jessica Alba, never nude in the movie, despite playing a stripper) degrade herself nightly, and then watching her go over the edge by mutilating herself to get back at her "daddy," a powerfully corrupt politician (played by the great Powers Boothe).

Predictably stylish and comic-book garish, *Sin City: A Dame to Kill For* is okay if you're really into the graphic novels and loved the first film, but it's disappointing for being more than a little lackluster and for not allowing its characters to shine the way they should. Mickey Rourke was great in the first film, but here he's sort of a novelty, and supporting or cameo roles (from the likes of Bruce Willis, Joseph Gordon-Levitt, Rosario Dawson, and Ray Liotta) mostly fall flat or ring false. There's stuff to like here, but somehow it's missing the freakish elements that made the first one stand out.

Sister Street Fighter

1974 (Diamond DVD) (CD)

"I don't like race horses, so I keep killers. This is my private zoo. It amuses me. It's as much fun as a car load of gorillas."

Lee Long (Hiroshi Miyauchi) is a drug agent and martial arts champion who goes missing while on an investigation. His sister Tina (Sue Shiomi), arrives to pick up where he left off. As she gets closer to finding out the truth, drug smuggler Kaki (Bim Amatsu) hires a group of killers, all trained in different styles of martial arts, to kill her. Luckily, she has the help of Lee Long's martial arts school and their best student Sonny Hibachi (Sonny Chiba). She discovers her brother is still alive and attempts to rescue him but she can't do it alone. She brings along a couple of the students, including Sonny, to fight their way into the compound and get him out alive.

Sister Street Fighter is nothing more than a name and has no connection at all to the Sonny Chiba series of films. Even though star Sue Shiomi (*Dragon Princess*) appeared in some of those films, this is a brand-new character. Chiba himself appears in the film but not as his most famous character Terry Tsuguri. This is mostly just an extended cameo for him, but it's all good since his appearances all involve him beating the britches off some baddie. Director Kazuhiko Yamaguchi (*Karate for Life*) keeps the story simple, overloaded with action, and is smart enough to pit the heroes up against fighters with various fighting styles to give the audience a unique view of what the martial arts world has to offer. The original cut of the film runs five to six minutes longer than the censored US version, though it has been recently made available uncut by Brentwood.

6 Bullets

2012 (Sony DVD) (djm)

"I know you mean well, but you're not a cop. You're a soldier, and this is not Africa or Afghanistan. You might be used to collateral damage, but I'm not!"

Jean-Claude Van Damme's second film with director Ernie Barbarash (*Assassination Games*) has him playing a mercenary named Samson Gaul, who takes a job recovering a young boy from a human trafficking ring in Eastern Europe. He rescues the boy, but ends up being the cause of the deaths of several other children. This puts him in a deep depression. He sees the ghosts of two girls he accidentally killed, and he turns to alcohol for solace. Years pass and he has opened up a small butcher shop (this film was originally titled *The Butcher*) and has no interest in being a part of the world any longer. When a UFC-type American fighter named Fayden (Joe Flanigan from *Stargate: Atlantis*) comes to Romania with his family to fight a championship match, his preteen daughter is kidnapped by the same human trafficking ring. Fayden is desperate to find his girl, and when he hears about the local butcher who used to specialize in mercenary work, he turns to the embittered ex-mercenary. Gaul has no interest in the job until his son, a local cop (played by Van Damme's real-life son Kristopher Van Varenberg) convinces him to do it.

Barbarash seems to understand the roles Van Damme is really comfortable with playing. Van Damme is morose, depressed, and angry in this movie, and the physicality in his acting here is used to good effect. There's plenty of action, and Van Damme shines in another solid entry in his later direct-to-video features. As in *Assassination Games*, the tone here is grim and serious, and there's rarely a moment of levity. At times, I found it difficult to accept that Van Damme's character can be ultra prepared when in action and can seemingly be at several locations simultaneously, but you have to just roll with these things.

INTERVIEW:
ERNIE BARBARASH
(djm)

The direct-to-video action market isn't thriving the way it used to, but the few filmmakers who continue making films in this market are dedicated to delivering the best films with the best action stars who are still working in that market. Ernie Barbarash is such a director. His films Assassination Games (2011) and Six Bullets (2012) both star Jean-Claude Van Damme, and he's found a niche in a dying market. Barbarash seems to have a grasp on how to make a solid vehicle film with one of the best action stars in the world, and the future holds more films of this type from him. He's already finished two more action films: Falcon Rising (2014) with Michael Jai White and Pound of Flesh (2015) with Van Damme.

Ernie, how did you get started in the movie business?

I started out doing theater. I was doing theater since I was fourteen years old. I always wanted to direct theater. All my degrees are in theater directing. When I got out of graduate school in New York in the early '90s, I got attached to direct a show. It was supposed to be a big Broadway thing, and then it got postponed, and I was suddenly out of work. I was a Canadian citizen at the time, and I didn't have a green card, and then I was like, "Holy crap!" There was a Canadian film company that had just opened an office in New York. They needed somebody to read scripts. I'd never done anything in film other than a little bit of casting in TV stuff. So I started working for that little film company, and that company eventually became Lionsgate. After a couple of months working for them, they offered me a job as a development executive. I had other theater stuff coming up, and they asked me, "What would it take to come work with us?" I said, "Well, if you help me get a green card . . . " They said, "Yeah, sure." That company, which used to be called Cinepix, had done a movie with Gary Daniels and guys like that, and their big thing was that they had done *SnakeEater* with Lorenzo Lamas. They became my film school. I was younger, I was single, I was willing to travel, and I spoke a few different languages. Suddenly, I became the guy who would go to a set in Montreal or the Ukraine. I remember it was like the Wild West in the Ukraine. You would hand out cash in a paper bag. That was nuts. It was weird. I started out producing, but I had started out as a theater director, so I came from that creative part of it. The low-budget work with Cinepix . . . it led to me becoming a producer on *American Psycho* and a producer on a Peter Bogdanovich movie called *The Cat's Meow*. It was fun. I was a producer who worked for a living. I was on set, working with the director and sometimes fighting with the director. You had to learn to make do with what you had. I got into directing film after about eight years of producing for Lionsgate. I was in the final sound mix of a movie that I had co-written called *Hyper Cube*. I was sitting in the mix with my boss, and I said, "Hey, I have an idea for another *Cube* movie. If I pitch it to you and you like it, will you let me direct it?" He was like, "Yeah, sure." Three weeks later I had a deal to do *Cube Zero*, which was the first movie I directed. It was a hell of an experience. I was like, "Good God, can I really direct?" As a producer, I was getting really frustrated with the job because I was a highly paid babysitter. Did I want to send the rest of my life saying "No" to

directors? If I was going to stay in the industry, I wanted to write and direct my own work. It was a great opportunity I got from Lionsgate. I've never looked back. I've been writing and directing for more than ten years now. Somehow, I've survived as a freelancer in this industry. I have respect for anyone who's done that as a freelancer. It's one thing to be a trust-fund kid and direct. If you make movies for a living in this economy . . . it's very different than doing it as a hobby. I wish I'd had that opportunity. I'd love to take two years to put together a film. One of the reasons why Shakespeare's and Molière's work has survived all these years is because they cared about their audience. They had to. If it didn't work for the audience, they didn't work. So it wasn't all about pleasing themselves, it was about creating something that was good, something that practically worked.

After you'd done a few of these direct-to-video action films, do you know who your audience is?

It's funny. I'm very, very slowly—thanks to the Internet and social media—I'm a tiny bit in touch with the fans. Sometimes you think you know. My mother-in-law is a huge Van Damme and Seagal fan. She's a completely different demographic than the guys who write to you online. The only way you sort of know the audience is when I'm contacted online. They seem to come from all walks of life.

Do you think teenagers know who Van Damme and Seagal are anymore?

I only know this through Facebook, but I see really young faces who "like" their movies. I grew up watching a lot of Van Damme's stuff on VHS. I remember watching *Timecop* and *Lionheart*. *Hard Target*. They had a real brutal honesty about them. As a filmmaker and as a moviegoer, I personally need a more sophisticated plot sometimes. The audience has seen a lot of movies, and they're much more sophisticated than they used to be. In a way, what I find in the edit room, I feel like the audience is way ahead of me. The first twenty minutes need to be compressed into five because they *get* it. It was a thrill a few years back when a producer said, "Hey, we're about to do a Van Damme movie. You want to meet him?" I met him on the phone. It was great.

Let me go back a second. You mentioned that you're a freelancer and how hard that is. One of the reasons why I'm doing interviews with guys like you is because I can see how hard you're all working. It seems like a labor of love—not just for the money—but guys like Van Damme are still in shape, they're working hard, harder now than they ever have before.

They absolutely are. In a way, they have to. Anyone who works on low-budget genre movies has to love it. We all get paid, but nobody feels that they're paid enough. These aren't $150 million dollar movies where you work on a movie and you don't have to work for a few more years. Your next job is in a couple of months or in a few weeks. The actors are incredibly dedicated. Van Damme is in incredible shape. Scott Adkins

too. They do physical work like dancers. You can't go and do these movies unless you really train. They're dedicated. It's not even how you look. It's how your body moves. One of the keys to having a good working relationship with your lead actors is you have to be part of the process. You have to listen to them. You've got to work with them from the very beginning at the script stage. You have to involve them. You have to treat them like adults. I find that people treat them like children. Again, I find that everybody wants to coddle them. Everybody wants to say yes to them. Unless they're comatose, they can smell it a mile away. You just have to be genuine. I find that most actors don't want a director who says "Yes" to everything. They want feedback. That's my job. They're looking for a professional who will give their honest opinion. The filmmaker also has to be the audience. It is key to be honest with the actor. With JC, on 6 *Bullets*, we had a first draft, and we both had issues with the draft. What happens with these movies is that they're very market driven. Especially in this insane economy we're in.

Explain that.

For example: There are presales that go on. The movies get financed because the distributors worldwide will want *this* movie with Van Damme with *this* story. At any given point, because the number of actors in this range who are known names, these names can drive foreign sales. It's a small group of people, actually. You know that the hot box-office star is wanted by every studio. But for movies like the ones I do, vehicle guys . . . there are agencies that are looking to make movies with "X" actor. They're trying to get their script out there. People undervalue the story and the script. Unless you are going to offer the actor a huge studio release, and I don't think anyone is guaranteeing a huge studio release these days . . . Everything is market driven. There's a reason why these movies don't get written well initially. It's because somebody says, "I need to make an offer to Van Damme by next Friday. Who's got something?" Suddenly, there's a mad panic because Van Damme is saying "Yes" to a movie. Or it's Seagal saying "Yes" to a movie.

So all of a sudden a bunch of scripts show up?

Well, I only see it when it shows up to me. But I find that they're really rushed. I'm a writer too.

So, hold on: Do these scripts, for example, have echoes of Van Damme or whoever in them? Are they tailor-made for the stars?

Often, they are, but often they're not. There's a great script right now that I'm trying to make with Van Damme. It has a part written specifically for him. It's a brilliant story. I can't disclose what it is, but it's written for him. It's got his cadence, his background, it's got everything he loves to do. But so often it's not. Sometimes they're written for somebody who's a lot older or a lot younger, or it's written to take place in the South, but it doesn't work . . . the joke with the older Van Damme movies is how do they figure out his accent? Also, there's the economics of it . . . it comes down to the amount of shooting days you have. I will shoot almost anywhere in the world to shoot where we get the most amount of shooting days. You give me twenty-four to thirty days, I'll shoot anywhere. You can't make an "action" movie in sixteen days. In sixteen days, you can shoot a maybe okay Hallmark movie. I've done those, too. If you want me to really kill the actors, it'll go a lot faster. (Laughing.) It's the physical things that take time. On the schedules we have for some of these movies, the time we would have on a bigger budget to shoot a fight sequence is four times what we would get. You really feel like you need three days to shoot some things, and you end up getting only half a day. You can yell and scream, but that's what you signed on for. Some directors spend much more time on the fights than anything else. It's a double-edged sword because yes, you have a couple of really great fights, but there will be no story or acting to follow. That's the biggest challenge.

Scott Adkins told me that his fight scene with Jason Statham in *Expendables 2* was shot in just a few hours, and that both he and Statham were upset about that because they wanted to do a much longer and more complicated fight. And that's a hundred million dollar movie.

I wonder why. It looked great. Scott Adkins is a consummate pro. He does his own stunts. Other than if you're putting him in a burning car and blowing it up. Scott moves incredibly fast. He's very precise. In a good way, he's very demanding about it. All these guys are like that. It's stage combat, so they want to know where the camera will be and what angle you're going to use. I'm surprised about that fight on *Expendables 2*. You never have enough time. People say to me, "Oh, you wouldn't have enough time even if you had a hundred days!" Give me a hundred days, and we'll see. Someone smarter than me said, "If you're not directing the schedule, the schedule is directing you."

What I like about the later Van Damme movies, and the two you've done with him so far, is that he's delving more into the acting and less into the action. There's always just enough action in them, though.

There has to be because that's what you're selling. I always fight to have as much story as possible. The number one issue is that the audience wants to know what happens next. I'm not saying we're 100 percent successful on these movies, but that's what we strive for. The story is key. This is the conversation I have with fight choreographers all the time: The fights and the fight sequences have an arc—they have a beginning, a middle, and an end. Otherwise the action just stops if there is no story. You're just going, "Okay, who's going to win here?" I want you to think, "Okay, this guy's winning, how is our hero going to get out of that?" It's still a story.

Is Van Damme still cool with doing fights?

He's in incredible shape. When he's actually shooting, he's a very instinctual person. Because the schedule is so compressed, there are times where he'll do a little fight, and he'll say, "Do this piece with the double because I want to

Director Ernie Barbarash gives Jean-Claude Van Damme direction on *6 Bullets*.

go concentrate on this next thing where I have a monologue." In *6 Bullets*, there are entire sequences where it's just him fighting. There's one sequence where we had to shoot and I *had* to see his face. So often, it's not so much up to the actor whether they want a double or not. You shoot according to necessity and according to the schedule, or you're not shooting a movie.

Talk about working with Van Damme. What has been your experience with him so far?

You know what I love about Van Damme? He's a genuinely nice person. He's not a crazy, ego-driven guy. I've found him to be a very nice person. He's an actor. Sometimes he has his emotional highs and lows when he's working because you're asking him to go through highs and lows. He really does care about the work. Once he's psyched about it, he's 100 percent go, go, go. He really does care about the story. He does want to talk a lot during prep. They're working on four movies in a row, and the director is on this one movie for half a year. He really cares. I'm very lucky in that I've never worked with an actor who just phones it in. He looks at the script through his character. Sometimes he does a lot of movies so you have to disconnect him from the last thing he did. I find that he's an instinctive guy. He likes to do a lot of work in post, like in the ADR stage.

Well, that's cool. Steven Seagal won't do most of his ADR. He gets dubbed over by someone who sounds nothing like him.

That's what I've heard.

How many takes can you get out of Van Damme?

Um . . .

As many as it takes?

Yeah.

Does he ever refuse a take?

No. Sometimes he'll go, "What the fuck do you need another one for?!" Then I explain it, and he'll go, "Okay, okay, okay." He's not a morning person. With him, he's good for late morning through early into the next morning. Part of it has to do with that he travels so much. He has jet lag all the time.

When does he have time to work out?

He works out like crazy. He always works out. He'll call me while we're shooting, and he'll be like, "Can you start on something else? I'm still at the gym." I'll be like, "Yeah, okay."

Talk about the roles you've directed him in. He tends to play a lot of lonely, morose characters.

I don't know what it is, but someone else pointed that out to me. I think he'd be great in a comedy. He would do great in something like *Kindergarten Cop*. He's not a morose guy. He just did a comedy called *Welcome to the Jungle*. I hear he's really good in it. He's really good at playing those morose characters. They create good drama. He chooses his own material. People are always fighting to get him in their thing.

Can you give me a rough estimate on how much *Assassination Games* and *6 Bullets* cost to produce?

I think they were five million dollars and under. You never really know what the real bottom line is. Both of them were shot in twenty-four days. We wouldn't be able to shoot them in North America in that amount of time, which is why we go to Romania or Thailand.

Talk about working in Romania and Thailand.

I love working in Romania. I was born in Eastern Europe, so I love the food and I love the people. I have two kids, so it's hard to be away from home. The crews are great, the locations are great. Often with these budgets you don't get to explore the lush countrysides because you're putting up the entire cast and crew. Part of the fun of this job is getting to travel around the world. With Romanian actors, you encounter an accent problem. For bigger roles, you end up bringing in actors from England. Van Damme is always there when you need him. He's incredibly available. You can call him day or night on his cell about anything. He'll call you back, he'll text you, he'll Skype you. If he's ever late, he apologizes.

Wow. If only Steven Seagal were like that. He pops up now and again in his movies.

That's what I hear. Van Damme is picky about what he does, too. I've worked with his kids before, too. I surprised him with a role for Kristopher, his son, because I like Kristopher—he's good to work with. But there was also a role for his daughter. We came up with that role over a few days. I told him that I'd like to have her in the movie, too, but I wanted her to really be in the movie with a real part. He's very protective of his family. You'd think, "Oh, he's just Jean-Claude Van Damme, he's just a fighting guy." But he gets archetypes. He talks in those terms in big, universal terms. Many actors come in and they're like, "Where do you want me to stand?"

The two films you did with Van Damme are pretty grisly in terms of showing the aftereffects of horrible violence.

I figure maybe it's me. I don't think violence should be clean. Some movies go too far and it's pornography violence. Violence is bad. I just go with how I'm envisioning it. I don't think I went too far with these two films. Maybe I'm wrong . . .

Well, some of the images in these films sort of taint the films and it ends up putting a different spin on the typical Van Damme-type genre. These movies definitely feel like they're set in the real world. They're not PG-13 action movies, you know what I mean?

It's funny. No one has asked me to make a PG-13 action movie. I wish they would. My daughter is nine, and she watches PG-13 movies. I'm dying to make a movie that my kids can watch. My son is six. He loves *The Forbidden Kingdom*. There was a trend recently where everything was slow-mo, where the blood spurts were stylized. I found that boring after a while. I find that that stuff glorifies terrible things. With *Assassination Games*, we were going for the very real Krav Maga style. The fastest way to kill somebody. It felt more realistic. In *6 Bullets*, Van Damme came up with different stuff. He brought in a Belgian knife-fighter, self-defense instructor to choreograph the opening fight. Van Damme loved that. But with all these movies, I wish we had more time.

Do you watch Van Damme's other movies to kind of gauge where he's at?

I'm so busy usually. I saw *Expendables 2*. Scott Adkins was so good in that, but he was so underused. All those guys are great. I want to see Van Damme in *Dragon Eyes*. I have to keep working. When I'm home, it's hard for me to watch anything. I have not seen a lot of Van Damme's other movies, but I have read many of the scripts he's done.

I've noticed that Van Damme tends to work with directors he's worked with before.

It's really great for actors and directors to collaborate, but they don't always have to keep working together. I think it's unhealthy. Part of the whole work is a pretty emotional thing. You're at war together. You can't be at war together all the time. Why would Van Damme want to work with the same director all the time? Why would I want to work with the same actor all the time? Maybe he trusts me. They're trusting you to do as good a movie as you can. It's interesting. When he says "Yes" to a movie, it means work for 200 people. When I'm asked if the script is good or bad and if it works or doesn't work, I always tell them what I really think. That's what I get paid to do. I'm not going to tell him or anyone else, "It's wonderful, it's great!" when it's not.

Be honest with me, then. What are your thoughts on how *Assassination Games* turned out?

It looked great. I loved the cast. I wished we had more time to shoot it and more time to work on the script. I think the story is a little too convoluted. There were kinks that we should have smoothed out before we shot it.

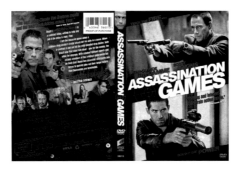

DVD artwork for *Assassination Games*. Author's collection.

DVD artwork for *6 Bullets*. Author's collection.

How about *6 Bullets*?

With *6 Bullets*, the story is a little clearer. I don't think we had as specific a visual style, but we didn't want to repeat ourselves. We had the same DP. We on purpose decided we weren't going to have the desaturated look. We wanted more color. With *6 Bullets*, the script was more solid, even if it was a little predictable. It's not like we had six months to write it. I wish that the end of it had more time to throw more of Van Damme towards the bad guys and the problems he solves at the end. We had a real hard time securing a location for the end. We ended up going to a real prison in Bucharest. They had Van Damme come in and talk to the prisoners and sign autographs. He talked about his life and inspired everyone. I wished someone had taken a video of it. That prison had real constraints. We were supposed to shoot certain sequences in certain areas of that place, but we were told in the morning that those areas were off limits for the day. That didn't help. The weather screws you, too.

Talk about working with Scott Adkins.

He's an incredible fighter and a really good actor. I would love to do more movies with him. I'm so glad he's in the *Expendables* movie. He's incredibly underused. He was great. At first, I have to admit, I was very reluctant to cast Scott. I was sent all these YouTube links to his fights, but I was like, "But can he act?" I'd never seen any of his movies. Then I saw his audition, and he *could* act. He's a dream. He has no ego. It's so rare. *And* he's a great fighter! He was very careful about his performance in *Assassination Games*.

He and Van Damme have done a number of movies together. How were they together?

They were great. They had a really good relationship. Scott was very respectful towards Van Damme, and Van Damme was really nice to Scott. We had to shoot some of their scenes together very quickly. They just got in there and worked. They were comfortable together. I was asked why Scott Adkins didn't play the Joe Flannigan role in *6 Bullets*. I don't think Scott would have wanted to instantly do another Van Damme movie, and vice versa. I wanted to shake it up. I keep in touch with both of those guys. I would love to do more movies with both of them.

I find it interesting that *Assassination Games* was briefly released in some theaters.

Sony put it out. There is always the hope that somebody will release it in theaters, but you never know. It doesn't really matter. It's just about doing good work. If I just started churning these out, I wouldn't get to make any more movies. I might be able to do one or two more movies and then that's it. Trust me, once in a while an actor can phone it in, but a director can't. I hear stories of directors who are alcoholics or whatever, and I marvel at that.

Who keeps track of the money that these movies make? I'd love to see the numbers of the revenue these movies generate. Somebody is obviously happy with your two Van Damme movies because you'll make more movies of that type.

I guess. They must be making money. Once in a while I get residual checks. I met the distributor for the company that had a lot of the Eastern European territories for *Assassination Games*. We had dinner when we were prepping *6 Bullets*. They were thrilled. They made really good money. They told me that Van Damme and Seagal are still the hottest names in the former Soviet Union. You can still get more money for a Van Damme or Seagal movie than you can for a whole bunch of other people. Which is great. Action translates better than anything else around the world. I love doing what I'm doing, and if I can make a living doing it, then that's great.

The 6th Day

2000 (Sony DVD) (CD)

"When I told you to screw yourself, I didn't mean for you to take it literally."

In a future where the cloning of pet animals has become routine, family man Adam Gibson (Arnold Schwarzenegger) is still against the process, not fully trusting if the cloned critters are safe or not. He and his partner Hank (Michael Rappaport) are pilots who have their own chartering business. They're hired by Michael Drucker (Tony Goldwyn) to take him on a ski trip. Drucker just so happens to be the man behind the company responsible for the cloning. Adam is supposed to be the one flying him but gives the duty to Hank when he learns that his daughter's dog has passed away. He considers getting her a Re-Pet, a clone created from the DNA of the animal. When Adam gets home, he finds a clone of himself celebrating his birthday with his family. A group of agents show up to kill him, as the cloning of human beings is illegal, and all of a sudden, Adam finds himself hunted for being one-too-many Adams. He escapes and heads to Replacement Technologies to learn the truth behind this nightmare, and with the aide of his doppelgänger, they get into some action together.

Arnold Schwarzenegger usually fares pretty well when he takes on projects that combine action with science fiction. *The 6th Day* is good but is by far his weakest ever in the genre. Arnold plays two versions of the same character, a gimmick that works a while, but then one might realize that the twin performance movies should just be given to Jean-Claude Van Damme. The movie does entertain but falters a bit in the action department, which doesn't really ramp up until the film is almost halfway over. He is accompanied by a terrific cast that includes Robert Duvall (*Jack Reacher*), Michael Rooker (*Replicant*), and Terry Crews (*The Expendables*) in his first film role. The film features some fantastic effects, and the makeup work during the finale is superb. This isn't a bad film, just sort of weak with Arnold delivering the goods when he needs to. Directed by Roger Spottiswoode, who worked with Stallone on the infamous *Stop! Or My Mom Will Shoot!*

Skin Trade

2015 (Magnet DVD) (djm)

Victor Dragovic (Ron Perlman) is in the *Skin Trade*, with a crime empire that spans all over the world, and he's at the top of the most wanted.

Dolph Lundgren in *Skin Trade*, a Magnet release. Courtesy of Magnet Releasing.

Tony Jaa in *Skin Trade*, a Magnet release. Courtesy of Magnet Releasing.

Dolph Lundgren and Tony Jaa in *Skin Trade*, a Magnet release. Courtesy of Magnet Releasing.

Thai detective Tony (Tony Jaa from *Ong-Bak*) is fighting to save the lives of kidnapped women in Thailand, while Detective Nick Cassidy (Dolph Lundgren, who produced and co-wrote the story) is fighting Dragovic's evil on the homefront in the US. When Nick kills one of Dragovic's sons in a raid, Dragovic has Nick's wife killed and his teenage daughter taken and interred into the skin trade (sex slavery, for the uninformed). Nick is wounded and hospitalized, but he goes renegade by going on a revenge spree throughout Asia, trying to topple Dragovic's empire single-handedly. Framed for a murder committed by a colleague named Reed (Michael Jai White from *Falcon Rising*), Nick is hunted by Tony, who doesn't realize that they are both working towards the same goal. When Nick and Tony eventually team up against Dragovic and Reed (who is in Dragovic's pocket), the ante is upped and the game is on!

A passion project for Lundgren, who once considered directing this, *Skin Trade* has enough going for it to get a recommendation, but for some reason the energy level is low and aside from two stellar fight scenes (one between Lundgren and Jaa and the other between Jaa and Jai White), the movie has an odd lack of momentum that should have been corrected somehow in the editing room. Lundgren looks more grizzled than ever (he even has a scarred face through most of the movie), and Jaa makes a much more satisfying English language transition here than he did in *Fast and Furious 7*. Jai White is relegated to a glasses-wearing secondary villain, but his fight scene with Jaa makes all the amends in the world. The movie ends as if there could be a sequel. Let's hope there is one. Also starring Cary-Hiroyuki Tagawa and Peter Weller in supporting roles. Directed by Ekachai Vekrongtham.

INTERVIEW:

DOLPH LUNDGREN

(djm)

Before his breakout, star-making role as Ivan Drago in Rocky IV *(1985), Swedish-born Dolph Lundgren had been in the military in his younger years and had practiced karate and competed professionally before obtaining a master's degree in chemical engineering. He was also the European heavyweight karate champion (1980–1981), so by the time he stumbled onto acting and became a sensation, he'd already*

Dolph Lundgren in *Skin Trade*, a Magnet release. Courtesy of Magnet Releasing.

lived a storied life. He's maintained a very steady and successful career as an action star over the last thirty years, and he's written several of his own films and directed a few as well. He's outlasted many of his peers and kept himself in incredible shape, and he truly is one of the greatest and most undervalued action stars of all time. Here he discusses aspects of his career and the release of his latest film Skin Trade, *which he wrote, produced, and starred in alongside Tony Jaa and Michael Jai White.*

As I understand it, you tried to make *Skin Trade* for seven years. What was it about this project that had you so determined to make it?

I wrote the script many years ago when I was involved in directing some movies; I'd been thinking about some projects to do. I read an article about these girls in Mexico who'd been trafficked. They were left by the traffickers in a van, and they all suffocated and died. That was an interesting incident in real life, and I hadn't seen anything like that before. I wrote the script, but then I set it aside and never thought it would get made. I came to Thailand to do another film [called *A Man Will Rise*] with Tony Jaa, for just a couple weeks. And then I did one week on a Thai movie—for some reason I ended up doing a Thai comedy—but I met Tony and I thought, Wait a second . . . He wanted to make a deal where I could be in one of his movies if he could be in one of my movies. Basically, that's how I rewrote the script. It was originally set in Eastern Europe, and so I switched it to Thailand. We got it financed. When I started working on the script, it was just another script. Once I'd done research, I realized that trafficking is a huge crime. I was surprised that it's the second largest criminal enterprise in the world. There are thirty million slaves all over the world, even here in America.

Talk a little bit about your time working with Tony Jaa. When did you first become aware of him and his work, and when you finally got down to filming your fight scenes, how were those scenes to film?

I hadn't seen his films before, so I of course watched them and saw that he was very skilled. I've done fights with Jet Li and Van Damme, and guys like that, so I know it's cool to have somebody that can fight because you can actually work with them. You don't have to use a bunch of doubles. Our fight was complicated because Tony and I had to do it ourselves. We had to get together and work it out. There were too many languages spoken, and our fight never would have gotten done if we hadn't done it ourselves.

Personally, I found your second fight with Tony in the film to be one of the most satisfying fights I've ever seen you involved in. How would you compare it to some of your other on-screen fights, say with Jet Li in _The Expendables_?

Well, we knew we had to do this scene, and in the movie we're on opposite sides, but we're actually on the same side. [The fights] are in the script, but it wasn't written to be such a big fight. We made it bigger. Tony had his ideas, and he had some guys working with him. I had one person working with me. Basically it came down to us going through it step by step to eliminate the middlemen. Otherwise you get so many people involved and have so many different moves, and it could have taken us six months. Finally, we just got together on the weekend and worked out the main beats. On the day, it changed as well because he likes to do his own stunts. It's kinda dangerous. A lot of times the stunt guy would want to do it, but Tony would show up and want to do it himself. He would do another flip in a different direction. The DP would go, "Oh, shit!" But I think it worked out okay. It certainly ranks up there in my book. I've fought Van Damme and Jet Li and some other people.

Michael Jai White has a solid role in the movie. He tells me that you had originally thought to have him in the role that Tony plays. As a fan, I would have loved to see you and Michael fight on screen, but that didn't happen.

Yeah, me too. Michael Jai is a great martial artist. We study the same style of karate. He's a champion. I used to be a champion back in the day in Europe. He is tremendous in the movie. He's about my size, and he can jump and spin and do roundhouse kicks. I went, "Hey, wait a second! He shouldn't be able to do that. It's not physically possible!" He's one of those guys, and he's very good in this.

You left _Skin Trade_ open-ended. Are you planning to continue the story?

I don't know. I thought it married the action fare with good subject matter. The original script, it was less action and more of a thriller. Because of the cast and the financing, that's how it ended up. There're some scenes in the film that are memorable, and I hope that in a few years you'll remember the film because of those things. I think maybe we could continue with it.

There are rumors of an _Expendables_ TV series. Will you be leading the show with Terry Crews?

I don't think we'll be the leads of the series because I don't think they want to pay us! I think they'll get somebody else. We may show up and do something on it. Sly might too. (In Sly's voice:) "Tall guys in the back!" I think Tony would be great [for _The Expendables_], but I don't know. Sly is the boss.

In your words, what is your idea of a successful collaboration when you're producing, directing, and starring in a film?

Well, you've got to listen to everybody. If you're in some kind of power position, you have to realize that you're going to benefit if you listen to everybody. Anybody can have a good idea. Use it. Take it. You can use it to make the best film possible for the audience.

Is there a certain aspect about filmmaking that you prefer above any others?

I like editing, but I also like writing and rewriting things. I hate to write on a blank page. It sucks. If there's something I've worked on that I've put away for a while, I can rewrite it and shape it and that's fun. Editing is fun too. It's like being an engineer—you're moving parts around to try to get some final result. There are so many options. When you're filming, it's hard work and you're trying to get things done on time. There's a lot of pressure.

What were some of the most difficult things to film while you were there in Thailand?

Just working outdoors, moving extras around because there's a language difficulty. There are marketplace areas where we have to spend time moving people around. Most of the extras in Thailand, it's their first time in a movie and they're excited about meeting Tony Jaa.

Is there anyone you'd like to do a movie with and is there a genre you haven't done that you'd like to try?

I'd like to work with Arnold [Schwarzenegger]. I know him pretty well. I'd like to do a historical movie because I like history. I like World War II movies.

You just shot _War Pigs,_ didn't you?

Yeah, I just did a World War II picture with Mickey Rourke. It was pretty cool. I play a French Legionnaire. I'm attached to an infantry unit to teach the GI's how to fight the Germans. It's not a big movie, but it has a lot of heart.

I really like that Magnet is releasing _Skin Trade_ to some theaters. I consider you a theatrical star.

Me too! It's been a slow way back. I hadn't been on the big screen for about ten–fifteen years between _Johnny Mnemonic_ and _The Expendable_s. There's a certain presence that kept me going all these years. _War Pigs_, from what I've heard, will get a theatrical release as well.

You continue to amaze and make your fans happy by starring in these great martial arts action films. What keeps you coming back for more, and is there anything you'd like to say to your fans?

Bills! You gotta do something for a living, and I've got a few things I want to produce and direct and expand a little bit. It's taking me a while to do it. It's taken me years to figure it out.

Michael Jai White in _Skin Trade_, a Magnet release. Courtesy of Magnet Releasing.

INTERVIEW:

MICHAEL JAI WHITE (djm)

For a man with such an incredible physique and body mass, Michael Jai White should not be able to do the things he does on screen. With astounding abilities in the martial arts, he's a force to be reckoned with, a one-of-a-kind action star who goes from the "B"-action movie world (with films like Undisputed II: Last Man Standing, _2006,_ Blood and Bone, _2009) to "A"-list films like_ Why Did I Get Married? _(2007) and_ The Dark Knight _(2008) with relative ease. He has black belts in seven different martial arts (Shotokan karate, taekwondo, Okinawan kobudo, Goju-Ryu karate, Tang Soo Do, wushu, and Kyokushin karate) and twenty-six competitive titles to his credit. Michael Jai White is one of the very best action stars making films in the genre today, and frankly, he should be getting more recognition for his work. With his latest film,_ Skin Trade _(2015), Jai White portrays the villain opposite Dolph Lundgren and_ Ong-Bak _star Tony Jaa, whom he shares an incredible fight scene with in the finale._

In the last year or so, I've seen you fight some great on-screen fights. In _Falcon Rising,_ you fight Lateef Crowder, a capoeirista, and in _Skin Trade_ you have an incredible fight scene with Tony Jaa, who is famous for his Muay Thai. Talk a little bit about how you're able to adapt your martial arts styles for different projects where you go up against different martial artists and their own styles.

The style will change depending on the character. According to the fight within the character's personality. I let that dictate. It's like two musicians. You make different types of music, but there're two of you. It's always about the character. I've done eight different styles, and I have my own particular style, a fighting method that I've developed. Depending on the character, I use aspects of what I've learned. With _Falcon Rising_, my character is a combat veteran, so he fights more deadly and direct. With _Blood and Bone_, it had more of a sport aspect to it, more street fighting. It all depends on the character.

Your fight with Tony in _Skin Trade_ was impressive. How were you two able to work that scene out?

Tony Jaa and I created a lot of our fight right before we shot it. There's this whole area where we fought inside this long room, and we created it ten minutes before we shot it. We just had this idea and we ran with it. We blocked it out and told the cameras to follow us. We just did it.

Did the lack of time you had to prepare and coordinate that fight hinder the fight itself? Would more time to coordinate the fight have made it a better fight? Or was the fight as good as it could have been?

I think we made it as good as it could have been because we created something that was right in the moment. It felt real. Sometimes when you have a lot more time, it's neat, but it feels very staged and organized. Some of the stuff that Tony and I were doing was actually real. It's like you want those happy accidents. We can do things on such a level and we have a great deal of control, and even mistakes wind up looking like they were supposed to happen. Just like any good acting scene. When someone does something unexpected, the other person adapts. It's a little bit more special.

When he hits your glasses off your face, that was a "Oh, snap!" moment. Was that for real? Did he actually hit you in the face and knock your glasses off, or was that staged?

Well, it was created. In the moment, I was like, "Oh, wow, it would be great if my glasses fell off." Then we had to try to make that happen. I was wrenching my neck trying to get them to come off. I don't know which take we used, but I know we tried to get them to fly off with a wire one time, but I think we just timed it right. Those are the things I'm talking about. You create that in moment. You don't come up with that early on. Usually, with a movie like that, you lose your glasses anyway.

It's fantastic that Tony is finally making his transition into the English-speaking world. What was it like for you to work with him?

We've been friends for a while. He's probably the most exemplary example of a martial artist that I've ever known. Not only is he amazingly talented, but he embodies what the spirit of martial arts is more than anyone else I've known. That's honesty. He's a fabulous person. It was a pleasure to work with him and I'm honored to call him my friend. The martial arts are not supposed to just develop somebody to whip somebody else's ass. It's supposed to develop the whole person. There are spiritual aspects of the martial arts where there's a balance of nature, a humbleness, a discipline. He really embodies that. I don't think I've ever heard him say a bad thing about another human being. How is that not of the highest level of humanity? This is one of the things that the martial arts are supposed to teach you; it's supposed to teach you this. It's supposed to make you an exemplary citizen of the world. I think he embodies that.

Unfortunately, we don't get to see you fight Dolph Lundgren in the film. Was that ever discussed?

No, I don't think it even came up. It had to be organic to the story. If we wound up fighting, it might have been a little strange, story-wise. Maybe we'll get a chance to do that some other time in the future. (Laughing.)

Did it ever concern you that you were playing the villain in _Skin Trade_, or were you perfectly at ease with that?

I'm at ease in this situation. There was a time where Dolph considered me as the Tony Jaa character. When we found out that there was a way to do this in the Far East, it made sense to get Tony Jaa to play that role, and I was just happy to be a part of it.

You do all kinds of work in the motion picture business, Michael. You do comedies, dramas, even voice-over work. But you sprinkle in some fantastic martial arts action movies in between. When you find an action script that you like, what is it you look for that gets you excited? When I look at something like _Skin Trade_, your part is a supporting one, and I would imagine that it doesn't look like much on paper for you, but when we're watching you in the film, it all makes sense because of how you portray your character.

With this one, it was a chance to work with Tony. It was a chance to be a part of a project with somebody I really believe in. I wanted to help in any way I could. I think he's one of the best in the world. Secondly, I enjoy working. I enjoy doing action movies. There's going to be a time when I can't do these anymore. I'm going to be too old. So, it worked out with my schedule. It was a great opportunity for me to get involved. I was happy to do it.

Who is someone you would love to do a movie fight with that you haven't fought yet?

One guy who I would love to work with is Donnie Yen. I regard him really high on the level of martial arts and action. I love the fact that he seems to evolve every time I see him. He would be the guy I would like to work with. He seems to be a perfectionist as well. I think I could learn a lot from him.

Have you done a fight on screen that really stands out for you as being a highlight?

Dolph Lundgren and Tony Jaa in _Skin Trade_, a Magnet release. Courtesy of Magnet Releasing.

Well, I wish the missing footage from my fight with Steven Seagal in _Exit Wounds_ could rear its head. We actually had quite an expensive fight scene together, but a lot of it got cut out. It got a little fancy, but I always wanted to see the other stuff that got cut out.

You directed a solid martial arts action movie called _Never Back Down 2_. Are you planning to come back to direct another film at some point?

Well, I'm actually going to start pre-production on a project in a couple weeks . . .

You have fans all over the world, Michael. Is there anything you would like to say to them?

Well, hopefully they'll continue to support me. I have a lot of really exciting projects in the works, and I'm about to embark on developing my own brand. What I want to do is pretty much what Tyler Perry has done. With the help of my fan base, I can get this done. I plan on doing a sequel to _Blood and Bone_ and _Black Dynamite_, but I'm trying to get my fans out for crowd funding to bring these things to life.

INTERVIEW:
TONY JAA
(djm)

When Tony Jaa (real name: Japanom Yeerum) crossed international lines with his stunning film Ong-bak _(2003), an action star was born. Using Muay Thai boxing and taekwondo, Jaa is a fearless force in action and martial arts cinema the likes of which the world hasn't seen since Jackie Chan crossed over with his "No fear, no stuntman, no equal" film_ Rumble in the Bronx _(1995). Jaa makes it very clear that he does not use stuntmen or body doubles in his films, and in fact he had gotten his start as a body double for Robin Shou in_ Mortal Kombat: Annihilation _(1997). In the decade that followed_ Ong-bak, _Jaa only made a handful of other films—including unrelated sequels to_ Ong-bak _set in ancient times—but the years ahead have already been slated with new films targeted at Western audiences starring Jaa, including_ A Man Will Rise _(2016, opposite Dolph Lundgren),_ Skin Trade _(2015, opposite Lundgren and Michael Jai White), and the blockbuster_ Fast and Furious 7 _(2015). During a press tour for_ Skin Trade, _Jaa was gracious enough to answer some questions I asked._

Tony Jaa in _Skin Trade_, a Magnet release. Courtesy of Magnet Releasing.

You've worked with Dolph Lundgren on two movies now—*Skin Trade* and the upcoming *A Man Will Rise*. Talk a little bit about working with Dolph. How familiar were you with his work before working with him for the first time?

I saw a number of Dolph's films including *Rocky IV* and *Showdown in Little Tokyo*. He was very cool. Dolph is a real professional, and had a real passion for *Skin Trade*. He is an accomplished martial artist so we had a lot of fun on our action scenes.

You have several incredible fight scenes in *Skin Trade.* You fight Dolph twice in the film and then later you fight Michael Jai White. Were there some challenges for you in incorporating your own style of martial arts against Dolph's and Jai White's own styles in those scenes you shared?

Not really, we practiced a lot and each of us had our own style, so it came down to choreography, and of course we had a great action coordinator with Diyan Hristov.

This has been a great year for you in appearing in big, Westernized films. You play a villain in *Fast and Furious 7,* and now you're appearing as a hero in *Skin Trade*. Would you like to say anything about your transition from Thai action films and into English-speaking films?

It has been a dream come true. It was also a challenge, as I had to learn English in the last two years. I enjoy the range of stories, style, and production potential that foreign films have.

You're a huge star in Thailand, with some great films like the *Ong-Bak* trilogy and the two *Tom Yum Goong* movies to your credit. How has your native country responded to your work in *Fast and Furious 7* and *Skin Trade?*

People have been very kind to me and very supportive. I feel like I am representing Thailand, and I always want to show what Thais can do and put our best foot forward.

Michael Jai White spoke very highly of you when I interviewed him. He told me that you are the most exemplary example of a martial artist that he's ever known. Would you talk a little bit about your journey through the martial arts and how you're able to incorporate your philosophy and discipline in some of your films?

First, Michael Jai White is amazing—he is truly amongst the best of the best. My background is grounded in Muay Thai and Muay boran, although I have learned a number of other disciplines. I started when I was eight years old, so this has become a way of life for me. I also learned acrobatics and in the movies I incorporate that into my style. It has been fun having the chance to try to develop my own style, and it is certainly something I have enjoyed doing.

What would you like to say about your role in *Skin Trade?*

It was unlike anything I have done before. The action was within my zone of comfort. The acting demands were different and I had a chance to show more of what I could do. Speaking in English was also relatively new for me, and I needed to practice to make sure my acting conveyed the proper emotions.

You have fans all over the world, Tony. What would you like to say to them?

I would say thanks very much for your support. I really, really appreciate it.

Skin Traffik

2015 (Inopia Films DVD) (CD)

"I'll tell you what, I don't have time to do this slowly, so I'll just make it painful."

Bradley (Gary Daniels) is one of the best. He's a hitman who always finishes his job and completes a mission. He takes a meeting with Vogel (Mickey Rourke), a man he's been paid to assassinate. Vogel has some vital information on disc that Bradley needs to retrieve for his employers. What was meant to be a simple hit turns into a mess when the blood of Vogel's innocent pregnant daughter is on his hands. Bradley turns his back on the hitman life, trying to live with his horrible mistake. But his neighborhood is turning to shit, and outside his apartment he witnesses the horrible beating of two young prostitutes who were forced into the life. This proves to be far too much for him to handle so he explodes back into the routine he swore to escape. After piling up some collateral damage, he's led to an organization overseen by the vicious man known only as The Executive (Eric Roberts) and his crony X (Ara Paiaya). It won't be easy but maybe if he can take them down and earn back some of the humanity he's lost.

From a story standpoint, *Skin Traffik* has the right idea. Sadly, things sort of fall apart just as things get going. This is no fault of the performers, though, and in fact, Gary Daniels (*Misfire*) is the glue holding this thing together. The ensemble cast is amazing and features the likes of Daniels, Mickey Rourke (*Bullet*), Eric Roberts (*Best of the Best*), and several other big names. When watching the film you will quickly realize something just isn't right. First, the always entertaining Rourke is saddled with one of the most ridiculous looking wigs ever featured on screen. An eyebrowless Michael Madsen appears to creep us out, and the car chases are all sped up (queue up the "Benny Hill" theme). Director Ara Paiaya (*Dubbed and Dangerous* trilogy) fared much better when he infused comedy with action; *Skin Traffik* is meant to be dramatic, but it never works. Daniels delivers a few solid fight scenes, including one with Paiaya. The choreography is great but the editing is horrible and noticeably choppy. It offers some mildly entertaining moments but all the big names show up mostly for just cameos. It's not a highpoint on Daniels' resume, but fans should check it out regardless.

Skinny Tiger, Fatty Dragon

1990 (Tai Seng DVD) (CD)

"Never do anything inhuman or there's no difference between you and an animal."

A triad gang is ruling Hong Kong with an iron fist until two hardboiled cops come along and put a dent in their business. First off, Fatty (Sammo Hung) and Baldy (Karl Maka) foil a jewel heist when they accidentally invade a woman's changing room. After getting in a bit of trouble, they continue investigating the gang but don't exactly use legal tactics to do so. To cover their tracks they pose as robbers themselves, sealing their fate as eternal enemies of the triads. Soon the people they care about are being attacked, and their only option is to go at the triad full force and stop them once and for all.

This movie is first and foremost a really goofy and politically incorrect comedy. Women are smacked around and treated poorly (at least for a portion of the film). Much of the humor is really funny but at least half of it gets lost in translation. Sammo Hung (*Eastern Condors*) never fails to impress; he is such a large man and his agility is unbelievable. If you're a fan of the films he made during this era then you will know what to expect. The comedy overshadows the action but the finale inside the old warehouse unleashes the excitement we all want to see. Not a classic, but it does have many great moments. Loosely based on the film *Running Scared* from Peter Hyams. Directed by Lau Kar-Wing (*City Cops*).

The Slams

1973 (Warner DVD) (djm)

Curtis Hook (Jim Brown from *Slaughter*) and a bunch of other guys pull of a heist that yields a million and a half in cash. Just before he's caught, he stashes the money, and he's put in "the slams." With his compatriots killed, Hook has the whole cut to himself, but the place he stored the money is going to be demolished soon so he's got to get a plan together if he's ever going to see his payday. First, he's got to make some deals on the inside because everyone is out to kill him for a piece of that payday, and then he's got to get word out on the outside that he's planning to escape. With corrupt prison guards and killer convicts at his back, and an impending deadline looming over him, Hook has got to cast his line or sink.

A solid exploitation movie with grittiness to spare, *The Slams* wouldn't have worked if just any actor had filled the title role. With Jim Brown in the center, it sparks to life and when other characters encounter him or mess with him, he shows them who's boss. Foul, violent, and rough, it fits right in with other prison action films and does them one better by having an action star in it who shines. Directed by Jonathan Kaplan, who much later did films like *Bad Girls* and *Unlawful Entry*.

S

Slaughter

1972 (MGM DVD) (djm)

"You're really far out, you know that? I mean, we go out to that house and let them know we're looking to get killed, and all of a sudden, you're sitting on top of the world like you're king shit, man. You're weird, Slaughter, I mean . . . goddammit, you're just weird!"

When an ex-Green Beret's family is killed by the mafia, he retaliates 100 fold by not only hunting down those responsible, but by pretty much ending the mafia altogether. The Green Beret is Slaughter (Jim Brown), a suave James Bond-style badass who looks just as good gambling in casinos as he does smashing thugs or mowing them down with bullets. He's good with the ladies, too, and in the middle of his crusade to "slaughter" the Mafioso who ended his family, mob henchman Dominic Hoffo (Rip Torn) loses his main squeeze Ann (Stella Stevens) to Slaughter's irresistible charms.

I almost don't want to consider this movie blaxploitation just because Jim Brown is the star. It feels like a movie that could star anyone of his era, someone like Charles Bronson, William Smith, Yul Brynner, Burt Reynolds, or whoever. The fact that Jim Brown is the star gives it a whole different status, I suppose, but this is a solid action movie either way, and Jim Brown really came into his own as an action star around this time when he began headlining films instead of co-starring in them. The movie has some nice moments for him, and he emerges as a strong leading star, with action scenes and sensual scenes galore, which he handles with ease. Like his contemporary Fred Williamson, he carried a "franchise" around the same time period. *Slaughter* had a sequel, and Williamson had his Tommy Gibbs movies *Black Caesar* and *Hell Up in Harlem*. *Slaughter* was directed by Jack Starrett, who had a small role in *First Blood*.

Slaughter's Big Rip-Off

1973 (MGM DVD) (djm)

"Nothing's gonna happen to me. I'm Slaughter, baby. The baddest cat that ever walked Earth. And besides, I'm going to do it to them before they do it to me."

Ex-Green Beret veteran Slaughter (Jim Brown) returns in this sequel to fight the mob again after they try to kill him in a failed assassination attempt, which leaves his friends dead. He adopts some secret agent tactics and picks up some allies—a detective and a pimp—who help him accomplish some tasks to get to the heart of the mafia. The head Mafioso this time is played by Ed McMahon, and his henchman is played by the hulking Don Stroud (from *License to Kill*), with

THE MOB PUT THE FINGER ON SLAUGHTER
...so he gave them the finger right back-- curled tight around a trigger!

JIM BROWN in SLAUGHTER'S BIG RIPOFF

SAMUEL Z. ARKOFF ..... AMERICAN INTERNATIONAL
ED McMAHON · DON STROUD · GLORIA HENDRY · RICHARD WILLIAMS BROCK PETERS
SAMUEL Z. ARKOFF · CHARLES JOHNSON · DON WILLIAMS · MONROE SACHSON · GORDON DOUGLAS

'SLAUGHTER'S BIG RIPOFF'

Theatrical poster for *Slaughter's Big Ripoff*. Author's collection.

whom Slaughter has two major fights. Slaughter has plenty of time to romance some pretty ladies again, but when his main squeeze Marcia (Gloria Hendry from *Live and Let Die*) is threatened to the point of death, he really steamrolls through his objectives to "do it to them" before they do it to him.

Slaughter's Big Rip-Off doesn't really go the bigger and better route, but instead kind of does the same thing as its predecessor without adding anything new. There's a set-up for another sequel to be set in Paris, but that one was never made. The DVD version has a different soundtrack than the theatrical release, which had music by James Brown. Fans of Jim Brown might feel the need to see this one more than others. It's average. Directed by Gordon Douglas.

Slow Burn

1989 (Arena VHS) (CD)

"Scarpelli's gonna find out what a crazy bastard I am."

Antonio Scarpelli (William Smith) is the top mobster in town, and his family has been dueling with a rival Chinese family. The cops are moving in and they want to put an end to this war. When Detective Murphy (Ivan Rogers from *Ballbuster*) loses his partner in the crossfire, he goes off the rails and starts training to take them down himself. Luckily, he meets Gino (Scott Anderson), an undercover cop who lost his family to Scarpelli's hitman, Renzetti (Anthony James). Murphy learns Renzetti was the one who pulled the trigger in his partner's murder as well. Together they will set up the mob, and they'll watch all of them fall.

There's no way in hell you could scoff at a film starring William Smith (*Platoon Leader*) as an Italian mobster with an accent like nothing you've ever heard. Even Ivan Rogers (also in *On Fire*) appears to be having a good time. The film tends to creep along like a turtle but there're a few great moments well worth witnessing. The film is surprisingly bloody and features some killer squibs, even launching blood on the camera lens. Rogers gets to slap a few people around and toss a guy out the back of a moving van onto the hood of a police car. Ivan Rogers is a unique personality, and the film actually plays out as a solid action thriller (even if it does drag a little). Director John Eyres was the perfect man to bring this story to the screen. He really knows action and helmed the first three *Shadowchaser* films, never disappointing with the appropriately titled *Slow Burn*.

Snake Eater

1988 (Lionsgate DVD) (djm)

"You're a fuckin' menace to society! The Marines are right—you can't take orders! You're an oddball! You're some kind of nutcase! Turn in your badge— you're on suspension!"

This is the film that put Lorenzo Lamas (formerly of TV's *Falcon Crest* and the dance movie *Body Rock*) on the map as a bona fide action star. He stars as a goofball badass named Jack Kelly, an ex-Marine crack commando fighter who has joined the police force. His methods are so radical and bizarre that he's put on suspension, and while on leave, his parents are murdered by evil, inbred hicks in the Everglades, and his sister is taken captive. His only order of business is to track down his teenage sister and hunt and kill her captors. Like Rambo, he sets traps in the woods and uses stealth, brute force, and cunning to thin out the herd until he faces the leader of the pack: a thick brute named Junior, who's planned to breed with his sister.

An odd, whimsical charm keeps *Snake Eater* fun and interesting right up until the conclusion. Lamas makes a solid action hero, and the fact that he's more comical than badass in the film makes the film that much more fascinating because when he does turn on the brutality, we can clearly see that he's the real thing. Lamas's character rides a motorcycle in the film, and the characters he would go on to play in other films (and in his long-running TV series *Renegade*) would also ride motorcycles, which is telling considering that Lamas is a motorcycle enthusiast. Director George Erschbamer also directed the two sequels and the film *Final Round*, also starring Lamas.

Lorenzo Lamas, the Renegade, in Los Angeles, California. Photo by david j. moore.

INTERVIEW:
LORENZO LAMAS
(djm)

Recognized worldwide for his extensive body of work in motion pictures and television series, Lorenzo Lamas—the son of actors Fernando Lamas and Arlene Dahl—segued from daytime soaps and TV's Falcon Crest *into a career as a full-time action star. After starring in the panned breakdance movie* Body Rock *(1984),* Lamas *headlined in the martial arts action film* Snake Eater *(1989), and he never looked back. The* Snake Eater *sequels (1990, 1992) helped him solidify his longhaired, motorcycle-riding kickboxing persona that he perfected in the five-season running program* Renegade *(1992–1997), co-starring his then-wife Kathleen Kinmont. Some of his other notable work includes the Thomas Ian Griffith-penned kickboxing opus* Night of the Warrior *(1991) and the short-lived series* The Immortal *(2000-2001). Now in his mid-50s, Lamas has moved on from starring in action films—partly because the genre has simply moved on without him. He left his mark, and the genre wouldn't quite be the same without the incredible amount of content he contributed to it.*

How did you make the jump from *Body Rock* to *Snake Eater?* You went from a dance movie to an action movie, and you stuck with action from then on.

I always wanted to be an action star. Always. I told my agent this about two years before *Falcon Crest* was ending. I told him to start looking for action movies for me to do. He said, "Okay." I did *Body Rock* because I had a chance at a motion picture career. It was a chance to do a movie that was released theatrically. It was pretty much a guaranteed theatrical release. So that's why I wanted to do it. The last movie I had done just prior to *Body Rock* that was released theatrically was a movie called *Take Down*, about a high-school wrestler who was failing school. Edward Herrmann played the coach. I had high hopes for that movie. That was about 1978. The problem with that movie was that it was a Disney movie. Buena Vista released it. We were their first PG film, and they did not know how to market it. It was before Disney became Touchstone. We were the first movie out of the gate for Disney doing a PG movie. It had a horrible publicity campaign. It played for

two weekends, and then they pulled it. Not long after that, along comes *All the Right Moves* with Tom Cruise, which was the same story about a football player. I really felt that I was gypped by Disney. So I wanted to do this breakdancing movie because breakdancing was a huge craze. The problem with *Body Rock* was that we came after *Beat Street* and *Breakin'*, and we were the last horse to leave the gate. That was it. I grew up watching Bruce Lee and David Carradine and Chuck Norris. Even Sean Connery. I just loved that type of character. I watched *Thunderball* because it had judo in it. I studied judo at the Y. My dad drove me to judo lessons after school when I was in the third grade. So I told my agent to find me an action film. He found a company up in Canada that was making these low-budget movies, a company called Cinepix. I was sent a script called *Snake Eater*.

It's a great title.

Well, I hated the title. I said, "Who's going to come to a movie called *Snake Eater*?" It sounds like a porn film. But I really liked the character Jack Kelly in it. It was a way for me to start developing an action career. At that point—in 1989—I'd been in taekwondo for ten years. I had a black belt in taekwondo. I started to use some of my skills and tried to incorporate martial arts in the movie. I just love karate and the ability to choreograph fights. I worked with a stunt coordinator, and they were able to use the skills that I had. We worked with a stuntman who did the fights with me. It was a lot of fun. So I did the *Snake Eater* movie, and they wanted me to do another one. Then we did a third one. It became a thing. In between seasons of *Falcon Crest* I would go and do these action movies. In the '90s, it really hit its zenith because those straight-to-video movies were kicking ass. Everybody was looking for those off-the-shelf action movies.

So *Snake Eater* wasn't a theatrical release? It went straight to video?

Snake Eater had a theatrical release. In Montreal. They flew me up for the premier. I'm thinking red carpet, paparazzi. There were four people in the theater. And it was the kind of theater that had four other theaters in it. It was hilarious. It pretty much went straight to video. But it did very, very well. The reason why Stephen Cannell wanted me for *Renegade* is because I had such a strong foreign name in the straight to video marketplace. My movies did really well

VHS artwork for *SnakeEater*. Author's collection.

overseas. *Renegade* he knew was going to be big bank overseas to the foreign television stations.

You developed this persona throughout your action movie career: the long hair, the motorcycles, the gorgeous women at your side, and I felt like the *Snake Eater* movies were the testing ground for that image.

In the first *Snake Eater* I had a Harley. That was before *Renegade*. After *Renegade* happened, I had to keep my hair long. Even when I did my movies like *Midnight Man, Bounty Tracker, Final Round*, I was still on *Renegade*. I did those during hiatus. I couldn't cut my hair off! I had to kind of keep a similar look. They were kind of different characters—kind of. Cops. The movies didn't have the wealth of great script writing.

But that's okay.

And the characters weren't very dimensional. You know? That wasn't what they were trying to do with these movies. These movies were just action movies.

I don't watch these movies hoping that they'll have great stories or scripts. I watch these kinds of movies because of the star in them. That's the whole reason why they exist.

Exactly. And they knew that. The distributors knew that. I knew that. They were just a lot of fun to do. But I had to keep my hair long in all of them because if I cut my hair after season three of *Renegade*, I would look completely different.

And what about the motorcycles? That's a motif with you. In at least one, you were a motorcycle mechanic, and in others you just rode motorcycles. And the kickboxing themes were just incidental.

I just like to ride. I always have. I got my driver's license at sixteen, and at seventeen I was out on the street riding. My dad hated it. He thought I was going to kill myself. I almost did. I was really young and stupid. I was racing up Mulholland like two nights a week. I woke up in the hospital, I couldn't talk. It messed up my speech. I haven't gone down since then. That was a long time ago.

It seems like you made more of these action movies than any of the other guys doing action movies around the same time. Plus, you did several TV series at the same time. Tons of material. I look at your movies and I watch *Renegade* and *The Immortal* and I go, "How did he do all this?" How do you maintain a life and do all these movies and twenty-two episodes a season every year?

Well. There are certain things in my life that suffered, obviously. I had kids that I barely saw. If I had to do it over again, I would definitely take time off. But . . . I like to work. I like the experience of working with friends on every movie. It's just hard to say no.

Were these movies designed for you or were they existing scripts that came to you?

They were scripts that I was offered. But I had some influence in the writing of them. A lot of them were tailored for me. Not so much the plot, but certain characteristics of the leading character. They'd kind of work it out so that they were more fitting for me. If the character was an FBI agent, they'd change it to being a cop because of my hair. No real plot changes.

In many of the movies you made, there was a lot of stuff going on. Explosions, hardware, stunts. Today, I don't think those movies would be made. If they're made today, they're very cheap, but back then it seemed like they were spending some millions on these things.

Keep in mind that a lot of these movies were shot up in Canada. We were pretty much cowboys up there. There wasn't a lot of government involvement in shooting movies up in Canada back then. They had a firearms guy on the set, they had an explosives guy on the set, and they were very good at what they did. A lot of these guys were ex-military. We used full loads in our weapons. A full load is what you would actually use in a bullet. It's still spitting out lead. A blank is a bullet. It looks like a bullet, it has gunpowder, but it shoots out a paper wad instead of a slug. The size of the load determines the velocity or the power of the discharge. A lot of companies now are using electric guns. Guns that simulate on picture a live round. You look at the picture and the pistol will have sparks flying out, some smoke, but there's no kick and there's no sound. It's so lame. That's what it's gone to now. Most motion picture companies will not get insurance if they're using bullet rounds, shells, casings. They can't get licenses to do it. But back in the day when I was doing these movies, we were shooting casings with full loads of gunpowder . . . because *it looks really good*. There's a natural recoil to it. Also, the explosions and stuff. We were lighting fifty-five gallon drums of gasoline! Those were our explosions! We were using gas! Now, it's all CGI. They'll CGI stuff in there. I'll give you an example of how frickin' dangerous it was in the '90s doing these movies. In '94, I did a movie called *Bad Blood*. I had a ponytail. That movie had some *big* explosions. They were using some heat in that movie. I was supposed to run through . . . I'm killing all these bad guys in a warehouse . . .

I know exactly what you're talking about: You're running and there's these explosions behind you . . .

. . . all these explosions behind me . . .

Dude, you're back is on fire!

So we rehearsed this, and I basically ran through a row of gas drums. In the rehearsals, the special-effects guy just goes, "Bang!" I had already run through these rows of gas before he called "Bang!" I said, "You can step it up a little bit. You can hit the switch about two seconds before the last rehearsal." He hit the switch three seconds before the last rehearsal. When he hit the switch,

I was in between the last four drums of gas that were going off. So he hit the switch, the gas drums blew, and I feel this intense heat on my back. The flames are actually surrounding me. So I run by camera, and the camera guy goes, "Is there something on fire?" I said, "I think *I* am!" And I was! My shirt was on fire, my hair was on fire! I fell to the ground and , , ,

It's on camera, dude! You can see it!

(Laughing.) That was it! It was dangerous. We didn't have the best special-effects guys money could buy. Let's put it that way. We had the best special-effects guys that low-budget movie money could buy.

How long were the shoots for these movies, generally? Was there much preparation?

These movies were done in six weeks.

Did some of these movies blur into each other for you? Some of them are very similar.

I can't tell any of them apart. It's funny that I can't. Except for the *Snake Eaters*. The Jack Kelly character. He was different.

Do you have a favorite movie that you did?

I'll be honest with you. My favorite movie was the one I co-produced. It was called *Night of the Warrior*. It was also the movie where I had the best fights.

That's my favorite of all your movies.

That was the first movie I did with James Lew.

Tell me why that's your favorite.

It tried to be too many things, and it got lost in the process. It tried to be a smart action movie, and there wasn't a market for a smart action movie on video store shelves. I say smart, because the character I played was a photographer. He was taking pictures of dire circumstances on the streets of LA. Trying to get his photography accepted and seen and embraced by a person who would buy it for a gallery. It's not really a strong foundation to build a martial arts action film. A guy who wants to be a photographer. It's weird. And then they got a guy who was a very creative music video director to direct the movie. He had a great eye. It was too eccentric.

But I love it. It was off-beat, quirky, and kinky. Such a weird combination for an action movie. Another weird thing is that Thomas Ian Griffith wrote that script. What's the story with that?

He wrote it for himself. He and I and the producer were all studying taekwondo together. Thomas was enjoying a rather successful career as an actor, and he's also a very good writer. He wrote that script and showed it to Mike Erwin, the producer, and Mike came to me with it and said, "We want to get this movie funded. Would you help us produce it?" I said, "Sure." We couldn't get financing in place with Thomas. So Thomas—graciously—stepped aside as the lead

Video release poster for *Night of the Warrior*. Author's collection.

and we went back out there with me in the lead and we got financing for it. We just switched. I became the star, and Thomas became the executive producer on it.

Did that create a fissure between you guys?

No. To this day. I think it's the most generous thing . . . I think it would be like Sylvester Stallone saying, "Okay, Michael Douglas, you can play *Rocky*. I'll just step aside." It was an incredibly selfless thing to do. He believed in the script so much. We all did. He really wanted it to be made. Period.

That movie felt personal. It had your wife and it had your mom in it.

Yeah. I really put in everything I could creatively to make that movie one of the better ones. I had hopes for it going theatrical. Especially when we cast Anthony Geary as the villain. He was so good in that part. He has a huge soap opera following. We just didn't get the theatrical. We sold it to Trimark. They did an okay distribution. It did all right.

You dabbled in directing. You did *CIA II*, and you did some episodes of *Renegade*. What made you decide to go in that direction and how come you didn't continue in that direction?

I decided to go in that direction because I'd always wanted to direct. I haven't been fortunate enough to pursue it because the industry knows that I'm an actor and not a director. There's a lot of directors who need the work, so they're going to hire someone who they know is a director rather than hire an actor who wants to direct. I don't want to speak for anybody, but Mario van Peebles is a very good director. He doesn't direct enough probably because people think

S

of him as an actor and not as a director. Listen, this business is like any other business. The same five people do the same five jobs every time. They hire the same five actors to play the same characters, movie after movie, after movie. It's difficult to break into that cloistered club.

Are there any directors for whom you've worked that you would like to mention?

Sidney Furie. He directed me in a movie that I actually cut my hair for. I thought that this movie was really going to break out and go theatrical. The movie was *The Rage* with Gary Busey, and Roy Scheider played my boss in the CIA. I had to cut my hair because the character was a CIA operative. They weren't going to change the script. Sidney Furie directed a celebrated movie with Diana Ross called *Lady Sings the Blues*. He's a very, very prolific director. He gave me the best advice that almost anybody has ever given me in terms of performance. Basically he said, "Read it off the page. Don't try to do too much with it. It's there. Just read it. Read it and believe it." Jane Wyman said the same thing to me. The way he directed . . . I learned so much from him. I did that movie in '96, so I had already directed a little bit. It really shaped my directing style.

Talk about some of the co-stars you've worked with. You've fought a lot of guys. People like Matthias Hues, James Lew, and Jesse Ventura.

Jesse Ventura. (Laughing.) He was a lot of fun. The guy is built like an oak. The fight we did on an episode of *Renegade* was out in the woods and the ground was uneven with branches and rocks and shit, and I always try to clear the rocks out. When you're out in a non-controlled environment there's shit you can fall on and hurt you. Like rocks that are partially buried that you don't see until you fall on them because a little corner of it is sticking out of the ground. So what we try to do before we shoot or rehearse is basically landscape the area where we're going to be fighting on. You check for rocks and glass—there's glass everywhere, even in the woods! How is there fucking glass in the fucking woods? So we landscaped the whole area, but it's still uneven. He's such a towering human. I'm 6 foot 2, and Jesse is probably 6 foot 5, 6 foot 6, and fifteen years ago, he was still in really good shape. He was strong. We rehearsed this fight, and it was like chopping down a tree. That's how we choreographed it: Like I was chopping down a tree. He'd throw a punch, I'd duck and kick one side of his leg. He'd throw another punch, I'd duck and kick another side of his leg. This went on back and forth like three or four times, like chopping down a tree. I got up to his knees because in the last kick he'd dropped. Then, I was going to go behind him and get him in a choke and choke him out. First of all, he wasn't reacting to my kicks. I wasn't kicking him because you can't make contact or you'll hurt somebody, right? So I was giving him movie kicks. He wasn't feelin' it. So I was having to put more hip into it so he'd feel it. So I started kicking him a little harder, but he still wasn't reacting. He's a wrestler. These guys really pound on each other to get a reaction. They need to feel something. So I started to really put something into these roundhouse kicks. Now he's moving a little bit. "Oh, okay." By the end of the master shot, I'm beat, I'm really exhausted. (Laughing.) Ah, man. So I get behind him and I've got a choke on him, but it's not a real choke. I'm working on him. I could control it a little bit, but with the acting and the moving around, I don't want to hurt his neck. You need to control the pressure. He's got his hand in there, but he forgets and slips his hand in there and now I've got him in a real choke, and he's still running around with me on his back! Like I'm a monkey on his back! I'm going like, *Okay, where are we going with this*? It wasn't supposed to go like this. He's supposed to go down and I'm supposed to check his pockets, but he's not going out. So I put it on a little tighter. *A little tighter*. But he doesn't fall down. Finally, he gets it, and goes, "Oh." I was really trying to choke this guy out. He didn't have any safety at all. He's such a monster of a man. They say wrestling is fake. Get in the ring with them if you think it's fake.

Talk about the transition period from your peak in the '90s to what you're up to these days.

The market is totally gone for me. I'm fifty-five years old. I'm doing comedy now. I did two short films for *Funny or Die*. It broke the ice for me to do comedy. They cast me in a Nickelodeon TV show. Slapstick, loud humor. I shot a show for Spike called *The Joe Schmo Show*.

You parody your image. Are you okay with that?

Oh, absolutely. I think the more an action star can parody himself, the more he'll be accepted by today's audience. That's why *The Expendables* was so good. Because those guys all kind of send themselves up. They made fun of themselves. That's what people want to see. I'm not into being a serious martial arts star anymore. I'm good with that. I enjoyed it. I set out to become an action star, and I did. Now, this is another chapter of my life. I want to do comedy.

You're best known for *Renegade.* Anything you want to say about working on that show?

It was the best opportunity I ever had. It was my own show. It was the first series where I carried it. I got a chance to direct. I got a chance to produce. It's so rare to get a chance to do a show where you have so much influence. If I never get another series for the rest of my life, I'm happy because I got that one. That was it.

How about the show *Immortal?*

You know, there could have been so much to that show. It's a little sad to think about that show. They didn't really know which direction to go with that show. Was it a parody of sci-fi movies, or was it straight action? What's it going to be? If you watch it, you don't really know who my character is. You know that he's a 400-year-old slayer, but they had things that happened in the series that were supposed to be funny. It wasn't really well defined.

You did a movie that was similar to *Highlander* called *The Swordsman*. You worked well with swords.

That went okay.

I have a question about *Gladiator Cop: The Swordsman II.*

I wasn't in it.

I know, right?

I sued them.

Good.

I'll tell you what happened. I was reading the trades one day and I saw a double page ad, announcing *The Swordsman II* with a big ass picture of my ugly face. I didn't do this movie. I called my agent. I said, "Pick up the trades today. Did you know we did a movie last summer called *Swordsman II*?" My agent goes, "No . . ." That was pretty ballsy. We contact the producer, we say, "You will have a lawsuit if you do not pay Lorenzo for the same amount that you paid him on the first movie. I want that in cash, and I want it today, or we will sue you for defamation of character, or whatever." They did. They paid me for that. But I didn't do that movie. They paid me to be quiet.

Talk about allowing your character to die in *Final Round.* This was a first for you.

That's the whole story of this movie. I'm too old to fight. I have to coach Michael Worth, and I want him to succeed me. I'm an action star, but I like to think once in a while I can do a movie that has a couple of good scenes. So I thought to do this movie would be great. Joseph Merhi, the producer, wanted that. They wanted the character to die, and I thought that was a really interesting thing to do in an action movie like that. Gary Daniels was in it, and he went on to do four or five PM movies.

You've done all kinds of movies now. You've delved into the horror and sci-fi genre over the past decade or so.

I would definitely do a horror movie. I've never really done a horror movie.

Incubus?

That was so cheap. My friend directed that, and he asked me to do that as a favor. I don't really count that. I'd love to do something like *The Walking Dead.*

Anything you want to say to your fans?

Thanks for hanging in there. I hope that everybody can make the transition to my comedy. I've had a lot of positive feedback from the people who saw *The Joe Schmo Show*. Some of my fans from the old days, they liked it. They thought it was great.

Snake Eater II: The Drug Buster

1990 (Lionsgate DVD) (djm)

This second entry in the *Snake Eater* trilogy, starring Lorenzo Lamas, goes off the reservation a bit and treads into parody territory. Police officer Soldier Kelly (Lamas) kills a drug dealer (in cold blood) in an alley and he's arrested and put on trial. He's happy to plead guilty, but his attorney gets him an insanity plea, and he's put in a mental institution for rehabilitation. While there, his group therapy consists of telling his stories with all of the other crazy people locked up with him. He quickly realizes that the institution is never really that secure, so he leaves at night and continues his quest to rid the streets of drugs. When he comes back every morning, it isn't difficult to convince his doctor (an attractive, gullible woman) that's he's not really crazy, just intent on carrying out his own brand of justice.

Most of the film is set in the hospital, so it becomes clear that this *Snake Eater* won't have the action/adventure feel and texture of the first film, which is a disappointment. Soldier Kelly is even more off-kilter and wacky in this film, but that only makes the movie more silly and less badass. It's the sort of picture and set-up that movies like *Last Action Hero* and *National Lampoon's Loaded Weapon* were quick to spoof. *Snake Eater III* was much better and should be seen following Part 1. George Erschbamer directed.

Snake Eater III . . . His Law

1992 (Lionsgate DVD) (djm)

More in tune to the original than Part 2 was, *Snake Eater III* continues the saga of Soldier Kelly (Lorenzo Lamas), who is put on suspension from the police force *again* following a wacky incident where he saves a waitress from a robber wanting to raid the till. While on suspension, he becomes a private eye, and his first assignment is to track down some bikers who kidnapped and raped a college girl over an extended period of time. Her parents want revenge, and Kelly and his sidekick (a no-nonsense cowboy) do some detective work and find where the bikers in question hang out and take their captive women to rape them. The final act involves rigging the bikers' motorcycles with grenades and plowing into their headquarters with a wrecking truck.

Lamas's character in this entry highly resembles Martin Riggs, the character Mel Gibson played in the *Lethal Weapon* series. He is unpredictable, likable, and borderline bipolar, which makes him a fun character to watch. Much more entertaining than Part 2, this final film in the *Snake Eater* trilogy gives Lamas a good foil: a thug named Goose, played by wrestler Scott "Bam Bam" Bigelow, who has a fun scene where he's shot in the foot after he challenges Lamas to a fight. George Erschbamer directed all three films in the series.

Snitch

2013 (Summit DVD) (djm)

Hard-working, blue-collar businessman John Matthews (Dwayne Johnson) has a strained relationship with his teenaged son (Rafi Gavron), but when his son is set up for a drug-related crime he didn't commit, Matthews goes to great lengths to make sure he won't be in prison for the greater part of his life. Matthews makes a deal with a hard-nosed district attorney (Susan Sarandon) and goes undercover in the DEA to set up an untouchable drug kingpin known as El Topo (Benjamin Bratt). Matthews is clearly in over his head, and his brawn and gruff demeanor don't really help him in saving his son from a grisly fate in prison. He has to rely on fortitude and an uneasy alliance with an ex-con (Jon Bernthal) to save his son's life.

Marketed like an action movie, *Snitch* is yet another cop-out for Dwayne "The Rock" Johnson as far as being misrepresented as an action star. This, along with *Faster*, really show that he isn't interested in making a full commitment to being the action star he has the potential to be. *Snitch* has all the dramatics and intense confrontations of an episode of *The Shield* or *The Sons of Anarchy*, but it's as far from being an action movie as *The Tooth Fairy*. It was directed by ex-stuntman Ric Roman Waugh, who worked on *They Live, Tango and Cash,* and *Universal Soldier* in a stunt capacity, and directed the good film *Felon* with Val Kilmer. He displays some skill as a director, and stages a good car/truck chase on a freeway involving Johnson, but the film is woefully devoid of action. It's a sign of the times.

Soda Cracker

(a.k.a. **The Kill Reflex**)

1989 (MGM DVD) (djm)

> "Soda's not going to stop
> unless we give him a funeral
> —so let's *give* him a funeral!"

A slight variation on *Dirty Harry*, *Soda Cracker* stars Fred Williamson (who also directed and produced) as Detective Soda, whose longtime partner is assassinated by a sniper in the middle of a crowd. Soda is assigned a new partner (played by *Octopussy*'s Maud Adams), who can appreciate his quest for vengeance, but their captain is constantly at Soda's jugular because of it. Their investigation leads them to an obvious suspect: A snarky mob henchman, played by Bo Svenson, who has ties to corruption in the police department. Soda's perception of who his partner was begins to change as buried secrets are unveiled, and new dangers present themselves as he digs deeper.

A *Soda Cracker* franchise might have been interesting, but Williamson's direction is loose and free, resulting in a mostly unbelievable detective actioner that falls apart by the end. We know who the bad guys are, so there's no suspense. We know that Maud Adams will fall for Williamson, so there's little left in the plot department to play out in a surprising way. The action scenes are absurd. Williamson is severely wounded in the climax (and so is Svenson), but they keep fighting as virile men, trading punches, gunshots, and kicks. Some of the action set pieces (one involves a remote-control helicopter) are ridiculous. I liked what this movie was going for, but it's a mess. Williamson, however, is imminently likable in it.

Soldier Boyz

1995 (HBO VHS) (djm)

Fans of Michael Dudikoff need to check this one out. He plays a badass Marine named Toliver who runs a prison in LA, and he has lunch on the floor with the general population every day. He gets an offer from a billionaire to go to Vietnam to rescue his daughter, who was taken captive by some bandits while she was there on business. At first, Toliver isn't interested, but then he gets the idea to recruit some of the toughest, most worthless convicts in his prison to go on this rescue mission. It's a bad idea to begin with because he doesn't even bother training them, but he goes ahead and handpicks five men and one woman for the job. All six of them are hungry at the prospect that they will all receive Presidential pardons for their job if they come back alive, and so off they go to Vietnam with not a single day of training! Toliver knows what he's in for, so once they land in the jungle, he challenges all six of them to a fight to get the tension over with, and after three of them fail in their one-on-ones, they get on with the mission. From then on, they all have to rely on each other for their survival, and they have to learn to trust each other and get past their issues and hatreds. Toliver, it turns out, picked the right six cons to rescue the girl.

Here's the deal. This is a completely ridiculous premise, and it worked better in *Band of the Hand* because the kids in that movie weren't sent off to Vietnam, and at least *they* were trained to fight before they faced their enemy, but *Solider Boyz* amazingly works. Dudikoff was never better in another film. He's tough, resilient, and I actually believed that he was that character. The action is pretty good, too. There are some "holy crap!" moments, and the film ends up feeling more like an adventure than a war movie. Louis Morneau (*Bet Your Life*) directs this with a strong hand, and it's probably both his and Dudikoff's best work. Cary-Hiroyuki Tagawa co-stars as the leader of the bandits. He's typically serious and no-nonsense.

S

Soldier of Vengeance

(a.k.a. **True Justice: Soldier of Vengeance**)

2012 (Studiocanal DVD R2) (djm)

"We kill the bad guys before they kill us . . . with extreme prejudice."

Task force leader Elijah Kane (Steven Seagal) experiences a tragedy within his team when one of the members is shot dead by a Russian assassin during a raid. When Kane realizes that he was actually the target, he decides to disband his team and start from scratch. With team tryouts on his agenda while going after an old adversary—Nikolai (Gil Bellows), who's behind bars, but still involved in hunting Kane down—Kane has his hands full making sure justice is served.

The seventh entry in the series of DVD movies compiled from Seagal's *True Justice* program, *Solider of Vengeance* is an interesting departure when compared to the earlier films because his character is working more or less on his own rather than relying on his team, which usually makes up for a lot of the time. He's angrier than usual, and he shoots bad guys dead without hesitating. Most of the time in the earlier films, he gives the bad guys time to reconsider their actions, but this time he's not that nice. If you're coming into the series cold with this entry, you'll be fine because it's a restart. Written and directed by Keoni Waxman, who's worked with Seagal on many of his recent pictures including *Maximum Conviction* and *Force of Execution*.

Sons of Thunder

1999 (NOV) (djm)

During Seasons 5 and 6 of *Walker, Texas Ranger*, starring Chuck Norris, two younger characters were introduced—a Dallas PD detective named Carlos Sandoval (played by Marco Sanchez) and an Army sergeant protégé of Walker's named Trent Malloy (played by James Wicek). These two characters got their own short-lived TV series called *Sons of Thunder*, which was created by both Chuck and Aaron Norris. The spin-off features both Carlos and Trent starting up a private detective agency, where they help people and solve murders, with help from Walker and his partner Trivette (Clarence Gilyard) and the district attorney Alex Cahill (Sheree J. Wilson), who were all mainstay characters on *Walker, Texas Ranger*. The first episode has the two private eyes catching a serial killer, and the second one has them catching a rapist. Other episodes follow suit, with plenty of action.

Canceled after only six episodes, *Sons of Thunder* might be considered Chuck Norris's "lost *Walker* episodes," but the focus is never on him, but on the two young male stars that take

the baton and carry it. Norris's presence in the show is more of a blessing on the show's behalf, and he shows up maybe twice in each episode to offer pointers, to train the guys, or to give the guys some back up. He never really gets in on the action, so if you're hoping for the typical roundhouse kicking he does on every episode of *Walker*, you might be disappointed. Strangely, this show has never been released on video, but bootlegs are floating around.

Soul of Chiba

(a.k.a. **Soul of Bruce Lee**)

1977 (VideoAsia DVD) (CD)

"When a man concentrates his life force he becomes a machine of incredible power."

The Young Man With No Name (*The Street Fighter*'s Sonny Chiba) worships his master. One day without reason, someone appears and kills his master in cold blood. Chiba chases down the assailant only to find it's another student known as Samuan (Yasuyoshi Shikamura). The two battle it out, but Chiba is defeated. Afterward, he trains and trains so that the next time they meet the result will be different. With Samuan rising in the underground drug world, Chiba will have to count on help from an undercover police officer (Tadashi Yamashita a.k.a. Bronson Lee). The two of them are unlikely partners: One's a cop, and the other is a drug-addicted martial artist. The two of them put their differences aside to uncover the truth and tear down the local drug cartel.

What the hell is happening in this movie? There are so many bizarre martial arts films but this one has to be somewhere at the top. Japanese legend Sonny Chiba once again proves he's a force to be reckoned with while scaring the living crap out of his fans. *Soul of Chiba* is out of this world, a film where men are possessed by monkeys, Tadashi Yamashita (*American Ninja*) uses his arm as a bow, and Chiba straps himself into some sort of electric device that looks more like a corset and violently shakes his ass directly into the camera. Thankfully, there's an abundance of wild and frenetic martial arts, kung fu theater–style. Chiba is such a powerhouse that all the silliness just falls by the wayside.

The Soul of Nigger Charley

1973 (Blax Film DVD) (CD)

"Quiet down or this lazy nigger is going to blow your goddamn heads off."

After the Civil War ends, all the slaves have been set free. Some white men just can't deal with that fact and have decided to take matters into their

own hands. They've been traveling from town to town and rounding up former slaves with the intention of selling them to plantation owners in Mexico. Charley (Fred Williamson) has now become a folk hero; the kids want to be him, and their parents all worship him. He's tired of all the killing and wants to put an end to it once and for all. He learns of a train carrying $100,000 in gold, so he and Toby (D'Urville Martin) put together a posse to rob the train. His plan is to use the gold to buy the slaves before they are sold off to the Mexicans. If the plan fails, then he will have to find a way to carry on with the mission regardless.

This film is a sequel to *The Legend of Nigger Charley* and doesn't quite live up to its predecessor. *Soul* has a bigger budget, a bigger cast, and more action, but it somehow fails to capture the magic that made the first picture so special. Williamson never misses a beat and once again delivers a great performance. His character has lightened up a bit and the anger that fueled him in the first film has conspicuously disappeared. A shootout is always around the corner in this movie but *still* the film is tame in comparison to what we usually see from Williamson. Director Larry Spangler (*Joshua*, also with Williamson) directed.

Soul of the Avenger

(a.k.a. **For Life or Death**)

1997 (MTI VHS) (djm)

A superhuman martial arts warrior named Kaan (James Lew from *Blood For Blood*) has a legion of enemies, but his chief adversary is a witch named Ling Li (Nancy Kwan) and her henchman Sir Xavier (Richard Norton from *Mr. Nice Guy*), who want to see him banished to the spirit world. In their epic battle, Kaan is killed, but not before he transfers his essence and spirit to a homeless vagrant named Earl (Mark Pelligrino, who would later play Lucifer on *Supernatural*), who begins to experience striking dreams, visions, and spiritual revelations. Earl—possessed by Kaan—goes on a quest through Los Angeles (where the movie was shot and takes place) to find someone to help guide him through his spirit tribulations because Ling Li and Sir Xavier are hunting him. He finds Zani (Karen Sheperd from *Operation Golden Phoenix*), a martial arts sentinel, who is able to help him channel Kaan through a mystic spirit monk (played by Gerald Okamura) and bring Kaan out of Earl so that the ultimate showdown between good and evil can take place.

I started watching *Soul of the Avenger* at four a.m. one Sunday, and by five-thirty, my brain was melting. It was great to see people like James Lew, Richard Norton, Karen Sheperd, and Gerald Okamura jump around through puffs of smoke, fighting ninjas, and casting shadows in the LA nights where and when the movie was shot, but to call this a coherent, feasible action film with redeeming qualities wouldn't be quite correct. The writer/director Steven W. Kaman had the camera all over the place, shooting forced perspective shots to make the ninjas look like they're flying around, but what's going

S

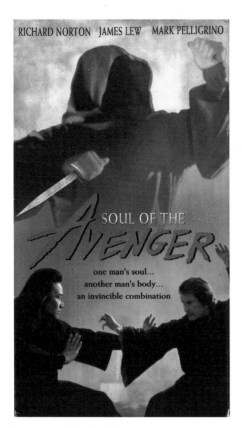

VHS artwork for *Soul of the Avenger*. Author's collection.

on here? No idea. It should be mentioned that Kaman was the cinematographer for a handful of '80s porno titles. Benny "The Jet" Urquidez and Nils Allen Stewart appear in cameo action roles.

South Beach

1992 (Prism VHS) (CD)

Mack Derringer (Fred Williamson) is a former NFL hero who is now working as a private investigator. He gets plenty of help from his old pro pals Jake (Peter Fonda) and Lenny (Gary Busey). Mack's ex-wife Jennifer (Vanity) is running a phone sex business when someone only known as "Billy" harasses her. Things quickly become serious when girls are dropping dead, leaving her with no choice other than to go to Mack for help. He'll do whatever he can, but he has found himself in hot water and framed for a murder he didn't commit. His old college pal Detective Coleman (Robert Forster) wants to help him . . . if only things didn't look so rough for Mack. His buddies are highly devoted to him, and they risk their own lives to help clear his name while he tries to figure out who's stalking Jennifer.

As far as dream casts go, you can't get much better than this ensemble. With people like Fred Williamson (*Black Cobra*), Robert Forster (*The Delta Force*), Peter Fonda (*Escape from L.A.*), and Gary Busey (*Under Siege*) on board, it's a wonder why it hasn't been properly discovered. They take this ridiculous script and shape it into a highly entertaining film. Once again Williamson jumps behind the camera to direct himself and gives us a film full of action and sex, which is nothing less than we expect from him. Though

it's predominantly a thriller, there are several shootouts and Fred isn't afraid to unleash his *hai-yah!* on a group of baddies. No one handles the lady action quite like Fred, and when the ladies come a knockin', he's ready to do the rockin'. This is a fun flick with a surprise appearance by Sam Jones from *Flash Gordon* and *The Highwayman*.

Space Mutiny

1988 (Echo Bridge DVD) (CD)

"Will you allow him to spoil your ambitions for a greater future?"

The Southern Sun is a spaceship that has been soaring through space for decades, trying to find a new planet to inhabit. Commander Kalgan (John Philip Law) is ready to call it quits, and has his own idea of where they should go. He joins forces with a group of pirates and uses the ship's police force to hijack the *Sun* and change course. When shuttle pilot Dave Ryder (*Cage*'s Reb Brown) almost loses his life when his shuttle crashes, but he manages to make it on board the *Sun* and realizes that something is afoot. He sets out to find the truth and return the *Sun* to its original course and stop Kalgan from completing his mad mission.

Space Mutiny is considered by many to be one of the worst films ever made, and they may not be too far off. Things happen in this film that should just never happen. All of the space action is reused footage from the original *Battlestar Galactica* series—people die only to appear as an extra in the next scene, and the list just goes on. The story I've heard is that director David Winters (*Rage to Kill*) had to take a leave for a family emergency and the film went on without him. At the center of this mess is the fantastic Reb Brown. He isn't to blame—he has fun blowing things up with his laser blaster and knocking a few guys around with his unique brand of fisticuffs. The film was a total bomb but received a new lease on life when the comedy series *Mystery Science Theater 3000* spoofed the film in an episode airing in 1997, proving to be one of the more popular episodes. No matter how bad it may be, *Space Mutiny* is here to stay. South African action star James Ryan from *Kill or Be Killed* is also in it.

Spawn

1997 (New Line DVD) (CD)

"You sent me to hell, Jason! I'm here to return the favor!"

Al Simmons (Michael Jai White) is an assassin for the government. When he takes on a top-secret assignment he's double-crossed by Jason Wynn (Martin Sheen), the leader of the government agency he works for. Simmons is burned to a crisp and is sent to hell. The devil makes him an offer: If he leads hell's army he will return him to Earth so that he can once again see the love of his life, Wanda

(Teresa Randle). When he returns, five years have passed and everyone has moved on without him. He meets an evil clown known as The Violator (a scene-stealing John Leguizamo) who tries to teach him and lead him down the path of evil. Meanwhile, Wynn is planning mass destruction with the release of a new chemical weapon known as Heat 16. Burnt from head to toe, Simmons discovers and learns to use his newfound powers (as well as call upon some killer armor) to betray the devil and bring Wynn down in the process.

When released theatrically, *Spawn* was a mild hit for New Line Cinema. Critics bashed it, and comic fans were split over it. For an actor who made his first appearance in a Troma film, Michael Jai White proved to everyone that he could carry a big-budget Hollywood action picture. While his martial arts talents were not fully used in the movie, his presence was definitely felt. *Spawn* has always been one of the darker superheroes and the film was watered down in order to get a PG-13 rating, although the home video release is "R". Jai White spends most of the picture in prosthetic burn makeup, but there's no mistaking who he is. There's action a-plenty, but the martial arts is limited to a few short moments. He's in the *Spawn* armor for the entire finale (with weak CGI effects surrounding him) so we don't get to experience the identity he has molded for himself in the films he has done since. His next notable role was opposite Jean-Claude Van Damme in *Universal Soldier: The Return*. Directed by Mark A.Z. Dippe.

Special Forces
(a.k.a. **Black Sea Raid**)

2000 (Spartan DVD) (CD)

"Do not attempt to interfere in our work. You can have the money, or you can have death."

Rick Halsey (Daniel Bernhardt) is a CIA agent approached by an old friend for help on a mission. But his friend is murdered, leaving Rick with unanswered questions and a need to go ahead with the mission. His superior can't sanction it but gives Rick his support. A Russian nuclear scientist name Natalya (Marina Mogilevskaya) is being held, and he needs to assemble a team to go behind enemy lines to rescue her. Once she is safe in their care, she reveals information of serious importance: She knows the location of a nuclear missile being sold into the black market. Rick and his team need to intercept the missile, but the greed of others on his team may cost them their lives.

Special Forces is a very low-budget affair but in all honesty, the film contains all the elements an action fan could want. Right from the get-go, the audience is treated with martial arts fighting, explosions, thousands of spent shells, and burning baddies. Daniel Bernhardt (from the *Bloodsport* sequels) is at the center of most the action and has several opportunities to show off his skills. It's nowhere near his best work, but it's still entertaining. He never really gets to show off fully since there is no real one-on-one fight.

S

The movie comes in at a trim eighty-two minutes with the majority of that time being some sort of action. Some of the dubbing from the supporting players may be a bit distracting so focus on the action and this one will be a good time-killer. Directed by Jeno Hodi (*American Kickboxer 2*).

Special Forces

2002 (First Look DVD) (djm)

Fans of *The Expendables* should have a good time with this very similar action film, directed by Isaac (*Ninja*) Florentine. An American female journalist is taken captive by a cutthroat group in Eastern Europe and a special forces commando unit led by Marshall Teague goes in to rescue her. The unit is assisted by a rogue British agent (Scott Adkins in an early role) who saves their butts more than once.

What makes this movie work is the casting. Teague and his commandos are all played by tough-looking badasses, and Adkins all but steals the show. He has an incredible fight scene with one of the lead villains, and it was this movie that got him in through Nu Image's door. Thanks to Florentine, Adkins would soon climb the action movie ladder, later co-starring beside the likes of Michael Jai White, Jean-Claude Van Damme, and Dolph Lundgren, and then having his own vehicle films like *Ninja*. *Special Forces* is precisely what it intends to be, and then some. It's typical of its type, but if you've seen anything else by Florentine then you know you're going to get just a little more than you might expect.

Special ID

2013 (Well Go USA DVD) (CD)

Detective Chen (Donnie Yen) has spent a major portion of his career deep undercover. He looks and acts the part, so much so that his boss is beginning to wonder if he has crossed over for good. While undercover, he had mentored Sonny (Andy On) who has just made his way back to China after spending three years in America. Sonny kills a mob leader and has plans to take over the criminal underworld in his country. Chen is reassigned from Hong Kong to China to help catch Sonny. He's paired up with female cop Fang Jing (Jing Tian), and the two don't see eye to eye. She treats him like he's a real criminal and it isn't until they are facing death that she learns to trust him. Through their trust, Chen begins to feel more like a cop again and wants to close this case, hoping that he can leave his undercover past behind.

After a string of period and fantasy flicks, this was supposed to be Donnie Yen's (*Flashpoint*) big return to modern action films. Sadly, the film was plagued by turmoil behind the scenes, which seems to have affected the final outcome. This was a very different performance for Yen, and the departure in style and character served him well. There are many great action scenes in the film, and Yen is always right in the center of them. His fighting technique is very different from what we are used to seeing from him. At times he almost seems like a madman flailing blindly at anything, when he is actually just using anything he can to survive. It

was also a nice surprise to see him using grappling techniques usually found in an MMA movie. With age creeping up on him (he was nearly fifty when this was shot), it's nice to know he still has what it takes and that he's able to try new things and mix it up a bit. While the story falters, the action still delivers top-notch excitement. Directed by Clarence Fok (*The Iceman Cometh*).

The Specialist

1994 (Warner DVD) (djm)

An explosives specialist named Ray Quick (Sylvester Stallone) is a sort of assassin for hire, but he only chooses certain jobs that require his particular expertise. A sultry woman named May Munro (Sharon Stone) comes to him and asks him to do a job for her: Kill a Mafioso patriarch (Rod Steiger), his son (Eric Roberts), and some of their hired thugs one by one as punishment for the pain she's endured for most of her life when her mother and father were viciously murdered in front of her as a child. Quick is careful and hesitant as he begins to trust her, but as he comes to see that she's genuine, he takes on the job and begins his assassinations. In the process of the killings, he gets the attention of a former colleague in the special forces, a slimy psychotic named Trent (James Woods), who is working with the mafia *and* with the bomb squad to find the assassin who's been killing with explosives. As Quick falls in love/lust with May, she reveals to him that she's not a woman he can trust, and when it's revealed that she's working with Trent to root out his former colleague/nemesis, Quick turns up the heat and sets the charges to burn.

Ultra slick and star powered, *The Specialist* marks the first time Stallone engaged in erotic scenes with a co-star, and Sharon Stone certainly wasn't shy or new to this sort of thing. Her chemistry with Sly on screen is good, and the sexy Miami atmosphere and smoky John Barry score give the film an extra dose of noir-swelter that helps it achieve a unique status as an *erotic* action picture. There are decent action set-ups and lots of explosions, and Stallone's performance is pretty good, despite an awkward scuffle in a bus with some ruffians who refuse to give up a seat to a pregnant lady. The movie's co-stars—James Woods and Eric Roberts—really spice the movie up with their presence, and without them the movie would be a little lackluster. The theme song "Turn the Beat Around" by Gloria Estefan was a huge hit on the radio and continues to get airplay. Director Luis Llosa also did *Sniper*.

Spectre

2005 (Sony DVD) (djm)

"You're a kite dancing in a hurricane, Mr. Bond."

After the events in *Skyfall* left him in tears, James Bond (Daniel Craig) goes to Mexico City to hunt down an assassin, which was the final mission

"M" (Judi Dench) gave him. With that mission accomplished, a whole can of worms is opened as Bond edges closer to the shadowy terrorist organization known as Spectre. which begins to reveal itself and the puppet master who is running the show. It seems that all of the supe villains from the Craig/Bond universe are all connected, and someone from Bond's own past has orchestrated "all of his pain" since he was a young lad. As the clues point Bond to the beautiful daughter of a former nemesis of his, Bond begins to be pursued by a powerful henchman named Mr. Hinx (professional wrestler turned action star Dave Bautista) who is above and beyond his superior in the physical class, but with some well-timed luck, Bond and his new lover Madeleine (Lei Seydoux), the daughter of his old nemesis, get the better of Hinx and are able to step into the stratosphere of the master class villain Franz Oberhauser (a.k.a. Blofeld, played by Christoph Waltz), who is just hours away from clinching a worldwide net of surveillance technology that would put the planet under his watchful eye.

Following the worst 007 movie of all time, *Spectre* only had one task, as far as I was concerned, and that was to be better in any way, shape, or form than *Skyfall*. It succeeded. It doesn't have a bone-headed, head-hanging sensibility to it the way that *Skyfall* did, and Bond emerges much more heroic and in tune to what has made him a beloved cinematic hero since the 1960s, while retaining the globetrotting, romantic, and thrilling aspects of the long-running franchise. Casting the hulking Bautista (who filmed this while *Guardians of the Galaxy* was killing it at the box office) was a stroke of genius, as he proves himself to be a worthy (and silent until his only line, "Shit!") henchman in the vein of Jaws from *The Spy Who Loved Me* and *Moonraker*. Every time he's on screen—and he gets plenty of screen time—you pay attention, and it would be great if they brought him back again for another Craig entry if Craig decides to continue his tenure as Bond. From director Sam Mendes.

Spitfire

1995 (Vidmark VHS) (djm)

A James Bond-type supersecret agent named Richard Charles (Lance Henriksen) is being hunted by global villains for some launch codes he possesses, and the villains kill one of his former lovers to get his attention. His lover confesses to him as she dies (with her boobs hanging out of her dress) that they had a daughter together, which is news to him. He does some investigating and finds his long-lost daughter in Italy where she is competing in the Olympics as a gymnast. His adversaries find him and capture him, threatening to kill his daughter if he doesn't reveal where the launch codes are. Around this point, his daughter Charlie Chase (real-life gold medal gymnast Kristie Phillips) becomes aware of the danger around her, and she flees to Hong Kong with a wily journalist named Rex (Tim Thomerson), who is sort of a surrogate father to her. They are pursued, chased, attacked, and captured, but Charlie manages to surprise everyone with her unique martial arts abilities, which combine gymnastics and kung fu. She saves the day, the world, and makes it back to the Olympics just in time to win the gold.

Writer/director Albert Pyun (*Kickboxer 2, Knights*) was very prolific during the 1980s and 1990s, and he was known for working with real-life champions of martial arts and personalities strong enough to have action movies centered around them. His star in *Spitfire*, Kristie Phillips (a Louisiana native with red hair and an incredible gymnast physique), doesn't really have action star potential, and as rough as her acting is, Pyun makes the best of it by showcasing her real-life abilities and surrounding her with a good cast. The spoofy nature of the film is hard to like, though. It's got a goofy tone, and it never takes itself seriously, which I feel is wrong for the movie. It could have been a flipside to *Gymkata* with a female lead, but instead it's something totally oddball and weird. The foreign locations (Hong Kong and Italy) are genuine and nice looking, and there are scenes of boat chases, helicopters in pursuit, and even a jetpack getaway. There is a title song sequence in the style of the 007 movies, and several original pop songs on the soundtrack. Phillips never made another movie.

The Split

1968 (Warner DVD) (djm)

Following his supporting roles in *The Dirty Dozen* and *Dark of the Sun*, NFL player Jim Brown starred in this heist thriller featuring him as the even-headed McClain, a man with a plan to rob the LA Coliseum during a football match. He handpicks a crackerjack crew to help him do the job, played by Donald Sutherland, Jack Klugman, Ernest Borgnine, and Warren Oates. After their heist (their take is over a half a million) is a success, their loot is stolen by an outside party, and McClain's crew turns against him. He joins a cop (played by Gene Hackman) to try to reclaim the cash.

Relying on character development and suspense more than action, *The Split* is a solid enough vehicle for star Brown, who has a great knockabout fight scene with Borgnine early on. An abrupt, unsatisfying ending ruins what might have been a class act caper movie. Directed by Gordon Flemying.

S Spoiler

1998 (York DVD) (djm)

An incarcerated prisoner named Roger Mason (Gary Daniels) is put through the wringer as he is mistreated by the system. He serves his time for being a "spoiler," but when for mild infractions he is given longer stretches of time, he eventually becomes a guinea pig and is put in stasis for decades at a time at the whim of the courts. After being tormented by the fact that his daughter is growing up in leaps and bounds as he is brought out of stasis, he decides to stage escapes from prison to make his way to her, but inevitably he gets caught within a day or two of being free. Punished without mercy by the courts, Mason is virtually rendered an invisible man to the world, as he is constantly given more extreme sentences. A the end, he breaks out a final time to visit his daughter who is by now an old woman, and he visits her just before she dies of old age.

Pretty grim for a direct-to-video action movie starring Gary Daniels (*Recoil, American Streetfighter*), *Spoiler* is a low-rent iteration of the much cooler *Fortress*, starring Christopher Lambert, who in another book might be considered an action star. Daniels throws some kicks and stuff here, but he's basically a punching bag for his captors, who endlessly torture him. "B" action star Bryan Genesse (*Traitor's Heart, Street Justice*) has a small supporting role at the beginning of the film, and he fights Daniels. They also appeared together in Isaac Florentine's *Cold Harvest*. *Spoiler* was directed by Jeff Burr.

Spy

2015 (Fox DVD) (CD)

"I once used defibrillators on myself. I put shards of glass in my fuckin' eye. I've jumped from a high-rise building using only a raincoat as a parachute and broke both legs upon landing, I still had to pretend I was in a fucking Cirque du Soleil show! I've swallowed enough microchips and shit them back out again to make a computer."

Rick Ford (Jason Statham) is hell-bent on revenge. He has relocated to the United States and found permanent residence as a spy for the CIA. When his friend and fellow spy Bradley Fine (Jude Law) is murdered while on assignment, he's ready to head out of the office and make everyone pay. Instead, the assignment is given to matronly desk jockey Susan Cooper (Melissa McCarthy). She lacks any real experience, but the suspect they're after, Rayna Boyanov (Rose Byrne), has no clue who Susan is or who she works for. She will have to infiltrate Rayna's inner circle in order to get the intel she needs to track down the nukes Fine died trying to protect. Ford isn't one to take a backseat; he'll be armed and ready to make sure Susan succeeds in her mission.

After trudging through the two-hour-plus runtime, you will need to go back and watch something more befitting Jason Statham's talents. *Spy* is just a ludicrous concept any way you try looking at it; it is just a showcase for the so-called talents of actress Melissa McCarthy (*The Heat*). Statham creates a few mild moments of laughter but for the fan's money, he's just wasted in the film. The supporting cast of the film was fantastic and the more enjoyable moments of the movie belonged to the likes of Statham, Jude Law, Rose Byrne, and Allison Janney. Director Paul Feig (*Bridesmaids*) has his strengths, but sadly, casting Jason Statham in this film was a mistake. His character is almost a parody of his image, despite giving him the best action moments in the film. On the plus side, maybe the exposure a film like this will give Statham has helped to gain him new fans—but was it worth it? You decide. (Or maybe just trust us.)

Spy Kids 3-D: Game Over

2003 (Dimension DVD) (CD)

Pint-sized spy Juni Cortez (Daryl Sabara) has given up the 007-type lifestyle to pursue a career as a private investigator. He's down on his luck but getting back into the spy game isn't in the cards until the president (George Clooney) calls to tell him his sister Carmen (Alexa Vega) has been captured in cyberspace by a villain known as The Toymaker (Sylvester Stallone) who was imprisoned there by the OSS (Organization of Super Spies) to make him pay for his crimes. While inside, The Toymaker creates a virtual-reality video game called *Game Over*. It's developed to have five levels, and the fifth and final level is an unwinnable trap, designed to be the villain's escape route. Juni agrees to go into the game to bring his sister out and to shut down the game before the Toymaker can break free.

This third film in the kid-friendly series is every bit as fun as the previous two (if you like this sort of thing). The presence of series regulars (Antonio Banderas, Carla Gugino, Alexa Vega) are diminished to nothing more than cameos. This hurts the picture a bit but with the addition of superstar Sylvester Stallone (in a career rut after several hard flops in a row), it more than makes up for their absence. Every moment Stallone is on screen, he appears to be having a blast. The film is full of adventure with Juni and his pals battling all sorts of different creatures, all courtesy of Stallone's Toymaker character, so he's indirectly involved in all the action. While the critics have predominantly slammed this film series, director Robert Rodriguez (*Machete Kills*) isn't afraid to just let loose and let everyone play around and have a good time. Just imagine what Quentin Tarantino could do with Stallone in a movie.

The Spy Next Door

2010 (Lionsgate DVD) (CD)

Bob Ho (Jackie Chan) is a Chinese agent working with the CIA. He has one final mission to take down Poldark (Magnus Scheving). When it's all said and done, he wants to make a commitment to his girlfriend Gillian (Amber Valletta). She has three children who don't exactly care for Bob, so when Gillian has an emergency arise, Bob sees it as an opportunity to grow closer to the kids. It ends up being much tougher than he expected: Bob's friend at the agency, Colton (Billy Ray Cyrus), sends him a top-secret file that accidentally gets intercepted by the children. Poldark has escaped and is tracking the file, which leads him to Bob and the kids. Bob gets the kids to safety and has to deal with the threat before anyone gets hurt.

Hardcore Jackie Chan (*First Strike*) fans may scoff at *The Spy Next Door*, but it's actually a sweet and fun family film. The relationship between Chan and Valletta is never convincing for a moment, but the relationship between him and the kids is. The humor is obviously aimed at the youngsters but there's a couple of laugh-out-loud moments for everyone. The movie is a bit light on fighting with the exception of the finale and a backyard scuffle. They're meant to be more humorous than anything.

Chan does his usual shtick—using whatever he can find around him as a weapon like a ladder, chair, bicycle, and a pool net. It's all light family entertainment and a safe watch with the kiddies. Directed by frequent family film director Brian Levant (*Jingle All the Way*).

Star Wars Episode I: The Phantom Menace

1999 (Fox DVD) (CD)

"At last we will reveal ourselves to the Jedi. At last we will have revenge."

A long time ago, in a galaxy far, far away, a "Sith" Lord had received orders from Darth Sidious (Ian McDiarmid) to find the recently escaped Padme Amidala (Natalie Portman), the queen of Naboo, to bring her to him. This Sith Lord is known as Darth Maul (Ray Park) and he makes his way to the planet of Tatooine to find her. Locating her isn't so difficult, but getting his hands on her proves to be the real challenge since she is being protected by Jedi Master Qui-Gon Jinn (Liam Neeson) and his apprentice Obi-Wan Kenobi (Ewan McGregor). Maul isn't the type of Sith Lord to give up easily, so he confronts Jinn, who escapes with his life, but now Jinn and the rest of the Jedis know the Order of the Sith Lord isn't extinct. Maul follows them to the planet Naboo where he must face both Jinn and Kenobi in a duel to the death.

Everyone has already formed their opinion of the prequel trilogy but this first film introduced two characters who were memorable for completely different reasons: One is the much maligned Jar Jar Binks and the other is fan favorite Darth Maul as portrayed by wushu gold medalist Ray Park (*G.I. Joe: The Rise of Cobra*). Following in the footsteps of Darth Vader isn't an easy task but Park is able to bring a truly menacing and unique character to life. He wields a double-sided light saber, is draped in a black hood, and his demonic red visage gives the franchise a face. The two most athletic and exciting light saber duels in the film both feature Park. From the one-on-one fight in the sands of Tatooine to the two-on-one extravaganza on Naboo, Park's athleticism is amazing and is the only reason to ever revisit George Lucas's unnecessary return to a galaxy we grew up in. Park would later become a fixture in big-budget action adventure films, but only in a supporting, masked capacity. It's a shame, since he clearly deserves to be recognized in more action/martial arts roles.

Stash House

2012 (Warner DVD) (CD)

"I was really hoping you weren't gonna say that, David. You see, I bet someone twenty dollars that you two wouldn't find that stash tonight. I guess I lost."

David (Sean Farris) has a surprise for his wife, Amy (Brianna Evigan), on her birthday: he's found the perfect house for them. It's everything they've wanted and together they sign the papers, beginning the rest of their lives in the new home. They accidentally discover a breakaway wall only to find the shelves are lined with heroin. Not knowing what to do, they decide to go get help when they're quickly confronted by two men: Spector (Dolph Lundgren) and Jaffe (Jon Huertas). David and Amy will do anything to protect each other from the vicious attacks these men attempt. The house is almost like a barricade with surveillance, bulletproof windows, and rooms that can be locked down. Maybe if they play their cards right, they will find a way to use the house to their advantage and escape with their lives.

Stash House is a huge disappointment. Relative newcomer Sean Farris has proven he can handle an action film with lead roles in *Never Back Down* and *The King of Fighters*, so it's a shame he wasn't used in that manner. Throwing action legend Dolph Lundgren (*Red Scorpion*) into the mix for whatever reason and not using him to his full potential is a huge mistake. This is just a by-the-numbers thriller that shouldn't be considered an "action" movie by any means, despite the fact that it was part of the "After Dark Action" film festival (it played theatrically for a week). Directed by Eduardo Rodriguez, who also did *El Gringo* (starring Scott Adkins), which was also part of the "After Dark Action" fest in 2012.

Steel

1997 (Warner DVD) (djm)

"Well, I'll be damned. John Henry Irons has turned himself into the Man of Steel."

A metallurgist contractor named John Henry Irons (NBA pro Shaquille O'Neal) makes a mortal enemy in a dishonorably discharged soldier named Nathaniel Burke (Judd Nelson), who uses a weapon on the field that Irons helped to create. With plans to incite chaos in the streets with modified weapons based on designs Irons had a hand in fashioning, Burke builds himself up to be a quasi-super villain on the streets of Los Angeles, and when Irons realizes that his creations are partly the cause of the mayhem all around him, he builds himself a radical suit of armor and becomes a masked avenger known as Steel.

A huge bomb when it was released a year after Shaq's genie comedy, *Kazaam*, *Steel* is a well-produced adaptation of a DC comic book from director Kenneth Johnson, the developer of hit TV shows like *V* and *The Incredible Hulk*. Shaq, in his first and thus far only outing as an action star, does what he can with his limited acting abilities, but he works his charm and his likable persona into a passable role where he pokes fun at his basketball star image. He towers over his co-stars and tosses villains around like they weigh nothing. If something like this were to be made today, it would probably bomb just as bad as it did in 1997.

Steele Justice

1987 (Paramount VHS) (djm)

"He isn't being recruited: He's being unleashed!"

Martin Cove's answer to *Rambo* has him playing a badass 'Nam vet named John Steele. In Nam, Steele crossed paths with a Viet Cong general (Soon-Tek Oh) who was given asylum by the US. Years later, Steele is a burnout cop, whose best friend and partner, Lee (Robert Kim), is killed by a drug cartel, run by Oh, who has used his political influence to gain power on the streets. The general has a cadre of rough and ready bodyguards and "yes men," some of whom are played by action film's greatest Asian actors and stuntmen (Al Leong and Peter Kwong among them). Ronny Cox plays Steele's boss, who understandably can't keep a leash around his officer, but it's amazing that no one has the balls to fire Steele because he's *out of control*! Steele arms himself with all sorts of guns and artillery, and in the film's best scene he shoots his gorgeous wife (Sela Ward) at point-blank range for getting in his way (turns out, it was part of his plan).

Steele Justice belongs on a short list of insane action films. Other films on the list might include *Stone Cold, Invasion USA, On Deadly Ground, Tango and Cash,* and *Death Wish 3.* People like John Steele only exist in action films from the 1980s and early 1990s. That's a good thing. Cove is fun in a role he must have enjoyed playing. The Vietnam scenes are goofy and almost slapstick. Just before he kills someone, he says his tagline, "Good morning!" Robert Boris was the director.

Steele's Law

1991 (Liberty DVD) (CD)

"Halt—police! Shit . . . it doesn't work in Dallas, either."

John Steele (Fred Williamson) is one tough S.O.B. He's a former Green Beret who now makes a living as a cop in Chicago. He's in for a big surprise when his captain calls him in for a meeting. Two FBI agents are waiting for him, and they need his assistance with a case. The Iraqi Ambassador is making his way to Texas for the final stop on his tour, and there is intelligence suggesting an assassination attempt will be made. The suspect is Joe Keno (Doran Ingram), a man Steele has hunted before. The FBI sends him to Dallas, Texas, to let him loose so he can work his magic and find this lunatic before he kills again.

We can file this one alongside all the other classic movies Fred Williamson (*Mr. Mean*) starred in. The planets all aligned for *Steele's Law*, allowing the Hammer to run rampant all over Texas. There's an abundance of Fred-kwondo, endless shootouts, and he always makes time to deliver the hammer to the ladies. Bo Svenson (*Inglorious Bastards*) makes a notable appearance as the captain of the police force in

S

Texas. Their rapport together is quite refreshing and brilliant to see. It should be no surprise to know Williamson was responsible for the story and directed himself in the picture. He's one of those directors who wisely knows his limitations and is able to focus on his strengths. This is grade "A" entertainment for the "B"-movie mindset.

Stick

1985 (Universal DVD) (djm)

Moke: "What the fuck you lookin' at?"
Sitck: "I never seen anybody with bunny eyes before."

Ernest Stickley (Burt Reynolds) gets out of the slammer and visits his former cellmate, who is running drugs in the Everglades. On a drug/cash exchange, his buddy is murdered in front of him by a psychopathic albino who goes by "Moke" (famed stuntman Dar Robinson). Stick escapes and lays low by charming himself into the good graces of a multimillionaire buffoon named Barry (George Segal), who has ties to a drug cartel and movie producers, and also has money to burn. Barry takes a shine to Stick, who in turn takes a shine to Barry's business associate Kyle (Candice Bergen), and just like that Stick has become a major player in Barry's world of high rollers. When Moke finds Stick living in the lap of luxury, his boss (Charles Durning) orders a hit on Stick, but Stick doesn't turn the other cheek when struck—he turns up the heat and goes full gallop!

Based on a book by Elmore Leonard, *Stick* is a great vehicle for star/director Reynolds, who was at the peak of his stardom here. After his superlative *Sharkey's Machine*, Reynolds should have kept climbing, but instead he made too many lazy vehicle films like *Stroker Ace* and *Cannonball Run* that helped sink his star. Reynolds cast stuntman Dar Robinson in the crucial role of Moke (who is a great movie villain), and it was an inspired casting choice, as Robinson hadn't really had much experience as an actor at this point. Robinson, who was one of the great high-fall stuntmen experts of all time, gets to tussle with Reynolds, and ultimately do what he did best in his final scene in the film. *Stick* is an excellent little action film, but it's also a great place to get acquainted with one of the most daring stuntmen who ever lived. For more of Dar in front of the camera, see *Cyclone*.

St. Ives

1976 (Warner DVD) (djm)

A gumshoe named Raymond St. Ives (Charles Bronson) based out of a dumpy hotel is hired by a beautiful woman named Janet Whistler (Jacqueline Bisset), who works for a retired notorious thief. The thief—Abner Procane (John Houseman)—has had his diary stolen, and he needs St. Ives to retrieve it for him. St. Ives takes the job, but as soon as he tries to make an exchange with the blackmailer, the blackmailer turns up dead, and just like that St. Ives is on the police watch list because he was at the

scene of the crime. He stays on the case so long as Procane continues to pay him, but every errand he goes on ends with someone's death, or an attempt on his own life. One scene has him being harassed by some goons (played by Jeff Goldblum and Robert England), and he gets thrown down an elevator shaft, but being as in shape as he is, he manages to save his own life and get the better of the goons.

A breezy private-eye thriller with some comedic elements, *St. Ives* is perfect action fodder for fans of Bronson, and some of the best scenes in the film don't really involve action. There's a scene at the end where he lifts the lovely Bisset in his arms and tosses her in a swimming pool (she's not as sweet as she seems in the movie), and it's just a throwaway moment, but in the context of the film and the way Bronson does it, it is classic. This is not essential Bronson viewing, but any real fan should get around to it at some point. This was director J. Lee Thompson's first film with Bronson, but they would make many more together. Their next film was *The White Buffalo*, and then *Cabo Blanco*.

Stone Cold

1991 (MGM DVD) (djm)

A standout in the genre, *Stone Cold* was the first film Brian (The Boz) Bosworth starred in following his career as an NFL linebacker. Here he plays an on-suspension cop named Joe Huff who is asked by the FBI to go deep undercover in a motorcycle gang to bring down their operation. He becomes

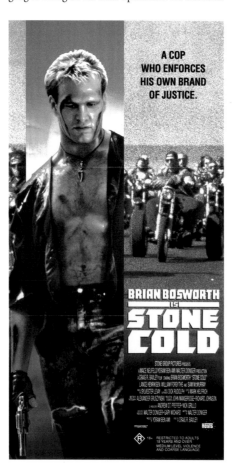

A COP
WHO ENFORCES
HIS OWN BRAND
OF JUSTICE.

BRIAN BOSWORTH
**STONE
COLD**

Australian poster for *Stone Cold*. Author's collection.

John Stone, a smooth and cool biker who quickly gains the trust of the gang's leader, Chains Cooper (a superlative Lance Henriksen), much to the aggravation of Chain's right-hand man, Ice (William Forsythe). Stone becomes Chain's trusted right hand, privy to the deepest and ugliest goings-on in the gang until his identity is compromised. Chains plan to attack the courts of Washington, a huge operation that involves his entire gang, a helicopter assault, and a bombing, and Stone must save the day. The climax involves motorcycles in the Capitol building, a jousting competition (sort of), and a motorcycle slamming into a helicopter (in the air!). It's amazing.

I love *Stone Cold*. Bosworth made a fantastic action star, and it's a mystery why his star faded so quickly. He made a handful of good action movies like *Back in Business* and *One Man's Justice*, but he eventually began starring in movies that didn't deserve him. Director Craig R. Baxley (*Action Jackson*) gives *Stone Cold* a verve no other director could have given it, and it's filled with great moments, one-liners, and badass character moments. It literally is as iconic as any great movie starring Chuck Norris, Steven Seagal, or even Stallone and Schwarzenegger. This is one of the good ones. It's a perfect vehicle for an underrated action star.

The Stone Killer

1973 (Sony DVD R2) (djm)

Cop: "What hit him?"
Torrey: "A complete state of death."

Right from the start of *The Stone Killer* a pace of verve and unparalleled grittiness set a striking mood, and my eyes were glued to the screen. Charles Bronson plays a renegade detective named Lou Torrey who bulldozes his way through his cases, and when he gets the chance, he goes out into the field to find, chase, and kill the bad guys if the dominoes fall that way. I mean, seriously: We see Torrey shoot guys down point-blank, run over a dude with a car while chasing him on the wrong side of the street, and mowing scum down while in a helicopter! Torrey is the type of cop who could tell Dirty Harry a few things about how to be even more badass. The plot concerns a Mafioso named Vescari (Martin Balsam), who has planned a revenge on other mafia dons for the past forty years. As his plan comes to the attention of Torrey, it's a race to stop the massacre he has in mind, but first Torrey has to find and stop/kill the Vietnam veterans Vescari has hired to carry out the massacre, and *then* get to the point where he can nail Vescari and the other members of the mafia who are responsible for the string of deaths around town.

Complicated, but vibrant from one frame to the next, *The Stone Killer* relies on slick editing and in-your-face violence to sell it, and it's a shame movies this intense and gritty (with stars like Bronson in the center) aren't made anymore. Bronson is fantastic in it. He punches dudes out, he runs, he drives, he splits hairs with everyone in the film. It's intense, but not for everyone's

S

tastes. Even Bronson's most devoted fans might have a little difficulty with it. Director Michael Winner also did the first three *Death Wish* films with Bronson, among others.

Stoner

1974 (Shout Factory DVD) (djm)

"The Happy Pill" is sweeping the world by storm. Genetically modified by a drug cartel in Hong Kong, the pill is instantly addictive and causes euphoria and an insatiable horniness that goes over real well with sex cults and pimps all over the planet. A gonzo cop named Joe Stoner (George Lazenby) goes off the rails when his younger sister ODs from the drug, and he tracks the cartel's origins in Hong Kong and single-handedly tries to topple the kingpin (named Mr. Chin, if anyone cares), but just when he's about to be overwhelmed by his reckless endeavor, he's aided by a Taiwanese female cop named Angela (played by *Enter the Dragon*'s Angela Mao Ying), who has a similar agenda to bring the cartel down. Stoner with his chop sockie skills and Angela with her hapkido abilities manage to be a great team and rid the world of The Happy Pill.

A grindhouse movie any way you look at it, *Stoner* is exactly the movie it wants to be. and it's a success if you want to see a former James Bond spend most of two hours throwing little Chinese guys over his shoulders. Lazenby has a great fight scene with Sammo Hung, who plays a villain, and Mao Ying takes on dozens of guys, too. There's sex, nudity, hallucinations, funky music, and kung fu galore. This was once going to star Bruce Lee, Sonny Chiba, and Lazenby. Soak *that* in. Directed by Feng Huang. From Golden Harvest.

Stop! Or My Mom Will Shoot!

1992 (Universal DVD) (djm)

A buddy cop movie featuring a badass cop and his elderly mother can only have one title, and one title only for all eternity, and *Stop! Or My Mom Will Shoot!* is it. LA detective Joe Bomowski (Sylvester Stallone post *Oscar* and pre *Cliffhanger*) receives an unwelcome surprise when his pint-sized mom (Estelle Getty from *The Golden Girls*) comes to town to live with him for a few weeks. She shows off his naked baby pictures, walks in on him showering, and embarrasses him every second of every day until she turns out to be a witness to a murder. She aides him in finding the gun-running scum who are responsible for some serious crime in LA, and she surprises him when she turns out to be a credible witness . . . and a good partner!

This was the movie that almost ruined Stallone's career, and it set him back decades in terms of it being a punchline and a blemish on his record. It was produced by Ivan Reitman, who had found much success with making Arnold Schwarzenegger into a comedic action star, but after the flop that was *Oscar* the previous year, Stallone all but abandoned comedy until many years later when he did *Grudge Match* with Robert DeNiro. As far as entertainment value goes, *Stop!* is as lightweight as cop comedies go, and Stallone's

enthusiasm wanes from the get-go. There's a lot of Getty's shtick to fill two much longer movies, and at less than ninety minutes, *Stop!* runs out of gas long before it's over. An action finale doesn't really help. Roger Spottiswoode directed. He worked with Schwarzenegger on *The 6th Day*.

Storm Catcher

1999 (Sony DVD) (CD)

Jack Holloway (Dolph Lundgren) is a family man who is incredibly devoted to his country. He's the only man who can fly the new top-secret military aircraft known as the Storm Catcher. When the aircraft is stolen, the military immediately suspects Holloway. Though he's innocent, all of the evidence is pointing to him. While being transported by the military, his van is attacked. He's able to escape and make his way to his family. The only other person he can turn to is his old pal Lt. Sparks (Mystro Clark). Sparks looks into the group that attacked Holloway when being transported and learns of their dark secret as well as the plans they have in store to start a war on American soil. Holloway fights his way through the group until he becomes the key to fulfilling their goal.

This film is a middle-of-the-road flick for Lundgren (*The Joshua Tree*), who had been starring in a string of unsatisfying pictures at the time. There are several solid action scenes here: The best one has him using a futon as a weapon. With several exciting shootouts, it's a shame the aerial action looked so cheap and tacky. Director Anthony Hickox (who also did Lundgren's *Jill the Ripper*) does the best he can with the budget and resources he was given, though it just wasn't quite enough.

Straight Line

1990 (Cabin Fever VHS) (djm)

A white supremacy group that calls itself "The Future" is terrorizing a city where a black man is running for mayor. The group inducts young, impressionable white men to join their cause, and when a woman hires private detective T. S. (Too Strong) Turner (played by Mr. T) to help crack down on the mayhem, T. S. literally grins at the opportunity because he's had it up to here with the racism and prejudice. As T. S. begins to mentor a recent inductee to The Future, he realizes that the problem is manifold and that violence and assassination are on their agenda. With T. S. on the case, The Future doesn't look too bright!

Simplistic and by the numbers, *Straight Line* is an interesting little vehicle for Mr. T, who at this time was still considered a superstar after his star-making stint on *The A-Team*, but he doesn't get to do nearly as much as he should, which is a shame, because he looks great in it and he has plenty of energy to fuel this otherwise pedestrian plot. The movie was shot for television, but some of the violence verges on being "R"-rated. If you're a hardcore fan of Mr. T, then *Straight Line* should be something to see, but it's underwhelming. He deserved better vehicles. Directed by George Mihalka.

Stranded

2009 (E One DVD R2) (djm)

A French commando unit is dispatched to the Algerian desert (circa, 1960) to check out a downed plane, and during the mission, the unit runs afoul of some AWOL Algerian rebels, who fire on them. The French soldiers (one of whom is played by Cyril Raffaelli from *District B13* and the sequel *District 13: Ultimatum*) retreat into the thick of the unforgiving desert and wind up in a forsaken village inhabited by a cult of priestesses who are guarding the outlying areas from a supernatural element. One by one, the soldiers succumb to the evil creatures, and the Algerian rebels wind up fighting side by side with the French soldiers to keep the ancient *djinn* monsters from taking them all alive.

The synopsis I just wrote makes the movie sound 100 percent better than it is. Slow, uninvolving, not scary, and almost entirely action-free, *Stranded* (lame, boring title) should have been a great vehicle for co-star Raffaelli who could have used some martial arts on the possessed soldiers who hunt and kill other soldiers in their unit, but for the most part, he runs, hides, and snivels just like the rest of his team. If this had been made in America it wouldn't have been so glum. Stick to the energetic and exciting *District B13* movies (which, incidentally, are also French). Directed by Sandra and Hugues Martin.

The Stranger

1994 (Columbia Tri-Star VHS) (djm)

"I've no doubt you were justified doing what you did out there. I mean, those bastards were pimples on the buttcheeks of humanity, but you've been here less than six hours, and I've got four dead bodies on my hands. You want to give us your side of the story?"

Real-life kickboxing champ Kathy Long (from Albert Pyun's *Knights*) is cast as the hero in *The Stranger*. She plays a ghost known as The Stranger, who rides into a dustbowl town on a motorcycle, looking for revenge on those who raped and murdered her. Andrew Divoff (from *Nemesis 4*) plays the motorcycle gang leader who was chiefly responsible for her rape and death, and his cronies (played by the likes of Danny Trejo and Nils Allen Stewart) hang around him, waiting to be ordered to do something heinous. When The Stranger rides into town seeking revenge she doesn't waste any time in making sure the scumbags who plague the area know she's there. She wears skimpy attire and invites men to call her a bitch, and when they do, she shows no mercy. The sheriff of the town is a former lover of hers, and even he's at a loss as to how to handle her. She helps a homeless girl find a home, and when she's done revenging, she rides off into the sunset.

S

Video release poster for *The Stranger*. Author's collection.

Kathy Long, who was so interesting and cool to watch in *Knights* is given a one-note role to work with, and she's never any fun in *The Stranger*. Her humorless line deliveries and one-track minded mission in the film give the proceedings a heaviness that ultimately sinks the entire film. The action and fight scenes aren't special, either, which is a shame. A cool western-style score by Kevin Kiner helps a little, but not enough. Long next appeared opposite Richard Norton in *Under the Gun*. Directed by Fritz Kiersch.

The Stranger

2010 (Anchor Bay DVD) (CD)

"I didn't mind screwing the Tijuana cartel, that was my job. But I'm not gonna die for a few lousy bucks."

Steve Austin is a mysterious stranger who has amnesia. He has no idea why he is doing what he's doing or where he's going. The only thing he remembers is the phone number of Grace Bishop (Erica Cerra). He has no idea who she is or why he knows her number but he calls her. She wants to help him to get his memory back but it's proving much harder than expected since there are people everywhere trying to kill him. There also happens to be a large sum of government money that this stranger has hidden away but doesn't know much about. He's haunted by a past that he can't remember. If he wants to have a future, he must come to terms with his loss and stop those who want him dead.

WWE star Steve Austin (*The Package*) is the type of action guy who may be a bit limited by his range as an actor. That isn't necessarily a bad thing if his director(s) are working within those parameters, but with *The Stranger*, Austin seems a

bit miscast in the lead. He has more of an everyman charm, a blue-collar tough guy who likes to drink a beer and be a smart ass. There's enough action here to please most of his fans, but the problem is that he seems a bit uncomfortable in the role. The spark that makes Austin special just isn't there. There's some hand-to-hand brawling and a few shootouts, but watch how he holds his handguns in the film: it just doesn't look right. The script had potential but was plagued by several problems, one being that the title character's name is Tom Thomachevsky, which is ridiculous. Director Robert Lieberman (*Fire in the Sky*) made some questionable decisions when assembling the picture. The opening felt out of place, there's poor (digital) cinematography, and the action scenes rarely build any excitement or maintain momentum. Austin isn't to blame here; he did the best he could in a film that just wasn't meant for him.

Stranglehold

1994 (New Concord DVD) (djm)

By-the-numbers action fare with Jerry Trimble as a badass Secret Service agent tasked to guard a Congresswoman as she tours a chemical plant. When terrorists (led by smarmy Vernon Wells from *Commando*) take over the plant and hold the Congresswoman hostage, Trimble springs into action, *Die Hard*-style.

Most of the film's short running time (seventy-three minutes) is set in and around the chemical compound, so the setting gives Trimble an advantage. There are lots of bars he can climb and chains and wires he can heroically swing from. His character is 100 percent good, and he has a one-track mind, which makes him boring. The villains, who threaten to unleash a virus if they aren't paid millions of dollars, are fairly uninteresting too. The fact that the movie just isn't very good isn't Trimble's fault. Roger Corman produced it and Cirio Santiago directed it. For better Trimble/Corman/Santiago results, see *Live by the Fist*.

Strategic Command

1997 (Platinum DVD) (CD)

"You may not like me but don't think for one second I'm not prepared to do my job. I was commanding missions while you were learning your ABCs. So why don't you just shut up and start acting like a leader."

Bromax-360 is a deadly chemical weapon created by the US government, and it's kept under lock and key in an FBI research lab. A group of terrorists, led by Carlos Gruber (Richard Norton), break into the facility to steal as much of the Bromax as they can. What they aren't expecting is to be interrupted by former Marine and current FBI chemical weapon designer Rick Harding (Michael Dudikoff). Gruber fights him off and gets away clean, but the FBI is ready to do whatever it takes to find them. When journalists board a flight with the vice president,

they're hijacked by Gruber's gang, which threatens to unleash the chemical weapon all over California. Harding heads up a special forces team to sneak on board and try to defuse the situation, but the stakes are far higher for him when he realizes his wife, Michelle (Amanda Wyss), is one of the hostages.

The first thing to come to mind when watching *Strategic Command* is just how similar it is to *Executive Decision*, a film released less than a year earlier. What sets it apart is just how cool the cast is. It's led by action movie legends Michael Dudikoff (*Avenging Force*) and Richard Norton (*Sword of Bushido*) and has names like Paul Winfield, Amanda Wyss, and Bryan Cranston in supporting role. Dudikoff and Norton face off twice during the picture and both scenes don't disappoint. It should be mentioned that these two also appeared in another film called *Black Thunder*, and that Norton was Dudikoff's stunt double in the original *American Ninja*. As predictable as it may be, when in the hands of such a great genre director like Rick Jacobson (who made a slew of movies with Don "The Dragon" Wilson), we get to see all-American hero Dudikoff doing what he does best.

Street Crimes

1992 (Madacy DVD) (djm)

Tony: "If I'd blown those guys away instead of handling them with my fists—*that*—that would have made me a hero, right?"
Brian: "No, not a hero."

Brian (Dennis Farina) and Tony (Michael Worth) are partners with a street beat on the force. Brian is the seasoned one and Tony is still wet behind the ears, but Tony has something none of the other cops have: martial arts skills. Tony is over exuberant when he's on the job—he sprints, runs, tackles bad guys, gets in brawls with gang bangers, and sometimes even drops his gun by accident. Brian saves his life at least once, but a scene early in the film shows how Tony, because of the way he deals with robbers and murderers, becomes a hero in the media. On the side, Tony tries to reignite interest in the local youth center by having kickboxing matches, and it doesn't take long for the undesirable element to challenge Tony to fights, which he accepts. The youth center becomes a hot spot for scum, and so Tony has to up his game in the ring if he's going to keep his department looking good. Brian isn't sure how to handle Tony at first, and when Tony asks his blind daughter out on a date, their dynamic shifts in a noticeable way.

A smart script with snappy, intelligent dialogue and a fantastic performance from Farina really elevates *Street Crimes* shoulders above most of its contemporaries. It goes on a little too long, with a drawn-out concluding fight between Worth and a local crime lord, but this is pretty good stuff for fans of early '90s action/martial arts fare. From PM Entertainment and director Stephen Smoke (who worked with Worth on *Final Impact*), *Street Crimes* was Worth's second film out of the gate, and while he seems a little too young to be playing a rookie cop, I still liked it and highly recommend it to anyone who likes these kinds of movies. It was filmed in ten days!

The Street Fighter
1974 (Diamond DVD) (djm)

Sonny Chiba's biggest and most infamous hit *The Street Fighter* is an outstanding effort in the genre. Chiba plays a ruthless mercenary named Takuma Tsurugi (or Terry for short), who takes a job offered to him by the mob. His task is to help a convicted prisoner escape from prison, and when he accomplishes his task, the second half of his payment is withheld, which sends him in a rage. He goes after the mob in a systematic fashion, and the results leave a trail of bodies and carnage the likes of which no character in the movie has ever seen or heard of before. Terry has flashbacks to his harsh life as a child that help explain his uncompromising nature as an adult.

A grindhouse classic, *The Street Fighter* features Sonny (real name Shin'ichi Chiba) in his crazed, fire-breathing glory. His technique as a fighter involves heavy, focused breathing, and wildly enthusiastic bursts of rage, and when he fights guys, they usually end up dead with gushing wounds in their necks, eyes, or skulls. Much like the classic anime show *Fist of the North Star* (which came much later), *The Street Fighter* centers around a brutal killing-machine hero, whose mystic art as a fighter is comparable to a god-like avenger. No one stands a chance against Terry the street fighter. The closing scene (a great fight in the middle of a storm on a ship) ends with the promise of a sequel *Return of the Street Fighter*. Director Shigehiro Ozawa directed this and the immediate sequels.

Street Fighter
1994 (Universal DVD) (djm)

Universal's big Christmas release of 1994, Steven E. de Souza's adaptation of Capcom's beloved videogame tanked hard when audiences realized it was a turkey. Jean-Claude Van Damme plays Colonel Guile, the guy in charge of taking down a megalomaniacal dictator named Bison (Raul Julia in his last movie) who uses mutagens and mind control tactics to help him create an unstoppable army. In the mix is a batch of martial arts fighters (the stock characters from the game fans expected to see like Chun-Li, Ken, Vega, and Ryu) who get

in on the adventure (but mostly get in the way), even though the movie only really needed Guile to save the day. What a mess.

Street Fighter (Van Damme's first PG-13 movie) had a troubled production, and it's easy to see the problems on screen. The script by de Souza (who wrote *Die Hard*!) is terrible, Van Damme had a hard time with the dialogue, there're too many characters, and the action is clunky. The finale is okay, but what this movie really feels like is a 1950s monster movie with some martial arts thrown in. Maybe kids will like it. I saw it at Christmas 1994 and went home angry. It hasn't aged well.

Street Fighter: Assassin's Fist
2014 (Funimation DVD) (CD)

"The man I face: my closest friend, my brother in arms, and my greatest rival. We both fight to win but right now it's not enough. Something has changed."

Ryu (Mike Moh) and Ken (Christian Howard) are the two sole students of Sensei Goken (Akira Koieyama). They are being taught the lost art of ansatsuken (Assassin's Fist). This style of martial art allows them to harness their chi to open up special abilities. The two of them train their whole lives together and live as brothers, but once their training reaches a certain level, they begin to lose sight of the brotherhood and become enemies. Goken is proud of his disciples, but he harbors a secret in his past, one he keeps from them as long as he can until his past shows up on his doorstep and he can't hide anymore.

This was originally a twelve-episode web series before being released onto DVD in a single feature format. *Street Fighter: Assassin's Fist* is the most faithful representation of the video game series you will find. The acting by the leads is adequate and the effects work used for their special abilities is decent enough to pass. Mike Moh (*Robin-B-Hood*) and Christian Howard (*Green Street 3*) convincingly portray two fan favorite characters, giving them life, and they deliver some very well executed fight scenes. They pay particular attention to giving the audience the signature moves from the video games and they never look corny or goofy. Action star Joey Ansah (also in *Green Street 3*) directed the series as well as appeared in the movie as another fan-favorite character, Akuma. The story is left open ended, and it appears as if the web series was successful enough to warrant what would be considered a second season.

The Streetfighter's Last Revenge
1974 (Diamond DVD) (CD)

"Bull, what I'd like to do right now is cut your goddamn balls off and then send them to you as a birthday present."

Terry Sugury (Sonny Chiba) is the guy people call when they need some dirty work done. He's tough, mean, and will kick your ass without hesitation. He's hired to find a cassette tape with a secret formula for synthetic heroin, saving the producers and suppliers a ton of money. The tape, however, will only work in conjunction with a second tape still on the loose. Terry's double-crossed and the tape falls into the wrong hands. Never to fail a job, Terry quickly puts the pieces together and sets out to find the tape and destroy those who crossed him.

The Streetfighter's Last Revenge is an empty shell of what the first two films in the series were. This doesn't make it a bad film, per se, but it just doesn't measure up as a worthy sequel. Viewing it as a separate entity gives it a bit of footing to stand on its own. There's some unintentional hilarity, heavy doses of karate, and a Mexican mercenary in a giant sombrero. The film lacks the ultra violence and gore of the first two but there's nonstop action throughout. Sonny Chiba (*Dragon Princess*) is so intense during the action scenes one might wonder if his head might explode with all his "hoo-ing" and "hah-ing." Tons of fun and action packed, view this one separately from the rest, and you'll have yourself a campy good time.

Street Fighter: The Legend of Chun-Li
2009 (Fox DVD) (CD)

"I want you to send Bison a message. Tell him the schoolgirl's grown up."

As a young child, Chun-Li (Kristin Kreuck from TV's *Smallville*) witnesses her father being abducted. She grows up without him and becomes an accomplished pianist. After a concert she finds someone has given her a scroll written in Chinese. Just days later, she loses her mother to cancer. With nothing left to lose, she goes on a quest to learn what the scroll means and to find out what happened to her father. She learns in the scroll that she must find a man in Bangkok named Gen (Robin Shou). After a fight with thugs, Gen finds her and takes her to his home, informing Chun-Li he knows who took her father: Bison (Neal McDonough), a crime syndicate leader with plans to wipe out the competition. With additional training from Gen, she will have the strength to take down Bison and his syndicate as well as learn the truth about what happened to her father.

If ever there was a film no one really cared to see, *Street Fighter: The Legend of Chun-Li* could very well be it. It suffers from horrible miscasting and is guilty of underusing certain performers who should have had a larger showcase. One person who emerged unscathed is Robin Shou (*Mortal Kombat, Death Cage*). He brings some much-needed authenticity to the picture when the cast is stuffed with fine actors who just don't seem to fit in a martial arts action film. Shou has several showcase moments as Gen, the mentor of Chun-Li. The film is meant to be a prequel of sorts to the *Street Fighter* videogames but it fails at capturing their spirit. It also bears no kinship (other than

The masked villain Vega (Jay Tavare) in *Street Fighter*. Author's collection.

franchise familiarity) to the 1994 film starring Jean-Claude Van Damme. Rising action star Tim Man (*Kill 'Em All, Ninja 2: Shadow of a Tear*) has a small role, and Hong Kong film legend Cheng Pei-Pei (*Come Drink With Me*) is also featured. Directed by Andrzej Bartkowiak (*Romeo Must Die, Cradle 2 the Grave*).

Street Hunter

1990 (RCA VHS) (djm)

"The more people I meet, the more I like my dog."

Steve James wrote and starred in this vehicle for himself. He plays a bounty hunter named Logan Blade, who wears a duster and a cowboy hat in the urban jungles of Manhattan. He has a sidekick Doberman pincher, and he lives in a booby-trapped van. Some Colombians (led by a pint-sized loudmouth, played by John Leguizamo) have muscled into the drug scene, which angers the Italian mob, and suddenly there is a street war. Leguizamo hires an insane militant (Reb Brown, who quotes a lot of war facts from history) to be his right-hand man, but Brown ends up taking charge and giving Logan Blade and the Italian mafia the hardest time. Blade and the militant have a hand-to-hand fight scene, and luckily Blade is an apt martial artist.

Steve James shone brightly in almost every part he played, and he shines here too, but the film itself is foul and nondescript. Reb Brown makes an interesting, but baffling villain, and it

VHS artwork for *Street Hunter*. Author's collection.

was nice to see these two guys go head to head. They were just about evenly matched. The film was directed by John A. Gallagher.

Street Justice

1991–1993 (VEI DVD) (djm)

For two seasons (forty-three episodes total), *Street Justice* packed a wallop on television. It starred Carl Weathers (from *Predator* and *Action Jackson*) and Bryan Genesse (who would later star in *Traitor's Heart* and *Cold Harvest*) as unlikely buddies in an urban city setting. Weathers played Vietnam vet Adam Beaudreaux, a hard-nosed detective with a heart of gold who is reunited with the much younger Grady Jameson (Genesse), a ward of Adam's in Vietnam after Grady's missionary parents were killed during the war. When the war was over, they got separated and Grady lived in squalor in Eastern Asia, searching for his adopted father/brother Adam. When he finally finds Adam living in the US as a cop/bartender, Grady once again becomes a part of his life and becomes a sort of deputized partner on the police force, helping him solve crimes and fighting bad guys. Grady learned some martial arts in Asia, and handles himself really well beside Adam, who uses brute force.

It's really strange that *Street Justice* isn't better known these days. The drama is pretty intense and the action is pretty great, considering they did the episodes fairly quickly. Weathers keeps the show grounded in reality, while Genesse shows off his martial arts skills and constantly gets himself in trouble. Most of the episodes (especially in the first season) are pretty great, and if you pay attention, you'll see some cool guest stars like Billy Blanks, Carrie Ann Moss, and even Salma Hayek. My favorite episodes had flashbacks to Vietnam or dealt with Vietnam vet characters. If you're a fan of Weathers or have never heard of Genesse, you've got to get your hands on this show. From Stephen J. Cannell, who also did *Renegade* with Lorenzo Lamas and *Cobra* with Michael Dudikoff.

INTERVIEW:

BRYAN GENESSE

(djm)

Canadian-born actor-turned-action-star Bryan Genesse got his start in the '80s teen sex comedy Loose Screws (1985), *and later transitioned into action-oriented projects, using his taekwondo and hung gar kung fu skills in the TV series* Street Justice (1991–1993), *co-starring Carl Weathers, and in motion pictures such as* Night Siege: Project Shadowchaser (1994) *and* Cold Harvest (1999), *both of which were produced by Nu Image, one of the leading production companies of action and martial arts films throughout the 1990s and into the new millennium. Starring alongside fellow peers in the industry like Gary Daniels and Frank Zagarino, Genesse built a solid reputation in the business and worked heavily in the genre until an on-set accident badly injured him and forced him into early retirement.*

Watching *Loose Screws,* you'd never think you'd go on to be one of Nu Image's action stars. Never in a million years. You're this teen sex comedy guy, and then you end up being one of the martial arts action stars of the '90s. How did *that* happen?

I was actually in a dress in one scene in *Loose Screws,* so I don't think Avi [Lerner at Nu Image] quite saw me in that way. (Laughing.) I got *Street Justice,* that's what happened. I was living in New York City, auditioning for stuff there. I had auditioned for this soap opera called *The Bold and the Beautiful.* When I was auditioning for that, I went out for it like everyone else did, and seven months later I get a call back—it was a long time later. They wanted me to go from New York to LA I was like "For what?" I didn't even remember it. So I ended up getting that part on *The Bold and the Beautiful.* What ended up happening is that I choreographed some of the fight scenes on that show. That's what started the martial arts choreography for me. I was able to do it. I love doing martial arts. I've been doing them my whole life. I started when I was around thirteen years old.

What's your background in martial arts?

I started with taekwondo, which I have a black belt in. That was very big at the time. It wasn't Olympic taekwondo, it was more of a combat taekwondo. That's what I started with. I went to hung gar kung fu and got a black belt in that. Then I did a bunch of different things—a year or two here or there doing different things like kenpo, and then I did Muay Thai for many, many years here in LA. I did judo and got a brown belt. I started jiu jitsu, Brazilian jiu jitsu, and I'm working on my black belt for that. The classic kicks I did come from taekwondo. I watched the classic guys during my time growing up who did those kicks and thought, *Oh, I can do that! I can do what Van Damme does—I can do the splits!* I thought maybe I could get into that as well.

You mentioned *Street Justice,* which was a great show you did with Carl Weathers. Talk about how you got that program and some of your experiences working on it. There's an incredible amount of action that goes on in it for an episodic show.

From *Bold and the Beautiful* I went to *Street Justice.* Carl was already attached. Once I got hired, what they said to me was that this was like *Lethal Weapon.* One character is a cop, and my character wasn't a cop. My character who isn't a cop is a martial artist, so he isn't bound by the law, by the other one is bound by the law. Sometimes you have to bend the law. It was a great concept. We had Billy Blanks come in as a guest and other great people, too. That was a lot of fun. It was exhausting. Honestly, it was a lot of work. I was choreographing as well. You work long hours, but you get paid very well, so . . . it's what we love to do. It was a difficult process to do all of the fighting, all of the acting, all the choreography, all that stuff. By the second year, they turned it around to be a little bit more of a drama. The buyers still wanted the action, and I still wanted to do the action, but Carl wanted it to

S

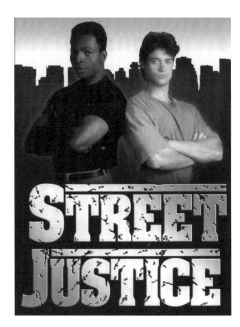

DVD artwork for *Street Justice*. Author's collection.

Frank Zagarino and Bryan Genesse in Nu Image's *Terminal Impact*. Author's collection.

be a little bit more dramatic. The show changed a bit. That's probably—unfortunately—what brought about its demise. It was sold as an action series, but it became more of a drama. I wish it had gone on a little bit longer.

How did your relationship with Nu Image begin? Was it because someone at Nu Image saw Street Justice?

I got hired for a project called *Project Shadowchaser* with Nu Image. I did not know Nu Image, and I didn't even audition for it. My agent got me hired based on my tape. They needed someone to go to South Africa to do an audition, but I couldn't be there because I was in Italy doing promotions for *Bold and the Beautiful*. Nu Image saw my action reel from *Street Justice*, and that's how I got hired. I went from Italy to South Africa. That started my career with Nu Image.

That was a great time for guys like you and Frank Zagarino, Michael Dudikoff, and David Bradley. You were all prolific during that period. You guys were all very fortunate to have been a part of that wave of direct-to-video action movies. You shot movies all over the world. Talk about making movies during that time.

Nu Image has grown massively. At the time, it was really cool to go to South Africa to shoot these movies. Nu Image had bought an amusement park, and that was their soundstage and where we shot everything. They'd purchased this park that was going to shut down. It had large buildings and open land. If they needed a pool, they had a pool; it was very cool to be on this land. I don't know how many acres it was, but they had this facility. At that time, everything was pretty basic, but as they got bigger, they grew and grew. The facilities got better, the Winnebagoes got better, everything got better. We were there to make these films. You could see that these films were shot quickly and got out there fairly quickly. In Japan and in

other countries, they actually went to theaters, but in the US they didn't so much. Mine didn't. My movies sold well in Japan, so they asked me to do more movies with them right away. I did *Project Shadowchaser,* and then *Terminal Impact,* and then *Live Wire: Human Timebomb.* I did those three right away, almost back-to-back. I would come home and then I'd have to go back out right away and do another one. It would have been great to become like a Jean-Claude Van Damme. I was hoping that I could have been groomed for that. Unfortunately, it didn't happen for me to his level. Nu Image works with Jean-Claude on *The Expendables* and other things now.

You also did a movie called Traitor's Heart. Do you want to mention that one?

Danny Lerner directed that. He asked me to do that as a favor, which I would have been happy to do anyway. The budget wasn't as big on that, but I said, "Of course I'll do it!" It was his first directorial gig, and he knew that I would make his life easy on that. It was great to work with it. He'd produced movies with me before, but he'd never directed. He had the reins. It was fun to work with him.

One of the most important movies you were in was Cold Harvest, the Isaac Florentine/Gary Daniels movie you did.

Cold Harvest was a riot! Great director, Isaac Florentine. He's a fabulous director. I loved working with him, and I hope I can work with him again. Gary Daniels is a great martial artist. They included me in there, so we had two good martial artists working together. You have great choreography—they brought in fabulous choreographers who'd worked with Jackie Chan. They were fuckin' awesome! As a choreographer, I got to learn a lot. It helped me grow. I did a lot of my hung gar stuff in that movie. They asked me what styles I did, and they showed me how to work that in. Fighting with Gary was great. He's such a professional. You see those fight scenes, and they're just great. Those fight scenes were shot over two and three days each. I'd never had the luxury of that before. A lot of fight scenes I'd been involved with a lot of fight scenes that looked pretty good that were shot in four hours. People don't believe it, but it's true.

I don't know if I'm speaking for anyone else, but what I saw you do in Cold Harvest makes me wonder why you didn't rise to stardom after that. What do you think happened?

Thank you. One thing that happened was that I was injured very badly on a movie called *Nature Unleashed: Fire,* which was the last film I starred in. I tore my hamstring in two places, I blew my knee, I serrated my back muscles on set. What people don't know is that when I finished that film . . . I told the director that I couldn't walk. I was in a full cast from groin all the way to my ankles bent at forty-five degrees to keep my hamstring from bleeding out. I couldn't fly home because I could have gotten an embolism from the amount of blood from the torn hamstring, so I couldn't fly. We'd been shooting for about a week and a half, and they would have lost a million or so dollars if they didn't complete the film with me, so I had to complete the film. They would carry me in and I would be a talking head. They had doubles for me even for the walking scenes. It was done very well. I would do my lines, but I wasn't in the whole movie. Unfortunately, I had to move to Canada for health care to get operations and stuff like that, so that's why I disappeared. I just had to recoup. It took almost ten years for that to happen.

Was there martial arts in that movie? What happened to you that you injured yourself so bad?

(Laughing.) I've gotta tell you, David, I've done so many films where I've done martial arts . . . I did a simple judo throw on one of the stuntmen. We did it, and it was no problem. We rode motorcycles in that film, and the wardrobe department built motocross pants for me instead of buying them. They built them and instead of using molded plastic for the knees, they put *steel* in the knees. The steel locked my knee in place. When I put them on, I said, "Guys, I can't even move in these. You've got to buy me pants. These don't work!" We had to shoot the scene, and I said, "Lemme see if I can do this. I'll throw a couple punches, and I'll throw the guy, but I can't do a major fight scene in these pants. Let's do that." So that's what we did. On the third take, I threw my knee, and basically my foot came to my face and bent the wrong way. All you heard was SNAP SNAP, which was basically my hamstrings snapping, and my back muscles were shot. A bunch of fun stuff happened. I went to the hospital. That was an interesting part of my life.

Well, okay, that explains some things . . .

Yeah. Where I am now is that I'm doing Brazilian jiu jitsu, which I couldn't do for years because of my injury. I can protect myself. I don't throw a lot of kicks anymore. I can, but I don't really do it repetitively. It changed my life. I'm a real estate agent now. It wasn't drugs, it wasn't alcohol. It was a very bad injury. It ended up being a big problem.

Bryan, you were an action star. What was that like for you?

It's exciting to be a part of a movement like that. As an actor, you are given incredible gifts. We get paid very well to do what we love to do. To go out in public and be recognized for something you love to do—like martial arts—was a phenomenal thing for me. To remain humble through that is the most

S

important thing. How lucky was I to be able to build those life experiences? I had all that. I would have loved to grow a little more as an action star, but I wasn't able to because of the injury. Prior to my injury, I did like eight or nine films with Nu Image, and it was fun to do better and better films and to be able to travel around the world to do that. I've seen some of my peers experience large success. There was always a movement that was moving me toward this dream that I had.

Is there anything you want to say to your fans who remember you from your days on *Street Justice* or from your films?

Thank you very much for the support. On Facebook, I get a lot of people who are fans of the show and they tell me that I had a big impact on their life in getting them into martial arts. Thank you. You helped me keep on the straight and narrow and helped me be a good role model, and if I helped you get into martial arts, then that's really the greatest gift to me. Don't write me off! I'm almost sixty years old, but I'm in darn good shape. Thank you for the opportunity, David.

Street Knight

1993 (Cannon VHS) (djm)

"Yeah, you're some hero:
A regular knight in shining armor."

Kenpo specialist Jeff Speakman from *The Perfect Weapon* returned to the big screen with *Street Knight*, which was his last theatrical release. He stars as a PTSD-plagued ex-cop named Jake Barrett who now works as an auto mechanic in LA Whenever people in the neighborhood have troubles with the gangs, they turn to him for help. A young woman named Rebecca (Jennifer Gatti) is looking for her brother, who's been missing for a few days, and she thinks it might have something to do with a gang war going on in the streets. As Barrett begins his investigation, he finds that a group of heavily funded men are secretly inciting a war between the black gangs and the Hispanic gangs. He quickly garners the respect of both sides of the gangs, while getting undue attention from the villains who are to blame for all the deaths. He also saves Jennifer's brother, and the police department asks him to re-instate as an officer of the law. The last motion picture produced by Cannon (directed by Albert Magnoli), *Street Knight* was a step down from the Paramount-released *The Perfect Weapon*. It has long stretches without fighting, and the plot is weak. When Speakman engages in fighting, he's a wonder to behold, but there's just not enough of it to go around. Still, he should be proud of the film and the fact that it was a notable theatrical release. He looks great in it, and he plays a

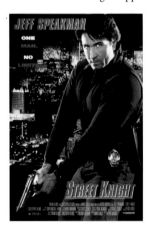

Theatrical poster for the last Cannon film *Street Knight*. Author's collection.

stalwart hero. He quotes Arnold Schwarzenegger at the precise moment when he should have created his own catchphrase, but I'll let bygones be bygones. He made *Deadly Outbreak* and *The Expert* next.

Street Law

1994 (Image DVD) (djm)

Lawyer John Ryan (played by Jeff Wincott from *Open Fire*) loses his livelihood after he borrows money from gangsters to keep his practice afloat. He's disbarred and disgraced, and soon a former friend of his—ex-con Louis Calderone (Paco Christian Prieto from *Only the Strong*) is all but demanding that he come work for him, but at nearly the cost of his soul. John takes a stand and defends his honor by using his skills as a martial artist to fight for money and to sharpen his skills so that when he goes up against Louis in a one-on-one bout, he'll be up to par.

Sleazy and mean-spirited, *Street Law* has as preposterous a plot as a "B" action movie can possibly have (a disbarred lawyer who fights in underground martial arts tournaments for money? Really?), but that's not where it goes wrong. It has a distinct misogynistic tone and all of the characters—including the one the hero plays—are unappealing and debased. Wincott is an interesting action star and if you see him in the right vehicle, he's fantastic. *Street Law* isn't a great place to start with him. Damien Lee (*Agent Red* with Dolph Lundgren) directed. He also did *No Exit* with Wincott.

Streets of Rage

1994 (Image DVD) (djm)

A former special forces commando named Melody Sails (Mimi Lessos) becomes a journalist for a small-time newspaper in Los Angeles, and her first big assignment is to write a story about children living on the streets. While trying to develop trust with some of the homeless kids she comes across, she is appalled to learn that a child prostitution ring is happening, and when a teenage girl turns up dead as a result, she sets her sights on the head of the organization, despite the fact that her boss at the newspaper tries to talk her out of it. Melody uses her military training and deadly kickboxing abilities to render the child exploiters powerless against her, and she puts herself at risk for trying to save the kids being exploited.

Shot on a very low budget (it's noticeable), *Streets of Rage* is really just about watching Lessos kick ass and, in one scene, shed her clothes for a gratuitous shower scene. The plot, script, and lighting are all fairly poor, but I won't complain because I feel like I got my money's worth. Lessos scripted. She starred in

Personal Vendetta next. The director is credited as "Aristide Sumatra," which is a pseudonym for Richard Elfman, the director of the cult movie *Forbidden Zone*.

Street Wars (a.k.a. True Justice: Street Wars)

2010 (Optimum DVD R2) (djm)

Elijah Kane (Steve Seagal) and his crew of undercover cops in Seattle are on a case involving a deadly drug that kills anyone who takes it for the first time. Young people are dropping dead at nightclubs over the course of several nights, and Kane is out to get the supplier of the drug before anyone else takes the pills. During the course of their investigation, Kane ends up killing the nephew of a mobster, who swears vengeance on Kane in particular, and as a way to get at him, the mobster kidnaps several members of Kane's crew, including an asthmatic father-to-be.

This is the third compilation movie from Steven Seagal's TV series *True Justice*. It bears the brand of television, with very little bloodletting or profanity (which is fine), but it's hard to watch it as a movie. The fact that two episodes were connected together gives it a disjointed effect, but Seagal fans should like it. It's better than some of his direct-to-video movies. *Lethal Justice* is the next compilation in the series. Directed by Wayne Rose.

Strike Commando

1987 (Revok DVD) (djm)

"Where your air force has failed, my strike commandos won't! They'll see you through!"

The amount of influence *Rambo: First Blood Part II* had on this Italian effort is immediately obvious. Reb Brown (*Mercenary Fighters*) stars as Michael Ransom, the strike commando. His superior, played by Christopher Connelly, is the back-stabbing bureaucrat who leaves him behind enemy lines during a mission to take out a Viet Cong base. Ransom is captured, tortured, and beaten down by a big, buff Russian who kills his cellmate and leaves the body in the cell with him for months. Ransom begins deteriorating until a female Russian takes pity on him. Ransom escapes, fights the Russian and knocks out his teeth, and goes to the American base and shoots up the place in anger. Later, he tracks his superior down in central Asia and gets his revenge.

Fans of Vietnam action films might get a kick out of the outrageousness of this exploitation entry. The violence is more extreme and outlandish than in the first three *Rambo* pictures, and the score is a typically cool synth job. Reb Brown made a lot of Vietnam action-type films. He was also in *RoboWar*, a rip-off of

S

Predator, which was directed by Bruno Mattei, who directed this film. Certain scenes and whole sections of this were directly ripped off from *Rambo II*.

Strike Force

(a.k.a. **The Librarians**)

2003 (Lionsgate DVD) (CD)

"Gather up your shit, Merry Christmas, and get the fuck out of my house!"

Simon (William Forsythe), Toshko (Daniel Bernhardt), and G-Man (Amaury Nolasco) are a team of mercenaries who call themselves "The Librarians." An old friend of Simon's contacts him for help when his granddaughter goes missing. After doing some investigating, the mercenaries find themselves slipping into a dark world of underground fighting, drugs, and the murder of young women. The ruthless Marco (Andrew Divoff) and his sidekicks Ringo (Christopher Atkins) and Ciro (Matthias Hues) are behind it all. Simon takes his men deep undercover and plans on hitting the bad guys hard and ending their reign of terror.

Aside from being too talky, *Strike Force* is damn entertaining and has one great moment action fans will not want to miss. There's an extended fight scene between action heroes Daniel Bernhardt (*G2*) and Matthias Hues (*No Retreat No Surrender*). These two titans face off about halfway through the film, each showcasing his own style of fighting while still making time to get a little dirty on the ground with some effective grappling techniques. Bernhardt has some other great moments including letting some loud mouth asshole talk crap to him, and he keeps himself calm until just the right moment. William Forsythe (*Stone Cold*) is one of the great character actors and this was a rare lead role. He also produced and co-wrote the film with director Mike Kirton (*The Last Marshal*).

Striker

1987 (AIP VHS) (djm)

Mercenary John "Striker" Slade (Frank Zagarino) is bamboozled into undertaking a Rambo-esque mission to Nicaragua to rescue a captured American journalist, played by John Phillip Law. His contact in the war-torn, chaotic Nicaragua is a foxy militant (Melonee Rodgers), who is a lot like the doomed female character in *Rambo: First Blood Part II* in that she's vulnerable, but good with a machine gun. Together, they traverse rivers, traipse through jungles, and get shot at and clobbered by enemy soldiers. Slade, however, isn't a man to go down easily, and even though he fails his mission (and says, "I hate violence" at the end), he lives to fight another day.

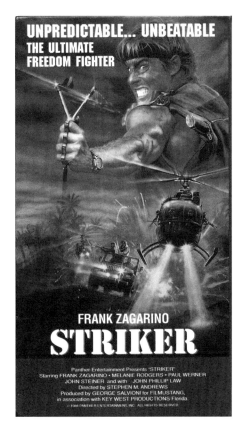

VHS artwork for *Striker*. Author's collection.

From the Italian exploitation film market and director Enzo G. Castellari (*1990: Bronx Warriors*), *Striker* has an undeniable appeal to fans of one-man army movie adventures. For one, *Striker's* weapon of choice is a slingshot that chucks small exploding bombs! Zagarino had just broken out on his own to pursue a career in action movies (he'd previously co-starred in the sword and sorcery flick *Barbarian Queen*), and *Striker* was his first solo vehicle out of the gate. It's pretty good if you like these Italian-made actioners, and there were a slew of these types of movies made during the era. Reb Brown from *Yor: Hunter From the Future* made a ton of these, too—stuff like *Strike Commando* and *Last Flight to Hell*. The sequel to *Striker* (also with Zagarino) is called *Project: Eliminator*.

Strike Zone

2000 (NOV) (CD)

"Covert ops is not a game. Things go wrong, people get hurt, and yes, missions do not get accomplished."

Alex Goddard (Billy Drago) is a former military pilot who defects from the United States and plots to sell a nuclear guidance systems device to various countries. While trying to gather intelligence, Rebecca Lamport (Sonia Satra) is captured by Goddard's people and held hostage in a secret base. Her father, Admiral Lamport (Richard Lynch) wants her returned safely so he reassembles his special team of Navy Seals, led by Rick Burns (Frank Zagarino) who is

also one of Rebecca's former flames. To aid in the mission, Lamport also recruits hotshot pilot Dunk Stevens (Joe Lara). The thing about Dunk is that he used to date Rebecca. He and Rick are constantly bumping heads, but they realize the fate of the world (as well as bringing Rebecca back alive) is more important than their petty feud. They set their differences aside long enough to do what needs to be done.

Strike Zone is by far the best film that action star Frank Zagarino collaborated on with J. Christian Ingvordsen (all four *Airboss* movies with Zags). This film (like the *Airboss* series) is chock full of stock footage and ridiculous-looking miniatures, but all is forgiven when the pair of Zagarino and Joe Lara (*Hologram Man*) light up the screen. The two have a great chemistry, trade some funny quips, and smack up each other. Having guys like Richard Lynch (playing a good guy) and Billy Drago rounding out the supporting cast, you have the recipe for solid entertainment. It moves along at a brisk pace while still allowing time for your eyes to roll when picking out stock footage scenes. These films might actually be perfect for developing some sort of drinking game to accompany them. Take a shot every time you see a stock shot, a double when you see the shot repeated—it would be a blast (or a mess)! This one is a must-see and it's absolutely F-U-N . . . FUN!! Zagarino and Lara can also be seen together in *Warhead*.

Stunt Rock

1978 (Code Red DVD) (JAS)

"*Death Wish* at 120 decibels"

Brian Trenchard-Smith's *Stunt Rock* follows Australian real-life stuntman Grant Page as he visits Hollywood, hangs out with the theatrical metal band Sorcery (think Blue Oyster Cult meets Kiss), and explains to a nay-saying journalist (Margaret Gerard) that being a stuntman is more about calculated risks than reckless living. The film highlights a parade of dangerous stunts with a nifty use of split-screens, and there are extended passages of faux concert footage that incorporate magic tricks, fire, and even a battle between Merlin the Wizard and Satan. Some of the stunt footage is borrowed from other films, but that just adds to the clunky charm of this 1970s grindhouser.

Stunt Rock is a furiously fun time capsule of a film, and a tribute to unsung stuntmen who put their lives on the line in the name of entertainment. This is not to say it suits all tastes. Virtually plotless, the movie chugs along on the strength of Grant Page's amiable demeanor and searing stunt work. Throw in an equal dose of *Spinal Tap*-esque '70s heavy metal, and you have the full meal (cheese included). Highly recommended for midnight movie fans. Director Trenchard-Smith and star Page also collaborated on the action films *Deathcheaters* and *The Man From Hong Kong*.

S

443

Submerged

2005 (Sony DVD) (CD)

"There's some sick shit
up in here, alligator."

After a group of commandos is captured and then brainwashed at a decrepit facility, a small group of Secret Service agents kill an ambassador and then turn their weapons upon themselves. The government decides they should unleash mercenary Chris Cody (Steven Seagal) to clean up the mess. He's currently in a military prison with his team, and they're offered full pardons if they succeed with their new mission. Dr. Adrian Lehder (Nick Brimble) has mastered the art of brainwashing, using it to control soldiers for his own plans. The captured commandos, led by Colonel Sharpe (Gary Daniels), have switches, and once they are flicked on, they immediately do his bidding. In this case, they take over a submarine, leaving Cody and his team to try to stop them before they can go after Lehder.

Submerged is another poor excuse of an action film. Sadly, it's brought down by the inclusion of star Seagal (Hard to Kill), who never for one second looks like he's in the moment. This is another one of his direct-to-video movies where he was too busy after filming to loop his own dialogue and much of it was done by another voice actor who sounds nothing like him. There's very little fighting but plenty of rounds are spent and all sorts of things are blown up real good. Gary Daniels (Forced to Fight) is completely wasted in the film. He has a very short and unimpressive fight with Seagal, which is to be expected. The story isn't terrible and director Anthony Hickox (Blast) injects a bit of style into the film. The only real standout is Vinnie Jones (Mean Machine), who walks away with the best dialogue and action scenes. Without the participation of Mr. Seagal, this may have actually been a better film. Don E. Fontleroy, who later directed Seagal in Mercenary For Justice and Urban Justice, was brought in mid-production to film Seagal's close-ups and pick-ups.

Subterfuge

1996 (Avalanche DVD) (djm)

A passenger plane is shot out of the sky and crashes into the Black Sea. Russia sends a squad of agents to retrieve a mysterious black box from the wreckage, but they have a problem locating the wreckage. The American government sends a former agent—now a devil-may-care scuba instructor—to find the black box before the Russians do. Jonathan Slade (Matt McColm) refuses the gig at first, but the government has leverage in that his brother is a computer-hacking cyber thief and they hold that against him so he'll do the job. Plunged into action, Slade joins another agent on the job named Alex (Amanda Pays), whom he feels crowds his style, but eventually they fall for each other whilst dodging bullets and baddies.

McColm (a Hollywood stuntman and kenpo black belt) is given a slightly better vehicle here to star in than his previous one, Red Scorpion 2, but the film still isn't as good as it could have been. The action is passable and his fight scenes are okay, but the movie needed more punch and pizzazz. Action fans and admirers of action stars may have a good time with it. I thought it was merely average. Directed by Herb Reed, who also worked with Mike Norris on Survival Game.

Suburban Commando

1991 (New Line DVD) (CD)

"How the hell was I supposed to know that you were some sort of alien Rambo with psycho enemies?"

Shep Ramsey (Terry "Hulk" Hogan) is an interstellar crime fighter who is constantly saving the universe. He's ordered to take some down time and let his ship recharge, which will take several weeks. He's not happy about it but lands his ship on Earth. He finds an apartment to rent so he can regroup. Charlie Wilcox (Christopher Llyod) and his family are tight on money and have converted their shed into an apartment. Charlie gets pushed around by everyone (except his family) and is sort of a wimp. With Shep living in the apartment, Charlie begins to suspect there's something different about him. When he discovers Shep's secret, the two must team up to stop two vicious bounty hunters from space and Shep's arch nemesis whom he thought was dead.

Suburban Commando has been a punchline for years now, even during Hulk Hogan's (Mr. Nanny) wrestling resurgence in the early 2000s. The surprising news is the film is actually pretty funny. It's a ridiculous concept but Hogan manages to bring a certain charm to this film. There's plenty of action, and he has a genuine chemistry with Christopher Lloyd (Back to the Future), which helps to bring the laughs. Of course, the fights are pretty harmless but Hogan does fight Mark Halloway in the film (wrestling fans might know him better as the legendary Undertaker). There's a good chance you may find yourself laughing out loud on more than one occasion—there are things to laugh at and laugh with. To top it off, kids will love it. For all of its shortcomings, Suburban Commando is a really fun time. Director Burt Kennedy (Dirty Dingus McGee) may be better known for his work on popular television shows from the '80s or his westerns.

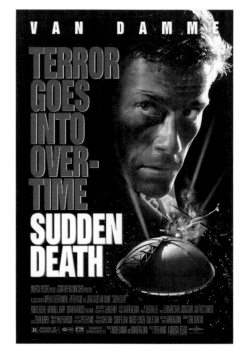

Theatrical poster for Sudden Death. Author's collection.

Sudden Death

1995 (Universal DVD) (djm)

Following a traumatic incident that left a young girl dead, fireman Darren McCord (Jean-Claude Van Damme) transitions into a fire inspector, now divorced and trying to kindle relationships with his two young kids. On his son's birthday, he surprises him with tickets to a hockey game, the final game of the season. Having seated his two children in their seats, McCord goes about his inspection duties, but something huge is going down: The vice president of the United States is watching the game from a private booth, and terrorists have taken him hostage, rigging the entire arena with bombs as a backup plan. When McCord realizes that his daughter is among the hostages, he turns into a one-man Die Hard machine, getting the job done when the Secret Service and all of the policemen in the area falter at their duties.

Slick for a relatively low-budget studio film, Sudden Death is a rock-solid Die Hard riff, with Van Damme completely capable as an everyman turned into an action-tastic hero. The fights in the film aren't necessarily outrageous or over-the-top: instead, they come in spurts and play out in a believable fashion. Powers Boothe (Rapid Fire, Extreme Prejudice) scores big as the leader of the terrorists. Action fans in general should enjoy this one; Van Damme followers won't have anything to complain about. Originally intended as a film for Denzel Washington, this was released in theaters at the height of the Christmas season in 1995 and was drowned by the competition. It marked Van Damme's second collaboration with director Peter Hyams.

Sunland Heat

2004 (MTI DVD) (CD)

Jennifer (Alex Van Hagen) is married to millionaire Daniel Howard (Jay Richardson), a man who enjoys underground fighting. Since she's a world-class fighter, he plans to use her to make himself money by forcing her to fight. That's when the unthinkable happens and she's forced to kill someone in the ring. Disgusted with her husband and her actions, she takes her daughter and leaves for Brazil to get away from it all. Daniel isn't going to let this fly and sends his henchman John Paul (Andre Lima) to get her back. Jennifer has bonded with a photographer named Matthews (fight choreographer J. J. Perry) and the two of them are ready to fight their way out of Daniel's grasp.

Sunland Heat is just one big mess from a story standpoint since budget constraints forced director Halder Gomez to cut out some important stuff. We're treated to the usual wooden acting found so frequently in these types of films, but if you're watching it for the acting then you might want to rethink your priorities. While the action may be sparse, the fights are very well executed and exciting. There's an especially good one with Andre Lima (from *Beyond the Ring*) and J. J. Perry (from *And Now You're Dead* with Shannon Lee) when they meet up for the second time. Alex Van Hagen made her one and only film with this flick and at least makes an impression with one memorable fight during a flashback. The movie is short enough, and it won't do anyone any harm to watch it.

Supercop: Police Story III

1992 (Dimension DVD) (djm)

Jackie Chan once again plays Inspector Chan in the popular (and rightfully so) *Police Story* series that feature death-defying stunts, incredible martial arts action, and slapstick comedy. Chan is assigned an undercover assignment to help a notorious criminal named Panther (Wah Yuen) escape from a prison labor camp and to infiltrate his gang with the ultimate mission being to bring Panther's higher-up boss, Chaibat (Kenneth Tsang), to justice. Chan is partnered with another "supercop," Inspector Yang (Michelle Yeoh), to pose as his sister, and once the two of them begin traveling with Panther's

Publicity still from *Supercop*. Author's collection.

Hanging from a helicopter in *Supercop*, featuring Jackie Chan. Author's collection.

Michelle Yeoh and Jackie Chan in Stanley Tong's *Supercop*. Author's collection.

gang, they get into some serious situations that require them to think on their toes. On a trip to Thailand with Panther and Chaibat, an arms deal goes bad, and all of a sudden the two inspectors find themselves in the middle of a *Rambo*-type action scenario involving exploding huts, rocket launchers, and dynamite-packed bulletproof vests. The finale features Chan jumping off the roof of a building to a dangling ladder from a helicopter, and Yeoh riding a speeding motorcycle on the top of a train. It doesn't get much better than this.

Two versions of this picture exist. The original Chinese release runs about ninety-five minutes, while the dubbed Dimension theatrical release from 1996 runs about seven minutes shorter. I am reviewing the original Chinese version, though the US cut is still perfectly suitable entertainment. More *Police Story* movies followed. Yeoh reprised her role in *Supercop 2* (with a cameo by Chan), which is also known as *Police Story III: Supercop 2*. Chan returned as Inspector Chan in *First Strike*. Stanley Tong directed.

Supercop 2

1993 (Dimension DVD) (djm)

Inspector Yang (Michelle Yeoh) did such a good job enforcing the law on her last mission (see the first *Supercop* for more on that) that her department has given her accolades and a task to take down a gang of thieves, whose violent crime sprees are rocking Hong Kong. As she closes in on the ringleaders, she realizes that her own boyfriend is one of the top guys in the gang.

Technically, this is the fourth entry in the *Police Story* franchise, and a short goofy cameo with Jackie Chan (in drag!) solidifies the connection, but coming after the incredible *Supercop*, this entry is a massive misstep and sets the franchise back by fathoms. Star Yeoh is a force to be reckoned with in most of her films, but here she's reduced to an emotional wreck where her relationship conflicts take center stage over the action set pieces, most of which are perfunctory and pedestrian. She has a beat-down with a huge guy three times her size in the climax, but compared to the first film, which had one jaw-dropping scene after another, this entry is negligible. Stanley Tong, who did the first film, directed. Followed by *First Strike*.

Jackie Chan as Inspector Chan, the Supercop. Author's collection.

Supercop is chock full of fights. Author's collection.

Superfights

1995 (Seasonal Film Corporation VHS) (djm)

If you've never heard of this movie, it's probably because the distribution for it on VHS was poor. It similar to *The Karate Kid* and *No Retreat, No Surrender*, and it deserves an honorable mention for kicking more ass than those movies. A teen named Jack Cody (Brandon Gaines, a one-hit wonder) thinks he's the boss of martial arts, and he goes out one night and saves a pretty Asian girl from being mugged. She takes him home and introduces him to her grandfather, who happens to be a wise kung fu master, complete with a wispy white beard and mop. The old man sees Jack for what he is: a petulant kid whose vanity and know-it-all attitude can infect his granddaughter. Jack has to humble himself and ask for the old man's wisdom and guidance to become a better fighter. Meanwhile, a video of Jack's rescue goes viral on the news and he becomes a hero. A producer of an *American Gladiators*-type show sees the video and wants Jack to be on it. When Jack agrees, he virtually signs his soul away because what he doesn't know is that the producer (Keith Vitali from *Revenge of the Ninja* and *American Kickboxer*) is pumping his contestants full of drugs and demands that they join his illegal operation of drug running. Jack faces even more temptation when the show's token Amazon (Kelly Gallant from *Talons of the Eagle* and *TC 2000*) seduces him into the operation. Is Jack a hero or not? He asks himself the question and when he decides to do the right thing, it makes for some really intense fight scenes.

This movie's got some layers. It's silly and about as basic as an episode of a Saturday morning cartoon (always with a moral at the end), but amazingly, it feels like a junior *Rocky*, and it's much harder than a PG-rated *Karate Kid* spinoff. The star, Brandon Gaines, only did this one movie, but he'd been a real-life karate champ beforehand. Keith Vitali plays the villain well, and his final fight with Gaines is incredible. Chuck Jeffreys (*Bloodmoon*) is in it too. The director, Tony Leung (Siu-Hung Leung), also directed *Bloodmoon* with Gary Daniels and Vitali.

Supreme Champion

2010 (Phase 4 DVD) (djm)

Sub-par shot-on-video nonsense stars MMA champion Stephan Bonnar as a decorated war veteran named Troy who's turned to prize fighting for money. A former flame of his comes to him asking for his help: She's in for a lot of money to a gambling tycoon named Lucien Gallows (Daniel Bernhardt), and she's now his property. Troy goes straight to the source, but quickly realizes that he's in over his head. Gallows puts Troy through an obstacle course of fights just to get to the point where he can speak to him face to face, and when they speak, Gallows make it very clear that if his girl is going to walk away, then Troy will have to participate in a life-or-death game (also known as *The Most Dangerous Game* or *Hard Target*, depending on what source the filmmakers stole from). Troy plays the game (with some friends—former vets like him), and they win. The final fight between Troy and Gallows is disappointing.

Low rent all the way, *Supreme Champion* may have a real-life MMA fighter as its "star," but Bonnar has nothing worth watching as an action guy. He's stiff, boring, and unconvincing as the "next big thing." Bernhardt is okay as the villain, but he plays a character with terminal brain cancer, so he doesn't get in the action much. The actresses in the film all look like former strippers, and indeed several key scenes in the film take place at a "gentleman's club." Ted Fox, who wrote, produced, and directed, also co-stars as one of the vets who comes to the hero's aide. The whole film is tacky. Watch for Oleg Taktarov from *Predators* in a supporting role.

Surf Ninjas

1993 (New Line DVD) (CD)

Johnny (Ernie Reyes Jr.) and Adam (Nicolas Cowan) are two adopted teenage brothers living in LA with their father Mac (John Karlen). They enjoy blowing off school so they can go out and catch some waves with their best friend Iggy (Rob Schneider). Their seemingly normal life is about to be turned upside-down when they are attacked by ninjas, only to be saved by the mysterious, eye patch-wearing Zatch (Ernie Reyes Sr.). The boys' father is kidnapped and they learn about their past. The truth is that they're the sons of the King of Patusan who was overthrown by the evil Colonel Chi (Leslie Nielson) and it's their destiny to go back to their home and restore order to the once-peaceful land. But first they will have to learn how to use their secret abilities and Johnny meets Ro-May (Kelly Hu), the girl who his family has chosen to be his wife.

When *Surf Ninjas* was released in theaters, critics were not very kind to the film. It seems that most critics tend to forget how a movie like this was meant to be fun. For all of the silliness that goes on in it, there's also some fantastic action on display courtesy of both Ernie Reyes Jr. (*The Rundown*) and his legendary father, Ernie Reyes Sr. (*Art of Submission*), who also served as the fight choreographer. Watching father and son fighting side by side is a blast. While some of the humor may only be funny to a preteen, the action is universal and more than competent. Reyes Jr. displays some highly impressive acrobatics and why he hasn't yet become a bigger action star is beyond comprehension. The Reyeses also appeared on screen together in *The Ultimate Fight*. Directed by Neal Israel (*Combat High*).

Survival Game

1987 (Media VHS) (djm)

"We're not talking survival camp here, boy. We're talking real ammo. Real blood and guts!"

After starring in *Born American*, Mike Norris (son of Chuck) headlined this actioner where he plays a college-aged kid named Michael Hawkins who spends his days at a camp where paintballers and weekend warriors come to play survival games. He's good at survival techniques and staying fit and ready for action, but his Vietnam vet boss thinks he's wasting his potential. When a nearby correctional facility releases a well-known convict named Dave Forrest (Seymour Cassell) after nearly two decades of incarceration, Dave's daughter C. J. (Deborah Goodrich) is thrilled to have her father back, but Dave isn't out a full day before he's kidnapped by some thugs who think Dave knows where a stash of millions of dollars is (money he accrued before going to prison). C. J. needs someone's help immediately if she wants to save her father, and Hawkins is the nearest thing to a hero she can find. Using his instincts as a survivalist and as a proficient martial artist, young Hawkins is able to come to his full potential and save the day.

Survival Game could have easily been a better movie. Mike Norris should have been a bigger action star, but most of the movies he did were underwhelming and didn't capitalize on his abilities. It's too bad, because this movie (even more so than *Born American*) had a really good idea, but it didn't flow the way it should have. First of all, having his character saddled with nagging parents was a bad idea. He should have been a young renegade, an orphan, or a soldier on leave or something. Second, the action scenes are weak. There're a few decent little fight scenes, but there's not enough to go around. Lastly, this movie needed a really good bad guy. Instead, we get a handful of generic goons who hassle the main characters. There are similar movies to *Survival Game* like *The Zero Boys* and *Edge of Honor* that are fantastic . . . and those didn't even have action stars in them! This was directed by Herb Freed and produced by Gideon Amir, who wrote the story for the original *American Ninja*.

SWAT: Warhead One

2004 (Tous DVD) (CD)

A Navy SEAL team attempts to thwart a group of terrorists who are stealing a nuclear warhead. The leader of the SEALS, Luc Remy (Olivier Gruner), tries his best to wrangle them in, only to lose the battle. Eight years later, Luc is now living in Los Angeles, heading up a SWAT team. While on a raid, one of his members is killed and the drug peddlers get away. While the SWAT team has their image tarnished in the public eye, the police captain assigns news reporter Dick Danvers (Mel Novak) to shadow them. Luc isn't happy but he

S

brings Dick into his world where he is about to face a deadly threat. The nuke has re-emerged and terrorists have taken over the hospital where Luc's ex-wife works. He leads his team right into the belly of the beast in order to save the entire Los Angeles area from nuclear devastation.

While Olivier Gruner (from *Angel Town* and *Savate*) always manages to add a bit of flare to the films he's been saddled with over the past decade or so, there's no denying the entertainment value of his films has diminished. The budget for this film was non-existent and the martial arts action was sparse. The film opens with promise, with Gruner laying waste to some terrorists with his fists and a nifty knife fight, then things go south from there. We don't see much more action until the finale, and it doesn't quite match the battles we saw earlier. We do get to see character action star/stuntman James Lew (*The Circuit III*) in a fighting flashback and Gerald Okamura (*Big Trouble in Little China*) is the big bad terrorist. Sadly, we never get to see him duke it out with Gruner. This is a disappointing effort from director Carribo Seto (an alias for David Huey who helmed *Full Impact* with Gary Daniels).

Sweepers

1998 (Image DVD) (CD)

"Have you always been this much of an asshole or did you take lessons?"

In Angola, Christian Erickson (Dolph Lundgren) leads a team of people who sweep the fields for land mines, making it safe for the locals who live there. While doing a routine search, rebels attack the nearby village where Christian's eleven year-old son is. He has no clue the boy is there and he's killed by a mine. Five years later, Michelle Flynn (Claire Stansfield) and her team fly to Angola to stop the spread of a vicious new type of mine called the A6. Terrorists have been using it in the US and the manufacturing plant seems to be in the area. When her team gets too close, they're killed, leaving her with one option: seek out Christian Ericson for help. He's reluctant at first but when another child is injured he doesn't have a choice. Once he begins to uncover who is actually behind the mines and what is being done with a trainload of them, he will have to come to terms with his own demons and stop the villain (played by *Passenger 57*'s Bruce Payne) responsible.

The first twenty to thirty minutes of *Sweepers* offers up non-stop action. From shootouts to fist fights, Dolph Lundgren (*Bridge of Dragons*) is completely in his element. He has a rugged coolness and being a bit of a jerk makes this character a memorable one for him. Then things slow down for just a bit before we're treated with a fantastic final act filled with adrenaline-pumping action. One moment that really connects is when Lundgren chases a train on a motorcycle, jumps onto the train, only to slide across the surface while wasting bad guys. It's an absolutely blissful moment and *Sweepers* is just another reason why he is one of the greatest action heroes of all time. The director is Keoni

Waxman (under the pseudonym Darby Black), who would go on to helm many Steven Seagal movies and the film *Hunt to Kill* with "Stone Cold" Steve Austin.

Swelter (a.k.a. Duels)

2014 (Well Go USA) (djm)

A casino heist goes south, and four guys out of the five-man crew get caught straight off the bat, but one of them—Bishop (Lennie James)—gets shot in the head and is rescued by an alcoholic doctor (Alfred Molina) and is nursed back to health. Bishop (who had the entire ten million dollars in loot) has amnesia, but his strong will and demeanor is enough to get him the job as sheriff of a middle-of-nowhere town about a hundred miles outside of Las Vegas, and for the next ten years he performs his job the best he can, but with a nagging sense of danger lurking at every corner. When his old crew comes searching for him, the town is turned upside-down as Bishop must face off with his former associates, who have spent the last ten years in prison, planning their revenge on him. Cole (Grant Bowler) and his right-hand man Stillman (a nice supporting turn by Jean-Claude Van Damme) aren't going anywhere until they jog Bishop's memory and reclaim their millions in cash.

2014 was an interesting year for Van Damme. His appearances in *Welcome to the Jungle* and *Enemies Closer* were strong (and memorable) supporting roles, and his part in *Swelter* is just as indelible, but this time, he sheds every ounce of vanity you think he's ever had and he simply . . . *acts*. That isn't to say that he doesn't get physical, because he does, but if you think he's going to be the hero of this movie, you'll be pretty surprised when he reveals himself to be an understated bad guy with more than his share of pathos. The movie itself might once have featured him as the star (which is easy to imagine), but it becomes that much more interesting because he isn't the lead. It's worth seeing if just to watch him step down and let others do the heavy lifting. I wasn't crazy about the movie itself, but then again, I just wanted to see JC get in on the action. Directed by Keith Parmer.

The Sword of Bushido

1990 (MIA DVD) (djm)

Zac Connors (Richard Norton) is on a quest to find an ancient Japanese sword, once the property of his grandfather, who served in World War II. Zac—a former Navy SEAL—is certainly formidable in martial arts and survival, so when he begins his expedition into Eastern Asia, where he believes the sword rests (along with his grandfather's body), he's ready for any dangers that might befall him. A Yakuza gangster finds out about his mission and coveting the sacred sword for himself, he sends killers and ninja assassins to retrieve the sword from Connors should he recover it. Connors is ready to take all comers!

Any movie with Richard Norton (from *Equalizer 2000* and *Mr. Nice Guy*) is worth watching, and *The Sword of Bushido* actually gets better as it goes along. It's got a serious, no-nonsense tone and when the action picks up steam, it's presented with unflinching violence and conviction. Norton is in amazing shape, and his final scene with the Yakuza boss (played by Toshishiro Obata from *Showdown in Little Tokyo* and *Teenage Mutant Ninja Turtles*) is excellent. Directed by Adrian Carr.

Sword of Heaven

1985 (Trans World Entertainment VHS) (djm)

"This man is a skilled fighter! Now move out! And kill him!"

In ancient times, a comet hits the Earth and monks find the lump of space metal and forge a sword that would be prized and passed on from generation to generation within one family for hundreds of years. This . . . is the Sword of Heaven. In the present day, the sword is stolen from Japan and taken to Los Angeles, and the owner of the sword, Toshiro Kobiashi, comes to LA looking for it. By happenstance, another Japanese man named Tadashi (Tadashi Yamashita from *American Ninja* and *Gymkata*) watches Toshiro get into a mortal fight with the men who stole his sword, and Tadashi gets in on the fight and kills all the villains, which deeply impresses Toshiro, who is mortally wounded. Sensing that Tadashi is a modern-day samurai, Toshiro bestows the Sword of Heaven on him as an anointing, and when Tadashi takes the sword, trouble follows him wherever he goes.

Shot on a very low budget, but resembling a Channel 5 afternoon movie from 1988, *Sword of Heaven* is great if you think Sho Kosugi's TV series *The Master* was something special. Made for guys who were ingrained in the ninja movement of the 1980s, this is a movie with very little sophistication, but hey, it's got Tadashi Yamashita(!) and a glowing blue sword, so how much more awesome can a movie get? Yamashita, who had memorable roles in "B" martial arts movies from the Cannon era, is given his one-hit-wonder movie, and I'd be proud of it if I were he, despite the fact that he has an extended fight scene in drag. Also starring Bill Wallace (as a bad guy). Written by James Bruner, who scripted some of Chuck Norris's best movies like *Invasion U.S.A.* and *The Delta Force*. Directed by Byron Meyers.

S

Sword of Honor

1996 (Platinum DVD) (CD)

"True, but people don't look at cops like heroes anymore. That's why I like working with the kids at the martial arts school. At least they look up to me."

Johnny (Steven Vincent Leigh) and Alan (Jeff Pruit) have been partners on the force for years, and the time has come for one of them to turn in his badge. Alan is ready to be a full-time teacher at his sister's martial arts school. A group of thieves has found the auction house where a multi-million-dollar sword is being kept and they're going to break in and get it. Johnny gets called out to investigate and Alan wants one last piece of the action for his final day. Things go south quickly: The thieves make off with the sword, and Alan is murdered. Johnny can't let his friend's killer run free so he quickly begins his own investigation, even though his captain has removed him from the case. Alan's killer will soon wish he had never crossed this high-kicking cop with an attitude.

Steven Vincent Leigh (usually a supporting player in low-budget action movies like *Deadly Bet*) never quite reached leading man status, but *Sword of Honor* shows what he was capable of as a lead. He usually played a patsy or a villain, but here he successfully carries the entire picture on his shoulders as the hero. The film is molded in such a way that he gets into some sort of action situation every five to ten minutes. His character Johnny isn't safe anywhere. He gets attacked at the party store, the gym, and even at a damn hot dog stand. He punches and kicks his way out of every situation like a pro, and Leigh is great in it. There's also a standout car chase culminating in an epic crash and explosion. Leigh gives a solid acting performance making *Sword of Honor* a worthy action flick. Director Robert Tiffe manages to shape a generic script into decent late-night entertainment.

The Swordsman

1992 (Alliance VHS) (djm)

In the tradition of *Highlander*, this detective film starring Lorenzo Lamas features themes of reincarnation, mysticism, and a hint of the supernatural. Lamas plays a cop named Andrew who has dreams and visions (accompanied by severe seizures) of a former life and events from ancient history. He's on a murder case dealing

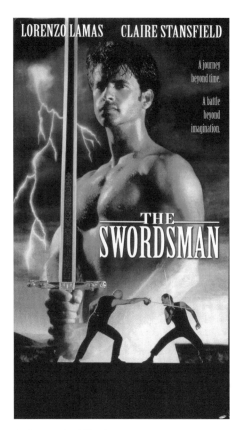

VHS artwork of *The Swordsman*. Author's collection.

with a stolen sword—and not just any sword, but Alexander the Great's sword. Every time Andrew touches a dead body or blood, he sees past events unfolding and his boss thinks he's crazy. In his spare time, Andrew is a master swordsman and joins a fencing class taught by a shady millionaire named Stratos (Michael Champion), who takes a shine to him and introduces him to an underground sword-fighting club where players fight to the death. Andrew, a cop on the edge, enters the ring and wins a fight, but refuses to kill his opponent, which causes Stratos not to trust him. Further events lead Andrew to fall in love with an archaeologist (and sword expert) named Julie (Claire Stansfield), who knows some things about the stolen sword. The climax of the film has Andrew pitted against Stratos for the fate of the sword, which Stratos is in possession of.

Written and directed by Michael Kennedy, who later made *Talons of the Eagle* and *Red Scorpion 2*, this is a well-shot and edited action-type film with martial arts and swordplay, but it needed more of a punch in its center to be a fully entertaining picture. It was edited by Nick Rotundo, who would go on to helm the sequel, as well as a suspiciously similar film called *G2*, starring Daniel Bernhardt.

Sworn to Justice

1996 (MTI DVD) (djm)

After a home invasion that left her loved ones murdered, police detective Janna Dane (Cynthia Rothrock) wakes up with a head wound at the hospital. As she recuperates, she begins to realize that she has extra-sensory visions and psychic powers as a side effect of her trauma. She begins a new job working for the police in a different capacity: solving crimes as a psychic and testifying in court by touching murder weapons and forensic evidence. The one crime she has yet to solve is the one that left her family slaughtered by home invaders. By day, she is a model citizen, and by night, she goes out looking for crimes to quell as they occur. She falls in love with a cute guy (Kurt McKinney from *No Retreat, No Surrender*), who is a good match for her, but her drama gets a little too intense for him at some point, and she's left to her own devices when she finally figures out who is to blame for the tragedy in her life.

Sworn to Justice is an almost-but-not-quite-good-enough vehicle for Rothrock, who produced. The set-up is all good, and it might almost be considered a failed pilot for a TV series, but the tone is iffy and uneven. Her first fight in a warehouse with some goons is tracked with silly music, and there are gag comedy sound effects that upset the film's intentions. Subsequent fight scenes are not treated as such, which is confusing. Rothrock shows more of a sensual side than we've seen from her before, and she's featured in several soft sex scenes. She's a sport, as usual, but the director, Paul Maslak, mars the movie with his unsure hand. He's known for writing several Don Wilson movies including *Out For Blood, Red Sun Rising,* and *Blackbelt*. Mako, Walter Koenig, and Brad Dourif have small supporting roles.

Tactical Force

2011 (Vivendi DVD) (djm)

SWAT team captain Tate (Steve Austin) is ordered to take his team to an abandoned warehouse to perform some training exercises, but while there they stumble upon two rival gangs, who are in a dispute. The SWAT team is not only outnumbered but also without ammunition because the guns they're using are filled with blanks. The gangs surround them and kill one of them, and Tate and his team have to fight to survive.

Slightly similar in theme to the superior films *Trespass* and *Judgment Night*, *Tactical Force* is a huge disappointment on every front. Shot on crappy digital video and directed like a music video (quick cuts, bombastic music and noise, etc.), it completely lowers the bar for its good cast. Aside from Austin, there's Michael Jai White (*Blood and Bone*), Darren Shahlavi (*Bloodmoon*), Peter Kent (Arnold Schwarzenegger's stunt double for many years), and Keith Jardine (MMA fighter, also in *Recoil* with Austin). The best fight scenes in the film are intercut with other fights, which is a major deficit. Austin fights Kent in one scene, and then he fights Jardine in a later scene. Jai White fights Shahlavi in a hallway. Unfortunately, even the fight scenes can't salvage this turkey. Directed by Adamo Paulo Cultraro.

Tagteam

1991 (NOV) (djm)

Bobby: "Rick?"
Rick: "Yeah?"
Bobby: "I think we just body-slammed the truck."

Professional tag team wrestlers Bobby Youngblood (Jesse Ventura) and Rick McDonald (Roddy Piper) are booted out of wrestling for winning a match they were supposed to lose, and on a lark they decide they want to become police officers. They go to the academy, pass the tests (much to everyone's surprise), and in no time they're assigned to protect a murder witness at a safe house. The witness (played by Jennifer Runyon) is targeted for death by the men whom she can identify in court, and in a weak moment, she runs away from the safe house, which puts Bobby and Rick in a bad situation. Suspended from duty, they take to the streets to find the witness, and when they find her, they first must deal with the thugs who want to kill her. They tag each other into the fight when each gets tired or overwhelmed.

Designed as a pilot for a never-realized television series, *Tagteam* is a fun bit of nostalgia for fans of its two wrestling stars. Many of the guys they come up against (note the scene in the supermarket where they foil a robbery) are real wrestlers, and there are some familiar faces that show up to get smashed around. Piper and Ventura made a good team, and it's understandable why the show wasn't picked up, but it's still a good time. The entire pilot is available to view on YouTube complete with the original commercials. Directed by Paul Krasny.

Take a Hard Ride

1975 (Shout Factory DVD) (djm)

A spaghetti western/blaxploitation/kung fu hybrid, *Take a Hard Ride* stars Jim Brown, Fred Williamson, Jim Kelly, and Lee Van Cleef. Brown plays a trail boss named Pike, who's on an honorable mission to deliver $87,000 to a crew of men who deserve to be paid, but along the way over thousands of miles of desert, he encounters various sorts who want to rob him of his rucksack full of cash. He takes on an uneasy sidekick partnership with a suave gambler named Tyree (Williamson), and when they take on a *third* sidekick/partner named Kashtok (Kelly), a mute black man who has been raised by American Indians, their dynamic improves because Kashtok is formidable in martial arts. They encounter ruffians, bandits, and bounty hunters, led by the hawkish Kiefer (Van Cleef), and it's a hard ride indeed for them if they're ever going to make it to their destination alive with all of their money.

Filmed at the Canary Islands in Spain, *Take a Hard Ride* is a fun western adventure with plenty of action and *just enough* martial arts in it (courtesy of the underused Kelly) to satisfy a cross-pollination of fans of several different genres. This is really Brown's and Williamson's film, though, and that's fine because they're both really good in it. A fantastic score by Jerry Goldsmith helps the movie out immensely. Williamson, Brown, and Kelly also appeared together in *Three the Hard Way* and *One Down, Two to Go*. Williamson and Brown reunited years later in the all-star party *Original Gangstas*. Antonio Margheriti directed *Take a Hard Ride*.

Talons of the Eagle

1992 (Key DVD) (djm)

This was the first and best of three movies Billy Blanks did with Jalal Merhi. All three of them (*TC 2000* and *Expect No Mercy* were the others) weren't very memorable. This one tries to be a buddy cop movie. Blanks is a DEA agent who joins with a vice detective (Merhi) to capture an evil gangster named Li (James Hong). They gain his trust by enlisting in a life-or-death martial arts tournament, and by happenstance, they save Li's life from an assassin. Li puts them on staff and they have an ally in the woman Li is sleeping with (Priscilla Barnes), who also happens to be an undercover agent. Li's main henchman is played by Matthias Hues. There's a long, drawn-out fight at the end between Blanks and Hues.

Video store shelves were crammed with movies like *Talons of the Eagle* throughout the 1990s. This is precisely the sort of movie that helped define the straight-to-video mentality of action and martial arts films. The market for this sort of movie was there: Movies like this were made by the dozen for very little money, and they were rented out daily. The problem with this type of movie—and this movie in particular—is that repeat viewings really aren't going to improve upon the first impression. These movies are just barely *good enough* to watch once, though the potential is there for a really good movie. Billy Blanks certainly had the build and abilities to be a major "A"-list action star, but the movies he did like *Talons of the Eagle* disappoint because the directors he worked with just couldn't use him to the best of his abilities. The best films he did were with Roddy Piper (*Back in Action* and *Tough and Deadly*). This one was directed by Michael Kennedy. Merhi worked with James Hong again on *Operation Golden Phoenix*.

Tango and Cash

1989 (Warner DVD) (djm)

"If it isn't Tango, it's Cash. Tango and Cash! Cash and Tango! These two cops are driving me crazy! We *have* to do something about this!"

The quintessential overblown action movie of the 1980s stars two of the best action guys in two of their worst roles. Lt. Raymond Tango (Sylvester Stallone) is a prim and proper cop who plays the stock market and dresses in designer clothes, while his "competition" is Lt. Gabriel Cash, a streetwise rapscallion who is constantly perturbed to find that his busts are beneath Tango's headlines. A seasoned mastermind of the criminal underworld named Perret (Jack Palance doing what Jack Palance did best), concocts a grand scheme to frame both Tango and Cash for murder, coercion, and police brutality, and it mind-bogglingly works. The public turns against them, their departments shun them, and they're sent to prison. Instead of the minimum-security club Med vacation they were expecting, they're sent to a maximum-security hellhole filled with hardened cons they personally sent away. They're met with extreme hostility, and they're cornered, tortured, and are sure to die if they don't come up with a plan of escape. Their escape is quite easy: after only a day and a night in incarceration, they manage a great exodus, and when they get themselves hooked up with an arsenal and a ridiculous RV armed for WWIII, they invade Perret's compound and level it.

If you're a lover of action movies, it's impossible *not* to like *Tango and Cash*. That said, it's the whole reason why *Last Action Hero* exists. It's virtually a spoof of the genre, but it's about as sincere as can be. Stallone is on full-tilt comedy mode, and if you've seen *Oscar* and *Stop! Or My Mom Will Shoot!* then you know he's not at his best when he's trying to be funny. Russell, however, is great in an impossible role. He matches Stallone's swagger and actually seems to make the preposterous plot and absurdity all around him feel *right*. The best scenes of the film come from Russell, but anyone watching this film thinking it's going to be a *Cobra* or a *Rambo* is going to be floored by its triple-barreled ransacking of the genre. It's no wonder that the genre began to be lampooned after it.

T

Brion James, James Hong, Robert Z'Dar, and Philip Tan populate the familiar cast. Andrey Konchalovskiy directed it after he made the incredible *Runaway Train*. Albert Magnoli (*Street Knight*) took over directing duties when Konchalovskiy walked. A synth-heavy music score by Harold Faltermeyer helps root the film in the '80s. Written by Randy Feldman, who also wrote *Nowhere to Run*, starring Jean-Claude Van Damme.

Tapped Out

2013 (Lionsgate DVD) (djm)

When Michael was a young lad, he watched as his parents were murdered at the hands of a tattooed carjacker. Seven years later, orphaned Michael (played by five-time World Karate Champion Cody Hackman) is headed for trouble, and his grandfather is having a difficult time raising him. His last chance at redeeming himself and going down the straight and narrow path comes when he's ordered to perform so many hours of community service, and he serves it out at a martial arts dojo run by Reggie (Michael Biehn, who also produced). Reggie takes a shine to Michael, and so does Reggie's pretty niece, and just like that Michael is learning discipline and martial arts training. Coincidentally, he sees the man who he is sure murdered his parents—at a mixed martial arts cage match—and he focuses all of his rage and discipline into training hard so that he can jump in the cage and begin working his way up the circuit to face the man who made him an orphan.

Speckled with real MMA and UFC fighters like Anderson Silva, Lyoto Machida, and Krzysztof Soszynski (who plays the villain), *Tapped Out* is a solid coming-of-age drama with well choreographed and convincing fights, starring a real-deal champion. Though the DVD box art is mostly misleading—Silva and Machida only make cameos—it hearkens back to the days of *No Retreat, No Surrender* and *The Karate Kid*, though it makes no bones about being gritty and "R"-rated. I liked it. Star Hackman also came up with the story. From director Allan Ungar.

The Tattoo Connection

1978 (World Northal DVD) (CD)

A group of thieves steals a very valuable diamond in Hong Kong. The insurance company is at a loss, and they send the only person they can think of to investigate and return it: Lucas (Jim Kelly), a former CIA agent who's also a master martial artist. Tin-Hao (Tao-Liang Tan) has had enough of the criminal life and wants to leave with the woman he loves. Lucas and Tin-Hao make an uneasy alliance and fight the gangsters who stand in their way of getting what they most require.

The Tattoo Connection is a ridiculously low-budgeted film that sends Jim Kelly (*Enter the Dragon*) to Hong Kong to find a priceless diamond. As a marketing ploy, the film is also known as *Black Belt Jones 2*, so just remember, it's not a sequel. This particular version was dubbed

in English, which is sort of a weird experience. Nonetheless, the film is a fast-paced actioner with large doses of unintentional humor, impressive kung fu fighting, and a plethora of nubile Asian beauties baring their assets to the camera. It's sort of shocking how much nudity is actually in the film. Kelly has several fight scenes where he is able to show just how truly talented a fighter he is. It's mostly hand-to-hand stuff but at one point, Kelly gets to show off with a staff. There is a certain rhythm to the fight sequences that's only seen in martial arts films from that era, and it's sorely missed. Also, for fight film fans, Kelly reunites with his *Enter the Dragon* co-star Bolo Yeung with whom he shares a solid fight scene during the finale. The movie sort of ends rather abruptly, but it's an overall fun film with a good action performance by Kelly. Directed by Tso Nam Lee.

TC 2000

1993 (Universal VHS) (CD)

In a future where the rich have built their sanctuary beneath the surface in a place known as UnderWorld, Jason Storm (Billy Blanks) along with his lovely partner Zoey Kinsella (Bobbie Phillips) are tracker/communicators (TC 2000) who are there to protect them from what lies above. SurfaceWorld is occupied by thieves and gangs who are constantly trying to invade the UnderWorld. The Earth has begun to heal itself (years of pollution have torn up the ozone layer), and the Controller (Ramsay Smith) knows this. He has hatched a plan to wipe out the entire population of SurfaceWorld by releasing a chemical weapon into the atmosphere. When a gang of hooligans, led by vicious gangster Niki Picasso (Jalal Merhi), infiltrates the UnderWorld, the game is changed. They kill Zoey, leaving the Controller the perfect opportunity to hatch a plan that involves resurrecting her as the TC 2000X. She is programmed to charm Picasso and use him as a stepping stone to release the chemical. Meanwhile, Storm has been framed and is on the run. He hides out in SurfaceWorld where he befriends Master Sumai (Bolo Yeung). Together they must prevent the elimination of SurfaceWorld inhabitants by stopping Picasso, Zoey, and the Controller's forces, led by strongman Bigalow (Matthias Hues).

One thing Billy Blanks can never be accused of is making a dull film. The action is almost nonstop and there seems to be a fight scene every five to ten minutes, which is why we watch these films in the first place. The story wasn't all that interesting and mostly a hodgepodge of ideas from different films. The most exciting thing about *TC 2000* is the fact that Bolo Yeung is *not* the villain. Seeing him in action fighting alongside Blanks is a treat. Both men are given the chance to show off their fighting abilities (acting and language skills, not so much). Phillips is the sole beauty among the brawn but really isn't given much to do during the film's last half. Merhi and Hues (depending on how you feel about them) are solid in their respective roles. The music is generic and the sets look drab. If the wardrobe in this film is any indication to what we have to look forward

to in the world's future, I'll check out early. There are a few unintentionally funny moments (most notably Matthias Hues in short shorts and combat boots) that just add to the charm that is *TC 2000*.

Teenage Mutant Ninja Turtles II: The Secret of the Ooze

1991 (New Line DVD) (djm)

Quickly produced in the wake of the success of the first Ninja Turtles movie (which came out the previous year), *The Secret of the Ooze* is more silly and cartoonish. The turtles—Raphael, Donatello, Michaelangelo, Leonardo—are up against the revived Shredder, who has secured himself the last canister of toxic "ooze" to make some mutant creatures of his own. Helping the turtles out is a pizza delivery teenager named Keno, who is played by the amazing Ernie Reyes Jr. from *The Last Dragon* and *Red Sonja*. The five of them battle Shredder's Foot Clan and the mutant monsters he creates.

As far as sequels go, this one is purely a cash-in on the much-better first entry, but if it wasn't for Ernie Reyes Jr., it wouldn't have much life at all. Reyes Jr. is so talented as a martial artist that it astonishes me that he wasn't given more parts to play in movies. Watching him in this junky flick should clue you in that Hollywood dropped the ball somewhere. He's awesome. His next movie was *Surf Ninjas*. Kenn Scott (later the star of *Showdown*) plays Raphael. Toshishiro Obata co-stars. Michael Pressman directed.

Tekken

2010 (Anchor Bay DVD) (CD)

In the future, war has destroyed the territories and the corporations now run everything. *Tekken* is the top of them all. When Jin (John Foo) witnesses the death of his mother at their orders in Anvil (the slums outside the corporations), he wants revenge on all those responsible, especially Heihachi (Cary-Hiroyuki Tagawa) and Kazuya Mishima (Ian Anthony Dale). Jin meets up with Steve Fox (Luke Goss) who acts as a mentor and gets him into a tournament hosted by Tekken. Together, with the help of the beautiful Christie Monteiro (Kelly Overton), they enter into the tournament and surprise everyone. With the metallically enhanced champion Bryan Fury (Gary Daniels) in Kazuya's corner, their fight is just beginning, and it won't be easy to bring them all down.

Tekken is a movie that may divide audiences but it has a certain type of charm that I really enjoyed. Director Dwight Little (*Rapid Fire*) is no stranger to action and knows how to film a fight scene. The script and story are weak, the characters are mostly one-dimensional, and the editing during some of the action scenes was too hyperkinetic, but he still manages to make a fairly solid film. That said, the overall production design of the picture is outstanding. The depressing darkness of life outside the tournament contrasts well with the bright and colorful world within it. The original music by John Hunter is loud and heavy, raising your adrenalin level for the action. The fights would have been nothing without the expert choreography by Cyril Raffaelli (also star of the excellent *District B-13* films). They are fast and furious with each character having a very unique style. As in many film adaptations of video games, there is usually a heavy dose of miscasting but *Tekken* manages to do it right. John Foo (*House of Fury, Universal Soldier: Regeneration*) is perfectly cast as Jin Kazama. He is full of energy and has a youthful charm with leading man potential. Ian Anthony Dale (*Mortal Kombat: Legacy*) plays his main nemesis Kazuya and does everything a good villain should do. The best fight goes to Jin and Bryan Fury (Daniels, perfectly cast). The rest of the cast is equally impressive with Kelly Overton, Cary-Hiroyuki Tagawa, and underused Cung Le (*Dragon Eyes*) and Luke Goss (*Death Race 2 and 3*). Goss can elevate anything that he appears in and just needs to find that one project that will send him to superstardom. Though *Tekken* makes a few missteps, it's still a blast from start to finish.

Tekken 2: Kazuya's Revenge

2014 (SP Distribution DVD) (CD)

"Tekken . . . my empire. Let them come. He will come."

A young man (Kane Kosugi from *Ninja 2: Shadow of a Tear*) wakes up in a hotel room with no recollection of how he ended up there or who he is. He's immediately attacked by unknown assailants, and he's shocked to find out he's an expert fighter. He's quickly caught and recruited into an underground organization and trained to be an assassin. If he does what they ask, he will eventually earn his freedom. He begins to fall for his innocent neighbor Aura (Paige Lindquist) and begins to question his motives. After a confrontation with former assassin Bryan Fury (Gary Daniels), he learns the organization is evil. With the help of Rhona (Kelly Wenham), his handler, they set out to bring it all tumbling down. *Tekken* videogame fans will not like this movie. It essentially ignores the first feature film and doesn't even come close to following anything in the video games. Only two actors return from the previous entry—Cary-Hirouki Tagawa as Heihachi and Gary Daniels as Bryan Fury. The thing is, they only appear in cameo roles. One thing this film does prove is that Kane Kosugi (also in *Revenge of the Ninja* with his father Sho) should be a much bigger action star. His portrayal of Kazuya elevates the poor material, and he shows plenty of fire in the action scenes. The fight between Kazuya and Bryan Fury is cut horribly short, leaving you wanting more. Instead of an ultimate showdown, we're given a final fight between two unimportant henchmen. If *Tekken* is *Street Fighter* (1994) then *Tekken 2: Kazuya's Revenge* is *Street Fighter: The Legend of Chun Li*. Directed by cinematographer

Wych Kaos. The fights were choreographed by Brahim Achabbakhe, who also worked on *Ninja 2: Shadow of a Tear* with Kosugi.

Telefon

1977 (Warner DVD) (djm)

A conspiracy thriller that riffs on *The Manchurian Candidate*, *Telefon* (based on a novel by Walter Wager) stars Charles Bronson as a KGB agent who is tasked with saving the world from WWIII. A rogue KGB agent named Dalchimsky (Donald Pleasence) has stolen a list of names of sleeper agents living ordinary lives throughout the US, and he is systematically making calls to each name on the list, "waking them up," so that they can perform their suicide mission of terror. Almost all of the people on the list are stationed near a US military base, and it won't be long before the US government realizes that the seemingly random attacks are all connected to the KGB, which is where Major Grigori Borzov (Bronson) comes into play. He and his partner (played by Lee Remick) must get to Dalchimsky before the situation gets completely out of hand, but the trick is to predict which name will be next on his list so that they can more or less be prepared to stop or intercept his call.

A fairly engaging Cold War thriller, with Bronson in a nicely balanced role where he shows calculated cool and menace at the same time, *Telefon* isn't much of an action film, though if anyone wants to see Bronson choke Donald Pleasence to death with his bare hands, then look no further. Peter Hyams contributed to the script, while Don Siegel (*Dirty Harry*) directed.

10 to Midnight

1983 (MGM DVD) (djm)

An impotent, good-looking slasher is targeting beautiful young women in LA, and his trademark is that he kills in the nude and manages to set up perfect alibis. The detective on his trail is Leo Kessler (Charles Bronson), whose daughter becomes the perverted maniac's next intended target. The killer, Warren Stacey (an indelible Gene Davis), doesn't fool Kessler when he's interrogated the first time, and so the stage is quickly set for a tête-à-tête between the two because they're both aware of whom their enemy is. When Kessler senses that the justice system may favor Stacey's case, Kessler plants false evidence on him, and when that tactic turns out a bust, Kessler takes it one step further . . . *with his gun!*

This movie literally scarred me as a child. I saw it when I was pretty young, and I remember thinking, *Why is that man running around naked in the streets, and why is Charles Bronson chasing him?* No studio in Hollywood would ever make *10 to Midnight* today, but in 1983, Cannon did, and there's no going back! For an '80s Bronson picture, it's really special. Bronson, while generally pretty sedentary in the film, is entirely forceful and macho as Kessler, a seasoned and protective detective/father, and

it's a perfect role for him for that time. It's not quite a *Death Wish* sequel (it's smarter) or one of the *Death Wish* emulators he made at Cannon during the period (it's better), and it feels pretty comfortable in a kinky alternate parallel to the era of teen slashers that were flooding the market concurrently. With Bronson on the outskirts, busting down the world of the killer at the center, it's pretty unique as an action movie. Technically, it's more of a thriller, but whatever. It's good. J. Lee Thompson (*Murphy's Law, The Evil That Men Do*, both with Bronson) directed.

Ten Zan: The Ultimate Mission

1988 (NOV) (djm)

A village in Eastern Asia is plagued by a warlord who abducts their young women and kills their strongest men. The warlord—Jason (Mark Gregory from *Delta Force Commando*)—is working with a mad scientist to create a master race by manipulating the DNA of the women he abducts, and his experiments and abductions have gotten out of control, so much so that the villages band together and hire an American mercenary named Lou (Frank Zagarino from *Striker*) to help them get rid of the warlord. Lou flies to Italy for a rendezvous meeting with the ambassadors of the Asian governments, but he's intercepted by Jason's personal assistant (the foxy Sabrina Siani), who distracts him enough to get the drop on him and kidnap him. He's taken to be tortured, but he's rescued by an old buddy named Ricky (Romano Kristoff), and together they're an unstoppable team against the mad scientist and warlord.

A low-rent action movie from Italy's prime years as an exploitation movie factory, *Ten Zan* is good viewing for purveyors of war movies where everyone shoots machine guns and throws grenades, but only the bad guys get blown away. Strangely, I watched this the same night I saw *Expendables 3* in a theater, and I got an overwhelming sense of déjà vu. Zagarino fans will be happy with it. This was the final film to be directed by Fernando Baldi (under the name Ted Kaplan).

Terminal Impact

(a.k.a. **Cyborg Cop 3**)

1995 (Image DVD) (djm)

Two federal marshals, Max and Saint ("B" action princes Frank Zagarino and Bryan Genesse), are not just best friends and roommates—they're the best in the business despite coming off as immature beer-drinking macho guys who eat lots of junk food and watch the news together and leer at the hot newscaster. Their latest gig sort of coincides with a story that the hot newscaster Evelyn Reed (Jennifer Miller) is pursuing: A corporation in South Africa has been testing cybernetic technology in human soldiers, and their latest experiment has the government curious. Evelyn and her cameraman go for the story while Max and Saint go to protect/save her

T

when she dupes the corporation after witnessing the murder of her cameraman at the hands of a cyborg soldier. She steals a valuable trigger device that controls the cyborgs, and the deadly terminators hunt her down, but luckily she has the two marshals to back her up and save the day.

In its execution, *Terminal Impact* ends up feeling and looking like a live Universal Studios theme park stunt show, with explosions, stunt work, live humans being flung halfway across the screen, and gunfire galore, all set to corny humor and dialogue. It's fun for what it is, and Zagarino (*Project: Shadowchaser*) and Genesse (*Street Justice*) are a good pair, but neither one of them really emerges completely heroic in the film. It's like they're playing two characters from *Three Men and a Baby*, and when they throw kicks, shoot guns, or whatever action-oriented things they perform in the film, it's kinda cartoonish. A bombastic finale at a junkyard is lively. From Nu Image. Directed by Yossi Wein, who was the cinematographer on *Cyborg Soldier* (a.k.a. *Cyborg Cop 2*).

Terminal Justice

(a.k.a. **Cybertech P.D.**)

1996 (Echo Bridge DVD) (djm)

Set in a future (2008!) where virtual reality is a big deal, *Terminal Justice* stars Lorenzo Lamas (from TV's *Renegade*) as a cop named Bobby Chase, who moonlights as a bodyguard to a sexy movie star named Pamela Travis (Kari Wuhrer), who has a bootlegged virtual reality sex program that everyone seems to have enjoyed. When Bobby's partner is killed in a botched takedown, he goes into a deep funk where Pamela finds him vulnerable and consolable in her embrace. As Bobby comes back from the brink, he begins focusing his attention on a strange series of killings of women who look the same—exactly the same, in fact—and that leads him to a virtual reality game/program designer (played by Chris Sarandon) who clones women for his programs, then tosses them out after mutilating them and using them for his perverse pleasure. His next target is Pamela Travis, but Bobby Chase is there to rescue her and save her life.

Made during Lamas's run on *Renegade*, *Terminal Justice*—from director Rick King, who had made *Kickboxer 3*—is pretty good if you're a fan of its star, but if you've only dabbled with *Renegade* or various few other movies with Lamas, it might not be the best place to begin with him. I really liked him in this. He seemed more mature and seasoned as an action star, and he scaled back the martial arts and kept his performance on a mostly even keel. It's a physical performance to be sure, but it's not a movie packed with explosions and close-encounter fights. If it had been made with someone like Don "The Dragon" Wilson, there would have been kicking in every other scene, so take that as you will.

Terminal Rush

1996 (Blast Films DVD) (djm)

A group of terrorists take over the Hoover Dam in Nevada and demand millions or they will blow it all to hell. Tough rez cop Jacob Harper (Don "The Dragon" Wilson) steps into action and gets himself into the mix. Head terrorist Dekker (Michael Anderson Jr.) has his right-hand-man Bartel (Roddy "Rowdy" Piper) do his best to defend their position. Some big explosions and lots of gunfire and close-quarter combat attempt to engage the viewer in a *Die Hard*-esque exercise.

At turns, *Terminal Rush* looks expensive and cheap all at the same time. The major explosions and actual footage in and around the Hoover Dam compel me to believe that the movie had a budget, but other scenes of characters chatting in ugly compartmentalized sets reciting terrible dialogue get me thinking that the movie was shot in under a week. Whatever the case, it veers too far in either direction, and it never manages to be a solid action film, despite its marquee stars. Wilson delivers an on-par performance, while Piper seems to be hamming it up, complete with a Hamburglar look (painted black-eye mask for no reason). Their climactic fight is more of a scuffle, so if you're hoping to get a spectacular Wilson on Piper fight, you may be slightly disappointed. Damien Lee, who worked with Jesse Ventura on *Abraxis* and with Michael Dudikoff on *Moving Target*, directed it. Incidentally, Don Wilson made a movie called *Moving Target* as well.

The Terminator

1984 (MGM DVD) (MJ)

"Hey, buddy. You got a dead cat in there, or what?"

The Terminator tells the story of two soldiers from the year 2029 who travel back in time and arrive in present-day Los Angeles. One is a man (played by Michael Biehn). The other is a machine—The Terminator (played by Arnold Schwarzenegger). Both have arrived for the same reason: To find a woman named Sarah Connor (Linda Hamilton)

The T-100 Terminator, played by Arnold Schwarzenegger. Author's collection.

Arnold Schwarzenegger plays The Terminator. Author's collection.

He's from the future. He's The Terminator, featuring Arnold Schwarzenegger. Author's collection.

who is responsible for the future of humanity. One is here to destroy her. The other is here to protect her. Which one will find her first?

Released in October 1984, *The Terminator* was one of the first films to meld the action and science fiction genres successfully and was greatly rewarded for it at the box office. This success was even more significant because the film was produced independently and not by any of the major studios of the day. The testament to the film's great success are the infinite number of rip-offs it spawned immediately after its release as producers all over the world struggled to duplicate its formula for success. This is the film that helped cement Schwarzenegger's status as an action star and introduced the world to writer/director James Cameron, who succeeded at finding the right balance between the action and science fiction elements of the story, writing characters the audience could relate to and care for right away and casting the film with mostly unknown actors at the time, actors who would become genre favorites overnight in the wake of the film's success. Initially conceived with a different actor in mind to play The Terminator (Lance Henriksen), Schwarzenegger took on the role and immediately made it his own, a role that had a bare minimum of dialogue but required someone with a significant physical presence or the plot would not be able to sustain itself. While Schwarzenegger plays it straight for the entire film, his performance still contains all of the elements that would make him a worldwide star in the years to come. *The Terminator* also showed that writer/director James Cameron could make a great innovative action film that looked infinitely more expensive than the film actually cost. It is a talent that would serve him greatly on his future projects.

Terminator 2: Judgment Day

1991 (Lionsgate DVD) (MJ)

"I need your clothes, your boots, and your motorcycle."

Released seven years after the runaway box-office success of *The Terminator*, audience expectations were incredibly high for this bigger and more expansive sequel. The world had changed in many ways since 1984. In the meantime, director James Cameron had continued his success with *Aliens* and *The Abyss*. Arnold Schwarzenegger continued to triumph at the box office with every new film, including recent triumphs with *Kindergarten Cop* and *Total Recall* in 1990. In another filmmaker's hands, a high-profile sequel like this could have been a catastrophe but for James Cameron, it was a challenge to improve his craft with more resources at his disposal than ever before. *Terminator 2* picks up the threads of Sarah Connor's (played by a toned Linda Hamilton) life ten years later. Currently incarcerated in a state sanitarium while her son, John (played by newcomer Edward Furlong), has grown up in foster care, she has lost touch with him and possibly with reality. Skynet, the artificial intelligence responsible for driving the extermination of humanity in 2029, sends another more advanced and more powerful Terminator (the T-1000, played by Robert Patrick) back to the present to kill John Connor while he is still a child, which will prevent him from organizing the resistance in 2029. Unknown to Skynet, the resistance has reprogrammed a Terminator (a T-101, played by Schwarzenegger) and sent it back in time as well to protect John at all costs. Which one will find John first?

At the heart of the success of *Terminator 2: Judgment Day* is the creative partnership between director James Cameron and star Arnold Schwarzenegger. Both men were not interested in simply remaking the first film but were seeking ways to challenge themselves creatively and to entertain an audience, using all the filmmaking tools at their disposal. While the film relies heavily on the audience's knowledge of the first film, the writers are constantly looking to challenge the audience's expectations of the characters while also supporting the film's anti-war message. As with other Cameron films, the action alone does not drive the film. The characters drive the action that drives the film. *Judgment Day* was also an excellent showcase for Schwarzenegger to show people how much he had grown as an actor since the first film. The picture also includes an incredible performance from Linda Hamilton, who completely physically transformed herself to meet the demands of playing Sarah Connor, and also gave Robert Patrick a plum, breakout role.

Terminator 3: Rise of the Machines

2003 (Warner DVD) (MJ)

"Talk to the hand."

It's hard to believe after the gargantuan box-office success of *Terminator 2: Judgment Day* in 1991 that a sequel was not immediately forthcoming. And yet this is what happened, with director James Cameron and star Arnold Schwarzenegger moving on and continuing to find success working on other projects. Even after reuniting in 1994 for *True Lies*, it seemed as if the ship had already sailed on future installments. Twelve years later, though, the Terminator would keep his promise and Schwarzenegger returned to play the role that made him an international star. *T3* tells the continuing story of John Connor, now a young adult adrift in life in more ways than one. With Judgment Day seemingly averted, John (now played by actor Nick Stahl) lives off the grid, with no records of his existence, no attachments, no piece of information that could be used by SkyNet to initiate another attempt on his life. Unknown to John, though, SkyNet is now being developed as an artificial intelligence by the US government but no longer shackled to any hardware after transforming itself into a computer virus and has begun to slowly infect other computer networks and assume control. With this knowledge, SkyNet sets another plan in motion to eliminate any opposition from the human resistance, arriving in the form of another Terminator from the future, the T-X, played by newcomer Kristanna Loken. With no current information available to help in locating John Connor, the T-X has been tasked with eliminating multiple targets that will eventually form the core of the human resistance. Anticipating this, the resistance also sends back another T-101 (Schwarzenegger) to protect John and one other unique individual from the T-X. And so the doomsday clock begins again, with the future of the human race in the balance . . .

When Arnold returned to play the Terminator again, the world was a different place. The star underwent a voluntary procedure in 1997 to correct a congenital heart valve condition. His legendary grip over the box office had begun to loosen as films like *End of Days, The 6th Day,* and *Collateral Damage,* yielded diminishing returns. With box-office returns slowing down, the star began to contemplate spending more time in politics. Married at the time to Maria Shriver, a member of the legendary Kennedy family, Schwarzenegger had also become known as a vocal supporter of social causes, especially in the state of California. In October of 2003, Schwarzenegger was elected governor of California, and he would hold the office until 2011. *Rise of the Machines* would be his last starring role until his return in 2013 with *The Last Stand.* The script for *ROTM* is incredibly well constructed, taking into account the passage of time between the two films and acknowledging the audience's familiarity with the events of the previous two films; it plays with

their expectations, while also challenging them. One of the tenets of the previous films is that the future is not set and there is the possibility of changing one's fate. With *T3*, the filmmakers tell the audience flat-out in the first act of the film that this is no longer true. Judgment Day is unavoidable now and this marked a major shift in the tone of the franchise, one which may have proven too great an obstacle for enjoying the film as it sets the stage for an unexpected ending.

The Terminators

2009 (The Asylum DVD) (CD)

"I feel pain, I feel anger, I feel what I believe is compassion. Will I know when I die?"

Sometime in the near future, cyborgs have become commonplace in everyday life. The most common model is the TR-4 (played by Paul Logan from *The Ultimate Game*), and it's used as a laborer. Their program gets manipulated and every single TR-4 turns against humankind and begins to attack Earth. Small-town sheriff Reed Carpenter (A. Martinez) leads a small group of survivors on a mission to prevent the TR-4s from doing any more damage. No matter what they do, it appears that the evil cyborgs are unstoppable until they meet Kurt Ross (Jeremy London), a mysterious man with the only weapon powerful enough to stop them. With his knowledge to destroy them comes a checkered past and secrets to shock everyone.

Don't be fooled by the title (though The Asylum hopes you will be). This film is more akin to the resurrected *Battlestar Galactica* than to *The Terminator* films. If you're someone who can't get enough of action star Paul Logan (also seen in *Ballistica*) then you will want to savor every moment of the film since he plays *all* of the TR-4s and pops up everywhere. He's a killing machine who tends to rip his victim's guts out when convenient and is just as comfortable running at top speed with a blazing gun in his hand. The film is fast-paced, entertaining, and boasts better than expected special effects. This is still the sole directorial effort for director Xavier S. Puslowski, although he's made a career out of being an assistant director on numerous Asylum projects.

Terminator: Genisys

2015 (Paramount DVD) (djm)

"I'm old, not obsolete."

Judgment day happens in 1997, as we've seen in the original two *Terminator* movies. In 2017, Skynet—the all-encompassing, machine-run juggernaut that tries to eradicate humanity—is amazingly losing the war against the human resistance, led by John Connor (Jason Clarke), a pseudo prophet/

T

unstoppable soldier who was taught how to defeat Skynet by his mother since he was a child. He leads his army to overtake a Skynet stronghold where the machines have sent a T-800 Terminator (Arnold Schwarzenegger) back in time to 1984 to kill John's mother Sarah (Emilia Clarke) before she ever gives birth to John. John sends his right-hand man Kyle Reese (Jai Courtney) to the same time to stop the T-800, but there's a ripple in the time continuum at the moment when he travels through time: He sees John being attacked by another Terminator, and in that moment Reese begins having memories he never had before. Up to that point, this is all filler material we knew from the previous entries in this franchise, but as soon as Reese finds himself back in 1984, everything is topsy-turvy. Sarah Connor is not a waitress, but a prepared soldier who has been protected since childhood by "Pops," another T-800 (played by Schwarzenegger). When Reese and the other T-800 land in 1984, Pops and Sarah are ready to receive them, setting the course of a whole new series of events that lead up to a vastly different timeline where Judgment Day doesn't occur until 2017 upon the launch of a computer program called Genisys, which is essentially Skynet. Adding to the complications in the time continuum are a T-1000 (Byung-hun Lee) and an altered John Connor, who has become a sort of T-X (from Terminator 3) with a sinister agenda.

A lot of fans of this series are going to be upset by the meddling with the original story threads that James Cameron set with the first two films, but if you've followed this franchise as far as *Terminator Salvation* and *The Sarah Connor Chronicles*, then *Genisys* is just one step further. It's not as set piece–oriented as *Terminator 3* or as character-driven as the first two films, but I actually enjoyed the film for trying to carry the *Terminator* mythos onward for a new generation. The plot is confusing, but it makes sense if you simply accept the one new plot twist that turns John Connor into a villain. I took issue with the too-clean and indistinct Jai Courtney being cast as Kyle Reese, and Jason Clarke isn't very interesting either. Emilia Clarke is able to remind us of Linda Hamilton, which is a plus, and Schwarzenegger as the aged Terminator model is a major asset. The movie moves a little too fast, with action scenes that erupt sometimes simply to keep the plot moving, but overall this is a totally agreeable entry in one of the most integral post-apocalyptic franchises in movie history. Lorne Balfe's score is better and more memorable than the last two scores from the previous two films. Alan Taylor (*Thor: The Dark World*) directed.

T-Force
1994 (Platinum DVD) (CD)

"To obey authority in this case would contradict self-preservation."

A group of terrorists, led by Samuel Washington (Vernon Wells), seizes control of the British embassy in downtown LA. They have no trouble killing hostages to further their cause and the only option the authorities have is to send in the Terminal Force. They're a group of cyborgs

(called "cybernauts") programmed specifically to be the perfect law enforcers. The leader of the cybernaut team, Adam (Evan Lurie from *American Kickboxer 2*), takes things too far and believes the human authorities are now his enemy. He takes out the rest of the terrorists (and some hostages, too) before going on a rampage with the rest of his team . . . except for one. Cain (Bobby Johnston) realizes Adam's outlook is tainted and goes to the police to help them stop the angry cyborgs. He's paired with veteran Lt. Jack Floyd (Jack Scalia) who hates these machines with a passion. Cain will have to prove his intentions to Jack and the two will have to trust each other if they're to stop Adam from killing anyone else.

There's nothing like watching a film where all of the action is real. *T-Force* wastes no time at all jumping right in it with monster-sized explosions, thousands of blanks, squibs, simple animatronics, and a healthy dose of martial arts action to wet the thirsty palate. Evan Lurie (a popular "B" star during the '90s with titles like *Double Impact* and *Tiger Claws II* to his credit) plays the villain, and he looks like he's having fun. He gets to blow things up, attempt procreation with a female cyborg, *and* beat the spit out of anyone trying to get in his way, with his cyborg sidekick played by bodybuilder Deron McBee (*The Killing Zone*). PM Entertainment and director Richard Pepin (*Escape from Alaska*) didn't set out to make high art; they aimed to entertain and *T-Force* never fails on that front.

That Man Bolt
1973 (Universal DVD) (djm)

A defining moment for star Fred Williamson, *That Man Bolt* showcases him as a James Bond-type agent/mercenary named Jefferson Bolt, a world-traveled adventurer with martial arts skills, a suave sense of style, and pithy comebacks and one-liners. It starts with him incarcerated in Hong Kong where he's recruited by a British agent who has a job for him: Transport a suitcase of supposedly counterfeit cash to Mexico City. He takes the job and is forthwith released from prison, and in no time he's neck-deep in danger and intrigue. Men are chasing him, women are falling for him, and even his most trusted colleague is working against him. Who can do such a job? That man Bolt!

Fans of Williamson will most likely hold this film in high regard, shoulders above many of his other pictures. If Williamson is an action star generally unfamiliar to you, this is a wonderful place to start. He had Universal behind him with this one, and the production values are solid, giving audiences the most bang for its buck. It's a decent 007 riff, with its own spin on the genre, and Williamson more than delivers on the action

Jefferson Bolt (Fred Williamson) is laying the hammer down in *That Man Bolt*. Author's collection.

front. He kicks, he chops, he runs and shoots and romances. It's got everything. It was directed by Henry Levin and David Lowell Rich.

They Live
1988 (Shout Factory DVD) (djm)

"I have come here to chew bubblegum and kick ass . . . and I'm all out of bubblegum."

A vagrant in an increasingly corporate American world, John Nada (Roddy Piper) wanders into Los Angeles, looking for work. He finds a gig for a week as a construction worker and makes a hesitant friendship with Frank (Keith David), who also seems to be a vagabond. Nada camps at a settlement for the homeless, and he stumbles onto a resistance group that makes illegal broadcasts on television, stating that there is a force at work in the world that cannot be seen with ordinary eyes, that humanity is living under the oppression of a deep and sinister power that dwells among humans. Nada puts on a pair of ordinary-looking sunglasses and suddenly, the truth is revealed: Aliens have colonized Earth and have enslaved humanity, hypnotizing them to the point of complete submission and servitude. Nada joins the resistance and tries to enlist Frank to join in, and when they've become a unified force, they are a faction to be reckoned with.

Some might assert that *They Live* is director John Carpenter's most subversive, politically charged film, but it's also a pretty damn fine action film too. Casting Piper in the lead role was a stroke of genius, and Carpenter is able to adapt Piper's professional wrestling persona and harness it, making Piper a verifiable action star. The centerpiece fight scene between Piper and David has become a high mark in fight choreography for a reason: It's expertly choreographed by Jeff

Theatrical poster for *That Man Bolt*. Author's collection.

Imada, and Carpenter captures every punch, slam, and kick without missing a beat. Sadly, Piper was never able to ride the wave *They Live* started for him, but he became a mainstay in direct-to-video action films, many of which didn't deserve him. *They Live* has become his signature film, and rightly so.

INTERVIEW:
RODDY PIPER
(djm)

Since he was in his teens, Roddy Piper has always been regarded as a badass. From his early days as a fighter and pro wrestler (as WWE's "Rowdy" Roddy Piper), he was one of the very first professional wrestlers to make the crossover to Hollywood to star in major motion pictures. He starred in the cult post-apocalyptic movie Hell Comes To Frogtown (1988), *and then shortly after got the call from John Carpenter to star in* They Live (1988), *which remains Piper's best-known work as an actor. While some action stars and athletes find success in "vehicle" movies that are perpetuated by success, Piper struggled to maintain a steady stream of hits after* They Live, *and therefore returned to pro-wrestling. He continued to make films within different genres, but of course it's action films that most people loved to see him star in. He passed away in 2015.*

At what point did you decide to segue into movies from wrestling?

When I was a young kid in Los Angeles, I was working in the Olympic Auditorium. This would have been the '70s. I was the light heavyweight champion of the world. There was a very famous man, who at one time was the toughest man in the world—not according to him, but according to everybody else. His name was "Judo" Gene LeBell. He trained Bruce Lee, Chuck Norris, and myself, and he had twenty-four black belts. He is 79 years old and every Monday he's still on the mats. I might have been seventeen or eighteenish, and Henry Winkler did a movie called *The One and Only*, which Carl Reiner directed. I was there working with Judo Gene, who was a professional wrestler and was stunt coordinating on the film, and he said to Reiner, "Hey, put this kid in it." I played the part of

He's here to kick ass and chew bubblegum . . . and he's all out of bubblegum. Roddy Piper in *They Live*. Author's collection.

Leatherneck Joe Brady. I'd never been in a film, or even thought about being in one. Just for reference: I never had any aspirations of being a professional actor, in any entertainment. That came by accident. Making a film didn't interest me at the time, but Judo Gene asked me to be in the scene with Henry Winkler. I even got a close-up. The director said out loud during my scene, "We've got another Robert Redford here." He tried to get me to go in the movies. That's how I got my first big break. That director was Carl Reiner. I didn't have much of a part in that movie, but they kept playing the scene I was in over and over. It's just like everything in my life. It just kind of happened.

You did a movie called *Body Slam* with Tanya Roberts in the early '80s. Do you remember anything interesting about that shoot?

Yeah, Hal Needham directed that. He was one of the greatest stuntmen ever, but I think he was relatively new on the directing scene. He was a great guy. He never missed a set call, but that set got wild. They wanted to make a movie about pro wrestlers. Dirk Benedict was in it. You know, it was getting away from where I wanted to go at that point in my career. I was trying to completely distance myself and start playing better characters, and they asked me to get some other wrestlers on the movie. They had so many other guys from my business that it got to be very wild on the set. It wasn't as professional as it could have been.

How did the film *Hell Comes to Frogtown* come your way?

In 1983 or 1984, there was this movie called *Hell Comes to Frogtown*, and Cyndi Lauper's manager said to me, "Hey, come on over here and do this movie." I didn't read the script, I just went over and talked to the director, Donald Jackson. It was an awkward meeting. As soon as I said I liked it, I got the part.

***Frogtown* looks like a fairly low-budget movie. I mean it has to be because Donald G. Jackson made it . . .**

(Laughing.) I didn't think anyone would see it. It was about frogs! Mutant frogs. I just thought, *yeah, okay.* I was on top of the world at that time—in my mind. So I went and did it, and I didn't get along with the director *at all.* There was this one instance where in this scene I was tied up. The director decided to do another take, and he went off to do something, and I was like, "Hey, untie me here." He just kind of remarked, "Hey, you're getting paid enough." I said, "Hey, I can kick your fuckin' ass from here." It was that kind of rapport. Again, I was a young kid when I got out of this wild business of wrestling, and here I was doing a movie getting the kind of feedback that I wasn't used to.

Video release poster for *Hell Comes to Frogtown*. Author's collection.

Was it difficult adjusting your wrestling persona to fit into the confines of a movie and being on location?

When I did it, I'd never had an acting lesson or anything. But I had fun. It was all in the desert, there were a lot of pretty ladies. I had fun making it, regardless of the director. They did a second one without me, and it bombed. I never thought the first one would sell so many copies. (Laughing.) But it did! Every time I see it on the shelf, I buy them so nobody else can see them. (Laughing.) Not really, but I've thought of it.

So let me get this straight: Have you ever actually watched the film?

Yes. Once. It was interesting. After I had watched it and had done *They Live*, I compared the two. Once I'd gotten to *They Live*, I'd done acting classes to understand the art of acting, to catch up. The classes had begun putting controls on me because acting is a completely different art. Action is the opposite. Pro wrestling is *explosive.* Acting is *implosive.* So I took a look at the two films, and I wished I'd been a little freer in *They Live* as I'd been in *Frogtown*. I wasn't down on myself in *Frogtown* because I was just being me, and sometimes that's the best thing for me.

So what did I think of *Frogtown*?

It's a hokey little movie. Kind of cute. I got a lot of guys teasing me about it. I'm not ashamed of it, really. What didn't bother me was the innocence of me coming into it as an artist or an actor. There were some moments in it where I was really in the moment. *They Live* got so complicated, and I'd wished I'd put a little more Sam Hell into Nada.

T

Were you at all aware of who Donald G. Jackson was when you made the film? When he was alive, he was making some pretty lowbrow movies. *Hell Comes to Frogtown* **is probably the "biggest" movie he ever made.**

No, I had no idea who he was. I went to the meeting because Cyndi Lauper's manager, who was also my manager at the time, set it up for me.

You had some cool co-stars in the film. Can you talk a little bit about working with Sandahl Bergman, Rory Calhoun, and William Smith?

Sure. Rory Calhoun played the character who taught me about sludge. I went through the whole movie, and I really liked him. We got along good. We'd talk and talk, and then after the movie was finished, I realized that I'd had no idea that when I was a kid I used to watch Rory Calhoun on TV when he was a cowboy. I went, "Jeepers! That was the guy I hung out with on the set with every day?!" I would have told him, "I watched you on TV when I was a kid!" Sandahl Bergman was real sweet. There was nobody in the cast I didn't get along with. It was more from the director that I might have had a problem with. It was like, *Oh, great, we've got a jock coming to do a movie.* That's what he was thinking. He wasn't giving me respect. *Oh great, we've got a phony wrestler coming to do this movie, isn't that great?* But you hired me! So, the people in the cast were great. It was out in the desert, so it was really hot. It's difficult to make a movie. Long hours. First time, I'm rolling hard.

What about William Smith? He's a tough guy.

William Smith, he was telling me during the movie that he used to do bombing missions in the war because it was extra money. He was an arm wrestler, or something. He had a little bit of a testosterone attitude. He was a little . . . I don't know if I want to use the word jealous, but he was . . . there wasn't great chemistry between him and I. But I had very few scenes with him.

After *Frogtown,* **you starred in the film most people remember you from,** *They Live.* **Can you talk a little bit about working under John Carpenter's wing and how he directed you?**

John Carpenter saw *Hell Comes to Frogtown.* He reached out to me to do *They Live.* He spent a lot of time with me. We did a lot of prep for the movie, in writing the script. I would talk to him, and we would get into lengthy conversations. The first thing about John Carpenter: He had me watch *The Quiet Man* with John Wayne and Maureen O'Hara. At the time, that was the longest fight scene in cinema history. John wanted the longest fight in cinema history, and the best fight as possible in cinema history. That was one thing he wanted to accomplish. The other thing was that he created the character Nada after me, and the word 'nada' means 'nothing' in Spanish. He named me that because you don't know anything about John Nada. You don't know where he came from, you didn't know what he was about. I wore my wedding ring during the whole shoot, which was something I did quite often, just to tell my family that I love

them, and he allowed me to keep it on because it brought more mystique to the character. Why was he wearing a wedding ring? That's what made John Nada so interesting: It's because you didn't know anything about him and you were trying to learn as much as you could. One of John's directions to me was that I could ask him anything all day and all night until we got to principle photography, and then we gotta roll. So I took that opportunity. I took an acting class in Hollywood, and I did something that most actors couldn't believe that I did, which was that after I got the part in *They Live,* I'd shoot videos of my scenes in the acting class, and I'd bring them back to John, and ask him, "What do you think?" I guess actors, once they get the part, they would've never done that in case the director might say, "Wait a second, I think I got the wrong guy." I was innocent. Maybe naïve is a better word. John had a lot of respect for a guy who would do that and bring it back. He saw my dedication to it. One of the things that happened on *They Live* was that John had his people and his crew from his other movies, and there became a jealousy factor that became quite strong. They felt that John was spending so much time with me and trying to make this movie great, and that meant that he wasn't spending as much time with them. It was a hard shoot. Very difficult, hard shoot. I think it took six weeks to shoot it. They had me on this regimen where I was down from my 235 pounds to about 201. Every morning I had to get up at four a.m., go into the sauna for an hour, then when I hit the set they had a sink full of ice and water, and I had to soak my face in it for thirty minutes. As soon as I got to the set there were all these things that one of the people from John's crew was making me go through, and towards the end of the movie I would get in the sauna—and I saunaed so much that I wasn't sweating anymore, it was just burning my skin. This person was forming this jealousy towards me, and so there were long, long hours on the set. I was keeping it in my heart. I was trying to do the best I could under the circumstances.

How was the infamous fight scene to shoot?

The fights in the film were choreographed by Jeff Imada, but fighting is something from *my* job. Keith David was a wonderful guy. He was extremely trustful with me during that fight. It is the longest fight in cinema history. It's in the *Guinness Book of World Records.* They took five minutes off in the editing, too! So that was a couple of things that John wanted to accomplish in the movie. John had just finished *Big Trouble in Little China,* and that was John's first big-budget movie, and it didn't do well at the box office, and he told me that he needed a hit. There was that pressure, too. It wasn't like everyone was having fun and having a great time.

Did the wrestling world support you becoming an actor?

When I went into *They Live,* the wrestling world got angry at me. At the time, I'd just finished *Wrestlemania 3,* which had the largest indoor crowd in America—93,000 people at the Pontiac Silverdome. I think it still holds the record. I retired and said "I'm going to Hollywood to

make movies," so I'd made the commitment. With that said, John Carpenter said to me, "I want you to be my John Wayne, and I want to be your John Ford, and I want to do movies with you." But there was so much hassle on the set that we didn't continue with it. Because of that, and because I had children and I needed to make big money, I had to go back to professional wrestling at that time. For me, it was a deep wound. I was on my way to do this thing. When *They Live* came out it was the number one movie at the box office the week it came out. The other two movies were *Everybody's All-American* with Dennis Quaid and *U2: Rattle and Hum,* and on Friday night that weekend, U2 blocked off Hollywood Boulevard and did a free concert to pump the movie, and I thought, "We're dead meat." And sure as heck, *They Live* became the number one movie that weekend, which was very cool.

How does each director you've worked with adapt your unique physicality and fighting style into each project you've worked on? In other words, how are you able to translate your unique styles as an "action" actor into each role you star in?

I've been fortunate with John and some of the others. They realize that that's my department. Being unorthodox in not shooting fights in the way they would've normally in the movie world, where they set up and say "You can go this far and we'll cut," I remember my scene with Keith where he would be throwing camera punches and miss me, but as he'd pull his fist back, he'd catch me in the eye. Finally, I said, "Whoa, whoa, whoa." I called Carpenter aside, and said, "Listen to me: Trust me. Let Keith and I go for it." And I said, "Keith, from the neck down, just go ahead and hit me. Let's take the fight as far as we possibly can in each cut." It did something that was unusual, and I watch it now and I can see that it was a completely different fight from what I've normally seen in cinema fights. It was a fight between two friends. It had to match the arc of the script. So, as opposed to martial arts films where you have a story and all of a sudden you go into a hundred and eighty foot punches and kicks and moves and whatever, this was completely different. Every punch and every move would count as it would in real time. Because we went as far as we possibly could, I think we did it in three back-to-back takes. Pushed it as far we could. Okay, cut. Push it as far as we could. Cut again. What that did was

Keith David and Roddy Piper star in *They Live.* Author's collection.

After one of the greatest fight scenes in movie history, these two guys (Roddy Piper and Keith David) become allies in *They Live.* Author's collection.

it kept a certain energy up in the fight that you don't normally get. And then, of course, the next day we came back and had to come in for things where we had to have mats and stuff in the alley. When Keith and I got right into the fight, we kind of knew where we were going, but at the same time, when I grabbed him and punched him boom boom boom and tackled him, I was just doing that and Keith was good enough to keep up with me. I would whisper to him here and whisper to him there. They had never seen fight choreography in that way before. But it worked out the best for me and the best for the movie.

Is that how it went for some of your other action films like *Back in Action* and *Tough and Deadly*, which you did with Billy Blanks?

Ah, Billy Blanks. When I did one of those with Billy, he was coming up with a new system of exercise. He was trying to come up with a name for it, and it turned out to be Tae Bo. On the set and in-between, we were talking about his new system. Billy is a very good martial artist. When you have somebody of that caliber, you go, "Okay, let's go." I can remember one time with Billy and I, we had a scene where there was a four-foot wall and we had to go into some tables and I can remember Billy grabbing me and going, "Okay, we're gonna go, we're gonna go for it, right?" I said, "Yeah, Billy, we're gonna go for it. I'll be there." When they said "Action," away we went. And we went *hard.* We're two fighters, we're two athletes. We weren't afraid of getting hurt. So those fights were easier than the *They Live* fights, but they also had to be a little sharper because we had to pick up the speed. I was in professional wrestling, and he was a professional martial artist. He's a wonderful guy. We understood what we were trying to get down.

Richard Norton was one of your co-stars in *Tough and Deadly.* Do you remember working with Norton?

Oh, yes. He's a great guy. Same as Billy. We all came from the same background. We got along great. It was like the boys just sitting around. We didn't have any problems at all.

Back in Action and Tough and Deadly almost feel like a franchise together, or a series. Were they pitched as a double feature for you and Blanks?

Well, we did *Back in Action* first and it seemed to work so well, and so we rolled right into the second one. I played a detective named Elmo Freech in *Tough and Deadly.* Because the first one went so well, we went into the second one and the producers were really excited about it. It was about the time when the video market was huge, but it started dropping. So after we did the second one, the producers Shapiro and Glickenhaus, decided that we had lost the financial flow of the Billy Blanks/Roddy Piper team. Otherwise, I think we would have done another few in the *Lethal Weapon* style. They were getting better and better, and we enjoyed working together.

Why was it decided that these two films would go directly to video and not to theaters? They look and feel like big theatrical films.

That was a decision the producers made. Direct-to-video was less money for them. It's more prestigious to be released to theaters, but that's the way that they ran their company at the time. They were making a lot of money doing it in this format. By the time the second one was finished, they saw how good they were getting and they wanted to do another one for theaters, but that's when their company broke down. The whole market changed.

Were you disappointed that the movies you were making at this time were going directly to video?

Absolutely. I was very disappointed. I was at the top of my career in pro wrestling, and I said at *Wrestlemania 3* that I was retiring and going to Hollywood. I quit. I fully intended to carry on an acting career, but what happened after *They Live* with the problems on the set, then with the Shapiro/Glickenhaus movies not making the theaters like *They Live* did . . . you know, I had kids. The wrestling world was already angry at me for doing *They Live.* They felt like I'd betrayed them. The Hollywood world didn't like me because *Oh, great: Another jock coming in who wants to be an actor.* So, I got used to not being liked quite a bit. But it didn't deter me in my work, it just made it a little difficult.

You were actually ahead of the curve as far as crossing over because now all of those wrestlers have done it and continue trying to do it.

Yeah, I was the first pro wrestler to star in a major motion picture, being Universal Pictures, and it was the number one hit of the weekend. I'm not saying it was *Gone With the Wind.* It was an accomplishment to come out with a number one movie. I so much had my heart into it. I'd been fighting maybe fourteen years by that time, and I had my heart into it big-time going into Hollywood. My family lived in Portland, Oregon, and to relocate my family to Hollywood . . . my kids were in school and we were having trouble with that, and WWF (now

WWE) was calling, and I made some money on *They Live*, and as disappointed as I was, I needed it to happen *quickly*, and I needed to roll from *They Live* to the next one. But then John Carpenter, you know, he didn't follow up with what he said, and the thing with Shapiro/Glickenhaus didn't continue, so I had to make a bad decision. I went back to wrestling. One good thing that happened was that because I was the first wrestler to do that, when I came back to the WWF, I was even stronger than when I left, which was a godsend to me. It put me in a position that no other wrestler had been in. I got so much anger from the WWF at the time, that Hulk Hogan and Vince McMahon countered *They Live* by checking into a hotel room for a week and wrote *No Holds Barred*, and that's why that movie was made with Hogan. *They Live* beat it. (Laughing.) Sorry about that.

After the two you did with Billy Blanks, you became a pretty big name on the direct-to-video market. You did some other action films like *Last to Surrender,* which paired you up with Han Soo Ong, a Chinese action star. Do you have anything to say about this film or any of the others you've done since?

Yeah, but I like to consider *They Live* an "A" movie, or a "B plus" movie, and it was definitely going in the right direction. I wanted to star in the biggest movies I could be in. When I did the two with Billy and they went directly to video, it was like "I'm losing ground here." They weren't paying anywhere close to what I could make in professional wrestling. I love my kids so much, and they're perfect, but I had to make a choice because I didn't have the time to sit around and schmooze in Hollywood, and so that's why I went back to wrestling. I did a couple of movies in Canada, but they were just using me and my name to make a quick buck. I wasn't getting the scripts that I needed, and also, my own lack of knowledge and my ignorance of how Hollywood business worked, I didn't understand the process of it. I was like, "Let's make another one, let's make another one." It doesn't quite work that way. It was a very low point in my life when I had to go back into professional wrestling. I really wanted to make my mark in Hollywood. I never made a 100 million-dollar movie, and obviously I could have made much more doing a movie like that, but all the best plans laid by mice and men . . . it didn't work out. Guy's got a family. That's the most important thing in this life. I did what a dad had to do.

How about some of your other films? How about *The Shepherd* (a.k.a. *CyberCity*) which co-starred C. Thomas Howell? Any thoughts or comments?

It rings a bell, but it's not coming to me.

It was a Roger Corman production.

Oh, okay. Um, again, when I was doing these movies, I was realizing that I was going downhill after *They Live.* It started to kill my enthusiasm. I could feel that I was losing my grip on the Hollywood industry. Not to say that I didn't do my best on every one of them. If I could have gone from

They Live and as John laid out in the beginning where we were going to make movies together that were tailored to me at that time, we would have gone much further ahead. But these other films that you're talking about . . . I was still trying to make it work. When the final cuts of these movies came out and the way they publicized them and the distribution . . . it's all about money. It's a business. I'm looking at how much damage I'm doing to myself as a commodity, so all those things were playing into what was going on with these films.

Have you reconciled with Carpenter? It sounds like you hold a little bit of a . . .

Absolutely, I do. Obviously, I've seen him since, and I say, "Hey, John." The script girl, the continuity girl on *They Live* had a big problem with me. I reminded her of her brother. Whatever that means. So when I left and went back to wrestling, this person started to make up a whole lot of stories. One of the stories was that because they were making me lose all that weight, I got so mad at them that I took off after them and they ran and I was chasing them. I had never heard this story until seven years later when I was asked to sit down and talk about the movie with the director. Then I had just heard the story, and I got angry because I realized that Hollywood was putting out the negatives on Rod for no reason. I said to John, "Hey, John. What is this bullshit?" He says, "Oh, I remember we were around catering, and there was goofing around and she was chasing you." I said, "No, I don't remember that, but I have a question for you: What the fuck was she gonna do if she caught me?" And silence. I said, "You stop that bullshit now." So that camp was being big shots, and I drew back. Whatever they were saying wasn't true, and Hollywood being a small village, and me back in wrestling, they were believing it. I finally said, "What was the problem?" And John finally said to me, "It was ninety-five percent that person's fault." Well, what was my five percent? Because he took a guy that got into pro wrestling at five years old. One of the most wireless types of entertainment that you could get. Very demanding, very guttural. And they took me and wanted me to be this Hollywood guy, calm, and schmooze here and schmooze there. That was really hard to do after fourteen years of wrestling. I'd have to do the math. I started wrestling in '69 and *They Live* was '88. I didn't know the rules. "One of the reasons you got me, John, was because I was known all over the world and I'd had this rough exterior as John Wayne did." So I got into this Hollywood thing where I left and all these people start talking about you behind your back, all these bullshit stories. I'm in another world and I'm not hearing them. Vince McMahon came to me while I was shooting *They Live* and told me "If you give me four weeks, I'll get another movie at the same money." I said, "Not with John Carpenter directing, you won't." He got very angry. And again, John told me that he wanted me to be his John Wayne. So he took this rough piece of coal to turn it into a diamond, but I was pretty wild because that was my job. You can't expect a guy to change in six to eight weeks. Hollywood's Hollywood. So I went back to wrestling, and I hung in there. If I hadn't, I don't know where I'd be now. So, yeah, I do. I hold animosity.

What kind of roles are you looking for these days? I still see that you're working in movies. It seems like you appear in several movies a year.

I want to play roles that go against the impression people have of me. I'd love to play Lenny in *Of Mice and Men*. I'd love to play Quasimodo. I'd like to play an AIDS patient. Something with depth that gets away from "I'm gonna kick your ass!" I haven't had an opportunity to really show my acting skills. I have that word out. I have overcome all the negativities, I'm on a whole different level. I'm looking for scripts that will allow me to put my best artistic talents forward and people will go, "Oh, shit. That was Roddy Piper?" and they will have respect for me as an artist.

Is there anything else you'd like to say or add about your career in movies or in wrestling?

The only thing I'd like to say is I have not done my best work yet. I am determined to go there and in the next three or four years you're going to see me do some stuff that you'll be proud of. With wrestling, I was a big, dumb wrestler back in those days. I hated that. I came fit for the world playing the bagpipes when I was fourteen. I can play just about every musical instrument. I wrote a book. I want to be known as an artist, not Roddy Piper, the wrestler. They don't call me Roddy Piper the bagpipe player, or Roddy Piper the dad, or Roddy Piper the author, it's always Roddy Piper the wrestler, and I understand that, but part of the artist gets overlooked. I want them to see the range in me. I have a big, dark side to me. There's one movie coming up called *Video Store* that's about a guy who owns an old video store, and I play him with a lot of prosthetics and I'll be hobbling around. So, okay, yeah. Give me something like that. I understand they're remaking *They Live*, and I wouldn't mind coming down from the mountain and doing a cameo for that because it's my movie. I'm not against the lone, quiet, kick ass, Billy Jack characters, but I want to be able to diversify and be able to play really solid roles.

(Editor's note: In 2015, "Rowdy" Roddy Piper was taken from the world too soon. He passed away from a heart attack in his sleep and left a legion of fans mourning in his wake.)

Think Big

1989 (Media VHS) (djm)

Twin brothers Peter and David Paul from *The Barbarians* are cast as perpetual "foul-up" truck drivers Rafe and Victor, whose latest pickup lands them in a pickle when they find out that they also have a stowaway. Their unwanted passenger is a sixteen-year-old runaway girl named Holly (Ari Meyers) who happens to be a genius and working for the government on a secret weapon. She convinces the likable and harmless twins to transport her across the country, not realizing that she's caused a major situation. The government has hired goons to capture her, and the buffed out twins have to save her life while also dealing with a situation of their own: They're late on their truck

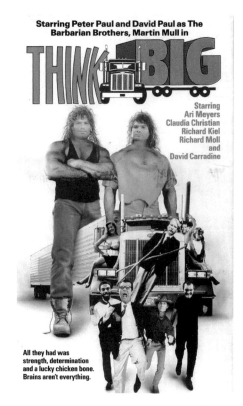

VHS artwork for *Think Big*. Author's collection.

payments and a repo man (David Carradine) is on their trail, hoping to repossess their ride when they're not in it.

Harmless family-oriented fare from director Jon Turtletaub (who later became a major director in Hollywood), *Think Big* is one of several benign vehicles starring the brothers Paul. Their juvenile humor should still appeal to young kids, but adults might grow weary of them within the first five minutes of the movie. They're certainly distinctive to look at, but sadly the same can't be said of most of their movies. Richard Kiel (Jaws from *The Spy Who Loved Me*) has a supporting role as a goon. The twins starred in *Double Trouble* next.

13 Dead Men

2003 (York Home Entertainment) (CD)

"Man, don't thank me for shit!
Man, you don't owe me nothing, man!
We not friends!"

When jewel thief Malachi (Latin martial artist Ashley Tucker) ends up on death row for a murder he didn't commit, he has to endure horrors by corrupt Warden Kowalski (David Weininger) on a daily basis. Malachi has a secret, and Kowalski wants to know where a stash of diamonds are hidden. Sympathetic guard DeLuca (Mia Riverton) doesn't agree with how he is being treated and wants to help. Malachi gives her a number of an old friend of his named Santos (Lorenzo Lamas) who may be his only hope. Santos reluctantly agrees and decides to hatch a plan with his old crew to break Malachi out of prison. Of course, things don't go according to plan and quickly turn south. Malachi decides to bring inmate Caj (Mystikal) into the fold but trusting him may or may not be a mistake.

13 Dead Men is a DTV action film from veteran director Art Camacho (*Gangland*) that fails to stir up much (if any) excitement. Working with a tight budget and a script that makes little sense, this film is problematic coming out of the gates. There's an interesting cast in place, but as a whole, the team players weren't used properly or to their full potential. With seasoned performer Lorenzo Lamas on board, it should have been much better than it was. He emerged from the film unscathed and does his best to make it interesting. He plays a laid-back thief who can get the job done when needed. The characters are all really one-dimensional, and Lamas gives Santos a pinch more life than expected. The majority of the fighting in the film lies with Tucker battling inmates in the prison yard. The choreography is competent, but it just doesn't do anything to impress. Though many of the actors are real martial artists, I don't feel they were given the opportunity to shine in any capacity. Rapper Mystikal is a major presence in the movie, but his character almost felt pointless to the plot and was written only to include a rap artist in the film. The music in the picture ranges from rap to metal and may be the most entertaining aspect of the project. You could do worse if you're a fan of Lamas.

This Girl is Badass!!

2011 (Magnet DVD) (djm)

Jeeja Yanin from *Chocolate* and *Phoenix Rising* plays a bicycle courier named Jukkalan, who takes side jobs as a drug runner for several competing crime syndicates, and whenever she encounters a dangerous situation, she always surprises her attackers because she's a dynamo martial artist and an adept bike rider. She can fight and ride her way out of any tight spot . . . until she gets on the nerves of both competing syndicates. With help from her ex-cop uncle and a goofy neighbor who has a crush on her, she manages to bring both sides crashing down around her.

Jeeja Yannin took a nosedive when she starred in *This Girl is Badass!!* It's a cheap shot full of dopey, bad humor and lackluster fight choreography, and her performance is beholden to a terrible script that clearly disrespects the martial arts genre and spits on her two previous star-making films. Luckily, she recovered from this fiasco and co-starred with Tony Jaa in the sequel to *The Protector*. Directed by Phetthai Wongkhamlao.

Three Days to a Kill

1992 (HBO VHS) (djm)

An ambassador is kidnapped by a South American drug lord named Perez (Henry Silva), and a mercenary named Calvin Sims (Fred "The Hammer" Williamson) becomes attached to a mission to rescue him. Sims requests a demolition expert named Rick Masters (Bo Svenson) to help him, but first a deal must be arranged to get Masters out of prison. Once they are teamed up, Sims and Masters make contact with an exotic dancer who is the former mistress of Perez, and the little leeway she has with her former lover goes a long way—she is also the mother of Perez's only son. Sims plans an ambush at a compound retreat south of the border, and a showdown commences.

Redundant and unimaginative, Williamson's *Three Days to a Kill* isn't going to raise any eyebrows or spark any interest from casual fans of his. As both the director and the star, Williamson strokes his ego in the film (which is fine), but there's so little that he does to convince me that this movie was worth making in the first place. It's a time-filler, and while I can say the same thing about many movies I actually like in the same genre, I can't say the same about this one. The best scene in the movie involves a fight between Williamson and co-star Sonny Landham (from *Predator* and *Action Jackson*), who plays Silva's right-hand man. Landham, a criminally underused actor/tough guy from the VHS-era, has the most memorable scenes in this picture. Williamson and Svenson starred alongside each other several times, most notably in *Inglorious Bastards*.

3 Ninjas:

High Noon at Mega Mountain

1998 (Sony DVD) (CD)

"Why did you use your head to hit my feet?"

The *3 Ninjas* are back! Rocky (Mathew Botuchis), Colt (Michael J. O'Laskey II), and Tum Tum (J. P. Roeske II) have a day planned with their neighbor Amanda (Chelsey Earlywine) to visit the Mega Mountain theme park. The kids are all having a great time until the park is overrun by Medusa (Loni Anderson) and her evil gang of ninjas. She demands ten million dollars, threatening that if she doesn't get it, accidents might start happening within the park. The kids all want to help save the day but they can't do it on their own. The kids might be tough but this is their most dangerous adventure and a little help could go a long way: Making his final appearance at the park is kid show star Dave Dragon (Hulk Hogan). They enlist the help of Dragon to foil Medusa's plans and rescue the people being held in the park.

A grown adult should never sit down to watch this film alone. It's little tough to sit through. Children, however, may have lots of fun with it. The dialogue is corny, and the story is ludicrous. Hulk Hogan does seem to be having fun in his role as a television star who is about to lose his show. The action is pretty harmless, and there's plenty of it. Hogan shows off his wrestling skills as well as throwing some unexpected high kicks. The three children are all really talented martial artists and fight often. Again, this film aims to entertain eight-year-olds so the action is all over-the-top goofiness. This isn't Hogan's finest hour but it's still fun to watch if you have young children. The other entries in the *3 Ninjas* series may have their merits, but none of them have an "action star" to support them.

Theatrical poster for *Three the Hard Way*. Author's collection.

Three the Hard Way

1974 (Warner DVD) (djm)

A hackneyed plot about a white supremacy group planning to commit genocide by eliminating the African American race through careful scientific murder by way of poisoning the water supply is really what *Three the Hard Way* is about, but if you think about it for more than a few seconds, it just falls apart. Focus instead on the three superstars in it: Jim Brown (from *Rio Conchos*), Fred Williamson (from *That Man Bolt*), and Jim Kelly (from *Black Belt Jones*) unite for the first of three on-screen pairings in this hokey action movie that at least gets its stars involved in some good action. Brown plays a music producer named Jimmy who is alerted to the wild, nefarious plot I mentioned above, and he calls in his buddies Jagger (Williamson) and Mister Keyes (a cool Kelly), who come in and stage a raid on the racist group who have kidnapped Jimmy's girlfriend for some kind of leverage. Explosions, gunfire, and chop sockie ensue.

From Gordon Parks Jr., who directed the blaxploitation perennial *Super Fly*, *Three the Hard Way* is good enough action fare for fans of its stars, but it's pretty disposable and forgettable, especially if you've seen their next pairing, *Take a Hard Ride*, which put them all in a western environment and had better results. Still, I had fun watching it, despite how silly it was. If you want to go further with these studies, check out *Black Dynamite*, which is a spoof of this movie.

Three Tough Guys

(a.k.a. **Tough Guys**)

1974 (Blax DVD) (CD)

After the vicious murder of his close friend, Father Charlie (Lino Ventura) decides he can't live with himself if he doesn't do some investigating of his own. He learns the murder was tied to a huge chunk of cash gone missing. Father Charlie may be fast with his fists but these thugs are more than he can handle alone. Luckily, former cop Lee (Isaac Hayes) is around to help a man when he's down. Together, they get down and dirty with the criminal element on the seedy streets of Chicago until they find the killer and the dough. They will have to move fast since low-rent crime lord Joe Snake (Fred Williamson) is trying to sniff the greenbacks out for himself and he's willing to kill anyone to get it.

Fred Williamson (*Mr. Mean*) fans will be sorely disappointed in *Three Tough Guys* for one reason only: There just isn't enough of him. We all know one of the three tough guys in the title refers to Williamson, but in this picture we don't get to see how tough he is. The real Fred Williamson we're all familiar with would never get himself knocked out by a priest with a bowling pin. It just feels wrong when we know the real man would take that bowling pin and shove it right up the other guy's ass. In addition to starring, Isaac Hayes also composed the killer score for this flick directed by Duccio Tessari (*Beyond Justice*). It's a decent enough film, but it needs more of The Hammer.

Thunderbolt
1995 (New Line DVD) (djm)

A mostly humorless martial arts action film with competitive speed racing at its center, *Thunderbolt* stars Jackie Chan as a former professional racer who has become a mechanic. While Chan is working on some cars, a well-known criminal named Cougar (Thorsten Nickel) speeds by his workstation, causing a ruckus. Sensing an opportunity to apprehend him, Chan jumps in a car and chases him down, managing to assist the authorities in his capture. Cougar isn't in prison long, though, and when he's out, he takes it personally that Chan interfered, and he makes it his top priority to strike back by ruining Chan's business and—even worse—kidnapping Chan's sisters and psychologically tormenting Chan by forcing him to race him in a media-hyped championship. Chan takes the challenge and races the guy, leading to an adrenalin-charged finale where Chan leaves all precaution behind in the race of his life.

A long running time and a lack of humor dampens this otherwise adequate outing for star Chan, who is purported to have used stunt doubles heavily during the course of this movie. Honestly, I didn't really notice anything awkward or untrue about any of the fight scenes; everything was more or less up to par with other films he'd done during this period, but it's still not one of his more memorable or best movies. Some of the racing scenes are really snappy, though, and the movie's finest moments involve Chan in the driver's seat. Director Gordon Chan also made *The Medallion* with Jackie and *Fist of Legend* with Jet Li.

Thunderground
1989 (SGE VHS) (djm)

A gem of a movie, *Thunderground* is an old-fashioned tale about a homeless boxer named Bird (played by Paul Coufos, reprising his role from *Busted Up*), who meets a scrapper named Casey (a wonderful Margaret Langrick) on the road. Casey hustles for cash to get by, and her wit and endearing attitude appeals to Bird, whose luck had all but run out before meeting her. When Casey realizes that Bird is a good fighter, she gets him involved in bum fights for dollars and change, and there's a rumor going around that the champion of bare-knuckle boxing is looking for a new challenger. The Man (wrestler Jesse Ventura) is sort of a myth and legend the way everyone on the road talks about him, but Bird isn't worried about anything other than where his next meal is coming from, so he goes with Casey to New Orleans to challenge The Man. Their climactic fight is pretty impressive, but the movie really hangs on the relationship between Bird and Casey.

Every once in a blue moon, a movie blindsides me with its genuine appeal and good nature. *Thunderground* is such a film. I thought it was going to be about Jesse Ventura's character, but Ventura only has a glorified cameo in the picture. Coufos, who didn't have much of a career as an action star, is great in the lead role, and I kept wondering why he didn't do more movies in this vein. He was also in *Dragonfight* and *Cold Vengeance*. Damien Lee (*Abraxis*) wrote and produced this, and David Mitchell (*Mask of Death, Last to Surrender*) directed.

Thunder in Paradise
1994 (NOV) (djm)

At the peak of his action movie career, Terry "Hulk" Hogan starred in *Thunder in Paradise*, a "PG"-rated TV series that featured him as a former Navy SEAL named R.J. "Hurricane" Spencer, a massively muscled mercenary for hire who uses a jet-propelled speedboat armed with rockets and lasers to accomplish his missions. His partner Bru (a buffed-out Chris Lemmon, son of Jack) provides comedy relief and together they are a fun-loving team. In order to keep his business afloat, R.J. has to marry a rich debutante named Megan (Felicity Waterman), who also must be married by a deadline, or she loses her resort hotel in Hawaii. Once they marry, R.J. learns to love her young daughter Jessica, and when Megan is written off the show (she dies off screen), R.J. adopts Jessica, and her godfather Edward (Patrick Macnee) shows up from time to time to complicate things. In the meanwhile, R.J. and Bru go on secret missions, some involving treasure hunts, fighting modern-day pirates, dictators, ninjas, and even a couple of criminal masterminds who use virtual reality to mind-control a massive brute to do their dirty work.

I watched *Thunder in Paradise* when it played on TV, and even when I watch it now as an adult, I have a soft spot for it. Hogan is in magnificent condition, and he doesn't shy

away from being as physical on the show as he's allowed. The show is incredibly fluffy and lots of footage of girls in bikinis is used as filler when things get boring. Some episodes have cool co-stars like Loren Avedon, Cary-Hiroyuki Tagawa, Sam Jones, Peter Kent, Richard Lynch, and Terry Funk. Lionsgate put out a three-disc DVD set that collects several two-part episodes. The entire series is only offered by bootleggers.

Thunderkick
2008 (Sky Dragon DVD) (djm)

Once upon a time, *Thunderkick* would have been shot on 35mm film (maybe 16mm), found its way to a VHS distributor, and ended up on some shelves at mom-and-pop video stores all over the world. In 2008, a real martial artist from England named Gary Wasniewski got some of his friends together and made a movie in what seems like someone's backyard—they shot it on a cheap digital video camera, had a screenplay that probably took a few days to write (maybe a day, I dunno), and they ordered some pizzas and fed the actors who probably worked for a couple of weekends. Maybe some people got paid. I have no idea. But here's what happens in the movie: Wasniewski plays a guy named Sean Kane who comes to LA to visit his sifu, played by Leo Fong, who also wrote and "produced." Fans of Fong take note: Fong is indeed in the movie, playing a guy who Fong can play. There's no stretch on his part. When Leo Fong's in a movie, and when you're watching that movie, then you know better than anyone that you're in for a movie with Leo Fong. So there it is. He's in *Thunderkick*. Get ready. Anyway, Kane is looking for his master, but his master has become a cook for a religious cult, whose leader is having homeless people kidnapped and harvested for their organs in the black market. When Kane comes calling, they want to harvest his organs, too, so he fights them and saves his old sifu, who has also been marked for the operating table. There's lots of running, and Wasniewski seems pretty tall, so when he kicks, it looks good, but after he kicks, he immediately starts running again, so he's not like the other action stars who stick around to face his enemies. He runs. It's funny.

Thunderkick and its sequels, *The Kill Factor* and *Extreme Counterstrike*, are pretty much the final word on "vehicle" action films starring a virtual unknown. Wasniewski, who is an accomplished martial artist, has a good kick, and he has a modicum of *something* that makes him special, but he's the perfect example of a guy who

Gary Wasniewski stars as Sean Kane in *Thunderkick*, featuring Leo Fong, right. Courtesy of Gary Wasniewski.

wasn't satisfied with just the black belts or the competitions. He wanted to be in movies, and good for him. Other guys like Y. K. Kim (*Miami Connection*) or Il Lim (*Acts of Violence*) have some martial arts abilities and manage to get a movie off the ground, and they're slotted into this "so bad they're great" category. Wasniewski is so far off the radar that they'd have to invent a category just for him. I admire him for making *Thunderkick* and his other movies. Good for him for aligning himself with Leo Fong. Make more movies, Gary, and I'll keep watching them. Ron Hall from *Triple Impact* has a cameo fight with Gary here. Not quite the best scene of the movie, but close.

Thunder Mission (a.k.a.
Raiders of Losing Treasure)
1992 (Tai Seng VHS) (CD)

After the death of their father, two half-sisters (one of them being former Japanese bodybuilder Nishiwaki Michiko) learn he had a large estate and they're about to inherit it. Annie (Michiko) has no real interest in the inheritance and would rather dip her toes in the computer software business. But she soon meets a man who is somehow involved in a murder, and she finds herself fighting for her life when some evil entity is out to get her and her sister. Oh: and the inheritance might have something to do with it as well.

This movie is for the Nishiwaki Michiko (also seen in *City Cops*) fans who have always wanted to see her in a lead hero role. The fans know these were almost non-existent for her so to see her step up and take control is a treat. Too bad the film is pretty much incomprehensible from a story standpoint; at least the action is cool. She has all sorts of run-ins with various types of bad guys, including some ninjas. I wouldn't call the action above average, but it manages to stay entertaining to a degree. The rest of the film just feels like it's slopped together with random scenes and ideas. A more comprehensive script could have given the film a boost. Directed by Yao Wang, who never made another feature.

Thuppakki
2012 (AP International DVD) (CD)

"After breaking my hand and with the protection of so many you are still scared to undo my handcuffs and hit me, right? I like that fear."

Jagadish (Vijay) has made a trip home to Mumbai to visit his family and meet the woman his parents have arranged for him to marry. The meeting with Nisha (Kajal Aggarwal) doesn't go

quite as planned so they call the arrangement off. When crossing paths again later, they realize both were pretending to be people they weren't and are actually perfect for one another. The romance will have to be put on hold when Jagadish witnesses the bombing of a bus where dozens of innocent people are killed. He tracks down the bomber only to learn he is just a small part of a large terrorist operation. Jagadish sets out to stop several more bombings, enraging the cell's leader (*Commando: A One Man Army*'s Vidyut Jamwal) and sending him off on a killing spree only he can stop.

Vidyut Jamwal (also in *Bullet Raja*) is right at home playing the villain and has quite a presence in the film. It seems as if he was kept on a pretty tight leash for this film for fear of him outshining leading man Vijay. He does have a solid fight scene with the actor to wrap up the film, and it's a good one. Action star Vidyut wasn't allowed to let loose like he has on numerous occasions before (and after). Regardless, it's a good film (*really* long), and has one of the coolest mass assassinations I've seen in a film. This one has at least half a dozen song and dance numbers, so be prepared to shake you rump in your seat to the catchy little numbers. *Thuppakki* was the top-grossing Tamil film of 2012 and was remade twice in 2014 (one of those was by the director of this version, AR Murugadoss).

Ticker
2001 (Artisan DVD) (CD)

"Now listen to me, man. You're just gonna have to go beyond hope and fear. Don't get attached to living or dying, or anything else, and understand that death is just another stage on the playground."

Detective Ray Nettles (Tom Sizemore) is on a routine investigation with his partner Art "Fuzzy" Rice (Nas) when Fuzzy is killed by terrorist Swann (Dennis Hopper), who recently bombed a senator's house. Swann escapes from Nettles, but Swann's girlfriend Claire (Jaime Pressly) is detained. More than anything, he wants Claire back and is willing to risk it all to do so. Nettles teams up with the head of the bomb squad, Frank Glass (Steven Seagal), and together they try to find a lead that will land them Swann. In a fit of rage, Swann threatens to detonate bombs throughout the city until Claire is released. With the clock ticking, Glass and Nettles set out to save the city from destruction.

With the amount of star power that appears in the Nu Image-produced *Ticker*, you would think that the film would be much better than it ends up being. It's hard to tell what exactly went wrong but there's no question that it just doesn't work. Sizemore (*Heat*) is front and center in the film. His performance is solid, even though the material was rather cliché and dry. Steven Seagal (in his second direct-to-video film after *The*

Patriot) kind of plays this one rather laid back. He spends the majority of the film sitting in a chair or trying to dish out philosophical advice to Sizemore's troubled character. What he doesn't do is partake in much action. There were only one or two poorly choreographed fight scenes that were nothing but a couple of throws and punches. Even the great Dennis Hopper (*Speed*) stumbles, playing a bomber who has an Irish accent that tends to come and go. Rap artists Nas (*Rush Hour 3*) and Ice-T (*New Jack City*) both appear in the film. It's a shame that neither of them do anything to further their careers really and one has to wonder why Ice-T even bothered to be in the film since he only shows up for a few very short moments. Fairing slightly better in their roles were Jaime Pressly (*DOA: Dead or Alive*) and Peter Greene (*Under Siege 2: Dark Territory*). This was a strange departure for director Albert Pyun who has been rather vocal about how much he dislikes the film in this form and pieced together a director's cut for his fans.

...tick...tick...tick
1970 (Warner DVD) (CD)

"Next time you go into the hardware store you stay away from the disinfectant aisle. You stay away from that disinfectant, you hear me? 'Cuz you aint nothing but a bug!"

Jim Price (Jim Brown) is the newly elected sheriff of a small town in Mississippi called Colusa. He's a family man, married with two children, and wants nothing more than to uphold the law. He's fair, honest, and one of the good ones. The problem is that the townsfolk aren't happy with him being elected . . . because he's black. In his first few days on the job he has to deal with the rape of a young girl, the death of a child, and a bunch of people spewing nasty comments and threatening his life. The only people on his side are the mayor and former sheriff John Little (George Kennedy), who is dealing with his own set of threats for losing. These two men have sworn to uphold the law and the events they face will test their boundaries.

This is an important film and one far deserving of more attention. Jim Brown (*Slaughter's Big Rip-off*) is absolutely mesmerizing in the lead role. He's such a positive and strong figure and just owns the screen. There's very little action in the film but when you watch Brown, you know he wants to kick someone's ass, though he refrains, keeping himself composed. It deals with some serious subject matters and tastefully addresses many issues that were of import during that time period. Director Ralph Nelson skillfully builds the tension, stringing you along, and delivers a satisfying conclusion. It's not the type of role or film you would expect to see Brown in but I'm thankful that he chose it.

T

Tiger Claws

1992 (Universal VHS) (djm)

"They think it's some kind of game: They've never looked death in the eye."

The first in a trilogy starring Jalal Merhi and Cynthia Rothrock, *Tiger Claws* is a basic kung fu cops versus kung fu killer movie. Bolo Yeung plays a serial killer known as The Death Dealer. His victims are martial arts champions, and he slays them with a swipe of his "tiger claws." Merhi, as Detective Richards, goes undercover in a tiger cult to learn the art of tiger-style martial arts, and his partner, Masterson (Rothrock) hangs back and lets her partner do all the heavy lifting. The finale gives all three of the stars an opportunity to showcase their styles. Surprisingly, the villain isn't killed at the end, which made a sequel a possibility. Each sequel followed four years after the previous one.

Kelly Makin directed this from a script by J. Stephen Maunder, who directed the sequels. This is the best of the trilogy, but it's still a little anemic. Rothrock's role was diminished more and more as the films went on. Merhi became more the focus, which is obvious considering that he produced them.

INTERVIEW:
JALAL MERHI
(djm)

Brazilian-born Lebanese martial artist-turned action star Jalal Merhi came in on the action and martial arts movie craze at its peak when VHS was king. A shrewd businessman who sold his lucrative jewelry business to become a full-time movie producer, action star, and filmmaker, Merhi went straight for the starring role with his self-financed films Fearless Tiger *(a.k.a. Black Pearls, 1991), Tiger Claws (1991), and Talons of the Eagle (1992). He had a nice gig at Universal, which was distributing his films for a few years, and then as the video market begin changing, Merhi went the independent route, and then eventually dropped out of action films altogether. Action fans and critics have derided his performances across the board, but*

Jalal Merhi in Santa Monica, California. Photo by david j. moore.

his contributions to the genre are important, and his perspective on the business side of the genre is integral.

Jalal, how did you get your first movie, *Black Pearls*, off the ground? What was your life like before this movie came together?

Black Pearls was a combination of situations that came together. I was in a martial arts tournament, and I won the grand championship. There was a producer there, and he was looking for martial arts experts to use in a movie, and I think it was called *Honor*. He picked me and asked if I could meet him in his office. We met, I went there, and he picked me to be the main villain for the movie. I was to be a Middle Eastern terrorist. I got to know him more, then he picked a bunch of other martial artists, and it took him three or four months. I met the other producers and the structure was in place, everything was in place. I was very busy with my life at the time. He did not know what I did. I was running a kung fu school, and then I saw that project go downhill. I saw from his mistakes. I was a young businessman. By age twenty-three, I was a self-made millionaire with my own money. I knew what to do. So I called him and I told him to come to my office and let's chat. I told him that I could see his problems and that the investors were on his back, so I lent him some money. I knew how I could get the value back. I was also a jeweler by trade, which was a family business. He comes in, and he thought I worked there. Then he realized what I am. I had studied film in Toronto, and my professor told me that with my accent and my ethnicity that I would never make it and that I should find another job. The rest of the students at that school were dreamers and had no concept, and I felt that everyone was non-realistic about what they were doing. I left. Being in business and meeting this producer got me into the group. They respected me somehow. I had two students who were studying film and, gradually, one thing led to another and they started writing a script and came up with some ideas. I hired the first crew, and it showed my lack of knowledge, but they were wonderful artists, but the film went twice the budget they gave me. They came to me and said, "With $600,000, we can make this." We were shooting on film. The $600,000 passed and still we didn't have a full film yet. Some shots, some action, we would spend a whole evening shooting establishing shots and by three in the morning we would come down to the action. So we couldn't cover it. The film lacked what I wanted, which was the action feel. It didn't have the grittiness I wanted. But it had a certain sweetness to it.

Yeah, it had an innocence to it.

Yes. We did the film, and I still needed a cameo for it. A friend of one of my students was a martial arts star from Hong Kong. Through him and some other people, we went to Hong Kong and shot some other scenes on a mountain. We met Bolo [Yeung] there, and he did some scenes. He made a nice deal. He was very helpful. He carried equipment, but he didn't want to do any action scenes. He only wanted to do a demonstration for a certain amount of money. So we did that scene up there. He played the Master.

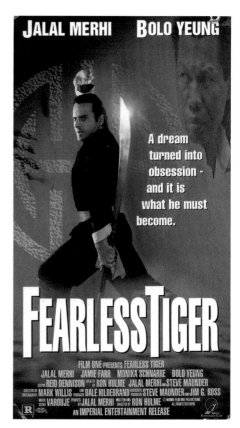

VHS artwork for *Fearless Tiger*. Author's collection.

What year was that?

1988. Officially it came out in 1991 in Canada. Then we had to do a re-edit.

But that was years later. You're talking about the *Fearless Tiger* version, right?

Yes. Once the first one came out, we did not bad. Then, we got the eye of a couple of distributors in the US, and they said, "Can you give us something more gritty?" So we went and shot a few scenes.

At this point, did you see yourself making movies as a career?

Not yet. To me, it was a dream come true. We all dream as a kid, and I remember watching Bruce Lee. To me it was a wake-up call. As a kid, I loved Batman because he could do multiple fighting. Because of Batman and so on, my family let me learn martial arts. Later, I joined Japanese karate. Martial arts have been a part of me since a very early age.

Where were you born?

I was born in Brazil. My parents are Lebanese.

One of the reasons I wanted to talk to you is because you have an unusual background. As far as I know, you're the only Lebanese action star. You say you were born in Brazil. Were you ever into capoeira?

Later. I was already older when that became big. I did jiu jitsu. I'm not very musically inclined, and I'm flexible, and I have the ability to do capoeira, but no.

When you did *Tiger Claws* with Cynthia Rothrock and Bolo Yeung, was *Black Pearls* the only movie you'd done at that point?

Yeah.

That trilogy is basically your trilogy. You're the star. Rothrock is the sidekick, which is interesting because she's usually the lead. Talk about *Tiger Claws* and how you were able to sell yourself as the star.

Don't forget that I knew Cynthia from competition days. We did the same circuits. She was higher on the food chain. With Cynthia, I didn't have to convince as much. We were friends. We had the concept, and she shot the promo. To me, I believe it's an equal role for her, but at the same time, it's mainly my role. At the time, I had Cineplex Odion, a big distributor. I was personal friends with the head of Cineplex at the time. Cynthia saw that I wasn't someone just walking in from the streets. I had access from everything. She came into Toronto and shot the promo and we took it to Universal. I ended up doing four films with Universal. I did *Tiger Claws, Talons of the Eagle, TC 2000,* and *Operation Golden Phoenix.* As long as they were doing that genre, and then they quit doing that genre, which was fine. They did well with them, and I did well with them. It was good. *Tiger Claws* was something good. They liked the grittiness of it. It was more hardcore. I did *Tiger Claws* for cheaper than I did *Black Pearls.* By then I knew what I was doing.

How come you didn't direct it?

No, I wasn't ready. In the middle of *Tiger Claws,* once I'd gotten the deal from Universal and international distributors, there was money on the table—real money—and by that time I'd already spent two and a half million of my own money setting up the whole thing. I made a decision that I wanted to go heart and soul into it. It was only money. I was still single. I jumped into it. I sold my share of my business, I sold everything. When the soldiers go to the other side of the shore, they burned all their ships. They had the sea behind them, the enemy in front of you, and they are going to make it or not. To me, I had to do it this way. When I believe in something, I move forward and I don't look back.

Video Poster for *Tiger Claws*. Author's collection.

You started off by telling me that your first role was supposed to be a Middle Eastern terrorist. I've seen all your movies, and you've never played anything remotely like that until this day. You usually play a cop or a detective. Why be the heroic cop all the time?

There are two things I did. I always tried not to kill my opponent as much as possible.

Yeah, you're right. In *Tiger Claws,* you put the villain in a police car and it ends. That was different.

That was very intentional. The distributors were always, "No, they've got to die." But I hated the idea of having to kill my opponent. I did not like that. I also try not to show as much blood. I would get depressed if we put too much blood. After a while, I knew that people would see that this is just a martial arts movie, I don't have to have gore and heads blown away. I feel that I fit in this type of role, being the good guy that wants to protect the law. It's funny, in the script for *Tiger Claws 4*—I still haven't made it—this one changes my character. He goes to the dark side for whatever reason because it's a development of that character. I'm not against going there. To control violence, you become more violent. I did not want to be that.

You played the villain in *TC 2000,* which was different for you.

Yeah.

Over the years when you were on a roll with these movies, you continued to work with the same group of people. In addition to Rothrock, you worked with Billy Blanks and Bolo Yeung, not to mention many supporting players. Even your composer Varouje worked on almost all of your films. Tell me about that. You have a little community, a family who works with you from movie to movie.

You've got to be faithful to your people. When Lionsgate first launched, the person who took it public was Jeff Sackman. Jeff and I were very good friends. He was in my wedding, and I was in his. I remember his superiors. Behind the guy is always other guys with money. I was offered to get rid of my crew because they thought they could take me to the next level. They thought that keeping my crew would keep me at the same level. I refused. Maybe people would say that was a mistake. I don't know. Maybe they could have dropped me and then I have no one from the past for the future. I've seen this happen. I like to be faithful to those who work with me. They were making a living with me. Many of them, I gave them places to live—literally. Even when I didn't have a production going on. If I'd let them go, other production companies would think . . .

if you look at them, they all started with me. If you look at Varouje, he started with me. I got him his first job. I carried many others. As much as I could until I started to get hurt myself. For years and years I kept the same people because I knew the moment I let them go, they would have a hard time finding a place anywhere else. It was a fun time.

What was Lionsgate's definition of "the next level" for you?

It would have been me moving to LA and started work, surrounding me with bigger names.

Like . . . Van Damme, or someone like that?

No, more actors' names. I'm like a Van Damme, but on a smaller level. So how do you go to the next level? You bring in *actors*, not action guys. I was offered that. Let's take the budget from this number to *this* number. Maybe I was ignorant about the market. I did say no to a couple of things from the right people. I didn't know they were the right people. I've made that mistake. I also know exactly when my career stopped.

When?

When the collapse of the video market happened. Like everyone else. Just before that, I said no to a couple of people, who I won't name. I'm okay with that. I've been married for twenty years now, and happy. I know that if I did say yes to those couple of things, I wouldn't be happily married now. You need time to spend with your family and kids. I've seen a lot of my friends, some of who are major stars, bigger in the action world than me, and I saw how they lost it. I was there when they made the wrong choice that evening. The wife would be there on the set, they leave, and somebody else comes in later, "Hey, you want to come with us? We're doing this and this." I never really went in those cycles and circles. I don't really drink much.

Let's talk about the video market. The late '80s and early '90s were the best times for guys like you. Oliver Gruner, Don Wilson, Rothrock. You all thrived and made movie after movie after movie. Talk about working and living during that time and being a part of that movement.

It was a special world. Many of my films went out theatrical in many places. *Talons* and *Tiger Claws* . . . and *TC* were released in limited markets. In South America and Brazil, *Talons* was number five in theaters. In the Middle East, all of them went theatrical. In Europe, I had some go theatrical. I have all the master prints in my basement. I have prints in Spanish and prints in English. I have some French prints, too. We will be mastering them into HD soon. One thing I kept . . . I own all the rights. I don't think any other star owns the rights to their films. So that's different. For a period of time, I stuck with my family. Then I went into television. I've been doing a conspiracy show. With the market changing . . . every trip has an end. The customer didn't change. What changed is that executives were all buying each other out. They became too big to worry about the smaller films.

T

In the last days of Blockbuster, movies like my *Circuit* films were starting to lose their grip. Mainly because the digital world was becoming stronger. In a way, it's leveling the playing field because everyone can go shoot something. But, you don't really have a platform to sell it. When we had VHS and DVD—and most of my films are on laserdisc—there was a specific place you could go to. There was a market there. Universal took me and Imperial took *Black Pearls* and turned it into *Fearless Tiger*, which they took me on tour for across the US. I went to Nashville at exhibitions, and I miss that. Everyone should miss that. It's a different world. Different people are becoming stars. The format is different too now. We're so lucky that we were a part of that. It was not an easy wave. I was at the markets all the time, and I saw people selling themselves that could have been somebody, but they never became anything. And some did. *Expect No Mercy* was supposed to be Olivier Gruner and myself, not Billy Blanks. Then Olivier came in and his nose was broken—he had just done *Savate*—and he felt that maybe he shouldn't do it because of his nose. I love Olivier. He's a friend. He had a contract with Imperial, and they were selling me his contract. The lead bad guy was going to be Gary Daniels. I had a verbal deal with Gary, and I love Gary—he's wonderful—but the distributor did not want him. They brought me the guy who played Tarzan, and they said that he was going to be a big star. I said, "Well, I like Gary." I don't think Gary speaks to me until now because of that. It's unfortunate. They overruled me. The guy who they made me use did not go far. Gary did. That's the difference. At that time, these movies were so strong and influential. Sometimes executives make the worst decisions. They did get involved.

Talk about your martial arts abilities and how you were able to adapt your style to the styles of your co-stars like Billy Blanks or Darren Shahlavi, or whoever. Do you feel like you represented your martial arts skills well on film?

No, and no, and no. Being a producer is draining. You'll see me arguing and talking about things with some crew or managing how things are moved around. Then I have to now go jump in and be an actor, and that was my biggest disservice I did to myself. That's why when those producers wanted to move me to the next level, they told me that I would just do this one thing: Acting. I did suffer from it. When a director . . . most of them did not know martial arts, they'd say, "You think you know everything? Go do it." So I never got direction. Doing that, when all the lights are on you, and you're carrying it on both sides of the camera, and there's only so much money . . . if you make a mistake you can't reshoot. I would worry about the others more than I would worry about me. David Carradine told me, "Jalal, you're too generous." I said, "What do you mean?" He said, "You allow the guy next to you to steal your light." He said, "If there's a lady over there, you allow her to walk through. If there is a camera—no!—*you* walk through." By the time I got that, it was the early 2000s, so it was too late!

During that period, you did a couple of things with Darren Shahlavi. *G.O.D.* was one of the movies you did.

Great guy. I did *Sometimes a Hero* with him, too. It's a good film for him.

Darren is a premier action guy. He's fantastic. When I saw that fight scene between you and him in *G.O.D.* I was so disappointed. It didn't feel like a complete fight to me. That fight scene made me mad. I'm not trying to insult you here.

No, no. I know better than you do.

That's one of the things I wanted to bring up about you. I've read a lot of harsh criticisms about you, but I'm here to lift you up. Sometimes the fight scenes in your movies just don't feel right.

I know exactly what it is. I'm the first critic of myself. We shot *G.O.D.* in eleven days. Okay? The director was a first-time director, but I loved the script. He came to the set—and I liked the guy—with one camera. He had in mind what he wanted to shoot, but the way he had it would have taken much longer. I said, "No." He got really flustered. When you fight the director, now he doesn't give a damn what he's doing. I haven't used him since. He had no knowledge of what we were doing. We had to do all those scenes there you mentioned in one afternoon. It was a nice location, but we had to be out of there by sunset. We didn't get everything we needed. Again, I only blame myself. There was no time. That fight between him and I—and he's a good fighter, and at that time he was still up and coming—we rehearsed it and went inside and the sun was going down. We had one crack at it. You move on. There's no coverage. No excuse, but that's what it is. That could have been a nice, big set-up. Similar to what we had on *Tiger Claws 2* with Bolo and the other guy. You just run out of time.

How about your fight with Anthony DeLongis in *Expect No Mercy*? That was an okay fight.

On the roof? That was not bad. Again, all the explosions and that fight were all done in one night. It's fine, it's there. No excuses. I shouldn't have done that. When I watch that . . . everyone says, "When I see you, oh, you've got it. I know what you've done in tournaments, and you've never lost a tournament, so what happened?" I know what happened. What happened is condense twenty days of shooting, and there's no time to be the actor and the producer. If I had a chance to relive that life, I would get somebody I can trust to do that producing job. I even blew up my own car on *Black Pearls* because we needed to blow up a car. The car I ordered did not show up, so I blew up my car. Things like this. You do what you need to do.

Let me ask you about the two movies you did with David Bradley. *Crisis* and *Expect to Die*. These were two of his very last movies. You directed those movies. I was surprised that David Bradley was not used to the best of his abilities in those movies.

He didn't want to.

Why?

He didn't want to be the martial artist anymore. He was going through a transition period. David is a wonderful person. I don't know where he is now. It breaks my heart. He sold his beautiful house and toured the world, and I think he lost something inside. I don't like thinking about it. He was a real passionate, good person. He has negatives in Hollywood. He had everything it took to be a big star. In *Crisis*, he didn't want to do any fights. Since he wouldn't do martial arts, we decided that he would fight like a brawler. We shot it in eleven days. One location. Three days of those days, he was missing. With *Expect to Die*, again, he did not want to use martial arts. He wanted to be the villain. No fights. Same thing. That was the deal with him. That film, I originally had Shannon Tweed as the woman, and Billy Blanks was going to be the bad guy. That was the initial cast.

You latest films are *The Circuit* films, three of them, with Olivier Gruner. These came out at the right time, right when MMA was coming in.

In *G.O.D.* you'll notice that Gruner didn't want to fight. I allowed him to do that. Some of them don't want to fight all the time; they want to be an actor, and that's fine. He did a great performance. He trusted me because of that movie. We talked about doing an underground fight movie. I like that he was looking to be more than a martial artist, and he wanted to try different styles of fighting. I used my own money, we did it for very little money. We had a cast of wonderful people. Loren Avedon, and the others, and I told them how much money I had for it and we would shoot for a few days, and they said, "Sure!" Everyone came in. I never abused anyone—I never used anyone for free a day in my life. They were all paid. Olivier was amazing. Very fit. He worked very hard. I think we did well. It was released on DVD and VHS and we were # 5 and #7 in the first two weeks. We did very well.

Was it an immediate decision to do two more?

Yes. By the time we got Part 3 off the ground, the market was changing. My international distributor got sick, and he passed away. A few things went south. It's got some nice stuff. We did a good job with it. I think it's a nice movie. It works. I'd like to go back and re-edit it someday.

What are your final comments about being an action star?

It's a trip. Just growing up not being in North America . . . everything is a gift. I'm thankful. In certain instances, I was too kind and I allowed things to weaken my projects, but I don't regret a thing. If I could employ everybody I employed before, I would employ them all again. I have at least two or three scripts, but there's no market. It would be committing financial suicide. I know Stallone did it. I admire what he did. Sometimes, you put so much into something that something else is left behind. Either family or kids, and it does come back to haunt you. But I don't regret a day.

I've seen some nice reports, and I've seen some critical. I don't fault the critics, but some of them are just nasty for no reason. They've got their own problems. If it makes them feel better, then fine. Sometimes if you can't do it, it's easy to criticize somebody else. It takes balls to go out and do it. I admire what you're doing, writing this book. That way, you go around it in a different way. Anyone who takes the bull by the horn, it's amazing. I'm still in the business, all these years later.

Tiger Claws 2

1996 (Platinum DVD) (djm)

Bolo Yeung returns as The Death Dealer who slashes his victims with "Tiger Claws," and he is broken out of prison to join a cult that plans to cross dimensions. On the case are detectives Richards (Jalal Merhi) and Masterson (Cynthia Rothrock) who are working in two different states, but come together when they both seem to be after the same killer. There's lots of gunfire and not enough action from Rothrock, who takes a big backseat to Merhi. He produced this film, and he gave himself the biggest role and the most fight scenes. The ending is cryptic and leaves room for another sequel. The sequel that followed didn't really continue the thread.

This one is about on par with the first film. It's cheap but entertaining as far as this type of film goes. Evan Lurie co-stars as a tough villain who has some fight scenes, and he later co-starred with Merhi in *Expect to Die*, but as usual, Merhi wins his fights despite the fact that he appears outmatched by some of his opponents. J. Stephen Maunder, a frequent collaborator of Merhi's, directed this.

Tiger Claws III:
The Final Conflict

2000 (New Concord DVD) (djm)

"Can someone tell me what the hell is going on here? We've got four dead bodies, but not *one* Chinese master!"

By this third and last entry in the *Tiger Claws* series, the production quality was relegated to Roger Corman-esque status, and while still entertaining to some degree, it had lost whatever spark that made the first two tolerable. Instead of picking up right where the cryptic ending of Part 2 left off, it goes in a different direction. Richards (Jalal Merhi, still promoting himself as a star) and Masterson (Cynthia Rothrock, still not being used enough in this series) are partners again, and they face a threat even greater than The Death Dealer (Bolo Yeung, who is absent). Loren Avedon, as a sort of cultist, unleashes

three otherworldly beings who resemble in attitude and powers the three storms in *Big Trouble in Little China* or the three Kryptonian criminals from *Superman 2*. His purpose for unleashing these three beings is never made clear, and he wastes their power on shaking some Chinese restaurants down for cash. They obey his orders and he flaunts them around town like a brand new car, which seems like a waste to me. When Richards and Masterson face them for the first time, Masterson is killed (off screen!), and so we're left with Richards to carry the movie. He seeks the help of a Chinese master named Jin (Carter Wong, who played one of the three storms in *Big Trouble*) to teach him how to defeat the three supernatural beings and their master. The conclusion is a huge disappointment, even though it brings Rothrock back from the dead.

J. Stephen Maunder directed this (he also did part 2) in collaboration with Merhi, who at this point still thought he was going to be a big martial arts action star. He cast Avedon as the villain again (see *Operation Golden Phoenix*), but Avedon isn't used to the best of his abilities. The same thing can be said of Rothrock, who is tossed aside in this movie, which is a crime.

Tiger Heart

1995 (PM Entertainment VHS) (djm)

"You're going to need a lot more than the Karate Kid to save you!"

T. J. Roberts from *The Power Within* and *Magic Kid* stars in this family-friendly martial arts movie from PM Entertainment. Roberts plays a high-school graduate named Eric who has one last summer before heading off to college, but his neighborhood is under siege by a ruthless real estate developer who wants to run everyone in the neighborhood out of town and out of business so that he can swoop in and buy the land cheaply. Eric is right in the middle of kindling a romance with a local girl (Jennifer Lyons) whose uncle owns a convenience store when thugs come around, causing trouble. Kid or not, Eric is a powerhouse of a fighter, and when the thugs go back to their boss with their tails between their legs, the developer hires more guys to assault Eric and his girlfriend. It's a good thing Eric is good friends with his sensei (played by Art Camacho) because he's going to need the backup!

Kinda fun for kids and kids at heart, *Tiger Heart* is a little more deadly and dangerous than stuff like *3 Ninjas*, which is more for the *Home Alone* crowd. Branded with a PG-13 rating because of some bloodless, but hard enough violence, *Tiger Heart* is a good vehicle for child star Roberts, who was an in-house name for PM. I liked it, but others might be dismissive towards it. Matthias Hues has a cameo. Directed by Georges Chamchoum.

Tiger Street

1998 (Chang Sam DVD R3) (djm)

Tiger Sun (Julian Lee from *My Samurai*) is an escaped political prisoner from North Korea who was imprisoned for illegally teaching taekwondo to students. He breaks out of his prison, flees to America, and finds a job in construction. He makes friends with a schoolteacher, who's just experienced a great tragedy in his classroom: One of his students committed suicide in class after taking hard drugs he bought from another student in class. The school is turned upside-down, and the schoolteacher has an idea to hire Tiger as an extracurricular P.E. teacher who would instruct the troubled kids in taekwondo and hopefully give their lives a little direction. Tiger accepts, and in no time at all, the school's collected GPA crawls up, and kids are excited to learn again. The local drug lord isn't pleased with the "Say no to drugs" campaign in the neighborhood, and he targets Tiger for death, but every person he sends his way ends up beat up and sent packing. Tiger's not going to go down lightly, and even when his emissaries destroy his car and corner him and beat him to a pulp, he gets back up and keeps fighting for his school's honor. The only way the drug lord can deal with his problem is to face Tiger himself, and on the very day Tiger is supposed to lead his class in a martial arts tournament, he must engage in an ultimate showdown with his enemy and set the neighborhood straight.

After *Fatal Revenge* and *My Samurai*, Julian Lee starred in this earnest and good-hearted action film that has fair production values and good fights. It's not going to make jaded movie watchers and hardcore action fans happy, but if you're looking to discover a fringe action star with more than enough honest-to-goodness appeal, then give it a go and discover why I really like Julian Lee. He's got kind of a goofy, awkward screen presence, but that's just who he is. He's only playing himself, and that's the best part of watching him in his films. He was in *Dragon and the Hawk* next. This was directed by Timothy Ryerson.

Time Burst: The Final Alliance

1989 (AIP VHS) (djm)

An obvious riff on *Highlander*, this quickie AIP release stars one-movie-wonder Scott David King as an immortal drifter through time named Urbane (seriously). His martial arts guru and trainer is Master, played by martial arts mascot and mainstay Gerald Okamura, who takes up the most space on the VHS box cover. Urbane has harnessed the secret of some sacred tablets that grant eternal life, but in true *Highlander* fashion, there can be only one person walking around on Earth at a time who has the secret of immortality. This contradicts Master's plan because he is supposed to be the only immortal, but his pupil Urbane upsets the balance of things, thus creating a rift between them through the ages. Also involved is a government agency that has discovered Urbane's secret (he isn't exactly subtle; he goofs around after being shot down and scares people in the morgue where he wakes up from death), and some action/martial arts chases ensue.

Almost entirely negligible as an entry in this book, *Time Burst* is really only notable for co-starring Okamura, whose presence adds a touch of "action star" to this otherwise pedestrian effort from director Peter Yuval, who co-founded Action International Pictures (AIP). For similar results on the *Highlander* riff, see *The Swordsman* with Lorenzo Lamas and *G2* with Daniel Bernhardt.

Timecop

1994 (Universal DVD) (DH)

"I'm still kicking, I must be on Broadway!"

Following a steady stream of low-budget (yet money-making) martial arts films, Belgium's Muscles From Brussels Jean-Claude Van Damme was ready to join Arnold Schwarzenegger and Sylvester Stallone as kings of the action film. But break out attempts in Carolco's *Universal Soldier*, Sony's *Nowhere to Run* and Universal's *Hard Target* failed to launch Wham Bam Van Damme into the upper echelon of cinematic tough guys. Universal was confident that with a decent budget and promotional push, Van Damme could break into the "A"-list and recruited him for the Dark Horse Comics adaptation of *Timecop*. Beginning in a 1994 where time travel is a reality, JCVD

The Timecop Walker (Jean-Claude Van Damme) does the splits in his kitchen. Author's collection.

Bad guys come calling on the Timecop. Author's collection.

Jean-Claude Van Damme demonstrates his kick in the Peter Hyams film *Timecop*. Author's collection.

Two Timecops: Walker (Jean-Claude Van Damme) and Fielding (Gloria Reuben). Author's collection.

Walker (Jean-Claude Van Damme) faces the future (or is it the past?) with McComb (Ron Silver) in *Timecop*. Author's collection.

plays Max Walker, former Washington, DC, cop turned Time Enforcement Commission officer, who travels through various eras to bring down illegal time-jumpers. After his wife is mysteriously killed, grizzled 2004 Max faces off with diabolical presidential candidate Aaron McComb (Ron Silver) who is traveling back in the time stream to raise fifty million dollars for his election campaign.

Directed by *Outland* and *Running Scared*'s Peter Hyams, *Timecop* was Van Damme's biggest, classiest, and most ambitious film to date. In the first twenty minutes we go from the Civil War to 1994 to 1929 and 2004 without missing a beat. By this time JCVD was trying to leave his pure kickboxing image behind, so there are fights with sticks, knives, wrenches, axes, future guns, and more, but also his trademark high kicks, a butt shot (in a sex scene where he shows more skin than lovely co-star Mia Sara), and the splits (used to duck an attack from a lamp and before jumping up onto a counter to

avoid being electrocuted). The science and time travel methods don't quite add up; a painful and harrowing rocket pod ride racing towards a brick wall sends you to the past, and yet a simple click of a button brings you back to the present . . . and the end climax kind of slumps as 1994 and 2004 versions of Max battle thugs in and around the house during a rain storm, much of it in the dark as per Hyam's usual underlit D.P. style. However, Van Damme really puts effort into his performance to play the young, naive version and older, hardened self in a real studio picture complete with familiar and talented co-stars and a seasoned director. This would become his highest-grossing film. *Best of the Best*'s James Lew pops up in a not very good on Van Damme's part knife fight, while *Evil Dead* and *Spider-Man* helmer Sam Raimi produced. Hyams would next direct *Sudden Death* with JC.

Timecop 2: The Berlin Decision

2003 (Universal DVD) (djm)

"Drop the gun or your timeline is over!"

Ryan Chang, a "timecop" working for the agency that polices time travel through different time lines, kills the wife of a fellow timecop, who goes rogue. Chang (Jason Scott Lee) is by-the-book all the way, and when his fellow cop Branson Miller (Thomas Ian Griffith) and his wife try to disrupt the time continuum in Nazi Germany, Chang must go with his instinct and try to stop them from causing untold damage in the future. When Miller's wife is slain, Miller really goes into villain mode and travels through time to kill Chang as a child to prevent his wife's death in the future, but Chang follows him through time to stop him. At eighty-one minutes, the movie doesn't really have much more to offer.

A drastic step down from the Van Damme vehicle from 1994, *The Berlin Decision* is every bit the direct-to-video effort that it is. Cheap, desperately boring, and devoid of real action, it at least has Thomas Ian Griffith (from *Excessive Force*) in a derivative villain role, and in the last ten minutes of the picture, he has a martial arts fight scene with star Scott Lee, who tears off his own shirt and tries to impress his nemesis with his martial arts prowess. It's a desperate, last-ditch effort to engage a hopelessly bored audience. Directed by Stephen Boyum.

Timelock

1996 (MTI DVD) (CD)

"You know, I have only ever read about stuff like this happening. Who would'a thought?"

In the future, a group of inmates are being transported to a distant penal colony when they rebel against their captors. Villum (Jeffrey Meek from *Raven*) and his cronies have a plan in place to upload a virus into the computer system of the prison, freeing all of the inmates. His plan is to bust out one of the worst criminals on the colony, McMasters (Jeff Speakman of *The Perfect Weapon*), blow the planet to bits, and make their escape back to Earth. The only people standing in their way are pilot Jessie Teegs (Maryam D'Abo) and Jack Riley (Arye Gross), a computer hacker and embezzler. They are an unlikely duo willing to do whatever it takes to stop the violent attack on the planet.

With special effects straight out of *Plan 9*, *Timelock* is a waste of really good talent. With martial artists Jeff Speakman (also in *Memorial Day*) and Jeffrey Meek (also in *Mortal Kombat: Conquest*), there should have been a major showdown between the two titans, but instead they fight Ayre Gross (*Hexed*)! Now, nothing against Gross, but seriously?! Speakman and Meek only get to sling a sword around a bit and throw a few kicks, so it's a huge disappointment knowing they are both essentially wasted in this junker. Director Robert Munic (TV's *NightMan*) delivers what he can but it's just never enough. Also in the cast are genre favorites Ricco Ross (*Death Wish 3*) and Martin Kove (*The Karate Kid*) who soften the blow, but they just can't save you from the pain.

T.K.O.
2007 (Lionsgate DVD) (CD)

"Motherfucker, ain't you supposed to be on a mountain top hibernating or some shit?"

The time of year has come again to prepare for the big tournament. Martin (Paul Green) kills the brother of Zendo (Andre McCoy) in order to bring Zendo out of hiding and to force him to fight. At the same time, Mick (Daz Crawford) is trying to find a fighter of his own. Their boss Warren (Joel King) is going to get rid of one of them after the tournament. Whoever has the winning fighter will stay on and take over the business of running the very lucrative fight syndicate. Zendo returns to town with vengeance in mind, only he doesn't know who killed his brother or who he should trust. With no one trusting anyone, the only way to settle anything is in the ring. Mick learns the truth behind Martin's twisted plan to bury him and finds wisdom and strength in the women who care for him.

TKO is a huge mess from a story standpoint. There's an abundance of characters with no development and they sort of weave in and out of the story with very little to no logic. As far as the acting goes, it doesn't fare much better than the story. What *is* good about the film are some solidly choreographed fight scenes. Sadly, the film lacks any real focus. Daz Crawford has one short fight at the beginning of the film, and Andre McCoy is very impressive in several different scenes. The action just isn't really enough to enjoy *T.K.O.*, since little else about it makes sense. The end is

aggravating and odd, so this is a film to watch strictly for the fights, or not at all. Directed by Declan Mulvey, who has worked as a stuntman on many big Hollywood productions.

T.N.T.
1997 (Lionsgate DVD) (djm)

A covert, fringe organization (known as "The Organization") recruits a badass named Nate Spears, a French Canadian, who engages in two missions, the second of which ends with a woman and child dead at his hands. Spears (Olivier Gruner) quits and flees, negating to relay his plans to his superior (Eric Roberts) or anyone else on his team. Time passes, and he's realigned his path in life, has found a woman to love, and is just beginning to make friends when he realizes that The Organization has been after him ever since he deserted. When mercenary soldiers arrive in the small town he's living in, he quickly adjusts his path to survival mode and protecting those he cares about. Luckily the sheriff in town (country star Randy Travis) is on his side, because he'll need backup when the guns start going off.

A minor effort for star Gruner (from *Nemesis* and *Mercenary*), *T.N.T.* doesn't stand up to scrutiny much, but at least Gruner is allowed to engage in some fights and passably flashy action scenes. What's interesting is that the director was Robert Radler, who directed the first two *Best of the Best* films. His alumni from those films, Eric Roberts and Simon Rhee (Philip's brother), appear in this film in smaller roles, and Sam Jones (from *Flash Gordon* and *Hard Vice*) also shows up. Anyone interested in Gruner might get something out of *T.N.T.*, but passing fans of these types of movies will be disappointed.

To Be the Best
1993 (PM VHS) (djm)

Eric Kulhane (Michael Worth from *Final Impact*) is a semi-retired kickboxer, whose domineering father and trainer (Martin Kove from *The Karate Kid*) has plans for him to compete in a world championship, whose favored fighter to win is from China. Kulhane, who has attitude problems and never refuses a fight or a challenge, goes to Las Vegas for the fight, and he's met with a proposal by a ruthless gambler: take a dive for more money than he's ever received for a fight before. Kulhane refuses the proposal, but when the gambler threatens the lives of his father and his fiancée, he seriously considers taking the fall. Meanwhile, the Chinese fighter (Steven Vincent Leigh) learns to respect Kulhane despite their checkered history and intense rivalry, and when Kulhane ultimately decides to fight his best fight ever—and win—he's got to step out of the ring to fight the fight of his life for his loved ones' sake.

Fairly standard and of its time, *To Be the Best* has echoes of so many other kickboxing championship movies of the period, most notably the first two *Best of the Best* entries. The

casting is almost clichéd, but there's nothing wrong with the casting, per se, it's just . . . expected. Martin Kove as the father/trainer? Check. Michael Worth as the star? Check. Steven Vincent Leigh as the Asian rival, destined to lose to the hero? Check. Everything about *To Be the Best* is familiar, and there's nothing that helps it rise above its contemporaries. A *Die Hard*-esque helicopter stunt at the beginning came out of nowhere, but it definitely got my attention. From PM Entertainment and director Joseph Merhi (*Magic Kid*, *Riot*).

INTERVIEW:
MICHAEL WORTH
(djm)

*With a black belt in Tang Soo Do karate and skills in Jeet Kune Do and escrima (a Filipino martial art), Michael Worth has his own unique fighting style on screen. Blessed with good looks and a memorable on-screen presence, he landed his first action film—*Final Impact*, co-starring Lorenzo Lamas—at the age of eighteen. Since that film, he starred in a handful of low-budget martial arts action films like* To Be the Best *(1993),* Fist of Iron *(1995), and Isaac Florentine's extravaganza* U.S. Seals II *(2001). His largest body of work was a co-starring role on the action program* Acapulco H.E.A.T. *(1993–1996), where he was able to showcase his martial arts in every episode. In latter years, Worth has scaled back the action and focused his attention on more personal, heartfelt projects where he has more creative control, but fans of action stars will most certainly hope for his return to the action and martial arts genres.*

You were eighteen when you landed your first role in *Final Impact*. How did that happen for you at such a young age?

I'd just gotten to LA about a year before. I was auditioning like everybody else. It was really the first time I'd gone in for a martial arts film. At that time, I was really training a lot, so I was superexcited. I didn't come to the business to be a martial arts actor. The first place I went to when I came down to LA was to Dan Inosanto's studio. I went right into it. I wanted to do some fight movies. I got called in for this movie—at the time it was called *The Flying Dutchman* because there was a technique I was going to have where Lorenzo Lamas's character teaches me this move

Michael Worth in Glendale, California. Photo by david j. moore.

called The Flying Dutchman, and I can't learn it until the very end—so I got called in, and I guess Don Wilson was originally going to play that part. They wanted Don and Lorenzo to be in it. For whatever reason, Don didn't do it. He had just done *Ring of Fire* for PM Entertainment. I went in there and I was in the waiting room with everybody, and I got called into the audition room, and all of a sudden there was Lorenzo and Kathleen Kinmont. The director was in there and Eric Lee was in there. I recognized most of them, so I was getting nervous. I went in there and ate it up and had a great time. Later that day Eric Lee called me up and he goes, "You've got to come in for rehearsals!" I said, "For what?" He was like, "Oh, for the movie." I was like, "I got it?" He goes, "Oh, they didn't call you yet? Oh, I'll call you back!" He jumped the gun a little bit, but that's how I found out I got it.

That was a great time for "B" martial arts action stars and studios like PM Entertainment. Talk a little bit about that.

PM Entertainment has served—for me as a filmmaker—as my number one school. I learned so much from watching them make movies at that time. Now, to this day, when I'm making films as a producer and as a director and as a writer even, I'm remembering and recalling and using their techniques and approaches. When I did *Final Impact* I had no idea how to make a film. I was expecting that I was going to get paid enough money to go buy a house. (Laughing.) I was thinking all these things in my head. We went to Vegas to shoot it. I drove out with Lorenzo and Kathleen in a car. We didn't fly. We drove. The rest of the crew drove behind us in a van. We shot stuff along the way. We were in Baker and Barstow and we stopped and filmed a couple of scenes for the movie. We showed up in Vegas -and before we even got to our hotel—we just pulled into a hotel parking lot and shot the scene where I'm walking out of my hotel and Lorenzo's sitting on a car and we almost fight each other. That was the first thing we shot within the first ten minutes of arriving in Vegas. It was like that. It was constant. I had never been to Vegas before. My character had never been to Vegas before. I got to play into my naiveté. That was a time when these "B" movies were still being shown in theaters. *Final Impact* played in theaters. Kathleen Kinmont and I would go running into theaters and sit in the back and see people's reactions. It was great.

Where are you from?

I grew up in Philadelphia. Then I moved to Chesapeake Bay. Then to Northern California.

Growing up, what types of martial arts did you study before coming to LA?

The very first martial art I learned was aikido. I was ten years old. A few years later, I got into Northern Shaolin. Very, very traditional. It was a pretty interesting base. Then I started entering into karate tournaments.

When you were making *Final Impact,* did you feel like a career as an action star might actually be possible for you?

I didn't necessarily want to be an action star. I definitely knew that I wanted to be in film. From the get-go, I was very interested in what everybody was doing on the set. I love film in general. I knew my limitations of my own abilities. I didn't want to overdo myself. Bruce Lee was my inspiration as a martial artist. I wasn't necessarily interested in replicating him on film. Spencer Tracy and Steve McQueen were more my inspiration for me being in the business than martial arts were, but I loved martial arts. I love the combat and I love the training and I love what it does for my health. When I did *Final Impact*, I did get the bug. I wanted to get better with the fighting. They asked me to do three more films. *Street Crimes* was next. With Dennis Farina. It was very similar to *Final Impact.* We did it in ten days. I think I made $4,500 on *Final Impact.* Lorenzo got paid fifteen or twenty. It was before *Renegade.* I can't remember. Kathleen only got six or seven. We were all struggling at the time. Even Lorenzo. I think he used all his money from that movie to buy his motorcycle. I'm not sure if that's true or not. Both of them were really supportive of me. They knew the ins and outs of this kind of filmmaking. That's how they did it. The next one I did they paid me a little more and a little more. It wasn't a ton of money.

What was Joseph Merhi like to work with as a director?

Joe was great. He and Rick Pepin were a good team. Joe directed and Pepin did the cinematography. They were constantly together. Joe is a very low-key guy. He laughs a lot because he keeps everybody at ease. PM Entertainment was making a movie a month at the time. They had to match Don Wilson's pay to Roger Corman's. At that point, PM was paying a lot more. They owned soundstages by then. They did a movie with Gary Daniels called *Rage*, and they'd built this huge set, and normally they wouldn't do that—they would just rent a space somewhere. Eventually, they did a movie with Van Damme called *Desert Heat.* There were a lot of problems by then and they stopped PM Entertainment.

You fought Gary in *Final Impact.*

Yeah, that was my first fight on screen.

Gary has gone on to have an impressive career and he's still making these types of movies. Your career path went a slightly different way, but did you ever look at Gary or other peers and see anything that you could have done differently?

It wasn't a bother to me. I had the option to do that. I could have followed that path. I'm not saying I could have been successful doing that or not. I had opportunities. I felt like I was being tested. Am I going to go down this route and do this martial arts thing for a while and maybe rise up and then people say about me, "Oh, he's that older martial arts guy." I didn't want people to

say that about me. Should I just start rejecting some of it and take a risk doing TV and more episodic guest spots and do more indie films where I'm not fighting and instead showing my range as an actor? When these other guys would get work, I was happy as hell for them. I loved it. I'd hang out with them on sets. I used to go to Don's sets. Just sit there and talk with him. Gary and I used to run into each other at signings. There's an element of competition with some of these guys because they've come out of competition. For me, that was never my goal. Right now—the last couple of years—have been the best time for me. I've been doing exactly what I've been wanting to do. I've got a film company I'm putting together, and ironically the first thing we're doing is a martial arts film.

Was a sequel ever discussed for *Final Impact?*

Yes, actually, but they were bummed that they killed off Lorenzo in it. What's funny about that is that they showed it in Cannes, and I got a call from Joseph real early in the morning, and he was so excited, "Mike, I just want to tell you we just showed the movie and the buyers came out crying after Lorenzo died! We're so happy! Why'd we kill him?"

Talk about the show you did called *Acapulco Heat.* It ran for two seasons. You had a major role in it as the martial arts guy.

An actor named Vince Murdocco, who had been in a bunch of martial arts action movies, was reading for this show called *Acapulco Heat.* I went over to his house and helped him audition for it. He went and read for it. A month or two later, I got called in for the same part and I went in and read for it. I got the role. They had done a demo for the sales reel and Keith Cooke was in the sales reel with me. Keith and I were working together when I first started in the business. We were going to star in a movie called *19* about nineteen-year-olds who went to Vietnam. *Acapulco Heat* was an amazing experience. It was my first time as a regular on a series, and it was shot in Mexico. As a martial artist, I was used to going to the set and doing my own fighting. What happened was I was showing up on set—I think it was the third day—and I'm going to do a fight scene and I'm walking through the hotel and I see a second unit filming a fight scene and a guy is wearing my wardrobe being thrown around the room by a couple of women. I'm like, "What are they doing down there?" They go, "Oh, they're shooting your fight scenes." "How can they be shooting my fight scenes? I'm sitting right here!" They were shooting it in a way where all they really needed was a shot of my face, and I walked over and looked at the choreographer, who had staged this scene in the John Wayne style, with a punch and a throw, and I walked up to him, and I said, "Hey, guys, can we sit down and discuss these fights? Let me do them. If you light me on fire, we can bring a stuntman, but anything else let me do." The first season had a huge cast. By the time we did the second season, they whittled it down to four of us. There was about ten to twelve of us in the first year.

How was the show for your career?

I was gone six months of the year shooting it, so I missed a lot of work, but when I came back I got a lot more television. I did *Fists of Iron* after the first season of *Acapulco Heat*. I got called for that right away.

You worked with Matthias Hues on that one.

I'd seen Matthias in that movie with Dolph, *I Come in Peace*, and I said to myself, *Oh, this guy is going to be the biggest jerk*. Sometimes you get these preconceived ideas. He shows up on set and he's the nicest, sweetest guy you've ever met! A giant teddy bear. I enjoyed working with him."

Your director on *U.S. Seals 2* was Isaac Florentine. He takes a lot of care in how he shoots his scenes.

Why Isaac's so great is because he's a martial artist. That guy loves martial arts. He was on set practicing karate. He always wanted to talk about martial arts. He's so interested in the history of it. The first time I met him was at the audition, and I read the part, and then he said, "Can you show me some martial arts?" I started doing my traditional kung fu stuff. He was asking me if I knew any Shotokan, and I did know a little bit. He said, "Good, good, good—that's good Michael! I want you to go home and watch *Once Upon a Time in the West*!" He started telling me about Charles Bronson. I went home and started thinking, I think he wants to give me this part. I got a call two or three days later and I got the part. It was shot in Bulgaria. It was like doing a fight a day. Fights every single day.

Talk about doing some of your later projects like *Ghost Rock*.

I didn't want to go down the route where I did twenty kickboxing movies. It was already happening to me where I'd go to auditions and people would go, "Oh, hey, you're in those karate movies!" That's not the impression I wanted to put out there. I was thinking longevity. Even Jean-Claude wasn't jumping at the top of the bandwagon anymore. I was concerned about that. Thank God we have *The Expendables* now. I left my agency. I forced myself to find films I wanted. The only way I could get money for *Ghost Rock* was to put martial arts in it. They said, "You've got to fight people in it." So I said, "Okay, then let's make it a martial arts western." We had no idea what we were doing. We made it for $400,000. It was crazy. We had three units going at the same time. We had forty-five people in the cast. We shot it in old Tucson. All the money came from doctors and lawyers, all pooled together. I literally went to doctors' offices, trying to raise money. It was crazy. At one point I wanted to direct it, but I stuck with being the writer. I just watched the process. I learned a lot from the failures of the movie and what did work. I brought Jeff Fahey and Gary Busey, who were friends at the time, and they helped get it off the ground. The next thing I put together

was a movie called *God's Ears*. It's a drama based on this autistic kid on a basketball team who's always kept on the sidelines, but the two main players on the team were injured, so they stuck him in the game and he got the highest scoring points than any other team members in the history of the team. I thought it was a great story, but I changed it to boxing. He's a guy that everyone's rejecting, but he has this skill.

Say something to your fans. If there's anyone out there who's ever cared about you and your films, what would you like to say to them?

I want to say that I definitely care about this genre. I pulled back from it to give myself the ability to have a long career so that I can come back and keep doing it. When I go out and do these— and whether they fail or if they're successful —I'm always out there trying to do something interesting or different. I'm always conscious of the fact that people pay to see these movies, so I want to leave something behind me and be proud of some of the things I've done. As proud as I am of *God's Ears*, I want to feel like it's just the start of the kind of quality of the sort of things that I want to do. The action genre is an art form. They're always trying to find a way to escalate it, and I want to do that, too.

Today You Die

2005 (Sony DVD) (djm)

Steven Seagal stars in one of his (slightly) better straight-to-video efforts as a thief named Harlan, who has a soothsayer for a girlfriend. She warns him not to take his next job, which is to drive an armored truck after picking up a "delivery." He takes the job anyway, and he soon finds out that his girlfriend was right: The whole thing is a set-up to blame him for a robbery of millions of dollars. He gets into a bad accident, but he manages to hide the money before he's caught. He's sent to prison and he's immediately accosted by other inmates who've been paid to rough him up for information, but since he's Steven Seagal no one can touch him. He makes an alliance with another inmate named Ice Cool (rapper Treach), who manages to orchestrate their escape via helicopter (by way of a prison riot distraction). Once on the outside, Harlan and Ice Cool work together to find out who set him up, and by the end, it's all good.

From director Don E. Fontleroy (also the cinematographer), who worked with Seagal on the films *Mercenary For Justice* and *Urban Justice*, this outing shows a nicer, more amiable Seagal than usual, but he's just as deadly with his hands. Most of the fight scenes feature a double (we never see Seagal's face in most of the shots), but it's not a big deal for me with this film. I liked seeing him in a cool role, and he has some funny lines that made me laugh. Future kid star Chloe Grace Moretz (from *Kick Ass*) has a small role. James Jew and Jerry Trimble have bit roles as guys with guns. It was produced by Nu Image/Millennium.

Tomorrow Never Dies

1997 (MGM DVD) (CD)

The Carver Media Group Network is racing to the top of world coverage with groundbreaking news—and it's news before it even happens. Elliot Carver (Jonathon Price) is trying to become the most powerful man in the media and begins engineering events to incite a third world war. After sinking a British sub and stealing a missile from the wreckage to use against China, his plan is on the verge of coming to fruition. There's only one person with the skills and gadgets to prevent the world from becoming a battleground. There's only one super spy, who needs no introduction, who will risk it all to bring down Elliot Carver by any means necessary, and her name is Colonel Wai Lin (Michelle Yeoh in her English language debut). With the help of British agent James Bond (Pierce Brosnan), the two of them will travel continents while risking everything to protect the world.

Michelle Yeoh (*Project S*) single-handedly redefined what it is to be a Bond girl. She's sexy, funny, and most importantly she can hold her own in a gunfight. When it comes down to hand-to-hand combat, Bond better re-evaluate his techniques since she could and would whoop his ass. To this day, Yeoh's character Wai Lin is the only formidable female partner 007 has ever had. She has her own featured fight scene and is every bit Bond's equal. Yeoh and Brosnan have an excellent rapport and the film kicks into high gear when they finally team up to bring down Price, who hits it out of the park as the duo's nemesis. Director Roger Spottiswoode (who later did *The 6th Day* with Schwarzenegger) refused to allow Yeoh to do her own stunts even though she requested to do so. Pierce Brosnan's second outing as Bond is by far his most exciting. It's a shame Yeoh wasn't given the chance to carry her own franchise spinoff from this.

Tooth Fairy

2010 (Fox DVD) (CD)

"You can't handle the Tooth!
And that's the Tooth, the whole Tooth and nothing but the Tooth! I pledge allegiance to the Tooth."

Derek Thompson (Dwayne Johnson) is a former pro-hockey player who is trying to keep his name alive in the minor leagues. They call him "The Tooth Fairy" since he has a streak for knocking his opponents' teeth out. When his girlfriend's daughter leaves a tooth for the Tooth Fairy, she can't seem to find the money anywhere. In his insensitivity, he threatens to tell her there's no such thing as the Tooth Fairy. His girlfriend, Carly (Ashely Judd), scolds him and he goes home. When he wakes up, he finds himself in Tooth Fairy land and he has been sentenced to live as a fairy for two weeks, going on assignments and collecting teeth from children. He has to learn what it means to a child

T

to have dreams. If he succeeds, he can have his life back. He has to keep the truth from Carly and her kids while developing a bond with her son who is having troubles of his own.

If Hulk Hogan was *Mr. Nanny*, then Dwayne "The Rock" Johnson can be the *Tooth Fairy*. This isn't exactly the type of film Johnson should have been anxious to do. Most of the humor is only appealing to youngsters and he is far too talented to be wasting his time on stuff like this. He had proven himself as a box-office draw by this point, even doing a far superior family film with *Journey 2: The Mysterious Island*. He spends most of the film being an unlikable character, running from cats and dogs and parading in a tutu. The only real action in the film is sports related, and it's all pretty harmless. With his current trajectory, it appears Johnson has learned from this misstep and has headed in the right direction, starring in PG-13-rated fare like *Fast Five*, *G.I. Joe: Retaliation*, and *Snitch*. Directed by Michael Lembeck (*The Santa Clause III*).

Top Dog

1995 (Artisan DVD) (djm)

Slightly better than the trailer, *Top Dog* was a late-out-of-the-gate buddy cop/dog movie, starring Chuck Norris in his last theatrical action movie until he made a cameo in *Expendables 2*. As clichéd as it is, it's still watchable due to Chuck's persona and physicality. He plays a cop named Jake Wilder, who is assigned a new partner, a scruffy dog named Reno, whose previous cop partner was killed in the line of duty. Reno, who was wounded, is the smartest cop on the force

A publicity shot from *Top Dog*. Author's collection.

Jake Wilder (Chuck Norris) roundhouses a thug in *Top Dog*. Author's collection.

Chuck Norris plays Jake Wilder in *Top Dog*. Author's collection.

(or so they say), and he has about as likable a personality as a movie dog can. Together, they're on a case involving a white supremacist group, who plans to bomb a racial unification rally in Los Angeles. Typical stuff ensues, and by the end, Wilder owes Reno his life.

After Tom Hanks and Jim Belushi both had their turn making cop/dog buddy movies, Chuck Norris gave it a go with this lark of a movie. It was shot in between seasons of *Walker, Texas Ranger*, and it has a rushed, uninspired tone, without any surprises. It amazed me that it was given a theatrical release (it grossed just over five million), as it feels like a movie made for television. Reno, the dog, slightly ups the ugly quotient for movie dogs, and his co-star, Chuck, while fit, looks bored. Aaron Norris directed.

Total Reality

1997 (York DVD) (CD)

"What the fuck? What the fucking fuck? Get me the fuck off this ship!"

Rand (David Bradley) is a soldier in the distant future, one who is fighting what he believes to be the good fight. When his commanding officer kills thousands of innocent people, Rand does what he feels is right and kills him. After landing himself in prison, he's given the chance to go back in time and take out two rebels who have a mission of their own: to kill the man responsible for writing the cultish book led to the miserable future. Once he lands in 1998, he will face many difficult and moral choices. He only has forty-eight hours to carry out his mission; if he fails, the microchip implanted inside him will explode. If he succeeds, he will change the future. It's a race through time and space with Rand willing to change the events of the past in order to save the future.

Total Reality was one of the last films David Bradley (*Blood Warriors*, *Cyborg Cop*) starred in before disappearing from the business altogether. It's not the proper send-off he should have had or deserved. The story was fairly well conceived (though a bit familiar) and Bradley has always been such a likable lead that even with the shortcomings, it's still a pretty entertaining affair. There's an abundance of gunfire and explosions, but director Philip Roth (*Velocity*

Trap and *Interceptor Force* with Olivier Gruner) failed to use him or his wicked mad martial art skills in a film where it could have only helped the picture. There's only one short fight, acting as a teaser for what we are missing out on. The only thing left to say is that David Bradley is an action hero and we, as fans, want him back.

To the Death

1992 (Cannon VHS) (djm)

Kickboxing champion Rick Quinn (John Barrett) retires at the peak of his condition, and he tries living a quiet life with his wife, but a scuzzy millionaire named Le Braque (Robert Whitehead) wants him to fight in his underground high-stakes fight ring. After refusing Le Braque several times, Quinn's wife is killed in a car explosion, sending Quinn into a deep depression and an alcoholic haze. Months later, Quinn is living in dilapidated squalor at pay-by-the-day motels, and Le Braque comes back to him with an offer of fighting in his ring for peanuts. With nothing left to lose, Quinn joins the circuit and quickly learns that Le Braque is an evil man, staging to-the-death fights for millions, and in the first fight Quinn realizes that he's become a prisoner in Le Braque's world. Unable to escape and without a friend on the outside to help him, Quinn makes an ally with another fighter named Denard (Michel Qissi from *Kickboxer*), who was once his mortal enemy when they were prize fighters. When they're both faced with death if they lose in Le Braque's ring, they become friends and teammates against the armed guards in Le Braque's tournament stadium.

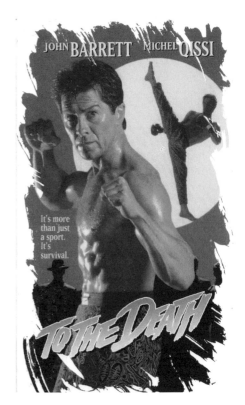

VHS artwork for *To the Death*. Author's collection.

John Barrett's career as an action star had a small chug of energy when the revamped Cannon Films gave him the lead roles in this film and in *American Kickboxer*, but as fate would have it, he wasn't able to sustain a stream of vehicles to continue on. At forty-plus years old, he looks like a seasoned pro in *To the Death*, and it's immediately clear that he is putting forth everything he has, but the problem with this film and with *American Kickboxer* is that he's playing characters that aren't interesting or even very sympathetic. His acting is okay as far as acting goes, but it's difficult for me to see him as the star of these films. *To the Death* has so little going for it—the villain is a caricature, the fights are pedestrian, the budget is noticeably low—that it desperately needs a charismatic star to carry it, and Barrett doesn't quite cut it. It's too bad because I wanted to like this one. A rap theme song opens and closes it. Filmed in South Africa. Directed by Darrell James Roodt.

The Touch
(a.k.a. **The Martial Touch**)
2002 (Miramax DVD) (CD)

Yin Fay (Michelle Yeoh) has taken over the family business since her father passed away. Her family is a renowned group of acrobats who put on an amazing show. What no one knows is they are also the protectors of an ancient relic worth millions. The relic is hidden deep within the desert so no one could ever find it. Yin's ex-boyfriend Eric (Ben Chaplin) returns to see her but he has become a master thief. His former boss Karl (Richard Roxburgh) wants the relic for himself and knows Eric has ties to the family. After Yin refuses to help, Karl kidnaps her younger brother and his girlfriend, forcing them to lead the way to the relic. Yin and Eric quickly team up to get her brother back and to protect the relic from Karl and his goons.

Director Peter Pau is best known as an Academy Award–winning cinematographer (*Crouching Tiger, Hidden Dragon* is on his credits), and he directed this film for Miramax as a co-production between several Asian companies. The picture boasts some stunning cinematography, especially of some mountain ranges that had never been filmed before. Michelle Yeoh (*Royal Warriors, Tomorrow Never Dies*) is never one to disappoint an audience. There are many problems within the narrative of the film and it features some dodgy effects during the finale, but every moment she's in action, she shows she is one of the most graceful screen fighters of all time. Every movement she makes just flows with precision and beauty. The movie tries to emulate the type of adventure associated with something like the Indiana Jones movies or even *Tomb Raider*. It also continues the trend of casting comedian Dane Cook (*Simon Sez*) as an over-the-top annoyance, but Yeoh's grace and presence make it all worthwhile.

Tough and Deadly
1994 (Universal VHS) (djm)

Roddy Piper and Billy Blanks made a good team. This is their second (and last) action film together, and it's not bad. Blanks plays a CIA operative code-named Quicksilver because he has amazingly fast reactionary skills and knows karate. When he is knocked out and lands in a hospital, a "skip tracer" named Elmo Freech (Piper) happens to be in the same ward of the hospital while trying to hustle himself some business. While Freech is checking the new arrival out in his room, some killers come to murder the unconscious Blanks, but they are interrupted by Freech, who is hiding behind a curtain. Freech becomes even more interested in Quicksilver's history when he can't find any trace of his records or fingerprints in the system. When Quicksilver wakes up, Freech takes him to his own house for safekeeping, which seems crazy to me, but he's Roddy Piper, so it's cool. They try to get to know each other, but Quicksilver can't remember anything—not even his own name, so they get off to an awkward start. They bond by exercising and going to bars and getting into fights (they always win), and later, they get into a fight with each other because Freech wants to test out Quicksilver's karate skills. Bad idea.

The story is stock stuff with rogue government agents and drugs, but the only thing that matters is that there's more action and fighting than usual for movies of this type. Piper and Blanks are given equal screen time and both are allowed to showcase their physical abilities. The comedy is there, and some of it works, and both of the guys look great and seem to be having fun. It's too bad this and *Back in Action* didn't get theatrical releases. They might be two of the best-looking direct-to-video action films from the early 1990s. They definitely give the viewers their money's worth. The music and locations leave a little to be desired, though. Lots of standard underscoring and synthesizers set to backdrops like warehouses and city streets and bars. This was a Shapiro/Glickenhaus production, directed by Steve Cohen. Richard Norton has some scenes as a bad guy.

The Tournament
2009 (Dimension DVD) (CD)

"Thirty seconds . . . Twenty-four hours . . . one rule: Kill or die. Ladies and gentleman, place your bets. The Tournament has begun!"

Every seven years, a tournament takes place that pits thirty of the world's greatest assassins against one another in a fight to the death. They have twenty-four hours to yield a winner, and if by then there is a standstill, then an explosive device (planted into each participant earlier) will detonate. There's ten million at stake, so everyone is out to win. Former champion Joshua (Ving Rhames) reluctantly enters the game to find out which player killed his wife. Lai Lai Zhen (Kelly Hu) wants to leave the covert killing life behind and hopes to win the tournament and do so. She ends up partnered with reluctant player Father MacAvoy (Robert Carlyle), a drunken priest who accidentally consumes one of the tracking devices. At every turn, someone is out for blood, with all the proceedings being watched by high rollers placing bets, all moderated by the twisted mastermind Powers (Liam Cunningham).

The Tournament is a blood-drenched action film with enough carnage to please the most jaded of viewers. The story is simple, the characters are thin, but there's enough going on that you won't mind. It appears like the action was done without the help of digital effects (with just a few minor things) and used plenty of squibs, buckets of blood, amazing stunts, and severed body parts. Kelly Hu (*The Scorpion King*) is a terrific action heroine and should be doing more films like this. She has a great fight scene with real-deal action star Scott Adkins (*Ninja, Special Forces*), who has an incredibly small role as a Russian assassin. As usual, Adkins is fantastic, so it's a shame he barely has ten minutes of screen time. That said, he's featured on the DVD box art, which says something. Very few action films are made like this anymore, and director Scott Mann gets this one right.

Trained to Kill
1989 (Prism VHS) (djm)

A Vietnam vet named Ed (Chuck Connors) goes to Cambodia to rescue his long-lost son Samnaug (Glen Eaton from *The Last Dragon*), and his rescue is underscored with heroic war music and a *Missing in Action*-esque action scene involving a helicopter and an M134 machine gun, so the prologue of the movie is pretty exciting. When Ed takes Samnaug home, Ed's older son Matt (Frank Zagarino) greets his new brother with friendship and love, and everything is great until an old war buddy of Ed's named Ace (Henry Silva) comes looking for something Samnaug supposedly smuggled out of Cambodia. Ace has three badass henchmen (played by Robert Z'Dar, Marshall Teague, and the great Harold Diamond, the star of *Killing American Style*), who harass Ed's family and eventually kill Ed and his wife and kidnap Matt's wife and hold her for ransom. Matt and Samnaug train in martial arts together, and go on a seek and destroy mission, to right wrongs and bring balance back to their family.

A real nice surprise for fans of these low-grade action/martial arts movies, *Trained to Kill* has such a great cast and some really good action in it that it's strange that it hasn't been given more notice. Though Zagarino (from *Striker* and *Project Shadowchaser*) is given top billing and has his face on the video box, the movie is really an ensemble piece, with nice action roles for Eaton and Diamond, who both shine. Diamond was a real-life kickboxing champ, and his biggest claim to fame is stick fighting with Stallone in *Rambo III*. A solid effort all the way. Directed by H. K. Dyal, who would go on to make *Project Eliminator* with Zagarino next.

T

Traitor's Heart

1999 (Image DVD) (CD)

Nick Brody (Bryan Genesse) lives a seemingly normal life with his wife Maggie (Kimberley Kates) and son Sean (Michael Stark) in New York. Then one evening Sean gets lost at a crowded fireworks display, sending Nick in a panic as he looks for him. The man who helps Sean find Nick feels like they have met before. Nick wouldn't remember since he lost his memory five years previously in a helicopter accident. From then on, things go downhill and Nick witnesses the murder of a second man who is trying to warn him about their past. It becomes apparent that there was a major cover-up of something that happened five years ago and the people closest to him are hiding the truth. All the secrets and lies are threatening to destroy the one thing he cares most about in the world: his family . . . and he will do anything to keep them together.

Traitor's Heart was sort of a surprise since it's pretty light on the action but it actually has a rather compelling story that's sold with ease by the underrated Bryan Genesse (*Cold Harvest*). His performance in the film was unexpectedly strong. At times, it felt like it might be a sort of *Bourne Identity*-type of film but at the core it's ultimately about family. When the betrayals are revealed, you find yourself feeling for him. His character is quite likable, and Genesse is much more versatile than he's given credit for. It's light on action but high on suspense. Danny Lerner made his directorial debut for Nu Image with this film (he has since gone on to produce films like *The Expendables*).

Transformed

2005 (Sky Dragon Entertainment DVD) (djm)

"You're the lowest of the low! You're a social cancer!"

Some drug dealers are trying to recruit a bunch of kids in the neighborhood, and Pastor Debra (Shirlee Knudson) takes it personally. She tries using good sense and the Word of God to rebuke the drug dealers and the local drug lord Cholo (played by stuntman Ken Moreno), but they laugh her off. She's visited by a guardian angel (played by Leo Fong, who also wrote, produced, and directed this), who assists her in fending off the thugs and saving the children. Also in the mix is a "cleaner," who calls himself The Hammer (Fred Williamson).

I dunno, guys. I watch stuff like *Transformed*, trying to keep my happy face on, desperately formulating the best, most respectful way to write a review that praises its performers, but this one's tough. *Transformed* is about as earnest as they get, with good intentions worn openly on its cheap, torn sleeves. I love Leo Fong, but I can't recommend his endeavor here. There was most certainly a script because I can hear the writing,

and it's bad. Real bad. The movie looks like it was filmed entirely without permits, stealing scenes at Universal Studios, Disneyland, and various other public places where the camera captures the actors going through their motions, but the entire effort feels forced and strained to the point of breaking. Fred Williamson shot his scenes in two days, and when he fights guest actor Tadashi Yamashita (from *American Ninja*) at the end, it's embarrassing for both actors, who deserve better material and much more rehearsal. Leo Fong is undoubtedly a whiz at getting movies made with a wallet full of twenties, but after *Transformed* and a few of those Gary Wasniewski pictures he did, I'm thinking maybe it's time for retirement.

The Transporter

2002 (Fox DVD) (djm)

The Transporter blindsided me when I first saw it in theaters. Up until that point in his career, Jason Statham had mostly co-starred in action-type movies like *Ghosts of Mars, The One* (with Jet Li), and *Lock, Stock, and Two Smoking Barrels*. Nothing prepared me for what he does in *The Transporter*. He plays an ex-special forces soldier living in the French Mediterranean, taking no-questions-asked transport jobs in his modified BMW for cash. One such job requires him to transport a squirming package to a designated location, but he breaks his own rules and opens the package, finding a cute Chinese woman (Shu Qi) bound and gagged inside, which leads to a series of events that basically spells doom for

Frank Martin Jason Statham) doesn't need a shirt when he fights because he's The Transporter. Author's collection.

Jason Statham stars as The Transporter in his breakout action movie. Author's collection.

She ain't heavy, she's his cargo. Jason Statham shoulders Shu Qi like nobody's business in *The Transporter*. Author's collection.

him if he doesn't turn the tables and fight back. With a French inspector on his case (played by François Berléand who would go on to appear in the sequels *and* a spinoff TV series), Frank goes after the guy who put a hit out on him (Matt Schulze from *The Fast and the Furious*), and tries to uncover a plot concerning a shipment of human cargo from China. As it turns out, Frank isn't just a transporter—he's a martial arts dynamo, the likes of which the special forces probably has never before or since produced.

This is the movie that made Statham an action star. Even if he's not a genuine martial artist (he was, however, a professional swimmer), he had me fooled for years until someone in the know told me he's not what is generally regarded as "the real thing." As far as I'm concerned, Statham is the real deal, and after this movie solidified his on-screen persona and crafted an action star image for him, he's pretty much stayed within the genre. When people think of Jason Statham, *The Transporter* is what comes to mind. If this had been made five years earlier, it would have been a great vehicle for Jean-Claude Van Damme. Corey Yuen (*No Retreat, No Surrender*) directed from Luc Besson's and Robert Mark Kamen's screenplay.

Transporter 2

2005 (Fox DVD) (djm)

Frank Martin, the enigmatic "Transporter," played by Jason Statham, is back, and this time his "package" is a young boy whom he is paid

Hitwoman Lola (Kate Nauta) and The Transporter Frank Martin (Jason Statham) face off in *Transporter 2*. Author's collection.

The agile Transporter Frank Martin (Jason Statham) protects his car from thugs in *Transporter 2*. Author's collection.

Jack (Hunter Clary) is "the package" and Frank Martin (Jason Statham) is The Transporter in *Transporter 2*. Author's collection.

to drive to and from school every day for a prestigious political family in Miami. When a terrorist named Chellini (Alessandro Gassman) plans an elaborate scheme to inject the boy with a toxin—which would inevitably be passed on to his politically connected father—Frank must race against the clock to find the antidote and make sure the deadly poison isn't passed on to other politicos at a summit meeting. Amongst those whom Frank must deal with: a nearly naked lingerie-wearing vixen strapped with Uzis named Lola (Kate Nauta), and a legion of toughs who prove to be not tough enough when faced with the heroic Transporter.

Even more successful than the first film, *Transporter 2* remains Statham's biggest solo-starring hit, and as a follow-up, it's more of the same, but reaches slightly more into a broader, mass-appeal stratum by turning its hero into a surrogate dad figure instead of a romantic lothario/secret agent type. The stunts and martial arts battles are plentiful, and in its eighty-seven-minute running time, the movie rarely stops to take a breather. It's fun. Corey Yuen (director of the first film) was the action director this time, while Louis Leterrier directed from Luc Besson's and Robert Mark Kamen's script.

Transporter 3
2008 (Lionsgate DVD) (djm)

Trying to enjoy the good life, Frank Martin—a.k.a. "The Transporter" (played by Jason Statham)—is forced back into his old ways when a terrorist demands that he transport a

French poster for *Transporter 3*. Author's collection.

woman from one locale to the next, which is just a ruse to keep the woman in transit while the terrorist forces a politico to sign a shady deal that would ensure tons of nuclear waste would be illegally disposed of for a period of time. Martin's precious cargo is, in fact, the politico's only daughter (a hot number played by Natalya Rudakova), and Frank's only enforced stipulation is that he never leave her side *or* the side of his brand-spanking-new and modified Audi, which is geared to explode if Frank steps too far away from it. So this time The Transporter is literally glued to his car, which makes some of the ensuing action and chase scenes a bit tricky since he's got to be in and/or around his ride to make progress on his mission.

Under a new distributor, the *Transporter* series shifted gears subtly, which is fine for most fans of Statham and of the franchise, but I felt like this one was more tired and less inventive than the first two. It's lengthier by nearly twenty minutes than the other two, and while it feels like a kindred spirit to those, it lacks the sense of fun that made me enjoy the others so much. The villain is played by Robert Knepper, and he's good, but for some reason the fight scenes and the stunt set-ups lacked an imaginative spark. Remember the scene in the first one where Statham dumped a bunch of oil on the ground to fight some guys and used bike pedals to hop around them? That's what this movie needs—a fight scene like that. Statham himself looks a little bored this time around, and it's easy to see why. He hasn't returned to this franchise since. A cable TV series starring Chris Vance (not an action star) carried on the adventures of Frank Martin. Olivier Megaton (*Taken 2*) directed this entry from Luc Besson's and Robert Mark Kamen's script.

Treasure Raiders
2007 (Maverick DVD) (djm)

A Scottish archaeology professor named Michael (Steven Brand) is teaching a course in Moscow, and he's edging closer to a lost gospel that the Knights Templar were entrusted to keep safe. To fund his searches, he street races at night, and the king of the racing circuit is a mercenary-turned-bodybuilding crime lord named Wolf (Alexander Nevsky from *Moscow Heat*). Michael challenges Wolf to an offer he can't refuse: He will bet $50,000 against the amulet Wolf wears around his neck in an upcoming street race. Wolf takes the offer, and he takes a shine to Michael because of his audacity, but when neither of them win the race, they band together to find the lost Templar treasure. In the background of their treasure hunt is a rival crime syndicate who is after Wolf, as well as a shadowy collegiate benefactor named Pierre (a slumming David Carradine) who is after the Templar treasure for himself.

With more action, flash, and bang than *Moscow Heat*, *Treasure Raiders* is pretty fun stuff, and if you're coming into it having never seen Nevsky in *Moscow Heat*, then you'll be floored by how much of a ringer he is for a young Arnold Schwarzenegger. Nevsky doesn't have the confidence, the swagger, or the can't-lose attitude Arnold did in his early years, but it's fun watching Nevsky in the film. He has a fight scene in a nightclub where he takes out about a dozen guys, and later on he has a couple of shootouts. The movie is a little confused about what it wants to be—is it *National Treasure* or is it *The Fast and the Furious*? It's a little bit of both with a buff dude in the center. Directed by Brent Huff, who was almost an action star himself once upon a time.

The Trial of Billy Jack
1974 (Image DVD) (JAS)

"If there is absolutely no way you can get out of taking a terrible beating, the only sensible thing to do is get in the first lick!"

Director Tom Laughlin and wife/co-star Delores Taylor continue the saga of spiritual warrior Billy Jack in a heady dose of genrefied, post-Nixon social commentary. After Billy Jack is released from prison for "involuntary manslaughter," he engages in a vision quest with the local Native Americans to continue his journey toward spiritual clarity. Meanwhile, the nearby school he helped defend in the previous film (see: *Billy Jack*) is in further political trouble. The students' aggressive journalism exposes the manipulation of the native tribal leaders by crooked politicians. On top of that, an abused child protected by the school is sent back to his abusive father. Eventually, all of these opposing forces require Billy Jack to step in and kick ass, which he does in his established hapkido style.

T

The *Trial of Billy Jack* is arguably the lengthiest low-budget action film of all time. Clocking in at 170 minutes, it is a stamina tester for even a die-hard action completist. That's not to say it's a bad film. It has an earnest dose of effective social commentary and dramatic pathos that is accumulatively effective for those with patience. Director and star Tom Laughlin took a lot of criticism for the pretentiousness of the Billy Jack series, but credit must be given for his overreaching. The finale is fittingly bleak for the era. Much like the *Kung Fu* television series of the same time, the protagonist resorts to fighting in small, necessary doses. This befits the character arc of a man for whom violence offers no glory. This is heavy-handed, Watergate-era hippie action for pacifists. Definitely worth a look for genre fans.

Triple Impact

1992 (AIP VHS) (djm)

"Okay, that's better. I see there's about twelve of you. The three of us. That makes it about a fair fight. Get you some."

A pointless prologue in the Vietnam war sets the tone for this goofball action adventure in the tradition of *No Retreat, No Surrender II*. Some soldiers find an ancient treasure in the jungles of Nam, and several decades later a treasure hunter uses the surviving veterans to help him lead an expedition back to Asia to find the treasure. Somehow, two bumbling low-rent kickboxers (Dale "Apollo" Cook and Ron Hall) get mixed up in the adventure, and later on another kickboxer (Bridgett "Baby Doll" Riley) joins their expedition.

The novelty of watching these particular real-life kickboxing champions trying to act in this movie might turn some viewers off. Cook isn't known for being a good actor, but there's something strangely old-fashioned about him. In this film, he appears to be having a fun time acting goofy and silly, and while others might hate his performance, I paid close attention to him. I actually saw something special there, but many people won't see it. His co-stars (with the exception of Hall, who is about on par with him) don't fare so well, though. Riley is no Cynthia Rothrock, and she clearly isn't comfortable in front of a camera, and the villains are pretty terrible. The entire film is comedic and intentionally silly. The director, David Hunt, produced other films with Cook.

True Lies

1994 (Fox DVD) (MJ)

"We will tell the whole world that we speak the truth. No force can stop us now . . . We're cool, we're badasses . . . blah, blah, blah."

Following the significant box-office failure of *Last Action Hero* in 1993, fans of Arnold Schwarzenegger had strong hopes for a return to greatness with his next film and they were not disappointed with *True Lies*, which offered, among other things, a reteaming of Schwarzenegger with director James Cameron, after their successful (and profitable) collaborations on *The Terminator* and *Terminator 2: Judgment Day*. *True Lies* tells the story of Harry Tasker (Schwarzenegger), a computer salesman and devoted husband to Helen (Jamie Lee Curtis) and loving father to Dana (Eliza Dushku). Harry is living a double life. He is really a secret agent for the United States government and he travels the world dealing with potential threats to the country. Finding herself bored and lonely while Harry is away on his frequent trips, Helen begins to have an affair with a used car salesman (a hilarious Bill Paxton) who has been conning her into thinking he might be a spy. When Harry starts to figure out what Helen has been up to, he sets out to win her back. At the same time, his agency has been tracking the movements of Crimson Jihad, a terrorist network, and it looks like they have succeeded in getting an atomic bomb onto United States soil. As both of his worlds collide, Harry has to find a way to stop the terrorists from detonating the bomb and win back the love of his wife and daughter.

Another step forward in the creative evolution of Arnold Schwarzenegger, *True Lies* provided him with an opportunity to make an action film that would appeal to all ages of his enormous fan base. Schwarzenegger gets to play the action star and gets to show off his skills as a comedian and an actor with the role of Harry Tasker. Cameron surrounds Arnold with an excellent supporting cast, including Jamie Lee Curtis as his wife, Tom Arnold (an unlikely casting choice), Charlton Heston as his boss at the agency, and Art Malik as the leader of the Crimson Jihad, in addition to Cameron veteran Bill Paxton as the scuzzy used car salesman who tries to con Helen. *True Lies* also has superb production design to rival any James Bond film, as evidenced by the riveting action set piece that opens up the film. Also in the same year, Arnold would reunite with director Ivan Reitman (*Twins*) and actor Danny De Vito for the pregnant man comedy *Junior*.

True Vengeance

1997 (FM VHS) (djm)

In the late 1990s, John Woo's influence was becoming obvious in American action movies, such as this one. *True Vengeance* stars Daniel

Bernhardt (*Bloodsport 2-4*, *Parker*) as Henry Griffin, an ex-SEAL who worked as an assassin for the Yakuza. Years later, the Yakuza demands that he do another job, but he refuses. They take his daughter and force him to do it. Once the job is done, they try to kill him, and he gets angry enough to go after his daughter's kidnappers. He suits up and shoots dozens of people as he trailblazes his way to the top Yakuza kingpin. The Yakuza call upon Griffin's former nemesis, The Specialist (Miles O'Keeffe from the *Ator* movies), to stop him. Their final fight is with samurai swords.

The director, David Worth, worked with many action stars throughout the 1980s and 1990s. He was involved with *Bloodsport* and *Kickboxer* with Jean-Calude Van Damme, the *Lady Dragon* films with Cynthia Rothrock, and *Chain of Command* with Michael Dudkioff. He also was his own director of photography. He did a great job with the camera work on *True Vengeance*, but some of the supporting cast members are terrible. Bernhardt is one of the unheralded and unsung action stars. His acting is a little rough here, but he grew into his look and became more comfortable as an actor as he got older. *True Vengeance* is one of his best vehicles.

Turn It Up

2000 (New Line DVD) (CD)

It's not easy getting off the mean streets of Brooklyn, just ask Diamond (Pras, a rapper), a young man with dreams of being a rap star. He, along with his pal Gage (Ja Rule, another rapper) are running drugs for crime lord Mr. B (Jason Statham). The money they earn turns into studio time for Diamond, who is working hard on his first album. With money running out, Gage (who is also acting as Diamond's manager) robs a man for $100,000 to invest into the album. What he doesn't know is the guy he robs is working for Mr. B and the money he stole belongs to him. After reconnecting with his father and finding out he has a baby on the way, Diamond begins to see life differently and wants to change his ways. The problem is that Mr. B isn't going to let this go and will create far bigger problems for the duo to deal with.

Jason Statham (*Crank*) plays a small but pivotal role in this film, and he's a great villain. This really isn't a straight-up action film, but it does have some pretty violent shootouts, one of which involves Statham. He doesn't get to show off any of his physical skills except for when he roughs up Ja Rule (*The Fast and the Furious*) a bit for stealing his money. The movie itself is mostly a drama about getting off the streets with a couple of action scenes thrown in for good measure. Statham fans will enjoy his villainous turn but don't expect much more from the film. It was directed by Robert Adetuyi.

The Tuxedo

2002 (DreamWorks DVD) (CD)

"When I look at you, I have a wet dream!"

Jimmy Tong (Jackie Chan) is nothing but a driver for a millionaire named Clark Devlin (Jason Isaacs). Devlin is a top agent who keeps his identity secret from Tong. When Devlin becomes injured, Tong goes back to his home and happens to don the man's tuxedo. It's a state-of-the art suit that can be controlled by a watch, giving Tong superhero-like abilities. A bit of mistaken identity occurs, and Tong finds himself paired with inexperienced agent Del Blaine (Jennifer Love Hewitt) who believes him to be Devlin. Together they seek the terrorist group that is out to poison the world's water supply using genetically enhanced insects. Dietrich Banning (Ritchie Coster) is the mastermind behind the operation and when he finds out about the suit, he will do anything to get his hands on it.

For longtime Jackie Chan fans, *The Tuxedo* is terribly painful to watch. There are a few inspired moments but overall it's an incredibly weak film that may only be appealing to youngsters. For whatever reason, Chan, in most of his Hollywood productions, was never really able to inspire. He is assisted by wires and CGI here, which takes some getting used to if you are familiar with his past films. Not everything is augmented, and there are some fun moments with the typical fighting we love to see from him, but just not enough. The comedy elements of the film are hit and miss, with Chan being his usual charming self. Jennifer Love Hewitt (*I Know What You Did Last Summer*) tries her hardest but no matter how hard she tries, she's really miscast and out of her element. Coster (*The Dark Knight*) is a decent-enough villain, but the final showdown could have been much more exciting had it focused on a one-on-one battle with the two men in their enhanced suits. Instead, things get really silly and farcical. Also making appearances in the film are Debi Mazar (*Goodfellas*) and Peter Stormare (*The Last Stand*). If handled correctly, *The Tuxedo* could have been a great film. The concept and story (by James Bond scribe Michael G. Wilson) are certainly fun, but in the hands of first-time feature director Kevin Donovan, it's a borderline fiasco. Chan has made some truly epic and classic films that will stand the test of time. *The Tuxedo* isn't one of them.

12 Rounds

2009 (Fox DVD) (djm)

John Cena's second theatrical vehicle, *12 Rounds*, was dumped to theaters by 20th Century Fox without any fanfare, trailers, or promotion, and it's perplexing because Cena was on an upward trajectory after his auspicious debut film *The Marine*. Renny Harlin, the Finnish director of *Die Hard 2: Die Harder, Cliffhanger,* and *The Long Kiss Goodnight* was hired to direct *12 Rounds*, but a PG-13 rating and a "safe" action

star like Cena pretty much neutered Harlin's outrageous style in lieu of bloodless, generic action (even the "extreme cut" on video is tame). All that said, *12 Rounds* is acceptable because Cena is good in it, but it's a little surprising how restrained the whole movie is. It copies *Die Hard With a Vengeance* and *Speed*: Cena plays a beat cop named Danny Fisher who single-handedly captures a mastermind criminal running around New Orleans, and in his capture, the terrorist's wife is killed. One year later, Danny is a detective, and he gets a phone call from Miles Jackson (Aidan Gillen), the escaped mastermind who has planned his revenge on Danny for the whole year. Jackson has kidnapped Danny's girlfriend and he forces Danny to play a game of "12 rounds," each round more deadly and impossible to beat. Think back on *Die Hard With a Vengeance* where Bruce Willis and Samuel Jackson had to run around New York playing "Simon says." Same thing happens here. One stage has Danny trying to stop a runaway railcar (an homage to *Speed*), and other stages have him jumping out of buildings, escaping busted elevators, and trying to defuse bombs.

What *12 Rounds* really needed was a badass villain. Renny Harlin, who's made some great action movies with awesome villains, should have known this. The bigger the hero, the more intense and memorable the villain should be. That's not the case here, unfortunately. Cena is so huge and muscular that it's a little hard to buy him as a beat cop, but there are a few key scenes where his brawn is required to maintain the course that the bad guy has set for him. Basically, *12 Rounds* is an incredibly familiar sort of action movie, and Cena is okay in it, but I can easily see almost any leading man in Hollywood playing the same part just as well—or better—than he did. Can't you see Nicolas Cage or Colin Farrell doing the same thing? Cena was in the wrestling movie *Legendary* next.

12 Rounds: Reloaded

2013 (Fox DVD) (djm)

An EMT named Nick (Randy Orton) is on a date with his wife when a drunk driver crashes into another car on the road, and Nick is at the right place at the right time to do some good before an ambulance arrives on the scene. He does his best to save some lives, but several people involved in the crash expire. A year later, Nick is working one night when a mysterious caller to his cell phone demands he participate in a "12-round" game where he must jump to dangerous tasks on a timed scale, and if he refuses at any stage of the game, his wife will be killed. One of his first tasks is to pick up a young sidekick, who happens to be the man who was drunk and driving on that fateful day a year ago. The caller is a vengeful man whose wife was killed that night, and he holds Nick and the young man responsible for her death. While running through the rounds, Nick gets the attention of the police (he's breaking all sorts of laws out of necessity), and a detective on his trail suspects that Nick is a pawn in a much bigger game than anyone could suspect.

A virtual rehash of the theatrical release starring John Cena, *Reloaded* is a direct-to-video exercise with a much smaller budget, which means no exploding helicopters, no big names in the cast, and a by-the-numbers script that leaves no elbow room for its leading star, who tries his hardest to get in the spirit of things. WWE Entertainment has given Randy Orton his shot at being an action hero here, but it's just not a fair chance because they've cast him as a runner-up to Cena, who was given a much better opportunity in a bigger (and better) film. *Reloaded* is as "R" rated as it gets with hard profanity, but the violence and action is still restrained, and Orton doesn't have the charisma or screen presence to make an indelible impression. I'd be down for more movies starring Orton (who reminds me a little of early Dolph Lundgren), but I hope they're better than this one. Directed by Roel Reine, who also did *The Marine 2*, another WWE movie.

12 Rounds 3: Lockdown

2015 (Lionsgate DVD) (djm)

"Eight rounds, six bad guys. I'm liking the odds."

Good concepts for action movies can be found out there. *Die Hard* had a great one, and then there were the riffs on *Die Hard* like *Under Siege, Speed, Passenger 57,* and every other "guy gets stuck in a place with terrorists" movie. No matter how many times it gets knocked off, it's still a great idea. By the time the PG-13 rated WWE film *12 Rounds* (starring John Cena) was released, the riffing got to the point where the riff was lifting the idea of the third film in the *Die Hard* franchise, and while the idea of a guy being forced to run around a city, doing impossible tasks for a terrorist, is fairly sound, it was never an idea that anyone should have been copying, but it was what it was, and it gave us another big-screen effort from the hulked-out John Cena, who to this day has never been given the vehicle film he needs to have to make him a full-fledged action star.

The first *12 Rounds*, from director Renny Harlin (who did the far superior *Die Hard 2: Die Harder*), was bogged down by bloodless action, safe scripting, and a woefully weak villain who never stood a chance against Cena, who at least on the surface looks like a beast. When WWE eventually decided to spin *12 Rounds* into an in-name only sequel franchise like they were doing with *The Marine* (which was another PG-13 Cena-starring vehicle), they'd moved on to the next tier of in-house wrestling stars and gave Randy Orton his shot at the title with the direct-to-video *12 Rounds 2: Reloaded*. With Orton off shooting *The Condemned 2*, the next guy in line to headline another *12 Rounds* movie was Dean Ambrose (a.k.a. Jonathan Good).

Ambrose doesn't really look like much and hardly has the appearance of a wrestler (he never takes off his shirt in this film, so it's hard to tell), but he's got that everyman look to him, a little less like John McClane, a little more like the character

Jason Patrick played in, say, *Speed 2: Cruise Control*. That's a fair comparison. Ambrose is playing a cop named Shaw, who's just returned to work after an extended leave following a shooting that got his partner killed and got him wounded. Everyone on the force is jittery around him, and no one is able to make eye contact with him because at this point he seems like damaged goods. I like it so far. Another cop—whom we know is a sociopathic dirty detective named Burke (played by Roger E. Cross) —is a loose cannon everyone in the department loves, and to say that he makes up his own rules using his badge as a license to kill is an understatement. He has a squad of dirty cops at his beck and call, and the lady police chief eats out of the palm of his hand. It's perplexing because Shaw gets a bad rap for doing his job safely, but Burke is a celebrity for being all over the map. It's the antithesis of the cliché cop scenario, and so when things get wonky after Shaw realizes that Burke and his pals are dirty when he comes across a memory stick with damning evidence, the concept that the whole movie rests on kicks in. Instead of having Burke force Shaw to go through twelve grueling rounds of tasks throughout the city the way *Die Hard With a Vengeance* and the first two *12 Rounds* movies did, Shaw gets stuck in the police station (which is several stories high) after Burke pulls the fire alarm, instigating a mandatory evacuation so that the building is empty. Burke and his dirty cop friends (there seems to be nearly a dozen of them) take over the building, shut the electricity off, man the video cameras, and jam the radio signals so that no calls can come in or out, making sure that Shaw is a cornered animal with only his sidearm—with twelve rounds of ammunition—as his weapon. That's the idea this movie has, and while there's a seed of a good thought there, you have to realize that in reality that idea is ridiculous and moronic.

On the inside of the building you've got one cop with only twelve rounds of bullets to kill off just as many bad cops who've locked him in, and they're working their way towards him in groups, in pairs, and in singles, and while that sounds kind of okay, you keep thinking to yourself that this is taking place in a POLICE STATION where there might be other weapons stashed all over the place! Even after the hero shoots down and kills the bad guys, there will be OTHER WEAPONS to pick up and use, but he never thinks to pick up another weapon or go through some jackets and hanging belts for more clips. And what is happening on the outside of the police station? Does the fire department ever show up? No. When the other cops who've evacuation the station keep hearing gunfire in their place of work, do they ever do anything? No. The SWAT team is eventually called when it becomes apparent that Shaw has supposedly lost his mind and is killing other cops, but when do they enter the building? In the last five minutes of the ninety-minute movie.

Once Shaw is locked in and the gimmick of the film takes effect, the movie becomes a joke that isn't funny. I lost track of all the police men and women who are killed in the proceedings. Does Burke honestly believe for one second that he'll get away with the things he does in the movie? Does anyone in the film ever for one second consider the consequences of the mess they make? There's a scene where a bunch of guys shoot up the air vents in their own station.

You know what I thought when that happened? That's going to cost the department thousands of dollars in repairs. It gets to the point where the bad guys start picking up grenades to throw at Shaw, and nothing I could do could stop me from trying to reason through what these characters were thinking.

I love it when someone tries to make a new action star. A real-deal action star, the kind that comes from professional sports, martial arts, or wrestling. I'm always there to cheer the new guy or gal on, hoping that they'll find the perfect movie that fits them like a glove the way *The Perfect Weapon* was tailor-made for Jeff Speakman. That's what I'm talking about—that serendipitous occasion when the stars align and bring forth the chosen one to carry forth the hallowed baton into action movie history. Honestly, I'd never heard of Dean Ambrose before. I'm not into wrestling, but I trust the WWE to introduce us to guys who will last the test of time—big dudes like Hulk Hogan, Steve Austin, and Dwayne Johnson. It's not a terrible thing that Ambrose got the thankless gig of starring in the third entry in a second rate franchise. I mean, think about it. After Michael Dudikoff passed on doing *American Ninja 3: Blood Hunt*, David Bradley came into the picture and lasted a good while, starring in solid action and martial arts films, and carried the *American Ninja* franchise into its fifth and final entry. I'm not sure what kind of future Ambrose has in action films, but if *12 Rounds 3: Lockdown* is his only outing, then he got the short end of the baton. It's not his fault the movie is awful, and it's not even his fault that the movie has choppy, thrown-together action scenes. The director —Stephen Reynolds—should have taken a look at the junky, lazy script and said something before taking the job. WWE signed off on it and allowed this to happen, and it's by far the worst film from their canon—worse even than you can imagine. I've seen them all—and most of them in theaters (*12 Rounds 3: Lockdown* was released theatrically in a limited spread)—but this one is the pits. It makes the first *12 Rounds* (which was mediocre) look fantastic by comparison. That, my friends, is bad news.

24 Hours to Midnight

1985 (AIP VHS) (djm)

A woman named Devon Grady (Cynthia Rothrock) is in the witness protection program, and she's devastated when her husband is murdered by White Powder Chan's goons. White Powder Chan (Stack Pierce) is the head of a billion-dollar drug empire, and all he wants is to do away with Devon, a material witness who could put him away behind bars. Enraged by his hubris and disregard of the law, Devon dons a ninja suit and systematically slaughters all of White Powder Chan's men, leaving him for last. On her trail are two detectives, who follow the trail of carnage she leaves behind.

Sounds good, right? First of all, you've got Cynthia Rothrock as a ninja! Second, you've got Stack Pierce (a black actor) playing a character named White Powder Chan! Third, the title's kind of cool, yeah? Here's what the movie is *really* like: Rothrock only shot a few scenes for this film, and her scenes (two of which are fight scenes) are

repeated over and over. Every time we see her in the ninja suit, it's not her, but a body double. Add to that the fact that her voice was dubbed over by Brinke Stevens, and all that's left of Rothrock are those few scenes that are replayed. The story is ludicrous and was most likely fashioned around Rothrock's few moments. The title doesn't have anything to do with the rest of the movie. So what's left? A pile of junk. Steer clear of this time-waster. Rothrock completists should probably avoid it. Directed by Leo Fong, who made a slew of ninja pictures throughout the 1980s. He also has a small role in this film as "Mr. Big."

Twin Dragon Encounter

1986 (Vidmark VHS) (djm)

If you've never seen Michael and Martin McNamara in action, you're missing out. The McNamaras (mustachioed twins) starred in two movies and appeared in *Back in Action* with Billy Blanks and Roddy Piper, but their two starring vehicles—*Twin Dragon Encounter* and *Dragon Hunt*—are amazing motion pictures. In real life they made names for themselves in the kickboxing world and ran their own martial arts studio, and they got a fire in their guts to be movie stars and made these two movies where they basically play themselves. The movies are homegrown action pictures featuring the twins running around forests, saving their girlfriends, and defeating "a private army" run by a crazed blond villain who chomps on cigars. The twins chop wood, crack jokes, and get in the action and hit *hard*. When they kick guys in the face it looks real. They drive ATVs, shoot arrows, and encourage their girlfriends to do karate. They do all this to a synth rock score with original songs.

I dunno, man. I like the McNamaras, but I can't really tell you why. Their movies are laughably bad, earnest to a fault, and completely sincere as far as I can tell. I like these guys because they're being entirely honest. They think they're making awesome stuff, and in a way they did. It's obvious that they worked hard, but it's also obvious that they see themselves as mighty warriors. And that's cool with me. I'd rather watch *Twin Dragon Encounter* and *Dragon Hunt* again than rewatch most of the direct-to-video movies Steven Seagal made. No contest. The McNamaras made a (small) mark in the world of martial arts action movies, and I salute them. Nice going, guys. Directed by Paul Dunlop.

Twin Dragons

1992/1999 (Dimension DVD) (djm)

Released in 1992 in Hong Kong, but in 1999 in the US by the Weinsteins in a slightly shorter version, *Twin Dragons* stars Jackie Chan as twins who never knew the other one existed until their worlds collide when they're adults. One of them grew up with prestige and culture and became a famous orchestra conductor, while the other one had none of that and became a martial arts–proficient car mechanic. When their paths nearly cross one day, they manage to confuse their girlfriends, and through funny circumstances, their girls end up with the wrong brothers, which begins a chain reaction of mistaken identities and major foul-ups where the brothers don't realize what's going on until they both inadvertently end up fighting bad guys for reasons they never quite comprehend. In one scene the mechanic brother ends up on stage in front of thousands who have come to watch him conduct a concert, and he does a sort of kung fu version of conducting, which brings down the house. Later, his brother the conductor gets into fights he can't win, which confuses the bad guys who thought he could kick their asses.

The right balance of slapstick and action gives *Twin Dragons* a solid foundation to build from, and the results are pretty satisfying. The comedy was never *too* silly and the action was never *too* serious, so fans of Chan's greater body of work will feel right at home. It's all in good fun, and newcomers to Hong Kong action films or to Jackie Chan should have a good time. Directing duties were split between Ringo Lam (*Maximum Risk*) and Tsui Hark (*Double Team*). Weird trivia: Michael and Martin McNamara, the kickboxing twin action stars of *Twin Dragon Encounter* and *Dragon Hunt*, sued the distribution company for copyright infringement over the phrase "Twin Dragons" when this was released to theaters in North America.

Twins

1988 (Universal DVD) (djm)

"We're twins! We're basically the same!"

A scientific experiment involving gene manipulation and selective breeding produces twins: Julius and Vincent. They are separated at birth, and decades later, Julius (Arnold Schwarzenegger), who has been raised with the utmost care and comfort with culture, class, and extreme physical training, learns that he has a twin brother somewhere in the world. He leaves the island where he was raised and embarks on a trip to Los Angeles, where his twin, Vincent (Danny DeVito), is living as a scoundrel and small-time crook. When they meet, it's of course a comedy of big proportions as Julius tries to convince Vincent that they're "basically the same." They go on a road trip together with two girlfriends in tow (Chloe Webb and Kelly Preston), and they get into some trouble with an assassin who sets his sights on Vincent, whose latest car theft has landed him a top-secret engine in the trunk worth five million bucks. It's up to Julius—with his incredible strength and physical prowess—to protect him. Once that's all done, they begin to like (and even love) each other, and their final step is to come to terms with who they are and to find their mother.

It was a genius move to give Arnold a comedy vehicle, and *Twins* is a perfect fit for him. Director Ivan Reitman (who also did Arnold's successive comedies, *Kindergarten Cop* and

Junior) allows Arnold to be himself and show off his physical awesomeness while fitting in some laughs. The danger and intrigue in the movie is very PG-rated, but that's fine. It's fun for the family. Arnold is quite the comedian. For years, he talked about doing *Triplets* with DeVito and Eddie Murphy.

Twin Sitters

1994 (Sony DVD) (djm)

"You boys really did a job on those hoods. Where did you learn to handle yourselves like that? Military?"
"Nah, we were fat kids. Fat kids either got to learn how to fight or learn how to hurt. We got tired of hurtin'."

Peter and David Paul star as Peter and David Falcone, two overbearing and bumbling twin brothers who have a talent in the culinary arts but don't have the capital to open up a restaurant of their own. They do, however, have enough money to make payments on an obscenely large monster truck, which they drive around town, and their ridiculous wardrobe implies that they have money to burn. They're at a park one afternoon where a botched kidnapping/hit on a whistle-blower takes place, and they end up saving the lives of some civilians and discouraging the hitmen/kidnappers. It turns out that a businessman named Hillhurst (Jared Martin) is in the process of testifying against a slimy tycoon named Leland Stromm (former James Bond actor George Lazenby), and now that Hillhurst has a hit on his head, he needs protection for his nephews, who are also in danger. He hires the muscle-headed Falcone twins to babysit his twin(!) nephews (Christian and Joseph Cousins), who are obviously inspired by the Macaulay Culkin character from *Home Alone*. The kids wreak havoc for the kid-at-heart Falcones (lots of pratfalls, pranks, and jokes) until the Falcones find a way into their hearts. When the hitmen and thugs come calling, it's basically *3 Ninjas* and *Home Alone*.

Twin Sitters was the swan song for the Barbarian brothers, and rightfully so. By this stage, they had become jokes, and their juvenile attempts at humor are painful at times to watch and listen to, but it's hard to be a hater. It's amazing that they were able to last as long as they did, but what's even more amazing is that this movie followed on the footsteps of the extremely similar *Mr. Nanny*, starring Hulk Hogan. That movie has virtually the same premise and script and the same African American actress (Mother Love) in the same role. If there are any hardcore fans of the Barbarian brothers, *Twin Sitters* should be a heaping portion of goodness, but for all others, it's grating, ridiculous, and an affront to the medium. To top it off, there was a soundtrack release with songs performed by the Pauls. Directed by John Paragon, who also did *Double Trouble*, a slightly better movie starring the twins.

Two Wrongs Make a Right

1987 (Unicorn Home Video VHS) (JS)

Ivan Rogers is more than just a martial arts master and obscure action guy—he's a veritable self-made, movie-minded renaissance man. Rogers had a stint in the music business but soon grew tired of the lifestyle and found himself returning to one of his other major interests: karate! He found success in the kickboxing circuit and gained some recognition with a world rating, eventually leading him to be noticed by a Videodisc distribution company by the name of INEDCO Productions that wanted him to create an educational home video instructional on karate and self-defense. Rogers would write, produce, and star in what would become *Karate and Self-Defense: Step-by-Step Instructions from Black Belt Master Ivan Rogers*. This experience was all Ivan needed to invigorate and propel his passion for writing, producing and starring in films. Though he's not as prolific as some (and his films are decidedly independent productions), his general enterprise and persistence in the face of adversity (which he faced plenty of once he entered the movie biz) is something to be noted and applauded.

Two Wrongs Make a Right is an exemplary passion project for Rogers as he wrote, produced, and starred in this palatable but ultimately routine crime drama. The plot is simple and thematically threadbare: Rogers plays the perpetually calm and cool, essentially stoic club owner Fletcher Quinn. When he refuses to give the mob some dough (for "real estate" purposes), they waltz into his club with a blaze of bullets, killing his friends and patrons alike. Quinn gives chase with a gun in hand, only to see his friend killed in cold blood, and then have a cop come up behind him with the assumption that he's the perp. Things settle down at the club, but Quinn's got a chip on his shoulder from a previous incident where the cops couldn't nail down the guy who murdered his father. So what'd he do? He took the law into his own hands. And that's exactly what he's gonna do again!

The standards are mostly all here in *Two Wrongs*: incompetent cops, loathsome mob goons, a bored nympho at the mob base, and the stoic, hardened anti-hero played by Rogers. The problem? There's just no action. There's one unimpressive bar brawl, an off-screen girlfriend beating, and some brief hand-busting bottle torture . . . but that's it. This one never made it to DVD, probably attributed to problems with distribution rights and the fact that this movie is pretty flat. Unicorn Video VHS Collector enthusiasts will want to track this one down (along with another Rogers flick called *Crazed Cop*), as it's apt to be relegated to an analog-only existence forevermore.

T

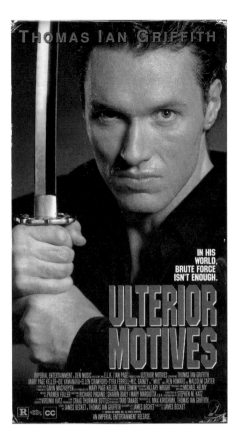

VHS artwork for Imperial's *Ulterior Motives*. Author's collection.

Ulterior Motives

1993 (Imperial VHS) (djm)

This is an intriguing action/thriller from Imperial Entertainment that showcases Thomas Ian Griffith as a charming hero of questionable integrity. He plays a private eye named Jack Blaylock, whose office is literally at a booth in a Japanese restaurant whose past is muddled with previous run-ins with the law and a prison record. A reporter named Erica (Mary Page Keller, Griffith's real-life wife) comes to him with a job. Will he help her steal some government documents from the Yakuza, who seem to be dealing in espionage? Of course he will, and when they encounter some resistance, he uses his kenpo martial arts to quell all issues. Erica is onto a big story, but she places her trust in the wrong people. It turns out that Jack is working for her corrupt uncle who has hired Jack to kill his niece if she gets too close to the heart of his corruption, which involves hiring Japanese men to pose as Yakuza to confuse her. When Jack is ordered to murder Erica, he turns on his employer and saves Erica's life. When she realizes that he isn't what he seems to be and has been lying to her all along, she knows he is a man of murky intent. The ending is surprisingly effective, as Jack is forced to run from the law, alone and wounded.

Griffith's character makes an interesting case study in this film. He's heroic, but we see him do bad things here. He smiles a lot, which made me nervous. There are plenty of scenes with him fighting, and his signature weapon in the film is a sword, which he uses a few times, once to chop a dead woman to pieces. The chemistry between the actors is good, and the

tone should pique your interest. This was not the movie I thought it was going to be. James Lew (from *The Perfect Weapon*) has a small role. Directed by James Becket.

The Ultimate Fight

(a.k.a. **The Process**)

1998 (Lionsgate DVD) (djm)

Ernie Reyes Jr. from *Teenage Mutant Ninja Turtles II: The Secret of the Ooze* and his famous martial arts instructor father Ernie Reyes Sr. collaborated for this throwaway little action movie that takes place in and around one location, a farmhouse in the country. Reyes Jr. directed his dad and his younger brother Lee (from *American Ninja 5*) here, and what ended up happening is that Reyes Jr. got to have some fun with a camera while directing his friends and family in a homemade movie with a barely-there plot. Reyes Jr. plays a smart-aleck named Jesse, who is out one night and gets in a fight with some punks. He's saved by an immigrant stick fighter named Pinoy (Shishir Inocalla) from the Philippines, and they strike up a friendship. Jesse takes him home to meet his dad (Reyes Sr.) and some of his pals, and while in the introductory stage of getting acquainted with each other, the gang that they defeated comes calling on them, overwhelming the farmhouse and threatening to kill everyone within. Meanwhile, there's a pointless subplot about a neo-Nazi drug lord (played by a ridiculous Corin Nemic) out to get Pinoy for reasons of his own.

Paper-thin and aggressively unappealing, *The Ultimate Fight* is a blight on the house of Reyes, simply because Ernie Jr., who's shown so much promise over the years in films like *Surf Ninjas* (no classic) and *The Rundown*, devoted himself to writing, directing, and starring in this embarrassing movie. The fight scenes are okay, but if that's all you're getting then it's basically a showreel. The character he plays verges on vexatious, and the tone throughout is decidedly misogynistic and vile. I've always been a fan of Reyes Jr. This is not a movie his fans should see.

Ultimate Force

2005 (BCI DVD) (djm)

A government science program takes soldiers and experiments on them, and one soldier/police officer named Axon Rey—code name "Sphinx"—fails a mission by showing mercy. As punishment he's sent to an island where other disgraced soldiers are dropped. Once on the island, Axon (played by Croatian UFC fighter Mirko Cro-Cop Filipovic) must battle each soldier to the death and make his way back to civilization to get revenge on the covert organization that put him in this position.

There's a really good movie somewhere within *Ultimate Force*, but it's not easy to find. It was filmed in Eastern Europe in English with associates of Filipovic's, many of whom were a part of an anti-terrorist unit that Filipovic

was once a member of. The action scenes are quick and anticlimactic, and Filipovic—while genuine—is a bit of a wet blanket on screen. The digital photography is washed out, and the color seems to have been drained out. The whole movie is on the depressing side, which is strange considering that this could have been a new *Universal Soldier* with vibrant action and stunt work. As it stands, it's a limp addition to the canon of crossovers from UFC. Despite all that, it's of interest to fans of the genre. Some viewers will like it more than I did. Written and directed by Mark Burson.

The Ultimate Game

2001 (T Entertainment DVD) (djm)

A secret martial arts team competition is held once a year on a private island, and the prize for the winning team is a million dollars to split amongst themselves. A family man named Jack (J. D. Rifkin, who didn't pursue more films after this) is invited to participate, but he first needs to convince his wife and son that fighting (possibly to the death) is a good move for their family. After that, he must assemble a team of the best fighters he can find, and once he's got a mostly complete team, he realizes that someone is trying to kill him and stop him before he even reaches the island. Several attempts are made on his life, and being the martial arts expert that he is, he's able to survive the attacks and prepare to face the reality that this will be the fight of his life. A separate team of fighters, led by a deadly hit man named Slater (Paul Logan from *Blazing Force*), has assembled all of their fighters, but one of them—Rick (T. J. Storm from *Black Cobra*)—defects when he realizes that his team is sponsored by a corrupt businessman who has targeted Jack and his crew for death. Rick joins Jack's team, and once their unit is complete, they go to the private island and begin fighting the other teams in organized fights. The fight to the finish between Jack and Slater reveals who has the most honor and which team deserves the million-dollar cash prize.

Simplistic and sincere (maybe to a fault), *The Ultimate Game* is precisely the sort of film you are expecting it to be, and while it's a little on the late side for kickboxing tournament movies, it at least has three central stars who are obviously from the world of martial arts. Star Rifkin has a big, muscular frame and is able to do his flips and kicks with a smile on his face, while Logan and Storm (who choreographed all the fights) each get more than their share of screen time to showcase their unique brands of martial arts. The movie's silly, but if you're reading this book, then at some point in your list-making for films to watch you should put it somewhere towards the bottom and catch up with it some day. Directed by Jack Kaprielian and Kevin Derek.

Ultimate Prey

2000 (Digiview DVD) (CD)

"Men have been hunters since they've been on this planet. And these men have hunted every kind of prey there is, and now finally they graduate to the ultimate prey . . . men."

Jon Brant (Benjamin Maccabee) is a family man and a workaholic. He busts his ass every day to try to make ends meet. Then, one day, things take a wrong turn for him. Business is slow, and his boss is forced to lay him off until things pick up. To add insult to injury, he comes home early from work only to find his wife in bed with another man. In his moment of darkness, there's a tiny light shining: a phone call from a man named Richard Walton (Joe Estevez) offering him a high-paying job. He quickly meets up with the mysterious man only to be drugged. When he wakes up, he finds himself trapped with a small group of people. They find out they're to be hunted by men who have paid good money to do so. Jon isn't about to go down like this and has a few aces up his sleeve, and before you know it, the hunted becomes the hunter.

Benjamin Maccabee (*Deadly Eyes*) is 100 percent the real deal. After spending four years in the Israeli military, this jack of all trades decided to try his hand at making movies. *Ultimate Prey* has Maccabee pulling quadruple duty as actor, director, producer, and writer. There's nothing really interesting about the story—it's essentially another retelling of *The Most Dangerous Game* but Maccabee is such an interesting individual, *Ultimate Prey* becomes essential viewing for those who enjoy swimming in a "B"-movie ocean of entertainment. If low-tech weapons, martial arts action, and squibless shootouts are your thing, you may enjoy this.

Ultimate Target

(a.k.a. **Ides of March**)

2000 (NOV) (CD)

"Whoo, damn, do not go down there, you know what I'm talkin' about? I dropped a motherfucking bomb down that motherfucker. I'll tell you what man, Angelo better be hooking up some more butt wipe in that motherfucker. I wore that shit thin—damn! What? What, I smell like shit or something?"

Thomas Cane (Gary Daniels) has what appears to be a simple life. He works hard and has a loving wife and daughter, but he's keeping a secret from them. You see, Thomas is a hitman; he earns his living killing people. He works for a corporation of hired killers, and they're an interesting bunch. He only associates with them when he has to, so it comes as no real surprise that he's double-crossed them in order to get out of the life. The only way he and his family will ever be able to live a normal life is if he takes them all out on his own. He sends his family to a safe place while he prepares for the battle of a lifetime.

Ultimate Target is a difficult movie to find, released only on DVD in Greece. The film experienced financial troubles and was never properly finished. Knowing this, the sloppy editing, awkward pacing, and uneven tone should be expected. This is a Gary Daniels (*Fist of the North Star, Recoil*) film with action choreographed by Akihiro Noguchi (*Drive*), so it's worth seeking it out. Daniels delivers where it counts with several set pieces to showcase some wickedly furious action. It tries to have a quirky sense of humor (some of it works, most of it doesn't), most notably in the scenes featuring Christopher Stapleton (*Black Friday*) and John Koyama (*High Voltage*). It's hard to criticize director Darren Doane because this wasn't his final vision of the film—the producers put it together and we'll never get the chance to see a true final version of it. What we do have is a group of cool actors (Michael Madsen, David Fralick, and George Cheung also star) in a patchwork picture that wants to be a martial arts *Pulp Fiction*.

The Ultimate Weapon

1998 (Avalanche DVD) (djm)

"... so . . . we're kinda like the good guys here."

In a period of making "R"-rated action movies, Terry "Hulk" Hogan starred in several similar straight-to-video (or straight-to-cable) movies where he had shortly cropped dark hair. In *The Ultimate Weapon*, he plays a disgruntled mercenary named Ben Cutter who is haunted by an earlier mission where he failed to protect a young girl. On his latest mission, he realizes that the men paying him are terrorists, and after he accomplishes his job and gets paid, he turns against them, inciting a war with them. The terrorists (IRA guys) go after his family—namely his estranged stripper daughter—and Cutter has to quickly reconnect with her if he's going to have a chance in saving her. Along for the ride is his new partner (who's the son of a former friend and ally) and Cutter's girlfriend, who is exasperated with him for being a complete loser at relational conflicts. Cutter's got his hands full, basically.

Fans of Hulk Hogan may want to stick with his family-friendly movies instead of venturing into the generic hallways of his "R"-rated career. His *Shadow Warrior* movies weren't spectacular and *The Ultimate Warrior*—which feels related to those—is basically more of the same, but without the cool supporting cast. Jon Cassar, who made the two *Shadow Warrior* movies, directed.

Undefeatable

1993 (Hen's Tooth DVD) (djm)

Kristi Jones (Cynthia Rothrock) tropes around the streets with her (Asian) gang, looking for fights for quick cash. She uses her winnings to pay for her sister to go to college, and when a psychotic kickboxing champion fixates on her sister and brutally murders her, Jones goes on a rampage in search of the killer. A martial arts–proficient detective (John Miller from *Honor and Glory*) is constantly at odds with Jones, but when he gets the picture that she's closer to finding the killer than he is, they team up. The killer (played by Don Niam, who is memorable here) has a mother complex and kills women who look like his abused wife, and he's incredibly intimidating when he fights, so when he goes up against Jones and the detective, the fight is worthwhile.

Godfrey Ho (Hall), who worked with Rothrock more than any other director, made this slasher/martial arts hybrid. Some of the scenes are unintentionally humorous, but Rothrock and Miller made a good screen team. They fought against each other in *Honor and Glory*. Niam plays the psycho role really well, and it's strange that he didn't go on to other things. Same goes for Miller, who clearly had a handle on martial arts, and physically, he looks great on screen. Rothrock delivers a performance worthy of her solid reputation, and the pace of the film is certainly satisfactory. Horror fans might be interested to see some of the gore scenes, but martial arts and Rothrock fans should be pleased.

Undercurrent

1998 (Avalanche DVD) (CD)

"Do you know what a lifer once told me in prison, Eddie? He said, 'When you take everything away that a man's got, he's got nothing left to lose.' So what the fuck do I have to lose by blowing your fat fucking head off?"

Mike Aguayo (Lorenzo Lamas) is a former police officer fresh out of prison for extortion. He's a pretty straight shooter, taking the fall for his mentor, Eddie (Frank Vincent). He travels to Puerto Rico to work with Eddie at an upper-class strip club. This is Puerto Rico, and there's always more ways to make money, so Eddie introduces Mike to Carlos Rivera (Philip Anthony-Rodriguez), a businessman with a proposition for him. He wants to get rid of his wife so he offers Mike $250,000 to seduce her, just long enough to get pictures of the indiscretion. Mike agrees, only to help Eddie clear a debt with Carlos. When Mike finally does meet Renee Rivera (Brenda Strong), things get far more complicated than he ever expected and the twists, turns, and double-crosses begin.

Undercurrent is more of an erotic thriller than an action film. Lamas turns in a strong performance and helps to make the film rather engaging. He doesn't really partake in much

U

fighting; a punch or elbow slam here and there is about the extent of it. Most of the action he gets is from the female persuasion, and there's plenty of skin on display. The movie has a gorgeous backdrop and the flamenco-inspired score adds to the tone. If you're not expecting a bunch of typical Lamas-style martial arts action and explosions, this one's got its moments. From director Frank Kerr.

Undercut

2004 (The Stunt People DVD) (djm)

A government-hired American ninja named Eric (played by Eric Jacobus) loses his job after he botches a terrorist takedown. Eric's replacement is a Chinese ninja named Andy (Andy Leung), who flaunts his new position to the despondent Eric. In no time at all, Eric can't pay his bills, loses his apartment, can't afford to cure his ailing dog, and spirals into depression. When his dog dies, he decides to go after Andy and fight him to the death, and maybe—just maybe—get his old job back with the government. When the two ninjas fight their issues out, the government fires them both, and they decide to form an alliance together and work for the French government.

The Stunt People is a cool production company that showcases working-class martial artists and allows them to shine in completely independent short films and feature-length films that are shot on shoestring budgets. Eric Jacobus, a hapkido specialist who would go on to write, direct, and star in the stellar *Death Grip*, is the lead guy in this goofy short film (thirty-four minutes), and even though it's a comedy, he's still able to show off his impressive skills in the martial arts. It's a little too silly of a film for my tastes, but years later he would do some great stuff, including the fantastic short film *Rope-a-Dope*. If you end up discovering Jacobus at some point in your travels through action stars, *Undercut* might not be the best place to affirm his potential, but it's fun if you're in the right frame of mind. Written and directed by Stephen Reedy.

Underdog Kids

2015 (Anchor Bay DVD) (djm)

Billed as "action adventure for the whole family," Phillip Rhee's PG-rated *Karate Kid*-inspired outing *Underdog Kids* is Rhee's first film since 1998's *Best of the Best IV: Without Warning*. For those unfamiliar with Rhee, he built for himself a small niche in martial arts and action cinema as the man who created the *Best of the Best* franchise that spanned a little more than a decade and had four entries. For a while there it seemed like he would go on to have a great career as an action star, but he withdrew himself from the scene, and only now has reemerged with this family-friendly riff on his own *Best of the Best* pictures.

Rhee plays Jimmy "The Lightning Bolt," a former MMA champion who suffered a serious injury in a car crash, and he rides into his old neighborhood on his motorcycle to reconnect with the owner of the gym he used to frequent. It turns out that his instructor—an old codger who also runs the community center—is trying to work with some ragtag kids from the neighborhood, each one of them a misfit child with his or her own hang-ups. One kid is overweight and gets bullied by his father (played by Beau Bridges), one is having problems with his single mother, and another one is known around town as "Psycho," but deep down he's just a stutterer who happens to have some talent in the martial arts. Jimmy sees some potential in these children, and since he's in a lull in his career he agrees to train them in the martial arts and get them ready for the big tournament on the horizon. The rival team is coached by an old nemesis of Jimmy's, so the climax has some resonance in a *Karate Kid* sort of way when the misfit kids actually turn out to be a better and more honorable team than their rivals.

Writer/director/producer/star Rhee has always had his heart in the right place when it comes to trying to tell stories with a message. The first *Best of the Best* set the template of where he was at in his life at the time, and it's basically his take on *Rocky*, and it's easily the best work he's ever done as an actor and writer, and it's also one of the very few movies that can almost bring me to tears. The second *Best of the Best* film got a little off-track with the over-the-top violence, but Rhee's character remained honorable and true to himself, retaining Rhee's own integrity as a screenwriter and performer. The third and fourth *Best of the Best* films were his training ground as a director and while those pictures lost what made the first two films so integral to the martial arts genre, they gave Rhee a chance to explore action rather than the martial arts, and he always tried to inject some humanity and humility into his character.

With *Underdog Kids*, the story is as tried and true as the Disney-fied sports film can be. This is a story everyone has seen: from *The Mighty Ducks* to *McFarland U.S.A.*, but with Rhee's own spin with his background in taekwondo and the martial arts, the movie somehow feels just about fresh. The message is simple and some families will really take to it, while more sophisticated viewers will be bored by it. It's interesting how audiences (particularly of action films in general) have moved on from enjoying movies with real martial arts action stars to gorging themselves on films saturated with overly complicated editing techniques and special effects because *Underdog Kids* is a back-to-basics movie with a limited budget that families might actually appreciate if they would give it a chance. Granted, the movie descends into cliché and—goodness help me—fart jokes, but it's got a real-deal action star in the center of it in a coach-relegated role who has simmered down in his maturity and acts as a shepherd to a bunch of unruly children who are damn lucky to have someone like him teaching them how to kick and defend themselves from bullies. *Underdog Kids* isn't going to ignite Rhee's career, but I'm thrilled to see him back in front of the camera.

Underground

2007 (City Lights DVD) (CD)

"With a total of $1.2 million staked on this tournament, the fighters are competing for a 500,000-pound prize. The winning backer will also receive 500,000. The remaining 200,000 . . . well . . . let's call it a handling fee."

In the seemingly harmless suburbs of the United Kingdom, a group of wealthy investors are putting the money together to host an underground martial arts tournament. Each of the six investors handpicks two fighters for their team. The fighters have all been found from various walks of life: teachers, ex-cons, police, models, etc., and they're given the opportunity to win five hundred thousand pounds. Fighters are paired off in an elimination-style tournament. The investors have their own side bets, and together they will decide who fights who. With so much money on the line, as long as the fighters put on a good show, the investors will continue to put on the brutal show. The cast is filled with up-and-coming stuntmen-turned-actors including Mark Strange from *The Medallion* and Joey Ansah, who fought Jean-Claude Van Damme in *Alien Uprising*.

Underground is such a strange film; there's little to no character development, and the story doesn't get much simpler. We get plenty of character stereotypes, and there's very little dialogue spoken by the fighters. Their main job is to fight, and they do plenty of it. The action is neatly choreographed, with each fighter using his or her own distinct style. They're only identified by their professions and only as the film progresses do we learn anything about them personally (mostly what it is they're fighting for). Eventually the characters become three-dimensional people and then they begin to show they have a conscience. It's a decent enough film; sometimes it works and sometimes it doesn't but it does display some promising talent. Director Chee Keong Chung (*Bodyguard: A New Beginning*) at least attempted something different and even with mixed results, it manages to be entertaining.

Under Siege

1992 (Warner DVD) (MJ)

"I'll tell you what. I'll carry everything, if you kill whoever we run into, all right?"

After one of the most confident debuts in the history of action cinema in 1988 with *Above the Law*, Steven Seagal continued to increase his profile in the industry with successful entries at the box office such as *Marked For Death* and *Out For Justice*. For his next film, Seagal reunited with director Andrew Davis after their successful collaboration on *Above the Law*. *Under Siege* takes place on the U.S.S. *Missouri* en route from Hawaii to San Francisco for decommissioning. By coincidence, the captain's birthday falls on one of the days the ship is at sea and one of his executive officers has been planning a surprise party for him. Unknown to the captain and the crew, the party is being used as an opportunity to land mercenaries on the *Missouri* and hijack it, with the intention of selling off its inventory of nuclear weapons to the highest bidder. After the ship has been taken over, the mercenaries discover that one member of the crew is unaccounted for, the captain's personal cook, Casey Ryback (Seagal). As they begin to search the ship for him and their men start to disappear, it becomes obvious that this man is more than just a cook.

Pitched to WB studio executives as "*Die Hard* on a boat," *Under Siege* was probably one of the easiest pitch meetings of all time. Steven Seagal had proven to be a reliable bet at the box office and Andrew Davis had established himself as a reliable director of action films and thrillers, having just directed Gene Hackman and Tommy Lee Jones in *The Package,* and with another project in development with the studio, a feature film version of *The Fugitive. Under Siege* would mark Seagal's greatest success at the box office, exposing him to a much wider audience than he'd ever had and would cement his status as an action star. It's easy to see why. The film was shot aboard the U.S.S. *Alabama* while it was docked in Mobile Bay, Alabama, and was made with the full support of the US Navy, which immediately gives the film an authenticity many action films do not normally have. Davis cast the film with strong personalities, starting with Tommy Lee Jones as William Stranix, a rogue CIA operative who is the architect of the plan to hijack the *Missouri* and sell off its payload. Stranix is a doppelganger to Seagal's character Casey Ryback, a former Navy SEAL captain with a similar Intelligence background who lost his rank after striking a superior officer. *Under Siege* is the rare Seagal film that offers an antagonist that might actually pose a believable threat to the hero. The cast also includes other strong personalities such as Gary Busey and Nick Mancuso, along with several actors that Andrew Davis is known to use in all of his films, and many of them would gather together again for *The Fugitive*, Davis's next film.

Under Siege 2: Dark Territory

1995 (Warner DVD) (djm)

"*This* I'm trained for."

In the summer of 1995, Steven Seagal was about to launch what would be the most expensive production he would ever star in. The sequel to his biggest hit to date, *Under Siege 2: Dark Territory* carries on the tradition started by *Die Hard* where terrorists take over a relatively small space and are systematically taken out by a hero who has found himself in the wrong place at the right time. Part-time cook and full-time Navy SEAL badass Casey Ryback (Seagal) is on a train

with his niece Sarah (teenaged Katherine Heigl) when terrorists hijack the train and use it as a mobile operating base while they commandeer a particle beam to blow up cities from space. Washington and the entire eastern seaboard are threatened with obliteration, and while billions of dollars are processed for ransom, Ryback goes to work on the terrorists. In charge is a computer geek named Travis Dane (Eric Bogosian), whose mercenary commandos are led by Penn (Everett McGill). Mercenaries under Penn's command are played by Patrick Kilpatrick (*Death Warrant*) and Peter Greene (*Fist of the Warrior*), and it's fun seeing them get dispatched throughout the film. A heavy-duty climax involving explosions, a train collision on a bridge, and a helicopter escape relies extensively on special effects, but it's a grand finale.

Seagal's knack for sensitivity and soft-spoken wisdom in the midst of wrist snapping and neck breaking is on full-fledged display here, but the plot doesn't really require much from him or from the audience for that matter. By this point in Seagal's career, it was already expected of him to deliver exactly what he had become known for, and in that case, *Dark Territory* delivers. Not as big of a hit as the first film, it might have needed a slightly more interesting marketing campaign, but audiences pretty much got what they paid for. A rich score by Basil Poledouris helps things out immensely. New Zealander Geoff Murphy (*Freejack*) directed.

Under the Gun

1995 (Image DVD) (djm)

A former hockey player star named Frank Torrance (Richard Norton) goes into the nightclub business, but in order to pay his bills he's had to dip into a life of crime, which brings all sorts of characters into his place of business. He's got the mob in the waiting room while the police are on the phone, and he's having a difficult time juggling his priorities. The best way he knows to handle tough customers is to use his martial arts, and most of the time he gets the best of the situation. When his debts get out of hand, he dabbles a bit in drug running, but that too gets out of hand when corrupt police officers begin investigating his affairs. At the breaking point, he gets a visit from an old friend (played by real-life kickboxing champ Kathy Long from *The Stranger*), and for a while she's able to help him fight off all comers, but when she's killed, Torrance is all alone and in the middle of a mess he might be too exhausted to handle.

With a film noir vibe and a simple-enough premise, *Under the Gun* gives Norton the center stage, and he's great in what might be considered an anti-hero role. The entire film is set in and around one central location (the nightclub under renovations), so there's definitely a low-budget sensibility to the proceedings, but fans of Norton will be pleased. Kathy Long's role is basically a cameo, but when she violently exited, I was shocked. Sorry for the spoiler. Written and directed by Matthew George.

Undisputed

2002 (Miramax DVD) (CD)

"Because I put people in body bags and get paid a lot of money for it. Because I'm a big, bad, black motherfucker, that's why nobody believes me."

George "The Iceman" Chambers (Ving Rhames) is the world heavyweight boxing champ and on top of the world until he finds himself in prison on a rape charge. He's stripped of his title, and his fans are turning against him. Boxer Monroe Hutchen (Wesley Snipes), also incarcerated, was on his way to fame and fortune and threw it all away in an uncontrollable moment of jealous rage. In prison, he keeps to himself most of the time, even when there's a moment or two to gain himself a bit of notoriety. Old-school gangster Mendy Ripstein (Peter Falk) calls the shots behind bars and pulls together a match between the two titans. Even though they are in prison, the corruption from the higher-ups and the guards is so pronounced that the deals being offered can't be refused. Hutchen does it for the pride and Chambers sees it as a chance to make a deal for an early release. Both men are ready to fight, and the best man will win.

Undisputed is never about the action, it's all about the build-up. It's the tension and anticipation to the big fight driving the picture. When the moment finally arrives, it's sort of bittersweet and just a tiny bit underwhelming. Wesley Snipes (*Drop Zone*) was in fantastic shape for this film and fights like a pro. His character is at peace with his situation, and it's a strong dramatic turn for the actor. Ving Rhames (*Pulp Fiction*) is a complete beast. His character is despicable, and the audience wants to see him fall. When the actual fight plays out, there's no way it lives up to the hype and build-up. It should have put audiences on the verge of frenzy when it plays out, but it just never does. Veteran action director Walter Hill (*Extreme Prejudice*) builds the excitement but fails to follow it through to the end. The film was followed by two superior sequels, *Undisputed II: Last Man Standing* and *Undisputed III: Redemption,* both directed by Isaac Florentine. Michael Jai White played Chambers in the first sequel.

Undisputed II:
Last Man Standing

2006 (New Line DVD) (CD)

While in Russia, George "Iceman" Chambers (Michael Jai White) finds himself framed and thrown into a gulag prison where he's expected to compete in the underground prison fights. The champion is prisoner Yuri Boyka (Scott Adkins), who wants nothing more than to get his hands on the American. Chambers is busy learning about humility while Boyka has focused all his energy on Chambers. When Chambers loses a match, his drive and attitude change and the training will never stop until he meets Boyka fair and square in the ring. There is a ton of money on the line and both men have a vendetta that needs settling.

In a very rare instance, *Undisputed II: Last Man Standing* is a far better film than the original. It's a sequel to the 2002 Walter Hill-directed film that starred Wesley Snipes and Ving Rhames. This one is directed by Isaac Florentine (*High Voltage*), and he undeniably knows how to shoot action. He is arguably one of the best directors working in the genre today. J. J. Perry (*Haywire*) choreographs the fights with a no-nonsense manner that's both stylish and brutal. Michael Jai White (*Blood and Bone*) takes over the George "Iceman" Chambers role (originally played by Ving Rhames) and runs away with it. There is so much energy in his performance that his character (who comes off as somewhat unlikable during the first part of the film) goes through some major transformations during the film. He learns to become a better man due to the experience he is forced to go through. To see him go head to head with Boyka is nothing short of true excitement. Scott Adkins (*Ninja*) owns the role of Boyka. He is absolutely vicious from his first introduction to the final showdown. Not only are both men incredible fighters, but they are portrayed by actors who are better than many would expect them to be, giving us a story that is simple yet emotionally charged. Some terrific supporting performances from Eli Danker (*Wanted: Dead or Alive*), Ben Cross (*The Russian Specialist*), Mark Ivanir (*The Delta Force 3*), and Ken Lerner (*Hit List*), help make *Undisputed II* a triumph. In 2010, Scott Adkins reprised his role in the second sequel, *Undisputed III: Redemption*.

INTERVIEW:
SCOTT ADKINS
(djm)

British martial arts wonder Adkins started his career as a supporting stunt player in Hong Kong action films and got the attention of Israeli director Isaac Florentine, who gave him a plum supporting role in the film Special Forces (2003), *which led to a long collaborative relationship. Adkins has co-starred in a number of films with Jean-Claude Van Damme and Dolph Lundgren, but he became a breakout action star in Florentine's* Undisputed II: Last Man Standing (2006), *co-starring Michael Jai White. Known for his incredible kicks and flips as well as his on-screen presence as an actor, Adkins continues to ride the wave of action movie stardom in films like* Universal Soldier: Day of Reckoning (2012) *and* Ninja: Shadow of a Tear (2013).

Are you ready to talk about action movies?

Always ready. Born ready.

I feel like you're the last action hero, Scott.

Really?

Scott Adkins as Casey, the Ninja. Courtesy of Nu Image, Inc.

I do. It's hard enough for anyone to break into the action movie world, but these days it's even more difficult.

Yeah.

How in the world were you able to accomplish what you've been able to accomplish in this late stage of the game?

I know exactly what you're saying, yeah. I can tell you know a lot about it just from saying that because I feel that if I was doing this in the '80s or the '90s, it would have been so much easier for me. I think because the industry's changed . . . I can remember the change with *The Matrix*, when Keanu Reeves could suddenly do kung fu. Quite convincingly, but obviously not as good as me and the other guys do it, but it was good enough for Hollywood to go, "All right, this is the way we can do it from now on." We've got Matt Damon and the Bourne films, and now we've got the superhero films that are all CGI-driven. You get a good actor and stuntman in a suit, and that's all you need, really. So the guys from the '80s and the '90s . . . they're gone. It's a different era. It's been really difficult. That's why, for me, my career has always risen, but it's been painstakingly slow. I've come up in this. It's been really difficult. It's interesting that you picked up on that, yeah.

You sort of snuck in the back door in Hollywood, didn't you? Through Hong Kong?

Yeah, I was over there as a stuntman, really. I got the opportunity to work with Jackie Chan and Yu Ping and Sammo Hung. I was lucky to do that at the very beginning of my career so that I could learn how to shoot action and learn fight sequences from the best guys in the world. I was just the guy running in from the left and getting punched by Jackie Chan and that was

it. I was "that guy." I never got to graduate to having my own one-on-one fight with Jackie Chan. I was just some white guy coming in to get beat up by the Chinese dude. But at the same time, in England, I was doing straight acting work in daytime soap operas and things like that. The two opposite sides of the spectrum in the industry, really. Eventually when I met Isaac [Florentine], that's when I was able to put the two together for the first time.

Isaac is almost single-handedly carrying the flag for "B" action movies right now. He's one of the only guys who are keeping these types of movies from becoming extinct.

Yeah, the two reasons are because of *The Matrix* and shaking the camera and all that, but also because the DVD market has crashed. You can download anything, and they lost so much money. The video market isn't as powerful as it used to be.

Talk a little bit about how you got into stunt work in Hong Kong.

I had a showreel, and I sent it over to Hong Kong. Bay Logan wrote a really good book called *Hong Kong Action Cinema*, and he's a British guy. He used to live in England, and then he moved to Hong Kong. I would always send my videos over to him, showreels from when I was about sixteen years old. He would always send back nice letters, really encouraging saying, "Keep working on it." I would always update my showreel as I got better, and I would send it to him. Eventually, he said, "They're making a movie called *Extreme Challenge*." This was 1999. I heard they were looking for some Caucasian martial arts stunt guys. I was supposed to send a video to a certain person, so I did. They flew me out to Hong Kong to be in that movie. It was strange because I never saw myself going into the Hong Kong film industry. I wasn't prepared to do that like so many English guys did. They flew me out there, and it was a snowball effect. As I finished it and was going back home, I stopped in Hong Kong because we shot it in China, and I auditioned for a film called *Black Mask 2*. I thought that I would be fighting Jet Li, or whatever. It turned out they were making a teaser trailer to presell the movie. They ended up putting me as Black Mask. I did all the martial arts stuff. There were three guys playing Black Mask. A Chinese singer named Hong Li, I think was his name, and another guy, and then they had me doing all the martial arts. They said they wanted it to have more of a Caucasian feel to it. So I did the film, and that's when I started to work with Jackie Chan, and it was a snowball effect. I became the new guy in Hong Kong, if you like.

Before going into the movie business and acting, what movies inspired you to really go into that direction?

I remember it completely. *Enter the Dragon* was always something that was in my mind. That was the film that was always on late at night on British television. You'd stay up late and watch it and then talk about it with your friends. Bruce Lee was always around. I don't remember the lightning bolt effect of that movie, but I remember Bruce Lee because he was always around in my life. What an amazing guy he was. I think I was twelve years old, I think it was 1988, and I was coming back home, I was walking back home from school, and I went into the local convenience store, and it had a small video selection, and I would always look through the videos, and I'll always remember seeing *Bloodsport*, starring "international martial artist sensation, Jean-Claude Van Damme." He was on the front with his muscles out, doing that pose, and I thought, *Oh, I've got to get this film!* But of course, in England, it's an eighteen certificate. I'm twelve years old, so I took the box, and I hid it behind some other videos, and I counted on walking back home and I told my mom, "Mom, we've got to get back down to the Circle K. You've got to get this video for me. It looks brilliant! It's called *Bloodsport*!" We went and got the video, and I must have watched it three times, one after the other. It completely blew me away. I was already a fan of Stallone and Schwarzenegger. I think why Van Damme impressed me so much is that he had the body of the Western heroes, but he had the martial arts of Bruce Lee. At this time, I didn't know who Jackie Chan was. His films had not been released in my country. I had seen him in *The Cannonball Run*, and I thought the Chinese guy was cool. I didn't know much about him. So Van Damme was the one after Bruce Lee. After I watched that film, I told my mother, "Mom, I know what I want to do with my life. I'm going to be a martial arts movie star."

Were you keeping up with the other Caucasian martial arts movies like *American Ninja* and *Gymkata?*

I was on top of all of it, yeah. I remember there was a time when a new "B" movie martial arts film would come out once a week. It was a brilliant time. You had your *China O'Brien*s, the *American Ninja*s with David Bradley doing his thing, and then there was Loren Avedon. I loved the *No Retreat, No Surrender* films because they had such a charm about them. The fights were always brilliant. Everything else was kind of cheesy and corny, but as a kid, I loved that stuff. I still like those films now. Some of these "B" movies were crap. If there was some fighting in there, I was all for it.

What's it like for you to meet and work with some of the heroes you looked up to when you were younger?

I remember the time I first met Van Damme. I'd gone to Los Angeles because he wanted to meet with me. He was thinking about producing a *Kickboxer* TV series, but it never happened. He wanted to meet with me. That was amazing. I was meeting my hero. There was no one more important to me, other than Bruce Lee. I've worked with Van Damme four times, and I know him very well.

Isaac told me a story about Van Damme being a little nervous working with you the first time on screen. But when you guys got into the groove of working together, he was impressed with you and told Isaac that you made him look great on screen. You guys obviously work very well together.

Being honest with you, I think Jean-Claude was concerned that I would upstage him in the martial arts. Let's be clear about this: We're standing on the shoulders of giants. The reason why I'm a better on-screen martial arts performer than Jean-Claude Van Damme—and I hope I'm not sounding arrogant or anything—the reason I am the way I am is because he's *inspired* me. When I started to train, looking at the kicks and things he could do—jumping 360 kicks—that's what I was learning to do at the age of fourteen. Then at fifteen, I could do it as good as him, you know? Then, inevitable, when I meet him, I'm going to be on the next level. We're all standing on the shoulders of giants. There're kids now doing martial arts stuff that I can't even believe. That's just the way it is. I think Jean-Claude was concerned about that. What made him change his mind was because I started in Hong Kong as the whipping boy. I know how to really sell a punch, I know how to find Jean-Claude's kick and take it and do a big spin and make him look good. He was my hero as a kid, so I wanted to give him as much of myself as I could. I wanted him to look as good as he possibly could. I was dying to do a fight scene with Van Damme, and make him look as good as he did in the *Bloodsport* and *Kickboxer* days. The truth was, at that point in his career, he wasn't really into doing the fight sequences anymore. I just wanted to please him. I guess I did.

Do you guys have a process of working together now?

It's not a plan that we've come up between ourselves. It's not like he's grooming me, or I'm his protégé. It's purely coincidental that we've worked together so many times. As you say, there're not many action guys around these days. They tend to put these action guys together—whether it's Van Damme and Dolph Lundgren . . . at one point, Vinnie Jones was going to star with Van Damme in *Weapon* [*Assassination Games*], but it didn't work out, so I got in the mix. I was making my way into a leading man and as an action guy. Then *Expendables* came along. It just made sense that that part—his right-hand man—was right for me. There was no conspiracy or anything like that.

Scott Adkins and Jean-Claude Van Damme in *Universal Soldier: Day of Reckoning.* Courtesy of Magnet Releasing.

I loved your stuff in *Expendables.* The pissing contest with Jason Statham. You were standing in front of the whole cast for your big scene with Statham, and then of course you have the end fight with Statham. How were you doing that day when you had your big scene in front of the whole cast?

I was pretty nervous, yeah. I was nervous. (Laughing.) The first AD on that film did something that really annoyed me. He would say, "Good luck, everybody! And . . . action!" As an actor, you're trying to be relaxed as possible. You don't want your heart jumping in your chest. Every time he'd say that, it would remind me that there was so much at stake. I'm looking over at Stallone and Statham and Dolph, and I'm intimidated. I'm an actor, and I want to do a good job, and I don't think that's the right thing to say, even if it's an action sequence. You don't want to tempt fate by saying, "Good luck, everybody." That used to piss me off. Every time he said, "Action!" it would make my heart jump. I knew the first take would be shit. I just needed to get it on the next one. That's what it's like being an actor. You need to be relaxed. I did another take, and I started to nail it, and it was good. Yeah, I was excited to do Uri Boyka [my character from *Undisputed 2* and *3*] for that movie because I knew that character, and it was a big stage so everyone is going to see it. I knew it would work, so I pretty much regurgitated it.

Since we're on *Expendables*, I wanted to be honest and say that I was a little disappointed by the fight you had with Statham because it was over so quickly.

(Long pause.) I don't want to speak badly about the producer because he gave me the job and all that, but we lost a half a day of shooting—first of all, we've only got two days to do the fight scene. It's not enough. Especially on a big-budget movie where they spend so much time setting up the lights. You lose tons of time doing that. They took half a day filming [Novak] Djokovic hitting bad guys with tennis balls. We all knew that this was never going to be in the movie. It was complete *stupidity*! So I was pissed off about that. At the end of the day . . . Stallone was pissed off about it, too. I read a little bit about it on the Internet, and they say that my fight with Jason was too short and the fight with Van Damme and Stallone is too short. It's a shame really. People expected more. It's a shame because we could have done such great stuff. Working with Jason was brilliant. He was pissed off, too, because we didn't have enough time. But, you know, what can we do?

Have you noticed a surge of interest in you after the release of *Expendables 2?*

Yeah, definitely. I get recognized much more now. It's a weird thing.

Let's talk a little bit about your first film with Isaac Florentine. This was *Special Forces*.

Isaac told me he wasn't trained—he just learned how to shoot movies by watching movies. The movies he enjoyed were the martial arts ones. He

U

knows how to frame movement. With Isaac, I sent him that showreel that I sent to everyone, and his partner watched it, and he told him, you've got to see this. He wasn't really interested because he'd seen so many bad ones. Eventually, he saw it and phoned me. He was going to be doing a movie with Van Damme called *The Tower*, but that didn't happen, but he said he wanted me to be in that movie. When *Special Forces* came together, he had that part specifically written for me so that I could bring the martial arts element to the movie. Isaac gave me jobs when no one else would. I owe everything to him, really.

Talk about working with Michael Jai White on *Undisputed 2*, which was another movie you did with Isaac.

Yeah, Michael can be quite intense, and obviously he looks pretty badass. When they offered me that part, they were talking about getting Dolph Lundgren to play Uri Boyka. That was how the part was written. I'm 5 foot 10. I didn't look like the part. Michael is so big that I had to put on muscle to play that part. I remember meeting Michael for the first time, and he looked me up and down, and was like, "Ah, shit, this kid's pretty short." We did these tricks to make me look taller in the movie. He's a good friend of mine, Michael. I was intimidated by him at first. To do a fight scene with someone like him is really easy because of timing because he understands the distance, the rhythm. What makes it easy sometimes is that you know that the other guy knows your technique. If you feel like the guy is forgetting what the next move is, you can't go 100 percent. I've never felt that way with Michael because he's such an accomplished martial artist. He's one of the few who can act.

The type of movie that *Undisputed 2* is had been out of style for a long time. When it showed up, it brought back the *Bloodsport*-type movie. Why do you think people like this type of movie, and why do you think that kind of movie went out of fashion for such a long time?

Those types of movies exist because people like fight scenes in film. If you do a tournament type of film, it's an excuse to have fight scenes. If you're doing a fight in a street, someone's just going to pull out a gun. So how do you answer that problem? Why aren't people pulling out guns? With a tournament film or a boxing film, you can just say it's a fight movie.

Speaking of guns, I saw your movie *El Gringo*. There's a lot of shooting in that movie. Talk about the dynamic of using your skills as a martial artist versus using guns on screen and learning how to make it look good.

What we tried to do with *El Gringo* was to try to make a fight scene out of the gun sequences. You'll notice that a lot of it is up close, where I'm turning the guy around and shooting through him and using him as a human shield. Then I'd kick him and shoot forward to the other guy. Then this guy comes around, and I grab him in an arm bar and blow his head off. It's kung fu with guns. For me, that's the way I wanted to

take it because that's what excites me. I wanted to keep the Scott Adkins vibe, but with the gunplay. And I think we did a great job. This film was shot quickly; we didn't have a lot of time to do it. It's okay to do it in a gym with plastic guns, but when you're doing it for real, the gun is firing and sometimes the gun jams, sometimes the squibs go off too soon or too late, and now the stunt guy has to change his costume to get the new squib put in, and it takes ages to do these types of films. With a fight sequence, if it didn't work, you just start again. The gun stuff, you're talking about reloading and squibs and the rest of it. I was happy with what we did on *El Gringo*, but the director cut the action too fast. You don't have time to actually see the punch land. I don't like the way they edited it at all. I would not have done that. That's a taste, that's a style. For whatever reason a lot of people think that *Bourne Ultimatum* style is a good way to go, but I think people that are in the know know that it isn't. You don't need to shake the camera and cut away quick to cover up my shortcomings because I can do it. I've proved that. Why edit it too quick? You don't need it.

You've worked on some big movies like *The Wolverine* and one of the Bourne movies. Have you noticed a difference in how these films are made versus how the low-budget action movies you've starred in are made?

I wouldn't say there's any difference in the directors, really. You haven't got as much time to make these smaller films. On the low-budget ones, you're really rushed. On the big-budget ones, you're thinking, *Man, what are they doing? Why can't they just hurry up?* (Laughing.) It seems like they have more time, but they're *wasting* time. I understand they need more time to light so that it'll look better. They *should* look better because it's going on the big screen. My experience with working on the Bourne film with Paul Greengrass—it was mainly just a fight sequence I was involved with. They had no clue how to shoot it properly. I'm not sitting here telling you that Paul Greengrass doesn't know what he's doing, because he's an incredible director and he knows how to tell a story, but he had a very valid point when he told me, "What you don't see, you believe more." That was when we were talking about a fight sequence. He had a valid point. It's also an action film. When you capture the beauty of the movement, of a technique, it looks brilliant. When you can do that, it only adds to that type of movie because it is an action movie. He could have had both, but he had his style, and I respect that.

How would you define an action hero? What is an action hero to you?

I don't know if I can define it. I can think of myself as a teenager, watching Van Damme and Stallone and Schwarzenegger. They are these bigger-than-life heroes. They're built like they are. You want to be as cool as them. They're so cool. They don't take any shit. They can do the things you want to do in life that you'd get locked up for. They stand up for the right reasons. The cool ones—the Han Solos and John Rambos—these guys don't take any shit. It's

complete escapism. Boys appreciate dudes with great fighting skills and awesome physiques. They inspired me to want to go to the gym and to change myself and to become fitter and be able to protect myself. I was fourteen years old and I got mugged on a bus by these guys. I just remember retreating to my garage every night and training. I turned my whole garage into a dojo. I had a Bruce Lee flag. It was like in *No Retreat, No Surrender* in my own life. I'd idolized these guys. What's great about Stallone is that he's an actor who transformed himself into this superhero-looking guy. I've always had a lot of respect for Stallone. Arnold got into it because he was a professional bodybuilder with this amazing physique. His head looks great from whatever angle you shoot it. Stallone does in a different way. For whatever reason, he looks powerful and brilliant. I remember seeing *Rambo III* and he was doing that stick fight and he threw some kicks. I was like, "Yeah! That looks great!" I'm sure he would have done more if he could. For me, a fight scene in a film is the purest form of cinema. All the elements come together. If it's done right, the story is already there. Then you've got the editing, you've got the angles, you're using blood and makeup, sometimes visual effects and pyrotechnics are used, smashing into the set dressing. All the elements are coming together. Cinema in its purest form.

Why do you think so many people and Hollywood in general looks down on these action movies?

Because most of them have shit stories. Occasionally, you get *The Matrix* or the Bourne movies.

I like that you've played both heroes and villains. You were the hero in *Ninja*, which I liked a lot. It felt like a hearkening back to the '80s.

Yeah, but I think we failed in a way. I'm not happy with my performance. The character was underwritten. My job as an actor is to take that underwritten character and breath life into it. I think I failed. The story was terrible in *Ninja*, but the action was great. That's why it doesn't work as well as *Undisputed*. The character of Boyka is really watchable, he's really engaging. You believe the journey that he's on. He's got something about him that makes you root for him. The story's not Shakespeare, is it, but it certainly works—it keeps you engaged. We put the fight sequences in it, and you've got a really great martial arts film. We didn't have that with *Ninja*.

Isaac Florentine's film *The Ninja*, featuring Scott Adkins. Courtesy of Nu Image, Inc.

Scott Adkins airborne in *Undisputed III*. Courtesy of Maroody Merav.

How did you discover Michael Shannon Jenkins, your co-star in *Undisputed 3*?

It was really difficult for Isaac to find that guy. He auditioned loads of actors. He auditioned him, and he really looked the part. He's a great actor. He didn't have the martial arts, but you needed a strong actor for that part. The rest of us could carry the film with the fight sequences. But he did a really good job anyway with the fight sequences because he's a physical guy. He really helped me out with my acting. He made me understand a lot.

How about The Latin Dragon—Marko Zaror? What was it like working with him?

Oh, he's a freak of nature! Six foot 3 and able to do all those crazy, crazy spinning kicks. He looks quite intimidating when you see him on film. I thought, *Oh God, this guy is going to be a bit rough and a bit nasty; I'll have to watch myself with him.* He's actually a lot like me, I found. He's easy going and he likes to joke around. He enjoys life. I'm sure people see me as Boyka and think I'm some crazy guy, too. That fight sequence we did in *Undisputed 3* was so good! He was willing to drill that fight scene with me every night that I came back from work. We went over it. We could do the whole thing in one go, full speed by the time it came to shoot it. It's a seven-minute long fight sequence.

Briefly talk about *Assassination Games.* It's a pretty grim movie for an action movie.

Yeah, it's pretty depressing. Wait until you see *Universal Soldier 4.* You won't be coming out of it doing high fives. It's a really good story. I hope people like it. You really don't know. I think it's a really interesting story, and it's really well thought out. It certainly takes it off in a different direction. The audience follows my character. He doesn't have a memory, he doesn't know who he is. He only has one memory in his head, and that's of Van Damme's character killing his wife and his child. He wakes up from a coma with only that memory in his head. Everything he learns, the audience learns it with him as he goes through the film. It's hard "R"-rated. I'm really proud of the film.

How's John Hyams to work with as a director?

Brilliant. He's really good. He gets it. He understands it. Just look at *Universal Soldier: Regeneration.* I can't think of a better action film than that in 2010. Him and Isaac should be doing studio pictures.

Scott Adkins in *Universal Soldier: Day of Reckoning.* Courtesy of Magnet Releasing.

Why do you think they're not doing studio pictures?

I honestly don't know.

How about you? Will you be doing any studio pictures anytime soon?

I'm trying my best. I'm in the new Kathryn Bigelow film, *Zero Dark Thirty.* It's not a massive role, but it's a step in the right direction. It's difficult.

Say something about doing something like *Zero Dark* or *Stag Night* where you're not doing martial arts. I was so let down when you got killed in *Stag Night.*

I know. I would be let down, too. It would be like watching Jeff Speakman in the second film he did, and I was like, "What?! No martial arts? Fuck you, Jeff Speakman!" But what are you going to do? At the end of the day, the industry's changed, and if I can't survive as an actor, I'm just going to be buried. That's the end of me. But I started acting when I was eighteen, and I've been to drama school and all the rest of it. I've always thought of myself as an actor first and a martial artist second. I'm aware that when I put both of them together that something special happens. That's what I'm hoping will put me where Jason Statham is. That's the goal.

You did a movie called *Re-Kill* that has been on the shelf for years. What's the deal with this movie?

I don't know what the deal is, and I'm waiting for it as well. They did a lot of reshoots, but not because it's a bad film, but because they thought it could go theatrical, so they wanted to make it even better. The concept's pretty cool. It's like an episode of *Cops.* The camera is following the "R"

division—the Reanimated Division—and there's been a zombie outbreak. We go out to where the zombies are, and the camera is following us as we rid the world of zombies. There are commercial breaks throughout the movie like they did in *RoboCop.* It was a lot of fun to film. I play a character you love to hate. He's a bit of a dick, but he's definitely the guy you want next to you if you're in a fight.

You also did an episode of *The Metal Hurlant Chronicles.* Say something about that.

It's a comic book. I knew it as *Heavy Metal.* David Fincher was going to make the film. Basically, these French producers got the rights, and I was just finishing *El Gringo,* and they didn't have a lot of money, but I found out that Larnell Stovall, who did the fights for *Undisputed 3* was doing it, Michael Jai White was involved, Matt Mullins, Darren Shahlavi, and I thought to myself, *This is a good opportunity to do some nice fight scenes.* I thought it would be fun to have a crack at it. We tried to do too much action than we had the time to do, to be honest. It's a bit cheesy like *Dr. Who.*

You've worked with Dolph Lundgren a number of times. How is he to work with?

Really down to earth. He doesn't bitch, he doesn't moan. He gets on with the job. He feels fortunate to have the job that he's got. He always turns up and works hard. He's turned out to be a good director, too, although I think he's happy to just be in front of the camera for a bit longer now. It's a lot of hard work to direct and star.

I heard that you've written something for yourself to star in.

Yeah, I've written something, but I don't want to talk about it. It's something that I'm getting the rights for. It's my dream project since I was fourteen years old.

Are there any action stars you've been paying attention to?

I love Tom Cruise. How about Tom Cruise?

Yeah, but I'm not going to include him as an action star. He's an actor.

I know what you mean—don't include him! What impresses me about Cruise is that he does his own stunts. He does his own stunts! It's crazy! I've got respect for that guy.

Is there anything else you'd like to add about being a rising action star?

I guess it's just nice to say that when I was a kid I decided that I wanted to go on this path. Everyone told me that I was never going to make it. That it couldn't be done. But I really, truly believe that if you really have the belief in yourself and that if you work hard enough that you can do whatever it is. Put your mind to it, and you can do it. Don't let anyone tell you that you can't do it. Just make sure you work hard for it.

Thank you, Scott. You're awesome.

Thanks, David. I really enjoyed it. I'm happy to be a part of a book like this. It means that I'm one of the guys.

Undisputed III: Redemption

2009 (New Line DVD) (djm)

Isaac Florentine's second *Undisputed* film turns the villain from part 2—Boyka, the Russian prisoner, played by Scott Adkins—into the guy you're rooting for. It's an interesting point of view. Boyka is now a disgraced cripple (his knee is shot from the last fight in Part 2), and he's a sort of Edmund Dantes from *The Count of Monte Cristo* this time. The corruption of the underground syndicate that holds kickboxing tournaments in prisons around the world has reached new levels. When Boyka re-enters the ring, he quickly becomes the new Russian favorite, and he's submitted into a win-or-die worldwide tournament, with the winner receiving a full pardon. The South American favorite is played by Marko Zaror (*Mandrill*, *Kiltro*), and the US competitor is played by Mykel Shannon Jenkins, whose intimidating attitude and boxing skills are certainly a threat to the other competitors. Before long, Adkins and Jenkins are having pissing contests, and not long after that, they become allies, but it gets tougher when their sponsors on the outside turn against them in favor of the promise of millions of dollars if they get behind Zaror, who has the sponsorship of the syndicate.

Florentine's visual finesse with the fight scenes and the almost-cinematic qualities of the rest of the film really elevate this picture above most of the mundane action and kickboxing films that have come and gone over the years. Along with Part 2, these *Undisputed* pictures remind us of what made movies like *Bloodsport* and *Lionheart* so special in the first place. Adkins is quite easily slipping into the "star" mode, and his subtle acting and powerhouse techniques as a martial artist are really interesting to watch. This is every bit the "B" movie, but "B" movies don't get much better or more compelling than this. Also featuring *capoeirista* Lateef Crowder, *who would play a significant part in the Michael Jai White film Falcon Rising.*

Universal Soldier

1992 (Lionsgate DVD) (djm)

Deveraux: "Scott: The war . . . it's over."
Scott: "Not for *me*. Not for *her*.
Not for *you*."

Before they were titans in action cinema, Jean-Claude Van Damme and Dolph Lundgren starred in this soft science-fiction action film that has profound implications and resonated enough with audiences that it was being sequalized twenty years later. In Vietnam, Sergeant Andrew Scott (Lundgren) goes ballistic and slaughters his entire platoon, including a whole village of innocents. The last member of his team—Luc Deveraux (Van Damme)—stands up to him, and in a fatal confrontation, they kill each other right there in the mire of the war field. They're zipped up in body bags, and in a blink of an eye, they wake up and find themselves in the present day (1992), on a team of "Universal Soldiers" (UniSol's), which is a top-secret government experiment that uses the corpses of long-dead soldiers to fight terrorism. With their memories supposedly wiped clean and their mandate to follow their orders implicitly, the UniSols work as a hive mind, until Deveraux begins having startling flashbacks that feature his fellow UniSol, Scott. Suddenly, both Deveraux and Scott act out of congress and go rogue, only Scott is entirely deranged and begins killing innocent people again. With a hopelessly clueless government team on their tail, Deveraux (along with a plucky and attractive reporter played by Ally Walker) must find out what happened to him during his twenty-year gap of being "dead," before Scott and his team of UniSol converts find him and kill him.

Surprisingly deep for a mass-market action picture with these two particular stars, *Universal Soldier* has layers of political intrigue and conspiracy, while still maintaining a course of blockbuster sensibilities with nice, widescreen cinematography and solid performances by an affecting Van Damme and a crazed Lundgren, who manages to give his ugly character a funny sense of humor. The Vietnam vet angle is fairly shocking in how it's handled, and the two sequels directed by Peter Hyams (*Regeneration* and *Day of Reckoning*) manage to follow the original thread to a subversive conclusion. Some of the other UniSols are played by Ralf Moeller (*Best of the Best II*), Tommy "Tiny" Lister (*No Holds Barred*), Simon Rhee (*Best of the Best*), and Eric Norris (youngest son of Chuck). The first sequel was called *Universal Soldier II: Brothers in Arms*, with Matt Battaglia playing Deveraux. The first official sequel with Van Damme reprising his role was called *Universal Soldier: The Return*. Rolland Emmerich directed the original, and Dean Devlin wrote the screenplay.

Universal Soldier: Day of Reckoning

2012 (Sony DVD) (djm)

Subversive and geared to explode upon contact, *Universal Soldier: Day of Reckoning* is without question the most intense and gut-punching action film of 2012. I would hesitate calling it an "action" film. Honestly, I don't even want to put a label on it. For better *and* worse, this is a mushroom cloud of such intensity that it blows away any preconceived notions you may have going into it. It's called "Universal Soldier" but it is something so completely radical and fearsome that it almost dares you to think that it is a "Universal Soldier" movie. This film goes so far beyond the "Universal Soldier" reservation that

it's basically a horror film with action undertones. That's almost a compliment. If *Apocalypse Now* were filtered through *Beyond the Black Rainbow* and retrofitted to accommodate Jean-Claude Van Damme and Dolph Lundgren to fit familiar roles, then *perhaps* you'd get the entirely progressive hybrid that *Day of Reckoning* is.

Scott Adkins (*Ninja*, *Undisputed 2* and *3*) is the star. He spends the length of the movie looking for the man he believes killed his family. That man is Luc Deveraux, played by Jean-Claude Van Damme. How can Van Damme, who is playing the same character from the previous entries in the franchise, be reduced to this, to a villain, to a supporting character? Good question, and one that the entire picture is dedicated to answering for the audience. Adkins is given a vehicle here to once again show to the world what he is capable of as both an actor and as an extraordinary martial artist and athlete. This is *his* movie, and he owns it. Dolph Lundgren is there, too, but he seems to be there almost as a mascot, to cheer on the other players as they move the story towards its clear and calculated destination. John Hyams, who also directed the previous *Universal Soldier* entry subtitled *Regeneration*, has laser-focused his vision to literally transform the *Universal Soldier* franchise into far graver territory than anyone else ever dreamed it could possibly dare go.

This picture is the hardest of the hardcore. It will shake action fans deeply. Fans of Van Damme and Lundgren may feel betrayed. Fans of Scott Adkins will rejoice. Newcomers to the *Universal Soldier* legacy will either be entirely disgusted by what they see or will have a fresh appreciation for what an "action" film can achieve. As for me, I was lucky enough to pretty much know what to expect. I had a feeling I was going to get gut-punched, so I was ready for the blow. If I'd gone in like a puppy in love with my action heroes, I'd have been incinerated by the pure nuclear blast that Hyams has dropped on the world. *Universal Soldier: Day of Reckoning* will kick your ass.

INTERVIEW:

JOHN HYAMS

(djm)

The Universal Soldier franchise soldiers on with the release of Universal Soldier 4: Day of Reckoning. *With a new protagonist (played by Scott Adkins) and familiar stars such as Jean-Claude Van Damme and Dolph Lundgren from the existing entries in the franchise,* Day of Reckoning *is guaranteed to challenge expectations. Director John Hyams, who also helmed* Universal Soldier 3: Regeneration, *has worked with Jean-Claude Van Damme on three consecutive films and with Strikeforce middleweight champion Cung Le on the film* Dragon Eyes. *Hyams, who is the son of prolific filmmaker Peter Hyams (who also directed Van Damme on* Timecop *and* Sudden Death*), is clearly a talent to be reckoned with, and with the release of* Day of Reckoning, *he proves once again that he has a style of his own.*

Director John Hyams on the set of *Universal Soldier: Day of Reckoning*. Courtesy of Magnet Releasing.

Dolph Lundgren takes direction from director John Hyams on the set of *Universal Soldier: Regeneration*. Courtesy of Maroody Merav.

Your father has worked with Jean-Claude Van Damme several times, and has in fact just finished working with him again on *Enemies Closer*. Your newest film *Universal Soldier: Day of Reckoning* is your third movie in a row with Van Damme. Were you at all present on the sets when your father was filming *Timecop* or *Sudden Death* back in the mid-1990s?

I really was not involved at all back then. In '94, I'd recently graduated college. I was living in New York City. At the time, I wasn't really involved in filmmaking. I'd studied fine art painting and sculpture. That was really what I wanted to pursue. I was painting and selling professionally. So I was in New York doing that. When I was younger, I spent a lot of time working with my dad. Almost all my jobs were on his sets. Whether it was pre-production, production, or post, I was always during my high-school years working with him, spending as much time on his sets as I could. When his association with Jean-Claude began with *Timecop*, I was never around for those. Actually, I visited the set of *Timecop* for one day of shooting. I was able to see one day of shooting, but I'd never met Jean-Claude at that time. I didn't see any shooting of *Sudden Death*. But all that served me later when I began developing a relationship with Jean-Claude. When I met him in fall/winter of 2008, it was the first time I'd met him or spoken with him.

How was it that you were chosen to direct *Universal Soldier: Regeneration*?

Originally, they had a different director involved. My dad was in talks with Moshe Diamant, the producer, about doing the film. It was a larger-budgeted movie that never ended up getting made. In the process of doing that, Moshe needed to get another Universal Soldier going. At the time, it might have been called A New Beginning, or something like that. They had a script for that movie, but they did not have either Jean-Claude's or Dolph Lundgren's agreement for that script as it was. Obviously, in order to get the money they needed for that movie, they needed the agreements of both of those guys. My dad struck up a deal with Moshe. He didn't want to direct the movie, but he said he would shoot the movie—he would be the DP on it. He would do that, and by doing so, they thought it might help attract Jean-Claude and would help stimulate the agreement to make the movie. My dad was involved before I was involved, and it had a different director.

Is it a big secret who the other director was?

I'm not even sure who the other director was. There were a couple different guys. Ultimately, because the movie was in flux and didn't have the two stars' agreement, my name was thrown in the mix. I don't know if my dad mentioned me to Moshe. I don't know if my dad was too thrilled about working with some other director . . . I don't know, it might not have gone so well. Maybe he thought of me, or maybe Moshe thought of me. Moshe had seen a documentary I'd done called *The Smashing Machine*. He was aware of me and what I could do. One way or the other, I got a call from Moshe, and he told me he was sending me the script for *Universal Soldier*, and that I needed to talk to Jean-Claude on the phone in a couple hours. I read the script that they had, which was the basic idea we used, which was the Chernobyl kidnapping of the kids aspect, but there were a lot of differences with what we ended up with. I had a long conversation with Jean-Claude, where he was just talking about ideas and things like that. Over the next month or two months, I realized that if I could get Jean-Claude and Dolph to both agree to the movie by whatever changes I proposed, then the movie would happen. So I set up for the next couple of months, working on the script, meeting with those guys, and eventually by getting their approval that's what won me the job. It was a hell of an education. I certainly understood some of the mechanical aspects of making a movie, but there's so much more to it in dealing with talent, in dealing with the power structure, doing the things you need to do to get a movie made. You don't just write your script and make your demands. It's more about somehow being in a position where you can execute your ideas and get people to understand what those ideas are in a way that makes them feel confident in your vision for the movie. If you've made several movies and you have a track record, they'll be more willing to place their trust in you. I'd really only done documentary work and some television, so there really wasn't a lot of fiction filmmaking that I'd had that was going to convince anyone of my ideas for this movie. Certainly in that case, just having my dad's presence on the set was something that helped.

What was the dynamic between the two of you—you and your father—while you were directing the film on location in Bulgaria?

The dynamic between myself and my dad was very much a DP/director dynamic. It really wasn't any different than that. We both had our ideas. Because he's the DP, he was more than happy to relinquish control. He really didn't want to be directing that movie. He didn't want the ultimate responsibility on that movie. He was there to help me execute my vision; if he disagreed with me, he'd tell me, and if I disagreed with him, then we would work it out. However, there's no doubt that having him there helped get Jean-Claude to agree to the movie. I'm not so sure he would have if he hadn't been involved. Not to mention, being in Bulgaria, being on a movie like this where the budgets are never what you need them to be. Having my dad involved helped us win a lot of battles that we might not have won if he hadn't been there. "Oh, we need a crane for this day," or "We need more lights," or "We need more time." All those things were from his influence, and I took advantage of that. It helped influence actors and producers, and my philosophy is that I don't care how anything gets done, I don't care who feels like they came up with the best idea, and I really don't care what people think of me on the set. That's a dangerous road to go on, to want to be the most popular guy on set, to want to be seen as a fun guy. Ultimately, when you're the director, you're the guy who's going to keep people there longer, you're the guy who makes them all do an extra take and make them miss the game that they wanted to go home to watch or miss the chance to tuck their kids in bed. Your decisions are best for the movie, but not necessarily the best decisions for everyone on set. Being popular on set isn't important. When the movie's over, everyone goes home, and you're living with it until it's finished. It's something I always had to remind myself. It doesn't matter what anyone thinks of me on set. I'd don't even care if people think it was really Peter Hyams who directed the movie and I was just riding his coattails. I knew in the end that it was just going to be me in the editing room dealing with post, with sound, with music, and I was going to putting this thing together, and what we came up with was either going to be embraced or not embraced. That's what we have to live with—that's what I have to live with forever. It's going to be out there forever. The only people I have to impress are the people who employed me, and beyond that, the audience. That's it. I work for the people who put the money up and for the audience. Not necessarily in that order. The people who put the money up might even hate you, but if the audience embraces you, then the producers learn to like you. That's what's going to determine your future employment. That's the hardest lesson to learn. Even on a low-budget film, you're still talking about millions of dollars. As a result, there's a lot of conflict. People have a lot riding on these things. They fear that you might not be making the right choice.

You must have felt that even more intensely with the new film *Day of Reckoning*. It looks so radically different than any of the other Universal Soldier films.

With *Universal Soldier: Day of Reckoning*, that's a perfect example—that's a movie the studio and people have not always felt entirely confident about until we started reading people's reactions

U

John Hyams (center) directs Jean-Claude Van Damme on the set of *Universal Soldier: Regeneration*. Courtesy of Maroody Merav.

to it. I didn't deliver to them *Regeneration Part 2*. I really went in a different direction. That certainly made some people nervous. We won't really know for sure until it's really out there, but so far it's been embraced by the fans and some members of the critical community, which helps. People who didn't like me maybe a month ago, maybe like me a little better right now.

You've done three movies in a row with Jean-Claude. Clearly you guys work well together and you've each placed a certain amount of trust in each other. What's that like, working with him?

After *Regeneration*, he trusted me. Every actor, first and foremost, doesn't want to be in something that's shitty. Number two, they don't want to be embarrassed or made a fool of. They don't want to feel that you're going to use their bad moments. They want you to use their good moments. In order to deliver any good

Jean-Claude Van Damme in *Universal Soldier: Day of Reckoning*. Courtesy of Magnet Releasing.

Andrei Arlovski and Jean-Claude Van Damme in *Universal Soldier: Day of Reckoning*. Courtesy of Magnet Releasing.

performance, they need to be free to do some takes where they don't have it right, where they deliver a bad performance on the way to the good one. So, that's part of the agreement and the trust. Let's be comfortable to go out there and fail and do things the long way, knowing that once we get it the right way, those are the moments we'll use. That frees you up as a performer a lot. JC, I assume, saw the final product and felt comfortable with what we came up with, so we've always had a good, easy working relationship.

Why was it decided to go directly to video for *Regeneration?* It certainly felt like a theatrical release, and it was a vast improvement over *Universal Soldier: The Return.*

It wasn't my decision. It was decided before we even made the movie, that it would be a direct-to-video movie. To release it theatrically requires some risk on the part of the people putting the money in. It costs something to release it theatrically. I think they all decided that it wasn't worth the risk. They couldn't lose releasing it directly to video. A lot of those things have to do with the track records of the performers. It involves a number of things. With *Regeneration*, we got a really positive reaction. I think it was beyond what they expected. They had very low expectations. They just wanted to make a profit, not lose money, and that was pretty much it. When all was said and done, it turned out that the reaction was far more positive than they anticipated. The bottom line is, I don't know if it would have gotten that reaction if it had been theatrically released. The fact that it was direct-to-video, it was released in this world of low expectations, and so when people saw it, a lot of them wrote about it and said, "Wow—I was expecting something that wasn't going to be very

Jean-Claude Van Damme stars as Luc Deveraux in *Universal Soldier: Regeneration*. Courtesy of Maroody Merav.

Luc Deveraux (Jean-Claude Van Damme), the original Universal Soldier, in action in *Universal Soldier: Regeneration*. Courtesy of Maroody Merav.

good, and it pleasantly surprised me." It was a blessing. It would have been nice to have gotten a theatrical release, but the decision had been made to go direct to video.

I find it curious that in the US, Magnet Releasing picked up *Day of Reckoning,* and they're going to release it in theaters simultaneously with a VOD release. Why wasn't Sony involved with *Day of Reckoning's* video release?

Sony is in it just for the home video. When the fourth one rolled around, the deal was basically the same. They told us, "This is going to be a direct-to-video movie." Even after the success of *Regeneration*, they told us that it would be a direct-to-video movie unless it proves itself otherwise. I realized that this time around, that if we wanted to go theatrical that it would take a little more effort on all of our parts to push that on them. I think when we had our finished product of *Day of Reckoning*, there may have been some people at Sony who thought, "Not only is this not going to be theatrically released, but we don't even like this movie." Some people at Sony weren't loving it because they'd thought we'd gone too far off the Universal Soldier reservation. They're saying it's not a straight action movie, it's kind of a sci-fi horror noir. Genre-wise, it's very different. Sony would not release it. Moshe and myself wanted to see it released theatrically, and Magnolia/Magnet saw it and wanted to release it and it fit right in with the kind of movies they release, so it was kind of a perfect marriage. I've been really pleased with what Magnet has been doing with it. It has a horror element to it, it's got some Cronenberg elements to it. It's almost like a Cronenberg interpretation of the Universal Soldier mythology. Magnet will release it in a number of cities and play it theatrically and will also play it on Video On Demand. There's also a 3D version. We shot it in 3D. We showed it at Fantastic Fest in 3D. It's been released in 3D in Germany already. I like the 2D version just as much. It's just a different way of looking at it. There's also the "unrated" version versus the "R" rated version. The theatrical version will most likely be the "R" rated version. On demand, you'll be able to choose which version you want to watch. When it comes out on DVD and Blu-Ray, it will be the "unrated" version. I prefer the "unrated" version.

How do you think audiences and fans of Jean-Claude are going to receive *Day of Reckoning?*

There's going to be a lot of people, some huge Van Damme fans, huge Universal Soldier fans, who are not going to be happy with this movie. In *Day of Reckoning*, Van Damme is not the protagonist. The Scott Adkins character is the protagonist. It in no way follows the formula of those other movies. To me, it was the logical conclusion after the end of *Regeneration*. When I was thinking about the next movie we were going to make, I really assumed that these were my contributions to the franchise, so whatever I do in this franchise should exist in a universe that makes sense in and of itself. It doesn't necessarily honor any other movie in the series except *Regeneration*. Since that was the last that

U

was made, I was going to take that ending into account and say, "Where would all this go from here?" After *Day of Reckoning*, they could hire someone else to go make another one, and say, "Okay, we're going to reboot the first one and start over." That option exists. As upset as some people get with the directors for some of these movies go, you have to remember there's no way you can kill a franchise. If people who are into this franchise and don't like the direction I've taken, well, that will bear itself out. They will make another movie and can reboot the original concept like Chris Nolan did with *Batman Begins*. He didn't have to honor what Tim Burton or Joel Schumacher did. Ultimately, I felt a responsibility to what we did on *Regeneration* and those ideas. So we took it in the direction we went because that's the best movie we could make under the budget and circumstances we had. That was the best way to go.

How did Van Damme and Lundgren react when you brought them *Day of Reckoning*?

Considering that his character changed so drastically—not only in the amount of screen time, but he moved from the protagonist role to the antagonist role—Van Damme was surprisingly on board. It was a big leap for him. However, I think my previous experiences with him and knowing that I wasn't out to do anything but honor him and his character and make everyone look as good as they can helped a great deal. The difference in his role this time wasn't to diminish him, but to take the character in a different direction. Jean-Claude is happy to do different things. He liked that this was a different challenge for him to play the character in a different way. He embraced it. Dolph, at first, did not necessarily embrace it. He sorta came around. The first script that I had turned in for this had gone even further off the reservation than the one that exists now. Sony thought I'd gone too far, and Dolph wasn't a big fan of it either. I really had to start from scratch and write a whole new script that was what we ended up with now. Dolph liked that better—he preferred it. We were on the same page with it. In hindsight, I think they were right. The script I had originally written didn't pick up right after *Regeneration*, but it took place many years, maybe twenty years later. *Day of Reckoning* takes place maybe five years later. My original idea took the technology that might have existed in that future world and went with that.

Is Dolph's role bigger in *Day of Reckoning* than it was in *Regeneration*?

Dolph's part is maybe a little bigger. It's comparable. Both Dolph's role and Jean-Claude's role are comparable in *Day of Reckoning*. Structurally, this film is almost a mystery. It's an amnesia story that focuses on Scott Adkins's character. The whole conceit of this movie was to change the perspective of the storytelling. All of the other Universal Soldier movies are from the government's perspective. In *Regeneration*, it was an international problem. The government needs to call someone to fix this problem. They call on this technology they created. I thought it would be more interesting to tell a new story

Andrei Arlovski and Dolph Lundgren in *Universal Soldier: Day of Reckoning*. Courtesy of Magnet Releasing.

Dolph Lundgren in *Universal Soldier: Day of Reckoning*. Courtesy of Magnet Releasing.

from the perspective of the weaponry, from the perspective of the monsters. The government in *Day of Reckoning* is a much more mysterious organization. We only see them as they come to the characters, and we're never really sure what their motivations are. By telling this story from their perspective, it requires that you see the whole story through the eyes of the protagonist named John, played by Adkins. Because we're seeing it through his perspective, it wouldn't allow for any other character to have as much screen time as that character. Like Jake Gittes moves through Chinatown, he comes in contact with other characters, and you never really know what anyone's intentions are until you get to the end. That kind of structure allowed me to place Van Damme's character, Luc Deveroux, in a more antagonistic role. He's the Harry Lime of the movie. From minute one of the movie, the story is really about finding him, and discovering what he has become and what his intentions are. The truth of it all, by the end he is actually the protagonist. He's the guy who the story is ultimately about. How we arrive there is through the vehicle of this other character, John.

Scott Adkins is fantastic. As far as I'm concerned he's one of the only new action guys who's worth paying attention to. He told me he'd been considered to play a part in *Regeneration*, but for whatever reason that didn't happen.

I love him. Yeah, he was considered. His name came up when we were casting *Regeneration*. I think it was for the role that Mike Pyle ended up playing. For one reason or another, it didn't work out. I remember being interested in him. There are a lot of factors at play when you're doing these things. Money, what they can afford for each character, what's put aside in the budget

for everyone. So that idea didn't last very long. At the time, I'd heard of him. I'd never seen a movie with him. I saw his highlights on the Internet. After that movie, I was setting about writing the script for *Day of Reckoning*, and Scott had contacted me on Facebook. He told me that he saw *Regeneration*, and he liked what I'd done, and we had a lot of mutual friends and co-workers. He'd done the *Undisputed* movies in Bulgaria, and I'd worked in Bulgaria, so we'd worked with a lot of the same stunt guys. So we struck up a Facebook friendship, and I told him that I'd admired what I'd seen of his work, but that I'd never actually watched any of his films. He sent me the DVD of *Undisputed III*, and I was incredibly impressed by what he was able to do physically and athletically. But also, very impressed that he actually had acting chops. That's always the thing when you're dealing with these kinds of movies—do you go with someone who can execute choreography and do the moves, or do you go with someone who can dramatically handle the scenes? One way or another, you're always tailoring the script and situations to fit the performer. But to me, it seemed by his performance in *Undisputed III*, by playing such an extreme character, I could see that he was very versatile. He could do a lot of things—dramatically and athletically. As we started going through the process of casting this movie, I remember thinking, "I really need an *actor* for this role." I didn't want a fighter or a stuntman, I wanted someone who could act, and if we would have to double him, then we would double him. I needed someone who could handle the role dramatically. The further along that road we went, I realized that we needed someone who could do both. Part of the allure of these movies is not just in dramatic performance, it's also *him* fighting. We were kind of anointing another action star. If he's going to be involved in this movie, it couldn't just be another actor who we would double in the fight scenes. It reached a point where Scott Adkins was the only guy we could think of that could combine all these elements and was relatively unknown in the United States, which helped as well. We wanted the audience to have their own sense of discovery with him. When you see the movie, he's not necessarily breaking out his repertoire until two-thirds into the movie. It was nice to watch him slowly reveal what he's capable of as the movie progressed. Scott did a brilliant job, and he's a real pleasure to work with. He's one of the hardest working guys I've ever worked with. He's an incredibly talented guy. He's so prepared, and that's when you realize that if he's able to perform at that level, to do the kind of things that he does, you *have* to be prepared—not just dramatically, but physically. He's basically a stuntman who can act. He's both. That's very rare.

Scott has worked with both Jean-Claude and Dolph on previous projects. Did they come to you beforehand and give him their blessing as a way of telling you he was able to handle the lead role?

Yeah, everyone vouched for him. As much as they vouched for him, you still had to be sensitive with the idea that all these guys have a

U

lot of pride in what they do, what they've done, and to have a fight in a movie where one guy loses to another guy, you know, people don't realize the amount of politics that can go into getting someone to agree to lose in a fight on screen to another person. So, there're a lot of negotiations that have to go into all of that. A lot of trust is required because for someone like Dolph or JC to have to capitulate to another performer, especially a guy like Scott, it's a guy who might be nipping at their heels if you looked at it one way . . . there has to be a lot of trust on a project like this and how it's all going to go down for guys like Dolph and JC to allow that to happen. I mean, Jean-Claude's done several movies with Scott, but in all of those, JC comes out on top.

There aren't many movies where Van Damme loses.

Yeah. So, what you'll see—and it's not for me to say whether he wins or loses—just see it.

You recently did another movie with Van Damme called *Dragon Eyes* that stars Cung Le. It's a pretty good movie. Talk a little bit about it.

Dragon Eyes was a completely different story. I was down in Louisiana, prepping *Universal Soldier: Day of Reckoning*. It was taking a long time to get it off the ground. There were a lot of negotiations going on with the script, going over who was going to be in the movie, and I'm sure they were trying to get the money together. I was down there, and the only way they were going to keep me down there was that they had to employ me. I couldn't afford to stay there, and they couldn't afford to keep me there. So, Signature Pictures and After Dark had this partnership where they were doing a bunch of pictures, and *Dragon Eyes* was one of them. So they came to me. They had the script, they had the locations, they had Cung Le, they had Van Damme, it was all ready to go. They came to me and said, "We need this movie to get made. We want you to direct it." The understanding was that it was something I would have to do in order to get *Universal Soldier 4* made. It was a very condensed preparation schedule. Once we officially started prep, we had two weeks and then we were shooting, and the shoot was only fifteen days, and they added a couple later. It was kind of the way you never want to go into something, but at the time it was a different kind of challenge for me. I've worked on condensed schedules before, and it was a chance to experiment with some things. Some technical ideas I'd been thinking about, I wanted to try these things out before I went out to make *Day of Reckoning*. It was a practice run. What happened was then I met Cung Le. I ended up talking to him, and I thought, "This guy is very committed to what he's doing here." He's an incredibly hard working guy, a great guy. He'd been in a number of movies, and he's also in *The Man With the Iron Fists*, which is going to be really good, but *Dragon Eyes* was a movie where he was going to be the lead, and he was going to be doing all the fight choreography. To me, it was a chance to work with this guy and realize his vision and get

some people involved who would bring stuff to the table. It was a very different type of scenario. How could we tell this existing story and tell it in a way that's maybe bringing a different flavor to the *Yojimbo*, *A Fistful of Dollars* story. We've seen this story before, so how do we do this story again that would make it stylistically different and just as entertaining as the previous versions? Same thing with *Day of Reckoning*.

From what I've seen of *Day of Reckoning*, it doesn't look or feel at all like what we've seen before.

Right. That was the thought with *Dragon Eyes*. Stylistically, it's much more of a comic book, graphic novel of a movie. It's two-dimensional. Archetypal characters, archetypal themes. On one hand, we have hard-hitting action, on the other hand, quite stylized as well. I had no idea how it was going to turn out.

Talk about working in the "vehicle" genre where the film is tailored to suit the skills and personas of the star or the athlete who wants to become an action star. Do you feel hindered by that, or do you embrace that sort of genre?

With the opportunities that I've been given, I feel like these three movies I've done so far are a "three-movie" chapter of my life, also a contained chapter. I'm proud of this chapter, I'm very glad I had the opportunity to make them, and wherever my career goes those movies will be the basis for whatever happens next. My career will be based off of those. I think what they taught me is that you don't always control the opportunities you have, and where you're given those opportunities, you have to make the most of them to present to the world what kind of filmmaker you want to be perceived as. I do feel like whatever I do next is going to have to present something different that I didn't present in those three movies. I can't really go back and do the same kind of movie like *Day of Reckoning* again. It doesn't mean I'll go and do a romantic comedy next, but I wouldn't be opposed to it. Every movie is a vehicle for someone. Whether it's a vehicle for Tom Cruise or a vehicle for Jean-Claude Van Damme, or a vehicle for Aaron Sorkin's script. In every movie, something is the star that needs to be served. Hopefully, your goal as a director is to be in a position one day where your contribution is what people are interested in seeing more than anything else. I am in a bit of a crossroads right now. I don't want to be heading in a direction of irrelevance. I need to do something for a different reason now. I need to do something different.

That's what I've found interesting about your dad's career. He's done all kinds of movies.

Yeah, he's done comedies, action movies . . . even early in his career he did dramas. The first thing he ever wrote, *T. R. Baskin*, was about a single woman living in the city, and it was a very different kind of story. In his mind, I think he's always had the philosophy that he can direct any kind of movie. It didn't matter what it was.

Is there anything else you'd like to say to fans of the *Universal Soldier* franchise?

Universal Soldier 4: Day of Reckoning . . . I want people to see this movie with an open mind. As I alluded to before, this isn't a definitive statement. This isn't the only story that can be told from this mythology. This franchise is bigger than me. It's probably even bigger than the actors in it. It's a set of characters. Just like Batman is bigger than Christian Bale. What I'm bringing to this storyline is obviously what interested me. If I look at *Regeneration* and *Day of Reckoning*, the parts of the story that interested me the most were the stories of the monsters themselves. To me, the true villain of *Regeneration* was the government scientist who created these monsters and played God. They created an enslaved race. I became very interested in the existential dilemma of the creation of someone that was created to be as human as possible but there's always something keeping them from experiencing things like the rest of us do. I thought that was an interesting area to explore. "Is there something missing, is there some kind of void in my soul?" In the case of *Day of Reckoning*, we're dealing with something where they literally have a void in their souls. They might not be aware of it, but it's about the process of discovering it. It's going to be about these characters coming into conflict with each other, but the root of the story has to come from someplace that is meaningful to you as a storyteller and as an audience. This is not the only story that can be told in this universe, but it is *a* story that can be told. It's just the story I wanted to tell.

Universal Soldier II: Brothers in Arms
1998 (TVA Films DVD) (djm)

Intended as a pilot for a proposed television series, *Brothers in Arms* picks up right when the original Roland Emmerich film ends, and explores the relationship between Luc Deveraux and the spunky reporter Veronica Roberts. Non-action star Matt Battaglia (who tries a little martial arts here, but fails miserably) fills Jean-Claude Van Damme's shoes, while Chandra West replaces Ally Walker. Deveraux and Roberts go on the run from the government spooks who have labeled them a threat in the media, and when Deveraux is captured, he's brainwashed (again) and becomes a mindless drone for a while until Roberts saves him by also rescuing his long-thought-dead brother Eric (played by real action star Jeff Wincott from *Mission of Justice*). Eric and his brother Luc try bonding even though they're both technically dead, so they have (at the very least) a common ground. The real villains in the movie are the government brass, led by Gary Busey, who spends most of his key scenes gunning down innocent soldiers and government employees.

A dismal attempt to revitalize the *Universal Soldier* name, this film feels rushed and compromised at every turn, and while it's pretty difficult to recast Van Damme, they did a terrible job by putting Matt Battaglia in the lead role. He doesn't even have a French accent! Wincott is usually great in whatever he's in, but here he barely has a chance to flex his muscles or do some martial arts. Overall, this movie is a waste. Followed by *Universal Soldier III: Unfinished Business*. *Universal Soldier: The Return*, starring Van Damme, was made and released in 1999, and it was his last theatrical release for nearly a decade. Directed by Jeffrey Woolnough.

Universal Soldier III: Unfinished Business

1999 (TVA Films DVD) (DL)

"What do you call that? Taekwon-don't?"

The third outing in the *Universal Soldier* series won't make much sense unless you've seen part two. But if you have, then you probably won't want to see part three. This one opens with an unhelpful recap of the previous movie featuring some random clips and enough Gary Busey to make us wish he was in this one, too. Once again the Universal Soldier program has been reactivated and dead warriors are being resurrected for nefarious purposes. Van Damme's Luc Deveraux returns, but he's shape-shifted into football player-turned-monotone actor Matt Battaglia. Partnered again with reporter Veronica Roberts (also recast from the original film), Luc races against time to expose the evildoers. Meanwhile Burt Reynolds collaborates with mad scientists to grow a clone of Luc's dead brother in an elaborate ploy to entrap the unstoppable Luc and blow him up good. Taekwondo black belt Jeff Wincott makes a glorified cameo as the test tube sibling, landing a few blows in a lop-sided battle with Battaglia before recognizing him as kin. They share a quick brotherly bear hug before Wincott gets nuked by Burt's cronies. Wincott fans be warned: he's seven minutes in and out despite prominent billing on the poster.

Universal Soldier 3 was written by Peter M. Lenkov (*Demolition Man*) and directed by Jeff Woolnough who went on to helm episodes of more respectable fare like *Dark Angel*, the revamped *Battlestar Galactica*, and *Vikings*. It's the back end of a two-part pilot designed to launch a regular series and does indeed look made for television. Action scenes are brief and by the numbers. Woolnough tries dressing things up with generous amounts of slow motion (including lots of the herky-jerky post production type) and a bizarre soundtrack of lyric-heavy rock songs that have nothing to do with what's happening. The real draw here is Burt Reynolds's spectacularly weird performance. Speaking with a half-assed Irish accent, he spends every scene chomping cigars that are probably the most expensive thing on screen. The ending hints at a future chapter featuring the Bandit himself as a Universal Soldier. Now that would be a sequel worth watching.

Universal Soldier: Regeneration

2009 (Sony DVD) (djm)

The *Universal Soldier* franchise gets a kick in the pants and a major shot of adrenaline in the arm with this revisionist entry from director John Hyams (son of Peter Hyams). A rehabilitated Luc Deveraux (Jean-Claude Van Damme) is slowly being reintegrated back into society, but he is forced to turn on the switch that will transform him into a killing machine once again when all efforts have failed to rescue the kidnapped son and daughter of an Eastern European diplomat. The dismantled "UniSol" project isn't as top secret as it used to be, and a terrorist organization that has kidnapped the diplomat's children are now employing one of the core developers of the UniSol program to ensure maximum effect in security and protection. In addition to having an army of disposable men, they have a single Universal Soldier (Andrei "The Pitbull" Arlovski) on their team, and he's unstoppable. When Deveraux is forced into action he is faced with his most difficult assignment: Save the children, diffuse a bomb, and eliminate the other UniSol. But there's something else: A cloned Andrew Scott (Dolph Lundgren reprising his role from the first film) is thrown into the mix, making his task that much more difficult.

Universal Soldier: Regeneration is an amazing achievement. It takes the virtually dead *Universal Soldier* franchise and brings it front and center in the action movie world and shows it off as a completely revamped and thrilling entity. It puts Van Damme in the center of one of his best and most deadly serious movies, and it should turn dormant fans back in his favor. As the "bad" Universal Soldier, Arlovsky isn't messing around, and his performance is all about his physicality. Lundgren is great for the little amount of time he's on screen. The script by Victor Ostrovsky is radically interesting, and the direction by Hyams is unbelievably intense. His father Peter (director of *Timecop* and *Sudden Death* with Van Damme) was the director of photography. The sequel is *Day of Reckoning*, starring Scott Adkins.

Universal Soldier: The Return

1999 (Sony DVD) (ZC)

The late '90s were mankind's intellectual and cultural outhouse. This statement may sound incendiary to those raised in the warm glow of *Saved by the Bell*, but I dare you to watch the second *Universal Soldier* movie and tell me I'm wrong. It's a bloodless amalgamation of cyberpunk, WWE posturing, Hallmark sentimentality, and small-screen would-be extremes, all set to an uncompromising nu-metal score complete with constipated gorilla vocals.

The screenwriters weren't concerned with the plot so I won't bother with it either. Basically, undead military man Luc Deveraux (Jean-Claude Van Damme) is back in the "UniSol"

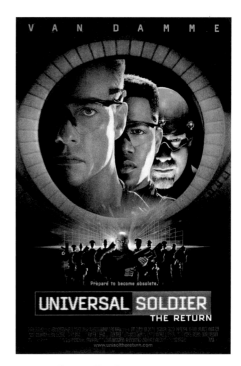

Universal Soldier: The Return theatrical poster. Author's collection.

system, working with the program's developers. He and his daughter are endangered when UniSol computer S.E.T.H. takes control of the government plant with near-SkyNet force, and Deveraux must ally with a hundred useless cops and a whiny female reporter to rage against the machine (I threw that one in there for you '90s apologists). When the other UniSols—including wrestler/non-actor Bill Goldberg—fail to carry out the sinister objective, S.E.T.H. assumes the human form of male physical ideal: Michael Jai White. While he and Van Damme kick each other reeeal good and make every effort to carry the film, it ultimately collapses under the weight of its own titanic nothingness.

Unleashed

2003 (Universal DVD) (djm)

A low-rent London underworld crime boss named Bart (Bob Hoskins) has something his competition doesn't have: Danny (Jet Li), a collared man-child, who is a beast when "unleashed," but a tame kitten when his collar is on. Bart uses him to rough up guys or to smash skulls in or simply as defense when needed, and Danny is a damaged innocent who doesn't realize what has been done to him over the years. When Bart's competition moves in on him and shoots him up and leaves him for dead, Danny has an incredibly rare opportunity to venture off on his own, and he ends up befriending an old blind piano repairman named Sam (Morgan Freeman), who takes him in under his wing and over the course of several months, Danny is treated like family, and he learns to trust and love, things he's never known before. By accident, Danny is discovered by some of Bart's associates, and he's forcefully brought before his "master" and, just like that, Danny's comfort and brief solace are stripped from him and he's thrust into an underground to-the-death fight circuit where he at first refuses to fight, but when he doesn't have a choice he fights with a newly found rage. He then turns on his "master" (a maimed Bart, who has become even more spiteful) and returns to his home and family with Sam and his kind step daughter, Victoria (Kerry Condon).

At turns brutal and genteel, *Unleashed* actually gives Jet Li a chance to act and play a character with depth, which is great. He's convincing as both the abused, brutish animal he's made to be and also as the innocent and kindly child-like man he is. Scripter Luc Besson worked well with Li, as he also wrote his best English-language film *Kiss of the Dragon*. Director Louis Leterrier (*Transporter 2*) packs in the action and gives the film a stark, chilling vibe throughout. In one scene Li fights four tournament fighters at once. One of those fighters is Scott Adkins, who would go on to become a household action star on his own.

Unrivaled

2010 (Lionsgate DVD) (CD)

"Only for the few minutes in the cage, I feel like I belong in this world. I might go down a 100 times but I'm bound and determined to get up 101 times."

Ringo Duran (Hector Echavarria) is an aging fighter who's down on his luck. He owes $20,000 to a small-time mobster and works in a strip club. He's been losing fights and has a bum shoulder. He doesn't have much faith in himself but his sidekick Link (Steven Yaffee) has enough for the both of them. He enters Ringo into a tournament that could lead him to a championship bout. At first, Ringo is against the tournament but with the support of Link, his girlfriend Kara (Jordan Madely), and his trainer Raphael (Nicholas Campbell), he decides to give it his all. The current champion (he's also part owner) of the top fighting league, Christopher Holland (Rashad Evans), wants Ringo taken out of the tournament as soon as possible and by any means necessary. The thing no one expects is how much heart Ringo truly has and it won't be as easy as they think it will be to get rid of him.

Unrivaled is a five-star action extravaganza that is aimed at a mostly male audience. There are constant breasts and beatings on display to hold the eyes of those with short attention spans. Thankfully, the film has some substance as well with a terrific performance by Hector Echavarria (*Los Bravos*). Much like his character, he puts his heart and soul into the role, and you will quickly find yourself rooting for him to succeed. He's in great shape and his fighting skills look top notch here. Much of the fighting is MMA style (it's a Tapout Film after all), but there are a couple of street fights where Hector is able to show off some different techniques. Several real-life MMA fighters appear in the film including Forrest Griffin (*Locked Down*), Keith Jardine, Nate Marquardt, and Rashad

Evans, who shines as the villain. Echavarria also served as the producer and contributed to the writing of the film. Director Warren Sonoda (*Ham & Cheese*) was able to take a standard and predictable underdog story and infuse it with energy and a thumping soundtrack to create an excellent action film.

Unstoppable

2004 (Sony DVD) (djm)

An ex-special ops soldier named Dean Cage (Wesley Snipes) is at a diner, waiting for a girlfriend, when he's mistakenly identified as a CIA target by a group of terrorists who inject him with an experimental drug. They abduct him after a brief chase, and the aftermath at the diner leaves a few clues for his girlfriend (an FBI agent) and the cops to follow. Cage is interrogated by his abductors, who think he's someone else, and their intent is to find out what he knows about the drug he's been injected with. The terrorists (who include Stuart Wilson, Kim Coates, and Mark A. Sheppard) have already stolen some of the drugs from a government facility, but they think that Cage has information about them and their plans, hence the rigmarole they go through to capture him. In the meanwhile, the drugs play havoc on Cage's body, and combined with his PTSD and the trauma he experienced in a recent war where his best friend was tortured to death, he has an extreme uphill battle to stay alive, escape, and find an antidote before he keels over and dies.

Unstoppable marks the first significant movie that Wesley Snipes starred in that went directly to video, and compared to the DTV movies that he starred in after this one, it feels closer to a theatrical feature. The action scenes are solid, and there's a good looking stunt where Snipes is dangling over an overpass as the big rig truck he's holding onto blows up and falls hundreds of feet to the ground in a glowing fireball. It's a neat scene, and some of this movie looks expensive, but what undoes the movie is a confusing plot, jump cuts, annoying hallucination scenes, and an overall lack of compelling direction. The director, David Carson, mostly has a history of directing episodic television, and his previous feature before this one was the straight-to-video Patrick Swayze movie *Letters from a Killer*. From Millennium.

Until Death

2006 (Sony DVD) (djm)

Skirting the edge of suicidal and heroic, detective Anthony Lowe (Jean-Claude Van Damme) has a mortal enemy: master criminal Callaghan (Stephen Rea). To cope with the stress of his job, Lowe seeks highs of various sorts, including shooting heroin and having sex with women he meets but doesn't know. After a fellow detective is murdered by Callaghan on Lowe's watch, he wages a personal vendetta against Callaghan, who wages one back. When Callaghan shoots Lowe in the skull, Lowe goes into a coma for

seven months while his pregnant wife (Selina Giles) moves on with another man. Finally, Lowe wakes up and rehabilitates himself with a newfound humility, and when Callaghan finds out that he's up and around, the game is on again as Callaghan has his wife kidnapped, with the hopes of drawing him out for a final one on one.

Van Damme has never been better as he is in *Until Death*. His role has several interesting arcs, and Van Damme (on a full career upswing) does an amazing job of playing it. His haggard, sickly appearance in the first half is matched by a nihilistic attitude, which completely changes when he wakes up from the coma. At that point, he's cleaner, slower, and even has a convincing speech impediment, which compliments his character's attempt to make amends with those he's wronged, including himself. Anyone who says Van Damme isn't a good actor should see this one after watching *JCVD* and try to stick to their original assessment. It's impossible to not see that he'd gotten really good at this point in his career. *Until Death* is one of his best. Directed by Simon Fellows, who also did *Second in Command* with Van Damme. From Millennium Films.

Urban Justice

2007 (Sony DVD) (djm)

If there was ever a movie to put Steven Seagal back on the big screen, it would have been *Urban Justice*. It's a back-to-basics and why-we-loved-him-in-the-first-place movie, and he's better in this than he was in half of his theatrical motion pictures, and certainly in all of his direct-to-video movies. He plays a guy named Simon Ballister, an angry and grieving man whose sole purpose in life is to find his son's killer. His son, an LA cop, was murdered in cold blood in the line of duty, and when Simon, the estranged father, enters the picture, the hood has something to fear. The small-time gangsters and thugs who cross paths with him have never seen or heard of anyone so badass and relentless. He hurts people so bad they never get up again, and he has a code few people understand. He's exactly the type of guy Steven Seagal should be playing more often, and without the bullshit that weighs down most of his direct-to-video movies.

Don't let the generic title and piss-poor box cover art dissuade you into thinking that this is just another cheapjack Steven Seagal movie. It's not. It's his best movie since *Out For Justice*. His fights are awesome, and as far as I can tell, he did his own stuff in it. The camera stays on his face, and there aren't too many "cheat" angles. He even kicks some guys, which shocked the hell out of me. He seems leaner, meaner, and more aggressive in this one, which fits the story. The bad guys (mostly thugs and gangbangers) haven't a clue how to deal with him. When the few people who seem to understand how deadly he is (guys like Danny Trejo and Eddie Griffin) actually meet him face to face, they just *understand*. This is the guy you don't mess with. The director, Don E. Fontleroy (who was also the director of photography), worked with Seagal to lesser effect on *Mercenary For Justice* and on *Today You Die*, which wasn't bad. Sadly, they've not made a movie together since *Urban Justice*.

Urban Warfare (a.k.a. True Justice: Urban Warfare)

2011 (Studiocanal DVD R2) (djm)

Seattle detective Elijah Kane (Steven Seagal) and his band of ultra elite cops are on the hunt for a rapist/sex offender, and in the meantime, Kane is being hunted down by some black ops goons. He suspects one of his own detectives of betraying him to al Qaeda, but the truth is slightly more interesting: When Kane was a black ops soldier in Afghanistan, he saved the life of an American soldier who was about to be beheaded in front of a death squad of al Qaeda soldiers. Kane not only killed all of the al Qaeda guys, but a camera filmed him doing the whole thing. When Kane figures out that al Qaeda has put a bounty on his head in Seattle, he calls on the soldier whose life he saved, and it turns out that the soldier has sold him out to the highest bidder. In the meanwhile, Kane's team of detectives solve the case of the sex offender (it was an administrator at a university) and they jump right into their next case, which involves a slew of vivisected female corpses. That case leads Kane and his team to a Russian mafia who are smuggling diamonds through the bodies of young women.

This is the sixth compilation from Steven Seagal's *True Justice* TV series. While taken out of context, it is a little disorienting in its abruptness, but if taken in the stream of the program, it makes a little bit more sense. A misleading title and DVD cover art aside, *Urban Warfare* has some nice little moments for Seagal. Directed by Keoni Waxman.

U.S. Marshals

1998 (Warner DVD) (CD)

"If everybody walks away breathing, everybody wins."

Mark Warren (Wesley Snipes) is a tow truck driver in Chicago and finds himself in a nasty accident. When he's retrieved from the wreckage, a concealed weapon is found and he's arrested. When the authorities check his fingerprints, they learn that he's wanted on federal murder charges. He ends up on a transport plane to New York where he's being extradited with several other prisoners. Overseeing the entire transportation is Deputy US Marshal Sam Gerard (Tommy Lee Jones). Things quickly go south when a Chinese assassin tries to shoot Warren, which depressurizes the cabin, forcing the plane to make a crash landing. Warren uses the opportunity to escape, and Gerard isn't

one to just let a man go. He learns Warren was wanted for killing two DSS agents, and he must team up with another one, Agent John Royce (Robert Downey Jr.), on the manhunt. With each step they grow closer to finding Warren, but as evidence is revealed, it looks like Warren may not be as guilty as he seemed. There's a much larger conspiracy being covered up, and Gerard and his team must use every resource they have to uncover the truth.

Even with a large ensemble cast, *U.S. Marshals* is still a one-man show. Tommy Lee Jones returns to his Academy Award–winning role of Sam Gerard from *The Fugitive* (a blockbuster starring Harrison Ford). This time, the fugitive he's after is portrayed by Wesley Snipes (one of Warner Brother's headlining action stars of the 1990s), and his innocence isn't as clear-cut as Ford's character was in the first film. Snipes spends most of the film running and hiding but has a few exciting moments of action to bring you to the edge of your seat. The script by John Pogue is weak, so it's the performances that drive the film and set it apart from other big-budget action thrillers. Even with guys like Snipes, Downey Jr., and Joe Pantoliano in the cast, the film depends on Jones, and he's brilliant. This was only the second film to be directed by veteran editor Stuart Baird, who previously helmed *Executive Decision*.

U.S. Seals 2

2001 (Artisan DVD) (CD)

After being betrayed by his best friend Chief Frank Ratliff (Damian Chapa), Lt. Casey Sheppard (Michael Worth) is ready to leave the Navy behind and retire from his SEAL team. Several years pass and Ratliff steals a nuclear warhead that he threatens to unleash unless the government pays him off. Shepard comes out of retirement and assembles a team to stop him. There's a leak of natural gas within the facility, and guns are not allowed to be fired anywhere near it. When the SEAL team breaches the compound, they will have to fight their way in with fists, swords, and chains if they want to stop Ratliff before he kills millions.

Director Isaac Florentine (*Cold Harvest*) almost never disappoints when it comes to action. *U.S. Seals 2* starts out pretty slow but if you hang in there, you will be rewarded with some fantastic fight scenes and stunt work rivaling most Hollywood films. Michael Worth (*Fists of Iron*) has never looked better. He really shows off his skill and agility in the Hong Kong–styled inspired action. Halfway through, the fighting kicks off with the entire SEAL team in a bloody battle against all of Ratliff's men. The choreography by Andy Cheng (*The Rundown*) is terrific and adrenaline fueled. *U.S Seals 2* also features one of the greatest death scenes for a villain ever committed to celluloid. Certain aspects of the film may be silly (sound effects, story) but after that first forty-five minutes, the action never lets up. When you pair Isaac Florentine with the production studio Nu Image, you really can't go wrong.

Vampire Assassin

2006 (Lionsgate DVD) (CD)

"He's so ugly he can break daylight with his fists!"

Police officer Derek (Ron Hall from *Triple Impact*) has lived his life fearing blood after witnessing a traumatic event as a child. Now, he must put the fear aside to go after a vicious crime figure known as Slovak (Mel Novak). He and his team raid Slovak's warehouse, only to have it blow up in his face. Derek, the lone survivor, learns Slovak is a vampire and seeks help from Master Kao (Gerald Okamura), a hunter ready to train him in the ancient art of vampire slaying. When it's time to face Slovak again, physically he will be prepared, but mentally, he may not be ready for what he will learn.

The level of enjoyment you get out of *Vampire Assassin* will rely solely on how you decide to view the film. If you take a serious approach, then you will realize it's quite possibly one of the worst films ever made. Or, you can decide to just have a few drinks with friends and allow the movie to bring a smile to your face. Ron Hall is a talented martial artist—there's no question about it. He fights his way through countless enemies doing his best Snipes impersonation. The effects were cheaply done, and it's hard to imagine the film being done on a budget of more than a few hundred dollars. With Hall pulling triple duty on the picture (director, writer, star), he was able to save some change. We are also treated to appearances by the great Gerald Okamura and Dolemite himself, Rudy Ray Moore. If you're looking for cheap, silly fun, then I guess it won't hurt you to give it a shot.

Vampire Effect

(a.k.a. The Twins Effect)

2003 (Sony DVD) (CD)

It's Jackie's (Jackie Chan) wedding day and he couldn't be more excited. All he wants is for his father to be impressed by his bride Ivy (Karen Mok) but things seem to be going sour. Before they even have a chance to say their vows, Ivy starts playing drinking games and ends up two sheets to the wind. To make matters worse, the best man loses the four-carat wedding ring. When the ceremony begins, the kindness of two strangers, Helen (Charlene Choi) and Kazaf (Edison Chen), allows him the chance to complete the ceremony by giving him a temporary ring. Several days later Kazaf is in dire need of help and Helen has no one to turn to: They're being hunted by a savage group of vampires and Jackie (an ambulance driver) is up for the challenge. Not believing what he is confronted with, he is quick to use his hands and feet to defeat the supernatural attackers.

Vampire Effect is way more fun than it should have been with spectacular fights, impressive visual effects, and a cast you can never

V

look away from. The film was directed by Dante Lam (*Beast Cops*) with help from Donnie Yen (*Ip Man*) handling the action department. Jackie Chan shows up to make a few jokes, gets chased in his ambulance by vampires on motorcycles, and seemingly fumbles through a fight with the undead. This will probably be the only time you'll see something like that from Chan, so savor it. The story is carried by the incredibly cute Cantopop duo Twins (Gillian Chung and Charlene Choi) in their film debut. It was the top box-office draw the year it was released and won several notable awards, including one for Donnie Yen and his action design. If you could turn an action film into a number one pop single, then this is it.

Vanishing Son

1994–1995 (NOV) (djm)

A witness to the Tiananmen Square massacre in China, Jian-Wa (Russell Wong) illegally immigrates to the United States with his brother Wago (Chi Muoi Lo) to seek political asylum. A proficient martial artist and studious musician (a violinist), Jian-Wa finds love and employment in the US while his brother Wago joins a crime syndicate and gets involved with murder, prostitution, and drugs. When his brother is murdered in a standoff, Jian-Wa is blamed for the death as well as the deaths of several government employees, and so he goes on the lam across the US as a vagrant. Two government agents hunt him as he goes from town to town, peacefully interfering with the lives of strangers. He falls in love over and over again, uses his martial arts to protect himself, and he visits old friends and distant relatives, always searching for a home.

Told over the course of four feature-length movies and a thirteen-episode TV series, *Vanishing Son* was part of Universal's "Action Pack" experiment to ignite television series. From creator Rob Cohen, this show was not only an outstanding attempt to show that Asians could carry a well-produced TV program with great action and stories, but also an exemplary vehicle for star Russell Wong, who fit the role gracefully and believably. Sadly, the show was short-lived and Wong did not go on to become the action star he should have. With his real-life skills in the martial arts, his talent for acting, and his good looks, he should have become one of the busiest action stars in the business, but it just didn't pan out for him. He would go on to star opposite Jet Li in both *Romeo Must Die* and *The Mummy: Tomb of the Dragon Emperor*. Strangely, *Vanishing Son* has yet to be released on home video. Find it if you can.

Velocity Trap

1998 (Sony DVD) (djm)

From the director of the post-apocalyptic films *Prototype X29A* and *A.P.E.X.*, *Velocity Trap* stars French action star Olivier Gruner of *Nemesis* and *Angel Town*. Set in outer space, Gruner plays a wrongfully accused police officer named Stokes who is aboard a ship that is threatened by thieves, and greater still, by an asteroid. His only ally is the ship's navigator, played by Alicia Coppola, and together they face a huge challenge: surviving The Velocity Trap.

With a cast of about a half a dozen or so, this bottom-of-the-barrel no-brainer gives Gruner almost nothing to do. He has one brief fight scene, which constitutes a waste of time for him as an action star and a waste of time for the viewer, who can do better with almost anything that premieres on the SyFy Channel. I listened to the commentary track of *Velocity Trap* and director Roth spends the entire time mocking his own film, and Gruner mocks it along with him. I rest my case.

Vendetta

2015 (Lionsgate DVD) (djm)

Here's the thing: Every time WWE Studios announces their next slate of movies featuring their in-house wrestling superstars, I get excited. I don't watch wrestling. Never have, never will, but the fact that WWE has built a roster of action-stars-in-waiting through wrestling entertainment in this downloadable age of cinema is a feat that only very few fans of action cinema can understand and appreciate. If you miss the days of The Cannon Group and the heyday of ninjas and mowing down bad guys with machine guns, then pay attention to WWE Studios and the art of the body slam because they're the Cannon of today. Since WWE tried to make John Cena an action star with the PG-13 rated *The Marine*, I've been on board with what they've been trying to do. While most of the films cater to the PG-13 demographic, the occasional hard "R"-rated entry gets out there like *The Condemned* with "Stone Cold" Steve Austin or the latter three entries in *The Marine* franchise. Basically, WWE has been testing the waters with their in-house stars with these relatively low-budget action films, and while the results have been all over the map, the intention is always there to create the next big deal in action movies the way they helped cultivate Dwayne "The Rock" Johnson and "Stone Cold" Steve Austin into mainstays in the genre outside of WWE's parameters.

John Cena—after four PG-13-rated WWE films (*The Marine, 12 Rounds, Legendary* and *The Reunion*)—failed to ignite a spark with fans of action movies because WWE played it too safe with him. We've gotten minor efforts with Adam "Edge" Copeland (*Bending the Rules*), Paul "Triple H" Levesque (*The Chaperone* and *Inside Out*), Randy Orton (a supporting role in *That's What I Am* and the lead in *12 Rounds 2: Reloaded*), Glenn "Kane" Jacobs (both *See No Evil* movies), Dylan "Hornswoggle"

Postl (*Leprechaun: Origins*), and some better entries with Ted DiBiase Jr. (*The Marine 2*), and hit-and-miss movies with Mike "The Miz" Mizanin (*Christmas Bounty* and *The Marine 3* and 4). The one guy I wasn't really paying attention to was Paul "The Big Show" Wight, who had headlined the goofy WWE comedy *Knucklehead*, but when it was announced that he would be starring in Jen and Sylvia Soska's *Vendetta* I got real interested because this would be the first time I would get to see the 7 foot tall Wight in a real action movie, and directed by the Soskas no less. The Soska twins have come from really edgy horror films, and while I didn't particularly care for their *See No Evil 2* film, I was definitely primed for what they would do in the action genre, and now that I've seen the hard "R"-rated *Vendetta* I can report back on the film and how "The Big Show" fared in his first real action piece.

Vendetta lays the groundwork for the rest of the movie in the first handful of scenes. Good cop Mason Danvers (Dean Cain, who tries real hard to be an action star here) busts bad guy Victor Abbot (Wight, who even on his knees stands almost as tall as Cain on his tiptoes) and his scuzzbag brother Griffin (Aleks Paunovic), but both brothers are released on a technicality the very next day. The first thing Victor does is go straight to Danvers's home and brutally murder his pregnant wife in a graphic scene that had my jaw gaping in surprise. Danvers shows up just a second after Victor has done his work, and the enraged cop shows shocking restraint by not killing him right there on the spot. That's where the movie pretty much drops the title of the film on you, and so I was ready for the next transition, which puts Danvers in full-on Punisher mode as he hunts down Griffin and some of his associates, killing all of them in cold blood in front of another cop just so that there's a witness to his crime. Danvers is quickly processed, declared guilty, and in seconds of screen time he's already in the slammer in the same penitentiary as Victor, who is running the place like a demented Bull Hurley (*Over the Top*, guys: pay attention) lording over the big house. Victor is so absolutely in charge that his minions skitter around him, afraid and in awe of his beastliness. When Danvers encounters him, though, he doesn't bat an eye, and in fact something deep and good has broken in Danvers's own soul and he has no other

Vendetta press release poster. Author's collection.

purpose in life other than to kill Victor and everyone who dares to be on his side. The vendetta is his mission, and nothing else matters. He gets jumped (but not raped), beaten, and thrown in the hole for weeks at a time, and yet he always comes back out to ambush and murder another of Victor's men until Victor runs to the oily warden (played by Michael Eklund who is on his sixth WWE release), who sees that Danvers is on a rampage and realizes that something must be done about it. The warden—who has a dark history with Victor—gives him some leeway to kill and

V

murder with extreme prejudice on his watch, but Danvers somehow always comes out on top until the climax when all hell breaks loose when there's a prison raid, with full-on chaos and pandemonium throughout the prison. The prisoners go on a feeding frenzy, tons of guards are slaughtered, and Danvers finally has his chance to go one-on-one with the mountainous Victor, who is a brick wall with legs.

There's a lot to like about *Vendetta*. The Big Show gets to showcase what a monster of a man he is. Sometimes he doesn't even have to move a muscle to beat a man down in this movie. When he's active, he throws guys around, pummels Dean Cain to a pulp, and he's a wonder to behold. He's technically an action star, but since he's not the hero, we're never rooting for him. The role that Dean Cain plays should have been played by somebody like Scott Adkins or once upon a time by Lorenzo Lamas or even Michael Dudikoff, but Cain does what he can (and a little more, surprisingly) with it, and he makes it work. If you won't watch this movie because Cain is in it, you're making a mistake. Watch it because The Big Show is in it, and Cain will win you over. The Soskas haven't forgotten their roots in horror, as this is easily the goriest film from WWE studios outside of maybe the first *See No Evil* movie. In *Vendetta*, characters are beaten to death, stabbed until their faces are unrecognizable, choked, bludgeoned, forced to commit suicide, shot, thrown off buildings, and crushed to death. This is like those prison movies from the '70s and '80s where they would even throw a crazed dwarf at the audience (Cannon's *Penitentiary III*, hello?) just to get a reaction from them. *Vendetta*—as corny as it is sometimes—really goes for broke and shakes up the pot WWE has been stewing for the last decade, and it's a jambalaya of exploitation goodness fans of these types of movies shouldn't be able to resist. I had a really good time with it. The Big Show has arrived, as far as I'm concerned, and I'm really looking forward to whatever WWE puts him in next.

Vengeance
(a.k.a. **Kid Vengeance**)
1977 (Miracle DVD) (CD)

"Get away from me, I can't stand the smell of you! I can't stand the smell of you stinking men!"

Isaac (Jim Brown) is out in the Wild West searching for gold and hoping to make it rich. He stumbles across a family that gives him a good meal and sends him on his way. Shortly after, the family runs afoul of McClain (Lee Van Cleef) and his gang of degenerates. The parents are brutally murdered while the daughter abducted. The only person left is the young boy named Tom (Leif Garrett) who witnesses the entire ordeal. He has a raging fire blistering inside him so he packs his stuff up and tracks the gang down. He can't do it all alone so he meets up again with Isaac who has had his gold stolen by the same gang. The two of them team up, and they're going to make these guys pay.

This is a surprisingly engaging story featuring top-tier performances from Jim Brown (*...tick... tick...tick*), Lee Van Cleef (*The Master*), and the young heartthrob of his day, Leif Garrett. Now, you might have to try really hard to stretch your imagination a bit in order to believe a little white boy like Garrett has to save Jim Brown, but other than this playful gripe, it's great cinema. Jim Brown gets to show off when it comes to the emotional finale. This was an early film from producers Menahem Golan and Yoram Globus (who both became mini moguls during their Cannon years) with skillful direction by Joseph Manduke.

Victory
(a.k.a. **Escape to Victory**)
1981 (Warner DVD) (djm)

Shot in between *Nighthawks* and *Rocky III*, John Huston's *Victory* stars Sylvester Stallone as a prisoner of war in World War II Germany. Stallone plays an American soldier named Hatch, who is building up to a big escape from the concentration camp, but when a German major named Von Steiner (Max Von Sydow) finds out that one of his prisoners—a Brit named Colby (Michael Caine)—was a famous soccer player, Von Steiner encourages Colby to form the best soccer team he can to compete against the German team to "boost morale." When Colby is given the go-ahead to create a team and begin training in earnest (with special treatment, extra rations, and better housing), Hatch ingratiates himself to Colby, with the hope that he can join the team. As it turns out, Hatch is a pretty good goalie, and as Colby's team (which includes real soccer star Pelé) gets into shape, a plan of mass escape from the allotted soccer field in Paris is formulated. It's going to be a great escape!

If you haven't seen *Victory* yet and you call yourself a fan of Stallone, you really need to see it. Lean, down-to-earth, and incredibly fit, Stallone shines in a Steve McQueen-type role that he rarely got a chance to play. His scenes on the soccer field are fun to watch, and his obvious inexperience as a player is evident, but kinda cool to behold. He plays well against co-star Caine (whom he would appear alongside again much later in *Get Carter*), and the whole PG-rated enterprise is endearing and old-fashioned.

Victory UK quad poster. Author's collection.

I highly recommend it. In addition to Pelé, more than a dozen professional soccer players appear in the film. Bill Conti's score is fantastic. Conti scored nine movies starring Stallone. This one was the fifth.

Vigilante
1983 (Blue Underground DVD) (djm)

"Hey. I don't know about you guys, but me, I've had it up to *here.* There are some forty-odd homicides a day on our streets. There are over two million illegal guns in this city. Man, that's enough guns to invade a whole damn country with! They shoot a cop in our city without even thinking twice about it! Now, come on. I mean, you guys ride the subway. How much more of this grief we gonna stand for? How many more locks we gotta put on our goddamn doors? Now, we ain't got the police, the prosecutors, the courts, or the prisons. I mean, it's *over.* The books don't balance. *We are a statistic.* Now, I'm tellin' you, you can't go to the corner and buy a pack of cigarettes after dark, because you know the punks and the scum own the street when the sun goes down, and our own government can't protect its own people. Then I say this, pal: You got a moral obligation, the right of self-preservation. Now you can run, you can hide, or you can start to live like human beings again. This is our Waterloo, baby! If you want your city back, you gotta take it! Dig it? *Take it!*"

William Lustig, the director of great grindhouse movies like *Maniac, Relentless,* and the *Maniac Cop* trilogy directed this slam-bang actioner that punches your gut and doesn't let you breathe before punching you again. Fred Williamson plays Nick, the leader of a vigilante group that hunts scumbags in the New York boroughs, and his friend Eddie (Robert Forster) is an honest factory worker, whose son is murdered and whose wife is maimed and brutally assaulted by a street gang. When the courts give the assailants a slap on the wrist, Eddie lashes out at the judge in court and is held in contempt and sent to prison for a short stint. He mulls his options over in prison, and the day he's released, he goes to Nick and joins the team of vigilantes and they go after the unpunished ruffians who ruined his life. With the police hunting *them*, Nick and Eddie plow through their nightly agenda, doing the work that no one else will.

Forceful, brutal, and intense, *Vigilante* is a great vehicle for Williamson even though Forster is really the star. Williamson gets the best moments (including the badass monologue that opens the film), and it's a shame there wasn't a *Vigilante 2* that featured more of him. A snappy, electronic score by Jay Chattaway is a highlight. Steve James and Woody Strode also appear in the movie in supporting roles.

V

The Villain

1979 (Sony DVD) (djm)

Before *Conan the Barbarian* and *The Terminator*, Arnold Schwarzenegger appeared in a few movies that had no idea what to do with him. In Hal Needham's zany western *The Villain*, Arnold plays a clean-cut (but buff) good guy named Handsome Stranger who saves a buxom beauty named Miss Charming Jones (a gorgeous Ann-Margret) from "the villain" Cactus Jack, played by Kirk Douglas. Handsome Stranger is so straight-laced and sweet that he's virtually virginal and clueless as to what effect he has on women around him, but Cactus Jack has him in his sights and spends the whole movie (all eighty-nine minutes of it, in fact) chasing after him like the Coyote in the old Road Runner cartoons. Pratfall after pratfall, Cactus Jack simply cannot catch up to Handsome Stranger and Miss Charming, but a switcheroo ending changes all that.

Filled with galumphing stunts and silly, cartoony music that overemphasizes the comedy, *The Villain* is pretty terrible, and Arnold plays it completely straight while everyone else around him is in full slapstick mode. Fans of his might want to see it for curiosity's sake, but it's just a blip on his career, and certainly not a necessary venture. It's interesting to see him in a western, performing some stunts (some courtesy of a double) on horses, but it's pretty much a waste of time. Kudos to John Milius and James Cameron for seeing the potential in him because *The Villain* doesn't do him any favors

Villa Rides!

1968 (Paramount DVD) (djm)

Yul Brynner is unrecognizable as Mexican revolutionary Pancho Villa, and Charles Bronson plays his trusty right-hand man Rodolfo Fierro, a ruthless (but likable) gunman who kills on whims. The revolution is in full swing when a downed American pilot named Lee Arnold (Robert Mitchum) ends up captured on Villa's turf. When Arnold manages to appeal to Villa's good senses, Arnold becomes a first-hand witness to the mayhem and methods to which Villa is willing to go through to attain his revolution.

Plodding, yet epic in scale, *Villa Rides!* might have been Oscar bait once upon a time, but the real (and only) treat of the film is seeing a chiseled Bronson in a delectable character role where he lines three guys up and shoots all three of them with a single bullet. Every time he's on screen, he commands your attention, which, while watching this film, will otherwise easily wane. Sam Peckinpah and Robert Towne wrote the screenplay, and Buzz Kulik directed.

Violence of Action (a.k.a. True Justice: Violence of Action)

2012 (Studiocanal DVD R2) (djm)

A Mexican cartel's money shipment is hijacked by a covert group calling itself "Quicksilver" and somehow security specialist Elijah Kane (Steven Seagal) gets involved. He follows the money trail and ends up going head to head with Quicksilver, which is a pretty easy (for him) task to accomplish. He gets a little sidetracked with a European gun-for-hire named Bojan (played by Darren Shahlavi), who proves to be a slightly more difficult challenge for Kane. Finally Kane and his dwindling team catch up to Bojan, who then is swiftly dispatched by Kane. Ironically, Kane delivers the stolen money back to the cartel, whom he has aligned himself with.

The ninth compilation of episodes from the *True Justice* TV series, *Violence of Action* is one of the good ones simply because it gives Steven Seagal a worthy adversary in Darren Shahlavi, who is always good as a bad guy in martial arts action movies. He's not just a throwaway villain here—he's able to give the character a little more dimension and the episodes allow him to flex his acting a little bit, while showing that he's a more than capable martial artist. He also fought Seagal in *Born to Raise Hell*. The next movie entry in this series is *Angel of Death*. This one was directed by Lauro Chartrand.

Violent City (a.k.a. The Family)

1970 (Anchor Bay DVD) (ZC)

Italian crime films got a tough rap, some of which was well deserved. The majority of them aimed for visceral thrills, delivering gunshots and car flips straight to the audience's gut, but made on the cheap-'n'-tawdry. But for every hundred or so Milanese gutter epics, there's one *Violent City*. Charles Bronson wasn't yet an American superstar in 1970, but European audiences had already recognized his power. Following his timeless performance in Sergio Leone's *Once Upon a Time in the West*, he was tapped for the lead in multiple European productions, most of which (*Cold Sweat*; *Rider on the Rain*) were modest at best. Sergio Sollima's *Violent City* is a monumental exception, and one that deserves much more attention than it's received.

Bronson is Jeff Heston, a once-untouchable gunman taken down by romantic betrayal (courtesy of Jill Ireland, Bronson's real-world wife). Heartbroken and imprisoned, he sketches out his ultimate vengeance. Minutes after his release, he's assassinating, beating and detonating his way back to dignity. But no matter how high the corpse tally rises, he still craves satisfaction, and he eventually clashes proverbial swords with the syndicate's top man (a shirtless Telly Savalas). Meanwhile, he and every other character are double-, triple- or quadruple-crossed, and the film's ruthless world is revealed to be worthy of its characters' paranoid misanthropy.

One can't discuss *Violent City* without mentioning the opening scene, a dialogue-free rampage through the winding cobblestone streets of small-town Italy, in which Bronson (or his stunt double driver) pilots a car up a flight of ancient stone stairs while evading gunfire. It's a pulse-pounding intro to our protagonist's survival skills, and it sets the pace for an unpredictable movie with refreshingly little conscience. Almost all of the scenes are shot as sweeping exteriors, allowing cinematographer Aldo Tonti to flex the impossible skills that he honed working with Fellini (*Nights of Cabiria*) and John Huston (*Reflections in a Golden Eye*). Ennio Morricone's score is among his best, adding massively to the tone, and igniting along with cars as they smash through brick walls. But nothing compares to *Violent City*'s climax, a calculated culmination of all the tension that came before, and my absolute favorite in Italian crime cinema.

Virtual Combat

1995 (Image DVD) (djm)

Set in a vague and cheap-looking future, *Virtual Combat* combines virtual reality elements and martial arts to make a wholly unsatisfying motion picture. Don "The Dragon" Wilson stars as David Quarry, a cop who chases espionage thieves and cyber smugglers who wheel and deal in the black market. The two most popular cyber programs involve cybersex or cyberfighting with gladiator-type fighters. A shady corporation creates living, breathing clones of two cybersex models to mass-produce later, but during the cloning process a deadly killer from a cyberfight game manages to have himself cloned in the real world, and once fully materialized, he goes on a killing spree. Quarry joins up with one of the cybersex clones, and they lie smack in the middle of the killer's path of carnage.

Since this is an Andrew Stevens picture, it seems definite that it will have that extra sleaze factor, which it has in spades. Nudity and soft-core sex play a big part in the film, and the action scenes are lightweight and don't carry much consequence. Wilson has two separate fights with Loren Avedon, who plays an incidental character (not the lead villain), but both fights are a letdown considering the possibilities. This feels more like a late-night Cinemax flick from the 1990s than a straight-up action movie.

Virus

1996 (Lionsgate DVD) (CD)

"She didn't sing it to me. It's not over, sir, not by a long shot."

The president's head of security Ken Fairchild (Brian Bosworth) travels to a national park in Oregon where a summit will be taking place to assess all security risks. Nearby, a tanker carrying a deadly virus crashes and the liquid escapes and leaks into the water stream. People quickly begin to fall ill, including Fairchild, and no one knows the cause. Fairchild meets a local veterinarian, Larraine (Leah Pinsent), who despite being infected, teams up with Fairchild to find the source of the spill and stop it from spreading. They learn it was an attempt to keep the president from speaking at the environmental summit, which is only a few hours away. They quickly learn there's a faction of the military behind the spill but they will need hard evidence in order to convince the president of what's happening. With time running out, they race through the wilderness to stop the virus from causing a mass infection.

Virus takes a little while before it gets trucking along but Brian Bosworth (*Stone Cold*) doesn't disappoint when it comes to laying out the bad guys. These can't really be called fight scenes when it's mostly the Boz obliterating the opposing forces with his killer clothesline or lightning-quick take downs. Some of these encounters really looked as if they hurt *bad*. The story is pretty much your typical government cover-up angle, and it serves the picture well. By setting the film in the wilderness, director Allan A. Goldstein (*Death Wish V*) gets some fantastic shots and sets up some interesting sequences. Leah Pinsent helps to bring out Bosworth's humorous side just a pinch, which the movie could've used more of. Bosworth himself is the sole reason to watch this picture, and he doesn't disappoint.

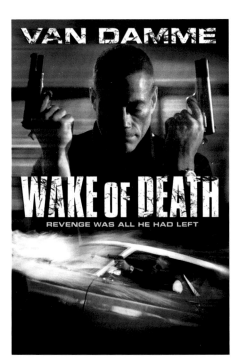

Wake of Death press release poster. Author's collection.

Wake of Death

2004 (Sony DVD) (CD)

"One man takes out three of your guys. I think that's a problem."

Ben Archer (Jean-Claude Van Damme) is a thug for a criminal organization, and he's ready to leave the life behind. The most important thing for him is keeping his wife and son safe. His wife Cynthia (Lisa King) is a worker for the INS who rescues a young girl named Kim (Valerie Tian) who was found with a group of immigrants. Cynthia takes her into their home to care for her. The girl's father is Sun Quan (Simon Yam), a vicious triad leader who is smuggling heroin into the country. Sun Quan wants his daughter back and kills Cynthia in the process. Ben's son Nicholas (Pierre Marais) escapes with Kim. Revenge is all Ben can think about. He sets off on a bloody rampage to avenge his wife's murder and keep his son and Kim safe.

Wake of Death is one of Jean-Claude Van Damme's (*Kickboxer*) best films. It's an outstanding action thriller that doesn't pull any punches and delivers the goods on every level. Van Damme gives a powerful performance as a man with a past who wants to protect his family. He proves that he can push the envelope with his range as an actor. There are plenty of fight scenes, bloody two-fisted shootouts, and a great motorcycle chase. Hong Kong veteran Simon Yam (*Full Contact*) is a brilliant performer. His body language and facial expressions can speak volumes; he's the perfect villain for the film. Director Philippe Martinez shows incredible skill behind the camera, fashioning a tense, exciting, and action-packed revenge film that deserves to be considered a minor classic. He took over the director's chair after Ringo Lam (*Maximum Risk*) left the project.

Walker, Texas Ranger

1993–2001 (Paramount DVD) (djm)

After a lucrative string of hard "R"-rated movies for The Cannon Group, Chuck Norris went out to pasture with *Walker, Texas Ranger*, a wildly successful TV program that lasted eight long seasons (with a total of 203 episodes!). Norris plays a variation of his role in *Lone Wolf McQuade*, but this time he's Cordell Walker, a part Native American Vietnam vet turned Texas Ranger who foils bad guys and terrorists on a weekly basis. His partner is former football pro James Trivette (Clarence Gilyard), who starts off as a fish out of water, but soon becomes

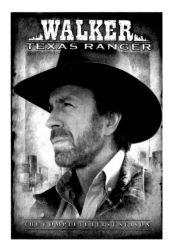

Walker, Texas Ranger DVD cover. Author's collection.

formidable back-up for Walker, who is always running horns-first into trouble. Their ally is the beautiful Alex Cahill (Sheree J. Wilson), a district attorney who has romantic feelings for Walker, but it takes a while for him to cozy up to her. After the sixth season, Walker and Trivette get more back-up with two rookie Rangers (played by Nia Peeples and Judson Mills), and there's a crossover in the eighth season with another show called *Martial Law*, which was Sammo Hung's vehicle show that only lasted two seasons.

Families and grandparents could watch and love *Walker, Texas Ranger*, as it targets them as their core audience. The violence is on a "PG" level, and every episode has Norris or his stunt double doing roundhouse kicks and punches, though the focus is never on action but instead on the characters who, up until about the fourth season, were appealing. When the show kept going like a juggernaut, the series took on a more corporate atmosphere, adding younger characters and dropping some of the older ones. By the second season, Norris himself sang the opening title song (wait until about midway through the second season for that), and his character became even more stoic and impenetrable. The first season is easily the best of the bunch, with a more vitalized and energetic Norris at the center, and the show itself felt more honest and akin to his film work than what would follow in the series. The pilot episode "One Riot, One Ranger" is often confused as a standalone movie, as it was released on video by Cannon in the mid 1990s. Walker would also appear in the short-lived TV series *Sons of Thunder*, which was spun off from *Walker*. There are a plethora of great guest stars that come and go on *Walker*. Just to name a few: Mike Norris, Richard Norton, James Lew, Cary-Hiroyuki Tagawa, Bob Wall, Martin Kove, Tommy "Tiny" Lister, Hulk Hogan, Brian Thompson, Kathy Long, Danny Trejo, and even Don "The Dragon" Wilson.

Walking Tall

2004 (MGM DVD) (djm)

A remake of the 1973 movie starring Joe Don Baker and the follow-ups starring Bo Svenson, this version of *Walking Tall* stars Dwayne "The Rock" Johnson as a recently returned war veteran named Chris Vaughn. His hometown is a shadow of what it once was: A casino is the sole source of income, and drugs, prostitution, and corruption have eaten away at the once-proud town. On his first day back, he goes to the casino with some friends, and over an infraction at one of the tables, he causes a ruckus, which results in him being brutally maimed and left for dead. After months in recuperation, he emerges with a bone to pick with the casino's owner, Jay Hamilton (Neil McDonough), who tries bribing him not to go

W

War veteran Chris Vaughn (Dwayne Johnson with the 2 × 4) and deputy Ray Templeton (Johnny Knoxville) usher a band of ruffians out of town in *Walking Tall*. Author's collection.

Walking Tall has a great shootout halfway through the film, featuring Dwayne Johnson and Ashley Scott. Author's collection.

Chris Vaughn (Dwayne Johnson) gets into a brawl at a casino in *Walking Tall*. Author's collection.

Neil McDonough and Dwayne Johnson duke it out with big sticks at the climax of *Walking Tall*. Author's collection.

Ray Templeton (Johnny Knoxville) takes up arms with Chris Vaughn (Dwayne Johnson) in *Walking Tall*. Author's collection.

to the authorities over his troubles, but Vaughn is a straight arrow, and his anger leads him down a path of controlled vengeance. Armed with a two-by-four, he demolishes the casino and breaks some bones of some hired thugs, and he's swiftly arrested and brought to trial for being a menace to society. In his trial, he sways the jury to his side by promising to clean up the town if he is elected sheriff, and so he's declared innocent, and in due course, he wins the election and becomes the town's new sheriff. Sporting a badge and his two-by-four, Vaughn does as promised, but it gets messy when Hamilton's underlings retaliate.

Between this movie (directed by Kevin Bray) and the films made in the '70s, there were a couple of good "B" action movies that told the same story. Jerry Trimble made *One Man Army* and Cynthia Rothrock made *China O'Brien*,

and both of those movies were just as fun as The Rock's *Walking Tall*, which bears the seal of approval as an official remake. It's short (eighty-six minutes with credits), and there's very little time for much other than action and set-up, so if you're looking for something very simple, easy to follow, and completely as advertised, then there's no reason why it won't make you happy. The Rock is good in it, and I like this better than his first film *The Rundown*, but it still feels compromised by a PG-13 rating. Co-starring Johnny Knoxville as one of the hero's buddies. Knoxville played a strikingly similar character in *The Last Stand*, starring Arnold Schwarzenegger. Two direct-to-video sequels/follow-ups called *Walking Tall: The Payback* and *Walking Tall: Lone Justice* starring Kevin Sorbo came in 2007.

War

2007 (Lionsgate DVD) (CD)

"It's you, isn't it? I remember your eyes, something real familiar about them. It's the one thing the surgeons can't change, can they? The eyes."

After his partner is killed by the vicious assassin known as Rogue (Jet Li), FBI agent Jack Crawford (Jason Statham) becomes obsessed with finding Rogue. It costs Crawford his family but he just can't let it go. Several years go by but eventually

Rogue resurfaces. Crawford is right there to greet him. He finds himself smack-dab in the middle of a mob war between the Yakuza and Triads. Rogue has his own reasons for pitting the two factions against one another while Crawford just uses it as an excuse to bring himself closer to stopping this assassin he has been trailing for years. When the two men eventually come face to face, the hatred they have for one another boils and everyone better move out of the way because these two explode with rage.

War isn't the big martial arts extravaganza many people may have expected from Li and Statham. There's plenty of action to be sure, except this one is filled with character and story. It's a fairly well-balanced mix and the two leads have great chemistry on screen (they've appeared together in five films so far). *War* is visually rich and fast-paced with an exciting cast to boot. Also in the cast are Sung Kang (*Fast Five*), John Lone (*The Hunted*) and Kane Kosugi (*Muscle Heat*). With all the car chases, shootouts, and fighting, each actor has his time to shine. The moment everyone may be waiting for is the showdown between Li and Statham. While there's some great stuff here, it just didn't quite meet expectations. The story (while very well done) feels like it was a set-up for a much bigger story. This still remains the only feature film directed by Philip G. Atwell.

Warhead

1996 (Vidmark VHS) (djm)

A terrorist named Craft (Joe Lara with a long, romantic ponytail) gets his hands on a nuclear missile and threatens to launch it on US soil to cleanse the world of corruption and oppression. A special forces team is assembled, and Tannen (Frank Zagarino) is the head of the team, and after his first bout with Craft, he has a lot to prove because Craft's strategy in an earlier encounter left Tannen licking his wounds. With the help of a female scientist who knows a thing or two about nuclear missiles, Tannen is able to get his team into a position to take Craft down, but a wrench is thrown into Tannen's mission when the scientist realizes that her father—a nuclear physicist—is working for Craft and has turned his heart against America.

A quickie Nu Image Production, *Warhead* feels like one of those *Operation Delta Force* movies, and it might as well be one, but as a stand-alone, it works on a nominal, numbing level where you absolutely must shut your brain down and let the gunfire, explosions, and karate fights just happen, because if you don't and if anybody else walks into the room when you're watching it, you'll be just a little embarrassed to explain why you're watching something so corny. Still, watching Zagarino beat the snot out of Joe Lara (who in another book might be considered an action star) is worth the price of a rental or a purchase. Directed by Mark Roper (who did *High Adventure* with Thomas Ian Griffith and *Queen's Messenger* with Gary Daniels).

War Pigs

2015 (Cinedigm DVD) (djm)

In the thick of World War II, Captain Jack Wosick (Luke Goss from *Death Race 2* and *3*) loses his whole squad (which includes UFC fighter Chuck Liddell in a cameo) in a mission that was doomed from the start. Wosick is commended for following bad orders, and his commanding officer, the Major (Mickey Rourke not looking so good) offers him another doomed mission, but only after promoting him. The mission is to spy out a new cannon the Germans are rumored to have built, and Wosick is given a new partner, a French Legionnaire named Hans Picault (Dolph Lundgren), who is to help him whip into shape a squadron of losers known as The War Pigs to go behind enemy lines and to report back what they see. After an extended training period (which takes up the greater part of the running time of the film), the platoon goes behind enemy lines deep into Nazi territory, and things go south when several of the War Pigs are captured. It's up to Wosick (who's on foot) and Picault (who hijacks a tank) to save the day, but instead of taking a passive approach to their mission, they end up blowing up the cannon real good for the hell of it.

A sort of send up of *The Dirty Dozen* done on a low budget, *War Pigs* is endearing, but lackluster. While I admire Luke Goss for what he's been able to accomplish in this downloadable age as an up-and-coming action star (with no skills in the martial arts or without any background in sports), he doesn't have much charisma or screen presence, which puts him in the deficit of anyone who stands next to him who has slightly more verve than he does. Anytime Lundgren is on screen in this movie, your eyes and attention immediately gravitate towards him, but Goss is the star of the movie even though he doesn't really deserve to be. As for the film itself, it doesn't have the energy it needs to retain any sort of action classic status. It's adequate, but not spectacular in any way. Rourke and Liddell are wasted in the film. By some miracle, this received a one-week theatrical engagement (which I saw) upon release. Directed by Ryan Little.

Warrior of Justice (a.k.a. Invitation to Die)

1995 (MP DVD) (CD)

"His last fight, he tore off the man's ears and held them up to the crowd."

George (Macedonian martial artist Jorgo Ognenovski) is a karate expert who is investigating the disappearance of his student Tony (Ian Jacklin from *Expert Weapon*). As he begins to discover information leading to the truth, an evil figure from his past appears to be the culprit: Verdugo (Jorge Rivero from *Fist Fighter*). Years ago the two had a confrontation,

and George left him scarred for life. He quickly learns that Verdugo has been running an underground fighting circuit and the losers are having their organs harvested. With guidance from his master (Richard Lynch) and against the wishes of his soon-to-be wife, he dives head-first into this brutal underworld to get the revenge his student Tony deserves.

Everything you shouldn't do when making an action flick was done when directors Mike Tristano (*Ultimate Prey*) and Jorgo Ognenovski (*Caged Fury*) pieced together this rotten little slice of cinema. Richard Lynch makes a cameo appearance as—wait for it—a long-haired martial arts master! Jorgo is a great fighter except that he seems to be more technical and stiff; he never really tries to adapt his style to be flashier on screen. The fights were horribly shot, using too many extreme close-ups, so essentially these guys are just flailing their arms (or swinging swords) at nothing, so no points there. The actress who plays Jorgo's lady spends the majority of the film in skimpy clothes, lingerie, or just buck-ass naked. This isn't a complaint, but she's playing a detective and her character seemed entirely unprofessional. There's enough action, though, to keep it fun, and appearances from Ian Jacklin (also in *Death Match*), Nils Allen Stewart (*Raw Target*), Nick Hill (*Bloodsport 2*), and Frank Dux (yep, the real Frank Dux) help.

War Wolves

2008 (Monarch DVD) (djm)

While engaging in combat in the Middle East with his special forces team, Jake Gabriel (Michael Worth from *Acapulco H.E.A.T.*) is infected with a deadly virus. A few years later, he's back home, trying to cope with PTSD, and he desperately tries to keep sane while working a dead-end job at a grocery store. He secretly suffers from the virus he contracted while at war, which, as it turns out, is the werewolf virus. He has no idea that he's being hunted by two separate groups: one group is a team of werewolf hunters (which includes John Saxon, Tim Thomerson, and Martin Kove), and the other group is his former special forces team, which has also succumbed to the werewolf virus. The other werewolves (who include three foxy female soldiers, who have embraced being werewolves) are out to force Jake to join them or die, and the hunters are out to kill him and any other creature that shows itself. As Jake fights the dormant monster within himself, he must also capitalize on his strengths as a man to protect his town and the people he has come to care about.

An odd mixture of quirky drama and hesitant action infused with a hybridized martial arts gives *War Wolves* a decidedly uneven tone, but fans of Michael Worth (who also wrote and directed this) should give it a go, as it allows him to experiment with his acting a little bit. This is not an action-packed creature feature, but when it has action, it's interesting to look at. The werewolves have an odd martial art all to themselves, and as they leap, jump, and flail around (aided by wires), they also engage in

martial arts combat. Some viewers will like this more than others. It's unusual. Worth has starred in his fair share of direct-to-video martial arts movie including *Fists of Iron* and *Ghost Rock*.

Way of the Black Dragon

1979 (BCI DVD) (djm)

Interpol agent Bill Eaton (Ron Van Clief) is in Hong Kong on a case involving some drug smugglers, and he comes to the aid of a drug mule named Allison who has become a slave of the cartel. Her brother (played by Carter Wong from *Big Trouble in Little China*) teams up with Bill to help his sister get out of the deadly drug and human trafficking trade. Both Bill and Allison's brother are martial arts experts, and their kung fu skills are needed when the cartel fights back.

Ron Van Clief (from *The Black Dragon*) doesn't show up for at least a half-hour into the film. His role is important, and fans of black action stars may want to track this film down, but it has a thick vein of misogyny running through it. Long scenes of female degradation and abuse play on and on, and most of the film is done in the grungy "grindhouse" style that might appeal to fans of those types of movies. Van Clief's acting in this one is questionable, but so what? He kicks ass in it. That's all that really matters. Chih Chen (Chan Chor) directed.

The Way of the Dragon (a.k.a. The Return of the Dragon)

1972 (Shout Factory DVD) (djm)

Tang Lung (Bruce Lee) is called upon by some friends living in Rome, and he visits them with the intention of helping them defend themselves from a crime syndicate that is moving in on his friends and their small restaurant business. The syndicate has made every effort to convince the Chinese running the restaurant to sell their business to them, but they refuse time and again, which is driving the syndicate to more forceful methods of persuasion. When Tan Lung arrives, he uses his "Chinese boxing" to dissuade the Italians from muscling his friends into submission, and when the Italians get desperate, they call upon a mercenary with martial arts skills (Chuck Norris) to go up against Tang Lung. Their final fight in the historic Colosseum is a little bit of motion picture magic, with two titans going full throttle against each other.

Comedic in tone throughout, *The Way of the Dragon* is mostly hokum and fluff until the incredible fight between Lee and Norris at the conclusion. Lee (who also directed) plays the film like it's a comedy, but Norris steps in with complete seriousness, which gives the movie some grounding. Their fight is spectacular. Lee also fights Bob Wall in a scene. A few snippets from the Norris/Lee fight were featured in the patchwork film *Game of Death*, which was released posthumously after Lee's death.

W

Weapons of Death

1981 (Synergy DVD) (djm)

A band of mercenaries are hired to kidnap a Chinese girl, whose family has some influence in Chinatown, and when she's taken, her half-brother Eric (Eric Lee from *Ninja Busters*) gets his closest friends and relatives to get her back and rain holy hell on the villains who took her. Along for the ride is the kidnapped girl's real father (a white dude who is some kind of soldier), and with an armory and massively insane martial arts powers on their side, the good guys go to war with the bad guys. Who are the bad guys? Some rapist bikers, some kung fu masters (including the always welcome Gerald Okamura), and some badass ninja chicks. Watching the final battle is like witnessing a horde of LARPers on a field going crazy.

An undeniable, goofy charm makes Paul Kyriazi's *Weapons of Death* fun viewing, but if you're looking for a modicum of seriousness or any realism, steer clear. This one's for fans of wild karate mayhem, and if you've never seen a movie with Eric Lee before (chances are you have and didn't know he was in it), you could start here, but you may want to try some of his other movies like *The Master Demon* instead. Kyriazi made this film in earnest, and some of his movies are great (see *Omega Cop*), but some of them are on the mediocre side (like *Death Machines*). He also did *Ninja Busters* with Lee and Okamura. Kyriazi also has a fun supporting role in *Weapons of Death* as one of the good guys.

Welcome to the Jungle

2013 (Universal DVD) (djm)

An ad agency's nerdy staff is sent on a mandatory morale-boosting trip to a jungle island with a guide named Storm (Jean-Claude Van Damme) to pump

Theatrical release poster for *Welcome to the Jungle*. Author's collection.

them up into shape. Storm's methodology involves screaming and yelling as a means to confidence building, but when he is attacked by a wild tiger and presumed dead, he leaves behind a completely unprepared group of city folk to fend for themselves without a way to get home. Good-hearted ad man Chris (Adam Brody) is practical and cautious, while his back-stabbing and obnoxious co-worker Phil (Rob Huebel) steps it up a notch and declares himself the leader of the group, setting absurd rules and regulations, which everyone around him seems to want to obey. He makes the women his sex slaves and the men subservient to his will. Chris and a few others retreat to another part of the island where they try desperately to come up with a plan to overthrow Phil's kingdom. Storm re-enters the picture and helps Chris save the day.

Cruel, misogynistic, and cheap, *Welcome to the Jungle* is notable only for having Van Damme in it, but even with him in it, the film is crippling to his image and doesn't do anyone else in it any favors. It's farcical and tries desperately to be shockingly funny, but it's painful to watch. Van Damme pokes fun at his persona, and he throws one kick at the end. His fans will be sorely disappointed. Directed by Rob Meltzer.

Whatever it Takes

1999 (Razor Digital DVD) (djm)

Don "The Dragon" Wilson and Andrew Dice Clay play undercover detectives in the world of exercise where illegal steroid use is causing bodybuilders to overdose. The steroid kingpin (Fred "The Hammer" Williamson) gets wind of their true identities, and their safety is compromised. When his men are dwindled to just a few after being killed by them, the kingpin does "Whatever It Takes" to get the cops off his back. The final scene has Wilson fighting Williamson in a slug match.

It's nice to see Don Wilson in a movie with other stars sharing the screen in equal measure. Everyone has the same amount of screen time, and even if you're not a big Dice Clay fan (I'm not), it's cool to see him muscling in on Wilson for attention because it gives the film a more natural, more interesting quality that many of Wilson's movies lack. Williamson has some screen time too—and in a rare villain role—but unfortunately, too much of his time is spent ogling a beautiful (and often naked) female co-star. He doesn't come across as a truly despicable or fascinating bad guy. The movie itself is mediocre, and the action is instantly forgettable, but fans of Wilson should enjoy it. Directed by Brady MacKenzie.

Wheels on Meals

1984 (Universe Laser and Video DVD) (djm)

Jackie Chan and Yuen Biao star as two buddies who run a food truck in Barcelona. They try romancing a beautiful pickpocket/call girl (Lola Forner), who is being hunted down by a gangster. The gangster's two right-hand men are played by Benny "The Jet" Urquidez and Keith Vitali, who are both given several incredible fight scenes with Chan and Biao. Along for the ride is a clueless private detective played by Sammo Hung, who also directed.

This has the feel of a Euro/Asian comic book. It's not a classic, but it's certainly a fun action film with Chan's and Hung's light touch. There are vehicular stunts aplenty, and the scenes with Urquidez and Vitali are the highlights. Some consider Chan and Urquidez's climactic showdown one of the greatest fight scenes of all time. Chan, Biao, and Urquidez also appeared together in *Dragons Forever*.

INTERVIEW:

KEITH VITALI

(djm)

Some guys in the action and martial arts movie scene don't have dozens of films on their resume, even though they should. Keith Vitali, a world karate Cchampion and US national karate champion for three consecutive years (1978–1980) is such a person. His first film was opposite Sho Kosugi in Cannon's Revenge of the Ninja *(1983), and then he had a plum role in the Jackie Chan movie* Wheels on Meals *(1984), which features one of the most incredible fight scenes in movie history. His few other films include* No Retreat, No Surrender 3: Blood Brothers *(1990) and the little-seen* Superfights *(1995). A renown martial artist and a bestselling author, Vitali seems content with the success that he's had.*

After you became a number one kickboxing champion, how did you get started in the movie business?

I was teaching in Atlanta at the time. My future wife said, "There's somebody on the phone that wants to speak with you." It was someone from Cannon films. I picked up the phone, and they said that they wanted to talk to me about starring in a movie. I had a friend who played pranks on me all the time, and so I said, "Nice try," and I hung up. The phone rings again, and my wife handed me the phone again. "I am in LA with Menahem Golan, and we want to offer you a three-picture deal." So we talked about it, and they flew me up to LA, and my first film ended up being *Revenge of the Ninja* with Sho Kosugi. What I asked them was how they found me in Atlanta, Georgia. They'd discovered me on the cover of a karate magazine. That was one my best years ever, and I was on the cover of seven or eight magazines that year. This was when I was competing. That's how I got that part.

So, you signed a three-picture deal with Cannon?

Yes, I did, but we only did one. I was getting ready to do my second one when they went under. I went to the Cannes Film Festival, and I was there because David Bradley and I were going to do a movie together, and we had the banner up, but unfortunately the movie didn't go through.

Between *Revenge of the Ninja* and the point when Cannon went bankrupt were a handful of years. Why such a long wait between your first movie and your potential second one?

I was doing other films. Cannon became involved in other movies, dance movies and other things. Because *Revenge of the Ninja* made a lot of money, and then the next film did a lot of money, they just went nuts. They went into producing "A" films instead of "B" films. They did one with Sylvester Stallone, and they lost a lot of money.

What was the David Bradley project going to be about?

I didn't even know we were supposed to be working together, and when I saw the billboard in Cannes, I thought, *Hey, that must be my next film!* The third film I had already auditioned for, I was to play twins: A good brother and an evil brother. I signed for that one, and I was really excited about that project.

You did a project with John Barrett called *American Kickboxer*. Talk about that one. It still bears the Cannon label.

Anant Singh was the producer. He was from India. For the first time in my experience, while we were filming he had sold the rights to the film. He said, "Congratulations: We sold the rights to the film." I didn't know if it was Cannon, but it may have been sold to Cannon later on. It was a very simple film. The interesting thing about the whole dichotomy about that film was that Brad Morris, who played the villain, and John Barrett did not like each other. Brad was a local South African actor. He was phenomenally talented and gifted. He and John did not get along. John was the star. I was the choreographer of the fights, and I played the sidekick of John Barrett. Having to choreograph fight scenes between these two . . . it was a very tough experience. They would get upset that I was giving one fighter more time than the other, or making one fighter look better than the other. I loved working with both of them, though. They were both extremely talented.

You should have been the star of *American Kickboxer*. It's obvious.

I thought I was going to be when I got out there. I was hired to be the star. There were last-minute negotiations going on, and I don't know what happened. John became the star, and we're

Chad Hunter (Keith Vitali) and BJ Quinn (Keith Barrett) in *American Kickboxer 1*. Courtesy of Keith Vitali.

friends to this day. We filmed in South Africa at the time when they released Nelson Mandela. During our production, he was released. The whole wall of press was there in Johannesburg. It was quite an experience.

I've always felt that your movie career was a little too short. You did some good ones like *Wheels on Meals* and *No Retreat, No Surrender 3*, but how come you didn't make more films? Why weren't you catapulted into the lead guy?

Well, I had a choice. I could have moved out to Los Angels and pursued it that way. I was told that that was what I really needed to do. I just decided not to do that. I stayed in Atlanta. I would have had to have been in LA for auditions, trying to get cast in films. I just took a whole other route. I did six or eight of them.

Well, you certainly worked with some of the best in the business. You started with Sho Kosugi, and then you worked with Jackie Chan next. Talk about that a little bit.

Sho is quite extraordinary because he truly believed he was a ninja. I used to joke with him all the time and say, "Sho, you're not a ninja." And he'd say, "Yes I am. I'm a ninja." (Laughing.) He was almost insanely infatuated with the weapons. Prior to the film, he'd built fifty, sixty weapons, which he'd incorporate into the film. He was so adamant. He was a tall Japanese man. You would see a total performer. When the film came out, while we were watching the film, he got up and ran to the projectionist and told him to turn the music up louder. Then with one minute to go, he would rush to the door, and when everyone was coming out through the doors, they could see him, the star of the film. He was so upset because people couldn't recognize him. They would walk by him, and he would go, "No! It's me!" He was so depressed about that.

You were great in *Revenge of the Ninja*. When I first saw it years ago, I thought for sure you had gone on and done at least twenty movies.

Well, thank you so much. I enjoyed the process. It was my first movie and I wasn't used to seeing how movies were made. While watching the production of it, I thought it was going to be the worst movie ever made. There was so much blood on the set. So much killing. I would question everything to myself. *Where did that blood come from? Where did that weapon come from? Am I the only one thinking this is over the top?* It *was* over the top. We were so fortunate that MGM took over the marketing of the film, and it was the first martial arts movie in history to be in every major theater in the United States. They took out full-page ads in every major newspaper in the United States. I went to two premieres for that movie. It was a big deal.

Benny "The Jet" Urquidez, Mike Genova, Jackie Chan, and Keith Vitali on the set of *Wheels on Meals*. Courtesy of Keith Vitali.

Mike, Jackie Chan, and Keith Vitali in Spain

After *Revenge,* you got *Wheels on Meals* with Jackie Chan. Talk about that.

A friend of mine named Pat Johnson was in Los Angeles and he was the fight choreographer for the film *Force: Five* with Joe Lewis, Richard Norton, and Benny Urquidez. The film was supposed to star not Joe Lewis, but Bill Wallace at first. Bill and I went to casting for that film at the same time. I didn't know what I was doing. I walked onto the set and met all the producers. There were about fifty of the best fighters in the world on that film. They were all phenomenal. That movie never went anywhere. I never even saw it in a video store. So years later, I got a call from Pat Johnson, "Hey, I've got a good friend who's producing a film with Jackie Chan, would you like to be in it?" I said, "Sure!" He goes, "Well, today's Wednesday. You've got to leave on Friday." Two days later, I was on a plane to Barcelona. I met Benny Urquidez there, and we'd known each other already. Then we met Jackie Chan. It was a great experience for us because Jackie was trying to work on his English all the time, so he spent a lot of time with us. He would talk to us. He would sing to us! In our culture, men don't sing a lot, but it didn't bother Jackie at all. He would just start singing. I would look over at Benny and go, "My goodness!" We both felt that we were on something special. He showed us a lot of his previous fight sequences. Benny and I thought that there was no way he could do all the phenomenal stuff he did and still live. The difference between that film and *Revenge of the Ninja* . . . when I was watching the filming on *Wheels on Meals*, I was amazed, I was impressed. I went, "Oh my God!" every single time any stunt was filmed or any fight scene was filmed. It was phenomenal. You have to take into account that the editing hadn't been done and the music wasn't in place. That's what makes a fight scene look phenomenal, but just watching the real thing and raw footage: The most incredible thing I've ever seen. Sammo Hung was in that, oh my gosh. Just phenomenal.

Was there a point around the time you did *Wheels on Meals* that you felt like you were progressing towards a career in action and martial arts films? Was there ever a point like that in your career as an action star?

Yeah, I was taking acting classes at the time. I flew out to Los Angles and took acting classes out there. I was taking my craft more seriously. I was starting to become a better actor. I was searching out other projects. I teamed up with a guy named Keith Strandberg, and we had worked with a company called Impact. You would pick a target that had a digital readout of the pounds of pressure you were hitting that target with. I was the spokesperson for that company, and I would go around to tournaments and demonstrate the power of my sidekicks. Keith and I became

W

good friends. He had written *No Retreat, No Surrender*, and discovered Jean-Claude Van Damme doing that film. And then he did the second one with Loren Avedon. He came to me and said, "I have a project for you. It's called *No Retreat, No Surrender 3*." I said, "Great." We shot it in Tampa, Florida. You can see that the fight scenes in that film were very close to the fight scenes in the Jackie Chan film. A lot of the same stunt people came from Jackie Chan's crew. High speed and the movement. The difference with those types of films is that it's not so much about the power, it's about the technique. They want to see fluidity. They want to see speed. The Americans want to see more of the raw power. They want to see the end result. They want to see the guy go down. I was producing a movie with Gary Daniels called *Bloodmoon*, and Gary was complaining to me through the whole time—and I understood him 100 percent—Gary was like, "If you kick someone one time, he's down." I talked to the director about it, and he was like, "No. I'm not making movies for you—Gary Daniels—I'm not making these movies for Western audiences. I'm making movies for the world. The world likes to see my type of films. If you kick someone in the head eighty-two times, still the guy gets back up every time." Gary looked at me and said, "If I kick a guy one time—one time—the guy's falling to the ground." That's the difference of the methodology of how they shoot films and choreograph films from a Hong Kong perspective and an American perspective.

No Retreat, No Surrender 3 was your big movie. You're pretty much the lead with Loren Avedon. That scene at the hangar was great.

It was an exciting film. It's very demanding working on a film like that. When I did *American Kickboxer* in South Africa, the pace was very laid back. You could even kick back and have a beer on set. But working on *No Retreat, No Surrender* with the Chinese director and the Chinese producers . . . the last scene in the movie took seven days to film, at twelve or thirteen hours per day. Sometimes you're so physically exhausted. To take that kind of pressure over and over and over again. When you're doing take after take after take, you have to be in ten times better shape than you are for a karate tournament, a full contact match. You might have to do a take or a kick fifty or sixty times! When I did a scene with Sammo Hung on *Wheels on Meals* I did a scene fifty times. I had to change my outfit twice. I might miss, Sammo might miss, the weapons might miss. For whatever reason, you have to do it over and over again. While doing *No Retreat, No Surrender* with Loren, there were intricate moves. We would be fighting one person and would have to choreograph almost like a dance. Our director had a great stunt team. If you watch the film very closely, you'll see me spin pirouettes and land on my back on a desk or something, but that isn't me—that's the stunt team. Most of the time, I did my own work.

How come Corey Yuen didn't direct that one? Why did Lucas Lowe direct it?

Well, I don't know. Lucas Lowe was so hard to work with. He was a little, five-foot Napoleon. He had that attitude. You couldn't suggest anything. He had his way all the time. It was very difficult. He was a tough director. And Loren and I had some friction between us on the set. When it's so demanding and you're working so many hours . . . it was a tough shoot.

Let's talk about *Superfights*. I love *Superfights!* This is a movie that not many people know about. You play the villain in that one. And the star of that movie, Brandon Gaines, was great in it. That was the only thing he ever did.

Yeah, Brandon. He was such a good actor. The sad reality was that he was not liked by the producer, the director, and the crew. They just didn't care for him. He was just breaking into film. They would say, "Don't say anything. Just do what you're told." Brandon was smarter than anyone on that set. He was a brainiac. He was a genius. He was the smartest guy I've ever known. He had total recall. He had seen *Revenge of the Ninja* as a child, and he remembered every line of dialogue from that movie. Sometimes, right before he would do one of his dramatic scenes, and right before the director would call "Action," he would start reciting *my* dialogue from *Revenge of the Ninja*. I liked the kid. He was wonderful, just a pleasure to work with. He would say, "Excuse me, but I need a break." And they would tell him, "No, you don't get a break." He would say, "No, I'm taking a break." And the director would say, "No, you have to work." He would say, "I can't throw kicks for several hours without stopping. I need fifteen minutes." They would throw temper tantrums and yell at him. I always felt bad for him. He was delightful. From a personal perspective, that was one of my favorite movies that I made. I thought the end fight scene in that movie was dynamic. I showed that movie to Keith Strandberg, and we took it to a festival. While that film was being screened, and I was standing in the back of the audience, which was about 100 producers and buyers from around the world. At the end of that film, they all stood up and gave it a standing ovation. They loved it. I loved it, too. I died in that film, but it was a great scene. I really enjoyed that film. We shot it in 105-degree weather in a warehouse, and in that warehouse we weren't allowed to turn on the air conditioning, so it got even hotter. They brought in blocks of ice, gigantic blocks of ice, and they had an industrial fan blow on it to cool us. They would shut it down and stop it and go back to shooting.

How come *Superfights* didn't get better distribution? I'd never heard of it until I started working on this book and began preparing to interview you.

That's a good point. I've wondered why. I know it did well overseas. We know it sold to international markets very well. We were disappointed that it didn't sell well here. I've seen it on TV

You worked with the same team on *Bloodmoon*, which was a Gary Daniels movie, right? You produced that one.

Right. Same team. Their English was very limited. Keith Strandberg was there, and he is fluent in Chinese. He can write it and speak it. Keith and I were a great team.

I was surprised and a little disappointed that you were barely in *Bloodmoon*. What was the story there?

I was a co-producer. From a SAG standpoint, I wasn't supposed to be in the film. I got fined for that. What happened was that the stunt team didn't show up that day. The fighters who were supposed to fight didn't show up. I said, "I'll be in the scene!" I got beat up in a very quick scene, but it was fun for me. I have very high respect for Gary Daniels. Also, Darren Shahlavi. They were two of the most talented athletes—not just martial artists—I've ever seen. They were just phenomenally built, they had stamina . . . there was nothing they couldn't do. They wanted to shoot everything themselves. Watching those fight scenes between those two . . . it was great.

How do you feel about how your movie career went? Any regrets?

Well . . . one time they offered me a part in *Teenage Mutant Ninja Turtles*, and I didn't think it was going to be that good. That was a big mistake. I would have sacrificed my family to move out to LA. I probably could have had a better career in entertainment, but I did well. From a fighter's perspective, I made it to the top of my . . . all my goals were reached. I did a handful of films. That was good enough for me. I still have aspirations to produce. Keith Strandberg and I still talk about it. I feel blessed that I was able to travel and represent my sport. I transitioned from that into the movie world, and from that I transitioned into writing. There's not much regret.

You wrote a couple of high-profile books. Say something about your career as a writer.

One of my students is a writer, and he and I had a concept of doing three technical books on martial arts. We sold the concept and Contemporary Books told us that these books were the template that they give every other writer who publishes with them. They're simple, they're right to the point and very well illustrated. I started that way. I got into my book, *Bullyproof Your Child*. I had this other concept that changed my life. One day, I was sitting with my son Travis and my daughter Jennifer, and my son was watching a movie, and I said, "Travis, why are you watching this film?" He said, "Because there's kids in it." He said, "Anything with kids in it, I like to watch." I've never agreed with the mentality with how martial arts instructors teach their kids. I thought I was one of the best experts and teachers of martial arts that kids could go to. I really understood that most of the time when kids are picked on, they're not picked on by "stranger danger," they're being picked on by a friend or a big brother. I hated that most martial arts self-defense surrounded around really violent techniques. Kick to the groin, go for the head, go for the eyes. I taught five-year-olds, six-year-olds, seven-year-olds. I didn't like the concept of telling a six-year-old to go for the eyes, especially when it was their big brother or big sister. I said to myself, *You know what I'm going to do? I'm going to produce a video. Something different that has never been seen.* So what I did was that night I wrote a little script out, no big deal. I called a friend of mine in the film world and asked him, "Would you mind getting a few of friends together, get some lighting equipment and a camera, and I'll pay you five thousand, or whatever, and I want to shoot this concept." He said, "Sure." He shows up the next day, and I pick up my son and daughter from school and get a few more kids, and I go to the schoolyard and all I do is shoot one day's shot. No big deal. One day of shooting. I had it edited with some music, and the next thing you know it's a final product. I thought it was all right. I make a couple phone calls and maybe two months later, that little venture I did—I was on *Oprah*. I was a guest expert with that video. I was on the front page of *USA Today*. I toured the country for a year, and I never sold that video to one karate school. Karate schools all know what's best for their students. My video was not made for martial artists. My videos are made for parents and for kids who were not into martial arts. It was a very mainstream venture. I sold them to Blockbuster, Toys R Us. I sold my video all over the country. I'm still the only video in that market, to this day. No one has reproduced or tried to copy my concept, ever.

When the Bullet Hits the Bone

1996 (New Horizons VHS) (CD)

Dr. Jack Davies (Jeff Wincott) has spent the better part of his life as an ER physician doing what he can to save people. He soon realizes there's not much he can do when drugs are taking over. He accidentally stumbles across a woman being roughed up, and he steps in. Little does he know that his life will change forever when he's shot and left for dead. He becomes obsessed with saving the woman, Lisa (Michelle Johnson), but there's not much he can do until his wounds have healed. He empties out his bank account and tosses his ID; he finds himself a couple of guns and goes to save her, stumbling into a world of drugs and corruption even he didn't know existed. He's going to start at the top and take out the bad seeds, one bullet at a time.

This film takes Jeff Wincott (*Martial Outlaw, Open Fire*) into a much grittier direction than most of us associate with the great action star. Gone are his trademark martial arts skills, using guns and his wits to drive the film instead. It wanted to be something akin to a John Woo film but gets nowhere close. It's still a good story and Wincott has always been a fine actor. You can tell he was pushing his acting skills and gives a damn fine performance. Even without the martial arts, there are some pretty brutal (and bloody) shootouts to keep action fans happy. Directed by Damian Lee (*Agent Red, Terminal Rush*), while Wincott served as an associate producer.

Jack Warden, Charles Bronson, and Will Sampson star in *The White Buffalo*. Author's collection.

The White Buffalo

1977 (MGM DVD) (djm)

Wild Bill Hickock (Charles Bronson) has nightmares of a monstrous, hulking white buffalo, and the specters haunt him. He is on a mission to find the legendary creature, hunt it down, and kill it. He and his friend Charlie Zane (a wily old Jack Warden) go out into the snowy wilderness—even braving Indian country—to find the creature. On their quest, Bill makes an alliance with an ostracized Indian chief named Crazy Horse (Will Sampson), who was kicked out of his tribe for crying when his child was killed by the white buffalo. Crazy Horse is on his own campaign to find and kill the monster, and so the three hunters join forces, hoping to find success even if it means being killed themselves by their quarry.

As a western, this J. Lee Thompson-directed picture has some stylized camera work and dialogue, not to mention some really good performances from the leads, but it feels more akin to a horror movie with its *Moby Dick/Jaws/ Razorback* vibe of creature feature-ish gore and violence. The white buffalo itself (a practical special effect of puppetry, but very scary and impressive) is a terror to behold, and seeing Bronson and his two cohorts attack it and slay it is a wonderful movie treat. Unlike any other Bronson vehicle (especially at the time when it was released), *The White Buffalo* has a haunting aspect to it that should appeal to interested parties. Bronson's next movie was *Telefon*.

White Cargo

1996 (Third Coast VHS) (CD)

"Skin like a baby and a body a king would pay a fortune to fuck. Yes, sir, a real waste. Smile baby, I'm about to make you immortal."

Joe Hargatay (former *American Ninja* David Bradley) is independently wealthy, owns a bar, plays guitar, and is also a detective with the police department, just because it's fun and he has the time. Things don't exactly seem so fun when he begins to investigate the murder of a model/escort, matching a series of recent cases.

The murders seem to have a connection to the triads and the Italian mob, but there are far more turns than he expected. Soon, his ex-wife finds herself wrapped up in the mess, forcing Joe to throw in his badge and take the law into his own hands.

What's great about *White Cargo* is the fact David Bradley (*American Ninja 3: Bloodhunt, Hard Justice*) just plays this character with such a calm and cool demeanor. He's all suited up, looking like a smooth player, ready for whatever comes his way. At first, the movie just seems to be your typical erotic thriller, but then you sort of get lost in Bradley's performance and you just can't turn your eyes away from the screen. Later in his movie career, he pretty much abandoned martial arts all together, but I'm happy to report that there's a couple of great scenes with him kicking ass and never once wrinkling his suit. The finale is by far the highlight when we get to see him team up with Shannon Tweed (*The Firing Line*) and Tommy Lister (*No Holds Barred*) for a bloody gun battle. There's also a fantastic shotgun blast that sends the victim soaring through the air. It's a standout moment and happens very quickly. This is the only film under director Daniel Reardon's belt.

White Fire

1984 (TWE VHS) (djm)

"Night or day, it doesn't matter! I want that White Fire . . . at *any* cost!"

Two orphaned children who have lived through a traumatic experience of seeing their parents murdered grow up to be adventurers living in Turkey. Boris (Robert Ginty) and Ingrid (Belinda Mayne) learn of the existence of the White Fire diamond, a jewel in the raw that's so big and enormous, that if it is touched, it burns flesh with its intensity. The White Fire resides deep in a diamond mine, and when its existence is known, treasure hunters seek it out. Boris's sister is killed, and as he mourns her death, he falls in love with a woman named Olga who looks a lot like Ingrid. To confuse mercenaries who are sent to follow Boris (he knows where the diamond is), Olga has her face reconstructed to look exactly like Ingrid, which is a plot point that gets creepier the more you think about it. Boris, in love (and making love) with Olga, fends off an advantageous mercenary named Barclay (Fred Williamson) who displays some martial arts abilities. In the end, Barclay and Boris (and Olga/Ingrid) have made an alliance.

Only in the 1980s exploitation film market could a movie like *White Fire* get made and released. It's confusing, confounding, and mind-bogglingly weird. Ginty (*The Exterminator*) is hardly an action star, but Williamson, who shows up somewhere around the halfway point, is definitely an action star and he exhibits enough action stuff in this film for it to qualify. Fans of bizarre movies and somewhat sick sexual situations (Ginty ogles and has sex with his sister, basically) will need to see this one. Williamson fans won't

W

really be satisfied. He and Ginty also appeared in the apocalyptic film *Warrior of the Lost World* together. Directed by Jean-Marie Pallardy.

White Light

1991 (Academy VHS) (V)

"Yes, for a dead man
he's very much alive."

We all know Martin Kove as the anti-Miyagi and leading proponent of leg-sweeping, but he can also be a Lorenzo Lamas or Treat Williams-esque leading man. In this thriller from the writer of *Heavenly Bodies*, he plays Sean Craig, a cop so deep undercover in the mob that the don throws him a huge birthday party and presents him with a fancy gun. This is also the night when the big bust is going down, so Craig takes the opportunity to point the gun at the kingpin's head and arrest and humiliate him in front of everyone. Though he has blown his own cover in front of the entire gang, he then decides to go home to his apartment, where he should've known he would immediately get shot. Here's where the gimmick comes in: during a near-death experience he meets and falls in love with a woman (Allison Hossack), apparently stuck in some dreamy residential purgatory. So when he's revived, Craig goes detecting to find out who this woman is and if he can save her (or solve her murder). The action is pretty standard. There's a brief shootout, a couple fights, one involving pretty good use of office equipment. But combining that with elements of *Flatliners*—he convinces a doctor (Martha Henry) to induce a coma so he can talk to his lady some more while crooked cops are trying to shoot him—is pretty novel.

White Light is not a great movie, but more watchable than I expected. There seems to be more effort put into the dialogue than in many "B" movies. Some of it is painfully self-conscious, but some of it is kind of clever. My favorite part is the opening when Craig is prepping his gangster alter ego who he later describes thusly: "Everyone liked Tony. He had bounce. Life." He smiles and checks his mustache and tux in the mirror, and I swear his version of a gregarious goodfella is really just a white Billy Dee Williams.

White Tiger

1995 (Keystone VHS) (djm)

DEA agents Mike (Gary Daniels) and John (Matt Craven) are best friends, and they're enjoying a vacation together with their families when they are called in on an emergency: A rogue Asian mobster named Victor Chow (Cary-Hiroyuki Tagawa) has turned his back on the mob and has a chance to be caught, but when Mike and John try apprehending him, John is killed, leaving Mike to stew in his rage. In his plan to go after Chow, Mike hooks up with an attractive girl named Jade (Julia Nickson) at a nightclub, and in the tryst,

Mike begins losing his focus on his vengeance. Jade, meanwhile, is a secret lover of Victor Chow, who has made sure that Mike is distracted with her while he moves in for a kill, but even Chow doesn't realize that Jade is working against him as well, as she has been hired by the Asian mob to assassinate him for being unruly. When Mike finds out that he has no idea who he's been sleeping with, things get complicated, resulting in an action-packed finale.

Surprisingly well directed (by Richard Martin) for a seemingly generic outing with Daniels, *White Tiger* has some good stuff going on. Daniels, as always, is solid in a martial-arts-type role with lots of fights, action, and physicality, and his co-stars Nickson and Tagawa also deliver decent performances. Tagawa gets into the action, with several close-quarter fights with Daniels. The scenery is nice, and some above-average stunts elevate this movie a notch above many others of its type. The big detriment to the film is a terrible techno-flavored score. *White Tiger* isn't too distinctive, but I enjoyed it. Daniels fans should check it out. Also with George Cheung, who killed Nickson on screen in *Rambo: First Blood Part II*.

White Tiger

2014 (NOV) (djm)

Petulant and stubborn American agent Michael Turner (Matt Mullins from *Bloodfist 2050*) has brought his wife to Thailand, but instead of delivering on the vacation he promised, he's investigating a warlord named Draco, who is well known for human trafficking. Turner and his father figure Conrad (kickboxing legend Joe Lewis), who has a history with Draco, spend their nights in Thailand hunting Draco and hounding his operation. When Conrad is killed while they're on a recon mission, Michael tells his wife to fly back home so that he can hunt Draco on his own. The Thai police recommend that he hire a mercenary named Bobby Pau (Don "The Dragon" Wilson in a great character role), who will help him find Draco on the Thai/Burmese border. Teamed up with the best, Michael has to cool his jets a little bit because he realizes that he's in over his head, and when they finally find Draco (played by Gigi Velicitat) and his henchmen (played by Cynthia Rothrock and Jawed El Berni from *Ninja II: Shadow of a Tear*), they incite a small war, culminating in explosions, martial arts battles, and truck chases.

Shot in 2012, but very similar to Isaac Florentine's *Ninja II: Shadow of a Tear*, *White Tiger* is perfectly suitable entertainment for fans of Don Wilson, Cynthia Rothrock, and those who are still unfamiliar with Matt Mullins, who ironically took over Wilson's *Bloodfist* franchise in 2005. The martial

arts fight scenes are top notch, and even though Mullins shows his inexperience as an actor here, he makes up for it with his fancy footwork and his concordant kicks and flips. The best aspect of the film is watching a seasoned Don Wilson play the *Rambo*-esque expatriate mentoring a young up-and-comer, and this might actually be one of his best roles. Rothrock, who has a few choice scenes, displays some flare in a rare villain turn, but if you're hoping that she's the star, you will be disappointed. Joe Lewis, who looked unhealthy in his scenes, died before this movie found a release. Directed by Toby Russell.

White Wall

2010 (Wellspring DVD) (CD)

A deadly disease has wiped out much of the human population, and there is no cure. A giant white wall is constructed to quarantine the infected on the outside. Shawn Kors (James Boss) appears to be just a janitor inside a medical facility. In actuality, he was raised in a child internment camp with a group of boys who became his brothers. Together they escaped only to lose touch as time went on. His brother Jude (Michael Teh) has ventured down a much darker path. He has planned to shut off the generators and tear the walls down. Shawn goes on a quest to find Jude and a cure for the virus. He can't go it alone so he reluctantly accepts help from Dryden (Gary Kohn) who proves himself to be more valuable than he appears. It's a long and dangerous journey that leads to devastating truths and a final battle that will pit brother against brother.

White Wall is a unique film. While it doesn't particularly work, it does manage to stray from the beaten path and travel a road less traveled. As a whole, I really don't feel like everything meshed particularly well but there are some really inspired moments that may make a trip to the *White Wall* worthwhile. The pacing of the film was a major issue. It felt overly slow, taking you out of the moment instead of building tension as it should have. Lots of time is spent in dark alleys or dark corridors that led to scenes that were difficult to make out. There isn't an

Poster artwork for James Boss's *White Wall*. Courtesy of James Boss.

abundance of dialogue and the story was barely an excuse to go forward. The backstory was more interesting, and it might have been more rewarding to follow that story than what ended up in the final product. With all that being said, director and star James Boss is just getting started. For a first-timer, he did many things well and right. As an actor, his weaknesses were exposed, but as an action and martial arts star, he shows tremendous promise. There are a few knife fights in the film, and the way they were handled was rather exciting. Close-quartered combat is hard to capture correctly and Boss did a terrific job showing

W

it to the audience. The intensity level was pretty high, and the actors really impressed with their styles. Michael Teh plays the antagonist Jude Black and gives the best acting performance in the film. *White Wall* will hopefully be a steppingstone for Boss. He has studied many different martial art styles and has his own take on how they should be presented on film. If he can learn from his missteps on his first feature, he may come back around and surprise us.

Who Am I? (a.k.a. Jackie Chan's Who Am I?)

1998 (Sony DVD) (djm)

"You want to know who I am?
I want to know who I am!"

A soldier and his entire squad of commandos are pawns for a covert spy group, and when the whole team is dispatched in an unexpected plane mishap, Jackie (Chan, that is) manages to jump out of the plane without a chute and ends up cracking his head and some bones on his way down as he hits jillions of tree branches before he meets the dirt. When he wakes up much later, he is in a hut somewhere in Africa, mending and being tended to by a tribe of natives, who immediately begin calling him Who Am I because that's the first thing he says to them. Over the course of months, he gets better, but he still can't remember his name or what he was doing in Africa. He ventures out of the village and saves the life of a car racer, which gets him media attention, and suddenly shady CIA guys and martial arts goons are out to get him because they think he knows something about a secret weapon that the covert spy group is after. The climax atop a skyscraper between Jackie and two bad guys is amazing.

Released to video in the US the same year that Jackie's *Rush Hour* was playing in theaters, *Who Am I?* is one of his most fun late '90s action pictures, but for some reason, it doesn't get talked about as much as some of the others like *Rumble in the Bronx*. The action doesn't really get going until about forty minutes into it, but once he starts moving and fighting, it's unrelenting and fun. Amusing throughout, this one deserves an audience. Directed by Jackie and Benny Chan.

Wild Card

2015 (Lionsgate DVD) (djm)

Nick Wild (Jason Statham) is an ex-special something-or-other soldier, living as a security specialist or "companion" right off the Vegas strip, taking two-bit jobs and biding his time until the day he can make just enough cash to leave it all behind and embark on a dream trip to Corsica. Everyone who's anyone knows who Nick is and what he's capable of, and it seems like he's helped out every waitress, housekeeping lady, and hooker who's ever had a problem because he's just that

kind of guy. Even the mob knows who he is, and they like him and respect him. If he ever makes an enemy, it's only because he's thought the whole thing through and is prepared to face the consequences. He gets two job prospects on the same day: a hooker friend of his named Holly (Dominik Garcia-Lorido) is brutally beaten and sexually assaulted by a wealthy client, and she asks him to help her get revenge, and on the flipside, a nebbish young businessman named Cyrus (Michael Angarano) asks Nick to show him around Vegas in the evening. The second client has no strings attached, but the first one is full of problems. Nick finds the scumbag who nearly killed Holly, and in order to teach him a lesson he'll never forget, he first has to take out his two bodyguards, which proves as easy as pie for Nick because that's what he's good at. With Holly present for the act of revenge, Nick leaves the snit (played by Milo Ventimiglia) humiliated and demoralized, but he also leaves with twenty-five grand, which he promptly takes to a casino and proceeds to have the lucky streak of his life, winning over a hundred grand at blackjack. With Cyrus as his witness, he tests his luck just a little too far and loses every penny in one devastating shot. And then the real trouble begins when a few days later the mob comes for him, based on the insinuations of the connected man whom he stole from and emasculated. What follows is what amounts to Nick's final stab at redemption that could either get him killed or land him a one-way ticket to a permanent vacation in Corsica.

A virtual scene-for-scene remake of *Heat* (1986) with Burt Reynolds, *Wild Card* is a small, understated character piece for action star Statham, who engages in three separate (and intense) close-quarter action scenes. Screenwriter William Goldman wrote both versions based on his novel *Heat*, and director Simon West, who worked with Statham on *The Mechanic* and *The Expendables 2* directed. Along with *Safe* and *Redemption* (a.k.a. *Hummingbird*), this is one of Statham's sleeper films, and it's a shame it wasn't given a bigger release because with a proper marketing push, it could have been a modest hit. This marks the third time Statham has starred in a remake. See also: *The Mechanic* (previously with Charles Bronson) and *Parker* (previously with Lee Marvin as Point Blank).

The Wild Pair

1987 (Media VHS) (djm)

Beau Bridges starred and directed this buddy/buddy cop action movie co-starring the massive Bubba Smith (professional football player and co-star of all of the *Police Academy* movies). Bridges plays an FBI guy named Joe Jennings, and Smith plays a narcotics cop named Benny Avalon, and they butt heads when they almost kill each other while working the same case. They're both pursuing a drug lord, but there's a much bigger picture that they don't see at first: The drug lord has aligned his forces with a paramilitary commando leader (played by Beau's father Lloyd), and together, the drug lord and the commando unit plan on launching some kind of attack, which can only be stopped by Joe and Benny.

VHS artwork for *The Wild Pair*. Author's collection.

Surprisingly sleazy and foul-mouthed for a lightweight action movie, *The Wild Pair* is the best action vehicle Bubba Smith ever got. In those *Police Academy* movies (which are not included in this book for review), he's basically just there for looks, but he never really got a chance to show what he could do in terms of action. Here he runs, shoots, slays, and beats the crap out of Beau in several scenes. He also shows rage, which is a lot more interesting than the stuff he showed as Hightower. Beau's flare for directing leans toward passable, but I'll give him credit for having a steady hand in staging some good action scenes. Bubba's next appearance in an action-oriented movie was in 1992's *My Samurai*.

Winners and Sinners

1983 (Fox DVD) (djm)

Some low-level convicts (one of whom is played by Sammo Hung) get paroled at the same time, and they're pretty much like the Five Stooges, all living under the same roof, planning schemes that don't pan out and ending up in trouble at the same time. They come upon a briefcase containing the mob's counterfeit money templates, and they bumble around, trying to do the right thing, but the mob comes after them, as do the cops. Two policemen (played by Jackie Chan and Yuen Biao, but mostly Chan) try to help the dumbbells out, and the results are slapsticky and actiony.

This is the first movie in the series that continued on with *My Lucky Stars*, featuring the same five morons (who know some kung fu) and

W

the cops whom they befriend. There's nothing notorious about any of the fight scenes here, but one memorable scene has Jackie roller-skating down a freeway while speeding cars zip around him. How he ends up on a motorcycle is one of the movie's best surprises. Other than that, this one is mainly for Chan and Hung's most hardcore fans. Sammo also directed it.

Without Mercy

1995 (Live VHS) (djm)

A soldier named John Carter (Frank Zagarino from *Striker*) is captured and tortured for several years in an East Asian country. When he's finally released, he has nothing but his incredible physique, which he puts to use in warehouse brawls for cash. He befriends an expatriate Vietnam vet named Wolf Larson (Martin Kove, who seemed to play this sort of role quite often in the 1990s), and they form a partnership that lasts only as long as Wolf manages to hide that he's an evil, lecherous scumbag who doesn't have John's best interests at heart. In the mix is a pretty young Asian woman who John crossed paths with before he was captured years ago, and as he falls in love with her, she too reveals that she doesn't especially have John's best interests at heart. With so much stacked up against him, it's a wonder John doesn't just hop on the next freighter as a stowaway to escape his miserable existence. The climax involves a helicopter/speedboat stunt that manages to halfway redeem an otherwise pedestrian action movie.

Very much in the vein of dozens of other direct-to-video action fare from the late 1980s through to the early-mid '90s, *Without Mercy* has a forlorn, empty quality to it that's hard to define. Zagarino is a capable action guy with a big, muscular frame, but you've got to put him in the right movie in the right role for him to shine. He's kind of a victim/sap in this movie, so it's hard to really consider him a badass of any kind. In fact, every time he gets in a fight in the movie, he gets pummeled just as bad as the guys he pummels. The stunt-filled chase at the end with the speedboat was really impressive, and it looked like Zagarino performed his own (very dangerous) stunts himself. Respect for you, Mr. Zagarino. Directed by Robert Anthony, who is actually Robert Chappell, the cinematographer of many of Errol Morris's documentaries.

Witness to a Kill

2001 (First Look DVD) (CD)

The Queen's messenger, Captain Strong (Gary Daniels), is called back in to duty for a mission to deliver some vital information for a top-secret meeting. He is also asked to watch over a woman named Monica (Eva Habermann), who is disguised as his escort. Once they have arrived in South Africa, they are immediately attacked by a group of mercenaries led by Karl Wolf (Nick Boraine). They escape and make it to their destination, where they are briefed on the situation. Strong originally thought the mercenaries were after what was locked in his case, but then realizes Monica has been keeping a secret from him. Also in tow is reporter (and former lover) Kristen Lee (Françoise Yip) who is trying to expose the corruption within the government. When all these people collide, double-crosses are revealed, and Strong is the man to set things straight.

Gary Daniels is a talented individual who always seems to find himself in material that is far beneath him. *Witness to a Kill* may not be one of his finer pictures but it still manages to be a solid piece of action entertainment. There are several fight scenes in the film. They should have been more drawn out, however, to extend the excitement. They are fast with a slight hint of some simple wirework. There may be a few quick cuts but the camera moves with the action allowing you to see everything. One standout fight has Daniels sparring with an assailant in a Michael Jackson mask atop a moving train. There is also a decent one-on-one showdown with the main villain Wolf, played by Nick Boraine (*Operation Delta Force 5*). The only problem I had with that sequence was that it was too short. There's no skimping on the action, which includes a car chase in an underground garage and plenty of gunfire. The story was interesting, though slightly predictable, and much of the dialogue was corny. Along for the ride was Françoise Yip (*Rumble in the Bronx*) and German actress Eva Habermann. What I did find sort of strange were some of the musical cues. The opening number was more of a jazz tune, and the end title sequence played some sort of mamba-type track that almost made it feel like the end of a comedy film. All in all, *Witness to a Kill* (a sequel to *Queen's Messenger*) was a fun viewing experience and fans of Daniels may enjoy it. The film was directed with style by Darrell Roodt (*Dangerous Ground*).

Wolf Warrior

2015 (WellGo USA DVD) (CD)

"You know, I've got to admit, you may not be the smartest soldier I've ever seen, but you are the bravest."

Leng Feng (Wu Jing) is a Chinese special forces sniper with impeccable marksmanship. During an intense showdown with terrorists, he disobeys a direct order, assassinating a man, and finds himself him in a military prison. Because of his reputation, he's quickly recruited by Commander Long Xiaoyun (Nan Yu) to an even more elite team known as the Wolf Warriors. While on a training mission with the Wolves, his team is attacked by a group of mercenaries led by Tom Cat (Scott Adkins). It seems the brother of the man he assassinated on that last mission wants his revenge. The Wolves are trapped in the woods without live ammunition and they're being picked off one by one. Leng Feng isn't about to allow his team to be murdered over the actions of his past, so he risks everything to save their lives.

The thing about Wolf Warrior is that it felt as if it were nothing but a buildup to the finale where it would be a final battle with Wu Jing (*Kill Zone*) fighting Scott Adkins (*The Expendables 2*). When the inevitable moment arrives, the results were a letdown considering how badly we wanted a proper payoff. This is not a bad movie, per se, but fans of its stars will be disappointed. There were no real surprises in the story, so action should have been used to elevate the picture but it just wasn't there. Wu Jing not only starred in the picture, he directed it as well. Directing isn't his strongest asset. Co-star Adkins does a very fine job as the villain, but again, there was so much more he could have done in the film if given the opportunity. This broke box-office records in its native China.

The Wrath of Vajra

2013 (Well Go USA DVD) (CD)

"A devil who slaughters the innocent is eternally trapped in suffering. He harms others, but himself also. He should become enlightened. This could still be considered merciful."

The Temple of Hades has plans for their enemies, a way to destroy China by kidnapping the children and training them as assassins. K-29 (Shi Yanneng) was part of this cult but left when he realized innocent people were being harmed. When the time arises for a tournament in which the winner would become the new Vajra (top fighter), K-29 returns to the cult to save the lives of all the children. The cult has grown strong and has a group of soldiers, led by Bill (Matt Mullins from *Kamen Right: Dragon Knight*), who are forced into fighting as well. K-29 teams up with them to devise a plot to move up the ranks and destroy the cult one by one, never forgetting their main goal, to do whatever it takes to save the young.

The Wrath of Vajra is a visually gorgeous martial arts film with amazing choreography and quite possibly a breakout role for first-time leading man Shi Yanneng (who was formerly a Shaolin monk). The producers of this film were also brilliant enough to bring in American action star Matt Mullins (who has done some impressive work in "B" movies like *Bloodfist 2050*) to fill one of the supporting roles. Mullins is given only one major fight scene, but it's exciting and hopefully it will be enough to show the world what he's capable of. This guy needs to find or be offered the perfect vehicle for his talents and hopefully this could be a springboard. Yanneng has had minor roles in films like *Dragon Tiger Gate* and *Ip Man*; this film is a showcase for him and he has never looked better. The choreography is tight and brutal, shot in a unique way that feels very fresh. The story is just bizarre enough to make this tournament fighting film stand out among the countless others. Director Wing-cheong Law (*Iceman*) is a man with a stunning visual flare, and *The Wrath of Vajra* is a movie to check out.

The Wrestler

2008 (Fox DVD) (DL)

"The only place I get hurt is out there. The world don't give a shit about me."

Mickey Rourke was in a career valley when he accepted the role of the washed up title character in *The Wrestler*. The resulting film and performance would reignite his career, leading to major parts in blockbusters like *Iron Man 2* and *The Expendables*. Rourke plays Randy "The Ram" Robinson, an '80s-era pro wrestling superstar so revered that he once had his own action figure and Nintendo game. Now Randy finds himself broke and broken, wrestling on the local underground circuit and hawking old VHS tapes of his glory days at low-rent autograph shows. With the twentieth anniversary of his most celebrated match approaching, Randy agrees to a rematch that could put him back on top. But when a heart attack nearly takes his life, he's warned by doctors to retire or face the inevitable consequences. Choosing retirement, he wrestles instead with ways to put the pieces of his shattered personal life back together.

A former pro boxer and Hollywood "A"-lister with self-professed demons of his own, Rourke likely found the role an all-too-comfortable fit. His Randy is a lonely and gentle soul performing as a pumped-up hero caricature for the benefit of his adoring fans. Rarely has there been a more perfect fusion of actor and character. Visionary director Darren Aronofsky (*The Fountain*) forgoes his usual stylistic flourishes in favor of a gritty, hand-held realism appropriate to the story. The brutally choreographed matches demonstrate that while pro wrestling may be theater, the physical damage done on stage is anything but faked. Rourke's career shift from athlete to actor makes *The Wrestler* relevant to this book. But even more relevant is the theme of former supermen struggling to stay relevant in a world that has moved on without them. Randy is not so different from many of our beloved action stars forced to constantly reinvent themselves to stay in the game. *The Wrestler* is a heartbreaking and powerful film with a career-defining (and maybe life-defining) performance by Rourke. It's his best work and one of the best films of its decade.

Wrong Side of Town

2010 (Lionsgate DVD) (djm)

"You know, I am really not having a good night tonight. Up until now, I think I've done a pretty good job of keeping my sense of humor. But I feel like I'm starting to lose it. So how about this? How about you take your gang of goofballs here and you get out of my way before you find out what happens when I lose my sense of humor?"

On a whim, Bobby Kalinowski (Rob Van Dam) takes his wife to a nightclub in the city to have a nice night out, and when she takes a while freshening up in the restroom at the club, he goes to find her. In the middle of being assaulted and raped by a young thug, his wife is helpless until her husband steps in and kills the guy in seconds, but pretty much by accident. The police are called, and the owner of the club is notified, and when he finds out that his son (the rapist) was killed, he goes berserk and puts a $100,000 bounty on his son's killer. The owner of the club is a well-known and feared crime lord, and so the call for Kalinowski's head goes out far and wide, ensuring that Kalinowski's drive home back to suburbia will be the longest trip of his life. But here's the catch: Kalinowski (who looks like someone you shouldn't mess with) is a badass former special forces commando, and when things get crazy during the night as he's surrounded, overwhelmed, and inundated with killers on his trail, he calls on a favor from his old war buddy Big Ronnie (Dave Bautista) to help him out and get him home safely.

I had zero expectations going into *Wrong Side of Town*. It looks like a throwaway Wal-Mart dump bin DVD (because it absolutely is one), with wrestler Dave Bautista prominently displayed on the cover, so when the movie turned out to be about Rob Van Dam's character, I was surprised. Van Dam (also a wrestler) just might turn out to be a halfway interesting action star if he lands the right vehicles. *Wrong Side of Town* is a big step in the right direction for him. When he's not being a badass in the movie, he's a flop, but when he's kicking ass or *about* to kick ass in it, he's great. The movie's big shortcoming (other than a piss-poor budget) is that it tries to be goofy and lighthearted when it should have stuck to the hardcore and gritty aspect of the story. It has echoes of movies like *Trespass*, *Judgment Night*, and *Jungleground* (with Roddy Piper), and it should please a certain demographic—those who like movies with guys like Bautista and Van Dam on the cover of DVDs. I enjoyed it. Van Dam's career outside of wrestling includes a few movies, stuff like *Bloodmoon*, *Black Mask 2*, and the exemplary *Superfights*. David DeFalco directed *Wrong Side of Town*.

X-treme Fighter

(a.k.a. **Sci-Fighter**)

2004 (MTI DVD) (djm)

Made about ten years too late to cash in on the virtual reality craze, Art Camacho's cornball *X-Treme Fighter* casts Don Wilson as a respected has-been fight champion named Jack Tanaka, whose son is going through a phase of rebellion. His son Brad (Daneya Mayid) is discovering girls and alcohol and his relationship with his father is getting rocky, mainly because his mother recently passed away. Jack's father is a video game developer, whose new game is called "Sci-Fighter" (this movie's original title), which is a virtual reality fight simulator. Brad plays the game and gets stuck in it due to a virus, and Jack has to enter the game and help his son beat the tough fighters on every level. Cynthia Rothrock and Lorenzo Lamas fill out mostly thankless supporting roles.

Camacho's gift as a director is that he has made friends with some cool "B" action stars and they are willing to make movies with him, but his films aren't endowed with the skills and budgets they need to be completely entertaining. It's a great idea to put Wilson, Rothrock, and Lamas in a movie together, but why put them together in a bloodless, PG-13 movie aimed at kids and teens? At the time when this film was released onto DVD, I'm fairly certain that there were less than a handful of kids and teens who knew who this film's stars were, and fewer still who cared to see all three of them in the same movie. So who is this film's audience? Fans of Lamas and Rothrock will be disappointed, and Wilson's fans *might* be willing to invest the cost of a rental or a purchase, but it certainly isn't worth watching more than once. It's hokey, outdated, and doesn't pack the punch it should. If Camacho has fans, this movie might be for them. Wilson made a similar film in 1995 (when virtual reality was "in") called *Virtual Combat*.

xXx

2002 (Sony DVD) (djm)

"You got a bazooka! Dude, stop thinking Prague police and start thinking PlayStation! Blow shit up!"

After the surprising success of *The Fast and the Furious,* star Vin Diesel and director Rob Cohen reunited on this hip riff on 007 movies. Diesel plays Xander Cage, a daredevil anarchist who does spectacular stunts while making a point to condemn bureaucratic hypocrisy as he's doing them. He's a likable lawbreaker, but the government snatches him out of his off-the-grid pad and throws him into a boot camp with the hope of turning him into a renegade secret agent. Out of all the recruits, he's the best of the bunch, and when his contact (Samuel L. Jackson, with a bad burn scar on his face) gives him the lowdown on his mission, Xander is attracted to

X

Xander Cage (Vin Diesel) is tortured and taunted by a drug runner with a machete, played by Danny Trejo in *xXx*. Author's collection.

There are death-defying stunts in Rob Cohen's *xXx*, starring Vin Diesel and Asia Argento. Author's collection.

The dynamic duo: Cynthia Rothrock (left) and Michelle Yeoh in *Yes, Madam!* Author's collection.

Vin Diesel is a secret agent with attitude in *xXx*. Author's collection.

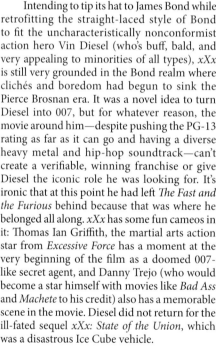

Xander Cage (Vin Diesel) has just been recruited by Agent Gibbons (Samuel L. Jackson) in *xXx*. Author's collection.

A hip riff on the 007 films, *xXx* stars Asia Argento as Yelena and Vin Diesel as Xander Cage. Author's collection.

the danger and the possibilities of being a real hero for once in his life. His mission is to go undercover in Russia and buddy up with some cold-hearted anarchists who may or may not be planning to decimate Europe with missiles armed with deadly chemicals. Since he's basically a celebrity amongst criminals, Xander fits right in . . . until his cover is blown and he has to perform some seriously death-defying stunts to stay alive, defuse the missiles, and win himself a sexy girlfriend (Asia Argento).

Intending to tip its hat to James Bond while retrofitting the straight-laced style of Bond to fit the uncharacteristically nonconformist action hero Vin Diesel (who's buff, bald, and very appealing to minorities of all types), *xXx* is still very grounded in the Bond realm where clichés and boredom had begun to sink the Pierce Brosnan era. It was a novel idea to turn Diesel into 007, but for whatever reason, the movie around him—despite pushing the PG-13 rating as far as it can go and having a diverse heavy metal and hip-hop soundtrack—can't create a verifiable, winning franchise or give Diesel the iconic role he was looking for. It's ironic that at this point he had left *The Fast and the Furious* behind because that was where he belonged all along. *xXx* has some fun cameos in it: Thomas Ian Griffith, the martial arts action star from *Excessive Force* has a moment at the very beginning of the film as a doomed 007-like secret agent, and Danny Trejo (who would become a star himself with movies like *Bad Ass* and *Machete* to his credit) also has a memorable scene in the movie. Diesel did not return for the ill-fated sequel *xXx: State of the Union*, which was a disastrous Ice Cube vehicle.

Yes, Madam!
1985 (Universe Laser and Video DVD) (djm)

"This foreign chick is very swift!"

The action gets going right away in Corey Yuen's *Yes, Madam!* Inspector Ng (Michelle Yeoh) is on a case retrieving a stolen strip of microfilm. The film is evidence against a surly and easily amused gangster, and by a series of events, a pair of bumbling (but likable) crooks manage to obtain the evidence, and before long, they're being chased by the gangster's goons. Ng seems to have the case under control when she is joined by Inspector Carrie Morris (Cynthia Rothrock), whose first scene in the movie is a knockout. The two inspectors hatch a plan to catch the gangster red-handed with the evidence, but to do that they have to set up the two likable crooks. The final showdown features Yeoh and Rothrock fighting off the gangster's bodyguards and assassins. It's a doozy.

A disposable plot and an easily forgettable script make *Yes, Madam!* an average viewing experience, but what makes the film work is the presence and enthusiasm of its two leads. Rothrock's character (as usual) is susceptible to sexist and racist remarks from her Asian counterparts, and she proves them all wrong with her amazing prowess as a fighter. Her period of making films in Hong Kong yielded her best fights on screen, and *Yes, Madam!* is proof positive that she was a force to be reckoned with. She later worked with Yuen again on *No Retreat No Surrender II* and *Above the Law*.

You Can't Win 'Em All

1970 (Creative DVD R2) (JAS)

You Can't Win 'Em All stars Tony Curtis and Charles Bronson as two American mercenaries in 1922 Turkey who are caught up in a political mission. Their charge is to safely transport three royal daughters of the Ottoman Empire along with some precious cargo to the ancient city of Smyrna. Along the way, the two are hoping to procure a fortune in gold that is among the items they are smuggling. With all this at stake, there is the expected double-crossing and general two-fisted mayhem among the heroes.

With a cartoonish slant towards its action, *You Can't Win 'Em All* is of note as a time capsule to the days when plausibility wasn't necessary to entertain an action audience. Unfortunately, this feels like the last gasp of the rip-roarin' barroom brawl days of cinema, and even the chemistry of Bronson and Curtis can't seem to save this from the doldrums. On a positive note, the cinematography is strong and there are some beautiful shots of Turkey. Co-starring Patrick Magee. Directed by Peter Collinson.

Zero Tolerance

2014 (Lionsgate DVD) (djm)

The beautiful daughter of a former paramilitary soldier named Johnny (Dustin Nguyen) is found naked and slain, floating in a Bangkok river. An old associate of his—now a cop—contacts him and tells him the bad news. The cop friend expects Johnny to go on a rampage while hunting for his daughter's killer, so he goes along with him, keeping him "legal" and within range. Their investigation leads them to the sleazy underbelly of Bangkok, and it doesn't take long for Johnny to find out that his daughter was a high-end prostitute who had worked her way into the hearts of gangsters, hoods, and pimps all over the city. The suspect list is piling up, but two key suspects are Sammy (Gary Daniels), a bartender/pimp who was in love with the girl, and Steven (Scott Adkins), a gangster who specialized in exploiting young girls to high rollers. Also in the mix is a gangster (Kane Kosugi in a cameo) and some unexpected suspects who knew Johnny's daughter very well. Johnny's penchant for violence and revenge gets out of control the further he delves into his daughter's sordid history, and the collateral damage becomes difficult for his cop buddy to maintain.

From director Wych Kaosayananda (also known as Kaos in his days as the director of *Ballistic: Ecks vs Sever*), *Zero Tolerance* has such a great line up of badass action stars in smaller roles. Daniels, who has three scenes in the film, turns in a surprisingly non-physical turn as a villain, and Adkins, who is featured on the poster, starts off being a sort-of hero, but ends up being yet another villain who faces off against Nguyen towards the climax. Kosugi only appears in a quick cameo, so fans of his will be blindsided by his in-and-out appearance. The structure of the film is wildly uneven, with plot threads being severed and then unexpectedly reignited much later. I seriously thought the movie was over fifty minutes into the picture, and when it continued on for more than thirty more minutes, I was sort of exhausted by the time it was over. This is Nguyen's movie all the way, so if you can't bear to stand the sight of your favorite action stars (Kosugi, Daniels, Adkins) fall at the hands of an inferior fighter, then be warned.

Z

INDEX OF ACTION STARS

(Titles in **bold** best represent the star on film.)

A

Kareem Abdul-Jabbar

b. 1947. At 7 foot 2, Kareem Abdul-Jabbar (real name: Ferdinand Lewis Alcindor) was certainly the tallest man to fight Bruce Lee on screen. An NBA player for the Milwaukee Bucks (1969–1975) and the LA Lakers (1975–1989), Abdul-Jabbar shot some key fight scenes with Bruce Lee for The Game of Death (1978), which was an incomplete film that was released several years after Lee's untimely death. Abdul-Jabbar made many other appearances in TV shows and motion pictures, but it was his scenes with Bruce Lee that will be most familiar to fans of action and martial arts films.

TITLE REVIEWED:
The Game of Death (1978)

Brahim Achabbakhe

b. 1984. One of the busiest, hardest-working stuntmen working today, Brahim Achabbakhe has the potential to emerge as a viable action star in his own right. From France, he is multilingual, is fit like nobody's business, and has already accrued dozens of credits, a good handful of them in front of the camera as an action actor. I watched him working on the set of Ninja II: Shadow of a Tear in Bangkok, and I was immeasurably impressed by his skill and professionalism.

TITLES REVIEWED:
Street Fighter: The Legend of Chun-Li (2009)
The Kick (2011)
The Mark (2012)
Kill 'Em All (2012)
The Mark 2: Redemption (2013)
Man of Tai Chi (2013)
Tekken 2: Kazuya's Revenge (2014)
Pound of Flesh (2015)

Scott Adkins

b. 1976. (See interview on pages 313 and 482..)

TITLES REVIEWED:
The Accidental Spy (2001)
Extreme Challenge (2001)
Black Mask 2: City of Masks (2002)
Special Forces (2003)
The Medallion (2003)
Unleashed (2005)
Pit Fighter (2005)
Undisputed II: Last Man Standing (2006)

The Shepherd: Border Patrol (2008)
The Tournament (2009)
Ninja (2009)
Undisputed III: Redemption (2010)
Assassination Games (2011)
El Gringo (2012)
The Expendables 2 (2012)
Universal Soldier: Day of Reckoning (2012)
Metal Hurlant Chronicles: King's Crown (2012)
Legendary: Tomb of the Dragon (2013)
Ninja 2: Shadow of a Tear (2013)
Green Street 3: Never Back Down (2013)
Zero Tolerance (2014)
Close Range (2015)
Wolf Warrior (2015)

Tiana Alexandra

b. 1961. Born Thi Thanh Nga, Tiana Alexandra became Bruce Lee's first female protégée through her husband, screenwriter Stirling Silliphant, who was a student of Lee's. It wasn't until the mid-80s that Alexandra was able to land a starring role in the sexy martial arts action movie Catch the Heat (1987), which wasn't a big enough hit to warrant more action films starring the Vietnamese martial artist/dancer.

TITLE REVIEWED:
Catch the Heat (1987)

Lyle Alzado

b. 1949. d. 1992. Massively muscular and intimidating-looking, Lyle Alzado played defensive lineman for the NFL from 1971 to 1991 for the Browns, the Raiders, and the Broncos. He acted in numerous films and television programs, but he starred in lead roles in only a handful of action-themed films. As an actor, he might be best known for his role as a psycho killer in the prison-themed horror film Destroyer (1988). He passed away from a brain tumor, which he attributed to his long-term steroid abuse.

TITLES REVIEWED:
Destroyer (1988)
Hangfire (1991)
Neon City (1991)

Dean Ambrose:

b. 1985. From WWE's roster of wrestlers-turned-action stars, Dean Ambrose (real name: Jonathan Good) was given his shot at movies with the woefully ill-conceived 12 Rounds 3: Lockdown, which is an in-name only sequel to the first 12 Rounds with John Cena. Ambrose doesn't have the hulked-out muscles professional wrestlers tend to flaunt, but his everyman-styled looks are a little disarming when he gets into the action. In the ring, he's known as "The Lunatic Fringe," which is a moniker that you'd never know from watching him in 12 Rounds 3. His performance was adequate in the film, but the film itself didn't give him a chance to succeed.

TITLE REVIEWED:
12 Rounds 3: Lockdown (2015)

Ken "Mr. Kennedy" Anderson

b. 1976. Ken Anderson is a distinguished professional wrestler with several championship titles under his belt. He has wrestled with Total Nonstop Action Wrestling (TNA) and World Wrestling Entertainment (WWE) under his "Mr. Kennedy" moniker. With his big bravado and stark, shortly cropped blonde hair, he has the makings of an action star, but to date, he has only starred in a single action film, the direct-to-video movie Behind Enemy Lines: Columbia (2009).

TITLE REVIEWED:
Behind Enemy Lines: Columbia (2009)

Kurt Angle

b. 1969. Not many action stars are known for being Olympic gold medal winners, but stocky and muscular Kurt Angle won a gold in 1996 for freestyle wrestling in the 220 pound weight category. He had a full career in WWF/WWE wrestling and has recently embarked on a career as an action star in low-budget direct-to-video movies. His movies haven't made much of an impression in the world of action, but he continues to make them, so obviously there's a market for them. All of his starring films have been directed (so far) by Bruce Koehler.

TITLES REVIEWED:
End Game (2009)
River of Darkness (2011)
Death From Above (2012)
Pain and Gain (2013)

DVD artwork for End Game. Author's collection.

Joey Ansah

b. 1982. The youngest person (at the time) in the UK to receive a black belt in ninjutsu, Joey Ansah has come a long way in a short period of time. He's appeared in an impressive line-up of movies as either a stunt performer or actor, and in Alien Uprising *(a.k.a.* U.F.O., *2012) he has a doozy of a donnybrook with Jean-Claude Van Damme. An up-and-coming action star, Ansah has everything he needs to make it, but the real test for him will be to survive in today's dying market for action stars.*

TITLES REVIEWED:

Underground (2007)
Alien Uprising (a.k.a. **U.F.O.**) (2012)
Green Street 3: Never Back Down (2013)
Street Fighter: Assassin's Fist (2014)

Andrei Arlovski

b. 1979. Andrei "The Pit Bull" Arlovski was born in the USSR and became a Sambo (Russian martial art) champion, later embarking on a career in the UFC. John Hyams cast him in Universal Soldier: Regeneration *(2009) and then in* Universal Soldier: Day of Reckoning *(2012), opposite the likes of Jean-Claude Van Damme, Dolph Lundgren, and Scott Adkins. Arlovski's screen presence and sheer, unbridled physicality when unleashed are a treat to see, and it would be fantastic to see him do more films.*

TITLES REVIEWED:

Universal Soldier: Regeneration (2009)
Universal Soldier: Day of Reckoning (2012)

Andrei Arlovski as the UniSol NGU in *Universal Soldier: Regeneration*. Courtesy of Maroody Merav.

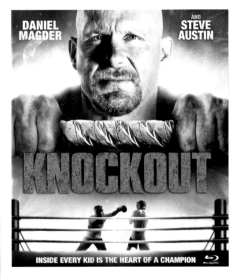

Blu Ray artwork for *Knockout*. Author's collection.

"Stone Cold" Steve Austin

b. 1964. A blue-collar dockworker before he became a professional wrestler who rose through the ranks and became a sensation, "Stone Cold" Steve Austin is known for his steely, stalwart looks, his shaved head and goatee, and his Texas drawl. WWE Entertainment gave him his breakout vehicle film, the hard "R"-rated The Condemned *(2007), which flopped at the box office and inevitably led Austin to starring in a slew of direct-to-video films, many of which weren't worth his talents. He co-starred alongside Sylvester Stallone and a league of major players in* The Expendables *(2010) and notoriously fractured Stallone's neck during their fight scene together. His later films feature him up against notable action star opponents such as Dolph Lundgren, Steven Seagal, and Danny Trejo.*

TITLES REVIEWED:

The Longest Yard (2005)
The Condemned (2007)
Damage (2009)
The Stranger (2010)
The Expendables (2010)
Hunt to Kill (2010)
Recoil (2011)
Knockout (2011)
Tactical Force (2011)
Maximum Conviction (2012)
The Package (2013)
Chain of Command (2015)

Loren Avedon

b. 1962. (See interview on page 321.)

TITLES REVIEWED:

Furious (1984)
L.A. Streetfighters (a.k.a. Ninja Turf) (1985)
No Retreat, No Surrender 2 (1987)
No Retreat, No Surrender 3: Blood Brothers (1990)
The King of the Kickboxers (1990)
Fighting Spirit (a.k.a. The King of the Kickboxers 2) (1992)
Thunder in Paradise (1994)
Operation Golden Phoenix (1994)
Virtual Combat (1995)
Carjack (1996)

Deadly Ransom (1998)
Martial Law (1999)
Tiger Claws III (2000)
Manhattan Chase (2000)
The Silent Force (2001)
The Circuit (2002)
Risk Factor (2015)

B

Blake Bahner

b. 1959. A handsome and busy actor throughout the late 1980s and early 1990s, Blake Bahner is notable for starring in the Roger Corman-produced sequel to Don "The Dragon" Wilson's Black Belt *in 1989. Bahner's "B"-action movie status is confirmed because of the string of action films he was in, but no confirmation has been provided for his martial arts record, despite the fact that the DVD box for* Black Belt II *states that he was the "W.K.F. World Kickboxing Champion." If this is true, then all the better.*

TITLE REVIEWED:

Black Belt II: Fatal Force (a.k.a. *Spyder*) (1989)

John Barrett

b. 1952. Having studied martial arts under Chuck Norris and receiving a black belt in American Tang Soo Do, John Barrett became a stunt coordinator on many of Norris's films before becoming an action star himself. After making small appearances in Norris's films The Octagon *(1980) and* Silent Rage *(1982), Barrett began securing notable roles in films like* Gymkata *(1985) and* Merchants of War *(1989). He then starred in two films for Cannon, the titles he will be most remembered for:* American Kickboxer 1

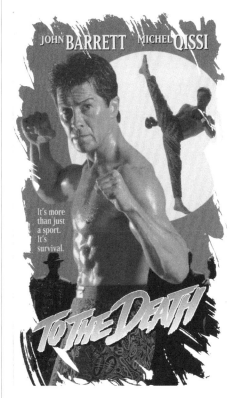

VHS artwork for *To the Death*. Author's collection.

(1991) and To the Death *(1992). Since then, he's gone on to create his own martial arts system known as American Martial Arts System, and has appeared in only a handful of action films and thrillers.*

Mike Bass

b. 1945. One of several NFL players who starred in the blaxploitation action film Brotherhood of Death *(1976), Mike Bass played defensive back and cornerback for the Detroit Lions (1967) and the Washington Redskins (1969–1975). Reportedly, Bass has never watched the film he starred in, stating that he wasn't happy with the script.*

Andy Bauman

b. 1941. Star of the 1988 AIP VHS release Night of the Kickfighters, *Andy Bauman holds a black belt in five different martial arts: Ja Shin Do, taekwondo, Tang Soo Do, Shotokan, and Chung Do Quan. He created the "Ja Shin Do" (path of self-belief) style, and is proficient in judo, boxing, and wrestling. Before starring in* Night of the Kickfighters,

VHS artwork for *Night of the Kickfighters.* Author's collection.

Bauman got his start in the movie business as a stuntman in several Sho Kosugi movies, including Ninja III: The Domination *(1983). Bauman currently owns and operates several fitness centers throughout Boston, Massachusetts.*

Video poster for *House of the Rising Sun.* Author's collection.

Dave Bautista

b. 1969. A WWE wrestling superstar of Greek and Filipino descent who briefly became an MMA fighter (and won his only fight), Dave Bautista is instantly recognizable for his imposing stature and build, sporting extensive body tattoos and a chiseled musculature. He's been building his career in action films, working his way from "B" films like Wrong Side of Town *(2010) and* House of the Rising Sun *(2011) to big-budget "A" pictures such as* Riddick *(2013) and* Guardians of the Galaxy *(2014), Bautista is on an upward trajectory that will help him achieve action movie stardom.*

Zoë Bell

b. 1978. (See interview on page 137.)

David Belle

b. 1973. Belle, a Frenchman, is credited as the inventor of parkour, a modern art of action involving sprinting, climbing, and rolling through any environment without using any safety equipment. Modern action films have adapted parkour to fit films like the Bourne series or the

James Bond films starring Daniel Craig. Belle has performed stunts in films like Transporter 2 *(2005) and* Babylon A.D. *(2008), but his best body of work can be seen in the films* District B13 *(2004) and* District 13: Ultimatum *(2009), both of which were produced and written by Luc Besson.*

Jimmy Bennett

b. 1975. Irish-born Jimmy Bennett wrote, directed, and starred in the martial arts action movie Fatal Deviation *(1998), which holds the record of being the first martial arts movie made entirely in Ireland. His follow-up role was as a supporting stuntman in the Don "The Dragon" Wilson movie* Moving Target *(2000), which was one of the first movies Roger Corman produced in Ireland. Bennett hasn't been able to sustain a starring career in these types of movies, but occasionally he'll pop up as a supporting stunt player.*

Michael Bernardo

b. 1964. A martial artist since the age of eight, Michael Bernardo trained heavily in karate and opened up his own studio, Bernardo Karate Academy, at the age of seventeen, while taking numerous championship titles in various circuits, including the National Tournament Circuit. He acted in a number of low-budget action and martial arts films throughout the 1990s, but his biggest roles were in the two Shootfighter *films (1993,1996), co-starring Bolo Yeung.*

Daniel Bernhardt

b. 1965. (See interview on page 178.)

Swiss action star Daniel Bernhardt in Santa Monica, California. Photo by david j. moore.

The Killing Grounds (a.k.a. *Children of Wax*)
Supreme Champion (2010)
Parker (2013)
John Wick (2014)

Yuen Biao (Biao Yuen)

b. 1967. Hong Kong martial artist and acrobat, Yuen Biao has been working in kung fu films since the early 1970s, and even doubled for Bruce Lee in Lee's posthumous film Game of Death *(1978)*. He picked up steam when he starred in movies like Knockabout *(1979)* and The Prodigal Son *(1981)*, which were solid vehicles films showcasing his martial arts abilities. In the mid-1980s, he starred alongside Jackie Chan and Sammo Hung in various films including Wheels on Meals *(1984)*, Shanghai Express *(1986)*, and Dragons Forever *(1988)*, but one of his standout films was Above the Law *(a.k.a.* Righting Wrongs*) (1986)*, co-starring Cynthia Rothrock and Karen Sheperd. Many consider Biao an underrated action star, and rightfully so.

TITLES REVIEWED:
Project A (1983)
Winners and Sinners (1983)
Wheels on Meals (1984)
My Lucky Stars (1985)
Shanghai Express (1986)
Above the Law (a.k.a. **Righting Wrongs**)
  (1986)
Eastern Condors (1986)
Dragons Forever (1988)
The Iceman Cometh (1989)
Robin B-Hood (2006)

Scott "Bam Bam" Bigalow

b. 1961. d. 2007. "Bam Bam" (as his wrestling fans knew him) was a distinctive-looking roughhouser—part Hell's Angel, part luchador— and while he didn't leave a large legacy of film behind, he did have many fans from his days as a professional wrestler. His most notable film role was as the villain in Snake Eater III: His Law *(1992)*, opposite Lorenzo Lamas. He also appeared in smaller roles in the comedies Major Payne *(1995)* and Joe's Apartment *(1996)*.

TITLE REVIEWED:
Snake Eater III: His Law (1992)

Billy Blanks

b. 1955. (See interview on page 49.).

TITLES REVIEWED:
Low Blow (1986)
Driving Force (1989)
Bloodfist (1989)
China O'Brien II (1990)
The King of the Kickboxers (1990)
The Master (1992)
Street Justice (1992)
Talons of the Eagle (1992)
TC 2000 (1993)
Showdown (1993)
Back in Action (1993)
Tough and Deadly (1995)
Balance of Power (a.k.a. **Hidden Tiger**)
  (1996)
Shadow Warriors (a.k.a. *Assault on Devil's Island*) (1997)
Martial Law (1999)

Michael Blanks

Brother to Billy Blanks, Michael appeared in several direct to video action and martial arts films. Not much is known about him, but he can be seen in small roles in movies such as Dragon Fire *(1993)* and Ring of Steel *(1994)*.

TITLES REVIEWED:
Dragon Fire (1993)
Ring of Steel (1994)
Bloodfist VI: Ground Zero (1995)
Expect No Mercy (1995)
The Circuit (2002)
The Circuit 2: The Final Punch (2002)

Stephan Bonnar

b. 1977. Stephan Bonnar is an MMA fighter and a two-time Golden Gloves champion in the super heavyweight division who made his film debut in the direct-to-video picture Supreme Champion *(2010)*, co-starring Daniel Bernhardt.

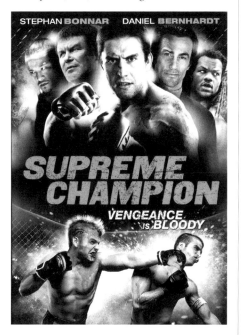

DVD artwork for *Supreme Champion*. Author's collection.

Bonnar, a proficient martial artist in jiu jitsu and taekwondo, was the star of Supreme Champion, though the movie wasn't able to rise above its low-budget pedigree, and as a result of the film's poor performance, Bonnar hasn't been able to sustain a career in films despite a brief appearance in the "A" picture Warrior *(2011)*.

TITLE REVIEWED:
Supreme Champion (2010)

Johnny Yong Bosch

b. 1976. Best known for his extensive work on The Mighty Morphin Power Rangers, *Johnny Yong Bosch, who is proficient in Shaolin kung fu, has co-starred in two notable martial arts action films:* Hellbinders *(2009)* with Ray Park and Death Grip *(2012)* with Eric Jacobus.

TITLES REVIEWED:
Hellbinders (2009)
Death Grip (2012)

James Boss

b. 1980. Not content merely to practice and study the martial arts, young actor James Boss—a Korean American and a third degree black belt in taekwondo—got his own film White Wall *(2010)* off the ground and financed independently, and eventually released to home video. Boss wrote, directed, and starred in the post-apocalyptic martial arts film, and made a name for himself. While the film had its shortcomings, Boss did something most aspiring actors and filmmakers only dream of by starring in his own martial arts action movie. We're still waiting for White Wall 2, James.

TITLE REVIEWED:
White Wall (2010)

Brian Bosworth

b. 1965. A sensation while he was an NFL linebacker for the Seattle Seahawks, Brian Bosworth (nicknamed "The Boz") made an auspicious action star debut in the outrageous Stone Cold *(1991)*, directed by Craig R. Baxley. Hailed as the next big action star, Bosworth rapidly descended into a direct-to-video career, headlining in about a half a dozen less-than-stellar pictures. His status as an action star, however, is forever minted because of Stone Cold, which remains his best film, and it truly is an action classic. Bosworth, a tall, distinctive-looking athlete, attempted to become a television star with the short-lived action series Lawless *(1997)*, which was cancelled virtually before it had a chance to begin.

TITLES REVIEWED:
Stone Cold (1991)
Blackout (a.k.a. *Midnight Heat*) (1996)
One Man's Justice (a.k.a. *One Tough Bastard*) (1996)
Virus (1996)
Back in Business (1997)
The Operative (2000)
Mach 2 (2001)
Phase IV (2002)
The Longest Yard (2005)

Revelation Road: The Beginning of the End (2013)
Revelation Road 2: The Sea of Glass and Fire (2013)

David Bradley cuts a striking profile as Sean Davidson, the American Ninja in *American Ninja 3: Blood Hunt*. Author's collection.

David Bradley

b. 1959. Texan David Bradley (real name: Bradley Simpson) was trained in kenpo, Shotokan karate, aikido, and tai chi, and became a karate champion. When Michael Dudikoff exited Cannon's American Ninja *franchise to pursue other films, Bradley stepped in and assumed the role of "The American Ninja," although he played a new character. Best known for his three* American Ninja *entries (*American Ninja 3: Blood Hunt, American Ninja 4: The Annihilation, *and* American Ninja 5*), Bradley went on to have a decent career as an action star in low-budget martial arts and action films. The director he worked with most was Sam Firstenberg who, ironically, was the director of the first two* American Ninja *pictures. Bradley garnered a bad reputation in Hollywood as being difficult to work with, and he gradually gravitated away from using his martial arts in movies, picking films that required him to act instead of getting in on the action. Some of his non-action film roles include the slasher* Lower Level *(1992) and the erotic thriller* Exit *(1996). He hasn't made a movie since the late 1990s.*

TITLES REVIEWED:

American Ninja 3: Blood Hunt (1989)
American Ninja 4: The Annihilation (1990)
American Samurai (1992)
American Ninja 5 (1992)
Cyborg Cop (1993)
Blood Warriors (1993)
Cyborg Cop II (a.k.a. *Cyborg Soldier*) (1994)
Outside the Law (a.k.a. *Blood Run*) (1994)
Hard Justice (1995)
Exit (1996)
White Cargo (1996)
Expect to Die (1997)
Total Reality (1997)
Crisis (1997)

Charles Bronson

b. 1926. d. 2003. Born Charles Buchinsky to Lithuanian parents, Bronson was a miner alongside his father, and later served in World War II in the air corps. With a perpetually lean, muscular, and sinewy frame, Bronson became

Theatrical poster for *Raid on Entebee*. Author's collection.

known as a physical actor (or an action star, if you like) as he picked up steam, starring in dozens of action-filled westerns, thrillers, and adventures. Cast in various ethnic roles where he played Native American Indians, Mexicans, and Russians, he was able to fill almost any role he took on. It wasn't until he was in his fifties that he became a full-fledged action star with the surprise hit Death Wish *(1974), which was the film he was most associated with throughout the rest of his career and life. In the early 1980s, he signed a multi-picture deal with The Cannon Group, and made ten films (including* Death Wish V: The Face of Death *(1993) in just over a decade for that studio. Bronson's persona was steely and stalwart, and he wasn't a man to mince words.*

TITLES REVIEWED:

The Dirty Dozen (1967)
Guns for San Sebastian (1968)
Villa Rides! (1968)
Once Upon a Time in the West (1968)
Honor Among Thieves (a.k.a. *Farewell, Friend*) (1968)
Rider on the Rain (1970)
You Can't Win 'Em All (1970)
Violent City (a.k.a. *The Family*) (1970)
Cold Sweat (1970)
Red Sun (1971)
Chato's Land (1972)
The Mechanic (1972)
The Stone Killer (1973)
Chino (1973)
Mr. Majestyk (1974)
Death Wish (1974)
Breakout (1975)
Hard Times (1975)
Breakheart Pass (1975)
St. Ives (1976)
From Noon Till Three (1976)
Raid on Entebbe (1976)
The White Buffalo (1977)
Telefon (1977)
Love and Bullets (1979)
Cabo Blanco (1980)
Borderline (1980)
Death Hunt (1981)
Death Wish II (1982)
10 to Midnight (1983)
The Evil That Men Do (1984)
Death Wish 3 (1985)
Murphy's Law (1986)
Assassination (1987)
Death Wish 4: The Crackdown (1987)
Messenger of Death (1988)
Kinjite: Forbidden Subjects (1989)

Dead to Rights (a.k.a. *Donato and Daughter*) (1993)
Death Wish V: The Face of Death (1993)
Family of Cops (1995)
Breach of Faith: Family of Cops II (1997)
Family of Cops III: Under Suspicion (1998)

Jim Brown

b. 1936. A pioneer action star for African Americans, Jim Brown began his career as a lacrosse star and then as a fullback for the Cleveland Browns (1957–1965), netting world records and Hall of Fame status. He segued into acting, co-starring in the western Rio Conchos *(1964), alongside Richard Boone and Stuart Whitman. His big coup as an action star was being included in the now-classic* The Dirty Dozen *(1967), alongside genre greats like Lee Marvin and Charles Bronson. In time, Brown became one of the first bona fide black action stars, starring in blaxploitation genre vehicles like* Slaughter *(1972),* Black Gunn *(1972), and* Slaughter's Big Rip-off *(1973). Brown was a mainstay in action and genre films for the next two decades, and remains an icon in the world of action stars.*

TITLES REVIEWED:

Rio Conchos (1964)
The Dirty Dozen (1967)
Dark of the Sun (1968)
Kenner (1968)
The Split (1968)
Ice Station Zebra (1968)
Riot (1969)
100 Rifles (1969)
...tick...tick...tick (1970)
El Condor (1970)
Slaughter (1972)
Black Gunn (1972)
Slaughter's Big Rip-off (1973)
I Escaped Devil's Island (1973)
The Slams (1973)
Three the Hard Way (1974)
Take a Hard Ride (1975)
One Down, Two to Go (1976)
Vengeance (a.k.a. *Kid Vengeance*) (1977)
Pacific Inferno (1979)
The Running Man (1987)
Crack House (1989)
Killing American Style (1990)
The Divine Enforcer (1992)
Original Gangstas (1996)
Mars Attacks! (1996)
On the Edge (2002)

Mike Brown

b. 1975. A professional mixed martial arts fighter and cage fighter since 2001, Mike Brown has a long and varied fight record, but finally made his transition into action films with the unfortunately abysmal Vietnam war action film The Bunker *in 2014. He plays a supporting role in the film opposite professional wrestler Ken Shamrock. Here's hoping in the future Brown finds better movie vehicles to star in.*

TITLE REVIEWED:

The Bunker (2014)

Reb Brown

b. 1948. (See interview on page 92.)

TITLES REVIEWED:
Captain America (1979)
Captain America II: Death Too Soon (1979)
Strike Commando (1987)
Robowar (1988)
Mercenary Fighters (1988)
Space Mutiny (1988)
The Firing Line (1988)
Cage (1989)
Last Flight to Hell (1990)
Street Hunter (1990)
Cage II (1994)

C

Lee Canalito

b. 1953. Sylvester Stallone was on a hot streak when he wrote, directed, and starred in the wrestling movie Paradise Alley in 1978. He cast professional heavyweight boxer Lee Canalito (whom he managed for a time) in his new film, and gave him what would amount to the lead role. When Paradise Alley *flopped in theaters and became one of Stallone's novelty films, Canalito wouldn't make another movie until 1989's* The Glass Jungle, *a very low-budget action picture from the still-forming PM Entertainment. By then, Canalito was no longer a young up-and-coming action star hopeful, but a retired undefeated boxer with twenty-one victories to his credit. His place in the world of action films is sidelined because not many fans of action films have ever heard of him.*

TITLES REVIEWED:
Paradise Alley (1978)
The Glass Jungle (1989)

Gina Carano

b. 1982. A breakout action star when director Steven Soderbergh hand-picked her to headline his film Haywire *(2011), Gina Carano had by then already become "The Face of Women's MMA," with an impressive record of seven wins and only one loss in professional women's mixed martial arts fighting. Since starring in* Haywire, *she's only appeared in a few films, but her potential as an action star is limitless.*

TITLES REVIEWED:
Blood and Bone (2009)
Haywire (2011)
Fast & Furious 6 (2013)
In the Blood (2014)
Extraction (2015)

Sean Carrigan

b. 1974. A one-hit wonder, Sean Carrigan who had a one-year stint as a professional boxer (1998–1999) has bounced around as an actor and a comedian, but when NBC hosted producer Joel Silver's reality program Next Action Star, Carrigan beat his male competition and became the victor of the contest (after going through various obstacle courses and trials throughout the show's single season), with the prize being a starring role in an action film, produced by Silver. Carrigan's sole contribution to feature films as the star was the made-for-TV effort Bet Your Life,

co-starring Billy Zane and Corinne Van Ryck de Groot, who was the show's female winner.

TITLE REVIEWED:
Bet Your Life (2004)

Fabian Carrillo

b. 1963. After immigrating to the United States with his family, Fabian Carrillo spent much of his childhood in inner-city dojos training to be the best he could be. He holds belts in multiple disciplines and was inducted into the Martial Arts Hall of Fame. The next logical step for a man with his talents was to leap onto the big screen. Making it into the movies was a long, tough road but all the persistence and hard work paid off when his solo vehicle Latin Dragon was released in 2004.

TITLES REVIEWED:
Champions (1998)
Latin Dragon (2004)
Double Tap (2015)

John Cena

b. 1977. A superstar of modern professional wrestling, John Cena is virtually a brand name unto himself, with merchandising, films, and even a rap album that sells simply because he's endorsed them. A "good guy" wrestler with a massive muscular frame and tons of WWE championship titles, Cena made his film debut in the WWE-sponsored picture The Marine (2006), which bore a PG-13 rating when it was released in theaters. Since then, he's only starred in a handful of films, all of which were also rated PG-13, which should indicate who his fan base is. With plenty of potential to become a full-fledged, no-holds-barred action star unhindered by a safe MPAA rating, Cena has yet to maximize on what he's capable of in terms of making action movies that should last the test of time.

Theatrical poster for *Legendary.* Author's collection.

TITLES REVIEWED:
The Marine (2006)
12 Rounds (2009)
Legendary (2010)
The Reunion (2011)
Scooby-Doo! WrestleMania Mystery (2014)

Jackie Chan

b. 1954. A comedian, a martial artist, and a daredevil of the most incredible sort, Jackie Chan has made an indelible mark in the action and martial arts genres. Trained in the China Drama Academy (otherwise known as "opera school"), Chan made small appearances in early '70s kung fu films, most notably Enter the Dragon, *opposite Bruce Lee in 1973. A little further on and Jackie was a full-fledged star, putting himself through rigorous routines where he became known for putting his life and safety on the line to entertain audiences. When he made his first international crossover with* The Big Brawl *(1980), Western audiences were lukewarm in receiving him and despite appearances in* The Cannonball Run *(1981), opposite major Hollywood stars, it would be quite some time before he would finally find his big break when his film* Rumble in the Bronx *became a surprise box-office hit in 1995 in the United States. Western audiences were finally ready to embrace him as an action star. Throughout his incredible career, Jackie has made some astoundingly awesome action films of unparalleled glory like* Police Story *(1985),* Supercop *(1992), and* Operation Condor *(1991), but it's his English language films like the* Rush Hour *trilogy (1998–2007) and* Shanghai Noon *(2000) that have garnered him millions of fans throughout the world and have given him crossover appeal. As he's slowed down and scaled back his physical feats on screen, he's begun acting in more dramatic roles, which is an interesting transition for him. Jackie Chan is a once-in-a-lifetime action star, and we'll never see his like again.*

Rumble in the Bronx brought Jackie Chan to America again, but in a bigger and better way. Author's collection.

Robert Chapin

b. 1964. The three films that Robert Chapin starred in featured him wielding swords, which is fitting since he was trained in stage combat and swordplay. A practitioner of several different martial arts including taekwondo, wushu, and the Filipino art known as kali (which specializes in weaponry), Chapin fit right in as an action star during the early 1990s when others of his ilk were able to write and star in their own vehicles if they had just the right amount of fighting skills and screen presence to pull it off. Since he dropped off the acting radar over a decade ago, he went in a completely different direction and became a visual effects artist for major motion pictures.

Tiger Hu Chen

b. 1982. A stunt and fight double for Keanu Reeves and Uma Thurman on several major films including The Matrix Reloaded and Kill Bill, Tiger Hu Chen got a major break when Reeves fashioned his directorial debut film Man of Tai Chi (2013) around him. A martial arts champion and the protégée of Yuen Wo Ping, Chen made an excellent leading action star in the Reeves film, and it will be interesting to see what he does next.

Sonny Chiba

b. 1939. A force of nature, Sonny (Shin'ichi) Chiba (real name: Sadao Maeda) has a roster of films that would take any movie watcher months to track down and watch, but there are great rewards to be found in his films. A martial artist skilled in judo, karate, kenpo, and ninjutsu, Chiba cut a swathe in the martial arts genre right around the time Bruce Lee had made his mark and left our world, but Chiba kept at it, churning out several movies a year. His movie The Streetfighter (1974) made such an indelible impression on viewers, that it spawned several sequels and spin-offs, and who can forget the X-ray punches? Chiba had his own brand of extreme violence in his films, and his style is inimitable.

Theatrical poster for *Man of Tai Chi*. Author's collection.

George Chung

Part self-deprecating comedian and part martial arts dynamo, George Chung sort of crept through the back door of the action movie scene in the mid-80s with independent martial arts movies starring the likes of Cynthia Rothrock, Richard Norton, Chuck Jeffreys, and Leo Fong. Chung not only acted in front of the camera but also wrote, produced, and directed several of the films he appeared in, most notably Fight to Win (1987) and Karate Cops (a.k.a. Hawkeye, 1988). As the film market shifted in the '90s, Chung left the industry behind to pursue other endeavors.

VHS artwork for *Karate Cops*. Author's collection.

Titles Reviewed:
Fight to Win (1987)
Karate Cops (a.k.a. **Hawkeye**) (1988)
Blood Street (1988)
Dragon Fight (1989)
Kindergarten Ninja (1994)

Dwight Clark
b. 1957. A former wide receiver and quarterback for the San Francisco 49ers, Dwight Clark chose the ultra low-budget movie Kindergarten Ninja (1994) as his one and only vehicle film. In the movie, he plays a philandering drunk, who is aided by the ghost of Bruce Lee and a blind martial artist to set his life straight and save a kindergarten class from drug dealers.

TITLE REVIEWED:
Kindergarten Ninja (1994)

Teagan Clive
b. 1959. Female bodybuilder and author Teagan Clive made several movie crossovers, with two straight-up action-oriented films to her credit: the post-apocalyptic Interzone (1987) and the Terminator-esque Alienator (1990). Her career in films tapered off soon thereafter, but female bodybuilders-turned-action stars are a rare breed, so here's to her.

TITLES REVIEWED:
Interzone (1988)
Alienator (1990)

Franco Columbu
b. 1941. Arnold Schwarzenegger's training partner and two-time Mr. Olympia winner, Franco Columbu was given his chance to star in an action film called Beretta's Island (1994), which featured him playing a fictional version of himself as a secret agent who goes back to his hometown in Sardinia, Italy (his real birthplace) to clean up the streets of thugs and drug pushers. Columbu has also made several very small appearances in some of Schwarzenegger's films, but Beretta's Island is pretty much it if you're looking to see him in action.

TITLE REVIEWED:
Beretta's Island (1994)

Dale "Apollo" Cook
b. 1958. (See interview on page 194.)

TITLES REVIEWED:
Fist of Glory (1991)
Blood Ring (1991)
Fist of Steel (a.k.a. **Eternal Fist**) (1992)
Triple Impact (1992)
American Kickboxer 2 (1993)
Double Blast (1994)
Raw Target (1995)
Blood Ring 2 (1995)

Keith Cooke
b. 1959. Keith Cooke (Hirabayashi) was an accomplished martial artist and competitor before embarking on an on-again, off-again career in action films. Trained in wushu, taekwondo, and karate, Cooke is a world champion in forms and weapons, and also holds distinguished titles in the martial arts world. Disappointingly, he hasn't made as many feature film appearances as he should have, so the few times he co-starred in films are small treasures, to be savored.

TITLES REVIEWED:
Picasso Trigger (1988)
China O'Brien (1990)
China O'Brien II (1990)
King of the Kickboxers (1990)
Heatseeker (1995)
Mortal Kombat (1995)
Beverly Hills Ninja (1997)
Mortal Kombat: Annihilation (1997)

Paul Coufos
b. 1952. The VHS box of Busted Up (1986) features a bare-chested Paul Coufos, fists raised, ready to knock your lights out. The film is about a down-on-his luck boxer, whose relationship with his wife is on the rocks, and the only thing that keeps him grounded is his ability to fight and earn a meager living. The sequel Thunderground (1989) has Coufos playing the same character, only he's drifting through life like a vagrant, making his way from one bare-knuckle back alley fight to the next, and Coufos shines in the role, making him a verifiable action star in this book despite the fact that he's not a crossover athlete or martial artist. He's got what it takes to be an action star, and it's a true shame that he didn't stick with the genre because he could have been one of the great ones.

TITLES REVIEWED:
Busted Up (1986)
Thunderground (1989)
Dragonfight (1990)
Cold Vengeance (a.k.a. *Sometimes a Hero*) (2003)

Randy Couture
b. 1963. Two-time UFC light-heavyweight champion and three-time UFC heavyweight champion Randy Couture retired from professional mixed martial arts fighting at forty-seven, but not before making his transition into action films. His first appearance was a bit role in the Jet Li film Cradle 2 the Grave (2003), but he's probably best known on film for his role as Toll Road in the Expendables trilogy (2010–2014). His solo vehicle Hijacked (2012) was a huge disappointment because it didn't capitalize on his talents and abilities, so the jury remains out on whether or not Hollywood will nurture Couture as a stand-alone action star. He's certainly capable of pulling it off.

TITLES REVIEWED:
Cradle 2 the Grave (2003)
Today You Die (2005)
No Rules (2005)

The Expendables (2010)
Hijacked (2012)
The Expendables 2 (2012)
Ambushed (2013)
The Expendables 3 (2014)

Daz Crawford
b. 1968. After a career in the Royal Air Force, Daz Crawford became an amateur boxer, ranking tenth in the world. He embarked on a career in action and martial arts films, two of which co-starred Andre "Chyna" McCoy. As the DVD market for action and martial arts films is currently waning, Crawford's career in this field is in limbo, as he hasn't made a notable feature in the genre in several years.

TITLES REVIEWED:
Blade II (2002)
Game Over (2005)
T.K.O. (2007)

Terry Crews
b. 1968. A busy actor since 2000, Terry Crews has a huge, muscular frame and has played all sorts of diverse characters, including the president of the United States in Mike Judge's classic Idiocracy (2006). A former NFL player with the LA Rams, the San Diego Chargers, the Washington Redskins, and the Philadelphia Eagles from the years 1991 to 1997, Crews eventually transitioned into films, with a small role in Arnold Schwarzenegger's The 6th Day (2000). He's probably best known to fans of action films for playing Hale Caesar in the Expendables trilogy (2010–2014), and it's a shame that he's not yet been given his own vehicle to star in. That said, he remains an extremely busy character actor in feature films and television shows equally.

TITLES REVIEWED:
The 6th Day (2000)
The Longest Yard (2005)
Get Smart (2008)
The Expendables (2010)
The Expendables 2 (2012)
The Expendables 3 (2014)

Lateef Crowder
b. 1977. A practitioner of capoeira, Lateef Crowder has represented his passion for that martial art in most of his film appearances, namely in The Protector (2005), opposite Tony Jaa, and in Falcon Rising (a.k.a. Favela, 2014), opposite Michael Jai White. Crowder is getting around, and he's being seen in more and more films, and in bigger projects, so keep your eyes open for him.

TITLES REVIEWED:
The Protector (a.k.a. **Tom Yum Goong**) (2005)
Never Surrender (2009)
Tekken (2010)
Undisputed 3: Redemption (2010)
The Girl From the Naked Eye (2012)
Falcon Rising (a.k.a. **Favela**) (2014)

D

Mark Dacascos

b. 1964. (See interview on page 329.)

TITLES REVIEWED:
American Samurai (1992)
Only the Strong (1993)
Double Dragon (1994)
Kickboxer 5 (1995)
Crying Freeman (1995)
Sabotage (1996)
DNA (1997)
Drive (1997)
Redline (1997)
Boogie Boy (1998)
Sanctuary (1998)
The Crow: Stairway to Heaven (1998-1999)
No Code of Conduct (1998)
The Base (1999)
China Strike Force (2000)
Brotherhood of the Wolf (2001)
Instinct to Kill (2001)
Cradle 2 the Grave (2003)
The Hunt for Eagle One (2006)
The Hunt for Eagle One: Crash Point (2006)
Alien Agent (2007)
I Am Omega (2007)
The Lost Medallion: The Adventures of Billy Stone (2013)
Mortal Kombat: Legacy II (2013)
The Extendables (2014)
Operation Rogue (2014)

Gary Daniels

b. 1963. (See interview on page 197.)

TITLES REVIEWED:
The Secret of King Mahi's Island (1988)
Final Reprisal (1988)
Ring of Fire (1991)
Capital Punishment (1991)
Final Impact (1992)
Deadly Bet (1992)

WHEN ACTION IS THE ONLY ANSWER

GARY DANIELS

MISFIRE

REVENGE COMES DEADLY

DVD artwork for *Misfire*. Author's collection.

Bloodfist IV: Die Trying (1992)
American Streetfighter (1992)
City Hunter (1993)
Full Impact (1993)
Knights (1993)
Firepower (1993)
Deadly Target (1994)
Fist of the North Star (1995)
Heatseeker (1995)
Rage (1995)
Hawk's Vengeance (1996)
White Tiger (1996)
Riot (1996)
Pocket Ninjas (1997)
Bloodmoon (1997)
Recoil (1998)
Spoiler (1998)
Cold Harvest (1999)
No Tomorrow (1999)
City of Fear (2000)
Fatal Blade (a.k.a. Gedo) (2000)
Delta Force One: The Lost Patrol (2000)
Ultimate Target (a.k.a. Ides of March) (2000)
Witness to a Kill (2001)
Black Friday (2001)
Queen's Messenger (2001)
Retrograde (2004)
Submerged (2005)
Reptilicant (2006)
Tekken (2010)
The Expendables (2010)
Hunt to Kill (2010)
Game of Death (2010)
The Lazarus Papers (2010)
Forced to Fight (2011)
The Mark (2012)
The Mark 2: Redemption (2013)
Misfire (2014)
Zero Tolerance (2014)
Skin Traffik (2015)

Anthony De Longis

b. 1950. A man of many talents, Anthony De Longis might be best known for his villainous role of Blade in Gary Goddard's Masters of the Universe (1987), but De Longis has had a fascinating career as a whip trainer, a sword master, a martial arts stunt and fight coordinator, and as an actor in tons of feature films and television shows. He trained Harrison Ford to use the whip in Indiana Jones and the Kingdom of the Crystal Skull (2008) and Michelle Pfeiffer in Batman Returns (1992), and his skills as a sword master have extended to projects like television's Highlander (1992–1998), Conan The Adventurer (1997), and The Queen of Swords (2000–2001). As a character actor and martial artist, De Longis has appeared in the sci-fi shows Battlestar Galactica (1978–1979), Babylon 5 (1994–1998), and Star Trek: Voyager (1995–2001), and has fought alongside or against action stars like Don "The Dragon" Wilson, Lorenzo Lamas, Joe Lewis, and Jalal Merhi, and amazingly, he's still in the game, having appeared in recent episodes of Justified and Grimm.

TITLES REVIEWED:
Jaguar Lives! (1979)
The A-Team (1984)
The Master (1984)
Renegade (1993)

CIA II: Target Alexa (1993)
Final Round (1994)
Cyber-Tracker 2 (1995)
Expect No Mercy (1995)
Fearless (2006)
Double Duty (2009)

Harold Diamond

Remember the first time we see John Rambo (Sylvester Stallone) in Rambo III (1988) where he's stick fighting a dude in Thailand? That dude was Harold Diamond (born Harold Roth), a Muay Thai fighter, a full-contact karate fighter, and a champion kickboxer with a collected total of eighty-four fights under his belt. Diamond starred or co-starred in a handful of other films, most notably Killing American Style (1990), which might be his best vehicle film, but he was also in two movies directed by Andy Sidaris, the king of T & A action movies. Diamond's final film was the lost movie Gypsy (1991), which will reportedly see the light of day from Cinema Epoch DVD in the near future.

TITLES REVIEWED:
Hard Ticket to Hawaii (1987)
Picasso Trigger (1988)
Rambo III (1988)
Trained to Kill (1989)
Killing American Style (1990)

Ted DiBiase Jr.

b. 1982. Following in the footsteps of his father, "The Million Dollar Man" Ted DiBiase, Ted DiBiase Jr. became a professional wrestler with WWE, and performed matches from 2008 to 2013, but retired to pursue other ventures. His only movie vehicle to date was the direct-to-video WWE-sanctioned picture The Marine 2 (2009), for which he performed all of his stunts, resulting in a minor injury that prevented him for returning to wrestling straightaway. His grandfather "Iron" Mike DiBiase was also a professional wrestler, and Ted Jr.'s two brothers Brett and Mike are now professional wrestlers as well.

TITLE REVIEWED:
The Marine 2 (2009)

Vin Diesel

b. 1967. A Hollywood success story after raising enough money to star and direct in an independent film called Strays (1997), Vin Diesel's (real name Mark Sinclair Vincent) next film was for Steven Spielberg after he saw that film and hand-picked him for a crucial role in Saving Private Ryan (1998). Diesel became a full-fledged action star when he starred in the back-to-back hits Pitch Black (2000) and The Fast and the Furious (2001). When Hollywood caught on that the thick-voiced and muscular Diesel was a viable choice to star in action-themed movies, he became a superstar by the time he headlined the films xXx (2002) and the family-oriented action hit The Pacifier (2005). Diesel hasn't rushed to do movie after movie, but instead has carefully planned his course, deciding to star in sequels to The Fast and the Furious and Pitch Black, which has ultimately been a savvy move, as he remains a bankable action star.

Renegade DEA agent Sean Vetter (Vin Diesel) is after the drug cartel that killed his wife in *A Man Apart*. Author's collection.

TITLES REVIEWED:

Pitch Black (2000)
The Fast and the Furious (2001)
xXx (2002)
A Man Apart (2003)
The Chronicles of Riddick (2004)
The Pacifier (2005)
Babylon A.D. (2008)
Fast and Furious (2009)
Fast Five (2011)
Fast & Furious 6 (2013)
Riddick (2013)
Guardians of the Galaxy (2014)
Fast and Furious 7 (a.k.a. *Furious 7*) (2015)
The Last Witch Hunter (2015)

Sean Donahue

b. 1966. Stuntman-turned-action star Sean Donahue got his start working for his father, director Patrick Donahue, on the action film Kill Squad *(1982), and then as the '80s passed, Patrick took on a handful of martial arts/action movies where he was the star. For whatever reason, his films didn't receive proper distribution and his star was not allowed to flourish, and therefore he remains one of the "forgotten" action stars of the 1990s. He's kept himself in shape, practices kuk sul do (a Korean martial art), and is planning his comeback as I write this.*

TITLES REVIEWED:

Blood Hands (1990)
King of the Kickboxers 2 (a.k.a. *Fighting Spirit*) (1992)
Roughcut (1994)
Parole Violators (1994)
Ground Rules (1997)
Shattered Dreams (1998)

Fred Dryer

b. 1946. A former NFL player who played for the New York Giants and then for thirteen years with the LA Rams, Fred Dryer struck paydirt when he landed the lead role in the massively popular television program Hunter, *which played for seven full seasons (over 150 episodes), and then years later was renewed for several movies-of-the-week. Dryer's only real feature film action vehicle was the New World Picture* Death Before Dishonor *(1987), which was also the film debut of future action star Sasha Mitchell.*

TITLES REVIEWED:

Hunter (1984–1991)
Cannonball Run II (1984)
Death Before Dishonor (1987)

Michael Dudikoff

b. 1954. (See interview on page 20.)

b. 1954. (See interview on page 20.)

TITLES REVIEWED:

American Ninja (1985)
Avenging Force (1986)
American Ninja 2: The Confrontation (1986)
Platoon Leader (1988)
River of Death (1989)
Midnight Ride (1990)
American Ninja 4: The Annihilation (1990)
The Human Shield (1991)
Rescue Me (1992)
Chain of Command (1994)
Cobra (1993–1994)
Cyberjack (1995)
Soldier Boyz (1995)
Bounty Hunters (1996)
Moving Target (1996)
Bounty Hunters 2: Hardball (1997)
Strategic Command (1997)
Crash Dive (1997)
Deadly Shooter (1997)
Freedom Strike (1998)
Counter Measures (1998)
Black Thunder (1998)
Musketeers Forever (1998)
Fugitive Mind (1999)
The Silencer (2000)
Ablaze (2000)
Gale Force (2002)
Quicksand (2002)
Stranded (a.k.a. *Black Horizon*) (2002)

Bill Duff

b. 1974. Former NFL player and current practitioner of Tang Soo Do, Bill Duff was also the host of The History Channel's The Human Weapon *(2007), which detailed worldwide martial arts styles. Jino Kang, the writer, director, and star of* Blade Warrior *(2000) cast Duff in his next film* Fist 2 Fist *(2011), which gave both martial artists their chance to shine in the spotlight. Since then, Duff has been fairly quiet on the action movie scene, but he certainly showed promise in that film.*

TITLE REVIEWED:

Fist 2 Fist (2011)

E

Glen Eaton

b. 1963. After appearing in a plum supporting role in the cult martial arts film The Last Dragon *(1985), Glen Eaton's only other action/martial arts film was the Frank Zagarino-starring* Trained to Kill *(1989), which gave Eaton his best role to date. Eaton, who is part Japanese, has practiced karate since the age of fourteen It's a mystery why he either chose not to continue making more action films or was not given the opportunity to.*

TITLES REVIEWED:

The Last Dragon (1985)
Trained to Kill (1989)

Hector Echavarria

b. 1969. Argentinian Hector Echavarria has been training in mixed martial arts since he was a child, and when he came to the US to pursue a career in action films, he formed his own production company and spearheaded his own films by writing, directing, and starring in them. Most of his films are very low budget, but many of them feature other real-life MMA and UFC fighters in small roles. Echavarria tends to give himself the best fights and the most attractive women in each of his films, and in his latest film Chavez: Cage of Glory *(2013, a theatrical release) he stars as a man given a shot at fighting in a championship MMA fight to pay for his sick son's mounting medical bills. Like him or not, Echavarria doesn't just sit around waiting for roles to come his way. He takes the initiative and fights the odds to make films he wants to make and star in.*

TITLES REVIEWED:

Extreme Force (2001)
Los Bravos (2001)
Cradle 2 the Grave (2003)
Confessions of a Pit Fighter (2005)
Never Surrender (2009)
Death Warrior (2009)
Unrivaled (2010)
Chavez: Cage of Glory (2013)

Anthony "Amp" Elmore

b. 1953. A devout Buddhist who lived by the Bushido Code as a young man, Anthony "Amp" Elmore became a kickboxer after being inspired by Bruce Lee's work in the television show The Green Hornet *(1967). Elmore, who combined elements of his heroes Muhammad Ali and Bruce Lee in his own fighting style, became a kickboxing champion and later made a feature film based on his life. The film—*Iron Thunder *(a.k.a.* Contemporary Gladiator, *1989)—remains his only effort in movies. Today, he runs a successful carpet business in Memphis, Tennessee.*

TITLE REVIEWED:

Iron Thunder (a.k.a. **Contemporary Gladiator**) (1989)

Rahsad Evans

b. 1979. The heavyweight winner of The Ultimate Fighter, Rashad Evans has an impressive MMA and UFC record with nineteen wins, one draw, and only three losses. He crossed over into low-budget action and martial arts films in 2009 with the Tapout-sponsored Death Warrior, *and his subsequent above-the-title movies have also been sponsored by Tapout. In the films he's been in, he co-stars with his MMA and UFC peers Keith Jardine and Quinton "Rampage" Jackson, amongst others.*

TITLES REVIEWED:

Death Warrior (2009)
Unrivaled (2010)
Locked Down (2010)

Corey Everson and director Sheldon Lettich on the set of *Double Impact*. Courtesy of Sheldon Lettich.

Corey Everson

b. 1959. Six-time Miss Olympia winner, Corrina (Corey) Everson made her auspicious action movie debut in the Jean-Claude Van Damme film Double Impact *(1991) where she played a butch henchwoman who grabs Van Damme's balls in their fight scene together. Everson would go on to co-star in the "B" martial arts action film* Ballistic *(1995), where she faced off against Marjean Holden in a to-the-death fight. Strangely, Everson would never get the stand-alone vehicle film she deserved.*

TITLES REVIEWED:
Double Impact (1991)
Renegade (1994)
Ballistic (1995)

F

Kevin "Kimbo Slice" Ferguson

b. 1974. From bouncer, to bodyguard, to street fighting, and then to a career in MMA, and then boxing, Kevin "Kimbo Slice" Ferguson has had a storied path to becoming an actor, and anyone who's ever seen him fight knows him instantly by his trademark beard and bad attitude. He's only been in a handful of films so far, but his brief appearances in them have been indelible.

TITLES REVIEWED:
Blood and Bone (2009)
Circle of Pain (2010)
Locked Down (2010)

Lou Ferrigno

b. 1951. Best known for portraying the green, enraged Hulk on the popular TV series The Incredible Hulk *(1977–1982), Lou Ferrigno has had a prestigious career as a professional bodybuilder (well documented in the documentary film* Pumping Iron, *1977), where he won several major titles including Mr. Universe (twice) and Mr. America. A little-known fact is that he also played professional football in the Canadian Football League. His career in action cinema hasn't been as extensive as it could have been, but he also starred in several sword and sorcery titles, including Cannon's* Hercules *(1983) and* Sinbad of the Seven Seas *(1989). To this day, Ferrigno (who is hearing impaired) remains a fixture in topics of bodybuilding, Marvel Comics, and crossovers into action films.*

Vietnam damaged Billy (Lou Ferrigno) forever in *Cage*. Author's collection.

TITLES REVIEWED:
The Incredible Hulk (1977–1982)
Desert Warrior (1988)
Cage (1989)
Liberty and Bash (1989)
Hangfire (1991)
Return to Frogtown (1992)
Cage II (1994)
Liberator (2012)

Mirko Cro Crop Filipovic

b. 1974. Mirko Cro Crop Filipovic is a Croatian boxer, kickboxer, and mixed martial arts fighter who got his chance to star in his own movie called Ultimate Force *(2005). That film featured several members of the Luko Anti Terrorist Unit, which Filipovic was once a member of. While the film didn't do much for his career, it does have several moments where he's able to showcase his abilities as a fighter, but the film was a disappointment.*

TITLE REVIEWED:
Ultimate Force (2005)

Michael Foley

b. 1954. A bit player in Lionheart *(1990),* Karate Cop *(1991), and a handful of other martial arts–themed movies, Michael Foley was given the starring role in the low-budget grindhouse actioner* The Divine Enforcer *in 1992, where he played a kickboxing vigilante priest. He would go on to have action roles in Isaac Florentine's* Desert Kickboxer *(1992) and just a few other action-oriented films before retiring to pursue a career in training soldiers in the US Army. With an extensive background in jiu jitsu, kenpo Chuan Fa, tai chi, and his specialty in Koden Kan karate, which he has practiced for more than thirty years, Foley's time as an action star was merely a footnote in his otherwise intensive career as both a student and a teacher of the martial arts.*

TITLES REVIEWED:
Lionheart (1990)
Karate Cop (1991)
The Divine Enforcer (1992)
Desert Kickboxer (1992)
Pushed to the Limit (1992)
Raven (1993)

Leo Fong in Burbank, California. Photo by david j. moore.

Leo Fong

b. 1928. A one-of-a-kind martial artist and author with a unique philosophy and approach to filmmaking, Leo Fong was inspired by Bruce Lee's example and began practicing Jeet Kune Do, which when added to his own skills in boxing and faith in Jesus Christ, gave him the wherewithal to create his own martial art Wei Kuen Do ("the way of the integrated fist"). Fong has been writing, directing, and starring in action and martial arts films since the early 1970s, and in several of the films he was in, he was the star. He played private eye Joe Wong in Low Blow *(1986) and in the sequel* Blood Street *(1988), opposite Richard Norton. Fong is a mainstay in low-budget exploitation action films, and even into his 80s he's still making the effort to produce and direct films.*

TITLES REVIEWED:
Murder in the Orient (1974)
Ninja Assassins (1978)
Blind Rage (1978)
Revenge of the Bushido Blade (a.k.a. *The Last Reunion* a.k.a. *Ninja Nightmare*) (1980)
Killpoint (1984)
Low Blow (1986)
Blood Street (1988)
Showdown (1993)
Cage II (1994)
Carjack (1996)
Transformed (2005)
Thunderkick (2008)

Jon Foo

b. 1982. Irish Chinese martial artist Jon Foo trained at the Shichahai School of Martial Arts in Beijing and has a background as a circus performer. He broke into the movie business by performing stunts in the Thai film The Protector *(2005) where he fought against Tony Jaa. It didn't take long for Foo to start landing lead roles in vehicle films like* Tekken *(2010) and* Bangkok Revenge *(2011). With youthful good looks and capable abilities as a martial artist, Foo is on course to have a long career in action films.*

Bren Foster

b. 1976. A taekwondo champion at a young age, British-born Bren Foster has only just recently emerged as an action star hopeful in this late age where action stars are a dying breed. He's co-starred with Steven Seagal in the back-to-back films Maximum Conviction (2012) and Force of Execution (2013), and in the latter film, he was virtually the star. With black belts in hapkido and Hwa Rang Do (a Korean martial art), and a fifth degree black belt in taekwondo, Foster has the looks, the talent, and the abilities to be a full-fledged action star.

Terry Funk

b. 1944. A true character of professional wrestling, Terry Funk (known as Chainsaw Charlie in the WWE) has made a few appearances in some movies and a few in TV shows. One of his earliest roles was a bit part in the Sylvester Stallone movie Paradise Alley (1978), and then in the Stallone film Over the Top (1987). Stallone would use Funk for stunt work on Rambo III (1988) and Rocky V (1990), but Funk's main forte (as always) was wrestling. His work in films is minor.

G

Fabien Garcia

One of the four founding members of a stunt and martial arts group known as The Z Team, Fabien Garcia is well versed in intensive martial arts training, and his skills in jiu jitsu, Viet vo dao, and wushu have translated quite well in his first feature film (which he also directed) Die Fighting (a.k.a. The Price of Success, 2014). With formal training at a Shaolin monastery, Garcia is poised to become a breakout action star.

Bryan Genesse

b. 1964. (See interview on page 440.)

Trevor Goddard

b. 1962. d. 2003. A British brute with a large, muscular frame and strong, rugged good looks, Trevor Goddard had a brief stint as a professional boxer before becoming an actor. His role in the Dolph Lundgren action film Men of War (1994) was a perfect vehicle for both tough guys, and Goddard would go on to play in roles opposite action stars like Roddy Piper and Hulk Hogan in various projects. Goddard tended to play screen villains in action and martial arts films because he was great at it. Sadly, he passed away from a drug overdose in 2003.

Bill Goldberg

b. 1966. A world championship Wrestling World heavyweight champion, Bill Goldberg has had a career as a professional wrestler for both the

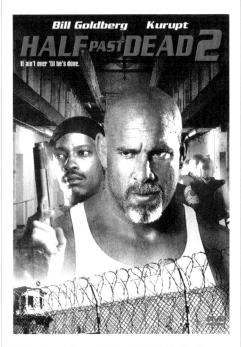

DVD artwork for Half Past Dead 2. Author's collection.

WCW and the WWE, and though he hasn't had an extensive career in motion pictures, he has made notable contributions to several action films including Universal Soldier: The Return (1999) and Half Past Dead 2 (2007). His fan base is more connected to him as a wrestler than as an action star, but his potential as a figure in action cinema—like so many of his peer crossover stars—is huge.

Thomas Ian Griffith

b. 1962. A multi-faceted action star who is also a highly talented screenwriter, Thomas Ian Griffith burst on the action scene when he played the villain role in The Karate Kid III (1989), but it would be a few years down the line when he would embark on a starring action career with the stellar Excessive Force (1993), which was a film he wrote for himself. His successive films certainly had merits, but he would never be able to match the intensity and vitality he displayed in that film. With a background in taekwondo and kenpo karate, Griffith's presence and fighting style on screen is always electric and unique unto himself. He also played villain roles in bigger "A" pictures like Kull the Conqueror (1995) and Vampires (1996). Of note: Griffith wrote the screenplay for Lorenzo Lamas's best film as an action star, Night of the Warrior (1991), which he intended as a vehicle for himself.

Olivier Gruner

b. 1960. (See interview on page 33.)

Interceptor Force (1999)
Crackerjack 3 (2000)
G.O.D. (2001)
Extreme Honor (2001)
The Circuit (2002)
The Circuit 2 (2002)
Interceptor Force (2002)
Deadly Engagement (2003)
SWAT: Warhead One (2004)
Crooked (2006)
The Circuit III: The Street Monk (2006)
Re-Generator (2010)
Sector 4: Extraction (2013)
The Chemist (2015)

H

Cody Hackman

b. 1987. A five-time world karate champion, Cody Hackman wrote the story for and co-produced Tapped Out *(2014), a mixed martial arts coming-of-age movie where he plays a young fighter who is mentored by several characters played by Michael Biehn and a real fighter played by Anderson Silva. In the film, Hackman goes up against Krzysztof Soszynski in the action-packed climax.*

TITLE REVIEWED:
> **Tapped Out** (2014)

Ron Hall

b. 1964. In the lower and middle echelon of martial arts action stars were guys like Dale "Apollo" Cook and Vince Murdocco, who made movie after movie for studios like AIP and PM Entertainment. Ron Hall, an African American martial artist with skills in Moo Duk Kwan (a Korean martial art) and wushu, co-starred in a number of low-budget action and martial arts films opposite Dale Cook, Gary Daniels, and Daniel Bernhardt in about a ten-year time span. Late in his career, he starred in and directed the Blade-*esque film* Vampire Assassin *(2005), though it didn't help him star in and direct other projects afterwards. Every time Hall appears on screen in a fight scene, viewers can expect some fancy footwork and acrobatics, and he made some of his co-stars look like they were standing still during their scenes together.*

TITLES REVIEWED:
> *Deadly Bet* (1992)
> **Triple Impact** (1992)
> *Full Impact* (1993)
> **Double Blast** (1994)
> **Raw Target** (1995)
> **Bloodsport II** (1996)
> *Pocket Ninjas* (1997)
> *Vampire Assassin* (2005)
> *Thunderkick* (2008)

Bong Soo Han

b. 1933. d. 2007. Widely considered "The Father of Hapkido," Bong Soo Han was incredibly influential in bringing that martial art to the United States, which in turn paved the way for Tom Laughlin to fashion his film Billy Jack *(1971) around hapkido's art and Han's philosophy. Han made several appearances in martial arts films, but his biggest role was in the movie* Kill the Golden Goose *(1979), opposite kenpo's founder, Ed Parker.*

TITLES REVIEWED:
> *The Trial of Billy Jack* (1974)
> **Kill the Golden Goose** (1979)
> *Force: Five* (1981)

Mickey Hardt

b. 1969. Swiss-born Mickey Hardt has been a martial artist since the age of eight, and his first major role in a martial arts-themed project was in the Jackie Chan film The Vampire Effect *(a.k.a.* The Twins Effect, *2003). After that, he shot the two Max Havoc (2004, 2006) movies back to back. One would have thought that after those two films he would have gone on to do more direct-to-video action films, but this being an era where DTV action films are a dying breed, it's no wonder that Hardt has struggled to find his action star legs.*

TITLES REVIEWED:
> *The Vampire Effect* (a.k.a. *The Twins Effect*) (2003)
> **Max Havoc: Curse of the Dragon** (2004)
> **Max Havoc: Ring of Fire** (2006)

Sam Hargrave

Up-and-coming stuntman and action star Sam Hargrave has come a long way in a relatively short time span. He won two Taurus World Stunt Awards for his work doubling Chris Evans as Captain America in Captain America: The Winter Soldier *(2014), but he's also accrued an impressive list of appearances in "B" action and martial arts films, including* Blood and Bone *(2009) and* The King of Fighters *(2010). His best work as a stunt double is in* Road House 2 *(2006), where he doubled Johnathon Schaech, simply because his work in that film was astounding and it was clear that he should have been the star instead of Schaech. Hargrave might very well transition into a major action star to watch out for.*

TITLES REVIEWED:
> *Crooked* (2006)
> *T.K.O.* (2007)
> *Angel of Death* (2009)
> *Blood and Bone* (2009)
> *Acts of Violence* (2010)
> *The King of Fighters* (2010)

Heath Herring

b. 1978. A UFC fighter who hilariously knocked out his opponent with one punch after being kissed on the lips before the fight started, Heath Herring has made several notable appearances in direct-to-video MMA movies like Never Surrender *(2009),* Circle of Pain *(2010), and* Beatdown *(2010). In most of those films, he hasn't been required to do more than make cameo appearances, but given the right vehicle, he could make an indelible impression the way he has in the ring in real life.*

TITLES REVIEWED:
> *Never Surrender* (2009)
> *Unrivaled* (2010)
> **Circle of Pain** (2010)
> *Beatdown* (2010)

Hulk Hogan stars as Mike McBride in *Shadow Warriors*. Author's collection.

Terry "Hulk" Hogan

b. 1953. A legend and an icon in professional wrestling, Hulk Hogan is as distinctive as they come. With a huge, muscular frame (at 6 foot 4), long, blond hair, and a trademark handlebar mustache, The Hulkster made his crossover debut in Sylvester Stallone's Rocky III *(1982), where he fought Rocky in a memorable exhibition match. A few years later he headlined in his own film* No Holds Barred *(1989), giving WWE (then, WWF) one of its first major movie superstars. In the movies that followed, Hogan stuck with family-friendly features, and even had his own TV series called* Thunder in Paradise *(1994), which was a riff on James Bond and Indiana Jones adventures on a weekly basis. In the late '90s, he dyed his hair brown and took on a trio of "R"-rated action films (Shadow Warriors 1 & 2, and The Ultimate Weapon) that had a harder edge than his previous features. For the most part, though, Hogan has kept within the bounds of his younger fan base (which is perpetuated from generation to generation), and he remains active in the wrestling world.*

TITLES REVIEWED:
> *Rocky III* (1982)
> **No Holds Barred** (1989)
> **Suburban Commando** (1991)
> *Mr. Nanny* (1993)
> **Thunder in Paradise** (1994)
> *The Secret Agent Club* (1996)
> *Santa With Muscles* (1996)
> *Shadow Warriors* (a.k.a. *Assault on Devil's Island*) (1997)
> *McCinsey's Island* (1998)
> *3 Ninjas: High Noon at Mega Mountain* (1998)
> *The Ultimate Weapon* (1998)
> *Shadow Warriors 2* (a.k.a. *Assault on Death Mountain*) (1999)
> *Walker: Texas Ranger* (2001)

Marjean Holden

b. 1964. A black belt in Wun Hop Kuen Do kung fu, Marjean Holden attempted to break into action films in the mid-90s with her starring film Ballistic *(1995), which featured her as a renegade cop going up against the likes of Michael Jai White and bodybuilder Corey Everson. The film was an adequate vehicle for Holden, but she wasn't able to sustain the momentum, and she has since gone into stunt work and supporting roles in other projects.*

Matthias Hues
b. 1959. (See interview on page 124.)

Sammo Hung
b. 1952. The rotund Sammo Hung has never ceased to amaze. For a jolly man with a fairly large belly, he should not be able to do even a smidgen of what he does when he gets his action star groove on. An amazing martial artist, stuntman, actor, and director, Sammo Hung Kam-Bo has been working steadily since his days at opera school, which is where he met his lifelong friends and associates Jackie Chan and Yuen Biao. He did not make a fully fledged international crossover until he came to the US to star in the fairly popular TV program Martial Law *(1998–2000)*, which was a riff on Chan's hit movie Rush Hour *(1998)*. Hung even got to do a few crossover episodes with Chuck Norris on his show Walker, Texas Ranger *in 2000*. Even into his later years, Hung has continued acting in action and martial arts movies, and his appearance in Ip Man 2: Legend of the Grandmaster *(2010)* is a great indication of what he's still able to accomplish.

Sammo Hung (on the ground) plays a minor character in *The Man From Hong Kong*. Author's collection.

I

Dan Inosanto
b. 1936. Filipino American Dan Inosanto studied Jeet Kune Do under Bruce Lee and mastered several disciplines of the martial arts, later forming The Inosanto Academy in Marina Del Rey. He has performed stunts on many films and has trained some notable actors in the martial arts. If you watch carefully, you can see him fight Steven Seagal with sticks in Out For Justice *(1991)*. For the most part, Inosanto has only made small appearances in a handful of films, but his legacy as a teacher and trainer is rich and much respected.

Steve Irwin
b. 1962. d. 2006. The one and only Steve Irwin was a daredevil and stuntman if there ever was one. He made a name for himself capturing crocodiles for the Queensland crocodile relocation program and hosted his own program The Crocodile Hunter on Animal Planet, which was spun off into a feature film The Crocodile Hunter: Collision Course *(2002)*, a stunt-filled, death-defying action adventure movie that will make your jaw drop. Irwin, playing a slightly fictionalized version of himself, manhandles deadly poisonous snakes, spiders, and live crocodiles, while dodging poachers, terrorists, and saving the world. Sadly, in life, Irwin met his untimely end while shooting footage for one of his shows when a stingray stung him in the heart. He might be considered a stretch as an action star, but no other action movie features the insane, near-death experiences as Irwin's Collision Course does in the spirit of entertainment.

J

Tony Jaa is Kham, The Protector. Author's collection.

Tony Jaa
b. 1976. (See interview on page 424.)

Ian Jacklin
b. 1968. A Canadian and North American kickboxing champion who later became a professional light heavyweight boxer, Ian Jacklin co-starred in a number of low-budget films starring the likes of Don "The Dragon" Wilson, Lorenzo Lamas, and Gary Daniels for studios such as Cine Excel, PM Entertainment, and Roger Corman's New Horizons. Jacklin got his chance to star in just a few films, namely Expert Weapon *(1993)* and Death Match *(1994)*. As the era of direct-to-video martial arts action films began to fade away, so too did Jacklin's appearances in films drop off.

Quinton "Rampage" Jackson

b. 1978. Former kickboxer, UFC fighter, and wrestler, Quinton "Rampage" Jackson worked his way through direct-to-video MMA fight movies like Confessions of a Pit Fighter (2005), Never Surrender (2009), and Death Warrior (2009) before landing a lead role in the big-budget redux of The A-Team (2010). As B. A. Baracus—the role that Mr. T originated—Jackson made the role his own and showed that he could help carry a movie. Although the film was not the runaway hit he needed, it gave him massive exposure and helped him establish his cred as an actor and action star.

TITLES REVIEWED:
Confessions of a Pit Fighter (2005)
Never Surrender (2009)
Death Warrior (2009)
The A-Team (2010)

Eric Jacobus, the star of *Death Grip*. Photo by david j. moore.

Glenn "Kane" Jacobs

b. 1967. (See interview on page 410.)

TITLES REVIEWED:
See No Evil (2006)
See No Evil 2 (2014)

Eric Jacobus

b. 1982. (See interview on page 132.)

TITLES REVIEWED:
Undercut (2004)
Immortal (2006)
Contour (2006)
Dogs of Chinatown (2010)
Death Grip (2012)
Mortal Kombat: Legacy II (2013)
Rope a Dope (2013)

Steve James

b. 1952. d. 1993. Everyone who ever worked with Steve James tells great stories about him. A New York native who got his start in the movie business as a stuntman, James soon became an actor and action star in his own right. A practitioner in Tiger Claw kung fu and an avid fan of martial arts movies and martial arts in general, he's best known for co-starring in films alongside Chuck Norris (in The Delta Force, 1986 and Hero and the Terror, 1988) and Michael Dudikoff (in American Ninja, 1985, Avenging Force, 1986, and American Ninja 2: The Confrontation,

Steve James plays the badass Curtis Jackson in *American Ninja*. Author's collection.

1987), but he also starred in action films like Riverbend (1989) and Street Hunter (1990). Though his life was cut short by cancer, Steve James left an indelible legacy in the world of action films.

TITLES REVIEWED:
American Ninja (1985)
The Delta Force (1986)
Avenging Force (1986)
American Ninja II: The Confrontation (1987)
Hero and the Terror (1988)
American Ninja 3: Blood Hunt (1989)
Riverbend (1989)
Street Hunter (1990)
Bloodfist V: Human Target (1994)

Vidyut Jamwal

b. 1980. Born in Jammu, India, Vidyut Jamwal has studied one of the oldest martial arts systems in the world (kalaripayattu) since he was three years old. His father had moved the family all over while he was growing up but Vidyut excelled in his training. He eventually had the opportunity to travel to dozens of countries to perform action scenes he created live on stage. Before moving into film, he decided to try his hand as a fashion model. Eventually, when he settled in Mumbai he auditioned for the film Force (2011), nabbing the lead villain role, thus setting his film career in motion. He took several minor roles in films like Oosaravelli (2011), Billa 2 (2012), and Thuppakki (2012) before getting his big break as an action lead in Commando: A One Man Force (2013). He's a vegetarian (and an active PETA supporter), a fitness guru, and has started a widespread movement to help teach women self-defense (crimes against women have become widespread recently in India).

TITLES REVIEWED:
Force (2011)
Oosaravelli (2011)
Thuppakki (2012)
Billa 2 (2012)
Bullet Raja (2013)
Commando: A One Man Army (2013)

Keith Jardine

b. 1975. Before embarking on a professional career in boxing and mixed martial arts fighting, Keith "The Dean of Mean" Jardine had been a miner and a bounty hunter. As he transitioned from prize fighting into motion pictures, he got slightly bigger and better roles in action films, most notably in

Recoil (2011), where he had a memorable face-off against "Stone Cold" Steve Austin. Jardine's plate is full with several roles in high-profile movies to be released in the near future.

TITLES REVIEWED:
Death Warrior (2009)
Unrivaled (2010)
Recoil (2011)
Tactical Force (2011)
John Wick (2014)

Roy Jefferson

b. 1943. An NFL player who co-starred in a single action movie—Brotherhood of Death (1976)—Roy Jefferson is best known for his seasons with the Pittsburgh Steelers (1965–1969), the Baltimore Colts (1970), and the Washington Redkins (1971–1976). He never made another movie.

TITLE REVIEWED:
Brotherhood of Death (1976)

Chuck Jeffreys

b. 1958. A multitalented martial artist with skills in nearly a dozen different styles (and multiple belts to prove it), Chuck Jeffreys got his start in low-budget action and martial arts movies and segued into stunt work and fight coordinating on "A"-list pictures like Gladiator (2000) and Spider-Man (2002). His work in front of the camera as an action star provided some very impressive martial artistry and comedic timing, and it should also be noted that Jeffreys bears a striking resemblance to Eddie Murphy, whom he worked with for a while as a bodyguard and body double.

TITLES REVIEWED:
Fight to Win (1987)
Karate Cops (a.k.a. **Hawkeye**) (1988)
Blood Street (1988)
Aftershock (1989)
Lockdown (1990)
Honor and Glory (1993)
Death Fight (a.k.a. **Rage**) (1994)
Superfights (1995)
Bloodmoon (1997)

Dwayne "The Rock" Johnson

b. 1972. A wrestling superstar who made the auspicious jump into feature films with a small role as "The Scorpion King" in the blockbuster The Mummy Returns (2001), Dwayne "The Rock"

Beck (Dwayne "The Rock" Johnson) is a badass in *The Rundown*. Author's collection.

Johnson has a fun, flamboyant persona and his massive fan base has only been too happy to follow him as his career in movies has flourished. His first venture into action cinema was the action adventure The Rundown (2003), which had a cameo by Arnold Schwarzenegger, who literally gave him his blessing in the quick scene by telling him, "Have fun." Having fun is what Johnson has been doing ever since, and while one might argue that his films cater more to family audiences than serious action fans, his place as an action star in this post-millennial world is cemented.

TITLES REVIEWED:
The Rundown (2003)
Walking Tall (2004)
Doom (2005)
Gridiron Gang (2006)
The Game Plan (2007)
Get Smart (2008)
Race to Witch Mountain (2009)
Tooth Fairy (2010)
The Other Guys (2010)
Faster (2010)
Fast Five (2011)
Journey 2: The Mysterious Island (2012)
Snitch (2013)
G.I. Joe: Retaliation (2013)
Empire State (2013)
Pain & Gain (2013)
Fast and Furious 6 (2013)
Fast and Furious 7 (2015)
San Andreas (2015)

Nathan Jones

b. 1969. Australian Nathan Jones truly is a giant. At 6 foot 11, he competed in the World Musclepower Championships, and later became a WWE wrestler. He's best known in films for his memorable roles in Jackie Chan's First Strike (1996), The Protector (2005), and The Condemned (2007). When he goes up against "Stone Cold" Steve Austin in that latter film, it's easy to see how intimidating he can be, and every time he's featured in a movie he usually commands your attention with his sheer size and screen presence. He is featured in a pivotal role in the upcoming Mad Max: Fury Road (2015).

TITLES REVIEWED:
Jackie Chan's First Strike (a.k.a. Police Story IV: First Strike) (1996)
The Protector (a.k.a. **Tom Yum Goong**) (2005)
Fearless (2006)
The Condemned (2007)
Muay Thai Giant (2008)

K

Jino Kang

b. 1960. (See interview on page 69.)

TITLES REVIEWED:
Blade Warrior (2001)
Fist 2 Fist (2011)
Weapon of Choice: Fist 2 Fist 2 (2014)

Jino Kang as Jack Lee in Fist 2 Fist 2: Weapon of Choice. Courtesy of Jino Kang.

Naomi Karpati

b. 1986. Born in Budapest, Hungary, Naomi Karpati relocated to Australia in 2008 and began training in kickboxing, stunt work, and Chinese boxing when she caught the eye of director James Richards, who began to fashion a movie around her. After several years of hard, punishing training, her first movie, Agent Provocateur (2012), was made and released, which showcased her natural fighting abilities. Though the film has not been received in the US yet, it will hopefully open doors for her to star in other action vehicles.

TITLE REVIEWED:
Agent Provocateur (2012)

Publicity still from Agent Provocateur, featuring kickboxer Naomi Karpati. Courtesy of James Richards.

A woman of action in Agent Provocateur, featuring Naomi Karpati. Courtesy of James Richards.

Jim Kelly

b. 1946. d. 2013. Jim Kelly was one of action cinema's most underused treasures, having starred or co-starred in less than a dozen films, most of which wasted his talents. His breakout role was in the classic Enter the Dragon (1973), opposite Bruce Lee, and from there his next few films were under the Warner Brothers banner. As he moved on, the quality of his projects lessened and it was difficult for him to make a comeback. A verifiable blaxploitation superstar and a martial arts dynamo with a middleweight karate champion title to his credit, Kelly also embarked on a professional tennis career in 1975. Sadly, he passed away in 2013 of cancer.

TITLES REVIEWED:
Enter the Dragon (1973)
Black Belt Jones (1974)
Three the Hard Way (1974)
Golden Needles (1974)
Take a Hard Ride (1975)
Hot Potato (1976)
One Down, Two to Go (1976)
Black Samurai (1977)
Death Dimension (1978)
Tattoo Connection (1979)

Leon Isaac Kennedy

b. 1949. (See interview on page 344.)

TITLES REVIEWED:
Fighting Mad (a.k.a. Death Force) (1978)
Penitentiary (1979)
Body and Soul (1981)
Penitentiary II (1982)
Lone Wolf McQuade (1983)
Knights of the City (1985)
Hollywood Vice Squad (1986)
Penitentiary III (1987)

Peter Kent

b. 1957. Body double to Arnold Schwarzenegger for nearly all of his movies from The Terminator (1984) to Jingle All the Way (1996), Peter Kent has appeared in a number of action films apart from his work with Arnold, most notably in the "Stone Cold" Steve Austin film Tactical Force (2011). With a resemblance to Arnold, Kent has performed some death-defying stunts on film, but it's important to note that he is an action star in his own right.

TITLES REVIEWED:
Mr. Nanny (1993)
Thunder in Paradise (1994)
Renegade (1994)

Cyber-Tracker 2 (1995)
The Crow: Stairway to Heaven (1999)
The 6th Day (2000)
Tactical Force (2011)
Angel of Death (a.k.a. *True Justice: Angel of Death*) (2012)

Gail Kim

b. 1976. Korean-born Gail Kim was a professional wrestler with WWE, and she won the women's championship at WWE in 2003, which led to her starring in the independently financed action movie Ninja's Creed *(a.k.a.* Royal Kill, *2009). Kim's role in that film was integral to the (incomprehensible) plot, but she's never made a movie since.*

TITLE REVIEWED:
Ninja's Creed (a.k.a. **Royal Kill**) (2009)

Kim Ho Kim

A practitioner of wushu, wing chun, and aikido, Kim Ho Kim made his first (and so far only) feature film Fighting Fish *(2004), which was a martial arts feature from the Netherlands.*

TITLE REVIEWED:
Fighting Fish (2004)

Y. K. Kim

b. 1956. When Young Kun Kim wrote, produced, starred, and co-directed Miami Connection *in 1987, he was a taekwondo champion and entrepreneur who almost went bankrupt after he financed that film. Relegated to obscurity,* Miami Connection *was resurrected more than twenty years later when Drafthouse Films redistributed it nationwide and gave the film its very first home video release. In the interim, Kim had become a widely heard motivational speaker, but he never made another film. When* Miami Connection *screened around the US, Kim attended many of the screenings, passing by the long lines of people who were waiting to see his film, shaking hands with everyone and thanking them for their support. The film became an underground sensation.*

TITLE REVIEWED:
Miami Connection (1987)

Vincent Klyn

b. 1960. New Zealander Vincent Klyn is best known for his surfing feats, but Albert Pyun inducted him into the world of action and martial arts films by casting him as the lead villain in the Jean-Claude Van Damme movie Cyborg *(1989). From that point on, Klyn became a mainstay in action films, and invariably he'd play the villain. In the straight-to-video movie* Ballistic *(1995), he had a memorable fight scene alongside Michael Jai White.*

TITLES REVIEWED:
Cyborg (1989)
Kickboxer 2: The Road Back (1991)
Bloodmatch (1991)
Nemesis (1992)
Knights (1993)
Double Dragon (1994)

Vincent Klyn (left) absorbs a kick from Jean-Claude Van Damme in *Cyborg*. Author's collection.

Ballistic (1995)
Ravenhawk (1996)
Night Hunter (1996)
Gangland (2001)
Max Havoc: Curse of the Dragon (2004)

Kane Kosugi

b. 1974. (See interview on page 384.)

TITLES REVIEWED:
Revenge of the Ninja (1983)
The Master (1984)
9 Deaths of the Ninja (1985)
Pray for Death (1985)
Black Eagle (1988)
Blood Heat (a.k.a. *Muscle Heat*) (2002)
DOA: Dead or Alive (2006)
War (2007)
Ninja Masters (2009)
Fight the Fight (2011)
Ninja 2: Shadow of a Tear (2013)
Tekken 2: Kazuya's Revenge (2014)
Zero Tolerance (2014)

Sho Kosugi

b. 1948. When The Cannon Group was pitched a ninja movie in 1980 by Mike Stone, the birth of the ninja craze that would inundate the 1980s had begun. Menahem Golan and Yoram Globus found their ninja in the 6 foot 1 Japanese martial artist Sho Kosugi. For the next handful of years, Kosugi would star in more than a half a dozen consecutive projects where he was cast as an unbeatable ninja, and he even created and crafted most of the weapons he would wield in each film. From Revenge of the Ninja *(1983) to* Black Eagle *(1988), Kosugi kept up his ninja persona until the*

The heroic Spike Shinobi (Sho Kosugi) in *9 Deaths of the Ninja*. Author's collection.

ninja craze petered out. In several of his projects, his two sons Kane and Shane would appear as his character's sons, and Kane would grow up to be an action star in his own right.

TITLES REVIEWED:
Enter the Ninja (1981)
Revenge of the Ninja (1983)
The Master (1984)
Ninja III: The Domination (1984)
9 Deaths of the Ninja (1985)
Pray for Death (1985)
Rage of Honor (a.k.a. **Top Fighter**) (1987)
Black Eagle (1988)
Blind Fury (1989)
Ninja Assassin (2009)

Martin Kove

b. 1946. Most people know Martin Kove as the sadistic sensei from The Karate Kid *(1984), but he's been in dozens of action and martial arts movies, and what's more, he's trained extensively in the martial arts, achieving black belts in kendō, Okinawa-Te, and Tiger kenpo. His best film as an action star is* Steele Justice *(1987), which is truly one of the greatest action movies to come out of the 1980s. Kove's career as an action star is ongoing and isn't limited to the '80s as so many of his peers, and he's worked with dozens of other action stars over the years like Sylvester Stallone, Olivier Gruner, Chuck Norris, Jeff Speakman, Don "The Dragon" Wilson, Frank Zagarino, Michael Worth, and Bolo Yeung. As he's gotten older, he's simmered down on the action front, but he's been busy playing character roles in action films and remains a very busy actor.*

TITLES REVIEWED:
The Karate Kid (1984)
Rambo: First Blood Part II (1985)
The Karate Kid Part II (1986)
Steele Justice (1987)
Hard Time on Planet Earth (1989)
The Karate Kid Part III (1989)
White Light (1991)
Project Shadowchaser (1992)
Firehawk (1993)
Shootfighter: Fight to the Death (1993)
Renegade (1993)
To Be the Best (1993)
Death Match (1994)
Walker, Texas Ranger (1995)
Mercenary (1996)
Without Mercy (1996)
Timelock (1996)
Shadow Warriors (a.k.a. *Assault on Devil's Island*) (1997)
Shadow Warriors 2 (a.k.a. *Assault on Death Mountain*) (1999)
Extreme Honor (2001)
Shattered Lies (2002)
Crooked (2006)
Max Havoc: Ring of Fire (2006)
Beyond the Ring (2008)
War Wolves (2009)
Ballistica (2009)
Bare Knuckles (2010)
Assassins Code (2011)
Tapped Out (2014)
The Extendables (2014)
The Chemist (2015)

Michelle "Mouse" Krasnoo

b. 1974. A supporting player in several direct-to-video martial arts action films starring the likes of Sasha Mitchell, Don "The Dragon" Wilson, and Jerry Trimble, Michelle "Mouse" Krasnoo had been a champion in competitive karate and holds a fifth degree black belt in Tang Soo Do. Her most notable role was in Kickboxer 4: The Aggressor (1994), but she's also produced and starred in her own fitness workout videos.

TITLES REVIEWED:
Blackbelt (1992)
Full Contact (1993)
Kickboxer 4: The Aggressor (1994)
Death Match (1994)
Thunderkick (2008)

Yasuaki Kurata

b. 1946. Japanese martial artist Yasuaki Kurata has had a great career in martial arts films. He's worked with the big ones: Jet Li, Bolo Yeung, Cynthia Rothrock, Yuen Biao, Jackie Chan, Sammo Hung, and many more. He starred in the English language film Bloodfight (1989), and then later fought Jet Li in a famous fight in Fist of Legend (1994). He is a seventh degree dan in karate, a third degree dan in judo, and a second dan in aikido, and he continues to work in films even until this very day.

TITLES REVIEWED:
My Lucky Stars 2: Twinkle, Twinkle My Lucky Stars (1985)
Shanghai Express (a.k.a. Millionaire's Express) (1986)
Eastern Condors (1987)
Bloodfight (1989)
Fist of Legend (1994)
Shinjuku Incident (2009)
The Wrath of Vajra (2013)

L

Dominick LaBanca

b. 1969. At ten years old, Dominick LaBanca began training in Okinawan karate and transitioned into Northern Shaolin kung fu. As he entered his twenties, he trained in wushu and Wing Chun and became a kickboxer. He lucked out and landed the starring role in the Roger Corman-produced movie Dragon Fire (1993), which was a riff on several other films Corman had produced, including Full Contact (1993), starring Jerry Trimble. LaBanca later had a single professional MMA fight in 2004, which he lost.

TITLE REVIEWED:
Dragon Fire (1993)

Lorenzo Lamas

b. 1958. (See interview on page 427.)

TITLES REVIEWED:
Detour to Terror (1980)
Snake Eater (1989)
Snake Eater II: The Drug Buster (1990)
Night of the Warrior (1991)
Killing Streets (1991)
Final Impact (1992)

The Swordsman (1992)
Snake Eater III: His Law (1992)
Renegade (1992–1997)
CIA: Code Name Alexa (1992)
Bounty Tracker (1993)
CIA II: Target Alexa (1993)
Final Round (1994)
Bad Blood (1994)
Blood for Blood (a.k.a. **Midnight Man**) (1995)
Gladiator Cop: The Swordsman II (1995)
Mask of Death (1996)
Terminal Justice (1996)
Good Cop, Bad Cop (a.k.a. Black Dawn) (1997)
The Rage (1997)
Undercurrent (1998)
The Immortal (2000–2001)
The Circuit 2: The Final Punch (2002)
Rapid Exchange (2003)
13 Dead Men (2003)
Latin Dragon (2004)
X-Treme Fighter (a.k.a. Sci-Fighter) (2004)
Lethal (2005)
18 Fingers of Death! (2006)
Atomic EDEN (2015)

Matthis Landwehr

b. 1980. (See interview on page 243.)

TITLES REVIEWED:
Kampfansage (a.k.a. **The Challenge**) (2005)
Death Train (2006)
Kingz (2007)
Arena of the Streetfighter (2012)

Tom Laughlin

b. 1931. d. 2013. The man who universally became associated with the fictional character known as Billy Jack, Tom Laughlin was a pioneer in the world of action and martial arts movies. With his radical politics and philosophical entreaties, Laughlin filtered his belief system and his adopted brand of martial arts (hapkido) into Billy Jack (1971), a kick in Hollywood's pants at a time when martial arts action stars really didn't exist yet. Laughlin had a style all his own—part Native American Indian, part martial arts dynamo—and he predated Steven Seagal by nearly twenty years, and yet their agenda was essentially the same: Save the environment and the native peoples while breaking some arms and necks. Laughlin extended the life of Billy Jack with several successful sequels that became even more politically minded, and he tried to resurrect the character in the '80s with the unfinished The Return of Billy Jack (1986), which remains unreleased. It should also be mentioned that Laughlin ran for president of the United States three times and wrote a number of books.

TITLES REVIEWED:
The Born Losers (1967)
Billy Jack (1971)
The Trial of Billy Jack (1974)
The Master Gunfighter (1975)
Billy Jack Goes to Washington (1977)

Cung Le

b. 1972. (See interview on page 156.)

TITLES REVIEWED:
Dark Assassin (2007)
Fighting (2009)
Tekken (2010)
Dragon Eyes (2012)
The Man With the Iron Fists (2012)
Puncture Wounds (2014)

Jerome Le Banner

b. 1972. A superheavyweight K-1 fighter, kickboxer, boxer, and professional wrestler, French-born Jerome Le Banner is a beast of a fighter, with dozens of victories to his credit. A black belt in judo and kyokushin, he was given his chance to shine in the low-budget French action drama Scorpion (2008), which cast him as the champion of an underground fight circuit.

TITLSE REVIEWED:
Scorpion (2008)
Babylon, A.D. (2008)

Brandon Lee

b. 1965. d. 1993. The son of perhaps the greatest martial artist who ever lived, Brandon Lee tried hard to live outside of his father Bruce's shadow. Bruce's legacy was overpowering to Brandon, but he was making his own way as both a martial artist and an actor, and just when his career was about to take off with The Crow (1994), his life was cut short by a fluke accident (a prop gun misfired a real slug from a blank discharge) on the set of that film. With only a handful of feature film credits, Brandon left a legacy that is comparable to his father's, but he left behind some solid work that deserves to be judged by its own merit.

TITLES REVIEWED:
Kung Fu: The Movie (1986)
Legacy of Rage (1986)
Laser Mission (1989)
Showdown in Little Tokyo (1991)
Rapid Fire (1992)
The Crow (1994)

Brandon Lee stars as Jake Lo in Rapid Fire. Author's collection.

Britton K. Lee

Not much is known about Korean martial artist Britton K. Lee, as he pretty much faded into obscurity after his solo starring film Ironheart

(1992) quietly arrived on VHS in the heyday of martial arts action movies. Lee, who produced the film, cast himself in the lead role, where he played a virtually untouchable cop proficient in the martial arts (taekwondo), who mows down the bad guys, including superior martial artists Richard Norton and Bolo Yeung. Interestingly enough, his brother Julian Lee—the star of the much better My Samurai (1992)—was one of the producers of Ironheart.

TITLE REVIEWED:
Fatal Revenge (1990)
Ironheart (1992)

Bruce Lee

b. 1940. d. 1973. Ask any action star who was brought up in the martial arts who their number one inspiration has been from the get-go, and almost every time they will point to Bruce Lee (real name Lee Jun Fan). Lee, who was born in San Francisco, was taught Wing Chun kung fu from the infamous sifu Yip Man (see the Ip Man movies starring Donnie Yen for more on that), and from there Lee developed his own style of martial arts known as jeet kun do. When he began his career in television and film, his breakout role was as Kato in The Green Hornet *(1966–1967), a short-lived superhero program that led to his scene-stealing role in the James Garner film* Marlowe *(1969). Once Lee began making kung fu films like* The Big Boss *(a.k.a.* Fists of Fury, *1971), his fame spread throughout Asia and beyond. No one had ever seen a martial arts powerhouse like Bruce Lee before (or after, for that matter), and after a few hits that broke the international barrier, he filmed his first English-language martial arts film* Enter the Dragon *(1973), which was released after his untimely death of brain swelling following a dosage of pain killers.* Enter the Dragon *had an impact of such magnitude that it not only made Lee a worldwide star (posthumously), but it created an entire genre and opened the floodgates of martial arts action films and kung fu crossovers that are still being felt today. Would-be Bruce Lee's and wannabe action stars have tried (and continue to try) to emulate Lee's spirit and fortitude on screen, but no one has ever come close to the legend and legacy he left behind.*

TITLES REVIEWED:
The Green Hornet (1966–1967)
Marlowe (1969)
The Big Boss (a.k.a. *Fists of Fury*) (1971)
Fist of Fury (a.k.a. *The Chinese Connection*) (1972)
The Way of the Dragon (a.k.a. **The Return of the Dragon**) (1972)
Enter the Dragon (1973)
The Game of Death (1978)

Chen Lee

b. 1939. d. 2005. Not much is known about Chen Lee (born Mioshini Akira Hayakawa), but he starred in a spaghetti western/martial arts hybrid called The Fighting Fist of Shanghai Joe *in 1973, co-starring Klaus Kinski, and he showcases some martial arts in the film, but there isn't enough information to really follow Lee, as his origins are mostly a mystery. It was said that he was*

discovered at a dojo in Japan, but the director of The Fighting Fist *remarked that he may have been a factory worker when he was discovered.*

TITLE REVIEWED:
The Fighting Fist of Shanghai Joe (a.k.a. **My Name is Shanghai Joe** a.k.a. **The Dragon Fights Back**) (1973)

Conan Lee

b. 1959. One of Conan Lee's first appearances in a movie was in the Robert Clouse cult classic Gymkata *(1985), and several years later he was in* Prince of the Sun *(1990) with Cynthia Rothrock. Most of Lee's films were Hong Kong kung fu movies, but he emerged again in the US with his directorial debut* Carjack *(1996), which co-starred Loren Avedon. He is also the creator of his own brand of martial arts known as "realistic fist."*

TITLES REVIEWED:
Gymkata (1985)
Eliminators (1986)
Prince of the Sun (1990)
Carjack (1996)
Lethal Weapon 4 (1998)

Eric Lee

b. 1948. A prolific martial arts action star and performer in dozens of action films, Eric Lee retired from competitive martial arts in the early 1970s. After that, he appeared in several films directed by Paul Kyriazi, including Death Machines *(1976),* The Weapons of Death *(1981), and* Ninja Busters *(1984). Over the last few decades, he's had roles in a number of films starring Don "The Dragon" Wilson, but his most memorable role might be in the film* The Master Demon *(1991), where he was the main star.*

TITLES REVIEWED:
The Weapons of Death (1981)
The Shinobi Ninja (1981)

DVD artwork for *The Master Demon*. Author's collection.

Ninja Busters (a.k.a. **Shadow Fight**) (1984)
Steele Justice (1987)
Ring of Fire (1991)
The Master Demon (1991)
Talons of the Eagle (1992)
Ring of Fire II: Blood and Steel (1993)
Death Match (1994)
Fists of Iron (1995)
Bloodsport 2 (1996)
Tiger Claws II (1996)
Sworn to Justice (1996)
The Accidental Spy (2001)
Redemption (2002)
X-Treme Fighter (a.k.a. *Sci-Fighter*) (2004)
The Chemist (2015)

Julian Lee

b. 1961. A gold medalist of the first taekwondo championship in South Korea, Julian Lee came to the US in the mid-'80s to make films. His first one was Fatal Revenge *(1990), a low-budget action exercise, which was soon followed up by Imperial's* My Samurai *(1992). Over two decades later, Lee has only made a handful of other starring films, but he's an endearing action/martial arts star, whose on-screen persona is inherently good and redeemable. Some viewers might write him off as a bad actor who stars in hokey movies, but if you study Lee himself rather than his films, you'll find an honest star in search of the right vehicles to exhibit his abilities and philosophies.*

TITLES REVIEWED:
Fatal Revenge (1990)
My Samurai (1992)
Tiger Street (1998)
Dragon and the Hawk (2001)
Little Bear and the Master (2008)
Assassins Code (2011)

Julian Lee from *My Samurai*. Courtesy of Julian Lee.

Shannon Lee

b. 1969. Shannon Lee, the only daughter of Bruce Lee and sister to Brandon Lee, sort of crept up on the action and martial arts communities by appearing in a handful of films, several of which she starred in. After strong supporting roles in Isaac Florentine's High Voltage (1997) and Cage II: The Arena of Death (1994), she starred in the Golden Harvest film And Now You're Dead (a.k.a. Enter the Eagles, 1998), and then in the quietly released Lessons For an Assassin (2003). While not an international superstar, Shannon Lee never set out to be anything more than what she accomplished, and her work deserves to be discovered.

TITLES REVIEWED:
Cage II: The Arena of Death (1994)
High Voltage (1997)
And Now You're Dead (a.k.a. **Enter the Eagles**) (1998)
Martial Law (1998)
Lessons For an Assassin (2003)

Steven Vincent Leigh

b. 1964. In the heyday of the direct-to-video action era of the 1990s, Steven Vincent Leigh made several key appearances in notable martial arts action films. A handsome, fit Asian with a distinctive face and impressive abilities in the martial arts, Leigh tended to play villains or sidekicks opposite the central star in the films he was in, but he had a shot at carrying his own film with Sword of Honor (1996). Since the early 2000s, he dropped out of the movie scene and pursued a career path in instructing fitness.

TITLES REVIEWED:
Ring of Fire (1991)
Deadly Bet (1992)
To Be the Best (1993)
Death Match (1994)
Blood For Blood (a.k.a. Midnight Man) (1995)
Sword of Honor (1996)
Redemption (2002)

Sugar Ray Leonard

b. 1956. One of the greatest boxers in history with world boxing championship titles and a gold medal to his name, Sugar Ray Leonard made his action film debut with PM Entertainment's Riot (1996), co-starring Gary Daniels. One of PM's best movies, Riot gave Leonard a chance to shine on screen, and perhaps one of the reasons why he didn't continue with a career in action films is because Riot was a relatively small, independent movie that didn't reach an especially wide audience.

TITLES REVIEWED:
Renegade (1995)
Riot (1996)

Al Leong

b. 1952. (See interview on page 369.)

TITLES REVIEWED:
Big Trouble in Little China (1985)
Steele Justice (1987)

Action Jackson (1988)
They Live (1988)
Aftershock (1989)
Savage Beach (1989)
Cage (1989)
Dark Angel (a.k.a. I Come in Peace) (1990)
Death Warrant (1990)
The Perfect Weapon (1991)
Rapid Fire (1992)
Hard Hunted (1992)
Renegade (1993)
Joshua Tree (a.k.a. Army of One) (1993)
Vanishing Son (1994)
Double Dragon (1994)
Deadly Target (1994)

Mimi Lesseos

b. 1964. (See interview on page 152.)

TITLES REVIEWED:
Final Impact (1992)
Pushed to the Limit (1992)
Beyond Fear (1993)
Streets of Rage (1994)
Personal Vendetta (1995)
Double Duty (2009)

DVD artwork for Personal Vendetta. Author's collection.

Paul "Triple H" Levesque

b. 1969. A WWE/WWF wrestling superstar, Paul "Triple H" Levesque has multiple wrestling title championships under his belt, and he has accrued millions of fans that know him strictly from wrestling. His first major crossover into film was as a bad guy in Blade: Trinity (2004), and it would be some years later when WWE Films would give him his shot at carrying a movie all on his own. In 2011, he starred in two PG-13 films for WWE: The Chaperone and Inside Out, both of which were theatrically released, but neither film really capitalized on Levesque's potential as a would-be action star. If given the right project

---

that won't shy away from violence or cater to a teen demographic, then he might have a fighting chance at being a force to contend with.

TITLES REVIEWED:
Blade: Trinity (2014)
The Chaperone (2011)
Inside Out (2011)
Scooby-Doo! WrestleMania Mystery (2014)

James Lew

b. 1952. (See interview on page 165).

TITLES REVIEWED:
Killpoint (1984)
L.A. Streetfighters (a.k.a. **Ninja Turf**) (1985)
Big Trouble in Little China (1985)
Action Jackson (1988)
Aftershock (1989)
Savage Beach (1989)
Ninja Academy (1989)
Best of the Best (1989)
Martial Law (1990)
The Perfect Weapon (1991)
Night of the Warrior (1991)
Raven (1992)
Mission of Justice (1992)
Warlords 3000 (1992)
Ulterior Motives (1993)
Renegade (1993)
American Ninja 5 (1993)
Showdown (1993)
Ring of Steel (1994)
Red Sun Rising (1994)
Timecop (1994)
Cage II (1994)
Walker, Texas Ranger (1994)
Blood for Blood (a.k.a. **Midnight Man**) (1995)
Ballistic (1995)
Excessive Force II: Force on Force (1995)
Night Hunter (1996)
Balance of Power (1996)
Soul of the Avenger (a.k.a. For Life or Death) (1997)
High Voltage (1997)
Boogie Boy (1998)
NightMan (1998)
Lethal Weapon 4 (1998)
Fatal Blade (a.k.a. Gedo) (2000)
Rush Hour 2 (2001)
Outside the Law (2002)
SWAT: Warhead One (2004)
Today You Die (2005)
18 Fingers of Death! (2006)
The Circuit III: Street Monk (2006)
Angel of Death (2009)
Ballistica (2009)
The Girl From the Naked Eye (2012)
G.I. Joe: Retalliation (2013)

Joe Lewis

b. 1944. d. 2012. The man who coined the phrase "American Kickboxing," Joe Lewis fought in the first kickboxing heavyweight title match in 1970, and would go on to be undefeated for his first twelve fights. Widely considered to be a pioneer in the sport (and perhaps the greatest), Lewis embarked on a short-lived career as a martial arts action star, which began with the globetrotting

Theatrical poster for *Jaguar Lives*. Author's collection.

007-styled film Jaguar Lives! *(1979). While it wasn't a hit, he tried again with the barely released* Force: Five *(1981), and then he made a few appearances (as villains) in several low-budget Asian-made films. His final film,* White Tiger, *was alongside Don "The Dragon" Wilson, Matt Mullins, and Cynthia Rothrock.*

TITLES REVIEWED:
Jaguar Lives! (1979)
Force: Five (1981)
Death Cage (1988)
Mr. X (1995)
Kill 'Em All (2012)
White Tiger (2014)

Jet Li

b. 1963. A wushu champion as a youngster, Jet Li was a prodigy at the martial arts. He began starring in films in his late teens, and tried early on making crossover films like The Master *(1992), but it wasn't until Joel Silver and Richard Donner brought him to America to star alongside Mel Gibson as the villain in* Lethal Weapon 4 *(1998) that Hollywood took notice and began using his icy cool demeanor and no-nonsense persona for fairly big-budget films like* The One *(2001) and* Cradle 2 the Grave *(2003). Li is universally recognized as an authority as an action star and martial artist, and while some of his best-known films like the* Once Upon a Time in China *trilogy and* Hero *(2002) are historical epics, his place as an urban action star is firmly established.*

Jet Li as Yin Yang in *The Expendables*.

Liu Jian (Jet Li) isn't messing around in *Kiss of the Dragon*. Author's collection.

TITLES REVIEWED:
Born to Defense (1986)
Dragon Fight (1989)
The Master (1992)
The Defender (1994)
Fist of Legend (1994)
The Enforcer (1995)
Meltdown (1995)
Dr. Wai in the Scriptures With No Words (1996)
Black Mask (1996)
Contract Killer (1998)
Lethal Weapon 4 (1998)
Romeo Must Die (2000)
Kiss of the Dragon (2001)
The One (2001)
Cradle 2 the Grave (2003)
Unleashed (a.k.a. **Danny the Dog**) (2005)
Fearless (2006)
War (2007)
The Forbidden Kingdom (2008)
The Mummy: Tomb of the Dragon Emperor (2008)
The Expendables (2010)
Expendables 2 (2012)
Badges of Fury (2013)
Expendables 3 (2014)

Lo Lieh

b. 1939. d. 2002. An Indonesian by birth, Lo Lieh (real name: Lida Wang) made his way to Hong Kong where he joined up with the Shaw brothers, becoming one of their very first superstars. As an early classic kung fu star, Lieh was able to star alongside Lee Van Cleef in the spaghetti western/kung fu hybrid Blood Money *(a.k.a.* The Stranger and the Gunfighter, *1974), which ironically is just a footnote in his very busy career as a kung fu star. A few of his better-known films are* The One-Armed Swordsman *(1976) and* The 36th Chamber of Shaolin *(1978).*

TITLES REVIEWED:
Blood Money (a.k.a. **The Stranger and the Gunfighter**) (1974)
Miracles (a.k.a. *Black Dragon*; a.k.a. *Mr. Canton and Lady Rose*) (1989)
Supercop: Police Story III (1992)

Il Lim

b. 1973. Born in Seoul, South Korea, Il Lim moved to Utah at an early age where he studied Moo Lim Do style hapkido from his father, grandmaster Kap Chul Lim. Honing his impressive physical skills, Lim became a well-respected martial arts

instructor, moving to Los Angeles to oversee his family's studio. He soon found work in student films and commercials (including a Tony Kaye Bank of America spot) before earning his SAG card for a small role in Heywood Gould's Double Bang *(2001). He then set to work writing, directing, and starring in his magnum opus* Acts of Violence, *which would receive a Southern Californian theatrical release in in 2010. He's currently at work on a faith-based martial arts film.*

TITLE REVIEWED:
Acts of Violence (2010)

Andre Lim

b. 1966. A seventh degree taekwondo black belt who competed professionally throughout Europe, Andre Lima also holds belts in Shotokan and Brazilian jiu jitsu. He made a few appearances in some low-budget action and martial arts movies, but he later starred in his own film Beyond the Ring *(2008), which remains his only starring vehicle.*

TITLES REVIEWED:
Red Sun Rising (1994)
Sworn to Justice (1996)
The Silent Force (2001)
Brazilian Brawl (2003)
Sunland Heat (2004)
Beyond the Ring (2008)

Tommy "Tiny" Lister

b. 1958. With a frightening visage and growling, scowling demeanor (partly due to the fact that he's blind in one eye), Tommy "Tiny" Lister hit the action movie scene hard when he co-starred opposite Hulk Hogan in the wrestling movie No Holds Barred *in 1989. As the demonic Zeus, Lister scared children all over America, and his role in that film set the tone for his future roles where he'd usually play a silent but menacing henchman who only had to growl to let anyone know that he wasn't to be messed with. As a way to promote* No Holds Barred, *Lister joined WWE (then WWF) and WCW wrestling, and his stint as a professional wrestler only lasted six months. His passion for bodybuilding was maintained over the next several decades as he continued to co-star or make appearances in action-star oriented films and television programs.*

TITLES REVIEWED:
Hard Time on Planet Earth (1989)
No Holds Barred (1989)
Think Big (1989)
9 1/2 Ninjas (1991)
Universal Soldier (1992)
Renegade (1993)
Walker, Texas Ranger (1993)
Immortal Combat (1994)
Men of War (1994)
Hologram Man (1995)
White Cargo (1996)
Santa's Slay (2005)
The Lazarus Papers (2010)

Zheng Liu

Hailed as "the next Bruce Lee" in an era when the world had pretty much given up on martial arts action stars, Zheng Liu quietly arrived via the low-

budget direct-to-video movie from Turbo/XLrator Media Blood Money (2012). Liu is a Shaolin monk trained since childhood in a monastery in China who can reportedly break steel bars over his skull. He was discovered in the monastery in an impromptu talent search for an upcoming movie, and his talents as a martial artist so impressed the director that he was given the lead role on the spot.

TITLE REVIEWED:
Blood Money (2012)

Paul Logan

b. 1973. It's not uncommon for action guys with huge potential to fall between the seams, and Paul Logan (unfortunately) is one of those guys. With the right look to be both a hero or a villain, with skills in kendō, aikido, jiu jitsu, and a black belt in Okinawa Goju-Ryu karate, and a background in stunt work and fight choreography, he's the ideal candidate to be a top-shelf action star, but with the reality of today's fledgling movie market and fluctuating medium on which films are now shot, productions aren't going after struggling would-be action stars who have not established themselves in "A" productions. Logan is one of the few guys working today in the low-budget and independent film market who deserves to be noticed, and it's actually a testament to his will that he's been working in the industry in multiple fields (acting, stunt performing, and appearing in action/martial arts roles) for several decades now.

TITLES REVIEWED:
Blazing Force (1996)
The Ultimate Game (2001)
Ballistica (2009)
The Terminators (2009)
Re-Generator (a.k.a. One Night) (2010)
Code Red (2013)

Howie Long

b. 1960. Pro football Hall of Famer Howie Long (all 6 foot, 5 inches of him) played for the Oakland/LA Raiders from 1981 to 1993, and a few years after that he landed a plum supporting role as John Travolta's henchman in John Woo's Broken Arrow (1996). Two years later, 20th Century Fox gave him his own vehicle film, the theatrically released Firestorm (1998), which cast him as a good-hearted firefighter in the middle of a forest fire with some escaped convicts who've forced him to lead them to safety. The film was a flop, which pretty much ensured that he wouldn't be getting another headlining film any time soon, but instead

Ex-NFL player Howie Long plays the heroic fireman Jesse in Firestorm. Author's collection.

of going the Brian Bosworth route (starring in direct-to-video movies), Long all but left movies behind and appeared in a string of successful commercials and commentating positions.

TITLES REVIEWED:
Broken Arrow (1996)
Firestorm (1998)
Dollar for the Dead (1998)

Kathy Long

b. 1964. A five-time world kickboxing champion with eighteen wins and only one loss to her record, Kathy Long is considered one of the top female sports athletes in history. In the early 1990s, she tried transitioning into movies, and it was a time when Cynthia Rothrock was the reigning female action star. When Long starred in her first big vehicle film Knights (1993), the market seemed ready to embrace her, but her next two films The Stranger (1995) and Under the Gun (1995) didn't give her much leverage to guarantee longevity in the business. She quit making action films altogether and she currently trains at a Tapout gym in Los Angeles.

TITLES REVIEWED:
Rage and Honor (1992)
Street Justice (1993)
Knights (1993)
The Stranger (1995)
Walker, Texas Ranger (1995)
Under the Gun (1995)

Dolph Lundgren

b. 1957 (See interview on page 422.)

TITLES REVIEWED:
Rocky IV (1985)
Red Scorpion (1988)
The Punisher (1989)
Dark Angel (a.k.a. I Come in Peace) (1990)

Exhausted? Never. Ready to fight? Always. Dolph Lundgren in Red Scorpion. Author's collection.

Cover-Up (1991)
Showdown in Little Tokyo (1991)
Universal Soldier (1992)
Joshua Tree (a.k.a. Army of One) (1993)
Pentathlon (1994)
Men of War (1994)
Johnny Mnemonic (1995)
Hidden Assassin (1995)
Silent Trigger (1996)
The Peacekeeper (1997)
Blackjack (1998)
The Minion (1998)
Sweepers (1998)
Bridge of Dragons (1999)
Storm Catcher (1999)
Jill the Ripper (2000)
The Last Warrior (a.k.a. The Last Patrol) (2000)
Agent Red (2000)
Hidden Agenda (2001)
Detention (2003)
Direct Action (2004)
Retrograde (2004)
The Defender (2004)
The Russian Specialist (a.k.a. **The Mechanik**) (2005)
Diamond Dogs (2007)
Missionary Man (2007)
Direct Contact (2009)
Command Performance (2009)
Universal Soldier: Regeneration (2009)
The Killing Machine (a.k.a. Icarus) (2010)
The Expendables (2010)
In the Name of the King 2: Two Worlds (2011)
Stash House (2012)
One in the Chamber (2012)
The Expendables 2 (2012)
Universal Soldier: Day of Reckoning (2012)
The Package (2012)
Legendary: Tomb of the Dragon (2013)
Battle of the Damned (2013)
Ambushed (a.k.a. Hard Rush) (2013)
Blood of Redemption (2013)
Puncture Wounds (2014)
Saf3 (2013–2014)
The Expendables 3 (2014)
4Got10 (2015)
Shark Lake (2015)
Skin Trade (2015)
War Pigs (2015)

Evan Lurie

b. 1966. New York-born Evan Lurie grew up in the arts scene during a period when Andy Warhol and Jean-Michel Basquiat were making their rounds, and with his passion for art and the martial arts, Lurie sought acting roles in Los Angeles. Finding only a bouncer job at a hot nightclub, he ejected a patron who was annoying a film producer's wife. When the producer and his wife left the club, the removed patron attacked them, and Lurie fended the man off, but found himself in jail for the effort (the man was an off-duty cop). He spent the night in jail, but the next morning the producer he saved had a car sent to pick him up, and he was offered a small role in Jean-Claude Van Damme's newest movie Double Impact (1991). From there, Lurie became a mainstay in low-budget martial arts action movies, and he even starred in a few like American Kickboxer 2 (1993) and Hologram Man

(1995). When his acting career dried up, he returned to his roots in fine art and opened up a successful gallery in Indiana, which continues to thrive.

TITLES REVIEWED:
Double Impact (1991)
Martial Law II: Undercover (1991)
Ring of Fire II: Blood and Steel (1993)
American Kickboxer 2 (1993)
T-Force (1994)
Hologram Man (1995)
Guns and Lipstick (1995)
Tiger Claws II (1996)
Expect to Die (1997)
Operation Cobra (a.k.a. *Inferno*) (1997)
Mortal Challenge (a.k.a. *Death Game*) (1997)

M

Ben Maccabee

b. 1966. Israeli-born Ben Macabee, who served four years in the Israeli army, holds a black belt in kung fu san soo, and used his martial arts abilities to fuel the stories of his low-budget starring films Enter the Blood Ring *(1995),* Broken Bars *(1995), and* Ultimate Prey *(2000). He has managed to continue producing small-scale action and martial arts films, against all odds and has kept himself in the game.*

TITLES REVIEWED:
Enter the Blood Ring (1995)
Broken Bars (1995)
Ultimate Prey (2000)
Moses: Fallen. In the City of Angels (2005)

Carlos Machado

b. 1963. The oldest of the Machado brothers and an eighth degree red and black belt in Brazilian jiu jitsu, Carlos co-starred with his four brothers in Leo Fong's low-budget actioner Brazilian Brawl *(2003).*

TITLES REVIEWED:
Walker, Texas Ranger (1996–1997)
Brazilian Brawl (2003)

Jean Jacques Machado

The fourth oldest of five brothers, Jean Jacques holds a seventh degree red and black belt in Brazilian jiu jitsu. His only appearance in a film is with his four brothers in the movie Brazilian Brawl *(2003).*

TITLE REVIEWED:
Brazilian Brawl (2003)

John Machado

The youngest of the Machado brothers, John is a seventh degree black belt in Brazilian jiu jiu jitsu and the Pan American Games Sambo champion (1993-1994). He appeared in Brazilian Brawl *(2003) alongside his four brothers, as well as co-starred in a handful of other "B" action films.*

TITLES REVIEWED:
Kickboxer 4: The Aggressor (1994)
Heatseeker (1995)
Walker, Texas Ranger (1996)
Brazilian Brawl (2003)

Rigan Machado

b. 1966. An eighth degree red and black belt in Brazilian jiu jitsu, Rigan is the third oldest of the Machado brothers. He has co-starred in a handful of low-budget martial arts movies, most notably in Brazilian Brawl *(2003), which also co-starred his four brothers.*

TITLES REVIEWED:
Kickboxer 4: The Aggressor (1994)
Brazilian Brawl (2003)
Confessions of a Pit Fighter (2005)
Beyond the Ring (2008)

Roger Machado

A 7th degree red and black belt in Brazilian jiu jitsu and the second oldest of the Machado brothers, Roger—like his brothers Carlos and Jean Jacques—hasn't done much in front of the camera, but he made an appearance on the TV show Walker, Texas Ranger *as well as co-starring in* Brazilian Brawl *(2003) with his four brothers.*

TITLES REVIEWED:
Walker, Texas Ranger (1996)
Brazilian Brawl (2003)

Lyoto Machida

b. 1978. Half Japanese/half Brazillian Lyoto Machida was a sumo champion in Brazil before embarking on a career in UFC fighting. He's thus far only made two notable appearances in action/martial arts films, most notably in Tapped Out *(2014), where he mentors the younger main character (played by Cody Hackman) in fighting the antagonist, played by Krzysztof Soszyski, also a professional UFC fighter.*

TITLES REVIEWED:
Unrivaled (2010)
Tapped Out (2014)

Cass Magda

b. 1959. A specialist in escrima, silat, kali, and Jeet Kune Do, Cass Magda was tapped to play the villain in the Gary Daniels film Hawk's Vengeance *(1996), and the following year as a good guy in the rarely seen movie* Blade Boxer *(1997). He coordinated the fights on several other "B" movies before giving up acting to instruct martial arts exclusively through his branches of martial arts studios throughout the world. His wife, Eleanor Academia, has also dabbled in action and martial arts films.*

TITLES REVIEWED:
Hawk's Vengeance (1996)
Blade Boxer (1997)

Tim Man

b. 1979. (See interview on page 316.)

b. 1979. (See interview on page 316.)

TITLES REVIEWED:
Street Fighter: The Legend of Chun-Li (2009)
Raging Phoenix (2009)
Kill 'Em All (2012)
Ninja II: Shadow of a Tear (2013)

Angela Mao (Ying)

b. 1950. A Hong Kong martial arts star who specialized in hapkido, Angela Mao (Ying) is best recognized for co-starring in Enter the Dragon *(1973) as Bruce Lee's sister. She worked her way up to starring in her own films, but only a few of them are considered international crossovers like* Stoner *(1974), which was an action film starring George Lazenby. Mao kept busy until she retired after starting a family.*

TITLES REVIEWED:
Enter the Dragon (1973)
Stoner (1974)
A Queen's Ransom (a.k.a. *International Assassin*) (1976)

Ron Marchini

b. 1946. A muscular martial arts champion throughout the 1960s and '70s, Ron Marchini's specialty was in Renbukai karate, and he's written several books about training in the art of it. He was an early "crossover" martial arts action star, starring in grindhouse movies made in the Philippines, and when he finally made his magnum opus Omega Cop *(1990), he was already well into his forties. Most of his films were very low-budget affairs, but if you know who he is and have seen at least one of his movies and enjoyed it, then clearly you're reading the right book.*

TITLES REVIEWED:
Murder in the Orient (1974)
Death Machines (1976)
Ninja Warriors (1985)
Jungle Wolf (a.k.a. *Forgotten Warrior*) (1986)
Return Fire: Jungle Wolf II (1988)
Omega Cop (1990)
Karate Cop (1991)
Karate Commando: Jungle Wolf 3 (1993)

John Matuszak

b. 1950. d. 1989. Most fondly remembered as playing the lovable Mongoloid Sloth in The Goonies *(1985), John Matuszak played a number of seasons for various NFL teams, including the Houston Oilers, the Houston Texans, the Kansas City Chiefs, the Washington Redskins, and the Oakland Raiders (1976–1982). He transitioned into motion pictures and television episodes in the early 1980s, and the year he died of heart failure in 1989, his best work as an action star was released with the film* One Man Force *(1989), where he starred as a bulldozing cop out for revenge for the death of his partner, played by Sam Jones. If the only thing you know Matuszak from is* The Goonies, *then you owe it to yourself to see him in* One Man Force.

TITLES REVIEWED:
The Goonies (1985)
Hunter (1986)
The A-Team (1986)
One Man Force (1989)

Deron McBee

b. 1961. A former American Gladiator known as "Malibu," Deron McBee has an impressive muscular physique that gives him an imposing appearance. Usually cast as a thug, bodyguard, or a villain of some kind, McBee has worked in the martial arts and action movie world since the early '90s, getting his break with a heroic starring role in The Killing Zone *(1991). The action world hasn't seen much of him since his role in the Chuck Norris film* The Cutter *in 2005, but his resume is full of action films so there's plenty of time to catch up before he makes another movie.*

TITLES REVIEWED:
The Killing Zone (1991)
Out for Blood (1992)
Ring of Steel (1994)
Immortal Combat (1994)
T-Force (1994)
Cage II (1994)
Enter the Blood Ring (1995)
Mortal Kombat: Annihilation (1997)
Deadly Currency (1998)
Martial Law (1998)
Walker, Texas Ranger (2000)
Instinct to Kill (2001)
Red Serpent (2003)
Latin Dragon (2004)
The Cutter (2005)

Matt McColm

b. 1965. An ideal choice to be an action star, Matt McColm has the looks, the martial arts abilities (in kenpo karate), a background in stunt work, and the wherewithal to carry a feature film all on his own, but (as fate would have it) the handful of projects he starred in didn't use him to the best of his capabilities. There was so much potential to his films Red Scorpion 2 *(1994),* Subterfuge *(1996), and* Body Armor *(1998), but the films themselves were underwhelming and left audiences wanting more action scenes with their underused star. His biggest body of work as the lead was in the TV series* NightMan *(1997-1999), which was a sort-of imitation of Batman. Of late, McColm has gone back to stunt work, where he continues working in major Hollywood blockbusters.*

Matt McColm stars in the direct-to-video movie *Red Scorpion 2*. Author's collection.

TITLES REVIEWED:
Red Scorpion 2 (1994)
Subterfuge (1996)
Acts of Betrayal (1997)
NightMan (1997-1999)
Body Armor (a.k.a. **The Protector**) (1998)
Cellular (2004)

Andre "Chyna" McCoy

b. 1966. Stuntman and fight coordinator Andre "Chyna" McCoy's big break came when he doubled Laurence Fishburne in The Matrix *(1999). McCoy, not content to simply work behind the scenes, began starring in low-budget action films throughout the world, namely in China. To date, he's only starred in a handful of films, but he's still at it and putting his best fists forward.*

TITLES REVIEWED:
The Ultimate Game (2001)
Pit Fighter (2005)
Game Over (2005)
T.K.O. (2007)
Project Purgatory (2010)

Kurt McKinney

b. 1962. Before he won the lead role in No Retreat, No Surrender *(1986), Kurt McKinney had achieved a black belt in taekwondo and had some amateur kickboxing fights. He turned down the sequel, and reportedly also turned down the opportunity to take over the American Ninja franchise when Michael Dudikoff vacated the lead role. When David Bradley took over the series, Bradley had a brief but lucrative career as a martial arts action star, but McKinney made his name in soap operas. The only other martial arts role he ever took on was opposite Cynthia Rothrock in* Sworn to Justice *(1996).*

TITLES REVIEWED:
No Retreat, No Surrender (1986)
Sworn to Justice (1996)

Kurt McKinney plays Jason Stillwell in *No Retreat, No Surrender*. Author's collection.

Rachel McLish

b. 1955. A striking individual with an impressive muscular figure, Rachel McLish is a two-time Ms. Olympia bodybuilder (1980, 1982) who was featured in the documentary Pumping Iron II: The Women *(1985). Some years later she segued into a short-lived career in action films, and her*

auspicious debut Aces: Iron Eagle III *(1992) was given a theatrical release. Four years later, she starred in Albert Pyun's* Ravenhawk *(1996), which cast McLish as a wrongly imprisoned Native American woman who, when released, seeks revenge on the men who killed her family and blamed her for the slayings. McLish should have made several more films, but for whatever reason, that wasn't in the cards for this brawny beauty.*

TITLES REVIEWED:
Aces: Iron Eagle III (1992)
Ravenhawk (1996)

Martin and Michael McNamara

b. 1950. The McNamara twins (also known as "The Twin Dragons") were inspired by Chuck Norris' Good Guys Wear Black (1978) to make their own films, but it proved to be a little bit of a challenge as the brothers are Canadian and the Canadian film industry wasn't producing action and martial arts movies in the early 1980s. Once they were able to get a fully financed film together—Twin Dragon Encounter (1986)—they were able to showcase their full contact kickboxing and kung fu skills, and they accrued a small following. Their second film, Dragon Hunt, (1990) never found proper distribution in the US, but they were able to land a cameo appearance in Back in Action (1993), where they fought Billy Blanks on screen. Their latest film The Right to Fight (2007) has been in legal limbo for close to a decade, but here's hoping it sees the light of day some time soon.

TITLES REVIEWED:
Twin Dragon Encounter (1986)
Dragon Hunt (1990)
Back in Action (1993)

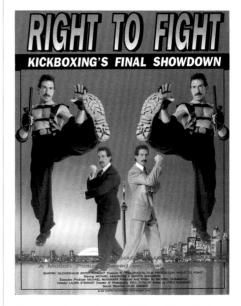

Promo for the unreleased *Right to Fight*. Author's collection.

Jeffrey Meek

b. 1959. Talk, dark, and handsome, Jeffrey Meek is an underrated action star that has done a variety of projects, but only a handful that capitalize on and showcase his abilities as a martial artist. With a black belt in aikido and taekwondo, Meek starred in the pilot of Remo Williams: The Adventure Continues (1988), but the pilot was never picked up for a series, and then later he starred in the martial arts-themed series Raven (1992–1993), which featured him as a samurai warrior looking for his long-lost son. He also appeared in the series Mortal Kombat: Conquest (1998–1999), which was yet another TV series that only lasted a single season.

TITLES REVIEWED:
Remo Williams: The Prophecy (1988)
Raven (1992–1993)
Timelock (1996)
Mortal Kombat: Conquest (1998–1999)
Code Name Phoenix (2000)

Jalal Merhi

b. 1967. (See interview on page 462.)

TITLES REVIEWED:
Fearless Tiger (a.k.a. *Black Pearls*) (1991)
Tiger Claws (1991)
Talons of the Eagle (1992)
TC 2000 (1993)
Operation Golden Phoenix (1994)
Expect No Mercy (1995)
Tiger Claws II (1996)
Expect to Die (1997)
Tiger Claws III (2000)
G.O.D. (2001)
The Circuit (2002)
The Circuit 2: The Final Punch (2002)
The Circuit III: Street Monk (2006)
Risk Factor (2015)

Nishiwaki Michiko

b. 1957. Japan's first woman's bodybuilding and power lifting champion, Nishiwaki Michiko also has an impressive line-up of films to her credit, but her most notable entries are My Lucky Stars (1985) with Jackie Chan and Sammo Hung and City Cops (1989) with Cynthia Rothrock. Despite her incredibly muscular frame, Michiko is an adept (and flexible) martial artist and stuntwoman, performing stunts for films like Kill Bill Vol. 2 (2004) and Mission Impossible III (2006).

TITLES REVIEWED:
My Lucky Stars (1985)
City Cops (1989)
Avenging Quartet (a.k.a. *Avenging Angels*) (1992)
Thunder Mission (1992)
Ghost Rock (2003)

John Miller

b. 1959. John Miller did two back-to-back action films with Cynthia Rothrock: Honor and Glory (1993) and Undefeatable (1993). In the former, he played the lead villain, and in the latter he played a good cop beside Rothrock. With a big, muscular frame, good looks, and powerful skills in the martial arts (he's an eighth generation master in hung fut kung fu and a weapons champion), he should have gone on to do more action movies,

John Miller plays a karate cop in Godfrey Ho's *Undefeatable*. Courtesy of John Miller.

but his career path went a different way and he never made another feature film.

TITLES REVIEWED:
Honor and Glory (1993)
Undefeatable (1993)

Stefanos Miltsakakis

b. 1960. If you've seen most of the movies starring Jean-Claude Van Damme, then you've also seen Stefanos Miltsakakis in action. An imposing Greek muscleman, Miltsakakis got his action star stats going in the Albert Pyun-directed film Cyborg (1989), and he continued appearing in notable features like Lionheart (1990) and Best of the Best II (1993), but his most memorable roles feature him fighting the lead stars in movies such as Maximum Risk (1996) and Bloodsport 4: The Dark Kumite (1999). He usually doesn't have any lines, but as a featured villain, he's impossible to forget. In the professional fight circuit, Miltsakakis fought three fights and won every fight. His specialty is Brazilian jiu jitsu.

TITLES REVIEWED:
Cyborg (1989)
The Master (1989)
Lionheart (1990)
Double Trouble (1992)
Best of the Best II (1993)
Martial Outlaw (1993)
T-Force (1994)
Fists of Iron (1995)
The Quest (1996)
Maximum Risk (1996)
Martial Law (1998)
Bloodsport 4: The Dark Kumite (1999)
Derailed (2002)

Sasha Mitchell

b. 1967. (See interview on page 248.)

TITLES REVIEWED:
Death Before Dishonor (1987)
Kickboxer 2: The Road Back (1991)
Kickboxer 3: The Art of War (1992)
Kickboxer 4: The Aggressor (1994)
Class of 1999 II: The Substitute (1994)
Gangland (2001)

Mike "The Miz" Mizanin

b. 1980. An Ultimate Pro wrestler and a WWE wrestling superstar, Mike "The Miz" Mizanin made his action star debut in WWE's direct-to-video film The Marine 3: Homefront (2013), which was enough of a hit for WWE to make another title in the franchise with Mizanin called The Marine 4: Moving Target (2014). At 6 foot 1, Mizanin isn't the hulking beast that John Cena (the star of the first Marine film is), but he's accrued a healthy fan base and a slowly-but-surely rising career as a WWE-sponsored action star.

TITLES REVIEWED:
The Marine 3: Homefront (2013)
Christmas Bounty (2013)
Scooby-Doo! WrestleMania Mystery (2014)
The Marine 4: Moving Target (2014)
Santa's Little Helper (2015)

Mike Moeller

b. 1976. (See interview on page 36.)

TITLES REVIEWED:
Kampfansage (a.k.a. *The Challenge*) (2005)
Ninja Masters (2009)
Arena of the Streetfighter (2012)
Atomic EDEN (2015)

Ralf Moeller

b. 1959. A hulking mass of muscle and brawn, Ralf Moeller (Möller) is a former Mr. Universe and the German bodybuilding champion of the

Phillip Rhee is Tommy Lee in *Best of the Best*, a movie he wrote. Author's collection.

International Federation of Bodybuilders. Also a champion boxer and a former professional swimmer, Moeller began his acting career in Albert Pyun's post-apocalyptic epic Cyborg (1989), where he played a flesh pirate. With a body and a screen presence like his, he was bound to land a big break, and that break was when he was cast as the villain in Best of the Best II (1993), where he memorably slays Chris Penn in front of a bloodthirsty audience. Moeller, a protégé of Arnold Schwarzenegger, has also appeared in a number of sword and sorcery titles like Conan: The Adventurer (1997), where he was an obvious choice to replace his compatriot.

TITLES REVIEWED:
Cyborg (1989)
Universal Soldier (1992)
Best of the Best II (1993)
The Bad Pack (1997)
Shark Alarm (a.k.a. ***Shark Attack in the Mediterranean***) (2004)

Mike Moh

b. 1983. A world champion in competitive taekwondo, Mike Moh got his start working with Jackie Chan in Robin-B-Hood (2006) and segued into stunt work and acting in the martial arts-filled TV series with Matt Mullins Kamen Rider: Dragon Knight (2009–2010). Moh, a fourth degree black belt in taekwondo, continues to pursue martial arts projects, and his latest work was in the web series-turned-feature Street Fighter: Assassin's Fist (2014), directed by fellow action star Joey Ansah.

TITLES REVIEWED:
Robin-B-Hood (2006)
Kamen Rider: Dragon Knight (2009-2010)
Street Fighter: Assassin's Fist (2014)

Mr. T

b. 1952. A flamboyant action hero and real-life personality, Mr. T (real name Laurence Tureaud) came on the scene really strong in the early 1980s when he appeared in Sylvester Stallone's Rocky III (1982) as the film's central protagonist. With his buff, bulky physique, Mohawk hairdo, heavy gold chains around his neck, and bad attitude, Mr. T announced his arrival as a contender. When he was in the US Army as an MP, he developed a reputation as someone not to be trifled with, and when he later became a bouncer at a nightclub, he

Mr. T pities the fool in *Penitentiary II*. Author's collection.

is reputed to have gotten in over 200 fights with unruly patrons and was sued repeatedly for beating up roustabouts (he never lost a case). He later became a bodyguard to high-paying clients like Steve McQueen, Muhammad Ali, and Joe Frazier, and he also won two Tough Man competitions back to back. After a brief stint as Hulk Hogan's tag-team partner in WrestleMania, he embarked on a lucrative acting career with action-centric roles, but the project that made him an icon was his role as B. A. Baracus on the massively popular show The A-Team, which ran for five seasons. As the '80s passed, so too did Mr. T's popularity, but he's still around "pitying the fool."

TITLES REVIEWED:
Penitentiary II (1982)
Rocky III (1982)
D.C. Cab (1983)
Mr. T (1983)
The A-Team (1983-1987)
Straight Line (1990)

Jeff Moldovan

b. 1953. d. 2013. Before creating his own unique systems in the martial arts, Jeff Moldovan trained extensively in the Indonesian art of Poekoelan Tjimindie Chuan Fa, which he helped to teach Dan Inosanto. After being devastated by Bruce Lee's death (with whom he'd hope to train), Moldovan traveled to Hawaii where he drifted and worked labor jobs, fighting on the streets for extra cash and experience. Later, he opened up the Chinese Boxing Institute in Pennsylvania and created a hybrid art of lung kune do and another fighting system called TLM's Fighting Chance Training System. Moldovan had worked as a bodyguard, a bouncer, a stuntman, actor, and a stunt coordinator, while also starring in a low-budget action film called Masterblaster (1987), which he also coordinated the fights on. He appeared in dozens more films and television episodes, but he rarely had the chance to star in features again. He tragically passed away in Venezuela in 2013 while teaching a seminar.

TITLES REVIEWED:
Knights of the City (1986)
Masterblaster (1987)

Matt Mullins

b. 1980. (See interview on page 241.)

TITLES REVIEWED:
Bloodfist 2050 (2005)
Adventures of Johnny Tao (2007)
Blood and Bone (2009)
Kamen Rider: Dragon Knight (2008–2010)
Mortal Kombat: Legacy: Season 1 (2011)
Metal Hurlant Chronicles: King's Crown (2012)
Wrath of Vajra (2013)
White Tiger (2014)

Vince Murdocco

b. 1966. A North American cruiserweight champion in kickboxing and a winner of a Japanese shoot boxing championship, Vince Murdocco got his start in the action movie business by co-starring in a slew of low-budget

films that headlined guys like Sasha Mitchell and Don "The Dragon" Wilson. Murdocco, a handsome, charismatic athlete and actor, got his chance to star in a low-budget action/martial arts film called L.A. Wars (1994), which featured him as a renegade cop on the loose in Los Angeles, and since stepping down as a front-and-center action star, he's gone into stunt work, contributing to big films such as 2012 (2009), The A-Team (2010), and The Grey (2011).

TITLES REVIEWED:
Kickboxer 2: The Road Back (1991)
Ring of Fire (1991)
Ring of Fire II: Blood and Steel (1993)
To Be the Best (1993)
Magic Kid II (1994)
L.A. Wars (1994)
Night Hunter (1996)
Sworn to Justice (1996)
Mortal Challenge (a.k.a. *Death Game*) (1997)

N

Alexander Nevsky

b. 1971. "The biggest bodybuilder in Russia" and a bestselling author of fitness books and articles throughout Russia, Alexander Nevsky (real name Aleksandr Kuritsyn) bears a striking resemblance to a young Arnold Schwarzenegger, and he knows it, too. His first notable crossover film Moscow Heat (2004) was an obvious nod to Red Heat (1988), and it was very clear that Nevsky holds Arnold in high regard as an inspiration. Nevsky's resemblance to Arnold is not a detriment, but rather a good selling point and place for him to build on, but with only two vehicle films that are worth mentioning to his name, he has an awful long way to go to prove himself as a successor to his idol. It should also be mentioned that he has been taught some martial arts and acting by both Chuck Norris and Steven Seagal.

TITLES REVIEWED:
Moscow Heat (2004)
Treasure Raiders (2007)

John Newton

b. 1965. John Newton's biggest claim to fame is starring as the iconic main character on TV's Superboy (1988–1989), and when he was replaced on that show, he went on to star in Isaac Florentine's first film Desert Kickboxer (1992), which used some of Newton's skills as a martial artist. His only other appearance in an action-related project was as a two-time guest star on Chuck Norris' Walker, Texas Ranger (1997).

TITLES REVIEWED:
Desert Kickboxer (1992)
Walker, Texas Ranger (1997)

Aaron Norris

b. 1951. The younger brother of Chuck, Aaron is best known for directing a number of his brother's films, but if you pay attention while watching some of Chuck's movies, you'll notice Aaron (who looks strikingly similar to his brother) in bit roles as a guard, a thug, or a punk. Lo and behold,

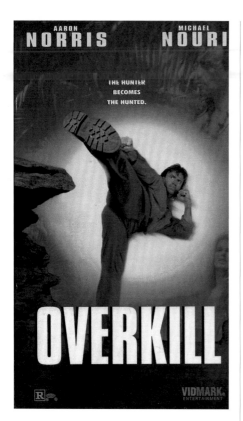

VHS artwork for *Overkill*. Author's collection.

Aaron stepped up to the plate and starred in a single action film called Overkill *(1996)*, which is extremely entertaining and shockingly similar to any of his brother's films of that period. It's uncanny at how similar Aaron was to his brother in that movie, and with his ninth degree black belt in Chun Kuk Do (his brother's own brand of martial arts), the two guys might as well be one. He never starred in another movie again, sadly.

TITLE REVIEWED:
   Overkill (1995)

Chuck Norris

b. 1940. Born Carlos Ray Norris, Chuck is a living legend. The first westerner to earn an eighth degree black belt in taekwondo, Norris has inspired countless up and coming martial artists, would-be action stars, and US troops all over the world with his support and admiration. He trained with Bruce Lee and infamously fought him on screen in The Way of the Dragon *(1972)*. Norris became an early "action star" before there was such a thing. With iconic roles such as the ones he played in great action projects like Missing in Action *(1984)*, Invasion U.S.A. *(1985)*, The Delta Force *(1986)*, and his best-known body of work Walker, Texas Ranger *(1993–2001)*, Norris became one of the greats as his fan base grew exponentially as his immensely popular TV series was syndicated all over the world. As he grew older, he veered away from his hard "R" rated days at Cannon, and he took on more family-oriented projects that celebrated life and his faith in Christianity. He is also a celebrated author and the inventor of the martial arts Chun Kuk Do ("the universal way") and American Tang Soo Do. He has all but retired from action films, and yet his legacy lives on vibrantly as his image and famous beard (with

Chuck Norris plays one of his most iconic roles as James Braddock in *Missing in Action*. Author's collection.

his celebrated one-liners and quips) have become a part of the pop culture lexicon.

TITLES REVIEWED:
   The Way of the Dragon (1972)
   The Game of Death (1973)
   Breaker! Breaker! (1977)
   Good Guys Wear Black (1978)
   A Force of One (1979)
   The Octagon (1980)
   An Eye For an Eye (1981)
   Silent Rage (1982)
   Forced Vengeance (1982)
   Lone Wolf McQuade (1983)
   Missing in Action (1984)
   Missing in Action 2: The Beginning (1985)
   Code of Silence (1985)
   Invasion U.S.A. (1985)
   The Delta Force (1986)
   Firewalker (1986)
   Braddock: Missing in Action III (1988)
   Hero and the Terror (1988)
   Delta Force 2: The Columbian Connection
      (1990)
   The Hitman (1991)
   Sidekicks (1992)
   Hellbound (1994)
   Walker, Texas Ranger (1993–2001)
   Top Dog (1995)
   Forest Warrior (1996)
   Logan's War: Bound by Honor (1998)
   Sons of Thunder (1999)
   The President's Man (2000)
   The President's Man: A Line in the Sand
      (2002)
   Bells of Innocence (2003)
   The Cutter (2005)
   The Expendables 2 (2012)

Mike Norris

b. 1963. Mike Norris's first few film appearances were in several of his father Chuck's films, including The Octagon *(1980)*, where he played a younger version of his dad. As Mike matured

and came into his own, he went to Scandinavia with the intention of becoming a stuntman, but instead landed the lead role in Renny Harlin's first film Born American *(1986)*, which was an inauspicious vehicle for Mike. He would go on to star in a handful of other straight-to-video action films, and would make several appearances on his father's hit show Walker, Texas Ranger throughout different seasons of its run. In recent years, Mike (who also practices martial arts and competed when he was younger) segued into the Christian movie market and produces, directs, and stars in films targeted for the evangelical market.

TITLES REVIEWED:
   The Octagon (1980)
   Born American (1986)
   Survival Game (1987)
   Delta Force 3: The Killing Game (1991)
   Death Ring (1992)
   Ripper Man (1995)
   Dragon Fury II (1996)
   Delta Force One: The Lost Patrol (2000)
   Walker, Texas Ranger (1993-2001)
   The Rage Within (2001)
   Bells of Innocence (2003)

Richard Norton

b. 1950. One of the great, unheralded action stars, Richard Norton has been in dozens of action films that feature him as the star or as a supporting player and stuntman, in roles that range from being the hero to being the villain. With a strong, fit physique and good looks, Norton—an Australian—had a black belt in karate at the age of seventeen and has gone on to teach at over 500 martial arts school around the world. He got his start in films in the Chuck Norris movie The Octagon *(1980)* and has since been in a number of projects with Norris, including more than half a dozen appearances in the popular series Walker, Texas Ranger *(1993–2001)*. Norton has shot films all over the globe, and many of his films were made in the Philippines, (the post-nuke films Equalizer 2000, Future Hunters, and

Publicity shot from the Vietnam action movie *Crossfire*, featuring Richard Norton. Courtesy of Richard Norton.

Raiders of the Sun, *for example), and others were shot in Hong Kong (films like* Shanghai Express, The Magic Crystal, *and* City Hunter, *amongst others). His most prolific on-screen partnership has been with Cynthia Rothrock, with whom he made eight films, and he's also worked with Jackie Chan, Sammo Hung, and Don "The Dragon" Wilson a number of times. His unending commitment to the martial arts continues to be an inspiration to would-be action stars and up-and-coming martial artists the worldwide over, and he's beginning to make a transition to stunt work and stunt coordinating in major films like* The Amazing Spiderman (2012) *and* Mad Max: Fury Road (2015).

TITLES REVIEWED:
The Octagon (1980)
Force: Five (1981)
Forced Vengeance (1982)
Gymkata (1985)
My Lucky Stars 2: Twinkle, Twinkle Lucky Stars (1985)
Shanghai Express (a.k.a. *Millionaire's Express*) (1986)
The Magic Crystal (1986)
Future Hunters (1986)
Fight to Win (1987)
Equalizer 2000 (1987)
Revenge of the Kickfighter (a.k.a. *Return of the Kickfighter*) (1987)
Crossfire (a.k.a. **Not Another Mistake**) (1988)
Blood Street (1988)
Hyper Space (1989)
Kick Fighter (a.k.a. **The Fighter**) (1989)
China O'Brien (1990)
China O'Brien II (1990)
The Sword of Bushido (1990)
Lady Dragon (1992)
Raiders of the Sun (1992)
Ironheart (1992)
Rage and Honor (1992)
City Hunter (1993)
Rage and Honor II (1993)
Death Fight (a.k.a. *Rage*) (1994)
Cyber Tracker (1994)
Tough and Deadly (1995)
Under the Gun (1995)
Strategic Command (1997)
Mr. Nice Guy (1997)
Soul of the Avenger (a.k.a. *For Life or Death*) (1997)
Black Thunder (1998)
Nautilus (2000)
Walker, Texas Ranger (1993–2001)
The Rage Within (2001)
Redemption (2002)
Road House 2: Last Call (2006)
Underdog Kids (2015)

⬤

Toshishiro Obata
b. 1948. Japanese swordsman Toshishiro Obata made a string of appearances in martial arts action films throughout the 1990s, namely in high-profile movies like Teenage Mutant Ninja Turtles II: The Secret of the Ooze *(1991) and* Showdown in Little Tokyo *(1991), and various other films where the Japanese Yakuza were featured as*

villains. *Rarely cast as a hero, Obata left acting behind altogether in the mid-90s to pursue his passion, which was to focus on sword arts, and he became the founder of the International Shin kendō Federation.*

TITLES REVIEWED:
China O'Brien II (1990)
Sword of Bushido (1990)
Teenage Mutant Ninja Turtles II: The Secret of the Ooze (1991)
Showdown in Little Tokyo (1991)
Rage and Honor (1992)
Ulterior Motives (1993)
Walker, Texas Ranger (1993)
Rising Sun (1993)
Demolition Man (1993)
Red Sun Rising (1994)

Jorgo Ognenovski
b. 1954. A black belt in Shotokan karate at nineteen years of age, Jorgo Ognenovski helped popularize martial arts in his home country, the Republic of Macedonia. He placed third in Europe and fifth in the world, and it was enough leverage for him to star in his own film Warrior of Justice *(1995), which he not only starred in, but wrote and co-directed as well.*

TITLE REVIEWED:
Warrior of Justice (1995)

Gerald Okamura
b. 1940. Hawaiian-born Gerald Okamura is a perennial action and martial arts star with several dozen feature film credits to his name. A practitioner of a variety of martial arts including kendō, aikido, judo, and taekwondo, Okamura is also a fifth degree black belt in kung fu san soo. With his trademark bald head and traditional Chinese master mustache and beard, he's an instantly recognizable performer, and much of the time, he's featured in nameless roles where he's featured in grappling fights with the star of the film. His starring roles in Ninja Academy *(1989),* Time Burst: The Final Alliance *(1989), and* The Power Within *(1995) are all great reminders that he's not just a bit player, but a star with potential to burn.*

TITLES REVIEWED:
The Octagon (1980)
Ninja Busters (a.k.a. **Shadow Fight**) (1984)
Sword of Heaven (1985)
Big Trouble in Little China (1985)
Aftershock (1989)
Ninja Academy (1989)
Time Burst: The Final Alliance (1989)
9 1/2 Ninjas (1991)
The Master Demon (1991)
Showdown in Little Tokyo (1991)
Samurai Cop (1991)
Ring of Fire (1991)
Capital Punishment (1991)
Deadly Bet (1992)
Rapid Fire (1992)
American Streetfighter (1992)
Ring of Fire II: Blood and Steel (1993)
Shootfighter: Fight to the Death (1993)
Full Impact (1993)

Firepower (1993)
Cage II (1994)
The Power Within (1995)
Soul of the Avenger (a.k.a. *For Life or Death*) (1997)
Blade (1998)
The Circuit 2: The Final Punch (2002)
Redemption (2002)
SWAT: Warhead One (2004)
Vampire Assassin (2005)
G.I. Joe: The Rise of Cobra (2009)
Hellbinders (2009)

Shaquille O'Neal
b. 1972. One of the most famous NBA basketball players of the last several decades, Shaquille O'Neal (Shaq) made his first film Blue Chips *in 1994, and his next two films had some action in them, so he's considered an "action star" by the standards of this book.* Kazaam *(1996) featured Shaq as a tough genie who helps out a bullied kid, and* Steel *(1997) is probably his best film because it features him as a pseudo-superhero who fights crime. Shaq's movies weren't hits, so he stuck to basketball (and also recorded a flop of a rap album), and only time will tell if he ever tries to make a go of action movies again someday.*

TITLES REVIEWED:
Kazaam (1996)
Steel (1997)

Han Soo Ong
Working his way up through small, supporting roles where he was cast as a fighter opposite the featured star of the film, Malaysian star Han Soo Ong finally got his chance to shine in the action picture Last to Surrender *(1999), opposite Roddy Piper. After his one shot as the star, Ong quit the business altogether and became a fitness instructor at a gym in Bangkok, Thailand.*

TITLES REVIEWED:
Kickboxer (1989)
The King of the Kickboxers (1990)
Bloodsport 2 (1996)
The Quest (1996)
Tiger Claws II (1996)
Last to Surrender (1999)

Victor Ortiz
b. 1987. Mexican American Victor Ortiz is a welterweight (formerly a light welterweight) boxer with twenty-nine (so far) wins out of thirty-six professional fights. He was handpicked to be a part of the new lineup for Sylvester Stallone's The Expendables 3 *(2014) alongside fellow fighter Ronda Rousey. Ortiz is just getting out of the gate as far as becoming an action star, and even though his role in* The Expendables 3 *was mostly relegated to the sidelines, his potential for success is intriguing and only time will tell if he can make it in the movie world.*

TITLE REVIEWED:
The Expendables 3 (2014)

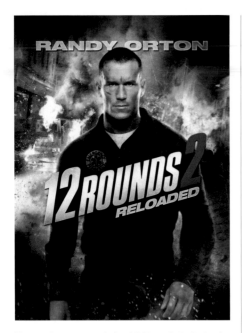

Press release artwork for *12 Rounds 2*. Author's collection.

Randy Orton

b. 1980. A third-generation pro wrestler and former Marine, 6 foot 5 Randy Orton is currently a WWE superstar, with just two (so far) starring films under his belt. WWE Studios started Orton off with a small role in the superlative coming-of-age drama That's What I Am (2011), and then came his vehicle film 12 Rounds 2: Reloaded (2013), which was basically a rehash of the first film starring John Cena. Orton is a diamond in the rough, and with the proper guidance, he could very well have the career that someone like Dolph Lundgren has had.

TITLE REVIEWED:
12 Rounds 2: Reloaded (2013)
The Condemned 2: Desert Prey (2015)

P

Grant Page

b. 1939. "Ozploitation" star Grant Page is a stuntman whose films The Man From Hong Kong (a.k.a. Dragon Files, 1975), Death Cheaters (1976), and Stunt Rock (1980) featured him engaging in insanely dangerous stunts, most of which would kill any normal man. But Grant Page is not a normal man, which is why director Brian-Trenchard Smith cast him in all three of these films and made him the star of the latter two. He has an undeniable action star quality and had a willingness to do nearly any feat that was required of him in these films, and those moments are immortalized on celluloid forever. It's a shame he didn't star in more movies.

TITLES REVIEWED:
The Man From Hong Kong (a.k.a. Dragon Files) (1975)
Deathcheaters (1976)
Stunt Rock (1980)
Mr. Nice Guy (1997)

Ara Paiaya

b. 1977. A British martial artist, stuntman, fight coordinator, and action star, Ara Paiaya (also known as "Bradley" Paiaya) has directed and starred in a handful of low-budget movies where he is the central lead. He also directed and appears in the upcoming Gary Daniels-headlining film Skin Traffik.

TITLES REVIEWED:
Dubbed and Dangerous trilogy (2001, 2003, 2004)
Death List (2006)
Maximum Impact (2008)
Skin Traffik (2015)

Ho-Sung Pak

b. 1968. Korean-born Ho-Sung Pak is a wushu champion who was inducted into the Black Belt Hall of Fame in 1991, before he started making films. His first big break in a movie was in The Legend of Drunken Master (1994), starring Jackie Chan, and he began making solo-starring vehicle films with Book of Swords (2007) and Fist of the Warrior (2007). To supplement his action star status, he has worked on major motion pictures as a stuntman and fight coordinator.

TITLES REVIEWED:
The Legend of Drunken Master (1994)
Epoch of Lotus (2000)
18 Fingers of Death! (2006)
Book of Swords (2007)
Fist of the Warrior (2007)
Game of Death (2010)

Ray Park

b. 1974. A gymnast and wushu champion, Scottish-born Ray Park gained worldwide notoriety when he was cast as the devilish Darth Maul in the blockbuster Star Wars Episode 1: The Phantom Menace (1999), which launched his career to a whole new level. He became an in-demand stunt performer and a featured actor in films that didn't always require him to say lines (G.I. Joe: The Rise of Cobra, 2009, G.I. Joe: Retaliation, 2013), but when he was given the chance to act as well as perform martial arts action in movies like Jinn (2014), he was able to show finally that he has a great screen presence as well as the ability to fight on screen without using a stunt double. The sky is the limit for Ray Park, who could very easily carry an entire movie all on his own.

TITLES REVIEWED:
Mortal Kombat: Annihilation (1997)
Star Wars Episode 1: The Phantom Menace (1999)
G.I. Joe: The Rise of Cobra (2009)
Hellbinders (2009)
The King of Fighters (2010)
G.I. Joe: Retaliation (2013)
Jinn (2014)

Ed Parker

b. 1931. d. 1990. The founder of kenpo karate, Ed Parker might be best known for teaching Jeff Speakman kenpo and for helping to choreograph some of the amazing fights in The Perfect Weapon (1991), but Parker also dabbled in front of the camera as a martial artist/actor. He starred in the seldom-seen Kill the Golden Goose (1979), and his role in the film is worthy of attention.

TITLE REVIEWED:
Kill the Golden Goose (1979)

David and Peter Paul

b. 1957. The ubiquitous "barbarian brothers" David and Peter Paul were a novelty in the 1980s when they had smallish roles in the Mr. T movie D.C. Cab (1983), and followed that up with a string of comedic action films that showcased their insanely huge muscles, infantile humor, and abilities as rap singers. After their stint with The Cannon Group's sword and sorcery spectacular The Barbarians (1987), they segued into the minor hit movies Think Big (1989), Double Trouble (1992), and Twin Sitters (1994). Never appearing in projects apart from one another, the barbarian twins hit the Hollywood bodybuilding scene and left their mark like no other pair of twin siblings did before or since. They exited the acting world behind and joined the "where are they now?" club, but after tracking them down for an interview, David Paul engaged in a discourse with us that revealed how dissatisfied he became with Hollywood and what executives and producers had made him and his brother out to be. Many years after moving on with their lives, the twins embarked on a new project called Faith Street Corner Tavern (2013), an art house film that documented Peter's real-life spiritual journey, and the movie was fascinating in its sincerity and willingness to be entirely honest and open about who these two brothers are today. It made it resoundingly apparent that the barbarian brothers aren't the same guys they were perceived to be decades ago. Unfortunately, they shied away at the last minute at a formal interview.

TITLES REVIEWED:
D.C. Cab (1983)
The Road Raiders (1989)
Think Big (1989)
Double Trouble (1992)
Twin Sitters (1994)

Video release poster for *Double Trouble*. Author's collection.

J. J. Perry

b. 1967. A former soldier in the US Army, an accomplished martial artist, stuntman, fight choreographer, and action star in his own right, J. J. Perry has been working steadily since the mid 1980s. Highly respected in the action and martial arts community, Perry has trained many movie stars to be in tip-top shape before the cameras roll, and if you look at his list of credits as a stuntman and fight coordinator, you'll be astonished at how much he's done. In front of the camera, he's just as accomplished, but ironically, not as recognized.

TITLES REVIEWED:
Full Impact (1993)
Bloodsport III (1996)
Mortal Kombat: Annihilation (1997)
Deadly Ransom (1998)
And Now You're Dead (a.k.a. *Enter the Eagles*) (1998)
Mortal Kombat: Conquest (1998–1999)
Martial Law (1998–2000)
Walker, Texas Ranger (2000)
The Rage Within (2001)
The Silent Force (2001)
Timecop 2: The Berlin Decision (2003)
Sunland Heat (2004)
Max Havoc: Curse of the Dragon (2004)
Today You Die (2005)
Adventures of Johnny Tao (2007)
The Shepherd (2008)
The Tournament (2009)
Haywire (2011)
Get the Gringo (2012)
Machete Kills (2013)

Kristie Phillips

b. 1972. The star of Albert Pyun's globetrotting spy action film Spitfire *(1995) was the 1986 US women's senior national all-around champion in women's gymnastics, Kristie Phillips. Though she missed her chance at the 1988 Olympics, she would later get her shot on the big screen opposite Tim Thomerson and Lance Henriksen in what would be her only appearance in an action movie. In the film she displays a hybridized martial art that incorporates her gymnastics, which will recall the unique martial arts in the Kurt Thomas (also a gymnast) film* Gymkata *(1985). Director Albert Pyun used the spunky Phillips to the best of her abilities in the film, and it's a shame that she didn't continue making more films.*

TITLE REVIEWED:
Spitfire (1995)

Roddy Piper

b. 1954. d. 2015 (See interview on page 455.)

TITLES REVIEWED:
Body Slam (1986)
Hell Comes to Frogtown (1988)
They Live (1988)
Tagteam (1991)
Back in Action (1993)
Immortal Combat (1994)
Tough and Deadly (1995)
No Contest (1995)
Jungleground (1995)
Marked Man (1996)

Terminal Rush (1996)
Sci-fighters (1996)
Dead Tides (1997)
The Bad Pack (1997)
First Encounter (1997)
Last to Surrender (1999)
Honor (2006)
Alien Opponent (2010)

Sue Price

b. 1965. The Schwarzenegger of female bodybuilders, Sue Price made her crossover from competitive bodybuilding (she competed in Ms. Olympia and various competitions including the National Physique Committee and the International Federation of Bodybuilding & Fitness throughout the 1990s) when she starred in a trio of direct-to-video sequels to Albert Pyun's Nemesis *(1992). She only made the three films (which were shot back to back), which is a shame because, while they featured her extensively on screen (and extensively nude in Part 4), she wasn't really given the best vehicle to make her mark on action cinema.*

TITLES REVIEWED:
Nemesis 2: Nebula (1995)
Nemesis 3: Time Lapse (1996)
Nemesis 4: Cry of Angles (1996)

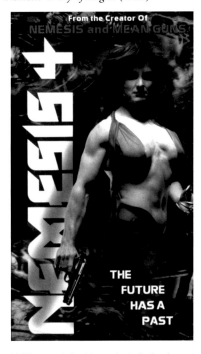

VHS artwork for *Nemesis 4*. Author's collection.

Paco Christian Prieto

b. 1955. Capoeirista Paco Christian Prieto (from Mexico) had his first gig in a movie opposite Jean-Claude Van Damme in Lionheart *(1990), and then he quickly graduated to lead villain in the Mark Dacascos film* Only the Strong *(1993). He only appeared in a handful of other action and martial arts films after that, but his abilities as a fighter on film make an impression.*

TITLES REVIEWED:
Lionheart (1990)
Only the Strong (1993)
Street Law (1995)
Champions (1998)

Abdel Qissi

b. 1960. Older brother to Michel Qissi, Abdel Qissi played the hulking beast who fights Jean-Claude Van Damme in the climax of Lionheart *(1990). Abdel, born in Morocco, was a boxer before becoming an actor, and he grew up in Brussels, where he was close friends with Van Damme, who would bring him on several of his projects much later, including* The Quest *(1996) and* The Order *(2001).*

TITLES REVIEWED:
Lionheart (1990)
The Quest (1996)
The Order (2001)

Michel Qissi

b. 1962. A childhood friend of Jean-Claude Van Damme, Michel Qissi played one of JC's greatest adversaries as Tong Po in Kickboxer *(1989). The Moroccan-born Qissi, who had been JC's trainer on Albert Pyun's* Cyborg *(1989) would go on to reprise his role in* Kickboxer 2: The Road Back *(1991) and direct two films of his own called* Eliminator Woman *(a.k.a.* Terminator Woman, *1993) with Karen Sheperd and Jerry Trimble, and* Extreme Force *(2001), starring Hector Echavarria. Michel will always be remembered for playing villains, but it might have been really interesting if he'd been given the chance to be the hero more often.*

TITLES REVIEWED:
Bloodsport (1988)
Kickboxer (1989)
Lionheart (1990)
Kickboxer 2: The Road Back (1991)
Bloodmatch (1991)
To the Death (1992)
Eliminator Woman (a.k.a. **Terminator Woman**) (1993)
Extreme Force (2001)
Los Bravos (2001)

Cyril Raffaelli

b. 1974. This French dynamo has done more stunt work behind the scenes in films than in front, but when he takes on centerpiece roles he's a powerhouse. Cyril Raffaelli was given his best gigs by writer/director/producer Luc Besson, who fashioned a film around his abilities as a martial artist. That film was District B13 (2004), which co-starred David Belle, the inventor of parkour, a fairly new pseudo martial art that incorporates running, jumping, climbing, and daredevil stunts. Raffaelli, an expert in Shotokan karate and wushu, also appeared as a silent henchman in Live Free or Die Hard *(2007).*

Crazed Inspector Richard (Tcheky Karyo) is on the hunt in *Kiss of the Dragon*. To his left is a henchman, played by Cyril Raffaelli. Author's collection.

TITLES REVIEWED:
Kiss of the Dragon (2001)
District B13 (2004)
District 13: Ultimatum (2009)
Stranded (2010)

Stacie Randall

Beautiful Stacie Randall had her shot at becoming a female action star at a time when Cynthia Rothrock and Kathy Long were still busy in the business of making action and martial arts movies. She was dating a producer, who managed to leverage her into the lead role of the straight-to-video actioner Excessive Force II: Force on Force *(1995), the unrelated sequel to the excellent Thomas Ian Griffith vehicle. She displayed an intensity usually not found in female action stars of her era, and her skills as a martial artist were questionable, but looked good on camera. Her next film was Jim Wynorski's action picture* The Assault *(1996), which wasn't a bad follow-up for her, but from then on she floundered as an action star and faded into obscurity soon thereafter.*

TITLES REVIEWED:
Excessive Force II: Force on Force (1995)
The Assault (1996)
First Encounter (1997)
Ticker (2001)

Ernie Reyes Jr.

b. 1972. A child action star who grew up to become a professional kickboxer with an undefeated record, Ernie Reyes Jr. came on the scene in 1985 with a small, but memorable role in The Last Dragon, *and he continued with the short-lived TV series* Sidekicks *(1986–1987) and then starred in* Teenage Mutant Ninja Turtles II: The Secret of the Ooze *(1991). Taught martial arts by his father Ernie Reyes Sr., he holds a fourth degree black belt in taekwondo, and continues working in the movie business in various capacities until this very day. Incidentally, he co-starred with his father in the films* Surf Ninjas *(1993) and* The Ultimate Fight *(a.k.a.* The Process, *1998).*

TITLES REVIEWED:
The Last Dragon (1985)
Sidekicks (1986-1987)
Teenage Mutant Ninja Turtles II: The Secret of the Ooze (1991)
Surf Ninjas (1993)
Paper Dragons (1996)

The Ultimate Fight (a.k.a. *The Process*) (1998)
Rush Hour 2 (2001)
The Rundown (2003)
Ninja Apocalypse (2014)

Phillip Rhee is Tommy Lee in *Best of the Best*, a movie he wrote. Author's collection.

Phillip Rhee

b. 1960. (See interview on page 58.).

TITLES REVIEWED:
Furious (1984)
L.A. Streetfighters (a.k.a. *Ninja Turf*) (1985)
Silent Assassins (1988)
Best of the Best (1989)
Best of the Best II (1993)
Best of the Best 3: No Turning Back (1995)
Best of the Best 4: Without Warning (1998)
Underdog Kids (2015)

Simon Rhee

b. 1957. Older brother to Phillip Rhee, Simon had won multiple martial arts championships before embarking on a career in movies. In fact, it was Simon—not Phillip—who was gearing to become an action star, but as events would play out, Phillip became the more recognized star, while Simon became more of a behind-the-scenes stunt performer and fight choreographer. That said, Simon has a list of credits a mile long, and if you watch his very first film, Furious *(1984), you'll see that he had the potential to be every bit the star that his brother became. With a seventh degree black belt in taekwondo and a fourth degree black belt in hapkido, Simon is a renowned instructor in the martial arts, as well as a very busy stuntman and actor.*

TITLES REVIEWED:
Furious (1984)
Silent Assassins (1988)
Best of the Best (1989)
Showdown in Little Tokyo (1991)
Universal Soldier (1992)
Best of the Best II (1993)

Bad Blood (1994)
T.N.T. (1997)
Lethal Weapon 4 (1998)
Martial Law (1998)
Clementine (2004)
18 Fingers of Death! (2006)
Ballistica (2009)
Game of Death (2010)

Branscombe Richmond

b. 1955. Native American Branscombe Richmond is one of TV's and film's most recognizable stuntmen and action stars. Usually seen with a mullet in biker clothes (or variations of leather jackets), Richmond might be best known for playing the second lead in the hit television program Renegade *(1992–1997), opposite Lorenzo Lamas. In addition to acting, Richmond is also a prolific stuntman, having taken the brunt of punishment from the likes of James Bond, Steven Seagal, Arnold Schwarzenegger, and plenty of other action icons.*

TITLES REVIEWED:
Kill the Golden Goose (1979)
Commando (1985)
The A-Team (1985–1986)
Action Jackson (1988)
Hunter (1986, 1988)
Hero and the Terror (1988)
Cage (1989)
Hard to Kill (1990)
The Perfect Weapon (1991)
Showdown in Little Tokyo (1991)
Aces: Iron Eagle III (1992)
Death Ring (1992)
Raven (1992)
Nemesis (1992)
Renegade (1992–1997)
CIA II: Target Alexa (1993)
Walker, Texas Ranger (1998)
Journey 2: The Mysterious Island (2012)

J. D. Rifkin

b. 1970. A fifth degree dan martial artist who specializes in taekwondo, full-contact kickboxing, and aikido, J. D. Rifkin tried to make a go of it in action and martial arts movies, but his single starring vehicle The Ultimate Game *(2001) didn't receive much notice when it was released directly to video during the decline of such films. He had previously appeared in a few other "B" action films and has performed some stunts on a few others, but Rifkin's passion is in instructing the martial arts, which is what he's been doing ever since leaving films behind altogether.*

TITLES REVIEWED:
Virtual Combat (1995)
Best of the Best 4: Without Warning (1998)
The Ultimate Game (2001)

George Rivero

b. 1938. Mexican film star George Rivero (born Jorge Pous Ribe) has been in dozens of films over the years, and with his cut physique and action star persona in many of his films, he has a Charles Bronson-esque quality about him. When he was in his early fifties he starred in his best action film

VHS artwork for *Counterforce*. Author's collection.

Fist Fighter *(1989), which he was easily able to carry as the star, and if that film is any indication to his abilities as an action star, then we missed out on having him blossom into a late-in-life superstar in the way that Bronson was able to do once* Death Wish *(1974) made him a star in his fifties. Rivero has a list of credits a mile long, but we only viewed those that began with* Counterforce *(1987).*

TITLES REVIEWED:
Counterforce (1987)
Fist Fighter (1989)
Death Match (1994)
Warrior of Justice (1995)
Guns and Lipstick (1995)

Ted Jan Roberts

b. 1979. An anomaly in this book, Ted Jan Roberts (T. J. Roberts, as he was usually billed) was a child action star who got his start with PM Entertainment and stayed with that company until he reached adulthood. At fourteen, he starred in the martial arts action film Magic Kid *(1993), co-starring Don "The Dragon" Wilson, and he continued making teen-centric action films that usually had a hard edge. His film* A Dangerous Place *(1995) was geared for teens, but with an "R"-rating, the film may not have reached its intended audience. With only a handful of films, T. J. made a mark on the genre that was dominated by adults, but his martial arts abilities measured up to many of his older peers.*

TITLES REVIEWED:
Magic Kid (1993)
Magic Kid II (1994)
A Dangerous Place (1995)

The Power Within (1995)
Masked Rider (1995-1996)
Tiger Heart (1996)

Dar Robinson

b. 1947. d. 1986. Widely regarded as one of the great stuntmen and stunt innovators in Hollywood history, Dar Robinson made several appearances as an actor in a few films, while also contributing some of the most awesome stunts ever captured on film for a number of other motion pictures. A high fall specialist, his stunts can be seen in Sharkey's Machine *(1981) and* Highpoint *(1982). His roles in* Stick *(1985) and in* Cyclone *(1987) are just a taste of what he was capable of as an actor/action star. He was tragically killed in a motorcycle accident during the shoot of a film called* Million Dollar Mystery *(1987). Richard Donner dedicated* Lethal Weapon *(1987) to his memory.*

TITLES REVIEWED:
Stick (1985)
Cyclone (1987)

Dennis Rodman

b. 1961. An infamous celebrity figure who played for the NBA (1986–2000), Dennis Rodman gained steam as a standout personality in the 1990s for his garish temper on the court and freakish antics off the court. Hollywood came calling, and his first action film was opposite Jean-Claude Van Damme and Mickey Rourke in Double Team *(1997), and soon after that he got his one and only shot at his own stand-alone action film* Simon Sez *(1999), which bombed at the box office. While notable as a novelty, Rodman couldn't maintain a career in films no matter how unusual he tried to be.*

TITLES REVIEWED:
Double Team (1997)
Simon Sez (1999)
Cutaway (2000)

Ivan Rogers

b. 1954. d. 2010. African American Ivan Rogers carved his own path as an action star. Before becoming an actor, he was a kickboxer for a brief period and he assembled a karate/self-defense video that was released on VHS and made him enough cash to venture into films. He wrote, produced, and directed a handful of martial arts/action films, with titles like Crazed Cop *(a.k.a.* One Way Out, *1986),* Two Wrongs Make a Right *(1987), and* Ballbuster *(1989), and then as the VHS era faded, so too did Rogers, despite trying to stay in the game with a smattering of sub-par action films.*

TITLES REVIEWED:
Crazed Cop (a.k.a. *One Way Out*) (1986)
Two Wrongs Make a Right (1987)
Slow Burn (1989)
Ballbuster (1989)
Karate Commando: Jungle Wolf 3 (1993)
On Fire (a.k.a. *Forgive Me Father*) (2001)

Cynthia Rothrock

b. 1957. (See interview on page 98.)

TITLES REVIEWED:
Yes, Madam! (1985)
24 Hours to Midnight (1985)
Shanghai Express (a.k.a. *Millionaire's Express*) (1986)
The Magic Crystal (1986)
Above the Law (a.k.a. **Righting Wrongs**) (1986)
Fight to Win (1987)
No Retreat, No Surrender 2 (1987)
The Inspector Wears Skirts (a.k.a. *Top Squad*) (1988)
The Blonde Fury (a.k.a. **Female Reporter**) (1989)
City Cops (1989)
China O'Brien (1990)
China O'Brien 2 (1990)
Martial Law (1990)
Prince of the Sun (1990)
Fast Getaway (1991)
Tiger Claws (1991)
Angel of Fury (1992)
Martial Law II: Undercover (1992)
Lady Dragon (1992)
Rage and Honor (1992)
Honor and Glory (1993)
Rage and Honor II (1993)
Irresistible Force (1993)
Lady Dragon 2 (1993)
Undefeatable (1993)
Fast Getaway II (1994)
Guardian Angel (1994)
Tiger Claws II (1996)
Sworn to Justice (1996)
Deep Cover (a.k.a. *Check Mate*) (1997)
Night Vision (1997)
Tiger Claws III (2000)
Manhattan Chase (2000)
Redemption (2002)
Outside the Law (2002)
X-Treme Fighter (a.k.a. *Sci-Fighter*) (2004)
Mercenaries (2014)
White Tiger (2014)
The Martial Arts Kid (2015)

Mickey Rourke

b. 1952. Mickey Rourke's career is all over the place. In addition to acting, he became an amateur boxer when he was fairly young and fought in thirty bouts, winning twenty-seven of them. In 1991 he started boxing professionally and for the next four years he fought eight bouts and called it quits when his face had been beaten beyond recognition. With a newly sculpted physique and a new face, Rourke became somewhat of an action star, with big roles in action-oriented projects like Double Team *(1997), opposite Jean-Claude Van Damme, and the direct-to-video actioner* Point Blank *(1998), which featured him doing butterfly kicks and backflips. His movie career floundered until he landed the once-in-a-lifetime comeback role in* The Wrestler *(2008), which was tailor-made for him. It's difficult to pinpoint Rourke's trajectory as an "action star," so we've picked only a handful of his latter-era films that personify his abilities as a sports crossover action star.*

Ronda Rousey

b. 1987. A powerhouse in the MMA world, Ronda Rousey got her start as a world junior judo competitor in the Olympics, and she won several gold medals before embarking on an astonishingly stellar career in the UFC. With thirteen fights (so far) and twelve wins, she remained undefeated until a shocking loss to Holly Holm in November 2015. She was cast in a plum role in The Expendables 3 opposite Sylvester Stallone, who made sure that she had plenty of screen time to show what she can do. It was just a teaser of what she's capable of, and if given the chance to carry a movie on her own like, say, Gina Carano has done, then Rousey might very well become the next great female action star. With a slate of action films already lined up, it is apparent that Hollywood will capitalize on her extraordinary talents in the years ahead.

Jeanette Roxborough

b. 1975. Jeanette Roxborough is a Canadian stuntwoman-turned-action star with her one-hit-wonder Bare Knuckles (2010). She's also a third degree black belt in Shotokan karate. She continues to work as a stunt player, but the world could do with Bare Knuckles 2 anytime.

James Ryan

b. 1958. Strikingly handsome James Ryan came on the scene from South Africa with the low-budget hit Kill or be Killed (1976), which featured a cavalcade of kung fu martial arts mayhem, and several years later Ryan followed that up with the drive-in cult classic sequel Kill and Kill Again (1981). While he was never quite able to break the barrier to become a full-fledged action star in the US, Ryan continued making action and martial arts films, mostly set in and around his native country. He also made a memorable appearance as the villain to Mark Dacascos's hero in Kickboxer 5 (1995).

S

Catya Sassoon

b. 1968. d. 2002. In the heyday of direct-to-video action and martial arts movies, Catya Sassoon—the daughter of famous hair stylist Vidal Sassoon—was chosen by Roger Corman to be his in-house female action star. He signed her to a five-picture deal, and her first film was Bloodfist IV: Die Trying (1992), starring Don "The Dragon" Wilson. Her next film was the starring role in Angelfist (1993), and she would only do one more film for Corman before she would tragically die from a drug overdose. It is worth noting that she was never officially trained as a martial artist, but she was being groomed and trained in the martial arts during her few years as an action star.

Tony Schiena

b. 1976. South African world karate champion and up-and-coming action star Tony Schiena is the star of Tapout's Circle of Pain (2010) and Locked Down (2010), both of which he also contributed fight choreography to. In addition to these accomplishments, Schiena also trains law enforcement officers and soldiers around the world in defensive tactics. If he is to continue making action and martial arts films, he might become one of the few to really watch out for.

Bob Schott

b. 1949. Former world arm wrestling champion Bob Schott played the bruiser Thorg in the classic martial arts movie Gymkata (1985), but he's also made appearances in various other "B" action films throughout the '80s and '90s. Schott dropped off the acting radar in the early '90s, but he'll always be associated with his role from Gymkata.

Arnold Schwarzenegger

b. 1947. The man who would eventually win the Mr. Olympia bodybuilding competition seven times (1970–1975, 1980), become the biggest box-office draw in the world, and then become

Arnold Schwarzenegger made a cameo appearance as Trench in *The Expendables*. Author's collection.

the governor of California (2003–2011) was born in a little village in Austria, would have a thick, nearly impenetrable accent, and brandished a last name that sounded like a sneeze. Arnold Schwarzenegger is a living legend and a titan among men, but more importantly he is one of the greatest action stars of all time. By the point he'd become a history-making bodybuilder (and an inspiration to millions), he'd established himself as a winner in every facet of his life. With accolades, honors, and a one-track mind for success, Arnold would create his own destiny, become a shrewd businessman, a best-selling author, and a movie star of such quality that the world had never seen before. As his films became blockbusters with titles such as The Terminator (1984), Commando (1985), and Predator (1987), the era of the modern action star was given validity and worth. Bigger, brawnier, and better was the new Hollywood standard when Arnold and Sylvester Stallone became the two action heroes which all others would follow and try to emulate. When Arnold left action films behind to pursue politics, the arena of action stars suffered immeasurably, and when he eventually returned to films with titles like The Last Stand (2013), Escape Plan (2013), and Sabotage (2014), his fan base had all but deserted him. His future as an action star in his twilight years remains uncertain, but his slate of to-be-released films include more Terminator films and a possible return to his iconic sword and sorcery franchise Conan in 2016.

Collateral Damage (2002)
Terminator 3: Rise of the Machines (2003)
The Rundown (2003)
Around the World in 80 Days (2004)
The Expendables (2010)
Expendables 2 (2012)
The Last Stand (2013)
Escape Plan (2013)
Sabotage (2014)
The Expendables 3 (2014)
Maggie (2015)
Terminator Genisys (2015)

Kenn Scott

b. 1970. The man who would play Raphael in Teenage Mutant Ninja Turtles II: The Secret of the Ooze (1991) would get his shot in front of the camera as an action star two years later in the Imperial action film Showdown (1993), opposite Billy Blanks. Scott made a great impression as an action star, showcasing his talents in the martial arts, but he would struggle to find more leading roles in other action films. Much later, he would transition into directing, and his film Adventures of Johnny Tao (2007) starred up-and-coming martial arts action star Matt Mullins.

TITLES REVIEWED:

Teenage Mutant Ninja Turtles II: The Secret of the Ooze (1991)
Shootfighter: Fight to the Death (1993)
Showdown (1993)
Sworn to Justice (1996)

Steven Seagal

b. 1952. Upon his arrival in Hollywood as a verifiable action star, Steven Seagal had already lived an interesting life. He spent many years as a young man training in the martial arts, namely aikido, and achieved a seventh dan degree and became the first westerner to operate an aikido dojo in Japan. In addition to aikido, he holds black

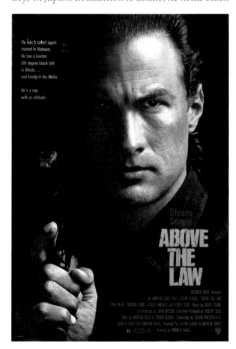

US theatrical poster for *Above the Law*. Author's collection.

belts in karate and judo, as well as being a kendō master. As his star rose with hit films like Above the Law (1988), Hard to Kill (1990), and Under Siege (1992), his persona and screen presence made an indelible impression on audiences because they'd never quite seen his like before. Tall, imposing, and soft spoken, Seagal tended to play ex-CIA agents, ex-Navy SEALs, ex-cops, or ex-assassins, and when in action he'd snap wrists, break necks, and slap guys around like nobody's business. By the time his star had fallen and he began making films that went directly to video, he'd put on extra pounds, stopped doing ADR work on many of his films, and lost ground as an action star. In his later years, he took on two notable television programs: the reality show Lawman (2009–2010), which featured him playing himself as a fully commissioned deputy in Jefferson Parish in Louisiana, and the action series True Justice (2010–2012), which was broken up into a dozen direct-to-video features. While he continues starring in action films and pursues other artistic ventures (he's a singer and recording artist, too), Seagal's fans continue to yearn for his big-screen comeback.

TITLES REVIEWED:

Above the Law (1988)
Hard to Kill (1990)
Marked for Death (1990)
Out for Justice (1991)
Under Siege (1992)
On Deadly Ground (1994)
Under Siege 2: Dark Territory (1995)
Executive Decision (1996)
The Glimmer Man (1996)
Fire Down Below (1997)
The Patriot (1998)
Exit Wounds (2001)
Ticker (2001)
Half Past Dead (2002)
The Foreigner (2003)
Out for a Kill (2003)
Belly of the Beast (2003)
Clementine (2004)
Out of Reach (2004)
Into the Sun (2005)
Submerged (2005)
Today You Die (2005)
Black Dawn (2005)
Mercenary for Justice (2006)
Shadow Man (2006)
Attack Force (2006)
Flight of Fury (2007)
Urban Justice (2007)
Pistol Whipped (2008)
Kill Switch (2008)
Against the Dark (2009)
Driven to Kill (2009)
The Keeper (2009)
A Dangerous Man (2009)
Machete (2010)
Born to Raise Hell (2010)
Deadly Crossing (a.k.a. *True Justice: Deadly Crossing*) (2010)
Dark Vengeance (a.k.a. *True Justice: Dark Vengeance*) (2010)
Street Wars (a.k.a. *True Justice: Street Wars*) (2010)
Lethal Justice (a.k.a. *True Justice: Lethal Justice*) (2010)
Death Riders (a.k.a. *True Justice: Death Riders*) (2011)

Urban Warfare (a.k.a. *True Justice: Urban Warfare*) (2011)
Soldier of Vengeance (a.k.a. *True Justice: Soldier of Vengeance*) (2012)
Blood Alley (a.k.a. *True Justice: Blood Alley*) (2012)
Violence of Action (a.k.a. *True Justice: Violence of Action*) (2012)
Angel of Death (a.k.a. *True Justice: Angel of Death*) (2012)
Dead Drop (a.k.a. *True Justice: Dead Drop*) (2012)
Deadly Assassin (a.k.a. *True Justice: Deadly Assassin*) (2012)
Maximum Conviction (2012)
Force of Execution (2013)
A Good Man (2013)
Gutshot Straight (2014)
Absolution (2015)

Darren Shahlavi

b. 1972. d. 2015. (See interview on page 232.)

TITLES REVIEWED:

Bloodmoon (1997)
Hostile Environment (a.k.a. *Watership Warrior*) (2000)
G.O.D. (2001)
Cold Vengeance (a.k.a. *Sometimes a Hero*) (2003)
Alien Agent (2007)
Ip Man 2 (2010)
Born to Raise Hell (2010)
Mortal Kombat: Legacy (2011)
Tactical Force (2011)
Metal Hurlant Chronicles: King's Crown (2012)
Dead Drop (a.k.a. *True Justice: Dead Drop*) (2012)
Violence of Action (a.k.a. *True Justice: Violence of Action*) (2012)
The Package (2012)
The Marine 3: Homefront (2013)
Metal Hurlant Chronicles: The Endomorphe (2014)
Pound of Flesh (2015)

Ken Shamrock

b. 1964. Ken Shamrock's statistics and records in professional wrestling and UFC fighting could take pages to write, but what matters is that he's been a mainstay in WWF (now WWE), in professional mixed martial arts, and in various other professional camps where competition is front and center. Unfortunately, his two forays into feature films haven't been as impressive as his life as a fighter and competitor. His latest film, The Bunker (2014), cast him as a deranged soldier in Vietnam who hunts down other American platoons and brutally murders them off one by one. It was a disgrace of a film, but if the right filmmaker sees his potential and is able to translate it properly in a film, then Shamrock will be given the chance to shine.

TITLES REVIEWED:

Champions (1998)
The Bunker (2014)

Karen Sheperd

b. 1961. (See interview on page 170.)

TITLES REVIEWED:
The Shinobi Ninja (1981)
Above the Law (a.k.a. **Righting Wrongs**) (1986)
Blood Chase (1989)
Mission of Justice (1992)
Eliminator Woman (a.k.a. **Terminator Woman**) (1993)
Operation Golden Phoenix (1994)
Soul of the Avenger (a.k.a. *For Life or Death*) (1997)
Boogie Boy (1998)

Robin Shou

b. 1960. A Hong Kong action star before making the crossover to the US to star in Mortal Kombat (1995), Robin Shou is a gold medalist for the national wushu team, and a four-time traditional forms champion. After his breakout role in Mortal Kombat, he made a handful of other action and martial arts movies, but late in his career he got another chance to shine in Mortal Enemies (2011), which gave him his first starring role in more than a decade.

TITLES REVIEWED:
Death Cage (1988)
Honor and Glory (1993)
Mortal Kombat (1995)
Beverly Hills Ninja (1997)
Mortal Kombat: Annihilation (1997)
18 Fingers of Death! (2006)
DOA: Dead or Alive (2006)
Death Race (2008)
Street Fighter: The Legend of Chun-Li (2009)
Mortal Enemies (2011)

Anderson Silva

b. 1975. This Brazilian mixed martial arts fighter holds several records in UFC. In addition to having sixteen consecutive wins, Anderson Silva also won ten title defenses. As he's begun the transition into films, his roles have been very minor in direct-to-video releases, but with a lauded professional fighting record and a "former UFC middleweight champion" label, it's quite possible that Silva will continue with acting and try his hand at starring in an action film all on his own.

TITLES REVIEWED:
Never Surrender (2009)
Tapped Out (2014)

O. J. Simpson

b. 1947. Born Orenthal James Simpson, O. J. had a great career as a running back for the Buffalo Bills (1969–1977) and the San Francisco 49ers (1978–1979) before he became a busy actor. He starred or co-starred in a slew of high-profile motion pictures and TV movies, but only a few of those are valid for the study of "action stars," so we've only included those few. O. J. became worldwide news when his wife Nicole Brown and her friend Ronald Goldman were found murdered, and he was notoriously put on trial and acquitted of the crime. Years later, he was convicted for robbery and kidnapping in Las Vegas, for which he is currently serving up to thirty-three years at the Lovelock Correctional Center in Nevada. Tarnished reputation aside, he was a great athlete and a notable actor/action star.

TITLES REVIEWED:
Firepower (1979)
Detour to Terror (1980)
Cocaine and Blue Eyes (1983)

Bubba Smith

b. 1945. d. 2011. Best known to movie fans as playing Hightower in all seven Police Academy movies, Bubba Smith (all 6 foot 7 inches of him) was an NFL defensive end/tackle for the Baltimore Colts (1967–1971), the Oakland Raiders (1973–1974), and the Houston Oilers (1975–1976) before crossing over into the movie business. He made numerous appearances on various television shows before landing a great role in the smash hit comedy Police Academy (1984), which spawned tons of sequels and spin-offs. We only reviewed the first entry in that series, but Smith (real name: Charles Aaron Smith) also co-starred in a handful of other action-oriented films that featured him in physical roles.

TITLES REVIEWED:
Police Academy (1984)
The Wild Pair (1987)
My Samurai (1992)
Down 'n Dirty (2001)

Simon Phoenix (Wesley Snipes) is a criminal mastermind in *Demolition Man*. Author's collection.

Wesley Snipes

b. 1962. (See interview on page 352.)

TITLES REVIEWED:
Passenger 57 (1992)
Boiling Point (1993)
Rising Sun (1993)
Demolition Man (1993)
Drop Zone (1994)
Money Train (1995)
Murder at 1600 (1997)
Futuresport (1998)
U.S. Marshals (1998)
Blade (1998)
The Art of War (2000)
Blade II (2002)
Undisputed (2002)
Unstoppable (2004)
Blade: Trinity (2004)

7 Seconds (2005)
The Marksman (2005)
Chaos (2005)
The Detonator (2006)
Hard Luck (2006)
The Contractor (2007)
The Art of War II: Betrayal (2008)
Game of Death (2010)
Gallowwalkers (2012)
The Expendables 3 (2014)
The Player (2015)

Joe Son

b. 1970. South Korean Joe Son appeared in a handful of "B" action and martial arts films starring the likes of Dolph Lundgren, Don "The Dragon" Wilson, Bolo Yeung, and Lorenzo Lamas. In all five of those films, he played a villain, and by the time he'd made Shootfighter II (1996), he had worked his way up to playing the lead villain. He had been a professional wrestler, kickboxer, and MMA fighter in the UFC, but he lost all five of his professional fights. In 2008, he was arrested on a charge of vandalism, and he was required to provide a DNA sample. When it was revealed that he had tortured and raped a nineteen-year-old woman in 1990, Son was charged with those crimes and convicted of torture. While serving his prison sentence, he murdered his cellmate in 2011. The last movie he made was Austin Powers: International Man of Mystery in 1997.

TITLES REVIEWED:
Joshua Tree (a.k.a. *Army of One*) (1993)
Shootfighter: Fight to the Death (1993)
Bloodfist V: Human Target (1994)
Bad Blood (1994)
Shootfighter II (1996)

Krzysztof Soszynski

b. 1977. Polish-born Krzysztof Soszynski is a UFC fighter and a TKO heavyweight champion who recently crossed over into films with a growing list of titles to his credit. After fighting Kevin James in the comedy Here Comes the Boom (2012), he appeared in the Dolph Lundgren/Steve Austin movie The Package (2012), and then in the MMA fight film Tapped Out (2014). Stay tuned for more films with Soszynski.

TITLES REVIEWED:
The Package (2012)
Tapped Out (2014)

Jeff Speakman

b. 1959. (See interview on page 348.)

TITLES REVIEWED:
Lionheart (1990)
The Perfect Weapon (1991)
Street Knight (1993)
Deadly Outbreak (1995)
The Expert (1995)
Timelock (1996)
Plato's Run (1997)
Escape From Atlantis (1997)
Scorpio One (1998)
Land of the Free (1998)
Memorial Day (1998)
Running Red (1999)

Cobretti (Sylvester Stallone) protects model Ingrid (Brigitte Nielsen) against the Night Slasher and his cult in *Cobra*. Author's collection.

Sylvester Stallone

b. 1946. It's interesting that of all the action stars covered in this book who've "crossed over" into films from the wide world of sports, martial arts, and various avenues where physicality played a major role in their careers, the same thing cannot be said of Sylvester Stallone, who—in essence—is the ultimate action star. When he sold his script for Rocky (1976), he made sure that no one else would star in it but himself, and it became the role that defined him. As the subsequent sequels were made, his physique became more sculpted, and his persona became bigger than the movies themselves. Sylvester Stallone was the first post-Vietnam era action star, and as his stardom solidified, so too did his boundless abilities to top himself in his brawn, bravado, and on-screen glory. When he took on the role of John Rambo in First Blood (1982), moviegoers eagerly identified with his portrayal of an ex-Green Beret 'Nam vet, who came home only to find prejudice and trouble with the locals, and as the Rambo sequels came, so too did the era of the action star boom and blossom. Throughout the last thirty-five years, Stallone's career has risen to the highest heights and fallen to lowest lows, but without fail, he's managed to prove that he's also the king of making a comeback. In his early sixties, he brought back his best characters in the stellar sequels Rocky Balboa (2006) and Rambo (2008), and all of a sudden a whole new generation was able to see and recognize just how essential Stallone is to the world of action entertainment on film. With his late-era Expendables films (2010–2014), Stallone has brought a host of the biggest and best action stars together to celebrate the genre and remind the world why action stars matter so much.

Cue Jerry Goldsmith's music: John Rambo (Sylvester Stallone) is about to be on the loose in *First Blood*. Author's collection.

TITLES REVIEWED:

Rocky (1976)
Paradise Alley (1978)
Rocky II (1979)
Nighthawks (1981)
Victory (1981)
Rocky III (1982)
First Blood (1982)
Rambo: First Blood Part II (1985)
Rocky IV (1985)
Cobra (1986)
Over the Top (1987)
Rambo III (1988)
Lock Up (1989)
Tango and Cash (1989)
Rocky V (1990)
Oscar (1991)
Stop! Or My Mom Will Shoot (1992)
Cliffhanger (1993)
Demolition Man (1993)
The Specialist (1994)
Judge Dredd (1995)
Assassins (1995)
Daylight (1996)
Cop Land (1997)
Get Carter (2000)
Driven (2001)
Eye See You (a.k.a. *Detox*) (2002)
Avenging Angelo (2002)
Spy Kids 3D: Game Over (2003)
Rocky Balboa (2006)
Rambo (2008)
The Expendables (2010)
The Expendables 2 (2012)
Bullet to the Head (2013)
Escape Plan (2013)
Grudge Match (2013)
The Expendables 3 (2014)
Creed (2015)

Jason Statham

b. 1967. One of the last and best action stars to rise in the post-millennial era, Jason Statham was a diver on the British National Diving Team before embarking on a very successful career in movies. His breakout role as an action star was in the Hong Kong/European hybrid The Transporter (2002), which spawned two sequels (so far) and remains his most recognizable role to date. With an immediately recognizable visage (bald, ruggedly handsome, with perpetual stubble on his face) and a distinctive British accent, Statham has been an incredibly busy man in the action world, sometimes making two to four films a year. Though not a martial artist in real life, his physicality and persona lend themselves quite nicely to the films he stars in.

Jason Statham stars as Arthur Bishop, The Mechanic. Author's collection.

TITLES REVIEWED:

Turn it Up (2000)
The One (2001)
Mean Machine (2001)
The Transporter (2002)
Italian Job (2003)
Cellular (2004)
Transporter 2 (2005)
Revolver (2005)
Chaos (2005)
Crank (2006)
War (2007)
The Bank Job (2008)
Death Race (2008)
Transporter 3 (2008)
Crank: High Voltage (2009)
The Expendables (2010)
The Mechanic (2011)
Blitz (2011)
Killer Elite (2011)
Safe (2012)
The Expendables 2 (2012)
Parker (2013)
Fast and Furious 6 (2013)
Redemption (a.k.a. **Hummingbird**) (2013)
Homefront (2013)
The Expendables 3 (2014)
Fast and Furious 7 (a.k.a. *Furious 7*) (2015)
Spy (2015)
Wild Card (**2015**)

Edward John Stazak

b. 1958. When Edward John Stazak was discovered while working as a bouncer for nightclubs in the early 1980s, he had already obtained a black belt in Karate Budokan International, a Japanese martial art founded in 1966. Stazak only starred in two films, both of which were for director Brian Trenchard-Smith: Day of the Panther (1988) and its sequel Fists of Blood (a.k.a. Strike of the Panther, 1988). Both were hits on video in Australia where they were produced, and Stazak quietly withdrew from making films altogether shortly thereafter.

TITLES REVIEWED:

Day of the Panther (1988)
Fists of Blood (a.k.a. *Strike of the Panther*) (1988)

Nils Allen Stewart

b. 1961. A longtime student of grappling and Hawaiian kenpo karate, Nils Allen Stewart is a formidable stuntman and a dependable tough guy. He's appeared in dozens of action and martial arts films, and he's immediately recognizable for his Mongolian-looking bald head, mustache, and long, braided ponytail. If you need a bad-looking dude to get his face smashed through plate glass, he's the guy to call.

TITLES REVIEWED:

Renegade (1993)
Firepower (1993)
On Deadly Ground (1994)
Double Dragon (1994)
Ballistic (1995)
The Stranger (1995)
Fist of the North Star (1995)
Warrior of Justice (1995)

Cyber Tracker 2 (1995)
Raw Target (1995)
Mercenary (1996)
Bloodsport 2 (1996)
The Quest (1996)
Mars (1997)
Soul of the Avenger (a.k.a. *For Life or Death*)
  (1997)
Deadly Shooter (a.k.a. *The Shooter*) (1997)
Martial Law (1998)
Whatever It Takes (1998)
Gangland (2001)
Undisputed (2002)
18 Fingers of Death! (2006)
The Last Sentinel (2007)
Fist of the Warrior (2007)

T. J. Storm

b. 1972. T. J. Storm (born Juan Ricardo Ojeda) has been active for several decades in the action and martial arts genres, starring in The Ultimate Game *(2001) and* Black Cobra *(2012), which both showcase his skills, among others, in taekwondo, ninjutsu, jiu jitsu, and Northern Shaolin kung fu. He's an underused talent, and it would take the right filmmaker to tap into his potential as a front-and-center action star.*

TITLES REVIEWED:
  Breathing Fire (1991)
  Dragon Fury (1995)
  Enter the Blood Ring (1995)
  Martial Law (2000)
  Epoch of Lotus (2000)
  The Ultimate Game (2001)
  Kamen Rider: Dragon Knight (2009)
  Black Cobra (2012)
  The Martial Arts Kid (2015)

Georges "Rush" St. Pierre

b. 1981. George "Rush" St. Pierre is a Canadian mixed martial artist who currently has the most wins in UFC history. His first foray into movies was in the Hector Echavarria film Never Surrender *(2009), and he worked with Echavarria again on the film* Death Warrior *(2009). St. Pierre's most recent appearance in a movie was in the blockbuster* Captain America: The Winter Soldier *(2014) where he vividly fought Cap in a memorable scene. St. Pierre's next appearance will be in the remake of* Kickboxer.

TITLES REVIEWED:
  Never Surrender (2009)
  Death Warrior (2009)

Mark Strange

b. 1973. A Euro-British full-contact champion and expert in Chin Woo, Mark Strange has been working quietly in various Hong Kong action and martial arts films for over a decade and has only in the last few years been able to land lead roles where the film is focused on him as the star. After appearing in several films with Jackie Chan, Strange starred in the direct-to-video action film Displaced *(2006), which has never gotten the attention it deserved.*

TITLES REVIEWED:
  Vampire Effect (a.k.a. *The Twins Effect*)
    (2003)
  The Medallion (a.k.a. *Highbinders*) (2003)
  Displaced (2006)
  Underground (2007)

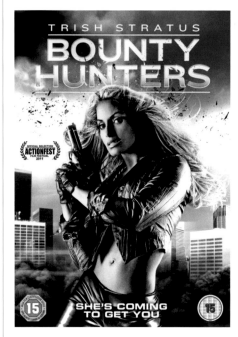

DVD artwork for *Bounty Hunters*. Author's collection.

Trish Stratus

b. 1975. With only one starring film to her credit, Trish Stratus was a WWE wrestler who became a very successful fitness model. Her film Bounty Hunters *(2011) was a direct-to-video action film that gave her a chance to show what she was capable of as an athlete, but unfortunately she wasn't able to leverage that film to make more features.*

TITLE REVIEWED:
  Bounty Hunters (2011)

T

Cary-Hiroyuki Tagawa

b. 1950. One of the most instantly recognizable screen villains in martial arts and action moviedom, Cary-Hiroyuki Tagawa has played more bad guys than he probably cares to admit, but the truth is that he does it very well. Usually cast as a Yakuza drug lord, henchman, or warlord, Tagawa has faced off against many of the great action heroes covered in this book including Jeff Speakman, Gary Daniels, Michael Dudikoff, Dolph Lundgren, Brandon Lee, Lorenzo Lamas, Chuck Norris, Olivier Gruner, Hulk Hogan, Sasha Mitchell, and Wesley Snipes. His scowl is practically enough to knock a man down. Whenever you know that he's going to be in the movie you're about to watch, you can rest a little easier because he's a consummate pro. Incidentally, he's developed his own martial art called chun shin, which is entirely without a physical fighting concept.

TITLES REVIEWED:
  Kickboxer 2: The Road Back (1991)
  The Perfect Weapon (1991)
  Showdown in Little Tokyo (1991)
  Nemesis (1992)
  Raven (1992)
  Renegade (1993)
  Rising Sun (1993)
  Thunder in Paradise (1995)
  Mortal Kombat (1995)
  Solider Boyz (1995)
  White Tiger (1996)
  Bridge of Dragons (1999)
  Walker, Texas Ranger (2000)
  The Art of War (2000)
  Tekken (2010)
  Black Cobra (2012)
  Mortal Kombat: Legacy II (2013)
  Ninja Apocalypse (2014)
  Tekken 2: Kazuya's Revenge (2014)

Taimak

b. 1964. (See interview on page 260.)

TITLES REVIEWED:
  The Last Dragon (1985)
  No More Dirty Deals (1993)
  Book of Swords (2007)

Oleg Taktarov

b. 1967. A two-time Russian Sambo champion, a Russian national judo champion and a jiu jitsu champion, and then later a UFC champ, Oleg Taktarov is a 100 percent badass, and with an impressive list of appearances in major motion pictures, he's also doing a fairly good job in the acting world. When looking over his films, though, only a handful of them really apply to what we're covering in this book, so we only included a few of his films here for review. This guy needs to star in his own action movie pronto.

TITLES REVIEWED:
  15 Minutes (2001)
  Red Serpent (2003)
  Supreme Champion (2010)
  Predators (2010)

Professor Toru Tanaka

b. 1930. d. 2000. Born Charles Kalani, Professor Toru Tanaka served in the US armed forces and later became a professional wrestler, with matches for WWF (now WWE). He embarked on a career in

Professor Toru Tanaka in *The Perfect Weapon*. Author's collection.

martial arts and action films, appearing in a whole bunch of movies starring everyone from Chuck Norris to Arnold Schwarzenegger. He usually played strong, silent henchman, and he always went down for the count at the hands of the hero.

TITLES REVIEWED:
An Eye For an Eye (1981)
Revenge of the Ninja (1983)
Missing in Action 2: The Beginning (1985)
Catch the Heat (1987)
The Running Man (1987)
Hyper Space (1989)
Martial Law (1990)
The Perfect Weapon (1991)
Last Action Hero (1993)
Hard Justice (1995)

Joe Taslim

b. 1981. Indonesian martial artist and gold medal winner for judo competitions, Joe Taslim came on the scene in Gareth Edwards' The Raid: Redemption (2011). His role as a SWAT team member beside the lead star Iko Uwais actually gave you a little hope that things would turn out all right for more than a few characters, but as the film would have it, Taslim's character died a grisly death. All that aside, his ability to carry a movie on his own extended to the film Dead Mine (2012). Skilled in silat, wushu, judo, and taekwondo, Taslim has everything he needs to make it on his own.

TITLES REVIEWED:
The Raid: Redemption (2011)
Dead Mine (2012)
Fast and Furious 6 (2013)

Kurt Thomas

b. 1956. The cult film Gymkata (1985), directed by Robert Clouse, is unlike any other martial arts action film ever made. Gold medal–winning gymnast Kurt Thomas, who was never able to compete in the Olympics due to a presidential boycott of the Moscow Olympics in 1980, starred as a gymnast who competes in a "most dangerous game" competition in Eastern Europe. The film's climax features the slight, but athletic Thomas straddling a pommel horse, using his "Thomas flairs" to fight off a pitchfork-wielding mob of crazies who are chomping at the bit to tear him to shreds. It's an indelible moment in the history of action and martial arts films simply because there's never been anything like it before or since. It truly is a pity that Thomas didn't make more films because it would have been interesting where he would have taken his "gymkata" skills in another feature. He currently runs a gymnastics school in Texas.

TITLE REVIEWED:
Gymkata (1985)

Mike Thomas

b. 1953. Former NFL player Mike Thomas's only movie credit is the blaxploitation action film Brotherhood of Death (1976), opposite several other NFL athletes. Thomas played six seasons with the NFL—with the Washington Redskins from 1975 to 1978 and with the San Diego Chargers from 1979 to 1980.

TITLE REVIEWED:
Brotherhood of Death (1976)

Brian Thompson plays the dreaded Night Slasher in the action thriller Cobra. Author's collection.

Brian Thompson

b. 1959. One of the great bad guys in action and martial arts movies, Brian Thompson was technically the very first person The Terminator killed on screen in The Terminator (1984), and he then co-starred in the Sylvester Stallone blockbuster Cobra (1986) as the vicious Night Slasher. Soon after, Thompson (who has a great face and voice) was starring in his own vehicle films like Commando Squad (1987) and Hired to Kill (1990), while still playing bad guys in films starring the likes of Jean-Claude Van Damme, Cynthia Rothrock, and the cast of Mortal Kombat: Annihilation (1997). Recently, he wrote, directed, and starred in the parody action movie The Extendables (2014). Thompson also holds a black belt in hapkido for good measure.

TITLES REVIEWED:
The Terminator (1984)
Cobra (1986)
Catch the Heat (1987)
Commando Squad (1987)
Lionheart (1990)
Hired to Kill (1990)
Renegade (1992)
Rage and Honor (1992)
Walker, Texas Ranger (1993)
Perfect Target (1997)
Mortal Kombat: Annihilation (1997)
The Order (2001)
Fist of the Warrior (2007)
The Extendables (2014)

Sven-Ole Thorsen

b. 1944. This bodybuilding champion and stuntman from Denmark holds multiple records in power lifting and a "Strongest Man in the World" record from 1981. He's been in nearly every movie starring Arnold Schwarzenegger, his good friend and colleague, but he's been in some films of his own where he (usually) plays a side or central villain, most notably in the films Abraxas, Guardian of the Universe (1990), opposite Jesse Ventura, and in No Exit (1995), opposite Jeff Wincott. Sven-Ole Thorsen is one of those guys who has appeared in dozens of action and martial arts films over the last thirty years, and you think to yourself, "There's that guy again!"

TITLES REVIEWED:
Raw Deal (1986)
Predator (1987)
The Running Man (1987)
Red Heat (1988)
Twins (1988)
Abraxas, Guardian of the Universe (1990)
Nowhere to Run (1993)
Last Action Hero (1993)
Hard Target (1993)
Cyborg 2 (1993)
On Deadly Ground (1994)
No Exit (1995)
Eraser (1996)
The Bad Pack (1997)
Best of the Best 4: Without Warning (1998)
Extreme Honor (2001)
Timecop 2: The Berlin Decision (2003)

Matthew Tompkins

b. 1967. Stuntman, martial artist, fight choreographer, and action star Matthew Tompkins cut his teeth while working with Chuck Norris on a number of episodes of Walker, Texas Ranger, and he was able to leverage his experience from that show into his starring vehicle film Killing Down (2006), which was a great calling card for him. Unfortunately, the film went largely unseen, but since then he's worked alongside Dolph Lundgren and Danny Trejo on several projects.

TITLES REVIEWED:
Walker, Texas Ranger (1993–1998)
Logan's War: Bound by Honor (1998)
Killing Down (2006)
Missionary Man (2007)
Bad Ass 2: Bad Asses (2014)

Danny Trejo

b. 1940. A criminal and drug addict before he was a teenager, Danny Trejo was serving hard time at San Quentin when he became a boxer. As a lightweight and welterweight fighter, he won several titles. When he was paroled, he stumbled into acting by showing up on the set of Runaway Train (1985) to support a fellow con who needed advice. When he was noticed on the set, Trejo was offered a job as an extra, and while there, he ended up training Eric Roberts, the star of the film, in boxing. Trejo hasn't stopped acting since. For twenty years, he appeared in smaller roles opposite dozens of stars, ranging from Charles Bronson to Steven Seagal, and when his second cousin Robert Rodriguez offered him the chance to star in his own film Machete (2010), which was spun off a faux trailer ahead of Grindhouse (2007), Trejo got a late-in-life star-making role that has propelled his career into hyper-drive ever since. At any given time, he has nearly a dozen films well into production, though not all of the films are "action" films per se, and not many of them feature Trejo in a lead role. Trejo reprised his Machete roll in Machete Kills (2013), but his best starring role to date was as a disgruntled Vietnam vet who cleans up his neighborhood in the theatrically released Bad Ass (2012). Trejo has certainly put in the mileage towards being an action star, and he deserves every success and accolade for turning his life around and making something of it.

Jerry Trimble

b. 1961. (See interview on page 272.)

Tonny Tulleners

The Marlboro Man of the martial arts, Tonny Tulleners was the 1965 middleweight international karate champion who beat Chuck Norris three (!) times in competition with his unbeatable Shotokan karate skills. As Norris took off with a successful movie career, Tulleners was left on the sidelines (probably by his own choice), but he starred in a single motion picture called Scorpion *(1987) from Crown International. Whether you like* Scorpion *or not (I do), it gave Tulleners his one and only chance to show that he was a badass on screen, and it's one of the great sorrows that he didn't make at least one more movie.*

Benny "The Jet" Urquidez

b. 1952. Benny Urquidez holds an outstanding kickboxing record: 200 wins and no losses. He won six world titles and successfully defended them over the course of twenty-four years. He is the longest reigning champion in professional sports history, which is incredible when you think about it. He began co-starring in feature films with the martial arts ensemble piece Force: Five *in 1981, and from there he worked with Jackie Chan (twice) and many other legends in the genre. He transitioned into stunt work and fight choreography on major motion pictures and just recently wrote his autobiography* The Jet, *which is a great account of his life. It's strange that he wasn't featured on camera more often as a front-and-center action guy, but it's great that we have what we've been given.*

Iko Uwais

b. 1983. When Welsh filmmaker Gareth Evans discovered Iko Uwais (real name: Uwais Qorny), Uwais had just become the Indonesian champion of silat in 2005. Evans gave Uwais the starring role in his low-budget action film Merantau *(2009), a gritty coming-of-age film that was equally a showcase for the star as it was for the filmmaker. Their next collaboration was the worldwide hit* The Raid: Redemption *(2011), which catapulted both of them into the public consciousness and was a great showcase for the silat martial art. Uwais has only made a few films thus far, but if his career path keeps going the way it's going, he'll be one of the best guys working in the business.*

Ron Van Clief

b. 1943. A Vietnam veteran, former police officer, and a tenth degree black belt in karate, Ron Van Clief was one of the first African American martial arts action stars, starring in a handful of "grindhouse" kung fu movies. His movies The Black Dragon *(1974) and* Way of the Black Dragon *(1979) are perfect examples of gonzo '70s kung fu movies, but what made them watchable is Van Clief himself. When he retired from acting*

Benny "The Jet" Urquidez in Burbank, California. Photo by david j. moore.

and competitive fighting, he trained secret service agents. Sounds like a badass to me.

Rob Van Dam

b. 1970. A professional wrestler who got the jump on doing movies quite a few years before many of his peers, Rob Van Dam made a good impression as a full-fledged action star in his late-in-his-career film Wrong Side of Town *(2010). His experience as both a wrestler and actor/performer in several films made with Hong Kong stunt teams paid off in that film, and it ended up being the best picture of his career. Since then, he's continued with wrestling, but the door remains open for him to give movies another go.*

Jean-Claude Van Damme

b. 1960. When Jean-Claude Van Damme (real last name: Van Varenberg) came on the scene with No Retreat, No Surrender *(1986), the film didn't have quite enough exposure to make much of a difference for him career-wise, but his next film* Bloodsport *(1988) became a phenomenon and not only launched him as the world's next big action star but virtually created the kickboxing genre and stimulated growth in the martial arts film market. There has always been something really unique about Van Damme ("The Muscles From Brussels") . . . his good looks and muscular frame almost contradict his grace and abilities to do 360 degree flying spin kicks and the splits, two trademark moves that were a requisite in each of his films for a long time. As he worked his way from* The Cannon Group, *which produced and distributed three of his early films (including* Bloodsport, Cyborg, *1989, and* Kickboxer, *1989) to the majors like Columbia and Universal, which both distributed his next block of films, Van Damme became one of the world's most popular martial arts action stars. After a string of box-office disappointments like*

Jean-Claude Van Damme in Newport Beach, California. Photo by david j. moore.

Double Team *(1997)* and Knock Off *(1998)*, he began making films that premiered on home video, and he spent a decade in direct-to-video limbo, where he was trying hard to stretch his acting chops while starring in low-budget films shot throughout Asia and Eastern Europe. At long last, he made an auspicious comeback with the semi-autobiographical action drama hybrid JCVD in 2008, but even then the film was off the mainstream grid. A supporting role as the villain in Expendables 2 *(2012)* ushered in a new era for Van Damme as a character actor where he was willing to play bad guys and play second fiddle to other actors and action stars. The truth is that he is an underrated actor and an underappreciated action star, who even with scandals and set backs, deserves to be praised for being an inspiration and role model for aspiring action stars all over the world.

TITLES REVIEWED:

No Retreat, No Surrender (1986)
Bloodsport (1988)
Black Eagle (1988)
Cyborg (1989)
Kickboxer (1989)
Lionheart (1990)
Death Warrant (1990)
Double Impact (1991)
Universal Soldier (1992)
Nowhere to Run (1993)
Hard Target (1993)
Timecop (1994)
Street Fighter (1994)
Sudden Death (1995)
The Quest (1996)
Maximum Risk (1996)
Double Team (1997)
Knock Off (1998)
Legionnaire (1998)
Universal Soldier: The Return (1999)
Desert Heat (1999)
The Order (2001)
Replicant (2001)
Derailed (2002)
In Hell (2003)
Wake of Death (2004)
Second in Command (2006)
The Hard Corps (2006)
Until Death (2007)
The Shepherd (2008)
JCVD (2008)
Universal Soldier: Regeneration (2009)

Assassination Games (2011)
Dragon Eyes (2012)
The Expendables 2 (2012)
Universal Soldier: Day of Reckoning (2012)
6 Bullets (2012)
Alien Uprising (a.k.a. *UFO*) (2012)
Welcome to the Jungle (2013)
Enemies Closer (2013)
Swelter (2014)
Jiang Bing Man (2015)
Pound of Flesh (2015)

Corinne Van Ryck De Groot

b. 1969. A professional boxer with eleven wins out of thirteen fights, Corinne Van Ryck De Groot was also the female winner of the Joel Silver reality-based TV series Next Action Star *(2004)*, which gave her the opportunity to co-star in Silver's Bet Your Life *(2004)*, a made-for-TV action movie. De Groot has also performed stunts on a number of television and movie projects, but to date Bet Your Life *is the only time she was able to show that she could be the world's "next action star."*

TITLE REVIEWED:

Bet Your Life (2004)

Dominique Vandenberg

b. 1969. A French Foreign Legionnaire for five years before becoming a professional Muay Thai kickboxer in Burma, Belgian-born Dominique Vandenberg broke into films as a stuntman and then became an action star, using his skills as a martial artist in front of the camera. Director Jesse Johnson gave him the lead role in Pit Fighter *(2005)*, and then continued to cast him in several other features. Vandenberg could easily carry more films if more directors would take notice.

TITLES REVIEWED:

Pit Fighter (2005)
Alien Agent (2007)

Jesse Ventura

b. 1951. Former wrestler Jesse Ventura (real name: James George Janos) joined the ripped-out cast of Predator *(1987)* and made a good enough impression that he was able to star or co-star in a handful of successive action films like The Running Man *(1987)*, Thunderground *(1989)*, and more notoriously Abraxis, Guardian of the Universe *(1990)*. After his era of making action films, Ventura became the mayor of Brooklyn Park, Minnesota, and then later he became the governor of Minnesota. He also wrote his autobiography, which was called I Ain't Got Time to Bleed.

TITLES REVIEWED:

Predator (1987)
The Running Man (1987)
Thunderground (1989)
Hunter (1985, 1990)
Abraxis, Guardian of the Universe (1990)
Tagteam (1991)
Renegade (1992)

Keith Vitali

b. 1955. (See interview on page 500.)

TITLES REVIEWED:

Revenge of the Ninja (1983)
Wheels on Meals (1984)
No Retreat, No Surrender 3: Blood Brothers (1990)
American Kickboxer 1 (1991)
Superfights (1995)
Bloodmoon (1997)

W

Bob Wall

b. 1939. With a plethora of black belts in various martial arts, Bob (Robert) Wall is most recognized for co-starring in several of Bruce Lee's most popular films, including Enter the Dragon *(1973)*. He would go on to make small appearances in a handful of other martial arts-oriented movies with Lee and Chuck Norris, but his film career more or less began and ended with Enter the Dragon. Wall holds ninth degree black belts (under Chuck Norris) in American Tang Soo Do and Chun Kuk Do, and black belts in Brazilian jiu jitsu, judo, Okinawan Okinawa-te, and Shōrin-ryū, amongst others. He was also the 1970 US professional karate champ.

TITLES REVIEWED:

The Way of the Dragon (1972)
Enter the Dragon (1973)
Black Belt Jones (1973)
The Game of Death (1978)
Firewalker (1986)
Hero and the Terror (1988)
Walker, Texas Ranger (1994-2001)
X-Treme Fighter (a.k.a. *Sci-Fighter*) (2004)
Blood and Bone (2009)

Bill Wallace

b. 1949. Bill "Superfoot" Wallace was a karate point fighter and competed against Chuck Norris and Joe Lewis, among others. When his karate career ended, he became a professional kickboxer and went on to win twenty-three straight fights, and he retired undefeated. Since that time, he co-starred in a string of martial arts action movies, starting with A Force of One *(1979)*, starring Norris. Wallace tended to play villains, and it suited him well.

TITLES REVIEWED:

A Force of One (1979)
Killpoint (1984)
Sword of Heaven (1985)
L.A. Streetfighters (a.k.a. **Ninja Turf**) (1985)
The Protector (1985)
Fight to Win (1987)
Silent Assassins (1988)
American Hunter (1989)
Los Bravos (2001)

Jimmy Wang Yu

b. 1944. A verifiable kung fu action star from the Hong Kong/Shaw brothers era with great titles like The One-Armed Swordsman *(1967)* and Master of the Flying Guillotine *(1976)* to his credit, (Jimmy) Wang Yu would make his

Wang Yu plays Inspector Fang Sing Leng in Brian Trenchard-Smith's *The Man From Hong Kong*. Author's collection.

English language crossover with the "Ozploitation" masterpiece The Man From Hong Kong (a.k.a. Dragon Files, 1975), directed by Brian-Trenchard Smith. He would go on to make only one more English language action film called Queen's Ransom (a.k.a. International Assassin, 1976), and then he would return to Hong Kong, making strictly Asian martial arts films, co-starring the likes of Jackie Chan and Donnie Yen. Incidentally, Yu was also a Hong Kong swimming champion.

TITLES REVIEWED:
The Man From Hong Kong (a.k.a. *Dragon Files*) (1975)
Queen's Ransom (a.k.a. *International Assassin*) (1976)
Shanghai Express (a.k.a. *Millionaire's Express*) (1986)
The Prisoner (a.k.a. *Island of Fire*) (1990)
Dragon (2011)

Gary Wasniewski

b. 1954. The very fact that men like Gary Wasniewski go after their dreams and try their hands at starring in action and martial arts films validates this entire book. Wasniewski is a practitioner of karate, taekwondo, and kickboxing, and he travels the world instructing students of martial arts. His first film Thunderkick (2008) was a collaboration between him and the great Leo Fong, and while the film basically remains in obscurity and has never been properly distributed, that didn't deter Wasniewski from making more movies. He's three movies deep into the genre, and here's hoping he makes at least three more.

TITLES REVIEWED:
Thunderkick (2008)
The Kill Factor (2010)
Extreme Counterstrike (2012)

Carl Weathers

b. 1948. (See interview on page 13.)

TITLES REVIEWED:
Bucktown (1975)
Rocky (1976)
Rocky II (1979)
Death Hunt (1981)
Rocky III (1982)
Rocky IV (1985)
Fortune Dane (1986)

Predator (1987)
Action Jackson (1988)
Dangerous Passion (1990)
Hurricane Smith (1992)
Street Justice (1991-1993)
Shadow Warriors (a.k.a. *Assault on Devil's Island*) (1997)
Shadow Warriors 2 (a.k.a. *Assault on Death Mountain*) (1999)

Victor Webster

b. 1973. An undefeated heavyweight kickboxer and taekwondo champion, Victor Webster has only just begun his path to action star status. He co-starred in a very physical role in the Steven Seagal film A Good Man (2013), and if that film is any indication, then hopefully we'll see much more of Webster in the future. At 6 foot 3, this Canadian actor has the chops to sustain a career in martial arts films if audiences will discover him.

TITLE REVIEWED:
A Good Man (2013)

Michael Jai White

b. 1967. (See Interview on page 423.)

TITLES REVIEWED:
Renegade (1993)
Full Contact (1993)
Ring of Fire III: Lion Strike (1994)
Ballistic (1995)
Spawn (1997)
Universal Soldier: The Return (1999)
Exit Wounds (2001)
Silverhawk (2004)
Undisputed II: Last Man Standing (2006)
Blood and Bone (2009)
Black Dynamite (2009)
Mortal Kombat: Legacy (2011)
Never Back Down 2: The Beatdown (2011)
Tactical Force (2011)
Black Dynamite: The TV Series (2011-2012)
Metal Hurlant Chronicles: King's Crown (2012)
Metal Hurlant Chronicles: The Endomorphe (2014)
Android Cop (2014)
Falcon Rising (a.k.a. *Favela*) (2014)
Chain of Command (2015)
Skin Trade (2015)

Paul "The Big Show" Wight

b. 1972. At 7 feet and 500 pounds, Paul "The Big Show" Wight is a mountain of a man, and one of the most popular professional wrestlers around. He's been involved with WCW and WWE/WWF for several decades now, but he's only just recently begun his foray into motion pictures. His direct-to-video movie Knucklehead (2010) was enough of a success to warrant his second crossover into film, the hardboiled action movie Vendetta (2015) from the Soska twins.

TITLE REVIEWED:
Jingle All the Way (1996)
Knucklehead (2010)
Vendetta (2015)

Fred Williamson

b. 1938. (See interview on page 335.)

TITLES REVIEWED:
Hammer (1972)
The Legend of Nigger Charley (1972)
Black Caesar (1973)
The Soul of Nigger Charley (1973)
That Man Bolt (1973)
Hell Up in Harlem (1973)
Tough Guys (1974)
Black Eye (1974)
Three the Hard Way (1974)
Boss Nigger (1975)
Bucktown (1975)
Take a Hard Ride (1975)
Mean Johnny Barrows (1976)
Adios, Amigo (1976)
No Way Back (1976)
Death Journey (1976)
Joshua (1976)
One Down, Two to Go (1976)
Mr. Mean (1977)
The Inglorious Bastards (1978)
Blind Rage (1978)
1990: Bronx Warriors (1982)
Vigilante (1983)
The New Barbarians (a.k.a. *Warriors of the Wasteland*) (1983)
The Last Fight (1983)
The Big Score (1983)
New Gladiators (1984)
Deadly Impact (1984)
White Fire (1984)
Foxtrap (1986)
The Messenger (1986)
Hell's Heroes (a.k.a. *Inglorious Bastards 2: Hell's Heroes*) (1987)
Black Cobra (1987)
Delta Force Commando (1988)
Deadly Intent (1988)
Black Cobra 2 (1989)
Soda Cracker (a.k.a. *The Kill Reflex*) (1989)
Black Cobra 3: The Manila Connection (1990)
Delta Force Commando II: Priority Red One (1990)
Detective Malone (a.k.a. *Black Cobra 4*) (1991)
Steele's Law (1991)
Three Days to a Kill (1992)
South Beach (1993)
Renegade (1994)
Silent Hunter (1995)
Original Gangstas (1996)
Night Vision (1997)
Blackjack (1998)
Whatever It Takes (1998)
Active Stealth (1999)
Down 'n Dirty (2001)
The Rage Within (2001)
On the Edge (2002)
Transformed (2005)
Crooked (2006)
Atomic EDEN (2015)

Don "The Dragon" Wilson
b. 1954. (See interview on page 387.)

TITLES REVIEWED:
Bloodfist (1989)
Bloodfist II (1990)
Ring of Fire (1991)
Future Kick (1991)
Bloodfist III: Forced to Fight (1992)
Blackbelt (1992)
Bloodfist IV: Die Trying (1992)
Out For Blood (1992)
Magic Kid (1993)
Ring of Fire II: Blood and Steel (1993)
Bloodfist V: Human Target (1994)
Cyber Tracker (1994)
Red Sun Rising (1994)
Ring of Fire III: Lion Strike (1994)
Bloodfist VI: Ground Zero (1995)
Virtual Combat (1995)
Bloodfist VII: Manhunt (1995)
Cyber Tracker 2 (1995)
The Power Within (1995)
Bloodfist VIII: Hard Way Out (1996)
Night Hunter (1996)
Terminal Rush (1996)
Operation Cobra (a.k.a. Inferno) (1997)
Whatever It Takes (1998)
The Capitol Conspiracy (a.k.a. The Prophet)
   (1999)
Moving Target (2000)
Walker, Texas Ranger (2001)
Redemption (2002)
X-Treme Fighter (a.k.a. Sci-Fighter) (2004)
Crooked (2006)
18 Fingers of Death! (2006)
The Last Sentinel (2007)
Liberator (2012)
White Tiger (2014)
The Martial Arts Kid (2015)
Underdog Kids (2015)

Jeff Wincott
b. 1956. An actor who segued into martial arts action films in the '90s, Jeff Wincott (brother of character actor Michael Wincott) became a stalwart mainstay in the direct-to-video action market during the era when these films were very popular and welcome with home video consumers. With a black belt in taekwondo, and an intense, astute presence on screen, his best moments in action usually involve him wielding kenpo sticks against a legion of bad guys. As the millennium approached, Wincott dropped out of action films for the most part and pursued acting in earnest.

TITLES REVIEWED:
Martial Law II: Undercover (1991)
Deadly Bet (1992)
Mission of Justice (1992)
Martial Outlaw (1993)
Open Fire (1994)
The Killing Man (a.k.a. The Killing Machine)
   (1994)
No Exit (1995)
Street Law (1995)
Last Man Standing (1995)
The Donor (1995)
When the Bullet Hits the Bone (1996)

Jeff Wincott plays Detective Sean Thompson in
Martial Law 2. Author's collection.

Future Fear (1997)
Universal Soldier II: Brothers in Arms (1998)
Universal Soldier III: Unfinished Business
   (1999)
Outside the Law (2002)

Carter Wong
b. 1947. Best known for his supporting role as one of the three storms in John Carpenter's Big Trouble in Little China (1985), Carter Wong (real name Chia-Ta Huang) has made a few international crossover films, beginning with Way of the Black Dragon (1979), starring Ron Van Clief. The greater and more essential portion of Wong's work can be found in a trove of Hong Kong martial arts movies made throughout the 1970s.

TITLES REVIEWED:
Way of the Black Dragon (1979)
Big Trouble in Little China (1985)
Hardcase and Fist (1989)
Tiger Claws III (2000)

Russell Wong
b. 1963. When Russell Wong landed the lead role in the groundbreaking martial arts action TV series Vanishing Son (1994–1995), he presented himself as a viable Asian action star, where there were so few at the time in the West. Vanishing Son was a great project for him, and he was able to show not only that he could be a romantic

leading actor, but that he could also showcase his skills in taekwondo, shoji ryu karate, and Fu-Jow Pai kung fu. Unfortunately, the show was canceled after a single season, and since then he has only appeared in a few other martial arts-centric projects, namely Romeo Must Die (2000) and The Mummy: Tomb of the Dragon Emperor (2008), both opposite Jet Li.

TITLES REVIEWED:
Vanishing Son (1994–1995)
Romeo Must Die (2000)
The Mummy: Tomb of the Dragon Emperor
   (2008)

Michael Worth
b. 1965. (See interview on page 467.)

TITLES REVIEWED:
Final Impact (1992)
Street Crimes (1992)
To Be the Best (1993)
Acapulco H.E.A.T. (1993-1996)
Fists of Iron (1995)
U.S. Seals II (2001)
Ghost Rock (2003)
Dual (2008)
War Wolves (2009)

Tadashi Yamashita
b. 1942. A tenth degree black belt in Kobayashi karate and Matayoshi Kobudo, Tadashi Yamashita might be best known as the "Black Star Ninja" from American Ninja (1985), but he's starred, co-starred, or appeared in a number of other martial arts action movies, and he's got the ability to leave a lasting impression. He's almost always cast as a badass ninja or mentor to a badass ninja, so next to Sho Kosugi, Yamashita is probably cinema's next-best casting choice to play a silent, hooded assassin.

TITLES REVIEWED:
Soul of Bruce Lee (1977)
The Octagon (1980)
The Shinobi Ninja (1981)
Gymkata (1985)
American Ninja (1985)
Sword of Heaven (1985)
Capital Punishment (1991)
American Ninja 5 (1993)
Rising Sun (1993)
Cage II (1994)
Carjack (1996)
Pocket Ninjas (1997)
Transformed (2005)

JeeJa Yanin
b. 1984. A rising star from Bangkok, Thailand, JeeJa Yanin (Vismitananda) is on the verge of a major breakthrough with her career. With awesome films like Chocolate (2008), Raging Phoenix (2009), and This Girl is Badass!! (2011) already under her belt, she was able to pair up with Tony Jaa for The Protector 2 (2013), a star who had already had his international breakthrough with Ong-bak (2003). With a third degree black belt in taekwondo and several guiding forces

working with her—including director Prachya Pinkaew who helped Jaa achieve stardom—we highly recommend you keep your eye on this one because her day is coming.

DVD artwork for *The Girl From the Naked Eye*. Author's collection.

Jason Yee

b. 1970. A Sanshou kickboxing champion who broke into the movie business by writing, directing, and starring in low-budget movies built around his abilities as a martial artist, Jason Yee has been working hard to put his own stamp on the action and martial arts genres since his first film Dark Assassin *(2007), co-starring Cung Le. The two films he's written, directed, and starred in have been very earnest attempts to reach fans of the genre, and if he continues on this path, he may yet find the fan base he deserves.*

Donnie Yen

b. 1963. As one of Asia's top action stars, Donnie Yen has been a part of the industry for over thirty years. He began his career as a stuntman before landing his first starring role in Drunken Tai Chi *(1984). Yen began practicing the martial arts at an early age and it was always a major part of his family life. His mother is a tai chi grandmaster and taught the discipline in Boston, Massachusetts. As a young teenager, he began to study various styles including boxing, wushu, Jeet Kune Do, hapkido, Wing Chun, and many others. He has turned his martial arts knowledge into a prolific film career with starring roles in films like* Kill Zone *(2005),* Flashpoint *(2007),and* Ip Man *(2008), and supporting roles in his first North American crossover films such as* Highlander: Endgame *(2000) and* Blade II *(2002). He's also known for being one of the best action choreographers in the business, mixing contemporary MMA fighting with traditional martial arts action. At middle age, Yen shows no signs of slowing down and has carved out his legacy in modern action cinema.*

Michelle Yeoh as Inspector Yang in *Supercop*. Author's collection.

Michelle Yeoh

b. 1962. Never officially trained as a martial artist, Michelle Yeoh—a Malaysian beauty queen who excelled at dancing—became one of Hong Kong's biggest female action stars with a string of knockout successes that included Yes, Madam! *(1985),* Royal Warriors *(a.k.a.* In the Line of Duty, *1986), and* Magnificent Warriors *(a.k.a.* Dynamite Fighters, *1987). She crossed over into English-language films with the blockbuster* Tomorrow Never Dies *(1997), which at the time was the most successful James Bond movie in history. She occasionally makes a film during her semi-retirement, but she remains one of the greatest female action stars God ever made.*

Bolo Yeung

b. 1946. An impossibly strong, silent villain in most of his film appearances, Bolo Yeung is a ten-time Hong Kong bodybuilding Champion who shot to international notoriety when he co-starred in Enter the Dragon *(1973) with Bruce Lee and John Saxon. For the next decade he was in dozens of martial arts films, and when he played the villain in* Bloodsport *(1988), he became a cult action star, and the ensuing decade gave him dozens more roles that typecast him as a vicious bad guy. Before he retired altogether, he was able to play a handful of "good guy" roles, but action and martial arts movie fans will always associate him as a henchman or movie brute.*

Ron Yuan

b. 1973. A multi-faceted martial artist, actor, fight choreographer, and stuntman, Ron Yuan has been heavily immersed in the martial arts and action communities for at least twenty-five years. He's appeared in dozens of low-budget action films and has been working on major Hollywood productions in various capacities. Guys like Yuan are why action and martial arts movies have great fight scenes in them: He works diligently alongside the stars and directors of many of the films he appears in to ensure maximum potential on screen. Case in point: Angel of Death *(2009) wouldn't be half as good as it is if his work with star Zoe Bell wasn't as inventive and hardcore on screen as it might've been under another fight coordinator's hands.*

The Art of War (2000)
Cradle 2 the Grave (2003)
Timecop 2: The Berlin Decision (2003)
Adventures of Johnny Tao (2007)
Fast & Furious (2009)
Blood and Bone (2009)
The Girl From the Naked Eye (2012)

Rick Yune

b. 1971. The fact that Rick Yune is not a bigger action star is a mystery. After co-starring in a few big hits like The Fast and the Furious *(2001) and* Die Another Day *(2002), Yune got his shot at carrying a martial arts action movie all on his own. That film was Jesse Johnson's* The Fifth Commandment *(2008), a surprisingly effective direct-to-video effort that Yune carried quite convincingly. With a background in taekwondo and a brief stint as a competitive Golden Gloves boxer, Yune certainly has the abilities to be a "next big action star," but his path has winded around and he's co-starred in various high-profile action films instead.*

TITLES REVIEWED:
The Fast and the Furious (2001)
Die Another Day (2002)
The Fifth Commandment (2008)
Ninja Assassin (2009)
The Man With the Iron Fists (2012)

z

William Zabka

b. 1965. When thinking of the bully from The Karate Kid *(1984), the words "action" and "star" don't usually come to mind, but the truth of the matter is that since that film, William Zabka has gone on to become a black belt in Tang Soo Do and has starred or appeared in a fair share of action and martial arts films, namely the two* Shootfighter *(1993, 1996) movies, co-starring Bolo Yeung. You've got to hand it to Zabka, who was hated throughout the 1980s for beating up poor Ralph Macchio . . . he transcended the bully role and became an action hero.*

TITLES REVIEWED:
The Karate Kid (1984)
Shootfighter: Fight to the Death (1993)
The Power Within (1995)
Shootfighter II (1996)
High Voltage (1997)
Interceptor Force (1999)
Ablaze (2000)
Gale Force (2002)

Frank Zagarino

b. 1959. For the guy who was Dolph Lundgren's workout partner in the exercise tape Maximum Potential *(1986), Frank Zagarino certainly went a long way as an action star in his own right. Tall, ripped out, and similar in complexion to the Swedish Dolph Lundgren, Zagarino (who was born in Los Angeles) got his action star legs going in Italian-made exploitation films like* Striker *(1988) and* Ten Zan: Ultimate Mission *(1988), and segued into action films made in South Africa like* The Revenger *(1989) and* Project Shadowchaser *(1992), all while retaining his own brand of what we call "Zagarate" martial arts. With one action film after another, he had one of the most prolific careers as an action star throughout the 1990s and beyond, and when he retired from films in 2008 he left a massive catalogue of "B" action films shot all throughout the world.*

TITLES REVIEWED:
Striker (1988)
Ten Zan: Ultimate Mission (1988)
Trained to Kill (1989)
The Revenger (1989)
Cy Warrior: Special Combat Unit (1989)
Project Eliminator (1991)
Project Shadowchaser (1992)
Blood Warriors (1993)
Project Shadowchaser II: Night Siege (1994)
Terminal Impact (a.k.a. *Cyborg Cop III*) (1995)
Never Say Die (1994)
Project Shadowchaser 3 (a.k.a. *Project Shadowchaser 3000*) (1995)
Without Mercy (1996)
Warhead (1996)
Alien Chaser (a.k.a. *Orion's Key*) (1996)
Operation Delta Force (1997)
The Apocalypse (1997)
Convict 762 (1997)
Airboss (1997)
Airboss II: Preemptive Strike (1998)
Deadly Reckoning (a.k.a. **The Company Man**) (1998)
Armstrong (1998)
The Protector (1998)
Fallout (1999)
No Tomorrow (1999)
The Guardian (2000)
Strike Zone (2000)
Airboss III: The Payback (2000)
Airboss 4: The X Factor (a.k.a. *Eco Warrior*) (2000)
Shattered Lies (2002)
Lethal (2005)
Little Bear and the Master (2008)

Marko Zaror

b. 1978. (See interview on page 293.)

TITLES REVIEWED:
Into the Flames (2002)
Chinango (2005)
Kiltro (2006)
Mirageman (2007)
Mandrill (2009)
Undisputed III: Redemption (2010)
Mitos y Leyendas: La nueva alianza (2010)
Machete Kills (2013)
Redeemer (2015)

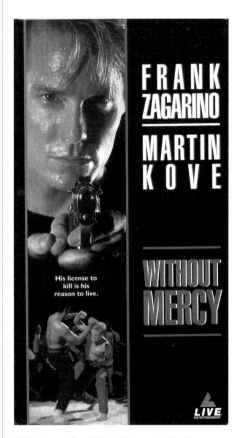

VHS artwork for *Without Mercy*. Author's collection.

A

Ablaze (2000)
Above the Law (a.k.a. Righting Wrongs) (1986)
Above the Law (1988)
Abraxas: Guardian of the Universe (1990)
Absolution (2015)
Acapulco H.E.A.T. (1993-1994, 1996)
The Accidental Spy (2001)
Aces: Iron Eagle III (1992)
Action Jackson (1988)
Active Stealth (1999)
Acts of Betrayal (1997)
Acts of Violence (2010)
Adios Amigos (1976)
Adventures of Johnny Tao (2007)
Aftershock (1989)
Against the Dark (2009)
Agent Provocateur (a.k.a. Agent Elite) (2012)
Agent Red (2000)
Airboss (1997)
Airboss II: Preemptive Strike (1998)
Airboss III: The Payback (2000)
Airboss 4: The X Factor (a.k.a. Eco Warrior) (2000)
Alien Agenda (2007)
Alienator (1990)
Alien Opponent (2011)
Alien Uprising (a.k.a. U.F.O.) (2012)
Ambushed (a.k.a. Hard Rush) (2013)
American Hunter (1989)
American Kickboxer (a.k.a. American Kickboxer 1) (1990)
American Kickboxer 2 (1993)
American Ninja (1985)
American Ninja 2: The Confrontation (1987)
American Ninja 3: Blood Hunt (1989)
American Ninja 4: Annihilation (1990)
American Ninja 5 (1992)
American Samurai (1992)
American Streetfighter (1992)
American Tigers (1996)
And Now You're Dead (a.k.a. Enter the Eagles) (1998)
Android Cop (2014)
Angelfist (1993)
Angel of Death (2007)
Angel of Death (a.k.a. True Justice: Angel of Death) (2012)
Angel of Fury (1992)
Angel Town (1990)
The Apocalypse (1997)
Arena of the Street Fighter (2012)
Armor of God (a.k.a. Operation Condor 2: The Armor of the Gods) (1986)
Armstrong (1998)
Around the World in 80 Days (2004)

Art of Submission (a.k.a. The Red Canvas) (2009)
The Art of War (2000)
The Art of War II: Betrayal (2008)
Assassination (1987)
Assassination Games (2011)
Assassins (1995)
Assassin's Code (2011)
The Assault (1997)
The A-Team (1983-1987)
The A-Team (2010)
Atomic EDEN (2015)
Attack Force (2006)
Automatic (1994)
Avenging Angelo (2002)
Avenging Force (1986)
Avenging Quartet (a.k.a. Avenging Angels) (1992)

B

Babylon A.D. (2008)
Back in Action (1994)
Back in Business (1997)
Bad Ass (2012)
Bad Ass 2: Bad Asses (2014)
Bad Asses on the Bayou (a.k.a. Bad Ass 3: Bad Asses on the Bayou (2015)
Bad Blood (1994)
Badges of Fury (2013)
The Bad Pack (1997)
Balance of Power (a.k.a. Hidden Dragon) (1996)
Ballbuster (1989)
Ballistic (1995)
Ballistica (2009)
Bangkok Revenge (2012)
The Bank Job (2008)
Bare Knuckles (2010)
The Base (1999)
Batman and Robin (1997)
Battle Creek Brawl (a.k.a. The Big Brawl) (1980)
Battle of the Damned (2013)
Beatdown (2010)
Behind Enemy Lines (1997)
Behind Enemy Lines: Colombia (2009)
The Bells of Innocence (2003)
Belly of the Beast (2003)
Bending the Rules (2012)
Beretta's Island (a.k.a. One Man Force) (1994)
Best of the Best (1989)
Best of the Best II (1992)
Best of the Best 3: No Turning Back (1995)
Best of the Best: Without Warning (1998)
Bet Your Life (2008)
Beverly Hills Ninja (1997)
Beyond Fear (1993)

Beyond Forgiveness (a.k.a. Blood of the Innocent) (1995)
Beyond the Ring (2008)
The Big Boss (a.k.a. Fists of Fury) (1971)
The Big Score (1983)
Big Trouble in Little China (1986)
Billa 2 (2012)
Billy Jack (1971)
Billy Jack Goes to Washington (1977)
Black Belt (1992)
Black Belt II: Fatal Force (a.k.a. Spyder) (1988)
Black Belt Jones (1974)
Black Caesar (1973)
The Black Cobra (a.k.a. Cobra Nero) (1987)
Black Cobra (2012)
The Black Cobra 2 (1988)
The Black Cobra 3 (1990)
Black Dawn (2005)
The Black Dragon (1974)
Black Dynamite (2008)
Black Dynamite (2011–2012)
Black Eagle (1988)
Black Eye (1973)
Black Friday (2001)
Black Gunn (1972)
Black Horizon (a.k.a. Stranded) (2002)
Blackjack (1998)
Black Mask (1996)
Black Mask 2: City of Masks (2001)
Black Out (a.k.a. Midnight Heat) (1996)
Black Point (2002)
Black Samurai (1977)
Black Thunder (1998)
Blade (1998)
Blade II (2002)
Blade Boxer (1997)
Blade: Trinity (2004)
Blade Warrior (2000)
Blazing Force (1996)
Blind Fury (1989)
Blind Rage (1978)
Blitz (2011)
The Blonde Fury (a.k.a. Female Reporter) (1989)
Blood Alley (a.k.a. True Justice: Blood Alley) (2012)
Blood and Bone (2009)
Blood Chase (1989)
Bloodfight (1989)
Bloodfist (1989)
Bloodfist II (1990)
Bloodfist III: Forced to Fight (1992)
Bloodfist IV: Die Trying (1992)
Bloodfist V: Human Target (1994)
Bloodfist VI: Ground Zero (1994)
Bloodfist VII: Manhunt (1995)
Bloodfist VIII: Hard Way Out (a.k.a. Hard Way Out) (1995)

Bloodfist 2050 (2005)
Blood For Blood (a.k.a. Midnight Man) (1994)
Blood Hands (1990)
Blood Heat (a.k.a. Muscle Heat) (2002)
Bloodmatch (a.k.a. Bloodchamp) (1991)
Blood Money (a.k.a. The Stranger and the Gunfighter) (1974)
Blood Money (2012)
Bloodmoon (1996)
Blood of Redemption (2013)
Blood Ring (1991)
Blood Ring 2 (1995)
Bloodsport (1987)
Bloodsport II (1996)
Bloodsport III (1996)
Bloodsport IV: The Dark Kumite (1999)
Blood Street (1988)
Blood Warriors (1993)
Body and Soul (1981)
Body Armor (1996)
The Bodyguard (a.k.a. Karate Chiba) (1976)
Body Slam (1986)
Boiling Point (1993)
Boogie Boy (1998)
Book of Swords (2007)
Borderline (1980)
Born American (1986)
The Born Losers (1967)
Born to Defense (1986)
Born to Raise Hell (2011)
Bounty Hunters (1996)
Bounty Hunters 2: Hardball (a.k.a. Hardball) (1997)
Bounty Hunters (2011)
Bounty Tracker (1992)
Braddock: Missing in Action III (1988)
Brazilian Brawl (2003)
Breach of Faith: A Family of Cops II (1997)
Breaker! Breaker! (1977)
Breakheart Pass (1975)
Breakout (1975)
Breathing Fire (1991)
Brick Mansions (2014)
Bridge of Dragons (1999)
Broken Arrow (1996)
Broken Bars (1995)
Brotherhood of Death (1976)
Brotherhood of the Wolf (2001)
Brutal Glory (1989)
Bucktown (1975)
Bullet (1996)
Bullet (2013)
Bullet Raja (2013)
Bullet to the Head (2013)
The Bunker (2013)
Busted Up (1986)

C

Cabo Blanco (1980)
Cage (1989)
Cage II: The Arena of Death (1994)
The Cannonball Run (1981)
Cannonball Run II (1984)
Capital Punishment (1991)
The Capitol Conspiracy (1998)
Captain America (1979)
Captain America II: Death Too Soon (1979)
Carjack (1996)
Catch the Heat (1987)
Cellular (2004)
Chain of Command (1993)
Chain of Command (2015)
Champions (1996)
Chaos (2005)
The Chaperone (2011)
Chato's Land (1972)
Chavez: Cage of Glory (2013)
Checkmate (a.k.a. Deep Cover) (1997)
The Chemist (2015)
Chinango (2005)
China O'Brien (1990)
China O'Brien 2 (1990)
China Strike Force (2000)
Chinese Zodiac (a.k.a. CZ 12) (2012)
Chino (1973)
Chocolate (2008)
Christmas Bounty (2013)
Chronicles of Riddick (2004)
Chuck Norris: Karate Kommandos (1986)
C.I.A. Code Name Alexa (1992)
C.I.A. Target Alexa (1993)
Circle of Pain (2010)
The Circuit (2002)
The Circuit 2 (2003)
The Circuit III: Street Monk (a.k.a. The Circuit 3: Final Flight) (2006)
City Cops (1989)
City Hunter (1992)
City of Fear (2000)
Class of 1999 II: The Substitute (1994)
Clementine (2004)
Cliffhanger (1993)
Close Range (2015)
Cobra (1986)
Cobra (1993)
Cocaine and Blue Eyes (1983)
Code Name Phoenix (2000)
Codename: Vengeance (1987)
Code of Silence (1985)
Code Red (2013)
Cold Harvest (1999)
Cold Sweat (1970)
Cold Vengeance (a.k.a. Sometimes a Hero) (2002)
Collateral Damage (2002)
Commando (1985)
Commando: A One Man Army (2013)
Commando Squad (1987)
Command Performance (2009)
The Condemned (2007)
The Condemned 2: Desert Prey (2015)
Confessions of a Pit Fighter (2005)
Contour (2007)
Contract Killer (a.k.a. Hitman) (1998)
The Contractor (2007)
Convict 762 (1997)
Cop Land (1997)
Counterforce (1987)
Counter Measures (1998)
Cover-Up (1991)
Crackerjack (1994)
Crackerjack 3 (1999)
Crack House (1989)
Cradle 2 the Grave (2003)
Crank (2006)

Crank 2: High Voltage (2009)
Crash Dive (1997)
Creed (2015)
Crime Story (1993)
Crisis (1997)
The Crocodile Hunter: Collision Course (2002)
Crooked (2006)
Crossfire (a.k.a. Not Another Mistake) (1988)
The Crow (1994)
The Crow: Stairway to Heaven (1998–1999)
Crying Freeman (1995)
Cutaway (2000)
The Cutter (2005)
Cyberjack (1995)
Cyber-Tracker (1993)
Cyber-Tracker 2 (1995)
Cyborg (1989)
Cyborg 2 (1993)
Cyborg Cop (1993)
Cyborg Cop 2 (a.k.a. Cyborg Soldier) (1994)
Cyclone (1987)
Cy Warrior: Special Combat Unit (1989)

D

Damage (2009)
A Dangerous Man (2009)
Dangerous Passion (1990)
A Dangerous Place (1994)
Dark Angel (a.k.a. I Come in Peace) (1990)
Dark Assassin (2006)
Dark of the Sun (1968)
Dark Vengeance (a.k.a. True Justice: Dark Vengeance) (2010)
Daylight (1996)
Day of the Panther (1987)
D.C. Cab (1983)
Dead Drop (a.k.a. True Justice: Dead Drop) (2012)
Dead in Tombstone (2012)
Deadly Assassin (a.k.a. True Justice: Deadly Assassin) (2012)
Deadly Bet (1992)
Deadly Crossing (2010)
Deadly Currency (1998)
Deadly Engagement (2003)
Deadly Impact (1984)
Deadly Intent (1988)
Deadly Outbreak (1995)
Deadly Ransom (1998)
Deadly Reckoning (a.k.a. The Company Man) (1998)
Deadly Shooter (a.k.a. The Shooter) (1997)
Deadly Target (1994)
Dead Mine (2012)
Dead Tides (1997)
Dead to Rights (a.k.a. Donato and Daughter) (1993)
Death Before Dishonor (1986)
Death Cage (1988)
Deathcheaters (1976)
Death Dimension (1978)
Death Fight (a.k.a. Rage) (1994)
Death From Above (2012)
Death Grip (2012)
Death Hunt (1981)
Death Journey (1976)
Death List (2006)
Death Machines (1976)
Death Match (1994)
The Death of Bruce Lee (a.k.a. Black Dragon's Revenge) (1975)
Death Proof (2007)
Death Race (2008)

Death Riders (a.k.a. True Justice: Brotherhood) (2011)
Death Ring (1993)
Death Train (2003)
Death Train (2006)
Death Warrant (1990)
Death Warrior (2009)
Death Wish (1974)
Death Wish II (1982)
Death Wish 3 (1985)
Death Wish 4: The Crackdown (1987)
Death Wish V: The Face of Death (1993)
The Defender (a.k.a. The Bodyguard From Beijing) (1994)
The Defender (2004)
The Delta Force (1986)
Delta Force Commando (1987)
Delta Force Commando 2 (1990)
Delta Force One: The Lost Patrol (a.k.a. D.F. One: The Lost Patrol) (1999)
Delta Force 2: The Columbian Connection (1990)
Delta Force 3: The Killing Game (1991)
Demolition Man (1993)
Derailed (2002)
Desert Heat (a.k.a. Inferno) (1999)
Desert Kickboxer (a.k.a. Desert Hawk) (1992)
Desert Warrior (1988)
Destroyer (1988)
Detective Malone (a.k.a. Black Cobra 4) (1991)
Detention (2003)
The Detonator (2005)
Detour to Terror (1980)
Diamond Dogs (2007)
Die Another Day (2002)
Die Fighting (a.k.a. The Price of Success) (2014)
Direct Action (2004)
Direct Contact (2009)
The Dirty Dozen (1967)
Displaced (2006)
District B13 (2004)
District 13: Ultimatum (2010)
The Divine Enforcer (1992)
DNA (1997)
DOA: Dead or Alive (2006)
Doberman Cop (1977)
Dogs of Chinatown (2010)
Dollar For the Dead (1998)
The Donor (1995)
Doom (2005)
Double Blast (1993)
Double Dragon (1994)
Double Duty (2009)
Double Impact (1991)
Double Tap (2011)
Double Team (1997)
Double Trouble (1991)
Down 'n Dirty (2001)
Dragon (Wu Xia) (2011)
Dragon and the Hawk (2000)
Dragon Eyes (2012)
Dragon Fight (1989)
Dragonfight (1990)
Dragon Fire (1993)
Dragon Fury (1995)
Dragon Fury 2 (1996)
Dragon Heat (a.k.a. Dragon Squad) (2005)
Dragon Hunt (1990)
Dragon Princess (1976)
Dragons Forever (1988)
Dragon Tiger Gate (2006)
Drive (1997)
Driven (2001)
Driven to Kill (2009)
Driving Force (1989)
Drop Zone (1994)

Dr. Wai in the Scriptures With No Words (1996)
Dual (2008)
Dubbed and Dangerous Trilogy (2001–2004)

E

Eastern Condors (1986)
Easy Money (1987)
18 Fingers of Death (2004)
El Condor (1970)
El Gringo (2012)
Eliminators (1986)
Eliminator Woman (a.k.a. Terminator Woman) (1992)
Empire State (2013)
End Game (2009)
End of Days (1999)
Enemies Closer (2014)
The Enforcer (a.k.a. My Father is a Hero) (1995)
Enter the Blood Ring (1995)
Enter the Dragon (1973)
Enter the Ninja (1981)
Entre Llamas (a.k.a. Into the Flames) (2002)
Epoch of Lotus (2000)
Equalizer 2000 (1987)
Eraser (1996)
Escape From Alaska (a.k.a. Avalanche) (1999)
Escape From Atlantis (1997)
Escape Plan (2013)
The Evil That Men Do (1983)
Excessive Force (1993)
Excessive Force II: Force on Force (1995)
The Executioner (1974)
The Executioner 2 (1974)
Executioners (1993)
Executive Decision (1996)
Exit (1996)
Exit Wounds (2001)
Expect No Mercy (1995)
Expect to Die (1997)
The Expendables (2010)
The Expendables 2 (a.k.a. The Expendables 2: Back For War) (2012)
The Expendables 3 (2014)
The Expert (1995)
Expert Weapon (a.k.a. American Dragon) (1993)
The Extendables (2014)
Extraction (2013)
Extraction (2015)
Extreme Challenge (2001)
Extreme Counterstrike (2012)
Extreme Force (2001)
Extreme Honor (2001)
An Eye For an Eye (1981)
Eye See You (a.k.a. Detox) (2002)

F

Falcon Rising (2014)
Fallout (1999)
Family of Cops (1995(1988))
Family of Cops III: Under Suspicion (1999)
Fast and Furious (2009)
Fast & Furious 6 (2013)
Fast & Furious 7 (2015)
The Fast and the Furious (2001)
Faster (2010)
Fast Five (2011)
Fast Getaway (1991)
Fast Getaway II (1994)
Fatal Blade (a.k.a. Gedo) (2000)
Fatal Deviation (1998)
Fatal Revenge (1990)
Fearless (2006)

Fearless Tiger (a.k.a. Black Pearls) (1991)
15 Minutes (2001)
The Fifth Commandment (2008)
Fighting (2009)
Fighting Fish (2004)
The Fighting Fist of Shanghai Joe (a.k.a. My Name is Shanghai Joe, a.k.a. The Dragon Fights Back) (1973)
Fighting Mad (a.k.a. Death Force) (1978)
Fight the Fight (2011)
Fight to Win (1987)
Final Impact (1992)
Final Reprisal (1988)
Final Round (1993)
Fire Down Below (1997)
Firehawk (1993)
Firepower (1979)
Firepower (1993)
Firestorm (1998)
Firewalker (1986)
The Firing Line (1988)
First Blood (1982)
First Encounter (1997)
Fist Fighter (1988)
Fist of Fury (a.k.a. The Chinese Connection) (1972)
Fist of Glory (1991)
Fist of Legend (1994)
Fist of Steel (a.k.a. Eternal Fist) (1992)
Fist of the North Star (1995)
Fist of the Warrior (2007)
Fists of Blood (a.k.a. Strike of the Panther) (1988)
Fists of Iron (1995)
Fist 2 Fist (2011)
Fist 2 Fist 2: Weapon of Choice (2014)
Flash Point (2007)
Flight of Fury (2007)
The Forbidden Kingdom (2008)
Force (2011)
Forced to Fight (2011)
Forced Vengeance (1982)
Force: Five (1981)
Force of Execution (2013)
A Force of One (1979)
The Foreigner (2002)
Forest Warrior (1996)
Fortune Dane (1986)
4Got10 (2015)
Foxtrap (1986)
Freedom Strike (1998)
From Noon Till Three (1976)
Fugitive Mind (1999)
Full Contact (1992)
Full Impact (a.k.a. American Streetfighter 2) (1993)
Furious (1984)
Future Fear (1997)
Future Hunters (1986)
Future Kick (1991)
Futuresport (1998)
Future War (1994)

G

Gale Force (2001)
Gallowwalkers (2013)
Game of Death (1978)
Game of Death (2010)
Game Over (2005)
The Game Plan (2007)
Gangland (2001)
Get Carter (2000)
Get Smart (2008)
Ghost Rock (2003)
G.I. Joe: Retaliation (2013)
G.I. Joe: The Rise of Cobra (2009)
The Girl From the Naked Eye (2011)
G.I. Samurai (a.k.a. Time Slip) (1979)
Gladiator Cop: The Swordsman II (1994)
The Glass Jungle (1989)

The Glimmer Man (1996)
Global Effect (2002)
Golden Needles (1974)
Golgo 13 (1977)
Good Cop, Bad Cop (a.k.a. Black Dawn) (1997)
Good Guys Wear Black (1977)
A Good Man (2013)
The Goonies (1985)
Gorgeous (1999)
The Green Hornet (1966)
Green Street 3: Never Back Down (2013)
Gridiron Gang (2006)
Grosse Point Blank (1996)
Ground Rules (1997)
Grudge Match (2013)
G2 (1999)
Guaranteed on Delivery (a.k.a. G.O.D.) (2001)
The Guardian (2000)
Guardian Angel (1994)
Guardians of the Galaxy (2014)
Guns and Lipstick (1995)
Guns For San Sebastian (1968)
Gutshot Straight (2014)
Gymkata (1985)

H

Half Past Dead (2002)
Half Past Dead 2 (2007)
Hammer (1972)
Hangfire (1991)
Hardcase and Fist (1989)
The Hard Corps (2006)
Hard Hunted (1992)
Hard Justice (1995)
Hard Luck (2006)
Hard Target (1993)
Hard Ticket to Hawaii (1987)
Hard Time on Planet Earth (1989)
Hard Times (1975)
Hard to Kill (1990)
Hawk's Vengeance (1996)
Haywire (2011)
Heart of Dragon (1985)
Heatseeker (1995)
Hellbinders (2009)
Hellbound (1993)
Hell Comes to Frogtown (1988)
Hell's Heroes (a.k.a. Inglorious Bastards 2: Hell's Heroes) (1987)
Hell Up in Harlem (1973)
Hercules in New York (a.k.a. Hercules Goes Bananas) (1970)
Hero and the Terror (1987)
The Heroic Trio (1993)
Hidden Agenda (2001)
Hidden Assassin (1995)
High Adventure (2001)
Highlander: Endgame (2000)
High Voltage (1997)
Hijacked (2012)
Hired to Kill (1990)
The Hitman (1991)
Hollow Point (1996)
Hollywood Vice Squad (1986)
Hologram Man (1995)
Homefront (2013)
Honor (2006)
Honor Among Thieves (a.k.a. Farewell, Friend) (1968)
Honor and Glory (1993)
Hostile Environment (a.k.a. Watership Warrior) (2000)
Hot Potato (1975)
House of the Rising Sun (2011)
The Human Shield (1992)
Hunter (1984-1991)
The Hunt for Eagle One (2006)

The Hunt For Eagle One: Crash Point (2006)
Hunt to Kill (2010)
Hurricane Smith (1992)
Hyper Space (1989)

I

I Am Omega (2007)
Ice Station Zebra (1968)
I Escaped Devil's Island (1973)
The Immortal (2000-2001)
Immortal (2006)
Immortal Combat (1993)
The Incredible Hulk (1978-1982)
Inglorious Bastards (1978)
In Hell (2003)
Inside Out (2011)
The Inspector Wears Skirts (1988)
Instinct to Kill (2001)
Interceptor Force (1999)
Interceptor Force 2 (2002)
Interzone (1987)
In the Blood (2014)
In the Name of the King 2: Two Worlds (2011)
Into the Sun (2005)
Invasion U.S.A. (1985)
Ip Man (2008)
Ip Man 2 (2010)
Ironheart (1992)
Iron Man 2 (2010)
Iron Thunder (a.k.a. Contemporary Gladiator) (1989)
Irresistible Force (1993)
Island of Fire (a.k.a. The Prisoner) (1990)
The Italian Job (2003)

J

Jackie Chan Adventures (2000–2005)
Jackie Chan's First Strike (a.k.a. Police Story 4: First Strike) (1997)
Jaguar Lives! (1979)
JCVD (2008)
Jian Bing Man (2015)
Jill the Ripper (2000)
Jingle All the Way (1996)
Jinn (2014)
Johnny Mnemonic (1995)
John Wick (2014)
Joshua (1976)
Joshua Tree (a.k.a. Army of One) (1993)
Journey 2: The Mysterious Island (2012)
Judge Dredd (1995)
Jungleground (1995)
Jungle Wolf (a.k.a. Forgotten Warrior/ a.k.a. The Wolf) (1986)

K

Kamen Rider: Dragon Knight (2009)
Kampfansage (a.k.a. The Challenge) (2005)
Karate Bear Fighter (1977)
Karate Bullfighter (a.k.a. Champion of Death) (1975)
Karate Commando: Jungle Wolf 3 (1993)
Karate Cop (1991)
Karate Cops (a.k.a. Hawkeye) (1988)
Karate For Life (1977)
The Karate Kid (2010)
The Karate Kid Part III (1989)
Karate Warriors (1976)
Kazaam (1996)
The Keeper (2009)
Kenner (1968)
The Kick (2011)
Kickboxer (1989)
Kickboxer 2: The Road Back (1991)
Kickboxer 3: The Art of War (1992)
Kickboxer 4: The Aggressor (1993)

Kickboxer 5: Redemption (1995)
Kick Fighter (a.k.a. The Fighter) (1989)
Kill and Kill Again (1981)
Kill 'Em All (2012)
Killer Elite (2012)
The Kill Factor (2009)
Killing American Style (1989)
Killing Down (2006)
The Killing Grounds (a.k.a. Children of Wax) (2007)
Killing Machine (1975)
The Killing Machine (2010)
The Killing Man (a.k.a. The Killing Machine) (1994)
Killing Streets (1991)
The Killing Zone (1991)
Kill or be Killed (1976)
Killpoint (1984)
Kill Switch (2008)
Kill the Golden Goose (1979)
Kill Zone (2005)
Kiltro (2006)
Kindergarten Cop (1990)
Kindergarten Ninja (1994)
The King of Fighters (2009)
The King of the Kickboxers (1990)
King of the Kickboxers 2 (a.k.a. Fighting Spirit) (1992)
Kingz (2007)
Kinjite: Forbidden Subjects (1989)
Kiss of the Dragon (2001)
Knights (1993)
Knights of the City (1985)
Knock Off (1998)
Knockout (2010)
Knucklehead (2010)
Kung Fu Killer (2015)
Kung Fu: The Movie (1986)

L

Lady Dragon (1992)
Lady Dragon 2 (1993)
Land of the Free (1998)
Laser Mission (a.k.a. Soldier of Fortune) (1989)
Last Action Hero (1993)
The Last Dragon (1985)
The Last Fight (1983)
Last Flight to Hell (1990)
Last Man Standing (1995)
The Last Witch Hunter (2015)
L.A. Streetfighters (a.k.a. Ninja Turf) (1985)
The Last Sentinel (2007)
The Last Stand (2013)
Last to Surrender (1999)
The Last Warrior (2000)
Latin Dragon (2004)
L.A. Wars (1994)
The Lazarus Papers (2010)
Legacy of Rage (1986)
Legendary (2010)
Legendary: Tomb of the Dragon (2013)
The Legend of Drunken Master (1994)
The Legend of Nigger Charley (1972)
Legend of the Dragon (2005)
Legend of the Fist: The Return of Chen Zhen (2010)
Legionnaire (1998)
Lessons for an Assassin (2001)
Lethal (2005)
Lethal Justice (a.k.a. True Justice: Lethal Justice) (2010)
Lethal Weapon 4 (1998)
Liberator (2012)
Liberty and Bash (1989)
Lionheart (1990)
Little Bear and the Master (2008)
Live by the Fist (1992)
Live Wire: Human Timebomb (1995)

Lockdown (1990)
Locked Down (2012)
Lock Up (1989)
Logan's War: Bound by Honor (1998)
Lone Tiger (1996)
Lone Wolf McQuade (1983)
The Longest Yard (2005)
Looney Tunes: Back in Action (2003)
Los Bravos (2001)
The Lost Medallion: The Adventures of
  Billy Stone (2013)
Love and Bullets (1978)
Low Blow (1986)

M
Machete (2010)
Machete Kills (2013)
Mach 2 (2001)
Maggie (2015)
Magic Crystal (1986)
Magic Kid (1992)
Magic Kid 2 (1994)
Magnificent Warriors (a.k.a. Dynamite
  Fighters) (1987)
A Man Apart (2003)
Mandrill (2009)
The Man From Hong Kong (a.k.a.
  Dragon Files) (1975)
Manhattan Chase (2000)
Man of Tai Chi (2013)
The Man With the Iron Fists (2012)
The Marine (2006)
The Marine 2 (2009)
The Marine 3 (2013)
The Marine 4 (2015)
The Mark (2012)
The Mark 2: Redemption (2013)
Marked For Death (1990)
Marked Man (1996)
The Marksman (2005)
Marlowe (1969)
Mars (1997)
Mars Attacks! (1996)
The Martial Arts Kid (2015)
Martial Law (1990)
Martial Law 2: Undercover (1991)
Martial Law (1998-2000)
Martial Outlaw (1993)
Masked Rider (1995-1996)
Mask of Death (1995)
The Master (a.k.a. The Master Ninja)
  (1984)
The Master (1989)
The Master Demon (1991)
The Master Gunfighter (1975)
Masterblaster (1985)
Max Havoc: Curse of the Dragon (2004)
Max Havoc: Ring of Fire (2006)
Maximum Conviction (2012)
Maximum Impact (2008)
Maximum Risk (1996)
McCinsey's Island (1997)
Mean Johnny Barrows (1976)
Mean Machine (2001)
The Mechanic (1972)
The Mechanic (2011)
The Medallion (a.k.a. Highbinders)
  (2003)
Meltdown (1995)
Memorial Day (1998)
Men of War (1994)
Merantau (2009)
Mercenaries (2014)
Mercenary (1996)
Mercenary II: Thick and Thin (1999)
Mercenary Fighters (1988)
Mercenary for Justice (2006)
Merchants of War (1989)
The Messenger (1986)
Messenger of Death (1988)

Metal Hurlant Chronicles: Second
  Chance (2014)
Metal Hurant Chronicles: The
  Endomorphe (2014)
Metal Hurlant Chronicles: The King's
  Crown (2012)
Miami Connection (1987)
Midnight Ride (1990)
The Minion (1998)
Miracles (a.k.a. Black Dragon, a.k.a. Mr.
  Canton and Lady Rose) (1989)
Mirageman (2007)
Misfire (2014)
Missing in Action (1984)
Missing in Action 2: The Beginning
  (1985)
Missionary Man (2007)
Mission of Justice (1992)
Mister T (1983-1986)
The Money Train (1995)
Mortal Challenge (1997)
Mortal Enemies (a.k.a. Pirate Brothers)
  (2011)
Mortal Kombat (1995)
Mortal Kombat: Annihilation (1997)
Mortal Kombat: Conquest (1998-1999)
Mortal Kombat: Legacy (2011)
Mortal Kombat: Legacy II (2013)
Moscow Heat (2004)
Moses: Fallen, In the City of Angels
  (2005)
Moving Target (1996)
Moving Target (2000)
Mr. Majestyk (1974)
Mr. Mean (1977)
Mr. Nanny (1993)
Mr. Nice Guy (1998)
Mr. X (1995)
Muay Thai Fighter (2008)
The Mummy: Tomb of the Dragon
  Emperor (2008)
Murder at 1600 (1997)
Murder in the Orient (1974)
Murphy's Law (1986)
Musketeers Forever (1998)
My Lucky Stars (1985)
My Lucky Stars 2: Twinkle, Twinkle
  Lucky Stars (1985)
My Samurai (1988)
The Myth (2007)
Myths and Legends: The New Alliance
  (2010)

N
Nature Unleashed: Fire (2004)
Nautilus (2000)
Nemesis (1992)
Nemesis 2: Nebula (1995)
Nemesis 3: Time Lapse (1996)
Nemesis 4: Death Angel (a.k.a. Nemesis
  4: Cry of Angels) (1996)
Neon City (1991)
Never Back Down 2: The Beatdown
  (2011)
Never Say Die (1994)
Never Surrender (2009)
The New Barbarians (a.k.a. Warriors of
  the Wasteland) (1983)
New Police Story (2004)
Nighthawks (1981)
Night Hunter (1996)
Night Man (1997-1999)
Night of the Kickfighters (1988)
Night of the Warrior (1991)
Night Vision (1997)
9 1/2 Ninjas (1991)
9 Deaths of the Ninja (1985)
1990: The Bronx Warriors (1982)
Ninja (2009)
Ninja: Shadow of a Tear (2013)

Ninja III: The Domination (1984)
Ninja Academy (1989)
Ninja Apocalypse (2014)
Ninja Assassin (2009)
Ninja Assassins (a.k.a. Enforcer From
  Death Row) (1978)
Ninja Busters (a.k.a. Shadow Fight)
  (1984)
Ninja Masters (2009)
Ninja's Creed (a.k.a. Royal Kill) (2009)
Ninja Warriors (1985)
No Code of Conduct (1998)
No Contest (1994)
No Exit (1995)
No Holds Barred (1989)
No More Dirty Deals (1993)
No Retreat, No Surrender (1985)
No Retreat, No Surrender 2 (1987)
No Retreat, No Surrender 3: Blood
  Brothers (1989)
No Rules (2005)
No Tomorrow (1999)
No Way Back (1976)
Nowhere to Run (1993)

O
The Octagon (1980)
Omega Cop (1990)
Once Upon a Time in the West (1969)
On Deadly Ground (1994)
The One (2001)
One Down, Two to Go (1976)
100 Rifles (1969)
One in the Chamber (2012)
One Man Army (1993)
One Man Force (1989)
One Man's Justice (a.k.a. One Tough
  Bastard) (1995)
On Fire (a.k.a. Forgive Me Father)
  (2001)
Ong-bak (2005)
Only the Strong (1993)
On the Edge (2002)
Oosaravelli (2011)
Open Fire (1994)
Operation Cobra (1997)
Operation Condor (a.k.a. Armor of God
  2) (1991)
Operation Delta Force (1997)
Operation Delta Force 3: Clear Target
  (1998)
Operation Golden Phoenix (1994)
Operation Rogue (2014)
The Operative (2000)
The Order (2001)
Original Gangstas (1996)
Orion's Key (1996)
Oscar (1991)
The Other Guys (2010)
Out For a Kill (2003)
Out for Blood (1992)
Out for Justice (1991)
Out of Reach (2004)
Outside the Law (a.k.a. Blood Run)
  (1994)
Outside the Law (2001)
Overkill (1995)
Over the Top (1987)

P
Pacific Inferno (1979)
The Pacifier (2005)
The Package (2012)
Pain and Gain (2013)
Paper Dragons (1996)
Paradise Alley (1978)
Parker (2013)
Parole Violators (1994)
Passenger 57 (1992)
The Patriot (1998)

Penitentiary (1979)
Penitentiary II (1982)
Penitentiary III (1987)
Pentathlon (1994)
Perfect Target (1996)
The Perfect Weapon (1991)
Personal Vendetta (1995)
Phase IV (2002)
Picasso Trigger (1988)
Pistol Whipped (2007)
Pitch Black (2000)
Pit Fighter (2005)
Platoon Leader (1988)
Plato's Run (1997)
The Player (2015)
Pocket Ninjas (1997)
Point Blank (1998)
Police Academy (1984)
Police Story (1985)
Police Story 2 (1988)
Police Story 2013 (2013)
Pound of Flesh (2015)
The Power Within (1995)
Pray For Death (1985)
Predator (1987)
Predators (2010)
The President's Man (2000)
The President's Man 2: A Line in the
  Sand (2002)
Prince of the Sun (1990)
The Prisoner (a.k.a. Island of Fire)
  (1990)
Project A (1983)
Project A 2 (1987)
Project Eliminator (1991)
Project Purgatory (2010)
Project Shadowchaser II: Night Siege
  (1994)
Project Shadowchaser III (a.k.a. Project
  Shadowchaser 3000) (1995)
The Protector (1985)
The Protector (1998)
The Protector (Tom Yum Goong) (2005)
The Protector 2 (Tom Yum Goong 2)
  (2013)
Puncture Wounds (a.k.a. A Certain Kind
  of Justice) (2014)
The Punisher (1989)
Pursuit (1991)
Pushed to the Limit (1992)

Q
Queen's Messenger (2001)
A Queen's Ransom (a.k.a. International
  Assassin) (1976)
The Quest (1996)
Quicksand (2002)

R
Race to Witch Mountain (2009)
Rage (1995)
The Rage (1997)
Rage and Honor (1992)
Rage and Honor II: The Hostile Takeover
  (1992)
Rage of Honor (a.k.a. Top Fighter)
  (1986)
Rage to Kill (1988)
The Rage Within (2001)
Raging Phoenix (2009)
Raid on Entebbe (1977)
The Raid: Redemption (2011)
The Raid 2 (a.k.a. The Raid 2: Berandal)
  (2014)
Raiders of the Sun (1992)
Rambo (a.k.a. John Rambo) (2008)
Rambo: First Blood Part II (1985)
Rambo III (1988)
Rapid Exchange (2003)
Rapid Fire (1992)

Raven (1992-1993)
Ravenhawk (1996)
Raw Deal (1986)
Raw Target (1995)
Raze (2013)
Ready to Rumble (2000)
Recoil (1998)
Recoil (2011)
Redeemer (2015)
Redemption (2002)
Redemption (a.k.a. Hummingbird) (2013)
Red Heat (1988)
Redline (1997)
Red Scorpion (1989)
Red Scorpion 2 (1994)
Red Serpent (2003)
Red Sun (1971)
Red Sun Rising (1994)
Re-Generator (2010)
Remo Williams: The Prophecy (1988)
Renegade (1992-1996)
Replicant (2001)
Reptilicant (2006)
Rescue Me (a.k.a. Street Hunter) (1992)
Retrograde (2004)
Return Fire: Jungle Wolf II (1988)
Return of the Street Fighter (1974)
Return to Frogtown (1992)
The Reunion (2011)
Revelation Road: The Beginning of the End (2013)
Revelation Road: The Sea of Glass and Fire (2013)
Revenge of the Kickfighter (a.k.a. Return of the Kickfighter) (1987)
Revenge of the Ninja (1983)
The Revenger (1990)
Revolver (2005)
Riddick (2013)
Rider on the Rain (1970)
Ring of Fire (1991)
Ring of Fire 2: Blood and Steel (1993)
Ring of Fire 3: Lionstrike (1994)
Ring of Steel (1994)
Rio Conchos (1964)
Riot (1969)
Riot (1996)
Ripper Man (1994)
Rising Sun (1993)
Risk Factor (2015)
Riverbend (1989)
River of Darkness (2010)
River of Death (1989)
Road House 2 (2006)
The Road Raiders (1989)
Roaring Fire (1982)
Robin-B-Hood (2006)
Robowar (1988)
Rocky (1976)
Rocky II (1979)
Rocky III (1982)
Rocky IV (1985)
Rocky V (1990)
Rocky Balboa (2006)
Romeo Must Die (2000)
Rome 2072: The New Gladiators (a.k.a. The New Gladiators) (1984)
Rope-a-Dope (2013)
Roughcut (1994)
Royal Warriors (a.k.a. In the Line of Duty) (1986)
Rumble in the Bronx (1995)
The Rundown (a.k.a. Welcome to the Jungle) (2003)
The Running Man (1987)
Running Red (1998)
Rush Hour (1998)
Rush Hour 2 (2001)
Rush Hour 3 (2007)

The Russian Specialist (a.k.a. The Mechanik) (2005)

S
Sabotage (1996)
Sabotage (2014)
Safe (2012)
Saf3 (2013)
Samurai Cop (1989)
San Andreas (2015)
Sanctuary (1997)
Santa's Little Helper (2015)
Santa's Slay (2005)
Santa With Muscles (1996)
Savage (1995)
Savage Beach (1989)
Savate (a.k.a. The Fighter) (1994)
Sci-Fighters (1996)
Scooby-Doo! WrestleMania Mystery (2014)
Scorpion (1987)
Scorpion (2008)
Scorpio One (1998)
Sea Wolf (a.k.a. Pirate's Curse) (2005)
Second in Command (2005)
The Secret Agent Club (1996)
The Secret of King Mahi's Island (1988)
Sector 4: Extraction (2013)
See No Evil (2006)
See No Evil 2 (2014)
7 Seconds (2005)
Shadow Man (2006)
Shadow Warriors (a.k.a. Assault on Devil's Island) (1997)
Shadow Warriors 2 (a.k.a. Assault on Death Mountain) (1999)
Shanghai Express (a.k.a. The Millionaire's Express) (1986)
Shanghai Knights (2003)
Shanghai Noon (2000)
Shark Alarm (a.k.a. Shark Attack in the Mediterranean) (2004)
Shark Lake (2015)
Shattered Dreams (1998)
Shattered Lies (2002)
The Shepherd: Border Patrol (2008)
Shinjuku Incident (2009)
The Shinobi Ninja (1981)
Shootfighter: Fight to the Death (1993)
Shootfighter 2 (1996)
Showdown (1993)
Showdown in Little Tokyo (1991)
Sidekicks (1986-1987)
Sidekicks (1992)
The Silencer (2000)
Silent Assassins (1988)
Silent Force (2001)
Silent Hunter (1995)
Silent Rage (1982)
Silent Trigger (1996)
Silverhawk (2005)
Simon Sez (1999)
Sin City (2005)
Sin City: A Dame to Kill For (2014)
Sister Street Fighter (1974)
6 Bullets (2012)
The 6th Day (2000)
Skin Trade (2015)
Skin Traffik (2015)
Skinny Tiger, Fatty Dragon (1990)
The Slams (1973)
Slaughter (1972)
Slaughter's Big Rip-Off (1973)
Slow Burn (1989)
Snake Eater (1988)
Snake Eater II: The Drug Buster (1990)
Snake Eater III . . . His Law (1992)
Snitch (2013)
Soda Cracker (a.k.a. The Killer Reflex) (1989)

Soldier Boyz (1995)
Soldier of Vengeance (a.k.a. True Justice: Soldier of Vengeance) (2012)
Sons of Thunder (1999)
Soul of Chiba (a.k.a. Soul of Bruce Lee) (1977)
The Soul of Nigger Charley (1973)
Soul of the Avenger (a.k.a. For Life or Death) (1997)
South Beach (1992)
Space Mutiny (1988)
Spawn (1997)
Special Forces (a.k.a. Black Sea Raid) (2000)
Special Forces (2002)
Special ID (2013)
The Specialist (1994
Spectre (2015)
Spitfire (1995)
The Split (1968)
Spoiler (1998)
Spy (2015)
Spy Kids 3D: Game Over (2003)
The Spy Next Door (2010)
Star Wars Episode 1: The Phantom Menace (1999)
Stash House (2012)
Steel (1997)
Steele Justice (1987)
Steele's Law (1991)
Stick (1985)
St. Ives (1976)
Stone Cold (1991)
The Stone Killer (1973)
Stoner (1974)
Stop! Or My Mom Will Shoot! (1992)
Storm Catcher (1999)
Straight Line (1990)
Stranded (2009)
The Stranger (1994)
The Stranger (2010)
Stranglehold (1994)
Strategic Command (1997)
Street Crimes (1992)
The Street Fighter (1974)
Street Fighter (1994)
Street Fighter: Assassin's Fist (2014)
The Streetfighter's Last Revenge (1974)
Street Fighter: The Legend of Chun-Li (2009)
Street Hunter (1990)
Street Justice (1991-1993)
Street Knight (1993)
Street Law (1994)
Streets of Rage (1994)
Street Wars (a.k.a. True Justice: Street Wars) (2010)
Strike Commando (1987)
Strike Force (a.k.a. The Librarians) (2003)
Striker (1987)
Strike Zone (2000)
Stunt Rock (1980)
Submerged (2005)
Subterfuge (1996)
Suburban Commando (1991)
Sudden Death (1995)
Sunland Heat (2004)
Supercop: Police Story III (1992)
Supercop 2 (1993)
Superfights (1995)
Supreme Champion (2010)
Surf Ninjas (1993)
Survival Game (1987)
SWAT: Warhead One (2004)
Sweepers (1998)
Swelter (a.k.a. Duels) (2014)
The Sword of Bushido (1990)
Sword of Heaven (1985)
Sword of Honor (1996)

The Swordsman (1992)
Sworn to Justice (1996)

T
Tactical Force (2011)
Tagteam (1991)
Take a Hard Ride (1975)
Talons of the Eagle (1992)
Tango and Cash (1989)
Tapped Out (2013)
The Tattoo Connection (1978)
TC 2000 (1993)
Teenage Mutant Ninja Turtles II: The Secret of the Ooze (1991)
Tekken (2010)
Tekken 2: Kazuya's Revenge (2014)
Telefon (1977)
10 to Midnight (1983)
Ten Zan: The Ultimate Mission (1988)
Terminal Impact (a.k.a. Cyborg Cop 3) (1995)
Terminal Justice (a.k.a. Cybertech P.D.) (1996)
Terminal Rush (1996)
The Terminator (1984)
Terminator 2: Judgment Day (1991)
Terminator 3: Rise of the Machines (2003)
The Terminators (2009)
Terminator Genisys (2015)
T-Force (1994)
That Man Bolt (1973)
They Live (1988)
Think Big (1989)
13 Dead Men (2003)
This Girl is Badass!! (2011)
Three Days to a Kill (1992)
3 Ninjas: High Noon at Mega Mountain (1998)
Three the Hard Way (1974)
Three Tough Guys (a.k.a. Tough Guys) (1974)
Thunderbolt (1995)
Thunderground (1989)
Thunder in Paradise (1994)
Thunderkick (2008)
Thunder Mission (a.k.a. Raiders of Losing Treasure) (1992)
Thuppakki (2012)
Ticker (2001)
...tick...tick...tick (1970)
Tiger Claws (1992)
Tiger Claws 2 (1996)
Tiger Claws 3: The Final Conflict (2000)
Tiger Heart (1995)
Tiger Street (1998)
Time Burst: The Final Alliance (1989)
Timecop (1994)
Timecop 2: The Berlin Decision (2003)
Timelock (1996)
T.K.O. (2007)
T.N.T. (1997)
To Be the Best (1993)
Today You Die (2005)
Tomorrow Never Dies (1997)
Tooth Fairy (2010)
Top Dog (1995)
Total Reality (1997)
To the Death (1992)
The Touch (a.k.a. The Martial Touch) (2002)
Tough and Deadly (1994)
The Tournament (2009)
Trained to Kill (1989)
Traitor's Heart (1999)
Transformed (2005)
The Transporter (2002)
Transporter 2 (2005)
Transporter 3 (2008)
Treasure Raiders (2007)

The Trial of Billy Jack (1974)
Triple Impact (1992)
True Lies (1994)
True Vengeance (1997)
Turn It Up (2000)
The Tuxedo (2002)
12 Rounds (2009)
12 Rounds: Reloaded (2013)
12 Rounds 3: Lockdown (2015)
24 Hours to Midnight (1985)
Twin Dragon Encounter (1986)
Twin Dragons (1992/1999)
Twins (1988)
Twin Sitters (1994)
Two Wrongs Make a Right (1987)

U

Ulterior Motives (1993)
The Ultimate Fight (a.k.a. The Process)
    (1998)
Ultimate Force (2005)
The Ultimate Game (2001)
Ultimate Prey (2000)
Ultimate Target (a.k.a. Ides of March)
    (2000)
The Ultimate Weapon (1998)
Undefeatable (1993)
Undercurrent (1998)
Undercut (2004)
Underdog Kids (2015)
Underground (2007)
Under Siege (1992)
Under Siege 2: Dark Territory (1995)
Under the Gun (1995)
Undisputed (2002)
Undisputed II: Last Man Standing
    (2006)
Undisputed III: Redemption (2009)
Universal Soldier (1992)
Universal Soldier: Day of Reckoning
    (2012)
Universal Soldier II: Brothers in Arms
    (1998)
Universal Soldier III: Unfinished
    Business (1999)
Universal Soldier: Regeneration (2009)
Universal Soldier: The Return (1999)
Unleashed (a.k.a. Danny the Dog) (2003)
Unrivaled (2010)
Unstoppable (2004)
Until Death (2006)
Urban Justice (2007)
Urban Warfare (a.k.a. True Justice:
    Urban Warfare) (2011)
U.S. Marshals (1998)
U.S. Seals 2 (2001)

V

Vampire Assassin (2006)
Vampire Effect (a.k.a. The Twins Effect)
    (2003)
Vanishing Son (1994–1995)
Velocity Trap (1998)
Vendetta (2015)
Vengeance (a.k.a. Kid Vengeance) (1977)
Victory (a.k.a. Escape to Victory) (1981)
Vigilante (1983)
The Villain (1979)
Villa Rides! (1968)
Violence of Action (a.k.a. True Justice:
    Violence of Action) (2012)
Violent City (a.k.a. The Family) (1970)
Virtual Combat (1994)
Virus (1996)

W

Wake of Death (2004)
Walker: Texas Ranger (1993–2001)
Walking Tall (2004)
War (2007)
Warhead (1996)
Warrior of Justice (a.k.a. Invitation to
    Die) (1995)
War Pigs (2015)
War Wolves (2008)
Way of the Black Dragon (1979)
The Way of the Dragon (a.k.a. The
    Return of the Dragon) (1972)
Weapons of Death (1981)
Welcome to the Jungle (2013)
Whatever It Takes (1999)
Wheels on Meals (1984)
When the Bullet Hits the Bone (1996)
The White Buffalo (1977)
White Cargo (1996)
White Fire (1984)
White Light (1991)
White Tiger (1995)
White Tiger (2014)
White Wall (2010)
Who Am I? (a.k.a. Jackie Chan's Who
    Am I?) (1998)
Wild Card (2015)
The Wild Pair (1987)
Winners and Sinners (1983)
Without Mercy (1995)
Witness to a Kill (2001)
Wolf Warrior (2015)
The Wrath of Vajra (2013)
The Wrestler (2008)
Wrong Side of Town (2010)

XYZ

X-Treme Fighter (a.k.a. Sci-Fighter)
    (2004)
xXx (2002)
Yes, Madam! (1985)
You Can't Win 'Em All (1970)
Zero Tolerance (2014)

ACKNOWLEDGMENTS & Thank-Yous

While writing *The Good, the Tough, and the Deadly: Action Stars and Their Movies*, I was amazed at how close the action and martial arts community was to each other. Everyone knew everybody in the business, and it was pure grace that led me to the right people, who kindly passed on contact information, spoke about me to other people, and just gave me as much help as I asked for in terms of getting in touch with people. This was a dream project, but I couldn't do it all by myself, and it was fun to share the dream with some of my contributing writers. I want to thank the following people for their encouragement, their willingness to go far beyond what I asked of them, and for helping to make this book a reality:

Eleanor Academia, Brahim Achabbakhe, Scott Adkins for the invitation to Thailand to visit the set of *Ninja II: Shadow of a Tear;* Marco Antonio, Ernie Barbarash, Keith Batcheller for the kickass cover art; Andy Bauman, Zoe Bell for being incredible; *Black Belt* magazine; Phil Blankenship for loving *Acts of Violence;* Martyn Burke, Gene Ching at *Kung Fu Tai Chi* magazine; Ross Clarkson, Gary Collinson at FlickeringMyth.com, Gary Conway, Norman Craver, Mark Dacascos for a great breakfast and lots of help along the way; Jeremie Damoiseau; Boaz Davidson at Millennium; Frank DeMartini at Millennium; Digital Conquest DVD; Erwin de Koning; John Di Nardo; Patrick Donahue; Sean Donahue; Scott Essman; Tim Everitt; Sam Firstenberg; a BIG thank you to Isaac Florentine; MV Gerhard at La La Land Records; Tobias Hohmann; Eric Jacobus for being awesome; Jesse Johnson; Joe Kane at *VideoScope* magazine; Jino Kang; Naomi Karpati; Leon Isaac Kennedy for being patient; Michael Klastorin for a bunch of stuff, but mainly for connecting me with Zoe Bell; Dominick La Banca; Julian Lee; James Lew for great spaghetti; Michael and Martin McNamara (The Twin Dragons!); Craig T. McNeely; Maroody Merav for taking great pictures; Simon Miller and his site ExplosiveAction.com; Jason Murphy; Richard Norton; Carrie Paul for great tips on how to survive in Thailand; Greg Rand; Tommy Reece; Revok.com; James Richards; Karen Sheperd; Leia

Sopeiki for the Laserdisc player; Jeff Speakman for the Kenpo lesson; Taimak; Brian Trenchard-Smith for helping me get in touch with Edward John Stazak; Michael Stradford; TwistedAnger.com; Matt Verboys (you rock, and thanks for the CDs!); Keith Vitali; Gary Wasneiwski; Stuart Watson; Thorsten Wedekind; and everyone else who helped provide me with contact info, lobby cards, posters, or words of encouragement.

I especially want to thank the following contributors, who spent time watching and reviewing movies for this book: Zack Carlson, Duvien Ho (and Dammaged Goods), Mike Joffe, Dustin Leimgruber, Mike McBeardo McPadden, Josh Schafer, Outlaw Vern (or just Vern, as he likes it), Jason Souza, and most of all Corey Danna, who worked incredibly hard at reviewing five movies a week for nearly two years, and for purchasing expensive lobby cards, sets, and posters from around the world to be used for this book. Also, a BIG thanks to Pete Schiffer at Schiffer Publishing, my editor Catherine Mallette, and lastly, thank you to the amazing Tina Libby who stuck with me through *World Gone Wild* and into *The Good, the Tough, and the Deadly.* Thank you, Tina, for seeing the potential of these books and helping me to offer them to the world.

Finally, thanks to my parents Graciela and William. You guys took me to see *Rambo: First Blood: Part II* three times in theaters. I think it all started there. To my wife, Kady Annette: I love you and thank you for your patience and support. To my son, Ronin Cricket: When we watch *American Ninja* and *Gymkata* together for the first time, I hope your world changes for the better. If not, don't sweat it: we'll watch *Predator* next. Thank you, one and all. Join me for the next adventure.

Dedicated to everybody who's watched any of the movies we reviewed in this book and once upon a time imagined themselves as action stars, and most of all, I dedicate this book to Sylvester Stallone and Arnold Schwarzenegger, whose movies made me dream. The dream should always stay alive.

Portions of the following interviews were previously published elsewhere:

Scott Adkins in *Black Belt* and on OutlawVern.com
Zoë Bell on TheActionElite.com
Reb Brown in *The Phantom of the Movies' VideoScope* magazine
Ross Clarkson on OutlawVern.com
Dale "Apollo" Cook in *World Gone Wild: A Survivor's Guide to Post-Apocalyptic Movies*
Mark Dacascos in *The Phantom of the Movies' VideoScope* magazine
Isaac Florentine in *Black Belt* and on OutlawVern.com
Mark Goldblatt in *Fangoria*
John Hyams on FlickeringMyth.com
Tony Jaa on KungFuTaiChi.com and The Phantom of the Movies' VideoScope Magazine
Glen "Kane" Jacobs on FlickeringMyth.com
Jesse Johnson on OutlawVern.com
Leon Isaac Kennedy in *The Phantom of the Movies' VideoScope* magazine
Kane Kosugi on OutlawVern.com
Lorenzo Lamas in *The Phantom of the Movies' VideoScope* magazine
Al Leong on TheActionElite.com
James Lew on TheActionElite.com
Dolph Lundgren on KungFuTaiChi.com and *The Phantom of the Movies' VideoScope* magazine
Tim Man on OutlawVern.com
Roddy Piper in *The Phantom of the Movies' VideoScope* magazine and in *World Gone Wild: A Survivor's Guide to Post-Apocalyptic Movies*
Ben Ramsey on OutlawVern.com
Cynthia Rothrock in *The Phantom of the Movies' VideoScope* magazine
Darren Shahlavi on KungFuTaiChi.com
Jeff Speakman on TheActionElite.com
Steve Wang on KungFuTaiChi.com
Michael Jai White on KungFuTaiChi.com and *The Phantom of the Movies' VideoScope* magazine
Don "The Dragon" Wilson in *The Phantom of the Movies' VideoScope* magazine